RESIDENTIAL AND LIGHT CONSTRUCTION

Ramsey/Sleeper

RESIDENTIAL AND LIGHT CONSTRUCTION

from

ARCHITECTURAL GRAPHIC STANDARDS

Eighth Edition

Edited by

JAMES AMBROSE

THE AMERICAN INSTITUTE OF ARCHITECTS

John Wiley & Sons, Inc.

New York / Chichester / Brisbane / Toronto / Singapore

The drawings, tables, data, and other information in this book have been obtained from many sources, including government organizations, trade associations, suppliers of building materials, and professional architects or architectural firms. The American Institute of Architects (AIA), the Architectural Graphic Standards Task Force of the AIA, and the publisher have made every reasonable effort to make this reference work accurate and authoritative, but do not warrant, and assume no liability for, the accuracy or completeness of the text or its fitness for any particular purpose. It is the responsibility of users to apply their professional knowledge in the use of information contained in this book, to consult the original sources for additional information when appropriate, and, if they themselves are not professional architects, to consult an architect when appropriate.

In recognition of the importance of preserving what has been written, it is a policy of John Wiley & Sons, Inc., to have books of enduring value published in the United States printed on acid-free paper, and we exert our best efforts to that end.

Library of Congress Cataloging in Publication Data:

Ramsey, Charles George, 1884–1963.
[Architectural graphic standards. Selections]
Ramsey/Sleeper residential and light construction: from Architectural graphic standards, eighth edition/edited by James Ambrose.
p. cm.
Includes bibliographical references and index.
ISBN 0-471-54371-3
1. Building—Details—Drawings. I. Sleeper, Harold Reeve, 1893–1960. II. Ambrose, James E. III. Title. IV. Title: Residential and light construction.
TH2031.A8425 1991
721′.022′2—dc20 90-29318
CIP

Printed in the United States of America

10 9 8 7 6 5 4 3 2 1

CONTENTS

PUBLISHER'S NOTE

Through eight editions spanning nearly 60 years, *Architectural Graphic Standards* has become *the* benchmark reference for the building design and construction professions. Originally the work of two authors, Charles Ramsey and Harold Sleeper, over the years *Architectural Graphic Standards* has continued to grow through the collaborative efforts of many publishing professionals at both Wiley and, since 1964, the American Institute of Architects.

Inevitably, the need to keep *Architectural Graphic Standards* the preeminent architectural graphic reference and its growth from some 233 pages to the 854 pages of the 8th edition has made the book too broad for some professionals who use the book for only a portion of its comprehensive contents. Reflecting the increasing specialization of professions in building design and construction, in recent years Wiley and the AIA have developed specialized versions of "the architect's bible" to respond to the changing needs of the book's users.

This volume is the latest result of our continuing effort to provide you, the user, with the essential information that only *Architectural Graphic Standards* can provide, and in the format most suitable for your needs. This special abridgement of the 8th edition, *Residential and Light Construction from Architectural Graphic Standards*, is designed for the building design and construction professional who specializes in small-scale construction.

Again the product of Wiley's long-time collaboration with the AIA, this volume is also the result of the expert editorial guidance of James Ambrose. In his 30 years as an educator, editor, and author, James Ambrose has consistently brought intelligence, insight, and clarity to the communication of complex technical information. His experience as the editor of Harry Parker's series of *Simplified Design Guides*, and as author of his own books on structural design topics, makes Jim an expert in assessing the specific needs of the small-scale construction professional.

We present this volume to you as part of our on-going effort to make the essential information of *Architectural Graphic Standards* available to the widest range of professional and academic readers in the most accessible and useful formats. Building on the example of excellence set by Ramsey and Sleeper, Wiley, together with the AIA, will continue to strive to serve the building design and construction professions with the very best in graphic information and design details.

KENNETH R. GESSER
Publisher
Professional, Reference, and Trade Group
John Wiley & Sons, Inc.

PREFACE

This abridged edition of the 8th edition of *Architectural Graphic Standards* has been developed for the purpose of providing a more concise reference for those persons whose interests are generally limited to the simpler forms of construction that are ordinarily associated with smaller buildings. This group includes most small architectural firms, and it is the general scope of activity of such design firms that is the primary basis for selection of the materials to be included from the 8th edition.

However, many others are also typically interested in this scope of work, including the engineers, landscape designers, interior designers, builders, building code reviewers, insurers, financers, and others who deal primarily with this type of construction. It is anticipated that these people may also find a more concise presentation to be useful and consider having their own copy, whereas they might not acquire the more extensive (and more expensive) 8th edition.

The 8th edition is indeed an extensive and rich source of reference materials and is well worth the investment for persons with broader scopes of concerns. Duplicating the contents of the 8th edition with a collection of other publications would assuredly cost the buyer several times the price of the single volume. This book does not pretend to replace the 8th edition; it instead extends access to a wider group of users whose interests are more specific.

This partial presentation of materials from the Ramsey and Sleeper book follows on other recent publications that have sought to extend the rich resource of this book, which has been in continuous publication since 1932, through eight editions.

In addition to the materials taken from the 8th edition of *Architectural Graphic Standards*, there are lists of references for additional information. Such lists are provided at the ends of the chapters, relating to the topics of the chapters. A list of general references—relating to the general topic of the book—is provided in the Reference section at the back of the book.

I must acknowledge the contributions of the many individuals and organizations who contributed to the development of the 8th edition. Developers of individual book pages are listed at the bottoms of the pages, and the many organizations providing book materials are listed in the Data Sources at the end of each chapter.

I must also acknowledge the contributions of the many generations of people—beginning with George Ramsey and Harold Sleeper—who made inputs to the development and contribution of this work over the almost 60 years of its publication. This includes the many authors, graphic artists, and editors, as well as the many people at the American Institute of Architects and John Wiley & Sons who worked on the several editions of the book.

For this book I am grateful for the contributions and support of my editors, Stephen Kliment and Everett Smethurst, and the many other editors and the marketing and production personnel at John Wiley & Sons, especially Robert J. Fletcher and Joseph Keenan.

I am also grateful for the support and direct assistance of my wife, Peggy, who did most of the work of redeveloping the extensive index—a major component of this book.

JAMES AMBROSE
Westlake Village, California
January, 1991

RESIDENTIAL AND LIGHT CONSTRUCTION

CHAPTER 1

GENERAL PLANNING AND DESIGN DATA

BED SIZES

TYPES	W	L
KING	72″	84″
QUEEN	60″	82″
DOUBLE	54″	82″
SINGLE	39″	82″
DAYBED	30″	75″
CRIB	30″	53″

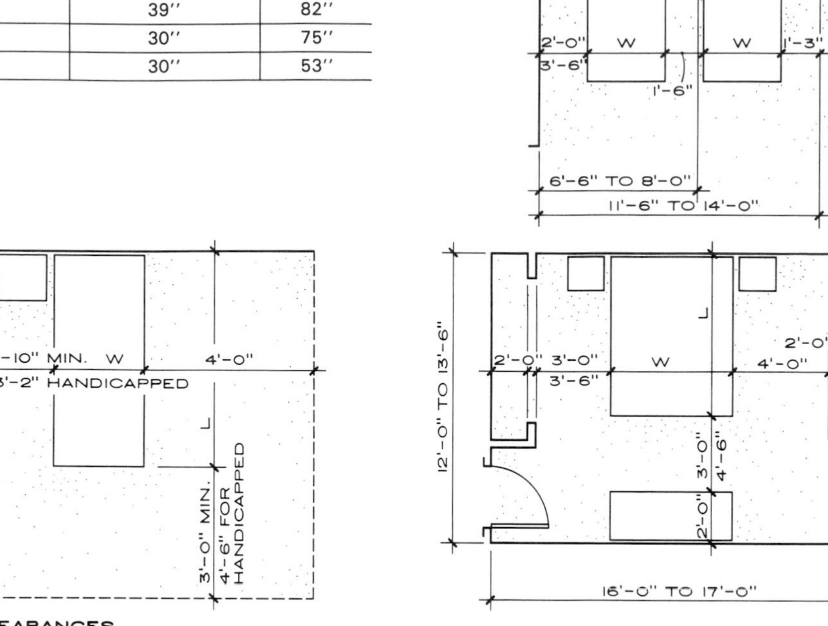

2'-0"
W
W
1'-3"
3'-6"
1'-6"
6'-6" TO 8'-0"
11'-6" TO 14'-0"
1'-10" MIN.
W
4'-0"
3'-2" HANDICAPPED
L
3'-0" MIN.
4'-6" FOR HANDICAPPED
12'-0" TO 13'-6"
2'-0" 3'-0"
3'-6"
W
L
2'-0"
4'-0"
3'-0"
4'-6"
2'-0"
16'-0" TO 17'-0"

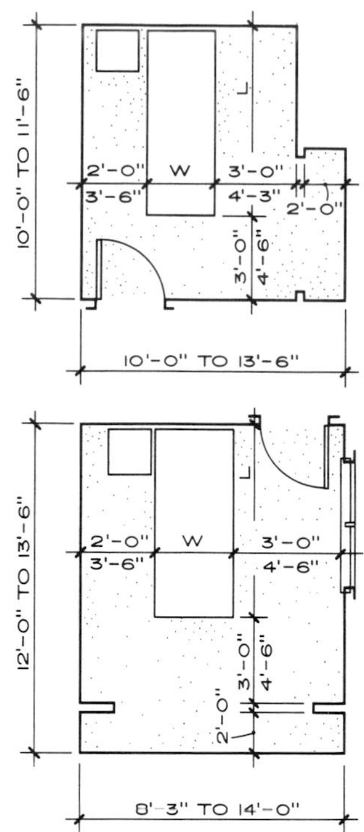

10'-0" TO 11'-6"
L
2'-0"
W
3'-0"
3'-6"
4'-3"
2'-0"
3'-0"
4'-6"
10'-0" TO 13'-6"
12'-0" TO 13'-6"
L
2'-0"
W
3'-0"
3'-6"
4'-6"
3'-0"
4'-6"
2'-0"
8'-3" TO 14'-0"

BED CLEARANCES

BEDROOM FURNITURE

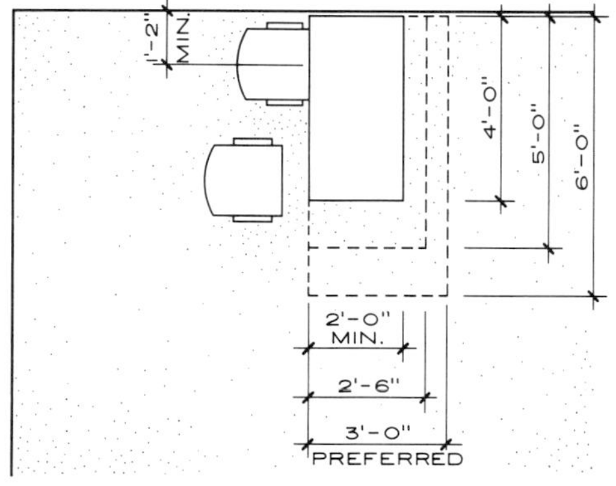

1'-2" MIN.
4'-0"
5'-0"
6'-0"
2'-0" MIN.
2'-6"
3'-0" PREFERRED

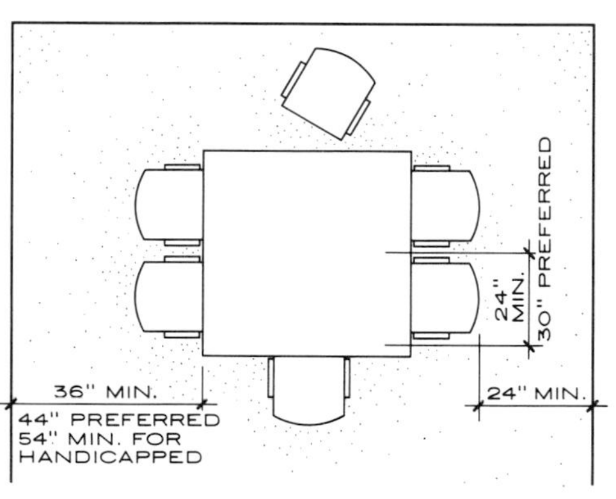

24" MIN.
30" PREFERRED
36" MIN.
44" PREFERRED
54" MIN. FOR HANDICAPPED
24" MIN.

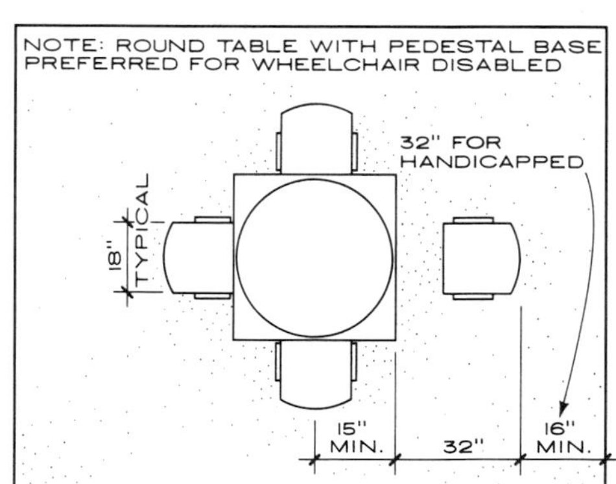

NOTE: ROUND TABLE WITH PEDESTAL BASE PREFERRED FOR WHEELCHAIR DISABLED
32" FOR HANDICAPPED
18" TYPICAL
15" MIN.
32"
16" MIN.

RECTANGULAR TABLES (IN.)

SIZE	SEAT	WHEELCHAIR
24 x 48	4	
30 x 48	4	2
30 x 60	4-6	2-4
36 x 72	4-6	4-6
36 x 84	6-8	6

SQUARE TABLES (IN.)

SIZE	SEAT	WHEELCHAIR
30 x 30	2	
36 x 36	2-4	
42 x 42	4	2 (TIGHT)
48 x 48	4-8	2
54 x 54	4-8	4

ROUND TABLES (IN.)

SIZE	SEAT	WHEELCHAIR
30	2	
36	2-4	
42	4-5	
48	5-6	2
54	5-6	4

DINING ROOM FURNITURE

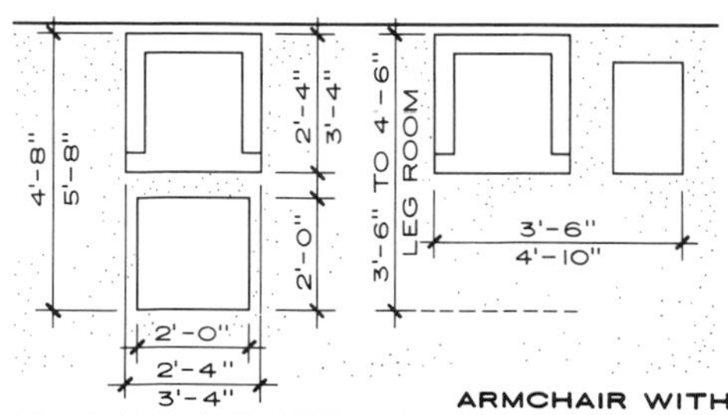

4'-8"
5'-8"
2'-4"
3'-4"
2'-0"
2'-0"
2'-4"
3'-4"
3'-6" TO 4'-6" LEG ROOM
3'-6"
4'-10"

ARMCHAIR AND OTTOMAN

ARMCHAIR WITH END TABLE

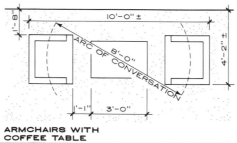

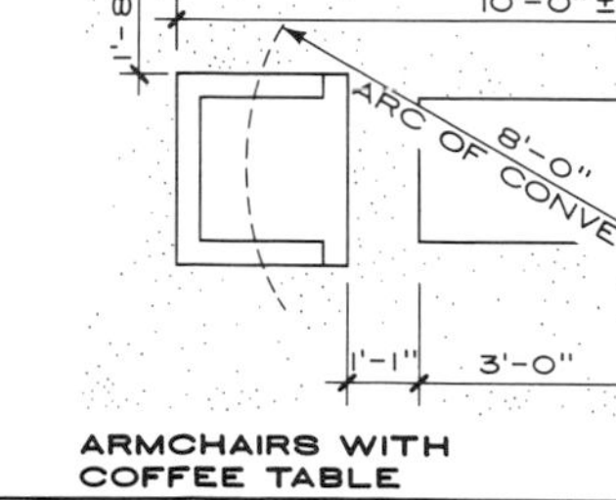

1'-8"
10'-0" ±
ARC OF CONVERSATION
8'-0"
4'-2" ±
1'-1"
3'-0"

ARMCHAIRS WITH COFFEE TABLE

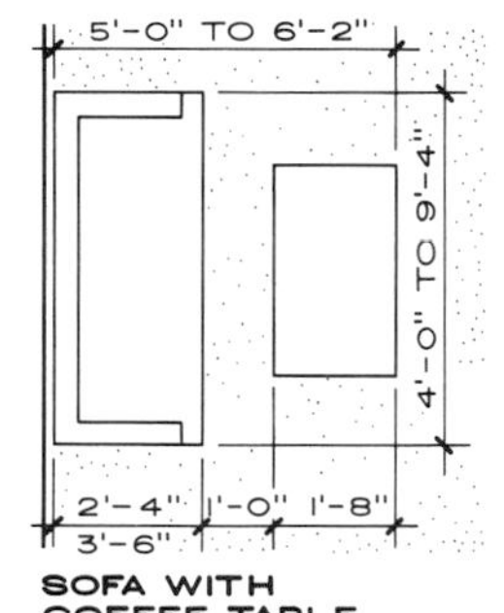

5'-0" TO 6'-2"
4'-0" TO 9'-4"
2'-4"
1'-0"
1'-8"
3'-6"

SOFA WITH COFFEE TABLE

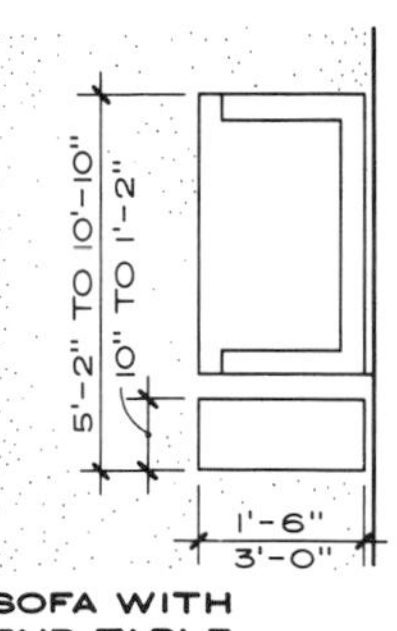

5'-2" TO 10'-0"
10" TO 1'-2"
1'-6"
3'-0"

SOFA WITH END TABLE

LIVING ROOM FURNITURE

Robin Andrew Roberts, AIA; Washington, D.C.
Arthur J. Pettorino, AIA; Hicksville, New York

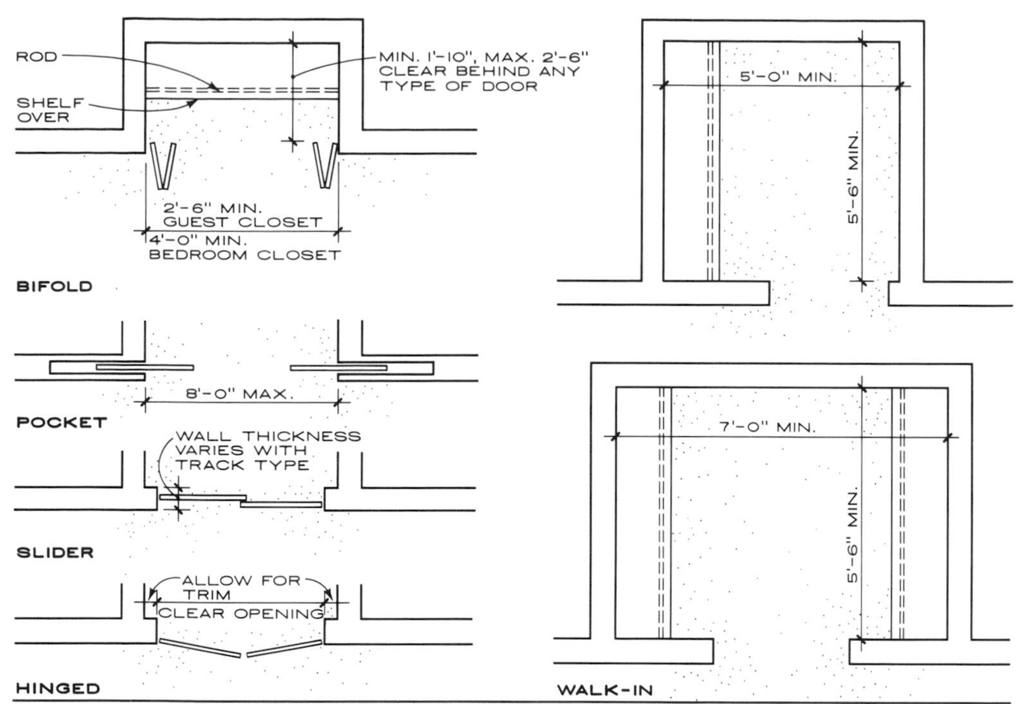
ROD
SHELF OVER
MIN. 1'-10", MAX. 2'-6" CLEAR BEHIND ANY TYPE OF DOOR
2'-6" MIN. GUEST CLOSET
4'-0" MIN. BEDROOM CLOSET
BIFOLD
8'-0" MAX.
POCKET
WALL THICKNESS VARIES WITH TRACK TYPE
SLIDER
ALLOW FOR TRIM
CLEAR OPENING
HINGED
5'-0" MIN.
5'-6" MIN.
7'-0" MIN.
5'-6" MIN.
WALK-IN

TYPICAL CLOSET PLANS

NOTES

1. No closet bifold door should exceed a 2 ft panel. Largest door stock in pocket and sliding door is 4 ft.
2. All closet doors should allow easy access to top shelves.
3. Doors for children's closets can be used as tackboards, chalkboards, or mirrors.
4. Consider use of hinged doors for storage fittings and mirrors.
5. Walk-in closets should be properly ventilated and lit.
6. Provide clear floor space at least 30 by 48 in. for wheelchair approach. Pole and shelf height is 54" maximum for handicapped.
7. Percentage of accessibility of closets varies with door types used: Bifold at 66⅔% min.; pocket at 100%; sliding at 50% or more; and hinged at 90% depending on hardware and door thickness.

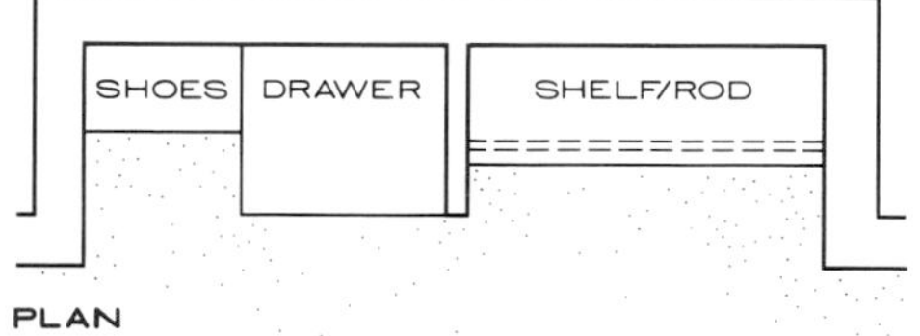
SHOES
DRAWER
SHELF/ROD
PLAN

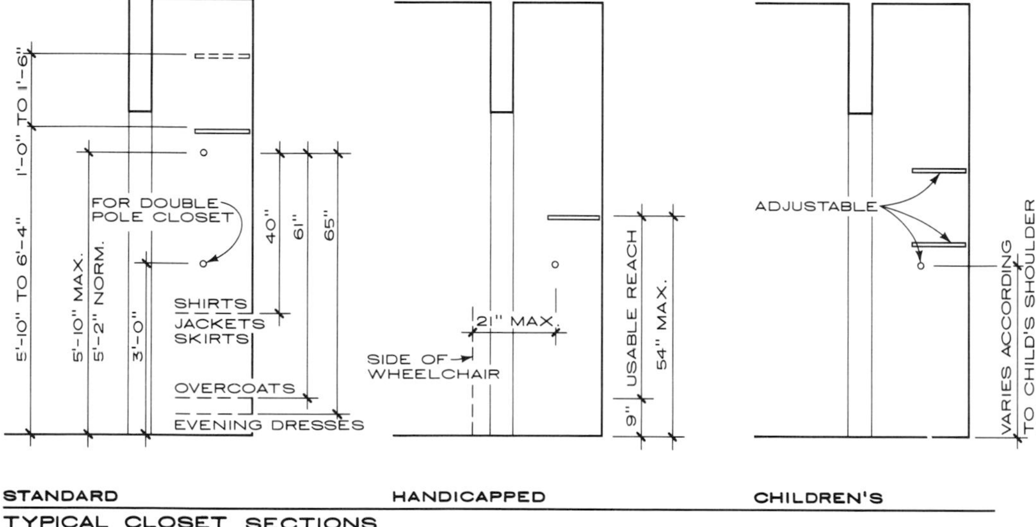
1'-0" TO 1'-6"
5'-10" TO 6'-4"
5'-10" MAX.
5'-2" NORM.
3'-0"
FOR DOUBLE POLE CLOSET
40"
61"
65"
SHIRTS
JACKETS
SKIRTS
OVERCOATS
EVENING DRESSES
STANDARD
21" MAX.
SIDE OF WHEELCHAIR
USABLE REACH
54" MAX.
9"
HANDICAPPED
ADJUSTABLE
VARIES ACCORDING TO CHILD'S SHOULDER HEIGHT
CHILDREN'S

TYPICAL CLOSET SECTIONS

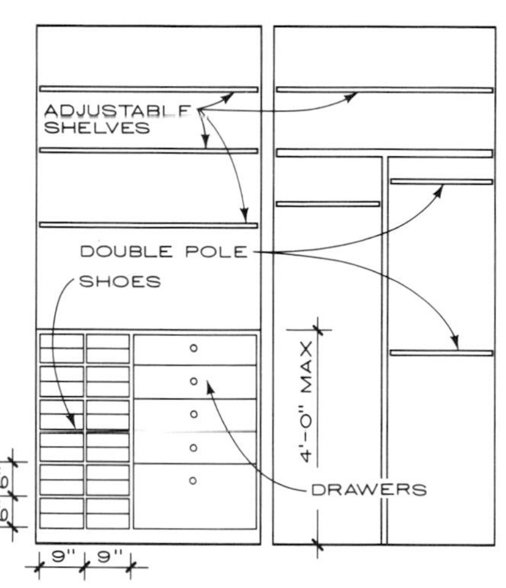
ADJUSTABLE SHELVES
DOUBLE POLE
SHOES
4'-0" MAX.
DRAWERS
6"
6"
9"
9"
ELEVATION

DIVIDED CLOSET

RESIDENTIAL STORAGE

SHELVING. Standard shelving sizes are 6, 8, 10, and 12 in., although shelving up to 18 in. deep is desirable for closet shelving. Shelving may be either fixed or adjustable.

DRAWERS. Typical drawers are from 16 to 24 in. deep, 12 to 36 in. wide, and 2 to 8 in. deep or deeper. Often built into casework, drawers may be of wood, metal, or molded plastic.

CLOSETS. Standard closet depth is 24 to 30 in. for clothing and 16 to 20 in. for linens.

BOXES. Closet storage fittings such as boxes and garment bags can be used for supplemental or seasonal storage.

Robin Andrew Roberts, AIA; Washington, D.C.
R. L. Speas, Jr.; Hugh N. Jacobsen, FAIA; Washington, D.C.

STORAGE REQUIREMENTS

BEDROOM. Allow 4 to 6 ft of hanging space per person. Allow 8 linear ft of hanging space for closets shared by 2 people. Allow 12 in. of hanging space for 6 suits, 12 shirts, 8 dresses, or 6 pairs of pants.

LINEN STORAGE. Place near bedrooms and bathrooms in a closet with 12 to 18 in. deep shelves. Supplemental storage in bins or baskets may be needed. Provide minimum 9 sq ft for 1–2 bedroom house; 12 sq ft for 3–4 bedroom house.

BATHROOMS. A mirrored wall cabinet 4 to 6 in. deep is typical bathroom storage, supplemented by space for supplies of soap, toothpaste, and other toiletries.

COATS. A closet near an entry door for coats and rainwear is desirable in most areas of the country. Provide extra 2 to 3 in. in depth for air circulation and added bulkiness of overcoats.

CLEANING EQUIPMENT. A closet at least 24 in. wide for storage of vacuum cleaners and household cleaning supplies is helpful. Locate closet near center of house and provide electrical outlet so vacuum can be left connected.

KITCHEN/DINING. See pages on kitchen planning for recommendations.

OTHER STORAGE. Most families have additional storage needs. For custom design work, these needs must be analyzed and storage planned. Storage rooms and attic and basement areas are possible supplemental storage locations.

KITCHEN SPACE PLANNING

The layouts shown here, together with their general area requirements, are based on studies of furniture, appliances, storage, and clearances for the average residential kitchen. They have been developed to accommodate work, storage, and floor areas required for various food preparation functions. The location and order of both appliances and associated work surfaces should be determined by physical limitations, traffic flow, individual preferences, and appliance type in determining kitchen size during the early planning stages. To simplify comparison of the various room types, basic sizes of furniture, appliances, and clearances have been standardized.

Storage: Minimum 18 sq ft of space for basic storage with an additional 6 sq ft/person served.

Work Flow: Work flow should move from refrigerator work center (A) to sink work center (B) to cooking work center (C), then to the serving spot. The total length of the work triangle (ABC) should average less than 23 lineal feet and never exceed 26 lineal feet.

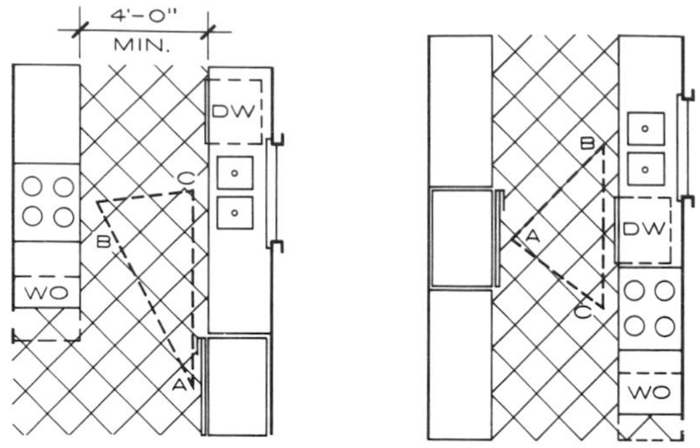

4'-0" MIN.

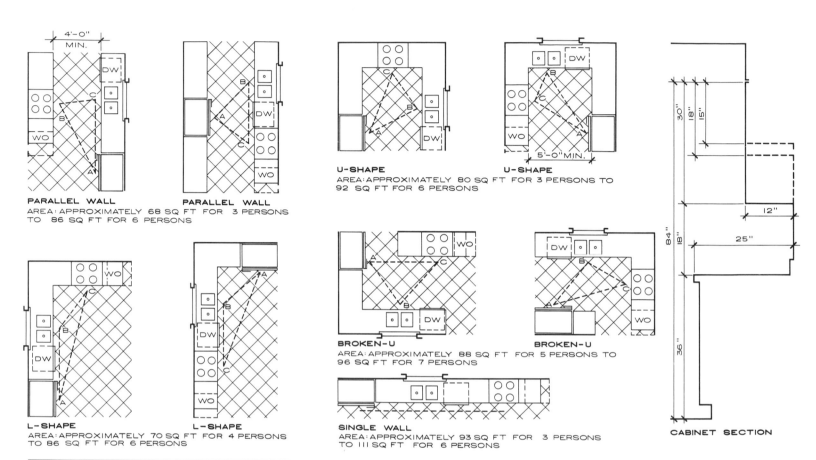

PARALLEL WALL   PARALLEL WALL

AREA: APPROXIMATELY 68 SQ FT FOR 3 PERSONS TO 86 SQ FT FOR 6 PERSONS

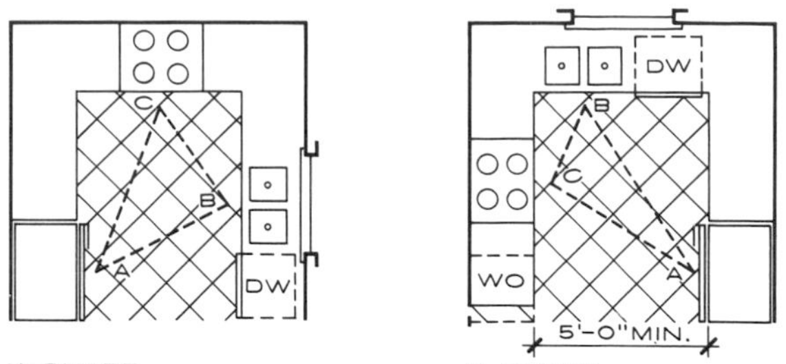

U-SHAPE   U-SHAPE

5'-0" MIN.

AREA: APPROXIMATELY 80 SQ FT FOR 3 PERSONS TO 92 SQ FT FOR 6 PERSONS

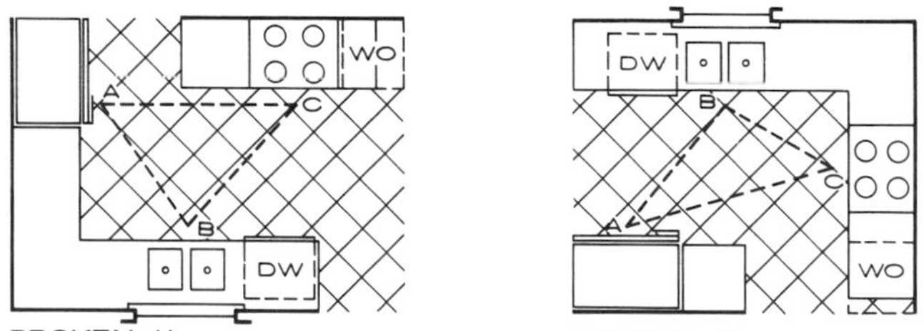

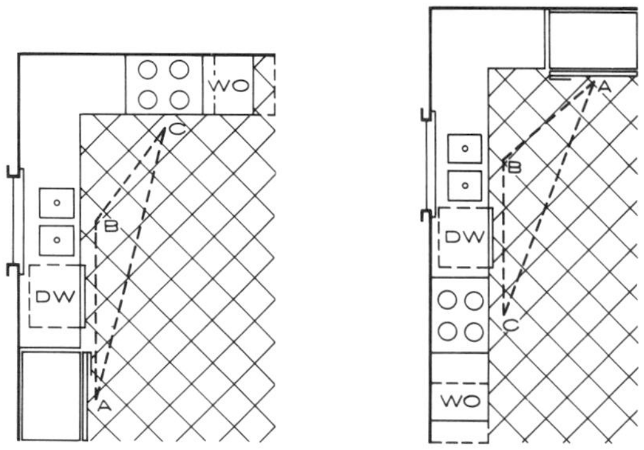

L-SHAPE   L-SHAPE

AREA: APPROXIMATELY 70 SQ FT FOR 4 PERSONS TO 86 SQ FT FOR 6 PERSONS

BROKEN-U   BROKEN-U

AREA: APPROXIMATELY 88 SQ FT FOR 5 PERSONS TO 96 SQ FT FOR 7 PERSONS

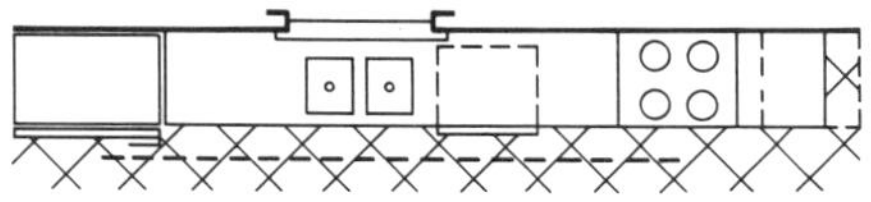

SINGLE WALL

AREA: APPROXIMATELY 93 SQ FT FOR 3 PERSONS TO 111 SQ FT FOR 6 PERSONS

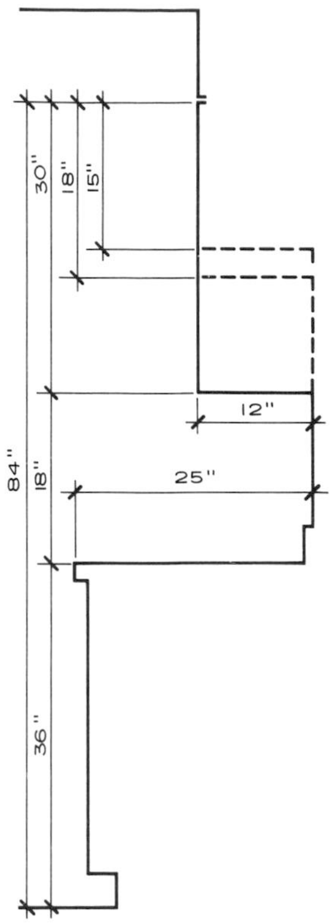

30" 18" 15" 84" 12" 25" 18" 36"

CABINET SECTION

RESIDENTIAL KITCHEN ARRANGEMENTS

NOTE: SMALL KITCHENS USUALLY HAVE UP TO 10 RUNNING FEET OF COUNTER AND EQUIPMENT. AVERAGE KITCHENS HAVE UP TO 20 RUNNING FEET OF THE SAME. USUAL EQUIPMENT INCLUDES UNDERCOUNTER REFRIGERATOR

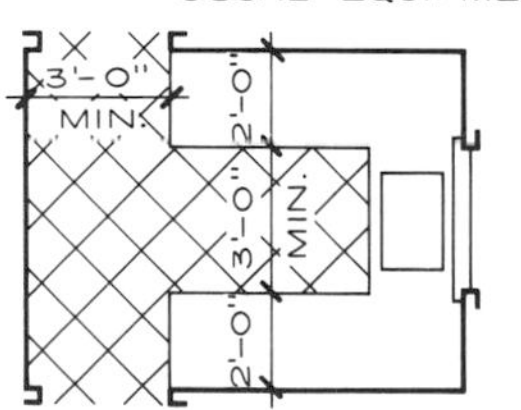
3'-0"
MIN.
2'-0"
3'-0"
MIN.
2'-0"

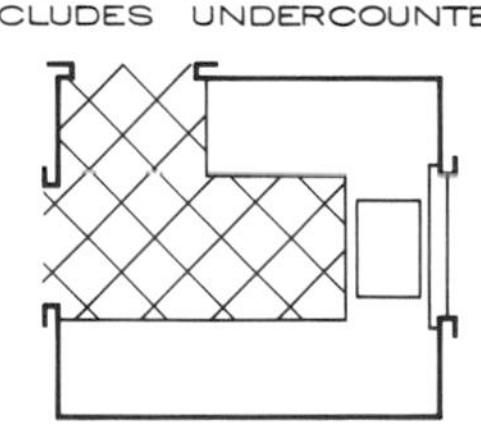

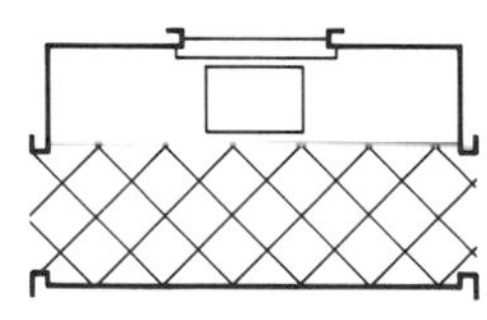

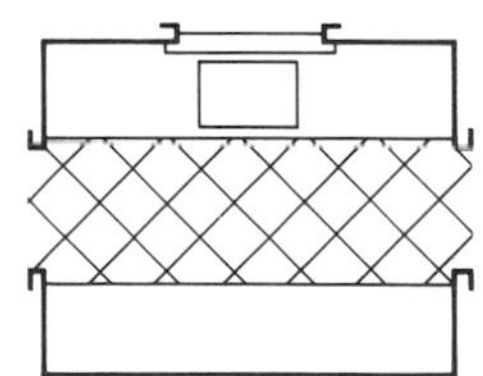

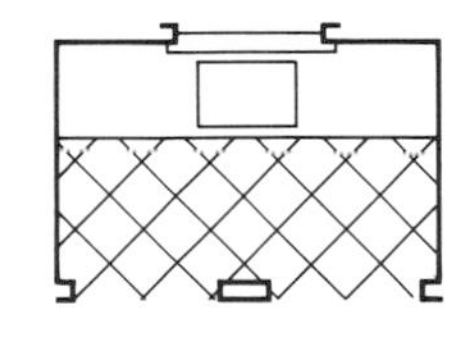

PANTRY TYPES

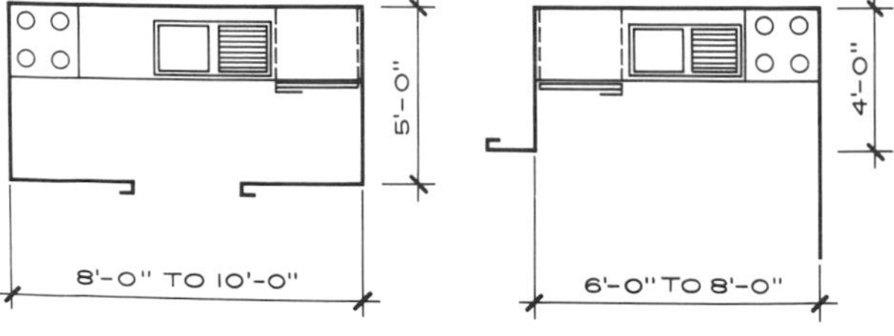
5'-0"
8'-0" TO 10'-0"
4'-0"
6'-0" TO 8'-0"

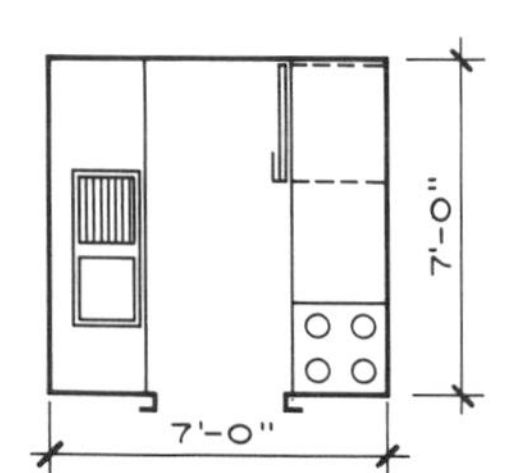
7'-0"
7'-0"

ABBREVIATIONS
DW = DISHWASHER
WO = WALL OVEN

KITCHENETTES

Robin Andrew Roberts, AIA; Washington, D.C.
R. E. Powe, Jr., AIA; Hugh N. Jacobsen, FAIA; Washington, D.C.

KITCHEN WORK CENTERS

A residential kitchen may be considered in terms of three interconnected work centers: A, B, and C, as shown below. Each encompasses a distinct phase of kitchen activity, and storage should be provided for the items that are most used in connection with each center.

The functions of the sink center are most common to the other two centers. It is recommended, therefore, that the sink center's location be convenient to each of the others (usually between them). The refrigerator center is best located near the entry and the range center near the dining area.

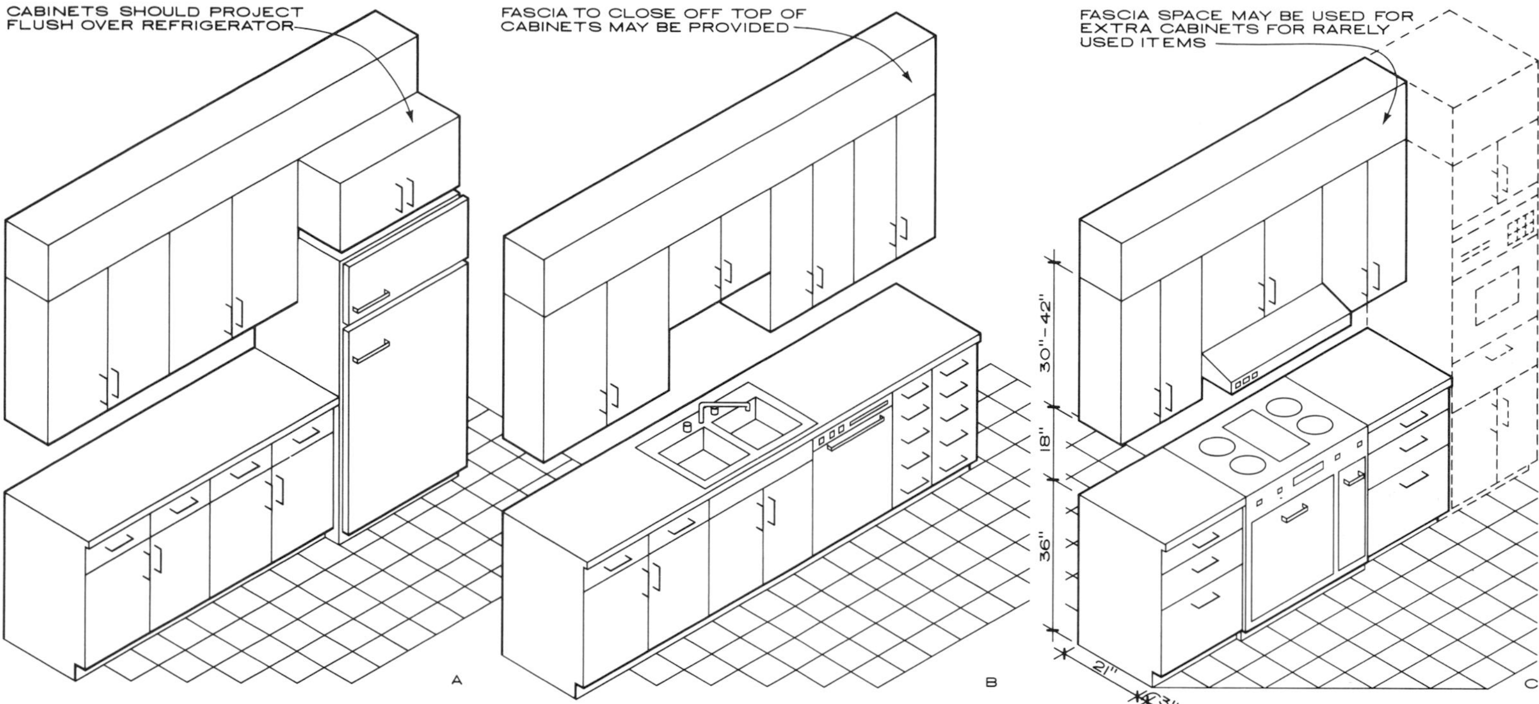
CABINETS SHOULD PROJECT FLUSH OVER REFRIGERATOR
FASCIA TO CLOSE OFF TOP OF CABINETS MAY BE PROVIDED
FASCIA SPACE MAY BE USED FOR EXTRA CABINETS FOR RARELY USED ITEMS
30"-42"
18"
36"
21"
3"
A
B
C

REFRIGERATOR CENTER
(Receiving and Food Preparation)

Provide storage for mixer and mixing bowls; other utensils: sifter, grater, salad molds, cake and pie tins, occasional dishes, condiments, staples, canned goods, brooms, and miscellaneous items.

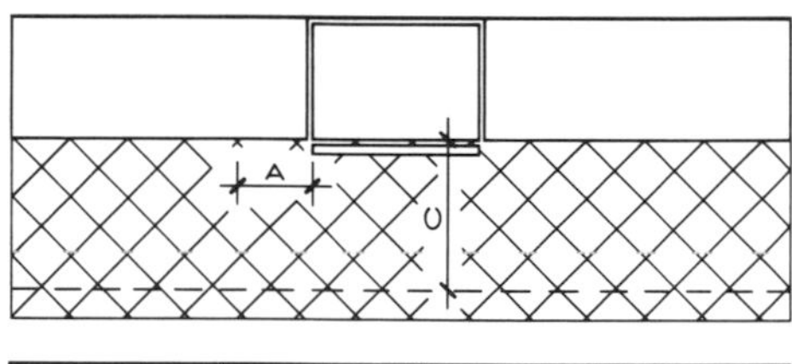
A
C

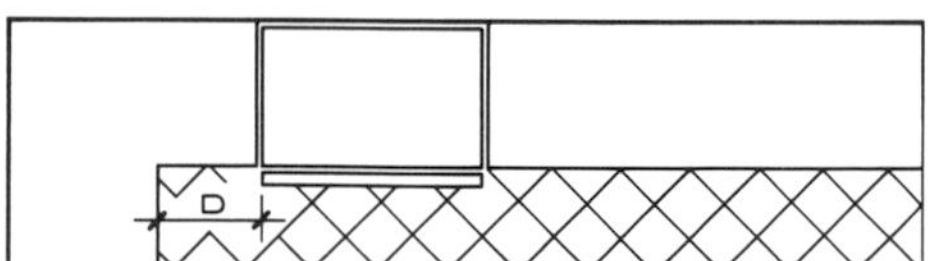
D

A = 15 in. minimum counter space at latch side of refrigerator for loading and unloading.

B = 18 in. minimum clearance between latch side of refrigerator and turn of counter.

C = 40 to 42 in. clearance from face of refrigerator to wall or facing counter.

SINK CENTER
(Food Preparation, Cleaning, and Cleanup)

Provide storage for everyday dishes, glassware, pots and pans, cutlery, silver, pitchers and shakers, vegetable bins, linen, towel rack, wastebasket, cleaning materials and utensils, garbage can or disposal, and dishdrain. Some codes require louvers or other venting provisions in the doors under enclosed sinks.

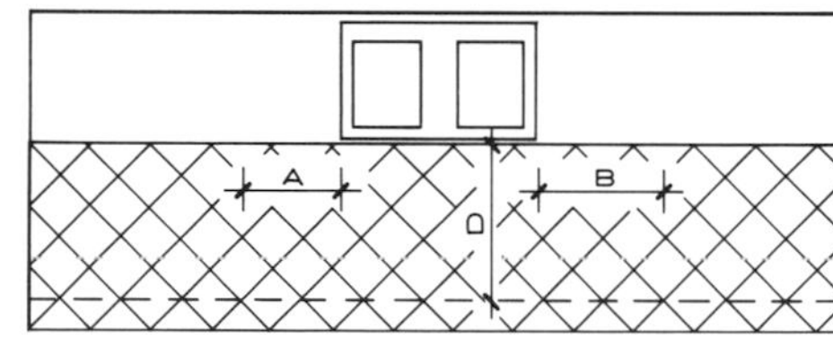
A
D
B

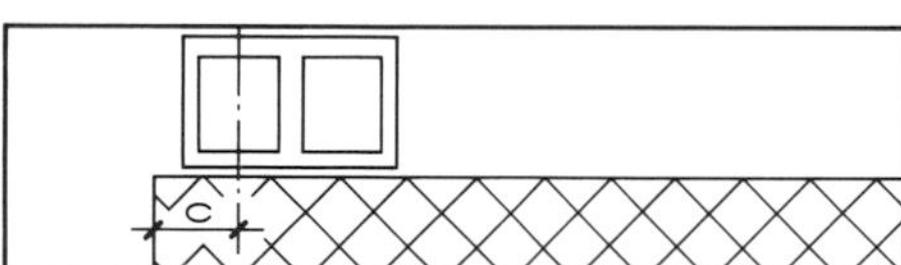
C

A = 18 to 36 in. counter space on side of sink.

B = 24 to 36 in. counter space on side of sink.

Provide 24 in. counter space at either right or left if dishwasher is used.

C = 14 in. minimum clearance between center of bowl and the turn of counter.

D = 40 to 42 in. minimum clearance from face of sink to wall or facing counter.

RANGE CENTER
(Cooking and Serving)

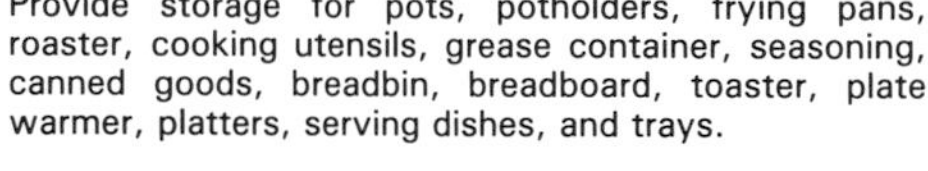

Provide storage for pots, potholders, frying pans, roaster, cooking utensils, grease container, seasoning, canned goods, breadbin, breadboard, toaster, plate warmer, platters, serving dishes, and trays.

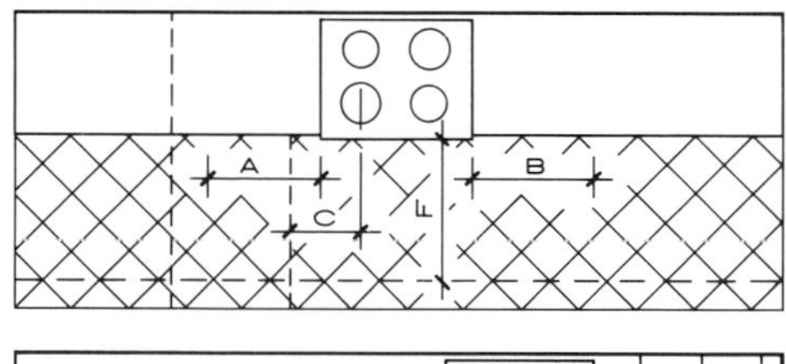
A
C
F
B

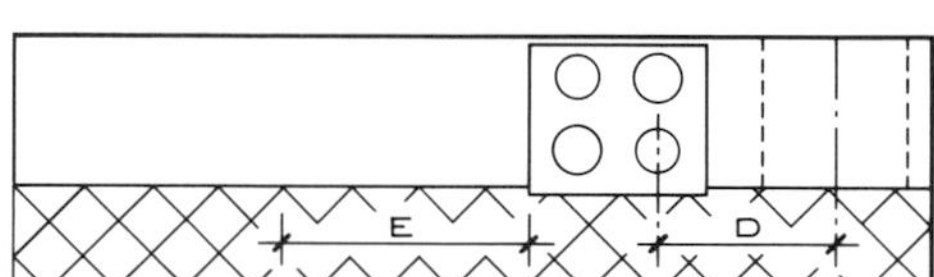
E
D

A, B = 18 to 24 in. counter space on either side of cooking facility.

C = 14 in. minimum clearance between center of front unit and the turn of counter.

D = 16 in. minimum clearance between center of front unit and nearest piece of high equipment or wall, or between center of wall oven and adjoining wall.

E = 36 to 42 in. counter space between range and nearest piece of equipment.

F = 40 to 42 in. clearance from face of range or oven to face of wall or facing counter.

CLEARANCES

KITCHENS FOR THE HANDICAPPED

The preferred cooktop and counter height is 30 to 33 in., but may be standard 36 in. Open floor space is necessary for wheelchair maneuverability; observe a 5 ft minimum turning radius. Smooth, nonskid flooring is required. Indoor–outdoor carpet is preferred, but difficult to maintain in a kitchen. Linoleum or vinyl tile is acceptable. Knee space is necessary under sink counter. Insulate pipes to avoid scalding. Provide cooktop controls at front to avoid reaching across hot surfaces. Wall ovens should preferably be set so that top of open oven door is 2 ft 7 in. above floor. Side-by-side refrigerator-freezer is preferred, although units with freezer on bottom are acceptable. Dishwashers should be front-loading.

Round tables with pedestal bases are preferred. A 4 ft diameter will accommodate two wheelchair users; a 4 ft 5 in. diameter will accommodate four wheelchair users.

Storage considerations for the wheelchair disabled include use of pegboard for pots, pans, and utensils. Vertical drawers in base cabinets allow for storage of food that would otherwise be out of reach of wheelchair users. Narrow shelving mounted to the backs of doors in cabinets or closets provides accessible storage for food and utensils.

Robin Andrew Roberts, AIA; Washington, D.C.
Arthur J. Pettorino, AIA; Hicksville, New York
R. E. Powe, Jr., AIA; Hugh N. Jacobsen, FAIA; Washington, D.C.

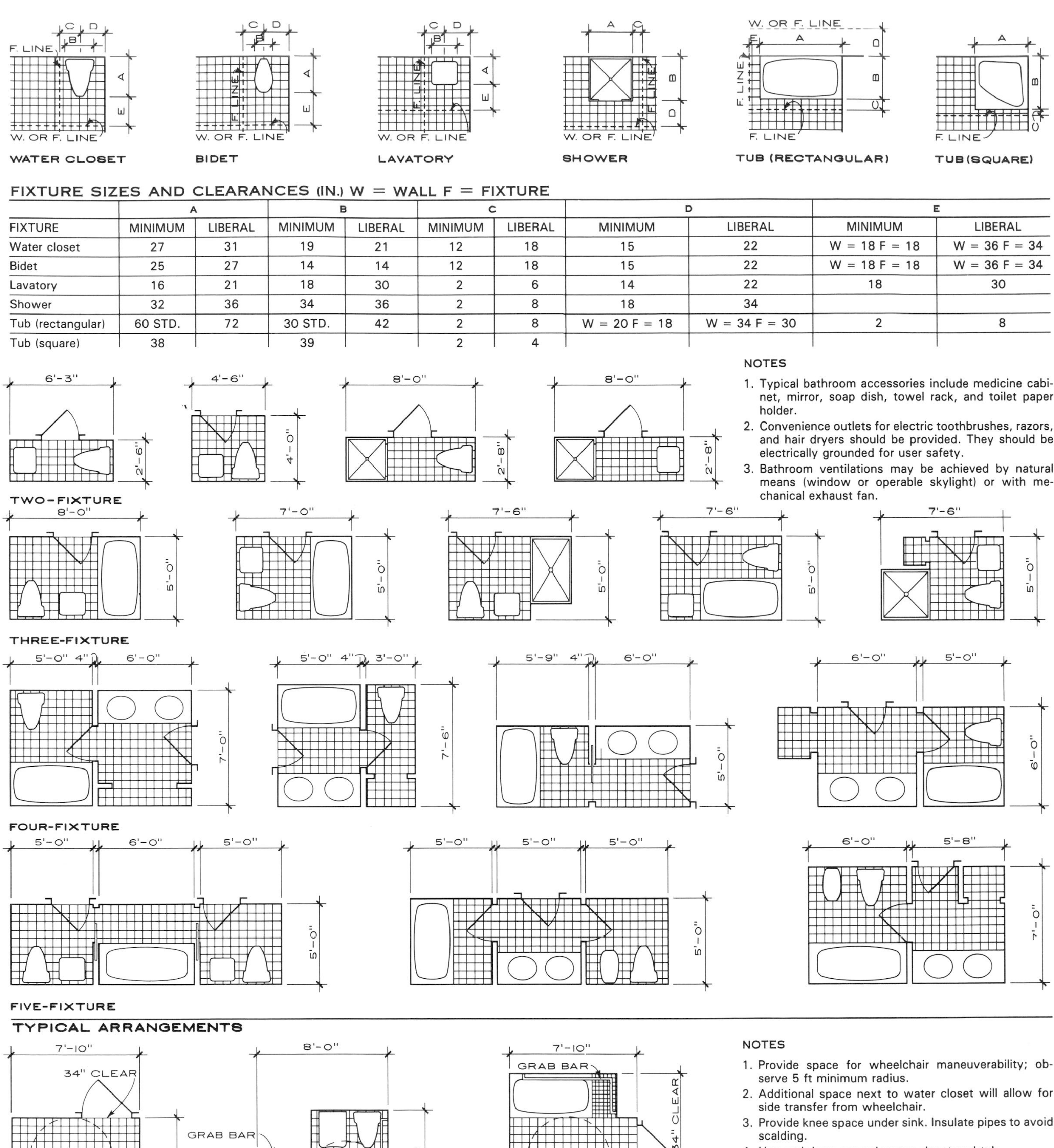

F. LINE
W. OR F. LINE
WATER CLOSET
BIDET
LAVATORY
SHOWER
TUB (RECTANGULAR)
TUB (SQUARE)
TWO-FIXTURE
THREE-FIXTURE
FOUR-FIXTURE
FIVE-FIXTURE

FIXTURE SIZES AND CLEARANCES (IN.) W = WALL F = FIXTURE

	A		B		C		D		E	
FIXTURE	MINIMUM	LIBERAL	MINIMUM	LIBERAL	MINIMUM	LIBERAL	MINIMUM	LIBERAL	MINIMUM	LIBERAL
Water closet	27	31	19	21	12	18	15	22	W = 18 F = 18	W = 36 F = 34
Bidet	25	27	14	14	12	18	15	22	W = 18 F = 18	W = 36 F = 34
Lavatory	16	21	18	30	2	6	14	22	18	30
Shower	32	36	34	36	2	8	18	34		
Tub (rectangular)	60 STD.	72	30 STD.	42	2	8	W = 20 F = 18	W = 34 F = 30	2	8
Tub (square)	38		39		2	4				

NOTES

1. Typical bathroom accessories include medicine cabinet, mirror, soap dish, towel rack, and toilet paper holder.
2. Convenience outlets for electric toothbrushes, razors, and hair dryers should be provided. They should be electrically grounded for user safety.
3. Bathroom ventilations may be achieved by natural means (window or operable skylight) or with mechanical exhaust fan.

TYPICAL ARRANGEMENTS

NOTES

1. Provide space for wheelchair maneuverability; observe 5 ft minimum radius.
2. Additional space next to water closet will allow for side transfer from wheelchair.
3. Provide knee space under sink. Insulate pipes to avoid scalding.
4. Use grab bars around water closet and tub.
5. Roll-in shower may replace tub and is more convenient for many wheelchair disabled.
6. Bathroom door to be minimum 32 in. clear opening and to swing outward. Use lever hardware on both sides.

ARRANGEMENTS FOR THE WHEELCHAIR DISABLED

Robin Andrew Roberts, AIA; Washington, D.C.
Arthur J. Pettorino, AIA; Hicksville, New York

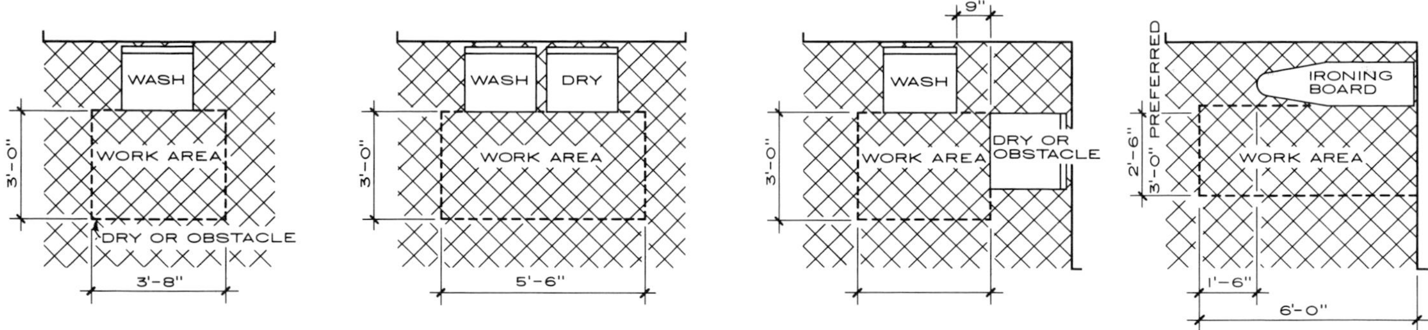
WASH
WORK AREA
DRY OR OBSTACLE
3'-0"
3'-8"
WASH
DRY
WORK AREA
3'-0"
5'-6"
9"
WASH
WORK AREA
DRY OR OBSTACLE
3'-0"
IRONING BOARD
WORK AREA
2'-6" 3'-0" PREFERRED
1'-6"
6'-0"

LAUNDRY EQUIPMENT CLEARANCES

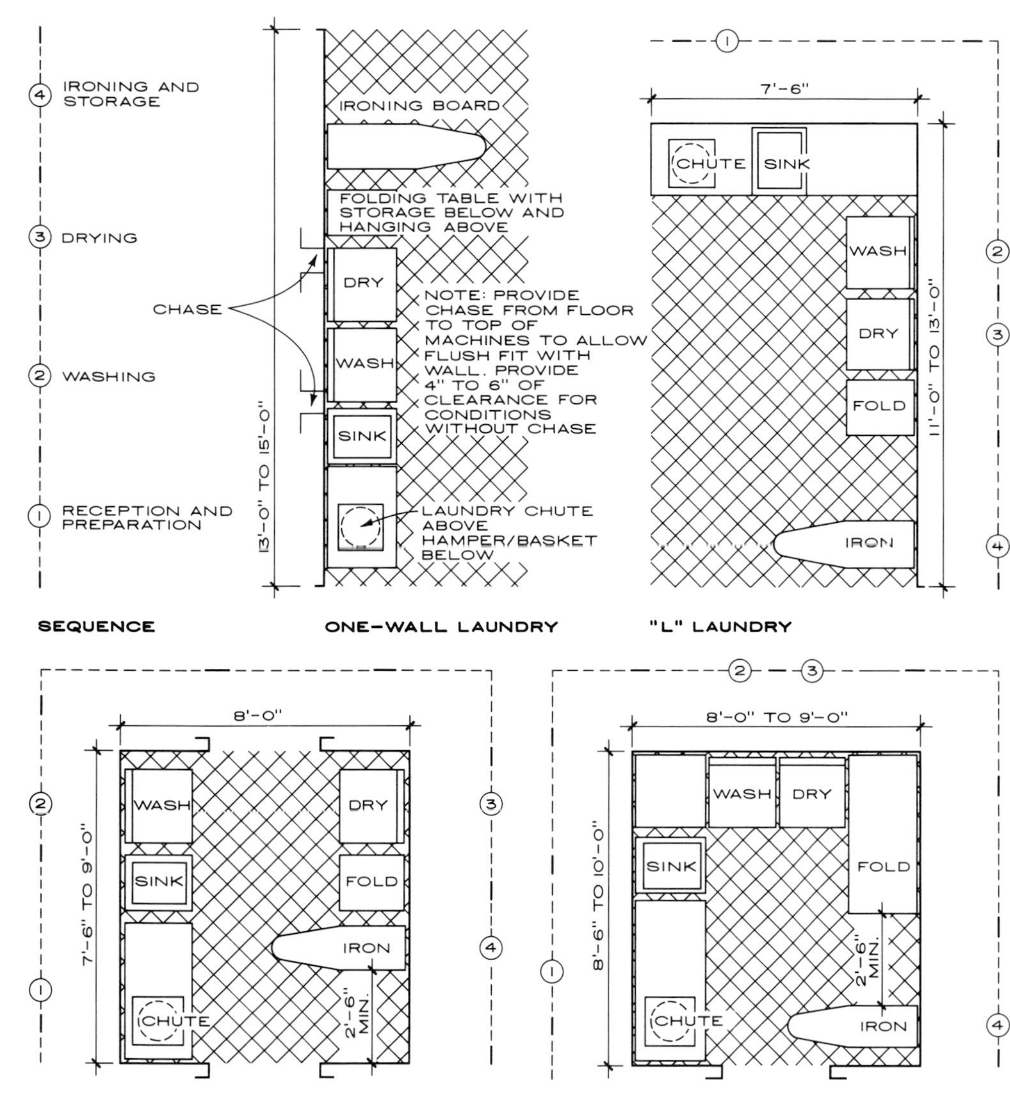
4 IRONING AND STORAGE
3 DRYING
CHASE
2 WASHING
1 RECEPTION AND PREPARATION
IRONING BOARD
FOLDING TABLE WITH STORAGE BELOW AND HANGING ABOVE
DRY
WASH
SINK
NOTE: PROVIDE CHASE FROM FLOOR TO TOP OF MACHINES TO ALLOW FLUSH FIT WITH WALL. PROVIDE 4" TO 6" OF CLEARANCE FOR CONDITIONS WITHOUT CHASE
LAUNDRY CHUTE ABOVE HAMPER/BASKET BELOW
13'-0" TO 15'-0"
7'-6"
CHUTE
SINK
WASH
DRY
FOLD
IRON
11'-0" TO 13'-0"
SEQUENCE
ONE-WALL LAUNDRY
"L" LAUNDRY
8'-0"
WASH
DRY
SINK
FOLD
IRON
CHUTE
7'-6" TO 9'-0"
2'-6" MIN.
8'-0" TO 9'-0"
WASH
DRY
SINK
FOLD
2'-6" MIN.
CHUTE
IRON
8'-6" TO 10'-0"
PARALLEL LAUNDRIES
"U" LAUNDRY

TYPICAL LAUNDRIES

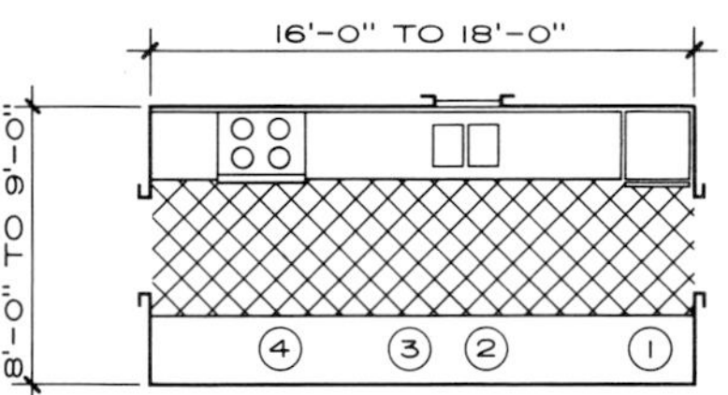
16'-0" TO 18'-0"
8'-0" TO 9'-0"

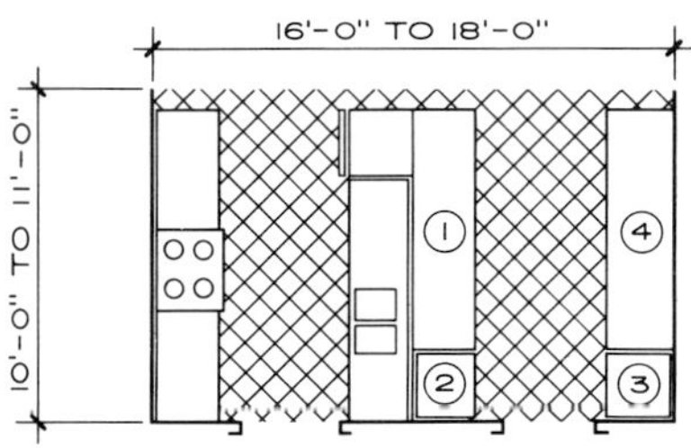
16'-0" TO 18'-0"
10'-0" TO 11'-0"

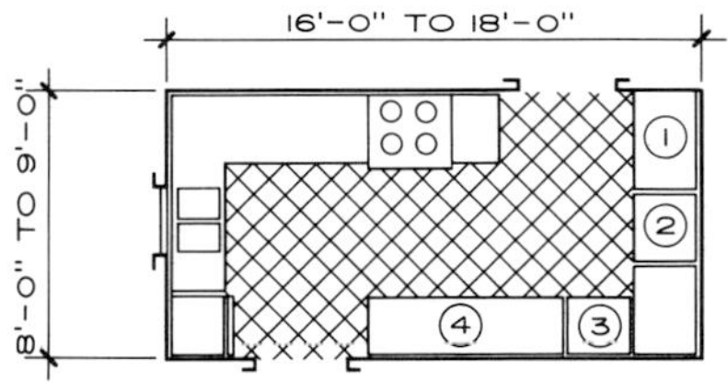
16'-0" TO 18'-0"
8'-0" TO 9'-0"

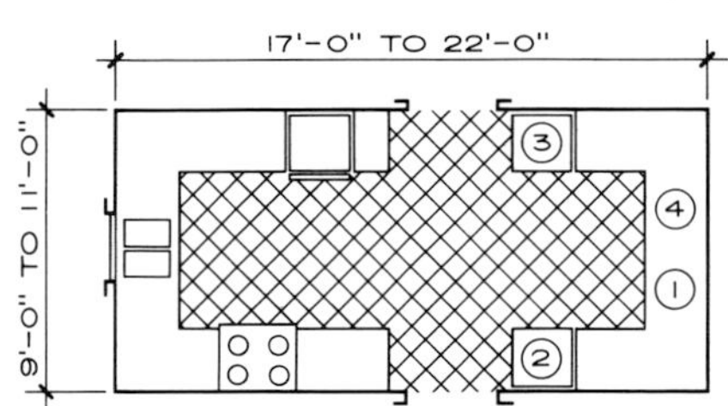
17'-0" TO 22'-0"
9'-0" TO 11'-0"

LAUNDRIES WITH KITCHEN

LAUNDRIES FOR THE HANDICAPPED

For the wheelchair disabled, having laundry facilities close to the kitchen combines several time-consuming activities with a minimum of movement from place to place.

The basic necessities for an accessible laundry facility are the following: front-loading automatic washer, dryer, storage shelving for supplies, lightweight steam iron, ironing board, and a surface for folding.

Laundry equipment controls are to be within high forward or side reach ranges. Controls shall be operable with one hand and not require tight grasping, pinching, or twisting of the wrist.

For an accessible laundry area, provide storage for supplies within high forward or side reach ranges and all working surfaces at a comfortable seated work height of 29 in. with knee clearance below.

APARTMENT HOUSE LAUNDRIES

In apartment houses, locate laundry rooms in the basement or on the ground floor of the building near necessary mechanical equipment, piping, and ventilation.

Locate laundry rooms on grade, to provide surfaces to absorb vibrations from operation and to not disturb the apartment dwellers.

Provide convenient access from dwelling units to laundry room. Incorporate into the laundry room design folding tables and vending machines for soap, bleach, and other laundry powders.

Provide the ability for visual inspection of the laundry room for the security of the users. Also, laundry rooms in large apartment buildings are public areas where apartment dwellers socialize and meet each other, so provide area to accommodate this necessary function.

Robin Andrew Roberts, AIA; Washington, D.C.
Arthur J. Pettorino, AIA; Hicksville, New York
R. E. Powe, Jr., AIA; Hugh N. Jacobsen, FAIA; Washington, D.C.

NOTES

Commercial kitchens usually are defined as those providing food to be consumed away from home. Typical of these are kitchens within restaurants, hotels and motels, cafeterias, snack bars and coffee shops, schools and colleges, office buildings, hospitals, and other institutions. The size, type, quantity, and layout of equipment in the kitchen and the related service areas are a direct function of the menu, amount of patronage, and the time in which the items are to be served.

The schematic drawings shown here do not attempt to present kitchen design solutions, but rather to familiarize the reader with typical characteristics of commercial kitchen design.

RECEIVING
DRY STORAGE
REFRIGERATED AND FROZEN STORAGE
PREPREPARATION
PREPARATION
WARE WASHING
POT WASHING
FINISH AND HOLDING PLATING
SERVING AND DINING

FUNCTIONAL FLOW DIAGRAM

NOTES

Workers and materials should travel minimum distances. They should proceed in a logical sequence with minimum crisscrossing and backtracking. Delay in processing and serving should be reduced to a minimum. Garbage and trash disposal facilities are required for all functions.

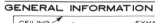

GENERAL INFORMATION

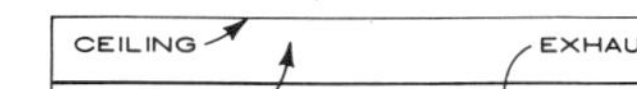
CEILING
EXHAUST VENTILATOR
CLOSURE PANEL

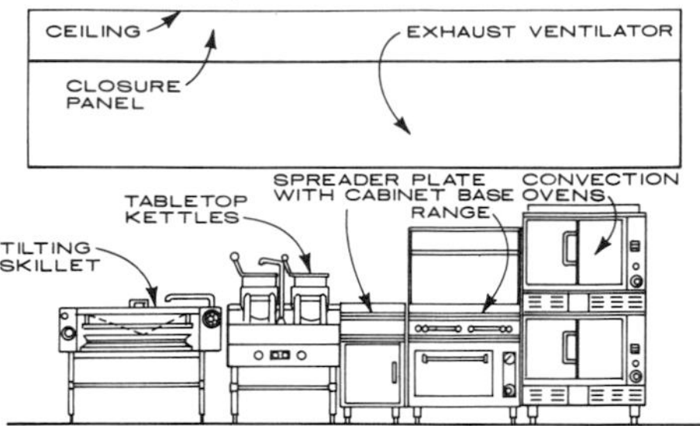
TILTING SKILLET
TABLETOP KETTLES
SPREADER PLATE WITH CABINET BASE
RANGE
CONVECTION OVENS

HOT FOOD PREPARATION AREA-ELEVATION

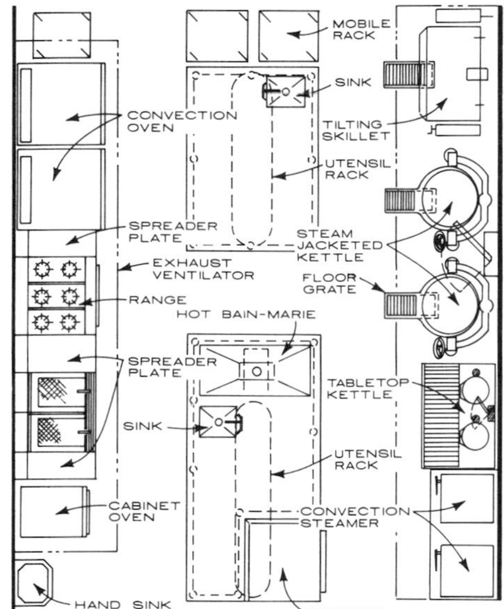
MOBILE RACK
SINK
CONVECTION OVEN
TILTING SKILLET
UTENSIL RACK
SPREADER PLATE
STEAM JACKETED KETTLE
EXHAUST VENTILATOR
FLOOR GRATE
RANGE
HOT BAIN-MARIE
SPREADER PLATE
TABLETOP KETTLE
SINK
UTENSIL RACK
CABINET OVEN
CONVECTION STEAMER
HAND SINK
FREEZER

HOT FOOD PREPARATION AREA-CAFETERIA/BANQUET

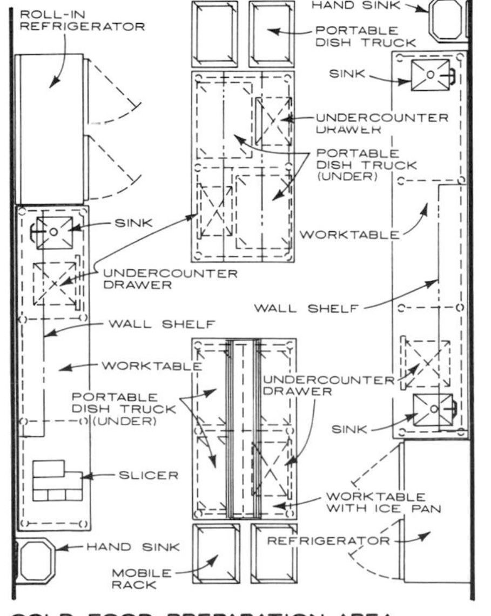
ROLL-IN REFRIGERATOR
HAND SINK
PORTABLE DISH TRUCK
SINK
UNDERCOUNTER DRAWER
PORTABLE DISH TRUCK (UNDER)
WORKTABLE
SINK
UNDERCOUNTER DRAWER
WALL SHELF
WALL SHELF
WORKTABLE
UNDERCOUNTER DRAWER
PORTABLE DISH TRUCK (UNDER)
SINK
SLICER
WORKTABLE WITH ICE PAN
HAND SINK
REFRIGERATOR
MOBILE RACK

COLD FOOD PREPARATION AREA-CAFETERIA/BANQUET

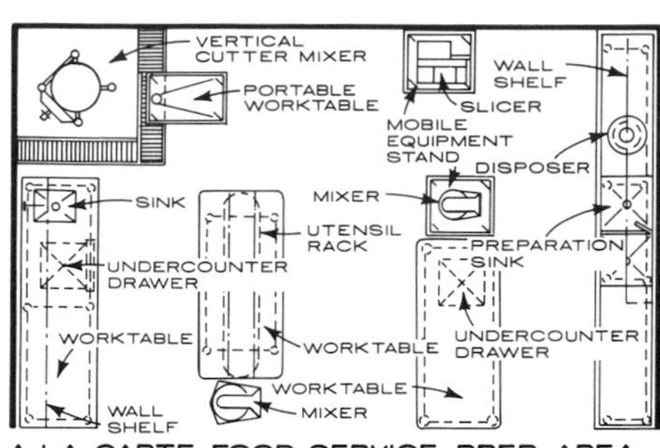
VERTICAL CUTTER MIXER
PORTABLE WORKTABLE
WALL SHELF
SLICER
MOBILE EQUIPMENT STAND
DISPOSER
SINK
MIXER
UTENSIL RACK
PREPARATION SINK
UNDERCOUNTER DRAWER
WORKTABLE
WORKTABLE
UNDERCOUNTER DRAWER
WORKTABLE
WALL SHELF
MIXER

A LA CARTE FOOD SERVICE PREP. AREA

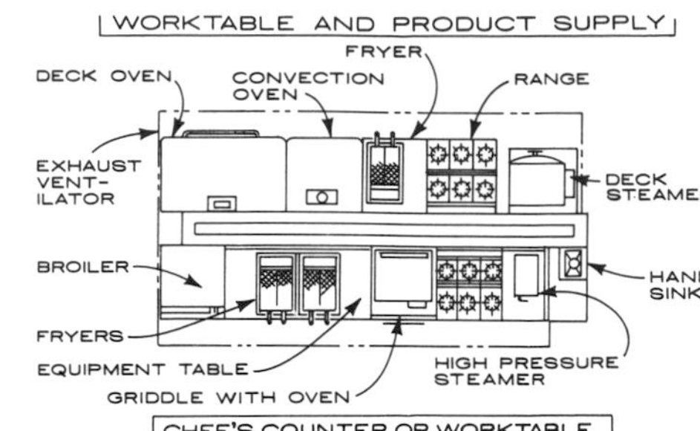
WORKTABLE AND PRODUCT SUPPLY
FRYER
DECK OVEN
CONVECTION OVEN
RANGE
EXHAUST VENTILATOR
DECK STEAMER
BROILER
HAND SINK
FRYERS
EQUIPMENT TABLE
HIGH PRESSURE STEAMER
GRIDDLE WITH OVEN
CHEF'S COUNTER OR WORKTABLE

HOT FOOD PREP. AREA–ISLAND TYPE

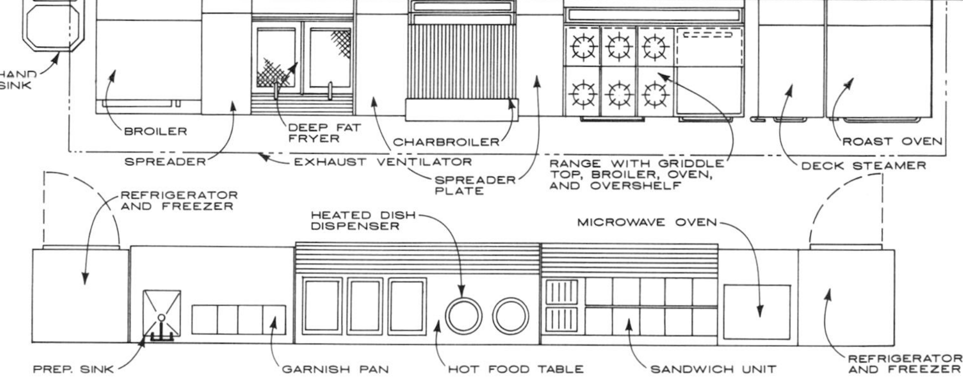
HAND SINK
BROILER
DEEP FAT FRYER
CHARBROILER
ROAST OVEN
SPREADER
EXHAUST VENTILATOR
SPREADER PLATE
RANGE WITH GRIDDLE TOP, BROILER, OVEN, AND OVERSHELF
DECK STEAMER
REFRIGERATOR AND FREEZER
HEATED DISH DISPENSER
MICROWAVE OVEN
PREP. SINK
GARNISH PAN
HOT FOOD TABLE
SANDWICH UNIT
REFRIGERATOR AND FREEZER

A LA CARTE FOOD SERVICE AREA

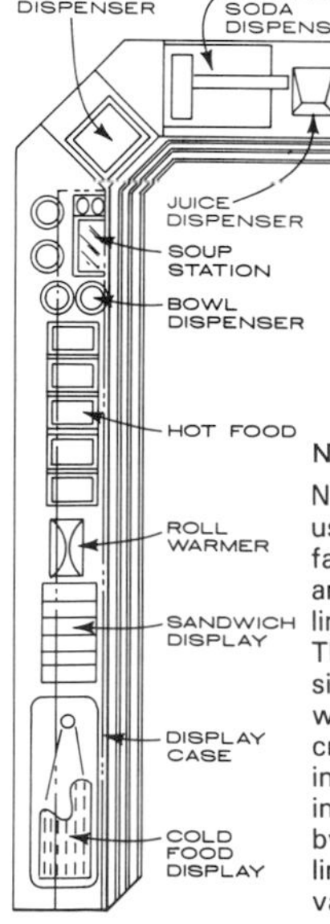
GLASS DISPENSER
ICE AND SODA DISPENSER
MILK DISPENSER
ICE CREAM AND SPOONS
JUICE DISPENSER
ICED TEA DISPENSER
CUP DISPENSER
COFFEE
SOUP STATION
BOWL DISPENSER
HOT FOOD
ROLL WARMER
SANDWICH DISPLAY
DISPLAY CASE
COLD FOOD DISPLAY

CAFETERIA

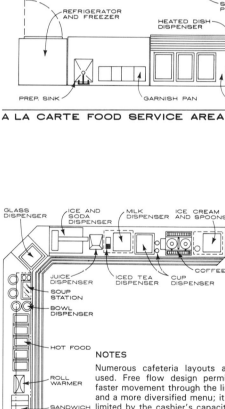

NOTES

Numerous cafeteria layouts are used. Free flow design permits faster movement through the line and a more diversified menu; it is limited by the cashier's capacity. The hollow square design, consisting of separate feeding lines with a central service facility, increases capacity without increasing staff. The straight line is used in low-volume operations limited by the cashier's capacity. Service line length is related directly to the variety of the menu.

RECOMMENDED STORAGE TEMPERATURES

1. DRY FOOD STORAGE: 65°F (15°C). Stored 4 in. off floor, 2 in. from wall.
2. COMMON STORAGE: 50°F to 60°F (10°C to 15°C).
3. FREEZER STORAGE: −10°F (−23°C).
4. REFRIGERATED STORAGE: 31°F to 40°F (−0.5°C to 4°C).

RECOMMENDED WARE WASHING TEMPERATURES

1. PRERINSE: 120°F to 140°F (49°C–60°C).
2. WASH: 140°F (60°C).
3. RINSE: 180°F (82°C) for 10 seconds. 170°F (77°C) for 30 seconds or longer.

(If sanitizing agent is used, 140°F (60°C) is acceptable for all ware washing functions.)

NOTE: Check local health codes for requirements.

VENTILATORS

Ventilators generally are required over all types of major cooking equipment. The exhaust system should be either a canopy type or high-speed backshelf exhaust. Grease should be removed through filters or internal centrifugal extraction. Fire extinguishing equipment must be installed in compliance with standard codes established by the National Fire Protection Association and local codes. The most commonly used systems are carbon dioxide and dry chemical extinguishing systems in conjunction with portable fire extinguishers. Water fog systems are being introduced and accepted in many areas.

Ventilator installations should cover completely the equipment being ventilated, with minimum overhangs on all sides regulated by national and local codes. Maximum floor to canopy height should be approximately 7 ft and the canopy from bottom to top should be 2 ft or more.

Cini-Grissom Associates, Inc.; Food Service Consultants; Washington, D.C.

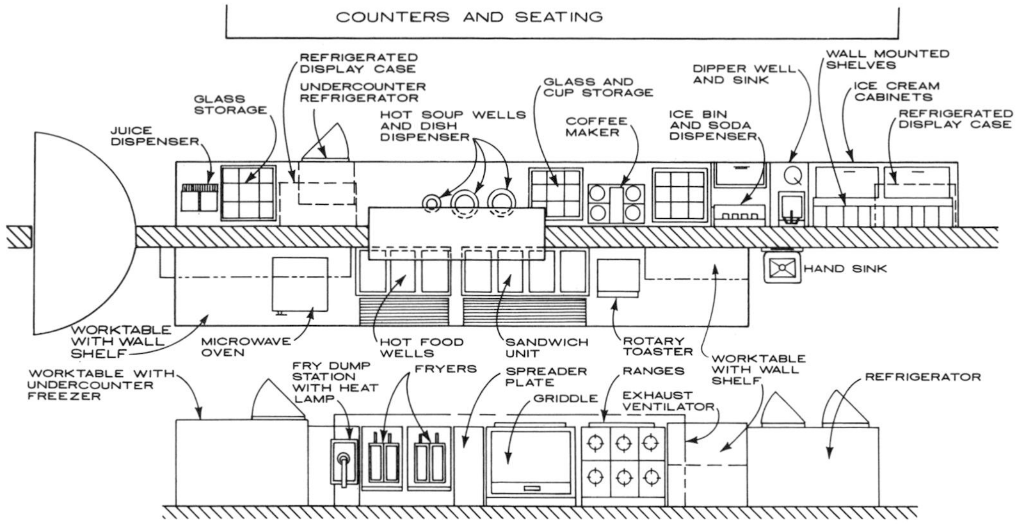

COUNTERS AND SEATING

REFRIGERATED DISPLAY CASE
UNDERCOUNTER REFRIGERATOR
GLASS STORAGE
JUICE DISPENSER
HOT SOUP WELLS AND DISH DISPENSER
GLASS AND CUP STORAGE
COFFEE MAKER
ICE BIN AND SODA DISPENSER
DIPPER WELL AND SINK
WALL MOUNTED SHELVES
ICE CREAM CABINETS
REFRIGERATED DISPLAY CASE
HAND SINK
WORKTABLE WITH WALL SHELF
MICROWAVE OVEN
HOT FOOD WELLS
SANDWICH UNIT
ROTARY TOASTER
WORKTABLE WITH WALL SHELF
WORKTABLE WITH UNDERCOUNTER FREEZER
FRY DUMP STATION WITH HEAT LAMP
FRYERS
SPREADER PLATE
GRIDDLE
RANGES
EXHAUST VENTILATOR
REFRIGERATOR

COFFEE SHOP KITCHEN AND SERVICE PANTRY

MOBILE HOT FOOD HOLDING UNIT
REACH-IN REFRIGERATOR
MOBILE RACK DISPENSERS
HOT FOOD SERVERS
MOBILE COVER DISPENSER
ICE CREAM DISPENSER
MILK DISPENSER
COFFEE URN
TRAYS
MOBILE DISH DISPENSER
COLD FOOD SERVER
TRAY CONVEYOR
TRAY STARTER STATION
HOT FOOD SERVERS
MOBILE DISH DISPENSERS
COLD FOOD SERVERS
COFFEE DISPENSER
BEVERAGE STAND
BEVERAGE SETUP
MOBILE RACK DISPENSERS
MOBILE HOT FOOD HOLDING UNIT
HAND SINK
ROLL-IN REFRIGERATORS

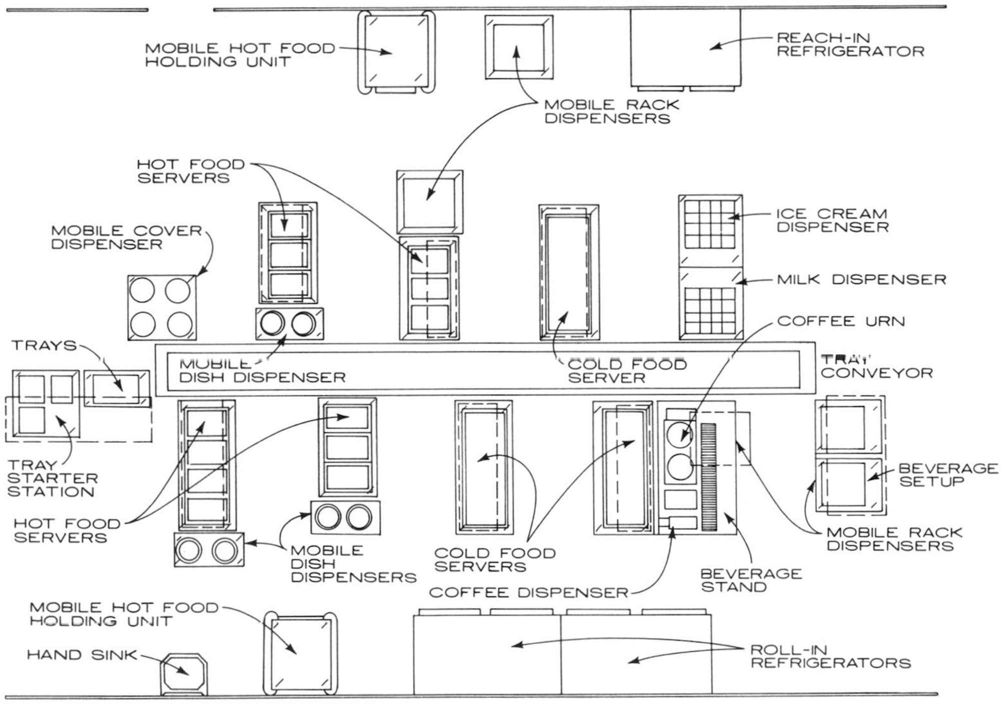

HOSPITAL PATIENT TRAY ASSEMBLY SYSTEM

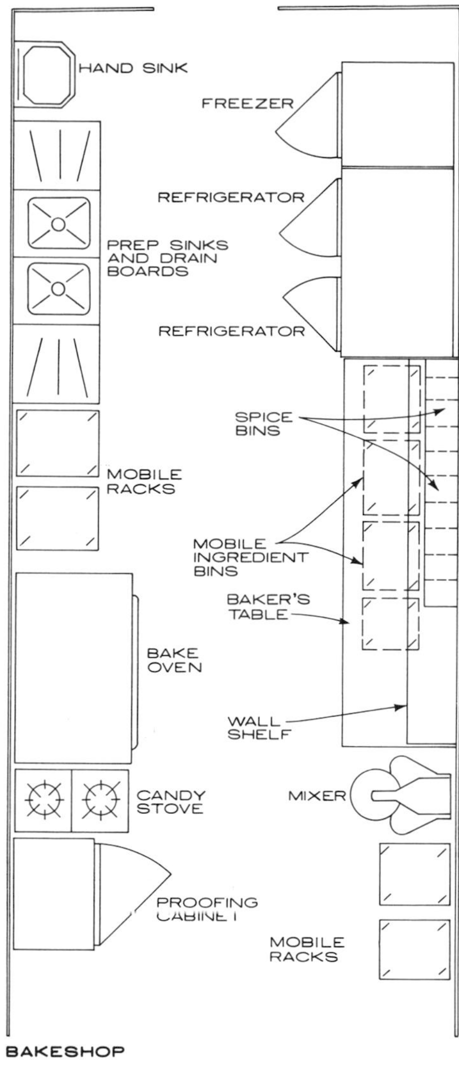
HAND SINK
FREEZER
REFRIGERATOR
PREP SINKS AND DRAIN BOARDS
REFRIGERATOR
SPICE BINS
MOBILE RACKS
MOBILE INGREDIENT BINS
BAKER'S TABLE
BAKE OVEN
WALL SHELF
CANDY STOVE
MIXER
PROOFING CABINET
MOBILE RACKS

BAKESHOP

NOTE

This tray assembly system is designed for trays made up in advance of service. It is used most commonly in hospitals, extended care facilities, and hospices. In some cafeteria situations, this design may be modified for reduced customer food handling. Because of the modular design, the system may accommodate a wide variety of menu items.

INSTITUTIONAL

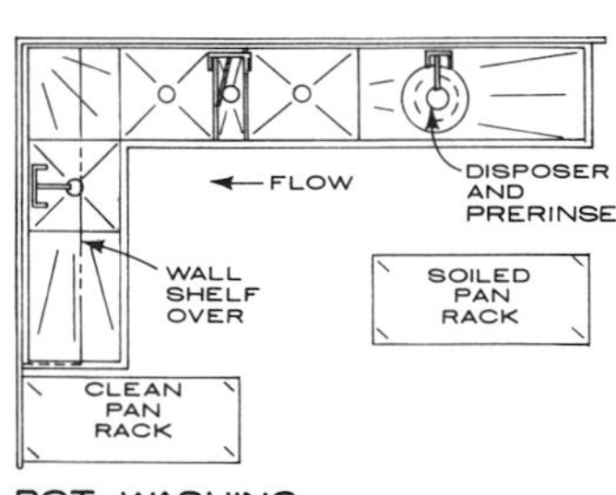
FLOW
DISPOSER AND PRERINSE
WALL SHELF OVER
SOILED PAN RACK
CLEAN PAN RACK

POT WASHING

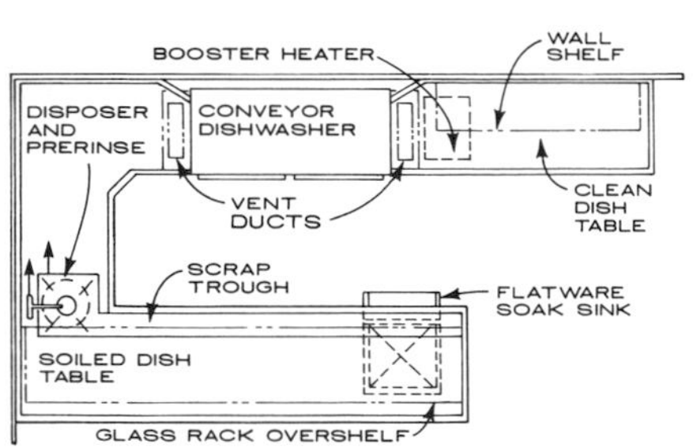
BOOSTER HEATER
WALL SHELF
DISPOSER AND PRERINSE
CONVEYOR DISHWASHER
VENT DUCTS
CLEAN DISH TABLE
SCRAP TROUGH
FLATWARE SOAK SINK
SOILED DISH TABLE
GLASS RACK OVERSHELF

U-SHAPED CONVEYOR TYPE

NOTE

The conveyor type dish machine is less costly than a circular system and has a larger volume capacity than a single compartment machine. Many table configurations are available.

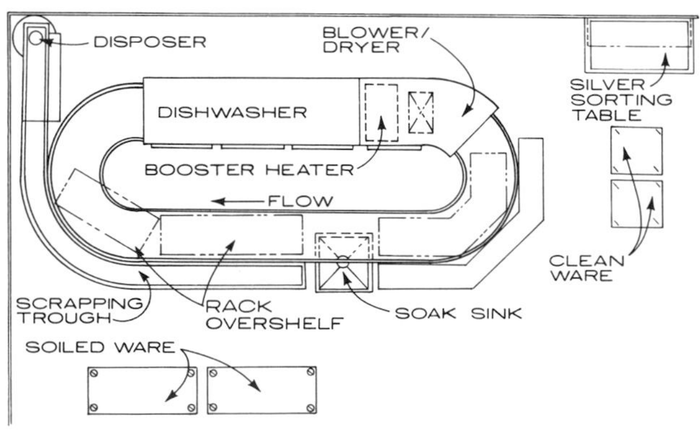
DISPOSER
BLOWER/ DRYER
DISHWASHER
SILVER SORTING TABLE
BOOSTER HEATER
FLOW
CLEAN WARE
SCRAPPING TROUGH
RACK OVERSHELF
SOAK SINK
SOILED WARE

CIRCULAR TYPE

NOTE

The circular system is overall less labor intensive than other designs. It is most useful in a large volume operation.

WARE WASHING SYSTEMS

Cini-Grissom Associates, Inc.; Food Service Consultants; Washington, D.C.

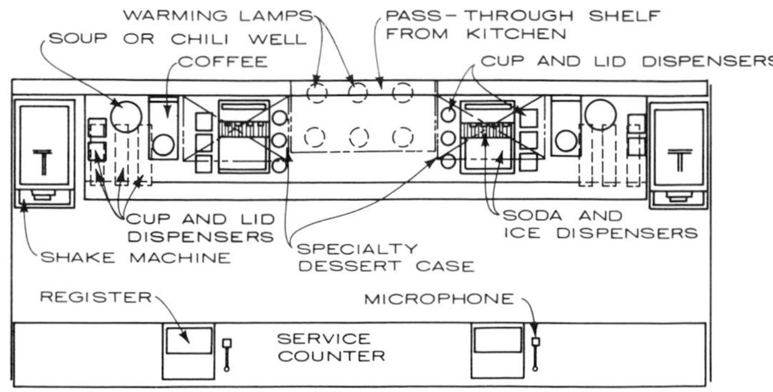
WARMING LAMPS
SOUP OR CHILI WELL
COFFEE
PASS-THROUGH SHELF FROM KITCHEN
CUP AND LID DISPENSERS
T
T
CUP AND LID DISPENSERS
SHAKE MACHINE
SPECIALTY DESSERT CASE
SODA AND ICE DISPENSERS
REGISTER
MICROPHONE
SERVICE COUNTER

BEVERAGE AND SERVICE COUNTER

NOTE

Design of the service counter depends on the number of stations required for efficient service and the amount of space available.

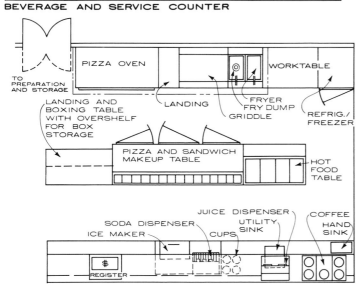

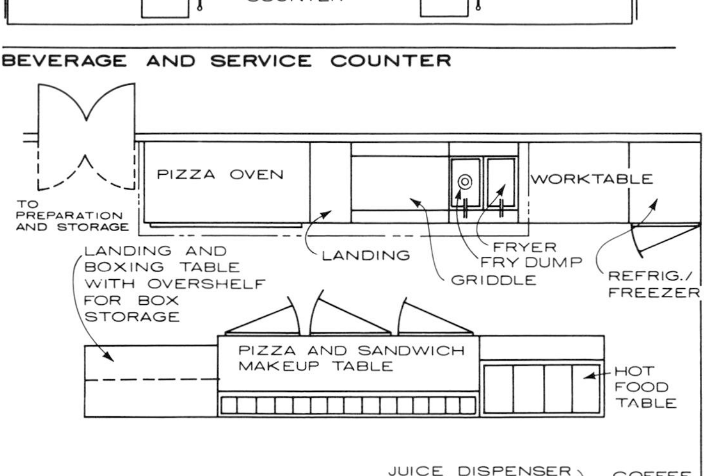
TO PREPARATION AND STORAGE
PIZZA OVEN
WORKTABLE
LANDING AND BOXING TABLE WITH OVERSHELF FOR BOX STORAGE
LANDING
FRYER
FRY DUMP
GRIDDLE
REFRIG./ FREEZER
PIZZA AND SANDWICH MAKEUP TABLE
HOT FOOD TABLE
JUICE DISPENSER
SODA DISPENSER
UTILITY SINK
COFFEE
HAND SINK
ICE MAKER
CUPS
$
REGISTER

PIZZA AND SANDWICH SHOP

NOTE

This type of operation has many variables. Sandwiches and hot entrees may or may not be offered. The equipment requirements are related directly to the menu, volume, and style of service.

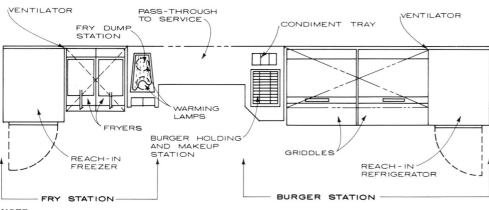

PASS-THROUGH WARMER
CHICKEN FRYER
FREEZER
DRY STORAGE
GRILLE
SLICER
SCALE
AU JUS
FRY STATION
TOASTER
COFFEE
SHAKES
ROAST BEEF
SALAD
CASHIER
REFRIGERATOR
TRAY SLIDE
DRINKS
PIE AND DESSERT DISPENSER
BURGERS
CHICKEN
CONDIMENTS
TRAYS

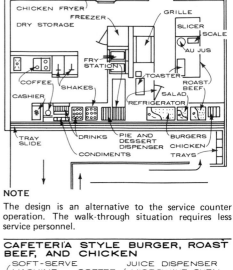

NOTE

The design is an alternative to the service counter operation. The walk-through situation requires less service personnel.

CAFETERIA STYLE BURGER, ROAST BEEF, AND CHICKEN

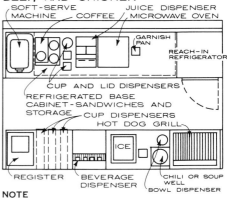

SOFT-SERVE MACHINE
COFFEE
JUICE DISPENSER
MICROWAVE OVEN
GARNISH PAN
REACH-IN REFRIGERATOR
CUP AND LID DISPENSERS
REFRIGERATED BASE CABINET-SANDWICHES AND STORAGE
CUP DISPENSERS
HOT DOG GRILL
ICE
REGISTER
BEVERAGE DISPENSER
CHILI OR SOUP WELL
BOWL DISPENSER

NOTE

Snack bars are found most commonly in stadiums, sports centers, and transportation terminals. They serve a limited menu with prepackaged foods. Most items will be prepared in a commissary situation.

SNACK BAR

VENTILATOR
PASS-THROUGH TO SERVICE
FRY DUMP STATION
CONDIMENT TRAY
VENTILATOR
WARMING LAMPS
FRYERS
BURGER HOLDING AND MAKEUP STATION
GRIDDLES
REACH-IN FREEZER
REACH-IN REFRIGERATOR
FRY STATION
BURGER STATION

NOTE

The area will vary depending on the menu and method of preparation. Alternate equipment would include a charbroiler, conveyor charbroiler, and more fry space for expanded fried menu items.

HAMBURGER AND FRENCH FRY PREPARATION AREA

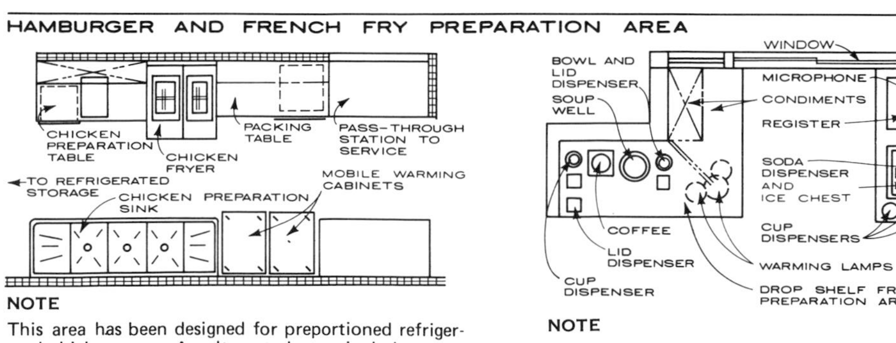
CHICKEN PREPARATION TABLE
PACKING TABLE
PASS-THROUGH STATION TO SERVICE
CHICKEN FRYER
TO REFRIGERATED STORAGE
MOBILE WARMING CABINETS
CHICKEN PREPARATION SINK
WINDOW
BOWL AND LID DISPENSER
SOUP WELL
MICROPHONE
CONDIMENTS
REGISTER
SODA DISPENSER AND ICE CHEST
COFFEE
LID DISPENSER
CUP DISPENSERS
CUP DISPENSER
WARMING LAMPS
DROP SHELF FROM PREPARATION AREA

NOTE

This area has been designed for preportioned refrigerated chicken parts. An alternate layout includes ovens for prebreaded, frozen portions.

CHICKEN PREPARATION

NOTE

The window serves the same menu as the inside operation. Service may be pass-window or bank-drawer type.

DRIVE-UP WINDOW

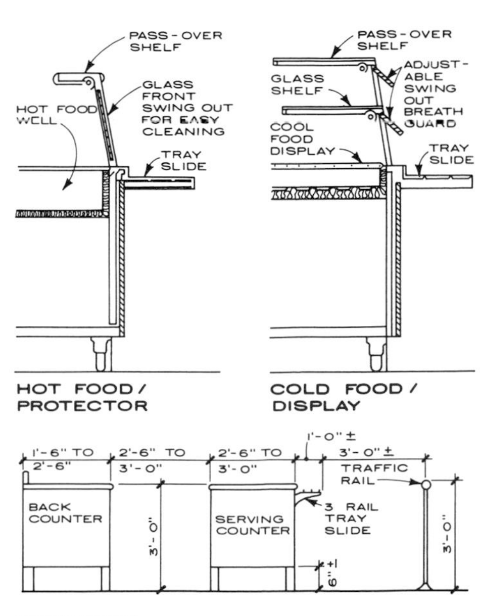
PASS-OVER SHELF
GLASS FRONT SWING OUT FOR EASY CLEANING
HOT FOOD WELL
TRAY SLIDE
PASS-OVER SHELF
GLASS SHELF
ADJUSTABLE SWING OUT BREATH GUARD
COOL FOOD DISPLAY
TRAY SLIDE
1'-6" TO 2'-6"
2'-6" TO 3'-0"
2'-6" TO 3'-0"
1'-0" ±
3'-0" ±
TRAFFIC RAIL
BACK COUNTER
SERVING COUNTER
3 RAIL TRAY SLIDE
3'-0"
6"±
3'-0"

HOT FOOD / PROTECTOR

COLD FOOD / DISPLAY

CAFETERIA COUNTERS

Cini-Grissom Associates, Inc.; Food Service Consultants; Washington, D.C.

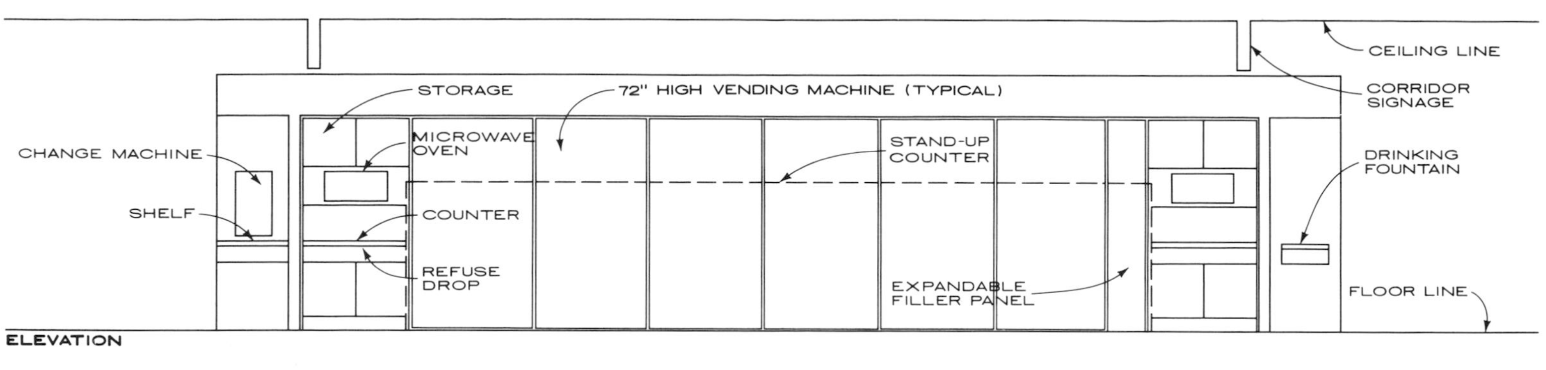
STORAGE
72" HIGH VENDING MACHINE (TYPICAL)
CEILING LINE
CORRIDOR SIGNAGE
CHANGE MACHINE
MICROWAVE OVEN
STAND-UP COUNTER
DRINKING FOUNTAIN
SHELF
COUNTER
REFUSE DROP
EXPANDABLE FILLER PANEL
FLOOR LINE
ELEVATION

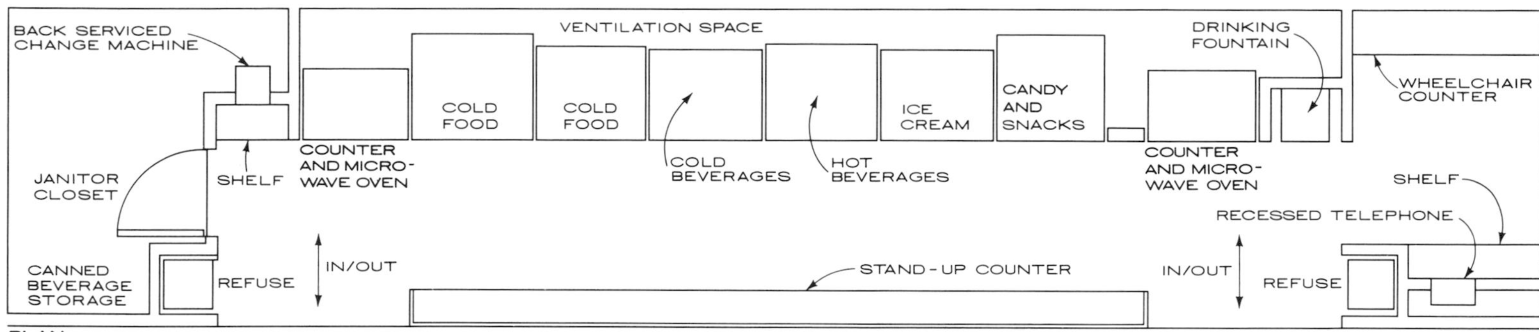
BACK SERVICED CHANGE MACHINE
VENTILATION SPACE
DRINKING FOUNTAIN
COLD FOOD
COLD FOOD
ICE CREAM
CANDY AND SNACKS
WHEELCHAIR COUNTER
JANITOR CLOSET
SHELF
COUNTER AND MICRO-WAVE OVEN
COLD BEVERAGES
HOT BEVERAGES
COUNTER AND MICRO-WAVE OVEN
SHELF
RECESSED TELEPHONE
CANNED BEVERAGE STORAGE
REFUSE
IN/OUT
STAND-UP COUNTER
IN/OUT
REFUSE
PLAN

TYPICAL CORPORATE OR INSTITUTIONAL VENDING AREA

NOTE

Refrigerated vending machines and microwave ovens require a rear wall clearance of up to 8 in. to permit cooling.

No hot water required. Some beverage dispensing units require a cold water line with a shut-off valve. Overflow waste disposes into internal bucket or tray.

A separate, 115 volt electrical circuit for each machine is suggested. Delivery amperages range from approximately 2 to 20 amps per machine.

Service access generally is from the front; some cigarette units require top access.

Some machines require patron to use both hands, make extended arm reach, or use more than minimal force to access some items or controls, all of which can make use by handicapped persons difficult. Consult local codes.

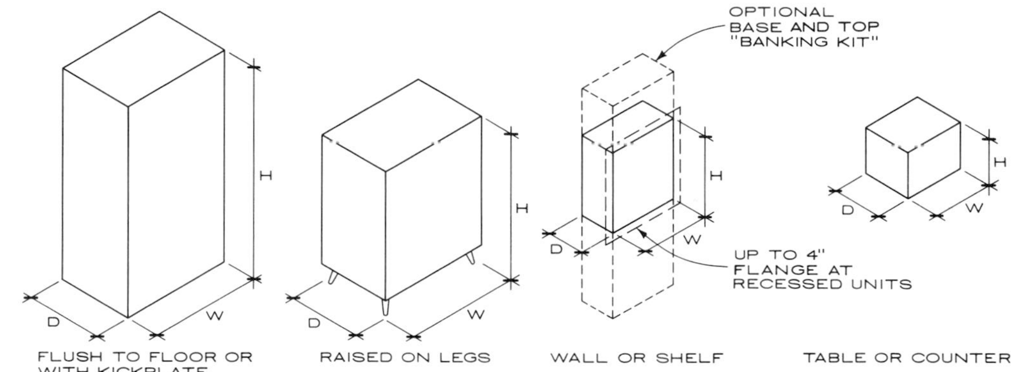
OPTIONAL BASE AND TOP "BANKING KIT"
H
D
W
UP TO 4" FLANGE AT RECESSED UNITS
FLUSH TO FLOOR OR WITH KICKPLATE
RAISED ON LEGS
WALL OR SHELF
TABLE OR COUNTER
F-FLOOR TYPE
W-WALL, SHELF, TABLE OR COUNTER TYPE

VENDING MACHINE TYPES

VENDING MACHINE DATA

		TYPICAL				APPROXIMATE RANGE							
						MINIMUM				MAXIMUM			
FOOD VENDING UNITS	TYPE	H (IN.)	W (IN.)	D (IN.)	LB.*	H (IN.)	W (IN.)	D (IN.)	LB.*	H (IN.)	W (IN.)	D (IN.)	LB.*
Cold Beverages	F	72	38 1/2	24 1/2	510	55 3/8	28 3/4	22 5/8	460	79 1/2	45 3/4	29 5/8	790
	W	35	28 3/4	10 3/4	125	35	28 3/4	10 3/4	125				
Hot Beverages	F	72	38	31	560	72	24	27 1/2	340	72	38	33	585
Cold Foods	F	72	35 1/2	31 1/2	720	72	35 1/4	30 1/4	647	72	41	35 5/8	950
Candy, Pastry, and Snacks	F	72	33	35	640	72	28	31	406	72	39	35 1/2	760
	W	25	24 7/16	24 5/8	100	25	24 7/16	24 5/8	100				

		TYPICAL				APPROXIMATE RANGE							
						MINIMUM				MAXIMUM			
OTHER UNITS	TYPE	H (IN.)	W (IN.)	D (IN.)	LB.*	H (IN.)	W (IN.)	D (IN.)	LB.*	H (IN.)	W (IN.)	D (IN.)	LB.*
Change	F	51 9/16	27 7/8	19 1/4	275	56	22 1/2	11	145	78	40		
	W	31 5/8	12 1/16	15 1/8	140	23 3/4	14 3/4	18 1/2	175	38 5/8	12 1/16	18 1/2	200
Cigarettes	F	51	38	21 1/4	410	50 1/2	32 1/2	21 1/4	300	72	36	25 1/4	485
Microwave oven	W	12 3/4	20 1/2	14 1/2	43					14 7/8	20 1/2	21	78
Microwave Oven with "banking kit"	F	72	25	31	204								
Postage Stamps	F	71	37 5/8										
	W	21 1/2	31 1/2										
Tickets	F	78	40										
	W												

*Net weight in pounds

William Xavier Fabis, Architect; San Francisco, California

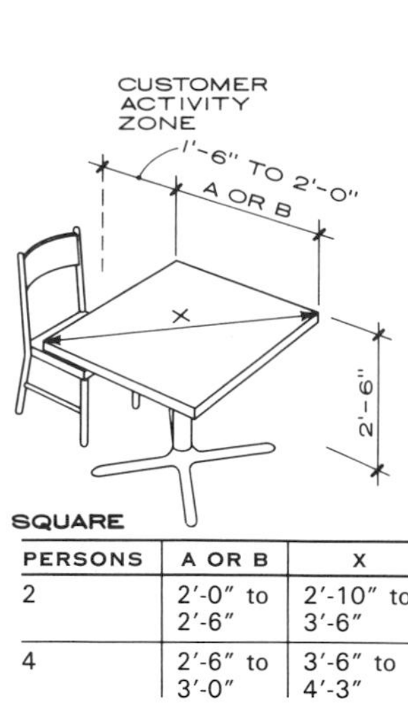
CUSTOMER ACTIVITY ZONE
1'-6" TO 2'-0"
A OR B
X
2'-6"

SQUARE

PERSONS	A OR B	X
2	2'-0" to 2'-6"	2'-10" to 3'-6"
4	2'-6" to 3'-0"	3'-6" to 4'-3"

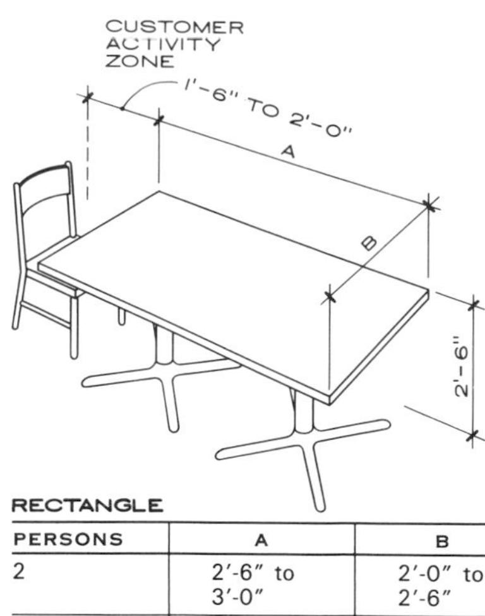
CUSTOMER ACTIVITY ZONE
1'-6" TO 2'-0"
A
B
2'-6"

RECTANGLE

PERSONS	A	B
2	2'-6" to 3'-0"	2'-0" to 2'-6"
2 (on one side)	3'-4" to 4'-0"	
6	5'-10" to 6'-0"	2'-6" to 3'-0"
8	6'-10" to 7'-0"	

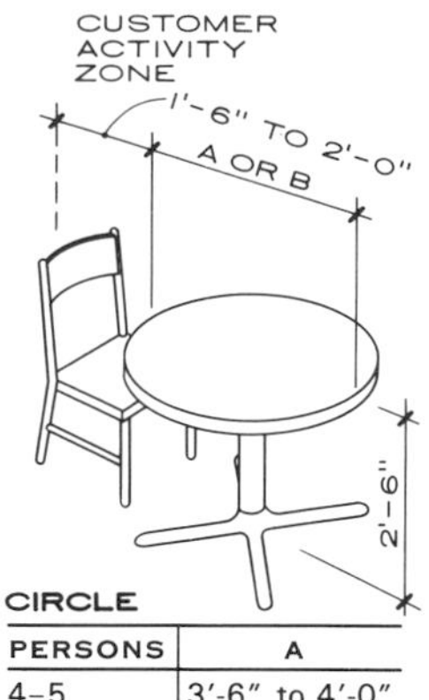
CUSTOMER ACTIVITY ZONE
1'-6" TO 2'-0"
A OR B
2'-6"

CIRCLE

PERSONS	A
4–5	3'-6" to 4'-0"
6–7	4'-6" to 5'-0"
7–8	5'-6" to 6'-4"
8–10	6'-0" to 7'-2"

TABLE

NOTES

Round tables are usually recommended only for seating 5 persons or more.

Dimension "A" depends on the perimeter (1'-10" to 2'-0" per person) necessary to seat required number. For cocktails, 1'-6" is sufficient.

Tables wider than 2 ft-6 in. will seat one at each end.

Minimum sizes are satisfactory for drink service; larger sizes for food. Tables with widespread bases are more practical than four-legged tables.

Tables and arrangements are affected by the type of operations and the style of service. The use of flaming trays, busing carts, high chairs for children, and handicapped access must be considered.

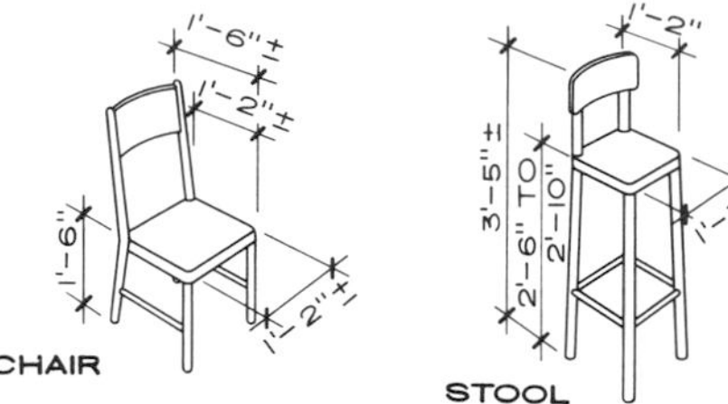
1'-6"±
1'-2"±
1'-6"
1'-2"±
CHAIR
1'-2"
3'-5"±
2'-6" TO 2'-10"
1'-3"
STOOL

AVERAGE CAPACITIES PER PERSON

TYPE OF ROOM	SQUARE FEET
Banquet	10-12
Cafeteria	12-15
Tearoom	10-14
Lunchroom/coffee shop	12-16
Dining room/restaurant	13-16
Specialty/formal dining	17-22

NOTE

Figures are general and represent minimum average dimensions. No maximum exists. Seating allowances and requirements may vary to suit individual operations.

A Seat back to seat back: 5'-0" to 6'-2"
B One person per side: 2'-0" to 2'-6"
Two persons per side: 3'-6" to 4'-6"
Recommended maximum for serving and cleaning: 4'-0"
C 3'-0" to 4'-0"
D 2'-6"
E 1'-6"
F 0 to 4"
G ± 1'-6"
H 2'-0" to 2'-6"

NOTE

Local regulations determine actual booth sizes. Tables are often 2 in. shorter than seats and may have rounded ends. Circular booths have overall diameter of 6'-4"+.

BOOTHS

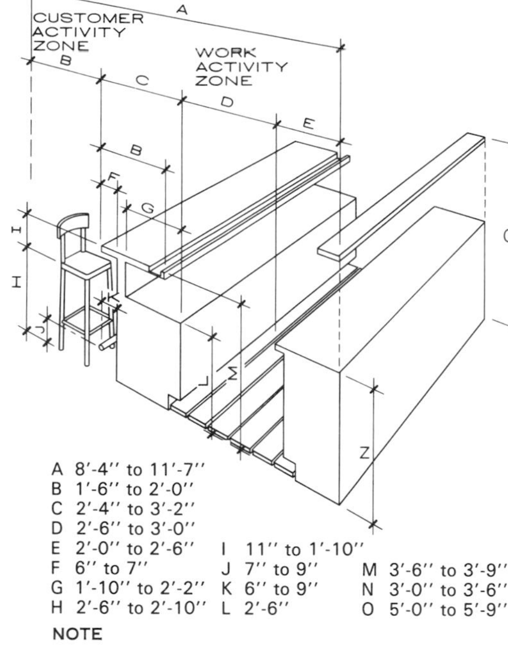
CUSTOMER ACTIVITY ZONE
WORK ACTIVITY ZONE
A
B
C
D
E
F
G
H
I
J
K
L
M
N
O

A 8'-4" to 11'-7"
B 1'-6" to 2'-0"
C 2'-4" to 3'-2"
D 2'-6" to 3'-0"
E 2'-0" to 2'-6"
F 6" to 7"
G 1'-10" to 2'-2"
H 2'-6" to 2'-10"
I 11" to 1'-10"
J 7" to 9"
K 6" to 9"
L 2'-6"
M 3'-6" to 3'-9"
N 3'-0" to 3'-6"
O 5'-0" to 5'-9"

NOTE

Ratio of counter stools to servers is 10:1.

GENERAL DESIGN CRITERIA

Service aisles: 30-42 in.

1. Square seating, 66 in. minimum between tables, 30 in. aisle plus two chairs back to back.
2. Diagonal seating, 36 in. minimum between corners of tables.
3. Wall seating, 30 in. minimum between wall and seat back.
4. Minimum of 30 in. for bus carts and flaming service carts.

Customer aisles:

1. Refer to local codes for restrictions on requirements.
2. Wheelchair requirements, 35-44 in. aisle.
3. Wall seating, 30 in. minimum between walls and table.

Tables:

1. Average 29 in. high.
2. Allow space around doors and food service areas.

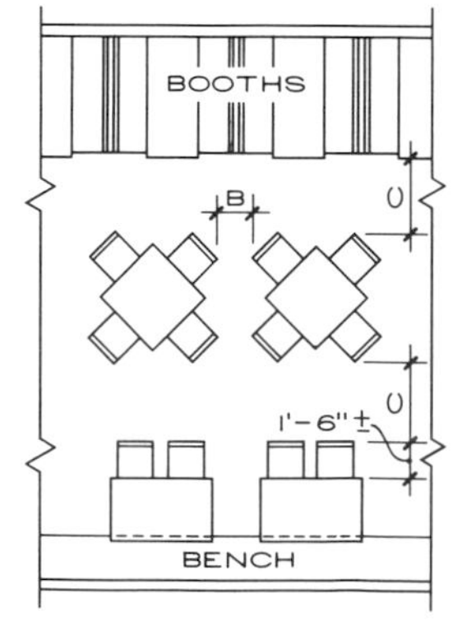
BOOTHS
B
C
1'-6"±
C
BENCH

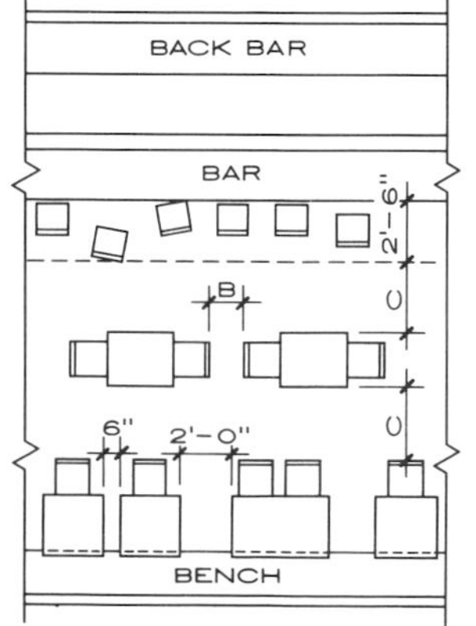
BACK BAR
BAR
2'-6"
B
C
6"
2'-0"
C
BENCH

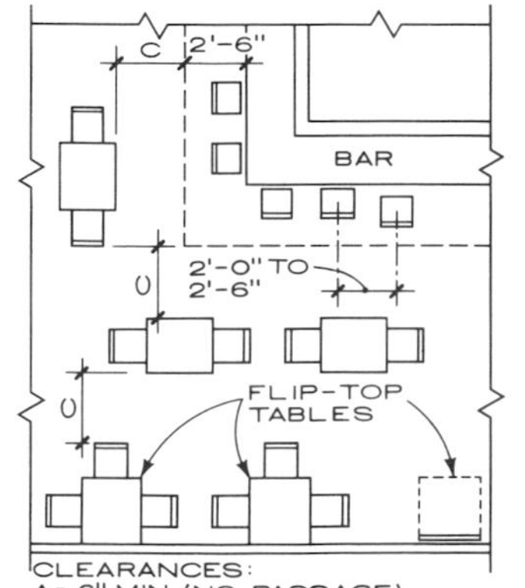
C
2'-6"
BAR
2'-0" TO 2'-6"
C
FLIP-TOP TABLES
C
CLEARANCES:
A= 6" MIN. (NO PASSAGE)
B= 1'-6" LIMITED PASSAGE
C= 2'-6" TO 3'-0" SERVICE AISLE

NOTE

All dimensions are minimum clearances. Seating layouts show general configurations and are not intended to depict any specific type of operation. Tables may be converted from square to round to enlarge seating capacity. Booth seating makes effective use of corner space.

TYPICAL SEATING ARRANGEMENTS

Richard J. Vitullo; Washington Grove, Maryland
Cini-Grissom Associates, Inc.; Food Service Consultants; Washington, D.C.

GENERAL

Conference rooms should be located for proximity to user groups within a building and for accessibility to outside guests. Since a conference room typically serves to communicate a firm's "image" to others, finishes are usually selected from higher quality materials to suggest a prominent and visible location. When a conference room functions as a multiuser or multigroup space, the position of access doors is altered and acoustical folding partitions or movable walls may be used. The designer should note the additional requirements imposed by building codes for assembly occupancy for larger rooms.

FINISHES

Carpeted floors, acoustical wall panels, or fabric wall coverings and acoustic ceilings should be used. Avoid using "attention-getting" patterns and colors on walls which may decrease focal emphasis of tables, seating, and speaker or projection area. All finishes should be carefully examined for flame spread and smoke-generated ratings.

LIGHTING

Parabolic lens fluorescent fixtures provide good general lighting with less glare. Directional fixtures such as track lighting may be used for presentation areas. Use dimming switches.

MECHANICAL

Provide a minimum of eight air changes per hour plus a minimum of 10 cu ft/min of outside air per person for odor-free air and good ventilation. Provide an exhaust system to be manually controlled from the room. Careful attention should be given to sound attenuation of diffusers.

TELECONFERENCING

The space and furniture requirements for teleconferencing are different from the typical conference room. All aspects are geared toward video camera requirements. Typically, the conference is held between groups in separate locations linked by video satellite. The standard layout includes two ceiling-mounted video cameras to cover the participants and an optional direct downward-aimed document camera, a projection television monitor (front or rear projecting) for the remote participants, and a control console which interfaces the video cameras, telephone, and satellite linkage. The room arrangement is such that all participants may view and be viewed simultaneously. Mixing presentation media (projection, boards, flip charts, etc.) becomes more difficult in teleconferencing, while the requirements for acoustics and ventilation remain unchanged from the typical conference room. Lighting must be in accordance with the requirements of the video system used.

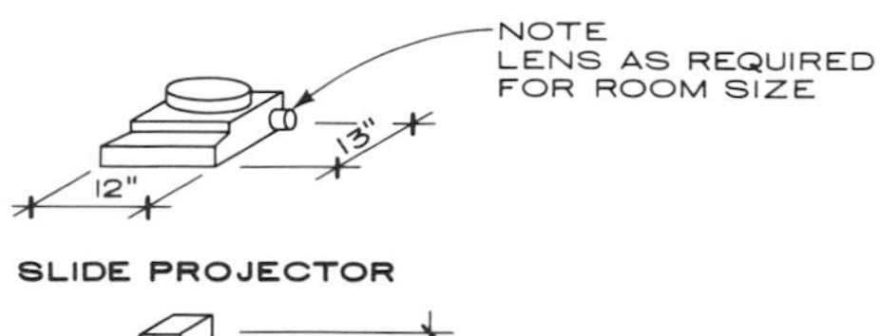

NOTE
LENS AS REQUIRED FOR ROOM SIZE
12"
13"

SLIDE PROJECTOR

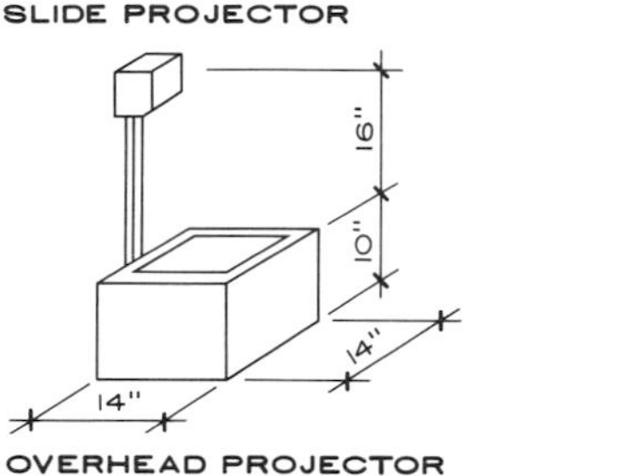

16"
10"
14"
14"

OVERHEAD PROJECTOR

PLASTIC LAMINATE OR WOOD SECTIONAL FOR LARGER SIZES
PEDESTAL TO MINIMIZE SEATING OBSTRUCTION

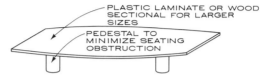

CONFERENCE TABLE
REFER TO FURNITURE SECTION FOR SIZE BASED ON SEATING

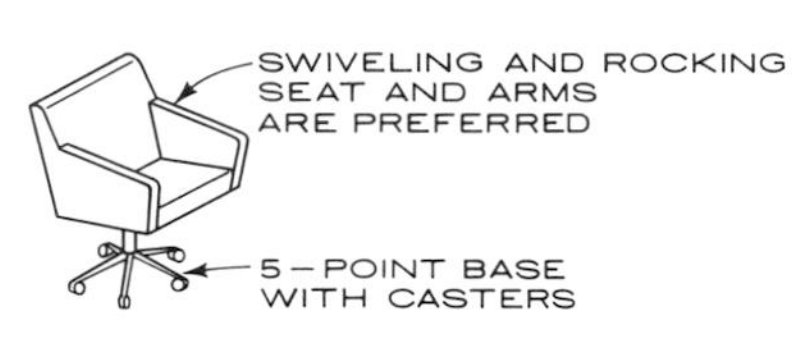

SWIVELING AND ROCKING SEAT AND ARMS ARE PREFERRED
5-POINT BASE WITH CASTERS

CHAIR

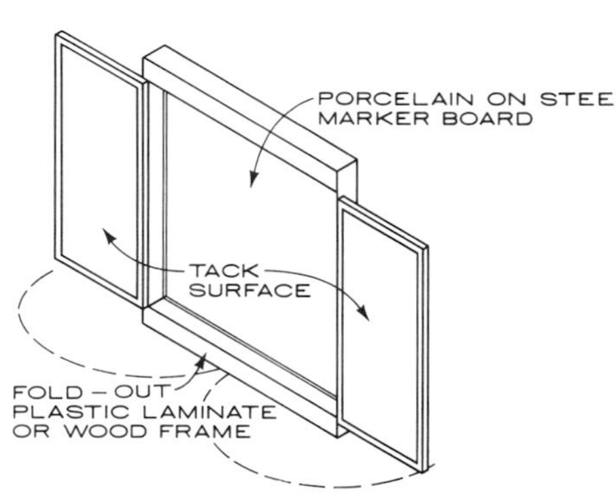

PORCELAIN ON STEEL MARKER BOARD
TACK SURFACE
FOLD-OUT PLASTIC LAMINATE OR WOOD FRAME

WALL-MOUNTED VISUAL CENTER

CONFERENCE ROOM FURNITURE AND EQUIPMENT

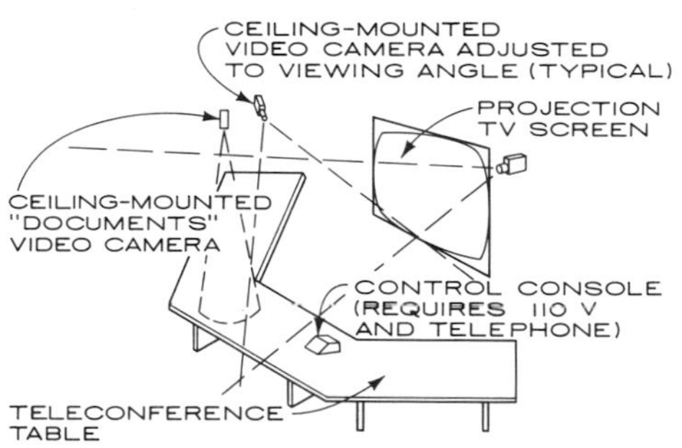

CEILING-MOUNTED VIDEO CAMERA ADJUSTED TO VIEWING ANGLE (TYPICAL)
PROJECTION TV SCREEN
CEILING-MOUNTED "DOCUMENTS" VIDEO CAMERA
CONTROL CONSOLE (REQUIRES 110 V AND TELEPHONE)
TELECONFERENCE TABLE

COMPONENTS OF A TYPICAL TELECONFERENCE ROOM

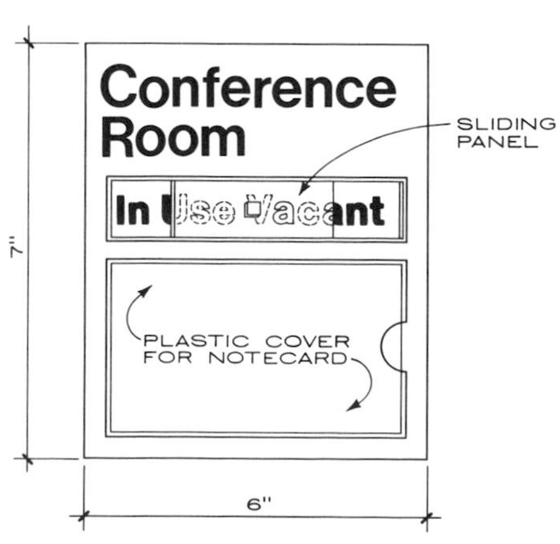

Conference Room
In Use Vacant
SLIDING PANEL
PLASTIC COVER FOR NOTECARD
7"
6"

GRAPHICS SILK SCREENED OR ROUTED INTO COLORED PLASTIC (TYPICAL)

CONFERENCE ROOM SIGN

WALLS STC 55 MIN.
TV
SINK BELOW
SLIDE PROJECTOR
STORAGE CABINET
COAT OR STORAGE CLOSET (TYPICAL)
20' CONFERENCE TABLE
OUTLINE OF TABLE FOR TELECONFERENCE
SIDE TABLE
WALL-MOUNTED VISUAL CENTER
24'-0"
WALL-MOUNTED REMOTE JACKS FOR MICROPHONE AND PROJECTOR
CEILING-MOUNTED PROJECTION SCREEN
110 V AND TELEPHONE OUTLET (TYPICAL)
34'-0"

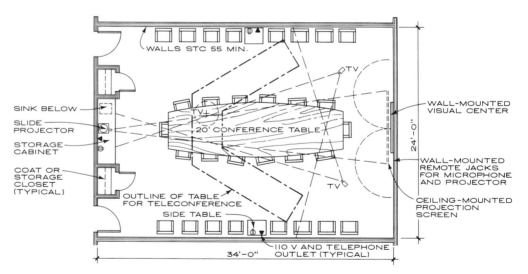

PLAN

NOTE

Components of both traditional and teleconferencing conference rooms are shown. The "board room" layout rendered here is not recommended for teleconferencing. See dashed layout, components at left, and general notes above.

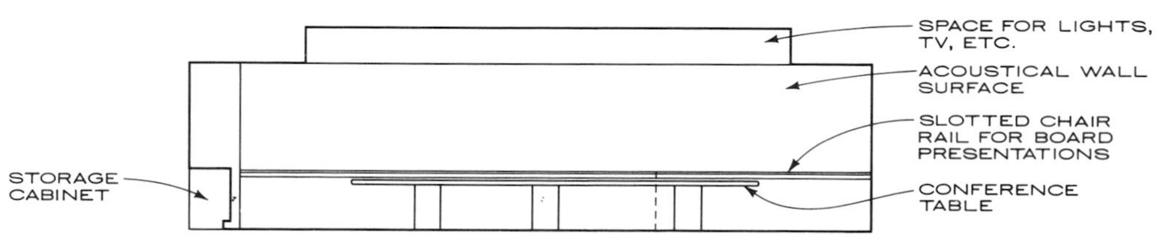

SPACE FOR LIGHTS, TV, ETC.
ACOUSTICAL WALL SURFACE
SLOTTED CHAIR RAIL FOR BOARD PRESENTATIONS
CONFERENCE TABLE
STORAGE CABINET

SECTION

TYPICAL CONFERENCE ROOM (25–30 PERSONS)

J. Kevin Lloyd, AIA; Barge, Waggoner, Sumner & Cannon; Nashville, Tennessee

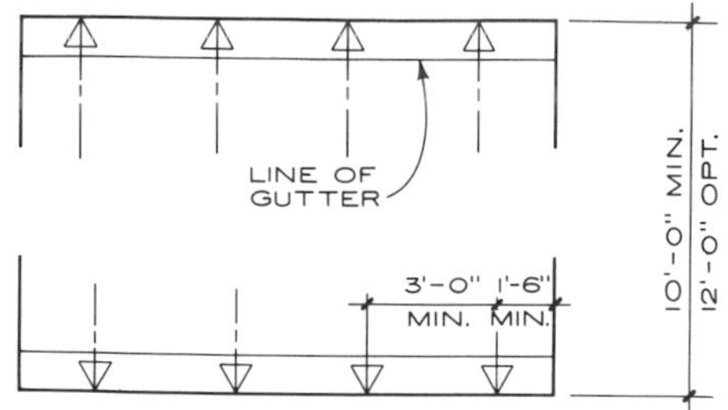
LINE OF GUTTER
3'-0" MIN.
1'-6" MIN.
10'-0" MIN.
12'-0" OPT.

PLAN

GROUP SHOWERS

There must be a sufficient number of shower heads. Educational facilities with time constraints should have 10 shower heads for the first 30 persons and 1 shower head for every 4 additional persons. In recreational facilities 1 shower head for each 10 dressing lockers is a minimum. Temperature controls are necessary to keep water from exceeding 110°F. Both individual and master controls are needed for group showers.

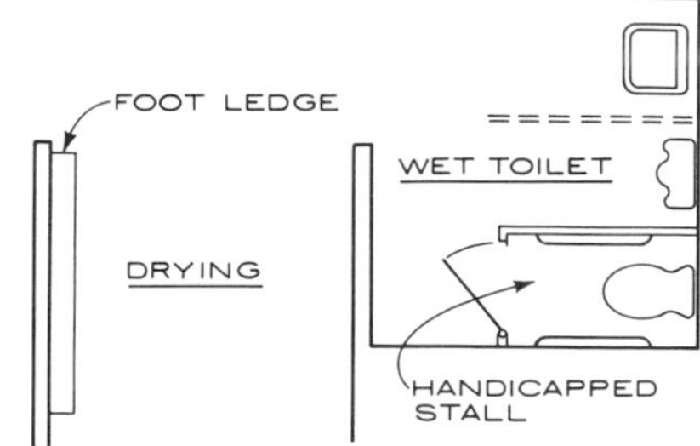
FOOT LEDGE
WET TOILET
DRYING
HANDICAPPED STALL

PLAN

DRYING ROOM AND WET TOILET

The drying room should have about the same area as the shower room. Provision for drainage should be made. Heavy duty towel rails, approximately 4 ft from the floor, are recommended. A foot drying ledge, 18 in. high and 8 in. wide as shown in the drawing, is desirable. An adjacent wet toilet is suggested. Avoid curbs between drying room and adjacent space. Towel service is desirable in a school. Size of area varies with material to be stored (can be used for distributing uniforms), with 200 sq ft usually being sufficient.

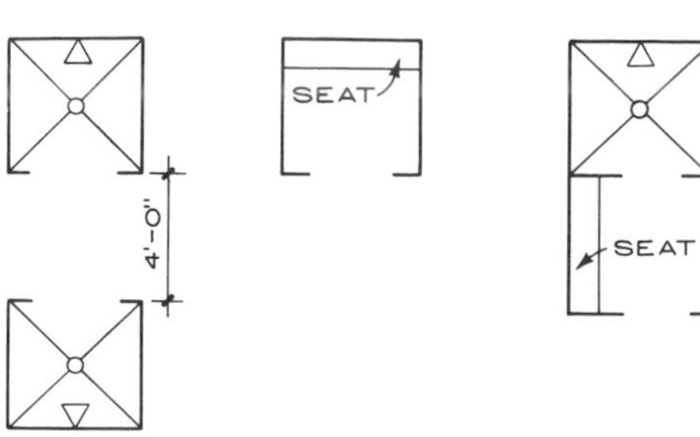
SEAT
4'-0"
SEAT

PLAN

INDIVIDUAL SHOWERS AND DRESSING ROOMS

INDIVIDUAL ROOMS	MINIMUM	OPTIMUM
Showers	3'-0" x 3'-6"	3'-6" x 3'-6"
Dressing Rooms	3'-0" x 3'-6"	3'-6" x 4'-0"

Individual dressing rooms and showers can be combined in a variety of configurations to obtain 1:1, 2:1, 3:1, and 4:1 ratios, respectively.

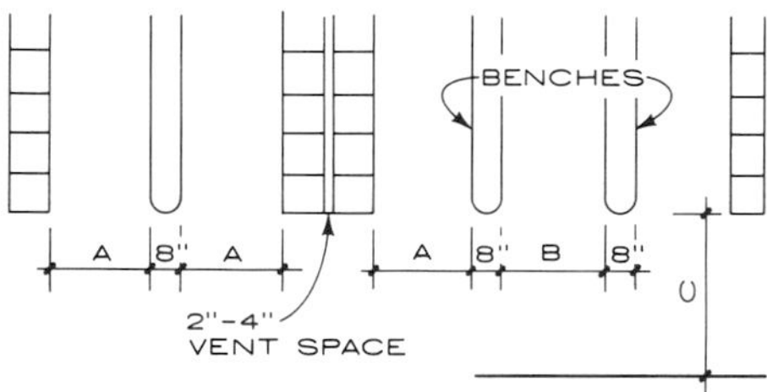
BENCHES
A
8"
A
A
8"
B
8"
C
2"-4"
VENT SPACE

PLAN

AISLE SPACE FOR DRESSING ROOM

AISLE SPACE

	A	B	C
Recreation	2'-2"	1'-8"	3'-6"
School	2'-6"	2'-6"	4'-0"

Bench should be minimum 8 in. in width and 16 in. from the floor. Traffic breaks 3 ft minimum wide should occur at maximum intervals of 12 ft. Main traffic aisle to be wider for large number of locker bays. Avoid lockers that meet at 90° corner.

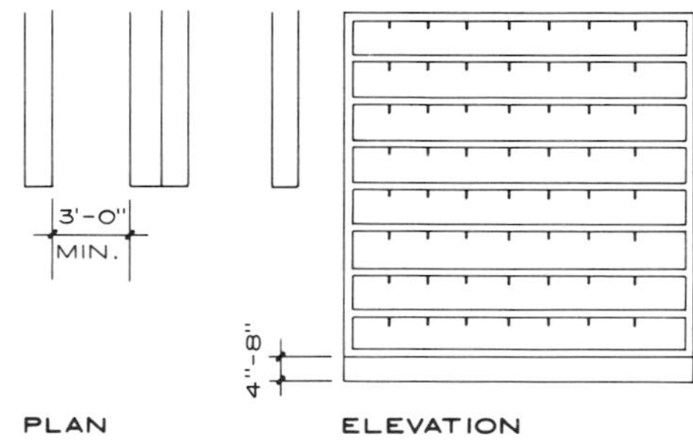
3'-0" MIN.
4'-8"

PLAN ELEVATION

BASKET ROOM AND BASKET RACK

Basket racks vary from 7 to 10 tiers in height. Wide baskets require 1 ft shelf space, small baskets 10 in. shelf space, both fit 1 to $1^1/_2$ ft deep shelf. Back-to-back shelving is 2 ft 3 in. wide. Height shelf-to-shelf is $9^1/_4$ in.

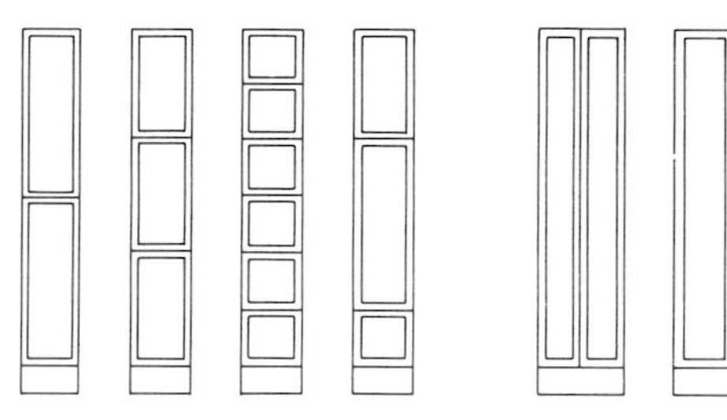

STORAGE DRESSING

LOCKERS

STANDARD SIZES

Width	9", 12", 15", 18"
Depth	12", 15", 18"
Height	60", 72" (overall)

For schools, standard storage locker is 9 in. or 12 in. x 12 in. x 12 in. to 24 in. One storage locker per student enrolled plus 10% for expansion. Standard dressing lockers are 12 in. x 12 in. x 60 in. or 72 in. Number of dressing lockers should be equal to the peak period load plus 10 to 15% for variation.

LOCKER ROOM FACILITIES

ITEMS TO BE PROVIDED

1. Fixed benches 16 in. high.
2. Lockers on raised base.
3. Locker numbering system.
4. Hair dryers—one per 20 lockers.
5. Mirrors at lavatory.
6. Makeup mirror and shelf.
7. Drinking fountain (height as required).
8. Bulletin board.
9. Dressing booths if required.
10. Full length mirror.
11. Clock.
12. Door signs.
13. Sound system speaker if required.
14. Lighting at mirrors for grooming.
15. Lighting located over aisles and passages.
16. Adequate ventilation for storage lockers.
17. Windows located with regard to height and arrangement of lockers.
18. Visual supervision from adjacent office.

RECOMMENDED MOUNTING HEIGHTS

Shower valve	4'-0"
Shower head	
Men	6'-6"
Women	6'-0"
Children	5'-0"
Hand dryer outlet	
Men	3'-8"
Women	3'-6"
Teenagers	3'-1"
Preteens	2'-8"
Hair dryer outlet	
Men	6'-0"
Women	5'-5"
Teenagers	5'-0"
Preteens	5'-0"
Clock	6'-6" min.
Robe hook	6'-3"
Towel bar	4'-0"

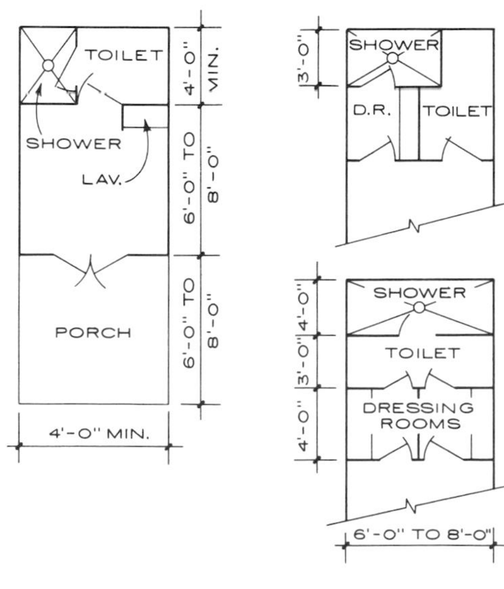
TOILET
SHOWER
LAV.
PORCH
4'-0" MIN.
6'-0" TO 8'-0"
6'-0" TO 8'-0"
4'-0" MIN.
3'-0"
SHOWER
D.R.
TOILET
SHOWER
TOILET
DRESSING ROOMS
4'-0"
3'-0"
4'-0"
6'-0" TO 8'-0"

CABANAS

YMCA Building and Furnishings Service; New York, New York

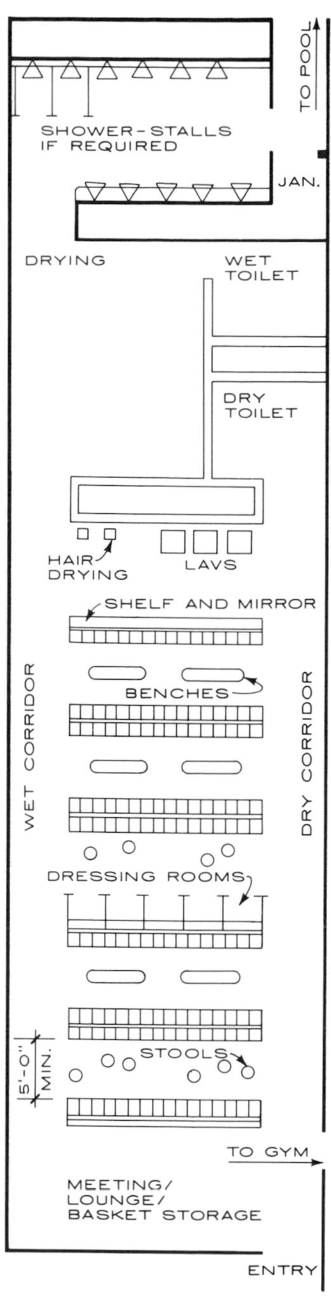
TO POOL
SHOWER-STALLS IF REQUIRED
JAN.
DRYING
WET TOILET
DRY TOILET
HAIR DRYING
LAVS
SHELF AND MIRROR
WET CORRIDOR
BENCHES
DRY CORRIDOR
DRESSING ROOMS
STOOLS
5'-0" MIN.
TO GYM
MEETING/ LOUNGE/ BASKET STORAGE
ENTRY

LOCKER/SHOWER UNIT

TO SERVE GYMNASIUM AND POOL

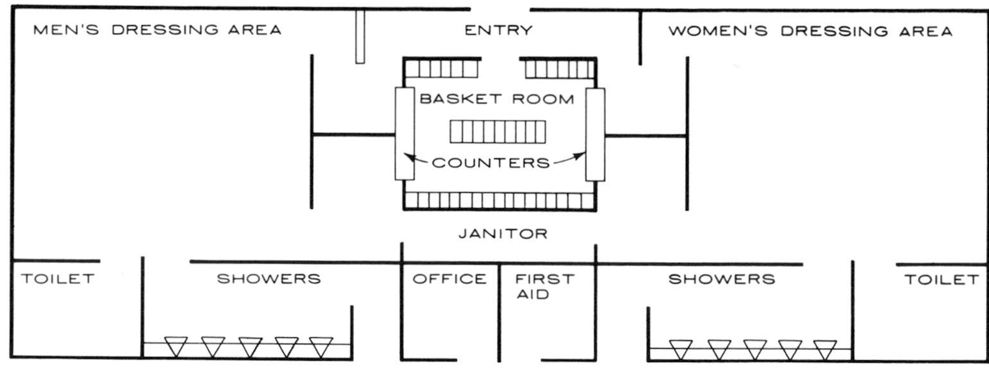
MEN'S DRESSING AREA
ENTRY
WOMEN'S DRESSING AREA
BASKET ROOM
COUNTERS
JANITOR
TOILET
SHOWERS
OFFICE
FIRST AID
SHOWERS
TOILET

DRESSING UNIT FOR POOL

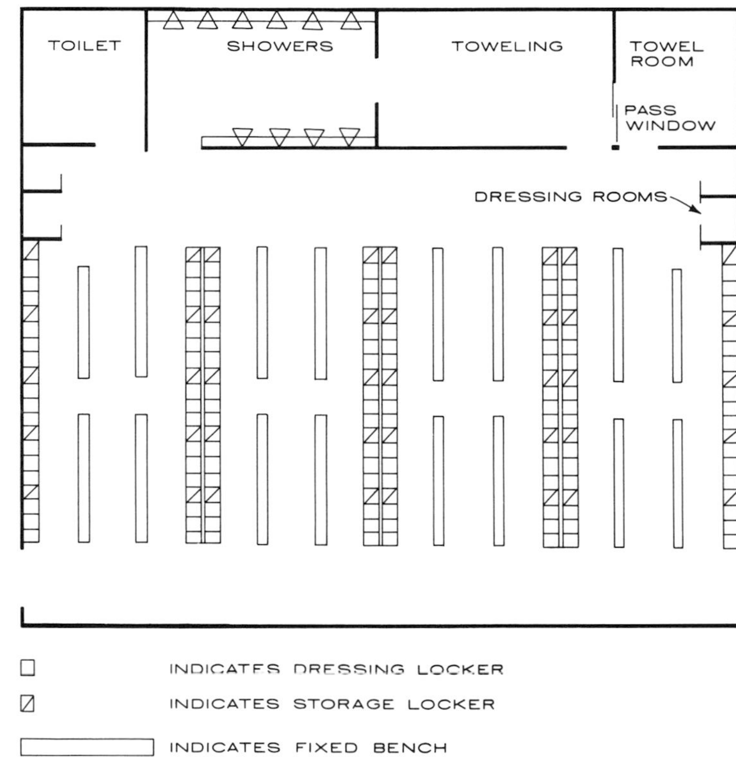
TOILET
SHOWERS
TOWELING
TOWEL ROOM
PASS WINDOW
DRESSING ROOMS
INDICATES DRESSING LOCKER
INDICATES STORAGE LOCKER
INDICATES FIXED BENCH

GYMNASIUM LOCKER ROOM

NOTES

The best arrangement of lockers is the bay system, with a minimum 4 ft circulation aisle at each end of the bays. Ordinarily, the maximum number of lockers in a bay is 16. Locate dry (shoe) traffic at one end of the bays and wet (barefoot) traffic at the other end. For long bays with a single bench, make 3 ft breaks at 15 ft intervals.

Supervision of school lockers is the easiest if they are located in single banks along the two long walls, providing one or more bays that run the length of the room.

The number of lockers in a locker room depends on the anticipated number of members and/or size of classes. Separate locker areas should be encouraged. In small buildings interconnecting doors provide flexibility and allow for the handling of peak loads.

Individual dressing and shower compartments may be required for women's and girls' locker and shower rooms and for men's clubs. A shower stall for the handicapped may also be required.

Basket storage, if included, is self-service. Maximum height is 8 tiers. A dehumidifying system should be provided to dry out basket contents overnight. Separate auxiliary locker rooms may be required. These may serve teams, part time instructors, the faculty, or volunteer leaders. A small room for the coach's use may be desirable.

The shower rooms should be directly accessible to the toweling room and the locker room that it serves. When a shower room is designed to serve a swimming pool, the room should be located so that all must pass through the showers prior to reaching the pool deck.

Separate wet and dry toilet areas are recommended. Wet toilets should be easily accessible from the shower room. When designed for use with a swimming pool, wet toilets should be located so that users must pass through the shower room after use of toilets.

Locker room entrance and exit doors should have vision barriers.

All facilities should be barrier free.

Floors should be of impervious material such as ceramic or quarry tile, with a Carborundum impregnated surface, and should slope toward the drains. Concrete floors (nonslip surface), if used, should be treated with a hardener to avoid the penetration of odors and moisture.

Walls should be of materials resistant to moisture and should have surfaces that are easily cleaned. All exterior corners in the locker rooms should be rounded.

Heavy duty, moisture resistant doors at locker room entrances and exits should be of sufficient size to handle the traffic flow and form natural vision barriers. Entrance/exit doors for the lockers should be equipped with corrosion resistant hardware.

Ceilings in shower areas should be of ceramic tile or other material impervious to moisture. Locker room ceilings should be acoustically treated with a material impervious to moisture and breakage. Floor drains should be kept out of the line of traffic where possible.

YMCA Building and Furnishings Service; New York, New York

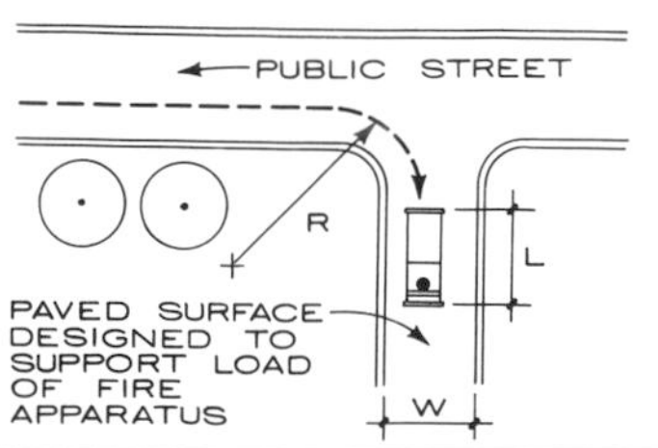
PUBLIC STREET
R
L
PAVED SURFACE DESIGNED TO SUPPORT LOAD OF FIRE APPARATUS
W

FIRE APPARATUS ACCESS

Fire apparatus (i.e., pumpers, ladder trucks, tankers) should have unobstructed access to buildings. Check with local fire department for apparatus turning radius (R), length (L), and other operating characteristics.

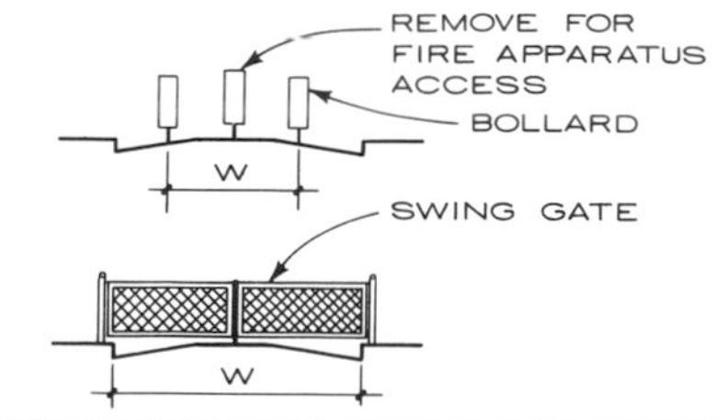
REMOVE FOR FIRE APPARATUS ACCESS
BOLLARD
W
SWING GATE
W

ACCESS OBSTRUCTIONS

Bollards used for traffic control and fences for security should allow sufficient open road width (W) for access by fire apparatus. Bollards and gates can be secured by standard fire department keyed locks (check with department having jurisdiction).

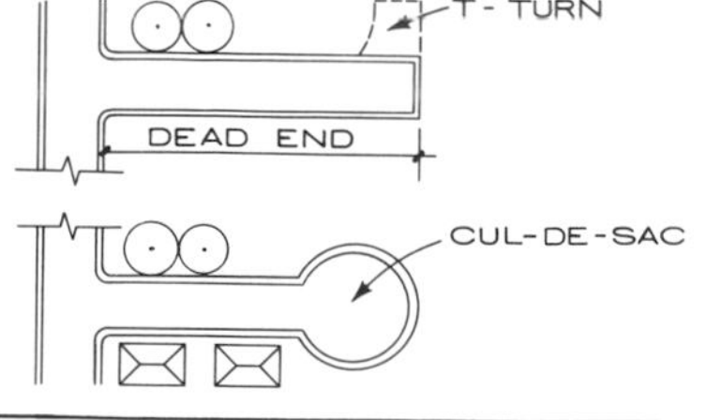
T - TURN
DEAD END
CUL-DE-SAC

DRIVEWAY LAYOUTS

Long dead ends (greater than 150 ft) can cause time consuming, hazardous backup maneuvers. Use t-turns, culs-de-sac, and curved driveway layouts to allow unimpeded access to buildings.

RESTRICTED ACCESS

Buildings constructed near cliffs or steep slopes should not restrict access by fire apparatus to only one side of the building. Grades greater than 10 percent make operation of fire apparatus difficult and dangerous.

FIRE DEPARTMENT RESPONSE TIME FACTOR

Site planning factors that determine response time are street accessibility (curbs, radii, bollards, T-turns, culs-de-sac, street and site slopes, street furniture and architectural obstructions, driveway widths), accessibility for firefighting (fire hydrant and standpipe connection layouts, outdoor lighting, identifying signs), and location (city, town, village, farm). Check with local codes, fire codes, and fire department for area regulations.

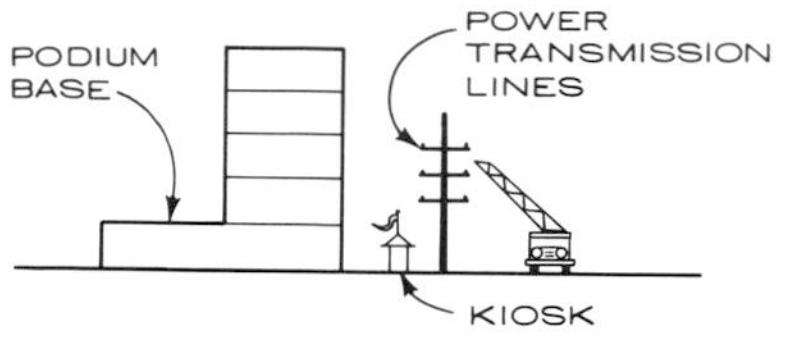
PODIUM BASE
POWER TRANSMISSION LINES
KIOSK

STREET FURNITURE AND ARCHITECTURAL OBSTRUCTIONS

Utility poles can obstruct use of aerial ladders for rescue and fire suppression operations. Kiosks, outdoor sculpture, fountains, newspaper boxes, and the like can also seriously impede fire fighting operations. Wide podium bases can prevent ladder access to the upper stories of buildings. Canopies and other nonstructural building components can also prevent fire apparatus operations close to buildings.

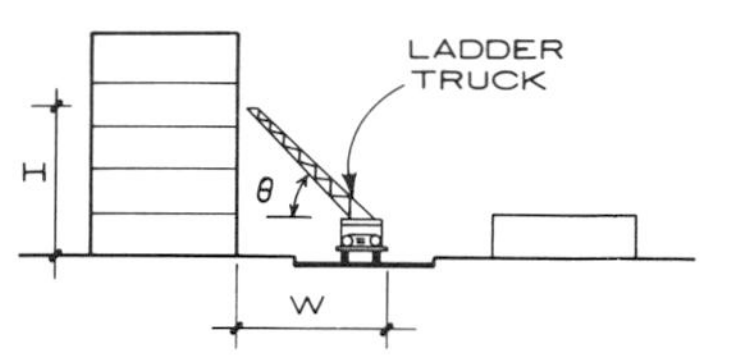
LADDER TRUCK
H
θ
W

DRIVEWAY WIDTHS

For full extension of aerial ladders at a safe climbing angle (θ), sufficient driveway width (W) is required. Estimate the required width in feet by: $W = (H - 6) \cot \theta + 4$, where preferred climbing angles are 60 to 80°. Check with local fire department for aerial apparatus operating requirements.

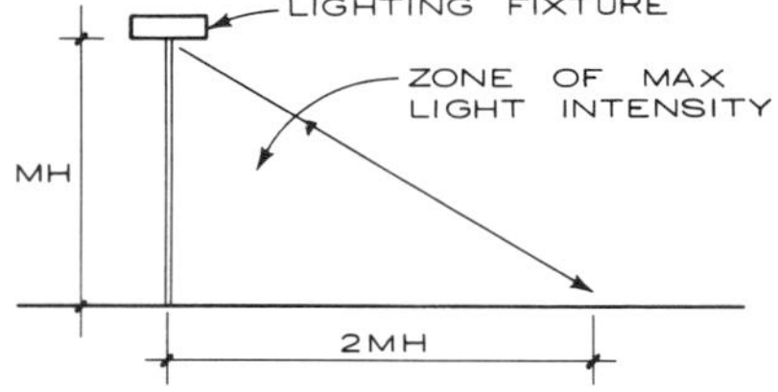
LIGHTING FIXTURE
ZONE OF MAX LIGHT INTENSITY
MH
2MH

OUTDOOR LIGHTING

Streets that are properly lighted enable fire fighters to locate hydrants quickly and to position apparatus at night. Avoid layouts that place hydrants and standpipe connections in shadows. In some situations, lighting fixtures can be integrated into exterior of buildings. All buildings should have a street address number on or near the main entrance.

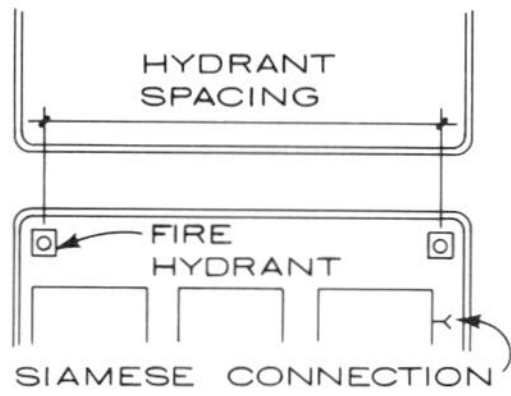
HYDRANT SPACING
FIRE HYDRANT
SIAMESE CONNECTION

FIRE HYDRANT AND STANDPIPE CONNECTION LAYOUT

Locate fire hydrants at street intersections and at intermediate points along roads so that spacing between hydrants does not exceed about 300 ft. (Check with local authority having fire jurisdiction for specific requirements.) Hydrants should be placed 2 to 10 ft from curb lines. Siamese connections to standpipes should be visible, marked conspicuously, and be within 200 ft of hydrant to allow rapid connection by fire fighters.

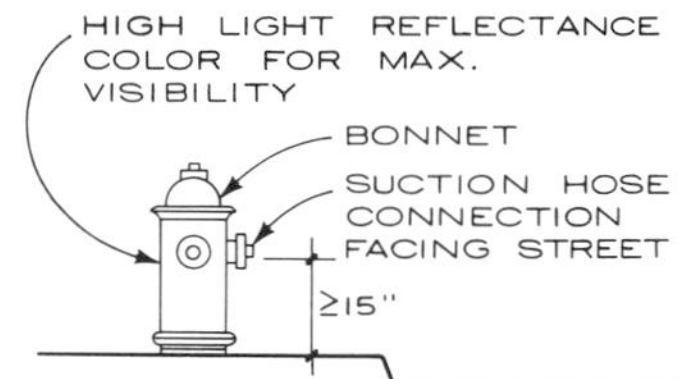
HIGH LIGHT REFLECTANCE COLOR FOR MAX. VISIBILITY
BONNET
SUCTION HOSE CONNECTION FACING STREET
≥15"

FIRE HYDRANT PLACEMENT

Fire hose connections should be at least 15" above grade. Do not bury hydrants or locate them behind shrubs or other visual barriers. Avoid locations where runoff water and snow can accumulate. Bollards and fences used to protect hydrants from vehicular traffic must not obstruct fire fighters' access to hose connections. Suction hose connection should usually face the side of arriving fire apparatus.

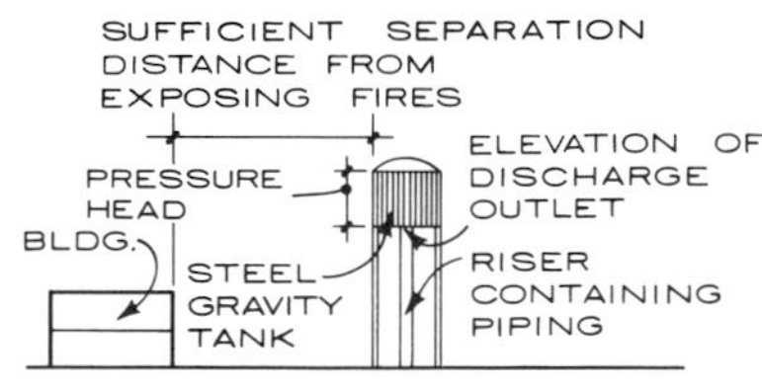
SUFFICIENT SEPARATION DISTANCE FROM EXPOSING FIRES
PRESSURE HEAD
ELEVATION OF DISCHARGE OUTLET
BLDG.
STEEL GRAVITY TANK
RISER CONTAINING PIPING

GRAVITY TANK

Gravity tanks can provide reliable source of pressure to building standpipe or sprinkler systems. Available pressure head increases by 0.434 psi/ft increase of water above tank discharge outlet. Tank capacity in gallons depends on fire hazard, water supply, and other factors. Tanks require periodic maintenance and protection against freezing during cold weather. Locations subject to seismic forces or high winds require special consideration. Gravity tanks also can be integrated within building design.

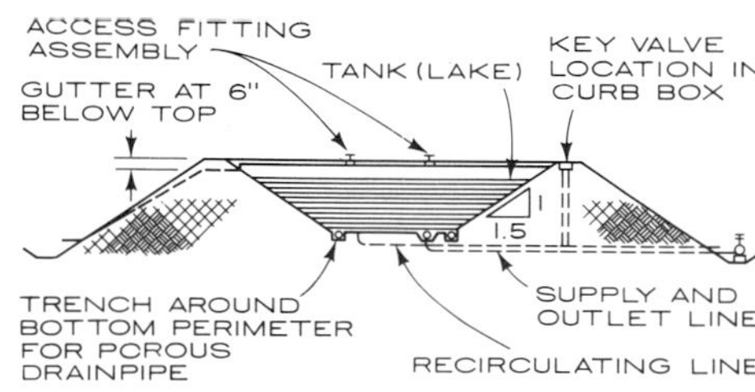
ACCESS FITTING ASSEMBLY
GUTTER AT 6" BELOW TOP
TANK (LAKE)
KEY VALVE LOCATION IN CURB BOX
1.5
1
TRENCH AROUND BOTTOM PERIMETER FOR POROUS DRAINPIPE
SUPPLY AND OUTLET LINE
RECIRCULATING LINE

ON-SITE LAKES

Man-made and natural on-site lakes are used for private firefighting in suburbs, on farms, and at resorts. Piped supply system (suction facilities) is preferred for its quantity flexibility, better maintenance, and accessibility. Man-made lakes such as reservoir liner are berm-supported or sunk in the ground. Lakes and ponds are natural water supplies dependent on the environment. See local codes, fire codes, and fire departments for on-site lake regulations.

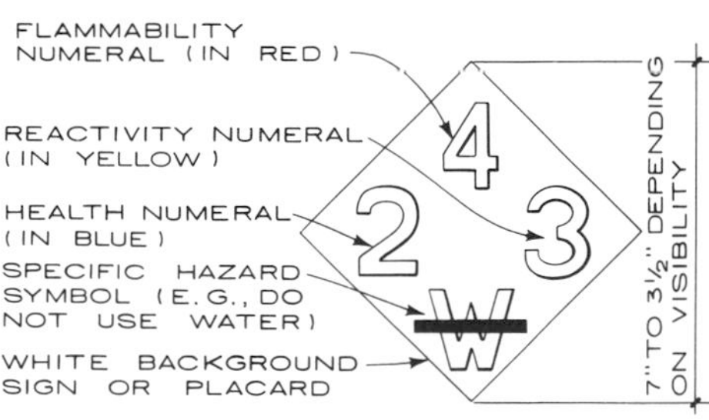
FLAMMABILITY NUMERAL (IN RED)
REACTIVITY NUMERAL (IN YELLOW)
HEALTH NUMERAL (IN BLUE)
SPECIFIC HAZARD SYMBOL (E.G., DO NOT USE WATER)
WHITE BACKGROUND SIGN OR PLACARD
4
2
3
W
7" TO 3½" DEPENDING ON VISIBILITY

NFPA 704 DIAMOND SYMBOLS

Standard diamond symbols provide information fire fighters need to avoid injury from hazardous building contents. 0 numeral is the lowest degree of hazard, 4 is highest. Locate symbols near building entrances. Correct spatial arrangement for two kinds of diamond symbols are shown. Consider integrating symbols with overall graphics design of building. (Refer to "Identification of the Fire Hazards of Materials," NFPA No. 704, available from the National Fire Protection Association.)

M. David Egan, P.E.; College of Architecture, Clemson University; Clemson, South Carolina
Nicholas A. Phillips, AIA; Lockwood Greene; New York, New York
National Fire Protection Association, see data sources

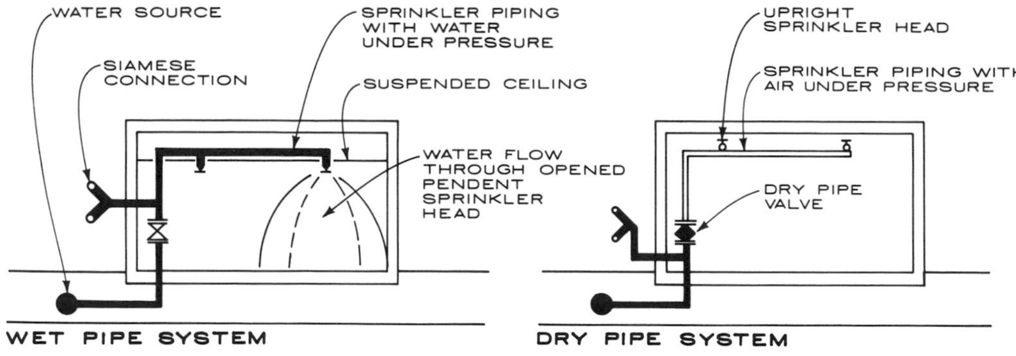
WATER SOURCE
SIAMESE CONNECTION
SPRINKLER PIPING WITH WATER UNDER PRESSURE
SUSPENDED CEILING
WATER FLOW THROUGH OPENED PENDENT SPRINKLER HEAD
UPRIGHT SPRINKLER HEAD
SPRINKLER PIPING WITH AIR UNDER PRESSURE
DRY PIPE VALVE

WET PIPE SYSTEM

DRY PIPE SYSTEM

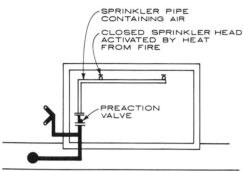

SPRINKLER PIPE CONTAINING AIR

CLOSED SPRINKLER HEAD ACTIVATED BY HEAT FROM FIRE

PREACTION VALVE

PREACTION SYSTEM

DELUGE VALVE

WATER FLOWS THROUGH ALL OPEN HEADS OR NOZZLES

DELUGE SYSTEM

SPRINKLER PIPING

CEILING

WATER DISCHARGE PATTERN

UP TO 20'-0" FOR SMALL, LIGHT-HAZARD OCCUPANCIES

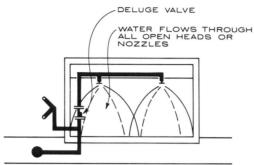

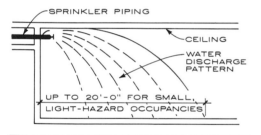

SIDEWALL SPRINKLER HEAD
(HORIZONTAL SIDEWALL SHOWN)

Piping can be unobtrusively installed along sides of exposed ceiling beams or joists. In small rooms, sidewall heads provide water discharge coverage without overhead piping.

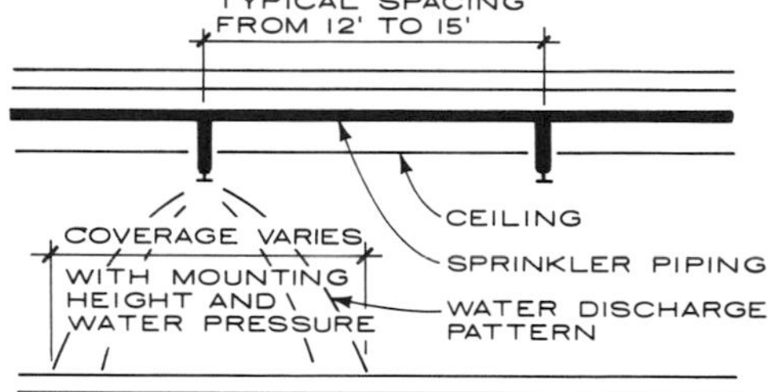
TYPICAL SPACING FROM 12' TO 15'
CEILING
SPRINKLER PIPING
COVERAGE VARIES WITH MOUNTING HEIGHT AND WATER PRESSURE
WATER DISCHARGE PATTERN

PENDENT SPRINKLER HEAD

Can be recessed in ceiling (e.g., coffered, modeled) or hidden above flat metal cover plate. (Flush sprinkler heads are also available.)

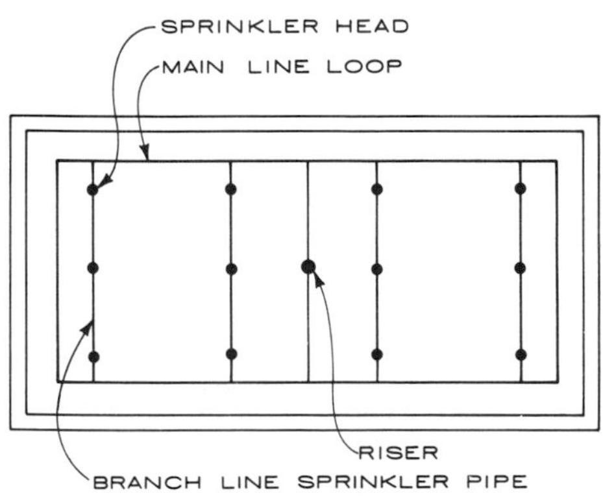
SPRINKLER HEAD
MAIN LINE LOOP
RISER
BRANCH LINE SPRINKLER PIPE

HYDRAULICALLY DESIGNED SPRINKLER SYSTEM LAYOUT

Loop provides water flow from two directions to operating sprinkler heads so pipe sizes will be small. Hydraulic calculations can assure delivery of adequate water flow and pressure throughout piping network to meet design requirements.

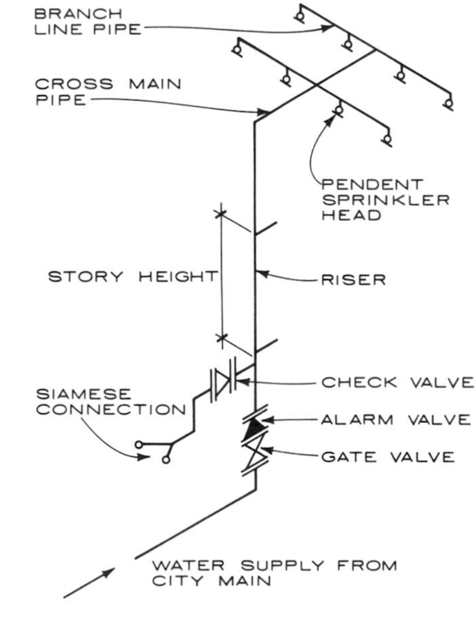
BRANCH LINE PIPE
CROSS MAIN PIPE
PENDENT SPRINKLER HEAD
STORY HEIGHT
RISER
CHECK VALVE
SIAMESE CONNECTION
ALARM VALVE
GATE VALVE
WATER SUPPLY FROM CITY MAIN

SPRINKLER SYSTEM RISER

TYPES OF SYSTEMS

WET PIPE: Piping network contains water under pressure at all times for immediate release through sprinkler heads as they are activated by heat from fire. Wet pipe system is the most widely used system, since water delivery here is faster than with a dry pipe system.

DRY PIPE: Piping network contains air (or nitrogen) under pressure. Following loss of air pressure through opened sprinkler head, dry pipe valve opens allowing water to enter piping network and to flow through opened sprinkler head (or heads). Used where piping is subject to freezing.

PREACTION: Closed head, dry system containing air in piping network. Preaction valve is activated by independent fire detection system more sensitive than sprinkler heads. The opened preaction valve allows water to fill piping network and to flow through sprinkler heads, as they are activated by heat from fire. Used where leakage or accidental discharge would cause serious damage.

DELUGE: Sprinkler heads (or spray nozzles) are open at all times and normally there is no water in piping network. Mechanical or hydraulic valves, operated by heat, smoke, or flame sensitive devices, are used to control water flow to heads by opening water control clapper. Deluge systems are special use systems, as water discharges from all heads (or nozzles) at the same time.

STANDPIPE AND HOSE: Dry standpipes are empty water pipes used by fire fighters to connect hoses in buildings to water sources such as ground level fire hydrants. Wet standpipes are water filled pipes permanently connected to public or private water mains for use by building occupants on small fires or by fire fighters.

FOAM: Used to suppress flammable liquid fires. Foam can be distributed by piping network to nozzles or other discharge outlets (e.g., tubes, troughs, chutes) depending on the hazard.

HALON (haloginated hydrocarbon): Can be used where water damage to building contents would be unacceptable. Piping network connects fixed supply of halon to nozzles that discharge uniform, low concentration throughout room. To avoid piping network, discharge cylinders may be installed throughout room or area. Though generally nontoxic, delayed discharge can cause problems by allowing decomposition of halon. Rapid detection is necessary.

CO_2 (carbon dioxide): Does not conduct electricity and leaves no residue after its use. Piping network connects fixed supply of CO_2 to nozzles that discharge CO_2 directly on burning materials where location of fire hazard is known (called "local application") or discharge CO_2 uniformly throughout room (called "total flooding"). In total flooding systems, safety requirements dictate advance alarm to allow occupants to evacuate area prior to discharge.

DRY CHEMICAL: Can be especially useful on electrical and flammable liquid fires. Powdered extinguishing agent, under pressure of dry air or nitrogen, commonly discharged over cooking surfaces (e.g., frying).

PREPARATION FOR SPRINKLER SYSTEMS

1. Begin planning sprinkler system at the very earliest design stages of project.
2. Determine hazard classification of building and type of system best suited for suppression needs.
3. Refer to national standards (NFPA), state and local codes.
4. Check with authority having jurisdiction:
   a. State and local fire marshals.
   b. Insurance Services Office (ISO).
   c. Insurance underwriting groups such as IRI, OIA, or FM (if they have jurisdiction).
5. Use qualified engineers to design system. Be sure water supply is adequate (e.g., by water flow tests). Integrate system with structural, mechanical, and other building services.
6. Check space requirements for sprinkler equipment. Sprinkler control room must be heated to prevent freezing of equipment.
7. Consider possible future alterations to building.

M. David Egan, P.E.; College of Architecture, Clemson University; Clemson, South Carolina

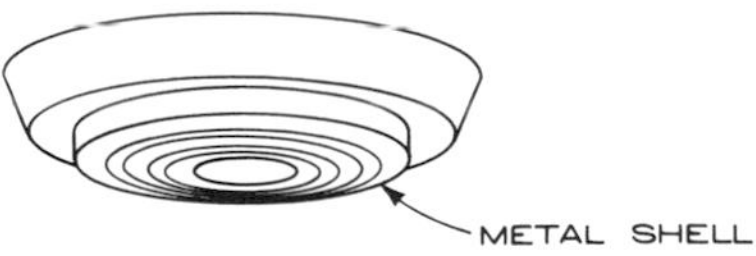
METAL SHELL

HEAT DETECTOR

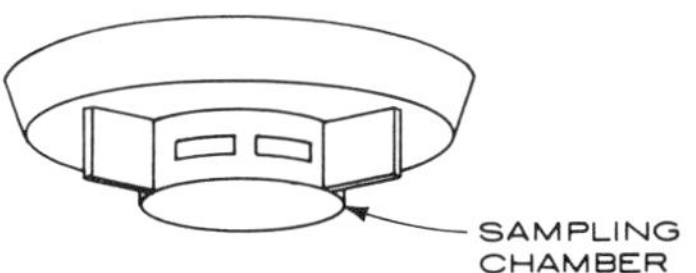
SAMPLING
CHAMBER

IONIZATION SMOKE DETECTOR

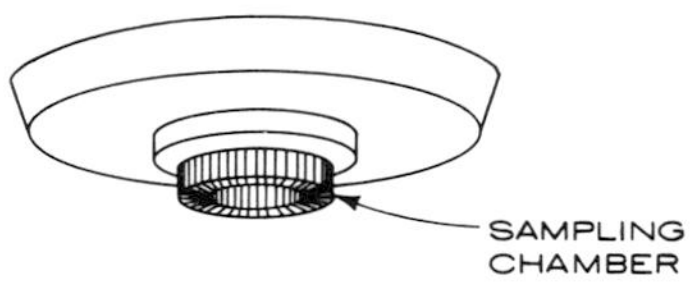
SAMPLING
CHAMBER

PHOTOELECTRIC SMOKE DETECTOR

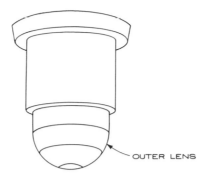

OUTER LENS

INFRARED FLAME DETECTOR

HEAT DETECTOR

Fixed temperature heat detectors (e.g., those rated at 135 to 197°F) use low melting point solder or metals that expand when exposed to heat to detect fire. Rate-of-rise heat detectors alarm when rate of temperature change exceeds about 15°F/min. Expansion of air in chamber with calibrated vent is used to detect rapidly developing fires. Devices are available with both rate-of-rise and fixed temperature detection features.

IONIZATION SMOKE DETECTOR

Ionization detectors use the interruption of small current flow between electrodes by smoke in ionized sampling chamber to detect fire. Dual chamber (with reference chamber exposed only to air temperature, pressure, and humidity) and single chamber detectors are available. Ionization detectors can be used in rooms and in air ducts to detect smoke in air distribution systems.

PHOTOELECTRIC SMOKE DETECTOR

Photoelectric smoke detectors use the scattering of light by smoke into view of photocell. Sources of light may be either incandescent lamp or light emitting diode (LED). Photoelectric detectors can be used in rooms and in air ducts to detect smoke in air distribution systems.

INFRARED FLAME DETECTOR

Infrared flame detectors respond to the high-frequency (IR) radiant energy from flames. Alarm is only triggered when IR energy flickers at rate which is characteristic of flames. Infrared detectors can be used in large open areas where rapid development of flaming conditions could occur (e.g., flammable liquids fire hazards).

FIRE AND SMOKE DETECTORS

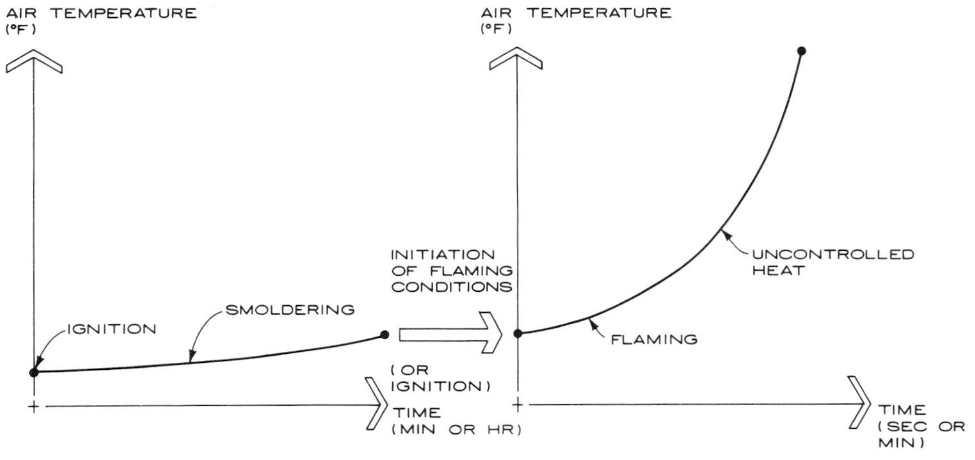
AIR TEMPERATURE
(°F)
IGNITION
SMOLDERING
INITIATION
OF FLAMING
CONDITIONS
(OR
IGNITION)
TIME
(MIN OR HR)
AIR TEMPERATURE
(°F)
FLAMING
UNCONTROLLED
HEAT
TIME
(SEC OR
MIN)

STAGES OF FIRE

Carefully match fire detectors to anticipated fire hazard (e.g., photoelectric smoke detectors for smoldering fires, ionization smoke detectors for flaming fires, infrared flame detectors for flash fires). The time-temperature curves show growth to hazardous conditions for smoldering, flaming, and uncontrolled heat stages of fire.

STAGES OF FIRE

LIVING ROOM
KITCHEN
DINING ROOM

BEDROOMS

SMOKE DETECTOR

RESIDENTIAL OCCUPANCY (WITH SINGLE SLEEPING AREA)

BED-
ROOMS
LIVING ROOM
KITCHEN
DINING ROOM
DEN
BED-
ROOMS
SMOKE DETECTOR

RESIDENTIAL OCCUPANCY (WITH SPLIT SLEEPING AREAS)

CHECKLIST FOR RESIDENTIAL FIRE DETECTION

1. Use smoke detectors to protect the following (in decreasing order of importance):
   a. Every occupied floor and basement.
   b. Sleeping areas and basement near stairs.
   c. Sleeping areas only.
2. Use heat detectors to protect remote areas (e.g., basement shops, attics) where serious fires could develop before smoke would reach smoke detector or in areas such as garages or kitchens where smoke detectors would be exposed to high smoke levels during normal conditions.
3. Locate smoke detectors on ceilings near center of rooms (or on the upper walls 6 to 12 in. from ceiling) where smoke can collect. In long corridors, consider using two or more detectors.
4. Use closer spacing between detectors where ceiling beams, joists, and the like will interrupt flow of smoke to detector.
5. Do not place smoke detectors near supply air registers or diffusers, or near return air grilles where return air could remove smoke from the area before it reaches detector.
6. For guidelines on fire detection for residences, refer to "Household Fire Warning Equipment," NFPA No. 74, available from the National Fire Protection Association.

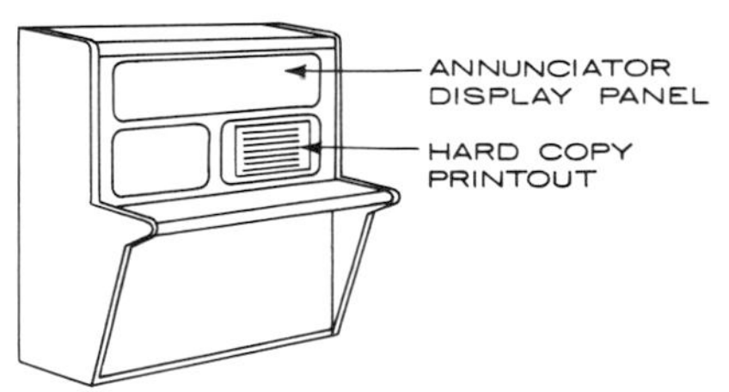
ANNUNCIATOR
DISPLAY PANEL
HARD COPY
PRINTOUT

AUTOMATED CONTROL CONSOLE

NOTE

When fire is detected (e.g., by smoke, heat, infrared detectors, or water flow indicators in sprinkler system piping), automated control systems immediately summon the fire department. Floor plans of fire area can be projected on annunciator display panel to pinpoint trouble spots. Controls can be designed to automatically shut down fan systems or activate fans and dampers for smoke removal and control. In addition, remote firefighter control panel, with telephone communication to control console and to each floor in building, can be used to control and monitor status of elevators, pumps and emergency generators, fans, dampers, and the like.

M. David Egan, P.E.; College of Architecture, Clemson University; Clemson, South Carolina

NOTES

The simplest fire alarm system is the self-contained, UL approved, residential smoke detector. It senses products of combustion, sounds an alarm, and signals when the battery needs replacement. Local fire departments campaign for their use in homes and apartments. They are required in motel and hotel rooms by local and/or state codes.

Where public safety is involved in schools, hospitals, office buildings, and other commercial establishments or institutions, more complex systems evolve. Although there are still applications for small hardwired and relay-operated alarm signaling systems, the trend is toward microprocessor-based digital multiplex systems that not only signal events, but initiate events. These may include conditioning fans and dampers for smoke control, closing fire doors and shutters, releasing locked doors, capturing elevators, and transmitting voice messages. Voice communication is required in "high-rise buildings" of specific group occupancies as defined by the BOCA Code. It is also recommended for large low-rise buildings to enhance life safety.

Fire alarm systems can be "stand alone" or a subsystem, integrated with security and building management functions. Processors and their peripheral equipment are generally located in a fully manned central command center accessible to arriving firemen. Depending on the degree of reliability desired, redundancy can be provided in wiring and processors, along with battery backup.

Transponder cabinets can be 36 in. wide x 8 in. deep. They must have battery backup, be UL approved, conform to NFPA No. 72, and may also require local approval. In small systems where only one cabinet may be required, all the functions required at the command center can be incorporated in the same cabinet and located in the main entrance lobby. In larger systems, remote cabinets are generally located in wiring closets throughout the building and can be provided with programmed intelligence to function independent of the central processor, should it fail.

Basic signaling systems can be:

NONCODED: Continuous sounding evacuation signal.

MASTER CODED: Four rounds of a repeating signal.

SELECTIVE CODED: Same as above except individual devices generate an assigned number code of up to three groups per round.

PRESIGNAL: Same as above except signals sound only at selected areas to prompt investigation. If hazard is determined, evacuation signal is initiated by key.

VOICE: Direct (by microphone) or automatic prerecorded messages are transmitted over speakers, following an "alert" signal.

FIRE
EMERGENCY
PHONE

Range in size from 4 to 12 in. diameter. Can be recessed behind a grille. Operation can be single stroke or continuous.

FIREMAN TELEPHONE JACK PLATE

Approximately 10 in. high x 7 in. wide with visual signal. Visual signal can be flashing light or stroke. Can be provided with directional sound projector.

SMOKE DETECTOR

MANUAL PULL STATION (F)
SMOKE DETECTOR (S)
DUCT SMOKE DETECTOR (S D)
THERMAL FIRE DETECTOR (F)
FLAME (UV) DETECTOR (F UV)
SPRINKLER FLOW SWITCH (WFS)
DRY PIPE PRESSURE SWITCH (SPS)
HALON SYSTEM ALARM (HCP)
FIRE PUMP ALARM (FPA)
VALVE TAMPER SWITCH (TS)
FIREMAN TELEPHONE (F)
FIREMAN TELEPHONE JACK (O)

TRANSPONDER PANEL
INITIATING CIRCUIT MODULE
SIGNAL TRANSMISSION MODULE
ANNUNCIATOR MODULE
BATTERY AND CHARGER MODULE
POWER SUPPLY MODULE
COMMUNICATION MODULE

(F) VIBRATING BELL OR GONG
(F) VIBRATING HORN
(F) FLASHING LIGHT OR STROBE
(F) MUNICIPAL CONNECTION
(DH) RELEASE DOOR HOLDER
(DR) RELEASE LATCH OR LOCK
(SD) CLOSE SMOKE DOOR
(ELC) CAPTURE ELEVATOR
(FC) CONTROL FAN
(DC) CONTROL DAMPER
(F) WALL FA SPEAKER
(F) CEILING FA SPEAKER

BUILDING MANAGEMENT SYSTEM INTERFACE
REDUNDANT OR LOOPED VOICE AND DATA LINES
MASTER TELEPHONE
PRINTER
REDUNDANT CENTRAL PROCESSOR
VOICE COMMUNICATION CONSOLE WITH TAPE DECK
ANNUNCIATOR PANEL
OPERATORS' TERMINAL

ELECTRONIC FIRE ALARM / COMMUNICATION SYSTEM FUNCTION DIAGRAM

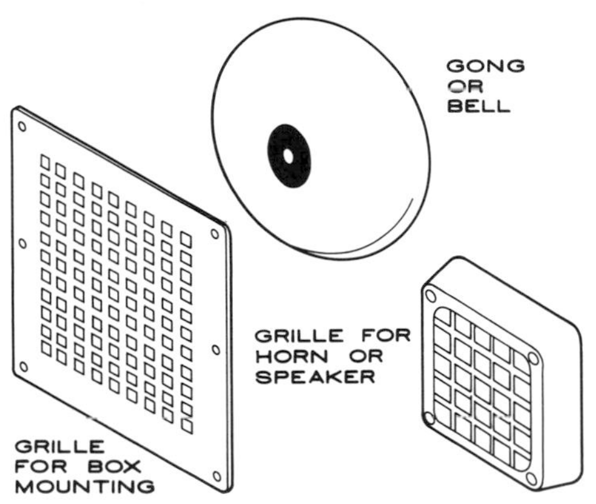
GONG OR BELL
GRILLE FOR HORN OR SPEAKER
GRILLE FOR BOX MOUNTING

Approximately 7 in. high x 5 in. wide surface or semi-flush mounted. Can be provided with break-glass (rod) feature. Operation can be coded or noncoded.

BELL AND COVERS

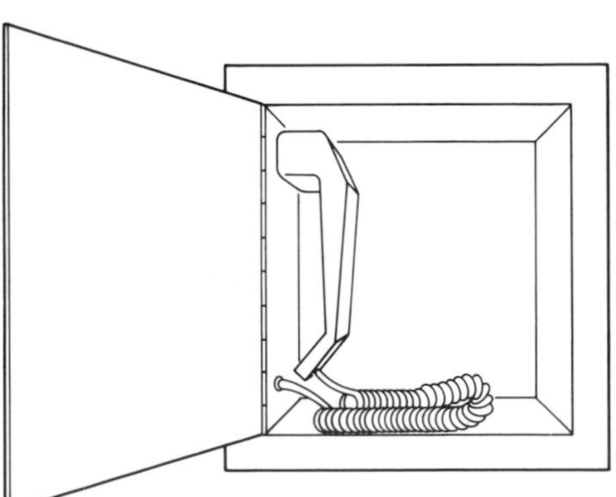

Standard single gang device plate size. Located at exit stair doors and elevator lobbies. Jack matches plug on phone carried by firemen.

FIREMAN TELEPHONE CABINET

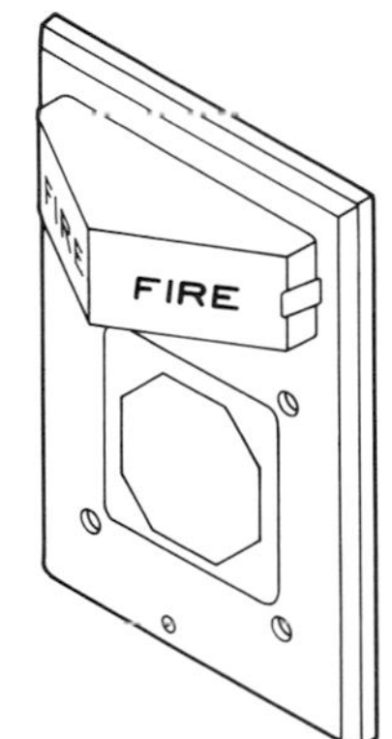
FIRE

Approximately 6 in. diameter, 5 in. high (maximum). Can be hardwired or electronically addressable. Operation can be ionization or photoelectric.

HORN / SPEAKER / VISUAL SIGNAL

PULL DOWN

Approximately 12 in. high x 10 in. wide x 3 in. deep, surface or flush. Provided in lieu of jack plates for a total system. Door can be glass or plastic pane.

MANUAL PULL STATION

Richard F. Humenn, P.E.; Joseph R. Loring & Associates, Inc., Consulting Engineers; New York, New York

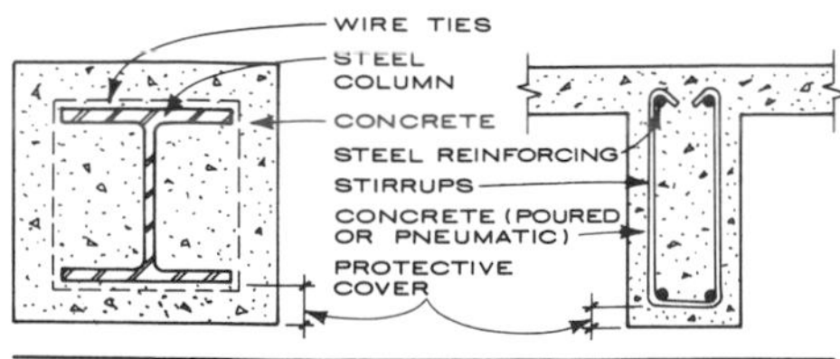
WIRE TIES
STEEL COLUMN
CONCRETE
STEEL REINFORCING
STIRRUPS
CONCRETE (POURED OR PNEUMATIC)
PROTECTIVE COVER

CONCRETE ENCASEMENT

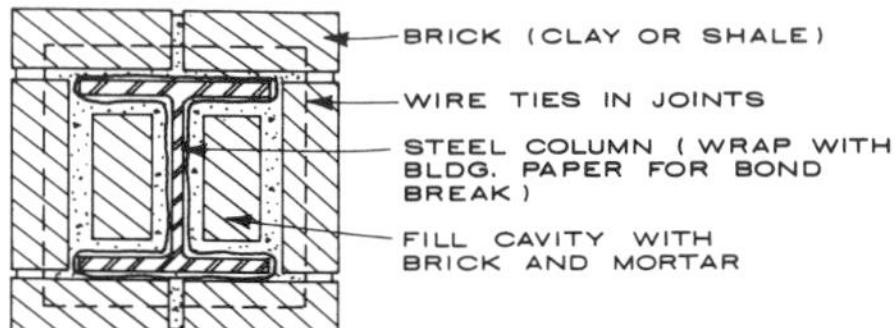
BRICK (CLAY OR SHALE)
WIRE TIES IN JOINTS
STEEL COLUMN (WRAP WITH BLDG. PAPER FOR BOND BREAK)
FILL CAVITY WITH BRICK AND MORTAR

MASONRY ENCLOSURE

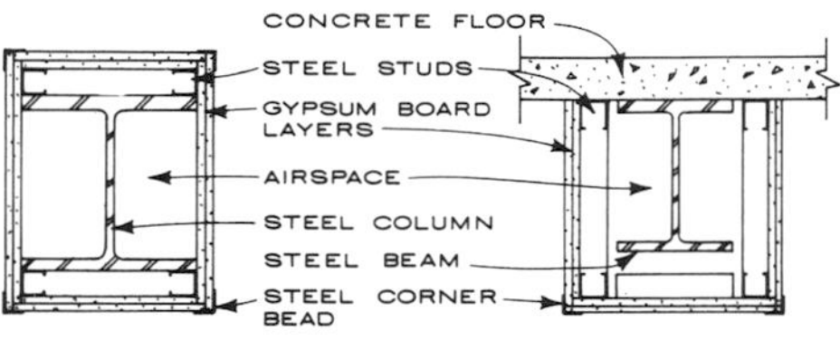
CONCRETE FLOOR
STEEL STUDS
GYPSUM BOARD LAYERS
AIRSPACE
STEEL COLUMN
STEEL BEAM
STEEL CORNER BEAD

GYPSUM MEMBRANE ENCLOSURE

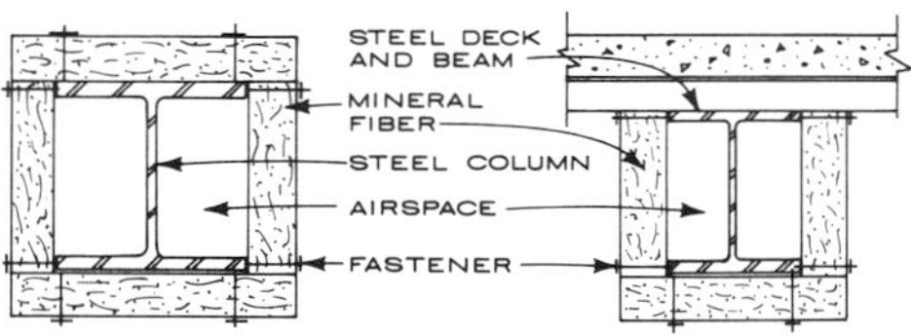
STEEL DECK AND BEAM
MINERAL FIBER
STEEL COLUMN
AIRSPACE
FASTENER

MINERAL FIBER MEMBRANE ENCLOSURE

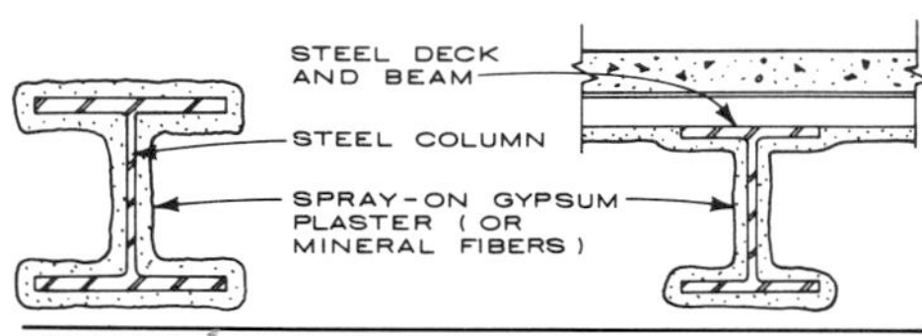
STEEL DECK AND BEAM
STEEL COLUMN
SPRAY-ON GYPSUM PLASTER (OR MINERAL FIBERS)

SPRAY–ON CONTOUR

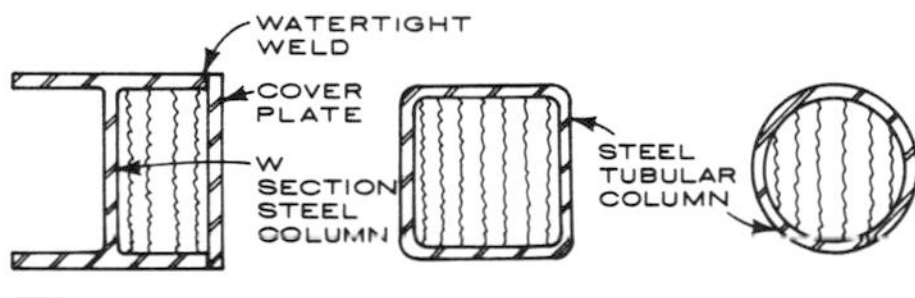
WATERTIGHT WELD
COVER PLATE
W SECTION STEEL COLUMN
STEEL TUBULAR COLUMN

LIQUID FILLED COLUMN

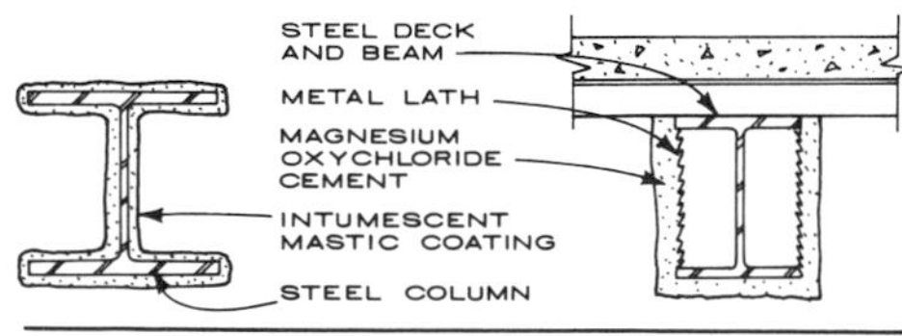
STEEL DECK AND BEAM
METAL LATH
MAGNESIUM OXYCHLORIDE CEMENT
INTUMESCENT MASTIC COATING
STEEL COLUMN

COATINGS

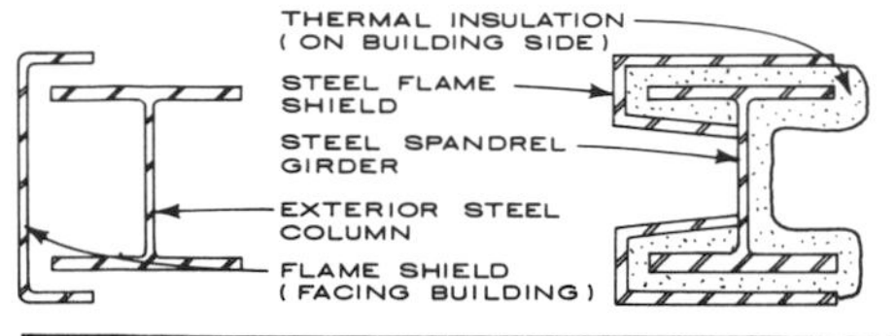
THERMAL INSULATION (ON BUILDING SIDE)
STEEL FLAME SHIELD
STEEL SPANDREL GIRDER
EXTERIOR STEEL COLUMN
FLAME SHIELD (FACING BUILDING)

FLAME SHIELDS

UNPROTECTED STEEL

At temperatures greater than 1000°F, mild steel loses about one half of its ultimate room temperature strength. Consequently, fire tests on steel beams and columns are terminated when the steel's surface temperatures reach a predetermined limit or when the applied design loading can no longer be sustained (specific alternate test procedures are given by ASTM Standard Methods E 119). Fire resistance ratings are expressed in terms of duration in hours of fire exposure to standard temperature conditions in a test furnace (e.g., 3/4 hr, 1 hr, 2 hr, 3 hr). For further information on fire resistance tests and fire protection of steel, see American Iron and Steel Institute's handbook, "Fire-Resistant Steel-Frame Construction."

CONCRETE ENCASEMENT

Achieved fire resistance for steel members encased in concrete depends on thickness of protective concrete cover, concrete mixture, and structural restraint (i.e., method of support and method of confining thermal expansion). Lightweight aggregate concrete has better fire resistance than normal weight concrete because of its higher moisture content and higher thermal resistance to heat flow. Heavier members require less cover for equivalent fire resistance, since they have greater mass. For data on columns encased in concrete, see National Fire Protection Association's "Fire Protection Handbook." Gunite, a mixture of cement, sand, and water, can be spray-applied by air pressure, but requires steel reinforcing. For exterior applications, reinforcing steel with less than 2 in. of concrete cover usually requires corrosion resistant primers.

MASONRY ENCLOSURE

Masonry materials (brick, concrete block, gypsum block, hollow clay tile) can be used to encase steel columns. The cores (or cells), which provide openings for reinforcing, also can be filled with mortar or insulating materials such as vermiculite to increase thermal resistance to heat flow. For data on fire resistance of masonry constructions, see National Concrete Masonry Association's "Fire Safety with Concrete Masonry."

GYPSUM MEMBRANE ENCLOSURE

Gypsum board or troweled plaster (e.g., vermiculite-gypsum, perlite-gypsum) or lath can be used to protect steel at building locations not exposed to moisture. Gypsum retards heat flow to steel by releasing chemically combined water (called "calcination") at temperatures above 180°F. To protect steel columns, gypsum board layers can be attached to steel studs by means of self-tapping screws or installed behind a galvanized or stainless sheet steel cover. For data on fire resistance of gypsum constructions, see Gypsum Association's "Fire Resistance Design Data Manual."

MINERAL FIBER MEMBRANE ENCLOSURE

When exposed to fire, mineral fiber (made from molten rock or slag) retards heat flow to steel because of its low thermal conductivity (it can withstand temperatures above 2000°F without melting). Mineral fiber requires a protective covering when exposed to outdoor conditions or the possibility of damage from accidental impact or abrasion.

SPRAY-ON CONTOUR

Spray-on applied cementitious mixtures (lightweight aggregate plasters with insulating fibers or vermiculite) or mineral fibers mixed with inorganic binders provide thermal barrier to heat from fire. The steel surface must be clean and free of loose paint, rust, oil, and grease before spraying, and a protective primer may be required. In addition, spraying should not be scheduled during cold conditions. Lightweight spray-on contours can be easily damaged during installation of nearby gas and water pipes, air ducts, and the like, and they are subject to flaking during normal use. Pins, studs, and other mechanical fasteners can be used to secure moisture or abrasion resistant protective finish coatings. Applications more than 2 in. thick generally require wire mesh or lath reinforcement.

LIQUID FILLED COLUMNS

During a fire the liquid, circulating by convection from fire floor columns, removes heat. Storage tanks or city water mains can be used to replace water converted to steam (vented by pressure relief valves or rupture discs). Pumps also may be used to avoid stagnant areas within an interconnected water circulation system of columns and piping. To prevent corrosion, use a rust inhibitor such as potassium nitrate. To prevent freezing in cold climates, use an antifreeze such as potassium carbonate. During construction, strict quality control is essential to achieve a watertight system.

COATINGS

Intumescent mastic coatings can be spray-applied like paint. When exposed to fire, the coating absorbs heat above about 300°F by expanding into a thick, lightweight thermal barrier more than about 150 times its initial thickness. This gas filled multicellular layer retards heat flow by releasing cooling gases and blocks off oxygen supply. Coatings should only be applied to steel surfaces that are free of dirt, scale, and oil. A multilayer system, consisting of intumescent mastic layers with glass fiber reinforcing between, is needed to achieve fire resistance ratings greater than 1 hr.

When exposed to heat, magnesium oxychloride cement retards heat flow to steel by releasing water of hydration at temperatures above about 570°F. Corrosion resistant priming may be required to assure proper adhesion of magnesium oxychloride to steel surfaces. In high intensity fires (e.g., flammable liquid or gas fires), magnesium oxychloride does not spall and the magnesium oxide residue acts as an efficient heat reflector.

FLAME SHIELDS

Steel flame shields can deflect heat and flames from burning building away from exterior structural steel members. For example, girder top and bottom flanges avoid direct flame impingement during fire by having flame shield protection with thermal insulation behind girder.

NOTES

1. Check prevailing building code for required fire resistance ratings of building constructions. Begin planning steel fire protection during the early stages of a project so that it can be integrated into building design. Consult early with authority having jurisdiction and insurance underwriting groups such as Industrial Risk Insurers, American Insurance Association, or Factory Mutual System.
2. Refer to fire resistance data based on ASTM E 119 test procedures from Underwriters' Laboratories, Factory Mutual, and other nationally recognized testing laboratories.
3. In general, fire resistance of constructions with cavity airspace (e.g., walls, floor-ceilings) will be greater than similar identical weight constructions without airspace.
4. If possible, locate cavity airspace on side of construction opposite potential fire exposure.
5. For most situations, fire resistance of constructions with thermal insulating materials such as mineral fiber and glass fiber in cavity airspace (e.g., doors, walls) will be greater than identical constructions without cavity insulation. Be careful, however, since adding thermal insulation to suspended floor-ceiling assemblies may lower fire resistance by causing metal suspension grid system to buckle or warp from elevated surface temperatures.
6. When plenum spaces above suspended ceilings are used for mechanical system return airflow, fire resistance of floor-ceiling assemblies will be diminished. Conversely, plenums under positive pressure from supply airflow can achieve greater fire resistances than under neutral pressure conditions (e.g., no air circulation in plenum).
7. For beams and columns, the higher the ratio of weight (e.g., pounds per unit length) to heated perimeter (i.e., surface area exposed to fire) the greater the fire resistance.
8. Beams and columns with membrane enclosure protection will have less surface area exposed to fire than identical members with spray-on applied contour protection. In addition, membrane enclosures (e.g., gypsum board, mineral fiber, magnesium oxychloride, or metal lath) form airspaces on both sides of W and S section webs.

M. David Egan, P.E.; College of Architecture, Clemson University; Clemson, South Carolina

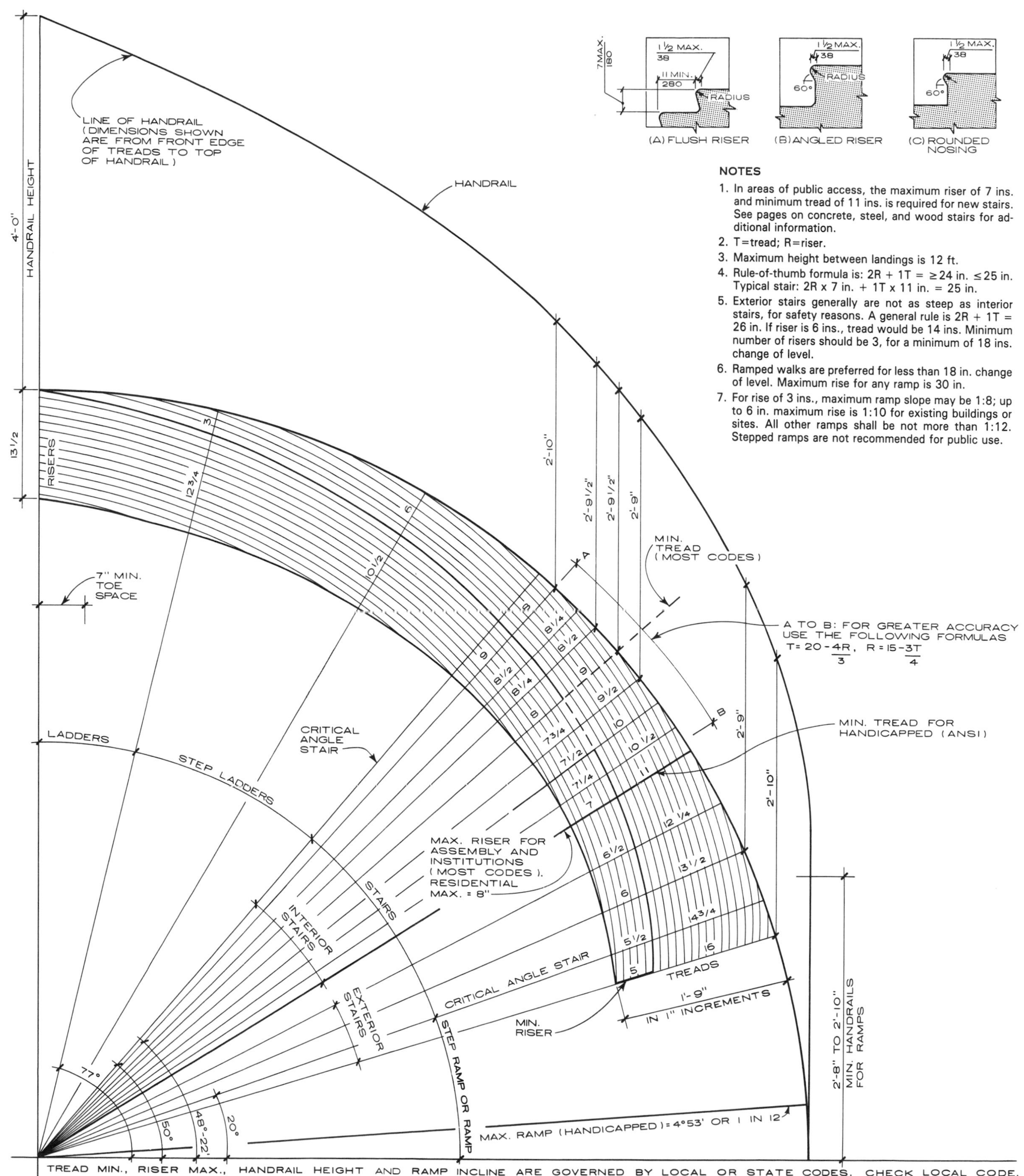

LINE OF HANDRAIL (DIMENSIONS SHOWN ARE FROM FRONT EDGE OF TREADS TO TOP OF HANDRAIL)
HANDRAIL
4'-0"
HANDRAIL HEIGHT
13 1/2
RISERS
7" MIN. TOE SPACE
LADDERS
STEP LADDERS
CRITICAL ANGLE STAIR
INTERIOR STAIRS
STAIRS
EXTERIOR STAIRS
CRITICAL ANGLE STAIR
STEP RAMP OR RAMP
MAX. RISER FOR ASSEMBLY AND INSTITUTIONS (MOST CODES). RESIDENTIAL MAX. = 8"
MIN. RISER
TREADS
1'-9"
IN 1" INCREMENTS
MIN. TREAD (MOST CODES)
A TO B: FOR GREATER ACCURACY USE THE FOLLOWING FORMULAS T= 20 - 4R/3, R = 15 - 3T/4
MIN. TREAD FOR HANDICAPPED (ANSI)
2'-10"
2'-9 1/2"
2'-9 1/2"
2'-9"
2'-9"
2'-10"
2'-8" TO 2'-10"
MIN. HANDRAILS FOR RAMPS
MAX. RAMP (HANDICAPPED) = 4°53' OR 1 IN 12
77°
50°
48°-22'
20°
7 MAX. 180
1 1/2 MAX. 38
11 MIN. 280
RADIUS
60°
(A) FLUSH RISER
(B) ANGLED RISER
(C) ROUNDED NOSING
TREAD MIN., RISER MAX., HANDRAIL HEIGHT AND RAMP INCLINE ARE GOVERNED BY LOCAL OR STATE CODES. CHECK LOCAL CODE.

NOTES

1. In areas of public access, the maximum riser of 7 ins. and minimum tread of 11 ins. is required for new stairs. See pages on concrete, steel, and wood stairs for additional information.
2. T=tread; R=riser.
3. Maximum height between landings is 12 ft.
4. Rule-of-thumb formula is: 2R + 1T = ≥24 in. ≤25 in. Typical stair: 2R x 7 in. + 1T x 11 in. = 25 in.
5. Exterior stairs generally are not as steep as interior stairs, for safety reasons. A general rule is 2R + 1T = 26 in. If riser is 6 ins., tread would be 14 ins. Minimum number of risers should be 3, for a minimum of 18 ins. change of level.
6. Ramped walks are preferred for less than 18 in. change of level. Maximum rise for any ramp is 30 in.
7. For rise of 3 ins., maximum ramp slope may be 1:8; up to 6 in. maximum rise is 1:10 for existing buildings or sites. All other ramps shall be not more than 1:12. Stepped ramps are not recommended for public use.

TREADS AND RISERS

Paul Vaughan, AIA; Charleston, West Virginia

FLOOR STRUCTURE ASSEMBLIES FOR ADDITIONAL INFORMATION CONSULT MANUFACTURERS' LITERATURE AND TRADE ASSOCIATIONS		DEPTH OF SYSTEM (IN.)	STANDARD MEMBER SIZES (IN.)	DEAD LOAD OF STRUCTURE (PSF)	SUITABLE LIVE LOAD RANGE (PSF)	SPAN RANGE (FT)	DIMENSIONAL STABILITY AFFECTED BY
WOOD JOIST	PLYWOOD SUBFLOOR; WOOD JOIST; CEILING	7-13	Nominal joist 2 x 6, 8, 10, and 12	5-8	30-40	Up to 18	Deflection
WOOD TRUSS OR PLYWOOD JOIST	PLYWOOD SUBFLOOR; PLYWOOD JOIST (OR WOOD TRUSS); CEILING	13-21	Plywood joists 12, 14, 16, 18, and 20	6-12	30-40	12-30	Deflection
WOOD BEAM AND PLANK	WOOD PLANK; WOOD BEAM	10-22	Nominal plank 2, 3, and 4	6-16	30-40	10-22	–
LAMINATED WOOD BEAM AND PLANK	WOOD PLANK; GLUE LAMINATED WOOD BEAM	8-22	Nominal plank 2, 3, and 4	6-20	30-40	8-34	–
STEEL JOIST	PLYWOOD SUBFLOOR; WOOD NAILER; STEEL JOIST; CEILING	9-31	Steel joists 8-30	8-20	30-40	16-40	Deflection
STEEL JOIST	CONCRETE SLAB; STEEL CENTERING; STEEL JOIST; CEILING	11-75	Steel joists 8-72	30-110	30-100	16-60 (up to 130)	Deflection
LIGHT-WEIGHT STEEL FRAMF	PLYWOOD SUBFLOOR; LIGHTWEIGHT STEEL FRAME; CEILING	7-12	Consult manufacturers' literature	6-20	30-60	10-22	–
STEEL FRAME	CONCRETE SLAB; STEEL CENTERING; STEEL BEAM; CEILING	9-15	–	35-60	30-100	16-35	Deflection
STEEL FRAME	CONCRETE TOPPING; PRECAST CONCRETE PLANK; STEEL BEAM; CEILING	8-16	Concrete plank 16-48 W 4-12 D	40-75	60-150	Up to 50 Generally below 35	Deflection and creep
PRECAST CONCRETE	CONCRETE TOPPING; PRECAST CONCRETE PLANK; CONCRETE BEAM	6-12	Concrete plank 16-48 W 4-12 D	40-75	60-150	Up to 60 Generally below 35	Deflection and creep
ONE-WAY CONCRETE SLAB	CONCRETE SLAB; CONCRETE BEAM	4-10	–	50-120	40-150	10-20 More with prestressing	–
TWO-WAY CONCRETE SLAB	CONCRETE SLAB; CONCRETE BEAM	4-10	–	50-120	40-250	10-30 More with prestressing	–
ONE-WAY RIBBED CONCRETE SLAB	CONCRETE SLAB; RIB (JOIST)	8-22	Standard pan forms 20 and 30 W 6-20 D	40-90	40-150	15-50 More with prestressing	Creep
TWO-WAY RIBBED CONCRETE SLAB	CONCRETE SLAB; RIB (JOIST)	8-22	Standard domc forms 19 x 19, 30 x 30 6-20 D	75-105	60-200	25-60 More with prestressing	Creep
CONCRETE FLAT SLAB	CONCRETE SLAB; DROP PANEL; CAPITAL; COLUMN	6-16	Min. slab thickness 5 without Drop panel, 4 with Drop panel	75-170	60-250	20-40 Up to 70 with prestressing	Creep
PRECAST DOUBLE TEE	CONCRETE TOPPING; PRECAST DOUBLE TEE	8-18	4', 5', 6', 8', and 10' W 6-16 D	50-80	40-150	20-50	Creep
PRECAST TEE	CONCRETE TOPPING; PRECAST SINGLE TEE	18-38	16-36 D	50-90	40-150	25-65	Creep
COMPOSITE	CONCRETE SLAB; WELDED STUD (SHEAR CONNECTOR); STEEL BEAM	4-6	–	35-70	60-200	Up to 35	Deflection
CONCRETE FLAT PLATE	COLUMN; CONCRETE FLAT PLATE	5-14	–	60-175	60-200	18-35 More with prestressing	Creep

Roger K. Lewis, FAIA, and Mehmet T. Ergene, Architect; Roger K. Lewis, FAIA, & Associates; Washington, D.C.

BAY SIZE CHARAC-TERISTICS	REQUIRES FINISHED FLOOR SURFACE	REQUIRES FINISHED CEILING SURFACE	SERVICE PLENUM	COMPARATIVE RESISTANCE TO SOUND TRANSMISSION		FIRE RESISTIVE RATING PER CODE AND UNDERWRITERS		CONSTRUC-TION TYPE CLASSIFI-CATION	REMARKS
				IMPACT	AIRBORNE	UNPRO-TECTED HOURS	MAXIMUM PROTECTED HOURS		
–	Yes	Visual or fire protection purposes	Between joists —one way	Poor	Fair	–	2 (combustible)	4B (A) 3C (B)	Economical, light, easy to construct. Limited to lowrise construction
–	Yes	Visual or fire protection purposes	Between trusses and joists —two ways	Poor	Fair	–	2 (combustible)	4B (A) 3C (B)	Close dimensional tolerances; cutting holes through web permissible
Maximum beam spacing 8′-0″	Optional	No	Under structure —one way	Poor	Fair	–	2	3A 6″ x 10″ frame min. 4″ planks min.	Most efficient with planks continuous over more than one span
–	Optional	No	Under structure —one way	Poor	Fair	–	2	3A 6″ x 10″ frame min. 4″ planks min.	–
Light joists 16″ to 30″ o.c. Heavy joists 4′-12′ o.c.	Yes	Visual or fire protection purposes	Between joists —two ways	Poor	Poor	–	1	3C (B)	–
Light joists 16″ to 30″ o.c. Heavy joists 4′-12′ o.c.	No	Visual or fire protection purposes	Between joists —two ways	Poor	Fair	–	1-3	1, 2 and 3	Economical system, selective partition placement required. Cantilevers difficult
–	Yes	Visual or fire protection purposes	Under structure	Poor	Poor	–	1	3C (B)	–
–	No	Visual or fire protection purposes	Under structure	Poor	Fair	1-3	1-4	1, 2, and 3	–
–	Optional	Visual or fire protection purposes	Under structure	Fair	Fair	–	1-4	1, 2, and 3	–
–	Optional	No	Under structure	Fair	Fair	2-4	3-4	1 and 2	–
–	No	No	Under structure	Good	Good	1-4	3-4	1 and 2	Restricted to short spans because of excessive dead load
L ≤ 1.33 W	No	No	Under structure	Good	Good	1-4	3-4	1 and 2	Suitable for concentrated loads, easy partition placement
–	No	No	Between ribs —one way	Good	Good	1-4	3-4	1 and 2	Economy through reuse of forms, shear at supports controlling factor
L ≤ 1.33 W	No	No	Under structure	Good	Good	1-4	3-4	1 and 2	For heavy loads, columns should be equidistant. Not good for cantilevers
L ≤ 1.33 W	No	No	Under structure	Good	Good	1-4	3-4	1 and 2	Drop panels against shear required for spans above 12 ft
–	Optional	Visual purposes; differential camber	Between ribs —one way	Fair	Good	2-3	3-4	1 and 2	Most widely used prestressed concrete product in the medium span range
–	Optional	Visual purposes; differential camber	Between ribs —one way	Fair	Good	2-3	3-4	1 and 2	Easy construction, lack continuity, poor earthquake resistance
–	No	Visual or fire protection purposes	Under structure	Good	Good	–	1-4	1, 2, and 3	–
L ≤ 1.33 W	No	No	Under structure	Good	Good	1-4	3-4	1 and 2	Uniform slab thickness, economical to form, easy to cantilever

Roger K. Lewis, FAIA, and Mehmet T. Ergene, Architect; Roger K. Lewis, FAIA, & Associates; Washington, D.C.

ROOF STRUCTURE ASSEMBLIES FOR ADDITIONAL INFORMATION CONSULT MANUFACTURER'S LITERATURE AND TRADE ASSOCIATIONS		DEPTH OF SYSTEM (IN.)	STANDARD MEMBER SIZES (IN.)	DEAD LOAD OF STRUCTURE (PSF)	SUITABLE LIVE LOAD RANGE (PSF)	SPAN RANGE (FT)	BAY SIZE CHARAC-TERISTICS	DIMENSIONAL STABILITY AFFECTED BY
WOOD RAFTER	PLYWOOD SHEATHING WOOD JOIST CEILING	5-13	Nominal rafters 2 x 4, 6, 8, 10, and 12	4-8	10-50	Up to 22	–	Deflection
WOOD BEAM AND PLANK	WOOD PLANK WOOD BEAM (OR LAMINATED BEAM)	8-22	Nominal planks 2, 3, and 4	5-12	10-50	8-34	Maximum beam spacing 8'-0"	–
PLYWOOD PANEL	PLYWOOD (STRESSED SKIN) PANELS	3¼ and 8¼	–	3-6	10-50	8-32	4'-0" modules	–
WOOD TRUSS	SHEATHING WOOD TRUSS CEILING	Varies (1'-12')	–	5-15	10-50	30-50	2'-8' between trusses	Deflection
STEEL TRUSS	STEEL DECK PURLIN STEEL TRUSS	Varies	–	15-25	10-60	100-200	–	Deflection
STEEL JOIST	CONCRETE STEEL CENTERING STEEL JOIST CEILING	11-75	Steel joists 8-72	10-28	10-50	Up to 96	Light joists 16"-30" o.c. Heavy joists 4'-12' o.c.	Deflection
STEEL JOIST	PLYWOOD DECK WOOD NAILER STEEL JOIST CEILING	10-32	Steel joists 8-30	8-20	10-50	Up to 96	Light joists 16"-30" o.c. Heavy joists 4'-12' o.c.	Deflection
STEEL JOIST	INSULATION STEEL DECK STEEL JOIST CEILING	11-75	Steel joists 8-72	6-24	10-50	Up to 96	–	Deflection
STEEL FRAME	PRECAST CONCRETE PLANK STEEL BEAM CEILING	4-12 plus beam depth	Concrete plank 16-48 W 4-12 D	40-75	30-70	20-60 Generally below 35	–	Deflection and creep
PRECAST CONCRETE	PRECAST CONCRETE PLANK CONCRETE BEAM	4-12 plus beam depth	Concrete plank 16-48 W 4-12 D	40-75	30-70	20-60 Generally below 35	–	Deflection and creep
ONE-WAY CONCRETE SLAB	CONCRETE SLAB CONCRETE BEAM	4-10 slab plus beam depth	–	50-120	Up to 100	10-25 More with prestressing	–	–
TWO-WAY CONCRETE SLAB	CONCRETE SLAB CONCRETE BEAM	4-10 slab plus beam depth	–	50-120	Up to 100	10-30 More with prestressing	L ≤ 1.33 W	–
ONE-WAY RIBBED CONCRETE SLAB	CONCRETE SLAB RIB (JOIST)	8-22	Standard pan forms 20 and 30 W 6-20 D	40-90	Up to 100	15-50 More with prestressing	–	Creep
TWO-WAY RIBBED CONCRETE SLAB	CONCRETE SLAB RIB (JOIST)	8-24	Standard dome forms 19 x 19, 30 x 30 6-20 D	75-105	Up to 100	25-60 More with prestressing	L ≤ 1.33 W	Creep
PRECAST TEE		16-36	16-36 deep	65-85	20-80	30-100	–	Creep
PRECAST DOUBLE TEE		6-16	4', 5', 6', 8', and 10' wide 6"-16" deep	35-55	25-60	20-75	–	Creep
CONCRETE FLAT PLATE	CONCRETE FLAT PLATE COLUMN	4-14	–	50-160	Up to 100	Up to 35 More with prestressing	L ≤ 1.33 W	Creep
CONCRETE FLAT SLAB	CONCRETE SLAB DROP PANEL CAPITAL COLUMN	5-16	Min. slab thickness 5 w/o } Drop 4 w/ } panel	50-200	Up to 100	Up to 40 More with prestressing	L ≤ 1.33 W Equal column spacing required	Creep
GYPSUM DECK	GYPSUM CONCRETE FORM BOARD SUBPURLIN CEILING	3-6	–	5-20	Up to 50	Up to 10	Up to 8' between subpurlins	Deflection and creep

Roger K. Lewis, FAIA, and Mehmet T. Ergene, Architect; Roger K. Lewis, FAIA, & Associates; Washington, D.C.

SUITABLE FOR INCLINED ROOFS	REQUIRES FINISHED CEILING SURFACE	SERVICE PLENUM	RELATIVE THERMAL CAPACITY	COMPARATIVE RESISTANCE TO SOUND TRANSMISSION		FIRE RESISTIVE RATING PER CODE AND UNDERWRITERS		CONSTRUCTION TYPE CLASSIFICATION	REMARKS
				IMPACT	AIRBORNE	UNPROTECTED HOURS	MAXIMUM PROTECTED HOURS		
Yes	For visual or fire protection purposes	Between rafters —one way	Low	Poor	Fair	–	2 (combustible)	4B (A) 3C (B)	
Yes	For fire protection purposes	Under structure —one way	Medium	Poor	Fair	–	2	3A 6" x 10" frame min. 4" plank min.	
Yes	No	Under structure only	Low	Poor	Fair	–	2	4B (A) 3C (B)	
Yes	For visual or fire protection purposes	Between trusses	Low	Poor	Fair	–	2 (combustible)	4B (A) 3C (B)	Truss depth to span ratio 1:5 to 1:10
Yes Pitched trusses usually used for short spans	For visual or fire protection purposes	Between trusses	Low	Fair	Fair	–	1-4	1, 2, and 3	Truss depth to span ratio 1:5 to 1:15
No	For visual or fire protection purposes	Between joists	Medium	Fair	Fair	–	1-4	1, 2, and 3	
Yes	For visual or fire protection purposes	Between joists	Low	Poor	Fair	–	1	1, 2, and 3	
Yes	For visual or fire protection purposes	Between joists	High	Excellent	Good	–	2	1, 2, and 3	
Yes	For visual or fire protection purposes	Under structure	High	Fair	Fair	–	1-4	1, 2, and 3	Easy to design; quick erection
Yes	No	Under structure	High	Fair	Fair	2-4	3-4	1 and 2	Provides finished flush ceiling. May be used with any framing system
No	No	Under structure	High	Good	Good	1-4	3-4	1 and 2	
No	No	Under structure	High	Good	Good	1-4	3-4	1 and 2	
No	For visual purposes	Between ribs —one way	High	Good	Good	1-4	3-4	1 and 2	
No	No	Under structure	High	Good	Good	1-4	3-4	1 and 2	Economy in forming; suitable for two-way cantilevering
Yes	For visual or fire protection purposes	Between ribs —one way	High	Fair	Good	2-3	3-4	1 and 2	Generally used for long spans
Yes	For visual or fire protection purposes	Between ribs —one way	High	Fair	Good	2-3	3-4	1 and 2	Most widely used prestressed concrete element.
No	No	Under structure	High	Good	Good	1-4	3-4	1 and 2	Uniform slab thickness; easy to form; suitable for vertical expansion of building
No	No	Under structure	High	Good	Good	1-4	3-4	1 and 2	Suitable for heavy roof loads
No	For visual or fire protection purposes	Under structure	High	Good	Good	–	2	1, 2, and 3	Provides resistance to wind and seismic loads

Roger K. Lewis, FAIA, and Mehmet T. Ergene, Architect; Roger K. Lewis, FAIA, & Associates; Washington, D.C.
DeChiara and Koppelman, see data sources

EXTERIOR WALL ASSEMBLIES — FOR ADDITIONAL INFORMATION CONSULT MANUFACTURERS LITERATURE AND TRADE ASSOCIATIONS		WALL THICKNESS (NOMINAL) (IN.)	WEIGHT (PSF)	VERTICAL SPAN RANGE (UNSUPPORTED HEIGHT) (FT)	WIND RESIST.	RACKING RESISTANCE	SERVICE PLENUM SPACE	HEAT TRANSMISSION COEFFICIENT (U-FACTOR) (BTU/HR · SQ FT · °F)
C. M. U.	C. M. U. (GRAVEL AGGREGATE)	8 12	55 85	Up to 13 Up to 20	Wind resistance depends on geographical location and height of building; wind velocity; wall material thickness, strength; workmanship; axial loads; and horizontal span. Design walls for both inward and outward pressures	Good	None	0.56 0.49
C. M. U. (INSULATED)	C. M. U. INSULATION INT. WALL FIN.	8 + 12 +	60 90	Up to 13 Up to 20		Good	Through insulation	0.21 0.20
C. M. U. AND BRICK VENEER (INSULATED)	BRICK VENEER C. M. U. INSULATION INT. WALL FIN.	4 + 4 + 4 + 8 +	75 100	Up to 13 (w/filled cavity) Up to 20 (w/filled cavity)		Good	Through insulation	0.19 0.18
CAVITY	BRICK VENEER CAVITY (MIN. 2") INSULATION (WATER REPELLENT) C. M. U. INT. WALL FIN.	4 + 2 + 4 4 + 2 + 8	75 100	Up to 9 Up to 13		Fair	None	0.12 0.11
C. M. U. AND STUCCO (INSULATED)	STUCCO C. M. U. INSULATION INT. WALL FIN.	8 +	67	Up to 13		Good	Through interior insulation	0.16
WOOD STUD	EXT. WALL FIN. SHEATHING WITH MOISTURE BARRIER WOOD STUD INSULATION WITH VAPOR BARRIER INT. WALL FIN	4 6	12 16	Up to 14 Up to 20 (L/d ≤ 50)		Poor to fair	Between studs	0.06 0.04
BRICK VENEER	BRICK VENEER SHEATHING WITH MOISTURE BARRIER WOOD STUD INSULATION WITH VAPOR BARRIER INT. WALL FIN.	4 + 4	52	Up to 14		Poor to fair	Between studs	0.07
METAL STUD	EXT. WALL FIN. METAL STUD AT 16" O.C. INSULATION WITH VAPOR BARRIER INT. WALL FIN.	4 5	14 18	Up to 13 Up to 17		Poor	Between studs	0.06 0.04
BRICK VENEER	BRICK VENEER SHEATHING WITH MOISTURE BARRIER METAL STUD AT 16" O.C. INSULATION WITH VAPOR BARRIER INT. WALL FIN.	4 + 4	54	Up to 15		Good	Between studs	0.07
INSULATED SANDWICH PANEL	METAL SKIN AIRSPACE INSULATING CORE METAL SKIN	5	6	See manufacturers' literature		Fair to good	None	0.05 See manufacturers' literature
CONCRETE	CONCRETE	8 12	92 138	Up to 13 (w/reinf. 17) Up to 20 (w/reinf. 25)		Excellent	None	0.68 0.55
CONCRETE (INSULATED)	CONCRETE INSULATION INT. WALL FIN.	8 +	97	Up to 13 (w/reinf. 17)		Excellent	Through insulation	0.13
CONCRETE AND BRICK VENEER (INSULATED)	BRICK VENEER CONCRETE INSULATION INT. WALL FIN.	4 + 8 +	112	Up to 13 (w/reinf. 17)		Excellent	Through insulation	0.13
PRECAST CONCRETE	CONCRETE (REINFORCED) INSULATION INT. WALL FINISH	2 + 4 +	23 46	Up to 6 Up to 12		Fair to good	Through insulation	0.99 0.85
PRECAST CONCRETE SANDWICH	CONCRETE INSULATION	5	45	Up to 14		Fair to good	None	0.14

GLASS	SEE INDEX UNDER "GLASS"			SIZE RANGE — MAXIMUM ALLOWABLE GLASS AREA	WIND LOAD	SHADING COEFFICIENT S.C.	
SINGLE GLAZING	1/4" GLASS	1/4	3.2	Four side supported Two side supported	110 SF @ 10 PSF 20 SF @ 60 PSF 40 SF @ 10 PSF 17 SF @ 60 PSF	Clear 0.94 Tinted 0.70 Reflective 0.44	Clear/tinted 1.1 Reflective 0.8–1.1
DOUBLE GLAZING	1/4" GLASS 1/4" CAVITY	3/4	6.4	Four side supported Heat strengthened	55 SF @ 30 PSF 28 SF @ 60 PSF 70 SF @ 80 PSF 30 SF @ 200 PSF		Clear/tinted 0.5–0.6 Reflective 0.3–0.6
TRIPLE GLAZING	1/4" GLASS 1/4" CAVITY	1 1/4	9.6	–			Clear/tinted 0.3–0.4 Reflective 0.2–0.4

Roger K. Lewis, FAIA, and Mehmet T. Ergene, Architect; Roger K. Lewis, FAIA, & Associates; Washington, D.C.

RESISTANCE TO EXTERIOR AIRBORNE SOUND TRANSMISSION	HAZARD CLASSIFICATION (FIRE)	FIRE RESISTIVE RATING PER CODE AND UNDERWRITERS (HRS)	CONSTRUCTION TYPE CLASSIFICATION	SUBCONTRACTORS REQUIRED FOR ERECTION (PLUS FINISHES)	EXTERIOR MAINTENANCE REQUIREMENTS	REMARKS
Fair to good	Classification provides data in regard to (1) flame spread, (2) fuel contributed, and (3) smoke developed during fire exposure of materials in comparison to asbestos-	2-4 4	1, 2, and 3	Masonry	Washing, repointing joints, painting, sand blasting	Properties of non-engineered masonry are drastically reduced
Fair to good	cement boards as zero and untreated red oak lumber as 100 when exposed to fire under similar conditions	2-4 4	1, 2, and 3	Masonry Carpentry Drywall	Washing, repointing joints, painting, sand blasting	
Excellent	FLAME SPREAD — FUEL CONTRIBUTED — SMOKE DEVELOPED Paint on CMU 5-25 — 0-5 — 0-10	3-4 4	1, 2, and 3	Masonry Carpentry Drywall	Washing, repointing joints, sand blasting	
Excellent	Gypsum board surfaced on both sides with paper 15 — 15 — 0	4	1, 2, and 3	Masonry Drywall (Carpentry)	Washing, repointing joints, sand blasting	Cavity increases heat storage capacity and resistance to rain penetration
Good	Gypsum board surfaced on both sides with paper, vinyl faced 25-35 — 0-10 — 15-45	2-4	1, 2, and 3	Masonry Drywall Lath and plaster (Carpentry)	Washing, painting, and restuccoing	The assembly is reversed for optimum energy conservation
Poor to fair	Untreated wood particle board 180 — 75 — 190	1 (combustible)	4	Carpentry Drywall (Lath and plaster)	Washing, painting, and replacing exterior finish	Exterior wall finishes: • wood, plywood, • aluminum siding • stucco
Good to excellent	Treated wood particle board with untreated wood face veneer 25-180 — 10-160 — 10-250	1-2 (combustible)	3B, C	Masonry Carpentry Drywall	Washing, repointing joints, sand blasting	
Poor to fair	Vermiculite acoustical plaster 10-20 — 10-20 — 0	1-2	1 (nonbearing) 2 and 3	Carpentry Drywall (Lath and plaster)	Washing, painting, and replacing exterior finish	Exterior wall finishes: • wood, plywood, • aluminum siding • stucco
Good to excellent	Glass fiber batts and blankets (basic) 20 — 15 — 20 (foil kraft faced)	1-2	1 (nonbearing) 2 and 3	Masonry Carpentry Drywall	Washing, repointing joints, sand blasting	
Poor to good; see manufacturers' literature	25 — 0 — 0 Treated lumber (Douglas fir) 15 — 10 — 0-5	See manufacturers' literature	See manufacturers' literature	Curtain walls —erection	Washing, steam cleaning, painting, replacing joint sealers	Temperature change critical Minimize metal through connections
Good	(Hemlock) 10-15 — 5-15 — 0 Laminated plastic (fr)	4 4	1, 2, and 3	Concrete work	Washing, sand blasting	Concrete walls have very high heat storage capacity
Good	20-30 — 0-15 — 5-30	4 4	1, 2, and 3	Concrete work Drywall (Carpentry)	Washing, sand blasting	
Excellent	NFPA CLASSIFICATION: CLASS — FLAME SPREAD — SMOKE DEVELOPED	4	1, 2, and 3	Concrete work Masonry Drywall (Carpentry)	Washing, repointing joints, sand blasting	
Poor to fair	A — 0-25 — 0-450 B — 26-75 — 0-450 C — 76-200 — 0-450 For lesser classifications, permitted in residential construction only,	— 1-3	1A (nonbearing) 1B, 2, and 3	Curtain walls —erection Drywall (Carpentry)	Washing, sand blasting, replacing joint sealers	Large size economical (fewer joints) units available with various finishes
Fair	refer to regulating agency guidelines	1-3	1A (nonbearing) 1B, 2, and 3	Curtain walls —erection	Washing, sand blasting, replacing joint sealers	8′ x 20′ max. size for concrete sandwich panels Plant quality control is very essential
Poor	—	—		Curtain walls —erection (Glazing)	Washing, replacing joint sealers, gaskets	Anchorage to building is critical Anchors must isolate wall to limit building movement transmitted to glass Wall design must limit wall movement transmitted to glass Mullions should accommodate movement through gaskets, sliding connections, etc.
Fair	—	—		Curtain walls —erection (Glazing)	Washing, replacing joint sealers, gaskets	
Good	—	—		Curtain walls —erection (Glazing)	Washing, replacing joint sealers, gaskets	

Roger K. Lewis, FAIA, and Mehmet T. Ergene, Architect; Roger K. Lewis, FAIA, & Associates; Washington, D.C.

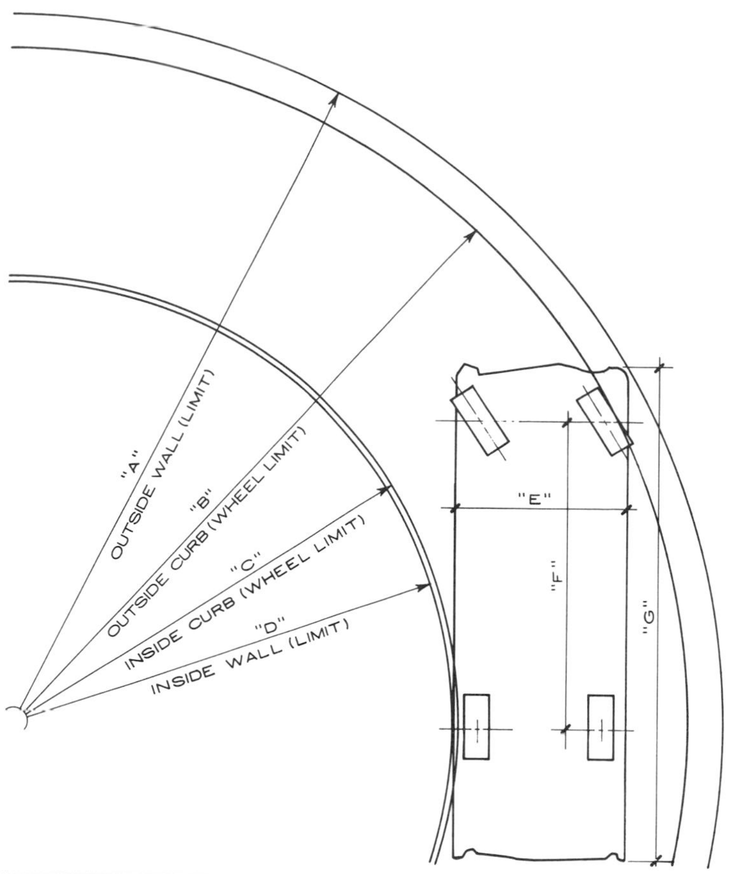
"A" OUTSIDE WALL (LIMIT)
"B" OUTSIDE CURB (WHEEL LIMIT)
"C" INSIDE CURB (WHEEL LIMIT)
"D" INSIDE WALL (LIMIT)
"E"
"F"
"G"

AMBULANCES AND HEARSES
DIMENSIONS AND TURNING RADII

MAKE OF CAR	A	B	C	D	E	F	G
BUICK	28'-9"	27'-3"	18'-4"	17'-10"	6'-0"	11'-7"	19'-2"
LINCOLN	30'-2"	28'-5"	18'-6"	18'-4"	6'-6"	11'-5"	19'-8"

Dimensions vary—verify with individual coach builder.

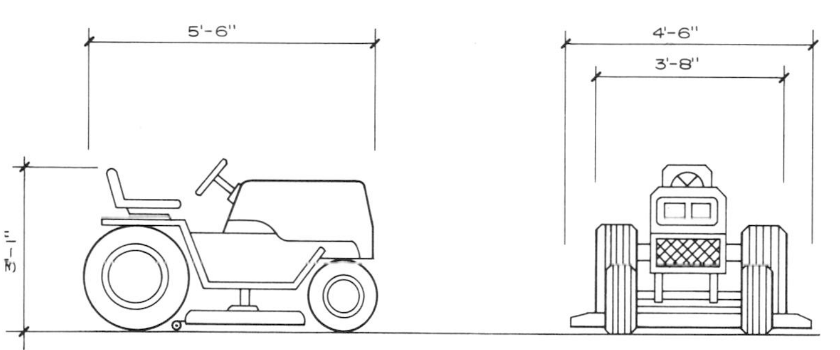
5'-6"
3'-1"
4'-6"
3'-8"

GARDEN TRACTOR

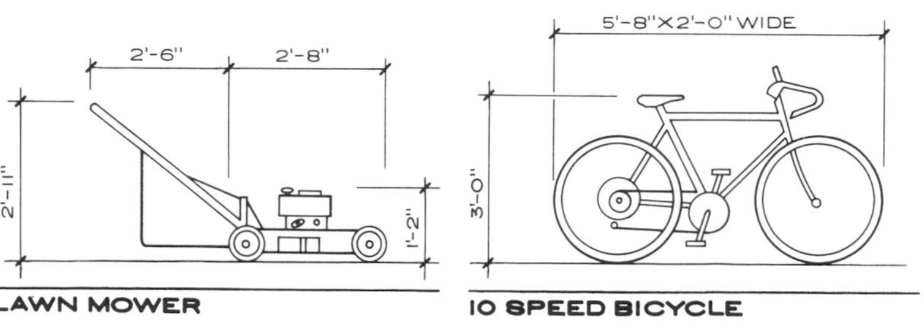
2'-6"
2'-8"
2'-11"
1'-2"
5'-8"X2'-0" WIDE
3'-0"

LAWN MOWER

10 SPEED BICYCLE

GOLF CARTS GASOLINE OR ELECTRIC POWER

3 WHEELS		4 WHEELS
46 3/4"	Overall Height	47 1/8"
10 3/4"	Floorboard Height	11 1/4"
27 3/4"	Seat Height	28 1/4"
102"	Length	102"
47"	Width	47"
68"	Wheel Base	68 3/4"
—	Front Wheel Tread	34"
34 5/8"	Rear Wheel Tread	34 5/8"
4 5/8"	Ground Clearance	4 5/8"
19'–6"	Clearance Circle	24'–0"

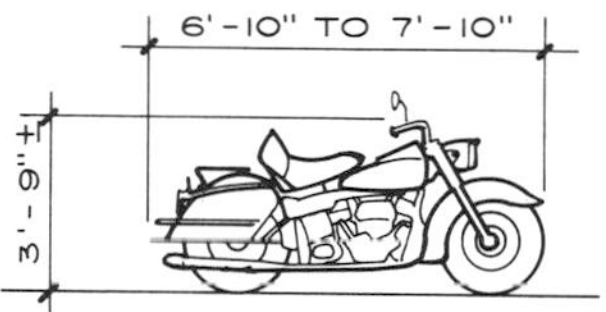
6'-10" TO 7'-10"
3'-9"±

WIDTH AT HANDLEBAR 2'-7" TO 3'-6"

When parked on stand motorcycle leans about 10° to 12°. Large vehicle requires about 3'–8" of space.

HEAVYWEIGHTS WEIGH FROM ABOUT 400 LB TO 661 LB

Consult manufacturers' information for width of motorcycle and sidecar.

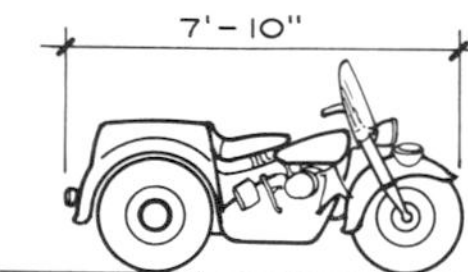
7'-10"

POLICE TRICYCLE WIDTH AT BOX 4'-0"±

HEAVYWEIGHT MOTORCYCLES

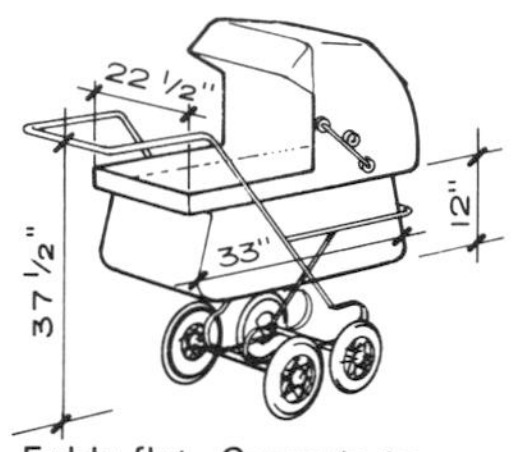
22 1/2"
12"
33"
37 1/2"

Folds flat. Converts to stroller. Body makes car bed.
BABY CARRIAGE

5'-9" TO 6'-10"

Handlebar width 23" and up.
Weight about 230 lb to about 300 lb

LIGHTWEIGHT MOTORCYCLE

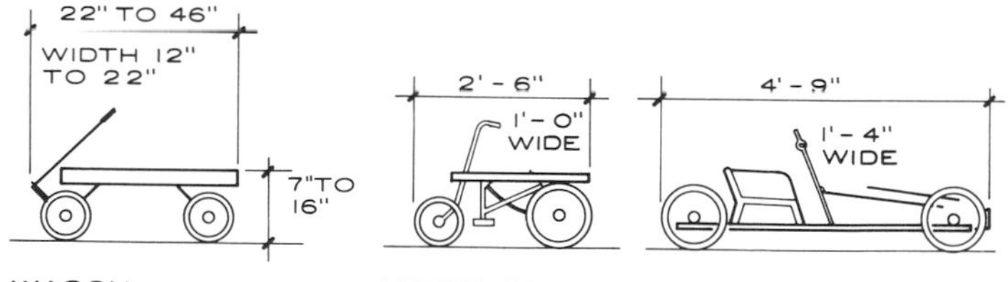
22" TO 46"
WIDTH 12" TO 22"
7" TO 16"
2'-6"
1'-0" WIDE
4'-9"
1'-4" WIDE

WAGON **KIDDIE CAR** **IRISH MAIL**

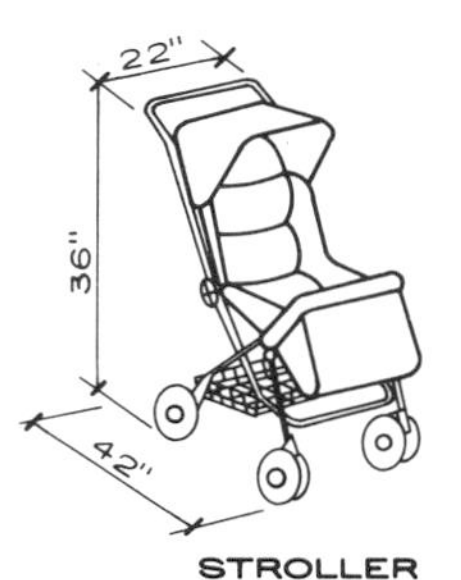
22"
36"
42"

STROLLER

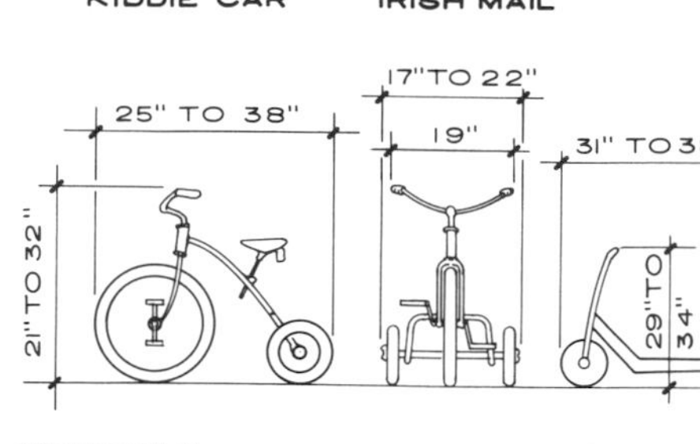
25" TO 38"
21" TO 32"
17" TO 22"
19"
31" TO 38"
29" TO 34"

TRICYCLE **SCOOTER**

Harold C. Munger, FAIA; Munger Munger + Associates Architects, Inc.; Toledo, Ohio
Foster C. Parriott; James M. Hunter & Associates; Boulder, Colorado

NOTE

Each design vehicle in Groups I, II, and III represents a composite of the critical dimensions of the real vehicles within each group below. Parking lot dimensions on the parking lot development page are based on these groups and dimensions. For parking purposes, both compact and standard size vehicles are in Group II. Turning dimensions R, R1, and C are shown on the private roads page.

DESIGN VEHICLE

GROUP I		SUBCOMPACTS
L	Length	13′-10″
W	Width	5′-5″
H	Height	4′-5″
WB	Wheelbase	8′-1″
OF	Overhang front	2′-6″
OR	Overhang rear	3′-9″
OS	Overhang sides	0′-7″
GW	Gross Weight	2100# to 2500#

GROUP II		COMPACTS
L	Length	14′-9″
W	Width	5′-8″
H	Height	4′-5″
WB	Wheelbase	8′-7″
OF	Overhang front	2′-8″
OR	Overhang rear	4′-3″
OS	Overhang sides	0′-8″
GW	Gross Weight	2300# to 2500#

GROUP III		INTERMEDIATE
L	Length	16′-8″
W	Width	6′-0″
H	Height	4′-6″
WB	Wheelbase	9′-0″
OF	Overhang front	2′-10″
OR	Overhang rear	4′-4″
OS	Overhang sides	0′-9″
GW	Gross Weight	2700# to 3200#

GROUP IV		LARGE CARS
L	Length	18′-5″
W	Width	6′-6″
H	Height	4′-9″
WB	Wheelbase	10′-2″
OF	Overhang front	2′-11″
OR	Overhang rear	4′-5″
OS	Overhang sides	0′-9″
GW	Gross Weight	3100# to 4030#

GROUP V		LARGE PICK-UP
L	Length	16′-4″
W	Width	6′-0″
H	Height	5′-8″
WB	Wheelbase	10′-5″
OF	Overhang front	2′-10″
OR	Overhang rear	4′-4″
OS	Overhang sides	0′-9″
GW	Gross Weight	3430#

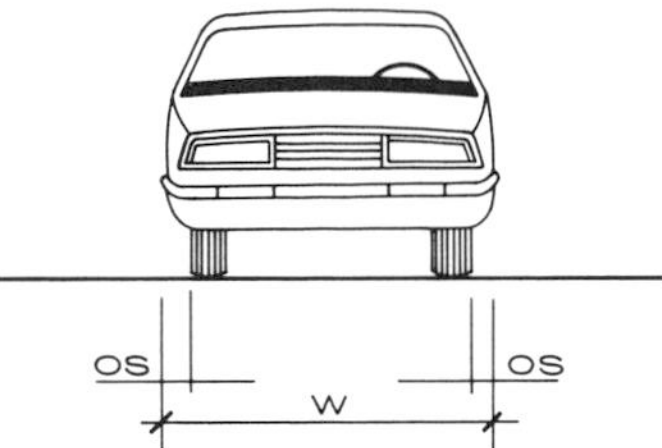
OS
OS
W

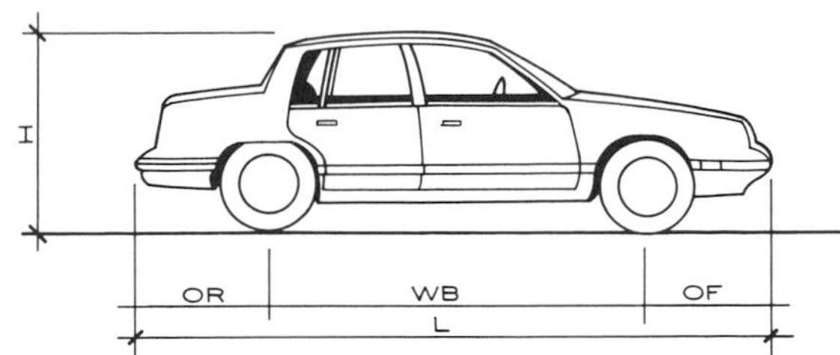
H
OR
WB
OF
L

NOTE

Angles shown below may vary depending on speed, load, tire pressure, and condition of shock absorbers.

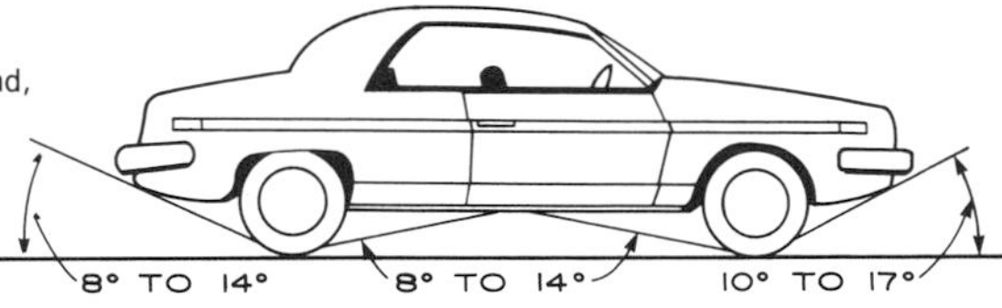
8° TO 14°
8° TO 14°
10° TO 17°

NOTE

Composite vehicle is shown with maximum wheelbase, front overhang, and rear overhang.

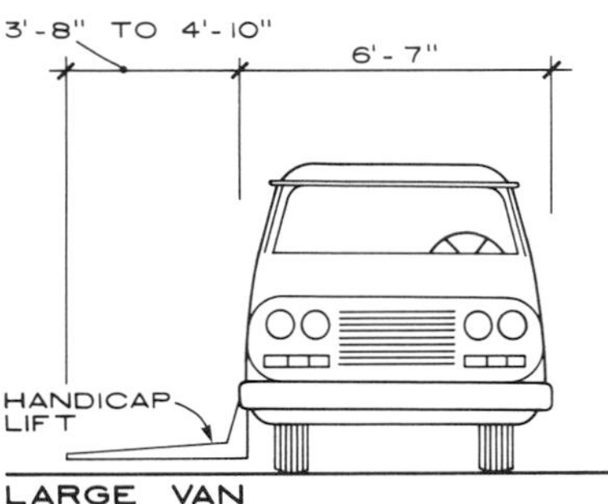
3′-8″ TO 4′-10″
6′-7″
HANDICAP LIFT

LARGE VAN

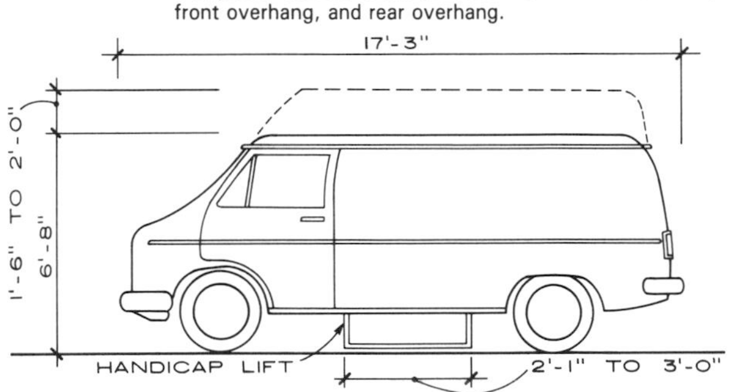
17′-3″
1′-6″ TO 2′-0″
6′-8″
HANDICAP LIFT
2′-1″ TO 3′-0″

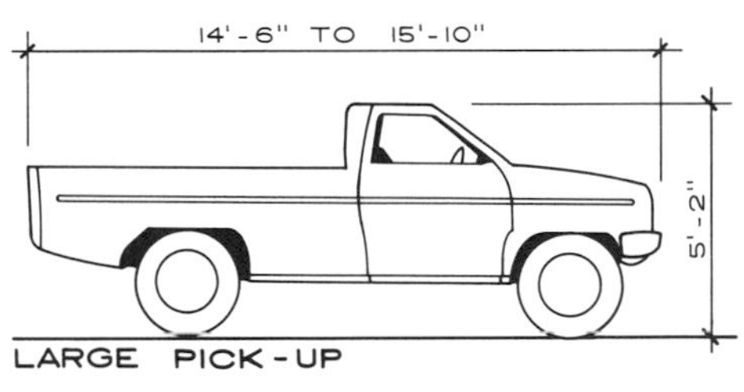
14′-6″ TO 15′-10″
5′-2″

LARGE PICK-UP

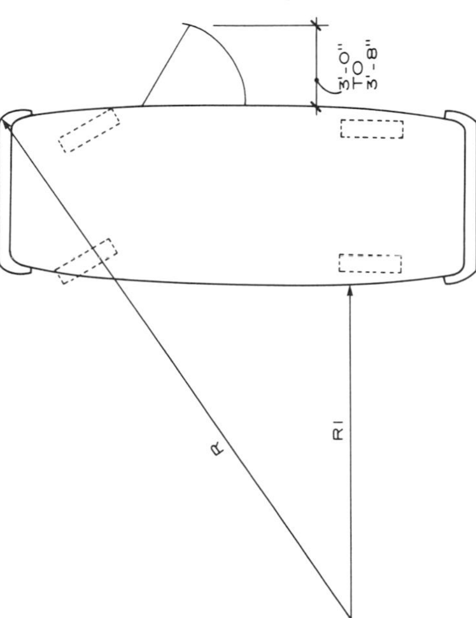
3′-0″ TO 3′-8″
R
R1

LARGE VEHICLE DIMENSIONS*

VEHICLE	(L) LENGTH	(W) WIDTH	(H) HEIGHT	(OR) OVERHANG REAR
Intercity bus	45′-0″	9′-0″	9′-0″	10′-1″
City bus	40′-0″	8′-6″	8′-6″	8′-0″
School bus	39′-6″	8′-0″	8′-6″	12′-8″
Ambulance	20′-10¼″	6′-11″	10′-0″	5′-4″
Paramedic van	21′-6″	8′-0″	6′-6″	4′-0″
Hearse	22′-1″	6′-8″	9′-3″	5′-4″
Airport limousine	22′-5¾″	6′-4″	5′-0″	3′-11″
Trash truck	28′-2″	8′-0″	11′-0″	6′-0″
U.P.S. truck	26′-3″	7′-11″	10′-8″	8′-5″
Fire truck	32′-0″	8′-0″	9′-8″	10′-0″

*Exact sizes of large vehicles may vary

For truck and trailer information, see pages on truck and trailer sizes.

NOTE

For dimensions A and D see page on private roads. Typically parking for handicapped area requires 20 ft. x 12 ft.

For further parking information, see pages on parking lot development and parking garages.

See local codes and standards for parking requirements, size, and quantity of parking spaces and number of spaces required for the handicapped.

Harold C. Munger, FAIA; Munger Munger + Associates Architects, Inc.; Toledo, Ohio
William T. Mahan, AIA; Santa Barbara, California

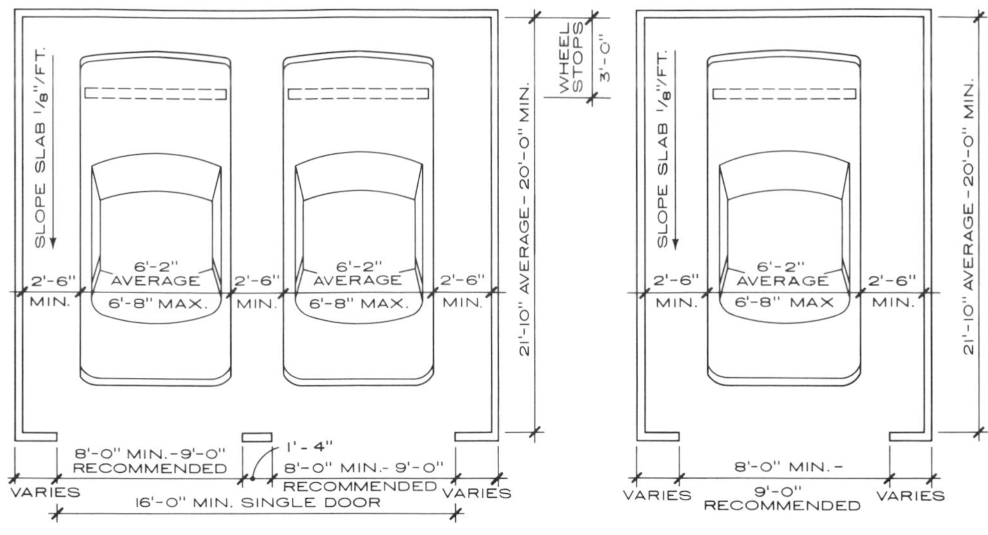
WHEEL STOPS 3'-0"
SLOPE SLAB 1/8"/FT.
2'-6" MIN.
6'-2" AVERAGE
6'-8" MAX.
21'-10" AVERAGE - 20'-0" MIN.
8'-0" MIN.-9'-0" RECOMMENDED
1'-4"
8'-0" MIN.- 9'-0" RECOMMENDED
VARIES
16'-0" MIN. SINGLE DOOR
8'-0" MIN. - 9'-0" RECOMMENDED

TWO-CAR GARAGE

ONE-CAR GARAGE

NOTES

1. Site location varies because of site constraints and design concept. Design considerations include circulation, visual safety for backing out, and visual consideration if garage is exposed to public view.
2. Garages may be enlarged to provide circulation ease by allowing spaces of 2 ft 6 in. minimum between all walls and other vehicles, and to provide space for work areas, photography laboratories, laundry room, and storage.
3. Garages may be attached directly to the house or be connected by a covered passage. Connection is preferable at or near the kitchen or utility area off the kitchen. If attached, refer to local code requirements.

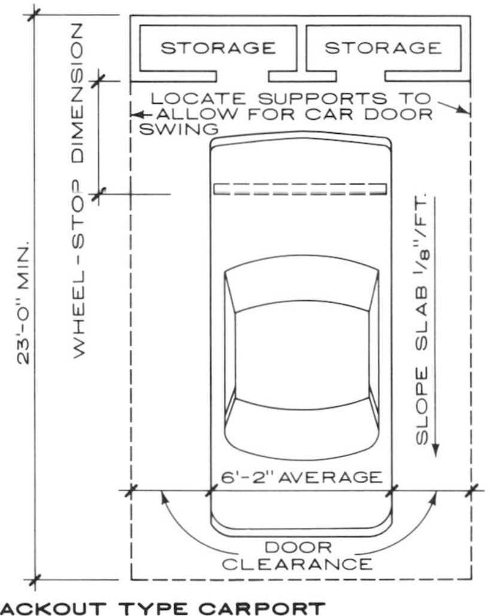
STORAGE
STORAGE
LOCATE SUPPORTS TO ALLOW FOR CAR DOOR SWING
WHEEL-STOP DIMENSION
23'-0" MIN.
SLOPE SLAB 1/8"/FT.
6'-2" AVERAGE
DOOR CLEARANCE

BACKOUT TYPE CARPORT

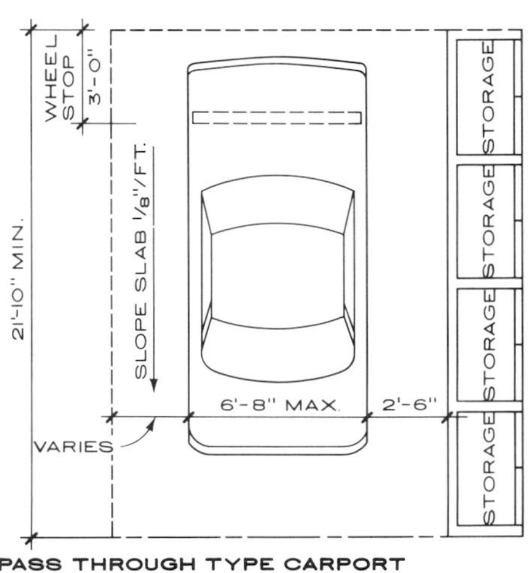
WHEEL STOP 3'-0"
21'-10" MIN.
SLOPE SLAB 1/8"/FT.
STORAGE
6'-8" MAX.
2'-6"
VARIES

PASS THROUGH TYPE CARPORT

CARPORTS

SECTIONAL DOOR SIZES

DOOR WIDTH	NUMBER OF PANELS ACROSS
To 8'-11''	2
9'-0''-11'-11''	3
12'-0''-14'-11''	4
15'-0''-17'-11''	5

NOTE: Doors up to 8'-6'' high require 4 sections.

HINGED GARAGE DOOR WIDTHS

OPENING	TWO-DOOR	THREE-DOOR	FOUR-DOOR
8'-0''	4'-0''	2'-8''	2'-0''
8'-6''	4'-3''	2'-10''	2'-1½''
9'-0''	4'-6''	3'-0''	2'-3''

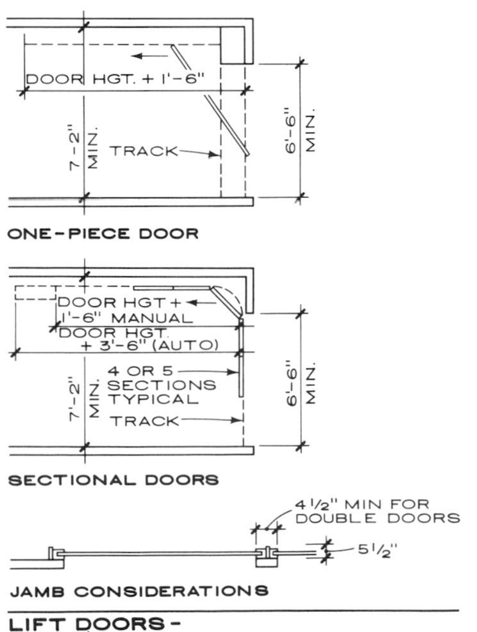
DOOR HGT. + 1'-6"
7'-2" MIN.
TRACK
6'-6" MIN.
DOOR HGT + 1'-6" MANUAL
DOOR HGT. + 3'-6" (AUTO)
4 OR 5 SECTIONS TYPICAL
TRACK
4 1/2" MIN FOR DOUBLE DOORS
5 1/2"

ONE-PIECE DOOR

SECTIONAL DOORS

JAMB CONSIDERATIONS

LIFT DOORS - MOST WIDELY USED - AUTOMATIC OPTIONAL

NOTE: HEIGHTS 6'-6", 6'-10", 7'-0", 7'-6" AND 8'-0"

2" TO 2'-2" CLEARANCE

20'-0" OPENING MAX

HINGED SECTION

JAMB CLEARANCE-WIDTH OF ONE SECTION
ANY OPENING

MULTIPLE DOORS - TWO OR MORE CARS

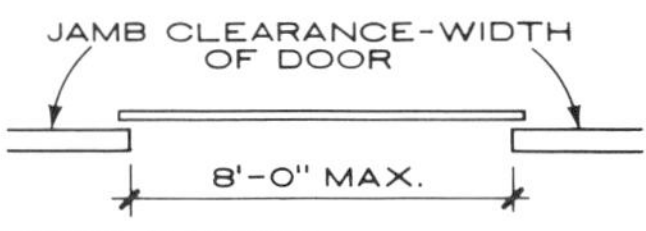
JAMB CLEARANCE-WIDTH OF DOOR
8'-0" MAX.

SINGLE DOOR

NOTE

6½ to 9 in. necessary from top of opening to ceiling (all sliding doors).

SLIDING DOORS

90°
180°
ANY OPENING

OFFSET HINGE-MULTI-LEAVE

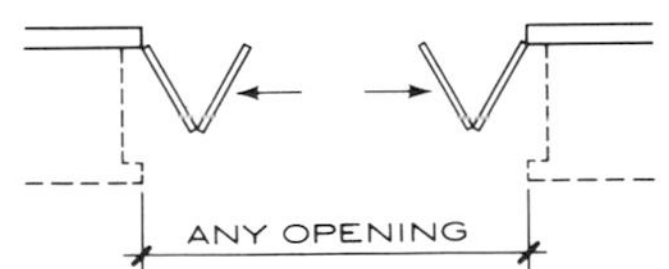
ANY OPENING

MULTIPLE HINGED DOOR TWO OR MORE CARS

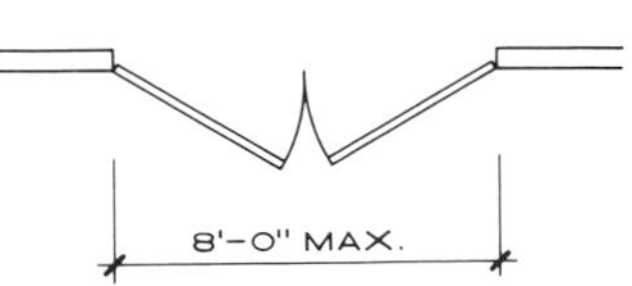
8'-0" MAX.

DOUBLE OR TRIPLE HINGED

NOTE

For multiple and offset hinged doors, swinging to one or both sides, hinged in or out, and used for two or more cars: 6½ to 11 in. necessary from top of opening to ceiling.

HINGED DOORS

William T. Cannady, FAIA; Houston, Texas
DeChiara and Koppelman, see data sources

6"
7'-2"
6"
3'-0"
6"
PASSENGER LOADING
3'-0"
2'-6"
2'-8"
2'-6"
3'-0"
WIDEN FOR ALL TURNS

CONCRETE RUNWAYS TO GARAGE

RAMP	APPROACH	APRON
4%	0% to 4%	0% to 2%
5%	0% to 3%	0% to 2%
6%	0% to 2%	0% to 2%
7%	0% to 1%	0% to 1%
8%	0%	0%

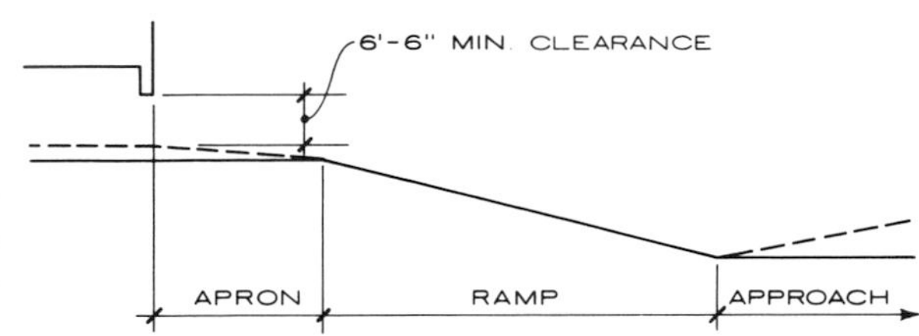
6'-6" MIN. CLEARANCE
APRON
RAMP
APPROACH

ROAD TO GARAGE RAMPS

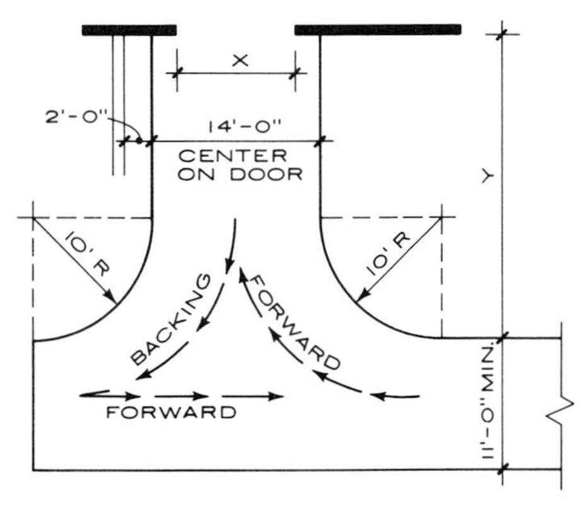
X
2'-0"
14'-0"
CENTER ON DOOR
Y
10' R
10' R
BACKING
FORWARD
FORWARD
11'-0" MIN.

90° IN—BACK OUT (1 CAR)

X	8'-9"	9'-0"	10'-0"	11'-0"	12'-0"
Y	25'-0"	24'-6"	23'-8"	23'-0"	22'-0"

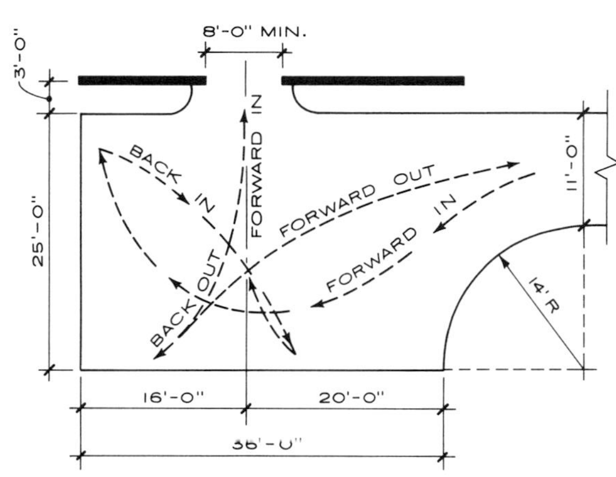
8'-0" MIN.
3'-0"
BACK IN
FORWARD IN
FORWARD OUT
FORWARD IN
BACK OUT
BACK OUT
25'-0"
11'-0"
14' R
16'-0"
20'-0"
36'-0"

NOTE

Three maneuver entrance for single car garage. Employ only when space limitations demand use. Dimensioned for large car.

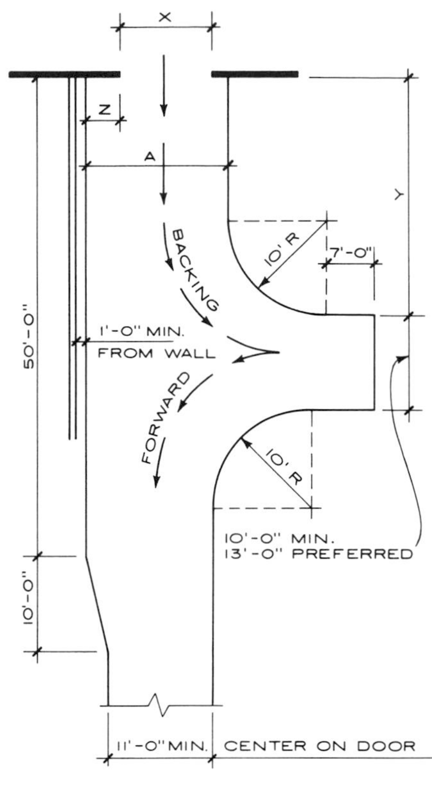
X
Z
A
Y
BACKING
10' R
7'-0"
1'-0" MIN. FROM WALL
FORWARD
10' R
50'-0"
10'-0"
10'-0" MIN.
13'-0" PREFERRED
11'-0" MIN.
CENTER ON DOOR

STRAIGHT IN—BACK OUT

X	9'-0"	10'-0"	12'-0"	16'-0"
Y	26'-0"	25'-0"	23'-6"	24'-0"
Z	3'-4"	3'-1"	2'-0"	3'-0"
A	14'-4"	14'-5"	14'-8"	20'-0"

PRIVATE DRIVEWAYS TO GARAGES

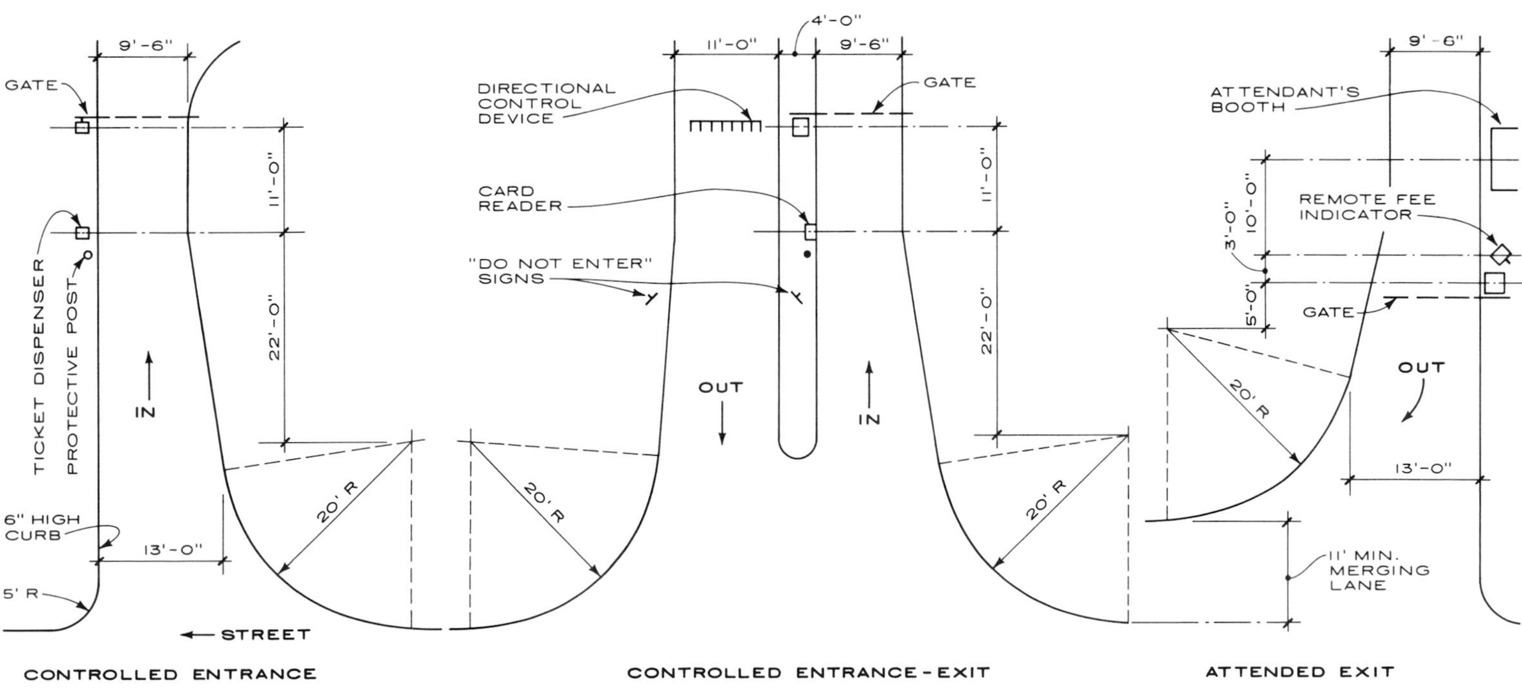
9'-6"
GATE
11'-0"
TICKET DISPENSER
PROTECTIVE POST
22'-0"
IN
6" HIGH CURB
13'-0"
20' R
5' R
STREET
DIRECTIONAL CONTROL DEVICE
CARD READER
"DO NOT ENTER" SIGNS
11'-0"
4'-0"
9'-6"
GATE
OUT
IN
11'-0"
22'-0"
20' R
20' R
9'-6"
ATTENDANT'S BOOTH
10'-0"
3'-0"
5'-0"
REMOTE FEE INDICATOR
GATE
OUT
20' R
13'-0"
11' MIN. MERGING LANE
CONTROLLED ENTRANCE
CONTROLLED ENTRANCE-EXIT
ATTENDED EXIT

DRIVEWAYS FOR PARKING FACILITIES

William T. Mahan, AIA; Santa Barbara, California

GENERAL NOTES

Examples shown are for easy driving at moderate speed. See the preceding page for vehicle dimensions (L, W, and OR). The "U" drive shown below illustrates a procedure for designating any drive configuration, given the vehicle's dimensions and turning radii. The T (tangent) dimensions given here are approximate minimums only and may vary with the driver's ability and speed.

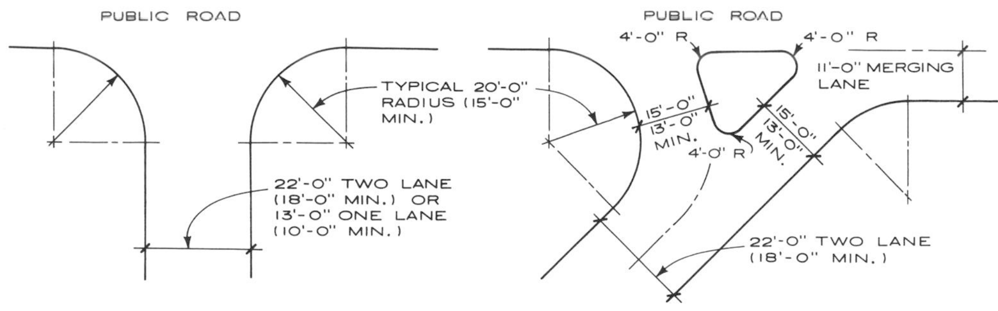
PUBLIC ROAD
TYPICAL 20'-0" RADIUS (15'-0" MIN.)
22'-0" TWO LANE (18'-0" MIN.) OR 13'-0" ONE LANE (10'-0" MIN.)
PUBLIC ROAD
4'-0" R
4'-0" R
11'-0" MERGING LANE
15'-0"
13'-0" MIN.
4'-0" R
15'-0"
13'-0" MIN.
22'-0" TWO LANE (18'-0" MIN.)

PRIVATE ROADS INTERSECTING PUBLIC ROADS

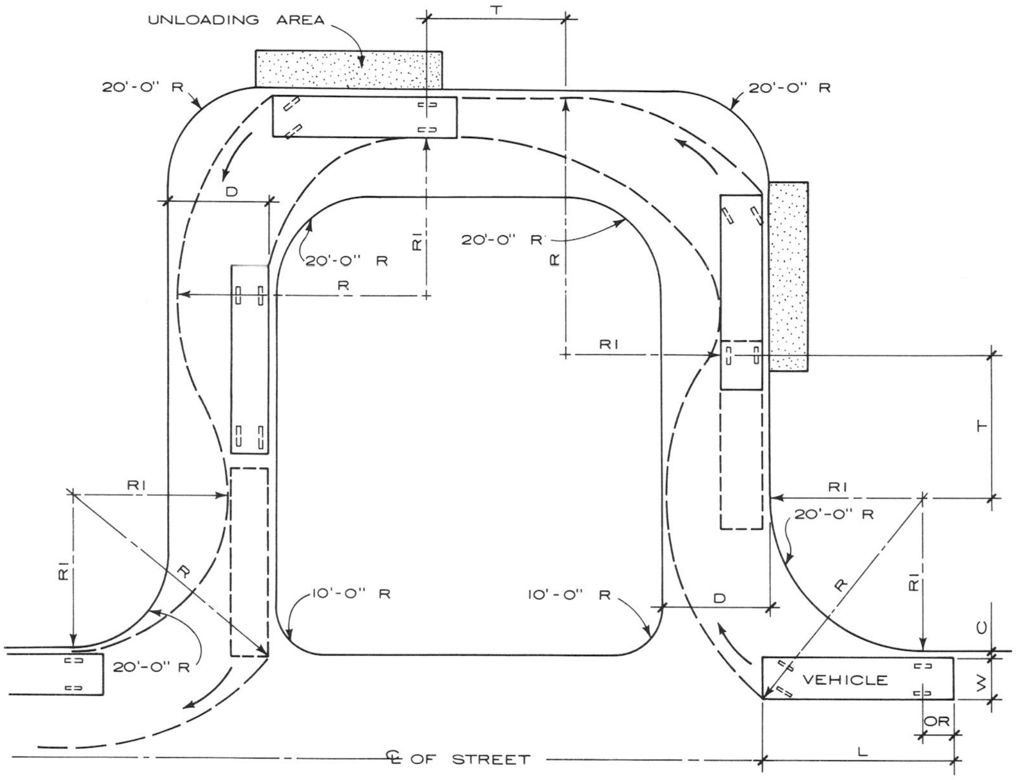

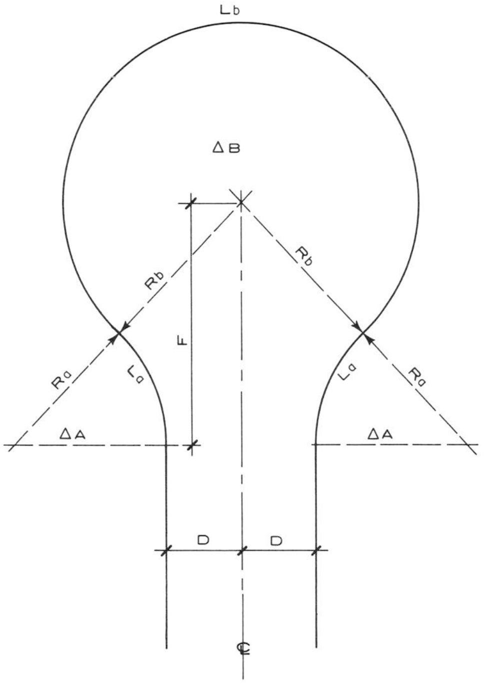

"U" DRIVE AND VEHICLE TURNING DIMENSIONS

VEHICLE	R	RI	T	D	C
Small car	19'-10"	10'-9"	12'-0"	10'-0'	6"
Compact car	21'-6"	11'-10"	15'-0"	10'-10"	7"
Standard car	22'-5"	12'-7"	15'-0"	11'-2"	8"
Large car	23'-0"	12'-7"	15'-0"	12'-0"	9"
Intercity bus*	55'-0"	33'-0"	30'-0"	22'-6"	1'-0"
City bus	53'-6"	33'-0"	30'-0"	22'-6"	1'-0"
School bus	43'-6"	26'-0"	30'-0"	19'-5"	1'-0"
Ambulance	30'-0"	18'-9"	25'-0"	13'-3"	1'-0"
Paramedic van	25'-0"	14'-0"	25'-0"	13'-0"	1'-0"
Hearse	30'-0"	18'-9"	20'-0"	13'-3"	1'-0"
Airport limousine	28'-3"	15'-1 1/2"	20'-0"	15'-1 1/2"	1'-0"
Trash truck†	32'-0"	18'-0"	20'-0"	16'-0"	1'-0"
U.P.S. truck	28'-0"	16'-0"	20'-0"	14'-0"	1'-0"
Fire truck	48'-0"	34'-4'	30'-0"	15'-8"	1'-0"

*Headroom = 14'.
†Headroom = 15'.

CUL-DE-SAC

	SMALL	LARGE
O	16'-0"	22'-0"
F	50'-11"	87'-3"
A	46.71°	35.58°
B	273.42°	251.15°
Ra	32'-0"	100'-0"
Rb	38'-0"	50'-0"
La	26'-1"	61'-8"
Lb	181'-4"	219'-2"

NOTE: R values for vehicles intended to use these culs-de-sac should not exceed Rb.

William T. Mahan, AIA; Santa Barbara, California

NOTE: Small car dimensions should be used only in lots designated for small cars or with entrance controls that admit only small cars. Placing small car stalls into a standard car layout is not recommended. Standard car parking dimensions will accommodate all normal passenger vehicles. Large car parking dimensions make parking easier and faster and are recommended for luxury, a high turnover, and use by the elderly. When the parking angle is 60° or less, it may be necessary to add 3 to 6 ft to the bay width to provide aisle space for pedestrians walking to and from their parked cars. Local zoning laws should be reviewed before proceeding.

RECOMMENDED RANGE OF STALL WIDTHS (SW)

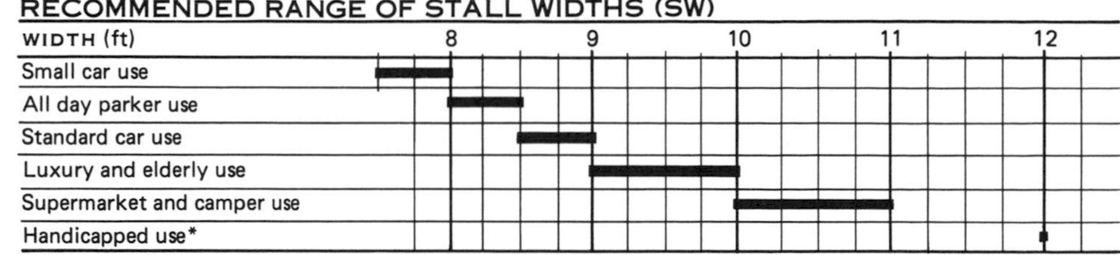
WIDTH (ft)
8
9
10
11
12
Small car use
All day parker use
Standard car use
Luxury and elderly use
Supermarket and camper use
Handicapped use*

*Minimum requirements = 1 or 2 per 100 stalls or as specified by local, state, or federal law; place convenient to destination.

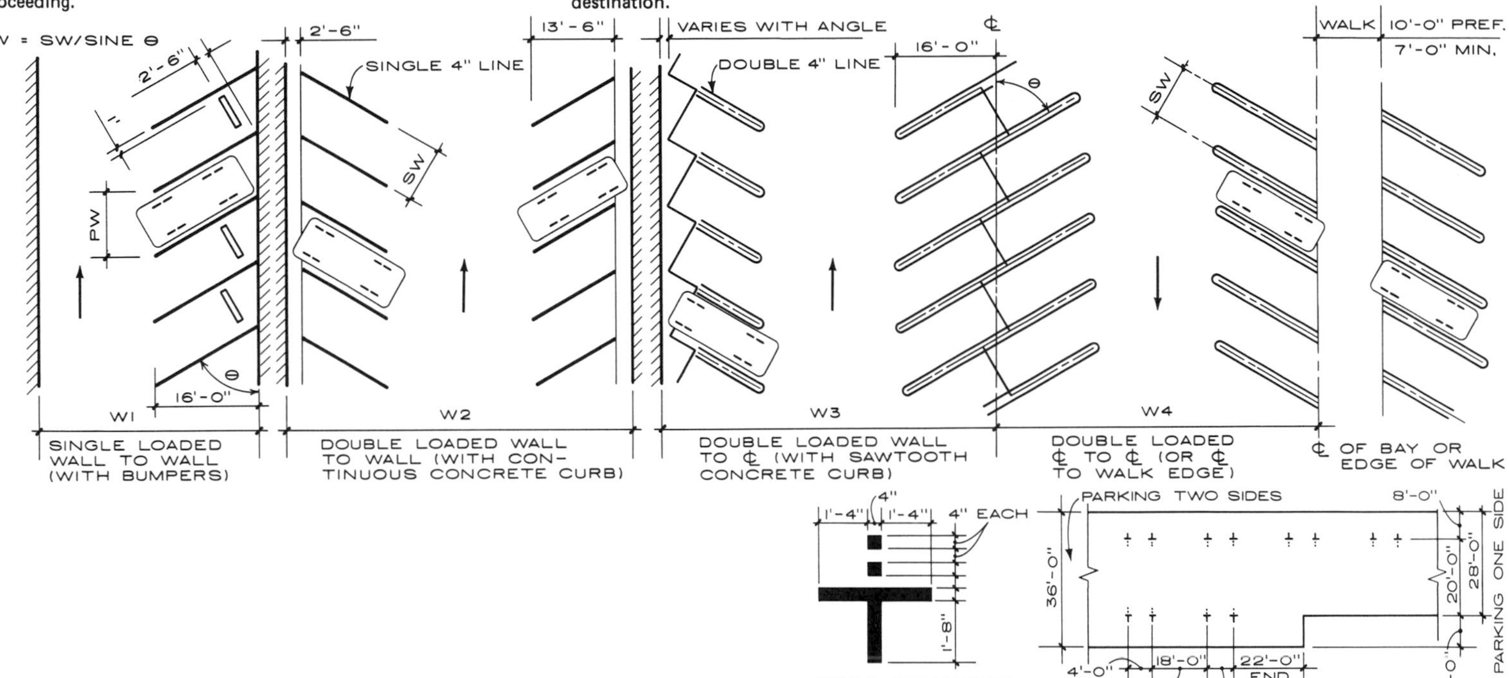
PW = SW/SINE θ
2'-6"
SINGLE 4" LINE
13'-6"
VARIES WITH ANGLE
16'-0"
DOUBLE 4" LINE
WALK
10'-0" PREF.
7'-0" MIN.
SW
PW
θ
16'-0"
W1
W2
W3
W4
SINGLE LOADED WALL TO WALL (WITH BUMPERS)
DOUBLE LOADED WALL TO WALL (WITH CONTINUOUS CONCRETE CURB)
DOUBLE LOADED WALL TO ℄ (WITH SAWTOOTH CONCRETE CURB)
DOUBLE LOADED ℄ TO ℄ (OR ℄ TO WALK EDGE)
℄ OF BAY OR EDGE OF WALK
4"
1'-4"
1'-4"
4" EACH
1'-8"
DETAIL "T" MARKER
PARKING TWO SIDES
8'-0"
36'-0"
20'-0"
28'-0"
PARKING ONE SIDE
4'-0"
18'-0"
22'-0"
TYPICAL STALL
4'-0"
END STALL
8'-0"

PARALLEL PARKING STALLS AND "T" MARKER DETAIL

PARKING DIMENSIONS IN FEET AND INCHES

			θ ANGLE OF PARK									
	SW	W	45°	50°	55°	60°	65°	70°	75°	80°	85°	90°
Group I: small cars	8'-0"	1	25'-9"	26'-6"	27'-2"	29'-4"	31'-9"	34'-0"	36'-2"	38'-2"	40'-0"	41'-9"
		2	40'-10"	42'-0"	43'-1"	45'-8"	48'-2"	50'-6"	52'-7"	54'-4"	55'-11"	57'-2"
		3	38'-9"	40'-2"	41'-5"	44'-2"	47'-0"	49'-6"	51'-10"	53'-10"	55'-8"	57'-2"
		4	36'-8"	38'-3"	39'-9"	42'-9"	45'-9"	48'-6"	51'-1"	53'-4"	55'-5"	57'-2"
Group II: standard cars	8'-6"	1	32'-0"	32'-11"	34'-2"	36'-2"	38'-5"	41'-0"	43'-6"	45'-6"	46'-11"	48'-0"
		2	49'-10"	51'-9"	53'-10"	56'-0"	58'-4"	60'-2"	62'-0"	63'-6"	64'-9"	66'-0"
		3	47'-8"	49'-4"	51'-6"	54'-0"	56'-6"	59'-0"	61'-2"	63'-0"	64'-6"	66'-0"
		4	45'-2"	46'-10"	49'-0"	51'-8"	54'-6"	57'-10"	60'-0"	62'-6"	64'-3"	66'-0"
	9'-0"	1	32'-0"	32'-9"	34'-0"	35'-4"	37'-6"	39'-8"	42'-0"	44'-4"	46'-2"	48'-0"
		2	49'-4"	51'-0"	53'-2"	55'-6"	57'-10"	60'-0"	61'-10"	63'-4"	64'-9"	66'-0"
		3	46'-4"	48'-10"	51'-4"	53'-10"	56'-0"	58'-8"	61'-0"	63'-0"	64'-6"	66'-0"
		4	44'-8"	46'-6"	49'-0"	51'-6"	54'-0"	57'-0"	59'-8"	62'-0"	64'-2"	66'-0"
	9'-6"	1	32'-0"	32'-8"	34'-0"	35'-0"	36'-10"	38'-10"	41'-6"	43'-8"	46'-0"	48'-0"
		2	49'-2"	50'-6"	51'-10"	53'-6"	55'-4"	58'-0"	60'-6"	62'-8"	64'-6"	65'-11"
		3	47'-0"	48'-2"	49'-10"	51'-6"	53'-11"	57'-0"	59'-8"	62'-0"	64'-3"	65'-11"
		4	44'-8"	45'-10"	47'-6"	49'-10"	52'-6"	55'-9"	58'-9"	61'-6"	63'-10"	65'-11"
Group III: large cars	9'-0"	1	32'-7"	33'-0"	34'-0"	35'-11"	38'-3"	40'-11"	43'-6"	45'-5"	46'-9"	48'-0"
		2	50'-2"	51'-2"	53'-3"	55'-4"	58'-0"	60'-4"	62'-9"	64'-3"	65'-5"	66'-0"
		3	47'-9"	49'-1"	52'-3"	53'-8"	56'-2"	59'-2"	61'-11"	63'-9"	65'-2"	66'-0"
		4	45'-5"	46'-11"	49'-0"	51'-8"	54'-9"	58'-0"	61'-0"	63'-2"	64'-10"	66'-0"
	9'-6"	1	32'-4"	32'-8"	33'-10"	34'-11"	37'-2"	39'-11"	42'-5"	45'-0"	46'-6"	48'-0"
		2	49'-11"	50'-11"	52'-2"	54'-0"	56'-6"	59'-3"	61'-9"	63'-4"	64'-8"	66'-0"
		3	47'-7"	48'-9"	50'-2"	52'-4"	55'-1"	58'-4"	60'-11"	62'-10"	64'-6"	66'-0"
		4	45'-3"	46'-8"	48'-5"	50'-8"	53'-8"	57'-0"	59'-10"	62'-2"	64'-1"	66'-0"
	10'-0"	1	32'-4"	32'-8"	33'-10"	34'-11"	37'-2"	39'-11"	42'-5"	45'-0"	46'-6"	48'-0"
		2	49'-11"	50'-11"	52'-2"	54'-0"	56'-6"	59'-3"	61'-9"	63'-4"	64'-8"	66'-0"
		3	47'-7"	48'-9"	50'-2"	52'-4"	55'-1"	58'-4"	60'-11"	62'-10"	64'-6"	66'-0"
		4	45'-3"	46'-8"	48'-5"	50'-8"	53'-8"	57'-0"	59'-10"	62'-2"	64'-1"	66'-0"

NOTE: θ angles greater than 70° have aisle widths wide enough for two-way travel.

William T. Mahan, AIA; Santa Barbara, California
Frederick J. Gaylord, AIA; McClellan/Cruz/Gaylord & Associates; Pasadena, California

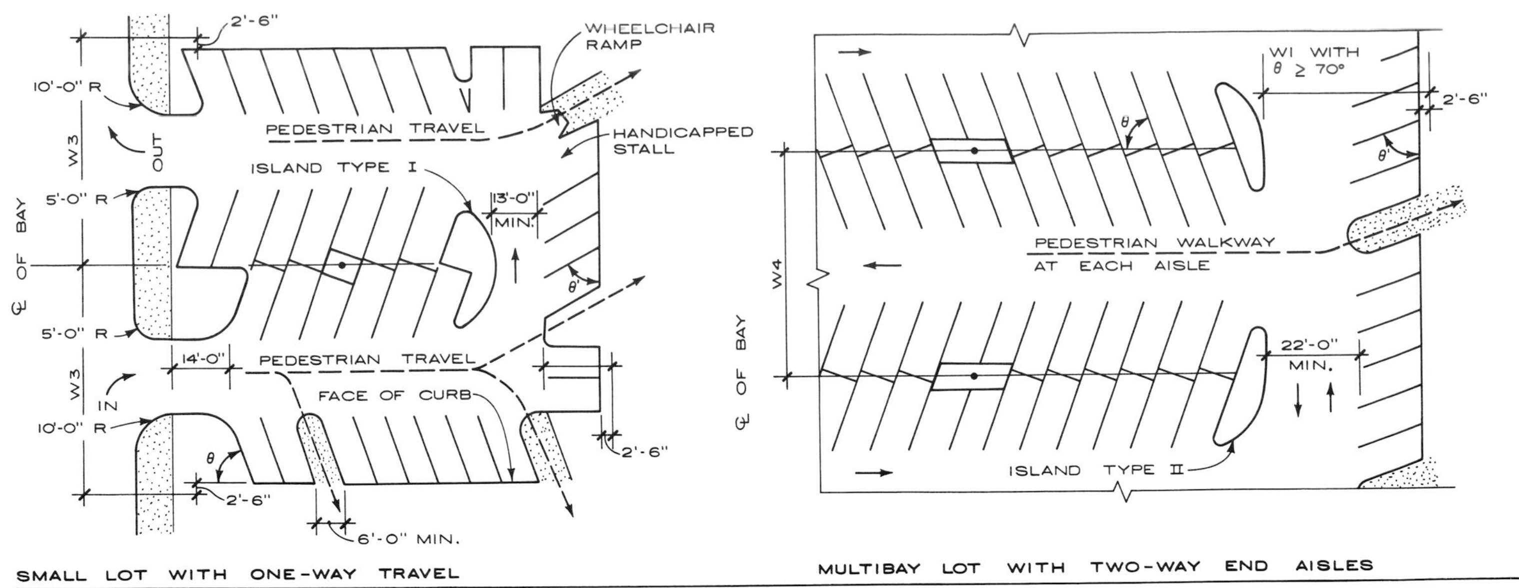
2'-6"
10'-0" R
WHEELCHAIR RAMP
PEDESTRIAN TRAVEL
OUT
W3
HANDICAPPED STALL
ISLAND TYPE I
5'-0" R
13'-0" MIN.
℄ OF BAY
θ'
5'-0" R
14'-0"
PEDESTRIAN TRAVEL
W3
IN
FACE OF CURB
10'-0" R
θ
2'-6"
2'-6"
6'-0" MIN.
WI WITH θ ≥ 70°
2'-6"
θ
θ'
W4
PEDESTRIAN WALKWAY AT EACH AISLE
℄ OF BAY
22'-0" MIN.
ISLAND TYPE II

SMALL LOT WITH ONE-WAY TRAVEL

MULTIBAY LOT WITH TWO-WAY END AISLES

TYPICAL PARKING LAYOUTS

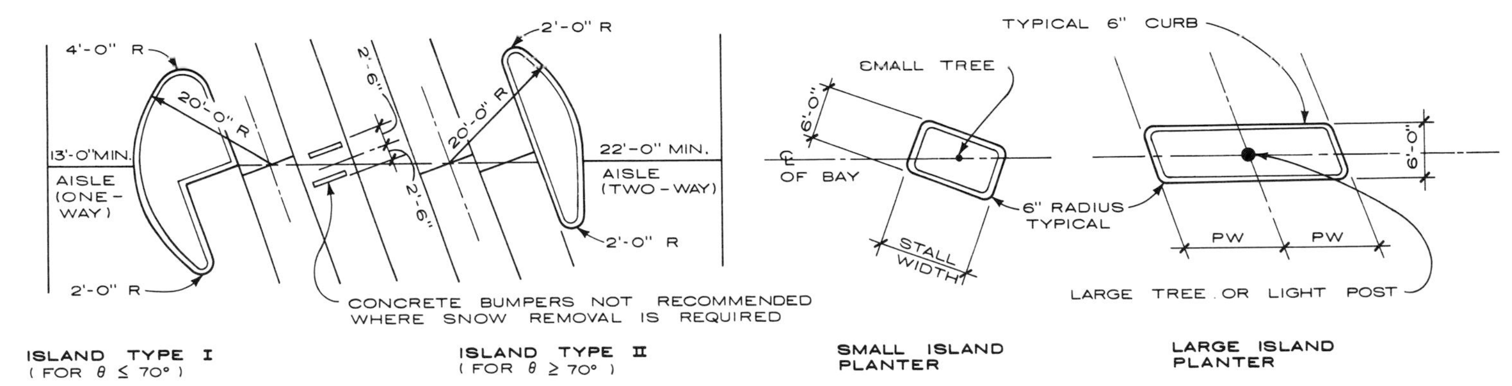
4'-0" R
20'-0" R
13'-0" MIN. AISLE (ONE-WAY)
2'-0" R
2'-6"
2'-6"
2'-0" R
20'-0" R
22'-0" MIN. AISLE (TWO-WAY)
2'-0" R
CONCRETE BUMPERS NOT RECOMMENDED WHERE SNOW REMOVAL IS REQUIRED
SMALL TREE
6'-0"
℄ OF BAY
6" RADIUS TYPICAL
STALL WIDTH
TYPICAL 6" CURB
6'-0"
PW
PW
LARGE TREE OR LIGHT POST

ISLAND TYPE I (FOR θ ≤ 70°)

ISLAND TYPE II (FOR θ ≥ 70°)

SMALL ISLAND PLANTER

LARGE ISLAND PLANTER

TYPICAL PLANTER ISLANDS

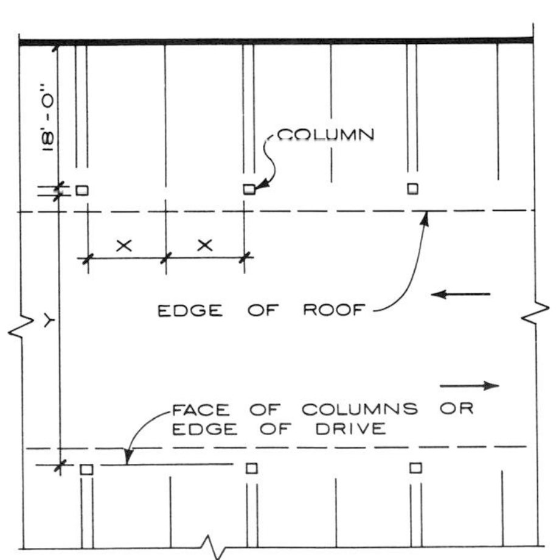
18'-0"
COLUMN
X
X
EDGE OF ROOF
Y
FACE OF COLUMNS OR EDGE OF DRIVE

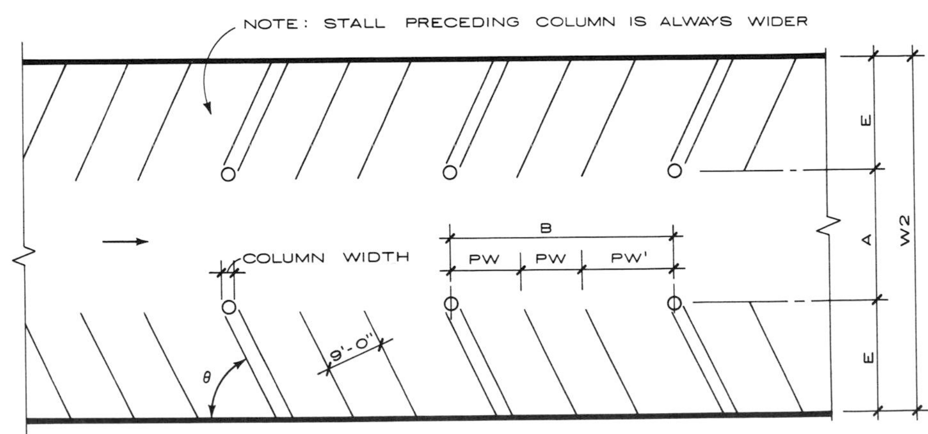
NOTE: STALL PRECEDING COLUMN IS ALWAYS WIDER
E
A
W2
E
B
COLUMN WIDTH
PW
PW
PW'
9'-0"
θ

TWO STALL 90° APARTMENT CARPORTS

X	9′-0″	10′-0″	11′-0″	12′-0″
Y	35′-0″	34′-0″	33′-0″	32′-0″

ANGLE PARKING WITH 3 STALLS PER COLUMN

θ	PW	PW′	W2	E	A	B	AREA/STALL
60°	10′-5″	13′-0″	55′-0″	18′-0″	19′-0″	33′-10″	310 sq ft
70°	9′-7″	11′-1″	59′-10″	18′-0″	23′-10″	30′-3″	302 sq ft
80°	9′-1″	10′-2″	63′-4″	18′-0″	27′-4″	28′-4″	300 sq ft

PARKING LAYOUTS WITH COLUMNS

William T. Mahan, AIA; Santa Barbara, California
Frederick J. Gaylord, AIA; McClellan/Cruz/Gaylord & Associates; Pasadena, California

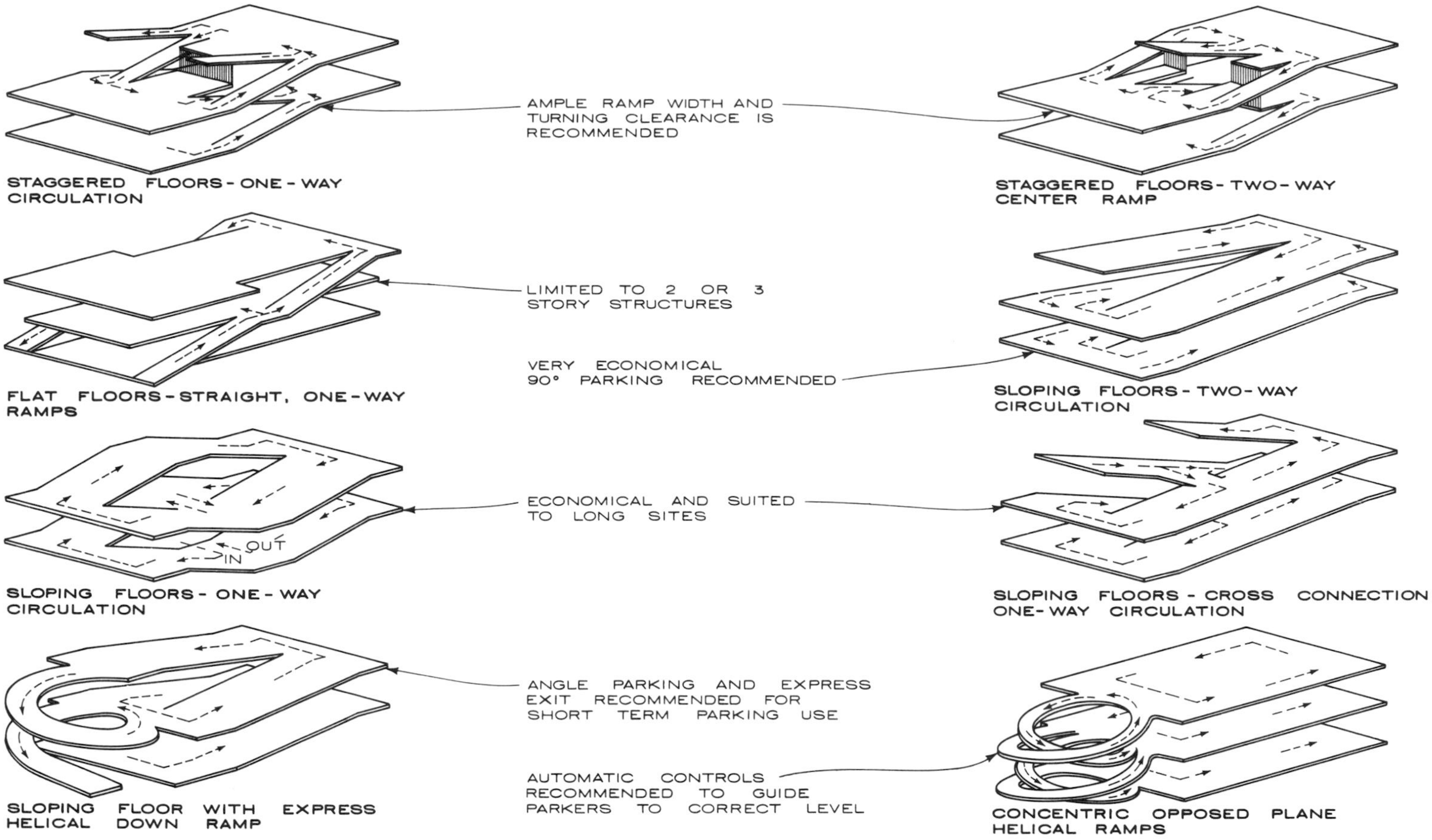

STAGGERED FLOORS - ONE - WAY CIRCULATION

AMPLE RAMP WIDTH AND TURNING CLEARANCE IS RECOMMENDED

STAGGERED FLOORS - TWO - WAY CENTER RAMP

FLAT FLOORS - STRAIGHT, ONE - WAY RAMPS

LIMITED TO 2 OR 3 STORY STRUCTURES

VERY ECONOMICAL 90° PARKING RECOMMENDED

SLOPING FLOORS - TWO - WAY CIRCULATION

SLOPING FLOORS - ONE - WAY CIRCULATION

OUT

IN

ECONOMICAL AND SUITED TO LONG SITES

SLOPING FLOORS - CROSS CONNECTION ONE - WAY CIRCULATION

SLOPING FLOOR WITH EXPRESS HELICAL DOWN RAMP

ANGLE PARKING AND EXPRESS EXIT RECOMMENDED FOR SHORT TERM PARKING USE

AUTOMATIC CONTROLS RECOMMENDED TO GUIDE PARKERS TO CORRECT LEVEL

CONCENTRIC OPPOSED PLANE HELICAL RAMPS

TYPICAL RAMP SYSTEMS

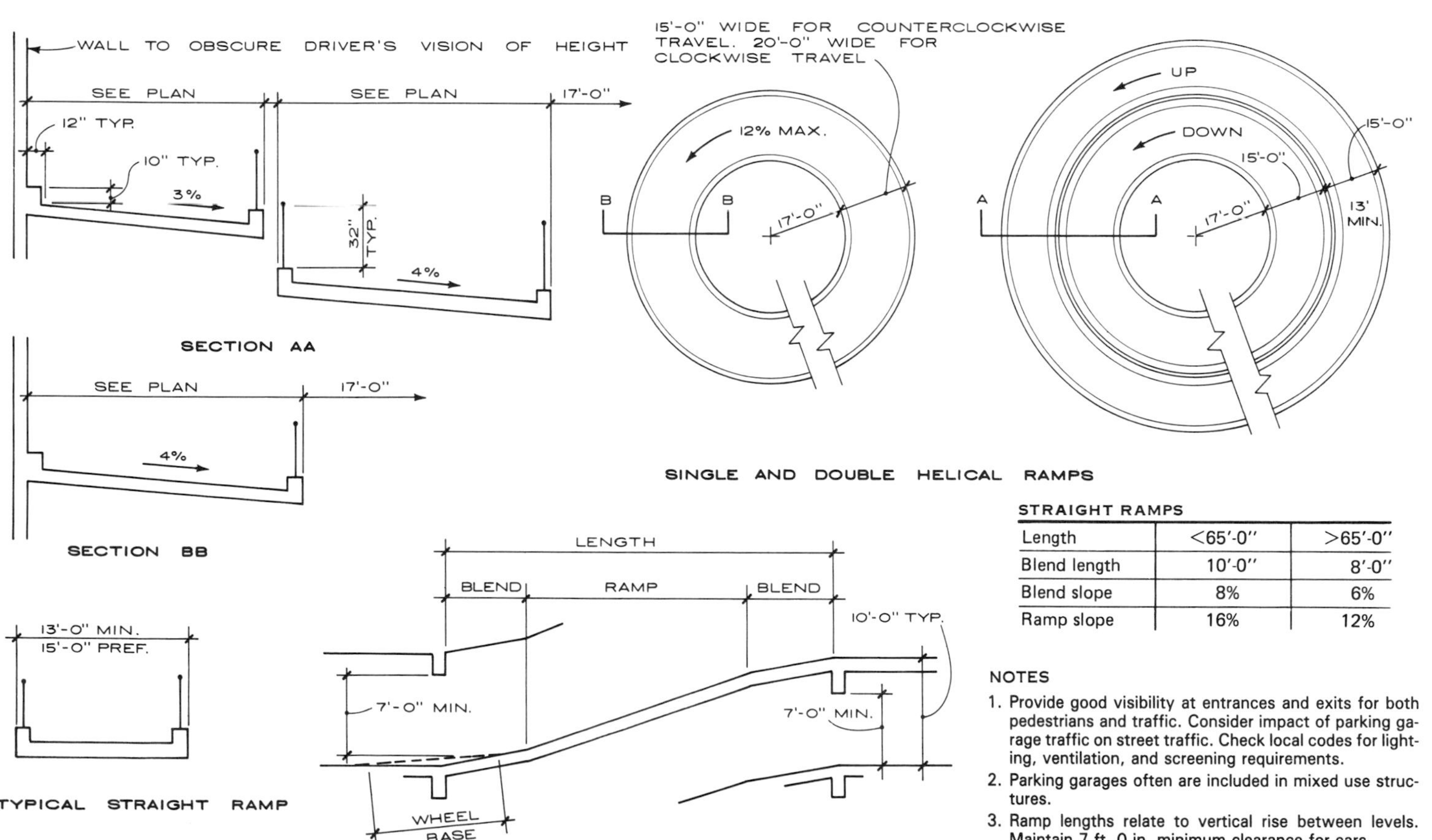
WALL TO OBSCURE DRIVER'S VISION OF HEIGHT
SEE PLAN
SEE PLAN
17'-0"
12" TYP.
10" TYP.
3%
32" TYP.
4%
SECTION AA
SEE PLAN
17'-0"
4%
SECTION BB
15'-0" WIDE FOR COUNTERCLOCKWISE TRAVEL. 20'-0" WIDE FOR CLOCKWISE TRAVEL
12% MAX.
B
B
17'-0"
UP
DOWN
15'-0"
15'-0"
A
A
17'-0"
13' MIN.
SINGLE AND DOUBLE HELICAL RAMPS
13'-0" MIN.
15'-0" PREF.
TYPICAL STRAIGHT RAMP
LENGTH
BLEND
RAMP
BLEND
10'-0" TYP.
7'-0" MIN.
7'-0" MIN.
WHEEL BASE

STRAIGHT RAMPS

	<65'-0"	>65'-0"
Length	<65'-0"	>65'-0"
Blend length	10'-0"	8'-0"
Blend slope	8%	6%
Ramp slope	16%	12%

NOTES

1. Provide good visibility at entrances and exits for both pedestrians and traffic. Consider impact of parking garage traffic on street traffic. Check local codes for lighting, ventilation, and screening requirements.
2. Parking garages often are included in mixed use structures.
3. Ramp lengths relate to vertical rise between levels. Maintain 7 ft. 0 in. minimum clearance for cars.

TYPICAL RAMP DETAILS

William T. Mahan, AIA; Santa Barbara, California

TRIPLE SEMITRAILER AND TRACTOR

MAXIMUM ALLOWABLE LENGTH
NOT PERMITTED, EXCEPT IN THOSE STATES LISTED BELOW

UNIT	STATE
90'-0" (each trailer 27'-0")	AK AZ
105'-0"	CO
105'-0"	ID
105'-0"	NV
105'-0"	OR
105'-0"	UT
65'-0"	IN
110'-0"	ND

DOUBLE SEMITRAILER AND TRACTOR

MAXIMUM ALLOWABLE LENGTH

UNIT	EACH TRAILER	STATE
60'-0"	28'-0"	GA, SC, VT, VA
61'-0"	—	UT
65'-0"	30'-0"	LA
65'-0"	28'-6"	MA, MN, NY, TX
65'-0"	28'-0"	DE, HI, MD, MO, NM, PA
65'-0"	—	ME, NB
70'-0"	28'-0"	CO, OK
75'-0"	28'-6"	CA, MT
75'-0"	28'-0"	ND
75'-0"	—	AK, OR
80'-0"	28'-6"	SD
85'-0"	—	WY
105'-0"	—	ID
—	30'-0"	MS
—	28'-6"	AL, AZ, IN, IA, KS, MI, TN, WI
—	28'-0"	AK, CT, DC, FL, KY, NH, NJ, NC, WV
—	27'-6"	RI
—	—	IL, NV, OH, WA

SEMITRAILER AND TRACTOR

MAXIMUM ALLOWABLE LENGTH

UNIT	EACH TRAILER	STATE
55'-0"	53'-0"	DC
55'-0"	48'-0"	MD
60'-0"	53'-0"	DE, WI
60'-0"	48'-0"	GA, NC, SC, VA, WV
60'-0"	45'-0"	MA, NY
60'-0"	—	MO, OR, VT
65'-0"	57'-0"	TX
65'-0"	53'-0"	OK
65'-0"	50'-0"	LA
65'-0"	48'-0"	HI, ME
65'-0"	—	CA, MN, NM, PA
70'-0"	48'-0"	AK
70'-0"	—	CO, NV
75'-0"	48'-0"	ID, MT
75'-0"	—	ND
80'-0"	53'-0"	SD
85'-0"	60'-0"	WY
—	53'-0"	NB, OH, IL, IN, IA, KS, KY
—	51'-0"	AZ
—	50'-0"	AL, MI, MS
—	48'-0"	AR, CT, FL, NH, NJ, RI, UT, WA
—	—	TN

STRAIGHT BODY TRUCKS

MAXIMUM ALLOWABLE LENGTH

UNIT	STATE
40'-0"	In all states, except those listed below
35'-0"	FL, KY, MA, NH, NJ, NY, NC, SC, WV
36'-0"	IN
42'-0"	IL
42'-6"	KS
45'-0"	LA, ME, SD, TX, UT
50'-0"	ND
60'-0"	CT, GA, VT, WY

L = SEE TABLE FOR MAX. LENGTH
AVERAGE = 70'-0" × 8'-0" WIDE
CITY TRACTOR OR ROAD TRACTOR
REAR SEMITRAILER 20'-0" TO 28'-0"
LEAD SEMITRAILER 20'-0" TO 28'-0" AVERAGE = 27'-0"
LG
RA
3'-0"
DOLLY CONVERTER
14'-0" MAX. AVERAGE 13'-6"

DOUBLE SEMITRAILER AND CITY TRACTOR

15'-0" TO 17'-0" (±) × 8'-0" WIDE
3'-0"
6'-2"
3'-4"
3'-0"
10' TO 12'
2'-0"

CITY TRACTOR

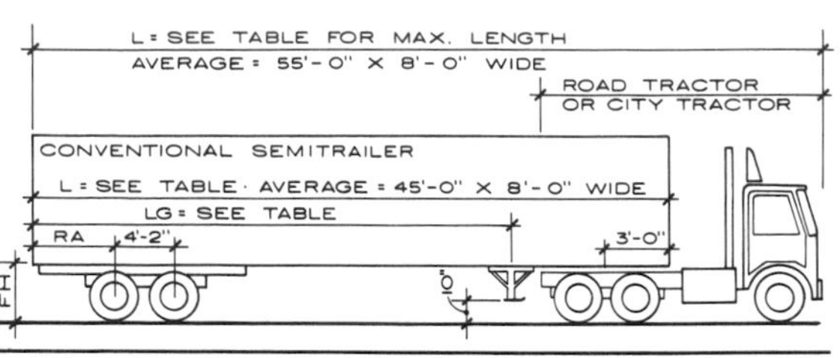
L = SEE TABLE FOR MAX. LENGTH
AVERAGE = 55'-0" × 8'-0" WIDE
ROAD TRACTOR OR CITY TRACTOR
CONVENTIONAL SEMITRAILER
L = SEE TABLE · AVERAGE = 45'-0" × 8'-0" WIDE
LG = SEE TABLE
RA
4'-2"
3'-0"
FH
10"

SEMITRAILER AND ROAD TRACTOR
TIRE SIZE APPROX. 41" ± DIA. × 10" ± WIDE

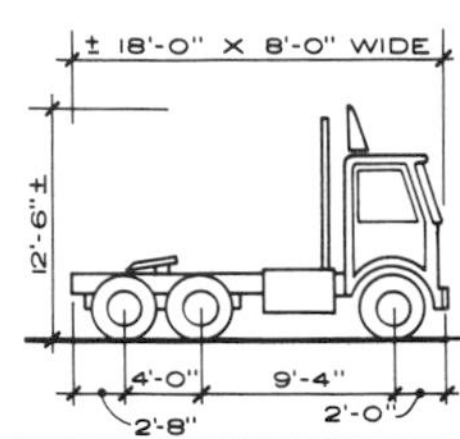
± 18'-0" × 8'-0" WIDE
12'-6" ±
4'-0"
9'-4"
2'-8"
2'-0"

ROAD TRACTOR

VEHICLE HEIGHT

MAXIMUM ALLOWABLE

TOTAL HEIGHT	STATE
13'-6"	In all states, except those listed below
13'-0"	FL
14'-0"	CA, ID, ME, NV, ND, OR, UT, WA, WY
14'-6"	CO, NB

VEHICLE WIDTH

MAXIMUM ALLOWABLE

TOTAL WIDTH	STATE
8'-6"	In all states, except those listed below
8'-0"	DE, DC, FL, IL, IA, KY, LA, MI, MO, NY, NC, PA, SC, TN, VA, WV

NOTE: Width is 8'-0" or 8'-6" according to state. Length and area restrictions vary with each state and locale. Verify exact dimensions and restrictions.

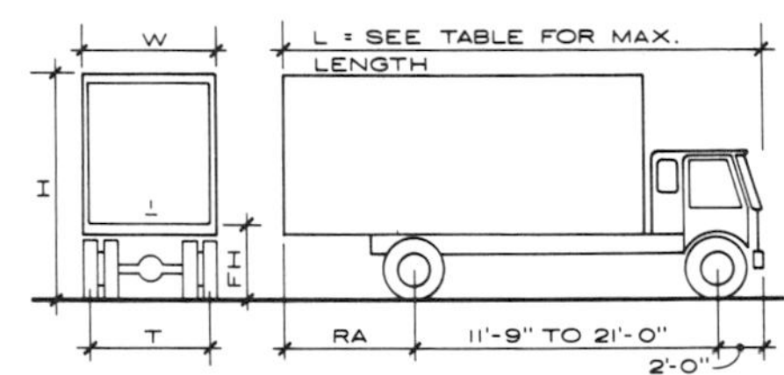
W
L = SEE TABLE FOR MAX. LENGTH
H
FH
T
RA
11'-9" TO 21'-0"
2'-0"

STRAIGHT BODY TRUCK

AVERAGE SEMITRAILER DIMENSIONS

	LENGTH (L)			
	27'-0"	40'-0"	45'-0"	REFRIG. 40'-0"
Floor height (FH)	4'-2"	4'-2"	4'-2"	4'-9"
Rear axle (RA)	3'-0"	5'-2"	5'-10"	4'-5"
Landing gear (LG)	19'-0"	30'-0"	34'-6"	29'-5"
Cubic feet (CU)	1564 ±	2327 ±	2620 ±	2113 ±

AVERAGE DIMENSIONS OF VEHICLES

	TYPE OF VEHICLES		
	DOUBLE SEMITRAILER	CONVENTIONAL SEMITRAILER	STRAIGHT BODY TRUCK
Length (L)	70'-0"	55'-0"	17'-0" to 40'-0"
Width (W)	8'-0"	8'-0"	8'-0"
Height (H)	13'-6"	13'-6"	13'-6"
Floor Height (FH)	4'-0" to 4'-6"	4'-0" to 4'-4"	3'-0" to 4'-0"
Track (T)	6'-6"	6'-6"	5'-10"
Rear Axle (RA)	3'-0" to 4'-0"	4'-0" to 12'-0"	2'-3" to 12'-0"

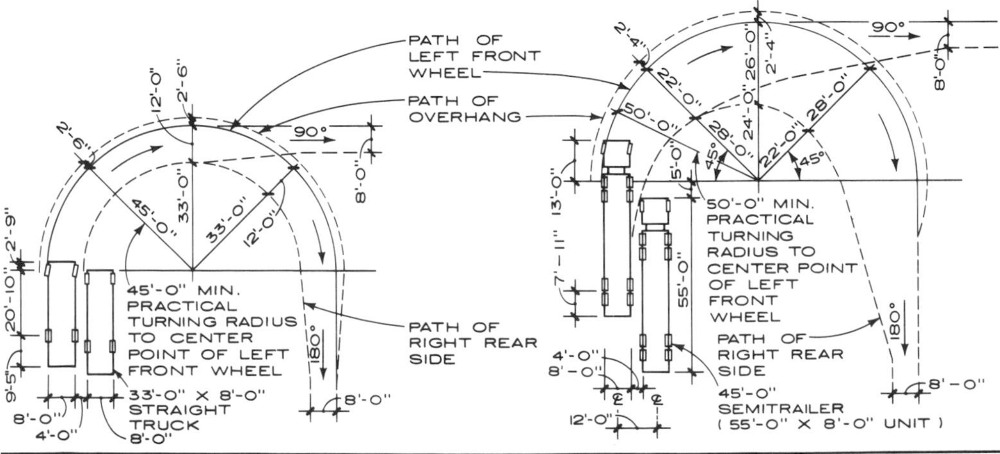
PATH OF LEFT FRONT WHEEL
PATH OF OVERHANG
PATH OF RIGHT REAR SIDE
45'-0" MIN. PRACTICAL TURNING RADIUS TO CENTER POINT OF LEFT FRONT WHEEL
33'-0" × 8'-0" STRAIGHT TRUCK
90°
180°
8'-0"
4'-0"
50'-0" MIN. PRACTICAL TURNING RADIUS TO CENTER POINT OF LEFT FRONT WHEEL
PATH OF RIGHT REAR SIDE
45'-0" SEMITRAILER (55'-0" × 8'-0" UNIT)
45°
12'-0"

33'-0" STRAIGHT BODY TRUCK MINIMUM PRACTICAL TURNING RADIUS OF 45'-0"

55'-0" SEMITRAILER AND TRACTOR COMBINATION MINIMUM PRACTICAL TURNING RADIUS OF 50'-0"

Robert H. Lorenz, AIA; Preston Trucking Company, Inc.; Preston, Maryland
The Operations Council, American Trucking Association; Washington, D.C.

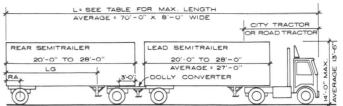

NOTES

1. Allow for off-street employee and driver parking.
2. Entrances and exits should be of reinforced concrete when excessive twisting and turning of vehicles are expected.
3. Average gate (swing or slide) 30 ft 0 in. wide for two-way traffic. People gate 5 ft 0 in. wide with concrete walkway 4 ft 0 in. to 6 ft 0 in. wide.
4. For yard security use a 6 ft 0 in. high chain link fence with barbed wire on top.
5. On-site fueling facilities are desirable for road units.
6. Provide general yard lighting from fixtures mounted on building or on 24 ft 0 in. high minimum poles at fence line. Mercury vapor or high pressure sodium preferred.
7. Tractor parking requires 12 ft 0 in. wide × 20 ft 0 in. long slot minimum. Provide motor heater outlets for diesel engines in cold climates.
8. Trailer parking requires 10 ft 0 in. wide slot minimum. Provide 10 ft 0 in. wide concrete pad for landing gear. Score concrete at 12 ft 0 in. o.c. to aid in correct spotting of trailer.
9. 4 ft 0 in. wide minimum concrete ramp from dock to grade. Slopes of 3 to 15% (10% average), score surface for traction.
10. Vehicles should circulate in a counterclockwise direction, making left hand turns, permitting driver to see rear of unit when backing into dock.
11. Double trailers are backed into dock separately.

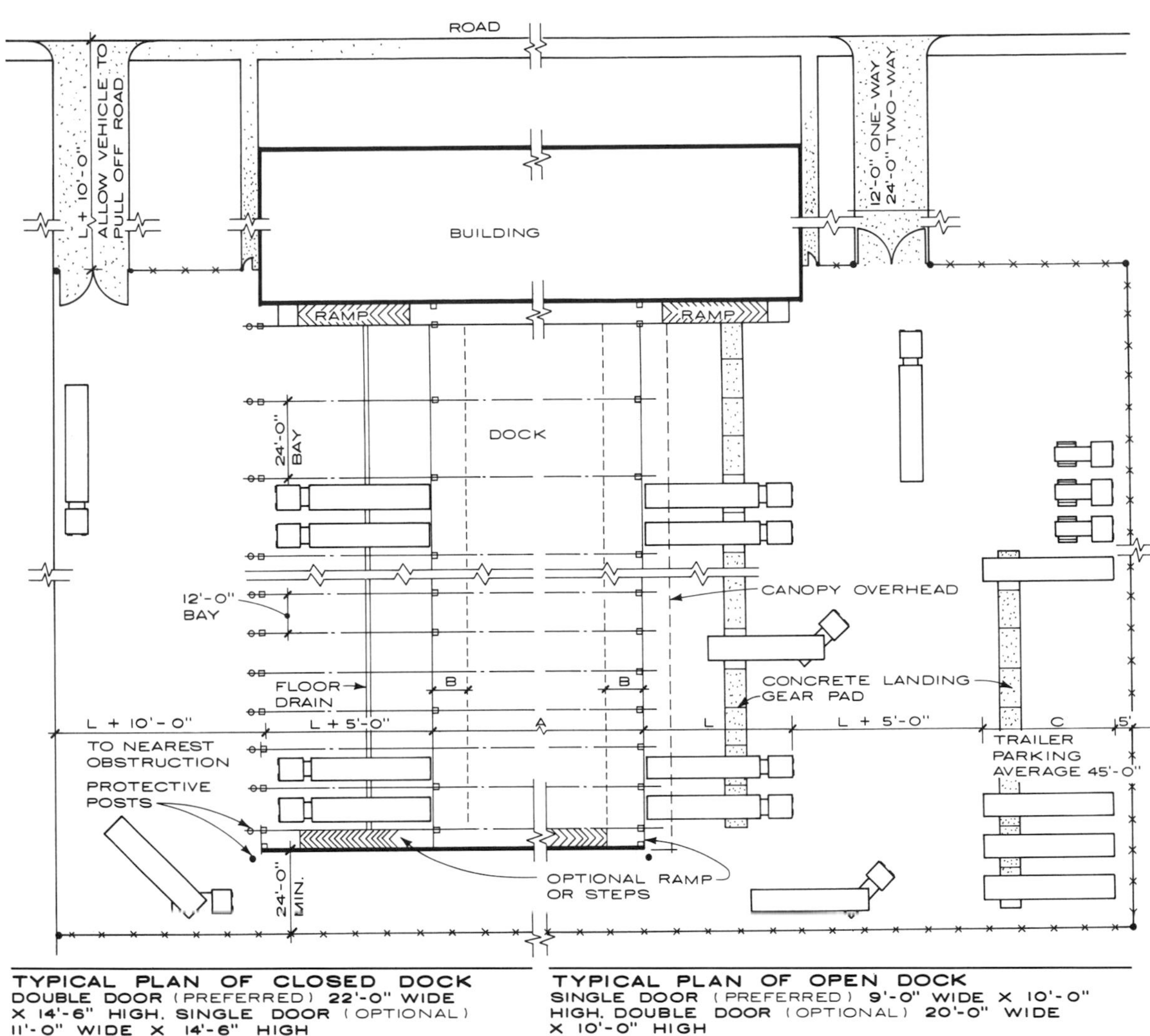
ROAD
L + 10'-0"
ALLOW VEHICLE TO PULL OFF ROAD
12'-0" ONE-WAY
24'-0" TWO-WAY
BUILDING
RAMP
RAMP
DOCK
24'-0" BAY
12'-0" BAY
CANOPY OVERHEAD
FLOOR DRAIN
B
B
CONCRETE LANDING GEAR PAD
L + 10'-0"
L + 5'-0"
A
L
L + 5'-0"
C
5'
TO NEAREST OBSTRUCTION
TRAILER PARKING AVERAGE 45'-0"
PROTECTIVE POSTS
OPTIONAL RAMP OR STEPS
24'-0" MIN.

TYPICAL PLAN OF CLOSED DOCK
DOUBLE DOOR (PREFERRED) 22'-0" WIDE × 14'-6" HIGH. SINGLE DOOR (OPTIONAL) 11'-0" WIDE × 14'-6" HIGH

TYPICAL PLAN OF OPEN DOCK
SINGLE DOOR (PREFERRED) 9'-0" WIDE × 10'-0" HIGH. DOUBLE DOOR (OPTIONAL) 20'-0" WIDE × 10'-0" HIGH

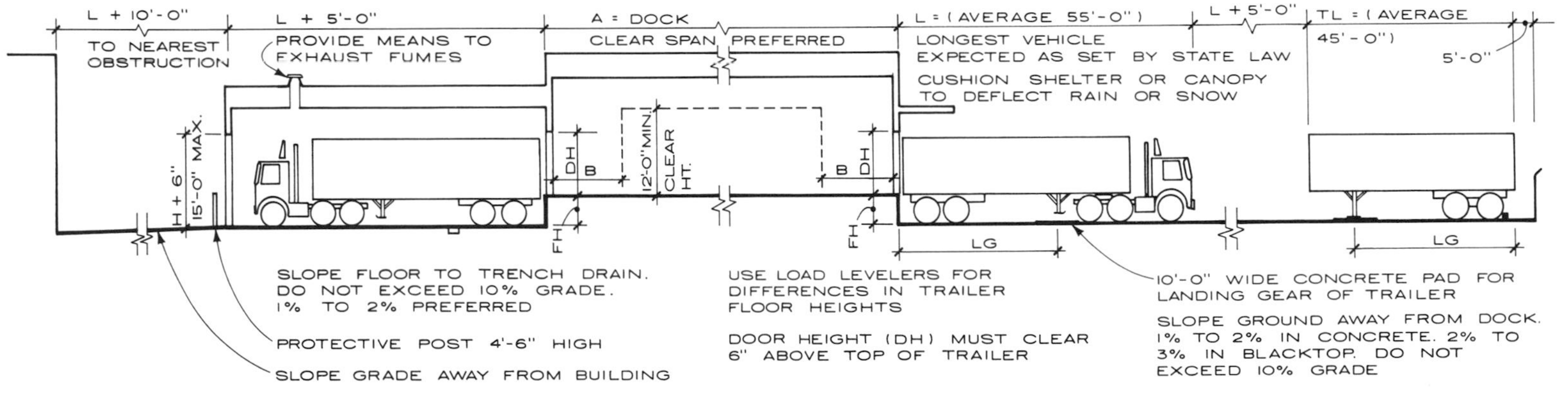
L + 10'-0"
TO NEAREST OBSTRUCTION
L + 5'-0"
PROVIDE MEANS TO EXHAUST FUMES
A = DOCK
CLEAR SPAN PREFERRED
L = (AVERAGE 55'-0")
LONGEST VEHICLE EXPECTED AS SET BY STATE LAW
L + 5'-0"
TL = (AVERAGE 45'-0")
5'-0"
CUSHION SHELTER OR CANOPY TO DEFLECT RAIN OR SNOW
H + 6"
15'-0" MAX.
DH
B
12'-0" MIN. CLEAR HT.
B
DH
FH
FH
LG
LG
SLOPE FLOOR TO TRENCH DRAIN. DO NOT EXCEED 10% GRADE. 1% TO 2% PREFERRED
PROTECTIVE POST 4'-6" HIGH
SLOPE GRADE AWAY FROM BUILDING
USE LOAD LEVELERS FOR DIFFERENCES IN TRAILER FLOOR HEIGHTS
DOOR HEIGHT (DH) MUST CLEAR 6" ABOVE TOP OF TRAILER
10'-0" WIDE CONCRETE PAD FOR LANDING GEAR OF TRAILER
SLOPE GROUND AWAY FROM DOCK. 1% TO 2% IN CONCRETE. 2% TO 3% IN BLACKTOP. DO NOT EXCEED 10% GRADE

TYPICAL SECTION OF CLOSED DOCK

TYPICAL SECTION OF OPEN DOCK

AVERAGE VEHICLE DIMENSIONS

LENGTH OF VEHICLE (L)	FLOOR HEIGHT (FH)	VEHICLE HEIGHT (H)
60 ft tractor trailer	4'-0" to 4'-6"	14'-0"
45 ft trailer	4'-0" to 4'-2"	13'-6"
40 ft straight body	3'-8" to 4'-2"	13'-6"
18 ft van	2'-0" to 2'-8"	7'-0"

NOTE: Refer to other pages for truck and trailer sizes.

AVERAGE WIDTHS OF DOCKS

TYPE OF OPERATION	TWO-WHEEL HAND TRUCK	FOUR-WHEEL HAND TRUCK	FORKLIFT TRUCK	DRAGLINE	AUTO SPUR DRAGLINE
Dock width (A)	50'-0"	60'-0"	60'-0" to 70'-0"	80'-0"	120'-0" to 140'-0"
Work aisle (B)	6'-0"	10'-0"	15'-0"	10'-0" to 15'-0"	10'-0" to 15'-0"

Robert H. Lorenz, AIA; Preston Trucking Company, Inc.; Preston, Maryland
The Operations Council, American Trucking Association; Washington, D.C.

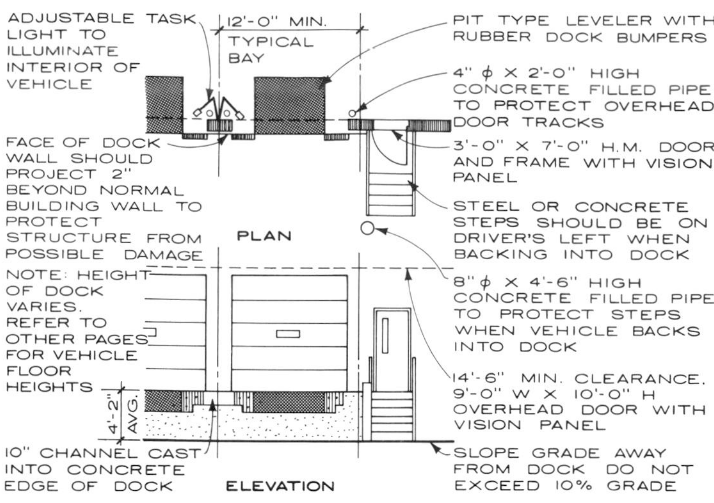
ADJUSTABLE TASK LIGHT TO ILLUMINATE INTERIOR OF VEHICLE
12'-0" MIN. TYPICAL BAY
PIT TYPE LEVELER WITH RUBBER DOCK BUMPERS
4" ϕ X 2'-0" HIGH CONCRETE FILLED PIPE TO PROTECT OVERHEAD DOOR TRACKS
FACE OF DOCK WALL SHOULD PROJECT 2" BEYOND NORMAL BUILDING WALL TO PROTECT STRUCTURE FROM POSSIBLE DAMAGE
3'-0" X 7'-0" H.M. DOOR AND FRAME WITH VISION PANEL
STEEL OR CONCRETE STEPS SHOULD BE ON DRIVER'S LEFT WHEN BACKING INTO DOCK
PLAN
NOTE: HEIGHT OF DOCK VARIES. REFER TO OTHER PAGES FOR VEHICLE FLOOR HEIGHTS
8" ϕ X 4'-6" HIGH CONCRETE FILLED PIPE TO PROTECT STEPS WHEN VEHICLE BACKS INTO DOCK
14'-6" MIN. CLEARANCE. 9'-0" W X 10'-0" H OVERHEAD DOOR WITH VISION PANEL
4'-2" AVG.
10" CHANNEL CAST INTO CONCRETE EDGE OF DOCK
ELEVATION
SLOPE GRADE AWAY FROM DOCK DO NOT EXCEED 10% GRADE

TYPICAL LOADING DOCK BAY

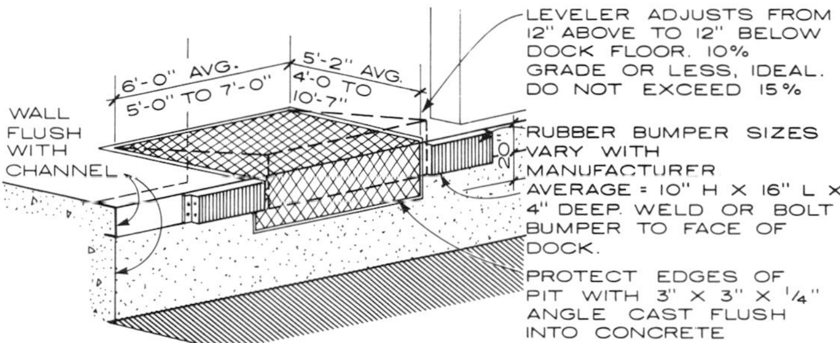
6'-0" AVG.
5'-0" TO 7'-0"
5'-2" AVG.
4'-0 TO 10'-7"
WALL FLUSH WITH CHANNEL
LEVELER ADJUSTS FROM 12" ABOVE TO 12" BELOW DOCK FLOOR. 10% GRADE OR LESS, IDEAL. DO NOT EXCEED 15%
20"
RUBBER BUMPER SIZES VARY WITH MANUFACTURER AVERAGE = 10" H X 16" L X 4" DEEP. WELD OR BOLT BUMPER TO FACE OF DOCK.
PROTECT EDGES OF PIT WITH 3" X 3" X 1/4" ANGLE CAST FLUSH INTO CONCRETE

Automatic or manual operation for high volume docks where incoming vehicle heights vary widely; must be installed in a preformed concrete pit. Exact dimensions provided by manufacturer.

PIT TYPE DOCK LEVELER

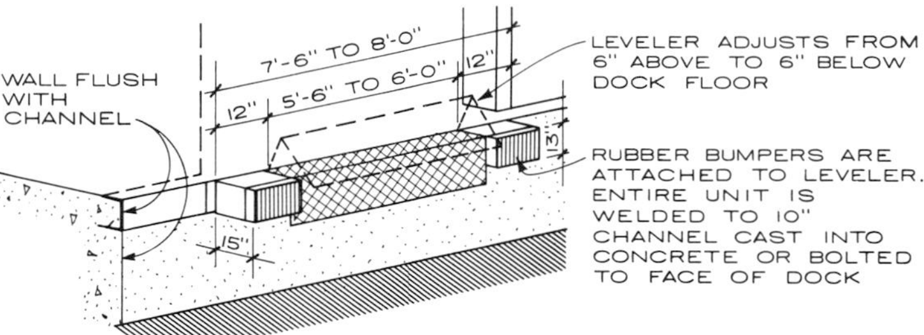
7'-6" TO 8'-0"
12"
5'-6" TO 6'-0"
12"
WALL FLUSH WITH CHANNEL
LEVELER ADJUSTS FROM 6" ABOVE TO 6" BELOW DOCK FLOOR
13"
15"
RUBBER BUMPERS ARE ATTACHED TO LEVELER. ENTIRE UNIT IS WELDED TO 10" CHANNEL CAST INTO CONCRETE OR BOLTED TO FACE OF DOCK

Manual operation for high or medium volume docks where pit type levelers are impractical or leased facilities are being used.

EDGE OF DOCK LEVELER

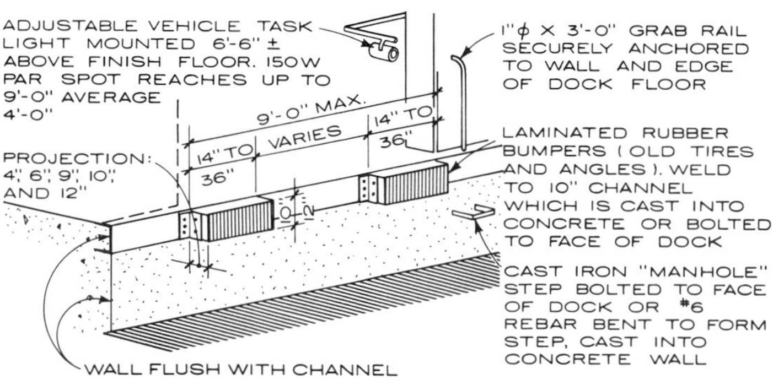
ADJUSTABLE VEHICLE TASK LIGHT MOUNTED 6'-6" ± ABOVE FINISH FLOOR. 150W PAR SPOT REACHES UP TO 9'-0" AVERAGE 4'-0"
PROJECTION: 4", 6", 9", 10", AND 12"
1"ϕ X 3'-0" GRAB RAIL SECURELY ANCHORED TO WALL AND EDGE OF DOCK FLOOR
9'-0" MAX.
14" TO 36"
VARIES
14" TO 36"
LAMINATED RUBBER BUMPERS (OLD TIRES AND ANGLES). WELD TO 10" CHANNEL WHICH IS CAST INTO CONCRETE OR BOLTED TO FACE OF DOCK
12"
CAST IRON "MANHOLE" STEP BOLTED TO FACE OF DOCK OR #6 REBAR BENT TO FORM STEP, CAST INTO CONCRETE WALL
WALL FLUSH WITH CHANNEL

Used for low volume docks where incoming vehicle heights do not vary. Use portable type leveler such as a throw plate.

LOADING DOCK WITHOUT LEVELER

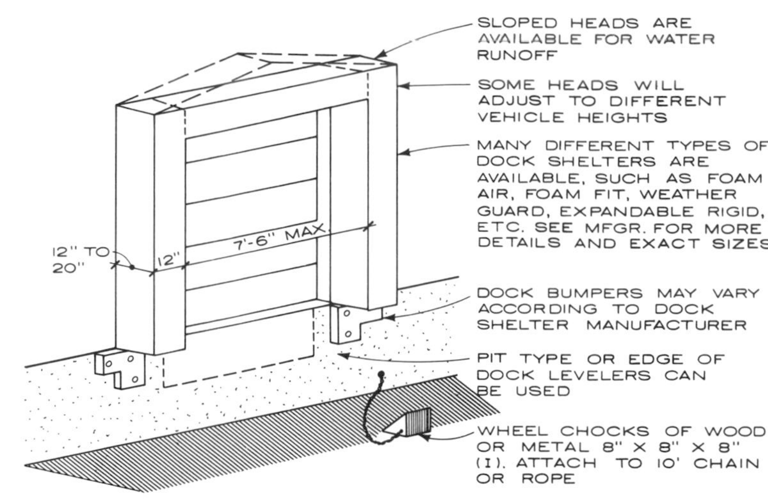
SLOPED HEADS ARE AVAILABLE FOR WATER RUNOFF
SOME HEADS WILL ADJUST TO DIFFERENT VEHICLE HEIGHTS
MANY DIFFERENT TYPES OF DOCK SHELTERS ARE AVAILABLE, SUCH AS FOAM AIR, FOAM FIT, WEATHER GUARD, EXPANDABLE RIGID, ETC. SEE MFGR. FOR MORE DETAILS AND EXACT SIZES
7'-6" MAX.
12" TO 20"
12"
DOCK BUMPERS MAY VARY ACCORDING TO DOCK SHELTER MANUFACTURER
PIT TYPE OR EDGE OF DOCK LEVELERS CAN BE USED
WHEEL CHOCKS OF WOOD OR METAL 8" X 8" X 8" (I). ATTACH TO 10' CHAIN OR ROPE

Provides positive weather seal; protects dock from wind, rain, snow, and dirt. Retains constant temperature between dock and vehicle.

CUSHIONED DOCK SHELTER

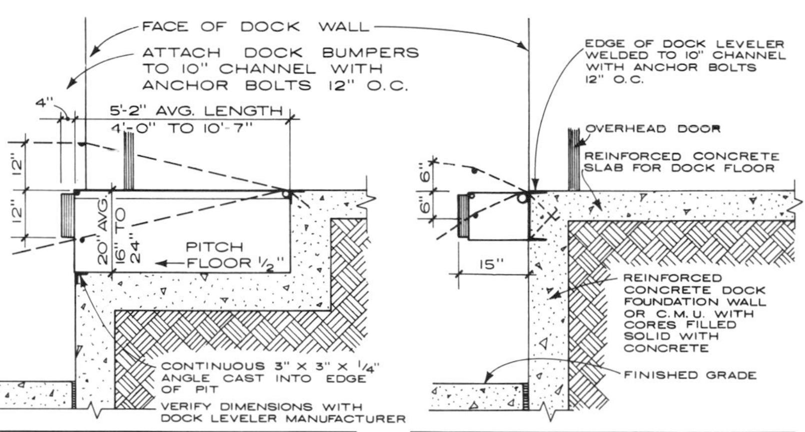
FACE OF DOCK WALL
ATTACH DOCK BUMPERS TO 10" CHANNEL WITH ANCHOR BOLTS 12" O.C.
4"
5'-2" AVG. LENGTH
4'-0" TO 10'-7"
12"
12"
20" AVG.
16" TO 24"
PITCH FLOOR 1/2"
CONTINUOUS 3" X 3" X 1/4" ANGLE CAST INTO EDGE OF PIT
VERIFY DIMENSIONS WITH DOCK LEVELER MANUFACTURER
EDGE OF DOCK LEVELER WELDED TO 10" CHANNEL WITH ANCHOR BOLTS 12" O.C.
OVERHEAD DOOR
REINFORCED CONCRETE SLAB FOR DOCK FLOOR
6"
6"
15"
REINFORCED CONCRETE DOCK FOUNDATION WALL OR C.M.U. WITH CORES FILLED SOLID WITH CONCRETE
FINISHED GRADE

SILL FOR PIT LEVELER

SILL FOR EDGE OF DOCK LEVELER

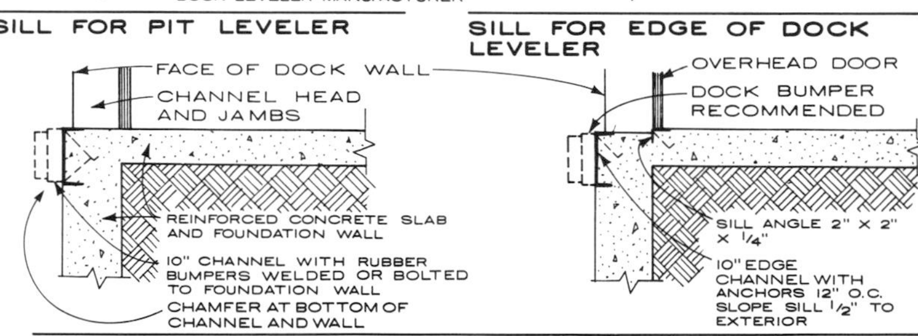
FACE OF DOCK WALL
CHANNEL HEAD AND JAMBS
REINFORCED CONCRETE SLAB AND FOUNDATION WALL
10" CHANNEL WITH RUBBER BUMPERS WELDED OR BOLTED TO FOUNDATION WALL
CHAMFER AT BOTTOM OF CHANNEL AND WALL
OVERHEAD DOOR
DOCK BUMPER RECOMMENDED
SILL ANGLE 2" X 2" X 1/4"
10" EDGE CHANNEL WITH ANCHORS 12" O.C. SLOPE SILL 1/2" TO EXTERIOR

DOCK SILL WITHOUT LEVELERS

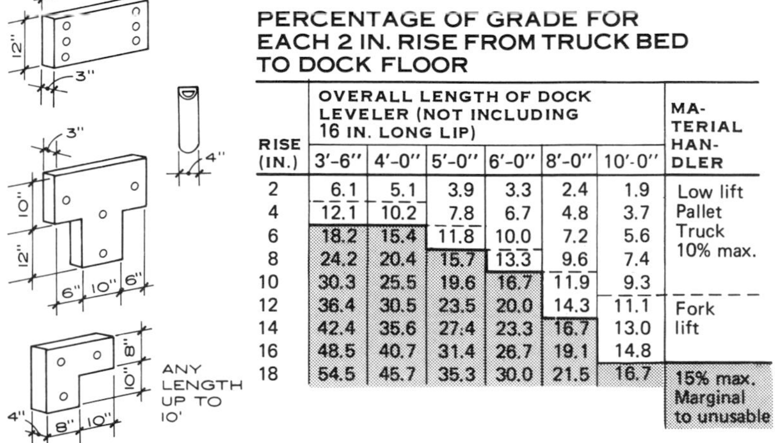
24"
12"
3"
3"
4"
10"
12"
6"
10"
6"
8"
10"
4"
8"
10"
ANY LENGTH UP TO 10'

MOLDED HARD RUBBER DOCK BUMPERS

PERCENTAGE OF GRADE FOR EACH 2 IN. RISE FROM TRUCK BED TO DOCK FLOOR

RISE (IN.)	OVERALL LENGTH OF DOCK LEVELER (NOT INCLUDING 16 IN. LONG LIP)						MATERIAL HANDLER
	3'-6"	4'-0"	5'-0"	6'-0"	8'-0"	10'-0"	
2	6.1	5.1	3.9	3.3	2.4	1.9	Low lift Pallet Truck 10% max.
4	12.1	10.2	7.8	6.7	4.8	3.7	
6	18.2	15.4	11.8	10.0	7.2	5.6	
8	24.2	20.4	15.7	13.3	9.6	7.4	
10	30.3	25.5	19.6	16.7	11.9	9.3	
12	36.4	30.5	23.5	20.0	14.3	11.1	Fork lift
14	42.4	35.6	27.4	23.3	16.7	13.0	
16	48.5	40.7	31.4	26.7	19.1	14.8	
18	54.5	45.7	35.3	30.0	21.5	16.7	15% max. Marginal to unusable

Robert H. Lorenz, AIA; Preston Trucking Company, Inc.; Preston, Maryland

ARCHITECTURAL AREA OF BUILDINGS

The architectural area of a building is the sum of the areas of the floors, measured horizontally in plan to the exterior faces of perimeter walls or to the centerline of walls separating buildings. Included are areas occupied by partitions, columns, stairwells, elevator shafts, duct shafts, elevator rooms, pipe spaces, mechanical penthouses, and similar spaces having a headroom of 6 ft and over. Areas of sloping surfaces, such as staircases, bleachers, and tiered terraces, should be measured horizontally in plan. Auditoriums, swimming pools, gymnasiums, foyers, and similar spaces extending through two or more floors should be measured once only, taking the largest area in plan at any level.

Mechanical penthouse rooms, pipe spaces, bulkheads, and similar spaces having a headroom less than 6 ft and balconies projecting beyond exterior walls, covered terraces and walkways, porches, and similar spaces shall have the architectural area multiplied by 0.50 in calculating the building gross area.

Exterior staircases and fire escapes, exterior steps, patios, terraces, open courtyards and lightwells, roof overhangs, cornices and chimneys, unfinished roof and attic areas, pipe trenches, and similar spaces are excluded from the architectural area calculations. Interstitial space in health care facilities is also excluded.

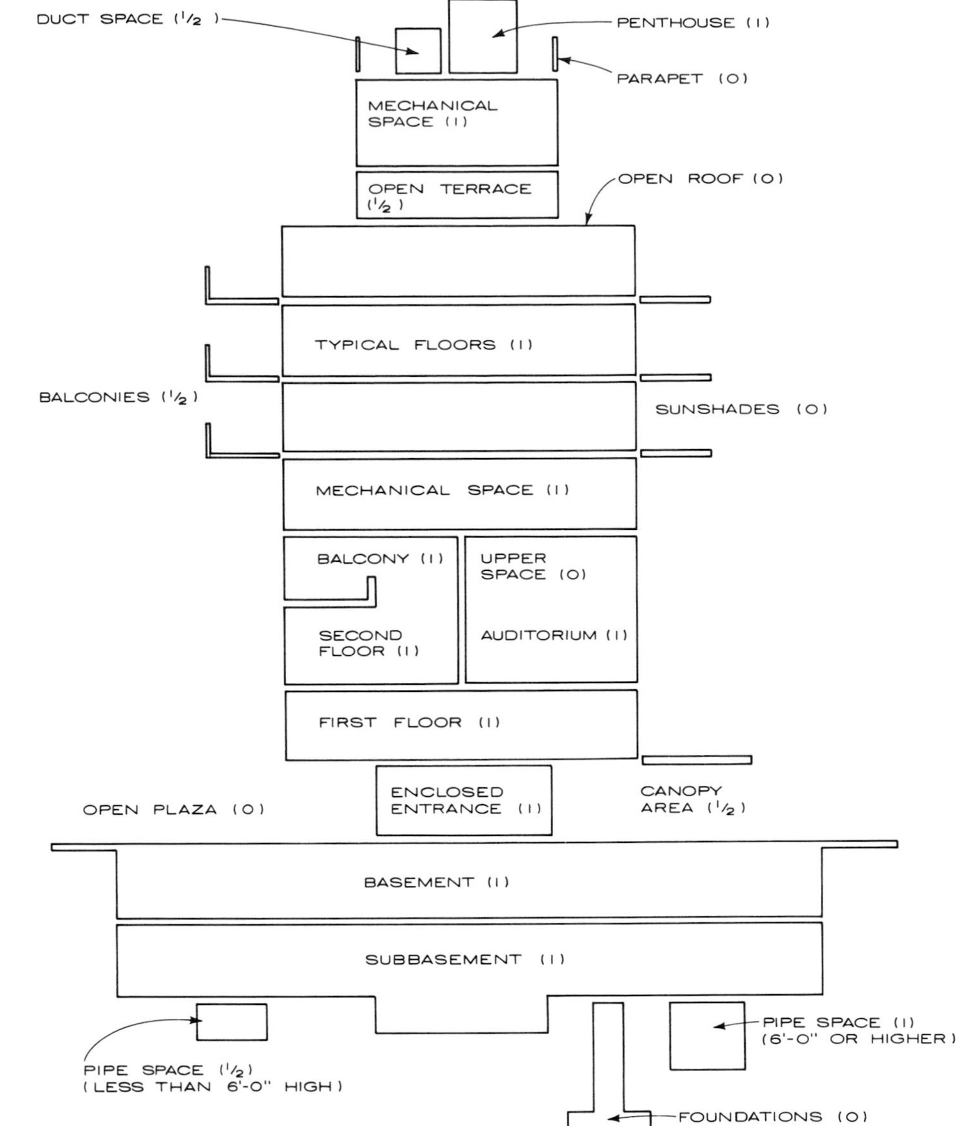
DUCT SPACE (1/2)
PENTHOUSE (1)
PARAPET (O)
MECHANICAL SPACE (1)
OPEN TERRACE (1/2)
OPEN ROOF (O)
TYPICAL FLOORS (1)
BALCONIES (1/2)
SUNSHADES (O)
MECHANICAL SPACE (1)
BALCONY (1)
UPPER SPACE (O)
SECOND FLOOR (1)
AUDITORIUM (1)
FIRST FLOOR (1)
OPEN PLAZA (O)
ENCLOSED ENTRANCE (1)
CANOPY AREA (1/2)
BASEMENT (1)
SUBBASEMENT (1)
PIPE SPACE (1)
(6'-0" OR HIGHER)
PIPE SPACE (1/2)
(LESS THAN 6'-0" HIGH)
FOUNDATIONS (O)

ARCHITECTURAL AREA DIAGRAM

ARCHITECTURAL VOLUME OF BUILDINGS

The architectural volume of a building is the sum of the products of the areas defined in the architectural area times the height from the underside of the lowest floor construction to the average height of the surface of the finished roof above, for the various parts of the building. Included in the architectural volume is the actual space enclosed within the outer surfaces of the exterior or outer walls and contained between the outside of the roof and the bottom of the lowest floor, taken in full: bays, oriels, dormers; penthouses, chimneys; walk tunnels; enclosed porches and balconies, including screened areas.

The following volumes are multiplied by 0.50 in calculating the architectural volume of a building; nonenclosed porches, if recessed into the building and without enclosing sash or screens; nonenclosed porches built as an extension to the building and without sash or screen; areaways and pipe tunnels; and patio areas that have building walls extended on two sides, roof over, and paved surfacing.

Excluded from the architectural volume are outside steps, terraces, courts, garden walls; light shafts, parapets, cornices, roof overhangs; footings, deep foundations, piling cassions, special foundations, and similar features.

NET ASSIGNABLE AREA

The net assignable area is that portion of the area which is available for assignment to an occupant, including every type of space usable by the occupant.

The net assignable area should be measured from the predominant inside finish of enclosing walls in the categories defined below. Areas occupied by exterior walls, partitions, internal structural, or party walls are to be excluded from the groups and are to be included under "construction area."

1. "NET ASSIGNABLE AREA": Total area of all enclosed spaces fulfilling the main functional requirements of the building for occupant use, including custodial and service areas such as guard rooms, workshops, locker rooms, janitors' closets, storerooms, and the total area of all toilet and washroom facilities.
2. "CIRCULATION AREA": Total area of all enclosed spaces which is required for physical access to subdivisions of space such as corridors, elevator shafts, escalators, fire towers or stairs, stairwells, elevator entrances, public lobbies, and public vestibules.
3. "MECHANICAL AREA": Total area of all enclosed spaces designed to house mechanical and electrical equipment and utility services such as mechanical and electrical equipment rooms, duct shafts, boiler rooms, fuel rooms, and mechanical service shafts.
4. "CONSTRUCTION AREA": The area occupied by exterior walls, partitions, structure, and so on.
5. "GROSS FLOOR OR ARCHITECTURAL AREA": The sum of areas 1, 2, 3, and 4 plus the area of all factored non- and semienclosed areas equal the gross floor area or architectural area of a building.

In commercial buildings constructed for leasing, net areas are to be measured in accordance with the "Standard Method of Floor Measurement," as set by the Building Owners and Managers Association (BOMA).

The net rentable area for offices is to be measured from the inside finish of permanent outer building walls, to the office or occupancy side of corridors and/or other permanent partitions, and to the center of partitions that separate the premises from adjoining rentable areas. No deductions are to be made for columns and projections necessary to the building.

The net rentable area for stores is to be measured from the building line in case of street frontages and from the inside finish of other outer building walls, corridor, and permanent partitions and to the center of partitions that separate the premises from adjoining rentable areas. No deductions are to be made for vestibules inside the building line or for columns and projections necessary to the building. No addition is to be made for projecting bay windows.

If a single occupant is to occupy the total floor in either the office or store categories, the net rentable area would include the accessory area for that floor of corridors, elevator lobbies, toilets, janitors' closets, electrical and telephone closets, air-conditioning rooms and fan rooms, and similar spaces.

The net rentable area for apartments is to be measured from the inside face of exterior walls, and all enclosing walls of the unit.

NOTE

Various governmental agencies have their own methods of calculating the net assignable area of buildings. They should be investigated if federal authority or funding apply to a project. Also, various building codes provide their own definitions of net and gross areas of building for use in quantifying requirements.

T. Edward Thomas; Hansen Lind Meyer, P.C.; Iowa City, Iowa

MINIMUM UNIFORMLY DISTRIBUTED LIVE LOADS

OCCUPANCY OR USE	LIVE LOAD (PSF)
Armories and drill rooms	150
Assembly halls and other places of assembly	
Fixed seats	60
Movable seats	100
Platforms (assembly)	100
Attics	
Nonstorage	25
Storage	80*
Bakeries	150
Balconies	
Exterior	100
Interior (fixed seats)	60
Interior (movable seats)	100
Bowling alleys, poolrooms, and similar recreational areas	75
Broadcasting studios	100
Catwalks	25
Cold storage rooms	
Floor	150
Roof	250
Corridors	
First floor	100
Other floors, same as occupancy served except as indicated	
Dance halls and ballrooms	100
Dining rooms and restaurants	100
Dormitories	
Nonpartitioned	80
Partitioned	40
File rooms	
Card	125*
Letter	80*
Fire escapes on multifamily or single family residential buildings only	100
Foundries	600†
Fuel rooms, framed	400†
Garages (passenger cars only). For trucks and buses use AASHO‡ lane load	50
Grandstands	100
Greenhouses	150
Gymnasiums, main floors and balconies	100
Hospitals	
Operating rooms, laboratories	60
Private rooms	40
Wards	40
Corridors, above first floor	80
Hotels (see Residential)	–
Kitchens, other than domestic	150†
Laboratories, scientific	100
Laundries	150†
Libraries	
Reading rooms	60
Stack rooms (books and shelving at 65 pcf) but not less than	150
Corridors, above first floor	80
Manufacturing	
Light	125
Heavy	250
Ice	300
Marquees	75
Morgues	125
Office buildings	
Office	50
Business machine equipment	100†
Lobbies	100
Corridors, above the first floor	80
File and computer rooms require heavier loads based on anticipated occupancy	
Penal institutions	
Cell blocks	40
Corridors	100
Printing plants	
Composing rooms	100
Linotype rooms	100
Paper storage rooms	§
Pressrooms	150†
Public rooms	100
Residential	
Multifamily houses	
Private apartments	40
Public rooms	100
Corridors	80
Dwellings	
First floor	40
Second floor and habitable attics	30
Uninhabitable attics	20
Hotels	
Guest rooms	40
Public rooms	100
Corridors serving public rooms	100
Rest rooms and toilet rooms	60
Schools	
Classrooms	40
Corridors	80
Sidewalks, vehicular driveways, and yards subject to trucking	250
Skating rinks	100
Stairs and exitways	100
Storage warehouses	
Light	125
Heavy	250
Hay or grain	300
Stores	
Retail	
First floor, rooms	100
Upper floors	75
Wholesale	125
Telephone exchange rooms	150†
Theaters	
Aisles, corridors, and lobbies	100
Orchestra floors	60
Balconies	60
Stage floors	100
Dressing rooms	40
Grid iron floor or fly gallery grating	60
Projection room	100
Transformer rooms	200†
Vaults, in offices	250*
Yards and terraces, pedestrians	100

*Increase when occupancy exceeds this amount.
†Use weight of actual equipment when greater.
‡American Association of State Highway Officials.
§Paper storage 50 lb/ft of clear story height.

LIVE LOAD

Live load is the weight superimposed by the use and occupancy of the building or other structure, not including the wind load, snow load, earthquake load, or dead load.

The live loads to be assumed in the design of buildings and other structures shall be the greatest loads that probably will be produced by the intended use or occupancy, but in no case less than the minimum uniformly distributed unit load.

THRUSTS AND HANDRAILS

Stairway and balcony railings, both exterior and interior, shall be designed to resist a vertical and a horizontal thrust of 50 lb/linear ft applied at the top of the railing. For one- and two-family dwellings, a thrust of 20 lb/ft may be used instead of 50 lb/ft.

CONCENTRATED LOADS

Floors shall be designed to support safely the uniformly distributed live load or the concentrated load in pounds given, whichever produces the greater stresses. Unless otherwise specified, the indicated concentration shall be assumed to occupy an area of 2½ feet square (6.25 ft^2) and shall be located so as to produce the maximum stress conditions in the structural members.

PARTIAL LOADING

The full intensity of the appropriately reduced live loads applied only to a portion of the length of a structure or member shall be considered if it produces a more unfavorable effect than the same intensity applied over the full length of the structure or member.

IMPACT LOADS

The live loads shall be assumed to include adequate allowance for ordinary impact conditions. Provision shall be made in structural design for uses and loads that involve unusual vibration and impact forces.

1. ELEVATORS: All elevator loads shall be increased 100% for impact, and the structural supports shall be designed within limits of deflection prescribed by American National Standard Safety Code for Elevators and Escalators, A17.1-1981, and American National Standard Practice for the Inspection of Elevators, Escalators, and Moving Walks (Inspector's Manual) A17.2-1979.
2. MACHINERY: For the purpose of design, the weight of machinery and moving loads shall be increased as follows to allow for impact: (a) elevator machinery, 100%; (b) light machinery, shaft or motor driven, 20%; (c) reciprocating machinery or power driven units, 50%; (d) hangers for floors or balconies, 33%. All percentages to be increased if so recommended by the manufacturer.
3. CRANEWAYS: All craneways, except those using only manually powered cranes, shall have their design loads increased for impact as follows: (a) a vertical force equal to 25% of the maximum wheel load; (b) a lateral force equal to 20% of the weight of trolley and lifted load only, applied one-half at the top of each rail; and (c) a longitudinal force of 10% of the maximum wheel loads of the crane applied at top of rail.

MINIMUM ROOF LOADS

1. FLAT, PITCHED, OR CURVED ROOFS: Ordinary roofs—flat, pitched, or curved—shall be designed for the live loads or the snow load, whichever produces the greater stresses.
2. PONDING: For roofs, care shall be taken to provide drainage or the load shall be increased to represent all likely accumulations of water. Deflection of roof members will permit ponding of water accompanied by increased deflection and additional ponding.
3. SPECIAL PURPOSE ROOFS: When used for promenade purposes, roofs shall be designed for a minimum live load of 60 psf; 100 psf when designed for roof garden or assembly uses. Roofs used for other special purposes shall be designed for appropriate loads, as directed or approved by the building official.

LIVE LOAD REDUCTION

In general, design live loads not in excess of 100 psf on any member supporting an area of 150 sq ft or more, except for places of public assembly, repair garages, parking structures, and roofs. The reduction shall not exceed the value of R from the following formulas:

$$R = .08(A-150)$$

$$R = 23(1 + D/L)$$

where R = reduction (%)
D = dead load per square foot of area supported by the member
L = live load per square foot of area supported by the member
A = area supported by the member.

In no case should the reduction exceed 60% for vertical members, nor 40 to 60% for horizontal members.

For live loads in excess of 100 psf, some codes allow a live load reduction of 20% for columns only.

CODES AND STANDARDS

The applicable building code should be referred to for specific uniformly distributed live load, movable partition load, special, and concentrated load requirements.

In addition to the specific code requirements, the designer must consider the effects of special loading conditions, such as moving loads, construction loads, roof top planting loads, and concentrated loads from supported or hanging equipment (radiology, computer, heavy filing, or mechanical equipment).

The live loads given in this table are obtained by reference to ANSI A58.1-1982.

David H. Holbert; Hansen Lind Meyer, P.C.; Iowa City, Iowa

GENERAL

Information to determine occupant load is from three model building codes in use in the United States:

1. Uniform Building Code (UBC), 1985 edition, copyright 1985, with permission of the International Conference of Building Officials, publisher.
2. BOCA National Building Code (BOCA), 1986 edition, copyright 1986, with permission of the Building Officials and Code Administrators International, Inc., publisher.
3. Standard Building Code (SBC), 1985 edition, copyright 1985, with permission of the Southern Building Code Congress International, Inc., publisher, with all rights reserved.

Occupant load generally is defined as the maximum capacity of a building or room given as the total number of people present at any one time. For occupant loads, generally it is assumed that all areas of a building will be occupied at the same time, with some exceptions noted in specific codes. For example, the UBC states: "Accessory use areas, which ordinarily are used only by persons who occupy the main areas of an occupancy, shall be provided with exits as though they are completely occupied, but their occupant load need not be included in computing the total occupant load of the building" [UBC-Sec. 3302.(a)].

Most codes require that to determine multiple use building or area occupancies, the occupant load (O.L.) be based on the use that produces the most occupants. For example, the occupant load for a school multiple use room, which also will be used for classroom activities (O.L. factor = 20), as well as for assembly space (O.L. factor = 15), is calculated using the 15 sq. ft. per occupant factor.

If buildings or areas contain two or more separate occupancies, the overall occupant load is determined by computing occupant loads for various areas and adding them together for an aggregate occupant load.

When calculating occupant load for areas with fixed seating in benches or pews, the number of occupants is based on one seat for each 18 in. of bench or pew. In dining areas with booth seating, the number of seats is based on 24 in. for each seat.

OCCUPANT LOADS

USE	MAXIMUM FLOOR AREA PER OCCUPANT (SQ. FT. PER OCCUPANT)		
	BOCA	SBC	UBC[1]
Assembly areas[2]—concentrated use (without fixed seats): auditoriums, bowling alleys[3], churches, dance floors, lodge rooms, reviewing stands, stadiums	7 net	7 net	7
Assembly areas—less concentrated use: conference rooms, dining/drinking areas, exhibit rooms, gymnasiums, lounges, stages[4]	15 net	15 net	15
Assembly areas—standing space	3 net	3 net	—
Business areas[7]	100 gross	100 gross	100
Courtrooms—(without fixed seats)	40 net	40 net	—
Daycare facilities	—	—	35
Dormitories	—	—	50
Educational			
classroom areas	20 net	20 net	20
shops and vocational rooms	50 net	50 net	50
Industrial areas[5]	100 gross	100 gross	200
Institutional[6]			
children's homes, homes for aged, nursing homes, sanitariums, hospitals	—	—	80
inpatient treatment areas	240 gross	240 gross	—
outpatient areas	100 gross	100 gross	—
sleeping areas	120 gross	120 gross	—
Kitchens (commercial)	—	—	300
Library			
reading rooms	50 net	50 net	50
stack areas	100 gross	100 gross	—
Lobbies (accessory to assembly area)	—	—	7
Locker rooms	—	—	50
Mechanical equipment areas	300 gross	300 gross	300
Mercantile[8]			
basements	30 gross	30 gross	20
ground floors	30 gross	30 gross	30
upper floors	60 gross	60 gross	50
storage, stockrooms, shipping areas	100 gross	100 gross	300[9]
Parking garages	200 gross	200 gross	200
Residential[10]	200 gross	200 gross	—
hotels and apartments	—	—	200
dwellings	—	—	300
Skating rinks[11]	—	15 net	—
rink area	—	—	50
deck	—	—	15
Storage areas	300 gross	300 gross	300
Swimming pools			
pool	—	—	50
deck	—	—	15
All other areas	—	—	100

TABLE NOTES

1. Both BOCA and SBC use net and gross floor areas to determine occupant load. UBC does not differentiate between gross and net areas.
2. Occupant loads for assembly areas with fixed seats are determined by the actual number of installed seats.
3. Occupant load calculations for bowling alleys under BOCA and SBC use 5 persons per alley in addition to tabular values indicated.
4. Stages are considered assembly areas—less concentrated use (15 sq. ft. per occupant) in UBC; not separately classified in BOCA or SBC.
5. UBC classifies industrial areas as manufacturing areas.
6. BOCA and SBC classify areas within institutional occupancies, UBC classifies by occupancy description only.
7. UBC classifies business areas as office occupancy.
8. UBC classifies mercantile areas as store-retail sales rooms.
9. UBC considers storage and stockroom areas as storage occupancy (300 sq. ft. per occupant).
10. BOCA and SBC do not separate hotel/apartment and dwelling occupancies.
11. BOCA does not classify separately skating rinks from other assembly areas—less concentrated use (15 sq. ft. per occupant). SBC does not separate areas within skating rinks.

EXITS

All three major codes use occupant loads to determine the size and number of required exits. Based on occupant loads and area usages, it is possible to determine the required exits, arrangement, and sizes of exit components. All three codes (BOCA, SBC, and UBC) consider an exit to be more than merely a door. Although specific definitions vary with each code, exits usually are considered to be continuous and unobstructed means of egress to a public way and may include such building elements as doors, corridors, stairs, balconies, lobbies, exit courts, etc. Elevators are not considered exits. Requirements for arrangements, size, and operation of exits vary; consult appropriate code for specific information.

MINIMUM EXITS BASED ON USAGE

USAGE	MINIMUM TWO EXITS REQUIRED WHERE O.L. IS AT LEAST:
Aircraft hangars	10
Auction rooms	20
Assembly areas	50
Children's homes and homes for the aged	6
Classrooms	50
Dormitories	10
Dwellings	10
Hospitals, sanitariums, and nursing homes	6
Hotels and apartments	10
Kitchens (commercial)	30
Library reading rooms	50
Locker rooms	30
Manufacturing areas	30
Mechanical equipment rooms	30
Nurseries for children (daycare)	7
Offices	30
Parking garages	30
School shops and vocational rooms	50
Skating rinks	50
Storage and stockrooms	30
Stores (retail sales rooms)	
basements	2 exits minimum
ground floors	50
upper floors	10
Swimming pools	50
Warehouses	30
All other	50

International Conference of Building Officials; Southern Building Code Congress International; Building Officials and Code Administrators International, Inc.; see data sources

James O. Rose, AIA; University of Wyoming; Laramie, Wyoming

REFERENCES

GENERAL REFERENCES

American National Standards Institute (ANSI)
ASTM Standards in Building Codes, American Society for Testing and Materials (ASTM)
BOCA National Building Code, Building Officials and Code Administrators International (BOCA)
Fire Protection Handbook, National Fire Protection Association (NFPA)
Minimum Guidelines and Requirements for Accessible Design, Architectural and Transportation Barriers Compliance Board
Southern Standard Building Code, Southern Building Code Congress (SBCC)
Uniform Building Code, International Conference of Building Officials (ICBO)

DATA SOURCES: ORGANIZATIONS

American Insurance Association, 20
American National Standards Institute (ANSI), 21, 40
American Society for Testing and Materials (ASTM), 20
American Society of Heating, Refrigerating and Air Conditioning Engineers (ASHRAE), 18, 19
Building Owners and Managers Association (BOMA), 39
Computer Parking Design, 33
Factory Mutual System, 17, 20
Grinnell Fire Protection Systems Company, 17
Industrial Risk Insurers, 20
National Automatic Sprinkler and Fire Control Association (NAFSCA), 17
National Building Code, American Insurance Association, 21
National Fire Protection Association (NFPA), 8, 18, 19
National Parking Association (NPA), 30
Northeastern Lumber Manufacturers Association (NELMA), 22, 24
Operations Council, American Trucking Association, 36, 37
Overhead Door Corporation, 30
Portland Cement Association (PCA), 22, 24
Simplex Time Recorder Company, 19
Underwriters Laboratories, Inc. (U.L.), 20
Young Mens Christian Association (YMCA), 14, 15
Zamboni Corporation, 28

DATA SOURCES: PUBLICATIONS

Basic Building Code, Building Officials and Code Administrators International (BOCA), 21
BOCA National Building Code, 1987, Building Officials and Code Administrators International (BOCA). Reprinted with permission of the publisher, 41
Concepts in Building Fire Safety, 1986, M. David Egan, Wiley, 17, 18, 20
Fire Protection Handbook, 15th ed., 1981, National Fire Protection Association (NFPA). Reprinted with permission of the publisher, 16, 20
Fire Resistance Design Data Manual, Gypsum Association, 20
Fire Safety with Concrete Masonry, National Concrete Masonry Association (NCMA), 20
Fire-Resistant Steel-Frame Construction, American Iron and Steel Institute (AISI), 20
Identification of the Fire Hazards of Materials, National Fire Protection Association (NFPA), 16
NFPA 13, Standard for the Installation of Sprinkler Systems, 1985 ed., National Fire Protection Association (NFPA), 17
Southern Standard Building Code, 1985 ed., Southern Building Code Congress (SBCC), 21, 41. Reprinted with permission, 41
Time-Saver Standards for Site Planning, 1966, Joseph De Chiara and Lee Koppelman, McGraw-Hill, 30
Uniform Building Code, 1982 ed., 1985 ed., International Conference of Building Officials (ICBO). Reprinted with permission, 41

CHAPTER **2**

SITEWORK

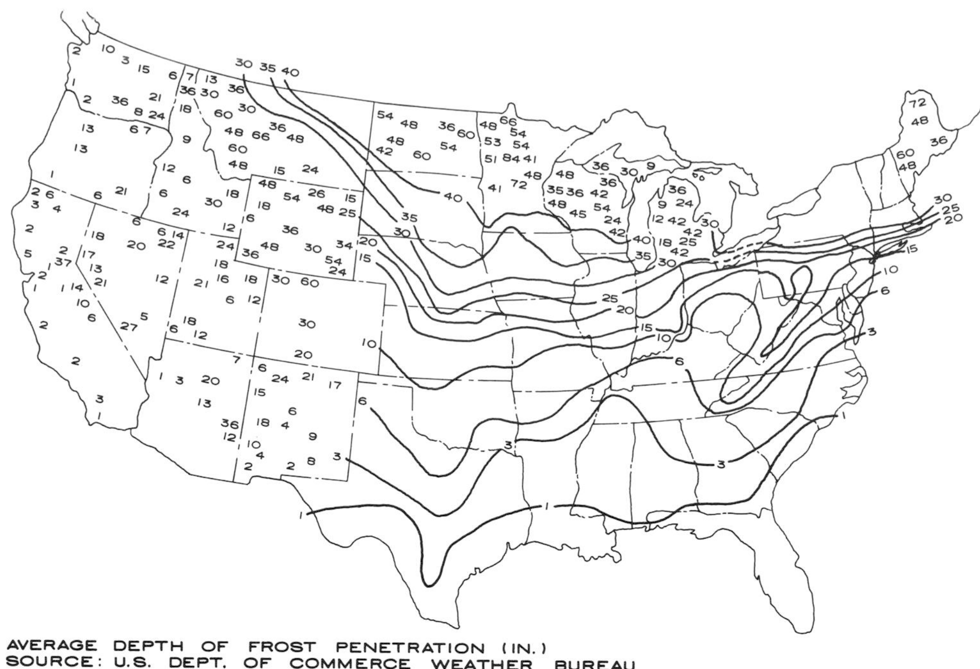

AVERAGE DEPTH OF FROST PENETRATION (IN.)
SOURCE: U.S. DEPT. OF COMMERCE WEATHER BUREAU

PRELIMINARY SUBSURFACE INFORMATION

A. Collect available information for soil, rock and water conditions, including the following:
   1. Topographic and aerial mapping.
   2. Geological survey maps and publications.
   3. Local knowledge (history of site development, experience of nearby structures, flooding, subsidence, etc.).
   4. Existing subsurface data (boreholes, well records, water soundings).
   5. Reconnaissance site survey.
   6. Previous studies.

B. Evaluate available information for site acceptability. If available data are insufficient, consult a geotechnical engineer to perform a limited subsurface investigation to gather basic information.

C. Consult geotechnical engineer for potential foundation performance at each site as part of the selection process.

DETAILED SUBSURFACE INFORMATION

After selection of a potential site a subsurface and laboratory test investigation should be carried out by a qualified geotechnical engineer before design is undertaken.

The investigation should provide an adequate understanding of the subsurface conditions and the information should be assessed to determine potential foundation behavior.

The engineer should evaluate alternative foundation methods and techniques in conjunction with the architect.

The engineer or architect should provide inspection during construction to ensure that material and construction procedures are as specified and to evaluate unexpected soil, rock, or groundwater conditions that may be exposed by excavations.

SOIL TYPES AND THEIR PROPERTIES

DIVISION	SYMBOLS: LETTER	SYMBOLS: HATCHING	SYMBOLS: COLOR	SOIL DESCRIPTION	VALUE AS A FOUNDATION MATERIAL	FROST ACTION	DRAINAGE
Gravel and gravelly soils	GW		Red	Well graded gravel, or gravel-sand mixture, little or no fines	Excellent	None	Excellent
	GP		Red	Poorly graded gravel, or gravel-sand mixtures, little or no fines	Good	None	Excellent
	GM		Yellow	Silty gravels, gravel-sand-silt mixtures	Good	Slight	Poor
	GC		Yellow	Clayey-gravels, gravel-clay-sand mixtures	Good	Slight	Poor
Sand and sandy soils	SW		Red	Well-graded sands, or gravelly sands, little or no fines	Good	None	Excellent
	SP		Red	Poorly graded sands, or gravelly sands, little or no fines	Fair	None	Excellent
	SM		Yellow	Silty sands, sand-silt mixtures	Fair	Slight	Fair
	SC		Yellow	Clayey sands, sand-clay mixtures	Fair	Medium	Poor
Silts and clays LL < 50	ML		Green	Inorganic silts, rock flour, silty or clayey fine sands, or clayey silts with slight plasticity	Fair	Very high	Poor
	CL		Green	Inorganic clays of low to medium plasticity, gravelly clays, silty clays, lean clays	Fair	Medium	Impervious
	OL		Green	Organic silt-clays of low plasticity	Poor	High	Impervious
Silts and clays LL > 50	MH		Blue	Inorganic silts, micaceous or diatomaceous fine sandy or silty soils, elastic silts	Poor	Very high	Poor
	CH		Blue	Inorganic clays of high plasticity, fat clays	Very poor	Medium	Impervious
	OH		Blue	Organic clays of medium to high plasticity, organic silts	Very poor	Medium	Impervious
Highly organic soils	Pt		Orange	Peat and other highly organic soils	Not suitable	Slight	Poor

NOTES
1. Consult soil engineers and local building codes for allowable soil bearing capacities.
2. LL indicates liquid limit.

Mueser, Rutledge, Johnston & DeSimone; New York, New York

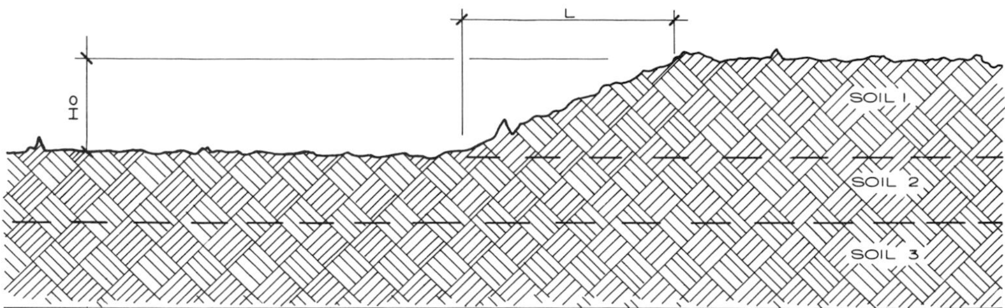
L
HO
SOIL 1
SOIL 2
SOIL 3
OPEN EXCAVATION

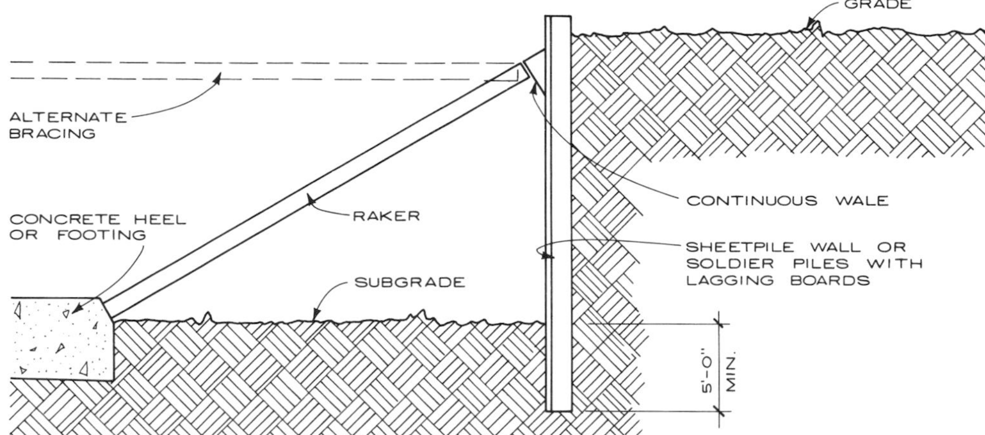
GRADE
ALTERNATE BRACING
CONCRETE HEEL OR FOOTING
RAKER
SUBGRADE
CONTINUOUS WALE
SHEETPILE WALL OR SOLDIER PILES WITH LAGGING BOARDS
5'-0" MIN.
BRACED EXCAVATION USING RAKERS

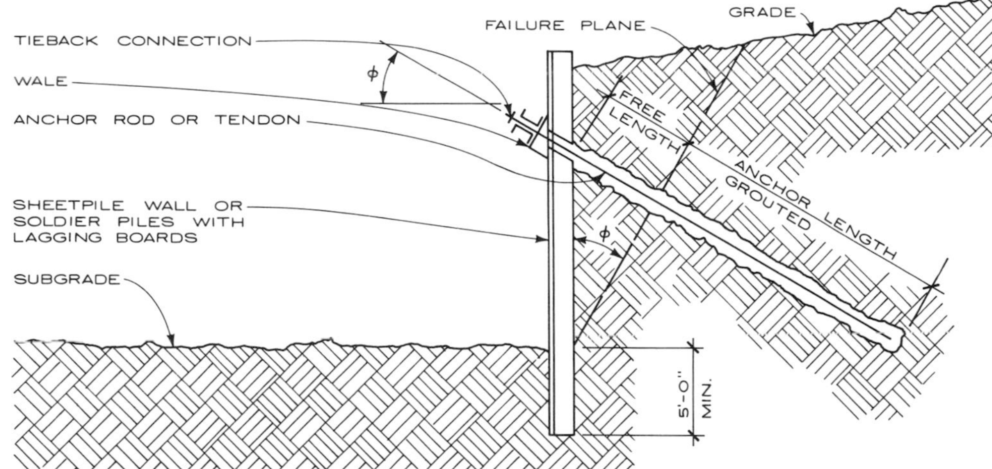
TIEBACK CONNECTION
WALE
ANCHOR ROD OR TENDON
SHEETPILE WALL OR SOLDIER PILES WITH LAGGING BOARDS
SUBGRADE
FAILURE PLANE
GRADE
FREE LENGTH
ANCHOR LENGTH GROUTED
5'-0" MIN.
BRACED EXCAVATION USING EARTH ANCHORS

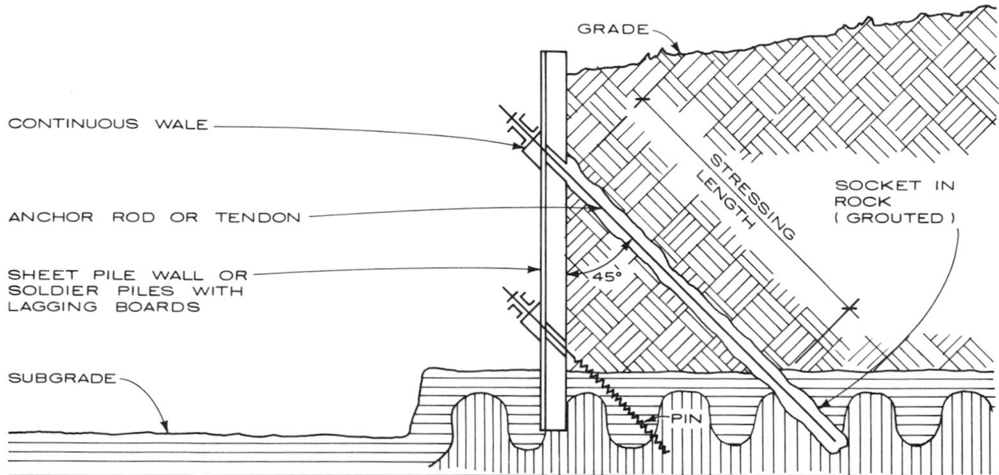
GRADE
CONTINUOUS WALE
ANCHOR ROD OR TENDON
SHEET PILE WALL OR SOLDIER PILES WITH LAGGING BOARDS
SUBGRADE
STRESSING LENGTH
SOCKET IN ROCK (GROUTED)
45°
PIN
BRACED EXCAVATION USING ROCK ANCHORS

EMBANKMENT STABILITY
CONSULT FOUNDATION ENGINEER

SOIL TYPES			L/H_O	REMARKS
S1	S2	S3		
Fill	Rock		>1.5	Check sliding of S1
Soft clay	Hard clay	Rock	>1.0	Check sliding of S1
Sand	Soft clay	Hard clay	>1.5	Check lateral displacement of S2
Sand	Sand	Hard clay	>1.5	
Hard clay	Soft clay	Sand	<1.0	Check lateral displacement of S2

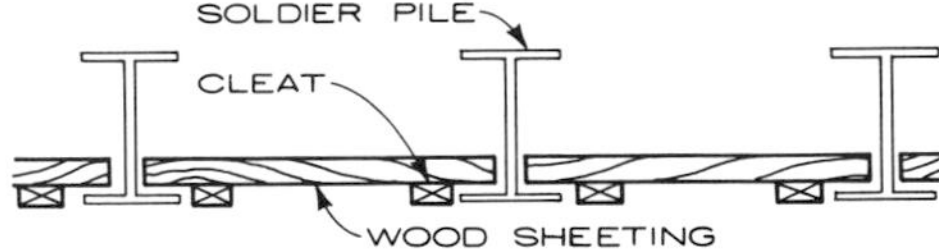
SOLDIER PILE
CLEAT
WOOD SHEETING
TIMBER LAGGING

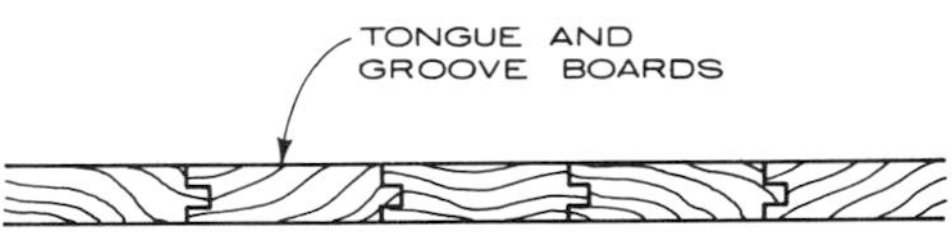
TONGUE AND GROOVE BOARDS
TIMBER SHEETING

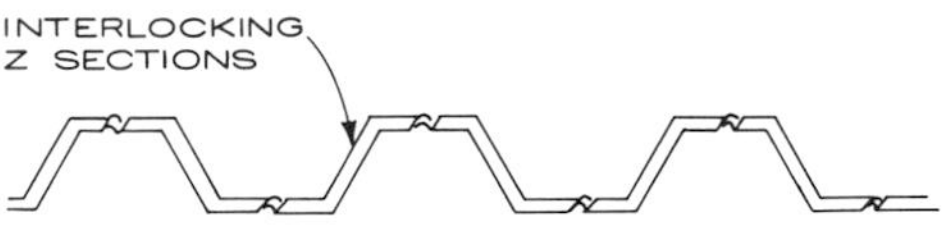
INTERLOCKING Z SECTIONS
STEEL SHEETING

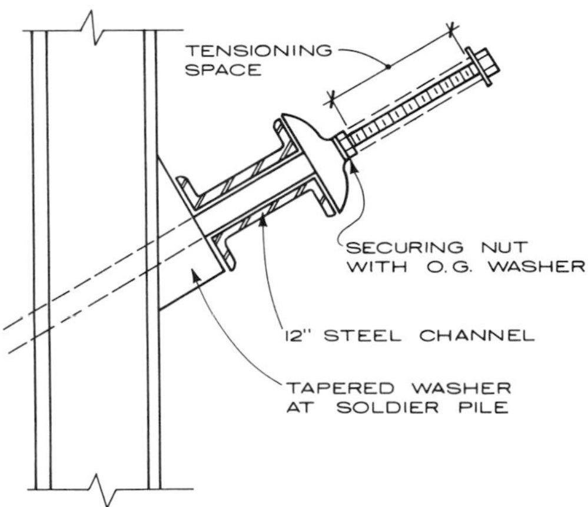
TENSIONING SPACE
SECURING NUT WITH O.G. WASHER
12" STEEL CHANNEL
TAPERED WASHER AT SOLDIER PILE
CHANNEL WALER DETAIL

NOTES

1. For shallow depths of excavation cantilever sheeting may be used, if driven to sufficient depth.
2. For deep excavations, several tiers of bracing may be necessary.
3. If subgrade of excavation is used for installation of spreadfootings or mats, proper dewatering procedures may be required to avoid disturbance of bearing level.
4. At times it may be possible to improve the bearing stratum by excavation of compressible materials and their replacement with compacted granular backfill.
5. For evaluation of problems encountered with sheeting and shoring, a foundation engineer should be consulted.
6. Local codes and OSHA regulations must be considered.
7. Proximity of utilities and other structures must be considered in design.

Mueser, Rutledge, Johnston & DeSimone; New York, New York

Embankment stabilization is required where extremely steep slopes exist that are subject to heavy storm water runoff. The need for mechanical stabilization can be reduced by intercepting the runoff, or slowing the velocity of the runoff down the slope. Diversions are desirable at the tops of slopes to intercept the runoff. Slopes can be shelved or terraced to reduce the velocity of runoff to the point where a major erosion hazard is avoided. Use an armored channel or slope drain if concentrated runoff down a slope must be controlled.

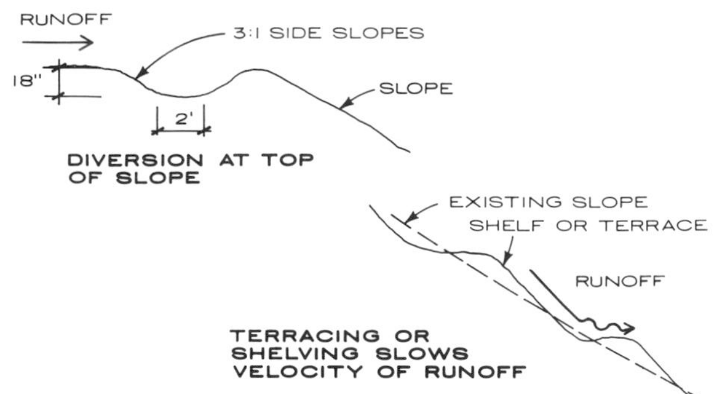
RUNOFF
3:1 SIDE SLOPES
18"
SLOPE
2'
DIVERSION AT TOP OF SLOPE
EXISTING SLOPE
SHELF OR TERRACE
RUNOFF
TERRACING OR SHELVING SLOWS VELOCITY OF RUNOFF

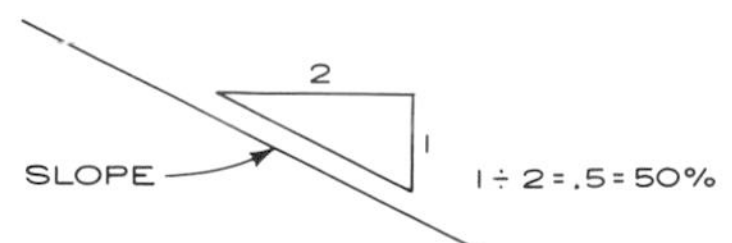
2
1
SLOPE
1 ÷ 2 = .5 = 50%

SOIL	GRADIENT	RATIO
Dry sand	33%	3:1
Loam	40%	2.5:1
Compacted clay	80%	1.25:1
Saturated clay	20%	5:1

MAX. GRADIENTS FOR BARE SOILS

SLOPE STABILIZATION WITH RIPRAP

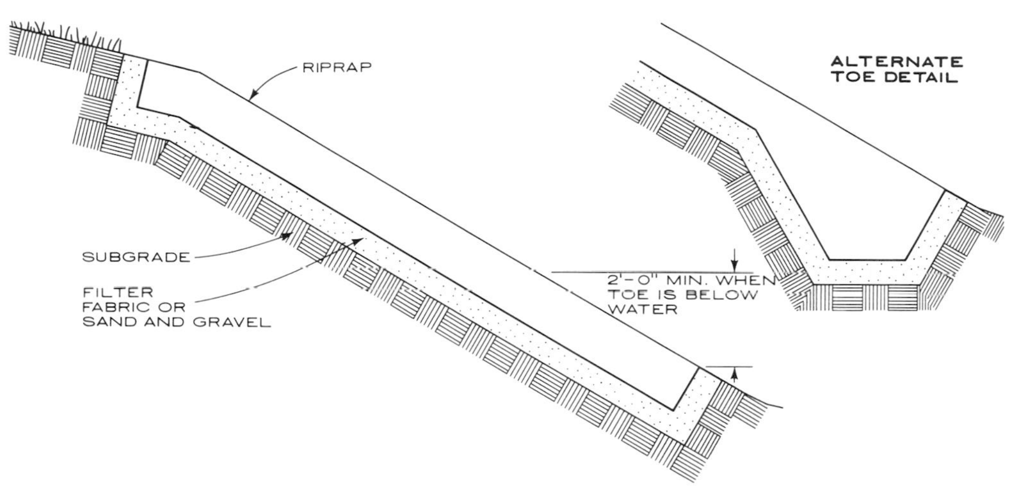
RIPRAP
ALTERNATE TOE DETAIL
SUBGRADE
FILTER FABRIC OR SAND AND GRAVEL
2'-0" MIN. WHEN TOE IS BELOW WATER

NOTE

A number of mechanical embankment stabilization materials are illustrated. Two important features all methods have in common are

1. Embedment of the toe and lateral limits to prevent undercutting and outflanking, and
2. Use of a granular or fabric filter to protect the soil beneath the protective layer from the effects of flowing water or existing groundwater.

RIPRAP EMBANKMENT WITH ALTERNATE TOE

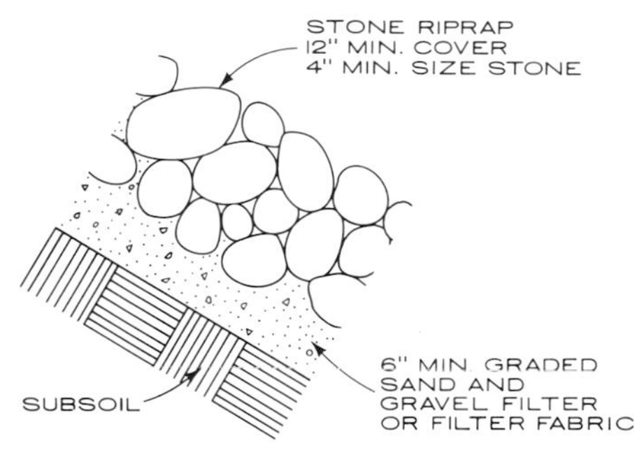
STONE RIPRAP
12" MIN. COVER
4" MIN. SIZE STONE
SUBSOIL
6" MIN. GRADED SAND AND GRAVEL FILTER OR FILTER FABRIC

STONE

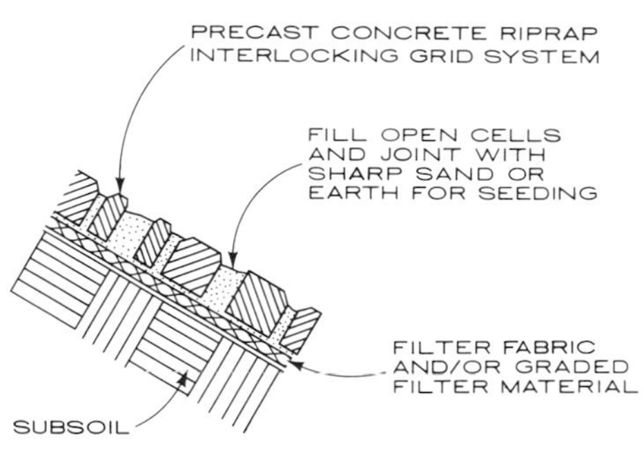
PRECAST CONCRETE RIPRAP INTERLOCKING GRID SYSTEM
FILL OPEN CELLS AND JOINT WITH SHARP SAND OR EARTH FOR SEEDING
FILTER FABRIC AND/OR GRADED FILTER MATERIAL
SUBSOIL

PRECAST CONCRETE

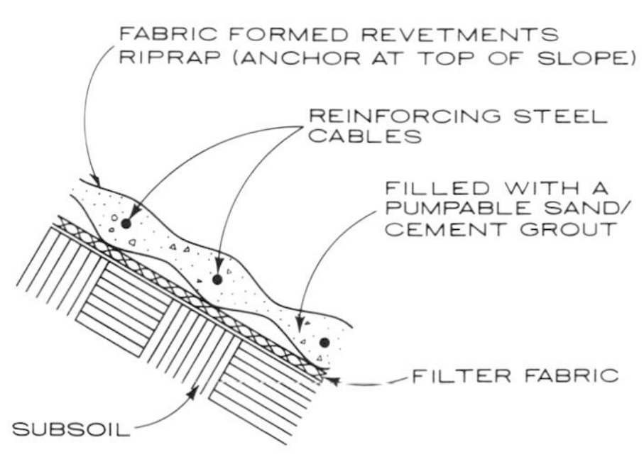
FABRIC FORMED REVETMENTS RIPRAP (ANCHOR AT TOP OF SLOPE)
REINFORCING STEEL CABLES
FILLED WITH A PUMPABLE SAND/ CEMENT GROUT
FILTER FABRIC
SUBSOIL

FABRIC FORMED REVETMENTS

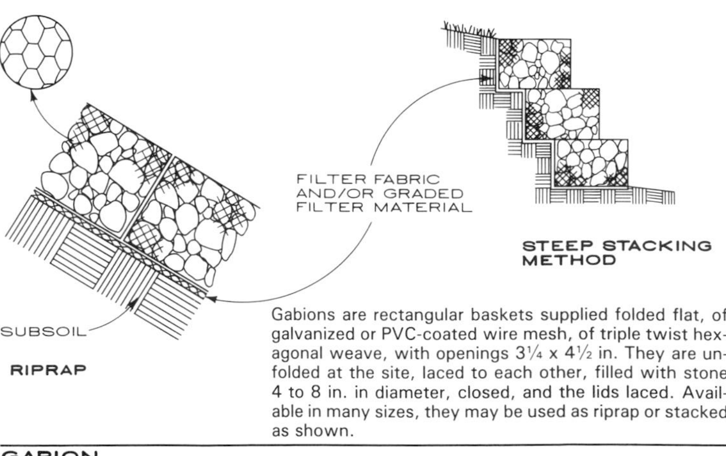
FILTER FABRIC AND/OR GRADED FILTER MATERIAL
STEEP STACKING METHOD
SUBSOIL
RIPRAP

Gabions are rectangular baskets supplied folded flat, of galvanized or PVC-coated wire mesh, of triple twist hexagonal weave, with openings $3^{1}/_{4}$ x $4^{1}/_{2}$ in. They are unfolded at the site, laced to each other, filled with stone 4 to 8 in. in diameter, closed, and the lids laced. Available in many sizes, they may be used as riprap or stacked as shown.

GABION

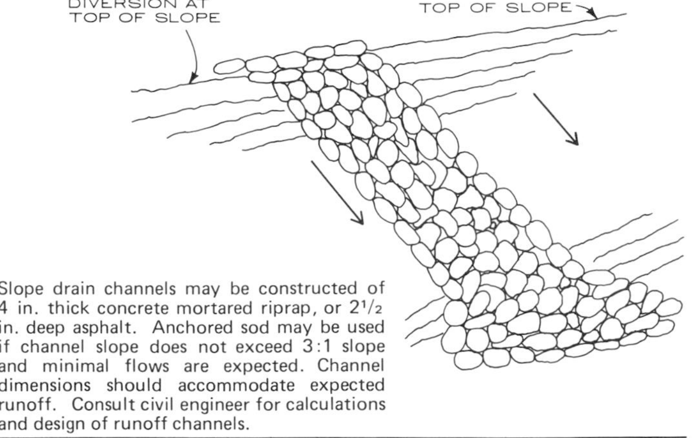
DIVERSION AT TOP OF SLOPE
TOP OF SLOPE

Slope drain channels may be constructed of 4 in. thick concrete mortared riprap, or $2^{1}/_{2}$ in. deep asphalt. Anchored sod may be used if channel slope does not exceed 3:1 slope and minimal flows are expected. Channel dimensions should accommodate expected runoff. Consult civil engineer for calculations and design of runoff channels.

SLOPE DRAIN

Derek Martin, FAIA; Pittsburgh, Pennsylvania
John M. Beckett; Beckett, Raeder, Rankin, Inc.; Ann Arbor, Michigan
James E. Sekela, PE; United States Army Corps of Engineers, Pittsburgh, Pennsylvania

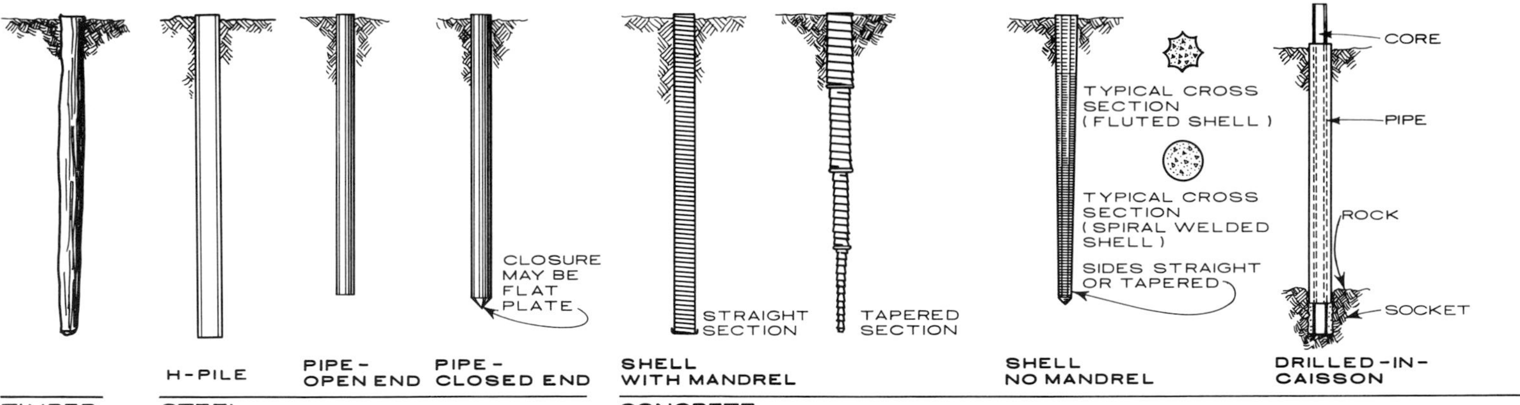
CLOSURE MAY BE FLAT PLATE
STRAIGHT SECTION
TAPERED SECTION
TYPICAL CROSS SECTION (FLUTED SHELL)
TYPICAL CROSS SECTION (SPIRAL WELDED SHELL)
SIDES STRAIGHT OR TAPERED
CORE
PIPE
ROCK
SOCKET
H-PILE
PIPE-OPEN END
PIPE-CLOSED END
SHELL WITH MANDREL
SHELL NO MANDREL
DRILLED-IN-CAISSON
TIMBER
STEEL
CONCRETE

NOTE: A mandrel is a member inserted into a hollow pile to reinforce the pile shell while it is driven into the ground.

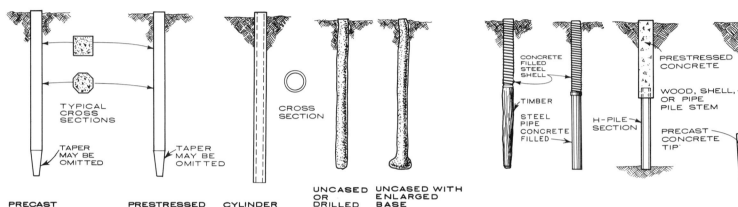

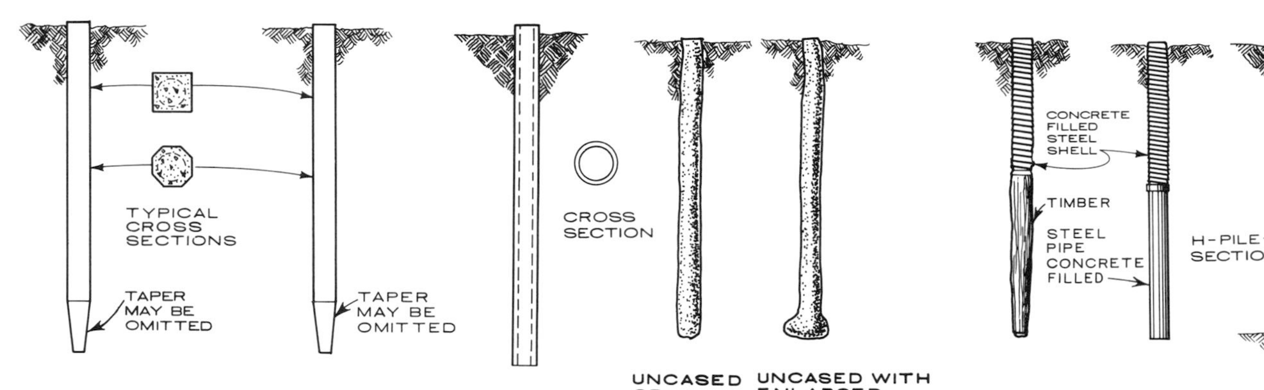
TYPICAL CROSS SECTIONS
TAPER MAY BE OMITTED
TAPER MAY BE OMITTED
CROSS SECTION
CONCRETE FILLED STEEL SHELL
TIMBER
STEEL PIPE CONCRETE FILLED
H-PILE SECTION
PRESTRESSED CONCRETE
WOOD, SHELL, OR PIPE PILE STEM
PRECAST CONCRETE TIP
PRECAST
PRESTRESSED
CYLINDER
UNCASED OR DRILLED
UNCASED WITH ENLARGED BASE
CONCRETE
COMPOSITE

GENERAL PILE DATA

PILE TYPE	MAXIMUM LENGTH (FT)	OPTIMUM LENGTH (FT)	SIZE (IN.)	MAXIMUM CAPACITY (TONS)	OPTIMUM LOAD RANGE (TONS)	USUAL SPACING
TIMBER	110	45-65	5-10 tip 12-20 butt	40	15-25	2′6″ to 3′0″
STEEL						
H-pile	250	40-150	8-14	200	50-200	2′6″ to 3′6″
Pipe—open end concrete filled	200	40-120	10-24	250	100-200	3′0″ to 4′0″
Pipe—closed end concrete filled	150	30-80	10-18	100	50-70	3′0″ to 4′0″
Shell—mandrel concrete filled straight or taper	100	40-80	8-18	75	40-60	3′0″ to 3′6″
Shell—no mandrel concrete filled	150	30-80	8-18	80	30-60	3′0″ to 3′6″
Drilled-in caisson concrete filled	250	60-120	24-48	3500	1000-2000	6′0″ to 8′0″
CONCRETE						
Precast	80	40-50	10-24	100	40-60	3′0″
Prestressed	200	60-80	10-24	200	100-150	3′0″ to 3′6″
Cylinder pile	150	60-80	36-54	500	250-400	6′0″ to 9′0″
Uncased or drilled	60	25-40	14-20	75	30-60	3′0″ to 3′6″
Uncased with enlarged base	60	25-40	14-20	150	40-100	6′0″
COMPOSITE						
Concrete—timber	150	60-100	5-10 tip 12-20 butt	40	15-25	3′0″ to 3′6″
Concrete—pipe	180	60-120	10-23	150	40-80	3′0″ to 4′0″
Prestressed concrete H-pile	200	100-150	20-24	200	120-150	3′6″ to 4′0″
Precast concrete tip	80	40	13-35	180	150	4′6″

NOTES

Timber piles must be treated with wood preservative when any portion is above permanent groundwater table.

Applicable material Specifications Concrete—ACL 318; Timber—ASTM D25: Structural Sections ASTM A36, A572 and A696.

For selection of type of pile consult foundation engineer.

Mueser, Rutledge, Johnston & DeSimone; New York, New York

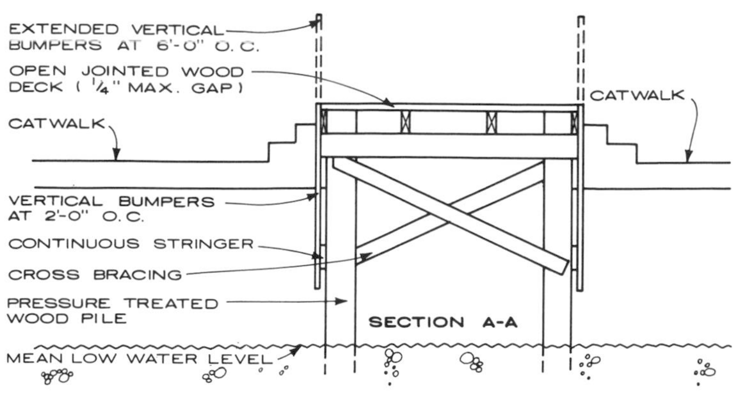
EXTENDED VERTICAL BUMPERS AT 6'-0" O.C.
OPEN JOINTED WOOD DECK (1/4" MAX. GAP)
CATWALK
CATWALK
VERTICAL BUMPERS AT 2'-0" O.C.
CONTINUOUS STRINGER
CROSS BRACING
PRESSURE TREATED WOOD PILE
SECTION A-A
MEAN LOW WATER LEVEL

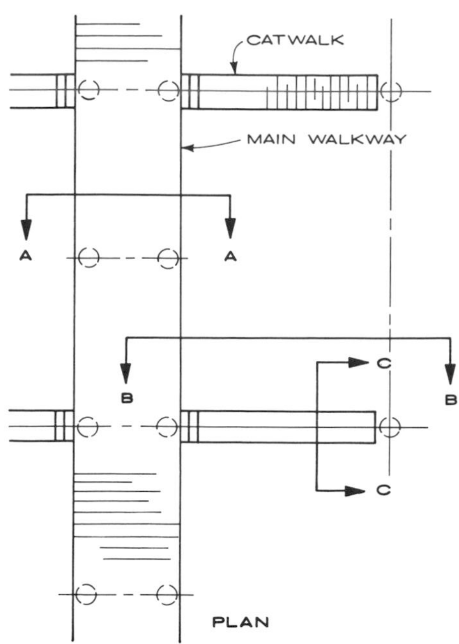
CATWALK
MAIN WALKWAY
A
A
B
B
C
C
PLAN

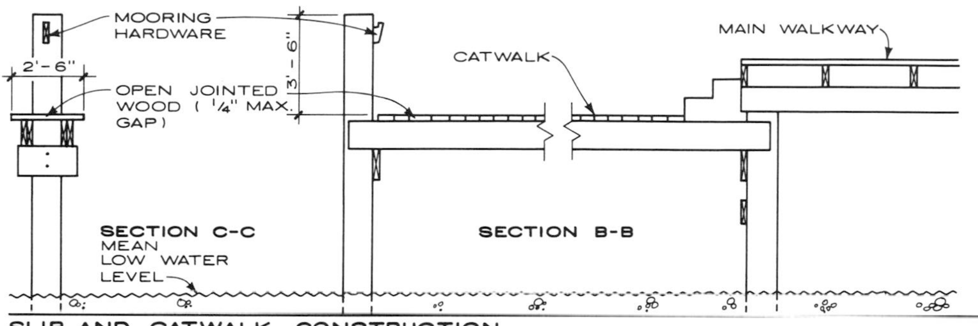
MOORING HARDWARE
2'-6"
3'-6"
OPEN JOINTED WOOD (1/4" MAX. GAP)
CATWALK
MAIN WALKWAY
SECTION C-C
MEAN LOW WATER LEVEL
SECTION B-B

SLIP AND CATWALK CONSTRUCTION

GENERAL NOTES

1. Wood marine construction must be pressure treated with a preservative. Wood preservatives for use in marine applications fall into two general categories, creosote and waterborne. To select a specific preservative from within these categories, the decaying agents must be identified. A preservative may then be chosen based on the recommendations of the American Wood Preservers Institute.
2. Waterborne preservatives are recommended for decks because creosote stains shoes and bare feet.
3. The preservatives selected should be approved by the Environmental Protection Agency.
4. Dock height above water is determined by average deck levels and probable water level. Maintain a 12 in. minimum dimension between water and deck. Floating docks may be required in tidal waters. Consult manufacturer for construction information.
5. Cross bracing should be minimized to avoid entanglement of swimmers.

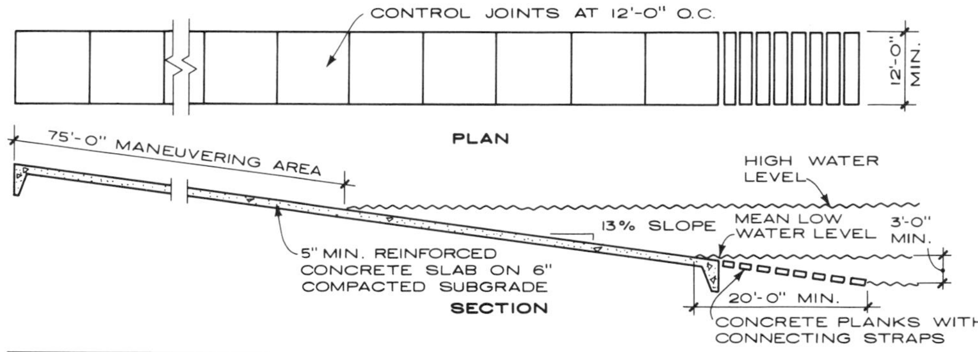
CONTROL JOINTS AT 12'-0" O.C.
12'-0" MIN.
PLAN
75'-0" MANEUVERING AREA
HIGH WATER LEVEL
13% SLOPE
MEAN LOW WATER LEVEL
3'-0" MIN.
5" MIN. REINFORCED CONCRETE SLAB ON 6" COMPACTED SUBGRADE
SECTION
20'-0" MIN.
CONCRETE PLANKS WITH CONNECTING STRAPS

BOAT LAUNCHING RAMP

LAUNCHING RAMPS

1. Launching ramps are for sheltered waters only.
2. A catwalk may be provided alongside the ramp.
3. Floating ramps may be required in tidal waters.

TABLE OF DIMENSIONS FOR SLIPS AND CATWALKS TO BE USED WITH PLAN DIAGRAM

LENGTH GROUP FOR BOAT	BEAM TO BE PROVIDED FOR	MIN. CLEAR WIDTH OF SLIP	GROSS SLIP WIDTH TYPE A	GROSS SLIP WIDTH TYPE B	GROSS SLIP WIDTH TYPE C	1ST CATWALK SPAN LENGTH D	2ND CATWALK SPAN LENGTH E	3RD CATWALK SPAN LENGTH F	DISTANCE G TO ANCHOR PILE
Up to 14'	6'–7"	8'–10"	10'–9"	10'–6"	11'–2"	12'–0"			17'–0"
Over 14' to 16'	7'–4"	9'–8"	11'–7"	11'–4"	12'–0"	12'–0"			19'–0"
Over 16' to 18'	8'–0"	10'–5"	12'–4"	12'–1"	12'–9"	14'–0"			21'–0"
Over 18' to 20'	8'–7"	11'–1"	13'–0"	12'–9"	13'–5"	8'–0"	8'–0"		23'–0"
Over 20' to 22'	9'–3"	11'–9"	13'–8"	13'–5"	14'–1"	10'–0"	8'–0"		25'–0"
Over 22' to 25'	10'–3"	13'–1"	15'–0"	14'–9"	15'–5"	10'–0"	8'–0"		28'–0"
Over 25' to 30'	11'–3"	14'–3"	16'–2"	15'–11"	16'–7"	10'–0"	10'–0"		33'–0"
Over 30' to 35'	12'–3"	15'–8"	17'–7"	17'–4"	18'–0"	12'–0"	10'–0"		38'–0"
Over 35' to 40'	13'–3"	16'–11"	18'–10"	18'–7"	19'–3"	12'–0"	12'–0"		43'–0"
Over 40' to 45'	14'–1"	17'–11"	19'–10"	19'–7"	20'–3"	14'–0"	12'–0"		48'–0"
Over 45' to 50'	14'–11"	19'–0"	20'–11"	20'–8"	21'–4"	9'–0"	9'–0"	10'–0"	53'–0"
Over 50' to 60'	16'–6"	21'–0"	22'–11"	22'–8"	23'–4"	11'–0"	11'–0"	12'–0"	63'–0"
Over 60' to 70'	18'–1"	23'–0"	26'–8"	24'–8"	25'–4"	11'–0"	11'–0"	12'–0"	73'–0"
Over 70' to 80'	19'–9"	24'–11"	28'–7"	26'–7"	26'–3"	11'–0"	11'–0"	12'–0"	83'–0"

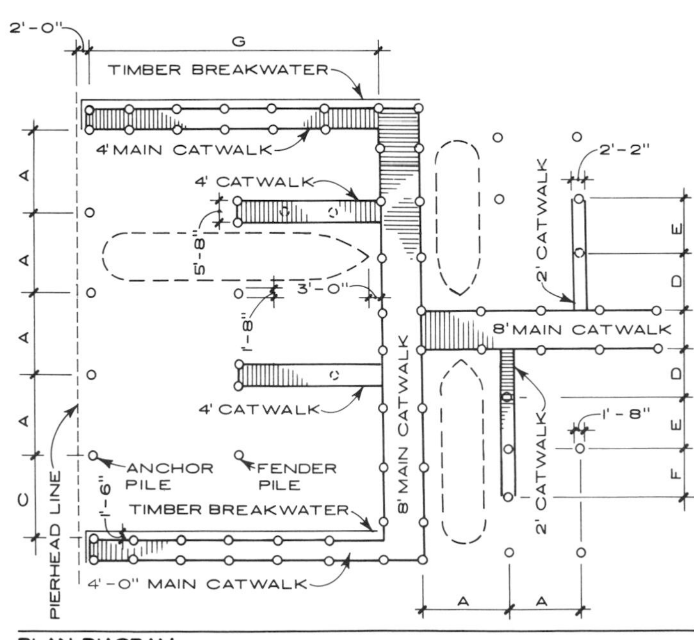
2'-0"
G
TIMBER BREAKWATER
4' MAIN CATWALK
4' CATWALK
5'-8"
3'-0"
1'-8"
2'-2"
2' CATWALK
8' MAIN CATWALK
4' CATWALK
1'-8"
ANCHOR PILE
FENDER PILE
1'-6"
TIMBER BREAKWATER
8' MAIN CATWALK
2' CATWALK
4'-0" MAIN CATWALK
PIERHEAD LINE
A
A
A
A
C
D
E
D
E
F
A
A

PLAN DIAGRAM

David E. Rose; Rossen/Neumann Associates; Southfield, Michigan

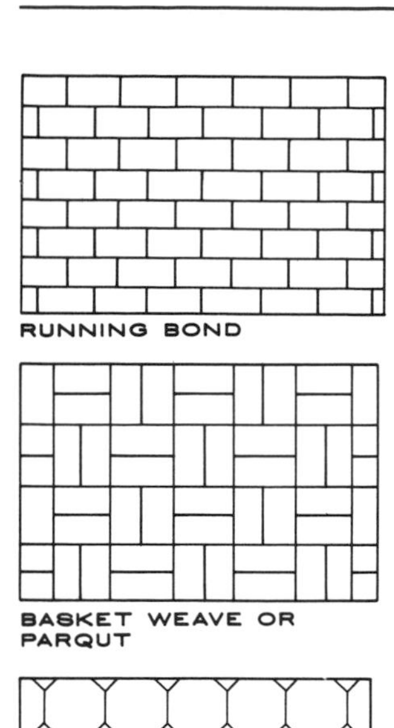
RUNNING BOND

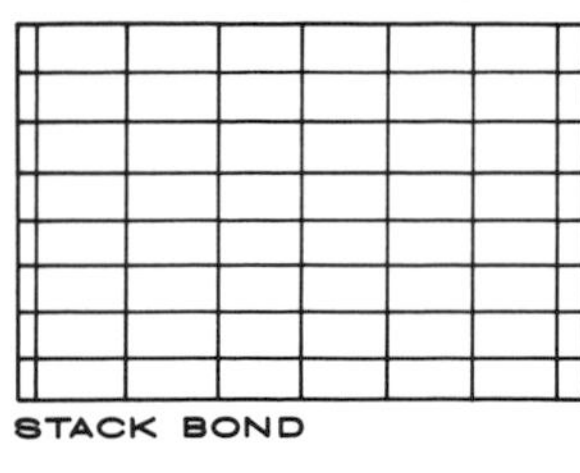
STACK BOND

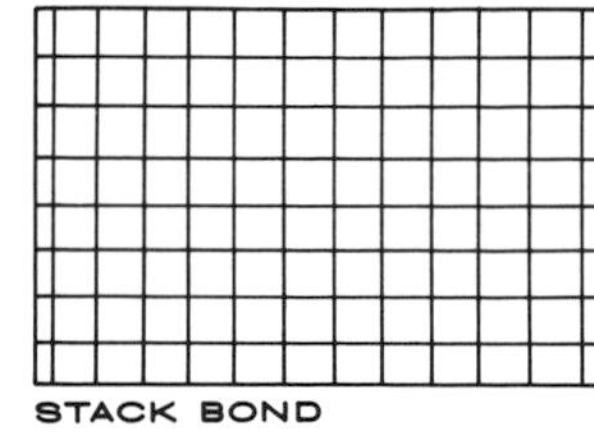
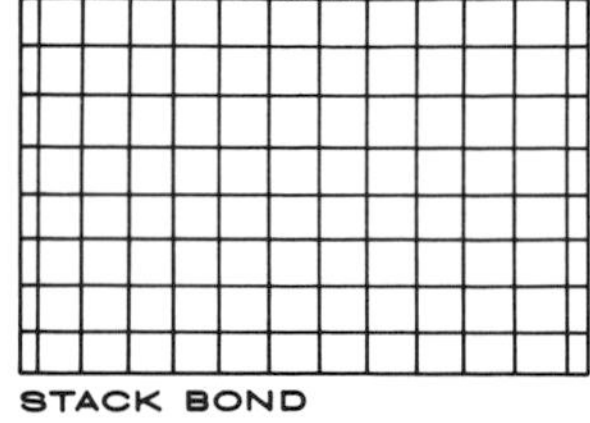
STACK BOND

BASKET WEAVE OR PARQUT

HERRINGBONE

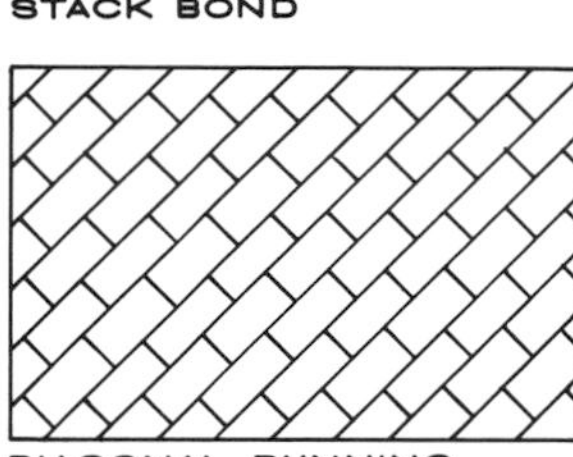
DIAGONAL RUNNING BOND

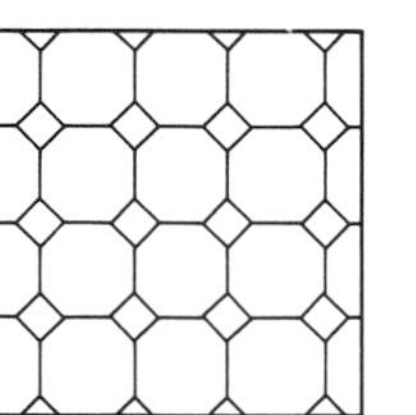
OCTAGON AND DOT

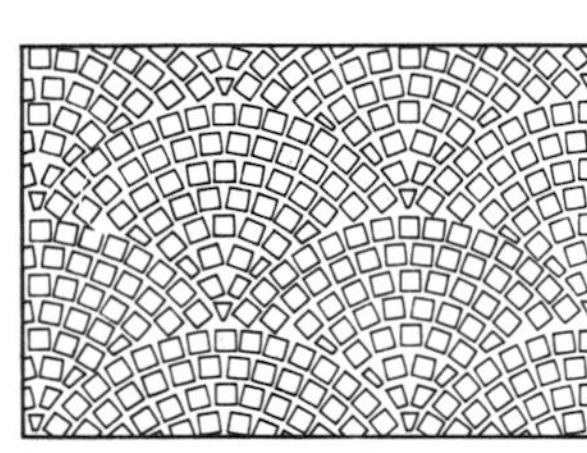
ROMAN COBBLE

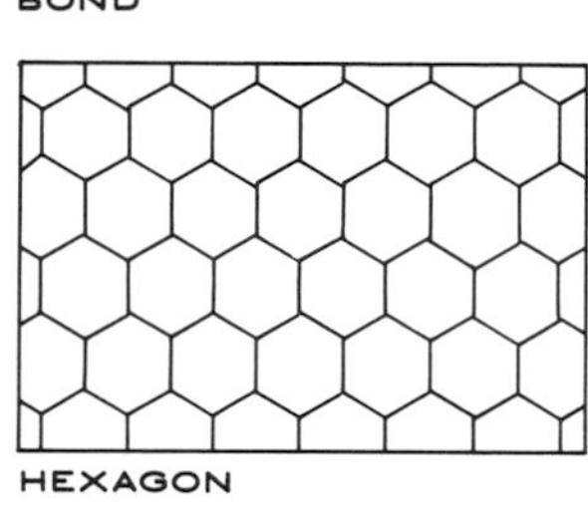
HEXAGON

UNIT PAVERS

TYPICAL UNIT PAVER TYPES AND NOMINAL SIZES

BRICK PAVERS: 4 in. x 4 in., 4 in. x 8 in., 4 in. x 12 in.; ½ in. to 2¼ in. thick.

PRESSED CONCRETE BRICKS: 4 in. x 8 in., 2½ in. to 3 in. thick.

PRESSED CONCRETE PAVERS: 12 in. x 12 in., 12 in. x 24 in., 18 in. x 18 in., 18 in. x 24 in., 24 in. x 24 in., 24 in. x 30 in., 24 in. x 36 in., 30 in. x 30 in., 36 in. x 36 in.; 1½ in. to 3 in. thick.

ASPHALT PAVERS: 5 in. x 12 in., 6 in. x 6 in., 6 in. x 12 in., 8 in. x 8 in., 8 in. hexagonal, 1¼ in. to 3 in. thick.

NOTES

1. Face brick, marble, and granite sometimes are used for paving.
2. See index for tile paver sizes and shapes.
3. Paving patterns shown often are rotated 45° for diagonal patterns.
4. Maximum 3 percent absorption for brick applications subject to vehicular traffic.
5. For pressed concrete and asphalt pavers subject to vehicular traffic, use 3 in. thickness.
6. Use modular size for brick paver patterns other than running and stack bond set with mortar joints. Use full size when set without mortar joints.

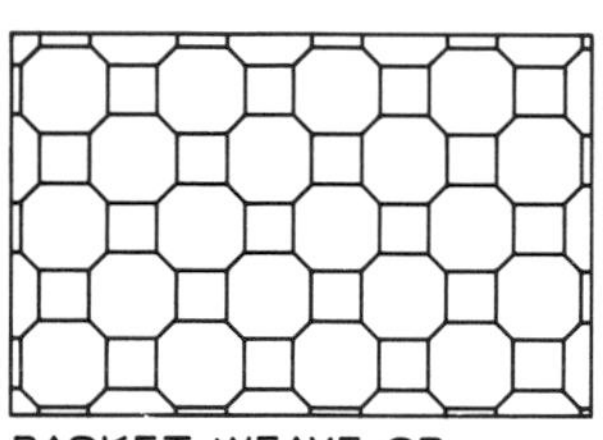
BASKET WEAVE OR PARQUET

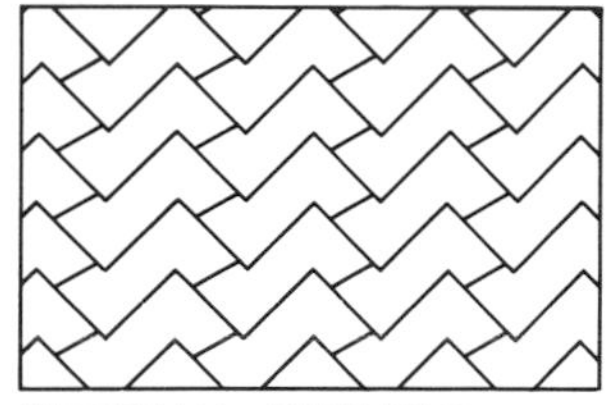
DIAGONAL RUNNING BOND

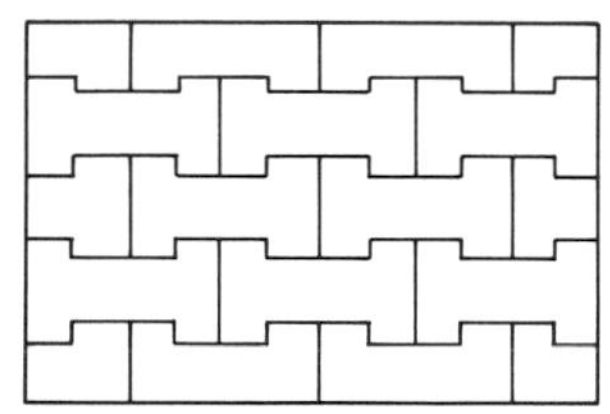
RUNNING BOND

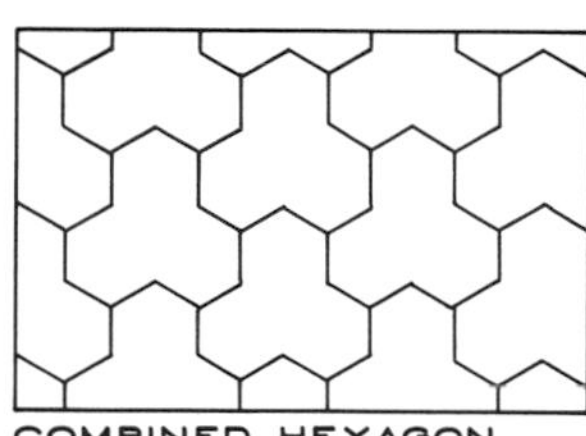
COMBINED HEXAGON

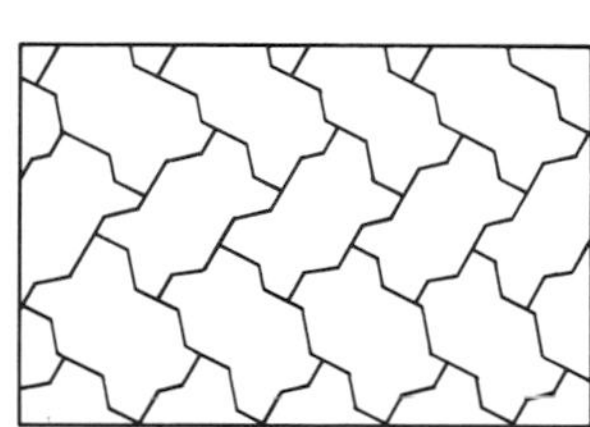
HERRINGBONE

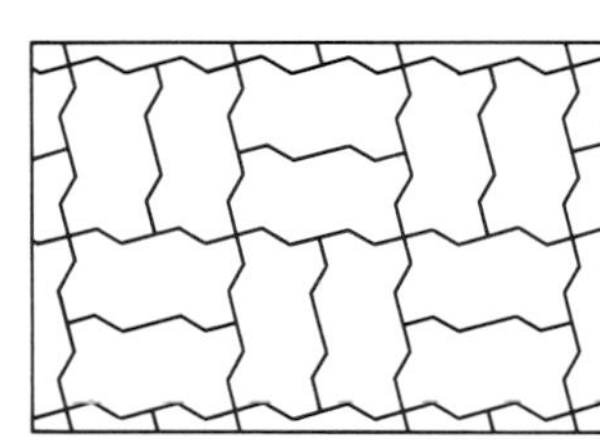
BASKET WEAVE

INTERLOCKING PAVERS

NOTES

1. Interlocking pavers are available in concrete, hydraulically pressed concrete, asphalt, and brick, and in different weight classifications, compressive strengths, surface textures, finishes, and colors. Consult local suppliers for availability.
2. Subject to manufacturer's recommendations and local code requirements, interlocking concrete pavers may be used in areas subject to heavy vehicle loads at 30 to 40 mph speeds.
3. Continuous curb or other edge restraint is required to anchor pavers in applications subject to vehicular traffic.
4. Concrete interlocking paver sizes are based on metric dimensions. Dimensions indicated are to nearest ⅛ in.
5. Where paver shape permits, herringbone pattern is recommended for paving subject to vehicular traffic.
6. Portions have been adapted, with permission, from ASTM C 939.

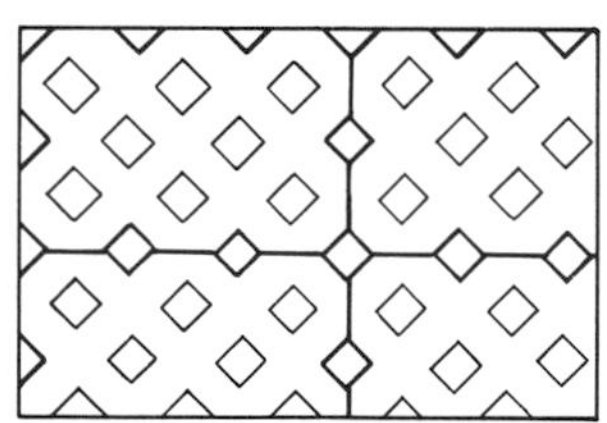
DIAGONAL SQUARES

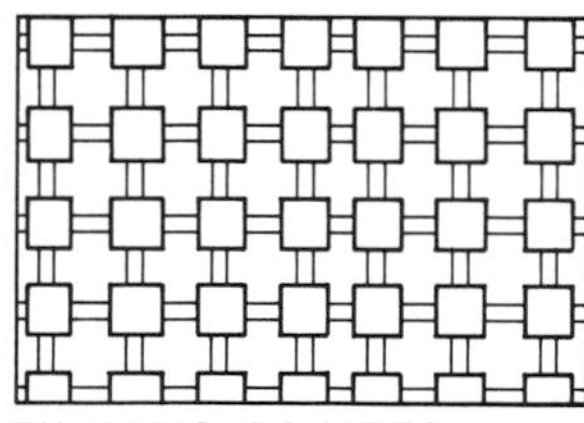
RUNNING SQUARES

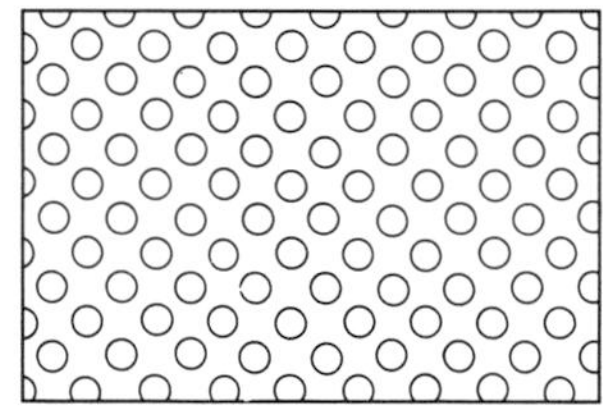
RINGS

GRASS PAVERS

NOTES

1. Appearance of grass pavers when voids are filled are shown by stipple to the right of the cut line. Voids may be filled with grass, a variety of ground cover, or gravel.
2. Grass pavers may be used to control erosion.
3. Herringbone pattern is recommended for concrete grass pavers subject to vehicular traffic.
4. Grass rings are available with close ring spacing for pedestrian use or wide ring spacing for vehicular use.

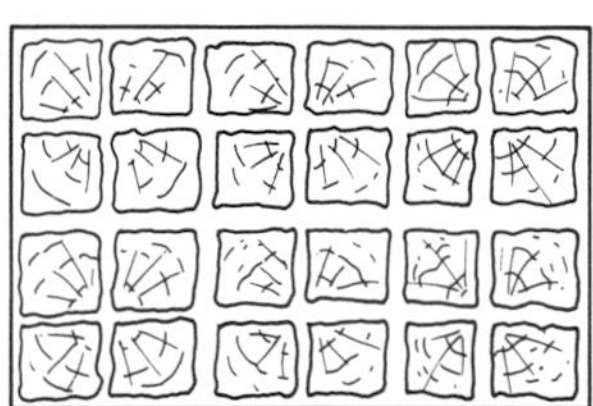
STACK BOND

RANDOM

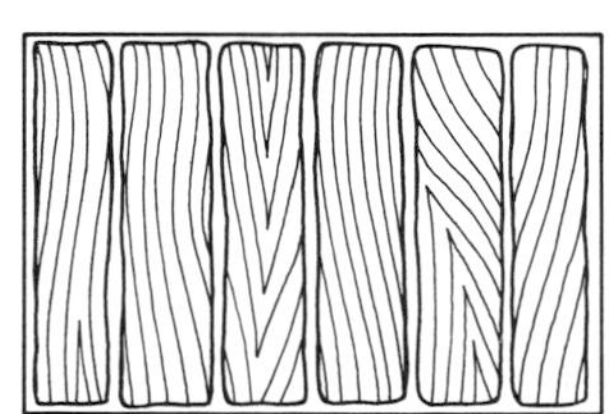
STACK BOND

BASKET WEAVE OR PARQUET

WOOD PAVERS

Jeffrey R. Vandevoort; Talbott Wilson Associates, Inc.; Houston, Texas

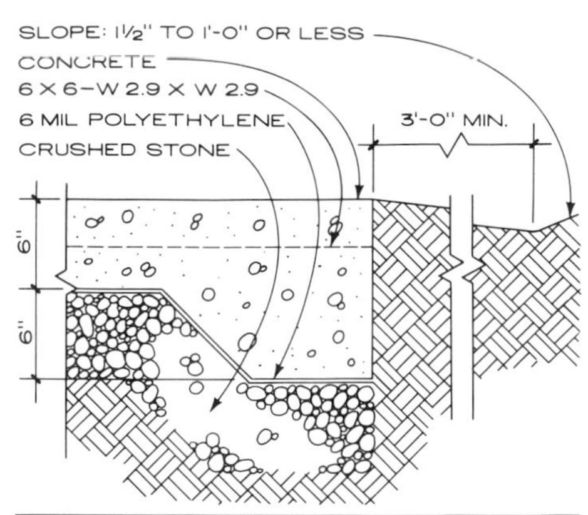
SLOPE: 1½" TO 1'-0" OR LESS
CONCRETE
6 X 6—W 2.9 X W 2.9
6 MIL POLYETHYLENE
CRUSHED STONE
3'-0" MIN.
6"
6"

CONCRETE PAVING WITHOUT CURB

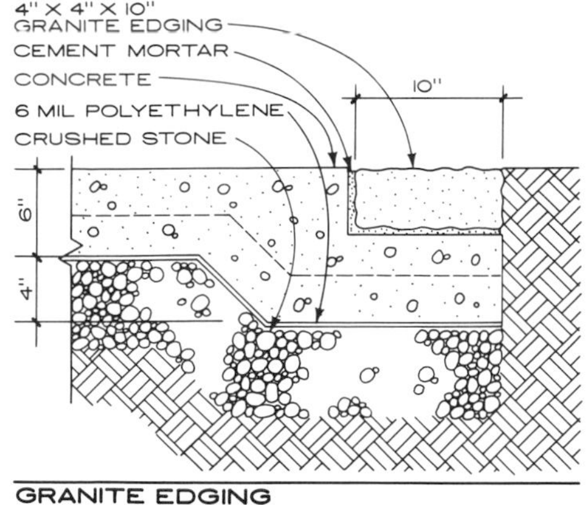
4" X 4" X 10"
GRANITE EDGING
CEMENT MORTAR
CONCRETE
6 MIL POLYETHYLENE
CRUSHED STONE
10"
6"
4"

GRANITE EDGING

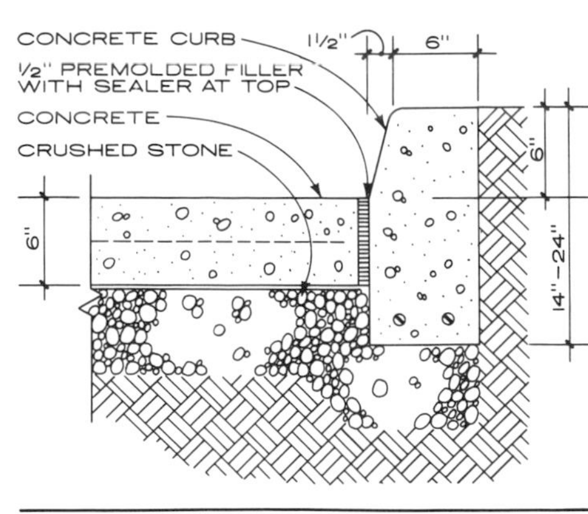
CONCRETE CURB
½" PREMOLDED FILLER
WITH SEALER AT TOP
CONCRETE
CRUSHED STONE
1½"
6"
6"
14"–24"
6"

SEPARATE CONCRETE CURB

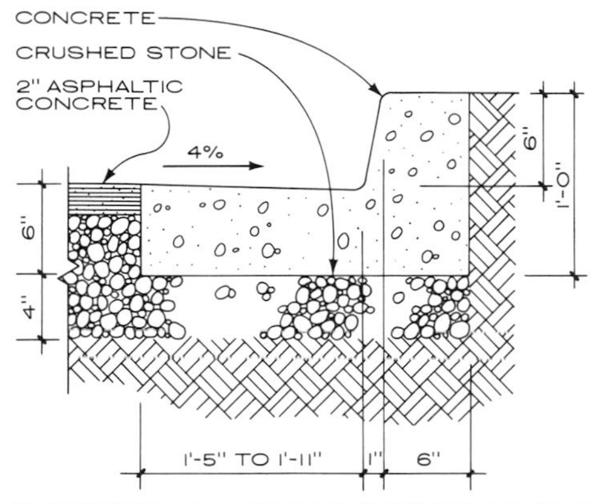
CONCRETE
CRUSHED STONE
2" ASPHALTIC
CONCRETE
4%
6"
1'-0"
6"
4"
1'-5" TO 1'-11"
1"
6"

CONCRETE CURB AND GUTTER

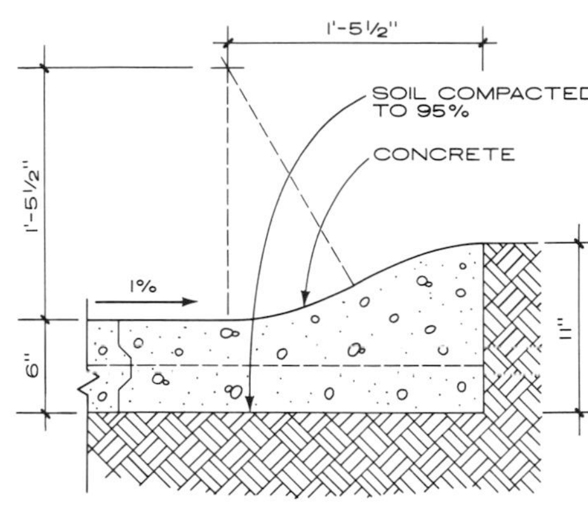
1'-5½"
SOIL COMPACTED
TO 95%
CONCRETE
1%
1'-5½"
6"
11"

MOUNTABLE CONCRETE CURB

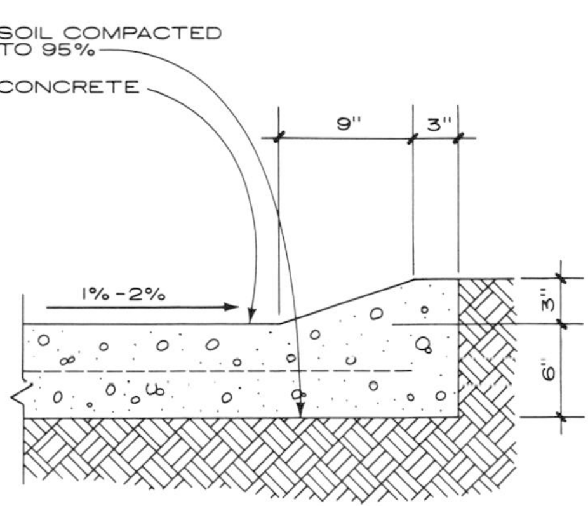
SOIL COMPACTED
TO 95%
CONCRETE
9"
3"
1%–2%
3"
6"

IOWA CONCRETE CURB

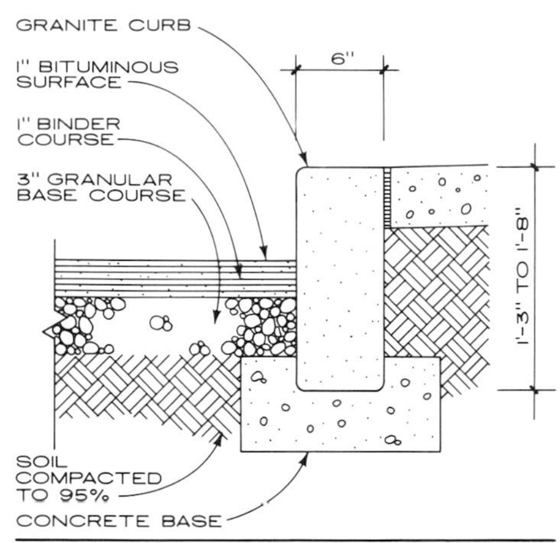
GRANITE CURB
1" BITUMINOUS
SURFACE
1" BINDER
COURSE
3" GRANULAR
BASE COURSE
6"
1'-3" TO 1'-8"
SOIL
COMPACTED
TO 95%
CONCRETE BASE

ASPHALT PAVING WITH STONE CURB

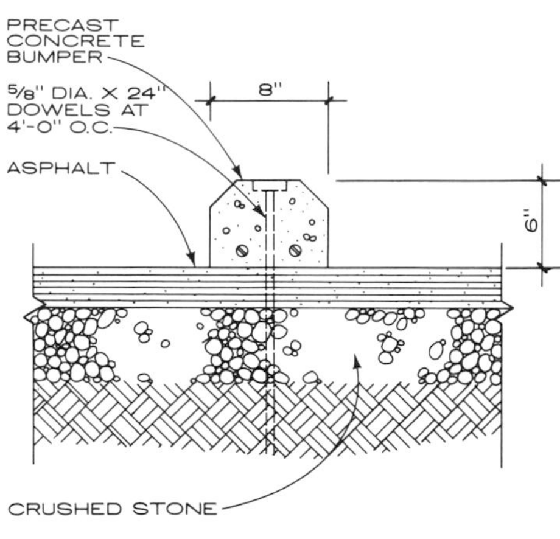
PRECAST
CONCRETE
BUMPER
5/8" DIA. X 24"
DOWELS AT
4'-0" O.C.
ASPHALT
8"
6"
CRUSHED STONE

ASPHALT PAVING WITH PRECAST CONCRETE BUMPER

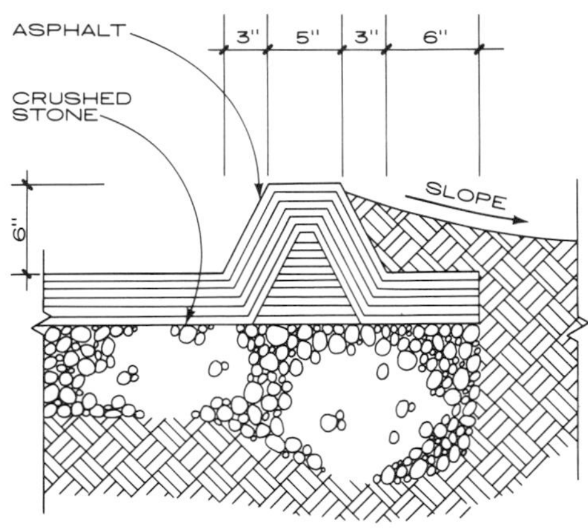
ASPHALT
CRUSHED
STONE
3"
5"
3"
6"
SLOPE
6"

NOT RECOMMENDED AS WHEEL STOP

ASPHALT CURB AND PAVING

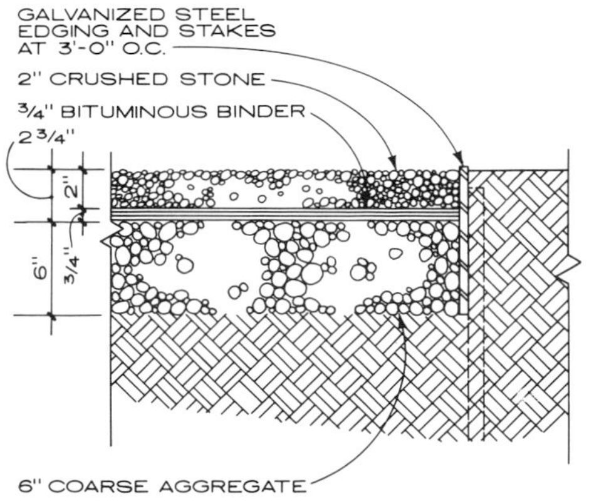
GALVANIZED STEEL
EDGING AND STAKES
AT 3'-0" O.C.
2" CRUSHED STONE
3/4" BITUMINOUS BINDER
2 3/4"
2"
3/4"
6"
6" COARSE AGGREGATE

CRUSHED STONE PAVING WITH METAL EDGE

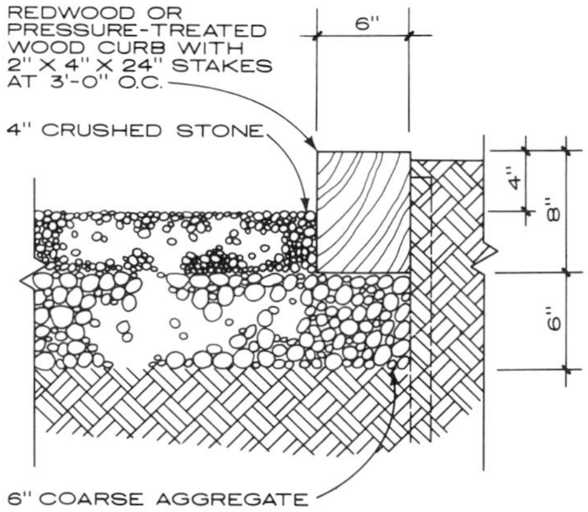

REDWOOD OR
PRESSURE-TREATED
WOOD CURB WITH
2" X 4" X 24" STAKES
AT 3'-0" O.C.
6"
4" CRUSHED STONE
4"
8"
6"
6" COARSE AGGREGATE

CRUSHED STONE PAVING WITH TIMBER CURB

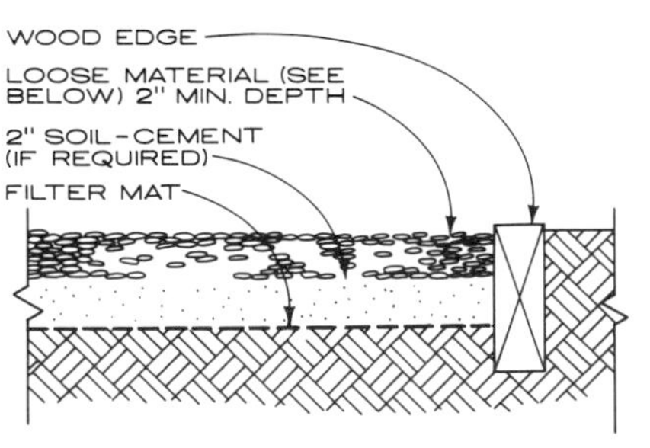
WOOD EDGE
LOOSE MATERIAL (SEE
BELOW) 2" MIN. DEPTH
2" SOIL-CEMENT
(IF REQUIRED)
FILTER MAT

LOOSE MATERIAL SIZES
WOOD CHIPS—1" NOMINAL
SHREDDED BARK MULCH
1/4" STONE CHIPS
3/4" PEA GRAVEL
1/2" DECOMPOSED GRANITE
3/4" CRUSHED STONE
1"-2" WASHED STONE

NOTE: ORGANIC MATERIALS WILL DECOMPOSE

LOOSE MATERIAL PAVING WITH WOOD EDGE

Francisco J. Menendez; Washington, D.C.
Richard J. Vitullo; Washington Grove, Maryland

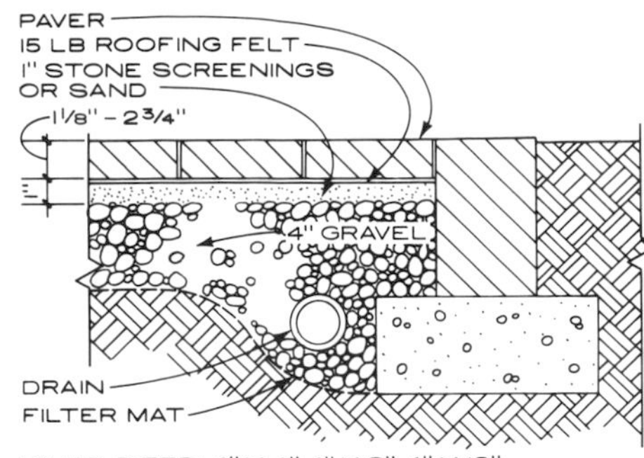
PAVER
15 LB ROOFING FELT
1" STONE SCREENINGS OR SAND
1 1/8" - 2 3/4"
4" GRAVEL
DRAIN
FILTER MAT

PAVER SIZES: 4" × 4", 4" × 8", 4" × 12", 6" × 6", 8" × 8", 12" × 12", 5 3/4", 8", AND 12" HEXAGON
PAVER THICKNESS: 1 1/8"-2 3/4"

BRICK, CLAY TILE, OR ASPHALT BLOCK PAVERS

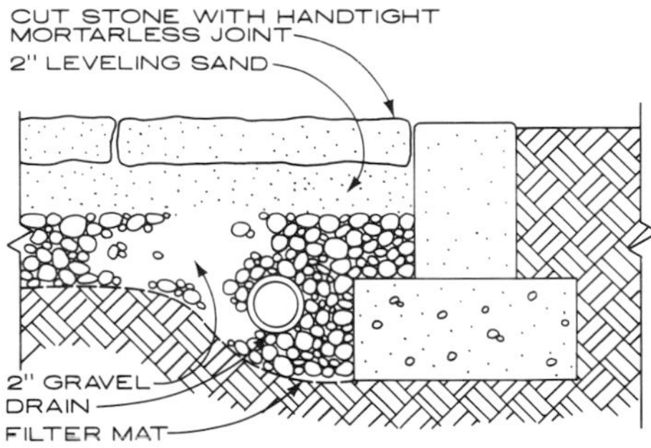
CONCRETE PAVER WITH HANDTIGHT MORTARLESS JOINT
2" SAND
FILTER MAT
2"-3" GRAVEL
DRAIN

PAVER SIZES: 12" × 12", 12" × 18", 18" × 18", 18" × 24", 24" × 36"
PAVER THICKNESS: 1 1/2"-2 1/2" PRECAST CONCRETE
TEXTURE: TROWEL FINISH, FLOAT FINISH, EXPOSED AGGREGATE FINISH

CONCRETE PAVERS AND LONDON WALKS

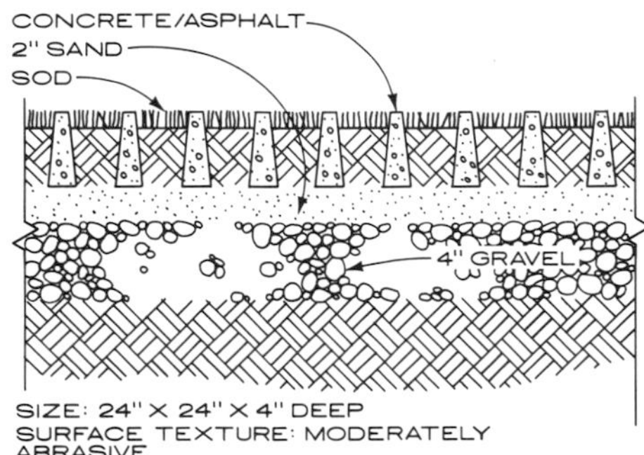
CUT STONE WITH HANDTIGHT MORTARLESS JOINT
2" LEVELING SAND
2" GRAVEL
DRAIN
FILTER MAT

STONE SIZES: 12" × 12", 12" × 18", 18" × 18", 18" × 24", 24" × 36", OR RANDOM SHAPES
STONE THICKNESS: 1"-2" CUT STONE
TEXTURE: HONED, NATURAL CLEFT, OR FLAME TREATED FOR NONSLIP FINISH

CUT STONE PAVERS

CONCRETE/ASPHALT
2" SAND
SOD
4" GRAVEL

SIZE: 24" × 24" × 4" DEEP
SURFACE TEXTURE: MODERATELY ABRASIVE
COLOR: STANDARD GRAY OR TAN
INSTALLED WITHOUT SLAB, MORTAR, OR GROUT. A PREFORMED LATTICE UNIT USED FOR STORM RUNOFF CONTROL, PATHWAYS, PARKING AREAS, AND SOIL CONSERVATION

GRID PAVING BLOCKS

UNIT PAVERS ON FLEXIBLE BASE

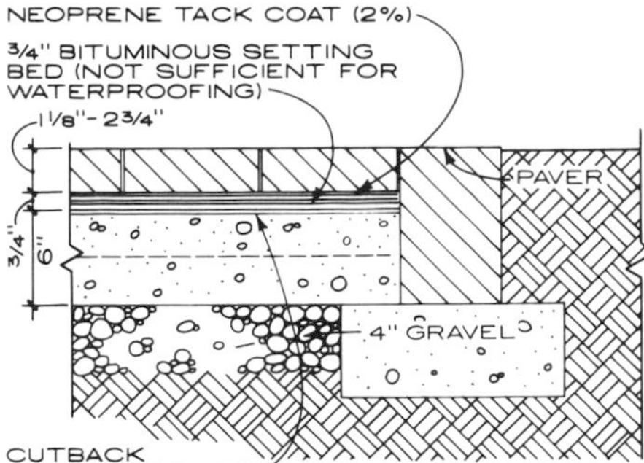
NEOPRENE TACK COAT (2%)
3/4" BITUMINOUS SETTING BED (NOT SUFFICIENT FOR WATERPROOFING)
1 1/8"-2 3/4"
PAVER
3/4"
6"
4" GRAVEL
CUTBACK ASPHALT PRIMER

WHERE WEATHER PERMITS, LATEX-MODIFIED MORTAR MAY BE USED FOR JOINTS AND SETTING BED

BRICK, CLAY TILE, OR ASPHALT BLOCK PAVERS

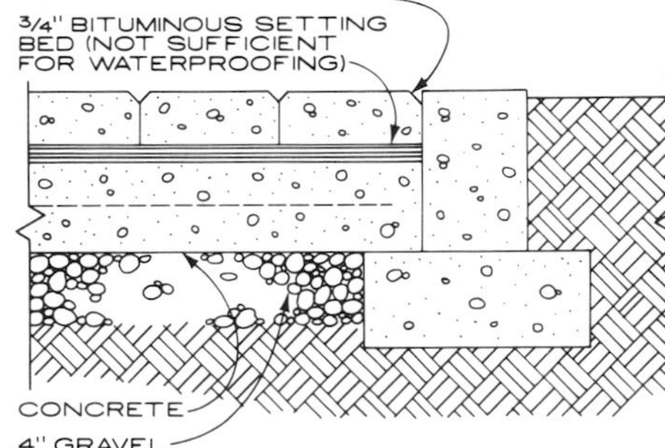
CONCRETE PAVER WITH HANDTIGHT MORTARLESS JOINT
3/4" BITUMINOUS SETTING BED (NOT SUFFICIENT FOR WATERPROOFING)
CONCRETE
4" GRAVEL

WHERE WEATHER PERMITS, LATEX-MODIFIED MORTAR MAY BE USED FOR JOINTS AND SETTING BED

CONCRETE PAVERS AND LONDON WALKS

CUT STONE PAVER WITH HANDTIGHT MORTARLESS JOINT
3/4" BITUMINOUS SETTING BED (NOT SUFFICIENT FOR WATERPROOFING)
4" GRAVEL
CONCRETE

SIZES: CAN BE SMALLER THAN FOR FLEXIBLE BASE WHERE WEATHER PERMITS LATEX-MODIFIED MORTAR. MAY BE USED FOR JOINT AND SETTING BEDS. JOINTS MAY BE STAGGERED OR RANDOM
STONE THICKNESS: 1/2" SLATE OR 1"-2" CUT STONE

CUT STONE PAVERS

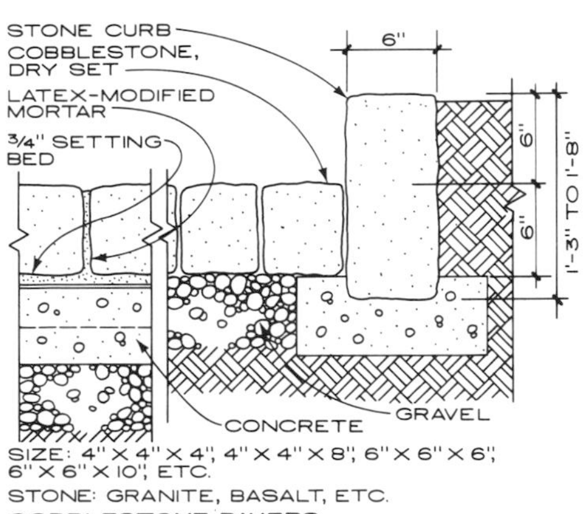
STONE CURB
COBBLESTONE, DRY SET
LATEX-MODIFIED MORTAR
3/4" SETTING BED
6"
6"
6"
1'-3" TO 1'-8"
CONCRETE
GRAVEL

SIZE: 4" × 4" × 4", 4" × 4" × 8", 6" × 6" × 6", 6" × 6" × 10", ETC.
STONE: GRANITE, BASALT, ETC.

COBBLESTONE PAVERS

UNIT PAVERS ON RIGID BASE

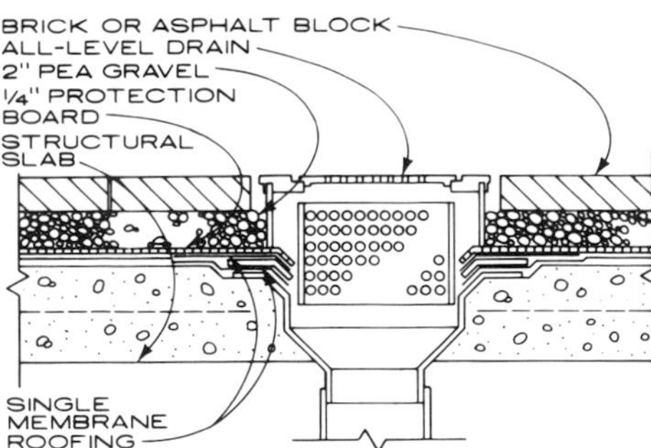
BRICK OR ASPHALT BLOCK
ALL-LEVEL DRAIN
2" PEA GRAVEL
1/4" PROTECTION BOARD
STRUCTURAL SLAB
SINGLE MEMBRANE ROOFING

FOR HEATED SPACES UNDER STRUCTURAL SLAB, USE CLOSED CELL INSULATION UNDER PAVERS

BRICK, CLAY TILE, ASPHALT BLOCK, CONCRETE, OR STONE PAVERS OVER UNINSULATED BASE

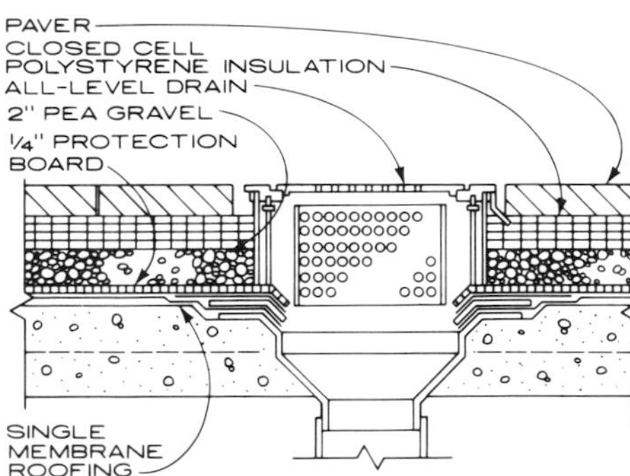
PAVER
CLOSED CELL POLYSTYRENE INSULATION
ALL-LEVEL DRAIN
2" PEA GRAVEL
1/4" PROTECTION BOARD
SINGLE MEMBRANE ROOFING

THIS SYSTEM SUITABLE FOR PEDESTRIAN TRAFFIC ONLY

BRICK, CLAY TILE, ASPHALT BLOCK, CONCRETE, OR STONE PAVERS OVER INSULATED BASE

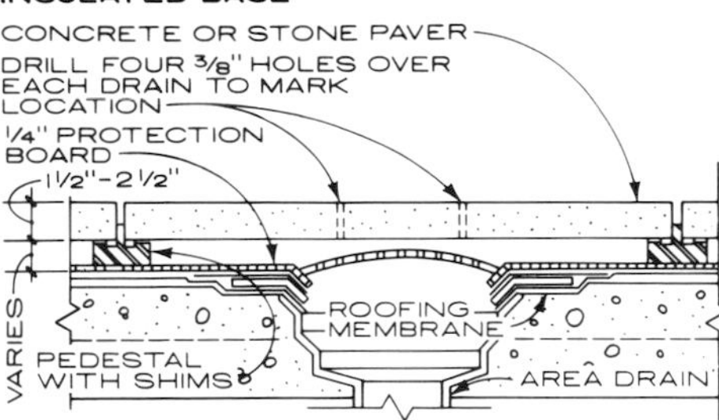
CONCRETE OR STONE PAVER
DRILL FOUR 3/8" HOLES OVER EACH DRAIN TO MARK LOCATION
1/4" PROTECTION BOARD
1 1/2"-2 1/2"
ROOFING MEMBRANE
VARIES
PEDESTAL WITH SHIMS
AREA DRAIN

FINISH SURFACE: LEVEL, JOINTS ACTING AS DRAINS
DRAINAGE SURFACE: SLOPE TO DRAIN 1/8"-1/4" PER FT
HEIGHT OF PEDESTALS: 1/2"-1 1/2"
PEDESTAL MATERIAL: NEOPRENE, METAL, VINYL, MORTAR
SHIMS: MULTIPLE OF 1/8"

CONCRETE OR CUT STONE PAVER ON PEDESTALS OVER UNINSULATED BASE

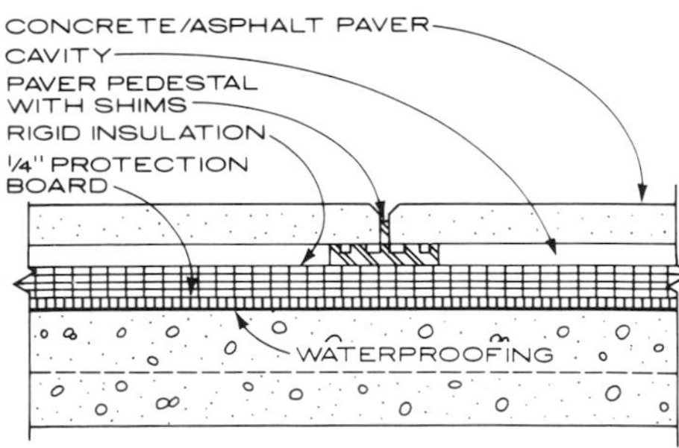
CONCRETE/ASPHALT PAVER
CAVITY
PAVER PEDESTAL WITH SHIMS
RIGID INSULATION
1/4" PROTECTION BOARD
WATERPROOFING

THIS SYSTEM IS SUITABLE FOR PEDESTRIAN TRAFFIC ONLY. RIGID INSULATION SHALL BE SUITABLE TO CARRY PEDESTRIAN LOADS
PEDESTAL MATERIAL: NEOPRENE, METAL, VINYL, MORTAR
SHIMS: SAME AS PEDESTAL MATERIAL

CONCRETE OR STONE PAVERS ON PEDESTALS OVER INSULATED BASE

UNIT PAVERS ON SUSPENDED BASE

GENERAL NOTES

1. Drainpipes may be omitted at well-drained areas.
2. Provide positive outflow for drainpipes.
3. Do not use unsatisfactory soil (expanding organic).
4. Satisfactory soil shall be compacted to 95%.
5. Flexible and suspended bases shown are for light duty only.
6. Edging width: 2, 4, 8, 12 in.; depth: 8, 12, 16, 24 in.
7. Footing of edging width: 8, 12, 16, 20 in.; depth: 6, 8 in.
8. If freezing, depth is deeper than bottom of footing; provide gravel at footing.

Charles A. Szoradi; Washington, D.C.
Richard J. Vitullo; Washington Grove, Maryland

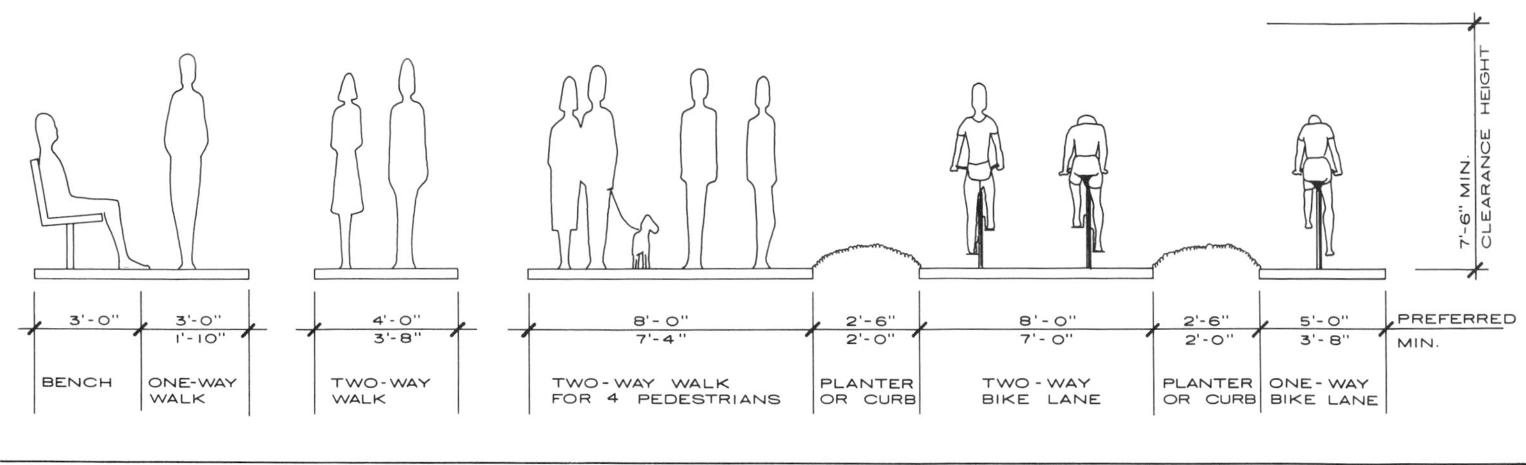

7'-6" MIN. CLEARANCE HEIGHT
3'-0"
3'-0" 1'-10"
4'-0" 3'-8"
8'-0" 7'-4"
2'-6" 2'-0"
8'-0" 7'-0"
2'-6" 2'-0"
5'-0" 3'-8"
PREFERRED
MIN.
BENCH
ONE-WAY WALK
TWO-WAY WALK
TWO-WAY WALK FOR 4 PEDESTRIANS
PLANTER OR CURB
TWO-WAY BIKE LANE
PLANTER OR CURB
ONE-WAY BIKE LANE

WALK AND BIKE LANE WIDTHS

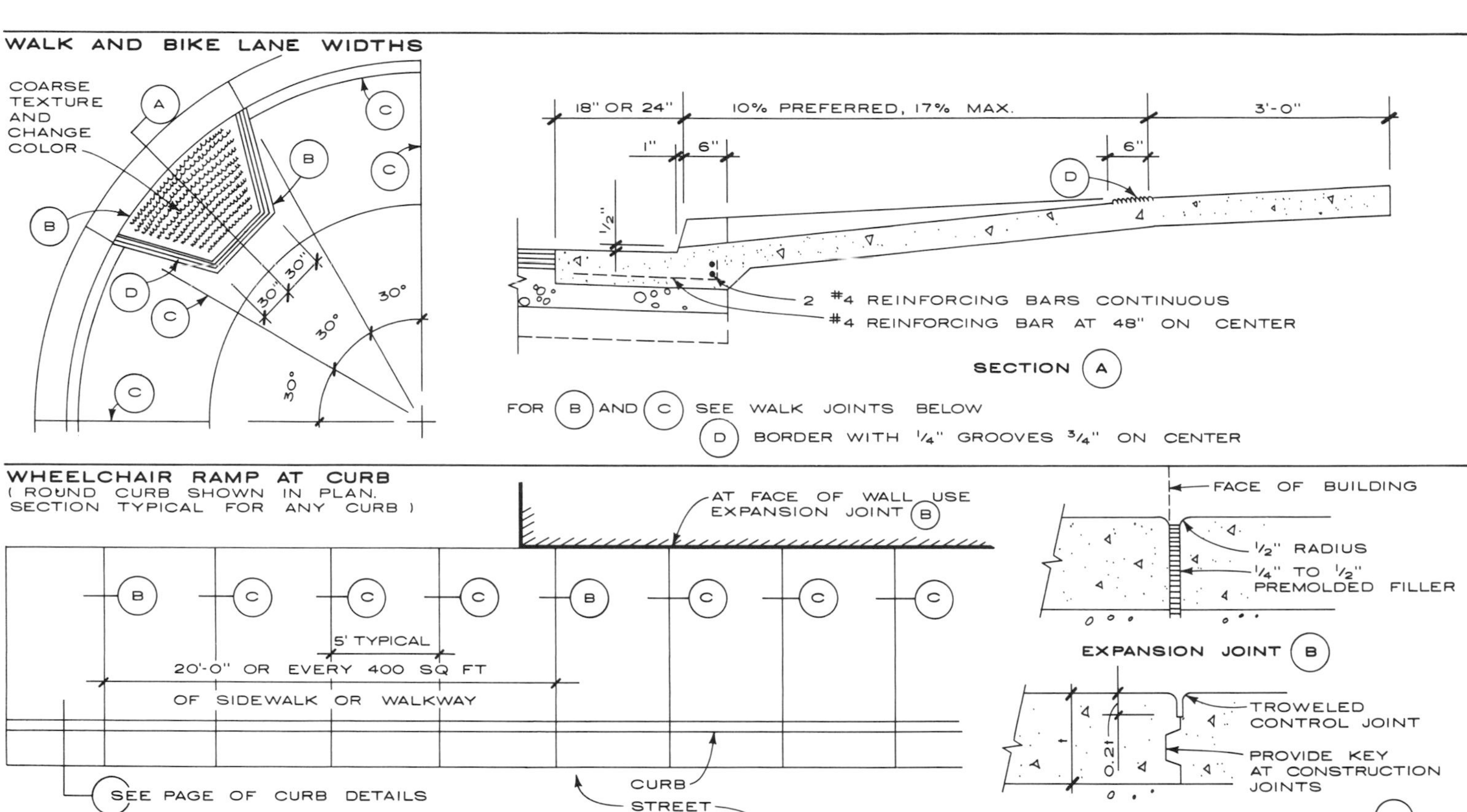

COARSE TEXTURE AND CHANGE COLOR
30°
18" OR 24"
10% PREFERRED, 17% MAX.
3'-0"
1"
6"
6"
1/2"
2 #4 REINFORCING BARS CONTINUOUS
#4 REINFORCING BAR AT 48" ON CENTER
SECTION (A)
FOR (B) AND (C) SEE WALK JOINTS BELOW
(D) BORDER WITH 1/4" GROOVES 3/4" ON CENTER
AT FACE OF WALL USE EXPANSION JOINT (B)
5' TYPICAL
20'-0" OR EVERY 400 SQ FT OF SIDEWALK OR WALKWAY
SEE PAGE OF CURB DETAILS
CURB
STREET
FACE OF BUILDING
1/2" RADIUS
1/4" TO 1/2" PREMOLDED FILLER
EXPANSION JOINT (B)
TROWELED CONTROL JOINT
PROVIDE KEY AT CONSTRUCTION JOINTS
0.2t
CONSTRUCTION CONTROL JOINT (C)

WHEELCHAIR RAMP AT CURB
(ROUND CURB SHOWN IN PLAN. SECTION TYPICAL FOR ANY CURB)

WALK AND CURB JOINTS

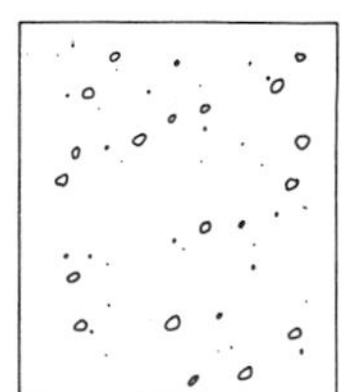

ROCK SALT

Spread on troweled surface and press in. Wash salt away after concrete hardens. Protect planting.

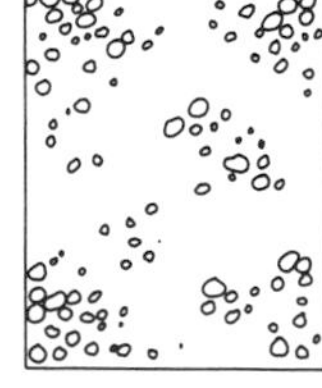

EXPOSED AGGREGATE

Seed aggregate uniformly onto surface. Embed by tamping. After setup, brush lightly and clean with spray. If using aggregate mix, trowel and expose by washing fines or use a retarder.

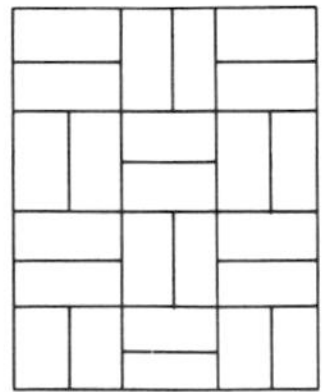

PRESSED OR STAMPED

Stock patterns are available. Use integral or dry shake colors. Joints may be filled with mortar.

BROOM SURFACE

Use stiff bristle for coarse texture. Use soft bristle on steel troweled surface for fine texture.

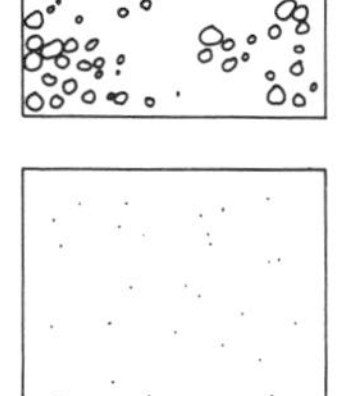

TROWELED

Use wood float for coarse texture. Use steel float for fine texture.

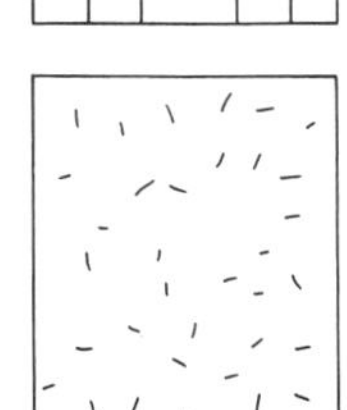

NONSLIP

Apply silicon carbide (sparkling) or aluminum oxide at 1/4 to 1/2 psf; trowel lightly.

WALK SURFACES AND TEXTURES

William T. Mahan, AIA; Santa Barbara, California

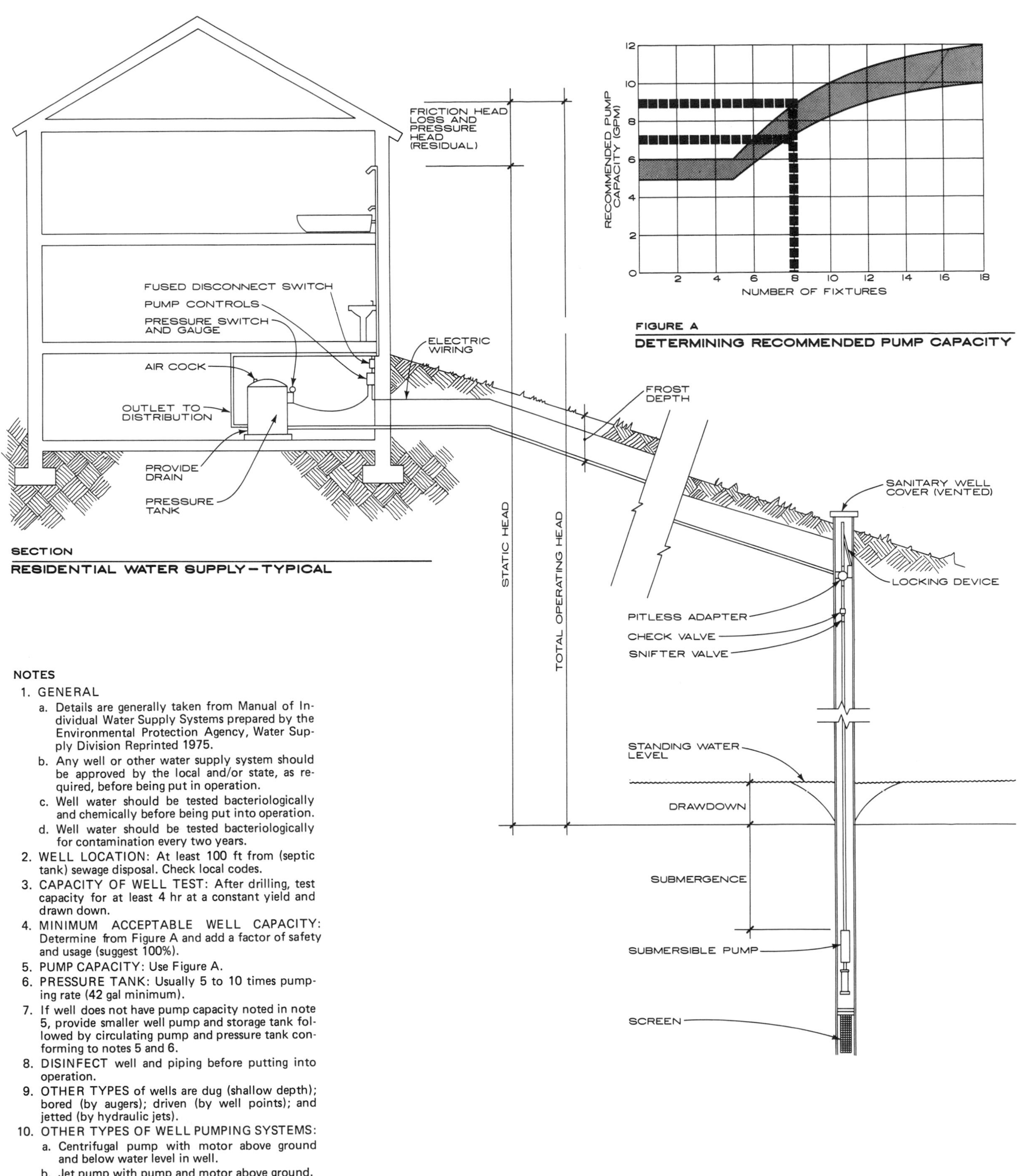

FRICTION HEAD LOSS AND PRESSURE HEAD (RESIDUAL)
FUSED DISCONNECT SWITCH
PUMP CONTROLS
PRESSURE SWITCH AND GAUGE
AIR COCK
OUTLET TO DISTRIBUTION
PROVIDE DRAIN
PRESSURE TANK
ELECTRIC WIRING
STATIC HEAD
TOTAL OPERATING HEAD
RECOMMENDED PUMP CAPACITY (GPM)
NUMBER OF FIXTURES
0
2
4
6
8
10
12
14
16
18
FROST DEPTH
SANITARY WELL COVER (VENTED)
LOCKING DEVICE
PITLESS ADAPTER
CHECK VALVE
SNIFTER VALVE
STANDING WATER LEVEL
DRAWDOWN
SUBMERGENCE
SUBMERSIBLE PUMP
SCREEN

SECTION

RESIDENTIAL WATER SUPPLY—TYPICAL

FIGURE A

DETERMINING RECOMMENDED PUMP CAPACITY

NOTES

1. GENERAL
   a. Details are generally taken from Manual of Individual Water Supply Systems prepared by the Environmental Protection Agency, Water Supply Division Reprinted 1975.
   b. Any well or other water supply system should be approved by the local and/or state, as required, before being put in operation.
   c. Well water should be tested bacteriologically and chemically before being put into operation.
   d. Well water should be tested bacteriologically for contamination every two years.
2. WELL LOCATION: At least 100 ft from (septic tank) sewage disposal. Check local codes.
3. CAPACITY OF WELL TEST: After drilling, test capacity for at least 4 hr at a constant yield and drawn down.
4. MINIMUM ACCEPTABLE WELL CAPACITY: Determine from Figure A and add a factor of safety and usage (suggest 100%).
5. PUMP CAPACITY: Use Figure A.
6. PRESSURE TANK: Usually 5 to 10 times pumping rate (42 gal minimum).
7. If well does not have pump capacity noted in note 5, provide smaller well pump and storage tank followed by circulating pump and pressure tank conforming to notes 5 and 6.
8. DISINFECT well and piping before putting into operation.
9. OTHER TYPES of wells are dug (shallow depth); bored (by augers); driven (by well points); and jetted (by hydraulic jets).
10. OTHER TYPES OF WELL PUMPING SYSTEMS:
    a. Centrifugal pump with motor above ground and below water level in well.
    b. Jet pump with pump and motor above ground.
    c. Direct or reciprocating pumps in the well with motor above ground.

FIGURE B

DRILLED WELL—SECTION

Jack L. Staunton, P.E.; Staunton and Freeman, Consulting Engineers; New York, New York

GENERAL NOTES

Seepage and runoff each require special engineering designs to protect against potential water damage. Drainage systems intercept and dispose of the water flow to prevent inordinate damage to an area or facility from seepage and direct runoff.

Subsurface drainage systems are designed to lower the natural water table, to intercept underground flow, and to dispose of infiltration percolating down through soils from surface sources. These systems typically are used under floors, around foundations, in planters, and under athletic fields and courts. Each system must be provided with a positive outfall either by pumped discharge or gravity drain above expected high water levels.

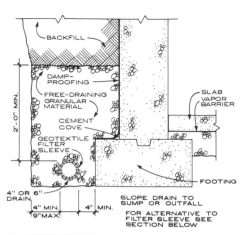

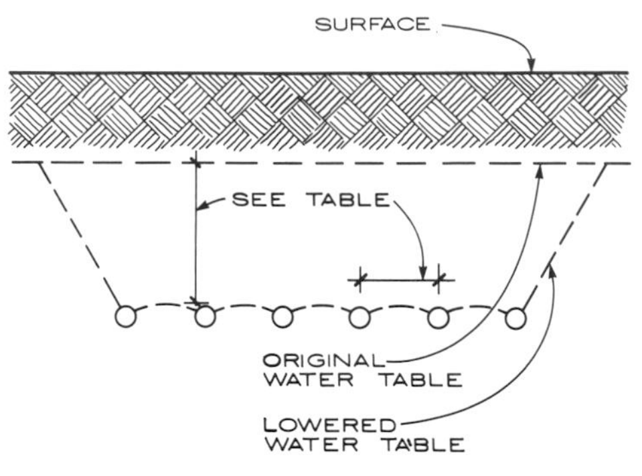
SURFACE
SEE TABLE
ORIGINAL WATER TABLE
LOWERED WATER TABLE

SECTION

Drain layout varies to meet need. May be grid, parallel, herringbone, or random pattern to fit topography.

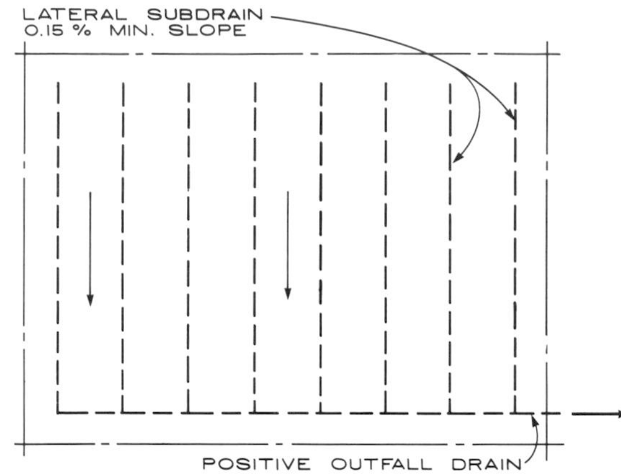
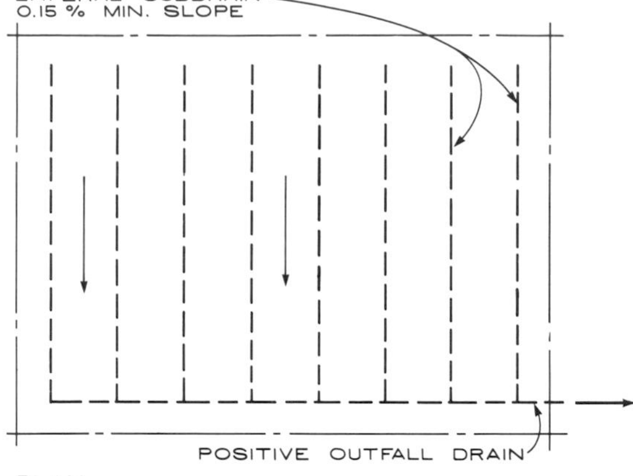
LATERAL SUBDRAIN 0.15 % MIN. SLOPE
POSITIVE OUTFALL DRAIN

PLAN

Depths indicated in table below are minimum range. Greater depths may be required to prevent frost heave in colder climates or where soils have a high capillarity.

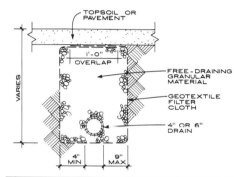

SLOPE DRAIN TO SUMP OR OUTFALL

FOR ALTERNATIVE TO FILTER SLEEVE SEE SECTION BELOW

FOOTING DRAIN

TYPICAL SECTION

If perforated drain is used, it should be installed with the holes facing down.

When used to intercept sidehill seepage, the bottom of the trench should be cut into underlying impervious material a minimum of 6 in.

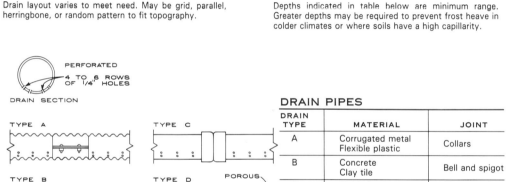

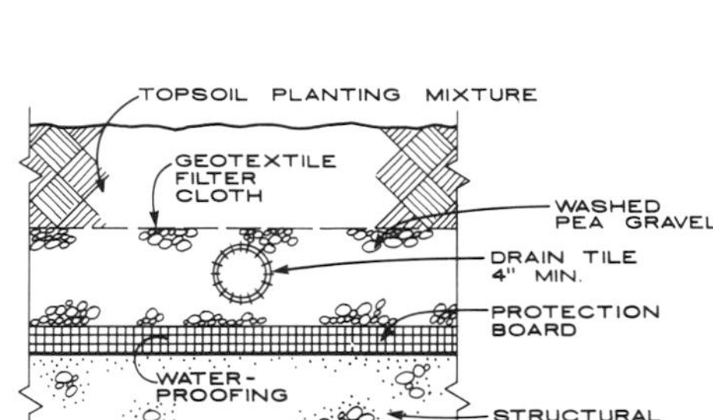
TOPSOIL PLANTING MIXTURE
GEOTEXTILE FILTER CLOTH
WASHED PEA GRAVEL
DRAIN TILE 4" MIN.
PROTECTION BOARD
WATER-PROOFING
STRUCTURAL SLAB

PLANTER DRAIN

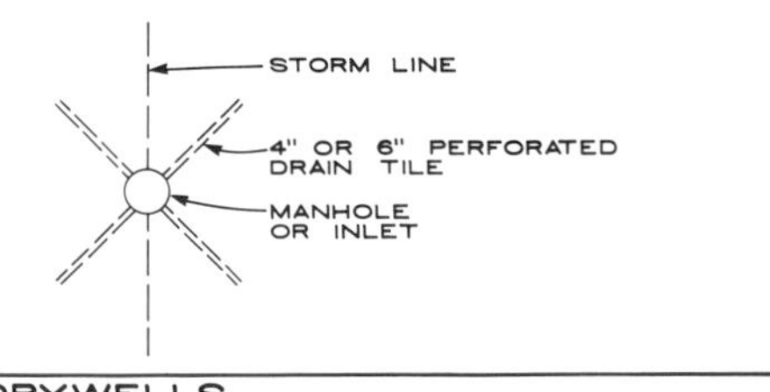
STORM LINE
4" OR 6" PERFORATED DRAIN TILE
MANHOLE OR INLET

DRYWELLS

Drywells provide an underground disposal system for surface runoff. Their effectiveness is in direct proportion to the porosity of surrounding soils, and they are efficient only for draining small areas. High rainfall runoff rates cannot be absorbed at the considerably lower percolation rates of most soils; the difference is stored temporarily in the drywell. Efficiency is reduced during extended periods of wet weather when receiving soils are saturated and the well is refilled prior to draining completely.

PERFORATED 4 TO 6 ROWS OF 1/4" HOLES

DRAIN SECTION

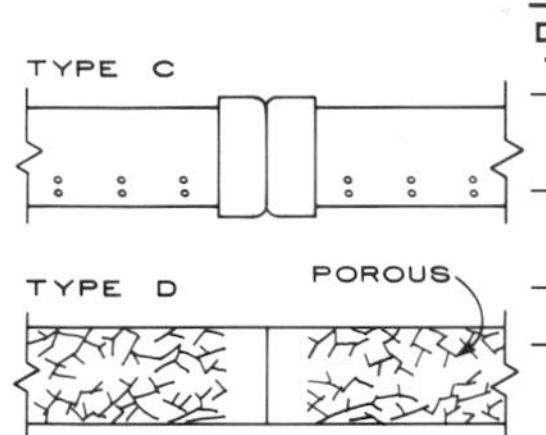
TYPE C
TYPE D
POROUS

DRAIN PIPES

DRAIN TYPE	MATERIAL	JOINT
A	Corrugated metal Flexible plastic	Collars
B	Concrete Clay tile	Bell and spigot
C	Rigid plastic	Sleeve socket
D	Porous concrete	Tongue and groove

SUBSURFACE DRAIN PIPES IN GENERAL USE

DEPTH AND SPACING OF SUBDRAINS RECOMMENDED FOR VARIOUS SOIL CLASSES

SOIL CLASSES	PERCENTAGE OF SOIL SEPARATES: SAND	SILT	CLAY	DEPTH OF BOTTOM OF DRAIN (FT.)	DISTANCE BETWEEN SUBDRAINS (FT.)
Sand	80-100	0-20	0-20	3-4 2-3	150-300 100-150
Sandy loam	50-80	0-50	0-20	3-4 2-3	100-150 85-100
Loam	30-50	30-50	0-20	3-4 2-3	85-100 75-85
Silt loam	0-50	50-100	0-20	3-4 2-3	75-85 65-75
Sandy clay loam	50-80	0-30	20-30	3-4 2-3	65-75 55-65
Clay loam	20-50	20-50	20-30	3-4 2-3	55-65 45-55
Silty clay loam	0-30	50-80	20-30	3-4 2-3	45-55 40-45
Sandy clay	50-70	0-20	30-50	3-4 2-3	40-45 35-40
Silty clay	0-20	50-70	30-50	3-4 2-3	35-40 30-35
Clay	0-50	0-50	30-100	3-4 2-3	30-35 25-30

Harold C. Munger, FAIA; Munger Munger + Associates Architects, Inc.; Toledo, Ohio
Kurt N. Pronske, P.E.; Reston, Virginia

SURFACE DRAINAGE SYSTEMS: Designed to collect and dispose of rainfall runoff. There are two basic types. One, a ditch/swale and culvert, or open system, is generally used in less densely populated and more open areas where natural surfaces predominate. In urbanized areas where much of the land is overbuilt, the second type is used—the pipe, inlet/catchbasin and manhole, or closed system. Combinations of the two are quite common where terrain and density dictate.

GENERAL NOTES

1. Lay out grades to allow safe flow away from building if drains becomes blocked.
2. It is generally more economical to keep water on surface as long as possible.
3. Consider the possibility of ice forming on surface when determining slopes for vehicles and pedestrians.
4. Determine which design criteria are set by code or governmental agency, such as intensity and duration of rain storm and allowable runoff.
5. Formulas given are for approx. only. A qualified engineer should be consulted to design the system.

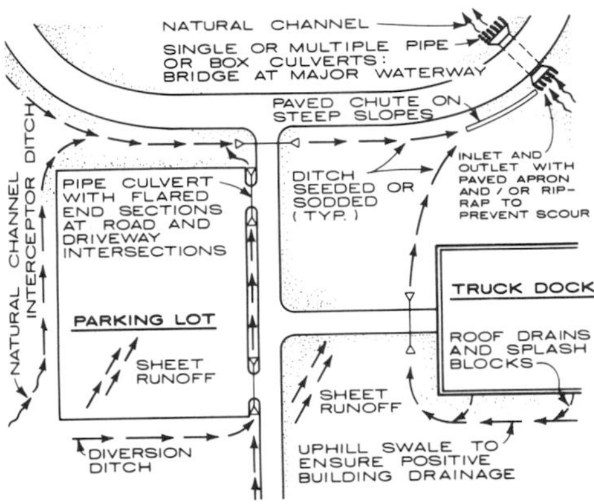
NATURAL CHANNEL
SINGLE OR MULTIPLE PIPE OR BOX CULVERTS: BRIDGE AT MAJOR WATERWAY
PAVED CHUTE ON STEEP SLOPES
NATURAL CHANNEL INTERCEPTOR DITCH
PIPE CULVERT WITH FLARED END SECTIONS AT ROAD AND DRIVEWAY INTERSECTIONS
DITCH SEEDED OR SODDED (TYP.)
INLET AND OUTLET WITH PAVED APRON AND / OR RIP-RAP TO PREVENT SCOUR
TRUCK DOCK
PARKING LOT
SHEET RUNOFF
ROOF DRAINS AND SPLASH BLOCKS
SHEET RUNOFF
DIVERSION DITCH
UPHILL SWALE TO ENSURE POSITIVE BUILDING DRAINAGE

OPEN SYSTEM

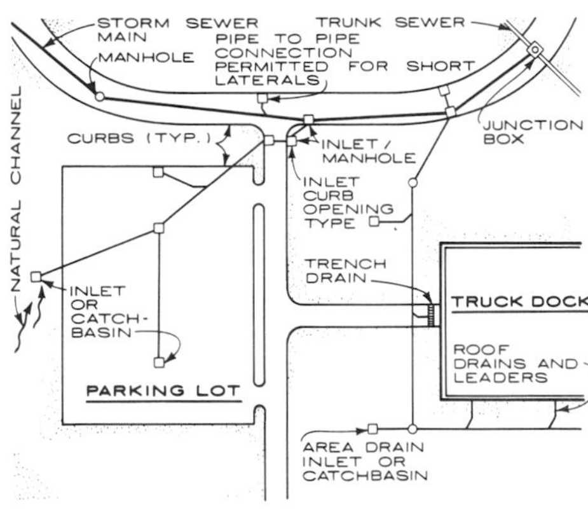
STORM SEWER MAIN
TRUNK SEWER PIPE TO PIPE CONNECTION PERMITTED FOR SHORT LATERALS
MANHOLE
NATURAL CHANNEL
CURBS (TYP.)
INLET / MANHOLE
JUNCTION BOX
INLET CURB OPENING TYPE
INLET OR CATCH-BASIN
TRENCH DRAIN
TRUCK DOCK
PARKING LOT
ROOF DRAINS AND LEADERS
AREA DRAIN INLET OR CATCHBASIN

CLOSED SYSTEM

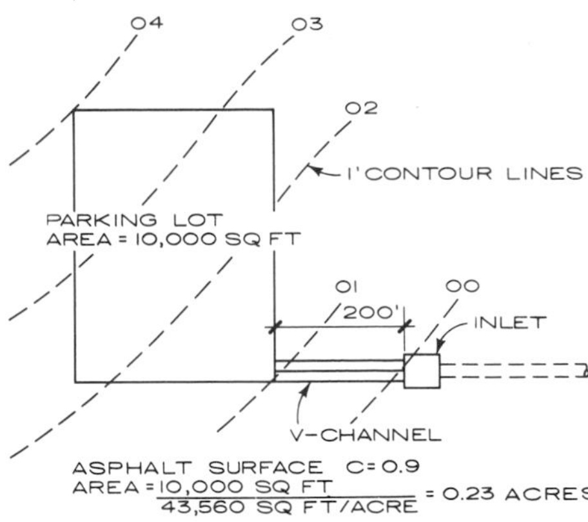
04
03
02
1' CONTOUR LINES
PARKING LOT
AREA = 10,000 SQ FT
01
00
200'
INLET
V-CHANNEL
ASPHALT SURFACE C = 0.9
AREA = 10,000 SQ FT / 43,560 SQ FT/ACRE = 0.23 ACRES

SITE PLAN—EXAMPLE

RATIONAL FORMULA

$Q = CIA$

Q = Flow (cu ft/sec)

C = From table (Approximate Values for C)

I = Intensity (in./hr)
Obtain from local code requirements

A = Area of site (acres)

EXAMPLE: Assume local code requires I = 5 in./hr

$Q = CIA$

$Q = 0.9(5)0.23$

$= 1.04$ cu ft/sec

= Approximate volume of water entering the V-channel per second from the parking lot

Note: Simplified method of calculation for areas of less than 100 acres.

APPROXIMATE METHOD FOR CALCULATING RUNOFF

APPROXIMATE VALUES FOR C

Roofs	0.95–1.00
Pavement	0.90–1.00
Roads	0.30–0.90
Bare soil	
Sand	0.20–0.40
Clay	0.30–0.75
Grass	0.15–0.60
Developed land	
Commercial	0.60–0.75
High-density residential	0.50–0.65
Low-density residential	0.30–0.55

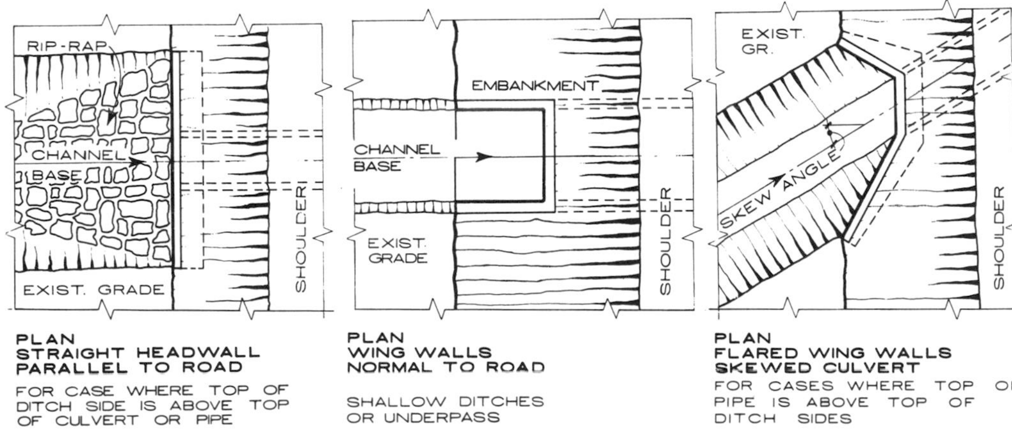
RIP-RAP
CHANNEL
BASE
EXIST. GRADE
SHOULDER
EMBANKMENT
CHANNEL BASE
EXIST. GRADE
SHOULDER
EXIST. GR.
SKEW ANGLE
SHOULDER

PLAN
STRAIGHT HEADWALL PARALLEL TO ROAD
FOR CASE WHERE TOP OF DITCH SIDE IS ABOVE TOP OF CULVERT OR PIPE

PLAN
WING WALLS NORMAL TO ROAD
SHALLOW DITCHES OR UNDERPASS

PLAN
FLARED WING WALLS SKEWED CULVERT
FOR CASES WHERE TOP OF PIPE IS ABOVE TOP OF DITCH SIDES

HEADWALL DESIGN AS CONTROLLED BY TOPOGRAPHY

n VALUES FOR MANNING FORMULA

CHANNEL SURFACE	n
Cast iron	0.012
Corrugated steel	0.032
Clay tile	0.014
Cement grout	0.013
Concrete	0.015
Earth ditch	0.023
Cut rock channel	0.033
Winding channel	0.025

NOTES

1. Determine velocity with Manning formula.
2. Check flow with formula $Q = Va$
   a = Cross-sectional area of water in sq ft.
3. For a given Q, adjust channel shape, size, and/or slope to obtain desired velocity (noneroding for earth and grass ditches, etc.)

MANNING FORMULA

$$V = \left(\frac{1.486}{n}\right) r^{0.67} S^{0.5}$$

= Velocity (ft/sec)

n = From table (n Values for Manning Formula)

r = Hydraulic radius
See Channel Properties for derivation of r

$$S = \text{Slope}\left(\frac{\text{drop in ft}}{\text{length in ft}}\right)$$

EXAMPLE: Assume concrete V-channel

W = 2 ft

h = 0.5 ft

S = 0.005 (see site plan—example)

r = 0.37 (calculated using V-channel properties)

$$V = \left(\frac{1.486}{0.015}\right)(0.37)^{0.67}(0.005)^{0.5}$$

= 2.6 ft/sec (see runoff velocity table)

CHECK FLOW

Q = Va (a from Channel Properties)

= 2.6 (0.5) = 1.3 cu ft/sec

1.04 cu ft/sec required from example above using the Rational Formula; therefore, flow is OK.

APPROXIMATE METHOD FOR SIZING CHANNELS

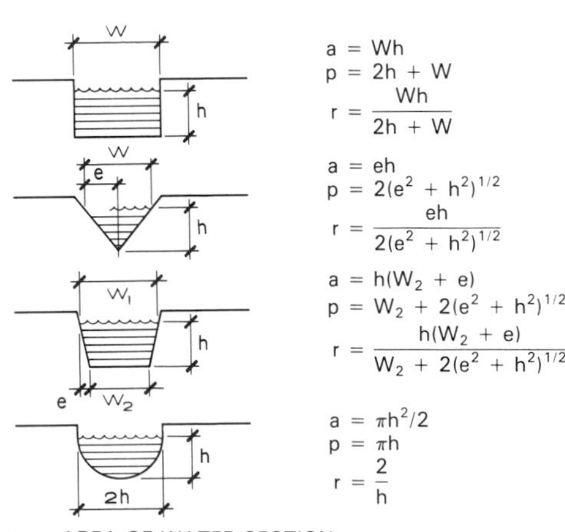
W
h
W
e
h
W_1
h
e
W_2
h
2h

$a = Wh$
$p = 2h + W$
$$r = \frac{Wh}{2h + W}$$

$a = eh$
$p = 2(e^2 + h^2)^{1/2}$
$$r = \frac{eh}{2(e^2 + h^2)^{1/2}}$$

$a = h(W_2 + e)$
$p = W_2 + 2(e^2 + h^2)^{1/2}$
$$r = \frac{h(W_2 + e)}{W_2 + 2(e^2 + h^2)^{1/2}}$$

$a = \pi h^2/2$
$p = \pi h$
$$r = \frac{2}{h}$$

a = AREA OF WATER SECTION
p = WETTED PERIMETER
r = a/p = HYDRAULIC RADIUS

CHANNEL PROPERTIES

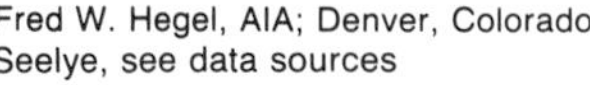
Fred W. Hegel, AIA; Denver, Colorado
Seelye, see data sources

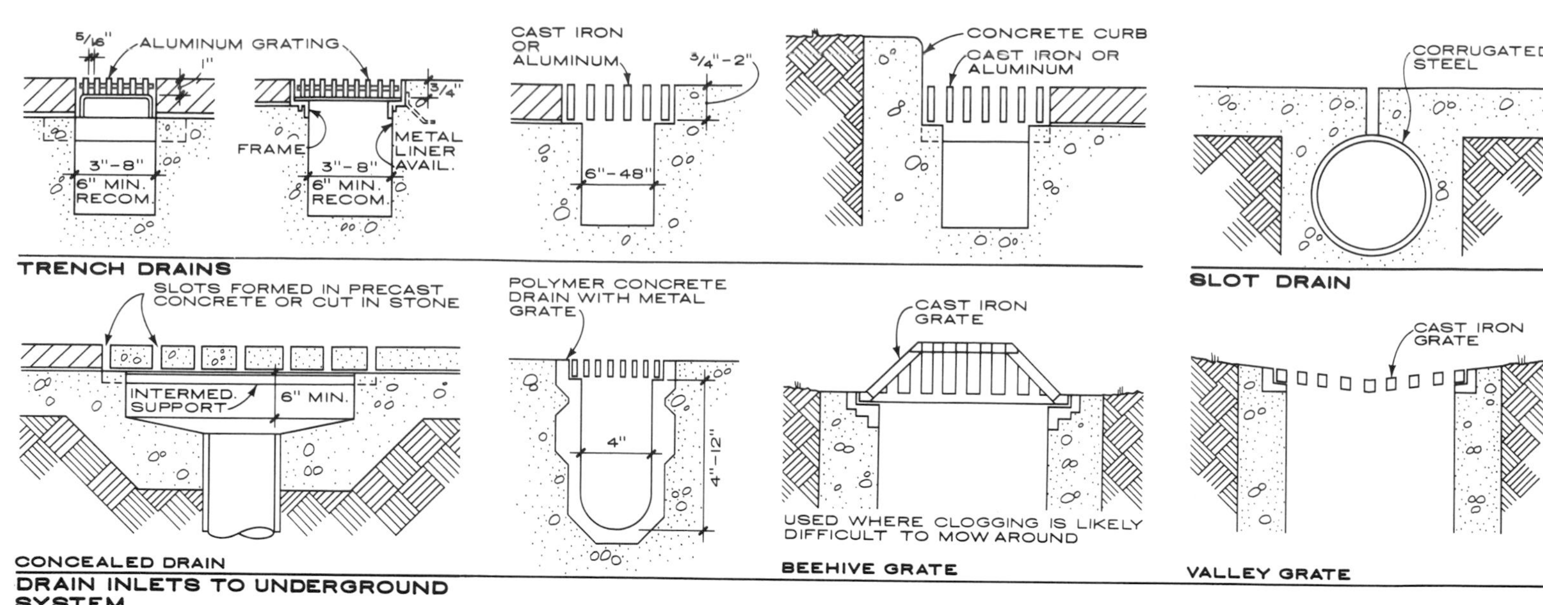
5/16"
ALUMINUM GRATING
1"
3/4"
FRAME
METAL LINER AVAIL.
3"–8"
6" MIN. RECOM.
CAST IRON OR ALUMINUM
3/4"–2"
6"–48"
CONCRETE CURB
CAST IRON OR ALUMINUM
CORRUGATED STEEL
TRENCH DRAINS
SLOT DRAIN
SLOTS FORMED IN PRECAST CONCRETE OR CUT IN STONE
INTERMED. SUPPORT
6" MIN.
POLYMER CONCRETE DRAIN WITH METAL GRATE
4"
4"–12"
CAST IRON GRATE
USED WHERE CLOGGING IS LIKELY DIFFICULT TO MOW AROUND
CONCEALED DRAIN
BEEHIVE GRATE
VALLEY GRATE

DRAIN INLETS TO UNDERGROUND SYSTEM

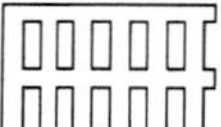
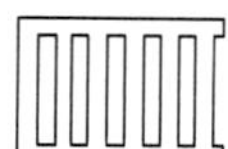
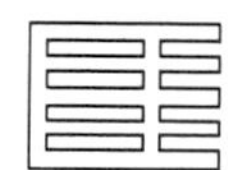
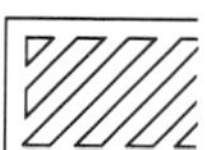

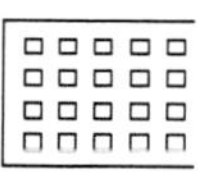

USE GRATING DESIGNED FOR EXTERIOR USE AND CORRECT WHEEL LOAD

GRATING DESIGNS—STANDARD

GRATE SIZING

Most gratings are oversized to prevent a buildup of water. See manufacturers' catalogs for free area.

Formula shown for sizing gratings is based on a given allowable depth of water (d) over the grating.

$Q = .66\ CA\ (64.4\ d)^{.5}$
A = Free area (square feet)
d = Allowable depth of water above grate (feet)
C = Orifice coefficient
.6 for square edges
.8 for round edges
.66 = Clogging factor

CHECK DAMS USED WHERE CHANNEL SLOPE AND VELOCITY WILL CAUSE EROSION

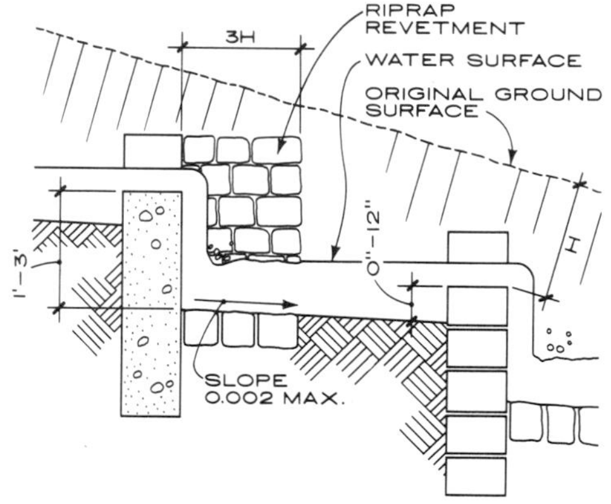
3H
RIPRAP REVETMENT
WATER SURFACE
ORIGINAL GROUND SURFACE
H
0"–12"
1'–3'
SLOPE 0.002 MAX.

CHECK DAMS

DETENTION

Check with local code requirements for control of storm water. Many require runoff to be maintained at predevelopment rates. This is accomplished with a detention facility upstream of a controlled outlet structure. The detention basin may be a structure or a paved or grass basin. If soil types permit, seepage may be used to dispose of runoff accumulated in a grass basin. The volume of detention required can be approximated by the following formula:

AMOUNT OF DETENTION:

$\text{Vol.} = (C_{dev.} - C_{hist.})AD$
D = Design storm depth (inches)
A = Area site (acres)
$C_{dev.}$ = C from table for developed land
$C_{hist.}$ = C from table for land prior to development

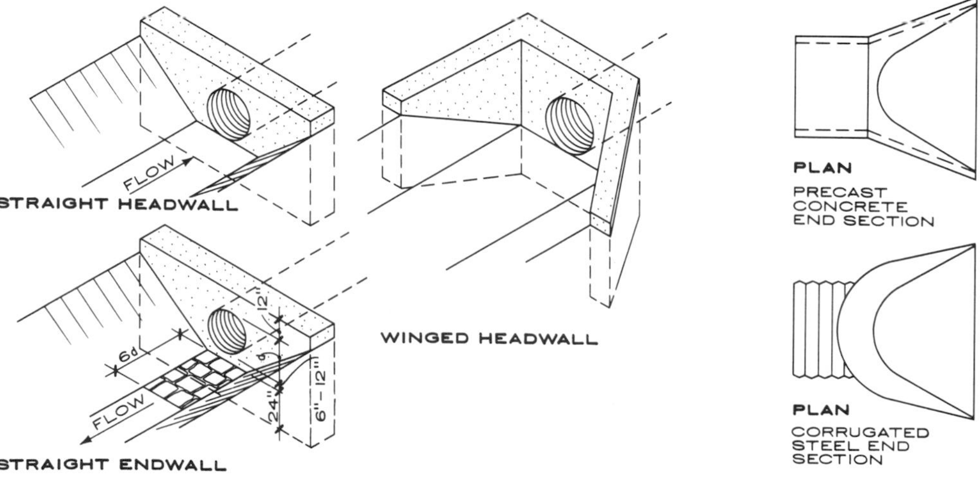
FLOW
STRAIGHT HEADWALL
WINGED HEADWALL
PLAN
PRECAST CONCRETE END SECTION
12"
6d
d
24"
6"–12"
FLOW
STRAIGHT ENDWALL
PLAN
CORRUGATED STEEL END SECTION

HEADWALLS AND ENDWALLS

SLOPES

DESCRIPTION	MIN. %	MAX. %	REC. %
Grass (mowed)	1	25	1.5–10
(athletic field)	.5	2	1
Walks (Long.)	.5	12*	1.5
(Transv.)	1	4	1–2
Streets (Long.)	.5	20	1–10
Parking	1	5	2–3
Channels			
Grass swale	1	8	1.5–2
Paved swale	.5	12	4–6

*8.3% max. for handicapped

RUN-OFF VELOCITY

VELOCITIES	MIN.	MAX.
CHANNEL	FT/SEC	FT/SEC
Grass	2	4
Concrete	2	10
Gravel	2	3
Asphalt	2	7.5
Sand	.5	1.5

Fred W. Hegel, AIA; Denver, Colorado
Seelye; Landphair and Klatt; see data sources

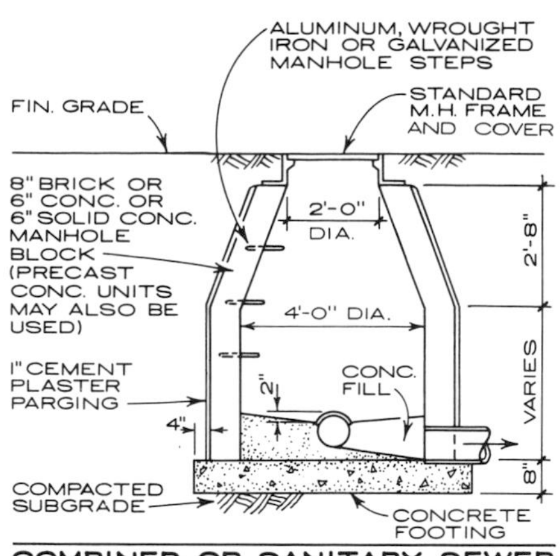
ALUMINUM, WROUGHT IRON OR GALVANIZED MANHOLE STEPS
FIN. GRADE
STANDARD M.H. FRAME AND COVER
8" BRICK OR 6" CONC. OR 6" SOLID CONC. MANHOLE BLOCK (PRECAST CONC. UNITS MAY ALSO BE USED)
2'-0" DIA.
4'-0" DIA.
1" CEMENT PLASTER PARGING
CONC. FILL
VARIES
COMPACTED SUBGRADE
CONCRETE FOOTING

COMBINED OR SANITARY SEWER MANHOLE

NOTES

1. Parging may be omitted in construction of storm sewer manholes.
2. Brick and block walls to be as shown for manholes up to 12 ft deep. For that part of manhole deeper than 12 ft, brick and block walls shall be 12 in. thick. Manholes over 12 ft deep shall have a 12 in. thick base.

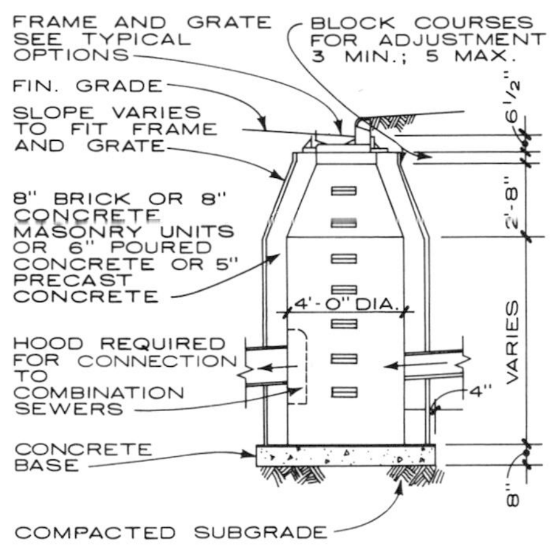
FRAME AND GRATE SEE TYPICAL OPTIONS
BLOCK COURSES FOR ADJUSTMENT 3 MIN.; 5 MAX.
FIN. GRADE
SLOPE VARIES TO FIT FRAME AND GRATE
8" BRICK OR 8" CONCRETE MASONRY UNITS OR 6" POURED CONCRETE OR 5" PRECAST CONCRETE
4'-0" DIA.
HOOD REQUIRED FOR CONNECTION TO COMBINATION SEWERS
VARIES
CONCRETE BASE
COMPACTED SUBGRADE

CATCH BASIN

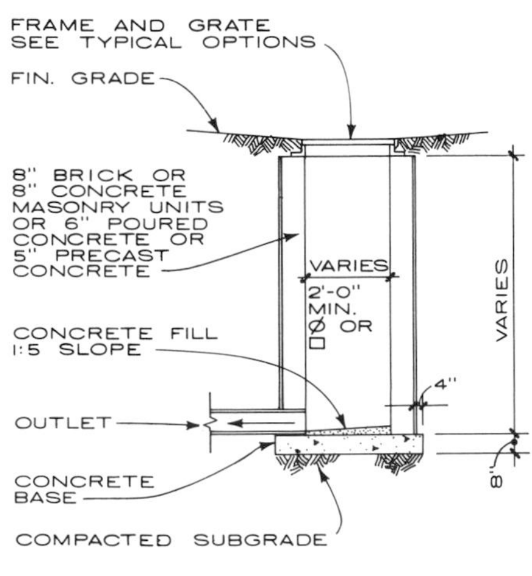
FRAME AND GRATE SEE TYPICAL OPTIONS
FIN. GRADE
8" BRICK OR 8" CONCRETE MASONRY UNITS OR 6" POURED CONCRETE OR 5" PRECAST CONCRETE
VARIES
2'-0" MIN. Ø OR □
CONCRETE FILL 1:5 SLOPE
OUTLET
CONCRETE BASE
COMPACTED SUBGRADE

INLET

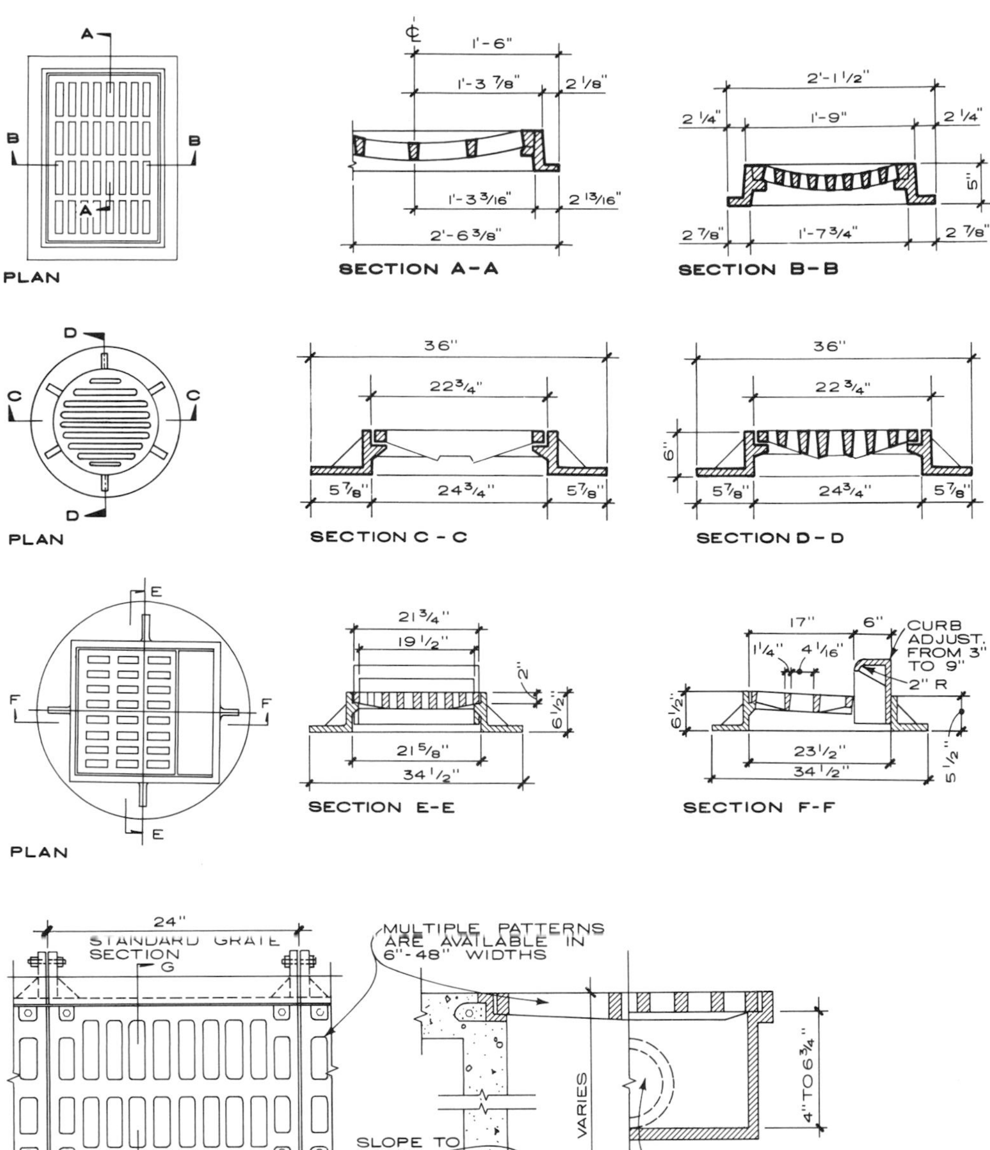
PLAN
SECTION A-A
SECTION B-B
SECTION C - C
SECTION D - D
SECTION E-E
SECTION F-F
CURB ADJUST. FROM 3" TO 9"
STANDARD GRATE SECTION
MULTIPLE PATTERNS ARE AVAILABLE IN 6"-48" WIDTHS
SLOPE TO DRAIN
OPTIONAL CAST IRON BASIN WITH END, SIDE, OR BOTTOM OUTLET, FOR GRATES 7"-24" WIDE
GRATES, WITHOUT BOLTS ARE AVAILABLE
PLAN—TRENCH DRAIN
SECTION G-G

TYPICAL FRAMES AND GRATES

NOTES

1. A great number of standard shapes and sizes of frames and grates are available. They are constructed of cast or ductile iron for light or heavy duty loading conditions. The available shapes are shown above: round, rectangular or square, and linear. In addition, grates may be flat, concave, or convex. Manufacturers' catalogs and local foundries should be consulted for the full range of castings.
2. Drainage structures with grated openings should be located on the periphery of traveled ways or beyond to minimize their contact with pedestrian or vehicular traffic. Grates that will be susceptible to foot or narrow wheel contact must be so constructed as to prevent penetration by heels, crutch and cane tips, and slim tires, but still serve to provide sufficient drainage. This can be done by reducing the size of each unit opening and increasing the overall size or number of grates. Where only narrow wheel use is expected, slotted gratings can be used if the slots are oriented transversely to the direction of traffic.

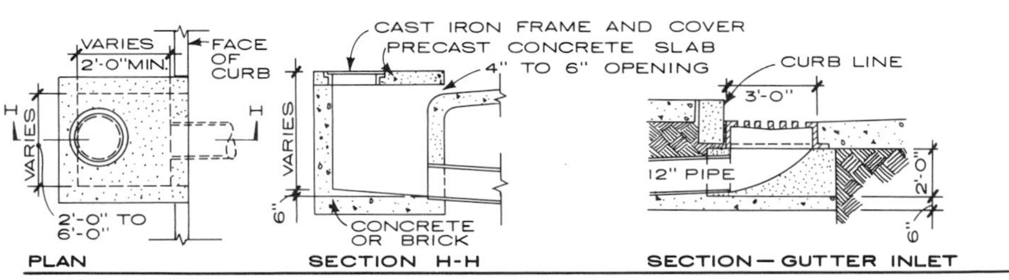
VARIES
2'-0" MIN.
FACE OF CURB
2'-0" TO 6'-0"
PLAN
CAST IRON FRAME AND COVER
PRECAST CONCRETE SLAB
4" TO 6" OPENING
CONCRETE OR BRICK
SECTION H-H
CURB LINE
3'-0"
12" PIPE
SECTION—GUTTER INLET

CURB INLET

Kurt N. Pronske, P.E.; Reston, Virginia

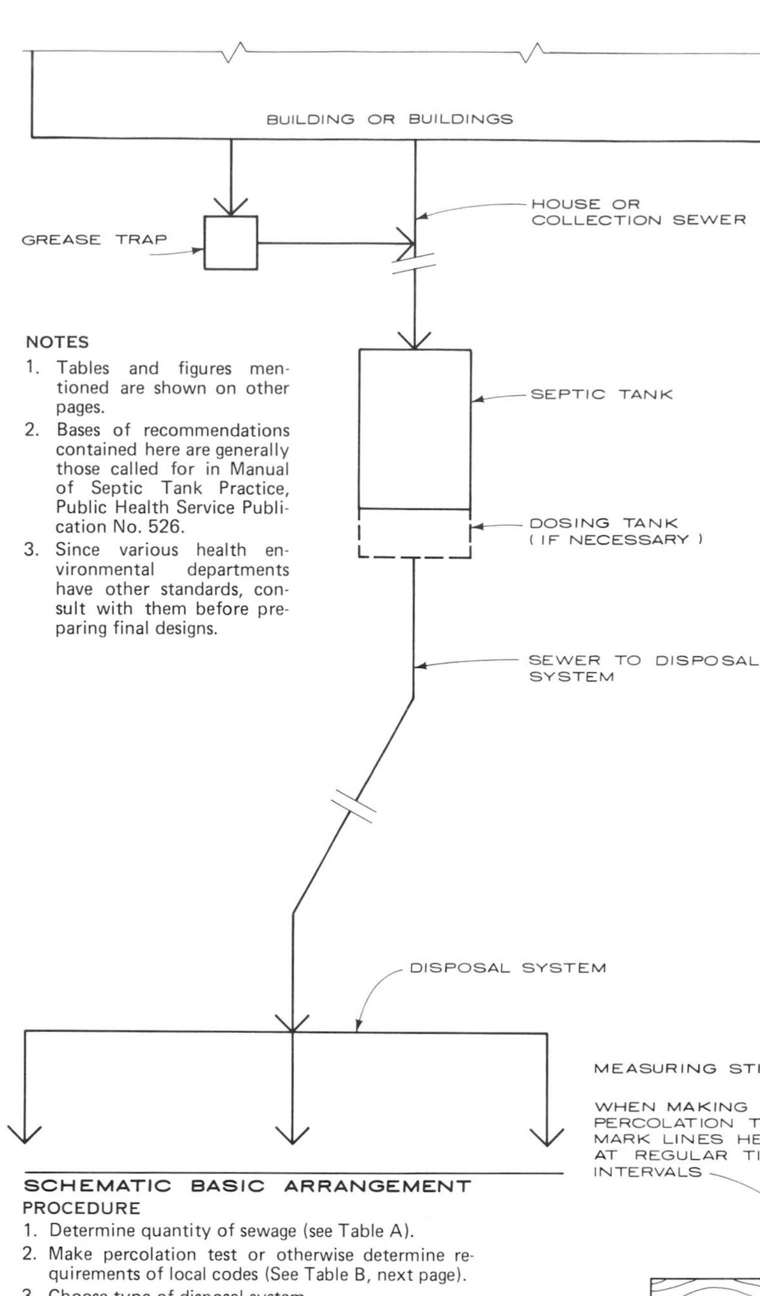
BUILDING OR BUILDINGS
GREASE TRAP
HOUSE OR COLLECTION SEWER
SEPTIC TANK
DOSING TANK (IF NECESSARY)
SEWER TO DISPOSAL SYSTEM
DISPOSAL SYSTEM

NOTES

1. Tables and figures mentioned are shown on other pages.
2. Bases of recommendations contained here are generally those called for in Manual of Septic Tank Practice, Public Health Service Publication No. 526.
3. Since various health environmental departments have other standards, consult with them before preparing final designs.

SCHEMATIC BASIC ARRANGEMENT

PROCEDURE

1. Determine quantity of sewage (see Table A).
2. Make percolation test or otherwise determine requirements of local codes (See Table B, next page).
3. Choose type of disposal system.
4. Layout disposal systems.
5. Design septic tank.
6. Use dosing tank, diversion box and/or trap where necessary.

MATERIALS

Piping may be salt glazed clay bell and spigot, tile pipe, asbestos cement or concrete bell and spigot. If near well or any other water supply, use cast iron.

Where trees or shrubs may cause root stoppage in clay pipe, use cast iron.

Use bituminous joints or rubber ring type joints for clay, concrete, or asbestos cement pipe; use lead for cast iron pipe.

SIZE

4 in. diameter for small installations; 6 in. is better in all cases.

GRADE

In northern latitudes, start sewer approximately 3 ft below grade. In southern latitudes, sewer may start just below grade.

PITCH

Pitch 4 in. sewer 1/4 in./ft minimum. Pitch 6 in. sewer 1/8 in./ft minimum.

TABLE A QUANTITIES OF SEWAGE FLOWS

TYPE OF ESTABLISHMENT	GALLONS PER PERSON PER DAY
Airports (per passenger)	5
Bathhouses and swimming pools	10
Camps	
Campground with central comfort stations	35
Day camps (no meals served)	15
Resort camp (night and day) with limited plumbing	50
Cottages and small dwelling with seasonal occupancy[1]	50
Country clubs (per resident member)	100
Country clubs (per nonresident member present)	25
Dwellings	
Boarding houses[1]	50
Multiple family dwellings (apartments)	60
Single family dwellings[1]	75
Factories (gallons per person, per shift, exclusive of industry wastes)	35
Hospitals (per bed space)	250+
Hotels with private baths (2 persons per room)[2]	60
Institutions other than hospitals (per bed space)	125
Laundries, self-service (gallons per wash, i.e., per customer)	50
Mobile home parks (per space)	250
Picnic parks (toilet wastes only, per picnicker)	5
Picnic parks with bathhouses, showers, and flush toilets	10
Restaurants (toilets and kitchen wastes per patron)	10
Restaurants (kitchen wastes per meal served)	3
Restaurants (additional for bars and cocktail lounges)	2
Schools	
Boarding	100
Day, with gyms, cafeteria, and showers	25
Service stations (per vehicle served)	10
Theaters	
Movie (per auditorium seat)	5
Drive-in (per car space)	5
Travel trailer parks with individual water and sewer hookups	100
Workers	
Day, at schools and offices (per shift)	15

NOTES

1. Two people per bedroom.
2. Use also for motels.

MEASURING STICK

WHEN MAKING PERCOLATION TEST MARK LINES HERE AT REGULAR TIME INTERVALS

BATTER BOARD OR OTHER FIXED REFERENCE POINT

PROCEDURE

First soak hole by filling at least 12 in. over gravel with water and continue to refill with water so that hole is soaked for 24 hr. After 24 hr adjust the depth of water over the gravel to approximately 6 in. Now measure the drop in water level over a 30 min period.

WATER SURFACE

6"

4" OR LARGER DIAMETER (HOLE MAY BE MADE WITH AN AUGER)

THE LOCATION AND ELEVATION OF THIS HOLE ARE APPROXIMATELY THE SAME AS DISPOSAL FIELD

2" LAYER OF GRAVEL

NOTE: THIS TEST IS RECOMMENDED BY THE ENVIRONMENTAL PROTECTION AGENCY. CHECK LOCAL REQUIREMENTS FOR OTHER TEST CONDITIONS

METHOD OF MAKING PERCOLATION TEST

Jack L. Staunton, P.E.; Staunton and Freeman, Consulting Engineers; New York, New York

TABLE B. ALLOWABLE RATE OF SEWAGE APPLICATION TO A SOIL ABSORPTION SYSTEM

PERCOLATION RATE [TIME (MIN) FOR WATER TO FALL 1 IN.]	MAXIMUM RATE OF SEWAGE APPLICATION (GAL/SQ FT/DAY)[1] FOR ABSORPTION TRENCHES,[2] SEEPAGE BEDS, AND SEEPAGE PITS[3]	PERCOLATION RATE [TIME (MIN) FOR WATER TO FALL 1 IN.]	MAXIMUM RATE OF SEWAGE APPLICATION (GAL/SQ FT/DAY)[1] FOR ABSORPTION TRENCHES,[2] SEEPAGE BEDS, AND SEEPAGE PITS[3]
1 or less	5.0	10	1.6
2	3.5	15	1.3
3	2.9	30[4]	0.9
4	2.5	45[4]	0.8
5	2.2	60[4, 5]	0.6

NOTES

1. Not including effluents from septic tanks that receive wastes from garbage grinders and automatic washing machines.
2. Absorption area is figured as trench bottom area and includes a statistical allowance for vertical sidewall area.
3. Absorption area for seepage pits is effective sidewall area.
4. Over 30 is unsuitable for seepage pits.
5. Over 60 is unsuitable for absorption systems.

If permissible, use sand filtration system. For subsurface sand filters use 1.15 gal/sq ft/day.

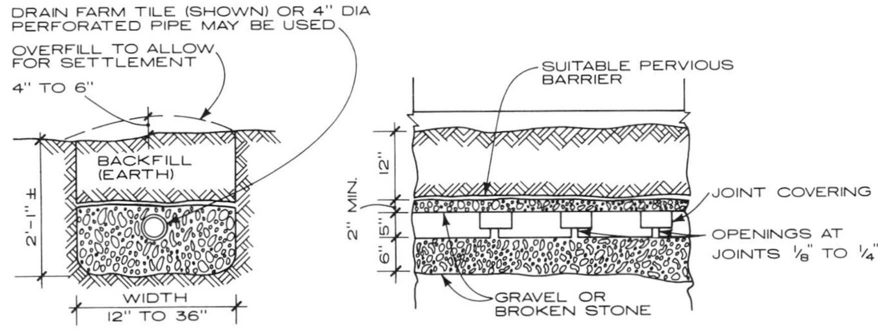
DRAIN FARM TILE (SHOWN) OR 4" DIA PERFORATED PIPE MAY BE USED
OVERFILL TO ALLOW FOR SETTLEMENT
4" TO 6"
BACKFILL (EARTH)
2'-1" ±
WIDTH 12" TO 36"
SUITABLE PERVIOUS BARRIER
12"
2" MIN.
5"
6"
JOINT COVERING
OPENINGS AT JOINTS 1/8" TO 1/4"
GRAVEL OR BROKEN STONE

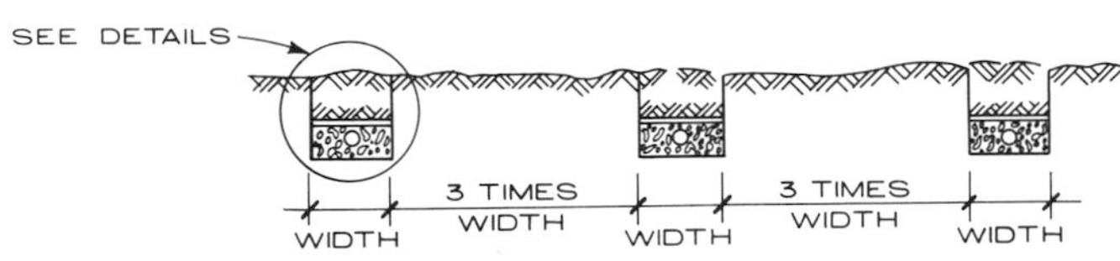
SEE DETAILS
WIDTH
3 TIMES WIDTH
WIDTH
3 TIMES WIDTH
WIDTH

ABSORPTION TRENCH SYSTEM DETAILS

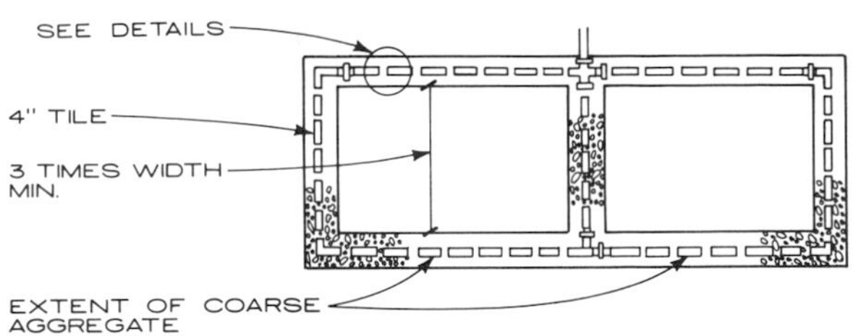
SEE DETAILS
4" TILE
3 TIMES WIDTH MIN.
EXTENT OF COARSE AGGREGATE

ABSORPTION TRENCH ARRANGEMENT FOR LEVEL GROUND FOR HOUSEHOLD DISPOSAL

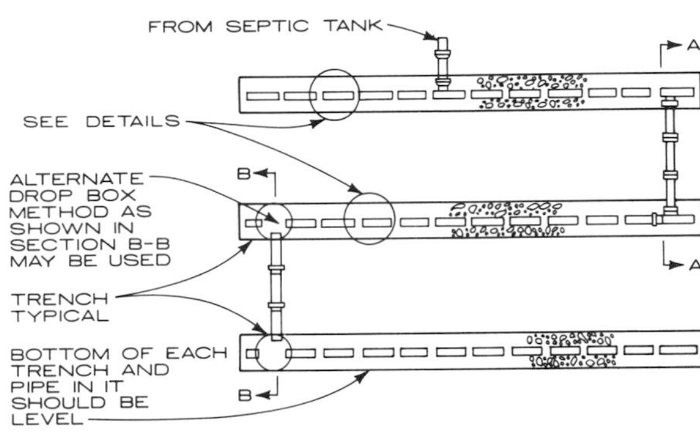
FROM SEPTIC TANK
A
SEE DETAILS
ALTERNATE DROP BOX METHOD AS SHOWN IN SECTION B-B MAY BE USED
B
A
TRENCH TYPICAL
BOTTOM OF EACH TRENCH AND PIPE IN IT SHOULD BE LEVEL
B
NOTE
INVERT OF THE OVERFLOW PIPE MUST BE AT LEAST 4" LOWER THAN INVERT OF THE SEPTIC TANK OUTLET

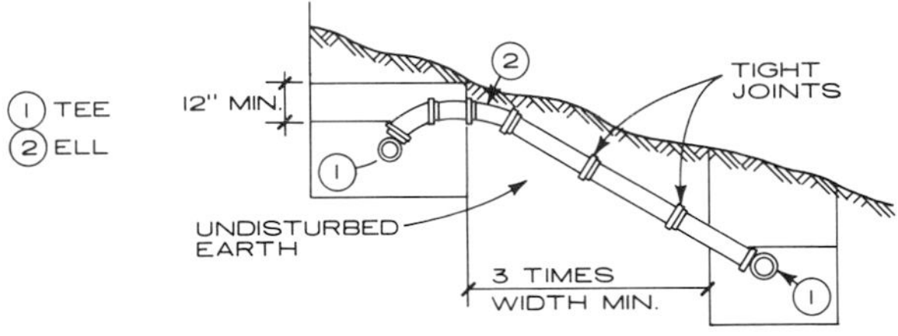
1 TEE
2 ELL
12" MIN.
TIGHT JOINTS
UNDISTURBED EARTH
3 TIMES WIDTH MIN.

SECTION A-A

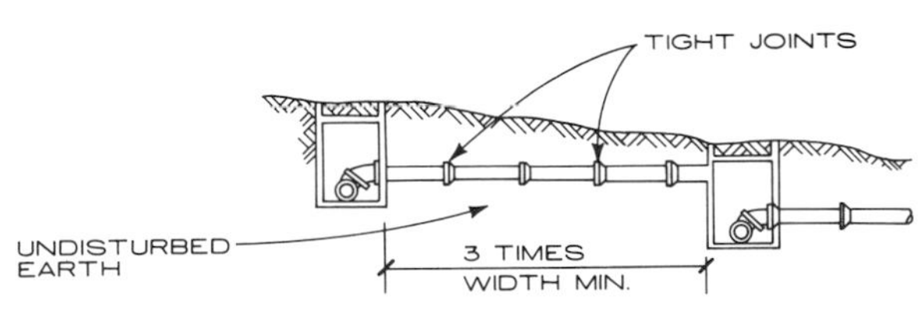
TIGHT JOINTS
UNDISTURBED EARTH
3 TIMES WIDTH MIN.
(ALTERNATE CONSTRUCTION)

SECTION B-B

ABSORPTION TRENCH ARRANGEMENT FOR HILLY SITE FOR HOUSEHOLD DISPOSAL

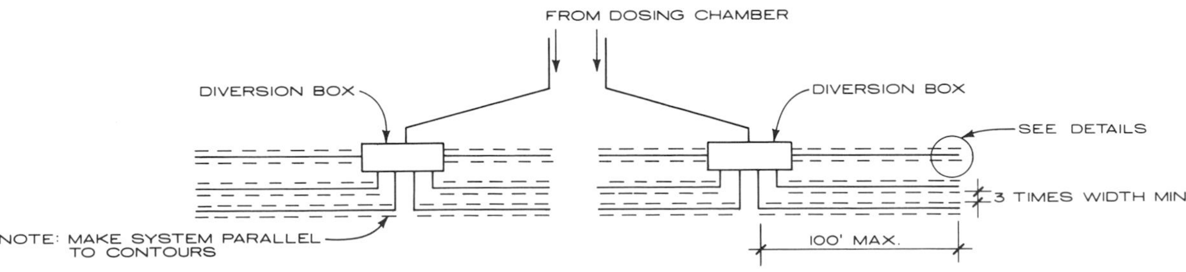
FROM DOSING CHAMBER
DIVERSION BOX
DIVERSION BOX
SEE DETAILS
3 TIMES WIDTH MIN.
NOTE: MAKE SYSTEM PARALLEL TO CONTOURS
100' MAX.

ABSORPTION TRENCH ARRANGEMENT FOR INSTITUTIONAL AND LIGHT COMMERCIAL DISPOSAL

Jack L. Staunton, P.E.; Staunton and Freeman, Consulting Engineers; New York, New York

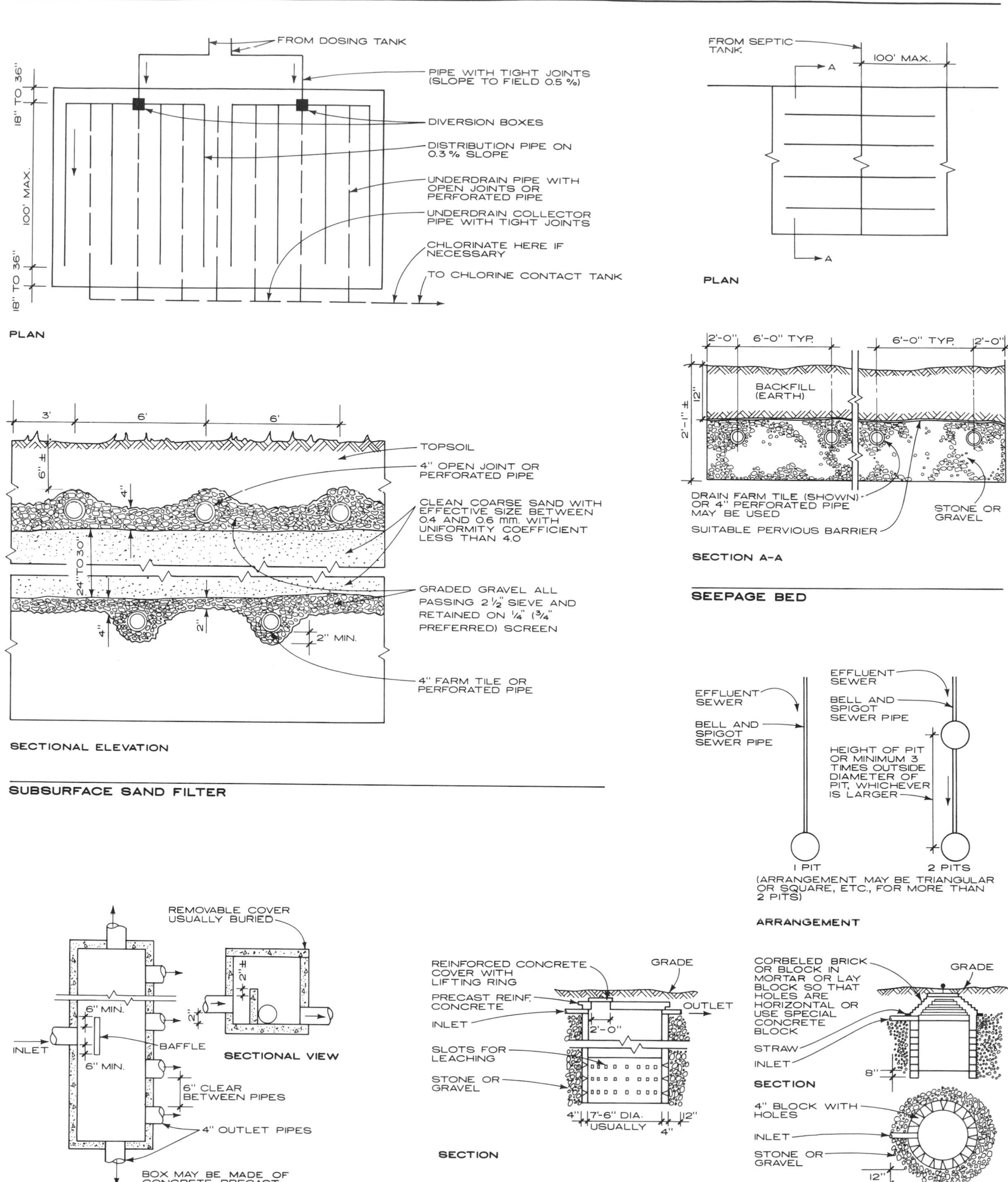
FROM DOSING TANK
PIPE WITH TIGHT JOINTS (SLOPE TO FIELD 0.5 %)
DIVERSION BOXES
DISTRIBUTION PIPE ON 0.3 % SLOPE
UNDERDRAIN PIPE WITH OPEN JOINTS OR PERFORATED PIPE
UNDERDRAIN COLLECTOR PIPE WITH TIGHT JOINTS
CHLORINATE HERE IF NECESSARY
TO CHLORINE CONTACT TANK
18" TO 36"
100' MAX.
18" TO 36"
PLAN
3'
6'
6'
TOPSOIL
6" ±
4" OPEN JOINT OR PERFORATED PIPE
4"
CLEAN COARSE SAND WITH EFFECTIVE SIZE BETWEEN 0.4 AND 0.6 mm. WITH UNIFORMITY COEFFICIENT LESS THAN 4.0
24" TO 30"
GRADED GRAVEL ALL PASSING 2 1/2" SIEVE AND RETAINED ON 1/4" (3/4" PREFERRED) SCREEN
4"
2"
2" MIN.
4" FARM TILE OR PERFORATED PIPE
SECTIONAL ELEVATION
SUBSURFACE SAND FILTER
FROM SEPTIC TANK
100' MAX.
A
A
PLAN
2'-0"
6'-0" TYP.
6'-0" TYP.
2'-0"
BACKFILL (EARTH)
12"
2'-1" ±
DRAIN FARM TILE (SHOWN) OR 4" PERFORATED PIPE MAY BE USED
SUITABLE PERVIOUS BARRIER
STONE OR GRAVEL
SECTION A-A
SEEPAGE BED
EFFLUENT SEWER
BELL AND SPIGOT SEWER PIPE
EFFLUENT SEWER
BELL AND SPIGOT SEWER PIPE
HEIGHT OF PIT OR MINIMUM 3 TIMES OUTSIDE DIAMETER OF PIT, WHICHEVER IS LARGER
1 PIT
2 PITS
(ARRANGEMENT MAY BE TRIANGULAR OR SQUARE, ETC., FOR MORE THAN 2 PITS)
ARRANGEMENT
REMOVABLE COVER USUALLY BURIED
6" MIN.
INLET
BAFFLE
6" MIN.
6" CLEAR BETWEEN PIPES
4" OUTLET PIPES
2" ±
2"
SECTIONAL VIEW
PLAN
BOX MAY BE MADE OF CONCRETE, PRECAST CONCRETE, CONCRETE BLOCK, OR BRICK
DIVERSION BOX
REINFORCED CONCRETE COVER WITH LIFTING RING
GRADE
PRECAST REINF. CONCRETE
OUTLET
INLET
2'-0"
SLOTS FOR LEACHING
STONE OR GRAVEL
4"
7'-6" DIA. USUALLY
4"
12"
SECTION
CORBELED BRICK OR BLOCK IN MORTAR OR LAY BLOCK SO THAT HOLES ARE HORIZONTAL OR USE SPECIAL CONCRETE BLOCK
GRADE
STRAW
INLET
8"
SECTION
4" BLOCK WITH HOLES
INLET
STONE OR GRAVEL
12"
PLAN OF 8" CONCRETE BLOCK PIT
SEEPAGE PITS

Jack L. Staunton, P.E.; Staunton and Freeman, Consulting Engineers; New York, New York

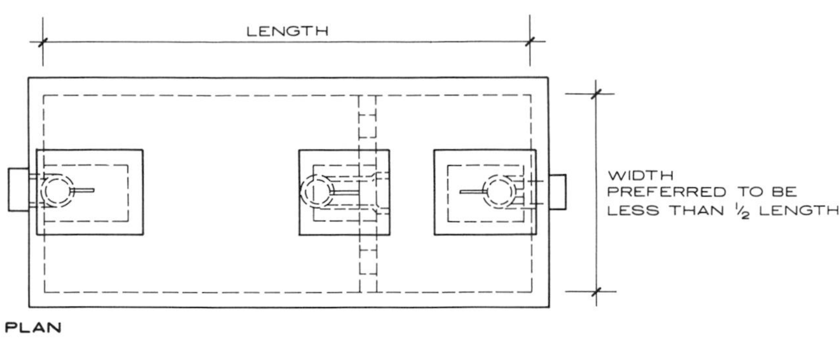
LENGTH
WIDTH
PREFERRED TO BE
LESS THAN ½ LENGTH

PLAN

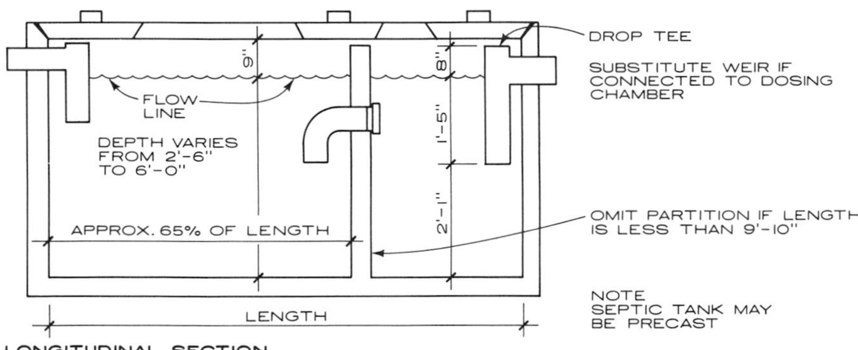
DROP TEE
SUBSTITUTE WEIR IF CONNECTED TO DOSING CHAMBER
9"
8"
FLOW LINE
DEPTH VARIES FROM 2'-6" TO 6'-0"
1'-5"
2'-1"
APPROX. 65% OF LENGTH
OMIT PARTITION IF LENGTH IS LESS THAN 9'-10"
LENGTH
NOTE
SEPTIC TANK MAY BE PRECAST

LONGITUDINAL SECTION

SEPTIC TANK

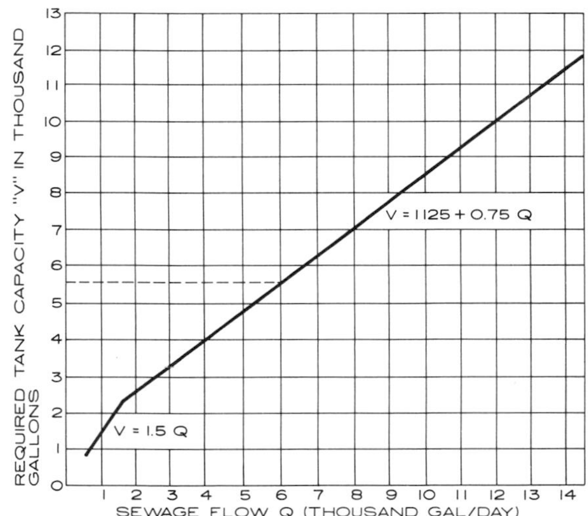
REQUIRED TANK CAPACITY "V" IN THOUSAND GALLONS
0
1
2
3
4
5
6
7
8
9
10
11
12
13
V = 1125 + 0.75 Q
V = 1.5 Q
1 2 3 4 5 6 7 8 9 10 11 12 13 14
SEWAGE FLOW Q (THOUSAND GAL/DAY)

DETERMINATION OF SEPTIC TANK VOLUME

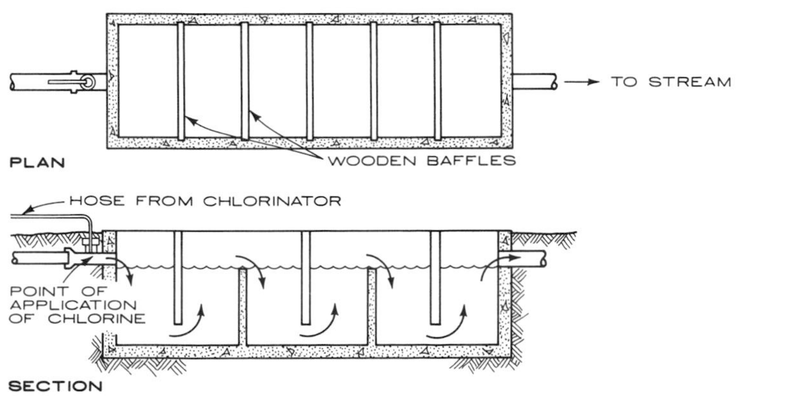
TO STREAM
WOODEN BAFFLES
HOSE FROM CHLORINATOR
POINT OF APPLICATION OF CHLORINE

PLAN

SECTION

CHLORINE CONTACT CHAMBER

Jack L. Staunton, P.E.; Staunton and Freeman, Consulting Engineers; New York, New York

NOTES
- DOSE FROM CHAMBER TO EQUAL ¾ OF FARM TILE OR PERFORATED PIPE IN ONE FIELD
- PIPES MAY BE SUBSTITUTED FOR SIPHONS IF CONDITION DICTATES

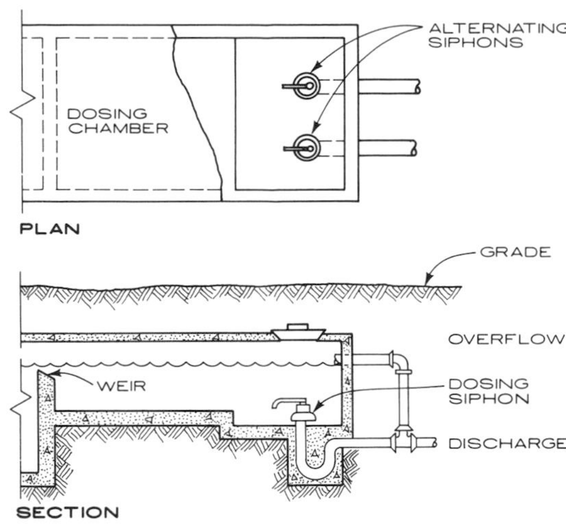
ALTERNATING SIPHONS
DOSING CHAMBER
PLAN
GRADE
OVERFLOW
WEIR
DOSING SIPHON
DISCHARGE

SECTION

DOSING CHAMBER WITH ALTERNATING SIPHONS

NOTE
GREASE TRAPS TO BE USED ONLY IF THEY ARE CLEANED DAILY

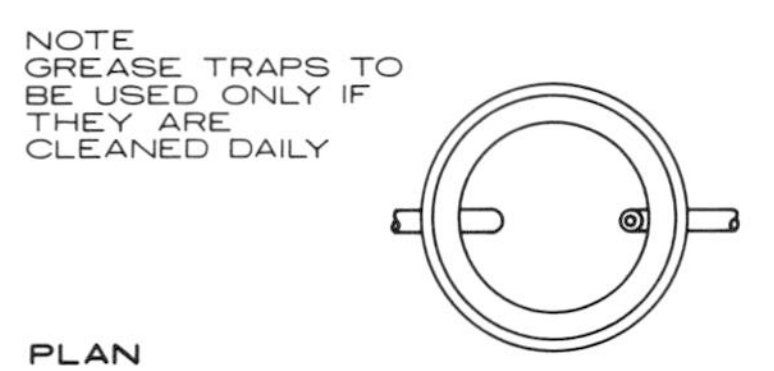

PLAN
(TOP REMOVED)

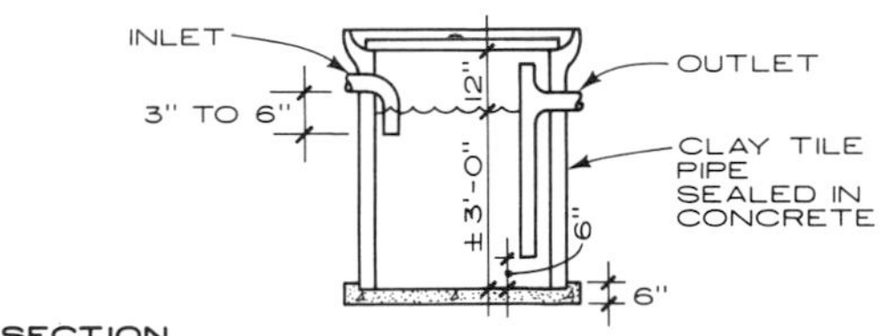
INLET
OUTLET
3" TO 6"
12"
±3'-0"
6"
CLAY TILE PIPE SEALED IN CONCRETE
6"

SECTION

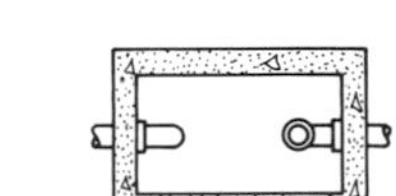

PLAN
(TOP REMOVED)

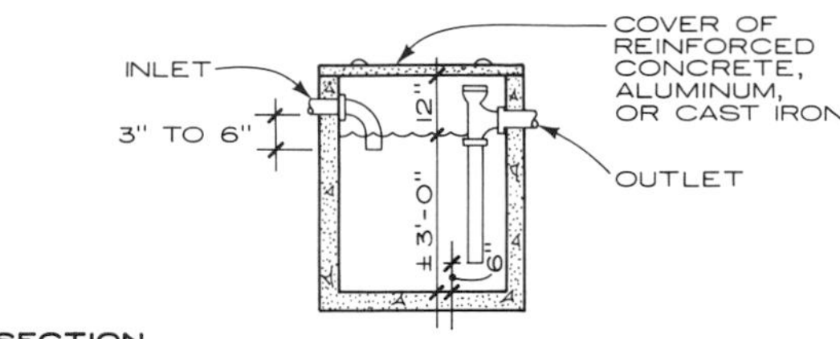
INLET
COVER OF REINFORCED CONCRETE, ALUMINUM, OR CAST IRON
3" TO 6"
12"
±3'-0"
6"
OUTLET

SECTION
CONCRETE BOX

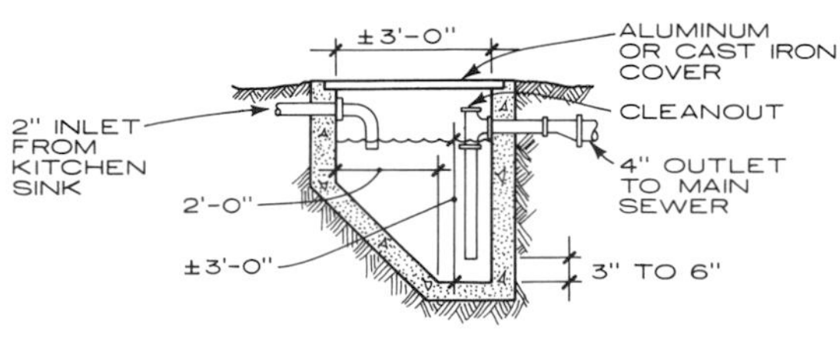
±3'-0"
ALUMINUM OR CAST IRON COVER
2" INLET FROM KITCHEN SINK
CLEANOUT
4" OUTLET TO MAIN SEWER
2'-0"
±3'-0"
3" TO 6"

TYPICAL GREASE TRAPS

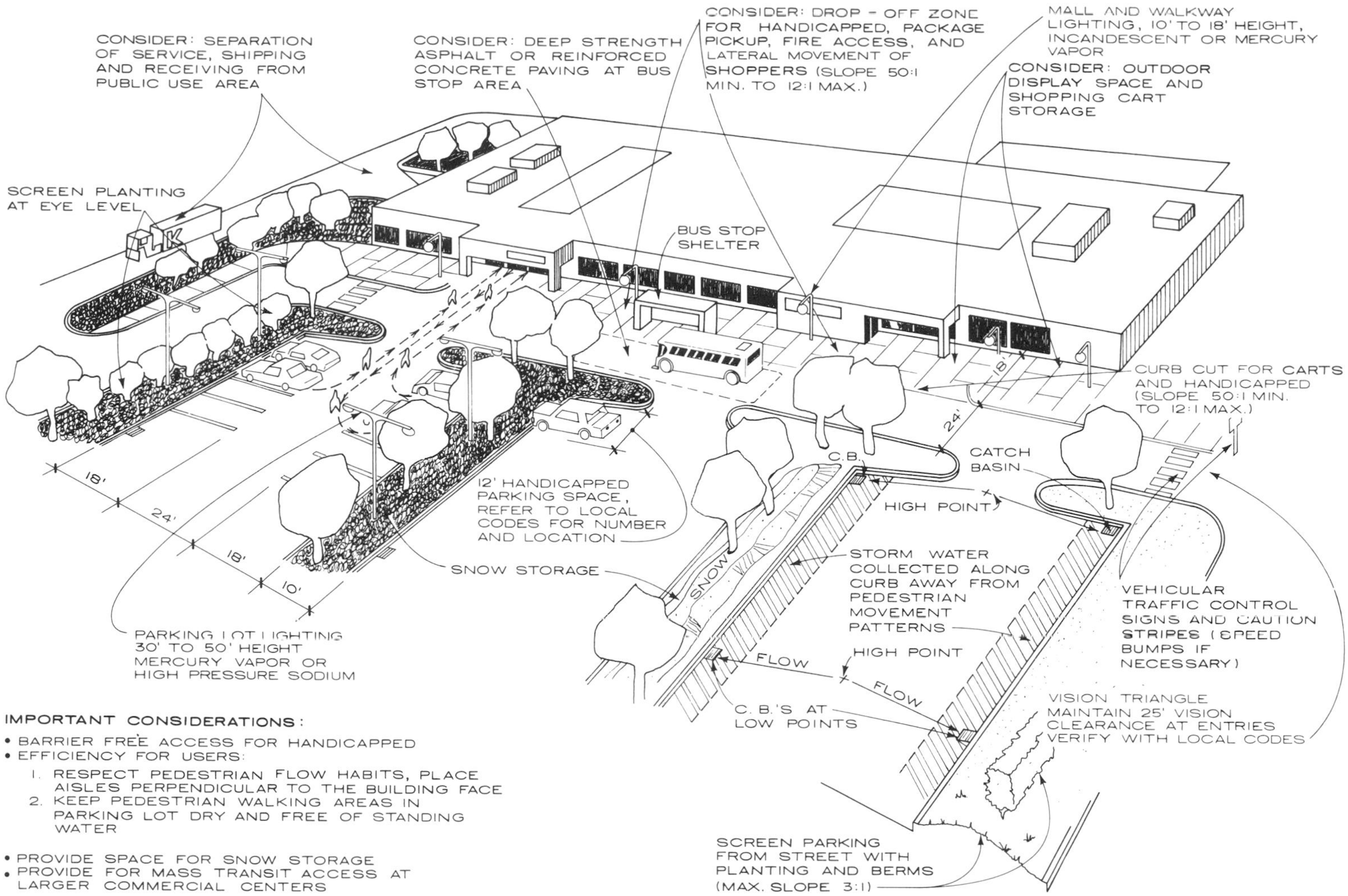

CONSIDER: SEPARATION OF SERVICE, SHIPPING AND RECEIVING FROM PUBLIC USE AREA

CONSIDER: DEEP STRENGTH ASPHALT OR REINFORCED CONCRETE PAVING AT BUS STOP AREA

CONSIDER: DROP - OFF ZONE FOR HANDICAPPED, PACKAGE PICKUP, FIRE ACCESS, AND LATERAL MOVEMENT OF SHOPPERS (SLOPE 50:1 MIN. TO 12:1 MAX.)

MALL AND WALKWAY LIGHTING, 10' TO 18' HEIGHT, INCANDESCENT OR MERCURY VAPOR

CONSIDER: OUTDOOR DISPLAY SPACE AND SHOPPING CART STORAGE

SCREEN PLANTING AT EYE LEVEL

BUS STOP SHELTER

CURB CUT FOR CARTS AND HANDICAPPED (SLOPE 50:1 MIN. TO 12:1 MAX.)

18'

24'

C.B.

CATCH BASIN

HIGH POINT

18'

24'

18'

10'

12' HANDICAPPED PARKING SPACE, REFER TO LOCAL CODES FOR NUMBER AND LOCATION

SNOW STORAGE

SNOW

STORM WATER COLLECTED ALONG CURB AWAY FROM PEDESTRIAN MOVEMENT PATTERNS

VEHICULAR TRAFFIC CONTROL SIGNS AND CAUTION STRIPES (SPEED BUMPS IF NECESSARY)

PARKING LOT LIGHTING 30' TO 50' HEIGHT MERCURY VAPOR OR HIGH PRESSURE SODIUM

FLOW

HIGH POINT

FLOW

C. B.'S AT LOW POINTS

VISION TRIANGLE MAINTAIN 25' VISION CLEARANCE AT ENTRIES VERIFY WITH LOCAL CODES

SCREEN PARKING FROM STREET WITH PLANTING AND BERMS (MAX. SLOPE 3:1)

IMPORTANT CONSIDERATIONS:

- BARRIER FREE ACCESS FOR HANDICAPPED
- EFFICIENCY FOR USERS:
  1. RESPECT PEDESTRIAN FLOW HABITS, PLACE AISLES PERPENDICULAR TO THE BUILDING FACE
  2. KEEP PEDESTRIAN WALKING AREAS IN PARKING LOT DRY AND FREE OF STANDING WATER
- PROVIDE SPACE FOR SNOW STORAGE
- PROVIDE FOR MASS TRANSIT ACCESS AT LARGER COMMERCIAL CENTERS

DESIGN CONSIDERATIONS

While efficiency (number of spaces per gross acres) is the major practical consideration in the development of parking areas, several other important design questions exist. Barrier free design is mandatory in most communities. Parking spaces for the handicapped should be designated near building entrances. Curb cuts for wheelchairs should be provided at entrances. The lots should not only be efficient in terms of parking spaces provided, but should also allow maximum efficiency for pedestrians once they leave their vehicles.

Pedestrians habitually walk in the aisles behind parked vehicles. This should be recognized in the orientation of the aisles to building entrances. When aisles are perpendicular to the building face, pedestrians can walk to and from the building without squeezing between parked cars with carts and packages. Pedestrian movement areas should be graded to avoid creating standing water in the paths of pedestrians. Space should be provided for snow storage within parking areas, if required.

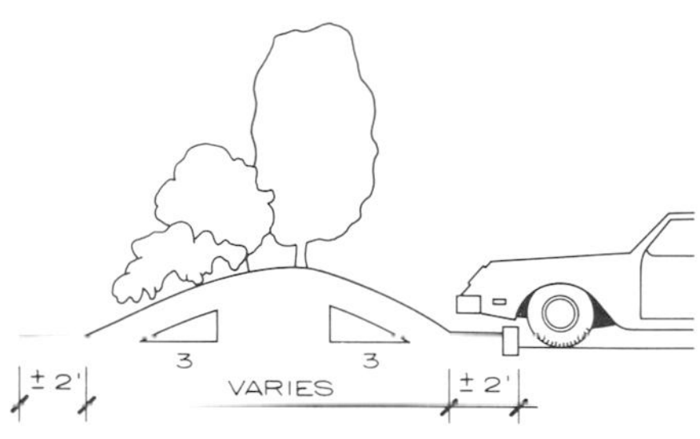
± 2'
3
VARIES
3
± 2'

BERM SECTION

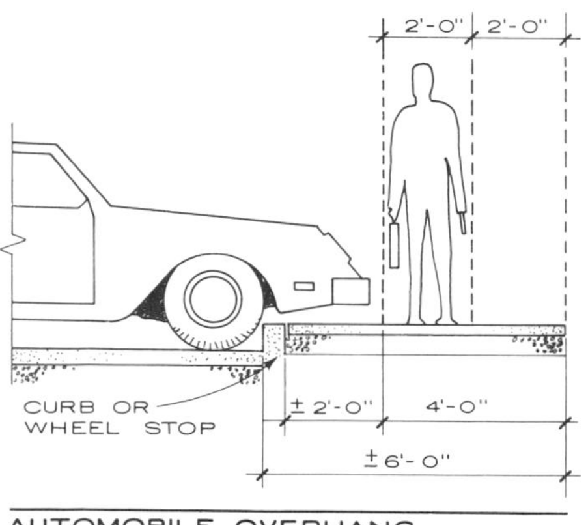
2'-0"
2'-0"
CURB OR WHEEL STOP
± 2'-0"
4'-0"
± 6'-0"

AUTOMOBILE OVERHANG REQUIREMENT

PLANTING CONSIDERATIONS

The distribution and placement of plants in parking areas can help to relieve the visually overwhelming scale of large parking lots. To maximize the impact of landscape materials, the screening capabilities of the plants must be considered. High branching canopy trees do not create a visual screen at eye level. When the landscaped area is concentrated in islands large enough to accommodate a diversified mixture of canopy and flowering trees, evergreen trees, and shrubs, visual screening via plants is much more effective. Planting low branching, densely foliated trees and shrubs can soften the visual impact of large parking areas. Consider the use of evergreens and avoid plants that drop fruit or sap.

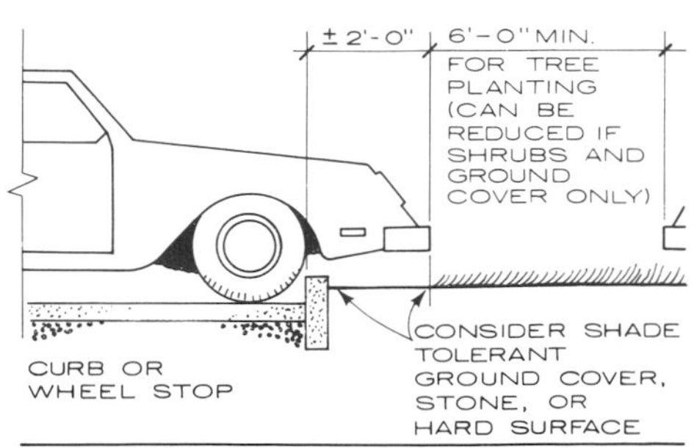
± 2'-0"
6'-0" MIN.
FOR TREE PLANTING (CAN BE REDUCED IF SHRUBS AND GROUND COVER ONLY)
CONSIDER SHADE TOLERANT GROUND COVER, STONE, OR HARD SURFACE
CURB OR WHEEL STOP

OVERHANGS IN PLANTING AREA

William H. Evans, AIA; San Antonio, Texas
Johnson, Johnson & Roy, Inc.; Ann Arbor, Michigan

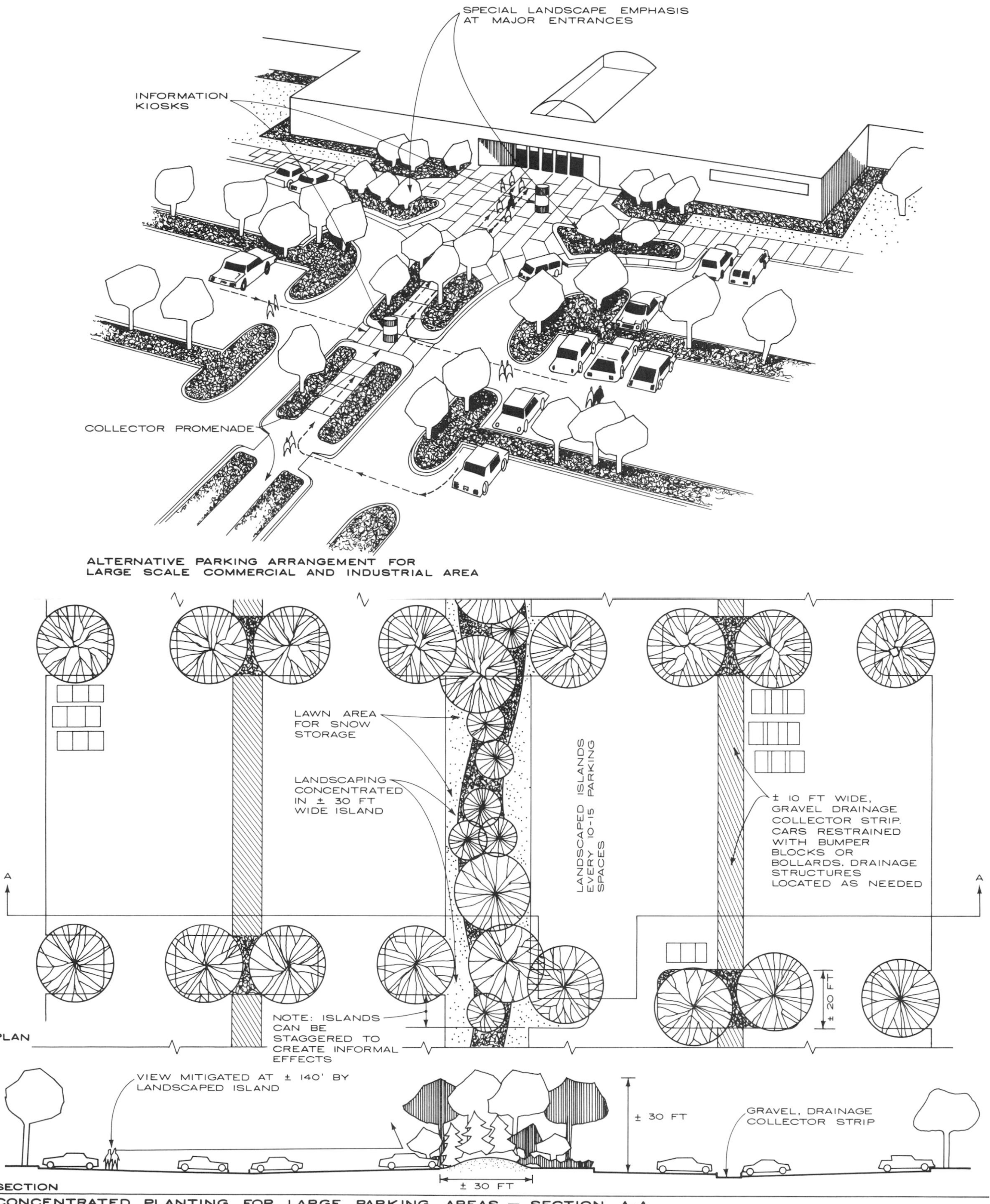
SPECIAL LANDSCAPE EMPHASIS AT MAJOR ENTRANCES
INFORMATION KIOSKS
COLLECTOR PROMENADE
ALTERNATIVE PARKING ARRANGEMENT FOR LARGE SCALE COMMERCIAL AND INDUSTRIAL AREA
LAWN AREA FOR SNOW STORAGE
LANDSCAPING CONCENTRATED IN ± 30 FT WIDE ISLAND
LANDSCAPED ISLANDS EVERY 10-15 PARKING SPACES
± 10 FT WIDE, GRAVEL DRAINAGE COLLECTOR STRIP. CARS RESTRAINED WITH BUMPER BLOCKS OR BOLLARDS. DRAINAGE STRUCTURES LOCATED AS NEEDED
A
A
NOTE: ISLANDS CAN BE STAGGERED TO CREATE INFORMAL EFFECTS
± 20 FT
PLAN
VIEW MITIGATED AT ± 140' BY LANDSCAPED ISLAND
± 30 FT
GRAVEL, DRAINAGE COLLECTOR STRIP
± 30 FT
SECTION

CONCENTRATED PLANTING FOR LARGE PARKING AREAS — SECTION A-A

Johnson, Johnson & Roy, Inc.; Ann Arbor, Michigan

VEHICULAR CONSIDERATIONS

There are strong differences between the perceptual performance of the driver and that of the pedestrian. Increasing speed imposes five limitations on man:

1. MAN'S CONCENTRATION INCREASES: While stationary or walking, a person's attention may be widely dispersed. When moving in an automobile, however, he or she concentrates on those factors that are relevant to the driving experience.
2. THE POINT OF CONCENTRATION RECEDES: As speed or motion increases, a person's concentration is directed at a focal point increasingly farther away.
3. PERIPHERAL VISION DIMINISHES: As the eye concentrates on detail at a point of focus a great distance ahead, the angular field of vision shrinks. This shrinking process is a function of focusing distance, angle of vision, and distance of foreground detail.
4. FOREGROUND DETAIL FADES INCREASINGLY: While concentrating on more significant distant objects, a person perceives foreground objects to be moving and increasingly blurred.
5. SPACE PERCEPTION BECOMES IMPAIRED: As the time available for perceiving objects decreases, specific details become less noticeable, making spatial perception more difficult.

With an increasing rate of motion, it becomes more and more important that copy, including illustrations and symbols, be created specifically for out-of-doors use and not merely rescaled from other media of communication. The safety of the motorist and passengers can depend on the clarity of messages conveyed by signs.

VEHICLE SPEEDS VERSUS LETTER HEIGHT ON TRAFFIC SIGNS

INITIAL SPEED	DISTANCE TRAVELED WHILE READING	DISTANCE TRAVELED WHILE SLOWING	TOTAL DISTANCE	SIZE OF COPY AT 65 FT/IN.
30 mph	110 ft	200 ft	310 ft	4.8 in.
40 mph	147 ft	307 ft	454 ft	7.0 in.
50 mph	183 ft	360 ft	543 ft	8.4 in.
60 mph	220 ft	390 ft	610 ft	9.4 in.

NOTE: It is recommended that street name signs have 4 in. letters in area where vehicle speeds are 30–35 mph. For speeds of 40 mph and over, a 5 in. letter size is recommended.

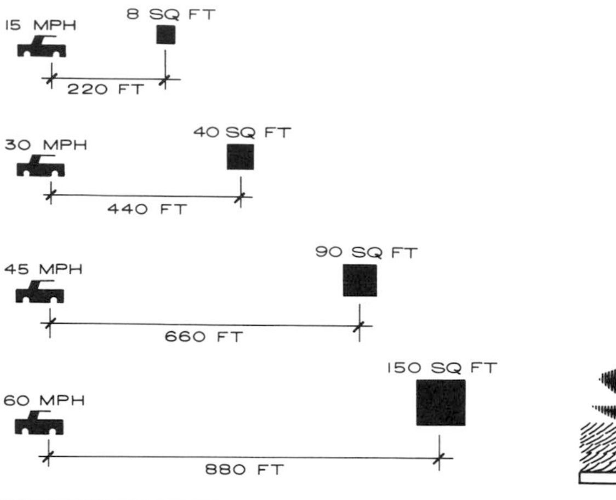
15 MPH
8 SQ FT
220 FT
30 MPH
40 SQ FT
440 FT
45 MPH
90 SQ FT
660 FT
60 MPH
150 SQ FT
880 FT

SPEED, SIGHT DISTANCE AND GRAPHIC SIZE RELATIONSHIPS

NOTE: LETTERS SHOULD CONSTITUTE APPROXIMATELY 40% OF GRAPHIC'S AREA

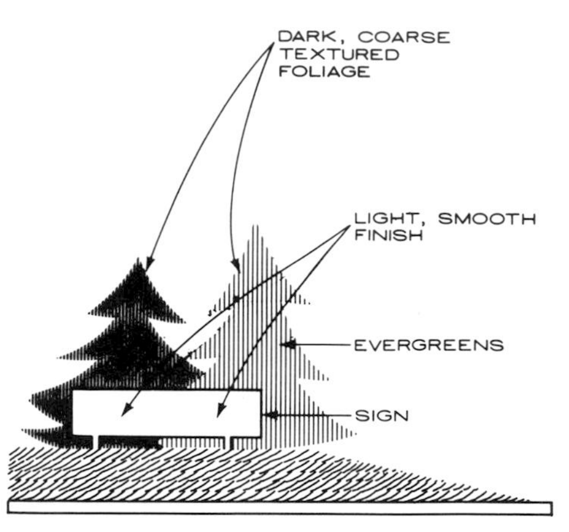
DARK, COARSE TEXTURED FOLIAGE
LIGHT, SMOOTH FINISH
EVERGREENS
SIGN

CONSIDER BACKGROUND WHEN CHOOSING COLOR AND MATERIALS

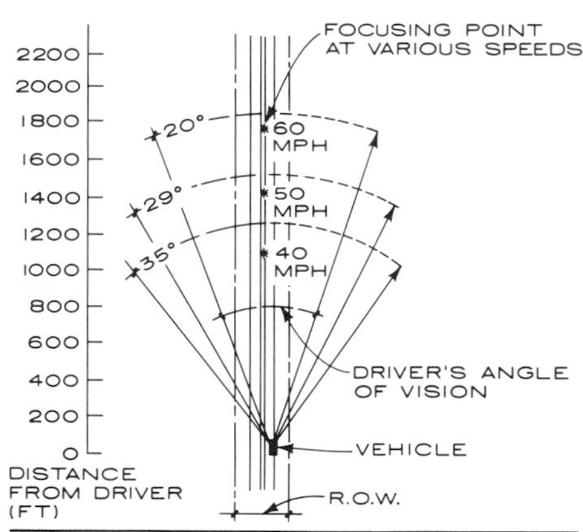
FOCUSING POINT AT VARIOUS SPEEDS
2200
2000
1800
1600
1400
1200
1000
800
600
400
200
0
20°
29°
35°
60 MPH
50 MPH
40 MPH
DRIVER'S ANGLE OF VISION
VEHICLE
R.O.W.
DISTANCE FROM DRIVER (FT)

RELATIONSHIP BETWEEN DRIVER'S FOCUSING POINT AND ANGLE OF VISION DOES NOT CONSIDER EFFECT OF PRECEDING TRAFFIC

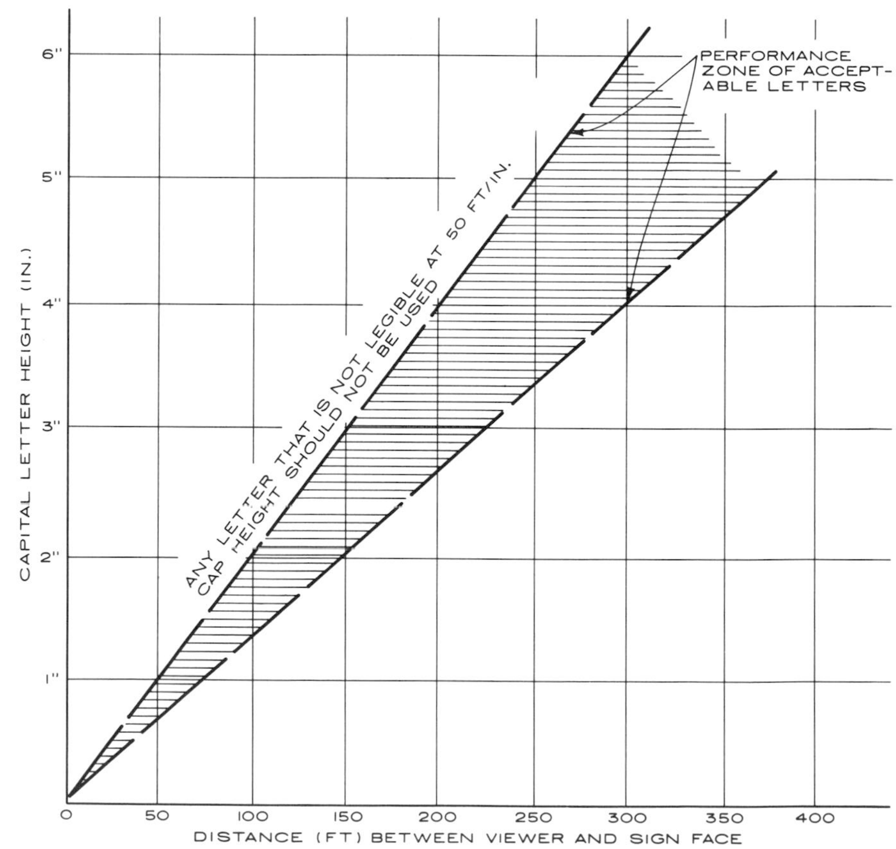
PERFORMANCE ZONE OF ACCEPTABLE LETTERS
ANY LETTER THAT IS NOT LEGIBLE AT 50 FT/IN. CAP HEIGHT SHOULD NOT BE USED
CAPITAL LETTER HEIGHT (IN.)
6"
5"
4"
3"
2"
1"
0
50
100
150
200
250
300
350
400
DISTANCE (FT) BETWEEN VIEWER AND SIGN FACE

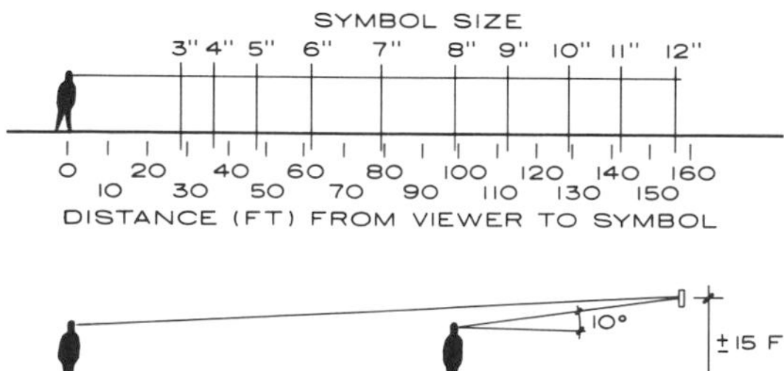
SYMBOL SIZE
3" 4" 5" 6" 7" 8" 9" 10" 11" 12"
0 20 40 60 80 100 120 140 160
10 30 50 70 90 110 130 150
DISTANCE (FT) FROM VIEWER TO SYMBOL

10°
±15 FT
EFFECTIVE VIEWING DISTANCE NOT MORE THAN 155 FT
EFFECTIVE VIEWING DISTANCE NOT LESS THAN 20 FT

PEDESTRIAN CONSIDERATIONS

NOTE

Under normal daylight conditions, with normal vision, and an angular distortion of 0° approximately 50 ft/in. of capital height can be taken as a guideline for minimal legibility, as seen from the chart.

Johnson, Johnson & Roy, Inc.; Ann Arbor, Michigan

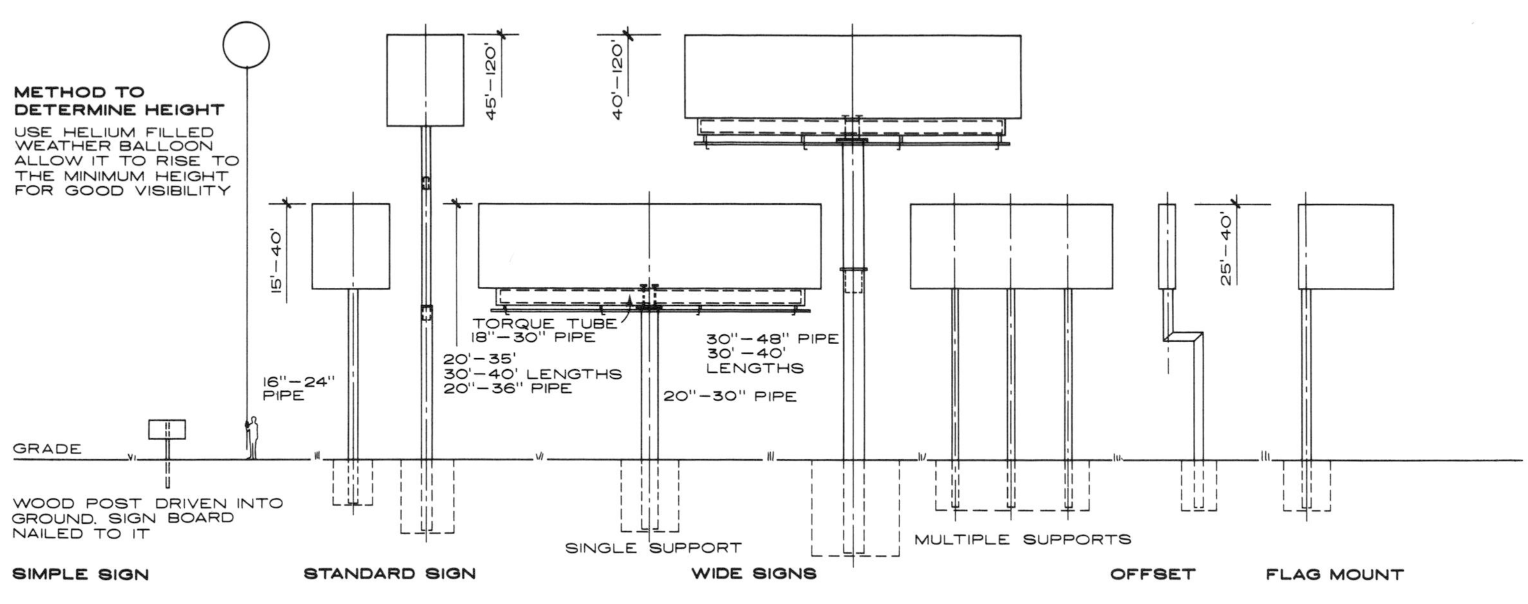
METHOD TO DETERMINE HEIGHT
USE HELIUM FILLED WEATHER BALLOON ALLOW IT TO RISE TO THE MINIMUM HEIGHT FOR GOOD VISIBILITY
45'–120'
40'–120'
15'–40'
TORQUE TUBE 18"–30" PIPE
20'–35'
30'–40' LENGTHS
20"–36" PIPE
30"–48" PIPE
30'–40' LENGTHS
20"–30" PIPE
16"–24" PIPE
25'–40'
GRADE
WOOD POST DRIVEN INTO GROUND. SIGN BOARD NAILED TO IT
SINGLE SUPPORT
MULTIPLE SUPPORTS
SIMPLE SIGN
STANDARD SIGN
WIDE SIGNS
OFFSET
FLAG MOUNT

TYPES OF SIGNS

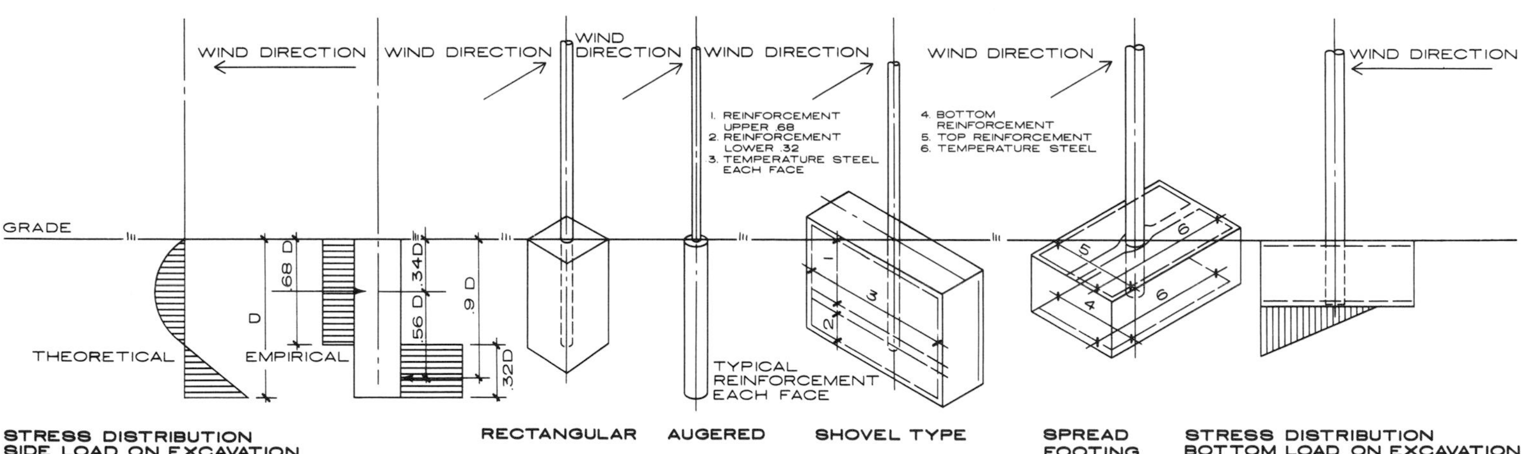
WIND DIRECTION
WIND DIRECTION
WIND DIRECTION
WIND DIRECTION
WIND DIRECTION
WIND DIRECTION
1. REINFORCEMENT UPPER .68
2. REINFORCEMENT LOWER .32
3. TEMPERATURE STEEL EACH FACE
4. BOTTOM REINFORCEMENT
5. TOP REINFORCEMENT
6. TEMPERATURE STEEL
GRADE
.68 D
D
.34D
.56 D
.9 D
.32D
THEORETICAL
EMPIRICAL
TYPICAL REINFORCEMENT EACH FACE
STRESS DISTRIBUTION SIDE LOAD ON EXCAVATION
RECTANGULAR
AUGERED
SHOVEL TYPE
SPREAD FOOTING
STRESS DISTRIBUTION BOTTOM LOAD ON EXCAVATION

FOOTING TYPES

STRUCTURAL DESIGN OF SIGNS

Signs are structurally designed primarily by wind forces and secondarily by gravitational forces. Wind forces are determined by wind speed, height, location, time interval for maximum wind (100 year, 50 year, etc.), gust factor, distribution on the surface, and codes. Although the basic wind load p is computed by the formula p = 0.00258 V where V = velocity of the wind in miles per hour, the factors that modify it vary in different regions by the codes that apply. Therefore wind loads are computed differently in different parts of the country. A state code may also be modified by a local ordinance, so a designer has to make sure that code requirements are met. By following the applicable code requirements utilizing wind maps, tables, and directions, the designer is able to determine the wind load per square foot acting on the sign surface in the locality in which the sign is being erected.

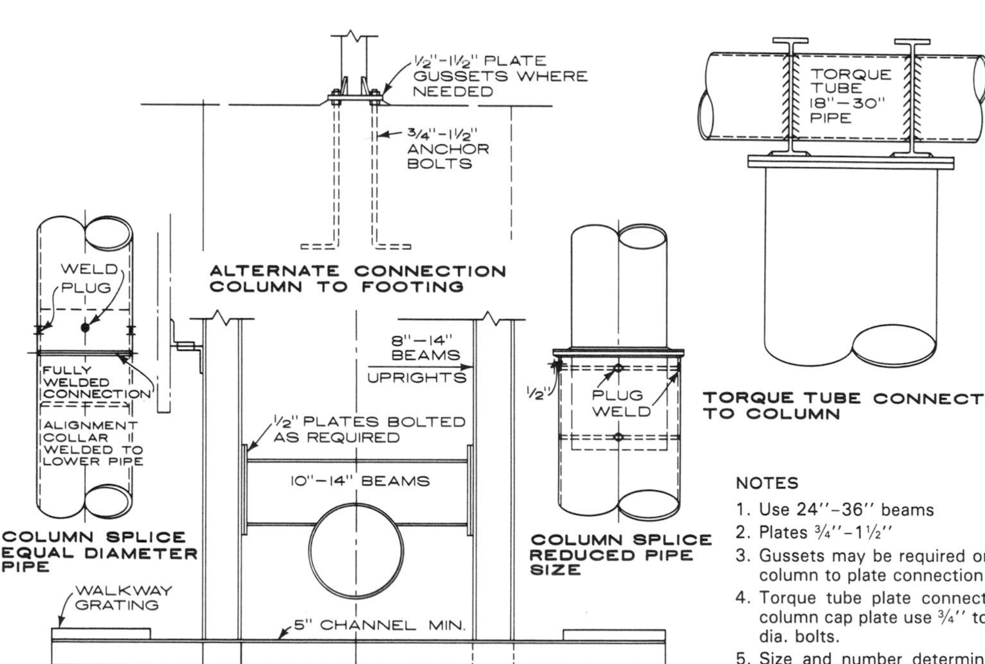
1/2"–1 1/2" PLATE GUSSETS WHERE NEEDED
3/4"–1 1/2" ANCHOR BOLTS
ALTERNATE CONNECTION COLUMN TO FOOTING
TORQUE TUBE 18"–30" PIPE
TORQUE TUBE CONNECTION TO COLUMN
WELD PLUG
FULLY WELDED CONNECTION
ALIGNMENT COLLAR WELDED TO LOWER PIPE
COLUMN SPLICE EQUAL DIAMETER PIPE
8"–14" BEAMS
UPRIGHTS
1/2" PLATES BOLTED AS REQUIRED
10"–14" BEAMS
WALKWAY GRATING
5" CHANNEL MIN.
UPRIGHT CONNECTION TO TORQUE TUBE
1/2"
PLUG WELD
COLUMN SPLICE REDUCED PIPE SIZE

NOTES

1. Use 24"–36" beams
2. Plates 3/4"–1 1/2"
3. Gussets may be required on pipe column to plate connection
4. Torque tube plate connected to column cap plate use 3/4" to 1 1/2" dia. bolts.
5. Size and number determined by design conditions

Leon Seligson, AIA; Columbus, Ohio

CONSIDERATIONS

The following factors must be considered when installing or renovating outdoor lighting systems:

1. In general, overhead lighting is more efficient and economical than low level lighting.
2. Fixtures should provide an overlapping pattern of light at a height of about 7 ft.
3. Lighting levels should respond to site hazards such as steps, ramps, and steep embankments.
4. Posts and standards should be placed so that they do not create hazards for pedestrians or vehicles.

NOTES

1. Because of their effect on light distribution, trees and shrubs at present height and growth potential should be considered in a lighting layout.
2. It is recommended to use manufacturer-provided lighting templates sized for fixture type, wattage, pole height, and layout scale.
3. Color rendition should be considered when selecting light source. When possible, colors should be selected under proposed light source.
4. Light pollution to areas other than those to be illuminated should be avoided.

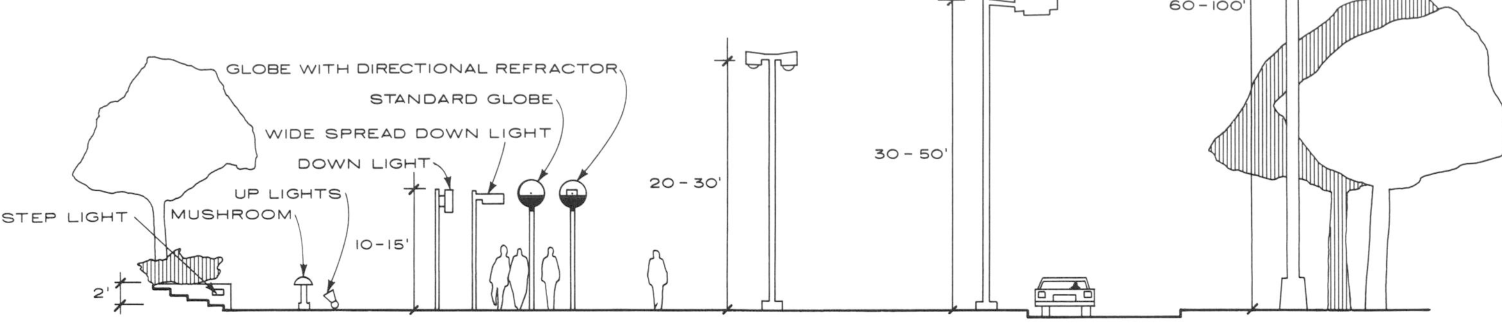
GLOBE WITH DIRECTIONAL REFRACTOR
STANDARD GLOBE
WIDE SPREAD DOWN LIGHT
DOWN LIGHT
UP LIGHTS
MUSHROOM
STEP LIGHT
2'
10-15'
20-30'
30-50'
60-100'

LOW LEVEL LIGHTING

1. Heights below eye level.
2. Very finite patterns with low wattage capabilities.
3. Incandescent, fluorescent, and high-pressure sodium, 5 to 150 watt lamps.
4. Lowest maintenance requirements, but highly susceptible to vandals.

MALL AND WALKWAY LIGHTING

1. 10 ft. to 15 ft. heights average for multiuse areas. Wide variety of fixtures and light patterns.
2. Mercury, metal halide, or high-pressure sodium, 70 to 250 watt lamps.
3. Susceptible to vandals.

SPECIAL PURPOSE LIGHTING

1. 20 ft. to 30 ft. heights average.
2. Recreational, commercial, residential, industrial.
3. Mercury, metal halide, or high-pressure sodium, 200 to 400 watt lamps.
4. Fixtures maintained by gantry.

PARKING AND ROADWAY LIGHTING

1. 30 ft. to 50 ft. heights average.
2. Large recreational, commercial, industrial areas, highways.
3. Mercury, metal halide, or high-pressure sodium, 400 to 1000 watt lamps.
4. Fixtures maintained by gantry.

HIGH MASTLIGHTING

1. 60 ft. to 100 ft. heights average.
2. Large areas—parking, recreational, highway interchanges.
3. Metal halide or high-pressure sodium, 1000 watt lamps.
4. Fixtures must lower for maintenance.

DEFINITIONS

A lumen is a unit used for measuring the amount of light energy given off by a light source. A footcandle is a unit used for measuring the amount of illumination on a surface. The amount of usable light from any given source is partially determined by the source's angle of incidence and the distance to the illuminated surface. See Chapter 1 on illumination.

NOTE

All exterior installations must be provided with ground fault interruption circuit.

RECOMMENDED LIGHTING LEVELS IN FOOTCANDLES

	COMMERCIAL	INTERMEDIATE	RESIDENTIAL
PEDESTRIAN AREAS			
Sidewalks	0.9	0.6	0.2
Pedestrian ways	2.0	1.0	0.5
VEHICULAR ROADS			
Freeway*	0.6	0.6	0.6
Major road and expressway*	2.0	1.4	1.0
Collector road	1.2	0.9	0.6
Local road	0.9	0.6	0.4
Alleys	0.6	0.4	0.2
PARKING AREAS			
Self-parking	1.0	–	–
Attendant parking	2.0	–	–
Security problem area	–	–	5.0
Minimum for television viewing of important interdiction areas	10.0	10.0	10.0
BUILDING AREAS			
Entrances	5.0	–	–
General grounds	1.0	–	–

*Both mainline and ramps.

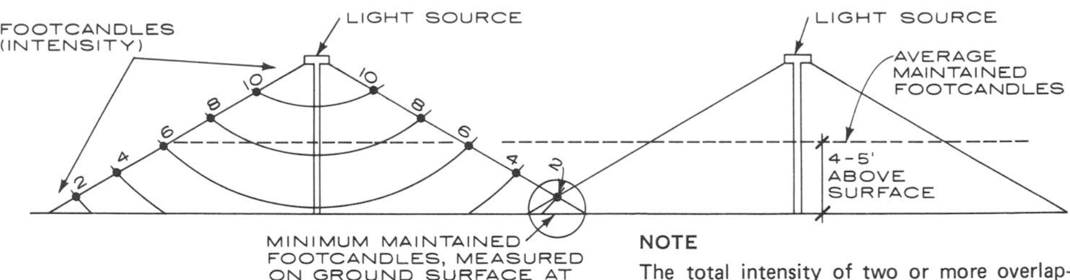
FOOTCANDLES (INTENSITY)
LIGHT SOURCE
2
4
6
8
10
MINIMUM MAINTAINED FOOTCANDLES, MEASURED ON GROUND SURFACE AT POINT OF LEAST ILLUMINATION
LIGHT SOURCE
AVERAGE MAINTAINED FOOTCANDLES
4-5' ABOVE SURFACE

NOTE

The total intensity of two or more overlapping light patterns equals the sum of their individual intensities.

MEASURING LIGHT INTENSITY IN FOOTCANDLES

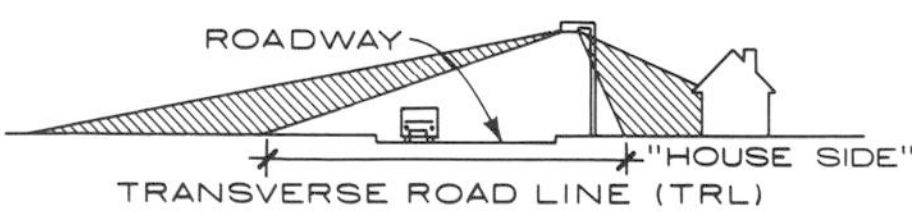
ROADWAY
"HOUSE SIDE"
TRANSVERSE ROAD LINE (TRL)

1. CUTOFF means that maximum of 10 percent of light source lumens fall outside of TRL area.
2. SEMICUTOFF means that maximum of 30 percent of light source lumens fall outside of the TRL area.
3. NONCUTOFF means that no control limitations exist.

CUTOFF TERMINOLOGY
(NOTE: "CUTOFF" IS MEASURED ALONG TRL.)

NOTE

Degree of cutoff is determined by one of the following:

(a) design of fixture housing
(b) incorporation of prismatic lens over light source
(c) addition of shield to fixture on "house side"

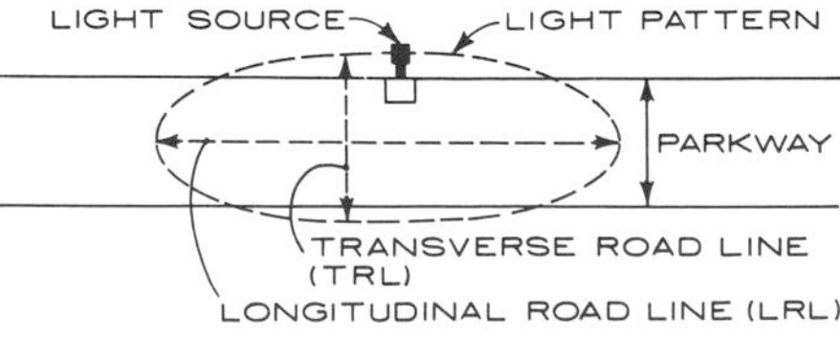
LIGHT SOURCE
LIGHT PATTERN
PARKWAY
TRANSVERSE ROAD LINE (TRL)
LONGITUDINAL ROAD LINE (LRL)

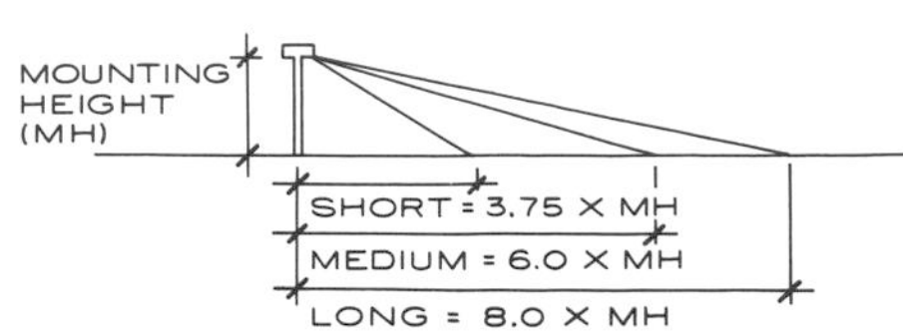
MOUNTING HEIGHT (MH)
SHORT = 3.75 X MH
MEDIUM = 6.0 X MH
LONG = 8.0 X MH

TYPES OF DISTRIBUTION
(NOTE: DISTRIBUTION IS MEASURED ALONG LRL)

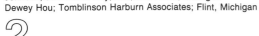

Johnson, Johnson & Roy, Inc.; Ann Arbor, Michigan
Dewey Hou; Tomblinson Harburn Associates; Flint, Michigan

BIKE PATH CLASSIFICATIONS

BIKE PATH (CLASS I BIKEWAY)

A bikeway physically separated from motorized vehicular traffic by an open space. It is located either within the roadway right-of-way or within an independent right-of-way (greenbelt).

BIKE LANE (CLASS II BIKEWAY)

A portion of a roadway that has been designated by lane stripes or traffic buttons, signs, or other pavement markings for the preferential or exclusive use of bicyclists.

BIKE ROUTE (CLASS III BIKEWAY)

A bikeway that shares the traffic right-of-way with motor vehicles and is designated only by signs. Bicycles are considered legal road vehicles, and bicyclists must obey all traffic laws. One-way bike travel only is permitted on a bike route.

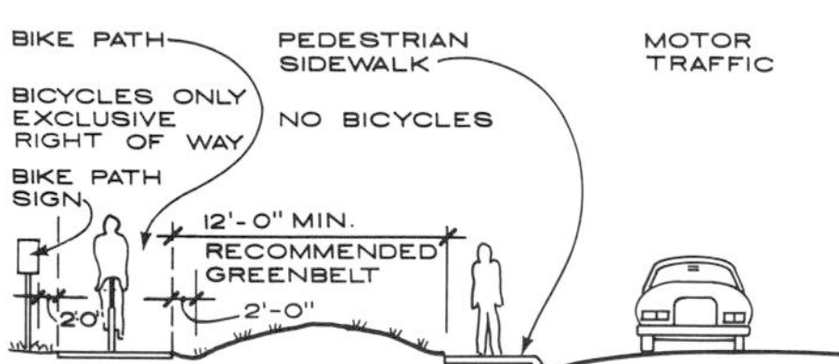
BIKE PATH
PEDESTRIAN SIDEWALK
MOTOR TRAFFIC
BICYCLES ONLY EXCLUSIVE RIGHT OF WAY
NO BICYCLES
BIKE PATH SIGN
12'-0" MIN. RECOMMENDED GREENBELT
2'-0"
2'-0"

CLASS I BIKEWAY

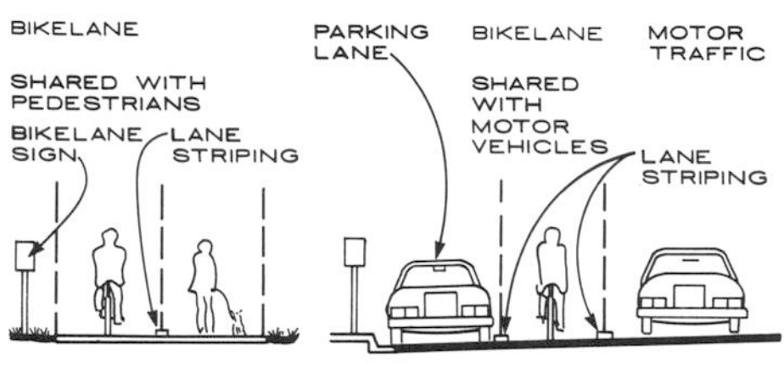
BIKELANE
PARKING LANE
BIKELANE
MOTOR TRAFFIC
SHARED WITH PEDESTRIANS
SHARED WITH MOTOR VEHICLES
BIKELANE SIGN
LANE STRIPING
LANE STRIPING

CLASS II BIKEWAY

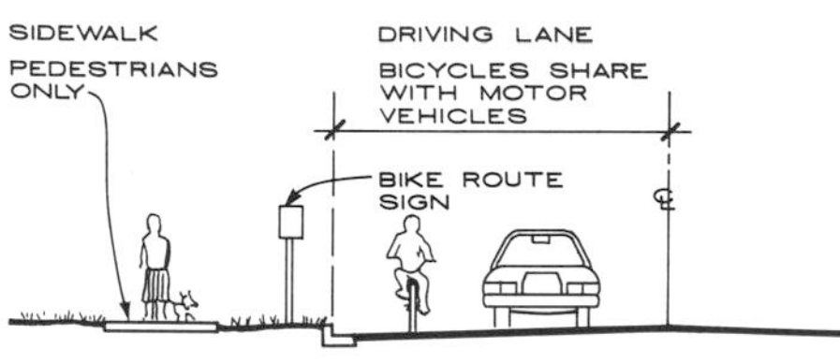
SIDEWALK
DRIVING LANE
PEDESTRIANS ONLY
BICYCLES SHARE WITH MOTOR VEHICLES
BIKE ROUTE SIGN

CLASS III BIKEWAY

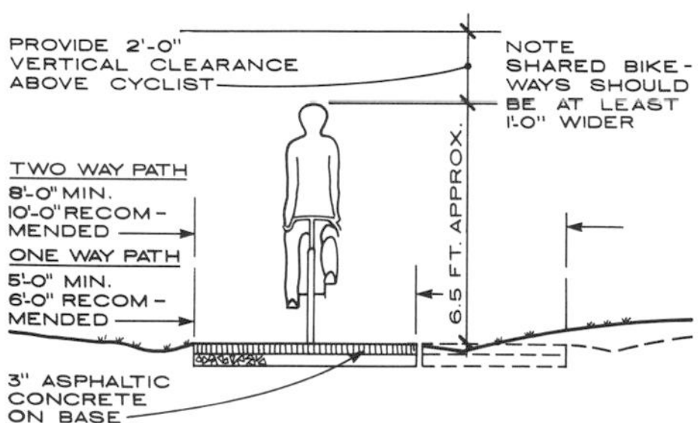
PROVIDE 2'-0" VERTICAL CLEARANCE ABOVE CYCLIST
NOTE SHARED BIKEWAYS SHOULD BE AT LEAST 1'-0" WIDER
TWO WAY PATH
8'-0" MIN.
10'-0" RECOMMENDED
ONE WAY PATH
5'-0" MIN.
6'-0" RECOMMENDED
6.5 FT. APPROX.
3" ASPHALTIC CONCRETE ON BASE

BIKEWAY CLEARANCE AND DIMENSIONS

HORIZONTAL, VERTICAL LAYOUT

Except in terrain where unavoidable, such as in mountains with numerous curves, long steep inclines should be avoided. Slopes of one percent to one-half percent have no significant effect on the use of bicycle paths by cyclists. Three percent slopes to 500 ft. are acceptable. Grades of six percent and more that are longer than 250 ft. will discourage bicycle path use except by expert cyclists using lightweight bicycles. Cyclists prefer straight or gently curving paths to circuitous, meandering paths.

PAVING SURFACE

Pavement must be smooth and durable, as 3 in. asphaltic concrete on a prepared subgrade or a minimum of 4 in. of crushed aggregate base (variable with climate and soil conditions). Concrete is satisfactory if it is well aligned. Tree root or frost heave displacement or differential settlement can create uneven paths in concrete unless doweling is provided.

TRAFFIC SAFETY

Class I Bikeways, with bicycles separated from motorized traffic, provide the most safety for cyclists. Class III Bikeways, dependent on signs, provide the least safety. They do not encourage bicycle use, but often are the only option in urban areas. On Class II and Class III Bikeways hazards can arise from suddenly opened doors of parked cars and from cross-traffic turning into driveways. Bikeways beside pedestrian walks may get interference as walkers stray onto the designated bikeway.

INTERSECTIONS

The major safety problem with bikeways is at grade intersections where motor vehicles, pedestrians, and cyclists converge or cross each other. The best solution is to provide a grade-separated intersection with an underpass or overpass planned as a part of a Class I Bikeway. Other possibilities include:

1. Provide a clearly defined mid-block crossing.
2. Merge bicycles and pedestrians a minimum of 100 ft. from four-way intersections using warning signs for both.
3. Provide warning signs for motorists approaching intersections where bikeways cross.
4. Provide and maintain adequate lighting.
5. Control planting and trimming of trees and plants to provide adequate intersection visibility.
6. Provide electronically activated signals for high traffic volume intersections.
7. At busy intersections or during peak traffic periods, restrict bicycle left turns.

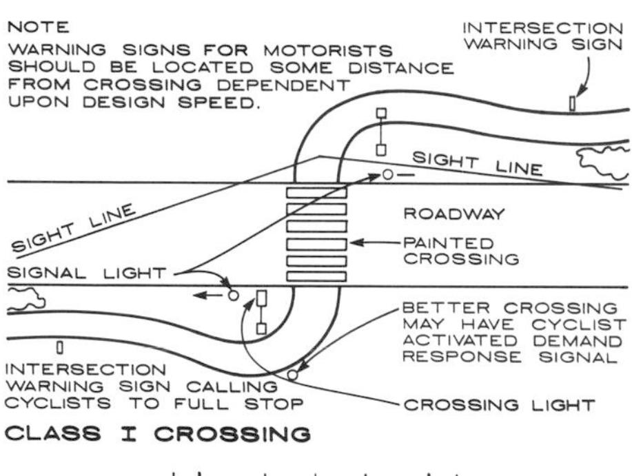
NOTE
WARNING SIGNS FOR MOTORISTS SHOULD BE LOCATED SOME DISTANCE FROM CROSSING DEPENDENT UPON DESIGN SPEED.
INTERSECTION WARNING SIGN
SIGHT LINE
SIGHT LINE
ROADWAY
PAINTED CROSSING
SIGNAL LIGHT
BETTER CROSSING MAY HAVE CYCLIST ACTIVATED DEMAND RESPONSE SIGNAL
INTERSECTION WARNING SIGN CALLING CYCLISTS TO FULL STOP
CROSSING LIGHT

CLASS I CROSSING

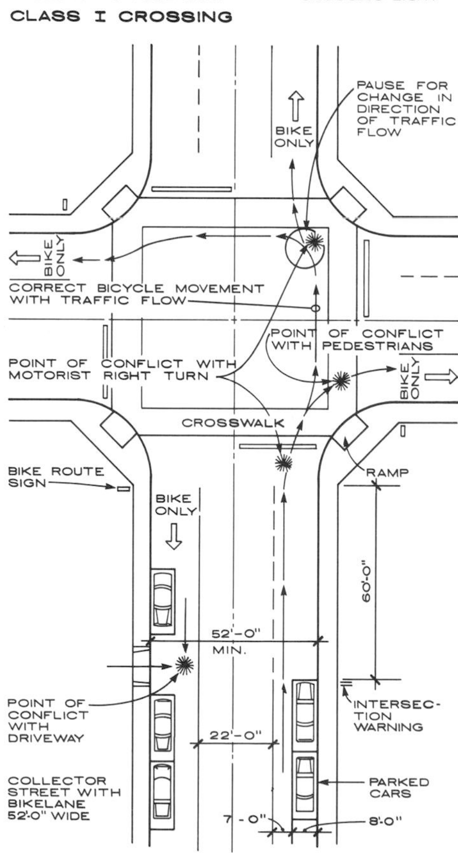
PAUSE FOR CHANGE IN DIRECTION OF TRAFFIC FLOW
BIKE ONLY
BIKE ONLY
CORRECT BICYCLE MOVEMENT WITH TRAFFIC FLOW
POINT OF CONFLICT WITH PEDESTRIANS
POINT OF CONFLICT WITH MOTORIST RIGHT TURN
BIKE ONLY
CROSSWALK
BIKE ROUTE SIGN
RAMP
BIKE ONLY
60'-0"
52'-0" MIN.
POINT OF CONFLICT WITH DRIVEWAY
INTERSECTION WARNING
22'-0"
COLLECTOR STREET WITH BIKELANE 52'-0" WIDE
PARKED CARS
7'-0"
8'-0"

CLASS II INTERSECTION

BICYCLE PARKING

Bicycle parking should be close to, but not obstructing, the main entrances to buildings. Where feasible, parking should be visible from the interior of a building or CCTV monitored. Good exterior lighting is important.

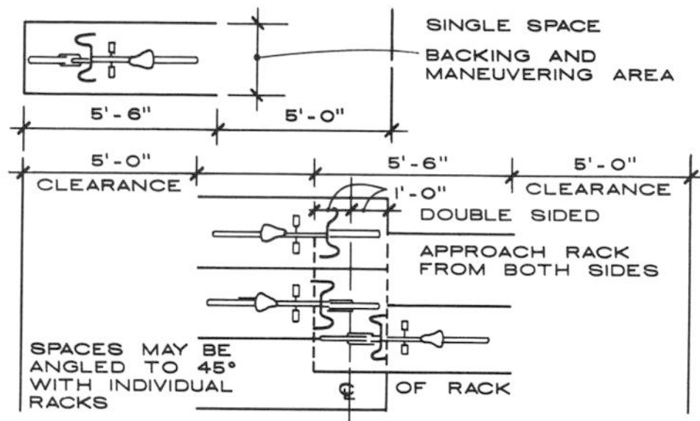
SINGLE SPACE
BACKING AND MANEUVERING AREA
5'-6"
5'-0"
5'-0" CLEARANCE
5'-6"
5'-0" CLEARANCE
1'-0"
DOUBLE SIDED
APPROACH RACK FROM BOTH SIDES
SPACES MAY BE ANGLED TO 45° WITH INDIVIDUAL RACKS
℄ OF RACK

BICYCLE PARKING SPACES

Theft of bicycles, bicycle wheels, and accessories has become a significant problem. All bicycle parking devices must have provisions for locking mechanisims. Cyclists usually provide the locks. Coin-operated locks also are available on some devices. Case-hardened chains or high strength cable with heavy duty padlocks, or bar locks must be accommodated at the parking device. Parking devices shown are classified by the amount of theft protection offered.

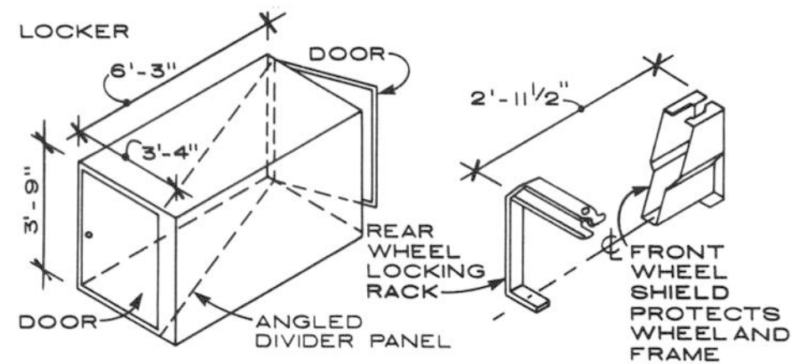
LOCKER
6'-3"
DOOR
2'-11½"
3'-4"
3'-9"
REAR WHEEL LOCKING RACK
FRONT WHEEL SHIELD PROTECTS WHEEL AND FRAME
DOOR
ANGLED DIVIDER PANEL

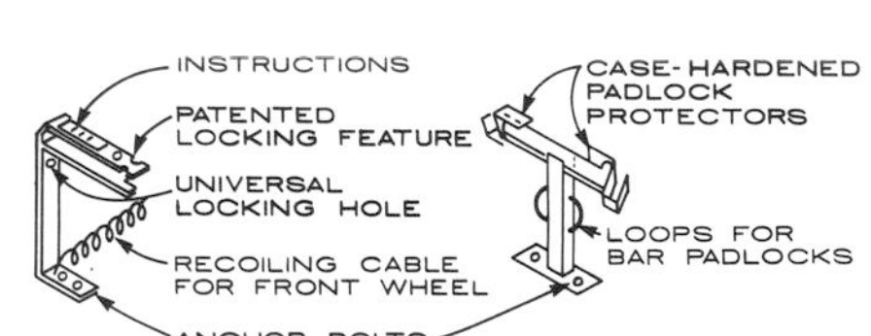
INSTRUCTIONS
PATENTED LOCKING FEATURE
CASE-HARDENED PADLOCK PROTECTORS
UNIVERSAL LOCKING HOLE
LOOPS FOR BAR PADLOCKS
RECOILING CABLE FOR FRONT WHEEL
ANCHOR BOLTS

TYPE A - HIGH PROTECTION

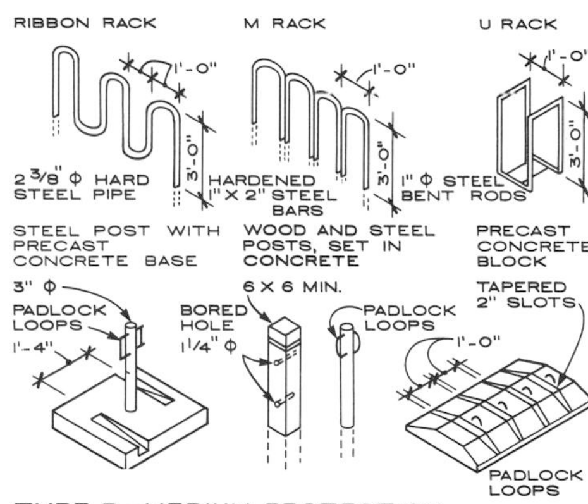
RIBBON RACK
M RACK
U RACK
1'-0"
1'-0"
1'-0"
3'-0"
3'-0"
3'-0"
2 3/8" Φ HARD STEEL PIPE
HARDENED 1" X 2" STEEL BARS
1" Φ STEEL BENT RODS
STEEL POST WITH PRECAST CONCRETE BASE
WOOD AND STEEL POSTS, SET IN CONCRETE
PRECAST CONCRETE BLOCK
3" Φ
6 X 6 MIN.
TAPERED 2" SLOTS
PADLOCK LOOPS
BORED HOLE 1 1/4" Φ
PADLOCK LOOPS
1'-4"
1'-0"
PADLOCK LOOPS

TYPE B - MEDIUM PROTECTION

All parking devices mentioned above must be constructed of hardened steel resistant to hacksaws and hammers. All must be anchored securely in concrete foundations or set with nonremovable bolts.

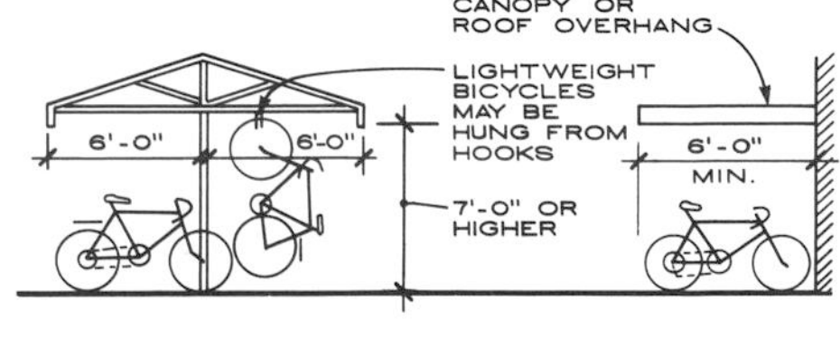
CANOPY OR ROOF OVERHANG
LIGHTWEIGHT BICYCLES MAY BE HUNG FROM HOOKS
6'-0"
6'-0"
6'-0" MIN.
7'-0" OR HIGHER

SHELTERS FOR BICYCLES

H. Thomas Wilson, AIA; Pasadena, California

Bicycle facilities designs courtesy of Rally Racks, Canterbury Designs, Brandir International, Sunshine U-Lok Corp.

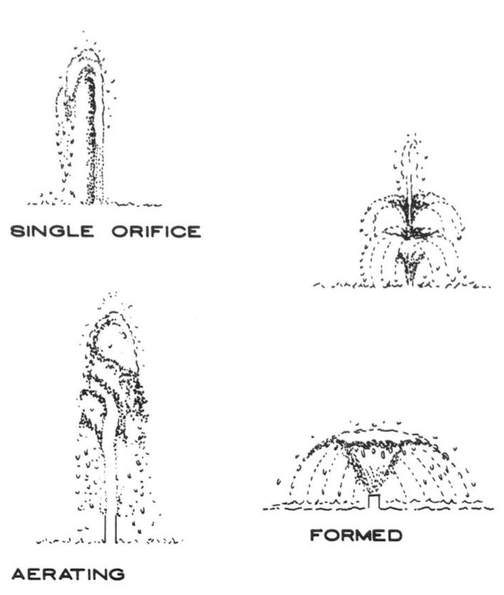
SINGLE ORIFICE
AERATING
FORMED

GENERAL JET TYPES

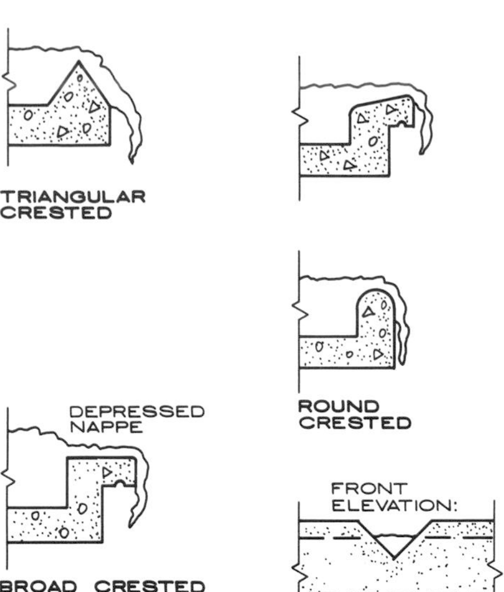
TRIANGULAR CRESTED
ROUND CRESTED
DEPRESSED NAPPE
BROAD CRESTED
FRONT ELEVATION:
'V' NOTCHED

WEIR SECTIONS

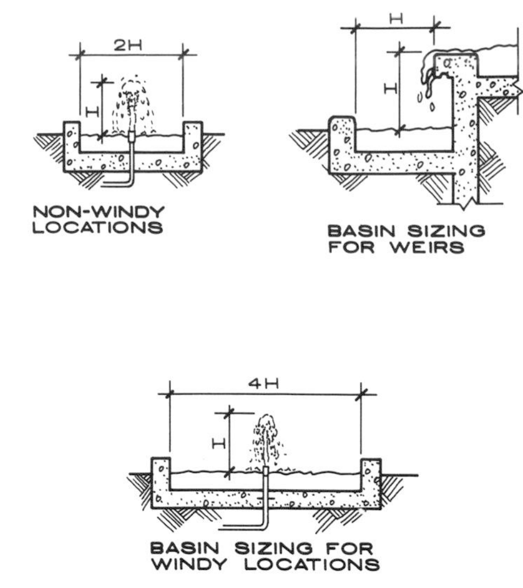
2H
H
NON-WINDY LOCATIONS
BASIN SIZING FOR WEIRS
4H
BASIN SIZING FOR WINDY LOCATIONS

BASIN SIZING FOR FOUNTAINS

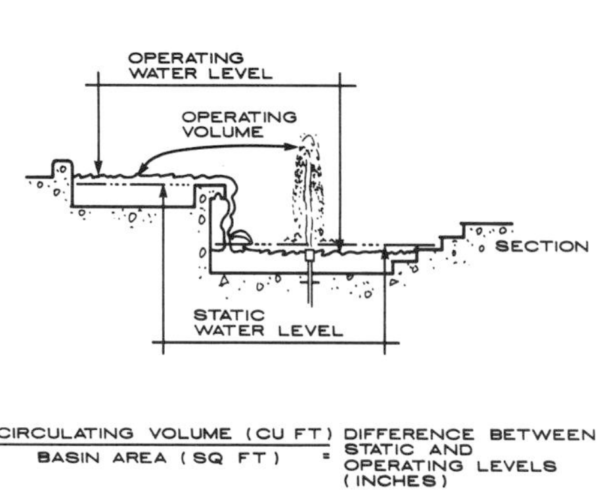
OPERATING WATER LEVEL
OPERATING VOLUME
SECTION
STATIC WATER LEVEL
CIRCULATING VOLUME (CU FT) / BASIN AREA (SQ FT) = DIFFERENCE BETWEEN STATIC AND OPERATING LEVELS (INCHES)

STATIC AND OPERATING LEVELS OF FOUNTAINS

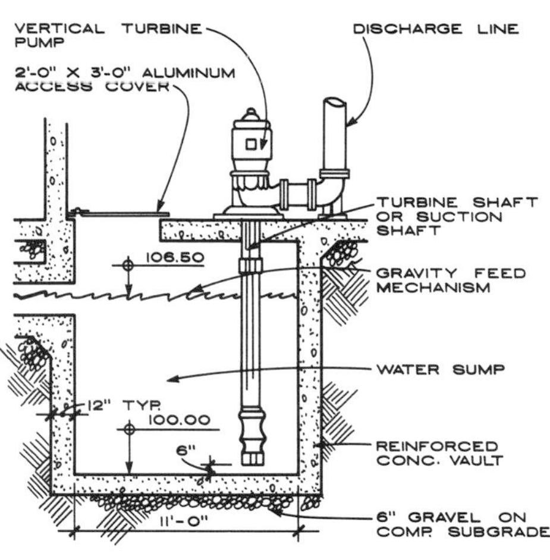
VERTICAL TURBINE PUMP
2'-0" X 3'-0" ALUMINUM ACCESS COVER
DISCHARGE LINE
TURBINE SHAFT OR SUCTION SHAFT
106.50
GRAVITY FEED MECHANISM
WATER SUMP
12" TYP
100.00
6"
REINFORCED CONC. VAULT
11'-0"
6" GRAVEL ON COMP. SUBGRADE

VERTICAL TURBINE PUMP

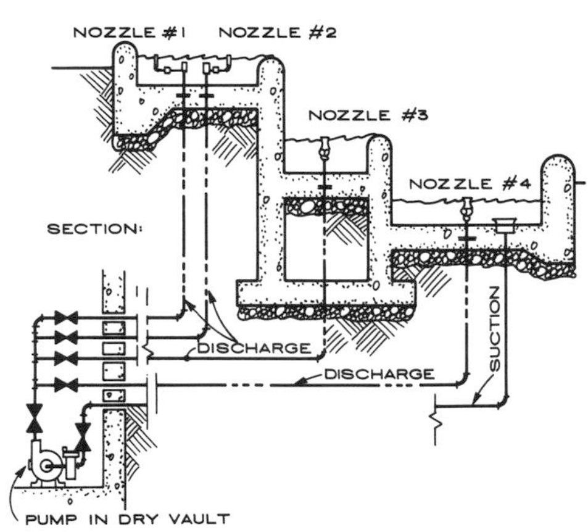
NOZZLE #1
NOZZLE #2
NOZZLE #3
NOZZLE #4
SECTION:
DISCHARGE
DISCHARGE
SUCTION
PUMP IN DRY VAULT

PIPE SCHEMATIC – DRY CENTRIFUGAL PUMP

PURPOSE

Fountains can provide the following site considerations or program elements:

1. Recreation
2. An altered environment to increase comfort
3. Image
4. Visual focal point
5. An activities focal point
6. To frame views
7. Acoustical control

FORMS

1. Held water in pools and ponds. Form and reflectivity are design considerations.
2. Falling water. The effect depends on water velocity, water volume, container surface, or the edge over or through which the water is moving.
3. Flowing water. The visual effect of the same volume of flowing water can be changed by narrowing or widening a channel, by placing objects in its path, by changing the direction of the flow, and by changing the slope and roughness of the bottom and sides.
4. Jets. An effect derived by forcing water into the air to create a pattern. Jet types include single orifice nozzles, aerated nozzles, and formed jets.
5. Surge. An effect created by a contrast between relatively quiet water and a surge (a wave or a splash), made by quickly adding water, by raising or lowering an object in the water, by moving an object back and forth through the water, or by introducing strong air currents.

OVERALL DESIGN CONSIDERATIONS

1. Scale. Size of the water feature in context to the surroundings.
2. Basin sizing: Width—consider fountain height and prevailing winds. Depth—consider weight (1 cu. ft. water = 62.366 lbs.). Safety—consider children playing near or in the pool. Cover—allow space for lights, nozzles, and pumps. Local codes may classify basins of a certain depth as swimming pools. Nozzle spray may be cushioned to prevent excessive surge.
3. Bottom appearance is important when clear water is maintained. It can be enhanced by patterns, colors, materials, three-dimensional objects, or textures. Dark bottoms increase reflectivity.
4. Edges or copings. In designing the water's edge, consider the difference between the operating water level and the static water level. Loosely defined edges (as in a pond) make movement into the water possible both visually and physically. Clearly defined edges (as in a basin) use copings to delineate the water's edge.
5. Lips and weirs—A lip is an edge over which flowing water falls. A weir is a dam in the water to divert the water flow or to raise the water level. If volume and velocity are insufficient to break the surface tension, a reglet on the underside of the edge may overcome this problem.

MATERIAL SELECTION CRITERIA

1. Waterproof
2. Crack resistant
3. Weather resistant, durable
4. Stain resistant
5. Workable material appropriate for intended effect

GENERATION OF WATER PRESSURE

1. Elevated dam structures, used in early fountains, are not feasible today.
2. Submersible pumps, used for low volume fountains only, are easy to install and require short pipe runs. The pump must be covered with water to operate correctly; it may be damaged if the water level drops. Vandalism can be a problem. Motors range from 1/20 to 1 horsepower.
3. Dry centrifugal pumps are used most commonly for larger water features. Motors range from 1/4 to 100 horsepower. The assembly consists of a pump, electric motor, suction line, and discharge line. The pump and motor are located in an isolated dry vault.
4. Vertical turbine pumps usually are more energy efficient than pumps with suction lines because the pump uses no energy to move the water to the pump. Water flows to the pump by gravity and thus reduces the amount of work exerted by the pump. The assembly consists of a pump and motor, a water sump in the equipment vault, a gravity feed mechanism to the pump, and a discharge line.

Barry R. Thalden, AIA; Thalden Corporation; St. Louis, Missouri

SPRINKLER SYSTEMS

Spray: For residential or commercial planting beds, shrub areas, ground covers, and trees. Available in various arc and strip patterns. 2 in. to 12 in. pop-up shrub heads common. Recommended operating pressure: 20-50 psi.

Stream rotor: For residential or commercial small to large turf areas, slopes, ground covers, and planting beds. Available in various arc patterns. 3 in. to 12 in. pop-up shrub heads common. Recommended operating pressure: 35-60 psi.

Rotory (gear driven): For residential or commercial large turf areas, sports fields, parks, and cemeteries. Available in various arc patterns. 2 in. to 4 in. pop-up and shrub heads common. Recommended operating pressure: 25-90 psi.

Agricultural: For dust control, ground cover, nurseries, and frost protection. Available in different trajectory angles and nozzle volumes. Recommended operating pressure: 20-100 psi.

Drip: For special residential, commercial, and agricultural problems such as hillsides or individual plantings, or where excessive runoff, overspray, and wasted water are problems. Recommended operating pressure: 10-40 psi.

DESIGN FACTORS

Supply line size, meter, available water pressure, code restrictions, type and scale of growing material, and soil conditions govern the type of system, spray heads, and pipe size used.

TYPES OF CONTROL SYSTEMS

Quick coupler: This system normally is under pressure. A key is inserted into a spray head where water is needed.

Manual: This system is turned on with a valve, all heads in place.

Automatic: The two basic types are hydraulic, in which the signal between the controller and the valves is transmitted through fluid pressure in control tubing, and electric, in which the signal is transmitted to the valves directly through buried wire. Electric is the more common system. It is operated from a central control unit.

PIPE

Polyvinyl chloride or polyethylene piping, easily cut and connected, commonly is used. Steel and copper pipe also are used. Pipe sleeves should be preset under walks and through walls for ease of installation and future extension of the system.

PRECIPITATION RATES

The amount of water applied to turf areas must be adjusted according to the species of grass, the traffic it receives, subsoil conditions, and surface gradient.

BACKFLOW PREVENTERS

A cross-connection device protects the potable water supply from contaminants caused by backsiphonage or backpressure. Many state and local plumbing codes require the use of such a device on an irrigation system. Types of cross-connections include atmospheric vacuum breakers, pressure vacuum breakers, double check valves, and reduced pressure valves.

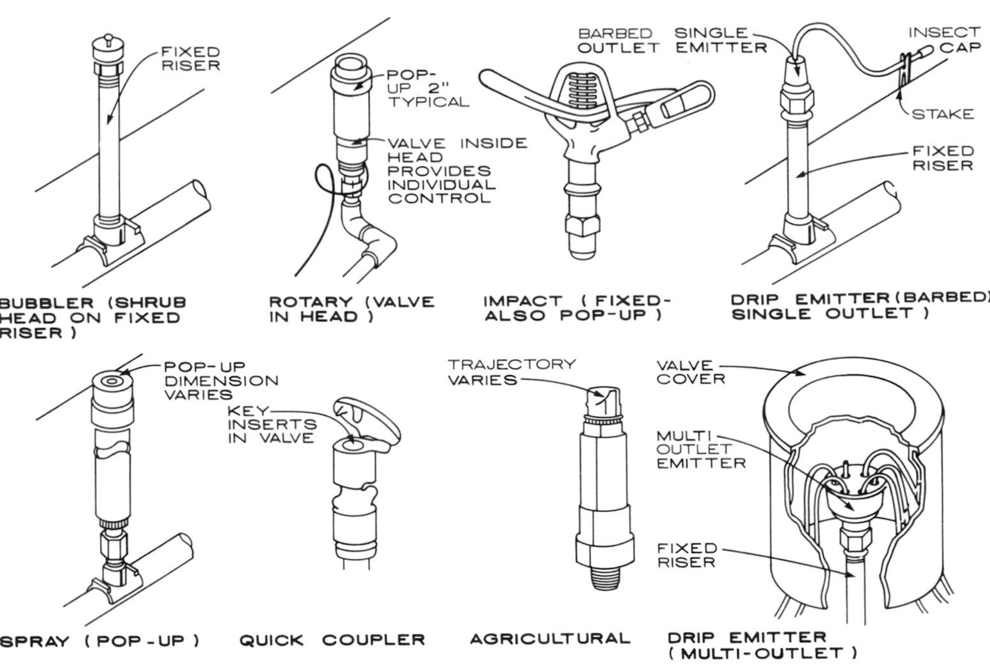
FIXED RISER
POP-UP 2" TYPICAL
VALVE INSIDE HEAD PROVIDES INDIVIDUAL CONTROL
BARBED OUTLET
SINGLE EMITTER
INSECT CAP
STAKE
FIXED RISER
POP-UP DIMENSION VARIES
KEY INSERTS IN VALVE
TRAJECTORY VARIES
VALVE COVER
MULTI OUTLET EMITTER
FIXED RISER

BUBBLER (SHRUB HEAD ON FIXED RISER) ROTARY (VALVE IN HEAD) IMPACT (FIXED-ALSO POP-UP) DRIP EMITTER (BARBED) SINGLE OUTLET)

SPRAY (POP-UP) QUICK COUPLER AGRICULTURAL DRIP EMITTER (MULTI-OUTLET)

SPRAY HEADS

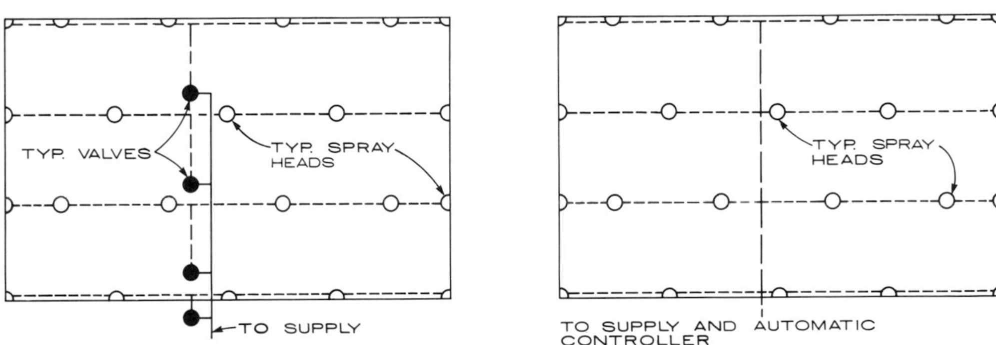
TYP. VALVES
TYP. SPRAY HEADS
TO SUPPLY
TYP. SPRAY HEADS
TO SUPPLY AND AUTOMATIC CONTROLLER

VALVE IN HEAD PROVIDES INDIVIDUAL HEAD CONTROL FOR MAXIMUM FLEXIBILITY TO FIT TURF USE, TOPOGRAPHY, AND SOIL.

BLOCK SYSTEM VALVE IN HEAD

TYPICAL LAYOUTS

35° TRAJECTORY
10° TRAJECTORY
0° TRAJECTORY

TYPICAL TRAJECTORIES

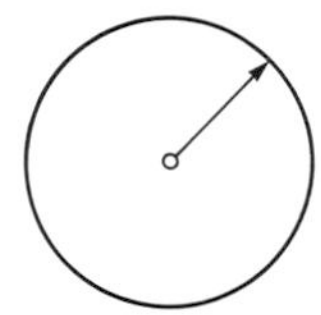

360° CIRCLE

OTHER TYPICAL PATTERNS AVAILABLE ARE 90°, 120°, 180°, 240°, AND 270°. SPECIAL ARCS ARE ALSO AVAILABLE

RADIUS DIMENSIONS VARY FROM 6' WITH SPRAY HEADS TO 100' WITH ROTARY HEADS.

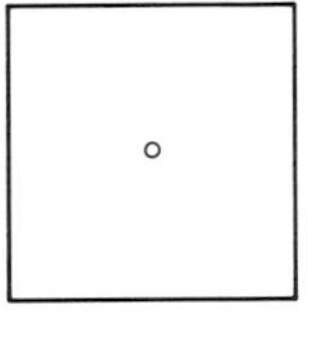

FULL SQUARE (SPECIAL)

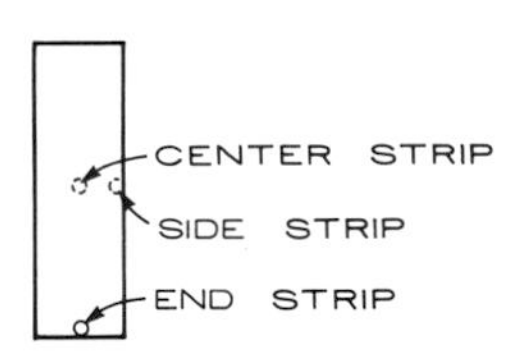
CENTER STRIP
SIDE STRIP
END STRIP

RECTANGLE (SPECIAL)

NOZZLE PATTERNS

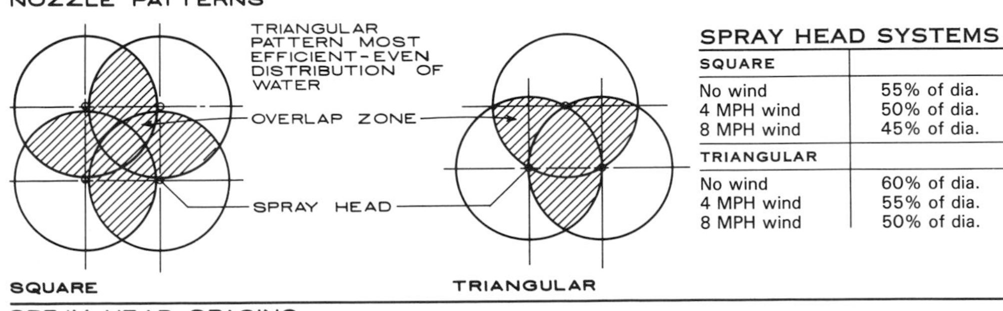
TRIANGULAR PATTERN MOST EFFICIENT-EVEN DISTRIBUTION OF WATER
OVERLAP ZONE
SPRAY HEAD

SPRAY HEAD SYSTEMS	
SQUARE	
No wind	55% of dia.
4 MPH wind	50% of dia.
8 MPH wind	45% of dia.
TRIANGULAR	
No wind	60% of dia.
4 MPH wind	55% of dia.
8 MPH wind	50% of dia.

SQUARE TRIANGULAR

SPRAY HEAD SPACING

Robert K. Sherrill; Wilkes, Faulkner, Jenkins & Bass; Washington, D.C.

GROWTH AND DEVELOPMENT

As children grow their physical abilities change, as does the scale of equipment that will challenge them. Physical growth is accommodated by social development resulting in different levels and types of interaction and activity. A child's play experience must be successful as well as challenging. Therefore play equipment should be designed and selected to meet the physical and intellectual requirements of groups that will use it. The height, distance between levels, and the ability and strength required to use the equipment should be scaled to the size and level of social and intellectual development of the child.

SINGLE UNIT VS. INTEGRATED PLAY EQUIPMENT

Many types of play equipment are designed to stand alone as units. While they may often be linked to other equipment, they are generally single activity items. Where space or other conditions limit the scope of development such equipment is useful. However, since activity proceeds in a continuous flow, integrated play areas have proved to be more successful than arrangements of individual items. Linking of equipment and equipment that combines several activities on one structure increase the options available to the user and tend to increase the interest and challenge.

PLAY COMPONENTS

Several basic elements are used to create play equipment. The most commonly employed include slides (standard, spiral, tube, rail, roller, and pole), swings (standard and tire), ladders (vertical, horizontal, chain net, cables, and arch), climbers (stepped wood posts, stacks, arch, chain, rungs, tire, and rope), and miscellaneous components (decks, panels, log rollers, spring pads, balance beams, parallel bars, rings, and clatter bridges).

INTEGRATED PLAY STRUCTURES

Manufacturers offer predesigned arrangements, using a variety of play components to provide a multitude of ways to serve groups of 5 to 75 children. These systems are available in timber and powder-coated steel. Both offer modular construction, ease of installation, durability, and a variety of accessories, most of which are common to each. Plan space requirements on the number of children expected to use such a structure at one time. Allot each child about 65 to 70 sq. ft., which includes a 4 ft. safety zone around the structure.

SAFETY CONCERNS

No playground or play activity is completely safe from all potential accidents because the element of risk is inherent in most play. To design an absolutely safe playground would remove all risk and thus would be counterproductive. Children would seek challenge elsewhere, usually where risk is unmanaged. As a goal, playground equipment should provide challenging activities in the safest way possible. Structures should be solidly built. Components should have rounded edges and corners. Metal fasteners should be covered or placed in recessed holes. Above all, playground equipment always should be installed on a bed of absorbing ground cover such as granulated pine bark (12 in. deep), pea gravel (10 in. deep), or sand (10 in. deep). Asphalt, packed dirt, or exposed concrete should never be an acceptable play surface. Manufacturers recommend a minimum of 4 ft. safety zone around the play area. Adequate seating space in clear view of all play equipment should be allotted for adults supervising children.

PLASTIC-COATED ALUM. ROLLERS WITH SELF-LUBRICATED NONMETALLIC BEARINGS
RECTANGULAR STEEL SIDE RAILS
ROLLER SLIDES CANNOT BE INSTALLED WHERE GRAVEL IS USED AS A GROUND COVER
ROLLER SLIDE
MOLDED STRUCTURAL FOAM PLASTIC (CAN BE STL)
MOLDED PLASTIC SEGMENTS - CURVED SECTIONS AVAILABLE
PIPE SUPPORT (COATED)
5" ⌀ STEEL TUBE (COATED)
SPIRAL SLIDE
TUNNEL SLIDE

ALSO AVAILABLE ARE STANDARD STAINLESS STEEL AND PLASTIC SLIDES. HEIGHTS AND LENGTHS VARY. CONSULT MANUFACTURERS' DATA FOR SPECIFIC AVAILABILITY AND INFORMATION.

SLIDES

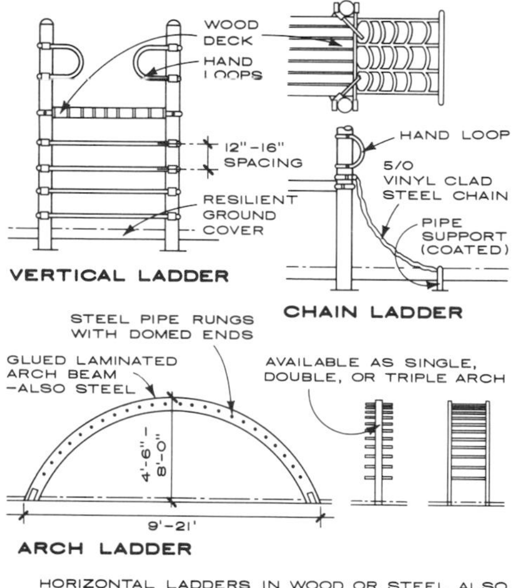

WOOD DECK
HAND LOOPS
12"-16" SPACING
RESILIENT GROUND COVER
VERTICAL LADDER
HAND LOOP
5/0 VINYL CLAD STEEL CHAIN
PIPE SUPPORT (COATED)
CHAIN LADDER
STEEL PIPE RUNGS WITH DOMED ENDS
GLUED LAMINATED ARCH BEAM -ALSO STEEL
AVAILABLE AS SINGLE, DOUBLE, OR TRIPLE ARCH
4'-6" - 8'-0"
9'-21'
ARCH LADDER

HORIZONTAL LADDERS IN WOOD OR STEEL ALSO ARE AVAILABLE IN VARIOUS DESIGNS.

LADDERS

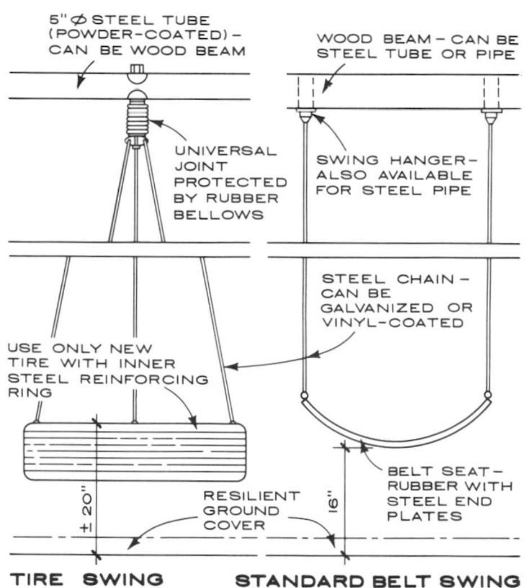

5" ⌀ STEEL TUBE (POWDER-COATED) - CAN BE WOOD BEAM
WOOD BEAM - CAN BE STEEL TUBE OR PIPE
UNIVERSAL JOINT PROTECTED BY RUBBER BELLOWS
SWING HANGER- ALSO AVAILABLE FOR STEEL PIPE
STEEL CHAIN - CAN BE GALVANIZED OR VINYL-COATED
USE ONLY NEW TIRE WITH INNER STEEL REINFORCING RING
BELT SEAT- RUBBER WITH STEEL END PLATES
RESILIENT GROUND COVER
±20"
16"
TIRE SWING
STANDARD BELT SWING

OPTIONAL SEATS FOR STANDARD SWING INCLUDE FULL OR PARTIAL BUCKET SEATS, FLAT MOLDED RUBBER SEATS, AND MOLDED CONTOUR CHAIRS.

SWINGS

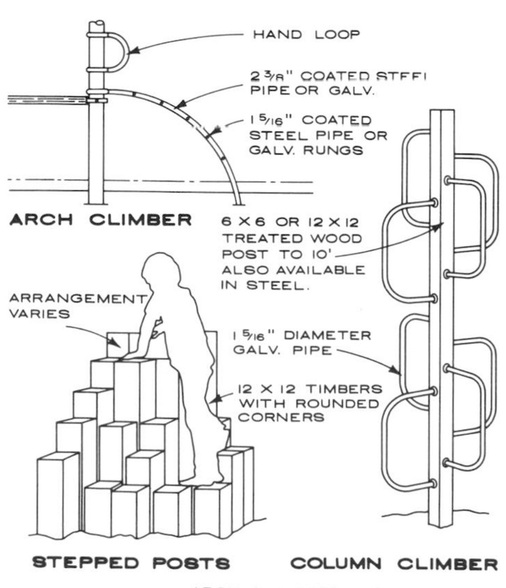

HAND LOOP
2 3/8" COATED STEEL PIPE OR GALV.
1 5/16" COATED STEEL PIPE OR GALV. RUNGS
ARCH CLIMBER
6 X 6 OR 12 X 12 TREATED WOOD POST TO 10' ALSO AVAILABLE IN STEEL.
ARRANGEMENT VARIES
1 5/16" DIAMETER GALV. PIPE
12 X 12 TIMBERS WITH ROUNDED CORNERS
STEPPED POSTS
COLUMN CLIMBER

ARCH CLIMBERS ALSO AVAILABLE IN TIMBER DESIGNS.

CLIMBERS

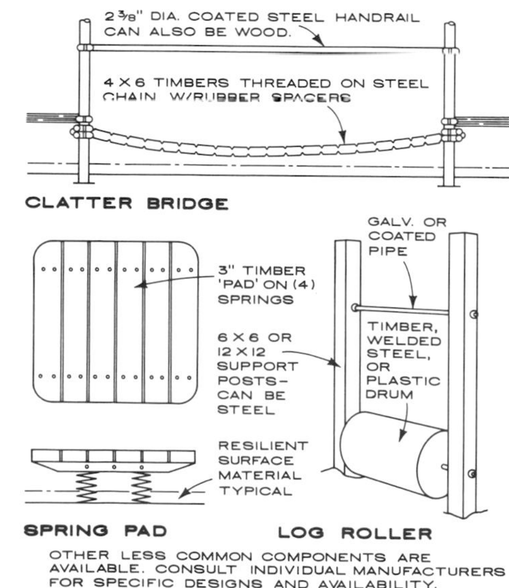

2 3/8" DIA. COATED STEEL HANDRAIL CAN ALSO BE WOOD.
4 X 6 TIMBERS THREADED ON STEEL CHAIN W/RUBBER SPACERS
CLATTER BRIDGE
3" TIMBER 'PAD' ON (4) SPRINGS
6 X 6 OR 12 X 12 SUPPORT POSTS- CAN BE STEEL
RESILIENT SURFACE MATERIAL TYPICAL
GALV. OR COATED PIPE
TIMBER, WELDED STEEL, OR PLASTIC DRUM
SPRING PAD
LOG ROLLER

OTHER LESS COMMON COMPONENTS ARE AVAILABLE. CONSULT INDIVIDUAL MANUFACTURERS FOR SPECIFIC DESIGNS AND AVAILABILITY.

MISCELLANEOUS

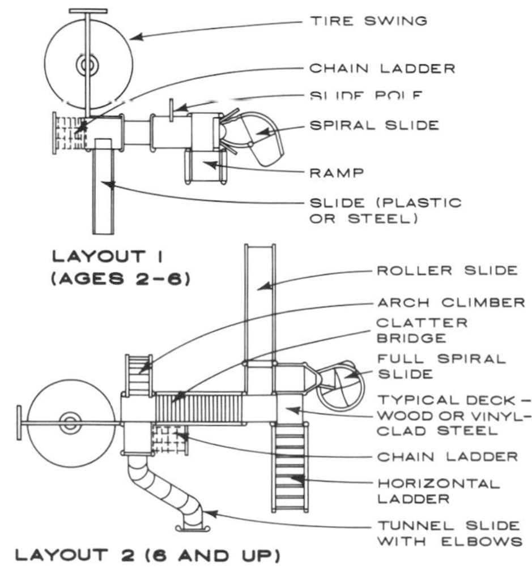

TIRE SWING
CHAIN LADDER
SLIDE POLE
SPIRAL SLIDE
RAMP
SLIDE (PLASTIC OR STEEL)
LAYOUT 1 (AGES 2-6)
ROLLER SLIDE
ARCH CLIMBER
CLATTER BRIDGE
FULL SPIRAL SLIDE
TYPICAL DECK - WOOD OR VINYL-CLAD STEEL
CHAIN LADDER
HORIZONTAL LADDER
TUNNEL SLIDE WITH ELBOWS
LAYOUT 2 (6 AND UP)

LAYOUTS SHOWN SERVE AS EXAMPLES ONLY. OPTIONAL LAYOUTS ARE PRACTICALLY INFINITE. CONSULT MANUFACTURERS' DATA FOR SPECIFIC ARRANGEMENTS.

INTEGRATED PLAYSYSTEMS

Robert K. Sherrill; Wilkes, Faulkner, Jenkins & Bass; Washington, D.C.

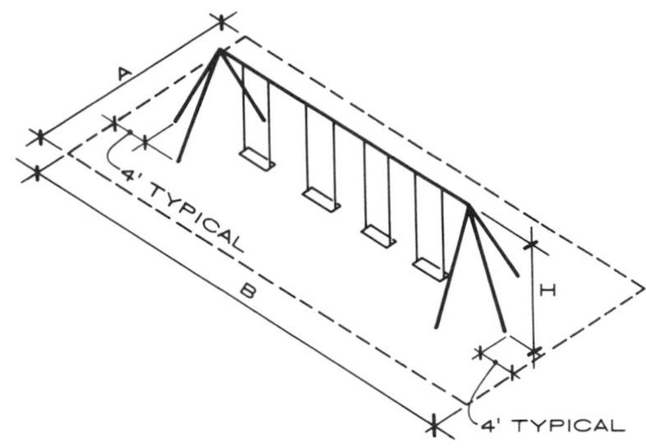
A
B
H
4' TYPICAL
4' TYPICAL

SWINGS

		SAFETY ZONE	
SWINGS	H (FT)	A (FT)	B (FT)
2	8	24	27
	10	28	27
	12	32	27
3	8	24	30
	10	28	30
	12	32	30
4	8	24	40
	10	28	40
	12	32	40
6	8	24	46
	10	28	46
	12	32	46
8	8	24	57
	10	28	57
	12	32	57
9	8	24	61
	10	28	61
	12	32	61

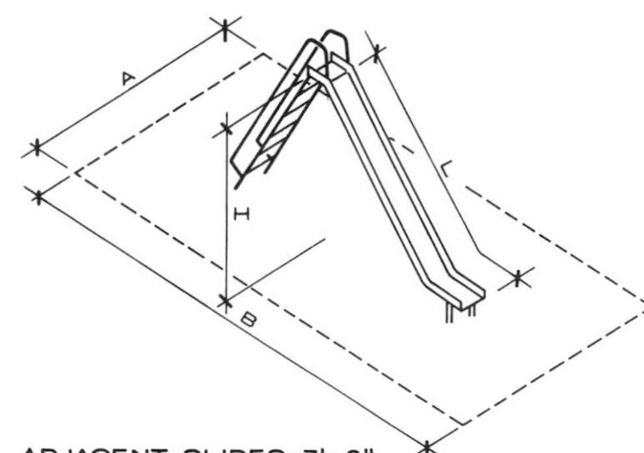
A
B
H
L

ADJACENT SLIDES: 7'-6" (CHUTES C.TO C.) OTHERS 10' O.C.

SLIDES

		SAFETY ZONE	
H	L	A	B
4	8	26	24
5	10	26	28
6	12	26	32
8	16	26	36

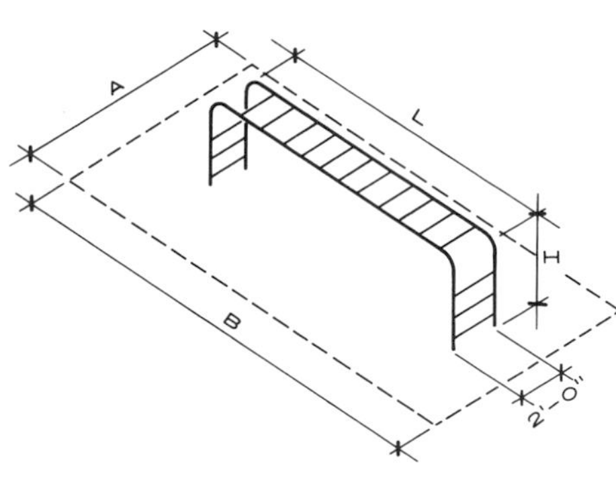
A
B
L
H
2'-0"

HORIZONTAL LADDER

		SAFETY ZONE	
H (FT-IN.)	L (FT-IN.)	A (FT)	B (FT)
6-6	12-6	14	25
7-6	16-0	14	30

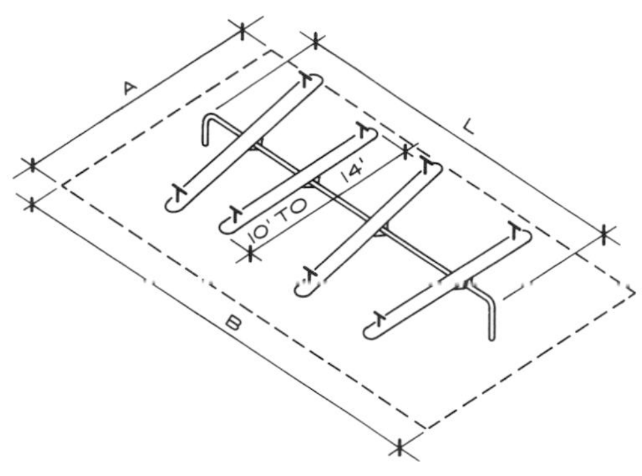
A
B
L
10' TO 14'

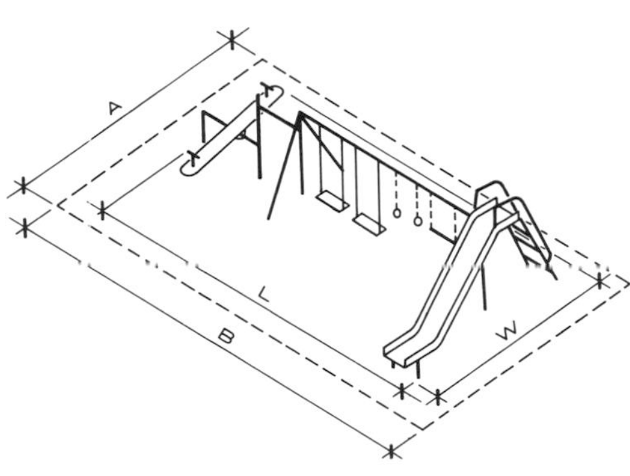
A
B
L
W

GENERAL PLANNING INFORMATION

EQUIPMENT	AREA (SQ FT)	CAPACITY (NUMBER OF CHILDREN)
Slide	450	4-6
Low swing	150	1
High swing	250	1
Horizontal ladder	375	6-8
Seesaw	100	2
Junior climbing gym	180	8-10
General climbing gym	500	15-20

SEESAWS

BOARDS	1	2	3	4	6
L	3	6	9	12	18
A	20	20	20	20	20
B	5	10	15	20	25

COMBINATION UNITS*

ENCLOSURE LIMITS
A = W + 12'-0" B = L + 6'-0"

*Types and no. of units are variable.

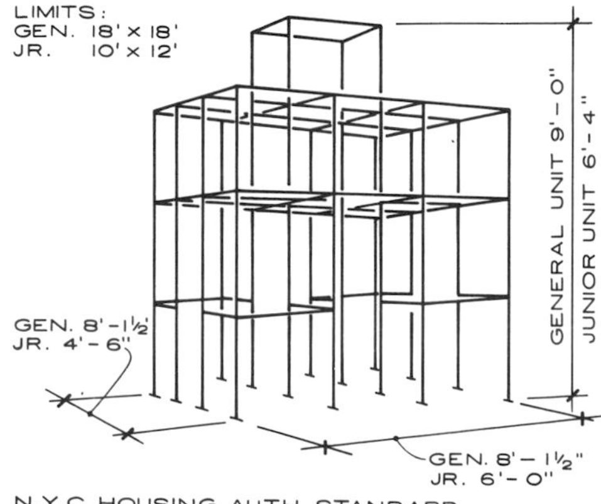
LIMITS:
GEN. 18' x 18'
JR. 10' x 12'
GENERAL UNIT 9'-0"
JUNIOR UNIT 6'-4"
GEN. 8'-1½"
JR. 4'-6"
GEN. 8'-1½"
JR. 6'-0"

N.Y.C. HOUSING AUTH. STANDARD

CLIMBING GYM

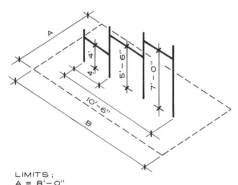

LIMITS;
A = 8'-0"
B = L + 6'-0" HEIGHTS ADJUSTABLE

HORIZONTAL BARS

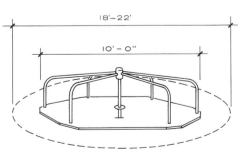

10 FT DIA. IS CONSIDERED STANDARD
OTHER DIA. = 6' AND 8'

SPIN AROUND

Robert K. Sherrill; Wilkes, Faulkner, Jenkins & Bass; Washington, D.C.
Vincent F. Nauseda; Sasaki, Dawson Associates, Inc.; Watertown, Massachusetts

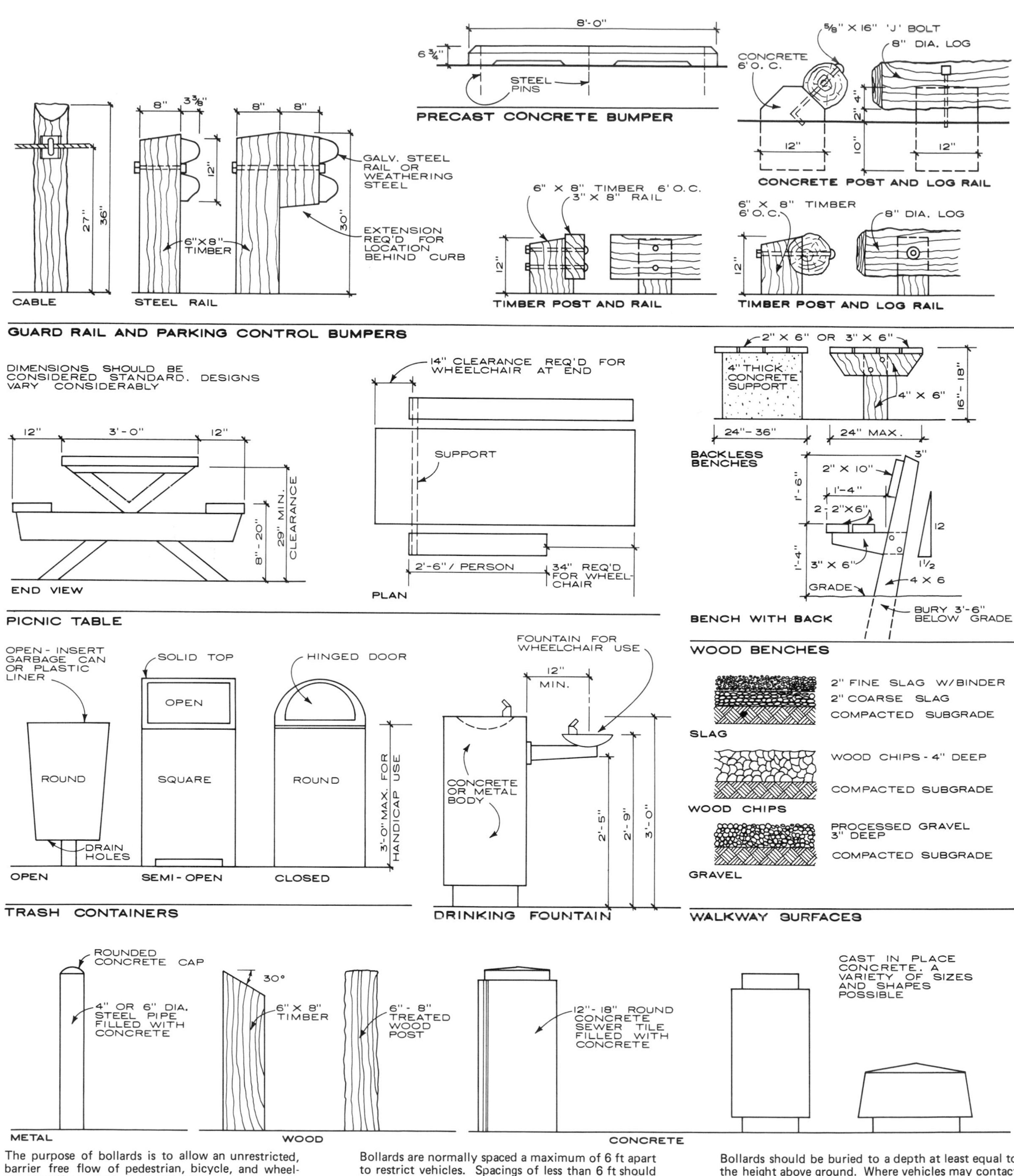
8'-0"
6 3/4"
STEEL PINS
PRECAST CONCRETE BUMPER
5/8" X 16" 'J' BOLT
8" DIA. LOG
CONCRETE 6' O. C.
2'-4"
12"
10"
12"
CONCRETE POST AND LOG RAIL
8"
3 3/8"
8"
8"
12"
GALV. STEEL RAIL OR WEATHERING STEEL
27"
36"
6"X8" TIMBER
30"
EXTENSION REQ'D FOR LOCATION BEHIND CURB
CABLE
STEEL RAIL
6" X 8" TIMBER 6' O.C.
3" X 8" RAIL
12"
TIMBER POST AND RAIL
6" X 8" TIMBER 6' O.C.
8" DIA. LOG
12"
TIMBER POST AND LOG RAIL
GUARD RAIL AND PARKING CONTROL BUMPERS
DIMENSIONS SHOULD BE CONSIDERED STANDARD. DESIGNS VARY CONSIDERABLY
12"
3'-0"
12"
8" - 20"
29" MIN. CLEARANCE
END VIEW
14" CLEARANCE REQ'D FOR WHEELCHAIR AT END
SUPPORT
2'-6" / PERSON
34" REQ'D FOR WHEEL-CHAIR
PLAN
PICNIC TABLE
2" X 6" OR 3" X 6"
4" THICK CONCRETE SUPPORT
4" X 6"
16" - 18"
24"- 36"
24" MAX.
BACKLESS BENCHES
3"
2" X 10"
1'-6"
1'-4"
2 - 2"X6"
12
1 1/2
1'-4"
3" X 6"
4 X 6
GRADE
BURY 3'-6" BELOW GRADE
BENCH WITH BACK
WOOD BENCHES
OPEN - INSERT GARBAGE CAN OR PLASTIC LINER
SOLID TOP
OPEN
HINGED DOOR
ROUND
SQUARE
ROUND
DRAIN HOLES
3'-0" MAX. FOR HANDICAP USE
OPEN
SEMI - OPEN
CLOSED
TRASH CONTAINERS
FOUNTAIN FOR WHEELCHAIR USE
12" MIN.
CONCRETE OR METAL BODY
2'-5"
2'-9"
3'-0"
DRINKING FOUNTAIN
2" FINE SLAG W/BINDER
2" COARSE SLAG
COMPACTED SUBGRADE
SLAG
WOOD CHIPS - 4" DEEP
COMPACTED SUBGRADE
WOOD CHIPS
PROCESSED GRAVEL 3" DEEP
COMPACTED SUBGRADE
GRAVEL
WALKWAY SURFACES
ROUNDED CONCRETE CAP
4" OR 6" DIA. STEEL PIPE FILLED WITH CONCRETE
30°
6" X 8" TIMBER
6" - 8" TREATED WOOD POST
12"- 18" ROUND CONCRETE SEWER TILE FILLED WITH CONCRETE
CAST IN PLACE CONCRETE. A VARIETY OF SIZES AND SHAPES POSSIBLE
METAL
WOOD
CONCRETE

The purpose of bollards is to allow an unrestricted, barrier free flow of pedestrian, bicycle, and wheelchair traffic, while restricting the passage of such vehicles as cars and trucks.

Bollards are normally spaced a maximum of 6 ft apart to restrict vehicles. Spacings of less than 6 ft should be determined in accordance with the height and mass of the unit for desired design effect.

Bollards should be buried to a depth at least equal to the height above ground. Where vehicles may contact the bollard, a concrete footing or encasement should be provided.

BOLLARDS

John M. Beckett; Beckett, Raeder, Rankin, Inc.; Ann Arbor, Michigan

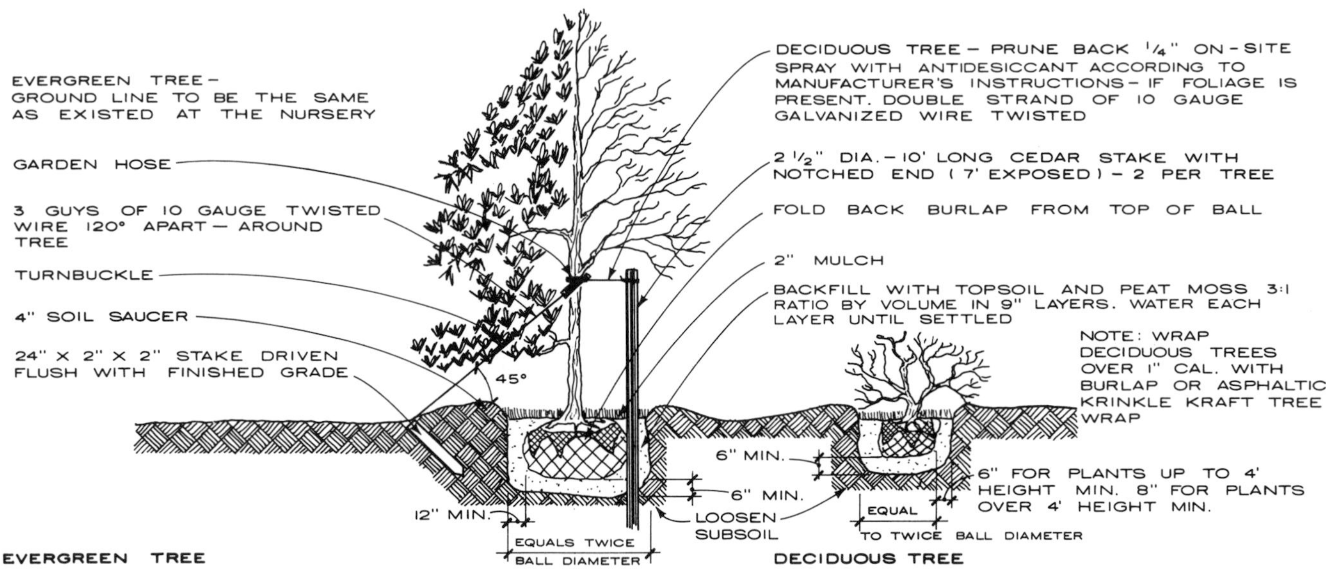
EVERGREEN TREE– GROUND LINE TO BE THE SAME AS EXISTED AT THE NURSERY
GARDEN HOSE
3 GUYS OF 10 GAUGE TWISTED WIRE 120° APART — AROUND TREE
TURNBUCKLE
4" SOIL SAUCER
24" X 2" X 2" STAKE DRIVEN FLUSH WITH FINISHED GRADE
45°
12" MIN.
EQUALS TWICE BALL DIAMETER
EVERGREEN TREE
DECIDUOUS TREE – PRUNE BACK 1/4" ON-SITE SPRAY WITH ANTIDESICCANT ACCORDING TO MANUFACTURER'S INSTRUCTIONS – IF FOLIAGE IS PRESENT. DOUBLE STRAND OF 10 GAUGE GALVANIZED WIRE TWISTED
2 1/2" DIA. – 10' LONG CEDAR STAKE WITH NOTCHED END (7' EXPOSED) – 2 PER TREE
FOLD BACK BURLAP FROM TOP OF BALL
2" MULCH
BACKFILL WITH TOPSOIL AND PEAT MOSS 3:1 RATIO BY VOLUME IN 9" LAYERS. WATER EACH LAYER UNTIL SETTLED
NOTE: WRAP DECIDUOUS TREES OVER 1" CAL. WITH BURLAP OR ASPHALTIC KRINKLE KRAFT TREE WRAP
6" MIN.
6" MIN.
LOOSEN SUBSOIL
6" FOR PLANTS UP TO 4' HEIGHT MIN. 8" FOR PLANTS OVER 4' HEIGHT MIN.
EQUAL TO TWICE BALL DIAMETER
DECIDUOUS TREE

PLANTING DETAILS — TREES AND SHRUBS

SHRUBS AND MINOR TREES BALLED AND BURLAPPED

HEIGHT RANGE (FT)	MINIMUM BALL DIAMETER (IN.)	MINIMUM BALL DEPTH (IN.)
1½–2	10	8
2–3	12	9
3–4	13	10
4–5	15	11
5–6	16	12
6–7	18	13
7–8	20	14
8–9	22	15
9–10	24	16
10–12	26	17

NOTE: Ball sizes should always be of a diameter to encompass the fibrous and feeding root system necessary for the full recovery of the plant.

STANDARD SHADE TREES—BALLED AND BURLAPPED

CALIPER* (IN.)	HEIGHT RANGE (FT)	MAXIMUM HEIGHTS (FT)	MINIMUM BALL DIAMETER (IN.)	MINIMUM BALL DEPTH (IN.)
½–¾	5-6	8	12	9
¾–1	6-8	10	14	10
1–1¼	7-9	11	16	12
1¼–1½	8-10	12	18	13
1½–1¾	10-12	14	20	14
1¾–2	10-12	14	22	15
2–2½	12-14	16	24	16
2½–3	12-14	16	28	19
3–3½	14-16	18	32	20
3½–4	14-16	18	36	22
4–5	16-18	22	44	26
5–6	18 and up	26	48	29

*Caliper indicates the diameter of the trunk taken 6 in. above the ground level up to and including 4 in. caliper size and 12 in. above the ground level for larger sizes.

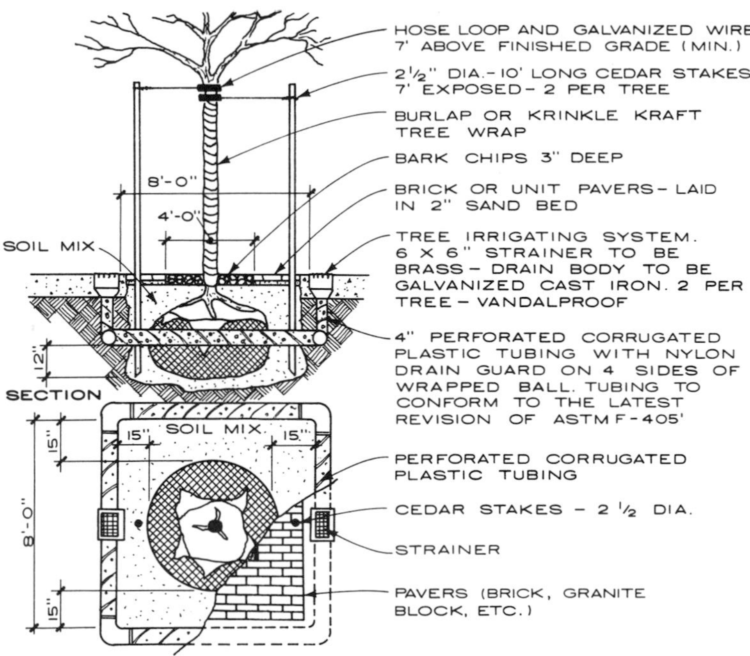
HOSE LOOP AND GALVANIZED WIRE 7' ABOVE FINISHED GRADE (MIN.)
2 1/2" DIA. – 10' LONG CEDAR STAKES 7' EXPOSED – 2 PER TREE
BURLAP OR KRINKLE KRAFT TREE WRAP
BARK CHIPS 3" DEEP
BRICK OR UNIT PAVERS – LAID IN 2" SAND BED
TREE IRRIGATING SYSTEM. 6 X 6" STRAINER TO BE BRASS – DRAIN BODY TO BE GALVANIZED CAST IRON. 2 PER TREE – VANDALPROOF
4" PERFORATED CORRUGATED PLASTIC TUBING WITH NYLON DRAIN GUARD ON 4 SIDES OF WRAPPED BALL. TUBING TO CONFORM TO THE LATEST REVISION OF ASTM F-405'
8'-0"
4'-0"
SOIL MIX
12"
SECTION
SOIL MIX
15"
15"
15"
8'-0"
15"
PERFORATED CORRUGATED PLASTIC TUBING
CEDAR STAKES – 2 1/2 DIA.
STRAINER
PAVERS (BRICK, GRANITE BLOCK, ETC.)
PLAN

PLANTING DETAIL — TREE IN PAVING

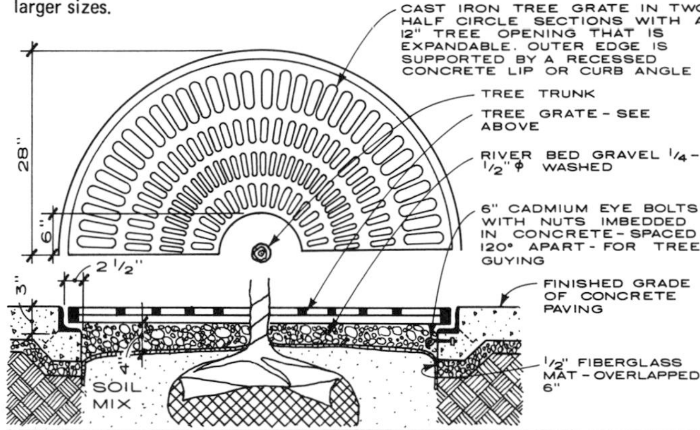
CAST IRON TREE GRATE IN TWO HALF CIRCLE SECTIONS WITH A 12" TREE OPENING THAT IS EXPANDABLE. OUTER EDGE IS SUPPORTED BY A RECESSED CONCRETE LIP OR CURB ANGLE
TREE TRUNK
TREE GRATE – SEE ABOVE
RIVER BED GRAVEL 1/4 - 1/2" φ WASHED
6" CADMIUM EYE BOLTS WITH NUTS IMBEDDED IN CONCRETE – SPACED 120° APART – FOR TREE GUYING
FINISHED GRADE OF CONCRETE PAVING
1/2" FIBERGLASS MAT – OVERLAPPED 6"
28"
6"
2 1/2"
3"
SOIL MIX

TREE GRATE DETAIL

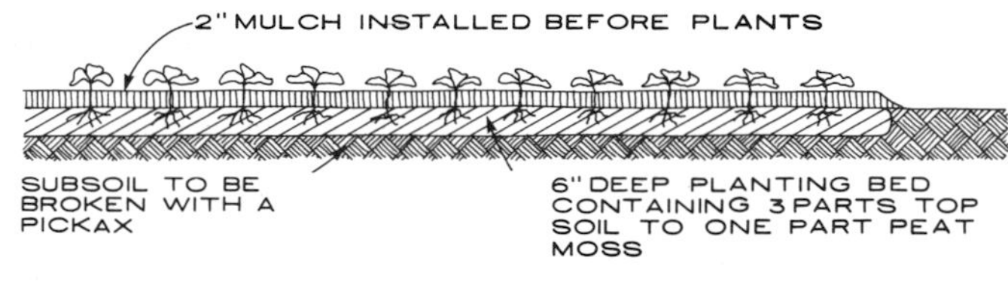
2" MULCH INSTALLED BEFORE PLANTS
SUBSOIL TO BE BROKEN WITH A PICKAX
6" DEEP PLANTING BED CONTAINING 3 PARTS TOP SOIL TO ONE PART PEAT MOSS

GROUND COVER PLANTING DETAIL
NOTE: GROUND COVERS SHOULD BE POT OR CONTAINER GROWN

A. E. Bye & Associates, Landscape Architects; Old Greenwich, Connecticut

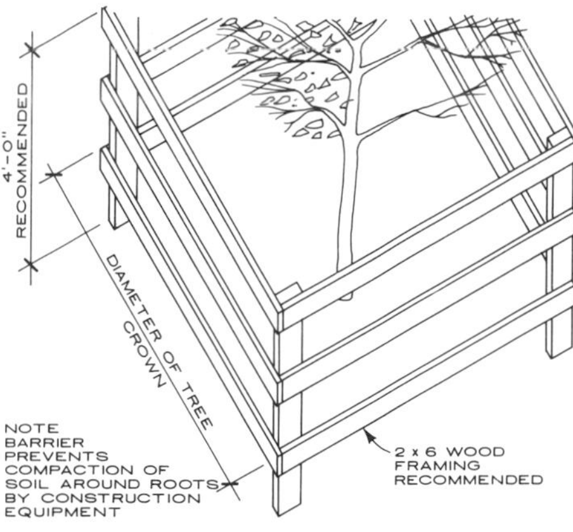
4'-0" RECOMMENDED
DIAMETER OF TREE CROWN
NOTE
BARRIER PREVENTS COMPACTION OF SOIL AROUND ROOTS BY CONSTRUCTION EQUIPMENT
2 x 6 WOOD FRAMING RECOMMENDED

TREE PROTECTION BARRIER

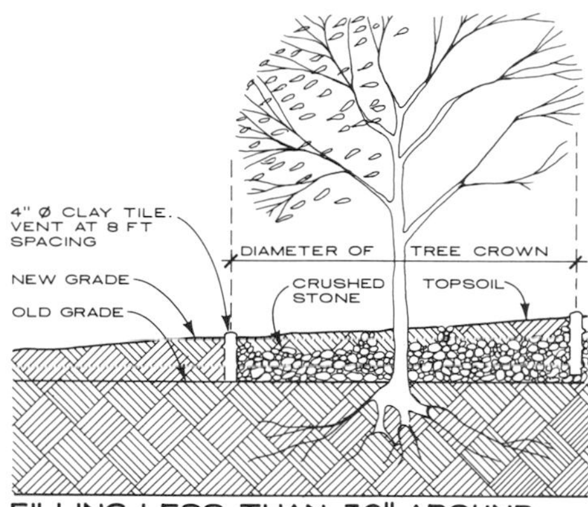
4" Ø CLAY TILE. VENT AT 8 FT SPACING
NEW GRADE
OLD GRADE
DIAMETER OF
TREE CROWN
CRUSHED STONE
TOPSOIL

FILLING LESS THAN 30" AROUND EXISTING TREE

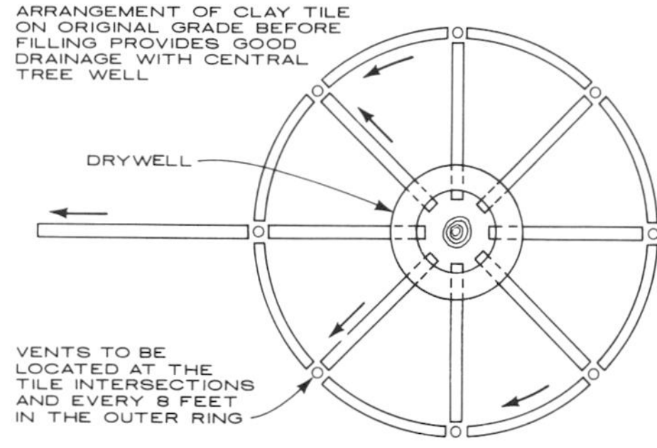
ARRANGEMENT OF CLAY TILE ON ORIGINAL GRADE BEFORE FILLING PROVIDES GOOD DRAINAGE WITH CENTRAL TREE WELL
DRYWELL
VENTS TO BE LOCATED AT THE TILE INTERSECTIONS AND EVERY 8 FEET IN THE OUTER RING

PLAN

FILLING OVER 30" AROUND EXISTING TREE

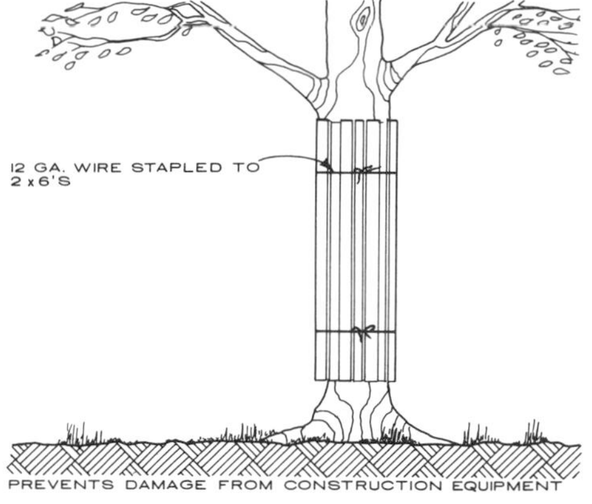
12 GA. WIRE STAPLED TO 2 x 6'S
PREVENTS DAMAGE FROM CONSTRUCTION EQUIPMENT

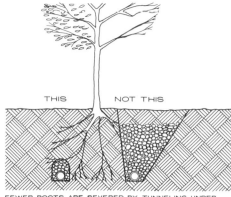

TREE TRUNK PROTECTION

CUTTING AROUND EXISTING TREES

Extreme care should be taken not to compact the earth within the crown of the tree. Compaction can cause severe root damage and reduce the air and water holding capacity of the soil.

If no surrounding barrier is provided, care should be taken not to operate equipment or store materials within the crown spread of the tree. If this area should be compacted, it would be necessary to aerate the soil thoroughly in the root zone immediately following construction. Certain tree species are severely affected by manipulation of the water table, and great care should be exercised to minimize this condition.

SPECIAL USE OF TREES

Trees for special uses should be branched or pruned naturally according to type. Where a form of growth is desired that is not in accordance with a natural growth habit, this form should be specified. For example:

1. BUSH FORM: Trees that start to branch close to the ground in the manner of a shrub.
2. CLUMPS: Trees with three or more main stems starting from the ground.
3. CUT BACK OR SHEARED: Trees that have been pruned back so as to multiply the branching structure and to develop a more formal effect.
4. ESPALIER: Trees pruned and trained to grow flat against a building or trellis, usually in a predetermined pattern or design.
5. PLEACHING: A technique of severe pruning, usually applied to a row or bosque of trees to produce a geometrically formal or clipped hedgelike effect.
6. POLLARDING: The technique in which annual severe pruning of certain species of trees serves to produce abundant vigorous growth the following year.
7. TOPIARY: Trees sheared or trimmed closely in a formal geometric pattern, or sculptural shapes frequently resembling animals or flowers.

THIS NOT THIS

FEWER ROOTS ARE SEVERED BY TUNNELING UNDER TREE THAN BY TRENCHING

UNDERGROUND UTILITIES NEAR EXISTING TREES

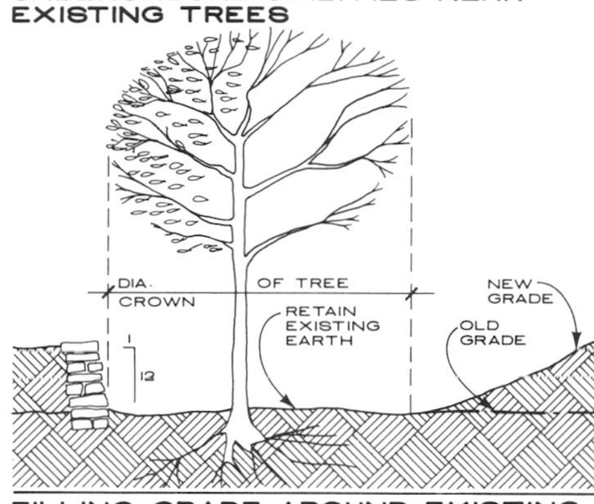
DIA.
CROWN
OF TREE
RETAIN EXISTING EARTH
NEW GRADE
OLD GRADE
12

FILLING GRADE AROUND EXISTING TREE

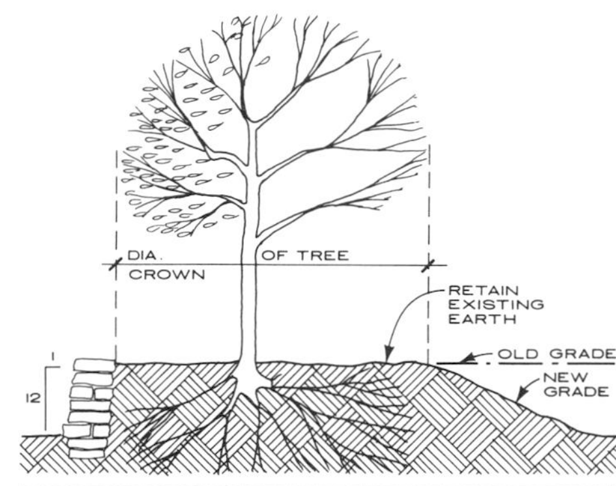
DIA.
CROWN
OF TREE
RETAIN EXISTING EARTH
OLD GRADE
NEW GRADE
12

CUTTING GRADE AROUND EXISTING TREE

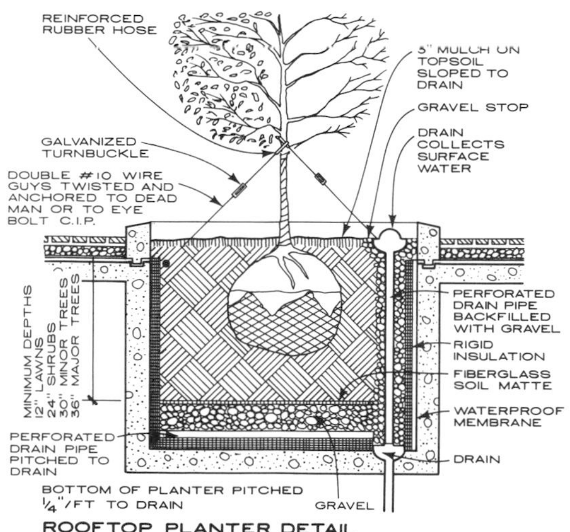
REINFORCED RUBBER HOSE
GALVANIZED TURNBUCKLE
DOUBLE #10 WIRE GUYS TWISTED AND ANCHORED TO DEAD MAN OR TO EYE BOLT C.I.P.
MINIMUM DEPTHS
12" LAWNS
24" SHRUBS
30" MINOR TREES
36" MAJOR TREES
PERFORATED DRAIN PIPE PITCHED TO DRAIN
3" MULCH ON TOPSOIL SLOPED TO DRAIN
GRAVEL STOP
DRAIN COLLECTS SURFACE WATER
PERFORATED DRAIN PIPE BACKFILLED WITH GRAVEL
RIGID INSULATION
FIBERGLASS SOIL MATTE
WATERPROOF MEMBRANE
DRAIN
BOTTOM OF PLANTER PITCHED 1/4"/FT TO DRAIN
GRAVEL

ROOFTOP PLANTER DETAIL

SELECTING PLANTS FOR ROOFTOPS

WIND TOLERANCE

Higher elevations and exposure to wind can cause defoliation and increased transpiration rate. High parapet walls with louvers screen wind velocity and provide shelter for plants.

HIGH EVAPORATION RATE

Drying effects of wind and sun on soil around planter reduce available soil moisture rapidly. Irrigation, mulches, moisture holding soil additives (perlite, vermiculite and peat moss), and insulation assist in reducing this moisture loss.

RAPID SOIL TEMPERATURE FLUCTUATION

The conduction capacity of planter materials tends to produce a broad range of soil temperatures. Certain plant species suffer severe root damage because of cold or heat. Use of rigid insulation lining planter alleviates this condition.

TOPSOIL

Topsoil in planters should be improved to provide the optimum growing condition. A general formula would add fertilizer (as per soil testing) plus 1 part peat moss or vermiculite (high water holding capacity) to 3 parts topsoil. More specific requirements for certain varieties of plants or grasses should be considered.

ROOT CAPACITY

Plant species should be carefully selected to adapt to the size of the plant bed. If species with shallow fibrous roots are used instead of species with a tap root system consult with nurseryman. Consider the ultimate maturity of the plant species in sizing planter.

PLANTING ON STRUCTURES

Jim E. Miller and David W. Wheeler; Saratoga Associates; Saratoga Springs, New York
Erik Johnson; Lawrence Cook and Associates; Falls Church, Virginia
Connecticut Coastal Management Program, see data sources

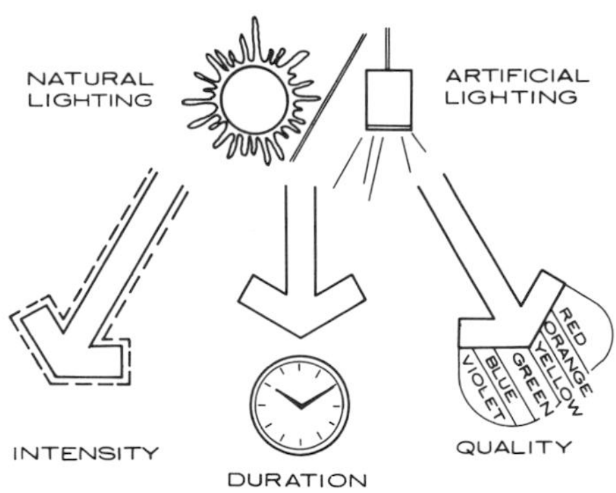
NATURAL LIGHTING
ARTIFICIAL LIGHTING
INTENSITY
DURATION
QUALITY
RED
ORANGE
YELLOW
GREEN
BLUE
VIOLET

INTERIOR PLANT LIGHTING FACTORS

LIGHTING DURATION NEEDS

1. Adequate lighting is the product of intensity times duration to yield "footcandle-hours"; therefore, compensation between the two exists (e.g., 300 ft-c x 12 hr = 360 ft-c x 10 hr).
2. Recommended rule of thumb: 10-12 hr of continuous lighting on a regular basis, 7 days a week.
3. Generally, it is believed that continuous 24 hr lighting period might be detrimental to plants, but no research bears this out and many projects are under this regime with no apparent bad effects.

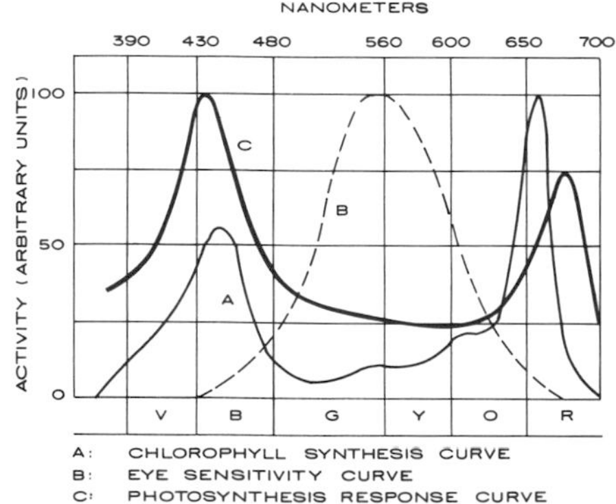
NANOMETERS
390 430 480 560 600 650 700
ACTIVITY (ARBITRARY UNITS)
100
50
0
C
B
A
V B G Y O R
A: CHLOROPHYLL SYNTHESIS CURVE
B: EYE SENSITIVITY CURVE
C: PHOTOSYNTHESIS RESPONSE CURVE

SPECTRAL ENERGY DISTRIBUTION CURVE SHOWING OPPOSING PLANT AND HUMAN EYE RESPONSES

LIGHT QUALITY NEEDS

1. Natural lighting is about twice as efficient as cool white fluorescent lighting for plant growth, because of sunlight's broad range spectrum (i.e., 200 ft-c of CWF = 95 ft-c of natural light).
2. Chlorophyll is most responsive to blue and red wavelength energy in the production of food. The human eye is least responsive to blue and red energy and most responsive to the green-yellow region of the spectrum.
3. High blue energy emitting sources are best for overall plant maintenance (stockier growth, dark green color, little elongation).
4. High red energy emitting sources produce lighter colored foliage, elongated growth, stragglier growth.
5. Designer must be cognizant of color rendition of source, as well as light quality, if lighting is to be used for both plant lighting and illumination. (See Lamp Responses table.)
6. Ultraviolet energy is believed to be somewhat helpful to the photosynthesis process, but is not considered necessary as an integral segment of plant lighting.

LIGHTING INTENSITY NEEDS

1. All plants desire good lighting, but many are tolerant and adaptable to lower light conditions.
2. Because most interior plants are native to areas with intensities of 10-14,000 ft-c, these plants must be "trained" through an acclimatization process of lowered light (2000-4000 ft-c), water and fertilizer levels for survival, and maintained appearance in the interior environment.
3. All plants have varying degrees of interior lighting intensity requirements, best understood as foot-candle (lumens/square foot) requirements.
4. Lighting intensity for plants must be planned and is not simply a footcandle measurement after the building is complete (i.e., footcandle meters are "after the fact" instruments).
5. Intensity must always be above the individual light compensation point for each plant variety, for survival. (LCP is the intensity point at which the plant utilizes as much food as it produces; hence no food storage. Eventually, the plant could die with no food backup.)
6. Recommended rule of thumb: design for a MINIMUM of 50 ft-c on the ground plane for fixed floor type of planters and 75 ft-c at desk height for movable decorative floor planters.
7. Flowering plants and flowers require extremely high intensities (above 2000 ft-c) or direct sunlight to bud, flower, or fruit, as well as lighting high in red and far-red energy.

RECOMMENDED LIGHTING SOURCES FOR PLANTS

Lighting sources are listed in order of priority, based on plant growth efficiency, color rendition preference, and energy efficiency.

CEILING HEIGHT	RECOMMENDED LIGHT SOURCE
10 ft and less	Daylight—sidewall glazing Cool white fluorescent Natural light fluorescent Incandescent Plant growth fluorescent
10-15 ft	Daylight Sidewall glazing Major glazing Skylights Metal halide lamp, phosphor coated Mercury lamp, deluxe white Mercury lamp, warm deluxe white High pressure sodium (if color rendition not a design factor) Quartz halogen lamp Incandescent
15 ft and greater	Daylight Sidewall glazing Major glazing Skylights Metal halide lamp, clear Metal halide lamp, phosphor coated Mercury lamp, deluxe white Mercury lamp, warm deluxe white High pressure sodium (if color rendition not a design factor) Quartz halogen lamp Incandescent

LAMP RESPONSES ON INTERIOR PLANTS

BULB	ROOM APPEARANCE	COLORS STRENGTHENED	COLORS GREYED	PLANT RESPONSES
CW WW	Neutral to cool Yellow to warm	Blue, yellow, orange Yellow, orange	Red Blue, green, red	Green foliage, stem elongates slowly, multiple side shoots, flower life long
GRO-PL	Purple to pink	Blue, red	Green, yellow	Deep green foliage, stem elongates very slowly, thick stems, multiple side shoots, late flowers on short stems
GRO-WS AGRO VITA	Warm Neutral to warm Neutral to warm	Blue, yellow, red Blue, yellow, red Blue, yellow, red	Green Green Green	Light green foliage, stem elongates rapidly, suppressed side shoots, early flowering on long stems, plant matures and dies rapidly
HG MH	Cool Cool green	Blue, green, yellow Blue, green, yellow	Red Red	Green foliage expands, stem elongates slowly, multiple side shoots, flower life long
HPS	Warm	Green, yellow, orange	Blue, red	Deep green, large foliage, stem elongates very slowly, late flowers, short stems
LPS	Warm	Yellow	All except yellow	Extra deep green foliage, slow, thick stem elongation, multiple side shoots, some flowering, short stems. Some plants require supplemental sun
INC INC-HG	Warm Warm	Yellow, orange, red Yellow, orange, red	Blue Blue	Pale, thin, long foliage, stems spindly, suppressed side shoots early, short-lived flowers

KEY

CW: cool white fluorescent.
WW: warm white fluorescent.
GRO-PL: Gro-Lux plant light.
GRO-WS: Gro-Lux wide spectrum.
AGRO: Agro-Lite.
VITA: Vita-Lite.
HG: mercury (all types).
MH: metal halide.
HPS: high pressure sodium.
LPS: low pressure sodium.
INC-HG: incandescent mercury.
INC-PL: incandescent plant light.

Richard L. Gaines, AIA; Plantscape House; Apopka, Florida

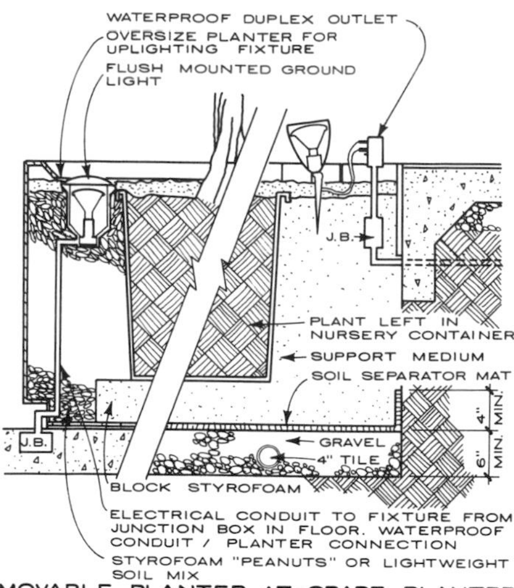
WATERPROOF DUPLEX OUTLET
OVERSIZE PLANTER FOR UPLIGHTING FIXTURE
FLUSH MOUNTED GROUND LIGHT
J.B.
PLANT LEFT IN NURSERY CONTAINER
SUPPORT MEDIUM
SOIL SEPARATOR MAT
GRAVEL
4" TILE
4" MIN.
6" MIN.
BLOCK STYROFOAM
ELECTRICAL CONDUIT TO FIXTURE FROM JUNCTION BOX IN FLOOR. WATERPROOF CONDUIT / PLANTER CONNECTION
STYROFOAM "PEANUTS" OR LIGHTWEIGHT SOIL MIX

MOVABLE PLANTER AT-GRADE PLANTER

UPLIGHTING / PLANTING DETAILS

UPLIGHTING AND ELECTRICAL NEEDS

1. May be of some benefit to plants, but inefficient for plant photosynthesis because of plant physiological structure. Chlorophyll is usually in upper part of leaf.
2. Uplighting should never be utilized as sole lighting source for plants.
3. Waterproof duplex outlets above soil line with a waterproof junction box below soil line are usually adequate for "atmosphere" uplighting and water fountain pumps.

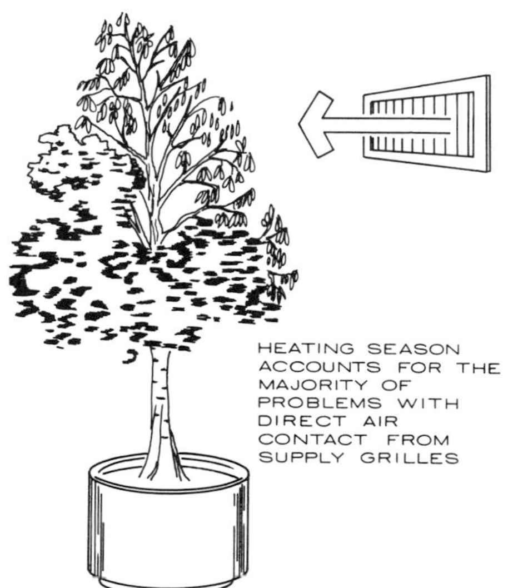
HEATING SEASON ACCOUNTS FOR THE MAJORITY OF PROBLEMS WITH DIRECT AIR CONTACT FROM SUPPLY GRILLES

FOLIAGE BURN FROM DIRECT HEAT CONTACT

HVAC EFFECT ON PLANTS

1. Air-conditioning (cooled air) is rarely detrimental to plants, even if it is "directed" at plants. The ventilation here is what counts! Good ventilation is a must with plants; otherwise oxygen and temperatures build up. Heat supply, on the other hand, when "directed" at plants, can truly be disastrous. Plan for supplies directed away from plants, but maintain adequate ventilation.
2. Extended heat or power failures of sufficient duration can damage plant health. The lower limit of temperature as a steady state is 65°F for plant survival. Brief drops to 55°F (less than 1 hr) are the lower limit before damage. Temperatures up to 85°F for only 2 days a week can usually be tolerated.
3. The relative humidity should not be allowed to fall below 30%, as plants prefer a relative humidity of 50-60%.

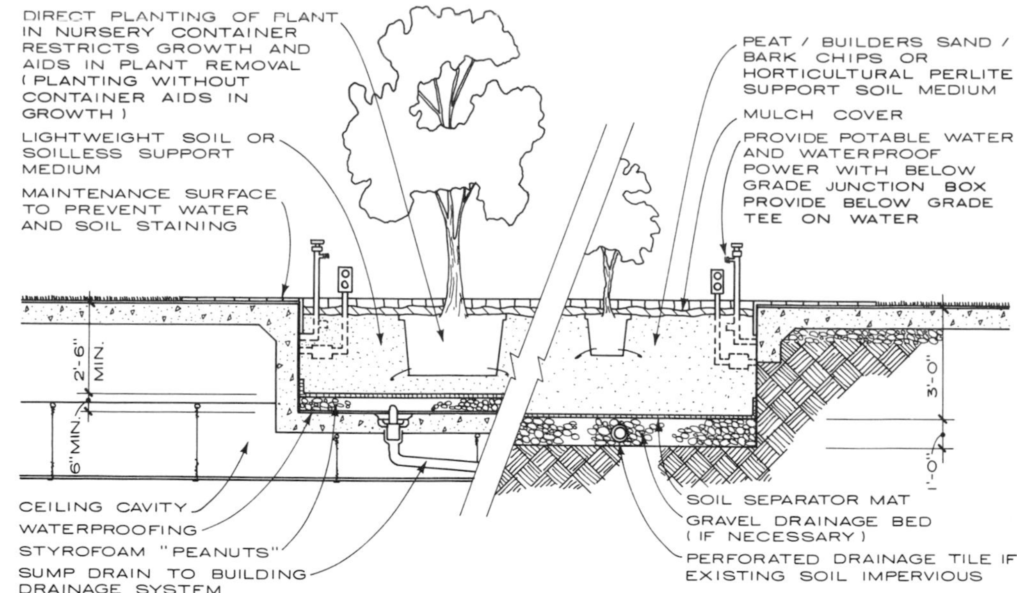
DIRECT PLANTING OF PLANT IN NURSERY CONTAINER RESTRICTS GROWTH AND AIDS IN PLANT REMOVAL (PLANTING WITHOUT CONTAINER AIDS IN GROWTH)
LIGHTWEIGHT SOIL OR SOILLESS SUPPORT MEDIUM
MAINTENANCE SURFACE TO PREVENT WATER AND SOIL STAINING
PEAT / BUILDERS SAND / BARK CHIPS OR HORTICULTURAL PERLITE SUPPORT SOIL MEDIUM
MULCH COVER
PROVIDE POTABLE WATER AND WATERPROOF POWER WITH BELOW GRADE JUNCTION BOX PROVIDE BELOW GRADE TEE ON WATER
2'-6" MIN.
6" MIN.
3'-0"
1'-0"
CEILING CAVITY
WATERPROOFING
STYROFOAM "PEANUTS"
SUMP DRAIN TO BUILDING DRAINAGE SYSTEM
SOIL SEPARATOR MAT
GRAVEL DRAINAGE BED (IF NECESSARY)
PERFORATED DRAINAGE TILE IF EXISTING SOIL IMPERVIOUS

ABOVE – GRADE PLANTER AT – GRADE PLANTER

FLOOR PLANTER DETAILS

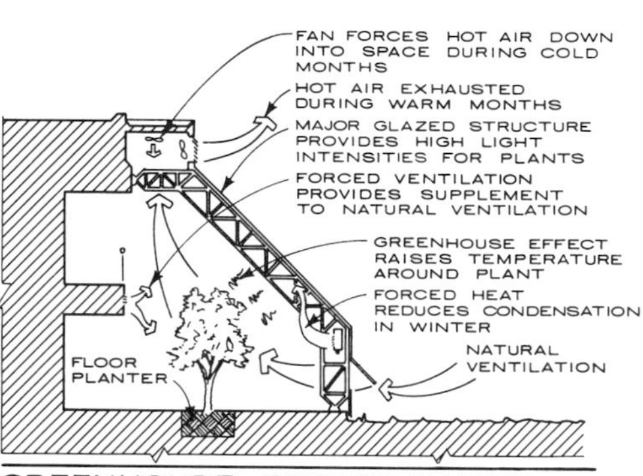
FAN FORCES HOT AIR DOWN INTO SPACE DURING COLD MONTHS
HOT AIR EXHAUSTED DURING WARM MONTHS
MAJOR GLAZED STRUCTURE PROVIDES HIGH LIGHT INTENSITIES FOR PLANTS
FORCED VENTILATION PROVIDES SUPPLEMENT TO NATURAL VENTILATION
GREENHOUSE EFFECT RAISES TEMPERATURE AROUND PLANT
FORCED HEAT REDUCES CONDENSATION IN WINTER
NATURAL VENTILATION
FLOOR PLANTER

GREENHOUSE EFFECT RAISES NEED FOR ADEQUATE VENTILATION

TEMPERATURE REQUIREMENTS

1. Most plants prefer human comfort range: 70-75°F daytime temperatures and 60-65°F nighttime temperatures.
2. An absolute minimum temperature of 50°F must be observed. Plant damage will result below this figure. Rapid temperature fluctuations of 30-40°F can also be detrimental to plants.
3. "Q-10" phenomenon of respiration: for every 10°C rise in temperature, plants' respiration rate and food consumption doubles.
4. Both photosynthesis and respiration decline and stop with time, as temperatures go beyond 80°F. Beware of the greenhouse effect!

WATER SUPPLY REQUIREMENTS

1. Movable and railing planters are often watered by watering can. Provide convenient access to hot and cold potable water by hose bibbs and/or service sinks (preferably in janitor's closet) during normal working hours, with long (min. 24 in.) faucet-to-sink or floor distances. Provide for maximum of 200 ft travel on all floors.
2. At-grade floor planters are usually watered by hose and extension wand. Provide hose bibbs above soil line (for maximum travel of 50 ft) with capped "tee" stub-outs beneath soil line. If soil temperature is apt to get abnormally low in winter, provide hot and cold water by mixer-faucet type hose bibbs.
3. High concentrations of fluoride and chlorine in water supply can cause damage to plants. Provide water with low concentrations of these elements and with a pH value of 5.0-6.0. Higher or lower pH levels can result in higher plant maintenance costs.

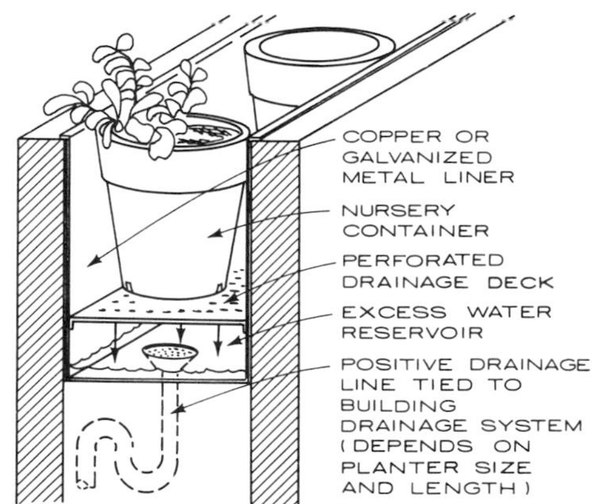
COPPER OR GALVANIZED METAL LINER
NURSERY CONTAINER
PERFORATED DRAINAGE DECK
EXCESS WATER RESERVOIR
POSITIVE DRAINAGE LINE TIED TO BUILDING DRAINAGE SYSTEM (DEPENDS ON PLANTER SIZE AND LENGTH)

RAILING PLANTER DETAIL

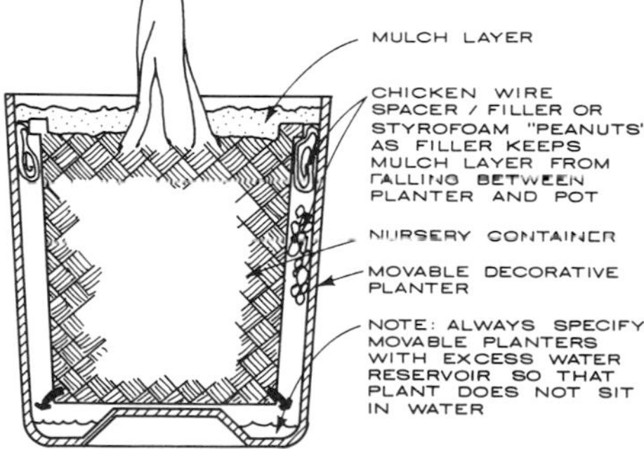
MULCH LAYER
CHICKEN WIRE SPACER / FILLER OR STYROFOAM "PEANUTS" AS FILLER KEEPS MULCH LAYER FROM FALLING BETWEEN PLANTER AND POT
NURSERY CONTAINER
MOVABLE DECORATIVE PLANTER
NOTE: ALWAYS SPECIFY MOVABLE PLANTERS WITH EXCESS WATER RESERVOIR SO THAT PLANT DOES NOT SIT IN WATER

MOVABLE DECORATIVE PLANTER DETAIL

STORAGE REQUIREMENTS

Provide a secured storage space of approximately 30 sq ft for watering equipment and other maintenance materials. It may be desirable to combine water supply and janitor needs in the same storage area.

AIR POLLUTION EFFECTS ON PLANTS

Problems result from inadequate ventilation. Excessive chlorine gas from swimming pool areas can be a damaging problem, as well as excessive fumes from toxic cleaning substances for floor finishes, etc. Ventilation a must here!

Richard L. Gaines, AIA; Plantscape House; Apopka, Florida

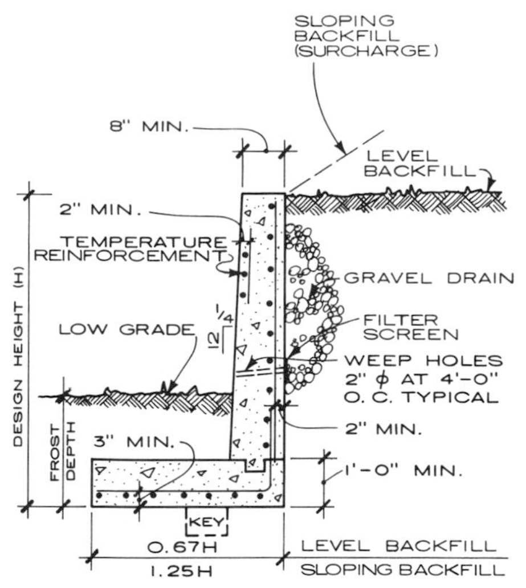
SLOPING
BACKFILL
(SURCHARGE)
8" MIN.
LEVEL
BACKFILL
2" MIN.
TEMPERATURE
REINFORCEMENT
GRAVEL DRAIN
LOW GRADE
FILTER
SCREEN
WEEP HOLES
2" ϕ AT 4'-0"
O. C. TYPICAL
2" MIN.
3" MIN.
1'-0" MIN.
DESIGN HEIGHT (H)
FROST
DEPTH
KEY
0.67H
1.25H
LEVEL BACKFILL
SLOPING BACKFILL

Place base below frost line. Dimensions are approximate.

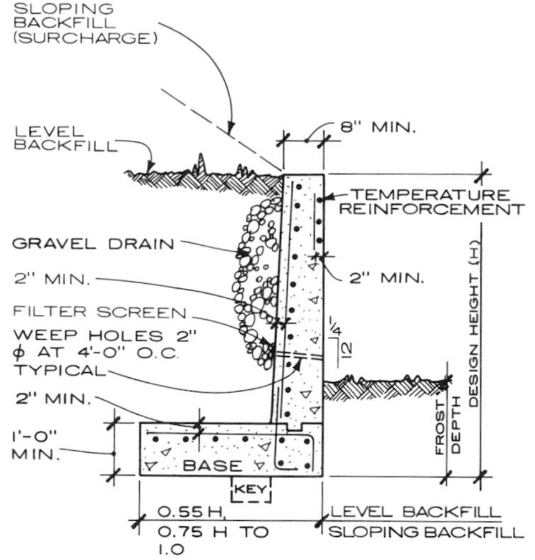
SLOPING
BACKFILL
(SURCHARGE)
LEVEL
BACKFILL
8" MIN.
TEMPERATURE
REINFORCEMENT
GRAVEL DRAIN
2" MIN.
2" MIN.
FILTER SCREEN
WEEP HOLES 2"
ϕ AT 4'-0" O.C.
TYPICAL
2" MIN.
1'-0"
MIN.
BASE
KEY
DESIGN HEIGHT (H)
FROST
DEPTH
0.55 H
0.75 H TO
1.0
LEVEL BACKFILL
SLOPING BACKFILL

Soil pressure at toe equals 0.2 times the height in kips per square foot. Dimensions are preliminary.

L TYPE RETAINING WALLS

GRAVITY RETAINING WALL

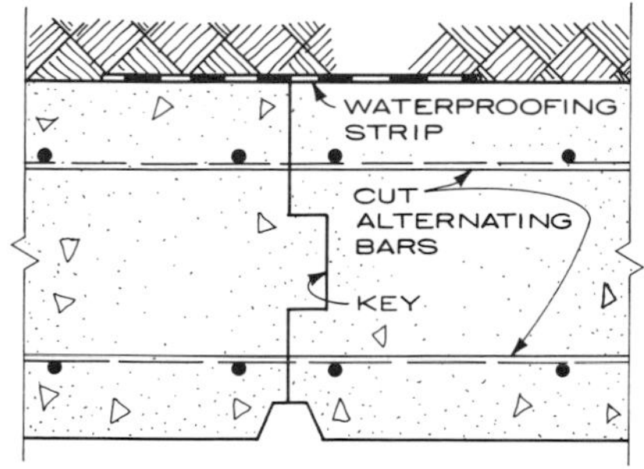
WATERPROOFING
STRIP
CUT
ALTERNATING
BARS
KEY

VERTICAL CONTROL JOINT

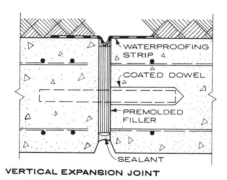

VERTICAL EXPANSION JOINT

RETAINING WALL JOINTS

NOTES

Provide control and/or construction joints in concrete retaining walls about every 25 ft and expansion joints about every fourth control and/or construction joint. Coated dowels should be used if average wall height on either side of a joint is different.

Consult with a structural engineer for final design of concrete retaining walls. An engineer's seal may be required for final design approval by local code officials.

Use temperature bars if wall is more than 10 in. thick.

Keys shown dashed may be required to prevent sliding in high walls and those on moist clay.

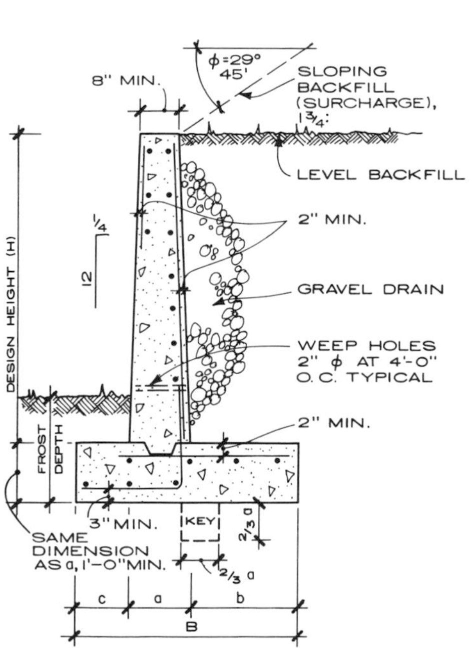
8" MIN.
ϕ=29°
45'
SLOPING
BACKFILL
(SURCHARGE),
1¾:1
LEVEL BACKFILL
2" MIN.
GRAVEL DRAIN
WEEP HOLES
2" ϕ AT 4'-0"
O. C. TYPICAL
2" MIN.
DESIGN HEIGHT (H)
FROST
DEPTH
3" MIN.
KEY
SAME
DIMENSION
AS a, 1'-0" MIN.
2/3 a
c
a
b
B

T TYPE RETAINING WALLS

PRELIMINARY DIMENSIONS

BACKFILL SLOPING ϕ = 29° 45' (1¾:1)				
APPROXIMATE CONCRETE DIMENSIONS				
HEIGHT OF WALL H (FT)	WIDTH OF BASE B (FT)	WIDTH OF WALL a (FT)	HEEL b (FT)	TOE c (FT)
3	2'-8"	0'-9"	1'-5"	0'-6"
4	3'-5"	0'-9"	2'-0"	0'-8"
5	4'-6"	0'-10"	2'-6"	1'-2"
6	5'-4"	0'-10"	2'-11"	1'-7"
7	6'-3"	0'-10"	3'-5"	2'-0"
8	7'-0"	1'-0"	3'-8"	2'-4"
9	7'-6"	1'-0"	4'-2"	2'-4"
10	8'-6"	1'-0"	4'-9"	2'-9"
11	11'-0"	1'-1"	7'-2"	2'-9"
12	12'-0"	1'-2"	7'-10"	3'-0"
13	13'-0"	1'-4"	8'-5"	3'-3"
14	14'-0"	1'-5"	9'-1"	3'-6"
15	15'-0"	1'-6"	9'-9"	3'-9"
16	16'-0"	1'-7"	10'-5"	4'-0"
17	17'-0"	1'-8"	11'-1"	4'-3"
18	18'-0"	1'-10"	11'-8"	4'-6"
19	19'-0"	1'-11"	12'-4"	4'-9"
20	20'-0"	2'-0"	13'-0"	5'-0"
21	21'-0"	2'-2"	13'-7"	5'-3"
22	22'-0"	2'-4"	14'-4"	5'-4"

BACKFILL LEVEL—NO SURCHARGE				
APPROXIMATE CONCRETE DIMENSIONS				
HEIGHT OF WALL H (FT)	WIDTH OF BASE B (FT)	WIDTH OF WALL a (FT)	HEEL b (FT)	TOE c (FT)
3	2'-1"	0'-8"	1'-0"	0'-5"
4	2'-8"	0'-8"	1'-7"	0'-5"
5	3'-3"	0'-8"	2'-2"	0'-5"
6	3'-9"	0'-8"	2'-5"	0'-8"
7	4'-2"	0'-8"	2'-6"	1'-0"
8	4'-8"	1'-0"	2'-8"	1'-0"
9	5'-2"	1'-0"	3'-2"	1'-0"
10	5'-9"	1'-0"	3'-7"	1'-2"
11	6'-7"	1'-1"	4'-1"	1'-5"
12	7'-3"	1'-2"	4'-7"	1'-6"
13	7'-10"	1'-2"	5'-0"	1'-8"
14	8'-5"	1'-3"	5'-5"	1'-9"
15	9'-0"	1'-4"	5'-9"	1'-11"
16	9'-7"	1'-5"	6'-2"	2'-0"
17	10'-3"	1'-6"	6'-7"	2'-2"
18	10'-10"	1'-6"	7'-1"	2'-3"
19	11'-5"	1'-7"	7'-5"	2'-5"
20	12'-0"	1'-8"	7'-10"	2'-6"
21	12'-7"	1'-9"	8'-2"	2'-8"
22	13'-3"	1'-11"	8'-7"	2'-9"

Kenneth D. Franch, AIA, PE; Phillips Swager Associates, Inc.; Dallas, Texas
Neubauer · Sohn, Engineers; Washington, D.C.

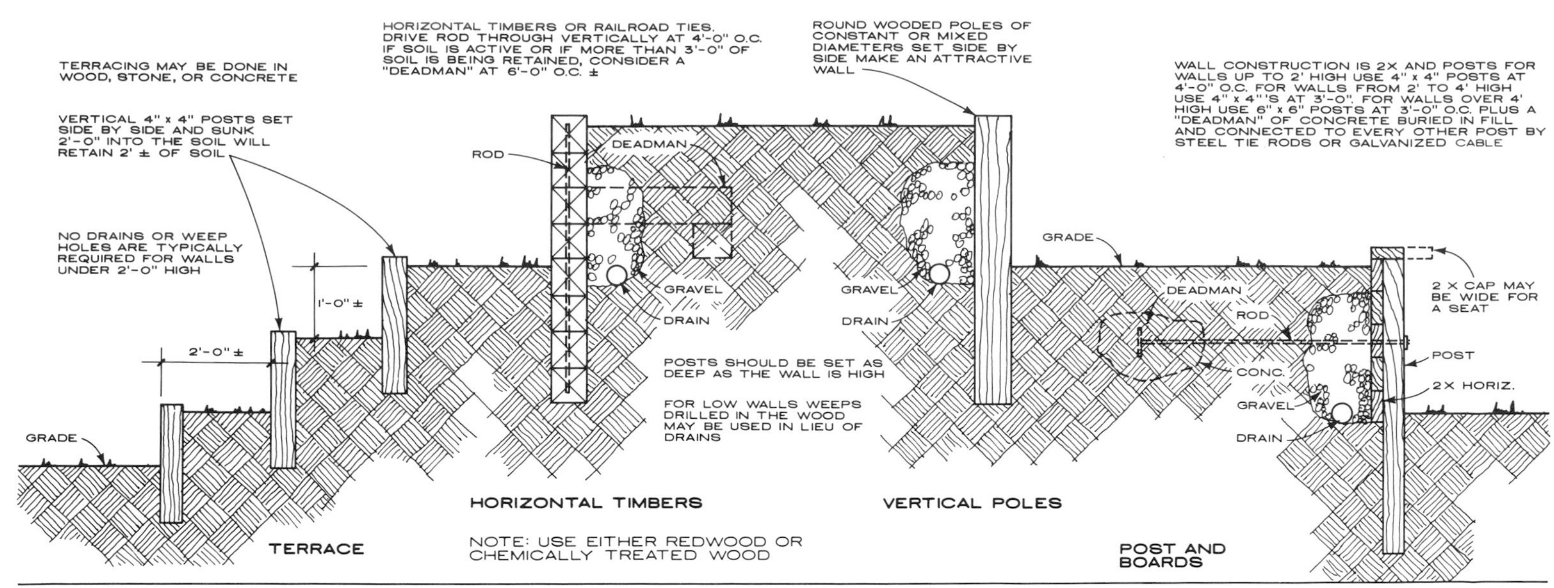
TERRACING MAY BE DONE IN WOOD, STONE, OR CONCRETE
VERTICAL 4" x 4" POSTS SET SIDE BY SIDE AND SUNK 2'-0" INTO THE SOIL WILL RETAIN 2' ± OF SOIL
NO DRAINS OR WEEP HOLES ARE TYPICALLY REQUIRED FOR WALLS UNDER 2'-0" HIGH
1'-0" ±
2'-0" ±
GRADE
TERRACE
HORIZONTAL TIMBERS OR RAILROAD TIES. DRIVE ROD THROUGH VERTICALLY AT 4'-0" O.C. IF SOIL IS ACTIVE OR IF MORE THAN 3'-0" OF SOIL IS BEING RETAINED, CONSIDER A "DEADMAN" AT 6'-0" O.C. ±
ROD
DEADMAN
GRAVEL
DRAIN
ROUND WOODED POLES OF CONSTANT OR MIXED DIAMETERS SET SIDE BY SIDE MAKE AN ATTRACTIVE WALL
GRAVEL
DRAIN
POSTS SHOULD BE SET AS DEEP AS THE WALL IS HIGH
FOR LOW WALLS WEEPS DRILLED IN THE WOOD MAY BE USED IN LIEU OF DRAINS
HORIZONTAL TIMBERS
VERTICAL POLES
NOTE: USE EITHER REDWOOD OR CHEMICALLY TREATED WOOD
WALL CONSTRUCTION IS 2X AND POSTS FOR WALLS UP TO 2' HIGH USE 4" x 4" POSTS AT 4'-0" O.C. FOR WALLS FROM 2' TO 4' HIGH USE 4" x 4"'S AT 3'-0". FOR WALLS OVER 4' HIGH USE 6" x 6" POSTS AT 3'-0" O.C. PLUS A "DEADMAN" OF CONCRETE BURIED IN FILL AND CONNECTED TO EVERY OTHER POST BY STEEL TIE RODS OR GALVANIZED CABLE
GRADE
DEADMAN
ROD
CONC.
GRAVEL
DRAIN
2 X CAP MAY BE WIDE FOR A SEAT
POST
2X HORIZ.
POST AND BOARDS

WOOD APPLICATIONS

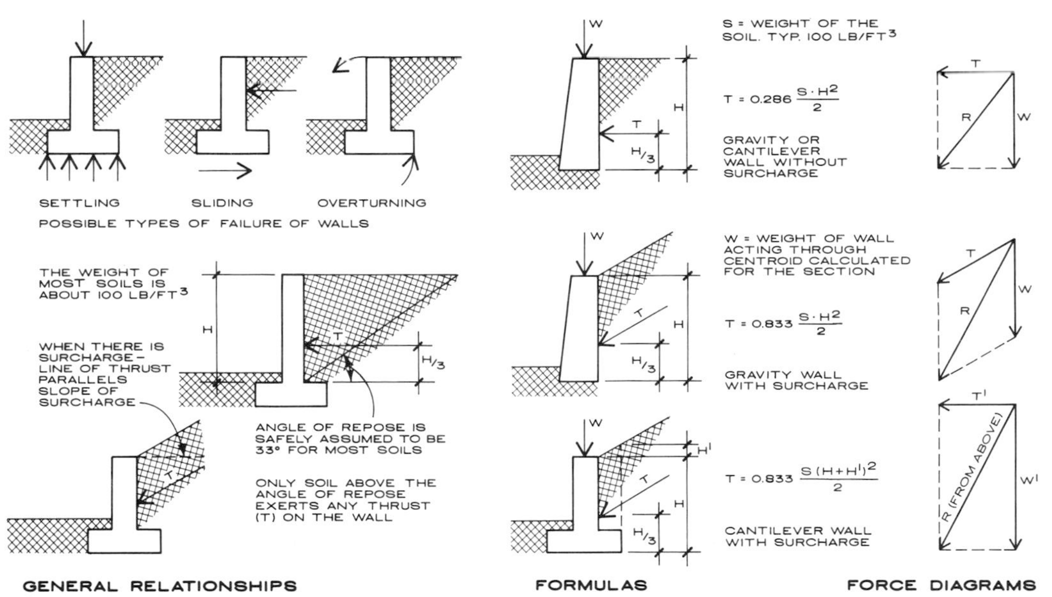
SETTLING
SLIDING
OVERTURNING
POSSIBLE TYPES OF FAILURE OF WALLS
THE WEIGHT OF MOST SOILS IS ABOUT 100 LB/FT3
WHEN THERE IS SURCHARGE - LINE OF THRUST PARALLELS SLOPE OF SURCHARGE
H
T
H/3
ANGLE OF REPOSE IS SAFELY ASSUMED TO BE 33° FOR MOST SOILS
ONLY SOIL ABOVE THE ANGLE OF REPOSE EXERTS ANY THRUST (T) ON THE WALL
GENERAL RELATIONSHIPS
W
S = WEIGHT OF THE SOIL. TYP. 100 LB/FT3
T = 0.286 S·H2/2
GRAVITY OR CANTILEVER WALL WITHOUT SURCHARGE
W = WEIGHT OF WALL ACTING THROUGH CENTROID CALCULATED FOR THE SECTION
T = 0.833 S·H2/2
GRAVITY WALL WITH SURCHARGE
H'
T = 0.833 S(H+H')2/2
CANTILEVER WALL WITH SURCHARGE
FORMULAS
R
R (FROM ABOVE)
T'
W'
FORCE DIAGRAMS

SLIDING

The thrust on the wall must be resisted. The resisting force is the weight of the wall times the coefficient of soil friction. Use a safety factor of 1.5. Therefore:

$$W(C.F.) \geq 1.5T$$

Average coefficients:

Gravel	0.6
Silt/dry clay	0.5
Sand	0.4
Wet clay	0.3

OVERTURNING

The overturning moment equals T(H/3). This is resisted by the resisting moment. For symmetrical sections, resisting moment equals W times (width of base/2). Use a safety factor of 2.0. Therefore:

$$M_R \geq 2(M_O)$$

SETTLING

Soil bearing value must resist vertical force. For symmetrical sections that force is W (or W′)/bearing area. Use a safety factor of 1.5. Therefore:

$$S.B. \geq 1.5(W/A)$$

STRUCTURAL DESIGN CONSIDERATIONS

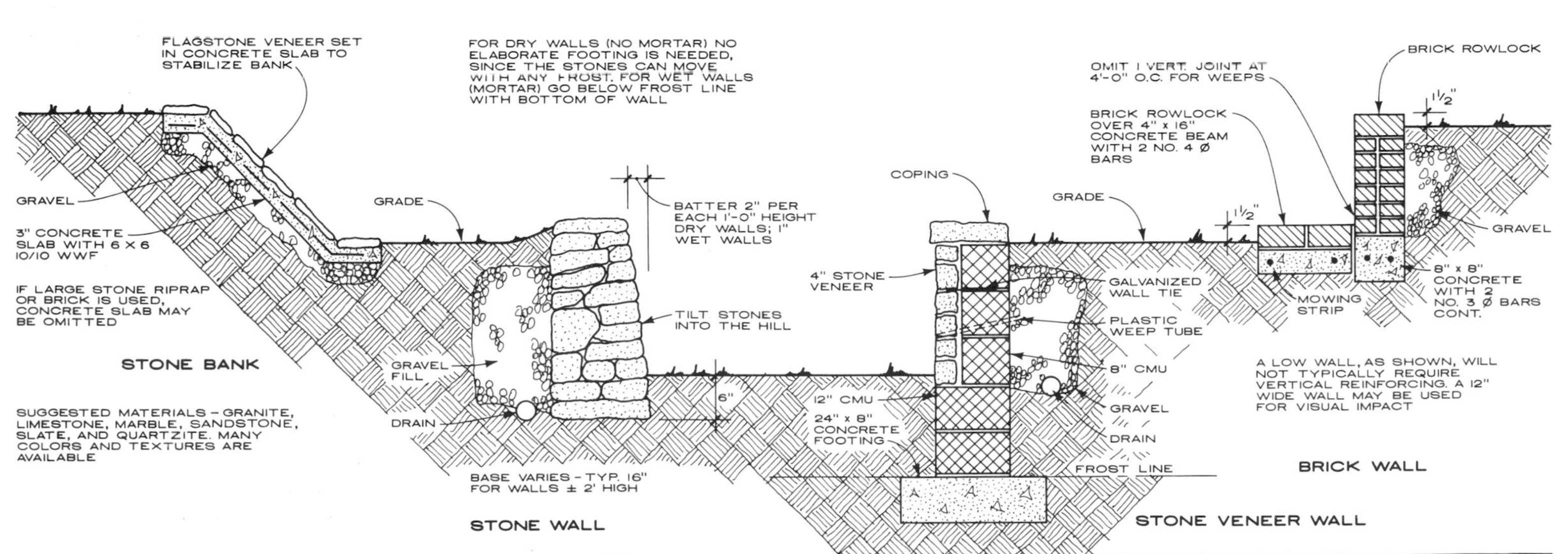
FLAGSTONE VENEER SET IN CONCRETE SLAB TO STABILIZE BANK
GRAVEL
3" CONCRETE SLAB WITH 6 X 6 10/10 WWF
IF LARGE STONE RIPRAP OR BRICK IS USED, CONCRETE SLAB MAY BE OMITTED
STONE BANK
SUGGESTED MATERIALS - GRANITE, LIMESTONE, MARBLE, SANDSTONE, SLATE, AND QUARTZITE. MANY COLORS AND TEXTURES ARE AVAILABLE
FOR DRY WALLS (NO MORTAR) NO ELABORATE FOOTING IS NEEDED, SINCE THE STONES CAN MOVE WITH ANY FROST. FOR WET WALLS (MORTAR) GO BELOW FROST LINE WITH BOTTOM OF WALL
GRADE
BATTER 2" PER EACH 1'-0" HEIGHT DRY WALLS; 1" WET WALLS
TILT STONES INTO THE HILL
GRAVEL FILL
DRAIN
6"
BASE VARIES - TYP. 16" FOR WALLS ± 2' HIGH
STONE WALL
COPING
4" STONE VENEER
12" CMU
24" x 8" CONCRETE FOOTING
GRADE
GALVANIZED WALL TIE
PLASTIC WEEP TUBE
8" CMU
GRAVEL
DRAIN
FROST LINE
STONE VENEER WALL
OMIT 1 VERT. JOINT AT 4'-0" O.C. FOR WEEPS
BRICK ROWLOCK OVER 4" x 16" CONCRETE BEAM WITH 2 NO. 4 Ø BARS
BRICK ROWLOCK
1 1/2"
GRAVEL
8" x 8" CONCRETE WITH 2 NO. 3 Ø BARS CONT.
MOWING STRIP
A LOW WALL, AS SHOWN, WILL NOT TYPICALLY REQUIRE VERTICAL REINFORCING. A 12" WIDE WALL MAY BE USED FOR VISUAL IMPACT
BRICK WALL

STONE AND MASONRY APPLICATIONS

Charles R. Heuer, AIA; Washington, D.C.

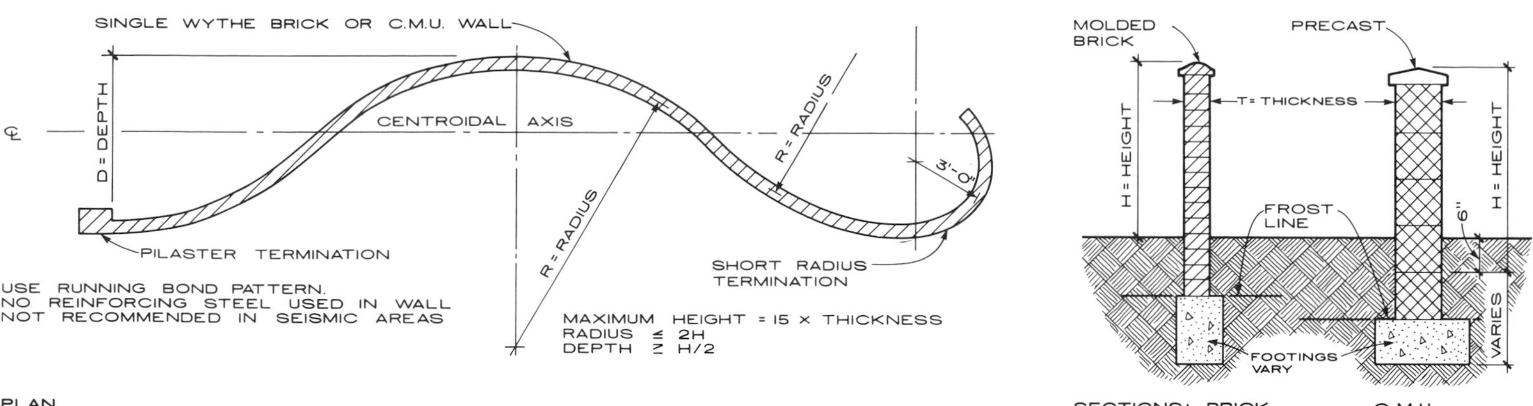

SINGLE WYTHE BRICK OR C.M.U. WALL
D = DEPTH
CENTROIDAL AXIS
R = RADIUS
R = RADIUS
3'-0"
PILASTER TERMINATION
SHORT RADIUS TERMINATION
USE RUNNING BOND PATTERN.
NO REINFORCING STEEL USED IN WALL
NOT RECOMMENDED IN SEISMIC AREAS
MAXIMUM HEIGHT = 15 × THICKNESS
RADIUS ≤ 2H
DEPTH ≥ H/2
MOLDED BRICK
PRECAST
T = THICKNESS
H = HEIGHT
H = HEIGHT
FROST LINE
6"
VARIES
FOOTINGS VARY

PLAN

SECTIONS: BRICK C.M.U.

SERPENTINE GARDEN WALLS

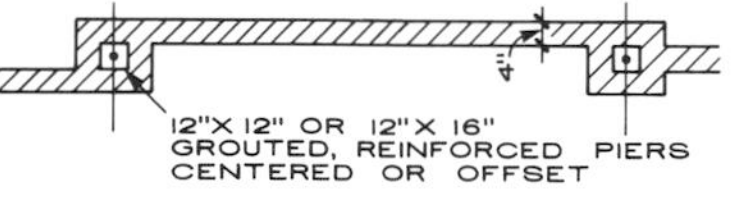

4"
12"X 12" OR 12"X 16" GROUTED, REINFORCED PIERS CENTERED OR OFFSET

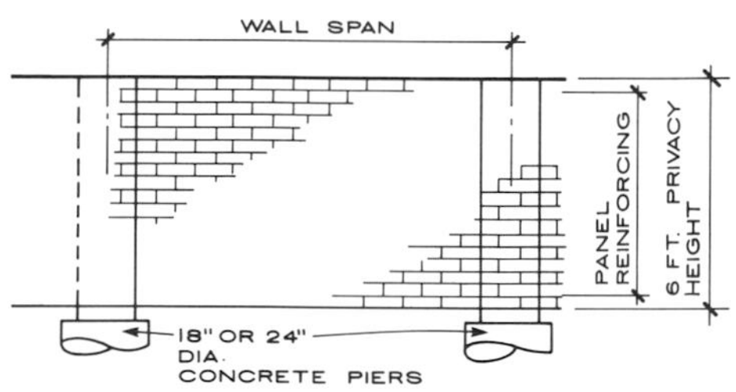

WALL SPAN
PANEL REINFORCING
6 FT. PRIVACY HEIGHT
18" OR 24" DIA. CONCRETE PIERS

REINFORCED WALLS

PANEL WALL REINFORCING STEEL

WALL SPAN (FT.)	VERTICAL SPACING* (IN.)								
	WIND LOAD 10 PSF			WIND LOAD 15 PSF			WIND LOAD 20 PSF		
	A	B	C	A	B	C	A	B	C
8	45	30	19	30	20	12	23	15	9.5
10	29	19	12	19	13	8.0	14	10	6.0
12	20	13	8.5	13	9.0	5.5	10	7.0	4.0
14	15	10	6.5	10	6.5	4.0	7.5	5.0	3.0
16	11	7.5	5.0	7.5	5.0	3.0	6.0	4.0	2.5

*A, two #2 bars; B, two 3/16 in. diameter wires; C, two 9-gauge wires.
NOTE: Wall spans between piers, no footing.

T = THICKNESS

L = LENGTH

NON-REINFORCED WALLS L/T RATIO

WIND PRESSURE (P.S.F.)	MAXIMUM LENGTH/THICKNESS RATIO
5	35
10	25
15	20
20	18
25	16
30	14
35	13
40	12

NON-REINFORCED WALLS WITH CONTINUOUS FOOTINGS

PIER AND PANEL GARDEN WALLS

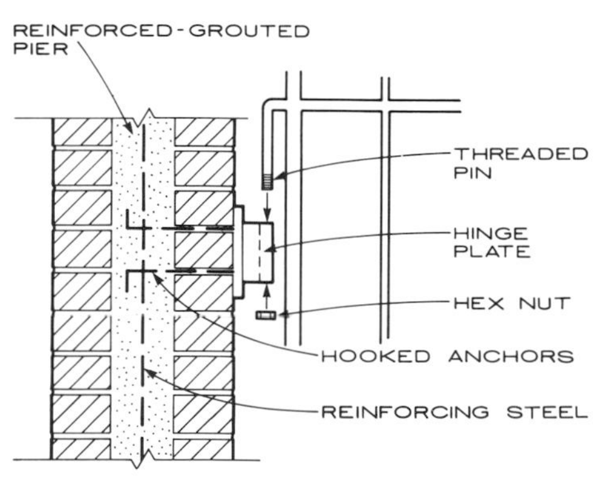

REINFORCED-GROUTED PIER
THREADED PIN
HINGE PLATE
HEX NUT
HOOKED ANCHORS
REINFORCING STEEL

HINGE DETAIL

IRON GARDEN GATE

ANALYSIS OF SECTIONS

M_o = OVERTURNING MOMENT

M_r = RESISTING MOMENT

W = WEIGHT OF WALL AND FOOTING (LB.)

P = WIND LOAD (LB./FT.^{2}) (FROM CODE)

$M_o = PL_1$ $M_r = WL_2$

FOR STABILITY $M_r \geq M_o$;

IF NOT, REDESIGN

CANTILEVER FOOTINGS ARE OFTEN USED AT PROPERTY LINES OR TO INCREASE RESISTANCE TO OVERTURNING. BE SURE TO CHECK FOR WIND FROM EITHER DIRECTION

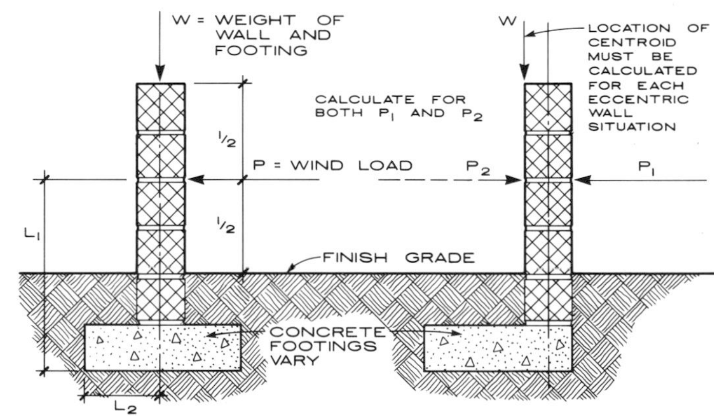

W = WEIGHT OF WALL AND FOOTING
W
LOCATION OF CENTROID MUST BE CALCULATED FOR EACH ECCENTRIC WALL SITUATION
CALCULATE FOR BOTH P1 AND P2
l/2
P = WIND LOAD
P2
P1
l/2
L1
FINISH GRADE
CONCRETE FOOTINGS VARY
L2

SYMMETRICAL CANTILEVER/ECCENTRIC

HORIZONTAL LOADING - FREESTANDING WALLS

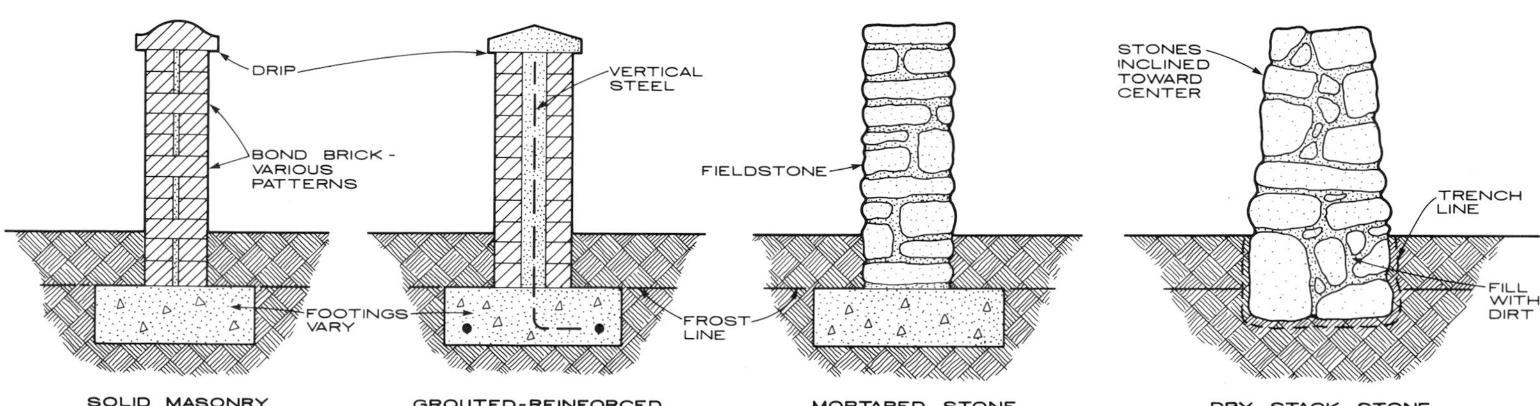

DRIP
VERTICAL STEEL
BOND BRICK - VARIOUS PATTERNS
FIELDSTONE
STONES INCLINED TOWARD CENTER
TRENCH LINE
FOOTINGS VARY
FROST LINE
FILL WITH DIRT

SOLID MASONRY GROUTED-REINFORCED MORTARED STONE DRY STACK STONE

FREESTANDING WALL TYPES

Christine Beall, AIA, CCS; Austin, Texas
Charles R. Heuer, AIA; Washington, D.C.

DIMENSIONS AND REINFORCEMENT

WALL	H	B	T	A	"V" BARS	"F" BARS
8"	3' 4"	2' 4"	9"	8"	#3 @ 32"	#3 @ 27"
	4' 0"	2' 9"	9"	10"	#4 @ 32"	#3 @ 27"
	4' 8"	3' 4"	10"	12"	#5 @ 32"	#3 @ 27"
	5' 4"	3' 8"	10"	14"	#4 @ 16"	#4 @ 30"
	6' 0"	4' 2"	12"	16"	#6 @ 24"	#4 @ 25"
12"	5' 4"	3' 8"	10"	14"	#4 @ 24"	#3 @ 25"
	6' 0"	4' 2"	12"	15"	#4 @ 16"	#4 @ 30"
	6' 8"	4' 6"	12"	16"	#6 @ 24"	#4 @ 22"
	7' 4"	4' 10"	12"	18"	#5 @ 16"	#5 @ 26"
	8' 0"	5' 4"	12"	20"	#7 @ 24"	#5 @ 21"
	8' 8"	5' 10"	14"	22"	#6 @ 8"	#6 @ 26"
	9' 4"	6' 2"	14"	24"	#8 @ 8"	#6 @ 21"

NOTE: See General Notes for design parameters.

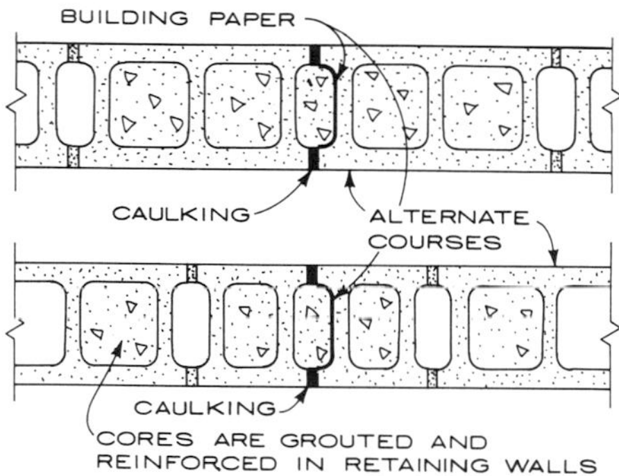
BUILDING PAPER
CAULKING
ALTERNATE COURSES
CAULKING
CORES ARE GROUTED AND REINFORCED IN RETAINING WALLS

SHEAR-RESISTING CONTROL JOINT

NOTE

Long retaining walls should be broken into panels 20 ft. to 30 ft. long by vertical control joints designed to resist shear and other lateral forces while permitting longitudinal movement.

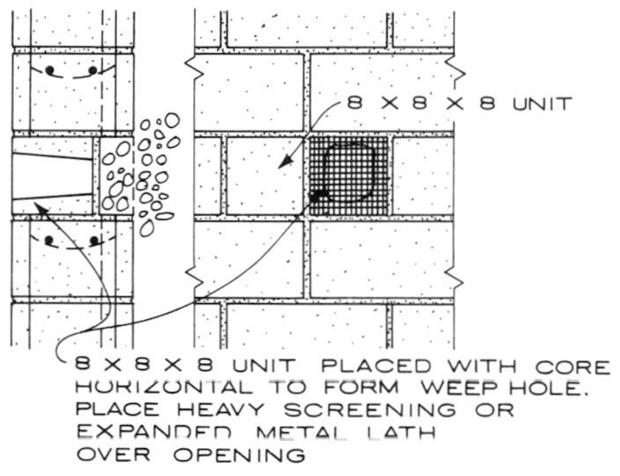
8 X 8 X 8 UNIT
8 X 8 X 8 UNIT PLACED WITH CORE HORIZONTAL TO FORM WEEP HOLE. PLACE HEAVY SCREENING OR EXPANDED METAL LATH OVER OPENING

ALTERNATE WEEP HOLE DETAIL

NOTE

Four inch diameter weepholes located at 5 to 10 ft spacing along the base of the wall should be sufficient. Place about 1 cu ft of gravel or crushed stone around the intake of each weephole.

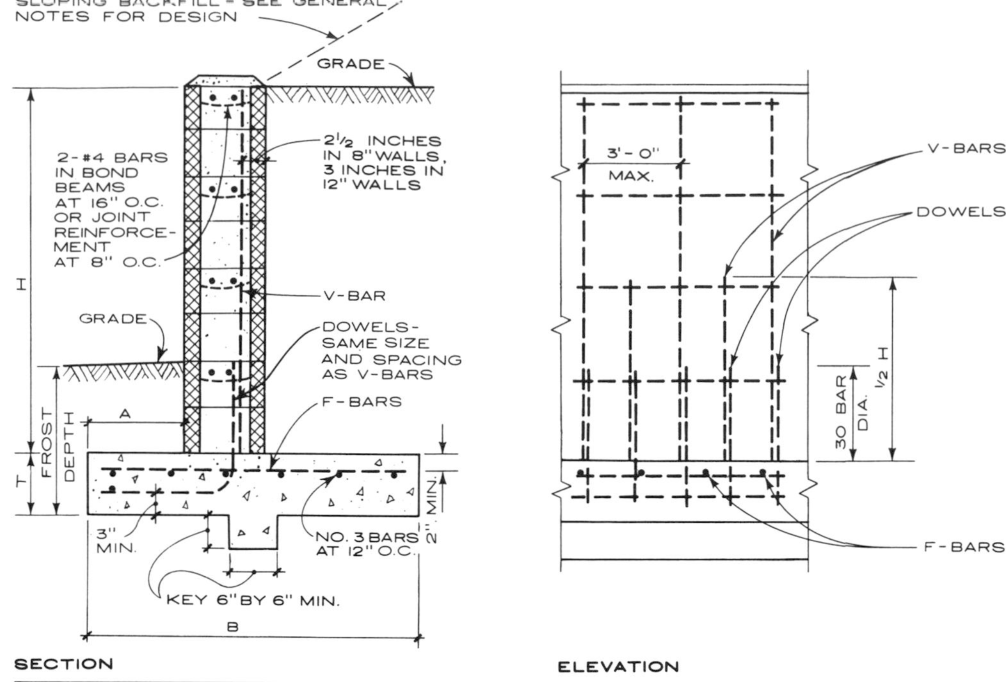
SLOPING BACKFILL - SEE GENERAL NOTES FOR DESIGN
GRADE
2-#4 BARS IN BOND BEAMS AT 16" O.C. OR JOINT REINFORCEMENT AT 8" O.C.
2½ INCHES IN 8" WALLS, 3 INCHES IN 12" WALLS
H
GRADE
V-BAR
DOWELS - SAME SIZE AND SPACING AS V-BARS
F-BARS
A
FROST DEPTH
T
2" MIN.
3" MIN.
NO. 3 BARS AT 12" O.C.
KEY 6" BY 6" MIN.
B
3'-0" MAX.
V-BARS
DOWELS
30 BAR DIA.
½ H
F-BARS
SECTION
ELEVATION

TYPICAL CANTILEVER RETAINING WALL

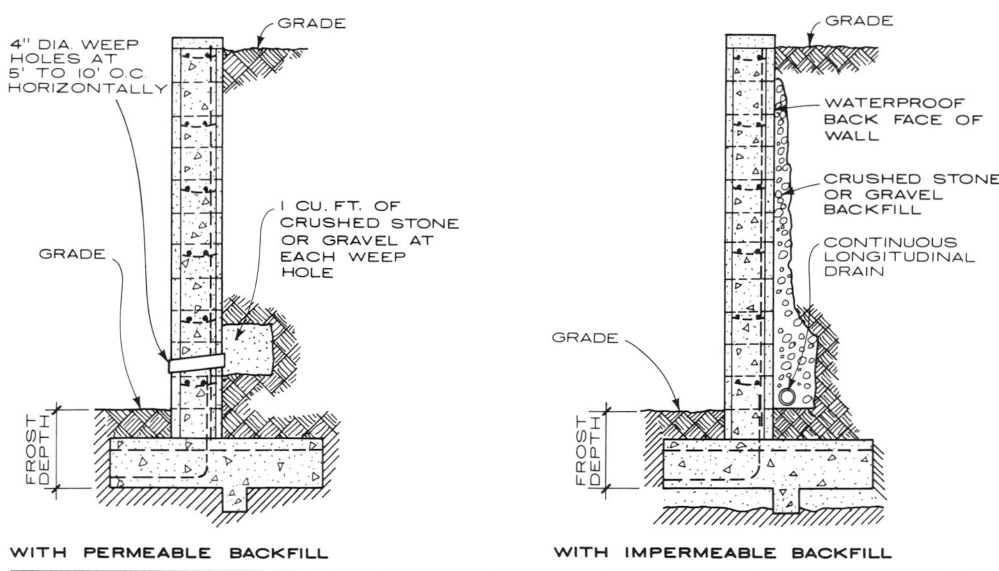
GRADE
4" DIA. WEEP HOLES AT 5' TO 10' O.C. HORIZONTALLY
1 CU. FT. OF CRUSHED STONE OR GRAVEL AT EACH WEEP HOLE
GRADE
FROST DEPTH
GRADE
WATERPROOF BACK FACE OF WALL
CRUSHED STONE OR GRAVEL BACKFILL
CONTINUOUS LONGITUDINAL DRAIN
GRADE
FROST DEPTH
WITH PERMEABLE BACKFILL
WITH IMPERMEABLE BACKFILL

DRAINAGE DETAILS FOR VARYING SOIL CONDITIONS

GENERAL NOTES

1. Materials and construction practices for concrete masonry retaining walls should comply with "Building Code Requirements for Concrete Masonry Structures (ACI 531)."
2. Use fine grout where grout space is less than 3 in. in least dimension. Use coarse grout where the least dimension of the grout space is 3 in. or more.
3. Steel reinforcement should be clean, free from harmful rust, and in compliance with applicable ASTM standards for deformed bars and steel wire.
4. Alternate vertical bars may be stopped at wall mid-height. Vertical reinforcement usually is secured in place after the masonry work has been completed and before grouting.
5. Designs herein are based on an assumed soil weight (vertical pressure) of 100 pcf. Horizontal pressure is based on an equivalent fluid weight for the soil of 45 pcf.
6. Walls shown are designed with a safety factor against overturning of not less than 2 and a safety factor against horizontal sliding of not less than 1.5. Computations in the table for wall heights are based on level backfill. One method of providing for additional loads due to sloping backfill or surface loads is to consider them as an additional depth of soil, that is, an extra load of 300 psf can be treated as 3 ft. of extra soil weighing 100 psf.
7. Top of masonry retaining walls should be capped or otherwise protected to prevent entry of water into unfilled hollow cells and spaces. If bond beams are used, steel is placed in the beams as the wall is constructed. Horizontal joint reinforcement may be placed in each joint (8 in. o.c.) and the bond beams omitted.
8. Allow 24 hours for masonry to set before grouting. Pour grout in 4 ft. layers, 1 hour between each pour. Break long walls into panels of 20 ft. to 30 ft. in length with vertical control joints. Allow 7 days for finished wall to set before backfilling. Prevent water from accumulating behind wall by means of 4 in. diameter weepholes at 5 ft. to 10 ft. spacing (with screen and graded stone) or by a continuous drain with felt-covered open joints combined with waterproofing.
9. Where backfill height exceeds 6 ft., provide a key under the footing base to resist the wall's tendency to slide horizontally.
10. Heavy equipment used in backfilling should not approach closer to the top of the wall than a distance equal to the height of the wall.
11. A structural engineer should be consulted for final design.

Kenneth D. Franch, AIA, PE; Phillips Swager Associates, Inc.; Dallas, Texas
Stephen J. Zipp, AIA; Wilkes and Faulkner Associates; Washington, D.C.

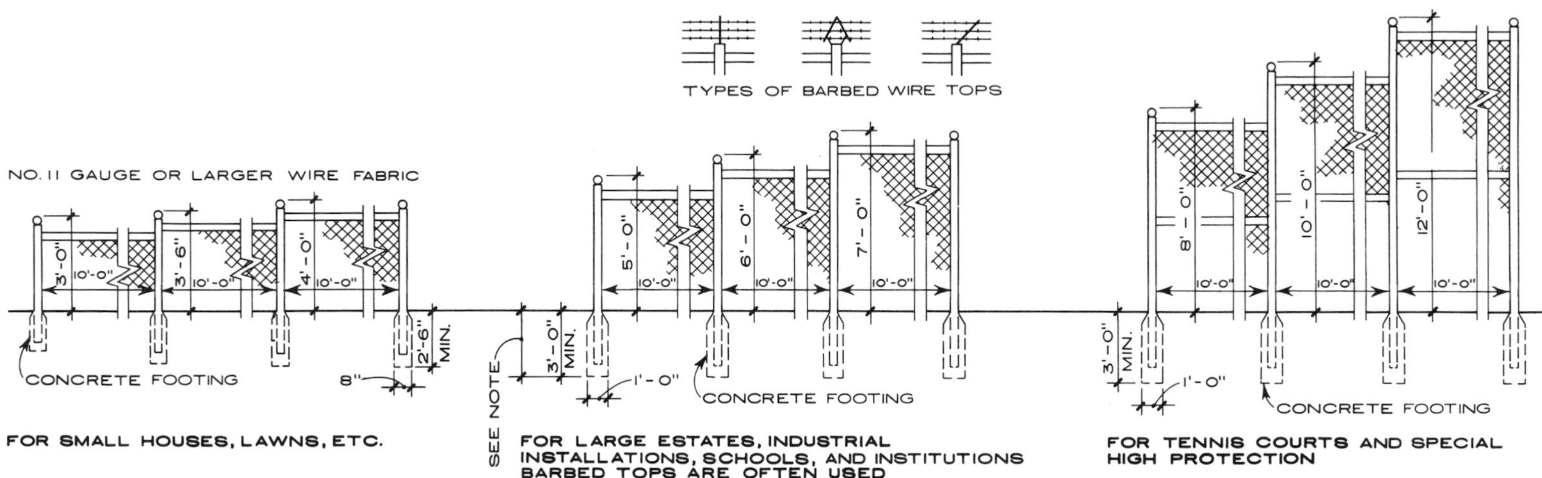
TYPES OF BARBED WIRE TOPS
NO. 11 GAUGE OR LARGER WIRE FABRIC
CONCRETE FOOTING
FOR SMALL HOUSES, LAWNS, ETC.
SEE NOTE
FOR LARGE ESTATES, INDUSTRIAL INSTALLATIONS, SCHOOLS, AND INSTITUTIONS BARBED TOPS ARE OFTEN USED
FOR TENNIS COURTS AND SPECIAL HIGH PROTECTION

HEIGHTS OF FENCES FOR VARIOUS USES

See note at middle right for depth of concrete footings.

MATERIALS

SIZES GIVEN ARE NOT STANDARD BUT REPRESENT THE AVERAGE SIZES USED

Wire gauge	Usually No. 11 or No. 9 W & M. For specially rugged use use No. 6. For tennis courts usually No. 11
Wire mesh	Usually 2″. For tennis courts usually $1^5/_8$″ or $1^3/_4$″ of chain link steel hot dip galvanized after weaving. Top and bottom salvage may be barbed or knuckled
Corner and end posts	For lawn fences usually 2″ O.D. For estate fences 2″ for low and $2^1/_2$″ for medium and 3″ O.D. for heavy or high For tennis courts 3″ O.D.
Line or intermediate posts	For lawn $1^3/_8$″ or 2″ O.D. round For estate etc. 2″, $2^1/_4$″, $2^1/_2$″ H or I sections For tennis courts $2^1/_2$″ round O.D. or $2^1/_4$″ H or I sections
Gate posts	The same or next size larger than the corner posts. Footings for gate posts 3′-6″ deep
Top rails	$1^5/_8$″ O.D. except some lawn fence may be $1^3/_8$″ O.D.
Middle rails	On 12′-0″ fence same as top rail
Gates	Single or double any width desired
Post spacing	Line posts 10′-0″ O.C., 8′-0″ O.C. may be used on heavy construction

O.D. = outside diameter.

POST SIZES FOR HEAVY DUTY GATES

A.S.A. SCHEDULE 40 PIPE SIZES	SWING GATE OPENINGS	
	SINGLE GATE	DOUBLE GATE
$2^1/_2$″	To 6′-0″	Up to 12′-0″
$3^1/_2$″	Over 6′ to 18′	Over 12′ to 26′
6″	Over 13′ to 18′	Over 26′ to 36′
8″	Over 18′ to 32′	Over 36′ to 64′

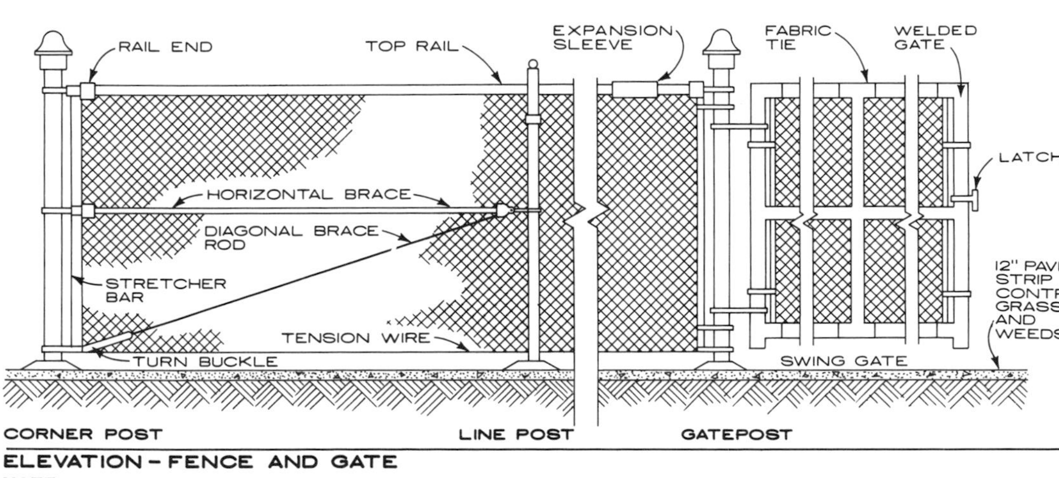
RAIL END
TOP RAIL
EXPANSION SLEEVE
FABRIC TIE
WELDED GATE
LATCH
HORIZONTAL BRACE
DIAGONAL BRACE ROD
STRETCHER BAR
TENSION WIRE
TURN BUCKLE
SWING GATE
12″ PAVED STRIP TO CONTROL GRASS AND WEEDS
CORNER POST
LINE POST
GATEPOST

ELEVATION – FENCE AND GATE

NOTE

For fences 5′-0″ and taller a horizontal or diagonal brace, or both, is used for greater stability. Post spacing should be equidistant and should not exceed 10′-0″ O.C.

CONCRETE FOOTING

Bottom of concrete footing to be set below frost line (see local code). Concrete footing sizes shown are the recommended minimum; they should be redesigned for conditions where soil is poor.

TYPES OF WIRE FABRIC MESH

VINYL-COATED: Suitable for residential, commercial or industrial applications.

Mesh sizes: 1, $1^1/_4$, $1^1/_2$, $1^3/_4$, and 2 in.

Gauge sizes: 11, 9, 6, and 3.

REDWOOD SLATS

Used for visual privacy and appearance. Suitable for homes, swimming pools, and gardens.

Mesh size: $3^1/_2$ x 5 in.

Gauge size: 9.

1. PREGALVANIZED: Should be restricted to such residential applications as residential perimeter fencing, swimming pool enclosures, private tennis courts, dog kennels, and interior industrial storage.
   Mesh sizes: $1^1/_2$, $1^3/_4$, and 2 in. Gauge sizes: 13, 11, and 9.
2. HOT DIPPED GALVANIZED: Suitable for highway enclosures, institutional security fencing, highway bridge enclosures, exterior industrial security fences, parking lot enclosures, recreational applications, and any other environment where resistance to abuse and severe climatic conditions exist.
   Mesh sizes: $1^1/_2$, $2^3/_4$, and 2 in. Gauge sizes: 9 and 6.

COATINGS

Protective coatings used on fencing, such as zinc and aluminum. Various decorative coatings can be applied including vinyl bonded and organic coatings available from most manufacturers.

SPECIAL FENCING

1. ORNAMENTAL: Vertical struts only—no chain link fabric required. Ideal for landscape or as barrier fence.
2. ELEPHANT FENCE: This fence can actually stop an elephant, hold back a rock slide, or bring a small truck to a halt. Size: 3 gauges x 2-in. mesh.
3. SECURITY FENCE: This fabric is nonclimbable and cannot be penetrated by gun muzzles, knives, or other weapons. Suitable as security barrier for police stations, prisons, reformatories, hospitals, and mental institutions. Mesh size: $^3/_8$ in. for maximum security, $^1/_2$ in. for high security, $^5/_8$ in. for supersecurity, and 1 in. for standard security.

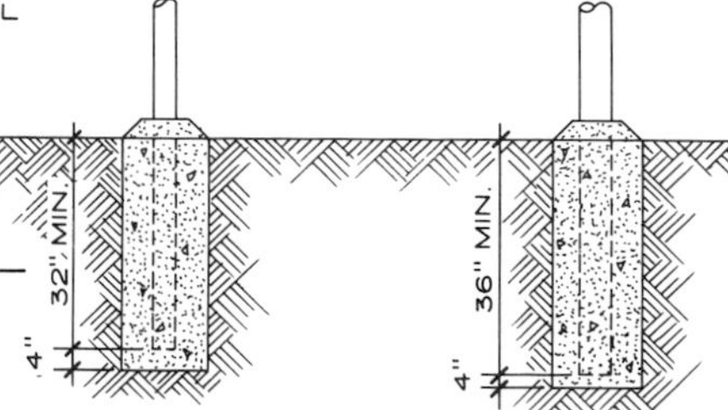
32″ MIN.
36″ MIN.
4″
LINE POST
CORNER AND GATEPOST

Charles Driesen; Ewing Cole Erdman & Eubank; Philadelphia, Pennsylvania

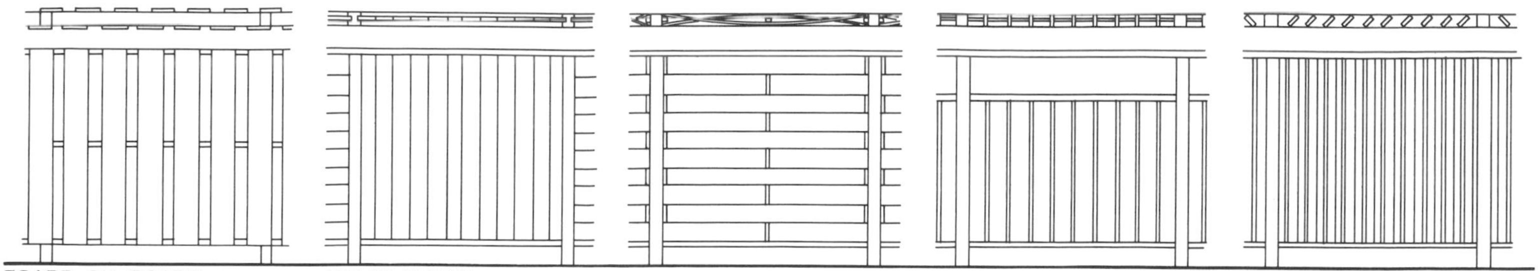

BOARD ON BOARD | SOLID BOARD | BASKETWEAVE | SOLID PANEL WITH STRIPS | LOUVERS

SOLID FENCE TYPES

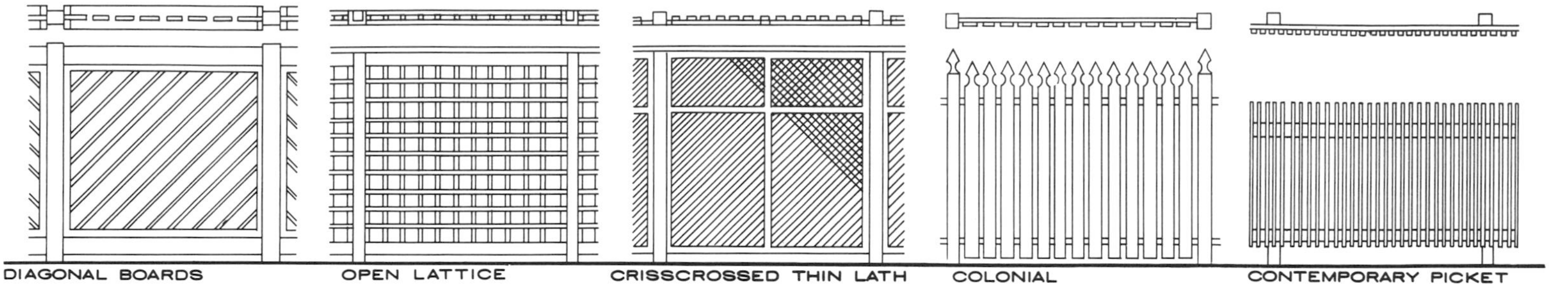

DIAGONAL BOARDS | OPEN LATTICE | CRISSCROSSED THIN LATH | COLONIAL | CONTEMPORARY PICKET

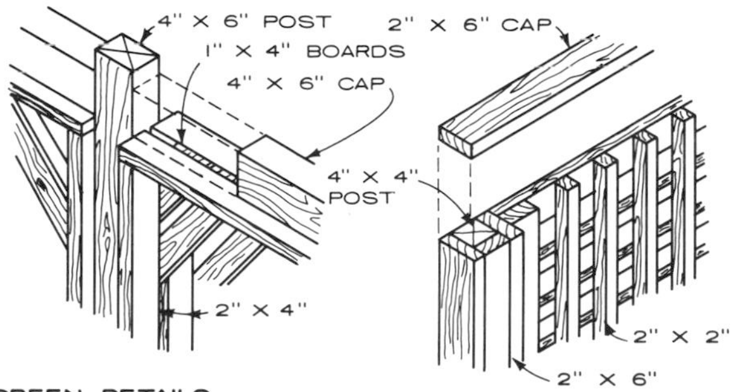

4" X 6" POST
2" X 6" CAP
1" X 4" BOARDS
4" X 6" CAP
4" X 4" POST
2" X 4"
2" X 2"
2" X 6"

SCREEN DETAILS

TOP RAIL OF POSTS MAY BE SLOPED 2% TO PROVIDE DRAINAGE

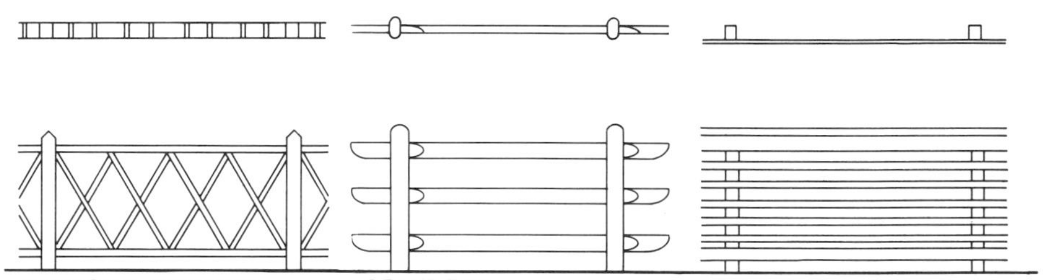

DIAMOND BRACING | SPLIT RAIL | POST AND BOARD

TRANSPARENT FENCES AND SCREENS

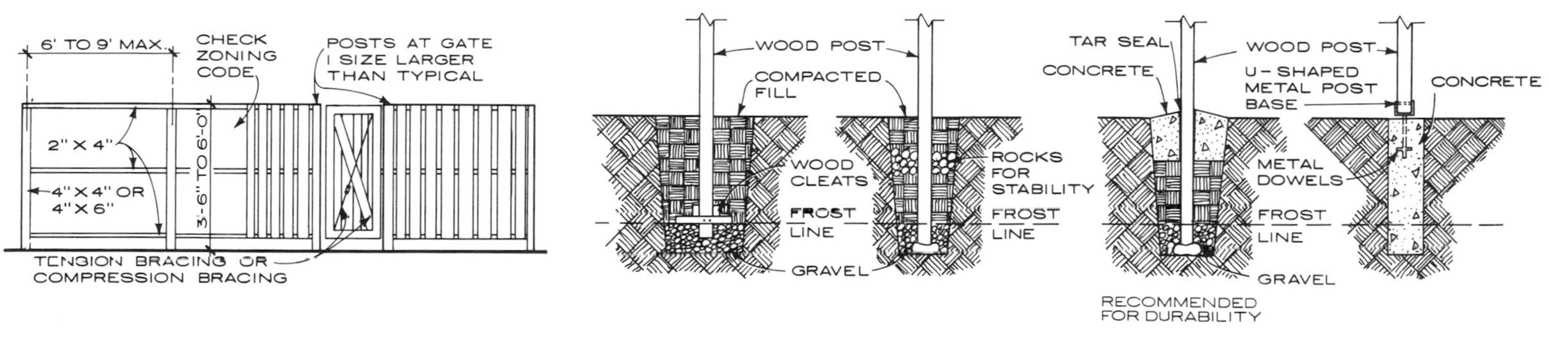
6' TO 9' MAX.
CHECK ZONING CODE
POSTS AT GATE 1 SIZE LARGER THAN TYPICAL
2" X 4"
4" X 4" OR 4" X 6"
3'-6" TO 6'-0"
TENSION BRACING OR COMPRESSION BRACING
WOOD POST
COMPACTED FILL
WOOD CLEATS
ROCKS FOR STABILITY
FROST LINE
GRAVEL
TAR SEAL
CONCRETE
WOOD POST
U-SHAPED METAL POST BASE
CONCRETE
METAL DOWELS
FROST LINE
GRAVEL
RECOMMENDED FOR DURABILITY

TYPICAL FENCE DIMENSIONS

FOOTING DETAILS

NOTES

When selecting a wood fence pattern, consider:

1. Site topography and prevailing wind conditions;
2. Architectural style of surrounding buildings and adjacent land use;
3. Required fence height and size of the property to be enclosed.

PURPOSE

Wood fences are used for security, privacy, and screening of outdoor spaces. Picket fences 3 ft. or 4 ft. high keep small children or small dogs in the yard. Board-on-board fences, by standards built taller, provide greater wind and view barriers. Acoustical fences are built to keep out sound and wind, and to provide privacy. Open lattice or louvered fences, usually a minimum of 4 ft. high with self-closing gates and latches, are used for swimming pool enclosures. A semitransparent wood screen often is used to enclose an outdoor room to avoid totally obstructing the view or restricting natural ventilation. Long, open fence patterns are used best at the property line to define boundaries or limit access to a site.

FASTENERS

Fasteners should be of noncorrosive aluminum alloy or stainless steel. Top quality, hot dipped galvanized steel is acceptable. Metal flanges, cleats, bolts, and screws are better than common nails.

Pressure-treated wood commonly is used for fencing. Certain species of nontreated woods, such as cedar and redwood heart, also are suitable. Refer to pages on wood uses in Chapter 6 for further information. Natural, stain, and paint finishes may be used.

Charles R. Heuer, AIA; Washington, D.C.

GENERAL INFORMATION AND TERMINOLOGY

Building layout requires a site plan that has been accurately drawn to a specific scale (e.g., 1 in. = 20 ft), showing all relevant information regarding: building outline (footprint) dimensioned location from the property lines, existing and new streets and curbs, above and below ground utilities, easements, all site improvements (other than the building footprint) such as driveways, retaining walls, and patios, and other features unique to the site. Existing and new contour lines, spot grade elevations, and bench marks should be shown on a site plan if there is not a separate grading plan. All information, especially building location, should be verified to conform to local codes and zoning ordinance requirements prior to layout.

1. Angles: The difference in direction of two intersecting lines.
2. Azimuths: Angles measured clockwise from any meridian, usually north; however, the National Geodetic Survey uses south.
3. Bearings: The acute angle between the meridian and a line, measured from north or south, toward east or west to give a reading of less than 90° (e.g., S 31° 13′ E).
4. Transit: A precise general-purpose surveying instrument primarily used for measuring horizontal (azimuth and bearing) angles, vertical (altitude) angles, and to run level lines. It can also be used to measure distances directly by subtense and stadia measurement.
5. Taping: Tape lengths are not guaranteed accurate. Certified tapes are those having their lengths verified at the National Bureau of Standards, checked at a temperature of 68°F at both 10 lb pull (fully supported) and 12 lb pull (ends supported). To obtain accurate measurements, the measured distance must be corrected for temperature differences. The coefficient of thermal expansion for steel tapes is 0.0000065/unit of length/°F. Invar tapes, made of special nickel steel alloy, do not need temperature corrections. A spring balance is used to measure standard pull. The tape must be horizontal and in true alignment.
6. Stadia measurement: A rapid, efficient method of measuring distances accurately enough for locating topographic details. The transit has two horizontal cross hairs, spaced equidistant from the center cross hair. The interval between hairs gives a vertical intercept of 1 ft on the rod for every 100 ft of distance to the rod; thus the distance to a point can be read directly by counting the number of hundredths of a foot between stadia hairs.
7. Subtense bar: The angle between targets is determined by using a transit reading to an accuracy of 1 sec of an arc or less. The horizontal distance from the transit to the bar is computed mathematically or read from a table.
8. Bench mark (BM): An established elevation point, used as a reference for survey purposes. Mean sea level is the national reference elevation. Local datum may exist in many areas.
9. Leveling: The process of finding the difference in elevations between points. The transit is set up approximately one-half the distance between the BM and the point to be determined. A back sight (BS) is taken on the BM and the height of instrument (HI) determined by reading the rod at the center cross hair (rod reading + BM + HI). The rod is then placed on the new point. A foresight is taken and the rod reading subtracted from HI to determine the elevation of the point (HI − rod reading = elevation in ft).
10. Leveling rods: Tall rods, usually wood, graduated in feet, tenths, and hundredths of a foot; or in metric using meters, centimeters, and millimeters.
11. Cadastral surveys: Surveys that are made to establish property boundary lines. Deed descriptions are essential parts of any document denoting ownership or conveyance of land. The basic rule of property lines and corners is that they shall remain in their original positions as established on the ground. This basic rule is important because most land surveys are resurveys. The original description may be followed, but this description is merely an aid to the discovery of the originally established lines and corners. Substantial discrepancies are frequently found. In some states, surveys are conducted on the metes and bounds principle, and in others, the basic subdivisions are rectangular. If boundaries to be described border an irregular line (a winding stream), the line can be located by a series of closely spaced perpendicular offsets from an auxiliary straight line.

John J. Hare, AIA; Haddonfield, New Jersey
Walter H. Sobel, FAIA, and Associates; Chicago, Illinois

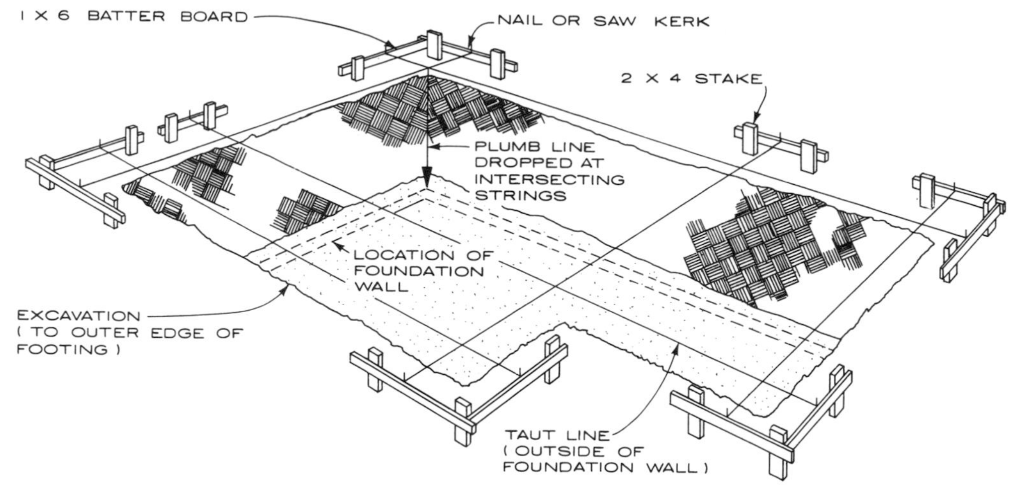
1 X 6 BATTER BOARD
NAIL OR SAW KERK
2 X 4 STAKE
PLUMB LINE DROPPED AT INTERSECTING STRINGS
LOCATION OF FOUNDATION WALL
EXCAVATION (TO OUTER EDGE OF FOOTING)
TAUT LINE (OUTSIDE OF FOUNDATION WALL)

NOTES

First locate the building in its correct relationship to the property lines. Set stakes at the building corners, using a transit to reestablish correct angles and steel tapes for distance measurements. Mark exact corner locations on the stake heads with finishing nails. Set offset stakes or batter boards 3 to 5 ft outside the corners to allow room for construction operations. Set batter boards at a predetermined elevation. Then project the location of the building corners to the tops of the batter boards and set nails. Stretch strings taut between nails to define the corners and outside wall lines. For small buildings, the elevation of the top of the footings can be located by measuring down from the strings. Strings sag over long distances and with changes in humidity, so for large buildings stakes indicating top of footings are set with the transit.

BUILDING LAYOUT PROCEDURES

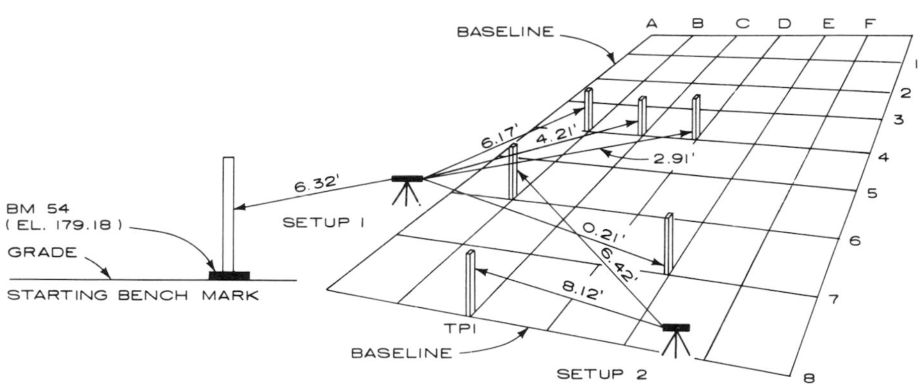
BASELINE
A B C D E F
1
2
3
4
5
6
7
8
6.17′
4.21′
2.91′
6.32′
BM 54 (EL. 179.18)
GRADE
STARTING BENCH MARK
SETUP 1
0.21′
6.42′
8.12′
TP1
BASELINE
SETUP 2

NOTES

A grid system can be used for identifying those points whose elevation is required. The transit is set where both the BM and the points on the grid can be observed. Sighting on the BM determines HI. Elevations of grid points can then be found by sighting the rod held at each point. The rod reading is subtracted from the HI to obtain the elevation of the point sighted (HI − rod reading = elevation point). Resight the BM periodically to assure the instrument has not moved. Contour lines are then sketched between elevation points by interpolation.

TOPOGRAPHIC SURVEY—GRID SYSTEM

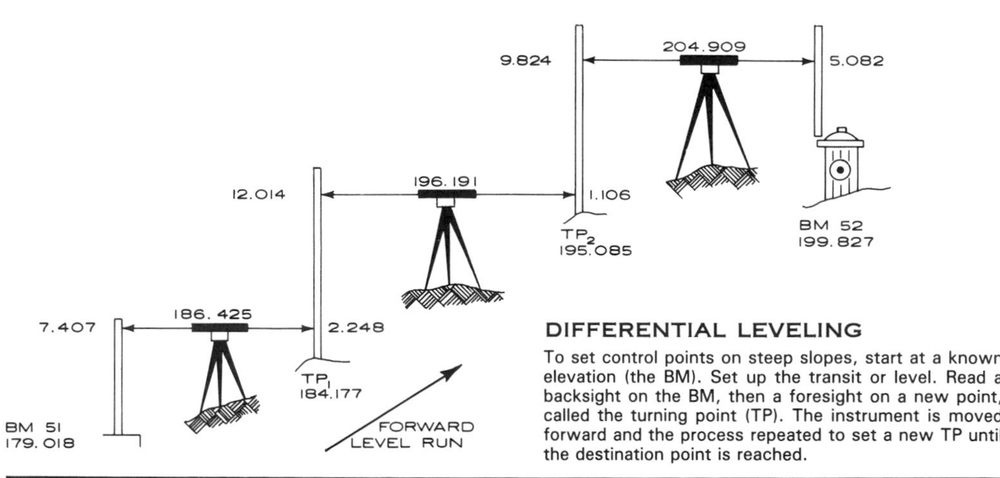
9.824
204.909
5.082
12.014
196.191
1.106
TP2
195.085
BM 52
199.827
7.407
186.425
2.248
TP1
184.177
BM 51
179.018
FORWARD LEVEL RUN

DIFFERENTIAL LEVELING

To set control points on steep slopes, start at a known elevation (the BM). Set up the transit or level. Read a backsight on the BM, then a foresight on a new point, called the turning point (TP). The instrument is moved forward and the process repeated to set a new TP until the destination point is reached.

DIFFERENTIAL LEVELING

REFERENCES

GENERAL REFERENCES

Building Foundation Design Handbook, 1988, K. Labs, J. Carmody, et al., Underground Space Center, Minneapolis

Concrete Basements for Residential and Light Construction, Portland Cement Association (PCA)

Energy Conserving Site Design, 1984, E. G. McPherson, American Society of Landscape Architects (ASLA)

Graphic Standards for Landscape Architecture, 1986, Richard Austin, Van Nostrand Reinhold

Handbook of Landscape Architectural Construction, American Society of Landscape Architects (ASLA)

Simplified Design of Building Foundations, 1988, James Ambrose, Wiley

Site Design and Construction Detailing, 1988, Theodore D. Walker, PDA Publishers

Site Details, 1989, Gregory W. Jameson and Michael A. Verson, Van Nostrand Reinhold

Time-Saver Standards for Landscape Architecture, 1988, Charles W. Harris and Nicholas T. Dines, McGraw-Hill

Time-Saver Standards for Site Planning, 1984, Joseph DeChiara and Lee E. Koppleman, McGraw-Hill

DATA SOURCES: ORGANIZATIONS

American Society for Testing and Materials (ASTM), 47, 49, 80

American Wood Preservers Institute (AWPI), 48

Architectural Press Limited, 48

Barry Pattern & Foundry Company, Inc., 56

California Redwood Association, 82

Canterbury Designs, Canterbury International, Inc., 67

Columbia Cascade Timber Company, 70

Contech Construction Products, Inc., 56

CONTECH—Construction Techniques, Inc., 46

Endicott Clay Products Company, 49

Environmental Protection Agency (EPA), 48, 58–61

Florist and Nursery Corps and Agricultural Engineering Laboratories, U.S. Department of Agriculture (USDA), 75

Gametime, Inc., 71

Grass Pavers Limited, 46

Hanover Prest-Paving Company, 49

Hastings Pavement Company, Inc., 49

Iron Mountain Forge, 70

Landscape Products, Inc., 48

Landscape Structures, Inc., 70, 71

Metalines, Inc., 56

National Cement Products, 46

National Concrete Masonry Association (NCMA), 80

Neenah Foundry Company, 56

Outdoor Advertising Association of America, Inc. (OAAA), 65

Pavestone Company, 49

Paving Stones of Texas, 49

Pee Dee Ceramics, 49

Playworld Systems, 70, 71

Polydrain, 56

Portland Cement Association (PCA), 48

Rally Racks, Inc., 67

Ritterings USA, Inc., 49

Sunshine U-lock Corporation, 67

Toro Company, 69

Underpinning and Foundation Construction, Inc., 47

Walker Porsowall Pipe Company, 54

Weather Bureau, U.S. Department of Commerce, 44

DATA SOURCES: PUBLICATIONS

Annual Book of ASTM Standards, American Society for Testing and Materials (ASTM), 49

Concrete Reinforcing Steel Institute Handbook, 1984 ed., Concrete Reinforcing Steel Institute (CRSI), 77

Construction Measurements, 2nd ed., 1988, B. Austin Barry, Wiley, 83

Data Book for Civil Engineers, Vol. 1: Design, 1945, Elwyn E. Seelye, Wiley. Reprinted with permission, 55, 56

Design for Landscape Architects, 1984, Albe E. Munsun, McGraw-Hill, 62

Developer's Handbook, Allen Carroll, Connecticut Coastal Management Program. Excerpted with permission, 62

Fountains and Pools, 1986, C. Douglas Aurand, PDA Publishers, 68

Handbook of Landscape Architectural Construction, American Society of Landscape Architects (ASLA), 52

Handbook of Landscape Architectural Construction, E. Byron McCulley and Joe D. Carpenter, Landscape Foundation Inc., 68

Interior Plantscaping: Building Design for Interior Foliage Plants, 1977, Richard L. Gaines, AIA; Architectural Record Books, 75, 76

Landscape Architecture, 1982, Linda Jewell, American Society of Landscape Architects Publication Board, 49

Landscape Architecture Construction, 1979, Harlow C. Landphair and Fred Klatt, Jr., Elsevier Science Publishing Co, Inc. Reprinted with permission, 55, 56

Light and Color, General Electric Company, 75

Manual of Individual Water Supply Systems, Environmental Protection Agency (EPA), 53

Manual of Septic Tank Practice, Public Health Service Publication No. 526, 58

Masonry Design and Detailing, 1984, Christine Beall, McGraw-Hill, 79

Pile Foundations, Robert D. Chelus, McGraw-Hill, 47

Site Design and Construction Detailing, 1978, Theodore Walker, PDA Publishers, 56

Turf Irrigation Manual, James A. Watkins, Telsco Industries, 69

CHAPTER 3

CONCRETE

CAST-IN-PLACE CONCRETE CONSTRUCTION; PRELIMINARY DATA

REINFORCED CONCRETE

Reinforced concrete consists of concrete and reinforcing steel; the concrete resists the compressive stresses and the reinforcing steel resists the tensile stresses.

Concrete is a mixture of hydraulic cement (usually portland cement), aggregate, admixtures, and water. The concrete strength develops by the hydration of the portland cement, which binds the aggregate together.

TYPES OF CEMENT

Five types of portland cement are manufactured to meet ASTM standards.

Type I is a general purpose cement for all uses. It is the most commonly used type.

Type II cement provides moderate protection from sulfate attack for concrete in drainage structures and a lower heat of hydration for concrete use in heavy retaining walls, piers, and abutments where heat buildup in the concrete can cause problems.

Type III cement provides high strengths at an early age, a week or less. Type III is used when rapid removal of forms is desired and in cold weather to reduce time of controlled curing conditions.

Type IV cement has a low heat of hydration and is used for massive concrete structures such as gravity dams.

Type V cement is sulfate-resisting cement for use where the soil and groundwater have a high sulfate content.

Pozzolans such as fly ash can be used to reduce the amount of cement in a concrete mix. Fly ash is a powdery residue resulting from combustion in coal-fired electric generating plants. It reacts chemically with calcium hydroxide produced by hydration to form cementitious compounds.

ADMIXTURES

Admixtures are various compounds, other than cement, water, and aggregates, added to a mixture to modify the fresh or hardened properties of concrete.

Air entraining admixtures disperse small air bubbles in the concrete, which improves the concrete's resistance to freezing and thawing and to scaling by deicing chemicals. Recommended total air contents are shown in Table 1 for different exposure conditions and for maximum size of aggregate.

Water reducing admixtures reduce the quantity of mixing water needed for a given consistency. Admixtures may delay the set time, and they also may entrain air.

Other mixtures are used to retard or to accelerate the set of concrete. Some accelerating admixtures contain chlorides that can cause corrosion of the reinforcing steel; therefore, they should be used with caution and only for very specific purposes. Some water reducing and accelerating admixtures may increase dry shrinkage.

Superplasticizers are high-range water reducers that can greatly affect the slump and strength of concrete. When used in concrete with normal water-cement ratios, they produce a high slump, flowable concrete that is easily placed. When used to reduce the water-cement ratio, the slump is not affected, but significantly higher than normal strengths are attained. When used to produce flowable concrete, the plasticizer's effect has a limited timespan.

AGGREGATES

The aggregate portion of a concrete mix is divided into fine and coarse aggregates. The fine aggregate generally is sand of particles less than ⅜ in. large. The coarse aggregate is crushed rock or gravel. Concrete weighs 135 pcf to 165 pcf. Lightweight aggregate is manufactured from expanded shale, slate, clay, or slag, and the concrete weighs from 85 pcf to 115 pcf.

Normal weight aggregates must meet ASTM Specification C33. Lightweight aggregates must meet ASTM Specification C330.

The aggregate represents 60 percent to 80 percent of the concrete volume, and the gradation (range of particle sizes) affects the amount of cement and water required in the mix, the physical properties during placing and finishing, and the compressive strength. Aggregates should be clean, hard, strong, and free of surface materials.

REINFORCING STEEL

Reinforcing steel, manufactured as round rods with raised deformations for adhesion and resistance to slip in the concrete, is available in several grades (yield strengths) and diameters manufactured to ASTM standards. Commonly used reinforcing rods have a yield strength of 60,000 psi available in sizes from #3 to #18, the size being the diameter in eighths of an inch. Reinforcing rods having a yield strength of 40,000 psi also are available in the smaller bar sizes. Welded wire mesh has yield strengths of 60,000 psi to 70,000 psi, and the wire is either plain or deformed.

Table 3 summarizes the various grades of reinforcing steel, and Figure 1 shows the system of reinforcing rod identification.

SLUMP TEST

The ASTM standard slump cone test is to determine only the consistency among batches of concrete of the same mix design; it should not be used to compare mixes of greatly different mix proportions. A slump test mold is a funnel-shaped sheet metal form. The slump mold is filled from the top in three levels, each level being tamped 25 times with a ⅝ in. diameter rod. The mold is removed slowly, allowing the concrete to slump down from its original height. The difference from the top of the mold to the top of the slumped concrete is the slump. There is no "right" slump consistency for all concrete work. It can vary from 1 in. to 6 in., depending on the specific requirements of the job. Table 2 lists typical slumps for various types of construction.

Workability is the ease or difficulty of placing, consolidating, and finishing the concrete. Concrete should be workable, but it should not segregate or bleed excessively before finishing.

CYLINDER TEST

A major problem with concrete tests is that the most important data, the compressive strength, cannot be determined until after curing has begun. This occasionally has caused the removal of deficient concrete several weeks after it was placed. A standard compression test is made in accordance with ASTM C39 by placing three layers of concrete in a cardboard cylinder 6 in. in diameter and 12 in. high. Each layer is rodded 25 times with a ⅝ in. diameter steel rod. The cylinder should be protected from damage but placed in the same temperature and humidity environment as the concrete from which the sample was obtained. At the end of the test curing time, usually 7 to 28 days, the concrete cylinder is removed from its form and tested in compression. The load at which the cylinder fails in compression is registered on a gauge in pounds, and the strength of the concrete is calculated in pounds per square inch.

PLACING CONCRETE

Concrete should be placed as near its final position as possible, and it should not be moved horizontally in forms because segregation of the mortar from the coarser material may occur. Concrete should be placed in horizontal layers of uniform thickness, each layer being thoroughly consolidated before the next layer is positioned.

Consolidation of concrete can be achieved either by hand tamping and rodding or by mechanical internal or external vibration. The frequency and amplitude of an internal mechanical vibration should be appropriate for the plastic properties (stiffness or slump) and space in the forms to prevent segregation of the concrete during placing. External vibration can be accomplished by surface vibration for thin sections (slabs) that cannot be consolidated practically by internal vibration. Surface vibrators may be used directly on the surface of slab or with plates attached to the concrete form stiffeners. External vibration must be done for a longer time (1 to 2 min.) than for internal vibration (5 to 15 sec.) to achieve the same consolidation.

TABLE 1. RECOMMENDED AIR CONTENT PERCENTAGE

NOMINAL MAXIMUM SIZE OF COARSE AGGREGATE (IN.)	EXPOSURE	
	MILD	EXTREME
⅜ (10 mm)	4.5	7.5
½ (13 mm)	4.0	6.0
¾ (19 mm)	3.5	6.0
1 (25 mm)	3.0	6.0
1½ (40 mm)	2.5	5.5
2 (50 mm)	2.0	5.0
3 (75 mm)	1.5	4.5

TABLE 2. RECOMMENDED SLUMPS FOR VARIOUS TYPES OF CONSTRUCTION

CONCRETE CONSTRUCTION	SLUMP (IN.)	
	MAXIMUM*	MINIMUM
Reinforced foundation walls and footings	3	1
Plain footings, caissons, and substructure walls	3	1
Beams and reinforced walls	4	1
Building columns	4	1
Pavements and slabs	3	1
Mass concrete	2	1

*May be increased 1 in. for consolidation by hand methods such as rodding and spading.

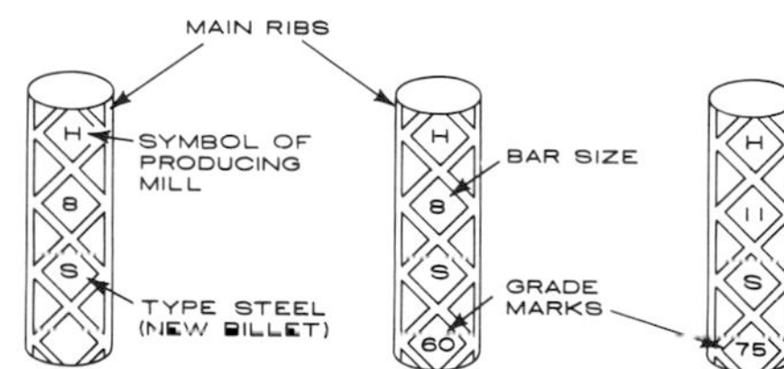
MAIN RIBS
SYMBOL OF PRODUCING MILL
BAR SIZE
TYPE STEEL (NEW BILLET)
GRADE MARKS

NUMBER SYSTEM — GRADE MARKS

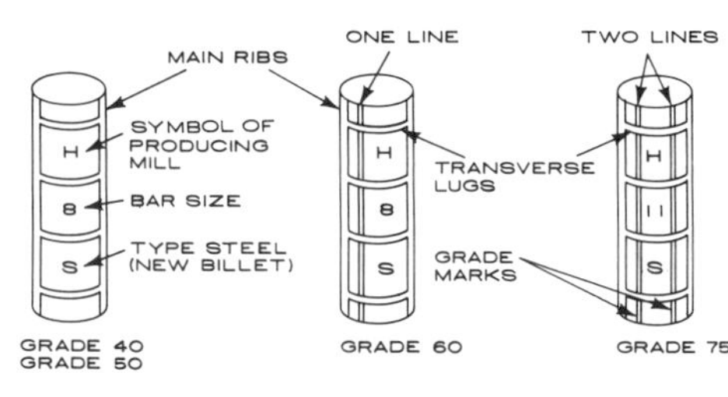
ONE LINE
TWO LINES
MAIN RIBS
SYMBOL OF PRODUCING MILL
BAR SIZE
TYPE STEEL (NEW BILLET)
TRANSVERSE LUGS
GRADE MARKS
GRADE 40
GRADE 50
GRADE 60
GRADE 75

LINE SYSTEM — GRADE MARKS

FIGURE 1. REINFORCING BAR IDENTIFICATION

TABLE 3. REINFORCING STEEL GRADES AND STRENGTHS

ASTM SPEC	YIELD STRENGTH (PSI)	ULTIMATE STRENGTH (PSI)	STEEL TYPE
New billet ASTM A-615			
Grade 40	40,000	70,000	S
Grade 60	60,000	90,000	
Rail steel ASTM A-616			
Grade 50	50,000	80,000	R
Grade 60	60,000	90,000	
Axle steel ASTM A-617			
Grade 40	40,000	70,000	A
Grade 60	60,000	90,000	
Deformed wire ASTM A-496			
Welded fabric	70,000	80,000	—
Cold drawn wire ASTM A-82			
Welded fabric W 1.2	56,000	70,000	
Size W 1.2	65,000	75,000	—

Quentin L. Reutershan, AIA, Architect; Potsdam, New York
Gordon B. Batson, P.E.; Potsdam, New York
Bob Cotton; W. E. Simpson Company Inc.; San Antonio, Texas

PROPERTIES OF CONCRETE

Concrete design strength generally is stated as a minimum compressive strength at 28 days of age for concrete in various structural elements. The normal 28-day compressive strength for commercial-ready mix concrete is 3,000 psi to 4,000 psi; however, higher strengths of 5,000 psi to 7,000 psi generally are required for pre- or post-tensioned concrete. Higher strengths of 10,000 to 12,000 psi may be required for highrise concrete structures.

A typical design mix for 3,000 psi concrete would be 517 lb. of cement (5½ sacks), 1,300 lb. of sand, 1,800 lb. of gravel, and 34 gal. of water (6.2 gal. per sack), which would yield one cu. yd. of concrete, the standard unit of measure.

Compressive strength depends primarily on the type of cement, water-cement ratio, and aggregate quality; the most important is the water-cement ratio. The lower the water-cement ratio, the greater the compressive strength for workable mixes.

When cement, aggregate, and water are mixed, the water starts hydrating, a chemical reaction independent of drying. Concrete does not need air to cure. It can set under water. Concrete sets or becomes firm within hours after it has been mixed, but curing, the process of attaining strength, takes considerably longer. The majority of strength is achieved in the first days of curing. Approximately 50 percent of the total compressive strength is reached in 3 days; 70 percent is reached in 7 days. The remaining 30 percent occurs at a much slower rate in the last 21 days. The concrete's compressive strength may continue to increase beyond the designed strength, as shown in Figure 2.

CURING AND PROTECTION

Two physical conditions profoundly affect concrete's final compressive strength and curing: temperature and the rate at which water used in mixing is allowed to leave the concrete. Optimum temperature for curing concrete is 73°F (22.8°C). Any great variance from this mark reduces its compressive strength. Freezing concrete during curing affects the compressive strength and reduces its weather resistance.

Proper curing is essential to obtain design strength. Moisture, at temperatures above 50°F, must be available for hydration, and the concrete must be protected against temperatures below 40°F during early curing. The longer the water is in the concrete, the longer the reaction takes place; hence, the stronger it becomes.

Moisture conditions can be maintained by spreading wet coverings of burlap or mats, waterproof paper, or plastic sheets over concrete; by placing plastic sheets on the ground before the slab is poured; by spraying liquid curing compound on the surface of fresh concrete; and by leaving the concrete in forms longer.

HOT AND COLD WEATHER CONSTRUCTION

Additional precautions are needed in hot and cold weather to ensure proper curing of the concrete. High temperatures accelerate hardening. More water is needed to maintain the mix consistency; more cement is required to prevent reduced strength from the added water. Chilled water or ice reduces the temperature of the aggregates, and admixtures can retard the initial set. Temperatures ranging from 75°F to 90°F are hot weather construction conditions.

In cold weather the concrete must be heated to above 40°F during placing and early curing, the first 7 days. Protection against freezing may be necessary for up to 2 weeks. This is accomplished by covering the concrete with plastic sheets and heating the interior space with a portable heater. Concrete floors should be protected from carbon dioxide by using specially vented heaters that conduct the exhaust away from the concrete. The time the concrete must be protected can be reduced by using Type III and IIIA cement; a low water-cement ratio; accelerator admixtures; and steam curing. Concrete never should be placed directly on frozen ground. Fresh concrete that has frozen during curing should be removed and replaced because frozen concrete containing ice crystals has very little strength.

PROPORTION OF STRUCTURAL ELEMENTS

Rules of thumb for approximating proportions of solid rectangular beams and slabs are one inch of depth for each foot of span, and the beam width is about two-thirds the depth. The area of steel varies from 1 percent to 2 percent of cross-sectional area of the beam or slab. Columns usually have higher steel percentages than beams. The maximum for columns is 8 percent of the cross-sectional area; however, common range is 3 percent to 6 percent.

DEFLECTIONS

Deflection is affected by shrinkage, load duration, and creep. Creep is the tendency of concrete to continue to deform under sustained load. The more sustained load that a member supports, the more it creeps. The ACI-318 sets minimum length-to-depth ratios for concrete members as shown on Table 6. When members meet or exceed these minimums, deflections usually will not be a problem, and they do not need to be calculated.

FORMWORK

Forming costs can account for 30 percent to 50 percent of a concrete structure. Economy can be gained through the repetitious use of forms. Usually it is cheaper to use one column size rather than to vary column sizes.

In sizing individual floor members, usually it is more economical to use wider girders that are the same depths as the joists or beams they support than to use narrow, deeper girders. Wall pilasters, lugs, and openings should be kept to a minimum since their use increases forming costs. All members should be sized so that readily available standard forms can be used instead of custom job-built forms.

SHORING

Floor framing forms are supported by temporary columns and bracing called shoring. Concrete must be cured for a minimum time or reach a specified percentage of its design strength before shores and forms can be removed.

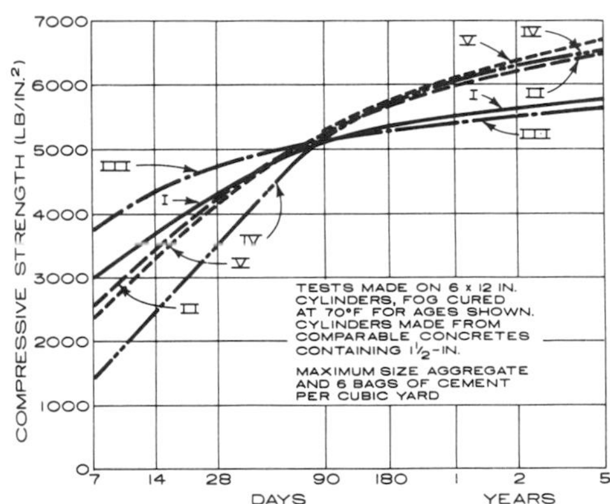

COMPRESSIVE STRENGTH (LB/IN²)
7000
6000
5000
4000
3000
2000
1000
0
I
II
III
IV
V
TESTS MADE ON 6 x 12 IN. CYLINDERS, FOG CURED AT 70°F FOR AGES SHOWN. CYLINDERS MADE FROM COMPARABLE CONCRETES CONTAINING 1½-IN.
MAXIMUM SIZE AGGREGATE AND 6 BAGS OF CEMENT PER CUBIC YARD
7
14
28
90
180
1
2
5
DAYS
YEARS

FIGURE 2. RATES OF STRENGTH DEVELOPMENT FOR CONCRETE MADE WITH VARIOUS TYPES OF CEMENT

TABLE 4. MAXIMUM WATER-CEMENT RATIOS FOR VARIOUS EXPOSURE CONDITIONS

EXPOSURE CONDITION	NORMAL WEIGHT CONCRETE, ABSOLUTE WATER-CEMENT RATIO BY WEIGHT
Concrete protected from exposure to freezing and thawing or application of deicer chemicals	Select water-cement ratio on basis of strength, workability, and finishing needs
Watertight concrete*	
In fresh water	0.50
In seawater	0.45
Frost resistant concrete*	
Thin sections; any section with less than 2-in. cover over reinforcement and any concrete exposed to deicing salts	0.45
All other structures	0.50
Exposure to sulfates*	
Moderate	0.50
Severe	0.45
Placing concrete under water	Not less than 650 lb of cement per cubic yard (386 kg/m³)
Floors on grade	Select water-cement ratio for strength, plus minimum cement requirements

*Contain entrained air within the limits of Table 1.

Bob Cotton; W. E. Simpson Company Inc.; San Antonio, Texas
Quentin L. Reutershan, AIA, Architect; Potsdam, New York
Gordon B. Batson, P.E.; Potsdam, New York

TABLE 5. MAXIMUM PERMISSIBLE WATER-CEMENT RATIOS FOR CONCRETE WHEN STRENGTH DATA FROM TRIAL BATCHES OR FIELD EXPERIENCE ARE NOT AVAILABLE

SPECIFIED COMPRESSIVE STRENGTH F'_c (PSI*)	MAXIMUM ABSOLUTE PERMISSIBLE WATER-CEMENT RATIO, BY WEIGHT	
	NON-AIR ENTRAINED CONCRETE	AIR ENTRAINED CONCRETE
2500	0.67	0.54
3000	0.58	0.46
3500	0.51	0.40
4000	0.44	0.35
4500	0.38	†
5000	†	†

NOTE: 1000 psi ≃ 7 MPa.
*28-day strength. With most materials, the water-cement ratios shown will provide average strengths greater than required.
†For strengths above 4500 psi (non-air entrained concrete) and 4000 psi (air entrained concrete), proportions should be established by the trial batch method.

ASTM, see data sources

TABLE 6. MINIMUM THICKNESS OF NON-PRESTRESSED BEAMS OR ONE WAY SLABS

	SIMPLY SUPPORTED	ONE END CONT.	BOTH ENDS CONT.	CANTILEVER
Solid One-Way Slabs	ℓ/20	ℓ/24	ℓ/28	ℓ/10
Beams or Ribbed One-Way Slabs	ℓ/16	ℓ/18.5	ℓ/21	ℓ/8

NOTE

Span length, l, is in inches. Values given are for members with normal weight concrete and Grade 60 reinforcement in construction not supporting or attached to partitions or other construction likely to be damaged by large deflections. For additional information, reference should be made to the American Concrete Institute Building Requirements for Reinforced Concrete (ACI 318).

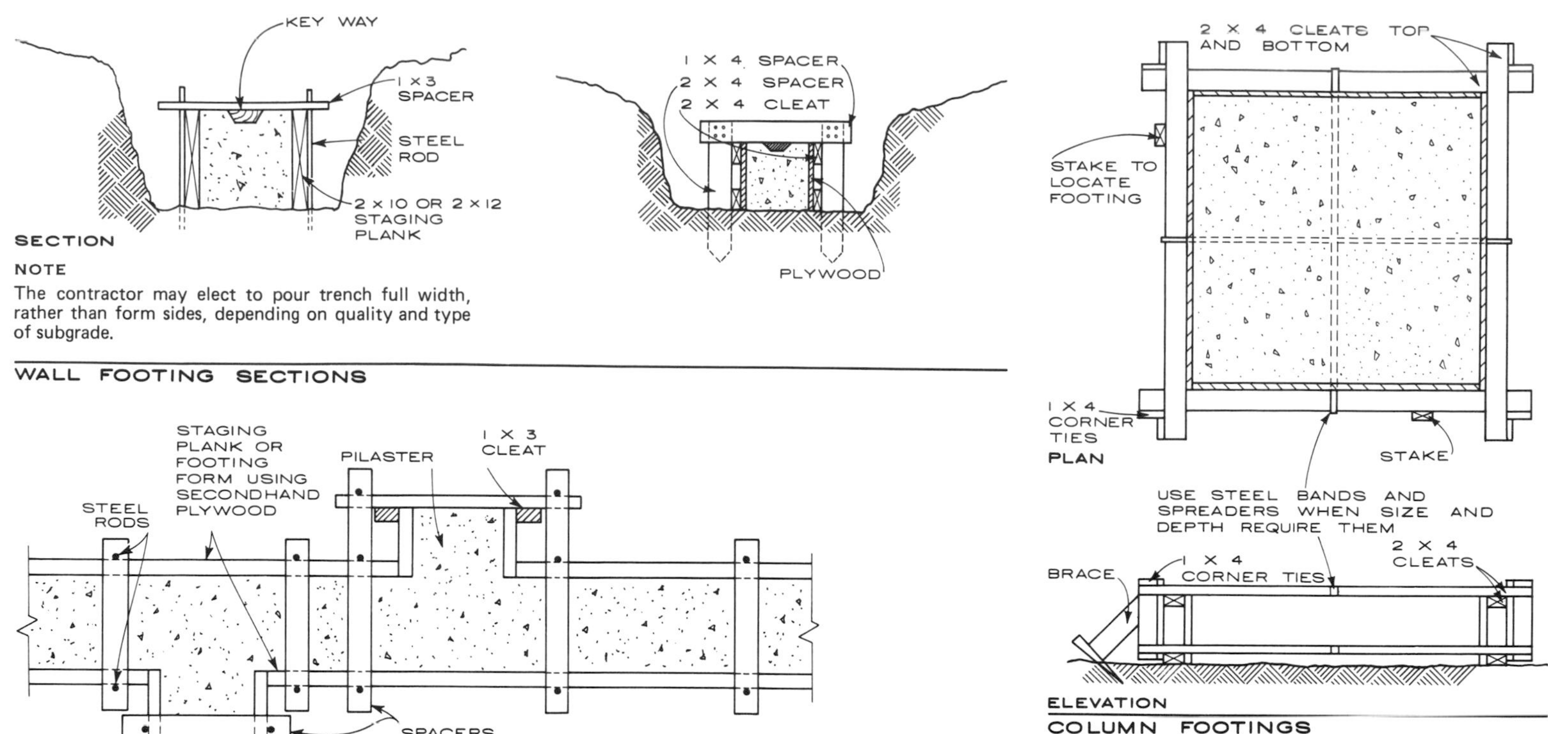
KEY WAY
1 x 3 SPACER
STEEL ROD
2 x 10 OR 2 x 12 STAGING PLANK
SECTION
1 X 4 SPACER
2 X 4 SPACER
2 X 4 CLEAT
PLYWOOD
2 X 4 CLEATS TOP AND BOTTOM
STAKE TO LOCATE FOOTING
1 X 4 CORNER TIES
PLAN
STAKE
USE STEEL BANDS AND SPREADERS WHEN SIZE AND DEPTH REQUIRE THEM
BRACE
1 X 4 CORNER TIES
2 X 4 CLEATS
ELEVATION

NOTE

The contractor may elect to pour trench full width, rather than form sides, depending on quality and type of subgrade.

WALL FOOTING SECTIONS

COLUMN FOOTINGS

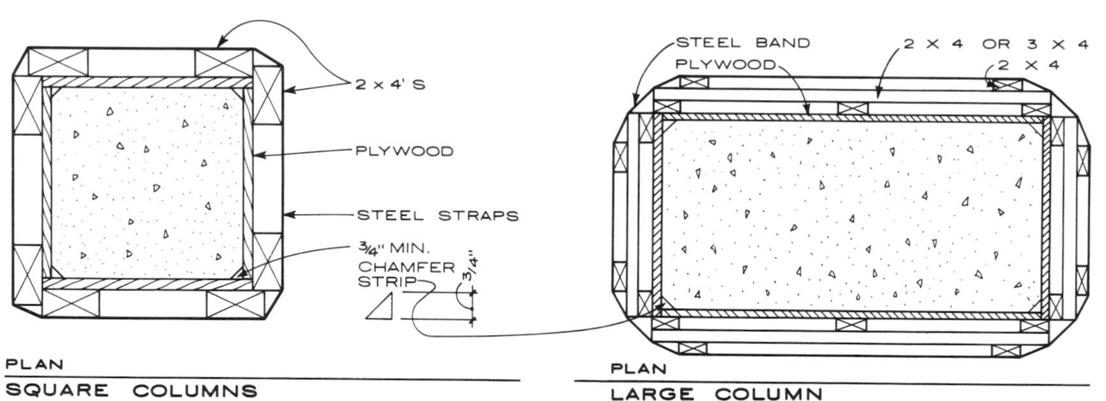
STAGING PLANK OR FOOTING FORM USING SECONDHAND PLYWOOD
PILASTER
1 X 3 CLEAT
STEEL RODS
SPACERS

PLAN OF WALL FOOTINGS

2 x 4' S
PLYWOOD
STEEL STRAPS
3/4" MIN. CHAMFER STRIP
3/4"
PLAN
STEEL BAND
PLYWOOD
2 X 4 OR 3 X 4
2 X 4
PLAN

SQUARE COLUMNS

LARGE COLUMN

NOTE

Height of column will change thickness and spaces of steel bands. Consult manufacturers' catalogs. Selection of sheathing (or plywood), type of column clamps (job built or patented metal types), and their spacing will depend on column height, rate of concrete pour (ft/hr), and concrete temperature (°F), as well as on whether the concrete is to be vibrated during pour. Consult design guides for correct selection of materials to ensure safe column forms.

It is recommended that chamfer strips be used at all outside corners to reduce damage to concrete when forms are removed.

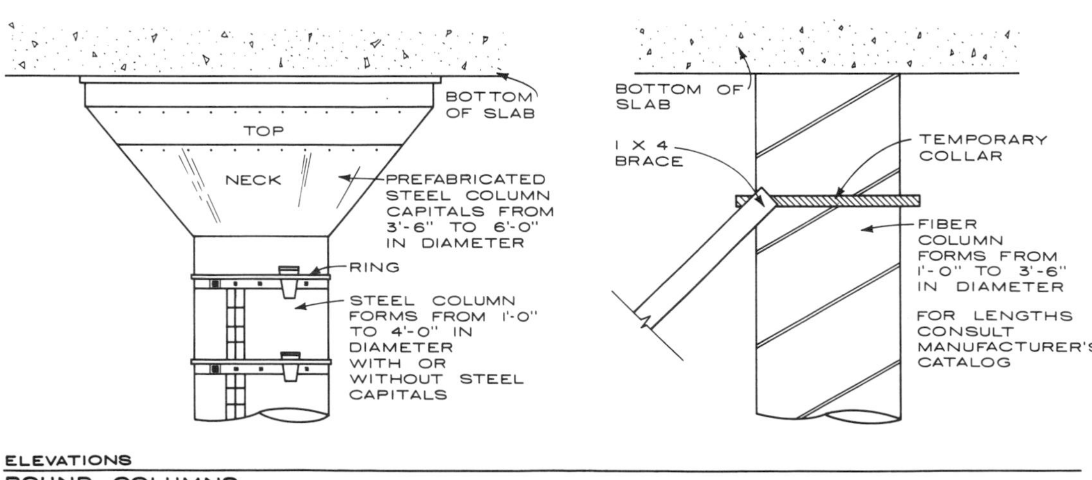
BOTTOM OF SLAB
TOP
NECK
PREFABRICATED STEEL COLUMN CAPITALS FROM 3'-6" TO 6'-0" IN DIAMETER
RING
STEEL COLUMN FORMS FROM 1'-0" TO 4'-0" IN DIAMETER WITH OR WITHOUT STEEL CAPITALS
BOTTOM OF SLAB
1 X 4 BRACE
TEMPORARY COLLAR
FIBER COLUMN FORMS FROM 1'-0" TO 3'-6" IN DIAMETER
FOR LENGTHS CONSULT MANUFACTURER'S CATALOG
ELEVATIONS

ROUND COLUMNS

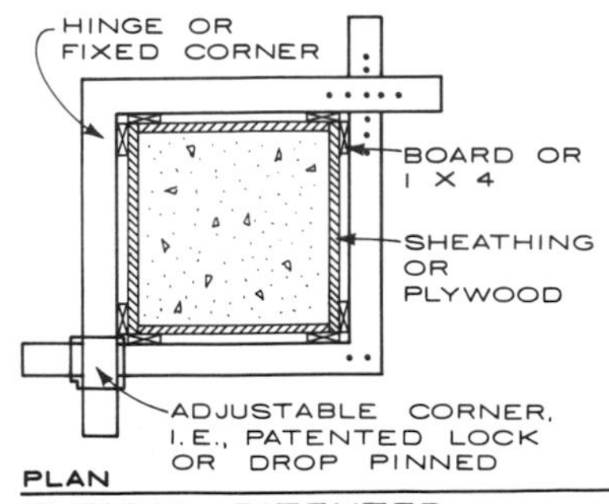
HINGE OR FIXED CORNER
BOARD OR 1 X 4
SHEATHING OR PLYWOOD
ADJUSTABLE CORNER, I.E., PATENTED LOCK OR DROP PINNED
PLAN

TYPICAL PATENTED COLUMN CLAMP

Tucker Concrete Form Co.; Malden, Massachusetts

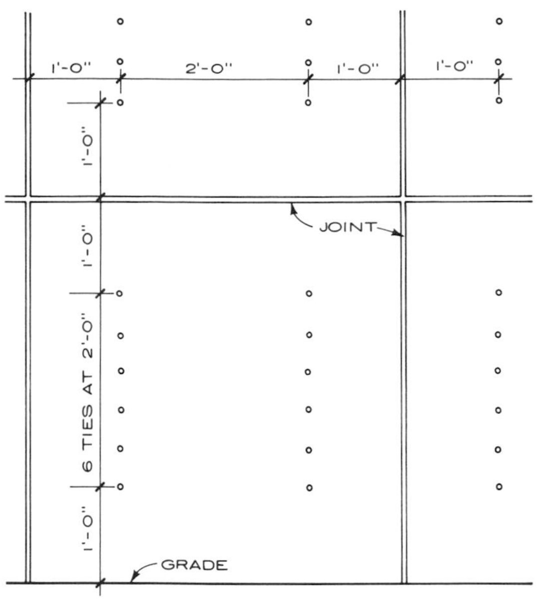

1'-0"
2'-0"
1'-0"
1'-0"
JOINT
6 TIES AT 2'-0"
GRADE

ELEVATION

EXPOSED CONCRETE WITH RUSTICATION STRIP (IF DESIRED)

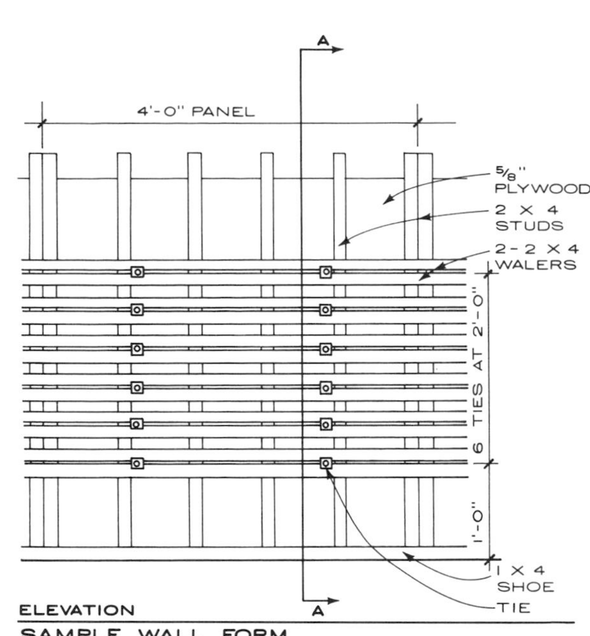

4'-0" PANEL
A
5/8" PLYWOOD
2 X 4 STUDS
2-2 X 4 WALERS
6 TIES AT 2'-0"
1'-0"
1 X 4 SHOE
TIE

ELEVATION

SAMPLE WALL FORM

Mortar-tight forms are required for architectural exposed concrete. Consult manufacturers' literature on the proper use of metal forms or plywood forms with metal frames.

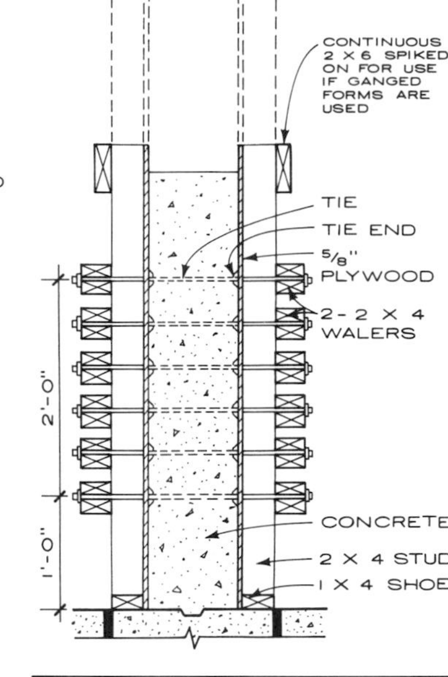

CONTINUOUS 2 X 6 SPIKED ON FOR USE IF GANGED FORMS ARE USED
TIE
TIE END
5/8" PLYWOOD
2-2 X 4 WALERS
2'-0"
1'-0"
CONCRETE
2 X 4 STUD
1 X 4 SHOE

SECTION A-A

The section above will change if there are any variations in the thickness of plywood used, the type and strength of ties, or the size of studs and walers.

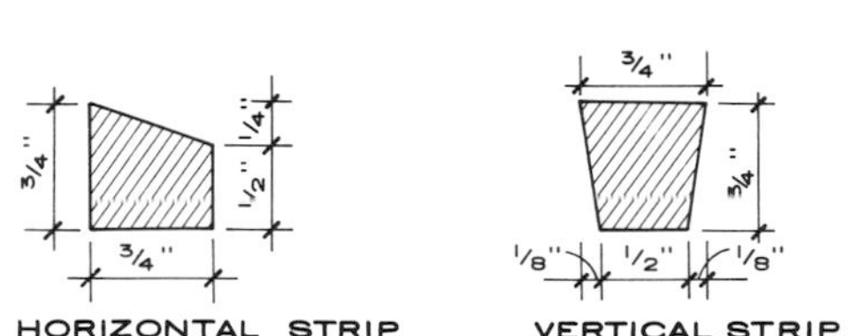

3/4"
1/4"
1/2"
3/4"
1/8"
1/2"
1/8"

HORIZONTAL STRIP   VERTICAL STRIP

RUSTICATION STRIPS

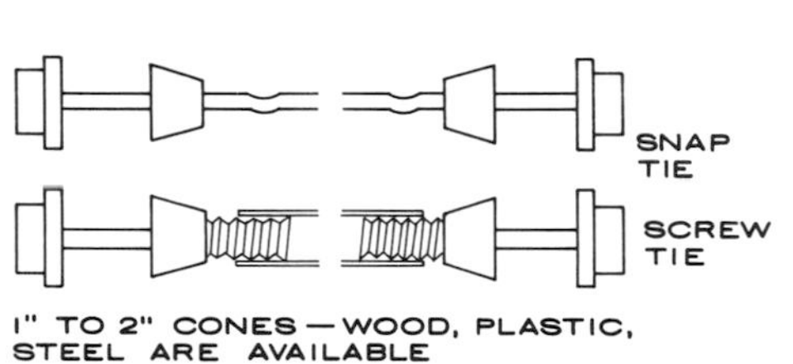

SNAP TIE
SCREW TIE

1" TO 2" CONES—WOOD, PLASTIC, STEEL ARE AVAILABLE

TYPICAL TIES

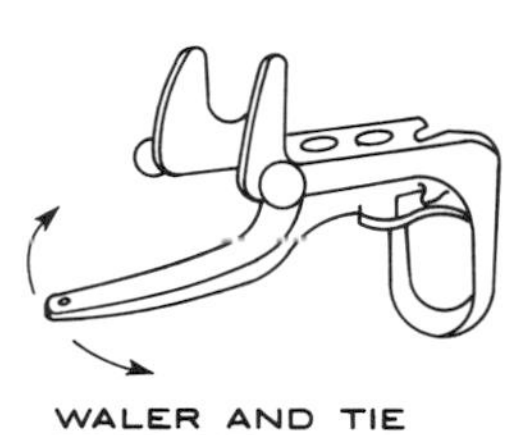

WALER AND TIE BRACKET   STRONG-BACK CAM

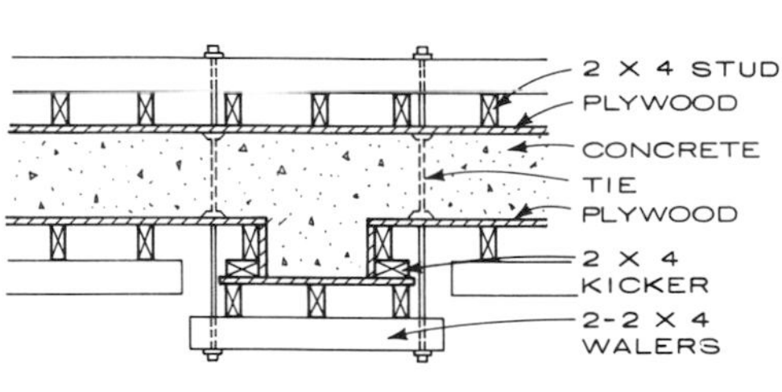

2 X 4 STUD
PLYWOOD
CONCRETE
TIE
PLYWOOD
2 X 4 KICKER
2-2 X 4 WALERS

PLAN

SMALL PILASTER

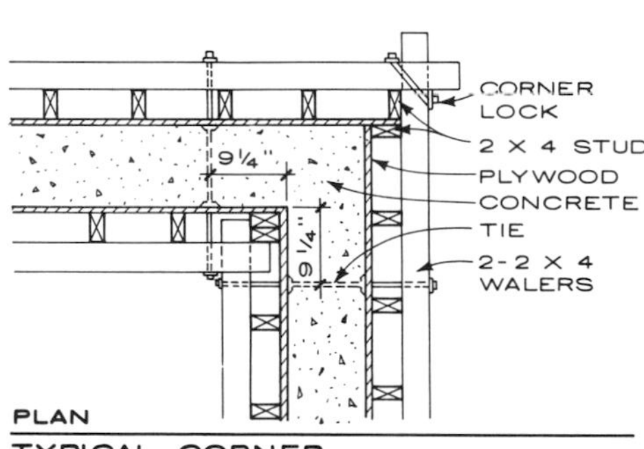

CORNER LOCK
2 X 4 STUD
PLYWOOD
CONCRETE
TIE
2-2 X 4 WALERS
9 1/4"
9 1/4"

PLAN

TYPICAL CORNER

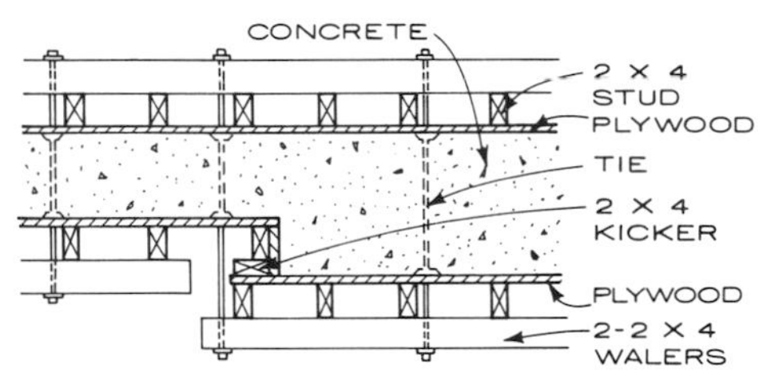

CONCRETE
2 X 4 STUD
PLYWOOD
TIE
2 X 4 KICKER
PLYWOOD
2-2 X 4 WALERS

TYPICAL WALL WITH OFFSET

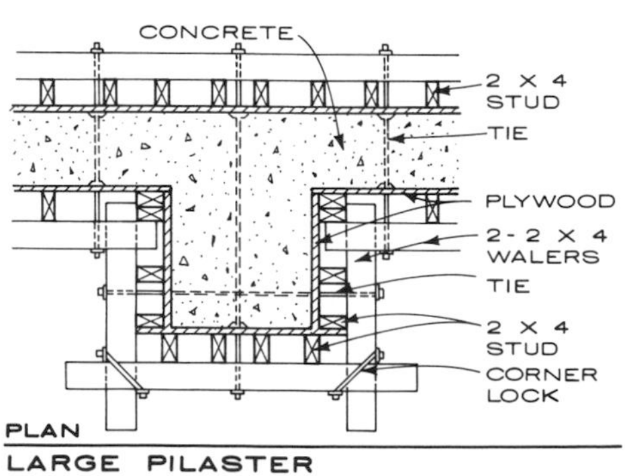

CONCRETE
2 X 4 STUD
TIE
PLYWOOD
2-2 X 4 WALERS
TIE
2 X 4 STUD
CORNER LOCK

PLAN

LARGE PILASTER

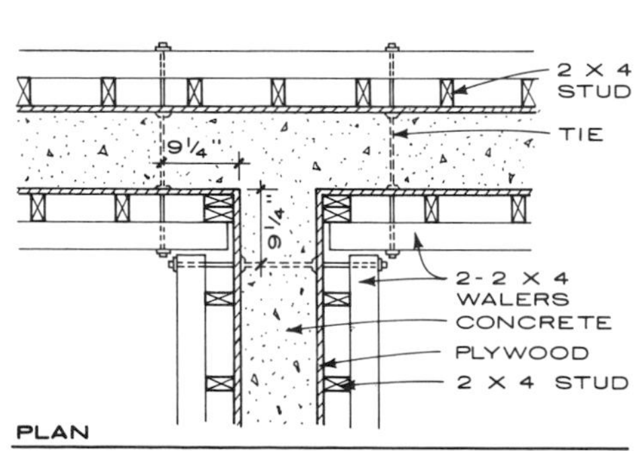

2 X 4 STUD
TIE
9 1/4"
9 1/4"
2-2 X 4 WALERS
CONCRETE
PLYWOOD
2 X 4 STUD

PLAN

TYPICAL "T" WALL JUNCTION

FORM DESIGN NOTES

1. Pressure depends on rate of pour (ft/hr) and concrete temperature (°F). Vibration of concrete is also a factor in form pressure.
2. Provide cleanout doors at bottom of wall forms.
3. Various types of form ties are on the market. Some are not suitable for architectural concrete work, i.e., they cannot be withdrawn from the concrete.
4. Various plastic cones 1 1/2 in. in diameter and 1/2 in. deep can be used and the holes are left ungrouted to form a type of architectural feature.
5. Consult manufacturers' catalogs for form design and tie strength information.

Tucker Concrete Form Co.; Malden, Massachusetts

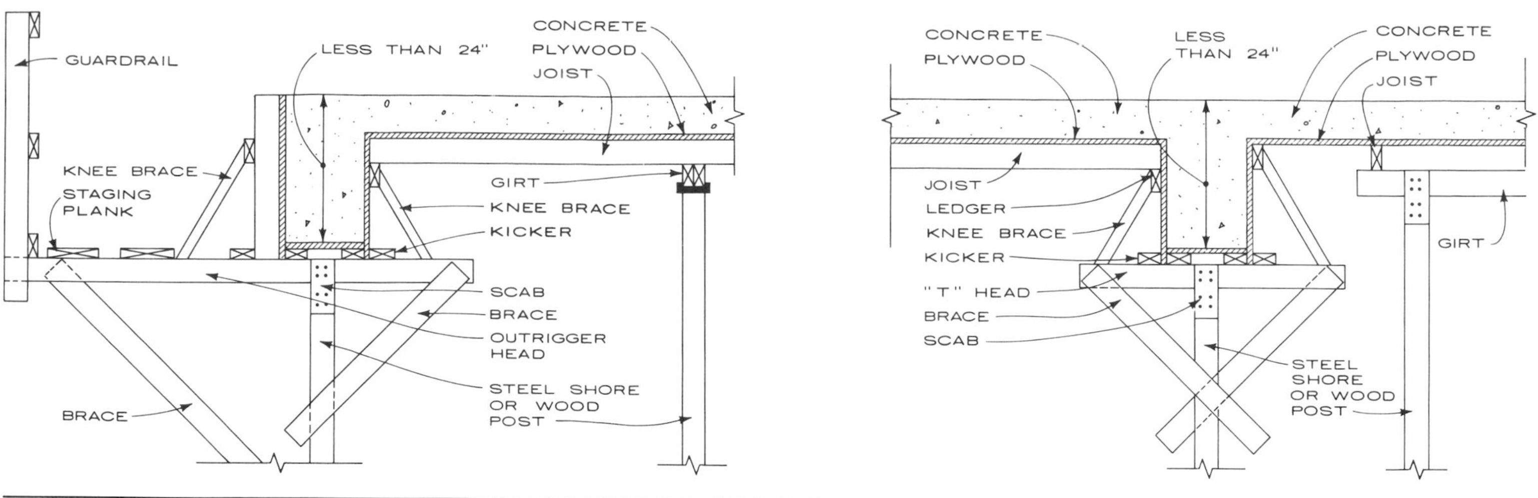
GUARDRAIL
LESS THAN 24"
CONCRETE
PLYWOOD
JOIST
KNEE BRACE
STAGING PLANK
GIRT
KNEE BRACE
KICKER
SCAB
BRACE
OUTRIGGER HEAD
STEEL SHORE OR WOOD POST
BRACE
CONCRETE
PLYWOOD
LESS THAN 24"
CONCRETE
PLYWOOD
JOIST
JOIST
LEDGER
KNEE BRACE
KICKER
"T" HEAD
BRACE
SCAB
GIRT
STEEL SHORE OR WOOD POST

TYPICAL SLAB AND SHALLOW BEAM FORMING

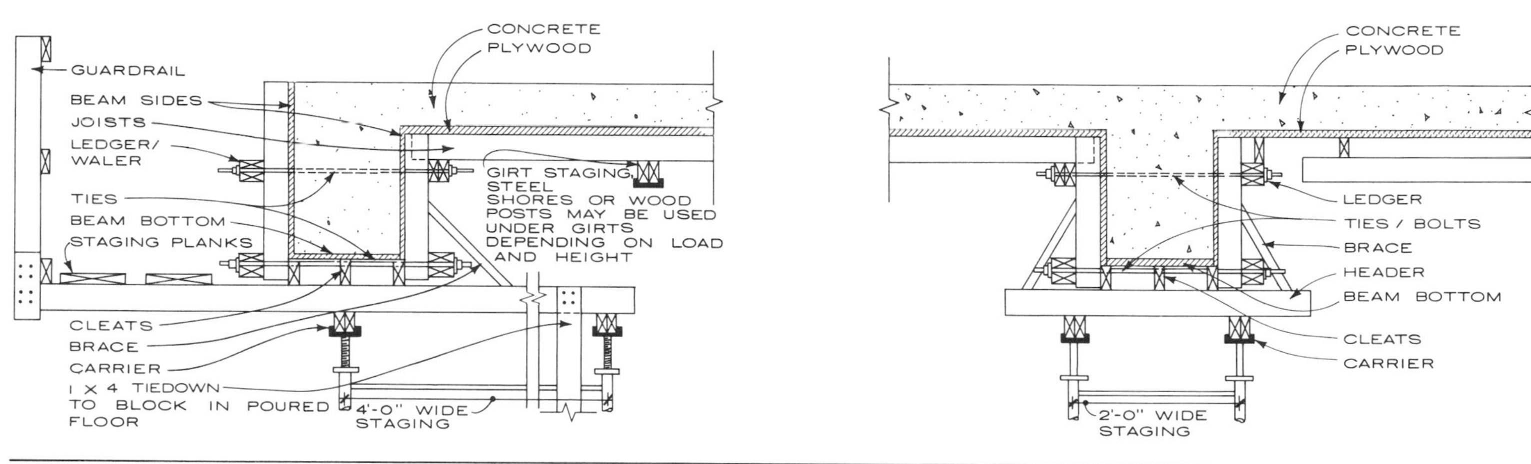
GUARDRAIL
CONCRETE
PLYWOOD
BEAM SIDES
JOISTS
LEDGER/ WALER
TIES
BEAM BOTTOM
STAGING PLANKS
GIRT STAGING, STEEL SHORES OR WOOD POSTS MAY BE USED UNDER GIRTS DEPENDING ON LOAD AND HEIGHT
CLEATS
BRACE
CARRIER
1 X 4 TIEDOWN TO BLOCK IN POURED FLOOR
4'-0" WIDE STAGING
CONCRETE
PLYWOOD
LEDGER
TIES / BOLTS
BRACE
HEADER
BEAM BOTTOM
CLEATS
CARRIER
2'-0" WIDE STAGING

TYPICAL SLAB AND HEAVY BEAM FORMING

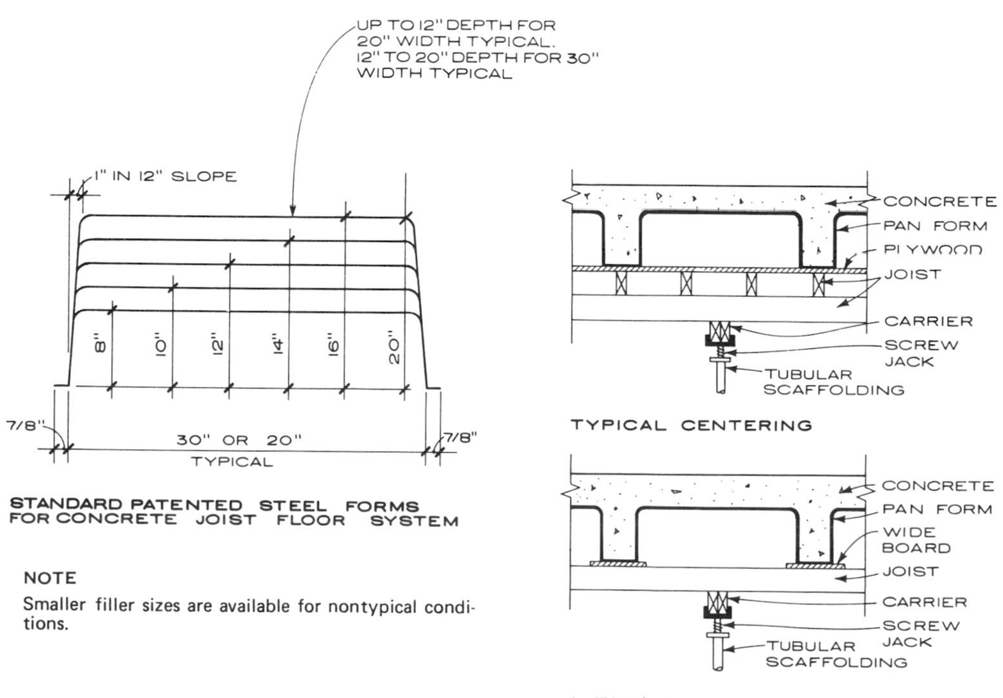
UP TO 12" DEPTH FOR 20" WIDTH TYPICAL. 12" TO 20" DEPTH FOR 30" WIDTH TYPICAL
1" IN 12" SLOPE
8"
10"
12"
14"
16"
20"
7/8"
30" OR 20"
TYPICAL
7/8"
CONCRETE
PAN FORM
PLYWOOD
JOIST
CARRIER
SCREW JACK
TUBULAR SCAFFOLDING
CONCRETE
PAN FORM
WIDE BOARD
JOIST
CARRIER
SCREW JACK
TUBULAR SCAFFOLDING

STANDARD PATENTED STEEL FORMS FOR CONCRETE JOIST FLOOR SYSTEM

TYPICAL CENTERING

ALTERNATE SYSTEM

NOTE

Smaller filler sizes are available for nontypical conditions.

NOTES

1. Staging, steel shores, or wood posts may be used under girts depending on loads and height requirements.
2. For flat slabs of flat plate forming, metal "flying forms" are commonly used.
3. Patented steel forms or fillers are also available for nontypical conditions on special order. See manufacturer's catalogs. Fiber forms, too, are on the market in similar sizes. Plywood deck is required for forming.
4. Plywood is usually 5/8" minimum thickness, Exposure 1.

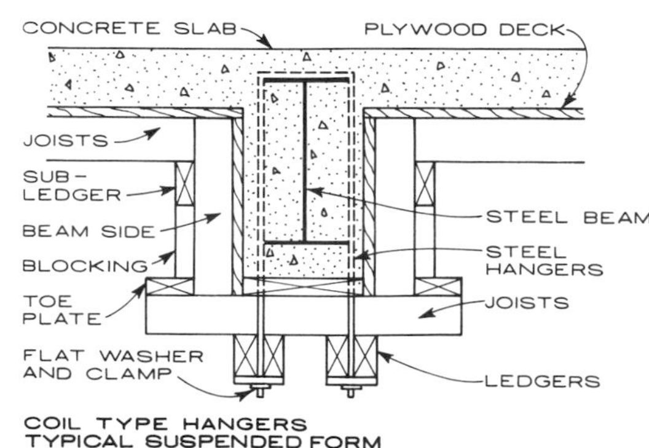
CONCRETE SLAB
PLYWOOD DECK
JOISTS
SUB-LEDGER
BEAM SIDE
BLOCKING
TOE PLATE
FLAT WASHER AND CLAMP
STEEL BEAM
STEEL HANGERS
JOISTS
LEDGERS

COIL TYPE HANGERS TYPICAL SUSPENDED FORM

Tucker Concrete Form Co.; Malden, Massachusetts

ASTM STANDARD REINFORCING BAR SIZES—NOMINAL DIAMETER

BAR SIZE DESIGNATION	WEIGHT PER FOOT		DIAMETER		CROSS-SECTIONAL AREA SQUARED	
	LB	KG	IN.	CM	IN.	CM
#3	0.376	0.171	0.375	0.953	0.11	0.71
#4	0.668	0.303	0.500	1.270	0.20	1.29
#5	1.043	0.473	0.625	1.588	0.31	2.00
#6	1.502	0.681	0.750	1.905	0.44	2.84
#7	2.044	0.927	0.875	2.223	0.60	3.87
#8	2.670	1.211	1.000	2.540	0.79	5.10
#9	3.400	1.542	1.128	2.865	1.00	6.45
#10	4.303	1.952	1.270	3.226	1.27	8.19
#11	5.313	2.410	1.410	3.581	1.56	10.07
#14	7.650	3.470	1.693	4.300	2.25	14.52
#18	13.600	6.169	2.257	5.733	4.00	25.81

COMMON STOCK STYLES OF WELDED WIRE FABRIC

	NEW DESIGNATION	OLD DESIGNATION	STEEL AREA PER FOOT				APPROXIMATE WEIGHT PER 100 SQ FT	
	SPACING—CROSS SECTIONAL AREA (IN.)—(SQ IN./100)	SPACING—WIRE GAUGE (IN.)—(AS & W)	LONGITUDINAL		TRANSVERSE			
			IN.	CM	IN.	CM	LB	KG
Rolls	6 x 6—W1.4 x W1.4	6 x 6—10 x 10	0.028	0.071	0.028	0.071	21	9.53
Rolls	6 x 6—W2.0 x W2.0	6 x 6—8 x 8 (1)	0.040	0.102	0.040	0.102	29	13.15
Rolls	6 x 6—W2.9 x W2.9	6 x 6—6 x 6	0.058	0.147	0.058	0.147	42	19.05
Rolls	6 x 6—W4.0 x W4.0	6 x 6—4 x 4	0.080	0.203	0.080	0.203	58	26.31
Rolls	4 x 4—W1.4 x W1.4	4 x 4—10 x 10	0.042	0.107	0.042	0.107	31	14.06
Rolls	4 x 4—W2.0 x W2.0	4 x 4—8 x 8 (1)	0.060	0.152	0.060	0.152	43	19.50
Rolls	4 x 4—W2.9 x W2.9	4 x 4—6 x 6	0.087	0.221	0.087	0.221	62	28.12
Rolls	4 x 4—W4.0 x W4.0	4 x 4—4 x 4	0.120	0.305	0.120	0.305	85	38.56
Sheets	6 x 6—W2.9 x W2.9	6 x 6—6 x 6	0.058	0.147	0.058	0.147	42	19.05
Sheets	6 x 6—W4.0 x W4.0	6 x 6—4 x 4	0.080	0.203	0.080	0.203	58	26.31
Sheets	6 x 6—W5.5 x W5.5	6 x 6—2 x 2 (2)	0.110	0.279	0.110	0.279	80	36.29
Sheets	4 x 4—W4.0 x W4.0	4 x 4—4 x 4	0.120	0.305	0.120	0.305	85	38.56

NOTES

1. Exact W-number size for 8 gauge is W2.1.
2. Exact W-number size for 2 gauge is W5.4.

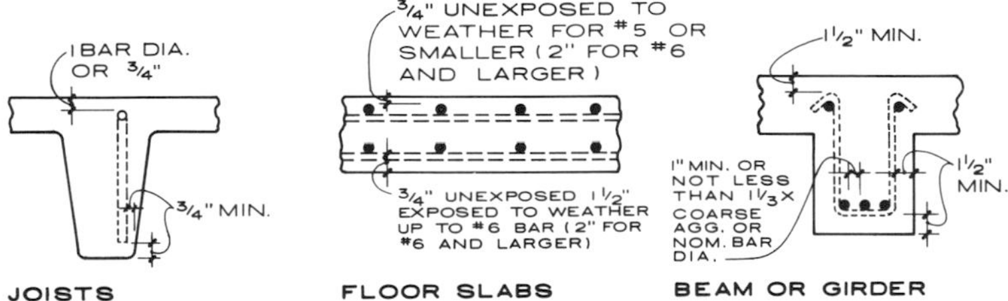

1 BAR DIA. OR 3/4"
3/4" MIN.
JOISTS
3/4" UNEXPOSED TO WEATHER FOR #5 OR SMALLER (2" FOR #6 AND LARGER)
3/4" UNEXPOSED 1 1/2" EXPOSED TO WEATHER UP TO #6 BAR (2" FOR #6 AND LARGER)
FLOOR SLABS
1 1/2" MIN.
1" MIN. OR NOT LESS THAN 1 1/3 X COARSE AGG. OR NOM. BAR DIA.
1 1/2" MIN.
BEAM OR GIRDER

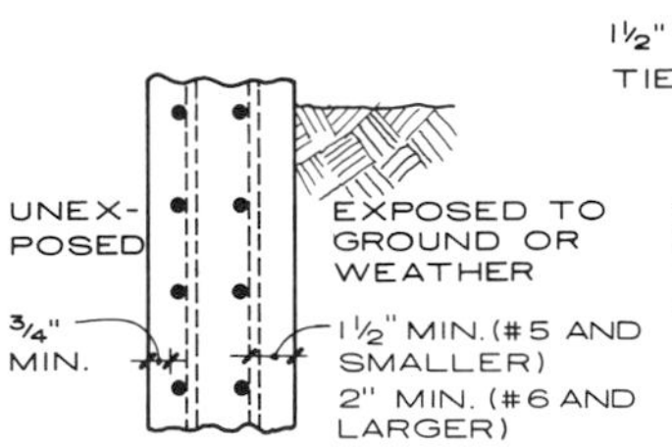

UNEXPOSED
EXPOSED TO GROUND OR WEATHER
3/4" MIN.
1 1/2" MIN. (#5 AND SMALLER)
2" MIN. (#6 AND LARGER)
WALLS

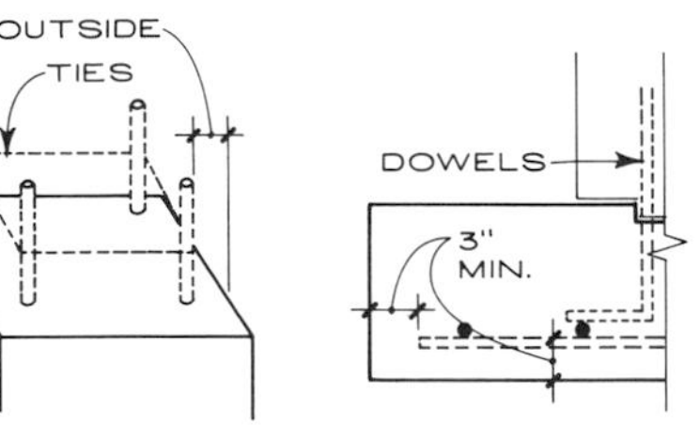

1 1/2" MIN. OUTSIDE TIES
TIES
COLUMNS

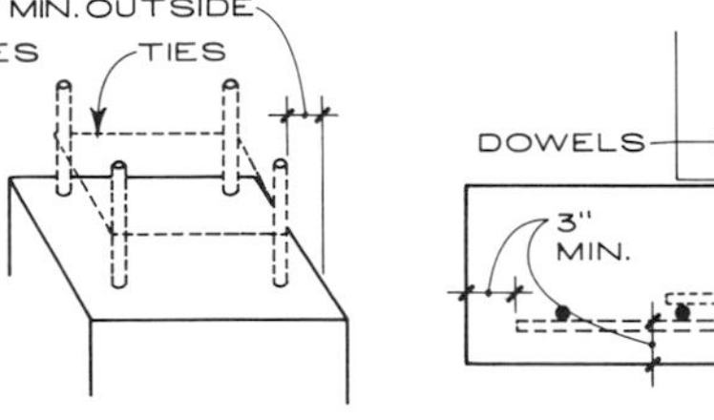

DOWELS
3" MIN.
FOOTINGS

PROTECTION FOR REINFORCEMENT

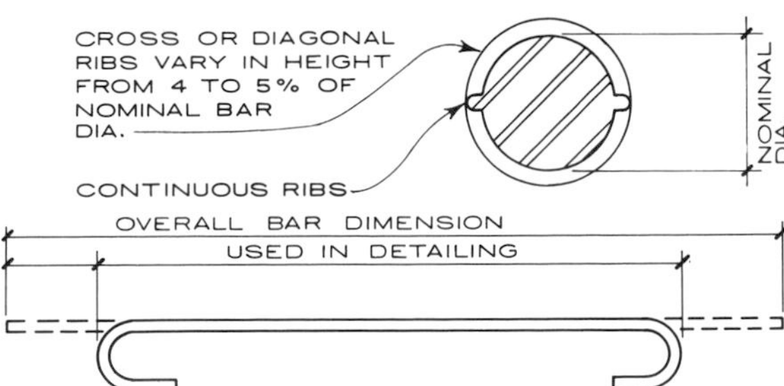

CROSS OR DIAGONAL RIBS VARY IN HEIGHT FROM 4 TO 5% OF NOMINAL BAR DIA.
CONTINUOUS RIBS
NOMINAL DIA.
OVERALL BAR DIMENSION
USED IN DETAILING

REINFORCING BAR DIMENSIONING

STANDARD STEEL WIRE SIZES AND GAUGES

A.S.&W GAUGE	DIAMETER		AREA SQUARED		WEIGHT PER FOOT	
	IN.	CM	IN.	CM	LB	KG
00	0.3310	0.8407	0.0860	0.5549	0.2922	0.1325
0	0.3065	0.7785	0.0738	0.4762	0.2506	0.1137
1	0.2830	0.7188	0.0629	0.4058	0.2136	0.0969
2	0.2625	0.6668	0.0541	0.3491	0.1829	0.0830
— (1/4")	0.2500	0.6350	0.0491	0.3168	0.1667	0.0756
3	0.2437	0.6190	0.0466	0.3007	0.1584	0.0718
4	0.2253	0.5723	0.0397	0.2561	0.1354	0.0614
5	0.2070	0.5258	0.0337	0.2174	0.1143	0.0518
6	0.1920	0.4877	0.0290	0.1871	0.0983	0.0446
7	0.1770	0.4496	0.0246	0.1587	0.0836	0.0379
8	0.1620	0.4115	0.0206	0.1329	0.0700	0.0318
9	0.1483	0.3767	0.0173	0.1116	0.0587	0.0266
10	0.1350	0.3429	0.0143	0.0922	0.0486	0.0220
11 (1/8")	0.1250	0.3175	0.0114	0.0736	0.0387	0.0176
12	0.1055	0.2680	0.0087	0.0561	0.0297	0.0135
13	0.0915	0.2324	0.0066	0.0426	0.0223	0.0101
14	0.0800	0.2032	0.0050	0.0323	0.0171	0.0078
15	0.0720	0.1838	0.0041	0.0265	0.0138	0.0063
16 (1/16")	0.0625	0.1588	0.0031	0.0200	0.0104	0.0047

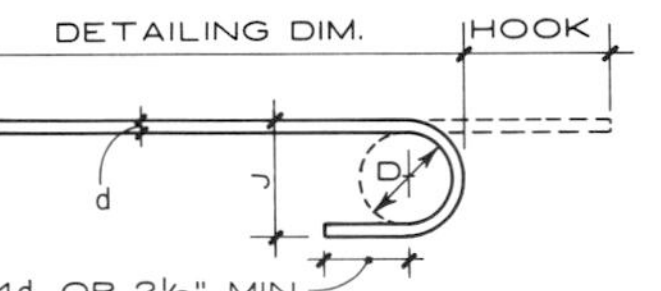

DETAILING DIM.
HOOK
d
D
J
4d OR 2 1/2" MIN.

180° HOOK

d = (1) Bar Diameter
D = 6d for No. 3 to No. 8 Bars
D = 8d for No. 9 to No. 11 Bars
J = D + 2d
H = 5d + D/2 (or) 2 1/2" + d + D/2 minimum

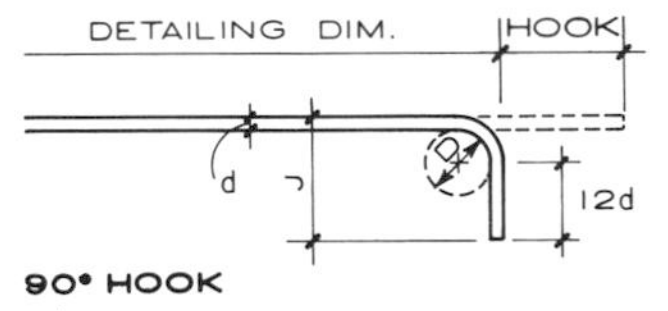

DETAILING DIM.
HOOK
d
J
D
12d

90° HOOK

d = (1) Bar Diameter
D = 6d for No. 3 to No. 8 bars
D = 8d for No. 9 to No. 11 bars
J = 13d + D/2

HOOK
6D OR 2 1/2" MIN.
DETAILING DIM.
D
d
℄ BEAM

135° HOOK STIRRUP — TIES SIMILAR

d = (1) Bar Diameter
D = 1 1/2" for No. 3
D = 2" for No. 4
D = 2 1/2" for No. 5
D = 6d for No. 6 to No. 8

STANDARD REINFORCING BAR HOOK DETAILS

LAP SPLICE REQUIREMENTS

1983 CODE IN BAR DIAMETERS

f'_y (KSI)	SPIRAL COLUMN	TIED COLUMN	LOOSE
40	15.0	16.6	20
50	18.75	20.75	25
60	22.5	24.9	30
75	32.6	36.2	43.5
80	36.0	39.9	48.0

LAP
BARS IN CONTACT
BEAM STIRRUPS OR COLUMN TIES REQUIRED IF WITHIN 6" OF AN OUTSIDE CORNER

NOTES

1. These requirements are for compression lap splices only.
2. Lap splice lengths are minimum for $f'_c \geq 3000$ psi.
3. Minimum lap is 12 in.
4. Maximum reinforcing bar size permitted in lap splice is No. 11.

TEMPERATURE REINFORCEMENT FOR STRUCTURAL FLOOR AND ROOF SLAB (ONE WAY) (IN PERCENTAGE OF CROSS-SECTIONAL AREA OF CONCRETE)

REINFORCEMENT		CONCRETE SLABS	
GRADE	TYPE		
40/50	Deformed bars	0.20%	Max. spacing five times slab thickness
—	Welded wire fabric	0.18%	
60	Deformed bars	0.18%	

Dave Keppler; Haver, Nunn and Collamer; Phoenix, Arizona

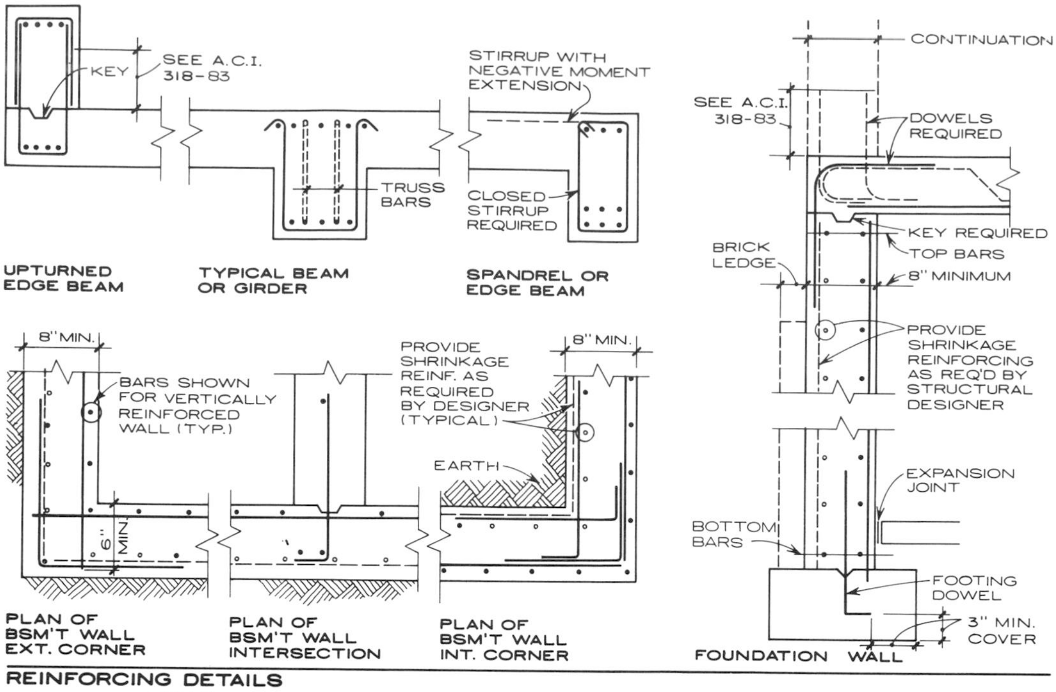

UPTURNED EDGE BEAM

TYPICAL BEAM OR GIRDER

SPANDREL OR EDGE BEAM

PLAN OF BSM'T WALL EXT. CORNER

PLAN OF BSM'T WALL INTERSECTION

PLAN OF BSM'T WALL INT. CORNER

FOUNDATION WALL

REINFORCING DETAILS

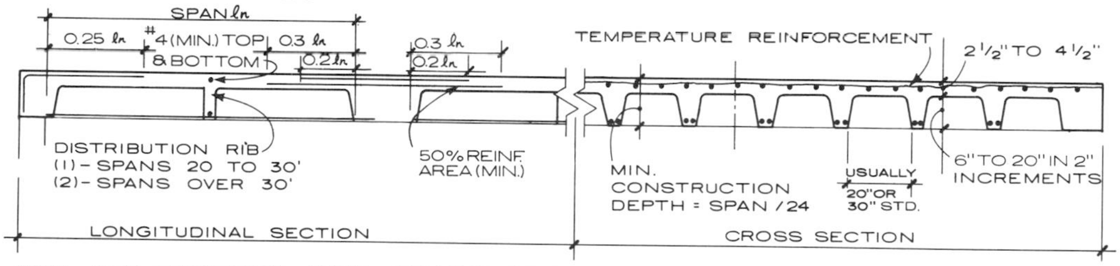

ONE-WAY CONCRETE JOIST CONSTRUCTION

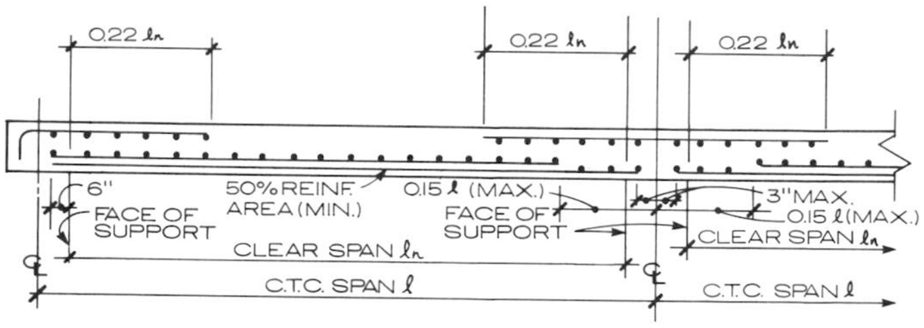

FLAT PLATE CONSTRUCTION – MIDDLE STRIP

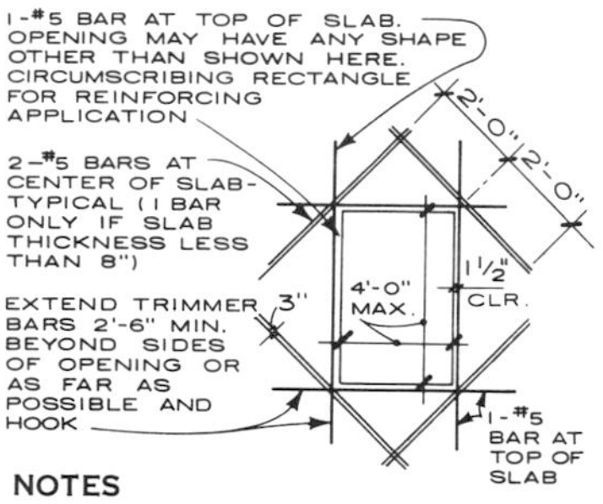

FLAT PLATE CONSTRUCTION – COLUMN STRIP

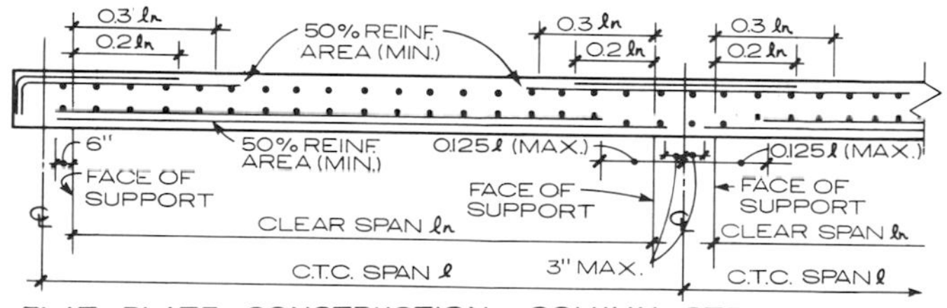

NOTES

1. Provide extra bars (not shown) parallel to sides of openings, equal to areas of interrupted slab bars. Extend full length of span or to top bars as applicable.
2. This detail is typical at openings up to 4 ft maximum dimensions except as otherwise shown.
3. Circular openings less than 18 in. diameter require no reinforcing.

OPENING IN SLAB OR WALL

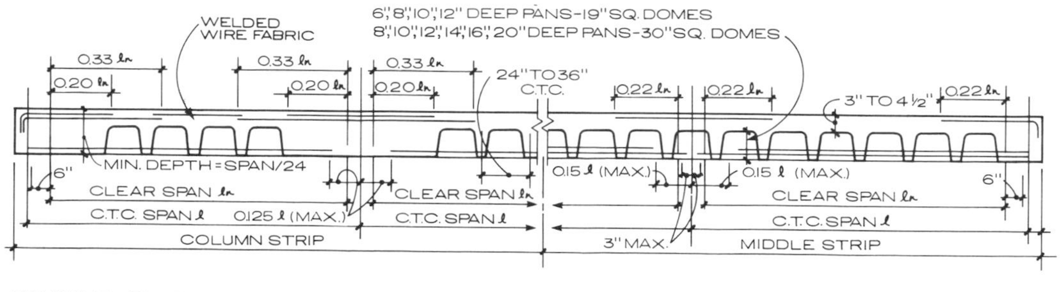

WAFFLE FLAT SLAB – SQUARE BAY CONSTRUCTION

CONCRETE FLOOR SYSTEMS

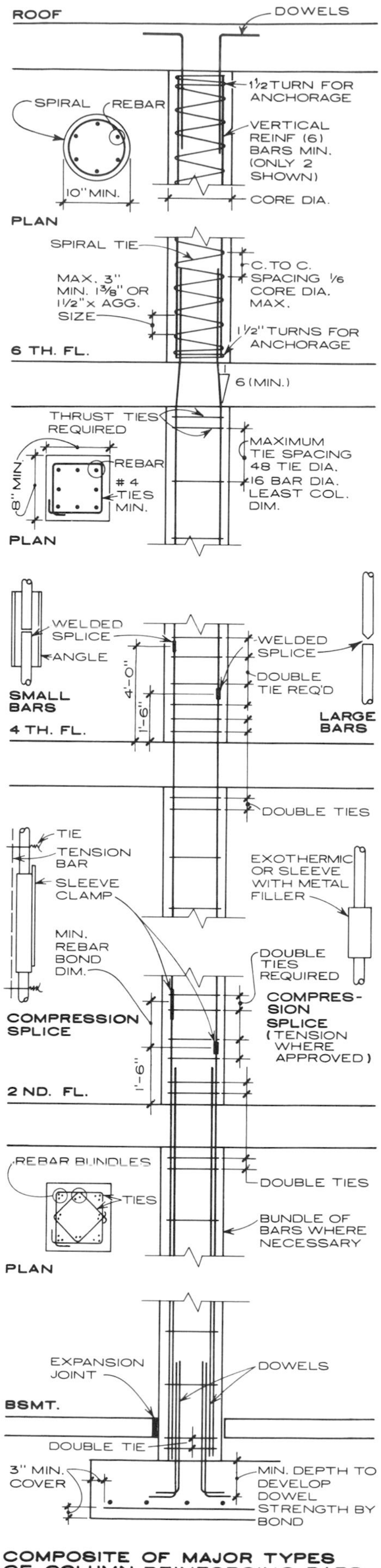

COMPOSITE OF MAJOR TYPES OF COLUMN REINFORCING BARS

Thomas A. Lines; Haver, Nunn and Collamer; Phoenix, Arizona
Kenneth D. Franch, AIA, PE; Phillips Swager Associates, Inc.; Dallas, Texas

GENERAL NOTES

Factors to consider in construction of all concrete slabs on grade include assurance of uniform subgrade, quality of concrete, adequacy of structural capacity, type and spacing of joints, finishing, curing, and the application of special surfaces. It is vital to design and construct the subgrade as carefully as the floor slab itself. The subgrade support must be reasonably uniform, and the upper portion of the subgrade should be of uniform material and density. A subbase, a thin layer of granular material placed on the subgrade, should be used in most cases to cushion the slab.

Wear resistance is directly related to concrete strength. A low water-cement ratio improves the surface hardness and finishability as well as internal strength of concrete. Low water-cement ratio, low slump, and well graded aggregates with coarse aggregate size as large as placing and finishing requirements will permit and enhance the quality of concrete.

Exterior concrete subjected to freeze-thaw cycles should have 6 to 8% entrained air. Reinforcement is unnecessary where frequent joint spacing is used. Where less frequent joint spacing is necessary, reinforcement is put in the top one third depth to hold together any shrinkage cracks that form. Control joint spacing of 15 to 25 ft square is recommended. Checkerboard pouring patterns allow for some shrinkage between pours, but the process is more costly and is not recommended for large areas. The total shrinkage process takes up to one year. Strip pouring, allowing for a continuous pour with control joints cut after concrete has set, is a fast economical method, recommended for large areas.

Three types of joints are recommended:

1. ISOLATION JOINTS (also called expansion joints): Allow movement between slab and fixed parts of the building such as columns, walls, and machinery bases.
2. CONTROL JOINTS: Induce cracking at preselected locations.
3. CONSTRUCTION JOINTS: Provide stopping places during floor construction. Construction joints also function as control and isolation joints.

   Sawcut control joints should be made as early as is practical after finishing the slab and should be filled in areas with wet conditions, hygienic and dust control requirements, or considerable traffic by hard wheeled vehicles, such as forklift trucks. A semirigid filler with Shore Hardness "A" of at least 80 should be used.

Concrete floor slabs are monolithically finished by floating and troweling the concrete to a smooth dense finish. Depressions of more than 1/8 in. in 10 ft or variations of more than 1/4 in. from a level plane are undesirable. Special finishes are available to improve appearance. These include sprinkled (shake) finishes and high strength concrete toppings, either monolithic or separate (two-stage floor).

A vaporproof barrier should be placed under all slabs on grade where the passage of water vapor through the floor is undesirable. Permeance of vapor barrier should not exceed 0.20 perms.

Generally the controlling factor in determining the thickness of a floor on ground is the heaviest concentrated load it will carry, usually the wheel load plus impact of an industrial truck. Because of practical considerations, the minimum recommended thickness for an industrial floor is about 5 in. For Class 1, 2, and 3 floors, the minimum thickness should be 4 in.

The floor thickness required for wheel loads on relatively small areas may be obtained from the table for concrete; an allowable flexural tensile stress (psi) can be estimated from the approximate formula $f_t = 4.6\sqrt{f'_c}$ in which f'_c is the 28-day concrete compressive strength. If f_t is not 300 psi, the table can be used by multiplying the actual total load by the ratio of 300 to the stress used and entering the chart with that value.

Assume that a 5000 psi concrete slab is to be designed for an industrial plant floor over which there will be considerable traffic—trucks with loads of 10,000 lb/wheel, each of which has a contact area of about 30 sq in. Assume that operating conditions are such that impact will be equivalent to about 25% of the load. The equivalent static load will then be 12,500 lb. The allowable flexural tensile stress for 5000 psi concrete is

$$4.6\sqrt{5000} = 325 \text{ psi}$$

The allowable loads in the table are based on a stress of 300 psi, so that the design load must be corrected by the factor 300/325. Thus 11,500 lb on an area of 30 sq in. requires a slab about 7 1/2 in. thick.

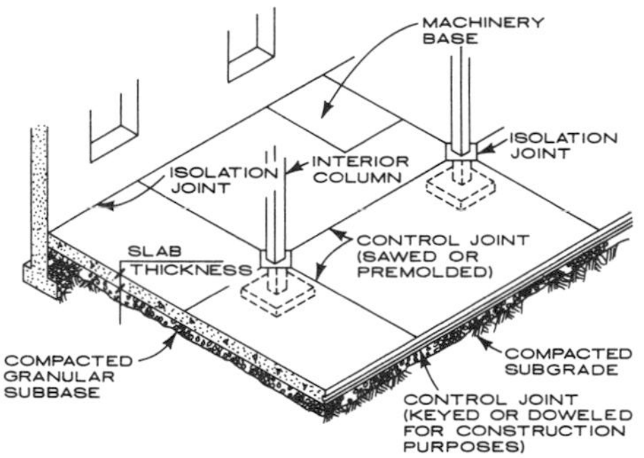

MACHINERY BASE
ISOLATION JOINT
INTERIOR COLUMN
ISOLATION JOINT
CONTROL JOINT (SAWED OR PREMOLDED)
SLAB THICKNESS
COMPACTED GRANULAR SUBBASE
COMPACTED SUBGRADE
CONTROL JOINT (KEYED OR DOWELED FOR CONSTRUCTION PURPOSES)

CONTROL JOINTS FOR A SLAB ON GRADE

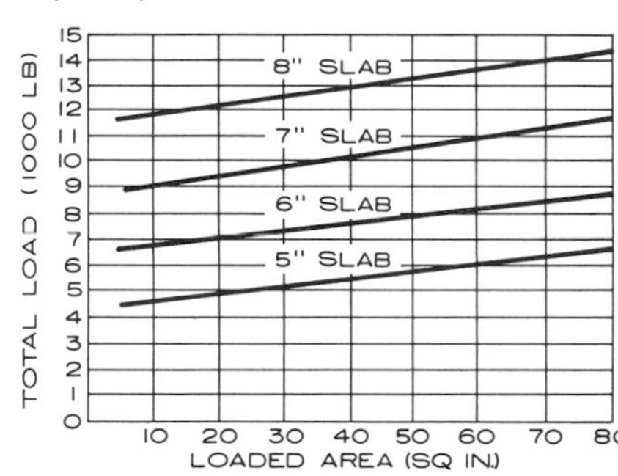

8" SLAB
7" SLAB
6" SLAB
5" SLAB
TOTAL LOAD (1000 LB)
0 1 2 3 4 5 6 7 8 9 10 11 12 13 14 15
10 20 30 40 50 60 70 80
LOADED AREA (SQ IN.)

MAXIMUM WHEEL LOADS FOR INDUSTRIAL FLOORS (FLEXURAL TENSILE STRESS = 300 PSI)

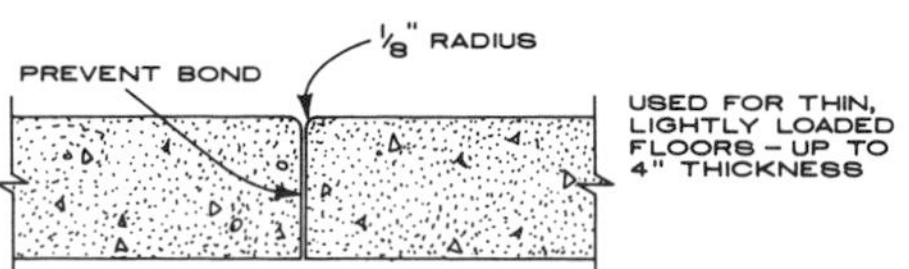

1/8" RADIUS
PREVENT BOND
USED FOR THIN, LIGHTLY LOADED FLOORS – UP TO 4" THICKNESS

BUTT TYPE CONSTRUCTION JOINT

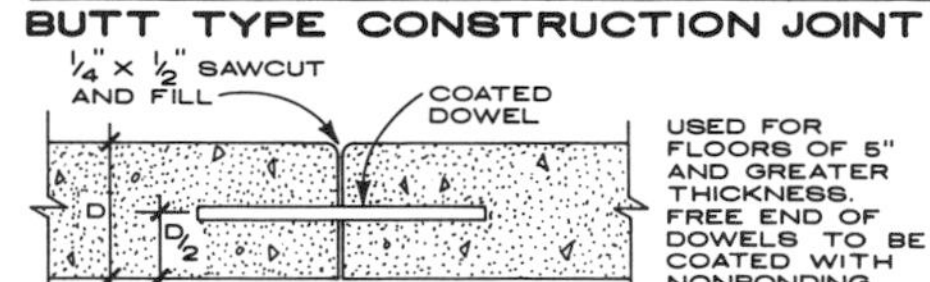

1/4" x 1/2" SAWCUT AND FILL
COATED DOWEL
D
D/2
USED FOR FLOORS OF 5" AND GREATER THICKNESS. FREE END OF DOWELS TO BE COATED WITH NONBONDING AGENT

BUTT TYPE CONSTRUCTION JOINT WITH DOWELS

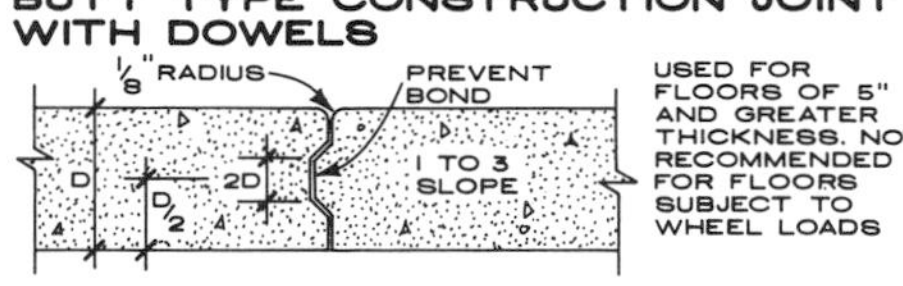

1/8" RADIUS
PREVENT BOND
D
2D
D/2
1 TO 3 SLOPE
USED FOR FLOORS OF 5" AND GREATER THICKNESS. NOT RECOMMENDED FOR FLOORS SUBJECT TO WHEEL LOADS

TONGUE AND GROOVE CONSTRUCTION JOINT

PLASTIC OR PREFORMED HARDBOARD STRIP
D/4
IF SAWCUT ONLY, FILL WITH SEALER (SHORE HARDNESS >80)
D
PLACED IN SLAB IMMEDIATELY AFTER POURING
INDUCED CRACK

SAWED OR PREMOLDED CONTROL JOINT FOR SLABS <4"

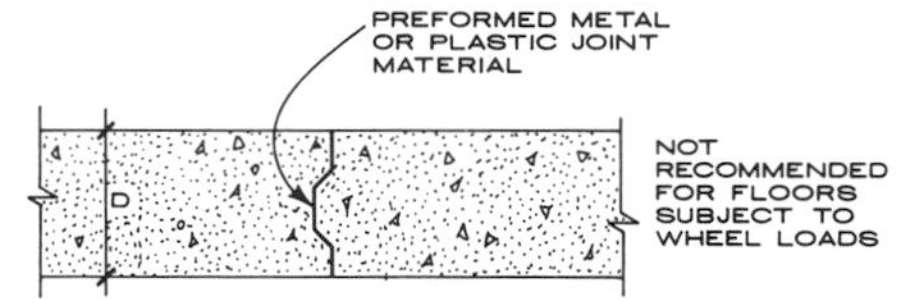

PREFORMED METAL OR PLASTIC JOINT MATERIAL
D
NOT RECOMMENDED FOR FLOORS SUBJECT TO WHEEL LOADS

TONGUE AND GROOVE CONTROL JOINT

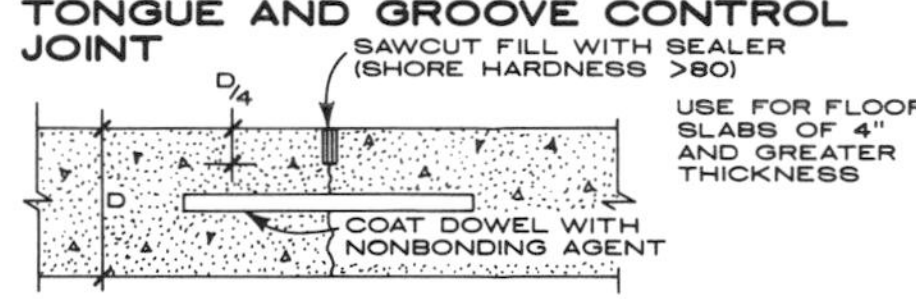

D/4
SAWCUT FILL WITH SEALER (SHORE HARDNESS >80)
D
USE FOR FLOOR SLABS OF 4" AND GREATER THICKNESS
COAT DOWEL WITH NONBONDING AGENT

CONTROL JOINT WITH DOWELS

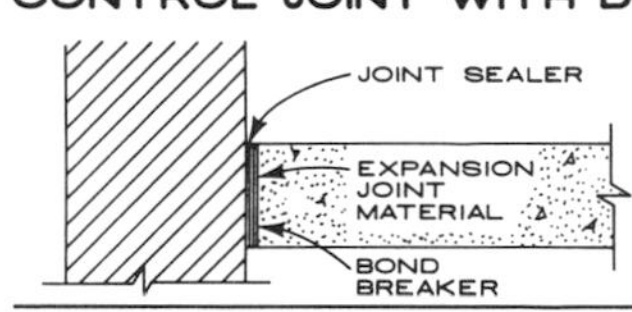

JOINT SEALER
EXPANSION JOINT MATERIAL
BOND BREAKER

ISOLATION JOINT

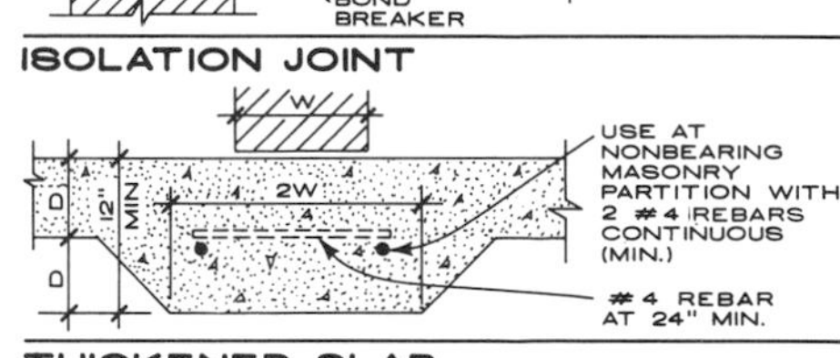

W
2W
D
12" MIN.
USE AT NONBEARING MASONRY PARTITION WITH 2 #4 REBARS CONTINUOUS (MIN.)
#4 REBAR AT 24" MIN.

THICKENED SLAB

CLASSIFICATION OF CONCRETE SLABS ON GRADE

CLASS	SLUMP RANGE (IN.)	MINIMUM COMPRESSIVE STRENGTH (PSI)	USUAL TRAFFIC	USE	SPECIAL CONSIDERATION	CONCRETE FINISHING TECHNIQUE
1	2-4	3500	Light foot	Residential or tile covered	Grade for drainage; plane smooth for tile	Medium steel trowel
2	2-4	3500	Foot	Offices, schools, hospitals, residential	Nonslip aggregate, mix in surface Color shake, special	Steel trowel; special finish for nonslip Steel trowel, color exposed aggregate
3	2-4	3500	Light foot and pneumatic wheels	Drives, garage floors, sidewalks for residences	Crown; pitch joints	Float, trowel, and broom
4	1-3	4000	Foot and pneumatic wheels	Light industrial, commercial	Careful curing	Hard steel trowel and brush for nonslip
5	1-3	4500	Foot and wheels—abrasive wear	Single course industrial, integral topping	Careful curing	Special hard aggregate, float and trowel
6	2-4	3500	Foot and steel tire vehicles—severe abrasion	Bonded two-course, heavy industrial	Base: textured surface and bond Top: special aggregate	Base: surface leveled by screeding Top: special power floats
7	1-3	4000	Same as Classes 3, 4, 5, 6	Unbonded topping	Mesh reinforcing; bond breaker on old concrete surface	—

Setter, Leach & Lindstrom, Inc.; Minneapolis, Minnesota

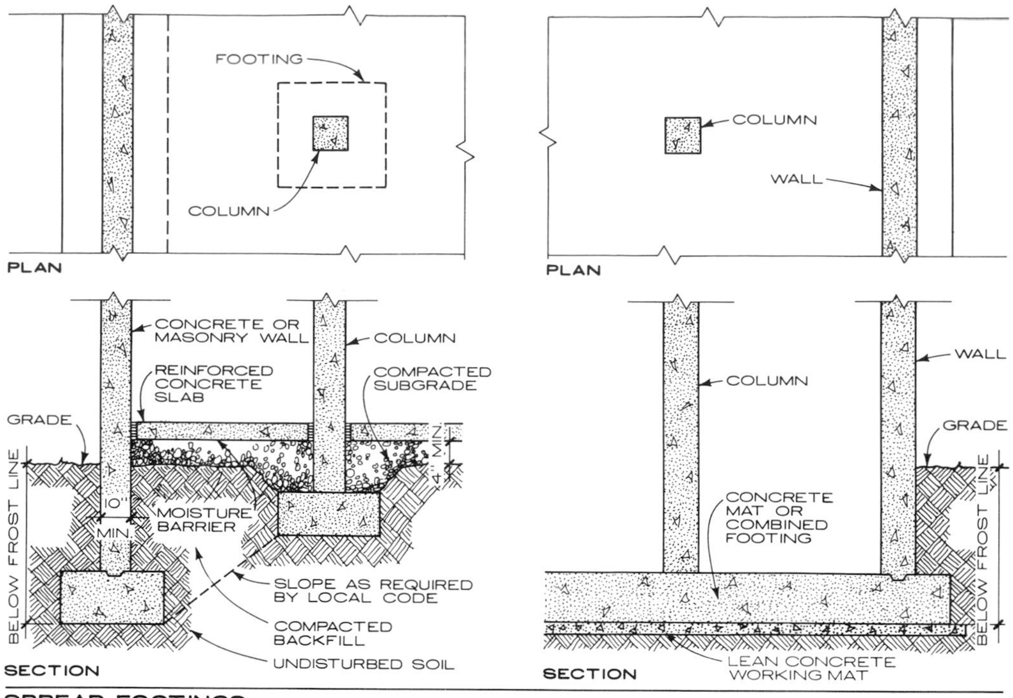

PLAN

FOOTING

COLUMN

SECTION

CONCRETE OR MASONRY WALL

COLUMN

REINFORCED CONCRETE SLAB

COMPACTED SUBGRADE

GRADE

4" MIN.

10" MIN.

MOISTURE BARRIER

BELOW FROST LINE

SLOPE AS REQUIRED BY LOCAL CODE

COMPACTED BACKFILL

UNDISTURBED SOIL

PLAN

COLUMN

WALL

SECTION

COLUMN

WALL

GRADE

CONCRETE MAT OR COMBINED FOOTING

BELOW FROST LINE

LEAN CONCRETE WORKING MAT

SPREAD FOOTINGS

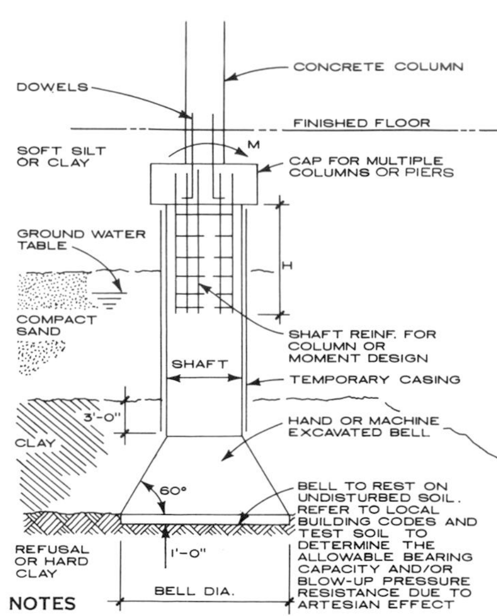

CONCRETE COLUMN
DOWELS
FINISHED FLOOR
M
SOFT SILT OR CLAY
CAP FOR MULTIPLE COLUMNS OR PIERS
GROUND WATER TABLE
H
COMPACT SAND
SHAFT REINF. FOR COLUMN OR MOMENT DESIGN
SHAFT
TEMPORARY CASING
3'-0"
HAND OR MACHINE EXCAVATED BELL
CLAY
60°
BELL TO REST ON UNDISTURBED SOIL. REFER TO LOCAL BUILDING CODES AND TEST SOIL TO DETERMINE THE ALLOWABLE BEARING CAPACITY AND/OR BLOW-UP PRESSURE RESISTANCE DUE TO ARTESIAN EFFECT
REFUSAL OR HARD CLAY
1'-0"
BELL DIA.

NOTES

1. H is a function of the passive resistance of the soil, generated by the moment applied to the pier cap.
2. Piers may be used under grade beams or concrete walls. For very heavy loads, pier foundations may be more economical than piles.

BELL PIER FOUNDATION

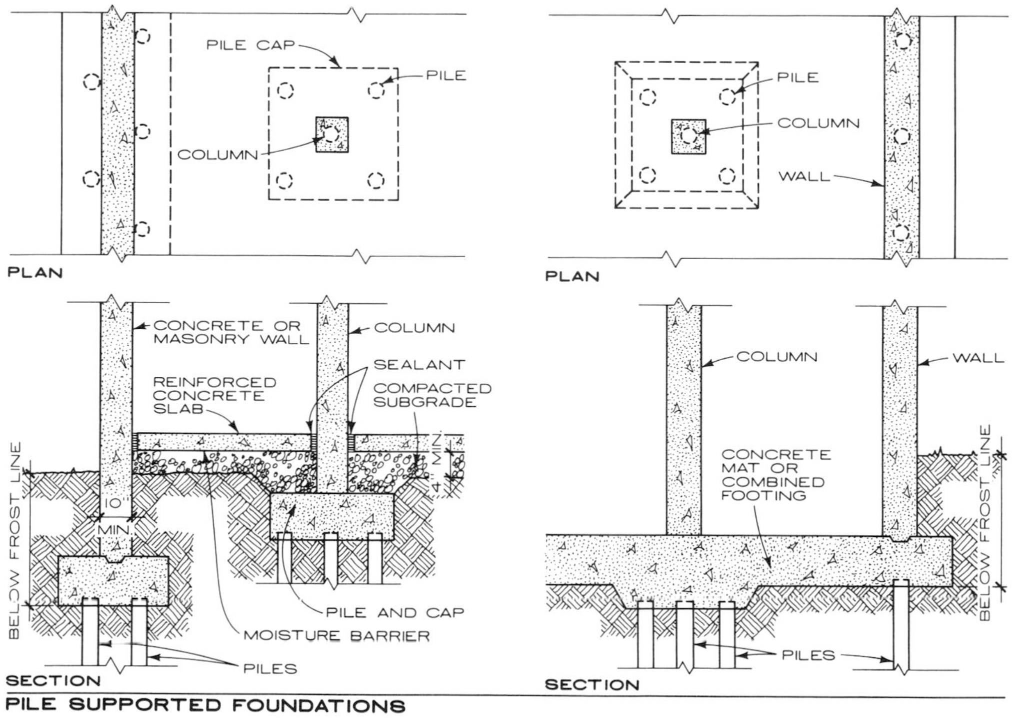

PLAN

PILE CAP

PILE

COLUMN

SECTION

CONCRETE OR MASONRY WALL

COLUMN

SEALANT

REINFORCED CONCRETE SLAB

COMPACTED SUBGRADE

4" MIN.

10" MIN.

BELOW FROST LINE

PILE AND CAP

MOISTURE BARRIER

PILES

PLAN

PILE

COLUMN

WALL

SECTION

COLUMN

WALL

CONCRETE MAT OR COMBINED FOOTING

BELOW FROST LINE

PILES

PILE SUPPORTED FOUNDATIONS

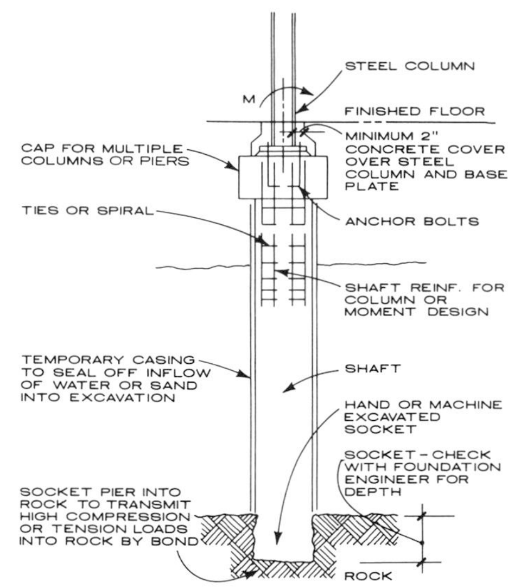

STEEL COLUMN
M
FINISHED FLOOR
MINIMUM 2" CONCRETE COVER OVER STEEL COLUMN AND BASE PLATE
CAP FOR MULTIPLE COLUMNS OR PIERS
ANCHOR BOLTS
TIES OR SPIRAL
SHAFT REINF. FOR COLUMN OR MOMENT DESIGN
TEMPORARY CASING TO SEAL OFF INFLOW OF WATER OR SAND INTO EXCAVATION
SHAFT
HAND OR MACHINE EXCAVATED SOCKET
SOCKET - CHECK WITH FOUNDATION ENGINEER FOR DEPTH
SOCKET PIER INTO ROCK TO TRANSMIT HIGH COMPRESSION OR TENSION LOADS INTO ROCK BY BOND
ROCK

NOTES

1. Pier shaft should be poured in the dry if possible, but tremie pours can be used with appropriate control.
2. Grout bottom of shaft against artesian water or sulphur gas intrusion into the excavation.

SOCKET PIER FOUNDATION

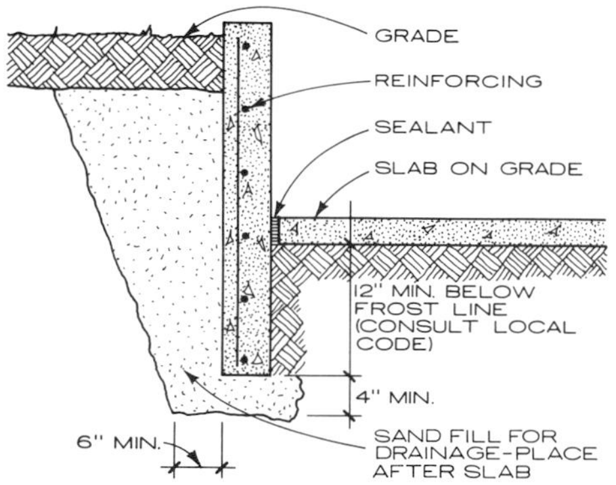

GRADE

REINFORCING

SEALANT

SLAB ON GRADE

12" MIN. BELOW FROST LINE (CONSULT LOCAL CODE)

4" MIN.

6" MIN.

SAND FILL FOR DRAINAGE-PLACE AFTER SLAB

AREAWAY WALL

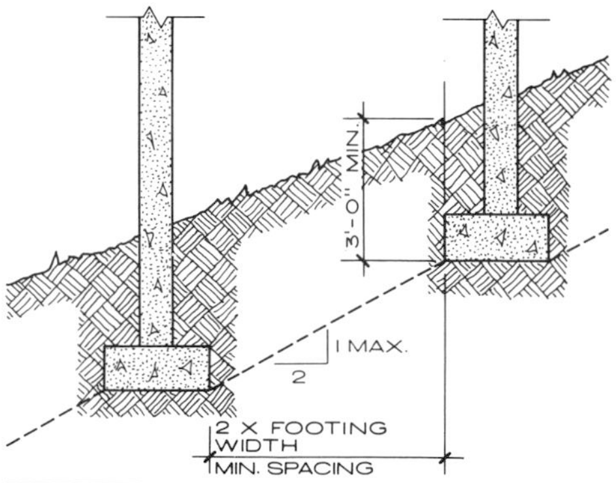

3'-0" MIN.

1 MAX.

2

2 X FOOTING WIDTH

MIN. SPACING

STEP FOOTINGS

MAX. STEEPNESS: 2 HORIZONTAL TO 1 VERTICAL

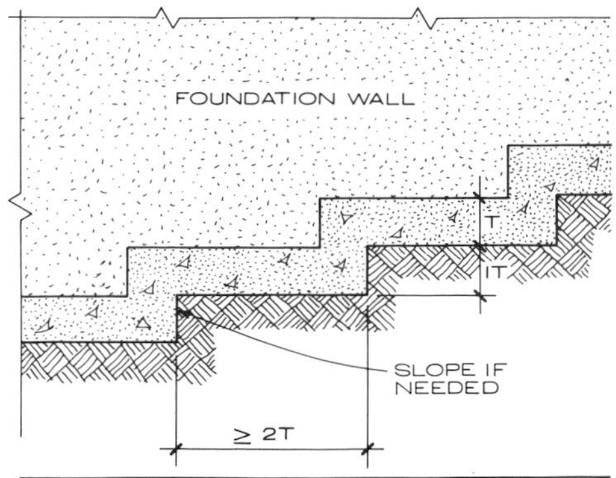

FOUNDATION WALL
T
T
SLOPE IF NEEDED
≥ 2T

STEP FOOTING (FOR CONTINUOUS WALL)

MAX. STEEPNESS: 2 HORIZONTAL TO 1 VERTICAL

Mueser, Rutledge, Johnston & DeSimone; New York, New York

NOTES

1. See page on stair dimensions for code requirements for stairs.
2. Structural designer to determine reinforcement and verify structural assumptions.

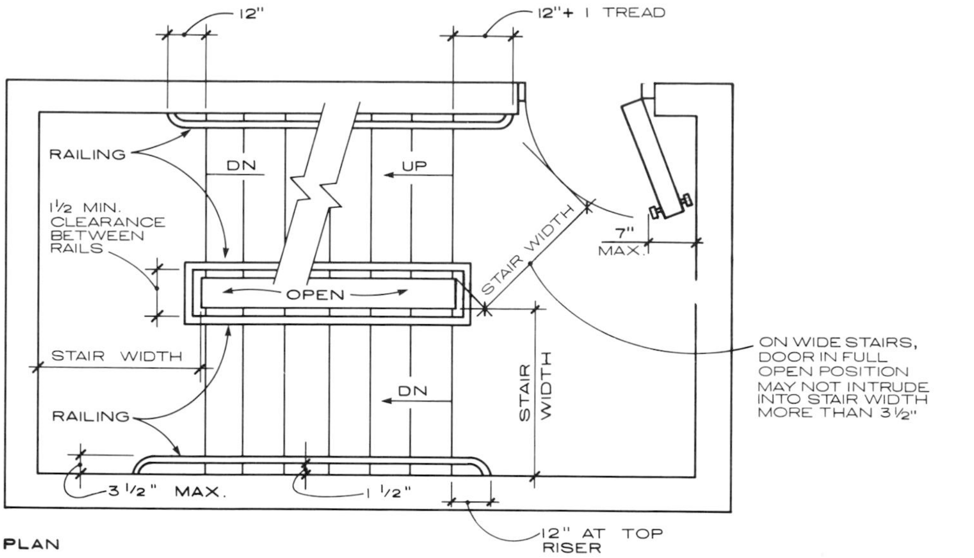

12"
12" + 1 TREAD
RAILING
DN
UP
1½ MIN. CLEARANCE BETWEEN RAILS
OPEN
STAIR WIDTH
7" MAX.
STAIR WIDTH
DN
STAIR WIDTH
RAILING
ON WIDE STAIRS, DOOR IN FULL OPEN POSITION MAY NOT INTRUDE INTO STAIR WIDTH MORE THAN 3½"
3½" MAX.
1½"
12" AT TOP RISER

PLAN

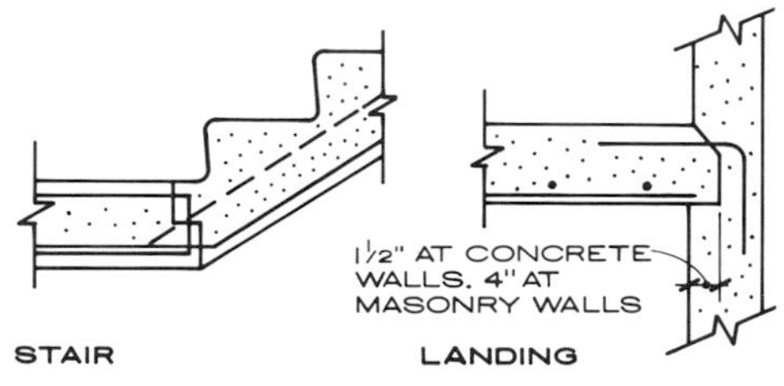

1½" AT CONCRETE WALLS, 4" AT MASONRY WALLS

STAIR

LANDING

SHEAR KEY DETAILS

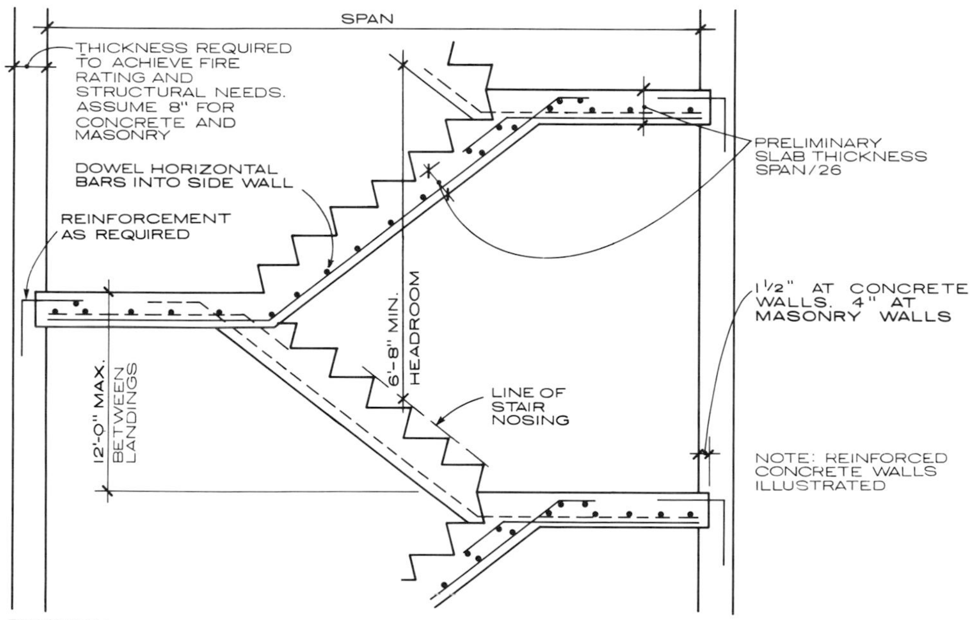

SPAN
THICKNESS REQUIRED TO ACHIEVE FIRE RATING AND STRUCTURAL NEEDS. ASSUME 8" FOR CONCRETE AND MASONRY
DOWEL HORIZONTAL BARS INTO SIDE WALL
REINFORCEMENT AS REQUIRED
PRELIMINARY SLAB THICKNESS SPAN/26
6'-8" MIN. HEADROOM
1½" AT CONCRETE WALLS, 4" AT MASONRY WALLS
12'-0" MAX. BETWEEN LANDINGS
LINE OF STAIR NOSING
NOTE: REINFORCED CONCRETE WALLS ILLUSTRATED

SECTION

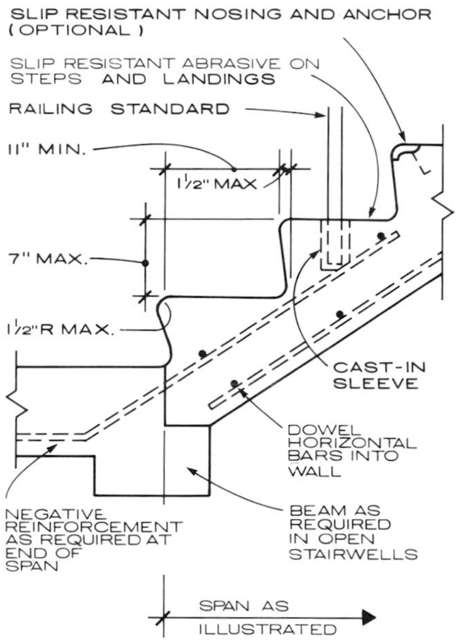

SLIP RESISTANT NOSING AND ANCHOR (OPTIONAL)
SLIP RESISTANT ABRASIVE ON STEPS AND LANDINGS
RAILING STANDARD
11" MIN.
1½" MAX
7" MAX.
½"R MAX.
CAST-IN SLEEVE
DOWEL HORIZONTAL BARS INTO WALL
NEGATIVE REINFORCEMENT AS REQUIRED AT END OF SPAN
BEAM AS REQUIRED IN OPEN STAIRWELLS
SPAN AS ILLUSTRATED

COMPOSITE DETAIL

U-TYPE CONCRETE STAIRS

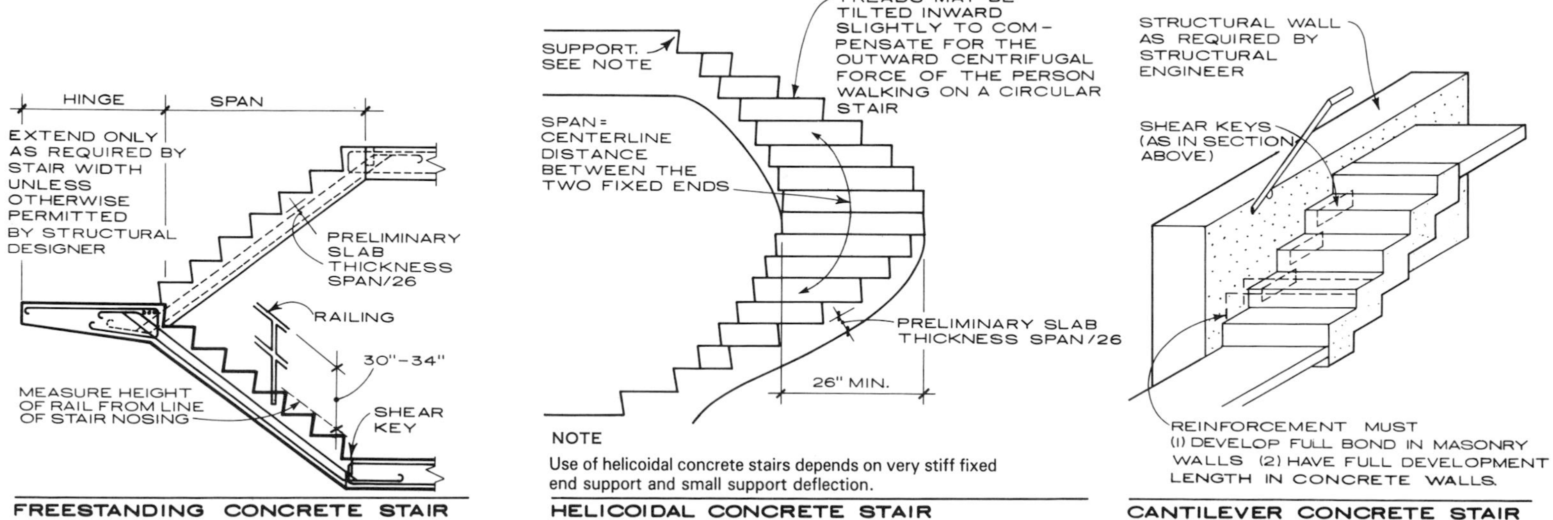
HINGE
SPAN
EXTEND ONLY AS REQUIRED BY STAIR WIDTH UNLESS OTHERWISE PERMITTED BY STRUCTURAL DESIGNER
PRELIMINARY SLAB THICKNESS SPAN/26
RAILING
30"-34"
MEASURE HEIGHT OF RAIL FROM LINE OF STAIR NOSING
SHEAR KEY
SUPPORT. SEE NOTE
TREADS MAY BE TILTED INWARD SLIGHTLY TO COMPENSATE FOR THE OUTWARD CENTRIFUGAL FORCE OF THE PERSON WALKING ON A CIRCULAR STAIR
SPAN = CENTERLINE DISTANCE BETWEEN THE TWO FIXED ENDS
PRELIMINARY SLAB THICKNESS SPAN/26
26" MIN.
STRUCTURAL WALL AS REQUIRED BY STRUCTURAL ENGINEER
SHEAR KEYS (AS IN SECTION ABOVE)
REINFORCEMENT MUST (1) DEVELOP FULL BOND IN MASONRY WALLS (2) HAVE FULL DEVELOPMENT LENGTH IN CONCRETE WALLS

NOTE

Use of helicoidal concrete stairs depends on very stiff fixed end support and small support deflection.

FREESTANDING CONCRETE STAIR

HELICOIDAL CONCRETE STAIR

CANTILEVER CONCRETE STAIR

Krommenhoek/McKeown & Associates; San Diego, California
Karlsberger and Associates, Inc.; Columbus, Ohio

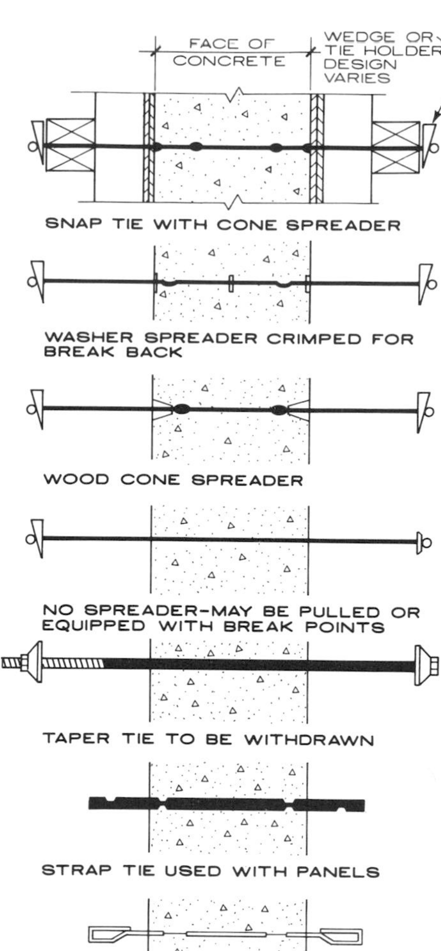
FACE OF CONCRETE
WEDGE OR TIE HOLDER DESIGN VARIES

SNAP TIE WITH CONE SPREADER

WASHER SPREADER CRIMPED FOR BREAK BACK

WOOD CONE SPREADER

NO SPREADER—MAY BE PULLED OR EQUIPPED WITH BREAK POINTS

TAPER TIE TO BE WITHDRAWN

STRAP TIE USED WITH PANELS

LOOP END TIE USED WITH PANELS

TYPICAL SINGLE MEMBER TIES

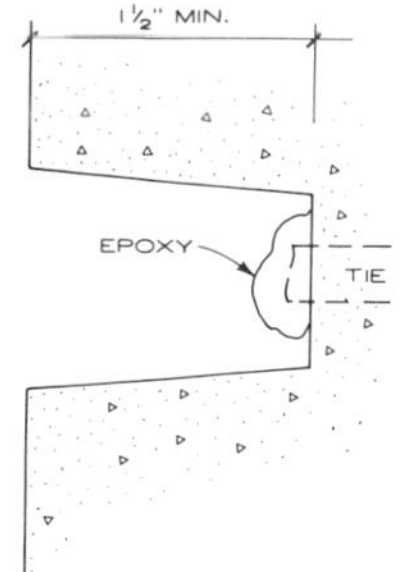
1½" MIN.
EPOXY
TIE

EPOXY OVER TIE

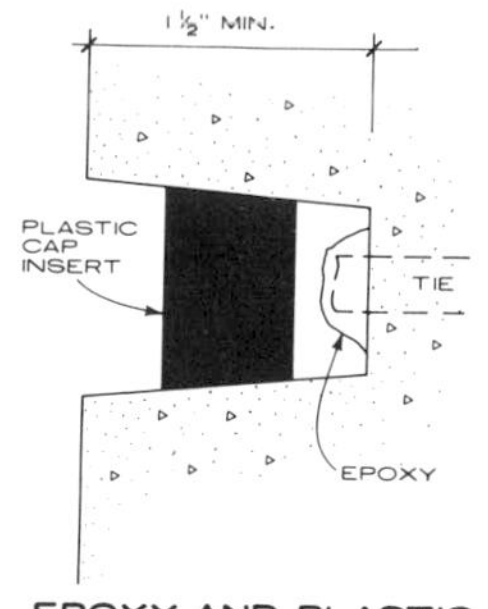
1½" MIN.
PLASTIC CAP INSERT
TIE
EPOXY

EPOXY AND PLASTIC CAP

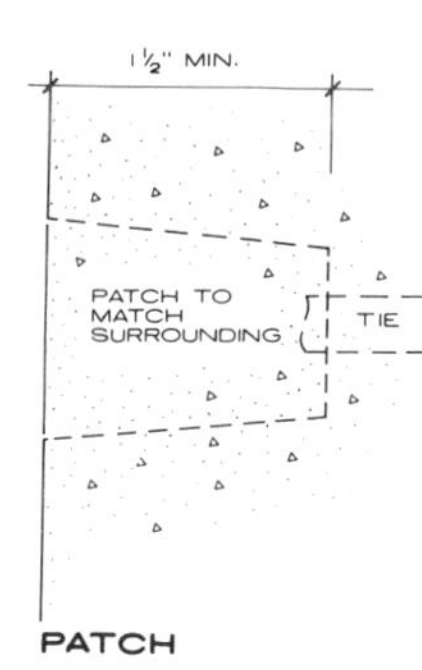
1½" MIN.
PATCH TO MATCH SURROUNDING
TIE

PATCH

TIE HOLE TREATMENT OPTIONS

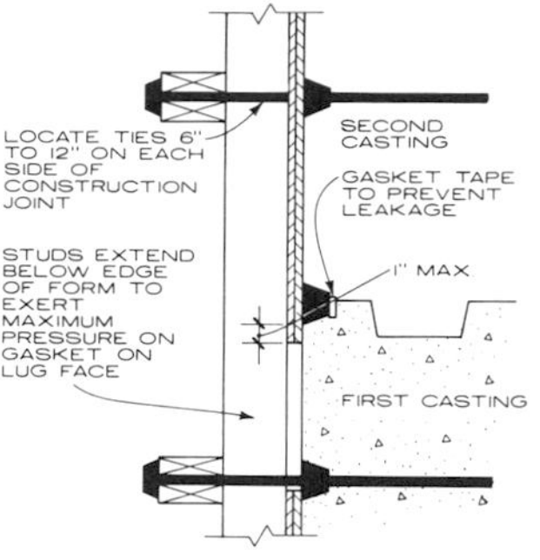
LOCATE TIES 6" TO 12" ON EACH SIDE OF CONSTRUCTION JOINT
SECOND CASTING
GASKET TAPE TO PREVENT LEAKAGE
STUDS EXTEND BELOW EDGE OF FORM TO EXERT MAXIMUM PRESSURE ON GASKET ON LUG FACE
1" MAX
FIRST CASTING

TYPICAL CONSTRUCTION JOINT

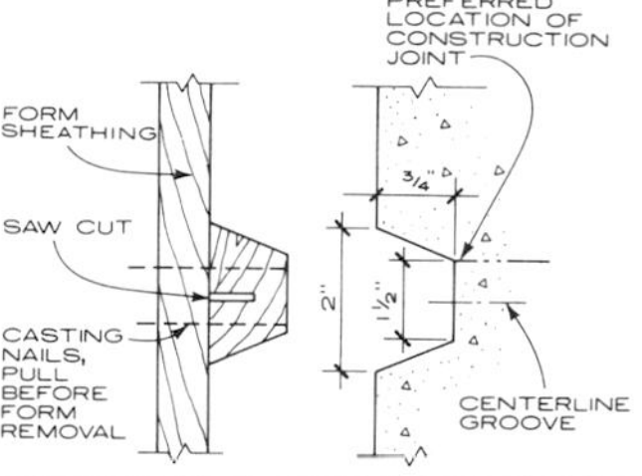
FORM SHEATHING
SAW CUT
CASTING NAILS, PULL BEFORE FORM REMOVAL
PREFERRED LOCATION OF CONSTRUCTION JOINT
3/4"
2"
1½"
CENTERLINE GROOVE

RUSTICATION AT CONSTRUCTION JOINT

CONCRETE SURFACES—GENERAL

The variety of architectural finishes is as extensive as the cost and effort expended to achieve them. There are three basic ways to improve or change the appearance of concrete:

1. Changing materials, that is, using a colored matrix and exposed aggregates.
2. Changing the mold or form by such means as a form liner.
3. By treating or tooling the concrete surface in the final stages of hardening.

The aim is to obtain maximum benefit from one of three features—color, texture, and pattern—all of which are interrelated. Color is the easiest method of changing the appearance of concrete. It should not be used on a plain concrete surface with a series of panels, since color matches are difficult to achieve. The exception is possible when white cement is used, usually as a base for the pigment to help reduce changes of color variation. Since white cement is expensive, many effects are tried with gray cement to avoid an entire plain surface. Colored concrete is most effective when it is used with an exposed aggregate finish.

FORM LINERS

1. Sandblasted Douglas fir or long leaf yellow pine dressed one side away from the concrete surface.
2. Flexible steel strip formwork adapted to curved surfaces (Schwellmer System).
3. Resin coated, striated, or sandblasted plywood.
4. Rubber mats.
5. Thermoplastic sheets with high gloss or texture laid over stone, for example.
6. Formed plastics.
7. Plaster of Paris molds for sculptured work.
8. Clay (sculpturing and staining concrete).
9. Hardboard (screen side).
10. Standard steel forms.
11. Wood boarding and reversed battens.
12. Square-edged lumber dressed one side.
13. Resawn wood boards.

RELEASE AGENTS

1. Oils, petroleum based, used on wood, concrete, and steel forms.
2. Soft soaps.
3. Talcum.
4. Whitewash used on wood with tannin in conjunction with oils.
5. Calcium stearate powder.
6. Silicones used on steel forms.
7. Plastics used on wood forms.
8. Lacquers used on plywood and plaster forms.
9. Resins used on plywood forms.
10. Sodium silicate.
11. Membrane used over any form.
12. Grease used on plaster forms.
13. Epoxy resin plastic used on plywood.

CATEGORIES OF COMMON AGGREGATE

1. QUARTZ: Clear, white, rose.
2. MARBLE: Green, yellow, red, pink, blue, gray, white, black.
3. GRANITE: Pink, gray, black, white.
4. CERAMIC: Full range.
5. VITREOUS/GLASS: Full range.

CRITICAL FACTORS AFFECTING SURFACES

DESIGN DRAWINGS should show form details, including openings, control joints, construction joints, expansion joints, and other important specifics.

1. CEMENT: Types and brands.
2. AGGREGATES: Sources of coarse and fine aggregates.
3. TECHNIQUES: Uniformity in mixing and placing.
4. FORMS: Closure techniques or concealing joints in formwork materials.
5. SLUMP CONTROL: Ensure compliance with design.
6. CURING METHODS: Ensure compliance with design.

TIES

A concrete tie is a tensile unit adapted to hold concrete forms secure against the lateral pressure of unhardened concrete. Two general types of concrete ties exist:

1. Continuous single member where the tensile unit is a single piece and the holding device engages the tensile unit against the exterior of the form. Standard types: working load = 2500 to 5000 lb.
2. Internal disconnecting where the tensile unit has an inner part with threaded connections to removable external members, which have suitable devices of securing them against the outside of the form. Working load = 6000 to 36,000 lb.

GUIDELINES FOR PATCHING

1. Design the patch mix to match the original, with small amount of white cement; may eliminate coarse aggregate or hand place it. Trial and error is the only reliable match method.
2. Saturate area with water and apply bonding agent to base of hole and to water of patch mix.
3. Pack patch mix to density of original.
4. Place exposed aggregate by hand.
5. Bristle brush after setup to match existing material.
6. Moist cure to prevent shrinking.
7. Use form or finish to match original.

CHECKLIST IN PLANNING FOR ARCHITECTURAL CONCRETE PLACING TECHNIQUES:

Pumping vs. bottom drop or other type of bucket.

1. FORMING SYSTEM: Evaluate whether architectural concrete forms can also be used for structural concrete.
2. SHOP DRAWINGS: Determine form quality and steel placement.
3. VIBRATORS: Verify that proper size, frequency, and power are used.
4. RELEASE AGENTS: Consider form material, color impact of agents, and possible use throughout job.
5. CURING COMPOUND: Determine how fast it wears off.
6. SAMPLES: Require approval of forms and finishes. Field mock-up is advised to evaluate appearance of panel and quality of workmanship.

D. Neil Rankins; SHWC, Inc.; Dallas, Texas

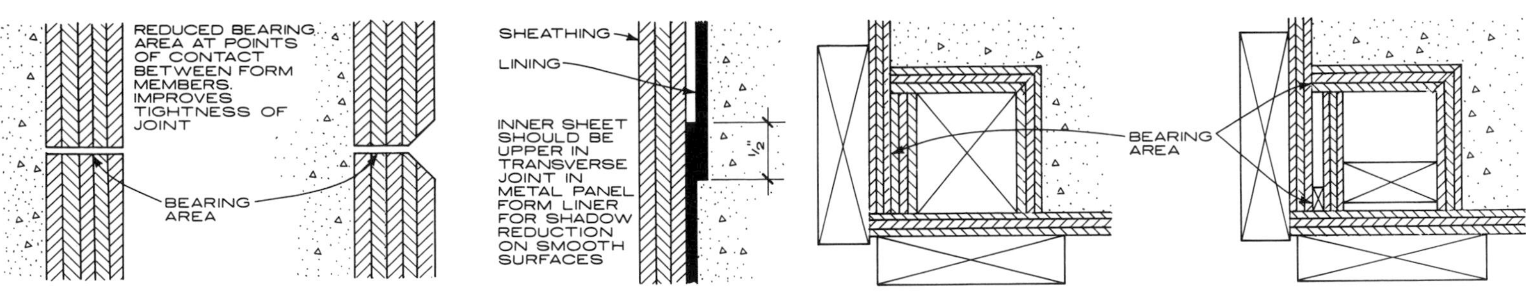
REDUCED BEARING AREA AT POINTS OF CONTACT BETWEEN FORM MEMBERS. IMPROVES TIGHTNESS OF JOINT
BEARING AREA
SHEATHING
LINING
INNER SHEET SHOULD BE UPPER IN TRANSVERSE JOINT IN METAL PANEL FORM LINER FOR SHADOW REDUCTION ON SMOOTH SURFACES
1/2"
BEARING AREA

USUAL RECOMMENDED LINER JOINT USUAL RECOMMENDED

FORM JOINTS

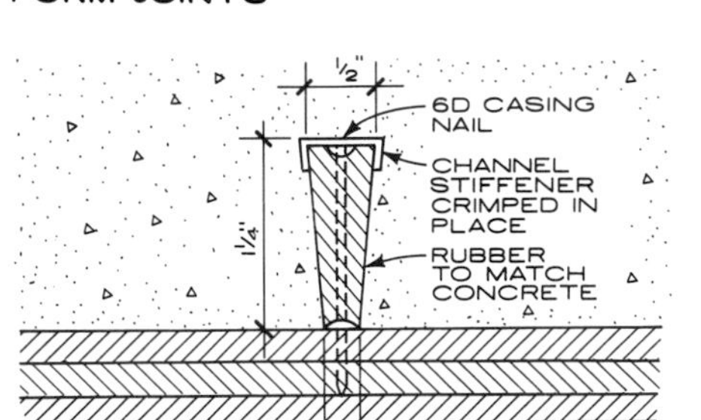
1/2"
6D CASING NAIL
CHANNEL STIFFENER CRIMPED IN PLACE
RUBBER TO MATCH CONCRETE
1 1/4"
1/4"

RUBBER FORM INSERT

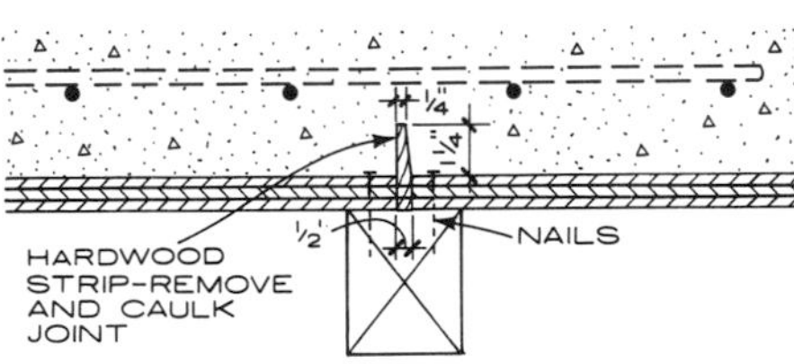
1/4"
1/2"
HARDWOOD STRIP–REMOVE AND CAULK JOINT
NAILS

WOOD FORM INSERT

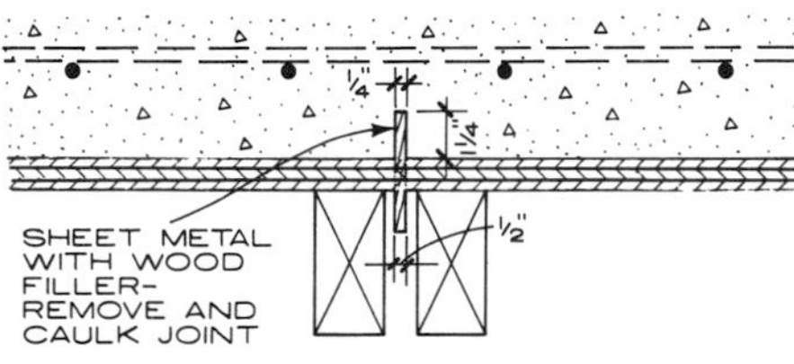
1/4"
1/4"
1/2"
SHEET METAL WITH WOOD FILLER–REMOVE AND CAULK JOINT

SHEET METAL FORM INSERT

CONTROL JOINTS

RUSTICATION (PREFERRED)

TAPED (MEDIUM LIGHT BLAST)

EPOXY ON 45° CUT

GASKETED

TONGUE AND GROOVED

SPLINED

IMPERVIOUS LINER (1/4" TO 3/8")

SHIPLAP

PLYWOOD BUTT JOINTS FOR EXPOSED AGGREGATE FINISHES

CATEGORIES OF ARCHITECTURAL CONCRETE SURFACES

CATEGORY	FINISH	COLOR	FORMS	CRITICAL DETAILS
1. As cast	Remains as is after form removal—usually board marks or wood grain	Cement first influence, fine aggregate second influence	Plastic best All others • Wire-brushed plywood • Sandblasted plywood • Exposed-grain plywood • Unfinished sheathing lumber • Ammonia sprayed wood • Tongue-and-groove bands spaced	Slump = 2½" to 3½" Joinery of forms Proper release agent Point form joints to avoid marks
2. Abrasive blasted surfaces A. Brush blast	Uniform scour cleaning	Cement plus fine aggregate have equal influence	All smooth	Scouring after 7 days Slump = 2½" to 3½"
B. Light blast	Sandblast to expose fine and some coarse aggregate	Fine aggregate primary coarse aggregate plus cement secondary	All smooth	10% more coarse aggregate Slump = 2½" to 3½" Blasting between 7 and 45 days
C. Medium exposed aggregate	Sandblasted to expose coarse aggregate	Coarse aggregate	All smooth	Higher than normal coarse aggregate Slump = 2" to 3" Blast before 7 days
D. Heavy exposed aggregate	Sandblasted to expose coarse aggregate 80% viable	Coarse aggregate	All smooth	Special mix coarse aggregate Slump = 0" to 2" Blast within 24 hours Use high frequency vibrator
3. Chemical retardation of surface set	Chemicals expose aggregate Aggregate can be adhered to surface	Coarse aggregate and cement	All smooth, glass fiber best	Chemical Grade determines etch depth Stripping scheduled to prevent long drying between stripping and washoff
4. Mechanically fractured surfaces, scaling, bush hammering, jackhammering, tooling	Varied	Cement, fine and coarse Aggregate	Textured	Aggregate particles 3/8" for scaling and tooling Aggregate particles
5. Combination/fluted	Striated/abrasive blasted/irregular pattern Corrugated/abrasive Vertical rusticated/abrasive blasted Reeded and bush hammered Reeded and hammered Reeded and chiseled	The shallower the surface, the more influence aggregate fines and cement have	Wood or rubber strips, corrugated sheet metal or glass fiber	Depends on type of finish desired Wood fluke kerfed and nailed loosely

D. Neil Rankins; SHWC, Inc.; Dallas, Texas

REFERENCES

GENERAL REFERENCES

ACI Detailing Manual, American Concrete Institute (ACI)

Building Code Requirements for Reinforced Concrete, American Concrete Institute (ACI)

CRSI Handbook, 1984, Concrete Reinforcing Steel Institute (CRSI)

Design and Typical Details of Connections for Precast and Prestressed Concrete, Precast/Prestressed Concrete Institute (PCI)

PCI Design Handbook: Precast and Prestressed Concrete, Precast/Prestressed Concrete Institute (PCI)

Structural Details for Concrete Construction, 1988, Morton Newman, McGraw-Hill

DATA SOURCES: ORGANIZATIONS

American Concrete Institute (ACI), 87, 91, 96, 97

American National Standards Institute (ANSI), 95

American Society for Testing and Materials (ASTM), 86, 87, 91. Reprinted with permission, 86, 87

Concrete Reinforcing Steel Institute (CRSI), 91, 92

Portland Cement Association (PCA), 86, 87, 93

DATA SOURCES: PUBLICATIONS

Annual Book of ASTM Standards, American Society for Testing and Materials (ASTM), 87

Basic Building Code, Building Officials and Code Administrators International (BOCA), 95

Building Code Requirements for Reinforced Concrete, American Concrete Institute (ACI), 87

CHAPTER 4

MASONRY

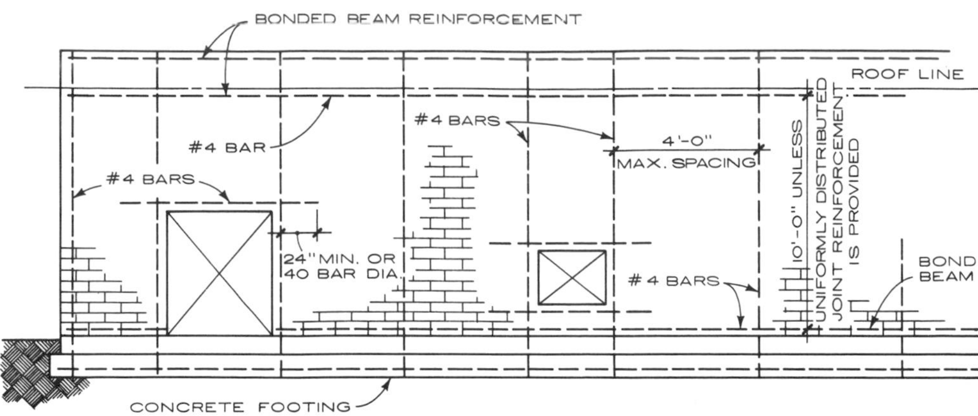

BONDED BEAM REINFORCEMENT
ROOF LINE
#4 BARS
4'-0" MAX. SPACING
#4 BAR
#4 BARS
10'-0" UNLESS UNIFORMLY DISTRIBUTED JOINT REINFORCEMENT IS PROVIDED
24" MIN. OR 40 BAR DIA.
#4 BARS
BOND BEAM
CONCRETE FOOTING

PARTIALLY REINFORCED LOAD-BEARING BRICK OR CMU WALL (SEISMIC ZONES 0, 1, AND 2)

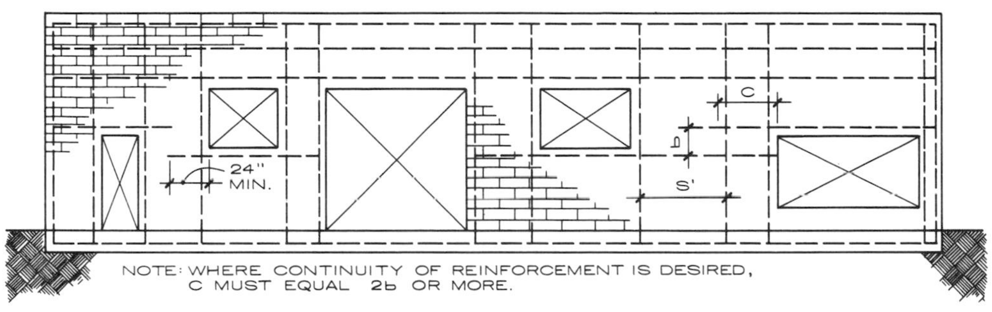

C
b
24" MIN.
S'
NOTE: WHERE CONTINUITY OF REINFORCEMENT IS DESIRED, C MUST EQUAL 2b OR MORE.

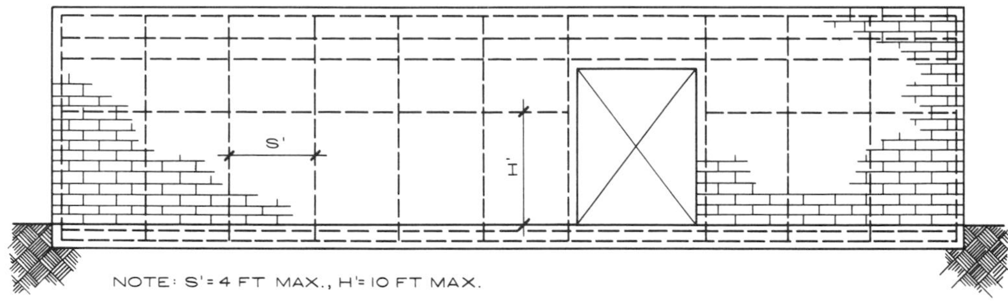

S'
H'
NOTE: S' = 4 FT MAX., H' = 10 FT MAX.

REINFORCED LOAD-BEARING BRICK OR CMU WALLS (SEISMIC ZONES 3 AND 4)

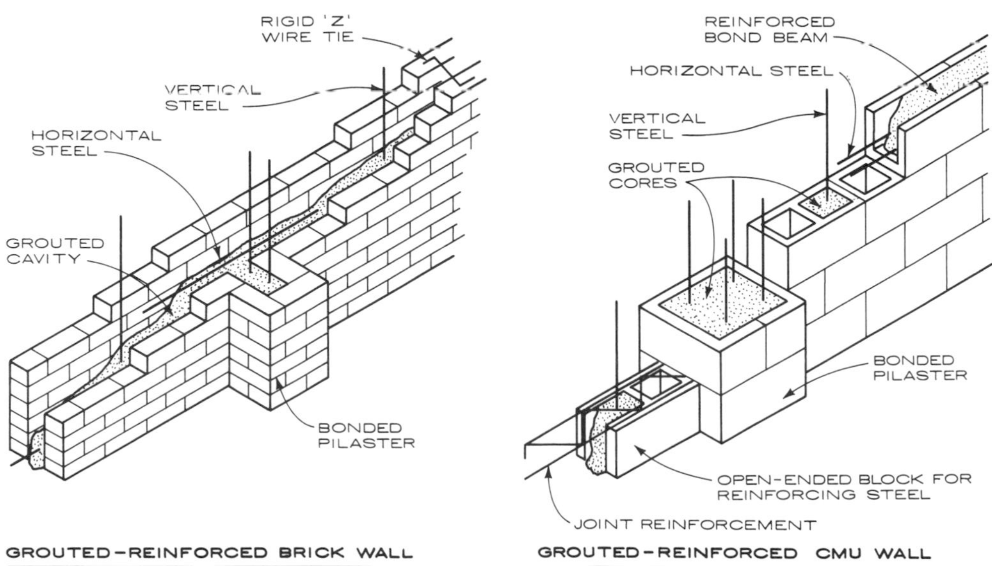

RIGID 'Z' WIRE TIE
VERTICAL STEEL
HORIZONTAL STEEL
GROUTED CAVITY
BONDED PILASTER
REINFORCED BOND BEAM
HORIZONTAL STEEL
VERTICAL STEEL
GROUTED CORES
BONDED PILASTER
OPEN-ENDED BLOCK FOR REINFORCING STEEL
JOINT REINFORCEMENT

GROUTED-REINFORCED BRICK WALL

GROUTED-REINFORCED CMU WALL

METHODS OF REINFORCING

LOAD-BEARING MASONRY

Engineered load-bearing masonry walls may be plain (unreinforced), partially reinforced, or reinforced. They may be single-wythe CMU or structural clay tile, multiwythe brick, or combinations of these materials. Reinforcing steel increases resistance to lateral loads and to buckling. Single-wythe brick masonry may be reinforced to function as panel wall or curtain wall systems, with relatively long spans between lateral supports.

ANCHORS AND REINFORCEMENT

Reinforced masonry uses standard deformed steel reinforcing bars, ASTM A615. Masonry wall ties should be rigid wire, minimum 3/16 in. diameter, rectangular where open cavity occurs, rectangular or Z-ties where cavity is grouted. Do not used crimped ties with water drip, as strength is considerably reduced. Horizontal joint reinforcement is used to control shrinkage cracking in CMU construction. It may be ladder or truss type design with optional tabs for fixed or adjustable veneer anchorage. Standard widths are 2 in. less than nominal wall thickness to permit a minimum 5/8 in. mortar cover at outside of joints. Longitudinal wires may be 10 gauge (light duty, interior only), 9 gauge (standard duty), 8 gauge (heavy duty), or 3/16 in. diameter (extra heavy duty).

Cross wires may be a different size, generally 12 gauge minimum. For corrosion resistance, joint reinforcement and ties should be hot-dip galvanized, ASTM A153.

HORIZONTAL AND VERTICAL STEEL

Some codes permit calculation of horizontal joint reinforcement as part of the steel required for certain types of load-bearing walls. Other codes require standard deformed reinforcing bars placed horizontally in bond beam courses or grouted cavities and vertically in grouted cores or cavities.

PARTIALLY REINFORCED MASONRY (SEISMIC ZONE 2)

Partially reinforced masonry (not permitted in seismic zones 3 and 4) uses a certain minimum of code-required steel (check local requirements), plus an additional 0.2 sq in. in cross section horizontally and vertically wherever engineering design analysis indicated that tensile stress is developed. Maximum spacing of vertical steel is 4 ft 0 in. Vertical steel must also be placed at each side of window and door openings and at all corners. Bond beam courses must be provided at top of footings, bottom and top of wall openings, below roof and floor lines, and at top of parapet walls.

REINFORCED MASONRY (SEISMIC ZONES 3 AND 4)

Walls designed as reinforced masonry must have a minimum area of steel equal to 0.002 times the cross-sectional area of the wall, not more than 2/3 of which (0.0007) may be placed in either direction. Maximum spacing principal reinforcement may not exceed 6 times the wall thickness or 48 in. o.c. Horizontal reinforcement must be provided in bond beam courses at top of footings, bottom and top of wall openings, below roof and floor lines, and at top of parapet walls. There must also be one #4 bar vertically at all window and door openings, extending at least 24 in. beyond the opening to prevent diagonal cracking at these planes of weakness. Only continuous reinforcement may be considered in computing the minimum area of steel provided.

PRECAUTIONS

Reinforcement must be lapped a minimum of 6 in. for continuity. Joint reinforcement, masonry ties, and steel wires located in mortar joints must be placed in the mortar bed and not directly on the masonry. CMU face shell bedding is acceptable except at grouted cores where cross-webs must also be bedded in mortar. Use spacers to hold vertical and horizontal reinforcement in proper alignment while grouting. Do not continue reinforcement through control or expansion joints. Do not place flashing in the same joint as reinforcement.

REFERENCES

Consult a structural engineer and local code requirements for design of grouted-reinforced masonry. For further technical information:

Masonry Design and Detailing, 2d ed. Christine Beall. New York: McGraw-Hill, 1987.

Technical Notes Series. Brick Institute of America.

TEK Series. National Concrete Masonry Association.

Christine Beall, AIA, CCS; Austin, Texas

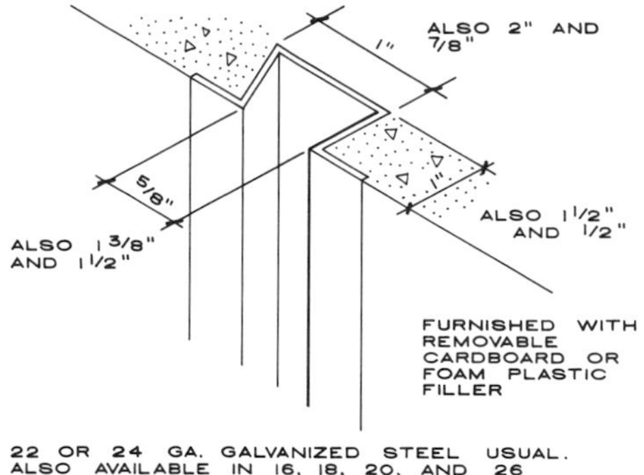
ALSO 2" AND 7/8"
1"
5/8"
ALSO 1 3/8" AND 1 1/2"
ALSO 1 1/2" AND 1/2"
1"
FURNISHED WITH REMOVABLE CARDBOARD OR FOAM PLASTIC FILLER
22 OR 24 GA. GALVANIZED STEEL USUAL. ALSO AVAILABLE IN 16, 18, 20, AND 26 GA. GALVANIZED STEEL AND STAINLESS STEEL, COPPER AND ZINC ALLOY

DOVETAIL SLOTS

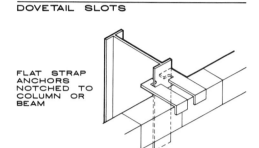

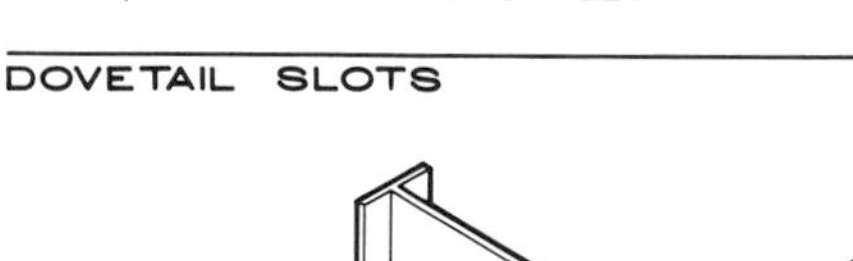
FLAT STRAP ANCHORS NOTCHED TO COLUMN OR BEAM

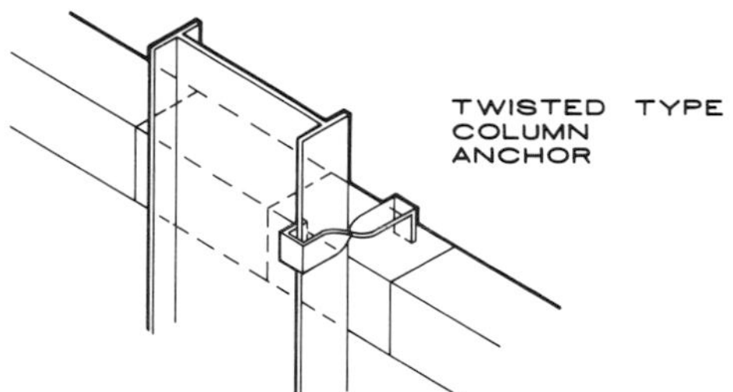
TWISTED TYPE COLUMN ANCHOR

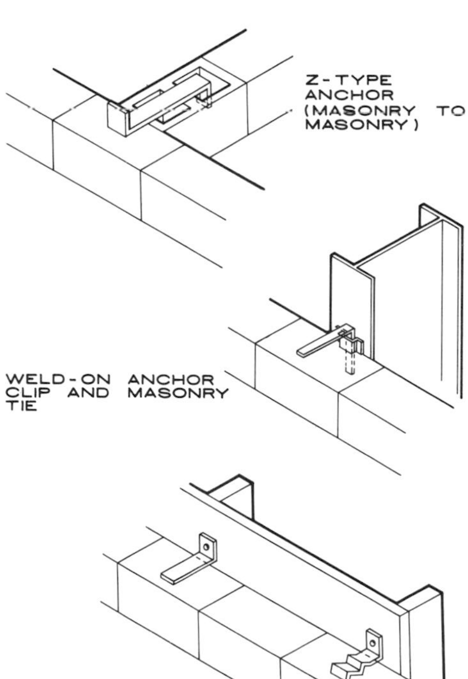
Z-TYPE ANCHOR (MASONRY TO MASONRY)
WELD-ON ANCHOR CLIP AND MASONRY TIE
VENEER ANCHORS (PLAIN AND CORRUGATED TYPES SHOWN)

MISCELLANEOUS ANCHORS

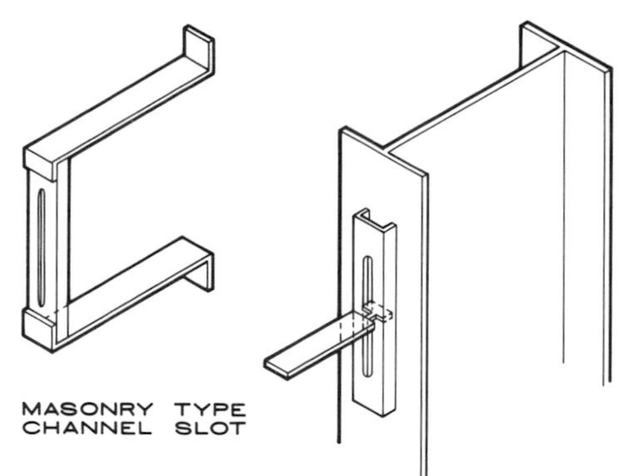
MASONRY TYPE CHANNEL SLOT
WELD-ON TYPE CHANNEL SLOT (WITH ANCHOR SHOWN)

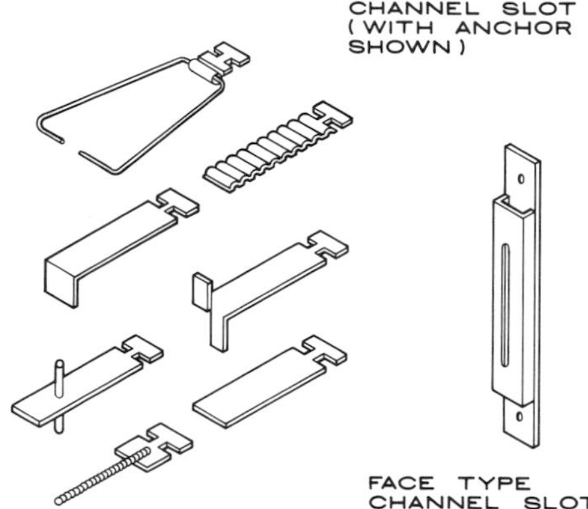
FACE TYPE CHANNEL SLOT
ANCHOR CONFIGURATIONS

CHANNEL SLOTS AND ANCHORS

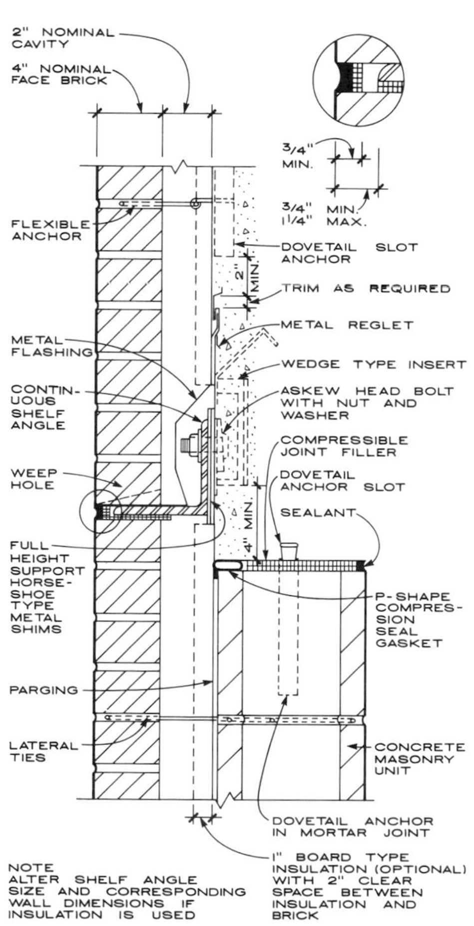
2" NOMINAL CAVITY
4" NOMINAL FACE BRICK
3/4" MIN.
3/4" MIN. 1 1/4" MAX.
FLEXIBLE ANCHOR
DOVETAIL SLOT ANCHOR
2" MIN.
TRIM AS REQUIRED
METAL REGLET
METAL FLASHING
WEDGE TYPE INSERT
CONTIN-UOUS SHELF ANGLE
ASKEW HEAD BOLT WITH NUT AND WASHER
COMPRESSIBLE JOINT FILLER
WEEP HOLE
DOVETAIL ANCHOR SLOT
SEALANT
4" MIN.
FULL HEIGHT SUPPORT HORSE-SHOE TYPE METAL SHIMS
P-SHAPE COMPRES-SION SEAL GASKET
PARGING
LATERAL TIES
CONCRETE MASONRY UNIT
DOVETAIL ANCHOR IN MORTAR JOINT
1" BOARD TYPE INSULATION (OPTIONAL) WITH 2" CLEAR SPACE BETWEEN INSULATION AND BRICK
NOTE
ALTER SHELF ANGLE SIZE AND CORRESPONDING WALL DIMENSIONS IF INSULATION IS USED

CAVITY WALL SHELF ANGLE SUPPORT

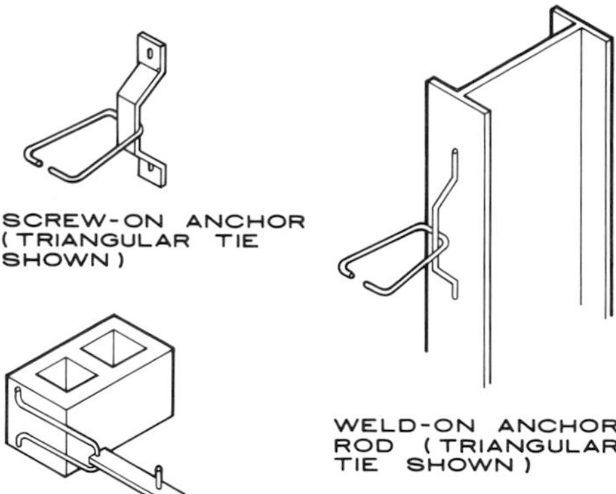
SCREW-ON ANCHOR (TRIANGULAR TIE SHOWN)
WELD-ON ANCHOR ROD (TRIANGULAR TIE SHOWN)
ADJUSTABLE U-BAR ANCHOR (FLAT TYPE PIN SHOWN)

1	Rectangular	Available with or without moisture drip in 3/16 in. or 1/4 in. mill or hot dipped galvanized steel; conforms to ASTM (A-82); space 16 in. vertically and 24 in. horizontally
2	Z	
3	Adjustable Z	
4	Mesh	1/2 in. mesh x 16 ga. hot dipped galvanized
5	Corrugated	mill or hot dipped galvanized steel 7/8 in. wide and 7 in. long; 12 to 28 ga.

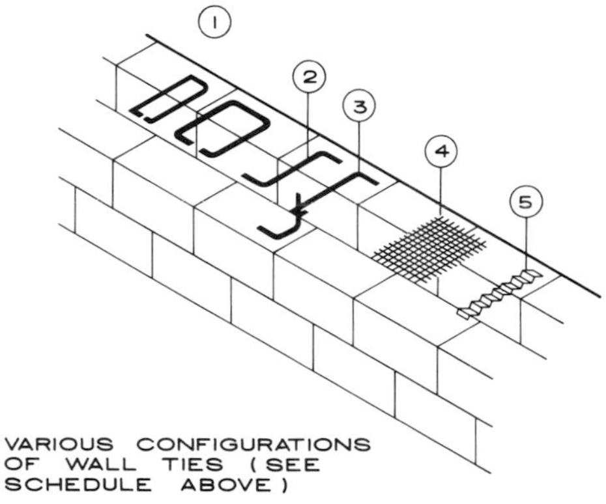
1
2
3
4
5
VARIOUS CONFIGURATIONS OF WALL TIES (SEE SCHEDULE ABOVE)

WIRE TIES

Masonry veneer and facing must be anchored to back-up construction. Codes usually require one anchor for 3 sq. ft. of surface area. Inserts usually are spaced 2 ft. on center horizontally, and ties usually are spaced 16 to 18 in. on center vertically. Spandrel beams over 18 in. deep require inserts and anchors for tying masonry facing to the beam. Most anchor systems permit differential movement in one or two directions. An anchoring system that allows movement only in the intended direction should be selected. See ASTM STP 778.

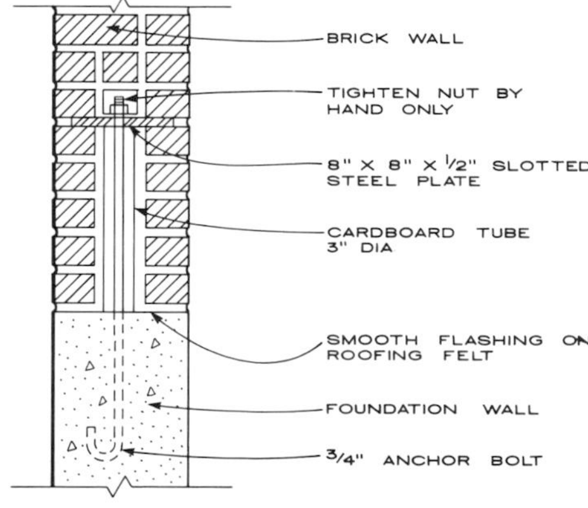
BRICK WALL
TIGHTEN NUT BY HAND ONLY
8" X 8" X 1/2" SLOTTED STEEL PLATE
CARDBOARD TUBE 3" DIA
SMOOTH FLASHING ON ROOFING FELT
FOUNDATION WALL
3/4" ANCHOR BOLT

WALL ANCHORAGE TO FOUNDATION

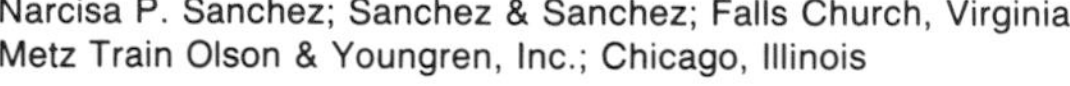
Narcisa P. Sanchez; Sanchez & Sanchez; Falls Church, Virginia
Metz Train Olson & Youngren, Inc.; Chicago, Illinois

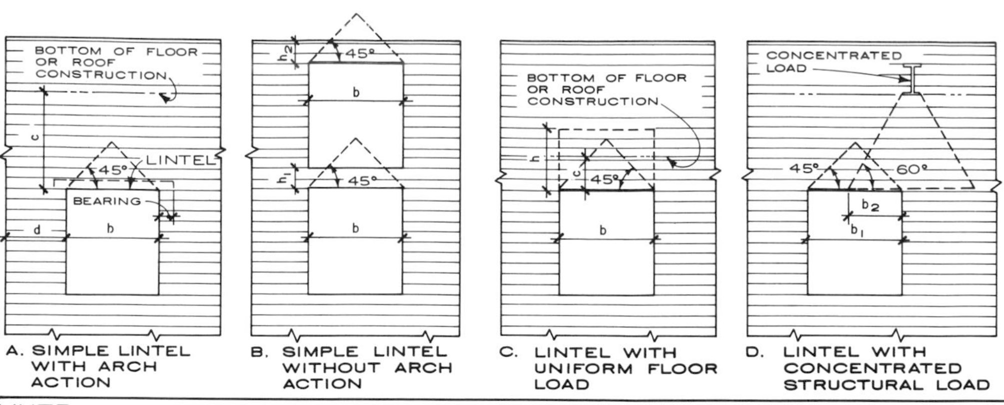
BOTTOM OF FLOOR OR ROOF CONSTRUCTION
LINTEL
BEARING
45°
c
d
b
h2
h1
BOTTOM OF FLOOR OR ROOF CONSTRUCTION
CONCENTRATED LOAD
60°
b2
b1
A. SIMPLE LINTEL WITH ARCH ACTION
B. SIMPLE LINTEL WITHOUT ARCH ACTION
C. LINTEL WITH UNIFORM FLOOR LOAD
D. LINTEL WITH CONCENTRATED STRUCTURAL LOAD

NOTES FOR LINTEL CONDITIONS

A. Simple lintel with arch action carries wall load only in triangle above opening:

$$c \geq b \quad \text{and} \quad d \geq b$$

B. Simple lintel without arch action carries less wall load than triangle above opening:

$$h_1 \text{ or } h_2 < 0.6b$$

C. Lintel with uniform floor load carries both wall and floor loads in rectangle above opening:

$$c < b$$

D. Lintel with concentrated load carries wall and portion of concentrated load distributed along length b_2.

LINTEL LOADING CONDITIONS (CONSULT STRUCTURAL HANDBOOK FOR DESIGN FORMULAS)

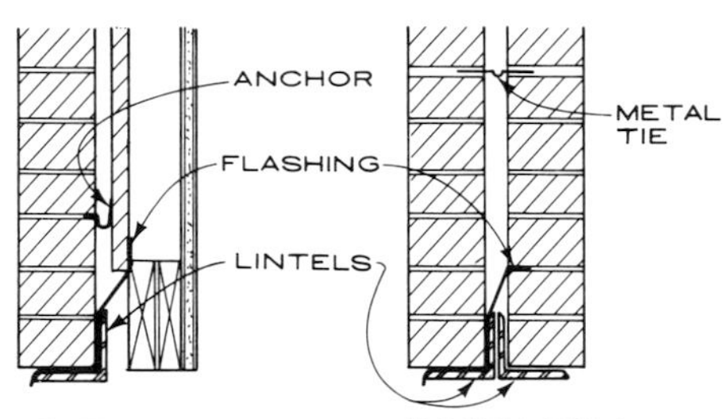
ANCHOR
METAL TIE
FLASHING
LINTELS
VENEER WALL
CAVITY WALL

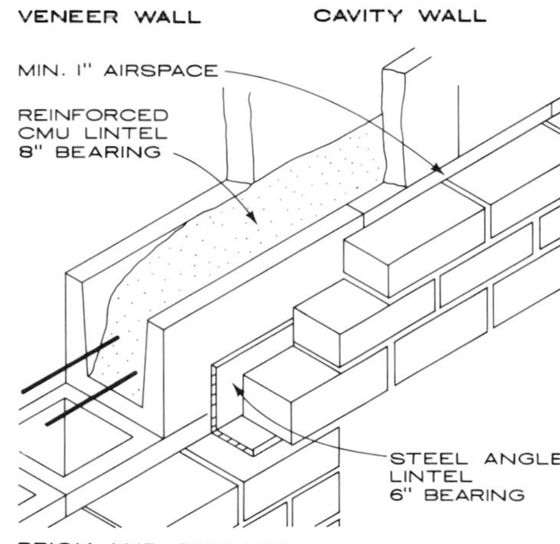
MIN. 1" AIRSPACE
REINFORCED CMU LINTEL 8" BEARING
STEEL ANGLE LINTEL 6" BEARING
BRICK AND CMU WALL

ALLOWABLE UNIFORM SUPERIMPOSED LOAD (IN LB) PER LINEAR FOOT FOR STEEL ANGLE LINTELS

HORIZONTAL LEG	ANGLE SIZE	WEIGHT PER FT. (LB)	SPAN IN FEET (CENTER TO CENTER OF REQUIRED BEARING) 3	4	5	6	7	8	9	10	11	12
3½	3 x 3½ x ¼	5.4	956	517	262	149	91	59				
	x 5/16	6.6	1166	637	323	184	113	73				
	x ⅜	7.9	1377	756	384	218	134	87	59			
3½	3½ x 3½ x ¼	5.8	1281	718	406	232	144	94	65			
	x 5/16	7.2	1589	891	507	290	179	118	80			
	x ⅜	8.5	1947	1091	589	336	208	137	93	66		
3½	4 x 3½ x ¼	6.2	1622	910	580	338	210	139	95	68		
	x 5/16	7.7	2110	1184	734	421	262	173	119	85	62	
	x ⅜	9.1	2434	1365	855	490	305	201	138	98	71	
	x 7/16	10.6	2760	1548	978	561	349	230	158	113	82	60
4	4 x 4 x 7/16	11.3	2920	1638	1018	584	363	239	164	116	85	62
	x ½	12.8	3246	1820	1141	654	407	268	185	131	95	70
3½	5 x 3½ x ¼	7.0	2600	1460	932	636	398	264	184	132	97	73
	x 5/16	8.7	3087	1733	1106	765	486	323	224	161	119	89
	x 7/16	12.0	4224	2371	1513	1047	655	435	302	217	160	120
	x ½	13.6	4875	2736	1746	1177	736	488	339	244	179	134
3½	6 x 3½ x ¼	7.9	3577	2009	1283	888	650	439	306	221	164	124
	x 5/16	9.8	4390	2465	1574	1090	798	538	375	271	201	151
	x ⅜	11.7	5200	2922	1865	1291	945	636	443	320	237	179
	x ½	15.3	6828	3834	2448	1695	1228	818	570	412	305	230
4	6 x 4 x ¼	8.3	3739	2099	1340	928	679	458	319	231	171	129
	x 5/16	10.3	4552	2556	1632	1129	827	562	391	283	209	158
	x ⅜	12.3	5365	3012	1923	1331	974	665	463	335	248	187
	x 7/16	14.3	6178	3469	2214	1533	1122	764	532	384	284	215
	x ½	16.2	6990	3925	2506	1734	1270	857	597	431	319	241

NOTE: Allowable loads to the left of the heavy line are governed by moment, and to the right by deflection. F_y = 36,000 psi. Maximum deflection 1/700. Consult structural engineer for long spans.

LOOSE STEEL LINTELS FOR MASONRY WALLS

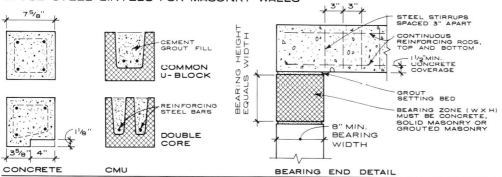

7⅝"
CEMENT GROUT FILL
COMMON U-BLOCK
REINFORCING STEEL BARS
DOUBLE CORE
1⅛"
3⅝" 4"
CONCRETE
CMU

3" 3"
STEEL STIRRUPS SPACED 3" APART
CONTINUOUS REINFORCING RODS, TOP AND BOTTOM
1½" MIN. CONCRETE COVERAGE
BEARING HEIGHT EQUALS WIDTH
GROUT SETTING BED
BEARING ZONE (W X H) MUST BE CONCRETE, SOLID MASONRY OR GROUTED MASONRY
8" MIN. BEARING WIDTH
BEARING END DETAIL

NUMBER AND SIZE OF REBARS REQUIRED

Precast Concrete and Reinforced CMU Lintels (no superimposed loads)

LINTEL TYPE	CLEAR SPAN (MAX)	8″ BRICK WALL (80 LB/SQ FT)	8″ CMU WALL (50 LB/SQ FT)
Reinforced concrete (7⅝″ square section)	4′-0″	4-#3	4-#3
	6′-0″	4-#4	4-#3
	8′-0″	4-#5	4-#4
CMU (7⅝″ square section) nominal 8 x 8 x 16 unit	4′-0″	2-#4	2-#3
	6′-0″	2-#5	2-#4
	8′-0″	2-#6	2-#5

NOTE: fc′ = 3000 psi concrete and grout
fy = 60,000 psi

PRECAST CONCRETE AND CMU LINTELS

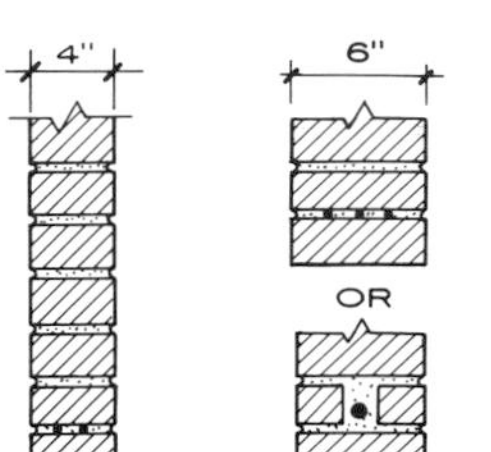
4"

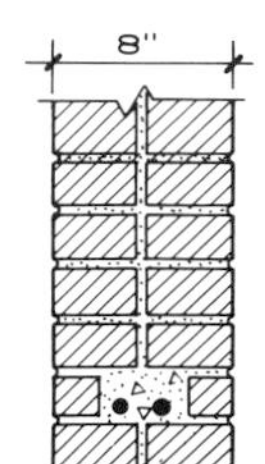
6"
OR

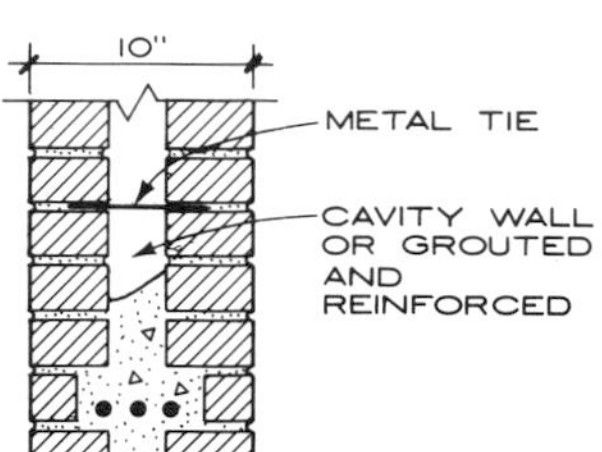
8"

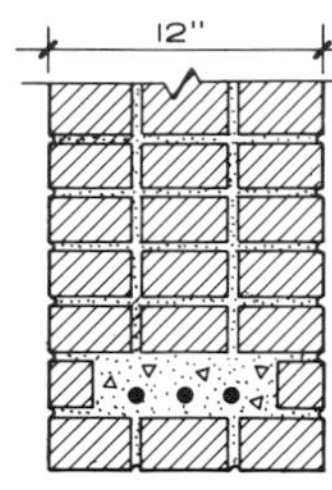
10"
METAL TIE
CAVITY WALL OR GROUTED AND REINFORCED
12"

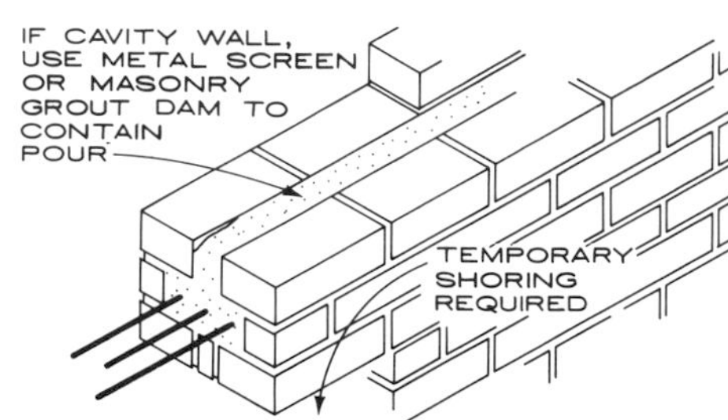
IF CAVITY WALL, USE METAL SCREEN OR MASONRY GROUT DAM TO CONTAIN POUR
TEMPORARY SHORING REQUIRED

REINFORCED BRICK LINTELS

Christine Beall, AIA, CCS; Austin, Texas
Metz, Train, Olson and Youngren, Inc.; Chicago, Illinois

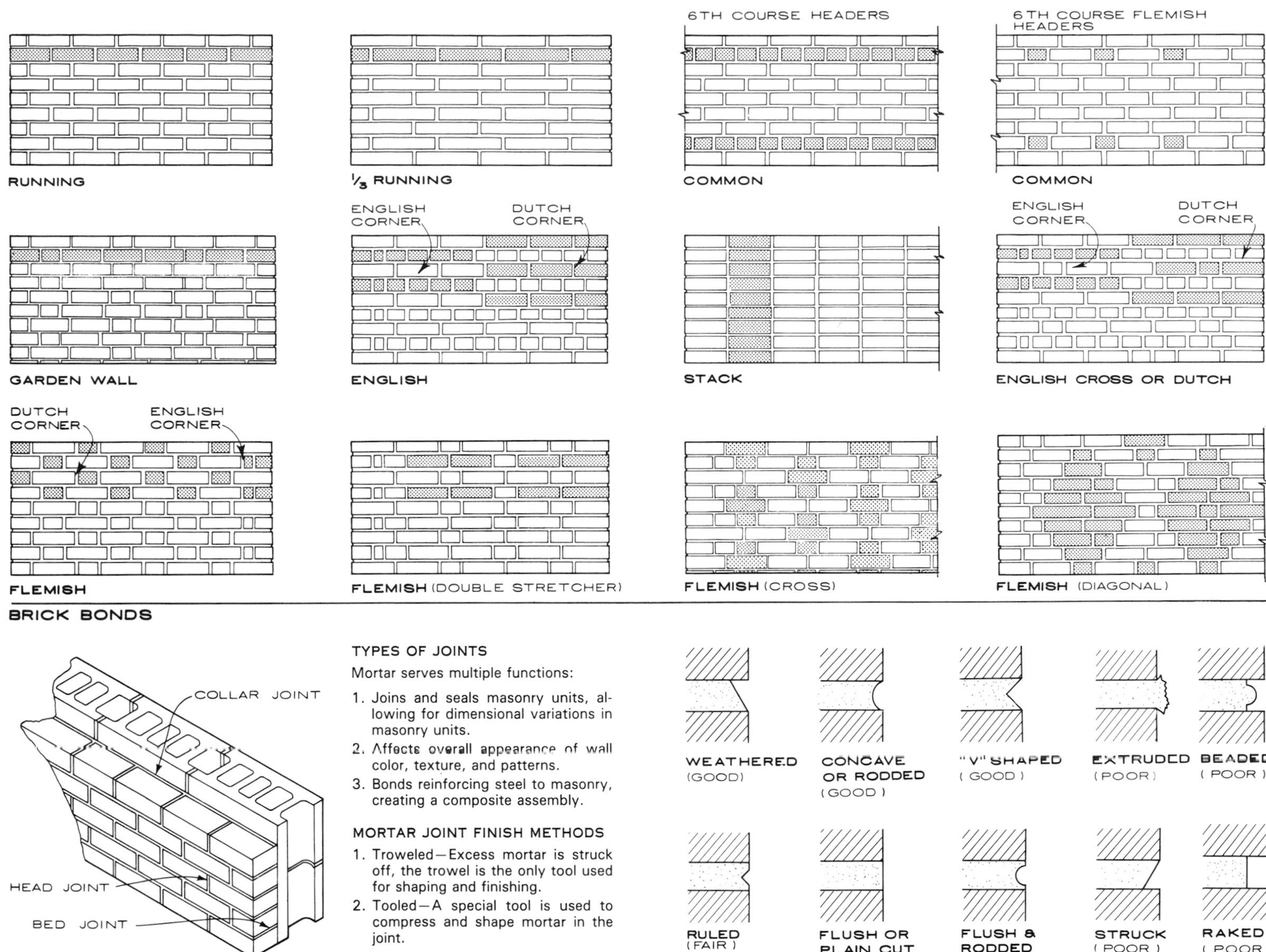
6TH COURSE HEADERS
6TH COURSE FLEMISH HEADERS
RUNNING
1/3 RUNNING
COMMON
COMMON
ENGLISH CORNER
DUTCH CORNER
ENGLISH CORNER
DUTCH CORNER
GARDEN WALL
ENGLISH
STACK
ENGLISH CROSS OR DUTCH
DUTCH CORNER
ENGLISH CORNER
FLEMISH
FLEMISH (DOUBLE STRETCHER)
FLEMISH (CROSS)
FLEMISH (DIAGONAL)
BRICK BONDS
COLLAR JOINT
HEAD JOINT
BED JOINT
TERMS APPLIED TO JOINTS
WEATHERED (GOOD)
CONCAVE OR RODDED (GOOD)
"V" SHAPED (GOOD)
EXTRUDED (POOR)
BEADED (POOR)
RULED (FAIR)
FLUSH OR PLAIN CUT (FAIR)
FLUSH & RODDED (FAIR)
STRUCK (POOR)
RAKED (POOR)
TYPES OF JOINTS (WEATHERABILITY)
BRICK JOINTS

TYPES OF JOINTS

Mortar serves multiple functions:

1. Joins and seals masonry units, allowing for dimensional variations in masonry units.
2. Affects overall appearance of wall color, texture, and patterns.
3. Bonds reinforcing steel to masonry, creating a composite assembly.

MORTAR JOINT FINISH METHODS

1. Troweled—Excess mortar is struck off, the trowel is the only tool used for shaping and finishing.
2. Tooled—A special tool is used to compress and shape mortar in the joint.

STRETCHER HEADER SOLDIER

SHINER ROWLOCK SAILOR

TERMS APPLIED TO VARIED BRICK POSITIONS

SIZES OF MODULAR BRICK

UNIT DESIGNATION	NOMINAL DIMENSIONS THICKNESS	HEIGHT	LENGTH	MODULAR COURSING
MODULAR	4″	2 2/3″	8″	3C = 8″
ENGINEER	4″	3 1/5″	8″	5C = 16″
ECONOMY	4″	4″	8″	1C = 4″
DOUBLE	4″	5 1/3″	8″	3C = 16″
ROMAN	4″	2″	12″	2C = 4″
NORMAN	4″	2 2/3″	12″	3C = 8″
NORWEGIAN	4″	3 1/5″	12″	5C = 16″
UTILITY[1]	4″	4″	12″	1C = 4″
TRIPLE	4″	5 1/3″	12″	3C = 16″
SCR BRICK	6″	2 2/3″	12″	3C = 8″
6″ NORWEGIAN	6″	3 1/5″	12″	5C = 16″
6″ JUMBO	6″	4″	12″	1C = 4″
8″ JUMBO	8″	4″	12″	1C = 4″
8″ SQUARE	4″	8″	8″	1C = 8″
12″ SQUARE	4″	12″	12″	1C = 12″

[1] Also called Norman Economy, General and King Norman.
*For special shapes contact local brick manufacturers.

Brick Institute of America; McLean, Virginia
Raso-Greaves An Architecture Corporation; Waco, Texas

GENERAL NOTES

1. Fire resistance ratings vary according to the ultimate composition of a masonry wall. Designers should refer to local codes to obtain this information.
2. Straight metal ties should be used in rigidly insulated masonry walls. Metal ties with drips should be used in noninsulated cavity masonry walls.
3. Water and vapor migration into a masonry wall may be controlled by designing a drainage-type wall or a barrier-type wall. Drainage walls are provided with damp course flashing and weep holes 24 in. o.c. just above the flashing. Barrier walls have a mortar-parged or fully grouted joint between wythes. Damp course flashing should also be used with the barrier-type wall. Most water migration occurs at mortar joints. Mortar selection should be based on the "initial" rate of absorption of the brick selected, as well as on regional weather conditions; mortars containing air-entering agents should be avoided.
4. All anchors, ties, and attachments should be stainless steel or of corrosion-resistant metal or be coated with such metal.
5. Block and brick quality varies throughout the industry. Masonry units should be chosen on the basis of availability, historical product quality of the manufacturer, strength, cost, and appearance. As with most construction assemblies, the final product will only be as good as the design and installation.

HEIGHT/THICKNESS RATIO OF MASONRY WALLS

BEARING CONDITION	TYPE 1	TYPE 2	TYPE 3
Maximum bearing wall height[1]	$\frac{H}{T} \le 18$	$\frac{H}{T} \le 18$	$\frac{H}{T} \le 18$
Maximum nonbearing wall height[1]	$\frac{H}{T} \le 20$	$\frac{H}{T} \le 20$	$\frac{H}{T} \le 20$
	TYPE 4	TYPE 5	TYPE 6
Maximum bearing wall height[1]	$\frac{H}{T} \le 18$	$\frac{H}{T} \le 25$	$\frac{H}{T} \le 25$
Maximum nonbearing wall height[1]	$\frac{H}{T} \le 20$	$\frac{H}{T} \le 48$	$\frac{H}{T} \le 48$
	TYPE 7	TYPE 8	TYPE 9
Maximum bearing wall height[1]	$\frac{H}{T} \le 25$	$\frac{H}{T} \le 18$[2]	$\frac{H}{T} \le 18$[2]
Maximum nonbearing wall height[1]	$\frac{H}{T} \le 48$	$\frac{H}{T} \le 20$[2]	$\frac{H}{T} \le 20$[2]

NOTES

1. Maximum unsupported wall heights should be determined by local codes. Formulas given are for planning purposes only and solutions should be verified by a structural engineer. In the formulas,
   H = height of wall (in feet)
   T = thickness of wall (in feet)
2. Resultant thickness is the net wall thickness of masonry units. Up to a 2 in. cavity may be used with this formula as long as the wythes are tied together with cavity wall ties.
3. Empirical formulas are taken from the 1982 Uniform Building Code.

PROPERTIES OF MASONRY WALL COMPONENTS

MATERIAL	WEIGHT (LB/SQ FT)	QUANTITY (100 SQ FT)[1]	U VALUE[2]	STC
4 in. brick	40	675 units	2.27	39
4 in. CMU	22	113 units	0.71	40
6 in. CMU	32	113 units	0.65	44
8 in. CMU	35	113 units	0.57	45
10 in. CMU	45	113 units	0.50	50
12 in. CMU	55	113 units	0.47	55
2 in. vermiculite (loose)	1.16	116 lb	0.22	—
2 in. perlite (loose)	1.08	108 lb	0.18	—
2 in. polystyrene (rigid)	0.58	100 sq ft	0.09	—
2 in. polyurethane (rigid)	0.25	100 sq ft	0.08	—
2 in. Airspace	—	—	0.40	4
Air film exterior[3]	—	—	4.76	—
Air film interior[4]	—	—	1.39	—

NOTES

1. Waste is not included, as this will vary with the job. A waste factor of 2–5% is often applied for masonry units.
2. U values are tabulated from various sources and represent an average value for the given material. Check with manufacturers for actual U values.
3. U value given is an average of both winter and summer winds.
4. U value given is an average of still air on all surface positions and direction of heat flow.

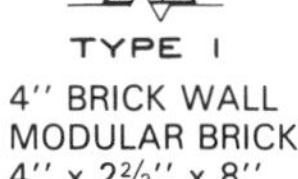

TYPE 1

4" BRICK WALL
MODULAR BRICK
4" x 2⅔" x 8"

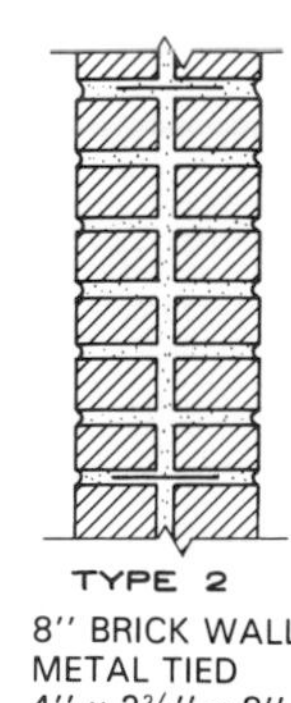

TYPE 2

8" BRICK WALL
METAL TIED
4" x 2⅔" x 8"

TYPE 3

CMU WALL

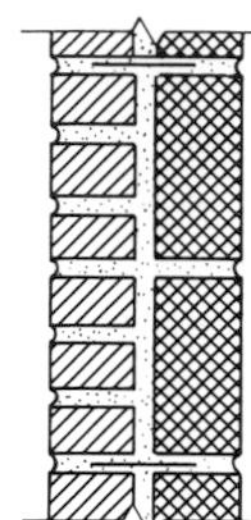

TYPE 4

4" MODULAR BRICK
4" CMU WALL
METAL TIED

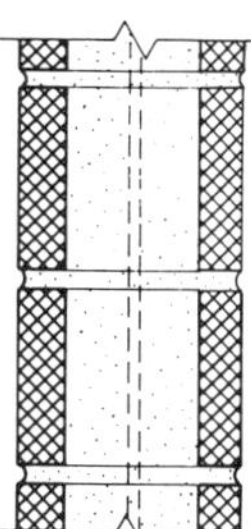

TYPE 5

REINFORCED
CMU WALL

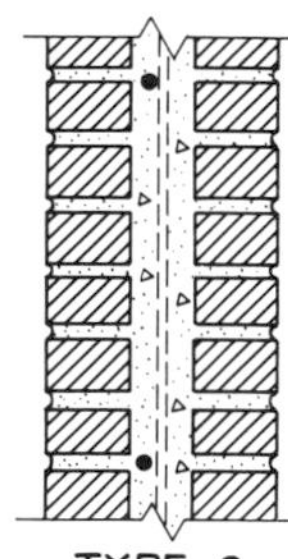

TYPE 6

REINFORCED
BRICK MASONRY
WALL (RBM)

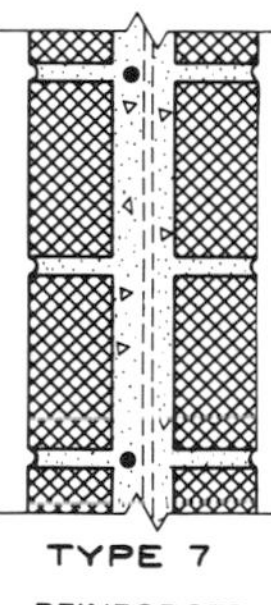

TYPE 7

REINFORCED
CMU WALL

TYPE 8

CAVITY WALL
SPLIT FACE CMU
AND CMU

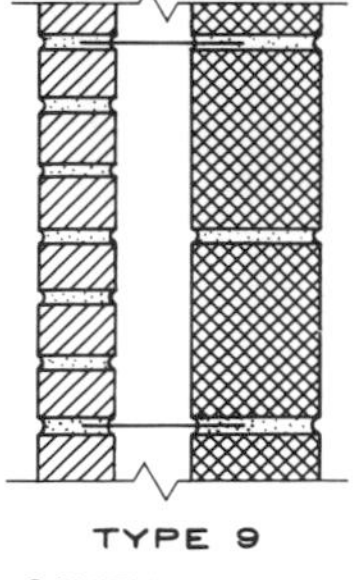

TYPE 9

CAVITY
WALL—BRICK
AND CMU

WALL TYPES

Charles L. Goodman, AIA; Everett I. Brown Company; Indianapolis, Indiana
Robert Joseph Sangiamo, AIA; New York, New York
Davis, Brody & Associates; New York, New York

International Conference of Building Officials, see data sources

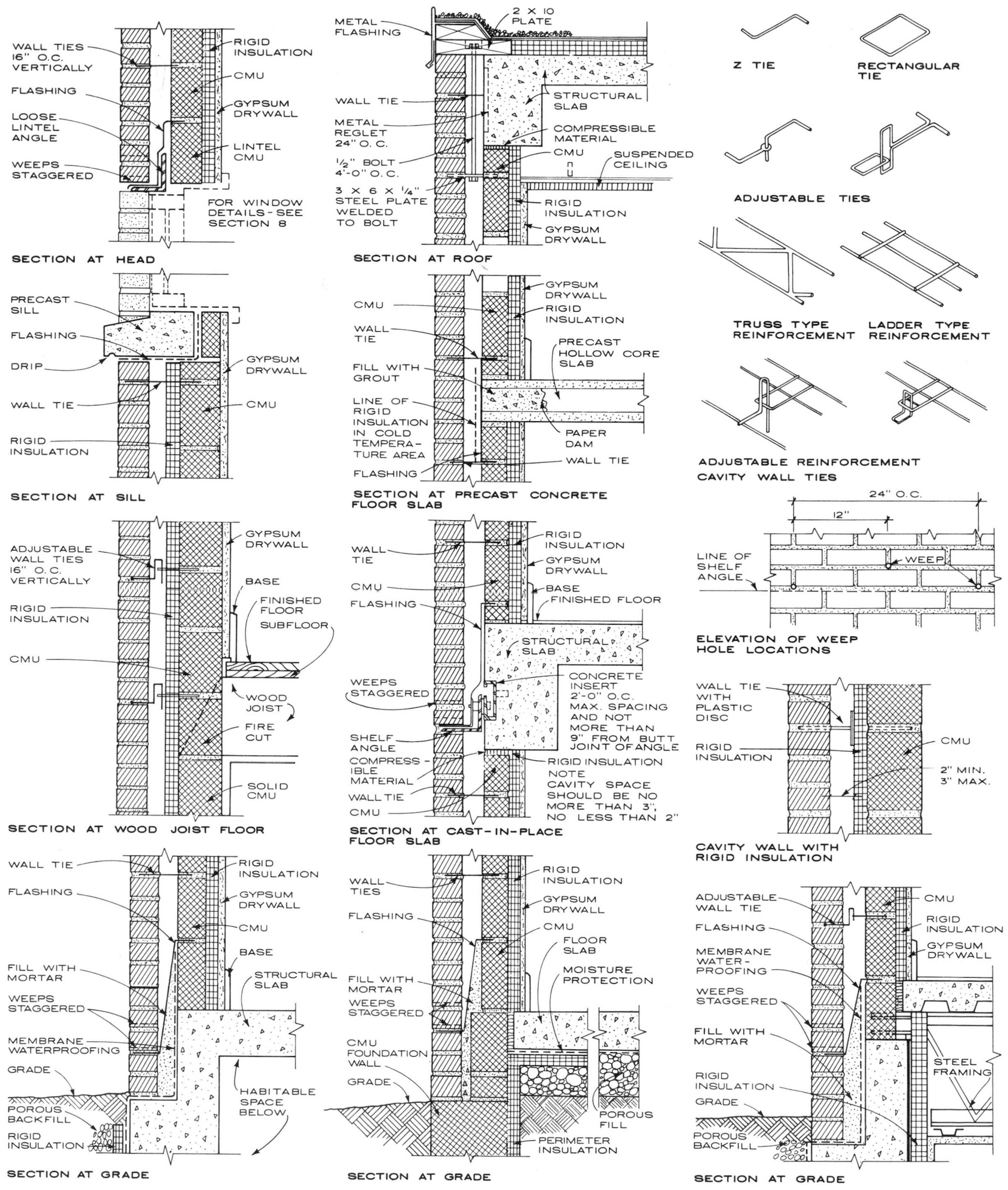
WALL TIES 16" O.C. VERTICALLY
FLASHING
LOOSE LINTEL ANGLE
WEEPS STAGGERED
RIGID INSULATION
CMU
GYPSUM DRYWALL
LINTEL CMU
FOR WINDOW DETAILS - SEE SECTION 8
SECTION AT HEAD
METAL FLASHING
2 X 10 PLATE
WALL TIE
METAL REGLET 24" O.C.
1/2" BOLT 4'-0" O.C.
3 X 6 X 1/4" STEEL PLATE WELDED TO BOLT
STRUCTURAL SLAB
COMPRESSIBLE MATERIAL
CMU
SUSPENDED CEILING
RIGID INSULATION
GYPSUM DRYWALL
SECTION AT ROOF
Z TIE
RECTANGULAR TIE
ADJUSTABLE TIES
TRUSS TYPE REINFORCEMENT
LADDER TYPE REINFORCEMENT
ADJUSTABLE REINFORCEMENT CAVITY WALL TIES
PRECAST SILL
FLASHING
DRIP
WALL TIE
RIGID INSULATION
GYPSUM DRYWALL
CMU
SECTION AT SILL
CMU
WALL TIE
FILL WITH GROUT
LINE OF RIGID INSULATION IN COLD TEMPERA-TURE AREA
FLASHING
GYPSUM DRYWALL
RIGID INSULATION
PRECAST HOLLOW CORE SLAB
PAPER DAM
WALL TIE
SECTION AT PRECAST CONCRETE FLOOR SLAB
24" O.C.
12"
LINE OF SHELF ANGLE
WEEP
ELEVATION OF WEEP HOLE LOCATIONS
ADJUSTABLE WALL TIES 16" O.C. VERTICALLY
RIGID INSULATION
CMU
GYPSUM DRYWALL
BASE
FINISHED FLOOR
SUBFLOOR
WOOD JOIST
FIRE CUT
SOLID CMU
SECTION AT WOOD JOIST FLOOR
WALL TIE
CMU
FLASHING
WEEPS STAGGERED
SHELF ANGLE
COMPRESS-IBLE MATERIAL
WALL TIE
CMU
RIGID INSULATION
GYPSUM DRYWALL
BASE
FINISHED FLOOR
STRUCTURAL SLAB
CONCRETE INSERT 2'-0" O.C. MAX. SPACING AND NOT MORE THAN 9" FROM BUTT JOINT OF ANGLE
RIGID INSULATION
NOTE CAVITY SPACE SHOULD BE NO MORE THAN 3", NO LESS THAN 2"
SECTION AT CAST-IN-PLACE FLOOR SLAB
WALL TIE WITH PLASTIC DISC
RIGID INSULATION
CMU
2" MIN. 3" MAX.
CAVITY WALL WITH RIGID INSULATION
WALL TIE
FLASHING
FILL WITH MORTAR
WEEPS STAGGERED
MEMBRANE WATERPROOFING
GRADE
POROUS BACKFILL
RIGID INSULATION
RIGID INSULATION
GYPSUM DRYWALL
CMU
BASE
STRUCTURAL SLAB
HABITABLE SPACE BELOW
SECTION AT GRADE
WALL TIES
FLASHING
FILL WITH MORTAR
WEEPS STAGGERED
CMU FOUNDATION WALL
GRADE
RIGID INSULATION
GYPSUM DRYWALL
CMU
FLOOR SLAB
MOISTURE PROTECTION
POROUS FILL
PERIMETER INSULATION
SECTION AT GRADE
ADJUSTABLE WALL TIE
FLASHING
MEMBRANE WATER-PROOFING
WEEPS STAGGERED
FILL WITH MORTAR
RIGID INSULATION
GRADE
POROUS BACKFILL
CMU
RIGID INSULATION
GYPSUM DRYWALL
STEEL FRAMING
SECTION AT GRADE

Robert J. Sangiamo, AIA; New York, New York
Davis, Brody & Associates; New York, New York

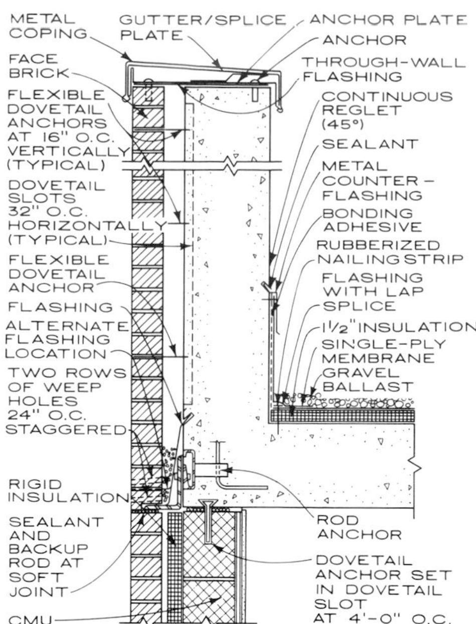
METAL COPING
GUTTER/SPLICE PLATE
ANCHOR PLATE
ANCHOR
FACE BRICK
THROUGH-WALL FLASHING
FLEXIBLE DOVETAIL ANCHORS AT 16" O.C. VERTICALLY (TYPICAL)
CONTINUOUS REGLET (45°)
SEALANT
DOVETAIL SLOTS 32" O.C. HORIZONTALLY (TYPICAL)
METAL COUNTER-FLASHING
BONDING ADHESIVE
RUBBERIZED NAILING STRIP
FLEXIBLE DOVETAIL ANCHOR
FLASHING WITH LAP SPLICE
FLASHING
1½" INSULATION
ALTERNATE FLASHING LOCATION
SINGLE-PLY MEMBRANE
TWO ROWS OF WEEP HOLES 24" O.C. STAGGERED
GRAVEL BALLAST
RIGID INSULATION
SEALANT AND BACKUP ROD AT SOFT JOINT
ROD ANCHOR
DOVETAIL ANCHOR SET IN DOVETAIL SLOT AT 4'-0" O.C.
CMU

CAVITY WALL AT CONCRETE PARAPET

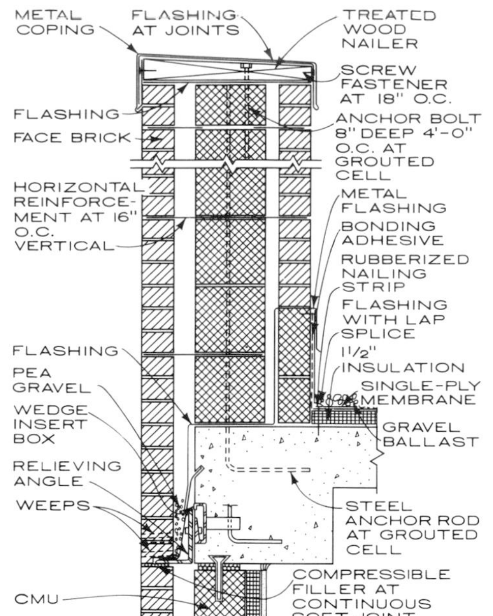
METAL COPING
FLASHING AT JOINTS
TREATED WOOD NAILER
SCREW FASTENER AT 18" O.C.
FLASHING
ANCHOR BOLT 8" DEEP 4'-0" O.C. AT GROUTED CELL
FACE BRICK
HORIZONTAL REINFORCEMENT AT 16" O.C. VERTICAL
METAL FLASHING
BONDING ADHESIVE
RUBBERIZED NAILING STRIP
FLASHING WITH LAP SPLICE
FLASHING
1½" INSULATION
PEA GRAVEL
SINGLE-PLY MEMBRANE
WEDGE INSERT BOX
GRAVEL BALLAST
RELIEVING ANGLE
WEEPS
STEEL ANCHOR ROD AT GROUTED CELL
CMU
COMPRESSIBLE FILLER AT CONTINUOUS SOFT JOINT

PARAPET WALL WITH DOUBLE CAVITY

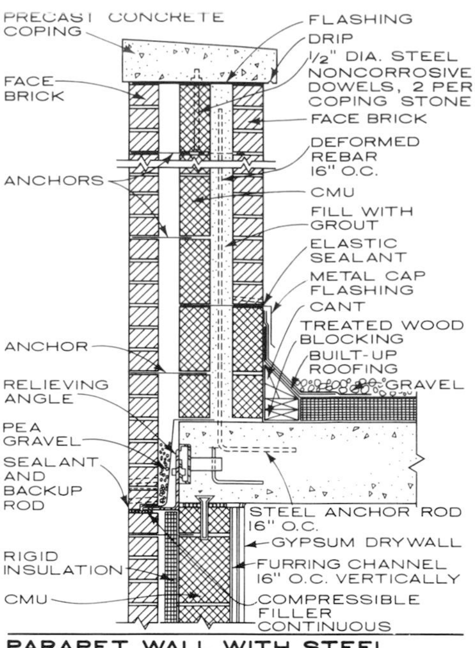
PRECAST CONCRETE COPING
FLASHING
DRIP
½" DIA. STEEL NONCORROSIVE DOWELS, 2 PER COPING STONE
FACE BRICK
FACE BRICK
DEFORMED REBAR 16" O.C.
ANCHORS
CMU
FILL WITH GROUT
ELASTIC SEALANT
METAL CAP FLASHING
CANT
TREATED WOOD BLOCKING
ANCHOR
BUILT-UP ROOFING
GRAVEL
RELIEVING ANGLE
PEA GRAVEL
SEALANT AND BACKUP ROD
STEEL ANCHOR ROD 16" O.C.
GYPSUM DRYWALL
RIGID INSULATION
FURRING CHANNEL 16" O.C. VERTICALLY
CMU
COMPRESSIBLE FILLER CONTINUOUS

PARAPET WALL WITH STEEL REINFORCING

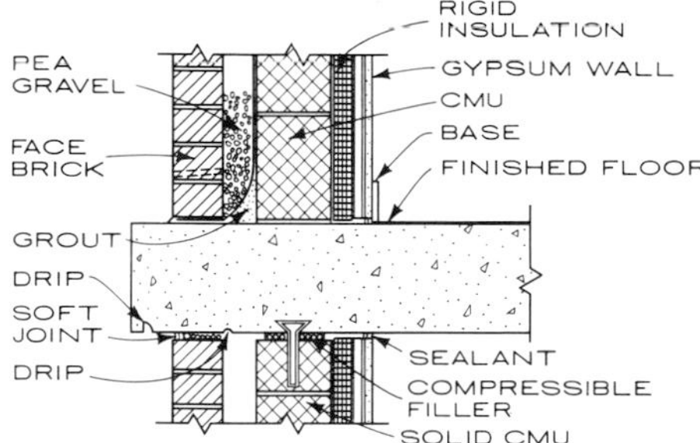
RIGID INSULATION
PEA GRAVEL
GYPSUM WALL
CMU
FACE BRICK
BASE
FINISHED FLOOR
GROUT
DRIP
SOFT JOINT
DRIP
SEALANT
COMPRESSIBLE FILLER
SOLID CMU

EXPOSED SLAB DETAIL

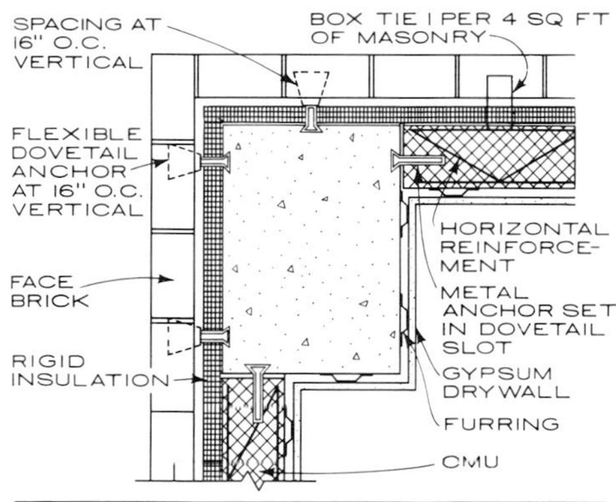
SPACING AT 16" O.C. VERTICAL
BOX TIE I PER 4 SQ FT OF MASONRY
FLEXIBLE DOVETAIL ANCHOR AT 16" O.C. VERTICAL
HORIZONTAL REINFORCEMENT
FACE BRICK
METAL ANCHOR SET IN DOVETAIL SLOT
RIGID INSULATION
GYPSUM DRYWALL
FURRING
CMU

DOVETAIL ANCHORS AT CORNER

GENERAL NOTES

1. Relieving angles should be designed to limit deflection to 1/700 of span between wedge inset centerlines.
2. The horizontal reinforcing whose primary purposes are to prevent cracks in the mortar of the CMU wythe of masonry and aid in spanning wind load to supports should also be used to attach the brick masonry ties. The ties are required only to transfer forces due to positive and negative wind pressure on the brick wythe of the CMU wythe.
3. "Z" type masonry ties should not be used with hollow CMU masonry.
4. Type S mortar should be used where the winds are greater than 80 miles per hour.
5. Exterior brick should conform to the requirements of ASTM-216.
6. The exterior wythe of brick masonry should be panelized by the use of horizontal and vertical control joints.
7. Control joint sizes should accommodate the following Brick Institute of America Formula Technical Note 18A:

$$w = [0.0002 + 0.000004\ (T\ max. - T\ min.)]\ L$$

where: L = length of wall in inches
T max. = maximum mean wall temperature in degrees Fahrenheit
T min. = minimum mean wall temperature in degrees Fahrenheit
w = total expansion of wall in inches

Actual joint width in masonry is determined by anticipated movement times the limit of compressibility and expandability of the sealant. Typically for polysulfide sealants one multiplies anticipated movement by four, and for urethane sealants by two. Consult manufacturers' recommendations for the actual products proposed for use.

8. When the structural frame of a building is of reinforced concrete, horizontal control joints must also accommodate the dimensional change due to anticipated shrinkage and creep of the concrete columns.
9. Aligning vertical control joints with the window jambs is good practice for economy.
10. The number of vertical control joints required should be doubled at the parapet, and vertical control joints should also be added at 5 to 10 ft from each corner.
11. CMU masonry and brick masonry should not be exposed on the same parapet, as the CMU expands and contracts at different rates than the brick masonry, causing parapet cracking.
12. The spacing and size of the vertical reinforcing in a parapet are a function of parapet height wall and local wind pressure. For high-rise buildings, structural design is required.
13. For lateral support requirements consult local codes.
14. Refer to Brick Institute of America Technical Note 21, Brick Masonry Cavity Walls, for additional information.

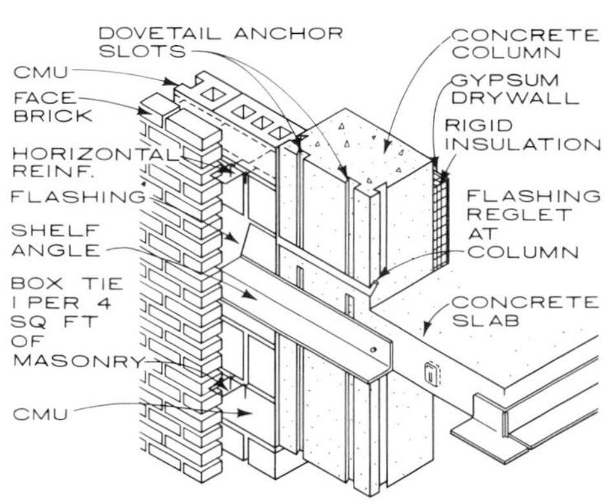
DOVETAIL ANCHOR SLOTS
CONCRETE COLUMN
CMU
GYPSUM DRYWALL
FACE BRICK
RIGID INSULATION
HORIZONTAL REINF.
FLASHING
FLASHING REGLET AT COLUMN
SHELF ANGLE
BOX TIE I PER 4 SQ FT OF MASONRY
CONCRETE SLAB
CMU

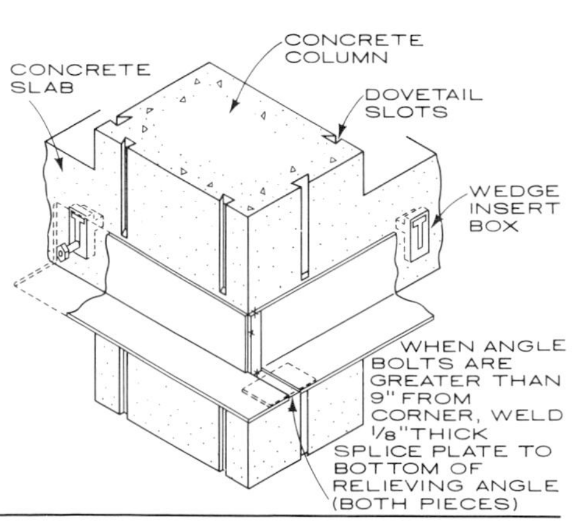
CONCRETE COLUMN
CONCRETE SLAB
DOVETAIL SLOTS
WEDGE INSERT BOX
WHEN ANGLE BOLTS ARE GREATER THAN 9" FROM CORNER, WELD ⅛" THICK SPLICE PLATE TO BOTTOM OF RELIEVING ANGLE (BOTH PIECES)

SHELF ANGLE AT CORNER COLUMN

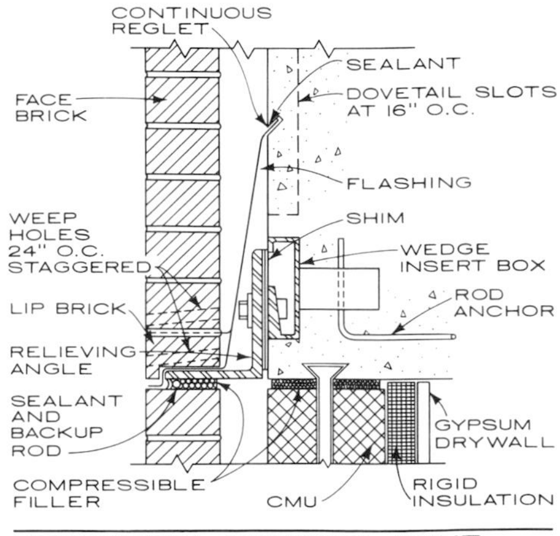
CONTINUOUS REGLET
SEALANT
FACE BRICK
DOVETAIL SLOTS AT 16" O.C.
FLASHING
SHIM
WEEP HOLES 24" O.C. STAGGERED
WEDGE INSERT BOX
LIP BRICK
ROD ANCHOR
RELIEVING ANGLE
SEALANT AND BACKUP ROD
GYPSUM DRYWALL
COMPRESSIBLE FILLER
CMU
RIGID INSULATION

HORIZONTAL CONTROL JOINT

Theodore D. Sherman; Lev Zetlin Associates, Inc.; New York, New York
Robert J. Sangiamo, AIA; New York, New York
Davis, Brody & Associates; New York, New York

GENERAL NOTE: VERMICULITE SHOULD NOT BE USED TO FILL CAVITY WALLS

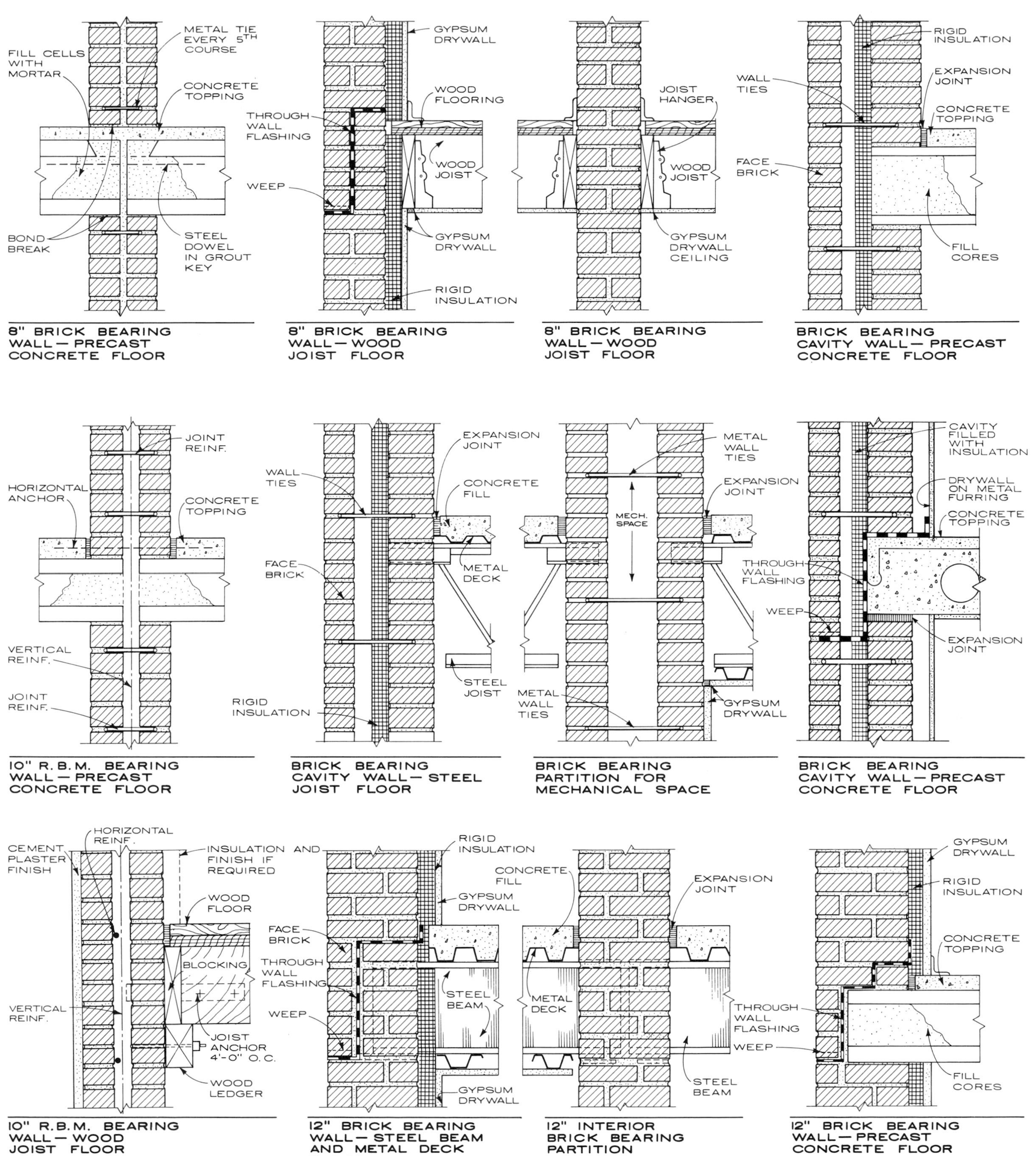
FILL CELLS WITH MORTAR
METAL TIE EVERY 5TH COURSE
CONCRETE TOPPING
BOND BREAK
STEEL DOWEL IN GROUT KEY
8" BRICK BEARING WALL—PRECAST CONCRETE FLOOR
GYPSUM DRYWALL
WOOD FLOORING
THROUGH WALL FLASHING
WOOD JOIST
WEEP
GYPSUM DRYWALL
RIGID INSULATION
8" BRICK BEARING WALL—WOOD JOIST FLOOR
JOIST HANGER
WOOD JOIST
GYPSUM DRYWALL CEILING
8" BRICK BEARING WALL—WOOD JOIST FLOOR
RIGID INSULATION
WALL TIES
EXPANSION JOINT
CONCRETE TOPPING
FACE BRICK
FILL CORES
BRICK BEARING CAVITY WALL—PRECAST CONCRETE FLOOR
JOINT REINF.
HORIZONTAL ANCHOR
CONCRETE TOPPING
VERTICAL REINF.
JOINT REINF.
10" R.B.M. BEARING WALL—PRECAST CONCRETE FLOOR
EXPANSION JOINT
WALL TIES
CONCRETE FILL
FACE BRICK
METAL DECK
STEEL JOIST
RIGID INSULATION
BRICK BEARING CAVITY WALL—STEEL JOIST FLOOR
METAL WALL TIES
EXPANSION JOINT
MECH. SPACE
METAL WALL TIES
GYPSUM DRYWALL
BRICK BEARING PARTITION FOR MECHANICAL SPACE
CAVITY FILLED WITH INSULATION
DRYWALL ON METAL FURRING
CONCRETE TOPPING
THROUGH WALL FLASHING
WEEP
EXPANSION JOINT
BRICK BEARING CAVITY WALL—PRECAST CONCRETE FLOOR
CEMENT PLASTER FINISH
HORIZONTAL REINF.
INSULATION AND FINISH IF REQUIRED
WOOD FLOOR
BLOCKING
VERTICAL REINF.
JOIST ANCHOR 4'-0" O.C.
WOOD LEDGER
10" R.B.M. BEARING WALL—WOOD JOIST FLOOR
RIGID INSULATION
CONCRETE FILL
GYPSUM DRYWALL
FACE BRICK
THROUGH WALL FLASHING
STEEL BEAM
WEEP
GYPSUM DRYWALL
12" BRICK BEARING WALL—STEEL BEAM AND METAL DECK FLOOR
EXPANSION JOINT
METAL DECK
THROUGH WALL FLASHING
WEEP
STEEL BEAM
12" INTERIOR BRICK BEARING PARTITION
GYPSUM DRYWALL
RIGID INSULATION
CONCRETE TOPPING
FILL CORES
12" BRICK BEARING WALL—PRECAST CONCRETE FLOOR

Robert Joseph Sangiamo, AIA; New York, New York
Davis, Brody & Associates; New York, New York

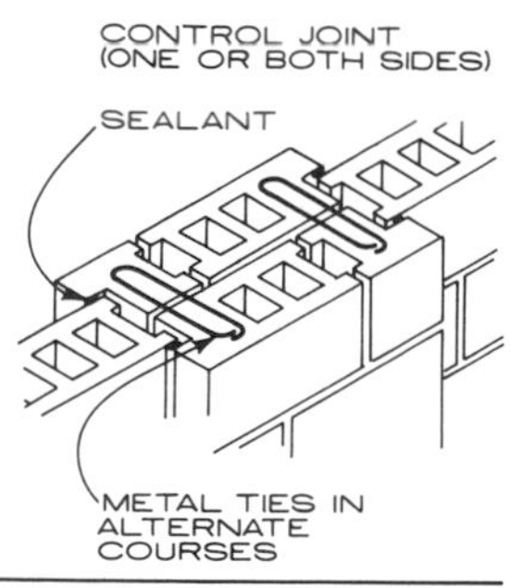
CONTROL JOINT (ONE OR BOTH SIDES)
SEALANT
METAL TIES IN ALTERNATE COURSES

CONTROL JOINT AT PIER

CONTROL JOINTS
TYPICAL HORIZONTAL JOINT REINFORCEMENT
FILLER ROD AND SEALANT

FLUSH WALL AND PLASTER CONTROL JOINTS

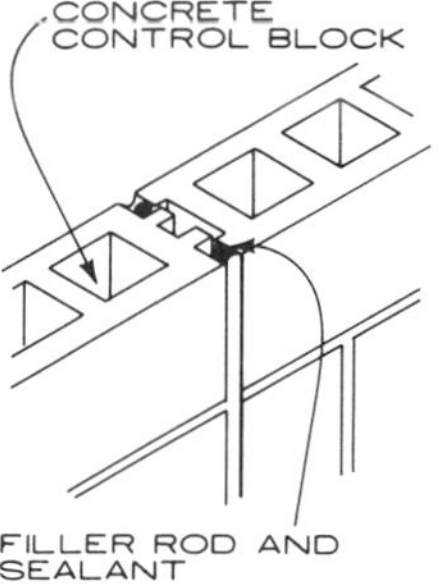
CONCRETE CONTROL BLOCK
FILLER ROD AND SEALANT

CONTROL JOINT BLOCK

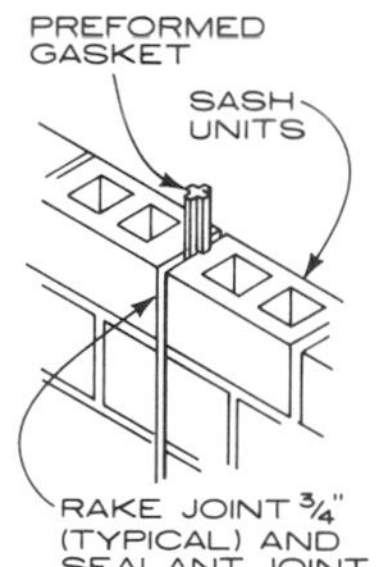
PREFORMED GASKET
SASH UNITS
RAKE JOINT 3/4" (TYPICAL) AND SEALANT JOINT

BUILDING FELT ON ONE SIDE ONLY OR COAT OF ASPHALT PAINT
CORE FILLED WITH MORTAR FOR LATERAL STABILITY AND SEALANT

FLUSH WALL CONTROL JOINTS

PRINCIPLES

Masonry materials expand and contract in response to temperature changes. Dimensional changes also occur in masonry because of moisture variations. To compensate for these dimensional changes and thus control cracking in masonry, keep the following in mind:

1. Proper product specifications and construction procedures limit moisture related movements. For example, Type I moisture controlled concrete masonry units are manufactured to minimize moisture related movement.
2. Proper steel reinforcing, including horizontal joint reinforcing, increases the tensile resistance of masonry walls.
3. Properly placed expansion joints and control joints accommodate movement and provide for controlled crack locations.

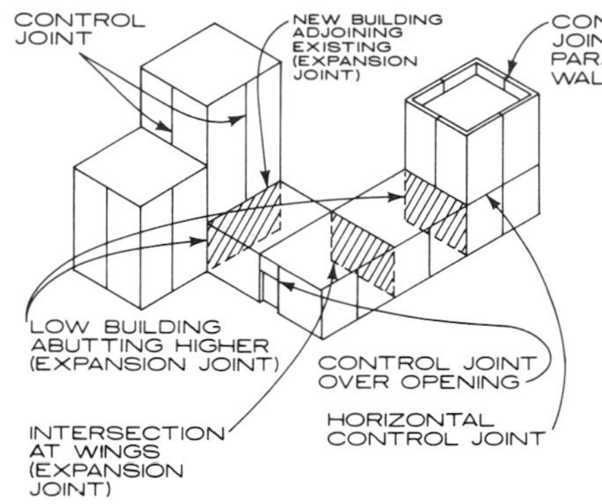
CONTROL JOINT
NEW BUILDING ADJOINING EXISTING (EXPANSION JOINT)
CONTROL JOINT THROUGH PARAPET WALL
LOW BUILDING ABUTTING HIGHER (EXPANSION JOINT)
CONTROL JOINT OVER OPENING
INTERSECTION AT WINGS (EXPANSION JOINT)
HORIZONTAL CONTROL JOINT

LOCATION OF CONTROL AND EXPANSION JOINTS

CONTROL JOINT SPACING FOR MOISTURE CONTROLLED ASTM C90 TYPE I BLOCK UNITS

RECOMMENDED SPACING OF CONTROL JOINTS	VERTICAL SPACING OF JOINT REINFORCEMENT			
	NONE	24"	16"	8"
Expressed as ratio of panel length to height (L/H)	2	$2^1/_2$	3	4
Panel length (L) not to exceed (regardless of height (H))	40'	45'	50'	60'

EXPANSION JOINTS

The purpose of expansion joints is to relieve tension and compression between separate portions of a masonry wall resulting from temperature and/or moisture induced dimensional movements.

Exterior and interior masonry wythes of cavity walls should be connected with flexible metal ties. Horizontal expansion joints should be located below shelf angles or structural frames supporting masonry walls or panels. Shelf angles should contain sufficient interruptions to accommodate thermal movements. Horizontal expansion joints (soft joints, slip channel, etc.) should also be provided above exterior masonry walls or panels abutting structural frames and at interior non-load-bearing masonry walls abutting the underside of floor or roof structures above.

CONTROL JOINTS

The purpose of control joints is to provide tension relief between individual portions of a masonry wall that may change from their original dimensions. They must provide for lateral stability across the joint and contain a through wall seal.

Control joints should be located in long straight walls, at major changes in wall heights, at changes in wall thickness, above joints in foundations, at columns and pilasters, at one or both sides of wall openings, near wall intersections, and near junctions of walls in L, T, or U shaped buildings. Joints should continue through roof parapets.

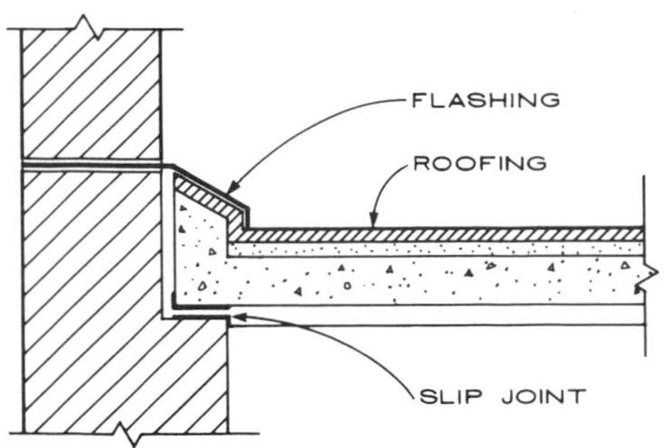
FLASHING
ROOFING
SLIP JOINT

PARAPET AND RIGID ROOF SLAB

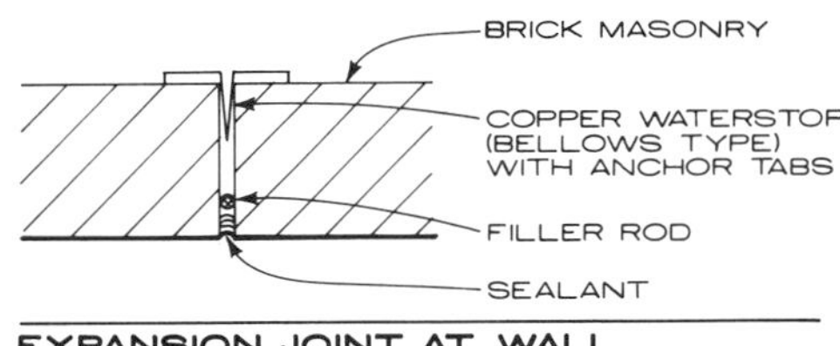
BRICK MASONRY
COPPER WATERSTOP (BELLOWS TYPE) WITH ANCHOR TABS
FILLER ROD
SEALANT

EXPANSION JOINT AT WALL

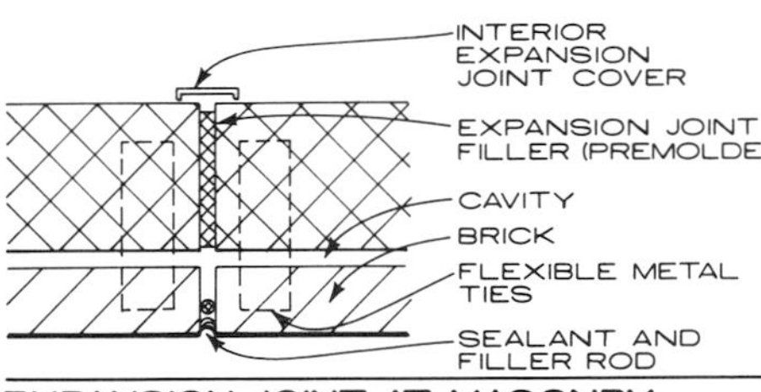
INTERIOR EXPANSION JOINT COVER
EXPANSION JOINT FILLER (PREMOLDED)
CAVITY
BRICK
FLEXIBLE METAL TIES
SEALANT AND FILLER ROD

EXPANSION JOINT AT MASONRY CAVITY WALL

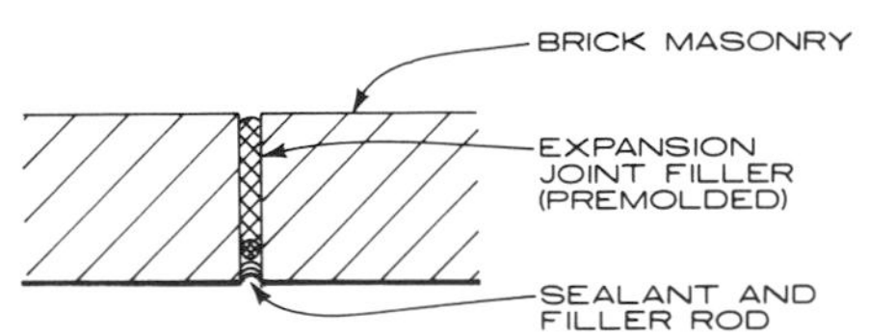
BRICK MASONRY
EXPANSION JOINT FILLER (PREMOLDED)
SEALANT AND FILLER ROD

EXPANSION JOINT AT WALL

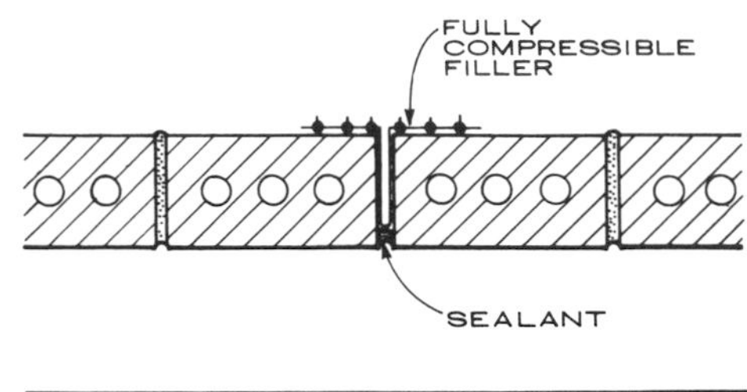
FULLY COMPRESSIBLE FILLER
SEALANT

WALL EXPANSION JOINT

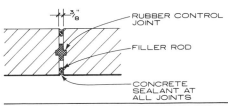

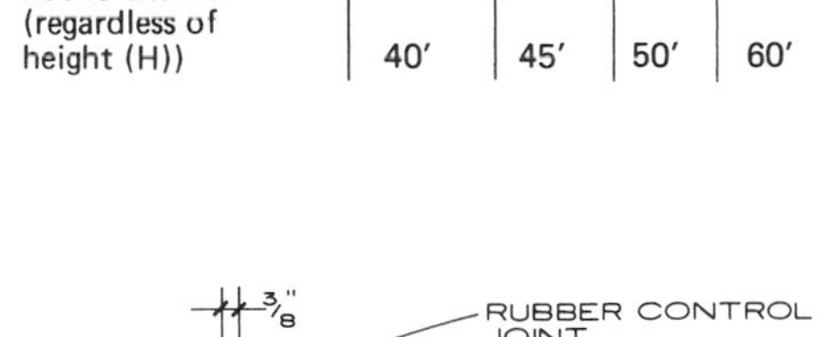
3/8"
RUBBER CONTROL JOINT
FILLER ROD
CONCRETE SEALANT AT ALL JOINTS

CONTROL JOINT AT STRAIGHT WALL

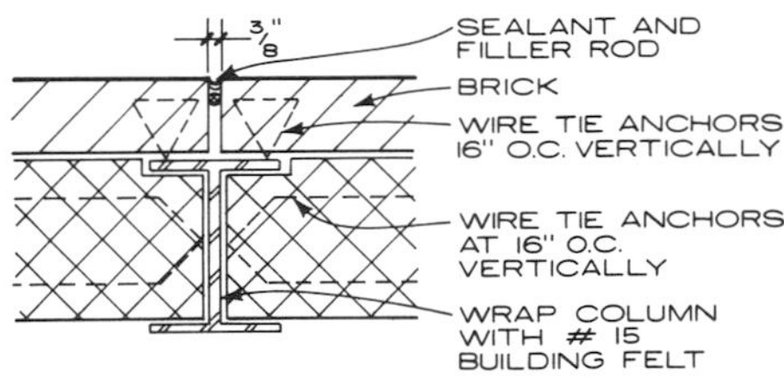
3/8"
SEALANT AND FILLER ROD
BRICK
WIRE TIE ANCHORS 16" O.C. VERTICALLY
WIRE TIE ANCHORS AT 16" O.C. VERTICALLY
WRAP COLUMN WITH # 15 BUILDING FELT

CONTROL JOINT AT STEEL COLUMN

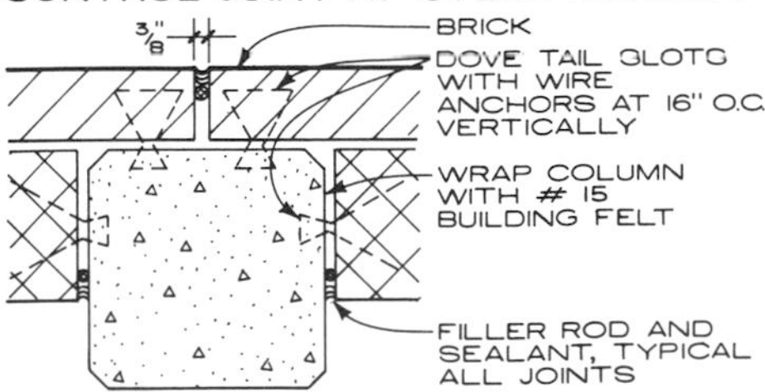
3/8"
BRICK
DOVE TAIL SLOTS WITH WIRE ANCHORS AT 16" O.C. VERTICALLY
WRAP COLUMN WITH # 15 BUILDING FELT
FILLER ROD AND SEALANT, TYPICAL ALL JOINTS

CONTROL JOINT AT CONCRETE COLUMN

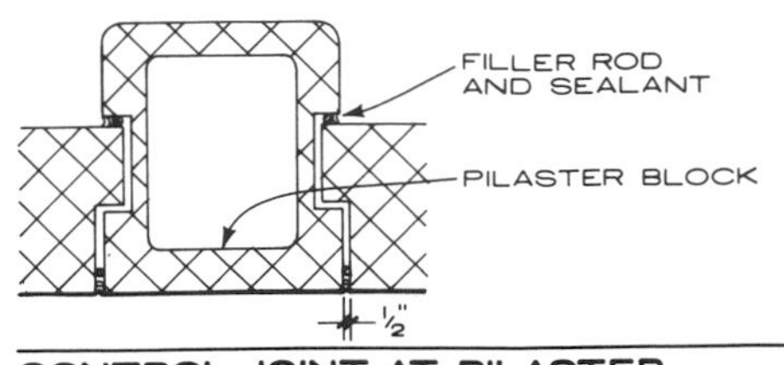
FILLER ROD AND SEALANT
PILASTER BLOCK
1/2"

CONTROL JOINT AT PILASTER

Setter, Leach & Lindstrom, Inc.; Minneapolis, Minnesota

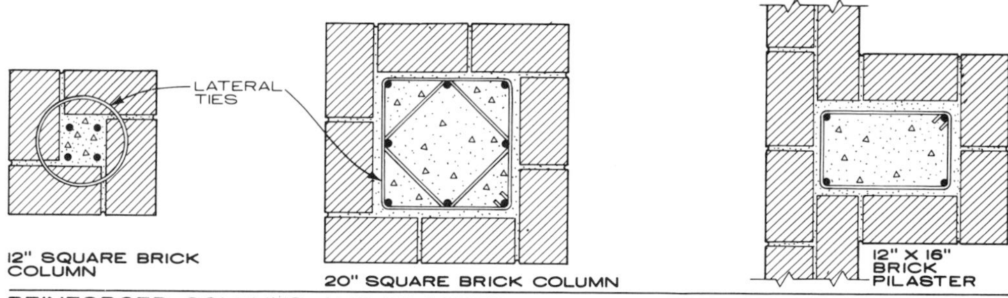
LATERAL TIES
12" SQUARE BRICK COLUMN
20" SQUARE BRICK COLUMN
12" X 16" BRICK PILASTER

REINFORCED COLUMNS AND PILASTER

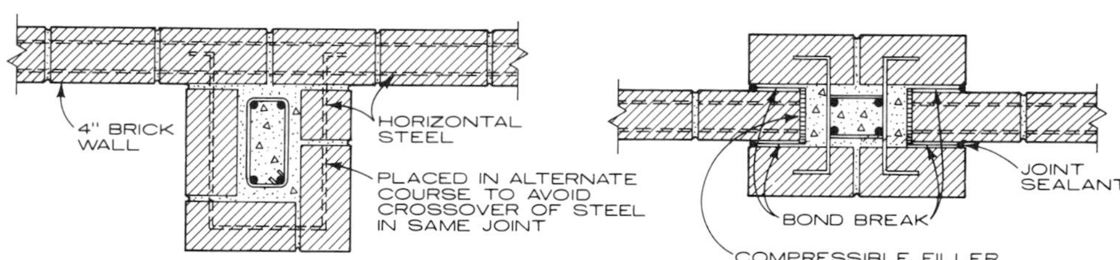
4" BRICK WALL
HORIZONTAL STEEL
PLACED IN ALTERNATE COURSE TO AVOID CROSSOVER OF STEEL IN SAME JOINT
JOINT SEALANT
BOND BREAK
COMPRESSIBLE FILLER

REINFORCED BRICK MASONRY COLUMN

REINFORCED BRICK MASONRY PILASTER

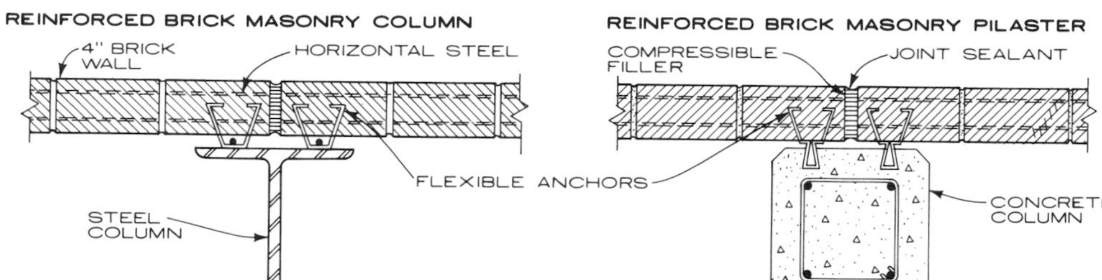
4" BRICK WALL
HORIZONTAL STEEL
COMPRESSIBLE FILLER
JOINT SEALANT
FLEXIBLE ANCHORS
STEEL COLUMN
CONCRETE COLUMN

STEEL COLUMN

REINFORCED CONCRETE COLUMN

BRICK CURTAIN WALL AND PANEL WALL REINFORCEMENT AND ANCHORAGE

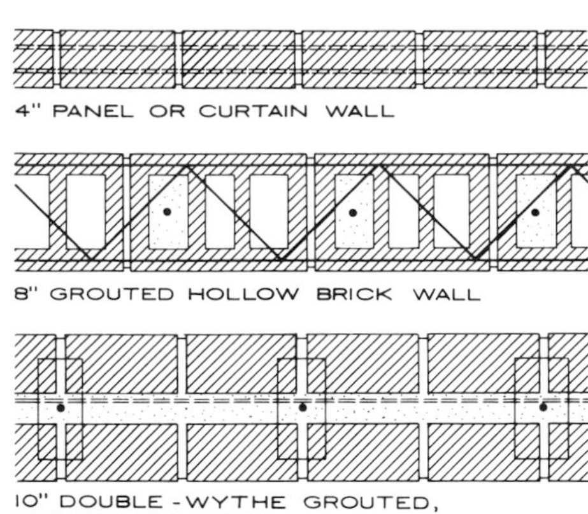
4" PANEL OR CURTAIN WALL
8" GROUTED HOLLOW BRICK WALL
10" DOUBLE-WYTHE GROUTED, REINFORCED BRICK WALL

WALL TYPES

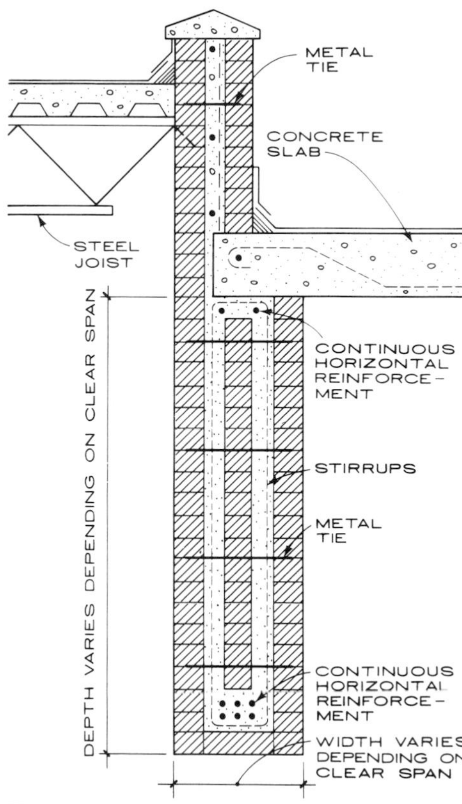
METAL TIE
CONCRETE SLAB
STEEL JOIST
DEPTH VARIES DEPENDING ON CLEAR SPAN
CONTINUOUS HORIZONTAL REINFORCE-MENT
STIRRUPS
METAL TIE
CONTINUOUS HORIZONTAL REINFORCE-MENT
WIDTH VARIES DEPENDING ON CLEAR SPAN

REINFORCED BRICK BEAM

TYPICAL RETAINING WALL DESIGN VALUES

H	B	L	D BARS	V BARS	F BARS
2'-0"	1'-9"	1'-10"	#3 @ 40"		#3 @ 40"
2'-6"	1'-9"	2'-4"	#3 @ 40"		#3 @ 40"
3'-0"	2'-0"	2'-10"	#3 @ 40"		#3 @ 40"
3'-6"	2'-0"	3'-4"	#3 @ 40"		#3 @ 40"
4'-0"	2'-4"	1'-4"	#3 @ 27" #4 @ 40"	#3 @ 27" #3 @ 40"	#3 @ 27" #3 @ 40"
4'-6"	2'-8"	1'-6"	#3 @ 19" #4 @ 35"	#3 @ 38" #3 @ 35"	#3 @ 19" #3 @ 35"
5'-0"	3'-0"	1'-8"	#3 @ 14" #4 @ 25" #5 @ 40"	#3 @ 28" #3 @ 25" #4 @ 40"	#3 @ 14" #3 @ 25" #4 @ 40"
5'-6"	3'-3"	1'-10"	#3 @ 11" #4 @ 20" #5 @ 31"	#3 @ 22" #4 @ 40" #4 @ 31"	#3 @ 11" #3 @ 20" #4 @ 31"
6'-0"	3'-6"	2'-0"	#3 @ 8" #4 @ 14" #5 @ 20"	#3 @ 16" #4 @ 28" #5 @ 40"	#3 @ 8" #3 @ 14" #4 @ 20"

NOTE: For convenience, this table was developed to aid the nondesigner in a typical application. However, materials must meet these additional minimum requirements:

1. Brick strength in excess of 6000 psi in compression.
2. Steel design tensile strength, F_s, of 20,000 psi.
3. No surcharge.

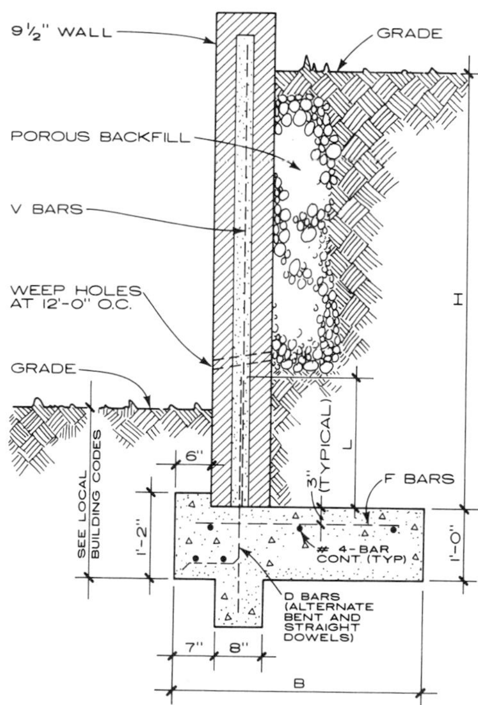
9½" WALL
GRADE
POROUS BACKFILL
V BARS
WEEP HOLES AT 12'-0" O.C.
GRADE
H
L (TYPICAL)
3"
6"
F BARS
SEE LOCAL BUILDING CODES
1'-2"
1'-0"
#4-BAR CONT (TYP)
D BARS (ALTERNATE BENT AND STRAIGHT DOWELS)
7"
8"
B

LOW BRICK MASONRY RETAINING WALL (LESS THAN 6'-0")

NOTE

Consult a qualified engineer and local code requirements for design of all grouted, reinforced masonry construction.

The design of load-bearing masonry buildings is based on a rational analysis of the magnitude, line of action, and direction of all forces acting on the structure. Dead loads, live loads, lateral loads, and other forces such as those resulting from temperature changes, impact, and unequal settlement are considered. The combination of loads producing the greatest stresses is used to size the members. Reinforced masonry is used where compressive, flexural, and shear stresses are greater than those permitted for unreinforced or partially reinforced masonry. The minimum amount of steel reinforcing required by code is designed for seismic zones 3 and 4 where high winds or earthquake activity subject buildings to severe lateral dynamic loads. Reinforcing steel adds ductility and strength to the wall, which then bears the load with minimum deflection and maximum damping of the earthquake energy. For further technical information:

Masonry Design and Detailing, 2nd edition. Christine Beall. New York: McGraw-Hill, 1987.

Recommended Practice for Engineered Brick Masonry. Brick Institute of America. McLean, VA, 1969.

Reinforced Masonry Design. R. Schneider and W. Dickey. New York: Prentice-Hall, Inc., 1980.

Technical Notes Series. Brick Institute of America.

Christine Beall, AIA, CCS; Austin, Texas
John R. Hoke, Jr., AIA, Architect; Washington, D.C.

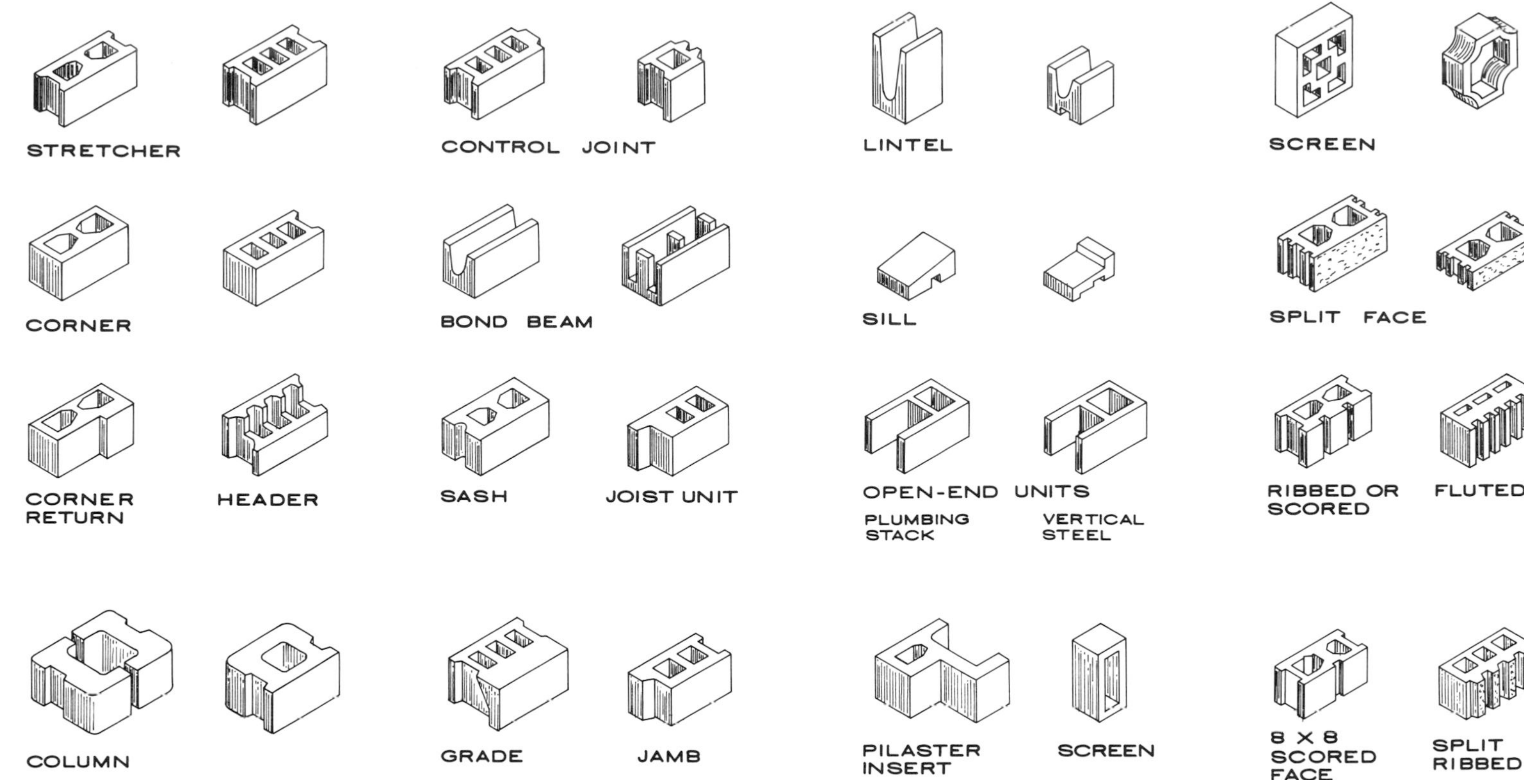
STRETCHER
CONTROL JOINT
LINTEL
SCREEN
CORNER
BOND BEAM
SILL
SPLIT FACE
CORNER RETURN
HEADER
SASH
JOIST UNIT
OPEN-END UNITS
PLUMBING STACK
VERTICAL STEEL
RIBBED OR SCORED
FLUTED
COLUMN
GRADE
JAMB
PILASTER INSERT
SCREEN
8 X 8 SCORED FACE
SPLIT RIBBED

TYPICAL CONCRETE MASONRY UNIT SHAPES

CONCRETE MASONRY UNIT SPECIFICATIONS AND FIRE RESISTANCE DATA

1. A solid (load bearing) concrete block is a unit whose cross-sectional area in every plane parallel to the bearing surface is not less than 75% of the gross cross-sectional area measured in the same plane. (ASTM C145–75.)
2. A hollow concrete block is a unit whose cross-sectional area in every plane parallel to the bearing surface is less than 75% of the gross cross-sectional area measured in the same plane. (ASTM C90–75.)
3. Actual dimension is 3/8 in. less than nominal shown.
4. All shapes shown are available in all dimensions given in chart except for width (W) which may be otherwise noted.
5. Because the number of shapes and sizes for concrete masonry screen units is virtually unlimited, it is advisable for the designer to check on availability of any specific shape during early planning.
6. Screen units should be of high quality, even though they seldom are employed in load bearing construction. When tested with their hollow cells parallel to the direction of the load, screen units should have a compressive strength exceeding 1000 psi of gross area; a quality of concrete unit comparable to "Specifications for Hollow Load-Bearing Concrete Masonry Units" ASTM C90–75.
7. Building codes are quite specific in the degree of fire protection required in various areas of buildings. Local building regulations will govern the concrete masonry wall section best suited for specific applications. Fire resistance ratings of concrete masonry walls are based on fire tests made at Underwriters' Laboratories, Inc., National Bureau of Standards, Portland Cement Association, and other recognized laboratories. Methods of test are described in ASTM E119 "Standard Method of Fire Tests of Building Construction and Materials."
8. The fire resistance ratings of most concrete masonry walls are determined by heat transmission measured by temperature rise on the cold side. Fire endurance can be calculated as a function of the aggregate type used in the block unit, and the solid thickness of the wall, or the equivalent solid thickness of the wall when working with hollow units.
9. Equivalent thickness of hollow units is calculated from actual thickness and the percentage of solid materials. Both needed items of information are normally reported by the testing laboratory using standard ASTM procedures, such as ASTM C140 "Methods of Sampling and Testing Concrete Masonry Units." When walls are plastered or otherwise faced with fire resistant materials, the thickness of these materials is included in calculating the equivalent thickness effective for fire resistance. Estimated fire resistance ratings shown in the table are for fully protected construction in which all structural members are of incombustible materials. Where combustible members are framed into walls, equivalent solid thickness protecting each such member should not be less than 93% of the thicknesses shown. Plaster is effective in increasing fire resistance when combustible members are framed into masonry walls, as is filling core spaces with various fire resistant materials.
10. Walls and partitions of 1- to 4-hr ratings are governed by code requirements for actual or equivalent solid thickness computed on the percent of core area in the unit. Increasing the wall thickness or filling the cores with grout increases the rating. Units with more than 25% core area are classified as hollow, and the equivalent solid thickness must first be computed in order to determine the fire rating. Since core size and shape will vary, either manufacturer's data or laboratory test data must be used to establish exact figures. A nominal 8 in. hollow unit reported to be 55% solid would be calculated as follows: equivalent solid thickness = 0.55 x 7.625 in. (actual thickness) = 4.19 in. Lightweight aggregates such as pumice, expanded slag, clay, or shale offer greater resistance to the transfer of heat in a fire because of their increased air content. Units made with these materials require less thickness to achieve the same fire rating as a heavyweight aggregate unit.

NOMINAL DIMENSIONS OF TYPICAL CONCRETE MASONRY UNIT SHAPES

Height (H) = 4″, 8″

Length (L) = 8″, 12″, 16″, 24″

Width (W) = 4″, 6″, 8″, 10″, 12″

EQUIVALENT THICKNESS FOR FIRE RATING

	1 HR	2 HR	3 HR	4 HR
Expanded slag or pumice	2.1	3.2	4.0	4.7
Expanded clay or shale	2.6	3.8	4.8	5.7
Limestone, cinders, air-cooled slag	2.7	4.0	5.0	5.9
Calcareous gravel	2.8	4.2	5.3	6.2
Siliceous gravel	3.0	4.5	5.7	6.7

R VALUE OF SINGLE WYTHE CMU, EMPTY AND WITH LOOSE-FILL INSULATION*

NOMINAL UNIT THICKNESS (IN.)	CORES	DENSITY OF CONCRETE IN CMU (PCF)				
		60	80	100	120	140
4	insul.	3.36	2.79	2.33	1.92	1.14
	empty	2.07	1.68	1.40	1.17	0.77
6	insul.	5.59	4.59	3.72	2.95	1.59
	empty	2.25	1.83	1.53	1.29	0.86
8	insul.	7.46	6.06	4.85	3.79	1.98
	empty	2.30	2.12	1.75	1.46	0.98
10	insul.	9.35	7.45	5.92	4.59	2.35
	empty	3.00	2.40	1.97	1.63	1.08
12	insul.	10.98	8.70	6.80	5.18	2.59
	empty	3.29	2.62	2.14	1.81	1.16

*Vermiculite or perlite insulation.

Robert J. Sangiamo, AIA, and Davis, Brody & Associates; New York, New York
Christine Beall, AIA, CCS; Austin, Texas

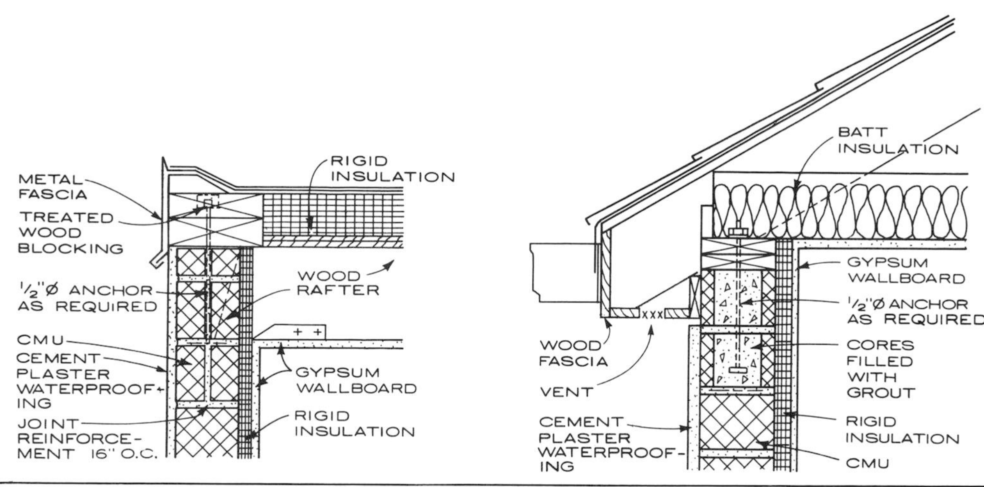
METAL FASCIA
TREATED WOOD BLOCKING
½"Ø ANCHOR AS REQUIRED
CMU
CEMENT PLASTER WATERPROOFING
JOINT REINFORCEMENT 16" O.C.
RIGID INSULATION
WOOD RAFTER
GYPSUM WALLBOARD
RIGID INSULATION
BATT INSULATION
WOOD FASCIA
VENT
CEMENT PLASTER WATERPROOFING
GYPSUM WALLBOARD
½"Ø ANCHOR AS REQUIRED
CORES FILLED WITH GROUT
RIGID INSULATION
CMU

WALL – ROOF ANCHORAGE

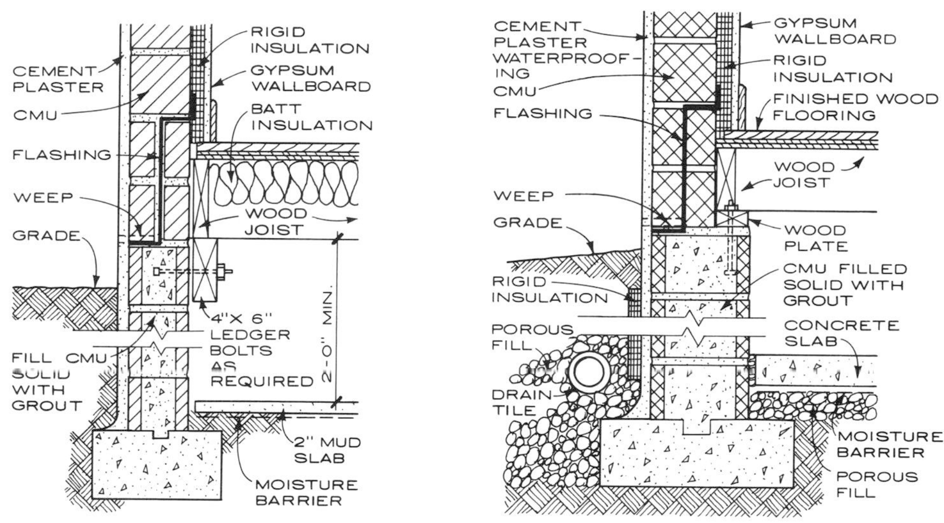
CEMENT PLASTER
CMU
FLASHING
WEEP
GRADE
FILL CMU SOLID WITH GROUT
RIGID INSULATION
GYPSUM WALLBOARD
BATT INSULATION
WOOD JOIST
4"X 6" LEDGER BOLTS AS REQUIRED
2'-0" MIN.
2" MUD SLAB
MOISTURE BARRIER
CEMENT PLASTER WATERPROOFING
CMU
FLASHING
WEEP
GRADE
RIGID INSULATION
POROUS FILL
DRAIN TILE
GYPSUM WALLBOARD
RIGID INSULATION
FINISHED WOOD FLOORING
WOOD JOIST
WOOD PLATE
CMU FILLED SOLID WITH GROUT
CONCRETE SLAB
MOISTURE BARRIER
POROUS FILL

FOUNDATION DETAILS

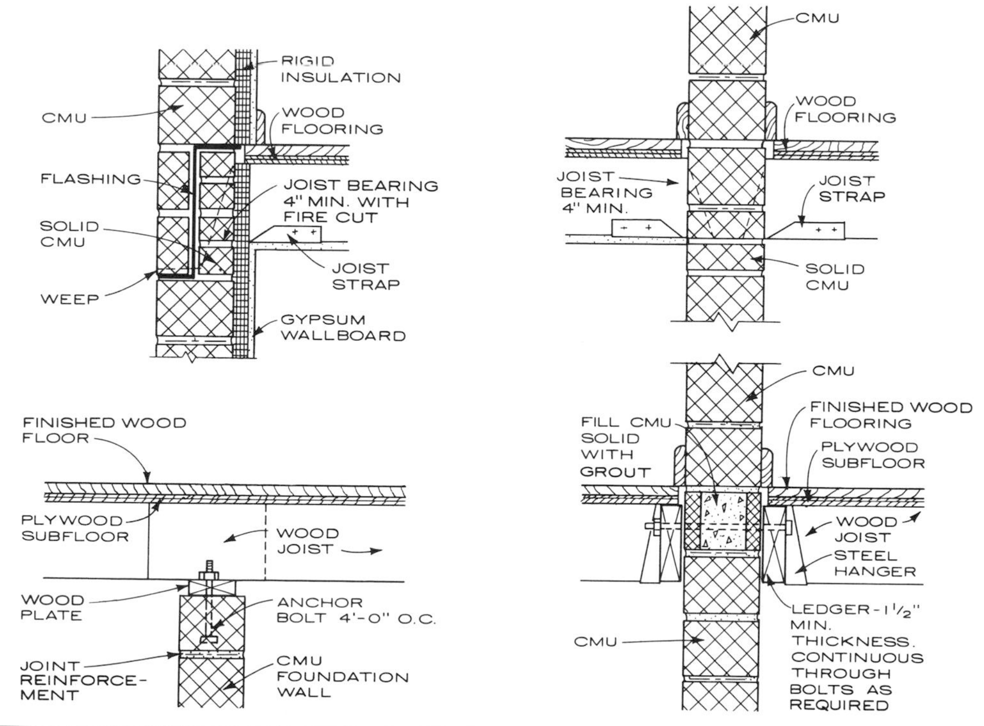
CMU
FLASHING
SOLID CMU
WEEP
RIGID INSULATION
WOOD FLOORING
JOIST BEARING 4" MIN. WITH FIRE CUT
JOIST STRAP
GYPSUM WALLBOARD
CMU
WOOD FLOORING
JOIST BEARING 4" MIN.
JOIST STRAP
SOLID CMU
FINISHED WOOD FLOOR
PLYWOOD SUBFLOOR
WOOD JOIST
WOOD PLATE
ANCHOR BOLT 4'-0" O.C.
JOINT REINFORCEMENT
CMU FOUNDATION WALL
CMU
FILL CMU SOLID WITH GROUT
FINISHED WOOD FLOORING
PLYWOOD SUBFLOOR
WOOD JOIST
STEEL HANGER
LEDGER-1½" MIN. THICKNESS, CONTINUOUS THROUGH BOLTS AS REQUIRED
CMU

WALL – FLOOR ANCHORAGE DETAILS

NOTES

Concrete masonry unit walls are susceptible to cracking due to the differential or restrained movements of building elements. These stresses may be controlled through reinforcement in the form of bond beams and horizontal joint reinforcing and through separation, as in control joints which accommodate movement of the wall.

In seismic zones, concrete masonry unit walls should be reinforced horizontally and vertically to resist the lateral forces acting nonconcurrently in the direction of each of the main axes of the building.

Reference state and local building codes and The National Concrete Masonry Association for design requirements and recommendations.

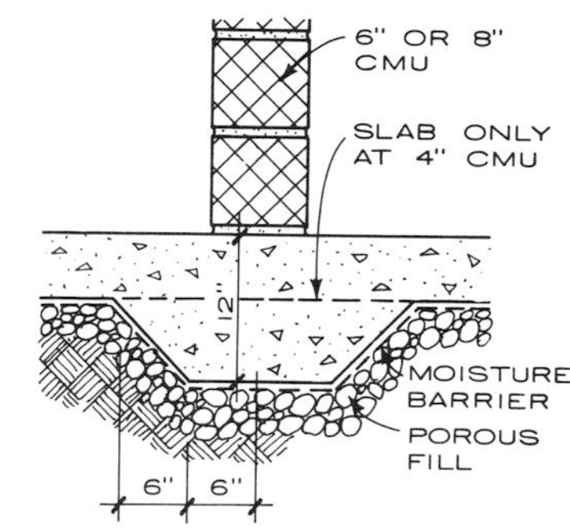
6" OR 8" CMU
SLAB ONLY AT 4" CMU
12"
MOISTURE BARRIER
POROUS FILL
6"
6"

NONBEARING WALL

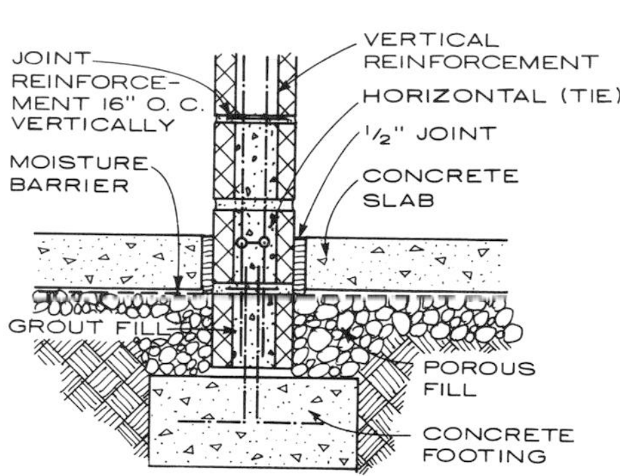
JOINT REINFORCEMENT 16" O. C. VERTICALLY
MOISTURE BARRIER
GROUT FILL
VERTICAL REINFORCEMENT
HORIZONTAL (TIE)
½" JOINT
CONCRETE SLAB
POROUS FILL
CONCRETE FOOTING

FOOTING DEPTH DETERMINED BY CODES

BEARING WALL

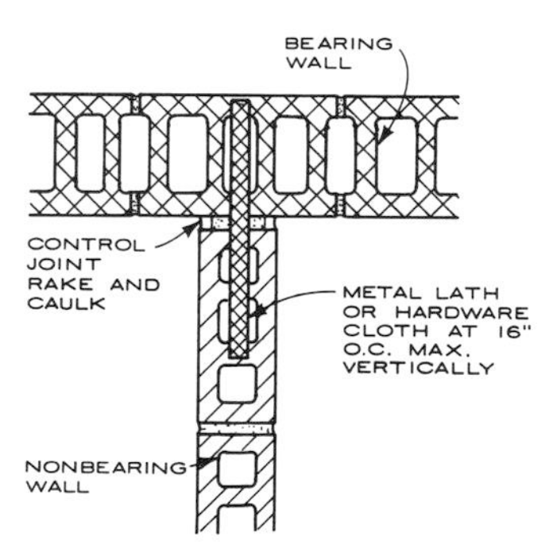
BEARING WALL
CONTROL JOINT RAKE AND CAULK
METAL LATH OR HARDWARE CLOTH AT 16" O.C. MAX. VERTICALLY
NONBEARING WALL

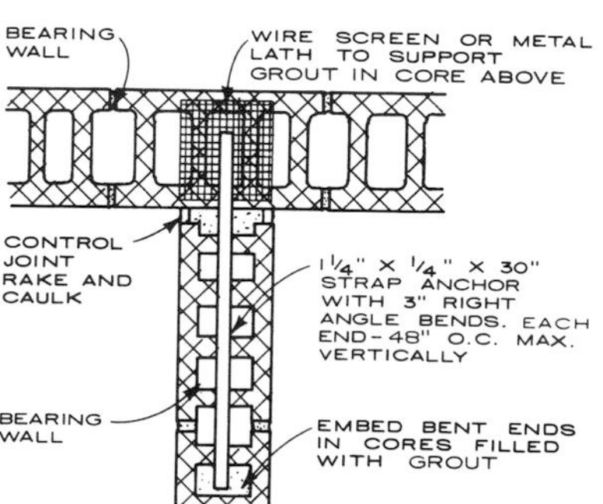
BEARING WALL
WIRE SCREEN OR METAL LATH TO SUPPORT GROUT IN CORE ABOVE
CONTROL JOINT RAKE AND CAULK
1¼" X ¼" X 30" STRAP ANCHOR WITH 3" RIGHT ANGLE BENDS. EACH END – 48" O.C. MAX. VERTICALLY
BEARING WALL
EMBED BENT ENDS IN CORES FILLED WITH GROUT

INTERSECTING WALL DETAILS

Robert J. Sangiamo, AIA; New York, New York
Davis, Brody & Associates; New York, New York
Ted B. Richey, AIA; The InterDesign Group; Indianapolis, Indiana

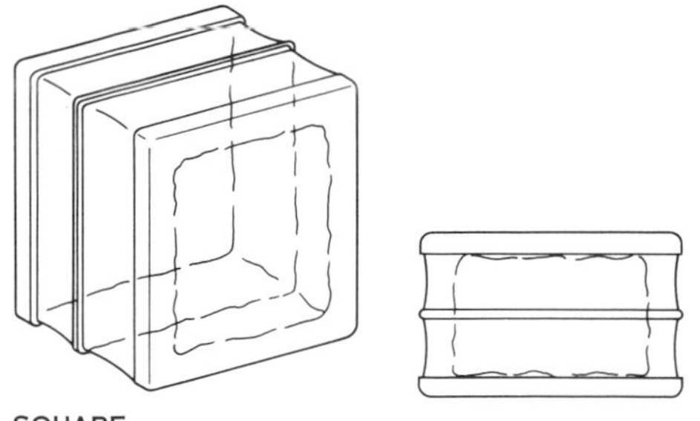

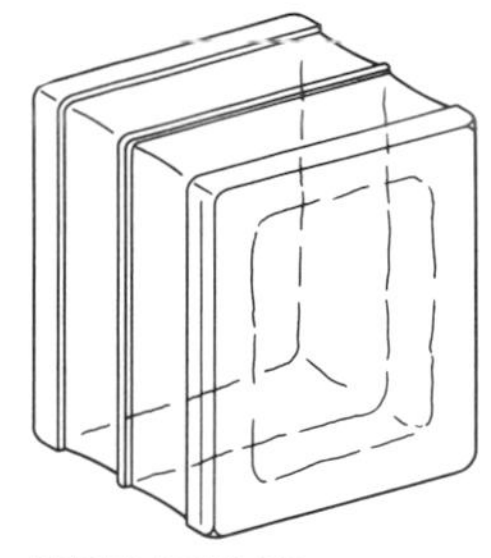

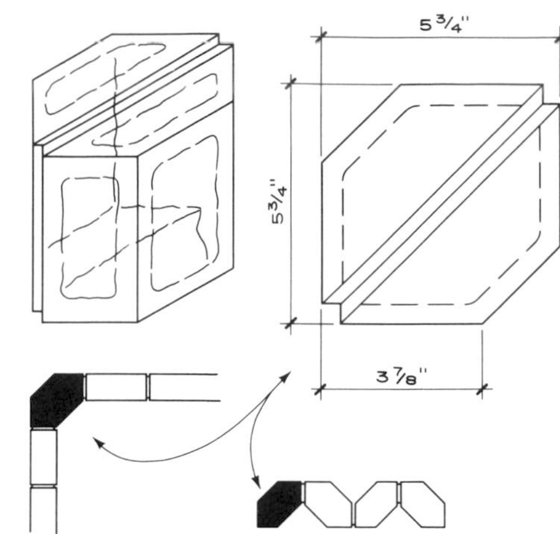
5 3/4"
5 3/4"
3 7/8"

SQUARE

4½ in. x 4½ in.
6 in. x 6 in. (5¾ in. x 5¾ in. actual)
7½ in. x 7½ in.
8 in. x 8 in. (7¾ in. x 7¾ in. actual)
9½ in. x 9½ in.
12 in. x 12 in. (11¾ in. x 11¾ in. actual)

115 mm x 115 mm
190 mm x 190 mm
240 mm x 240 mm
300 mm x 300 mm

Metric sizes are available from foreign manufacturers through distributors in the U.S.

RECTANGULAR

4 in. x 8 in. (3¾ in. x 7¾ in. actual)
6 in. x 8 in. (5¾ in. x 7¾ in. actual)
9½ in. x 4½ in.*

*240 mm x 115 mm

THICKNESSES

Square and rectangular glass block are available in thicknesses ranging from a minimum of 3 in. for solid units to a maximum of 4 in. for hollow units. Metric thicknesses range from 80 mm to 100 mm.

SPECIAL SHAPES (CORNERS)

A limited number of manufacturers have special shapes to execute corner designs. These units also may be placed together for varying patterns and forms.

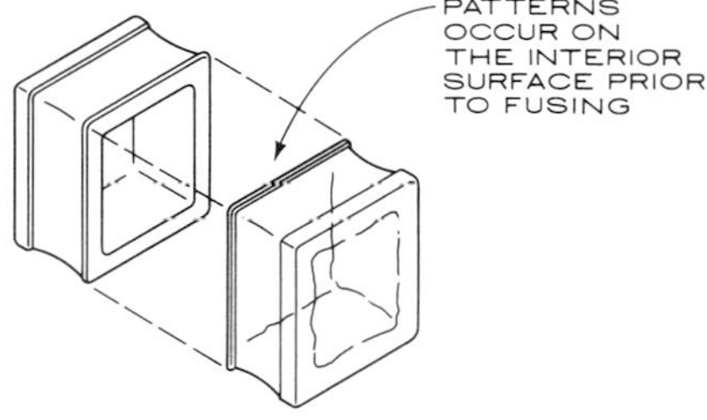
PATTERNS OCCUR ON THE INTERIOR SURFACE PRIOR TO FUSING

The basic glass block unit is made of two halves fused together with a partial vacuum inside. Faces may be clear, figured, or with integral relief forms.

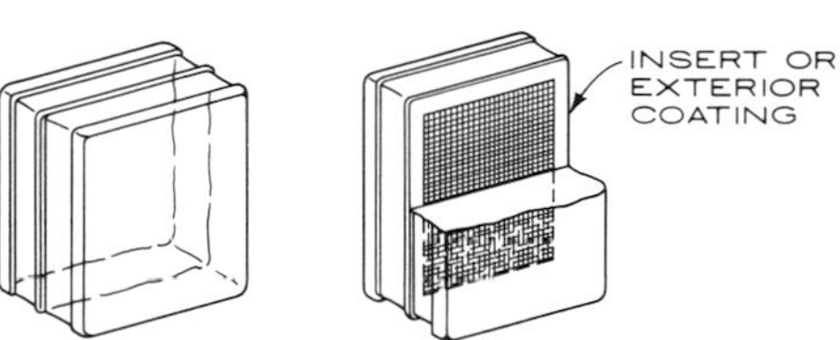
INSERT OR EXTERIOR COATING

Solid glass block units (glass bricks) are impact resistant and allow through vision.

Solar control units have either inserts or exterior coatings to reduce heat gain. Coated units require periodic cleaning to remove alkali and metal ions that can harm the surface coating. Edge drips are required to prevent moisture rundown on surface.

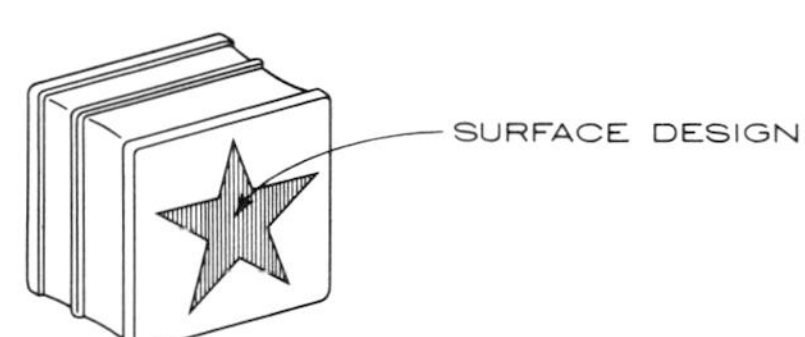
SURFACE DESIGN

Surface decoration may be achieved with fused-on ceramic, etching, or sandblasting. Glass block units may be split or shipped in halves in order to apply some decoration to the inside. Blocks then must be resealed. Resealed blocks will not perform the same under various stresses as factory sealed units. Placement in walls or panels should be limited to areas receiving minimum loading.

STANDARD BLOCK DESIGN

12" GLASS BLOCK
9½" GLASS BLOCK
8" GLASS BLOCK
7½" GLASS BLOCK
6" GLASS BLOCK
4½" GLASS BLOCK
4" GLASS BLOCK

32" 38½" 48½" 63" 65" 80" 96½"

5/8" OUTSIDE JOINT
1/8" OR 3/16" INSIDE JOINT

Curved walls may be constructed to the minimum radii (to the inside surface) indicated above. There are no maximum radii.

Table is based on an outside joint thickness of ⅝ in. and an inside joint thickness of ⅛ in. Some manufacturers prefer a minimum inside joint thickness of 3/16 in. Wider joints require a slightly larger radius.

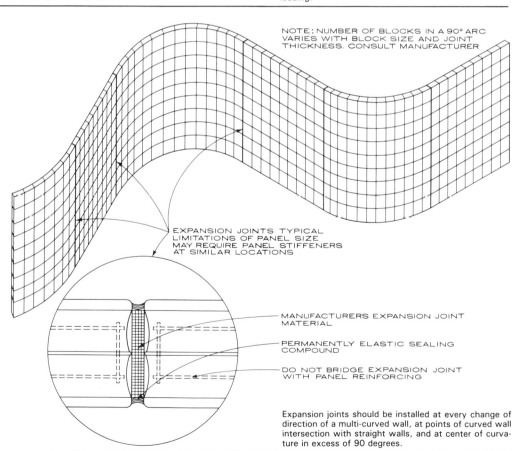

NOTE: NUMBER OF BLOCKS IN A 90° ARC VARIES WITH BLOCK SIZE AND JOINT THICKNESS. CONSULT MANUFACTURER

EXPANSION JOINTS TYPICAL LIMITATIONS OF PANEL SIZE MAY REQUIRE PANEL STIFFENERS AT SIMILAR LOCATIONS

MANUFACTURERS EXPANSION JOINT MATERIAL

PERMANENTLY ELASTIC SEALING COMPOUND

DO NOT BRIDGE EXPANSION JOINT WITH PANEL REINFORCING

Expansion joints should be installed at every change of direction of a multi-curved wall, at points of curved wall intersection with straight walls, and at center of curvature in excess of 90 degrees.

CURVED WALL DESIGN

Raso·Greaves An Architecture Corporation; Waco, Texas

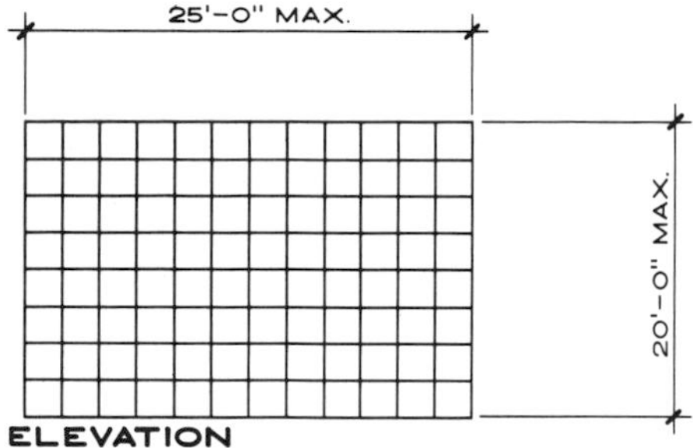
25'-0" MAX.
20'-0" MAX.
ELEVATION

NOTES

Area of exterior unbraced panel should not exceed 144 sq ft. Maximum size may be increased to 250 sq ft with the addition of mortared stiffeners.

Area of interior unbraced panel should not exceed 250 sq ft.

Panels are designed to be mortared at sill, with head and jambs providing for movement and settling. Deflection of lintel at head should be anticipated.

Consult manufacturers for specific design limitations of glass block panels. Thickness of block used also determines maximum panel size.

GLASS BLOCK PANEL

METAL ANCHORS SECURE GLASS BLOCK PANEL TO ADJACENT CONSTRUCTION (BEND WITHIN EXPANSION JOINT)

EXPANSION STRIP TO ALLOW FOR DIFFERENTIAL MOVEMENT

CLEAN SURFACES AFTER ERECTION WITH ORDINARY HOUSEHOLD SCRUB BRUSH WITH STIFF BRISTLES

HORIZONTAL JOINT REINFORCING AS REQUIRED FOR EACH INSTALLATION

FULL BED OF MORTAR TYPICALLY 1/4" WIDE AT FACE OF WALL
MORTAR TO BE TYPE S
OPTIMUM MIXTURE:
1 PART PORTLAND CEMENT
1/4 PART LIME
3 PARTS SAND

GLASS BLOCK PANEL COMPONENTS

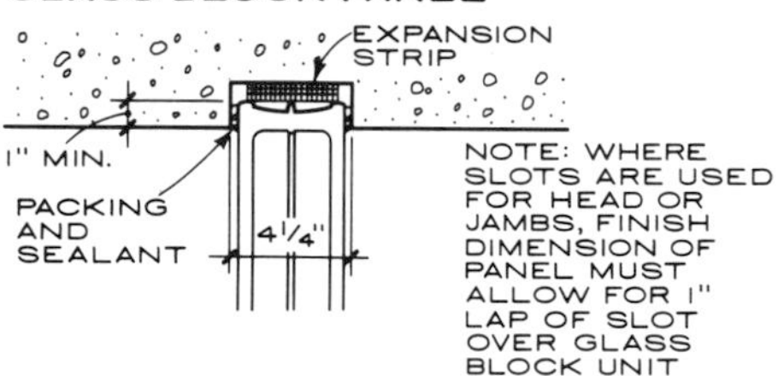
EXPANSION STRIP
1" MIN.
PACKING AND SEALANT
4 1/4"
NOTE: WHERE SLOTS ARE USED FOR HEAD OR JAMBS, FINISH DIMENSION OF PANEL MUST ALLOW FOR 1" LAP OF SLOT OVER GLASS BLOCK UNIT

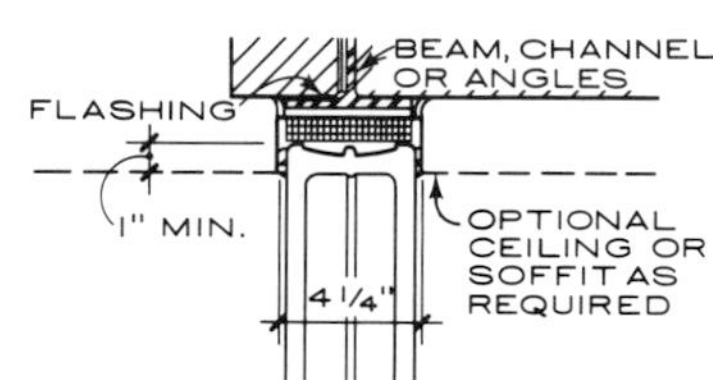
BEAM, CHANNEL OR ANGLES
FLASHING
1" MIN.
OPTIONAL CEILING OR SOFFIT AS REQUIRED
4 1/4"

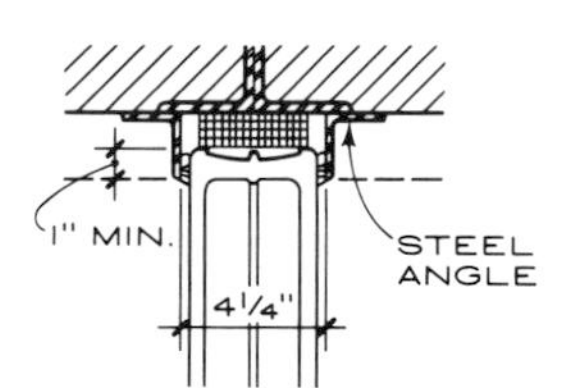
1" MIN.
4 1/4"
STEEL ANGLE

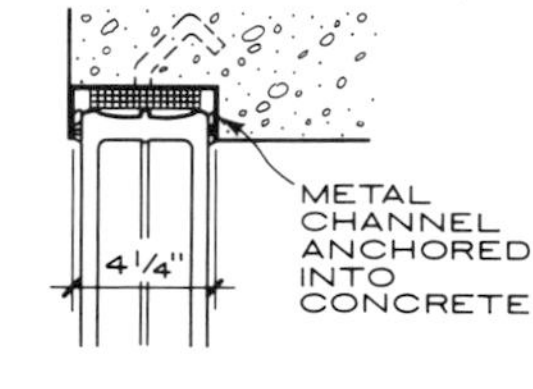
4 1/4"
METAL CHANNEL ANCHORED INTO CONCRETE

HEAD SECTIONS

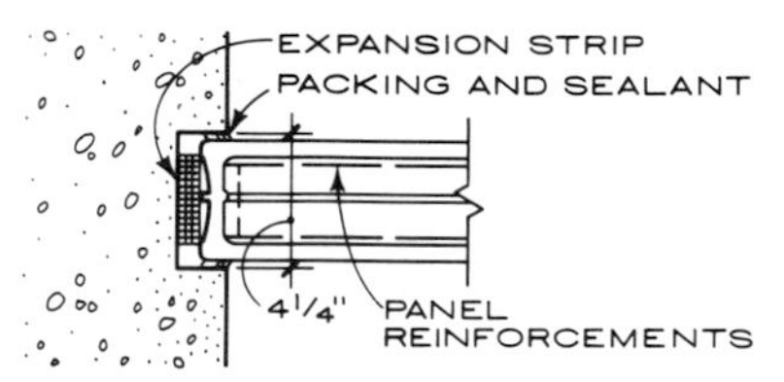
EXPANSION STRIP
PACKING AND SEALANT
4 1/4"
PANEL REINFORCEMENTS

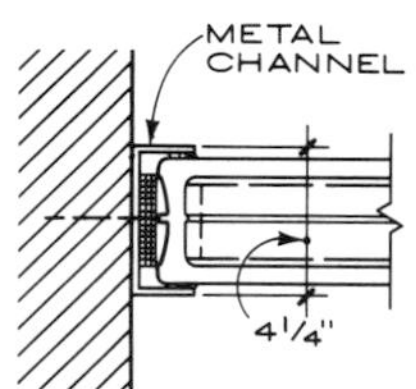
METAL CHANNEL
4 1/4"

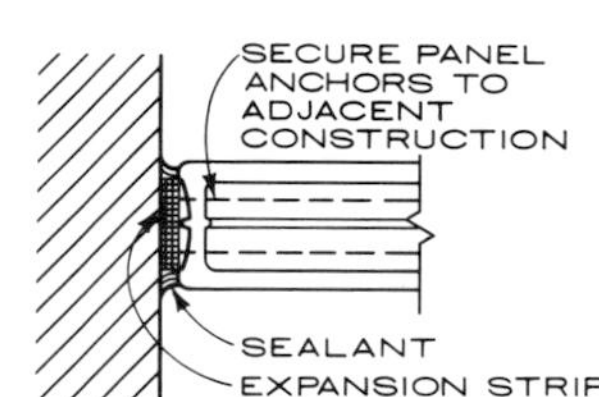
SECURE PANEL ANCHORS TO ADJACENT CONSTRUCTION
SEALANT
EXPANSION STRIP

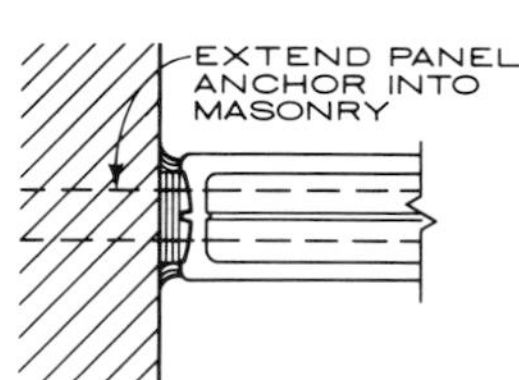
EXTEND PANEL ANCHOR INTO MASONRY

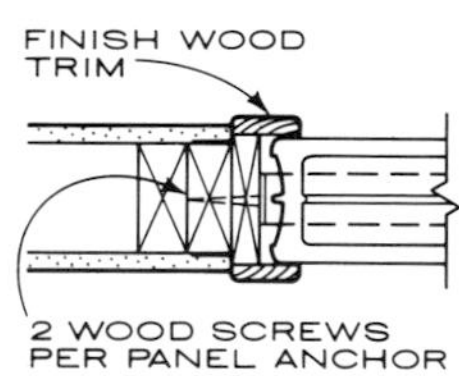
FINISH WOOD TRIM
2 WOOD SCREWS PER PANEL ANCHOR

JAMB SECTIONS

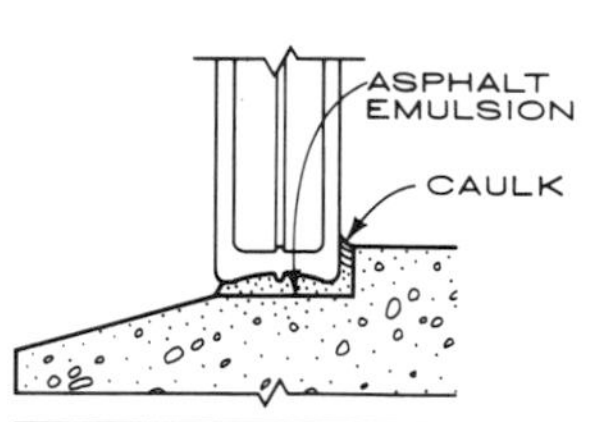
ASPHALT EMULSION
CAULK

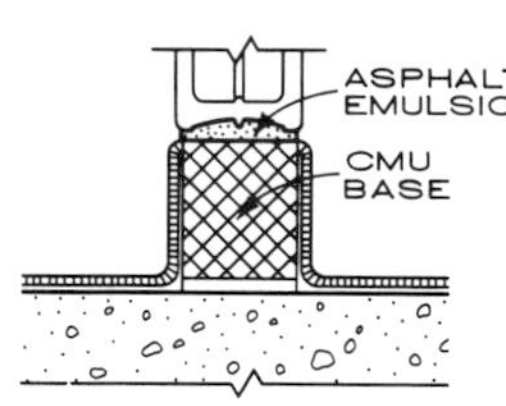
ASPHALT EMULSION
CMU BASE

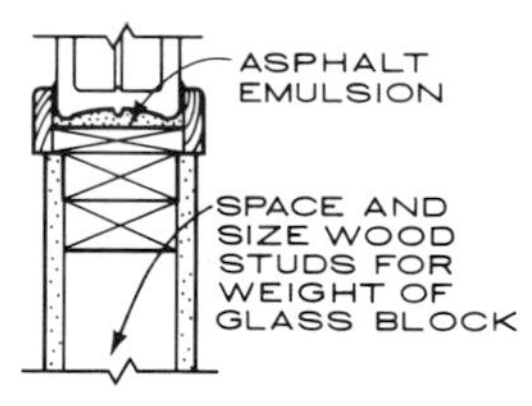
ASPHALT EMULSION
SPACE AND SIZE WOOD STUDS FOR WEIGHT OF GLASS BLOCK

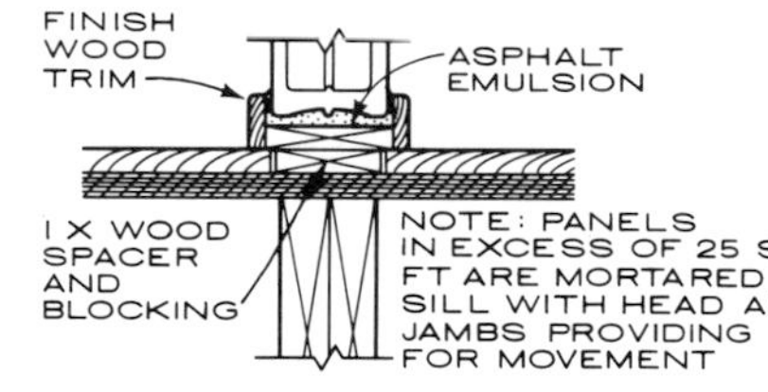
FINISH WOOD TRIM
ASPHALT EMULSION
1 X WOOD SPACER AND BLOCKING
NOTE: PANELS IN EXCESS OF 25 SQ FT ARE MORTARED AT SILL WITH HEAD AND JAMBS PROVIDING FOR MOVEMENT

SILL SECTIONS

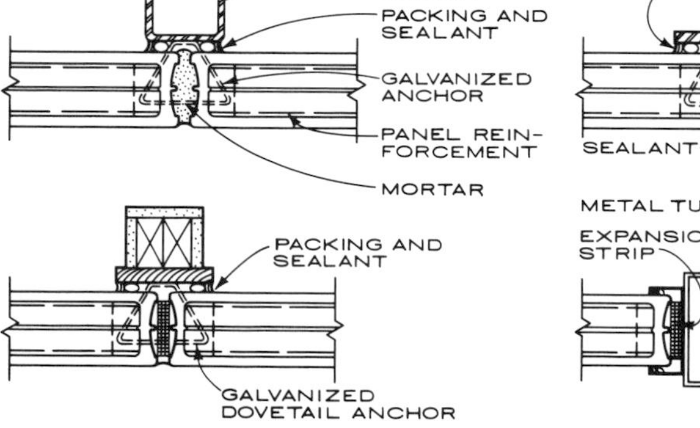
TUBE OR COLUMN
PACKING AND SEALANT
GALVANIZED ANCHOR
PANEL REINFORCEMENT
MORTAR
PACKING AND SEALANT
GALVANIZED DOVETAIL ANCHOR

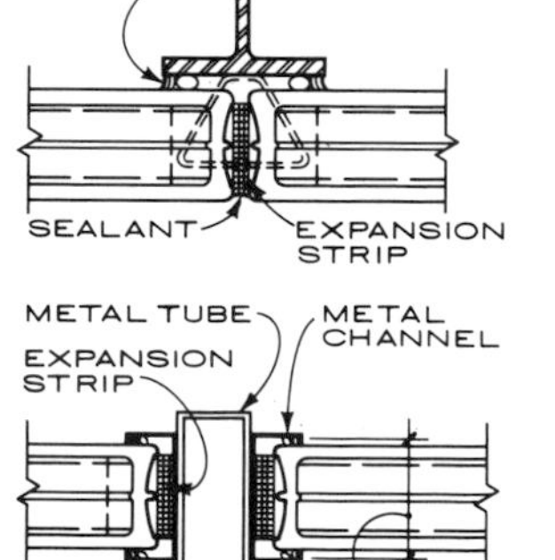
BACKER ROD AND SEALANT
SEALANT
EXPANSION STRIP
METAL TUBE
METAL CHANNEL
EXPANSION STRIP
4 1/4"

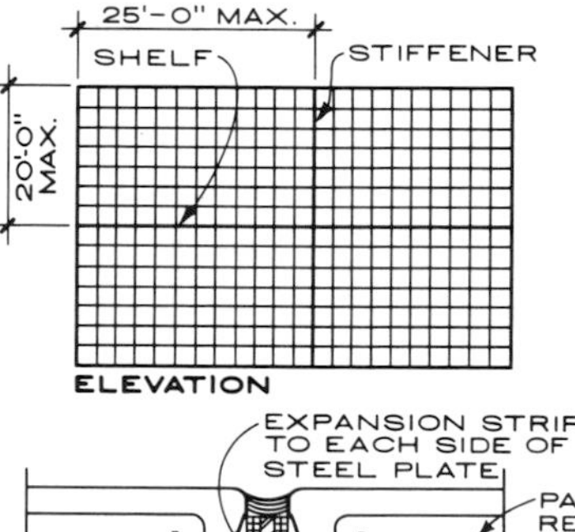
25'-0" MAX.
SHELF
STIFFENER
20'-0" MAX.
ELEVATION

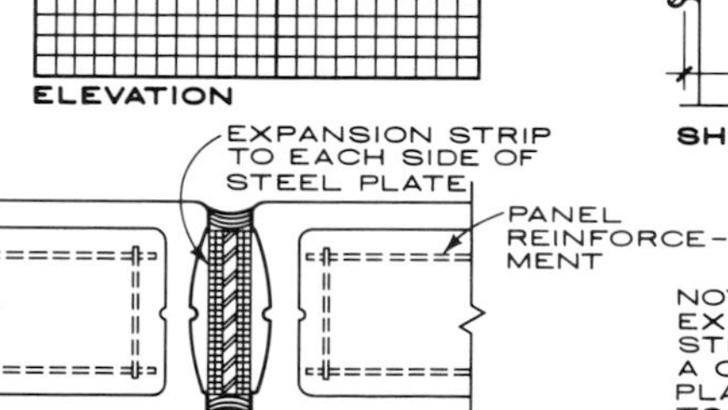
EXPANSION STRIP TO EACH SIDE OF STEEL PLATE
PANEL REINFORCEMENT

NOTE: PANELS WITH AN EXPANSION JOINT STIFFENER INCORPORATING A CONCEALED VERTICAL PLATE SHOULD BE LIMITED TO 10 FT MAX. HEIGHT

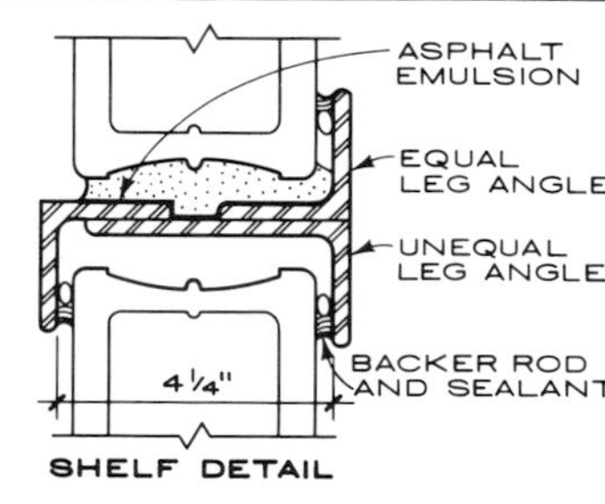
ASPHALT EMULSION
EQUAL LEG ANGLE
UNEQUAL LEG ANGLE
BACKER ROD AND SEALANT
4 1/4"

SHELF DETAIL

STIFFENER SECTIONS

Raso·Greaves An Architecture Corporation; Waco, Texas

GENERAL NOTES

Natural stone is used in building as a facing, veneer, and decoration. The major factors affecting the suitability and use of stone fall under two broad, but overlapping categories: physical and structural properties and aesthetic qualities. The three factors of building stone that most influence their selection by architects for aesthetic reasons are pattern, texture, and color. Consideration also should be given to costs, availability, weathering characteristics, physical properties, and size and thickness limitations.

Stone patterns are highly varied, and they provide special features that make building stone a unique material. Texture is varied, ranging from coarse fragments to fine grains and crystalline structures. Texture also varies with the hardness of minerals composing the stone. To accurately compare stone colors, the rock color chart published by the Geological Society of America (Boulder, CO) is recommended. Samples also may be used to establish acceptable color ranges for a particular installation.

Pattern, texture, and color all are affected by how the stone is fabricated and finished. Granites tend to hold their color and pattern, while limestone color and pattern changes with exposure. Textures may range from rough and flamed finishes to honed or polished surfaces. The harder the stone, the better it takes and holds a polish.

The three rock classes are igneous, sedimentary, and metamorphic. Common construction stones are marketed under the names given in the table below, although specialty stones such as soapstone and serpentine also are available. Each stone has various commercial grades. Limestone grades are A, statuary; B, select; C, standard; D, rustic; E, variegated; and F, old Gothic. Marble is graded A, B, C, or D on the basis of working qualities, uniformity, and flaws and imperfections. Only grade A highest quality stone should be used for exterior applications.

The physical characteristics of a particular stone must be suitable for its intended use. It is important to determine the physical properties of the actual stone being used rather than using values from a generic table, which can be very misleading. Considerations of the physical properties of the stone being selected include modulus of rupture, shear strength, coefficient of expansion, permanent irreversible growth and change in shape, creep deflection, compressive strength, modulus of elasticity, moisture resistance, and weatherability. Epoxy and polyester adhesives, often used with stone, are affected by cleanliness of surfaces to be bonded and ambient temperature. Curing time increases with cold temperatures and decreases with warmer temperatures.

With the introduction of new systems of fabrication and installation and recent developments in the design and detailing of stone cutting, support, and anchorage, costs are better controlled. Correct design of joints, selection of mortars, and use of sealants affect the quality and durability of installation. Adequate design and detailing of the anchorage of each piece of stone are required. The size and thickness of the stone should be established based on physical properties of the stone, its method of anchorage, and the loads it must resist. Appropriate safety factors should be developed based on the variability of the stone properties as well as other considerations such as imperfect workmanship, method of support and anchorage, and degree of exposure of the cladding installation. Relieving angles for stone support and anchorage may be necessary to preclude unacceptable compressive loading of the stone. The stone should be protected from staining and breakage during shipment, delivery, and installation.

Since stone cladding design and detailing vary with type of stone and installation, the designer should consult stone suppliers, stone-setting specialty contractors, industry standards (such as ASTM), and other publications to help select and implement a stone cladding system. Resource information is available in publications such as the Indiana Limestone Institute's Indiana Limestone Handbook and the Marble Institute of America's Dimensioned Stone, Volume 3.

STONE CLASSIFIED ACCORDING TO QUALITIES AFFECTING USE

CLASS	COLOR	TEXTURE	SPECIAL FEATURES	PARTINGS	HARDNESS	CHIEF USES
Sandstone	Very light buff to light chocolate brown or brick red; may tarnish to brown	Granular, showing sand grains, cemented together	Ripple marks; oblique color bands ("cross bedding")	Bedding planes; also fractures transverse to beds	Fairly hard if well cemented	General; walls; building; flagstone
Limestone	White, light gray to light buff	Fine to crystalline; may have fossils	May show fossils	Parallel to beds; also fractures across beds	Fairly soft; steel easily scratches	All building uses
Marble	Highly varied: snow white to black; also blue-gray and light to dark olive green; also pinkish	Finely granular to very coarsely crystalline showing flat-sided crystals	May show veins of different colors or angular rock pieces or fossils	Usually not along beds but may have irregular fractures	Slightly harder than limestone	May be used for building stone but usually in decorative panels
Granite (light igneous rock)	Almost white to pink-and-white or gray-and-white	Usually coarsely crystalline; crystals may be varicolored; may be fine grained	May be banded with pink, white or gray streaks and veins	Not necessarily any regular parting but fractures irregularly	Harder than limestone and marble; keeps cut shape well	Building stone, but also in paneling if attractively colored
Dark igneous rock	Gray, dark olive green to black; Laurvikite is beautifully crystalline	Usually coarsely crystalline if quarried but may be fine grained	May be banded with lighter and darker gray bands and veins	Not necessarily any regular parting but may fracture irregularly	About like granite; retains cut shape well	Building stone but also used in panels if nicely banded or crystalline
Lavas	Varies: pink, purple, black; if usable, rarely almost white	Fine grained; may have pores locally	Note rare porosity	Not necessarily any regular parting, as a rule, but some have parallel fractures	About as strong as granite; if light colored, usually softer	Good foundation and building stone; not decorative
Quartzite	Variable: white, buff, red, brown	Dense, almost glassy ideally	Very resistant to weather and impact	Usually no special parting	Very hard if well cemented, as usually the case	Excellent for building but hard to "shape"
Slate	Grayish-green, brick red or dark brown, usually gray; may be banded	Finely crystalline; flat crystals give slaty fracture	Some slates have color-fading with age	Splits along slate surface, often crossing color bands	Softer than granite or quartzite; scratches easily	Roofing; blackboards; paving
Gneiss	Usually gray with some pink, white or light gray bands	Crystalline, like granite, often with glassy bands (veins)	Banding is decorative; some bands very weak, however	No special parting; tends to break along banding	About like granite	Used for buildings; also may be decorative if banded

PHYSICAL PROPERTIES OF REPRESENTATIVE STONES

		IGNEOUS ROCK		SEDIMENTARY ROCK		METAMORPHIC ROCK	
PHYSICAL PROPERTY		GRANITE	TRAPROCK	LIMESTONE	SANDSTONE	MARBLE	SLATE
Composition—ultimate strength	(psi)	15,000-30,000	20,000	4,000-20,000	3,000-20,000	10,000-23,000	10,000-15,000
Composition—allowable working stress	(psi)	800-1,500		500-1,000	400-700	500-900	1,000
Shear—ultimate strength	(psi)	1,800-2,700		1,000-2,000	1,200-2,500	900-1,700	
Shear—allowable working stress	(psi)	200		200	150	150	
Tension—allowable working stress	(psi)	150		125	75	125	
Weight	(psf)	156-170	180-185	147-170	135-155	165-178	170-180
Specific gravity		2.4-2.7	2.96	2.1-2.8	2.0-2.6	2.4-2.8	2.7-2.8
Absorption of water (parts by weight)		1/750		1/38	1/24	1/300	1/430
Modulus of elasticity	(psi)	6-10,000,000	12,000,000	4-14,000,000	1-7,500,000	4-13,500,000	12,000,000
Coefficient of expansion	(psf)	0.0000040		0.0000045	0.0000055	0.0000045	0.0000058

NOTE: Particular stones may vary greatly from the average properties shown in this table. A particular stone's physical properties, as well as its allowable working values, always should be developed for each particular application.

The McGuire & Shook Corporation; Indianapolis, Indiana
Christine Beall, AIA, CCS; Austin, Texas

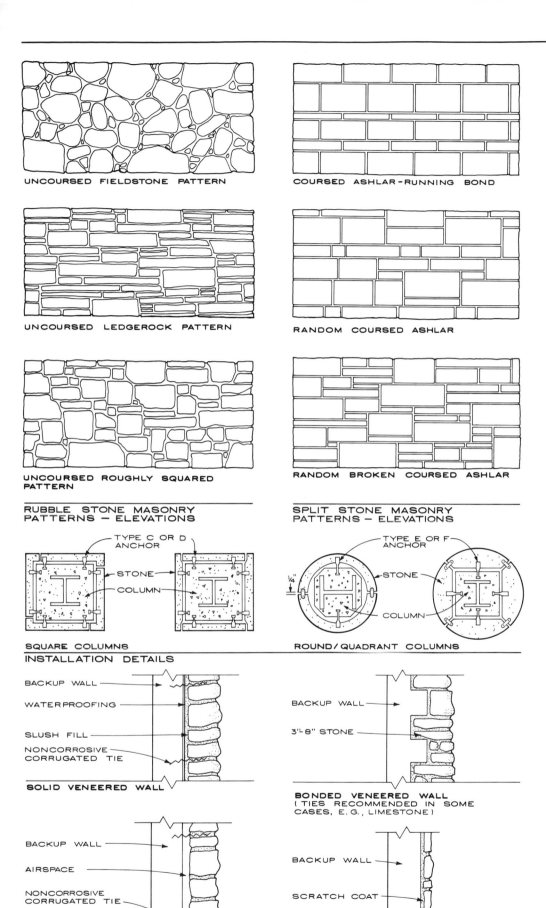

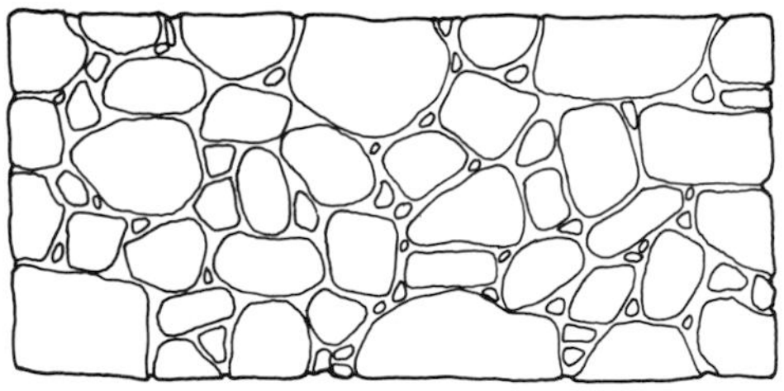

UNCOURSED FIELDSTONE PATTERN

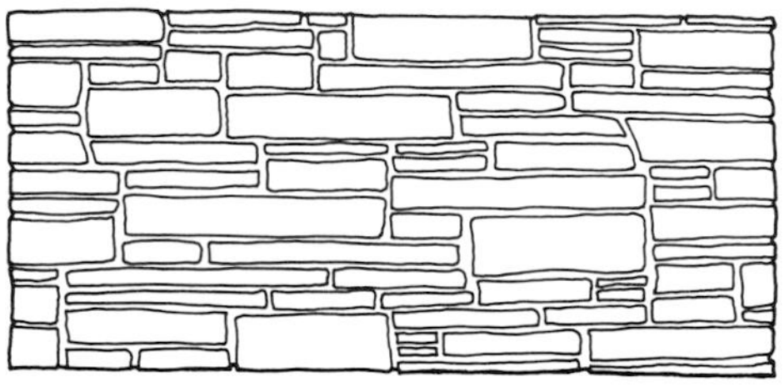

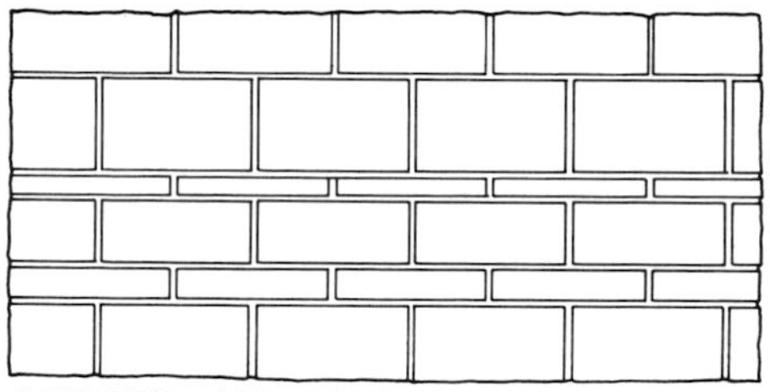

COURSED ASHLAR-RUNNING BOND

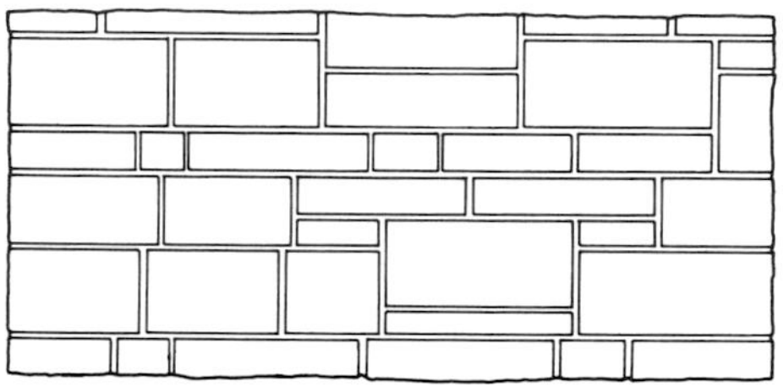

ONE-HEIGHT PATTERN (SINGLE RISE)

UNCOURSED LEDGEROCK PATTERN

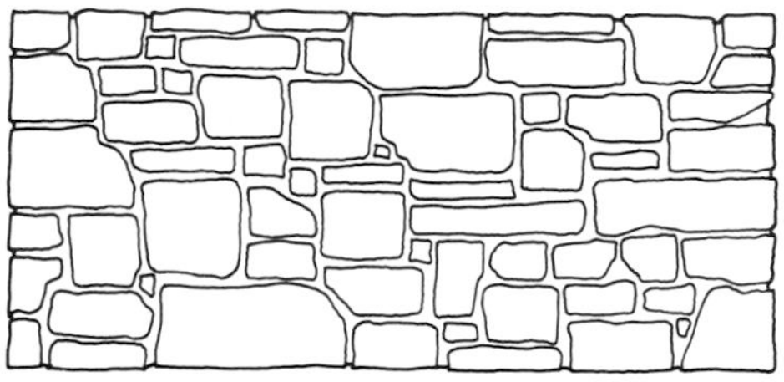

RANDOM COURSED ASHLAR

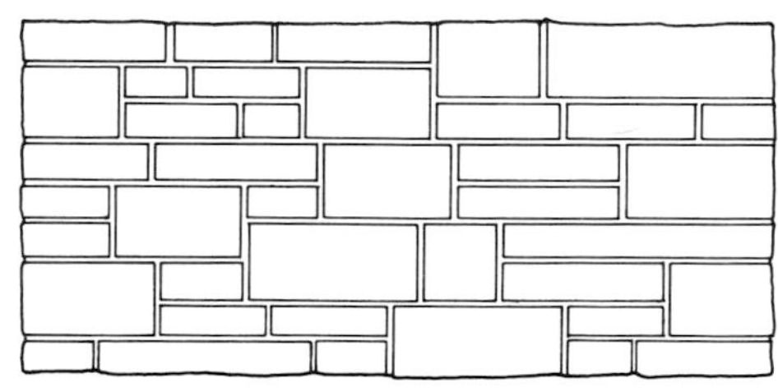

TWO-HEIGHT PATTERN (40% - 2 1/4"; 60% - 5")

UNCOURSED ROUGHLY SQUARED PATTERN

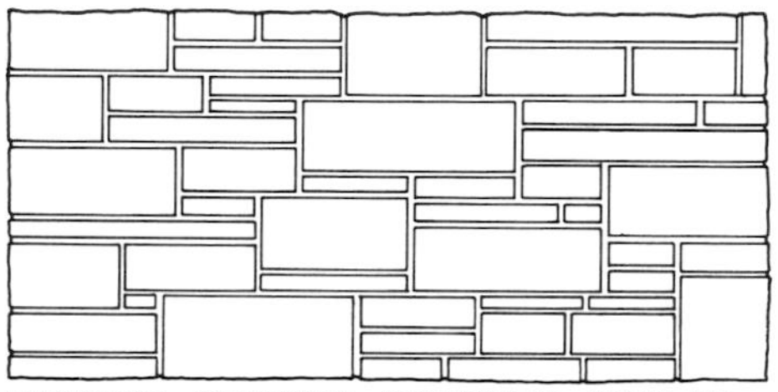

RANDOM BROKEN COURSED ASHLAR

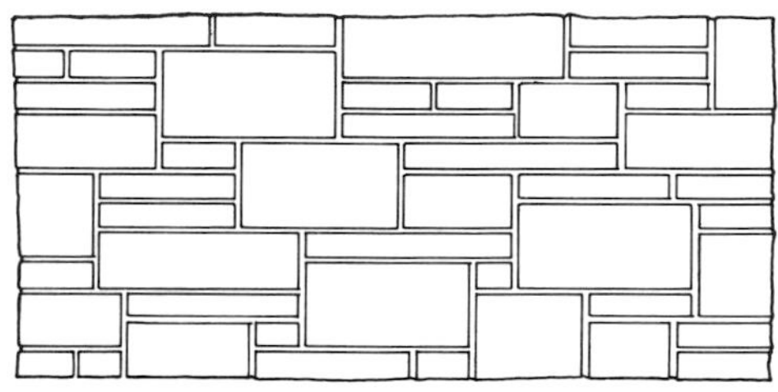

THREE-HEIGHT PATTERN (15% - 2 1/4"; 40% - 5"; 45% - 7 3/4")

RUBBLE STONE MASONRY PATTERNS — ELEVATIONS

SPLIT STONE MASONRY PATTERNS — ELEVATIONS

SPLIT STONE MASONRY HEIGHT PATTERNS — ELEVATIONS

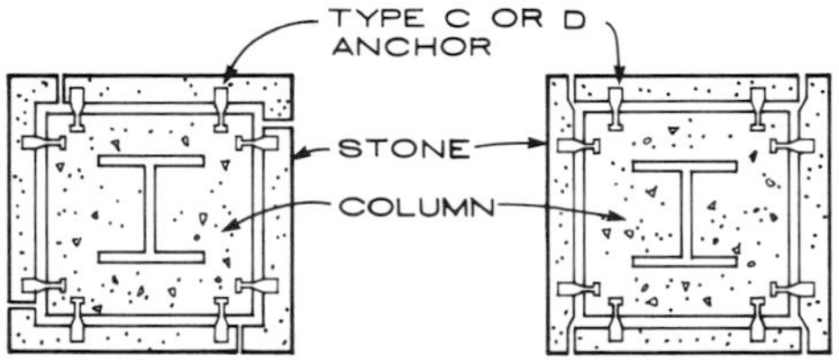

TYPE C OR D ANCHOR

STONE

COLUMN

SQUARE COLUMNS

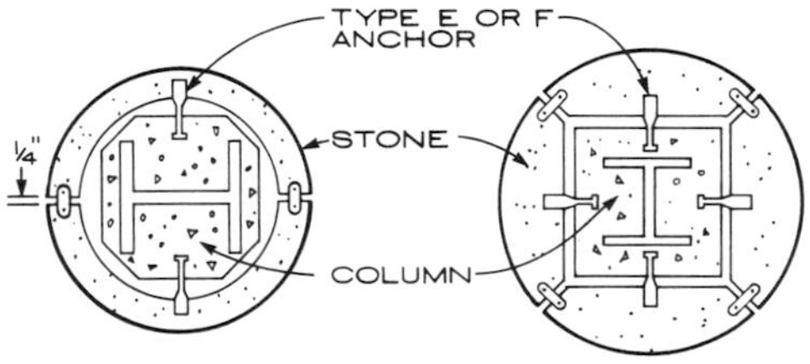

TYPE E OR F ANCHOR

1/4"

STONE

COLUMN

ROUND/QUADRANT COLUMNS

INSTALLATION DETAILS

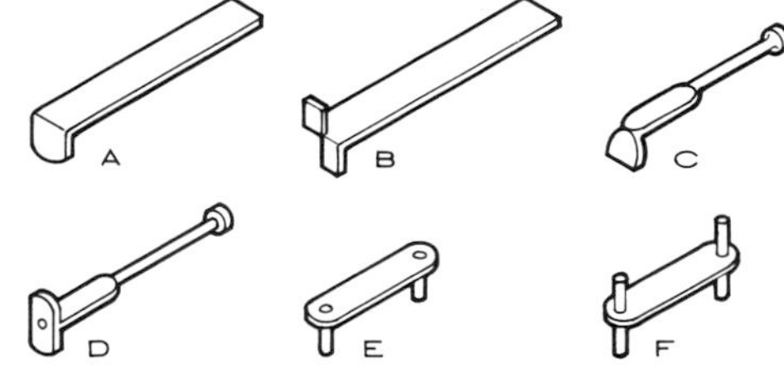
A
B
C
D
E
F

ANCHORS

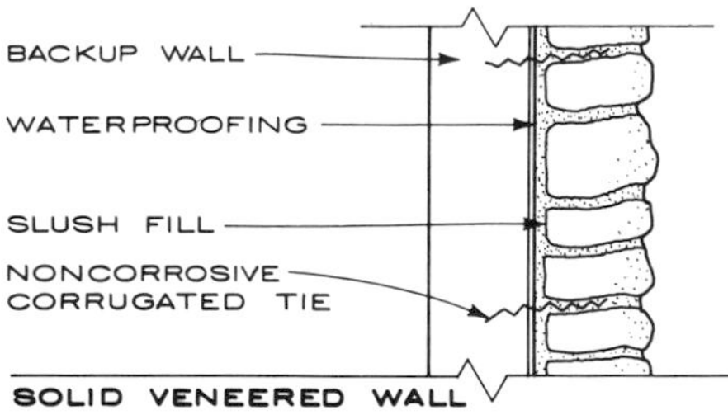

BACKUP WALL

WATERPROOFING

SLUSH FILL

NONCORROSIVE CORRUGATED TIE

SOLID VENEERED WALL

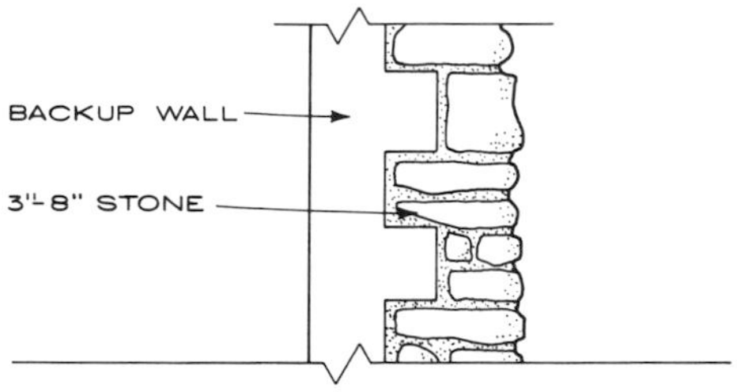

BACKUP WALL

3"-8" STONE

BONDED VENEERED WALL (TIES RECOMMENDED IN SOME CASES, E.G., LIMESTONE)

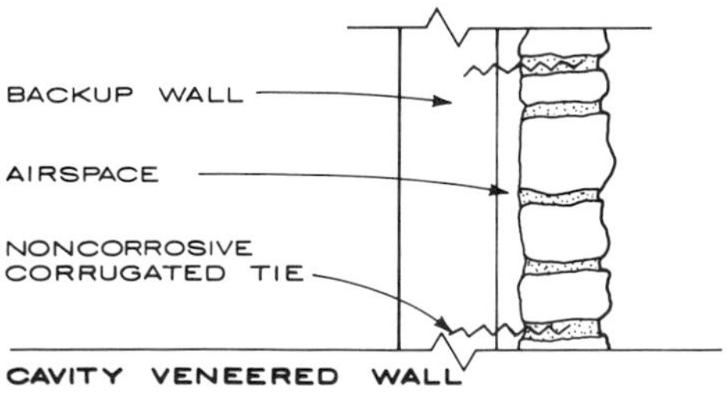

BACKUP WALL

AIRSPACE

NONCORROSIVE CORRUGATED TIE

CAVITY VENEERED WALL

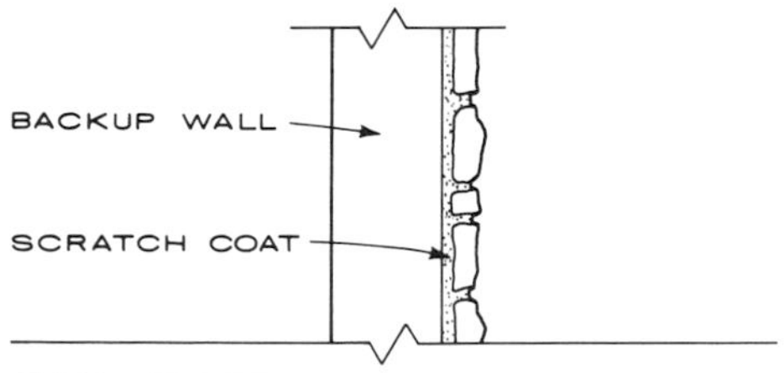

BACKUP WALL

SCRATCH COAT

THIN VENEERED WALL

TYPICAL WALL SECTIONS

NOTES

1. A course is a horizontal row of stone. Bond pattern is described by the horizontal arrangement of vertical joints. (See also Brickwork.) Structural bond refers to the physical tying together of load bearing and veneer portions of a composite wall. Structural bond can be accomplished with metal ties or with stone units set as headers into the backup.
2. Ashlar masonry is composed of squared-off building stone units of various sizes. Cut Ashlar is dressed to specific design dimensions at the mill. Ashlar is often used in random lengths and heights, with jointing worked out on the job.
3. All ties and anchors must be made of noncorrosive material. Chromium-nickel stainless steel types 302 and 304 and eraydo alloy zinc are the most resistant to corrosion and staining. Hot dipped galvanized is widely used, but is not as resistant, hence is prohibited by some building codes. Copper, brass, and bronze will stain under some conditions. Local building codes often govern the types of metal that may be used for stone anchors.
4. Nonstaining cement mortar should be used on porous and light colored stones. At all corners use extra ties and, when possible, larger stones. Joints are usually 1/2 to 1 1/2 in. for rough work and 3/8 to 3/4 in. for Ashlar.

Building Stone Institute; New York, New York
George M. Whiteside, III, AIA, and James D. Lloyd; Kennett Square, Pennsylvania
Alexander Keyes; Darrel Downing Rippeteau, Architect; Washington, D.C.

DOWELS
DRIP EDGE
FASCIA PANEL

COPING

BACKUP WALL
CLIP ANGLE WITH WELDED BAR TO RETAIN STONE
TWISTED STRAP
SELF-SUPPORTING STONE LINTEL

WINDOW HEAD

ROD ANCHOR
STONE VENEER
BACKUP WALL

WINDOWSILL

DOWEL
CLIP ANGLE

RELIEF ANGLE

CLIP ANGLE WITH WELDED BAR
HOOK ANCHOR

SOFFIT

SEALANT AND BACKER ROD
METAL ANCHOR

COLUMN ANCHOR

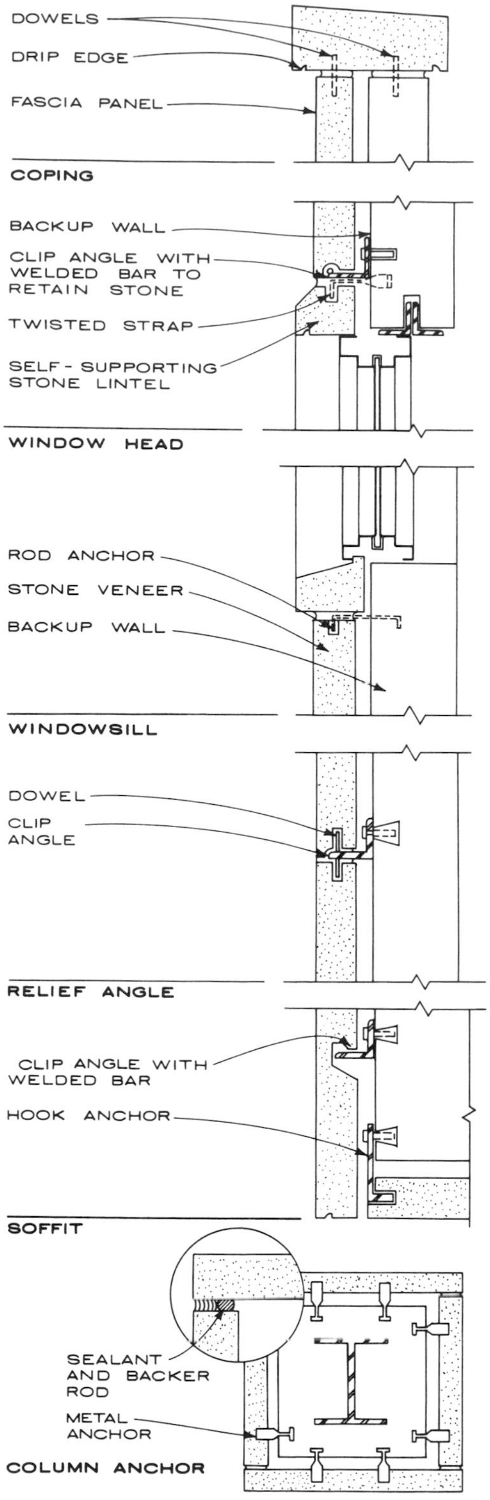

STONE VENEER ON CONCRETE WITH MASONRY BACKUP

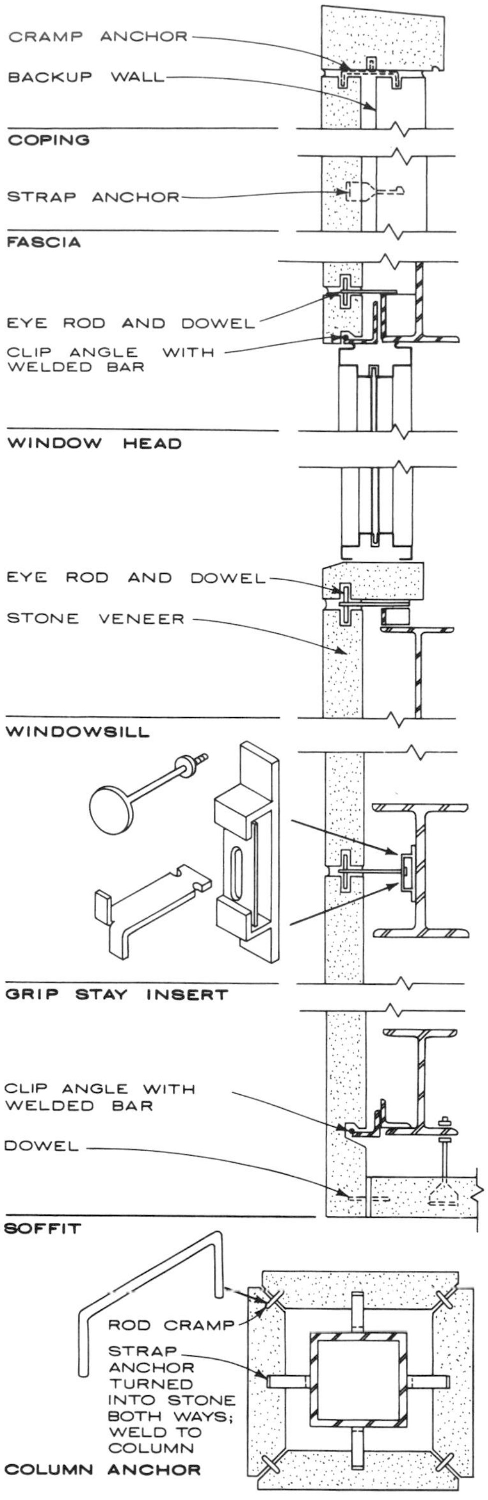

CRAMP ANCHOR
BACKUP WALL

COPING

STRAP ANCHOR

FASCIA

EYE ROD AND DOWEL
CLIP ANGLE WITH WELDED BAR

WINDOW HEAD

EYE ROD AND DOWEL
STONE VENEER

WINDOWSILL

GRIP STAY INSERT

CLIP ANGLE WITH WELDED BAR
DOWEL

SOFFIT

ROD CRAMP
STRAP ANCHOR TURNED INTO STONE BOTH WAYS; WELD TO COLUMN

COLUMN ANCHOR

STONE VENEER ON STEEL FRAME

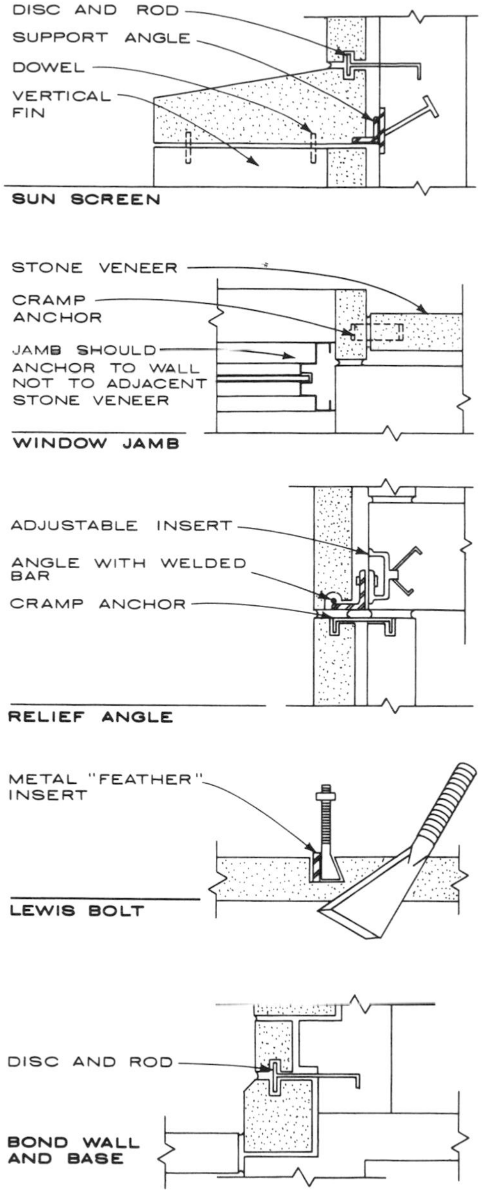

NOTES

1. Throughout this section, flashing, sealants, and other ancillary materials necessary for sound weatherproof construction sometimes have been omitted for clarity. See flashing and sealant details elsewhere.
2. Earlier editions of *Architectural Graphic Standards* give examples of classical molding details.
3. Allow for tolerances by including correct shimming to prevent installation fitting problems or performance failure.

DISC AND ROD
SUPPORT ANGLE
DOWEL
VERTICAL FIN

SUN SCREEN

STONE VENEER
CRAMP ANCHOR
JAMB SHOULD ANCHOR TO WALL NOT TO ADJACENT STONE VENEER

WINDOW JAMB

ADJUSTABLE INSERT
ANGLE WITH WELDED BAR
CRAMP ANCHOR

RELIEF ANGLE

METAL "FEATHER" INSERT

LEWIS BOLT

DISC AND ROD

BOND WALL AND BASE

STONE VENEER DETAILS; OPTIONS

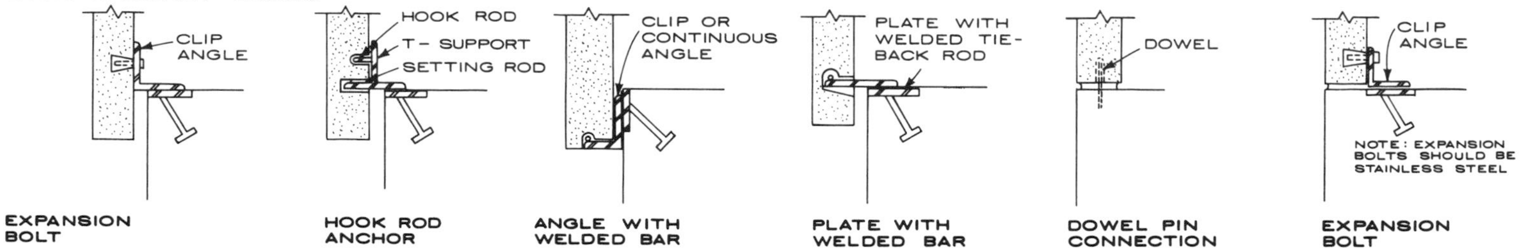

CLIP ANGLE

EXPANSION BOLT

HOOK ROD
T-SUPPORT
SETTING ROD

HOOK ROD ANCHOR

CLIP OR CONTINUOUS ANGLE

ANGLE WITH WELDED BAR

PLATE WITH WELDED TIE-BACK ROD

PLATE WITH WELDED BAR

DOWEL

DOWEL PIN CONNECTION

CLIP ANGLE

NOTE: EXPANSION BOLTS SHOULD BE STAINLESS STEEL

EXPANSION BOLT

BASE DETAILS

Building Stone Institute; New York, New York
George M. Whiteside, III, AIA, and James D. Lloyd; Kennett Square, Pennsylvania
Alexander Keyes; Darrel Downing Rippeteau, Architect; Washington, D.C.

STAINLESS STEEL DOWEL WITH HOOK ANCHOR
SEALANT AND FOAM ROD
SETTING BED
FLASHING
STONE VENEER

DOWEL CONNECTION
HORIZONTAL CONNECTION; DOWEL AND CRAMP
ANCHOR BOLT

COPINGS

ANCHOR DIMENSIONS

Standard flat stock anchors are made from strap 1 in. and 1¼ in. wide by ⅛ in., 3/16 in., and ¼ in. thick. Lengths vary up to 6 in., 8 in., 10 in. and 12 in. standards. Dovetail anchors are usually 4¼ in. overall with 3½ in. projection from face of concrete. Bends are ¾ in., 1 in., and 1¼ in.

Round stock anchors are made from stock of any diameter; ¼ in. and ⅜ in. are most common for rods; ⅛ in. (#11 gauge) through 3/16 in. (#6 gauge) for wire anchors; and ¼ in. and ⅜ in. are most common for dowels. Dowel lengths are usually 2 in. to 6 in.

Refer to page on 3 in. stone veneer for additional anchorage information.

Allow for tolerances by including correct shimming to prevent installation fitting problems or performance failure.

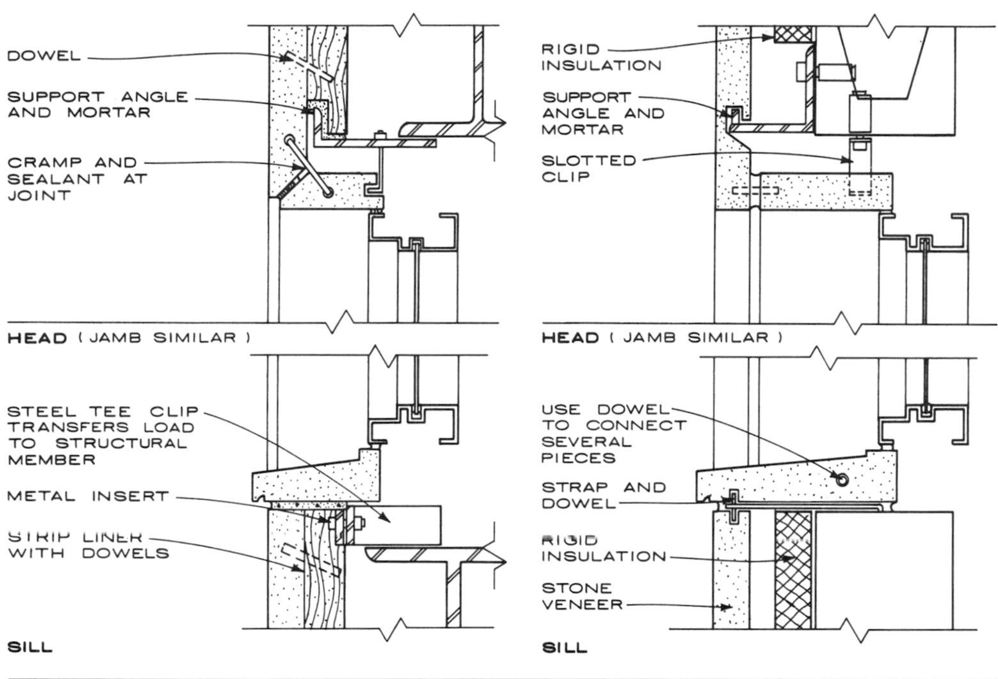
DOWEL
SUPPORT ANGLE AND MORTAR
CRAMP AND SEALANT AT JOINT
HEAD (JAMB SIMILAR)
RIGID INSULATION
SUPPORT ANGLE AND MORTAR
SLOTTED CLIP
HEAD (JAMB SIMILAR)
STEEL TEE CLIP TRANSFERS LOAD TO STRUCTURAL MEMBER
METAL INSERT
STRIP LINER WITH DOWELS
SILL
USE DOWEL TO CONNECT SEVERAL PIECES
STRAP AND DOWEL
RIGID INSULATION
STONE VENEER
SILL

WINDOW DETAILS

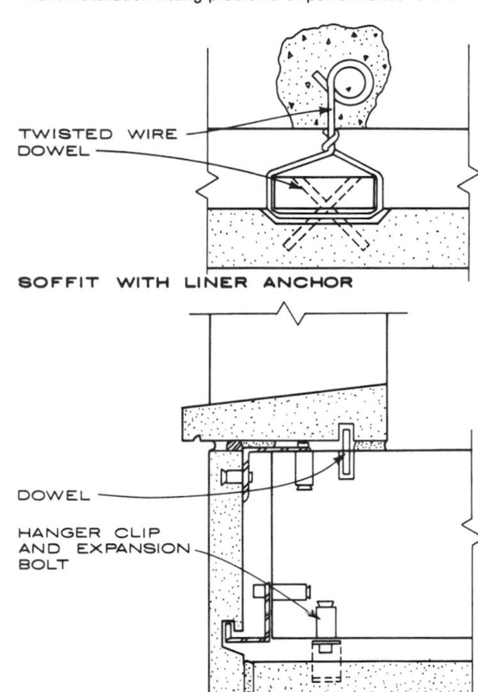
TWISTED WIRE DOWEL
SOFFIT WITH LINER ANCHOR
DOWEL
HANGER CLIP AND EXPANSION BOLT

SOFFIT AND SILL DETAIL

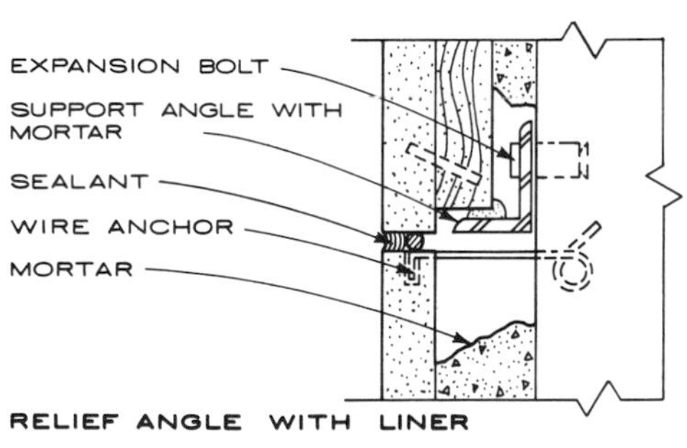
EXPANSION BOLT
SUPPORT ANGLE WITH MORTAR
SEALANT
WIRE ANCHOR
MORTAR

RELIEF ANGLE WITH LINER

EXPANSION BOLT
BAR WELDED TO ANGLE
SLOT ANCHOR
RIGID INSULATION

ANGLE SUPPORT WITH SHEAR RESISTANCE

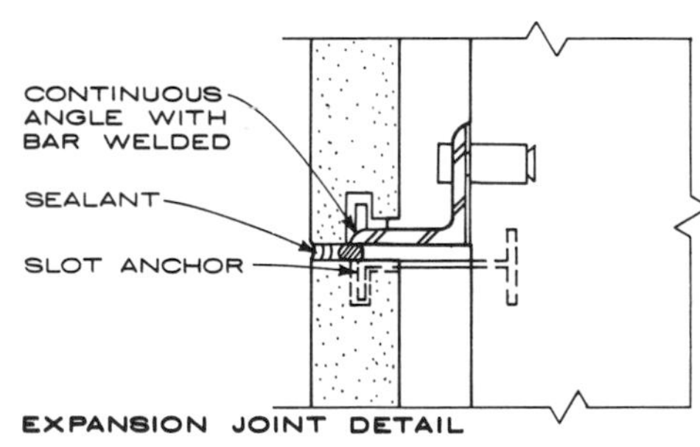
CONTINUOUS ANGLE WITH BAR WELDED
SEALANT
SLOT ANCHOR

EXPANSION JOINT DETAIL

RELIEF ANGLE SUPPORTS

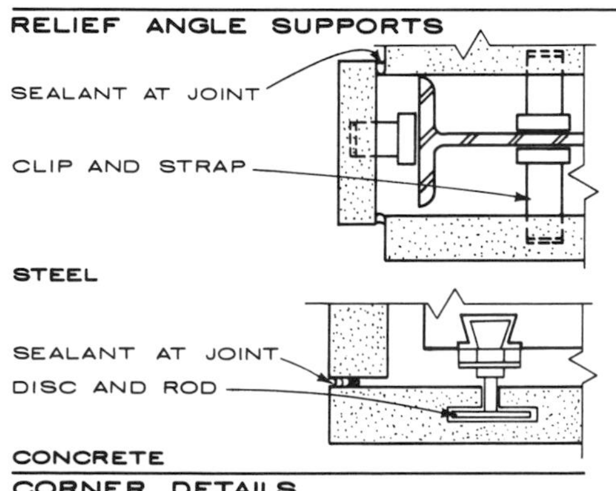
SEALANT AT JOINT
CLIP AND STRAP
STEEL
SEALANT AT JOINT
DISC AND ROD
CONCRETE

CORNER DETAILS

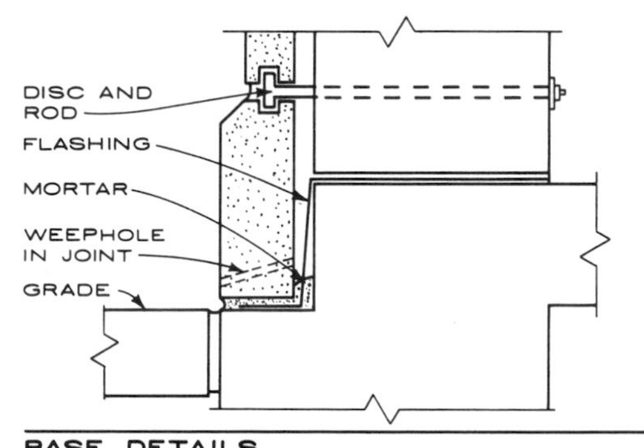
DISC AND ROD
FLASHING
MORTAR
WEEPHOLE IN JOINT
GRADE

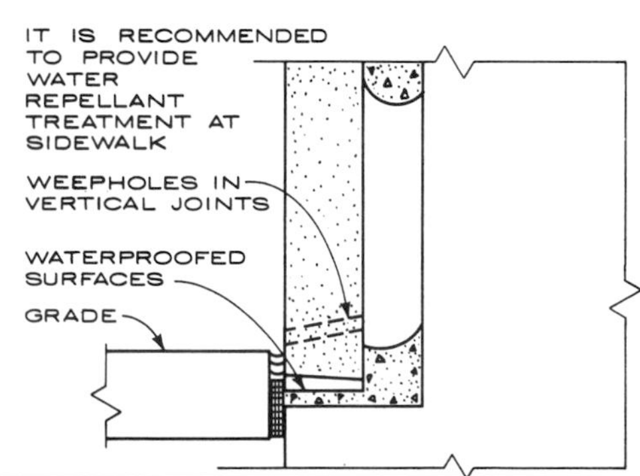
IT IS RECOMMENDED TO PROVIDE WATER REPELLANT TREATMENT AT SIDEWALK
WEEPHOLES IN VERTICAL JOINTS
WATERPROOFED SURFACES
GRADE

BASE DETAILS

Building Stone Institute; New York, New York
George M. Whiteside, III, AIA, and James D. Lloyd; Kennett Square, Pennsylvania
Alexander Keyes; Darrel Downing Rippeteau, Architect; Washington, D.C.

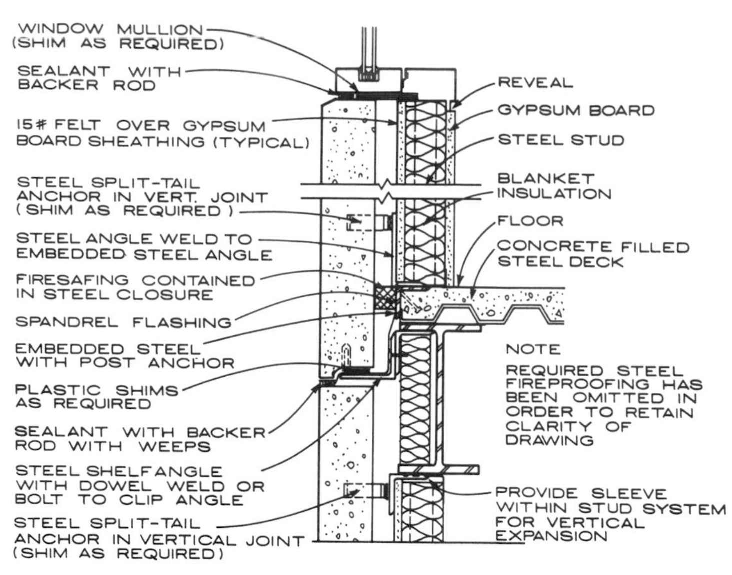
WINDOW MULLION (SHIM AS REQUIRED)
SEALANT WITH BACKER ROD
15# FELT OVER GYPSUM BOARD SHEATHING (TYPICAL)
STEEL SPLIT-TAIL ANCHOR IN VERT. JOINT (SHIM AS REQUIRED)
STEEL ANGLE WELD TO EMBEDDED STEEL ANGLE
FIRESAFING CONTAINED IN STEEL CLOSURE
SPANDREL FLASHING
EMBEDDED STEEL WITH POST ANCHOR
PLASTIC SHIMS AS REQUIRED
SEALANT WITH BACKER ROD WITH WEEPS
STEEL SHELF ANGLE WITH DOWEL WELD OR BOLT TO CLIP ANGLE
STEEL SPLIT-TAIL ANCHOR IN VERTICAL JOINT (SHIM AS REQUIRED)
REVEAL
GYPSUM BOARD
STEEL STUD
BLANKET INSULATION
FLOOR
CONCRETE FILLED STEEL DECK
NOTE
REQUIRED STEEL FIREPROOFING HAS BEEN OMITTED IN ORDER TO RETAIN CLARITY OF DRAWING
PROVIDE SLEEVE WITHIN STUD SYSTEM FOR VERTICAL EXPANSION

SECTION THROUGH HARD STONE PANEL AT WINDOW WALL

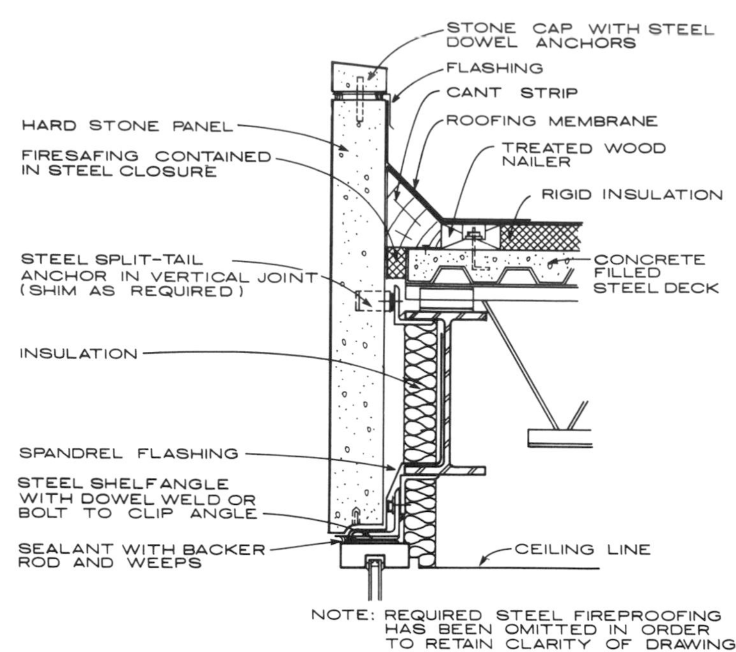
STONE CAP WITH STEEL DOWEL ANCHORS
FLASHING
CANT STRIP
ROOFING MEMBRANE
TREATED WOOD NAILER
RIGID INSULATION
HARD STONE PANEL
FIRESAFING CONTAINED IN STEEL CLOSURE
STEEL SPLIT-TAIL ANCHOR IN VERTICAL JOINT (SHIM AS REQUIRED)
CONCRETE FILLED STEEL DECK
INSULATION
SPANDREL FLASHING
STEEL SHELF ANGLE WITH DOWEL WELD OR BOLT TO CLIP ANGLE
SEALANT WITH BACKER ROD AND WEEPS
CEILING LINE
NOTE: REQUIRED STEEL FIREPROOFING HAS BEEN OMITTED IN ORDER TO RETAIN CLARITY OF DRAWING

SECTION THROUGH ROOF PARAPET AT HARD STONE PANEL

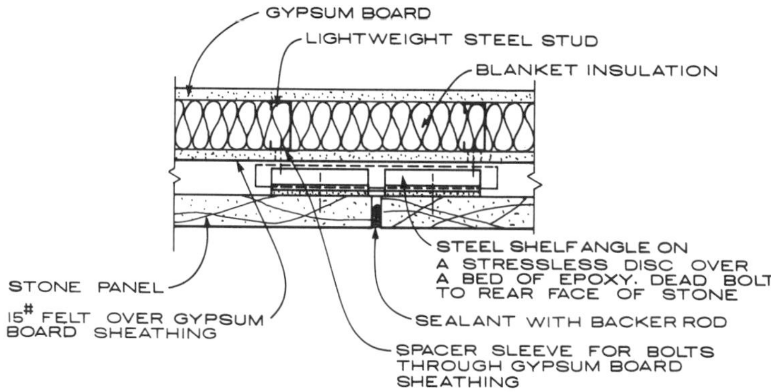
GYPSUM BOARD
LIGHTWEIGHT STEEL STUD
BLANKET INSULATION
STONE PANEL
15# FELT OVER GYPSUM BOARD SHEATHING
STEEL SHELF ANGLE ON A STRESSLESS DISC OVER A BED OF EPOXY. DEAD BOLT TO REAR FACE OF STONE
SEALANT WITH BACKER ROD
SPACER SLEEVE FOR BOLTS THROUGH GYPSUM BOARD SHEATHING

SECTION AT VERTICAL JOINT

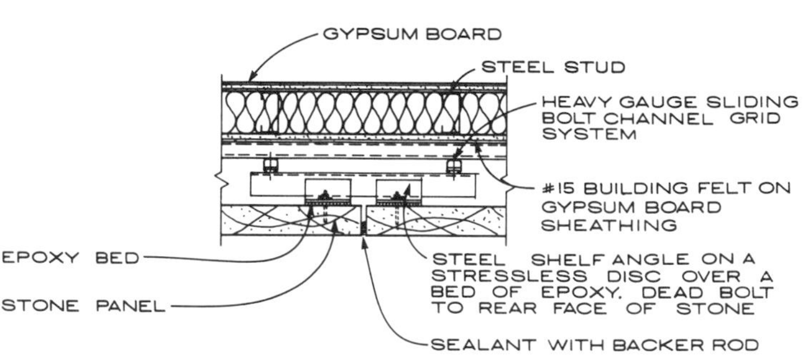
GYPSUM BOARD
STEEL STUD
HEAVY GAUGE SLIDING BOLT CHANNEL GRID SYSTEM
#15 BUILDING FELT ON GYPSUM BOARD SHEATHING
EPOXY BED
STONE PANEL
STEEL SHELF ANGLE ON A STRESSLESS DISC OVER A BED OF EPOXY. DEAD BOLT TO REAR FACE OF STONE
SEALANT WITH BACKER ROD

SECTION AT VERTICAL JOINT

NOTES

Use of the steel stud support system as shown requires an architect or engineer to develop adequate and realistic performance criteria, including thorough consideration of the long-term durability and corrosion resistance of light gauge members, mechanical fasteners, and other system components; provisions for adequate thermal movement; development of adequate system strength and stiffness; recognition of the structural interaction between the stone support system; and consideration of vapor retarders and flashing to control moisture migration. It also is important that adequate provisions be developed to ensure quality workmanship necessary to implement the system and to achieve the expected quality and durability.

The stone thickness depicted is a minimum of 1½ in. Thicker stone materials can use the same type of support system; however, engineering analyses of the system will be necessary to ensure proper performance and compliance with recommended design practices.

Design criteria for stone anchorage must include consideration of the particular stone's average as well as lowest strength values for safety, particularly at anchorage points. The proposed stone should be tested for adequate design properties and values. Stone anchorage size and location depend on establishing the particular stone's strength values, natural faults, and other properties; the stone's thickness and supported area; the expected lateral as well as gravity loading; and the amount of thermal movement to be accommodated.

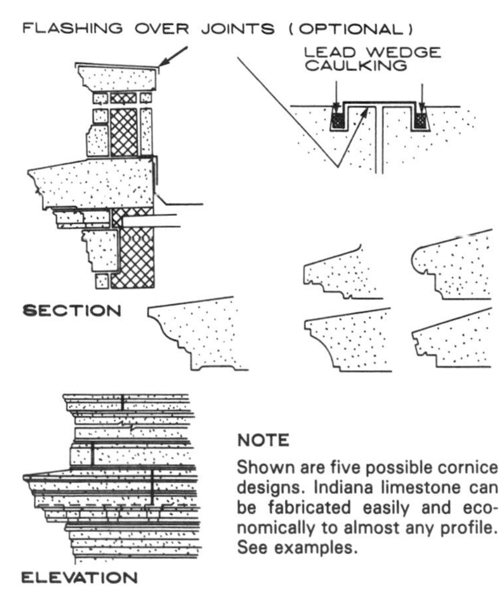
FLASHING OVER JOINTS (OPTIONAL)
LEAD WEDGE CAULKING
SECTION
ELEVATION

NOTE
Shown are five possible cornice designs. Indiana limestone can be fabricated easily and economically to almost any profile. See examples.

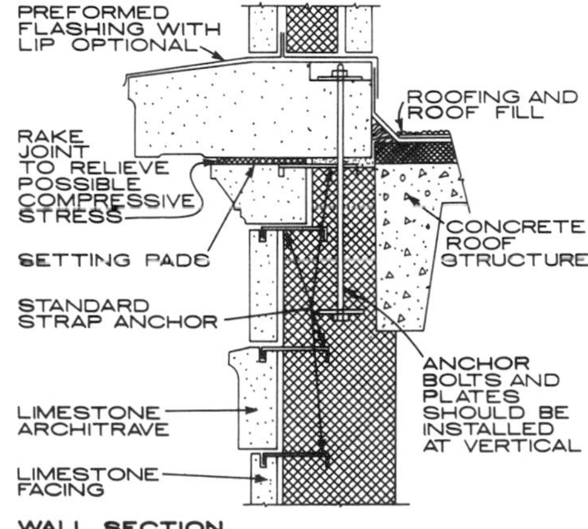
PREFORMED FLASHING WITH LIP OPTIONAL
ROOFING AND ROOF FILL
RAKE JOINT TO RELIEVE POSSIBLE COMPRESSIVE STRESS
SETTING PADS
CONCRETE ROOF STRUCTURE
STANDARD STRAP ANCHOR
ANCHOR BOLTS AND PLATES SHOULD BE INSTALLED AT VERTICAL
LIMESTONE ARCHITRAVE
LIMESTONE FACING

WALL SECTION

Shown here is the most common method of anchoring a cornice, which has a large enough projection to be unbalanced in the wall.

The bed joint immediately below the heavy cornice is open far enough back to remove any compressive stress that would have a tendency to break off stone below.

TRADITIONAL CORNICES

The Spector Group; North Hills, New York

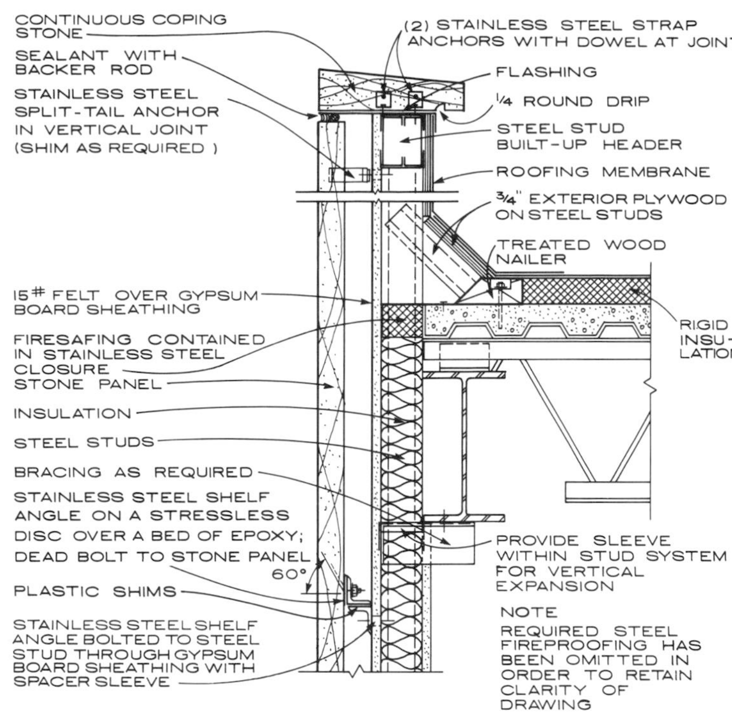
CONTINUOUS COPING STONE
SEALANT WITH BACKER ROD
STAINLESS STEEL SPLIT-TAIL ANCHOR IN VERTICAL JOINT (SHIM AS REQUIRED)
(2) STAINLESS STEEL STRAP ANCHORS WITH DOWEL AT JOINT
FLASHING
1/4 ROUND DRIP
STEEL STUD BUILT-UP HEADER
ROOFING MEMBRANE
3/4" EXTERIOR PLYWOOD ON STEEL STUDS
TREATED WOOD NAILER
15# FELT OVER GYPSUM BOARD SHEATHING
FIRESAFING CONTAINED IN STAINLESS STEEL CLOSURE
STONE PANEL
RIGID INSU-LATION
INSULATION
STEEL STUDS
BRACING AS REQUIRED
STAINLESS STEEL SHELF ANGLE ON A STRESSLESS DISC OVER A BED OF EPOXY; DEAD BOLT TO STONE PANEL
60°
PROVIDE SLEEVE WITHIN STUD SYSTEM FOR VERTICAL EXPANSION
PLASTIC SHIMS
STAINLESS STEEL SHELF ANGLE BOLTED TO STEEL STUD THROUGH GYPSUM BOARD SHEATHING WITH SPACER SLEEVE
NOTE
REQUIRED STEEL FIREPROOFING HAS BEEN OMITTED IN ORDER TO RETAIN CLARITY OF DRAWING

SECTION AT ROOF PARAPET AND WINDOWLESS WALL

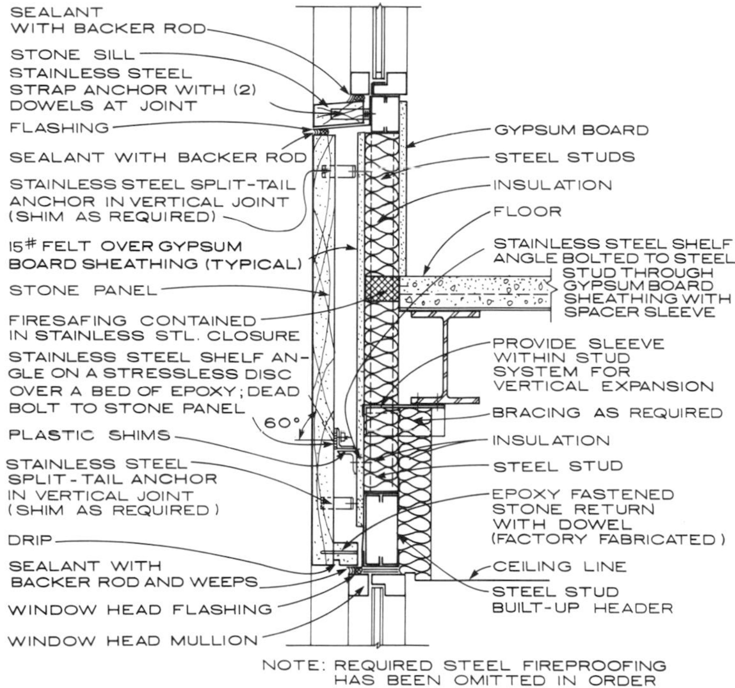
SEALANT WITH BACKER ROD
STONE SILL
STAINLESS STEEL STRAP ANCHOR WITH (2) DOWELS AT JOINT
FLASHING
GYPSUM BOARD
SEALANT WITH BACKER ROD
STEEL STUDS
STAINLESS STEEL SPLIT-TAIL ANCHOR IN VERTICAL JOINT (SHIM AS REQUIRED)
INSULATION
FLOOR
15# FELT OVER GYPSUM BOARD SHEATHING (TYPICAL)
STAINLESS STEEL SHELF ANGLE BOLTED TO STEEL STUD THROUGH GYPSUM BOARD SHEATHING WITH SPACER SLEEVE
STONE PANEL
FIRESAFING CONTAINED IN STAINLESS STL. CLOSURE
PROVIDE SLEEVE WITHIN STUD SYSTEM FOR VERTICAL EXPANSION
STAINLESS STEEL SHELF ANGLE ON A STRESSLESS DISC OVER A BED OF EPOXY; DEAD BOLT TO STONE PANEL
60°
BRACING AS REQUIRED
PLASTIC SHIMS
INSULATION
STAINLESS STEEL SPLIT-TAIL ANCHOR IN VERTICAL JOINT (SHIM AS REQUIRED)
STEEL STUD
EPOXY FASTENED STONE RETURN WITH DOWEL (FACTORY FABRICATED)
DRIP
SEALANT WITH BACKER ROD AND WEEPS
CEILING LINE
WINDOW HEAD FLASHING
STEEL STUD BUILT-UP HEADER
WINDOW HEAD MULLION
NOTE: REQUIRED STEEL FIREPROOFING HAS BEEN OMITTED IN ORDER TO RETAIN CLARITY OF DRAWING

STONE SPANDREL AT WINDOW HEAD AND SILL

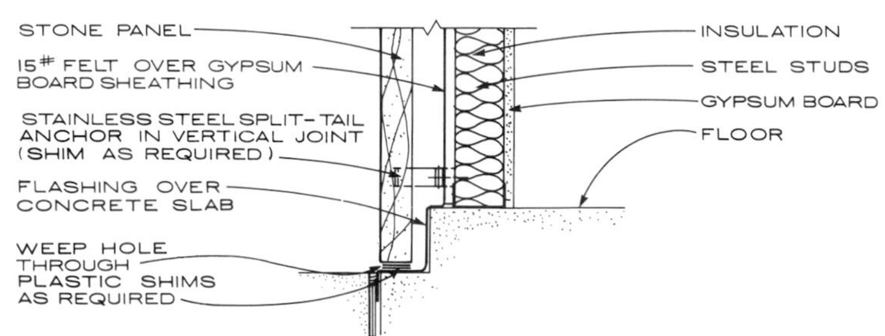
STONE PANEL
INSULATION
15# FELT OVER GYPSUM BOARD SHEATHING
STEEL STUDS
GYPSUM BOARD
STAINLESS STEEL SPLIT-TAIL ANCHOR IN VERTICAL JOINT (SHIM AS REQUIRED)
FLOOR
FLASHING OVER CONCRETE SLAB
WEEP HOLE THROUGH PLASTIC SHIMS AS REQUIRED

STONE SPANDREL AT GRADE

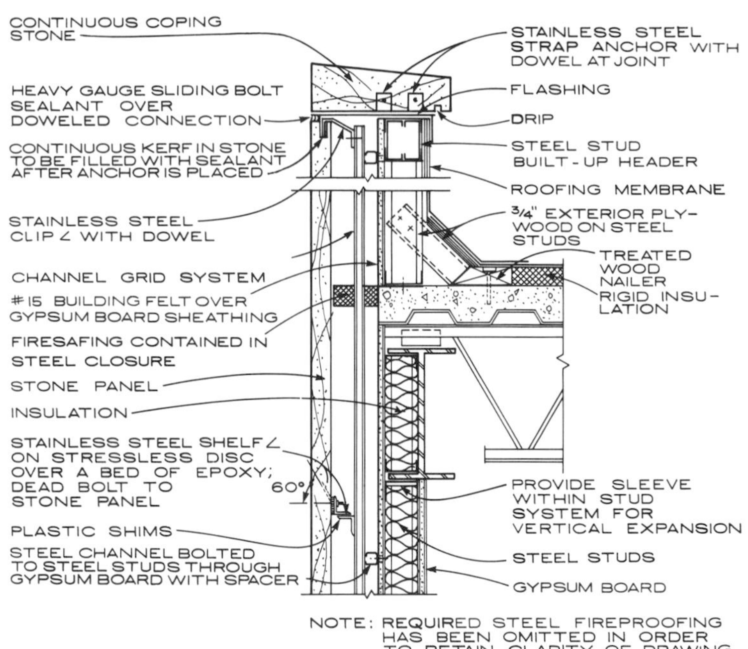
CONTINUOUS COPING STONE
STAINLESS STEEL STRAP ANCHOR WITH DOWEL AT JOINT
FLASHING
HEAVY GAUGE SLIDING BOLT SEALANT OVER DOWELED CONNECTION
DRIP
CONTINUOUS KERF IN STONE TO BE FILLED WITH SEALANT AFTER ANCHOR IS PLACED
STEEL STUD BUILT-UP HEADER
ROOFING MEMBRANE
STAINLESS STEEL CLIP ∠ WITH DOWEL
3/4" EXTERIOR PLY-WOOD ON STEEL STUDS
TREATED WOOD NAILER
CHANNEL GRID SYSTEM
RIGID INSU-LATION
#15 BUILDING FELT OVER GYPSUM BOARD SHEATHING
FIRESAFING CONTAINED IN STEEL CLOSURE
STONE PANEL
INSULATION
STAINLESS STEEL SHELF ∠ ON STRESSLESS DISC OVER A BED OF EPOXY; DEAD BOLT TO STONE PANEL
60°
PROVIDE SLEEVE WITHIN STUD SYSTEM FOR VERTICAL EXPANSION
PLASTIC SHIMS
STEEL STUDS
STEEL CHANNEL BOLTED TO STEEL STUDS THROUGH GYPSUM BOARD WITH SPACER
GYPSUM BOARD
NOTE: REQUIRED STEEL FIREPROOFING HAS BEEN OMITTED IN ORDER TO RETAIN CLARITY OF DRAWING

SECTION AT ROOF PARAPET AND WINDOWLESS WALL

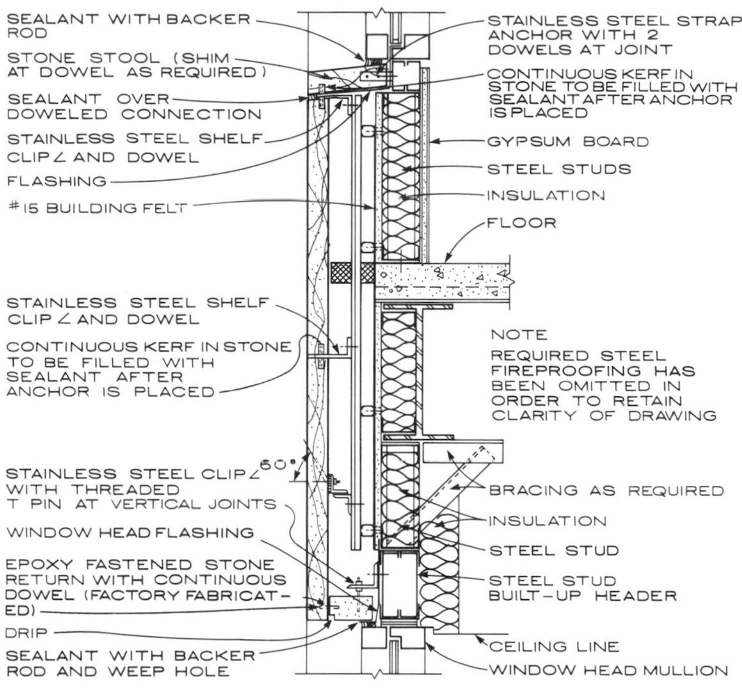
SEALANT WITH BACKER ROD
STAINLESS STEEL STRAP ANCHOR WITH 2 DOWELS AT JOINT
STONE STOOL (SHIM AT DOWEL AS REQUIRED)
CONTINUOUS KERF IN STONE TO BE FILLED WITH SEALANT AFTER ANCHOR IS PLACED
SEALANT OVER DOWELED CONNECTION
STAINLESS STEEL SHELF CLIP ∠ AND DOWEL
GYPSUM BOARD
FLASHING
STEEL STUDS
#15 BUILDING FELT
INSULATION
FLOOR
STAINLESS STEEL SHELF CLIP ∠ AND DOWEL
NOTE
CONTINUOUS KERF IN STONE TO BE FILLED WITH SEALANT AFTER ANCHOR IS PLACED
REQUIRED STEEL FIREPROOFING HAS BEEN OMITTED IN ORDER TO RETAIN CLARITY OF DRAWING
STAINLESS STEEL CLIP ∠ 60° WITH THREADED T PIN AT VERTICAL JOINTS
BRACING AS REQUIRED
INSULATION
WINDOW HEAD FLASHING
STEEL STUD
EPOXY FASTENED STONE RETURN WITH CONTINUOUS DOWEL (FACTORY FABRICAT-ED)
STEEL STUD BUILT-UP HEADER
DRIP
CEILING LINE
SEALANT WITH BACKER ROD AND WEEP HOLE
WINDOW HEAD MULLION

STONE SPANDREL AT WINDOW HEAD AND SILL

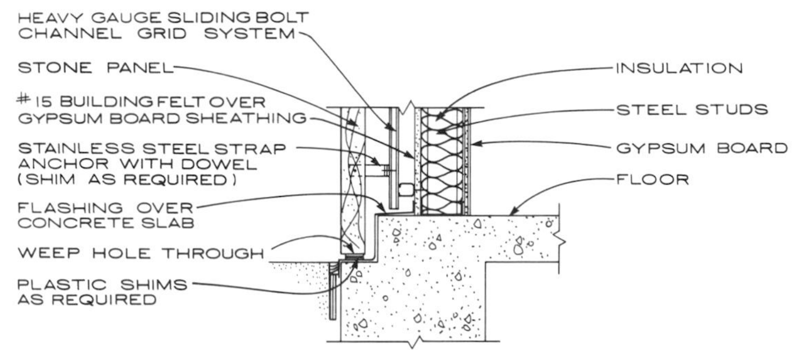
HEAVY GAUGE SLIDING BOLT CHANNEL GRID SYSTEM
STONE PANEL
INSULATION
#15 BUILDING FELT OVER GYPSUM BOARD SHEATHING
STEEL STUDS
STAINLESS STEEL STRAP ANCHOR WITH DOWEL (SHIM AS REQUIRED)
GYPSUM BOARD
FLOOR
FLASHING OVER CONCRETE SLAB
WEEP HOLE THROUGH
PLASTIC SHIMS AS REQUIRED

STONE SPANDREL AT GRADE

The Spector Group; North Hills, New York

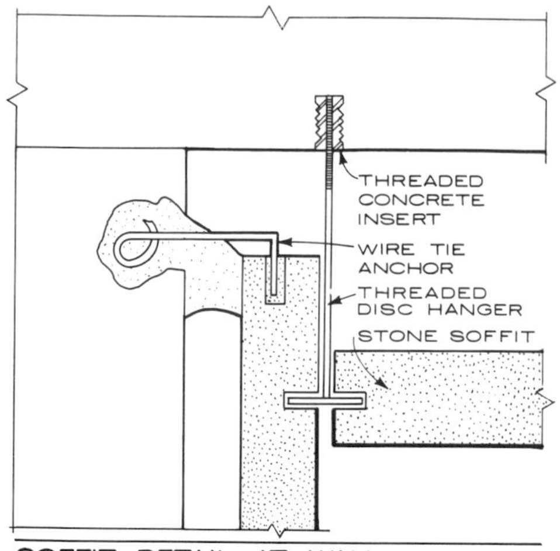

THREADED CONCRETE INSERT
WIRE TIE ANCHOR
THREADED DISC HANGER
STONE SOFFIT

SOFFIT DETAIL AT WALL

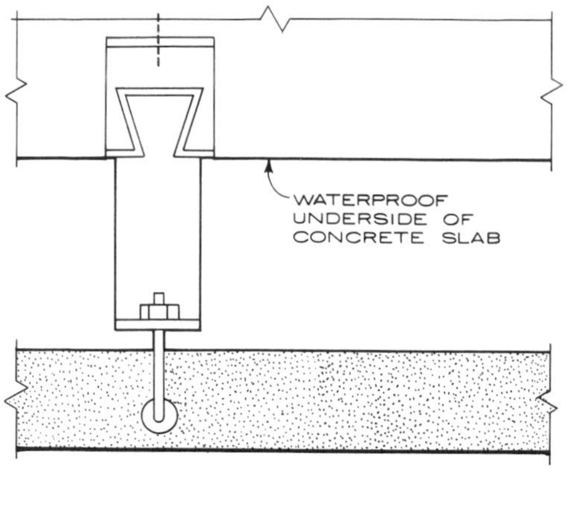

MORTAR
WIRE TIES
SEALANT
NOTE: WIRE ANCHORS CAN BE TIED AROUND A DOWEL INSERTED VERTICALLY INTO STONE

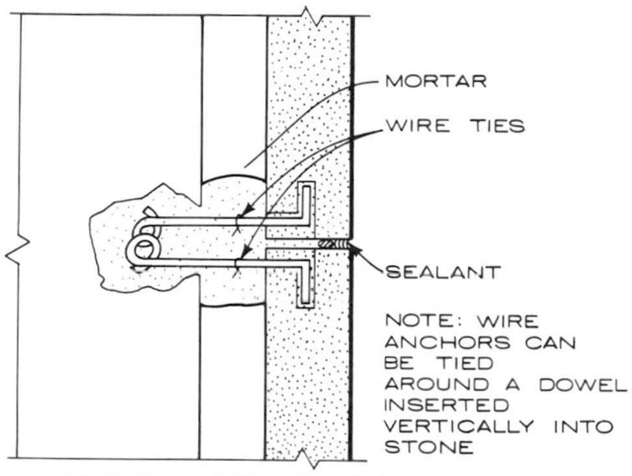

VERTICAL JOINT DETAIL - PLAN

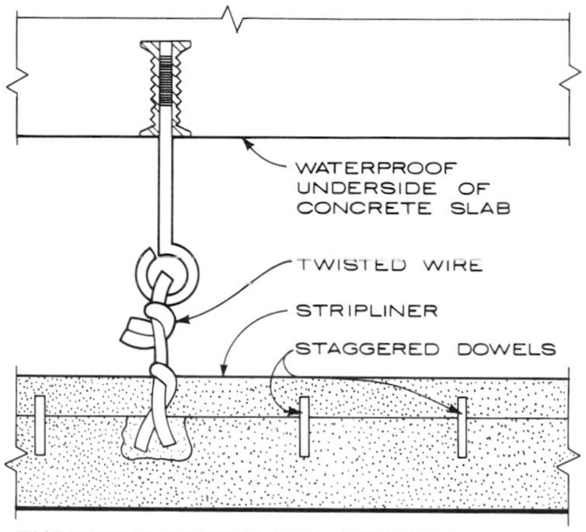

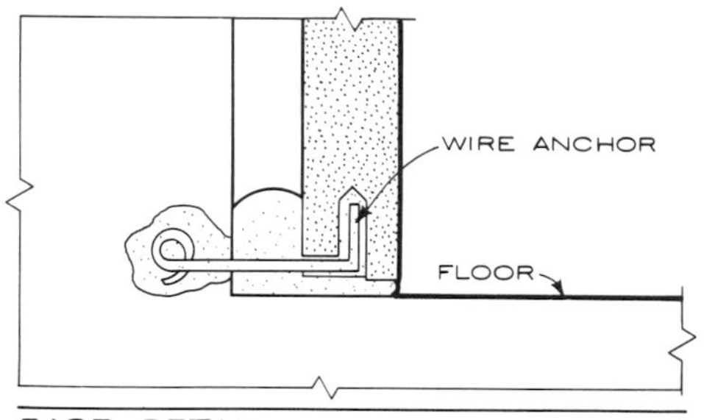

WIRE ANCHOR
FLOOR

BASE DETAIL

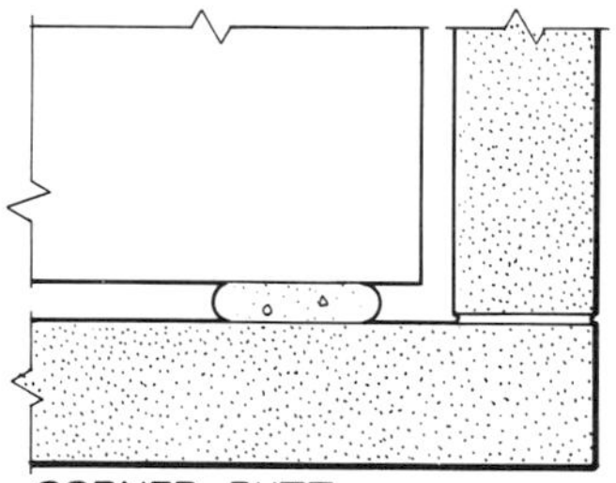

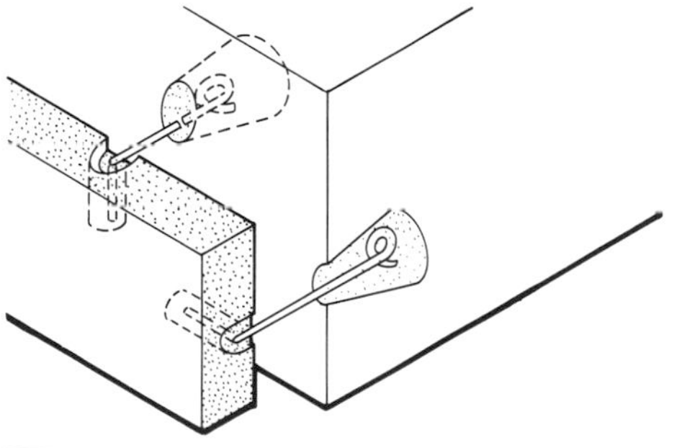

SIMPLE WIRE ANCHOR CONNECTION

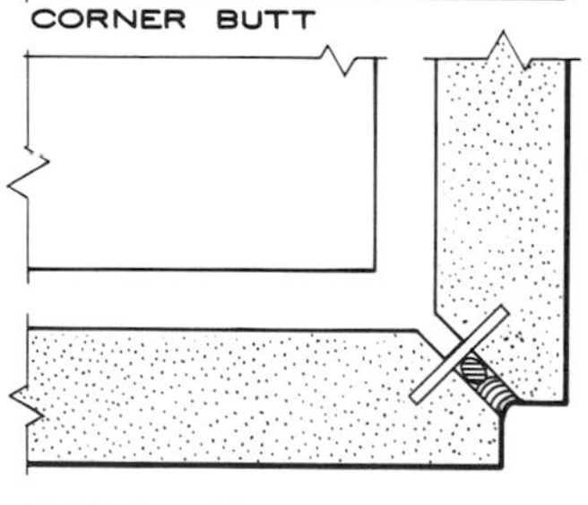

WIRE TIE
PLASTER SPOTS
2 X 2 BLOCKING
WOOD STUD
GYPSUM DRYWALL

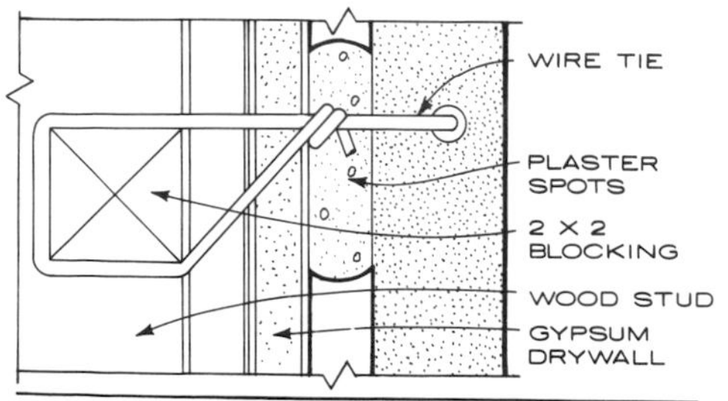

STONE PANEL ON WOOD STUDS

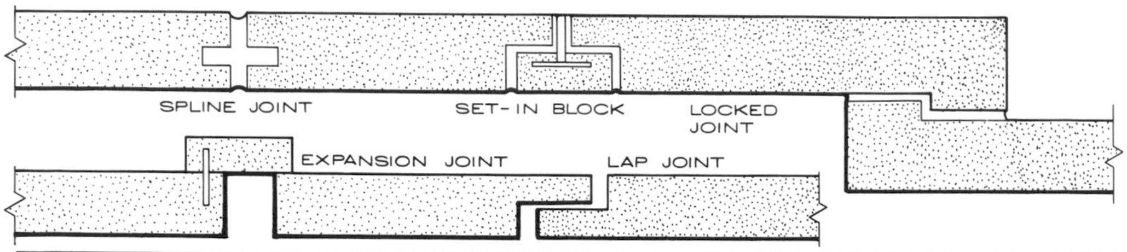

WATERPROOF UNDERSIDE OF CONCRETE SLAB

DOVETAIL STRAP WITH HOOK ROD ANCHOR

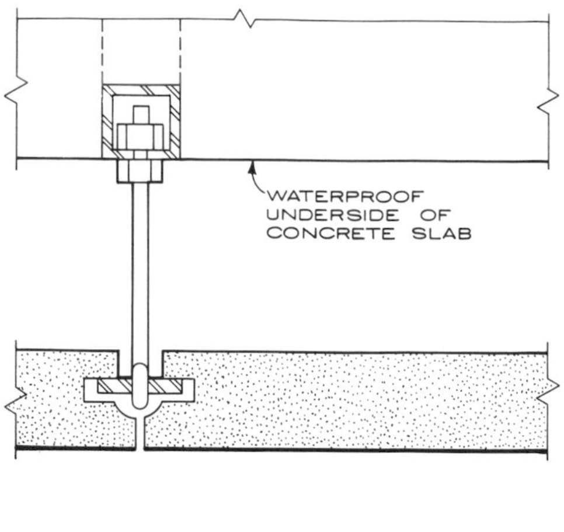

WATERPROOF UNDERSIDE OF CONCRETE SLAB

EYEBOLT AND DOWEL BOLTED TO THREADED CONCRETE INSERT

WATERPROOF UNDERSIDE OF CONCRETE SLAB
TWISTED WIRE
STRIPLINER
STAGGERED DOWELS

THREADED INSERT AND EYEBOLT

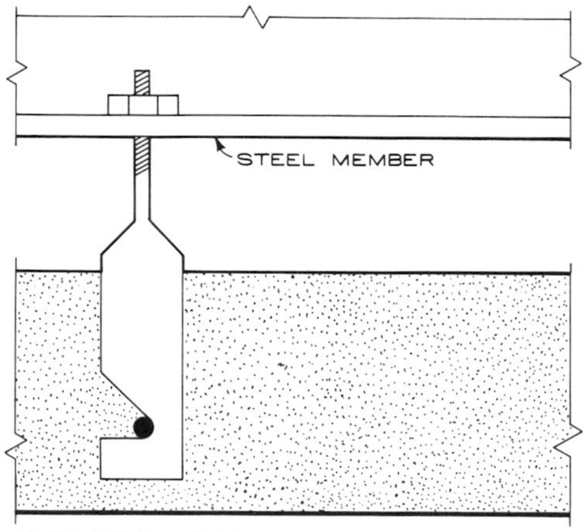

STEEL MEMBER

FLAT HOOK ANCHOR AND DOWEL

TYPICAL SYSTEMS FOR HANGING INTERIOR VENEER STONE

CORNER BUTT

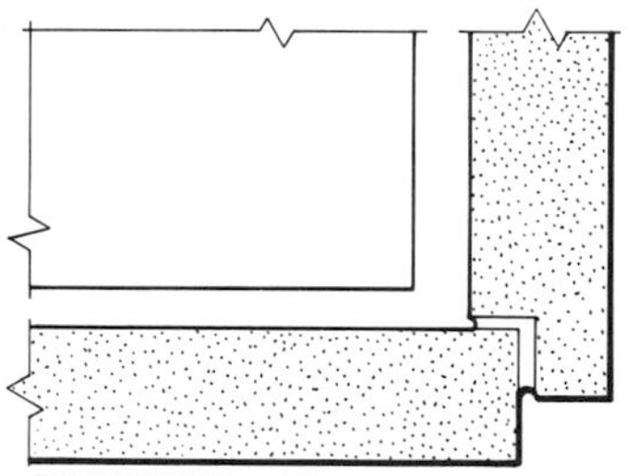

RABBETED CORNER

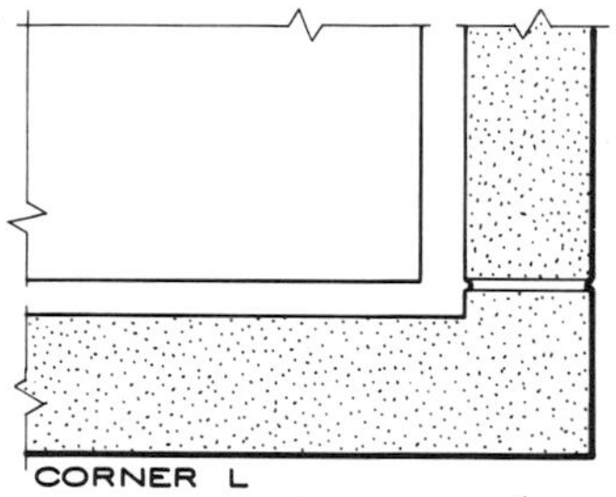

CORNER L

QUIRK MITER

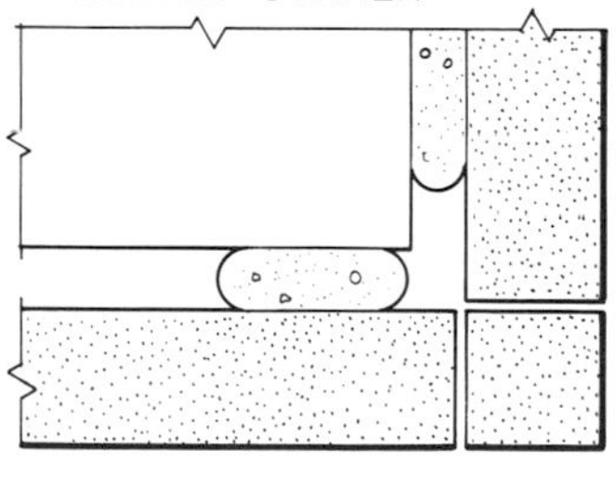

CORNER BLOCK

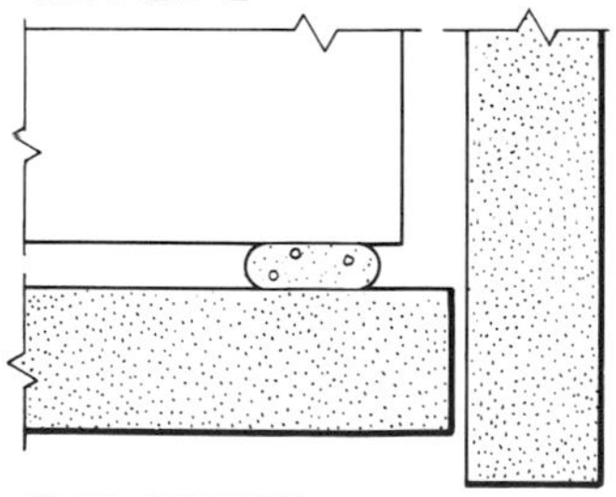

SLIP CORNER

TYPICAL CORNER DETAILS

SPLINE JOINT
SET-IN BLOCK
LOCKED JOINT
EXPANSION JOINT
LAP JOINT

TYPICAL HORIZONTAL JOINTS

Building Stone Institute; New York, New York
George M. Whiteside, III, AIA, and James D. Lloyd; Kennett Square, Pennsylvania
Alexander Keyes; Darrel Downing Rippeteau, Architect; Washington, D.C.

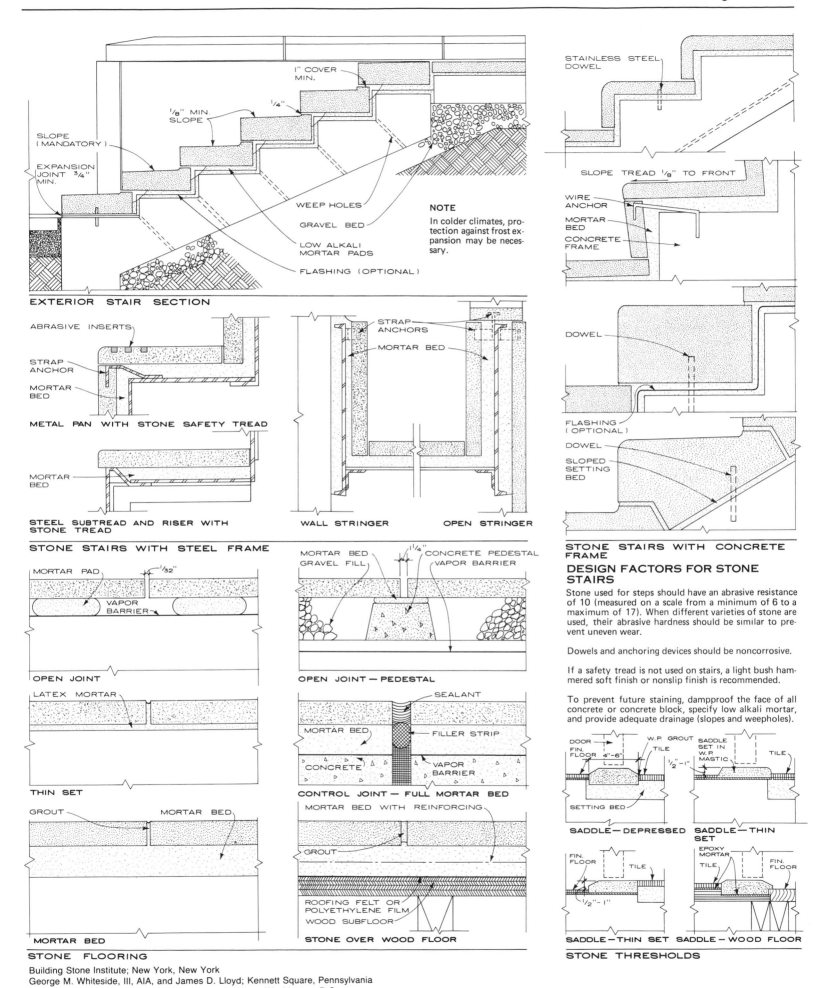

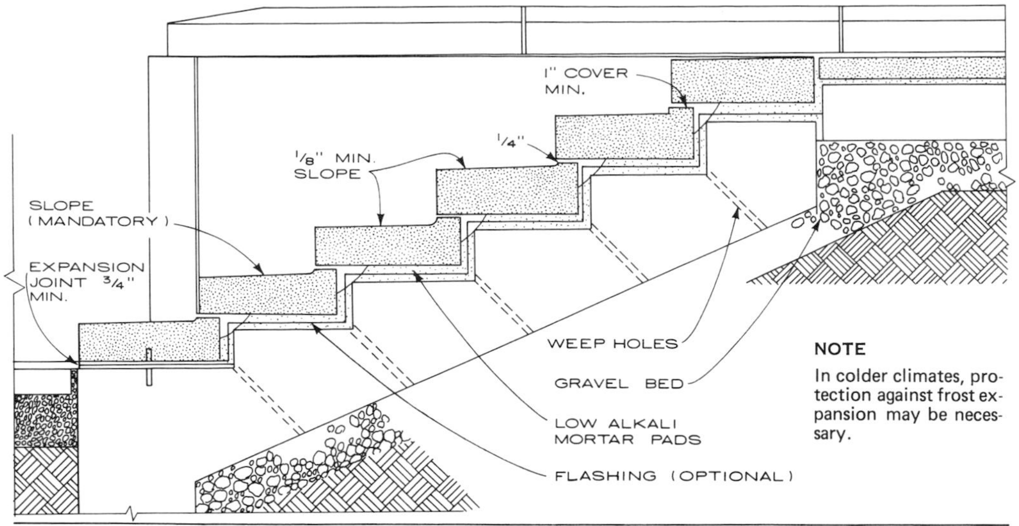

1" COVER MIN.
1/4"
1/8" MIN. SLOPE
SLOPE (MANDATORY)
EXPANSION JOINT 3/4" MIN.
WEEP HOLES
GRAVEL BED
LOW ALKALI MORTAR PADS
FLASHING (OPTIONAL)

NOTE

In colder climates, protection against frost expansion may be necessary.

EXTERIOR STAIR SECTION

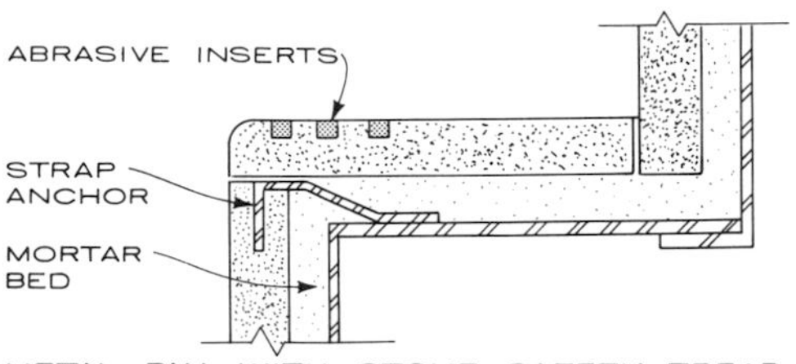

ABRASIVE INSERTS
STRAP ANCHOR
MORTAR BED

METAL PAN WITH STONE SAFETY TREAD

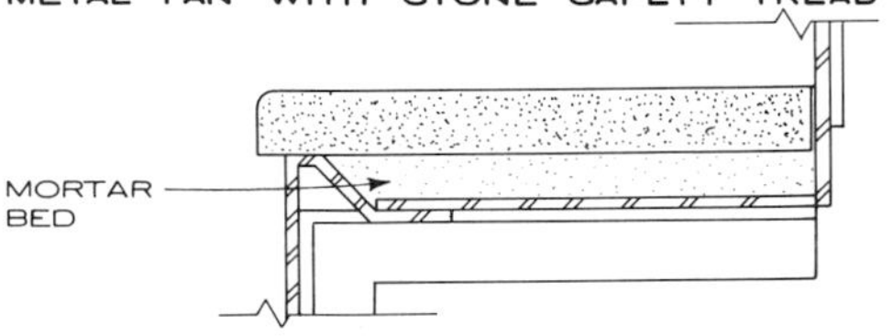

MORTAR BED

STEEL SUBTREAD AND RISER WITH STONE TREAD

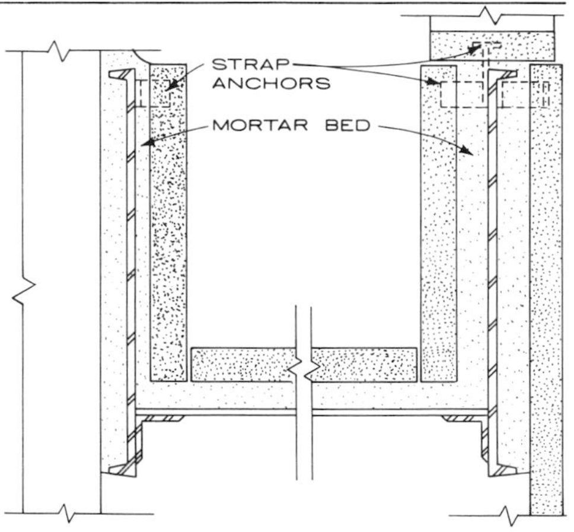

STRAP ANCHORS
MORTAR BED

WALL STRINGER

OPEN STRINGER

STONE STAIRS WITH STEEL FRAME

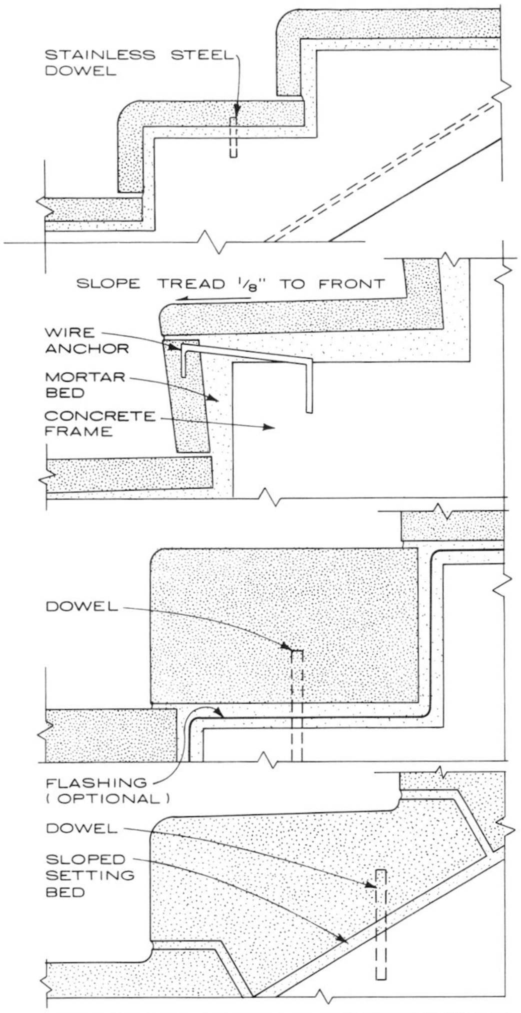

STAINLESS STEEL DOWEL
SLOPE TREAD 1/8" TO FRONT
WIRE ANCHOR
MORTAR BED
CONCRETE FRAME
DOWEL
FLASHING (OPTIONAL)
DOWEL
SLOPED SETTING BED

STONE STAIRS WITH CONCRETE FRAME

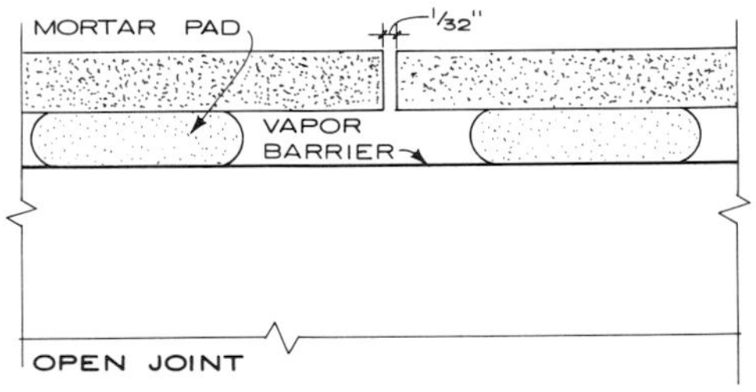

MORTAR PAD
1/32"
VAPOR BARRIER

OPEN JOINT

MORTAR BED
GRAVEL FILL
1 1/4"
CONCRETE PEDESTAL
VAPOR BARRIER

OPEN JOINT — PEDESTAL

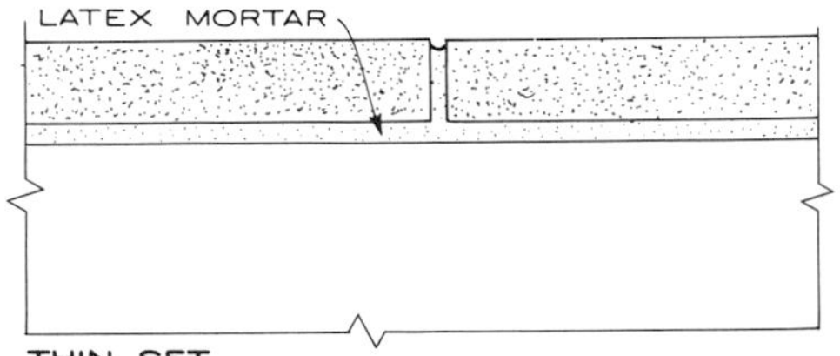

LATEX MORTAR

THIN SET

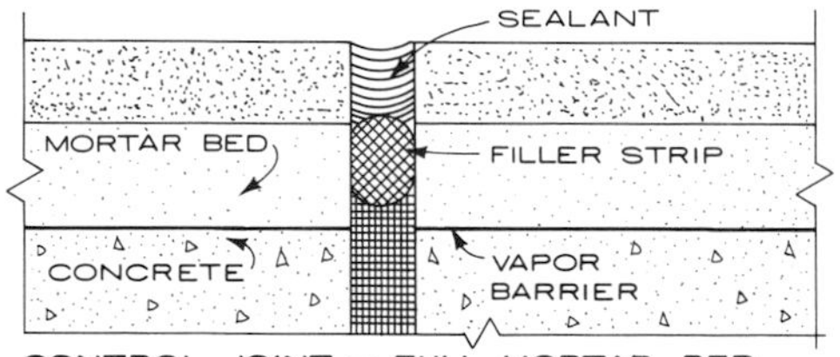

SEALANT
MORTAR BED
FILLER STRIP
CONCRETE
VAPOR BARRIER

CONTROL JOINT — FULL MORTAR BED

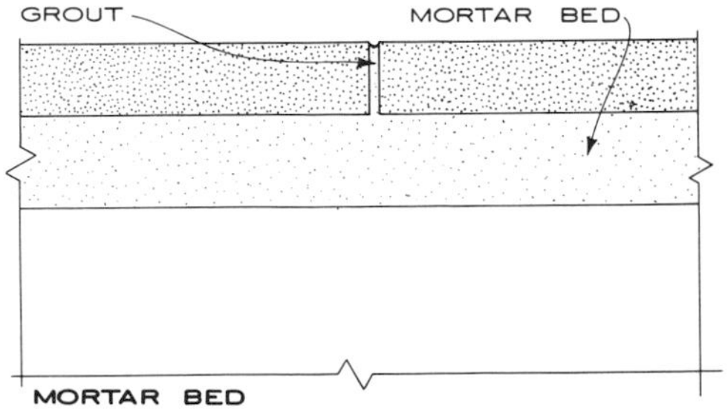

GROUT
MORTAR BED

MORTAR BED

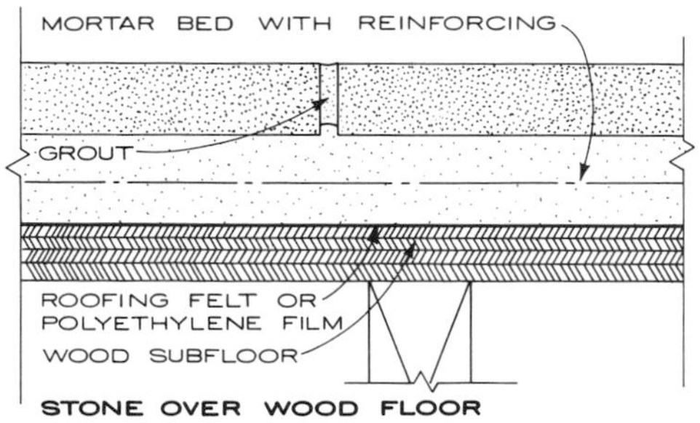

MORTAR BED WITH REINFORCING
GROUT
ROOFING FELT OR POLYETHYLENE FILM
WOOD SUBFLOOR

STONE OVER WOOD FLOOR

STONE FLOORING

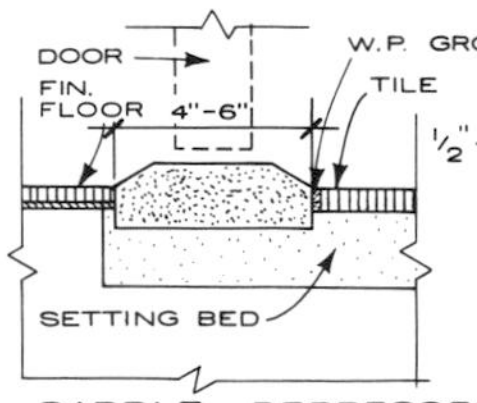

DESIGN FACTORS FOR STONE STAIRS

Stone used for steps should have an abrasive resistance of 10 (measured on a scale from a minimum of 6 to a maximum of 17). When different varieties of stone are used, their abrasive hardness should be similar to prevent uneven wear.

Dowels and anchoring devices should be noncorrosive.

If a safety tread is not used on stairs, a light bush hammered soft finish or nonslip finish is recommended.

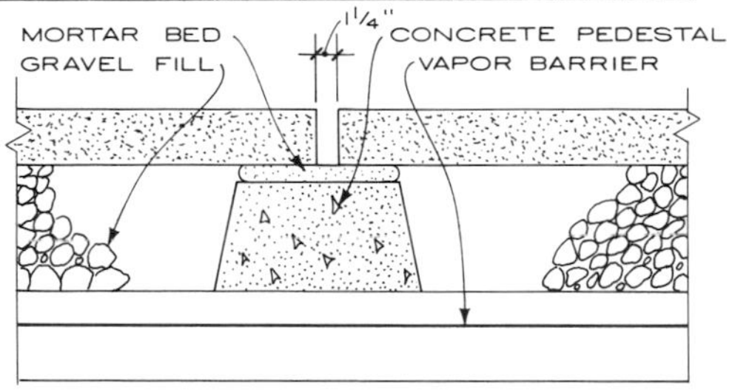

To prevent future staining, dampproof the face of all concrete or concrete block, specify low alkali mortar, and provide adequate drainage (slopes and weepholes).

DOOR
FIN. FLOOR
4"–6"
W.P. GROUT
TILE
1/2"–1"
SETTING BED

SADDLE—DEPRESSED

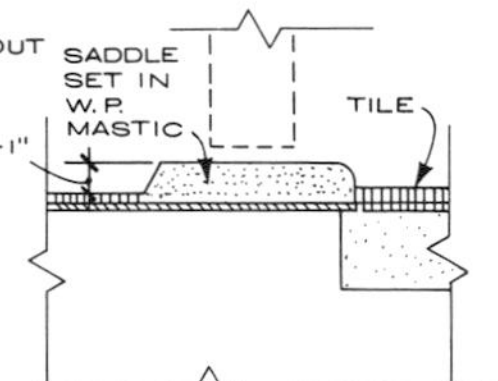

SADDLE SET IN W.P. MASTIC
TILE

SADDLE—THIN SET

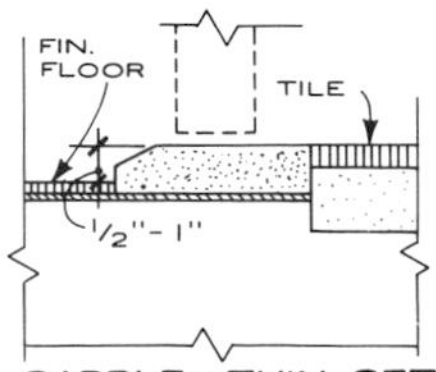

FIN. FLOOR
TILE
1/2"–1"

SADDLE—THIN SET

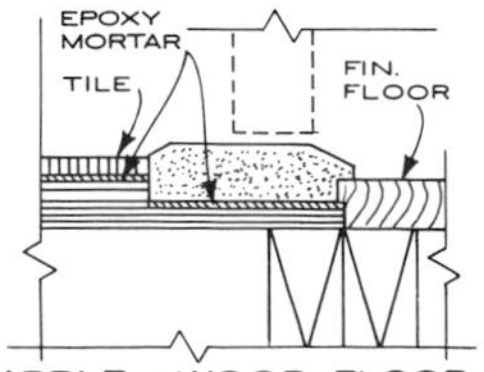

EPOXY MORTAR
TILE
FIN. FLOOR

SADDLE — WOOD FLOOR

STONE THRESHOLDS

Building Stone Institute; New York, New York
George M. Whiteside, III, AIA, and James D. Lloyd; Kennett Square, Pennsylvania
Alexander Keyes; Darrel Downing Rippeteau, Architect; Washington, D.C.

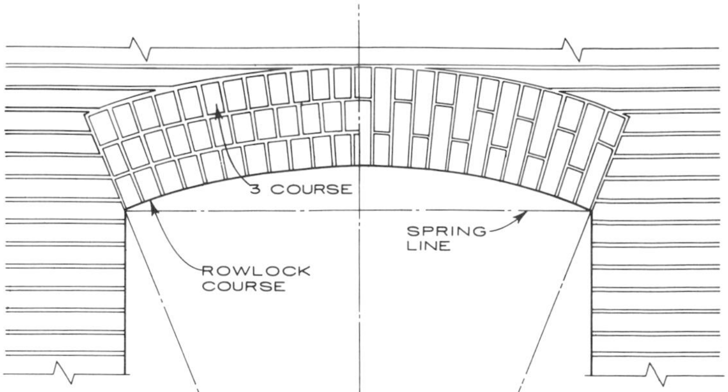

3 COURSE

SPRING LINE

ROWLOCK COURSE

SEGMENTAL

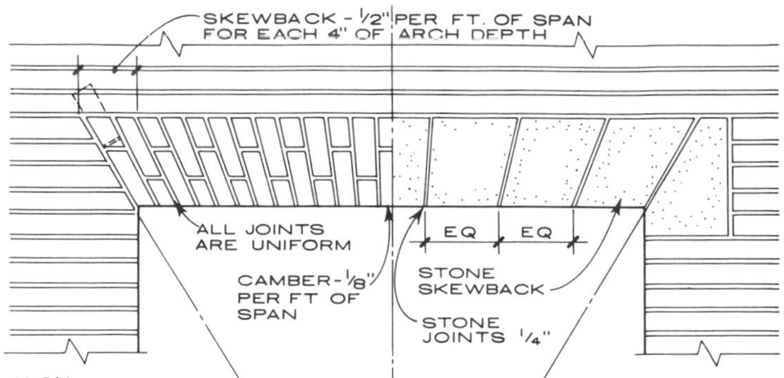

SKEWBACK - 1/2" PER FT. OF SPAN FOR EACH 4" OF ARCH DEPTH

ALL JOINTS ARE UNIFORM

EQ EQ

CAMBER - 1/8" PER FT OF SPAN

STONE SKEWBACK

STONE JOINTS 1/4"

JACK

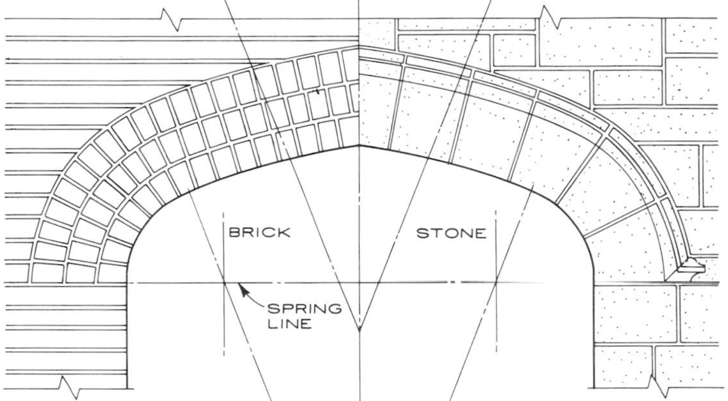

BRICK

STONE

SPRING LINE

TUDOR

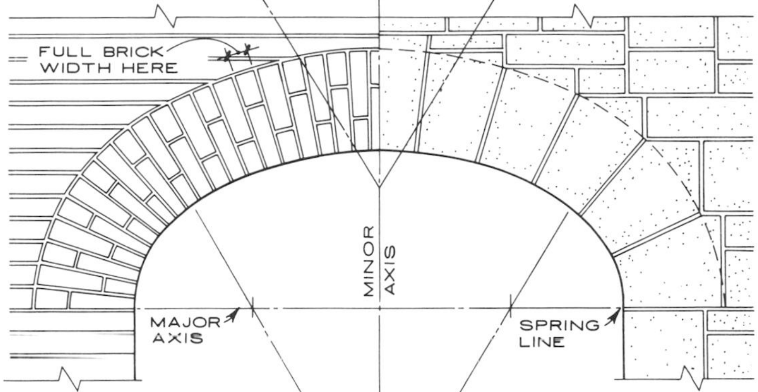

FULL BRICK WIDTH HERE

MINOR AXIS

MAJOR AXIS

SPRING LINE

ELLIPTICAL

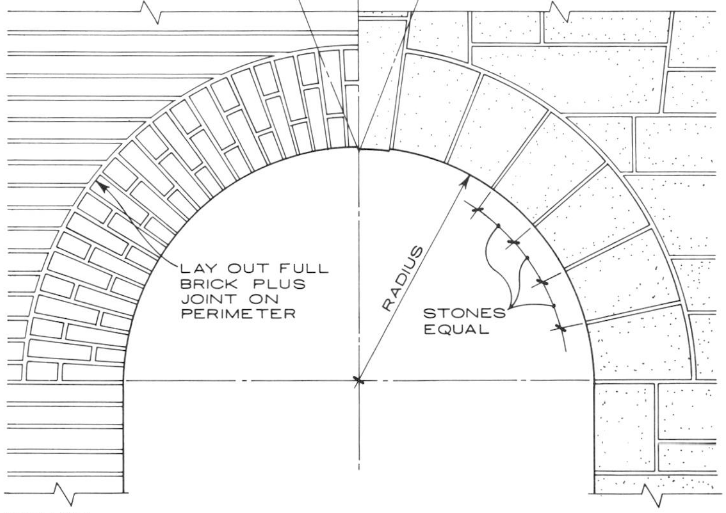

LAY OUT FULL BRICK PLUS JOINT ON PERIMETER

RADIUS

STONES EQUAL

ROMAN

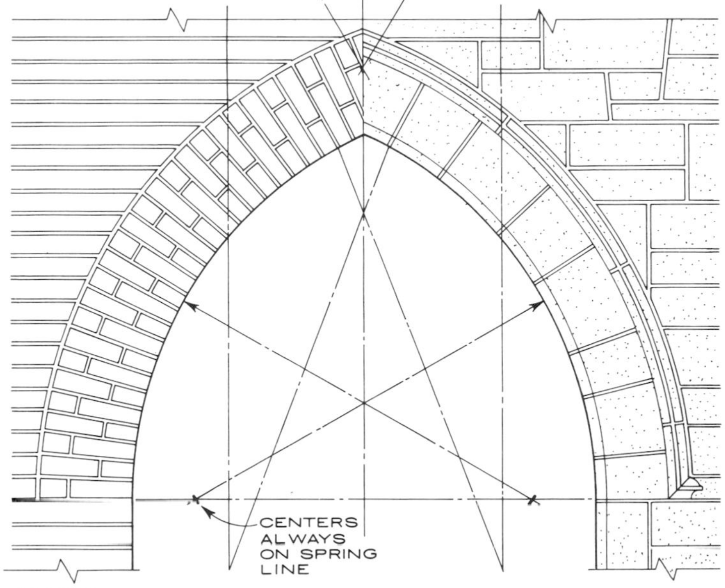

CENTERS ALWAYS ON SPRING LINE

GOTHIC

NOTE: Walls, piers, or abutments adjacent to masonry arches must be of sufficient strength to resist horizontal thrusts.

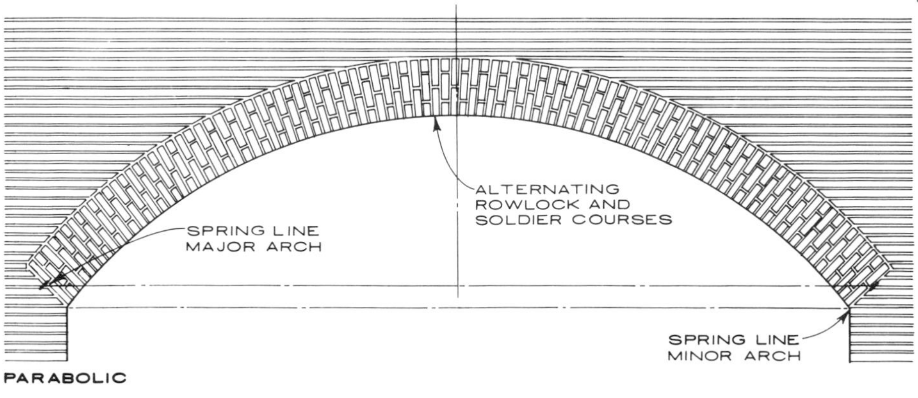

ALTERNATING ROWLOCK AND SOLDIER COURSES

SPRING LINE MAJOR ARCH

SPRING LINE MINOR ARCH

PARABOLIC

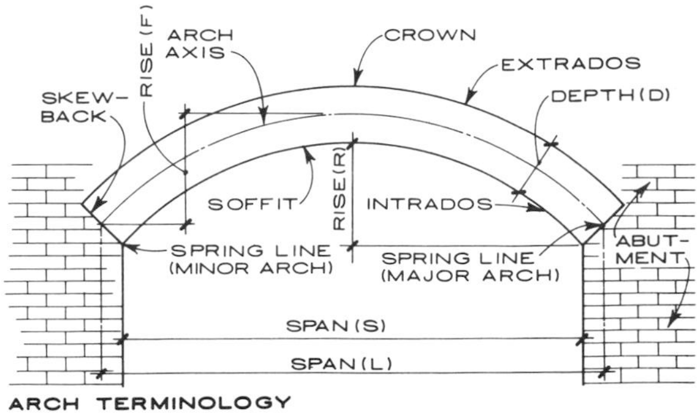

RISE (F)

ARCH AXIS

CROWN

EXTRADOS

SKEW-BACK

DEPTH (D)

RISE (R)

SOFFIT

INTRADOS

SPRING LINE (MINOR ARCH)

SPRING LINE (MAJOR ARCH)

ABUT-MENT

SPAN (S)

SPAN (L)

ARCH TERMINOLOGY

Brick Institute of America; Reston, Virginia

ATTIC

SECOND FLOOR

FIRE CLAY FLUE LINER

STRUCTURAL SUPPORT FOR FIRE CLAY FLUE LINER

SMOKE CHAMBER

SMOKE SHELF

DAMPER

FIRST FLOOR

INCLINED BACK WALL

FIREBRICK

THROAT

FIREPLACE

HEARTH

ASH DUMP

REINFORCED CONCRETE SLAB

OUTSIDE AIR INTAKE

BASEMENT

CLEAN-OUT DOOR

ASH PIT

REINFORCED CONCRETE FOOTING

SECTION

INTRODUCTION

A masonry chimney is usually the heaviest single part of a wood frame structure; therefore, it requires a special foundation. The same is true for masonry buildings where walls are not thick enough to incorporate the chimney or where the chimney is not designed into a masonry wall. Beyond the structural requirements, a fireplace and chimney must be designed so spaces and relationships between spaces sustain combustion and carry smoke away safely. Fireplace design is bound by various building and mechanical codes. The internal diagram of a working fireplace shows the several required parts and their vertical organization. Each part is illustrated further on succeeding pages. Other pages describe more efficient prefabricated fireplace units that incorporate air heating and circulating devices.

Most important in fireplace design is the location of the fireplace and chimney. It is best located at the center of the house to prevent heat loss to the exterior. For best efficiency, a fireplace should not be located opposite an outside door, near an open stairway leading to an upper floor, near a forced-air furnace, or near a return air register. Two factors primarily affect the chimney draft: height of the flue above the fireplace, and the pressure differential between the heated exhaust and cooler outside air.

The even combustion of wood fuel is improved by providing a measured supply of air, independent of room air, to the firebox. This is done by: installing an air duct from the exterior access to the ash dump, letting the ash door serve as a damper; or by providing a separate chase directly to the firebox. When a separate chase to the firebox is coupled with operable doors in the fireplace opening, the user can control the rate of combustion and maintain positive room air pressure; air infiltration and drafts are avoided.

DEFINITIONS

FLUE—Takes smoke from the smoke chamber to the outside. Flue area (in plan) is proportionally related to flue height and area of fireplace opening. A tight, lined flue is an important safety feature. Flue termination must be located according to codes. As an exterior building part, it requires weatherproofing.

SMOKE CHAMBER—Directs smoke into the flue by tapering up and in.

DAMPER—Allows throat size adjustment from fully open to tightly closed.

THROAT—Passes smoke from fireplace up into smoke chamber.

FIREPLACE—Where burning takes place. Size and proportions determine size of other components.

HEARTH—Extends fireplace floor beyond opening to protect room flooring from sparks, heat, and flames.

ASH DUMP—Operable louver in fireplace floor providing efficient ash removal. An air intake may be installed in the ash pit wall to introduce outside air into the fireplace via the ash dump.

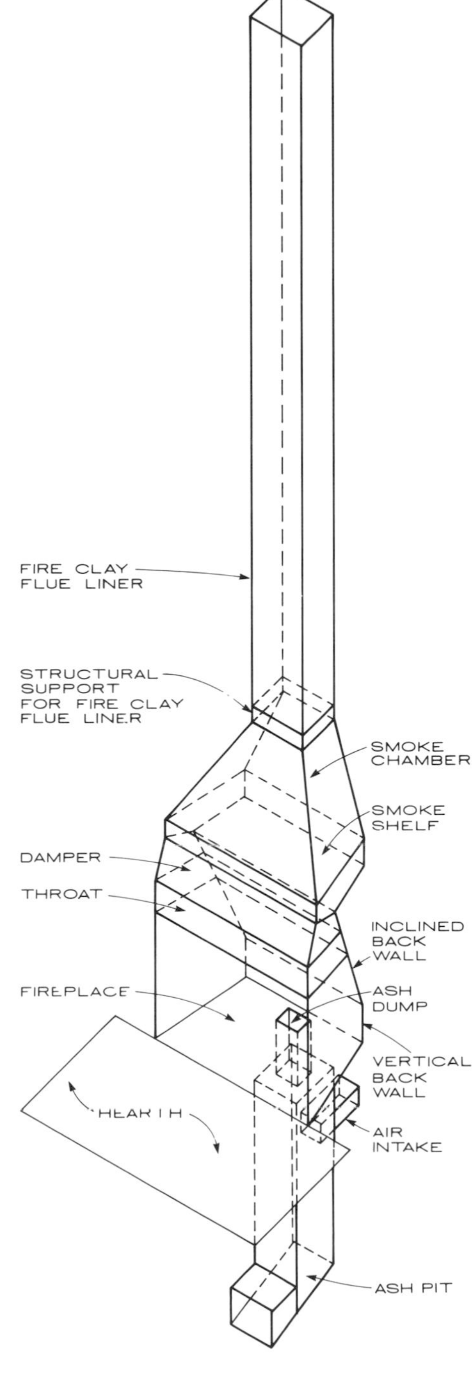
FIRE CLAY FLUE LINER
STRUCTURAL SUPPORT FOR FIRE CLAY FLUE LINER
SMOKE CHAMBER
SMOKE SHELF
DAMPER
THROAT
INCLINED BACK WALL
FIREPLACE
ASH DUMP
VERTICAL BACK WALL
HEARTH
AIR INTAKE
ASH PIT

SCHEMATIC DIAGRAM

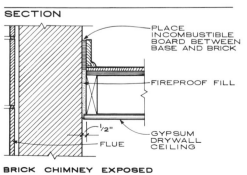

PLACE INCOMBUSTIBLE BOARD BETWEEN BASE AND BRICK

FIREPROOF FILL

1/2"

FLUE

GYPSUM DRYWALL CEILING

BRICK CHIMNEY EXPOSED

FLUE

STUD AND DRY WALL

POROUS NON-METALLIC, INCOMBUSTIBLE FILL

4"

2"

SHEET METAL OR LATH SUPPORT

BRICK CHIMNEY CONCEALED BEHIND A STUD WALL

INSULATION OF WOOD FRAMING MEMBERS AT A CHIMNEY

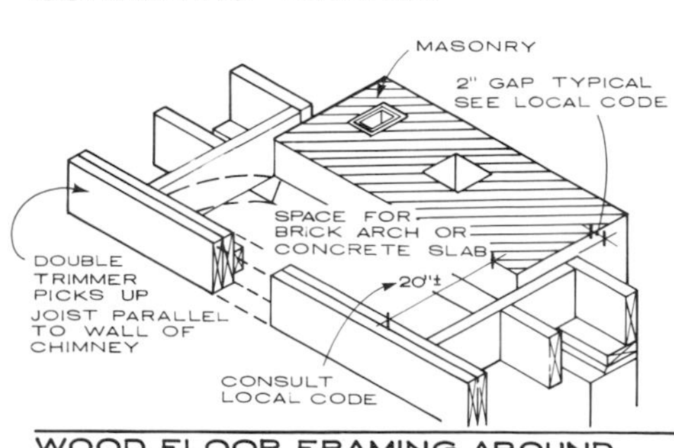
MASONRY
2" GAP TYPICAL SEE LOCAL CODE
SPACE FOR BRICK ARCH OR CONCRETE SLAB
DOUBLE TRIMMER PICKS UP JOIST PARALLEL TO WALL OF CHIMNEY
20"±
CONSULT LOCAL CODE

WOOD FLOOR FRAMING AROUND CHIMNEY AND HEARTH

Darrel Downing Rippeteau, Architect; Washington, D.C.
Timothy B. McDonald; Washington, D.C.

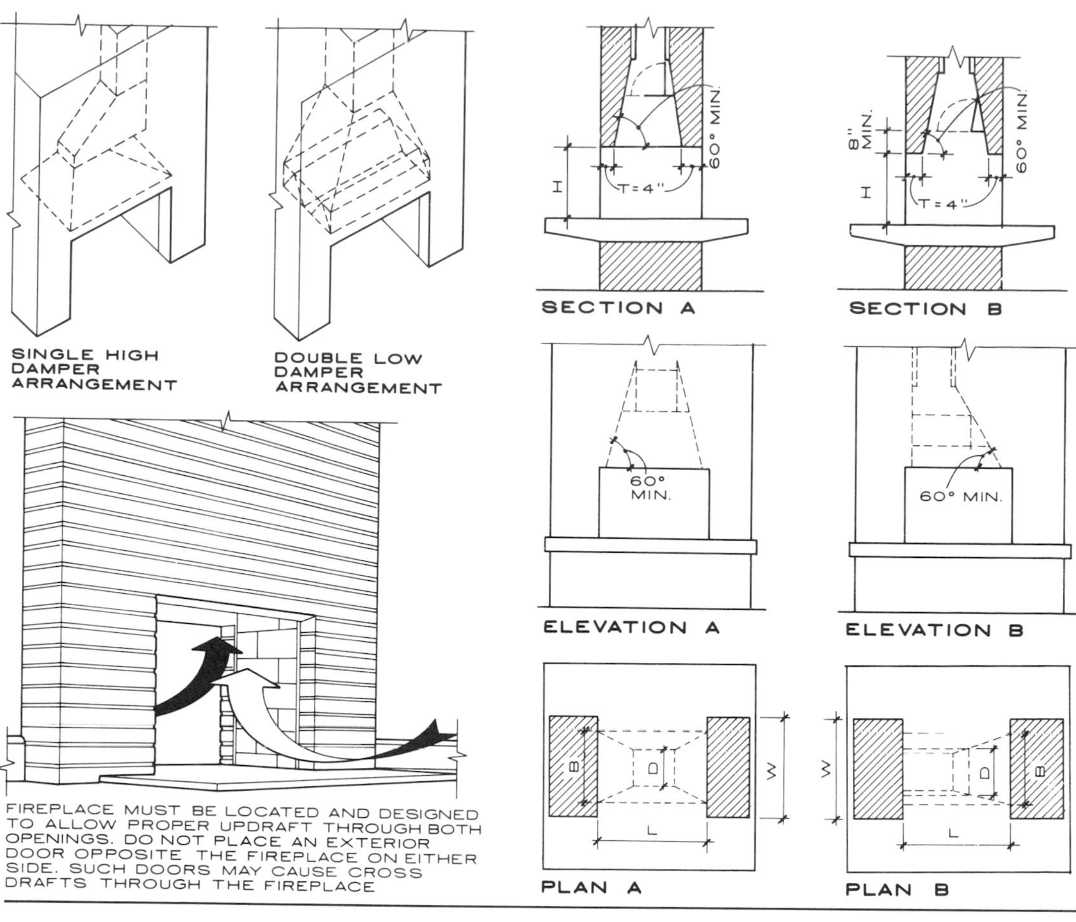
SINGLE HIGH DAMPER ARRANGEMENT
DOUBLE LOW DAMPER ARRANGEMENT
SECTION A
SECTION B
60° MIN.
8" MIN.
T=4"
H
ELEVATION A
ELEVATION B
PLAN A
PLAN B
B
D
W
L
FIREPLACE MUST BE LOCATED AND DESIGNED TO ALLOW PROPER UPDRAFT THROUGH BOTH OPENINGS. DO NOT PLACE AN EXTERIOR DOOR OPPOSITE THE FIREPLACE ON EITHER SIDE. SUCH DOORS MAY CAUSE CROSS DRAFTS THROUGH THE FIREPLACE

FIREPLACE OPEN FRONT AND BACK

FIREPLACE OPEN FRONT AND BACK

- H Height from top of hearth to bottom of facing.
- B (Depth of burning area) 5/8 H minus 8 in. but never less than 16 in.
- W (Width of fireplace) B + 2T.
- D (Damper at bottom of flue, see Section A) equal to free area of flue.
- D (Damper closer to fire, see Section B) equal to twice the free area of flue. Set damper a minimum of 8 in. from bottom of smoke chamber. Open damper should extend entire length of smoke chamber.

TYPICAL FIREPLACE DIMENSIONS

L	H	B	FLUE
28	24	16	13 x 13
30	28	16	13 x 18
36	30	17	18 x 18
48	32	19	20 x 24
54	36	22	24 x 24

NOTE: W should not be less than 24".

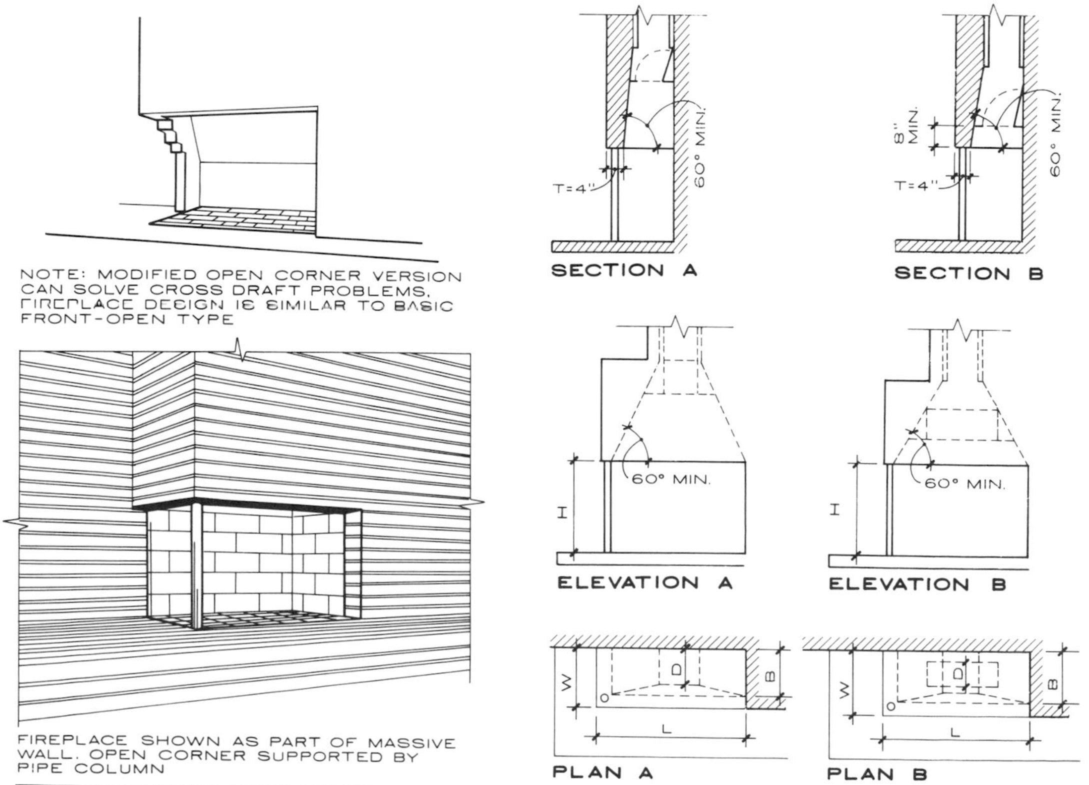
NOTE: MODIFIED OPEN CORNER VERSION CAN SOLVE CROSS DRAFT PROBLEMS. FIREPLACE DESIGN IS SIMILAR TO BASIC FRONT-OPEN TYPE
SECTION A
SECTION B
60° MIN.
8" MIN.
T=4"
H
ELEVATION A
ELEVATION B
PLAN A
PLAN B
W
D
B
L
FIREPLACE SHOWN AS PART OF MASSIVE WALL. OPEN CORNER SUPPORTED BY PIPE COLUMN

FIREPLACE OPEN FRONT AND SIDE

FIREPLACE OPEN FRONT AND SIDE

- H Height from top of hearth to bottom of facing.
- B (Depth of burning area) 2/3 H minus 4 in.
- W (Width of fireplace) B + T.
- D (Damper at bottom of flue, see Section A) equal to twice the free area of the flue. Set damper a minimum of 8 in. from bottom of smoke chamber.

TYPICAL FIREPLACE DIMENSIONS

L	H	B	FLUE
28	24	16	12 x 12
30	28	18	13 x 18
36	30	20	13 x 18
48	32	22	18 x 18

Darrel Downing Rippeteau, AIA, Architect; Washington, D.C.

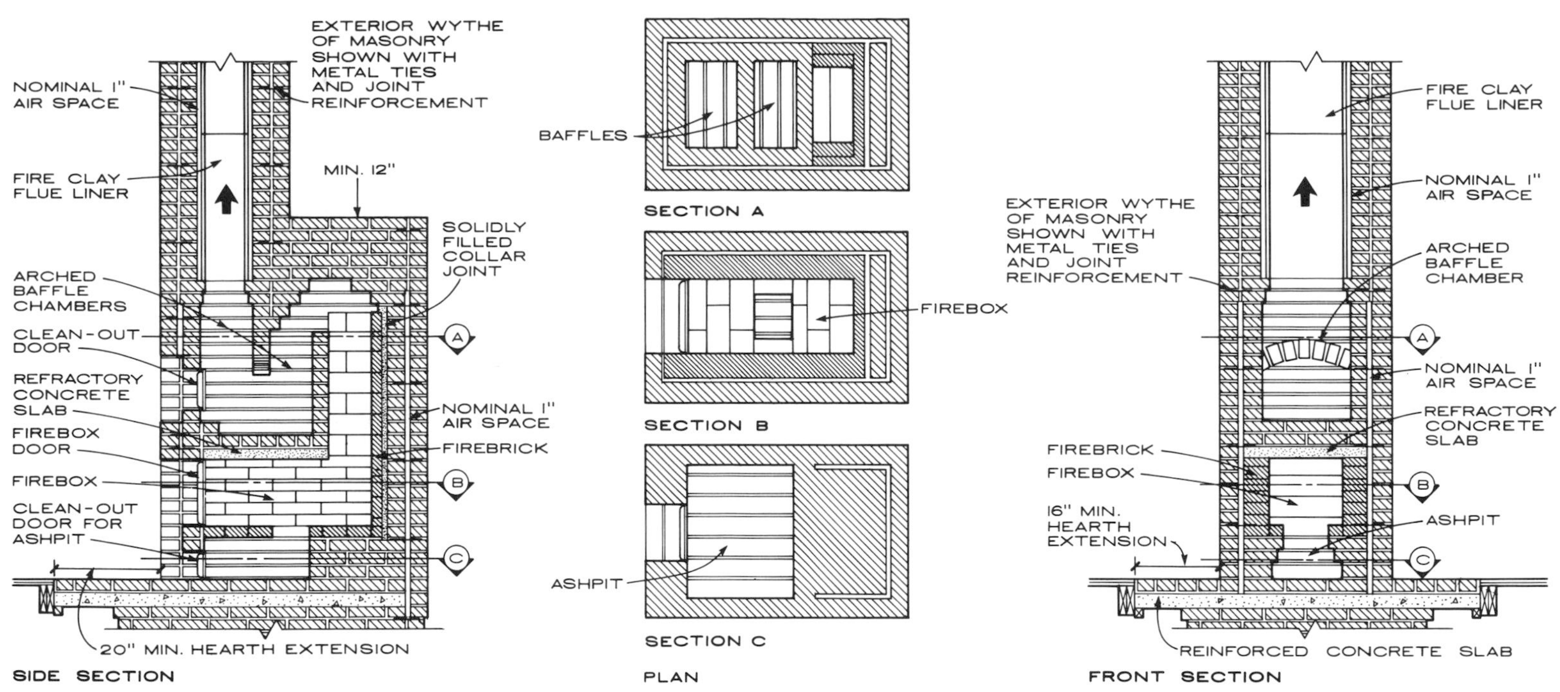
NOMINAL 1" AIR SPACE
EXTERIOR WYTHE OF MASONRY SHOWN WITH METAL TIES AND JOINT REINFORCEMENT
FIRE CLAY FLUE LINER
MIN. 12"
SOLIDLY FILLED COLLAR JOINT
ARCHED BAFFLE CHAMBERS
CLEAN-OUT DOOR
REFRACTORY CONCRETE SLAB
FIREBOX DOOR
FIREBOX
CLEAN-OUT DOOR FOR ASHPIT
NOMINAL 1" AIR SPACE
FIREBRICK
A
B
C
20" MIN. HEARTH EXTENSION
BAFFLES
SECTION A
FIREBOX
SECTION B
ASHPIT
SECTION C
FIRE CLAY FLUE LINER
NOMINAL 1" AIR SPACE
EXTERIOR WYTHE OF MASONRY SHOWN WITH METAL TIES AND JOINT REINFORCEMENT
ARCHED BAFFLE CHAMBER
NOMINAL 1" AIR SPACE
REFRACTORY CONCRETE SLAB
FIREBRICK
FIREBOX
16" MIN. HEARTH EXTENSION
ASHPIT
REINFORCED CONCRETE SLAB

SIDE SECTION — PLAN — FRONT SECTION

RUSSIAN MASONRY STOVE

INTRODUCTION

Brick masonry stoves are adapted from prototypes used in northern and eastern Europe and were used for a number of heating functions, including cooking. Masonry stoves utilize two basic principles to obtain high combustion and heating efficiencies, namely, controlled air intake to the combustion chamber/firebox, and a heat exchange system of baffle chambers through which the combustion gases are circulated.

FINNISH MASONRY STOVES

Finnish or contra-flow stoves are so called because heated air is forced from the top of the smoke chamber down through baffles on the sides of the stove while room air rises by convection along the exterior surface of the masonry. This allows for even heating of the masonry and efficient radiant heating of the room. The baffles converge below the firebox and open out to the flue from the base of the chimney.

RUSSIAN MASONRY STOVES

Russian stoves are typically deep with a small opening to the firebox with a system of either vertically or horizontally aligned baffles above, which replace the smoke chamber. After circulating through the baffle system exhaust gases pass directly into the flue. There is no decided advantage to either baffle alignment, though the horizontal system is easier to construct. Clean-outs are optional on either system, but are recommended to observe creosote build-up.

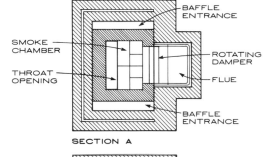

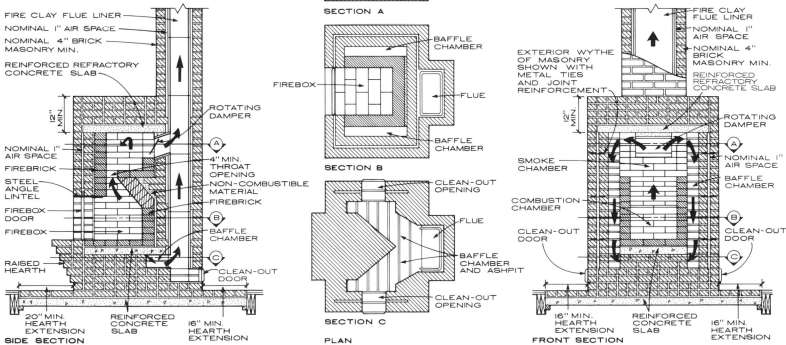

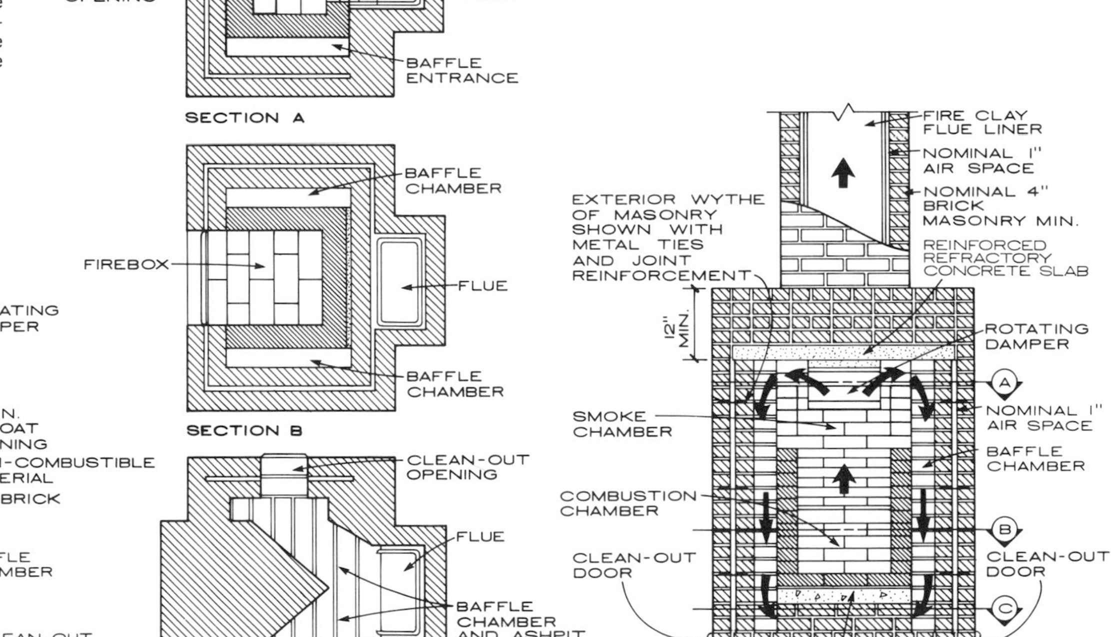
FIRE CLAY FLUE LINER
NOMINAL 1" AIR SPACE
NOMINAL 4" BRICK MASONRY MIN.
REINFORCED REFRACTORY CONCRETE SLAB
12" MIN
ROTATING DAMPER
NOMINAL 1" AIR SPACE
FIREBRICK
STEEL ANGLE LINTEL
4" MIN. THROAT OPENING
NON-COMBUSTIBLE MATERIAL
FIREBRICK
FIREBOX DOOR
FIREBOX
BAFFLE CHAMBER
RAISED HEARTH
CLEAN-OUT DOOR
20" MIN. HEARTH EXTENSION
REINFORCED CONCRETE SLAB
16" MIN. HEARTH EXTENSION
SMOKE CHAMBER
THROAT OPENING
BAFFLE ENTRANCE
ROTATING DAMPER
FLUE
BAFFLE ENTRANCE
SECTION A
FIREBOX
BAFFLE CHAMBER
FLUE
BAFFLE CHAMBER
SECTION B
CLEAN-OUT OPENING
FLUE
BAFFLE CHAMBER AND ASHPIT
CLEAN-OUT OPENING
SECTION C
FIRE CLAY FLUE LINER
NOMINAL 1" AIR SPACE
NOMINAL 4" BRICK MASONRY MIN.
EXTERIOR WYTHE OF MASONRY SHOWN WITH METAL TIES AND JOINT REINFORCEMENT
REINFORCED REFRACTORY CONCRETE SLAB
12" MIN
ROTATING DAMPER
NOMINAL 1" AIR SPACE
SMOKE CHAMBER
BAFFLE CHAMBER
COMBUSTION CHAMBER
CLEAN-OUT DOOR
CLEAN-OUT DOOR
A
B
C
16" MIN. HEARTH EXTENSION
REINFORCED CONCRETE SLAB
16" MIN. HEARTH EXTENSION

SIDE SECTION — PLAN — FRONT SECTION

FINNISH MASONRY STOVE

Timothy B. McDonald; Washington, D.C.

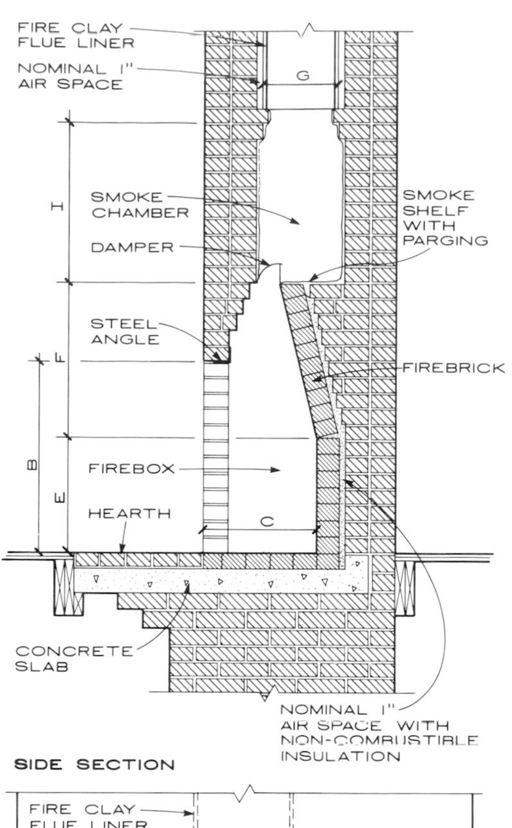

FIRE CLAY FLUE LINER
NOMINAL 1" AIR SPACE
G
H
SMOKE CHAMBER
DAMPER
SMOKE SHELF WITH PARGING
STEEL ANGLE
F
FIREBRICK
B
E
FIREBOX
HEARTH
C
CONCRETE SLAB
NOMINAL 1" AIR SPACE WITH NON-COMBUSTIBLE INSULATION

SIDE SECTION

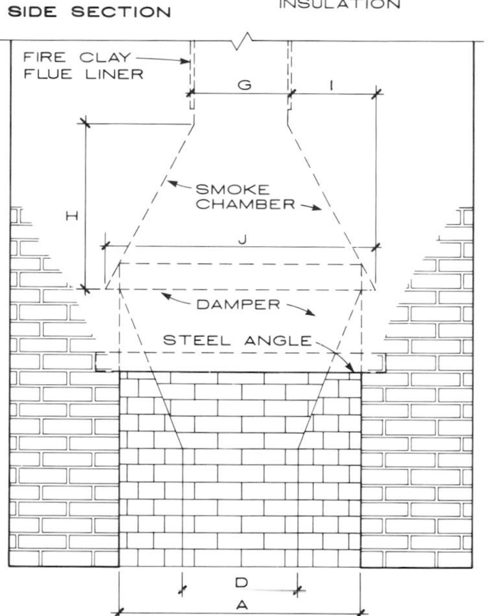

FIRE CLAY FLUE LINER
G
I
H
SMOKE CHAMBER
J
DAMPER
STEEL ANGLE
D
A

FRONT ELEVATION

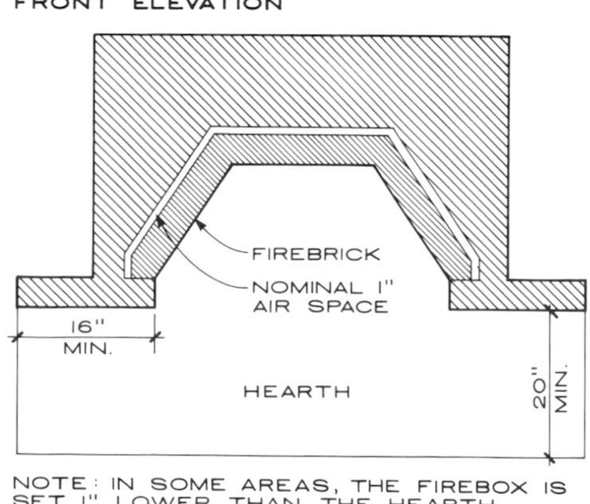

FIREBRICK
NOMINAL 1" AIR SPACE
16" MIN.
HEARTH
20" MIN.

NOTE: IN SOME AREAS, THE FIREBOX IS SET 1" LOWER THAN THE HEARTH

PLAN

RUMFORD FIREPLACE

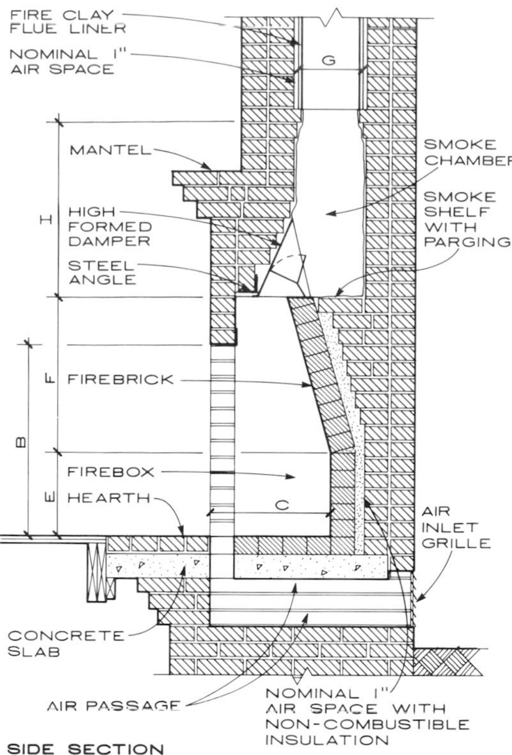

FIRE CLAY FLUE LINER
NOMINAL 1" AIR SPACE
G
MANTEL
SMOKE CHAMBER
SMOKE SHELF WITH PARGING
H
HIGH FORMED DAMPER
STEEL ANGLE
F
FIREBRICK
B
FIREBOX
E
HEARTH
C
AIR INLET GRILLE
CONCRETE SLAB
AIR PASSAGE
NOMINAL 1" AIR SPACE WITH NON-COMBUSTIBLE INSULATION

SIDE SECTION

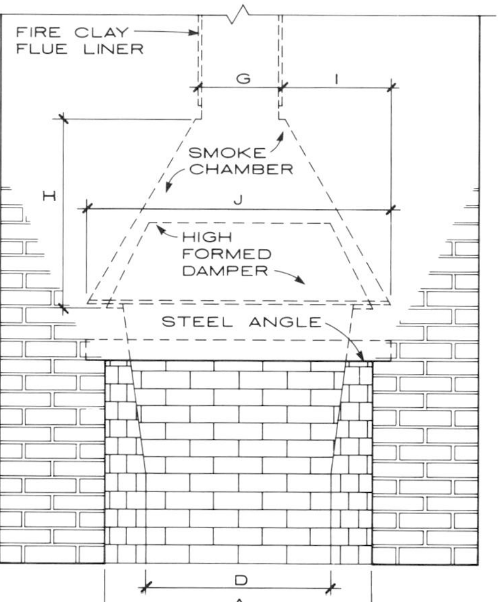

FIRE CLAY FLUE LINER
G
I
H
SMOKE CHAMBER
J
HIGH FORMED DAMPER
STEEL ANGLE
D
A

FRONT ELEVATION

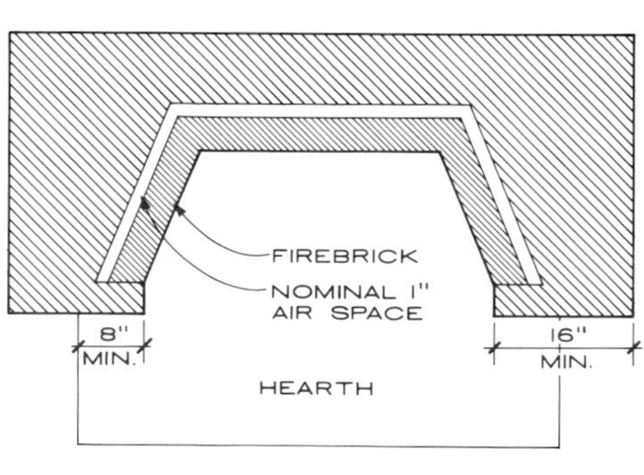

FIREBRICK
NOMINAL 1" AIR SPACE
8" MIN.
16" MIN.
HEARTH

PLAN

SINGLE FACE FIREPLACE

SINGLE FACED FIREPLACES

The design of single faced fireplaces has been well documented, thus a reasonably accurate set of design dimensions of fireplace openings, dampers and flue linings has been developed.

Single faced fireplaces can be efficient radiant heaters. The amount of heat radiated and reflected into the room is directly proportional to the masonry surface area exposed to the fire. The Rumford fireplace is a variation of the single faced fireplace with a shallow firebox, a high throat, and widely splayed sides, all features for optimal direct radiant heating.

In addition, the energy efficiency of new fireplaces can be improved by:

1. Placing the fireplace on the interior of the house, preferably as close to the center as possible.
2. Supplying outside air for combustion and maintenance of positive room pressure.
3. Providing glass screens to prevent unwanted air infiltration.

RECOMMENDED DIMENSIONS FOR WOOD BURNING FIREPLACES (IN.)

TYPICAL FIREPLACES

FIREPLACE OPENINGS			BACKWALL (INCLINED)			FLUE LINING (OUTSIDE DIM.)	SMOKE CHAMBER		
A	B	C	D	E	F	G	H	I	J
24	24	16	11	14	18	8 x 12	19	10	32
28	24	16	15	14	18	8 x 12	21	12	36
30	29	16	17	14	23	12 x 12	24	13	38
36	29	16	23	14	23	12 x 12	27	16	44
42	32	16	29	14	26	16 x 16	32	17	50
48	32	18	33	14	26	16 x 16	37	20	56
54	37	20	37	16	29	16 x 16	45	26	68
60	37	22	42	16	29	16 x 20	45	26	72
60	40	22	42	16	31	16 x 20	45	26	72
72	40	22	54	16	31	20 x 20	56	32	84

RUMFORD FIREPLACES

A	B	C	D	E	F	G	H	I	J
36	32	19	19	19	25	12 x 16	14	10	27
40	32	19	19	19	25	16 x 16	16	15	29
40	40	19	19	19	30	16 x 16	16	15	29
48	40	19	19	19	32	16 x 20	18	15	35
48	48	20	20	20	40	20 x 20	18	18	37
54	48	20	20	20	40	20 x 20	23	18	45
60	48	20	20	20	40	20 x 24	24	18	45

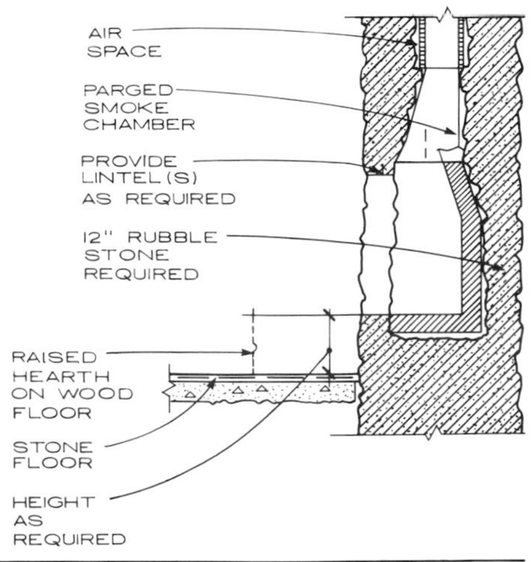

AIR SPACE
PARGED SMOKE CHAMBER
PROVIDE LINTEL (S) AS REQUIRED
12" RUBBLE STONE REQUIRED
RAISED HEARTH ON WOOD FLOOR
STONE FLOOR
HEIGHT AS REQUIRED

SIDE SECTION

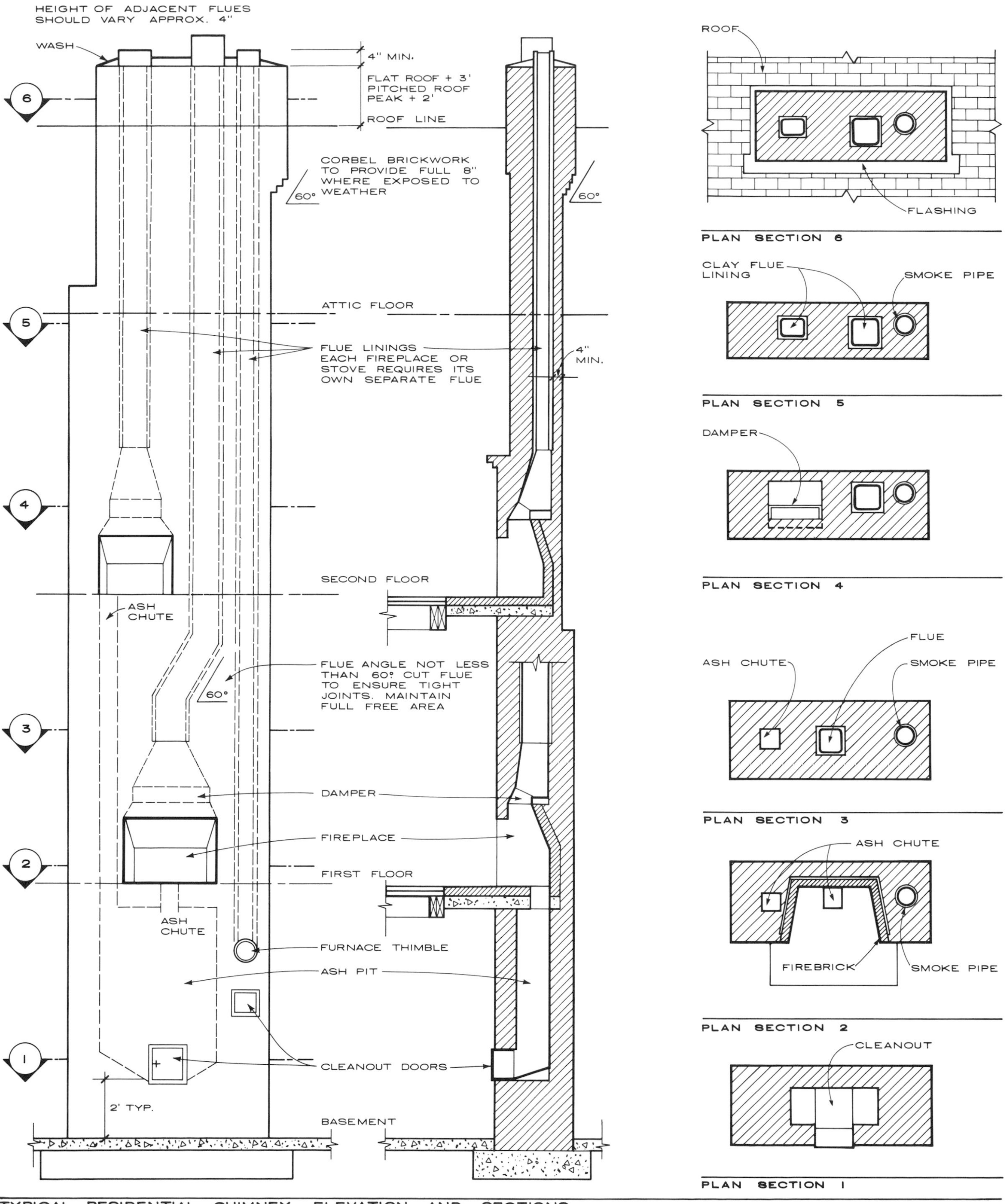
HEIGHT OF ADJACENT FLUES SHOULD VARY APPROX. 4"
WASH
4" MIN.
FLAT ROOF + 3'
PITCHED ROOF PEAK + 2'
ROOF LINE
CORBEL BRICKWORK TO PROVIDE FULL 8" WHERE EXPOSED TO WEATHER
60°
60°
ATTIC FLOOR
FLUE LININGS EACH FIREPLACE OR STOVE REQUIRES ITS OWN SEPARATE FLUE
4" MIN.
SECOND FLOOR
ASH CHUTE
FLUE ANGLE NOT LESS THAN 60° CUT FLUE TO ENSURE TIGHT JOINTS. MAINTAIN FULL FREE AREA
60°
DAMPER
FIREPLACE
FIRST FLOOR
ASH CHUTE
FURNACE THIMBLE
ASH PIT
CLEANOUT DOORS
2' TYP.
BASEMENT
6
5
4
3
2
1
ROOF
FLASHING
PLAN SECTION 6
CLAY FLUE LINING
SMOKE PIPE
PLAN SECTION 5
DAMPER
PLAN SECTION 4
FLUE
ASH CHUTE
SMOKE PIPE
PLAN SECTION 3
ASH CHUTE
FIREBRICK
SMOKE PIPE
PLAN SECTION 2
CLEANOUT
PLAN SECTION 1

TYPICAL RESIDENTIAL CHIMNEY ELEVATION AND SECTIONS

Darrel Downing Rippeteau, Architect; Washington, D.C.

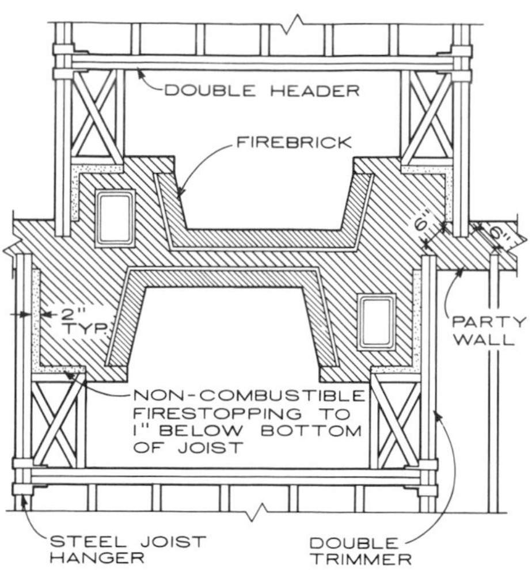
DOUBLE HEADER
FIREBRICK
2" TYP.
PARTY WALL
NON-COMBUSTIBLE FIRESTOPPING TO 1" BELOW BOTTOM OF JOIST
STEEL JOIST HANGER
DOUBLE TRIMMER

FIREPLACES BACK TO BACK IN PARTY WALL

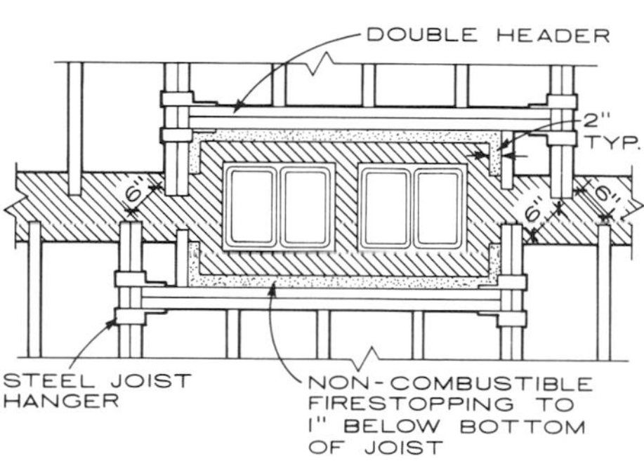
DOUBLE HEADER
2" TYP.
STEEL JOIST HANGER
NON-COMBUSTIBLE FIRESTOPPING TO 1" BELOW BOTTOM OF JOIST

CHIMNEY IN PARTY WALL

FIREPLACES CONSTRUCTED INTEGRALLY WITH BRICK PARTY WALL

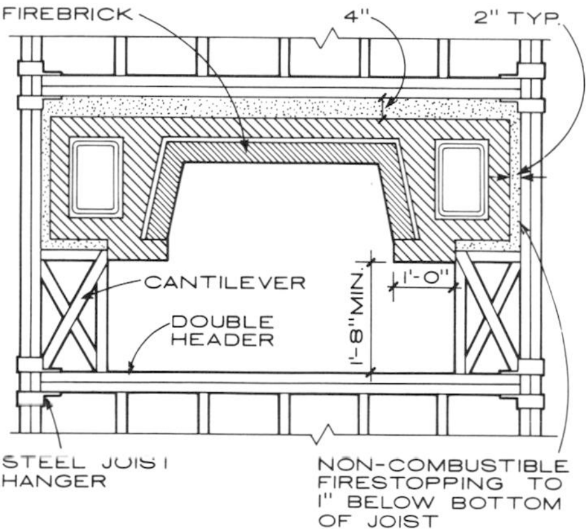
FIREBRICK
4"
2" TYP.
CANTILEVER
DOUBLE HEADER
1'-0"
1'-8" MIN.
STEEL JOIST HANGER
NON-COMBUSTIBLE FIRESTOPPING TO 1" BELOW BOTTOM OF JOIST

FLOOR FRAMING AT FIREPLACE

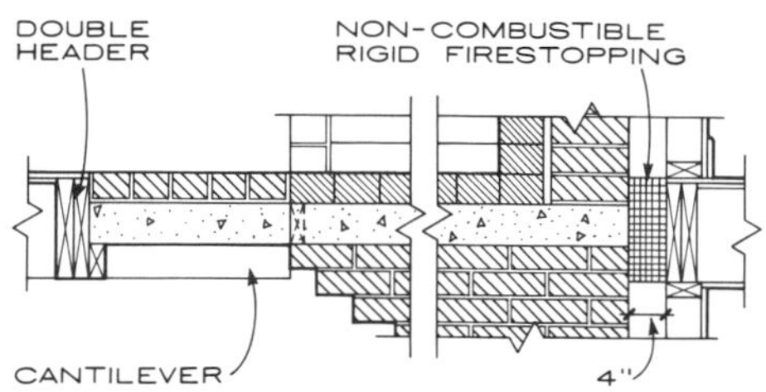
DOUBLE HEADER
NON-COMBUSTIBLE RIGID FIRESTOPPING
CANTILEVER
4"

FRAMING AT FIREPLACE HEARTH LEVEL

HEARTH FRAMING

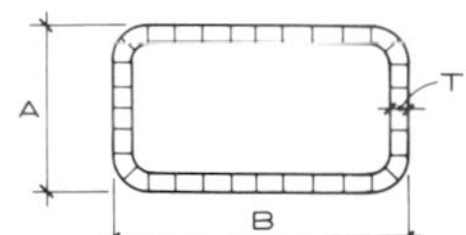
A
B
T

RECTANGULAR FLUE LINING (STANDARD)

AREA (SQ IN.)	A	B	T
51	8 1/2"	8 1/2"	5/8"
79	8 1/2"	13"	3/4"
108	8 1/2"	18"	7/8"
125	13"	13"	7/8"
168	13"	18"	7/8"
232	18"	18"	1 1/8"
279	20"	20"	1 3/8"
338	20"	24"	1 1/2"
420	24"	24"	1 1/2"

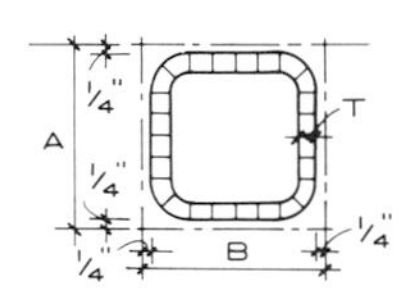
A
B
T

RECTANGULAR FLUE LINING (MODULAR)

AREA (SQ IN.)	A	B	T
57	8"	12"	3/4"
74	8"	16"	7/8"
87	12"	12"	7/8"
120	12"	16"	1"
162	16"	16"	1 1/8"
208	16"	20"	1 1/4"
262	20"	20"	1 3/8"
320	20"	24"	1 1/2"
385	24"	24"	1 5/8"

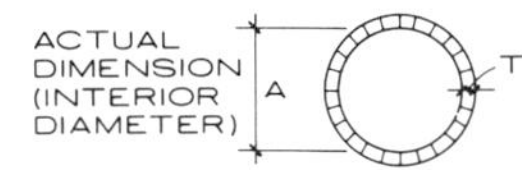
ACTUAL DIMENSION (INTERIOR DIAMETER)
A
T

ROUND FLUE LINING

AREA (SQ IN.)	A	T	LENGTH
47	8"	3/4"	2'-0"
74.5	10"	7/8"	2'-0"
108	12"	1"	2'-0"
171	15"	1 1/8"	2'-0"
240	18"	1 1/4"	2'-0"
298	20"	1 3/8"	2'-0"
433	24"	1 5/8"	2'-0"

CLAY FLUE LININGS

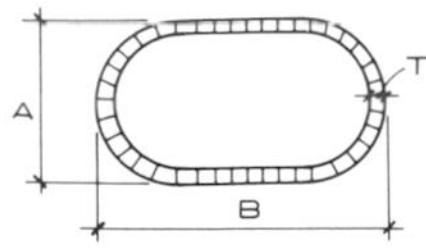
A
B
T

OVAL FLUE LINING

NOMINAL SIZE	AREA (SQ IN.)	A	B
8 1/2" x 13"	69	8 1/2"	12 3/4"
8 1/2" x 17"	87	8 1/2"	16 3/4"
10" x 18"	112	10"	17 3/4"
10" x 21"	138	10"	21"
13" x 17"	134	12 3/4"	16 3/4"
13" x 21"	173	12 3/4"	21"
17" x 17"	171	16 3/4"	16 3/4"
17" x 21"	223	16 3/4"	21"
21" x 21"	269	21"	21"

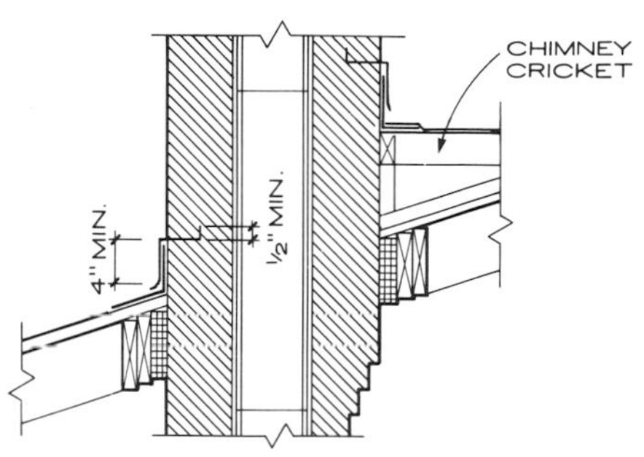
CHIMNEY CRICKET
4" MIN.
1/2" MIN.

INSULATION OF WOOD FRAMING MEMBERS AT A CHIMNEY

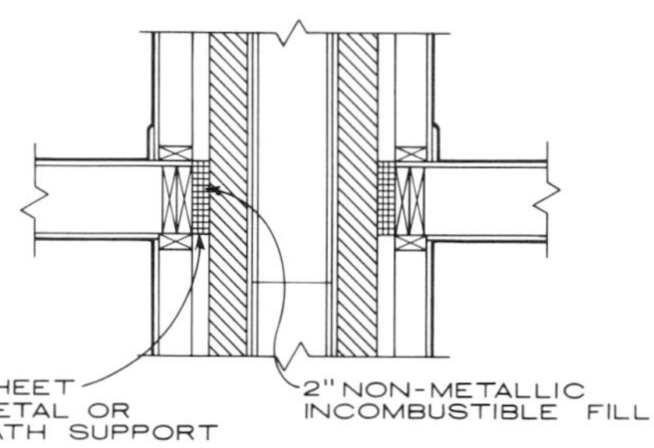
SHEET METAL OR LATH SUPPORT
2" NON-METALLIC INCOMBUSTIBLE FILL

BRICK CHIMNEY CONCEALED BEHIND STUD WALL

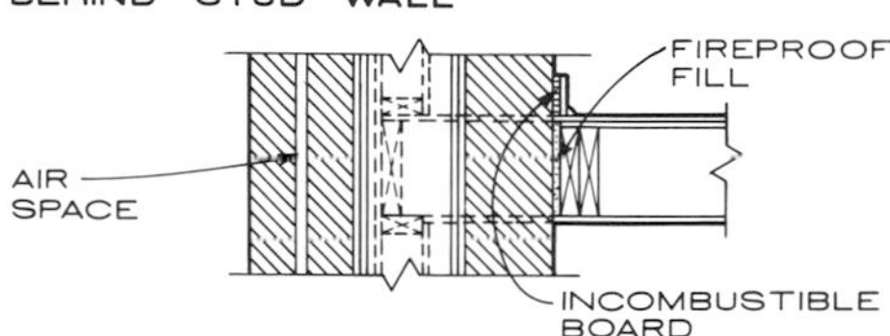
FIREPROOF FILL
AIR SPACE
INCOMBUSTIBLE BOARD

BRICK CHIMNEY EXPOSED

CHIMNEY FRAMING AND INSULATION

NOTES

1. Availability of specific clay flue lining shapes varies according to location. Generally, oval and round flue linings, used in construction with steel reinforcing bars, are available in the western states, while rectangular flue linings are found commonly throughout the eastern states. Check with local manufacturers for available types and sizes.
2. U.L. approved lightweight concrete flues are available in the western states in modular sizes 8 x 8 in. and 16 x 16 in.
3. Nominal flue size for round flues is interior diameter; nominal flue sizes for standard rectangular flues are the exterior dimensions and, for modular flue linings, the outside dimensions plus 1/2 in.
4. Areas shown are net minimum inside areas.
5. Wall thicknesses shown are minimum required. Flue dimensions vary ±1/2 in. about the nominal sizes shown.
6. All flue linings listed are generally available in 2 ft lengths. Verify other lengths with local supplier.
7. Fireplace flue sizes: One-tenth the area of fireplace opening recommended; one-eighth the area of opening recommended if chimney is higher than 20 ft and rectangular flues are used; one-twelfth the area is minimum required; verify with local codes.
8. Flue area should never be less than 70 sq in. for fireplace of 840 sq in. opening or smaller.

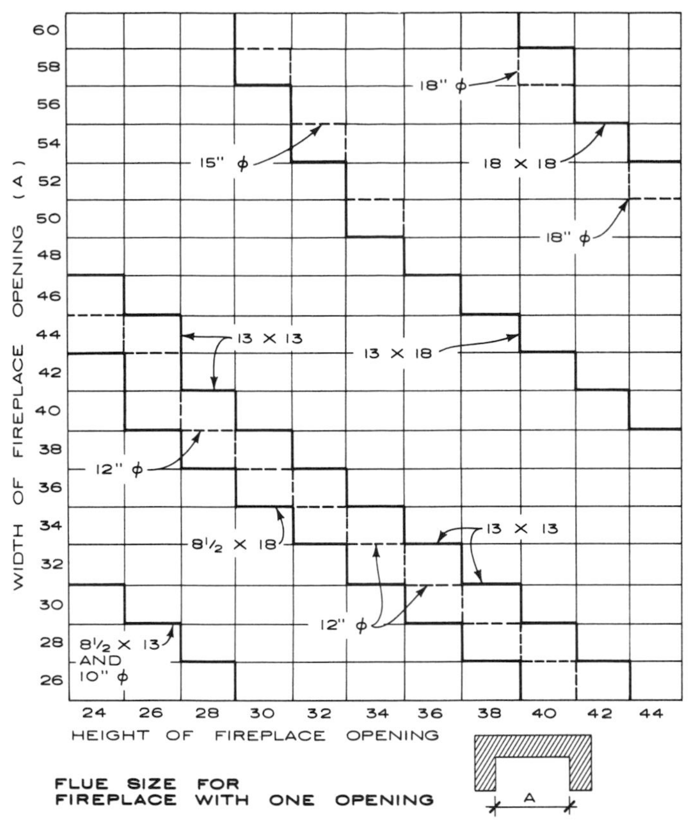
WIDTH OF FIREPLACE OPENING (A)
HEIGHT OF FIREPLACE OPENING
18" φ
15" φ
18 × 18
18" φ
13 × 13
13 × 18
12" φ
8½ × 18
13 × 13
12" φ
8½ × 13 AND 10" φ
A

FLUE SIZE FOR FIREPLACE WITH ONE OPENING

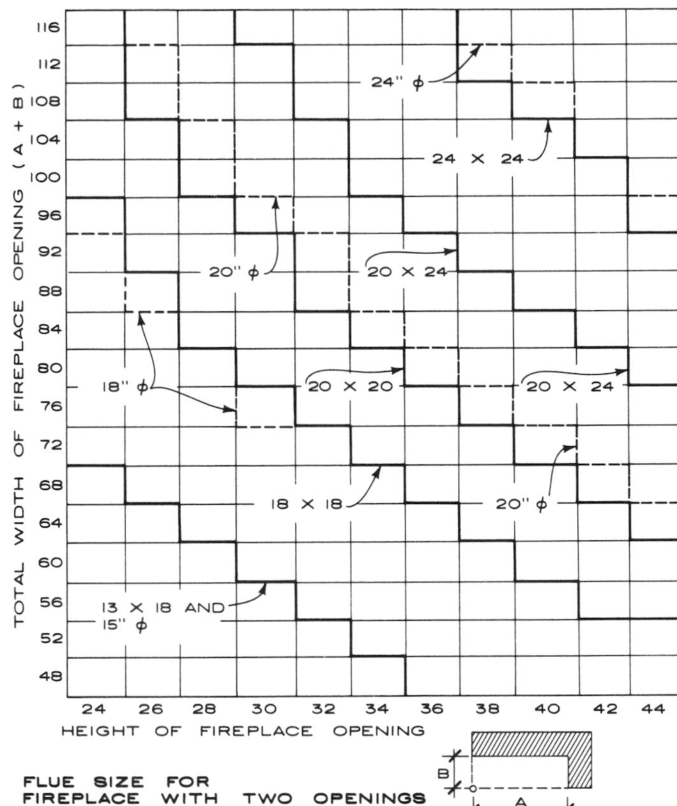
TOTAL WIDTH OF FIREPLACE OPENING (A + B)
HEIGHT OF FIREPLACE OPENING
24" φ
24 × 24
20" φ
20 × 24
18" φ
20 × 20
20 × 24
18 × 18
20" φ
13 × 18 AND 15" φ
A
B

FLUE SIZE FOR FIREPLACE WITH TWO OPENINGS

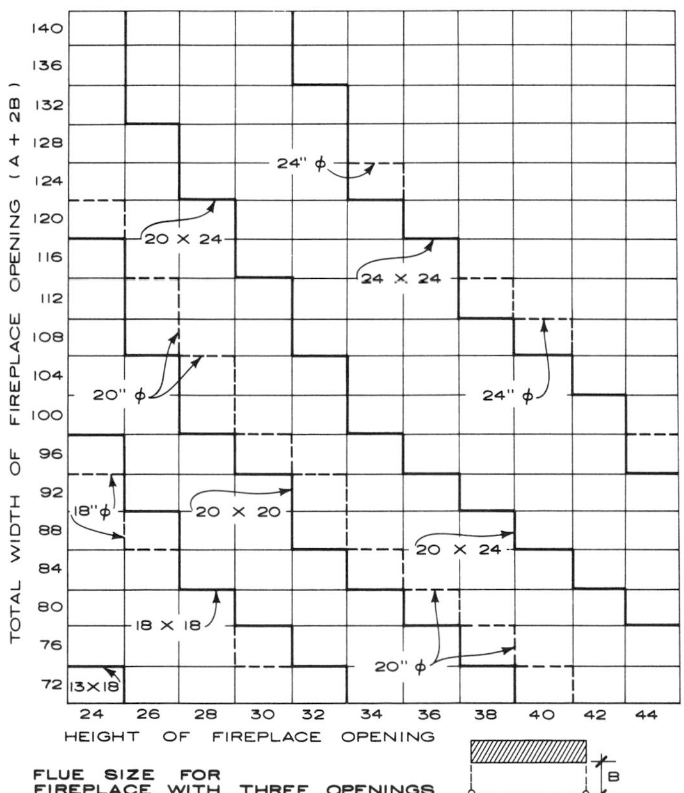
TOTAL WIDTH OF FIREPLACE OPENING (A + 2B)
HEIGHT OF FIREPLACE OPENING
24" φ
20 × 24
24 × 24
20" φ
24" φ
18" φ
20 × 20
20 × 24
18 × 18
20" φ
13×18
A
B

FLUE SIZE FOR FIREPLACE WITH THREE OPENINGS

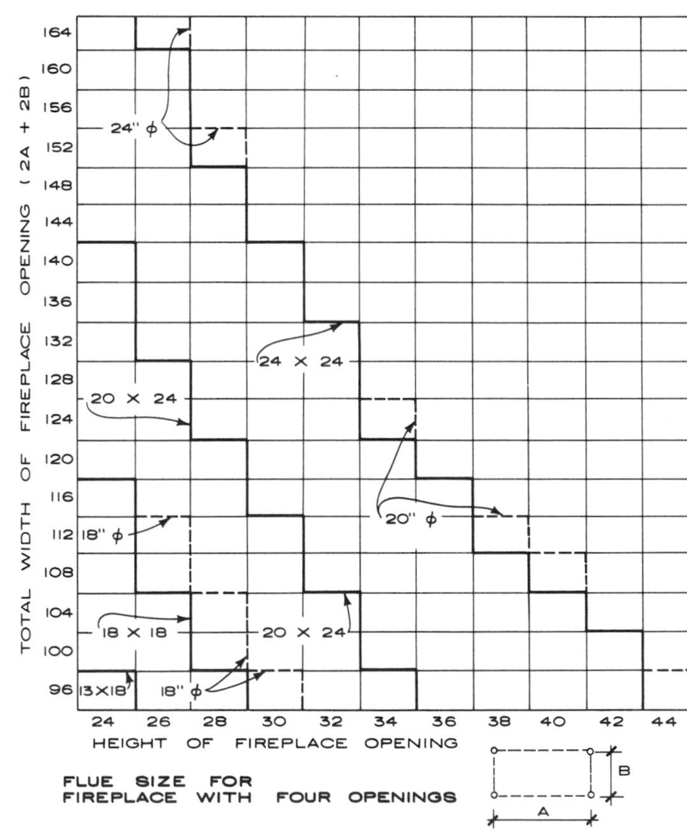
TOTAL WIDTH OF FIREPLACE OPENING (2A + 2B)
HEIGHT OF FIREPLACE OPENING
24" φ
24 × 24
20 × 24
20" φ
18" φ
18 × 18
20 × 24
13×18
18" φ
A
B

FLUE SIZE FOR FIREPLACE WITH FOUR OPENINGS

KEY

——— Rectangular flue.

– – – – Round flue.

Based on recommended sizes, 1/10 of fireplace area.

EXPLANATION

Flue size is indicated by the area of graph that lies within (or below) the designated solid or dashed line.

NOTES

Charts are based on minimum net inside area of standard rectangular and round terra cotta flue linings. Where rectangular (and round) flue designations coincide, the designation for rectangular flue is shown.

Alexander Keyes; Darrel Downing Rippeteau, Architect; Washington, D.C.

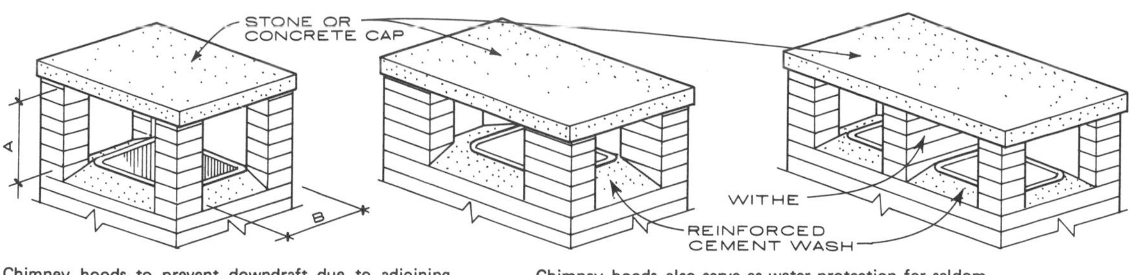
STONE OR CONCRETE CAP
A
B
WITHE
REINFORCED CEMENT WASH

Chimney hoods to prevent downdraft due to adjoining hills, buildings, trees, etc.

A should be $^{1}/_{4}$ greater than B in all hooded chimneys

Chimney hoods also serve as water protection for seldom used flues

Withe between flues is the best method of preventing downdraft

CHIMNEY HOODS

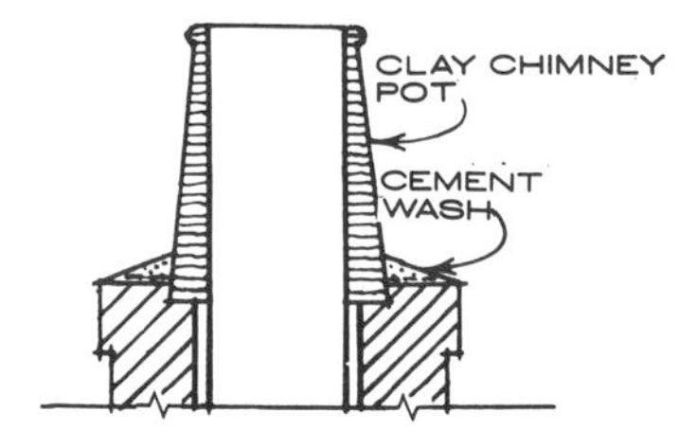
CLAY CHIMNEY POT
CEMENT WASH

CHIMNEY POT

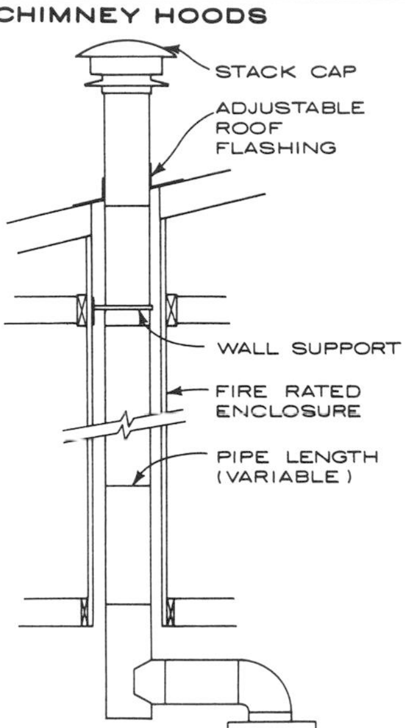
STACK CAP
ADJUSTABLE ROOF FLASHING
WALL SUPPORT
FIRE RATED ENCLOSURE
PIPE LENGTH (VARIABLE)

PREFAB METAL FLUE ASSEMBLY

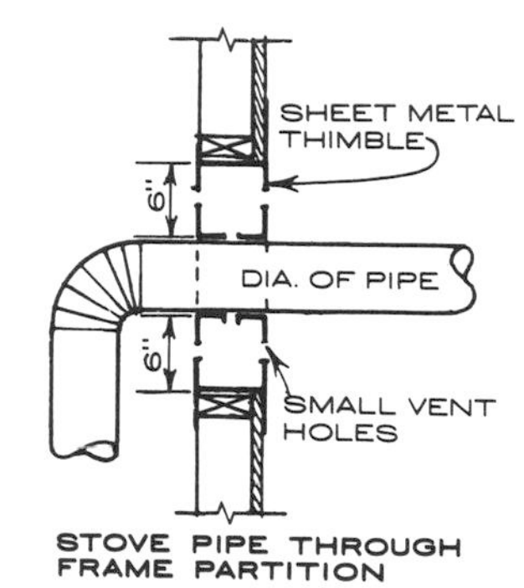
SHEET METAL THIMBLE
6"
DIA. OF PIPE
6"
SMALL VENT HOLES

STOVE PIPE THROUGH FRAME PARTITION

Metal chimneys, connections, and flues are designed to be assembled with other pipes and accessory parts of the same model without requiring field construction. Pipes are single, double, or triple metal walls separated by $^{1}/_{2}$ to 1 in. airspace. Sizes range from 3 to 14 in. I.D. round pipe and $4^{5}/_{6}$ in. oval pipe for use in 2 x 6 stud walls. Provide 1 to 2 in. clearance from enclosure walls and roof structure. Verify with manufacturer's listings for approved uses and specifications.

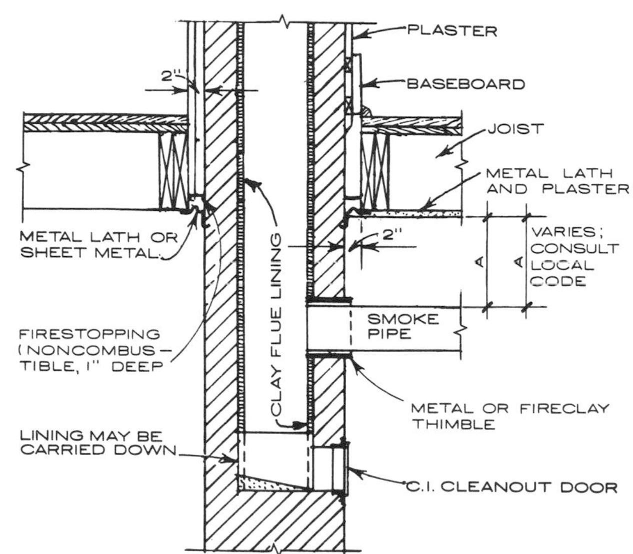
PLASTER
BASEBOARD
JOIST
METAL LATH AND PLASTER
2"
2"
METAL LATH OR SHEET METAL
A
A
VARIES; CONSULT LOCAL CODE
CLAY FLUE LINING
SMOKE PIPE
FIRESTOPPING (NONCOMBUS-TIBLE, 1" DEEP
METAL OR FIRECLAY THIMBLE
LINING MAY BE CARRIED DOWN
C.I. CLEANOUT DOOR

SMOKE PIPE FOR STOVES, H.W. HEATERS AND SMALL RANGES—CONNECTIONS AND CLEARANCES

FLUES, VENTS, AND SMOKE CONNECTIONS—RESIDENTIAL

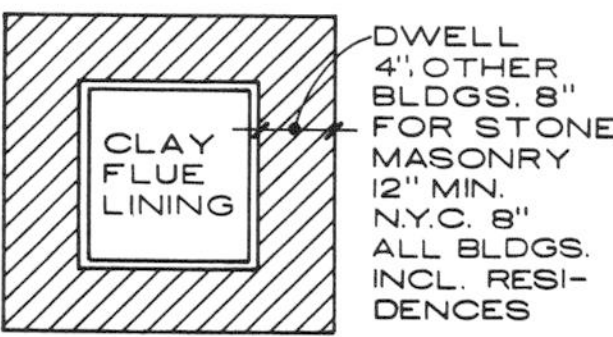
CLAY FLUE LINING
DWELL 4", OTHER BLDGS. 8" FOR STONE MASONRY 12" MIN. N.Y.C. 8" ALL BLDGS. INCL. RESIDENCES

Chimneys for stoves, cooking ranges, warm air, hot water and low pressure steam heating furnaces, low heat industrial appliances, portable type incinerators, fireplaces.

LOW HEAT APPLIANCES

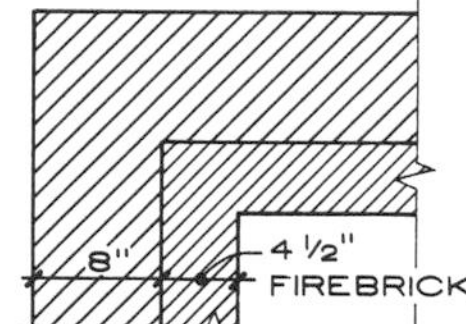
8"
4 1/2"
FIREBRICK

Chimneys for high pressure steam boilers, smokehouses, and other medium heat appliances other than incinerators. Continue firebrick up 25' min. N.Y.C. firebrick up 50' min.

MEDIUM HEAT APPLIANCES

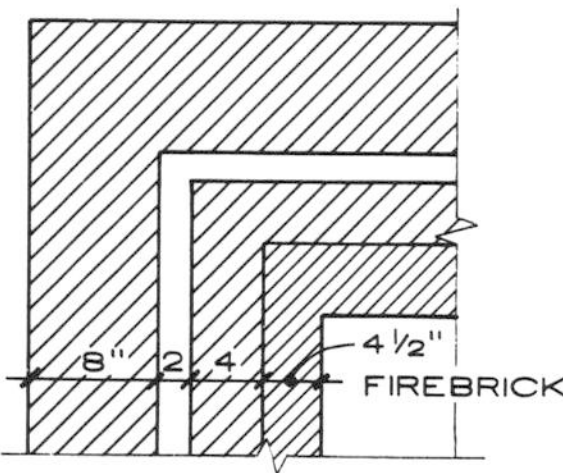
8"
2
4
4 1/2"
FIREBRICK

Chimneys for cupolas, brass furnaces, porcelain baking kilns, and other high heat appliances.

HIGH HEAT APPLIANCES

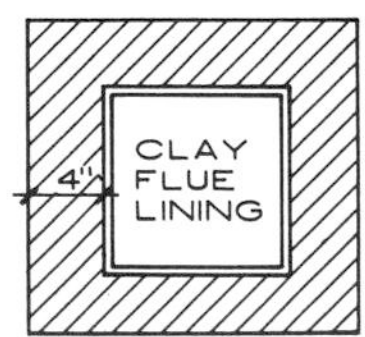
CLAY FLUE LINING
4"

For domestic type incinerators where firebox or charging compartment is not larger than 5 cu ft

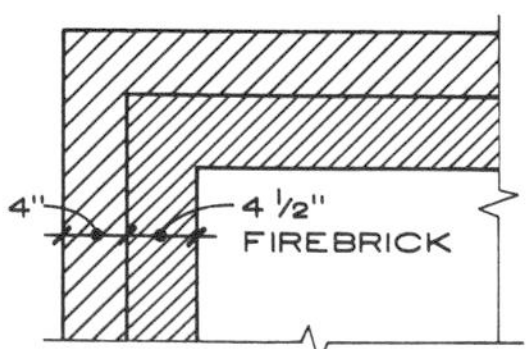
4"
4 1/2"
FIREBRICK

For apartment house type incinerators. Continue firebrick up 10' above roof of combustion chamber for grate area 7 sq ft or less; 40' above for grate area exceeding 7 sq ft.

FOR RESIDENCE BLDGS, INSTITUTIONAL BLDGS CHURCHES, SCHOOLS, & RESTAURANTS.

CHIMNEYS FOR INCINERATORS

CHIMNEY REQUIREMENTS—VARIOUS USE TYPES

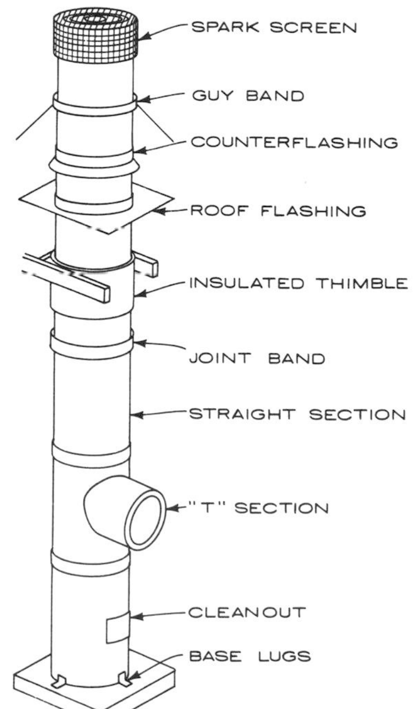
SPARK SCREEN
GUY BAND
COUNTERFLASHING
ROOF FLASHING
INSULATED THIMBLE
JOINT BAND
STRAIGHT SECTION
"T" SECTION
CLEANOUT
BASE LUGS

U.L. approved metal chimney systems with refractory linings are available in 10 to 60 in. I.D. in 4 ft lengths.

INDUSTRIAL CHIMNEY SYSTEM

Alexander Keyes; Darrel Downing Rippeteau, Architect; Washington, D.C.

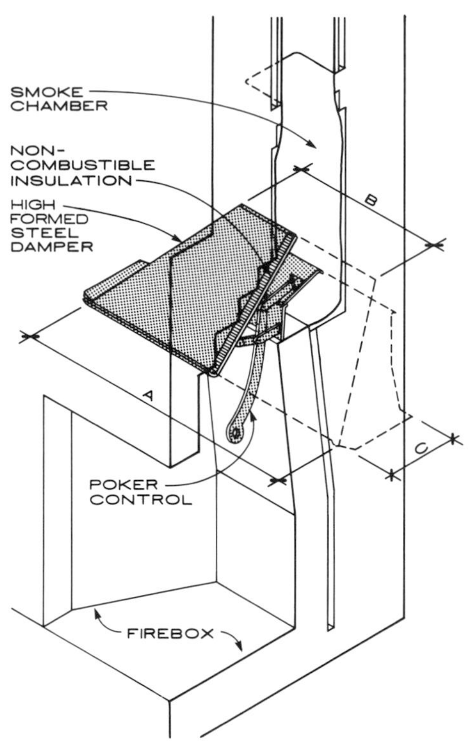
SMOKE CHAMBER
NON-COMBUSTIBLE INSULATION
HIGH FORMED STEEL DAMPER
B
A
C
POKER CONTROL
FIREBOX

HIGH FORMED DAMPER (IN.)

A	B	C
32	15¹/₄	9³/₄
36	19¹/₄	9³/₄
40	23¹/₄	9³/₄
44	27¹/₄	9³/₄
48	31¹/₄	9³/₄

HIGH FORMED DAMPERS provide correct ratio of throat-to-fireplace opening with an optional preformed smoke shelf, which can reduce material and labor requirements. They are useful for both single and multiple opening fireplaces.

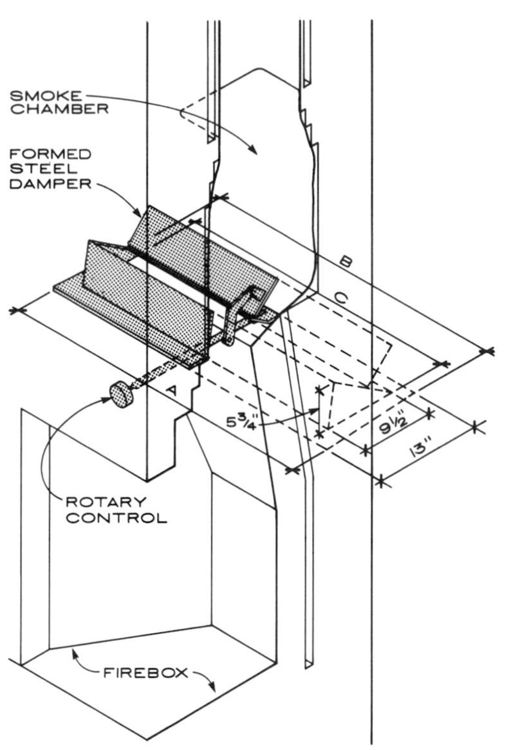
SMOKE CHAMBER
FORMED STEEL DAMPER
B
C
A
5¾"
9½"
13"
ROTARY CONTROL
FIREBOX

FORMED DAMPER (IN.)

WIDTH OF OPENING	DAMPER DIMENSIONS (IN.)		
	A	B	C
24 to 26	28¹/₄	26³/₄	24
27 to 30	32¹/₄	30³/₄	28
31 to 34	36¹/₄	34³/₄	32
35 to 38	40¹/₄	38³/₄	36
39 to 42	44¹/₄	42³/₄	40
43 to 46	48¹/₄	46³/₄	44
47 to 50	52¹/₄	50³/₄	48

FORMED STEEL DAMPERS are designed to provide the correct ratio of throat-to-fireplace opening, producing maximum draft. These dampers are equipped with poker type control and are easily installed.

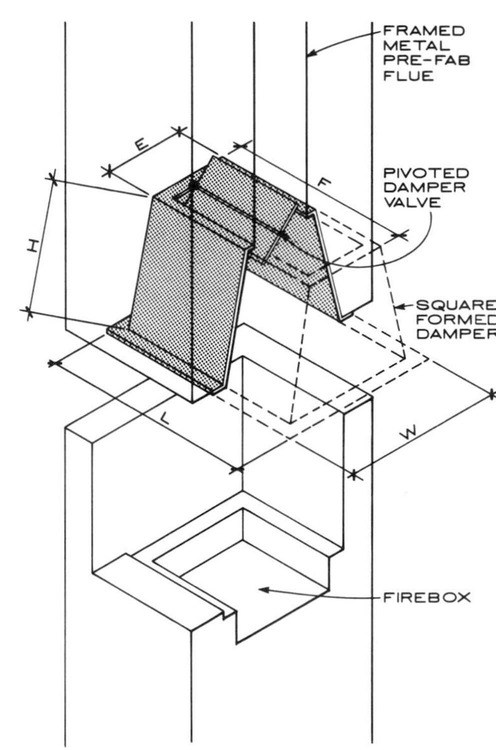
FRAMED METAL PRE-FAB FLUE
E
F
H
PIVOTED DAMPER VALVE
SQUARE FORMED DAMPER
L
W
FIREBOX

SQUARE FORMED DAMPER (IN.)

TOP OUTLET			OVERALL SIZE	
E	F	H	L	W
17	17	17	41	27
17	17	25	45	27
17	23	25	49	27

SQUARE FORMED DAMPERS have high sloping sides that promote even draw on all sides of multiple opening fireplaces. They are properly proportioned for a strong draft and smokefree operation.

FORMED STEEL DAMPERS

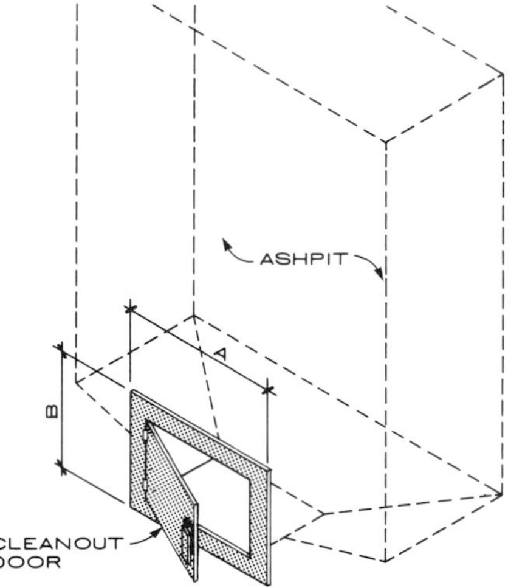
ASHPIT
A
B
CLEANOUT DOOR

DOOR DIMENSIONS (IN.)

A	B
6	8
8	8, 10
10	10, 12
12	8, 10, 12, 16, 18

CLEANOUT OR ASHPIT DOOR

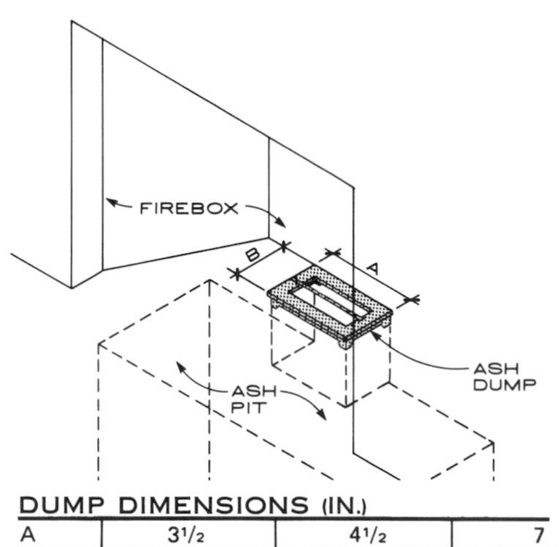
FIREBOX
B
A
ASH DUMP
ASH PIT

DUMP DIMENSIONS (IN.)

A	3¹/₂	4¹/₂	7
B	7	9	10

NOTE

Ash dumps and cleanout doors are available in heavy gauge steel or cast iron. See local manufacturers for available types and sizes.

ASH DUMP

NOTES

1. Locate bottom of damper minimum 6 to 8 in. from top of fireplace opening.
2. Mineral wool blanket allows for expansion of metal damper walls.
3. Dampers are available in heavy gauge steel or cast iron. Check with local suppliers for specific forms and sizes.
4. A cord of wood consists of 128 cu. ft or a stack 4 ft. high and 8 ft. wide, with logs 4 ft. long.
5. A face cord of wood consists of 64 cu ft, or a stack 4 ft high and 8 ft wide, with logs 2 ft long.
6. Logs are cut to lengths of 1 ft 4 in., 2 ft 0 in., 2 ft 6 in., and 4 ft. Allow 3 in. minimum clearance between logs and each side of fireplace.

Timothy B. McDonald; Washington, D.C.

REFERENCES

GENERAL REFERENCES

Architectural and Engineering Concrete Masonry Details for Building Construction, National Concrete Masonry Association (NCMA)
BIA Technical Notes on Brick Construction, Brick Institute of America (BIA)
Building Code Requirements for Masonry Structures, American Concrete Institute (ACI)
Dimensional Stone, Marble Institute of America
Indiana Limestone Institute of America, Inc., Handbook, Indiana Limestone Institute of America, Inc.
Masonry Design and Detailing, 2nd ed., 1987, Christine Beall, Prentice-Hall
Masonry Design Manual, Masonry Institute of America
Residential Masonry Fireplace and Chimney Handbook, 1989, James E. Amrhein, Masonry Institute of America
Structural Details for Masonry Construction, 1988, Morton Newman, McGraw-Hill

DATA SOURCES: ORGANIZATIONS

American Society for Testing and Materials (ASTM), 100, 108–110
Brick Institute of America (BIA), 102–104, 107–109, 122
Building Stone Institute (BSI), 114–117, 120, 121
Castellucci & Sons, Inc., 118, 119
Everett I. Brown Company, 104
Intrepid Enterprises, Inc., 118, 119
National Bureau of Standards (NBS), 110
National Concrete Masonry Association (NCMA), 110, 111
Pittsburg Corning Corporation, 112, 113
Portland Cement Association (PCA), 110
Rock Color Chart, Geological Society of America, 114
Solaris, 112, 113
Susquehanna Concrete Products, Inc., 130
Underwriters Laboratories, Inc., (U.L.), 110, 130

DATA SOURCES: PUBLICATIONS

American Standards Building Code for Masonry, American National Standards Institute (ANSI), 104
Masonry Accessories, National Wire Products Corporation, 101
Masonry Anchors and Ties, Heckman Building Products, 101
Masonry Design and Detailing, 1984, Christine Beall, AIA, 100, 102, 109, 110, 114
Shelf Angle Component Considerations in Cavity Wall Construction, C. J. Parise, American Society for Testing and Materials, 101
Uniform Building Code, 1982 ed., 1985 ed., International Conference of Building Officials (ICBO). Reprinted with permission of the publisher, 104

CHAPTER 5

METALS

NOTE: ALL WOOD SIZES ARE NOMINAL

ROUGH CARPENTRY	PENNY	INCHES	TYPE OF NAIL
1 in. thick stock	8	2½	Common nails
2 in. thick stock	16 to 20	3½ to 4	Common nails
3 in. thick stock	40 to 60	5 to 6	Common nails or spikes
Concrete forms	variable		Common or double-headed nails
Framing for general use and for large members	10, 16, 20, 60	3, 3½, 4, 6	Common nails or spikes depending on size of members
Toenailing studs, joists, etc.	10	3	Common nails
Spiking usual plates and sills	16	3½	Common nails
Toenailing rafters and plates	10	3	Common nails
Sheathing—roof and wall	8	2½	Common nails, may be zinc coated
Finished rough flooring	8	2½	Common nails, may be zinc coated
FINISH CARPENTRY			
Moldings—Sizes as required		7/8 to 1¼	Molding nails (brads)
Carpet strips, shoes	8	2½	Finishing or casing nails
Door window stops and members ¼ in. to ½ in. thick	4	1½	Finishing or casing nails
Ceiling, trim, casing, picture mold, base balusters and members ½ in. to ¾ in. thick	6	2	Finishing or casing nails
Ceiling, trim, casing, base, jambs, trim and members ¾ in. to 1 in. thick	8	2½	Finishing or casing nails
Doors and window trim, boards and other members 1 in. to 1¼ in. thick	10	3	Finishing or casing nails
Drop siding, 1 in. thick	7 or 9	2¼ or 2¾	Siding nails (7d), Casing nails (9d)
Bevel siding, ½ in. thick	6 or 8	2 or 2½	Finishing nails (6d), Siding nails (8d)
WOOD FLOORING			
See wood flooring page for nail sizes and types recommended			Cut steel, wire, finishing, wire casing, flooring brads, parquet and flooring nails
LATHING			
Wood lath	3	1¼	Blued lath nail
Gypsum lath	3	1¼	Blued common
Fiber lath			
Metal lath, interior		1	Blued lath nails, staples or offset head nails
Metal lath, exterior	3	1¼	Self-furring nails (double heads). Staple or cement coated
SHEATHING OR SIDING			
Fiber board ½ in. and 25/32 in.		1½ to 2	Galvanized roofing nail with 7/16 in. diameter head
Gypsum board ½ in.		1¾	Galvanized roofing nail 7/16 in. diameter head
Plywood 5/16 in. and 3/8 in. thick	6	2	Common nails
Plywood ½ in. and 5/8 in. thick	8	2½	Common nails
ROOFING & SHEET METAL			
Aluminum roofing	1	1¾ to 2½	Aluminum nail, neoprene washer optional
Asphalt shingles			Galvanized large head roofing
Copper cleats and flashing to wood			Copper wire or cut slating nails
Copper cleats and flashing to prevent joints			Barbed copper nails
Clay tile	4 to 6	1½ to 2	Copper nails
Prepared felt roofing		1 to 1¼	Zinc roofing nails or large head roofing nails (barbed preferred). Heads may be reinforced
Shingles, wood usual size for heavy butts	3 to 4 4 to 8	1¼ to 1½ 1½ to 2½	Zinc-coated, copper wire shingle, copper clad shingle, cut iron or cut steel
Slate	Use nails 1 in. larger than thickness of slate		Copper wire slating nail (large head). In dry climates zinc-coated or copper-clad nails may be used.
Tin, zinc roofing			Zinc-coated nails (roofing or slating)
Monel roofing			Monel nail
Nailing to sheet metal			Self-tapping screws, helical drive screws
TO CONCRETE OR CEMENT MORTAR			
See following pages of fastening devices			Concrete or cement nails (hardened), helical drive nails or drive bolts

NOTES

1. Thread sizes and lengths vary.
2. Hammer and powder-driven studs are intended for connections to concrete and steel. Refer to manufacturers' literature for specific applications.
3. Refer to building code provisions covering the use of powder-actuated devices. Some jurisdictions do not approve their use.
4. See ANSI A10.3 "Safety Requirements for Powder Actuated Fastening Systems" and OSHA regulations.

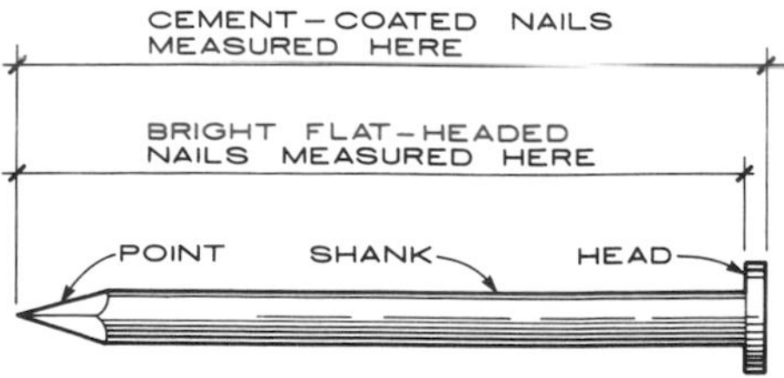
CEMENT—COATED NAILS MEASURED HERE
BRIGHT FLAT—HEADED NAILS MEASURED HERE
POINT
SHANK
HEAD

COMMON NAIL (STEEL WIRE)

COMMON NAIL (STEEL WIRE)

LENGTH	PENNY	GAUGE	DIAM. OF HEAD (IN.)	NAILS/LB.	SAFE WORKING RESISTANCE TO LATERAL SHEAR-LB.
1	2	15	11/64	847	
1¼	3	14	13/64	543	
1½	4	12½	¼	296	
1¾	5	12½	¼	254	
2	6	11½	17/64	167	48
2¼	7	11½	17/64	150	
2½	8	10¼	9/32	101	64
2¾	9	10¼	9/32	92.1	
3	10	9	5/16	66	80
3¼	12	9	5/16	66.1	96
3½	16	8	11/32	47.4	128
4	20	6	13/32	29.7	160
4½	30	5	7/16	22.7	
5	40	4	15/32	17.3	
5½	50	3	½	13.5	
6	60	2	17/32	10.7	

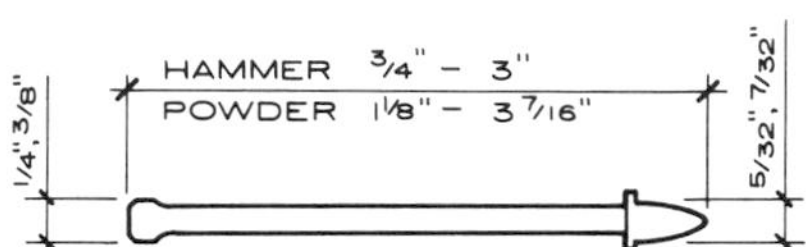
HAMMER ¾" – 3"
POWDER 1⅛" – 3 7/16"
¼", ⅜"
5/32", 7/32"

HAMMER-DRIVEN OR POWDER-DRIVEN PIN

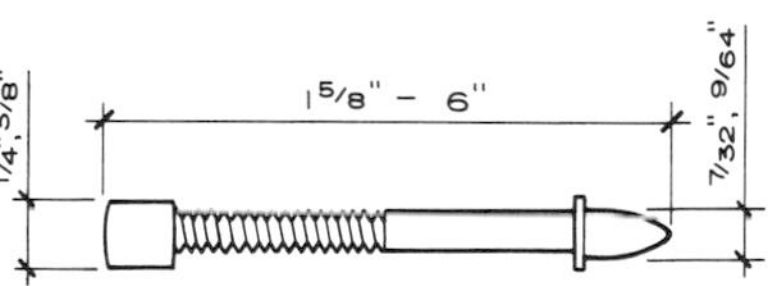
1⅝" – 6"
¼", ⅜"
7/32", 9/64"

POWDER-DRIVEN UTILITY HEAD THREADED STUD

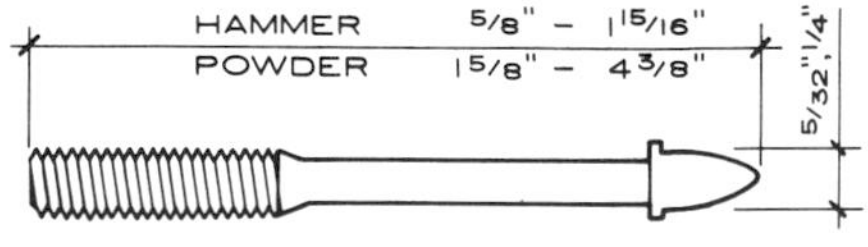
HAMMER ⅝" – 1 15/16"
POWDER 1⅝" – 4⅜"
5/32", ¼"

HAMMER-DRIVEN OR POWDER-DRIVEN HEADLESS THREADED STUD

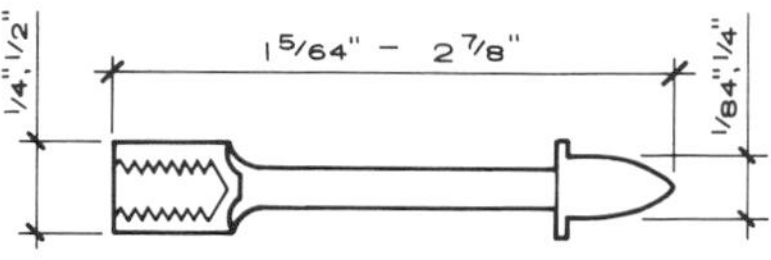
1 5/64" – 2⅞"
¼", ½"
1/64", ¼"

POWDER-DRIVEN INTERNALLY THREADED STUD

HAMMER- AND POWDER-DRIVEN FASTENERS

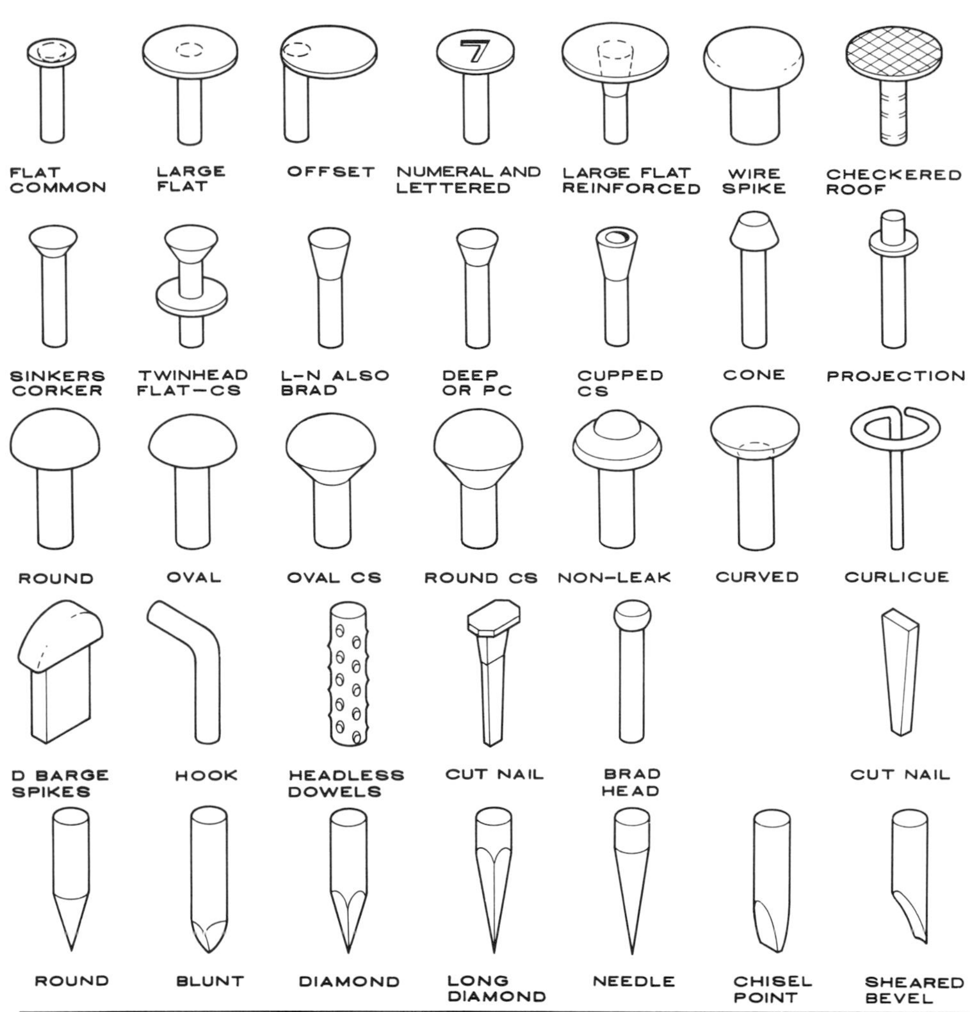
FLAT COMMON
LARGE FLAT
OFFSET
NUMERAL AND LETTERED
LARGE FLAT REINFORCED
WIRE SPIKE
CHECKERED ROOF
SINKERS CORKER
TWINHEAD FLAT—CS
L-N ALSO BRAD
DEEP OR PC
CUPPED CS
CONE
PROJECTION
ROUND
OVAL
OVAL CS
ROUND CS
NON-LEAK
CURVED
CURLICUE
D BARGE SPIKES
HOOK
HEADLESS DOWELS
CUT NAIL
BRAD HEAD
CUT NAIL
ROUND
BLUNT
DIAMOND
LONG DIAMOND
NEEDLE
CHISEL POINT
SHEARED BEVEL

TYPES OF NAIL HEADS AND NAIL POINTS

NOTES

1. Nail diameter, length, shape and surface affect holding power (withdrawal resistance and lateral resistance). See NFPA publications.
2. Materials: Zinc, brass, monel, copper, aluminum, iron or steel, stainless steel, copper bearing steel, muntz metal.
3. Coatings: Tin, copper, cement, brass plated, zinc, nickel, chrome, cadmium, etched acid, parkerized.
4. Forms: Smooth, barbed, helical, annular-ring.
5. Colors: Blue, bright, coppered, black (annealed).
6. Gauges shown are for steel wire (Washburn and Moen).
7. Abbreviations (for the following pages of nails only):

B = blunt	F = flat	O = oval
CS = countersunk	L = long	PC = pointing cone
D = diamond	N = narrow	R = round

FASTENER FINISHES AND COATINGS

COATINGS OR FINISH	USED ON:	COMMENTS
Anodizing	Aluminum	Excellent corrosion protection
Chromate: black, clear, colored	Zinc and cadmium plated	Colors usually offer better protection than clear
Cadmiumplate	Most metals	
Copperplate	Most metals	Electroplated, fair protection
Copper, brass, bronze	Most metals	Indoor, decorative finishes
Lacquering	All metals	Some specially designed for humid conditions
Lead-tin	Steel	Applied by hot-dip. Gives good lubrication to tapping screws.
Nickel, bright and dull	Most metals	Indoor; outdoor if at least .0005 in. thick
Phosphate rust preventative	Steel	Rustproofs steel. Oils increase corrosion resistance
Phosphate paint-base preparations	Steel, aluminum zinc plate	Chemical process for painting or lacquering
Colored phosphate coatings	Steel	Superior to regular phosphated or oiled surfaces
Rust preventatives	All metals	Usually applied to phosphate and black oxide finishes
Electroplated zinc or tin; electrogalvanized zinc; hot-dip zinc or tin	All metals	Zinc or Tin
Hot-dip aluminum	Steel	Maximum corrosion protection, withstands high temperatures

Timothy B. McDonald; Washington, D.C.

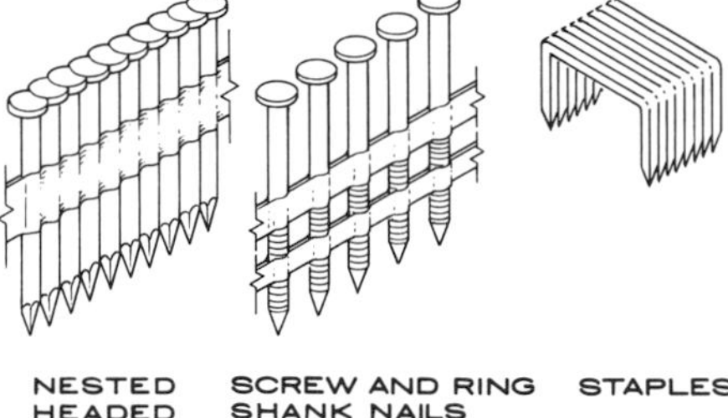
NESTED HEADED NAILS
SCREW AND RING SHANK NAILS
STAPLES

STAPLES AND NAILS FOR PNEUMATIC FASTENERS

ALLOWABLE LOADS FOR DESIGNED STRUCTURES

FASTENER	WIRE DIAMETER	WIRE GAUGE	PENETRATION INTO MAIN MEMBER	ALLOWABLE LOAD (LBS.) (6,7) LATERAL (4,5)	ALLOWABLE LOAD (LBS.) (6,7) WITHDRAWAL
T-nail	.097	12½	1⅛	52	29
T-nail	.113	11½	1¼	63	34
T-nail	.131	10¼	1½	78	39
T-nail	.148	9	1⅝	94	44
staple	.0625	16	1	52	36
staple	.072	15	1	64	42
staple	.080	14	1	75	46
staple	.0915	13	1	92	53
staple	.1055	12	1⅛	113	62

NOTES

1. Refer to Industrial Stapling and Nailing Technical Association, HUD-FHA Bulletin No. UM-25d (1973), for complete data.
2. Crown widths range from 3/16 in. to 1 in. Leg lengths vary from 5/32 in. to 3½ in. Gauge should be chosen for shear value needed.
3. Screw shank and ring shank nails have the same allowable loads as common nails.
4. Nested nails are manufactured with a crescent-shaped piece missing in the head.
5. For wood diaphragms resisting wind or seismic loading these values may be increased 30 percent in addition to the 33⅓ percent increase permitted for duration of load.
6. The tabulated allowable lateral values are for fasteners installed in Douglas Fir-Larch or Southern Pine.
7. Allowable values shall be adjusted for duration of load in accordance with standard engineering practices. Where metal side plates are used, lateral strength values may be increased 25 percent.
8. Withdrawal values are for fasteners inserted perpendicular to the grain in pounds per linear inch of penetration into the main member based on a specific gravity of approximately 0.545.

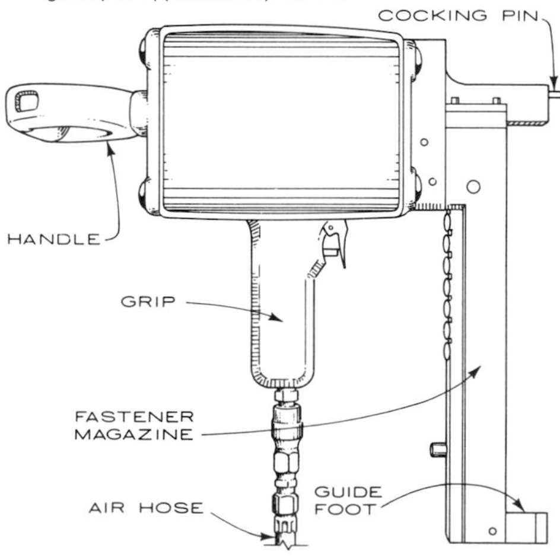
COCKING PIN
HANDLE
GRIP
FASTENER MAGAZINE
AIR HOSE
GUIDE FOOT

PNEUMATIC NAILERS AND STAPLERS

Pneumatic nailers and staplers, connected to compressors or CO_2 bottles, are capable of attaching a variety of fasteners to concrete and steel as well as wood. Consult manufacturer for special features and interchangeability of fasteners.

NAIL TYPE		SIZE	MATERIAL
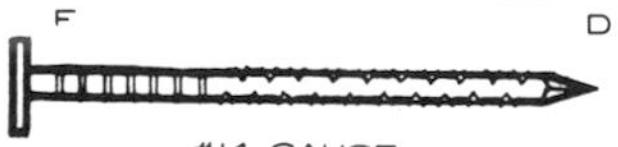 F D #14 GAUGE	BARBED NAILS	1/4" TO 1½"	CEMENT COATED, BRASS, STEEL
 LCSN D #14 GAUGE	CASING NAILS	2d TO 40d 6d TO 10d	BRIGHT, CEMENT COATED CUPPED HEADS AVAILABLE IN ALUMINUM
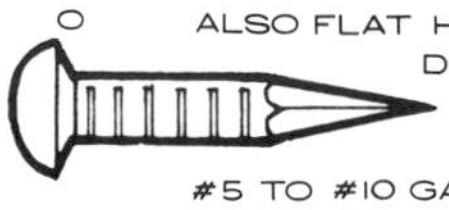 O ALSO FLAT HEAD CS D #5 TO #10 GAUGE	CEMENT NAILS ALSO CALLED CONCRETE NAILS AND HARDENED NAILS	1/2" TO 3"	SMOOTH, BRIGHT OIL QUENCHED
 LNF CUP HEAD AVAILABLE #15 TO #2 GAUGE	COMMON BRAD	2d TO 60d	BRIGHT–MAY BE SECURED WITH CUPPED HEAD, CEMENT COATED–USUALLY MADE IN HEAVY GAUGES
 F	CUT COMMON NAILS OR CUT COMMON SPIKE	2d TO 60d 20d TO 100d	STEEL OR IRON PLAIN OR ZINC COATED
 LNF D GAUGE	COMMON NAILS (SHINGLE NAILS)	2d TO 60d	COPPER–CLAD
 F D LIGHT GAUGE 095" HEAVY GAUGE 120"	COMMON BRASS WIRE NAILS	LIGHT GAUGE: 1/2", 1" TO 3½" HEAVY GAUGE: 3/4"–6"	BRASS, ALUMINUM
 F D 109 (ABOUT 12 GAUGE)	COMMON NAILS (SHINGLE NAILS)	5/8" TO 6"	COPPER WIRE, ALUMINUM
 F	STANDARD CUT NAILS (NON-FERROUS)	5/8" TO 6"	COPPER, MUNTZ METAL OR ZINC
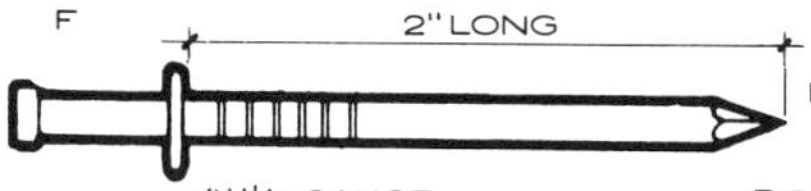 F 2" LONG D #11½ GAUGE	DOUBLE HEADED	1¾", 2", 2¼", 2½", 2¾", 3", 3½", 4", 4½"	BRIGHT, CEMENT COATED, MADE IN SEVERAL DESIGNS
 CUPPED HEAD AVAILABLE D MADE IN 5 DIAMETERS	DOWEL PINS	5/8" TO 2"	BARBED – CUPPED HEAD AVAILABLE
 O D MADE IN 3 GAUGES	ESCUTCHEON PINS	1/4" TO 2"	BRIGHT STEEL, BRASS PLATED, BRASS, ALSO NICKEL, SILVER, COPPER, ALUMINUM
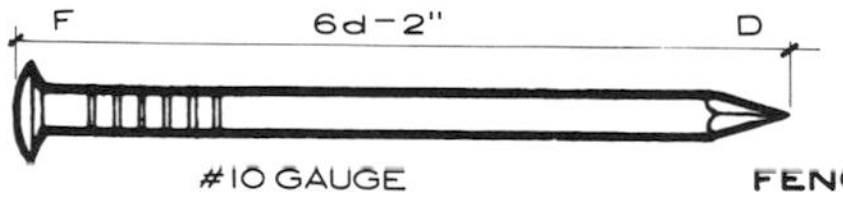 F 6d–2" D #10 GAUGE	FENCE NAILS	5d TO 20d	SMOOTH; BRIGHT, CEMENT COATED (GAUGE HEAVIER THAN COMMON)
 LNF D #15 GAUGE	FINISHING NAIL, WIRE	2d TO 20d	SMOOTH; CUPPED HEADS AVAILABLE (SMALLER GAUGE THAN USUAL COMMON BRAD)
	FINISHING NAILS	STANDARD: 3d TO 20d FINE: 6d TO 10d	CUT IRON AND STEEL
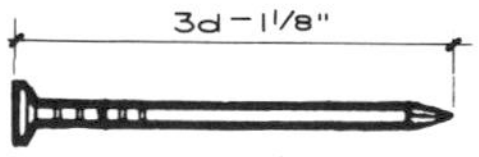 3d–1⅛" #15 & #16 GAUGE	FINE NAILS	2d & 2d EX.FINE 3d & 3d EX.FINE	BRIGHT–SMALLER GAUGE AND HEADS THAN COMMON NAILS
 PC B (ALSO WITH D. POINT) #14 GAUGE	FLOORING NAILS	3d TO 20d 6d TO 20d	BRIGHT AND CEMENT COATED (DIFFERENT GAUGE) CUPPED HEADS AVAILABLE
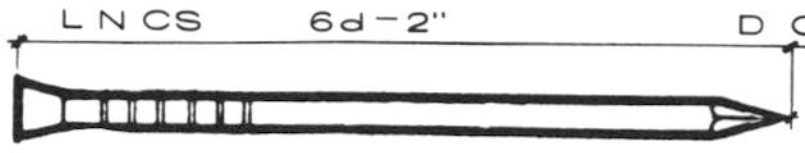 LNCS 6d–2" D OR BLUNT D #11 GAUGE	FLOORING BRAD	6d TO 20d	SMOOTH; BRIGHT AND CEMENT COATED CUPPED HEADS AVAILABLE

NAIL TYPE	SIZE	MATERIAL
NCSF 1 1/8" NEEDLE #15 GAUGE PARQUET FLOORING NAIL OR BRAD	1", 1 1/8", 1 1/4"	SMOOTH OR BARBED
FLOORING NAILS	4d TO 10d	IRON OR STEEL (CUT)
OVAL, - ALSO CS HEAD 1/4" HEAVY CHISEL HINGE NAILS	HEAVY: 1/4" TO 3/8" DIA. LIGHT-3/16" TO 1/4" DIA 1 1/2" TO 4" LONG	SMOOTH, BRIGHT OR ANNEALED
OVAL LONG D 3/16" LIGHT HINGE NAILS	HEAVY-1/4" DIA. LIGHT-3/16" DIA. 1 1/2" TO 3" ALSO TO 4"	SMOOTH, BRIGHT OR ANNEALED
F 3d - 1 1/8" D #15 GAUGE LATH NAILS (WOOD)	2d, 2d LIGHT, 3d, 3d LIGHT, 3d HEAVY 4d.	BRIGHT (NOT RECOMMENDED), BLUED OR CEMENT COATED
F CHECKERED, OVAL CHISEL OR D 3/16" - 1 1/4" GAUGE GUTTER SPIKES	6" TO 10"	STEEL, ZINC COATED
O R #6 1/2" GAUGE HINGE NAILS	1 1/2" TO 3"	STEEL, ZINC COATED
HOOK 1 1/8" #12 GAUGE LATH NAILS (METAL)	1 1/8"	BRIGHT, BLUED, ZINC COATED, ANNEALED
# 14 & #15 GAUGE LATH STAPLES	1" TO 1 1/2"	BRIGHT, BLUED, ZINC COATED, ANNEALED
OFFSET F D # 10 GAUGE LATH OFFSET HEAD NAILS FOR SELF FURRING METAL LATH	1 1/4" TO 1 3/4"	BRIGHT, ZINC COATED
F # 7 - # 9 GAUGE MASONRY NAILS USED FOR FURRING STRIPS CLEATS, PLATES	1/2" TO 4"	HIGH CARBON STEEL, HEATED & TEMPERED
NCSF NEEDLE #14 GAUGE MOLDING NAILS (BRADS)	7/8" TO 1 1/4"	SMOOTH, BRIGHT OR CEMENT COATED
1/2" D #9 OR #10 GAUGE PLASTER-BOARD NAILS USED ALSO FOR WALL-BOARD ROCK LATH (5/16" HEAD)	1" TO 1 3/4" 1 1/8" TO 1 1/2"	SMOOTH, BRIGHT OR CEMENT COATED, BLUED ALUMINUM
F D # 10 GAUGE ROOFING NAILS (STANDARD)	3/4" TO 2"	BRIGHT, CEMENT COATED, ZINC COATED BARBED
F 1" SQ. CUP REINFORCED D # 12 GAUGE ROOFING NAILS FOR BUILT-UP ROOFING	3/8" TO 2"	STEEL, ZINC COATED
UMBRELLA HEAD, FLAT HEAD AVAILABLE D # 9 TO # 10 GAUGE NEOPRENE WASHER ROOFING NAILS	1 1/2" TO 2 1/2"	STEEL, ZINC COATED
F 3/8" TO 1/2" D #8 TO,# 12 GAUGE ROOFING NAILS LARGE HEAD	3/4" TO 1 3/4" ALSO 2" 3/4" TO 2 1/2"	BARBED, BRIGHT OR ZINC COATED CHECKERED HEAD AVAILABLE ALUMINUM (ETCHED) NEOPRENE WASHER OPTIONAL

NAIL TYPE	SIZE	MATERIAL
F REINFORCED 5/8" DIA. 1 1/4" NEEDLE OR D #11 TO #12 GAUGE ALSO #10 GAUGE ROOFING NAILS LARGE HEAD	3/4" TO 1 1/4"	BRIGHT OR ZINC COATED
#10 GAUGE NON-LEAKING ROOFING NAIL	1 3/4" TO 2"	ZINC COATED, ALSO WITH LEAD HEADS
CUT SHEATHING NAILS	3/4" TO 3"	COPPER OR MUNTZ METAL
F LARGE HEAD AVAILABLE 1/4" TO 9/32" 5/16" DIA. #12 GAUGE D SHINGLE NAILS	3d TO 6d 2d TO 6d	SMOOTH, BRIGHT, ZINC, CEMENT COATED, LIGHT AND HEAVY ALUMINUM
CUT SHINGLE NAILS	2d TO 6d	IRON OR STEEL (CUT) PLAIN OR ZINC COATED
F D # 14 GAUGE SIDING NAILS	2d TO 40d 6d TO 10d	SMOOTH, BRIGHT OR CEMENT COATED SMALLER DIAMETER THAN COMMON NAILS ALUMINUM
F D # 11 GAUGE SIDING NAILS USED FOR FENCES, TANKS, GATES, ETC.	2 1/2" TO 3"	STEEL ZINC COATED
F 5/16" TO 3/8" SEVERAL GAUGES SLATING NAILS	3/8" HEAD 1" TO 2" SMALL HEADS 1" TO 2" COPPER WIRE 7/8"-1 1/2"	ZINC COATED, BRIGHT, CEMENT COATED, COPPER CLAD, COPPER
CUT SLATING NAILS, NON-FERROUS	1 1/4" TO 2"	COPPER, ZINC OR MUNTZ METAL
OVAL, SQUARE OR ROUND HEAD CHISEL POINT 1/4" TO 5/8" SQ. BARGE SPIKE, SQUARE	3" TO 12" ALSO 16"	PLAIN AND ZINC COATED USED FOR HARDWOOD
SQUARE OR DIAMOND HEAD 7/32" TO 1/8" DIA. CHISEL POINT 1/4" TO 5/8" SQ. BOAT SPIKE, SQUARE	3" TO 12"	PLAIN AND ZINC COATED USED FOR HARD WOOD
1" HEAD ROOF DECK NAILS	1" AND 1 3/4"	GALVANIZED - NAILS STEEL TUBE
F OR OCS D OR CHISEL POINT #6 TO 3/8" GAUGE ROUND WIRE SPIKES	10d TO 60d & 7" TO 12" ALSO 16"	SMOOTH, BRIGHT OR ZINC COATED

MACHINE BOLT ANCHORS AND SHIELDS (IN.)

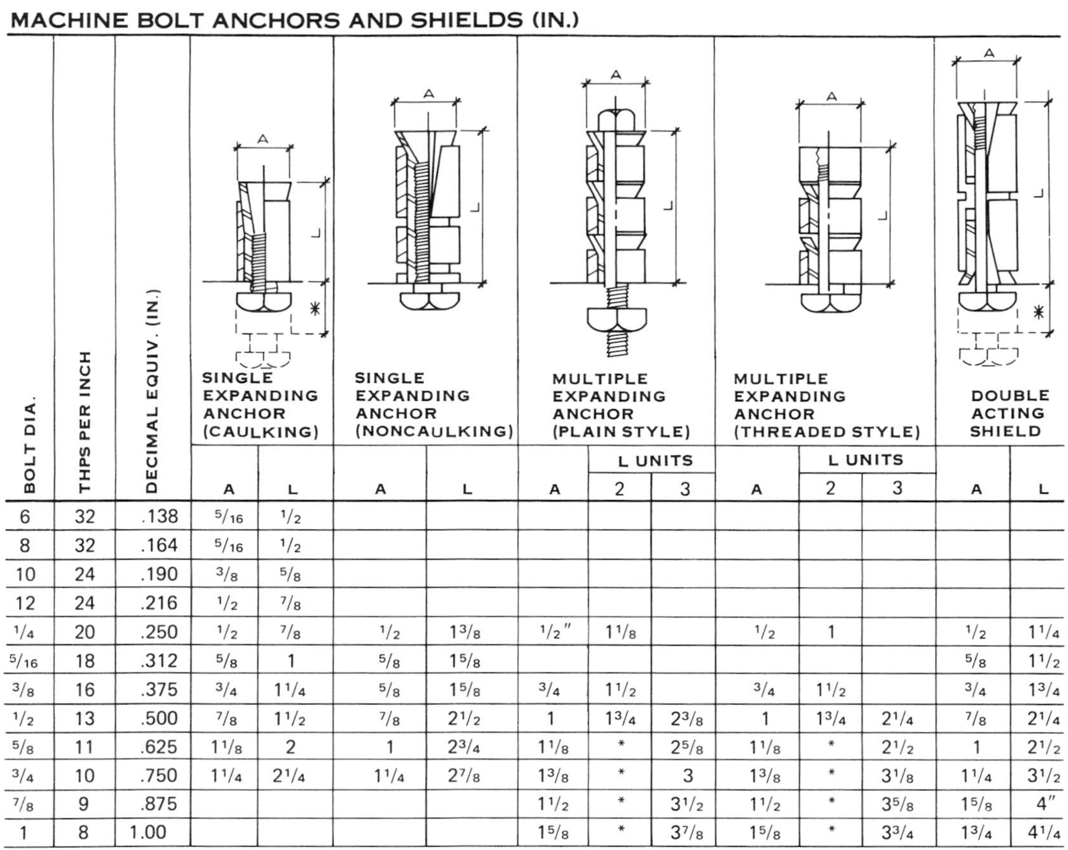

BOLT DIA.	THPS PER INCH	DECIMAL EQUIV. (IN.)	SINGLE EXPANDING ANCHOR (CAULKING)		SINGLE EXPANDING ANCHOR (NONCAULKING)		MULTIPLE EXPANDING ANCHOR (PLAIN STYLE)			MULTIPLE EXPANDING ANCHOR (THREADED STYLE)			DOUBLE ACTING SHIELD	
								L UNITS			L UNITS			
			A	L	A	L	A	2	3	A	2	3	A	L
6	32	.138	5/16	1/2										
8	32	.164	5/16	1/2										
10	24	.190	3/8	5/8										
12	24	.216	1/2	7/8										
1/4	20	.250	1/2	7/8	1/2	1 3/8	1/2"	1 1/8		1/2	1		1/2	1 1/4
5/16	18	.312	5/8	1	5/8	1 5/8							5/8	1 1/2
3/8	16	.375	3/4	1 1/4	5/8	1 5/8	3/4	1 1/2		3/4	1 1/2		3/4	1 3/4
1/2	13	.500	7/8	1 1/2	7/8	2 1/2	1	1 3/4	2 3/8	1	1 3/4	2 1/4	7/8	2 1/4
5/8	11	.625	1 1/8	2	1	2 3/4	1 1/8	*	2 5/8	1 1/8	*	2 1/2	1	2 1/2
3/4	10	.750	1 1/4	2 1/4	1 1/4	2 7/8	1 3/8	*	3	1 3/8	*	3 1/8	1 1/4	3 1/2
7/8	9	.875					1 1/2	*	3 1/2	1 1/2	*	3 5/8	1 5/8	4"
1	8	1.00					1 5/8	*	3 7/8	1 5/8	*	3 3/4	1 3/4	4 1/4

*Use of three units in these diameters is recommended.

NOTE

1. Extension sleeve for deep setting.
2. Expansion shields and anchors shown are representative of many types, some of which may be used in single or multiple units.
3. Many are threaded for use with the head of the screw outside, some with the head inside and some types require setting tools to install.
4. In light construction plastic expansion shields are used frequently.

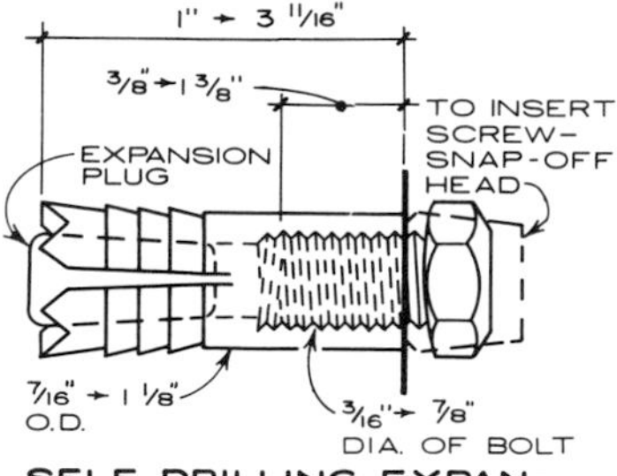

1" → 3 11/16"
3/8" → 1 3/8"
TO INSERT SCREW— SNAP-OFF HEAD
EXPANSION PLUG
7/16" → 1 1/8" O.D.
5/16" → 7/8" DIA. OF BOLT

SELF-DRILLING EXPANSION ANCHOR
(SNAP-OFF TYPE)

NOTE

1. Refer to manufacturers for size variations within the limits shown, and for different types of bolts.
2. The anchor is made of case hardened steel and drawn carburizing steel.

HOLLOW WALL ANCHORS

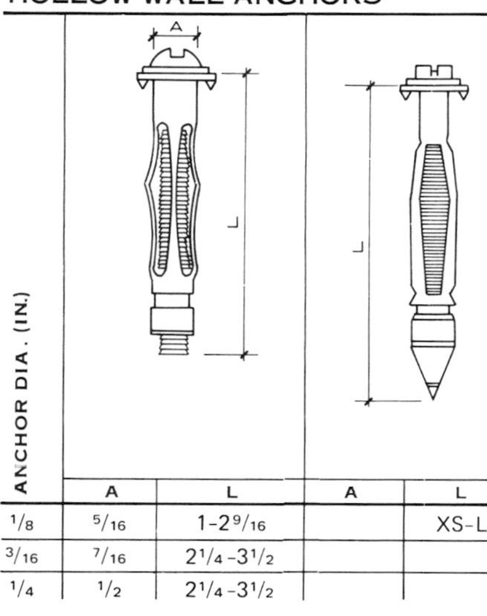

ANCHOR DIA. (IN.)	A	L	A	L
1/8	5/16	1-2 9/16		XS-L
3/16	7/16	2 1/4-3 1/2		
1/4	1/2	2 1/4-3 1/2		

SHIELDS FOR LAG BOLTS AND WOOD SCREWS (IN.)

LAG SCREW DIA. (IN.)	WOOD SCREW SIZES	DECIMAL EQUIV. (IN.)	LAG BOLT EXPANSION SHIELD			LEAD SHIELD FOR LAG BOLT OR WOOD SCREW	
				L			
			A	SHORT	LONG	A	L
	6	.138				1/4	3/4-1 1/2
	8	.164				1/4	3/4-1 1/2
	10	.190				5/16	1-1 1/2
	12	.216				5/16	1-1 1/2
1/4	14	.250	1/2	1	1 1/2	5/16	1-1 1/2
	16	.268				3/8	1 1/2
	18	.294				3/8	1 1/2
5/16	20	.320	1/2	1 1/4	1 3/4	7/16	1 3/4
3/8	24	.372	5/8	1 3/4	2 1/2	7/16	1 3/4
1/2		.500	3/4	2	3		
5/8		.625	7/8	2	3 1/2		
3/4		.750	1	2	3 1/2		

ONE PIECE ANCHORS (IN.)

ANCHOR SIZE AND DRILL SIZE	DECIMAL EQUIV. (IN.)	WEDGE ANCHOR		STUD ANCHOR		SLEEVE ANCHOR		
		L	MIN. HOLE DEPTH D	L	MIN. HOLE DEPTH D	L	MIN. HOLE DEPTH D	HEAD STYLE
1/4	.250	1 3/4-3 1/4	1 3/8	1 3/4-3 1/4	1 3/8	5/8-2 1/4	1/2-1 1/8	Acorn nut
5/16	.320					1 1/2-2 1/2	1 1/8	Hex nut
3/8	.375	2 1/4-5	1 3/4	2 1/4-6	1 5/8	1 7/8-3	1 1/2	"
1/2	.500	2 3/4-7	2 1/8	2 3/4-5 1/4	1 7/8	2 1/4-4	1 7/8	"
5/8	.625	3 1/2-8 1/2	2 5/8	3 3/8-7	2 3/8	2 1/4-6	2	"
3/4	.750	4 1/4-10	3 1/4	4 1/4-8 1/2	2 7/8	2 1/2-8	2 1/4-5 1/2	"
7/8	.875	6-10	3 3/4					
1	1.00	6-12	4 1/2					
1 1/4	1.25	9-12	5 1/2					

Sleeve anchors available in acorn nut, hex nut, flat head, round head, Phillips round head, and tie wire head styles.

MACHINE SCREW AND STOVE BOLT (INS.)

STOVE BOLT DIAM.	MACHINE SCREW DIAM.	ROUND HEAD	FLAT HEAD	FILLISTER HEAD	OVAL HEAD	OVEN HEAD
	2	1/8–7/8		1/8–7/8		
	3	1/8–7/8		1/8–7/8		
	4	1/8–1 1/2	40 N.C.	1/8–1 1/2		
	4	1/8–1 1/2	36 N.C.	1/8–1 1/2		1/8–3/4
1/8	5	1/8–2		1/8–2		3/8–2
	6	1/8–2		1/8–2		1/8–1
5/32	8	3/16–3		3/16–3		3/16–2
3/16	10	3/16–6		3/16–3		1/4–6
	12	1/4–3		1/4–3		
1/4	1/4	5/16–6		5/16–3		3/8–6
5/16	5/16	3/8–6		3/8–3		3/4–6
3/8	3/8	1/2–5		1/2–3		3/4–5
1/2	1/2	1–4				

Length intervals = 1/16 in. increments up to 1/2 in., 1/8 in. increments from 5/8 in. to 1 1/4 in., 1/4 in. increments from 1 1/2 in. to 3 in., 1/2 in. increments from 3 1/2 in. to 6 in.
NOTE: N.C. = Course thread

SCREW AND BOLT LENGTHS (INS.)

DIAMETER (INS.)	CAP SCREWS				BOLTS		
	BUTTON HEAD	FLAT HEAD	HEXAGON HEAD	FILLISTER HEAD	MACHINE BOLT	CARRIAGE BOLT	LAG BOLT
1/4	1/2–2 1/4		1/2–3 1/2	3/4–3	1/2–8	3/4–8	1–6
5/16	1/2–2 3/4		1/2–3 1/2	3/4–3 3/4	1/2–8	3/4–8	1–10
3/8	5/8–3		1/2–4	3/4–3 1/2	3/4–12	3/4–12	1–12
7/16	3/4–3		3/4–4	3/4–3 3/4	3/4–12	1–12	1–12
1/2	3/4–4		3/4–4 1/2	3/4–4	3/4–24	1–20	1–12
9/16	1–4		1–4 1/2	1–4	1–30	1–20	
5/8	1–4		1–5	1 1/4–4 1/2	1–30	1–20	1 1/2–16
3/4	1–4		1 1/4–5	1 1/2–4 1/2	1–30	1–20	1 1/2–16
7/8			2–6	1 3/4–5	1 1/2–30		2–16
1			2–6	2–5	1 1/2–30		2–16

Cap screws: Length intervals = 1/8 in. increments up to 1 in., 1/4 in. increments from 1 1/4 in. to 4 in., 1/2 in. increments from 4 1/2 in. to 6 in.

Machine and carriage bolts: Length intervals = 1/4 in. increments up to 6 in., 1/2 in. increments from 6 1/2 in. to 12 in., 1 in. increments over 12 in.

Lag bolt: Length intervals = 1/2 in. increments up to 8 in., 1 in. increments over 8 in.

ROUND

FLAT

OVAL

PAN

FILLISTER

TRUSS

HEX

WASHER

HEAD TYPES

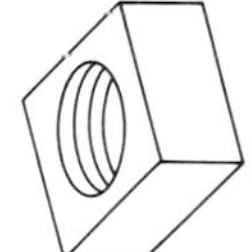
SQUARE

HEX

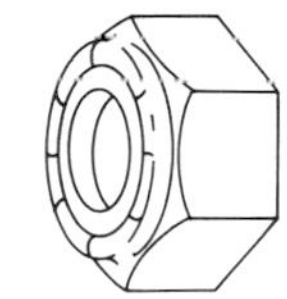
LOCK

CASTELLATED

CAP

WING

Self-locking nuts have a pin that acts as a rachet, sliding down the thread as the bolt is tightened, to prevent loosening from shock and vibration.

LOCK

NUTS

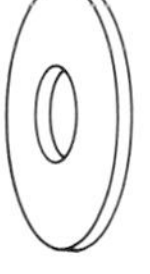
FLAT

LOCK (SPRING)

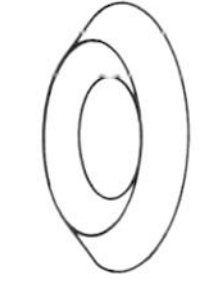
COUNTERSUNK

TOOTHLOCK (INTERNAL)

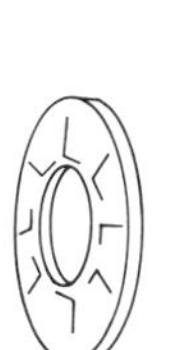
(EXTERNAL)

LOAD INDICATOR

The bolt's clamping force causes protrusions on the washer to flatten partially, closing the gap between the washer and the bolt head. Measurement of the gap indicates whether the bolt has been tightened adequately.

WASHERS

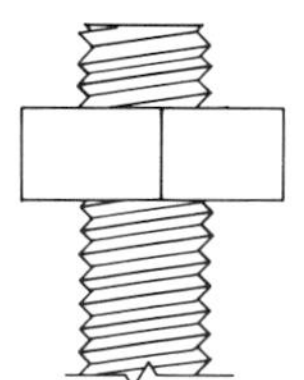

Fiberglass nuts and bolts are noncorrosive and nonconductive. Bolts are available in 3/8 in., 1/2 in., 5/8 in., 3/4 in., and 1 in. standard diameters.

FIBERGLASS NUTS AND BOLTS

High tension, stainless steel helical inserts are held in place by spring-like pressure, and they are used to salvage damaged threads. They also eliminate thread failure due to stress conditions.

HELICAL INSERTS

Interference body bolts are driven into reamed or drilled holes to create a joint in full bearing.

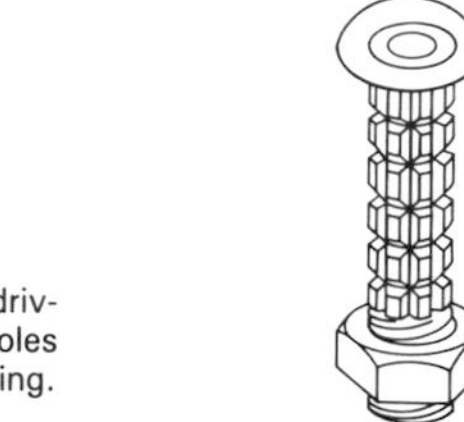

INTERFERENCE BODY BOLTS

D
T
L
C
E
F
A
EYE BOLT (CLOSED)

EYE BOLT (OPEN)

J - BOLT

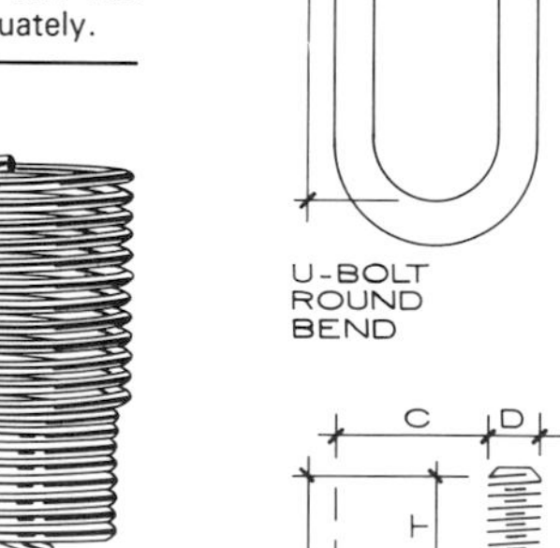
C
D
T
L
U-BOLT ROUND BEND

U-BOLT SQUARE BEND

HOOK BOLT ROUND BEND

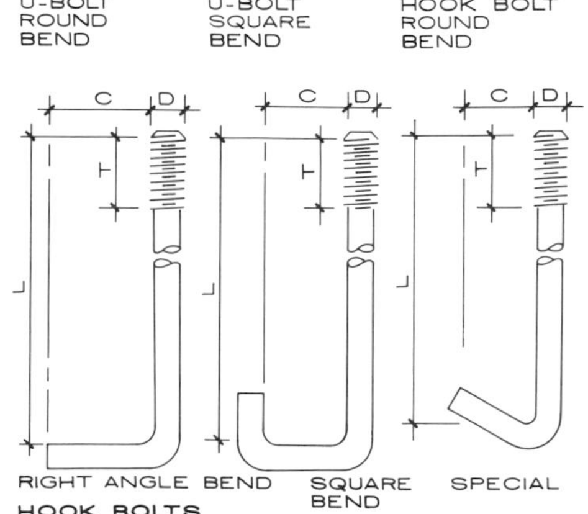
C
D
T
L
RIGHT ANGLE BEND

SQUARE BEND

SPECIAL

HOOK BOLTS

NOTES
1. Bent bolts are specialty items made to order.
2. D = bolt diameter; C = inside opening width; T = thread length; L = inside length of bolt; A = inside depth.

Timothy B. McDonald; Washington, D.C.

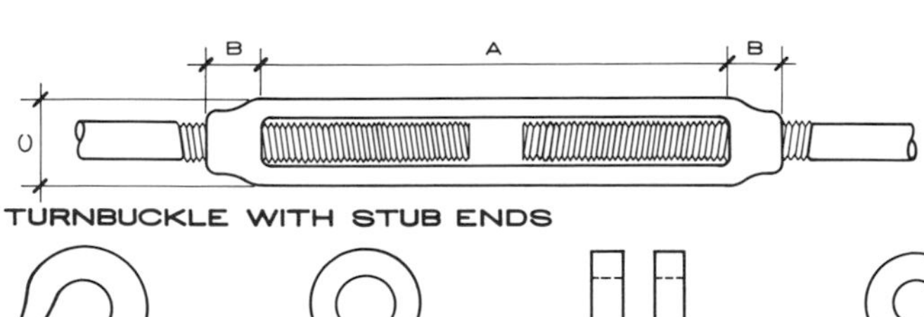
B
A
B
C
TURNBUCKLE WITH STUB ENDS

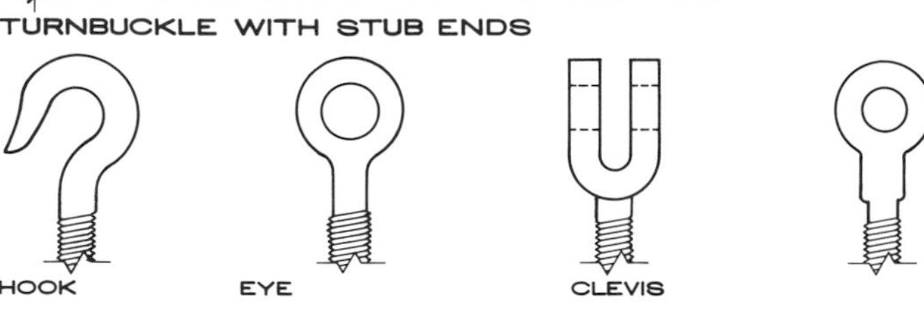
HOOK EYE CLEVIS

TURNBUCKLES (IN INCHES)

DIAMETER	1/4	5/16	3/8	1/2	5/8	3/4	7/8	1
DECI. EQUIV.	.250	.313	.375	.500	.625	.750	.875	1.00
	4	4 1/2	6″	6″	6″	6″	6″	6″
				9″	9″	9″		
A				12″	12″	12″	12″	12″
B	7/16	1/2	9/16	3/4	29/32	1 1/16	1 7/32	1 3/8
C	3/4	7/8	31/32	1 7/32	1 1/2	1 23/32	1 7/8	2 1/32

DIAMETERS OVER 1″ AVAILABLE, NOT ALWAYS STOCKED.

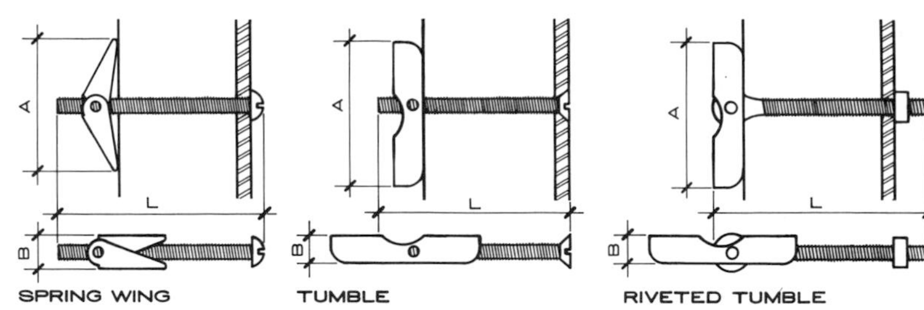
A
L
B
SPRING WING TUMBLE RIVETED TUMBLE

TOGGLE BOLTS (IN INCHES)

DIAMETER		1/8	5/32	3/16	1/4	5/16	3/8	1/2
DECIMAL EQUIV.		.138	.164	.190	.250	.313	.375	.500
	A	1.438	1.875	1.875	2.063	2.750	2.875	4.625
	B	.375	.500	.500	.688	.875	1.000	1.250
SPRING WING	L	2 – 4	2 1/2 – 4	2 – 6	2 1/2 – 6	3 – 6	3 – 6	4 – 6
	A	1.250	2.000	2.000	2.250	2.750	2.750	
	B	.375	.500	.500	.688	.875	.875	
TUMBLE	L	2 – 4	2 1/2 – 4	3 – 6	3 – 6	3 – 6	3 – 6	
	A		2.000	2.000	2.250	2.750	2.750	3.375
	B		.375	.375	.500	.625	.688	.875
RIVETED TUMBLE	L		2 1/2 – 4	3 – 6	3 – 6	3 – 6	3 – 6	3 – 6

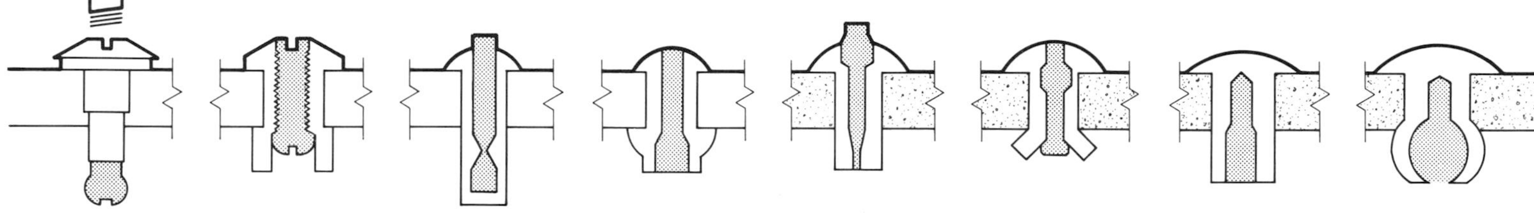
THREADED PULL MANDREL DRIVE PIN CHEMICALLY EXPANDED

BLIND RIVETS FOR USE IN A JOINT THAT IS ACCESSIBLE FROM ONLY ONE SIDE

ROUND

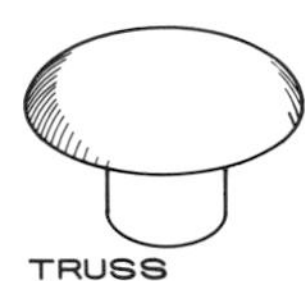
TRUSS

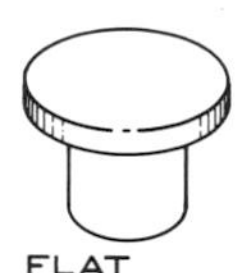
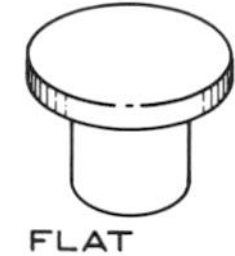
FLAT

COUNTERSUNK

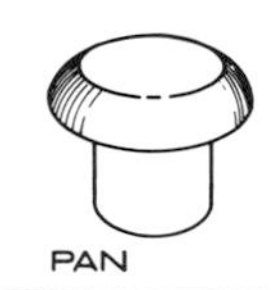
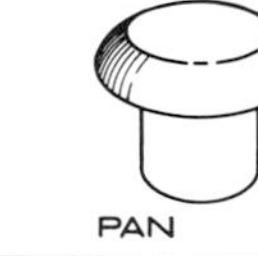
PAN

RIVETS

STANDARD RIVETS AVAILABLE WITH SOLID, TUBULAR AND SPLIT SHANKS OF STEEL, BRASS, COPPER, ALUMINUM, MONEL METAL AND STAINLESS STEEL; IN DIAMETERS OF 1/8″ TO 7/16″ AND LENGTHS OF 3/16″ TO 4 IN.

Self-drilling fasteners: used to attach metal to metal, wood, and concrete. Consult manufacturer for sizes and drilling capabilities.

SELF-DRILLING FASTENERS

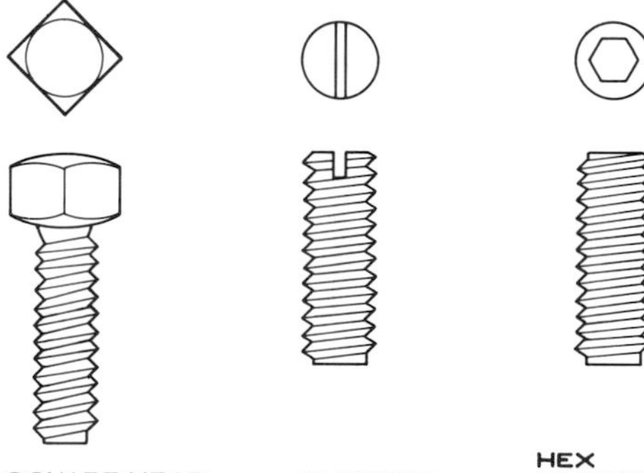
SQUARE HEAD SLOTTED HEX SOCKET

Set Screws: headless with socket or slotted top; made in sizes 4 in. to 1/2 in., and lengths 1/2 in. to 5 in. Square head sizes 1/4 in. to 1 in., and lengths 1/2 in. to 5 in.

SET SCREWS

SHEET METAL GIMLET POINT

Sheet metal gimlet point: hardened, self-tapping. Used in 28 gauge to 6 gauge sheet metal; aluminum, plastic, slate, etc. Usual head types.

SHEET METAL BLUNT POINT

Sheet metal blunt point: hardened, self-tapping. Used in 28 to 18 gauge sheet metal. Made in sizes 4 to 14 in usual head types.

THREAD CUTTING- CUTTING SLOT

Thread cutting, cutting slot: hardened. Used in metals up to 1/4 in. thick in sizes 4 in. to 5/16 in. in usual head types.

SHEET METAL & THREADING SCREWS

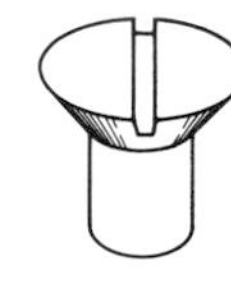
SLOTTED

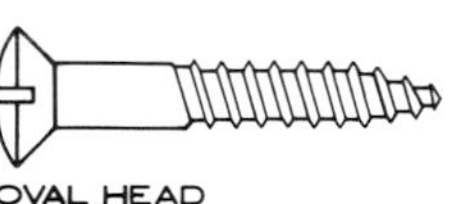
OVAL HEAD

ROUND HEAD

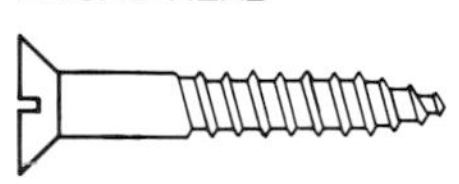

FLAT HEAD

PHILLIPS

FREARSON

WOOD SCREWS (IN IN.)

DIA.	DECI. EQUIV.	LENGTH
0	.060	1/4 – 3/8
1	.073	1/4 – 1/2
2	.086	1/4 – 3/4
3	.099	1/4 – 1
4	.112	1/4 – 1 1/2
5	.125	3/8 – 1 1/2
6	.138	3/8 – 2 1/2
7	.151	3/8 – 2 1/2
8	.164	3/8 – 3
9	.177	1/2 – 3
10	.190	1/2 – 3 1/2
11	.203	5/8 – 3 1/2
12	.216	5/8 – 4
14	.242	3/4 – 5
16	.268	1 – 5
18	.294	1 1/4 – 5
20	.320	1 1/2 – 5
24	.372	3 – 5

DRIVE TYPES

Timothy B. McDonald; Washington, D.C.

Composite construction combines two different materials or two different grades of a material to form a structural member that utilizes the most desirable properties of each material. Examples of composite construction are all around us but may go unrecognized as such. Perhaps the earliest composite structural unit was the mud brick reinforced with straw. Other common examples are: nineteenth century trusses of wood and iron; modern trusses and open web joists of wood and steel; reinforced concrete, which combines the tensile strength of steel with the compressive strength of concrete; cable supported concrete roofs and bridges; fiberglass reinforced plastics; wire reinforced safety glass; plywood; glued laminated wood beams.

Composite systems currently used in building construction include:

1. Concrete topped composite steel decks.
2. Steel beams acting compositely with concrete slabs.
3. Steel columns encased by or filled with concrete.
4. Open web joists of wood and steel or joists with plywood webs and wood chords.
5. Trusses combining wood and steel.
6. Hybrid girders utilizing steels of different strengths.
7. Cast-in-place concrete slab on precast concrete joists or beams.

To make two different materials act compositely as one unit they must be joined at their interface by one or a combination of these means:

1. Chemical bonding (concrete).
2. Gluing (plywood, glulam).
3. Welding (steel, aluminum).
4. Screws (sheet metal, wood).
5. Bolts (steel, wood).
6. Shear studs (steel to concrete).
7. Keys or embossments (steel deck to concrete, concrete to concrete).
8. Dowels (concrete to concrete).
9. Friction (positive clamping force must be present).

Individual elements of the composite unit must be securely fastened to prevent slippage with respect to one another. This principle can be demonstrated by bending a telephone book at its free edges and then trying to bend the book at its binding—the binding makes all the pages resist bending in a combined effort, unlike the free edges where pages slip and slide, offering little resistance.

The illustrations of composite systems show points of potential slippage, which occur where load is transferred from one element of the composite member to another.

Comparative designs are shown below for a floor beam and a roof joist to demonstrate possible reductions in structure weight and cost savings through use of composite design. Additional information on structural economy is presented in this chapter.

FLOOR: DEAD LOAD = 80 PSF
LIVE LOAD = 100 PSF
TOTAL = 180 PSF

ROOF: D.L. = 20 PSF
L.L. = 30 PSF
TOTAL = 50 PSF

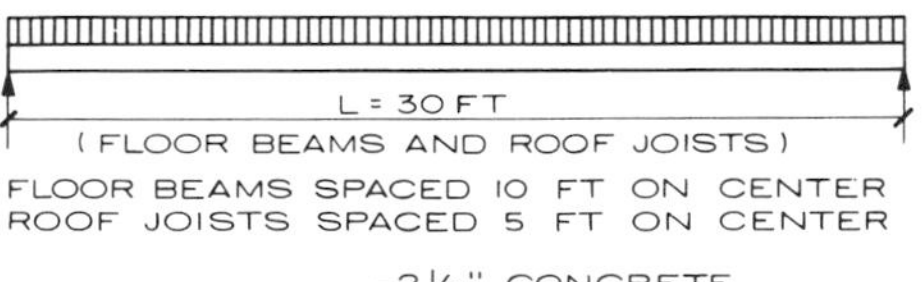
L = 30 FT
(FLOOR BEAMS AND ROOF JOISTS)

FLOOR BEAMS SPACED 10 FT ON CENTER
ROOF JOISTS SPACED 5 FT ON CENTER

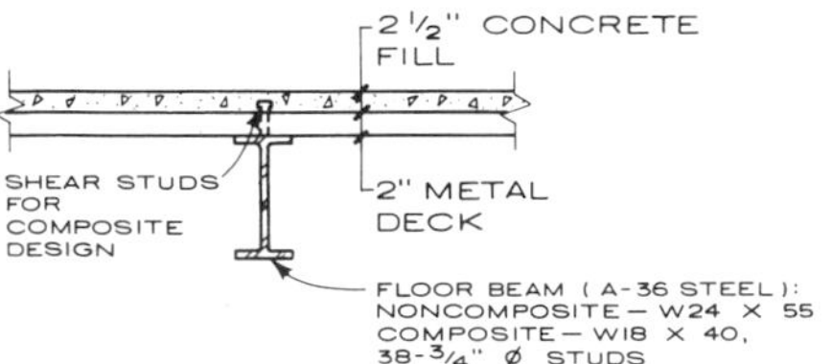
2 1/2" CONCRETE FILL
SHEAR STUDS FOR COMPOSITE DESIGN
2" METAL DECK
FLOOR BEAM (A-36 STEEL): NONCOMPOSITE — W24 × 55 COMPOSITE — W18 × 40, 38-3/4" ø STUDS

ROOF JOIST:
STEEL BEAM (A-36) — W14 × 22 #/FT
STEEL JOIST — 24J6 (9.9 #/FT) OR 20H5 (8.4 #/FT)
WOOD-STEEL JOIST — 26" DEEP (5 #/FT) DOUBLE 1.5" × 2.3" MICRO-LAM CHORDS, STEEL TUBE DIAGONALS — 1 1/2" TO 1" DIA.
(SEE DET. 4B ABOVE)

COMPARATIVE DESIGN EXAMPLE

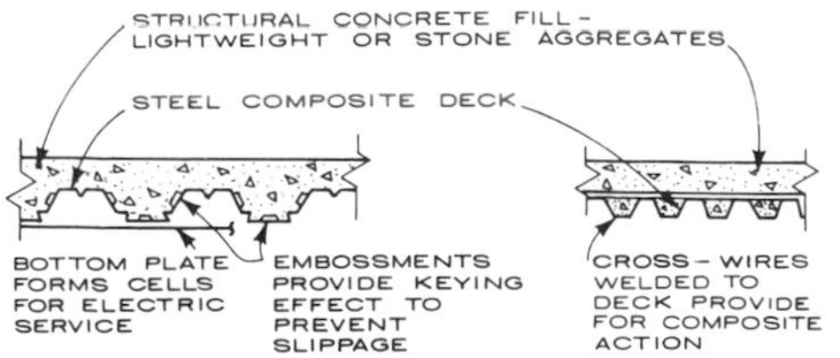
STRUCTURAL CONCRETE FILL - LIGHTWEIGHT OR STONE AGGREGATES
STEEL COMPOSITE DECK
BOTTOM PLATE FORMS CELLS FOR ELECTRIC SERVICE
EMBOSSMENTS PROVIDE KEYING EFFECT TO PREVENT SLIPPAGE
CROSS - WIRES WELDED TO DECK PROVIDE FOR COMPOSITE ACTION

1. CONCRETE TOPPED STEEL DECKING

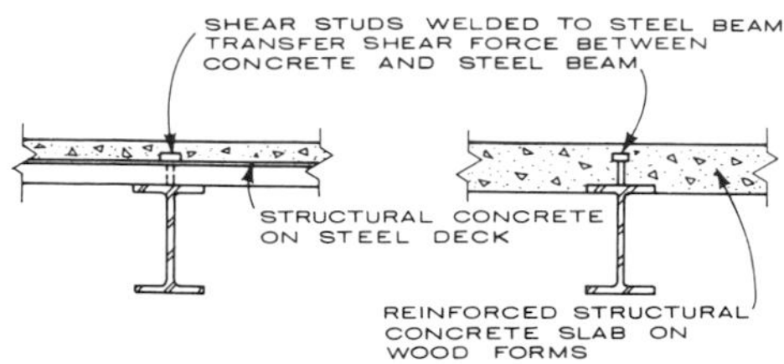
SHEAR STUDS WELDED TO STEEL BEAM TRANSFER SHEAR FORCE BETWEEN CONCRETE AND STEEL BEAM
STRUCTURAL CONCRETE ON STEEL DECK
REINFORCED STRUCTURAL CONCRETE SLAB ON WOOD FORMS

2. STEEL BEAM WITH STUD IN CONCRETE SLAB

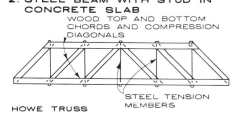

WOOD TOP AND BOTTOM CHORDS AND COMPRESSION DIAGONALS
STEEL TENSION MEMBERS
HOWE TRUSS

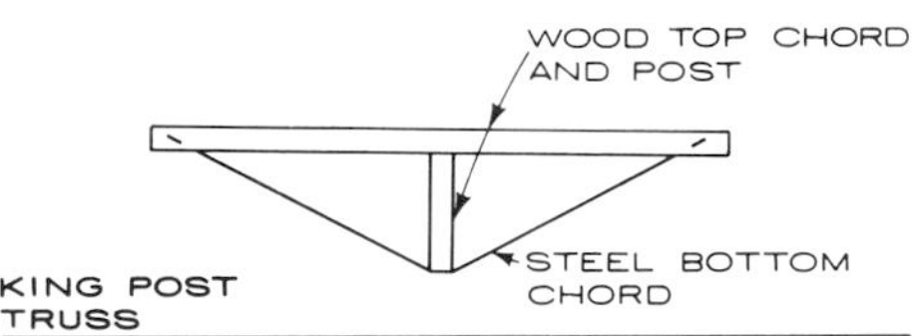
WOOD TOP CHORD AND POST
STEEL BOTTOM CHORD
KING POST TRUSS

5. WOOD AND STEEL TRUSSES

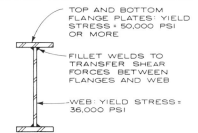

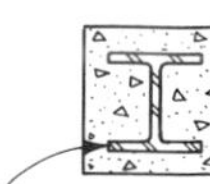

CONCRETE FILL BONDS TO STEEL PIPE OR TUBE
CONCRETE ENCASEMENT BONDS TO STRUCTURAL STEEL COLUMN AND REBARS FOR COMPOSITE ACTION

3. STEEL AND CONCRETE COLUMNS

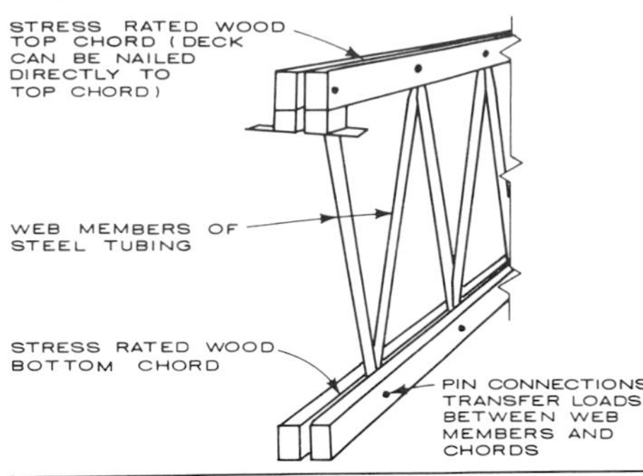
STRESS RATED WOOD TOP CHORD (DECK CAN BE NAILED DIRECTLY TO TOP CHORD)
WEB MEMBERS OF STEEL TUBING
STRESS RATED WOOD BOTTOM CHORD
PIN CONNECTIONS TRANSFER LOADS BETWEEN WEB MEMBERS AND CHORDS

4A. WOOD AND STEEL JOIST

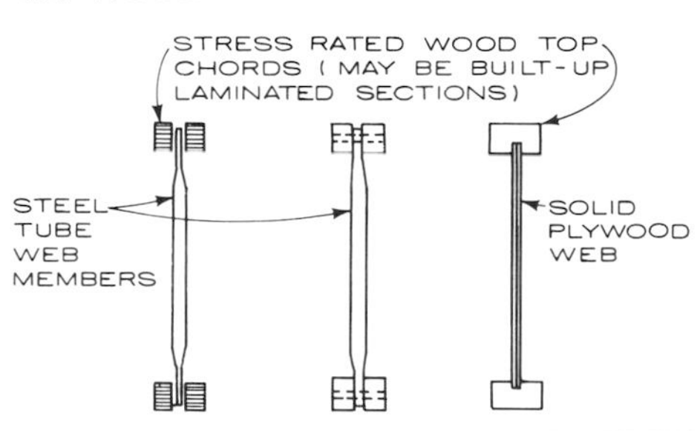
STRESS RATED WOOD TOP CHORDS (MAY BE BUILT-UP LAMINATED SECTIONS)
STEEL TUBE WEB MEMBERS
SOLID PLYWOOD WEB

4. TYPICAL COMPOSITE JOISTS

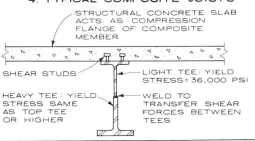

TOP AND BOTTOM FLANGE PLATES: YIELD STRESS = 50,000 PSI OR MORE
FILLET WELDS TO TRANSFER SHEAR FORCES BETWEEN FLANGES AND WEB
WEB: YIELD STRESS = 36,000 PSI

STRUCTURAL CONCRETE SLAB ACTS AS COMPRESSION FLANGE OF COMPOSITE MEMBER
SHEAR STUDS
LIGHT TEE: YIELD STRESS = 36,000 PSI
HEAVY TEE: YIELD STRESS SAME AS TOP TEE OR HIGHER
WELD TO TRANSFER SHEAR FORCES BETWEEN TEES

6A. HYBRID GIRDERS (USING DIFFERENT STRENGTH STEELS)

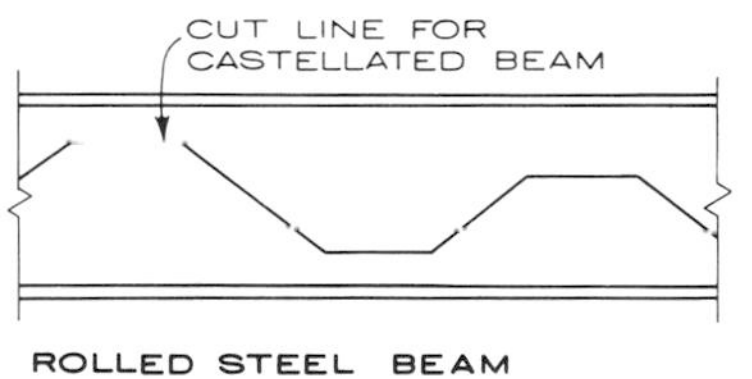
CUT LINE FOR CASTELLATED BEAM
ROLLED STEEL BEAM BEFORE CUTTING

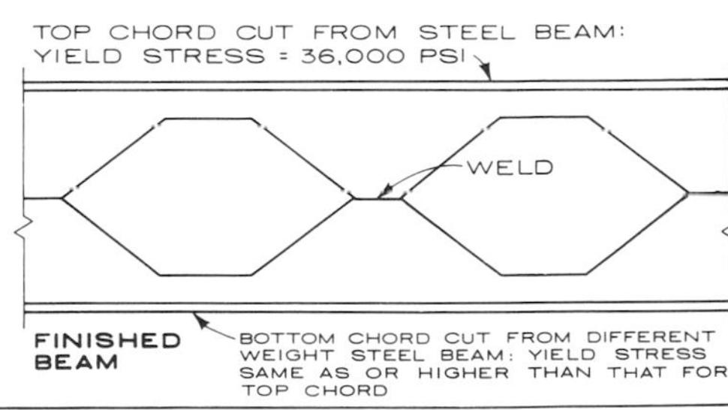
TOP CHORD CUT FROM STEEL BEAM: YIELD STRESS = 36,000 PSI
WELD
FINISHED BEAM
BOTTOM CHORD CUT FROM DIFFERENT WEIGHT STEEL BEAM: YIELD STRESS SAME AS OR HIGHER THAN THAT FOR TOP CHORD

6 CASTELLATED BEAMS

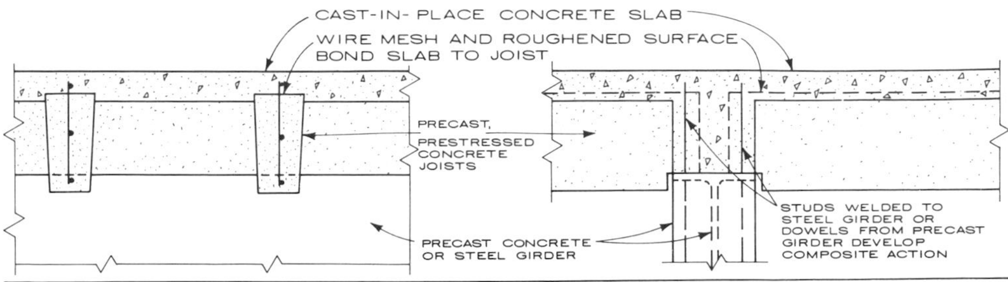
CAST-IN-PLACE CONCRETE SLAB
WIRE MESH AND ROUGHENED SURFACE BOND SLAB TO JOIST
PRECAST, PRESTRESSED CONCRETE JOISTS
PRECAST CONCRETE OR STEEL GIRDER
STUDS WELDED TO STEEL GIRDER OR DOWELS FROM PRECAST GIRDER DEVELOP COMPOSITE ACTION

7. REINFORCED CONCRETE SLAB AND PRECAST JOIST

Walter D. Shapiro, P.E.; Tor, Shapiro & Associates; New York, New York

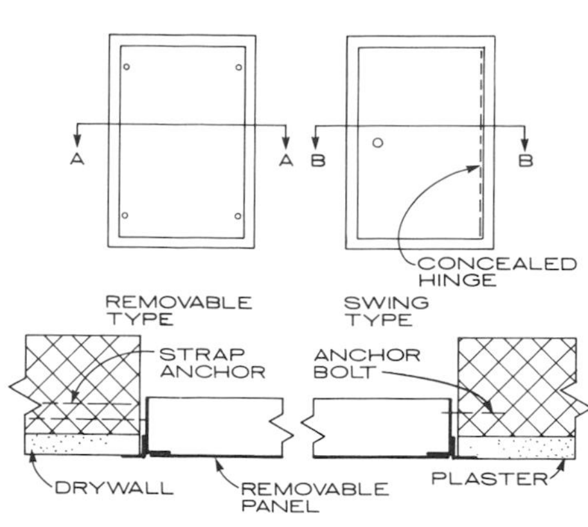
A
A
B
B
CONCEALED HINGE
REMOVABLE TYPE
SWING TYPE
STRAP ANCHOR
ANCHOR BOLT
DRYWALL
REMOVABLE PANEL
PLASTER

SECTION A-A

NOTES

1. Frames usually are set into building construction; doors are constructed to fit later. Doors may be hinged, set in with clips, or fastened with screws. Hinges may be butt or pivot, separate or continuous, surface or concealed. Assorted stock sizes range from 8 in. x 8 in. to 24 in. x 36 in.
2. Access panels should have a fire rating similar to the wall in which they occur. Access panels of more than 144 sq. ins. require automatic closers.
3. Minimum size for attic and crawl space access often is specified by building code.

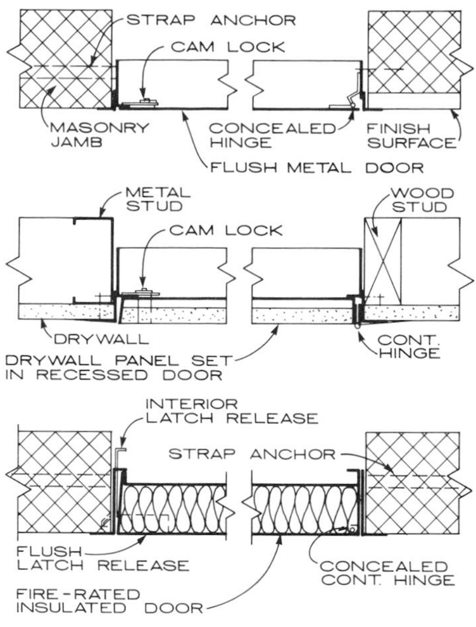
STRAP ANCHOR
CAM LOCK
MASONRY JAMB
CONCEALED HINGE
FINISH SURFACE
FLUSH METAL DOOR
METAL STUD
WOOD STUD
CAM LOCK
DRYWALL
CONT. HINGE
DRYWALL PANEL SET IN RECESSED DOOR
INTERIOR LATCH RELEASE
STRAP ANCHOR
FLUSH LATCH RELEASE
CONCEALED CONT. HINGE
FIRE-RATED INSULATED DOOR

SECTION B-B

ACCESS DOORS

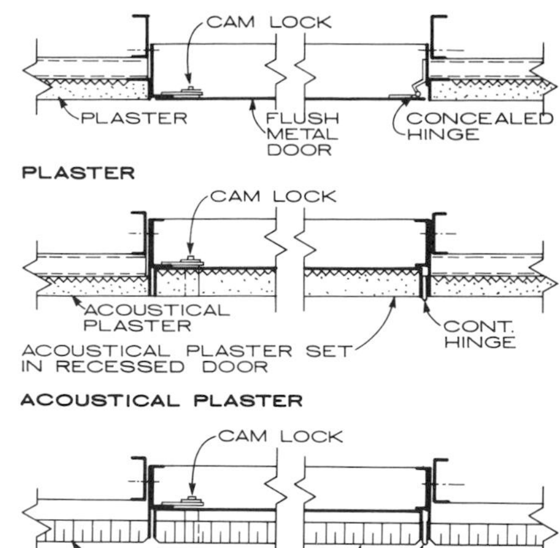
CAM LOCK
PLASTER
FLUSH METAL DOOR
CONCEALED HINGE
PLASTER
CAM LOCK
ACOUSTICAL PLASTER
ACOUSTICAL PLASTER SET IN RECESSED DOOR
CONT. HINGE
ACOUSTICAL PLASTER
CAM LOCK
ACOUSTICAL TILE
ACOUSTICAL TILE SET IN RECESSED DOOR
CONT. HINGE
ACOUSTICAL TILE

NOTES

1. Spring-operated, swingdown panels and swingup panels frequently are used for ceiling access.
2. Standard sizes range from 12 in. x 12 in. to 24 in. x 36 in.
3. Other finish ceiling panels are detailed similar to acoustical tiles.

CEILING ACCESS PANELS

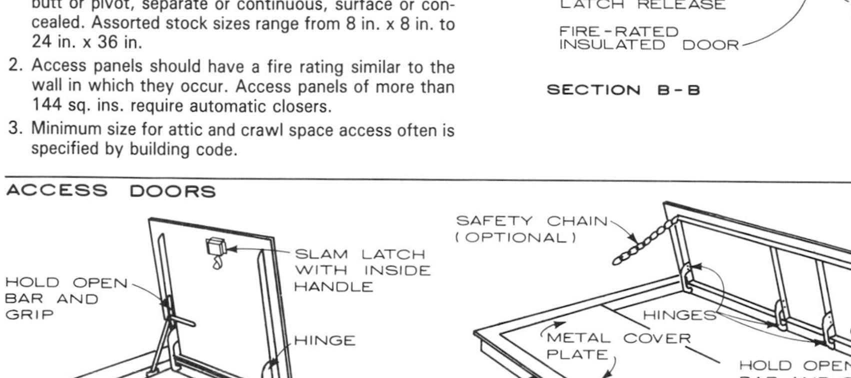
HOLD OPEN BAR AND GRIP
SLAM LATCH WITH INSIDE HANDLE
HINGE
C
C
EXTRUDED ALUMINUM FRAME
STEEL STRAP ANCHOR
SAFETY CHAIN (OPTIONAL)
HINGES
METAL COVER PLATE
HOLD OPEN BAR AND GRIP
C
C
REMOVABLE KEY WRENCH
ALUMINUM FRAME
STEEL STRAP ANCHOR

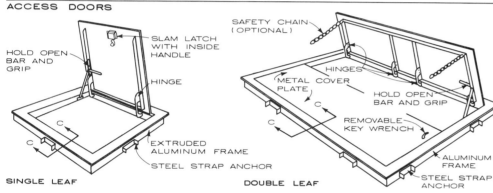

SINGLE LEAF

DOUBLE LEAF

1. MATERIAL: Steel or aluminum.
2. SIZES: Single leaf—2 ft. x 2 ft., 2 ft. 6 in. x 2 ft. 6 in., 2 ft. 6 in. x 3 ft., 3 ft. x 3 ft. Double leaf—3 ft. 6 in. x 3 ft. 6 in., 4 ft. x 4 ft., 4 ft. x 6 ft., 5 ft. x 5 ft.

Thickness "T" varies from 1/8 in. for resilient flooring to 3/16 in. for carpet; some manufacturers offer 3/4 in. for terrazzo and tile floor.

Double-leaf floor hatch is recommended for areas where there is danger a person could fall into the opening. Safety codes require that floor openings be protected. Check local codes for special requirements.

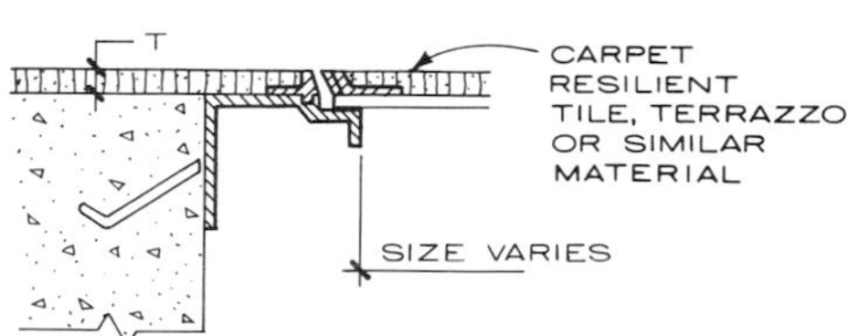
T
CARPET RESILIENT TILE, TERRAZZO OR SIMILAR MATERIAL
SIZE VARIES

FLOOR HATCH – SECTION C-C

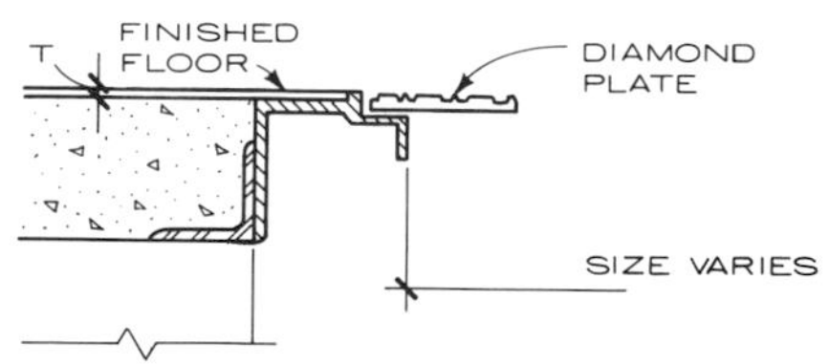
FINISHED FLOOR
T
DIAMOND PLATE
SIZE VARIES

FLOOR HATCH – SECTION C-C

FLOOR HATCHES

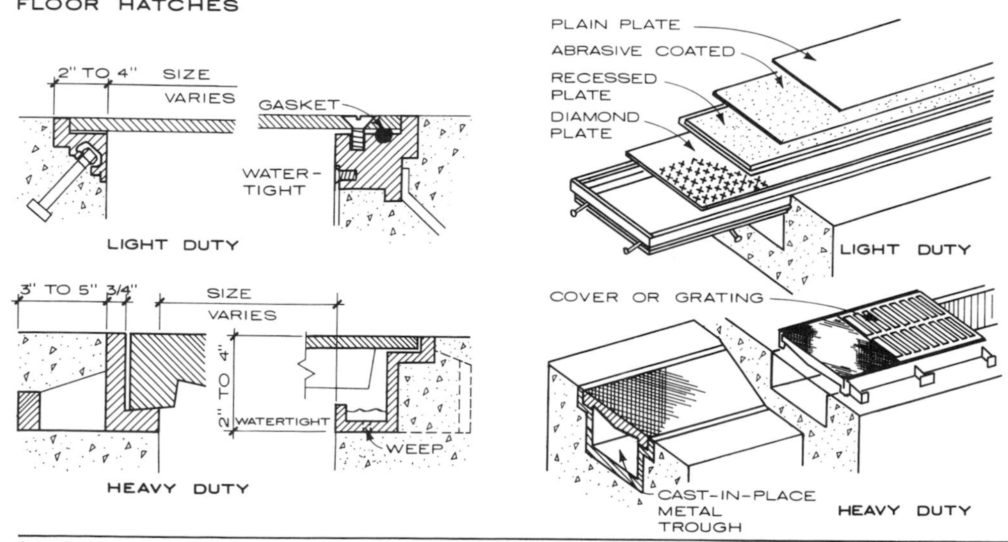
2" TO 4"
SIZE VARIES
GASKET
WATER-TIGHT
LIGHT DUTY
3" TO 5"
3/4"
SIZE VARIES
2" TO 4"
WATERTIGHT
WEEP
HEAVY DUTY
PLAIN PLATE
ABRASIVE COATED
RECESSED PLATE
DIAMOND PLATE
LIGHT DUTY
COVER OR GRATING
CAST-IN-PLACE METAL TROUGH
HEAVY DUTY

LIGHT-DUTY TRENCH COVERS

1. MATERIAL: Extruded aluminum.
2. SIZE: 2 in. to 36 in. wide. Side frames are available in cut length of 20 ft. stocks that can be spliced to any length. Recessed cover plates are available in 20 ft. stock; other covers are available in 10 ft. and 12 ft. stock.
3. Side frames normally are cast in concrete around trough form.

HEAVY-DUTY TRENCH COVERS

1. MATERIAL: Cast iron or ductile iron.
2. SIZES: Heavy duty cast iron trench covers should be planned carefully to use standard stock length to avoid cutting, or special length casting should be ordered.
3. STOCK COVER SIZE: To 48 in. wide and 24 in. long. Frames are manufactured in standard lengths of 24 in. or 36 in. depending on size and manufacturer. Cast iron troughs are 8 in. deep, 6 in. to 24 in. wide, and 48 in. in stock lengths.
4. Minimum grating size in walkways is specified in ANSI A117.1-1986.

TRENCH COVERS

Cohen, Karydas & Associates, Chartered; Washington, D.C.
Harold C. Munger, FAIA; Munger Munger + Associates Architects, Inc.; Toledo, Ohio

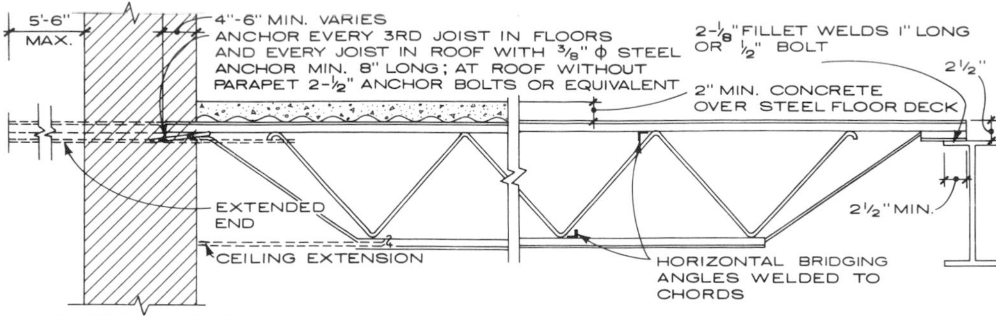

5'-6" MAX.
4"-6" MIN. VARIES
ANCHOR EVERY 3RD JOIST IN FLOORS AND EVERY JOIST IN ROOF WITH 3/8" ϕ STEEL ANCHOR MIN. 8" LONG; AT ROOF WITHOUT PARAPET 2-1/2" ANCHOR BOLTS OR EQUIVALENT
2-1/8" FILLET WELDS 1" LONG OR 1/2" BOLT
2 1/2"
2" MIN. CONCRETE OVER STEEL FLOOR DECK
EXTENDED END
2 1/2" MIN.
CEILING EXTENSION
HORIZONTAL BRIDGING ANGLES WELDED TO CHORDS

SECTION THROUGH JOIST BEARING

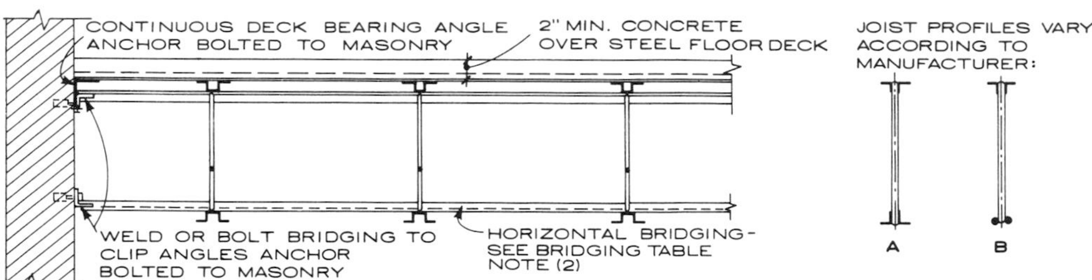

CONTINUOUS DECK BEARING ANGLE ANCHOR BOLTED TO MASONRY
2" MIN. CONCRETE OVER STEEL FLOOR DECK
JOIST PROFILES VARY ACCORDING TO MANUFACTURER:
A
B
WELD OR BOLT BRIDGING TO CLIP ANGLES ANCHOR BOLTED TO MASONRY
HORIZONTAL BRIDGING - SEE BRIDGING TABLE NOTE (2)

SECTION THROUGH JOISTS

PRELIMINARY JOIST SELECTION: The tables below are not to be used for final joist design but are intended as an aid in speeding selection of steel joists for preliminary design and planning. The final design must be a separate and thorough process, involving a complete investigation of the pertinent conditions. This page is not for that purpose. Consult structural engineer.

EXAMPLE: Assume a particular clear span. By assuming a joist spacing and estimating the total load a joist can immediately be selected from the table. Then proceed with preliminary design studies.

NOTES

1. Total safe load = live load + dead load. Dead load includes weight of joist. For dead loads and recommended live loads, see pages on weights of materials. Local codes will govern.
2. Span not to exceed a depth 24 times that of a nominal joist.
3. For more detailed information refer to standard specifications and load tables adopted by the Steel Joist Institute.

NUMBER OF ROWS OF BRIDGING (FT)

DISTANCES ARE CLEAR SPAN DIMENSIONS

CHORD SIZE[1]	1 ROW	2 ROWS	3 ROWS	4 ROWS[2]	5 ROWS[2]
#1	Up to 16	16–24	24–28	—	—
#2	Up to 17	17–25	25–32	—	—
#3	Up to 18	18–28	28–38	38–40	—
#4	Up to 19	19–28	28–38	38–48	—
#5	Up to 19	19–29	29–39	39–50	50–52
#6	Up to 19	19–29	29–39	39–51	51–56
#7	Up to 20	20–33	33–45	45–58	58–60
#8	Up to 20	20–33	33–45	45–58	58–60
#9	Up to 20	20–33	33–46	46–59	59–60
#10	Up to 20	20–37	37–51	51–60	
#11	Up to 20	20–38	38–53	53–60	
#12	Up to 20	20–39	39–53	53–60	

1. Last digit(s) of joist designation shown in load table below.
2. Where four or five rows of bridging are required, a row nearest the midspan of the joist shall be diagonal bridging with bolted connections at chords and intersections.

NOTES

The following information applies to both open web and long span steel joists.

JOIST DESIGNATION:

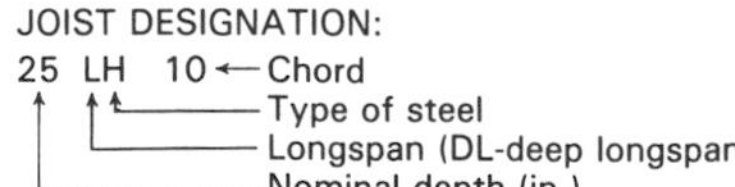

25 LH 10 ← Chord
Type of steel
Longspan (DL-deep longspan)
Nominal depth (in.)

For greater economy, the K-series joist replaced the H-series joist in 1986.

1. ROOF CONSTRUCTION: Joists are usually covered by steel deck topped with either rigid insulation board or lightweight concrete fill and built-up felt and gravel roof. Plywood, poured gypsum, or structural wood fiber deck systems can also be used with built-up roof.
2. CEILINGS: Ceiling supports can be suspended from or mounted directly to bottom chords of joists, although suspended systems are recommended because of dimensional variations in actual joist depths.
3. FLOOR CONSTRUCTION: Joists usually covered by 2 to 2 1/2 in. concrete on steel centering. Concrete thickness may be increased for electrical conduit or electrical/communications raceways. Precast concrete, gypsum planks, or plywood can also be used for the floor system.
4. VIBRATION: Objectionable vibrations can occur in open web joist and 2 1/2 in. concrete slab designs for open floor areas at spans between 24 and 40 ft, especially at 28 ft. When a floor area cannot have partitions, objectionable vibrations can be prevented or reduced by increasing slab thickness, joist spacing, or floor spans. Attention should also be given to support framing beams which can magnify a vibration problem.
5. OPENINGS IN FLOOR OR ROOF SYSTEMS: Small openings between joists are framed with angles of channel supported on the adjoining two joists. Larger openings necessitating interruption of joists are framed with steel angle or channel headers spanning the adjoining two joists. The interrupted joists bear on the headers.
6. ROOF DRAINAGE: Roof drainage should be carefully considered on level or near level roofs especially with parapet walls. Roof insulation can be sloped, joists can be sloped or obtained with sloping top chords in one or both directions, and overflow scuppers should be provided in parapet walls.

SELECTED LOAD TABLES: K SERIES—TOTAL SAFE UNIFORMLY DISTRIBUTED LOAD (LB/FT)

JOIST DESIGNATION		8	12	16	20	24	28	32	36	42	48	54	60
K SERIES f_s = 30,000 psi	8K1	550	444	246									
	10K1		550	313	199								
	12K3		550	476	302	208							
	14K4			550	428	295	216						
	16K5			550	550	384	281	214					
	18K6				550	473	346	264	208				
	20K7				550	550	430	328	259				
	22K9					550	550	436	344	252			
	24K9					550	550	478	377	276	211		
	26K10						550	549	486	356	272		
	28K10						550	549	487	384	294	232	
	30K11							549	487	417	362	285	231
	30K12							549	487	417	365	324	262

Note: Number preceding letter is joist depth; 14K4 is 14 in. deep.

Kenneth D. Franch, AIA, PE; Phillips Swager Associates, Inc.; Dallas, Texas
Setter, Leach & Lindstrom, Inc.; Minneapolis, Minnesota

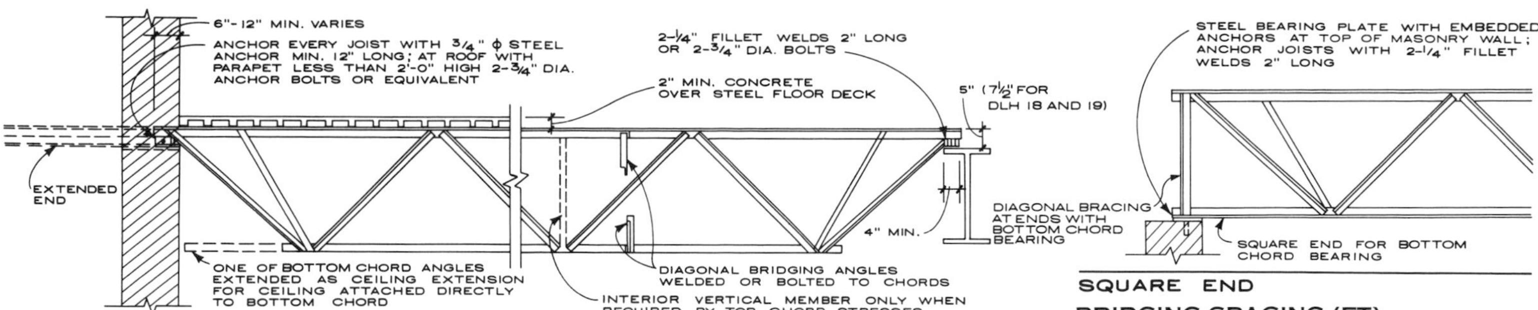
6"-12" MIN. VARIES
ANCHOR EVERY JOIST WITH 3/4" ϕ STEEL ANCHOR MIN. 12" LONG; AT ROOF WITH PARAPET LESS THAN 2'-0" HIGH 2-3/4" DIA. ANCHOR BOLTS OR EQUIVALENT
2-1/4" FILLET WELDS 2" LONG OR 2-3/4" DIA. BOLTS
2" MIN. CONCRETE OVER STEEL FLOOR DECK
5" (7 1/2" FOR DLH 18 AND 19)
EXTENDED END
4" MIN.
ONE OF BOTTOM CHORD ANGLES EXTENDED AS CEILING EXTENSION FOR CEILING ATTACHED DIRECTLY TO BOTTOM CHORD
DIAGONAL BRIDGING ANGLES WELDED OR BOLTED TO CHORDS
INTERIOR VERTICAL MEMBER ONLY WHEN REQUIRED BY TOP CHORD STRESSES
STEEL BEARING PLATE WITH EMBEDDED ANCHORS AT TOP OF MASONRY WALL; ANCHOR JOISTS WITH 2-1/4" FILLET WELDS 2" LONG
DIAGONAL BRACING AT ENDS WITH BOTTOM CHORD BEARING
SQUARE END FOR BOTTOM CHORD BEARING

SECTION THROUGH JOIST BEARING

SQUARE END

BRIDGING SPACING (FT)

LH CHORD SIZE†	MAXIMUM SPACING (FT)
02-09	11
10-14	16
15-17	21
DLH CHORD SIZE†	**MAXIMUM SPACING (FT)**
10	14
11-14	16
15-17	21
18-19	26

†Last two digits of joist designation shown in load tables.

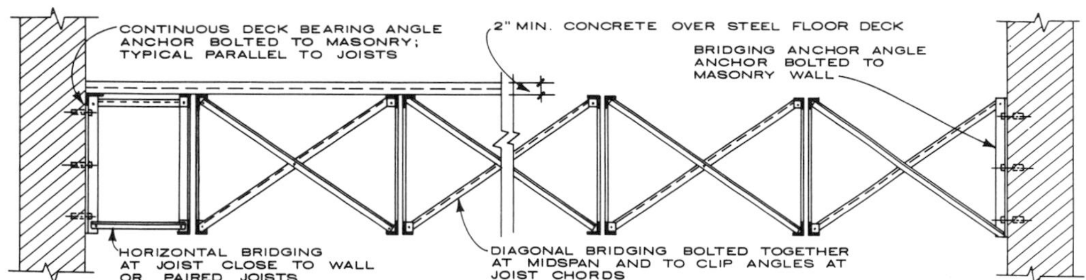
CONTINUOUS DECK BEARING ANGLE ANCHOR BOLTED TO MASONRY; TYPICAL PARALLEL TO JOISTS
2" MIN. CONCRETE OVER STEEL FLOOR DECK
BRIDGING ANCHOR ANGLE ANCHOR BOLTED TO MASONRY WALL
HORIZONTAL BRIDGING AT JOIST CLOSE TO WALL OR PAIRED JOISTS
DIAGONAL BRIDGING BOLTED TOGETHER AT MIDSPAN AND TO CLIP ANGLES AT JOIST CHORDS

SECTION THROUGH JOISTS

PRELIMINARY JOIST SELECTION

The tables below are not to be used for final joist design but are intended as an aid in speeding selection of steel joists for preliminary design and planning.

The final design must be a separate thorough process, involving a complete investigation of the pertinent conditions. This page is not for that purpose. Consult a structural engineer.

EXAMPLE

Assume a particular clear span. By assuming a joist spacing and estimating the total load a joist can immediately be selected from the table. Then proceed with preliminary design studies.

NOTES

1. Total safe load = live load + dead load. Dead load includes weight of joist. For dead loads and recommended live loads, see pages on weights of materials. Local codes will govern.
2. Span not to exceed 24 times depth of a nominal joist for roofs; 20 times depth for floors.
3. For more detailed information refer to standard specifications and load tables adopted by the Steel Joist Institute.

FIRE RESISTANCE RATINGS

TIME (HR)	FLOOR ASSEMBLIES	TIME (HR)	ROOF ASSEMBLIES
1 or 1 1/2	2" reinforced concrete, listed 1/2" (5/8" for 1 1/2 hr) acoustical tile ceiling, concealed ceiling grid suspended from joists	1	Built-up roofing on 2" structural wood fiber units, listed 3/4" acoustical ceiling tiles, concealed ceiling grid suspended from joists
	2" reinforced concrete, listed 1/2" acoustical board ceiling, listed exposed ceiling grid suspended from joists		Built-up roofing and insulation on 26 gauge min. steel deck, listed 5/8" acoustical ceiling boards, listed exposed ceiling grid suspended from joists
	2" reinforced concrete, listed 1/2" gypsum board ceiling fastened to joists		Built-up roofing over 2" vermiculite on centering, listed 1/2" acoustical ceiling boards, listed exposed ceiling grid suspended from joists
2	2 1/2" reinforced concrete, listed 5/8" acoustical tile ceiling, listed concealed ceiling grid suspended from joists		
	2 1/2" reinforced concrete, listed 1/2" acoustical board ceiling, listed exposed ceiling grid suspended from joists	2	Built-up roofing on 2" listed gypsum building units, listed 5/8" acoustical ceiling boards, listed exposed ceiling grid suspended from joists
	2" reinforced concrete, listed 5/8" gypsum board ceiling fastened to joists		Built-up roofing on 22 gauge min. steel deck, suspended 7/8" metal lath and plaster ceiling
	2 1/2" reinforced concrete, listed 1/2" gypsum board ceiling fastened to joists		

NOTE: Listed by Underwriters Laboratories or Factory Mutual approved, as appropriate. Ratings are the result of tests made in accordance with ASTM Standard E 119. A more complete list can be obtained from the SJI Technical Digest concerning the design of fire resistive assemblies with steel joists.

SELECTED LOAD TABLES: LH AND DLH SERIES—TOTAL SAFE UNIFORMLY DISTRIBUTED LOAD (LB/FT)

JOIST DESIGNATION		CLEAR SPAN (FT)												
		28	32	36	42	48	54	60	66	72	78	84	90	96
LH Series f_s = 30,000 psi	18LH05	581	448	355										
	20LH06	723	560	444										
	24LH07			588	446	343								
	28LH09				639	499	401							
	32LH10						478	389						
	36LH11							451	378	322				
	40LH12								472	402	346			
	44LH13										423	369		
	48LH14											444	390	346
		90	96	102	108	114	120	126	132	138	144			
DLH Series f_s = 30,000 psi	52DLH13	433	381	338										
	56DLH14			411	368									
	60DLH15				442	398	361							
	64DLH16					466	421	382						
	68DLH17							460	420					
	72DLH18								505	463	426			

NOTE: Number preceding letter is joist depth; 32LH10 is 32 in. deep.

Setter, Leach & Lindstrom, Inc.; Minneapolis, Minnesota

EXAMPLES OF THE MANY TYPES OF DECK AVAILABLE (SEE TABLES)

1. Roof deck.
2. Floor deck (noncomposite).
3. Composite floor deck interacting with concrete.
4. Permanent forms for self-supporting concrete slabs.
5. Cellular deck (composite or noncomposite).
6. Acoustical roof deck.
7. Acoustic cellular deck (composite or non-composite).
8. Electric raceway cellular deck.
9. Prevented roof deck (used with lightweight insulating concrete fill).

All metal floor and roof decks must be secured to all supports, generally by means of "puddle welds" made through the deck to supporting steel. Steel sheet lighter than 22 gauge (0.0295 in. thick) should be secured by use of welding washers (see illustration).

Shear studs welded through floor deck also serve to secure the deck to supporting steel. Power actuated and pneumatically driven fasteners may also be used in certain applications.

Side laps between adjacent sheets of deck must be secured by button-punching standing seams, welding, or screws, in accordance with manufacturer's recommendations.

Decks used as lateral diaphragms must be welded to steel supports around their entire perimeter to ensure development of diaphragm action. More stringent requirements may govern the size and/or spacing of attachments to supports and side lap fasteners or welds.

Roof deck selection must take into consideration construction and maintenance loads as well as the capacity to support uniformly distributed live loads. Consult current Steel Deck Institute recommendations and Factory Mutual requirements.

Floor deck loadings are virtually unlimited in scope, ranging from light residential and institutional loads to heavy duty industrial floors utilizing composite deck with slabs up to 24 in. thick. The designer can select the deck type, depth, and gauge most suitable for the application.

Fire resistance ratings for roof deck assemblies are published by Underwriters Laboratories and Factory Mutual. Ratings of 1 to 2 hr are achieved with spray-on insulation: a 1 hr rating with suspended acoustical ceiling and a 2 hr rating with a metal lath and plaster ceiling.

Floor deck assembly fire resistive ratings are available both with and without spray-applied fireproofing, and with regular weight or lightweight concrete fill. From 1 to 3 hr ratings are possible using only concrete fill—consult Underwriters Laboratory Fire Resistance Index for assembly ratings.

Consult manufacturer's literature and technical representatives for additional information. Consult "Steel Deck Institute Design Manual for Floor Decks and Roof Decks" and "Tentative Recommendations for the Design of Steel Deck Diaphragms" by the Steel Deck Institute.

ADVANTAGES OF METAL ROOF DECKS

1. High strength-to-weight ratio reduces roof dead load.
2. Can be erected in most weather conditions.
3. Variety of depths and rib patterns available.
4. Acoustical treatment is possible.
5. Serve as base for insulation and roofing.
6. Fire ratings can be obtained with standard assemblies.
7. Provide lateral diaphragm.
8. Can be erected quickly.
9. Can be erected economically.

ROOF DECK (ACOUSTICAL ROOF DECKS ARE AVAILABLE IN MANY OF THESE PROFILES - CONSULT MANUFACTURERS)

TYPICAL EXAMPLES	ECONOMICAL SPANS	USUAL WIDTH	MAX. LENGTH AVAILABLE
1½" NARROW RIB (6")	4'-6'	24" - 36"	36'- 42'
1½" INTERMEDIATE RIB (6")	5'- 7'	24"-36"	40'- 42'
1½" WIDE RIB (6")	6'- 9'	24"- 30"	32' - 42'
3" (8")	8'- 16'	24"	40'
4½"	15'- 18'	12"	32'
1½" (6")	7' - 11'	24"	32'
3⁵⁄₁₆"	10' - 20'	24"	40'
7½" (6", 4½", 3")	12'- 30'	12"	40'- 42'
7½" (6", 4½", 3")	13'- 33'	24"	40'

The use of vapor barriers on metal deck roofs is not customary for normal building occupancies. For high relative humidity exposure a vapor barrier may be provided as part of the roofing system, but the user should be aware of the great difficulties encountered in installing a vapor barrier on metal deck. Punctures of the vapor barrier over valleys might reduce or negate entirely the effectiveness of the vapor barrier.

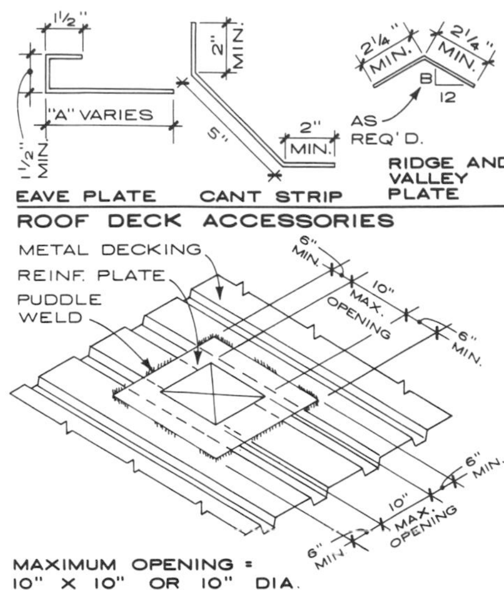
1½"
"A" VARIES
1½" MIN.
2" MIN.
5"
2" MIN.
2¼" MIN.
2¼" MIN.
B
12
AS REQ'D.
EAVE PLATE
CANT STRIP
RIDGE AND VALLEY PLATE
METAL DECKING
REINF. PLATE
PUDDLE WELD
6" MIN.
10" MAX. OPENING
6" MIN.
MAXIMUM OPENING = 10" X 10" OR 10" DIA.
ROOF DECK ACCESSORIES

REINFORCING PLATE

Small openings (up to 6 x 6 in. or 6 in. dia.) may usually be cut in roof or floor deck without reinforcing the deck. Openings up to 10 x 10 in. or 10 in. dia. require reinforcing of the deck by either welding a reinforcing plate to the deck all around the opening, or by providing channel shaped headers and/or supplementary reinforcing parallel to the deck span. Reinforcing plates should be 14 gauge sheets with a minimum projection of 6 in. beyond all sides of the opening, and they should be welded to each cell of the deck.

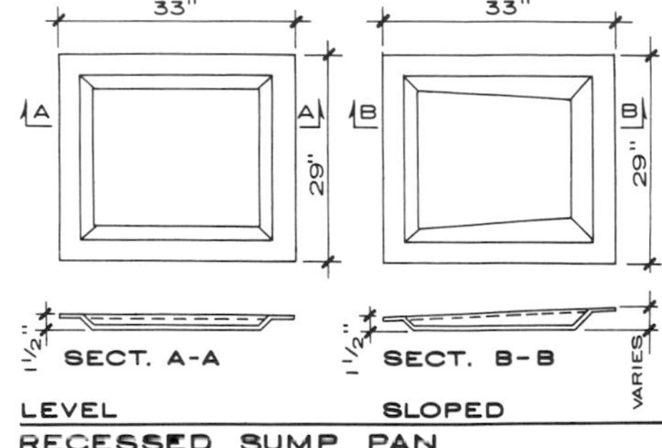
33"
33"
A
A
B
B
29"
29"
1½"
SECT. A-A
1½"
SECT. B-B
VARIES
LEVEL
SLOPED
RECESSED SUMP PAN

Preformed recessed sump pans are available from deck manufacturers for use at roof drains.

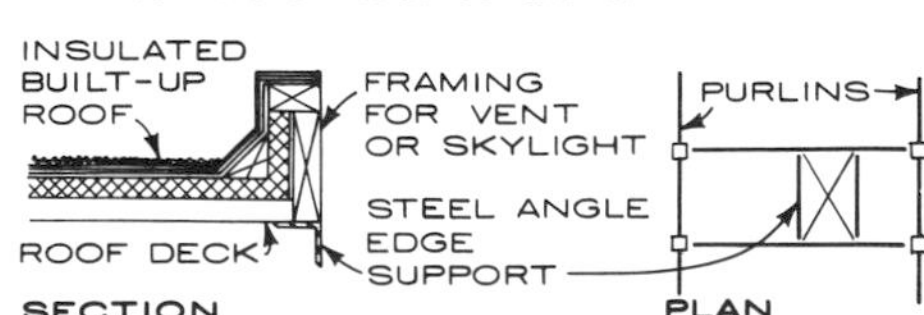
INSULATED BUILT-UP ROOF
FRAMING FOR VENT OR SKYLIGHT
STEEL ANGLE EDGE SUPPORT
ROOF DECK
PURLINS
SECTION
PLAN
FRAMED OPENING

Larger openings should be framed with supplementary steel members so that all free edges of deck are supported.

Roof-mounted mechanical equipment should not be placed directly on metal roof deck. Equipment on built-up or prefabricated curbs should be supported directly on main and supplementary structural members and the deck must also be supported along all free edges (see illustration). Heavy items such as cooling towers which must be elevated should be supported by posts extending through pitch pockets directly onto structural members below the deck. Openings through the deck may be handled as previously discussed.

Walter D. Shapiro, P.E.; Tor, Shapiro & Associates; New York, New York

FLOOR DECK – COMPOSITE WITH CONCRETE FILL

TYPICAL EXAMPLES	ECONOMICAL SPANS	USUAL WIDTH	MAX. LENGTH AVAILABLE
1 1/2"	4'-9'	30"	36'
2"	8'-12'	30"	40'-45'
3"	8'-15'	24"	40'
7 1/2", 6", 4 1/2", 3"	8'-24'	12"	40'

FLOOR DECK – COMPOSITE CELLULAR (ACOUSTIC DECK AVAILABLE IN SOME PROFILES; CONSULT MANUFACTURERS)

TYPICAL EXAMPLES	ECONOMICAL SPANS	USUAL WIDTH	MAX. LENGTH AVAILABLE
1 1/2", 6"	6'-12'	24"	40'
1 5/8"	6'-12'	24"	40'
2"	6'-12'	30"	36'-45'
3"	10'-16'	24"	40'
7 1/2", 6", 4 1/2", 3"	8'-24'	24"	40'

CORRUGATED FORMS FOR CONCRETE SLABS – NONCOMPOSITE

TYPICAL EXAMPLES	ECONOMICAL SPANS	USUAL WIDTH	MAX. LENGTH AVAILABLE
1/2"	1'-2'	96"	2'-6'
9/16"	1'-6"-3'	30"	40'
15/16"	3'-5'	29"	40'
1", 4"	3'-5'	28"	30'-40'
1 5/16", 4 1/2"	4'-9'	27"	30'-40'
2", 6"	7'-12'	24"	30'-40'

Walter D. Shapiro, P.E.; Tor, Shapiro & Associates; New York, New York

ADVANTAGES OF METAL FLOOR DECKS:

1. Provide a working platform, eliminating temporary wood planking in highrise use.
2. Composite decks provide positive reinforcement for concrete slabs.
3. Noncomposite and composite decks serve as forms for concrete, eliminate forming and stripping.
4. Fire ratings can be achieved without spray-on fire-proofing or rated ceilings.
5. Acoustical treatment is possible.
6. Electric raceways may be built into floor slab.
7. Economical floor assemblies.

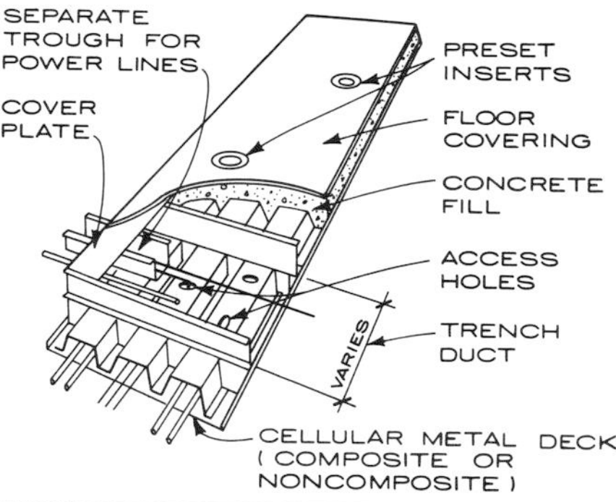
SEPARATE TROUGH FOR POWER LINES
COVER PLATE
PRESET INSERTS
FLOOR COVERING
CONCRETE FILL
ACCESS HOLES
TRENCH DUCT
VARIES
CELLULAR METAL DECK (COMPOSITE OR NONCOMPOSITE)

ELECTRICAL TRENCH DUCT

Electric raceways may be built into floor slabs by use of cellular deck or special units that are blended with plain deck. Two-way distribution is achieved by use of trench ducts that sit astride the cellular units at right angles. Use of trench ducts with composite floor deck may reduce or eliminate entirely the effectiveness of composite action at the trench duct. This is also true for composite action between steel floor beams and concrete fill. Trench duct locations must be taken into account in deciding whether composite action is possible.

Openings in composite deck may be blocked out on top of the deck and the deck can be burned out after the concrete has set and become self-supporting. Reinforcing bars can be added alongside openings to replace positive moment deck steel area lost at openings.

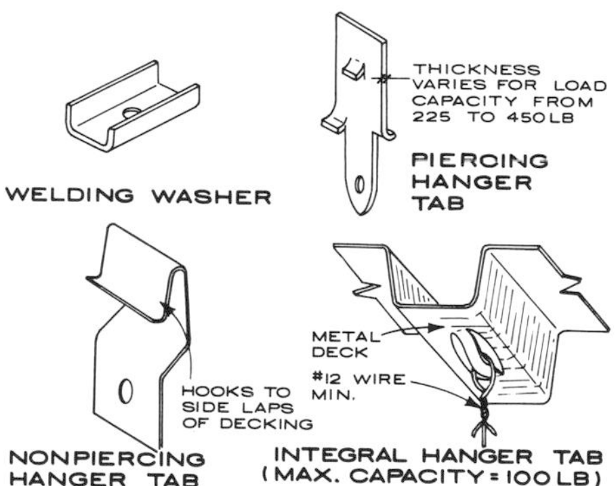
THICKNESS VARIES FOR LOAD CAPACITY FROM 225 TO 450LB
PIERCING HANGER TAB
WELDING WASHER
METAL DECK
#12 WIRE MIN.
HOOKS TO SIDE LAPS OF DECKING
NONPIERCING HANGER TAB
INTEGRAL HANGER TAB (MAX. CAPACITY=100LB)

DECKING ATTACHMENTS

A convenient and economical means for supporting lightweight acoustical ceilings is by attaching suspension system to hanger tabs at side laps, piercing tabs driven through deck, or prepunched tabs in roof deck (see illustrations above). These tabs and metal decks must not be used to support plaster ceilings, piping, ductwork, electric equipment, or other heavy loads. Such elements must be supported directly from structural joists, beams, girders, and so on, or from supplementary subframing, and not from metal deck.

ALLOWABLE LOADS FOR SIMPLE SPAN STEEL "C" JOISTS (LB/LINEAR FOOT) MADE OF 40 KSI MATERIAL

SPAN	SECTION (DEPTH/GAUGE)	SINGLE MEMBER: TOTAL ALLOWABLE LOAD	SINGLE MEMBER: ALLOWABLE LIVE LOAD	DOUBLE MEMBER: TOTAL ALLOWABLE LOAD	DOUBLE MEMBER: ALLOWABLE LIVE LOAD
8′	6″/18	201	189	402*	378
	6″/16	245	230	490	460
	6″/14	301	283	602	566
	8″/18	295	295	590*	590
	8″/16	359	359	718*	718
	8″/14	442	442	884*	884
	10″/16	506	506	1012*	1012
	10″/14	627	627	1254*	1254
10′	6″/18	129	97	258	194
	6″/16	157	118	314	236
	6″/14	193	144	386	288
	8″/18	188	186	376*	372
	8″/16	230	228	460*	456
	8″/14	283	280	566	560
	10″/16	326	326	652*	652
	10″/14	401	401	802*	802
12′	6″/18	89	56	178	112
	6″/16	109	68	218	136
	6″/14	134	83	268	166
	8″/18	131	108	262*	216
	8″/16	159	131	318	262
	8″/14	196	162	392	324
	10″/16	226	226	452*	452
	10″/14	278	278	556*	556
14′	6″/18	65	35	130	70
	6″/16	80	43	160	86
	6″/14	98	52	196	204
	8″/18	96	68	192	136
	8″/16	117	83	234	166
	8″/14	144	102	288	204
	10″/16	166	150	332*	300
	10″/14	204	184	408	368
16′	6″/18	50	23	100	46
	6″/16	61	28	122	56
	6″/14	75	35	150	70
	8″/18	73	45	146	90
	8″/16	89	55	178	110
	8″/14	110	68	220	136
	10″/16	127	100	254	200
	10″/14	156	123	312	246
18′	8″/18	58	32	116	64
	8″/16	71	39	142	78
	8″/14	87	48	174	96
	10″/16	100	70	200	140
	10″/14	123	86	246	172
20′	8″/18	47	23	94	46
	8″/16	57	28	114	56
	8″/14	70	35	140	70
	10″/16	81	51	162	102
	10″/14	100	63	200	126
22′	8″/18	39	17	78	34
	8″/16	47	21	94	42
	8″/14	58	26	116	52
	10″/16	67	38	134	76
	10″/14	82	47	164	94
24′	10″/16	56	29	112	58
	10″/14	69	36	138	72

NOTES

The tables on this page are not to be used for final design. They are intended to serve only as aids in the preliminary selection of members. Consult appropriate manufacturers' literature for final and/or additional information.

*Ends of members require additional reinforcing, such as by end clips.

Ed Hesner; Rasmussen & Hobbs Architects; Tacoma, Washington

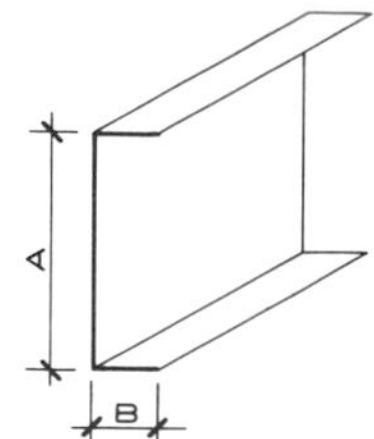
A
B

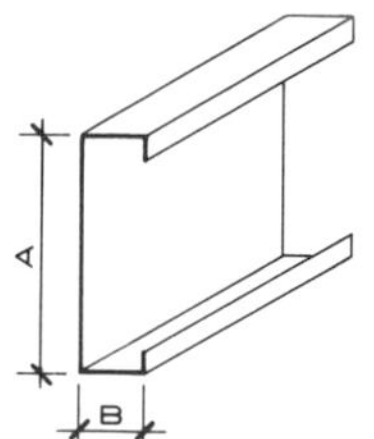
A
B

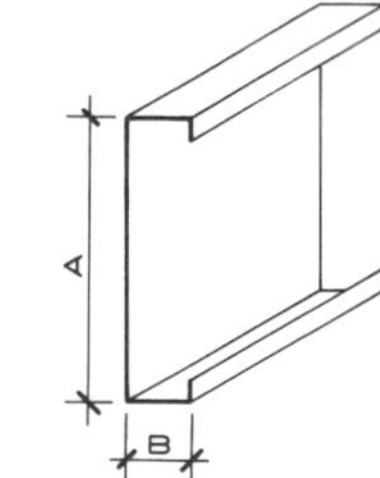
A
B

CHANNEL STUDS A	CHANNEL STUDS B	"C" STUDS A	"C" STUDS B	"C" JOISTS A	"C" JOISTS B
2½″	1″	2½″	1¼″	5½″	1⅞″
3¼″	1⅜″	3″	1⅜″	6″	1⅝″
3⅝″		3⅝″	1½″	7¼″	1¾″
4″		3¼″	1⅝″	8″	2″
6″		3½″		9¼″	2½″
		4″		10″	
		5½″		12″	
		6″			
		7½″			
		8″			

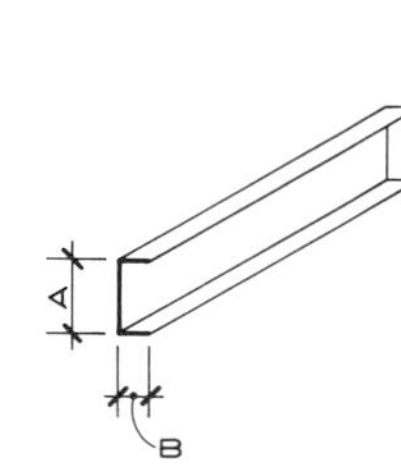
A
B

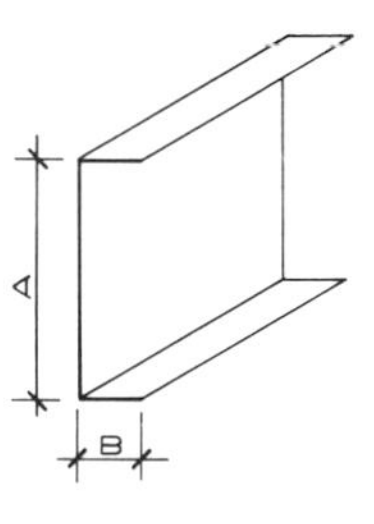
A
B

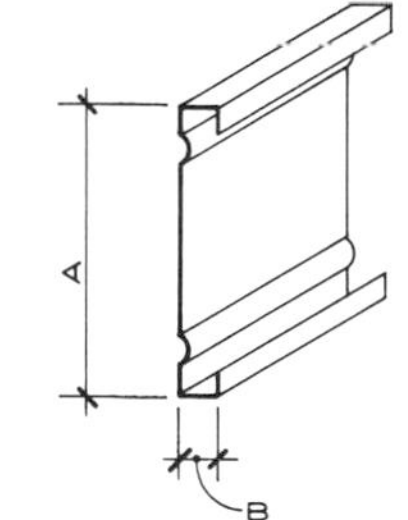
A
B

FURRING CHANNEL A	FURRING CHANNEL B	"C" JOIST CLOSURE A	"C" JOIST CLOSURE B	NESTABLE JOIST A	NESTABLE JOIST B
¾″	½″	5½″	1¼″	7¼″	1¾″
1½″	17/32″	6″		7½″	
		7¼″		8″	
		8″		9¼″	
		9¼″		9½″	
		10″		11½″	
		12″		13½″	
		Normally available in all joist sizes			

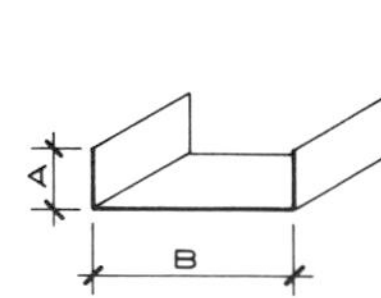
A
B

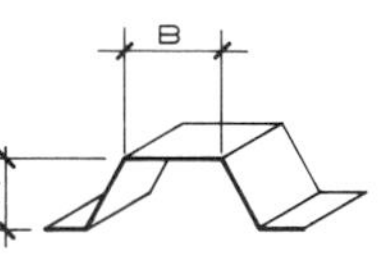
B
A

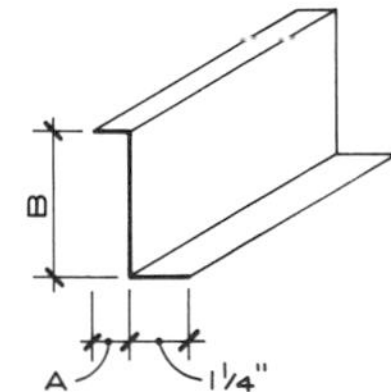
B
A
1¼"

RUNNER CHANNEL A	RUNNER CHANNEL B	FURRING HAT CHANNEL A	FURRING HAT CHANNEL B	"Z" FURRING A	"Z" FURRING B
¾″	2 11/16″	⅞″	1⅜″	¾″	1″
1″	3 13/16″	1½″	1¼″		1½″
1⅜″	3 7/16″				2″
1¼″	4 3/16″				3″
1½″	6 3/16″				
1¾″	8 3/16″				
3½″					

LIGHT GAUGE FRAMING MEMBERS

MEMBERS AVAILABLE IN 14, 16, 18, 20 & 22 GAUGE MATERIAL

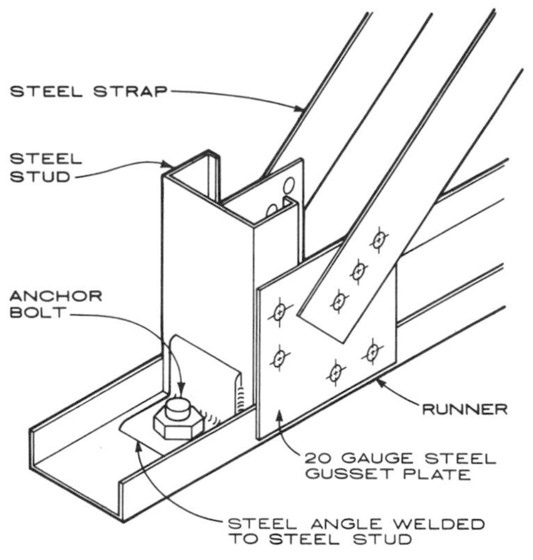
STEEL STRAP
STEEL STUD
ANCHOR BOLT
RUNNER
20 GAUGE STEEL GUSSET PLATE
STEEL ANGLE WELDED TO STEEL STUD

DIAGONAL STEEL STRAPPING

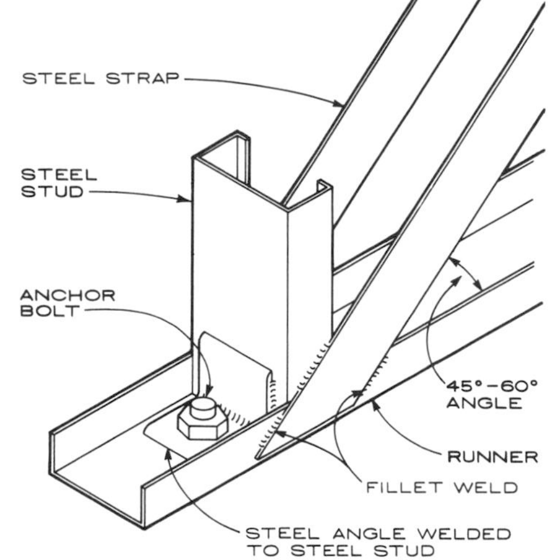
STEEL STRAP
STEEL STUD
ANCHOR BOLT
45°-60° ANGLE
RUNNER
FILLET WELD
STEEL ANGLE WELDED TO STEEL STUD

DIAGONAL STEEL STRAPPING

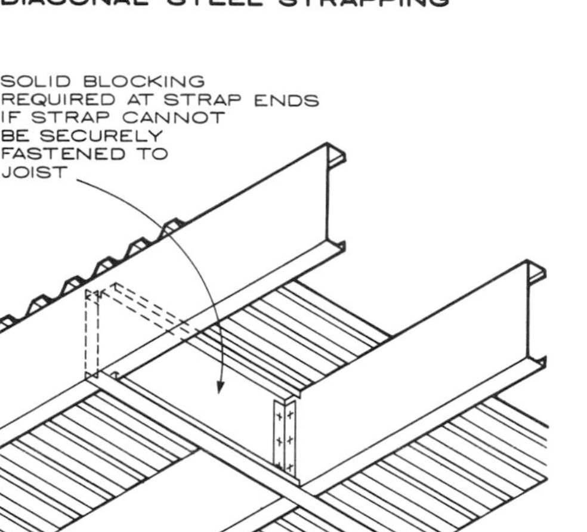
SOLID BLOCKING REQUIRED AT STRAP ENDS IF STRAP CANNOT BE SECURELY FASTENED TO JOIST
STEEL STRAPPING

JOIST BRACING

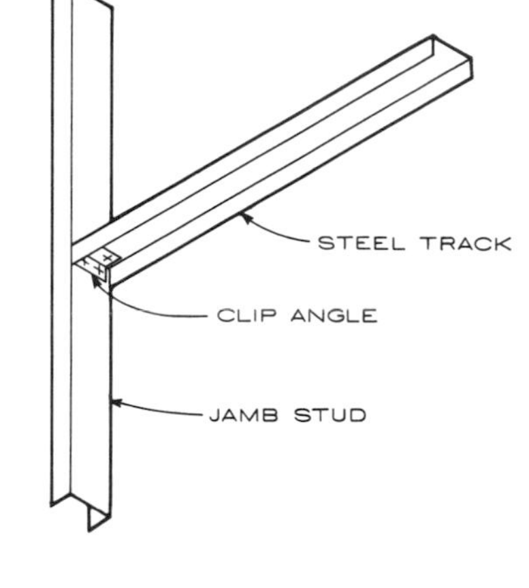
STEEL TRACK
CLIP ANGLE
JAMB STUD

SILL ATTACHMENT

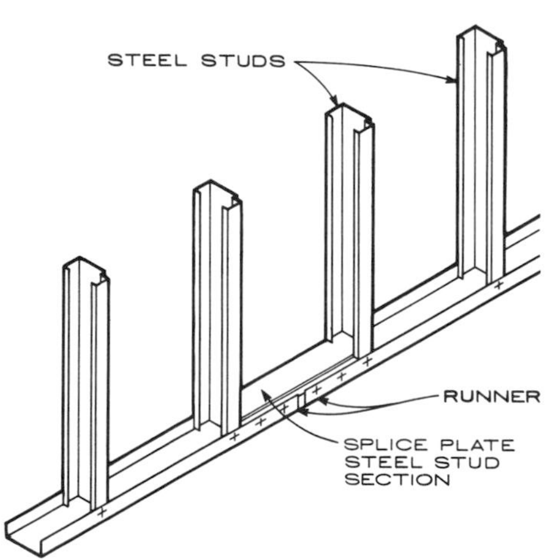
STEEL STUDS
RUNNER
SPLICE PLATE STEEL STUD SECTION

RUNNER SPLICE

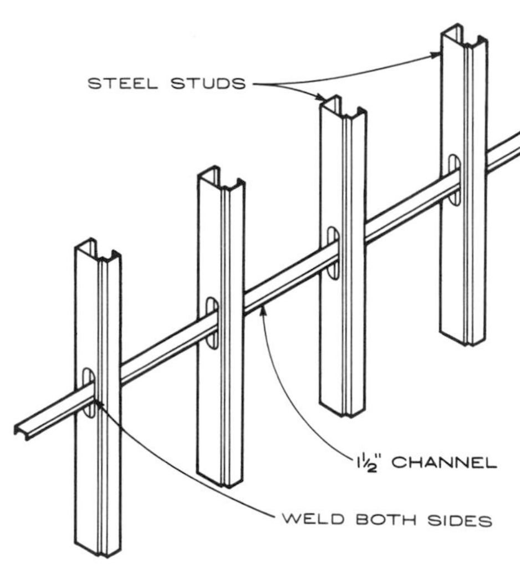
STEEL STUDS
1½" CHANNEL
WELD BOTH SIDES

HORIZONTAL BRACING

LIMITING HEIGHT TABLES FOR INTERIOR PARTITIONS AND CHASE WALL PARTITIONS

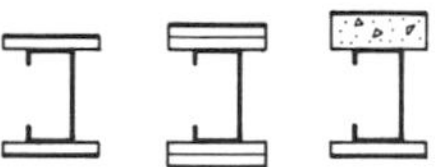

STUD WIDTH	STUD SPACING	ALLOW. DEFL.	PARTITION ONE LAYER	PARTITION TWO LAYERS	FURRING ONE LAYER
LIMITING HEIGHTS 25 GAUGE STEEL STUD ASSEMBLIES					
1 5/8″	16″	1/120	10′9″f	10′9″d	10′3″d
		1/240	9′6″d	10′6″d	8′3″d
	24″	1/120	8′9″f	8′9″f	8′9″f
		1/240	8′3″d	8′9″f	7′3″d
2 1/2″	16″	1/120	14′3″f	14′3″f	14′0″d
		1/240	12′6″d	13′6″d	11′0″d
	24″	1/120	11′6″f	11′6″f	11′6″f
		1/240	10′9″d	11′6″f	9′9″d
3 5/8″	16″	1/120	18′3″f	18′3″f	18′3″f
		1/240	16′0″d	17′0″d	14′6″d
	24″	1/120	15′0″f	15′0″f	15′0″f
		1/240	14′0″d	14′9″d	12′9″d
4″	16″	1/120	19′6″f	19′6″f	19′6″f
		1/240	17′3″d	18′3″d	15′9″d
	24″	1/120	16′0″f	16′0″f	16′0″f
		1/240	15′0″d	15′9″d	13′9″d
6″	16″	1/120	26′0″f	26′0″f	26′0″f
		1/240	23′0″d	24′0″d	21′6″d
	24″	1/120	21′3″f	21′3″f	21′3″f
		1/240	20′3″d	21′0″d	18′9″d
20 GAUGE STEEL STUDS ASSEMBLIES					
2 1/2″	16″	1/120	17′9″d	18′6″d	16′6″d
		1/240	14′0″d	14′9″d	13′0″d
	24″	1/120	15′6″d	16′3″f	14′6″d
		1/240	12′3″d	13′0″d	11′6″d
3 5/8″	16″	1/120	23′0″d	24′0″d	21′9″d
		1/240	18′3″d	19′0″d	17′3″d
	24″	1/120	20′0″d	20′9″f	19′0″d
		1/240	16′0″d	16′6″d	15′0″d
4″	16″	1/120	24′9″d	25′9″d	23′6″d
		1/240	19′6″d	20′3″d	18′9″d
	24″	1/120	21′6″d	22′0″f	20′6″d
		1/240	17′3″d	17′9″d	16′3″d
6″	16″	1/120	33′6″d	34′6″d	32′3″d
		1/240	26′6″d	27′6″d	25′6″d
	24″	1/120	29′3″d	29′6″f	28′0″d
		1/240	23′3″d	24′0″d	22′3″d
LIMITING HEIGHT 25 GAUGE CHASE WALL PARTITIONS					
1 5/8″	16″	1/120	15′3″f	15′3″f	
		1/240	13′3″d	14′6″d	
	24″	1/120	12′6″f	12′6″f	
		1/240	11′6″d	12′6″f	
2 1/2″	16″	1/120	20′3″f	20′3″f	
		1/240	17′6″d	19′0″d	
	24″	1/120	16′6″f	16′6″f	
		1/240	15′6″d	16′6″f	
3 5/8″	16″	1/120	25′9″f	25′9″f	
		1/240	22′9″d	24′3″d	
	24″	1/120	21′0″d	21′0″f	
		1/240	19′9″d	21′0″f	
2 1/2″ *	16″	1/120	24′3″d	25′9″d	
		1/240	19′3″d	20′6″d	
	24″	1/120	21′3″d	22′6″f	
		1/240	17′0″d	18′0″d	

NOTE

1. Limiting height for 1/2 in. or 5/8 in. thick panels and 5 psf uniform load perpendicular to partition or furring. Use one-layer heights for unbalanced assemblies. Limiting criteria: d-deflection, f-bending stress. Consult local code authority for limiting criteria.

* 20 Gauge chase wall partitions

Timothy B. McDonald; Washington, D.C.

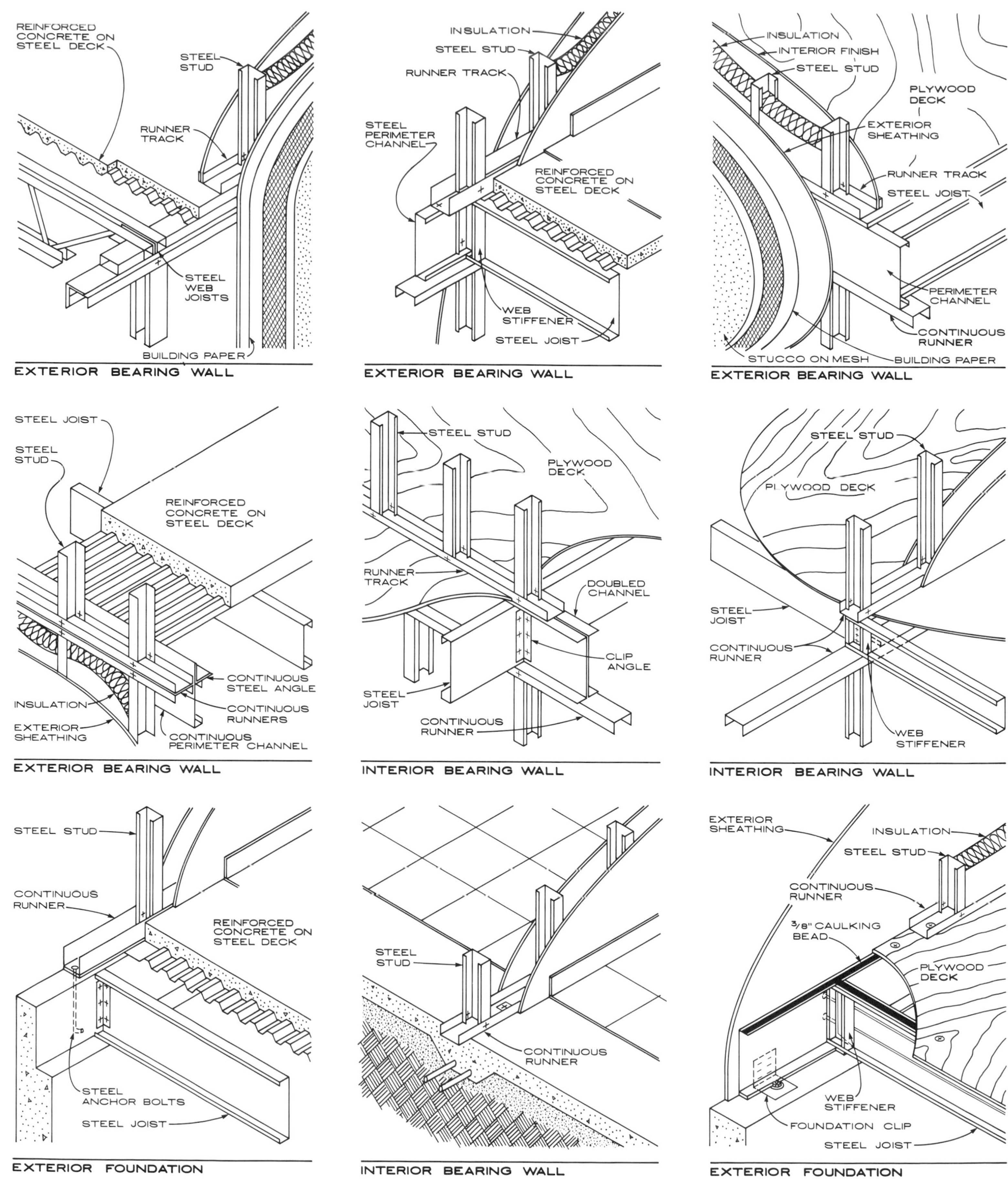
REINFORCED CONCRETE ON STEEL DECK
STEEL STUD
RUNNER TRACK
STEEL WEB JOISTS
BUILDING PAPER
EXTERIOR BEARING WALL
INSULATION
STEEL STUD
RUNNER TRACK
STEEL PERIMETER CHANNEL
REINFORCED CONCRETE ON STEEL DECK
WEB STIFFENER
STEEL JOIST
EXTERIOR BEARING WALL
INSULATION
INTERIOR FINISH
STEEL STUD
PLYWOOD DECK
EXTERIOR SHEATHING
RUNNER TRACK
STEEL JOIST
PERIMETER CHANNEL
CONTINUOUS RUNNER
STUCCO ON MESH
BUILDING PAPER
EXTERIOR BEARING WALL
STEEL JOIST
STEEL STUD
REINFORCED CONCRETE ON STEEL DECK
CONTINUOUS STEEL ANGLE
CONTINUOUS RUNNERS
INSULATION
EXTERIOR SHEATHING
CONTINUOUS PERIMETER CHANNEL
EXTERIOR BEARING WALL
STEEL STUD
PLYWOOD DECK
RUNNER TRACK
DOUBLED CHANNEL
CLIP ANGLE
STEEL JOIST
CONTINUOUS RUNNER
INTERIOR BEARING WALL
STEEL STUD
PLYWOOD DECK
STEEL JOIST
CONTINUOUS RUNNER
WEB STIFFENER
INTERIOR BEARING WALL
STEEL STUD
CONTINUOUS RUNNER
REINFORCED CONCRETE ON STEEL DECK
STEEL ANCHOR BOLTS
STEEL JOIST
EXTERIOR FOUNDATION
STEEL STUD
CONTINUOUS RUNNER
INTERIOR BEARING WALL
EXTERIOR SHEATHING
INSULATION
STEEL STUD
CONTINUOUS RUNNER
3/8" CAULKING BEAD
PLYWOOD DECK
WEB STIFFENER
FOUNDATION CLIP
STEEL JOIST
EXTERIOR FOUNDATION

Timothy B. McDonald; Washington, D.C.

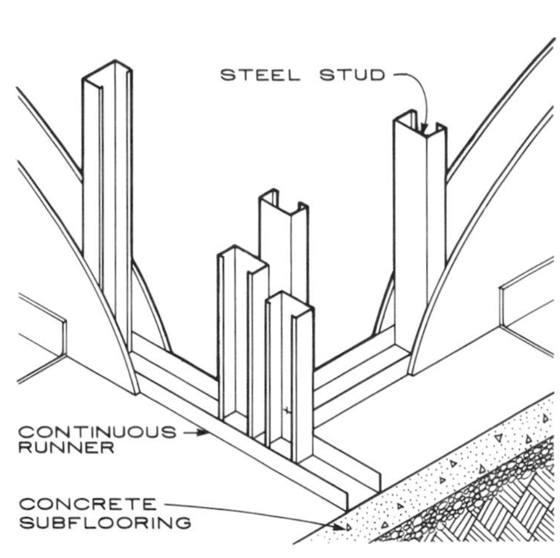
STEEL STUD
CONTINUOUS RUNNER
CONCRETE SUBFLOORING

PARTITION INTERSECTION

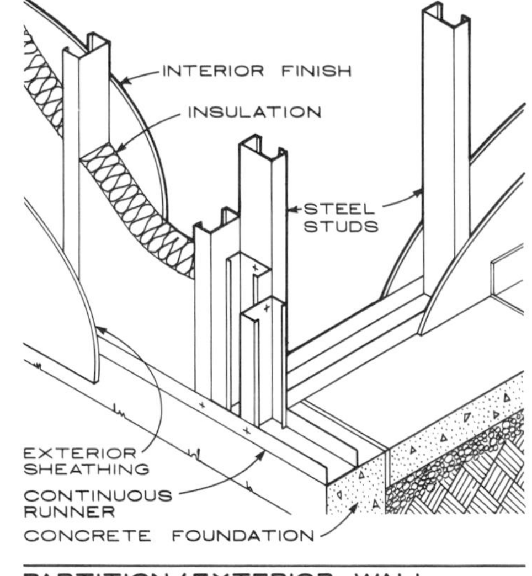
INTERIOR FINISH
INSULATION
STEEL STUDS
EXTERIOR SHEATHING
CONTINUOUS RUNNER
CONCRETE FOUNDATION

PARTITION / EXTERIOR WALL

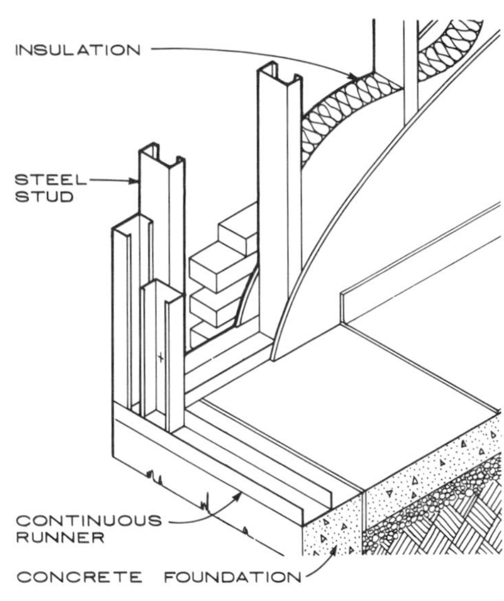
INSULATION
STEEL STUD
CONTINUOUS RUNNER
CONCRETE FOUNDATION

EXTERIOR CORNER

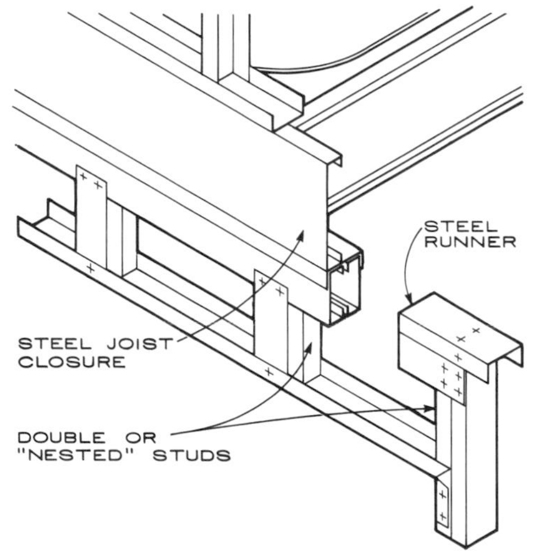
STEEL RUNNER
STEEL JOIST CLOSURE
DOUBLE OR "NESTED" STUDS

TWO MEMBER LINTEL

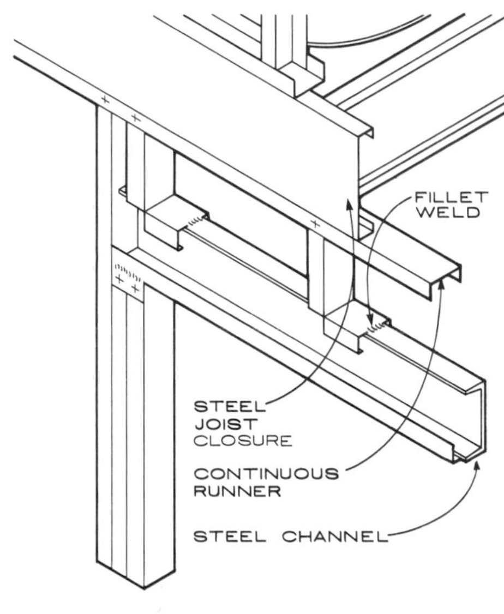
FILLET WELD
STEEL JOIST CLOSURE
CONTINUOUS RUNNER
STEEL CHANNEL

LONG SPAN LINTEL

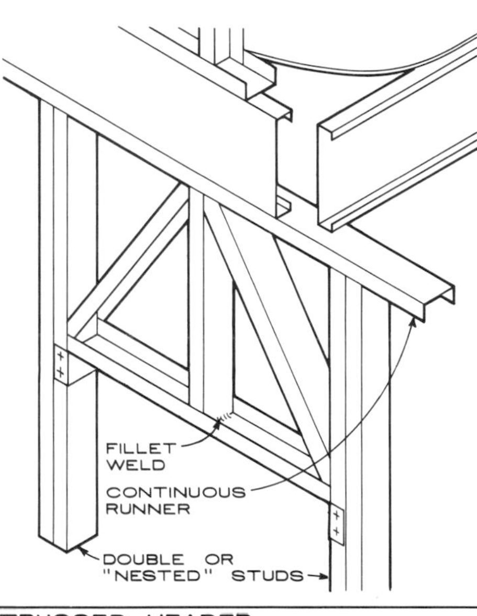
FILLET WELD
CONTINUOUS RUNNER
DOUBLE OR "NESTED" STUDS

TRUSSED HEADER

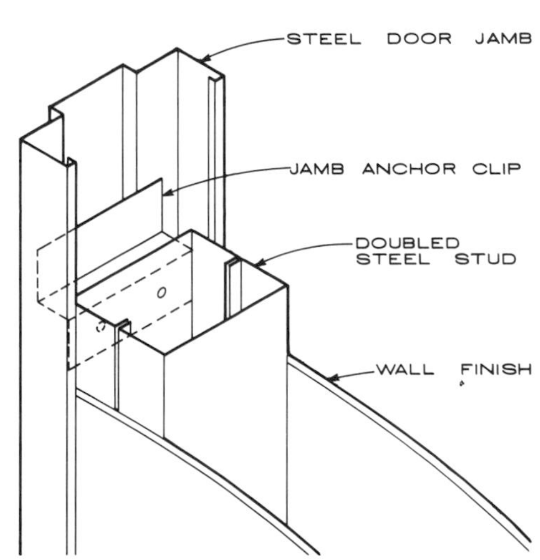
STEEL DOOR JAMB
JAMB ANCHOR CLIP
DOUBLED STEEL STUD
WALL FINISH

STUD-TO-DOOR BUCK

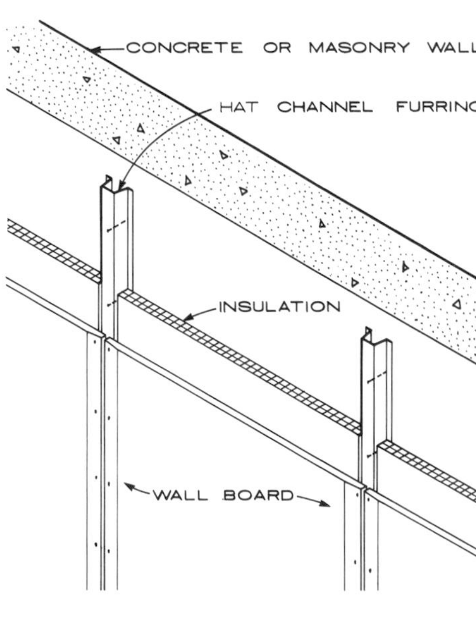
CONCRETE OR MASONRY WALL
HAT CHANNEL FURRING
INSULATION
WALL BOARD

FURRING

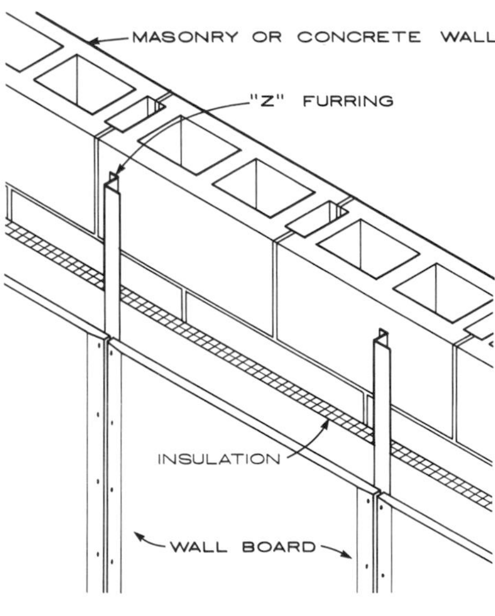
MASONRY OR CONCRETE WALL
"Z" FURRING
INSULATION
WALL BOARD

FURRING

Timothy B. McDonald; Washington, D.C.

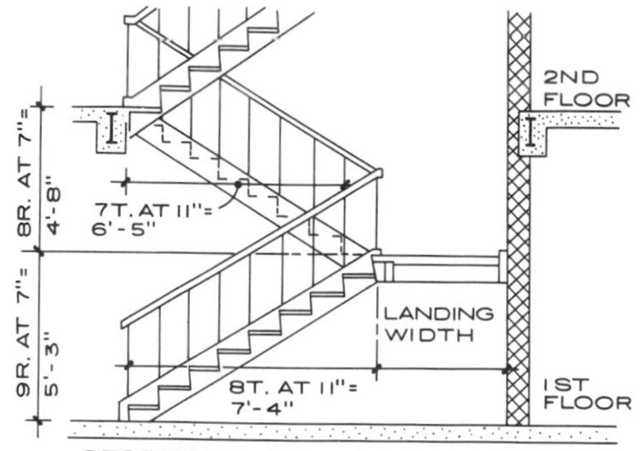

2ND FLOOR
9R. AT 7"= 5'-3"
8R. AT 7"= 4'-8"
7T. AT 11"= 6'-5"
LANDING WIDTH
8T. AT 11"= 7'-4"
1ST FLOOR

SECTION A - DIMENSIONS ARE SHOWN ONLY AS A GUIDE

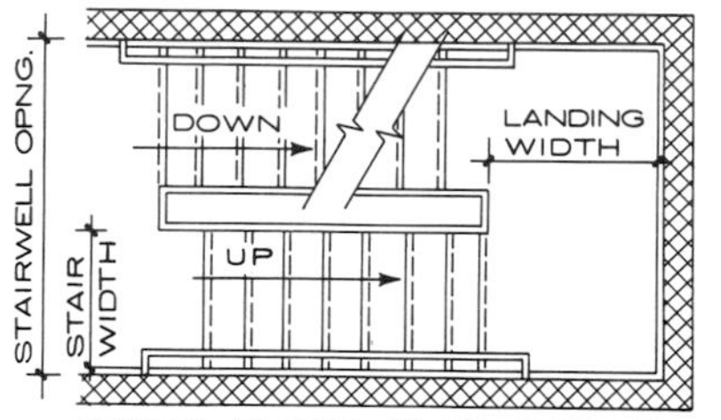

STAIRWELL OPNG.
STAIR WIDTH
DOWN
LANDING WIDTH
UP

UPPER FLOOR PLAN - WIDTHS AND CLEARANCES AS PER CODE

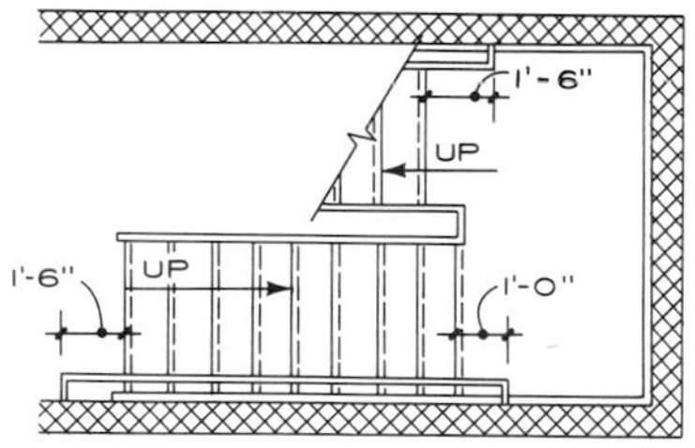

1'-6"
UP
1'-6"
UP
1'-0"

GROUND FLOOR PLAN - SHOWING HANDRAIL EXTENSIONS

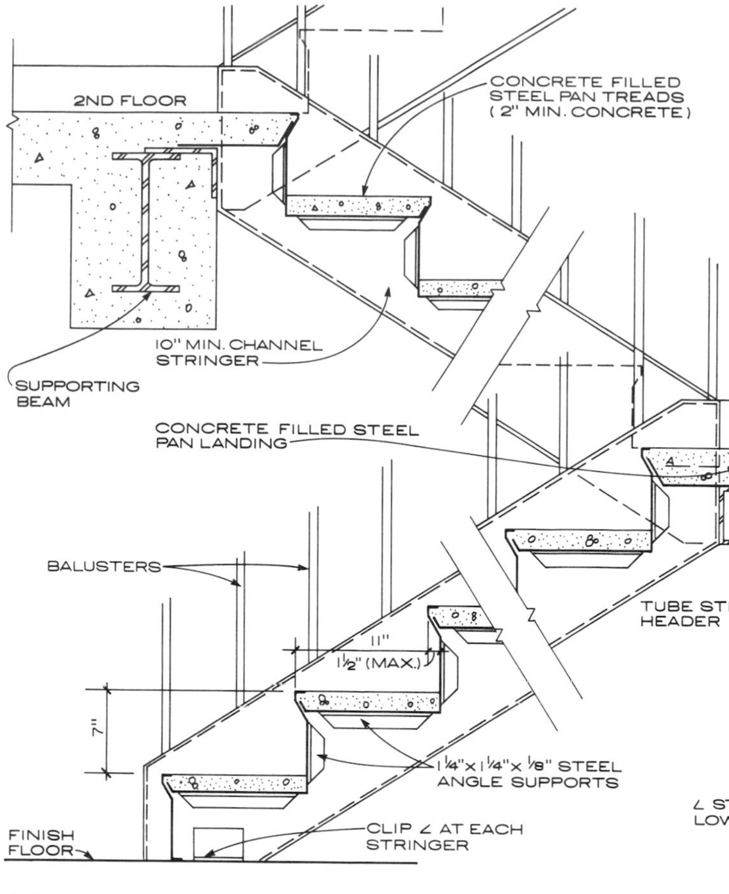

2ND FLOOR
CONCRETE FILLED STEEL PAN TREADS (2" MIN. CONCRETE)
10" MIN. CHANNEL STRINGER
SUPPORTING BEAM
CONCRETE FILLED STEEL PAN LANDING
BALUSTERS
TUBE STEEL HEADER
11"
1½" (MAX.)
7"
1¼"x1¼"x⅛" STEEL ANGLE SUPPORTS
FINISH FLOOR
CLIP ∠ AT EACH STRINGER

TYPICAL PAN TYPE CONSTRUCTION

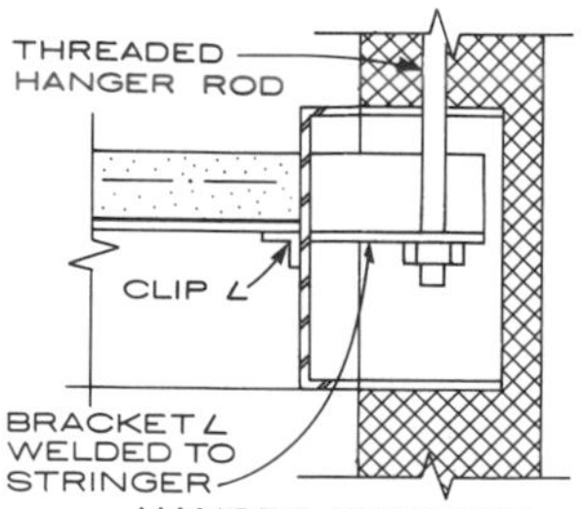

THREADED HANGER ROD
CLIP ∠
BRACKET ∠ WELDED TO STRINGER

HANGER SUPPORT

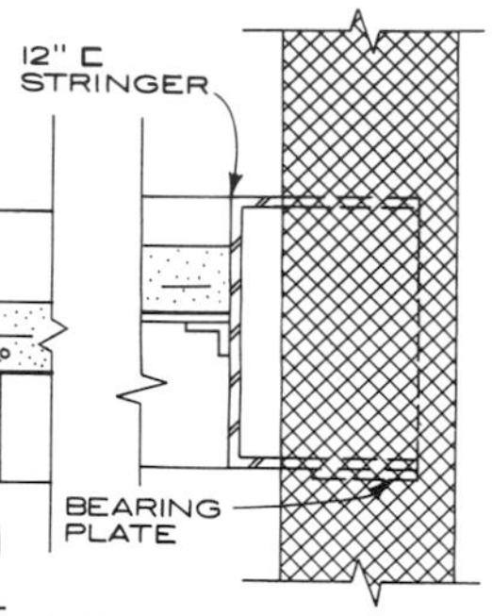

12" ⊏ STRINGER
BEARING PLATE

BEARING SUPPORT

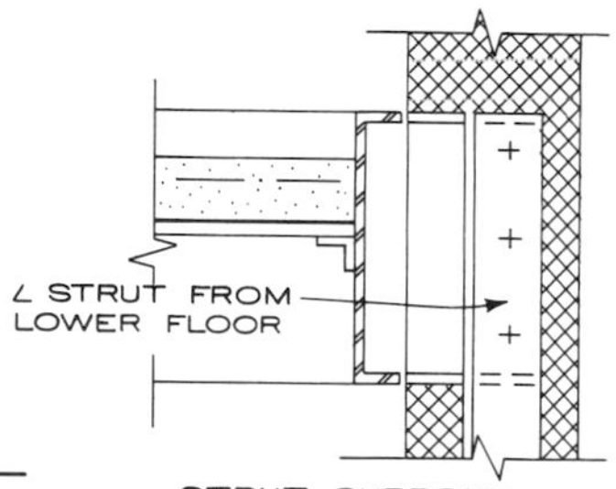

∠ STRUT FROM LOWER FLOOR

STRUT SUPPORT

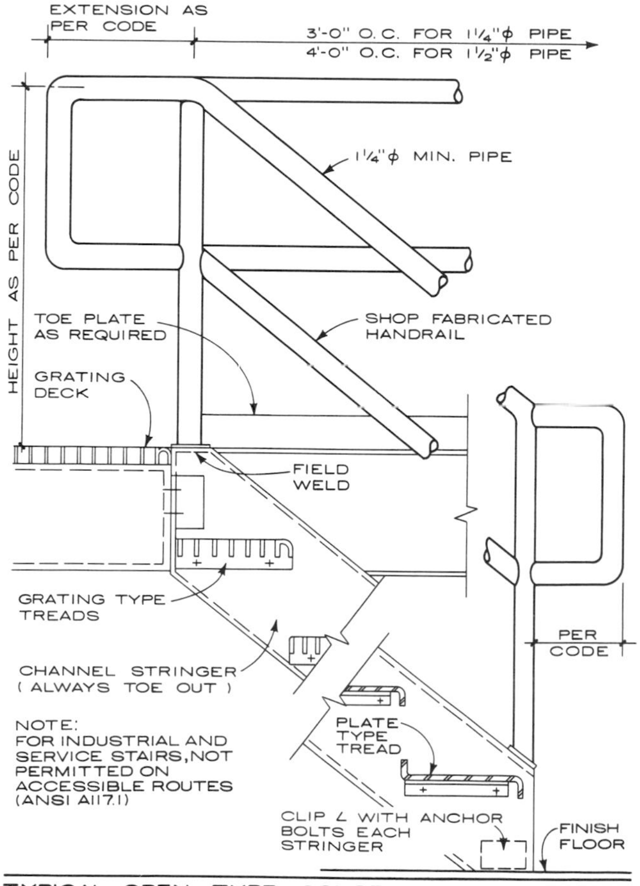

EXTENSION AS PER CODE
3'-0" O.C. FOR 1¼"φ PIPE
4'-0" O.C. FOR 1½"φ PIPE
HEIGHT AS PER CODE
1¼"φ MIN. PIPE
TOE PLATE AS REQUIRED
SHOP FABRICATED HANDRAIL
GRATING DECK
FIELD WELD
GRATING TYPE TREADS
CHANNEL STRINGER (ALWAYS TOE OUT)
PER CODE
PLATE TYPE TREAD
NOTE: FOR INDUSTRIAL AND SERVICE STAIRS, NOT PERMITTED ON ACCESSIBLE ROUTES (ANSI A117.1)
CLIP ∠ WITH ANCHOR BOLTS EACH STRINGER
FINISH FLOOR

TYPICAL OPEN TYPE CONSTRUCTION

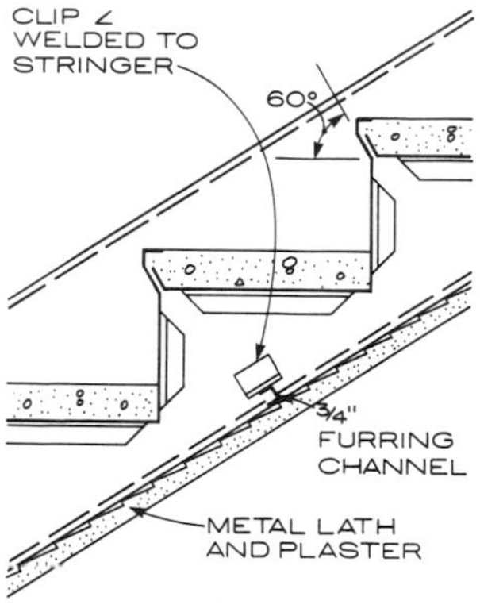

CLIP ∠ WELDED TO STRINGER
60°
¾" FURRING CHANNEL
METAL LATH AND PLASTER

PLASTER

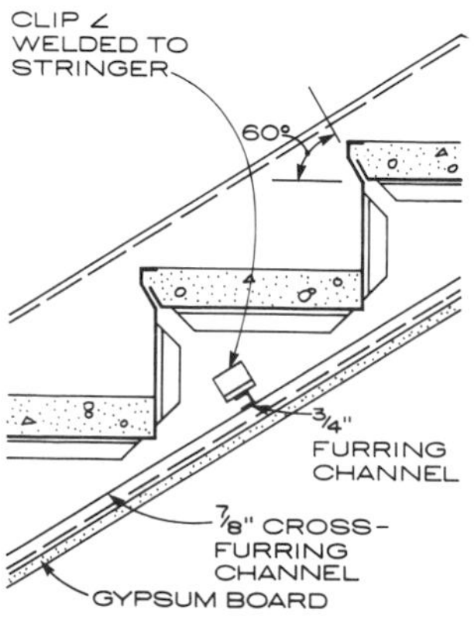

CLIP ∠ WELDED TO STRINGER
60°
¾" FURRING CHANNEL
⅞" CROSS-FURRING CHANNEL
GYPSUM BOARD

GYPSUM BOARD

SOFFIT DETAILS

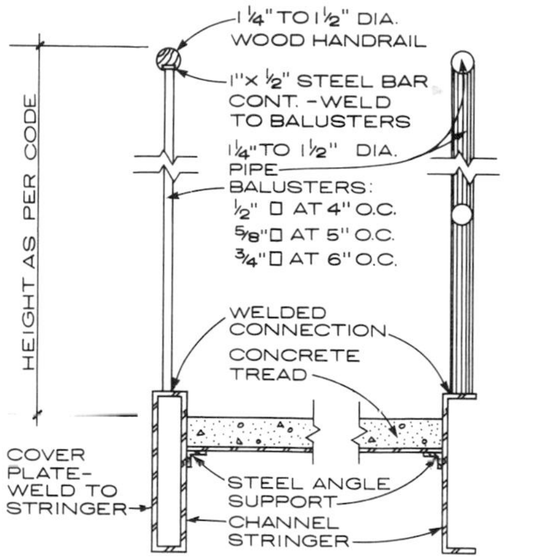

1¼" TO 1½" DIA. WOOD HANDRAIL
1"x ½" STEEL BAR CONT. - WELD TO BALUSTERS
1¼" TO 1½" DIA. PIPE
BALUSTERS:
½" □ AT 4" O.C.
⅝" □ AT 5" O.C.
¾" □ AT 6" O.C.
HEIGHT AS PER CODE
WELDED CONNECTION
CONCRETE TREAD
COVER PLATE-WELD TO STRINGER
STEEL ANGLE SUPPORT
CHANNEL STRINGER

STRINGER AND HANDRAIL SECTIONS

NOTE

Refer to applicable national, state, and local building codes for specific requirements as well as the standards established by ANSI 117.1, OSHA, and NFPA 1010 (Life Safety Code). Beyond these standards, special consideration should be given to stair surface texture, color, and lighting to improve stair safety. Further information may be obtained from the "Metal Stairs Manual" (National Association of Architectural Metal Manufacturers) and AIA's "Design for Aging: An Architect's Guide" (AIA Press, Washington, D.C., 1986).

Ted B. Richey, AIA; The InterDesign Group; Indianapolis, Indiana
John D. Harvey, AIA; Wheatley Associates; Charlotte, North Carolina

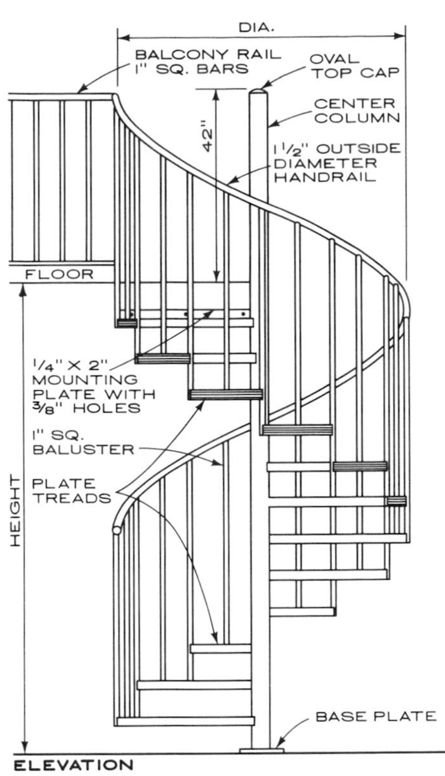

DIA.
BALCONY RAIL
1" SQ. BARS
OVAL
TOP CAP
CENTER
COLUMN
42"
1½" OUTSIDE
DIAMETER
HANDRAIL
FLOOR
¼" X 2"
MOUNTING
PLATE WITH
⅜" HOLES
1" SQ.
BALUSTER
PLATE
TREADS
HEIGHT
BASE PLATE

ELEVATION

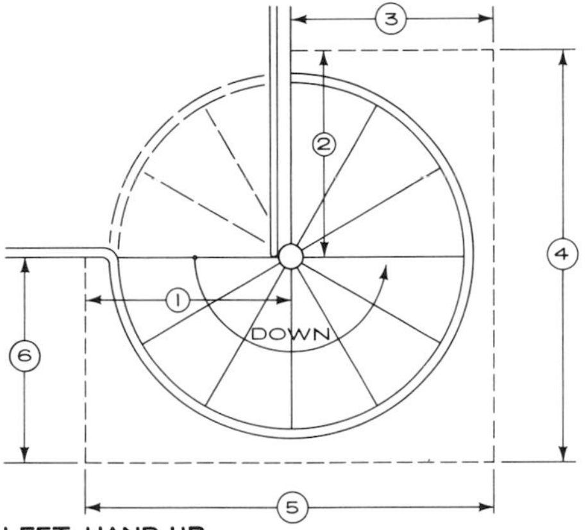

3
2
4
1
DOWN
6
5

LEFT-HAND UP
12 TREADS/CIRCLE 8" TO 9½" RISERS
MAY BE RIGHT-HAND UP

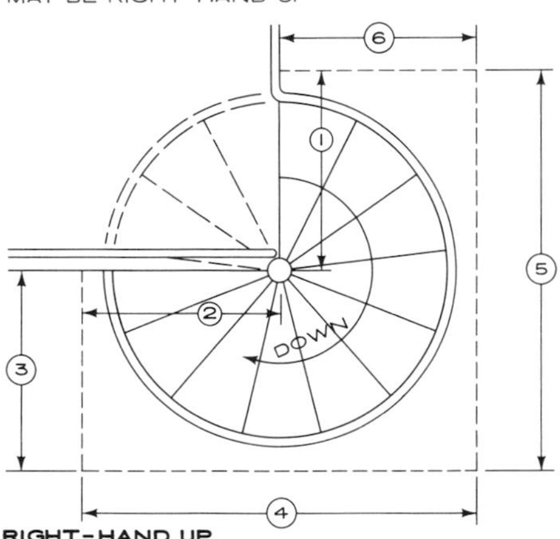

6
1
5
2
DOWN
3
4

RIGHT-HAND UP
13 TREADS/CIRCLE 7½" TO 8" RISERS
MAY BE LEFT-HAND UP

Framing dimensions are used when the stair passes through the flooring. The opening is "L" shaped, not square. For maximum head room, taper joist #2 45°. For standard 27° treads and 10 in. or over joist, delete one step to increase head room.

NOTES

1. Dimensions: Spiral stairs are manufactured in a variety of diameters. Larger diameters increase perceived comfort, ease of use, and safety.
2. Tread and platform materials: The most common materials are steel, aluminum, and wood. Steel and aluminum can be smooth plate, checker plate, pan type, and bar. A variety of hardwoods can be used, although many manufacturers use steel substructures to support the finish wood surface. Plywood usually is used under carpeting.
3. Factory finishes: Standard for exterior and wet area interiors are zinc-chromated rust inhibitor or hot-dipped galvanized. Other coatings are black acrylic enamel and black epoxy.
4. Handrails and balusters: A large variety of materials are available, including steel, aluminum, brass, bronze, wood, glass, and plastic laminate.
5. Platform dimensions usually are 2 in. larger than the stair radius. Various anchorage connections are available to suit the floor structure.
6. Refer to local and national codes for dimension and construction requirements and allowable uses.

SPECIFICATIONS (IN.)

Diameter	40	48	52	60	64	72	76	88	96
Center Column	4	4	4	4	4	4	4	6⅝	6⅝
Lb per 9 ft	205	220	235	250	265	310	325	435	485
Tread Detail A	4	4	4	4	4	4	4	6⅝	6⅝
Tread Detail B	18	22	24	28	32	34	36	42	48
27° Tread Detail C	9¼	11⅛	12⅛	13 15/16	14⅞	16¾	17⅝	20½	22 5/16
27° Tread Detail D	7⅝	8	8¼	8⅜	8½	8⅝	8¾	10	10½
30° Tread Detail C	10½	12 9/16	13⅝	15¾	16¾	18⅞	19⅞	23	25⅛
30° Tread Detail D	8½	8⅝	8¾	8⅞	9	9¼	9⅜	11⅜	11½
Landing Size	22	26	28	32	34	38	40	46	52

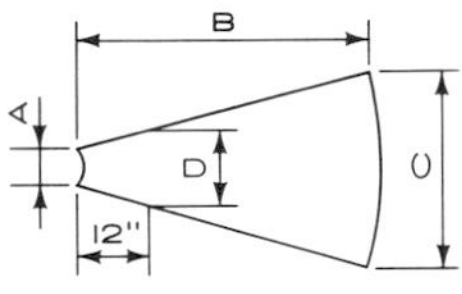

B
A
D
C
12"

TREAD DETAIL

27° RISER TABLE

FINISH FLOOR HEIGHT (IN.)	NUMBER OF STEPS	CIRCLE DEGREE
90 to 96	11	297°
97 to 104	12	324°
105 to 112	13	351°
113 to 120	14	375°
121 to 128	15	405°
129 to 136	16	432°
137 to 144	17	459°
145 to 152	18	486°
153 to 160	19	513°
161 to 168	20	540°

30° RISER TABLE

FINISH FLOOR HEIGHT (IN.)	NUMBER OF STEPS	CIRCLE DEGREE
85 to 95	9	270°
96 to 104	10	300°
105 to 114	11	330°
115 to 123	12	360°
124 to 133	13	390°
134 to 142	14	420°
143 to 152	15	450°
153 to 161	16	480°
162 to 171	17	510°
172 to 180	18	540°

FRAMING DIMENSIONS (IN.)

STAIR DIAMETER	1	2	3	4	5	6
40	20	20	24	44	44	24
48	24	24	28	52	52	28
52	26	26	30	56	56	30
60	30	30	34	64	64	34
64	32	32	36	68	68	36
72	36	36	40	76	76	40
76	38	38	42	80	80	42
88	44	44	48	92	92	48
96	48	48	52	100	100	52

SPIRAL STAIRS

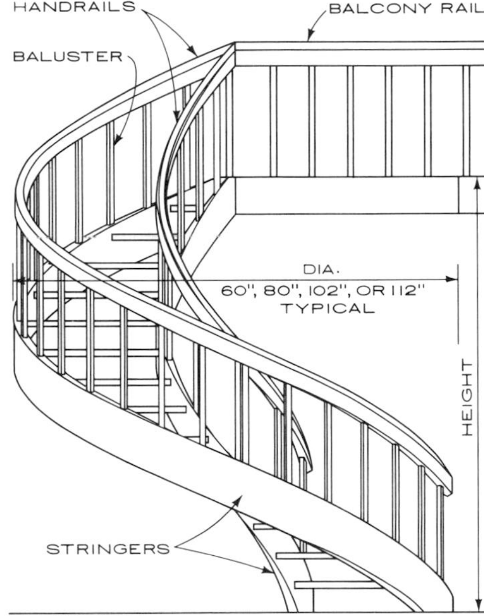

HANDRAILS
BALCONY RAIL
BALUSTER
DIA.
60", 80", 102", OR 112"
TYPICAL
HEIGHT
STRINGERS

ELEVATION

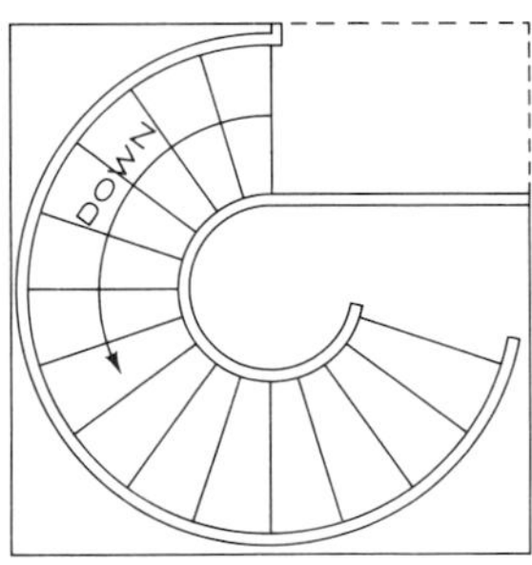

DOWN

PLAN

Design considerations are similar to those for spiral stairs. Made of fabricated steel tube one-piece stringer with treads bolted or welded to the stringer. Treads also are made of laminated wood. Numerous finishes are available, with wood the most common. Risers can be open or closed, and they can be carpeted.

CIRCULAR STAIRS

David W. Johnson; Washington, D.C.

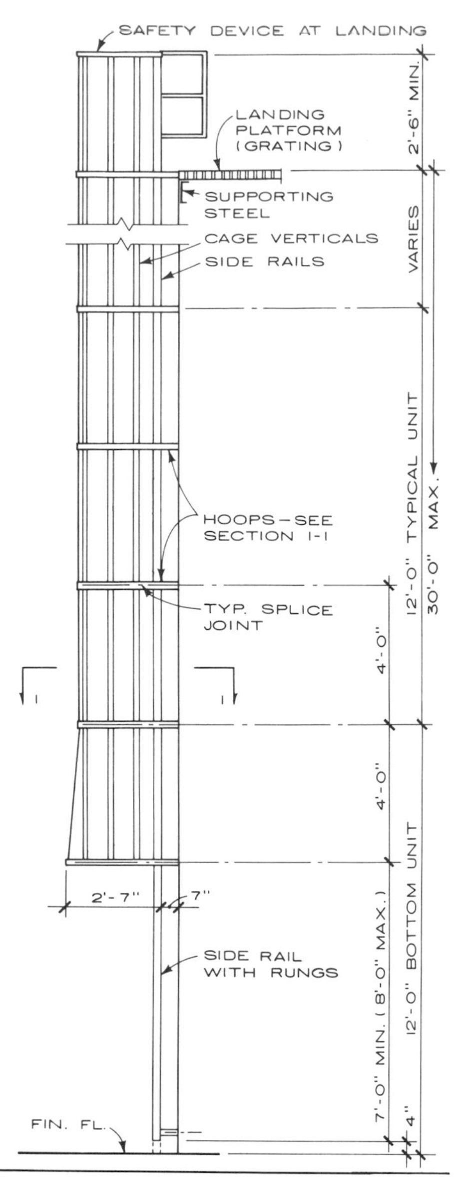
SAFETY DEVICE AT LANDING
LANDING PLATFORM (GRATING)
2'-6" MIN.
SUPPORTING STEEL
CAGE VERTICALS
SIDE RAILS
VARIES
HOOPS—SEE SECTION 1-1
TYP. SPLICE JOINT
12'-0" TYPICAL UNIT
30'-0" MAX.
4'-0"
4'-0"
2'-7"
7"
SIDE RAIL WITH RUNGS
7'-0" MIN. (8'-0" MAX.)
12'-0" BOTTOM UNIT
4"
FIN. FL.

TYPICAL SIDE ELEVATION
(EXTRUDED ALUMINUM LADDER)
MEETS OSHA REQUIREMENTS AND ANSI SPECIFICATIONS A 14.3

NOTE

All ladder safety devices such as those that incorporate lifebelts, friction brakes, and sliding attachments shall meet the design requirements of fire escape ladders; by U.S. Department of Labor-Occupational Safety and Health Administration.

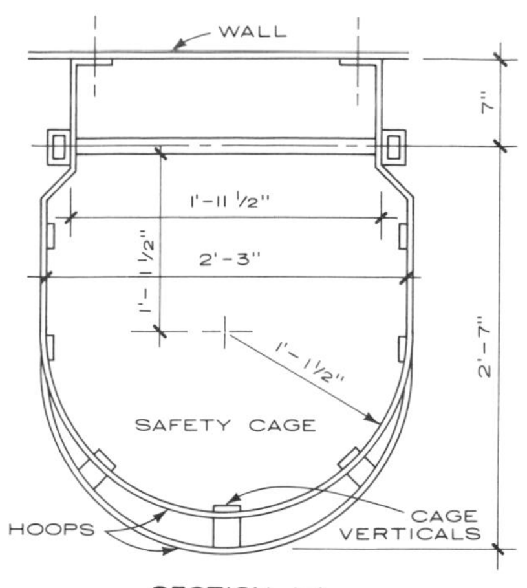
WALL
7"
1'-11 1/2"
2'-3"
1'-1 1/2"
1'-1 1/2"
2'-7"
SAFETY CAGE
HOOPS
CAGE VERTICALS

SECTION 1-1

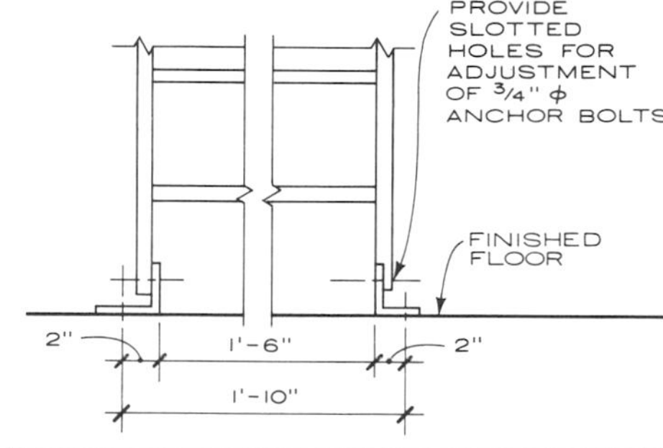
PROVIDE SLOTTED HOLES FOR ADJUSTMENT OF 3/4" ϕ ANCHOR BOLTS
FINISHED FLOOR
2"
1'-6"
2"
1'-10"

TYPICAL LADDER FOOTING CONNECTIONS

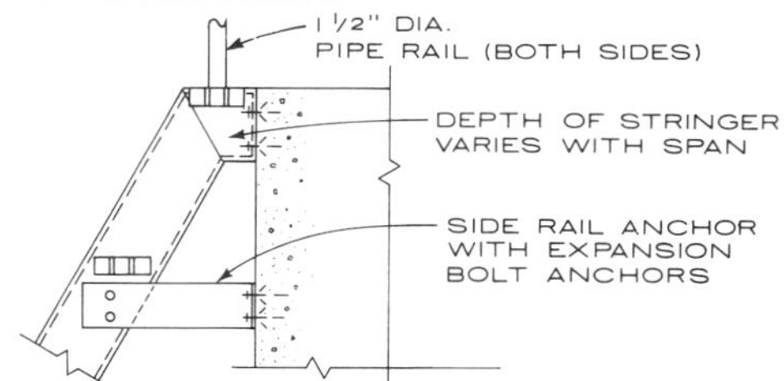
1 1/2" DIA. PIPE RAIL (BOTH SIDES)
DEPTH OF STRINGER VARIES WITH SPAN
SIDE RAIL ANCHOR WITH EXPANSION BOLT ANCHORS

SHIPS LADDER HEAD CONNECTION

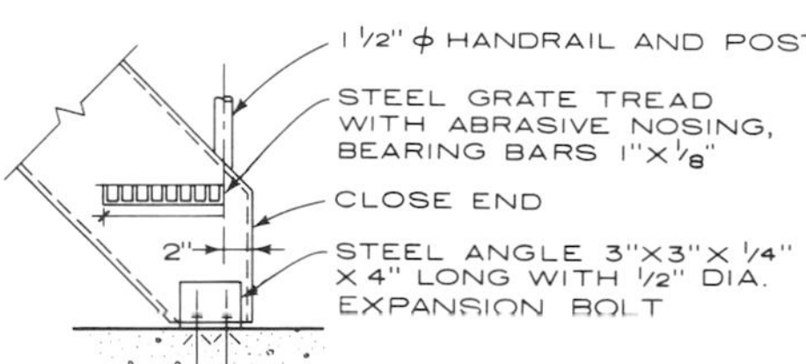
1 1/2" ϕ HANDRAIL AND POST
STEEL GRATE TREAD WITH ABRASIVE NOSING, BEARING BARS 1"x1/8"
CLOSE END
2"
STEEL ANGLE 3"X3"X 1/4" X 4" LONG WITH 1/2" DIA. EXPANSION BOLT

FIRE ESCAPE FOOTING CONNECTION

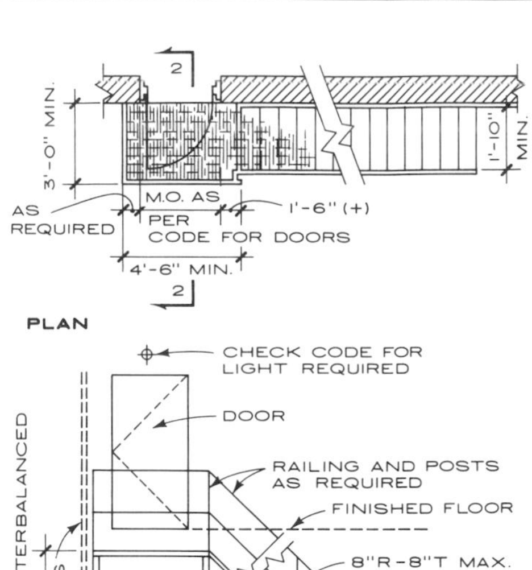
2
3'-0" MIN.
1'-10" MIN.
AS REQUIRED
M.O. AS PER CODE FOR DOORS
1'-6" (+)
4'-6" MIN.
2
CHECK CODE FOR LIGHT REQUIRED
DOOR
RAILING AND POSTS AS REQUIRED
FINISHED FLOOR
8"R-8"T MAX.
16'-0" MAX. IF COUNTERBALANCED OR DROP LADDER IS USED
10'-0" MIN. CLEARANCE
COUNTER-BALANCE
GRADE

PLAN

ELEVATION

NOTE: WEATHER PROTECTION FROM ICE AND SNOW IS REQUIRED IN SOME AREAS

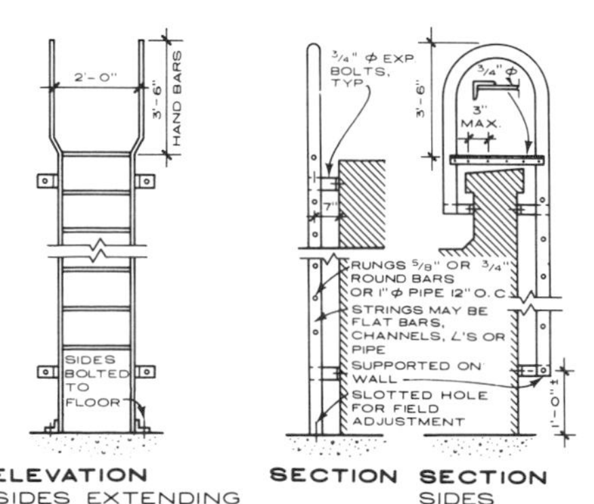
2'-0"
3'-6"
HAND BARS
SIDES BOLTED TO FLOOR
3/4" ϕ EXP BOLTS, TYP.
3'-6"
3/4" ϕ
3" MAX.
RUNGS 5/8" OR 3/4" ROUND BARS OR 1" ϕ PIPE 12" O.C.
STRINGS MAY BE FLAT BARS, CHANNELS, L'S OR PIPE
SUPPORTED ON WALL
SLOTTED HOLE FOR FIELD ADJUSTMENT
1'-0"

ELEVATION
SIDES EXTENDING ABOVE LANDING

SECTION

SECTION
SIDES OVER PARAPET

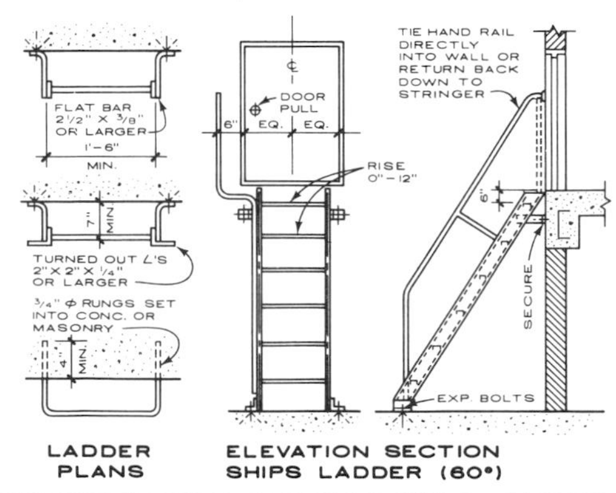
FLAT BAR 2 1/2" X 3/8" OR LARGER
1'-6" MIN.
7" MIN.
TURNED OUT L'S 2"X2"X 1/4" OR LARGER
3/4" ϕ RUNGS SET INTO CONC. OR MASONRY
4" MIN.
DOOR PULL
6"
EQ.
EQ.
TIE HAND RAIL DIRECTLY INTO WALL OR RETURN BACK DOWN TO STRINGER
RISE 0"–12"
6"
SECURE
EXP BOLTS

LADDER PLANS

ELEVATION SECTION
SHIPS LADDER (60°)

VERTICAL AND SHIPS LADDERS

NOTES

1. Freestanding stairways that are independently supported on steel columns with platforms at exits can be used on new and existing buildings. This type of exterior stair is subject to height limitations, occupancy classifications, and fire separation ratings.
2. Stairways supported on brackets attached to building walls with platforms at exits may be used for existing buildings, but only when outside stairways are not practical. This type of fire escape stair is subject to occupancy provisions: "Fire escape stairs may be used in existing buildings as permitted in applicable existing occupancy chapters but shall not constitute more than 50 percent of the required exit capacity" (NFPA 101 National Fire Code 1985, 5-2.8.1.4).
3. Slide fire escapes, used chiefly in institutional buildings, must be designed in accordance with state or local laws and ordinances. Frames for platforms can be angles or channels bolted to brackets; grating can be bolted or welded to the frame. Alternate brackets may be round or square steel, sized by a structural engineer.
4. Ships' ladder railings are 3/4 in., 1 in., or larger pipe railing on one or both sides, bolted or welded to strings. Tread may be channels, angles, bent plates, grating, or cast metals, with or without abrasives. Brackets are to be 2 1/2 in. x 3/8 in. or larger, and may be welded, bolted, or clamped to strings, but spaced not over 10 ft. Fastening to wall should be through bolts, bolts set in wall, or by expansion bolts. Rungs, 5/8 in. or 1/4 in. diameter bars, usually are set into holes in string and welded together.
5. Galvanic corrosion (electrolysis) potential between common flashing materials and selected construction materials should be considered.
6. Portable ladders, rope fire escapes, and similar emergency escape devices may be useful in buildings that lack adequate standard exits. Their use is not recognized by the Life Safety Code as satisfying requirements for means of egress. Many such devices are unsuited for use by aged or infirm persons or small children. Such devices may give a false sense of security and should not substitute for standard exit facilities.

Jan M. Sprawka; Symmes, Maini and McKee Associates, Inc.; Cambridge, Massachusetts
Max O. Urbahn Associates, Inc.; New York, New York
NFPA, see data sources

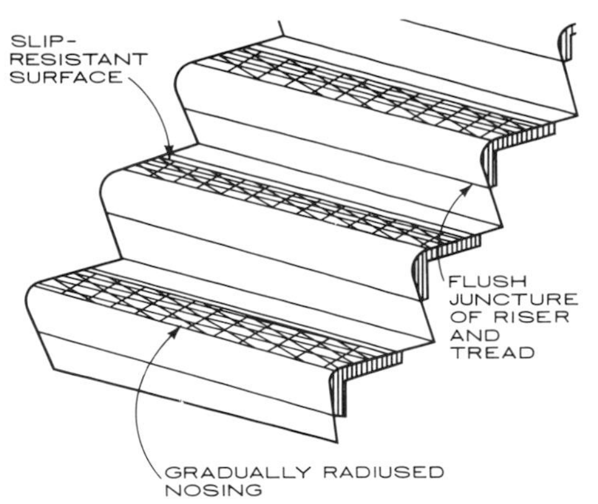
SLIP-
RESISTANT
SURFACE
FLUSH
JUNCTURE
OF RISER
AND
TREAD
GRADUALLY RADIUSED
NOSING
"SAFE" STAIR ELEMENTS

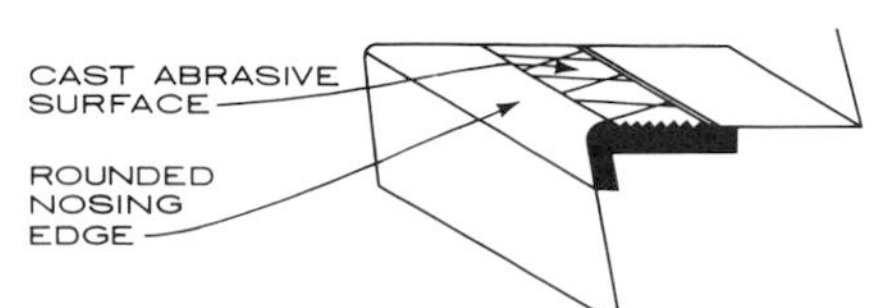
CAST ABRASIVE
SURFACE
ROUNDED
NOSING
EDGE
PREFERRED CAST METAL ABRASIVE NOSING

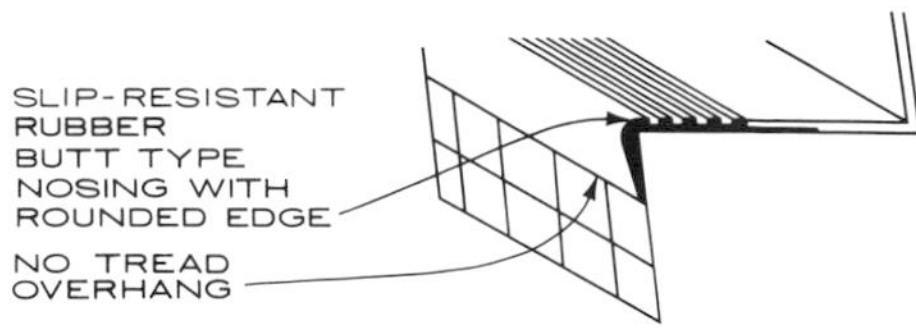
SLIP-RESISTANT
RUBBER
BUTT TYPE
NOSING WITH
ROUNDED EDGE
NO TREAD
OVERHANG
PREFERRED VINYL OR RUBBER NOSING

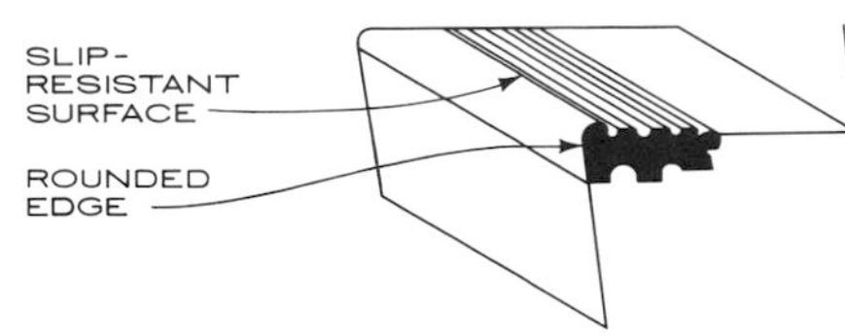
SLIP-
RESISTANT
SURFACE
ROUNDED
EDGE
PREFERRED CAST METAL NOSING FOR CONCRETE STAIR

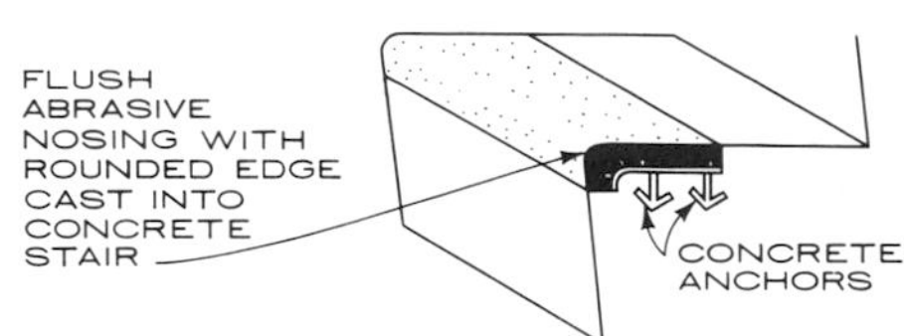
FLUSH
ABRASIVE
NOSING WITH
ROUNDED EDGE
CAST INTO
CONCRETE
STAIR
CONCRETE
ANCHORS
PREFERRED ABRASIVE EPOXY

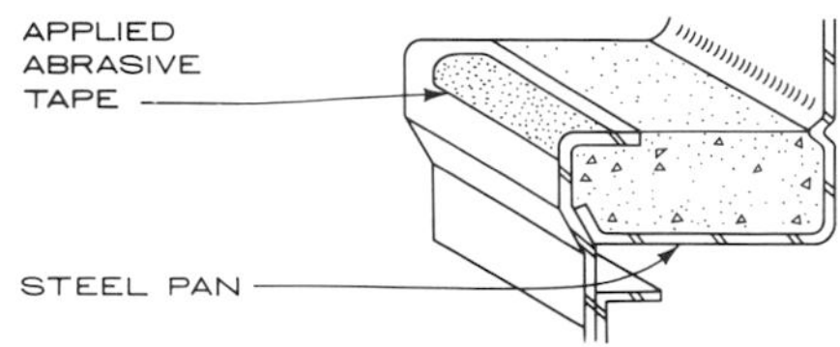
APPLIED
ABRASIVE
TAPE
STEEL PAN
PREFERRED ABRASIVE TAPE NOSING

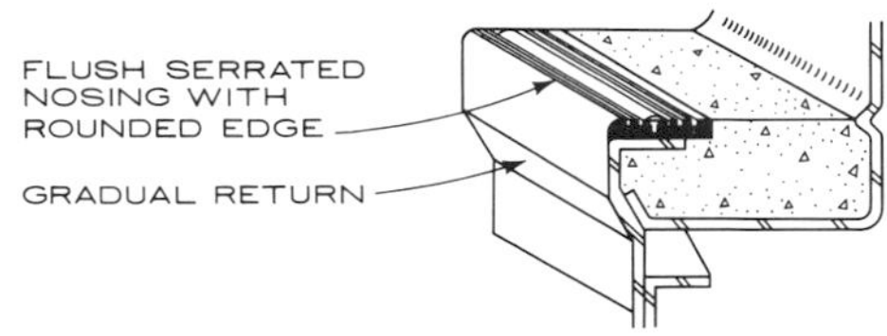
FLUSH SERRATED
NOSING WITH
ROUNDED EDGE
GRADUAL RETURN
PREFERRED STEEL SUBTREAD

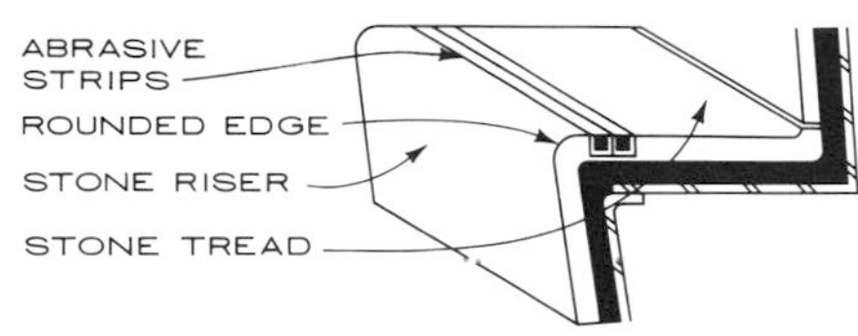
ABRASIVE
STRIPS
ROUNDED EDGE
STONE RISER
STONE TREAD
PREFERRED STONE TREAD

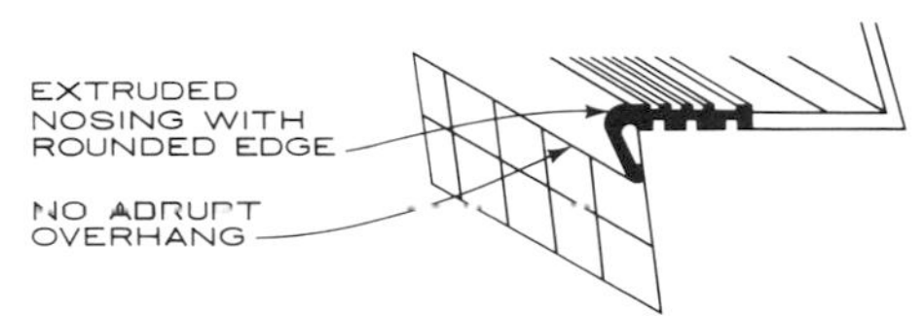
EXTRUDED
NOSING WITH
ROUNDED EDGE
NO ABRUPT
OVERHANG
PREFERRED ALUMINUM NOSING

TREAD AND RISER SIZES

Riser and tread dimensions must be uniform for the length of the stair. ANSI specifications recommend a minimum tread dimension of 11 in. nosing to nosing and a riser height of 7 in. maximum. Open risers are not permitted on stairs accessible to the handicapped.

TREAD COVERING

OSHA standards require finishes to be "reasonably slip resistant" with nosings of slip-resistant finish. Treads without nosings are acceptable provided that the tread is serrated or is of a definite slip-resistant design. Uniform color and texture are recommended for clear delineation of edges.

NOSING DESIGN

ANSI specifications recommend nosings without abrupt edges that project no more than 1½ in. beyond the edge of the riser. A safe stair uses a ½ in. radius abrasive nosing firmly anchored to the tread, with no overhangs and a clearly visible edge.

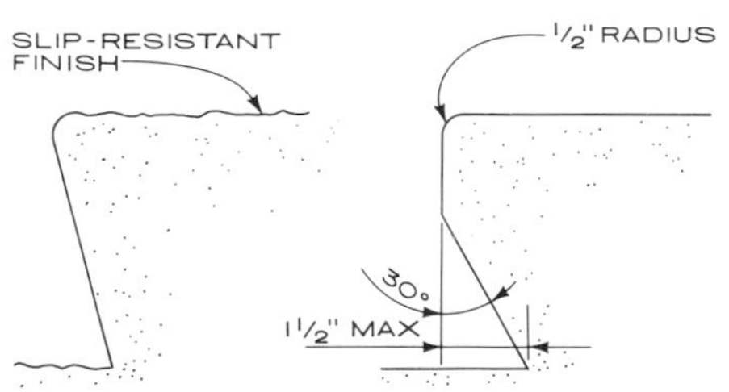
SLIP-RESISTANT
FINISH
½" RADIUS
30°
1½" MAX
ACCEPTABLE NOSING PROFILES

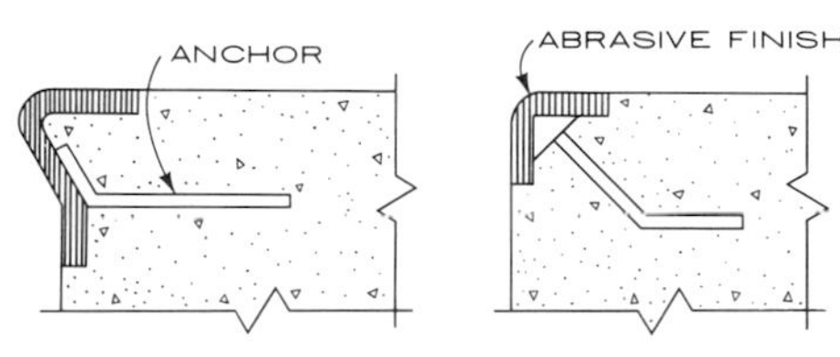
ANCHOR
ABRASIVE FINISH
PREFERRED CAST NOSINGS FOR CONCRETE

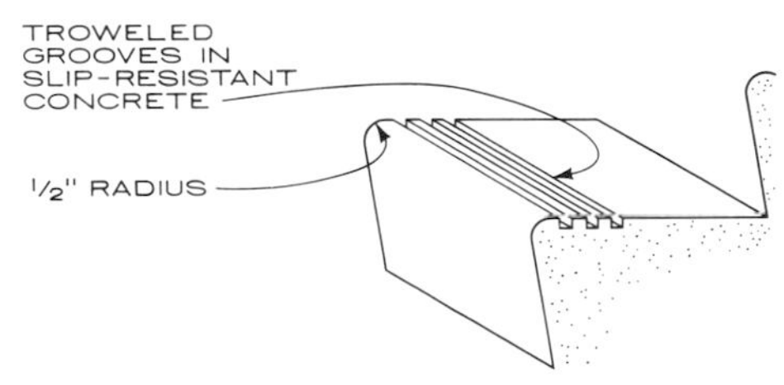
TROWELED
GROOVES IN
SLIP-RESISTANT
CONCRETE
½" RADIUS
PREFERRED CONCRETE TREAD

DESIGN OF A "SAFE" STAIR, USABLE BY THE PHYSICALLY HANDICAPPED

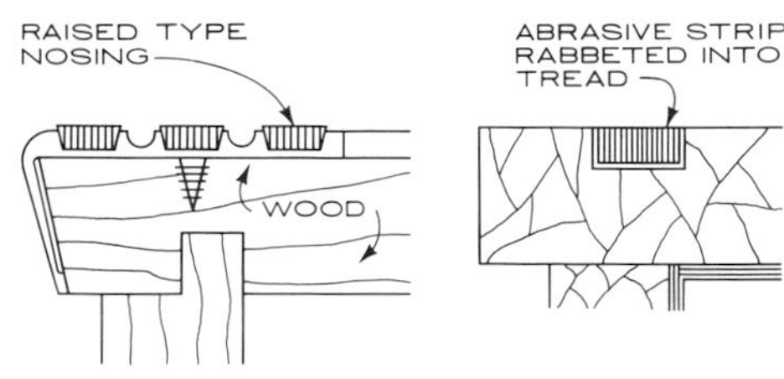
RAISED TYPE
NOSING
WOOD
ABRASIVE STRIP
RABBETED INTO
TREAD
OTHER ALUMINUM NOSINGS WITH ABRASIVE FILLER

NOTE

Cast nosings for concrete stairs are iron, aluminum, or bronze, custom-made to exact size. Nosings and treads come with factory-drilled countersunk holes, with riveted strap anchors, or with wing-type anchors.

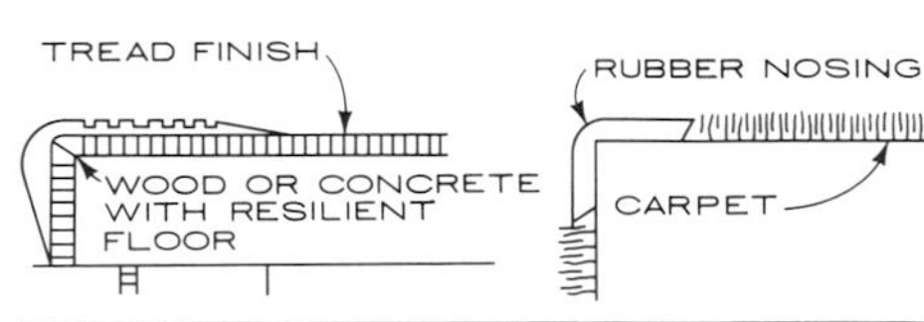
TREAD FINISH
WOOD OR CONCRETE
WITH RESILIENT
FLOOR
RUBBER NOSING
CARPET
OTHER SLIP-RESISTANT VINYL AND RUBBER NOSINGS

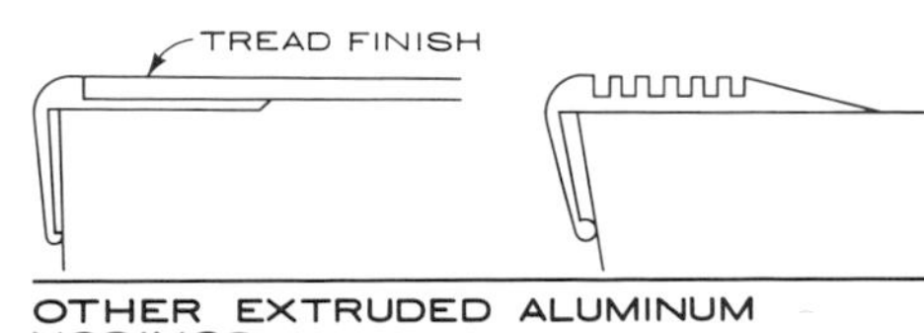
TREAD FINISH
OTHER EXTRUDED ALUMINUM NOSINGS

NOTE

Abrasive materials are used as treads, nosings, or inlay strips for new work and as surface-mounted replacement treads for old work. A homogeneous epoxy abrasive is cured on an extruded aluminum base for a smoother surface, or it is used as a filler between aluminum ribs.

Olga Barmine; Darrel Downing Rippeteau, Architect; Washington, D.C.
Krommenhoek/McKeown & Associates; San Diego, California

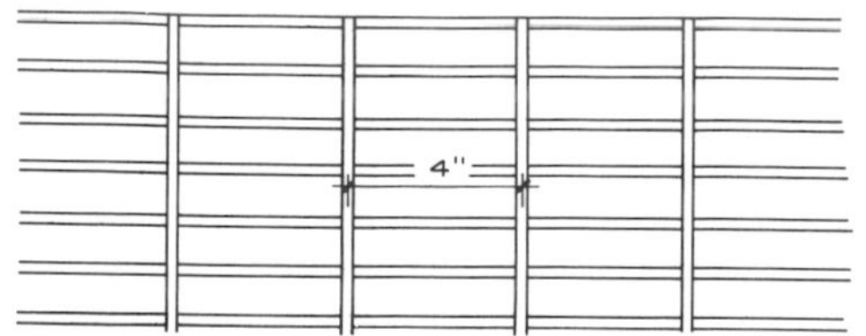
4"

WITH SPACER BARS WELDED 4" O.C.

2"

WITH SPACER BARS WELDED 2" O.C.

RECTANGULAR (WELDED OR PRESSURE LOCKED)

NOTES

Constructed of flat bearing bars of steel or aluminum I-bars, with spacer bars at right angles. Spacer bars may be square, rectangular, or of another shape. Spacer bars are connected to bearing bars by pressing them into prepared slots or by welding. They have open ends or perhaps ends banded with flat bars that are of about the same size as welded bearing bars. Standard bar spacings are 15/16 and 1 3/16 in.

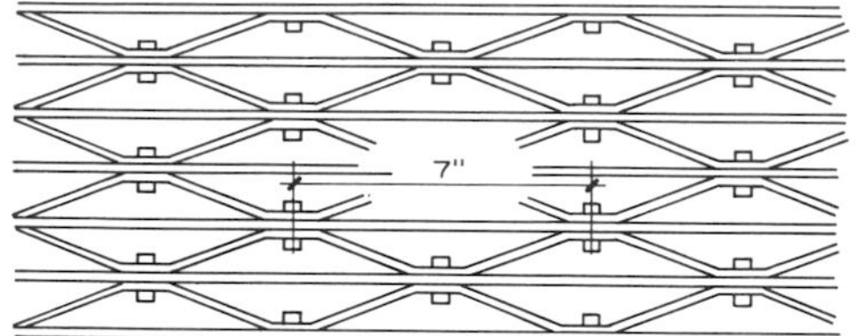
7"

WITH SPACER BARS RIVETED APPROX. 7" O.C.
USED FOR AVERAGE INSTALLATION

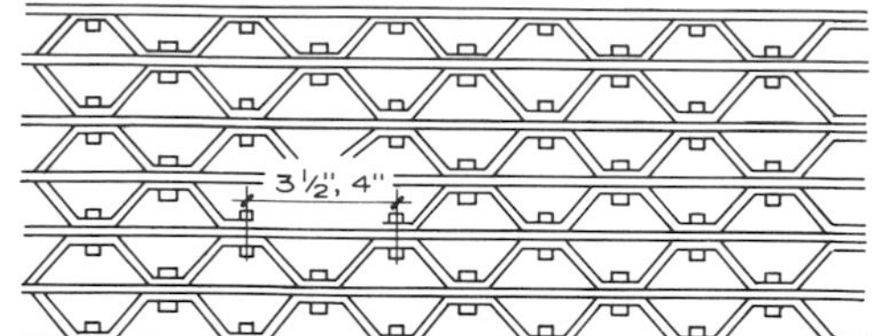
3 1/2", 4"

WITH SPACER BARS RIVETED 3 1/2" OR 4"
USED FOR HEAVY TRAFFIC AND WHERE WHEELED EQUIPMENT IS USED

RETICULATED (RIVETED)

NOTES

Flat bearing bars are made of steel or aluminum, and continuous bent spacer or reticulate bars are riveted to the bearing bars. Usually they have open ends or ends that are banded with flat bars of the same size as bearing bars, welded across the ends. Normal spacing of bars: 3/4, 1 1/8, or 2 5/16 in. Many bar gratings cannot be used in areas of public pedestrian traffic (crutches, canes, pogo sticks, women's shoes, etc.). Close mesh grating (1/4 in.) is available in steel and aluminum, for use in pedestrian traffic areas.

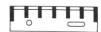

NOSING OF ANGLE AND ABRASIVE STRIP AND BAR ENDS

HEAVY FRONT AND BACK BEARING BARS AND BAR END PLATES

FLOOR PLATE NOSING, BAR END PLATES

NOSING OF CLOSELY SPACED BARS, ANGLE ENDS

CHECKER PLATE NOSING, BAR END PLATES

EXTRUDED ALUMINUM CORRUGATED NOSING, BAR END PLATES

TREADS

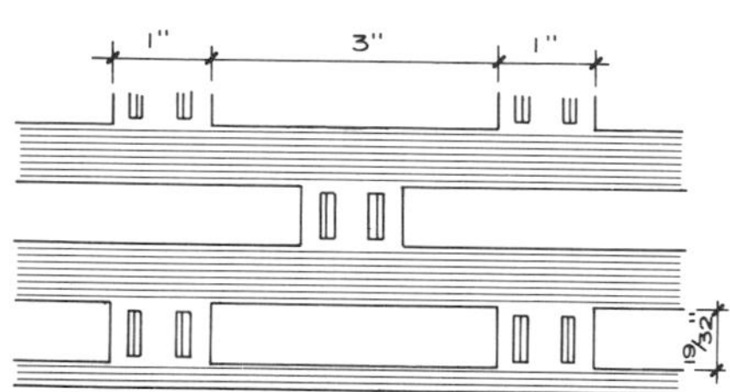
1"
3"
1"
19/32"

PLAN

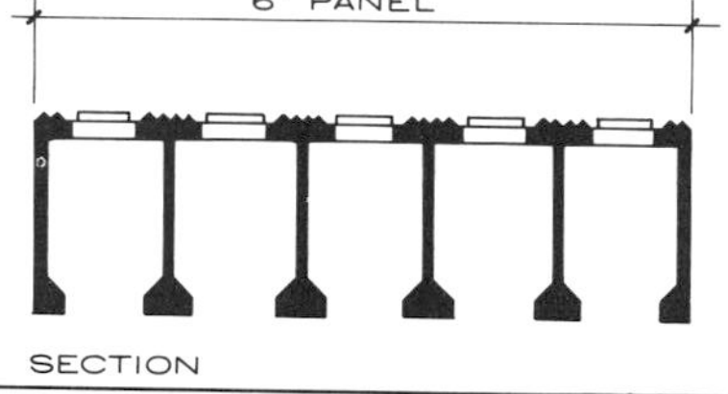
6" PANEL

SECTION

ALUMINUM PLANK

NOTES

Grating is extruded from aluminum alloy in one piece with integral I-beam ribs and can have a natural finish or be anodized. Top of surface may be solid or punched. Standard panel width is 6 in.

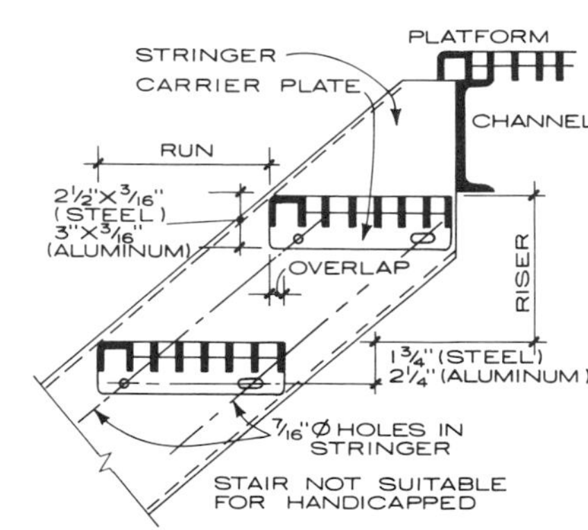
PLATFORM
STRINGER
CARRIER PLATE
CHANNEL
RUN
2 1/2"×3/16" (STEEL)
3"×3/16" (ALUMINUM)
OVERLAP
RISER
1 3/4" (STEEL)
2 1/4" (ALUMINUM)
7/16" Ø HOLES IN STRINGER
STAIR NOT SUITABLE FOR HANDICAPPED

STAIR STRINGER AND TREAD CARRIER

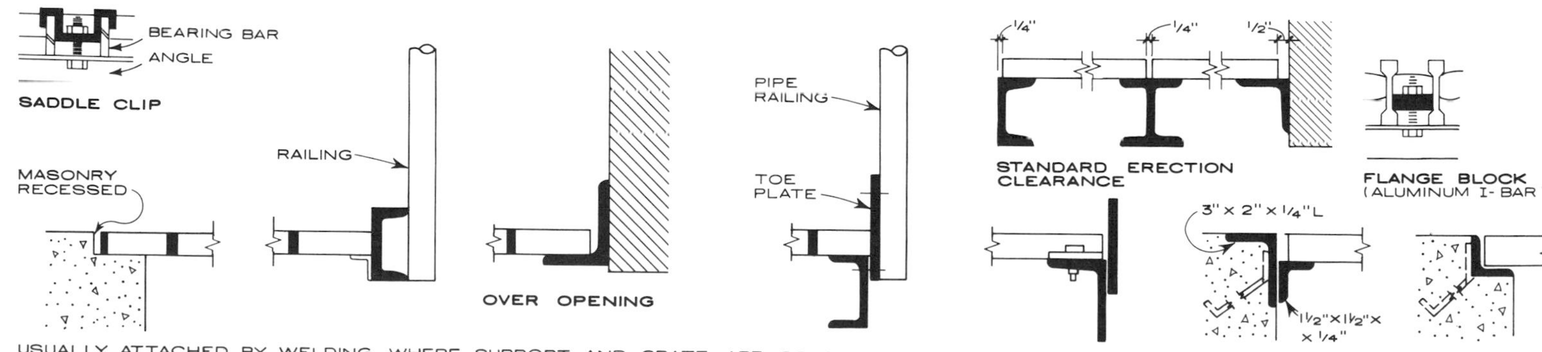
BEARING BAR
ANGLE
SADDLE CLIP
MASONRY RECESSED
RAILING
OVER OPENING
PIPE RAILING
TOE PLATE
1/4"
1/4"
1/2"
STANDARD ERECTION CLEARANCE
FLANGE BLOCK (ALUMINUM I-BAR)
3" × 2" × 1/4" L
1 1/2" × 1 1/2" × 1/4"

USUALLY ATTACHED BY WELDING, WHERE SUPPORT AND GRATE ARE CONSTRUCTED AS A UNIT

FIXED OR LOOSE GRATINGS

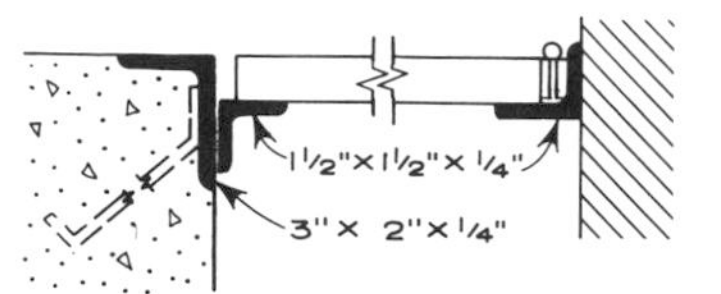
1 1/2"×1 1/2"×1/4"
3"× 2"×1/4"

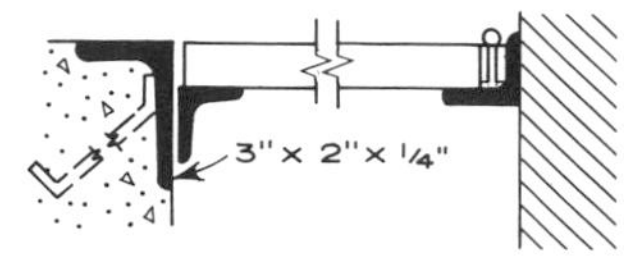
3"× 2"×1/4"

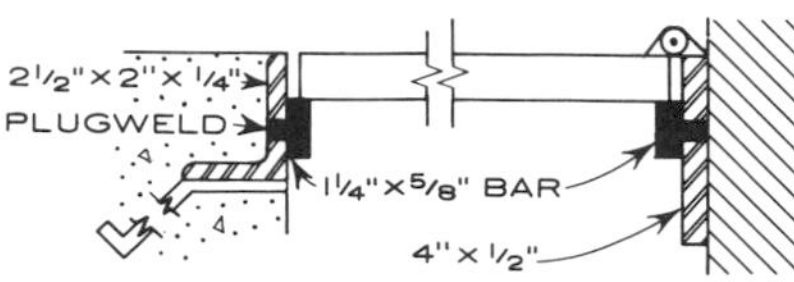
2 1/2"×2"×1/4"
PLUGWELD
1 1/4"×5/8" BAR
4"×1/2"

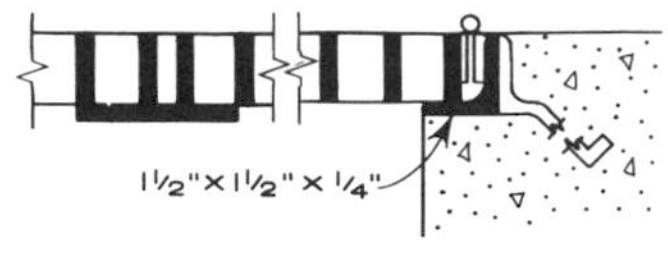
1 1/2"×1 1/2"×1/4"

SIZES OF ANGLES SUPPORTING GRATING DEPEND ON DEPTH OF GRATING BARS

HINGED AREA GRATINGS

Vicente Cordero, AIA; Arlington, Virginia

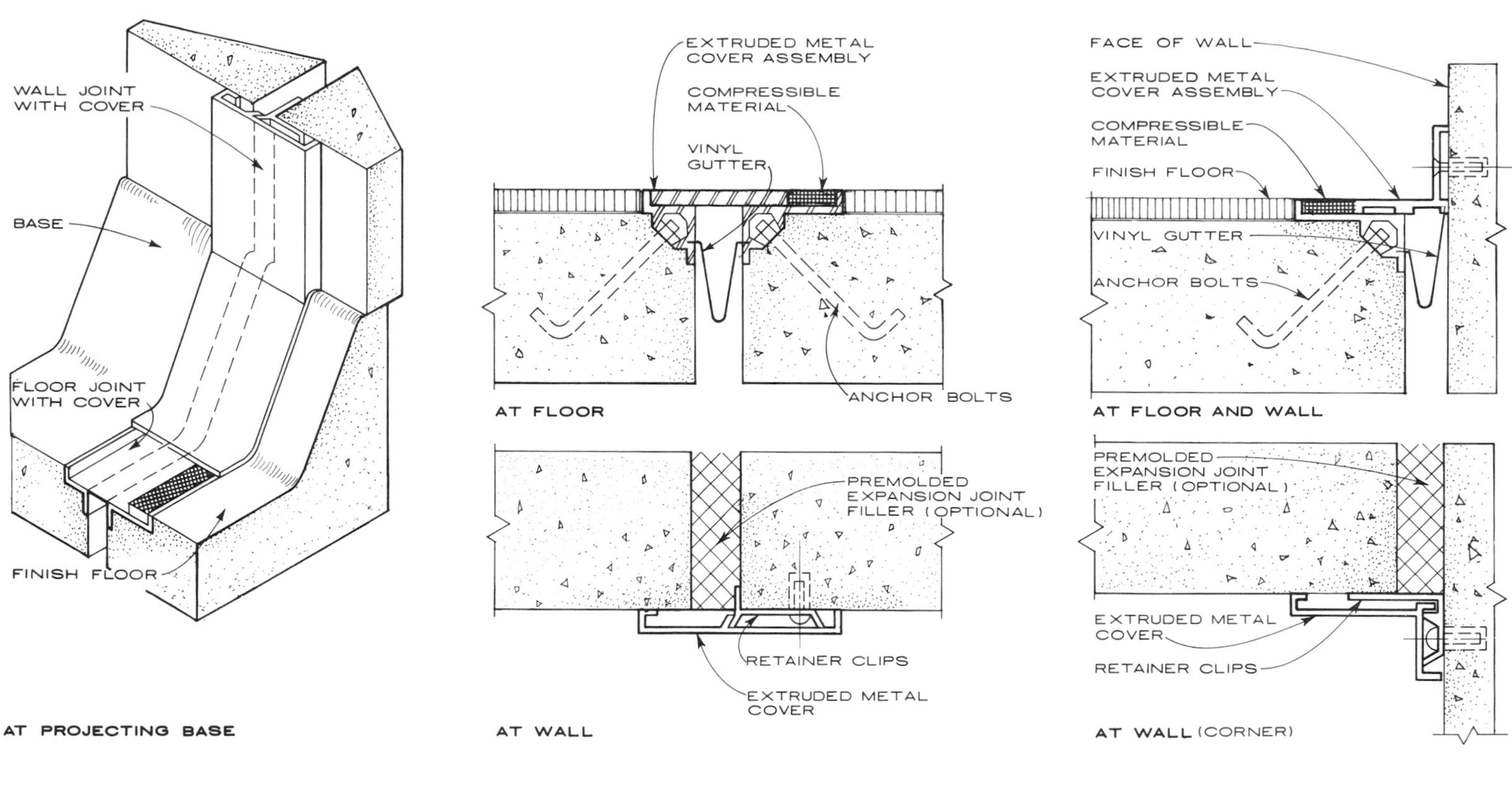
WALL JOINT WITH COVER
BASE
FLOOR JOINT WITH COVER
FINISH FLOOR
AT PROJECTING BASE
EXTRUDED METAL COVER ASSEMBLY
COMPRESSIBLE MATERIAL
VINYL GUTTER
ANCHOR BOLTS
AT FLOOR
PREMOLDED EXPANSION JOINT FILLER (OPTIONAL)
RETAINER CLIPS
EXTRUDED METAL COVER
AT WALL
FACE OF WALL
EXTRUDED METAL COVER ASSEMBLY
COMPRESSIBLE MATERIAL
FINISH FLOOR
VINYL GUTTER
ANCHOR BOLTS
AT FLOOR AND WALL
PREMOLDED EXPANSION JOINT FILLER (OPTIONAL)
EXTRUDED METAL COVER
RETAINER CLIPS
AT WALL (CORNER)

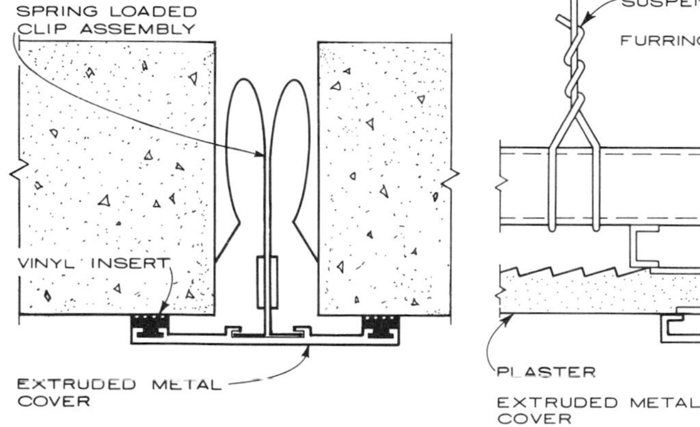
SPRING LOADED CLIP ASSEMBLY
VINYL INSERT
EXTRUDED METAL COVER

AT WALL OR CEILING

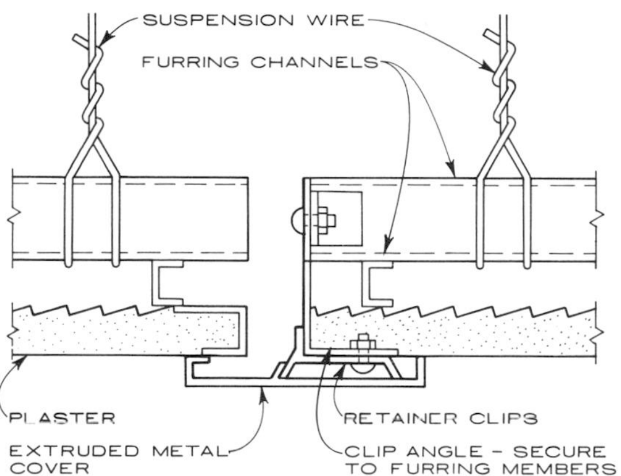
SUSPENSION WIRE
FURRING CHANNELS
PLASTER
EXTRUDED METAL COVER
RETAINER CLIPS
CLIP ANGLE - SECURE TO FURRING MEMBERS

AT SUSPENDED CEILING

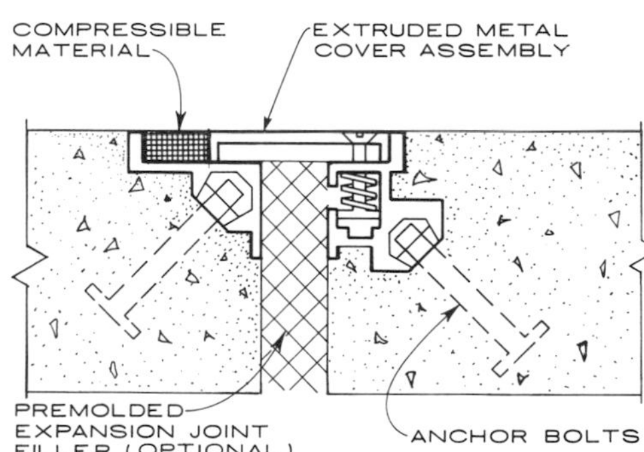
COMPRESSIBLE MATERIAL
EXTRUDED METAL COVER ASSEMBLY
PREMOLDED EXPANSION JOINT FILLER (OPTIONAL)
ANCHOR BOLTS

SEISMIC FLOOR JOINT COVER

NOTE

Expansion joint covers that will respond to differential movement, both laterally and horizontally, should be provided at joints in structures located where seismic action (earth tremors and quakes) may be expected or where differential settlement is anticipated.

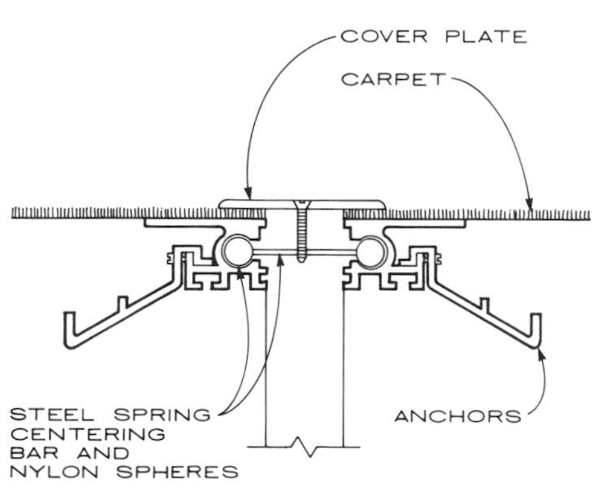
COVER PLATE
CARPET
STEEL SPRING CENTERING BAR AND NYLON SPHERES
ANCHORS

FLEXIBLE FLOOR JOINT COVER

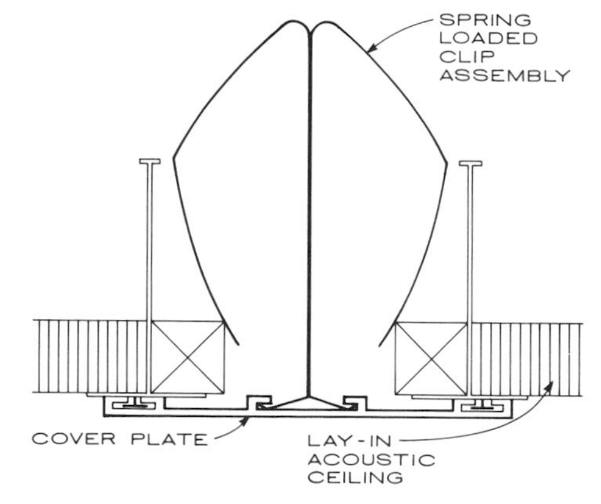
SPRING LOADED CLIP ASSEMBLY
COVER PLATE
LAY-IN ACOUSTIC CEILING

SUSPENDED ACOUSTIC CEILING

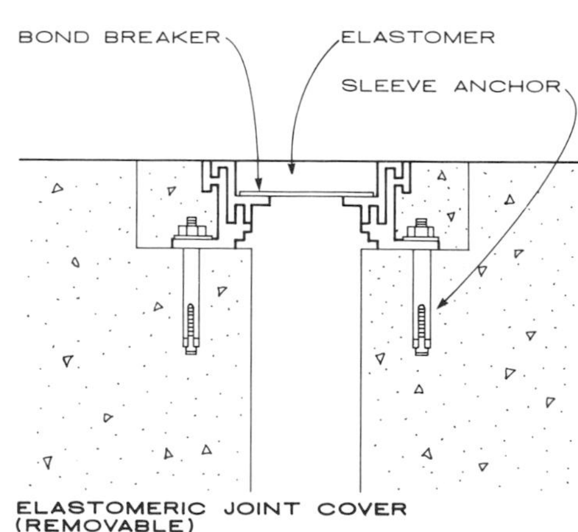
BOND BREAKER
ELASTOMER
SLEEVE ANCHOR

ELASTOMERIC JOINT COVER (REMOVABLE)

NOTE

A large selection of prefabricated assemblies to cover interior expansion joints are available from various manufacturers to satisfy most joint and finish conditions.

PREFABRICATED INTERIOR EXPANSION JOINT COVERS

Robert D. Abernathy; J. N. Pease Associates; Charlotte, North Carolina

GENERAL NOTES

Many variations of the typical types shown are available such as slanted, rounded, or tapered tops and ends; grooved, ribbed, fluted and shaped faces; as well as other decorative treatment.

Refer to the following sections for: a) Standard Metal Shapes b) Metal Stair Nosings

D.O.F. = DEPTH OF FACE

LEGEND

INDICATES BACK-UP MATERIAL (PLYWOOD, PLASTER OR OTHER DENSE SURFACE)

$^{13}/_{32}$" AND $^{11}/_{16}$" OVERLAP
7/8" → 1 3/8" D.O.F.

1/4" OVERLAP
3/4" → 1 1/4" D.O.F.

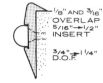

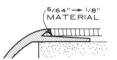

1/16" → 1/8" MATERIAL
5/8" → 1 1/2" D.O.F.

5/64" → 1/8" MATERIAL
13/16" → 1 3/32" D.O.F.

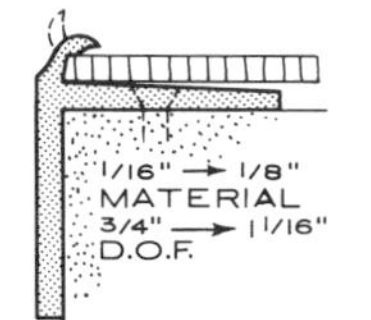

1/16" → 1/8" MATERIAL
3/4" → 1 1/16" D.O.F.

1/2" AND 5/8" OVERLAP
13/16" → 1 1/2" D.O.F.

3/16" AND 1/4" OVERLAP
5/16" → 2" D.O.F.

1/8" AND 3/16" OVERLAP
5/16" → 1/2" INSERT
3/4" → 1 1/4" D.O.F.

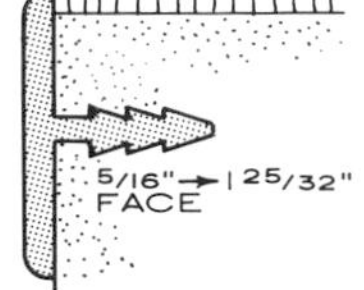

5/16" → 1 25/32" FACE

BUTT TYPE — OVERLAP TYPE — ROLL DOWN TYPE

CONCEALED FLANGES: TAPERED OR STRAIGHT

APPLIED AFTER TYPES

TEE TYPE

NOSINGS

5/64" → 1/8" MATERIAL

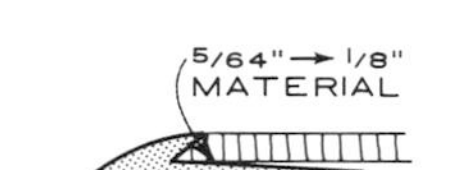

1/8" AND 1/4" UNDER FLANGE

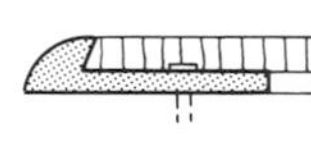

1/16" → 3/16" MATERIAL

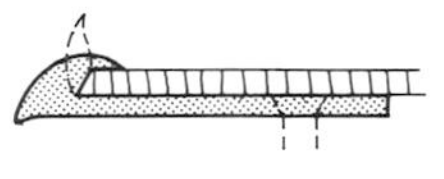

1/16" → 1/8" MATERIAL

1/8" AND 3/16" MATERIAL

1/8" AND 3/16" MATERIAL

SINK (FLAT RIM) OR DOORWAY: BUTT & ROLL DOWN TYPES
CONCEALED FLANGES: TAPERED OR STRAIGHT

BUTT TYPES

EDGINGS

3/32" → 5/32" MATERIAL
3/8" → 1 3/16" WIDTHS

EDGE BINDER
OVERLAP TYPES

3/4" → 1 9/32" WIDTHS

SEAM BINDER

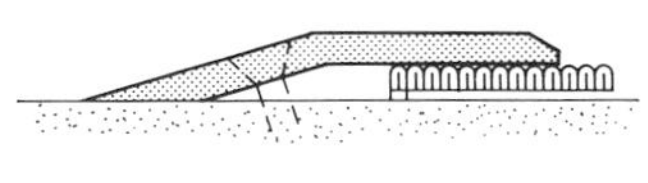

1" → 2 1/2" WIDTHS

OVERLAP TYPE
CARPET EDGE BINDERS

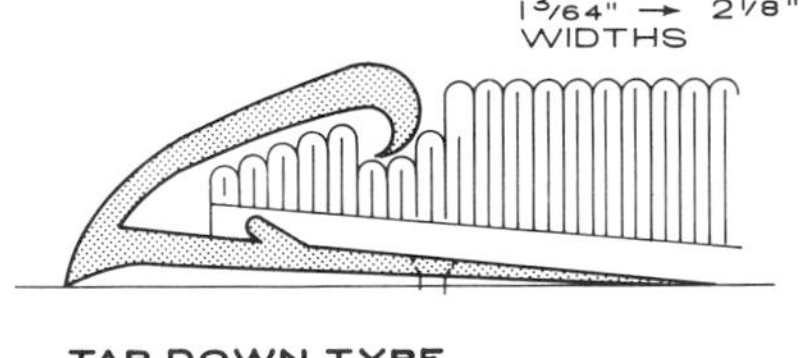

1 3/64" → 2 1/8" WIDTHS

TAP DOWN TYPE

EDGINGS

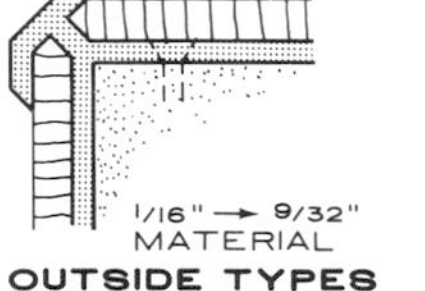

1/16" → 9/32" MATERIAL

1/32" → 1/4" MATERIAL

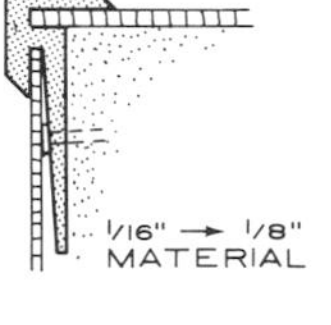

1/16" → 1/8" MATERIAL

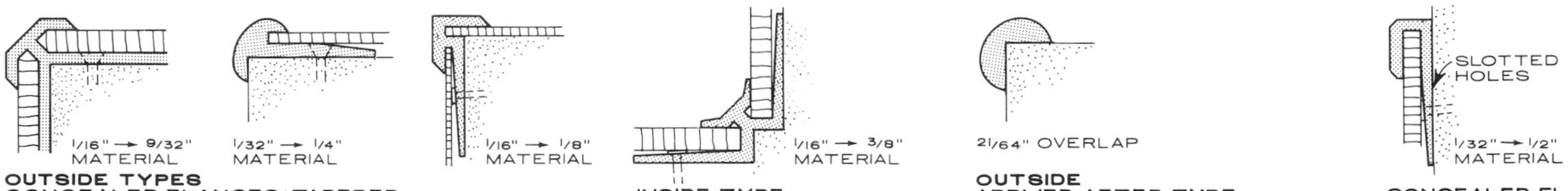

OUTSIDE TYPES
CONCEALED FLANGES: TAPERED

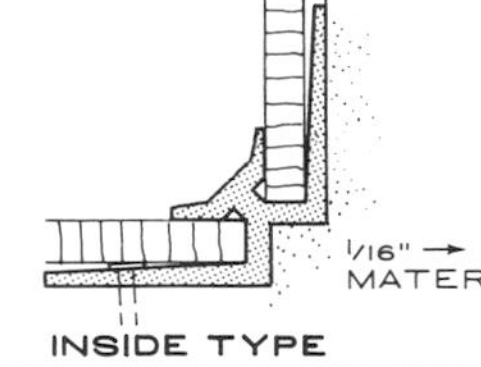

1/16" → 3/8" MATERIAL

INSIDE TYPE

21/64" OVERLAP

OUTSIDE
APPLIED AFTER TYPE

CORNERS

SLOTTED HOLES

1/32" → 1/2" MATERIAL

CONCEALED FLANGE

CAP MOLDING

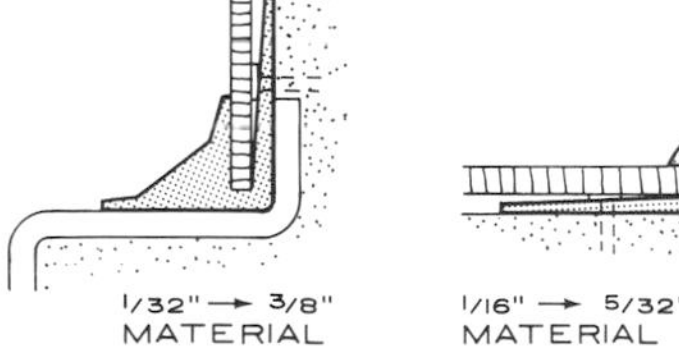

1/32" → 3/8" MATERIAL

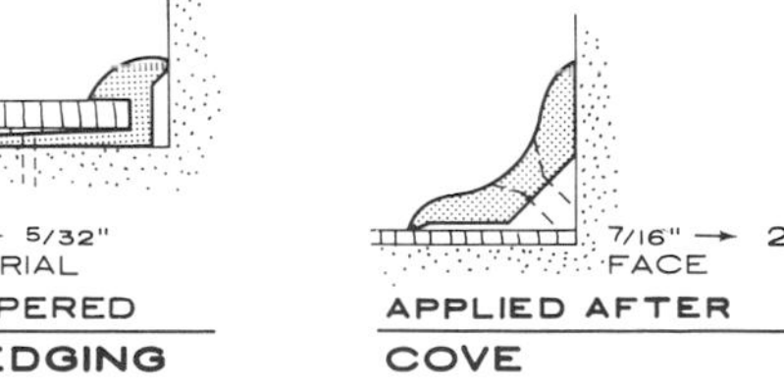

1/16" → 5/32" MATERIAL

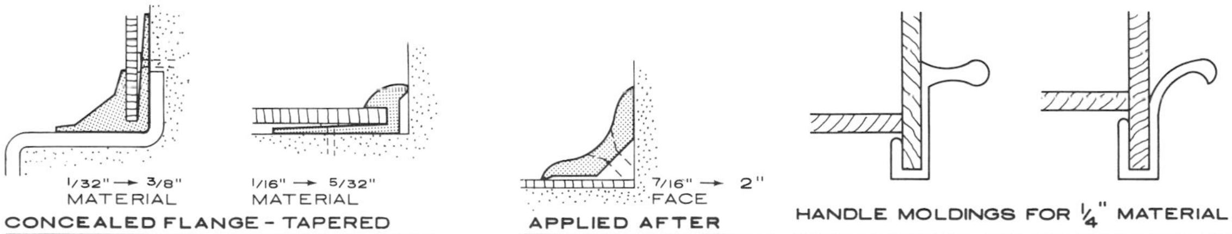

CONCEALED FLANGE - TAPERED

COVE AND BATHTUB EDGING

7/16" → 2" FACE

APPLIED AFTER

COVE

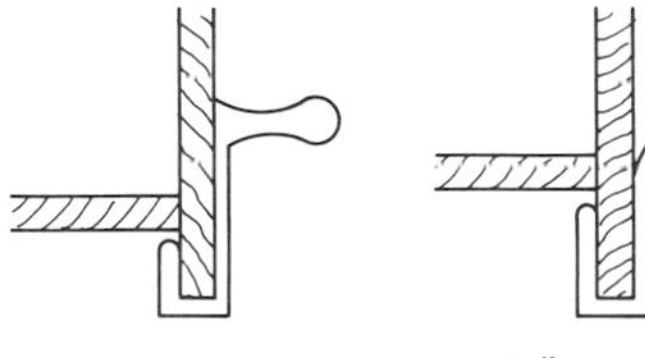

HANDLE MOLDINGS FOR 1/4" MATERIAL

SHOW CASE MOLDINGS

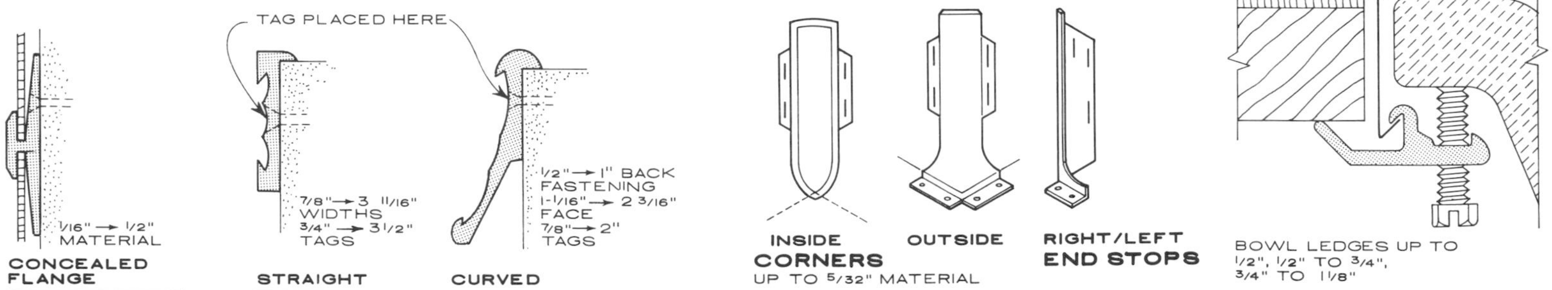

1/16" → 1/2" MATERIAL

CONCEALED FLANGE

DIVISION BAR

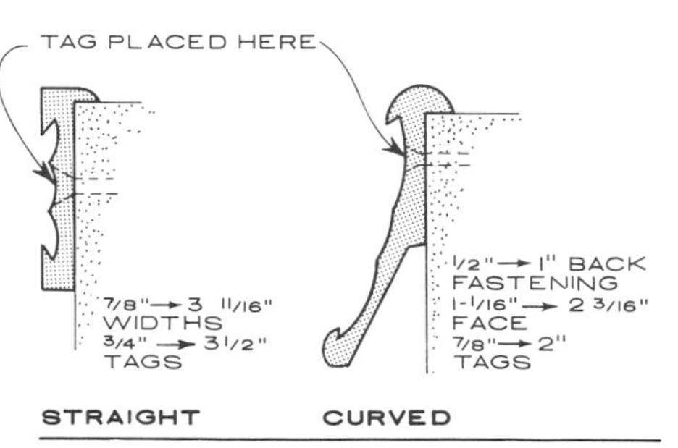

TAG PLACED HERE

7/8" → 3 11/16" WIDTHS
3/4" → 3 1/2" TAGS

1/2" → 1" BACK FASTENING
1-1/16" → 2 3/16" FACE
7/8" → 2" TAGS

STRAIGHT — CURVED

TAG MOLDINGS

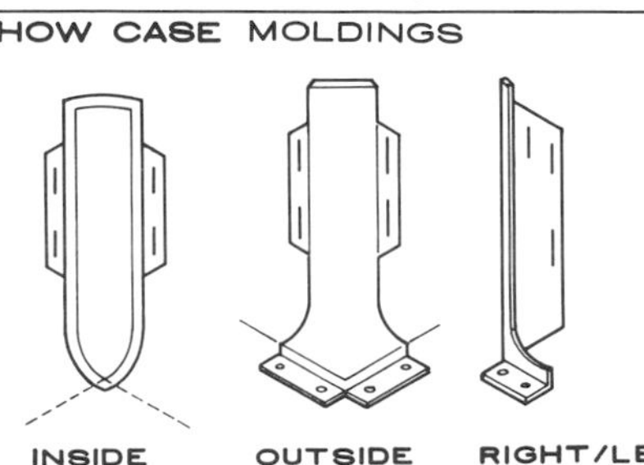

INSIDE — OUTSIDE
CORNERS
UP TO 5/32" MATERIAL

RIGHT/LEFT
END STOPS

COVE BASE

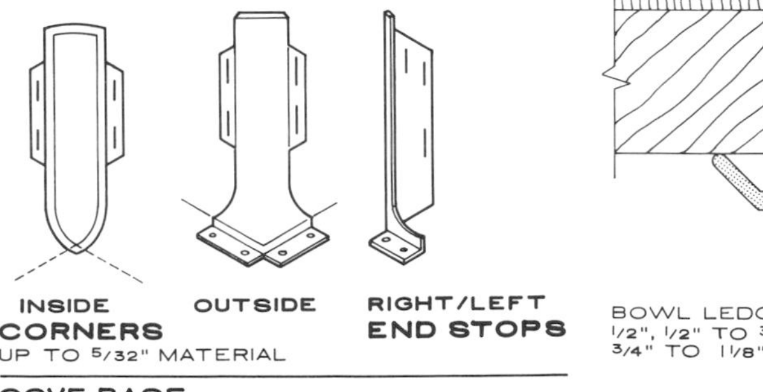

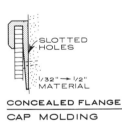

BOWL LEDGES UP TO 1/2", 1/2" TO 3/4", 3/4" TO 1 1/8"

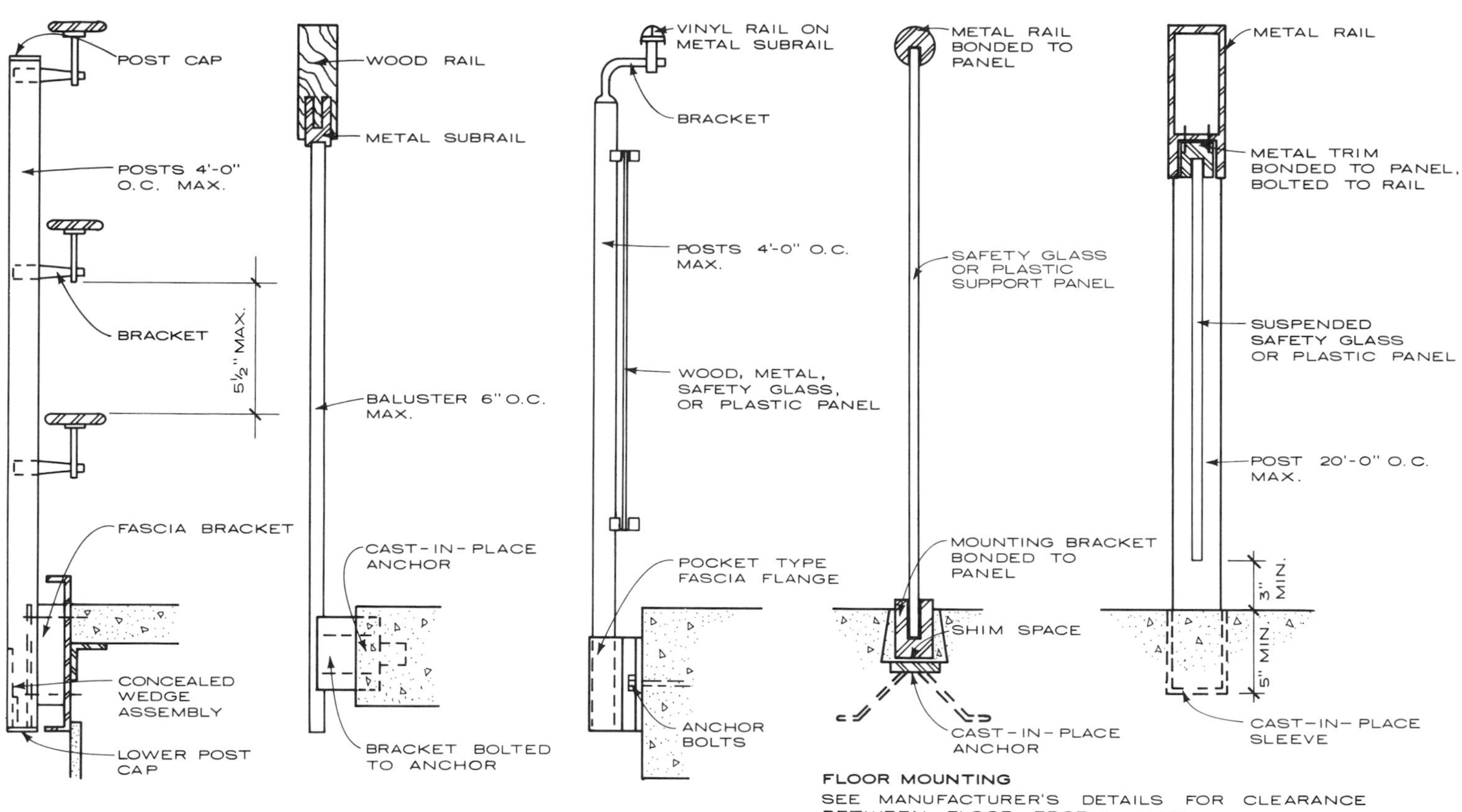
POST CAP
POSTS 4'-0" O.C. MAX.
BRACKET
5½" MAX.
FASCIA BRACKET
CONCEALED WEDGE ASSEMBLY
LOWER POST CAP
WOOD RAIL
METAL SUBRAIL
BALUSTER 6" O.C. MAX.
CAST-IN-PLACE ANCHOR
BRACKET BOLTED TO ANCHOR
VINYL RAIL ON METAL SUBRAIL
BRACKET
POSTS 4'-0" O.C. MAX.
WOOD, METAL, SAFETY GLASS, OR PLASTIC PANEL
POCKET TYPE FASCIA FLANGE
ANCHOR BOLTS
METAL RAIL BONDED TO PANEL
SAFETY GLASS OR PLASTIC SUPPORT PANEL
MOUNTING BRACKET BONDED TO PANEL
SHIM SPACE
CAST-IN-PLACE ANCHOR
METAL RAIL
METAL TRIM BONDED TO PANEL, BOLTED TO RAIL
SUSPENDED SAFETY GLASS OR PLASTIC PANEL
POST 20'-0" O.C. MAX.
3" MIN.
5" MIN.
CAST-IN-PLACE SLEEVE

FLOOR MOUNTING

SEE MANUFACTURER'S DETAILS FOR CLEARANCE BETWEEN FLOOR EDGE AND RAIL

SIDE MOUTING

CONSULT CODE FOR RAILING HEIGHT, POST RAIL, AND BALUSTER SPACING, AND LOADING REQUIREMENTS

TYPICAL POST AND RAIL DETAILS

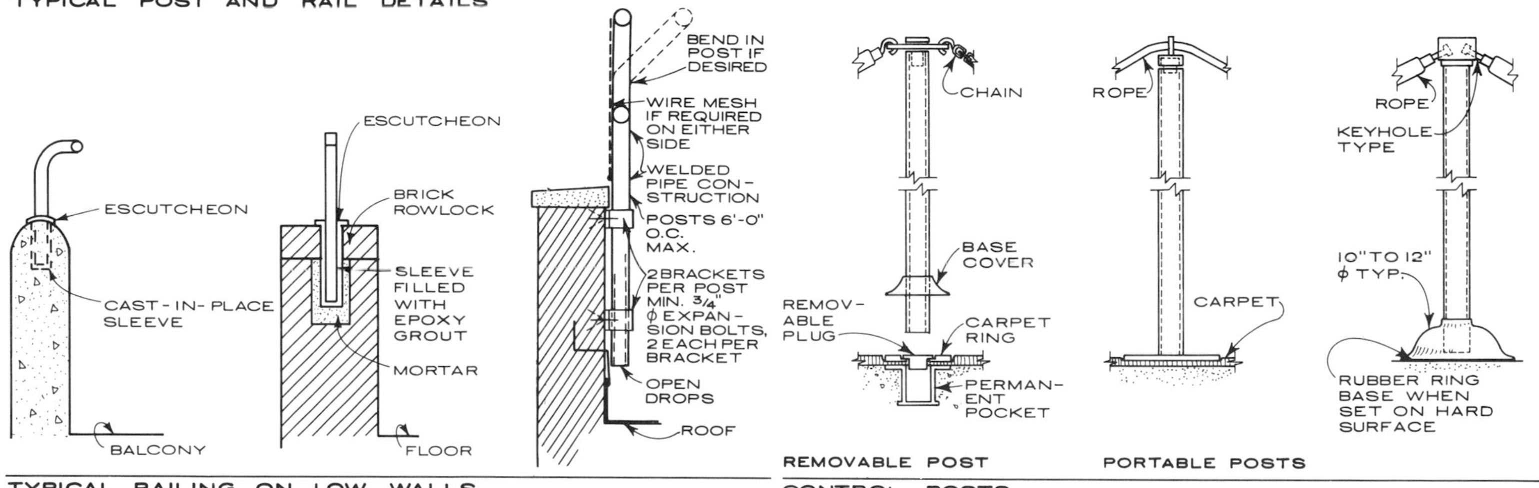
ESCUTCHEON
CAST-IN-PLACE SLEEVE
BALCONY
ESCUTCHEON
BRICK ROWLOCK
SLEEVE FILLED WITH EPOXY GROUT
MORTAR
FLOOR
BEND IN POST IF DESIRED
WIRE MESH IF REQUIRED ON EITHER SIDE
WELDED PIPE CONSTRUCTION
POSTS 6'-0" O.C. MAX.
2 BRACKETS PER POST MIN. ¾" ϕ EXPANSION BOLTS, 2 EACH PER BRACKET
OPEN DROPS
ROOF
CHAIN
BASE COVER
REMOVABLE PLUG
CARPET RING
PERMANENT POCKET
ROPE
CARPET
ROPE
KEYHOLE TYPE
10" TO 12" ϕ TYP.
RUBBER RING BASE WHEN SET ON HARD SURFACE

TYPICAL RAILING ON LOW WALLS

REMOVABLE POST **PORTABLE POSTS**

CONTROL POSTS

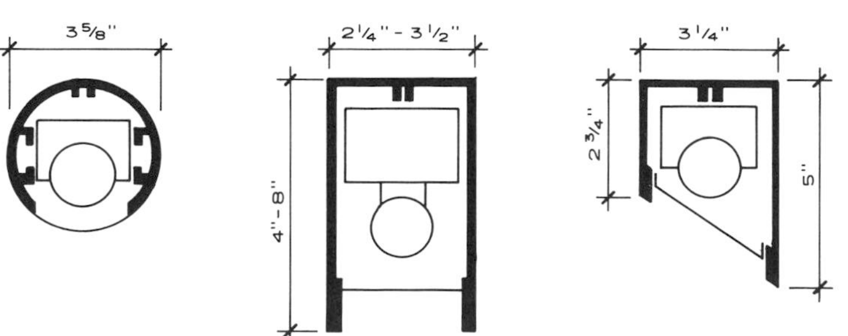
3⅝"
2¼" - 3½"
4'-8"
3¼"
2¾"
5"

FLUORESCENT FIXTURES AND PLASTIC DIFFUSERS, SMALLER HANDRAILS AVAILABLE WITH INCANDESCENT FIXTURES

LIGHTED HANDRAILS

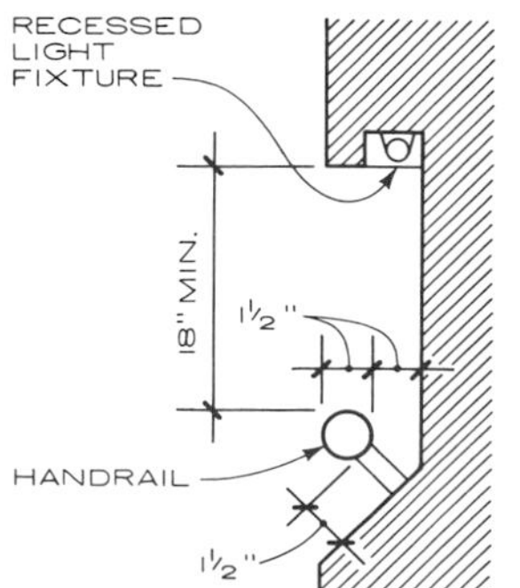
RECESSED LIGHT FIXTURE
18" MIN.
1½"
HANDRAIL
1½"

RECESSED HANDRAIL

GUIDELINES

Factors to consider for railing design include:

1. Follow all local code requirements, especially as they relate to handicap requirements, ramps, rail diameter, and rail clearances.
2. Verify allowable design stresses of rails, posts, and panels.
3. Verify the structural value of fasteners and anchorage to building structure for both vertical and lateral (horizontal) forces.
4. Requirements for uniform loading may vary from 100 to 200 lb/linear foot.
5. Requirements for concentrated loads, at any point along the rail, may vary from 200 to 300 lb.
6. Horizontal guardrail or rail at ramps is 42 in. above floor surface.
7. Guardrails and rails at stairs should be designed to prevent passage of a 6 in. diameter sphere, at any opening, in areas accessible to the public.
8. Refer to ASTM E-985 for additional information.

John McCartney, AIA; Washington, D.C.

REFERENCES

GENERAL REFERENCES

Architectural Metal Handbook, National Association of Architectural Metal Manufacturers

Design Manual for Composite Decks, Form Decks, and Roof Decks, Steel Deck Institute (SDI)

Fire-Resistant Steel Frame Construction, American Iron and Steel Institute (AISI)

Manual of Steel Construction, Allowable Stress Design, American Institute of Steel Construction (AISC)

Standard Specifications, Load Tables, and Weight Tables for Steel Joists and Joist Girders, Steel Joist Institute (SJI)

Structural Details for Steel Construction, 1988, Morton Newman, McGraw-Hill

Structural Steel in Architecture and Building Technology, 1988, Irvin Engel, Prentice-Hall

DATA SOURCES: ORGANIZATIONS

American Bolt, Nut and Rivet Manufacturers (ABNRM), 139

American Iron and Steel Institute (AISI), 148

American National Standards Institute (ANSI), 134, 143, 152, 155

American Society for Testing and Materials (ASTM), 145

Blumcraft of Pittsburg, 159

Factory Mutual System, 145, 146

Independent Nail and Packing Company, 134, 136–138

Irving Grating, IKG Industries, Harsco Corporation, 156

Julius Blum and Company, Inc., 159

Rawplug Company, Inc., 139

Red Head, ITT Phillips Drill Division, 139

Simplex Nails, Inc., 134, 136–138

Trus Joist Corporation, 142

Underwriters Laboratories, Inc. (U.L.), 145, 146

U.S. Steel Corporation, 148

Volume Indoor Parking, Inc., 142

Youngstown Aluminum Products, 158

DATA SOURCES: PUBLICATIONS

Architectural Metal Handbook, National Association of Architectural Metal Manufacturers, 152, 156

Design Manual for Floor Decks and Roof Decks, Steel Deck Institute (SDI), 146, 147

Life Safety Code, 5-2.8.1.4. NFPA 101, 1985, National Fire Protection Association. Reprinted with permission, 154

Standard Specifications Load Tables and Weight Tables for Steel Joists, Steel Joist Institute (SJI), 144, 145

CHAPTER 6

WOOD

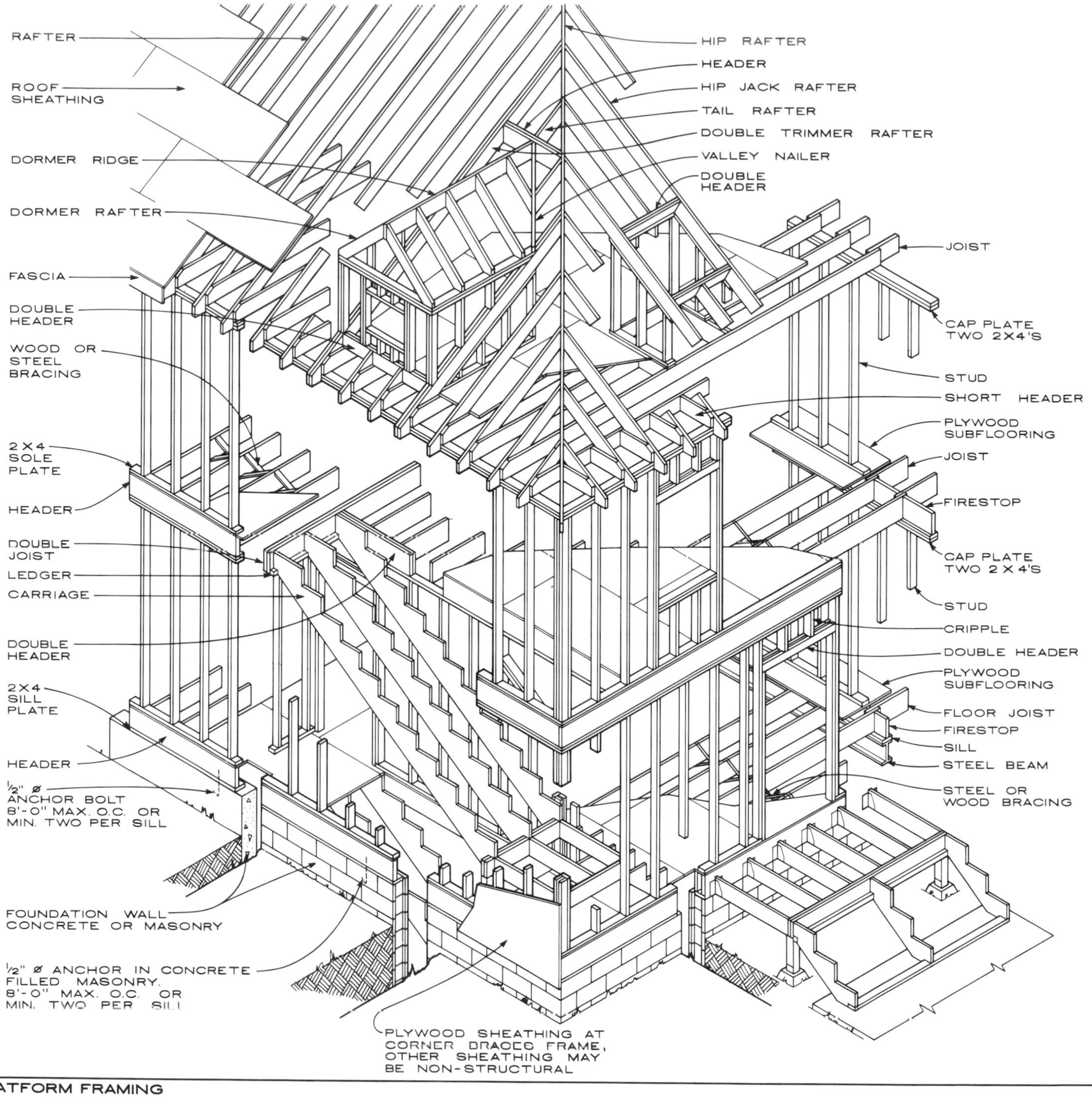

RAFTER
ROOF SHEATHING
DORMER RIDGE
DORMER RAFTER
FASCIA
DOUBLE HEADER
WOOD OR STEEL BRACING
2 X 4 SOLE PLATE
HEADER
DOUBLE JOIST
LEDGER
CARRIAGE
DOUBLE HEADER
2X4 SILL PLATE
HEADER
½" ø ANCHOR BOLT 8'-0" MAX. O.C. OR MIN. TWO PER SILL
FOUNDATION WALL CONCRETE OR MASONRY
½" ø ANCHOR IN CONCRETE FILLED MASONRY. 8'-0" MAX. O.C. OR MIN. TWO PER SILL
PLYWOOD SHEATHING AT CORNER BRACED FRAME, OTHER SHEATHING MAY BE NON-STRUCTURAL
HIP RAFTER
HEADER
HIP JACK RAFTER
TAIL RAFTER
DOUBLE TRIMMER RAFTER
VALLEY NAILER
DOUBLE HEADER
JOIST
CAP PLATE TWO 2X4'S
STUD
SHORT HEADER
PLYWOOD SUBFLOORING
JOIST
FIRESTOP
CAP PLATE TWO 2 X 4'S
STUD
CRIPPLE
DOUBLE HEADER
PLYWOOD SUBFLOORING
FLOOR JOIST
FIRESTOP
SILL
STEEL BEAM
STEEL OR WOOD BRACING

PLATFORM FRAMING

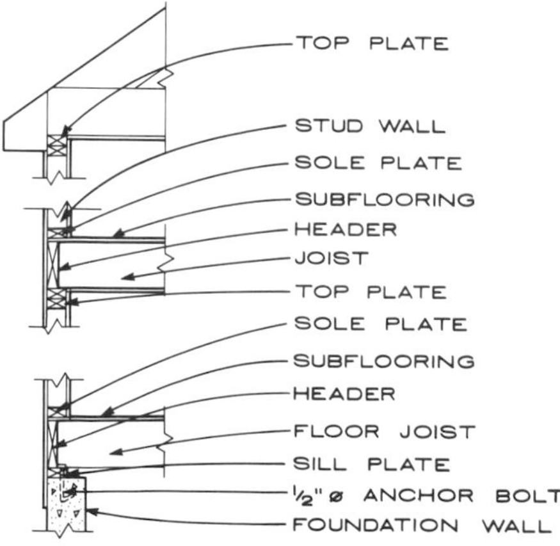
TOP PLATE
STUD WALL
SOLE PLATE
SUBFLOORING
HEADER
JOIST
TOP PLATE
SOLE PLATE
SUBFLOORING
HEADER
FLOOR JOIST
SILL PLATE
½" ø ANCHOR BOLT
FOUNDATION WALL

NOTES

WESTERN OR PLATFORM FRAMING

Before any of the superstructure is erected, the first floor subflooring is put down making a platform on which the walls and partitions can be assembled and tilted into place. The process is repeated for each story of the building. This framing system is used frequently .

FIRESTOPPING

All concealed spaces in framing, with the exception of areas around flues and chimneys, are to be fitted with 2 in. blocking arranged to prevent drafts between spaces.

EXTERIOR WALL FRAMING

One story buildings: 2 x 4's, 16 in. or 24 in. o.c.;
2 x 6's, 24 in. o.c.
Two and three stories: 2 x 4's, 16 in. o.c.;
2 x 6's, 24 in. o.c.

BRACING EXTERIOR WALLS

Because floor framing and wall frames do not interlock, adequate sheathing must act as bracing and provide the necessary lateral resistance. Where required for additional stiffness or bracing, 1 x 4's may be let into outer face of studs at 45° angle secured at top, bottom, and to studs.

BRIDGING FOR FLOOR JOISTS

May be omitted when flooring is nailed adequately to joist; however, where nominal depth-to-thickness ratio of joists exceeds 6, bridging would be installed at 8 ft. 0 in. intervals. Building codes may allow omission of bridging under certain conditions.

Steel bridging is available. Some types do not require nails.

Timothy B. McDonald; Washington, D.C.

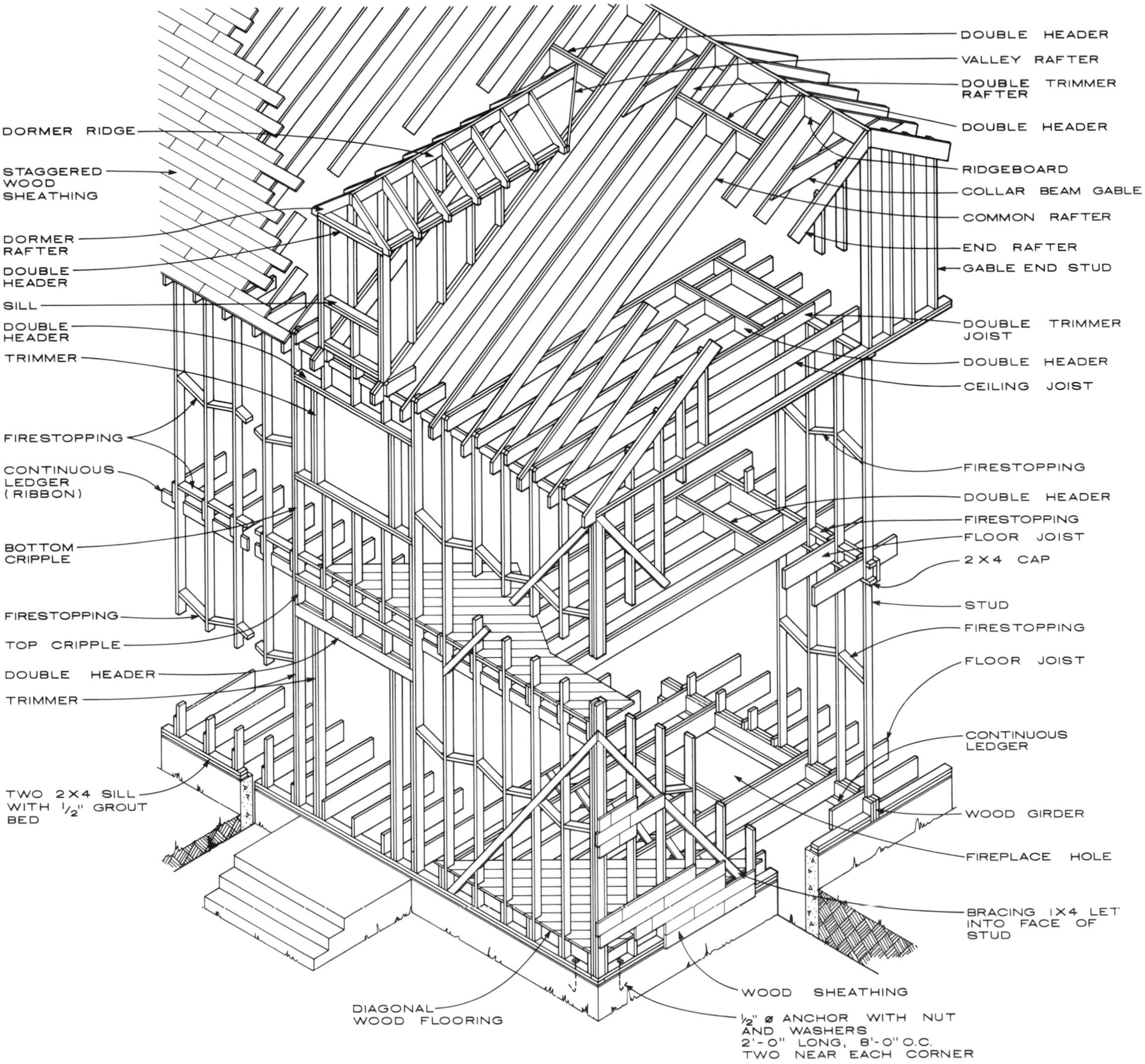

DOUBLE HEADER
VALLEY RAFTER
DOUBLE TRIMMER RAFTER
DOUBLE HEADER
RIDGEBOARD
COLLAR BEAM GABLE
COMMON RAFTER
END RAFTER
GABLE END STUD
DOUBLE TRIMMER JOIST
DOUBLE HEADER
CEILING JOIST
FIRESTOPPING
DOUBLE HEADER
FIRESTOPPING
FLOOR JOIST
2 X 4 CAP
STUD
FIRESTOPPING
FLOOR JOIST
CONTINUOUS LEDGER
WOOD GIRDER
FIREPLACE HOLE
BRACING 1X4 LET INTO FACE OF STUD
WOOD SHEATHING
½" ø ANCHOR WITH NUT AND WASHERS 2'-0" LONG, 8'-0" O.C. TWO NEAR EACH CORNER
DIAGONAL WOOD FLOORING
DORMER RIDGE
STAGGERED WOOD SHEATHING
DORMER RAFTER
DOUBLE HEADER
SILL
DOUBLE HEADER
TRIMMER
FIRESTOPPING
CONTINUOUS LEDGER (RIBBON)
BOTTOM CRIPPLE
FIRESTOPPING
TOP CRIPPLE
DOUBLE HEADER
TRIMMER
TWO 2X4 SILL WITH ½" GROUT BED

BALLOON FRAMING

NOTES

BALLOON FRAMING

Balloon Framing's principal characteristics are that wall studs and joists rest on an anchored sill, with the studs extending in one continuous piece from sill to roof. At the second floor level a ribbon is let into the studs. The floor joists rest on the ribbon and are fastened to the studs: supporting and tying the structure together. This type of framing can be found in older structures and is generally not used today.

FIRESTOPPING

The flue effect created by continuous studs from sill to roof make firestopping mandatory in this type of framing. Firestopping is provided at each floor level and at the mid wall level.

TYPICAL EXTERIOR WALL FRAMING

One story: 2 x 4's 16 in. o.c.
Two story: 2 x 4's 16 in. o.c.

BRACING EXTERIOR WALLS

There are no braces in the balloon frame itself; hence, two methods are used to provide lateral rigidity. Previously diagonal sheathing was used. The other method, sometimes used in conjunction with diagonal sheathing, is to let continuous 1 x 4's into the outer face of corner studs at a 45° angle, and fastened top, bottom, and to the studs.

BRIDGING FOR FLOOR JOISTS

May be omitted when flooring is properly nailed to joists. However, where nominal depth-to-thickness ratio of joists exceeds 6 bridging should be installed at 8 ft 0 in. intervals. (F.H.A. also allows omission of bridging under certain conditions—see F.H.A. publication No. 300, revised 1965.)

Steel bridging is available. Some types do not require nails.

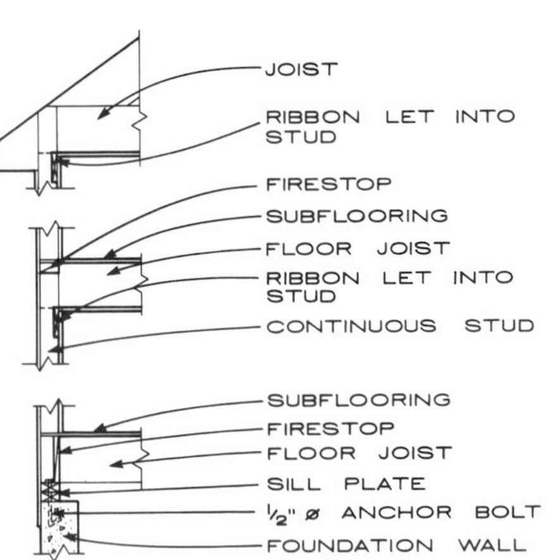
JOIST
RIBBON LET INTO STUD
FIRESTOP
SUBFLOORING
FLOOR JOIST
RIBBON LET INTO STUD
CONTINUOUS STUD
SUBFLOORING
FIRESTOP
FLOOR JOIST
SILL PLATE
½" ø ANCHOR BOLT
FOUNDATION WALL

Timothy B. McDonald; Washington, D.C.

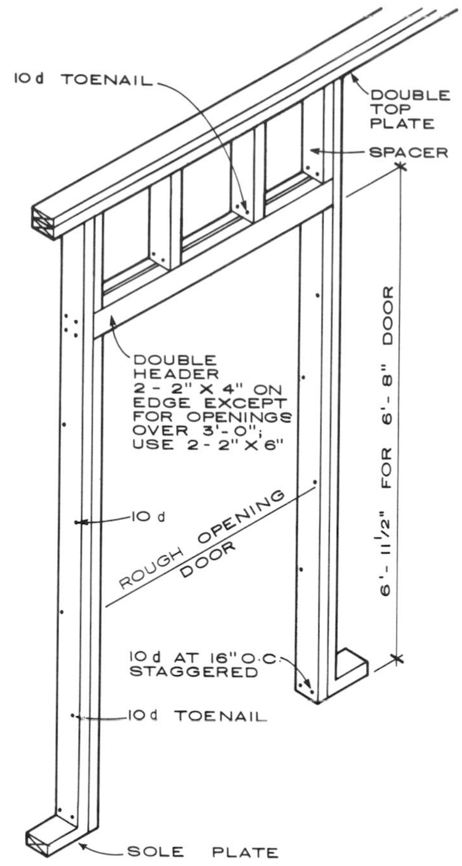

10d TOENAIL
DOUBLE TOP PLATE
SPACER
DOUBLE HEADER 2 - 2" X 4" ON EDGE EXCEPT FOR OPENINGS OVER 3'-0"; USE 2 - 2" X 6"
10 d
ROUGH OPENING DOOR
6'- 11 1/2" FOR 6'- 8" DOOR
10 d AT 16" O.C. STAGGERED
10 d TOENAIL
SOLE PLATE

DOOR OPENING

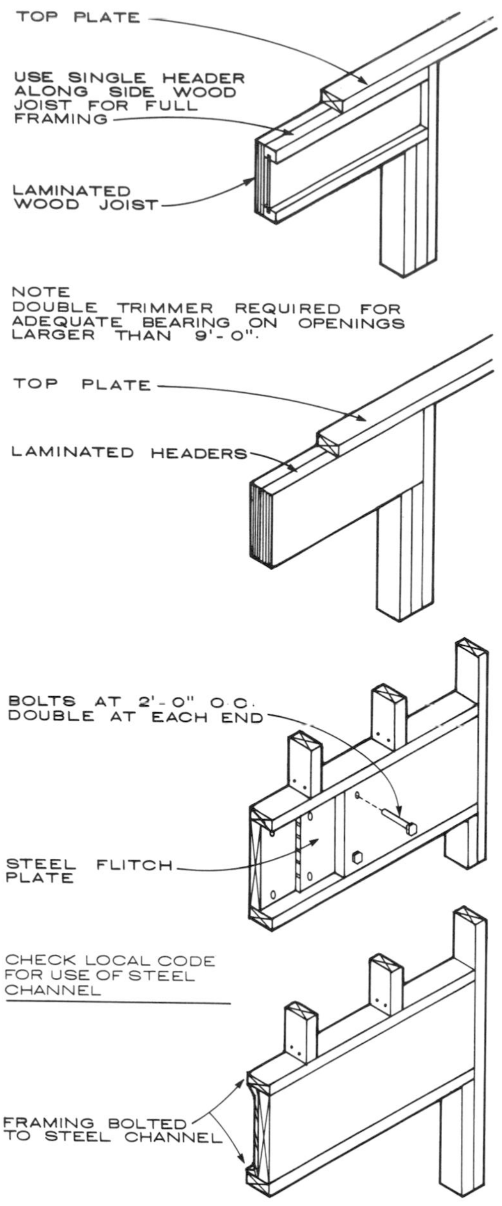

TOP PLATE
USE SINGLE HEADER ALONG SIDE WOOD JOIST FOR FULL FRAMING
LAMINATED WOOD JOIST
NOTE
DOUBLE TRIMMER REQUIRED FOR ADEQUATE BEARING ON OPENINGS LARGER THAN 9'-0".
TOP PLATE
LAMINATED HEADERS
BOLTS AT 2'-0" O.C. DOUBLE AT EACH END
STEEL FLITCH PLATE
CHECK LOCAL CODE FOR USE OF STEEL CHANNEL
FRAMING BOLTED TO STEEL CHANNEL

LINTELS FOR WIDE OPENINGS

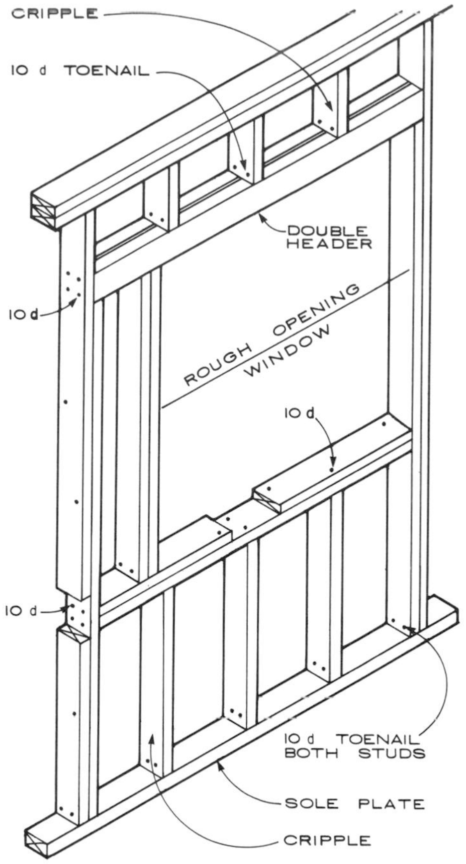

CRIPPLE
10 d TOENAIL
DOUBLE HEADER
10 d
ROUGH OPENING WINDOW
10 d
10 d
10 d TOENAIL BOTH STUDS
SOLE PLATE
CRIPPLE

WINDOW OPENING

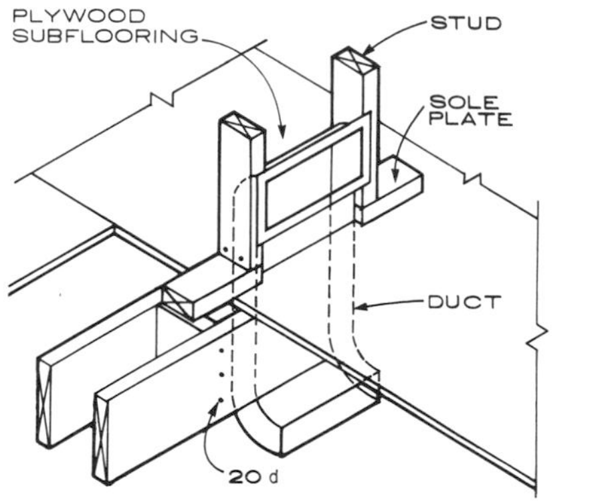

PLYWOOD SUBFLOORING
STUD
SOLE PLATE
DUCT
20 d

SMALL OPENING

NOTES

1. Steel lintels are selected from steel beam design tables on the basis of floor, wall, and roof openings.
2. Wood lintels over openings in bearing walls may be engineered as beams.
3. Composite beams, such as glued laminated beams, also are appropriate in some applications. Plywood box beams are used for garage doors. Steel flitch plates can add strength without adding extra width to a composite beam.
4. Check with local codes and standards for fire resistance requirements.

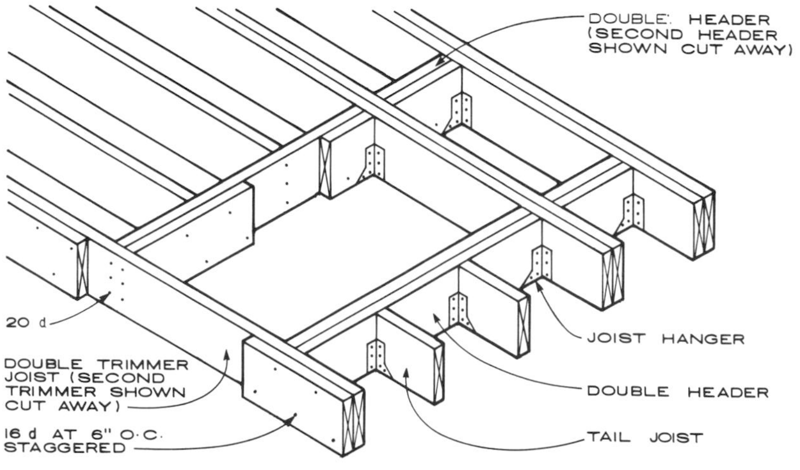

DOUBLE HEADER (SECOND HEADER SHOWN CUT AWAY)
20 d
DOUBLE TRIMMER JOIST (SECOND TRIMMER SHOWN CUT AWAY)
16 d AT 6" O.C. STAGGERED
JOIST HANGER
DOUBLE HEADER
TAIL JOIST

LARGE OPENING REMOVED FROM BEARING WALLS

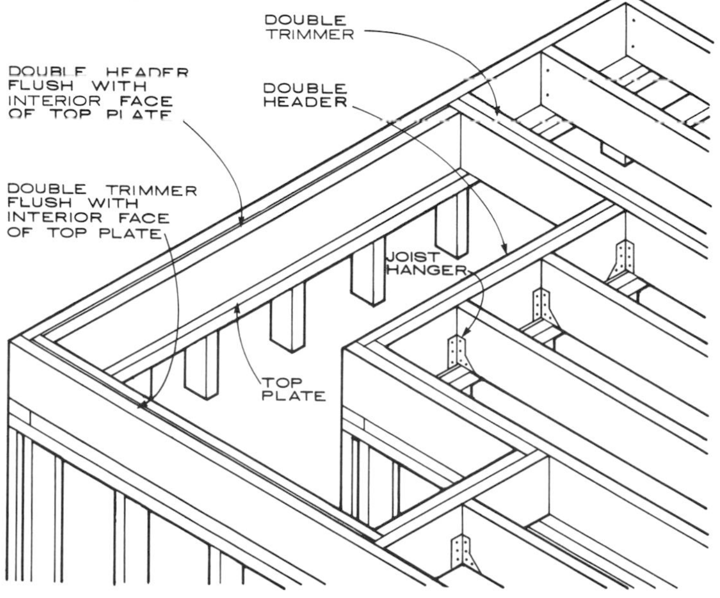

DOUBLE TRIMMER
DOUBLE HEADER
DOUBLE HEADER FLUSH WITH INTERIOR FACE OF TOP PLATE
DOUBLE TRIMMER FLUSH WITH INTERIOR FACE OF TOP PLATE
JOIST HANGER
TOP PLATE

STAIR OPENING AT EXTERIOR WALL

Joseph A. Wilkes, FAIA; Wilkes and Faulkner; Washington, D.C.

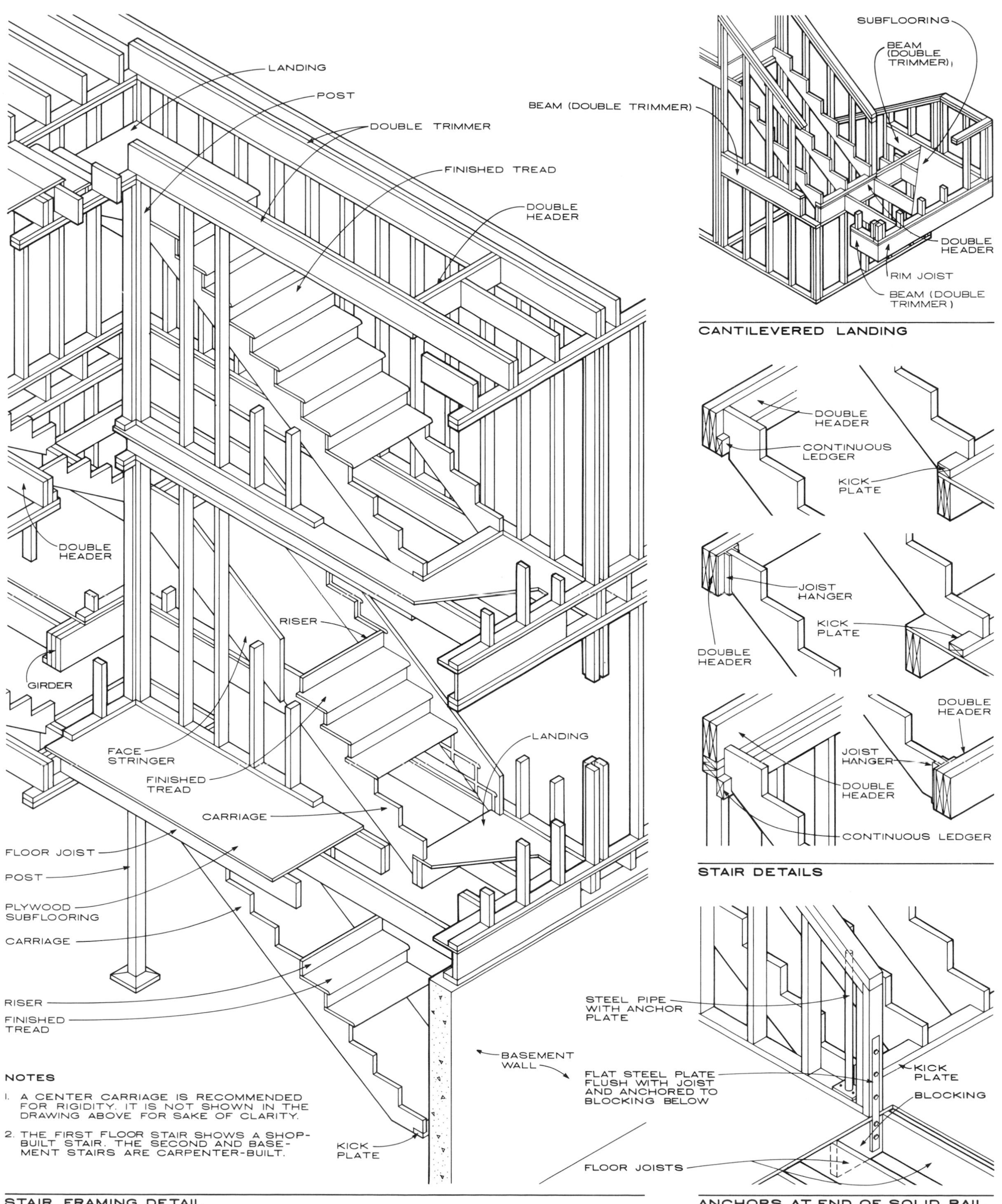
LANDING
POST
DOUBLE TRIMMER
FINISHED TREAD
DOUBLE HEADER
DOUBLE HEADER
RISER
GIRDER
FACE STRINGER
FINISHED TREAD
LANDING
CARRIAGE
FLOOR JOIST
POST
PLYWOOD SUBFLOORING
CARRIAGE
RISER
FINISHED TREAD
BASEMENT WALL
KICK PLATE
SUBFLOORING
BEAM (DOUBLE TRIMMER)
BEAM (DOUBLE TRIMMER)
DOUBLE HEADER
RIM JOIST
BEAM (DOUBLE TRIMMER)
CANTILEVERED LANDING
DOUBLE HEADER
CONTINUOUS LEDGER
KICK PLATE
JOIST HANGER
KICK PLATE
DOUBLE HEADER
DOUBLE HEADER
JOIST HANGER
DOUBLE HEADER
CONTINUOUS LEDGER
STAIR DETAILS
STEEL PIPE WITH ANCHOR PLATE
FLAT STEEL PLATE FLUSH WITH JOIST AND ANCHORED TO BLOCKING BELOW
KICK PLATE
BLOCKING
FLOOR JOISTS
ANCHORS AT END OF SOLID RAIL

NOTES

1. A CENTER CARRIAGE IS RECOMMENDED FOR RIGIDITY. IT IS NOT SHOWN IN THE DRAWING ABOVE FOR SAKE OF CLARITY.
2. THE FIRST FLOOR STAIR SHOWS A SHOP-BUILT STAIR. THE SECOND AND BASEMENT STAIRS ARE CARPENTER-BUILT.

STAIR FRAMING DETAIL

Timothy B. McDonald; Washington, D.C.

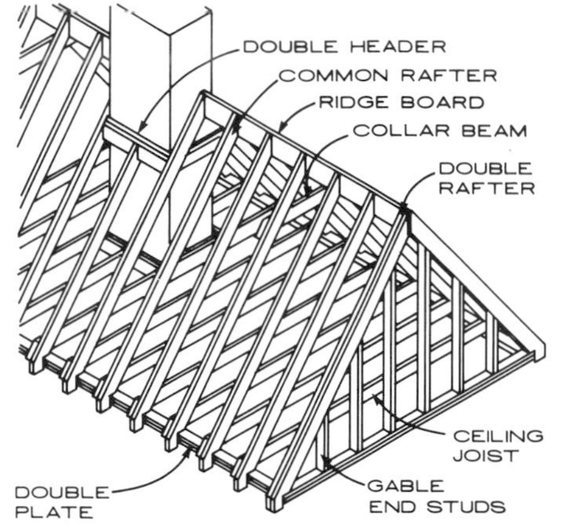
DOUBLE HEADER
COMMON RAFTER
RIDGE BOARD
COLLAR BEAM
DOUBLE RAFTER
CEILING JOIST
DOUBLE PLATE
GABLE END STUDS

GABLE ROOF

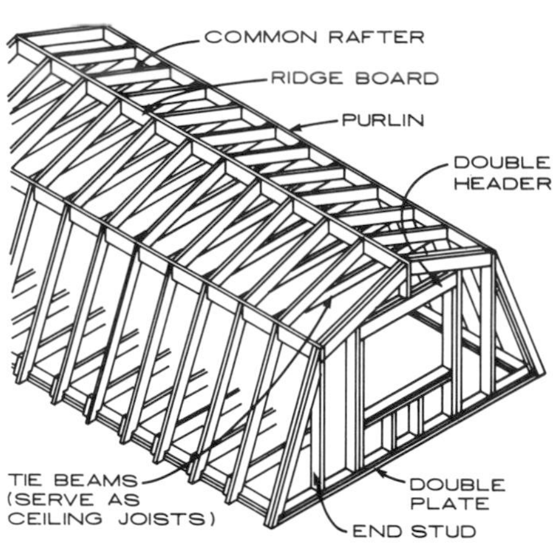
COMMON RAFTER
RIDGE BOARD
PURLIN
DOUBLE HEADER
TIE BEAMS (SERVE AS CEILING JOISTS)
DOUBLE PLATE
END STUD

GAMBREL ROOF

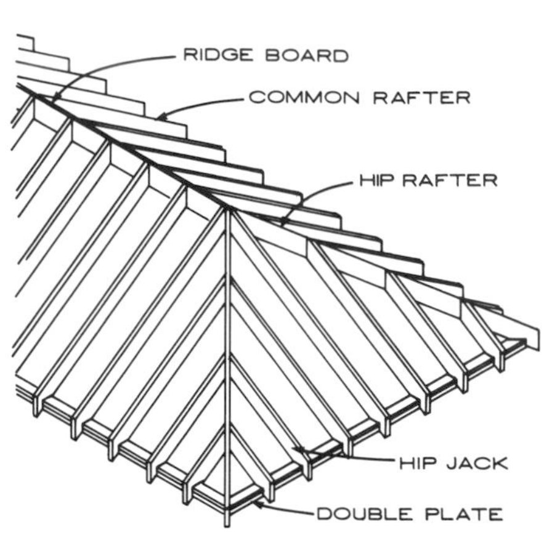
RIDGE BOARD
COMMON RAFTER
HIP RAFTER
HIP JACK
DOUBLE PLATE

HIP ROOF

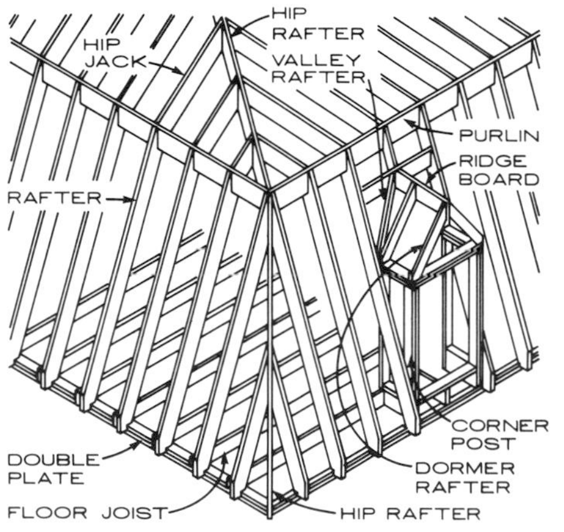
HIP RAFTER
HIP JACK
VALLEY RAFTER
PURLIN
RIDGE BOARD
RAFTER
CORNER POST
DOUBLE PLATE
DORMER RAFTER
FLOOR JOIST
HIP RAFTER

MANSARD ROOF

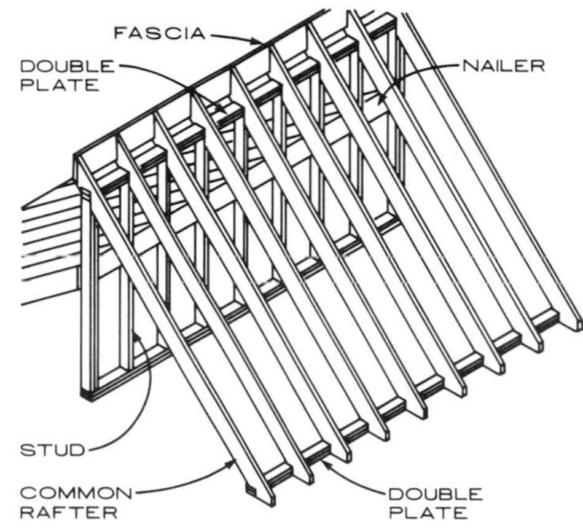
FASCIA
DOUBLE PLATE
NAILER
STUD
COMMON RAFTER
DOUBLE PLATE

SHED ROOF

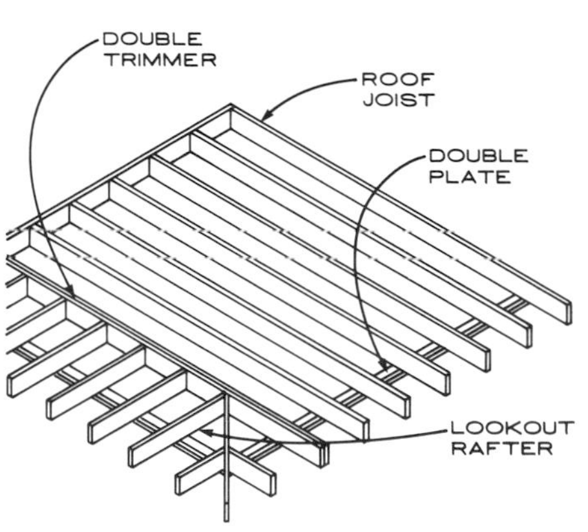
DOUBLE TRIMMER
ROOF JOIST
DOUBLE PLATE
LOOKOUT RAFTER

FLAT ROOF

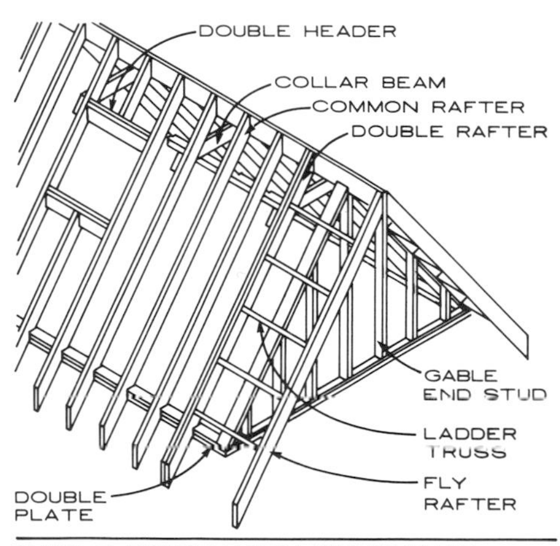
DOUBLE HEADER
COLLAR BEAM
COMMON RAFTER
DOUBLE RAFTER
GABLE END STUD
LADDER TRUSS
DOUBLE PLATE
FLY RAFTER

GABLE ROOF WITH OVERHANG

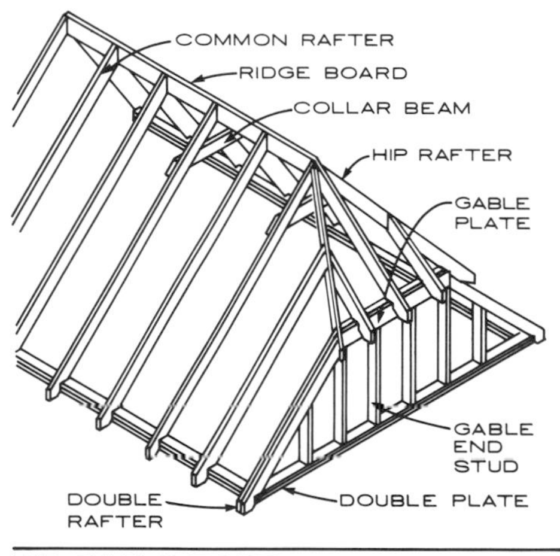
COMMON RAFTER
RIDGE BOARD
COLLAR BEAM
HIP RAFTER
GABLE PLATE
GABLE END STUD
DOUBLE RAFTER
DOUBLE PLATE

HIP GABLE ROOF

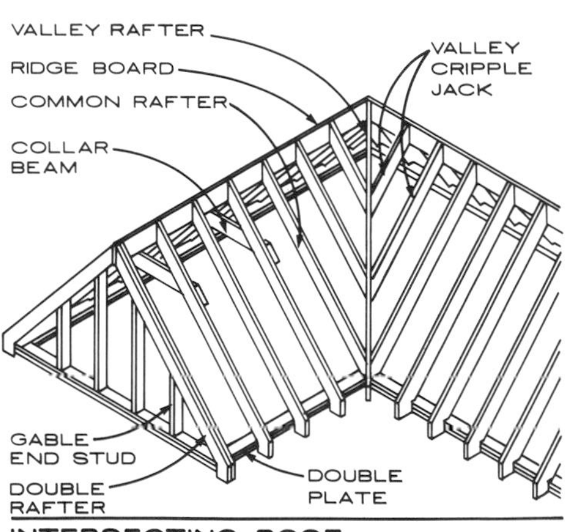
VALLEY RAFTER
RIDGE BOARD
COMMON RAFTER
VALLEY CRIPPLE JACK
COLLAR BEAM
GABLE END STUD
DOUBLE RAFTER
DOUBLE PLATE

INTERSECTING ROOF

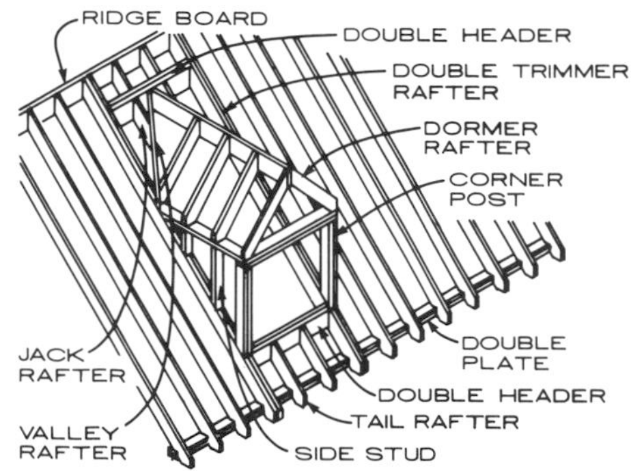
RIDGE BOARD
DOUBLE HEADER
DOUBLE TRIMMER RAFTER
DORMER RAFTER
CORNER POST
JACK RAFTER
DOUBLE PLATE
DOUBLE HEADER
TAIL RAFTER
VALLEY RAFTER
SIDE STUD

DORMER

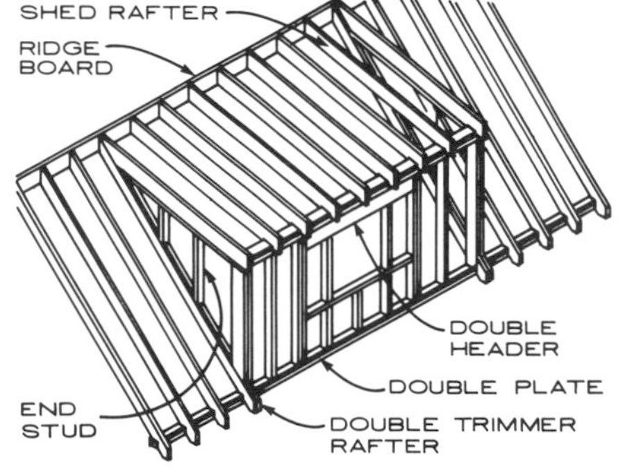
SHED RAFTER
RIDGE BOARD
DOUBLE HEADER
DOUBLE PLATE
END STUD
DOUBLE TRIMMER RAFTER

SMALL SHED DORMER

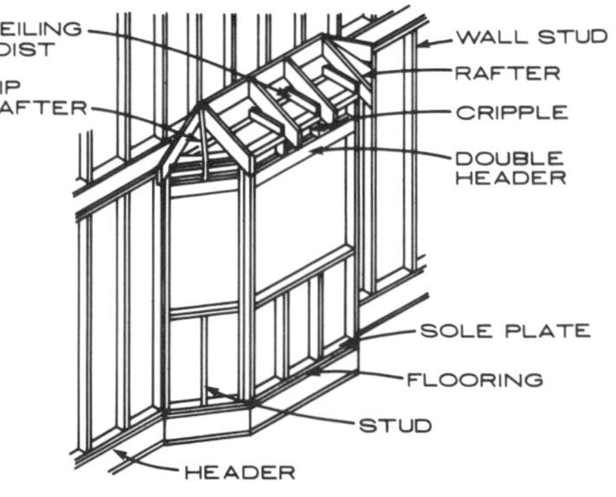
CEILING JOIST
WALL STUD
RAFTER
HIP RAFTER
CRIPPLE
DOUBLE HEADER
SOLE PLATE
FLOORING
STUD
HEADER

BAY WINDOW

Timothy B. McDonald; Washington, D.C.

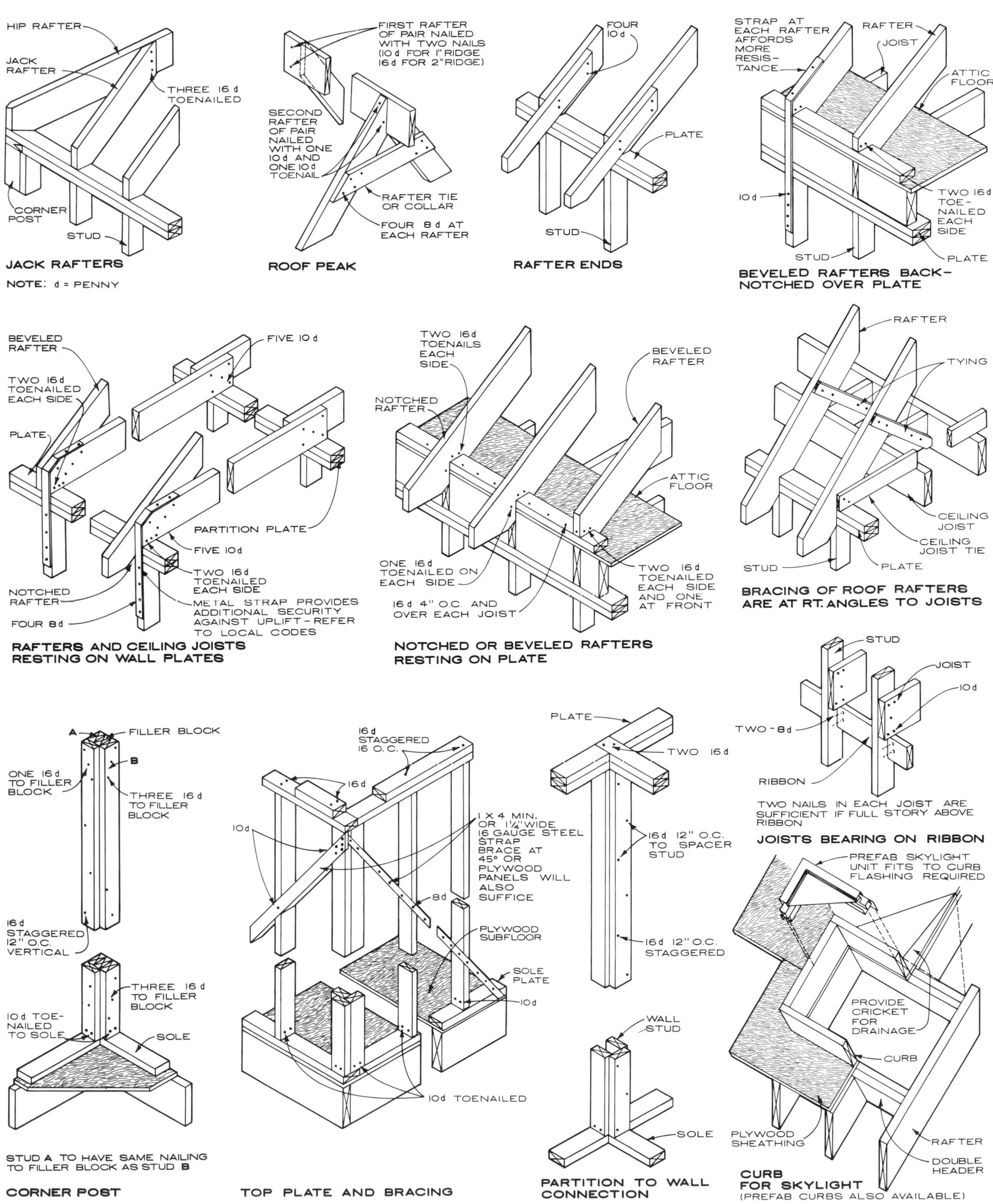
HIP RAFTER
JACK RAFTER
THREE 16d TOENAILED
CORNER POST
STUD
JACK RAFTERS
NOTE: d = PENNY
FIRST RAFTER OF PAIR NAILED WITH TWO NAILS (10d FOR 1" RIDGE 16d FOR 2" RIDGE)
SECOND RAFTER OF PAIR NAILED WITH ONE 10d AND ONE 10d TOENAIL
RAFTER TIE OR COLLAR
FOUR 8d AT EACH RAFTER
ROOF PEAK
FOUR 10d
PLATE
STUD
RAFTER ENDS
STRAP AT EACH RAFTER AFFORDS MORE RESIS-TANCE
RAFTER
JOIST
ATTIC FLOOR
10d
TWO 16d TOE-NAILED EACH SIDE
STUD
PLATE
BEVELED RAFTERS BACK-NOTCHED OVER PLATE
BEVELED RAFTER
TWO 16d TOENAILED EACH SIDE
PLATE
FIVE 10d
PARTITION PLATE
FIVE 10d
TWO 16d TOENAILED EACH SIDE
NOTCHED RAFTER
METAL STRAP PROVIDES ADDITIONAL SECURITY AGAINST UPLIFT-REFER TO LOCAL CODES
FOUR 8d
RAFTERS AND CEILING JOISTS RESTING ON WALL PLATES
TWO 16d TOENAILS EACH SIDE
NOTCHED RAFTER
BEVELED RAFTER
ATTIC FLOOR
ONE 16d TOENAILED ON EACH SIDE
16d 4" O.C. AND OVER EACH JOIST
TWO 16d TOENAILED EACH SIDE AND ONE AT FRONT
NOTCHED OR BEVELED RAFTERS RESTING ON PLATE
RAFTER
TYING
CEILING JOIST
CEILING JOIST TIE
STUD
PLATE
BRACING OF ROOF RAFTERS ARE AT RT. ANGLES TO JOISTS
STUD
JOIST
10d
TWO-8d
RIBBON
TWO NAILS IN EACH JOIST ARE SUFFICIENT IF FULL STORY ABOVE RIBBON
JOISTS BEARING ON RIBBON
A
FILLER BLOCK
B
ONE 16d TO FILLER BLOCK
THREE 16d TO FILLER BLOCK
16d STAGGERED 12" O.C. VERTICAL
THREE 16d TO FILLER BLOCK
10d TOE-NAILED TO SOLE
SOLE
STUD A TO HAVE SAME NAILING TO FILLER BLOCK AS STUD B
CORNER POST
16d STAGGERED 16 O.C.
16d
10d
1 X 4 MIN. OR 1¼" WIDE 16 GAUGE STEEL STRAP BRACE AT 45° OR PLYWOOD PANELS WILL ALSO SUFFICE
8d
PLYWOOD SUBFLOOR
SOLE PLATE
10d
10d TOENAILED
TOP PLATE AND BRACING
PLATE
TWO 16d
16d 12" O.C. TO SPACER STUD
16d 12" O.C. STAGGERED
WALL STUD
SOLE
PARTITION TO WALL CONNECTION
PREFAB SKYLIGHT UNIT FITS TO CURB FLASHING REQUIRED
PROVIDE CRICKET FOR DRAINAGE
CURB
PLYWOOD SHEATHING
RAFTER
DOUBLE HEADER
CURB FOR SKYLIGHT
(PREFAB CURBS ALSO AVAILABLE)

Joseph A. Wilkes, FAIA; Wilkes and Faulkner; Washington, D.C.

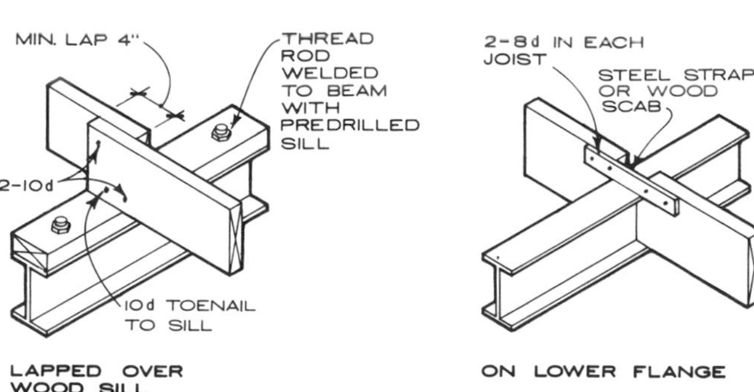
MIN. LAP 4"
THREAD ROD WELDED TO BEAM WITH PREDRILLED SILL
2-10d
10d TOENAIL TO SILL
2-8d IN EACH JOIST
STEEL STRAP OR WOOD SCAB

LAPPED OVER WOOD SILL

ON LOWER FLANGE

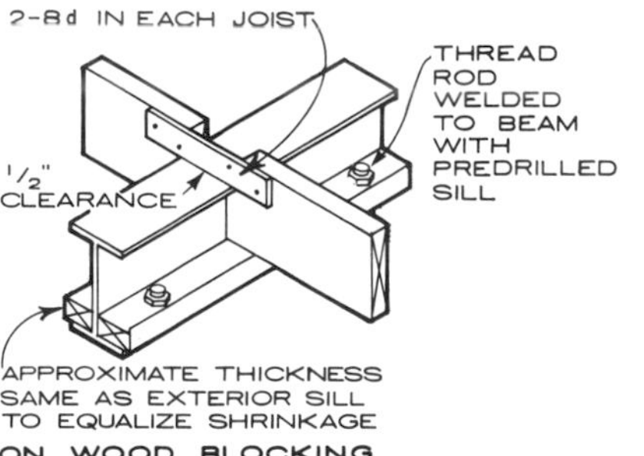
2-8d IN EACH JOIST
THREAD ROD WELDED TO BEAM WITH PREDRILLED SILL
1/2" CLEARANCE
APPROXIMATE THICKNESS SAME AS EXTERIOR SILL TO EQUALIZE SHRINKAGE

ON WOOD BLOCKING

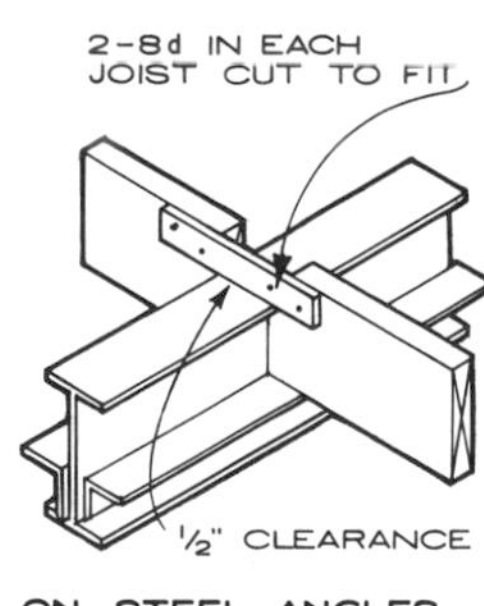
2-8d IN EACH JOIST CUT TO FIT
1/2" CLEARANCE

ON STEEL ANGLES

WOOD JOISTS SUPPORTED ON STEEL GIRDERS

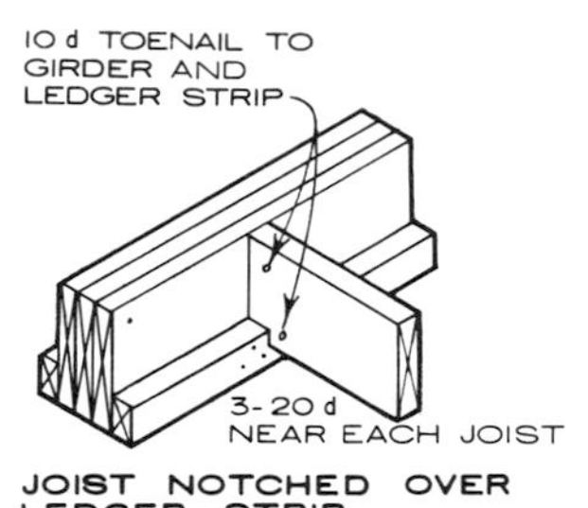
10d TOENAIL TO GIRDER AND LEDGER STRIP
3-20d NEAR EACH JOIST

JOIST NOTCHED OVER LEDGER STRIP
NOTCHING OVER BEARING NOT RECOMMENDED

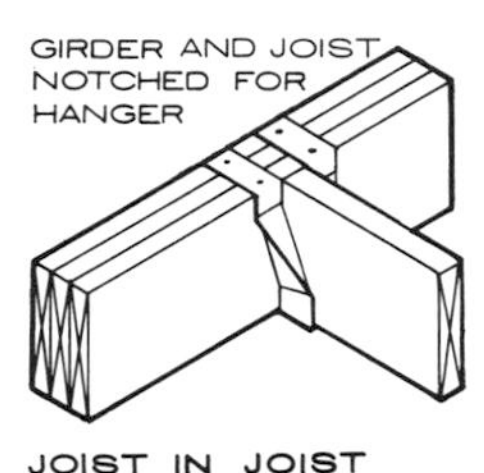
GIRDER AND JOIST NOTCHED FOR HANGER

JOIST IN JOIST HANGER IRON
ALSO CALLED STIRRUP OR BRIDLE IRON

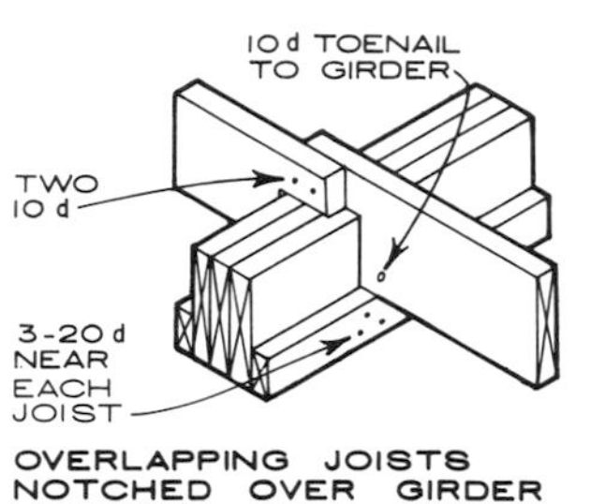
10d TOENAIL TO GIRDER
TWO 10d
3-20d NEAR EACH JOIST

OVERLAPPING JOISTS NOTCHED OVER GIRDER
BEARING ONLY ON LEDGER, NOT ON TOP OF GIRDER

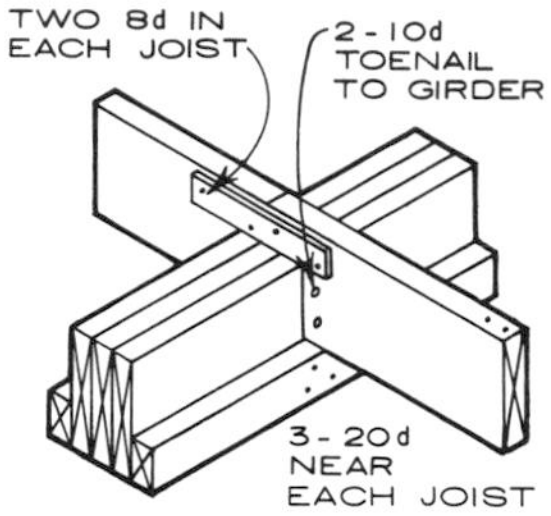

TWO 8d IN EACH JOIST
2-10d TOENAIL TO GIRDER
3-20d NEAR EACH JOIST

JOISTS NOTCHED OVER GIRDER
BEARING ONLY ON LEDGER, NOT ON TOP OF GIRDER

WOOD JOISTS SUPPORTED ON WOOD GIRDERS

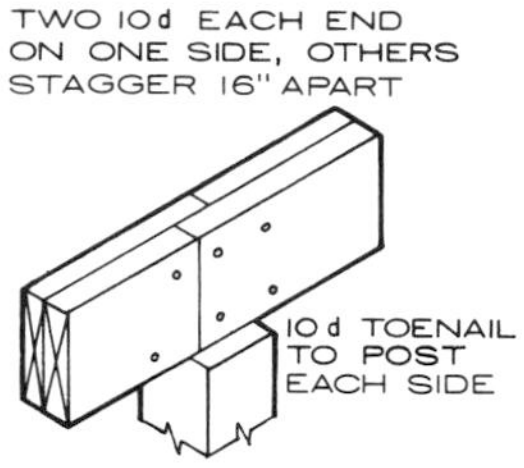

TWO 10d EACH END ON ONE SIDE, OTHERS STAGGER 16" APART
10d TOENAIL TO POST EACH SIDE

TWO PIECE GIRDER
GIRDER JOINTS ONLY AT SUPPORTS STAGGER JOINTS

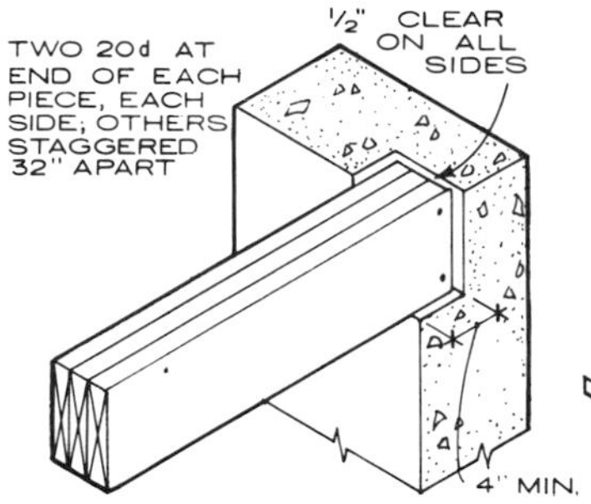

TWO 20d AT END OF EACH PIECE, EACH SIDE; OTHERS STAGGERED 32" APART
1/2" CLEAR ON ALL SIDES
4" MIN.

THREE PIECE GIRDER
FOR FOUR PIECE GIRDER: ADD NAILS

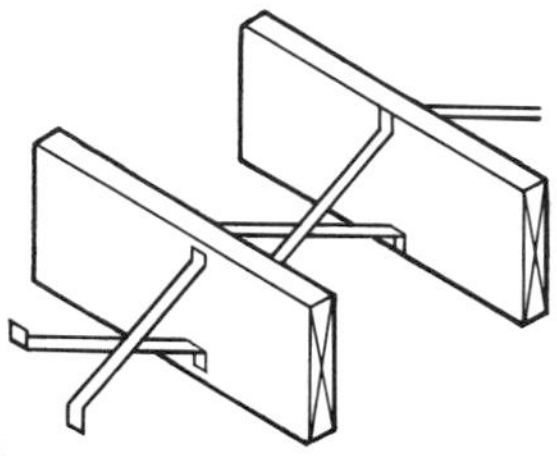

STEEL BRIDGING
SOME HAVE BUILT-IN TEETH, NEEDS NO NAILS

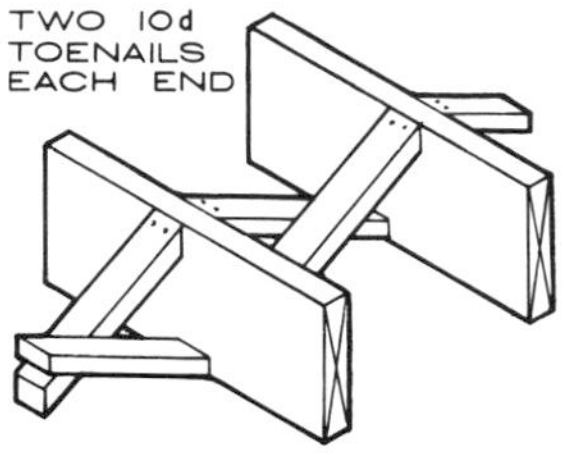

TWO 10d TOENAILS EACH END

1" X 3" CROSS BRIDGING
LOWER ENDS NOT NAILED, UNTIL SUBFLOORING IS LAYED

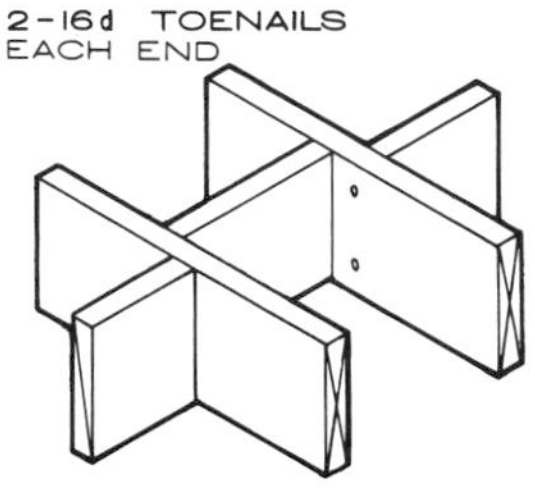

2-16d TOENAILS EACH END

SOLID BRIDGING
USED UNDER PARTITIONS FOR HEAVY LOADING STAGGER BOARDS FOR EASE OF NAILING

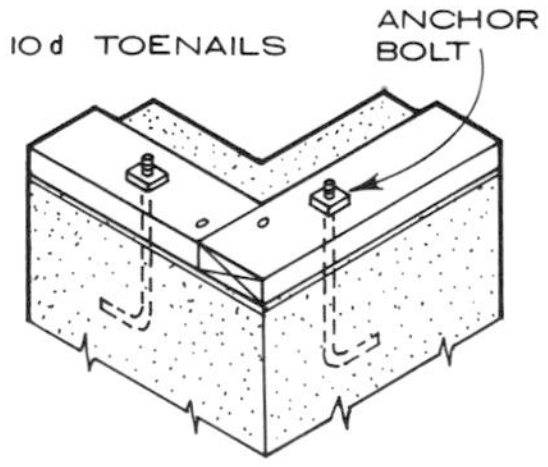

10d TOENAILS
ANCHOR BOLT

2 X 6 SILL

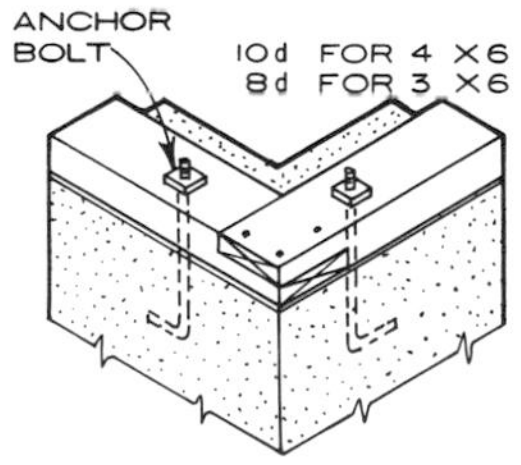

ANCHOR BOLT
10d FOR 4 X 6
8d FOR 3 X 6

3 X 6, 4 X 6 SILL
HALVED AT CORNERS

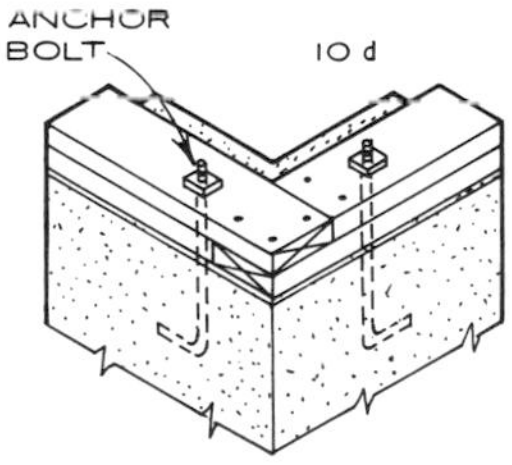

ANCHOR BOLT
10d

4 X 6 DOUBLE SILL
NAILS STAGGERED ALONG SILL 24" ON CENTER

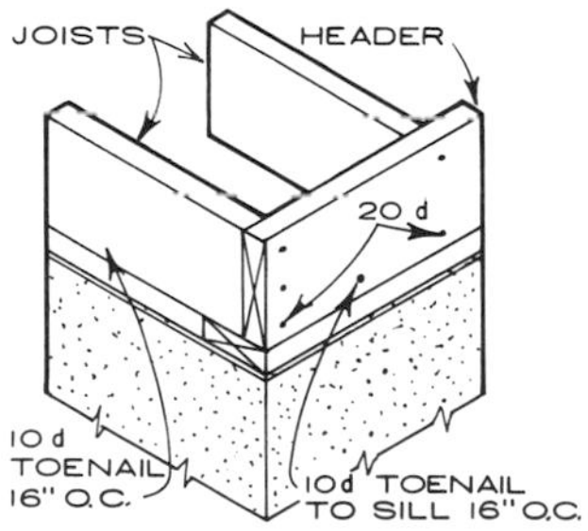

JOISTS
HEADER
20d
10d TOENAIL 16" O.C.
10d TOENAIL TO SILL 16" O.C.

PLATFORM FRAMING
TOENAIL TO SILL NOT REQUIRED IF DIAGONAL SHEATHING USED

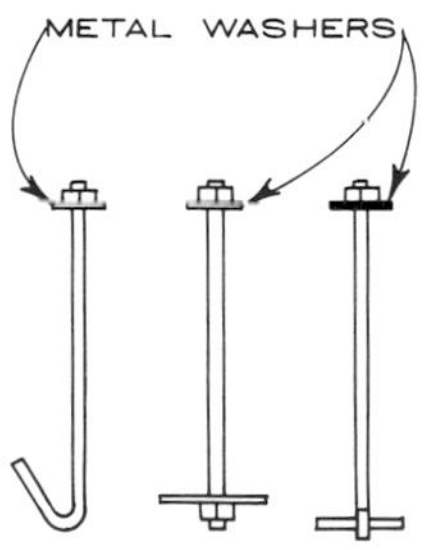

METAL WASHERS

TYPES OF SILL ANCHOR BOLTS

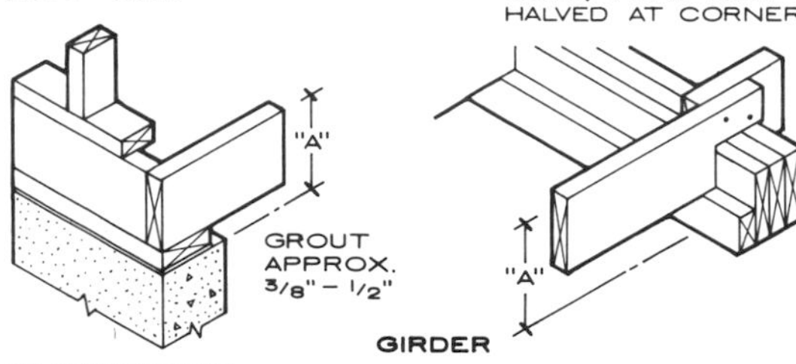

"A"
GROUT APPROX. 3/8" – 1/2"
"A"
GIRDER

SHRINKAGE
SELECT JOIST-GIRDER DETAIL THAT HAS APPROXIMATE SAME SHRINKAGE "A" AS THE SILL DETAIL USED

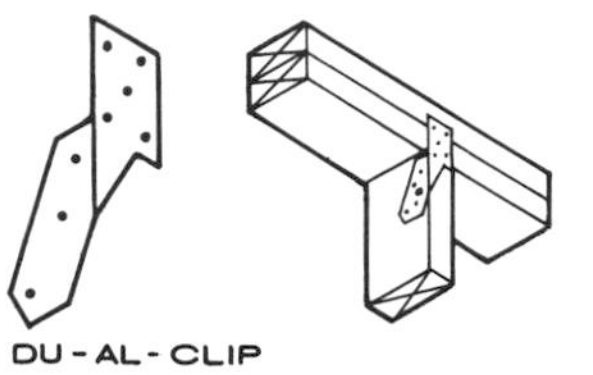

DU-AL-CLIP

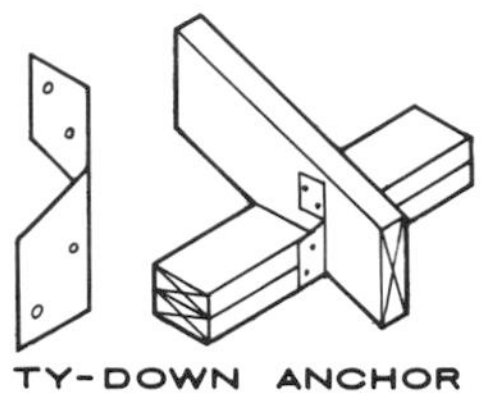

TY-DOWN ANCHOR

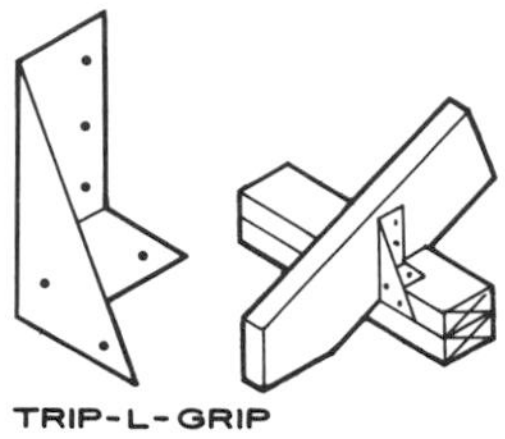

TRIP-L-GRIP

METAL FRAMING DEVICES
16-18 GAUGE ZINC COATED STEEL

Joseph A. Wilkes, FAIA; Wilkes and Faulkner; Washington, D.C.

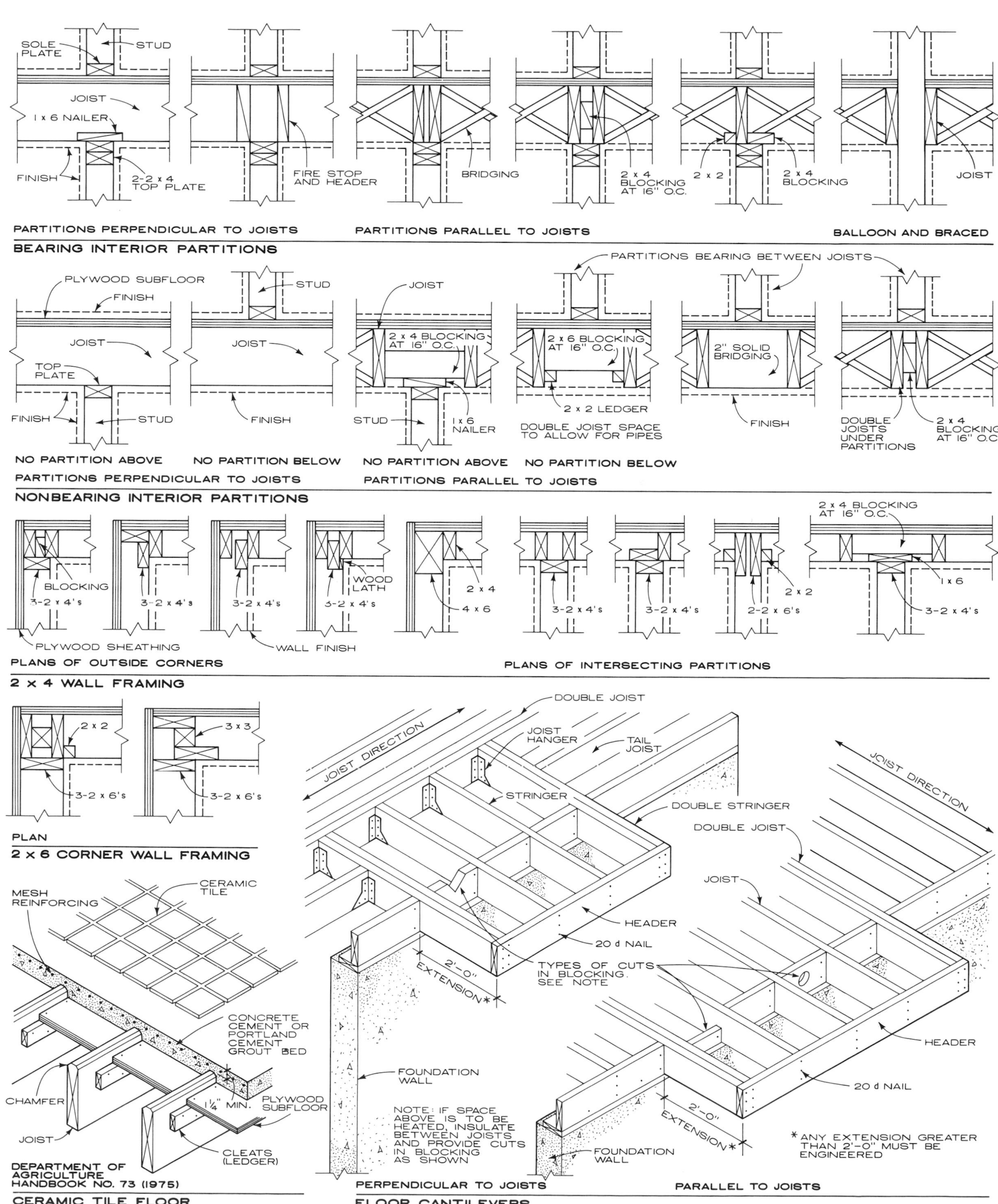
SOLE PLATE
STUD
JOIST
1 x 6 NAILER
FINISH
2-2 x 4 TOP PLATE
FIRE STOP AND HEADER
BRIDGING
2 x 4 BLOCKING AT 16" O.C.
2 x 2
2 x 4 BLOCKING
JOIST
PARTITIONS PERPENDICULAR TO JOISTS
PARTITIONS PARALLEL TO JOISTS
BALLOON AND BRACED
BEARING INTERIOR PARTITIONS
PLYWOOD SUBFLOOR
FINISH
STUD
JOIST
TOP PLATE
2 x 4 BLOCKING AT 16" O.C.
1 x 6 NAILER
PARTITIONS BEARING BETWEEN JOISTS
2 x 6 BLOCKING AT 16" O.C.
2 x 2 LEDGER
DOUBLE JOIST SPACE TO ALLOW FOR PIPES
2" SOLID BRIDGING
DOUBLE JOISTS UNDER PARTITIONS
2 x 4 BLOCKING AT 16" O.C.
NO PARTITION ABOVE
NO PARTITION BELOW
NO PARTITION ABOVE
NO PARTITION BELOW
PARTITIONS PERPENDICULAR TO JOISTS
PARTITIONS PARALLEL TO JOISTS
NONBEARING INTERIOR PARTITIONS
2 x 4 BLOCKING AT 16" O.C.
BLOCKING
3-2 x 4's
WOOD LATH
2 x 4
4 x 6
2 x 2
1 x 6
2-2 x 6's
PLYWOOD SHEATHING
WALL FINISH
PLANS OF OUTSIDE CORNERS
PLANS OF INTERSECTING PARTITIONS
2 x 4 WALL FRAMING
2 x 2
3 x 3
3-2 x 6's
PLAN
2 x 6 CORNER WALL FRAMING
MESH REINFORCING
CERAMIC TILE
CONCRETE CEMENT OR PORTLAND CEMENT GROUT BED
CHAMFER
1 1/4" MIN.
PLYWOOD SUBFLOOR
JOIST
CLEATS (LEDGER)
DEPARTMENT OF AGRICULTURE HANDBOOK NO. 73 (1975)
CERAMIC TILE FLOOR
JOIST DIRECTION
DOUBLE JOIST
JOIST HANGER
TAIL JOIST
STRINGER
DOUBLE STRINGER
DOUBLE JOIST
JOIST
HEADER
20 d NAIL
TYPES OF CUTS IN BLOCKING. SEE NOTE
2'-0" EXTENSION*
FOUNDATION WALL
NOTE: IF SPACE ABOVE IS TO BE HEATED, INSULATE BETWEEN JOISTS AND PROVIDE CUTS IN BLOCKING AS SHOWN
HEADER
20 d NAIL
*ANY EXTENSION GREATER THAN 2'-0" MUST BE ENGINEERED
PERPENDICULAR TO JOISTS
PARALLEL TO JOISTS
FLOOR CANTILEVERS

John Ray Hoke, Jr., AIA; Washington, D.C.

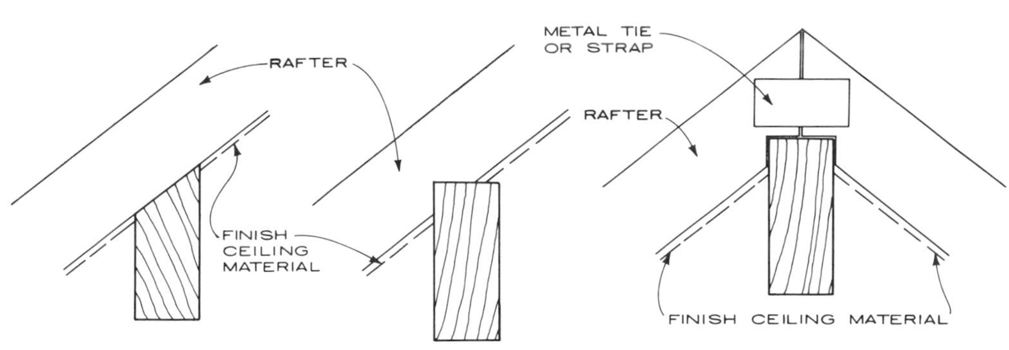
RAFTER
FINISH CEILING MATERIAL
METAL TIE OR STRAP
RAFTER
FINISH CEILING MATERIAL
SLOPED BEAM
BIRD'S MOUTH
RIDGE BEAM

EXPOSED BEAMS AT SLOPING RAFTERS

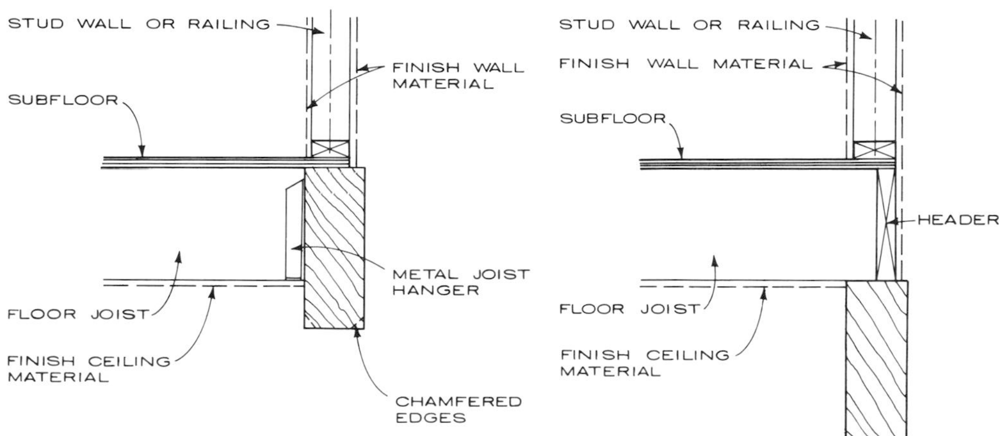
STUD WALL OR RAILING
FINISH WALL MATERIAL
SUBFLOOR
METAL JOIST HANGER
FLOOR JOIST
FINISH CEILING MATERIAL
CHAMFERED EDGES
STUD WALL OR RAILING
FINISH WALL MATERIAL
SUBFLOOR
HEADER
FLOOR JOIST
FINISH CEILING MATERIAL

EXPOSED BEAMS AT FLOORS

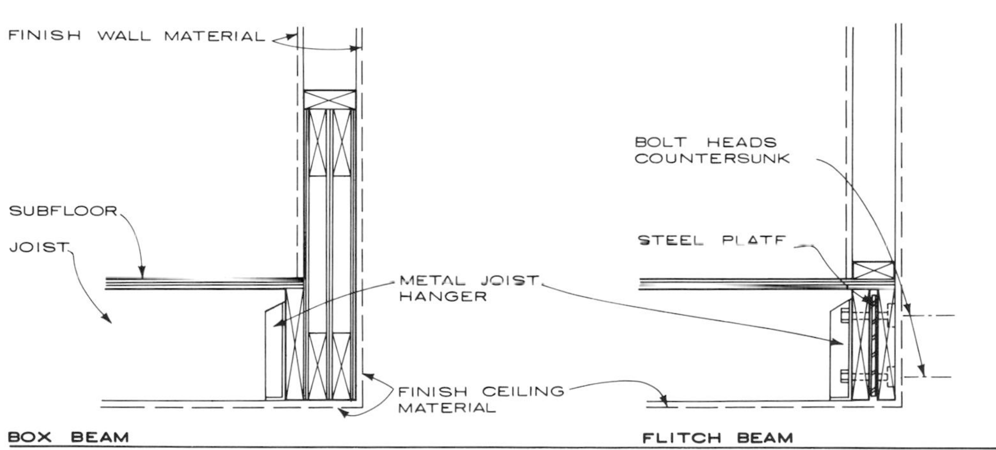
FINISH WALL MATERIAL
SUBFLOOR
JOIST
METAL JOIST HANGER
FINISH CEILING MATERIAL
BOLT HEADS COUNTERSUNK
STEEL PLATE
BOX BEAM
FLITCH BEAM

CONCEALED BUILT-UP BEAMS AT FLOORS

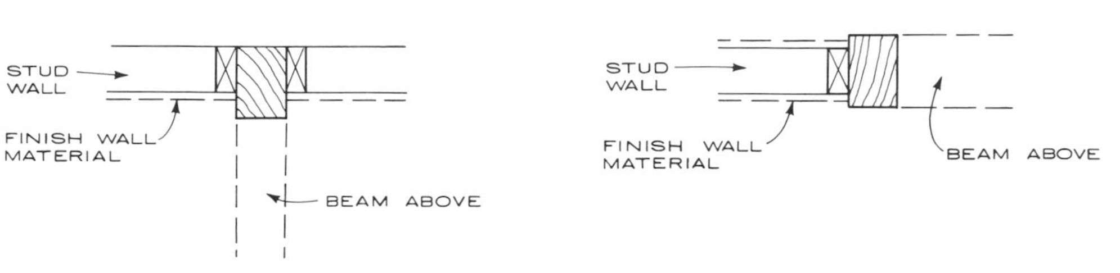
STUD WALL
FINISH WALL MATERIAL
BEAM ABOVE
STUD WALL
FINISH WALL MATERIAL
BEAM ABOVE

EXPOSED POSTS AT STUD WALLS

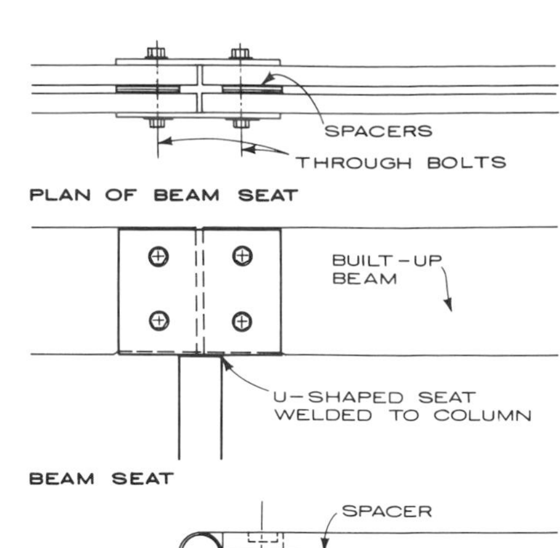
SPACERS
THROUGH BOLTS
PLAN OF BEAM SEAT
BUILT-UP BEAM
U-SHAPED SEAT WELDED TO COLUMN
BEAM SEAT
SPACER

PLAN OF INTERMEDIATE SEAT

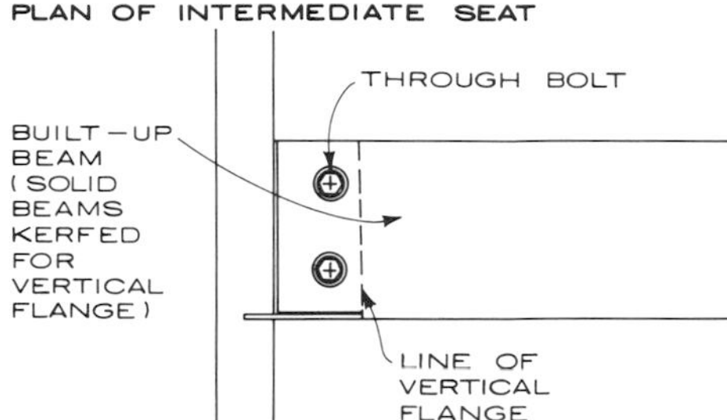
THROUGH BOLT
BUILT-UP BEAM (SOLID BEAMS KERFED FOR VERTICAL FLANGE)
LINE OF VERTICAL FLANGE

INTERMEDIATE BEAM SEAT

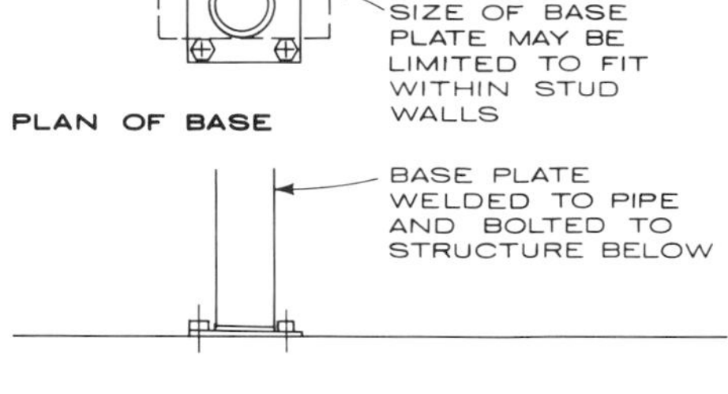
SIZE OF BASE PLATE MAY BE LIMITED TO FIT WITHIN STUD WALLS
PLAN OF BASE
BASE PLATE WELDED TO PIPE AND BOLTED TO STRUCTURE BELOW
BASE

STEEL PIPE COLUMNS

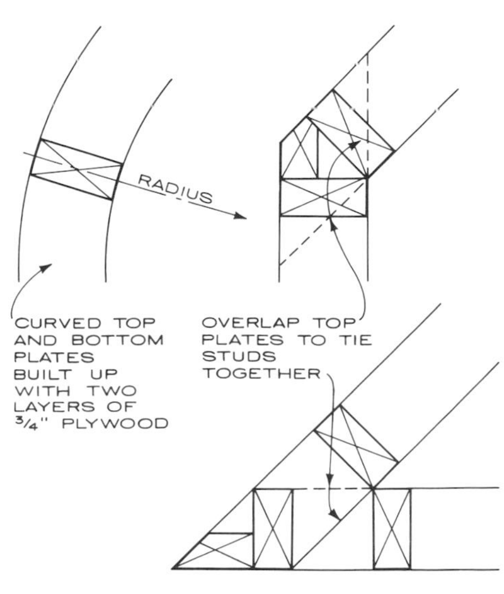
RADIUS
CURVED TOP AND BOTTOM PLATES BUILT UP WITH TWO LAYERS OF 3/4" PLYWOOD
OVERLAP TOP PLATES TO TIE STUDS TOGETHER

NON-RIGHT ANGLE WALL CORNERS

The Bumgardner Partnership/Architects; Seattle, Washington

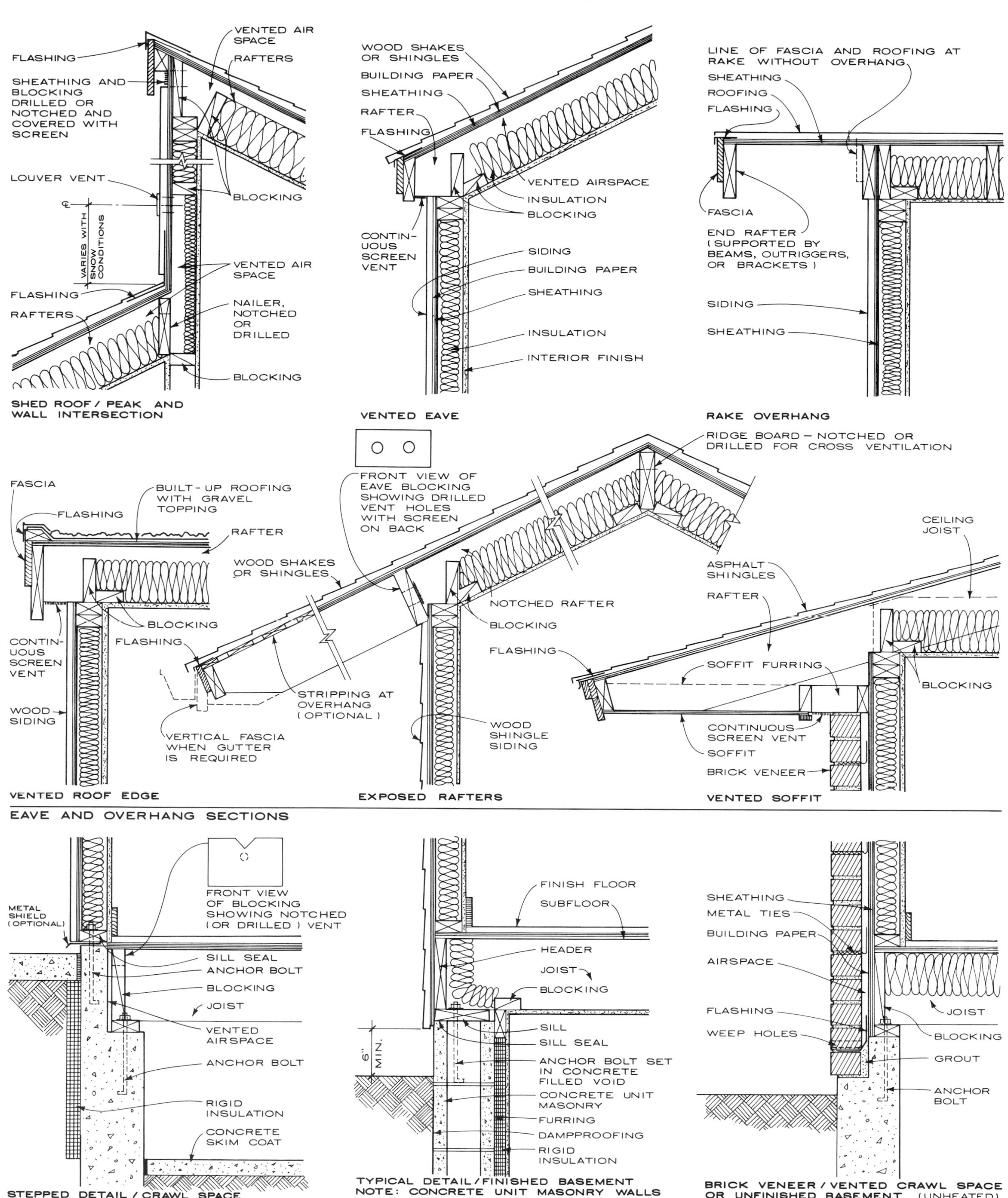
VENTED AIR SPACE
FLASHING
RAFTERS
SHEATHING AND BLOCKING DRILLED OR NOTCHED AND COVERED WITH SCREEN
LOUVER VENT
BLOCKING
VARIES WITH SNOW CONDITIONS
VENTED AIR SPACE
FLASHING
RAFTERS
NAILER, NOTCHED OR DRILLED
BLOCKING
SHED ROOF / PEAK AND WALL INTERSECTION
WOOD SHAKES OR SHINGLES
BUILDING PAPER
SHEATHING
RAFTER
FLASHING
VENTED AIRSPACE
INSULATION
BLOCKING
CONTINUOUS SCREEN VENT
SIDING
BUILDING PAPER
SHEATHING
INSULATION
INTERIOR FINISH
VENTED EAVE
LINE OF FASCIA AND ROOFING AT RAKE WITHOUT OVERHANG
SHEATHING
ROOFING
FLASHING
FASCIA
END RAFTER (SUPPORTED BY BEAMS, OUTRIGGERS, OR BRACKETS)
SIDING
SHEATHING
RAKE OVERHANG
RIDGE BOARD – NOTCHED OR DRILLED FOR CROSS VENTILATION
FRONT VIEW OF EAVE BLOCKING SHOWING DRILLED VENT HOLES WITH SCREEN ON BACK
FASCIA
BUILT-UP ROOFING WITH GRAVEL TOPPING
FLASHING
RAFTER
WOOD SHAKES OR SHINGLES
BLOCKING
FLASHING
CONTINUOUS SCREEN VENT
WOOD SIDING
VERTICAL FASCIA WHEN GUTTER IS REQUIRED
STRIPPING AT OVERHANG (OPTIONAL)
NOTCHED RAFTER
BLOCKING
FLASHING
WOOD SHINGLE SIDING
CEILING JOIST
ASPHALT SHINGLES
RAFTER
SOFFIT FURRING
BLOCKING
CONTINUOUS SCREEN VENT
SOFFIT
BRICK VENEER
VENTED ROOF EDGE
EXPOSED RAFTERS
VENTED SOFFIT
EAVE AND OVERHANG SECTIONS
METAL SHIELD (OPTIONAL)
FRONT VIEW OF BLOCKING SHOWING NOTCHED (OR DRILLED) VENT
SILL SEAL
ANCHOR BOLT
BLOCKING
JOIST
VENTED AIRSPACE
ANCHOR BOLT
RIGID INSULATION
CONCRETE SKIM COAT
STEPPED DETAIL / CRAWL SPACE
FINISH FLOOR
SUBFLOOR
HEADER
JOIST
BLOCKING
6" MIN.
SILL
SILL SEAL
ANCHOR BOLT SET IN CONCRETE FILLED VOID
CONCRETE UNIT MASONRY
FURRING
DAMPPROOFING
RIGID INSULATION
TYPICAL DETAIL / FINISHED BASEMENT
NOTE: CONCRETE UNIT MASONRY WALLS VARY WIDELY. CHECK LOCAL CODES
SHEATHING
METAL TIES
BUILDING PAPER
AIRSPACE
FLASHING
WEEP HOLES
JOIST
BLOCKING
GROUT
ANCHOR BOLT
BRICK VENEER / VENTED CRAWL SPACE OR UNFINISHED BASEMENT (UNHEATED)

FOUNDATION WALL SECTIONS

The Bumgardner Partnership/Architects; Seattle, Washington

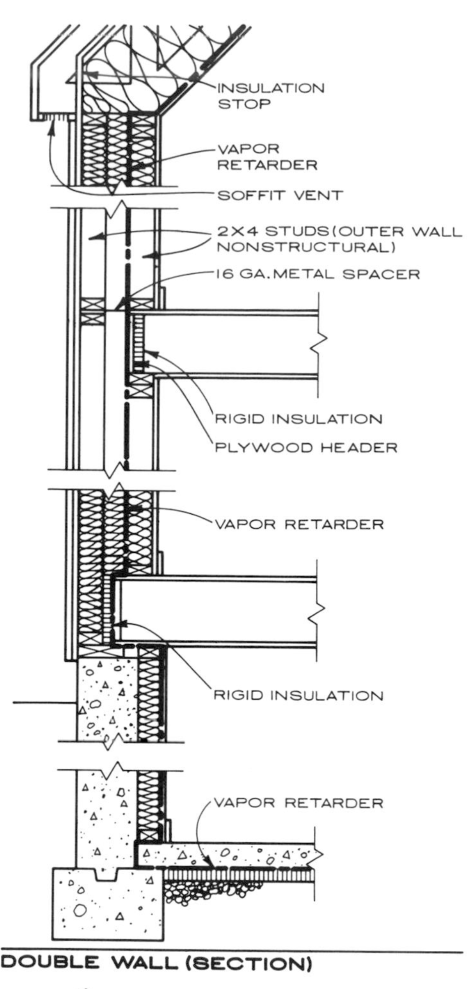
INSULATION STOP
VAPOR RETARDER
SOFFIT VENT
2×4 STUDS (OUTER WALL NONSTRUCTURAL)
16 GA. METAL SPACER
RIGID INSULATION
PLYWOOD HEADER
VAPOR RETARDER
RIGID INSULATION
VAPOR RETARDER

DOUBLE WALL (SECTION)

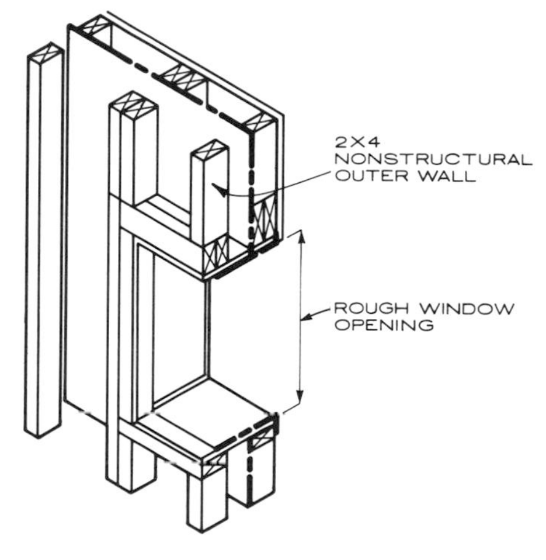
2×4 NONSTRUCTURAL OUTER WALL
ROUGH WINDOW OPENING

WINDOW DETAIL

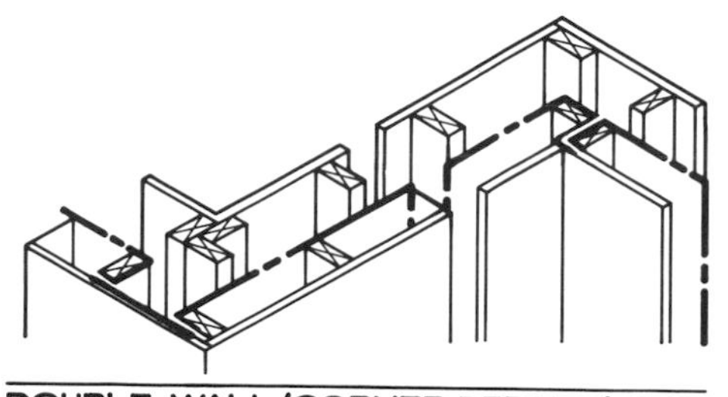

DOUBLE WALL (CORNER DETAILS)

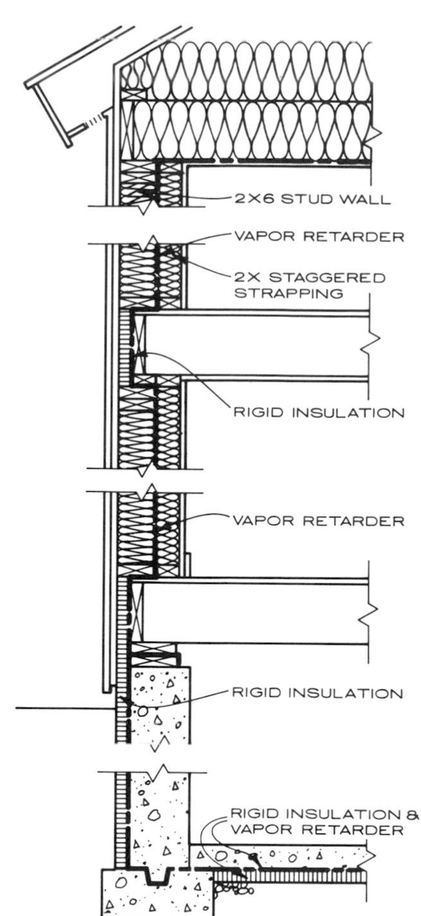
2×6 STUD WALL
VAPOR RETARDER
2X STAGGERED STRAPPING
RIGID INSULATION
VAPOR RETARDER
RIGID INSULATION
RIGID INSULATION & VAPOR RETARDER

STRAPPED WALL (SECTION)

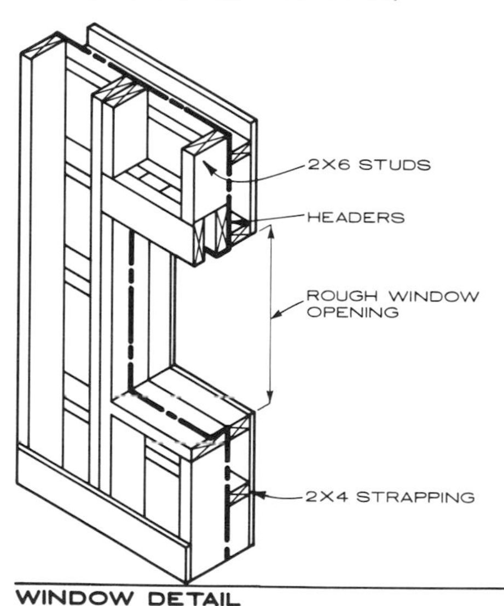
2×6 STUDS
HEADERS
ROUGH WINDOW OPENING
2×4 STRAPPING

WINDOW DETAIL

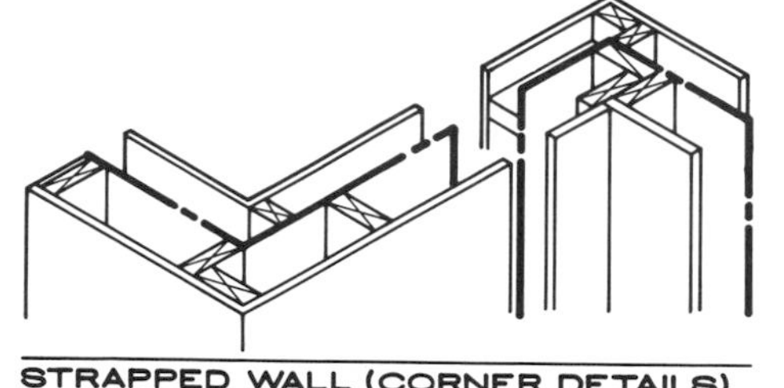

STRAPPED WALL (CORNER DETAILS)

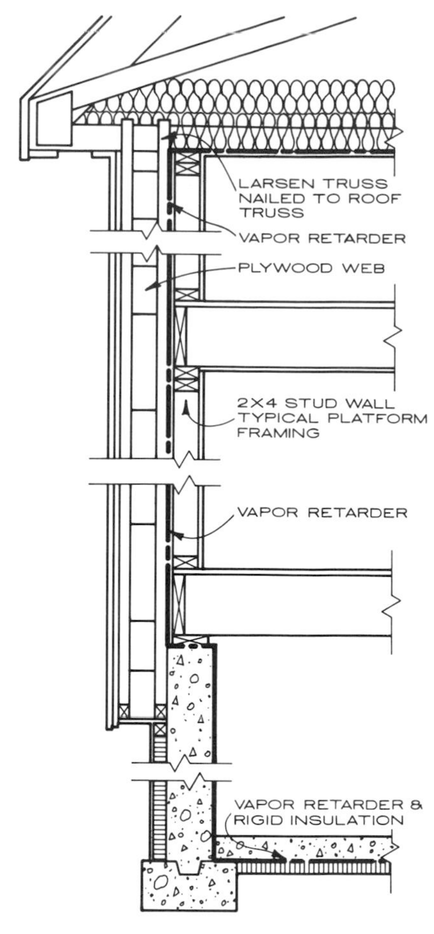
LARSEN TRUSS NAILED TO ROOF TRUSS
VAPOR RETARDER
PLYWOOD WEB
2×4 STUD WALL TYPICAL PLATFORM FRAMING
VAPOR RETARDER
VAPOR RETARDER & RIGID INSULATION

LARSEN TRUSS (SECTION)

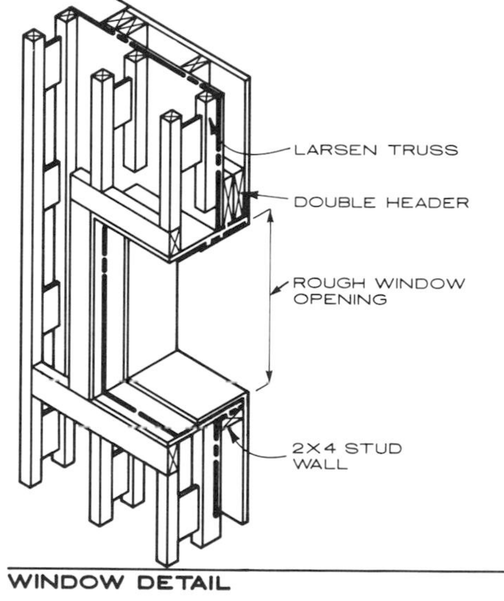
LARSEN TRUSS
DOUBLE HEADER
ROUGH WINDOW OPENING
2×4 STUD WALL

WINDOW DETAIL

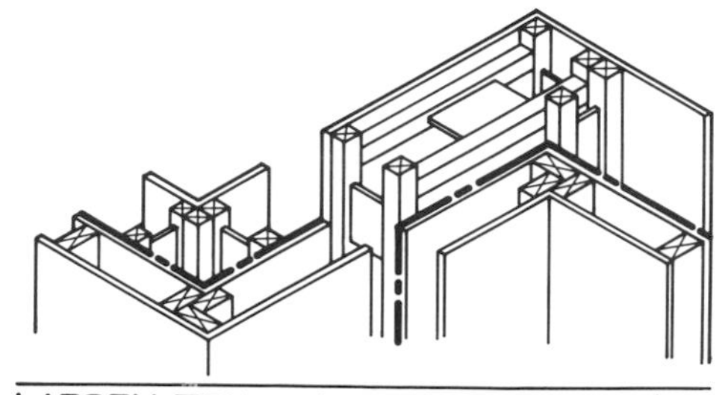

LARSEN TRUSS (CORNER DETAILS)

Timothy B. McDonald; Washington, D.C.

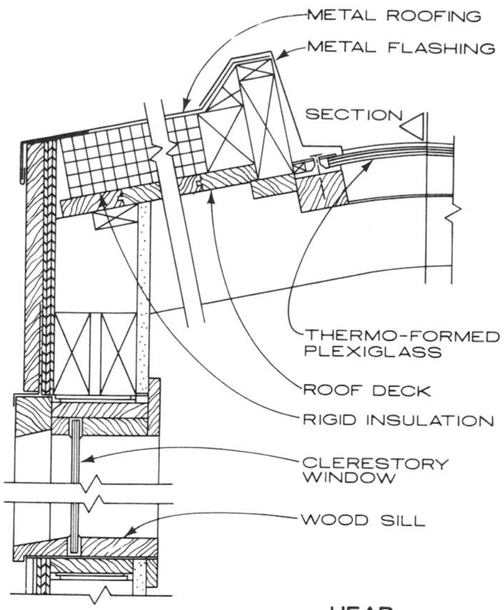

METAL ROOFING
METAL FLASHING
SECTION
THERMO-FORMED PLEXIGLASS
ROOF DECK
RIGID INSULATION
CLERESTORY WINDOW
WOOD SILL

HEAD

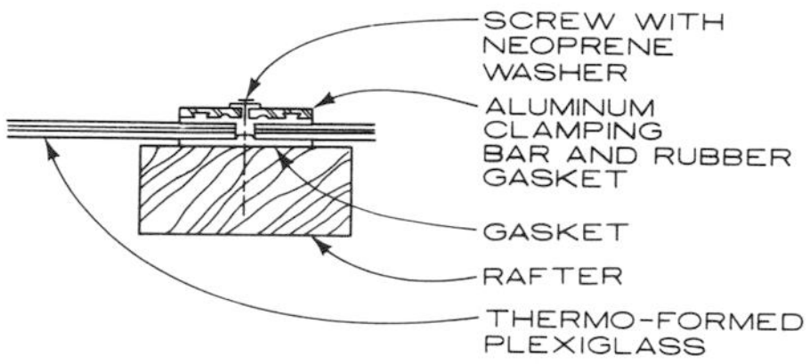

SCREW WITH NEOPRENE WASHER
ALUMINUM CLAMPING BAR AND RUBBER GASKET
GASKET
RAFTER
THERMO-FORMED PLEXIGLASS

SECTION

THERMO-FORMED PLEXIGLASS
SECTION
WOOD SILL
CASEMENT WINDOW

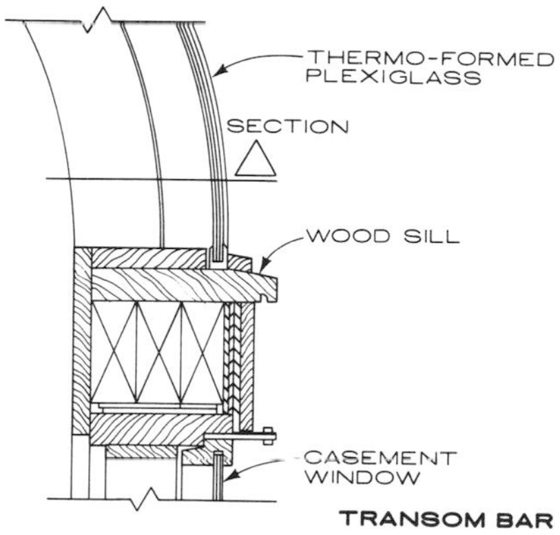

TRANSOM BAR

SUNSPACE DETAILS

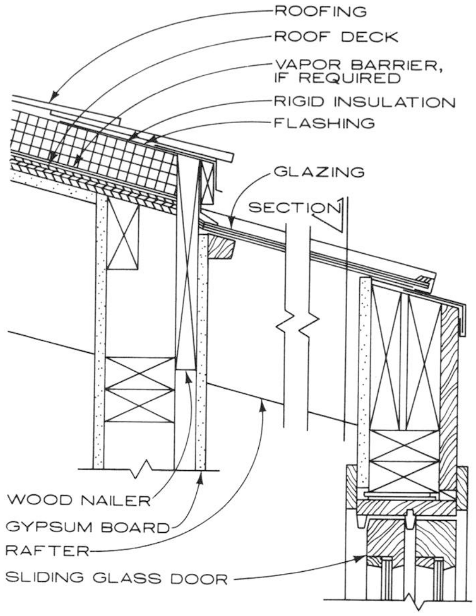

ROOFING
ROOF DECK
VAPOR BARRIER, IF REQUIRED
RIGID INSULATION
FLASHING
GLAZING
SECTION
WOOD NAILER
GYPSUM BOARD
RAFTER
SLIDING GLASS DOOR

SLOPING GLASS

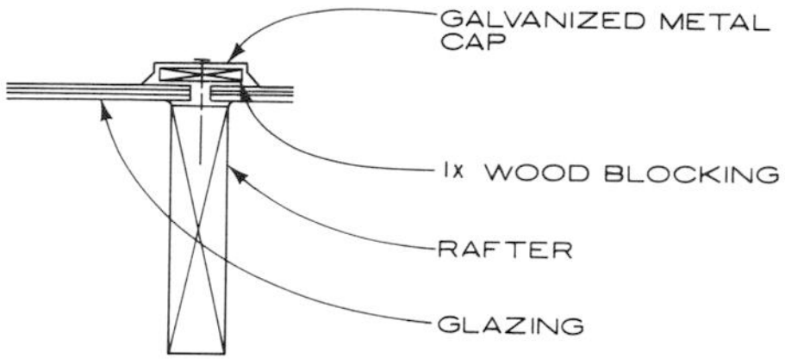

GALVANIZED METAL CAP
1x WOOD BLOCKING
RAFTER
GLAZING

SECTION

FIXED GLASS AT RAFTERS

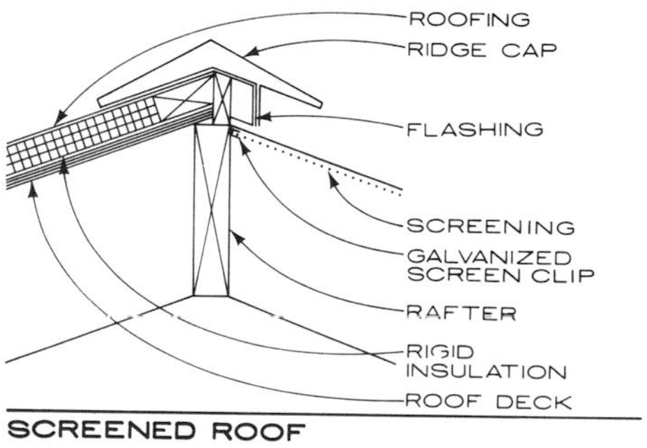

ROOFING
RIDGE CAP
FLASHING
SCREENING
GALVANIZED SCREEN CLIP
RAFTER
RIGID INSULATION
ROOF DECK

SCREENED ROOF

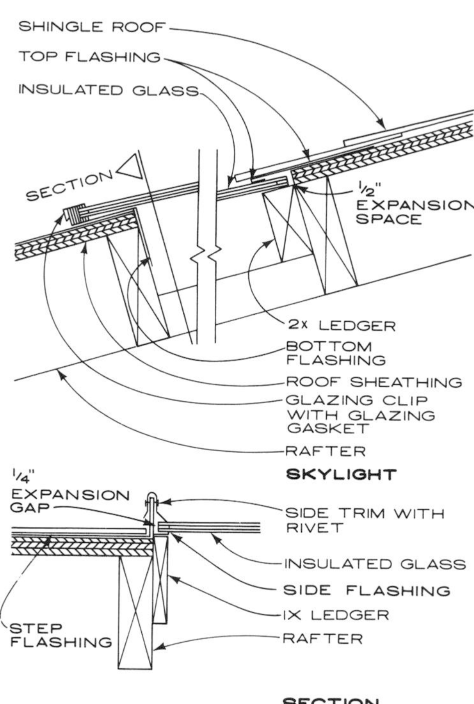
SHINGLE ROOF
TOP FLASHING
INSULATED GLASS
SECTION
1/2" EXPANSION SPACE
2x LEDGER
BOTTOM FLASHING
ROOF SHEATHING
GLAZING CLIP WITH GLAZING GASKET
RAFTER
SKYLIGHT
1/4" EXPANSION GAP
SIDE TRIM WITH RIVET
INSULATED GLASS
SIDE FLASHING
1X LEDGER
RAFTER
STEP FLASHING
SECTION

CURBLESS SKYLIGHT INSTALLATION

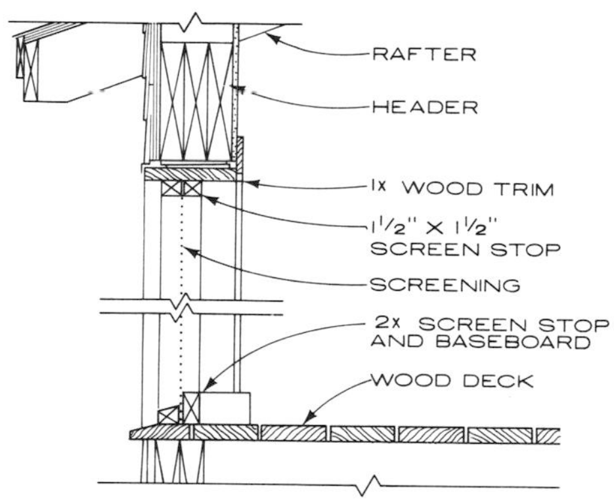
RAFTER
HEADER
1x WOOD TRIM
1 1/2" X 1 1/2" SCREEN STOP
SCREENING
2x SCREEN STOP AND BASEBOARD
WOOD DECK

SCREENED DECK

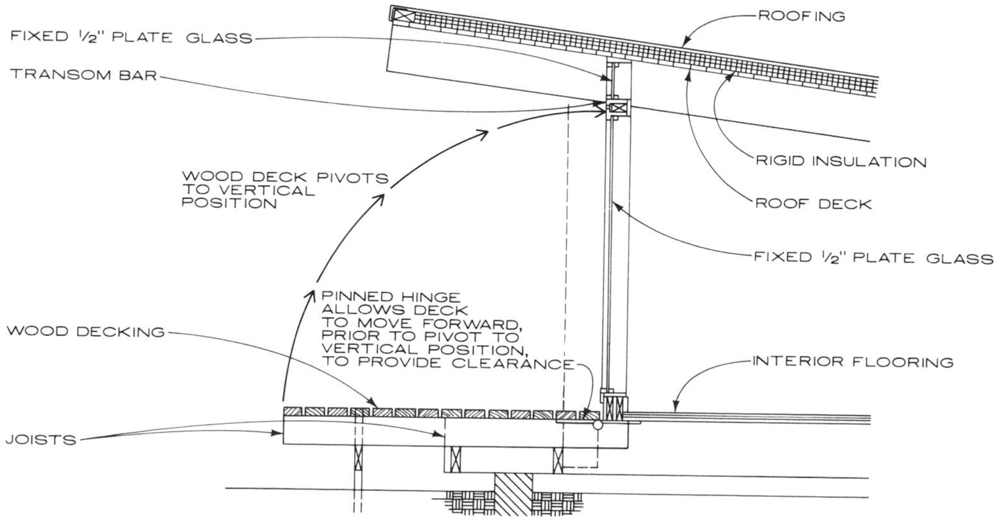

FIXED 1/2" PLATE GLASS
TRANSOM BAR
ROOFING
RIGID INSULATION
ROOF DECK
WOOD DECK PIVOTS TO VERTICAL POSITION
FIXED 1/2" PLATE GLASS
PINNED HINGE ALLOWS DECK TO MOVE FORWARD, PRIOR TO PIVOT TO VERTICAL POSITION, TO PROVIDE CLEARANCE
WOOD DECKING
INTERIOR FLOORING
JOISTS

WINDOW PROTECTION

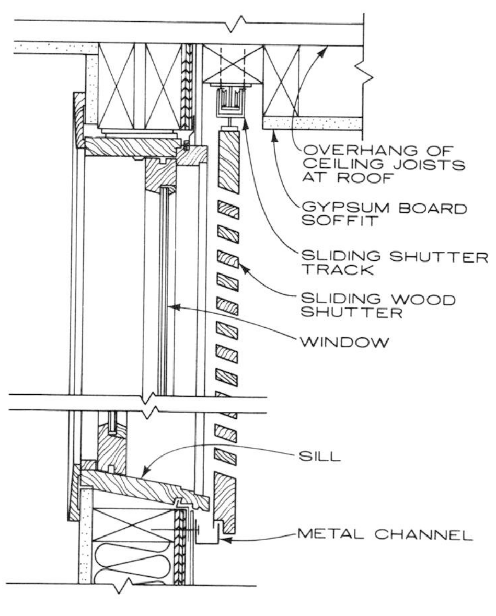
OVERHANG OF CEILING JOISTS AT ROOF
GYPSUM BOARD SOFFIT
SLIDING SHUTTER TRACK
SLIDING WOOD SHUTTER
WINDOW
SILL
METAL CHANNEL

SLIDING WOOD SHUTTERS

Daniel Tinney, AIA; The Russell Partnership, Inc.
Hoffman, see data sources

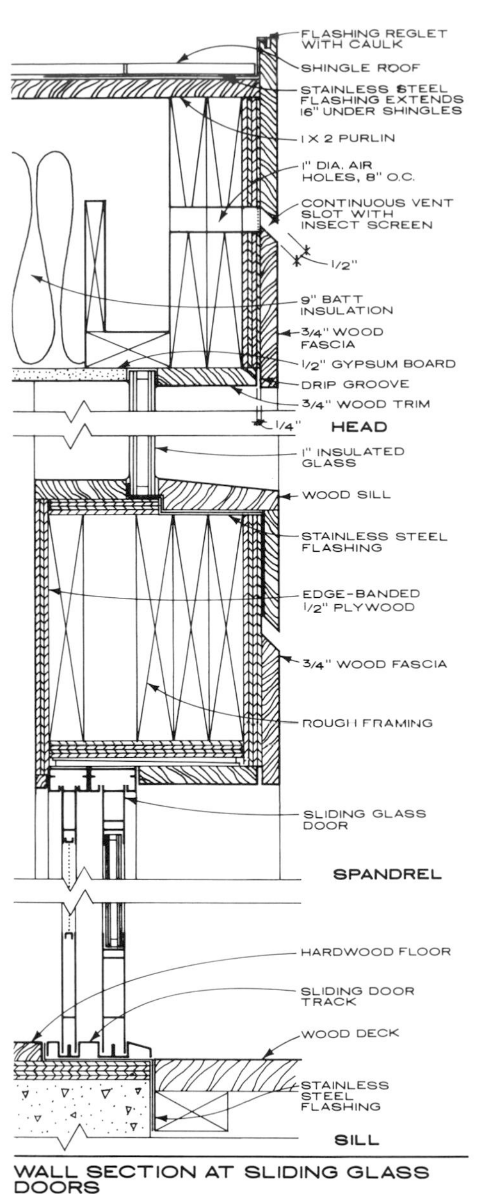
FLASHING REGLET WITH CAULK
SHINGLE ROOF
STAINLESS STEEL FLASHING EXTENDS 16" UNDER SHINGLES
1 X 2 PURLIN
1" DIA. AIR HOLES, 8" O.C.
CONTINUOUS VENT SLOT WITH INSECT SCREEN
1/2"
9" BATT INSULATION
3/4" WOOD FASCIA
1/2" GYPSUM BOARD
DRIP GROOVE
3/4" WOOD TRIM
1/4"
HEAD
1" INSULATED GLASS
WOOD SILL
STAINLESS STEEL FLASHING
EDGE-BANDED 1/2" PLYWOOD
3/4" WOOD FASCIA
ROUGH FRAMING
SLIDING GLASS DOOR
SPANDREL
HARDWOOD FLOOR
SLIDING DOOR TRACK
WOOD DECK
STAINLESS STEEL FLASHING
SILL

WALL SECTION AT SLIDING GLASS DOORS

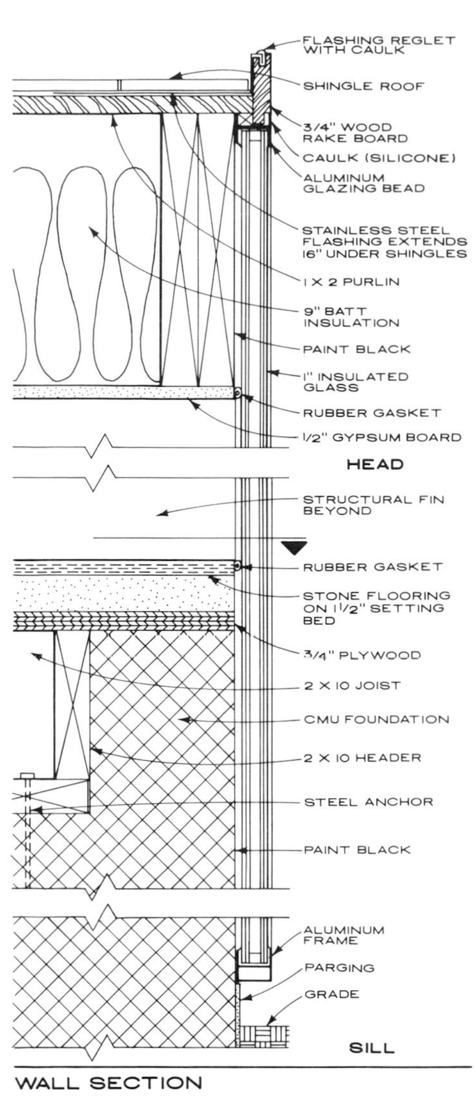
FLASHING REGLET WITH CAULK
SHINGLE ROOF
3/4" WOOD RAKE BOARD
CAULK (SILICONE)
ALUMINUM GLAZING BEAD
STAINLESS STEEL FLASHING EXTENDS 16" UNDER SHINGLES
1 X 2 PURLIN
9" BATT INSULATION
PAINT BLACK
1" INSULATED GLASS
RUBBER GASKET
1/2" GYPSUM BOARD
HEAD
STRUCTURAL FIN BEYOND
RUBBER GASKET
STONE FLOORING ON 1 1/2" SETTING BED
3/4" PLYWOOD
2 X 10 JOIST
CMU FOUNDATION
2 X 10 HEADER
STEEL ANCHOR
PAINT BLACK
ALUMINUM FRAME
PARGING
GRADE
SILL

WALL SECTION

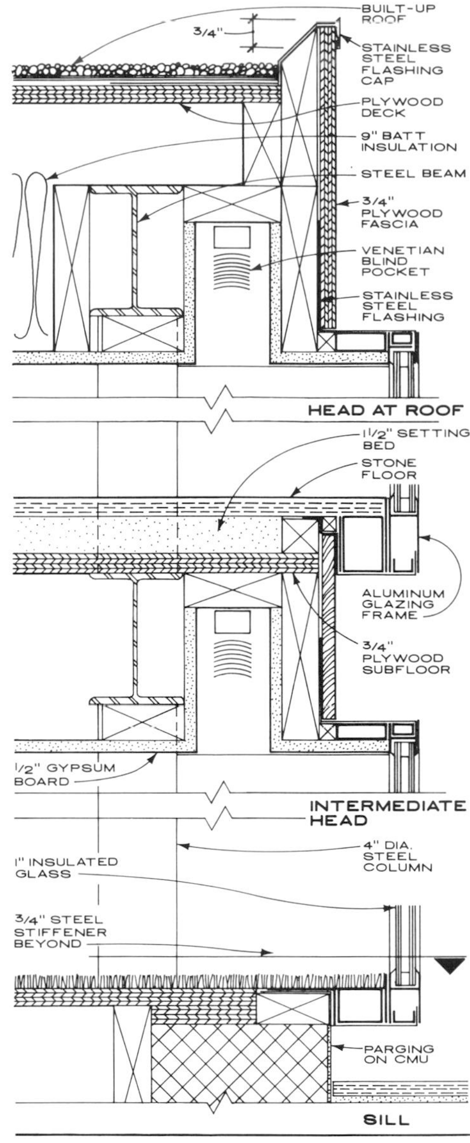
BUILT-UP ROOF
3/4"
STAINLESS STEEL FLASHING CAP
PLYWOOD DECK
9" BATT INSULATION
STEEL BEAM
3/4" PLYWOOD FASCIA
VENETIAN BLIND POCKET
STAINLESS STEEL FLASHING
HEAD AT ROOF
1 1/2" SETTING BED
STONE FLOOR
ALUMINUM GLAZING FRAME
3/4" PLYWOOD SUBFLOOR
1/2" GYPSUM BOARD
INTERMEDIATE HEAD
4" DIA. STEEL COLUMN
1" INSULATED GLASS
3/4" STEEL STIFFENER BEYOND
PARGING ON CMU
SILL

WALL SECTION

2"
ALUMINUM GLAZING BEAD
1" INSULATED GLASS
WOOD TRIM
STRUCTURAL STEEL FRAME
1/2" PLYWOOD
HINGED SHUTTER
2 X 4 STUD

CURTAIN WALL STRUCTURAL FIN

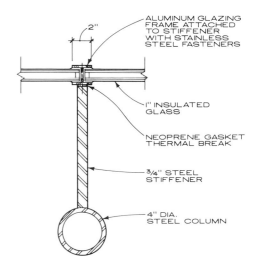

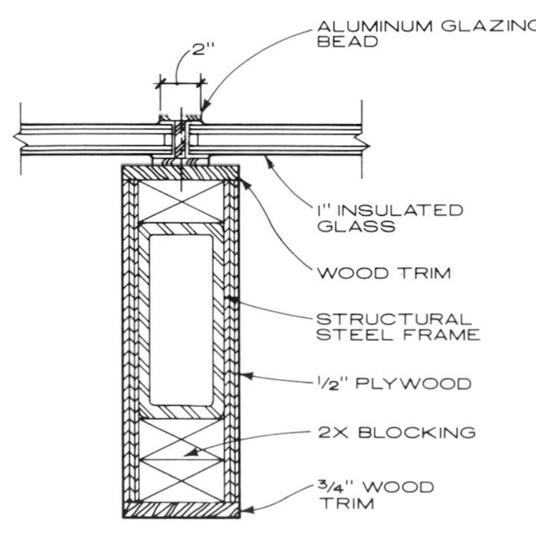
2"
ALUMINUM GLAZING BEAD
1" INSULATED GLASS
WOOD TRIM
STRUCTURAL STEEL FRAME
1/2" PLYWOOD
2X BLOCKING
3/4" WOOD TRIM

CURTAIN WALL STRUCTURAL FIN

2"

ALUMINUM GLAZING FRAME ATTACHED TO STIFFENER WITH STAINLESS STEEL FASTENERS

1" INSULATED GLASS

NEOPRENE GASKET THERMAL BREAK

3/4" STEEL STIFFENER

4" DIA. STEEL COLUMN

COLUMN WITH STIFFENER AT WINDOW WALL

Hugh Newell Jacobsen, FAIA; Washington, D.C.

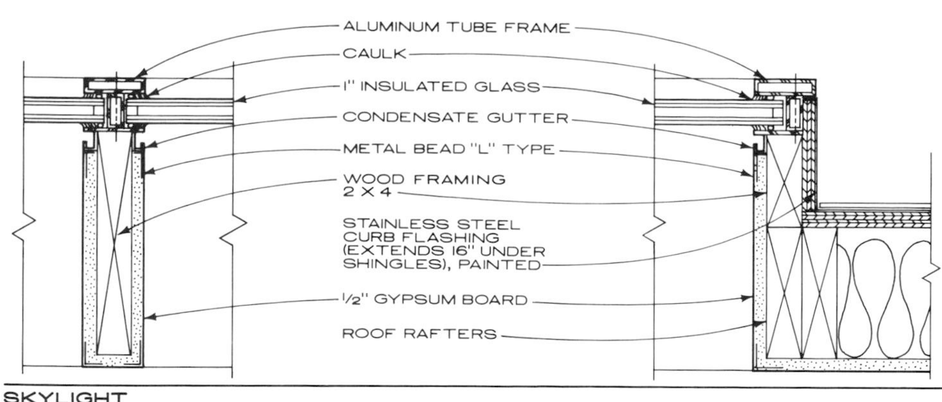
ALUMINUM TUBE FRAME
CAULK
1" INSULATED GLASS
CONDENSATE GUTTER
METAL BEAD "L" TYPE
WOOD FRAMING 2 X 4
STAINLESS STEEL CURB FLASHING (EXTENDS 16" UNDER SHINGLES), PAINTED
1/2" GYPSUM BOARD
ROOF RAFTERS

SKYLIGHT

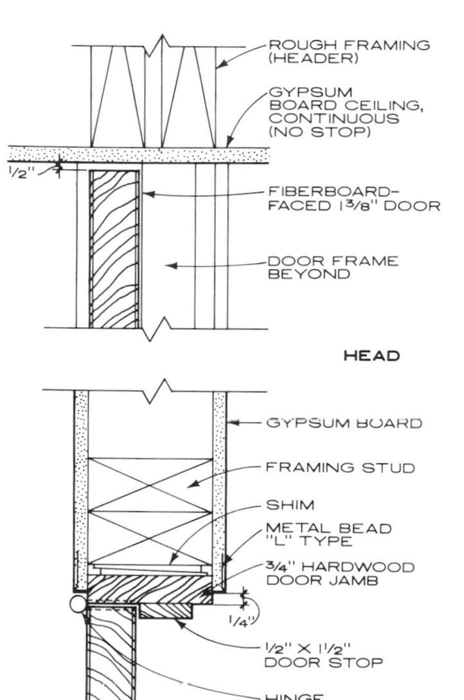
ROUGH FRAMING (HEADER)
GYPSUM BOARD CEILING, CONTINUOUS (NO STOP)
1/2"
FIBERBOARD-FACED 1 3/8" DOOR
DOOR FRAME BEYOND
HEAD
GYPSUM BOARD
FRAMING STUD
SHIM
METAL BEAD "L" TYPE
3/4" HARDWOOD DOOR JAMB
1/4"
1/2" X 1 1/2" DOOR STOP
HINGE
FIBERBOARD-FACED 1 3/8" DOOR
JAMB

TYPICAL INTERIOR DOOR

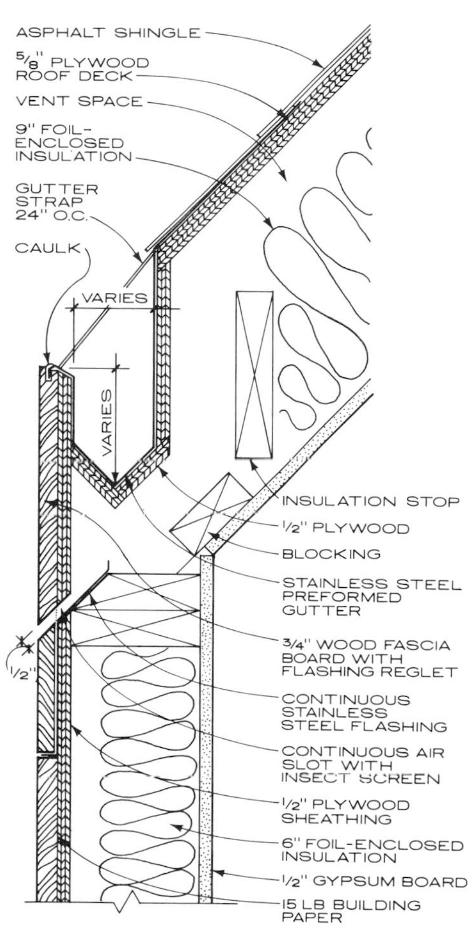
ASPHALT SHINGLE
5/8" PLYWOOD ROOF DECK
VENT SPACE
9" FOIL-ENCLOSED INSULATION
GUTTER STRAP 24" O.C.
CAULK
VARIES
VARIES
INSULATION STOP
1/2" PLYWOOD
BLOCKING
STAINLESS STEEL PREFORMED GUTTER
3/4" WOOD FASCIA BOARD WITH FLASHING REGLET
1/2"
CONTINUOUS STAINLESS STEEL FLASHING
CONTINUOUS AIR SLOT WITH INSECT SCREEN
1/2" PLYWOOD SHEATHING
6" FOIL-ENCLOSED INSULATION
1/2" GYPSUM BOARD
15 LB BUILDING PAPER

WALL SECTION AT CONCEALED GUTTER

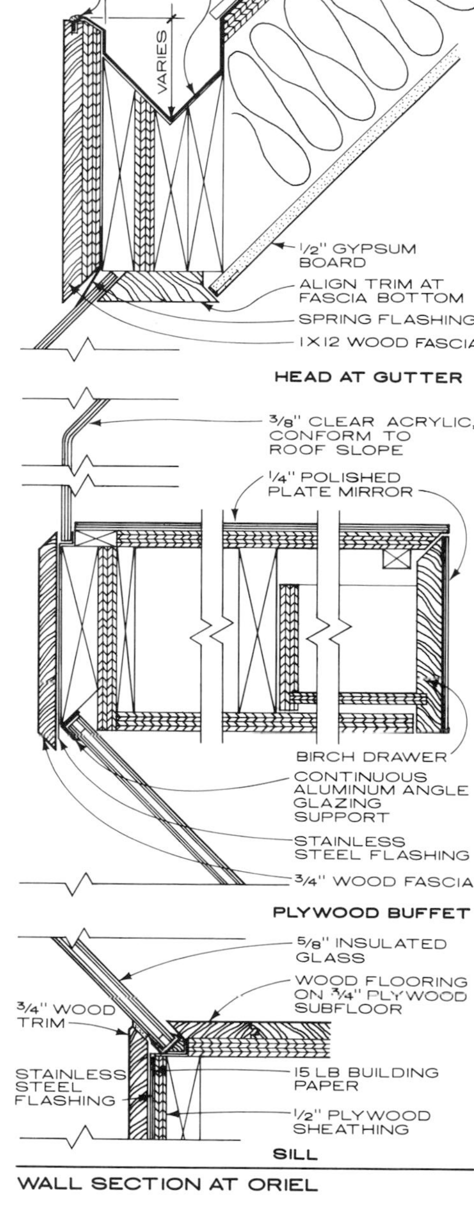
SHINGLE ROOF
9" FOIL-ENCASED INSULATION
INBOARD STAINLESS STEEL GUTTER
CAULK
VARIES
VARIES
1/2" GYPSUM BOARD
ALIGN TRIM AT FASCIA BOTTOM
SPRING FLASHING
1 X 12 WOOD FASCIA
HEAD AT GUTTER
3/8" CLEAR ACRYLIC, CONFORM TO ROOF SLOPE
1/4" POLISHED PLATE MIRROR
BIRCH DRAWER
CONTINUOUS ALUMINUM ANGLE GLAZING SUPPORT
STAINLESS STEEL FLASHING
3/4" WOOD FASCIA
PLYWOOD BUFFET
5/8" INSULATED GLASS
WOOD FLOORING ON 3/4" PLYWOOD SUBFLOOR
3/4" WOOD TRIM
STAINLESS STEEL FLASHING
15 LB BUILDING PAPER
1/2" PLYWOOD SHEATHING
SILL

WALL SECTION AT ORIEL

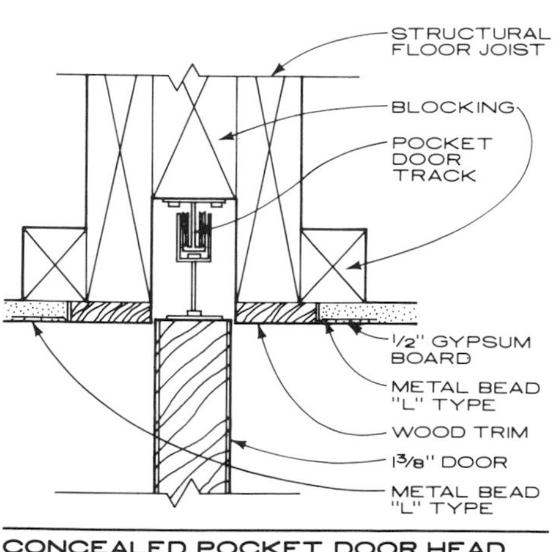
STRUCTURAL FLOOR JOIST
BLOCKING
POCKET DOOR TRACK
1/2" GYPSUM BOARD
METAL BEAD "L" TYPE
WOOD TRIM
1 3/8" DOOR
METAL BEAD "L" TYPE

CONCEALED POCKET DOOR HEAD

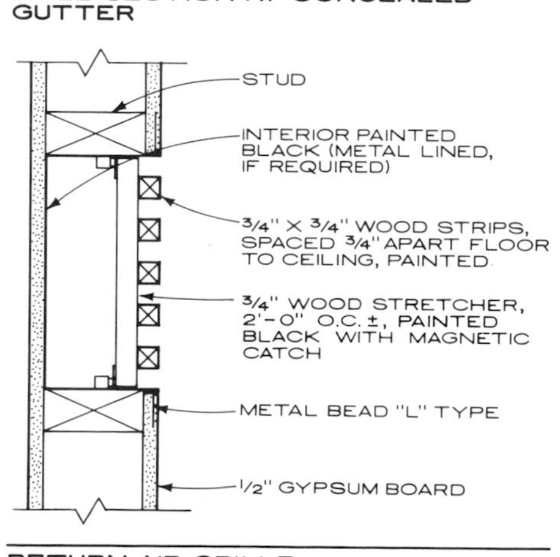
STUD
INTERIOR PAINTED BLACK (METAL LINED, IF REQUIRED)
3/4" X 3/4" WOOD STRIPS, SPACED 3/4" APART FLOOR TO CEILING, PAINTED
3/4" WOOD STRETCHER, 2'-0" O.C. ±, PAINTED BLACK WITH MAGNETIC CATCH
METAL BEAD "L" TYPE
1/2" GYPSUM BOARD

RETURN AIR GRILLE

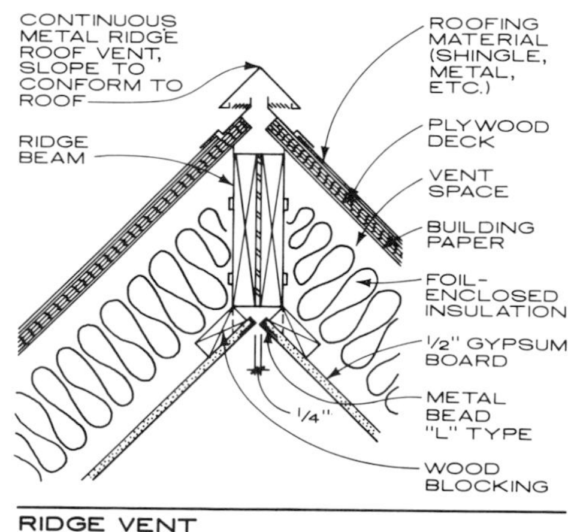
CONTINUOUS METAL RIDGE ROOF VENT, SLOPE TO CONFORM TO ROOF
RIDGE BEAM
ROOFING MATERIAL (SHINGLE, METAL, ETC.)
PLYWOOD DECK
VENT SPACE
BUILDING PAPER
FOIL-ENCLOSED INSULATION
1/2" GYPSUM BOARD
METAL BEAD "L" TYPE
1/4"
WOOD BLOCKING

RIDGE VENT

Hugh Newell Jacobsen, FAIA; Washington, D.C.

EXTERIOR TYPE PANELS

APPEARANCE (1, 3)		VENEER			THICKNESS (IN.)					
GRADE (2)	COMMON USES	F	M	B	1/4	5/16	11/32 3/8	15/32 1/2	19/32 5/8	23/32 3/4
A-A EXT APA (5)	Use where both sides are visible	A	C	A	•		•	•	•	•
A-B EXT APA (5)	Use where view of one side is less important	A	C	B	•		•	•	•	•
A-C EXT APA (5)	Use where only one side is visible	A	C	C	•		•	•	•	•
B-B EXT APA (5)	Utility panel with two solid faces	B	C	B	•		•	•	•	•
B-C EXT APA (5)	Utility panel. Also used as base for exterior coatings on walls and roofs	B	C	C	•		•	•	•	•
HDO EXT-APA (5)	High density overlay plywood has a hard, semi-opaque resin fiber overlay on both faces. Abrasion resistant. Use for concrete forms, cabinets, and countertops	A B	C	A B			•	•	•	•
MDO EXT APA (5)	Medium density overlay with smooth resin fiber overlay on one or two faces. Recommended for siding and other outdoor applications. Ideal base for paint	B	C	B C			•	•	•	•
303 SIDING EXT-APA (7)	Special surface treatment such as V-groove, channel groove, striated, brushed, rough sawn	(6)	C	C			•	•	•	
T1-11 EXT-APA (7)	Special 303 panel having grooves 1/4 in. deep, 3/8 in. wide, spaced 4 in. or 8 in. o.c. Other spacing optional. Edges shiplapped. Available unsanded, textured, and medium density overlay	A B C	C	C					•	
PLYRON EXT-APA	Hardboard faces both sides, tempered, smooth or screened	HB	C	HB				•	•	•
UNDER-LAYMENT C-C PLUGGED EXT-APA (5)	For application over structural subfloor. Provides smooth surface for application of resilient floor coverings where severe moisture conditions may be present. Touch-sanded	C	C	C			•	•	•	•
C-C PLUGGED EXT-APA (5)	For refrigerated or controlled atmosphere rooms. Touch-sanded	C	C	C			•	•	•	•
B-B PLYFORM CLASS I and CLASS II EXT-APA (4)	Concrete form grades with high reuse factor. Sanded both sides and mill-oiled unless otherwise specified. Special restrictions on species. Also available in HDO for very smooth concrete finish	B	C	B					•	•

PERFORMANCE RATED (3)		VENEER			THICKNESS (IN.)					
GRADE	COMMON USES	F	M	B	1/4	5/16	3/8	15/32 1/2	19/32 5/8	23/32 3/4
SHEATH-ING EXT-APA	Exterior sheathing panel for subflooring and wall and roof sheathing, siding on service and farm buildings. Manufactured as conventional veneered plywood	C	C	C		•	•	•	•	•
STRUC-TURAL I and II SHEATH-ING EXT-APA	For engineered applications in construction and industry where full exterior type panels are required. Unsanded. See Note 5 for species group requirements	C	C	C		•	•	•	•	•
STURDI-I-FLOOR EXT-APA	For combination subfloor underlayment under carpet and pad where severe moisture conditions exist, as in balcony decks. Touch-sanded and tongue and groove	C	C (11)	C					•	•

INTERIOR TYPE PANELS

APPEARANCE (1, 3)		VENEER			THICKNESS (IN.)					
GRADE (2) (12)	COMMON USES	F	M	B	1/4	5/16	11/32 3/8	15/32 1/2	19/32 5/8	23/32 3/4
N-N, N-A N-B INT-APA	Cabinet quality. For natural finish furniture. Special order items	N	C	NA B						•
N-D INT-APA	For natural finish paneling. Special orders	N	D	D	•					
A-A INT-APA	For applications where both sides are visible. Smooth face; suitable for painting	A	D	A	•		•	•	•	•
A-B INT-APA	Use where view of one side is less important but two solid surfaces are needed	A	D	B	•		•	•	•	•
A-D INT-APA	Use where only one side is visible	A	D	D	•		•	•	•	•
B-B INT-APA	Utility panel with two solid sides	B	D	B	•		•	•	•	•
B-D INT-APA	Utility panel with one solid side	B	D	D	•		•	•	•	•
Decorative panels-INT-APA	Rough sawn, brushed, grooved, or striated faces for walls and built-ins	A B C	D	D		•	•	•	•	
PLYRON INT-APA	Hardboard face on both sides, tempered smooth or screened for counters and doors	HB	C D	HB				•	•	•
UNDER-LAYMENT INT-APA (5)	For application over structural subfloor. Provides smooth surface for application of resilient floor coverings. Touch-sanded. Also available with exterior glue	C	C D	D			•	•	•	•
C-D PLUGGED INT-APA (5)	For built-ins, wall and ceiling tile backing, cable reels, walkways, separator boards. Not a substitute for UNDERLAYMENT or STURD-I-FLOOR as it lacks their indentation resistance. Touch-sanded. Also made with exterior glue	C	D	D			•	•	•	•

PERFORMANCE RATED (3, 8)		VENEER (13)			THICKNESS (IN.)					
GRADE	COMMON USES	F	M	B	1/4	5/16	3/8	15/32 1/2	19/32 5/8	23/32 3/4
SHEATH-ING EXP 1 and 2-APA	Commonly available with exterior glue for sheathing and subflooring. Specify Exposure 1 treated wood foundations	C	D	D		•	•	•	•	•
STRUC-TURAL I and II SHEATH-ING EXP 1-APA	Unsanded structural grades where plywood strength properties are of maximum importance. Made only with exterior glue for beams, gusset plates, and stressed-skin panels	C (10)	D (10)	D (10)		•	•	•	•	•
STURD-I-FLOOR EXP 1 and 2-APA	For combination subfloor and underlayment under carpet and pad. Specify Exposure 1 where moisture is present. Available in tongue and groove.	C	C D (11)	D					•	•
STURD-I-FLOOR 48 o.c. (2, 4, 1) EXP 1-APA (9)	Combination subfloor underlayment on 32 and 48 in. spans and for heavy timber roofs. Use in areas subject to moisture; or if construction may be delayed as in site built floors. Unsanded or touch-sanded as specified	C	C D	D						1 1/8

GENERAL NOTES

1. Sanded on both sides except where decorative or other surfaces specified.
2. Available in Group 1, 2, 3, 4, or 5 unless otherwise noted.
3. Standard 4 × 8 panel sizes; other sizes available.
4. Also available in Structural I.
5. Also available in Structural I (all plies limited to Group I species) and Structural II (all plies limited to Group 1, 2, or 3 species).
6. C or better for five plies; C Plugged or better for three-ply panels.
7. Stud spacing is shown on grade stamp.
8. Exposure 1 made with exterior glue, Exposure 2 with intermediate glue.
9. Made only in woods of certain species to conform to APA specifications.
10. Special improved grade for structural panels.
11. Special construction to resist indentation from concentrated loads.
12. Interior type panels with exterior glue are identified as Exposure 1.
13. Also available as nonveneer or composite panels.

Bloodgood Architects, PC; Des Moines and New York
American Plywood Association

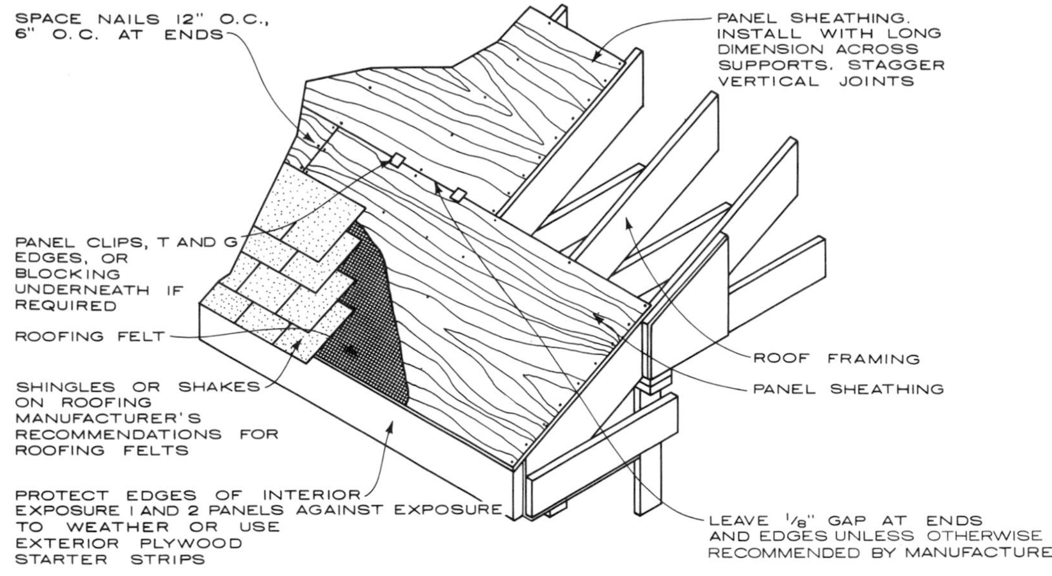
SPACE NAILS 12" O.C., 6" O. C. AT ENDS
PANEL SHEATHING. INSTALL WITH LONG DIMENSION ACROSS SUPPORTS. STAGGER VERTICAL JOINTS
PANEL CLIPS, T AND G EDGES, OR BLOCKING UNDERNEATH IF REQUIRED
ROOFING FELT
SHINGLES OR SHAKES ON ROOFING MANUFACTURER'S RECOMMENDATIONS FOR ROOFING FELTS
PROTECT EDGES OF INTERIOR EXPOSURE 1 AND 2 PANELS AGAINST EXPOSURE TO WEATHER OR USE EXTERIOR PLYWOOD STARTER STRIPS
ROOF FRAMING
PANEL SHEATHING
LEAVE 1/8" GAP AT ENDS AND EDGES UNLESS OTHERWISE RECOMMENDED BY MANUFACTURER

STRUCTURAL-USE PANEL ROOF SHEATHING

PANEL SHEATHING INSTALLED WITH LONG DIMENSION ACROSS STUDS, STAGGER VERTICAL JOINTS
LEAVE 1/8" GAP AT EDGES AND ENDS UNLESS OTHERWISE RECOMMENDED BY MANUFACTURER
SIDING MATERIAL
WALL FRAMING
SPACE NAILS 12" O.C., 6" O.C. AT EDGES
PANEL SHEATHING USED AS CORNER BRACING. INSTALL WITH LONG DIMENSION PARALLEL TO STUDS

STRUCTURAL-USE PANEL WALL SHEATHING

PLYWOOD ROOF SHEATHING

Plywood grades commonly used for roof (and wall) sheathing are A.P.A. rated sheathing with span ratings: 16/0, 20/0, 24/0, 24/16, 32/16, 40/20, 48/20; exposure durability classifications: Exterior, Exposure 1, Exposure 2. Refer to American Plywood Association recommendations for unsupported edges.

PLYWOOD WALL SHEATHING

Common grade is same as used in roof sheathing. Refer to American Plywood Association recommendations for unsupported edges.

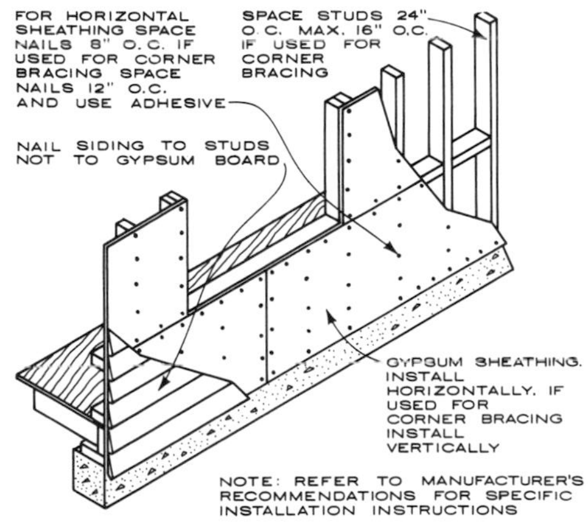
FOR HORIZONTAL SHEATHING SPACE NAILS 8" O.C. IF USED FOR CORNER BRACING SPACE NAILS 12" O.C. AND USE ADHESIVE
SPACE STUDS 24" O.C. MAX. 16" O.C. IF USED FOR CORNER BRACING
NAIL SIDING TO STUDS NOT TO GYPSUM BOARD
GYPSUM SHEATHING. INSTALL HORIZONTALLY. IF USED FOR CORNER BRACING INSTALL VERTICALLY
NOTE: REFER TO MANUFACTURER'S RECOMMENDATIONS FOR SPECIFIC INSTALLATION INSTRUCTIONS

GYPSUM WALL SHEATHING

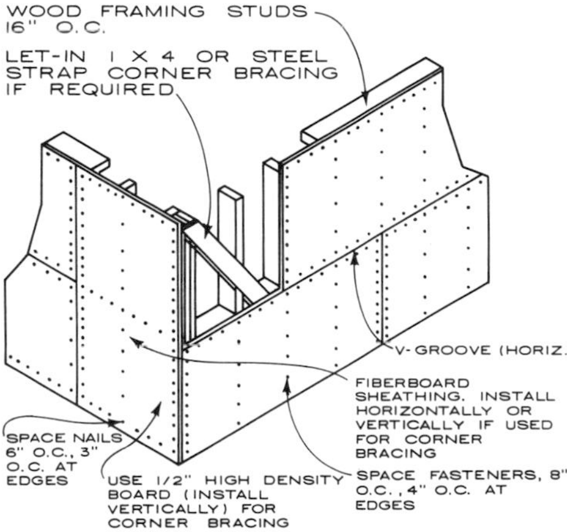
WOOD FRAMING STUDS 16" O.C.
LET-IN 1 X 4 OR STEEL STRAP CORNER BRACING IF REQUIRED
V-GROOVE (HORIZ.)
FIBERBOARD SHEATHING. INSTALL HORIZONTALLY OR VERTICALLY IF USED FOR CORNER BRACING
SPACE NAILS 6" O.C., 3" O.C. AT EDGES
USE 1/2" HIGH DENSITY BOARD (INSTALL VERTICALLY) FOR CORNER BRACING
SPACE FASTENERS, 8" O.C., 4" O.C. AT EDGES

FIBERBOARD SHEATHING

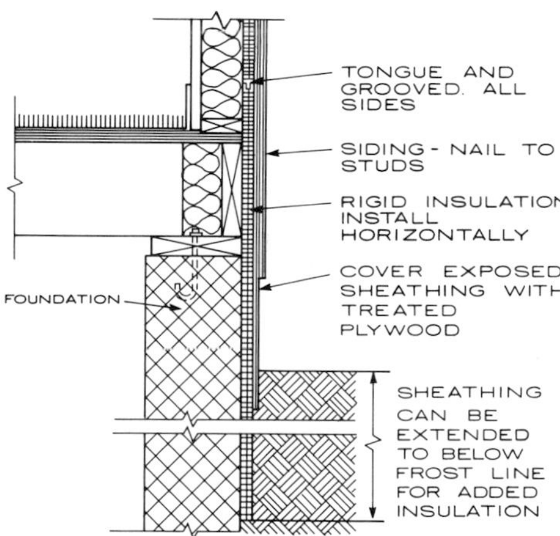
TONGUE AND GROOVED. ALL SIDES
SIDING - NAIL TO STUDS
RIGID INSULATION INSTALL HORIZONTALLY
COVER EXPOSED SHEATHING WITH TREATED PLYWOOD
FOUNDATION
SHEATHING CAN BE EXTENDED TO BELOW FROST LINE FOR ADDED INSULATION

PLASTIC SHEATHING

GYPSUM WALL SHEATHING

Fire rated panels are available in 1/2 and 5/8 in. thicknesses. Gypsum board is not an effective vapor barrier.

FIBERBOARD SHEATHING

Also called insulation board. Can be treated or impregnated with asphalt. Available in regular or 1/2 in. high density panels.

PLASTIC SHEATHING

Usually made of polyurethane or polystyrene. Can be considered an effective vapor barrier, hence wall must be effectively vented. All edges are usually tongue and groove.

SHEATHING MATERIALS

CHARACTERISTICS	PLYWOOD	GYPSUM	FIBERBOARD	PLASTIC
Nailable base	Yes	No	Only high density	No
Vapor barrier	No	No	If asphalt treated	Yes
Insulation R value (1/2 in. thickness)	1.2	0.7	2.6	6.25
Corner bracing provided	Yes	Yes (see manufacturer's recommendation)	Only high density	No
Panel sizes (ft.)	4 x 8, 4 x 9, 4 x 10	4 x 8, 4 x 10, 4 x 12, 4 x 14	4 x 8, 4 x 9, 4 x 10, 4 x 12	16 x 96, 24 x 48, 24 x 96
Panel thickness (in.)	5/16, 3/8, 7/16, 15/32, 1/2, 19/32, 5/8, 23/32, 3/4	1/4, 3/8, 1/2, 5/8	1/2, 25/32	3/4 to 6 (for roof)

Timothy B. McDonald; Washington, D.C.
John D. Bloodgood, Architects, P.C.; Des Moines, Iowa
American Plywood Association

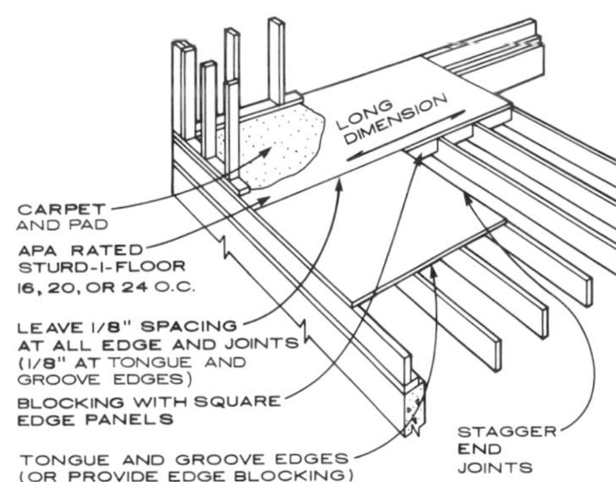
LONG DIMENSION
CARPET AND PAD
APA RATED STURD-I-FLOOR 16, 20, OR 24 O.C.
LEAVE 1/8" SPACING AT ALL EDGE AND JOINTS (1/8" AT TONGUE AND GROOVE EDGES)
BLOCKING WITH SQUARE EDGE PANELS
TONGUE AND GROOVE EDGES (OR PROVIDE EDGE BLOCKING)
STAGGER END JOINTS

APA RATED STURD-I-FLOOR

APA RATED STURD-I-FLOOR (1)

SPAN RATING (MAXIMUM JOIST SPACING) (IN.)	PANEL THICKNESS (2) (IN.)	FASTENING: NAIL SIZE AND TYPE	SPACING (IN.) PANEL EDGE (GLUE-NAILED (3) / NAILED ONLY)	SPACING (IN.) INTERMEDIATE (GLUE-NAILED (3) / NAILED ONLY)
16	19/32, 5/8, 21/32	6d Ring or Screw-Shank (4)	12 / 6	12 / 10
20	19/32, 5/8, 23/32, 3/4	6d Ring or Screw-Shank (4)	12 / 6	12 / 10
24	11/16, 23/32, 3/4	6d Ring or Screw-Shank (4)	12 / 6	12 / 10
	7/8, 1	8d Ring or Screw-Shank (4)	12 / 6	12 / 10
48 (2-4-1 Panels)	1 1/8	8d Ring or Screw-Shank (5)	6 / 6	(6) / (6)

STURD-I-FLOOR NOTES

1. For conditions not listed, see APA literature.
2. Use only APA Specification AFG-01 adhesives, properly applied. Use only solvent-based glues on non-veneered panels with sealed surfaces and edges.
3. 8d common nails may be substituted if ring- or screw-shank nails are not available.
4. 10d common nails may be substituted with 1 1/8 in. panels if supports are well seasoned.
5. Space nails 6 in. for 48 in. spans and 10 in. for 32 in. spans.

ALLOWABLE CLEAR SPANS FOR APA: GLUED FLOOR SYSTEM (1,4,5)

APA GLUED FLOOR SPANS

SPECIES GRADE	JOIST SIZE	16" o.c. (APA RATED STURD-I-FLOOR 16" OR 20" o.c.)	16" o.c. (APA RATED STURD-I-FLOOR 24" o.c.)	19.2" o.c. (APA RATED STURD-I-FLOOR 20" o.c.)	24" o.c. (APA RATED STURD-I-FLOOR 24" o.c.)
Douglas fir Larch-No. 2	2 x 6	10'-5"	10'-6"	9'-7"	8'-7"
	2 x 8	13'-7"	13'-10"	12'-7"	11'-3"
	2 x 10	17'-2"	17'-7"	16'-1"	14'-5"
	2 x 12	20'-9"	21'-5"	19'-7"	17'-6"
Douglas fir South-No. 1	2 x 6	9'-10"	10'-8"	9'-11"	9'-1"
	2 x 8	12'-9"	13'-8"	12'-8"	12'-0"
	2 x 10	16'-2"	17'-0"	15'-11"	15'-4"
	2 x 12	19'-7"	20'-5"	19'-1"	18'-4"
Hem-fir No. 1	2 x 6	10'-0"	10'-3"	9'-5"	8'-5"
	2 x 8	13'-1"	13'-7"	12'-5"	11'-1"
	2 x 10	16'-6"	17'-4"	15'-10"	14'-2"
	2 x 12	20'-0"	20'-10"	19'-3"	17'-2"
Mountain hemlock No. 2	2 x 6	9'-2"	9'-6"	8'-8"	7'-9"
	2 x 8	11'-11"	12'-7"	11'-6"	10'-3"
	2 x 10	15'-0"	16'-0"	14'-8"	13'-1"
	2 x 12	18'-2"	19'-2"	17'-9"	15'-11"
Southern pine KD No. 2	2 x 6	10'-2"	10'-8"	9'-9"	8'-8"
	2 x 8	13'-4"	14'-0"	12'-10"	11'-6"
	2 x 10	16'-10"	17'-8"	16'-4"	14'-8"
	2 x 12	20'-5"	21'-2"	19'-10"	17'-9"

John D. Bloodgood, Architects, P.C.; Des Moines, Iowa
American Plywood Association

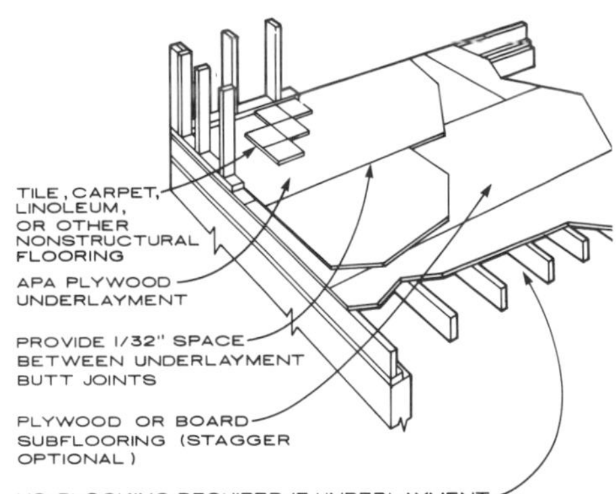
TILE, CARPET, LINOLEUM, OR OTHER NONSTRUCTURAL FLOORING
APA PLYWOOD UNDERLAYMENT
PROVIDE 1/32" SPACE BETWEEN UNDERLAYMENT BUTT JOINTS
PLYWOOD OR BOARD SUBFLOORING (STAGGER OPTIONAL)
NO BLOCKING REQUIRED IF UNDERLAYMENT JOINTS ARE OFFSET FROM SUBFLOOR JOINTS

PLYWOOD UNDERLAYMENT

PLYWOOD UNDERLAYMENT (1)

PLYWOOD GRADES AND SPECIES GROUP	APPLICATION (2)	MINIMUM PLYWOOD THICKNESS (IN.)
Groups 1, 2, 3, 4, 5 UNDERLAYMENT INT-APA (with interior or exterior glue), or UNDERLAYMENT EXT-APA (C-C plugged) EXT	Over smooth subfloor	1/4
	Over lumber subfloor or other uneven surfaces	11/32
Same grades as above, but Group 1 only	Over lumber floor up to 4 in. wide. Face grain must be perpendicular to boards	1/4

UNDERLAYMENT NOTES

1. For tile, carpeting, linoleum, or other nonstructural flooring. (Ceramic tile not recommended.)
2. Where floors may be subject to unusual moisture conditions, use panels with exterior glue (Exposure 1) or UNDERLAYMENT C-C Plugged EXT-APA. C-D Plugged is not an adequate substitute for underlayment grade, since it does not ensure equivalent dent resistance.
3. Recommended grades have a solid surface backed with a special inner ply construction that resists punch-through, dents, and concentrated loads.

UNDERLAYMENT NAILING SCHEDULE

Use 3d ring shank nails for underlayment up to 1/2 in. thickness, 4d for 5/8 in. and thicker. Use 16 gauge staples, except that 18 gauge may be used with 1/4 in. thick underlayment. Crown width should be 3/8 in. for 16 gauge staples, 3/16 in. for 18 gauge. Length should be sufficient to penetrate subflooring at least 5/8 in. or extend completely through. Space fasteners at 3 in. along panel edges and at 6 in. each way in the panel interior, except for 3/8 in. or thicker underlayment applied with ring shank nails. In this case, use 6 in. spacing along edges and 8 in. spacing each way in the panel interior. Unless subfloor and joists are of thoroughly seasoned material and have remained dry during construction, countersink nail heads below surface of the underlayment just prior to laying finish floors to avoid nail popping. If thin resilient flooring is to be applied, fill and thoroughly sand joints.

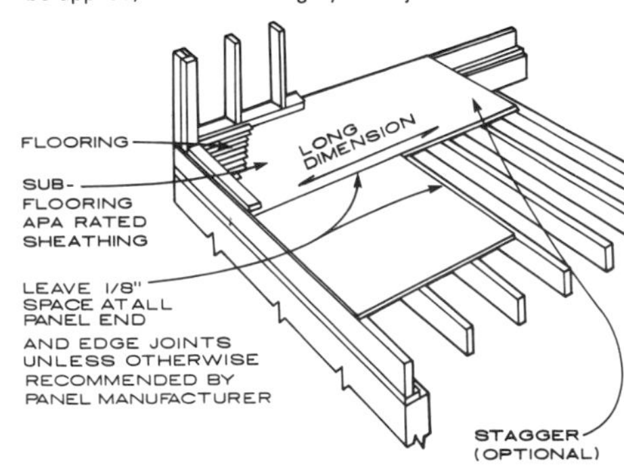
LONG DIMENSION
FLOORING
SUB-FLOORING APA RATED SHEATHING
LEAVE 1/8" SPACE AT ALL PANEL END AND EDGE JOINTS UNLESS OTHERWISE RECOMMENDED BY PANEL MANUFACTURER
STAGGER (OPTIONAL)

APA PANEL SUBFLOOR

APA PANEL SUBFLOORING (1)

PANEL SPAN RATING (OR GROUP NUMBER)	PANEL THICKNESS (IN.)	MAXIMUM SPACING (2, 3, 5) (IN.)
24/16	7/16, 1/2	16
32/16	15/32, 1/2, 5/8	16(4)
40/20	19/32, 5/8, 3/4, 7/8	20(4)
48/24	23/32, 3/4, 7/8	24
1 1/8 in. groups (1, 2)	1 1/8	32 (2x joists) 48 (4x joists)

SUBFLOORING NOTES

1. Applies to APA rated sheathing grades only.
2. The spans assume plywood continuous over two or more spans with long dimension across supports.
3. In some nonresidential buildings special conditions may require construction in excess of minimums given.
4. May be 24 in. if 25/32 in. wood strip flooring is installed at right angles to joists.
5. Spans are limited to the values shown because of the possible effect of concentrated loads.

SUBFLOORING NAILING SCHEDULE

For 7/16 in. panel, 16 in. span, use 6d common nails at 6 in. o.c. at panel edges, 10 in. o.c. at intermediate supports. For 15/32 in. to 7/8 in. panels, 16 in. to 24 in. spans, use 8d common nails at 6 in. o.c. at panel edges, 10 in. o.c. at intermediate supports. For 1 1/8 in. and 1 1/4 in. panels up to 48 in. span, use 10d common nails 6 in. o.c. at panel edges, and 6 in. at intermediate supports.

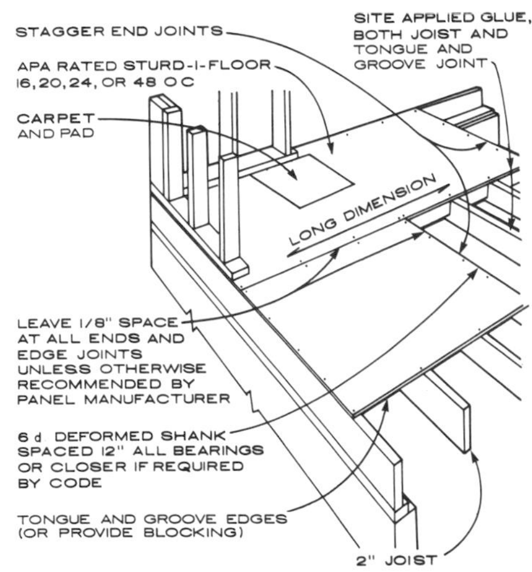
STAGGER END JOINTS
SITE APPLIED GLUE, BOTH JOIST AND TONGUE AND GROOVE JOINT
APA RATED STURD-I-FLOOR 16, 20, 24, OR 48 O C
CARPET AND PAD
LONG DIMENSION
LEAVE 1/8" SPACE AT ALL ENDS AND EDGE JOINTS UNLESS OTHERWISE RECOMMENDED BY PANEL MANUFACTURER
6 d DEFORMED SHANK SPACED 12" ALL BEARINGS OR CLOSER IF REQUIRED BY CODE
TONGUE AND GROOVE EDGES (OR PROVIDE BLOCKING)
2" JOIST

APA GLUED FLOOR SYSTEM

GLUED FLOOR NOTES

1. For complete information on glued floors, including joist span tables (based on building code criteria and lumber sizes), application sequence, and a list of recommended adhesives, contact the American Plywood Association.
2. Place APA STURD-I-FLOOR T&G across the joists with end joints staggered. Leave 1/8 in. space at all end and edge joints.
3. Although T&G is used most often, square edge may be used if 2 x 4 blocking is placed under panel edge joints between joists.
4. Based on live load of 40 psf, total load of 50 psf, deflection limited to 1/360 at 40 psf.
5. Glue tongue and groove joints. If square edge panels are used, block panel edges and glue between panels and between panels and blocking.

GLUED FLOOR NAILING SCHEDULE

Panels should be secured with power driven fasteners or nailed with 6d deformed shank nails, spaced 12 in. at supports. (8d common smooth nails may be substituted.)

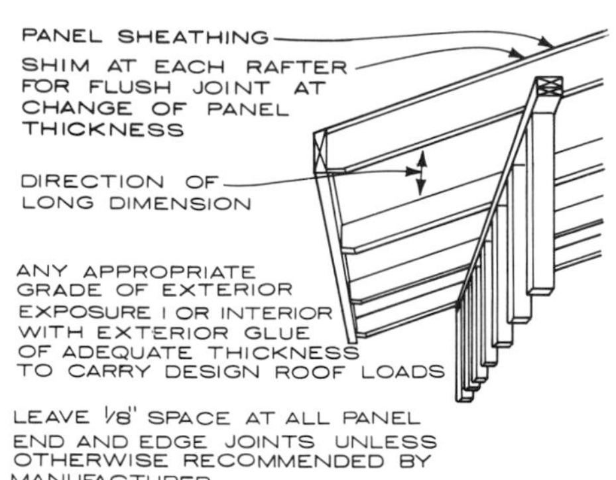
PANEL SHEATHING
SHIM AT EACH RAFTER FOR FLUSH JOINT AT CHANGE OF PANEL THICKNESS
DIRECTION OF LONG DIMENSION
ANY APPROPRIATE GRADE OF EXTERIOR EXPOSURE I OR INTERIOR WITH EXTERIOR GLUE OF ADEQUATE THICKNESS TO CARRY DESIGN ROOF LOADS
LEAVE 1/8" SPACE AT ALL PANEL END AND EDGE JOINTS UNLESS OTHERWISE RECOMMENDED BY MANUFACTURER

OPEN SOFFIT

EXTERIOR OPEN SOFFITS/ COMBINED CEILING DECKING (1)

PANEL DESCRIPTIONS, MINIMUM RECOMMENDATIONS	GROUP	MAXIMUM SPAN (IN.)
15/32" APA 303 siding 15/32" APA sanded	1, 2, 3, 4 1, 2, 3, 4	16
15/32" APA 303 siding 15/32" APA sanded 19/32" APA 303 siding 19/32" APA sanded	1 1, 2, 3 1, 2, 3, 4 1, 2, 3, 4	24
19/32" APA 303 siding 19/32" APA sanded 23/32" APA 303 siding 23/32" APA sanded	1 1 1, 2, 3, 4 1, 2, 3, 4	32 (2)
1 1/8" APA textured	1, 2, 3, 4	48 (2)

NOTES

1. Plywood is assumed to be continuous across two or more spans with face grain across supports.
2. For spans of 32 or 48 in. in open soffit construction, provide adequate blocking, tongue-and-groove edges, or other support such as panel clips. Minimum loads are at least 30 psf live load, plus 10 psf dead load.

NAILING SCHEDULE: For open soffits, use 6d common smooth, ring shank, or spiral thread nails for 1/2 in. or smaller thicknesses; use 8d nails for plywood 5/8 to 1 in. thick. Use 8d ring shank or spiral thread or 10d common smooth shank nails for 1 1/8 in. textured panels. Space nails 6 in. at panel edges, 12 in. at intermediate supports, except for 48 in. spans where nails should be spaced 6 in. at all supports.

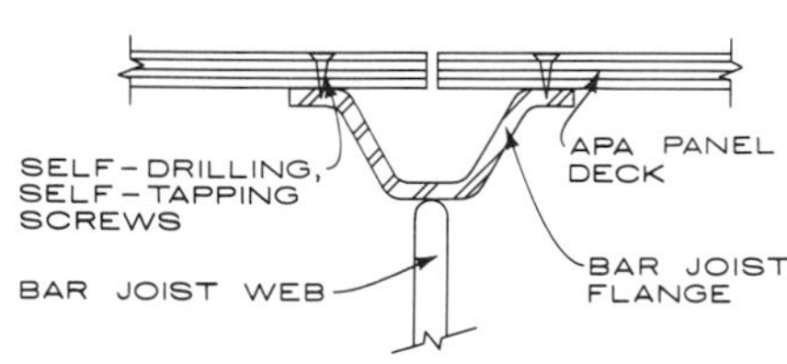
SELF-DRILLING, SELF-TAPPING SCREWS
APA PANEL DECK
BAR JOIST FLANGE
BAR JOIST WEB

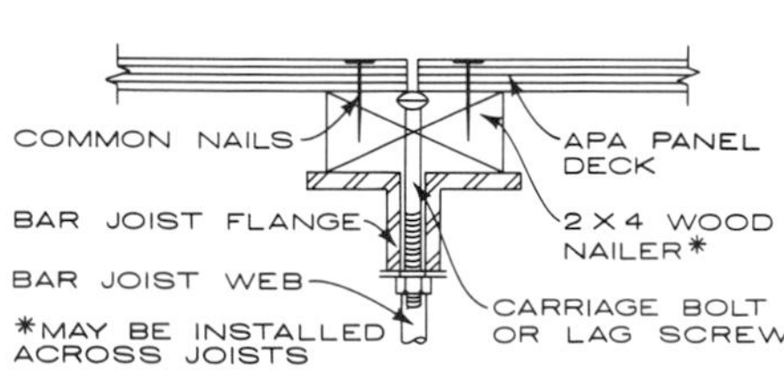
COMMON NAILS
APA PANEL DECK
BAR JOIST FLANGE
2 X 4 WOOD NAILER*
BAR JOIST WEB
CARRIAGE BOLT OR LAG SCREW
*MAY BE INSTALLED ACROSS JOISTS

CONNECTIONS TO OPEN WEB STEEL JOISTS

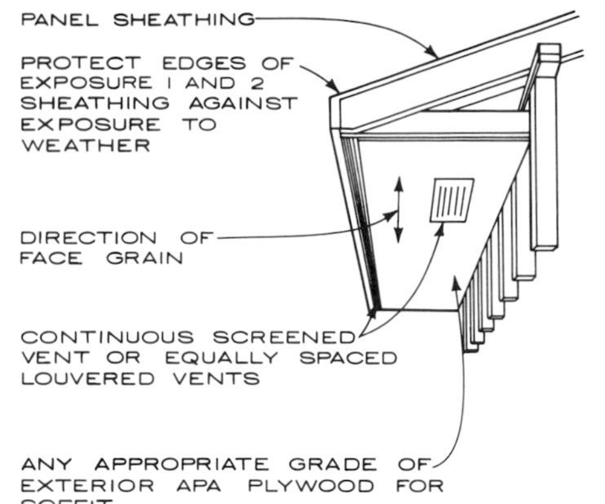
PANEL SHEATHING
PROTECT EDGES OF EXPOSURE I AND 2 SHEATHING AGAINST EXPOSURE TO WEATHER
DIRECTION OF FACE GRAIN
CONTINUOUS SCREENED VENT OR EQUALLY SPACED LOUVERED VENTS
ANY APPROPRIATE GRADE OF EXTERIOR APA PLYWOOD FOR SOFFIT

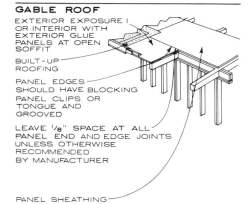

CLOSED SOFFIT

EXTERIOR CLOSED PLYWOOD SOFFITS

NOMINAL PLYWOOD THICKNESS	GROUP	MAXIMUM SPAN (IN.) ALL EDGES SUPPORTED
11/32" APA 303 siding or APA sanded	1, 2, 3, 4	24
15/32" APA 303 siding or APA sanded		32
19/32" APA 303 siding or APA sanded		48

NOTE: Plywood is assumed to be continuous across two or more spans with face grain across supports.

NAILING SCHEDULE: For closed soffits, use nonstaining box or casing nails, 6d for 11/32 and 15/32 in. panels and 8d for 19/32 in. panels. Space nails 6 in. at panel edges and 12 in. along intermediate supports.

LEAVE 1/8" SPACE AT ALL PANEL END AND EDGE JOINTS UNLESS OTHERWISE RECOMMENDED BY MANUFACTURER

ASPHALT, ASBESTOS, OR WOOD SHINGLES. FOLLOW MANUFACTURER'S RECOMMENDATIONS FOR ROOFING FELT

PANEL SHEATHING

PROTECT EDGES OF EXPOSURE I AND 2 PANELS AGAINST EXPOSURE TO WEATHER, OR USE EXTERIOR PLYWOOD STARTER STRIP

EXTERIOR PLYWOOD SOFFIT

PANEL CLIP

GABLE ROOF

EXTERIOR EXPOSURE I OR INTERIOR WITH EXTERIOR GLUE PANELS AT OPEN SOFFIT

BUILT-UP ROOFING

PANEL EDGES SHOULD HAVE BLOCKING PANEL CLIPS OR TONGUE AND GROOVED

LEAVE 1/8" SPACE AT ALL PANEL END AND EDGE JOINTS UNLESS OTHERWISE RECOMMENDED BY MANUFACTURER

PANEL SHEATHING

FLAT-LOW PITCHED ROOF

APA PANEL ROOF DECKING (1)

PANEL SPAN RATING	PANEL THICKNESS (IN.)	MAXIMUM SPAN (IN.) WITH EDGE SUPPORT	MAXIMUM SPAN (IN.) WITHOUT EDGE SUPPORT	NAIL SIZE AND TYPE	NAIL SPACING (IN.) PANEL EDGES	NAIL SPACING (IN.) INTERMEDIATE
12/0	5/16	12	12	6d common	6	12
16/0	5/16 3/8	16	16			
20/0	5/16 3/8	20	20			
24/0	3/8 7/16 1/2	24	20			
24/16	7/16 1/2	24	24			
32/16	15/32, 1/2	32	28			
32/16	5/8	32	28	8d common		
40/20	5/8 19/32, 3/4 7/8	40	32			
48/24	23/32, 3/4 7/8	48	36			
				STAPLING SPACES (IN.) LEG LENGTH	PANEL EDGES	INTERMEDIATE
(see above)	5/16"	(see above)		1 1/4"	4	8
	3/8"			1 3/8"		
	7/16", 15/32", 1/2"			1 1/2"		

NAILING SCHEDULE

Use 6d common smooth, ring shank, or spiral thread nails for plywood 1/2 in. thick or thinner and 8d for plywood to 1 in. thick. Use 8d ring shank or spiral thread or 10d common smooth for 2-4-1, and 1 1/8 in. panels. Space nails 6 in. at panel edges and 12 in. at intermediate supports, except for 48 in. or longer spans where nails should be spaced 6 in. at all supports.

NOTES

1. Apply to APA rated panel sheathing.
2. All panels will support at least 30 psf live load plus 10 psf dead load at maximum span. Uniform load deflection limit is 1/180 span under live load plus dead load, or 1/240 under live load only.
3. Special conditions may require construction in excess of the given minimums.
4. Panel is assumed to be continuous across two or more spans with long dimension across supports.

John D. Bloodgood, Architects, P.C.; Des Moines, Iowa
American Plywood Association

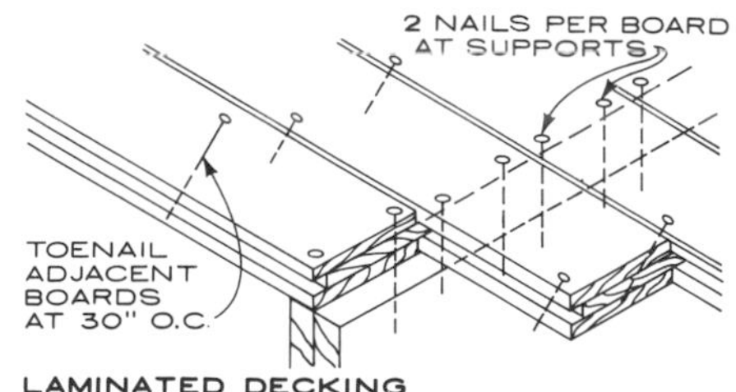
2 NAILS PER BOARD AT SUPPORTS
TOENAIL ADJACENT BOARDS AT 30" O.C.

LAMINATED DECKING

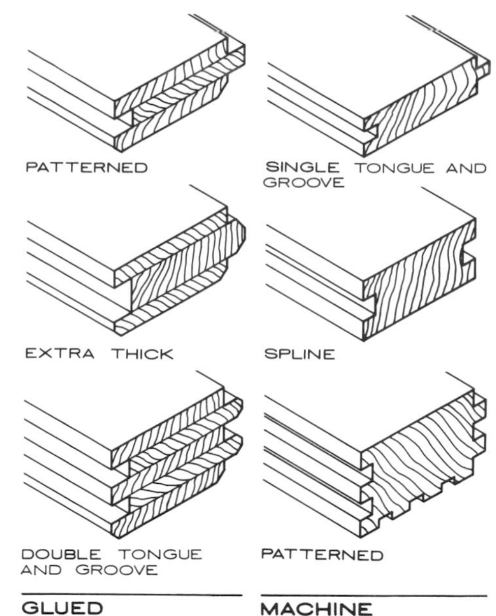
PATTERNED
SINGLE TONGUE AND GROOVE
EXTRA THICK
SPLINE
DOUBLE TONGUE AND GROOVE
PATTERNED

GLUED LAMINATED

MACHINE SHAPED

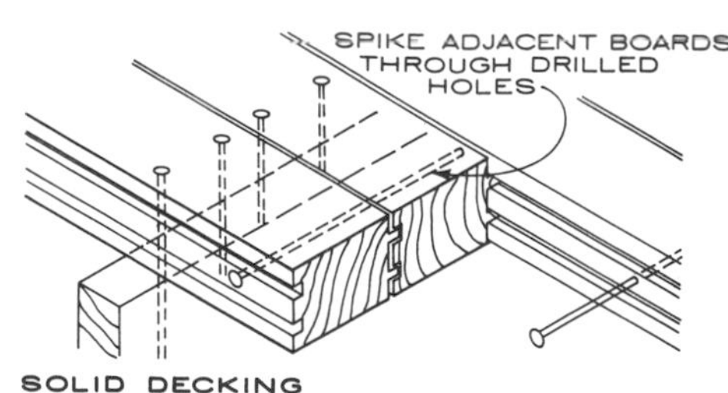
SPIKE ADJACENT BOARDS THROUGH DRILLED HOLES

SOLID DECKING

LAMINATED SIZES (IN.)

THICKNESS		WIDTH	
NOMINAL	ACTUAL	NOMINAL	ACTUAL
3	$2\frac{3}{16}$, $2\frac{1}{4}$	6,8	$5\frac{1}{4}$,7
3 STX	$2\frac{7}{8}$		
5	$3\frac{21}{32}$, $3\frac{13}{16}$		

MACHINE SHAPED SIZES (IN.)

THICKNESS		WIDTH	
NOMINAL	ACTUAL	NOMINAL	ACTUAL
2	$1\frac{1}{2}$	5,6,8,10,12	4, 5, $6\frac{3}{4}$, $8\frac{3}{4}$, $10\frac{3}{4}$
3	$2\frac{1}{2}$	6	$5\frac{1}{4}$
4	$3\frac{1}{2}$	6	$5\frac{1}{4}$

WEIGHT AND INSULATION VALUES

SPECIES	DECKING THICKNESS NOMINAL IN.	DECKING WEIGHTS PSF	DECKING ONLY R
Inland Red Cedar	3	4	4.00
	3 STX	5	5.02
	5	7	6.16
Cedar Face IWP/W Fir Core & Back	3	5	3.70
	3 STX	7	4.58
	5	8	5.59
White Fir Idaho White & Ponderosa Pine	3	5	3.58
	3 STX	7	4.47
	5	9	5.48
Douglas Fir	3	6	3.08
	3 STX	8	3.81
	5	11	4.63
Southern Pine	3	7	3.05
	3 STX	9	3.69
	5	12	4.63

NOTES

1. Insulation value may be increased with added rigid insulation.
2. Use of random lengths reduces waste.

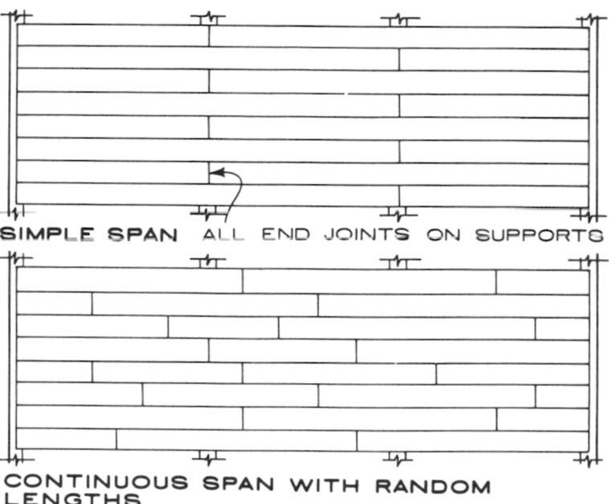
SIMPLE SPAN
ALL END JOINTS ON SUPPORTS
CONTINUOUS SPAN WITH RANDOM LENGTHS

LAMINATED DECK—ALLOWABLE UNIFORMLY DISTRIBUTED TOTAL ROOF LOADS GOVERNED BY DEFLECTION (1)

	SPAN IN FEET (2)	SOUTHERN PINE—E1.8 (3) F = 2640				INLAND RED CEDAR—E1.2 (INLAND RED CEDAR FACE AND BACK) F = 1590				PONDEROSA PINE—E1.3 INLAND RED CEDAR—E1.3 (IDAHO WHITE PINE OR WHITE FIR BACK) F = 1590				IDAHO WHITE PINE—E1.5 IDAHO WHITE FIR—E1.5 F = 1850				DOUGLAS FIR/LARCH—E1.8 F = 2640			
		SIMPLE SPAN END-JOINTS OVER SUPPORTS		RANDOM LENGTH CONTINUOUS OVER THREE OR MORE SPANS		SIMPLE SPAN END-JOINTS OVER SUPPORTS		RANDOM LENGTH CONTINUOUS OVER THREE OR MORE SPANS		SIMPLE SPAN END-JOINTS OVER SUPPORTS		RANDOM LENGTH CONTINUOUS OVER THREE OR MORE SPANS		SIMPLE SPAN END-JOINTS OVER SUPPORTS		RANDOM LENGTH CONTINUOUS OVER THREE OR MORE SPANS		SIMPLE SPAN END-JOINTS OVER SUPPORTS		RANDOM LENGTH CONTINUOUS OVER THREE OR MORE SPANS	
		1/180 PSF	1/240 PSF	1/180 PSF	1/240 PSF	1/180 PSF	1/240 PSF	1/180 PSF	1/240 PSF	1/180 PSF	1/240 .PSF	1/180 PSF	1/240 PSF	1/180 PSF	1/240 PSF	1/180 PSF	1/240 PSF	1/180 PSF	1/240 PSF	1/180 PSF	1/240 PSF
3 IN. NOMINAL	8	—	—	—	—	71	54	121	91	77	58	127(F)	98	89	67	151	113	107	80	181	136
	9	80	60	136	101	50	38	85	64	54	41	92	69	63	47	106	80	75	56	127	96
	10	59	44	99	74	37	27	62	46	40	30	67	50	46	34	77	58	55	41	93	70
	11	44	32	74	56	27	21	47	35	30	22	50	38	34	26	58	44	41	31	70	52
	12	33	25	57	42	21	16	36	27	23	17	39	29	26	20	45	34	32	24	54	40
	13	26	20	45	33	17	12	28	21	18	14	31	23	21	16	35	26	25	19	42	32
3 IN. STX	10	125	94	212	159	83	63	141	106	90	68	144(F)	115	104	78	168(F)	132	125	94	212	159
	11	94	70	159	119	63	47	106	79	68	51	115	86	78	59	132(F)	99	94	70	159	119
	12	72	54	122	92	48	36	82	61	52	39	88	66	60	45	102	77	72	54	122	92
	13	57	43	96	72	38	28	64	48	41	31	70	52	47	36	80	60	57	43	96	72
	14	46	34	77	58	30	23	51	39	33	25	56	42	38	28	64	48	46	34	77	58
	15	37	28	63	47	25	19	42	31	27	20	45	34	31	23	52	39	37	28	63	47
	16	31	23	52	39	20	15	34	26	22	17	37	28	25	19	43	32	31	23	52	39
	17	25	19	43	32	17	13	29	22	18	14	31	23	21	16	36	27	25	19	43	32
5 IN. NOMINAL	15	89	66	150	113	51	38	86	64	55	41	93	70	63	47	107	80				
	16	73	55	124	93	42	31	71	53	45	34	76	57	52	39	88	66				
	17	61	46	103	77	35	26	59	44	38	28	64	48	43	33	74	55				
	18	51	38	87	65	29	22	50	37	32	24	54	40	37	27	62	46				
	19	44	33	74	55	25	19	42	32	27	20	46	34	31	23	53	40				
	20	37	28	63	47	21	16	36	27	23	17	39	29	27	20	45	34				
	21	32	24	55	41	18	14	31	23	20	15	34	25	23	17	39	29				

SPAN TABLE NOTES

1. Values followed by (f) are governed by stress. Allowable loads for floors when governed by deflection are half of those listed in the 1/180 columns.
2. Span loads shown assume compliance to layup rules. Longer spans may require specific lengths differing from the standard shipment.
3. Custom Grade 3 in. and 5 in. Southern Pine deflection values are 83% of the E1.8 values shown. 3 in. STX Southern Pine values are equal to E1.5 Idaho White Pine values except when bending governs.
4. E = Modulus of elasticity psi.
5. Information derived from data supplied by the Potlatch Corporation.

Timothy B. McDonald; Washington, D.C.

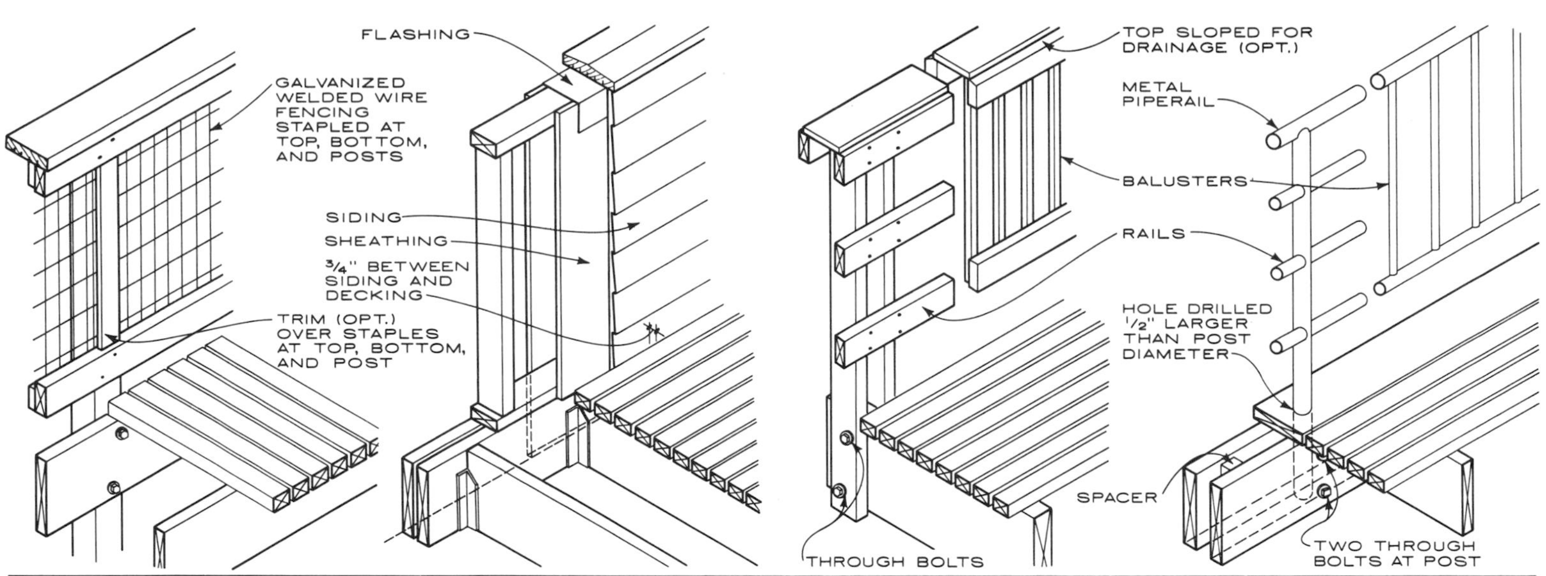

FLASHING
GALVANIZED WELDED WIRE FENCING STAPLED AT TOP, BOTTOM, AND POSTS
SIDING
SHEATHING
3/4" BETWEEN SIDING AND DECKING
TRIM (OPT.) OVER STAPLES AT TOP, BOTTOM, AND POST
TOP SLOPED FOR DRAINAGE (OPT.)
METAL PIPERAIL
BALUSTERS
RAILS
HOLE DRILLED 1/2" LARGER THAN POST DIAMETER
SPACER
THROUGH BOLTS
TWO THROUGH BOLTS AT POST

RAILINGS

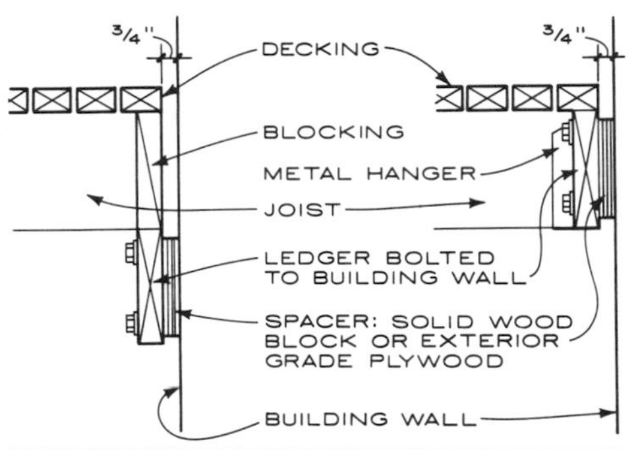

3/4"
DECKING
3/4"
BLOCKING
METAL HANGER
JOIST
LEDGER BOLTED TO BUILDING WALL
SPACER: SOLID WOOD BLOCK OR EXTERIOR GRADE PLYWOOD
BUILDING WALL

CONNECTIONS AT BUILDING WALL

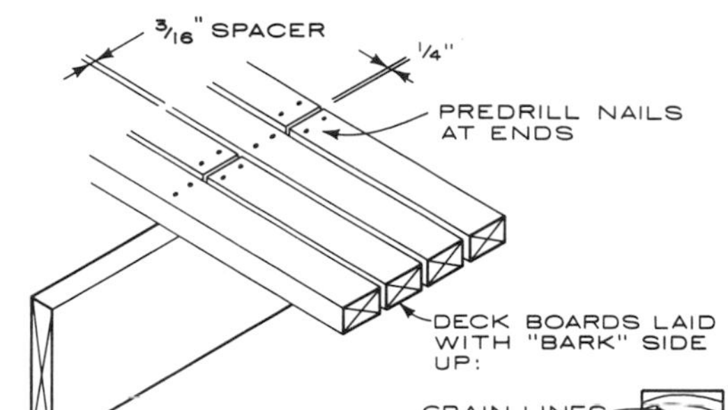

3/16" SPACER
1/4"
PREDRILL NAILS AT ENDS
DECK BOARDS LAID WITH "BARK" SIDE UP:
GRAIN LINES

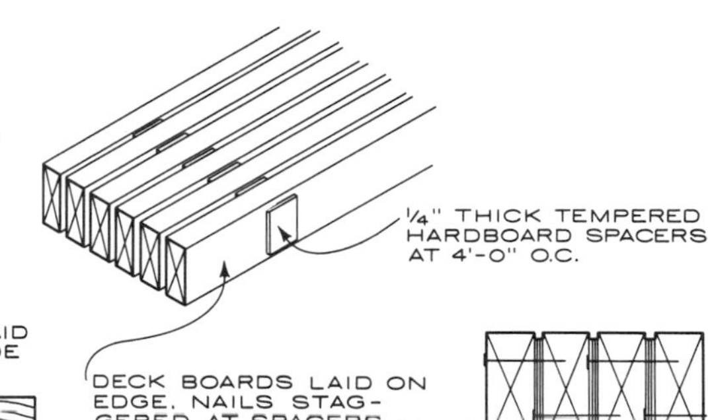

1/4" THICK TEMPERED HARDBOARD SPACERS AT 4'-0" O.C.
DECK BOARDS LAID ON EDGE, NAILS STAGGERED AT SPACERS

DECKING APPLICATIONS

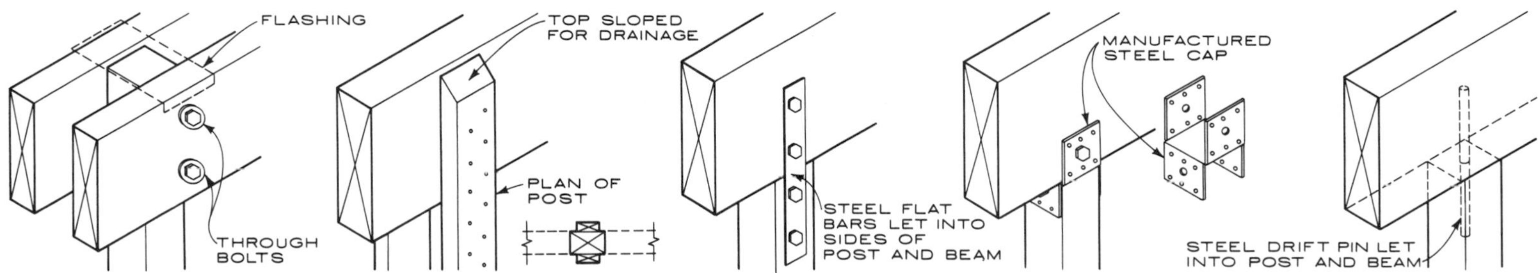

FLASHING
THROUGH BOLTS
TOP SLOPED FOR DRAINAGE
PLAN OF POST
STEEL FLAT BARS LET INTO SIDES OF POST AND BEAM
MANUFACTURED STEEL CAP
STEEL DRIFT PIN LET INTO POST AND BEAM

POST AND BEAM CONNECTIONS

RELATIVE COMPARISON OF VARIOUS QUALITIES OF WOOD USED IN DECK CONSTRUCTION

	DOUGLAS FIR—LARCH	SOUTHERN PINE	HEMLOCK FIR*	SOFT PINES†	WESTERN RED CEDAR	REDWOOD	SPRUCE	CYPRESS
Hardness	Fair	Fair	Poor	Poor	Poor	Fair	Poor	Fair
Warp resistance	Fair	Fair	Fair	Good	Good	Good	Fair	Fair
Ease of working	Poor	Fair	Fair	Good	Good	Fair	Fair	Fair
Paint holding	Poor	Poor	Poor	Good	Good	Good	Fair	Good
Stain acceptance‡	Fair	Fair	Fair	Fair	Good	Good	Fair	Fair
Nail holding	Good	Good	Poor	Poor	Poor	Fair	Fair	Fair
Heartwood decay resistance	Fair	Fair	Poor	Poor	Good	Good	Poor	Good
Proportion of heartwood	Good	Poor	Poor	Fair	Good	Good	Poor	Good
Bending strength	Good	Good	Fair	Poor	Poor	Fair	Fair	Fair
Stiffness	Good	Good	Good	Poor	Poor	Fair	Fair	Fair
Strength as a post	Good	Good	Fair	Poor	Fair	Good	Fair	Fair
Freedom from pitch	Fair	Poor	Good	Fair	Good	Good	Good	Good

*Includes West Coast and eastern hemlocks.
†Includes western and northeastern pines.
‡Categories refer to semitransparent oil base stain.

MAXIMUM SPAN OF DECK BOARDS

	FLAT		ON EDGE	
	1 x 4	2 x 2 (x3) (x4)	2 x 3	2 x 4
Douglas fir, larch, and southern pine	1'-4"	5'-0"	7'-6"	12'-0"
Hemlock-fir, Douglas-fir, southern	1'-2"	4'-0"	6'-6"	10'-0"
Western pines and cedars, redwoods, spruce	1'-0"	3'-6"	5'-6"	9'-0"

NOTES

Size and spacing of joists, posts, and beams may be selected according to other pages in chapter.

The Bumgardner Partnership/Architects; Seattle, Washington

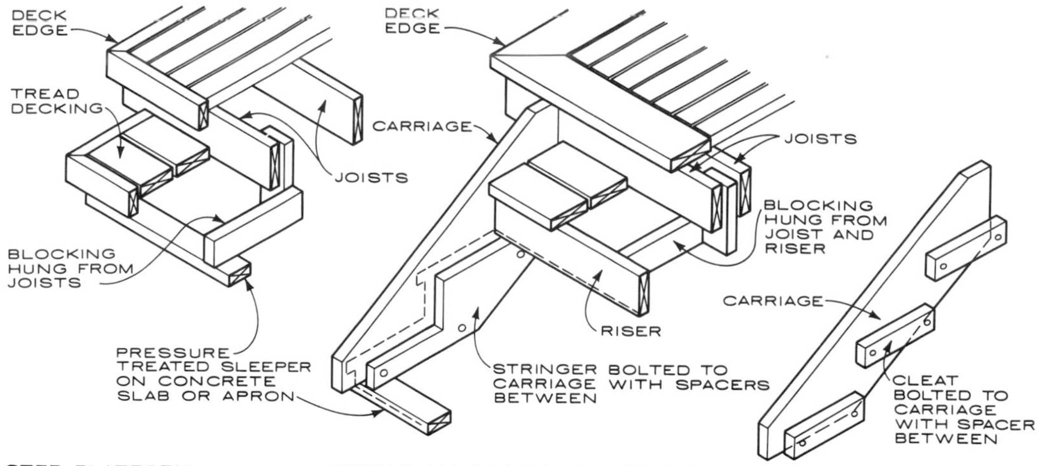

DECK EDGE
TREAD DECKING
JOISTS
BLOCKING HUNG FROM JOISTS
PRESSURE TREATED SLEEPER ON CONCRETE SLAB OR APRON

STEP PLATFORM

DECK EDGE
CARRIAGE
JOISTS
BLOCKING HUNG FROM JOIST AND RISER
RISER
STRINGER BOLTED TO CARRIAGE WITH SPACERS BETWEEN

STAIR CARRIAGE WITH STRINGER

CARRIAGE
CLEAT BOLTED TO CARRIAGE WITH SPACER BETWEEN

CARRIAGE WITH CLEATS

STEPS AND STAIRS

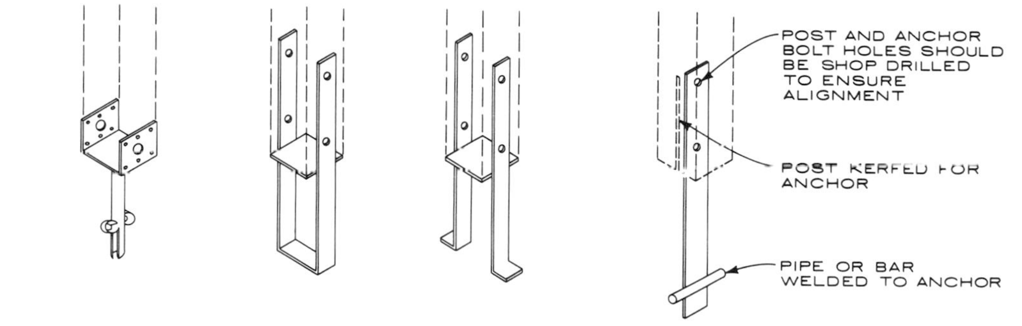

POST AND ANCHOR BOLT HOLES SHOULD BE SHOP DRILLED TO ENSURE ALIGNMENT
POST KERFED FOR ANCHOR
PIPE OR BAR WELDED TO ANCHOR

STANDARD MANUFACTURED

SHOP FABRICATED

STEEL POST ANCHORS

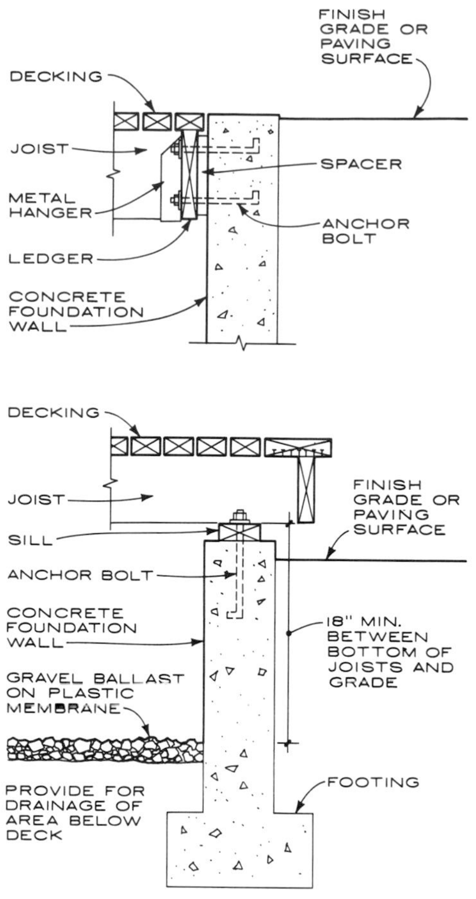

FINISH GRADE OR PAVING SURFACE
DECKING
JOIST
SPACER
METAL HANGER
ANCHOR BOLT
LEDGER
CONCRETE FOUNDATION WALL

DECKING
JOIST
FINISH GRADE OR PAVING SURFACE
SILL
ANCHOR BOLT
CONCRETE FOUNDATION WALL
18" MIN. BETWEEN BOTTOM OF JOISTS AND GRADE
GRAVEL BALLAST ON PLASTIC MEMBRANE
FOOTING
PROVIDE FOR DRAINAGE OF AREA BELOW DECK

LOW DECK EDGES

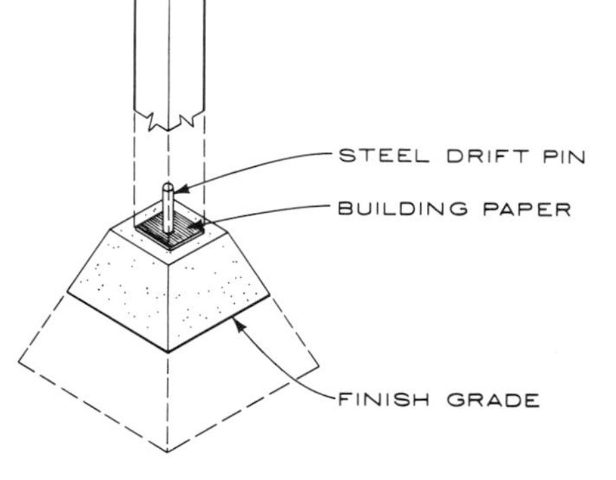
STEEL DRIFT PIN
BUILDING PAPER
FINISH GRADE

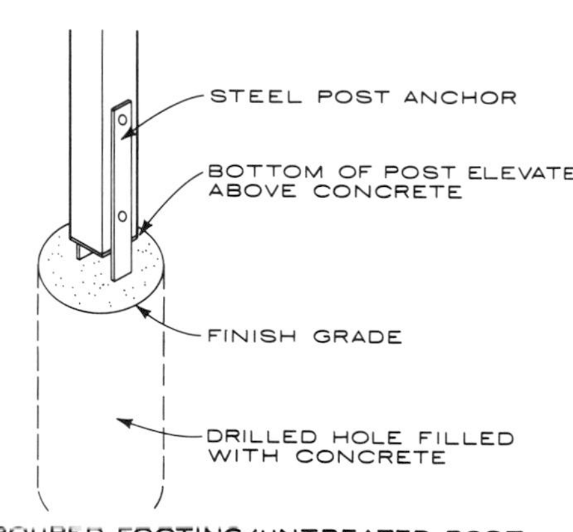
STEEL POST ANCHOR
BOTTOM OF POST ELEVATED ABOVE CONCRETE
FINISH GRADE
DRILLED HOLE FILLED WITH CONCRETE

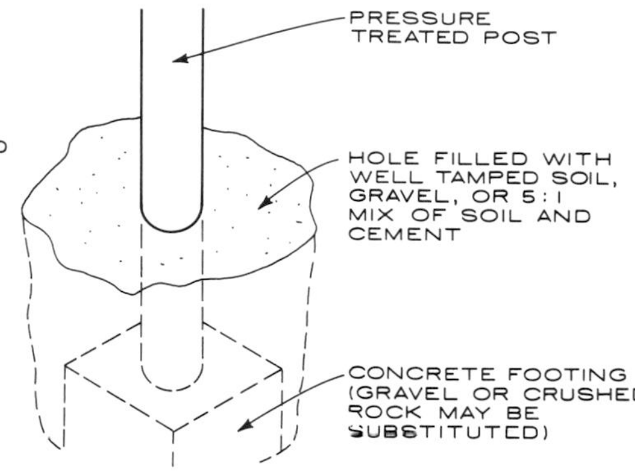
PRESSURE TREATED POST
HOLE FILLED WITH WELL TAMPED SOIL, GRAVEL, OR 5:1 MIX OF SOIL AND CEMENT
CONCRETE FOOTING (GRAVEL OR CRUSHED ROCK MAY BE SUBSTITUTED)

PRECAST CONCRETE PLINTH/UNTREATED POST

POURED FOOTING/UNTREATED POST

POURED OR PRECAST FOOTING/TREATED POST

POSTS AND FOOTINGS

FASTENERS

1. Smooth shank nails lose holding strength after repeated wet/dry cycles. Ring or spiral grooved shank nails are preferable.
2. Use galvanized or plated fasteners to avoid corrosion and staining.
3. To reduce board splitting by nailing: blunt nail points; predrill ($^3/_4$ of nail diameter); stagger nailing; place nails no closer to edge than one half of board thickness.
4. Avoid end grain nailing and toenailing if possible.
5. Use flat washers under heads of lag screws and bolts, and under nuts.

MOISTURE PROTECTION

1. All wood members should be protected from weather by pressure treatment or field application of preservatives, stains, or paints.
2. All wood in direct contact with soil must be pressure treated.
3. Bottoms of posts on piers should be 6 in. above grade.
4. Sterilize or cover soil with membrane to keep plant growth away from wood members so as to minimize moisture exchange.
5. Treat all ends, cuts, holes, and so on with preservative prior to placement.
6. Decking and flat trim boards, 2 x 6 and wider, should be kerfed on the underside with $^3/_4$ in. deep saw cuts at 1 in. on center to prevent cupping.
7. Avoid horizontal exposure of endgrain or provide adequate protection by flashing or sealing. Avoid or minimize joint situations where moisture may be trapped by using spacers and/or flashing, caulking, sealant, plastic roofing cement.

CONSTRUCTION

1. WOOD SELECTION: Usual requirements are good decay resistance, nonsplintering, fair stiffness, strength, hardness, and warp resistance. Selection varies according to local climate and exposure.
2. BRACING: On large decks, or decks where post heights exceed 5 ft, lateral stability should be achieved with horizontal bracing (metal or wood diagonal ties on top or bottom of joists, or diagonal application of decking) in combination with vertical bracing (rigid bolted or gusseted connections at top of posts, knee bracing, or "X" bracing between posts), and/or connection to a braced building wall. Lateral stability should be checked by a structural engineer.

The Bumgardner Partnership/Architects; Seattle, Washington

CEILING JOISTS—10 LB/SQ FT LIVE LOAD (GYPSUM WALLBOARD CEILING)

No attic storage and roof slope not steeper than 3 IN 12.

MAXIMUM ALLOWABLE LENGTHS L BETWEEN SUPPORTS

JOIST SIZE (NOMINAL) (IN.)	JOIST SPACING (NOMINAL) (IN.)	SPAN L LIMITED BY DEFLECTION AND F_b IS EXTREME FIBER STRESS				
		E =	1,000,000	1,200,000	1,400,000	1,600,000
2 x 4	12	L =	10-7	11-3	11-10	12-5
		F_b =	830	930	1030	1130
	16	L =	9-8	10-3	10-9	11-3
		F_b =	910	1030	1140	1240
	24	L =	8-5	8-11	9-5	9-10
		F_b =	1040	1170	1300	1420
2 x 6	12	L =	16-8	17-8	18-8	19-6
		F_b =	830	930	1030	1130
	16	L =	15-2	16-1	16-11	17-8
		F_b =	910	1030	1140	1240
	24	L =	13-3	14-1	14-9	15-6
		F_b =	1040	1170	1300	1420
2 x 8	12	L =	21-11	23-4	24-7	25-8
		F_b =	830	930	1030	1130
	16	L =	19-11	21-2	22-4	23-4
		F_b =	910	1030	1140	1240
	24	L =	17-5	18-6	19-6	20-5
		F_b =	1040	1170	1300	1420
2 x 10	12	L =	28-0	29-9	31-4	32-9
		F_b =	830	930	1030	1130
	16	L =	25-5	27-1	28-6	29-9
		F_b =	910	1030	1140	1240
	24	L =	22-3	23-8	24-10	26-0
		F_b =	1040	1170	1300	1420

NOTE: L in feet and inches; E and F_b in pounds per square inch as shown above.

DESIGN CRITERIA

1. Maximum allowable deflection = 1/240 of span length.
2. Live load of 10 lb/sq ft plus dead load of 5 lb/sq ft determine required fiber stress value.

CEILING JOISTS—20 LB/SQ FT LIVE LOAD (GYPSUM WALLBOARD CEILING)

Limited attic storage where development of future rooms is not possible.

MAXIMUM ALLOWABLE LENGTHS L BETWEEN SUPPORTS

JOIST SIZE (NOMINAL) (IN.)	JOIST SPACING (NOMINAL) (IN.)	SPAN L LIMITED BY DEFLECTION AND F_b IS EXTREME FIBER STRESS				
		E =	1,000,000	1,200,000	1,400,000	1,600,000
2 x 4	12	L =	8-5	8-11	9-5	9-10
		F_b =	1040	1170	1300	1420
	16	L =	7-8	8-1	8-7	8-11
		F_b =	1140	1290	1430	1570
	24	L =	6-8	7-1	7-6	7-10
		F_b =	1310	1480	1640	1790
2 x 6	12	L =	13-3	14-1	14-9	15-6
		F_b =	1040	1170	1300	1420
	16	L =	12-0	12-9	13-5	14-1
		F_b =	1140	1290	1430	1570
	24	L =	10-6	11-2	11-9	12-3
		F_b =	1310	1480	1640	1790
2 x 8	12	L =	17-5	18-6	19-6	20-5
		F_b =	1040	1170	1300	1420
	16	L =	15-10	16-10	17-9	18-6
		F_b =	1140	1290	1430	1570
	24	L =	13-10	14-8	15-6	16-2
		F_b =	1310	1480	1640	1790
2 x 10	12	L =	22-3	23-8	24-10	26-0
		F_b =	1040	1170	1300	1420
	16	L =	20-2	21-6	22-7	23-8
		F_b =	1140	1290	1430	1570
	24	L =	17-8	18-9	19-9	20-8
		F_b =	1310	1480	1640	1790

NOTE: L in feet and inches; E and F_b in pounds per square inch as shown above.

DESIGN CRITERIA

1. Maximum allowable deflection = 1/240 of span length.
2. Live load of 20 lb/sq ft plus dead load of 10 lb/sq ft determine required fiber stress value.

NOTE

For rafters, design values in F_b may be greater than the design values for normal duration of load, by the following amounts:

15% for 2 months' duration, as for snow.
25% for 7 days' duration, as for construction loading.

SPAN OF RAFTER
SPAN OF RAFTER

GAMBREL ROOF

COLLAR BEAM WITHIN THE UPPER 1/3
SPAN OF RAFTER
1/3
2/3

GABLE ROOF (SLOPE OVER 3 IN 12)

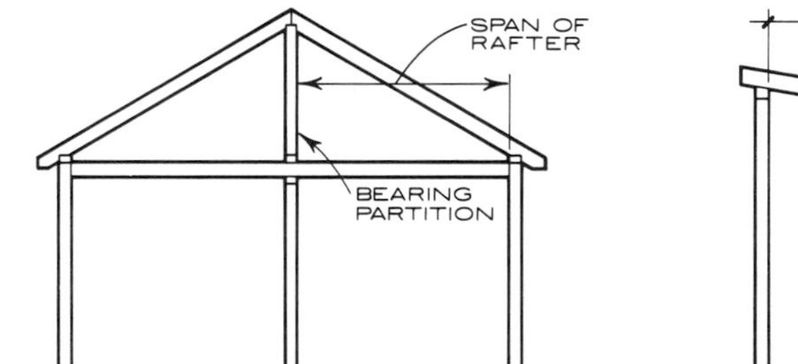
SPAN OF RAFTER
BEARING PARTITION

GABLE ROOF (SLOPE UNDER 3 IN 12)

SPAN OF RAFTER

LEAN-TO OR SHED ROOF

NOTE

(Applicable to this and the following pages on joist and rafter sizes.)

SPANS LIMITED BY DEFLECTION: Computed for the assumed loads to cause a deflection not exceeding 1/360 of the span. The weight of plaster itself was ignored in the assumed loads for the deflection computations, because the initial deflection from the dead load occurs before plaster sets. The influence of live loads, rather than dead loads, when the ratio of live to dead loads is relatively high, is the principal factor to be considered. Also with joisted floors, flooring and bridging serve to distribute moving or concentrated loads to adjoining members. The omission of the plaster weight in load assumption applies to deflection computations only; the full dead and live load is considered when computing for strength.

SPANS LIMITED BY BENDING STRENGTH OF PIECE: May be used where ceilings are not plastered and deflection is not objectionable.

E = modulus of elasticity
F_b = extreme fiber stress in bending
L = span length between supports

LIVE LOAD ASSUMPTIONS: Uniformly distributed.

PARTITIONS: Spans shown are computed for the given live load plus the dead load and do not provide for additional loads such as partitions. Where concentrated loads are imposed the spans should be recomputed to provide for them.

SECTION MODULUS

LUMBER SIZES (NOMINAL)	S (INCHES³)
2 x 3	1.56
2 x 4	3.06
2 x 6	7.56
2 x 8	13.41
2 x 10	21.39
2 x 12	31.64
3 x 6	12.60
3 x 8	21.90
3 x 10	35.65
3 x 12	52.73
3 x 14	73.15
4 x 4	7.15
4 x 6	17.65
4 x 8	30.66
4 x 10	49.91
4 x 12	73.82

SECTION MODULUS

$S = \frac{bd^2}{6}$

(INCHES³)

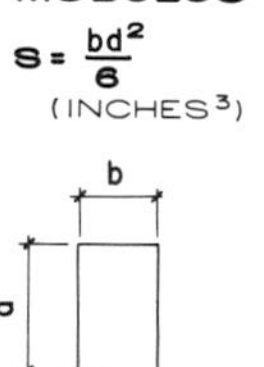
b
d

b AND d ARE ACTUAL DIMENSIONS

National Forest Products Association; Washington, D.C.

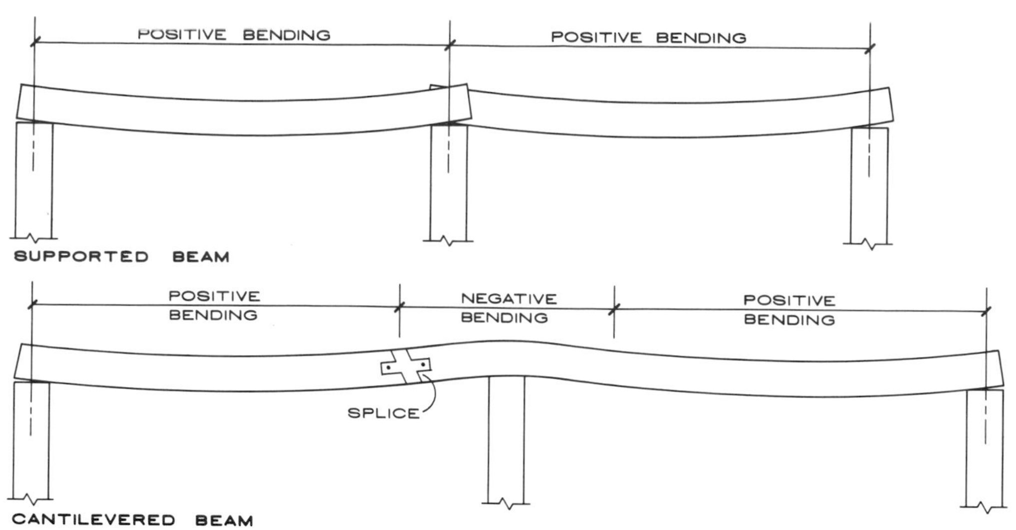
POSITIVE BENDING
POSITIVE BENDING
SUPPORTED BEAM
POSITIVE BENDING
NEGATIVE BENDING
POSITIVE BENDING
SPLICE
CANTILEVERED BEAM

SIMPLE FRAMING: This illustration shows the "positive" or downward bending that occurs in conventional framing with simple spans.

CANTILEVERED FRAMING: This illustration shows the combination of "positive" (downward) and "negative" (upward) bending that occurs with beams spliced at quarterpoint producing supported beam and cantilevered beam. The two types of bending counterbalance each other, which produces more uniform stresses and uses material more efficiently. In-line joists simplify plywood subflooring.

MOMENT SPLICE: Compression stress is taken in bearing on the wood through a steel compression plate. Tension is taken across the splice by means of steel straps and sheer plates. Side plates and straps are used to hold sides and tops of members in position. Shear is taken by shear plates in end grain. Bolts and shear plates are used as design and construction considerations require.

SIMPLE AND CANTILEVERED FRAMING

GROOVED PLANK MOLDED SPLINE

RABBETED PLANK BATTEN INSERT

GROOVED PLANK WITH SPLINE

GROOVED PLANK WITH EXPOSED SPLINE

SQUARE EDGE

TONGUE AND GROOVE

JOINT TYPES IN EXPOSED PLANK CEILINGS

DESIGN TABLE FOR NOMINAL 2 IN. PLANK

REQUIRED VALUES FOR FIBER STRESS IN BENDING (f) AND MODULUS OF ELASTICITY (E) TO SUPPORT SAFELY A LIVE LOAD OF 20, 30, OR 40 LB/SQ FT WITHIN A DEFLECTION LIMITATION OF ℓ/240, ℓ/300, OR ℓ/360.

SPAN (FT)	LIVE LOAD (PSF)	DEFLECTION LIMIT	TYPE A SINGLE SPAN f (PSI)	TYPE A E (PSI)	TYPE B DOUBLE SPAN f (PSI)	TYPE B E (PSI)	TYPE C THREE SPAN f (PSI)	TYPE C E (PSI)	TYPE D COMBINATION SINGLE AND DOUBLE SPAN f (PSI)	TYPE D E (PSI)	TYPE E RANDOM LAYUP f (PSI)	TYPE E E (PSI)
6	20	ℓ/240	360	576,000	360	239,000	288	305,000	360	408,000	360	442,000
		ℓ/300	360	720,000	360	299,000	288	381,000	360	509,000	360	553,000
		ℓ/360	360	864,000	360	359,000	288	457,000	360	611,000	360	664,000
	30	ℓ/240	480	864,000	480	359,000	384	457,000	480	611,000	480	664,000
		ℓ/300	480	1,080,000	480	448,000	384	571,000	480	764,000	480	829,000
		ℓ/360	480	1,296,000	480	538,000	384	685,000	480	917,000	480	995,000
	40	ℓ/240	600	1,152,000	600	478,000	480	609,000	600	815,000	600	886,000
		ℓ/300	600	1,440,000	600	598,000	480	762,000	600	1,019,000	600	1,106,000
		ℓ/360	600	1,728,000	600	717,000	480	914,000	600	1,223,000	600	1,327,000
7	20	ℓ/240	490	915,000	490	380,000	392	484,000	490	647,000	490	702,000
		ℓ/300	490	1,143,000	490	475,000	392	605,000	490	809,000	490	878,000
		ℓ/360	490	1,372,000	490	570,000	392	726,000	490	971,000	490	1,054,000
	30	ℓ/240	653	1,372,000	653	570,000	522	726,000	653	971,000	653	1,054,000
		ℓ/300	653	1,715,000	653	712,000	522	907,000	653	1,213,000	653	1,317,000
		ℓ/360	653	2,058,000	653	854,000	522	1,088,000	653	1,456,000	653	1,581,000
	40	ℓ/240	817	1,829,000	817	759,000	653	968,000	817	1,294,000	817	1,405,000
		ℓ/300	817	1,187,000	817	949,000	653	1,209,000	817	1,618,000	817	1,756,000
		ℓ/360	817	2,744,000	817	1,139,000	653	1,451,000	817	1,941,000	817	2,107,000
8	20	ℓ/240	640	1,365,000	640	567,000	512	722,000	640	966,000	640	1,049,000
		ℓ/300	640	1,707,000	640	708,000	512	903,000	640	1,208,000	640	1,311,000
		ℓ/360	640	2,048,000	640	850,000	512	1,083,000	640	1,449,000	640	1,573,000
	30	ℓ/240	853	2,048,000	853	850,000	682	1,083,000	853	1,449,000	853	1,573,000
		ℓ/300	853	2,560,000	853	1,063,000	682	1,345,000	853	1,811,000	853	1,966,000
		ℓ/360	853	3,072,000	853	1,275,000	682	1,625,000	853	2,174,000	853	2,359,000
	40	ℓ/240	1,067	2,731,000	1,067	1,134,000	853	1,144,000	1,067	1,932,000	1,067	2,097,000
		ℓ/300	1,067	3,413,000	1,067	1,417,000	853	1,805,000	1,067	2,145,000	1,067	2,621,000
		ℓ/360	1,067	4,096,000	1,067	1,700,000	853	2,166,000	1,067	2,898,000	1,067	3,146,000

Timothy B. McDonald; Washington, D.C.

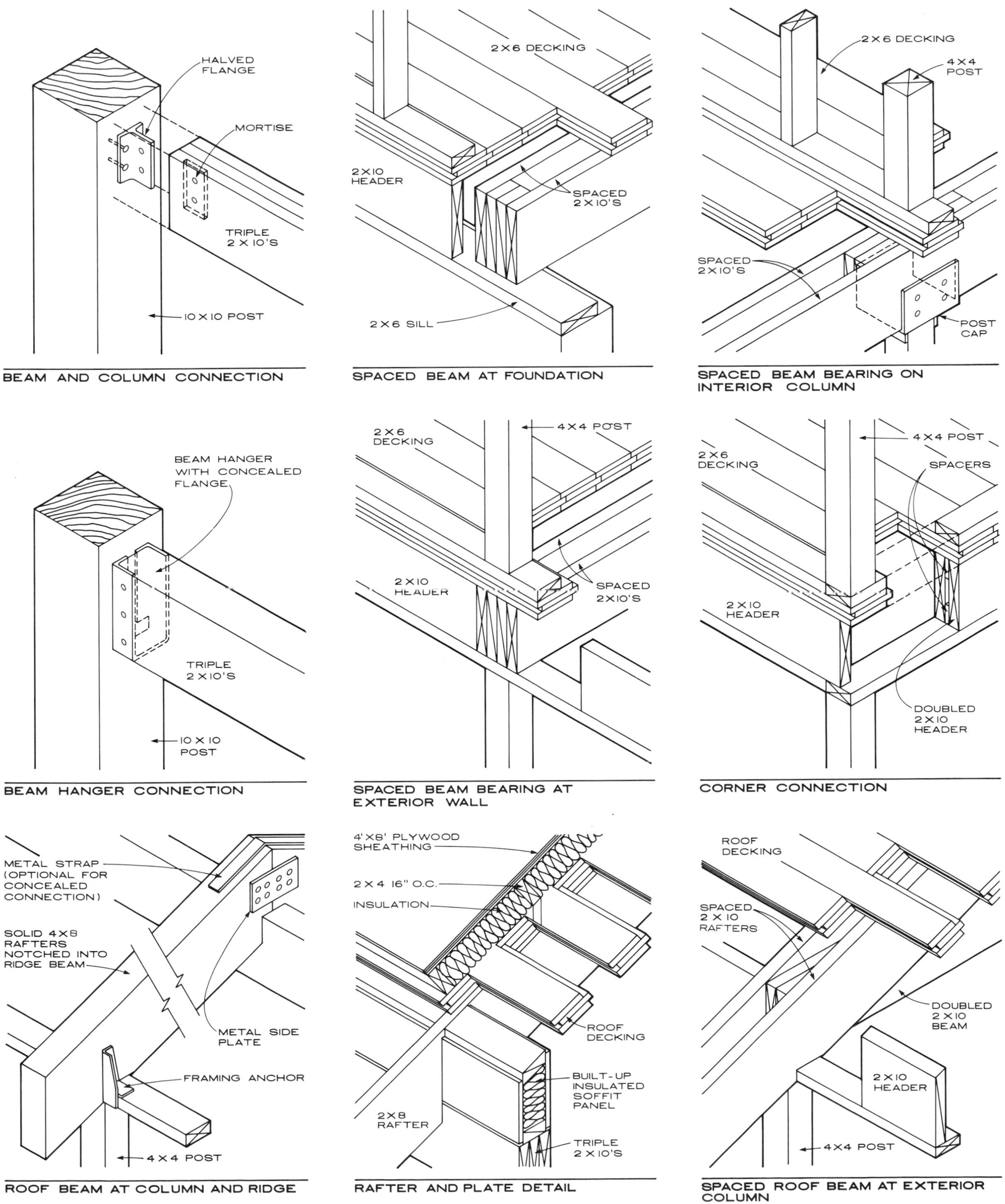
HALVED FLANGE
MORTISE
TRIPLE 2 X 10'S
10 X 10 POST
BEAM AND COLUMN CONNECTION
2 X 6 DECKING
2 X 10 HEADER
SPACED 2 X 10'S
2 X 6 SILL
SPACED BEAM AT FOUNDATION
2 X 6 DECKING
4 X 4 POST
SPACED 2 X 10'S
POST CAP
SPACED BEAM BEARING ON INTERIOR COLUMN
BEAM HANGER WITH CONCEALED FLANGE
TRIPLE 2 X 10'S
10 X 10 POST
BEAM HANGER CONNECTION
2 X 6 DECKING
4 X 4 POST
2 X 10 HEADER
SPACED 2 X 10'S
SPACED BEAM BEARING AT EXTERIOR WALL
2 X 6 DECKING
4 X 4 POST
SPACERS
2 X 10 HEADER
DOUBLED 2 X 10 HEADER
CORNER CONNECTION
METAL STRAP (OPTIONAL FOR CONCEALED CONNECTION)
SOLID 4 X 8 RAFTERS NOTCHED INTO RIDGE BEAM
METAL SIDE PLATE
FRAMING ANCHOR
4 X 4 POST
ROOF BEAM AT COLUMN AND RIDGE
4' X 8' PLYWOOD SHEATHING
2 X 4 16" O.C.
INSULATION
ROOF DECKING
BUILT-UP INSULATED SOFFIT PANEL
2 X 8 RAFTER
TRIPLE 2 X 10'S
RAFTER AND PLATE DETAIL
ROOF DECKING
SPACED 2 X 10 RAFTERS
DOUBLED 2 X 10 BEAM
2 X 10 HEADER
4 X 4 POST
SPACED ROOF BEAM AT EXTERIOR COLUMN

Timothy B. McDonald; Washington, D.C.

NOTES

1. Pole embedment depth depends on soil, slope and seismic zone.
2. Cross-bracing between poles may be required to resist lateral loads if shallow embedment. Treat all exposed surfaces with approved pressure treatment.
3. Pole notching for major beams can help align beams and walls that otherwise would be out of plumb due to pole warp. Notching improves bearing of major beams but weakens poles.
4. Roofs, walls and floors should be insulated to suit local climatic conditions. Wall and soffit insulation should meet continuously at the joint. Penetration of insulation should be minimal.
5. Various siding types can be used.
6. Dapping is a U.S. carpentry term for cutting wood to receive timber connectors.

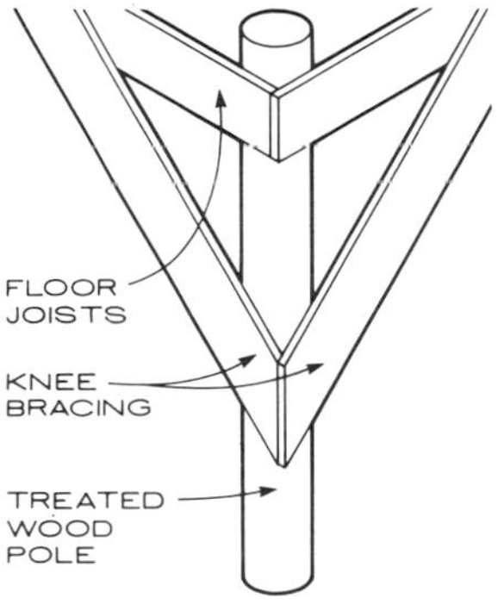

FLOOR JOISTS
KNEE BRACING
TREATED WOOD POLE

KNEE BRACING

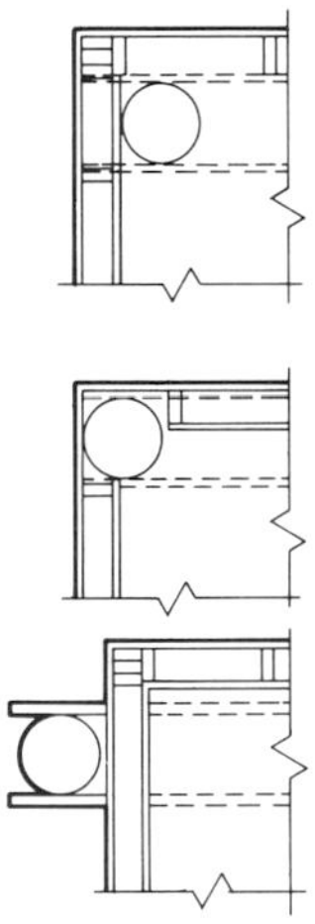

EXTERIOR WALL FRAMING OPTIONS

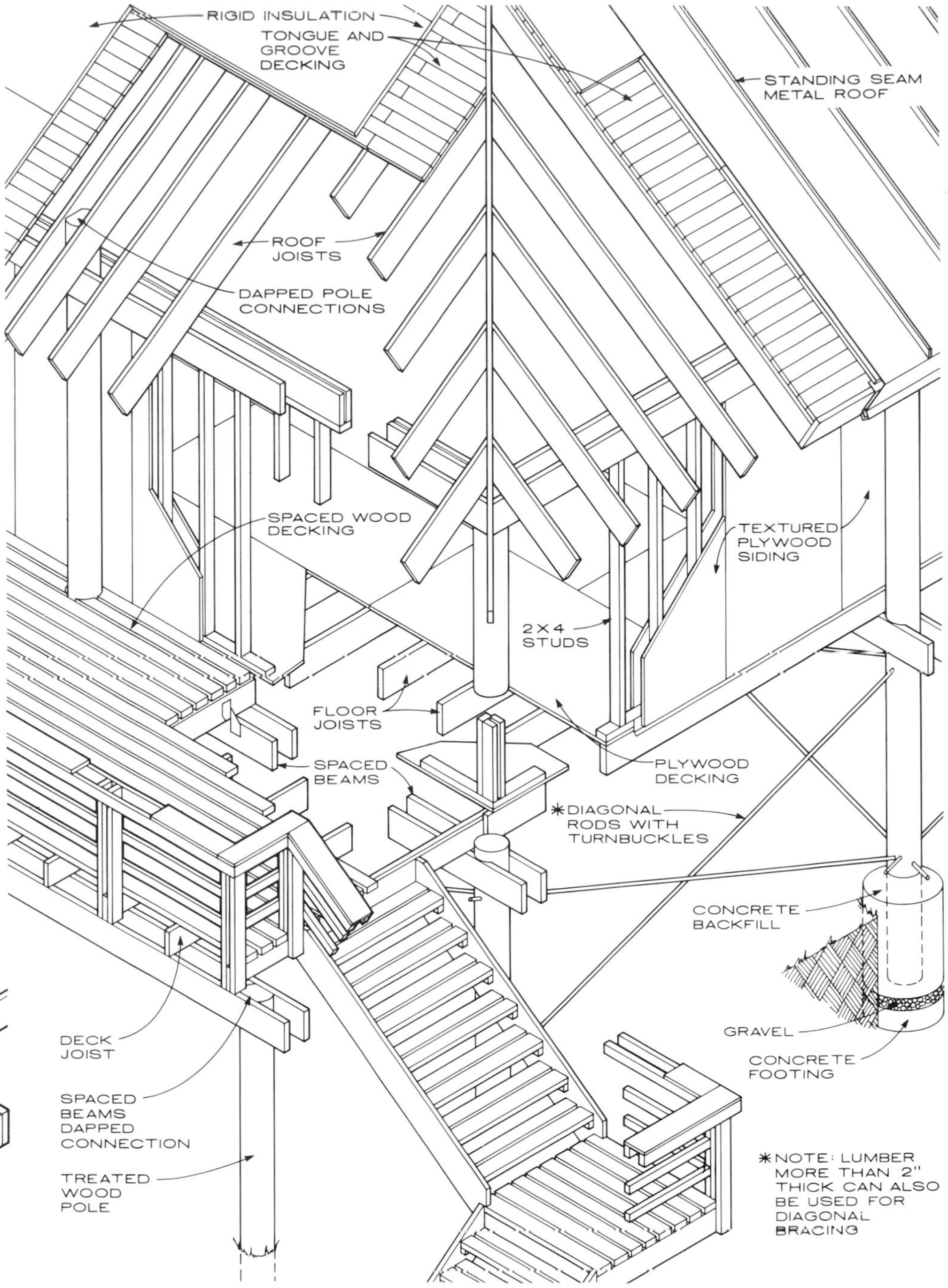

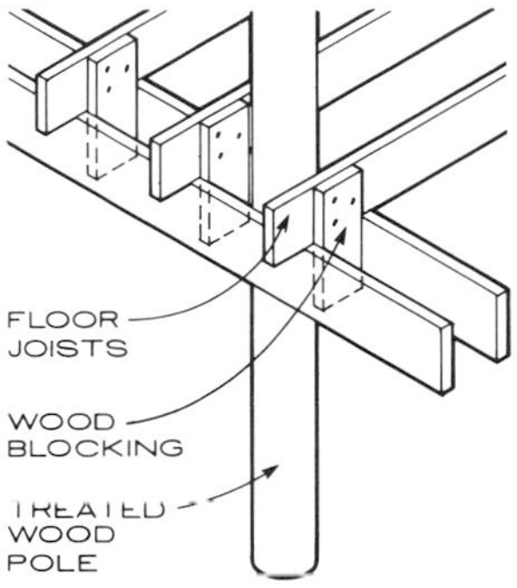

FLOOR JOISTS
WOOD BLOCKING
TREATED WOOD POLE

JOIST ANCHORS

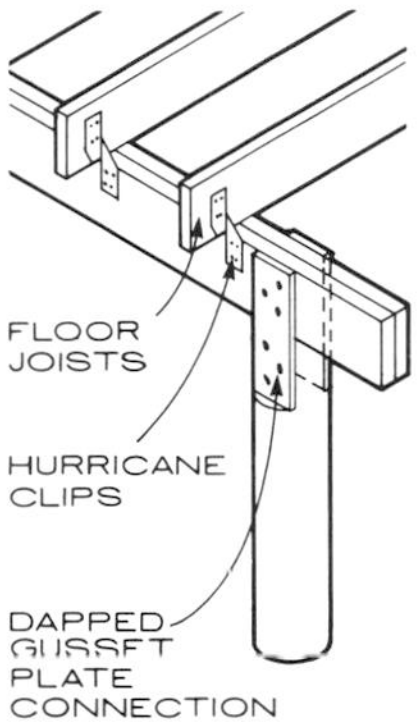

FLOOR JOISTS
HURRICANE CLIPS
DAPPED GUSSET PLATE CONNECTION

JOIST ANCHORS

RIGID INSULATION
TONGUE AND GROOVE DECKING
STANDING SEAM METAL ROOF
ROOF JOISTS
DAPPED POLE CONNECTIONS
SPACED WOOD DECKING
TEXTURED PLYWOOD SIDING
2×4 STUDS
FLOOR JOISTS
SPACED BEAMS
PLYWOOD DECKING
*DIAGONAL RODS WITH TURNBUCKLES
CONCRETE BACKFILL
GRAVEL
CONCRETE FOOTING
DECK JOIST
SPACED BEAMS DAPPED CONNECTION
TREATED WOOD POLE
*NOTE: LUMBER MORE THAN 2" THICK CAN ALSO BE USED FOR DIAGONAL BRACING

ISOMETRIC OF POLE HOUSE

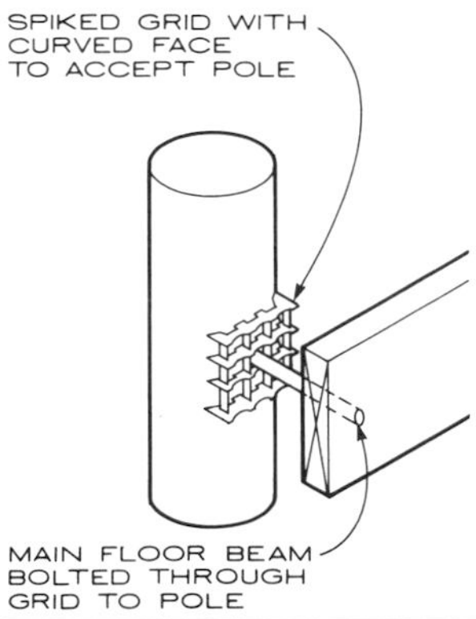

SPIKED GRID WITH CURVED FACE TO ACCEPT POLE
MAIN FLOOR BEAM BOLTED THROUGH GRID TO POLE

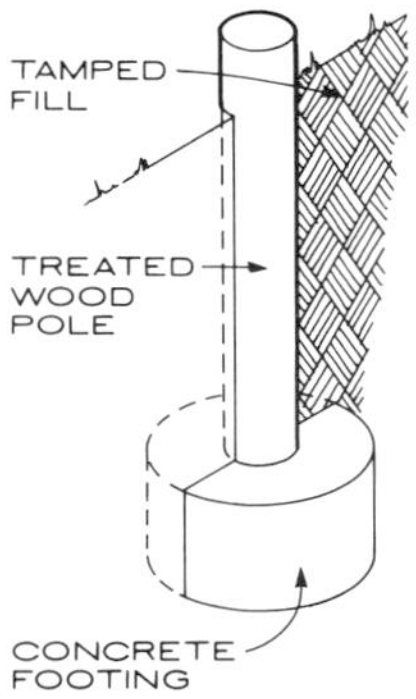

TAMPED FILL
TREATED WOOD POLE
CONCRETE FOOTING

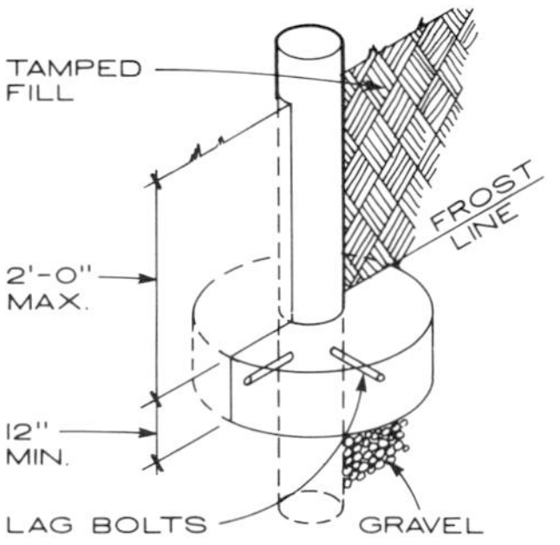

CONCRETE FOOTING

TAMPED FILL
FROST LINE
2'-0" MAX.
12" MIN.
LAG BOLTS
GRAVEL
FOR USE IN TEMPERATE CLIMATES (FROST LINE NO DEEPER THAN 2'-0")

REINFORCED CONCRETE COLLAR

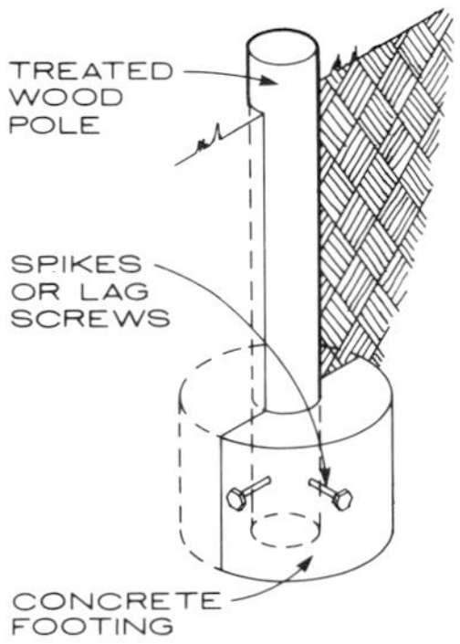

TREATED WOOD POLE
SPIKES OR LAG SCREWS
CONCRETE FOOTING

CONCRETE FOOTING WITH SPIKED ANCHORAGE

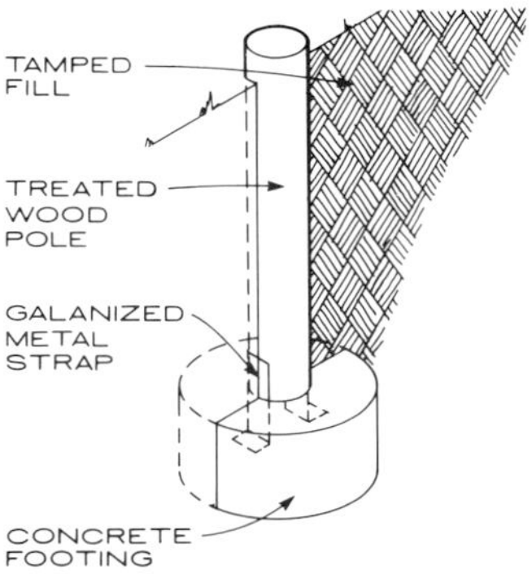

TAMPED FILL
TREATED WOOD POLE
GALANIZED METAL STRAP
CONCRETE FOOTING

CONCRETE FOOTING WITH STRAP ANCHOR

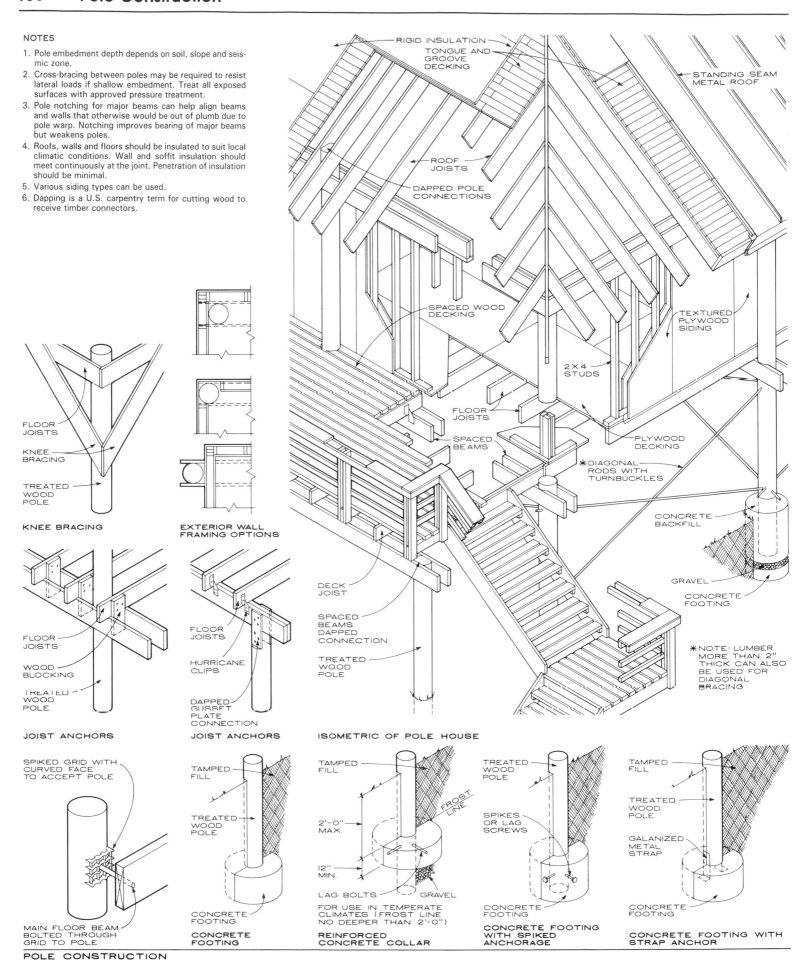

POLE CONSTRUCTION

Timothy B. McDonald; Washington, D.C.

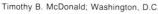

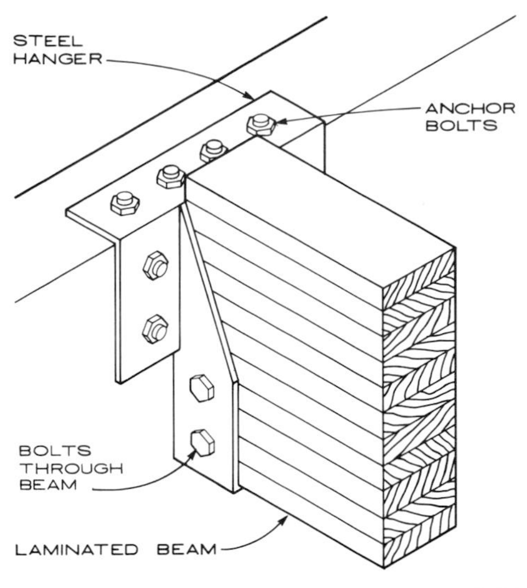
STEEL HANGER
ANCHOR BOLTS
BOLTS THROUGH BEAM
LAMINATED BEAM

BEAM HANGER

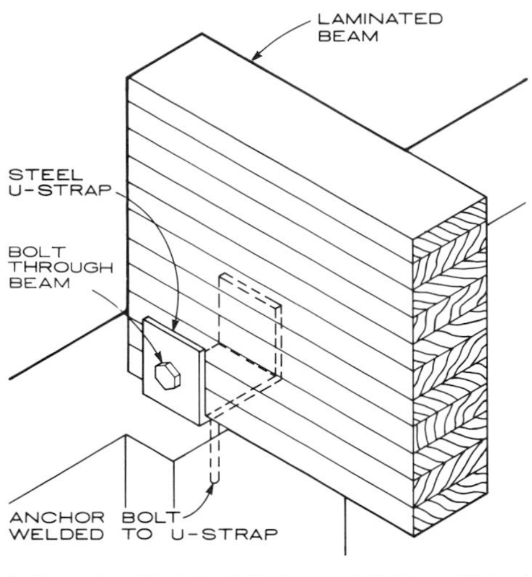
LAMINATED BEAM
STEEL U-STRAP
BOLT THROUGH BEAM
ANCHOR BOLT WELDED TO U-STRAP

BEAM ANCHOR

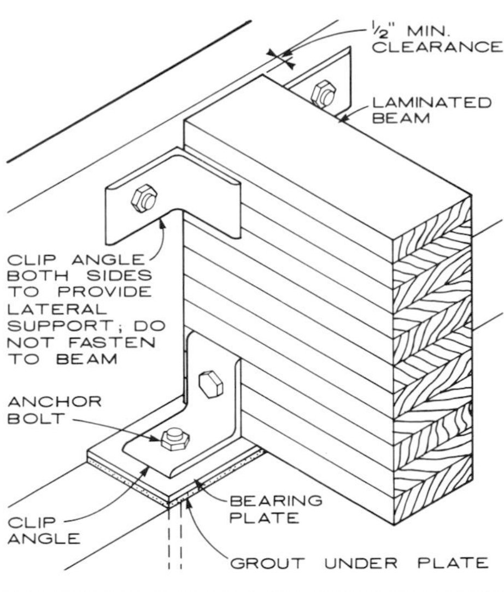
½" MIN. CLEARANCE
LAMINATED BEAM
CLIP ANGLE BOTH SIDES TO PROVIDE LATERAL SUPPORT; DO NOT FASTEN TO BEAM
ANCHOR BOLT
BEARING PLATE
CLIP ANGLE
GROUT UNDER PLATE

BEAM ANCHOR

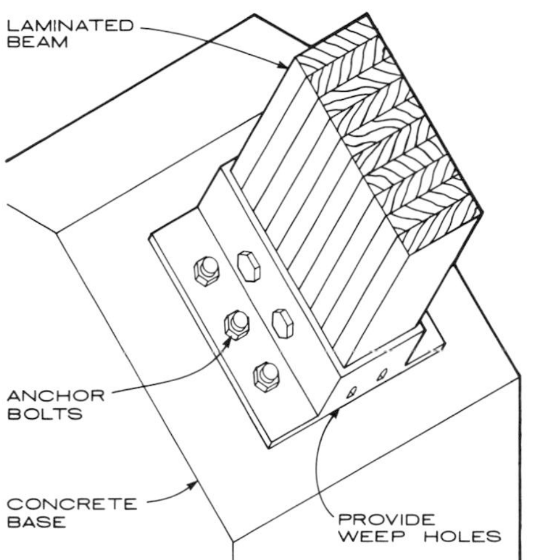
LAMINATED BEAM
ANCHOR BOLTS
CONCRETE BASE
PROVIDE WEEP HOLES

FIXED ARCH ANCHORAGE

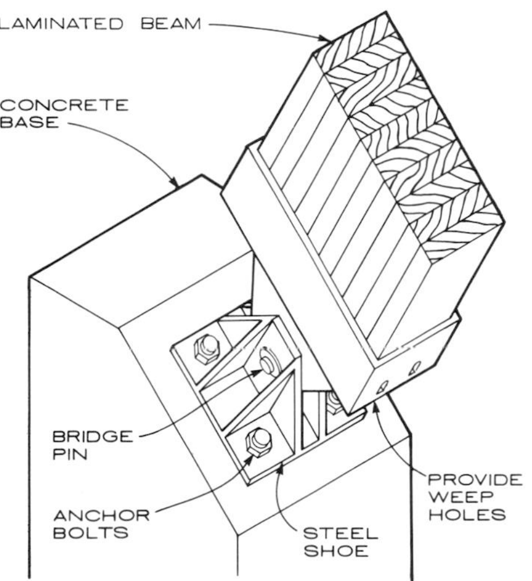
LAMINATED BEAM
CONCRETE BASE
BRIDGE PIN
ANCHOR BOLTS
STEEL SHOE
PROVIDE WEEP HOLES

TRUE HINGE ANCHORAGE FOR ARCHES

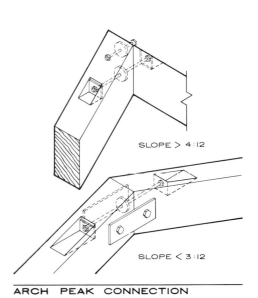

SLOPE > 4:12

SLOPE < 3:12

ARCH PEAK CONNECTION

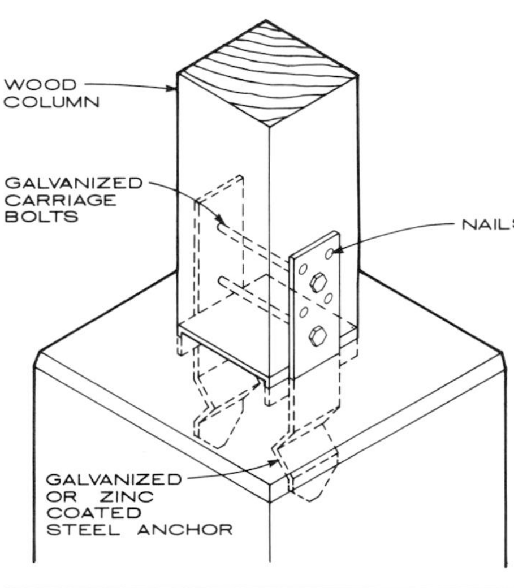
WOOD COLUMN
GALVANIZED CARRIAGE BOLTS
NAILS
GALVANIZED OR ZINC COATED STEEL ANCHOR

WET POST ANCHORAGE TO CONCRETE BASE

This detail is recommended for heavy duty use where moisture protection is desired. Anchor is set and leveled in wet concrete after screeding.

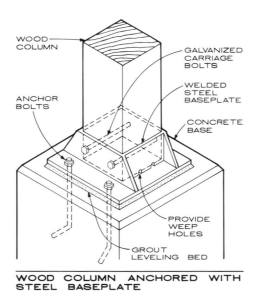

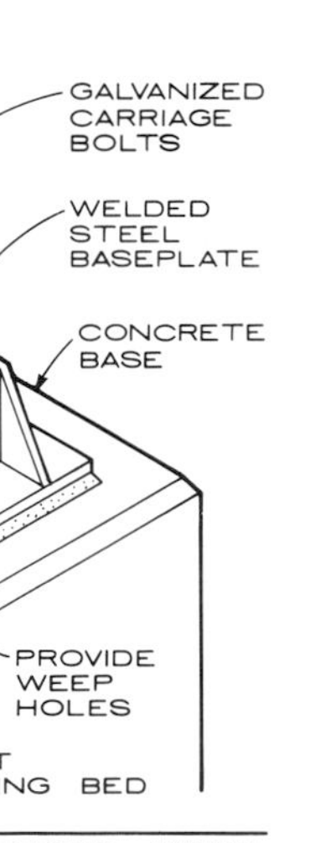
WOOD COLUMN
ANCHOR BOLTS
GALVANIZED CARRIAGE BOLTS
WELDED STEEL BASEPLATE
CONCRETE BASE
PROVIDE WEEP HOLES
GROUT LEVELING BED

WOOD COLUMN ANCHORED WITH STEEL BASEPLATE

WOOD COLUMN
BOLTS
CEMENT WASH
BEARING PLATE
STEEL U-STRAP
CONCRETE BASE

U-STRAP COLUMN ANCHORAGE TO CONCRETE BASE

This detail is recommended for industrial buildings and warehouses to resist both horizontal forces and uplift. Moisture barrier is recommended. It may be used with shear plates.

Timothy B. McDonald; Washington, D.C.

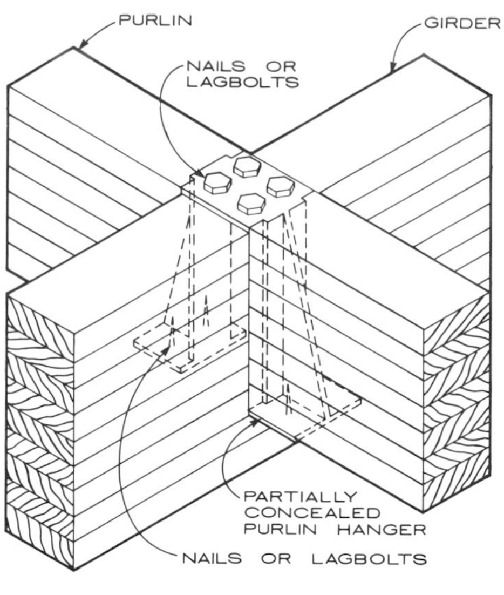

PURLIN
GIRDER
NAILS OR LAGBOLTS
PARTIALLY CONCEALED PURLIN HANGER
NAILS OR LAGBOLTS

BEAM TO PURLIN CONNECTION

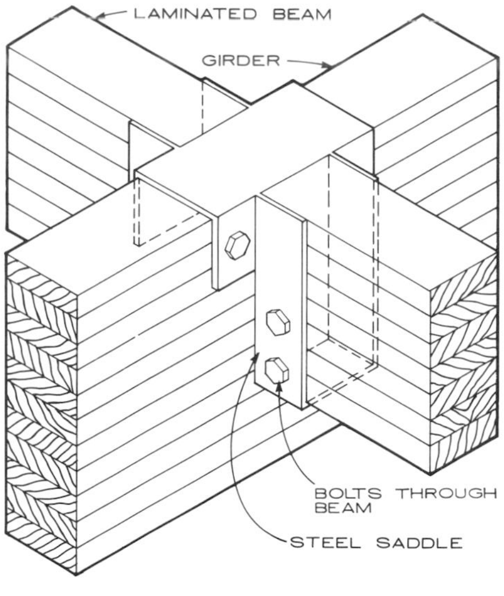

LAMINATED BEAM
GIRDER
BOLTS THROUGH BEAM
STEEL SADDLE

BEAM TO GIRDER CONNECTION

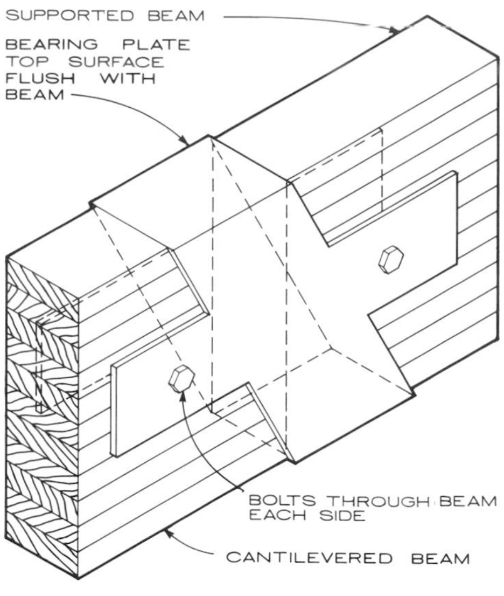

SUPPORTED BEAM
BEARING PLATE TOP SURFACE FLUSH WITH BEAM
BOLTS THROUGH BEAM EACH SIDE
CANTILEVERED BEAM

BEAM SPLICING

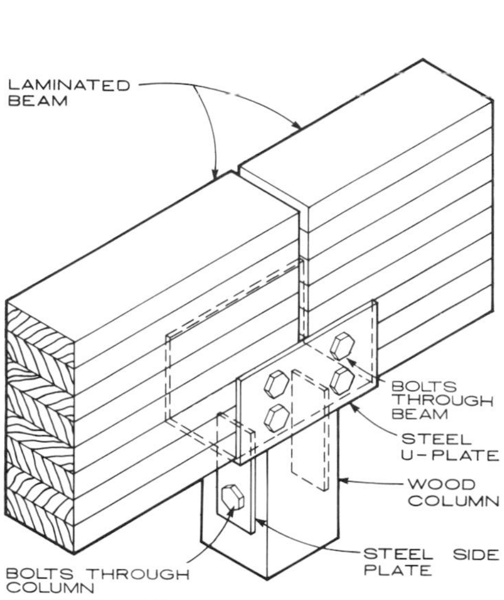

LAMINATED BEAM
BOLTS THROUGH BEAM
STEEL U-PLATE
WOOD COLUMN
STEEL SIDE PLATE
BOLTS THROUGH COLUMN

BEAM TO COLUMN CONNECTION

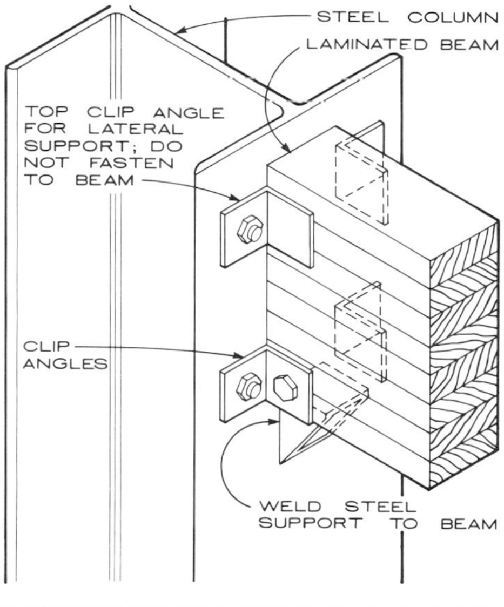

STEEL COLUMN
LAMINATED BEAM
TOP CLIP ANGLE FOR LATERAL SUPPORT; DO NOT FASTEN TO BEAM
CLIP ANGLES
WELD STEEL SUPPORT TO BEAM

BEAM TO COLUMN CONNECTION

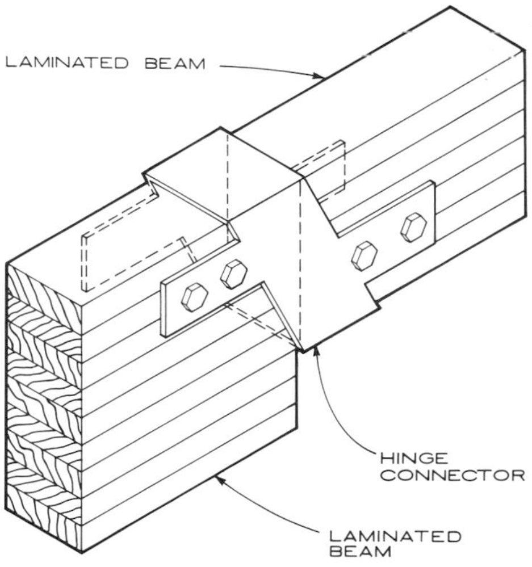

LAMINATED BEAM
HINGE CONNECTOR
LAMINATED BEAM

BEAM SPLICING

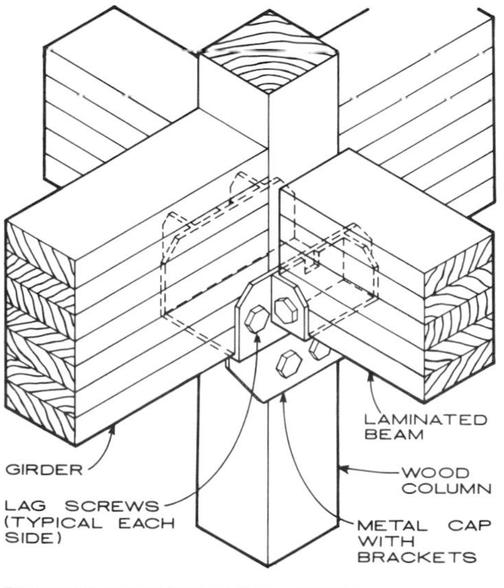

GIRDER
LAG SCREWS (TYPICAL EACH SIDE)
LAMINATED BEAM
WOOD COLUMN
METAL CAP WITH BRACKETS

METAL COLUMN CAP WITH BEAM SEATS

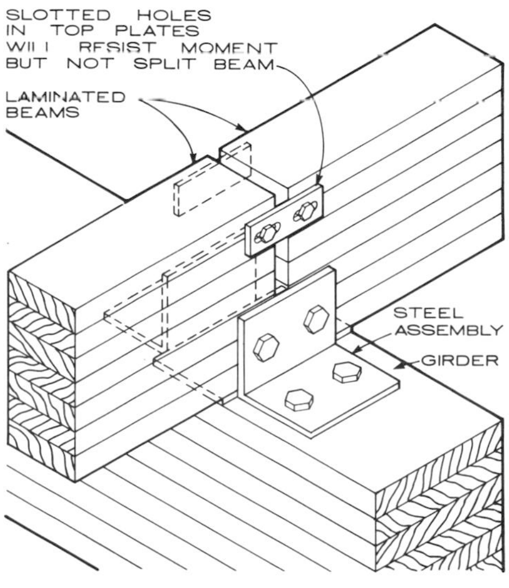

SLOTTED HOLES IN TOP PLATES WILL RESIST MOMENT BUT NOT SPLIT BEAM
LAMINATED BEAMS
STEEL ASSEMBLY
GIRDER

BEAM CONNECTION

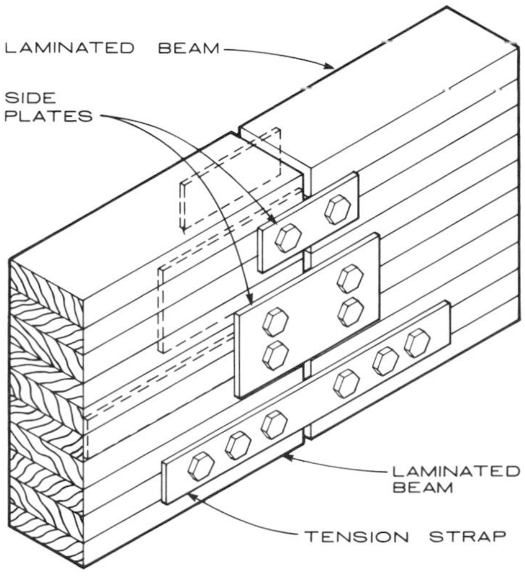

LAMINATED BEAM
SIDE PLATES
LAMINATED BEAM
TENSION STRAP

MOMENT SPLICING

Timothy B. McDonald; Washington, D.C.

NOTES

1. For light trusses (trussed rafters), average spacing is 2 ft. o.c., but varies up to 4 ft. o.c. The average combined dead and live loads is 45 lbs. per sq.ft. Spans, usually 20 ft. to 32 ft., can be up to 50 ft. in some applications.
2. Early in the design process, consult engineer or truss supplier for preengineered truss designs to establish the most economical and efficient truss proportions. Supplier may provide final truss engineering design.
3. Permanent and temporary erection bracing must be installed as specified to prevent failure of properly designed trusses.
4. Some locales require an engineer's stamp when prefab trusses are used. Check local codes.

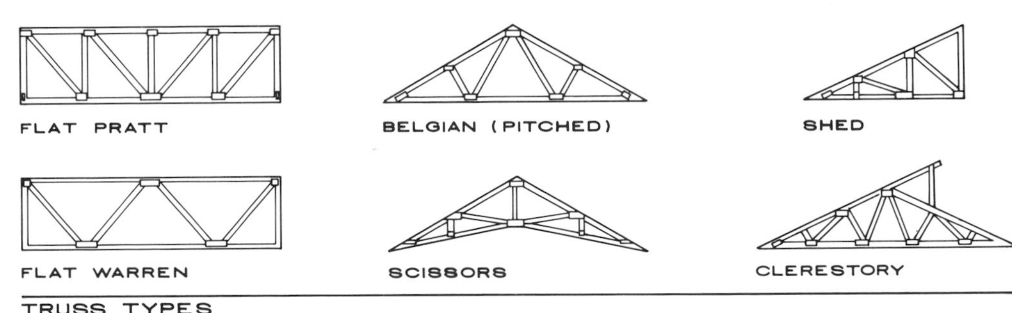
FLAT PRATT
BELGIAN (PITCHED)
SHED
FLAT WARREN
SCISSORS
CLERESTORY

TRUSS TYPES

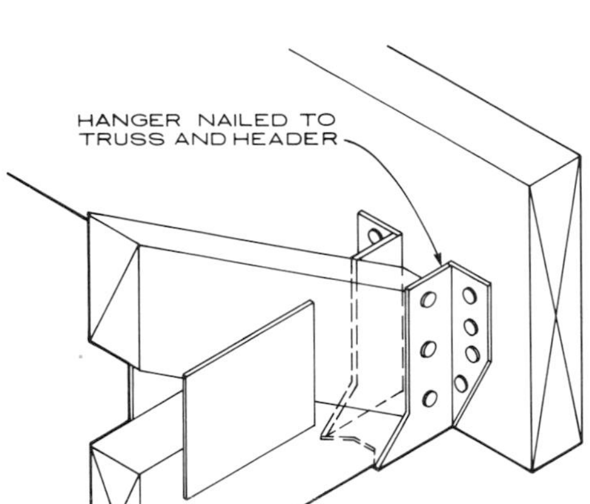
HANGER NAILED TO TRUSS AND HEADER

TRUSS HANGER (DETAIL)

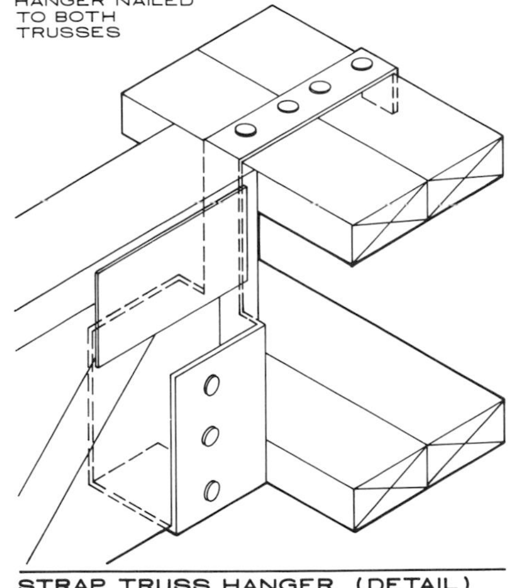
HANGER NAILED TO BOTH TRUSSES

STRAP TRUSS HANGER (DETAIL)

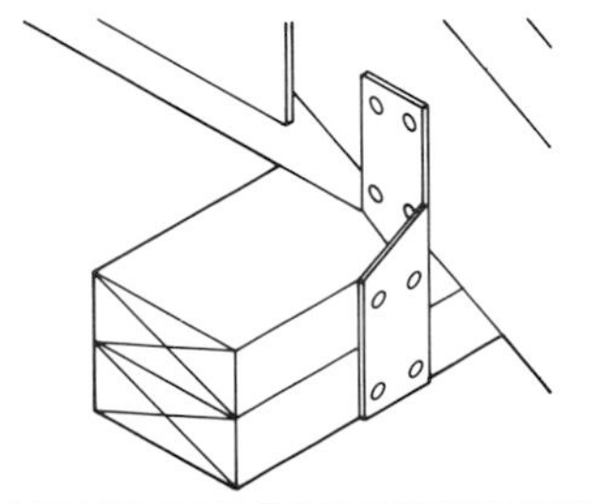

FRAMING ANCHOR (DETAIL)

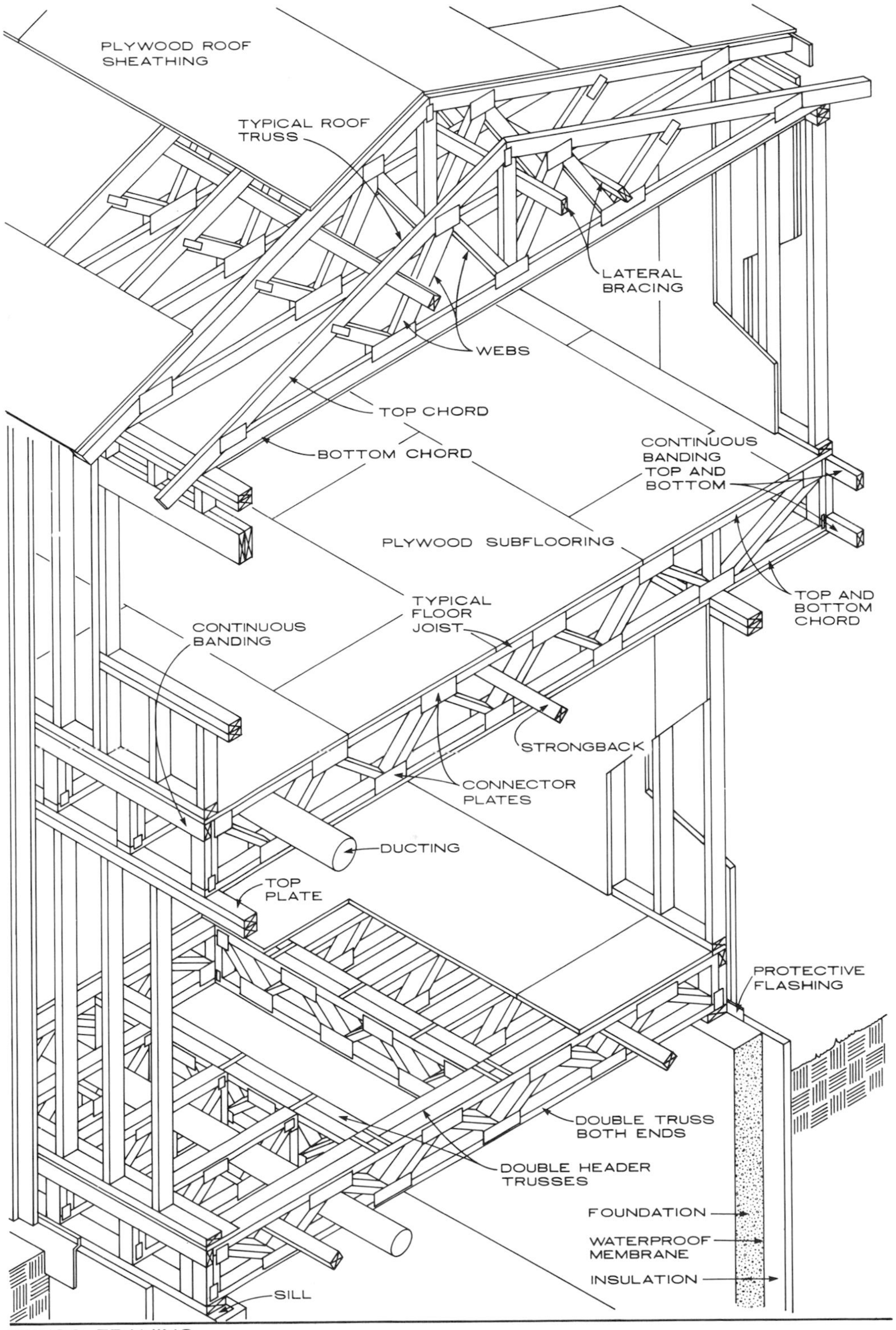

TRUSS FRAMING

Timothy B. McDonald; Washington, D.C.

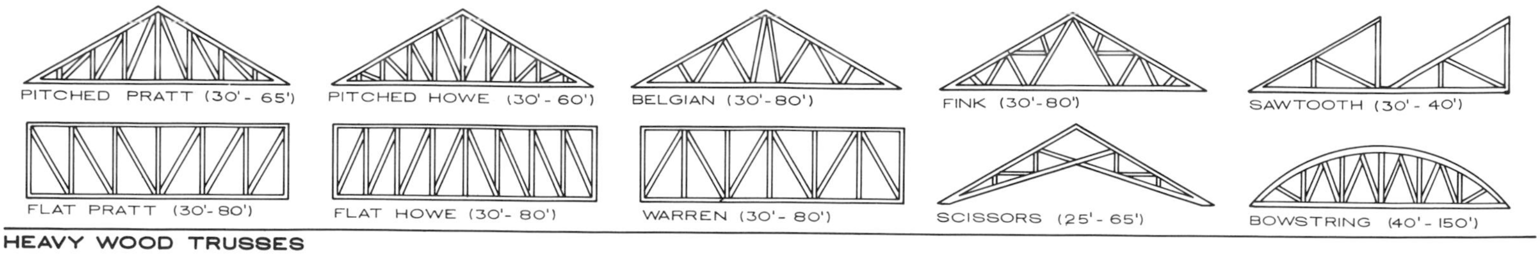

PITCHED PRATT (30'- 65')
PITCHED HOWE (30'- 60')
BELGIAN (30'-80')
FINK (30'-80')
SAWTOOTH (30'- 40')
FLAT PRATT (30'-80')
FLAT HOWE (30'- 80')
WARREN (30'- 80')
SCISSORS (25'- 65')
BOWSTRING (40'- 150')

HEAVY WOOD TRUSSES

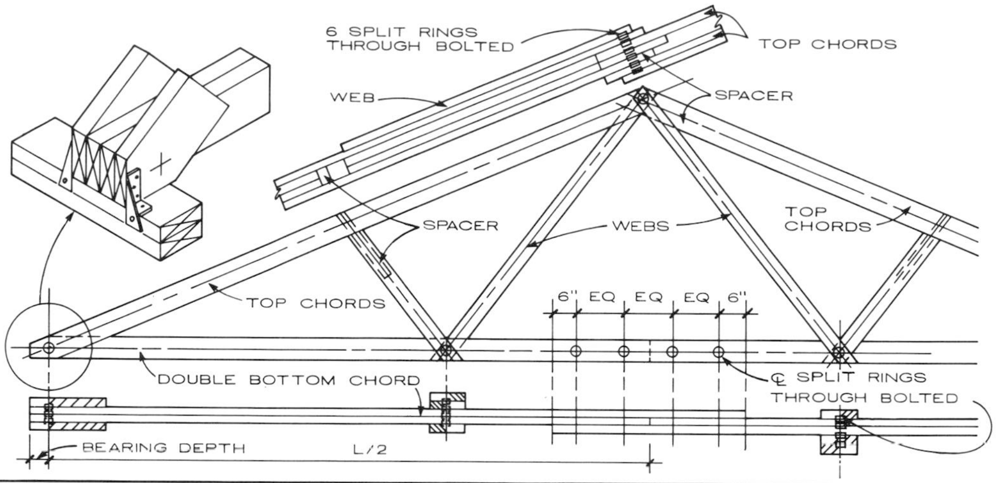

6 SPLIT RINGS THROUGH BOLTED
TOP CHORDS
WEB
SPACER
SPACER
WEBS
TOP CHORDS
TOP CHORDS
6" EQ EQ EQ 6"
DOUBLE BOTTOM CHORD
℄ SPLIT RINGS THROUGH BOLTED
BEARING DEPTH
L/2

PITCHED TRUSS

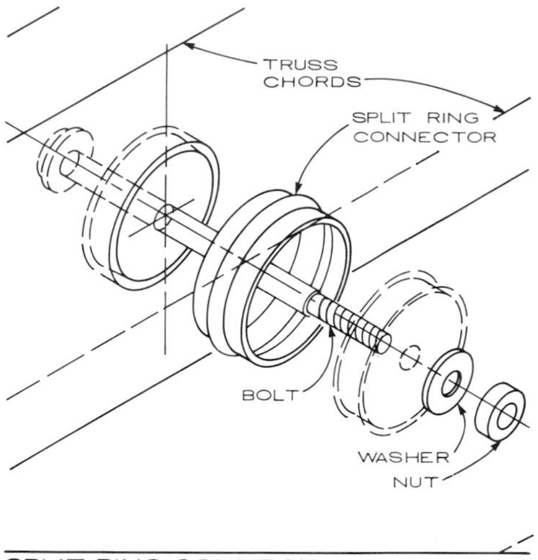

TRUSS CHORDS
SPLIT RING CONNECTOR
BOLT
WASHER
NUT

SPLIT RING CONNECTOR

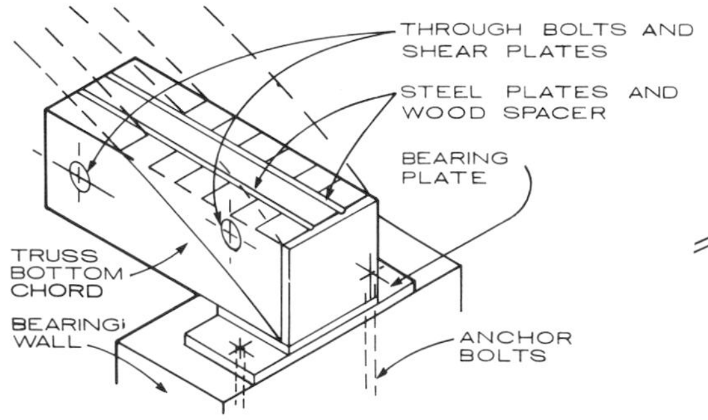

THROUGH BOLTS AND SHEAR PLATES
STEEL PLATES AND WOOD SPACER
BEARING PLATE
TRUSS BOTTOM CHORD
BEARING WALL
ANCHOR BOLTS

BOWSTRING TRUSS DETAIL

INSIDE DIAMETER	STEEL SIZE	BOLT SIZE	MINIMUM LUMBER SIZES: RING 1 SIDE	RING IN BOTH SIDES
2½"	¾" x 5/32"	½"	1" x 3½"	1½" x 3½"
4"	1" x 3/16"	¾"	1" x 5½"	1½" x 5½"

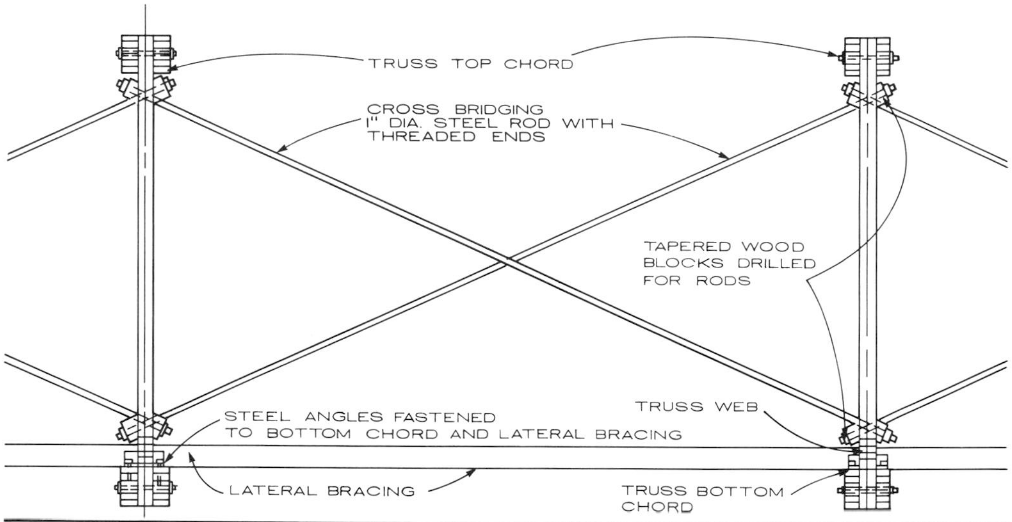

TRUSS TOP CHORD
CROSS BRIDGING 1" DIA. STEEL ROD WITH THREADED ENDS
TAPERED WOOD BLOCKS DRILLED FOR RODS
TRUSS WEB
STEEL ANGLES FASTENED TO BOTTOM CHORD AND LATERAL BRACING
LATERAL BRACING
TRUSS BOTTOM CHORD

SECTION–CROSS BRIDGING AND LATERAL BRACING

LAMINATED TOP CHORD
4-2 3/8" SHEAR PLATES WITH ¾" DIA. BOLT
LAMINATED WEB MEMBERS VERTICAL AND DIAGONAL
LAMINATED BOTTOM CHORD
10-4" DIA. SHEAR PLATES WITH 5-¾" DIA. BOLTS
SEE BEARING DETAIL ABOVE
6" 6"
6" 6"
4" 9" 9" 9" 9" 4"

SHEAR PLATE

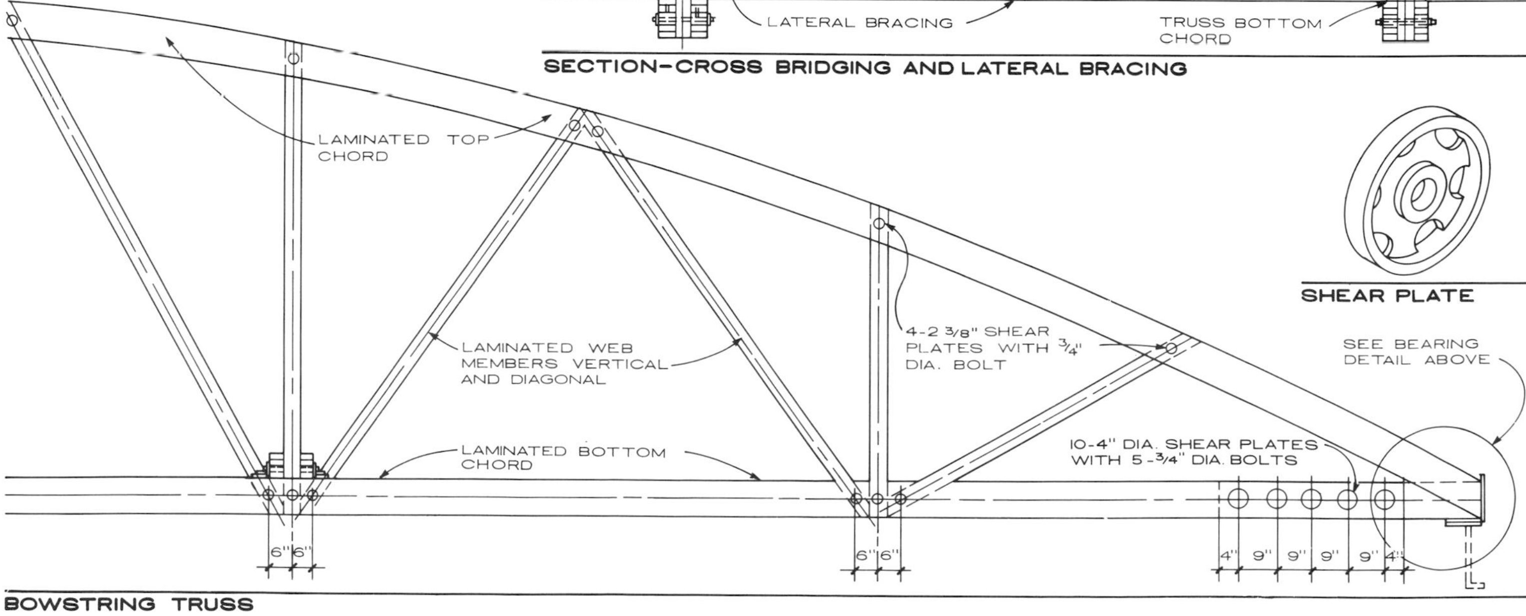

BOWSTRING TRUSS

Timothy B. McDonald; Washington, D.C.

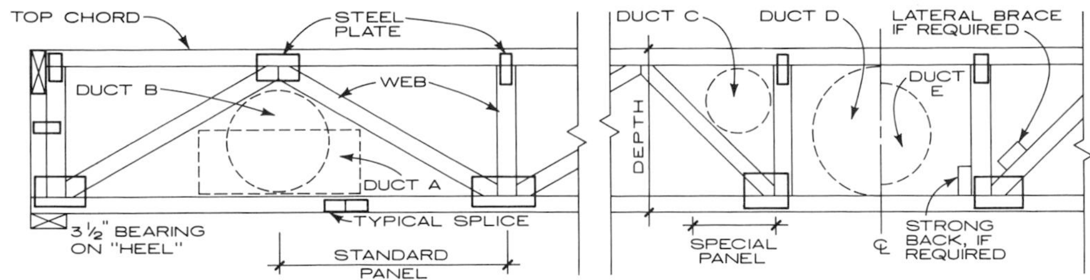
TOP CHORD
STEEL PLATE
DUCT B
WEB
DUCT A
TYPICAL SPLICE
3 ½" BEARING ON "HEEL"
STANDARD PANEL
DUCT C
DUCT D
LATERAL BRACE IF REQUIRED
DUCT E
DEPTH
SPECIAL PANEL
STRONG BACK, IF REQUIRED

RESIDENTIAL TYPE TRUSSED FLOOR JOIST STEEL PLATE CONNECTED

DUCT SIZES

Ease of running electrical and mechanical services through framing is a major advantage of trussed joists. Most manufacturers provide a large rectangular open panel at midspan; this void will generally accommodate a trunk line.

Sizes given here are approximations. Because web size and angles vary with different brands, the designer is cautioned to verify individual sizes carefully. Note that shape E is the duct that will fit in a flat truss with double chords top and bottom.

DEPTH OF TRUSS AND SIZE OF DUCTWORK

DEPTH	12"	16"	20"	24"
SHAPE				
A	4 x 9	6 x 12	7 x 13	8 x 14
B	7"	10"	12"	14"
C	5"	7"	8"	9"
D	9"	13"	17"	21"
E	6"	10"	14"	18"

WOOD TRUSSED RAFTERS SPANS FOR PRELIMINARY DESIGN

	RESIDENTIAL LIVE LOADS								
	FLOORS 55 PSF Ⓐ			ROOFS 40 PSF Ⓑ		55 PSF Ⓒ		(DOUBLE CHORDS) 55 PSF Ⓒ	
	TRUSSED RAFTERS SPACING (C TO C)								
DEPTH	12"	16"	24"	16"	24"	16"	24"	16"	24"
12"	23-6	21-0	17-1	24-0	21-4	21-11	18-2		
13"	24-11	22-0	17-11						
14"	26-4	22-11	18-8	27-5	23-3	24-5	19-10		
15"	27-7	23-10	19-5						
16"	28-7	24-9	20-1	30-3	25-0	26-4	21-4	31-10	27-10
18"	30-6	26-4	21-5	32-11	26-9	28-1	22-9	35-1	30-7
20"	32-4	27-11	22-8	34-8	28-0	29-7	23-11	38-1	33-1
22"	34-0	26-9	23-11						
24"	35-8	30-10	25-0	38-3	30-11	32-7	26-4	43-10	36-7
28"				41-6	33-6	35-5	28-7	49-2	39-11
32"				44-3	35-7	37-8	30-4	52-9	42-9
36"				47-0	37-10	40-1	32-3	56-3	45-7
48"								60-0	53-3

	COMMERCIAL LIVE LOADS								
	FLOORS 80 PSF Ⓓ			100 PSF Ⓔ			120 PSF Ⓕ		
	TRUSSED RAFTERS SPACING (C TO C)								
DEPTH	12"	16"	24"	12"	16"	24"	12"	16"	24"
12"	19-0	17-3	15-1	17-3	15-8	13-7	16-0	14-7	12-4
14"	21-4	19-4	16-6	19-4	17-7	14-9	18-0	16-4	13-6
16"	23-6	21-5	17-10	21-5	19-5	15-11	19-10	17-11	14-6
18"	25-8	23-4	19-0	23-4	21-0	17-0	21-8	19-2	15-6
20"	27-8	24-10	20-2	25-2	22-3	18-0	23-4	20-3	16-5
24"	31-6	27-5	22-2	28-5	24-6	19-10	25-11	22-4	18-1
16"*	27-7	25-1	21-11	25-1	22-9	19-11	23-2	21-2	18-5
24"*	38-0	34-6	30-1	34-6	31-4	27-4	32-0	29-1	25-1
32"*	47-1	42-9	36-1	42-9	38-10	32-3	39-8	36-1	29-5

Top chord live load	40 psf	20 psf	35 psf	60 psf	80 psf	100 psf
Top chord dead load	10 psf	10 psf	10 psf	10 psf	10 psf	10 psf
Bottom chord dead load	5 psf	10 psf	10 psf	10 psf	10 psf	10 psf
Total load	Ⓐ 55 psf	Ⓑ 40 psf	Ⓒ 55 psf	Ⓓ 80 psf	Ⓔ 100 psf	Ⓕ 120 psf

NOTES

1. Spans are clear, inside to inside, for bottom chord bearing. Values shown would vary very slightly for a truss with top chord loading.
2. Spans should not exceed 24 x depth of truss.
3. Designed deflection limit under total load is ℓ/240 for roofs, ℓ/360 for residential floors, and ℓ/480 for commercial floors.
4. Roof spans include a +15% short term stress.
5. Asterisk (*) indicates that truss has double chords, top and bottom.
6. Spans shown are for only one type of lumber; in this case—#2 Southern pine, with an f_b value of 1550. Charts are available for other grades and species. Lumber and grades may be mixed in the same truss, but chord size must be identical. Repetitive member bending stress is used in this chart.

Michael Bengis, AIA; Hopatcong, New Jersey

GENERAL

Monoplaner trusses are usually made up from 2 x 4 or 2 x 6 lumber. Spacing, normally 24 in. o.c., varies for special uses, especially in agriculture. Camber is designed for dead load only. Bottom chord furring generally is not required for drywall ceiling. Joints in plywood floor or roof should be staggered. Many trusses are approved by model codes, such as BOCA, ICBO, FHA, and SBC.

$$\text{CAMBER (USUAL)} = \frac{L(FT)}{60}$$

BRACING

Adequate bracing of trusses is vital. Sufficient support at right angles to plane of truss must be provided to hold each truss member in its designated position. Consider bracing during design, fabrication, and erection. In addition, provide permanent bracing/anchorage as an integral part of the building. Strongbacks are often used.

SMALL TO MEDIUM 20'-60'

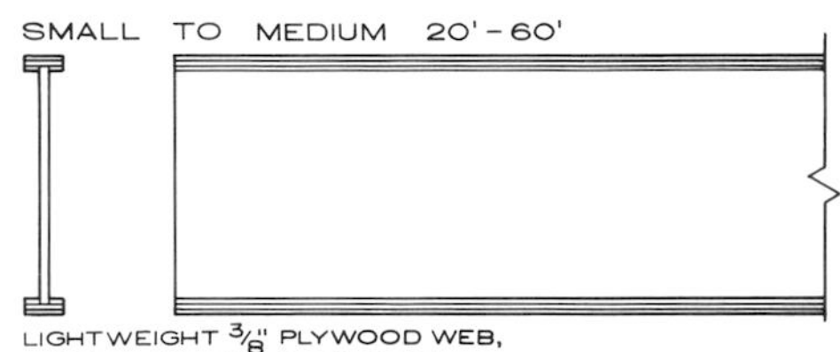

LIGHTWEIGHT 3/8" PLYWOOD WEB, 2 X 3 LAMINATED FLANGE

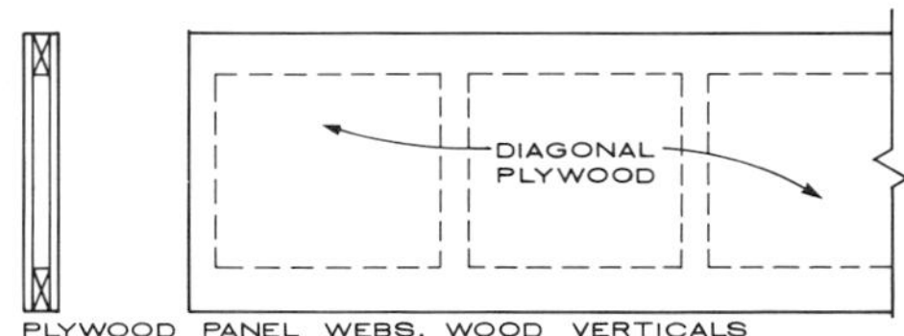
DIAGONAL PLYWOOD

PLYWOOD PANEL WEBS, WOOD VERTICALS

MEDIUM 40'-60'

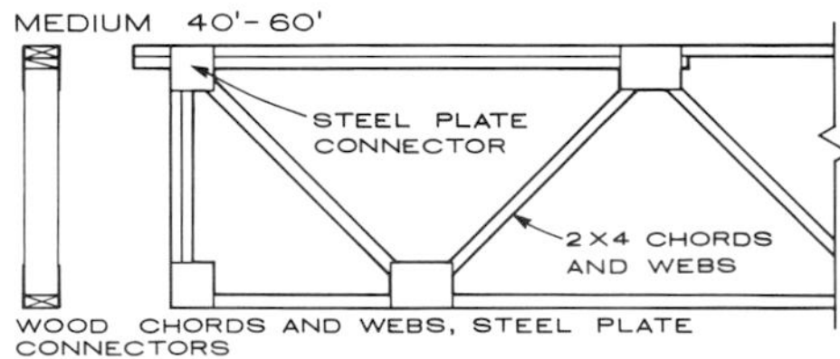
STEEL PLATE CONNECTOR
2 X 4 CHORDS AND WEBS

WOOD CHORDS AND WEBS, STEEL PLATE CONNECTORS

MEDIUM TO LONG 40'-80'

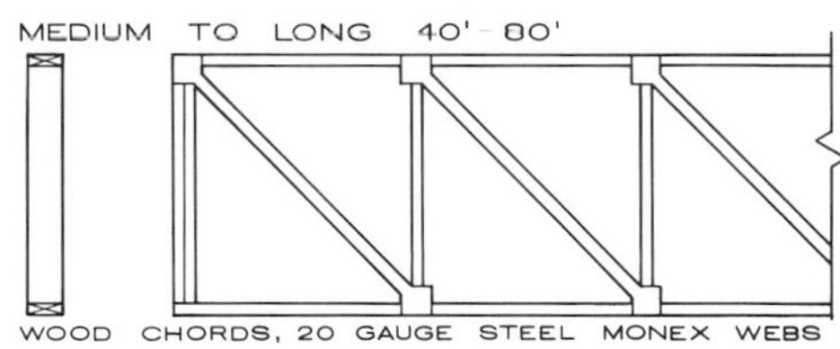

WOOD CHORDS, 20 GAUGE STEEL MONEX WEBS

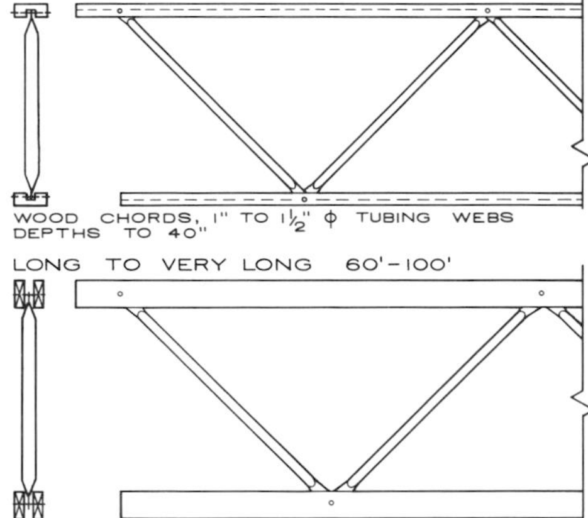

WOOD CHORDS, 1" TO 1½" φ TUBING WEBS DEPTHS TO 40"

LONG TO VERY LONG 60'-100'

DOUBLE 2 X 6 CHORDS, 2" φ WEBS DEPTH TO 63"

TYPES OF FABRICATED TRUSSES

6

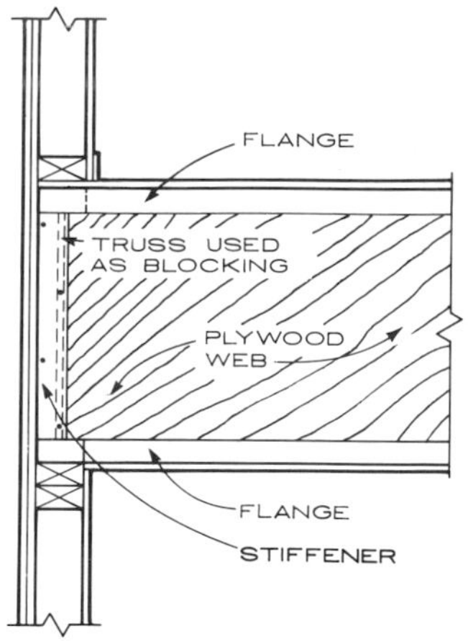

FLANGE
TRUSS USED AS BLOCKING
PLYWOOD WEB
FLANGE
STIFFENER

BEARING ON STUD WALL

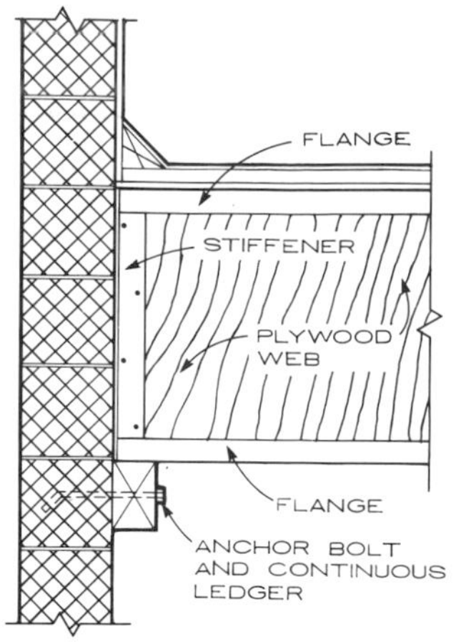

FLANGE
STIFFENER
PLYWOOD WEB
FLANGE
ANCHOR BOLT AND CONTINUOUS LEDGER

BEARING ON LEDGER

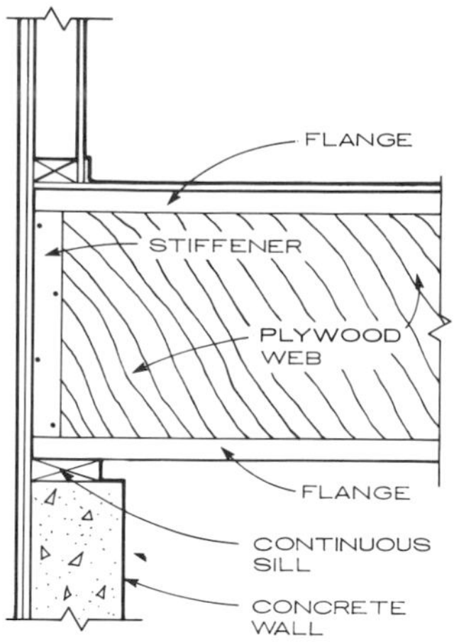

FLANGE
STIFFENER
PLYWOOD WEB
FLANGE
CONTINUOUS SILL
CONCRETE WALL

FOUNDATION

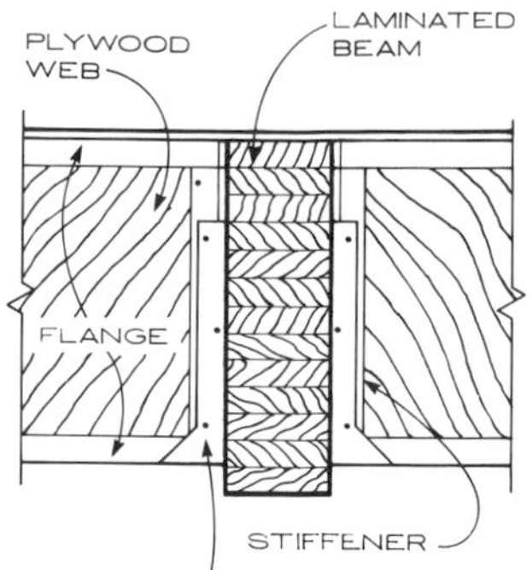

PLYWOOD WEB
LAMINATED BEAM
FLANGE
STIFFENER
JOIST HANGER

BOTTOM CHORD BEAM

PLYWOOD WEB TRUSS (WOOD CHORDS AND FLANGES)

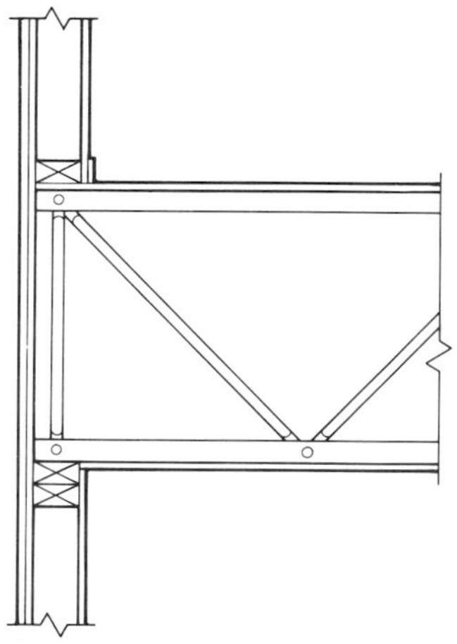

BOTTOM CHORD BEARING ON STUD WALL

CONTINUOUS NAILER FOR LATERAL SUPPORT
½" TYPICAL

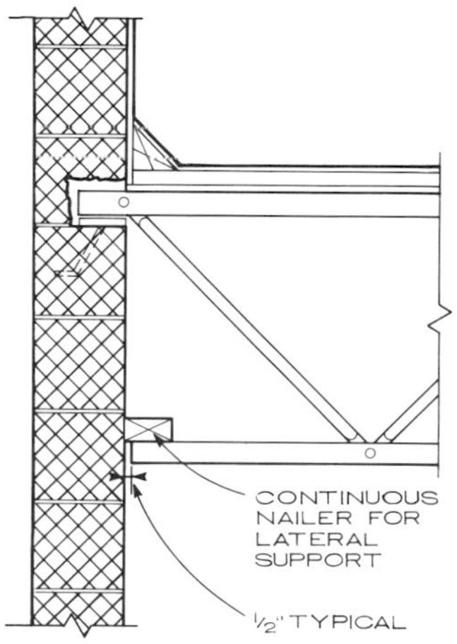

TOP CHORD BEARING–MASONRY WALL

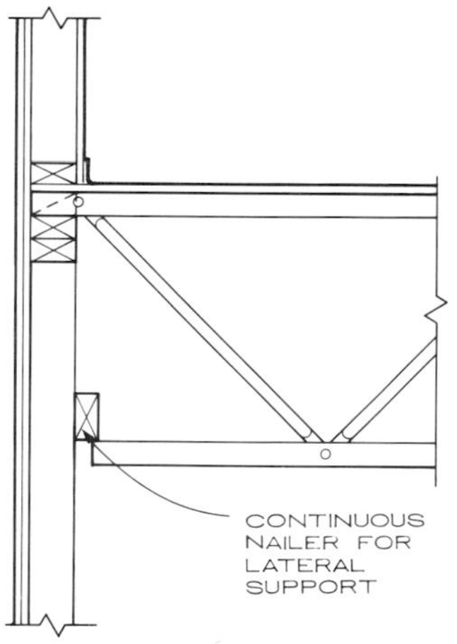

CONTINUOUS NAILER FOR LATERAL SUPPORT

TOP CHORD BEARING ON STUD WALL

CONTINUOUS NAILER FOR LATERAL SUPPORT

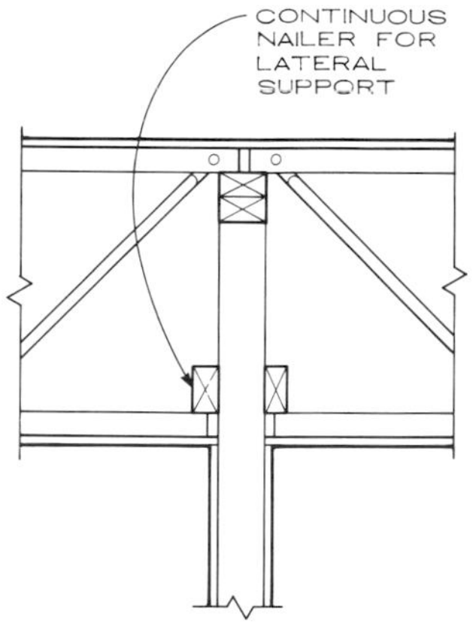

TOP CHORD BEARING

OPEN WEB TRUSS (STEEL WEB WOOD CHORD)

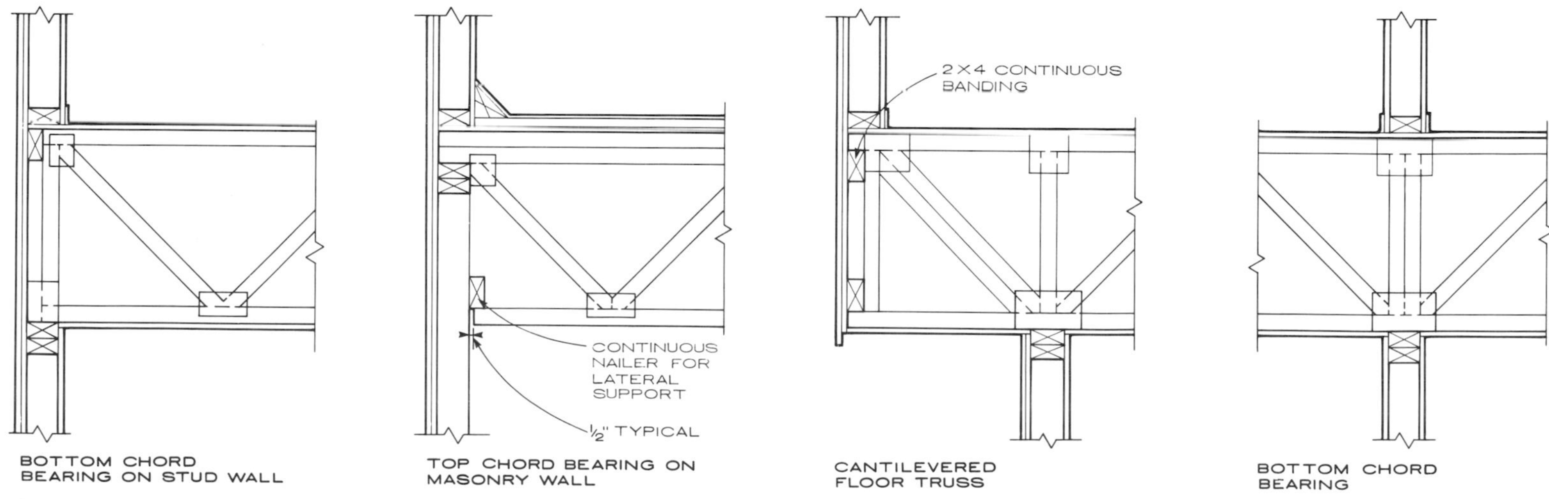
CONTINUOUS NAILER FOR LATERAL SUPPORT
½" TYPICAL
2×4 CONTINUOUS BANDING

BOTTOM CHORD BEARING ON STUD WALL

TOP CHORD BEARING ON MASONRY WALL

CANTILEVERED FLOOR TRUSS

BOTTOM CHORD BEARING

OPEN WEB TRUSS (WOOD CHORDS AND WEB, METAL PLATE CONNECTORS)

Timothy B. McDonald; Washington, D.C.

STRUCTURAL GLUED LAMINATED TIMBER

The term "structural glued laminated timber" refers to an engineered, stress-rated product made of appropriately selected and prepared wood laminations bonded with adhesives. The grain of all laminations is approximately parallel lengthwise. Laminations can be made of pieces end-joined to form any length, of pieces placed or glued edge-to-edge to make wider ones, or of bent pieces curved during gluing.

STANDARD DEPTHS

Dimensional lumber, surfaced to 1½ in. (38 mm), normally is used to laminate straight members and those curved members that have radii of curvature within the bending radius limitations for the species. Boards, surfaced to ¾ in. (19 mm), are recommended for laminating curved members when the bending radius is too short to permit the use of dimension lumber, provided that the bending radius limitations for the species are observed. Other lamination thicknesses may be used to meet special requirements.

STANDARD WIDTHS

Nominal width	in.	3	4	6	8	10	12	14	16
Net finished width	in.	2⅛	3⅛*	5⅛*	6¾	8¾	10¾	12¼	14¼
	mm	57	79	130	171	222	273	311	362

*3 in. and 5 in. for Southern pine.

CAMBER

Camber is curvature (circular or parabolic) made into structural glued laminated beams opposite the anticipated deflection movement. The recommended minimum camber is one and one-half times dead load deflection which, after plastic deformation has taken place, usually will produce a near level floor or roof beam under dead load conditions. Additional camber of slope may be provided to insure adequate drainage of roof beams. On level, long-span roof beams and floor beams of multistory buildings, additional camber may be needed to counter the optical illusion of the beam sagging.

FIRE SAFETY

The self-insulating qualities of heavy timber sizes create a slow burning characteristic. Good structural details, elimination of concealed spaces, and use of fire stops to interfere with the vertical passage of flames contribute to the fire performance of heavy timber construction in fire. While timber will burn, it retains its strength under fire longer than unprotected metals, which lose their strength quickly under extreme heat.

Building codes generally classify glued laminated timber as heavy timber construction if certain minimum dimensional requirements are met.

Fire retardant treatments may be applied to glued laminated timber but they do not substantially increase the fire resistance of heavy timber construction. When fire retardant treatments are used, the reduction of strength as related to type and penetration of treatment, the compatibility of treatment and adhesive, the use of special gluing procedures, the difficulty of application, and the effect on wood color and on fabricating procedures should be investigated.

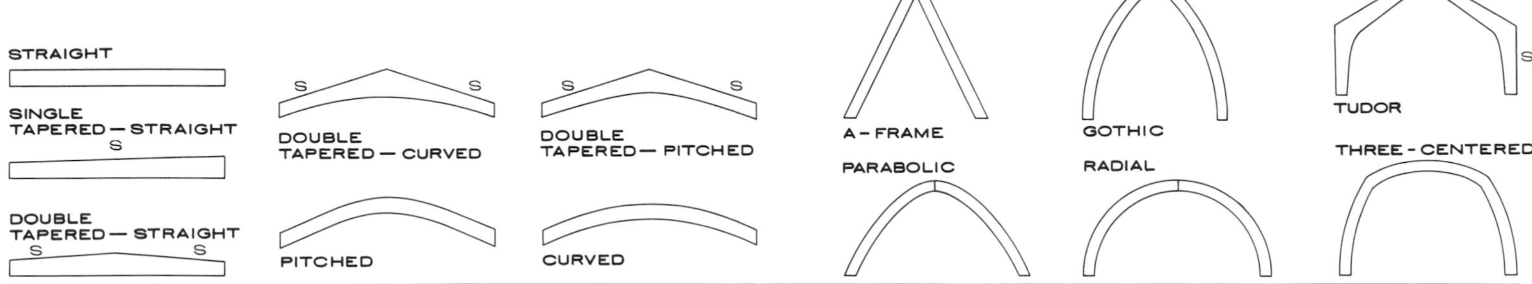
STRAIGHT
SINGLE TAPERED — STRAIGHT
S
DOUBLE TAPERED — STRAIGHT
S
S
S
S
DOUBLE TAPERED — CURVED
PITCHED
S
S
DOUBLE TAPERED — PITCHED
CURVED
A - FRAME
PARABOLIC
GOTHIC
RADIAL
S
S
TUDOR
THREE - CENTERED

STRUCTURAL GLUED LAMINATED TIMBER SHAPES

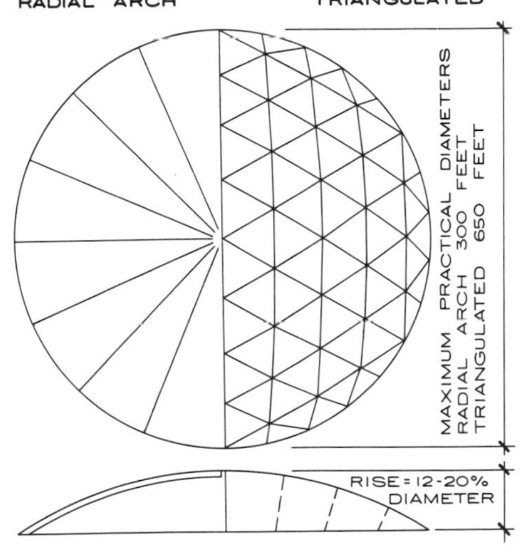
RADIAL ARCH
TRIANGULATED
MAXIMUM PRACTICAL DIAMETERS
RADIAL ARCH 300 FEET
TRIANGULATED 650 FEET
RISE = 12-20% DIAMETER

NOTES ON SHAPES

1. Beam names describe top and bottom surfaces of the beam. "S" designates a sawn or tapered surface. Sloped or pitched surfaces should be used on the tension side of the beam.
2. The three hinged arches and frames shown at right produce horizontal reactions requiring horizontal ties or modified foundations.
3. More complex shapes may be fabricated. Contact the American Institute of Timber Construction (AITC).

LAMINATED DOME SYSTEMS

The triangulated and the radial arch are the two basic types of structural glued laminated wood dome systems available. Both systems require a tension ring at the dome spring line to convert axial thrusts to vertical loads. Consideration must be given to the perimeter bond beam design since wind forces will produce loads in this member. The length of main members of the radial arch system, which must span a distance greater than half the dome diameter, limit the maximum practical dome diameter. The far smaller members of the triangulated dome result in the greater diameters. The triangulated system can be designed for five or more segments with an equal number of peripheral supports at each segment.

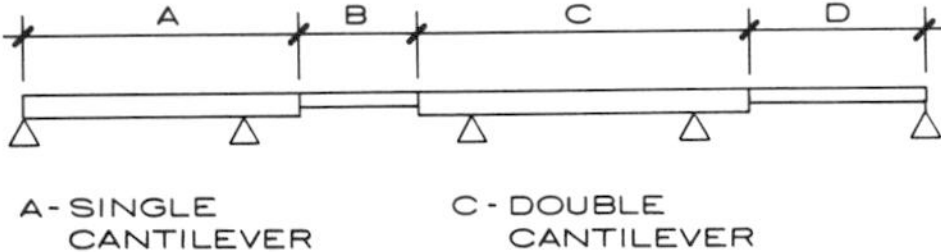
A
B
C
D
A - SINGLE CANTILEVER
B - SUSPENDED
C - DOUBLE CANTILEVER
D - SINGLE END SUSPENDED

CANTILEVERED AND CONTINUOUS SPAN SYSTEMS

Cantilever beam systems may be composed of any of the various types and combinations of beams shown above. Cantilever systems generally permit longer spans or larger loads per a given size member than do simple span systems. For economy, the negative bending moment at the support of a cantilevered beam should be equal in magnitude to the positive moment.

ALLOWABLE UNIT STRESS RANGES FOR STRUCTURAL GLUED LAMINATED-NORMAL DURATION OF LOADING

SPECIES	EXTREME FIBER IN BENDING	TENSION PARALLEL TO GRAIN	COMPRESSION PARALLEL TO GRAIN	HORIZONTAL SHEAR	COMPRESSION PERPENDICULAR TO GRAIN	MODULUS OF ELASTICITY
DRY CONDITIONS OF USE - MOISTURE CONTENT IN SERVICE LESS THAT 16%						
Douglas fir - larch	1600 to 2400	900 to 1600	1200 to 2400	165	560 to 650	1.5 to 1.8
Hem fir	1600 to 2400	800 to 1400	975 to 1750	155	375 to 500	1.4 to 1.5
Southern pine	1600 to 2400	900 to 1550	675 to 2300	200	560 to 650	1.4 to 1.8
California redwood	1600	875 to 1000	1350 to 1600	125	315	1.1
WET CONDITIONS OF USE FACTORS - MOISTURE CONTENT IN SERVICE 16% OR MORE (REQUIRES WET USE ADHESIVES)						
	0.800	0.800	0.730	0.875	0.530	0.833

Note: Multiply dry condition of use stress ranges by the above factors for corresponding wet conditions of use values

*For complete information see current American Institute of Timber Construction Publication AITC 117 - Design.

Thomas Hodne/Roger Kipp Architects, Planners, Inc.; Minneapolis, Minnesota

APPEARANCE GRADES

Structural glued laminated timber is produced in three appearance grades:

1. Industrial: For use where appearance is not a primary concern.
2. Architectural: For use where appearance is a factor.
3. Premium: For uses that demand the finest appearance.

These appearance grades do not modify design stresses, fabrication controls, grades of lumber used, or other provisions of the applicable standards. Descriptions of the three grades follow. A textured (rough sawn) surface may be called for instead of the surfacing described. In all grades, lamination will possess the natural growth characteristics of the lumber grade.

INDUSTRIAL APPEARANCE GRADE

Void filling on the edge of laminations is not required. The wide face of laminations exposed to view will be free of loose knots and open knot holes. Edge joints on the wide face will not be filled. Members will be surfaced two sides only, an occasional miss being permitted along individual laminations.

ARCHITECTURAL APPEARANCE GRADE

In exposed surfaces, knot holes and other voids measuring more than 3/4 in. (19 mm) will be replaced with clear wood inserts or a wood-tone colored filler. Inserts will be selected with reasonable care for similarity of the grain and color to the adjacent wood in the lamination. The wide face of laminations exposed to view will be free of loose knots and open knot holes. Voids greater than 1/16 in. (2 mm) wide in edge joints appearing on the wide face of laminations exposed to view will be filled. Exposed faces will be surfaced smooth. Misses are not permitted. The corners on the wide face of laminations exposed to view will be eased. Current practice for eased edges is for a radius between 1/8 in. (3 mm) and 1/2 in. (13 mm).

PREMIUM APPEARANCE GRADE

Similar to architectural grade except that in exposed surfaces, all knot holes and other voids will be replaced with wood inserts or a wood-tone colored filler as described for architectural grade. In addition, knots will be limited in size to 20 percent of the net face width of the lamination, with no more than two maximum size knots occurring in a 6 ft. (1.8 M) length of the exposed wide face of the laminations.

FINISHES

Available finishes for glued laminated timber include sealers, stains and paints.

End sealers retard moisture transmission and minimize checking and normally are applied to the ends of all members.

Surface sealers increase resistance to soiling, control grain raising, minimize checking, and serve as a moisture retardant. They fall within two classifications. Penetrating sealers provide limited protection and are suitable for use when the final finish requires staining or a natural finish. Primer and sealer coats provide maximum protection by sealing the surface of the wood, but should not be specified when the final finish requires a natural or stained finish. Wood color is modified by any sealer application. Wood sealers followed by staining will look different from stained untreated wood.

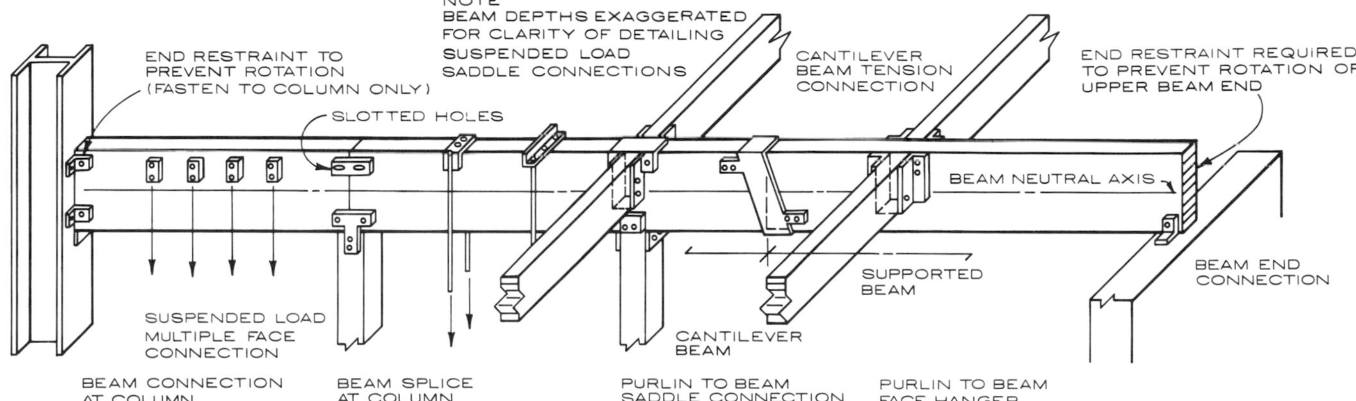
NOTE
BEAM DEPTHS EXAGGERATED
FOR CLARITY OF DETAILING
END RESTRAINT TO
PREVENT ROTATION
(FASTEN TO COLUMN ONLY)
SUSPENDED LOAD
SADDLE CONNECTIONS
CANTILEVER
BEAM TENSION
CONNECTION
END RESTRAINT REQUIRED
TO PREVENT ROTATION OF
UPPER BEAM END
SLOTTED HOLES
BEAM NEUTRAL AXIS
SUPPORTED
BEAM
BEAM END
CONNECTION
SUSPENDED LOAD
MULTIPLE FACE
CONNECTION
CANTILEVER
BEAM
BEAM CONNECTION
AT COLUMN
BEAM SPLICE
AT COLUMN
PURLIN TO BEAM
SADDLE CONNECTION
PURLIN TO BEAM
FACE HANGER

CONNECTION DESIGN

The design of connections for glued laminated timbers is similar to the design of connections for sawn lumber. Since glued laminated timbers often are much larger than sawn lumber and the loads transferred also are larger, the effect of increased size should be taken into account in the design of connections. In addition to being designed for strength to transfer loads, connections also should be designed to avoid splitting of the member and to accommodate swelling and shrinking of the wood.

BEAM END CONNECTIONS

Beam end connections should be designed to carry both induced horizontal and vertical loads. Bolts or fastenings at the end of the beam should be located toward the bottom of the beam so that the effect of shrinkage between the bottom of the beam and the fastening is minimized. Bolts or connectors located near or above the beam's neutral axis should not be used on large glued laminated beams or girders since the concentration of the tension perpendicular to grain due to restraint of shrinkage, and shear stresses acting at fasteners located in these beam areas tend to cause splitting of the member.

SUSPENDED LOADS

In cases where it is not possible for the suspending system to be carried on top of the beam, it is good practice to place the fastener above the neutral axis, particularly when other than light loading is involved or when a number of loads are to be suspended from the member. For heavy loads, a saddle detail placing loads directly on top of the beam is recommended.

Very light loads may be suspended near the bottom of a glued laminated timber. The distance above the beam bottom must be at least equal to the specified edge distance of the fastener used.

PURLIN TO BEAM CONNECTIONS

The preferred purlin to beam connection method is to transfer the end reaction by bearing perpendicular to grain in a saddle type connection extending over the beam top.

When the end reaction of the beam or purlin is relatively small, the hanger can be fastened to the face of the girder. The bolts or connectors in the main carrying beam or girder should be placed above the neutral axis of the member, and in the supported member should be placed near the bottom to avoid potential splitting.

SPLICE CONNECTIONS

At beam splice connections occurring over columns, it is important to allow for movement in the upper portions of the beam due to end rotation. Slotted connections will help to reduce the problem by allowing for some beam movement.

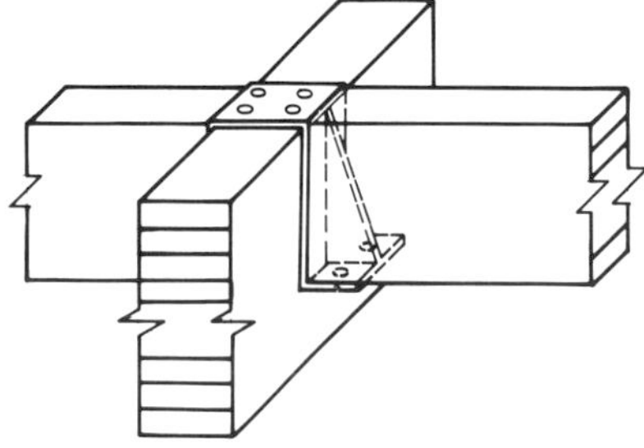

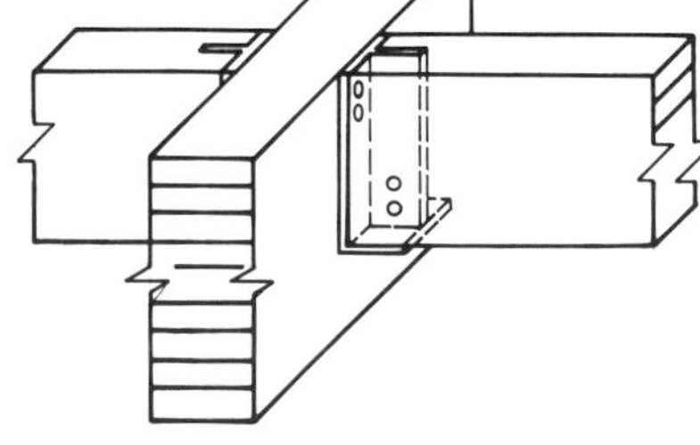

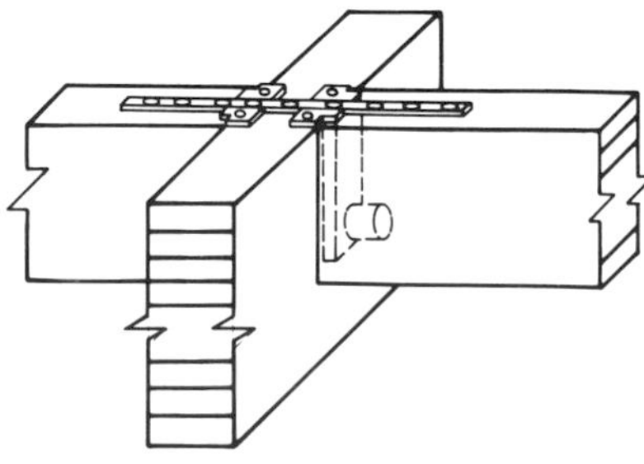

CONCEALED AND PARTIALLY CONCEALED PURLIN HANGERS

Partially concealed purlin hangers of the type shown to the left are used for normal loads. The center arrangement and the concealed hanger at the right are appropriate for relatively light loads. The concealed hanger at the right, as well as connections where the support plate at the base is notched into the beam, should be designed as notched beam reactions.

It is recommended that the support for the purlin be close to the bottom of the member to utilize the maximum effective area for shear. End fastenings should not include rows of bolts or other fasteners perpendicular to the grain. Glued laminated timbers, although relatively dry at the time of manufacture, may shrink when the members reach equilibrium moisture content in place. This may cause tension perpendicular to the grain and result in splitting.

Thomas Hodne/Roger Kipp Architects, Planners, Inc.; Minneapolis, Minnesota

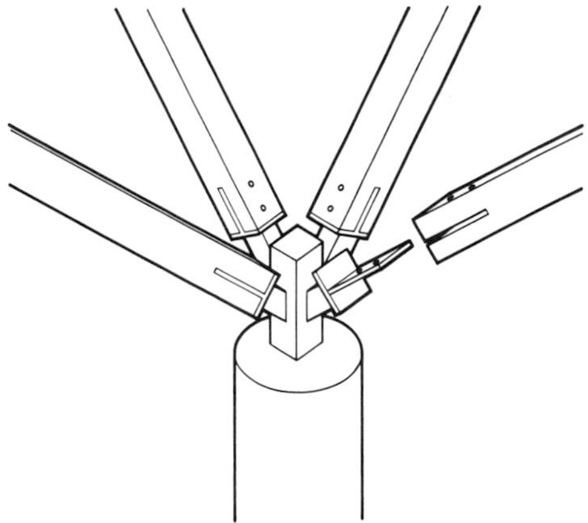

SPECIAL CONNECTIONS

The detail above is just one of a large variety of special connections and connection assemblies possible using structural glued laminated timber. It is critical that connections be designed carefully in accordance with good engineering practice.

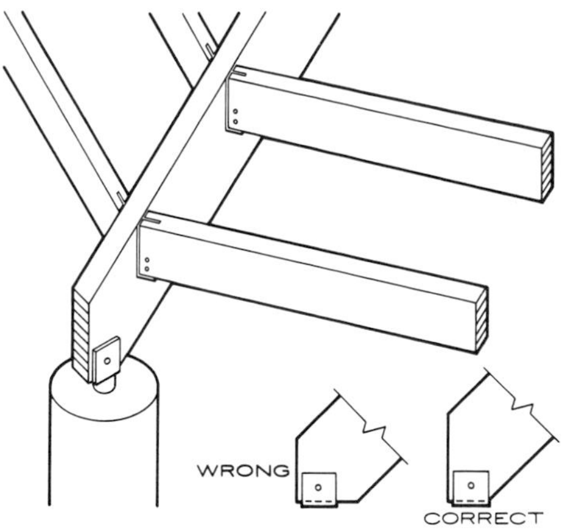
WRONG
CORRECT

NOTCHED BEARING CONDITIONS

An abrupt notch in the end of a wood member reduces the effective shear strength of the member and may permit a more rapid migration of moisture in the lower portion of the member causing potential splitting. This condition is similar to the incorrect detail above, but perhaps is not as evident. The shear strength of the end of the member is reduced and the exposed end grain also may result in splitting because of drying. At inclined beams, the taper cut should be loaded in bearing.

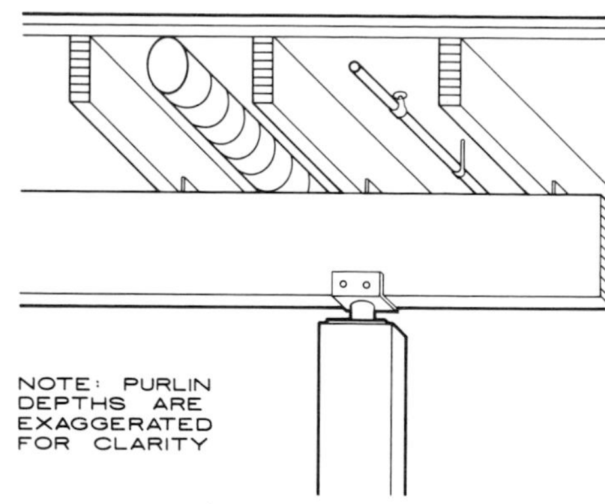
NOTE: PURLIN DEPTHS ARE EXAGGERATED FOR CLARITY

OVERLAY PURLIN-BEAM SYSTEM

The design of a structural glued laminated system in which the purlins frame over the top of the beams has the advantage of more easily accommodating the distribution of heating, cooling, and fire protection components. As with any timber structural design, beam and purlin end restraint, as well as overall system lateral stability, must be provided for.

GLUED LAMINATED COLUMNS

Structural glued laminated timber columns offer higher allowable stresses, controlled appearance, and the ability to fabricate variable sections. For simple rectangular columns, the slenderness ratio, or the ratio of the unsupported length between points of lateral support to the least column dimension, may not exceed 50. The least dimension for tapered columns is taken as the sum of the smaller dimension and one-third the difference between the smaller and greater dimensions. Spaced columns consist of two or more members with their longitudinal axes parallel, separated at the ends and at the midpoint by blocking, and joined at the ends by shear fastenings. The members are considered to act together to carry the total column load, and because of the end fixity developed, a greater slenderness ratio than that allowed for solid columns is permitted.

NOTES ON BEAM DESIGN CHART

1. Total load carrying capacity includes beam weight. Floor beams are designed for uniform loads of 40 psf live load and 10 psf dead load.
2. Allowable stresses: F_b = 2400 psi (reduced by size factor), F_v = 165 psi, E = 1,800,000 psi.
3. Deflection limits: roof = $^1/_{180}$, floor = $^1/_{360}$.
4. Values are for preliminary design purposes only. For more complete information see the AITC *Timber Construction Manual.*

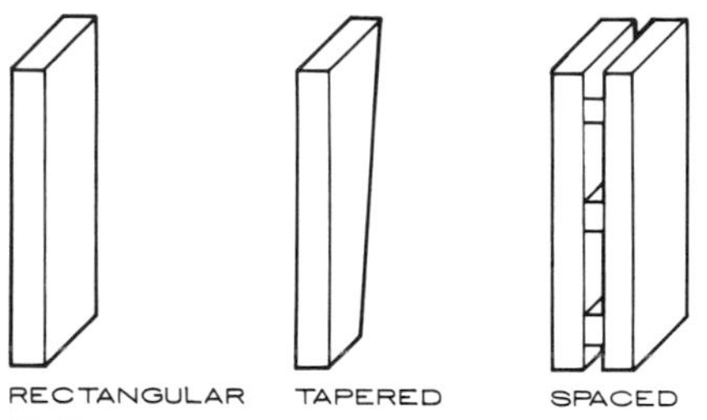
RECTANGULAR
TAPERED
SPACED

COLUMNS

LAMINATED FLOOR, ROOF BEAM, AND PURLIN DESIGN CHART—TYPICAL SINGLE SPAN SIMPLY SUPPORTED GLUED LAMINATED BEAMS (MEMBER SIZES IN INCHES)

SPAN (FT)	SPACING (FT)	TOTAL LOAD CARRYING CAPACITY (PSF) 30 PSF	35 PSF	40 PSF	45 PSF	50 PSF	55 PSF	FLOOR BEAMS 50 PSF
12	6	3 1/8 x 6	3 1/8 x 6	3 1/8 x 7 1/2	3 1/8 x 7 1/2	3 1/8 x 7 1/2	3 1/8 x 7 1/2	3 1/8 x 9
	8	3 1/8 x 6	3 1/8 x 7 1/2	3 1/8 x 9	3 1/8 x 9	3 1/8 x 9	3 1/8 x 9	3 1/8 x 10 1/2
	10	3 1/8 x 7 1/2	3 1/8 x 7 1/2	3 1/8 x 9	3 1/8 x 9	3 1/8 x 9	3 1/8 x 10 1/2	3 1/8 x 10 1/2
	12	3 1/8 x 7 1/2	3 1/8 x 9	3 1/8 x 9	3 1/8 x 9	3 1/8 x 10 1/2	3 1/8 x 10 1/2	3 1/8 x 12
16	8	3 1/8 x 9	3 1/8 x 9	3 1/8 x 10 1/2	3 1/8 x 10 1/2	3 1/8 x 12	3 1/8 x 12	3 1/8 x 13 1/2
	12	3 1/8 x 10 1/2	3 1/8 x 12	3 1/8 x 12	3 1/8 x 12	3 1/8 x 13 1/2	3 1/8 x 13 1/2	3 1/8 x 15
	14	3 1/8 x 12	3 1/8 x 12	3 1/8 x 13 1/2	3 1/8 x 13 1/2	3 1/8 x 15	3 1/8 x 15	3 1/8 x 15
	16	3 1/8 x 12	3 1/8 x 13 1/2	3 1/8 x 13 1/2	3 1/8 x 15	3 1/8 x 15	3 1/8 x 16 1/2	3 1/8 x 15
20	8	3 1/8 x 12	3 1/8 x 12	3 1/8 x 13 1/2	3 1/8 x 13 1/2	3 1/8 x 13 1/2	3 1/8 x 15	3 1/8 x 16 1/2
	12	3 1/8 x 13 1/2	3 1/8 x 13 1/2	3 1/8 x 15	3 1/8 x 16 1/2	3 1/8 x 16 1/2	5 1/8 x 13 1/2	5 1/8 x 15
	16	3 1/8 x 15	3 1/8 x 16 1/2	3 1/8 x 18	3 1/8 x 18	5 1/8 x 15	5 1/8 x 16 1/2	5 1/8 x 18
	20	3 1/8 x 16	3 1/8 x 18	5 1/8 x 15	5 1/8 x 16 1/2	5 1/8 x 16 1/2	5 1/8 x 18	5 1/8 x 18
24	8	3 1/8 x 13 1/2	3 1/8 x 15	3 1/8 x 15	3 1/8 x 16 1/2	3 1/8 x 16 1/2	3 1/8 x 18	5 1/8 x 19 1/2
	12	3 1/8 x 16 1/2	3 1/8 x 16 1/2	3 1/8 x 18	5 1/8 x 15	5 1/8 x 16 1/2	5 1/8 x 16 1/2	5 1/8 x 21
	16	3 1/8 x 18	5 1/8 x 16 1/2	5 1/8 x 16 1/2	5 1/8 x 18	5 1/8 x 18	5 1/8 x 19 1/2	5 1/8 x 24
	20	5 1/8 x 16 1/2	5 1/8 x 16 1/2	5 1/8 x 18	5 1/8 x 19 1/2	5 1/8 x 19 1/2	5 1/8 x 21	5 1/8 x 25 1/2
28	8	3 1/8 x 16 1/2	3 1/8 x 16 1/2	3 1/8 x 18	3 1/8 x 18	5 1/8 x 16 1/2	5 1/8 x 16 1/2	5 1/8 x 19 1/2
	12	3 1/8 x 18	5 1/8 x 16 1/2	5 1/8 x 18	5 1/8 x 18	5 1/8 x 18	5 1/8 x 19 1/2	5 1/8 x 21
	16	5 1/8 x 18	5 1/8 x 18	5 1/8 x 19 1/2	5 1/8 x 19 1/2	5 1/8 x 21	5 1/8 x 22 1/2	5 1/8 x 24
	20	5 1/8 x 18	5 1/8 x 19 1/2	5 1/8 x 21	5 1/8 x 22 1/2	5 1/8 x 24	5 1/8 x 25 1/2	5 1/8 x 25 1/2
32	8	3 1/8 x 18	5 1/8 x 16 1/2	5 1/8 x 18	5 1/8 x 18	5 1/8 x 18	5 1/8 x 19 1/2	5 1/8 x 21
	12	5 1/8 x 18	5 1/8 x 19 1/2	5 1/8 x 19 1/2	5 1/8 x 21	5 1/8 x 21	5 1/8 x 22 1/2	5 1/8 x 24
	16	5 1/8 x 19 1/2	5 1/8 x 21	5 1/8 x 22 1/2	5 1/8 x 22 1/2	5 1/8 x 24	5 1/8 x 25 1/2	5 1/8 x 27
	20	5 1/8 x 21	5 1/8 x 22 1/2	5 1/8 x 24	5 1/8 x 25 1/2	5 1/8 x 27	5 1/8 x 28 1/2	6 3/4 x 27
40	12	5 1/8 x 22 1/2	5 1/8 x 24	5 1/8 x 24	5 1/8 x 25 1/2	5 1/8 x 27	6 3/4 x 25 1/2	6 3/4 x 28 1/2
	16	5 1/8 x 24	5 1/8 x 25 1/2	5 1/8 x 27	5 1/8 x 28 1/2	6 3/4 x 27	6 3/4 x 28 1/2	6 3/4 x 31 1/2
	20	5 1/8 x 27	5 1/8 x 28 1/2	6 3/4 x 27	6 3/4 x 28 1/2	6 3/4 x 30	6 3/4 x 31 1/2	6 3/4 x 33
	24	5 1/8 x 28 1/2	6 3/4 x 27	6 3/4 x 28 1/2	6 3/4 x 31 1/2	6 3/4 x 33	6 3/4 x 34 1/2	6 3/4 x 36
48	12	5 1/8 x 27	5 1/8 x 28 1/2	5 1/8 x 30	5 1/8 x 30	6 3/4 x 28 1/2	6 3/4 x 30	6 3/4 x 33
	16	5 1/8 x 30	6 3/4 x 28 1/2	6 3/4 x 30	6 3/4 x 30	6 3/4 x 31 1/2	6 3/4 x 34 1/2	6 3/4 x 37 1/2
	20	6 3/4 x 28 1/2	6 3/4 x 30	6 3/4 x 31 1/2	6 3/4 x 34 1/2	6 3/4 x 36	6 3/4 x 37 1/2	8 3/4 x 36
	24	6 3/4 x 30	6 3/4 x 33	6 3/4 x 34 1/2	6 3/4 x 37 1/2	6 3/4 x 39	8 3/4 x 36	8 3/4 x 39
60	12	6 3/4 x 30	6 3/4 x 31 1/2	6 3/4 x 33	6 3/4 x 34 1/2	6 3/4 x 36	6 3/4 x 37 1/2	8 3/4 x 39
	16	6 3/4 x 33	6 3/4 x 34 1/2	6 3/4 x 36	6 3/4 x 39	8 3/4 x 36	8 3/4 x 37 1/2	8 3/4 x 42
	20	6 3/4 x 36	6 3/4 x 37 1/2	8 3/4 x 36	8 3/4 x 37 1/2	8 3/4 x 40 1/2	8 3/4 x 42	8 3/4 x 45
	24	6 3/4 x 39	8 3/4 x 36	8 3/4 x 39	8 3/4 x 42	8 3/4 x 43 1/2	8 3/4 x 45	8 3/4 x 48

Thomas Hodne/Roger Kipp Architects, Planners, Inc.; Minneapolis, Minnesota

GUIDELINES

1. Check current local building code regulations for requirements that may differ from the general recommendations shown or stated on this page.
2. Interior stair width: 3 ft (36 in.) minimum.
3. Minimum headroom should be 6 ft 8 in. as measured vertically from a diagonal line connecting tread nosings to the underside of the finished ceiling or stair landing directly above the stair run. Recommended headroom is 7 ft.
4. Only handrails and stair stringers may project into the required width of a stair.
   Handrail projection: 3½ in. maximum.
   Stringer projection: 1½ in. maximum.
5. The width of a landing or platform should be the same as the actual width of the stair.
6. Maximum vertical rise of stair between landings: 12 ft.
7. Maximum riser height: 7 in.
   Minimum riser height: 4 in.
   Minimum tread width: 11 in.
   Tolerances for variation in tread or riser dimension should not exceed $^3/_{16}$ in. for adjacent tread width or riser height. The maximum difference between the largest and smallest tread width or riser height for an entire flight of stairs should be $^3/_8$ in.
8. Height of handrail: 2 ft 6 in. to 2 ft 10 in. (at stair and landings). Handrails should be designed to be easily gripped and to fit the hand. Recommended diameter is 1½ in. for round handrail and similar size for elliptical or rounded edge square section. Handrails should be structurally designed so that both downward (vertical) and lateral (horizontal) thrust loads are considered.
9. Extensions of handrail at top and bottom of stair may affect total length of required run. Verify extensions required by local code before starting stair design.
10. Construction details on this page are for shop-built stairs reflecting Architectural Woodwork Institute Premium Grade Standards.

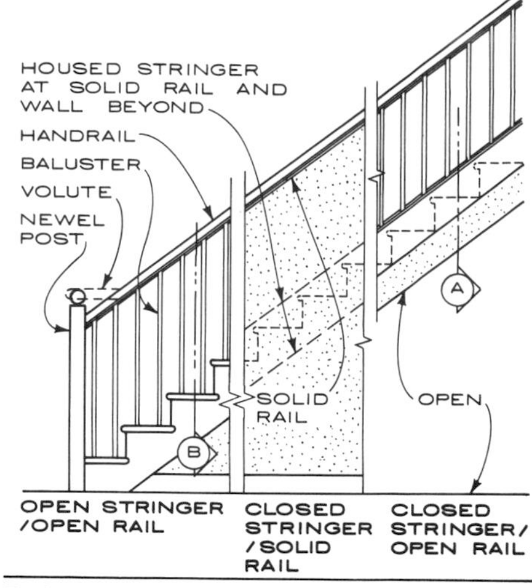
HOUSED STRINGER AT SOLID RAIL AND WALL BEYOND
HANDRAIL
BALUSTER
VOLUTE
NEWEL POST
SOLID RAIL
OPEN
A
B
OPEN STRINGER /OPEN RAIL
CLOSED STRINGER /SOLID RAIL
CLOSED STRINGER/ OPEN RAIL

ELEVATION OF FACE STRINGER

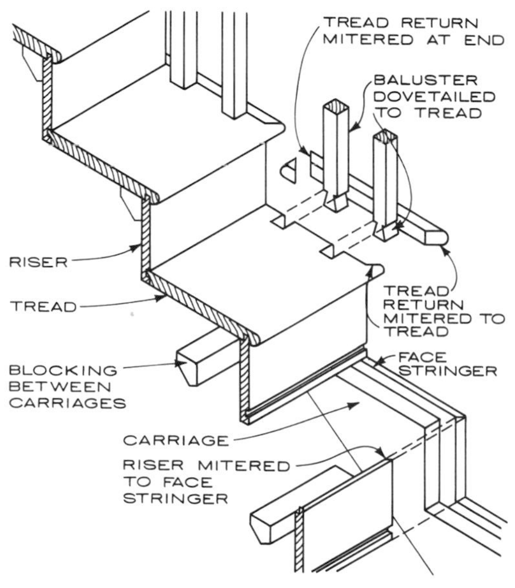
TREAD RETURN MITERED AT END
BALUSTER DOVETAILED TO TREAD
RISER
TREAD
TREAD RETURN MITERED TO TREAD
BLOCKING BETWEEN CARRIAGES
FACE STRINGER
CARRIAGE
RISER MITERED TO FACE STRINGER

BALUSTERS AND TRIM AT FACE STRINGER

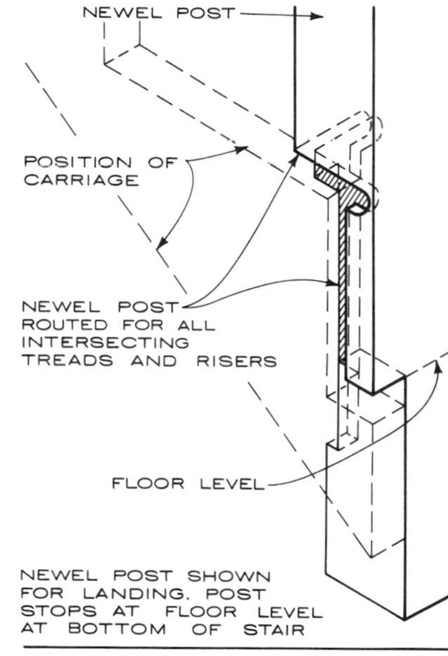
NEWEL POST
POSITION OF CARRIAGE
NEWEL POST ROUTED FOR ALL INTERSECTING TREADS AND RISERS
FLOOR LEVEL
NEWEL POST SHOWN FOR LANDING. POST STOPS AT FLOOR LEVEL AT BOTTOM OF STAIR

NEWEL POST

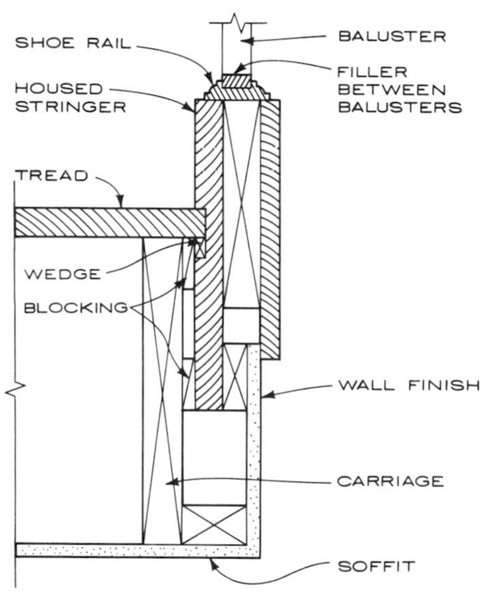
SHOE RAIL
BALUSTER
FILLER BETWEEN BALUSTERS
HOUSED STRINGER
TREAD
WEDGE
BLOCKING
WALL FINISH
CARRIAGE
SOFFIT

SECTION A

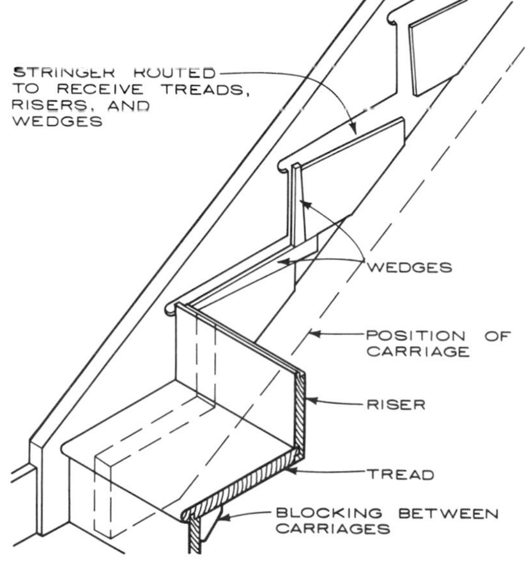
STRINGER ROUTED TO RECEIVE TREADS, RISERS, AND WEDGES
WEDGES
POSITION OF CARRIAGE
RISER
TREAD
BLOCKING BETWEEN CARRIAGES

TREADS AND RISERS AT HOUSED STRINGER

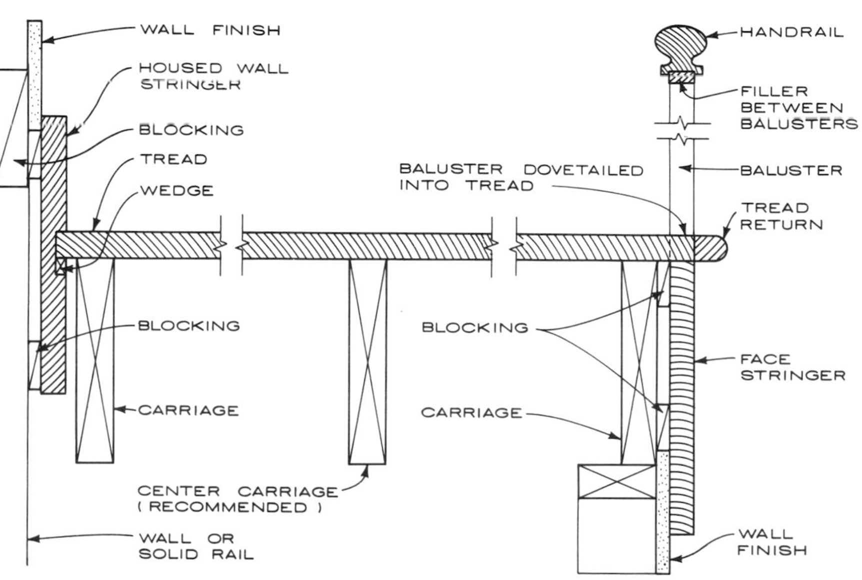
WALL FINISH
HOUSED WALL STRINGER
BLOCKING
TREAD
WEDGE
BLOCKING
CARRIAGE
CENTER CARRIAGE (RECOMMENDED)
WALL OR SOLID RAIL
BALUSTER DOVETAILED INTO TREAD
BLOCKING
CARRIAGE
HANDRAIL
FILLER BETWEEN BALUSTERS
BALUSTER
TREAD RETURN
FACE STRINGER
WALL FINISH

SECTION B

The Bumgardner Partnership/Architects; Seattle, Washington

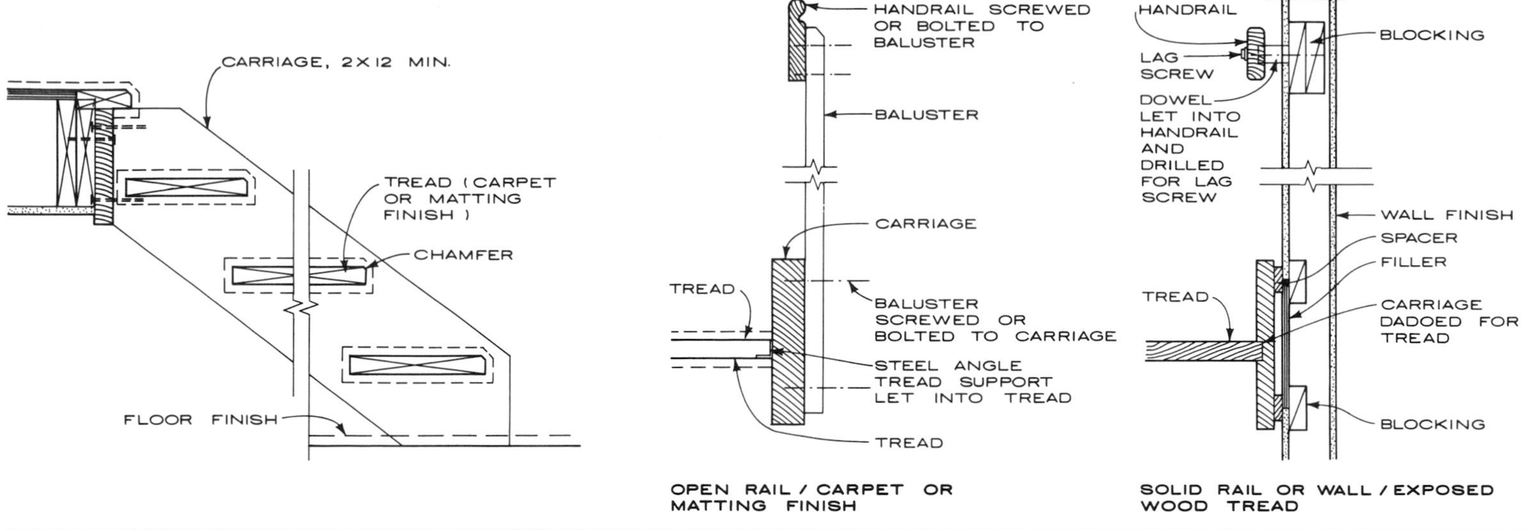
CARRIAGE, 2X12 MIN.
TREAD (CARPET OR MATTING FINISH)
CHAMFER
FLOOR FINISH
HANDRAIL SCREWED OR BOLTED TO BALUSTER
BALUSTER
CARRIAGE
TREAD
BALUSTER SCREWED OR BOLTED TO CARRIAGE
STEEL ANGLE TREAD SUPPORT LET INTO TREAD
TREAD
OPEN RAIL / CARPET OR MATTING FINISH
HANDRAIL
LAG SCREW
DOWEL LET INTO HANDRAIL AND DRILLED FOR LAG SCREW
BLOCKING
WALL FINISH
SPACER
FILLER
TREAD
CARRIAGE DADOED FOR TREAD
BLOCKING
SOLID RAIL OR WALL / EXPOSED WOOD TREAD

OPEN RISER STAIR

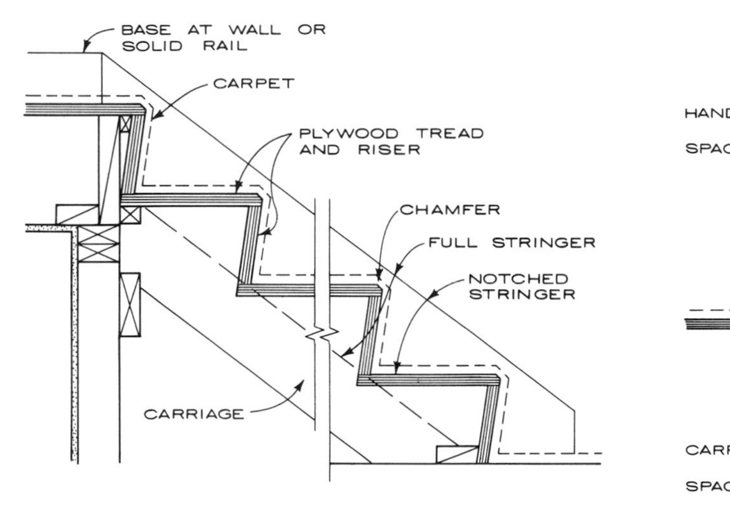
BASE AT WALL OR SOLID RAIL
CARPET
PLYWOOD TREAD AND RISER
CHAMFER
FULL STRINGER
NOTCHED STRINGER
CARRIAGE

CLOSED RISER STAIR/CARPET FINISH

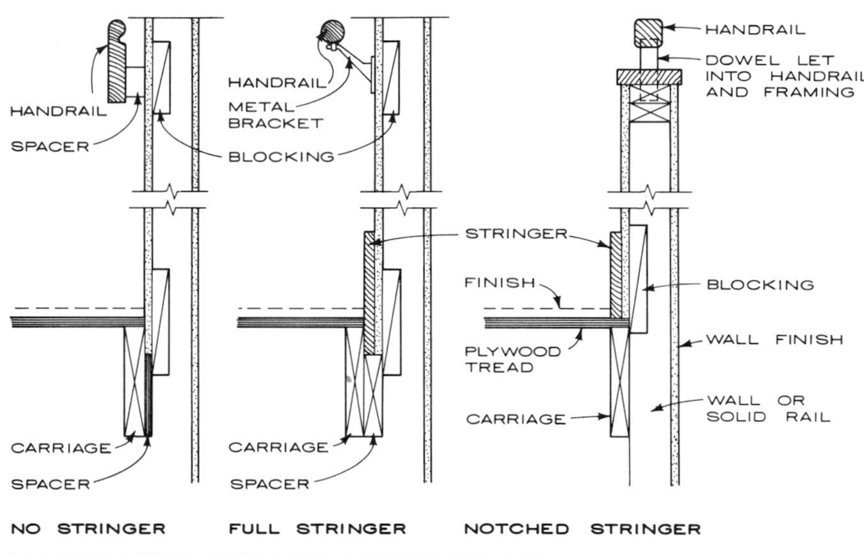
HANDRAIL
SPACER
CARRIAGE
SPACER
NO STRINGER
HANDRAIL
METAL BRACKET
BLOCKING
CARRIAGE
SPACER
FULL STRINGER
HANDRAIL
DOWEL LET INTO HANDRAIL AND FRAMING
STRINGER
FINISH
BLOCKING
PLYWOOD TREAD
WALL FINISH
CARRIAGE
WALL OR SOLID RAIL
NOTCHED STRINGER

CLOSED RISER STAIRS AT WALLS AND SOLID RAILING WALLS

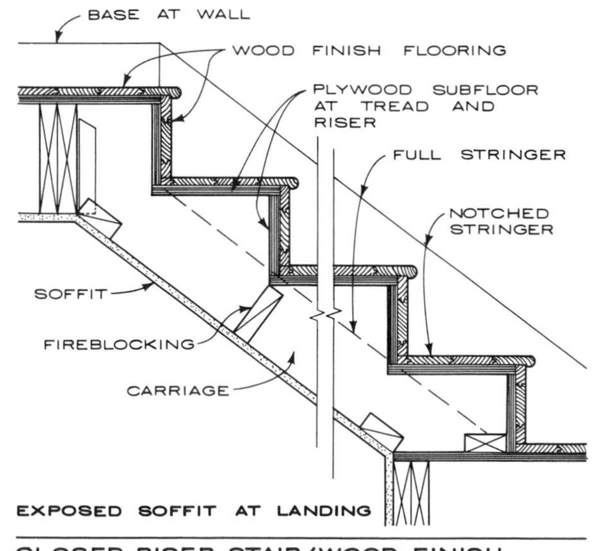
BASE AT WALL
WOOD FINISH FLOORING
PLYWOOD SUBFLOOR AT TREAD AND RISER
FULL STRINGER
NOTCHED STRINGER
SOFFIT
FIREBLOCKING
CARRIAGE
EXPOSED SOFFIT AT LANDING

CLOSED RISER STAIR/WOOD FINISH

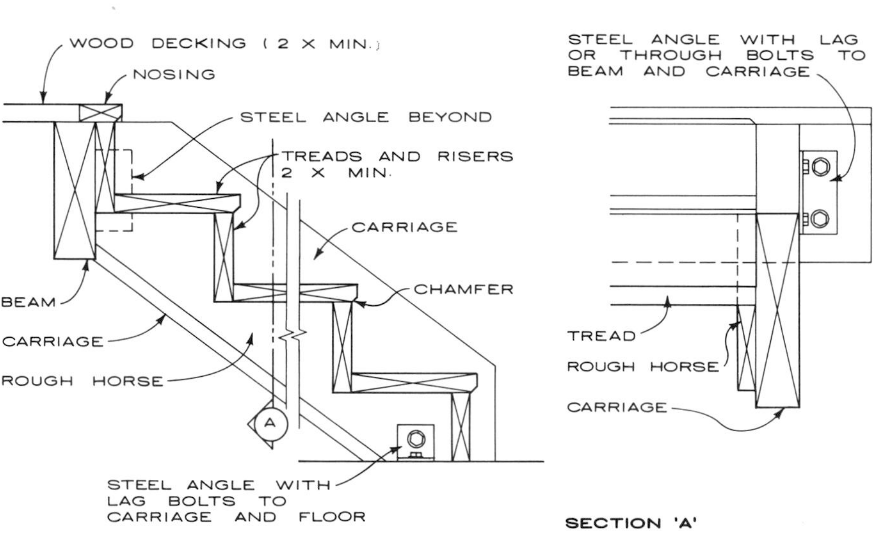
WOOD DECKING (2 X MIN.)
NOSING
STEEL ANGLE BEYOND
TREADS AND RISERS 2 X MIN.
CARRIAGE
CHAMFER
BEAM
CARRIAGE
ROUGH HORSE
A
STEEL ANGLE WITH LAG BOLTS TO CARRIAGE AND FLOOR
STEEL ANGLE WITH LAG OR THROUGH BOLTS TO BEAM AND CARRIAGE
TREAD
ROUGH HORSE
CARRIAGE
SECTION 'A'

HEAVY TIMBER STAIR

The Bumgardner Partnership/Architects; Seattle, Washington

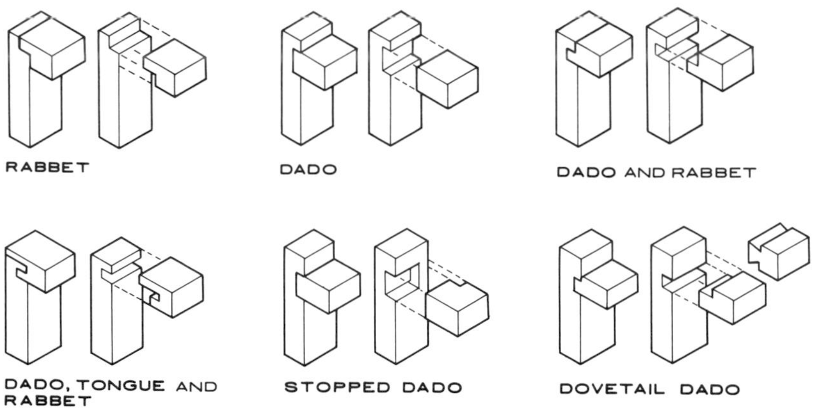

RABBET

DADO

DADO AND RABBET

DADO, TONGUE AND RABBET

STOPPED DADO

DOVETAIL DADO

RABBET AND DADO

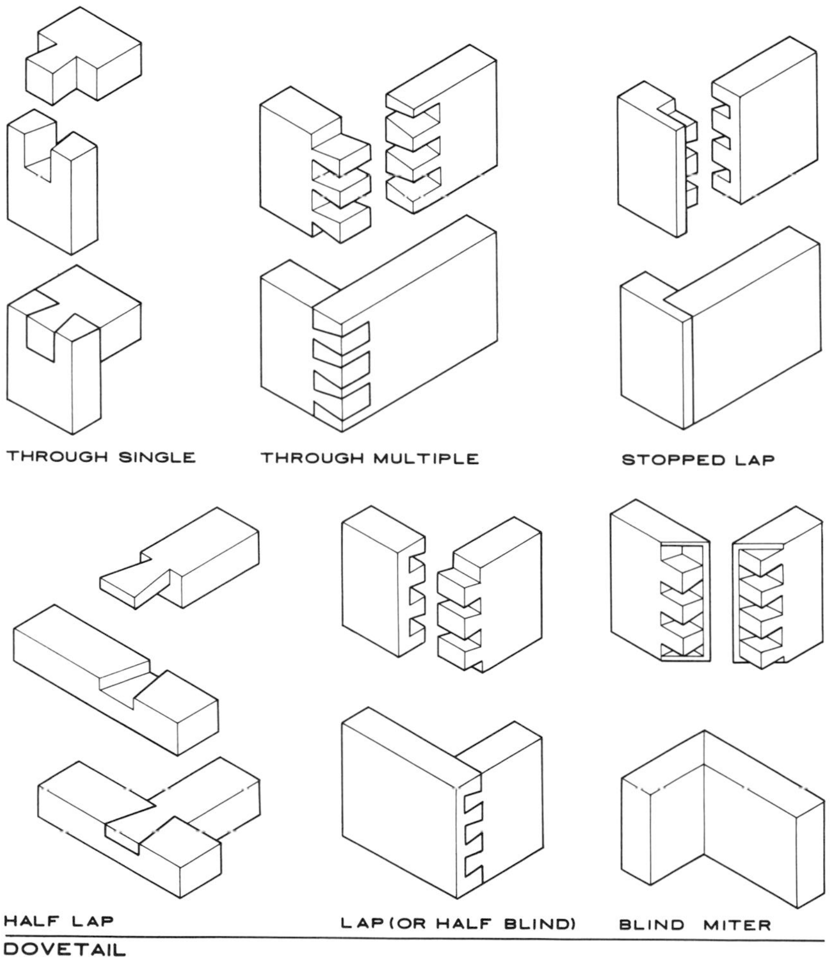

THROUGH SINGLE

THROUGH MULTIPLE

STOPPED LAP

HALF LAP

LAP (OR HALF BLIND)

BLIND MITER

DOVETAIL

NOTES

1. Wood joints may be grouped into three classes: (1) right angle joints, (2) end joints, and (3) edge joints.

2. End joints are used to increase the length of a wood member. By proper utilization of end joints short lengths can be used which might otherwise have been wasted.

3. Edge joints are used to increase the width of a wood member. By giving narrow widths greater use of narrow stock may result.

4. A rabbet (rebate) is a right angle cut made along a corner edge of a wood member. A dado is a rectangular groove cut across the grain of a wood member. If this groove extends along the edge or face of a wood member (being cut parallel to the grain) it is known as a plough (plow).

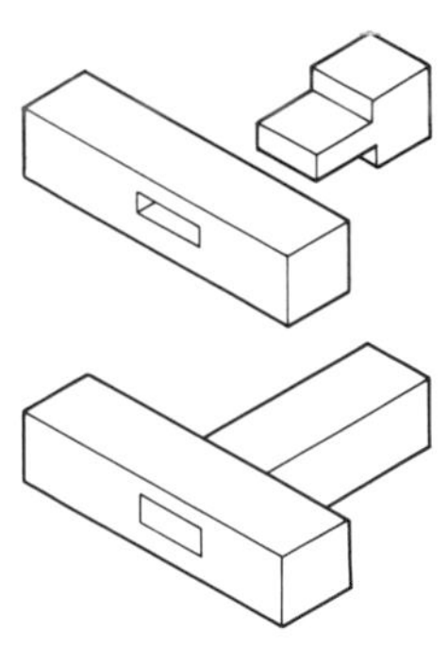

FULL (OR THROUGH)

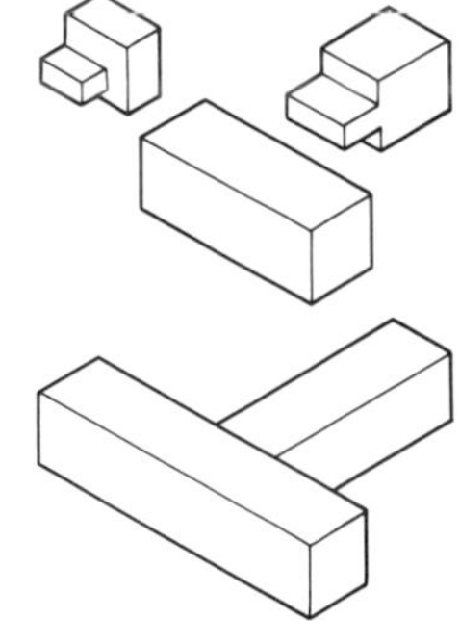

BLIND AND STUB

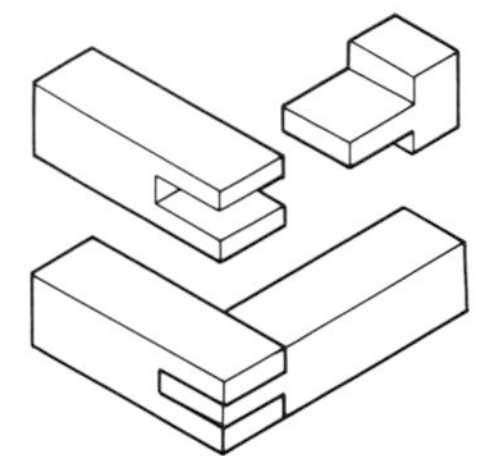

SHIP (OR OPEN)

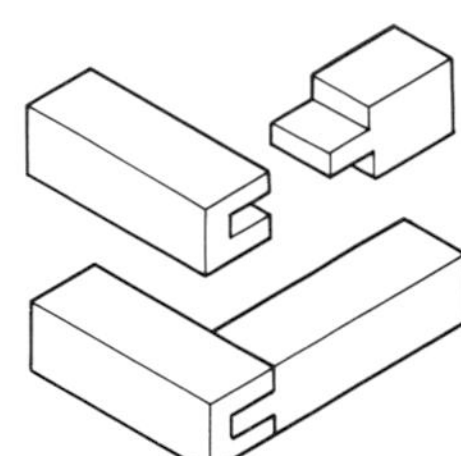

HALF BLIND

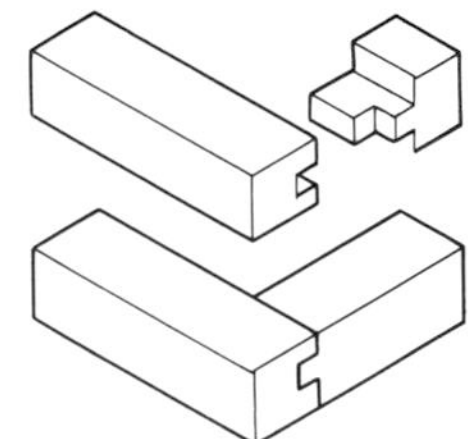

HAUNCH

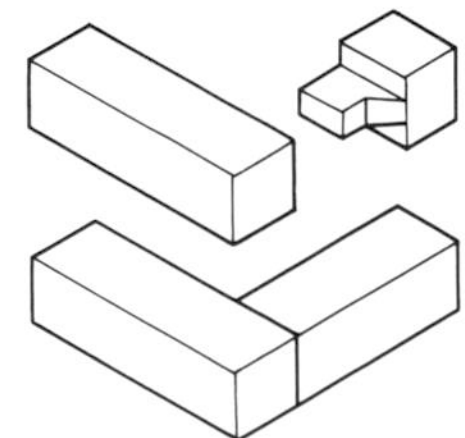

HAUNCH – BLIND

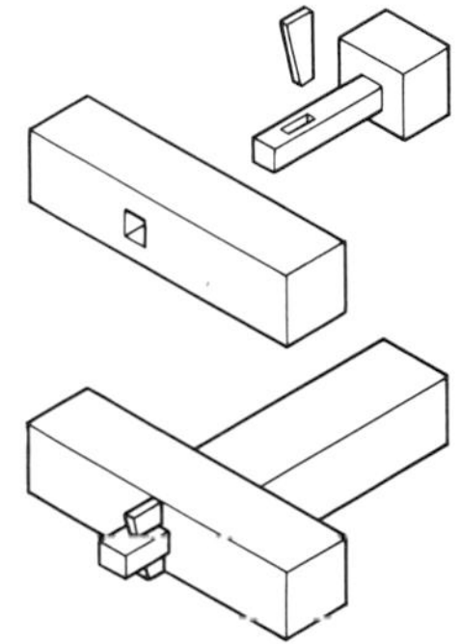

KEYED

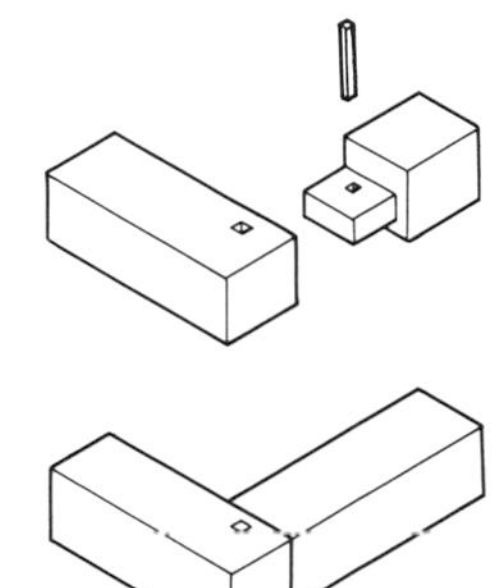

PINNED BLIND

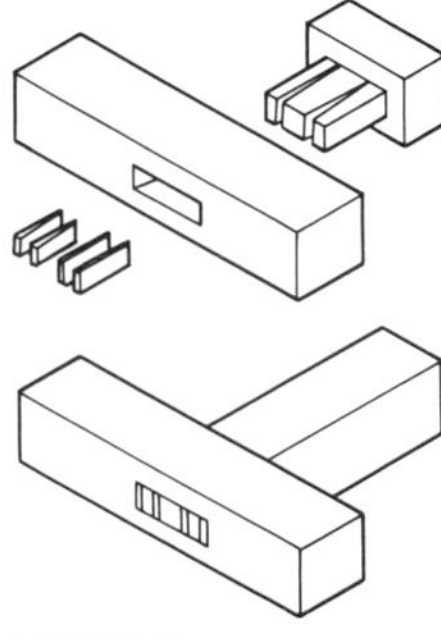

WEDGED

MORTISE AND TENON

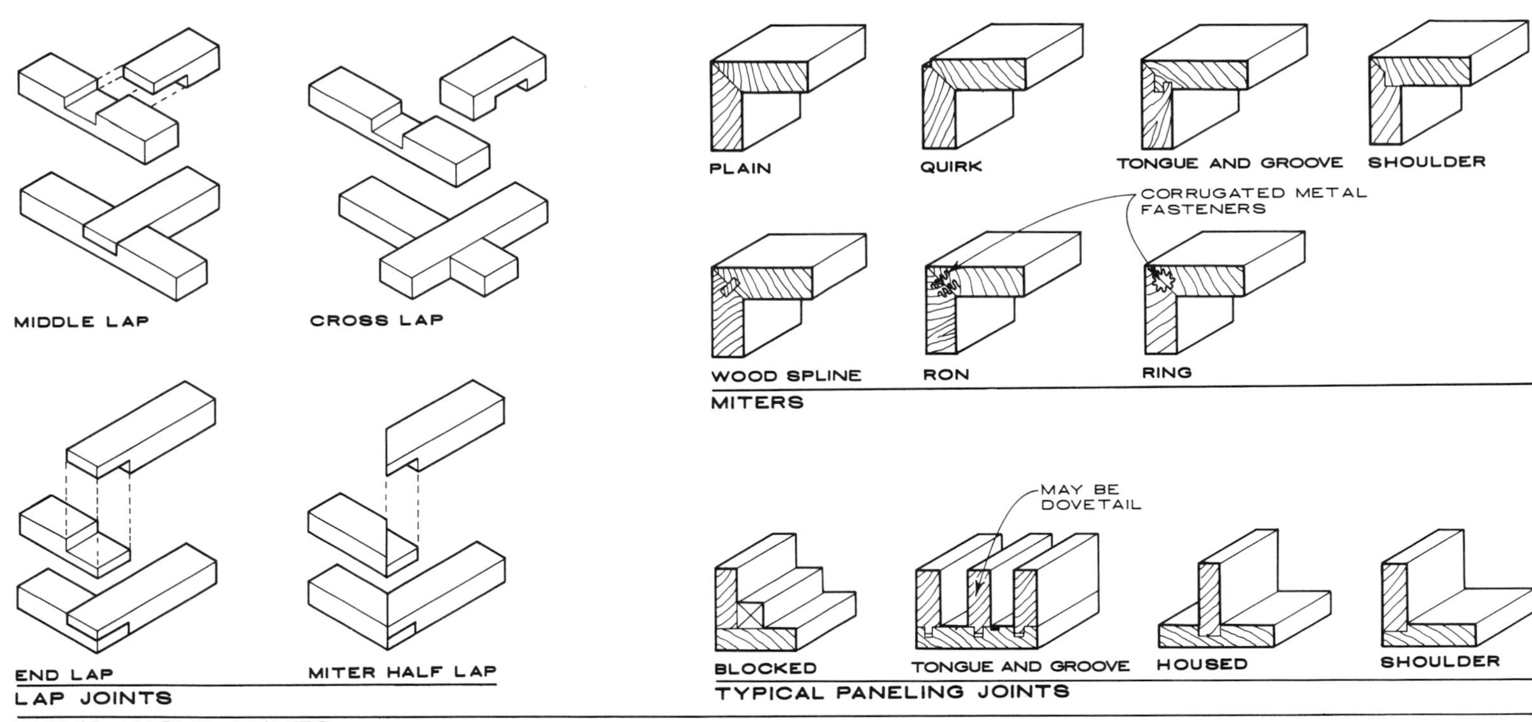
MIDDLE LAP
CROSS LAP
PLAIN
QUIRK
TONGUE AND GROOVE
SHOULDER
CORRUGATED METAL FASTENERS
WOOD SPLINE
RON
RING
MITERS
MAY BE DOVETAIL
END LAP
MITER HALF LAP
LAP JOINTS
BLOCKED
TONGUE AND GROOVE
HOUSED
SHOULDER
TYPICAL PANELING JOINTS

RIGHT ANGLE JOINTS

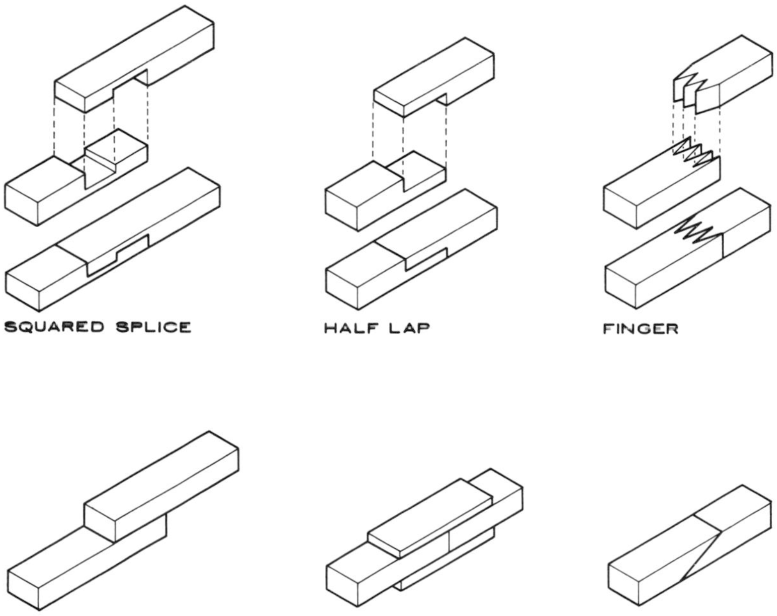

SQUARED SPLICE

HALF LAP

FINGER

LAP

SPLICE

SCARF

END JOINTS

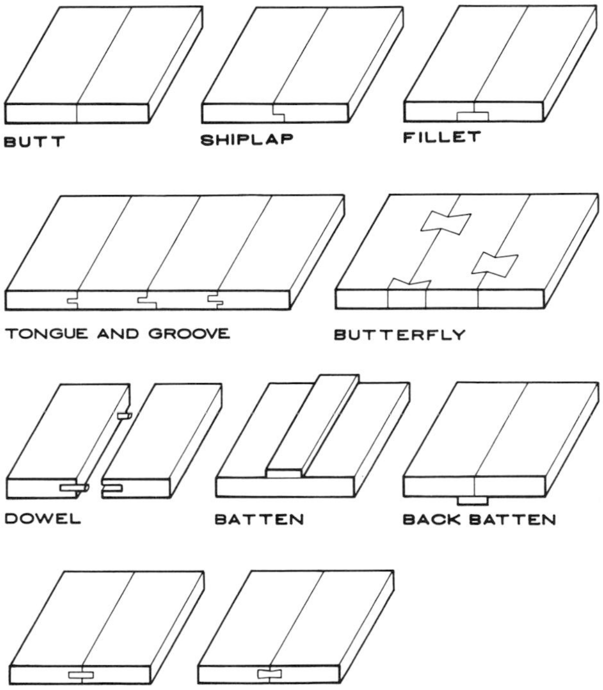

BUTT

SHIPLAP

FILLET

TONGUE AND GROOVE

BUTTERFLY

DOWEL

BATTEN

BACK BATTEN

SPLINE

BUTTERFLY SPLINE

EDGE JOINTS

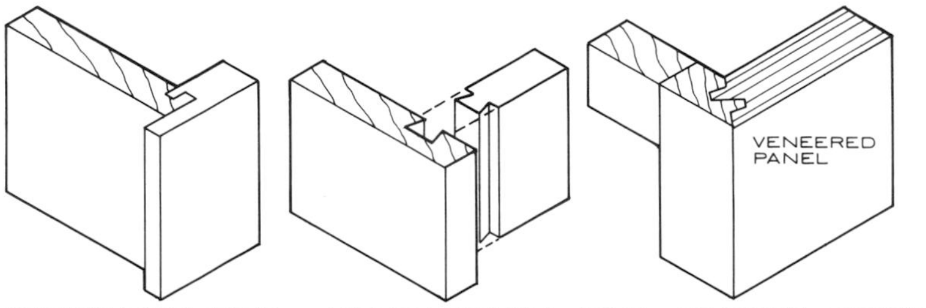

DRAWER LOCK JOINT

FRENCH DOVETAIL JOINT

MILLWORK CORNER

VENEERED PANEL

CORNER DETAILS

THROUGH DADO

STOP DADO

BLIND DADO

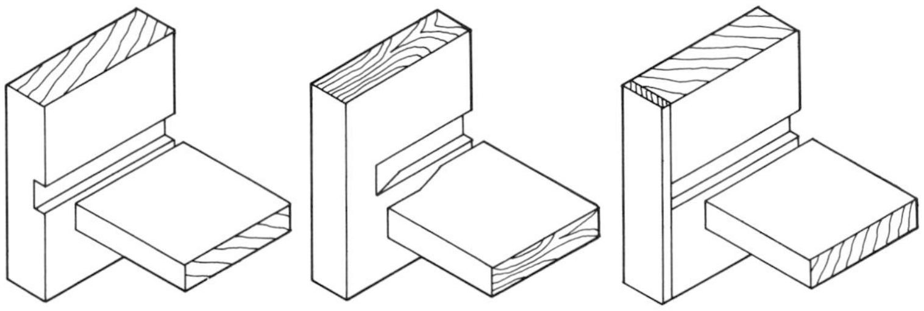

SHELF DETAILS

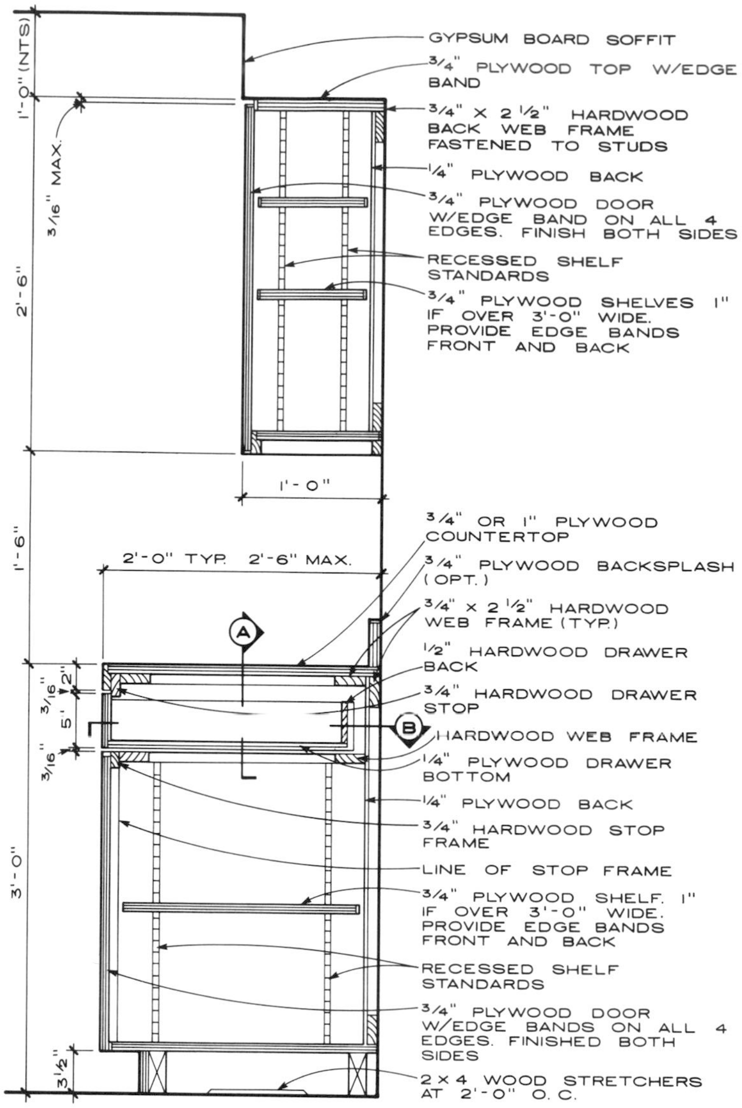

1'-0" (NTS)
3/16" MAX.
2'-6"
1'-6"
3'-0"
1'-0"
2'-0" TYP. 2'-6" MAX.
3/16"
1/2"
5"
3/16"
3 1/2"

GYPSUM BOARD SOFFIT
3/4" PLYWOOD TOP W/EDGE BAND
3/4" X 2 1/2" HARDWOOD BACK WEB FRAME FASTENED TO STUDS
1/4" PLYWOOD BACK
3/4" PLYWOOD DOOR W/EDGE BAND ON ALL 4 EDGES. FINISH BOTH SIDES
RECESSED SHELF STANDARDS
3/4" PLYWOOD SHELVES 1" IF OVER 3'-0" WIDE. PROVIDE EDGE BANDS FRONT AND BACK
3/4" OR 1" PLYWOOD COUNTERTOP
3/4" PLYWOOD BACKSPLASH (OPT.)
3/4" X 2 1/2" HARDWOOD WEB FRAME (TYP.)
1/2" HARDWOOD DRAWER BACK
3/4" HARDWOOD DRAWER STOP
HARDWOOD WEB FRAME
1/4" PLYWOOD DRAWER BOTTOM
1/4" PLYWOOD BACK
3/4" HARDWOOD STOP FRAME
LINE OF STOP FRAME
3/4" PLYWOOD SHELF. 1" IF OVER 3'-0" WIDE. PROVIDE EDGE BANDS FRONT AND BACK
RECESSED SHELF STANDARDS
3/4" PLYWOOD DOOR W/EDGE BANDS ON ALL 4 EDGES. FINISHED BOTH SIDES
2 X 4 WOOD STRETCHERS AT 2'-0" O.C.

SECTION THROUGH BASE AND WALL CABINETS

3/4" OR 1" PLYWOOD COUNTERTOP. WOOD VENEER WITH SHOULDER MITRE SHOWN
3/4" OR 2 1/2" HARDWOOD TOP WEB FRAME
1/2" HARDWOOD DRAWER SIDES
3/4" PLYWOOD END PANEL
CONSULT MANUFACTURER FOR DIMENSIONS AND SPECIFICATIONS OF DRAWER GLIDES
1/4" PLYWOOD DRAWER BOTTOM
3/4" PLYWOOD DIVIDER
HARDWOOD WEB FRAME

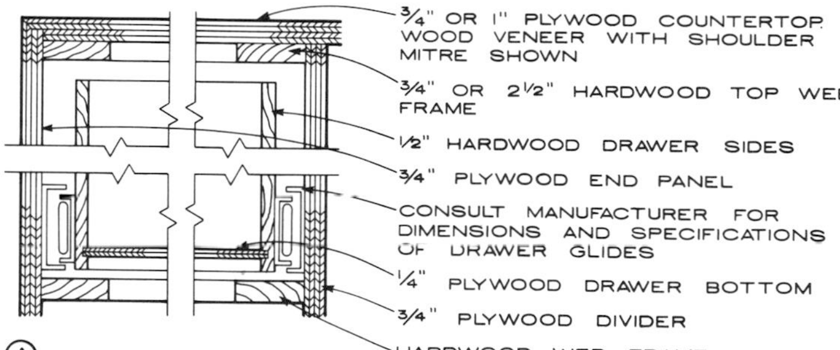

(A) SECTION THROUGH DRAWER

3/4" X 2 1/2" HARDWOOD BACK WEB FRAME
1/4" PLYWOOD BACK
1/2" HARDWOOD DRAWER BACK LET INTO DRAWER SIDES
3/4" PLYWOOD DIVIDER
1/2" HARDWOOD DRAWER SIDES
FRENCH DOVETAIL
HARDWOOD FRONT FRAME
3/4" PLYWOOD DRAWER FRONT WITH HARDWOOD EDGE BANDS ALL SIDES
3/16" MAX.

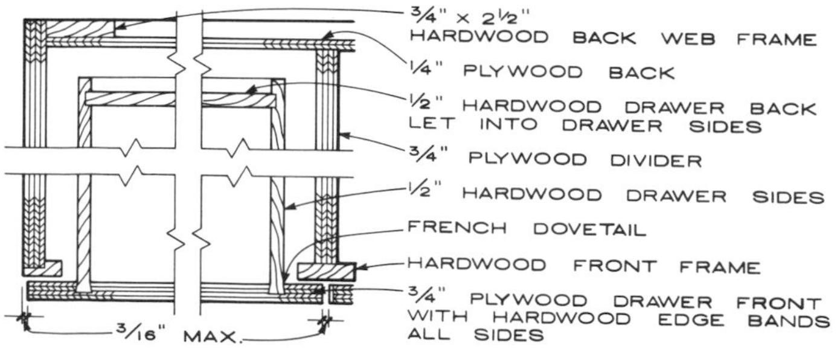

(B) PLAN OF DRAWER

CUSTOM GRADE (FLUSH OVERLAY TYPE)

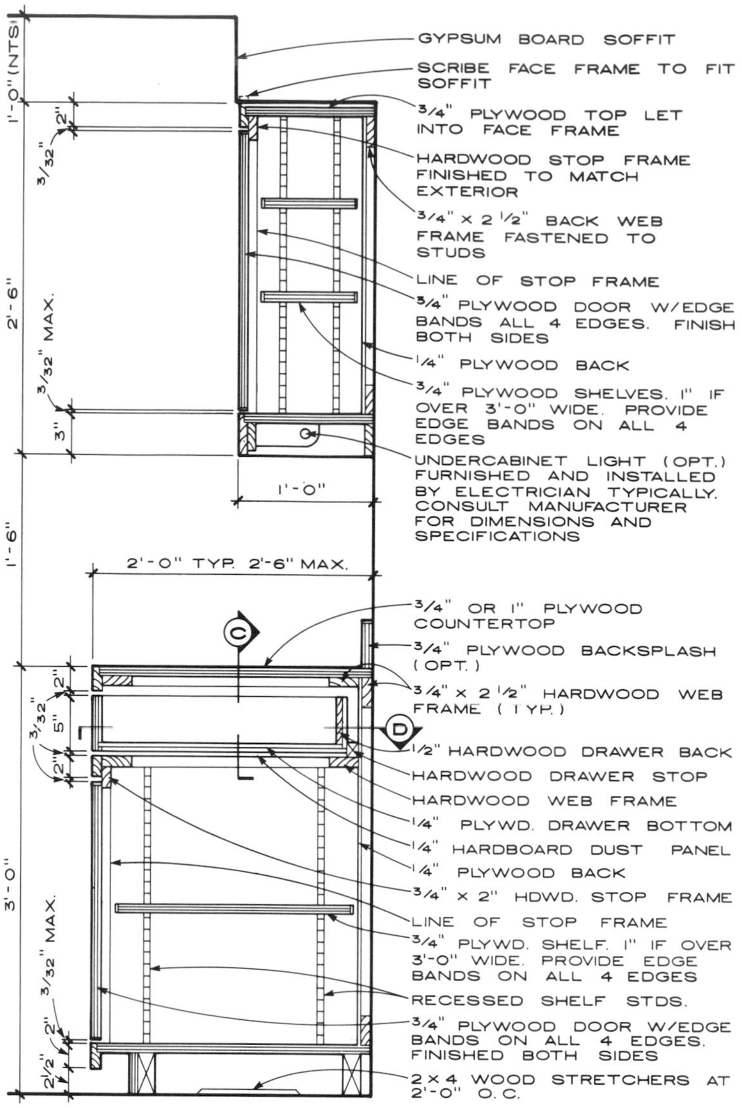

1'-0" (NTS)
2"
3/32"
2'-6"
3/32" MAX.
3"
1'-0"
1'-6"
2'-0" TYP. 2'-6" MAX.
2"
3/32"
5"
2"
3'-0"
3/32" MAX.
2"
2 1/2"

GYPSUM BOARD SOFFIT
SCRIBE FACE FRAME TO FIT SOFFIT
3/4" PLYWOOD TOP LET INTO FACE FRAME
HARDWOOD STOP FRAME FINISHED TO MATCH EXTERIOR
3/4" X 2 1/2" BACK WEB FRAME FASTENED TO STUDS
LINE OF STOP FRAME
3/4" PLYWOOD DOOR W/EDGE BANDS ALL 4 EDGES. FINISH BOTH SIDES
1/4" PLYWOOD BACK
3/4" PLYWOOD SHELVES. 1" IF OVER 3'-0" WIDE. PROVIDE EDGE BANDS ON ALL 4 EDGES
UNDERCABINET LIGHT (OPT.) FURNISHED AND INSTALLED BY ELECTRICIAN TYPICALLY. CONSULT MANUFACTURER FOR DIMENSIONS AND SPECIFICATIONS
3/4" OR 1" PLYWOOD COUNTERTOP
3/4" PLYWOOD BACKSPLASH (OPT.)
3/4" X 2 1/2" HARDWOOD WEB FRAME (TYP.)
1/2" HARDWOOD DRAWER BACK
HARDWOOD DRAWER STOP
HARDWOOD WEB FRAME
1/4" PLYWD. DRAWER BOTTOM
1/4" HARDBOARD DUST PANEL
1/4" PLYWOOD BACK
3/4" X 2" HDWD. STOP FRAME
LINE OF STOP FRAME
3/4" PLYWD. SHELF. 1" IF OVER 3'-0" WIDE. PROVIDE EDGE BANDS ON ALL 4 EDGES
RECESSED SHELF STDS.
3/4" PLYWOOD DOOR W/EDGE BANDS ON ALL 4 EDGES. FINISHED BOTH SIDES
2 X 4 WOOD STRETCHERS AT 2'-0" O.C.

SECTION THROUGH BASE AND WALL CABINETS

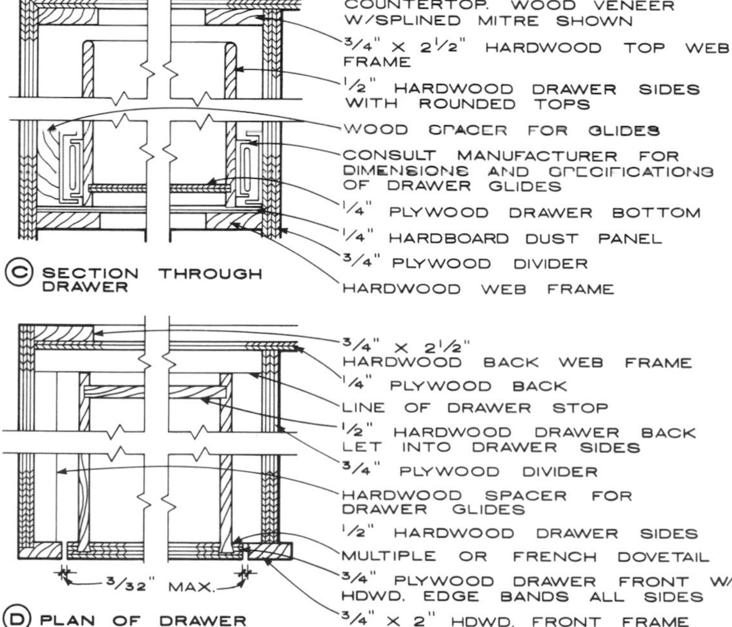
3/4" OR 1" PLYWOOD COUNTERTOP. WOOD VENEER W/SPLINED MITRE SHOWN
3/4" X 2 1/2" HARDWOOD TOP WEB FRAME
1/2" HARDWOOD DRAWER SIDES WITH ROUNDED TOPS
WOOD SPACER FOR GLIDES
CONSULT MANUFACTURER FOR DIMENSIONS AND SPECIFICATIONS OF DRAWER GLIDES
1/4" PLYWOOD DRAWER BOTTOM
1/4" HARDBOARD DUST PANEL
3/4" PLYWOOD DIVIDER
HARDWOOD WEB FRAME
(C) SECTION THROUGH DRAWER
3/4" X 2 1/2" HARDWOOD BACK WEB FRAME
1/4" PLYWOOD BACK
LINE OF DRAWER STOP
1/2" HARDWOOD DRAWER BACK LET INTO DRAWER SIDES
3/4" PLYWOOD DIVIDER
HARDWOOD SPACER FOR DRAWER GLIDES
1/2" HARDWOOD DRAWER SIDES
MULTIPLE OR FRENCH DOVETAIL
3/4" PLYWOOD DRAWER FRONT W/ HDWD. EDGE BANDS ALL SIDES
3/4" X 2" HDWD. FRONT FRAME
3/32" MAX.
(D) PLAN OF DRAWER

PREMIUM GRADE (EXPOSED FRONT FRAME TYPE)

John S. Fornaro, AIA; Columbia, Virginia

CABINET CLASSIFICATIONS

The Architectural Woodworking Institute classifies cabinets in three groups: economy, the lowest grade; custom, the average grade; and premium, the best grade. These details show the progression to higher quality and generally follow the AWI standards, but do not show all possible variations of cabinet details. Woodworking shops frequently set their own quality standards; thus many higher quality details can be found in lower quality work, and vice versa. Also, an architect's design may require crossover of details between the different quality groups.

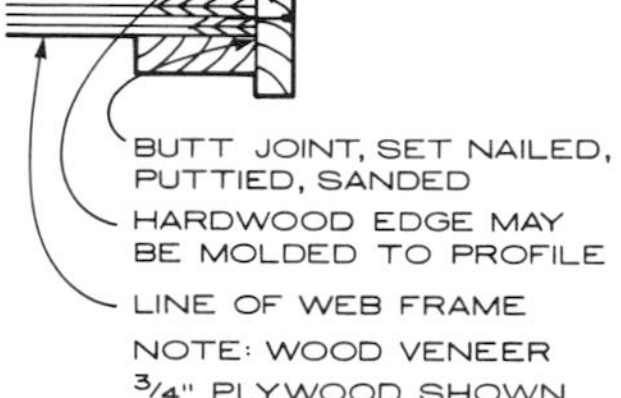

BUTT JOINT, SET NAILED, PUTTIED, SANDED
HARDWOOD EDGE MAY BE MOLDED TO PROFILE
LINE OF WEB FRAME
NOTE: WOOD VENEER 3/4" PLYWOOD SHOWN

ECONOMY GRADE

EDGE DETAIL

SHOULDER MITER SHOWN, TONGUE AND GROOVE MITER AND WOOD SPLINE MITER ALSO USED

LINE OF WEB FRAME

NOTE: WOOD VENEER 3/4" PLYWOOD SHOWN

CUSTOM GRADE

EDGE DETAIL

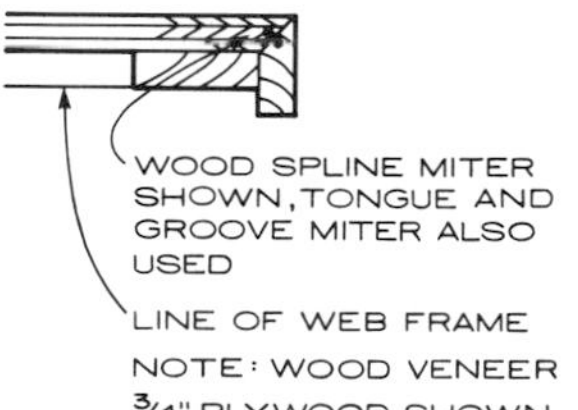

WOOD SPLINE MITER SHOWN, TONGUE AND GROOVE MITER ALSO USED
LINE OF WEB FRAME
NOTE: WOOD VENEER 3/4" PLYWOOD SHOWN

PREMIUM GRADE

EDGE DETAIL

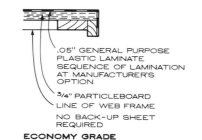

.05" GENERAL PURPOSE PLASTIC LAMINATE SEQUENCE OF LAMINATION AT MANUFACTURER'S OPTION

3/4" PARTICLEBOARD

LINE OF WEB FRAME

NO BACK-UP SHEET REQUIRED

ECONOMY GRADE

EDGE DETAIL

.05" GENERAL PURPOSE PLASTIC LAMINATE EDGES APPLIED BEFORE TOP.

3/4" PARTICLEBOARD

.02" BACK-UP SHEET FOR UNSUPPORTED AREAS OVER 6 SQ FT

CUSTOM GRADE

EDGE DETAIL

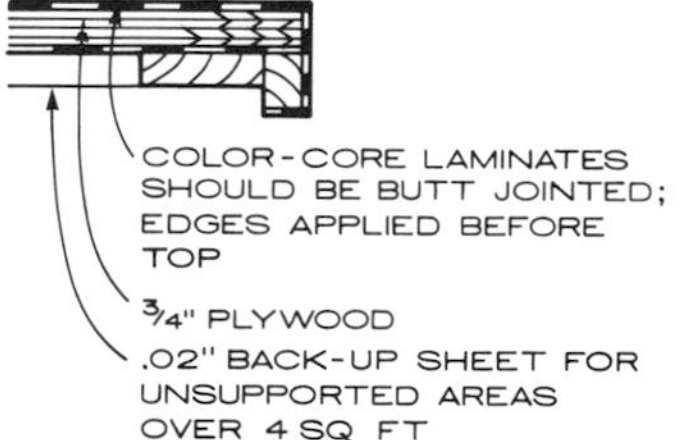

COLOR-CORE LAMINATES SHOULD BE BUTT JOINTED; EDGES APPLIED BEFORE TOP
3/4" PLYWOOD
.02" BACK-UP SHEET FOR UNSUPPORTED AREAS OVER 4 SQ FT

PREMIUM GRADE

EDGE DETAIL

SOAPSTONE, SLATE, OR MARBLE ON THIN-SET BED

2-LAYERS 3/4" PLYWOOD

PREMIUM GRADE

STONE COUNTER

POST-FORMED PLASTIC LAMINATE

CUSTOM OR ECONOMY GRADE

POST-FORMED COUNTER

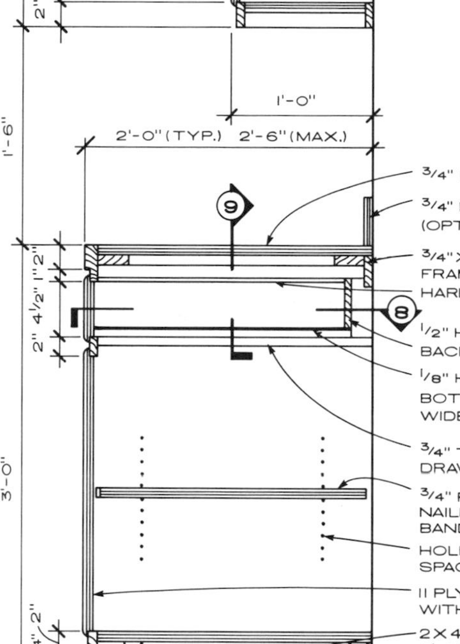

1'-0" (NTS)
2"
2'-6"
2"
1'-6"
1'-0"
2'-0" (TYP.) 2'-6" (MAX.)
1" 2"
2" 4 1/2"
3'-0"
2 1/4" 2"
9
8
GYPSUM BOARD SOFFIT (OPTIONAL)
3/4" X 2 1/2" HARDWOOD CLEAT FASTENED TO STUDS
11 PLY PLYWOOD LIPPED DOOR WITHOUT EDGE BANDING
3/4" PLYWOOD WITH NAILED AND GLUED EDGE BAND ON FRONT
1/8"-3/16" ϕ HOLES FOR SHELF SUPPORTS, CONSULT MANUFACTURER FOR DIMENSIONS
3/4" PLYWOOD COUNTERTOP
3/4" PLYWOOD BACKSPLASH (OPTIONAL)
3/4" X 2 1/2" HARDWOOD WEB FRAME
HARDWOOD TILT STRIP
1/2" HARDWOOD DRAWER BACK
1/8" HARDBOARD DRAWER BOTTOM. 1/4" IF OVER 1'-0" WIDE
3/4" THICK HARDWOOD DRAWER SUPPORT
3/4" PLYWOOD SHELF WITH NAILED AND GLUED EDGE BAND ON FRONT
HOLES FOR SHELF SUPPORT; SPACING OPTIONAL 1" TYPICAL
11 PLY PLYWOOD LIPPED DOOR WITHOUT EDGE BANDING
2X4 WOOD SLEEPER AT 2'-8" O.C.

ECONOMY GRADE

SECTION THROUGH BASE AND WALL CABINETS

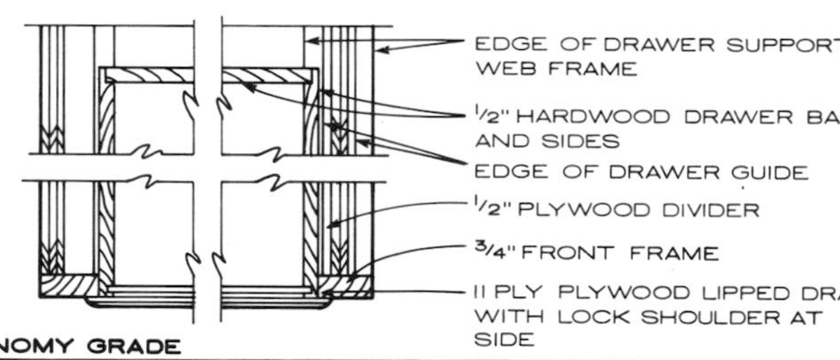

EDGE OF DRAWER SUPPORT WEB FRAME
1/2" HARDWOOD DRAWER BACK AND SIDES
EDGE OF DRAWER GUIDE
1/2" PLYWOOD DIVIDER
3/4" FRONT FRAME
11 PLY PLYWOOD LIPPED DRAWER WITH LOCK SHOULDER AT SIDE

ECONOMY GRADE

PLAN OF DRAWER (LIPPED DRAWER TYPE)

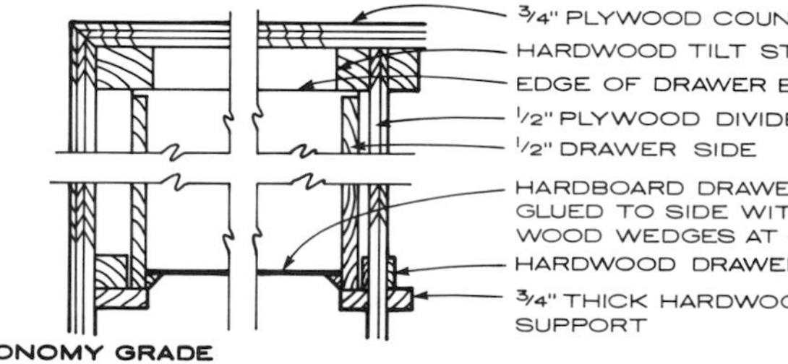

3/4" PLYWOOD COUNTERTOP
HARDWOOD TILT STRIP
EDGE OF DRAWER BACK
1/2" PLYWOOD DIVIDER
1/2" DRAWER SIDE
HARDBOARD DRAWER BOTTOM GLUED TO SIDE WITH 2" LONG WOOD WEDGES AT 6" O.C.
HARDWOOD DRAWER GUIDE
3/4" THICK HARDWOOD DRAWER SUPPORT

ECONOMY GRADE

SECTION THROUGH DRAWER

John S. Fornaro, AIA; Columbia, Virginia

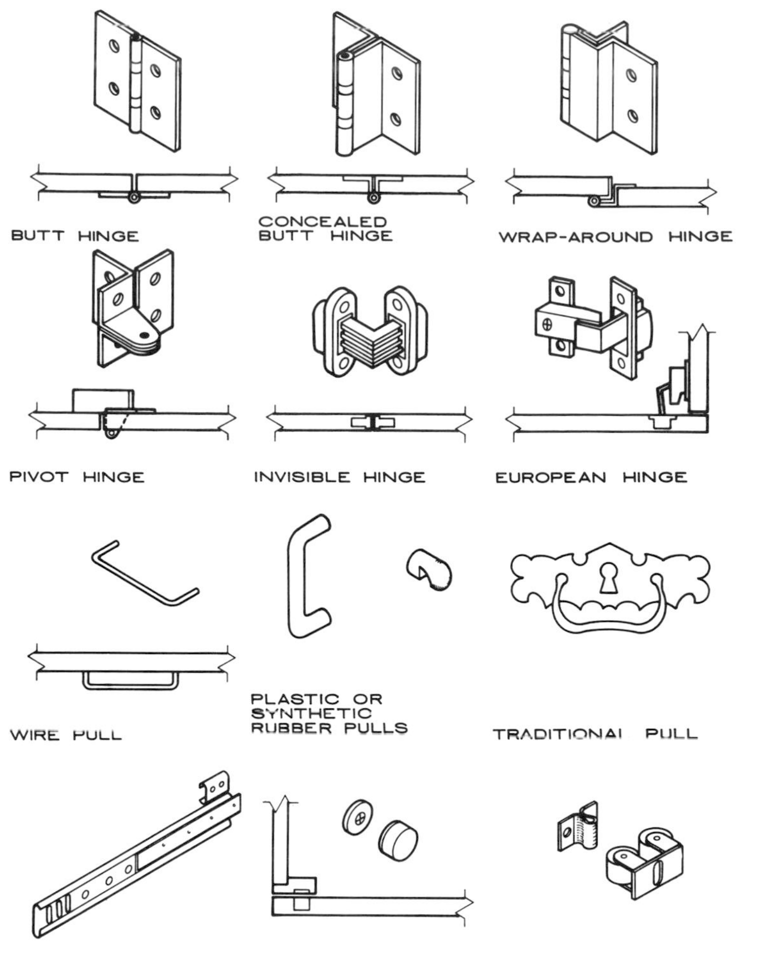

BUTT HINGE

CONCEALED BUTT HINGE

WRAP-AROUND HINGE

PIVOT HINGE

INVISIBLE HINGE

EUROPEAN HINGE

WIRE PULL

PLASTIC OR SYNTHETIC RUBBER PULLS

TRADITIONAL PULL

DRAWER GLIDE

MAGNETIC CATCH

FRICTION CATCH

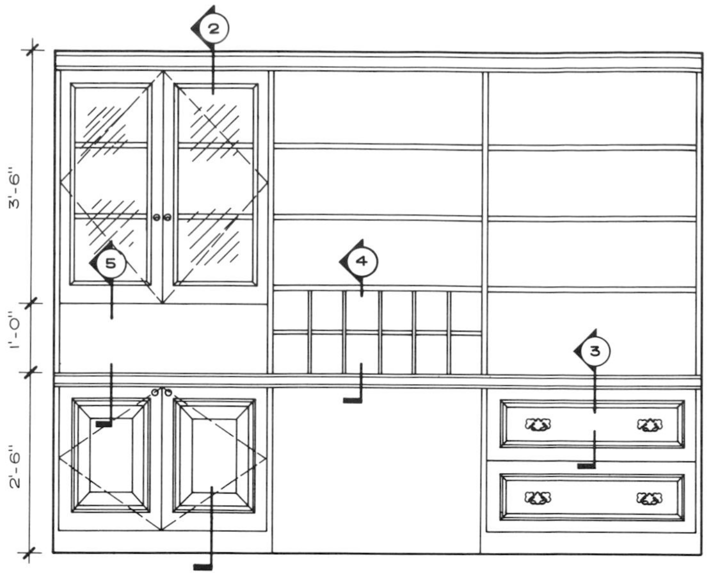

3'-6"
1'-0"
2'-6"

CUSTOM GRADE

① TRADITIONAL BUILT-IN CABINETRY

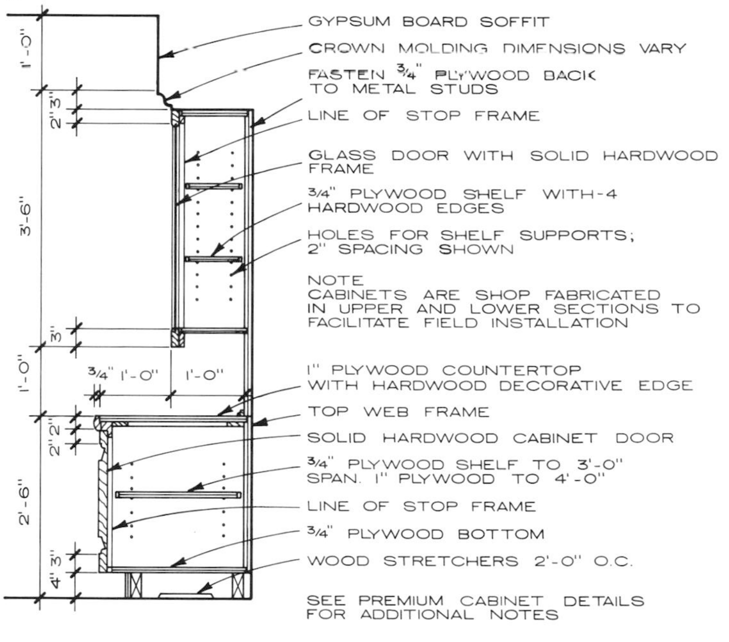

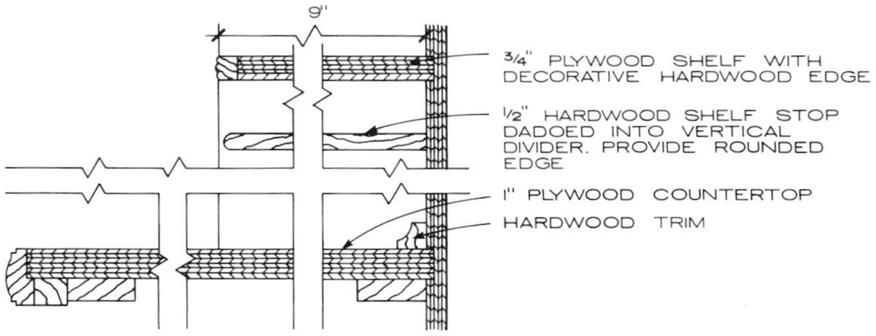

9"

3/4" PLYWOOD SHELF WITH DECORATIVE HARDWOOD EDGE

1/2" HARDWOOD SHELF STOP DADOED INTO VERTICAL DIVIDER. PROVIDE ROUNDED EDGE

1" PLYWOOD COUNTERTOP

HARDWOOD TRIM

④ SECTION THROUGH PIGEONHOLE

1'-0" 2" 3" 3'-6" 3" 1'-0" 3/4" 1'-0" 1'-0" 2" 2" 2'-6" 3" 4"

GYPSUM BOARD SOFFIT

CROWN MOLDING DIMENSIONS VARY

FASTEN 3/4" PLYWOOD BACK TO METAL STUDS

LINE OF STOP FRAME

GLASS DOOR WITH SOLID HARDWOOD FRAME

3/4" PLYWOOD SHELF WITH 4 HARDWOOD EDGES

HOLES FOR SHELF SUPPORTS; 2" SPACING SHOWN

NOTE
CABINETS ARE SHOP FABRICATED IN UPPER AND LOWER SECTIONS TO FACILITATE FIELD INSTALLATION

1" PLYWOOD COUNTERTOP WITH HARDWOOD DECORATIVE EDGE

TOP WEB FRAME

SOLID HARDWOOD CABINET DOOR

3/4" PLYWOOD SHELF TO 3'-0" SPAN. 1" PLYWOOD TO 4'-0"

LINE OF STOP FRAME

3/4" PLYWOOD BOTTOM

WOOD STRETCHERS 2'-0" O.C.

SEE PREMIUM CABINET DETAILS FOR ADDITIONAL NOTES

② SECTION THROUGH CABINETRY

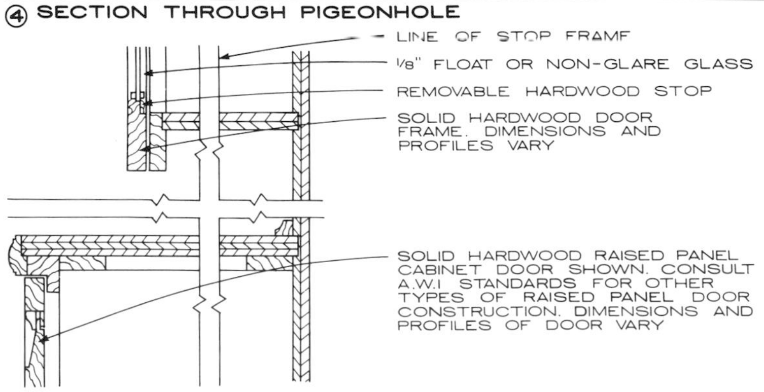

LINE OF STOP FRAME

1/8" FLOAT OR NON-GLARE GLASS

REMOVABLE HARDWOOD STOP

SOLID HARDWOOD DOOR FRAME. DIMENSIONS AND PROFILES VARY

SOLID HARDWOOD RAISED PANEL CABINET DOOR SHOWN. CONSULT A.W.I. STANDARDS FOR OTHER TYPES OF RAISED PANEL DOOR CONSTRUCTION. DIMENSIONS AND PROFILES OF DOOR VARY

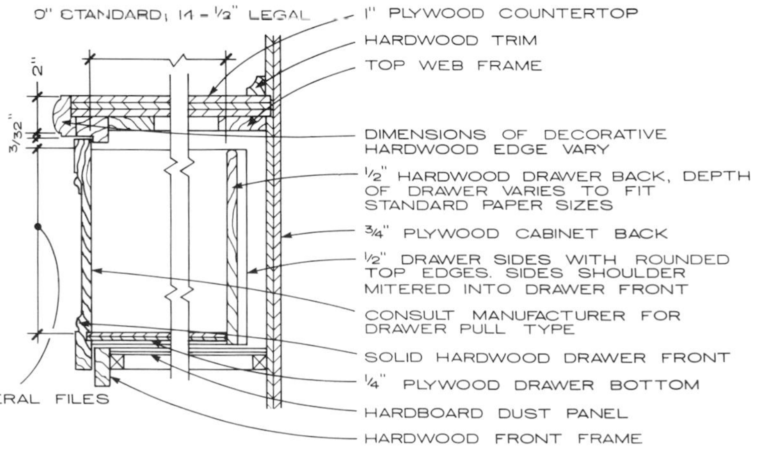

⑤ SECTION THROUGH GLASS AND WOOD DOOR

0" STANDARD; 14 - 1/2" LEGAL

2"

3/32"

1" PLYWOOD COUNTERTOP

HARDWOOD TRIM

TOP WEB FRAME

DIMENSIONS OF DECORATIVE HARDWOOD EDGE VARY

1/2" HARDWOOD DRAWER BACK, DEPTH OF DRAWER VARIES TO FIT STANDARD PAPER SIZES

3/4" PLYWOOD CABINET BACK

1/2" DRAWER SIDES WITH ROUNDED TOP EDGES. SIDES SHOULDER MITERED INTO DRAWER FRONT

CONSULT MANUFACTURER FOR DRAWER PULL TYPE

SOLID HARDWOOD DRAWER FRONT

1/4" PLYWOOD DRAWER BOTTOM

HARDBOARD DUST PANEL

HARDWOOD FRONT FRAME

10" FOR LATERAL FILES

③ SECTION THROUGH LATERAL FILE

John S. Fornaro, AIA; Columbia, Virginia

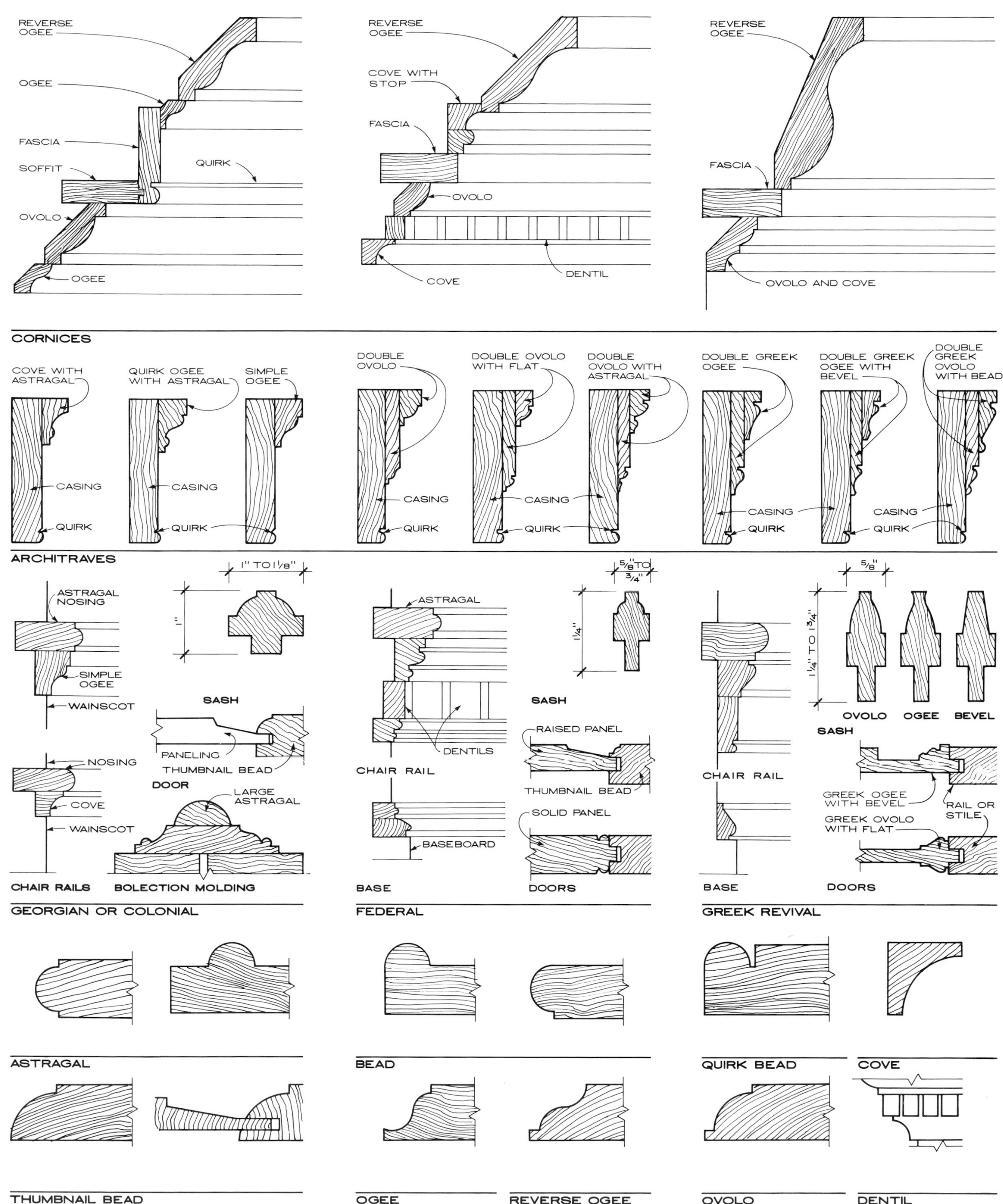

REVERSE OGEE
OGEE
FASCIA
SOFFIT
QUIRK
OVOLO
OGEE
REVERSE OGEE
COVE WITH STOP
FASCIA
OVOLO
COVE
DENTIL
REVERSE OGEE
FASCIA
OVOLO AND COVE
CORNICES
COVE WITH ASTRAGAL
QUIRK OGEE WITH ASTRAGAL
SIMPLE OGEE
DOUBLE OVOLO
DOUBLE OVOLO WITH FLAT
DOUBLE OVOLO WITH ASTRAGAL
DOUBLE GREEK OGEE
DOUBLE GREEK OGEE WITH BEVEL
DOUBLE GREEK OVOLO WITH BEAD
CASING
QUIRK
ARCHITRAVES
ASTRAGAL NOSING
SIMPLE OGEE
WAINSCOT
1" TO 1 1/8"
1"
SASH
PANELING
THUMBNAIL BEAD
DOOR
LARGE ASTRAGAL
NOSING
COVE
WAINSCOT
CHAIR RAILS
BOLECTION MOLDING
ASTRAGAL
DENTILS
CHAIR RAIL
BASEBOARD
BASE
5/8" TO 3/4"
1 1/4"
SASH
RAISED PANEL
THUMBNAIL BEAD
SOLID PANEL
DOORS
CHAIR RAIL
BASE
5/8"
1 1/4" TO 1 3/4"
OVOLO
OGEE
BEVEL
SASH
GREEK OGEE WITH BEVEL
RAIL OR STILE
GREEK OVOLO WITH FLAT
DOORS
GEORGIAN OR COLONIAL
FEDERAL
GREEK REVIVAL
ASTRAGAL
BEAD
QUIRK BEAD
COVE
THUMBNAIL BEAD
OGEE
REVERSE OGEE
OVOLO
DENTIL

Timothy B. McDonald; Washington, D.C.

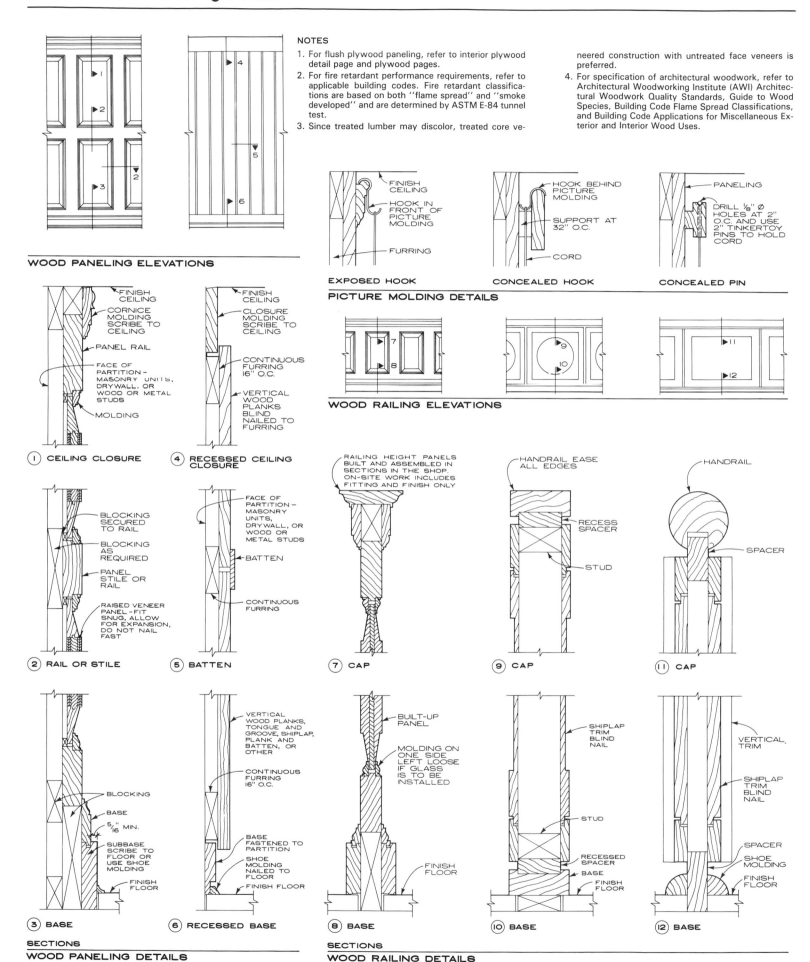

NOTES

1. For flush plywood paneling, refer to interior plywood detail page and plywood pages.
2. For fire retardant performance requirements, refer to applicable building codes. Fire retardant classifications are based on both "flame spread" and "smoke developed" and are determined by ASTM E-84 tunnel test.
3. Since treated lumber may discolor, treated core veneered construction with untreated face veneers is preferred.
4. For specification of architectural woodwork, refer to Architectural Woodworking Institute (AWI) Architectural Woodwork Quality Standards, Guide to Wood Species, Building Code Flame Spread Classifications, and Building Code Applications for Miscellaneous Exterior and Interior Wood Uses.

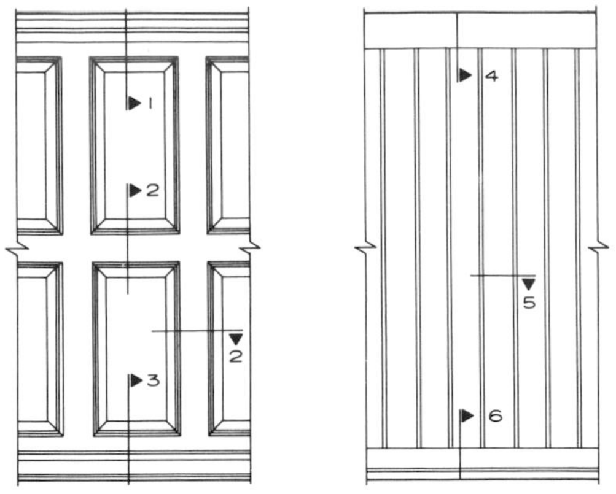

1
2
3
2
4
5
6

WOOD PANELING ELEVATIONS

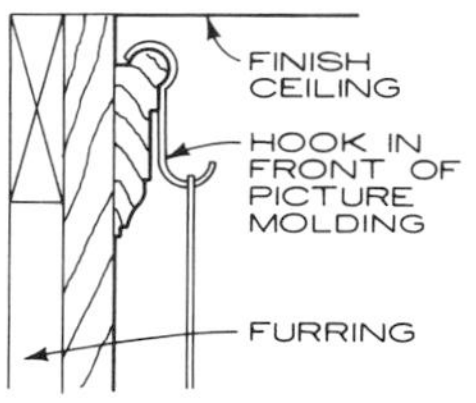

FINISH CEILING
HOOK IN FRONT OF PICTURE MOLDING
FURRING
HOOK BEHIND PICTURE MOLDING
SUPPORT AT 32" O.C.
CORD
PANELING
DRILL 1/8" Ø HOLES AT 2" O.C. AND USE 2" TINKERTOY PINS TO HOLD CORD

EXPOSED HOOK 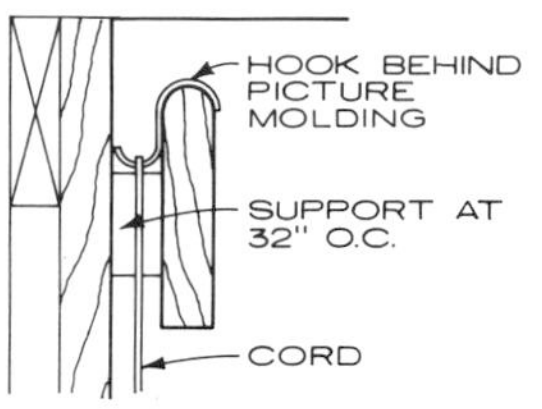 — CONCEALED HOOK 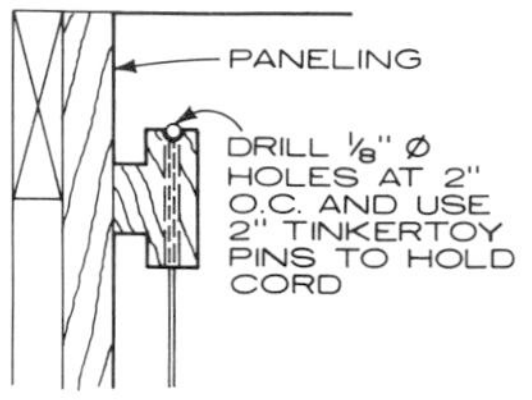 — CONCEALED PIN

PICTURE MOLDING DETAILS

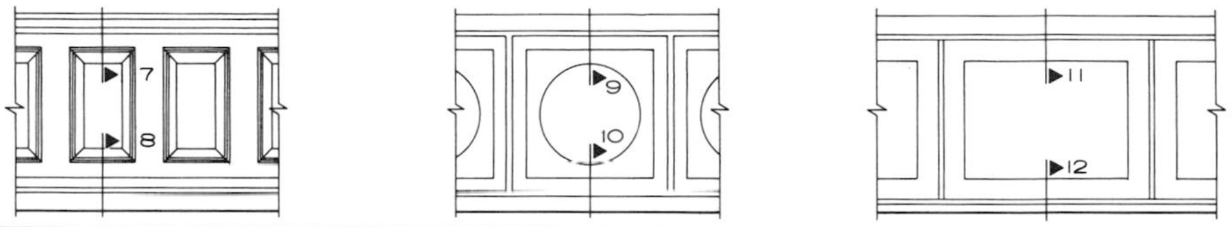

7
8
9
10
11
12

WOOD RAILING ELEVATIONS

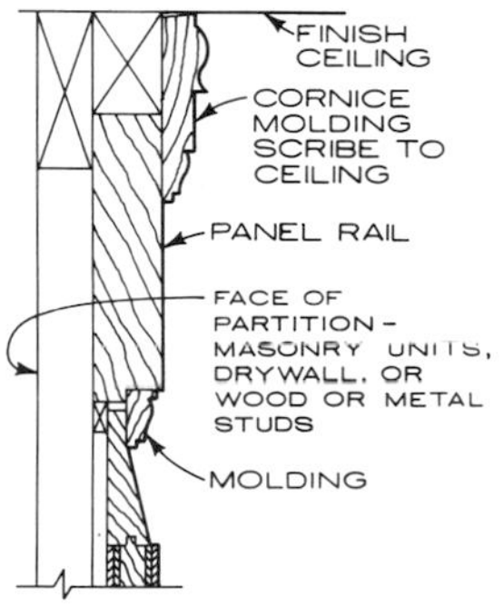

FINISH CEILING
CORNICE MOLDING SCRIBE TO CEILING
PANEL RAIL
FACE OF PARTITION - MASONRY UNITS, DRYWALL, OR WOOD OR METAL STUDS
MOLDING
FINISH CEILING
CLOSURE MOLDING SCRIBE TO CEILING
CONTINUOUS FURRING 16" O.C.
VERTICAL WOOD PLANKS BLIND NAILED TO FURRING

(1) CEILING CLOSURE

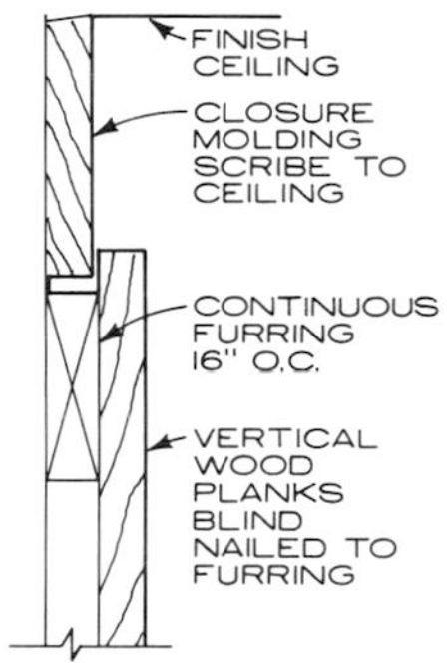

(4) RECESSED CEILING CLOSURE

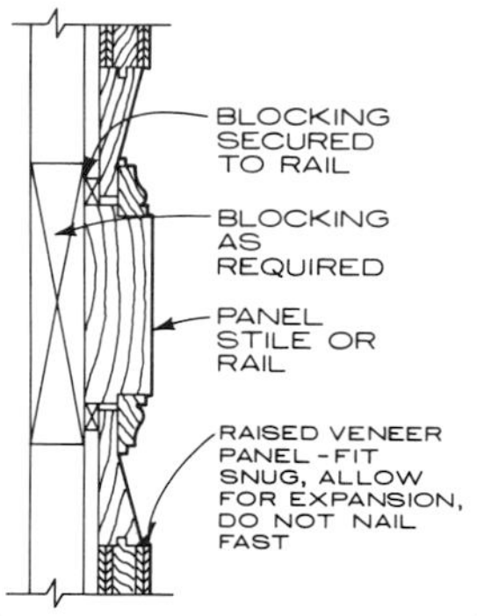

BLOCKING SECURED TO RAIL
BLOCKING AS REQUIRED
PANEL STILE OR RAIL
RAISED VENEER PANEL - FIT SNUG, ALLOW FOR EXPANSION, DO NOT NAIL FAST
FACE OF PARTITION - MASONRY UNITS, DRYWALL, OR WOOD OR METAL STUDS
BATTEN
CONTINUOUS FURRING

(2) RAIL OR STILE

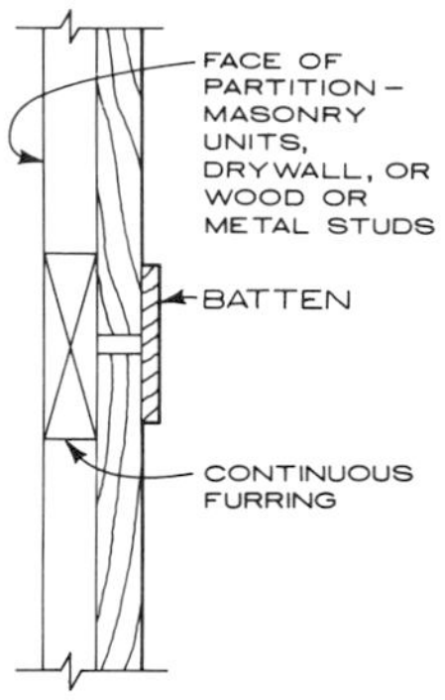

(5) BATTEN

BLOCKING
BASE
5/16" MIN.
SUBBASE SCRIBE TO FLOOR OR USE SHOE MOLDING
FINISH FLOOR
VERTICAL WOOD PLANKS, TONGUE AND GROOVE, SHIPLAP, PLANK AND BATTEN, OR OTHER
CONTINUOUS FURRING 16" O.C.
BASE FASTENED TO PARTITION
SHOE MOLDING NAILED TO FLOOR
FINISH FLOOR

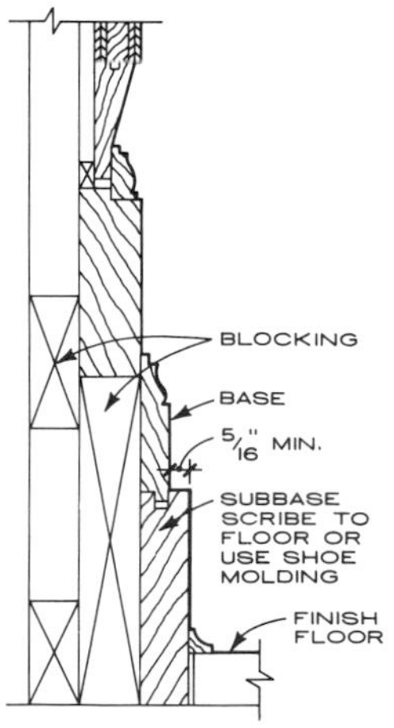

(3) BASE

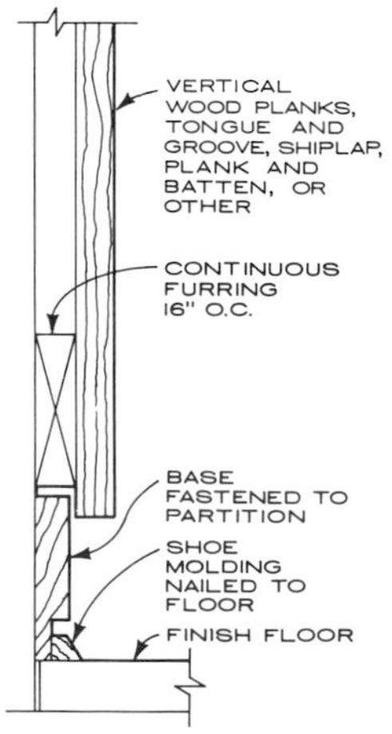

(6) RECESSED BASE

SECTIONS

WOOD PANELING DETAILS

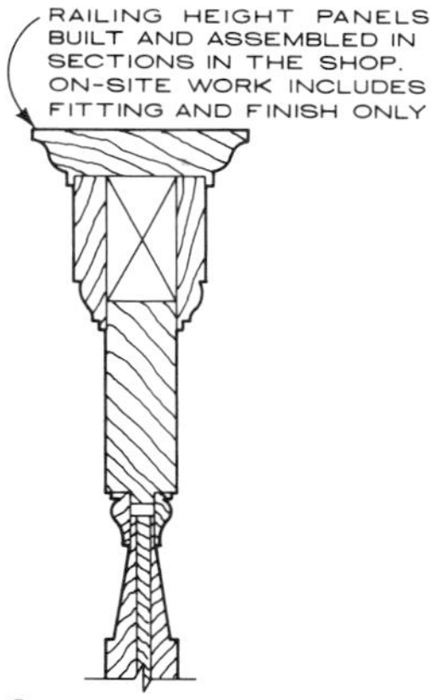

RAILING HEIGHT PANELS BUILT AND ASSEMBLED IN SECTIONS IN THE SHOP. ON-SITE WORK INCLUDES FITTING AND FINISH ONLY
HANDRAIL EASE ALL EDGES
RECESS SPACER
STUD
HANDRAIL
SPACER

(7) CAP

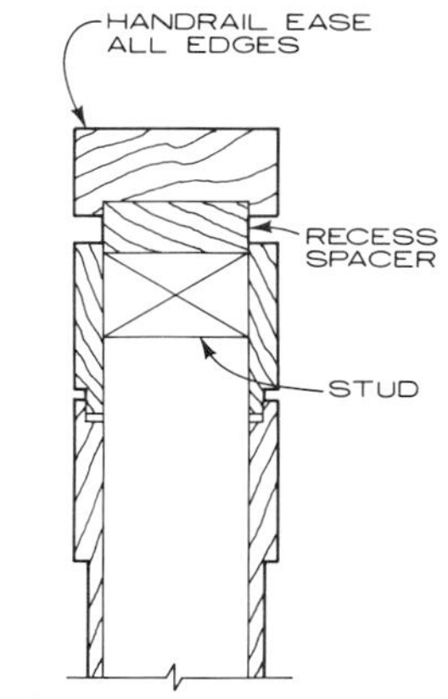

(9) CAP

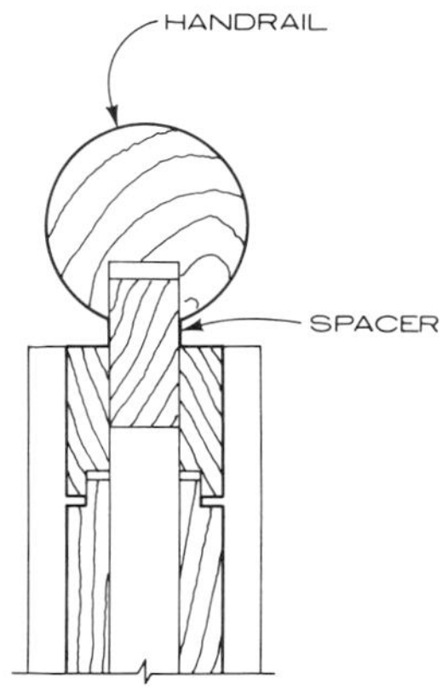

(11) CAP

BUILT-UP PANEL
MOLDING ON ONE SIDE LEFT LOOSE IF GLASS IS TO BE INSTALLED
FINISH FLOOR
SHIPLAP TRIM BLIND NAIL
STUD
RECESSED SPACER
BASE
FINISH FLOOR
VERTICAL TRIM
SHIPLAP TRIM BLIND NAIL
SPACER
SHOE MOLDING
FINISH FLOOR

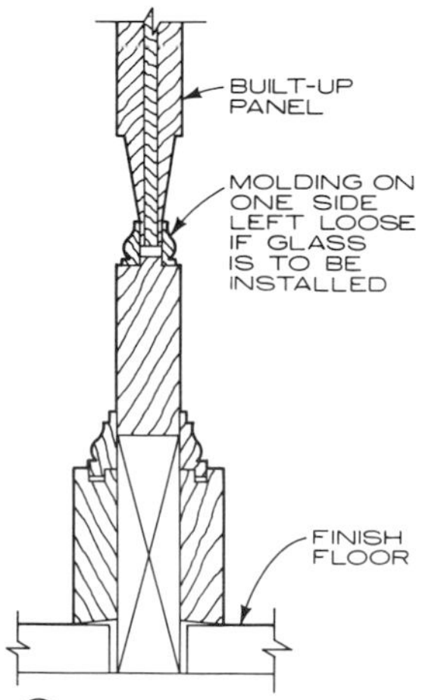

(8) BASE

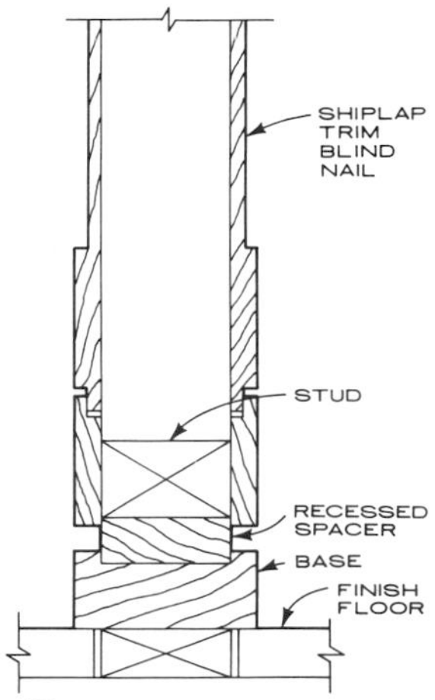

(10) BASE

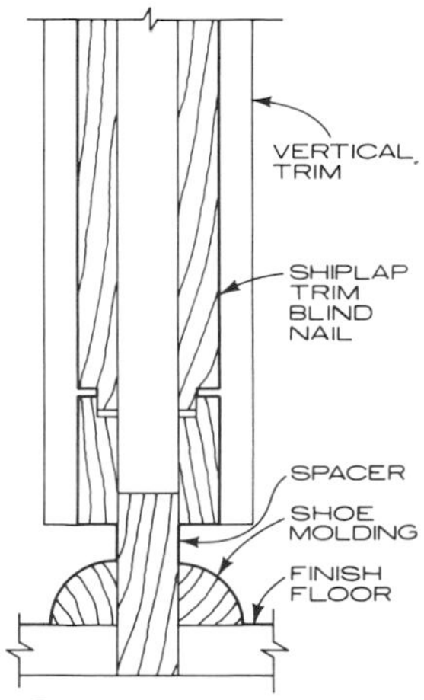

(12) BASE

SECTIONS

WOOD RAILING DETAILS

Charles Szoradi, AIA; Washington, D.C.

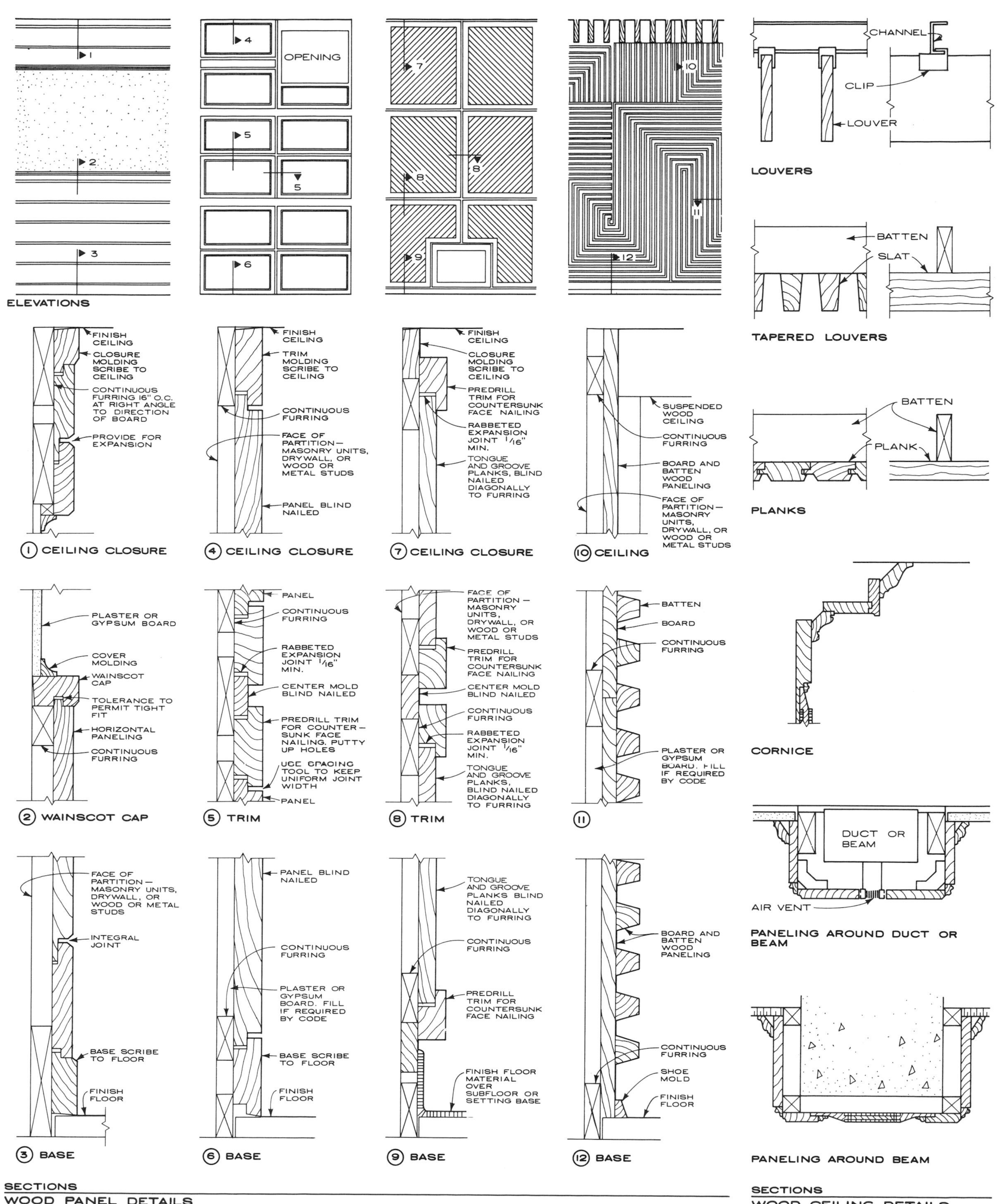

ELEVATIONS
OPENING
FINISH CEILING
CLOSURE MOLDING SCRIBE TO CEILING
CONTINUOUS FURRING 16" O.C. AT RIGHT ANGLE TO DIRECTION OF BOARD
PROVIDE FOR EXPANSION
1 CEILING CLOSURE
TRIM MOLDING SCRIBE TO CEILING
CONTINUOUS FURRING
FACE OF PARTITION— MASONRY UNITS, DRYWALL, OR WOOD OR METAL STUDS
PANEL BLIND NAILED
4 CEILING CLOSURE
PREDRILL TRIM FOR COUNTERSUNK FACE NAILING
RABBETED EXPANSION JOINT 1/16" MIN.
TONGUE AND GROOVE PLANKS, BLIND NAILED DIAGONALLY TO FURRING
7 CEILING CLOSURE
SUSPENDED WOOD CEILING
BOARD AND BATTEN WOOD PANELING
10 CEILING
PLASTER OR GYPSUM BOARD
COVER MOLDING
WAINSCOT CAP
TOLERANCE TO PERMIT TIGHT FIT
HORIZONTAL PANELING
2 WAINSCOT CAP
PANEL
CENTER MOLD BLIND NAILED
PREDRILL TRIM FOR COUNTER-SUNK FACE NAILING. PUTTY UP HOLES
USE SPACING TOOL TO KEEP UNIFORM JOINT WIDTH
5 TRIM
8 TRIM
BATTEN
BOARD
PLASTER OR GYPSUM BOARD. FILL IF REQUIRED BY CODE
11
INTEGRAL JOINT
BASE SCRIBE TO FLOOR
FINISH FLOOR
3 BASE
6 BASE
FINISH FLOOR MATERIAL OVER SUBFLOOR OR SETTING BASE
9 BASE
SHOE MOLD
12 BASE
SECTIONS
WOOD PANEL DETAILS
CHANNEL
CLIP
LOUVER
LOUVERS
SLAT
TAPERED LOUVERS
PLANK
PLANKS
CORNICE
DUCT OR BEAM
AIR VENT
PANELING AROUND DUCT OR BEAM
PANELING AROUND BEAM
SECTIONS
WOOD CEILING DETAILS

Charles Szoradi, AIA; Washington, D.C.

REFERENCES

GENERAL REFERENCES

Heavy Timber Construction Details, National Forest Products Association (NFPA)
National Design Specification for Wood Construction, National Forest Products Association (NFPA)
Typical Construction Details, American Institute of Timber Construction (AITC)
Timber Construction Manual, American Institute of Timber Construction (AITC)
Timber Design and Construction Sourcebook, 1989, Gotz, Hoor, Mohler, and Netterer, McGraw-Hill
Wood Engineering and Construction Handbook, 1989, Keith F. Faherty and Thomas G. Williamson, McGraw-Hill
Western Woods Use Book, Western Wood Products Association (WWPA)

DATA SOURCES: ORGANIZATIONS

American Institute of Timber Construction (AITC), 190, 193–195
American Plywood Association (APA), 176–179
American Society for Testing and Materials (ASTM), 204
Architectural Woodwork Institute (AWI), 196, 197, 204, 205
Automated Building Components, Inc., 191
Dow Chemical Company, 177
Federal Housing Administration (FHA), U.S. Department of Housing and Urban Development (HUD), 191
Hydro-Air Engineering, Inc., 191
Lumbermate, Inc., 191
Monex Corporation, 191
Potlatch Corporation, Wood Products Group, 180
Simpson Company, 181, 182, 189
Truss Plate Institute, 191
Weyerhaeuser Company, 180
Wood Fabricators, Inc., 191

DATA SOURCES: PUBLICATIONS

Basic Building Code, Building Officials and Code Administrators International (BOCA), 191
Bauen mit Holz, c. 1966, Kurt Hoffmann and Helga Griese, Verlag Julius Hoffman, Stuttgart, 173
Curbless Skylights, Rob Thallon, Fine Homebuilding, 173
National Design Specification for Wood Construction, National Forest Products Association, (NFPA), 183, 184
Southern Standard Building Code, Southern Building Code Congress (SBCC), 191
Southwest Sunspace, Valerie Walsh, Fine Homebuilding, 172
Uniform Building, 1982 ed., 1985 ed., International Conference of Building Officials (ICBO). Reprinted with permission of the publisher, 191

CHAPTER 7

THERMAL AND MOISTURE PROTECTION

BUILT-UP ROOFING

DECK OR SUBSTRATE	SURFACING	SLOPE (IN./FT)	BASE SHEET	PLYSHEETS	PLY BITUMEN (LB/SQ/PLY)	SURFACING BITUMEN (LB/SQ)	NOTES TO DESIGNER/SPECIFIER
Nonnailable decks or roof insulations (Consult manufacturer for approved types of roof insulation and recommendations for venting)[6]	Aggregate surface: Gravel: 400 lb/sq OR Slag: 300 lb/sq OR White marble chips: 400 lb/sq	Inclines up to ½:12	43 lb coated base spot mopped in asphalt to deck or solid mopped in asphalt to insulation[2]	3 coal tar saturated felts (perforated)	Coal tar @ 20–25	Coal tar @ 70–75	UL Class A on most deck and insulation types[1] Requires complete surfacing daily For ponded roofs, add 4th ply of felt and double flood and double gravel surface Base flashings must be installed in flashing cement Same configuration possible on slopes of ½-3 in./ft using Type III asphalt[5]
			Organic base felts 43 lb mopped. 43 lb coated base spot mopped in asphalt to deck or solid mopped in asphalt to insulation	3 organic felts (perforated)	Type II asphalt[3] @ 25	Type I asphalt[4] @ 60	
		Inclines up to ½:12	Fiberglass base spot mopped to deck or solid mopped to insulation	3 fiberglass plysheets, ASTM D2178 Type IV	Coal tar @ 25–30	Coal tar @ 75	UL Class A on most deck and insulation types[1] Roofing may be left up to 6 months before surfacing For ponded roofs, add plysheet and double flood and double gravel surface Base flashings must be installed in flashing cement
				3 fiberglass plysheets[7]	Type II asphalt @ 25	Type I asphalt @ 60	Same configuration possible on slopes of ½-3 in./ft using Type III asphalt[5]
	Mineral surface cap sheet (72–80 lb)	¼:12[5]	Fiberglass base spot mopped to deck or solid mopped to insulation	2 fiberglass plysheets	Type III asphalt @ 25–30	Asphalt @ 25–30 for cap sheet	UL Class A, B, or C depending on deck substrate, slope, and manufacturer[1] Consult manufacturer for specific regional requirements Proper application of mineral cap sheet requires warm weather Cold process fiberglass systems also possible; consult manufacturer
	Smooth surface	¼:12[5]	Fiberglass base spot mopped to deck or solid mopped to insulation	3 fiberglass plysheets	Type II asphalt @ 25–30	Asphalt/clay emulsion @ 6 gal/sq	UL Class A, B, or C depending on deck/substrate, slope, and manufacturer[1] Consult manufacturer for specific regional requirements Reflective coatings are recommended over smooth surface systems

NOTES

1. Underwriter's Laboratories test for Fire-Hazard Classification by assembling particular constructions using specific products of stated manufacturers; consult UL or the manufacturer to verify classifications for specific roofing systems for given project conditions.
   Class A: Not readily flammable under severe fire exposure and protects roof deck to high degree.
   Class B: Not readily flammable under moderate fire exposure and protects roof deck to moderate degree.
   Class C: Not readily flammable under light fire exposure and protects roof deck to slight degree.
   Only classes A and B are fire retardant.
2. On slopes up to ½ in./ft, apply asphalt and combine with felts to comply with ASTM D312.
3. For hot climates, use Type III instead of Type II, for higher softening point.
4. For hot climates, use Type III.
5. On slopes of 1 in./ft or greater, plies should be strapped (laid parallel to slope) and back nailed to prevent slippage, and Type III or Type IV asphalt should be used; if roofing is on roof insulation, wood insulation stops/nailers should be provided.
6. Vapor retarder under roof insulation is advisable for conditions having low outdoor temperatures (below 40°F) combined with high indoor relative humidity (above 44%). Allow vapor pressure to escape from between vapor retarder and roofing membrane by use of venting base sheets, vent stacks, or other methods recommended by manufacturer.
7. Three-ply or four-ply membrane system may be used. Number of plysheets to suit system selected.

ROLL ROOFING

TYPE	DESCRIPTION	SLOPE (IN./FT) MIN.	SLOPE (IN./FT) MAX.	WEIGHT (LB/SQ)	SIZE	UNDERLAY	FASTENERS	EXPOSURE	COLOR AND TEXTURE	U.L. RATING
Asphalt Roll Roofing	Smooth surface	0	6	50	36" x 36'		Nails and cement	33"	Black	C-wind resistant
				65						
	Mineral surface			90	36" x 36'					
	Double coverage fiberglass	1/2	4	60	36" x 36'			17"	Various color blends	A-wind resistant
	Fiberglass reinforced mineral fiber	1/8	4	75	36" x 72'				Black	B-wind resistant

Walter H. Sobel, FAIA, & Associates; Chicago, Illinois
Kent Wong; Hewlett, Jamison, Atkinson & Luey; Portland, Oregon; from data furnished by A. Larry Brown; Owens/Corning Fiberglas Corporation

BUILT-UP ROOFING (CONT.)

DECK OR SUBSTRATE	SURFACING	SLOPE (IN./FT)	BASE SHEET	PLYSHEETS	PLY BITUMEN (LB/SQ/PLY)	SURFACING BITUMEN (LB/SQ)	NOTES TO DESIGNER/SPECIFIER
Wood or other nailable decking (Over wood board decks, one ply of sheathing paper should be applied under base felt next to deck) (Consult manufacturers for approved decks and fasteners)	Gravel: 400 lb/sq OR Slag: 300 lb/sq OR White marble chips: 400 lb/sq	Inclines up to ½	43 lb coated base mechanically attached	3 coal tar saturated felts (perforated)	Coal tar @ 25	Coal tar @ 75	• U.L. Class A on most deck types (1) • Requires complete surfacing daily • For ponded roofs, add a 4th ply of felt and double flood and double gravel surface • Base flashings must be installed in flashing cement
			43 lb organic base felt mechanically attached	3 asphalt saturated felts	Type II asphalt @ 25	Type I asphalt @ 60	• Same configuration possible on slopes of ½-3 in./ft (2) using Type III asphalt
		Inclines up to ½	Fiberglas® base mechanically attached (3)	3 fiberglass plysheets ASTM D2178 Type IV (3)	Coal tar @ 25–30	Coal tar @ 75	• U.L. Class A on most deck types (1) • Roofing may be left up to 6 months before surfacing • For ponded roofs, add a 3rd ply of Perma-Ply R and double flood and double gravel surface • Base flashings must be installed in flashing cement
			Fiberglas® base mechanically attached (3)	3 fiberglass plysheets ASTM D2178 Type IV (3)	Type II asphalt @ 25	Type I asphalt @ 60–70	• Same configuration possible on slopes of ½-3 in./ft (2) using Type III asphalt
	Mineral surface cap sheet (72–80 lb)	¼-12 (2)	Fiberglass base mechanically attached	2 fiberglass plysheets, ASTM D2178 Type III or IV	Asphalt @ 25	Asphalt @ 30 for cap sheet	• U.L. Class A, B, or C depending on deck type, slope, and manufacturer (1) • Consult manufacturer for specific regional requirements for various types of plysheets • Fiberglass roofing may be left up to 6 months before surfacing • Proper application of mineral cap sheet requires warm weather
			43 lb organic base mechanically attached	2 fiberglass plysheets, ASTM D2178 Type III or IV	Asphalt @ 30	Asphalt @ 30 for cap sheet	
	Smooth surface	¼-12 (2)	Fiberglass base mechanically attached	3 fiberglass plysheets, ASTM D2178 Type III or IV; ASTM D250 Type II	Asphalt @ 25–30	Asphalt/clay emulsion @ 6 gal/sq	• U.L. Class A, B, or C depending on deck type, slope, and manufacturer (1) • Consult manufacturer for specific regional requirements • Reflective coatings are recommended over smooth surface systems

SHINGLES

TYPE	DESCRIPTION	SLOPE (IN./FT) MIN.	MAX.	WEIGHT (LB/SQ)[3]	SIZE	UNDERLAY	FASTENERS	EXPOSURE	COLOR AND TEXTURE	U.L. RATING
Asphalt Organic Felt[1,2]	3 tab	4	12	235	12″ x 36″	15 lb asphalt felt	Galvanized steel or aluminum roofing nails, or zinc-coated staples	5″	Various colors; granular texture	Class C fire resistant, wind resistant
	2 tab	4	12	300	12″ x 36″					
	Random edged	4	12	345	12″ x 36″				Varied; smooth	
	No cutout	2	12	290	12″ x 36″					
	Interlocking			180	19¾″ x 20½″			—	Varied; smooth	Class C fire resistant, wind resistant
	Basketweave			245	18½″ x 20″					
Fiberglass	Random edged Laminated Overlay	4	12	300	14″ x 35$\frac{9}{16}$″	15 lb asphalt felt	Galvanized steel or aluminum roofing nails, or zinc-coated staples	6″	Varied; smooth	Class A fire resistant, wind resistant
	3 tab	4	12	225	12″ x 36″			5″		
	2 tab	4	12	260	12″ x 36″			5″	Varied; granular texture	
	No cutout Random edged	4	12	225	12″ x 36¼″			5″	Varied; smooth	

NOTES

1. These shingles may be used on slopes down to 2 in./ft when over a two ply felt underlayment.
2. All shingles are self-sealing.
3. A SQUARE is a term used to describe 100 sq ft of roof area.

Walter H. Sobel, FAIA & Associates; Chicago, Illinois
Kent Wong; Hewlett, Jamison, Atkinson & Luey; Portland, Oregon; from data furnished by A. Larry Brown; Owens/Corning Fiberglas Corporation

SHINGLES AND ROOFING TILES

TYPE	DESCRIPTION	APPLICATION	SLOPE MINIMUM (IN./FT)	WEIGHT (LB/SQ)	UNDERLAY	FASTENERS	COLOR AND TEXTURE	SIZE (IN.) L X W	BUTT THICKNESS	EXPOSURE DATA
Wood: red cedar; most types and sizes available in cypress, redwood, white cedar; shakes	Handsplit and resawn	Roofs and sidewall panels for institutional, commercial, residential use	4	200–450	Spaced sheathing 30 lb felt interlayment with shakes	Corrosion resistant nails	Natural or various stains Various textures	Length 15–24 Width random	$\frac{1}{2}$–$\frac{3}{4}$ in.	5–7$\frac{1}{2}$ in.
	Taper split			260				Length 24 Width random	$\frac{1}{2}$ in.	10 in.
	Straight split			200–260				Length 18–24 Width random	$\frac{3}{8}$ in.	3 in. overlap
Wood: red cedar; most types and sizes available in cypress, redwood, white cedar; shingles	No. 1 Blue Label	Roofs and sidewall panels for institutional, commercial, residential use	4	None given	Open or solid sheathing Open sheathing shall be 1 x 4 or 1 x 6 in. boards	Corrosion resistant nails	Natural or various stains Various textures	Length 16	$\frac{3}{8}$ in.	5 in.
	No. 2 Red Label							18		5$\frac{1}{2}$ in.
	No. 3 Black Label							24		7$\frac{1}{2}$ in.
	No. 4							16		
	Undercoursing							18		
	No. 1 or No. 2 Rebutted-rejointed							16 18 24 Width random		
Clay tile	Shingle—flat	Institutional, commercial, residential	3	800–1600	One layer 30 lb or 45 lb felt over plywood	Noncorrosive copper nails	Various finishes	l w 15 x 7	$\frac{3}{8}$ in. minimum	Exposed length 6$\frac{1}{2}$ in. Exposed width 7 in.
	Interlocking flat			800				14 x 9	$\frac{7}{8}$ in. minimum	Exposed length 11 in. Exposed width 8$\frac{1}{4}$ in.
	French			940–1000				16$\frac{1}{4}$ x 9	2 in.	Exposed length 13$\frac{1}{8}$ in. Exposed width 8$\frac{1}{8}$ in.
	Spanish		4	850				13$\frac{1}{4}$ x 9$\frac{3}{4}$	$\frac{1}{2}$ in.	Exposed length 10$\frac{1}{2}$ in. Exposed width 8$\frac{1}{4}$ in.
Concrete[1]	Shingle—flat Barreled mission curved	Institutional, commercial, residential	4	950	One layer 30 lb felt over plywood	10 penny corrosion resistant galvanized copper, or colors stainless steel box nail	Various colors	13 x 16	1 in.	3 in. overlap
Slate	Commercial grade—smooth	Institutional, commercial, residential	4	700–800	One layer 30 lb asphalt saturated rag felt over plywood	Slaters hard copper wire nails cut copper, cut brass, or cut yellow metal slat nails	Blue-black	Various sizes	$\frac{3}{16}$, $\frac{1}{4}$ in.	3 in. overlap
	Quarry—run rough			825–3600					$\frac{3}{8}$, $\frac{1}{2}$, $\frac{3}{4}$ in.	

NOTES

1. Specifier should ask for concrete tile freeze-thaw test.
2. Underwriters Laboratories Standard UL 580 classifies roof deck assemblies as Class 30, Class 60, and Class 90. The nominal uplift pressures and wind velocities commonly related in technical studies and literature are the following:

RATING	NOMINAL UPLIFT PRESSURE	NOMINAL WIND VELOCITY
Class 30	30 psf	100 mph
Class 60	60 psf	142 mph
Class 90	90 psf	174 mph

Consult local manufacturer or agent for roofing system rating.

3. Underwriters Laboratories classifies prepared roof covering materials as Class A, B, or C. CLASS A includes roof coverings that are effective against severe fire exposure. Roof coverings of this class are then not readily flammable and do not carry or communicate fire; afford a fairly high degree of fire protection to the roof deck; do not slip from position; possess no flying brand hazard; and do not require frequent repairs in order to maintain their fire resisting properties.

Walter H. Sobel, FAIA, & Associates; Chicago, Illinois

SEAMED METAL ROOFING

TYPE	DESCRIPTION	MIN. SLOPE (IN./FT)	SIZE	THICKNESS	WEIGHT (LB/SQ)	UNDERLAY	FASTENER
Aluminum coated steel	Polyurethane insulation sandwiched between two layers of steel[1] standing seam	1/4	40" x 32'	2 1/2"	250	None	Panels are clipped to structurals, and interlocking seams sealed
Copper coated galvanized steel	Standing seam, pan, or roll method	3	20" x 30' max.	24 gauge	130	30 lb felt	Anchor clips and galvanized nails or screws
			22" x 30' max.				
Prepainted galvanized steel	Batten seam pan method	3	24" x 30' max.				
Zinc-copper titanium alloy	Batten or standing seam pan method	3	20", 24", or 28" x 8', 10', 12', or 14'	0.027"	100	Roofing felt	Galvanized U channel or L seam support spacer with screw or nails
Terne coated stainless[2,3,5]	Standing or batten seam	3	20", 24", 28", or 36" x 96", or 120"	0.015" or 0.018"	89	Roofing felt and rosin paper	TCS cleats and stainless steel nails
	Flat locked seam	1/2	20" x 28"				
Terne plate[4-6]	Batten seam	3	20" x 120" max.	26 gauge	62	Rosin paper	Terne cleats and roofing nails
	Standing seam	3	14", 20"	28 gauge			
			24" x 120" max.	30 gauge			
	Flat locked seam (wood deck only)	1/2	14" x 20"	28 gauge			
			20" x 28"	30 gauge			
	Horizontal seam (wood deck only)	3 1/2	24" x 96" max.	26 gauge			
				28 gauge			
Painted aluminum	Standing seam	1/2	12" x 60"–80"	0.032"	72.5	None	Anchor clips
			16" x 60"–80"	0.040"	90.4		

NOTES

1. This is a composite section providing structural deck, insulation, and weathertight roof. U value is 0.50; class I fire rating.
2. Terne coated steel is 304 nickel-chrome stainless steel covered on both sides with terne alloy (80% lead, 20% tin).
3. Terne coated steel can be painted without special preparation of the surface.
4. Terne plate is prime copper bearing steel coated with lead-tin alloy.
5. Expansion seams must be provided on runs exceeding 30 ft where both ends are free to move or exceeding 15 ft where ends are securely fastened.
6. Terne must be shop coated or painted one coat underside and primed and painted two coats on exposed side.

METAL SHINGLES AND TILES

TYPE	DESCRIPTION	APPLICATION	SLOPE MINIMUM (IN./FT)	WEIGHT (LB/SQ)	UNDERLAY	FASTENERS	COLOR AND TEXTURE	SIZE (IN.) L X W	BUTT THICKNESS	EXPOSURE DATA
Aluminum	California mission tile	Institutional, commercial, residential	3	48	One layer 30 lb asphalt saturated rag felt over plywood	Aluminum nails, screws	Tile red Burnt red	10 1/2 x 17 5 x 14	30 gauge aluminum	2 in. overlap
	Shake—shingle	Institutional, commercial, residential	4	36–88	One layer 30 lb felt over plywood	Anchor clip nailed	Various baked enamel finishes	12 x 48	Variable up to 1 3/16 in.	12 in.
Porcelain enamel on aluminum	Individual American method	Institutional, commercial, residential	3	225	One layer 30 lb felt plus 18 in. felt strips between tile	Special sealing nails supplied with tile	Various finishes	10 x 10	Prefinish for tiles custom fabricated to fit roof	

Walter H. Sobel, FAIA, & Associates; Chicago, Illinois

CORRUGATED AND CRIMPED ROOFING

TYPE		SLOPE MIN. (IN./FT)	MAX. SPAN (IN.)	WEIGHT (LB/ SQUARE)	SIZE	WEIGHT OR THICKNESS	EXPOSURE OR LAP	COLOR AND TEXTURE	FASTENER
Iron and steel or galvanized iron	2.67″ corrugations with 7/8, 3/4, or 1/2″ depth	3	81-51[1]	Uncoated from 548 to 69. Coated from 568 to 90. Add approx. 10% for 3″ corrugations	Width 34-5/8″, 39-1/8″, length 2-45′	Gauges 18-26	31 1/2, 36″, End lap 6″ min.	Uncoated galvanized or several colors of coatings	Corrosion resistant self-tapping screws, bolts, welded studs, power driven fasteners or nails in wood. All use neoprene washers
Protected metal (steel)[3]	Corrugated sheet 2.67″ corrugations with 3/4 or 1/2″ depth	(4)	88-44[1]	From 244 to 147	Width 33″ length to 12′	Gauges 18-24	29-3/4″ wide. End lap 6″ min.	Smooth black or several colors	Same as corrugated steel
	Mansard sheet, 6 beads per sheet				Width 30″ length to 12′				
	V-beam sheet, 5.4″ pitch and 1 5/8″ deep, 5 vees per sheet			From 278 to 167					
Aluminum	Corrugated sheet, 2.67″ corrugations, 7/8″ depth	3[6,7]	77-55[1] 91-64 102-72	42 56 70	Widths 35 or 48″, length 3-39′[1]	0.024 0.032 0.040 0.050	1 1/2″ corrugation side lap. 6″ min. end lap. 1 vee side lap[6]	Plain mill or stucco in natural and various colors of baked-on or porcelain enamel	Same as for corrugated steel, except use aluminum nails and sheet metal screws
	Curved corrugated sheet, same corrugations[5]			55.2	Width 33 3/4″, length 3-39′[1]	0.032			
	V-beam sheet, 4 7/8″ pitch and 1 5/8″ deep, top and bottom flats 3/4″		130-92[1] 152-107 173-122	58.4 72.2 90.3	Width 41 5/8″, length 3-39′[1]	0.032 0.040 0.050			
	Concealed clip panels (Reynolds Metals Co.)[7]			68.9 86.1 107.7	Width 13.35″, length 3-39′[1]	0.032 0.040 0.050	Width 12″, End lap 6″ min.	Stucco only; same colors as above	Clips with sheets locked at side laps
Corrugated fiberglass, wire-reinforced plastic	1 1/4″ corrugations, 1/4″ deep	3[6,7]	40-22[2]	Approx. 40	Width 26″ (max. 50″) length 4-39′	5, 6, 8 oz/sq ft	1, 1 1/2 or 2 corrugation side lap. 6″ min. end lap	Many colors, translucent opaque; or smooth or pebble finish.	Self-tapping screws, drive screws and nails. All with neoprene washers
	2 1/2″ corrugations, 1/2″ deep		65-32[2]		Widths 26″ (max. 50″) length 4-39′	4, 5, 6, 8, 10, 12 oz/sq ft			
	4.2″ corrugations, 1 1/16″ deep		72-50[2]		Widths 42, 50 3/8″, length 4-39′	5-12 oz/sq ft			
	2.67″ corrugations, 7/8″ deep		70-42[2]		Width 50″, length 4-39′	5-12 oz/sq ft			
	5-V crimp, 1/2″ deep		65-32[2]		Width 26″, length 4-39′	5-8 oz/sq ft			
	5.3-V crimp, 1″ deep		84-60[2]		Width 41 5/8, 45″, length 4-39′	5-12 oz/sq ft			
Corrugated glass or plastic, nonreinforced plastic[9]	2.67″ corrugations, 9/16″ deep	1	70-42[2]	Approx. 40	Width 50 1/2″, length 8, 10, 12, 15, 20′	5-8 oz/sq ft 1/4″ thick	1 corrugation side lap, 8″ min. end lap	Same as for reinforced plastic	Same as for reinforced plastic

NOTES

1. For 20 to 40 psf.
2. For 15 to 40 psf.
3. For use in chemical atmospheres. Panels are made of steel core, with both sides covered by a dry film at least 4 mils thick. The film has a special liquid resin coating, which is fused under high heat to a special corrosion resistant bond coat over chemically treated galvanized steel.
4. Corrugated and mansard sheets may be used on 4 in. min. slope with laps unsealed and on 3 in. min. slope with laps sealed. V-beam sheets may be used on 3 in. min. slope with laps unsealed and on 1 1/2 in. min. slope with laps sealed.
5. Minimum curvature radius 18 in.
6. Use 9 in. min. side laps on slopes from 2 to 3 in. Use 6 in. min. side laps on slopes above 3 in.
7. May be used on min. 1/2 in. slope only when one course used on slope. When more than one slope, the min. slope is 4 in.
8. Available in General Purpose, Type I, and Fire Retardant, Type II, except Type I has 5 oz weight only.
9. Used where economy and light weight are major considerations. Corrugated glass also available with installation requiring no side lap.

Walter H. Sobel, FAIA, & Associates; Chicago, Illinois

INSULATION

Many roof panel systems are available with foamed-in-place insulation. Their applications are subject to temperature limitations and various building codes, however. Check codes and manufacturers' fire ratings. Certain applications of roofing systems can also be applied directly over fiberglass batts.

VAPOR BARRIERS

To control a moderate level of relative humidity in living spaces, vapor resistant membranes must be utilized:

1. To control the moisture level within the structure.
2. To prevent moisture from passing through the insulation to a cold point where it can condense into water, possibly causing structural damage or rot. Provide condensate drainage.

WATER VAPOR MIGRATION

Water is present as vapor in indoor and outdoor air and as absorbed moisture in many building materials. Within the range of temperatures encountered in buildings water may exist in the liquid, vapor, or solid states. Moisture related problems may arise from changes in moisture content, from the presence of excessive moisture, or from the effects of changes of state such as freezing within wall insulation.

In the design and construction of buildings the behavior of moisture must be considered, including particularly the change from vapor to liquid (condensation). Such problems generally arise when moisture in relatively humid indoor air comes in contact with a cold surface such as a window or when the moisture migrates under the influence of vapor pressure differences through walls to enter a region of relatively low temperature where condensation can occur.

Moisture problems in residences generally occur in winter when the outdoor temperature and vapor pressure are low and there are many indoor vapor sources. These may include cooking, laundering, bathing, breathing, and perspiration from the occupants, as well as automatic washers and driers, dishwashers and humidifiers. All of these sources combine to cause vapor pressure indoors to be much higher than outdoors, so that the vapor tends to migrate outward through the building envelope. Vapor cannot permeate glazed windows or metal doors, but most other building materials are permeable to some extent. Walls are particularly susceptible to this phenomenon, and such migration must be prevented or at least minimized by the use of low permeability membranes known as vapor barriers, which should be installed as close as possible to the indoor surface of the building.

Water vapor migration is relatively independent of air motion within the building, since such migration depends primarily on vapor pressure differences. Migration always takes place from regions of higher vapor pressure toward spaces such as wall cavities where the vapor pressure will be lower. When surfaces below the local dewpoint temperature are encountered, condensation will occur and moisture droplets will form. If the local drybulb temperature is at or below 32°F, freezing will occur, which may lead to permanent structural damage.

Moisture in building materials usually increases their thermal conductance to a significant and unpredictable extent. Porous materials that become saturated with moisture lose most of their insulating capability and may not regain it when they dry out. Dust, which usually settles in airspaces, may become permanently affixed to originally reflective surfaces. Moisture migration by evaporation, vapor flow, and condensation can transport significant quantities of latent heat, particularly through fibrous insulating materials.

Positive steps should be taken to prevent migration of moisture in the form of vapor and accumulation in the form of water or ice within building components. Vapor barriers, correctly located near the source of the moisture, are the most effective means of preventing such migration. Venting of moisture laden air from bathrooms, laundry rooms, and kitchens will reduce indoor vapor pressure, as will the introduction of outdoor air with low moisture content.

BUILDING SECTION ANALYSIS FOR POTENTIAL CONDENSATION

Any building section may be analyzed by simple calculations to determine where condensation might occur and what might be done in selecting materials or their method of assembly to eliminate that possibility. The section may or may not contain a vapor barrier or it may contain a relatively imperfect barrier; the building section may include cold side materials of comparatively high resistance to the passage of vapor (which is highly undesirable and is to be avoided). With few exceptions, the vapor resistance at or near the warm surface should be five times that of any components. The table above gives permeances and permeability of building and vapor barrier materials. These values can be used in analyzing building sections by the following simple method:

- List the materials, without surface films or airspaces, in the order of their appearance in the building section, beginning with the inside surface material and working to the outside.
- Against each material list the permeance (or permeability) value from the table or a more accurate value if available from tests or manufacturers' data. Where a range is given, select an average value or use judgment in assigning a value based on the character and potential installation method of the material proposed for use.
- Start at the top of the list and note any material that has less permeance than the materials above it on the list. At that point the possibility exists that vapor leaking through the first material may condense on the second, provided the dew point (condensation point) is reached and the movement is considerable. In that case, provide ventilation through the cold side material or modify the design to eliminate or change the material to one of greater permeance.

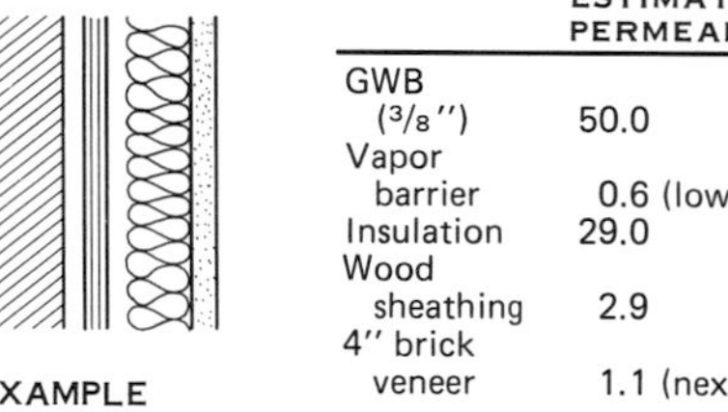

	ESTIMATED PERMEANCE
GWB (3/8")	50.0
Vapor barrier	0.6 (lowest)
Insulation	29.0
Wood sheathing	2.9
4" brick veneer	1.1 (next)

EXAMPLE

In this example the vapor barrier transmits 1 grain of moisture per square foot per hour for each unit of vapor pressure difference, and nothing else transmits less. However, since the cold brick veneer is nearly as low in permeance it is advisable to make certain that the vapor barrier is expertly installed, with all openings at pipes and with outlet boxes or joints carefully fitted or sealed. Alternatively, the brick veneer may have open mortar joints near the top and bottom to serve both as weep holes and as vapor release openings. They will also ventilate the wall and help to reduce heat gain in summer.

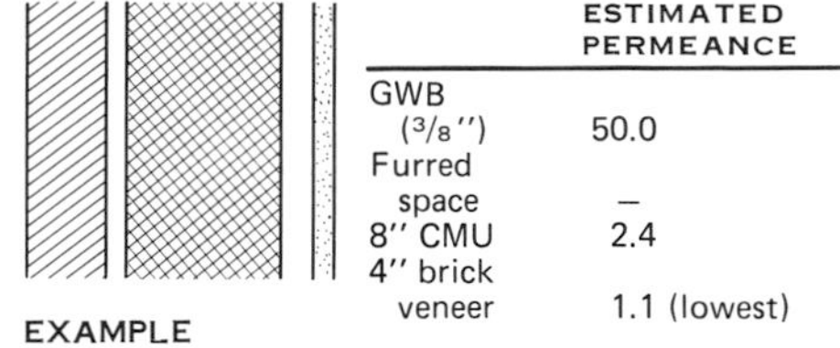

	ESTIMATED PERMEANCE
GWB (3/8")	50.0
Furred space	–
8" CMU	2.4
4" brick veneer	1.1 (lowest)

EXAMPLE

Vapor (under pressure) would easily pass through the interior finish, be slowed up by the concrete masonry unit, and be nearly stopped by the cold brick veneer. Unless this design is radically improved, the masonry will become saturated and may cause serious water stains or apparent "leaks" in cold weather. In addition, alternating freezing and thawing of condensation within the masonry wall can physically damage the construction.

PERMEANCE AND PERMEABILITY OF MATERIALS TO WATER VAPOR

MATERIAL	PERMEANCE (PERM)
MATERIALS USED IN CONSTRUCTION	
Concrete (1:2:4 mix)	3.2[5]
Brick-masonry (4 in. thick)	0.8-1.1
Concrete masonry (8 in. cored, limestone aggregate)	2.4
Plaster on metal lath (3/4 in.)	15
Plaster on plain gypsum lath (with studs)	20
Gypsum wallboard (3/8 in. plain)	50
Structural insulating board (sheathing quality)	20-50[5]
Structural insulating board (interior, uncoated, 1/2 in.)	50-90
Hardboard (1/8 in. standard)	11
Hardboard (1/8 in. tempered)	5
Built-up roofing (hot mopped)	0.0
Wood, fir sheathing, 3/4 in.	2.9
Plywood (Douglas fir, exterior glue, 1/4 in.)	0.7
Plywood (Douglas fir, interior, glue, 1/4 in.)	1.9
Acrylic, glass fiber reinforced sheet, 56 mil	0.12
Polyester, glass fiber reinforced sheet, 48 mil	0.05
THERMAL INSULATIONS	
Cellular glass	0.0[5]
Mineral wool, unprotected	29.0
Expanded polyurethane (R-11 blown)	0.4-1.6[5]
Expanded polystyrene—extruded	1.2[5]
Expanded polystyrene—bead	2.0-5.8[5]
PLASTIC AND METAL FOILS AND FILMS[2]	
Aluminum foil (1 mil)	0.0
Polyethylene (4 mil)	0.08
Polyethylene (6 mil)	0.06
Polyethylene (8 mil)	0.04
Polyester (1 mil)	0.7
Polyvinylchloride, unplasticized (2 mil)	0.68
Polyvinylchloride, plasticized (4 mil)	0.8-1.4

MATERIAL	PERMEANCE (PERM)
BUILDING PAPERS, FELTS, ROOFING PAPERS[3]	
Duplex sheet, asphalt laminated, aluminum foil one side (43)[4]	0.176
Saturated and coated roll roofing (326)[4]	0.24
Kraft paper and asphalt laminated, reinforced 30-120-30 (34)[4]	1.8
Asphalt-saturated, coated vapor-barrier paper (43)[4]	0.6
Asphalt-saturated, not coated sheathing paper (22)[4]	20.2
15-lb asphalt felt (70)[4]	5.6
15-lb tar felt (70)[4]	18.2
Single kraft, double infused (16)[4]	42
LIQUID APPLIED COATING MATERIALS	
Paint—two coats	
Aluminum varnish on wood	0.3-0.5
Enamels on smooth plaster	0.5-1.5
Primers and sealers on interior insulation board	0.9-2.1
Miscellaneous primers plus one coat flat oil paint on plastic	1.6-3.0
Flat paint on interior insulation board	4
Water emulsion on interior insulation board	30-85
Paint—three coats	
Exterior paint, white lead and oil on wood siding	0.3-1.0
Exterior paint, white lead-zinc oxide and oil on wood	0.9
Styrene-butadiene latex coating, 2 oz/sq ft	11
Polyvinyl acetate latex coating, 4 oz/sq ft	5.5
Asphalt cutback bastic	
1/16 in. dry	0.14
3/16 in. dry	0.0
Hot melt asphalt	
2 oz/sq ft	0.5
3.5 oz/sq ft	0.1

NOTES

1. The vapor transmission rates listed will permit comparisons of materials, but selection of values for vapor barrier materials should be based on rates obtained from the manufacturer or from laboratory tests. The range of values shown indicates variation among mean values for materials that are similar but of different density. Values are intended for design guidance only.
2. Usually installed as vapor barriers. If used as exterior finish and elsewhere near cold side, special considerations are required.
3. Low permeance sheets used as vapor barriers. High permeance use elsewhere in construction.
4. Bases (weight in lb/500 sq ft).
5. Permeability (PERM-in.).

Based on data from "ASHRAE Handbook of Fundamentals," 1981, Chapter 20.

Owen J. Delevante, AIA; Glen Rock, New Jersey
E. C. Shuman, P.E.; Consulting Engineer; State College, Pennsylvania

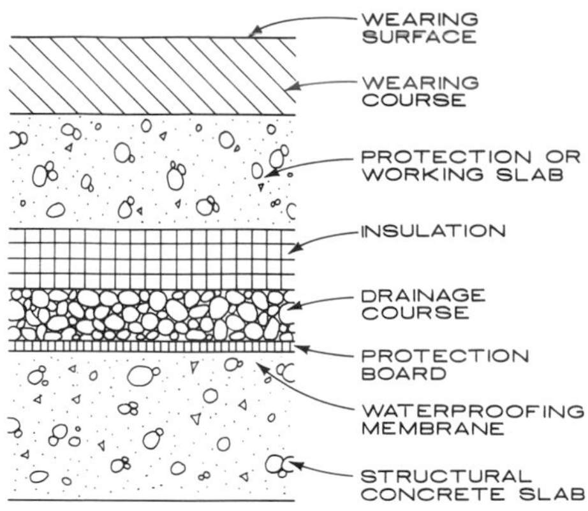
WEARING SURFACE
WEARING COURSE
PROTECTION OR WORKING SLAB
INSULATION
DRAINAGE COURSE
PROTECTION BOARD
WATERPROOFING MEMBRANE
STRUCTURAL CONCRETE SLAB

BASIC COMPONENTS OF WATERPROOFING SYSTEMS

GENERAL

The basic components, subsystems, and features for a building deck waterproofing system are the structural building deck or substrate to be waterproofed, waterproofing membrane, protection of membrane, drainage, insulation, and wearing course. See following pages for generic membrane applications.

SUBSTRATE

The substrate referred to is reinforced cast-in-place structural concrete. Precast concrete slabs pose more technical problems than cast-in-place concrete and the probability of lasting watertightness is greatly diminished and difficult to achieve because of the multitude of joints which have the capability of movement and must be treated accordingly.

The concrete used for the substrate should have a minimum density of 1762 kg/m^3 (110 lb/ft^3) and have a maximum moisture content of 8% when cured.

SLOPE FOR DRAINAGE

A monolithic concrete substrate slope of a minimum 11 mm/m (1/8 in./ft) should be maintained. Slope is best achieved with a monolithic structural slab and not with a separate concrete fill layer.

MEMBRANE

Detection of leakage can be a significant problem when the membrane is not bonded to the structural slab or when additional layers of materials separate it from the structural slab. Therefore, only membranes that can be bonded to the substrate should be used.

The membrane should be applied under dry, frost-free conditions on the surface as well as throughout the depth of the concrete slab.

When the membrane is turned up on a wall, it is preferable to terminate it above the wearing surface to eliminate the possibility of ponded surface water penetrating the wall above the membrane and running down behind it into the building.

Penetrations should be avoided wherever possible. For protection at such critical locations, pipe sleeves should be cast into the structural slab against which the membrane can be terminated.

Treatment at reinforced and nonreinforced joints depends on the membrane used. See following pages.

There are basically two concepts that could be considered in the detailing of expansion joints at the membrane level. These are the positive seal concept directly at the membrane level and the watershed concept with the seal at a higher lever than the membrane. Where additional safeguards are desired, a drainage gutter under the joint could be considered. Flexible support of the membrane is required in each case. Expansion joint details should be considered and used in accordance with their movement capability.

The positive seal concept entails a greater risk than the watershed concept, since it relies fully on positive seal joinery of materials at the membrane level, where the membrane is most vulnerable to water penetration. Since the precision required is not always attainable, this concept is best avoided.

The watershed concept, although requiring a greater height and more costly concrete forming, is superior in safeguarding against leakage, having the advantage of providing a water dam at the membrane level. However, if a head of water rises to the height of the materials joinery, this concept becomes almost as vulnerable as the positive seal concept. Therefore, drainage is recommended at the membrane level.

PROTECTION BOARD

The membrane should be protected from damage prior to and during the remainder of construction. Protection board should be applied after the membrane is installed. The proper timing of application after placement of the membrane is important and could vary with the type of membrane used. The manufacturer's printed instructions should be followed.

DRAINAGE SYSTEM

Drainage should be considered as a total system from the wearing surface down to the membrane, including use of multilevel drains.

Drainage at the wearing surface is generally accomplished in one of two ways:

1. By an open joint and pedestal system permitting most of the rainwater to penetrate rapidly down to the membrane level and subsurface drainage system, and
2. By a closed-joint system designed to remove most of the rainwater rapidly by slope to surface drains and to allow a minor portion to infiltrate to membrane.

A drainage course of washed, round gravel should be provided above the protection board, over the membrane. This permits water to filter to the drain and provides a place where it can collect and freeze without potential damage to the wearing course.

INSULATION

When required, insulation should be located above the membrane, but not in direct contact with it.

PROTECTION OR WORKING SLAB

A concrete slab could be placed soon after the membrane, protection board, drainage course, and insulation, if required, have been installed. It would serve as protection for the permanent waterproofing materials and insulation below, provide a working platform for construction traffic and storage of materials (within weight limits), and provide a substantial substrate for the placement of the finish wearing course materials near the completion of the project.

WEARING COURSE

The major requirements for the wearing course are a stable support of sufficient strength, resistance against lateral thrust, adequate drainage to avoid ponding of water, and proper treatment of joints.

Joints in which movement is anticipated should be treated as expansion joints.

Various proprietary compression seals are available that can be inserted into a formed joint under compression. Most of these, however, are not flush at the top surface and could fill up with sand or dirt.

Wet sealants are the materials most commonly used in moving joints at the wearing surface level. Dimension A is the design width dimension or the dimension at which the joint will be formed. The criterion normally used for determining this dimension with sealants capable of ±25% movement is to multiply the maximum expected movement in one direction by 4. Generally, this is expected to be about three-fourths of the total anticipated joint movement, but if there is any doubt, multiply the total anticipated joint movement by 4. It is better to have the joint too wide than too narrow. Dimension B (sealant depth) is related to dimension A and is best established by the sealant manufacturer. Generally, B is equal to A for widths up to 13 mm (1/2 in.), 15 mm (9/16 in.) for a 16 mm (5/8 in.) width, and 16 mm (5/8 in.) for 19 mm (3/4 in.) and greater widths. This allows some tolerance for self-leveling sealants.

Reference: ASTM C 898 and C 981. Highlights of text and figures are reprinted with permission from ASTM Committee C-24 of the American Society for Testing Materials.

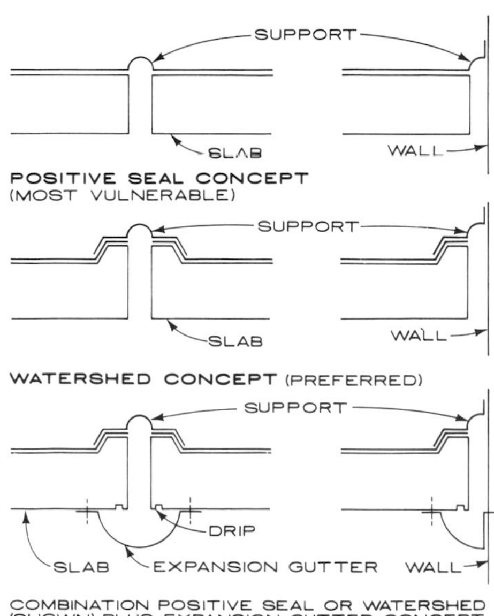
SUPPORT
SLAB
WALL
POSITIVE SEAL CONCEPT (MOST VULNERABLE)
SUPPORT
SLAB
WALL
WATERSHED CONCEPT (PREFERRED)
SUPPORT
DRIP
SLAB
EXPANSION GUTTER
WALL
COMBINATION POSITIVE SEAL OR WATERSHED (SHOWN) PLUS EXPANSION GUTTER CONCEPT (PROVIDES ADDITIONAL SAFEGUARD)

EXPANSION JOINT CONCEPTS AT MEMBRANE LEVEL

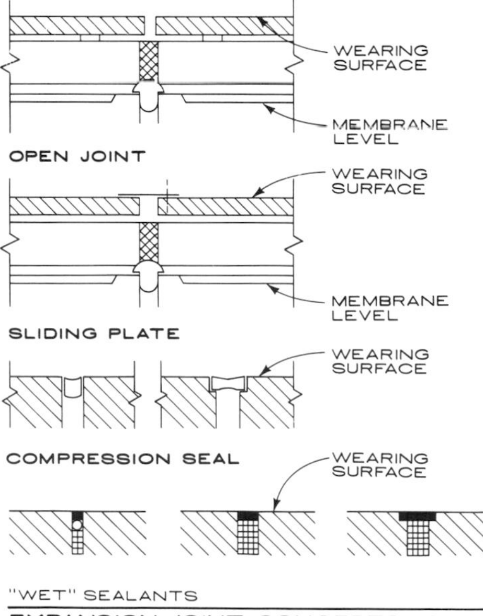
WEARING SURFACE
MEMBRANE LEVEL
OPEN JOINT
WEARING SURFACE
MEMBRANE LEVEL
SLIDING PLATE
WEARING SURFACE
COMPRESSION SEAL
WEARING SURFACE
"WET" SEALANTS

EXPANSION JOINT CONCEPTS AT WEARING SURFACE LEVEL

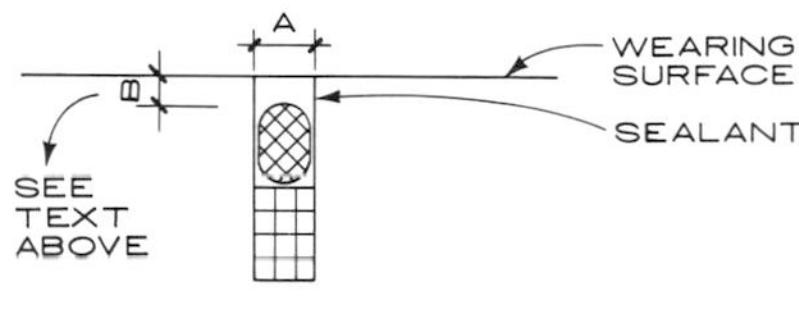
A
B
WEARING SURFACE
SEALANT
SEE TEXT ABOVE

FOR JOINTS UP TO 1/2" WIDE

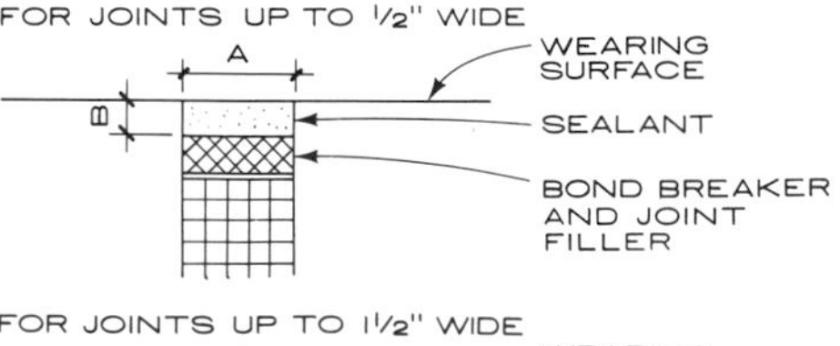
A
B
WEARING SURFACE
SEALANT
BOND BREAKER AND JOINT FILLER

FOR JOINTS UP TO 1 1/2" WIDE

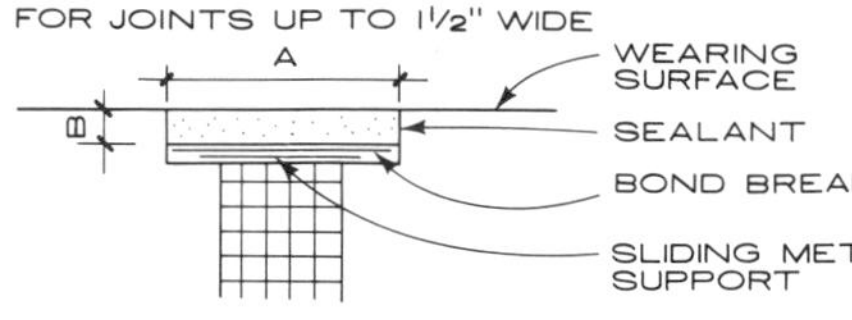
A
B
WEARING SURFACE
SEALANT
BOND BREAKER
SLIDING METAL SUPPORT

FOR JOINTS WIDER THAN 1 1/2"

SEE OTHER PAGES FOR JOINT DESIGN DIMENSIONS

WET SEALANT DETAILS AT WEARING SURFACE

Charles J. Parise, FAIA, FASTM; Smith, Hinchman & Grylls Associates, Inc.; Detroit, Michigan

SUBSTRATE

The building deck or substrate referred to is reinforced cast-in-place structural concrete.

The structural slab should have a finish of sufficiently rough texture to provide a mechanical bond for the membrane, but not so rough to preclude achieving continuity of the membrane across the surface.

The concrete should be cured a minimum of 7 days and aged a minimum of 28 days, including curing time, before application of the bituminous membrane. Curing is accomplished chemically with moisture and should not be construed as drying. Liquid or chemical curing compounds should not be used unless approved by the manufacturer of the built-up bituminous membrane as the material may interfere with the bond of the membrane to the structural slab.

MEMBRANE

A built-up bituminous waterproofing membrane consists of components joined together and bonded to its substrate at the site. The major membrane components include primers, bitumens, reinforcements, and flashing materials.

Surfaces to receive waterproofing must be clean, dry, reasonably smooth, and free of dust, dirt, voids, cracks, laitance, or sharp projections before application of materials.

Concrete surfaces should be uniformly primed to enhance the bond between the membrane and the substrate, so as to inhibit lateral movement of water.

The number of plies of membrane reinforcement required is dependent upon the head of water and strength required by the design function of the wearing surface. Plaza deck membranes should be composed of not less than three plies. The composition of the membrane is normally of a "shingle" or "ply-on-ply" (phased) construction.

For application temperatures, follow the recommendations of the manufacturers of the membrane materials.

Over reinforced structural slab joints, one ply of 6-in.-wide membrane reinforcement should be applied before application of the bituminous membrane.

Nonreinforced joints should receive a bead of compatible sealant in a recessed joint before application of the membrane.

At expansion joints, gaskets and flexible preformed sheets are required inasmuch as bituminous membranes have little or no movement capability. Since such materials must be joined to the bituminous membrane, the watershed concept should be used.

Reinforce all intersections with walls and corners with two layers of woven fabric embedded in hot bitumen.

Flashing membranes should extend above the wearing surface and the highest possible water level and not less than 150 mm (6 in.) onto the deck membrane.

The flashing should extend over the wall dampproofing or membrane waterproofing not less than 100 mm (4 in.).

Drains must be provided with a wide metal flange or base and set slightly below the drainage level. Metal flashing for the drain, if required, and the clamping ring should be set on the membrane in bituminous plastic cement. The metal flashing should be stripped in with a minimum of two plies of membrane reinforcement and three applications of bituminous plastic cement.

Penetrations through the membrane such as conduits and pipes should be avoided whenever possible. Penetrations must be flashed to a height above the anticipated water table that may extend above the wearing surface.

The built-up bituminous membrane should be protected from damage. Protection board should be placed on the waterproofing membrane when the final mopping is being placed. It will then be adhered to the membrane.

Reference: ASTM C 981. Highlights of text and figures are reprinted with permission from ASTM Committee C-24 of the American Society for Testing and Materials.

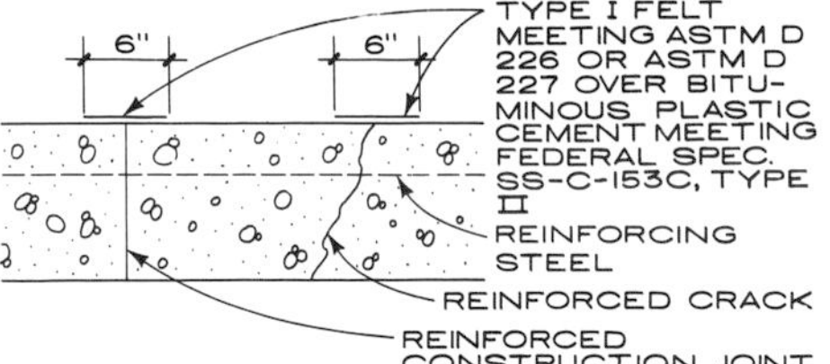
6"
6"
TYPE I FELT MEETING ASTM D 226 OR ASTM D 227 OVER BITUMINOUS PLASTIC CEMENT MEETING FEDERAL SPEC. SS-C-153C, TYPE II
REINFORCING STEEL
REINFORCED CRACK
REINFORCED CONSTRUCTION JOINT

TREATMENT AT REINFORCED JOINTS

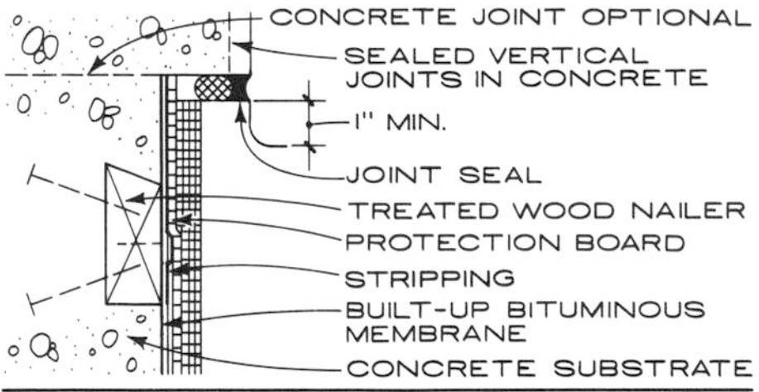
CONCRETE JOINT OPTIONAL
SEALED VERTICAL JOINTS IN CONCRETE
1" MIN.
JOINT SEAL
TREATED WOOD NAILER
PROTECTION BOARD
STRIPPING
BUILT-UP BITUMINOUS MEMBRANE
CONCRETE SUBSTRATE

TERMINAL CONDITION ABOVE FINISH GRADE ON CONCRETE WALL

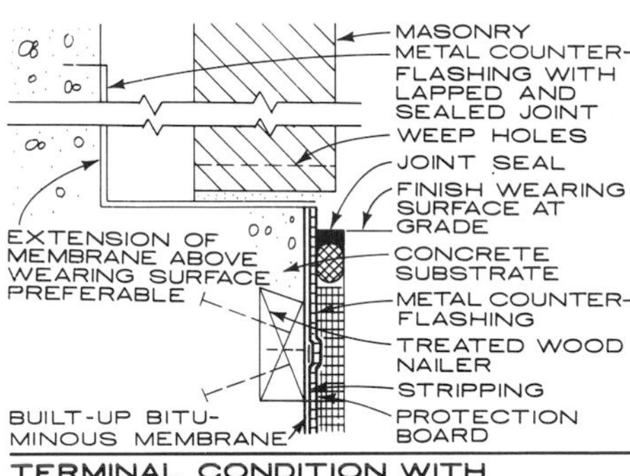
MASONRY
METAL COUNTER-FLASHING WITH LAPPED AND SEALED JOINT
WEEP HOLES
JOINT SEAL
FINISH WEARING SURFACE AT GRADE
EXTENSION OF MEMBRANE ABOVE WEARING SURFACE PREFERABLE
CONCRETE SUBSTRATE
METAL COUNTER-FLASHING
TREATED WOOD NAILER
STRIPPING
BUILT-UP BITUMINOUS MEMBRANE
PROTECTION BOARD

TERMINAL CONDITION WITH MASONRY ABOVE FINISH WEARING SURFACE AT GRADE

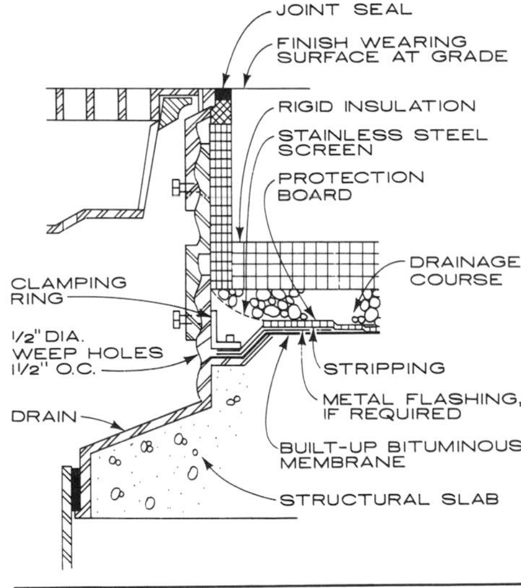
JOINT SEAL
FINISH WEARING SURFACE AT GRADE
RIGID INSULATION
STAINLESS STEEL SCREEN
PROTECTION BOARD
DRAINAGE COURSE
CLAMPING RING
1/2" DIA. WEEP HOLES 1 1/2" O.C.
STRIPPING
METAL FLASHING, IF REQUIRED
DRAIN
BUILT-UP BITUMINOUS MEMBRANE
STRUCTURAL SLAB

TERMINATION AT DRAIN

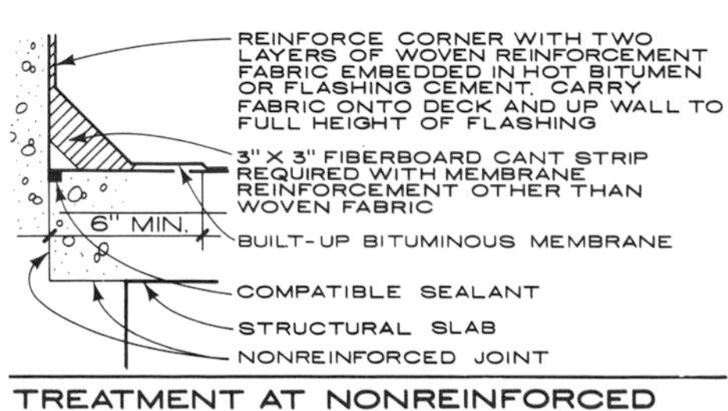
REINFORCE CORNER WITH TWO LAYERS OF WOVEN REINFORCEMENT FABRIC EMBEDDED IN HOT BITUMEN OR FLASHING CEMENT. CARRY FABRIC ONTO DECK AND UP WALL TO FULL HEIGHT OF FLASHING
3" X 3" FIBERBOARD CANT STRIP REQUIRED WITH MEMBRANE REINFORCEMENT OTHER THAN WOVEN FABRIC
6" MIN.
BUILT-UP BITUMINOUS MEMBRANE
COMPATIBLE SEALANT
STRUCTURAL SLAB
NONREINFORCED JOINT

TREATMENT AT NONREINFORCED JOINTS

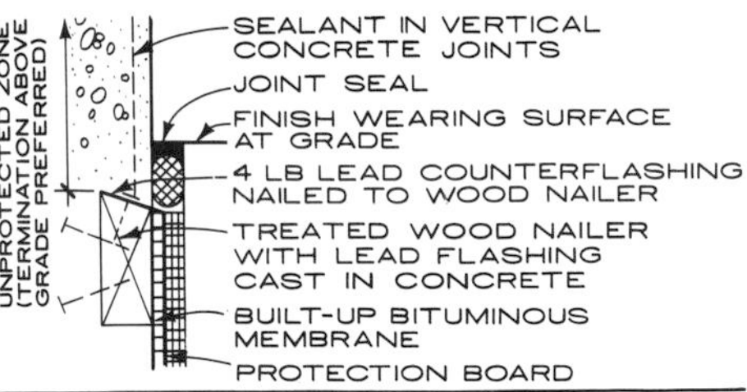
UNPROTECTED ZONE (TERMINATION ABOVE GRADE PREFERRED)
SEALANT IN VERTICAL CONCRETE JOINTS
JOINT SEAL
FINISH WEARING SURFACE AT GRADE
4 LB LEAD COUNTERFLASHING NAILED TO WOOD NAILER
TREATED WOOD NAILER WITH LEAD FLASHING CAST IN CONCRETE
BUILT-UP BITUMINOUS MEMBRANE
PROTECTION BOARD

TERMINAL CONDITIONS ON CONCRETE WALL BELOW FINISH WEARING SURFACE AT GRADE

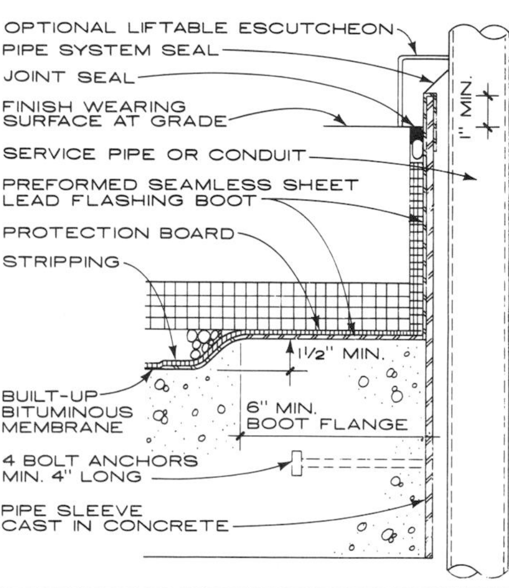
OPTIONAL LIFTABLE ESCUTCHEON
PIPE SYSTEM SEAL
JOINT SEAL
FINISH WEARING SURFACE AT GRADE
1" MIN.
SERVICE PIPE OR CONDUIT
PREFORMED SEAMLESS SHEET LEAD FLASHING BOOT
PROTECTION BOARD
STRIPPING
1 1/2" MIN.
BUILT-UP BITUMINOUS MEMBRANE
6" MIN. BOOT FLANGE
4 BOLT ANCHORS MIN. 4" LONG
PIPE SLEEVE CAST IN CONCRETE

TERMINATION AT PIPE PENETRATIONS

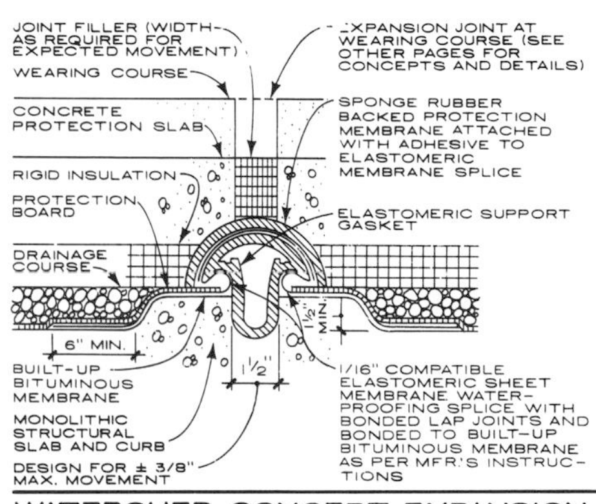
JOINT FILLER (WIDTH AS REQUIRED FOR EXPECTED MOVEMENT)
WEARING COURSE
EXPANSION JOINT AT WEARING COURSE (SEE OTHER PAGES FOR CONCEPTS AND DETAILS)
CONCRETE PROTECTION SLAB
SPONGE RUBBER BACKED PROTECTION MEMBRANE ATTACHED WITH ADHESIVE TO ELASTOMERIC MEMBRANE SPLICE
RIGID INSULATION
PROTECTION BOARD
ELASTOMERIC SUPPORT GASKET
DRAINAGE COURSE
1/2" MIN
6" MIN.
1/2"
BUILT-UP BITUMINOUS MEMBRANE
MONOLITHIC STRUCTURAL SLAB AND CURB
DESIGN FOR ± 3/8" MAX. MOVEMENT
1/16" COMPATIBLE ELASTOMERIC SHEET MEMBRANE WATERPROOFING SPLICE WITH BONDED LAP JOINTS AND BONDED TO BUILT-UP BITUMINOUS MEMBRANE AS PER MFR'S INSTRUCTIONS

WATERSHED CONCEPT EXPANSION JOINT

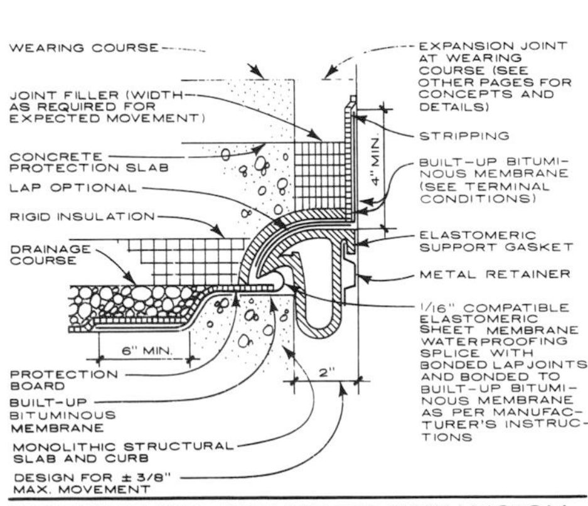
WEARING COURSE
EXPANSION JOINT AT WEARING COURSE (SEE OTHER PAGES FOR CONCEPTS AND DETAILS)
JOINT FILLER (WIDTH AS REQUIRED FOR EXPECTED MOVEMENT)
STRIPPING
CONCRETE PROTECTION SLAB
4" MIN.
LAP OPTIONAL
BUILT-UP BITUMINOUS MEMBRANE (SEE TERMINAL CONDITIONS)
RIGID INSULATION
ELASTOMERIC SUPPORT GASKET
DRAINAGE COURSE
METAL RETAINER
6" MIN.
2"
1/16" COMPATIBLE ELASTOMERIC SHEET MEMBRANE WATERPROOFING SPLICE WITH BONDED LAP JOINTS AND BONDED TO BUILT-UP BITUMINOUS MEMBRANE AS PER MANUFACTURER'S INSTRUCTIONS
PROTECTION BOARD
BUILT-UP BITUMINOUS MEMBRANE
MONOLITHIC STRUCTURAL SLAB AND CURB
DESIGN FOR ± 3/8" MAX. MOVEMENT

WATERSHED CONCEPT EXPANSION JOINT

Charles J. Parise, FAIA, FASTM; Smith, Hinchman & Grylls Associates, Inc.; Detroit, Michigan

NOTES

1. Consult a soils engineer to determine soil types and groundwater levels and their effect on selection of drainage and waterproofing methods.
2. Most membranes require a stable, rigid, and level substrate for their application. Generally a subslab (mudslab) is used when the membrane is below the structural slab. When placed on the structural slab, a protective cover, such as another concrete slab, is required.
3. Bentonite panels may be placed over level, well-compacted fill. Cover them with polyethylene film to prevent premature expansion from wet concrete placed over them. Note: Bentonite forms an impermeable barrier when confined by foundation backfill or by lagging or sheet piling. The material may swell, exerting pressure on adjacent construction. Consult with structural engineer and manufacturer to assure appropriate use and structural adequacy.
4. Protect the water-resistant membrane during construction and backfill operations by covering it with a protection course of parging or solid sheets of protection boards.
5. Some drainage membranes or composites may also serve as the protection course.
6. Footing drains recommended when groundwater level may rise above top of floor slab or when subject to hydrostatic pressure after heavy rain. The drainage composite conveys water to the drain, thus reducing hydrostatic pressure.
7. Water-resistant membrane of interior face of foundation wall only recommended when outside is not accessible.

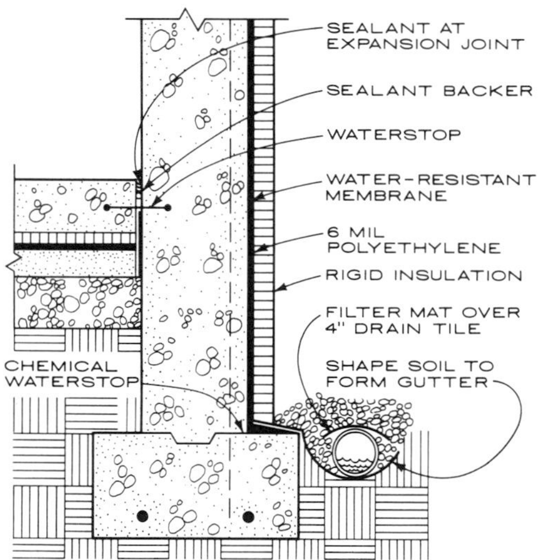
SEALANT AT EXPANSION JOINT
SEALANT BACKER
WATERSTOP
WATER-RESISTANT MEMBRANE
6 MIL POLYETHYLENE
RIGID INSULATION
FILTER MAT OVER 4" DRAIN TILE
SHAPE SOIL TO FORM GUTTER
CHEMICAL WATERSTOP

FOOTING WATER RESISTANCE-TYPE I

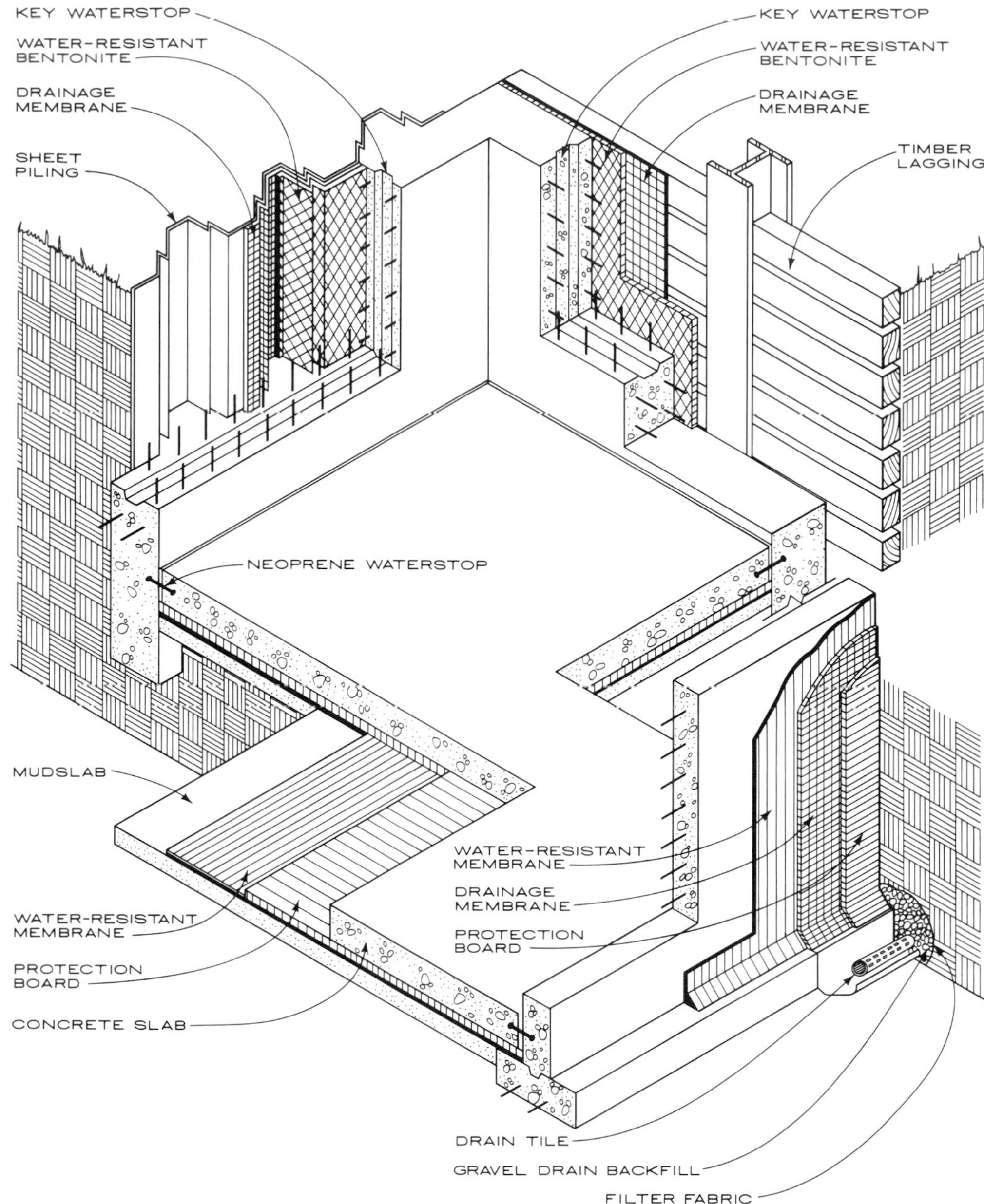
KEY WATERSTOP
WATER-RESISTANT BENTONITE
DRAINAGE MEMBRANE
SHEET PILING
KEY WATERSTOP
WATER-RESISTANT BENTONITE
DRAINAGE MEMBRANE
TIMBER LAGGING
NEOPRENE WATERSTOP
MUDSLAB
WATER-RESISTANT MEMBRANE
DRAINAGE MEMBRANE
PROTECTION BOARD
WATER-RESISTANT MEMBRANE
PROTECTION BOARD
CONCRETE SLAB
DRAIN TILE
GRAVEL DRAIN BACKFILL
FILTER FABRIC

FOUNDATION CONDITIONS

WATER RESISTANCE APPLICATIONS

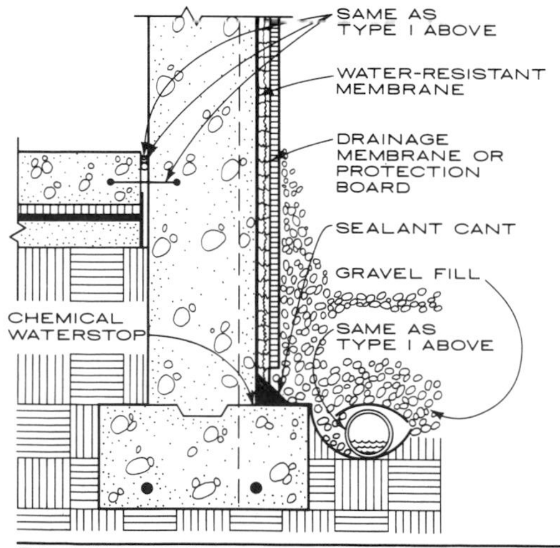
SAME AS TYPE I ABOVE
WATER-RESISTANT MEMBRANE
DRAINAGE MEMBRANE OR PROTECTION BOARD
SEALANT CANT
GRAVEL FILL
SAME AS TYPE I ABOVE
CHEMICAL WATERSTOP

FOOTING WATER RESISTANCE - TYPE 2

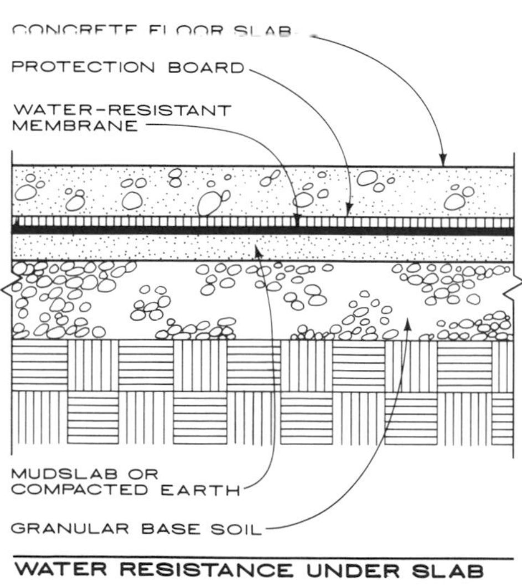
CONCRETE FLOOR SLAB
PROTECTION BOARD
WATER-RESISTANT MEMBRANE
MUDSLAB OR COMPACTED EARTH
GRANULAR BASE SOIL

WATER RESISTANCE UNDER SLAB

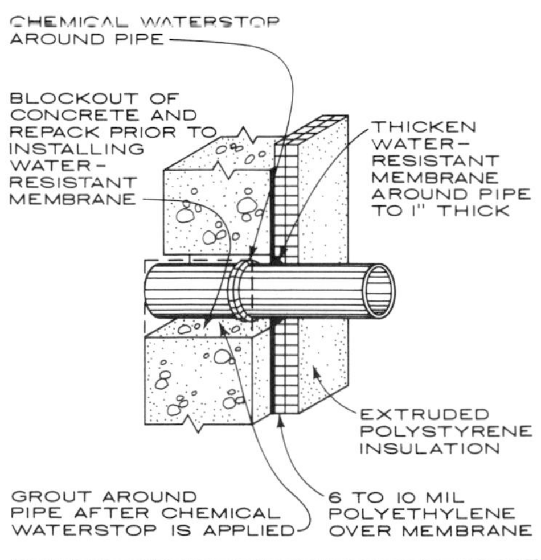
CHEMICAL WATERSTOP AROUND PIPE
BLOCKOUT OF CONCRETE AND REPACK PRIOR TO INSTALLING WATER-RESISTANT MEMBRANE
THICKEN WATER-RESISTANT MEMBRANE AROUND PIPE TO 1" THICK
EXTRUDED POLYSTYRENE INSULATION
GROUT AROUND PIPE AFTER CHEMICAL WATERSTOP IS APPLIED
6 TO 10 MIL POLYETHYLENE OVER MEMBRANE

PIPE PENETRATION AT WALL

Krommenhoek/McKeown & Associates; San Diego, California

RED CEDAR HANDSPLIT SHAKES

GRADE	LENGTH AND THICKNESS	DESCRIPTION
No. 1 handsplit and resawn	15″ starter-finish 18 x 1/2″ medium 18 x 3/4″ heavy 24 x 3/8″ 24 x 1/2″ medium 24 x 3/4″ heavy	These shakes have split faces and sawn backs. Cedar logs are first cut into desired lengths. Blanks or boards of proper thickness are split and then run diagonally through a bandsaw to produce two tapered shakes from each blank
No. 1 tapersplit	24 x 1/2″	Produced largely by hand, using a sharp bladed steel froe and a wooden mallet. The natural shinglelike taper is achieved by reversing the block, end-for-end, with each split
No. 1 straight	18 x 3/8″ side wall 18 x 3/8″ 24 x 3/8″	Produced in the same manner as tapersplit shakes except that by splitting from the same end of the block, the shakes acquire the same thickness throughout

18″ WIDE, 30 LB INTERLAYMENT OVER TOP PORTION OF EACH COURSE OF SHAKES
1 1/2″ MIN. OFFSET
RAFTERS
EXPOSURE
EXPOSURE X 2
1/4″ MIN.
1″ TO 1 1/2″
SPACED SHEATHING, 1″ x 4″ OR 1″ x 6″
DOUBLE STARTER COURSE
36″ WIDE 30 LB FELT STARTER STRIP

INSTALLATION OF SHAKES OVER SPACED SHEATHING (4 IN 12 MIN.)

RED CEDAR SHINGLES

	NO. 1 BLUE LABEL*			NO. 2 RED LABEL†			NO. 3 BLACK LABEL‡		
	MAXIMUM EXPOSURE RECOMMENDED FOR ROOFS								
ROOF PITCH	16″	18″	24″	16″	18″	24″	16″	18″	24″
3 in 12 to 4 in 12	3 3/4″	4 1/4″	5 3/4″	3 1/2″	4″	5 1/2″	3″	3 1/2″	5″
4 in 12 and steeper	5″	5 1/2″	7 1/2″	4″	4 1/2″	6 1/2″	3 1/2″	4″	5 1/2″

*Premium Grade: 100% heartwood, 100% clear, 100% edge grain, for highest quality.
†Intermediate Grade: not less then 10″ clear on 16″ shingles, 11″ clear on 18″ shingles, 16″ clear on 24″ shingles. Flat grain and limited sapwood permitted.
‡Utility Grade: 6″ clear on 16″ and 18″ shingles, 10″ clear on 24″ shingles. For economy applications.

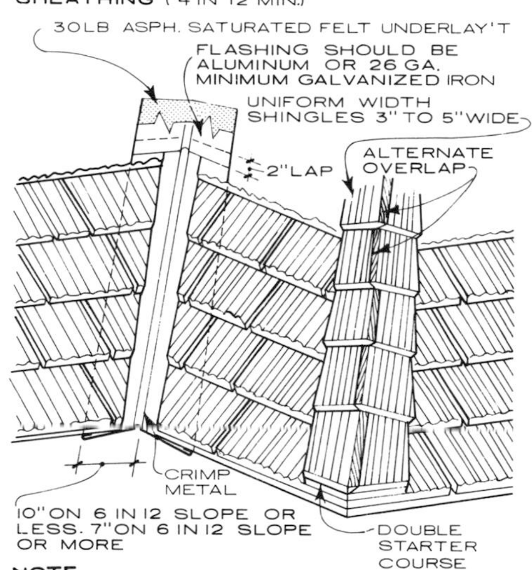

30LB ASPH. SATURATED FELT UNDERLAY'T
FLASHING SHOULD BE ALUMINUM OR 26 GA. MINIMUM GALVANIZED IRON
UNIFORM WIDTH SHINGLES 3″ TO 5″ WIDE
2″ LAP
ALTERNATE OVERLAP
CRIMP METAL
10″ ON 6 IN 12 SLOPE OR LESS. 7″ ON 6 IN 12 SLOPE OR MORE
DOUBLE STARTER COURSE

NOTE
Copper flashing should not be used with red cedar.

VALLEY HIP AND RIDGE APPLICATION OF SHAKES AND SHINGLES

UNDERLAYMENT AND SHEATHING

ROOFING TYPE	SHEATHING	UNDERLAYMENT	NORMAL SLOPE		LOW SLOPE	
Wood shakes and shingles	Solid or spaced	No. 30 asphalt saturated felt (interlayment)	4 in 12 and up	Underlayment starter course; interlayment over entire roof	3 in 12 to 4 in 12	Single layer underlayment over entire roof; interlayment over entire roof

NOTES
1. Shakes not recommended on slopes less than 4 in 12.
2. Breathing type building paper—such as deadening felt—may be applied over either type of sheating, although paper is not used in most applications.

SHINGLES AND SHAKES USED FOR ROOFING

EXPOSURE FOR SHINGLES AND SHAKES USED FOR SIDING

SHINGLE LENGTH	EXPOSURE OF SHINGLES	
	SGL. COURSE	DBL. COURSE
16″	6″ TO 7 1/2″	8″ TO 12″
18″	6″ TO 8 1/2″	9″ TO 14″
24″	8″ TO 11 1/2″	12″ TO 20″

SHINGLES
SHEATHING
NAILS
SHINGLE BACKER OR ASPHALT IMPREGNATED BACKER BOARD
1/2″
DOUBLE STARTER COURSE
TRIPLE STARTER COURSE

SINGLE COURSING APPLICATION **DOUBLE COURSING APPLICATION**

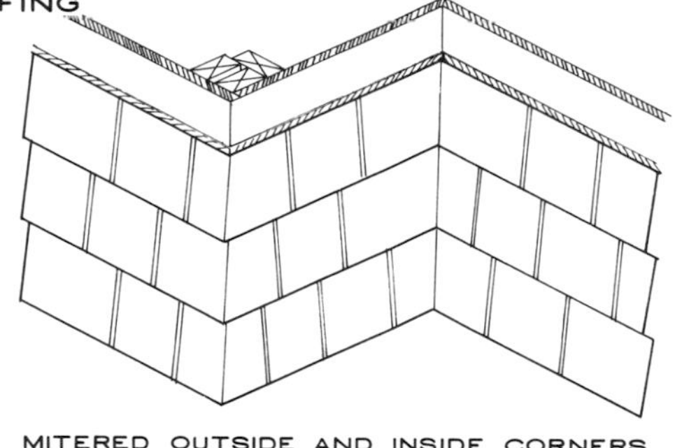

MITERED OUTSIDE AND INSIDE CORNERS (RECOMMENDED)

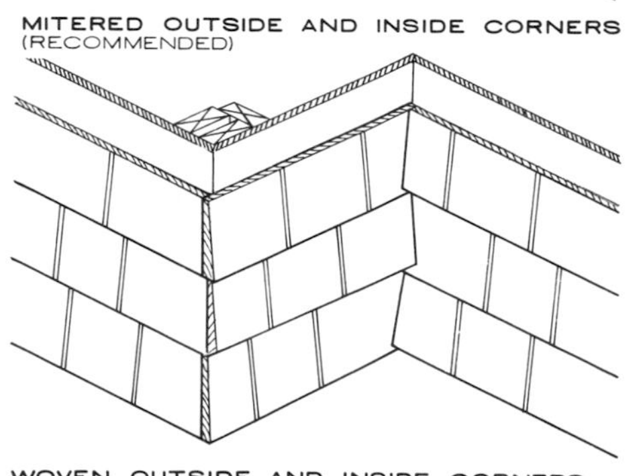

WOVEN OUTSIDE AND INSIDE CORNERS (MORE ECONOMICAL)

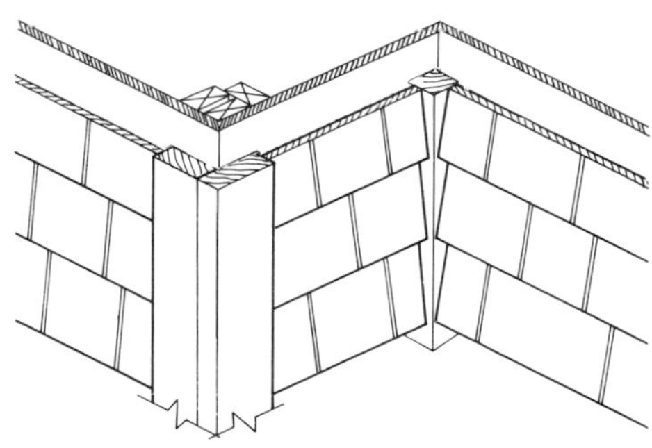

CORNER BOARDS OUTSIDE AND INSIDE CORNERS

NAILING (DEFORMED SHANK NON-FERROUS)

THICKNESS AND NAILS

16″ long	5 butts = 2″	3d
18″ long	5 butts = 2 1/4″	3d
24″ long	4 butts = 2″	4d
25″ to 27″	1 butt = 1/2″	5 or 6d
25″ to 27″	1 butt = 5/8″ to 1 1/4″	7 or 8d

SHEATHING NOTES

Sheathing may be strip-type, solid 1″ x 6″ diagonal type, plywood, fiberboard or gypsum. Horizontal wood nailing strips, 1″ x 2″, should be used over fiberboard and gypsum sheathing. Space strips equal to shingle exposure.

WOOD SHINGLES AND SHAKES FOR SIDING

Developed by Holroyd and Gray, Architects; Charlotte, North Carolina; from data furnished by Robert M. Stafford, P.E.; Consulting Engineer; Charlotte, North Carolina

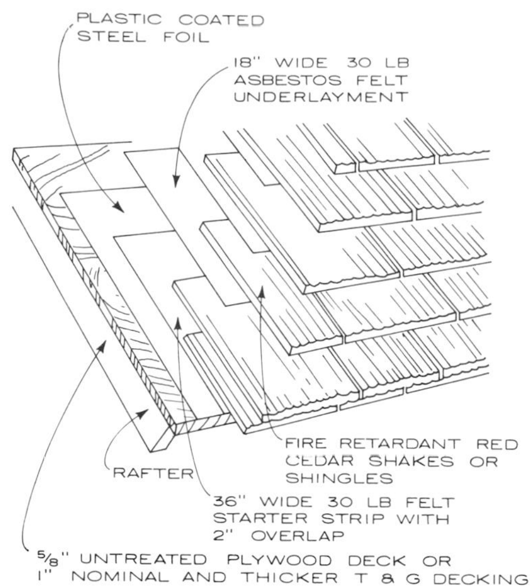

PLASTIC COATED STEEL FOIL
18" WIDE 30 LB ASBESTOS FELT UNDERLAYMENT
FIRE RETARDANT RED CEDAR SHAKES OR SHINGLES
RAFTER
36" WIDE 30 LB FELT STARTER STRIP WITH 2" OVERLAP
5/8" UNTREATED PLYWOOD DECK OR 1" NOMINAL AND THICKER T & G DECKING

FIRE RATED ROOF CONSTRUCTION

NOTES

In treating shakes, fire retardant chemicals are pressure impregnated into the wood cells, and chemicals are then fixed in the wood to prevent leaching. Treatment does not alter appearance. Fire retardant red cedar shakes are classified as Class C by U.L. With the addition of the deck constructed of 5/8 in. plywood with exterior glue or 1 in. nominal T&G boards, overlaid with a layer of approved asbestos felt lapped 2 in. on all joints and between each shake is an 18 in. wide strip of approved asbestos felt not exposed to the weather, Class B classification by U.L. is used. Decorative stains may be applied.

REMOVE OLD RIDGE COVERING. REPLACE WITH CEDAR BEVEL SIDING
1 X 4
OLD ROOFING
30 LB FELT
ROOF RAFTERS
REMOVE 6" WIDE STRIP OF OLD ROOFING. APPLY 1 X 6
METAL VALLEY SHEET 20" MIN. WIDTH
NEW CEDAR SHAKES USE LONGER NAILS TO PENETRATE SHEATHING

WOOD SHAKES APPLIED TO EXISTING ROOF

NOTES

Shakes can also be applied over any existing wall or roof. Brick or other masonry requires vertical frame-boards and horizontal nailing strips.

Over stucco, horizontal nailing strips are attached directly to wall. Nails should penetrate shading or studs. Over wood, apply shakes directly just as if on new sheathing.

NOMENCLATURE

16", 18" OR 24"
18" AND 24"
BUTT VARIES .40" TO .50"
SHINGLE (SAWN)
SHAKE (HANDSPLIT)
SECTION (SHINGLE)

Species: Shingles and shakes are available in red cedar, redwood, and tidewater red cypress.

GENERAL NOTES

1. Wood shingles and shakes are manufactured from wood species that are naturally resistant to water, sunlight, rot, and hail. They are typically installed in the natural state, although stains, primers, and paint may be applied.
2. Nails must be hot dipped in zinc or aluminum. Nail heads should be driven flush with the surface of the shingle or shake, but never into the wood.
3. Underlayment and sheathing should be designed to augment the protection provided by the shingles or shakes, depending on roof pitch and climate. For instance, a low pitched roof in an area subject to wind driven snow should have solid sheathing and an additional underlayment.

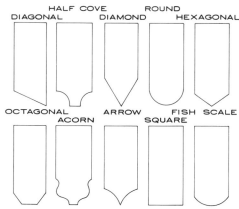

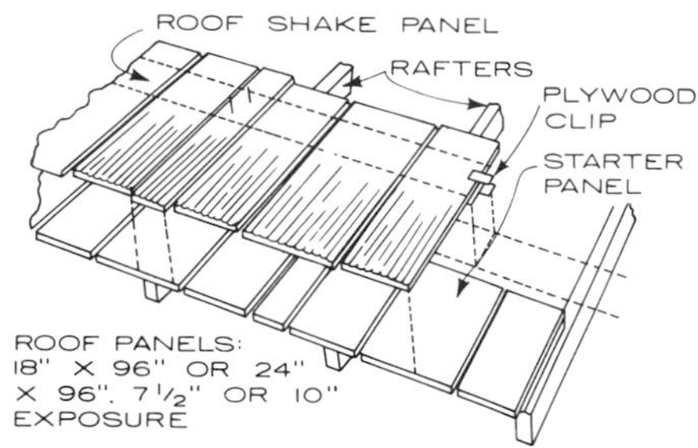

ROOF SHAKE PANEL
RAFTERS
PLYWOOD CLIP
STARTER PANEL
ROOF PANELS: 18" X 96" OR 24" X 96". 7 1/2" OR 10" EXPOSURE

NOTES

Shakes and shingles plus sheathing go up in one operation. 8 ft roof panels have 16 individual handsplit shakes bonded to 6 in. wide 1/2 in. plywood strip, which form a solid deck when the panels are nailed. A 4 to 12 in. or steeper roof pitch is recommended.

After application of starter panels, attach panels directly to rafters. Although designed to center on 16 or 24 in. spacing, they may meet between rafters. Use two 6d nails at each rafter.

ROOF PANEL

HALF COVE, DIAGONAL, DIAMOND, ROUND, HEXAGONAL
OCTAGONAL, ACORN, ARROW, SQUARE, FISH SCALE

NOTE

Fancy butt shingles are 5 in. wide and 7 1/2 in. long. Custom produced to individual orders.

FANCY BUTT RED CEDAR SHINGLES

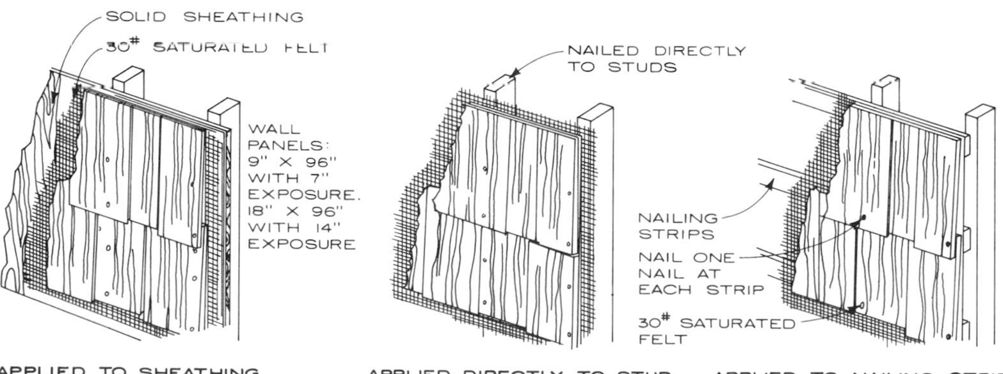

SOLID SHEATHING
30# SATURATED FELT
WALL PANELS: 9" X 96" WITH 7" EXPOSURE. 18" X 96" WITH 14" EXPOSURE
NAILED DIRECTLY TO STUDS
NAILING STRIPS
NAIL ONE NAIL AT EACH STRIP
30# SATURATED FELT
APPLIED TO SHEATHING
APPLIED DIRECTLY TO STUD
APPLIED TO NAILING STRIPS

NOTES

8 ft sidewall panels are of three-ply construction.

1. Surface layer of individual #1 grade shingles or shakes.
2. Cross binder core of plywood veneer.
3. Undercourse layer of shingle backing panels.

Panels can be applied to nailing strips or directly to studs where Code permits. Use 30 lb saturated fill lapped 3 in. vertically and horizontally. Stagger joints between panels. Matching sidewall or mansard style corners are available.

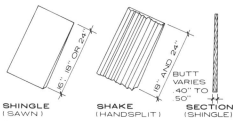

SIDEWALL PANELS

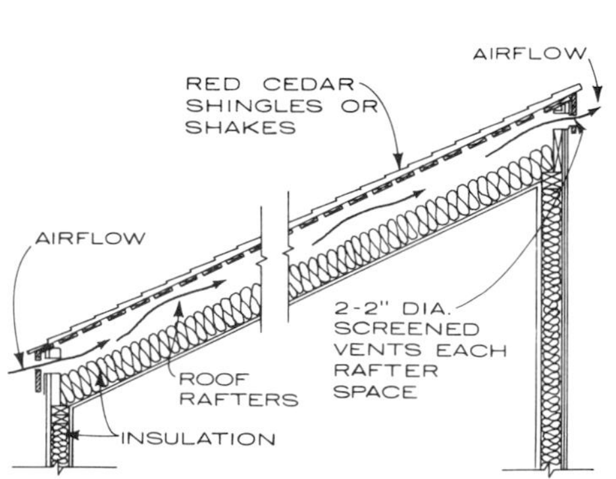

AIRFLOW
RED CEDAR SHINGLES OR SHAKES
AIRFLOW
ROOF RAFTERS
2-2" DIA. SCREENED VENTS EACH RAFTER SPACE
INSULATION

NOTE

A recommended ratio of total free area to adding area should not be less than 1 : 150 for adequate ventilation.

SECTION

VENTILATION OF ROOF

Robert E. Fehlberg, FAIA; CTA Architects Engineers; Billings, Montana

SCHEDULE OF UNDERLAYMENT

SLOPE	TYPE OF UNDERLAYMENT
Normal slope: 4 in 12 and up	Single layer of 15 lb asphalt saturated felt over entire roof
Low slope: 3 in 12 to 4 in 12	Two layers of 15 lb asphalt saturated felt over entire roof

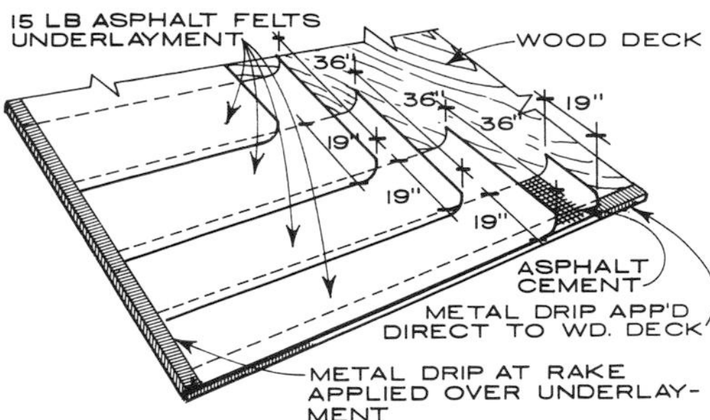

15 LB ASPHALT FELTS UNDERLAYMENT
WOOD DECK
36"
36"
36"
19"
19"
19"
19"
ASPHALT CEMENT
METAL DRIP APP'D DIRECT TO WD. DECK
METAL DRIP AT RAKE APPLIED OVER UNDERLAYMENT

Use only enough nails to hold underlayment in place until shingles are laid.

APPLICATION OF UNDERLAYMENT ON LOW SLOPE ROOFS

EAVES FLASHING STRIP PREVENTS BACKUP DAMAGE

ALL LAPS SHOULD BE OUTSIDE WALL LINE

24" MIN.

NORMAL SLOPE

DOUBLE UNDERLAYMENT CEMENTED TO PROVIDE EAVE FLASHING

UNDERLAYMENT TO OVERHANG METAL DRIP ¼ TO ⅜

36" MIN.

LOW SLOPE

EAVE FLASHING

EAVE FLASHING

Eave flashing is required wherever the January daily average temperature is 30°F or less or where there is a possibility of ice forming along the eaves.

NORMAL SLOPE—4 IN./FT OR OVER

A course of 90 lb mineral surfaced roll roofing or a course of 50 lb smooth roll roofing is installed to overhang the underlay and metal edge from ¼ to ⅜ in. Extend up the roof far enough to cover a point at least 24 in. inside the interior wall line of the building. When the overhang requires flashing wider than 36 in., the horizontal lap joint is cemented and located on the roof deck extending beyond the exterior line of the building.

LOW SLOPE—3 TO 4 IN./FT

Cover the deck with two layers of 15# asphalt saturated felt. Begin with a 19 in. starter course laid along the eaves, followed by a 36 in. wide sheet laid even with the eaves and completely overlapping the starter course. The starter course is covered with asphalt cement. Thereafter, 36 in. sheets are laid in asphalt cement, each to overlap the preceding course 19 in., exposing 17 in. of the underlying sheet.

The plies are placed in asphalt cement to a point at least 36 in. inside the interior wall line of the building.

SCHEDULE OF SHINGLE TYPES (1)

DESCRIPTION	DESIGN	MATERIAL	U.L. RATING	WEIGHT	SIZE
Three-tab square butt		Fiberglass Organic felts	A (4) C	205–225 lb/sq 235–300 lb/sq	36" x 12"
Two-tab square butt		Fiberglass Organic felts	A (4) C	260–325 lb/sq 300 lb/sq	36" x 12"
Laminated overlay (2)		Fiberglass Organic felts	A (3) C	300 lb/sq 330–380 lb/sq	36" x 14"
Random edge cut		Fiberglass Organic felts	A (3) C	225–260 lb/sq 250 lb/sq	36" x 12"

NOTE: Exposure 5", edge lap 2".

NOTES

1. Exposure 5 in., edge lap 2 in., for all designs.
2. More than one thickness for varying surface texture.
3. Many rated as wind resistant.
4. All rated as wind resistant.

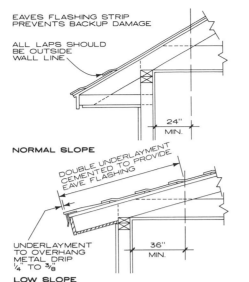

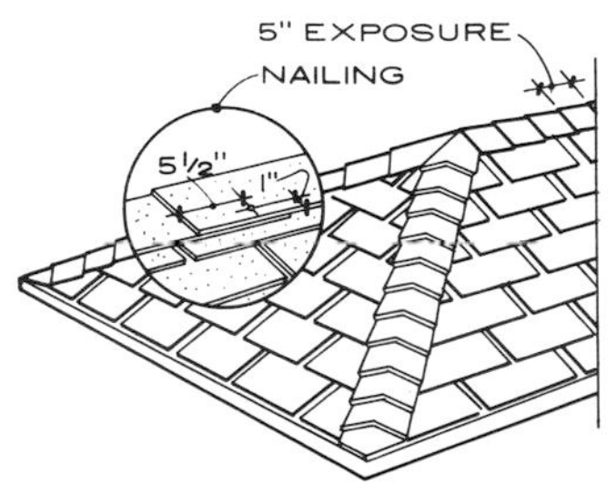

5" EXPOSURE
NAILING
5½"
1"

HIP AND RIDGE

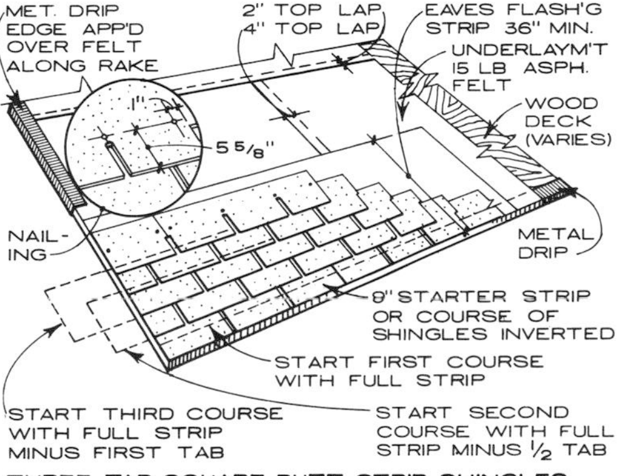

MET. DRIP EDGE APP'D OVER FELT ALONG RAKE
2" TOP LAP
4" TOP LAP
EAVES FLASH'G STRIP 36" MIN.
UNDERLAYM'T 15 LB ASPH. FELT
WOOD DECK (VARIES)
1"
5 ⅝"
NAILING
METAL DRIP
9" STARTER STRIP OR COURSE OF SHINGLES INVERTED
START FIRST COURSE WITH FULL STRIP
START THIRD COURSE WITH FULL STRIP MINUS FIRST TAB
START SECOND COURSE WITH FULL STRIP MINUS ½ TAB

THREE TAB SQUARE BUTT STRIP SHINGLES

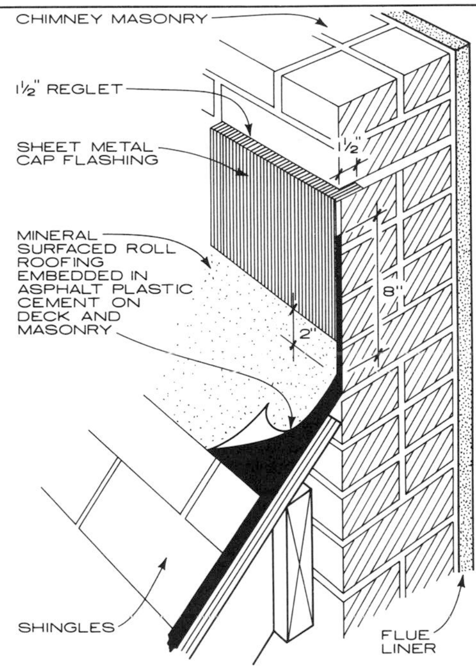

CHIMNEY MASONRY
1½" REGLET
SHEET METAL CAP FLASHING
1½"
MINERAL SURFACED ROLL ROOFING EMBEDDED IN ASPHALT PLASTIC CEMENT ON DECK AND MASONRY
8"
2"
SHINGLES
FLUE LINER

METHOD OF SECURING CAP FLASHING TO CHIMNEY MASONRY

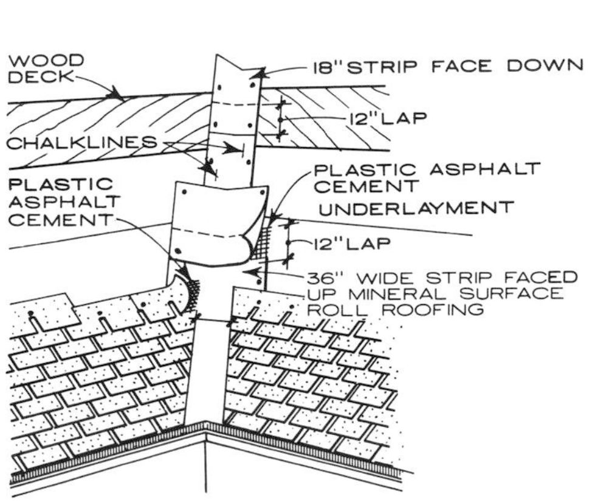

WOOD DECK
18" STRIP FACE DOWN
12" LAP
CHALKLINES
PLASTIC ASPHALT CEMENT
PLASTIC ASPHALT CEMENT
UNDERLAYMENT
12" LAP
36" WIDE STRIP FACED UP MINERAL SURFACE ROLL ROOFING

OPEN VALLEY

•Valley width should be 6" wide at ridge and spread wider at the rate of ⅛"/foot downward to eave. Establish valley width using chalkline from ridge to cove.

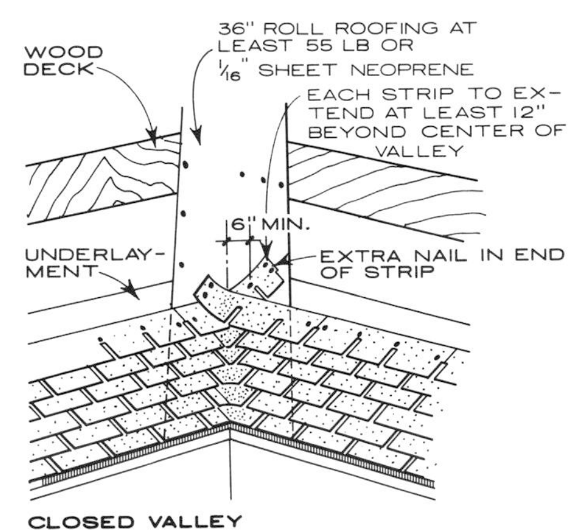

WOOD DECK
36" ROLL ROOFING AT LEAST 55 LB OR 1/16" SHEET NEOPRENE
EACH STRIP TO EXTEND AT LEAST 12" BEYOND CENTER OF VALLEY
UNDERLAYMENT
6" MIN.
EXTRA NAIL IN END OF STRIP

CLOSED VALLEY

APPLICATION DIAGRAMS

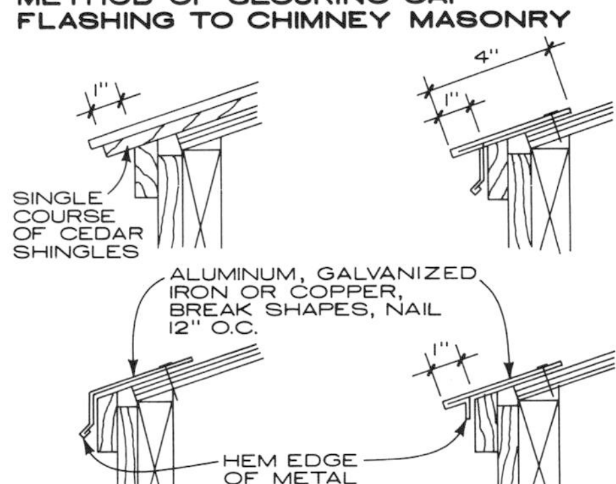

1"
4"
1"
SINGLE COURSE OF CEDAR SHINGLES
ALUMINUM, GALVANIZED IRON OR COPPER, BREAK SHAPES, NAIL 12" O.C.
1"
HEM EDGE OF METAL

DRIP EDGE DETAILS

SMOOTH

ANNULAR THREADED

SCREW THREADED

NAIL TYPES

NAILING OF SHINGLES RECOMMENDATION

DECK TYPE	NAIL LENGTH
1" Wood sheathing	1 ¼"
⅜" Plywood	⅞"
½" Plywood	1"
Reroofing over asphalt shingles	1 ¾"

Robert E. Fehlberg, FAIA; CTA Architects Engineers; Billings, Montana

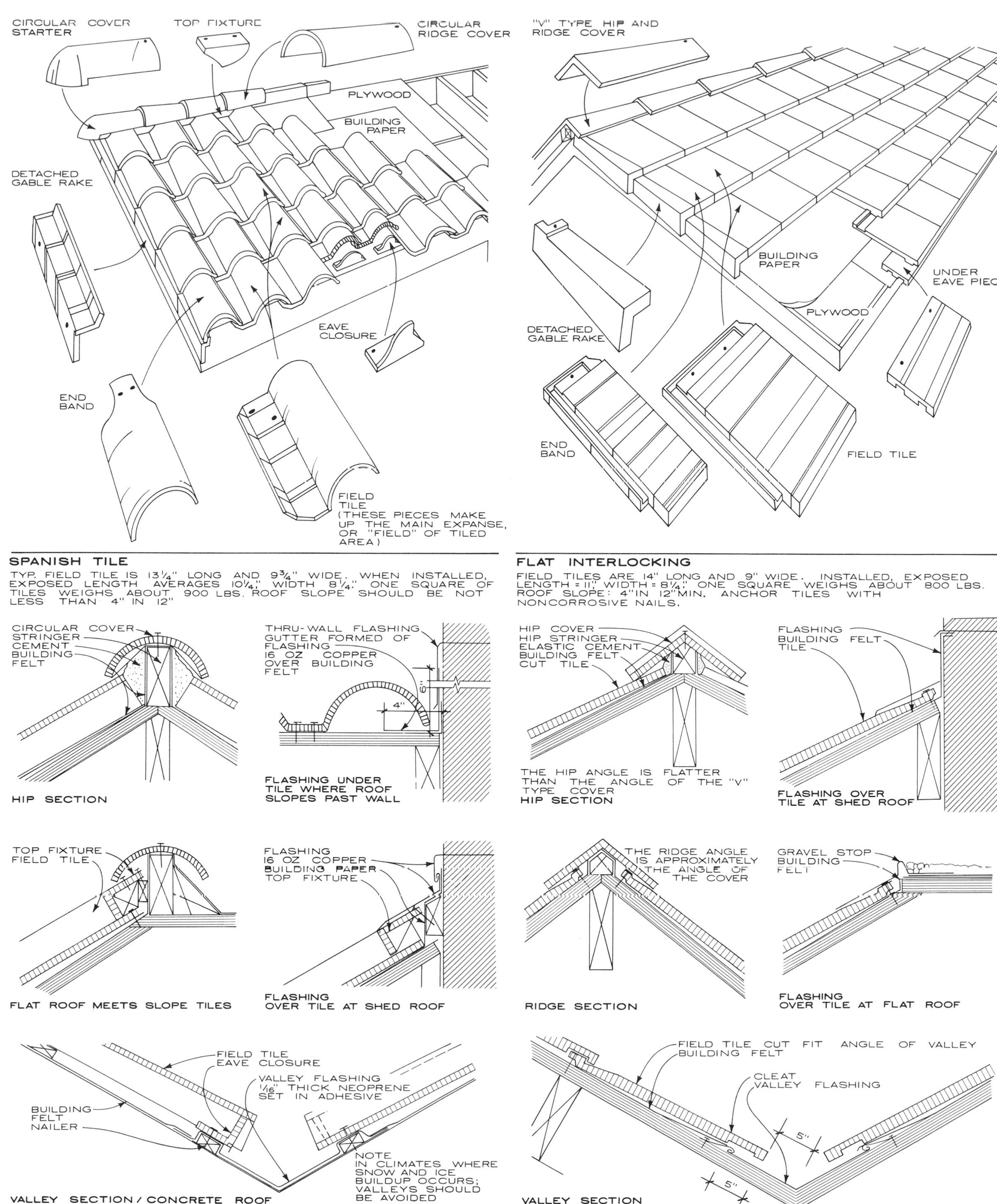
CIRCULAR COVER STARTER
TOP FIXTURE
CIRCULAR RIDGE COVER
PLYWOOD
BUILDING PAPER
DETACHED GABLE RAKE
EAVE CLOSURE
END BAND
FIELD TILE (THESE PIECES MAKE UP THE MAIN EXPANSE, OR "FIELD" OF TILED AREA)
"V" TYPE HIP AND RIDGE COVER
BUILDING PAPER
UNDER EAVE PIECE
PLYWOOD
DETACHED GABLE RAKE
END BAND
FIELD TILE
SPANISH TILE
TYP. FIELD TILE IS 13¼" LONG AND 9¾" WIDE. WHEN INSTALLED, EXPOSED LENGTH AVERAGES 10¼," WIDTH 8¼." ONE SQUARE OF TILES WEIGHS ABOUT 900 LBS. ROOF SLOPE SHOULD BE NOT LESS THAN 4" IN 12"
FLAT INTERLOCKING
FIELD TILES ARE 14" LONG AND 9" WIDE. INSTALLED, EXPOSED LENGTH = 11," WIDTH = 8¼." ONE SQUARE WEIGHS ABOUT 800 LBS. ROOF SLOPE: 4" IN 12" MIN. ANCHOR TILES WITH NONCORROSIVE NAILS.
CIRCULAR COVER
STRINGER
CEMENT
BUILDING FELT
HIP SECTION
THRU-WALL FLASHING
GUTTER FORMED OF FLASHING
16 OZ COPPER OVER BUILDING FELT
6"
4"
FLASHING UNDER TILE WHERE ROOF SLOPES PAST WALL
HIP COVER
HIP STRINGER
ELASTIC CEMENT
BUILDING FELT
CUT TILE
THE HIP ANGLE IS FLATTER THAN THE ANGLE OF THE "V" TYPE COVER
HIP SECTION
FLASHING
BUILDING FELT
TILE
FLASHING OVER TILE AT SHED ROOF
TOP FIXTURE
FIELD TILE
FLAT ROOF MEETS SLOPE TILES
FLASHING
16 OZ COPPER
BUILDING PAPER
TOP FIXTURE
FLASHING OVER TILE AT SHED ROOF
THE RIDGE ANGLE IS APPROXIMATELY THE ANGLE OF THE COVER
RIDGE SECTION
GRAVEL STOP
BUILDING FELT
FLASHING OVER TILE AT FLAT ROOF
FIELD TILE
EAVE CLOSURE
VALLEY FLASHING 1/16" THICK NEOPRENE SET IN ADHESIVE
BUILDING FELT
NAILER
NOTE
IN CLIMATES WHERE SNOW AND ICE BUILDUP OCCURS; VALLEYS SHOULD BE AVOIDED
VALLEY SECTION / CONCRETE ROOF
FIELD TILE CUT FIT ANGLE OF VALLEY
BUILDING FELT
CLEAT
VALLEY FLASHING
5"
5"
VALLEY SECTION

Darrel Downing Rippeteau, Architect; Washington, D.C.

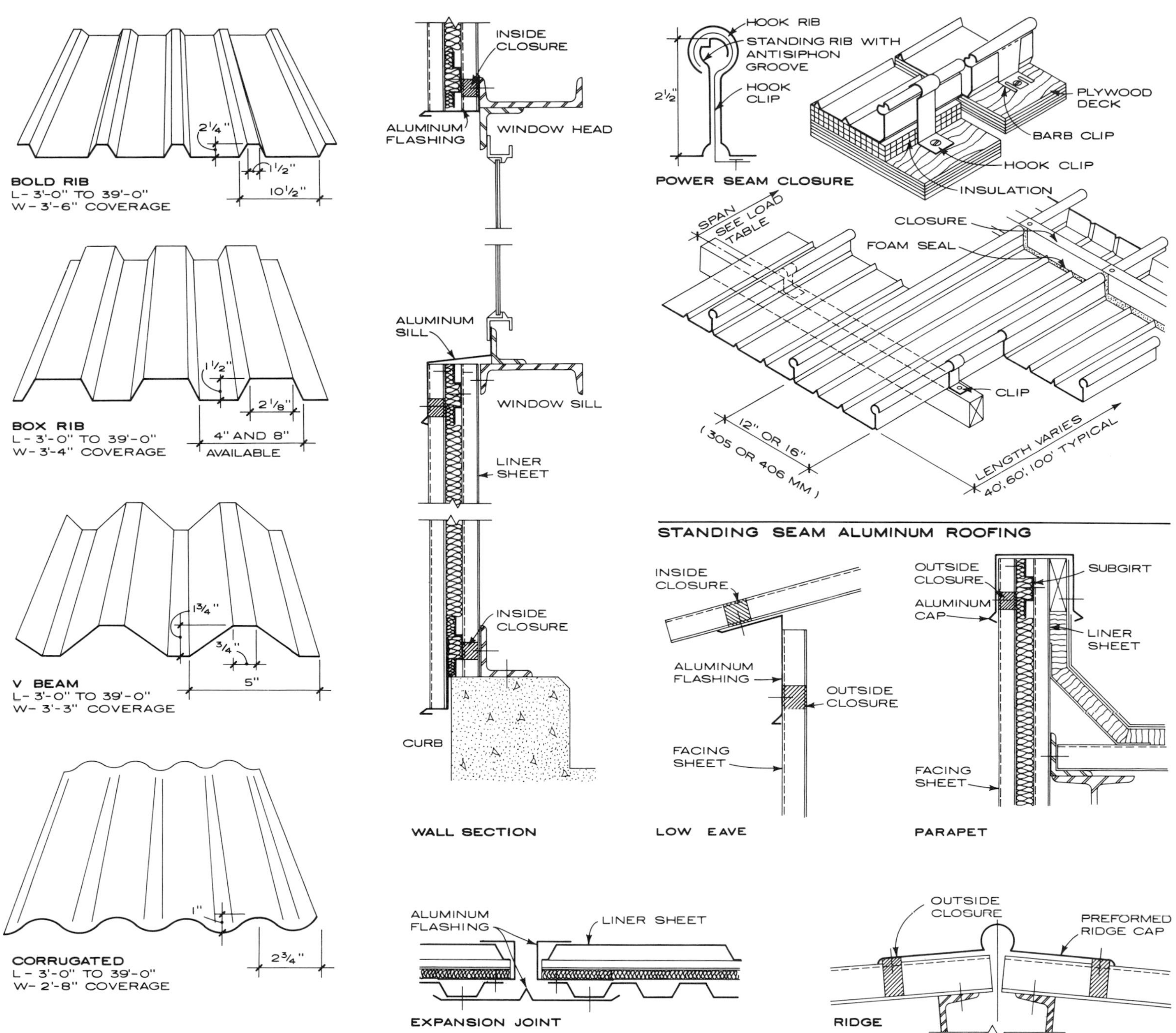

BOLD RIB
L - 3'-0" TO 39'-0"
W - 3'-6" COVERAGE
2¼"
1½"
10½"
BOX RIB
L - 3'-0" TO 39'-0"
W - 3'-4" COVERAGE
1½"
2⅛"
4" AND 8" AVAILABLE
V BEAM
L - 3'-0" TO 39'-0"
W - 3'-3" COVERAGE
1¾"
¾"
5"
CORRUGATED
L - 3'-0" TO 39'-0"
W - 2'-8" COVERAGE
1"
2¾"
INSIDE CLOSURE
ALUMINUM FLASHING
WINDOW HEAD
ALUMINUM SILL
WINDOW SILL
LINER SHEET
INSIDE CLOSURE
CURB
WALL SECTION
HOOK RIB
STANDING RIB WITH ANTISIPHON GROOVE
HOOK CLIP
2½"
POWER SEAM CLOSURE
PLYWOOD DECK
BARB CLIP
HOOK CLIP
INSULATION
SPAN SEE LOAD TABLE
CLOSURE
FOAM SEAL
CLIP
12" OR 16" (305 OR 406 MM)
LENGTH VARIES 40', 60', 100' TYPICAL
STANDING SEAM ALUMINUM ROOFING
INSIDE CLOSURE
ALUMINUM FLASHING
OUTSIDE CLOSURE
FACING SHEET
LOW EAVE
OUTSIDE CLOSURE
ALUMINUM CAP
SUBGIRT
LINER SHEET
FACING SHEET
PARAPET
ALUMINUM FLASHING
LINER SHEET
EXPANSION JOINT
OUTSIDE CLOSURE
PREFORMED RIDGE CAP
RIDGE

FORMED ALUMINUM ROOFING AND SIDING

NOTES

1. Endlaps for roofing and siding shall be at least 6 in. and fastened at every rib. Two fasteners may be required when designing for a negative (uplift) loading condition.
2. Minimum sidelaps shall be equal to one rib or corrugation and laid away from prevailing wind. Fasteners shall be spaced a maximum of 12 in. on center for all types of roofing and siding.
3. For roofing, fasteners shall pierce only the high corrugation. For siding, fasteners shall pierce either the high or low corrugation. Consult manufacturer for proper sheet metal fasteners and accessories.
4. Minimum slopes for sheet roofing are as follows:
   a. 1 in. depth corrugated—3 in 12.
   b. 1½ in. depth ribbed—2 in 12.
   c. 1¾ in. v-corrugated—2 in 12.
5. See page on Metal Walls for insulation details and fire rated wall assemblies.

MAXIMUM SPAN TABLE FOR FORMED ALUMINUM ROOFING AND SIDING (IN.)

DESIGN LOAD (PSF)	BOLD RIB		4" BOX RIB		V BEAM		CORRUGATED		STANDING SEAM	
	0.032 IN. THICK	0.040 IN. THICK	0.032 IN. THICK	0.040 IN. THICK	0.032 IN. THICK	0.040 IN. THICK	0.032 IN. THICK	0.040 IN. THICK	0.032 IN. THICK	0.040 IN. THICK
20	95	123	100	120	131	151	90	98	103	124
30	77	100	82	98	107	124	73	80	86	104
40	67	87	71	85	92	107	64	69	77	92
50	60	76	63	76	83	96	57	62	70	83

NOTE: Values are based on uniform positive (downward) and walking loads on single span only.

John A. Schulte; Hellmuth, Obata & Kassabaum, Inc.; St. Louis, Missouri

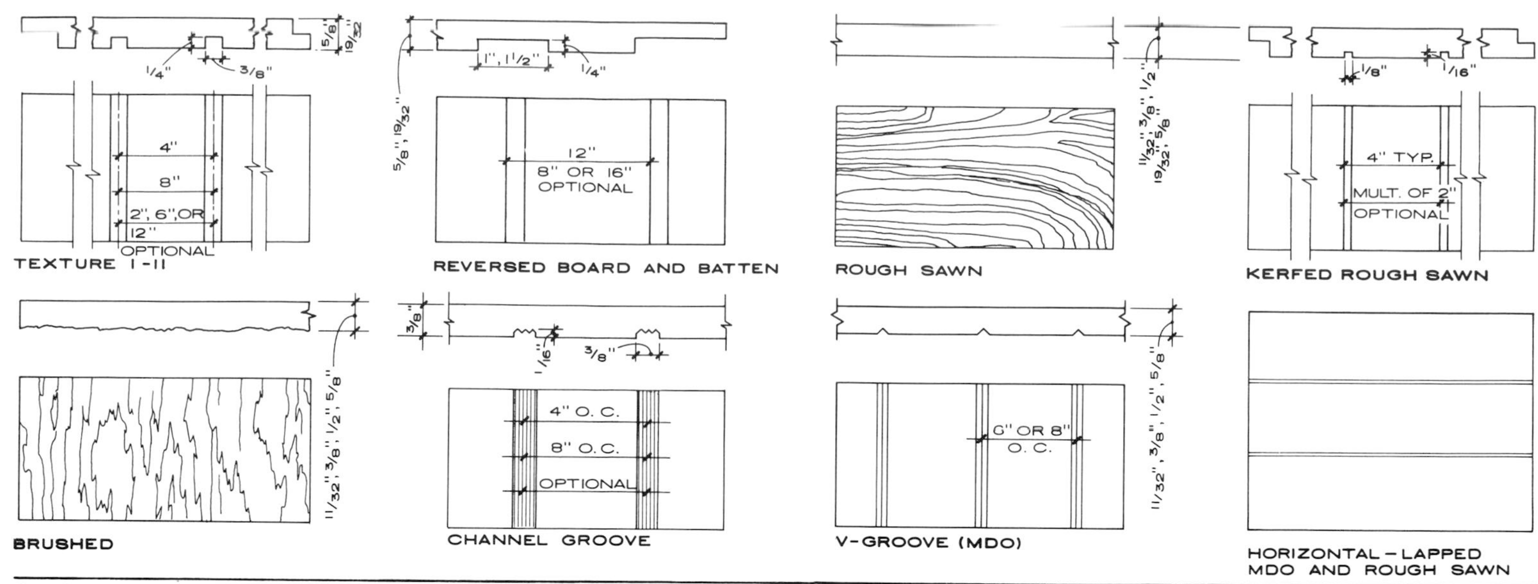

1/4"
3/8"
5/8"
19/32"
4"
8"
2", 6", OR 12"
OPTIONAL
TEXTURE 1-11
1", 1 1/2"
1/4"
5/8", 19/32"
12"
8" OR 16"
OPTIONAL
REVERSED BOARD AND BATTEN
11/32", 3/8", 1/2", 19/32", 5/8"
ROUGH SAWN
1/8"
1/16"
4" TYP.
MULT. OF 2"
OPTIONAL
KERFED ROUGH SAWN
11/32", 3/8", 1/2", 5/8"
BRUSHED
3/8"
1/16"
3/8"
4" O.C.
8" O.C.
OPTIONAL
CHANNEL GROOVE
6" OR 8" O.C.
11/32", 3/8", 1/2", 5/8"
V-GROOVE (MDO)
HORIZONTAL - LAPPED MDO AND ROUGH SAWN

PLYWOOD SIDING 303 AND T1-11 (303 SPECIAL)

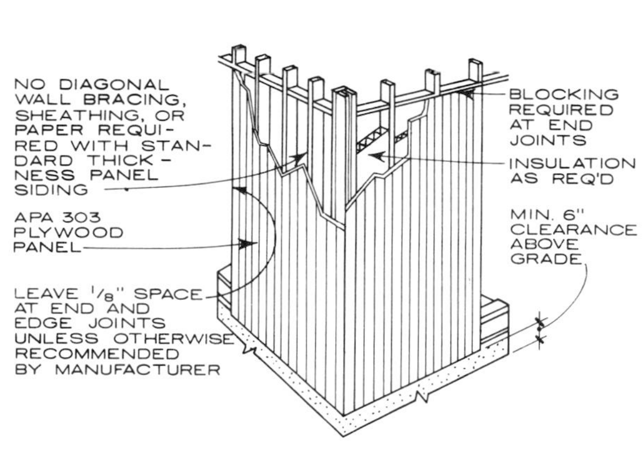

NO DIAGONAL WALL BRACING, SHEATHING, OR PAPER REQUIRED WITH STANDARD THICKNESS PANEL SIDING
APA 303 PLYWOOD PANEL
LEAVE 1/8" SPACE AT END AND EDGE JOINTS UNLESS OTHERWISE RECOMMENDED BY MANUFACTURER
BLOCKING REQUIRED AT END JOINTS
INSULATION AS REQ'D
MIN. 6" CLEARANCE ABOVE GRADE

PANEL SIDING VERTICAL APPLICATION

Medium density overlay (MDO) plywood lap siding: standard thickness is 3/8 in. in lengths to 16 ft on order; standard widths are 12 or 16 in.

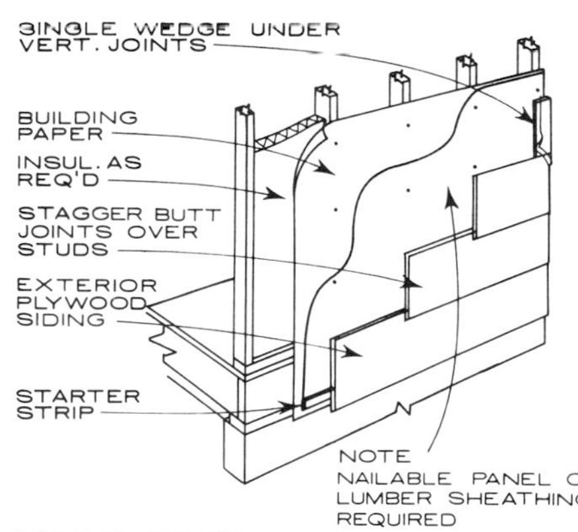

SINGLE WEDGE UNDER VERT. JOINTS
BUILDING PAPER
INSUL. AS REQ'D
STAGGER BUTT JOINTS OVER STUDS
EXTERIOR PLYWOOD SIDING
STARTER STRIP
NOTE
NAILABLE PANEL OR LUMBER SHEATHING REQUIRED

PLYWOOD LAP SIDING APPLICATION

1/8" SPACING AT ALL PANEL EDGES

CAULK VERTICAL JOINTS OR BACK WITH BUILDING PAPER

2 X 4 BLOCKING AT HORIZONTAL JOINTS

6" MIN. CLEAR ABOVE GRADE

MAY USE BATTENS TO CONCEAL BUTT JOINTS

PANEL SIDING HORIZONTAL

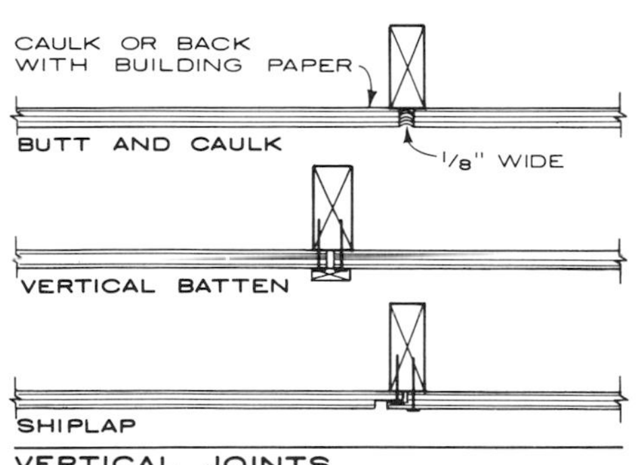

CAULK OR BACK WITH BUILDING PAPER
BUTT AND CAULK
1/8" WIDE
VERTICAL BATTEN
SHIPLAP

VERTICAL JOINTS

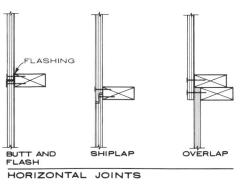

FLASHING

BUTT AND FLASH

SHIPLAP

OVERLAP

HORIZONTAL JOINTS

APA STURD-I-WALL CONSTRUCTION RECOMMENDATIONS (SIDING DIRECT TO STUDS AND OVER NONSTRUCTURAL SHEATHING)

PLYWOOD PANEL SIDING DESCRIPTION (ALL SPECIES GROUPS)	NOMINAL THICKNESS (IN.)	MAX. STUD SPACING (IN.) FACE GRAIN VERTICAL	MAX. STUD SPACING (IN.) FACE GRAIN HORIZONTAL	NAIL SIZE (USE NONSTAINING BOX, SIDING, OR CASING NAILS (1)(2)	NAIL SPACING (IN.) PANEL EDGES	NAIL SPACING (IN.) INTERMEDIATE
APA MDO EXT	11/32 and 3/8	16	24	6d for panels 1/2″ thick or less 8d for thicker panels	6(4)	12
	1/2 and thicker	24	24			
APA 303 siding 16 o.c. EXT (including T1-11)	11/32 and thicker	16	24			
APA 303 siding—24 o.c. EXT	15/32 and thicker (3)	24	24			

NOTES

1. If siding is applied over sheathing thicker than 1/2 in. use next regular nail size. Use nonstaining box nails for siding installed over foam insulation sheathing.
2. Hot-dipped or hot-tumbled galvanized steel nails are recommended for most siding applications. For best performance, stainless steel nails or aluminum nails should be considered. APA tests also show that electrically or mechanically galvanized steel nails appear satisfactory when plating meets or exceeds thickness requirements of ASTM A641 Class 2 coatings and is further protected by yellow chromate coating.
3. Only panels 15/32 in. and thicker which have certain groove depths and spacings qualify for 24 in. o.c. Span Rating.
4. For braced wall section with 11/32 in. or 3/8 in. siding applied horizontally over studs 24 in. o.c.

MINIMUM BENDING RADII FOR PLYWOOD PANELS PANEL THICKNESS (IN.)	1/4	3/8	1/2	5/8	3/4
Across grain (ft)	2	3	6	8	12
Parallel to grain (ft)	5	8	12	16	20

NOTES

The types of plywood recommended for exterior siding are: A.P.A. grade trademarked medium density overlay (MDO), Type 303 siding or Texture 1-11 (T1-11 special 303 siding). T1-11 plywood siding is manufactured with 3/8 in. wide parallel grooves and shiplapped edges. MDO is recommended for paint finishes and is available in variety of surfaces. 303 plywood panels are also available in a wide variety of surfaces. The most common A.P.A. plywood siding panel dimensions are 4 x 8 ft but the panels are also available in 9 and 10 ft lengths, lap siding to 16 ft.

John D. Bloodgood, Architect, P.C.; Des Moines, Iowa
American Plywood Association

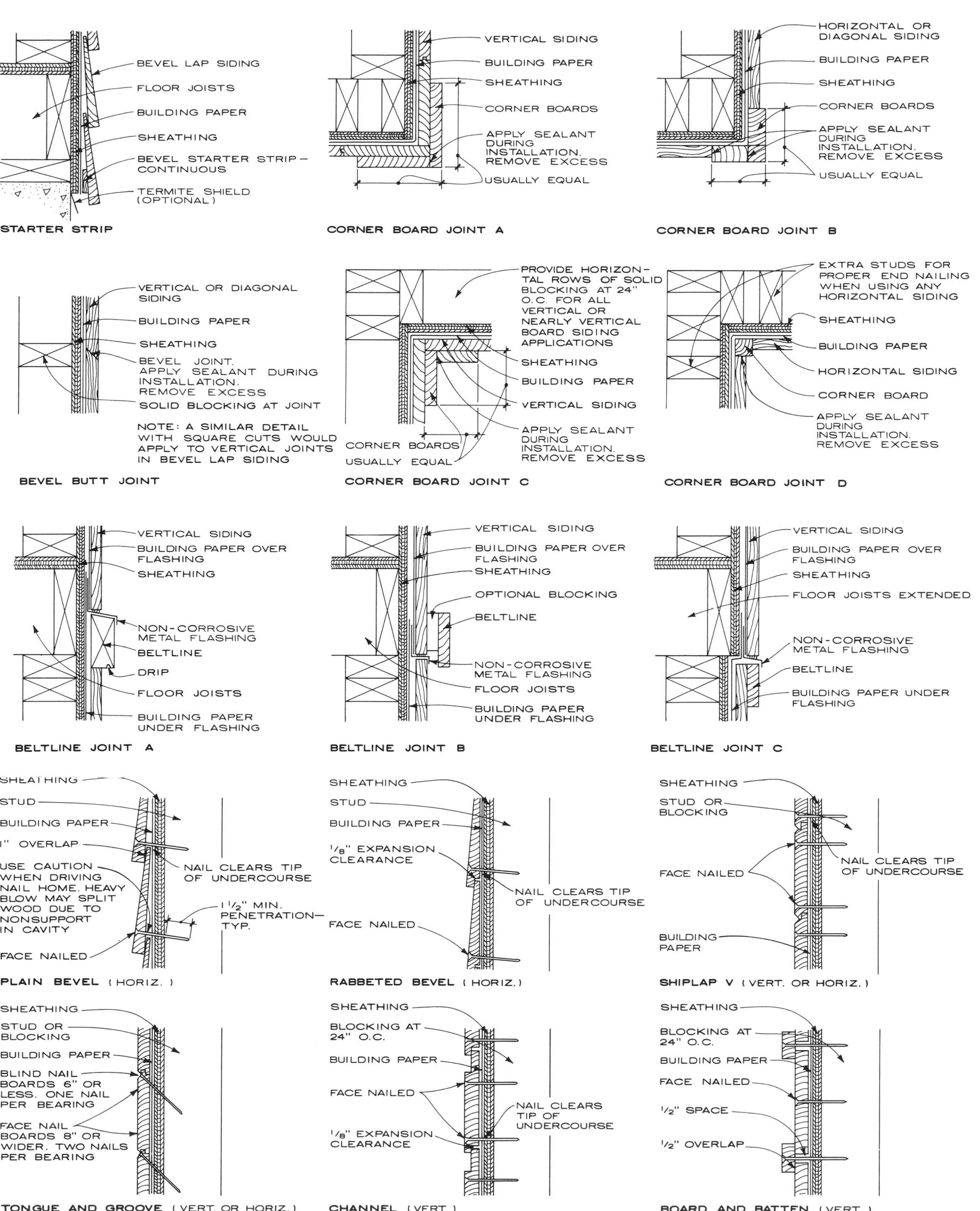
BEVEL LAP SIDING
FLOOR JOISTS
BUILDING PAPER
SHEATHING
BEVEL STARTER STRIP – CONTINUOUS
TERMITE SHIELD (OPTIONAL)
STARTER STRIP
VERTICAL SIDING
BUILDING PAPER
SHEATHING
CORNER BOARDS
APPLY SEALANT DURING INSTALLATION. REMOVE EXCESS
USUALLY EQUAL
CORNER BOARD JOINT A
HORIZONTAL OR DIAGONAL SIDING
BUILDING PAPER
SHEATHING
CORNER BOARDS
APPLY SEALANT DURING INSTALLATION. REMOVE EXCESS
USUALLY EQUAL
CORNER BOARD JOINT B
VERTICAL OR DIAGONAL SIDING
BUILDING PAPER
SHEATHING
BEVEL JOINT. APPLY SEALANT DURING INSTALLATION. REMOVE EXCESS
SOLID BLOCKING AT JOINT
NOTE: A SIMILAR DETAIL WITH SQUARE CUTS WOULD APPLY TO VERTICAL JOINTS IN BEVEL LAP SIDING
BEVEL BUTT JOINT
PROVIDE HORIZONTAL ROWS OF SOLID BLOCKING AT 24" O.C. FOR ALL VERTICAL OR NEARLY VERTICAL BOARD SIDING APPLICATIONS
SHEATHING
BUILDING PAPER
VERTICAL SIDING
APPLY SEALANT DURING INSTALLATION. REMOVE EXCESS
CORNER BOARDS
USUALLY EQUAL
CORNER BOARD JOINT C
EXTRA STUDS FOR PROPER END NAILING WHEN USING ANY HORIZONTAL SIDING
SHEATHING
BUILDING PAPER
HORIZONTAL SIDING
CORNER BOARD
APPLY SEALANT DURING INSTALLATION. REMOVE EXCESS
CORNER BOARD JOINT D
VERTICAL SIDING
BUILDING PAPER OVER FLASHING
SHEATHING
NON-CORROSIVE METAL FLASHING
BELTLINE
DRIP
FLOOR JOISTS
BUILDING PAPER UNDER FLASHING
BELTLINE JOINT A
VERTICAL SIDING
BUILDING PAPER OVER FLASHING
SHEATHING
OPTIONAL BLOCKING
BELTLINE
NON-CORROSIVE METAL FLASHING
FLOOR JOISTS
BUILDING PAPER UNDER FLASHING
BELTLINE JOINT B
VERTICAL SIDING
BUILDING PAPER OVER FLASHING
SHEATHING
FLOOR JOISTS EXTENDED
NON-CORROSIVE METAL FLASHING
BELTLINE
BUILDING PAPER UNDER FLASHING
BELTLINE JOINT C
SHEATHING
STUD
BUILDING PAPER
1" OVERLAP
USE CAUTION WHEN DRIVING NAIL HOME. HEAVY BLOW MAY SPLIT WOOD DUE TO NONSUPPORT IN CAVITY
FACE NAILED
NAIL CLEARS TIP OF UNDERCOURSE
1 1/2" MIN. PENETRATION–TYP.
PLAIN BEVEL (HORIZ.)
SHEATHING
STUD
BUILDING PAPER
1/8" EXPANSION CLEARANCE
NAIL CLEARS TIP OF UNDERCOURSE
FACE NAILED
RABBETED BEVEL (HORIZ.)
SHEATHING
STUD OR BLOCKING
FACE NAILED
NAIL CLEARS TIP OF UNDERCOURSE
BUILDING PAPER
SHIPLAP V (VERT. OR HORIZ.)
SHEATHING
STUD OR BLOCKING
BUILDING PAPER
BLIND NAIL BOARDS 6" OR LESS. ONE NAIL PER BEARING
FACE NAIL BOARDS 8" OR WIDER. TWO NAILS PER BEARING
TONGUE AND GROOVE (VERT. OR HORIZ.)
SHEATHING
BLOCKING AT 24" O.C.
BUILDING PAPER
FACE NAILED
NAIL CLEARS TIP OF UNDERCOURSE
1/8" EXPANSION CLEARANCE
CHANNEL (VERT.)
SHEATHING
BLOCKING AT 24" O.C.
BUILDING PAPER
FACE NAILED
1/2" SPACE
1/2" OVERLAP
BOARD AND BATTEN (VERT.)

Jerry Graham; CTA Architects Engineers; Billings, Montana

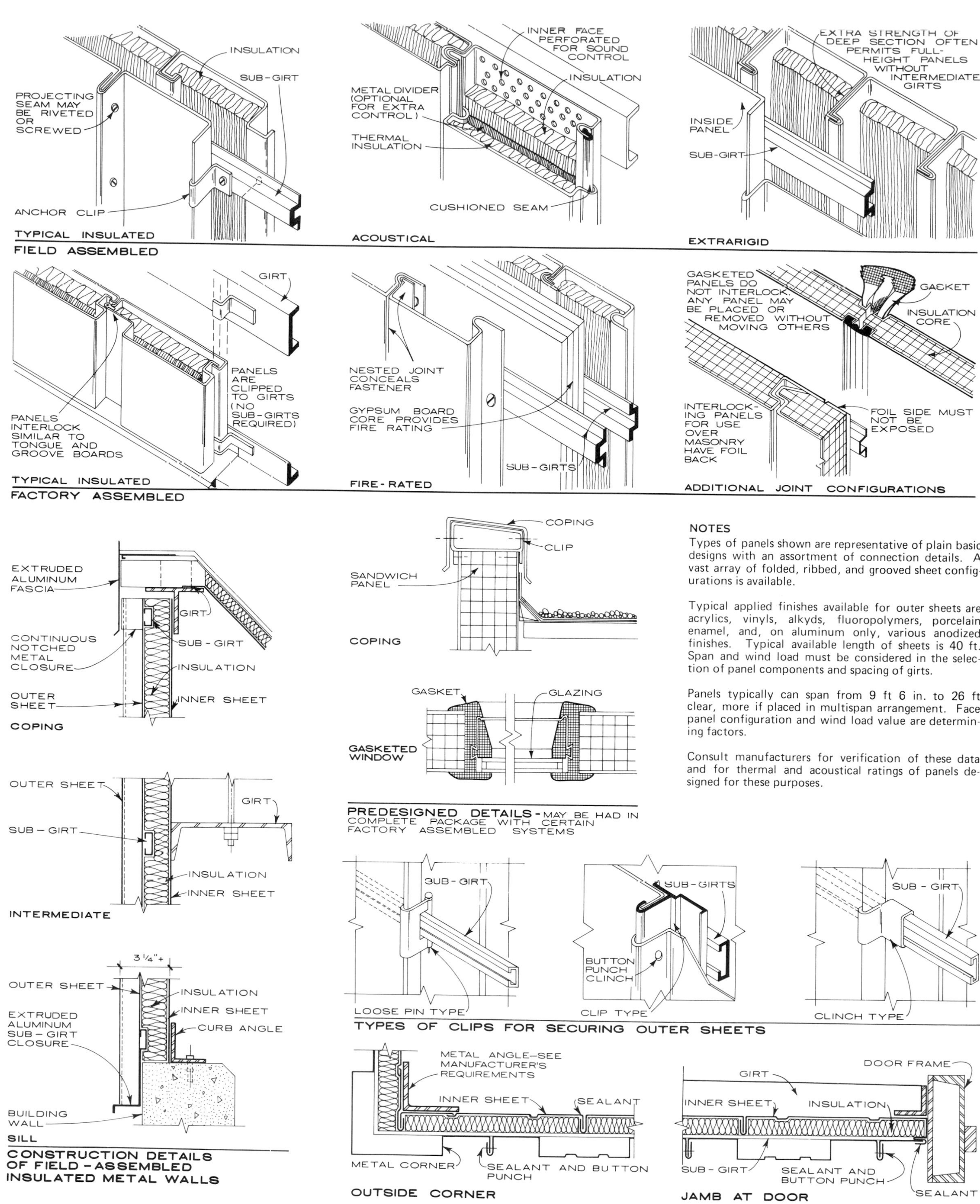
INSULATION
SUB-GIRT
PROJECTING SEAM MAY BE RIVETED OR SCREWED
ANCHOR CLIP
TYPICAL INSULATED FIELD ASSEMBLED
INNER FACE PERFORATED FOR SOUND CONTROL
INSULATION
METAL DIVIDER (OPTIONAL FOR EXTRA CONTROL)
THERMAL INSULATION
CUSHIONED SEAM
ACOUSTICAL
EXTRA STRENGTH OF DEEP SECTION OFTEN PERMITS FULL-HEIGHT PANELS WITHOUT INTERMEDIATE GIRTS
INSIDE PANEL
SUB-GIRT
EXTRARIGID
GIRT
PANELS ARE CLIPPED TO GIRTS (NO SUB-GIRTS REQUIRED)
PANELS INTERLOCK SIMILAR TO TONGUE AND GROOVE BOARDS
TYPICAL INSULATED FACTORY ASSEMBLED
NESTED JOINT CONCEALS FASTENER
GYPSUM BOARD CORE PROVIDES FIRE RATING
SUB-GIRTS
FIRE-RATED
GASKETED PANELS DO NOT INTERLOCK. ANY PANEL MAY BE PLACED OR REMOVED WITHOUT MOVING OTHERS
GASKET
INSULATION CORE
INTERLOCKING PANELS FOR USE OVER MASONRY HAVE FOIL BACK
FOIL SIDE MUST NOT BE EXPOSED
ADDITIONAL JOINT CONFIGURATIONS
EXTRUDED ALUMINUM FASCIA
GIRT
CONTINUOUS NOTCHED METAL CLOSURE
SUB-GIRT
INSULATION
OUTER SHEET
INNER SHEET
COPING
OUTER SHEET
GIRT
SUB-GIRT
INSULATION
INNER SHEET
INTERMEDIATE
3 1/4"+
OUTER SHEET
INSULATION
INNER SHEET
EXTRUDED ALUMINUM SUB-GIRT CLOSURE
CURB ANGLE
BUILDING WALL
SILL
CONSTRUCTION DETAILS OF FIELD-ASSEMBLED INSULATED METAL WALLS
COPING
CLIP
SANDWICH PANEL
COPING
GASKET
GLAZING
GASKETED WINDOW
PREDESIGNED DETAILS - MAY BE HAD IN COMPLETE PACKAGE WITH CERTAIN FACTORY ASSEMBLED SYSTEMS
SUB-GIRT
LOOSE PIN TYPE
SUB-GIRTS
BUTTON PUNCH CLINCH
CLIP TYPE
SUB-GIRT
CLINCH TYPE
TYPES OF CLIPS FOR SECURING OUTER SHEETS
METAL ANGLE-SEE MANUFACTURER'S REQUIREMENTS
INNER SHEET
SEALANT
METAL CORNER
SEALANT AND BUTTON PUNCH
OUTSIDE CORNER
DOOR FRAME
GIRT
INNER SHEET
INSULATION
SUB-GIRT
SEALANT AND BUTTON PUNCH
SEALANT
JAMB AT DOOR

NOTES

Types of panels shown are representative of plain basic designs with an assortment of connection details. A vast array of folded, ribbed, and grooved sheet configurations is available.

Typical applied finishes available for outer sheets are acrylics, vinyls, alkyds, fluoropolymers, porcelain enamel, and, on aluminum only, various anodized finishes. Typical available length of sheets is 40 ft. Span and wind load must be considered in the selection of panel components and spacing of girts.

Panels typically can span from 9 ft 6 in. to 26 ft clear, more if placed in multispan arrangement. Face panel configuration and wind load value are determining factors.

Consult manufacturers for verification of these data and for thermal and acoustical ratings of panels designed for these purposes.

FACING MATERIALS AVAILABLE

1. Aluminum.
2. Aluminized steel.
3. Galvanized steel.

FINISHES AVAILABLE

1. Anodized aluminum.
2. 50% silicone–modified polyester baked enamel paint.
3. Fluorocarbon baked enamel paint.
4. Porcelain enamel on aluminized steel.

INSULATING VALUES	MAX. U FACTOR
2 in. urethane core	0.065
3 in. honeycomb core	0.41
2 in. honeycomb with fill	0.107

NOTE

Some codes restrict the use of the urethane core panel. The honeycomb panels are more acceptable.

Urethane panel = 25 flame spread rating
Honeycomb panel = 15 flame spread rating
See manufacturer for span tables.

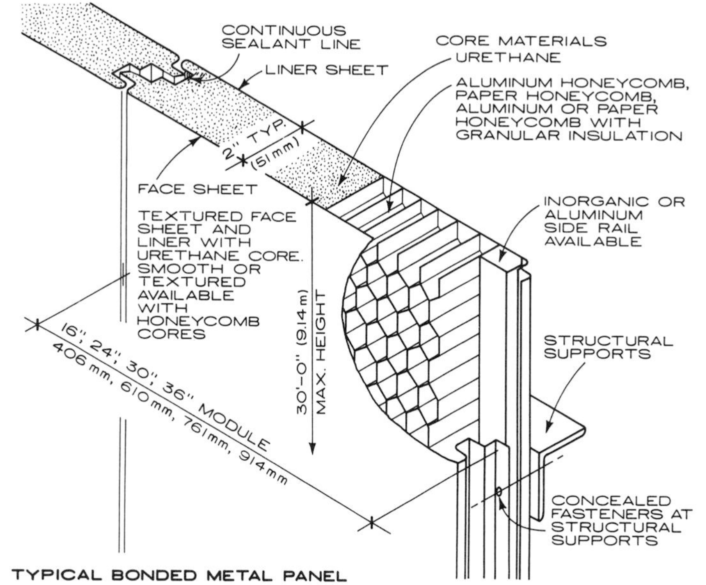
CONTINUOUS SEALANT LINE
LINER SHEET
CORE MATERIALS URETHANE
ALUMINUM HONEYCOMB, PAPER HONEYCOMB, ALUMINUM OR PAPER HONEYCOMB WITH GRANULAR INSULATION
2" TYP. (51 mm)
FACE SHEET
TEXTURED FACE SHEET AND LINER WITH URETHANE CORE. SMOOTH OR TEXTURED AVAILABLE WITH HONEYCOMB CORES
INORGANIC OR ALUMINUM SIDE RAIL AVAILABLE
16", 24", 30", 36" MODULE 406 mm, 610 mm, 761 mm, 914 mm
30'-0" (9.14 m) MAX. HEIGHT
STRUCTURAL SUPPORTS
CONCEALED FASTENERS AT STRUCTURAL SUPPORTS

TYPICAL BONDED METAL PANEL

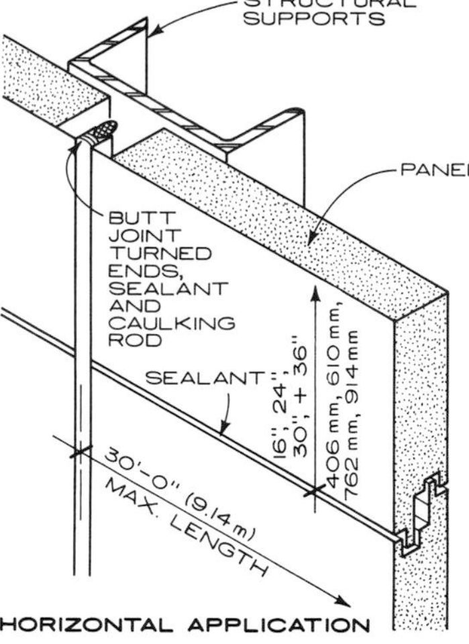
STRUCTURAL SUPPORTS
PANEL
BUTT JOINT TURNED ENDS, SEALANT AND CAULKING ROD
SEALANT
16", 24", 30", + 36"
406 mm, 610 mm, 762 mm, 914 mm
30'-0" (9.14 m) MAX. LENGTH

HORIZONTAL APPLICATION

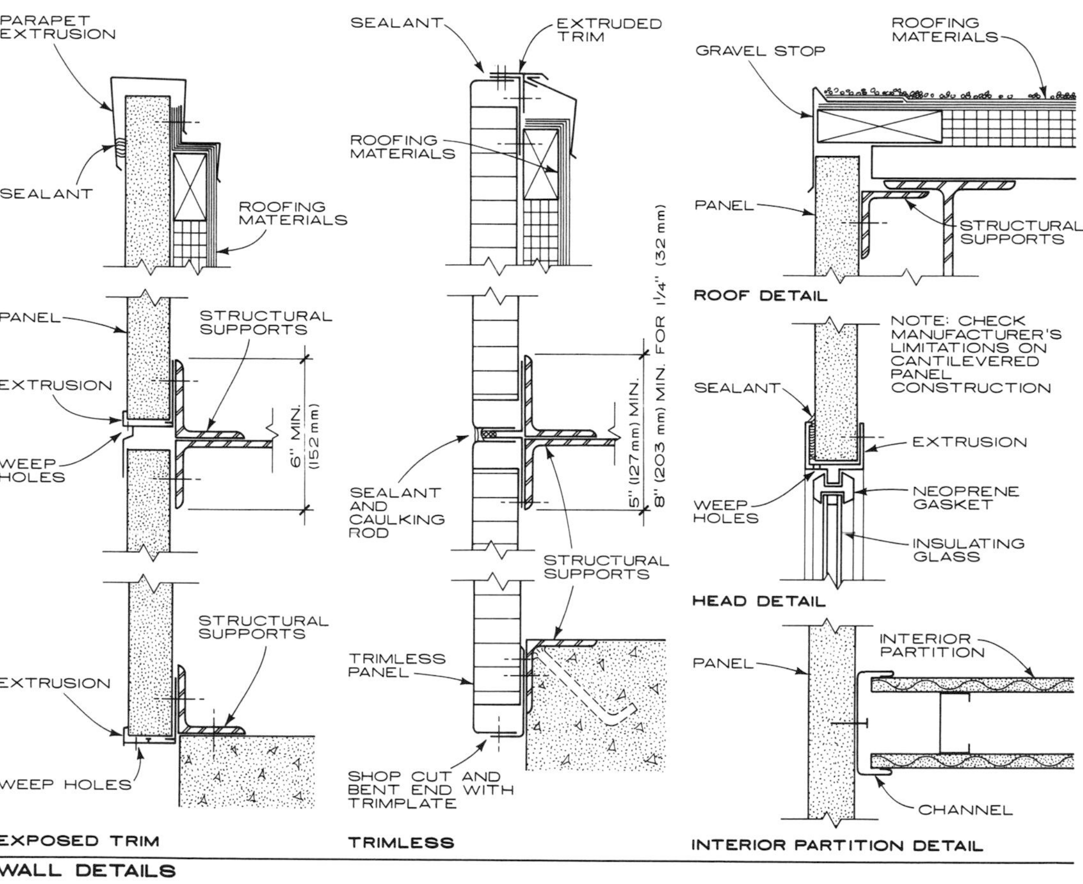
PARAPET EXTRUSION
SEALANT
ROOFING MATERIALS
PANEL
STRUCTURAL SUPPORTS
EXTRUSION
WEEP HOLES
6" MIN. (152 mm)
STRUCTURAL SUPPORTS
EXTRUSION
WEEP HOLES
EXPOSED TRIM
SEALANT
EXTRUDED TRIM
ROOFING MATERIALS
SEALANT AND CAULKING ROD
5" (127 mm) MIN.
8" (203 mm) MIN. FOR 1¼" (32 mm)
STRUCTURAL SUPPORTS
TRIMLESS PANEL
SHOP CUT AND BENT END WITH TRIMPLATE
TRIMLESS
GRAVEL STOP
ROOFING MATERIALS
PANEL
STRUCTURAL SUPPORTS
ROOF DETAIL
NOTE: CHECK MANUFACTURER'S LIMITATIONS ON CANTILEVERED PANEL CONSTRUCTION
SEALANT
EXTRUSION
WEEP HOLES
NEOPRENE GASKET
INSULATING GLASS
HEAD DETAIL
PANEL
INTERIOR PARTITION
CHANNEL
INTERIOR PARTITION DETAIL

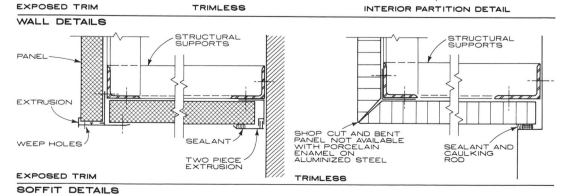

WALL DETAILS

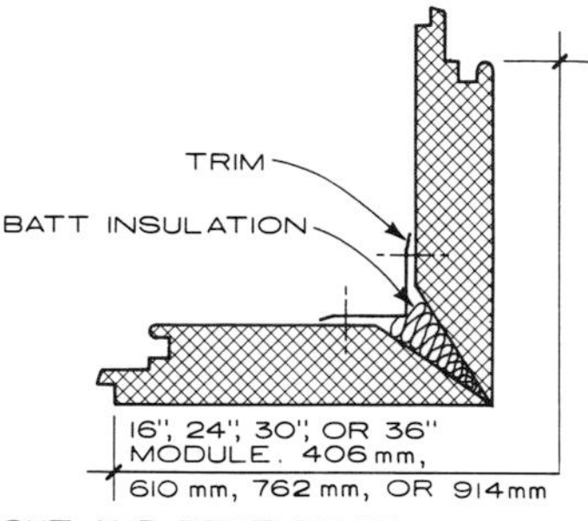
TRIM
BATT INSULATION
16", 24", 30", OR 36" MODULE. 406 mm, 610 mm, 762 mm, OR 914 mm

CUT AND BENT PANEL

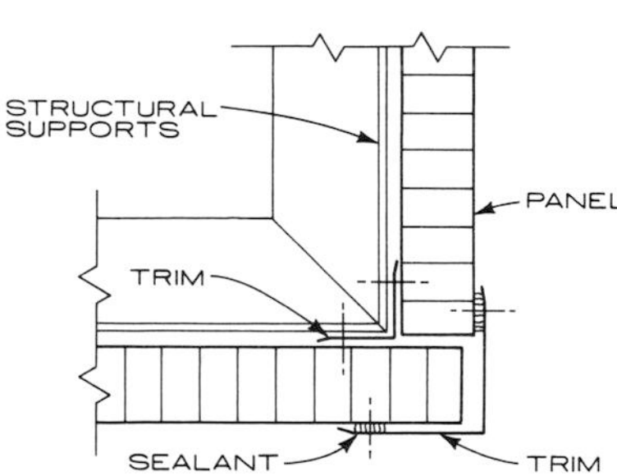
STRUCTURAL SUPPORTS
PANEL
TRIM
SEALANT
TRIM

EXPOSED TRIM

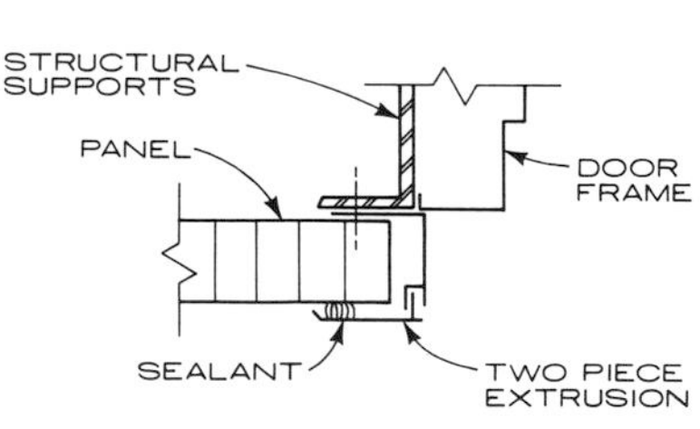
STRUCTURAL SUPPORTS
PANEL
DOOR FRAME
SEALANT
TWO PIECE EXTRUSION

DOOR JAMB

PANEL

STRUCTURAL SUPPORTS

EXTRUSION

WEEP HOLES

SEALANT

TWO PIECE EXTRUSION

EXPOSED TRIM

STRUCTURAL SUPPORTS

SHOP CUT AND BENT PANEL NOT AVAILABLE WITH PORCELAIN ENAMEL ON ALUMINIZED STEEL

SEALANT AND CAULKING ROD

TRIMLESS

SOFFIT DETAILS

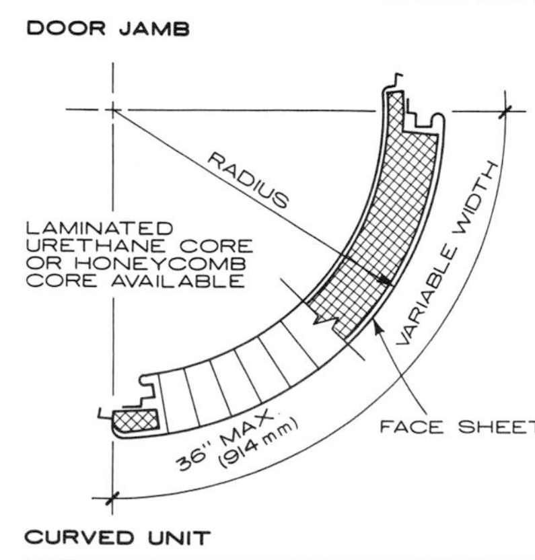
RADIUS
LAMINATED URETHANE CORE OR HONEYCOMB CORE AVAILABLE
VARIABLE WIDTH
36" MAX. (914 mm)
FACE SHEET

CURVED UNIT

CORNER DETAILS

John A. Schulte; Hellmuth, Obata, & Kassabaum, Inc.; St. Louis, Missouri

NOTE

Polyvinyl chloride (PVC) is a semirigid material that requires the addition of plasticizers to fabricate a flexible roofing membrane. PVC exhibits excellent weldability for making lap joints or attaching to PVC clad metal flashing.

TYPES OF MEMBRANE

Unreinforced sheet
Sheet reinforced with fiberglass or polyester

METHOD OF MANUFACTURE

Calendering
Spread coating
Extruding

GENERAL

Single ply roofing systems are also referred to as flexible sheet roofing systems. Consult manufacturers for specific requirements regarding materials selection and installation requirements. Compatibility of materials comprising total roofing system is essential.

MATERIAL PROPERTIES

Thickness: Typically 48 and 60 mil; 45 mil minimum

Color: Typically gray; other colors available

Contaminants to avoid: Bitumen, oils, animal fats, and coal tar pitch. See manufacturer's chemical resistance list.

Minimum standards: ASTM has developed standard test methods to evaluate the materials properties of PVC roof membranes. These test results form a useful basis for comparing various PVC membranes. ASTM's standard specification establishes minimum performance criteria for tensile strength, elongation, tear resistance, heat aging, weathering, and water absorption.

INSTALLATION

General guidelines: It is recommended that all roofing materials be installed on roofs with positive slope to drainage. Check with manufacturers regarding their specific requirements.

Lap joining methods: Hot air or solvent weld

Flashing methods: Membrane or PVC coated metal

Types of preformed accessories available: Inside and outside corners; pipe stacks

Weather restrictions during installation: 0°–120°F temperature range. Substrates and welding/bonding surfaces must be dry.

Method of repair: Clean surface; hot air or solvent weld of PVC patch

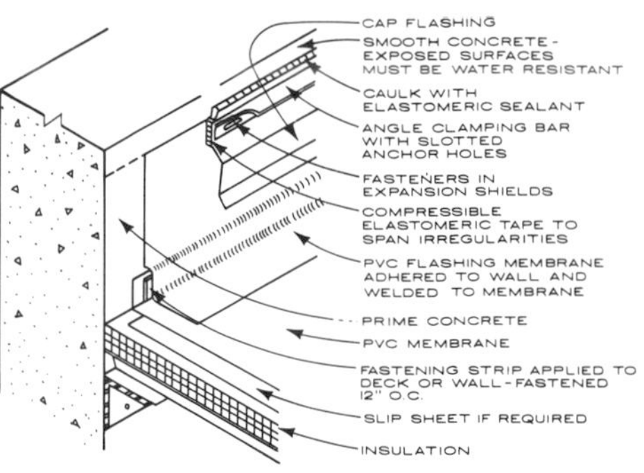
CAP FLASHING
SMOOTH CONCRETE - EXPOSED SURFACES MUST BE WATER RESISTANT
CAULK WITH ELASTOMERIC SEALANT
ANGLE CLAMPING BAR WITH SLOTTED ANCHOR HOLES
FASTENERS IN EXPANSION SHIELDS
COMPRESSIBLE ELASTOMERIC TAPE TO SPAN IRREGULARITIES
PVC FLASHING MEMBRANE ADHERED TO WALL AND WELDED TO MEMBRANE
PRIME CONCRETE
PVC MEMBRANE
FASTENING STRIP APPLIED TO DECK OR WALL-FASTENED 12" O.C.
SLIP SHEET IF REQUIRED
INSULATION

TYPICAL PARAPET FLASHING

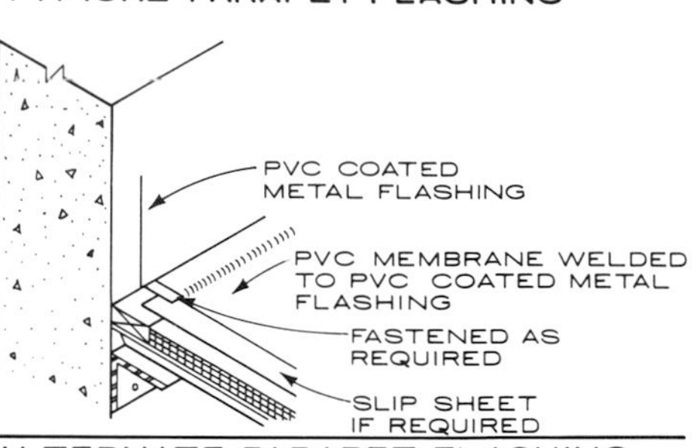
PVC COATED METAL FLASHING
PVC MEMBRANE WELDED TO PVC COATED METAL FLASHING
FASTENED AS REQUIRED
SLIP SHEET IF REQUIRED

ALTERNATE PARAPET FLASHING

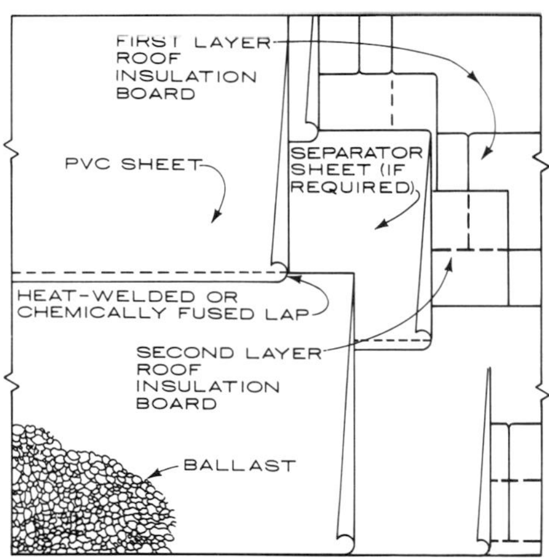
FIRST LAYER ROOF INSULATION BOARD
PVC SHEET
SEPARATOR SHEET (IF REQUIRED)
HEAT-WELDED OR CHEMICALLY FUSED LAP
SECOND LAYER ROOF INSULATION BOARD
BALLAST

Membrane sheets are laid loose over roof insulation (also laid loose) and secured at the perimeter and around penetrations only. The membrane is then covered with a ballast of river-washed stones (typically 10 lb/sq ft) or appropriate pavers.

This system works efficiently with insulation approved by the membrane manufacturer and on roofs with a slope not exceeding 2 in 12.

LOOSE-LAID BALLASTED SHEETS

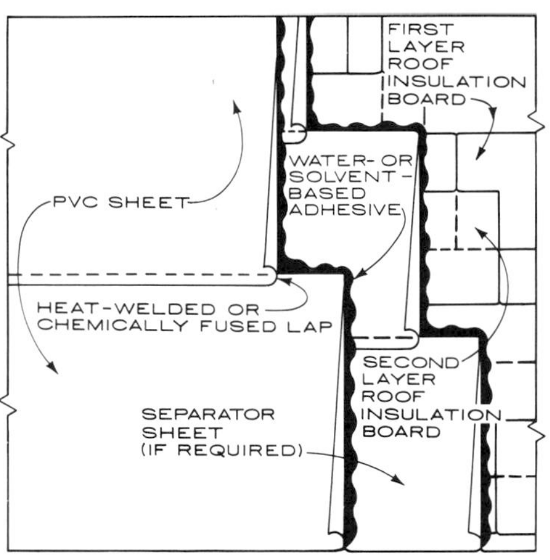
FIRST LAYER ROOF INSULATION BOARD
WATER- OR SOLVENT-BASED ADHESIVE
PVC SHEET
HEAT-WELDED OR CHEMICALLY FUSED LAP
SECOND LAYER ROOF INSULATION BOARD
SEPARATOR SHEET (IF REQUIRED)

For system with no slope limitations which secures membrane to substrate with bonding adhesive and by mechanically fastening the membrane to perimeter and penetrations. System is appropriate for contoured roofs and roofs that cannot withstand weight of ballasted system.

Membrane can be directly applied to deck surface of concrete, wood surfaces, or be applied to compatible insulation that is mechanically fastened to the deck.

FULLY ADHERED SHEETS

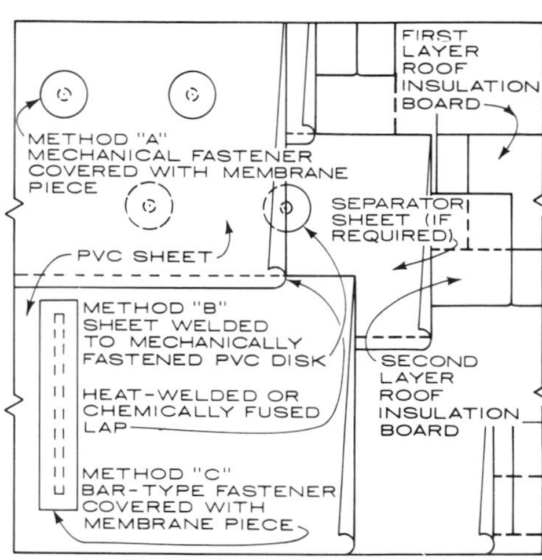
FIRST LAYER ROOF INSULATION BOARD
METHOD "A" MECHANICAL FASTENER COVERED WITH MEMBRANE PIECE
SEPARATOR SHEET (IF REQUIRED)
PVC SHEET
METHOD "B" SHEET WELDED TO MECHANICALLY FASTENED PVC DISK
HEAT-WELDED OR CHEMICALLY FUSED LAP
METHOD "C" BAR-TYPE FASTENER COVERED WITH MEMBRANE PIECE
SECOND LAYER ROOF INSULATION BOARD

A mechanically anchored roof system is appropriate for roofs that cannot carry the additional load of ballasted roof systems. Systems are available with fasteners that penetrate the membrane or that require no membrane penetration.

The membrane is anchored to the roof using metal bars or individual clips, and it may be installed over concrete, wood, metal, or compatible insulation.

MECHANICALLY ATTACHED SHEETS

Membrane sheets are laid loose over a sloped roof deck and with the insulation on top of it. When the roof deck is dead level, tapered roof insulation is either loose laid or mechanically attached under the membrane to achieve positive slope to drainage. In either instance, a layer of insulation is placed over the membrane and held in place by one of two methods: Either a loose fabric is laid over the insulation, with a minimum of 10 lb/sq ft of ballast laid over the fabric, or insulation with an integrally bonded concrete facing is used in place of the fabric and loose ballast. Membrane manufacturers should be consulted for their approved insulation list. In this roofing system, the membrane is protected from year-round temperature extremes, direct exposure to weather, and damage from other sources. The heat gain or loss is just the same as if the insulation were installed under the membrane. Since the waterproofing membrane is placed on the warm side of the insulation, it functions as a vapor retarder. For high humidity conditions with a dead level roof deck utilizing tapered insulation, a separate vapor barrier should be placed directly beneath the tapered insulation to prevent condensation.

PROTECTED MEMBRANE SHEET

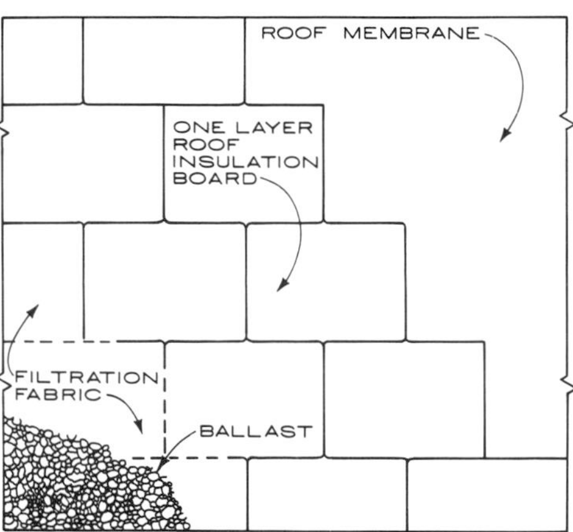
ROOF MEMBRANE
ONE LAYER ROOF INSULATION BOARD
FILTRATION FABRIC
BALLAST

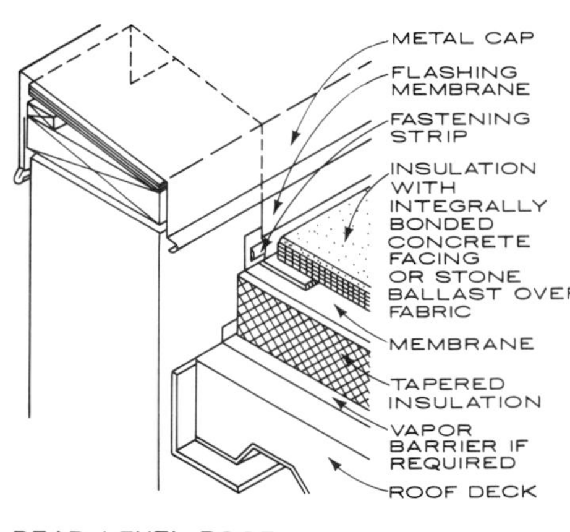
METAL CAP
FLASHING MEMBRANE
FASTENING STRIP
INSULATION WITH INTEGRALLY BONDED CONCRETE FACING OR STONE BALLAST OVER FABRIC
MEMBRANE
TAPERED INSULATION
VAPOR BARRIER IF REQUIRED
ROOF DECK

DEAD LEVEL ROOF

CTA Architects Engineers; Billings, Montana

NOTES

There are three generic installation methods for EPDM roofing:

1. Fully Adhered: Membrane roofing is rolled onto the substrate and allowed to relax. Underside is then fully coated with bonding adhesive. After both surfaces are tacky, the membrane is pressed onto the substrate with a push broom. Adjoining sheets must overlap at least 3 in., with laps spliced and cemented. Membrane is mechanically secured at perimeter and penetration edges. Flashing protects all edges, openings, and penetrations.
2. Loose Laid: Roofing in this application is laid loose over the substrate, either deck or rigid insulation, and ballasted in place. It is positioned without stretching, allowed to attain its natural shape, and adjacent sheets spliced with adjoining sheets overlapping at least 3 in. Sheets are cemented and rolled together to seal seams. The membrane is mechanically secured at perimeter and penetration edges, and flashing is installed. For ballast, a sufficient amount of river-washed gravel is laid over the membrane to provide 10 lb/sq ft of weight. As an alternate, a precast roof paver system is applied to hold the roofing membrane.
3. Mechanically Fastened: Membrane roof is directly attached to the roof deck with mechanical fasteners. The substrate is anchored to the roof deck, and the fasteners either go through both membrane and insulation or only go through the insulation and deck, with the membrane held down by retainer and cap over the base. Sealant protects against moisture.

Many EPDM membranes are field surfaced to improve resistance to weathering and fire, or to enhance appearance.

GENERAL NOTES

EPDM elastomeric roofing is synthesized from ethylene, propylene, and a small amount of diene monomer. Manufactured sheets range in thickness from 30 to 60 mils.

Advantages: EPDM roofing exhibits a high degree of resistance to ozone, ultraviolet, extreme temperature and other elements, and degradation from abrasion. It is resilient, strong, elastic, and less prone to cracking and tearing when compared to other forms of membrane roofing.

Disadvantages: Application methods, specific formulas and configurations for adhesives, fasteners, and coatings are unique with each system manufactured. Materials, design, and appropriate use vary widely. Close supervision and regular inspection by manufacturer are a requirement. Labor cost and time allotted for installation may vary.

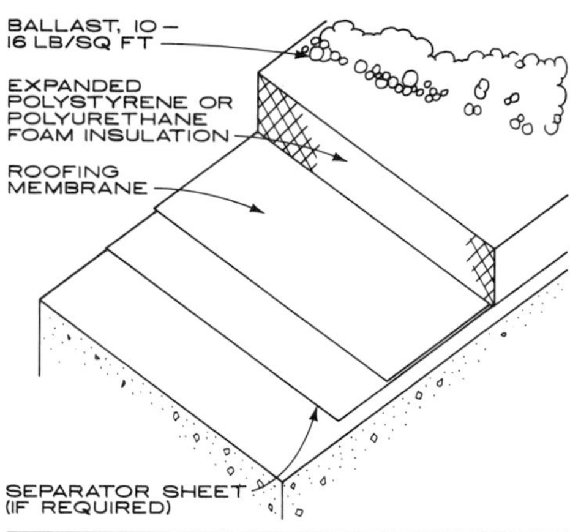
BALLAST, 10 – 16 LB/SQ FT
EXPANDED POLYSTYRENE OR POLYURETHANE FOAM INSULATION
ROOFING MEMBRANE
SEPARATOR SHEET (IF REQUIRED)

INSULATED ROOF MEMBRANE APPLICATION

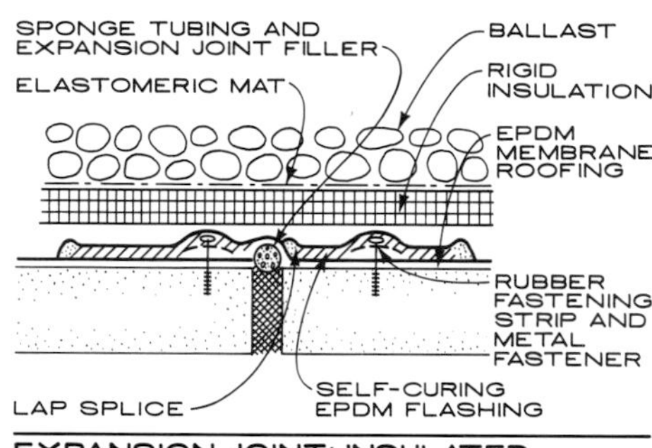
SPONGE TUBING AND EXPANSION JOINT FILLER
ELASTOMERIC MAT
BALLAST
RIGID INSULATION
EPDM MEMBRANE ROOFING
RUBBER FASTENING STRIP AND METAL FASTENER
LAP SPLICE
SELF-CURING EPDM FLASHING

EXPANSION JOINT: INSULATED ROOF MEMBRANE BALLASTED

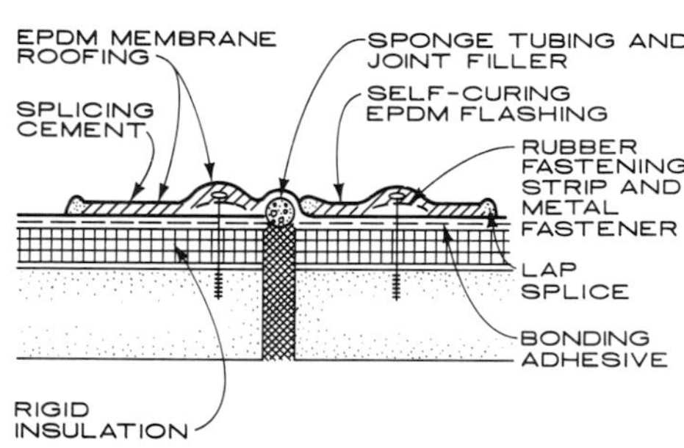
EPDM MEMBRANE ROOFING
SPLICING CEMENT
SPONGE TUBING AND JOINT FILLER
SELF-CURING EPDM FLASHING
RUBBER FASTENING STRIP AND METAL FASTENER
LAP SPLICE
BONDING ADHESIVE
RIGID INSULATION

EXPANSION JOINT: FULLY ADHERED ROOF MEMBRANE

PARAPET CAP AND CLEAT
EPDM MEMBRANE FLASHING–EXTEND UNDER PARAPET CAP USING LONGEST PIECES PRACTICAL
RUBBER FASTENING STRIP–ATTACH TO PARAPET OR WALL
SEALANT
FASTENER
BONDING ADHESIVE
RIGID INSULATION AND ROOF DECK

FULLY ADHERED ROOF AT PARAPET OR WALL

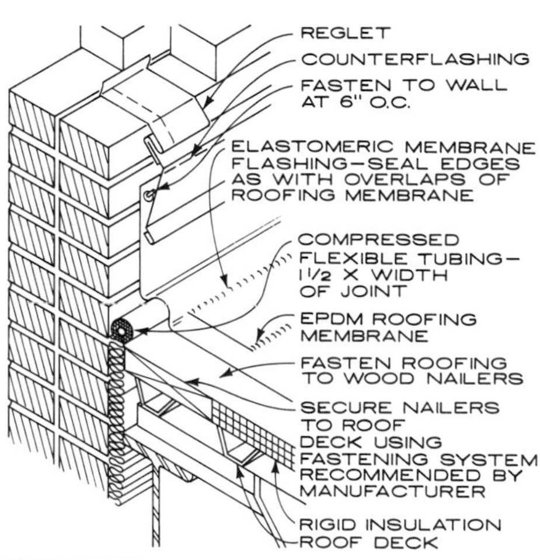
REGLET
COUNTERFLASHING
FASTEN TO WALL AT 6" O.C.
ELASTOMERIC MEMBRANE FLASHING–SEAL EDGES AS WITH OVERLAPS OF ROOFING MEMBRANE
COMPRESSED FLEXIBLE TUBING– 1 1/2 X WIDTH OF JOINT
EPDM ROOFING MEMBRANE
FASTEN ROOFING TO WOOD NAILERS
SECURE NAILERS TO ROOF DECK USING FASTENING SYSTEM RECOMMENDED BY MANUFACTURER
RIGID INSULATION
ROOF DECK

ROOF EDGE AT NONSUPPORTING WALL

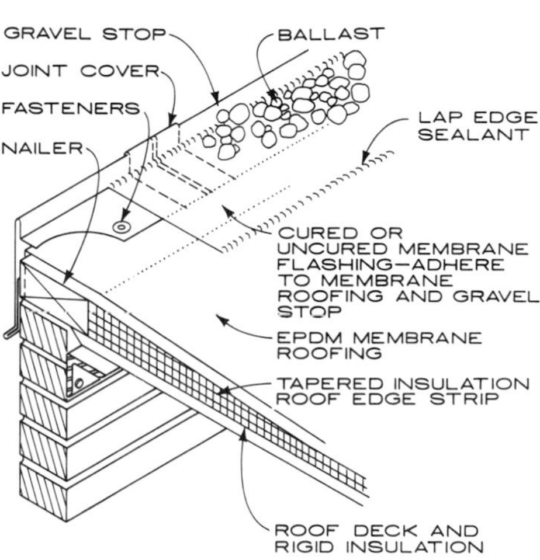
GRAVEL STOP
JOINT COVER
FASTENERS
NAILER
BALLAST
LAP EDGE SEALANT
CURED OR UNCURED MEMBRANE FLASHING–ADHERE TO MEMBRANE ROOFING AND GRAVEL STOP
EPDM MEMBRANE ROOFING
TAPERED INSULATION ROOF EDGE STRIP
ROOF DECK AND RIGID INSULATION

LIGHT METAL ROOF EDGE

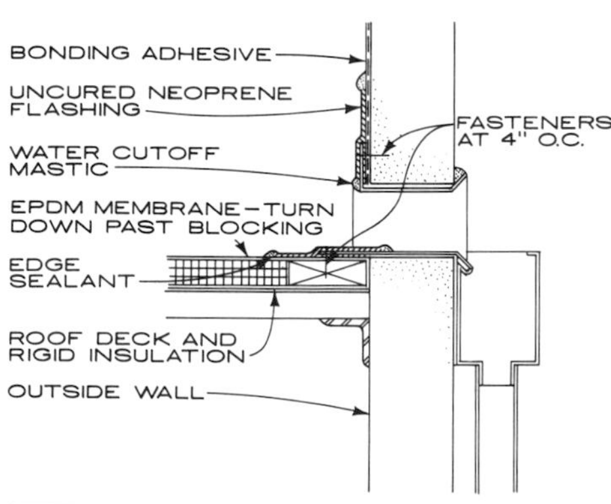
BONDING ADHESIVE
UNCURED NEOPRENE FLASHING
WATER CUTOFF MASTIC
EPDM MEMBRANE–TURN DOWN PAST BLOCKING
EDGE SEALANT
ROOF DECK AND RIGID INSULATION
OUTSIDE WALL
FASTENERS AT 4" O.C.

FULLY ADHERED ROOF SCUPPER

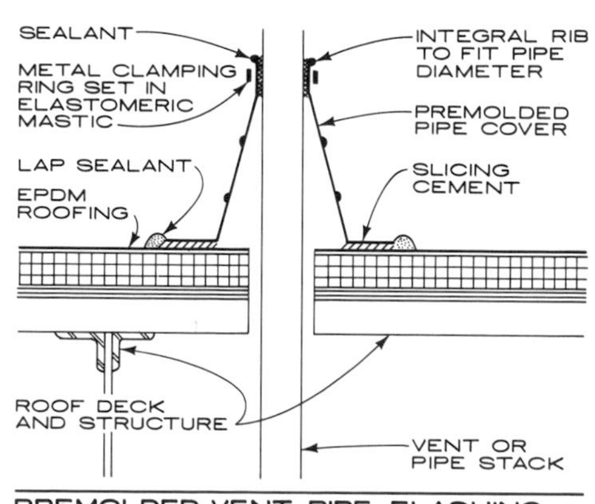
SEALANT
METAL CLAMPING RING SET IN ELASTOMERIC MASTIC
LAP SEALANT
EPDM ROOFING
ROOF DECK AND STRUCTURE
INTEGRAL RIB TO FIT PIPE DIAMETER
PREMOLDED PIPE COVER
SLICING CEMENT
VENT OR PIPE STACK

PREMOLDED VENT PIPE FLASHING

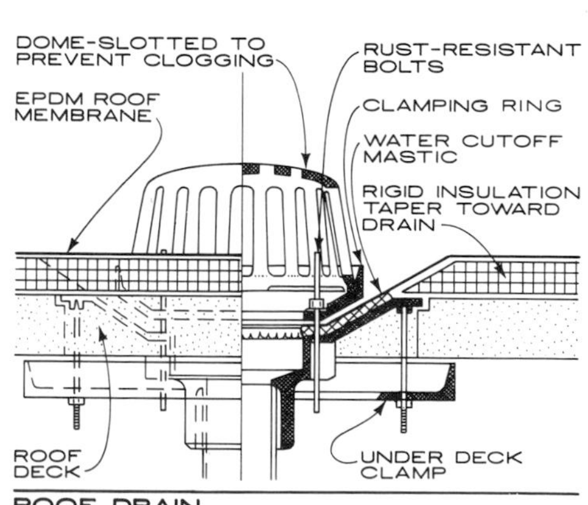
DOME-SLOTTED TO PREVENT CLOGGING
EPDM ROOF MEMBRANE
ROOF DECK
RUST-RESISTANT BOLTS
CLAMPING RING
WATER CUTOFF MASTIC
RIGID INSULATION TAPER TOWARD DRAIN
UNDER DECK CLAMP

ROOF DRAIN

Catherine A. Broad; Washington, D.C.

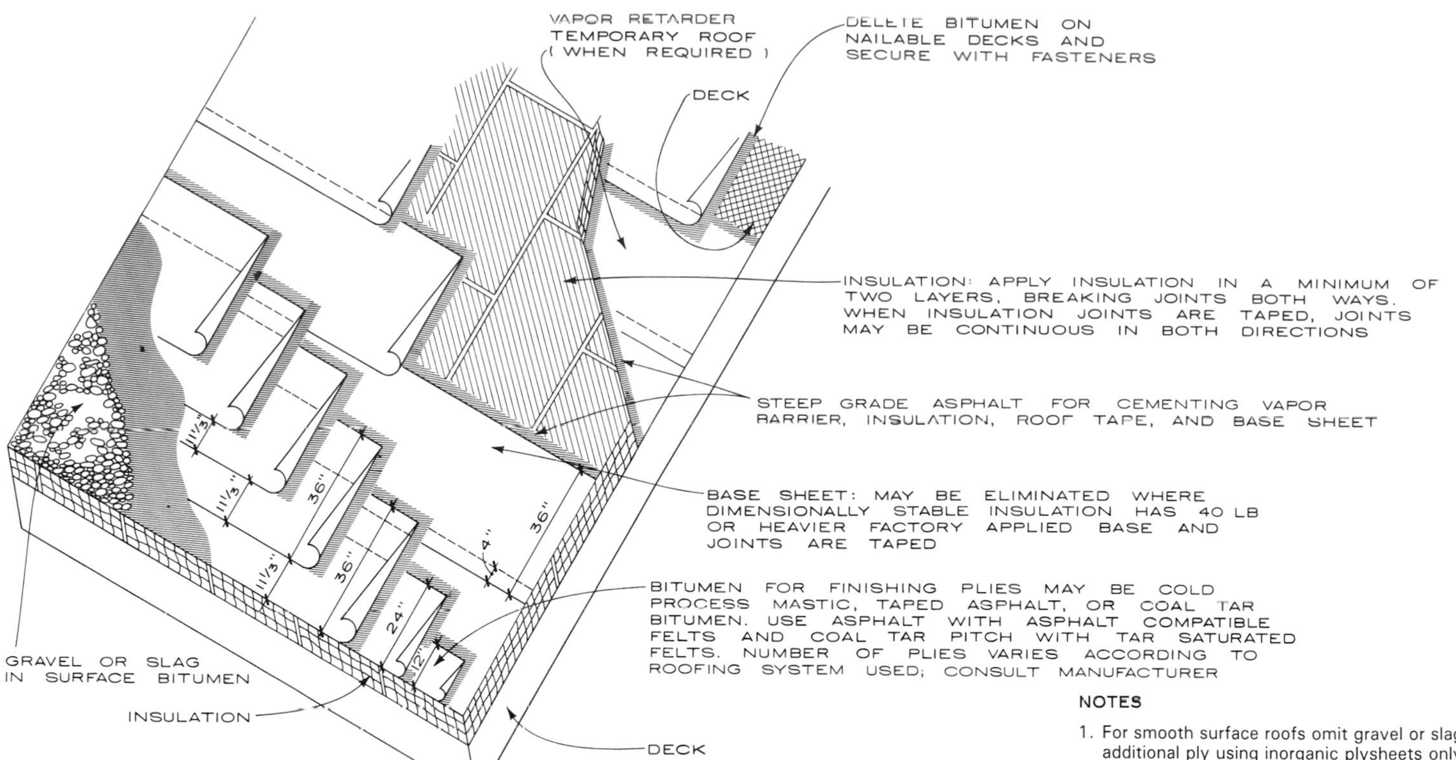
VAPOR RETARDER TEMPORARY ROOF (WHEN REQUIRED)
DELETE BITUMEN ON NAILABLE DECKS AND SECURE WITH FASTENERS
DECK
INSULATION: APPLY INSULATION IN A MINIMUM OF TWO LAYERS, BREAKING JOINTS BOTH WAYS. WHEN INSULATION JOINTS ARE TAPED, JOINTS MAY BE CONTINUOUS IN BOTH DIRECTIONS
STEEP GRADE ASPHALT FOR CEMENTING VAPOR BARRIER, INSULATION, ROOF TAPE, AND BASE SHEET
BASE SHEET: MAY BE ELIMINATED WHERE DIMENSIONALLY STABLE INSULATION HAS 40 LB OR HEAVIER FACTORY APPLIED BASE AND JOINTS ARE TAPED
BITUMEN FOR FINISHING PLIES MAY BE COLD PROCESS MASTIC, TAPED ASPHALT, OR COAL TAR BITUMEN. USE ASPHALT WITH ASPHALT COMPATIBLE FELTS AND COAL TAR PITCH WITH TAR SATURATED FELTS. NUMBER OF PLIES VARIES ACCORDING TO ROOFING SYSTEM USED; CONSULT MANUFACTURER
GRAVEL OR SLAG IN SURFACE BITUMEN
INSULATION
DECK
11 1/3"
11 1/3"
11 1/3"
36"
36"
36"
24"
12"
4"

NOTES

1. For smooth surface roofs omit gravel or slag and add additional ply using inorganic plysheets only.
2. On slopes over 1 in./ft all felts along top edge must usually be strapped and back-nailed.
3. When vapor retarder is used, edges of felt should be turned up to a height of 2 in. above cant strip at vertical surfaces. Felts should overlap all roof edges a minimum of 6 in. before application of roofing. 6 in. of felt must be re-turned over the insulation and mopped solidly.

20 YEAR TYPE BUILT-UP ROOF OVER INSULATION

NOTES

1. Over nonnailable deck or insulation omit rosin paper and cement with asphalt. Nailing strips must be provided.
2. Minimum slope for organic felt: ½ in./ft.
3. Minimum slope for fiberglass felt: 0 in./ft.
4. Consult manufacturer for spacing of nails for particular roofing system.

STAGGER NAILS AT 12" O.C.
NAILABLE DECK
ROSIN PAPER (OVER WOOD, EXCEPT PLYWOOD)
ASPHALT BETWEEN PLIES OF 15 LB FELT. ASPHALT TYPE (I, II, III, OR IV) DETERMINED BY ROOF SLOPE
MINERAL SURFACE ROOFING. 2" SIDE LAPS IF SELVAGE IS UNGRANULATED; 3" SIDE LAPS IF SELVAGE IS GRANULATED
STEEP GRADE ASPHALT
6"
18"
12"
12"
12"
17"
36"
18"

MINERAL SURFACE BUILT-UP ROOF

SCHEDULE OF FELT OVERLAP (INCHES)

Organic base sheet	4
Fiberglass or base sheet	2
2-ply felts/plysheets	19
3-ply felts/plysheets	24⅔
4-ply felts/plysheets	27½
Fiberglass mineral	3 if selvage granulated
Surface cap sheet	2 if selvage granulated

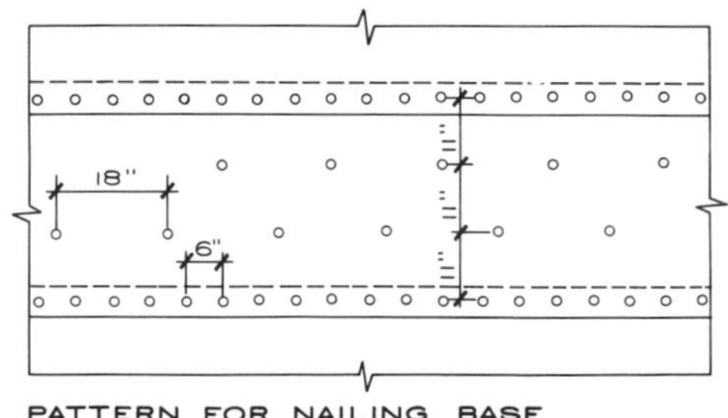
18"
6"
11"
11"
11"

PATTERN FOR NAILING BASE SHEET OR VAPOR RETARDER OVER NAILABLE DECK

Kent Wong; Hewlett, Jamison, Atkinson & Luey; Portland, Oregon
Developed by Angelo J. Forlidas, AIA; Charlotte, North Carolina; from data furnished by Robert M. Stafford, P.E., Consulting Engineer; Charlotte, North Carolina

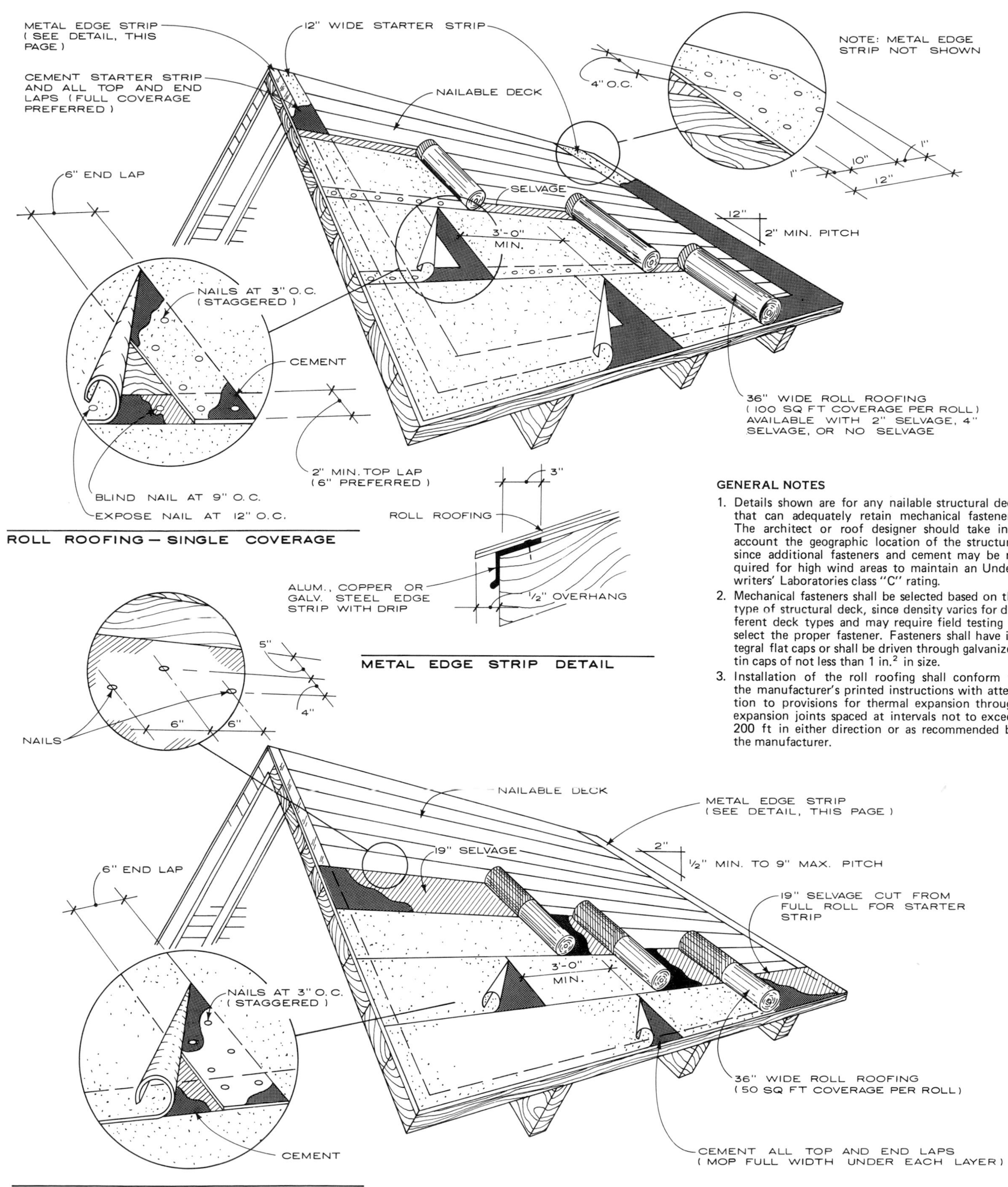
METAL EDGE STRIP (SEE DETAIL, THIS PAGE)
12" WIDE STARTER STRIP
NOTE: METAL EDGE STRIP NOT SHOWN
CEMENT STARTER STRIP AND ALL TOP AND END LAPS (FULL COVERAGE PREFERRED)
NAILABLE DECK
4" O.C.
6" END LAP
SELVAGE
10"
1"
1"
12"
3'-0" MIN.
12"
2" MIN. PITCH
NAILS AT 3" O.C. (STAGGERED)
CEMENT
36" WIDE ROLL ROOFING (100 SQ FT COVERAGE PER ROLL) AVAILABLE WITH 2" SELVAGE, 4" SELVAGE, OR NO SELVAGE
2" MIN. TOP LAP (6" PREFERRED)
3"
BLIND NAIL AT 9" O.C.
EXPOSE NAIL AT 12" O.C.
ROLL ROOFING
ALUM., COPPER OR GALV. STEEL EDGE STRIP WITH DRIP
1/2" OVERHANG
5"
4"
6"
6"
NAILS
NAILABLE DECK
METAL EDGE STRIP (SEE DETAIL, THIS PAGE)
2"
19" SELVAGE
1/2" MIN. TO 9" MAX. PITCH
6" END LAP
19" SELVAGE CUT FROM FULL ROLL FOR STARTER STRIP
3'-0" MIN.
NAILS AT 3" O.C. (STAGGERED)
36" WIDE ROLL ROOFING (50 SQ FT COVERAGE PER ROLL)
CEMENT
CEMENT ALL TOP AND END LAPS (MOP FULL WIDTH UNDER EACH LAYER)

ROLL ROOFING — SINGLE COVERAGE

METAL EDGE STRIP DETAIL

ROLL ROOFING — DOUBLE COVERAGE CONCEALED NAILING

GENERAL NOTES

1. Details shown are for any nailable structural deck that can adequately retain mechanical fasteners. The architect or roof designer should take into account the geographic location of the structure, since additional fasteners and cement may be required for high wind areas to maintain an Underwriters' Laboratories class "C" rating.
2. Mechanical fasteners shall be selected based on the type of structural deck, since density varies for different deck types and may require field testing to select the proper fastener. Fasteners shall have integral flat caps or shall be driven through galvanized tin caps of not less than 1 in.^{2} in size.
3. Installation of the roll roofing shall conform to the manufacturer's printed instructions with attention to provisions for thermal expansion through expansion joints spaced at intervals not to exceed 200 ft in either direction or as recommended by the manufacturer.

James E. Phillips; AIA, Liles/Associates/Architects; Greenville, South Carolina

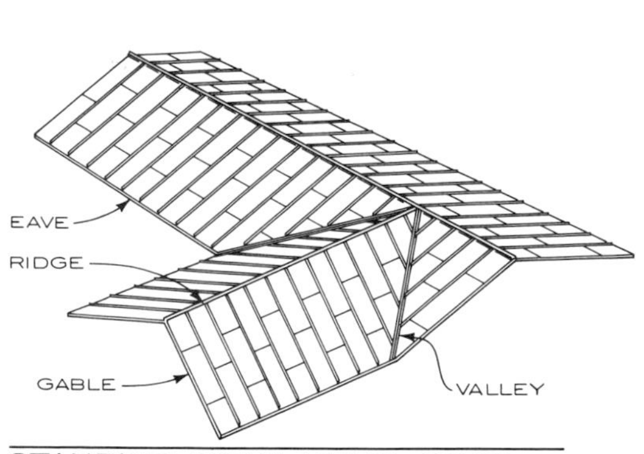
EAVE
RIDGE
GABLE
VALLEY

STANDING SEAM METAL ROOF

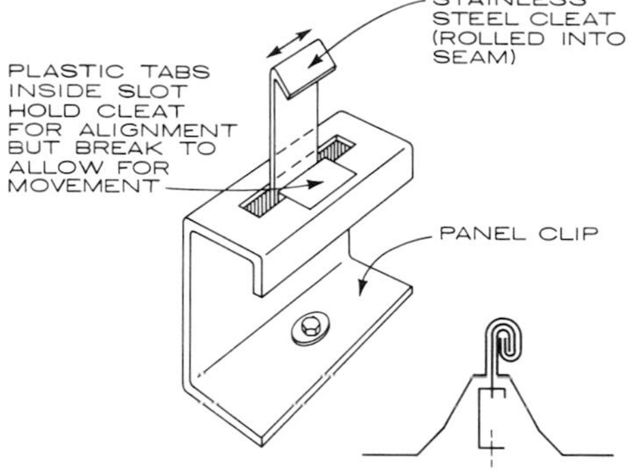
STAINLESS STEEL CLEAT (ROLLED INTO SEAM)
PLASTIC TABS INSIDE SLOT HOLD CLEAT FOR ALIGNMENT BUT BREAK TO ALLOW FOR MOVEMENT
PANEL CLIP

NOTES

To allow for expansion and contraction movement in roof panels, some manufacturers set movable cleats into a stationary panel clip system. The cleat is held in position in the center of a slot in the panel clip by two temporary plastic tabs. This allows for correct alignment of the cleat with the roof panel. Once the cleat has been rolled into the panel seam, it will move with the roof panel by forcing the plastic tabs to break under movement pressure.

MOVABLE CLEAT

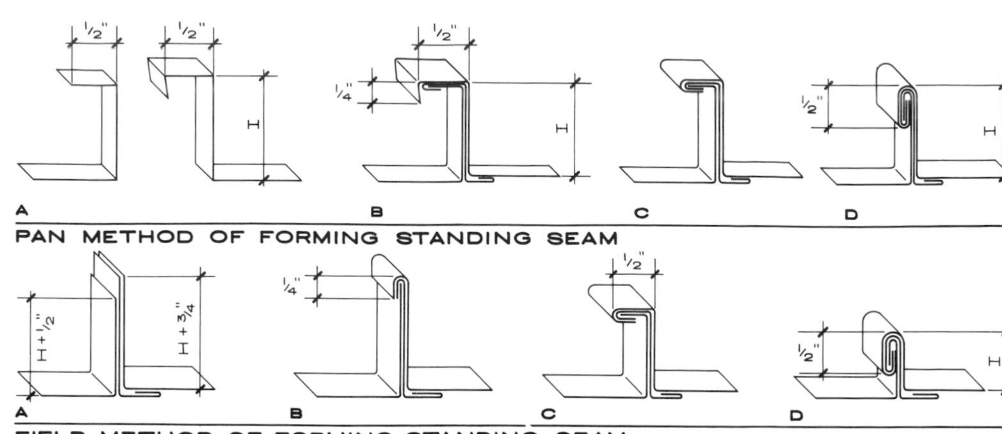
1/2"
1/4"
H
A
B
C
D
H + 1/2"
H + 3/4"

PAN METHOD OF FORMING STANDING SEAM

FIELD METHOD OF FORMING STANDING SEAM

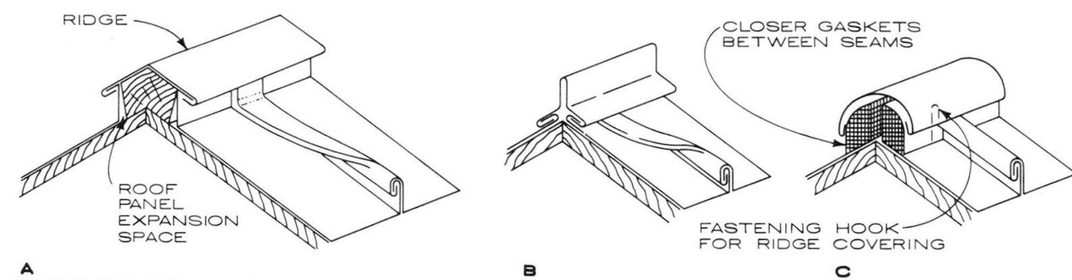
RIDGE
ROOF PANEL EXPANSION SPACE
CLOSER GASKETS BETWEEN SEAMS
FASTENING HOOK FOR RIDGE COVERING
A
B
C

RIDGE CONSTRUCTION

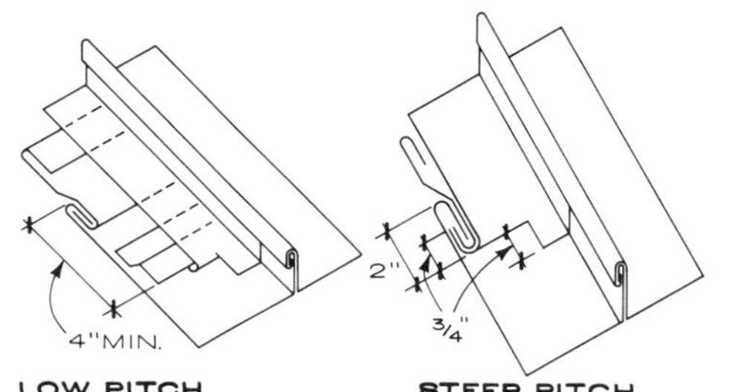
4" MIN.
2"
3/4"
LOW PITCH
STEEP PITCH

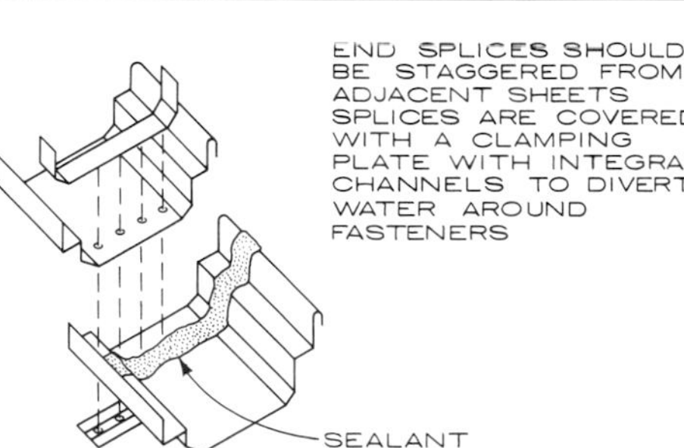
END SPLICES SHOULD BE STAGGERED FROM ADJACENT SHEETS SPLICES ARE COVERED WITH A CLAMPING PLATE WITH INTEGRAL CHANNELS TO DIVERT WATER AROUND FASTENERS
SEALANT

TRANSVERSE SEAM AND PANEL SPLICE

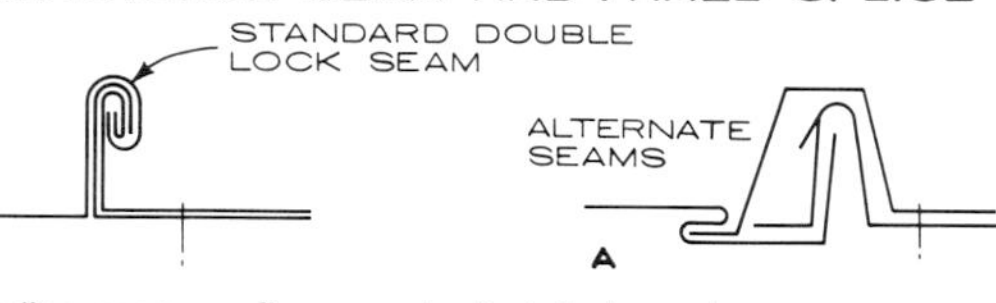
STANDARD DOUBLE LOCK SEAM
ALTERNATE SEAMS
A

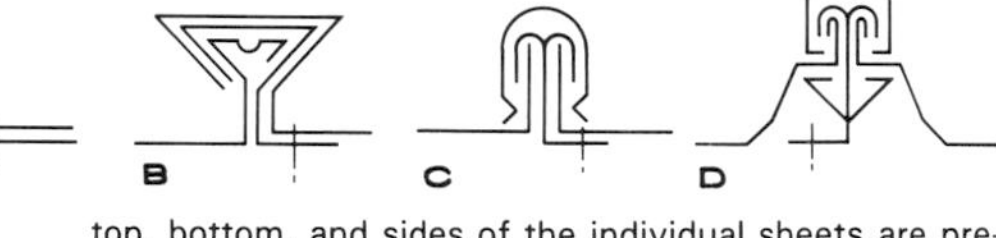
B
C
D

NOTES

Roof panels secured at the eave expand up the slope of the roof. Depending on the length of the roof panel, an engineered distance should be left between the end of roof panels on each side of the ridge, thereby allowing for expansion at the ridge. In cases of a very long run of roof panels (usually in excess of 200 ft), expansion joints will be required at other points in addition to the ridge. Any blocking at the ridge should be cut at an angle to provide a space for the panels to bend into when expanding (as in ridge detail A). Ridge coverings can be formed or bowed to move with the expansion of the roof panels (as in ridge details B and C). In addition, the seams can either be flattened or left upright. Upright seams require a closing gasket or panel between seams.

Standing seam roofing may be installed on slopes as gentle as 1/4 in./ft. Because of the architectural appearance of the roof system, it is more commonly used on steeper roof slopes, allowing the panels to be seen as part of the overall design.

The spacing of seams may vary within reasonable limits to suit the architectural style of a given building. Preformed sheets (as used with preengineered metal buildings) have seam locations set by locations of prepunched holes in the structural framing members.

The two methods of forming a standing seam are the pan method and the roll method. In the pan method, the top, bottom, and sides of the individual sheets are preformed to allow locking together at each edge. Seams at the top and bottom of each sheet are called transverse seams. In the roll method, a series of long sheets are joined together at their ends with double flat lock seams. These field-formed seams can be executed either manually or with a seaming machine (a wheeled electronic device which runs along the sheet joint forming the seam).

In either method, cleats (spaced as recommended by the manufacturer) are formed into the standing seam. Seam terminations are usually soldered.

STANDING SEAM METHODS AND SHAPES

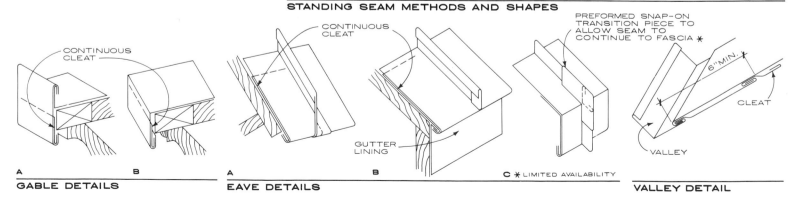

CONTINUOUS CLEAT

A B

GABLE DETAILS

CONTINUOUS CLEAT

GUTTER LINING

PREFORMED SNAP-ON TRANSITION PIECE TO ALLOW SEAM TO CONTINUE TO FASCIA *

A B C * LIMITED AVAILABILITY

EAVE DETAILS

6" MIN.

CLEAT

VALLEY

VALLEY DETAIL

Raso-Greaves An Architecture Corporation; Waco, Texas
Straub, VanDine, Dziurman/Architects; Troy, Michigan
Emory E. Hinkel, Jr.; A. G. Odell, Jr. and Associates; Charlotte, North Carolina

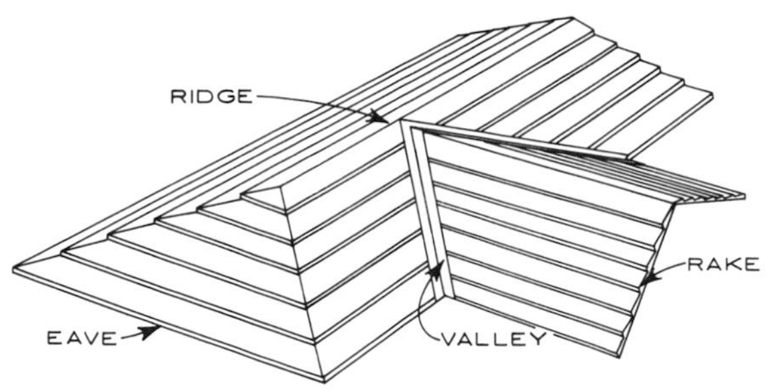
RIDGE
RAKE
EAVE
VALLEY

BERMUDA TYPE METAL ROOF

RECOMMENDED GAUGES OR WEIGHTS FOR PAN WIDTHS

WIDTH OF SHEET (IN.)	WIDTH OF PAN "D" (IN.)	COPPER (OZ)	GALVANIZED STEEL (GAUGE)	STAINLESS STEEL (GAUGE)	PAINTED TERNE 40 LB COATING
20	16½	16	26	28	0.015 IN.
22	18½	16	26	28	0.015 IN.
24	20½	16	26	26	0.015 IN.
26	22½	20	24	26	0.0178 IN.
28	24½	20	24	26	0.0178 IN.

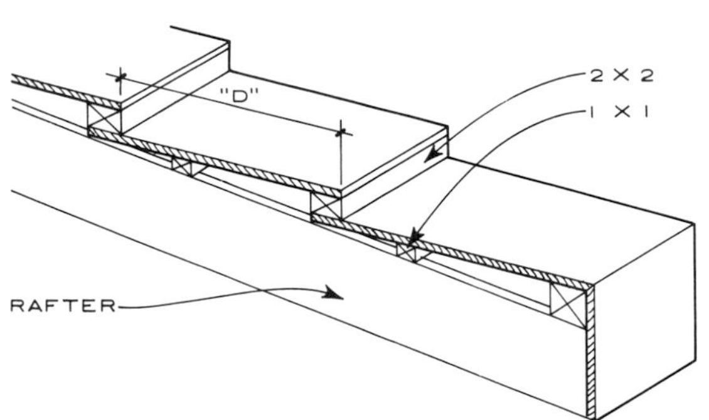
"D"
2 X 2
1 X 1
RAFTER

DETAIL 1-WOOD FRAMING

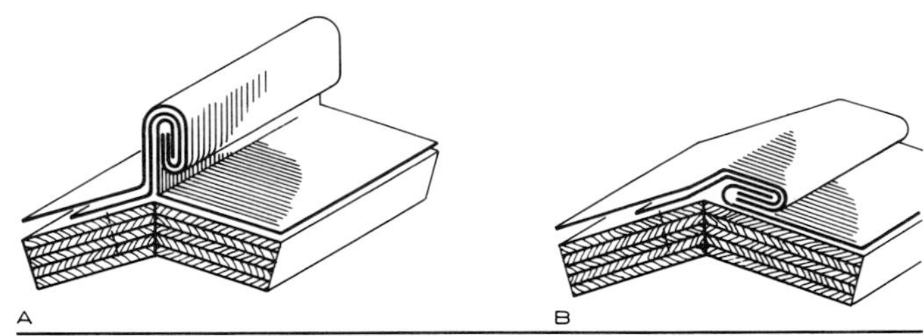
A
B

DETAIL 2-SEAM TYPES AT HIP OR RIDGE

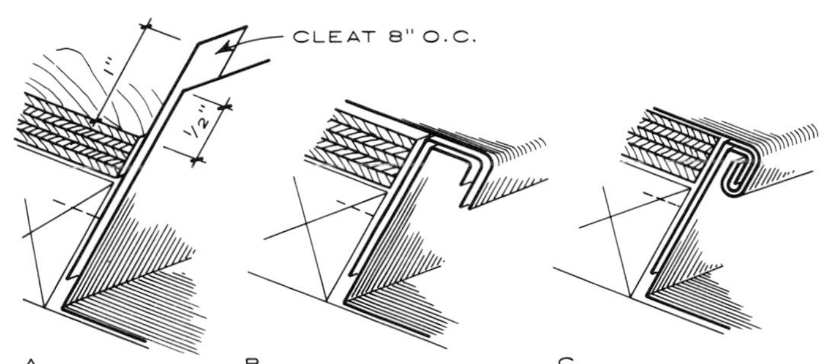
CLEAT 8" O.C.
1"
1/2"
A
B
C

DETAIL 3-CONSTRUCTION AT BATTEN

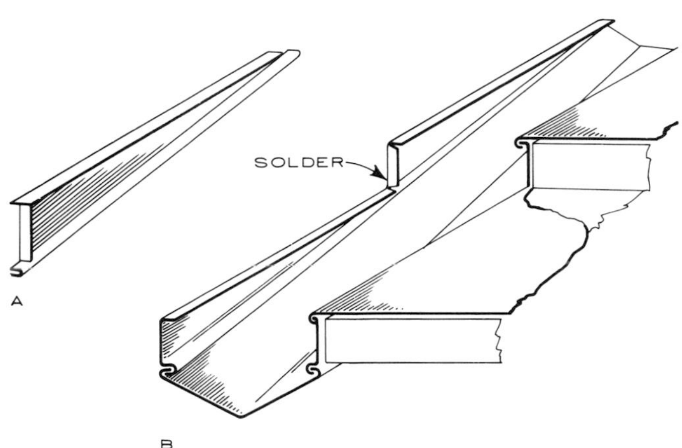
SOLDER
A
B

DETAIL 4-CONSTRUCTION AT CLOSURE AND VALLEY

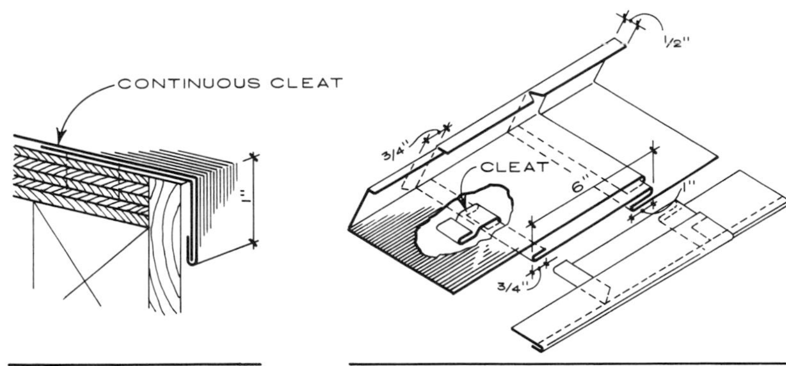
CONTINUOUS CLEAT
1"
CLEAT
6"
3/4"
1"
1/2"
3/4"

DETAIL 5-EAVE

DETAIL 6-EXPANSION JOINT

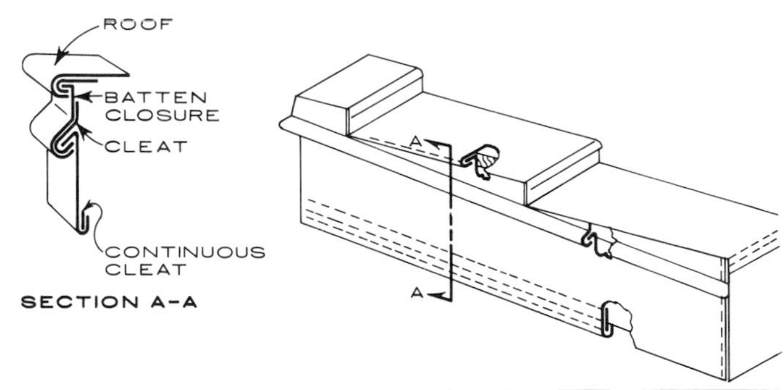
ROOF
BATTEN CLOSURE
CLEAT
CONTINUOUS CLEAT
SECTION A-A
A
A

DETAIL 7-CONSTRUCTION AT RAKE

NOTES

1. The Bermuda roof may be used for roofs having a slope greater than $2^1/_2$ in./ft. Wood framing must be provided as shown in detail 1. Dimension "D" and gauge of metal will depend on the size of sheet used. See chart. Consult general notes on metal roofs for recommended surface preparation.
2. Bermuda roof is applied beginning at the eave. The first pan is hooked over a continuous cleat as shown in detail 5. The upper portion of the first and each succeeding pan is attached as shown in detail 3. Cleats spaced on 8 in. centers are nailed to batten as in A of detail 3. Joint is developed as shown in B of detail 3 and malleted against batten as shown in C of detail 3. All cross seams are single locked and soldered except at expansion joints. Cross seams should be staggered. Expansion joints should be used at least every 25 ft and formed as shown in detail 6. Roofing is joined at hip or ridge by use of a standing seam as shown in A of detail 2. Seam may be malleted down as shown in B of detail 2.
3. Detail 4 shows the method of forming valleys. Valley sections are lapped 8 in. in direction of flow. Individual closures for sides of valley are formed as shown in A of detail 4 and must be soldered as indicated in B of detail 4. A method of terminating the roof at rake is shown in detail 7. The face plate (optional) is held in place by continuous cleats at both top and bottom. The batten closure is formed as a cleat to hold edge of roof pan as shown in section A-A of detail 7.

See also Metal Roofs for general notes.

Straub, VanDine, Dziurman/Architects; Troy, Michigan
Emory E. Hinkel, Jr.; A. G. Odell, Jr. and Associates; Charlotte, North Carolina

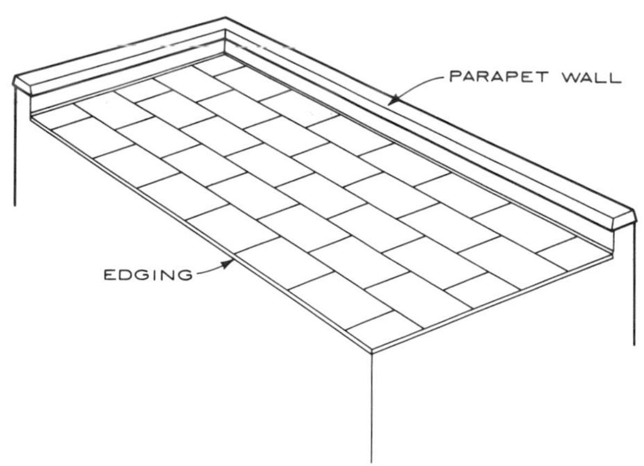
PARAPET WALL
EDGING

FLAT SEAM ROOF

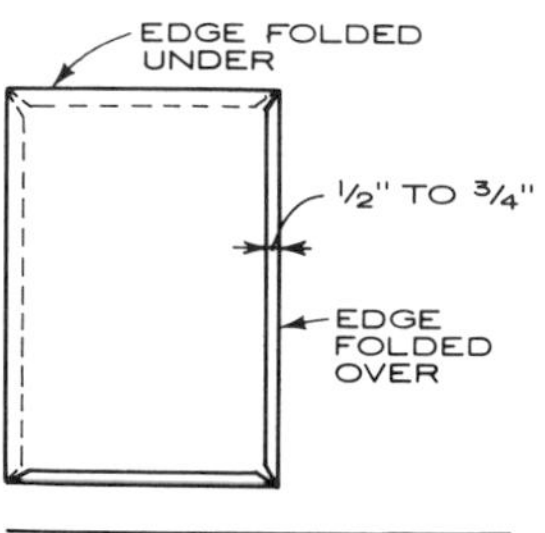
EDGE FOLDED UNDER
1/2" TO 3/4"
EDGE FOLDED OVER

DETAIL 1- ROOFING SHEET

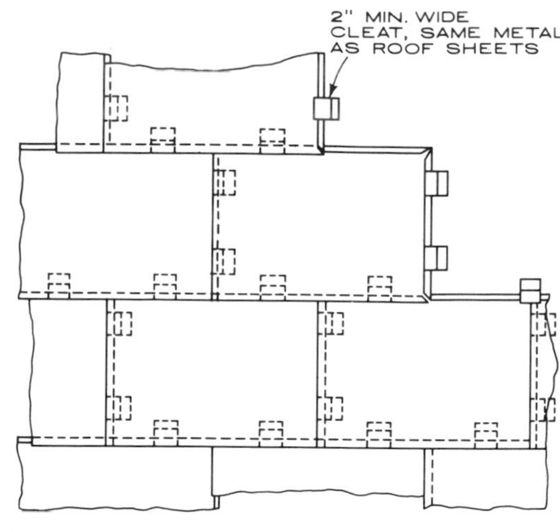
2" MIN. WIDE CLEAT, SAME METAL AS ROOF SHEETS

DETAIL 2- FLAT SEAM ROOF

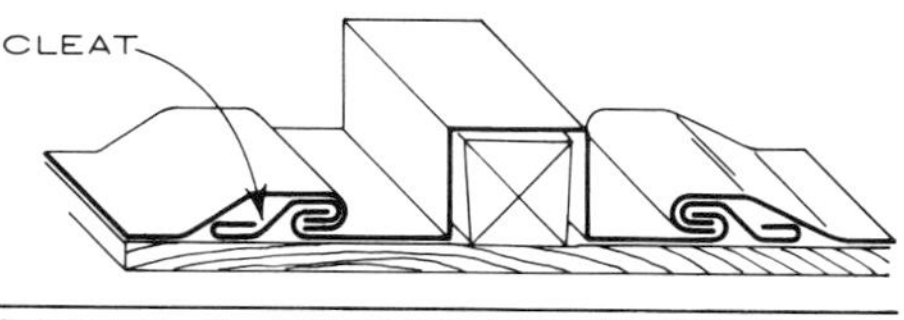
CLEAT

DETAIL 3- EXPANSION BATTEN

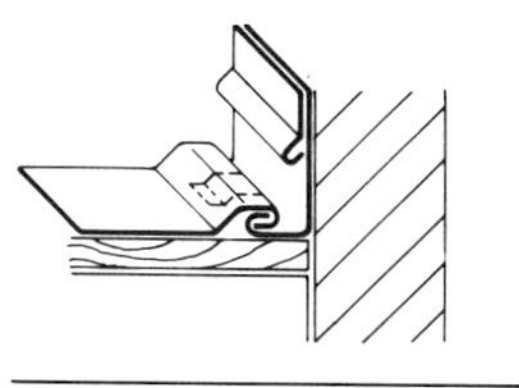

DETAIL 4- JUNCTION AT PARAPET WALL

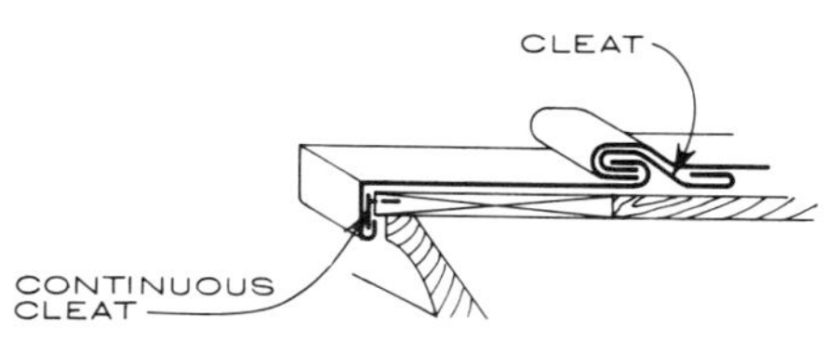
CLEAT
CONTINUOUS CLEAT

DETAIL 5- ROOF EDGE

NOTES

1. The flat seam method of roofing as illustrated is most commonly used on roofs of slight pitch or for the covering of curved surfaces such as towers or domes.
2. The joints connecting the sheets of roofs having a pitch greater than 1/2 in./ft may be sealed with caulking compound or white lead. The joints of roofs having a pitch of less than 1/2 in./ft must be malleted and thoroughly sweated full with solder.
3. Roofs of slight pitch should be divided by expansion batten as shown in detail 3, into sections not exceeding maximum total areas of 30 ft^2.
4. Consult general notes on metal roofs for recommended surface preparation.
5. The metal sheets may be pretinned if required, 1 1/2 in. back from all edges and on both sides of the sheet. Pans are formed by notching and folding the sheets as shown in detail 1.
6. The pans are held in place by cleating as shown. After pans are in place, all seams are malleted and soldered or sealed.
7. Detail 4 shows the junction of a roof and a parapet wall. Metal base flashing is cleated to deck on 2 ft centers and extended up wall; 8 in. pans are locked and soldered to base flashing. Metal counter flashing covers 4 in. of the base flashing. Detail 5 illustrates the installation of flashing at edge of roof. Flashing is formed as shown and attached to the face by a continuous cleat nailed on 1 ft centers and cleated to the roof deck. Pans are locked and soldered or sealed to the flashing. See also general notes below.

GENERAL NOTES

1. Detail drawings for metal roof types are diagrammatic only. The indication of adjoining construction is included merely to establish its relation to the sheet metal work and is not intended as a recommendation of architectural design. Any details that may suggest an architectural period do not limit the application of sheet metal to that or any other architectural style.
2. For weights of metals and roof slopes, see data of the Sheet Metal and Air Conditioning Contractors' National Association and recommendations of manufacturers.
3. Metals used must be of a thickness or gauge heavy enough and in correct proportion to the breadth and scale of the work. Provide expansion joints for freedom of movement.
4. Prevent direct contact of metal roofing with dissimilar metals that cause electrolysis.
5. A wide range of metals, alloys, and finishes are available for metal roofing. The durability as well as the maintenance requirements of each should be taken into consideration when selecting roofing.
6. The surface to receive the metal roofing should be thoroughly dry and covered by a saturated roofing felt in case of leakage due to construction error or wind driven moisture. A rosin paper should be applied over the felt to avoid bonding between felt and metal.
7. Many of the prefabricated batten and standing seam devices are not as watertight as with conventional methods and are therefore more suitable for steeply pitched roofs and mansards.

Straub, VanDine, Dziurman/Architects; Troy, Michigan
Emory E. Hinkel, Jr.; A. G. Odell, Jr. and Associates; Charlotte, North Carolina

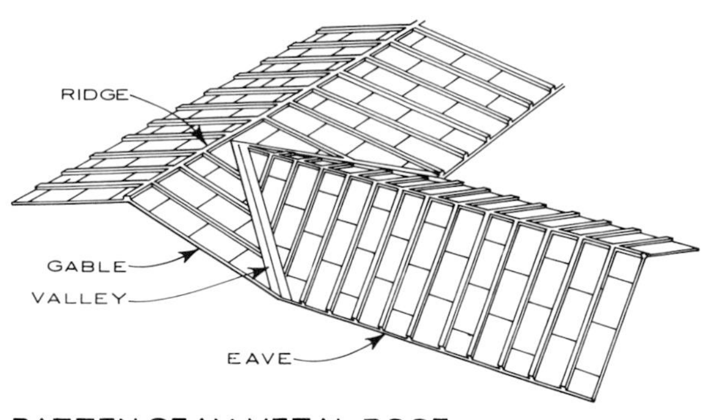
RIDGE
GABLE
VALLEY
EAVE
BATTEN SEAM METAL ROOF

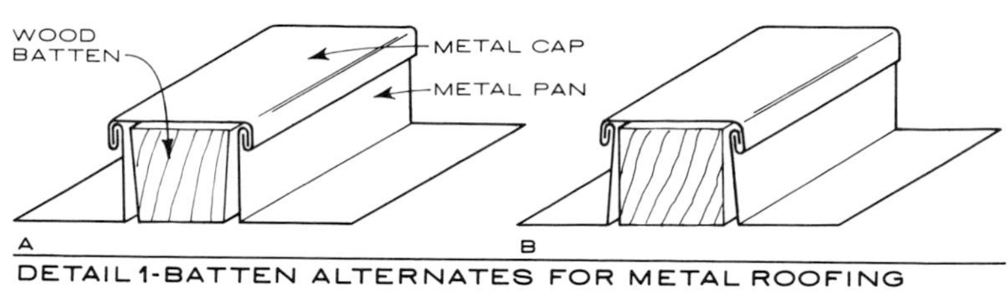
WOOD BATTEN
METAL CAP
METAL PAN
A
B
DETAIL 1-BATTEN ALTERNATES FOR METAL ROOFING

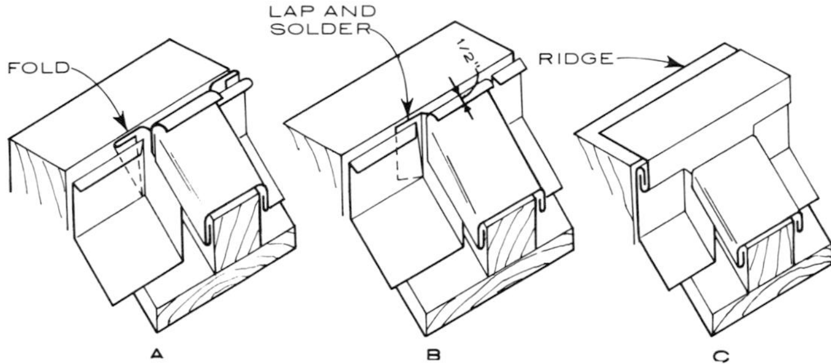
FOLD
LAP AND SOLDER
1/2"
RIDGE
A
B
C
DETAIL 2 - RIDGE CONSTRUCTION

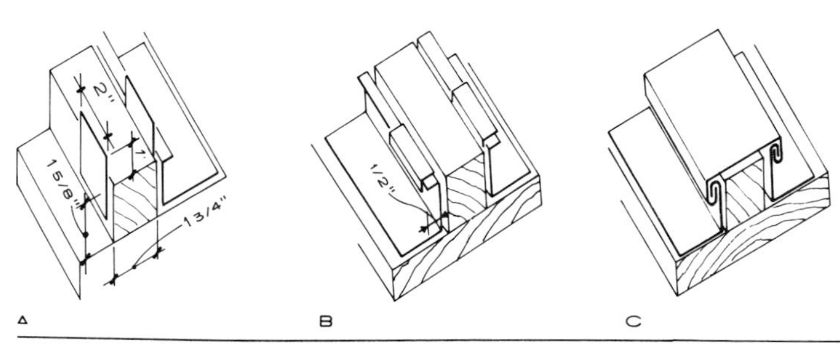
2"
1"
1 5/8"
1 3/4"
1/2"
A
B
C
DETAIL 3 - BATTEN JOINT CONSTRUCTION

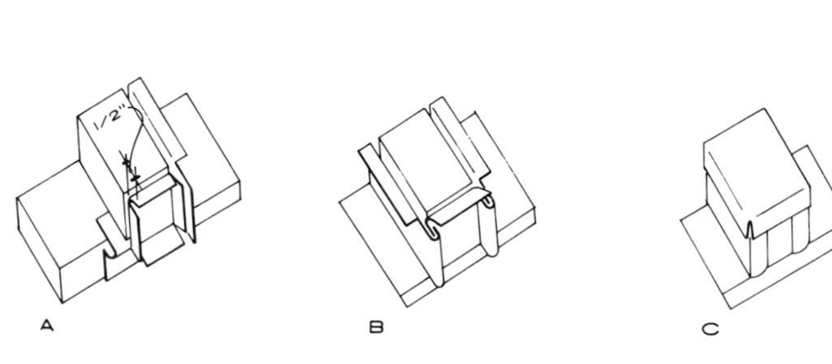
1/2"
A
B
C
DETAIL 4 - BATTEN CAP CONSTRUCTION

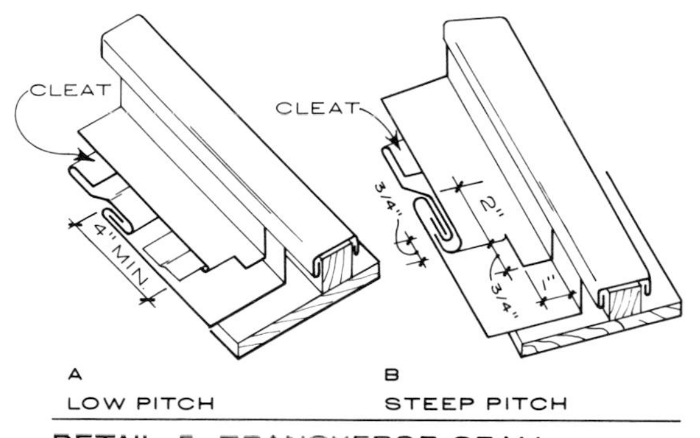
CLEAT
CLEAT
4" MIN
3/4"
2"
1"
3/4"
A
LOW PITCH
B
STEEP PITCH
DETAIL 5 -TRANSVERSE SEAM

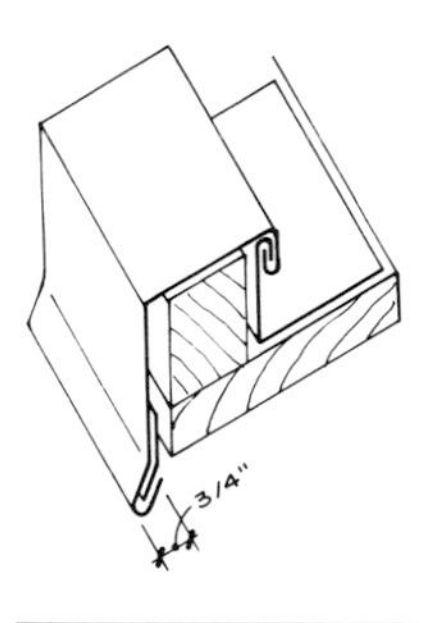
3/4"
DETAIL 6 - GABLE

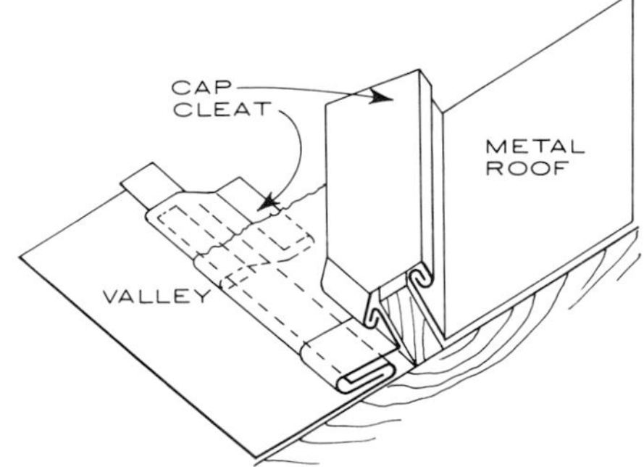
CAP
CLEAT
METAL ROOF
VALLEY
DETAIL 7 - VALLEY

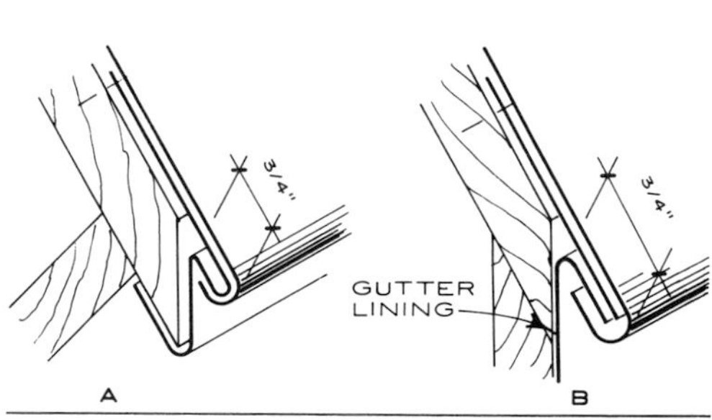
3/4"
3/4"
GUTTER LINING
A
B
DETAIL 8 - EAVES

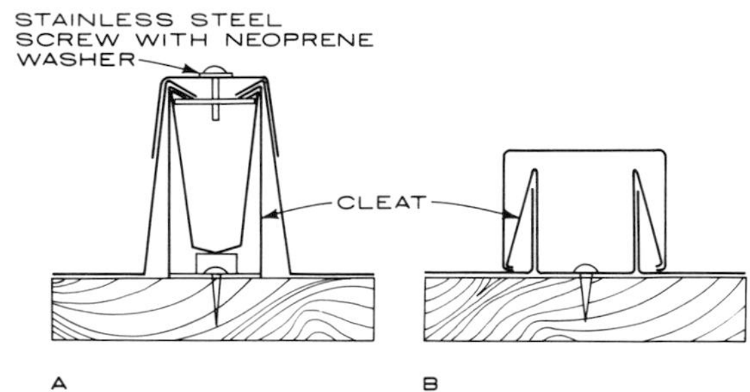
STAINLESS STEEL SCREW WITH NEOPRENE WASHER
CLEAT
A
B
DETAIL 9 - PREFABRICATED BATTENS

NOTES

1. Batten seam roofing may be applied on slopes of 3 in./ft or greater. If the surface to receive the roofing is other than wood, the battens should be bolted into place. All batten fasteners must be countersunk into battens. See general notes on Metal Roofs for recommended surface preparation.
2. The spacing of the wood battens may vary within reasonable limits to suit the architectural style and scale of the building, but the recommended maximum distance is 20 in. between battens. Care should be taken to space the battens in such a manner that waste of metal is held to a minimum. Battens may be shaped as shown in A or B of detail 1. A is preferred, since it automatically makes allowance for expansion. When battens shown in B are used, care must be taken to provide for expansion by bending the metal where it meets the batten at greater than 90°.
3. Sheets are formed into pans with each side turned up $2^1/_8$ in. A $^1/_2$ in. flange is turned toward the center of the pan as shown in B of detail 3. At lower end of the pan, the sheet is notched and a hook edge is formed as in A or B of detail 5. For low pitched roofs the upper end of the sheet is formed as in A of detail 5. On steeper roofs the upper end is formed as shown in B of detail 5. Pans are installed, starting at the eave, and held in place with cleats spaced not over 12 in. on center as shown in A of detail 3. Each pan is hooked to the one below it and cleated into place. After pans are in place, a cap is installed over the batten as shown in B and C of detail 3.
4. A number of manufacturers have developed metal roofing systems using several prefabricated devices. A and B of detail 9 show two common prefabricated battens in use.
5. See also Standing Seam Metal Roofing for details on combination batten and standing or flat seam roofing. See also Metal Roofs for general notes.

Straub, VanDine, Dziurman/Architects; Troy, Michigan
Emory E. Hinkel, Jr.; A. G. Odell, Jr. and Associates; Charlotte, North Carolina

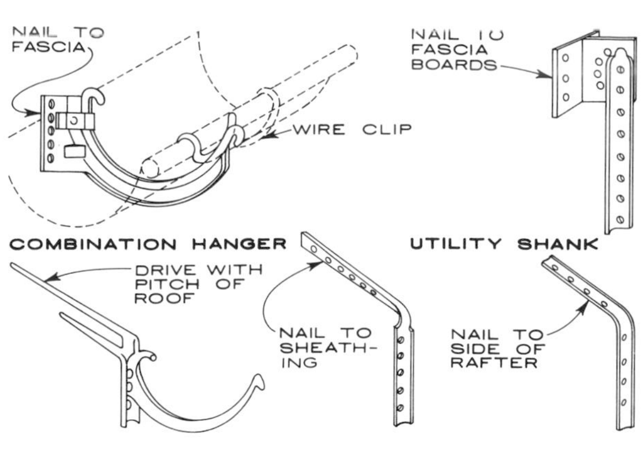
NAIL TO FASCIA
NAIL TO FASCIA BOARDS
WIRE CLIP
COMBINATION HANGER
UTILITY SHANK

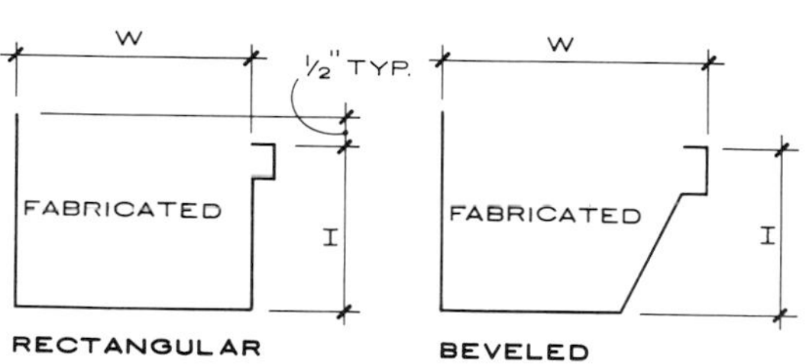
DRIVE WITH PITCH OF ROOF
NAIL TO SHEATHING
NAIL TO SIDE OF RAFTER

DRIVE HANGER VARIOUS SHANKS

SHANK AND CIRCLE HANGERS

Available in malleable and wrought copper, bronze, stainless steel and aluminum. Only a sampling of the wide variety of shapes available is shown. See mfrs. literature.

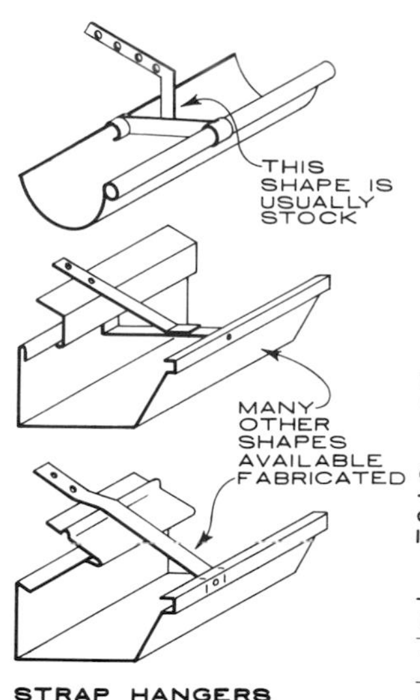
THIS SHAPE IS USUALLY STOCK

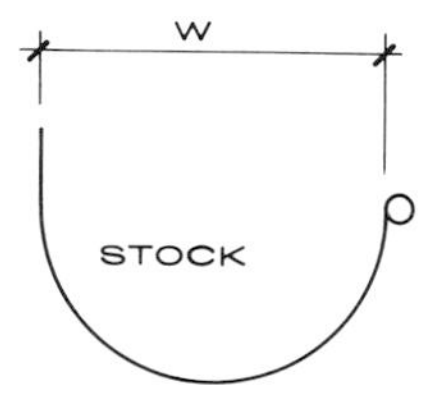
MANY OTHER SHAPES AVAILABLE FABRICATED

STRAP HANGERS

NOTE: Gutter hangers are normally spaced 3′–0″ O.C. Reduce to 1′–6″ O.C. where ice and snow are long lasting.

BRACKET HANGER

Various shapes are available.

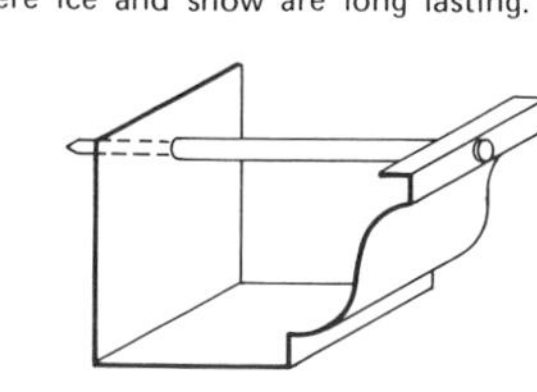

SPIKE AND FERRULE

Not recommended if girth is over 15 in.

GUTTER BRACKET OR STRAP SIZES

GIRTH INCHES	GALV. STEEL INCHES	COPPER INCHES	ALUM. INCHES	STAINLESS INCHES
UP TO 15	1/8 x 1	1/8 x 1	3/16 x 1	1/8 x 1
15 TO 20	3/16 x 1	1/4 x 1	1/4 x 1	1/8 x 1 1/2
20 TO 24	1/4 x 1 1/2	1/4 x 1 1/2	1/4 x 2	1/8 x 2

GUTTER HANGERS

W ½″ TYP. FABRICATED I — RECTANGULAR

W FABRICATED I — BEVELED

W STOCK I — OGEE OR STYLE "K"

W STOCK — SEMICIRCULAR OR HALF - ROUND

OGEE OR STYLE "K"	
2 1/2″ H x 3″ W	
2 3/4″ H x 4″ W	G A
3 3/4″ H x 5″ W	G A
4 3/4″ H x 6″ W	G
5 1/4″ H x 7″ W	
6″ H x 8″ W	

SEMICIRCULAR OR HALF - ROUND	
4″ W	G
5″ W	G A
6″ W	G A
7″ W	G
8″ W	G

NOTE: Stock sizes—G = galvanized, A = aluminum.

METAL GUTTER NOTES

Various sizes and other shapes available.

Always keep front ½ in. lower than back of gutter.

Do not use width less than 4 in. except for canopies and small porches. Minimum ratio of depth to width should be 3 to 4.

METAL GUTTER SHAPES AND SIZES

NOTES

1. Continuous gutters may be formed at the installation site with cold forming equipment, thus eliminating joints in long runs of gutter.
2. Girth is width of sheet metal from which gutter is fabricated.
3. Sizes listed in table to the left but not marked stock are available on special order.
4. Aluminum and galvanized steel are more commonly used, whereas copper and especially stainless steel are least used.
5. All jointing methods are applicable to most gutter shapes. Lap joints are more commonly used. Seal all joints with mastic or by soldering. Lock, slip, or lap joints do not provide expansion.
6. See SMACNA Architectural Sheet Metal Manual for gutter sizing and details.

EXPANSION JOINTS

Expansion joints should be used on all straight runs over 40 ft. In a 10 ft section of gutter and a 100° temperature change linear expansion will be:

EXPANSION OF METAL GUTTERS IN 40 FT

METAL	COEFFICIENT OF EXPANSION	MOVEMENT
Aluminum	.00128	.15 in.
Copper	.00093	.11 in.
Galvanized steel	.0065	.08 in.

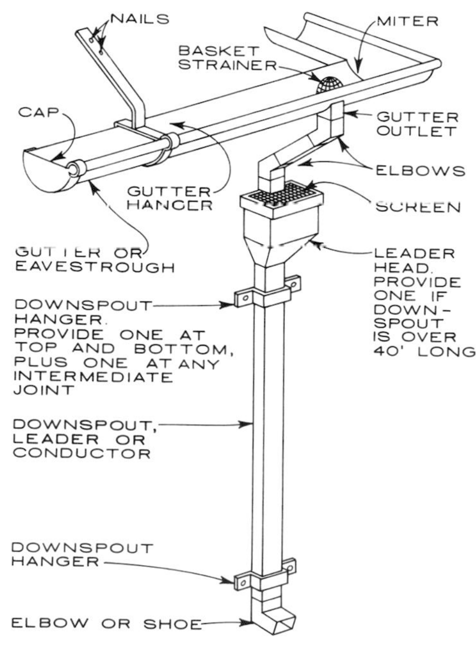
NAILS
MITER
BASKET STRAINER
CAP
GUTTER OUTLET
ELBOWS
GUTTER HANGER
SCREEN
GUTTER OR EAVESTROUGH
LEADER HEAD. PROVIDE ONE IF DOWN-SPOUT IS OVER 40′ LONG
DOWNSPOUT HANGER. PROVIDE ONE AT TOP AND BOTTOM, PLUS ONE AT ANY INTERMEDIATE JOINT
DOWNSPOUT, LEADER OR CONDUCTOR
DOWNSPOUT HANGER
ELBOW OR SHOE

PARTS OF A GUTTER

NOTE

PVC plastic gutter and downspout parts are similar to metal. See manufacturers' data for shapes and sizes.

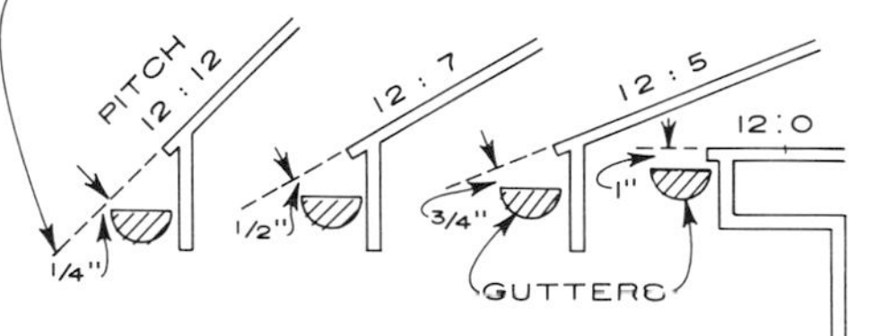
DASH LINE INDICATES ROOF SLOPE
PITCH 12 : 12
12 : 7
12 : 5
12 : 0
1/4″
1/2″
3/4″
1″
GUTTERS

Gutters should be placed below slope line so that snow and ice can slide clear. Steeper pitch requires less clearance.

PLACING OF GUTTERS

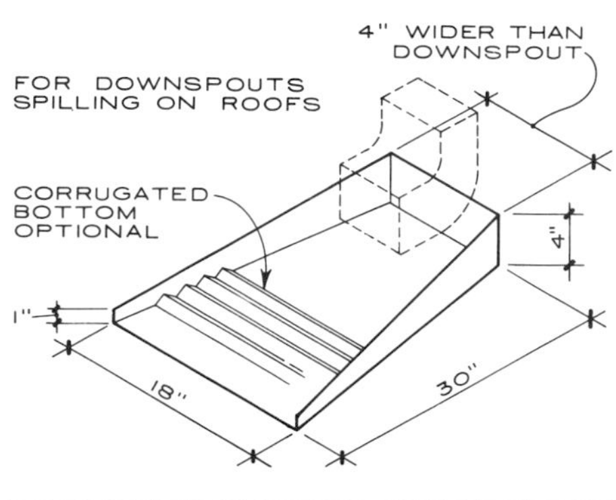
4″ WIDER THAN DOWNSPOUT
FOR DOWNSPOUTS SPILLING ON ROOFS
CORRUGATED BOTTOM OPTIONAL
4″
1″
18″
30″

SPLASH PAN

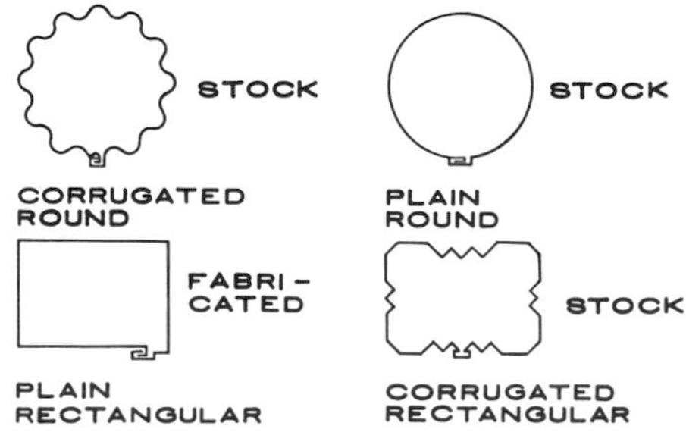
STOCK
STOCK
CORRUGATED ROUND
PLAIN ROUND
FABRICATED
STOCK
PLAIN RECTANGULAR
CORRUGATED RECTANGULAR

NOTES

Space downspouts 20 ft min., 50 ft max., generally. Extreme max. 60 ft.

Do not use size smaller than 7.00 in area except for canopies.

Corrugated shapes resist freezing better than plain shapes.

Elbows available: 45°, 60°, 75°, 90°.

Jones/Richards and Associates; Ogden, Utah
Lawrence W. Cobb; Columbia, South Carolina

WIDTH OF RECTANGULAR GUTTERS FOR GIVEN ROOF AREAS AND RAINFALL INTENSITIES

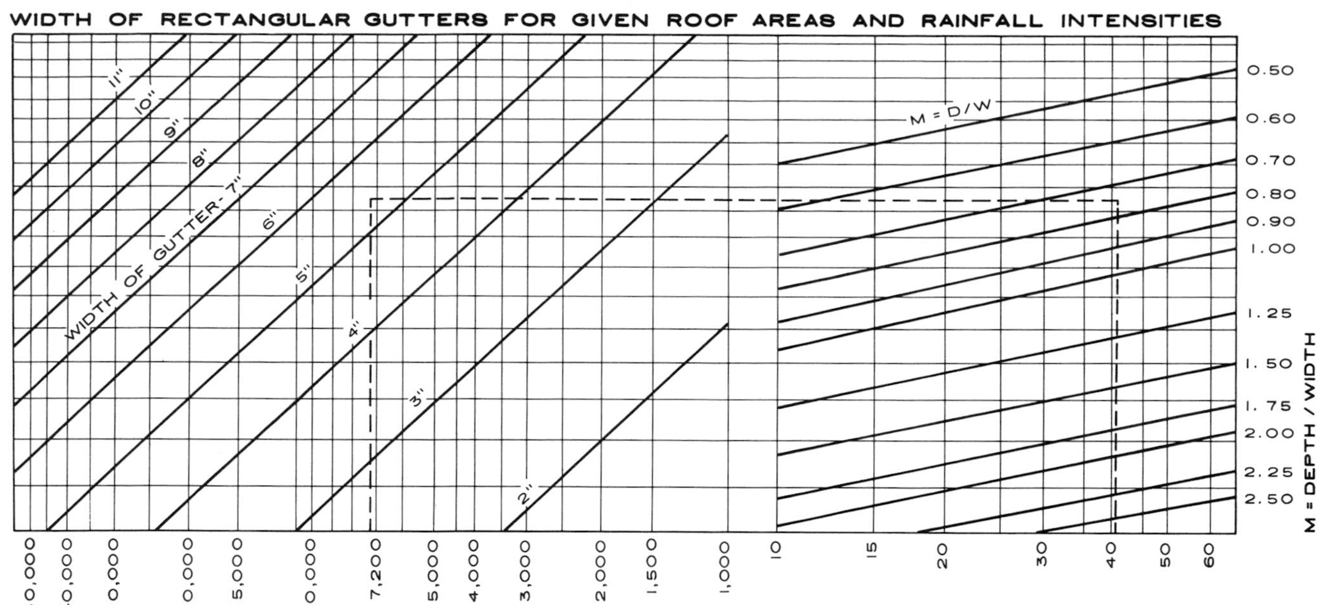

11"
10"
9"
8"
WIDTH OF GUTTER-7"
6"
5"
4"
3"
2"
M = D/W
0.50
0.60
0.70
0.80
0.90
1.00
1.25
1.50
1.75
2.00
2.25
2.50
M = DEPTH / WIDTH
50,000
40,000
30,000
20,000
15,000
10,000
7,200
5,000
4,000
3,000
2,000
1,500
1,000
10
15
20
30
40
50
60
IA = RAINFALL INTENSITY X AREA
L = LENGTH OF GUTTER IN FEET

NOTE

The terms "leader," "conductor," and "downspout" all mean the same thing.

SAMPLE PROBLEM

To size rectangular gutter for a building 120 x 30 ft. located in New York City. This building has a flat roof with a raised roof edge on three sides. A gutter is to be located on one of the 120 ft. sides. So that each section of gutter will not exceed 50 ft., three downspouts will be used with 2 gutter expansion joints. The area to be drained by each section of gutter will be 1200 sq. ft., the rainfall intensity from map below is 6 in., the length of each gutter section is 40 ft., and the ratio of gutter depth to width is 0.75. On chart above find the vertical line representing L = 40. Proceed vertically along this line to its intersection with the oblique line representing M = 0.75. Pass horizontally to the left to intersect the vertical line representing IA = 7200. The point of intersection occurs between the oblique line representing gutter widths of 5 and 6 in. The required width of gutter is, therefore, 6 in. and its depth need be only 4 $^1/_2$ in.

DESIGN AREAS FOR PITCHED ROOFS

PITCH	FACTOR
LEVEL TO 3 IN./FT.	1.00
4 TO 5 IN./FT.	1.05
6 TO 8 IN./FT.	1.10
9 TO 11 IN./FT.	1.20
12 IN./FT.	1.30

NOTE: When a roof is sloped neither the plan nor actual area should be used in sizing drainage. Multiply the plan area by the factor shown above to obtain design area.

INFLUENCE OF GUTTER SHAPE ON DESIGN

1. RECTANGULAR GUTTERS

Use graph at top of page.

2. IRREGULAR SHAPES

Determine equivalent rectangular size and use same method.

3. SEMICIRCULAR GUTTERS

First size downspout from tables below. Then use gutter 1 inch larger in diameter.

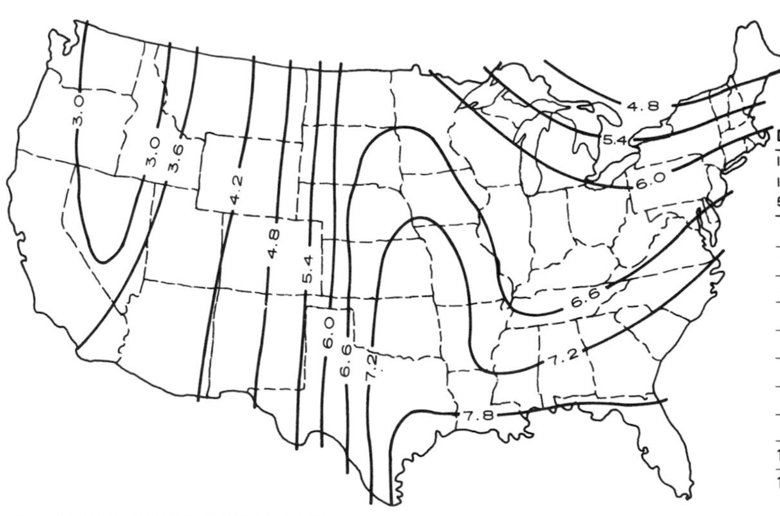

3.0
3.0
3.6
4.2
4.8
5.4
6.0
6.6
7.2
7.8
4.8
5.4
6.0
6.6
7.2

RAINFALL INTENSITY MAP

NOTE

Map shows hourly rainfall intensity in inches per hour for 5 minute periods to be expected once in 10 years. Normally this is adequate for design, but some storms have been twice as intense in some areas. See local records.

DOWNSPOUT CAPACITY

INTENSITY IN IN./HR. LASTING 5 MIN.	SQ.FT. ROOF/ SQ.IN. DOWNSPOUT
2	600
3	400
4	300
5	240
6	200
7	175
8	150
9	130
10	120
11	110

GENERAL NOTES

Most gutters are run level for appearance. However, a slope of $^1/_{16}$ in. per foot is desirable for drainage.

For residential work allow 100 sq. ft. of roof area per 1 sq. in. of downspout.

DOWNSPOUT SIZES

TYPE	AREA SQ.IN.	NOM. SIZE IN.	ACT. SIZE IN.
PLAIN ROUND	7.07	3	3
	12.57	4	4
	19.63	5	5
	28.27	6	6
CORR. ROUND	5.94	3	3
	11.04	4	4
	17.72	5	5
	25.97	6	6
CORR. RECT.	3.80	2	$1^3/_4 \times 2^1/_4$
	7.73	3	$2^3/_8 \times 3^1/_4$
	11.70	4	$2^3/_4 \times 4^1/_4$
	18.75	5	$3^3/_4 \times 5$
PLAIN RECT.	3.94	2	$1^3/_4 \times 2^1/_4$
	6.00	3	2 x 3
	12.00	4	3 x 4
	20.00	5	$3^3/_4 \times 4^3/_4$
	24.00	6	4 x 6

Lawrence W. Cobb; Columbia, South Carolina

MINIMUM THICKNESS (GAUGES OR WEIGHT) FOR COMMON FLASHING CONDITIONS

MATERIALS \ CONDITIONS	BASE COURSE	WALL OPENINGS HEAD AND SILL	THROUGH WALL AND SPANDREL	CAP AND BASE FLASHING	VERTICAL AND HORIZONTAL SURFACES	ROOF EDGE RIDGES AND HIPS	CRICKETS VALLEY OR GUTTER	CHIMNEY PAN	LEDGE FLASHING	ROOF PENETRATIONS	COPING WIDTH: UP TO 12"	COPING WIDTH: ABOVE 12"	EDGE STRIPS	CLEATS	NOTE
Copper	10 oz	10 oz	10 oz	16 oz	16 oz	16 oz	16 oz	16 oz	16 oz	16 oz	16 oz	20 oz	20 oz	16 oz	
Aluminum	0.019"	0.019"	0.019"	0.019"	0.019"	0.019"	0.019"	0.019"	0.019"	0.040"	0.032"	0.040"	0.024"	⊠	Note 6
Stainless steel	30 GA	30 GA	30 GA	26 GA	30 GA	26 GA	26 GA	30 GA	26 GA	26 GA	26 GA	24 GA	24 GA	⊠	Note 5
Galvanized steel	26 GA	26 GA	26 GA	26 GA	26 GA	24 GA	24 GA	26 GA	24 GA	24 GA	24 GA	22 GA	26 GA	22 GA	Note 2
Zinc alloy*	0.027"	0.027"	0.027"	0.027"	0.027"	0.027"	0.027"	0.027"	0.027"	0.027"	0.027"	0.032"	0.040"	0.027"	Note 4
Lead	3#	2½#	2½#	2½#	3#	3#	3#	3#	3#	3#	3#	3#	3#	3#	Note 3
Painted terne	40#	40#	40#	20#	40#	20#	40#	20#	40#	40#	⊠	⊠	20#	40#	Note 8
elastomeric sheet; fabric-coated metal	See Note 7			⊠	⊠	⊠	⊠	⊠	See Note 7		⊠	⊠	⊠	⊠	Note 7

GENERAL NOTES

1. All sizes and weights of material given in chart are minimum. Actual conditions may require greater strength.
2. All galvanized steel must be painted.
3. With lead flashing use 16 oz copper cleats. If any part is exposed, use 3# lead cleats.
4. Coat zinc with asphaltum paint when in contact with redwood or cedar. High acid content (in these woods only) develops stains.
5. Type 302 stainless steel is an all purpose flashing type.
6. Use only aluminum manufactured for the purpose of flashing.
7. See manufacturer's literature for use and types of flashing.
8. In general, cleats will be of the same material as flashing, but heavier weight or thicker gauge.
9. In selecting metal flashing, precaution must be taken not to place flashing in direct contact with dissimilar metals that cause electrolysis.
10. Spaces marked ⊠ in the table are uses not recommended for that material.

GALVANIC CORROSION (ELECTROLYSIS) POTENTIAL BETWEEN COMMON FLASHING MATERIALS AND SELECTED CONSTRUCTION MATERIALS

FLASHING MATERIALS \ CONSTRUCTION MATERIALS	COPPER	ALUMINUM	STAINLESS STEEL	GALVANIZED STEEL	ZINC	LEAD	BRASS	BRONZE	MONEL	UNCURED MORTAR OR CEMENT	WOODS WITH ACID (REDWOOD AND RED CEDAR)	IRON/STEEL
Copper		●	●	◑	●	◑	◑	◑	◑	○	○	●
Aluminum			○	○	○	◑	●	●	○	●	●	◑
Stainless steel				◑	●	◑	●	●	●	○	○	◑
Galvanized steel					○	○	◑	◑	◑	○	◑	◑
Zinc alloy						○	●	●	●	○	●	●
Lead							◑	◑	◑	●	○	○

● Galvanic action will occur, hence direct contact should be avoided.
◑ Galvanic action may occur under certain circumstances and/or over a period of time.
○ Galvanic action is insignificant, metals may come into direct contact under normal circumstances.

GENERAL NOTE: Galvanic corrosion is apt to occur when water runoff from one material comes in contact with a potentially reactive material.

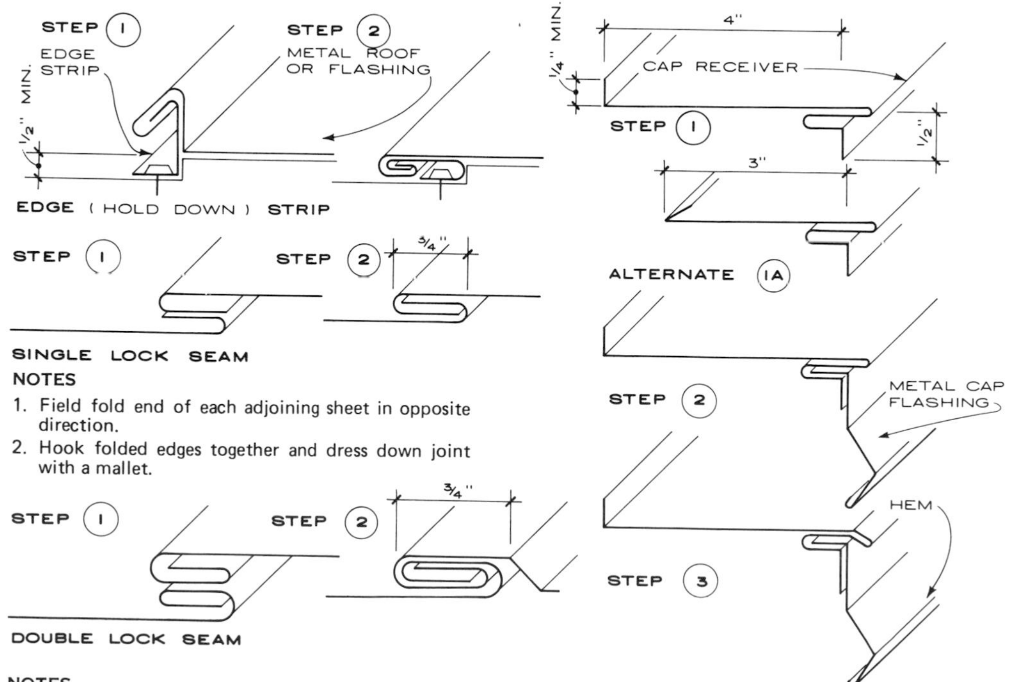
STEP 1
EDGE STRIP
1/2" MIN.
STEP 2
METAL ROOF OR FLASHING
EDGE (HOLD DOWN) STRIP
STEP 1
STEP 2
3/4"
SINGLE LOCK SEAM
STEP 1
STEP 2
3/4"
DOUBLE LOCK SEAM
1/4" MIN.
4"
CAP RECEIVER
STEP 1
1/2"
3"
ALTERNATE 1A
STEP 2
METAL CAP FLASHING
HEM
STEP 3
DEVELOPMENT OF CAP FLASHING

NOTES

1. Field fold end of each adjoining sheet in opposite direction.
2. Hook folded edges together and dress down joint with a mallet.

NOTES

1. Double fold end of each adjoining sheet in opposite direction with bar folder.
2. Slide edges together and dress down joint with a mallet.

NOTE

Hem in cap flashing recommended for stiffness; but may be omitted if heavier gauge material used.

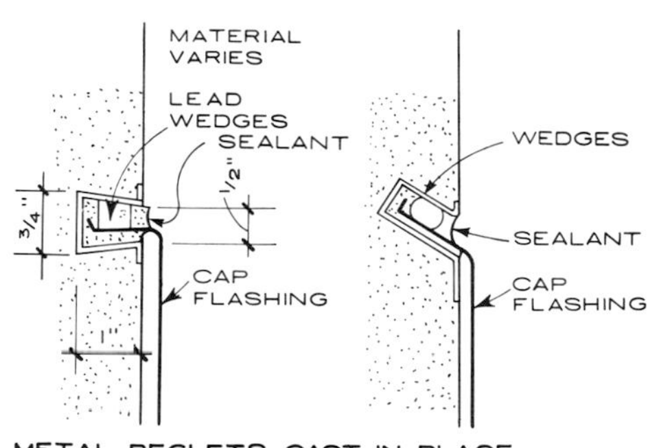
MATERIAL VARIES
LEAD WEDGES
SEALANT
1/2"
3/4"
1"
CAP FLASHING
WEDGES
SEALANT
CAP FLASHING
METAL REGLETS CAST IN PLACE

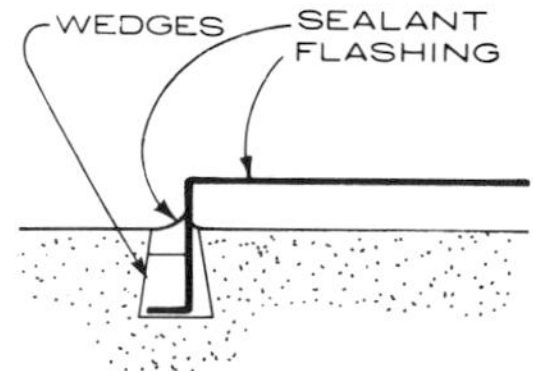
WEDGES
SEALANT
FLASHING
REGLET SAWED IN MATERIAL

TYPICAL REGLETS

NOTE

Various types of metal reglets are available for cast in place and masonry work; see manufacturer's literature. Where material permits, reglets may be sawn. Flashing is secured in reglets with lead wedges at max. 12" o.c., fill reglet with nonhardening water-resistant compound.

Michael Scott Rudden, The Stephens Associates P.C.—Architects; Albany, New York

DEFINITIONS

BASE FLASHINGS are essentially a continuation of the built-up roofing membrane at the upturned edges, applied in an operation separate from the application of the roof membrane itself.

CAP FLASHINGS (COUNTERFLASHINGS) are normally made of sheet metal and shield the exposed top of the base flashing. Some nonmetallic cap flashings are made of felts, and are made water-resistant with flashing cement.

CONCEALED FLASHINGS are invisible from the exterior or interior of the building. Metal sheet or foil, fabric, plastic, or various combinations of these materials may be used, depending on climate and structural requirements.

EXPOSED FLASHINGS are exposed to view and affect the aesthetics of the building. Metals are almost entirely used. Attention must be paid to the corrosive potential between dissimilar metals.

NOTES

1. Select flashing that is flexible for molding to flashing supports and can withstand expected thermal, wind, and structural movement. Provide expansion joints in place of flashing as required by conditions.
2. Consult manufacturer's literature for choice of flashing materials and details.
3. Avoid sharp bends in bituminous base flashings. Use cant strips with 45° maximum bend.
4. Provision for differential movement between roof deck and wall is recommended.
5. Ribbed or embossed through wall flashing is not recommended for earthquake areas.
6. Base flashing should extend 8 to 12 in. above highest anticipated waterline. Metal counterflashings should lap base flashing at least 4 in. minimum. Lap all vertical joints.
7. At cavity walls with more than 3/4" space between wythes, use flashing of type that provides mechanical bond.

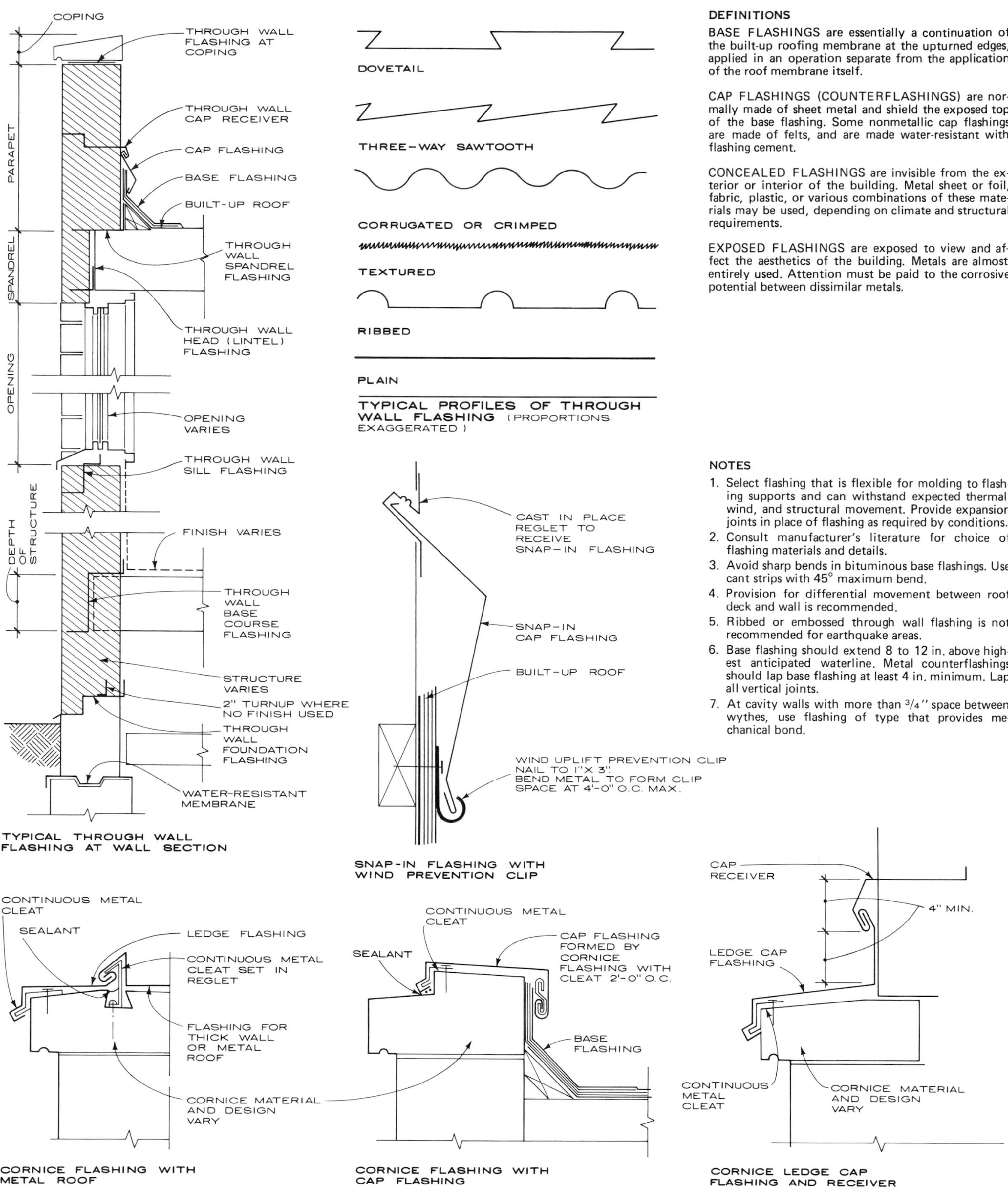
COPING
THROUGH WALL FLASHING AT COPING
THROUGH WALL CAP RECEIVER
CAP FLASHING
BASE FLASHING
BUILT-UP ROOF
PARAPET
SPANDREL
THROUGH WALL SPANDREL FLASHING
THROUGH WALL HEAD (LINTEL) FLASHING
OPENING
OPENING VARIES
THROUGH WALL SILL FLASHING
DEPTH OF STRUCTURE
FINISH VARIES
THROUGH WALL BASE COURSE FLASHING
STRUCTURE VARIES
2" TURNUP WHERE NO FINISH USED
THROUGH WALL FOUNDATION FLASHING
WATER-RESISTANT MEMBRANE
DOVETAIL
THREE-WAY SAWTOOTH
CORRUGATED OR CRIMPED
TEXTURED
RIBBED
PLAIN
CAST IN PLACE REGLET TO RECEIVE SNAP-IN FLASHING
SNAP-IN CAP FLASHING
BUILT-UP ROOF
WIND UPLIFT PREVENTION CLIP NAIL TO 1"X 3". BEND METAL TO FORM CLIP SPACE AT 4'-0" O.C. MAX.
CONTINUOUS METAL CLEAT
SEALANT
LEDGE FLASHING
CONTINUOUS METAL CLEAT SET IN REGLET
FLASHING FOR THICK WALL OR METAL ROOF
CORNICE MATERIAL AND DESIGN VARY
CONTINUOUS METAL CLEAT
SEALANT
CAP FLASHING FORMED BY CORNICE FLASHING WITH CLEAT 2'-0" O.C.
BASE FLASHING
CAP RECEIVER
4" MIN.
LEDGE CAP FLASHING
CONTINUOUS METAL CLEAT
CORNICE MATERIAL AND DESIGN VARY

TYPICAL THROUGH WALL FLASHING AT WALL SECTION

TYPICAL PROFILES OF THROUGH WALL FLASHING (PROPORTIONS EXAGGERATED)

SNAP-IN FLASHING WITH WIND PREVENTION CLIP

CORNICE FLASHING WITH METAL ROOF

CORNICE FLASHING WITH CAP FLASHING

CORNICE LEDGE CAP FLASHING AND RECEIVER

CORNICE FLASHING

Michael Scott Rudden, The Stephens Associates P.C.—Architects; Albany, New York

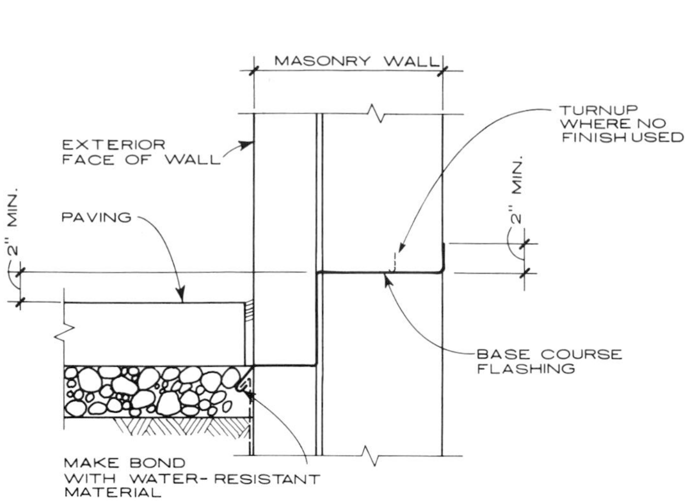
MASONRY WALL
TURNUP WHERE NO FINISH USED
EXTERIOR FACE OF WALL
2" MIN.
PAVING
2" MIN.
BASE COURSE FLASHING
MAKE BOND WITH WATER-RESISTANT MATERIAL
BASE COURSE AT PAVING AND WALL

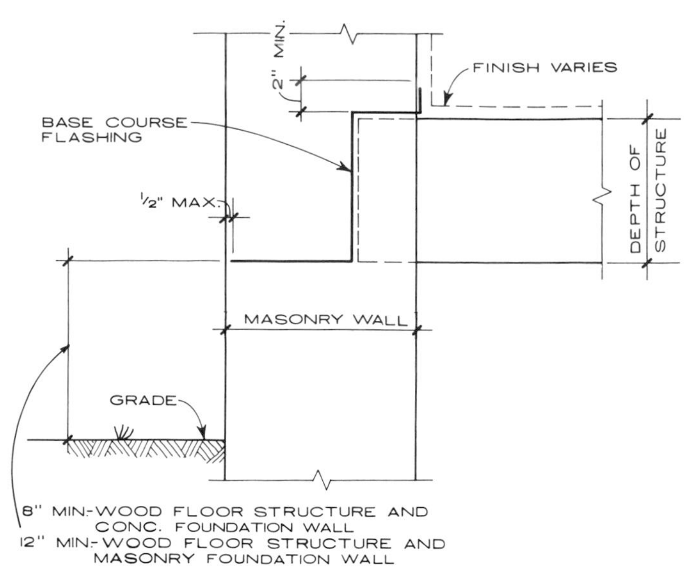
2" MIN.
FINISH VARIES
BASE COURSE FLASHING
½" MAX.
DEPTH OF STRUCTURE
MASONRY WALL
GRADE
8" MIN-WOOD FLOOR STRUCTURE AND CONC. FOUNDATION WALL
12" MIN-WOOD FLOOR STRUCTURE AND MASONRY FOUNDATION WALL
BASE COURSE AT FLOOR CONSTRUCTION

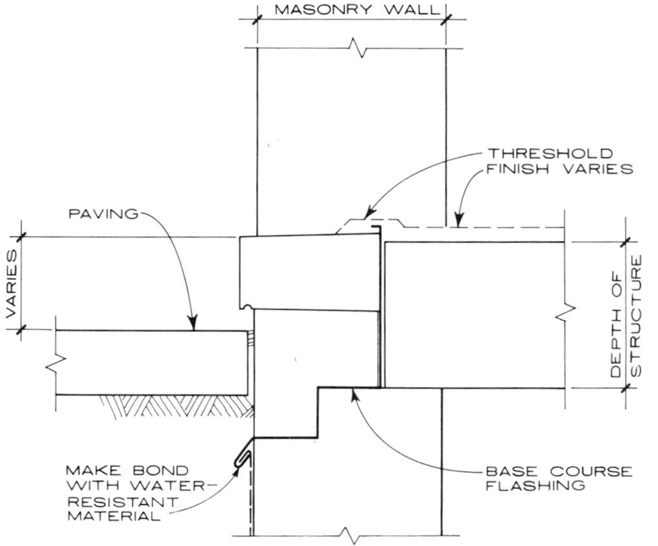
MASONRY WALL
THRESHOLD
FINISH VARIES
PAVING
VARIES
DEPTH OF STRUCTURE
MAKE BOND WITH WATER-RESISTANT MATERIAL
BASE COURSE FLASHING
BASE COURSE AT SILL OF MASONRY CONSTRUCTION

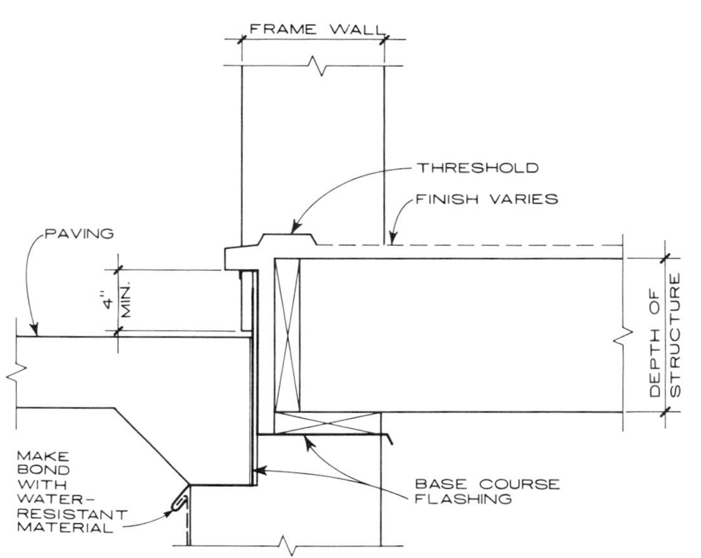
FRAME WALL
THRESHOLD
FINISH VARIES
PAVING
4" MIN.
DEPTH OF STRUCTURE
MAKE BOND WITH WATER-RESISTANT MATERIAL
BASE COURSE FLASHING
BASE COURSE AT SILL OF FRAME CONSTRUCTION

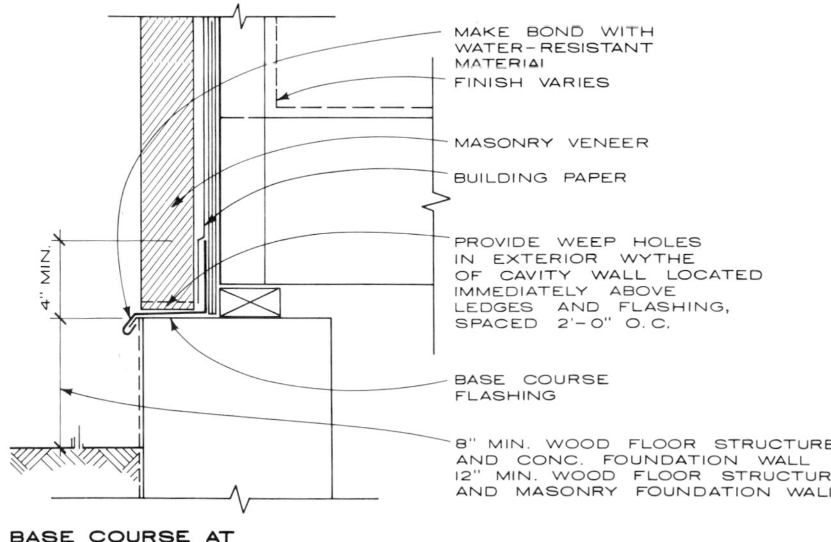
MAKE BOND WITH WATER-RESISTANT MATERIAL
FINISH VARIES
MASONRY VENEER
BUILDING PAPER
PROVIDE WEEP HOLES IN EXTERIOR WYTHE OF CAVITY WALL LOCATED IMMEDIATELY ABOVE LEDGES AND FLASHING, SPACED 2'-0" O. C.
4" MIN.
BASE COURSE FLASHING
8" MIN. WOOD FLOOR STRUCTURE AND CONC. FOUNDATION WALL
12" MIN. WOOD FLOOR STRUCTURE AND MASONRY FOUNDATION WALL
BASE COURSE AT MASONRY VENEER

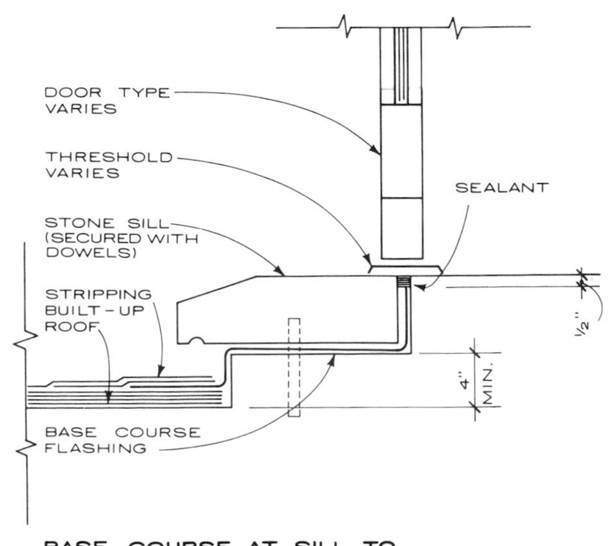
DOOR TYPE VARIES
THRESHOLD VARIES
SEALANT
STONE SILL (SECURED WITH DOWELS)
STRIPPING
BUILT-UP ROOF
½"
4" MIN.
BASE COURSE FLASHING
BASE COURSE AT SILL TO BUILT-UP ROOF

Michael Scott Rudden, The Stephens Associates P.C.—Architects; Albany, New York

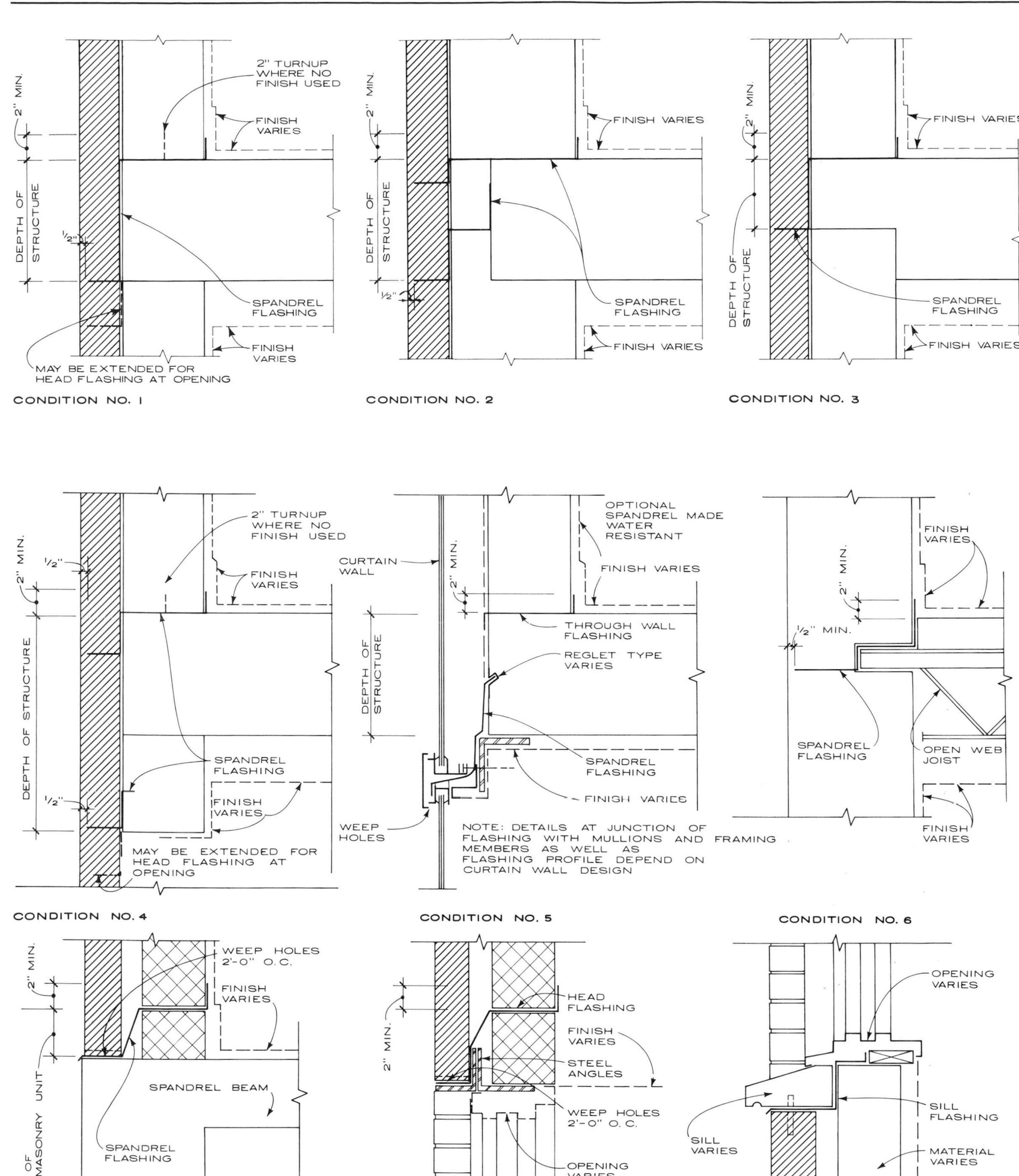
2" MIN.
DEPTH OF STRUCTURE
1/2"
2" TURNUP WHERE NO FINISH USED
FINISH VARIES
SPANDREL FLASHING
FINISH VARIES
MAY BE EXTENDED FOR HEAD FLASHING AT OPENING
CONDITION NO. 1
2" MIN.
DEPTH OF STRUCTURE
1/2"
FINISH VARIES
SPANDREL FLASHING
FINISH VARIES
CONDITION NO. 2
2" MIN.
DEPTH OF STRUCTURE
FINISH VARIES
SPANDREL FLASHING
FINISH VARIES
CONDITION NO. 3
2" MIN.
1/2"
DEPTH OF STRUCTURE
1/2"
2" TURNUP WHERE NO FINISH USED
FINISH VARIES
SPANDREL FLASHING
FINISH VARIES
MAY BE EXTENDED FOR HEAD FLASHING AT OPENING
CONDITION NO. 4
CURTAIN WALL
2" MIN.
DEPTH OF STRUCTURE
OPTIONAL SPANDREL MADE WATER RESISTANT
FINISH VARIES
THROUGH WALL FLASHING
REGLET TYPE VARIES
SPANDREL FLASHING
FINISH VARIES
WEEP HOLES
NOTE: DETAILS AT JUNCTION OF FLASHING WITH MULLIONS AND FRAMING MEMBERS AS WELL AS FLASHING PROFILE DEPEND ON CURTAIN WALL DESIGN
CONDITION NO. 5
2" MIN.
1/2" MIN.
FINISH VARIES
SPANDREL FLASHING
OPEN WEB JOIST
FINISH VARIES
CONDITION NO. 6
2" MIN.
HEIGHT OF CONC. MASONRY UNIT
WEEP HOLES 2'-0" O.C.
FINISH VARIES
SPANDREL BEAM
SPANDREL FLASHING
FINISH VARIES
CONDITION NO. 7
2" MIN.
HEAD FLASHING
FINISH VARIES
STEEL ANGLES
WEEP HOLES 2'-0" O.C.
OPENING VARIES
HEAD FLASHING
OPENING VARIES
SILL VARIES
SILL FLASHING
MATERIAL VARIES
FINISH VARIES
SILL FLASHING

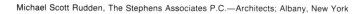

Michael Scott Rudden, The Stephens Associates P.C.—Architects; Albany, New York

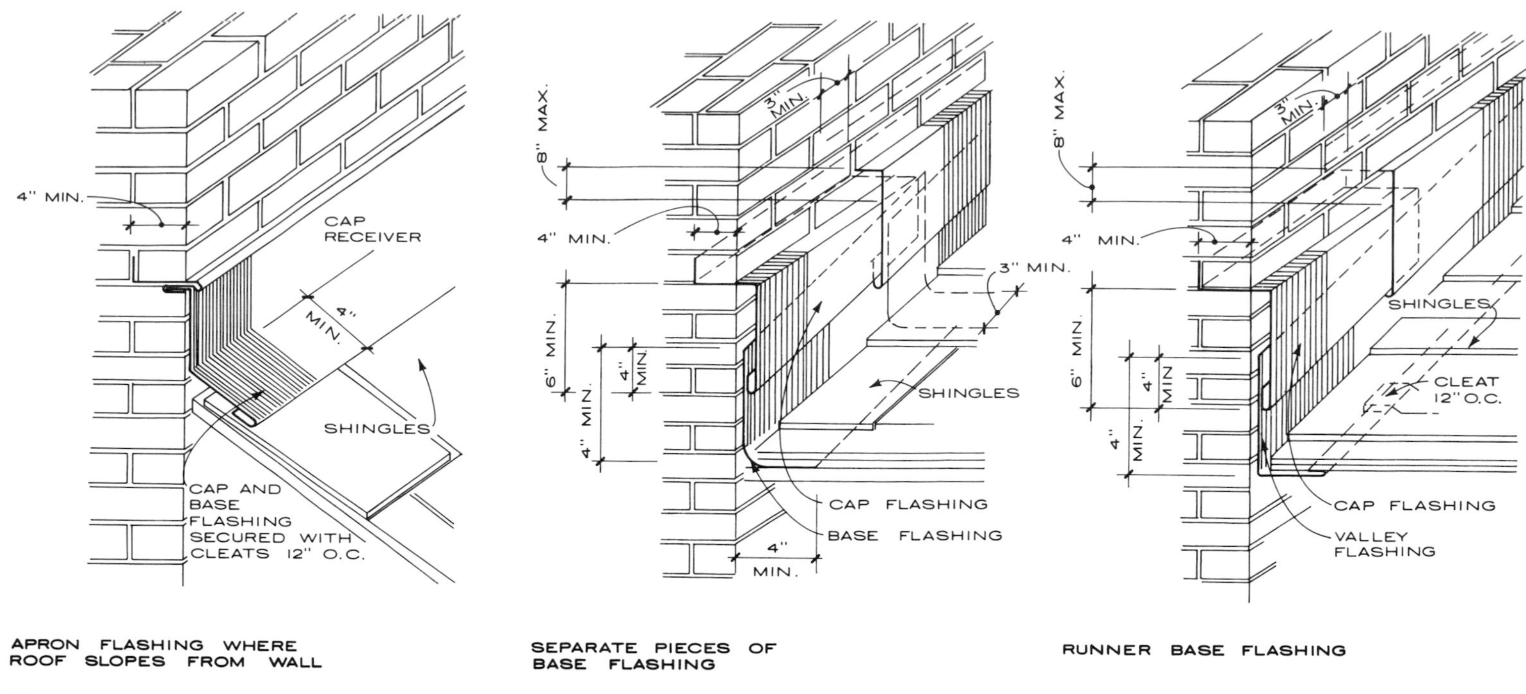
4" MIN.
CAP RECEIVER
4" MIN.
SHINGLES
CAP AND BASE FLASHING SECURED WITH CLEATS 12" O.C.
8" MAX.
3" MIN.
4" MIN.
3" MIN.
6" MIN.
4" MIN.
4" MIN.
SHINGLES
CAP FLASHING
BASE FLASHING
4" MIN.
8" MAX.
3" MIN.
4" MIN.
SHINGLES
6" MIN.
4" MIN.
4" MIN.
CLEAT 12" O.C.
CAP FLASHING
VALLEY FLASHING

APRON FLASHING WHERE ROOF SLOPES FROM WALL

SEPARATE PIECES OF BASE FLASHING

RUNNER BASE FLASHING

PITCHED ROOF WITH WALL FLASHING

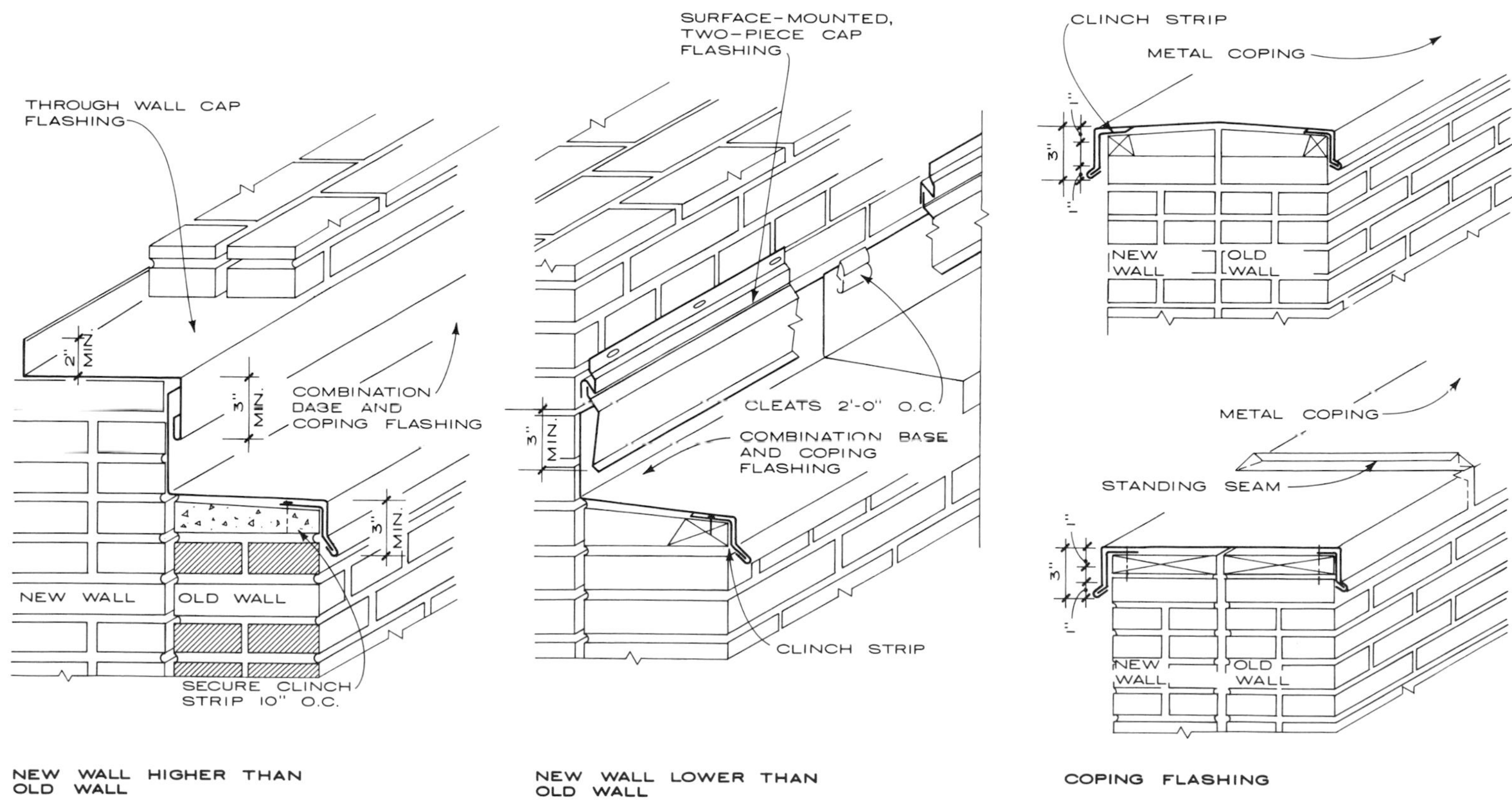
THROUGH WALL CAP FLASHING
2" MIN.
3" MIN.
COMBINATION BASE AND COPING FLASHING
3" MIN.
NEW WALL
OLD WALL
SECURE CLINCH STRIP 10" O.C.
SURFACE-MOUNTED, TWO-PIECE CAP FLASHING
CLEATS 2'-0" O.C.
3" MIN.
COMBINATION BASE AND COPING FLASHING
CLINCH STRIP
CLINCH STRIP
METAL COPING
1"
3"
1"
NEW WALL
OLD WALL
METAL COPING
STANDING SEAM
1"
3"
1"
NEW WALL
OLD WALL

NEW WALL HIGHER THAN OLD WALL

NEW WALL LOWER THAN OLD WALL

COPING FLASHING

NEW WALL TO OLD WALL FLASHING

NOTE

Through wall flashing not recommended in earthquake areas.

Michael Scott Rudden, The Stephens Associates P.C.—Architects; Albany, New York

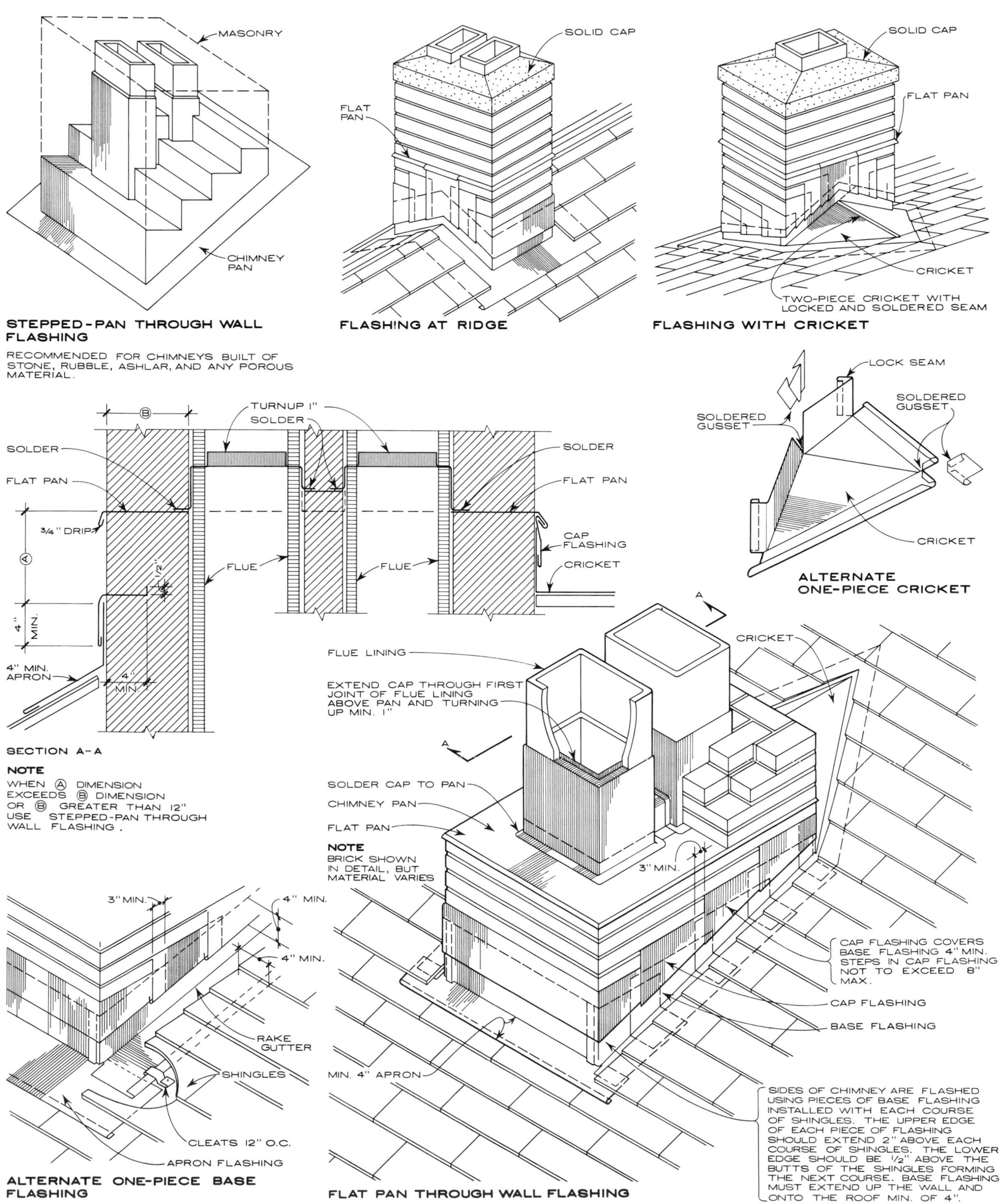
MASONRY
CHIMNEY PAN
STEPPED-PAN THROUGH WALL FLASHING
RECOMMENDED FOR CHIMNEYS BUILT OF STONE, RUBBLE, ASHLAR, AND ANY POROUS MATERIAL.
SOLID CAP
FLAT PAN
FLASHING AT RIDGE
SOLID CAP
FLAT PAN
CRICKET
TWO-PIECE CRICKET WITH LOCKED AND SOLDERED SEAM
FLASHING WITH CRICKET
TURNUP 1"
SOLDER
SOLDER
FLAT PAN
3/4" DRIP
FLUE
FLUE
SOLDER
FLAT PAN
CAP FLASHING
CRICKET
4" MIN.
4" MIN. APRON
4" MIN.
1/2"
SECTION A-A
NOTE
WHEN Ⓐ DIMENSION EXCEEDS Ⓑ DIMENSION OR Ⓑ GREATER THAN 12" USE STEPPED-PAN THROUGH WALL FLASHING.
LOCK SEAM
SOLDERED GUSSET
SOLDERED GUSSET
CRICKET
ALTERNATE ONE-PIECE CRICKET
FLUE LINING
EXTEND CAP THROUGH FIRST JOINT OF FLUE LINING ABOVE PAN AND TURNING UP MIN. 1"
CRICKET
SOLDER CAP TO PAN
CHIMNEY PAN
FLAT PAN
NOTE
BRICK SHOWN IN DETAIL, BUT MATERIAL VARIES
3" MIN.
CAP FLASHING COVERS BASE FLASHING 4" MIN. STEPS IN CAP FLASHING NOT TO EXCEED 8" MAX.
CAP FLASHING
BASE FLASHING
MIN. 4" APRON
SIDES OF CHIMNEY ARE FLASHED USING PIECES OF BASE FLASHING INSTALLED WITH EACH COURSE OF SHINGLES. THE UPPER EDGE OF EACH PIECE OF FLASHING SHOULD EXTEND 2" ABOVE EACH COURSE OF SHINGLES. THE LOWER EDGE SHOULD BE 1/2" ABOVE THE BUTTS OF THE SHINGLES FORMING THE NEXT COURSE. BASE FLASHING MUST EXTEND UP THE WALL AND ONTO THE ROOF MIN. OF 4".
FLAT PAN THROUGH WALL FLASHING
3" MIN.
4" MIN.
4" MIN.
RAKE GUTTER
SHINGLES
CLEATS 12" O.C.
APRON FLASHING
ALTERNATE ONE-PIECE BASE FLASHING

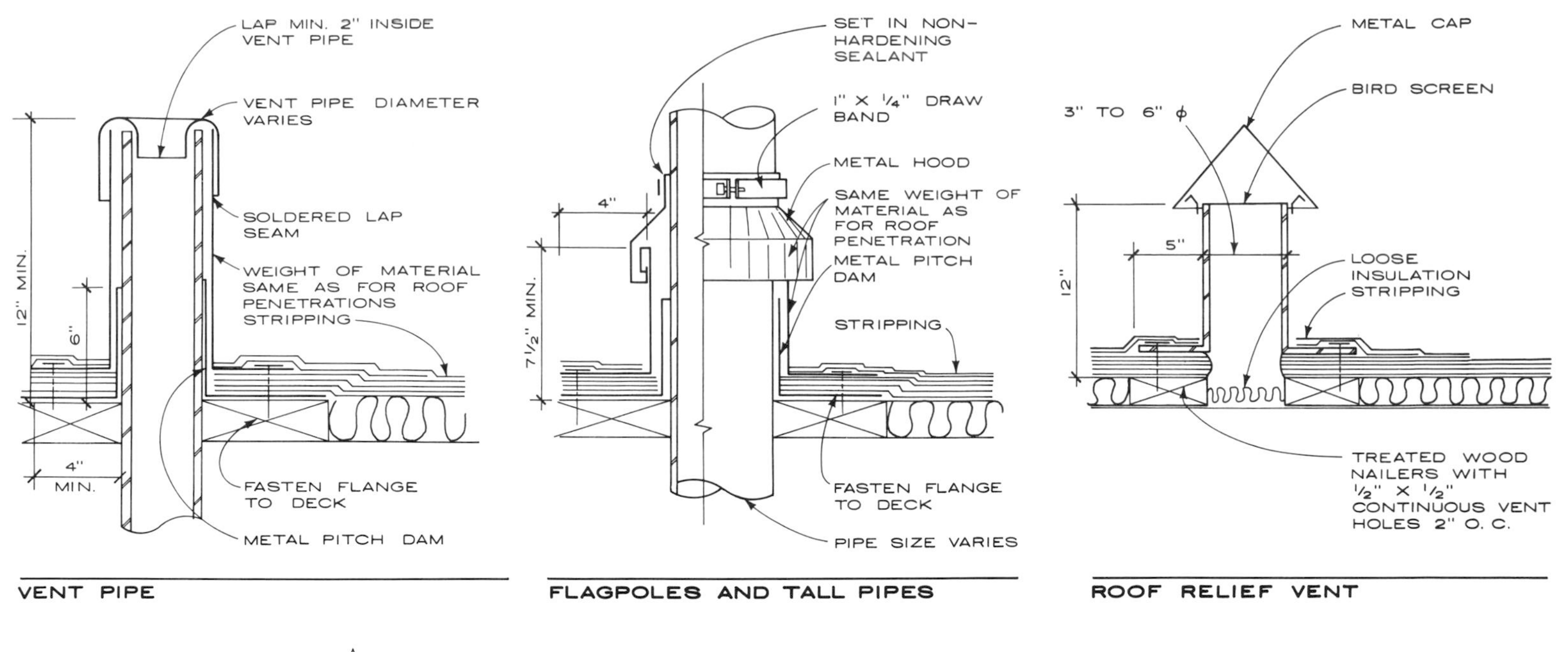
LAP MIN. 2" INSIDE VENT PIPE
VENT PIPE DIAMETER VARIES
SOLDERED LAP SEAM
WEIGHT OF MATERIAL SAME AS FOR ROOF PENETRATIONS
STRIPPING
12" MIN.
6"
4" MIN.
FASTEN FLANGE TO DECK
METAL PITCH DAM
VENT PIPE
SET IN NON-HARDENING SEALANT
1" X 1/4" DRAW BAND
METAL HOOD
SAME WEIGHT OF MATERIAL AS FOR ROOF PENETRATION
METAL PITCH DAM
STRIPPING
4"
7 1/2" MIN.
FASTEN FLANGE TO DECK
PIPE SIZE VARIES
FLAGPOLES AND TALL PIPES
METAL CAP
BIRD SCREEN
3" TO 6" ϕ
5"
12"
LOOSE INSULATION STRIPPING
TREATED WOOD NAILERS WITH 1/2" X 1/2" CONTINUOUS VENT HOLES 2" O. C.
ROOF RELIEF VENT

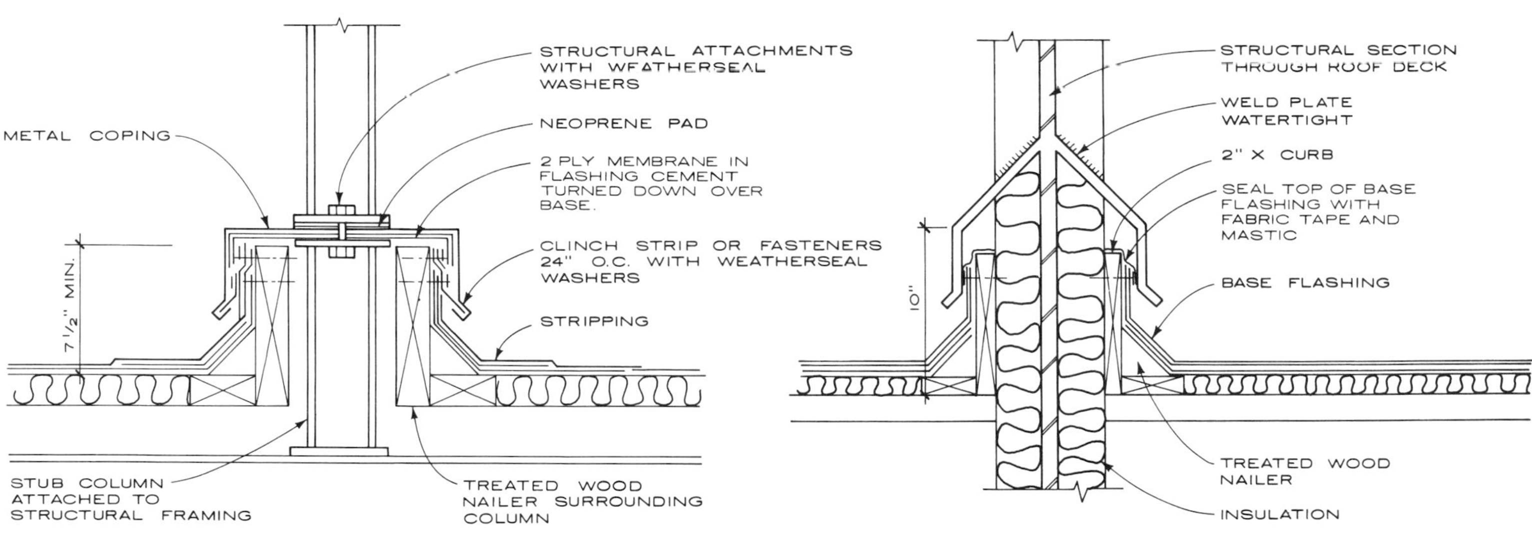
STRUCTURAL ATTACHMENTS WITH WEATHERSEAL WASHERS
METAL COPING
NEOPRENE PAD
2 PLY MEMBRANE IN FLASHING CEMENT TURNED DOWN OVER BASE.
CLINCH STRIP OR FASTENERS 24" O.C. WITH WEATHERSEAL WASHERS
STRIPPING
7 1/2" MIN.
STUB COLUMN ATTACHED TO STRUCTURAL FRAMING
TREATED WOOD NAILER SURROUNDING COLUMN
STRUCTURAL SECTION THROUGH ROOF DECK
WELD PLATE WATERTIGHT
2" X CURB
SEAL TOP OF BASE FLASHING WITH FABRIC TAPE AND MASTIC
BASE FLASHING
10"
TREATED WOOD NAILER
INSULATION

FUTURE COLUMNS, SIGN SUPPORTS, AND STEEL ANGLES

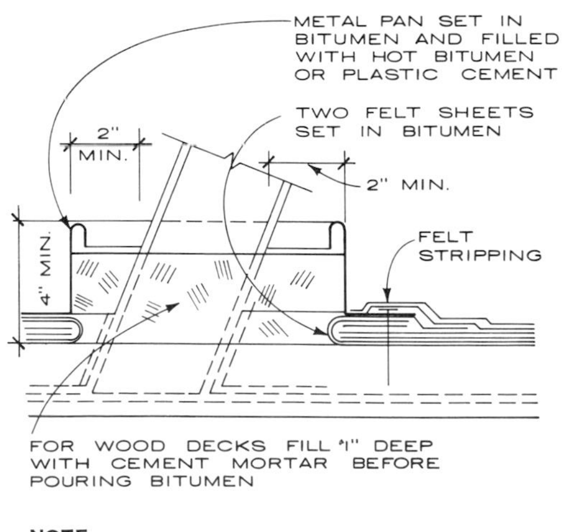
METAL PAN SET IN BITUMEN AND FILLED WITH HOT BITUMEN OR PLASTIC CEMENT
TWO FELT SHEETS SET IN BITUMEN
2" MIN.
2" MIN.
FELT STRIPPING
4" MIN.
FOR WOOD DECKS FILL 1" DEEP WITH CEMENT MORTAR BEFORE POURING BITUMEN

NOTE

Whenever possible avoid the use of pitch pockets in favor of curbs with base and cap flashing around the penetrating member.

PITCH POCKET

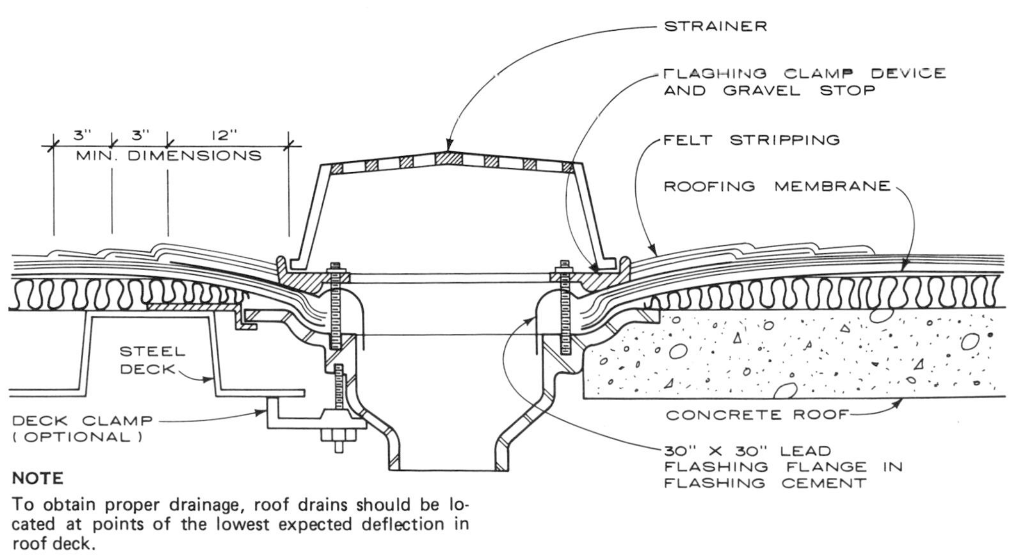
STRAINER
FLASHING CLAMP DEVICE AND GRAVEL STOP
FELT STRIPPING
ROOFING MEMBRANE
3" 3" 12"
MIN. DIMENSIONS
STEEL DECK
DECK CLAMP (OPTIONAL)
CONCRETE ROOF
30" X 30" LEAD FLASHING FLANGE IN FLASHING CEMENT

NOTE

To obtain proper drainage, roof drains should be located at points of the lowest expected deflection in roof deck.

ROOF DRAIN

Michael Scott Rudden, The Stephens Associates P.C.—Architects; Albany, New York

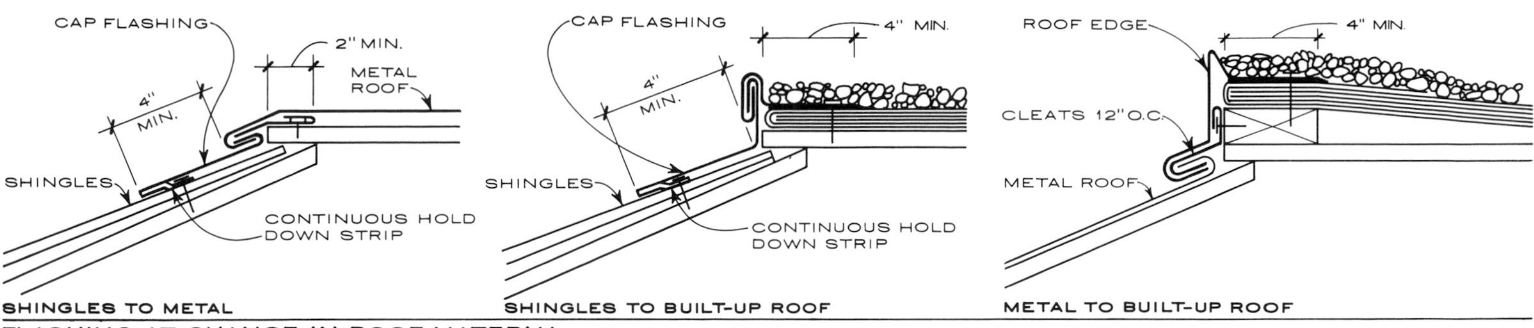
CAP FLASHING
2" MIN.
METAL ROOF
4" MIN.
SHINGLES
CONTINUOUS HOLD DOWN STRIP
CAP FLASHING
4" MIN.
4" MIN.
SHINGLES
CONTINUOUS HOLD DOWN STRIP
ROOF EDGE
4" MIN.
CLEATS 12" O.C.
METAL ROOF

SHINGLES TO METAL

SHINGLES TO BUILT-UP ROOF

METAL TO BUILT-UP ROOF

FLASHING AT CHANGE IN ROOF MATERIAL

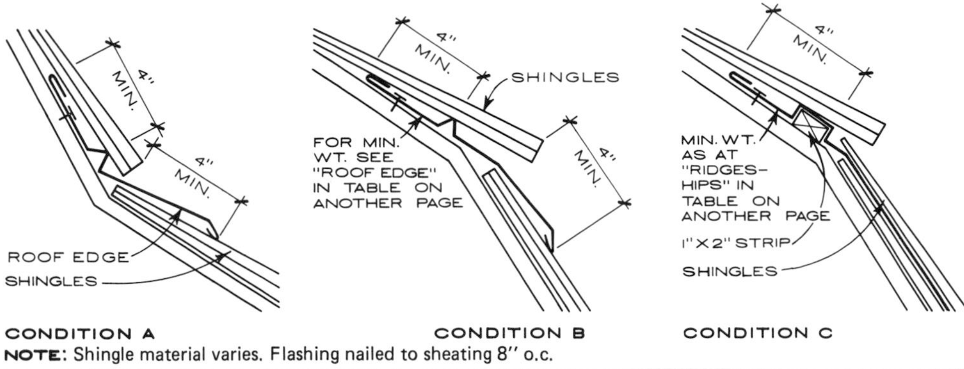
4" MIN.
4" MIN.
ROOF EDGE
SHINGLES
4" MIN.
SHINGLES
FOR MIN. WT. SEE "ROOF EDGE" IN TABLE ON ANOTHER PAGE
4" MIN.
4" MIN.
MIN. WT. AS AT "RIDGES-HIPS" IN TABLE ON ANOTHER PAGE
1" X 2" STRIP
SHINGLES

CONDITION A

CONDITION B

CONDITION C

NOTE: Shingle material varies. Flashing nailed to sheating 8" o.c.

FLASHING OF BREAK IN SLOPE OF SHINGLE ROOFS

SHINGLE MATERIAL VARIES

5" MIN.

CLEATS 2'-0" O.C.

PROVIDE 1" "V" CRIMP FOR SLOPES LESS THAN 6/12

5" MIN.

VALLEY FLASHING

EQUAL SLOPES

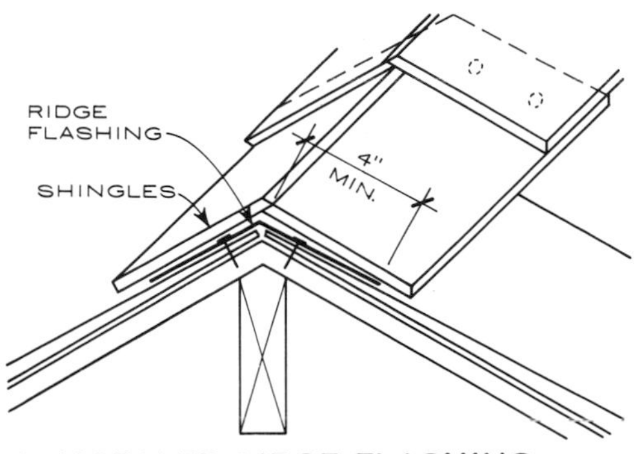
RIDGE FLASHING
SHINGLES
4" MIN.

CONCEALED RIDGE FLASHING

NOTE

Ridge flashing formed in 10' lengths and lapped 4". Flashing is nailed to sheathing after shingles are installed, then flashing is covered with ridge shingles.

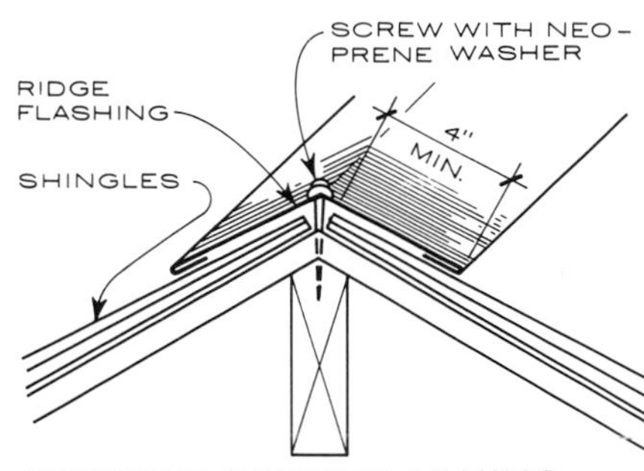
SCREW WITH NEO-PRENE WASHER
RIDGE FLASHING
SHINGLES
4" MIN.

EXPOSED RIDGE FLASHING

NOTE

Ridge flashing formed in 10' lengths and lapped 4".

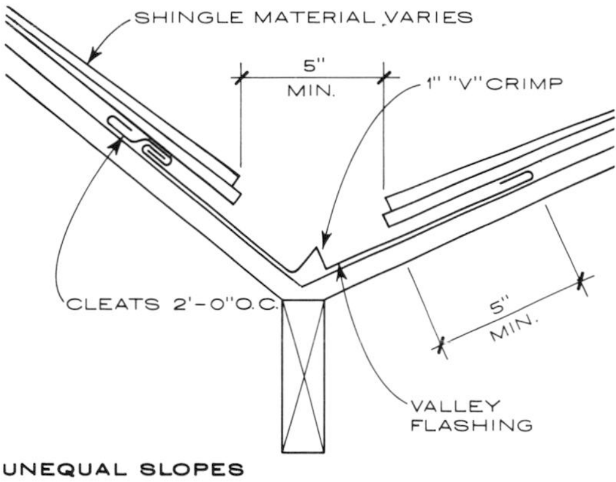
SHINGLE MATERIAL VARIES
5" MIN.
1" "V" CRIMP
CLEATS 2'-0" O.C.
5" MIN.
VALLEY FLASHING

UNEQUAL SLOPES

OPEN VALLEY FLASHING

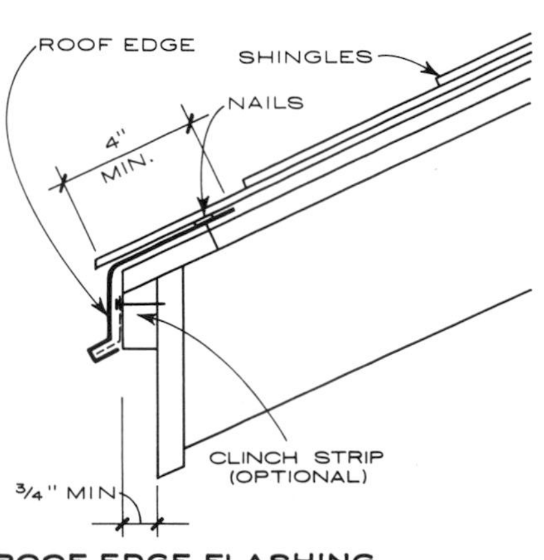
ROOF EDGE
SHINGLES
NAILS
4" MIN.
CLINCH STRIP (OPTIONAL)
3/4" MIN.

ROOF EDGE FLASHING

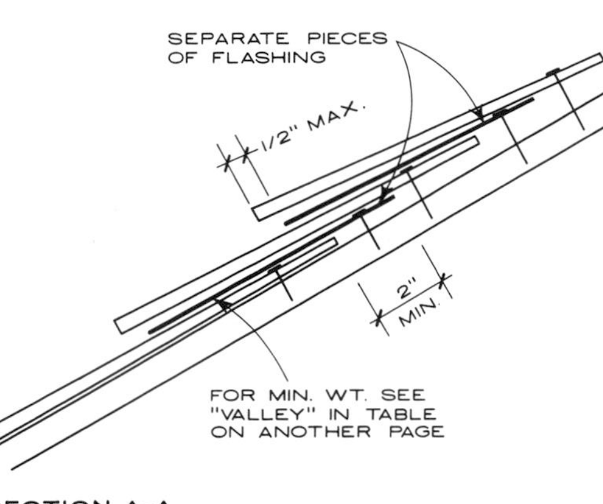
SEPARATE PIECES OF FLASHING
1/2" MAX.
2" MIN.
FOR MIN. WT. SEE "VALLEY" IN TABLE ON ANOTHER PAGE

SECTION A-A

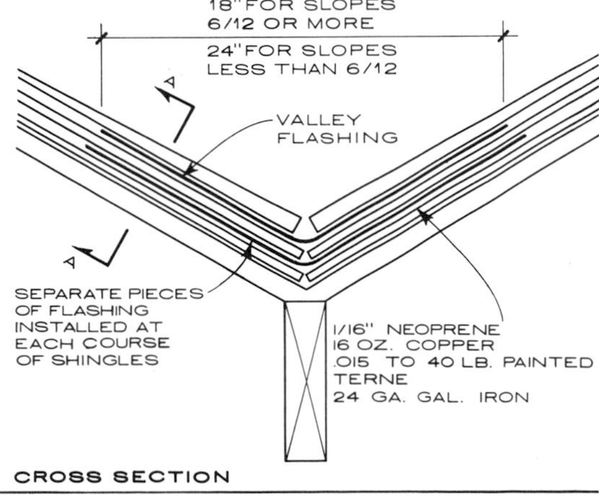
18" FOR SLOPES 6/12 OR MORE
24" FOR SLOPES LESS THAN 6/12
A
VALLEY FLASHING
A
SEPARATE PIECES OF FLASHING INSTALLED AT EACH COURSE OF SHINGLES
1/16" NEOPRENE
16 OZ. COPPER
.015 TO 40 LB. PAINTED TERNE
24 GA. GAL. IRON

CROSS SECTION

CONCEALED VALLEY FLASHING

Michael Scott Rudden, The Stephens Associates P.C.—Architects; Albany, New York

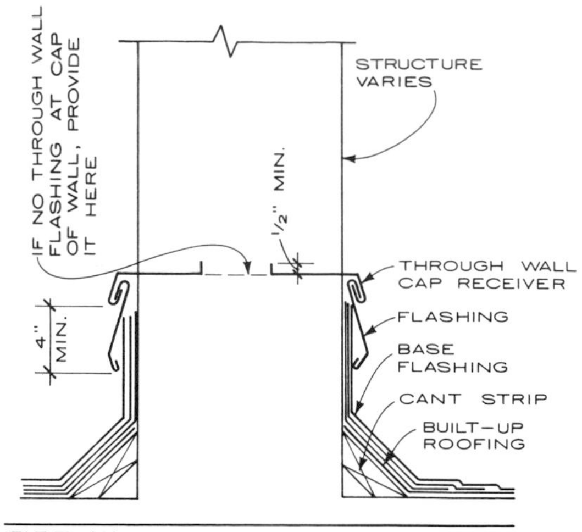

IF NO THROUGH WALL FLASHING AT CAP OF WALL, PROVIDE IT HERE
STRUCTURE VARIES
1/2" MIN.
4" MIN.
THROUGH WALL CAP RECEIVER
FLASHING
BASE FLASHING
CANT STRIP
BUILT-UP ROOFING

FIRE WALL

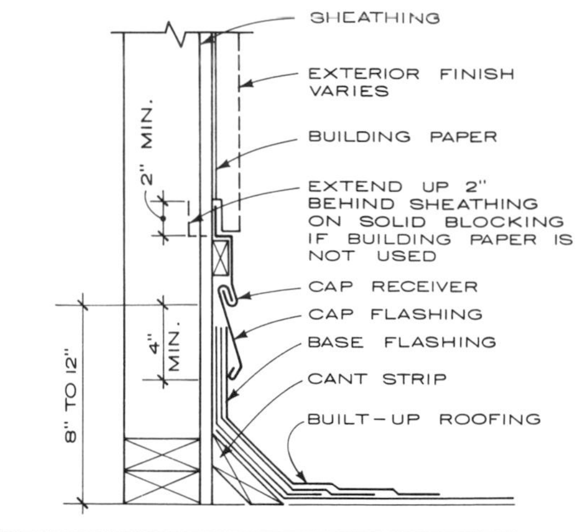

SHEATHING
EXTERIOR FINISH VARIES
BUILDING PAPER
EXTEND UP 2" BEHIND SHEATHING ON SOLID BLOCKING IF BUILDING PAPER IS NOT USED
CAP RECEIVER
CAP FLASHING
BASE FLASHING
CANT STRIP
BUILT-UP ROOFING
2" MIN.
4" MIN.
8" TO 12"

FRAME WALL

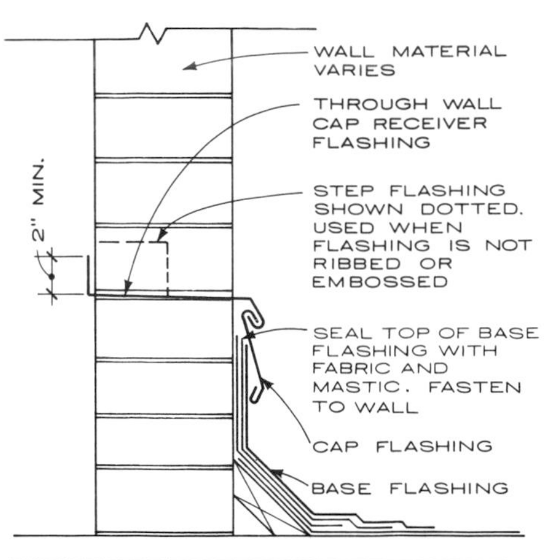

WALL MATERIAL VARIES
THROUGH WALL CAP RECEIVER FLASHING
STEP FLASHING SHOWN DOTTED. USED WHEN FLASHING IS NOT RIBBED OR EMBOSSED
SEAL TOP OF BASE FLASHING WITH FABRIC AND MASTIC. FASTEN TO WALL
CAP FLASHING
BASE FLASHING
2" MIN.

MASONRY WALL

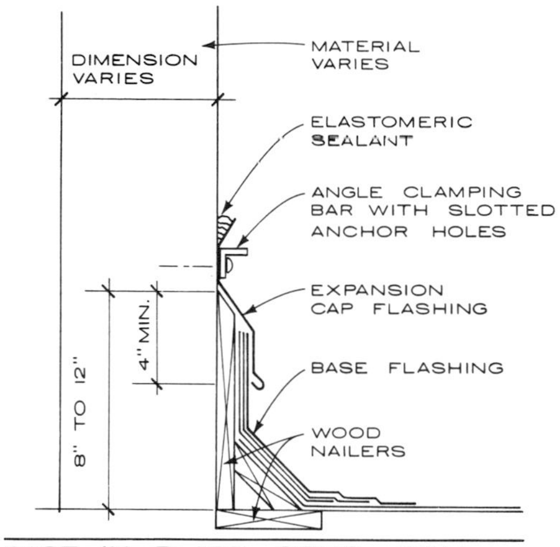

DIMENSION VARIES
MATERIAL VARIES
ELASTOMERIC SEALANT
ANGLE CLAMPING BAR WITH SLOTTED ANCHOR HOLES
EXPANSION CAP FLASHING
BASE FLASHING
WOOD NAILERS
4" MIN.
8" TO 12"

CAST IN PLACE CONC. WALL

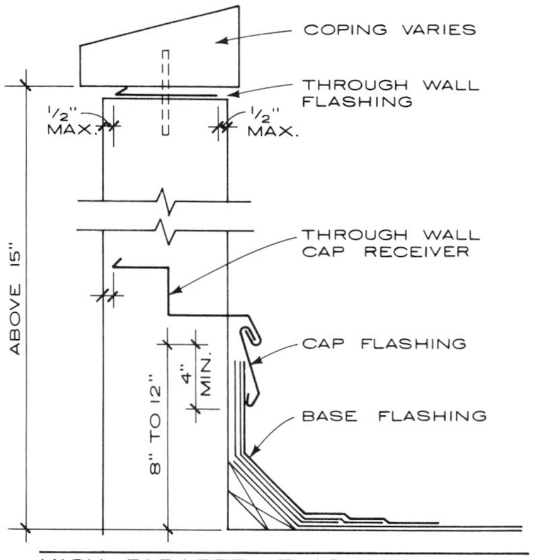

COPING VARIES
THROUGH WALL FLASHING
1/2" MAX.
1/2" MAX.
THROUGH WALL CAP RECEIVER
CAP FLASHING
BASE FLASHING
ABOVE 15"
8" TO 12"
4" MIN.

HIGH PARAPET FLASHING

COPING VARIES
THROUGH WALL CAP RECEIVER
1/2" MAX.
METAL STANDING SEAM PARAPET LINER
CLEAT AT STANDING SEAM
BASE FLASHING
ABOVE 15"
8" TO 12"
4" MIN.

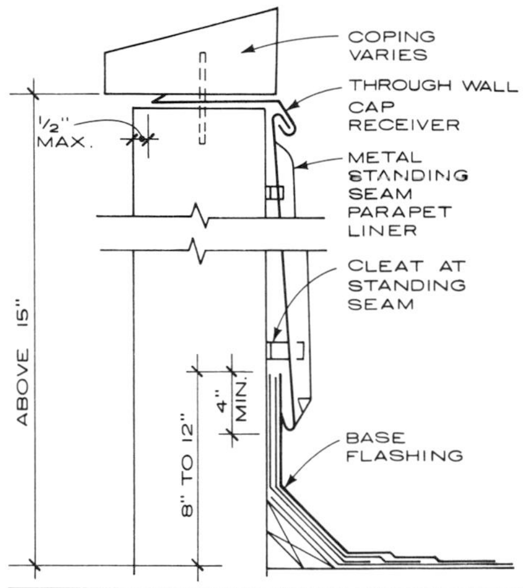

HIGH PARAPET WITH LINING

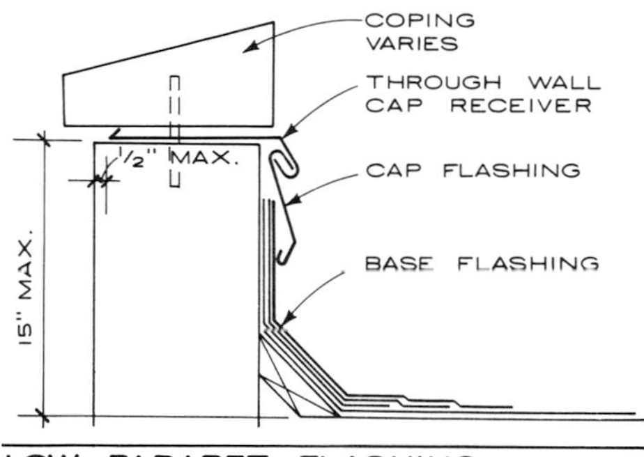
COPING VARIES
THROUGH WALL CAP RECEIVER
1/2" MAX.
CAP FLASHING
BASE FLASHING
15" MAX.

LOW PARAPET FLASHING

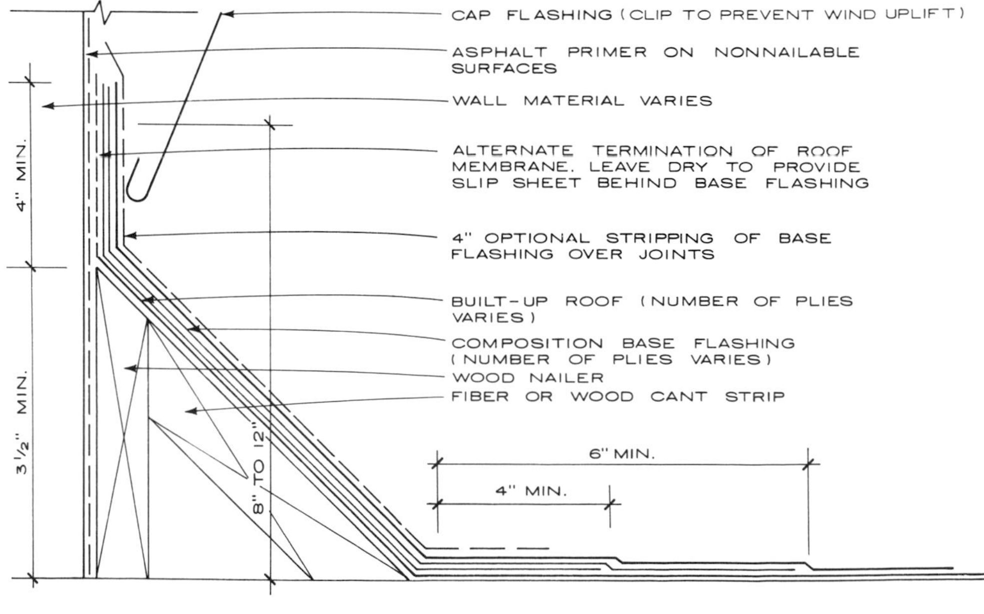
CAP FLASHING (CLIP TO PREVENT WIND UPLIFT)
ASPHALT PRIMER ON NONNAILABLE SURFACES
WALL MATERIAL VARIES
ALTERNATE TERMINATION OF ROOF MEMBRANE. LEAVE DRY TO PROVIDE SLIP SHEET BEHIND BASE FLASHING
4" OPTIONAL STRIPPING OF BASE FLASHING OVER JOINTS
BUILT-UP ROOF (NUMBER OF PLIES VARIES)
COMPOSITION BASE FLASHING (NUMBER OF PLIES VARIES)
WOOD NAILER
FIBER OR WOOD CANT STRIP
4" MIN.
3 1/2" MIN.
8" TO 12"
6" MIN.
4" MIN.

TYPICAL BASE FLASHING

GENERAL NOTES

1. Select flashing that is flexible for molding to flashing supports and that can withstand expected thermal, wind, and structural movement. Provide expansion joints in place of flashing as required by conditions.
2. Consult manufacturer's literature for choice of flashing materials and details.
3. Avoid sharp bends in bituminous base flashings. Use cant strips with 45° maximum bend.
4. Provision for differential movement between roof deck and wall is recommended.
5. A ribbed or embossed pattern should be used for all through wall flashing. Through wall flashing is not recommended for earthquake areas.
6. Base flashing should extend 8 to 12 in. above highest anticipated waterline. Metal counterflashing should lap base flashing by at least 4 in. Lap all vertical joints.

Michael Scott Rudden, The Stephens Associates P.C.—Architects; Albany, New York

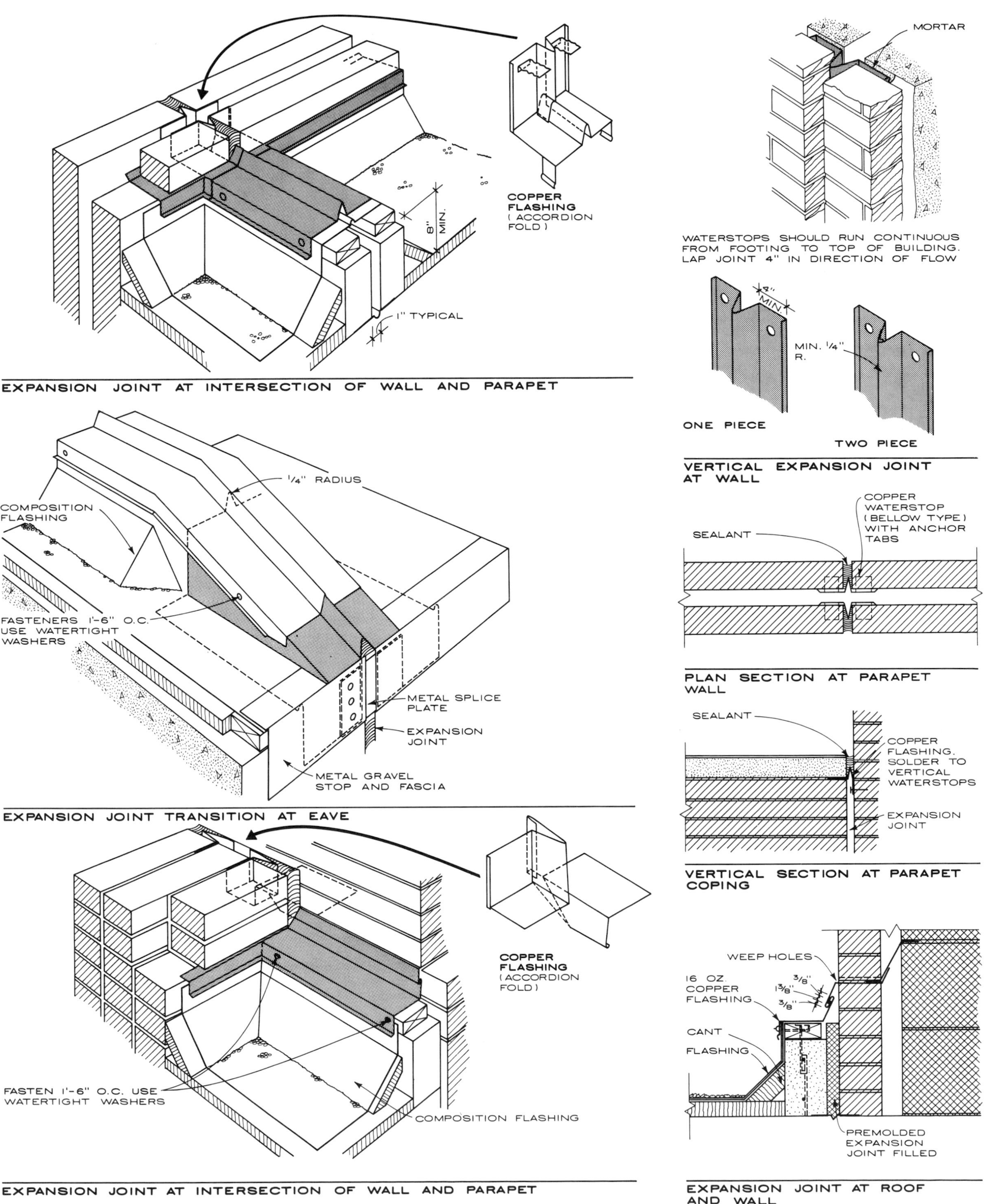
COPPER FLASHING (ACCORDION FOLD)
8" MIN.
1" TYPICAL
EXPANSION JOINT AT INTERSECTION OF WALL AND PARAPET
MORTAR
WATERSTOPS SHOULD RUN CONTINUOUS FROM FOOTING TO TOP OF BUILDING. LAP JOINT 4" IN DIRECTION OF FLOW
4" MIN
MIN. 1/4" R.
ONE PIECE
TWO PIECE
VERTICAL EXPANSION JOINT AT WALL
1/4" RADIUS
COMPOSITION FLASHING
FASTENERS 1'-6" O.C. USE WATERTIGHT WASHERS
METAL SPLICE PLATE
EXPANSION JOINT
METAL GRAVEL STOP AND FASCIA
EXPANSION JOINT TRANSITION AT EAVE
SEALANT
COPPER WATERSTOP (BELLOW TYPE) WITH ANCHOR TABS
PLAN SECTION AT PARAPET WALL
SEALANT
COPPER FLASHING. SOLDER TO VERTICAL WATERSTOPS
EXPANSION JOINT
VERTICAL SECTION AT PARAPET COPING
COPPER FLASHING (ACCORDION FOLD)
FASTEN 1'-6" O.C. USE WATERTIGHT WASHERS
COMPOSITION FLASHING
EXPANSION JOINT AT INTERSECTION OF WALL AND PARAPET
WEEP HOLES
16 OZ. COPPER FLASHING
3/8"
1 3/8"
3/8"
CANT
FLASHING
PREMOLDED EXPANSION JOINT FILLED
EXPANSION JOINT AT ROOF AND WALL

CTA Architects Engineers; Billings, Montana

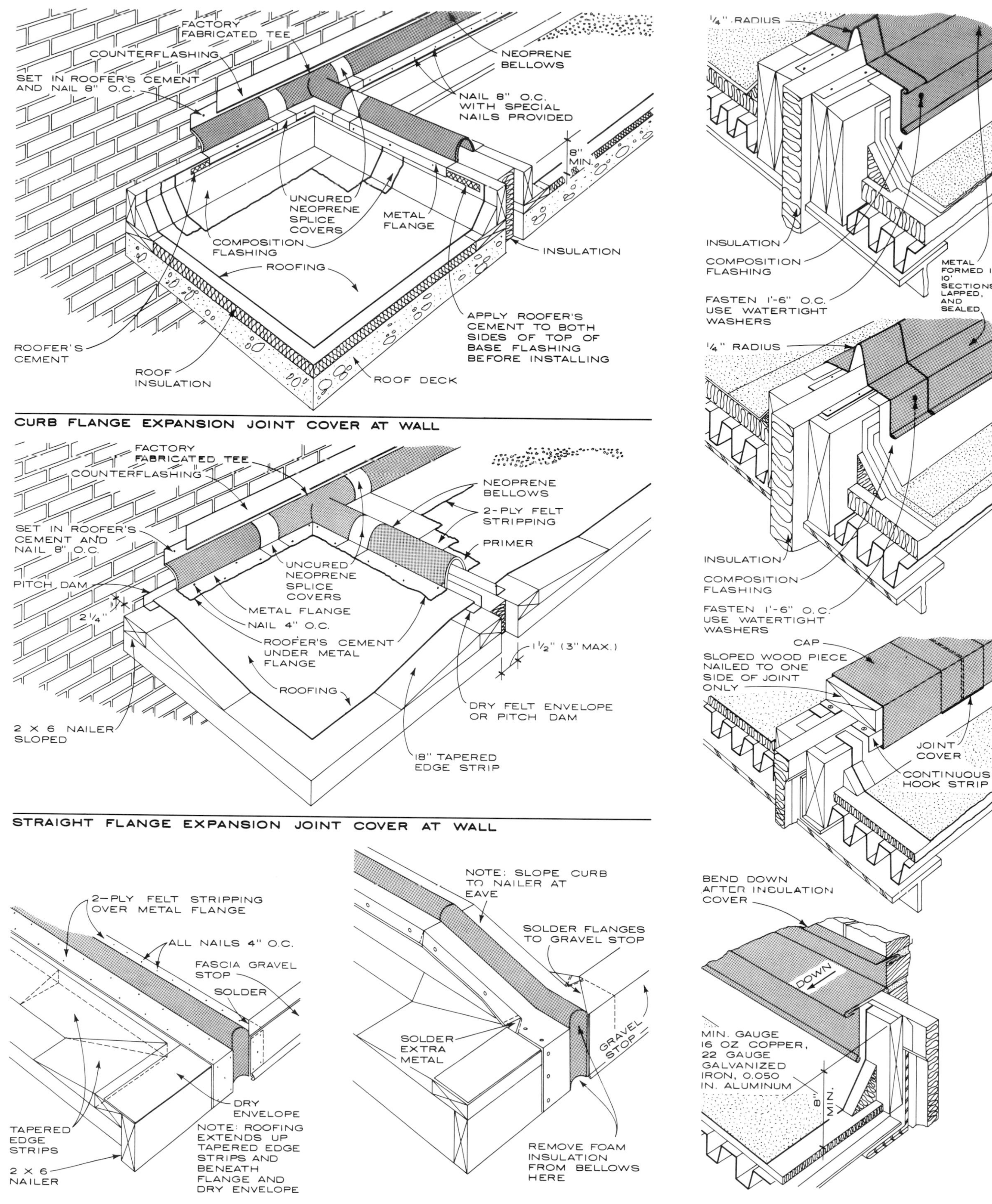

FACTORY FABRICATED TEE
COUNTERFLASHING
SET IN ROOFER'S CEMENT AND NAIL 8" O.C.
NEOPRENE BELLOWS
NAIL 8" O.C. WITH SPECIAL NAILS PROVIDED
8" MIN.
UNCURED NEOPRENE SPLICE COVERS
METAL FLANGE
COMPOSITION FLASHING
INSULATION
ROOFING
APPLY ROOFER'S CEMENT TO BOTH SIDES OF TOP OF BASE FLASHING BEFORE INSTALLING
ROOFER'S CEMENT
ROOF INSULATION
ROOF DECK
CURB FLANGE EXPANSION JOINT COVER AT WALL
FACTORY FABRICATED TEE
COUNTERFLASHING
SET IN ROOFER'S CEMENT AND NAIL 8" O.C.
NEOPRENE BELLOWS
2-PLY FELT STRIPPING
PRIMER
PITCH DAM
2 1/4"
UNCURED NEOPRENE SPLICE COVERS
METAL FLANGE
NAIL 4" O.C.
ROOFER'S CEMENT UNDER METAL FLANGE
1 1/2" (3" MAX.)
ROOFING
DRY FELT ENVELOPE OR PITCH DAM
2 x 6 NAILER SLOPED
18" TAPERED EDGE STRIP
STRAIGHT FLANGE EXPANSION JOINT COVER AT WALL
1/4" RADIUS
INSULATION
COMPOSITION FLASHING
FASTEN 1'-6" O.C. USE WATERTIGHT WASHERS
METAL FORMED IN 10' SECTIONS, LAPPED, AND SEALED
1/4" RADIUS
INSULATION
COMPOSITION FLASHING
FASTEN 1'-6" O.C. USE WATERTIGHT WASHERS
CAP
SLOPED WOOD PIECE NAILED TO ONE SIDE OF JOINT ONLY
JOINT COVER
CONTINUOUS HOOK STRIP
2-PLY FELT STRIPPING OVER METAL FLANGE
ALL NAILS 4" O.C.
FASCIA GRAVEL STOP
SOLDER
DRY ENVELOPE
TAPERED EDGE STRIPS
2 x 6 NAILER
NOTE: ROOFING EXTENDS UP TAPERED EDGE STRIPS AND BENEATH FLANGE AND DRY ENVELOPE
STRAIGHT FLANGE AT GRAVEL STOP
NOTE: SLOPE CURB TO NAILER AT EAVE
SOLDER FLANGES TO GRAVEL STOP
SOLDER EXTRA METAL
GRAVEL STOP
REMOVE FOAM INSULATION FROM BELLOWS HERE
CURB FLANGE AT GRAVEL STOP
BEND DOWN AFTER INSULATION COVER
CAP
DOWN
MIN. GAUGE 16 OZ COPPER, 22 GAUGE GALVANIZED IRON, 0.050 IN. ALUMINUM
8" MIN.
BUILDING EXPANSION JOINTS

CTA Architects Engineers; Billings, Montana

RECOMMENDED MINIMUM GAUGES GRAVEL STOP–FASCIA

D (MAX.) (IN.)	GALVANIZED STEEL (GAUGE)	COPPER (OZ.)	ALUMINUM (IN.)	ZINC ALLOY (IN.)	STAINLESS STEEL (GAUGE)
4	24	16	0.025	0.020	26
5	24	16	0.032	0.027	26
6	22	20	0.040	0.027	24
7	22	20	0.040	–	22
8	20	20	0.050	–	20

RECOMMENDED MINIMUM GAUGES FOR COPING

WIDTH OF COPING TOP (IN.)	GALVANIZED STEEL (GAUGE)	STAINLESS STEEL (GAUGE)	ALUMINUM (IN.)	COPPER (OZ.)
Through 12	24	26	0.232	16
13 to 18	22	24	0.040	20

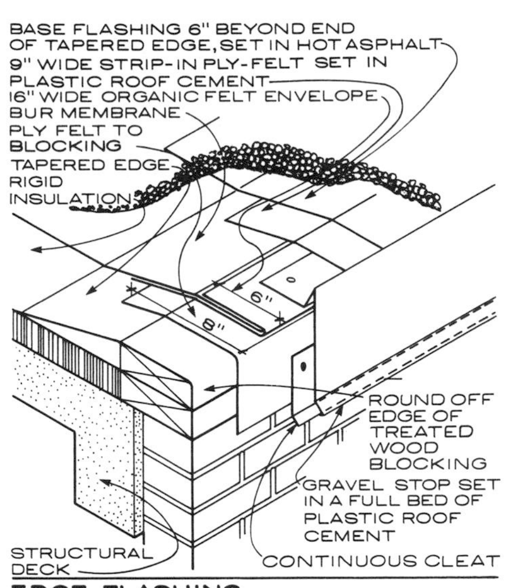
BASE FLASHING 6" BEYOND END OF TAPERED EDGE, SET IN HOT ASPHALT
9" WIDE STRIP-IN PLY-FELT SET IN PLASTIC ROOF CEMENT
16" WIDE ORGANIC FELT ENVELOPE
BUR MEMBRANE
PLY FELT TO BLOCKING
TAPERED EDGE
RIGID INSULATION
6"
8"
ROUND OFF EDGE OF TREATED WOOD BLOCKING
GRAVEL STOP SET IN A FULL BED OF PLASTIC ROOF CEMENT
STRUCTURAL DECK
CONTINUOUS CLEAT

EDGE FLASHING

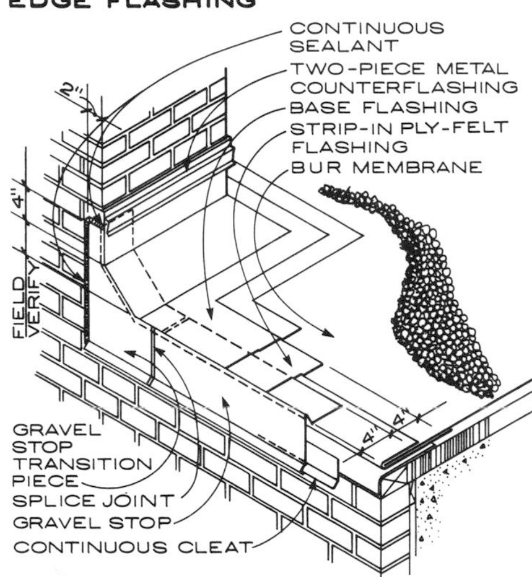
CONTINUOUS SEALANT
TWO-PIECE METAL COUNTERFLASHING
BASE FLASHING
STRIP-IN PLY-FELT FLASHING
BUR MEMBRANE
2"
4"
FIELD VERIFY
4"
4"
GRAVEL STOP TRANSITION PIECE
SPLICE JOINT
GRAVEL STOP
CONTINUOUS CLEAT

GRAVEL STOP TRANSITION

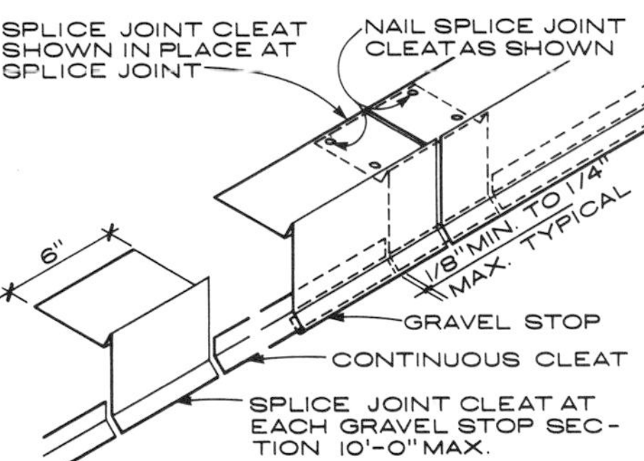
SPLICE JOINT CLEAT SHOWN IN PLACE AT SPLICE JOINT
NAIL SPLICE JOINT CLEAT AS SHOWN
6"
1/8" MIN. TO 1/4" MAX. TYPICAL
GRAVEL STOP
CONTINUOUS CLEAT
SPLICE JOINT CLEAT AT EACH GRAVEL STOP SECTION 10'-0" MAX.

GRAVEL STOP SPLICE JOINT

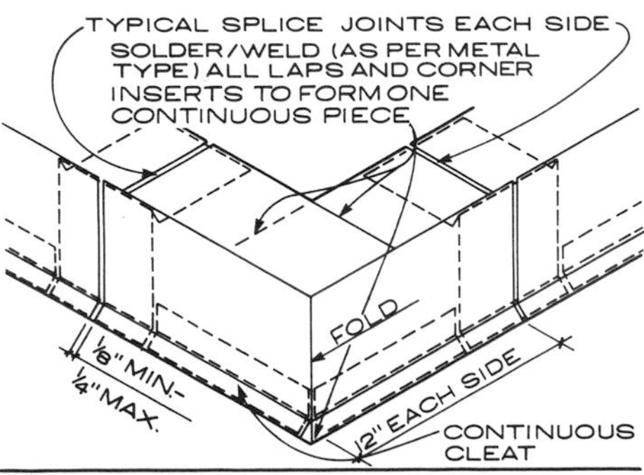
TYPICAL SPLICE JOINTS EACH SIDE
SOLDER/WELD (AS PER METAL TYPE) ALL LAPS AND CORNER INSERTS TO FORM ONE CONTINUOUS PIECE
FOLD
1/8" MIN.-1/4" MAX.
12" EACH SIDE
CONTINUOUS CLEAT

GRAVEL STOP OUTSIDE CORNER FABRICATION

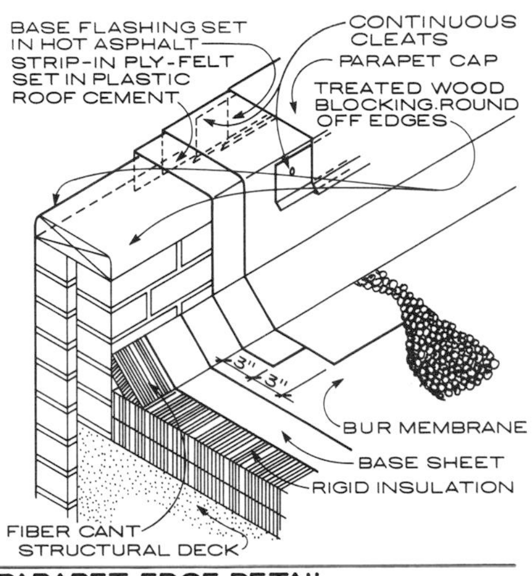
BASE FLASHING SET IN HOT ASPHALT
STRIP-IN PLY-FELT SET IN PLASTIC ROOF CEMENT
CONTINUOUS CLEATS
PARAPET CAP
TREATED WOOD BLOCKING. ROUND OFF EDGES
3"
3"
BUR MEMBRANE
BASE SHEET
RIGID INSULATION
FIBER CANT
STRUCTURAL DECK

PARAPET EDGE DETAIL

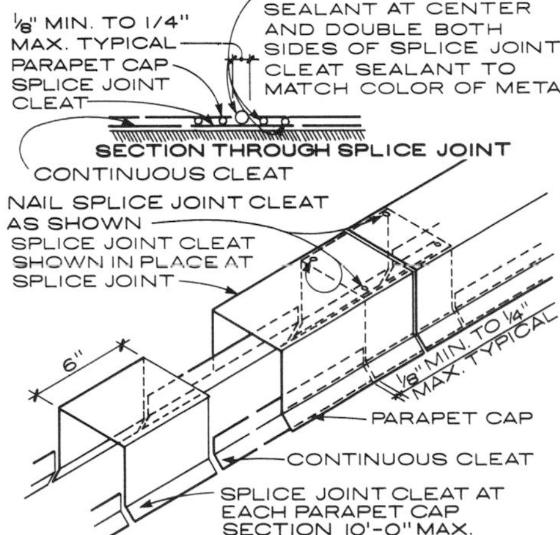
1/8" MIN. TO 1/4" MAX. TYPICAL
PARAPET CAP
SPLICE JOINT CLEAT
CONTINUOUS BEAD OF SEALANT AT CENTER AND DOUBLE BOTH SIDES OF SPLICE JOINT CLEAT SEALANT TO MATCH COLOR OF METAL
SECTION THROUGH SPLICE JOINT
CONTINUOUS CLEAT
NAIL SPLICE JOINT CLEAT AS SHOWN
SPLICE JOINT CLEAT SHOWN IN PLACE AT SPLICE JOINT
6"
1/8" MIN. TO 1/4" MAX. TYPICAL
PARAPET CAP
CONTINUOUS CLEAT
SPLICE JOINT CLEAT AT EACH PARAPET CAP SECTION 10'-0" MAX.

PARAPET CAP SPLICE JOINT

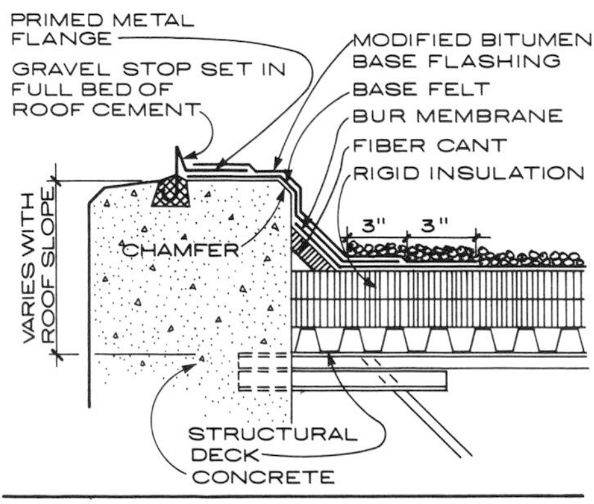
PRIMED METAL FLANGE
GRAVEL STOP SET IN FULL BED OF ROOF CEMENT
MODIFIED BITUMEN BASE FLASHING
BASE FELT
BUR MEMBRANE
FIBER CANT
RIGID INSULATION
3"
3"
VARIES WITH ROOF SLOPE
CHAMFER
STRUCTURAL DECK
CONCRETE

EDGE DETAIL

USER GUIDES TO FLASHING METAL SELECTION

Each commonly used flashing metal has distinctive characteristics, uses, and limitations. Thickness of materials is a function of material size, aesthetic consideration (prevention of oil-canning), and wind uplift due to metal movement during violent storms.

GALVANIZED STEEL

Galvanized steel flashings should be a minimum of 24 gauge with a G-90 galvanized coating. Of commonly used flashing metals, galvanized steel probably is the most common and least expensive. Although galvanized flashing metal may be left exposed, generally it is painted to further protect the steel from corrosion. Before it is painted, galvanized metal must be prepared. Plain galvanized material chemically etched in the field is preferred for surfaces to be painted. Factory etching, in which the metal is dipped in an acid bath, etches it on all sides. As a result, exposed edges often rust. Field etching is preferred because only the surfaces to be painted are etched. After etching, the surface should be primed and finish painted, preferably with two coats.

Galvanized steel is easy to solder, low in cost, and easy to work. All flashing metal transitions and terminations should be soldered fully for permanent installation; however, this should not be done at metal flashing joints where movement caused by thermal expansion is expected or at building expansion joints.

STAINLESS STEEL

Stainless steel has many advantages of other steel products, yet generally is corrosion resistant and can be field soldered to accommodate difficult transitions and terminations. If the mill finish appearance is unacceptable, stainless steel may be painted after installation with primer and finish coat.

COPPER

Copper also is a lifetime, relatively maintenance-free material. It can be soldered and molded easily, making it adaptable to complicated transitions and plane changes. Its terminations should be soldered fully. Runoff from the metal can stain adjoining building materials. Generally, copper is softer than other flashing metals and has a moderate expansion coefficient higher than steel, but less than aluminum.

ALUMINUM

Aluminum is a permanent material that corrodes slowly; however, it oxidizes and pits over time, depending on exposure. Since aluminum only can be welded, field connections can be difficult. Although corners can be prefabricated, some plane changes may be difficult. Aluminum has a high expansion and contraction coefficient compared with other flashing metals.

Joseph J. Williams, AIA; A/R/C Associates Inc.; Orlando, Florida

FRAMING

Skylights are available as preassembled units, stock or custom designed, shipped to the site ready to be installed, as assemblies of units, or framed assemblies of stock components, prefabricated off site and then site assembled. Skylight framing systems should provide complete control of both condensation and water infiltration.

Exterior gutter systems should be as simple and functional as possible. Design must take into account compatibility of materials and provision of positive slope for drainage.

The supporting structure, as well as the enclosure itself, must be engineered to carry the total resultant forces of the particular live load, wind load, and dead load in accordance with all building codes.

Framed skylights require somewhat greater mullion widths when glazed with acrylics, due to the expansion and contraction characteristics of plastics that must be taken up at the glazing connection.

Mullion spacing for framed skylights and dimensional limitations on skylight assemblies are governed by building codes responding to the glazing material specified. Maximum widths of glass vary with type:

1. Wire glass—60 in.
2. Laminated glass—48 in.
3. Tempered glass—72 in.

Other factors limiting size are

1. Requirements for positive drainage of rain water
2. Snow and wind loading
3. Condensate gutters in the body of the skylight assembly as well as at its perimeter

Mount on built-up curb with frame and counterflashing. Curb minimum height is 8 in. above roof structure. Prefabricated curbs are available with or without insulation.

Energy efficiency may be increased by use of double and triple glazing and with frames that have thermal breaks. These items will also reduce the probability of condensation.

All skylight units must be securely attached to the roof assembly which may require structural or miscellaneous steel frames at openings in deck.

GLAZING

The thickness, size, and geometric profile of all glass and acrylic glazing material should be carefully selected for compliance with building codes and manufacturer's recommendations.

The following glazing materials are available:

1. Formed acrylic with mar-resistant finish
2. Formed acrylic or flat acrylic
3. Polycarbonates
4. Tempered glass or laminated glass
5. Clear polished wire glass
6. Textured, obscure wire glass

Excessive expansion and contraction of acrylic glazing may cause "rolling" of the sealant between metal framing, causing shifting of glazing material out of the joint.

1:5
LOW RISE

1:3
MEDIUM RISE

1:2
HIGH RISE

The minimum rise to span on curved structures of framed skylights for vaulted and dome shapes is 22%.

Tinted acrylics should be limited to ¼ in. thickness for economy. A combination fiberglass sheet and aluminum frame system which has high insulating and excessive light diffusion may be an economic consideration.

Proper glazing methods have an important influence. Exposed gasketing is subject to material breakdown due to ultraviolet rays of the sun. Small valleys created at the bottom of sloped glazing and horizontal glazing cap will hold water.

Mar-resistant coatings for plastics should be specified if frequent cleaning or heavy pedestrian contact is anticipated.

Glazing with high-performance insulated glass units provides important energy savings and offers the architect numerous functional and aesthetic design choices, but initial cost may be high.

CTA Architects Engineers; Billings, Montana

FINISHES

Finishes for aluminum components are available in the following:

1. Mill finish
2. Clear anodized
3. Duranodic bronze or black
4. Acrylic enamel
5. Fluorocarbons

CONDENSATION

Double glazing and thermal break framing will minimize condensation.

Usually a separation is made where the glazing member is bolted into the framing member by use of a nonheat conductive material.

Insulated assemblies reduce condensation and energy losses.

Thermalized design will help in preventing excessive condensation buildup on the frame of domed skylight units, minimizing corrosion, staining, and general maintenance.

Incorporate a continuous condensation gutter to collect and store moisture until it evaporates.

BUILDING SECURITY

Resistance to forced entry through skylight should include

1. Provision to prevent disassembly of framing from the exterior
2. Elimination of snap-on materials
3. Melting point of glazing: Acrylics can be easily burned through with a torch
4. Use of metal security screens or burglar bars welded to steel angle frame directly below skylight

ENVIRONMENTAL CONTROL

In determining the desired form and size of the skylight unit/assembly, consideration should be given to

1. Environmental conditions, including orientation and the resulting winter and summer solar penetration angles in the given geographic location.
2. Prevailing wind's direction and force
3. Precipitation quantity and patterns
4. Topography and landscaping (trees/shades/leaves)
5. Coordination of the area of skylight with the HVAC system

Views into and out of the building through clear skylights are affected by

1. Overhanging trees and adjacent buildings
2. Nearby street lights
3. Other parts of the same building
4. Views into building from adjacent higher areas (privacy).

The more a formed plastic dome is raised, the greater its ability to refract light of the low early morning and late afternoon sun, which maximizes the use of natural light, but increases the solar heat gain.

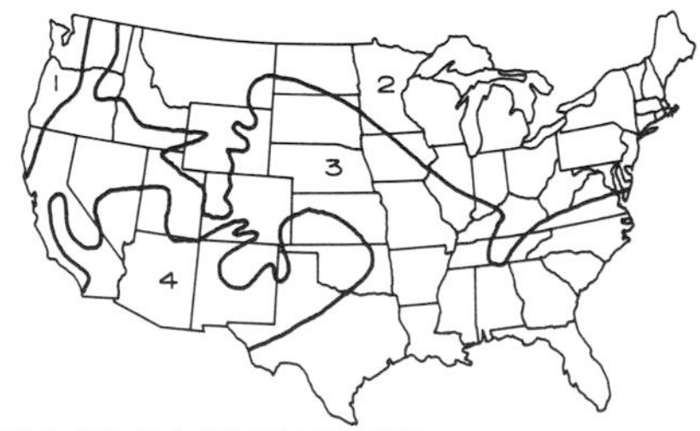
1
2
3
4

AVAILABLE LIGHT ZONES

PERCENTAGE OF ROOF AREA REQUIRED FOR SKYLIGHTING

LIGHT ZONE	LIGHT DESIGN LEVELS		
	30 FT-C	60 FT-C	120 FT-C
1	3.3	5.2	13.3
2	2.8	4.3	10.8
3	1.8	3.2	6.9
4	1.5	2.8	4.0

SKYLIGHTS WITH MOVABLE SECTIONS

Skylights can be designed with movable sections for those locations where a combination indoor–outdoor open-to-the-sky condition is desired. The movable sections are of two basic designs:

1. Complete skylight assemblies of double pitch or barrel vault configurations that roll open horizontally along a track.
2. Individual skylight roof panels of an overall double-pitched enclosure which are normally designed so that the top half slides down over the lower half to open the upper portion of roof.

Consideration should be given to motors, tracks, and other operating parts.

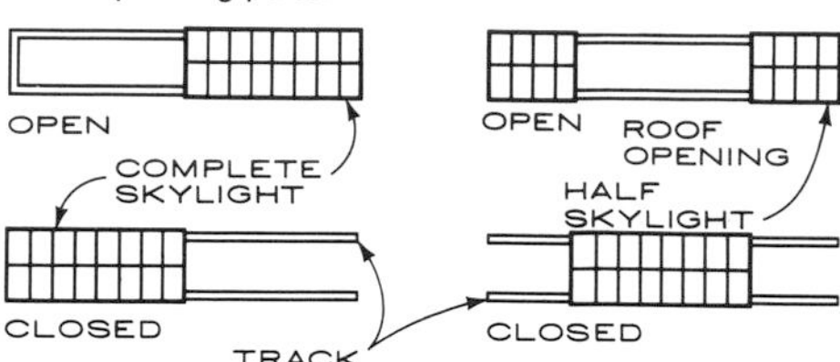
OPEN
COMPLETE SKYLIGHT
CLOSED
TRACK
SINGLE UNIT DESIGN 1
OPEN
ROOF OPENING
HALF SKYLIGHT
CLOSED
DOUBLE UNIT DESIGN 2

MOVABLE SKYLIGHT PLANS

GLASS AND PLASTIC STRUCTURES

Greenhouses, pool enclosures, and covered walkways are applications of skylight assemblies as complete envelopes. Available forms are domes, arches, barrel vaults, and single and double pitch. Lean-to enclosures are available with straight eaves, curved eaves, vertical sides, or slanted sides.

Framing may be of steel, aluminum, or wood, with a variety of glazing options. Secondary component options include doors, operable sash, louvers, shades, blinds, and ventilators. Envelopes are preengineered for specific live and wind loads, which should be checked against requirements of building codes.

FIRE AND SMOKE VENTING

In certain building types and occupancies fire and smoke units that open automatically due to fire-induced temperature increase are required. Their function is to permit the smoke to escape and lower temperatures at floor level.

A sufficient number of vents must be distributed over the entire roof area to assure reasonably early venting of a fire regardless of its location. The size and spacing of the vents must be determined for each building, depending upon

1. Size of building
2. Its particular use or combination of uses
3. The degree of hazard involved

Smoke venting is based upon movement of a specific number of cubic feet of air per minute through the fire vents. Building codes give required capacities, size, and spacing for various types of vents.

Typical roof vent area requirements are:

0.67% of roof area for low heat release occupancies
1% of roof area for moderate heat release occupancies
2% of roof area for high heat release occupancies

Roof vents may be required over stairs, elevator hoistways, atriums, and high hazard occupancies to offer explosion relief, as well as for stages and areas behind the proscenium in theaters.

In determining the number of vents to be used to satisfy the total required venting area, recognize that venting can be better accomplished by several small units than by a few larger ones (NFPA #204). The size of the vent required is based upon its opened area, about equal to its frame size.

Consider also the spacing of vents in relation to interior spaces and their uses, proximity to exits, and their use in providing daylighting. Fire vents may also function as skylights when glazed.

Fire vents may also function as skylights when glazed.

SIZES AND SPANS

2 ft 6 in. to 7 ft 7 in., with dome rise from 10 to 24 in.

GLAZING

1. Generally acrylic, but other glazing available.
2. Single and double glazed normal, triple available.
3. Clear, tinted transparent, and white translucent.
4. Scratches are difficult to remove from acrylic.

FRAMING

1. Self-flashing, with or without integral curb.
2. Insulated curbs available.
3. Areas where excessive snow loading occurs may require additional reinforcement. Consult manufacturer.
4. Skylight—No structural framing within unit.

REMARKS

1. Circular shape may make roofing seal more difficult.
2. Some visual distortion due to curvature of glazing.
3. Side wall installation possible.

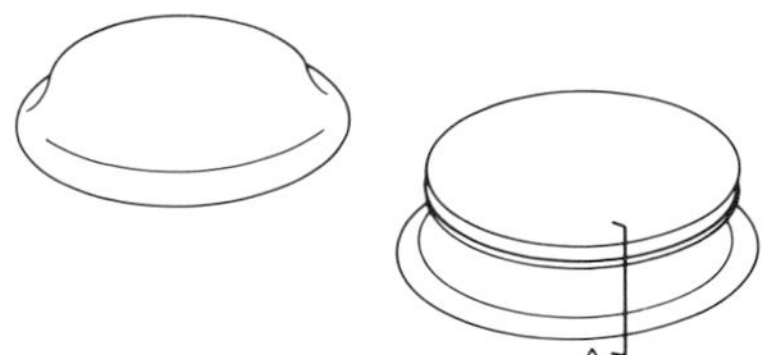
A

DOME-CIRCULAR

SIZES AND SPANS

Square from 2 ft 0 in. to 10 ft 0 in.; rectangular from 2 ft 0 in. to 5 ft 0 in. wide by 4 ft 0 in. to 8 ft 0 in. long, with dome rise from 8 to 22 in.

GLAZING

1. Acrylic, polycarbonate, glass fiber reinforced.
2. Single and double normal, triple glazing available.
3. Clear, tinted transparent, and white translucent.

FRAMING

1. See framing notes for circular dome skylight.
2. Self-flashing flanged available for pitched roof.

REMARKS

1. Steel security grill inserts available.
2. Explosion relief domes are available.
3. Louvered curbs available to allow skylight to act as ventilator without being opened.

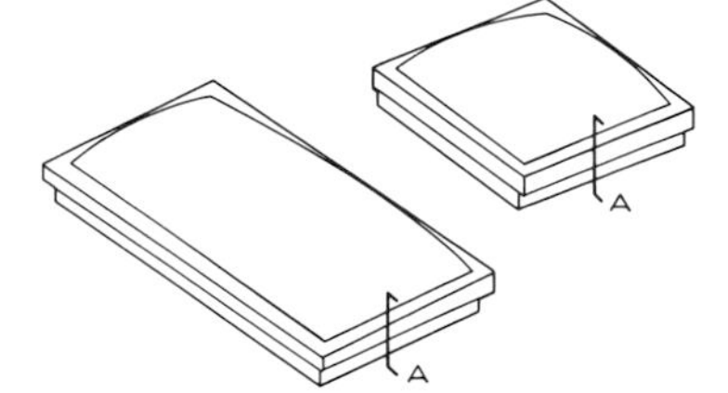
A
A

DOME-SQUARE AND RECTANGULAR

SIZES AND SPANS

2 ft 6 in. to 8 ft 0 in., with dome rise from 8 to 22 in.

GLAZING

1. Acrylic and polycarbonate typical.
2. Clear, tinted transparent, and white translucent.
3. Single and double normal.
4. Low visual distortion.

FRAMING

1. See framing notes for circular dome skylight.
2. Triangular base frame available.
3. Octagonal frame with curved dome glazing possible.
4. Normally designed for level roof application.

REMARKS

1. Sealed double domes available from some manufacturers.
2. Secondary dome under pyramid is normally curved.

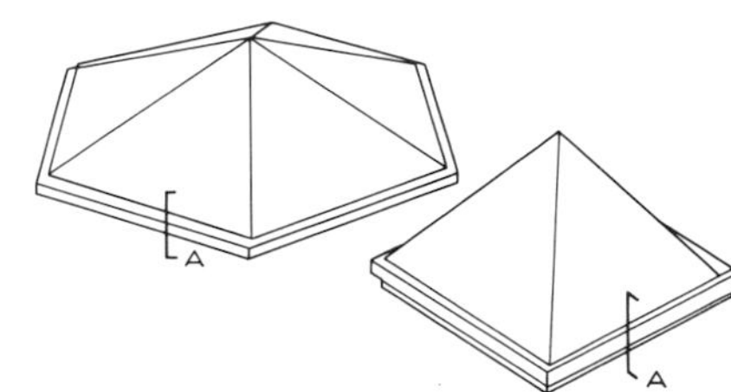
A
A

DOME-POLYGON AND PYRAMID

SIZES AND SPANS

Square 1 ft 2 in. to 4 ft 0 in.; rectangular from 2 ft 0 in. to 4 ft 0 in. wide to 4 ft 8 in. long.

GLAZING

1. Double glazed, insulating glass typical.
2. Tempered, laminated, and wire glass available.
3. Clear and tinted transparent normal.
4. Minimum visual distortion.

FRAMING

1. Operable sash: Hinged, pivoted, or sliding types.
2. Lockable frames available.
3. Aluminum and wood frames commonly available.
4. Skylight—No structural framing within unit.

REMARKS

1. Premanufactured screens and shades available.
2. Electric remote control opening operation optional.

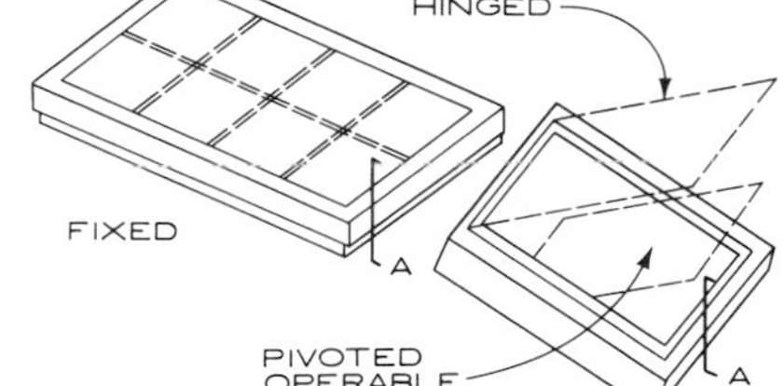
HINGED
FIXED
A
PIVOTED OPERABLE
A

FLAT PANEL-FIXED AND OPERABLE

SIZES AND SPANS

1. 2 ft 0 in. to 10 ft 0 in. wide by any length; rise from 6 to 14 in. or higher as width increases.
2. Larger widths available with vertical ends only.

GLAZING

1. Acrylic and polycarbonate typical.
2. Single or double available.
3. Clear, tinted, and white transluscent.

FRAMING

1. May be installed in series (with structural supports).
2. Expansion and contraction clearances must be considered at frame as size of unit increases.
3. Skylight—No structural framing within unit.

REMARKS

1. Quarter round vault (lean-to) available.
2. May also be used as exterior entry canopy.

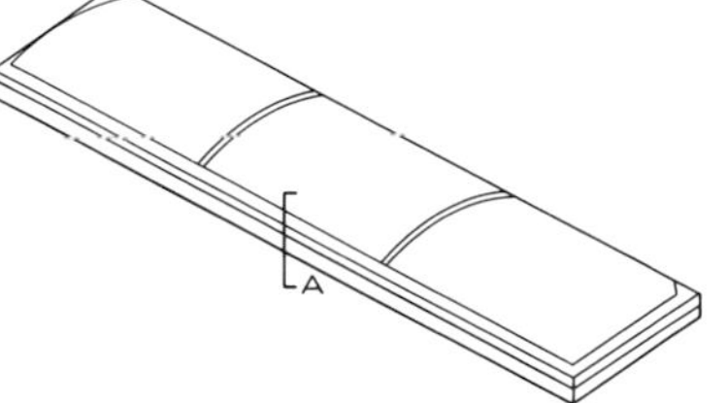
A

VAULT

SIZES AND SPANS

1. Length and width—almost any design requirement.
2. Variable pitch; up to 4 ft 0 in. along single slope.

GLAZING

1. Generally acrylic, but polycarbonate available.
2. Single or double.
3. Clear, tinted, or white transluscent.
4. Ends may be vertical glazed or hipped.

FRAMING

1. Integral condensation gutters with frame.
2. Expansion and contraction clearances may be needed.
3. Skylight—No structural framing within unit.

REMARKS

Normally used to provide natural light to interior spaces. May be used as exterior entry canopy and walkway protection.

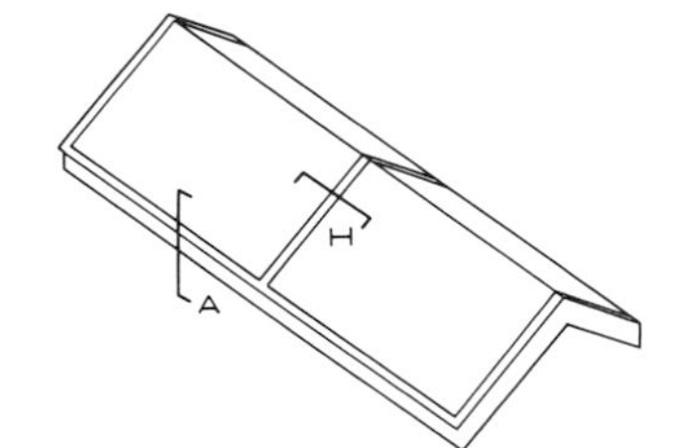
A
H

RIDGE

SIZES AND SPANS

Vertical wall and slope to 28 ft 0 in.; rafter spacing of 2, 3, and 4 ft, with glazing lengths of 4, 6, and 8 ft typical.

GLAZING

1. All types of glazing for flat panels; cold formed or thermoplastic for curved shapes.
2. Safety glass or plastic recommended.

FRAMING

1. Tubular or I-beam construction available.
2. May be custom sized to meet retrofit requirements.
3. Glazed structure—Framing within unit is structural to support glazed panels.

REMARKS

1. Shop drawings desirable for these structures.
2. Check local code for requirements of all glazing.

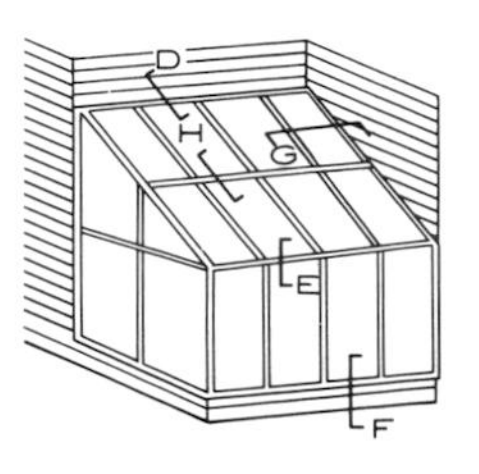
D
H
G
E
F

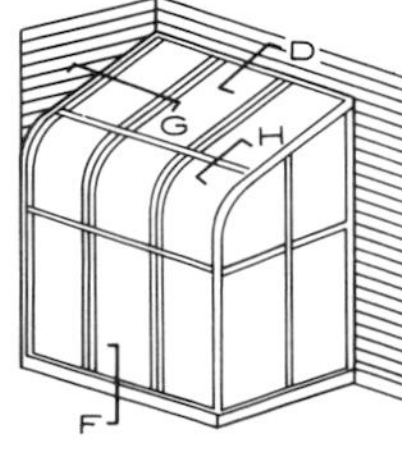
D
G
H
F

SHED

CTA Architects Engineers; Billings, Montana
Wheeler & Guay Architects PC; Alexandria, Virginia

SIZES AND SPANS

Custom sizes from 3 to 10 ft square, factory assembled. Grid more economical with larger units. Uninterrupted spans of 60 by 90 ft not unusual. Long-span grid networks require a perimeter gutter system to control watersheds.

GLAZING

All types of glazing for flat panels; cold-formed or thermoformed plastic for curved shapes.

FORMS

1. Flat panels used typically for low-pitched roof.
2. Domed units available from most manufacturers.

FRAMING

1. Tubular or I-beam construction available.
2. Glazed structure—framing within unit is structural to support glazed panels.

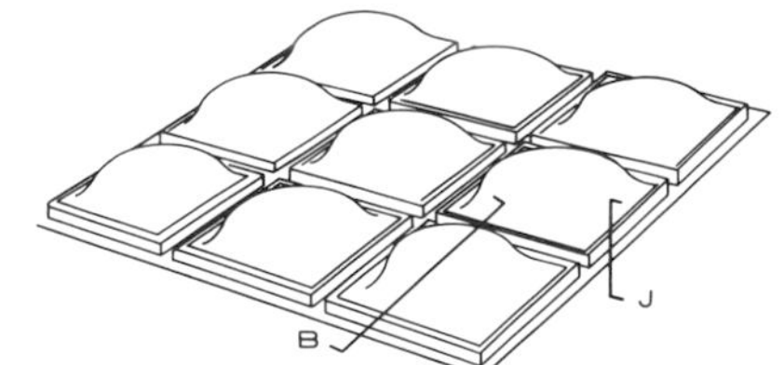
J
B

MULTIPLE GRID

SIZES AND SPANS

45 ft across, maximum used. Consult manufacturer before designing custom polygons.

GLAZING

1. All types applicable. Metal panel inserts available.
2. Thickness determined by load and environmental factors.

FORMS

A variety obtainable with varying facets constructed by joining straight framing sections.

FRAMING

1. Tubular and I-beam construction available.
2. Glazed structure—framing within unit is structural to support glazed panels.

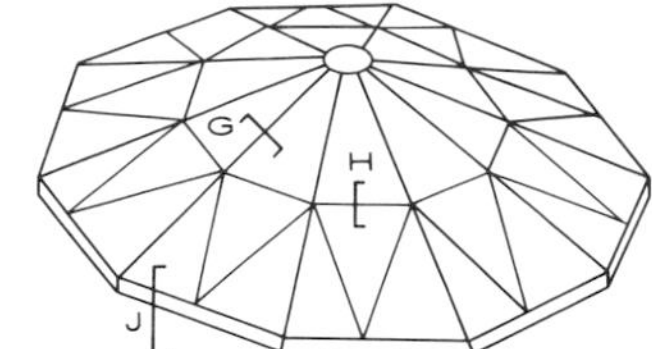
G
H
J

POLYGON

SIZES AND SPANS

10–24 ft usual; available in spans to 300 ft in both static and rollaway structures.

GLAZING

Only plastic glazing materials used. Cold-formed or thermoformed plastic, depending on strength requirements.

FORMS

Can be fabricated to most radii provided rise/span ratio is minimum 22%.

FRAMING

1. Number of curved framing sections can vary within same loading conditions.
2. Glazed structure—framing is structural.

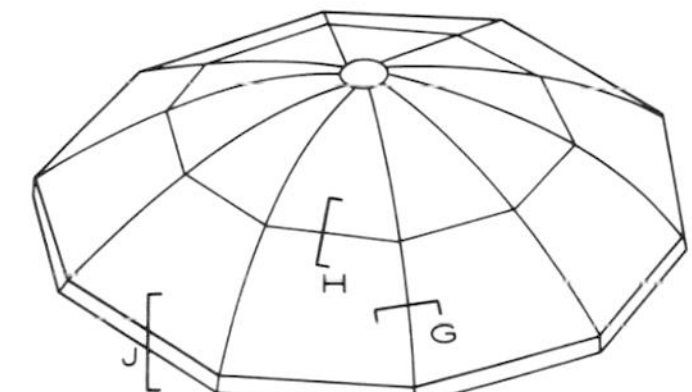
H
G
J

DOME

SIZES AND SPANS

1. Lean-to most economical for up to 20 ft 0 in. common. Slopes vary from 10° to 60°.
2. 40 ft spans possible if rafter depth increased.

GLAZING

1. All types applicable. Insulated glass is tempered.
2. Plastic or safety glass most common.

FORMS

1. Lean-to most commonly used.
2. For double pitch, hip (ridge) detail may vary.
3. Vertical or hip end possible.

FRAMING

1. Tubular or I-beam construction available.
2. Glazed structure—framing within units is structural.

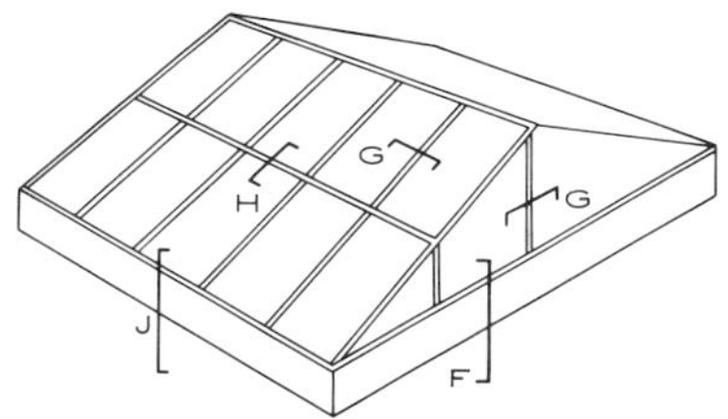
G
H
G
J
F

SINGLE OR DOUBLE PITCH

SIZES AND SPANS

1. Common sizes—10–40 ft, standard; one piece thermoformed units up to 10 by 10 ft available.
2. Curb load increases as size increases.

GLAZING

1. All types applicable. Insulated glass is tempered.
2. Plastic or safety glass most common.

FORMS

Three and four sided; standard slopes up to 45°. Maintain minimum rise of 15°.

FRAMING

1. Standard aluminum framing.
2. Many custom framing configurations possible.
3. Glazed structure—framing within unit is structural.

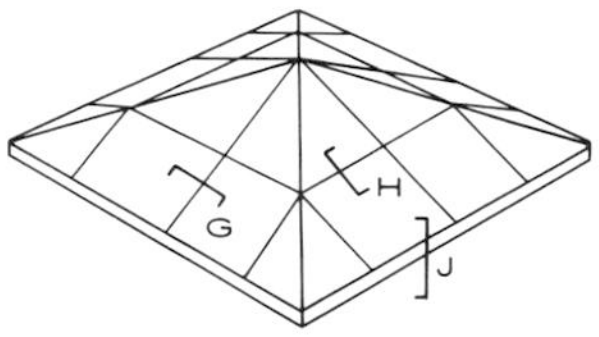

PYRAMID

SIZES AND SPANS

1. 15–25 ft most economical. Up to 40 ft used.
2. Height and width can be customized.

GLAZING

1. All types applicable.
2. Plastic or safety glass most common.
3. Insulated glass usually tempered.

FORMS

Can be used as single or multiple units; hipped gable ends also available.

FRAMING

1. Tubular or I-beam construction available.
2. Use structural gutter network with multiple units.
3. Glazed structure—framing is structural.

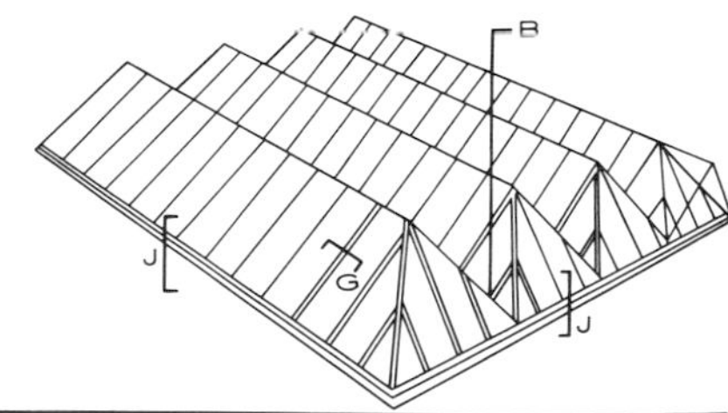
B
J
G
J

MULTIPLE RIDGE

SIZES AND SPANS

1. 10–40 ft most common. Up to 60 ft available.
2. As width increases, cross purlins become necessary.

GLAZING

1. Plastic glazing materials typical. Glass available in segmented vaults.
2. Glazed panel normally 4 ft wide maximum.

FORMS

Rises from 10 to 50%; 22% most economical.

FRAMING

1. Tubular or I-beam construction available.
2. Glazed structure—framing within unit is structural to support glazed panels.

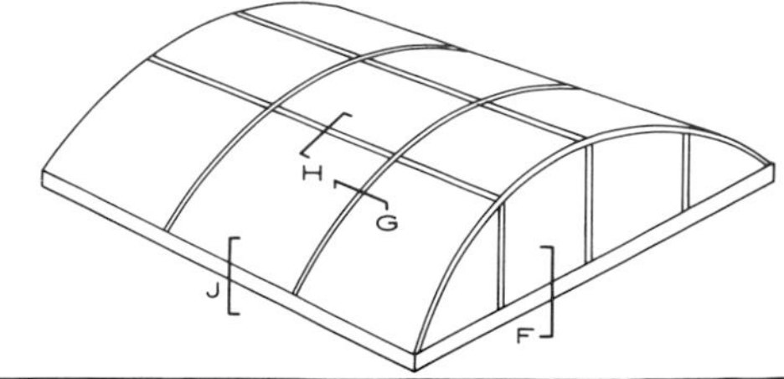
H
G
J
F

BARREL VAULT

CTA Architects Engineers; Billings, Montana
Wheeler & Guay Architects PC; Alexandria, Virginia

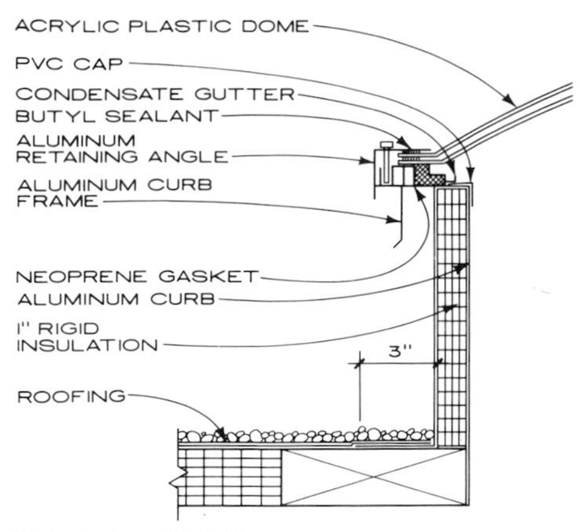
ACRYLIC PLASTIC DOME
PVC CAP
CONDENSATE GUTTER
BUTYL SEALANT
ALUMINUM RETAINING ANGLE
ALUMINUM CURB FRAME
NEOPRENE GASKET
ALUMINUM CURB
1" RIGID INSULATION
3"
ROOFING

INSULATED CURB

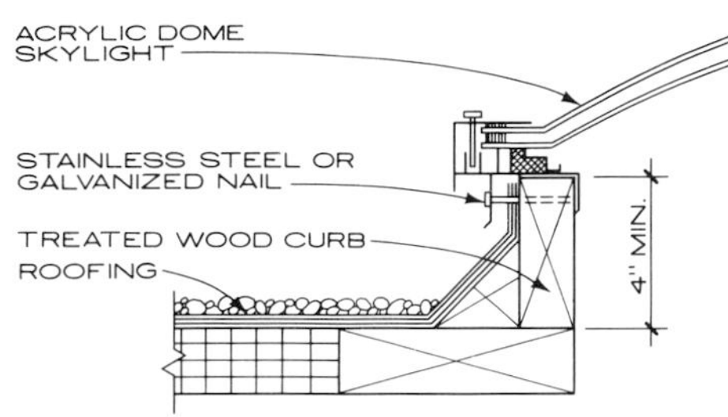
ACRYLIC DOME SKYLIGHT
STAINLESS STEEL OR GALVANIZED NAIL
TREATED WOOD CURB
ROOFING
4" MIN.

WOOD CURB

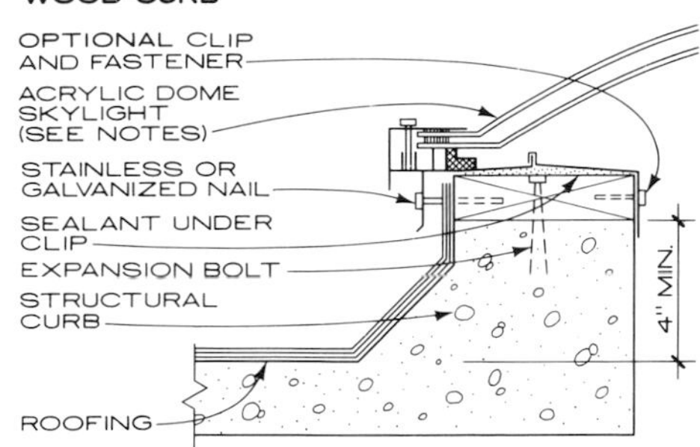
OPTIONAL CLIP AND FASTENER
ACRYLIC DOME SKYLIGHT (SEE NOTES)
STAINLESS OR GALVANIZED NAIL
SEALANT UNDER CLIP
EXPANSION BOLT
STRUCTURAL CURB
ROOFING
4" MIN.

CONCRETE CURB

DETAIL A: CURB TYPES

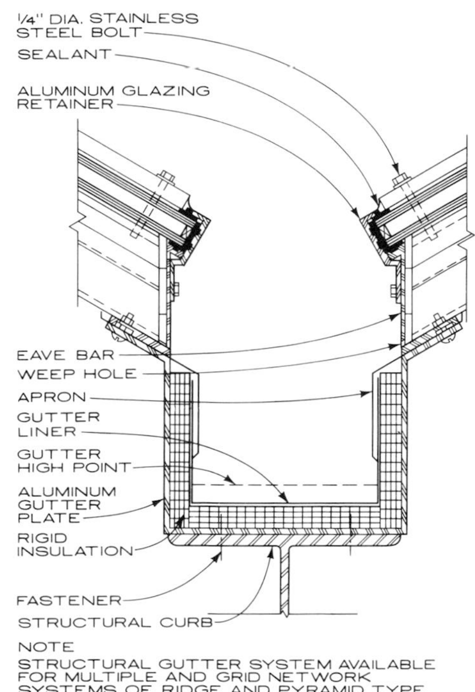
1/4" DIA. STAINLESS STEEL BOLT
SEALANT
ALUMINUM GLAZING RETAINER
EAVE BAR
WEEP HOLE
APRON
GUTTER LINER
GUTTER HIGH POINT
ALUMINUM GUTTER PLATE
RIGID INSULATION
FASTENER
STRUCTURAL CURB

NOTE
STRUCTURAL GUTTER SYSTEM AVAILABLE FOR MULTIPLE AND GRID NETWORK SYSTEMS OF RIDGE AND PYRAMID TYPE ENCLOSURES

DETAIL B: GUTTER

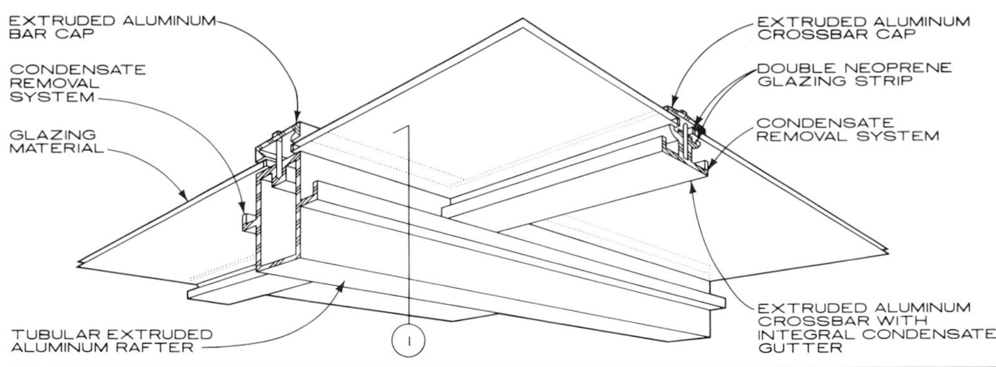
EXTRUDED ALUMINUM BAR CAP
CONDENSATE REMOVAL SYSTEM
GLAZING MATERIAL
TUBULAR EXTRUDED ALUMINUM RAFTER
EXTRUDED ALUMINUM CROSSBAR CAP
DOUBLE NEOPRENE GLAZING STRIP
CONDENSATE REMOVAL SYSTEM
EXTRUDED ALUMINUM CROSSBAR WITH INTEGRAL CONDENSATE GUTTER
1

DETAIL C: TYPICAL TUBULAR ALUMINUM FRAMING

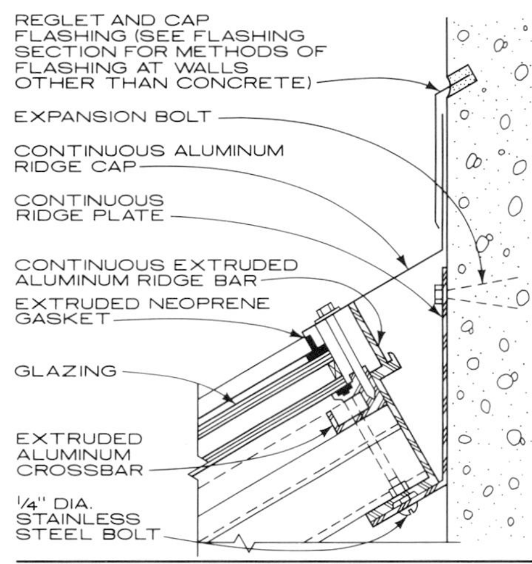
REGLET AND CAP FLASHING (SEE FLASHING SECTION FOR METHODS OF FLASHING AT WALLS OTHER THAN CONCRETE)
EXPANSION BOLT
CONTINUOUS ALUMINUM RIDGE CAP
CONTINUOUS RIDGE PLATE
CONTINUOUS EXTRUDED ALUMINUM RIDGE BAR
EXTRUDED NEOPRENE GASKET
GLAZING
EXTRUDED ALUMINUM CROSSBAR
1/4" DIA. STAINLESS STEEL BOLT

DETAIL D: RIDGE AT SHED

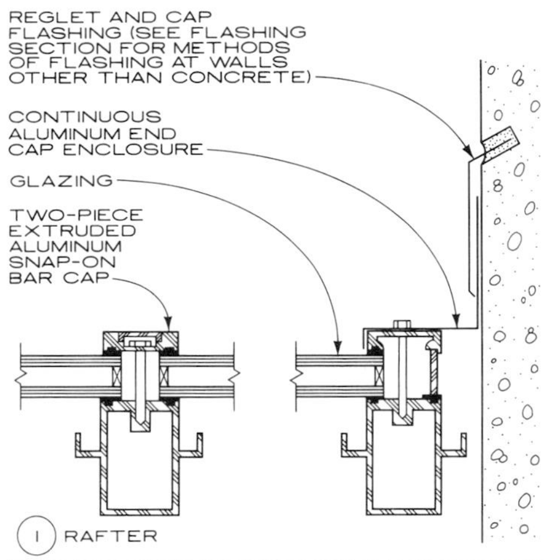
REGLET AND CAP FLASHING (SEE FLASHING SECTION FOR METHODS OF FLASHING AT WALLS OTHER THAN CONCRETE)
CONTINUOUS ALUMINUM END CAP ENCLOSURE
GLAZING
TWO-PIECE EXTRUDED ALUMINUM SNAP-ON BAR CAP
1 RAFTER

DETAIL G: RAFTER AND END WALL

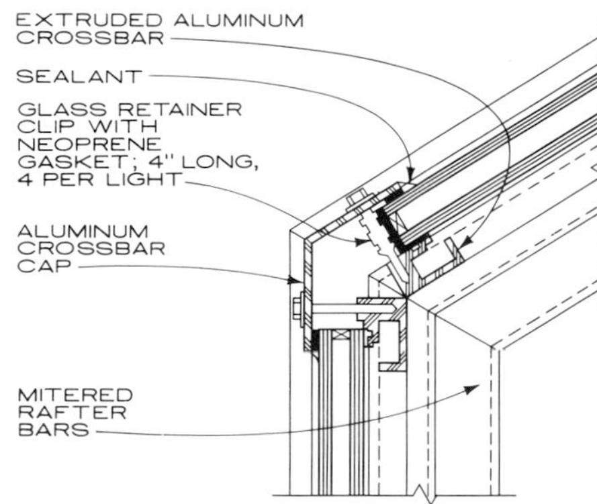
EXTRUDED ALUMINUM CROSSBAR
SEALANT
GLASS RETAINER CLIP WITH NEOPRENE GASKET; 4" LONG, 4 PER LIGHT
ALUMINUM CROSSBAR CAP
MITERED RAFTER BARS

DETAIL E: KNEE EDGE

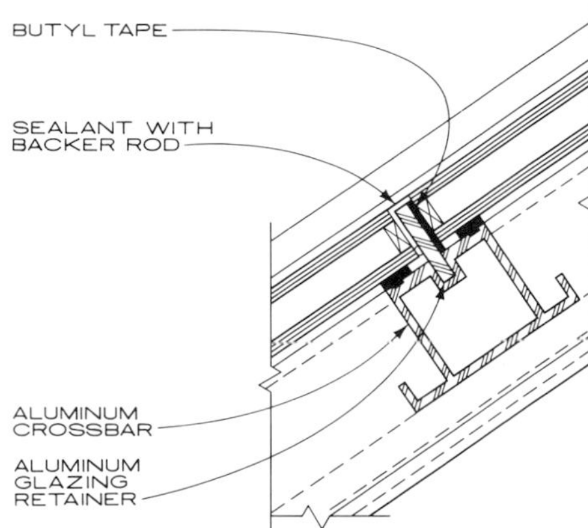
BUTYL TAPE
SEALANT WITH BACKER ROD
ALUMINUM CROSSBAR
ALUMINUM GLAZING RETAINER

DETAIL H: BUTT GLAZING

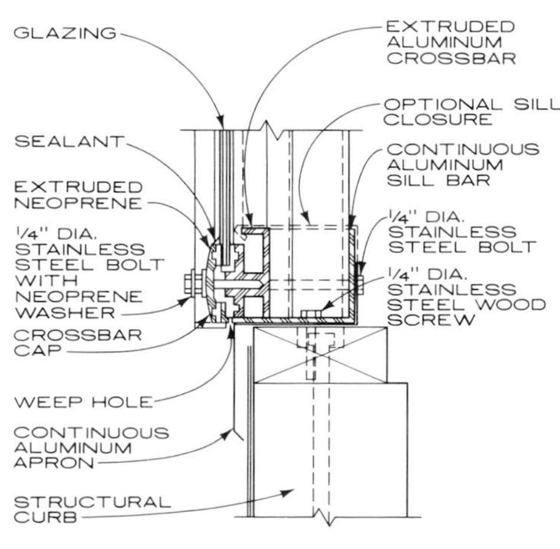
GLAZING
SEALANT
EXTRUDED NEOPRENE
1/4" DIA. STAINLESS STEEL BOLT WITH NEOPRENE WASHER
CROSSBAR CAP
WEEP HOLE
CONTINUOUS ALUMINUM APRON
STRUCTURAL CURB
EXTRUDED ALUMINUM CROSSBAR
OPTIONAL SILL CLOSURE
CONTINUOUS ALUMINUM SILL BAR
1/4" DIA. STAINLESS STEEL BOLT
1/4" DIA. STAINLESS STEEL WOOD SCREW

DETAIL F: VERTICAL SILL

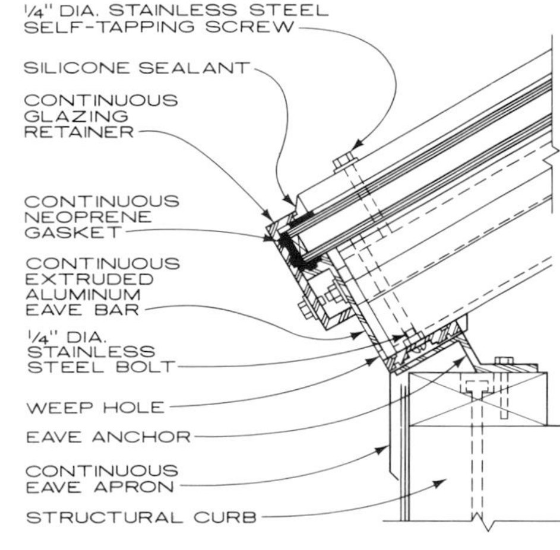
1/4" DIA. STAINLESS STEEL SELF-TAPPING SCREW
SILICONE SEALANT
CONTINUOUS GLAZING RETAINER
CONTINUOUS NEOPRENE GASKET
CONTINUOUS EXTRUDED ALUMINUM EAVE BAR
1/4" DIA. STAINLESS STEEL BOLT
WEEP HOLE
EAVE ANCHOR
CONTINUOUS EAVE APRON
STRUCTURAL CURB

DETAIL J: EAVE OR SILL

CTA Architects Engineers; Billings, Montana
Wheeler & Guay Architects PC; Alexandria, Virginia

REFERENCES

GENERAL REFERENCES

The NRCA Roofing and Waterproofing Manual, National Roofing Contractors Association (NRCA)

Architectural Sheet Metal Manual, Sheet Metal and Air Conditioning Contractors National Association

Fundamentals of Building Insulation, Insulating Board Institute

Manual of Built-Up Roofing Systems, 2nd ed., 1982, C.W. Griffin, McGraw-Hill

DATA SOURCES: ORGANIZATIONS

Aluminum Company of America (Alcoa), 211, 212, 221, 225

American Plywood Association (APA), 222

American Society for Testing and Materials (ASTM), 208, 209, 214, 215, 226

American Society of Heating, Refrigerating and Air Conditioning Engineers (ASHRAE), 213

Architectural Engineering Products Company, 211, 233

Asphalt Roofing Manufacturers Association (ARMA), 219

Ball Metal and Chemical Company, 211

Binkey Company, 212

Bird and Son, Inc., 211

Buckingham-Virginia State Corporation, 210

Carlisle Corporation, 227

Celotex Corporation, 246

Certain-Teed Corporation, 219

Fisher Skylights, Inc., 248–251

Follansbee Steel Corporation, 211

GAF Corporation, 209

H. H. Robertson Company, 225

Johns-Manville Sales Corporation, 209, 219, 247

Kaiser Aluminum and Chemical Sales, Inc., 211, 221

Koppers Company, Inc., 210, 217

Lasco Industries, 212

Long Fir Gutter Company, 234

Ludowici-Celadon Company, 210, 220

MM Systems Corporation, 233

Monier Company, 211

National Roofing Contractors' Association (NRCA), 227, 240–243, 245, 246

National Steel Products Company, 211

Owens-Corning Fiberglas Corporation, 208, 209

Perma Clad Industries, 233

Red Cedar Shingle and Handsplit Shake Bureau (RCSHSB), 210, 217, 218

Shakertown Corporation, 210, 217, 218

Steelite, Inc., 212

Underwriters Laboratories, Inc. (U.L.), 208–212, 229

DATA SOURCES: PUBLICATIONS

Architectural Sheet Metal Manual, Sheet Metal and Air Conditioning Contractors' National Association, Inc. (SMACNA), 231–234, 236–247

Bob Bates Associates, Various Foundation Waterproofing Methods and Conditions, 216

Underground Waterproofing, Brent Anderson, WEBCO Publishing, Inc., 216

CHAPTER 8

DOORS AND WINDOWS

INTRODUCTION:

The following is a selection of hollow metal details from various manufacturers. They are in no way intended to favor a manufacturer or a product. Details vary. Consult manufacturers literature.

Hollow metal is divided into a frame section and a door section. The frame section can be used with wood doors. Both sections are complete in themselves.

NOMENCLATURE

Active Leaf	The door leaf of a pair in which the lock is normally installed.
Astragal (overlapping)	A vertical molding attached to the meeting edge of one leaf of a pair of doors for protection against weather conditions and to retard passage of smoke, flame and gasses.
Astragal (split)	A vertical molding attached to both leaves at a pair of doors at the meeting edge for protection against weather conditions.
Barrier Screen	See Smoke Screen.
Beveled Edge	The edge at a door that is not at a 90° angle to the face of the door (std. bevel is 1/8" in 2").
Blank Jamb	Vertical member of frame without hardware preparation. Used when doors are furnished with push and pull hardware or surface mounted strikes and single active floor hinges.
Borrowed Light	Four-sided frame prepared for glass installation in field.
Bullnose Trim	The face & jamb width joined by a radius rather than a 90° break.
Cabinet Jamb	Frame in three or more pieces applied as the finished frame over rough buck.
Cap	See Soffit.
Cased Opening	Frame section which does not have any stops.
Covemold Frame	Frame having contour faces (exposed) simulating contour of wood frame.
Cut-Out	A preparation for hardware and/or accessories.
Double Acting Door	Type of door prepared for pivot or spring type hinge permitting the door to swing 90° in either direction.
Double Egress Frame	Double rabbeted double frame prepared to receive two single-acting doors swinging in opposite directions.
Dutch Door	Door having two separate leaves, one hung above the other. Shelf on lower leaf, optional.
Face	Exposed part of frame parallel to face of wall.
Filler Plate	A blank plate used to fill mortised cutouts.
Flat Frame	Frame having flat faces exposed.
Floor Clearance	Distance between bottom of door and finished floor.
Glass Stop	Fixed trim on a glass tight door against which glass is set.
Glazing Bead	A removable trim at glazing opening to hold glass securely in place.
Hand	Term used to designate direction in which door swings.
Handing	The swinging of the door e.g., right hand or left hand. To determine the hand of a door, view the door from the outside. The side that the hinges are on is the hand of the door. If the door swings away from the viewer, the hand is a regular hand, i.e. right or left hand. If the door swings to the viewer, the door is reverse swing, i.e. right hand reverse swing or left hand reverse swing.
Head	Horizontal frame member at top of door opening or top member of transom frames.
Header	See Head.
Hinge Backset	Distance from edge to hinge to stop on frame.
Hinge Filler Plate	Plate installed for a hinge cut-out when no hinge is required.
Inactive Leaf	The door leaf in a pair of doors which is normally held closed by top and bottom bolts.
Jamb	Vertical frame member; between door and glass or wall; between glass and door or wall. See also Mullion.
Jamb Depth	Over-all width of frame section.
Knock Down (KD) Frame	Door frame furnished by manufacturer in three or more basic parts for assembly in field.
Lock Backset	Distance from edge of door to centerline of cylinder or knob.
Masonry Box	See Plaster Guard.
Mortise Preparation	Reinforcing drilling and tapping for hardware which is to be mortised into door or frame.
Mullion	Vertical or horizontal frame member; between glass and glass, or door and door.
Muntin	Non-structural member used to subdivide an open area in frame or door.
Opening Size	Size of frame opening measured between rabbets and finished floor.
Plaster Guard	Metal shield attached behind hinge and strike reinforcement to prevent mortar or plaster from entering mounting holes.
Reveal	That part of the backband which extends beyond finished wall.
Reveal	Distance from face of frame to surface of finished wall.
Reversing Channel	See End Channel.
Reverse Bevel	Refers to hand of door or lock when doors swing to outside.
Rough Opening	Size of wall opening into which frame is installed.
Rubber Silencer	A part attached to the stop of a frame to cushion the closing of door.
Section Width	See Jamb Depth.
Single Acting Door	Type of door prepared for a pivot type or spring-type single-acting hinge permitting the door to swing 90° in one direction only.
Smoke Screen	A door frame combined with sidelights on either or both sides of door openings, including transom opening when and if required.
Soffit	Underside of stop on frame.
Split Jambs	Frames with jamb width in two pieces.
Stilts	See Floor Struts.
Stop	Part of frame against which door closes or glass rests.
Strike Stile	Vertical member of an inactive door leaf which receives the strike.
Strut Guide	Metal piece attached inside throat of frame which guides and holds ceiling strut to frame (usually incorporated in clip).
Sub Buck	See Rough Buck.
Surface Hardware Preparation	Reinforcing or machining or both, for hardware which is applied to surface of door or frame in field.
Top & Bottom Cap	Horizontal channel used in doors which do not have a flush top or bottom.
Transom Bar	The part of a transom frame which separates the top of the door from the transom.
Trim	(1) See face. (2) An applied face.
Trimmed Opening	See Cased Opening.

James W. G. Watson, AIA; Ronald A. Spahn and Associates; Cleveland Heights, Ohio

GENERAL

Fire door assemblies are used for the protection of openings in fire-rated walls. The assembly consists of a fire door, frame, and hardware. Each component is crucial to the overall performance of the assembly as a fire barrier.

NFPA 80 is a national standard to establish the degree of fire protection required at a given opening. Fire doors and frames are classified by the duration of test exposure (hourly rating) and the class of opening the assembly is intended for (letter designation).

Additional information is available in Chapter 7 of the NFPA "Fire Protection Handbook."

TYPES OF OPENINGS

1. CLASS A (3-hour doors): Openings in fire walls and in walls that divide a single building into fire areas.
2. CLASS B (1- or 1½-hour doors): Openings in enclosures of vertical communications through buildings and in 2-hour rated partitions providing horizontal fire separations.
3. CLASS C (¾-hour door): Openings in walls or partitions between rooms and corridors having a fire resistance rating of 1 hour or less.
4. CLASS D (1½-hour door): Openings in exterior walls subject to severe fire exposure from outside of the building.
5. CLASS E (¾-hour door): Openings in exterior walls subject to moderate or light fire exposure from outside of the building.

½- and ⅓-hour doors are used for smoke control in corridor walls.

TYPES OF DOORS

Typical construction for swinging fire doors:

1. COMPOSITE fire doors consist of wood, steel, or plastic sheets bonded to and supported by a solid core material.
2. HOLLOW METAL fire doors are of flush or panel design with not less than 20 gauge steel face.
3. METAL CLAD fire doors are of flush or panel design consisting of metal covered wood cores or stiles and rails and insulated panels covered with steel of 24 gauge or lighter.
4. SHEET METAL fire doors are formed of 22 gauge or lighter steel and are corrugated, flush sheet, or panel design.
5. TINCLAD fire doors consist of a wood core with a terne plate or galvanized steel facing (#30 or #24 gauge).
6. WOOD core-type doors consist of wood, hardboard, or plastic face sheets bonded to a wood block or wood particleboard core material with untreated wood edges.

TYPES OF FRAMES

Fire-rated door frames can be factory or field assembled. All frames must be adequately anchored at the jambs and floor per the manufacturers' specifications.

1. WOOD: Head and jamb members, with or without solid transom panel (20 minute maximum rating).
2. LIGHT GAUGE METAL FRAME: Head and jamb members with or without transom panel made from aluminum (45 minute maximum rating) or light gauge steel (1½ hour maximum rating). Frame is installed over finished wall.
3. PRESSED STEEL (HOLLOW METAL): Head and jamb members, with or without solid or glazed transoms or sidelights made from 18 gauge or heavier steel (3 hour maximum rating). This frame is required for most metal doors.

HARDWARE

Door hardware is either provided by the builder or furnished by the manufacturer. Generally the door and frame must be prepared to receive hardware by the manufacturer to insure that the integrity of the fire-rated assembly is maintained.

Fire doors are hung on steel ball bearing hinges. A fire door must close and latch at the time of a fire. Labeled automatic latches and door closers can be self-operated or controlled by failsafe devices that activate in a fire situation. Pairs of doors require coordinators with astragals to ensure both doors close. Gasketing to seal the head and jambs should be provided where smoke control is required.

FLUSH METAL DOOR, NO GLASS PERMITTED
TYPICAL MAX. CLEARANCES
⅛" AT JAMBS
¾" AT NONCOMBUSTIBLE FLOOR
⅜" AT NONCOMBUSTIBLE SILL

CLASS A (3HR) AND CLASS D (1½HR)

MAXIMUM DOOR SIZES (HOLLOW METAL, ALL CLASSES)

Single door	4 x 10 ft with labeled single-point or 3-point latching device. 4 x 8 ft with fire exit hardware.
Pair of doors	8 x 10 ft active leaf, with labeled single-point or 3-point latching device. inactive leaf, with labeled 2-point latching device or top and bottom bolts. 8 x 8 ft with fire exit hardware.

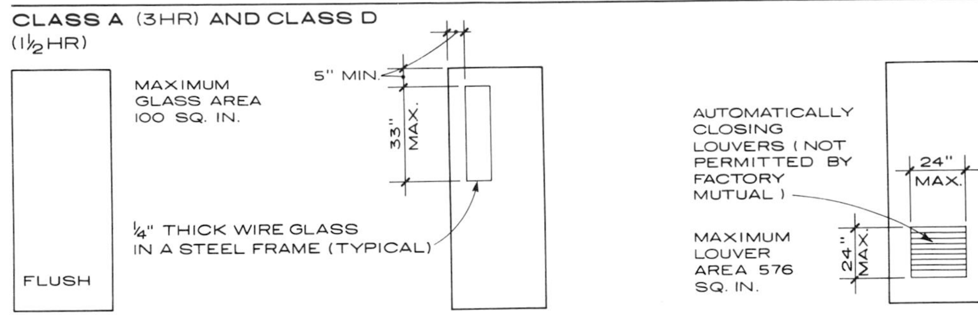
FLUSH
MAXIMUM GLASS AREA 100 SQ. IN.
5" MIN.
33" MAX.
¼" THICK WIRE GLASS IN A STEEL FRAME (TYPICAL)
AUTOMATICALLY CLOSING LOUVERS (NOT PERMITTED BY FACTORY MUTUAL)
24" MAX.
MAXIMUM LOUVER AREA 576 SQ. IN.
24" MAX.

CLASS B (1 OR 1½ HR)

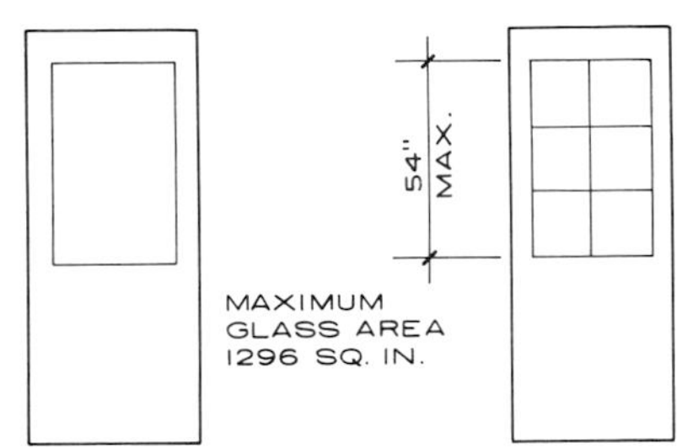
54" MAX.
MAXIMUM GLASS AREA 1296 SQ. IN.

HINGE REQUIREMENTS (ALL CLASSES)

All hinges or pivots must be steel. Two hinges are required on doors up to 5 ft in height and an additional hinge is required for each additional 2 ft 6 in. of door height or fraction thereof. The same requirement holds for pivots.

CLASS C (¾ HR), CLASS E (¾HR) AND SMOKE CONTROL DOORS (½ AND ⅓ HR)

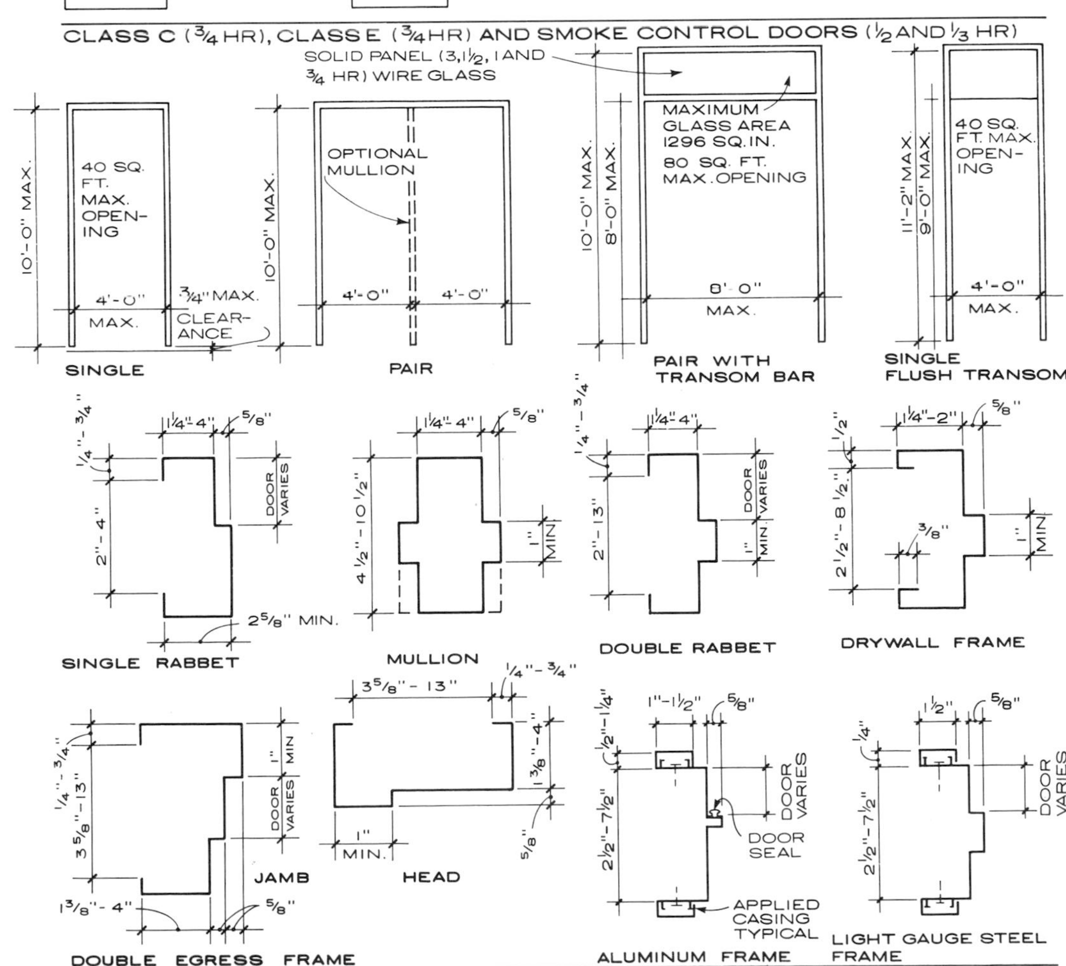
SOLID PANEL (3,1½, 1 AND ¾ HR) WIRE GLASS
10'-0" MAX.
40 SQ. FT. MAX. OPEN-ING
4'-0" MAX.
¾" MAX. CLEAR-ANCE
SINGLE
10'-0" MAX.
OPTIONAL MULLION
4'-0"
4'-0"
PAIR
10'-0" MAX.
8'-0" MAX.
MAXIMUM GLASS AREA 1296 SQ.IN.
80 SQ. FT. MAX. OPENING
8'-0" MAX.
PAIR WITH TRANSOM BAR
11'-2" MAX.
9'-0" MAX.
40 SQ. FT. MAX. OPEN-ING
4'-0" MAX.
SINGLE FLUSH TRANSOM
1¼"-4"
⅝"
¼"-¾"
2"-4"
DOOR VARIES
2⅝" MIN.
SINGLE RABBET
4½"-10½"
1" MIN.
MULLION
2"-13"
DOUBLE RABBET
1¼"-2"
2½"-8½"
⅜"
DRYWALL FRAME
3⅝"-13"
¼"-¾"
1" MIN
1⅜"-4"
JAMB
DOUBLE EGRESS FRAME
1" MIN.
1⅜"-4"
HEAD
1"-1½"
½"-1¼"
2½"-7½"
DOOR SEAL
APPLIED CASING TYPICAL
ALUMINUM FRAME
½"
¼"
LIGHT GAUGE STEEL FRAME

FIRE-RATED STEEL FRAMES–ELEVATIONS AND DETAILS

Thomas Emme, AIA; Albert C. Martin & Associates; Los Angeles, California
William G. Miner, AIA; Architect; Washington, D.C.
NFPA, see data sources

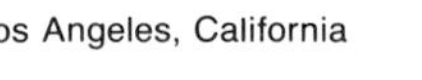

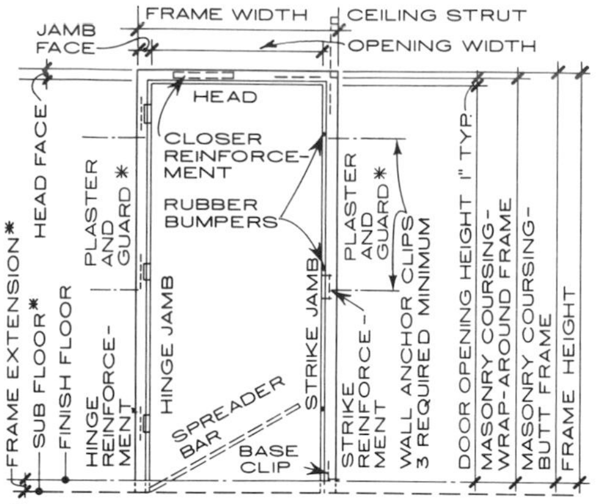

JAMB FACE
FRAME WIDTH
CEILING STRUT
OPENING WIDTH
HEAD
CLOSER REINFORCEMENT
RUBBER BUMPERS
HEAD FACE
FRAME EXTENSION*
SUB FLOOR*
FINISH FLOOR
PLASTER AND GUARD *
HINGE REINFORCEMENT
HINGE JAMB
SPREADER BAR
BASE CLIP
STRIKE JAMB
STRIKE REINFORCEMENT
PLASTER AND GUARD *
WALL ANCHOR CLIPS 3 REQUIRED MINIMUM
DOOR OPENING HEIGHT 1" TYP.
MASONRY COURSING-WRAP-AROUND FRAME
MASONRY COURSING-BUTT FRAME
FRAME HEIGHT

*REQUIRED EXCEPT IN DRYWALL CONSTRUCTION

STANDARD STEEL FRAME

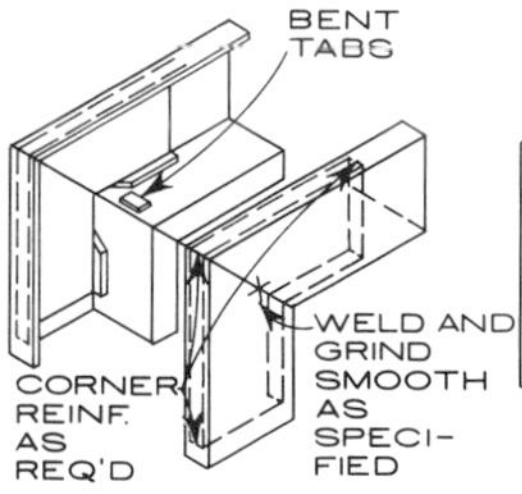

BENT TABS
CORNER REINF. AS REQ'D
WELD AND GRIND SMOOTH AS SPECIFIED

CORNER CONSTRUCTION

CORNER REINF. AS REQ'D

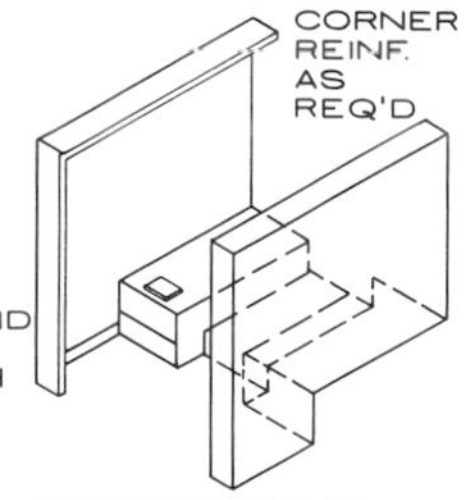

CORNER WITH VARIABLE FACES

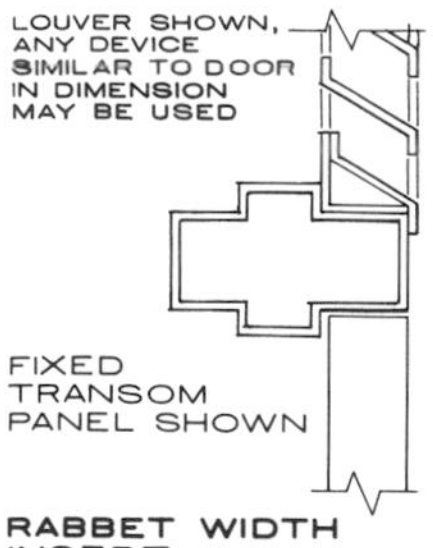

LOUVER SHOWN, ANY DEVICE SIMILAR TO DOOR IN DIMENSION MAY BE USED
FIXED TRANSOM PANEL SHOWN

RABBET WIDTH INSERT

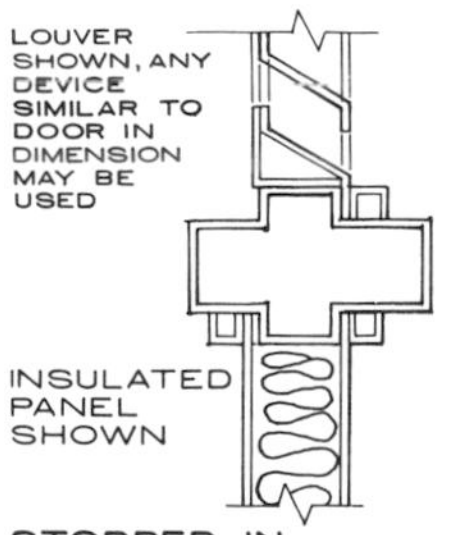

LOUVER SHOWN, ANY DEVICE SIMILAR TO DOOR IN DIMENSION MAY BE USED
INSULATED PANEL SHOWN

STOPPED-IN INSERT

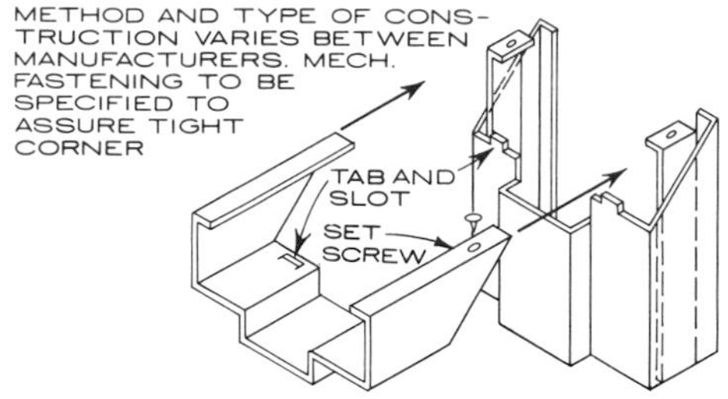

METHOD AND TYPE OF CONSTRUCTION VARIES BETWEEN MANUFACTURERS. MECH. FASTENING TO BE SPECIFIED TO ASSURE TIGHT CORNER
TAB AND SLOT
SET SCREW

KNOCK DOWN FRAME CORNER CONSTR.

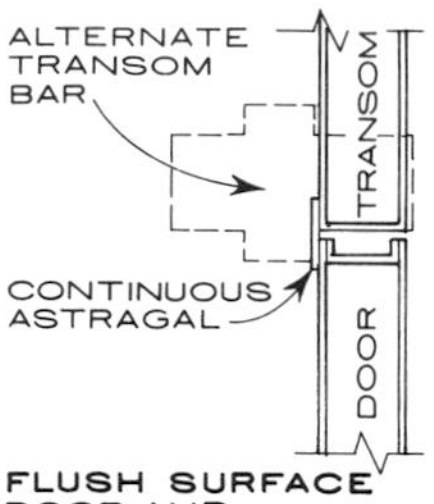

ALTERNATE TRANSOM BAR
TRANSOM
CONTINUOUS ASTRAGAL
DOOR

FLUSH SURFACE DOOR AND TRANSOM

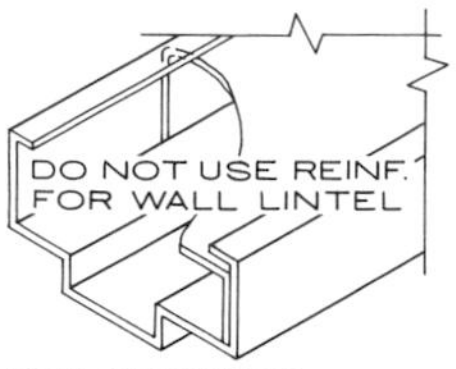

DO NOT USE REINF. FOR WALL LINTEL
FOR OPENINGS GREATER THAN 42" WIDE

STANDARD HEAD WITH REINFORCEMENT

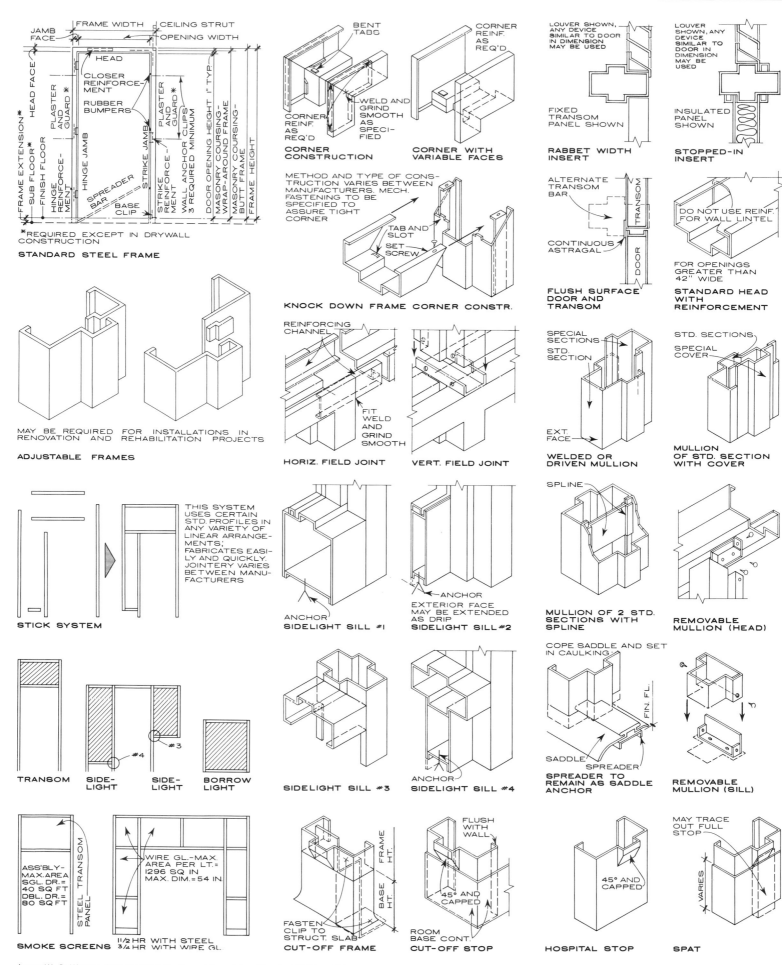

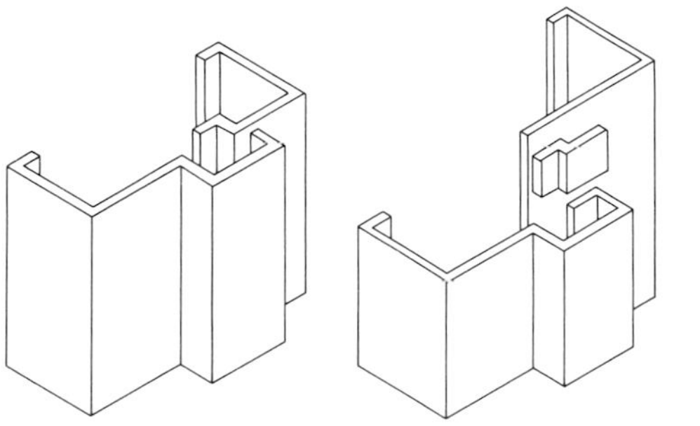

MAY BE REQUIRED FOR INSTALLATIONS IN RENOVATION AND REHABILITATION PROJECTS

ADJUSTABLE FRAMES

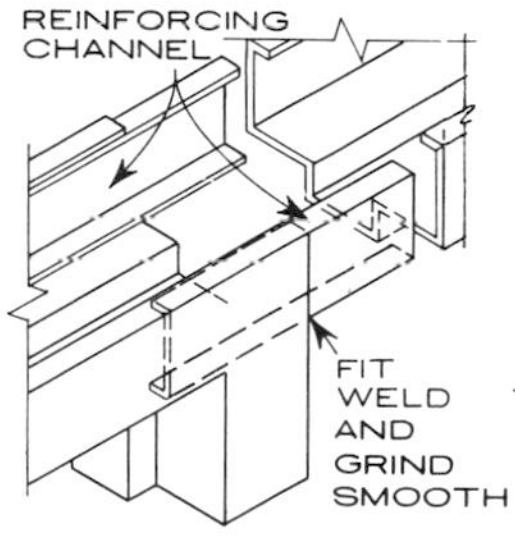

REINFORCING CHANNEL
FIT WELD AND GRIND SMOOTH

HORIZ. FIELD JOINT

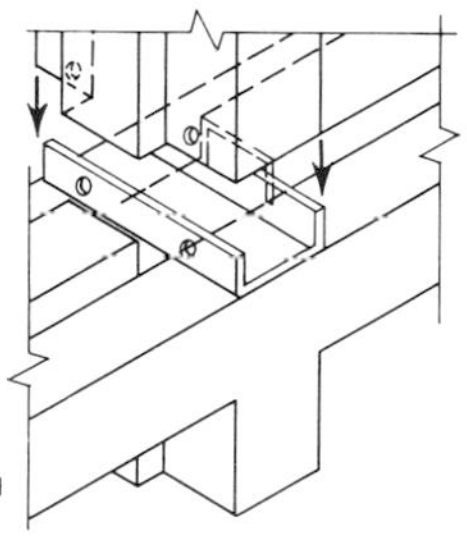

VERT. FIELD JOINT

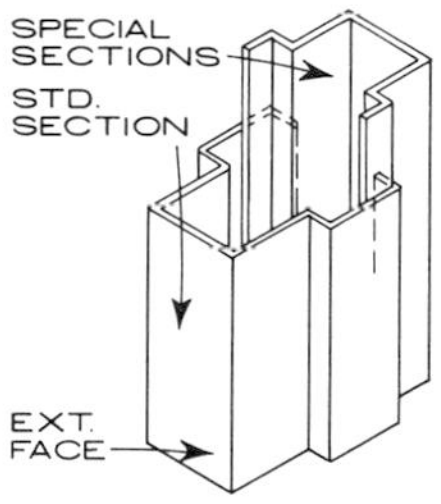

SPECIAL SECTIONS
STD. SECTION
EXT. FACE

WELDED OR DRIVEN MULLION

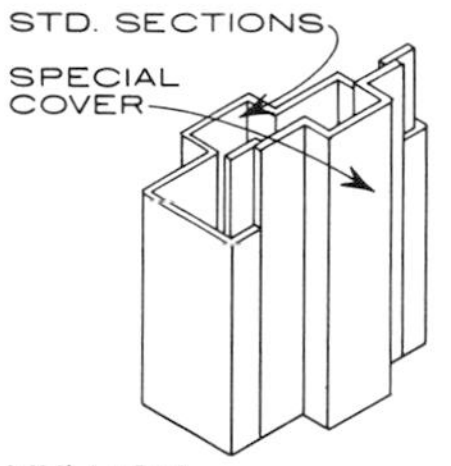

STD. SECTIONS
SPECIAL COVER

MULLION OF STD. SECTION WITH COVER

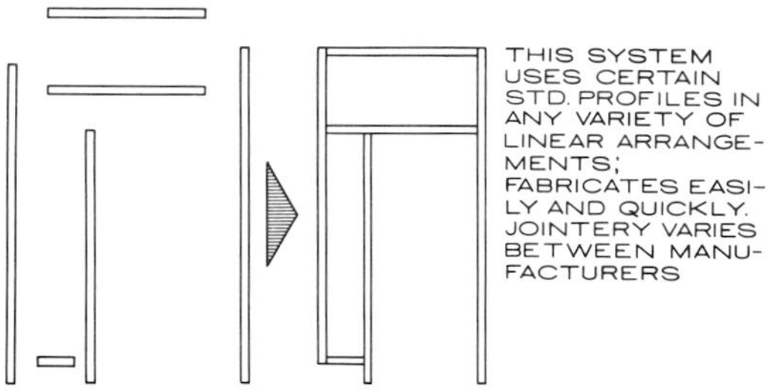

THIS SYSTEM USES CERTAIN STD. PROFILES IN ANY VARIETY OF LINEAR ARRANGEMENTS; FABRICATES EASILY AND QUICKLY. JOINTERY VARIES BETWEEN MANUFACTURERS

STICK SYSTEM

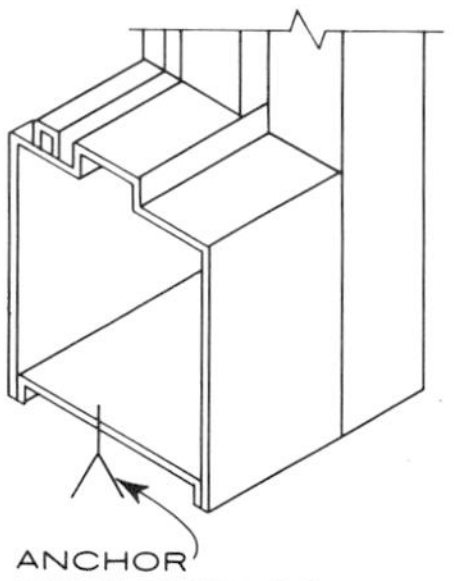

ANCHOR

SIDELIGHT SILL #1

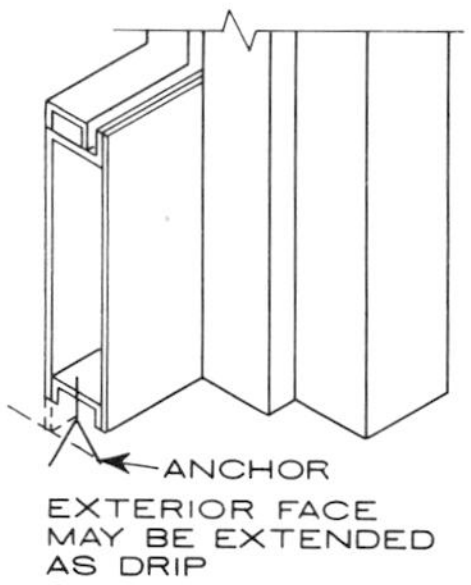

ANCHOR
EXTERIOR FACE MAY BE EXTENDED AS DRIP

SIDELIGHT SILL #2

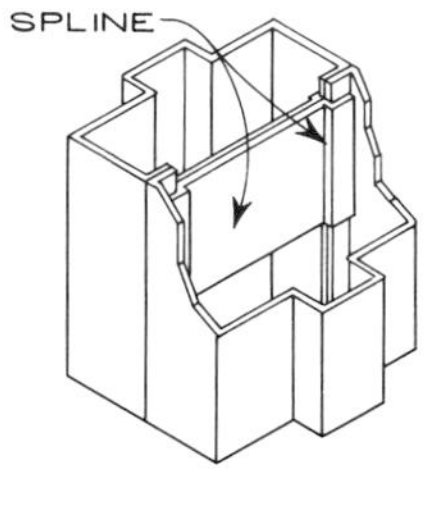

SPLINE

MULLION OF 2 STD. SECTIONS WITH SPLINE

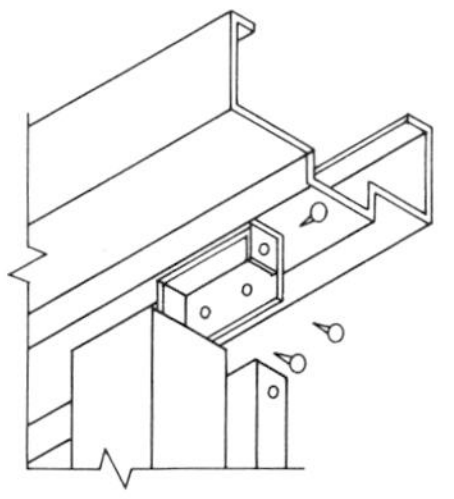

REMOVABLE MULLION (HEAD)

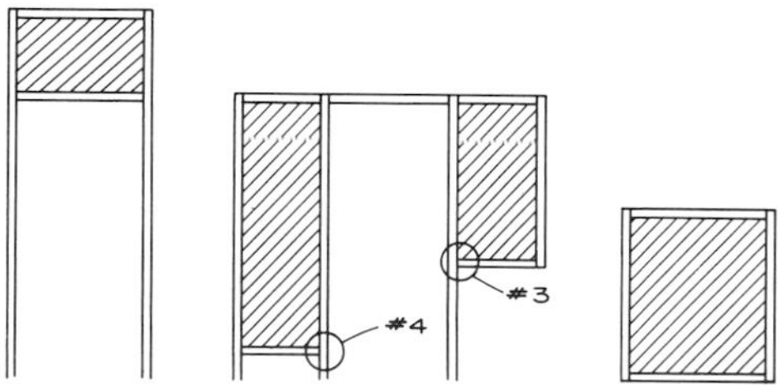

#4
#3

TRANSOM **SIDE-LIGHT** **SIDE-LIGHT** **BORROW LIGHT**

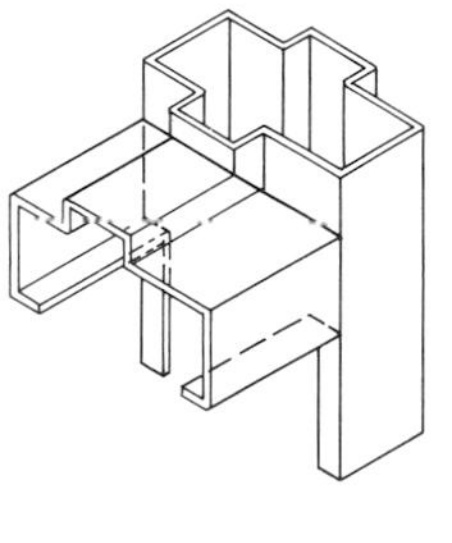

SIDELIGHT SILL #3

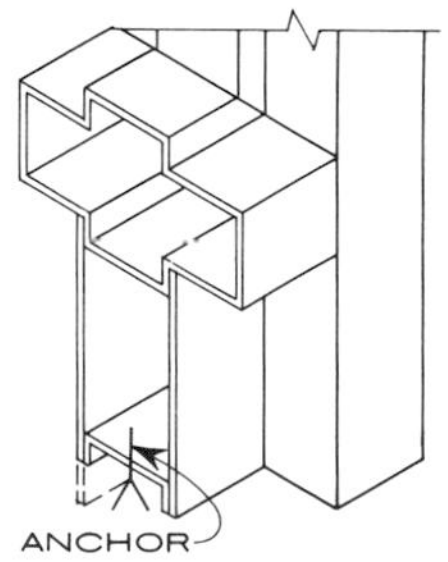

ANCHOR

SIDELIGHT SILL #4

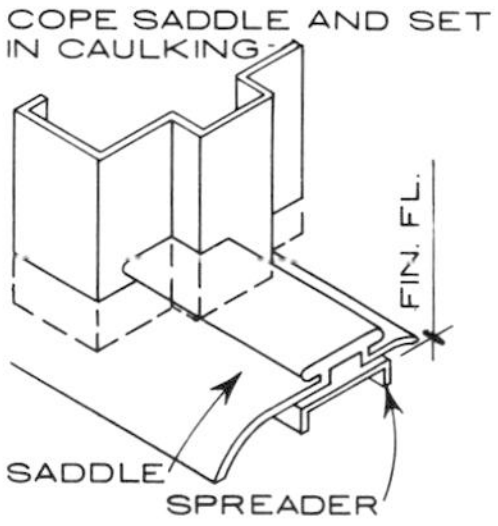

COPE SADDLE AND SET IN CAULKING
FIN. FL.
SADDLE
SPREADER

SPREADER TO REMAIN AS SADDLE ANCHOR

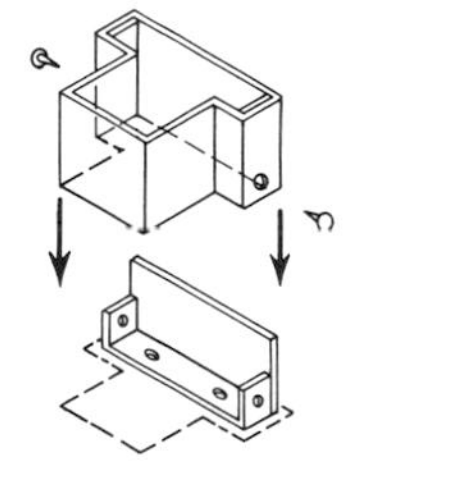

REMOVABLE MULLION (SILL)

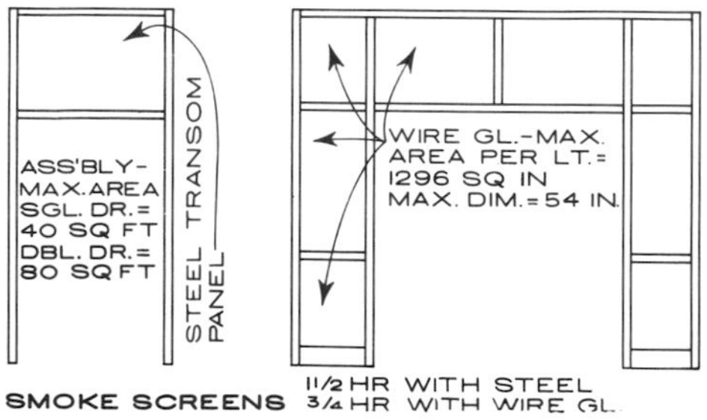

ASS'BLY-MAX.AREA SGL. DR.= 40 SQ FT DBL. DR.= 80 SQ FT
STEEL TRANSOM PANEL
WIRE GL.-MAX. AREA PER LT.= 1296 SQ IN MAX. DIM.= 54 IN.

SMOKE SCREENS 1 1/2 HR WITH STEEL, 3/4 HR WITH WIRE GL.

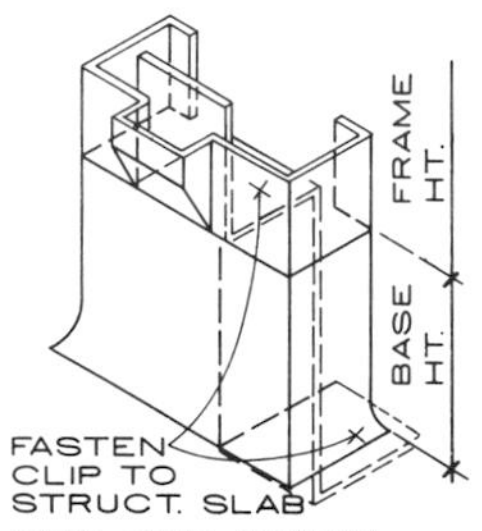

FRAME HT.
BASE HT.
FASTEN CLIP TO STRUCT. SLAB

CUT-OFF FRAME

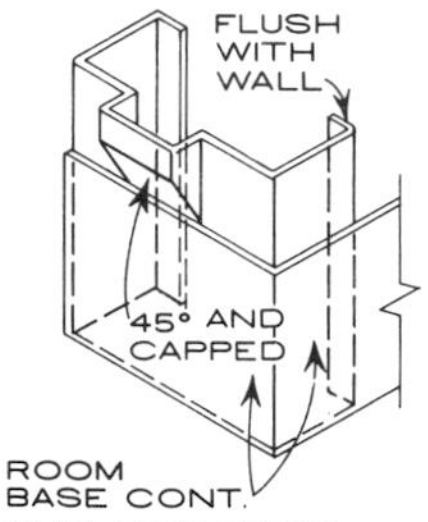

FLUSH WITH WALL
45° AND CAPPED
ROOM BASE CONT.

CUT-OFF STOP

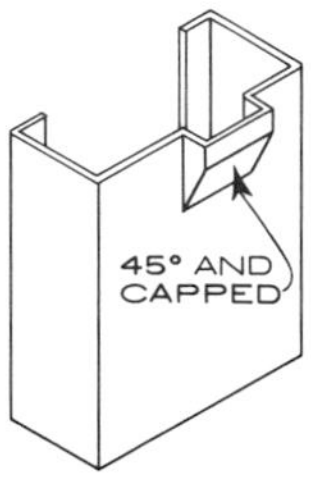

45° AND CAPPED

HOSPITAL STOP

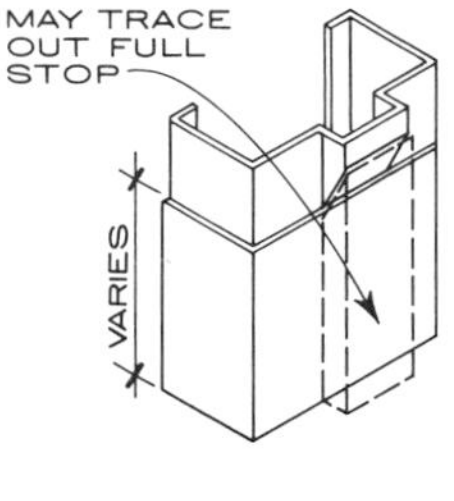

MAY TRACE OUT FULL STOP
VARIES

SPAT

James W. G. Watson, AIA; Ronald A. Spahn and Associates; Cleveland Heights, Ohio

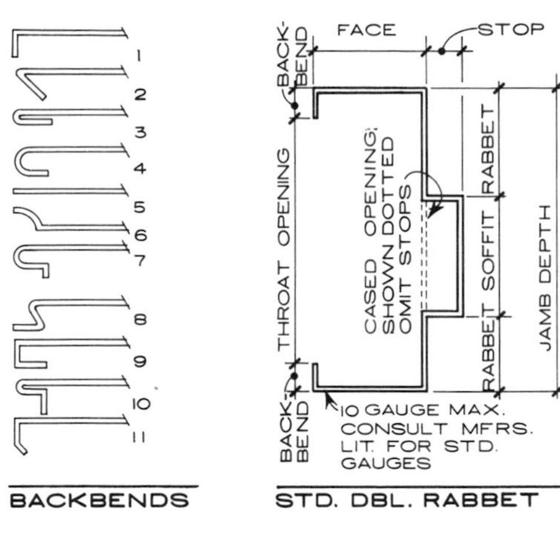
1
2
3
4
5
6
7
8
9
10
11
FACE
STOP
BACK-BEND
THROAT OPENING
CASED OPENING; SHOWN DOTTED OMIT STOPS
RABBET
SOFFIT
RABBET
JAMB DEPTH
BACK-BEND
10 GAUGE MAX.
CONSULT MFRS.
LIT. FOR STD.
GAUGES

BACKBENDS

STD. DBL. RABBET

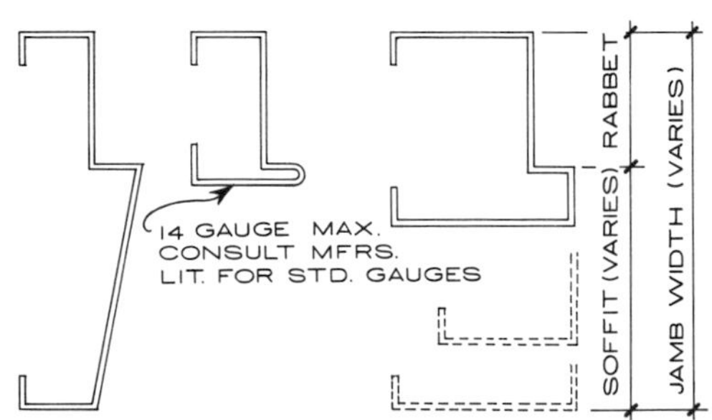
14 GAUGE MAX.
CONSULT MFRS.
LIT. FOR STD. GAUGES
RABBET
SOFFIT (VARIES)
JAMB WIDTH (VARIES)

VARIOUS SINGLE RABBETS

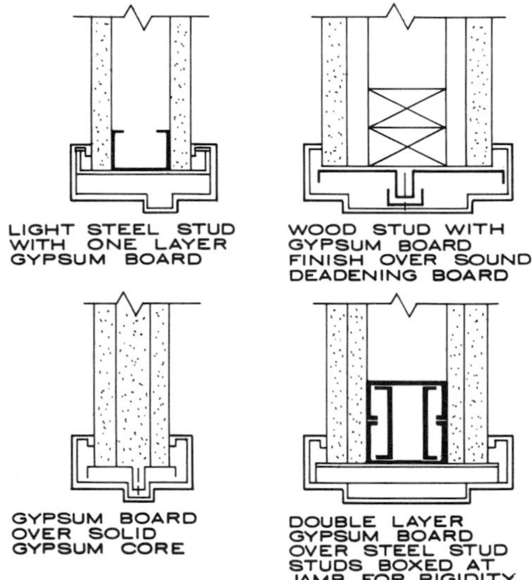
LIGHT STEEL STUD WITH ONE LAYER GYPSUM BOARD
WOOD STUD WITH GYPSUM BOARD FINISH OVER SOUND DEADENING BOARD
GYPSUM BOARD OVER SOLID GYPSUM CORE
DOUBLE LAYER GYPSUM BOARD OVER STEEL STUD STUDS BOXED AT JAMB FOR RIGIDITY

DRYWALL INSTALLATIONS

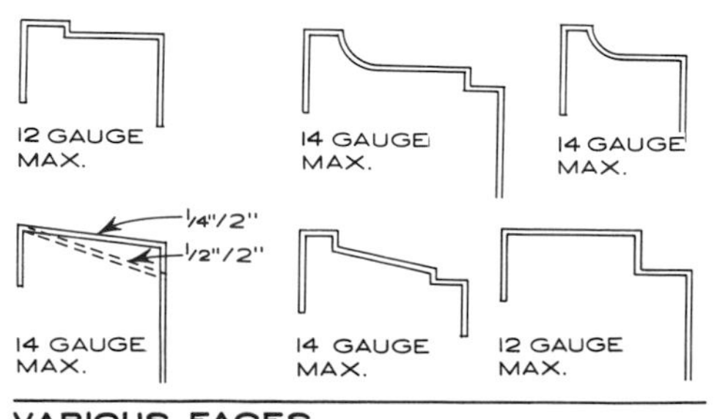
12 GAUGE MAX.
14 GAUGE MAX.
14 GAUGE MAX.
1/4"/2"
1/2"/2"
14 GAUGE MAX.
14 GAUGE MAX.
12 GAUGE MAX.

VARIOUS FACES

VARIOUS STANDARD PROFILES

JAMB DEPTH	2¾	3	3¾	4¾	5½	5¾	6¾	7¾	8¾	12¾
RABBET [3]	SINGLE RABBET ONLY			1 15/16 STD. FOR 1¾" DOOR						
SOFFIT [3]										
RABBET [3]				1 9/16 STD. FOR 1⅜" DOOR						
BACKBEND	½	7/16	½	½	¾	½	½	½	½	½
THROAT	1¾	2⅛	2	3¾	4	4¾	5¾	6¾	7¾	11¾

NOTES

1. Many others available. Consult mfrs. list for dimensions and options.
2. Depths vary in 1/8" increments to 12 3/4" max.
3. Omit stops for cased opening frames.
4. Std. stop 5/8", 1/2" min. + std. face 2", 1" min.

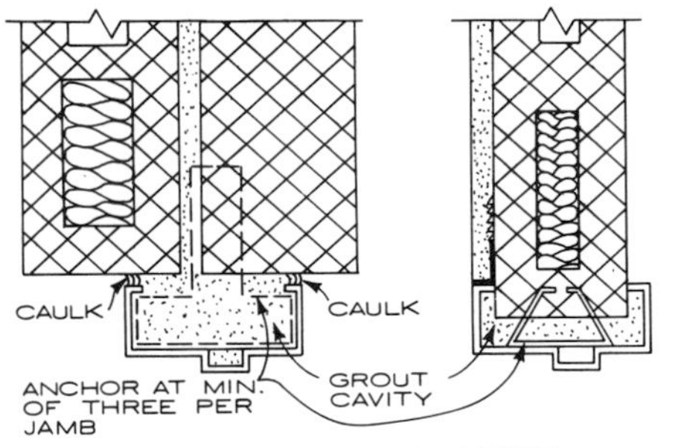

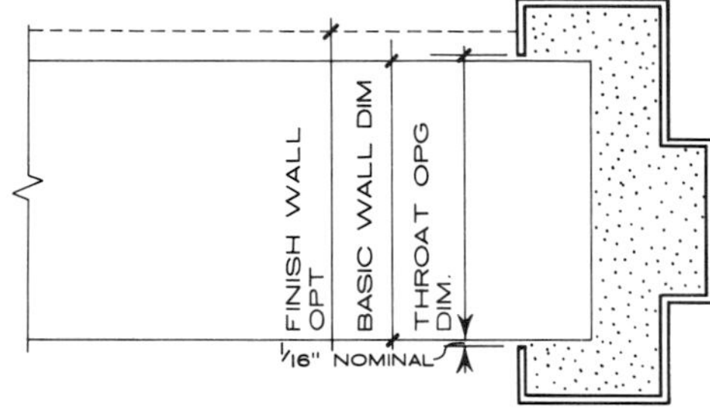
FINISH WALL OPT
BASIC WALL DIM
THROAT OPG DIM.
1/16" NOMINAL

1. Basic wall dim. < throat opening dim. Fin wall mat'l (dotted may encroach on backbend).
2. Anchors appropriate for wall constr. Req'd. min. 3 per jamb.
3. Fill frame w/mortar or plaster as used in wall.
4. Grout frame, backbend at masonry wall.
5. Backbend may vary as selected.

WRAP-AROUND FRAMES

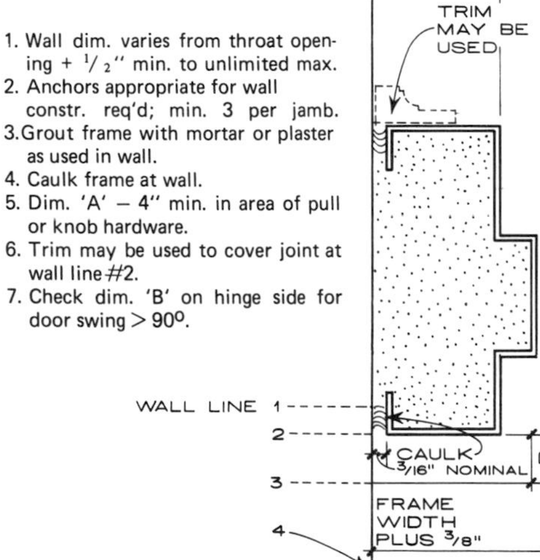
A
TRIM MAY BE USED
WALL LINE 1
2
3
4
CAULK
3/16" NOMINAL
B
FRAME WIDTH PLUS 3/8"

1. Wall dim. varies from throat opening + 1/2" min. to unlimited max.
2. Anchors appropriate for wall constr. req'd; min. 3 per jamb.
3. Grout frame with mortar or plaster as used in wall.
4. Caulk frame at wall.
5. Dim. 'A' – 4" min. in area of pull or knob hardware.
6. Trim may be used to cover joint at wall line #2.
7. Check dim. 'B' on hinge side for door swing > 90°.

BUTT FRAME

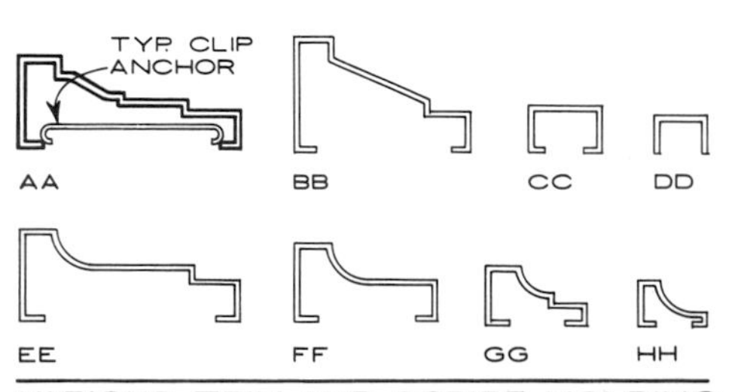
TYP. CLIP ANCHOR
AA
BB
CC
DD
EE
FF
GG
HH

VARIOUS TRIM AND SCRIBE MOLDING

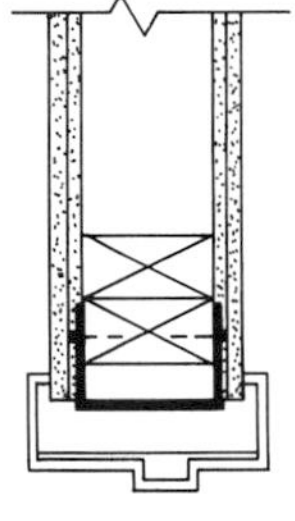
CAULK
CAULK
ANCHOR AT MIN. OF THREE PER JAMB
GROUT CAVITY

BUTTED TO MASONRY

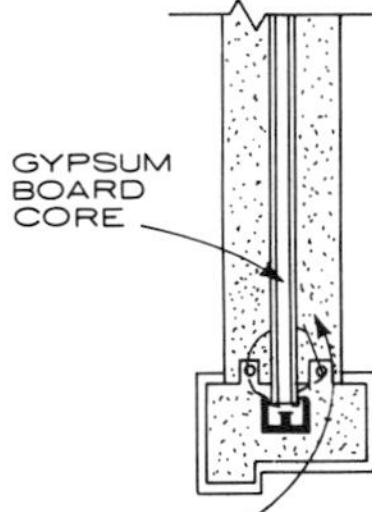

CONCRETE MASONRY UNIT WITH PLASTER FINISH

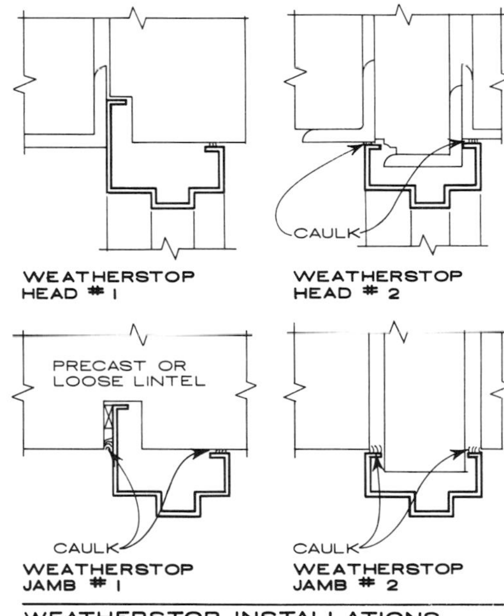
GYPSUM BOARD CORE
PLASTER
WOOD STUD WITH PLASTER ON PLASTER LATH
SOLID PLASTER
VARIOUS INSTALLATIONS
CAULK
WEATHERSTOP HEAD # 1
WEATHERSTOP HEAD # 2
PRECAST OR LOOSE LINTEL
CAULK
CAULK
WEATHERSTOP JAMB # 1
WEATHERSTOP JAMB # 2

WEATHERSTOP INSTALLATIONS

NOTES

1. Some details vary between manufacturers.
2. Stock frames stocked in warehouse prior to receipt of order. Certain profiles are warehoused locally.
3. Standard frames manufactured from existing jigs and tooling upon receipt of order. Certain profiles are readily available.
4. Custom frames manufactured in response to specific dimensional requirements of a particular customer. Custom profiles are available with relative delay.
5. Selection should reflect anticipated requirements of construction schedule.
6. Certain detail features will constitute a custom frame, verify with manufacturer.

James W. G. Watson, AIA; Ronald A. Spahn and Associates; Cleveland Heights, Ohio

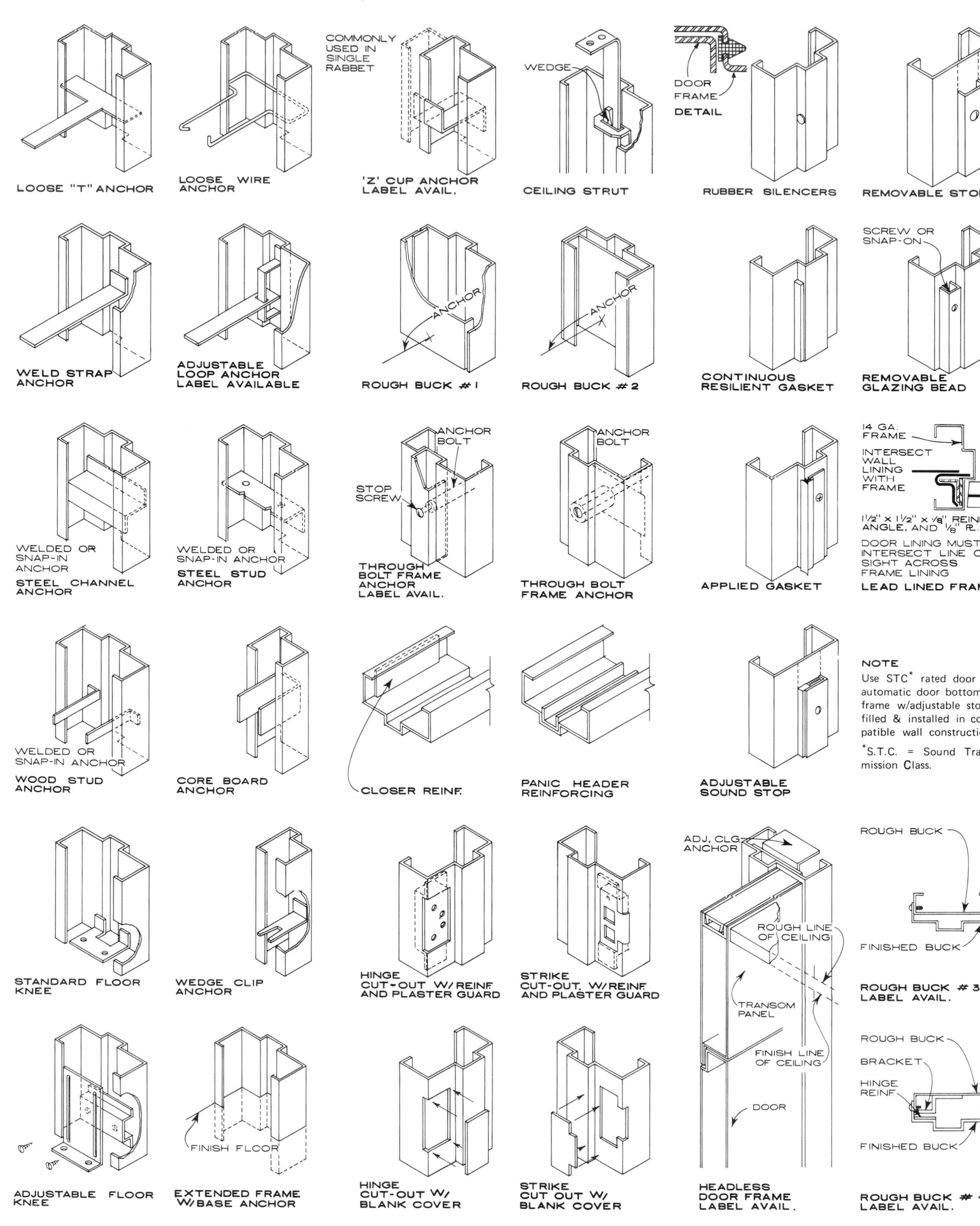

LOOSE "T" ANCHOR
LOOSE WIRE ANCHOR
COMMONLY USED IN SINGLE RABBET
'Z' CUP ANCHOR LABEL AVAIL.
WEDGE
CEILING STRUT
DOOR FRAME
DETAIL
RUBBER SILENCERS
REMOVABLE STOP
WELD STRAP ANCHOR
ADJUSTABLE LOOP ANCHOR LABEL AVAILABLE
ANCHOR
ROUGH BUCK # 1
ANCHOR
ROUGH BUCK # 2
CONTINUOUS RESILIENT GASKET
SCREW OR SNAP-ON
REMOVABLE GLAZING BEAD
WELDED OR SNAP-IN ANCHOR
STEEL CHANNEL ANCHOR
WELDED OR SNAP-IN ANCHOR
STEEL STUD ANCHOR
ANCHOR BOLT
STOP SCREW
THROUGH BOLT FRAME ANCHOR LABEL AVAIL.
ANCHOR BOLT
THROUGH BOLT FRAME ANCHOR
APPLIED GASKET
14 GA. FRAME
INTERSECT WALL LINING WITH FRAME
1 1/2" x 1 1/2" x 1/8" REINF. ANGLE, AND 1/8" PL.
DOOR LINING MUST INTERSECT LINE OF SIGHT ACROSS FRAME LINING
LEAD LINED FRAME
WELDED OR SNAP-IN ANCHOR
WOOD STUD ANCHOR
CORE BOARD ANCHOR
CLOSER REINF.
PANIC HEADER REINFORCING
ADJUSTABLE SOUND STOP
NOTE
Use STC* rated door w/ automatic door bottom & frame w/adjustable stops; filled & installed in compatible wall construction.
*S.T.C. = Sound Transmission Class.
STANDARD FLOOR KNEE
WEDGE CLIP ANCHOR
HINGE CUT-OUT W/ REINF. AND PLASTER GUARD
STRIKE CUT-OUT. W/ REINF. AND PLASTER GUARD
ADJ. CLG. ANCHOR
ROUGH LINE OF CEILING
TRANSOM PANEL
FINISH LINE OF CEILING
DOOR
HEADLESS DOOR FRAME LABEL AVAIL.
ROUGH BUCK
FINISHED BUCK
ROUGH BUCK # 3 LABEL AVAIL.
ADJUSTABLE FLOOR KNEE
FINISH FLOOR
EXTENDED FRAME W/BASE ANCHOR
HINGE CUT-OUT W/ BLANK COVER
STRIKE CUT OUT W/ BLANK COVER
ROUGH BUCK
BRACKET
HINGE REINF.
FINISHED BUCK
ROUGH BUCK # 4 LABEL AVAIL.

James W. G. Watson, AIA; Ronald A. Spahn and Associates; Cleveland Heights, Ohio

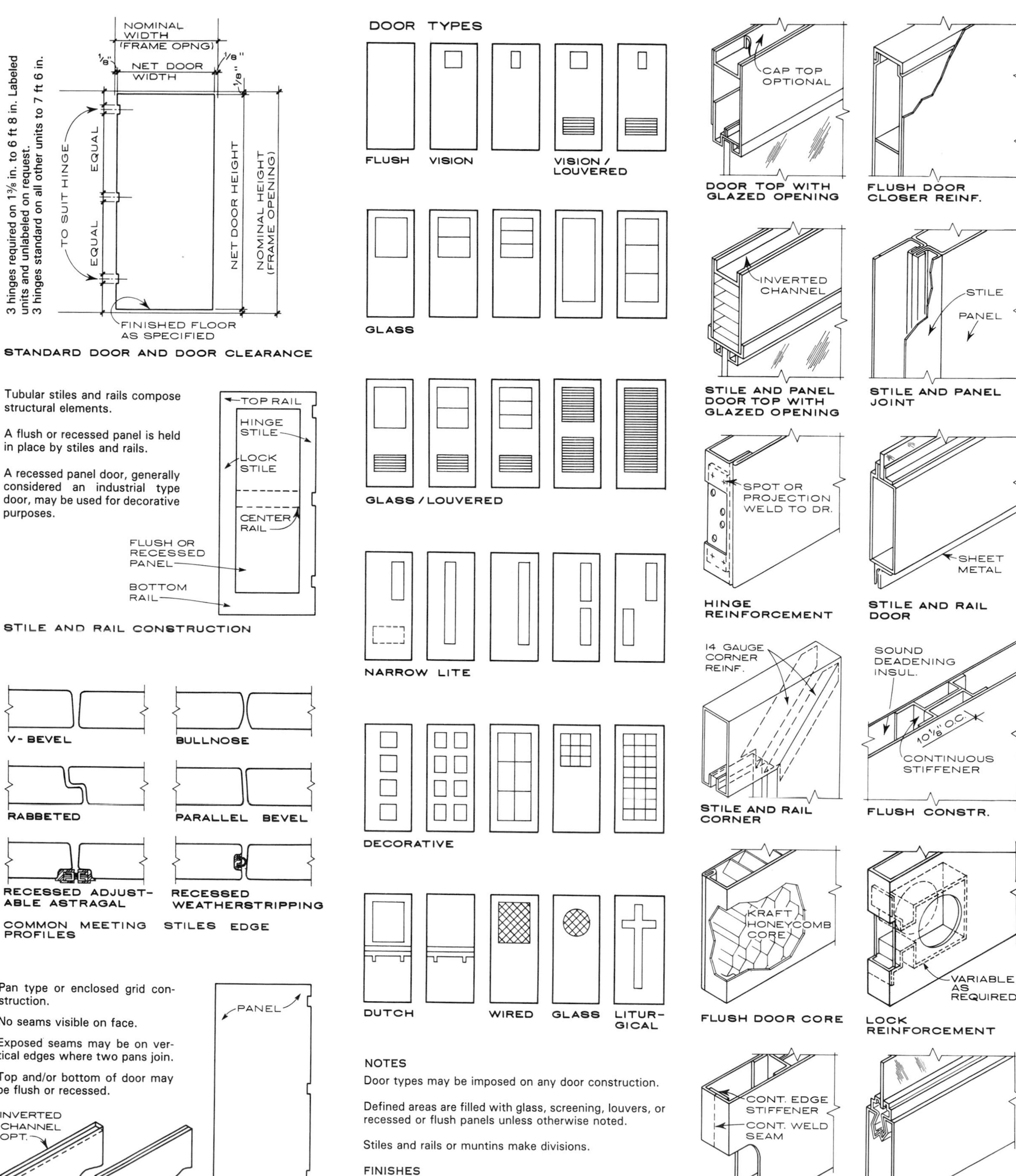

NOMINAL WIDTH (FRAME OPNG)
1/8"
1/8"
NET DOOR WIDTH
1/8"
TO SUIT HINGE
EQUAL
EQUAL
NET DOOR HEIGHT
NOMINAL HEIGHT (FRAME OPENING)
FINISHED FLOOR AS SPECIFIED
3 hinges required on 1 3/8 in. to 6 ft 8 in. Labeled units and unlabeled on request. 3 hinges standard on all other units to 7 ft 6 in.
STANDARD DOOR AND DOOR CLEARANCE
Tubular stiles and rails compose structural elements.
A flush or recessed panel is held in place by stiles and rails.
A recessed panel door, generally considered an industrial type door, may be used for decorative purposes.
TOP RAIL
HINGE STILE
LOCK STILE
CENTER RAIL
FLUSH OR RECESSED PANEL
BOTTOM RAIL
STILE AND RAIL CONSTRUCTION
V-BEVEL
BULLNOSE
RABBETED
PARALLEL BEVEL
RECESSED ADJUSTABLE ASTRAGAL
RECESSED WEATHERSTRIPPING
COMMON MEETING STILES EDGE PROFILES
DOOR TYPES
FLUSH
VISION
VISION / LOUVERED
GLASS
GLASS / LOUVERED
NARROW LITE
DECORATIVE
DUTCH
WIRED
GLASS
LITURGICAL
CAP TOP OPTIONAL
DOOR TOP WITH GLAZED OPENING
FLUSH DOOR CLOSER REINF.
INVERTED CHANNEL
STILE AND PANEL DOOR TOP WITH GLAZED OPENING
STILE
PANEL
STILE AND PANEL JOINT
SPOT OR PROJECTION WELD TO DR.
HINGE REINFORCEMENT
SHEET METAL
STILE AND RAIL DOOR
14 GAUGE CORNER REINF.
STILE AND RAIL CORNER
SOUND DEADENING INSUL.
10 1/8" O.C.
CONTINUOUS STIFFENER
FLUSH CONSTR.
KRAFT HONEYCOMB CORE
FLUSH DOOR CORE
VARIABLE AS REQUIRED
LOCK REINFORCEMENT

Pan type or enclosed grid construction.

No seams visible on face.

Exposed seams may be on vertical edges where two pans join.

Top and/or bottom of door may be flush or recessed.

INVERTED CHANNEL OPT.

PANEL

SEAMLESS FULL FLUSH

FLUSH CONSTRUCTION

NOTES

Door types may be imposed on any door construction.

Defined areas are filled with glass, screening, louvers, or recessed or flush panels unless otherwise noted.

Stiles and rails or muntins make divisions.

FINISHES

Standard: primed and/or galvanized
Paint: baked enamel
Applied: vinyl clad
Textured, embossed: stainless steel, aluminum
Polished: stainless steel

CONT. EDGE STIFFENER

CONT. WELD SEAM

FLUSH DOOR BOTTOM AND EDGE CONST.

STILE AND RAIL DOOR BOTTOM CONST.

James W. G. Watson, AIA; Ronald A. Spahn and Associates; Cleveland Heights, Ohio

MINIMUM GAUGES FOR COMMERCIAL STEEL DOORS

ITEM	GAUGE NO.	EQUIVALENT THICKNESS (IN.)
Door frames	16	0.0598
Surface applied hardware reinforcement	16	0.0598
Doors—hollow steel construction		
Panels and stile	18	0.0478
Doors—composite construction		
Perimeter channel	18	0.0478
Surface sheets	22	0.0299
Reinforcement		
Surface applied hardware	16	0.0598
Lock and strike	16	0.0598
Hinge	10	0.1345
Flush bolt	16	0.0598
Glass molding	20	0.0359
Glass muntins	22	0.0299

MINIMUM GAUGES FOR INTERIOR STEEL DOORS

ITEM	GAUGE NO.	EQUIVALENT THICKNESS (IN.)
Door frames, 1 3/8 in. thick	18	0.0478
Door frames, 1 3/4 in. thick	16	0.0598
Stiles and panels	20	0.0359
Reinforcement		
Lock and strike	16	0.0598
Hinge	11	0.1196
Closer	14	0.0747

NOTES

1. The steel door tables represent minimum standards published by the U.S. Department of Commerce for standard stock commercial, 1 3/4 in. thick steel doors and frames, and flush type interior steel doors and frames (doors not more than 3 ft in width).
2. Specifications for custom hollow metal doors and frames are published by the National Association of Architectural Metal Manufacturers. Standards may also vary according to location or the agency—always consult with the local authorities and/or agencies to determine what they require. Doors must be selected according to the project requirements such as frequency of usage, type of traffic, conditions required by the enclosed space, and environmental conditions.

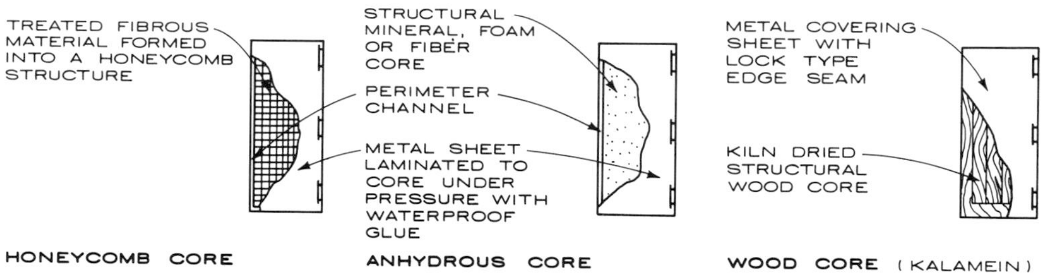
TREATED FIBROUS MATERIAL FORMED INTO A HONEYCOMB STRUCTURE
STRUCTURAL MINERAL, FOAM OR FIBER CORE
PERIMETER CHANNEL
METAL SHEET LAMINATED TO CORE UNDER PRESSURE WITH WATERPROOF GLUE
METAL COVERING SHEET WITH LOCK TYPE EDGE SEAM
KILN DRIED STRUCTURAL WOOD CORE

HONEYCOMB CORE — ANHYDROUS CORE — WOOD CORE (KALAMEIN)

NONMETALLIC CORE DOORS

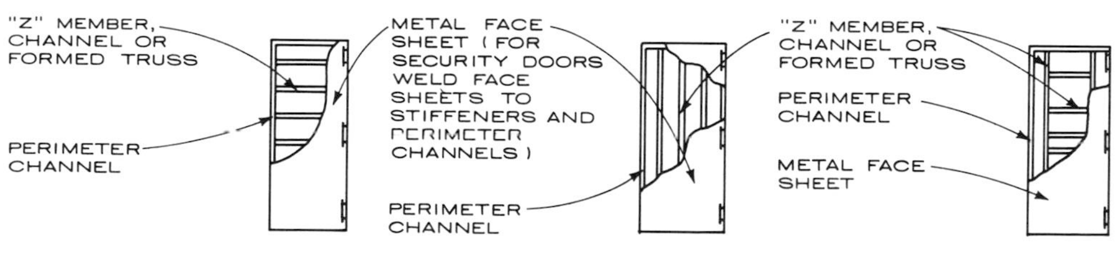
"Z" MEMBER, CHANNEL OR FORMED TRUSS
PERIMETER CHANNEL
METAL FACE SHEET (FOR SECURITY DOORS WELD FACE SHEETS TO STIFFENERS AND PERIMETER CHANNELS)
PERIMETER CHANNEL
"Z" MEMBER, CHANNEL OR FORMED TRUSS
PERIMETER CHANNEL
METAL FACE SHEET

HORIZONTAL STIFFENERS — VERTICAL STIFFENERS — GRID STIFFENERS

STIFFENED CORE DOORS (HEAVY DOORS) NORMALLY SOUND DEADENED OR INSULATED

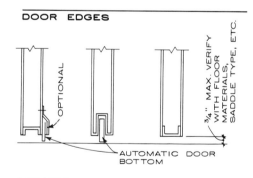

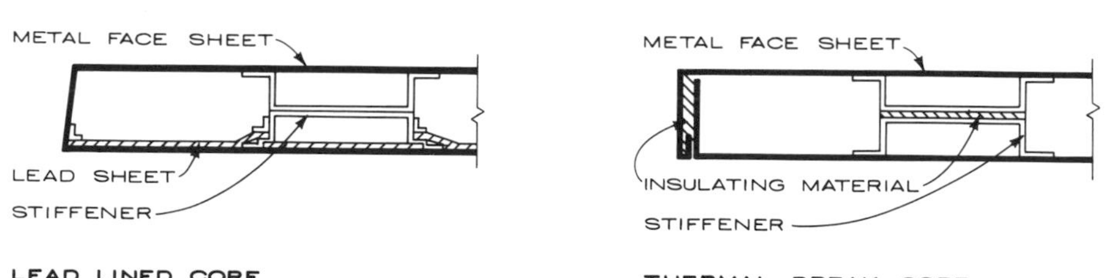
METAL FACE SHEET
LEAD SHEET
STIFFENER
METAL FACE SHEET
INSULATING MATERIAL
STIFFENER

LEAD LINED CORE — THERMAL BREAK CORE

SPECIAL CORE DOORS

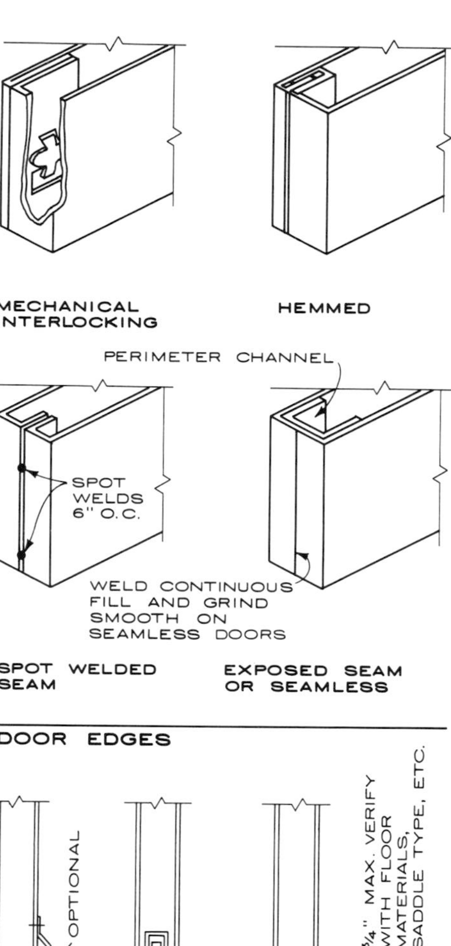
MECHANICAL INTERLOCKING
HEMMED
PERIMETER CHANNEL
SPOT WELDS 6" O.C.
WELD CONTINUOUS FILL AND GRIND SMOOTH ON SEAMLESS DOORS
SPOT WELDED SEAM
EXPOSED SEAM OR SEAMLESS

DOOR EDGES

OPTIONAL
3/4" MAX. VERIFY WITH FLOOR MATERIALS, SADDLE TYPE, ETC.
AUTOMATIC DOOR BOTTOM

DOOR BOTTOMS

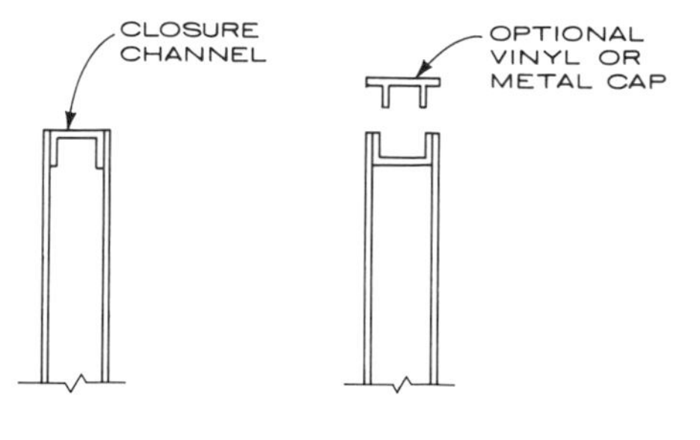
CLOSURE CHANNEL
OPTIONAL VINYL OR METAL CAP

DOOR TOPS

Kelly Sacher & Associates; Architects Engineers Planners; N. Babylon, New York

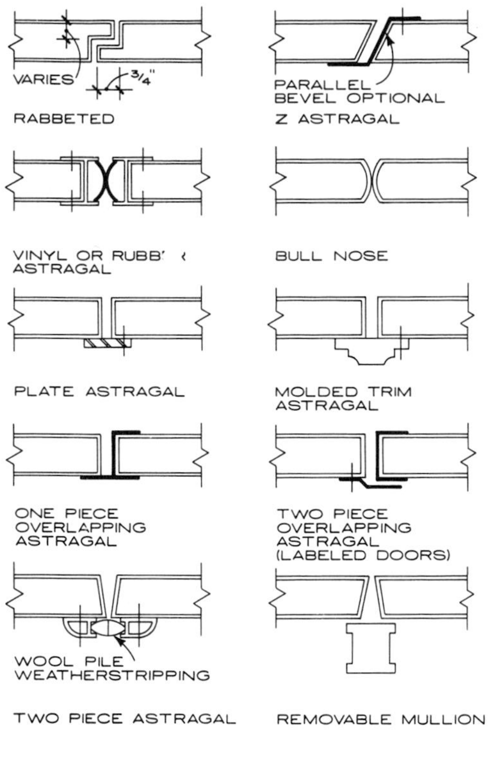

VARIES
3/4"
RABBETED

PARALLEL
BEVEL OPTIONAL
Z ASTRAGAL

VINYL OR RUBBER ASTRAGAL

BULL NOSE

PLATE ASTRAGAL

MOLDED TRIM ASTRAGAL

ONE PIECE OVERLAPPING ASTRAGAL

TWO PIECE OVERLAPPING ASTRAGAL (LABELED DOORS)

WOOL PILE WEATHERSTRIPPING

TWO PIECE ASTRAGAL

REMOVABLE MULLION

NOTE: V BEVELS ARE OPTIONAL

MEETING STILES

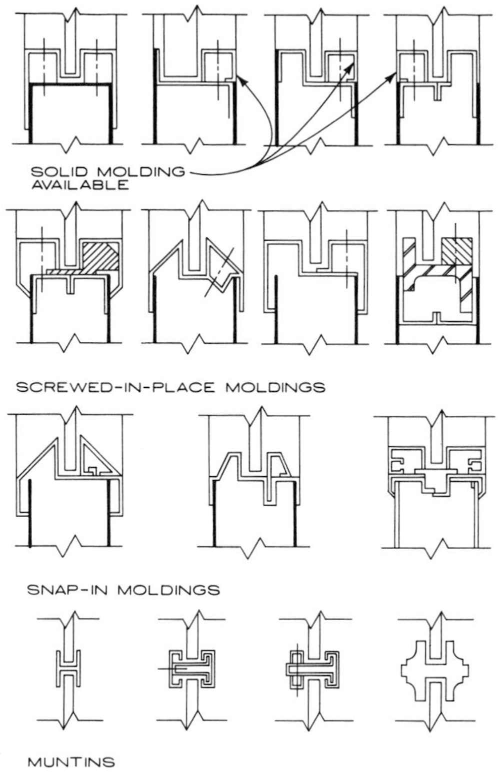

SOLID MOLDING AVAILABLE

SCREWED-IN-PLACE MOLDINGS

SNAP-IN MOLDINGS

MUNTINS

GLAZING DETAILS

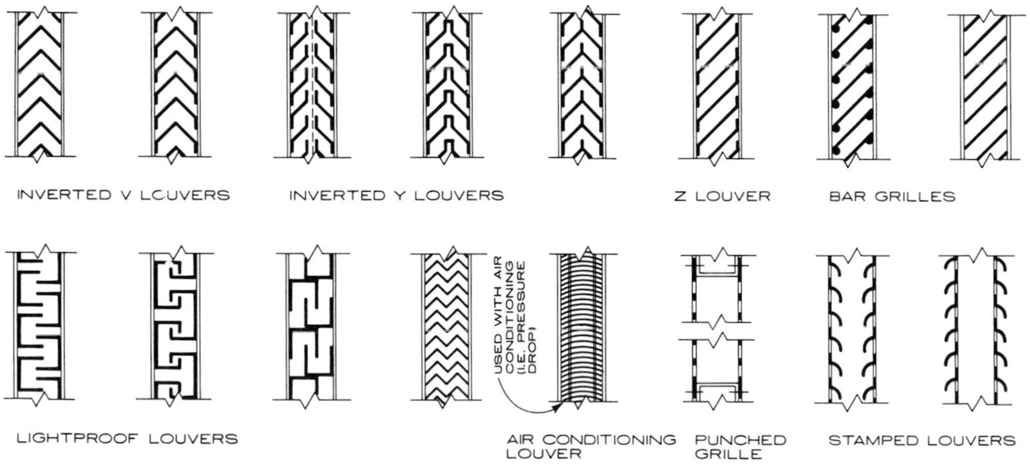

INVERTED V LOUVERS

INVERTED Y LOUVERS

Z LOUVER

BAR GRILLES

LIGHTPROOF LOUVERS

USED WITH AIR CONDITIONING (I.E. PRESSURE DROP)

AIR CONDITIONING LOUVER

PUNCHED GRILLE

STAMPED LOUVERS

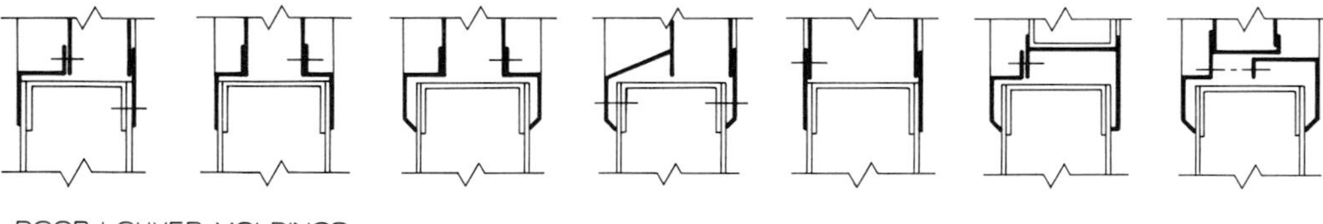

DOOR LOUVER MOLDINGS

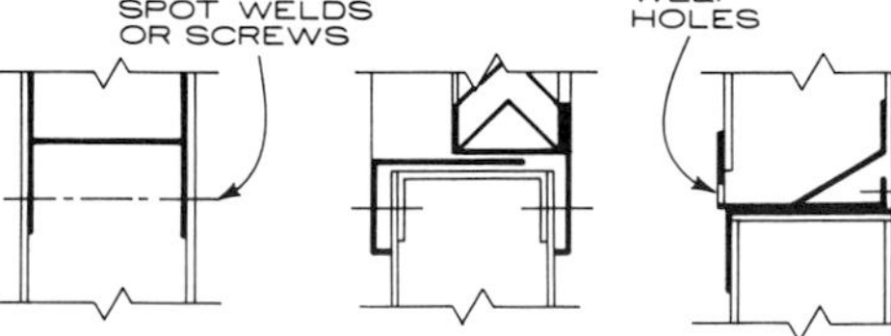
SPOT WELDS
OR SCREWS
WEEP
HOLES

DOOR LOUVER MOLDINGS

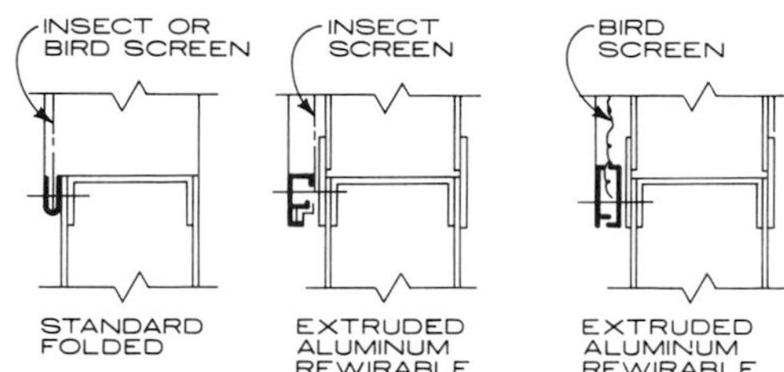
INSECT OR
BIRD SCREEN
INSECT
SCREEN
BIRD
SCREEN
STANDARD
FOLDED
EXTRUDED
ALUMINUM
REWIRABLE
EXTRUDED
ALUMINUM
REWIRABLE

DOOR SCREENS

LOUVERS AND VENTS

Kelly Sacher & Associates; Architects Engineers Planners; N. Babylon, New York

MATERIALS

Hollow metal doors are available in various steel gauges according to where and how they will be used. The following gradings should be used only as guidelines in selecting doors for a particular project. Local codes and governing authorities establish minimum gauges, which should always be consulted.

GRADE	GAUGE
Residential	20 gauge and lighter
Commercial	16 and 18 gauge
Institutional	12 and 14 gauge
High security	Steel plate

Some manufacturers will custom make moldings and muntins to meet a specific design, as long as there is sufficient quantity involved.

For security, the exterior moldings on exterior doors should be welded into the door and all exposed fasteners should be tamperproof.

For fire ratings of hollow metal doors and requirements for fire doors see other pages in this series.

FINISH

Hollow metal doors should receive at least one shop coat of rust inhibitive primer before they are delivered to the job site. In very corrosive atmospheres, such as saltwater beach locations, it is advisable to have the doors and frames hot dipped galvanized for additional protection.

Doors are available from several manufacturers, with factory applied paint finishes in various colors.

GLAZING

The size and type of glass permitted in fire rated doors is determined by local building codes and governing authorities having jurisdiction. The following table should only be used as a guide:

DOOR RATING	GLAZING REQUIREMENTS
*A—3 hr	No glazing permitted
*B—1 1/2 hr	100 sq in. of glazing per door leaf
C—3/4 hr	Max. 1296 sq in. of glazing per light. Max. dim. per light = 54 in. Min. dim. per light = 3 in.
*D—1 1/2 hr	No glazing permitted
E—3/4 hr	Max. 720 sq in. of glazing per light. Max. dim. per light = 54 in.

NOTE: Available on composite doors only. A, B, and D doors are available with Heat Transmission Ratings of 250°F or 650°F, or are not rated.

LOUVERS AND VENTS

Door louvers are available extruded, formed, and stamped in various metals and configurations; operable with or without a fusible link. Punched, stamped, and bar grilles are also available.

The percentage of free area for louvers depends on the louver blade thickness, spacing, and type. For this information consult the manufacturer's catalogs.

Door louvers and grilles are available prefinished, without moldings, and with moldings attached at the factory on one or both sides.

Insert screens are often used in conjunction with louvers or grilles; they may be used by themselves as well, however, in some applications. Screen material is available in various grid and wire sizes and materials.

GENERAL NOTES FOR ALL WOOD DOORS

Kiln dried wood, moisture content @ 6–12%.

Type 1 doors: Fully waterproof bond ext. and int.
Type 11 doors: Water resistant bond. Interior only.

Tolerances: Height, width, thickness, squareness and warp per NWMA STANDARDS and vary with solid vs. built-up construction.

Prefit: Doors @ 3/16" less in width and 1/8" less in height than nominal size, ± 1/32" tolerance, with vertical edges eased.

Premachining: Doors mortised for locks and cut out for hinges when so specified.

Premium: For transparent finish. Good/custom: For paint or transparent finish. Sound: For paint, with 2 coats completely covering defects.

FLUSH WOOD DOORS

CORE MATERIAL
SOLID CORES

Wood block, single specie, @ 2 1/2" max. width, surfaced two sides, without spaces or defects impairing strength or visible thru hdwd. veneer facing.

HOLLOW CORES

Wood, wood derivative, or class A insulation board.

TYPES OF WOOD FACES

Standard thickness face veneers @ 1/16"–1/32", bonded to hardwood, crossband @ 1/10"–1/16". Most economical and widely used, inhibits checking, difficult to refinish or repair face damage, for use on all cores.

1/8" Sawn veneers, bonded to crossband, easily refinished and repaired.

For use on staved block and stile and rail solid cores. 1/4" Sawn veneers: same as 1/8" but without crossband on stile and rail solid cores with horizontal blocks. Decorative grooves can be cut into faces.

LIGHT & LOUVER OPENINGS

Custom made to specifications. Wood beads and slats to match face veneer. 5" min. between opening and edge of door.

Hollow core: Cut-out area max. 1/2 height of door. Door not guaranteed with openings greater than 40%. Exterior doors: Weatherproofing required to prevent moisture from leaking into core.

FACTORY FINISHING

Partial: Sealing coats applied, final job finish.
Complete: Requires prefit and premachining.

SPECIAL FACING

High or medium-low density overlay faces of phenolic resins and cellulose fibers fused to inner faces of hardwood in lieu of final veneers as base for final opaque finish only.

1/16" min. laminated plastic bonded to 1/16" min. wood back of two or more piles.

1/8" hardboard, smooth one or two sides.

SPECIAL CORES
SOUND INSULATING DOORS

Thicknesses 1 3/4", 2 1/4". Transmission loss rating C Stc 36 for 1 3/4", 42 for 2 1/4". Barrier faces separated by a void or damping compound to keep faces from vibrating in unison. Special stops, gaskets, and threshold devices required. Mfrs. requirements as to wd. frames and wall specs.

FIRE RATED DOORS

3/4 hr "C" label and 1 hr "B" label-maximum size 4'0" x 10'0".
1 1/2 hr "B" label-maximum size 4'0" x 9'0". All doors 1 3/4" minimum thickness.

LEAD LINED DOORS

See U/L requirements. Optional location within door construction of 1/32" to 1/2" continuous lead sheet from edge to edge which may be reinforced with lead bolts or glued.

GROUNDED DOORS

Wire mesh located at center of core, grounded with copper wire through hinges to frame.

TYPES OF HOLLOW CORE DOORS

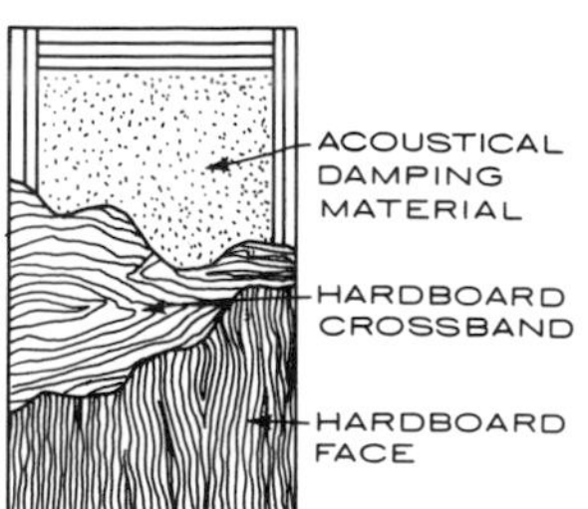
ACOUSTICAL DAMPING MATERIAL
HARDBOARD CROSSBAND
HARDBOARD FACE

ACOUSTICAL DOOR

Uses gasketed stops and neoprene bottom seals to cut sound transmission.

HONEYCOMB FIBER

INSTITUTIONAL: With cross rail.
INTERIOR: Without cross rail. Uniform core of honeycomb fiber to form 1/2" air cells.

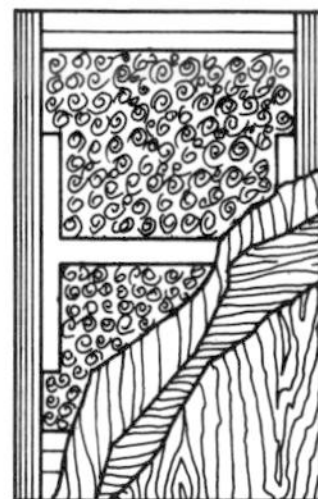

IMPLANTED BLANKS

Spirals or other forms separated or joined, implanted between & supporting outer faces of door.

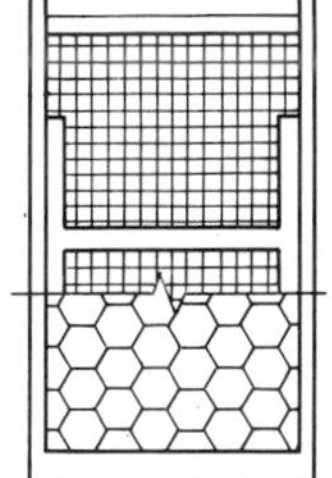

MESH

Interlocked, horizontal & vertical strips, equally spaced, notched into stiles, or expandable cellular or honey-comb core.

TYPES OF SOLID CORES

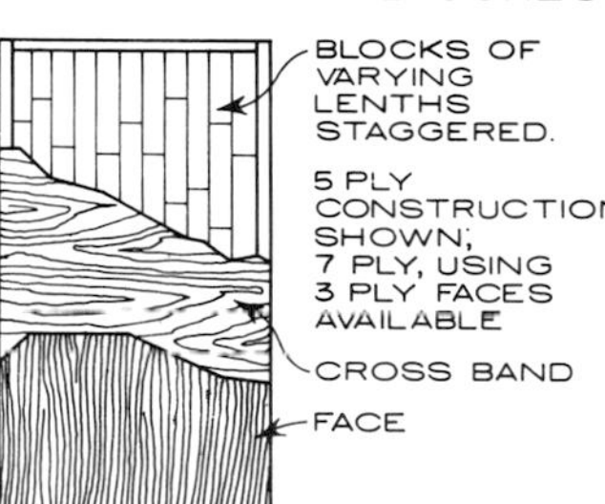
BLOCKS OF VARYING LENTHS STAGGERED.
5 PLY CONSTRUCTION SHOWN; 7 PLY, USING 3 PLY FACES AVAILABLE
CROSS BAND
FACE

CONTINUOUS BLOCK STAVED CORE

Bonded staggered blocks bonded to face panels. Most widely used & economical solid core.

FRAMED BLOCK STAVED CORE

Non-bonded staggered blocks laid up within stile rail frame, bonded to face panels.

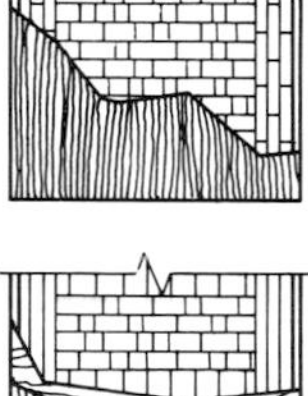

STILE AND RAIL

Horizontal blocks when cross banding is not used. Vertical panel blocks when cross banding is used.

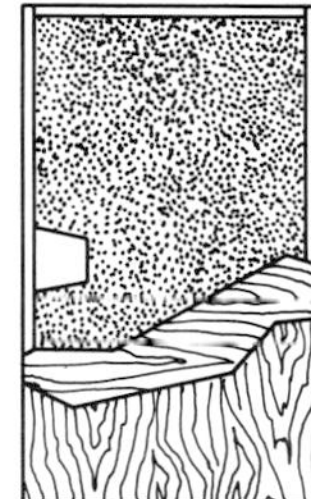

PARTICLE BOARD

Extremely heavy, more soundproof, economical door, available in hardwood face veneer or high pressure laminate face.

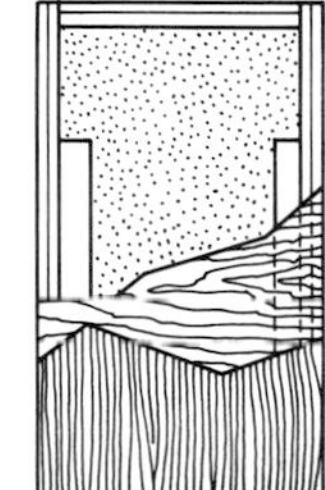

MINERAL COMPOSITION

Lightest weight of all cores. Details, as cut-outs, difficult. Low screw holding strength.

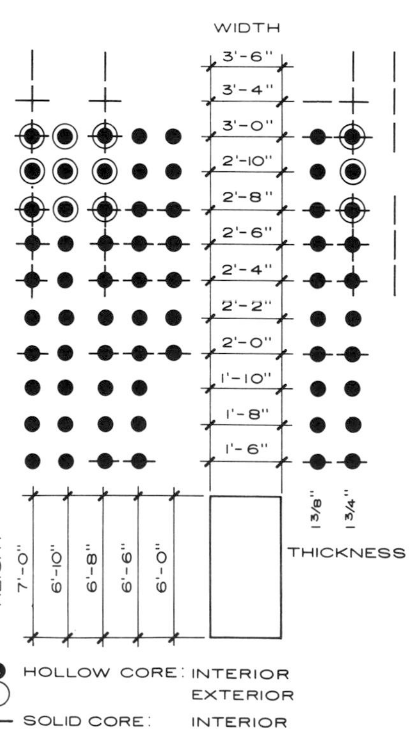
WIDTH
3'-6"
3'-4"
3'-0"
2'-10"
2'-8"
2'-6"
2'-4"
2'-2"
2'-0"
1'-10"
1'-8"
1'-6"
HEIGHT
7'-0"
6'-10"
6'-8"
6'-6"
6'-0"
1 3/8"
1 3/4"
THICKNESS
HOLLOW CORE: INTERIOR
EXTERIOR
SOLID CORE: INTERIOR
EXTERIOR

STANDARD SIZES

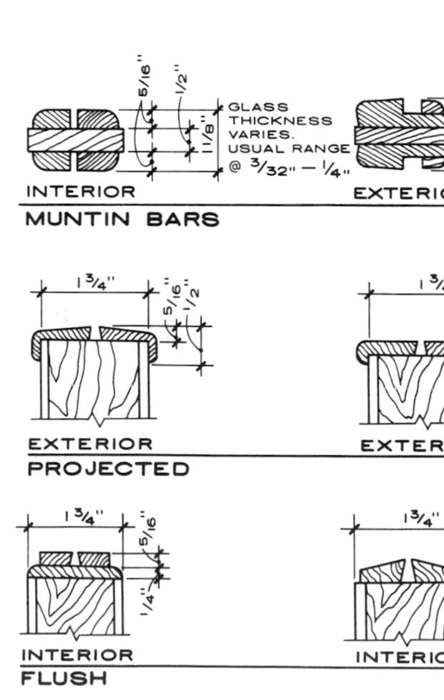
5/16"
1/2"
1 1/8"
GLASS THICKNESS VARIES. USUAL RANGE @ 3/32" – 1/4"
1/4"
1/16"
15/16"
INTERIOR
EXTERIOR
MUNTIN BARS
1 3/4"
5/16"
1/2"
1 3/4"
EXTERIOR
EXTERIOR
PROJECTED
1 3/4"
5/16"
1/4"
1 3/4"
INTERIOR
INTERIOR
FLUSH

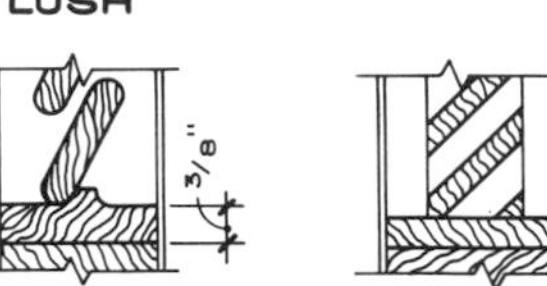
3/8"

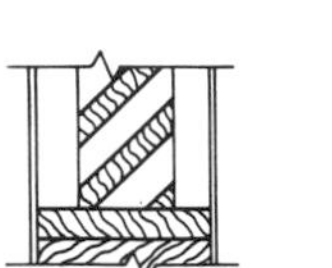

ROUND EDGE FLAT SLAT SIGHTPROOF

LOUVERS · METAL LOUVERS ALSO AVAILABLE

STOCK OPENING AND LOUVER DETAIL

NOTES

CONSTRUCTION

Solid or built-up stiles, rails, and vertical members or mullions, doweled as in NWWDA standard. Stock material includes ponderosa pine or other Western pine, fir, hemlock, or spruce, and hardwood veneers. Hardboard, metal, and plastic facings available in patterns simulating panel doors.

GRADES

Premium (select) grade: for natural, clear, or stained finish. Exposed wood free of defects that affect appearance.

Standard grade: for opaque finishes. Defects, discoloration, mixed species, and finger joints permitted if undetectable after finishing.

BUILT-UP MEMBERS

Core as in solid core of flush doors. Edge and end strips as in flush doors. Face veneer: hardwood at 1/8 in. minimum.

PANELS

Flat: 3-ply hardwood or softwood. Raised—two sides: solid hardwood or softwood built-up of two or more plies. Doors 1 ft 6 in. wide and narrower are one panel wide.

STICKING, GLASS STOPS, AND MUNTINS

Cove, bead, or ovolo; solid, matching face.

GLAZING

Must be safety glazing. Insulated (dual) glazing is available.

THICKNESS

Interior doors: 1 3/8 in.
Exterior doors: 1 3/8 in. or 1 3/4 in.
Storm and screen doors: 1 1/8 in.

See index for other door types and door hardware.

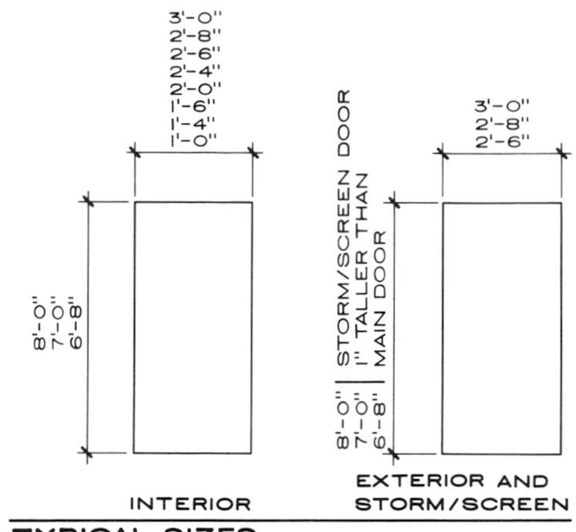
3'-0"
2'-8"
2'-6"
2'-4"
2'-0"
1'-6"
1'-4"
1'-0"
8'-0"
7'-0"
6'-8"
STORM/SCREEN DOOR 1" TALLER THAN MAIN DOOR
3'-0"
2'-8"
2'-6"
INTERIOR
EXTERIOR AND STORM/SCREEN

TYPICAL SIZES

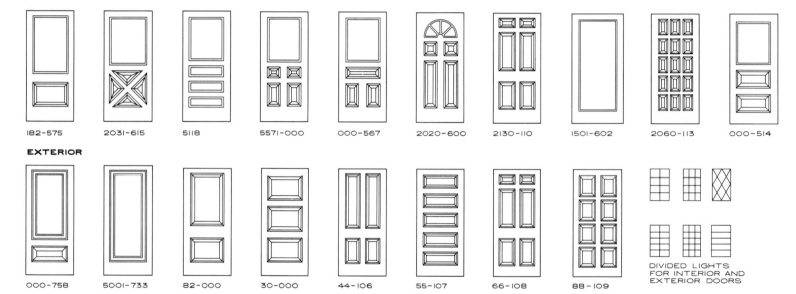

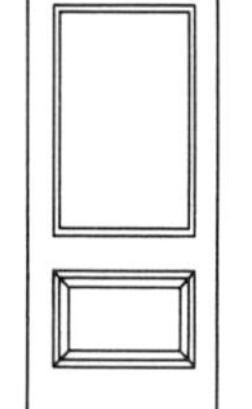
182-575

2031-615

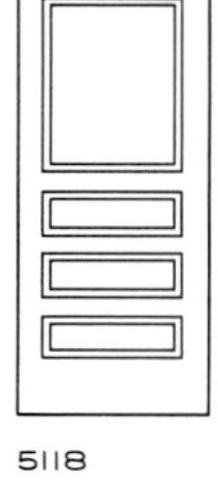
5118

5571-000

000-567

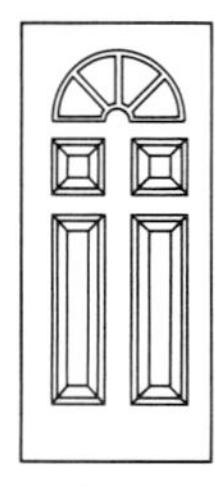
2020-600

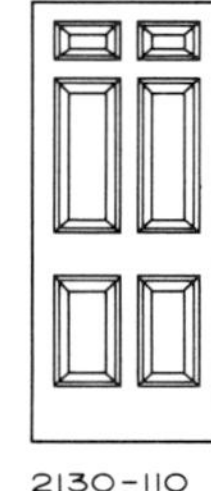
2130-110

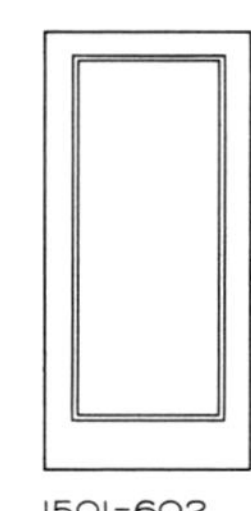
1501-602

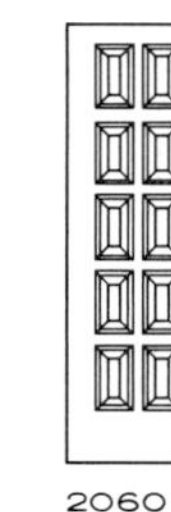
2060-113

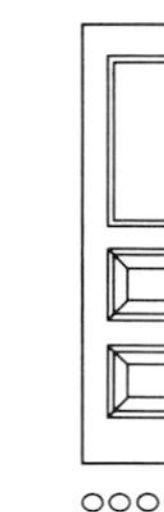
000-514

EXTERIOR

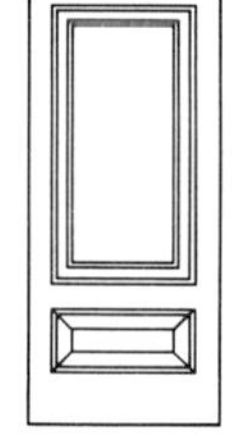
000-758

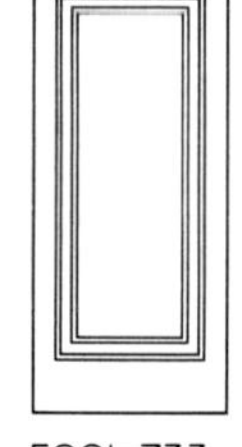
5001-733

SCREEN/STORM

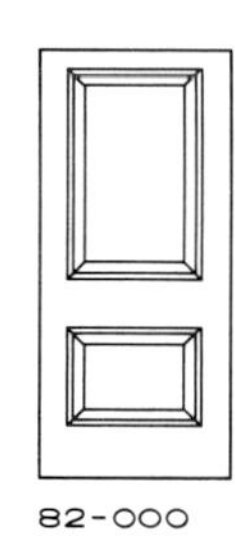
82-000

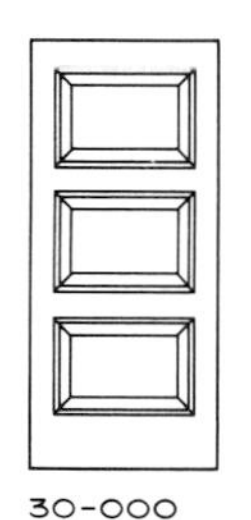
30-000

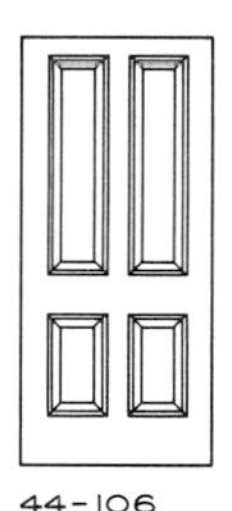
44-106

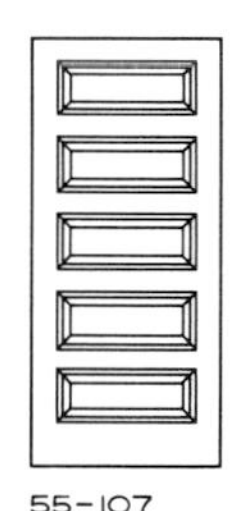
55-107

66-108

88-109

INTERIOR

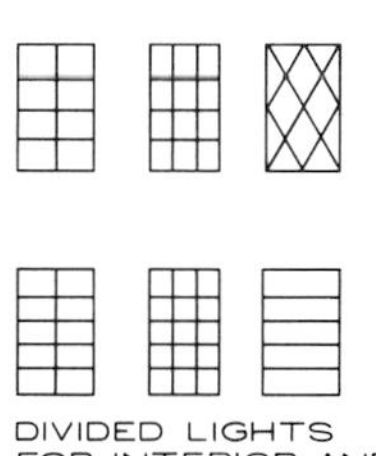
DIVIDED LIGHTS FOR INTERIOR AND EXTERIOR DOORS

SELECTED STANDARD DOOR TYPES (NUMBERS CORRESPOND TO NWWDA STANDARD)

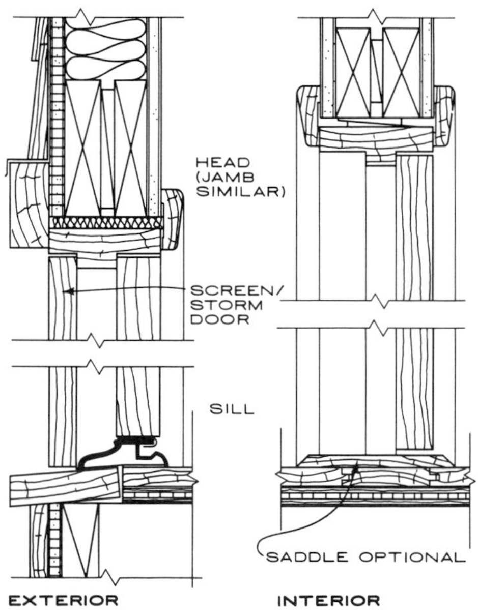
HEAD (JAMB SIMILAR)
SCREEN/ STORM DOOR
SILL
SADDLE OPTIONAL
EXTERIOR
INTERIOR

DOOR FRAMES

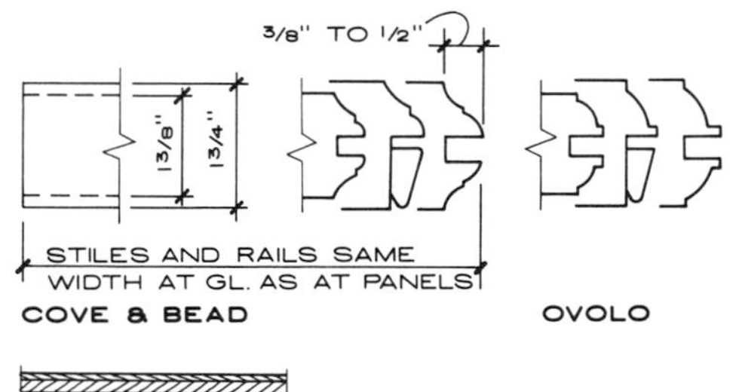
3/8" TO 1/2"
1 3/8"
1 3/4"
STILES AND RAILS SAME WIDTH AT GL. AS AT PANELS
COVE & BEAD
OVOLO

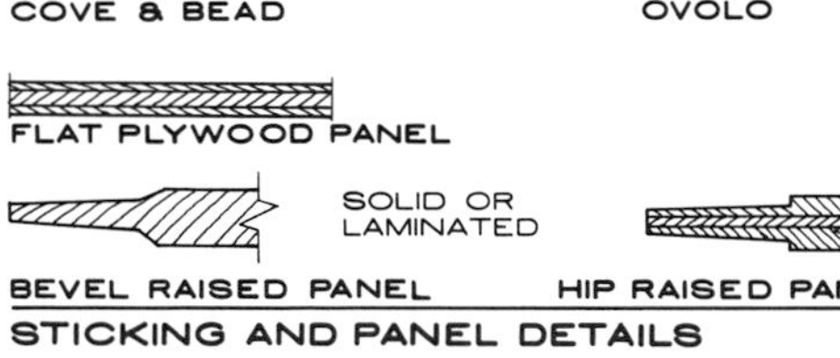
FLAT PLYWOOD PANEL
SOLID OR LAMINATED
BEVEL RAISED PANEL
HIP RAISED PANEL

STICKING AND PANEL DETAILS

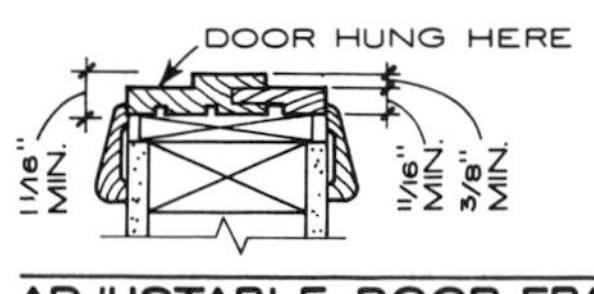
DOOR HUNG HERE
1/16" MIN.
1/16" MIN.
3/8" MIN.

ADJUSTABLE DOOR FRAME

NOTES

Top operable alone or with bottom using joining hardware.

Can swing in or out.

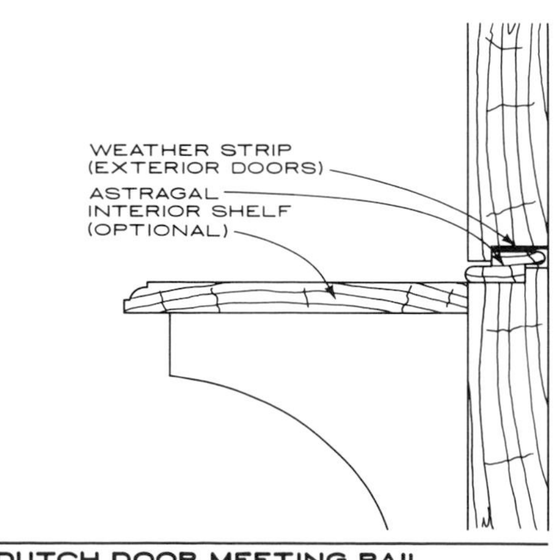
WEATHER STRIP (EXTERIOR DOORS)
ASTRAGAL
INTERIOR SHELF (OPTIONAL)

DUTCH DOOR MEETING RAIL

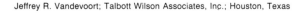

Jeffrey R. Vandevoort; Talbott Wilson Associates, Inc.; Houston, Texas

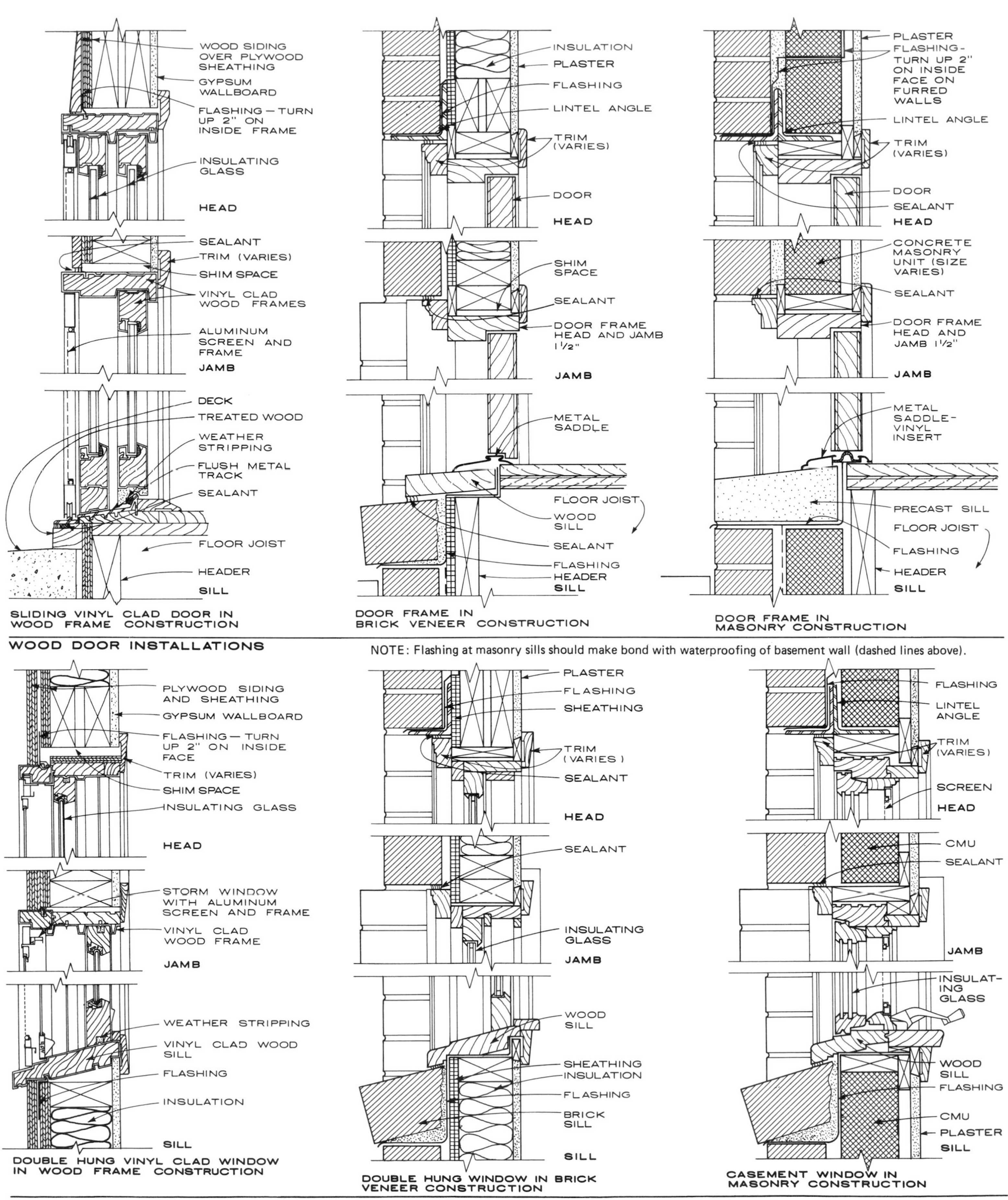
WOOD SIDING OVER PLYWOOD SHEATHING
GYPSUM WALLBOARD
FLASHING — TURN UP 2" ON INSIDE FRAME
INSULATING GLASS
HEAD
SEALANT
TRIM (VARIES)
SHIM SPACE
VINYL CLAD WOOD FRAMES
ALUMINUM SCREEN AND FRAME
JAMB
DECK
TREATED WOOD
WEATHER STRIPPING
FLUSH METAL TRACK
SEALANT
FLOOR JOIST
HEADER
SILL
SLIDING VINYL CLAD DOOR IN WOOD FRAME CONSTRUCTION
INSULATION
PLASTER
FLASHING
LINTEL ANGLE
TRIM (VARIES)
DOOR
HEAD
SHIM SPACE
SEALANT
DOOR FRAME HEAD AND JAMB 1 1/2"
JAMB
METAL SADDLE
FLOOR JOIST
WOOD SILL
SEALANT
FLASHING
HEADER
SILL
DOOR FRAME IN BRICK VENEER CONSTRUCTION
PLASTER
FLASHING- TURN UP 2" ON INSIDE FACE ON FURRED WALLS
LINTEL ANGLE
TRIM (VARIES)
DOOR
SEALANT
HEAD
CONCRETE MASONRY UNIT (SIZE VARIES)
SEALANT
DOOR FRAME HEAD AND JAMB 1 1/2"
JAMB
METAL SADDLE- VINYL INSERT
PRECAST SILL
FLOOR JOIST
FLASHING
HEADER
SILL
DOOR FRAME IN MASONRY CONSTRUCTION
WOOD DOOR INSTALLATIONS
NOTE: Flashing at masonry sills should make bond with waterproofing of basement wall (dashed lines above).
PLYWOOD SIDING AND SHEATHING
GYPSUM WALLBOARD
FLASHING — TURN UP 2" ON INSIDE FACE
TRIM (VARIES)
SHIM SPACE
INSULATING GLASS
HEAD
STORM WINDOW WITH ALUMINUM SCREEN AND FRAME
VINYL CLAD WOOD FRAME
JAMB
WEATHER STRIPPING
VINYL CLAD WOOD SILL
FLASHING
INSULATION
SILL
DOUBLE HUNG VINYL CLAD WINDOW IN WOOD FRAME CONSTRUCTION
PLASTER
FLASHING
SHEATHING
TRIM (VARIES)
SEALANT
HEAD
SEALANT
INSULATING GLASS
JAMB
WOOD SILL
SHEATHING
INSULATION
FLASHING
BRICK SILL
SILL
DOUBLE HUNG WINDOW IN BRICK VENEER CONSTRUCTION
FLASHING
LINTEL ANGLE
TRIM (VARIES)
SCREEN
HEAD
CMU
SEALANT
JAMB
INSULAT- ING GLASS
WOOD SILL
FLASHING
CMU
PLASTER
SILL
CASEMENT WINDOW IN MASONRY CONSTRUCTION
WOOD WINDOW INSTALLATIONS

SWINGING DOOR ASSEMBLIES

A door, in addition to providing a portal for entry, should resist unwanted intruders. This resistance can be accommodated by requiring that all exterior doors comply with ANSI/ASTM standard F476-76 Standard Test Methods for Security of Swinging Door Assemblies. The security of a door assembly depends not only on the lock but also on the strike, buck, hinge, door, and even the surrounding wall.

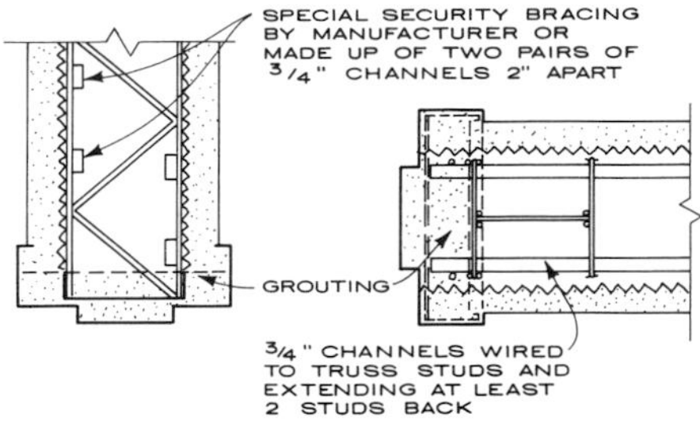
SPECIAL SECURITY BRACING BY MANUFACTURER OR MADE UP OF TWO PAIRS OF 3/4" CHANNELS 2" APART
GROUTING
3/4" CHANNELS WIRED TO TRUSS STUDS AND EXTENDING AT LEAST 2 STUDS BACK

HEAD JAMB

DOOR BUCK DETAIL

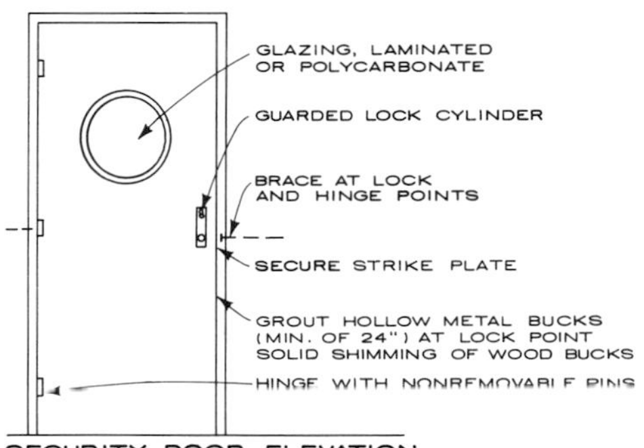
GLAZING, LAMINATED OR POLYCARBONATE
GUARDED LOCK CYLINDER
BRACE AT LOCK AND HINGE POINTS
SECURE STRIKE PLATE
GROUT HOLLOW METAL BUCKS (MIN. OF 24") AT LOCK POINT SOLID SHIMMING OF WOOD BUCKS
HINGE WITH NONREMOVABLE PINS

SECURITY DOOR ELEVATION

NOTE: Brace at lock point is essential; brace at hinge points for additional security. If two hinges, braces required at both; if three hinges, brace only at middle hinge. Braces should extend two studs back.

SUGGESTED MATERIALS AND METHODS FOR DOORS

1. GRADE 40: Hollow metal steel doors, 16 gauge.
2. GRADE 30: Hollow metal, 18 gauge; flush wood, lumber core, 1 3/4 in. thick.
3. GRADE 20: Flush wood, particle core, 1 3/4 in. thick, lock block of dense solid wood at least 6 in. wide x 24 in. high. Hinge blocks, 6 in. wide, x 12 in. high.
4. GRADE 10: Flush wood, particle core, 1 3/4 in. thick; wood panel door with minimum thickness of panel at 1/2 in. including rebate, stiles minimum dimension 1 3/4 x 6 in.

FRAME

The stiffness of the bucks is critical; wood bucks should be a minimum of 2 in. thick and have solid, secure shims for 24 in. at the locking point and 12 in. at each hinge point; stops should be milled integral with the buck; wood bucks for Grade 20 should be of hard wood premium grade; Grade 20 bucks should be 16 gauge steel; Grade 40 bucks should be 15 gauge steel; all steel bucks should be grouted full.

WALL

Fire stops or braces should be located at the lock point and each hinge point—for one stud space at Grade 10, two stud spaces for Grade 20 and above; if wood studs appear, plywood sheathing should be used on both sides of the studs for two stud spaces to each side of the doorway; if it is a masonry wall, grout all space between frame and wall.

GRADE SELECTION FACTORS

The following items should be considered when designing and selecting components for an entrance door:

1. LOCATION: If the doorway is hidden from public view, or if security lighting is not provided, a higher grade is required than that normally used in the area.
2. ACCESS: If entry is controlled by a guard or protected by a detection device, a lower grade should be adequate.
3. USE: If the doorway provides access to particularly valuable or desirable property, a higher grade is required.
4. TYPE: In a double door, each door should be tested. If the door has solid or glazed panels make sure they meet the test requirements; mail slots are not recommended in the door.

GRADE 10

Minimum security level; adequate for single family residential buildings located in stable, comparatively low crime areas.

GRADE 20

Low to medium security level; provides security for residential buildings located in average crime rate areas or for apartments in both low and average crime rate areas.

GRADE 30

Medium to high security level; provides security for residential buildings located in higher than average crime rate areas or for small commercial buildings in average or low crime rate areas.

GRADE 40

High security level; provides security for commercial buildings located in medium to high crime rate areas.

SLIDING DOOR UNITS

Sliding glass doors are a particular concern in securing a building. Performance requirements specified in the NILECJ-STD-0318, Physical Security of Sliding Glass Door Units should be complied with.

The locking devices should include vertical rod, or lever bolts, at top and bottom; the frame should be solid or reinforced at the locking points; the stile must also be reinforced at the lock points. The operating panels should be designed so that they cannot be lifted out of their tracks when in the locked position.

Glazing and other components should be installed from the inside so that entry cannot be gained by disassembly. As with windows and other doors, a hidden location requires a higher grade.

FIXED PANEL SECURED ON THE INSIDE

OPERABLE DOOR SECURED AGAINST LIFTOUT

PROVIDE LEVER BOLT AT TOP AND BOTTOM WITH 1" MINIMUM THROW

INTERLOCKING MEETING STILE

HEAVY DUTY LOCK WITH HOOK TYPE HARDENED DEAD BOLT

GROUT FRAME FULL OR BRACE SOLID FROM FLOOR TO 12" ABOVE LOCK

POLYCARBONATE OR LAMINATED GLASS

SLIDING GLASS DOOR

WINDOW FORCED ENTRY DESIGN CRITERIA

EXTERIOR DESIGN ELEMENTS

1. The following items should be considered when designing and selecting windows:
   LOCATION: If accessible (residential: 12 ft vertical, 6 ft horizontal; commercial: 18 ft vertical, 10 ft horizontal) and hidden from public view, a higher grade is required.
   PROTECTED: If windows are protected by a detection device (such as shutters, security screens, or bars), the window grade could be irrelevant. If security screens, bars, or shutters are used, requirements for fire exiting must be met.
2. The existence of windbreaks near a building may provide cover for intruders.
3. The use of shades and window coverings may deter intruders, depending on the ease of removal of these devices or the noise from breakage. The use of lockable shutters or rolldown blinds is very effective.
4. WINDOW UNITS: Window units should at least comply with ANSI/ASTM F 588-79 Standard Test Methods for Resistance of Window Assemblies to Forced Entry for a minimum grade performance and with NILECJ-STD-0316, Physical Security of Window Units, for higher grade performance.
5. As with a door assembly, the security of a window does not rely on the lock alone.

FRAME DESIGN ELEMENTS

1. A rigid frame and sash is important to resist prying and should be removable from the inside only.
2. The quality of the hardware and its placement and anchorage are critical to security. Exposed removable hinges should not be used.
3. Special attention must be given to the use of weather stripping, since this can permit insertion of wires to unlock windows.

GLAZING DESIGN ELEMENTS

1. Multiple glazing systems provide a greater hazard to entry/exit through broken-out windows.
2. Reflective glazing impedes outside daytime surveillance.

MATERIALS AND METHODS FOR WINDOWS

1. Grade 40: Very heavy fixed frames with laminated glass over 1/4 in. thick or security screen, bars, or shutters with special locking device.
2. Grade 30: Heavy duty sash with laminated glass over 1/4 in. thick or polycarbonate glazing 1/4 in. thick. Lock should include at least two heavy duty dead locking bolts.
3. Grade 20: Heavy duty sash with laminated glass or polycarbonate glazing; if wood, sash must be reinforced or heavy; double locks required.
4. Grade 10: Regular glazing in commercial sash with double locks; can be wood frame.

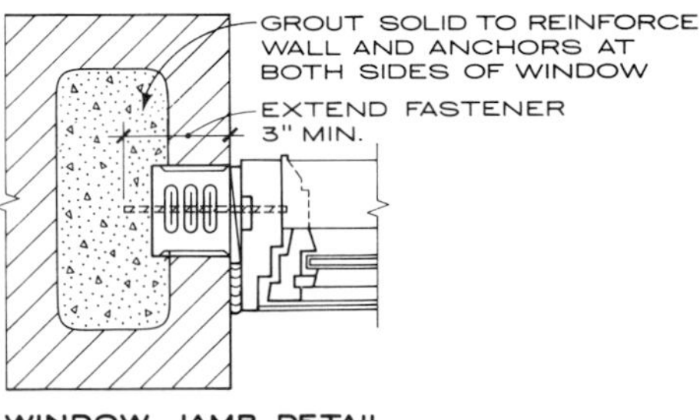
GROUT SOLID TO REINFORCE WALL AND ANCHORS AT BOTH SIDES OF WINDOW
EXTEND FASTENER 3" MIN.

WINDOW JAMB DETAIL

John Stroik, Architect, and Porter Driscoll, AIA, Architect; Center for Building Technology, National Bureau of Standards; Washington, D.C.
William G. Miner, AIA; Washington, D.C.

GENERAL

Comprehensive, effective site security provides deterrents to hostile acts, barriers to unauthorized entry, access/egress control, detection of unauthorized entry or exit, and positions for security personnel. Design of the system includes:

1. Perimeter physical barriers preventing penetration by intruders and vehicles
2. Entry/exit control
3. Protective lighting
4. Standoff distance from blasts
5. Intrusion detection, alert, and notification
6. Guard posts and guard walls

Perimeter and site security are augmented by a comprehensive building security system.

SITE ACCESS

A screening facility at perimeter access points should be considered in high risk areas to detect explosives, firearms, and other weapons. A sally port detains vehicles for inspection and prevents other vehicles from gaining access by tailgating.

A protected guard booth should be located so that the guard can control entry/exit of pedestrians and vehicles. Guard booths in high risk areas should be constructed to appropriate ballistic and forced entry resistant standards. Where extensive vehicle inspection is required, a roving guard should augment guards in the booth.

PERIMETER PROTECTION

Perimeter security addresses issues of protection against forced entry by unauthorized personnel and vehicles, and against explosive blast.

PERSONNEL BARRIERS: FENCES AND WALLS

Walls and opaque fences to deter and resist intruders should be smooth-faced with no easy foot or handholds, and be a minimum 9 ft high. Open fencing should be constructed of vertical elements with 9 ft minimum between horizontal elements.

SITE SECURITY LIGHTING

A comprehensive system of security lighting should include illumination of the perimeter, structures within, and site passageways.

Continuous lighting using fixed luminaires to flood an area with overlapping cones of light is most common. Lighting across an area makes it difficult for intruders to see inside the area. Controlled lighting, which adjusts light to fit a particular strip inside and/or outside the perimeter, is less intrusive to adjacent properties.

Auxiliary standby lighting is turned on if suspicious activity is detected. Movable lighting supplements continuous or standby lighting.

EXPLOSIVE BLAST RESISTANCE

The most effective protective measure against explosive blast is to maximize the standoff distance from perimeter barriers to buildings or other assets. Blast walls are of limited effectiveness.

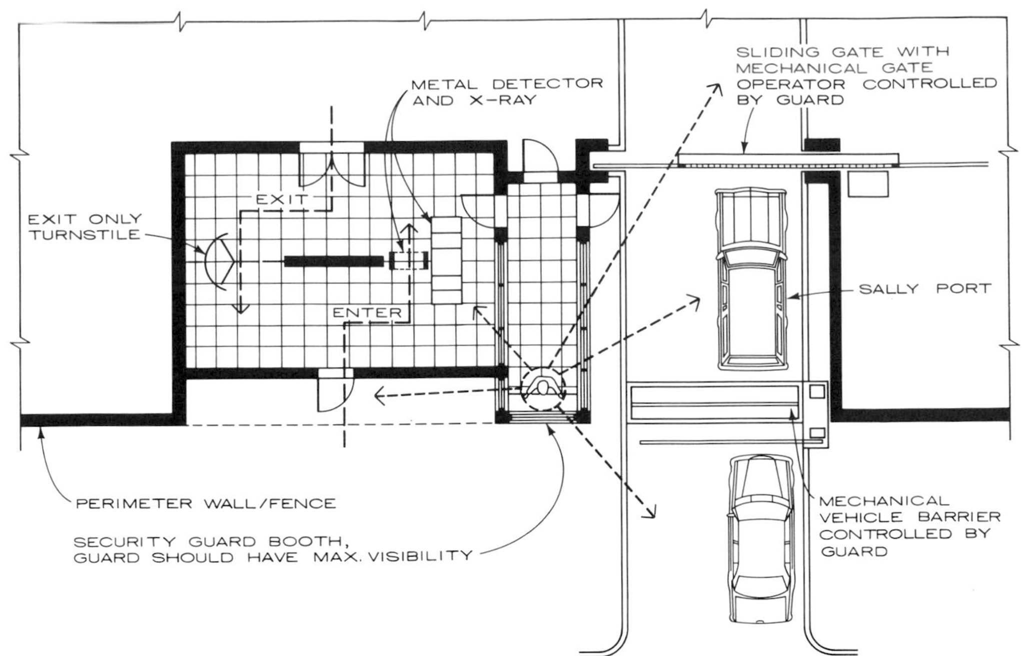

METAL DETECTOR AND X-RAY
SLIDING GATE WITH MECHANICAL GATE OPERATOR CONTROLLED BY GUARD
EXIT
EXIT ONLY TURNSTILE
ENTER
SALLY PORT
PERIMETER WALL/FENCE
SECURITY GUARD BOOTH, GUARD SHOULD HAVE MAX. VISIBILITY
MECHANICAL VEHICLE BARRIER CONTROLLED BY GUARD

SITE ACCESS DIAGRAM

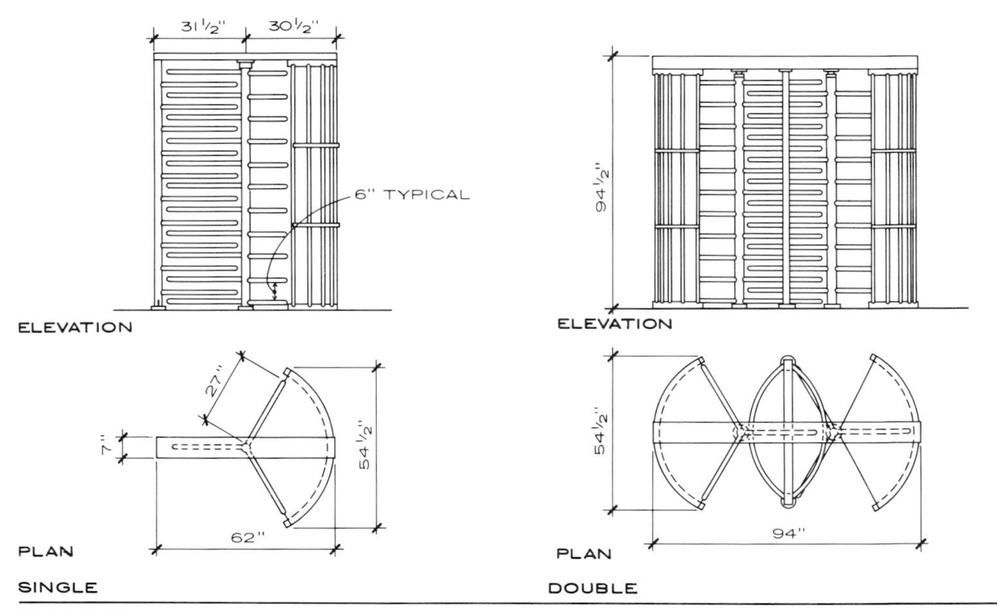

31½"
30½"
6" TYPICAL
ELEVATION
27"
7"
54½"
62"
PLAN
94½"
ELEVATION
54½"
94"
PLAN

SINGLE

DOUBLE

TURNSTILES

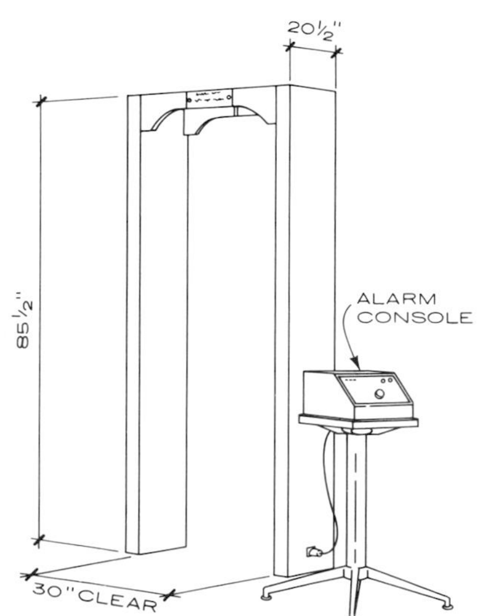

20½"
85½"
ALARM CONSOLE
30" CLEAR

WALK THROUGH METAL DETECTOR

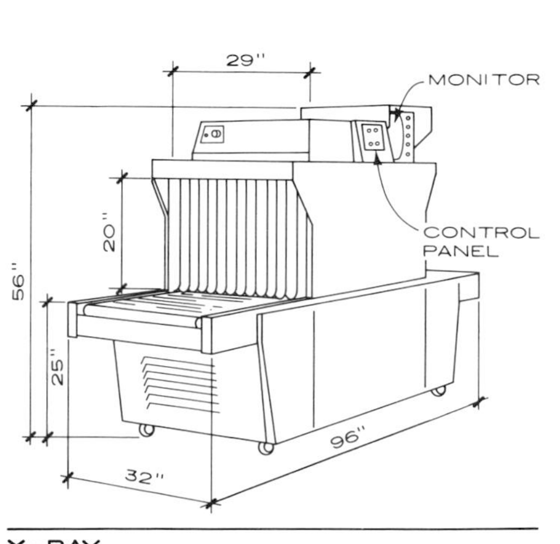

29"
MONITOR
CONTROL PANEL
20"
56"
25"
32"
96"

X-RAY

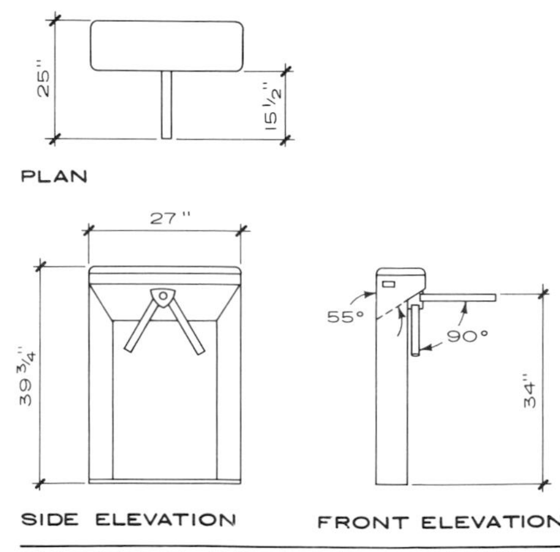

25"
15½"
PLAN
27"
39¾"
55°
90°
34"
SIDE ELEVATION
FRONT ELEVATION

TURNSTILE WITH CARD READER

Edwin Daly, AIA; Joseph Handwerger, Architects; Washington, D.C.
William G. Miner, AIA; Washington, D.C.

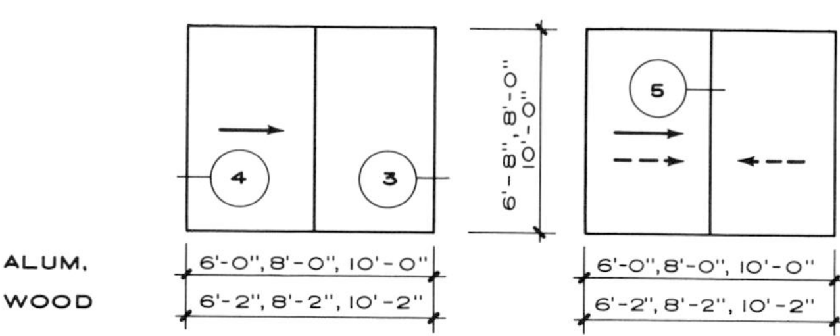

4
3
6'-8", 8'-0"
10'-0"
ALUM.
6'-0", 8'-0", 10'-0"
WOOD
6'-2", 8'-2", 10'-2"
5
6'-0", 8'-0", 10'-0"
6'-2", 8'-2", 10'-2"

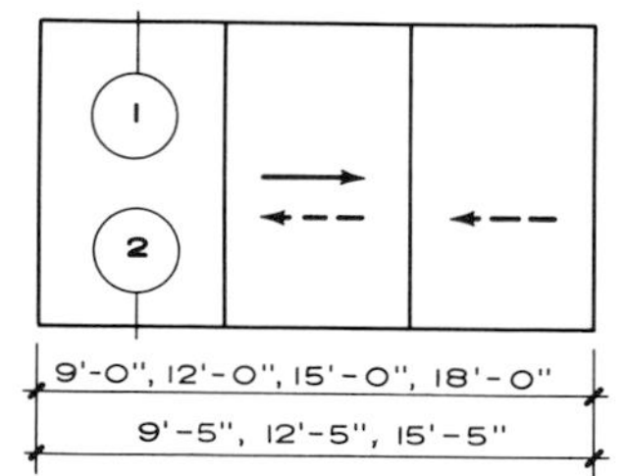

1
2
9'-0", 12'-0", 15'-0", 18'-0"
9'-5", 12'-5", 15'-5"

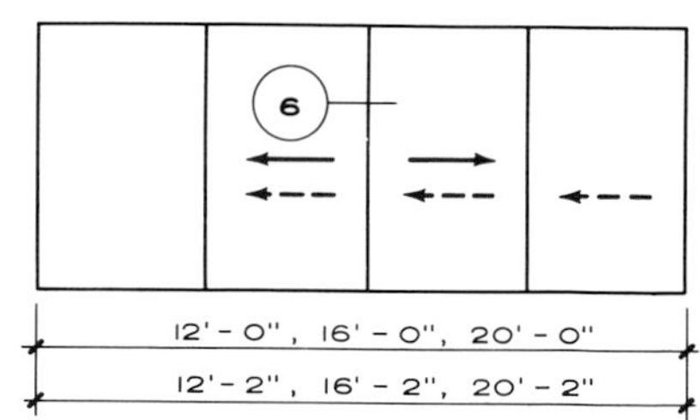

6
12'-0", 16'-0", 20'-0"
12'-2", 16'-2", 20'-2"

RESIDENTIAL SLIDING DOOR DIMENSIONS
DIMENSIONS SHOWN ARE NOMINAL STOCK SIZES

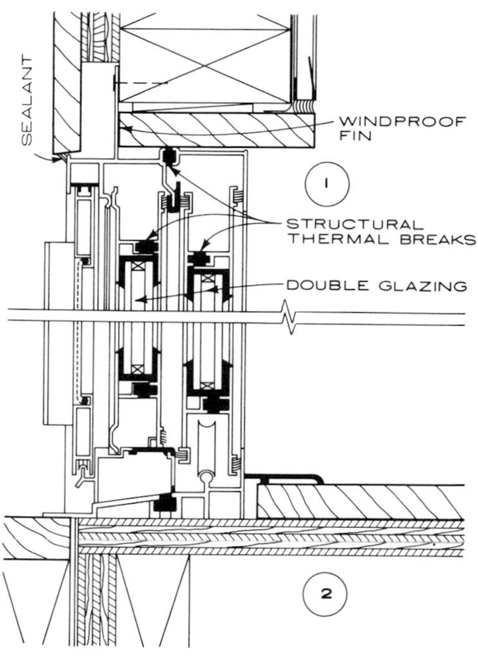

SEALANT
WINDPROOF FIN
1
STRUCTURAL THERMAL BREAKS
DOUBLE GLAZING
2

NOTES

1. Residential sliding door dimensions shown are nominal stock sizes. Custom sizes are available in accordance with individual manufacturing limitations and availability of glass sizes.
2. Details shown are for wood frame construction. Interior and exterior finishes and trim are optional. See manufacturer's data for typical installation details.
3. Tempered glass should always be used to reduce the chance of breakage and to avoid dangerous glass shards if breakage occurs.
4. Screens are available for all doors. Details show screens on the exterior for both the metal and wood doors. Consult individual manufacturer's literature to determine if screens are interior only, exterior only, or available either way.
5. Energy conservation is enhanced through the use of structural thermal breaks in aluminum sliding doors along with windproof mounting fins and double glazing. Standard aluminum sliding doors are also available.
6. See manufacturer's data for special sizes, locking devices, finishes, and specific limitations.

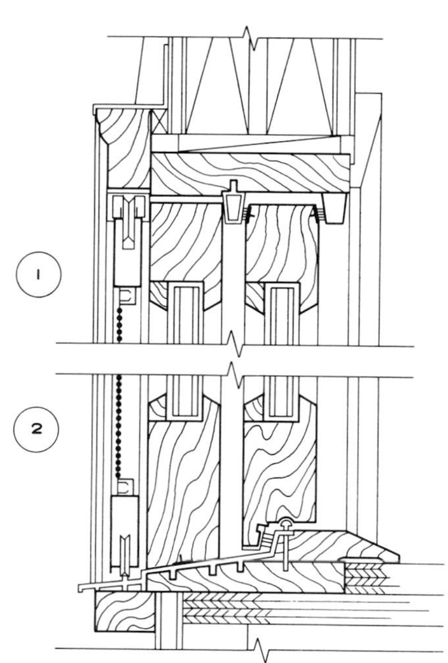

1
2

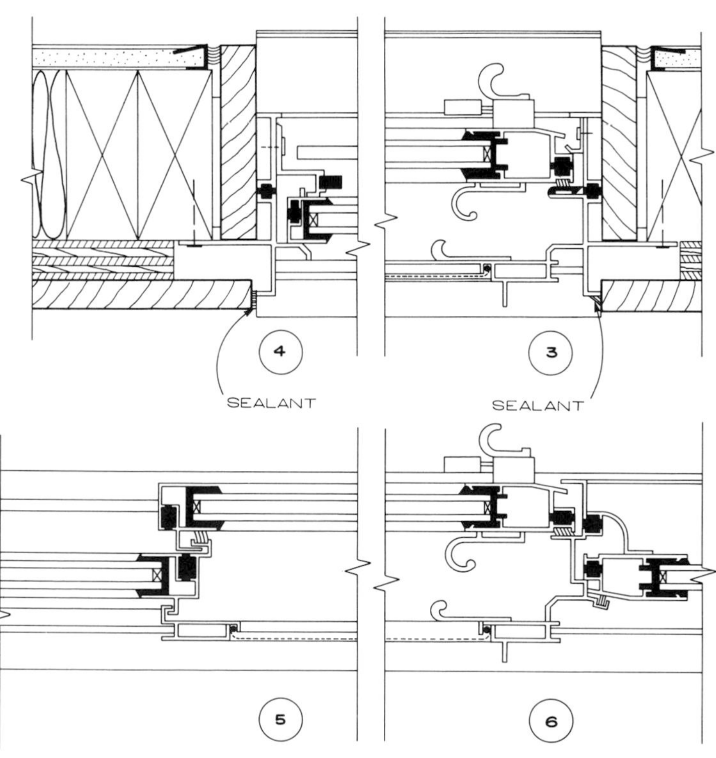

4
SEALANT
3
SEALANT
5
6

ALUMINUM SLIDING DOOR DETAILS WITH ENERGY CONSERVATION FEATURES

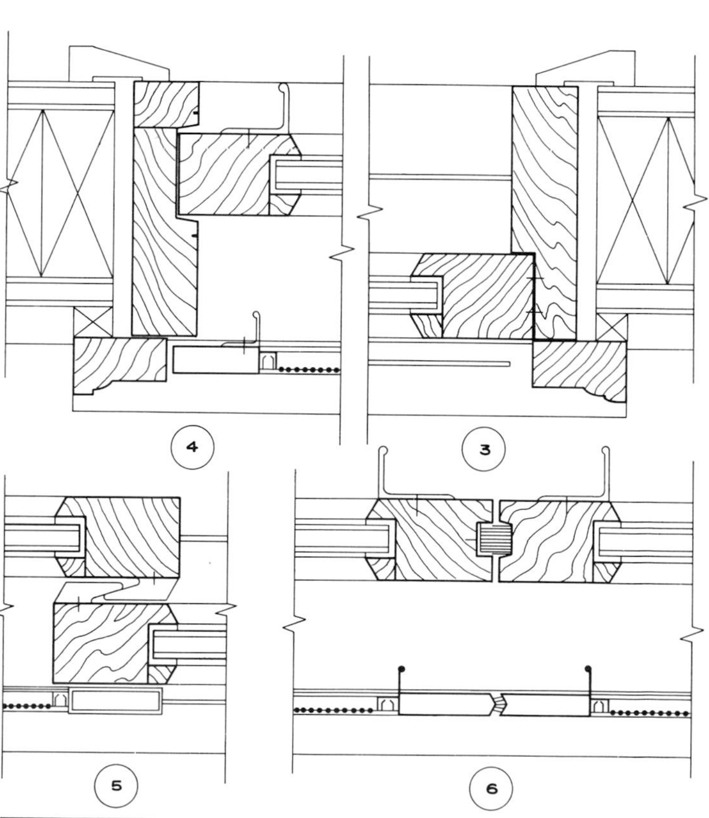

4
3
5
6

WOOD SLIDING DOOR DETAILS

Leo A. Daly; Architecture-Engineering-Planning; Omaha, Nebraska

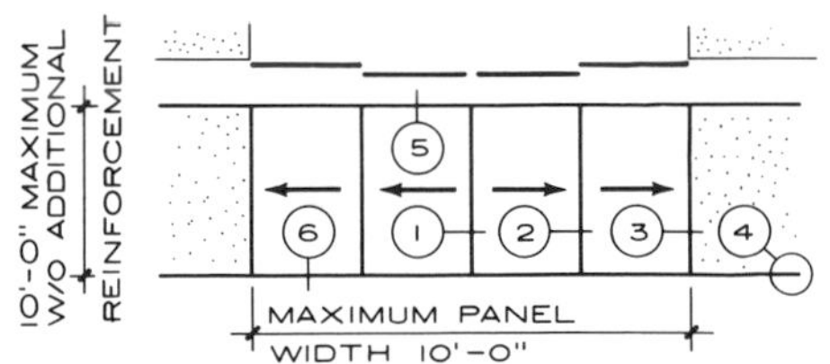
10'-0" MAXIMUM W/O ADDITIONAL REINFORCEMENT
MAXIMUM PANEL WIDTH 10'-0"

BYPASS DOOR ELEVATION

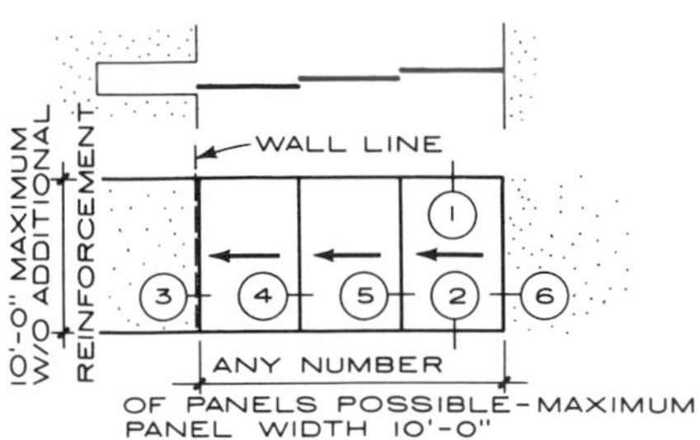
10'-0" MAXIMUM W/O ADDITIONAL REINFORCEMENT
WALL LINE
ANY NUMBER OF PANELS POSSIBLE-MAXIMUM PANEL WIDTH 10'-0"

POCKET DOOR ELEVATION

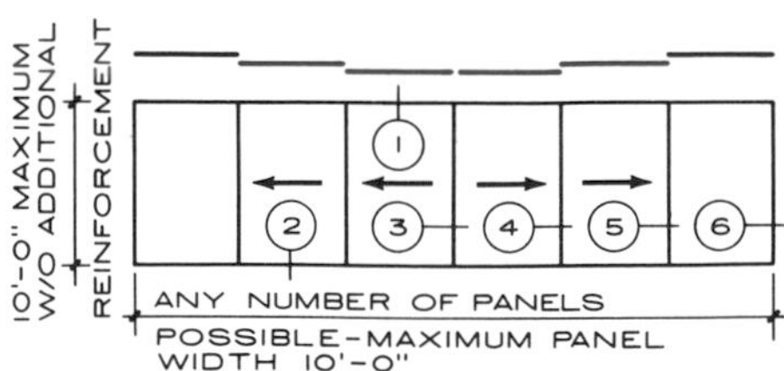
10'-0" MAXIMUM W/O ADDITIONAL REINFORCEMENT
ANY NUMBER OF PANELS POSSIBLE-MAXIMUM PANEL WIDTH 10'-0"

MULTIPLE SLIDING DOOR ELEVATION

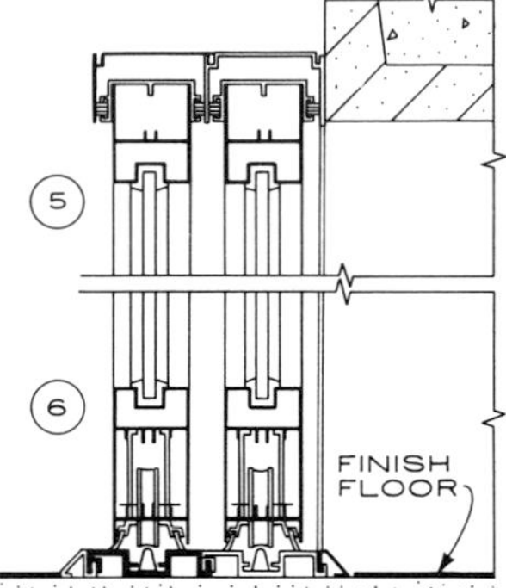
FINISH FLOOR

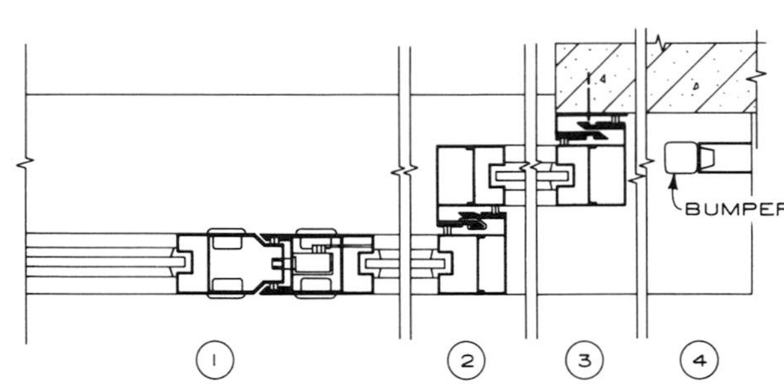
BUMPER

BYPASS DOOR DETAILS

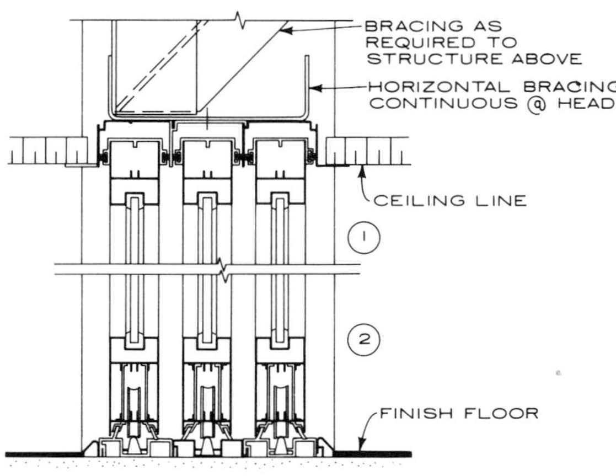
BRACING AS REQUIRED TO STRUCTURE ABOVE
HORIZONTAL BRACING CONTINUOUS @ HEAD
CEILING LINE
FINISH FLOOR

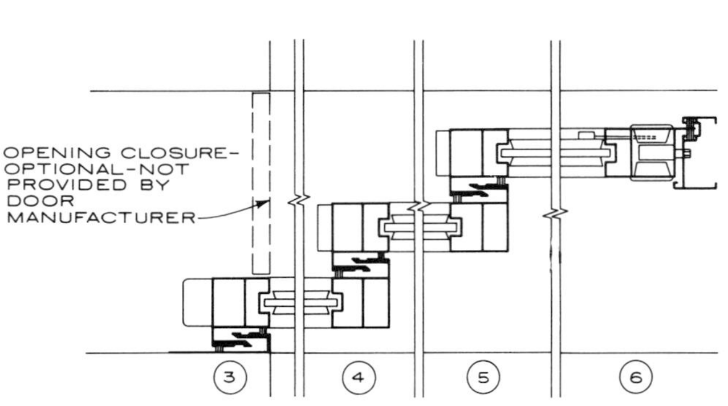
OPENING CLOSURE-OPTIONAL-NOT PROVIDED BY DOOR MANUFACTURER

POCKET DOOR DETAILS

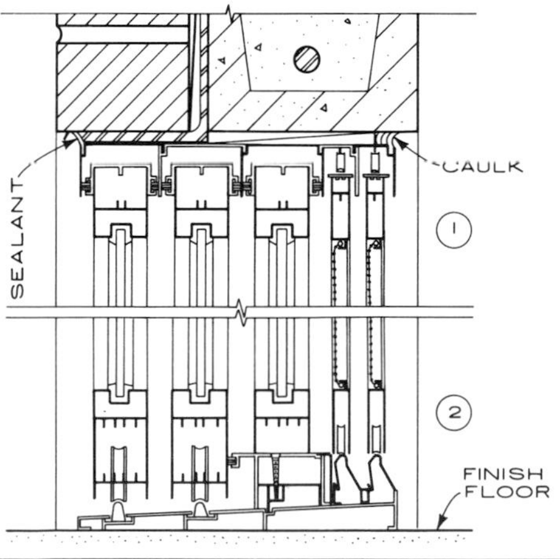
SEALANT
CAULK
FINISH FLOOR

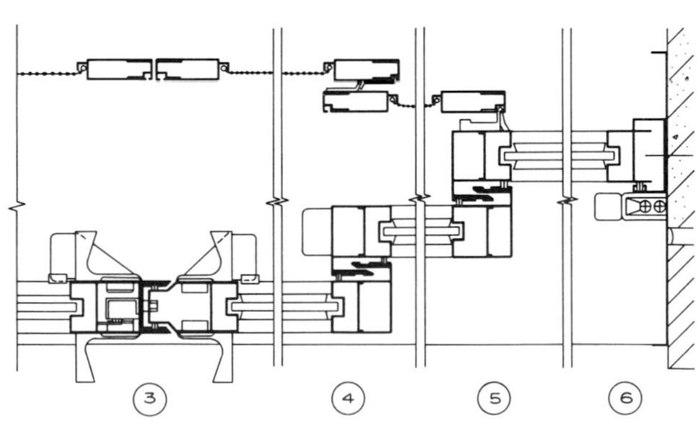

MULTIPLE SLIDING DOOR DETAILS

NOTES

1. Details shown are for masonry construction. Interior and exterior finishes are optional. Consult manufacturer's data for typical installation details.
2. Screens are available for all doors if required. Where shown, the details indicate screens on the interior. Consult specific manufacturer's literature to determine if screens are available for interior only, exterior only, or both. Glazing should be of safety glass, tempered, or insulating glass. Maximum manufacturable sizes of individual glass types will be the governing factor in determining maximum panel sizes. Consult industry standards for applicable data.
3. Consult manufacturer's data for available sizes, locking devices, and finishes.

Leo A. Daly; Architecture-Engineering-Planning; Omaha, Nebraska

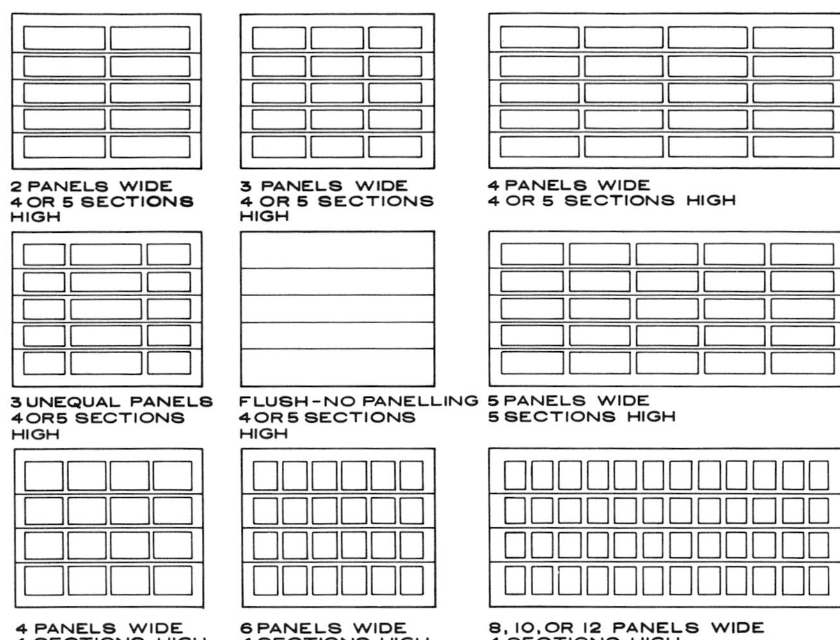
2 PANELS WIDE
4 OR 5 SECTIONS
HIGH
3 PANELS WIDE
4 OR 5 SECTIONS
HIGH
4 PANELS WIDE
4 OR 5 SECTIONS HIGH
3 UNEQUAL PANELS
4 OR 5 SECTIONS
HIGH
FLUSH-NO PANELLING
4 OR 5 SECTIONS
HIGH
5 PANELS WIDE
5 SECTIONS HIGH
4 PANELS WIDE
4 SECTIONS HIGH
6 PANELS WIDE
4 SECTIONS HIGH
8, 10, OR 12 PANELS WIDE
4 SECTIONS HIGH

Panel and section dimensions are set in the factory to provide overall door dimensions that meet the design requirements. Manufacturers will recommend the optimum number of panels and sections to best accommodate specific dimensional ranges. Heights range up to 20 ft, widths to 30 ft (approximate).

WOOD DOORS STANDARD STOCK DESIGNS

NOTE

Glazed panels may be located as desired. 3 section doors also available. Other stock designs and sizes available varying with manufacturers.

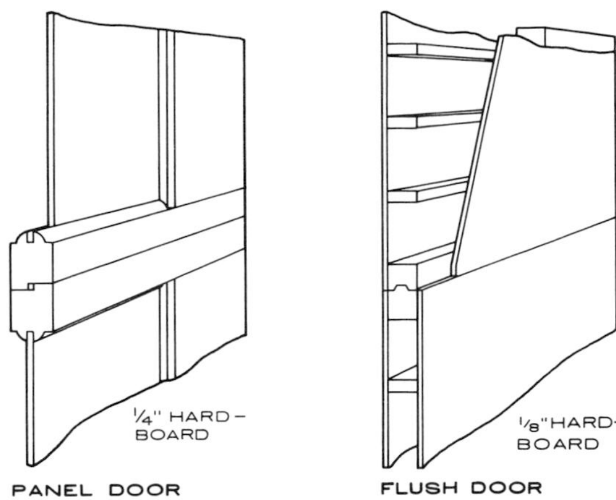
¼" HARD-
BOARD
⅛" HARD-
BOARD
PANEL DOOR
FLUSH DOOR

TYPICAL DETAILS OF WOOD DOORS

All doors available with torsion or extension spring counterbalance.

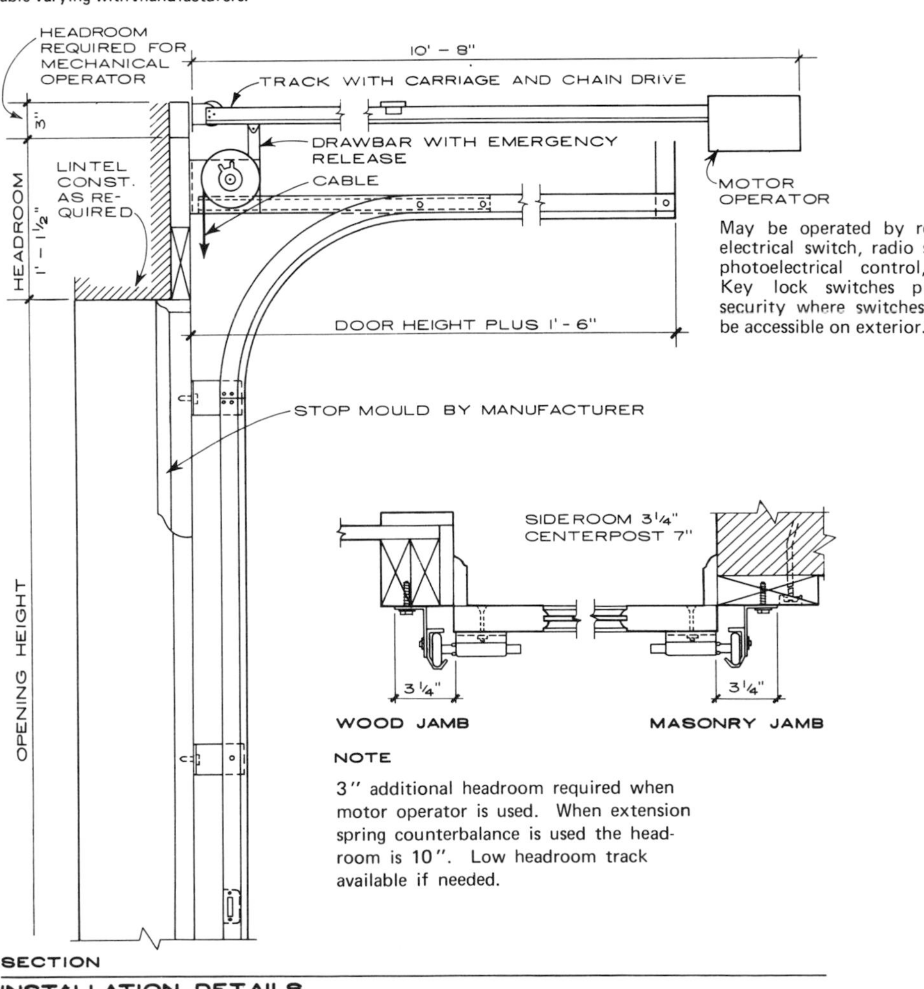
HEADROOM
REQUIRED FOR
MECHANICAL
OPERATOR
10' - 8"
TRACK WITH CARRIAGE AND CHAIN DRIVE
3"
DRAWBAR WITH EMERGENCY
RELEASE
CABLE
LINTEL
CONST.
AS RE-
QUIRED
HEADROOM
1' - 1½"
MOTOR
OPERATOR
DOOR HEIGHT PLUS 1' - 6"
STOP MOULD BY MANUFACTURER
OPENING HEIGHT
SIDEROOM 3¼"
CENTERPOST 7"
3¼"
3¼"
WOOD JAMB
MASONRY JAMB
SECTION

May be operated by remote electrical switch, radio signal, photoelectrical control, etc. Key lock switches provide security where switches must be accessible on exterior.

NOTE

3" additional headroom required when motor operator is used. When extension spring counterbalance is used the headroom is 10". Low headroom track available if needed.

INSTALLATION DETAILS

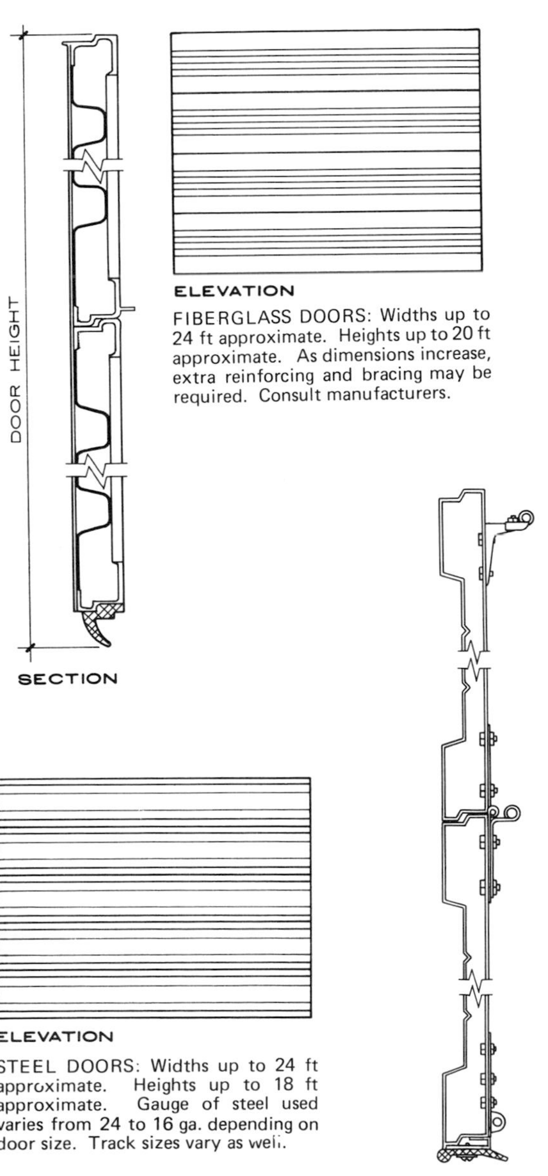
DOOR HEIGHT
SECTION
ELEVATION
ELEVATION
SECTION

FIBERGLASS DOORS: Widths up to 24 ft approximate. Heights up to 20 ft approximate. As dimensions increase, extra reinforcing and bracing may be required. Consult manufacturers.

STEEL DOORS: Widths up to 24 ft approximate. Heights up to 18 ft approximate. Gauge of steel used varies from 24 to 16 ga. depending on door size. Track sizes vary as well.

FIBERGLASS AND STEEL DOORS

Eugene Patrick Holden, AIA; Dale E. Selzer, AIA, Architect; Dallas, Texas

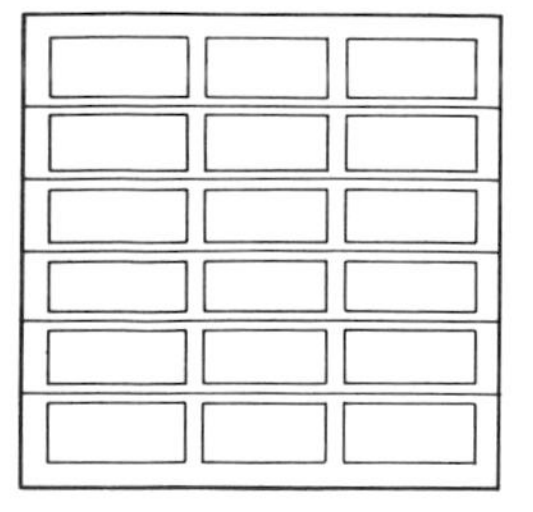

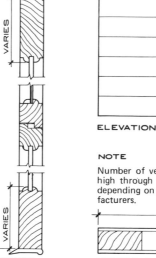

ELEVATION

SIZE LIMITATIONS

2" Track—not to exceed 240 sq. ft., 24'–2" wide or 16'–1" high.

3" Track—not to exceed 600 sq. ft., 33'–2" wide or 25'–1" high.

Wood doors are easily repaired, but are more susceptible to moisture and heat damage than are metal and fiberglass doors.

NOTE

Number of panels varies from 2 for an 8'–6" wide door, through 14 for widths from 30'–4" to 33'–3"; number of vertical sections varies from 4 for doors up to 8'–6" high through 13 sections for doors from 24'–2" to 25'–1" high. Number of panels and sections depends on increments in height and width established by manufacturer.

DOOR WIDTH
VARIES
DOOR HEIGHT
VARIES

HORIZONTAL SECTION

SECTION

WOOD PANEL DOOR

ELEVATION

SIZE LIMITATIONS

2" Track—not to exceed 240 sq. ft., 24'–2" wide or 16'–1" high.

3" Track—not to exceed 600 sq. ft., 33'–2" wide or 25'–1" high.

MATERIAL

1/8" hardboard secured with waterproof adhesive on both sides of 1 1/2" wood frame. Pressure bonded between the hardboard walls are thick, tough waterproof core strips of styrofoam.

NOTE

Number of vertical sections varies from 4 for doors up to 7'–0" high through 15 sections for doors from 24'–7" to 25'–1" high, depending on increments in height established by particular manufacturers.

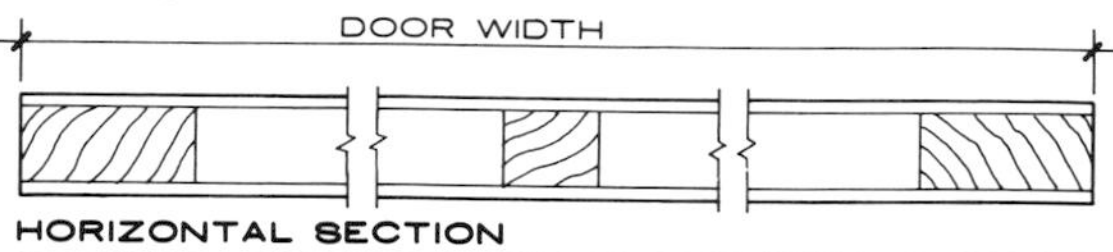
DOOR WIDTH
DOOR HEIGHT

HORIZONTAL SECTION

SECTION

FLUSH WOOD DOOR

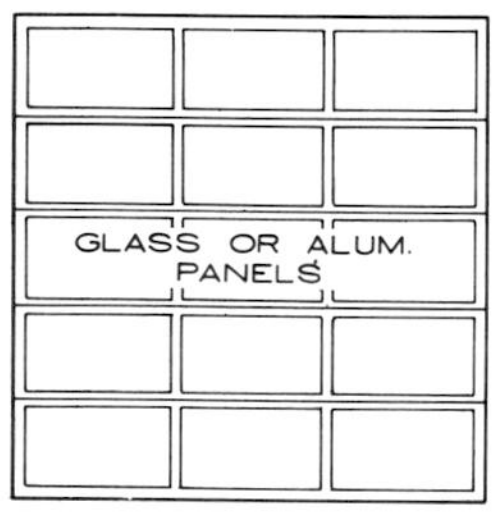
GLASS OR ALUM. PANELS

ELEVATION

SIZE LIMITATIONS

2 in. track is not to exceed 240 sq. ft. or 20 ft. 2 in. wide or 16 ft. 1 in. high. Rails and stiles are of extruded aluminum. Stiles and rails are bolted with 1/4 in. rods for the length of the stile.

This and other doors are available with slats. Check manufacturer's literature.

NOTE

Number of panels varies from 2 for doors up to 8'–11" wide, through 6 for widths from 18'–0" to 20'–2"; number of vertical sections varies from 4 for doors up to 8'–6" high, through 8 sections for doors from 14'–2" to 16'–1" high. Number of panels and sections depends on increments in height and width established by manufacturer.

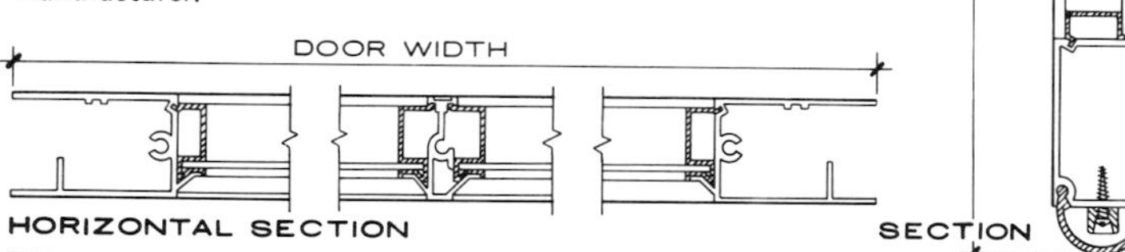
DOOR WIDTH
DOOR HEIGHT

HORIZONTAL SECTION

SECTION

PANORAMIC ALUMINUM

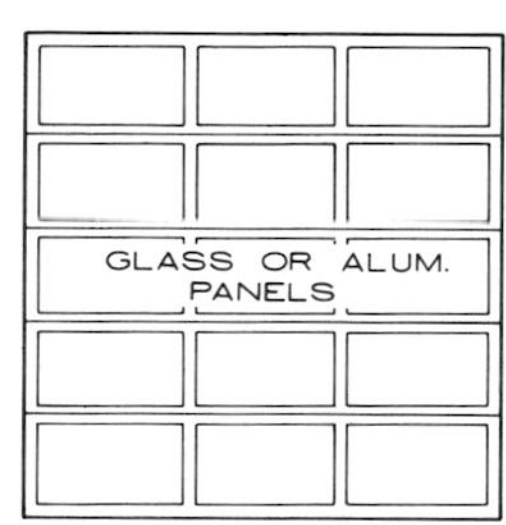
GLASS OR ALUM. PANELS

ELEVATION

SIZE LIMITATIONS

2" Track—not to exceed 336 sq. ft. 24'–2" wide or 16'–1" high.

3" Track—not to exceed 384 sq. ft., 24'–2" wide or 16'–1" high.

Stiles and rails of extruded aluminum. Stiles are bolted to rails with 1/4" rods the length of the stile.

NOTE

Number of panels varies from 2 for doors up to 8'–11" wide through 8 for widths from 21'–0" to 23'–11"; number of vertical sections varies from 4 for doors up to 8'–6" high, through 8 sections for doors from 14'–2" to 16'–1" high. Number of panels and sections depends on increments in height and width established by manufactures.

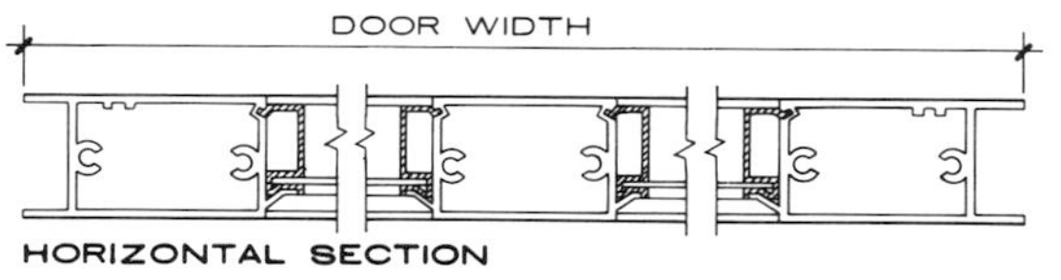
DOOR WIDTH
DOOR HEIGHT

HORIZONTAL SECTION

SECTION

HEAVY DUTY ALUMINUM

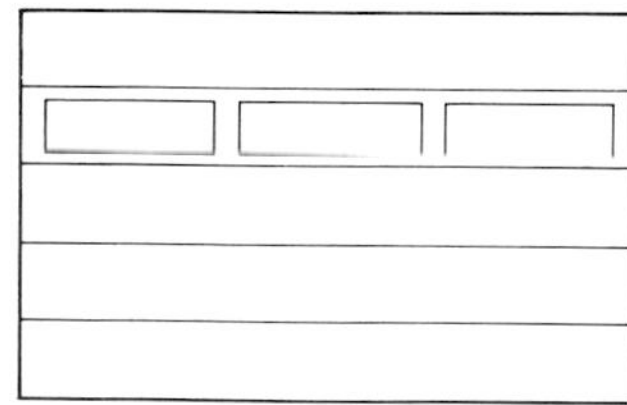

ELEVATION

SIZE LIMITATIONS

2 in. track is not to exceed 180 sq. ft. or 16 ft. 2 in. wide or 14 ft. 1 in. high. 3 in. track is not to exceed 450 sq. ft. or 33 ft. 2 in. wide or 22 ft. 1 in. high.

This and other doors are available with varying amounts of insulation. Check manufacturer's literature.

NOTE

Number of panels varies from 2 for doors up to 9'–11" wide through 10 for widths from 31'–11" to 33'–2"; number of vertical sections varies from 5 for doors up to 8'–0" high, through 14 sections for doors from 20'–11" to 22'–1" high. Number of panels and sections depends on increments in height and width established by particular manufacturers.

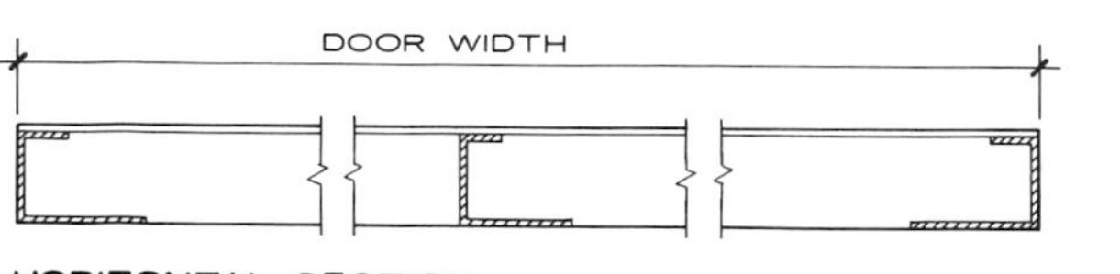
DOOR WIDTH
DOOR HEIGHT

HORIZONTAL SECTION

SECTION

16 GAUGE STEEL DOOR

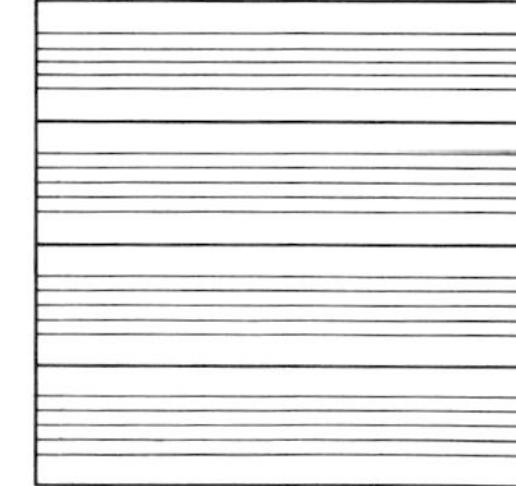

ELEVATION

SIZE LIMITATIONS

2" Track—not to exceed 340 sq. ft., 26'–2" wide or 16'–1" high.

3" Track—optional.

Stiles and rails made of extruded aluminum.

Doors made of fiberglass fastened to both the rails and stiles.

NOTE

Number of stiles varies from 2 for doors up to 12'–2" wide, through 7 for widths from 22'–3" to 26'–2"; number of vertical sections varies from 4 for doors up to 8'–1" high, through 8 sections for doors from 14'–2" to 16'–1" high. Number of stiles and sections depends on increments in height and width established by particular manufacturers.

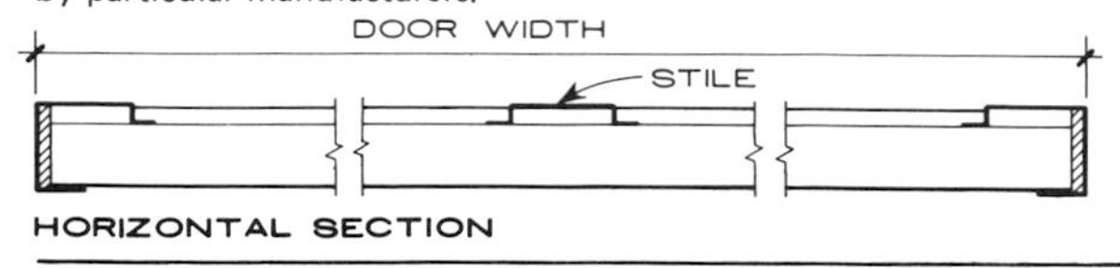
DOOR WIDTH
STILE

HORIZONTAL SECTION

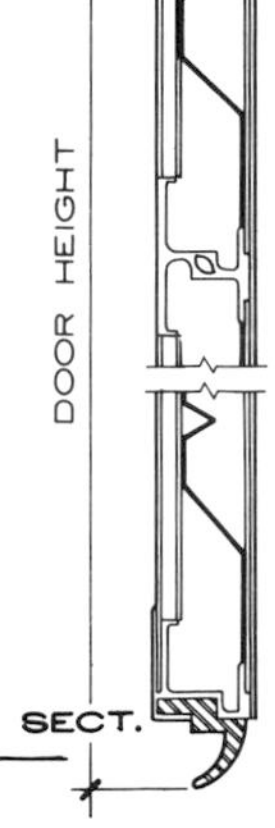
DOOR HEIGHT

SECT.

FIBERGLASS

Eugene Patrick Holden, AIA; Dale E. Selzer, AIA, Architect; Dallas, Texas

CENTER STILE		SECTION	
DOOR WIDTH	NO. OF STILES	DOOR HEIGHT	NO. OF SECTIONS
to 8′-2″	2	to 8′-1″	4
8′-3″ to 12′-2″	3	8′-2″ to 10′-1″	5
12′-3″ to 16′-2″	4	10′-2″ to 12′-1″	6
16′-3″ to 19′-2″	5	12′-2″ to 14′-1″	7
19′-3″ to 22′-2″	6	14′-2″ to 16′-1″	8
22′-3″ to 26′-2″	7	16′-2″ to 18′-1″	9
		18′-2″ to 20′-1″	10
		20′-2″ to 22′-1″	11
		22′-2″ to 24′-1″	12

ELEVATION

SIZE LIMITATIONS FOR STANDARD SIZES ON STANDARD TRACK:
20 gauge, 3 in. track—not to exceed 600 sq. ft., 33 ft. 2 in. wide or 24 ft. 1 in. high.
24 gauge, 2 in. track—not to exceed 340 sq. ft., 26 ft. 2 in. wide or 16 ft. 1 in. high.

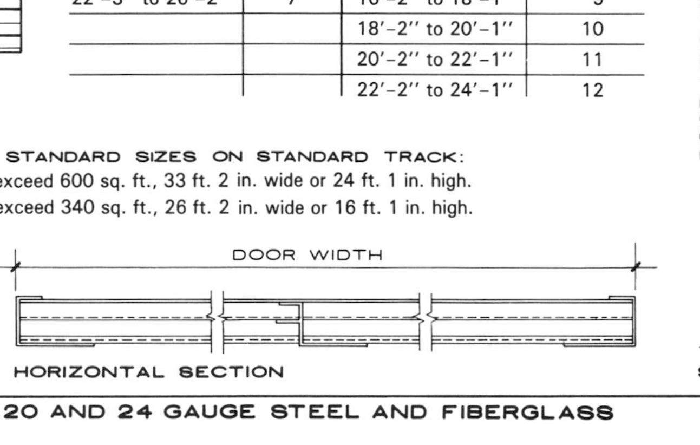
DOOR WIDTH

HORIZONTAL SECTION

DOOR HEIGHT

SECTION

GENERAL INFORMATION

1. Standard commercial doors are designed to 20 lbs. per sq. ft. wind load.
2. All doors are available with sash sections or sash openings in standard section.
3. Doors are available using 20 gauge or 24 gauge steel sections on the top and bottom and intermediate fiberglass sections.
4. Larger openings can be enclosed by using 2 or more doors with removable or swing-up center posts. When the center posts are removed or raised, the entire opening is clear.
5. Larger size doors can be manufactured with special engineering.
6. Consider the range of energy-conscious options now available, such as weatherstripping and anti-infiltration hoods.
7. In some applications doors may require specific fire ratings. Check local building codes.
8. Doors are available with built-in pass-through doors, vision panels, insulation, and many other options. Check manufacturers' literature for availability.

COMBINED DOOR - 20 AND 24 GAUGE STEEL AND FIBERGLASS

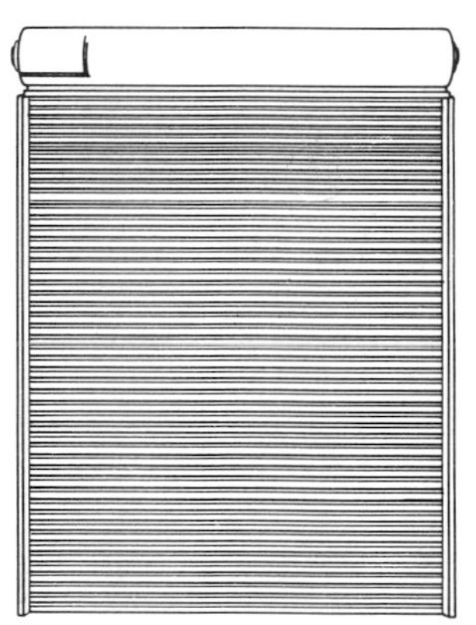

CURTAIN
Available in sizes listed below.

GRILLE
Maximum push-up grille sizes: 95 sq. ft. in steel, 130 sq. ft. in aluminum.

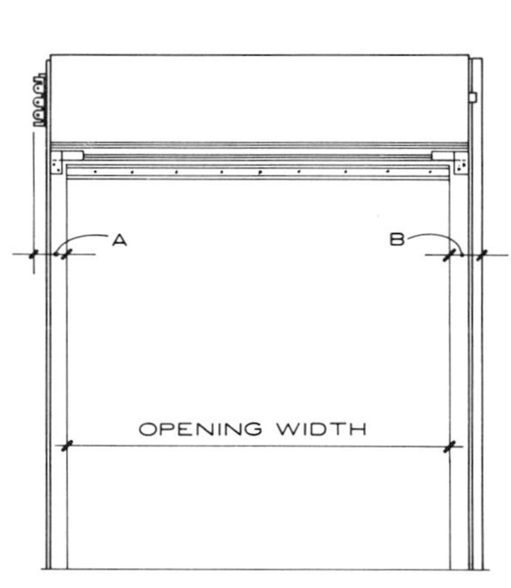
A
B
OPENING WIDTH

FRAME ELEVATION

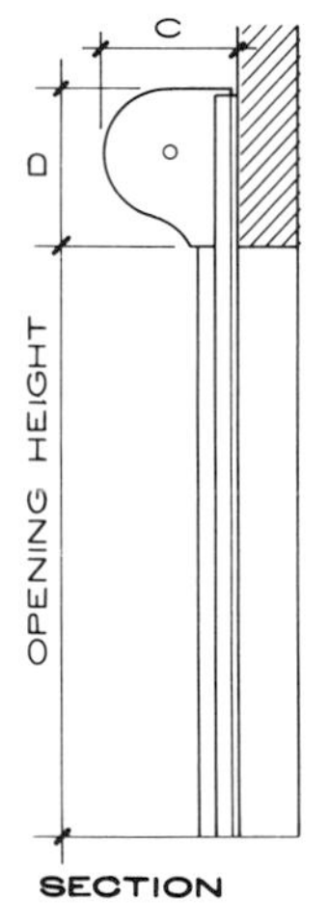
C
D
OPENING HEIGHT

SECTION

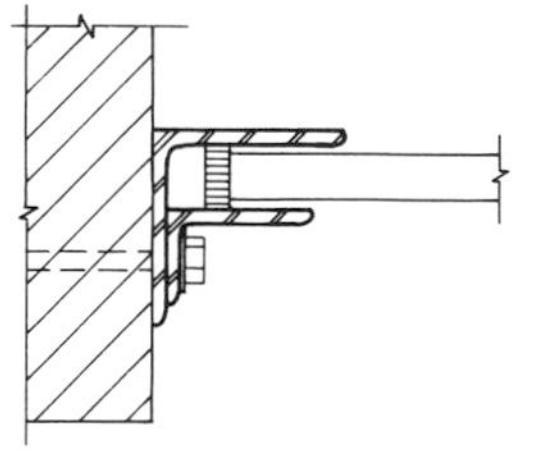

JAMB MOUNTED, STEEL

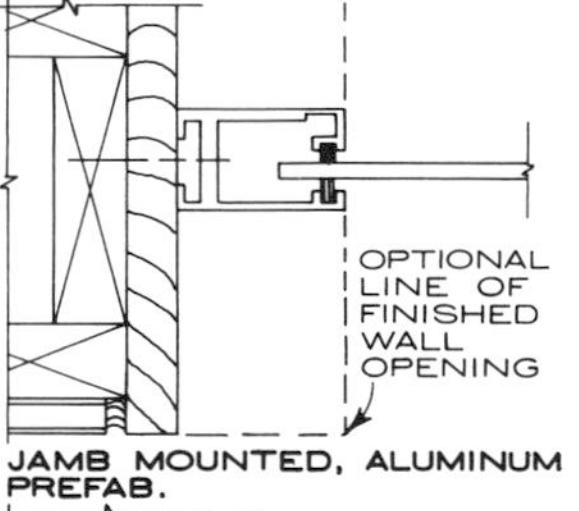
OPTIONAL LINE OF FINISHED WALL OPENING

JAMB MOUNTED, ALUMINUM PREFAB.

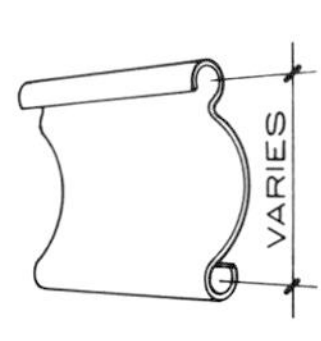

FLAT SLAT
Provides best weather protection.

ROLLED SLAT
VARIES
Available in galvanized, stainless steel and aluminum.

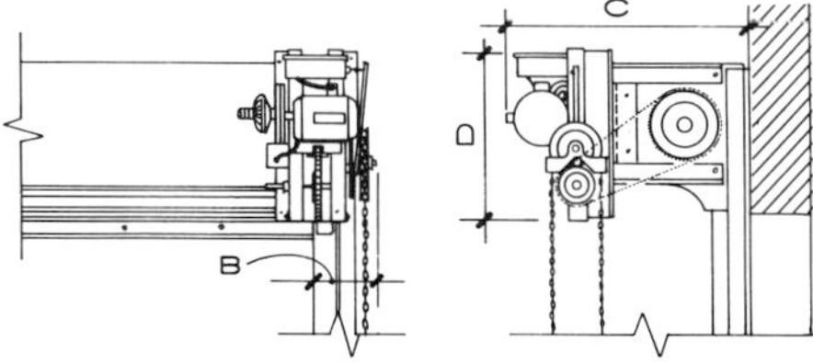
B
C
D

FRONT OF HOOD MOUNTED OPERATOR
Refer to manufacturers' literature for dimensions.

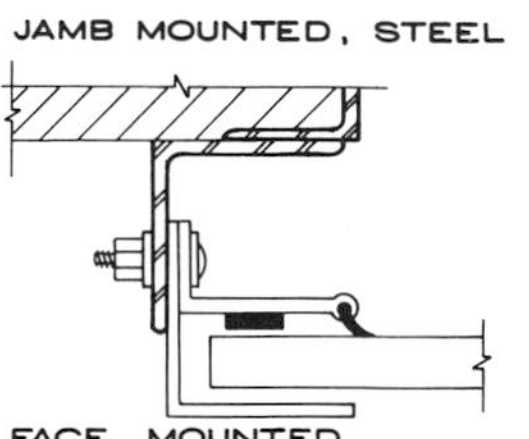

FACE MOUNTED, WEATHER STRIPPED

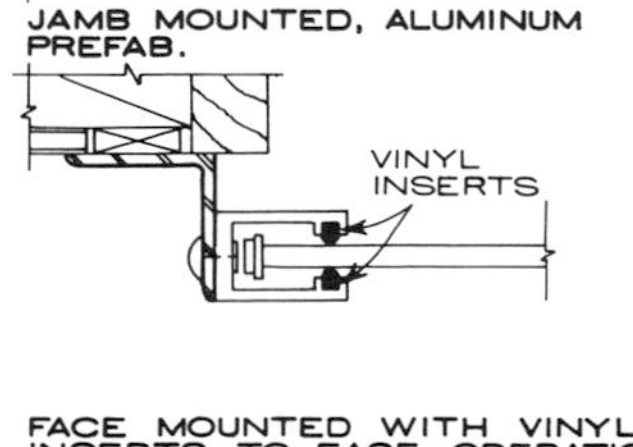
VINYL INSERTS

FACE MOUNTED WITH VINYL INSERTS TO EASE OPERATION

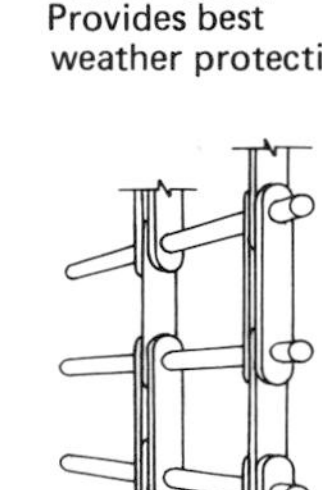

ROLLING GRILLE

GUIDE DETAILS (THESE VARY AMONG MANUFACTURERS)

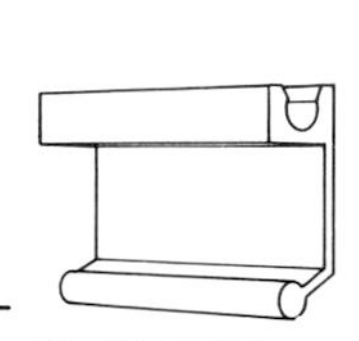

EXTRUDED ALUMINUM SLAT
For use with rolling counter doors.

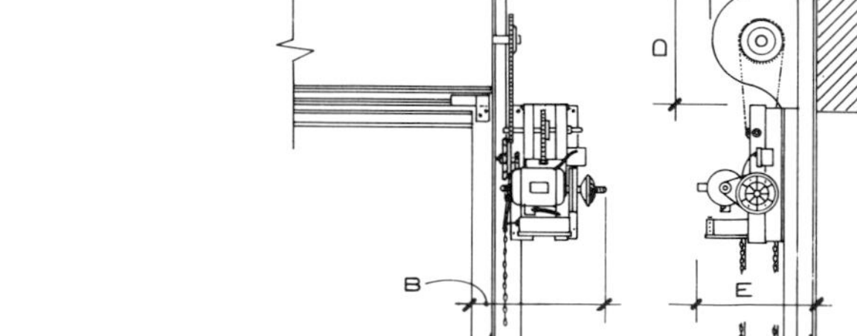
B
C
D
E

WALL MOUNTED OPERATOR
Refer to manufacturers' literature for dimensions.

NOTE

Doors and grilles are manufactured in a wide range of sizes. Many makers provide standard products up to approximately 30 ft high and 33 ft wide. Larger items may require special engineering. Operator dimensions A, B, C, D, and E vary with size and type of rolling door. Small units may be obtained in preassembled form.

ROLLING METAL DOORS & GRILLES

Eugene Patrick Holden, AIA; Dale E. Selzer, AIA, Architect; Dallas, Texas

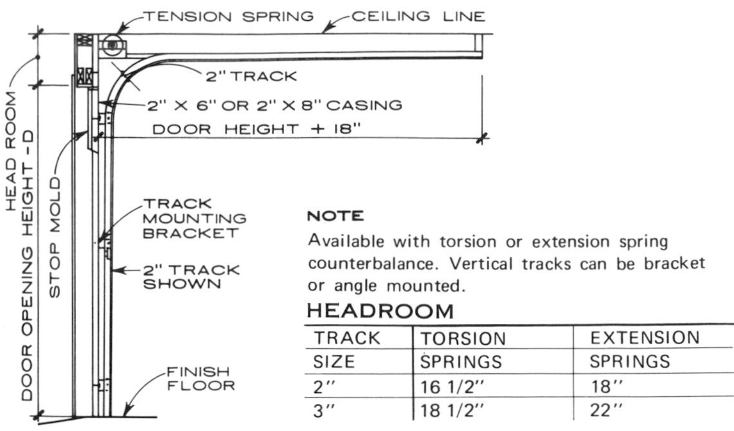

TENSION SPRING
CEILING LINE
2" TRACK
2" X 6" OR 2" X 8" CASING
DOOR HEIGHT + 18"
HEAD ROOM
DOOR OPENING HEIGHT - D
STOP MOLD
TRACK MOUNTING BRACKET
2" TRACK SHOWN
FINISH FLOOR

NOTE

Available with torsion or extension spring counterbalance. Vertical tracks can be bracket or angle mounted.

HEADROOM

TRACK SIZE	TORSION SPRINGS	EXTENSION SPRINGS
2″	16 1/2″	18″
3″	18 1/2″	22″

STANDARD HEADROOM TRACK - 2" OR 3"

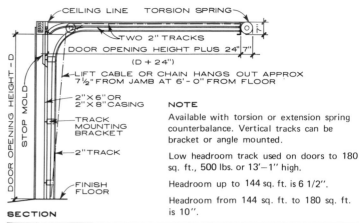

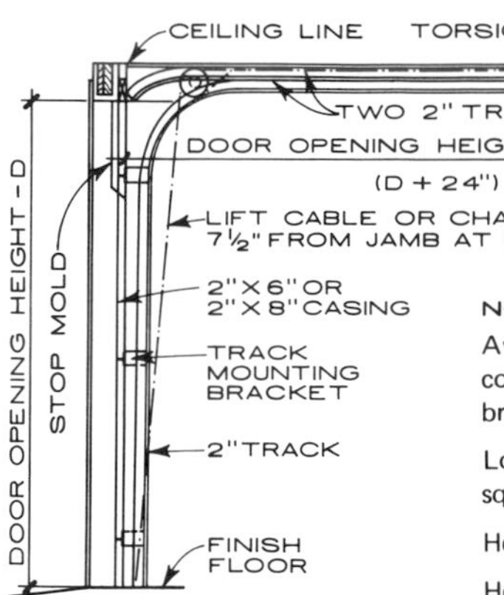

CEILING LINE
TORSION SPRING
7"
TWO 2" TRACKS
DOOR OPENING HEIGHT PLUS 24"
(D + 24")
LIFT CABLE OR CHAIN HANGS OUT APPROX 7½" FROM JAMB AT 6'-0" FROM FLOOR
2"X6" OR 2"X8" CASING
TRACK MOUNTING BRACKET
2" TRACK
FINISH FLOOR
DOOR OPENING HEIGHT - D
STOP MOLD
SECTION

NOTE

Available with torsion or extension spring counterbalance. Vertical tracks can be bracket or angle mounted.

Low headroom track used on doors to 180 sq. ft., 500 lbs. or 13′–1″ high.

Headroom up to 144 sq. ft. is 6 1/2″.

Headroom from 144 sq. ft. to 180 sq. ft. is 10″.

LOW HEADROOM TRACK - 2"

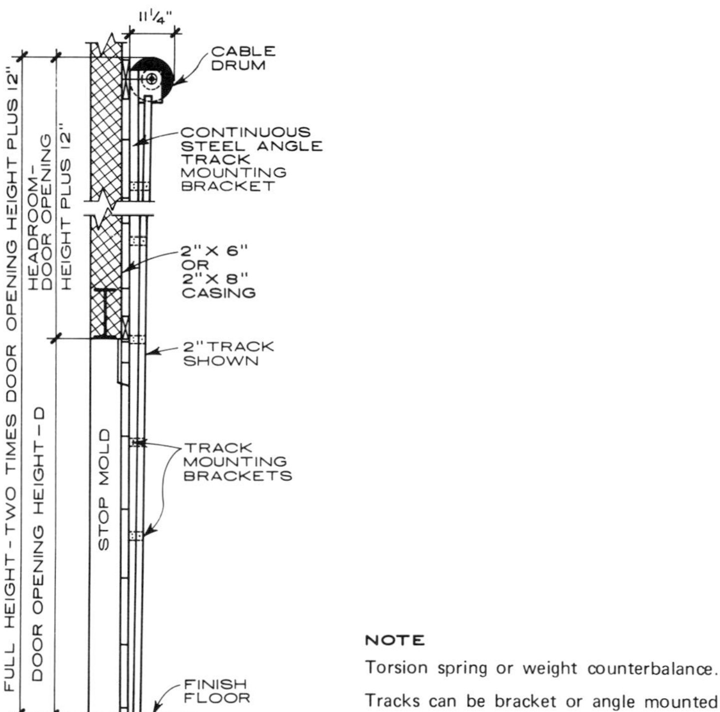

1 1/4"
CABLE DRUM
CONTINUOUS STEEL ANGLE TRACK MOUNTING BRACKET
2" X 6" OR 2" X 8" CASING
2" TRACK SHOWN
TRACK MOUNTING BRACKETS
FINISH FLOOR
FULL HEIGHT - TWO TIMES DOOR OPENING HEIGHT PLUS 12"
HEADROOM- DOOR OPENING HEIGHT PLUS 12"
DOOR OPENING HEIGHT - D
STOP MOLD

NOTE

Torsion spring or weight counterbalance.

Tracks can be bracket or angle mounted.

FULL VERTICAL TRACK - 2" OR 3"

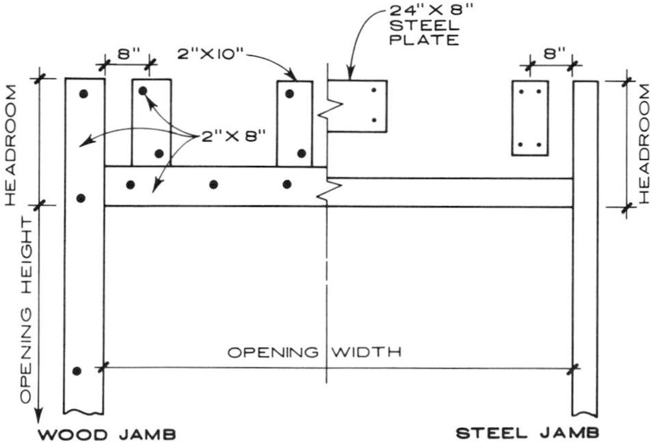

24" X 8" STEEL PLATE
8"
2"X10"
2"X8"
HEADROOM
OPENING HEIGHT
OPENING WIDTH
WOOD JAMB
STEEL JAMB

All pads and plates to be flush with wood or steel jambs.

Wide or heavy doors which require more than two springs will require pads additional to those shown in the above detail.

INTERIOR ELEVATION OF DOOR OPENING

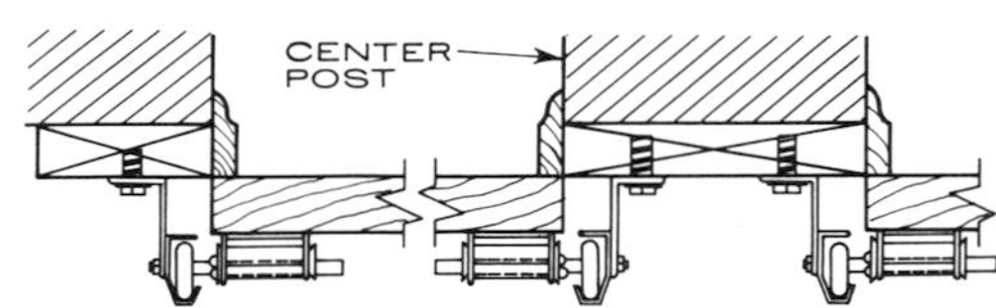

CENTER POST
WOOD JAMBS

NOTE

For weight counterbalance doors, additional sideroom is required.

See note for asterisk at Table for Steel Jamb sideroom below.

SIDEROOM

TRACK SIZE	SIDEROOM	FOR DOORS		CENTER POST
2″	3″	to 12′–1″ high		6″
2″	3 1/2″	12′–2″ to 14′–1″	*	7″
2″	4 1/2″	14′–2″ to 16′–1″	*	9″
3″	5″	to 320 sq. ft.	*	10″
3″	5 1/2″	over 320 sq. ft.	*	11″

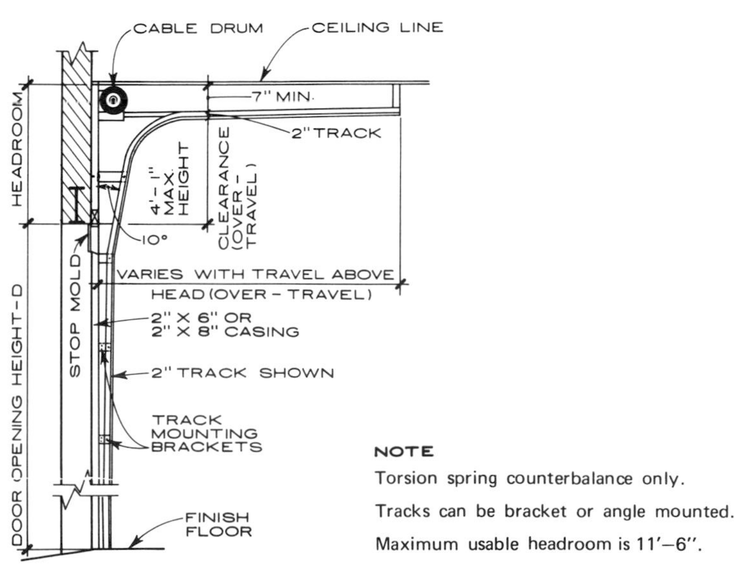

CABLE DRUM
CEILING LINE
7" MIN.
2" TRACK
HEADROOM
4'-1" MAX HEIGHT
CLEARANCE (OVER - TRAVEL)
10°
VARIES WITH TRAVEL ABOVE HEAD (OVER - TRAVEL)
2" X 6" OR 2" X 8" CASING
2" TRACK SHOWN
TRACK MOUNTING BRACKETS
FINISH FLOOR
DOOR OPENING HEIGHT - D
STOP MOLD

NOTE

Torsion spring counterbalance only.

Tracks can be bracket or angle mounted.

Maximum usable headroom is 11′–6″.

LIFT CLEARANCE TRACK - 2" OR 3"

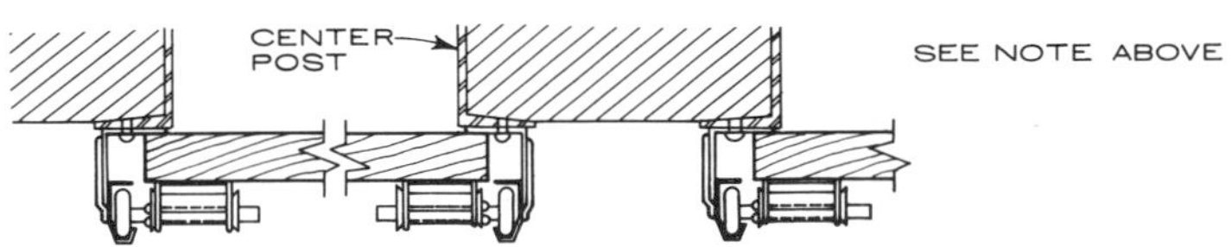

CENTER POST
SEE NOTE ABOVE
STEEL JAMBS

SIDEROOM

TRACK SIZE	SIDEROOM	FOR DOORS		CENTER POST
2″	4″	to 12′–1″ high		8″
2″	4 1/2″	12′–2″ to 14′–1″	*	9″
2″	5 1/2″	14′–2″ to 16′–1″	*	11″
3″	6″	to 320 sq. ft.	*	12″
3″	7″	over 320 sq. ft.	*	14″

* 16 ga. steel doors over 168 sq. ft. Use 3″ angle mounted track with 7″ sideroom, 14″ center post.

Eugene Patrick Holden, AIA; Dale E. Selzer, AIA, Architect; Dallas, Texas

NOTE

If door is not electric operated, a chain hoist is recommended for all doors exceeding 160 sq. ft. or 13′–0″ high. For 16 ga. steel use chain hoist on doors exceeding 120 sq. ft. or 12′–0″ high.

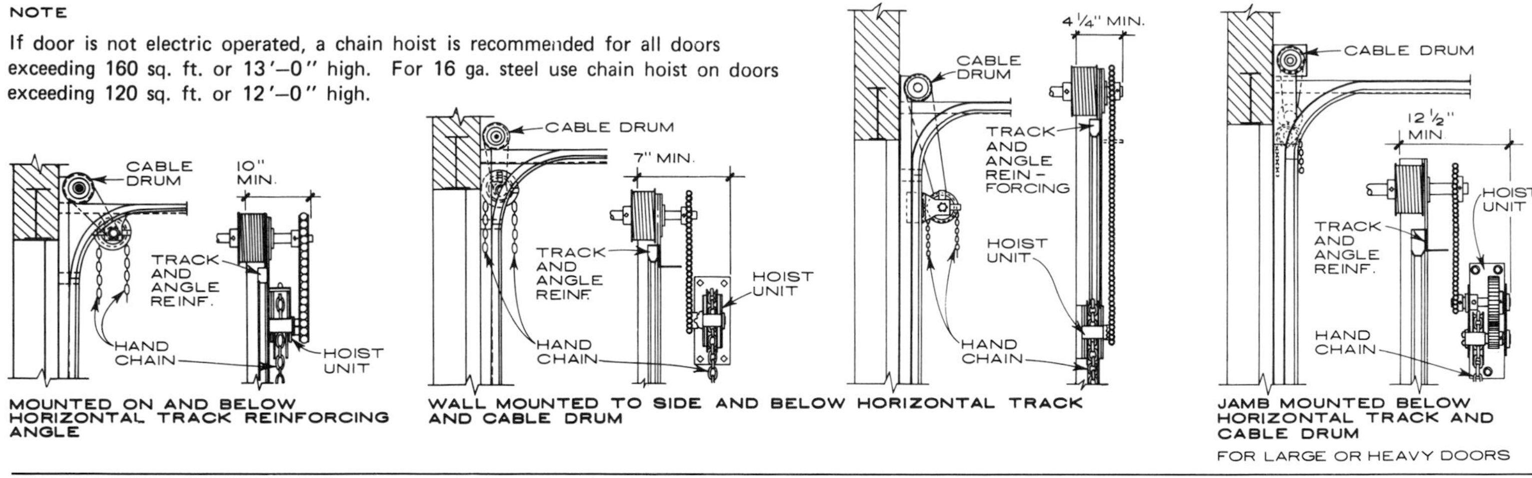
CABLE DRUM
10" MIN.
TRACK AND ANGLE REINF.
HAND CHAIN
HOIST UNIT
CABLE DRUM
7" MIN.
TRACK AND ANGLE REINF.
HOIST UNIT
HAND CHAIN
4 1/4" MIN.
CABLE DRUM
TRACK AND ANGLE REIN-FORCING
HOIST UNIT
HAND CHAIN
CABLE DRUM
12 1/2" MIN.
HOIST UNIT
TRACK AND ANGLE REINF.
HAND CHAIN

MOUNTED ON AND BELOW HORIZONTAL TRACK REINFORCING ANGLE

WALL MOUNTED TO SIDE AND BELOW HORIZONTAL TRACK AND CABLE DRUM

JAMB MOUNTED BELOW HORIZONTAL TRACK AND CABLE DRUM

FOR LARGE OR HEAVY DOORS

CHAIN HOIST OPERATORS - MINIMUM SIDE ROOM CLEARANCE

NOTE: All chain hoist operators require additional sideroom clearance. Operator may be mounted on left or right side as shown; on the left greater sideroom is required. Dimensions shown are from door jamb to projection of operator.

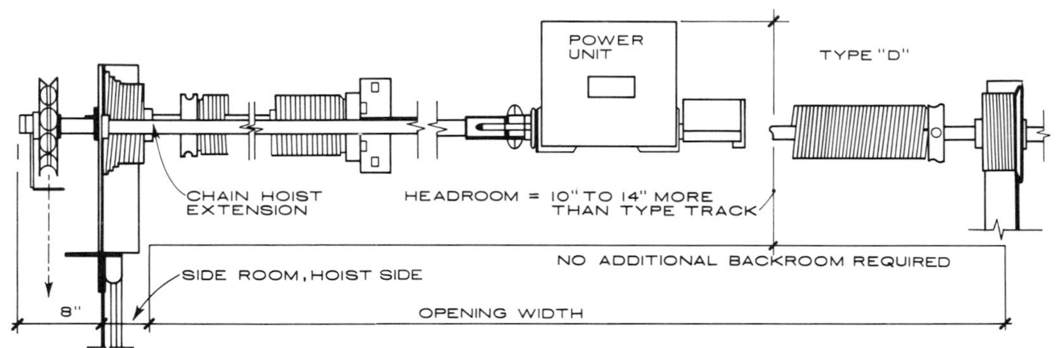
POWER UNIT
TYPE "D"
CHAIN HOIST EXTENSION
HEADROOM = 10" TO 14" MORE THAN TYPE TRACK
NO ADDITIONAL BACKROOM REQUIRED
SIDE ROOM, HOIST SIDE
8"
OPENING WIDTH

CENTER MOUNTED OPERATOR

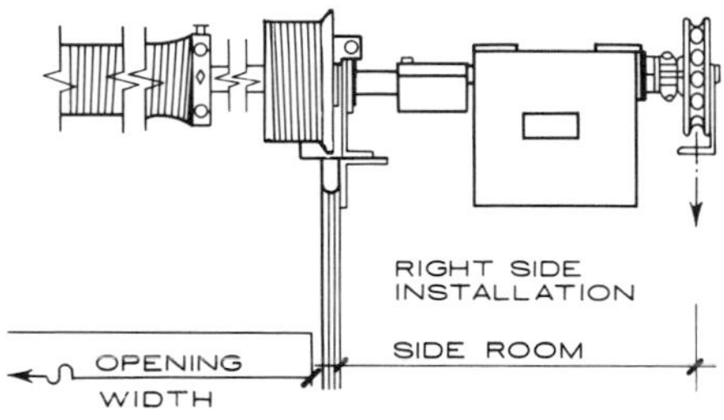
RIGHT SIDE INSTALLATION
OPENING WIDTH
SIDE ROOM

SIDEROOM WIDTHS FOR HEAVY COMMERCIAL USE – 20" FOR 2" TRACK AND 21" FOR 3" TRACK. FOR INDUSTRIAL USE, WIDTHS ARE 23" FOR 2" TRACK AND 24" FOR 3" TRACK

SIDE MOUNTED OPERATOR

NOTES
CENTER MOUNTED

Same principle as side mounted operator except power unit is located on front wall above door opening. No additional sideroom is needed. Needs from 10″ to 18″ additional headroom; 3″ additional sideroom on chain hoist side.

NOTES
SIDE MOUNTED

Power unit is mounted on inside front wall to the right or left of the door and is connected to the crosshead shaft with a drive chain and sprockets or an adjustable coupling. Power is applied to the shaft to raise the door. The door closes by its own weight with the speed controlled by the operator.

No extra headroom required. Needs 20″ to 24″ of sideroom on mounting side. Side mounted operators are available with direct coupled or chain drive, depending on installation condition.

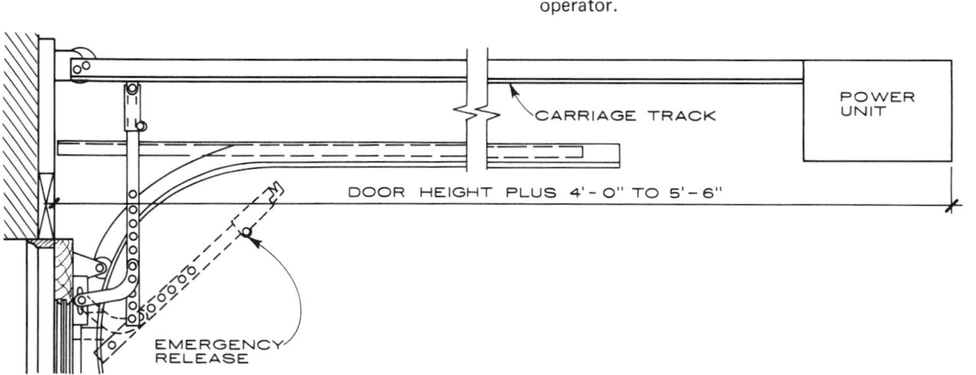
POWER UNIT
CARRIAGE TRACK
DOOR HEIGHT PLUS 4'-0" TO 5'-6"
EMERGENCY RELEASE

DRAWBAR TYPE OPERATOR

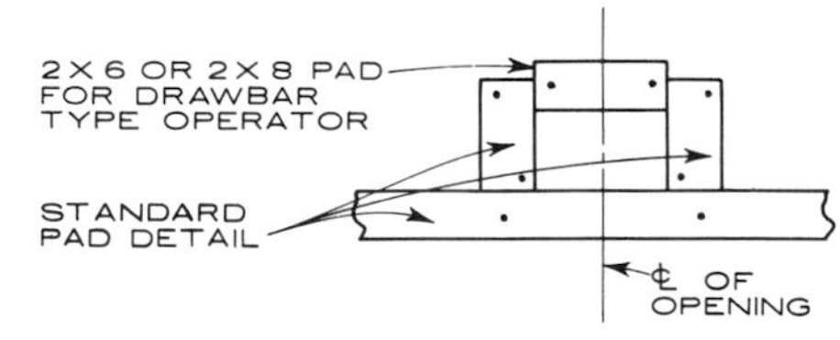
2 X 6 OR 2 X 8 PAD FOR DRAWBAR TYPE OPERATOR
STANDARD PAD DETAIL
℄ OF OPENING

PAD DETAIL FOR DRAWBAR TYPE OPERATORS

NOTE

Power unit is mounted between, above and to the rear of horizontal tracks of door. A chain-driven carriage slides forward and back in its own tracks, which run from power unit to front wall above door. An arm linking the carriage and the door applies force to open and close the door as the carriage moves backward and forward. Door requires a minimum of 2″ additional head room above tracks plus 1″ to 3 1/2″ more at power unit. No additional sideroom is required.

Drawbar type is not recommended for use on extra large doors nor with lift clearance track installations. Emergency chain hoists are not normally used on drawbar type operators.

ELECTRIC MOTOR OPERATORS

Available in all standard voltages, frequency and phase. Control can be by 2 or 3 button push button station, pull switches, photoelectric, radio control (single or multiple), time delay closing and/or reversing or stop only safety switch. For Operator Selector chart see manufacturers data.

Eugene Patrick Holden, AIA; Dale E. Selzer, AIA, Architect; Dallas, Texas

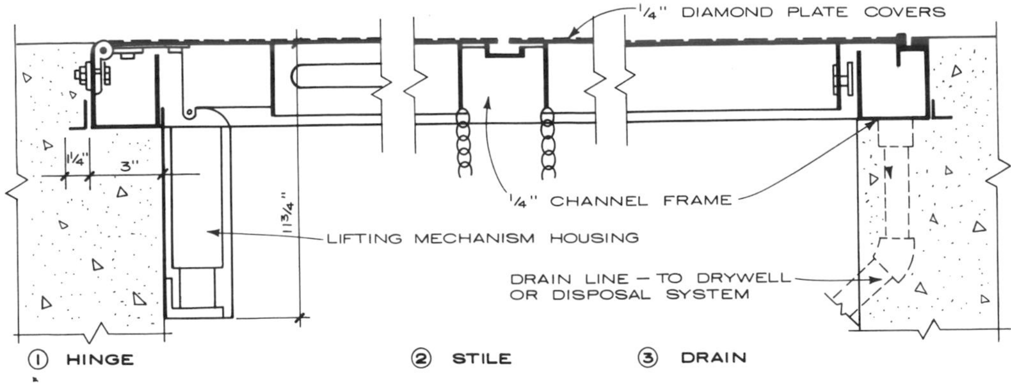
1/4" DIAMOND PLATE COVERS
1 1/4"
3"
11 3/4"
1/4" CHANNEL FRAME
LIFTING MECHANISM HOUSING
DRAIN LINE — TO DRYWELL OR DISPOSAL SYSTEM
① HINGE
② STILE
③ DRAIN

DETAILS

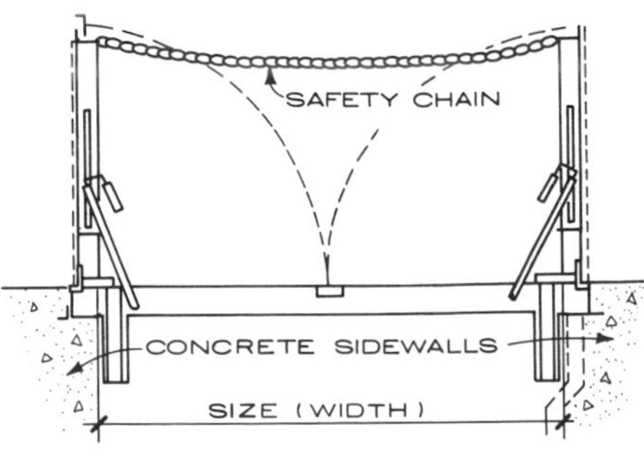
SAFETY CHAIN
CONCRETE SIDEWALLS
SIZE (WIDTH)

SECTION

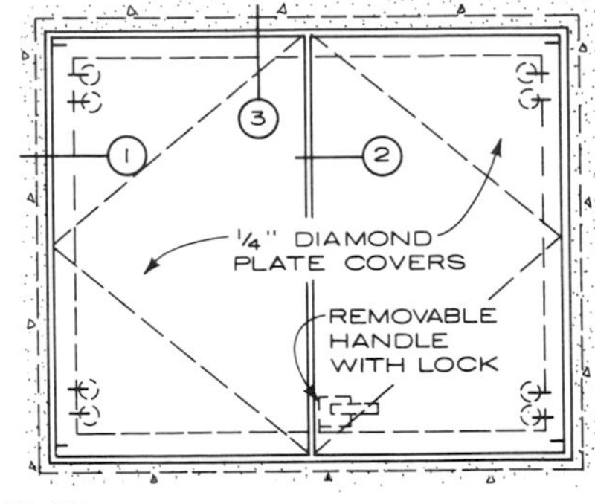
1/4" DIAMOND PLATE COVERS
REMOVABLE HANDLE WITH LOCK

PLAN

SIDEWALK DOORS are available in single and double leaf openings. Single leaf doors range in size from 2 ft to 3 ft 6 in. in 6 in. increments. Double leaf doors range in size from 4 to 6 ft in 1 ft increments. Special sizes are available.

Units are constructed in steel or aluminum. The door leafs are made of 1/4 in. diamond plate and are reinforced to withstand 300 psf of live load. Doors can be reinforced for greater loading conditions. The channel frames are made of 1/4 in. steel or aluminum with an anchor flange around the perimeter. Each door leaf is equipped with forged brass hinges, stainless steel pins, spring operators, and an automatic hold-open arm with release handle and is locked with a concealed snap lock. A drain coupling is provided to drain the internal gutter system. Safety chains are required to protect the opening.

SIDEWALK DOOR

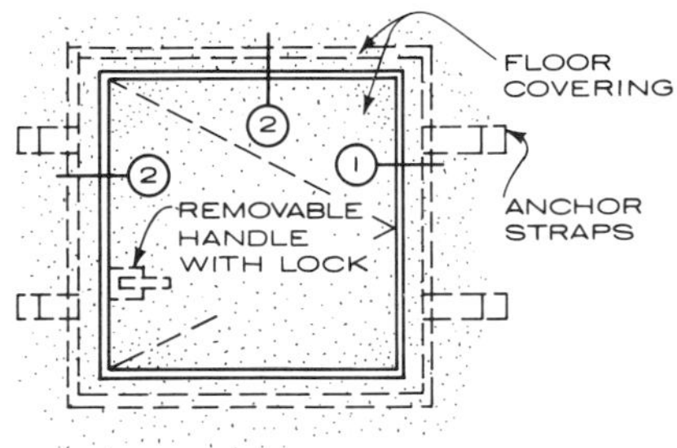
FLOOR COVERING
ANCHOR STRAPS
REMOVABLE HANDLE WITH LOCK

PLAN

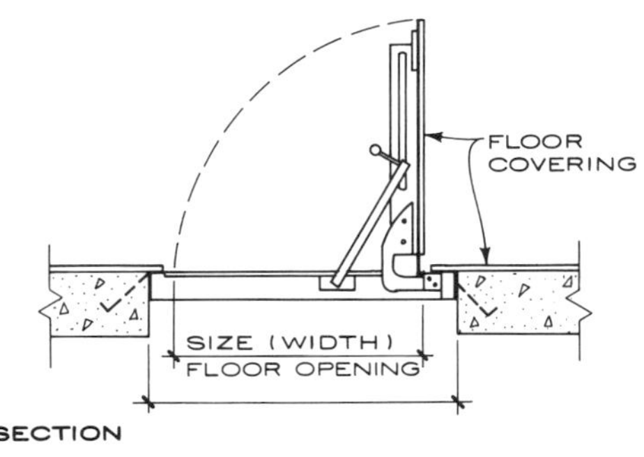
FLOOR COVERING
SIZE (WIDTH)
FLOOR OPENING

SECTION

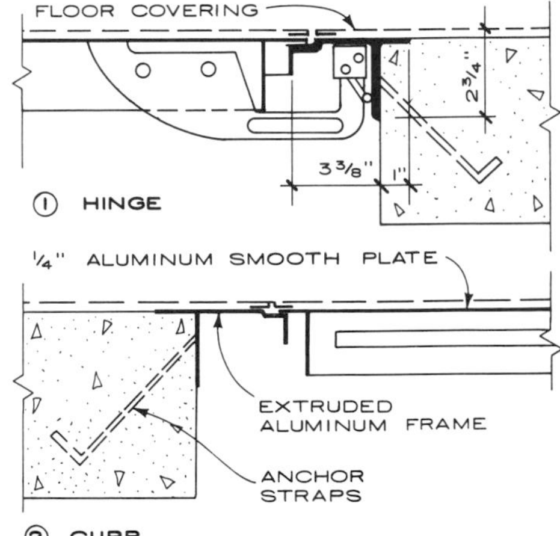
FLOOR COVERING
2 3/4"
3 3/8"
1"
① HINGE
1/4" ALUMINUM SMOOTH PLATE
EXTRUDED ALUMINUM FRAME
ANCHOR STRAPS
② CURB

FLOOR DOORS are available in single and double leaf openings. Single leaf doors range in size from 2 ft to 3 ft 6 in. in 6 in. increments. Double leaf doors range in size from 4 to 6 ft in 1 ft increments. Special sizes are available. Units are constructed in aluminum.

The door leafs are made of 1/4 in. extruded aluminum. Doors are made to accept 1/8 or 3/16 in. flooring. Each leaf has cast steel hinges and torsion bars. Doors open by a removable handle and are locked with a concealed snap lock.

FLOOR DOOR

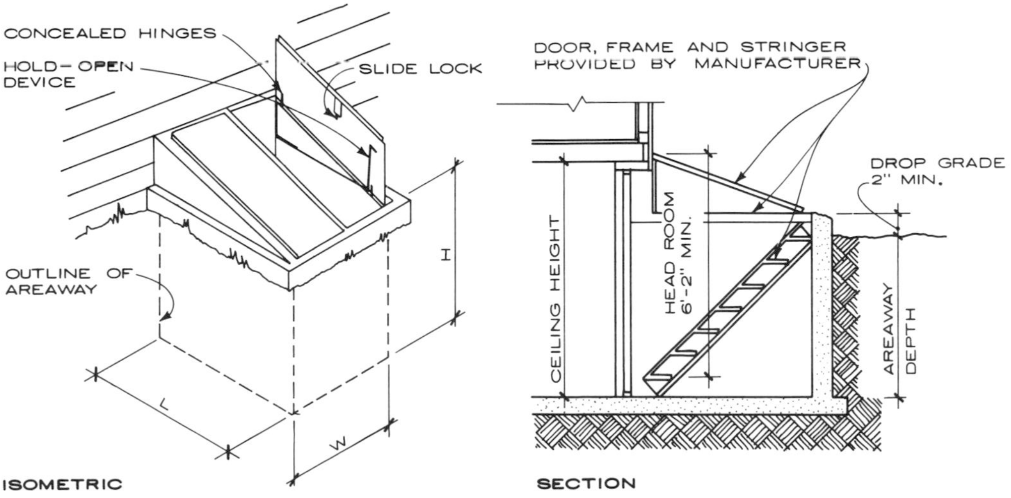
CONCEALED HINGES
HOLD-OPEN DEVICE
SLIDE LOCK
OUTLINE OF AREAWAY
H
L
W
DOOR, FRAME AND STRINGER PROVIDED BY MANUFACTURER
DROP GRADE 2" MIN.
CEILING HEIGHT
HEAD ROOM 6'-2" MIN.
AREAWAY DEPTH

ISOMETRIC

SECTION

CELLAR DOOR DIMENSIONS

TYPE	LENGTH	WIDTH	HEIGHT
S/L	3'-7 1/4"	4'-3"	4'-4"
O	4'-10"	3'-11"	2'-6"
B	5'-4"	4'-3"	1'-10"
C	6'-0"	4'-7"	1'-7 1/2"

AREAWAY DIMENSIONS (INSIDE)

TYPE	LENGTH	WIDTH	HEIGHT
S/L	3'-4"	3'-8"	3'-5 1/4"
O	4'-6"	3'-4"	4'-9 3/4"
B	5'-0"	3'-8"	5'-6"
C*	5'-8"	4'-0"	6'-2 1/4"

*Type C door can have a deeper areaway dimension with the use of stringer extensions.

CELLAR DOOR

Ronald C. Olech; SRGF, Inc., Architects; Champaign, Illinois

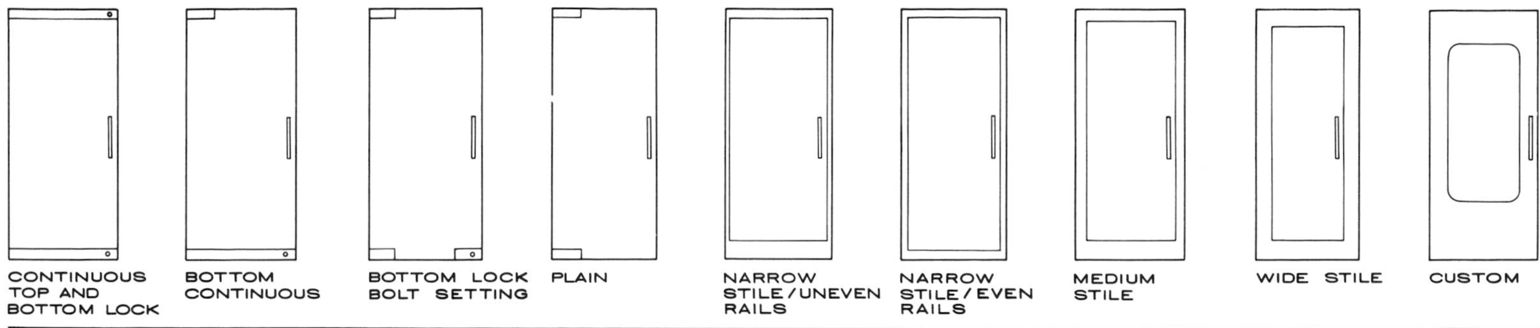
CONTINUOUS TOP AND BOTTOM LOCK
BOTTOM CONTINUOUS
BOTTOM LOCK BOLT SETTING
PLAIN
NARROW STILE / UNEVEN RAILS
NARROW STILE / EVEN RAILS
MEDIUM STILE
WIDE STILE
CUSTOM

DOOR TYPES - NOTE: DOORS WITH NARROW STILES SHOULD NOT BE USED IN HEAVILY TRAFFICKED AREAS.

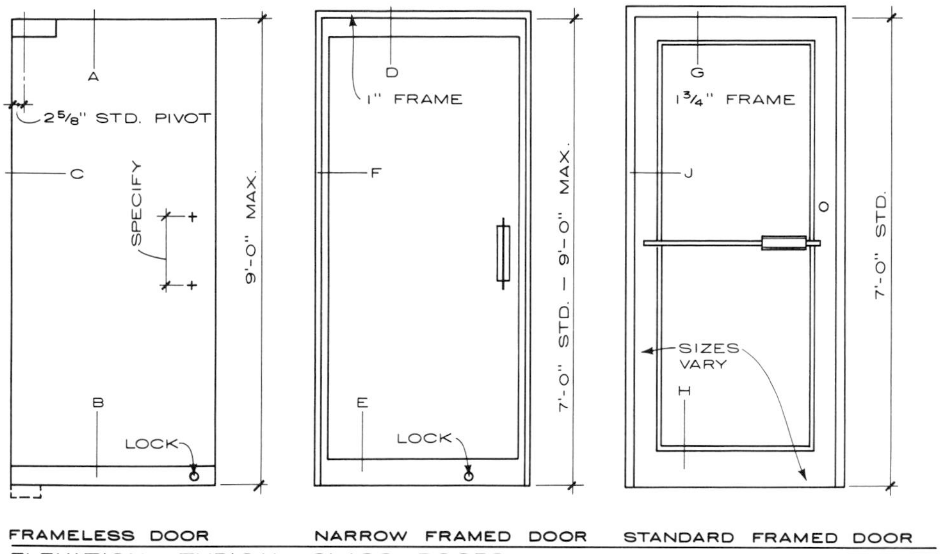

A
2 5/8" STD. PIVOT
C
SPECIFY
9'-0" MAX.
B
LOCK

D
1" FRAME
F
7'-0" STD. - 9'-0" MAX.
E
LOCK

G
1 3/4" FRAME
J
SIZES VARY
H
7'-0" STD.

FRAMELESS DOOR

NARROW FRAMED DOOR

STANDARD FRAMED DOOR

ELEVATION—TYPICAL GLASS DOORS

CLOSED POSITION
PARTLY OPEN
COMPLETELY OPEN

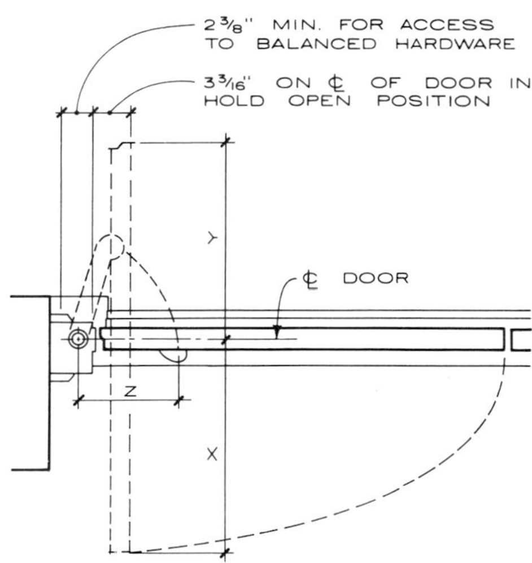
2 3/8" MIN. FOR ACCESS TO BALANCED HARDWARE
3 3/16" ON ℄ OF DOOR IN HOLD OPEN POSITION
Y
℄ DOOR
Z
X

PLAN

BALANCED DOOR

TRANSOM BAR OR HEAD JAMB

HEAD SECTION A

SILL SECTION B

CLEARANCE

3/16"

CHECKING HINGE

1"

HEAD SECTION D

SILL SECTION E

HEAD SECTION G

SILL SECTION H

1/8" CLEARANCE WHEN CLOSED OR OPEN AT ANY POSITION

JAMB SECTION C

JAMB SECTION F

JAMB SECTION J

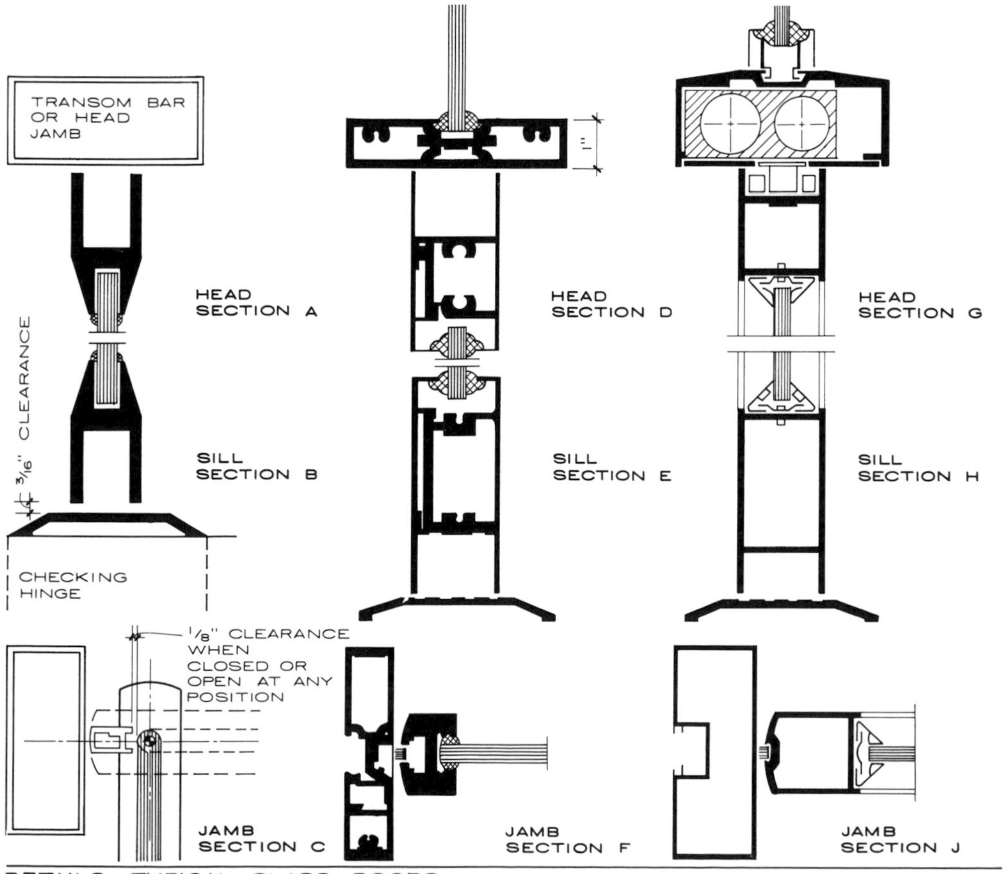

DETAILS—TYPICAL GLASS DOORS

SPACE REQUIREMENTS—VARIOUS DOOR WIDTHS (IN.)

	34	36	38	40	42	44
X	21 1/4	23 1/4	25 1/4	23 1/4	25 1/4	27 1/4
Y	12 3/4			16 1/4		
Z	7 1/8			8 7/8		

NOTES

1. Consult applicable codes for safety requirements, glass size, thickness, and tempering.
2. Frameless 1/2 in. glass doors are available in clear, grey, or bronze tints in sizes up to 60 in. x 108 in. Frameless 3/4 in. glass doors are available only in clear tint in sizes up to 48 in. x 108 in.
3. Consult manufacturer's data on structural adequacy for required loads and for frames and transom bars reinforcement.
4. Aluminum doors and frames are available in all standard aluminum finishes in sizes up to 6 ft. x 7 ft.
5. Frameless doors may not permit adequate weatherstripping. The use of frameless doors in exterior walls in northern climates should be evaluated for energy efficiency and comfort.

G. Lawson Drinkard, III, AIA; The Vickery Partnership, Architects; Charlottesville, Virginia

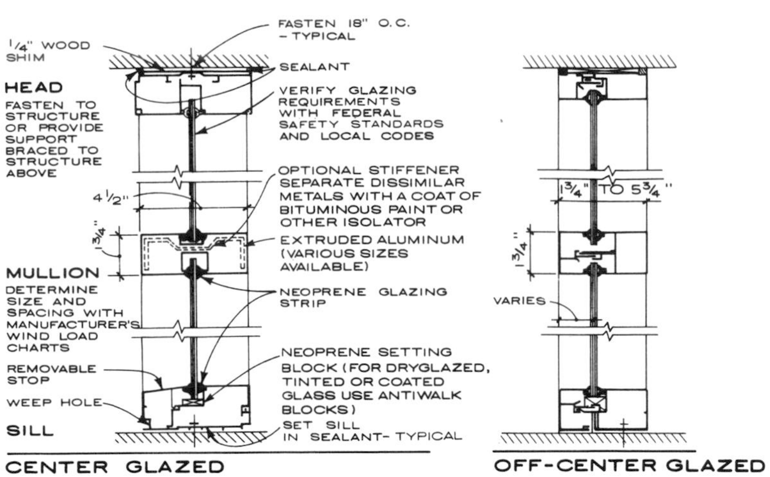
FASTEN 18" O.C. - TYPICAL
1/4" WOOD SHIM
SEALANT
HEAD
FASTEN TO STRUCTURE OR PROVIDE SUPPORT BRACED TO STRUCTURE ABOVE
VERIFY GLAZING REQUIREMENTS WITH FEDERAL SAFETY STANDARDS AND LOCAL CODES
OPTIONAL STIFFENER
4 1/2"
SEPARATE DISSIMILAR METALS WITH A COAT OF BITUMINOUS PAINT OR OTHER ISOLATOR
1 3/4"
EXTRUDED ALUMINUM (VARIOUS SIZES AVAILABLE)
MULLION
DETERMINE SIZE AND SPACING WITH MANUFACTURER'S WIND LOAD CHARTS
NEOPRENE GLAZING STRIP
NEOPRENE SETTING BLOCK (FOR DRYGLAZED, TINTED OR COATED GLASS USE ANTIWALK BLOCKS)
REMOVABLE STOP
WEEP HOLE
SILL
SET SILL IN SEALANT- TYPICAL
1 3/4" TO 5 3/4"
1 3/4"
VARIES

CENTER GLAZED

OFF-CENTER GLAZED

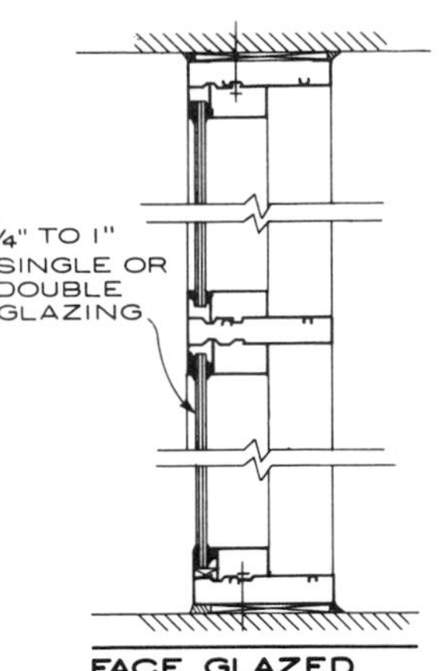
1/4" TO 1" SINGLE OR DOUBLE GLAZING

FACE GLAZED

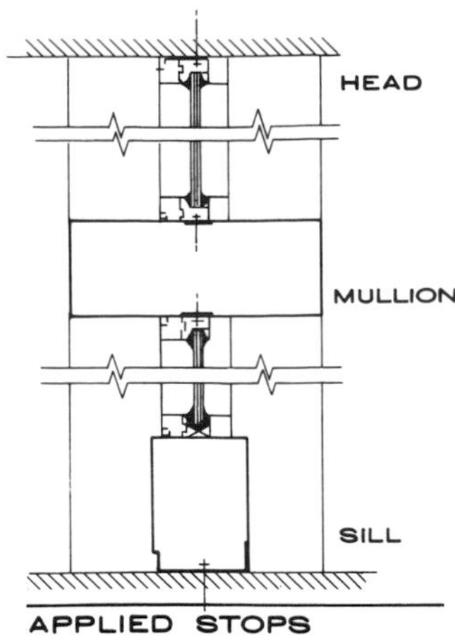
HEAD
MULLION
SILL

APPLIED STOPS

NOTES

1. Review tinted and coated glass applications and details to eliminate possibility of thermal breakage due to shading devices and shadow patterns.
2. Review setting block spacing, size, and hardness to prevent glass slippage and breakage.
3. Weep holes are required at sill for double glazing.
4. Refer to manufacturer's current recommendations for specific applications.
5. Other materials such as hollow metal or wood can be used for custom work and in saltwater atmospheres where aluminum will corrode.
6. Various aluminum anodized color finishes are available. Class I (0.7 mil) or Class II (0.4 mil) in black, bronze, or clear are standard with most manufacturers.
7. To extend life of aluminum and to reduce tendency of surface pitting, wash aluminum periodically with water and mild detergent.
8. Glass edges mitered at corners are not recommended. Maximum vertical span for butt glazing is 10 ft. x 8 ft. wide.
9. Mullions are clear glass. Tinted or coated glass lights may be considered for small areas. Maximum vertical span is 30 ft.

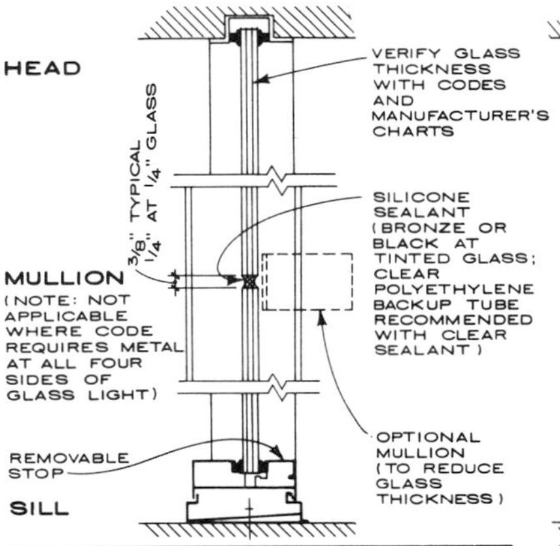

HEAD

VERIFY GLASS THICKNESS WITH CODES AND MANUFACTURER'S CHARTS

3/8" TYPICAL AT 1/4" GLASS

SILICONE SEALANT (BRONZE OR BLACK AT TINTED GLASS; CLEAR POLYETHYLENE BACKUP TUBE RECOMMENDED WITH CLEAR SEALANT)

MULLION (NOTE: NOT APPLICABLE WHERE CODE REQUIRES METAL AT ALL FOUR SIDES OF GLASS LIGHT)

REMOVABLE STOP

SILL

OPTIONAL MULLION (TO REDUCE GLASS THICKNESS)

BUTT GLAZED WITH FLUSH HEAD AND JAMB

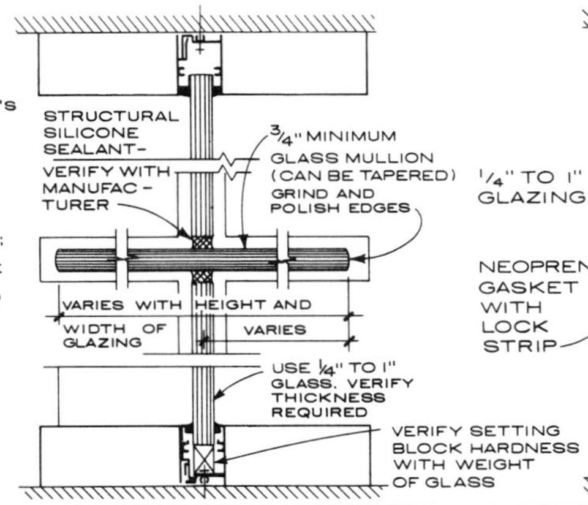

STRUCTURAL SILICONE SEALANT- VERIFY WITH MANUFACTURER

3/4" MINIMUM GLASS MULLION (CAN BE TAPERED) GRIND AND POLISH EDGES

VARIES WITH HEIGHT AND WIDTH OF GLAZING

VARIES

USE 1/4" TO 1" GLASS. VERIFY THICKNESS REQUIRED

VERIFY SETTING BLOCK HARDNESS WITH WEIGHT OF GLASS

GLASS MULLION

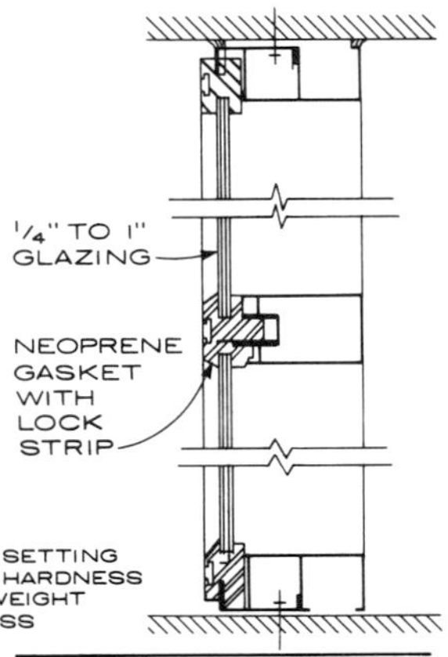

1/4" TO 1" GLAZING

NEOPRENE GASKET WITH LOCK STRIP

GASKET GLAZED

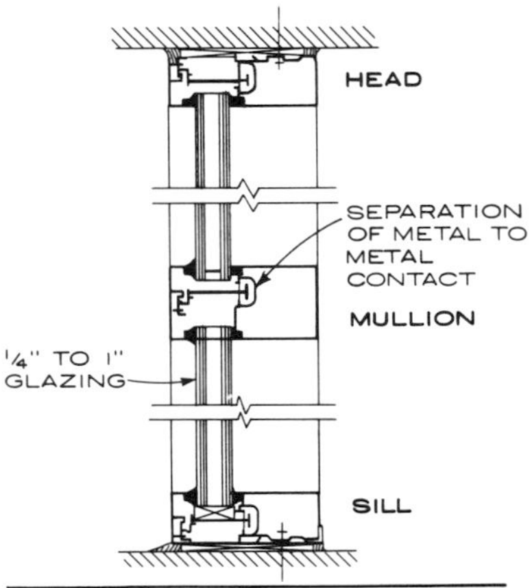

HEAD

SEPARATION OF METAL TO METAL CONTACT

MULLION

1/4" TO 1" GLAZING

SILL

THERMAL GLAZING

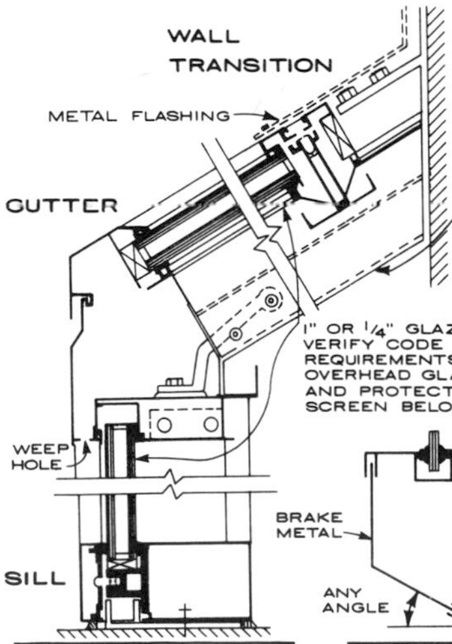

WALL TRANSITION

METAL FLASHING

GUTTER

RAFTER SIZE AND REINFORCING DETERMINED BY SPAN

1" OR 1/4" GLAZING. VERIFY CODE REQUIREMENTS FOR OVERHEAD GLAZING AND PROTECTIVE SCREEN BELOW

WEEP HOLE

SILL

SLOPED GLAZING

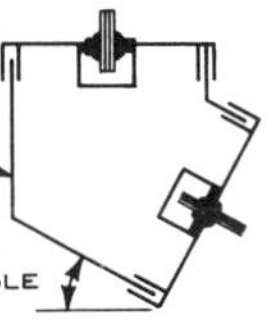

BRAKE METAL

ANY ANGLE

ANGLED CORNER

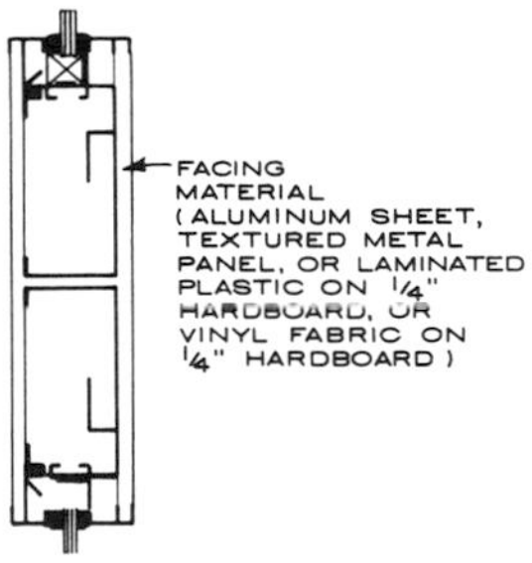

FACING MATERIAL (ALUMINUM SHEET, TEXTURED METAL PANEL, OR LAMINATED PLASTIC ON 1/4" HARDBOARD, OR VINYL FABRIC ON 1/4" HARDBOARD)

HORIZONTAL MUNTIN

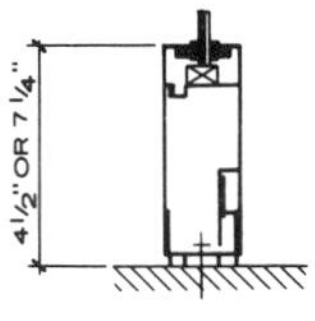

4 1/2" OR 7 1/4"

BULKHEAD SILL

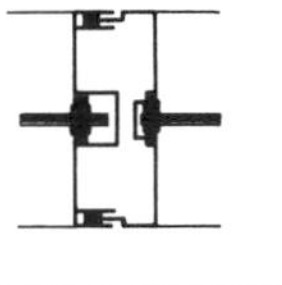

EXPANSION MULLION

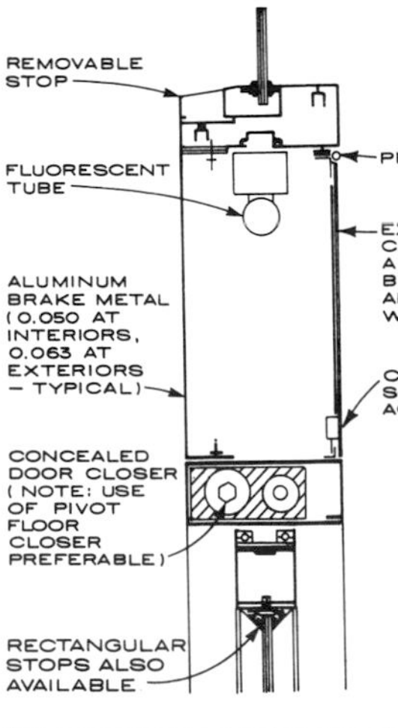

REMOVABLE STOP

PIANO HINGE

FLUORESCENT TUBE

EXIT SIGN CUT OUT OF ALUMINUM BRAKE METAL AND BACKED WITH PLASTIC

ALUMINUM BRAKE METAL (0.050 AT INTERIORS, 0.063 AT EXTERIORS - TYPICAL)

CATCH WITH SCREWDRIVER ACCESS HOLE

CONCEALED DOOR CLOSER (NOTE: USE OF PIVOT FLOOR CLOSER PREFERABLE)

RECTANGULAR STOPS ALSO AVAILABLE

DOOR TRANSOM WITH CLOSER AND ILLUMINATED EXIT SIGN

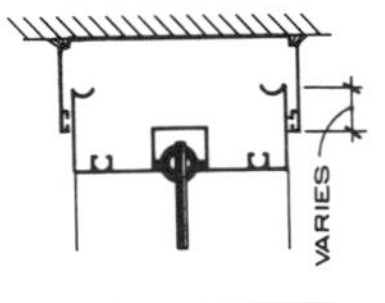

VARIES

HEAD WITH RECEPTOR

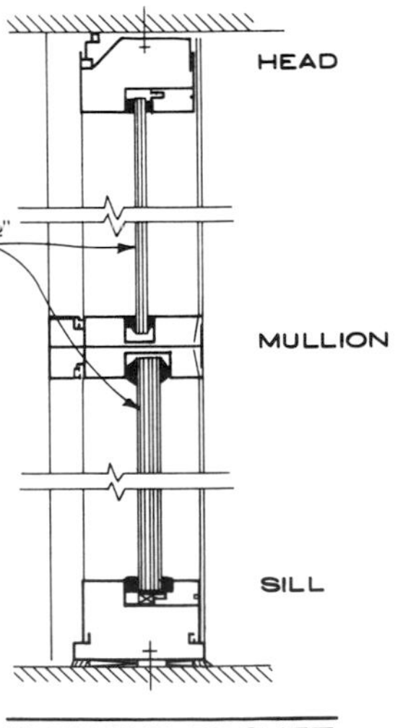

HEAD

1/4" TO 1 1/2" GLAZING

MULLION

SILL

VARIABLE POCKET GLAZING

Care should be taken to protect the public from the possibility of overhead glass breakage.

Higher bulkheads can be built up with aluminum tubing and applied stops. Locate expansion mullions 20 ft o.c.

Use receptor for deflection or dimensional tolerance problems.

O'Leary Terasawa Takahashi DeChellis & Chaffin, AIA Architects; Los Angeles, California

PROJECTED

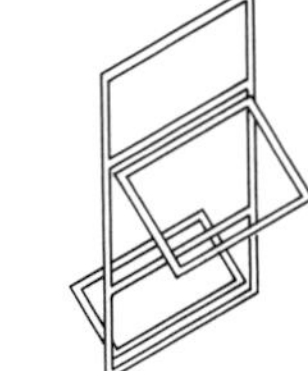

This is the workhorse of metal windows, available in many combinations of fixed and operating sash. Usually the lowest light will project in and the upper vents project out for maximum comfort and convenience. However, the flexibility of substituting fixed lights for vents and omitting muntins permits a variety of configurations.

Available in various weights, these windows are frequently used in institutional, commercial, and industrial projects. They will receive single or double glazing, from inside or outside. A wide assortment of hardware has been developed to meet almost every need, including special accessories for manual or mechanical operation of sash above normal reach.

SECURITY

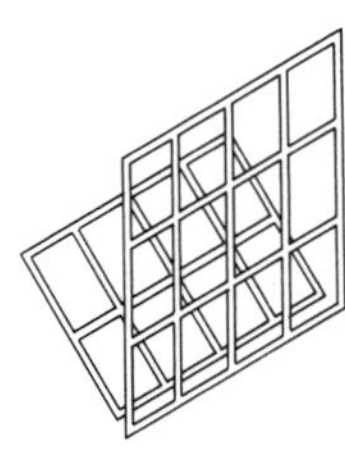

Another variation of the projected sash, this window provides an integral grill permitting ventilation but restricting the size of an object that can pass through the window. Used in institutions requiring detention or tight security against outside entry, this sash minimizes the psychological, installation, and maintenance problems associated with a separate grill.

DOUBLE HUNG

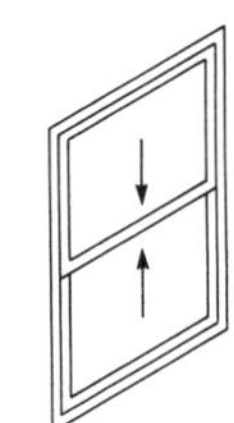

The traditional window of the United States wood window industry, metal double hung windows are finding wide application in projects where economy and flush window treatment are paramount. Single hung windows, which provide a fixed light in lieu of the top sash, are employed where economy is particularly critical. Triple hung windows are another variation, providing three operating sash for ease of operation in tall windows.

SLIDING

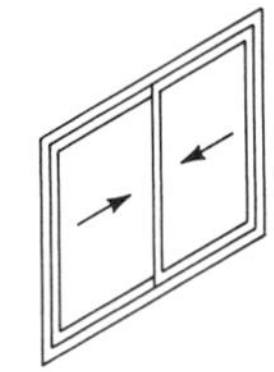

Horizontally sliding or rolling sash provide flush interior and exterior wall surfaces without the need for counterbalancing hardware intrinsic in the double hung window. Initially they were popular as economical sash in residential applications; the sliding window industry has subsequently made substantial product improvements. Their inherent weatherproofing problems have been overcome with careful engineering and workmanship utilizing heavier members. Generally speaking, horizontally or squarely proportioned sash will operate more smoothly than tall, narrow sash. Most manufacturers apply full width insect screens on the exterior.

COMBINATION

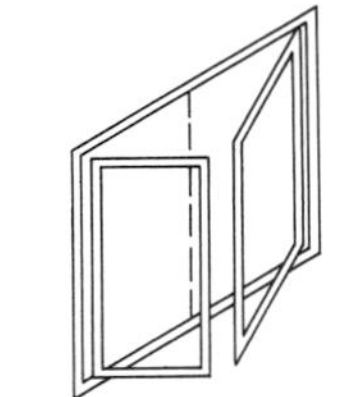

An economical variation of the projected sash that is used where light more than ventilation is desired. Size and height of this type of window will determine its usability as a fire escape in dwelling units and small offices. It may not be used as a fire escape in buildings classified for public assembly such as schools. Operating vents may be designed to project in or out. Insect screens pose different problems in both situations.

CASEMENT

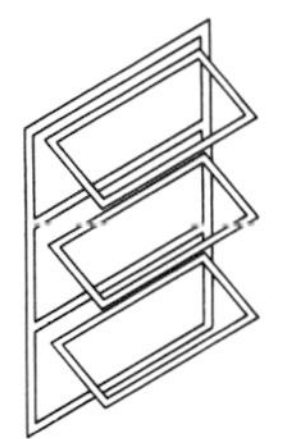

Consisting of vertically proportioned sash that swing outward, somewhat like a door, casement windows offer an aesthetic appeal not furnished by other window types. Insect screens are necessarily placed on the inside. Thus underscreen mechanical operators are usually provided. Otherwise the screen would have to be hinged or equipped with wickets for access to manual pulls.

AWNING

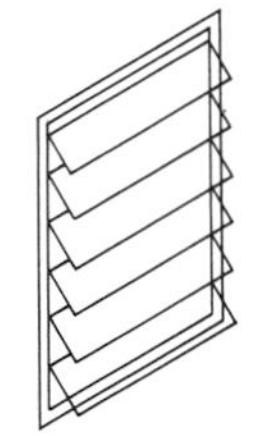

A window that has grown in popularity from its Southern residential origins, an awning window offers 100% ventilation combined with a degree of rain protection not attainable with casement sash. Awning sash can be fully weatherstripped and will readily receive double glazing or storm sash. Since their inherent horizontal proportions are not currently in vogue, their use has diminished recently. Insect screens are mounted in the interior, and rotary operators are standard.

JALOUSIE

When the individual sash depth of the awning window is reduced to the point where it becomes, in effect, an operating louver, horizontal sash members are unnecessary. This has a profound effect on appearance and the ability to provide weatherstripping. Most often found in residences and commercial work, particularly where ventilation is most desirable, jalousie windows are not as widely used as most other sash. Sash widths are limited to the free span capability of the blade materials (usually glass, wood, or metal). Storm sash are readily available and, in some instances, are an integral part of the jalousie. Insect screens are necessarily placed on the interior, with operating hardware usually placed at normal hand height.

PIVOTED

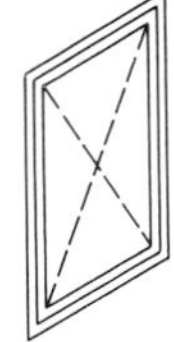

Popular in multistory, air-conditioned commercial buildings, horizontally or vertically pivoting sash are used only for maintenance. Though they usually rotate 90°, some manufacturers produce a sash that rotates 180°. Effective weatherstripping is mandatory in both cases. Wind action on walls of highrise structures must be considered in sash design. Top or side hung sash are also produced by some manufacturers for occasional opening of fixed sash.

GENERAL NOTES

1. Most types are readily available in steel or aluminum. Steel sash tend to be more rigid and have thinner sight lines. They will be galvanized and/or bonderized and primed prior to finishing if so specified. While aluminum sash may be more economical and may offer greater inherent corrosion resistance, they have greater thermal expansion and conductance. Both are available in a variety of finishes.
2. All operating sash are regularly mulled to fixed sash, thus providing for economy, appearance, and a variety of functions.
3. Thoughtful selection of glazing material is as important as window type selection. Plastic glazing materials generally have greater coefficients of thermal expansion than glass, requiring deeper glazing legs and stops.
4. Effective thermal isolation requires double glazing (some manufacturers offer triple glazing or dual sash), continuous weatherstripping, and a "thermal break" in aluminum sash for colder climates.
5. Many manufacturers produce more than one quality window. SWI criteria for various weights of steel sash are useful in making comparisons. Current criteria for aluminum sash are based on performance of a tested specimen, hence require careful consideration unless the manufacturer has a well established reputation.
6. Many manufacturers have ceased using "stock sizes" and produce only custom work. Consequently, special shapes and configurations are easier to obtain, particularly in monumental or commercial grades. Some manufacturers also produce specialized windows that are sound resistant, contain venetian blinds, and so on. Since there is little correlation between the manufacturers' dimensioning systems, individual consultation is imperative where dimensions are critical.
7. Residential grades are somewhat more standardized, generally based on available dimensions of welded edge insulating glass.
8. Muntins, either simulating or forming small glass lights, are usually available for residential sash, if desired.
9. Installation details must take into account internal condensation in most climates. Hardware selection must consider insect screens as well as mounting heights, operating convenience, security, and so on.
10. Most codes have a minimum light and ventilation, minimum wind load resistance, and maximum thermal transmittance requirements, as well as minimum egress provisions from residential sleeping space. All these factors may affect window selection.
11. Prefinished window frames are generally installed after contiguous masonry rather than being built in.

William A. Klene, AIA, Architect; Herndon, Virginia

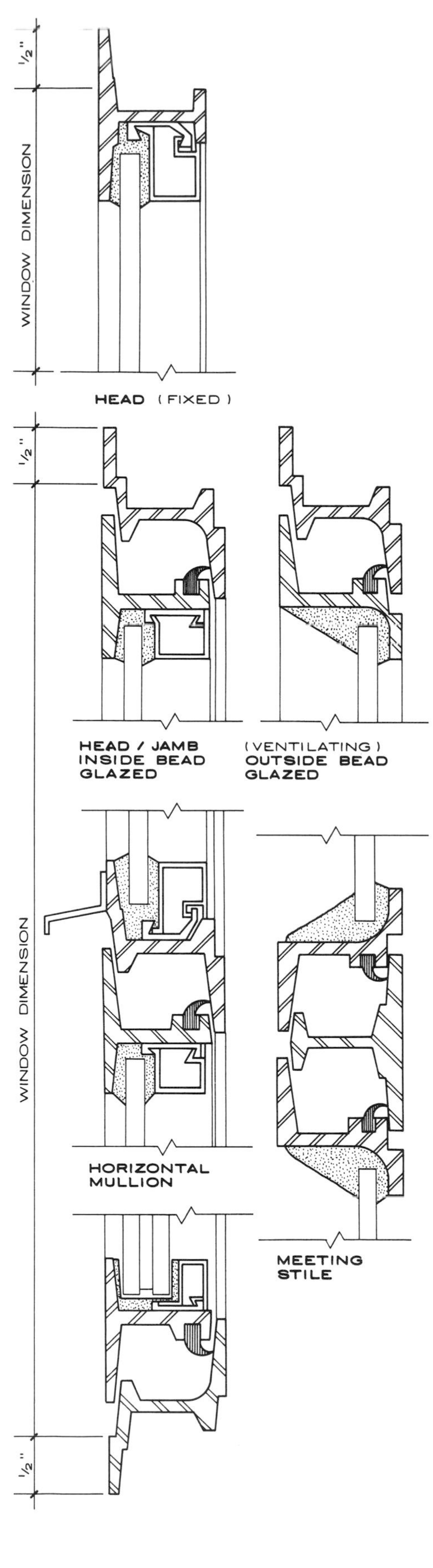

1/2"
WINDOW DIMENSION
HEAD (FIXED)
1/2"
HEAD / JAMB INSIDE BEAD GLAZED
(VENTILATING) OUTSIDE BEAD GLAZED
WINDOW DIMENSION
HORIZONTAL MULLION
MEETING STILE
1/2"

STEEL SASH CONSTRUCTION

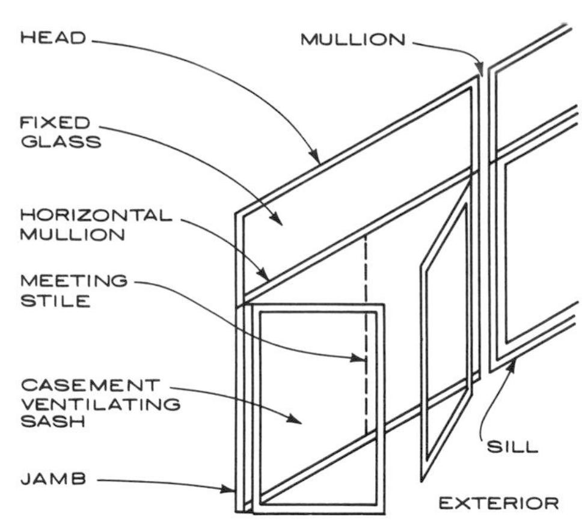

HEAD
MULLION
FIXED GLASS
HORIZONTAL MULLION
MEETING STILE
CASEMENT VENTILATING SASH
JAMB
SILL
EXTERIOR

WINDOW NOMENCLATURE

NOTES

1. Window sizes and dimensioning methods, as listed, are not uniform for all manufacturers. Some manufacturers have no stock sizes, producing only custom work. Check with those who supply sash for each geographical area.
2. In general, heavier grades of windows offer greater configuration flexibility. Larger operating sash can be produced with heavier members than with lighter members. Thus the fixed lights shown for taller steel sash can be avoided, if desired.
3. Insect screens are necessarily installed on the interior and must be taken into account when selecting hardware.
4. The raindrip indicated on the horizontal mullion may be required at ventilating heads if sash is placed flush with exterior face of wall.
5. Drawings or specification must contain the following information: window size and location, installation details, sills, stools, flashing, sealing, and anchors; sash material and finish; glazing material; glazing method (tape, putty, or bead, inside or outside); weatherstripping, insect screen material, and hardware.

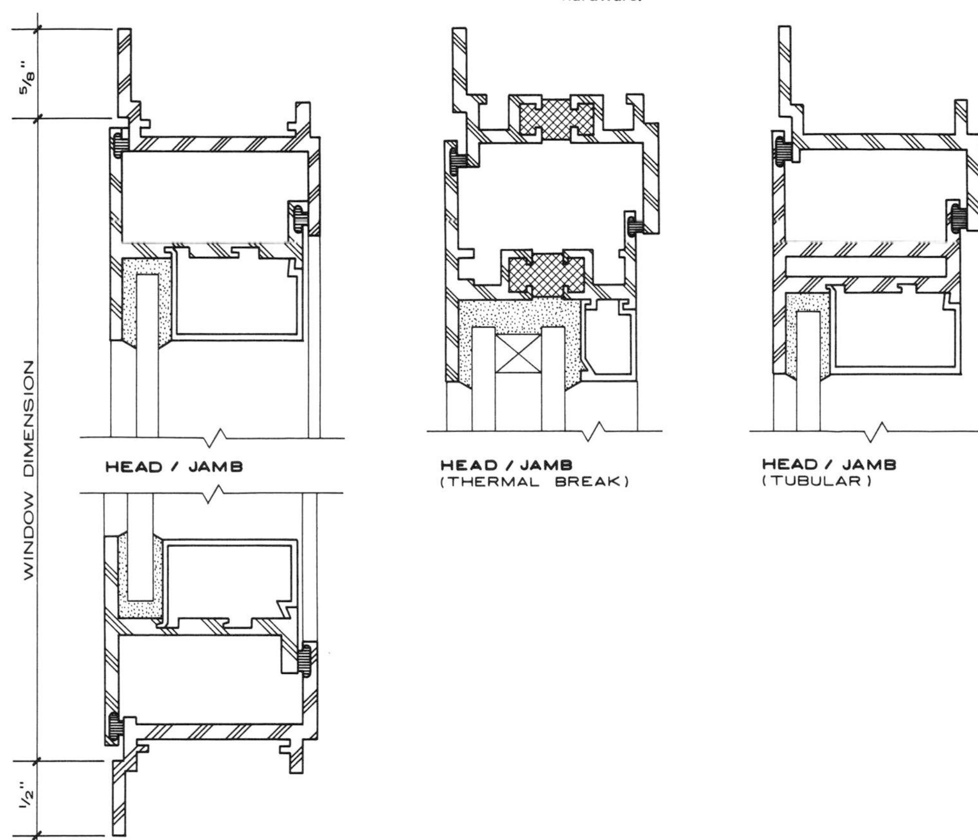

5/8"
WINDOW DIMENSION
HEAD / JAMB
HEAD / JAMB (THERMAL BREAK)
HEAD / JAMB (TUBULAR)
1/2"
SILL

ALUMINUM SASH CONSTRUCTION

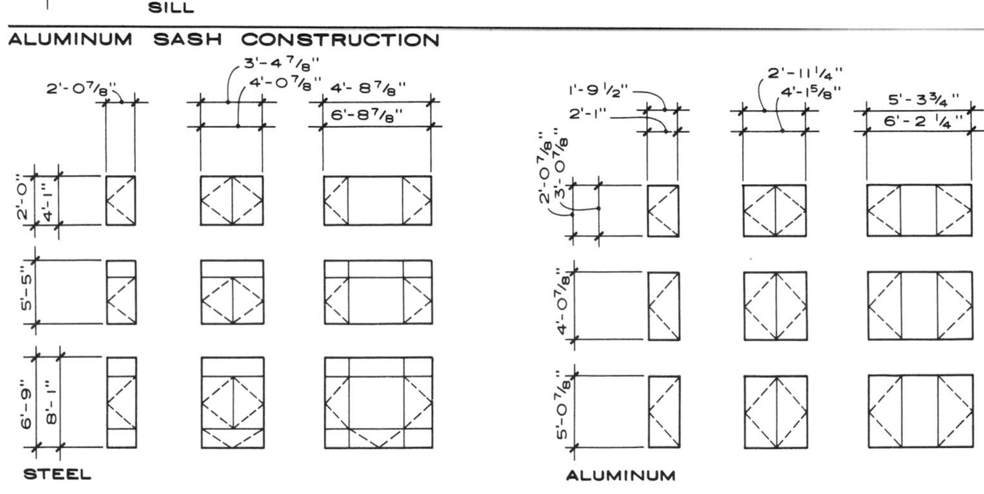

2'-0 7/8"
3'-4 7/8"
4'-0 7/8"
4'-8 7/8"
6'-8 7/8"
2'-0"
4'-1"
5'-5"
6'-9"
8'-1"
STEEL
1'-9 1/2"
2'-1"
2'-11 1/4"
4'-1 5/8"
5'-3 3/4"
6'-2 1/4"
2'-0 7/8"
3'-0 7/8"
4'-0 7/8"
5'-0 7/8"
ALUMINUM

WINDOW SIZES

William A. Klene, AIA, Architect; Herndon, Virginia

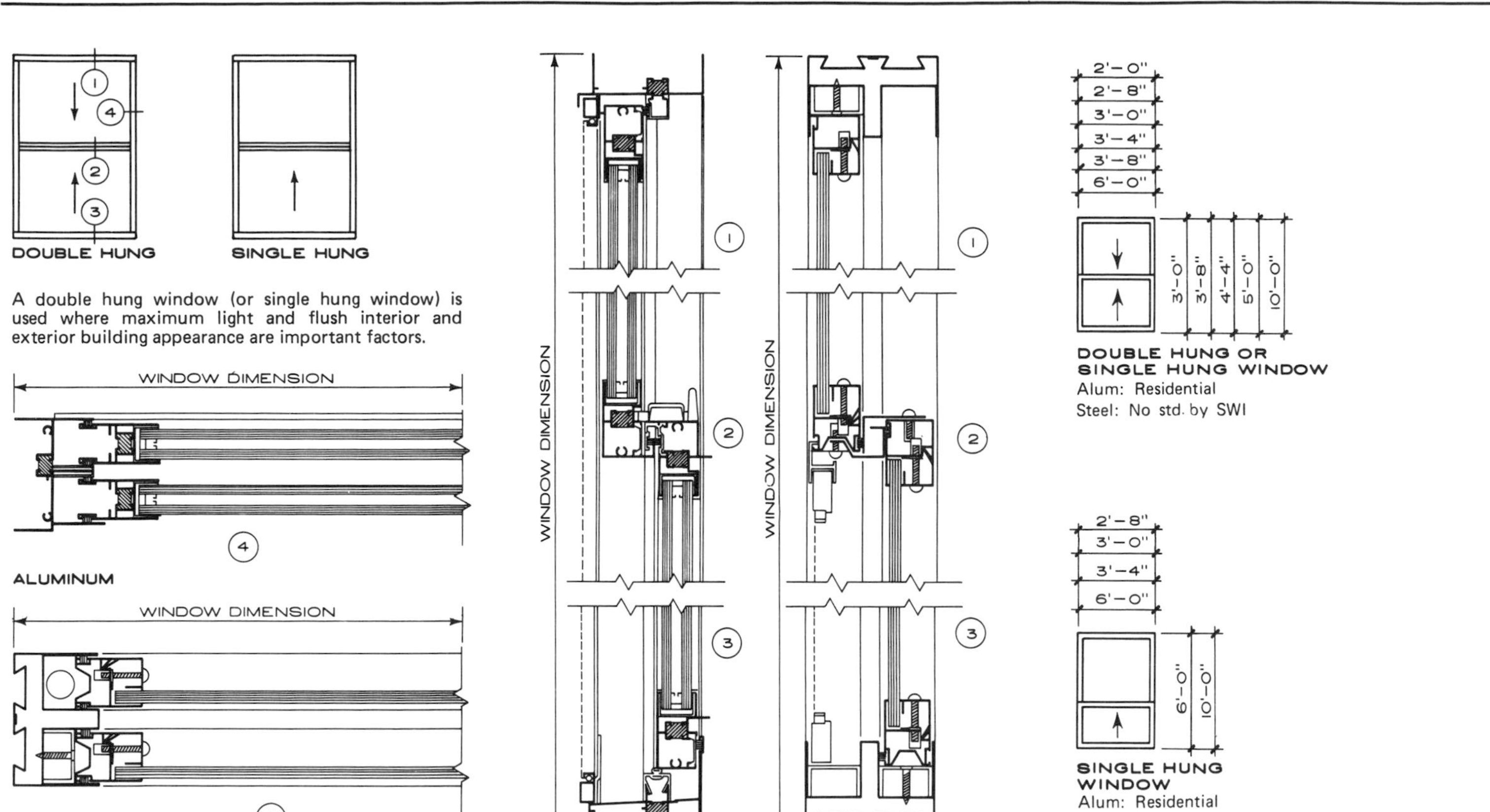
DOUBLE HUNG
SINGLE HUNG
WINDOW DIMENSION
ALUMINUM
WINDOW DIMENSION
STEEL
WINDOW DIMENSION
ALUMINUM
WINDOW DIMENSION
STEEL
2'–0"
2'–8"
3'–0"
3'–4"
3'–8"
6'–0"
3'–0"
3'–8"
4'–4"
5'–0"
10'–0"
2'–8"
3'–0"
3'–4"
6'–0"
6'–0"
10'–0"

A double hung window (or single hung window) is used where maximum light and flush interior and exterior building appearance are important factors.

DOUBLE HUNG OR SINGLE HUNG WINDOW
Alum: Residential
Steel: No std. by SWI

SINGLE HUNG WINDOW
Alum: Residential
Steel: No std. by SWI

JAMB SECTIONS

VERTICAL SECTIONS

SINGLE AND DOUBLE HUNG WINDOWS

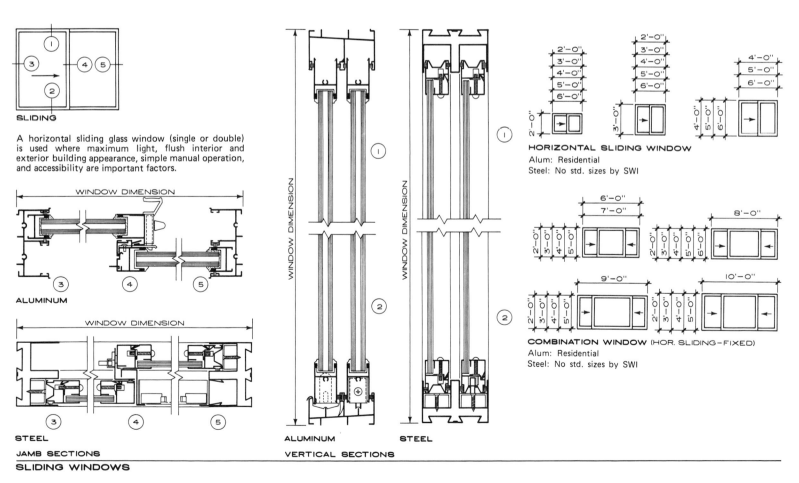

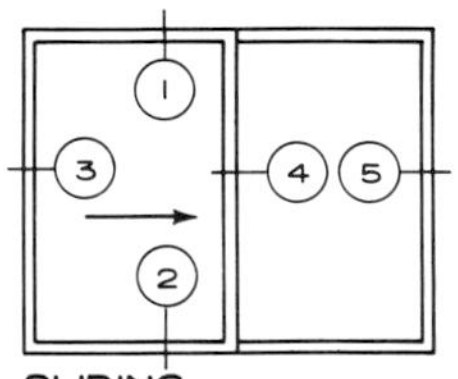

SLIDING

A horizontal sliding glass window (single or double) is used where maximum light, flush interior and exterior building appearance, simple manual operation, and accessibility are important factors.

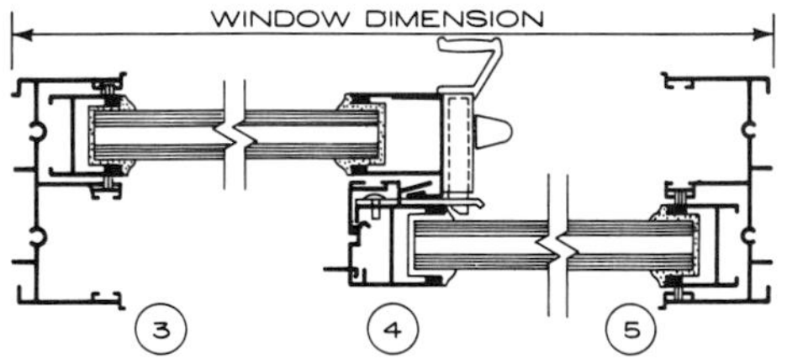

WINDOW DIMENSION

ALUMINUM

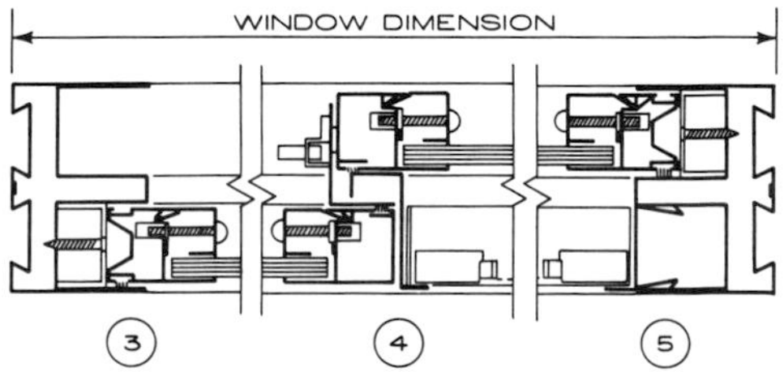

WINDOW DIMENSION

STEEL

JAMB SECTIONS

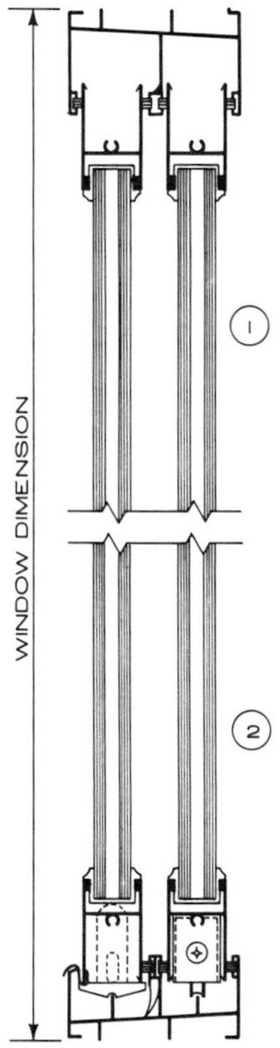

WINDOW DIMENSION

ALUMINUM

WINDOW DIMENSION

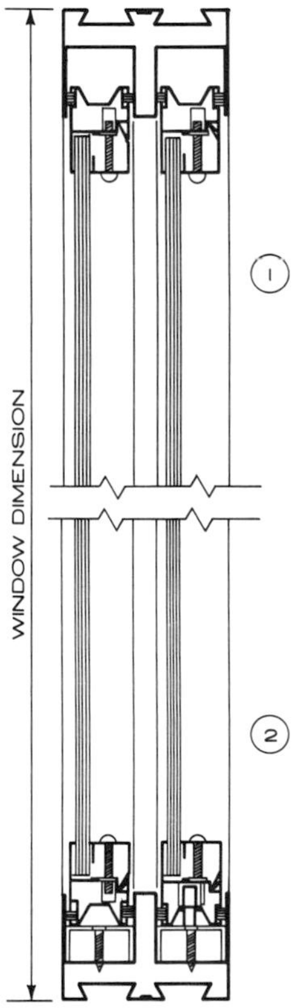

STEEL

VERTICAL SECTIONS

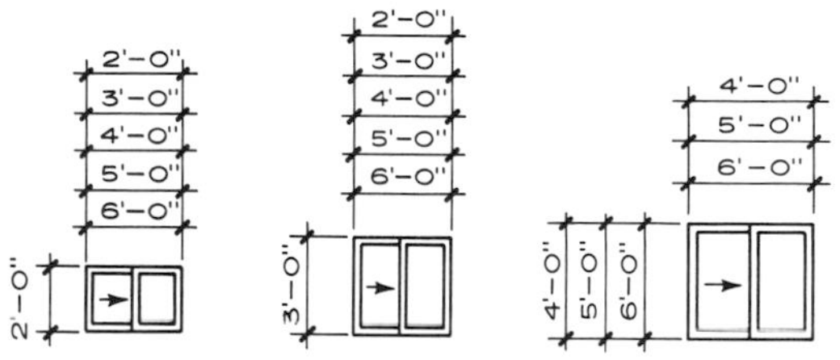

2'–0" 3'–0" 4'–0" 5'–0" 6'–0"

2'–0" 3'–0" 4'–0" 5'–0" 6'–0"

4'–0" 5'–0" 6'–0"

HORIZONTAL SLIDING WINDOW
Alum: Residential
Steel: No std. sizes by SWI

6'–0" 7'–0" 8'–0" 9'–0" 10'–0"

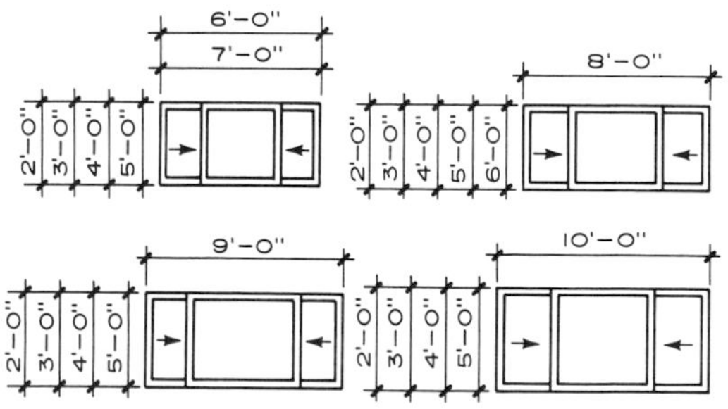

COMBINATION WINDOW (HOR. SLIDING–FIXED)
Alum: Residential
Steel: No std. sizes by SWI

SLIDING WINDOWS

David W. Johnson; Washington, D.C.

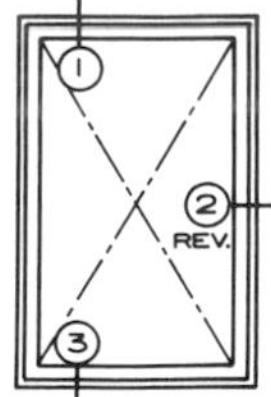
1
2
REV.
3

ELEVATION

NOTE

A reversible window is used mostly in multistory, air conditioned buildings where window washing from the interior is desired. It is normally opened for cleaning only; however, it may be combined with a hopper if ventilation is required.

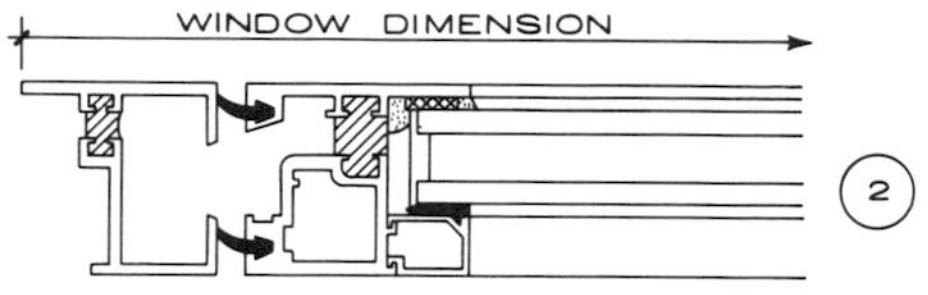
WINDOW DIMENSION
2

ALUMINUM

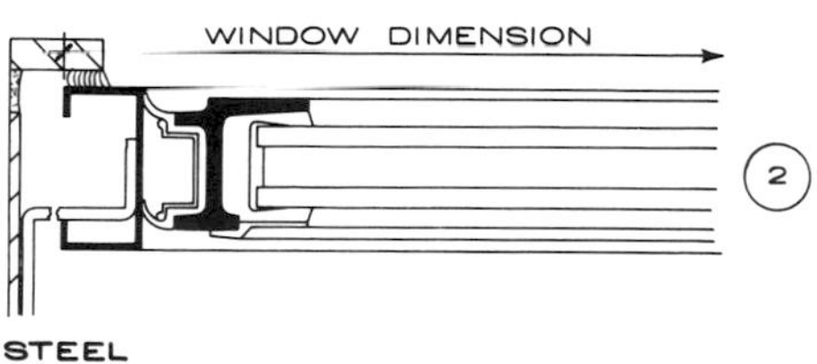
WINDOW DIMENSION
2

STEEL

JAMB SECTIONS

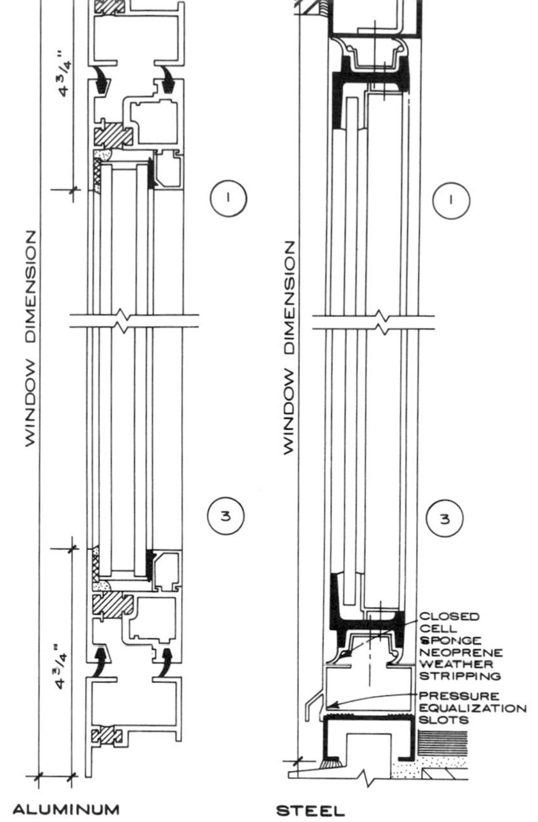
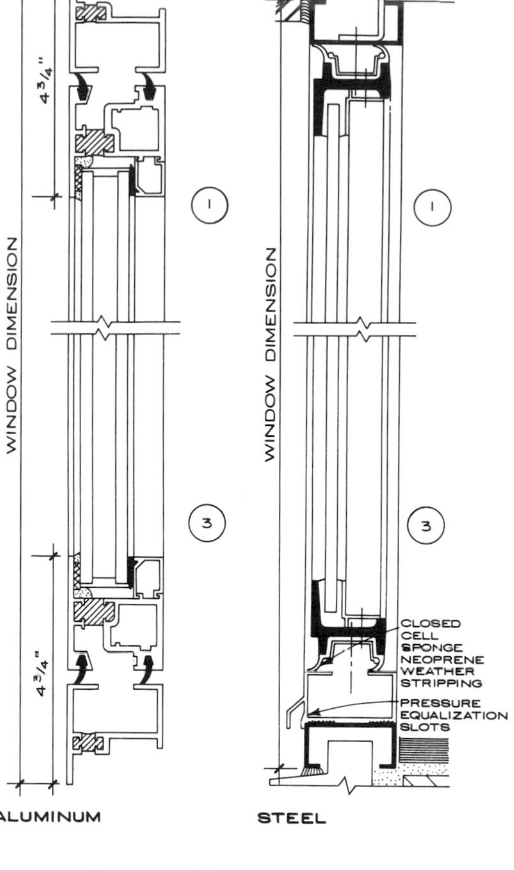
$4^3/_4$"
WINDOW DIMENSION
1
3
$4^3/_4$"
WINDOW DIMENSION
1
3
CLOSED CELL SPONGE NEOPRENE WEATHER STRIPPING
PRESSURE EQUALIZATION SLOTS

ALUMINUM

STEEL

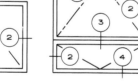

VERTICAL SECTIONS

REVERSIBLE WINDOWS

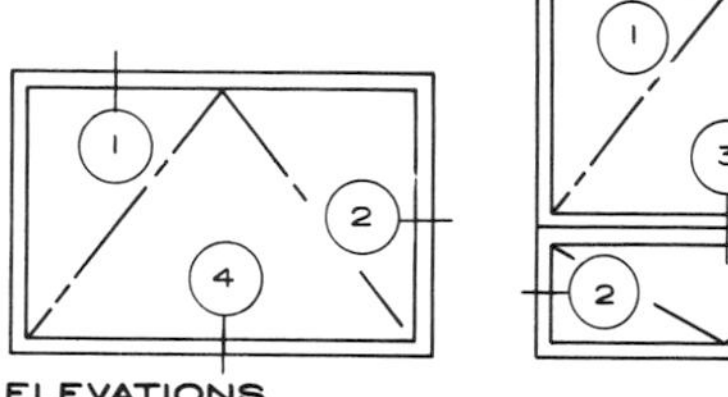
1
2
4
1
2
3
2
4

ELEVATIONS

NOTE

A projected (special) window is used mostly in multistory, air conditioned buildings where window washing from the interior is desired. It is normally opened for cleaning only; however, it may be combined with a hopper if ventilation is required. For such use see alternate above.

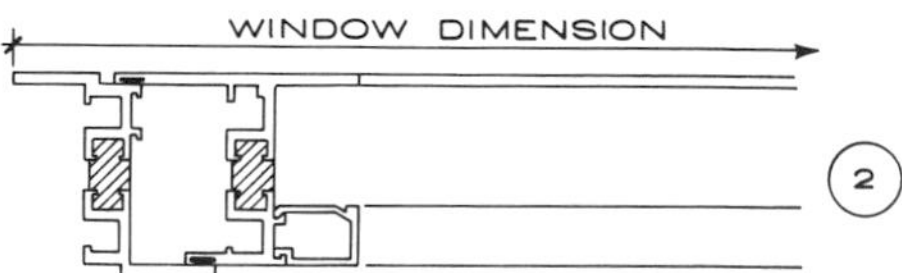
WINDOW DIMENSION
2

ALUMINUM

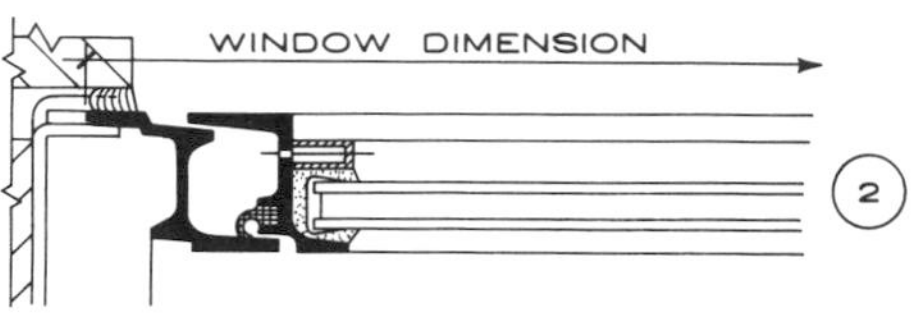
WINDOW DIMENSION
2

STEEL

JAMB SECTIONS

$3^{13}/_{16}$"

1

WINDOW DIMENSION

$5^5/_{16}$"

3

$3^5/_8$"

4

ALUMINUM

WINDOW DIMENSION

1

3

4

STEEL

VERTICAL SECTIONS

PROJECTED WINDOWS

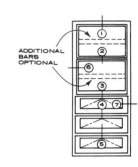

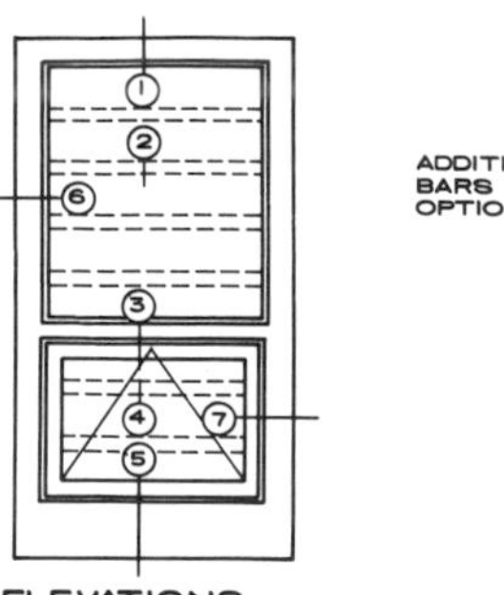
1
2
6
3
4
7
5
ADDITIONAL BARS OPTIONAL
1
2
6
3
4
7
5

ELEVATIONS

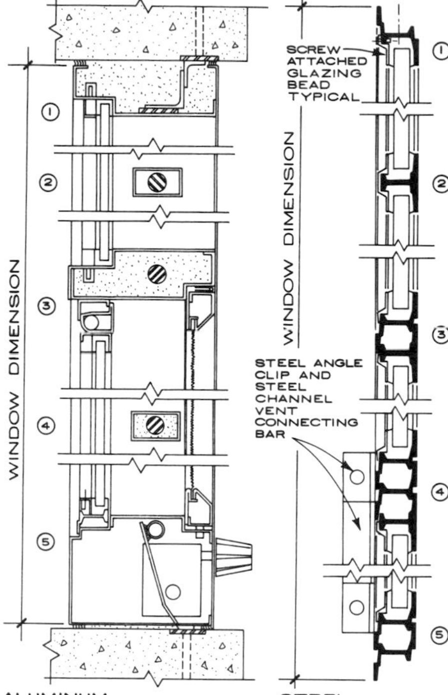
1
2
3
4
5
WINDOW DIMENSION
SCREW ATTACHED GLAZING BEAD TYPICAL
1
WINDOW DIMENSION
2
3
STEEL ANGLE CLIP AND STEEL CHANNEL VENT CONNECTING BAR
4
5

ALUMINUM

STEEL

VERTICAL SECTIONS

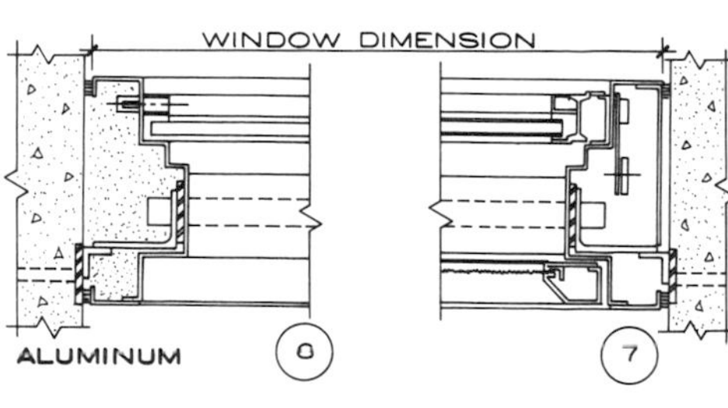
WINDOW DIMENSION

ALUMINUM 6 7

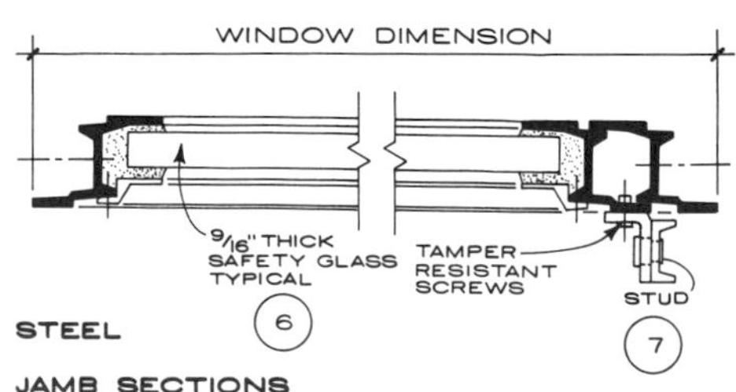
WINDOW DIMENSION
$^9/_{16}$" THICK SAFETY GLASS TYPICAL
TAMPER RESISTANT SCREWS
STUD

STEEL 6 7

JAMB SECTIONS

NOTES

1. Housing sill frame size varies with manufacturer of window operator.
2. Muntin and mullion tubes are 12 gauge maximum and 14 gauge medium security, grouted full, and contain a $^7/_8$ in. diameter tamper resistant bar.
3. Tempered glass is $^1/_2$ in. on exterior side.
4. Horizontal tube/bars to have maximum spacing of 5 in.

SECURITY WINDOWS

David W. Johnson; Washington, D.C.

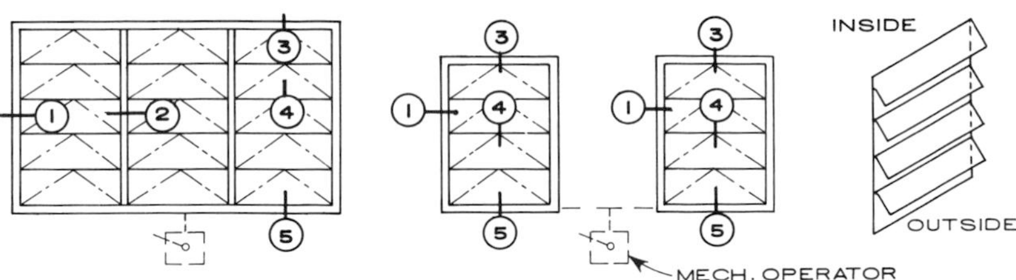
INSIDE
OUTSIDE
MECH. OPERATOR

AWNING

AN AWNING WINDOW is one whose movable units consist of a group of hand operated or gear operated outward projecting ventilators, all of which move in unison. It is used where maximum height and ventilation is required in inaccessible areas such as upper parts of gymnasiums or auditoriums. Hand operation is limited to one window only, while a single gear operator may be connected to two or more awning windows, and may be motorized.

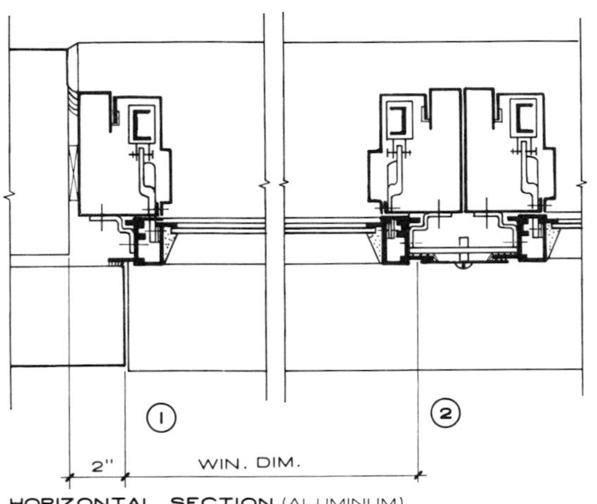
2"
WIN. DIM.

HORIZONTAL SECTION (ALUMINUM)

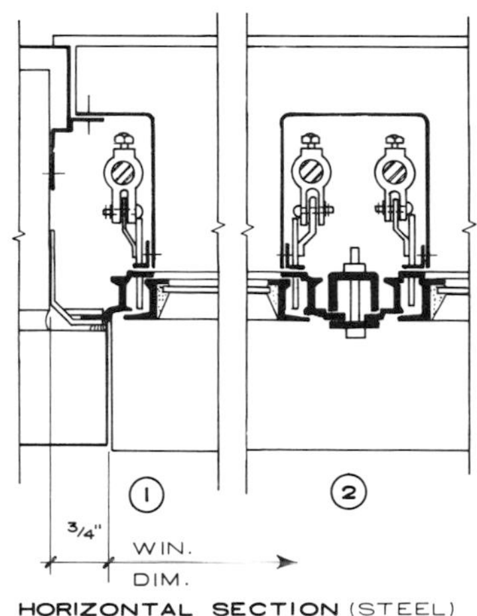
3/4"
WIN. DIM.

HORIZONTAL SECTION (STEEL)

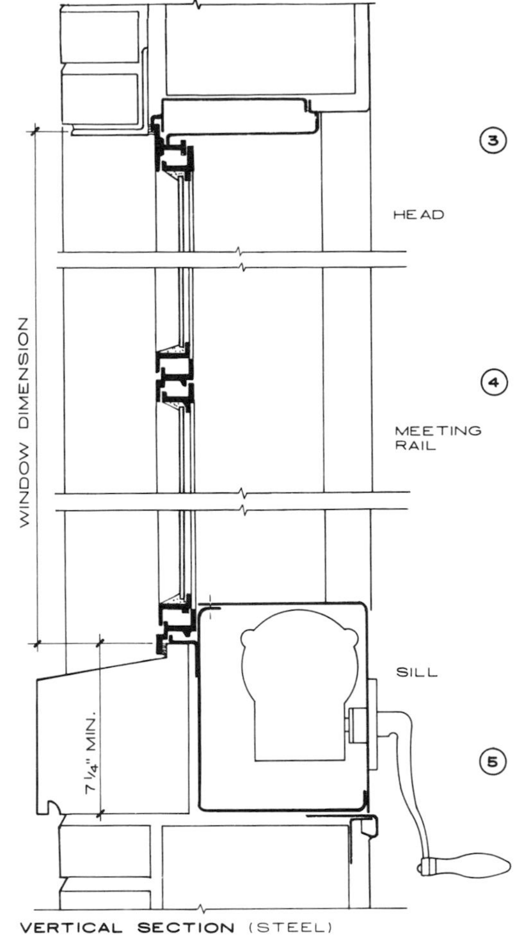
HEAD
MEETING RAIL
SILL
WINDOW DIMENSION
7 1/4" MIN.

VERTICAL SECTION (STEEL)

AWNING WINDOWS

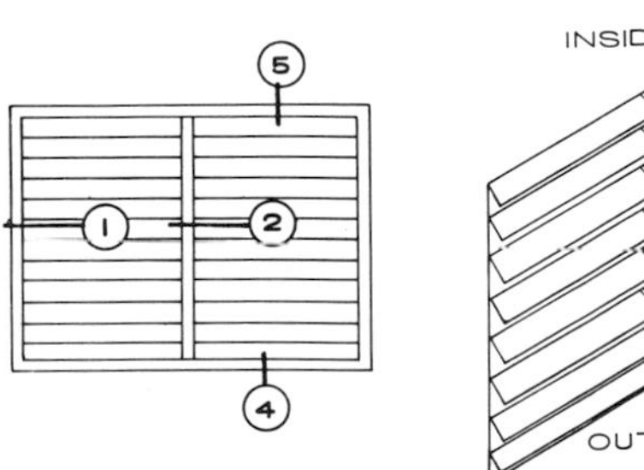

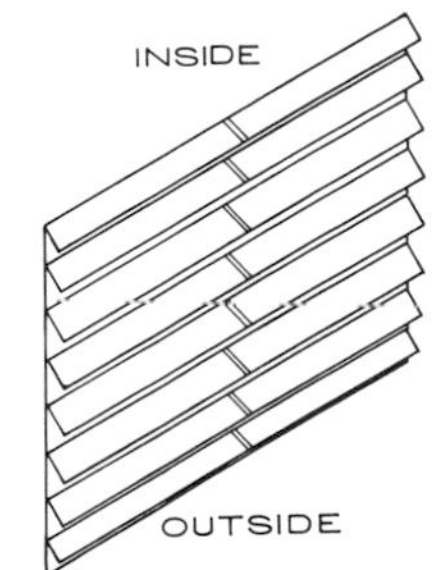
INSIDE
OUTSIDE

JALOUSIE

A JALOUSIE WINDOW (ALUMINUM) consists of a series of operable overlapping glass louvers which pivot in unison. It may be combined in the same frame with a series of operable opaque louvers for climate control. It is used mostly in residential type constructions in southern climates, where maximum ventilation and flush exterior and interior appearance is desired.

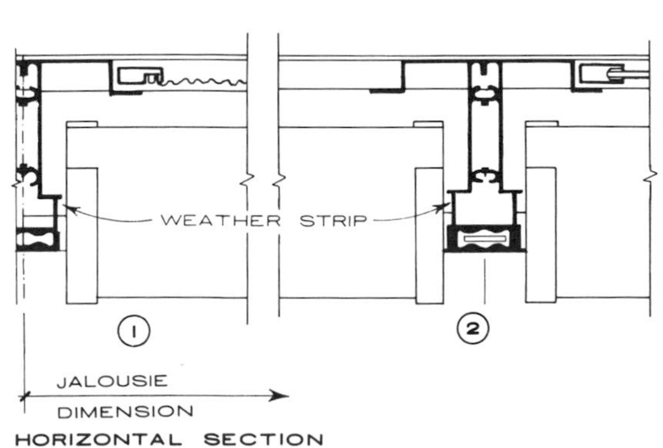
WEATHER STRIP
JALOUSIE DIMENSION

HORIZONTAL SECTION

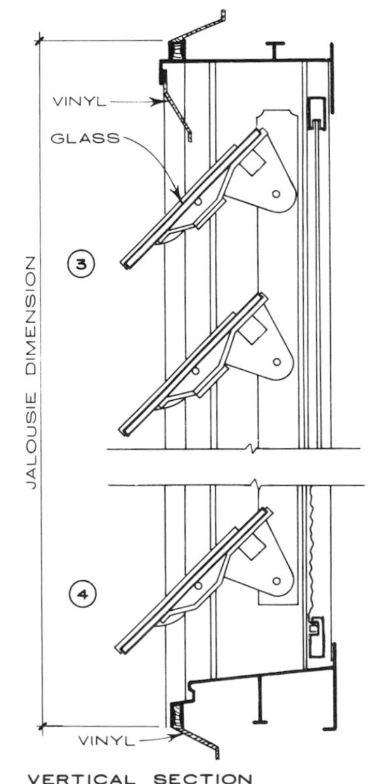
VINYL
GLASS
JALOUSIE DIMENSION
VINYL

VERTICAL SECTION

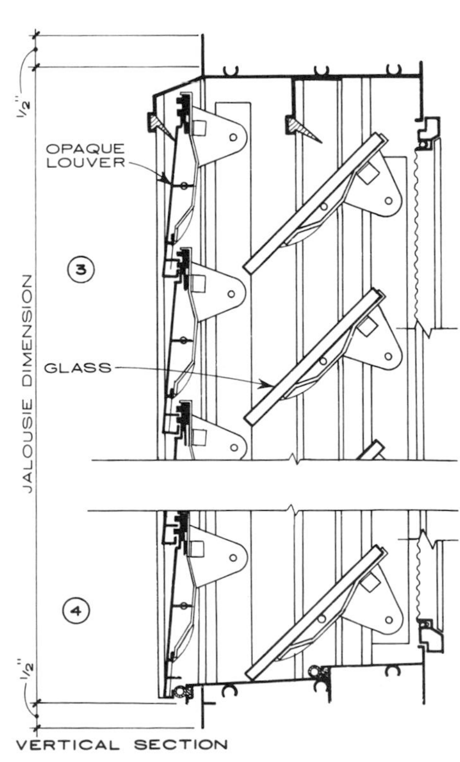
1/2"
OPAQUE LOUVER
GLASS
JALOUSIE DIMENSION
1/2"

VERTICAL SECTION

JALOUSIE WINDOWS

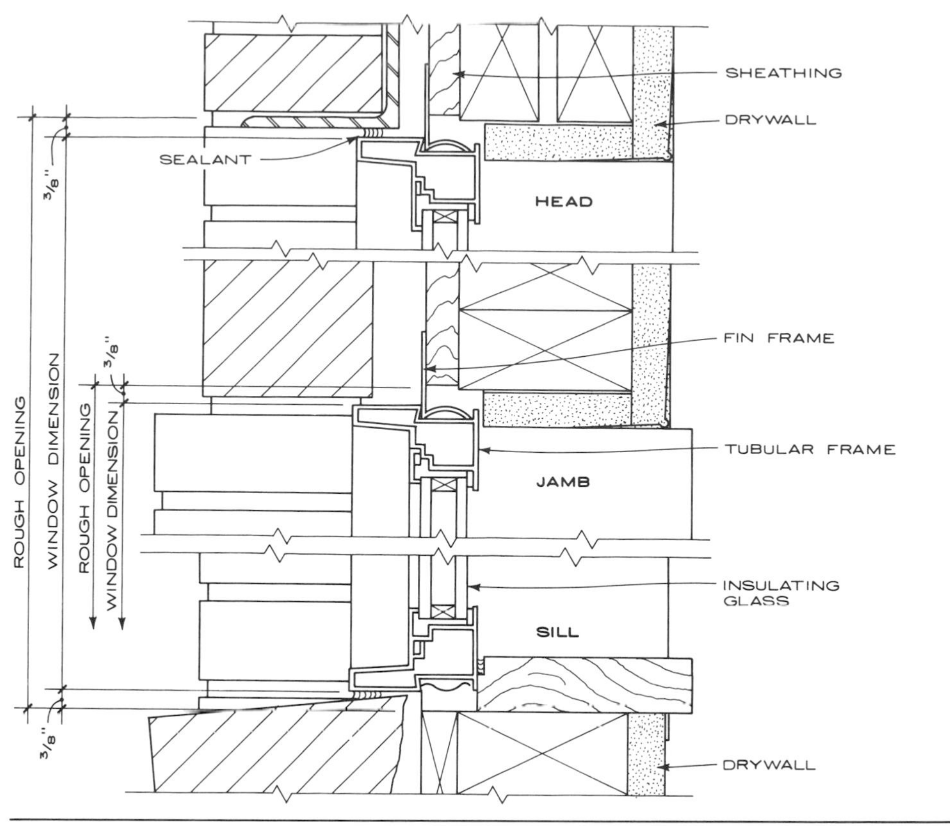
SHEATHING
DRYWALL
SEALANT
3/8"
HEAD
FIN FRAME
TUBULAR FRAME
JAMB
INSULATING GLASS
SILL
DRYWALL
ROUGH OPENING
WINDOW DIMENSION
ROUGH OPENING
WINDOW DIMENSION
3/8"
3/8"

BRICK VENEER ON WOOD FRAME WALL

WOOD FRAME WALL

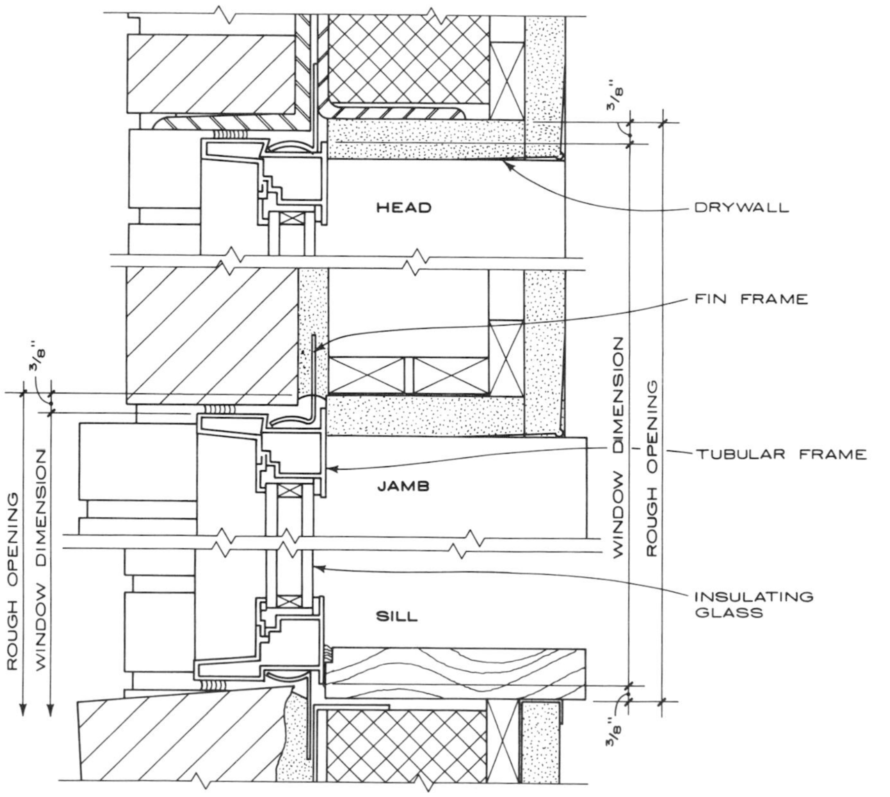
3/8"
HEAD
DRYWALL
FIN FRAME
3/8"
TUBULAR FRAME
JAMB
WINDOW DIMENSION
ROUGH OPENING
INSULATING GLASS
SILL
ROUGH OPENING
WINDOW DIMENSION
3/8"

MASONRY WALL

CONCRETE WALL

NOTES

1. Fins and interior casings are available to meet various installation requirements. Interior trims are available in depths of 2 to 10 in., in 1/2 in. increments.
2. Thermal-break type extrusions are available. Consult with manufacturers for sizes and shapes.

Nicanor A. Alano, Architect; Tacoma, Washington

TYPICAL OPERATING HARDWARE FOR METAL WINDOWS

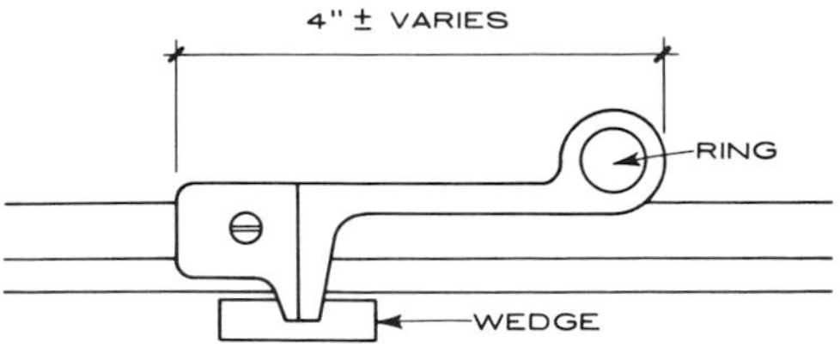
4" ± VARIES
RING
WEDGE

TYPICAL (CAM) LOCKING HANDLE

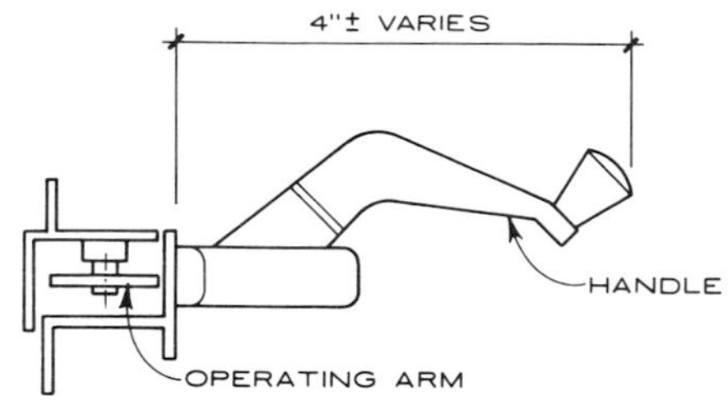
4"± VARIES
HANDLE
OPERATING ARM

TYPICAL CRANK (ROTO) OPERATOR

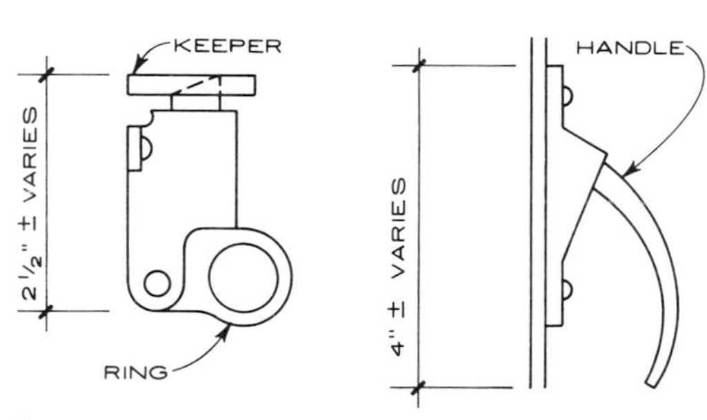
KEEPER
2½" ± VARIES
RING
HANDLE
4" ± VARIES

TYP. SPRING CATCH TYP. LOCKING HANDLE

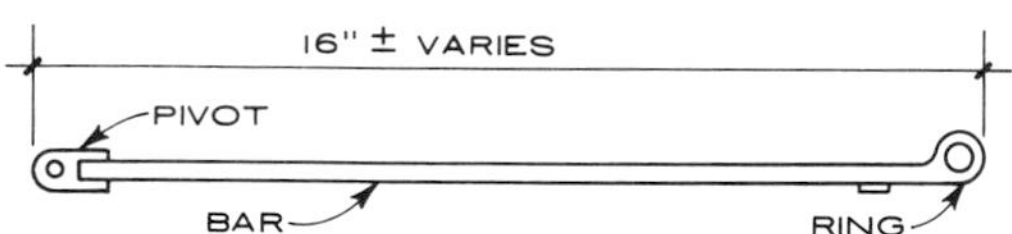
16" ± VARIES
PIVOT
BAR
RING

TYPICAL STAY BAR (PUSH BAR)

OTHER TYPES OF HARDWARE

1. Concealed cam hardware.
2. Hardware with removable handles for A.C. buildings. Also key locks.
3. Sliding window hardware.
4. D. H. window hardware (sweeplock).
5. Telescoping adjuster.
6. Chain, pole & cord operated hardware.
7. Hardware for security windows.
8. Heavy duty, electrical powered hardware for group window control.

FINISHES INCLUDE

1. Steel: diecast, lacquered & painted.
2. Aluminum: wide range of finishes and colors. Generally match window finish.
3. Bronze
4. White bronze & nickel bronze

Charles F. D. Egbert, AIA, Architect; Washington, D.C.

EXTRUDED ALUMINUM SILLS

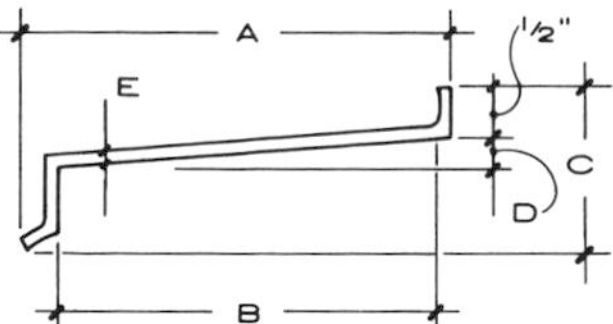
A
½"
E
C
D
B

For Lug Sills
Extend into brick joints at window jambs and allow 1/4" space for expansion at ends.

For Continuous Sills
At joints allow 1/4" to 3/8" expansion and flash joints.

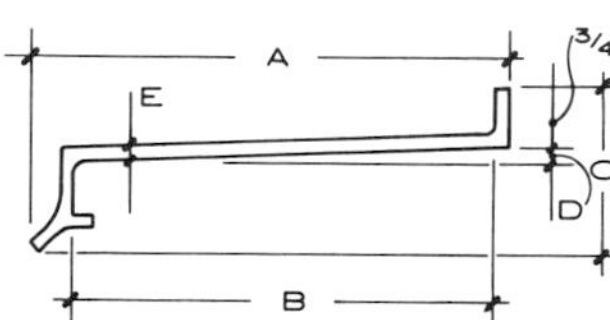
A
¾"
E
C
D
B

Used for continuous line of windows. Provide 1/4" to 3/8" expansion space at jamb or butt joints of continuous sills.

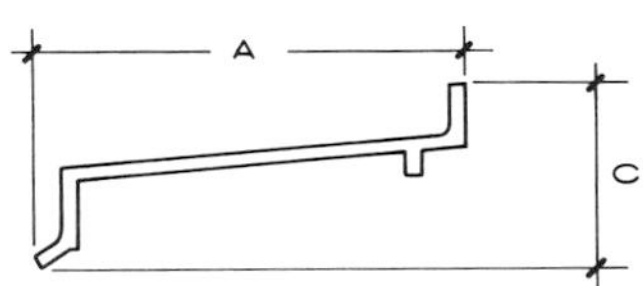
A
C

A	B	C	D	E	Std. No.*
3 7/16"	3"	1 9/16"	3/16"	3/32"	37734
3 29/32"		1 1/2"			P-3684
3 15/16"	3 1/2"	1 19/32"	7/32"	3/32"	37735
4 13/32"		1 17/32"			P-3683
4 7/16"	4"	1 5/8"	1/4"	3/32"	37736
4 7/8"		1 9/16"			3686
4 15/16"	4 1/2"	1 21/32"	9/32"	3/32"	37737
5 3/8"		1 9/16"			3687
5 7/16"	5"	1 11/16"	5/16"	3/32"	37738
5 7/8"		1 5/8"			3685
5 15/16"	5 1/2"	1 23/32"	11/32"	3/32"	37739
9 1/16"	8 1/2"	1 31/32"	7/32"	5/32"	37745
3 1/2"	2 3/4"	1 13/16"	3/16"	1/8"	54684
4"	3 1/4"	1 27/32"	7/32"	1/8"	54685
4 1/2"	3 3/4"	1 7/8"	1/4"	1/8"	54686
					9558
5"	4 1/4"	1 29/32"	9/32"	1/8"	54687
					13008
5 1/2"	4 3/4"	1 15/16"	5/16"	1/8"	54688
					13009
6"	5 1/4"	1 31/32"	11/32"	1/8"	54689
6 9/16"	5 3/4"	2"	3/8"	5/32"	54690
7 9/16"	6 3/4	2 1/16"	7/16"	5/32"	54691
8 1/8"	7 1/4"	2 5/32"	15/32"	3/16"	54692
9 1/8"	8 1/4"	2 7/32"	17/32"	3/16"	54693
3 1/2"		1 9/16"			P-3692
4"		1 19/32"			P-3691
4 1/2"		1 5/8"			P-3690
5"		1 21/32"			P-3126
5 1/2"		1 11/16"			P-3127
6"		1 23/32"			P-3128
9 1/16"		1 29/32"			P-3230

Sills may be made to fit posts or mullions, and may be mitered at corners. Sills over eight feet in length should have central anchorage to keep them in proper position.

* Non-warehouse items

Refer to aluminum manufacturers catalogs.

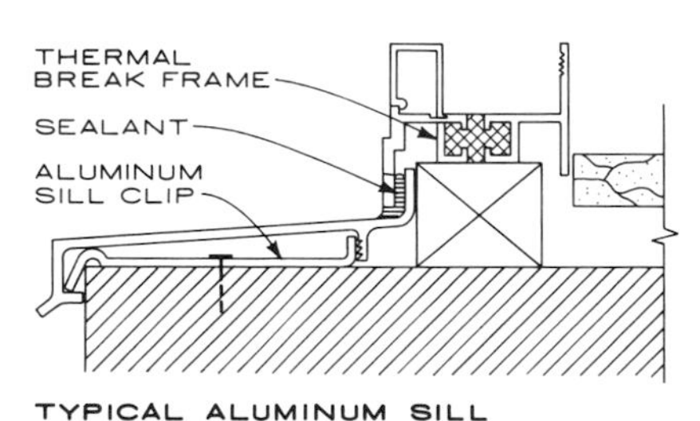
THERMAL BREAK FRAME
SEALANT
ALUMINUM SILL CLIP

TYPICAL ALUMINUM SILL

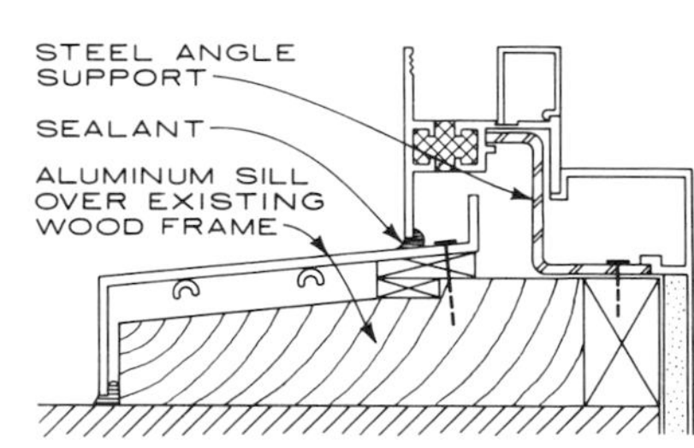
STEEL ANGLE SUPPORT
SEALANT
ALUMINUM SILL OVER EXISTING WOOD FRAME

REPLACEMENT SILL

INSTALLATION DETAILS

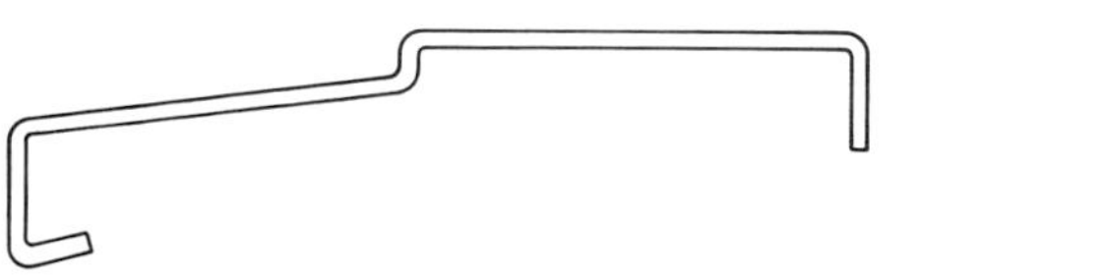

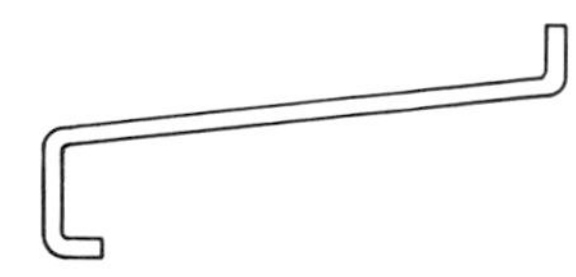

TYPICAL FORMED METAL SILLS
SHAPES MADE TO ORDER

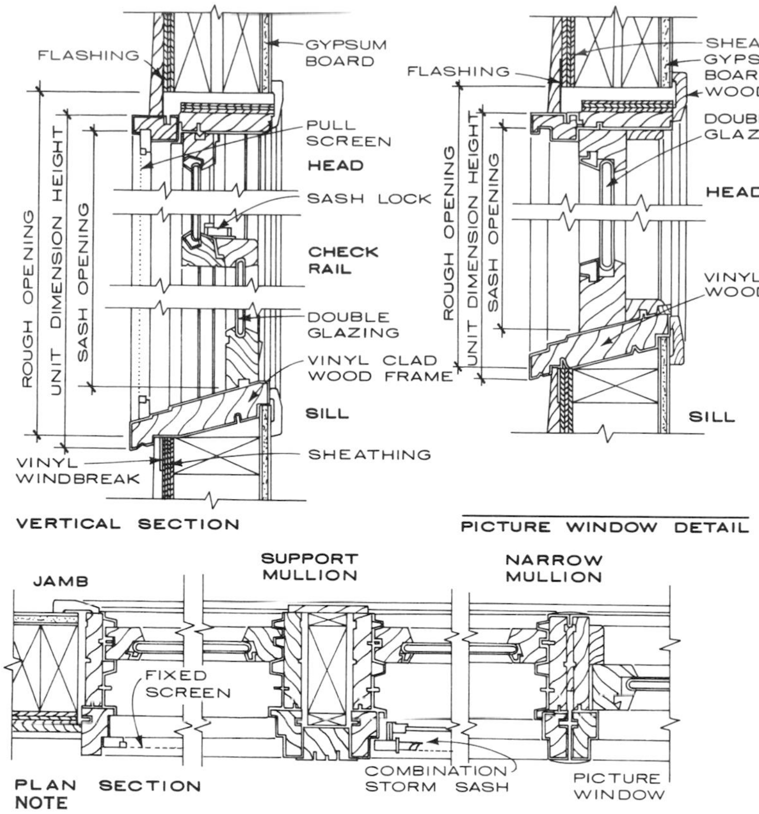

FLASHING
GYPSUM BOARD
PULL SCREEN
HEAD
SASH LOCK
CHECK RAIL
DOUBLE GLAZING
VINYL CLAD WOOD FRAME
SILL
SHEATHING
VINYL WINDBREAK
ROUGH OPENING
UNIT DIMENSION HEIGHT
SASH OPENING

VERTICAL SECTION

SHEATHING
GYPSUM BOARD
FLASHING
WOOD TRIM
DOUBLE GLAZING
HEAD
VINYL CLAD WOOD FRAME
SILL
ROUGH OPENING
UNIT DIMENSION HEIGHT
SASH OPENING

PICTURE WINDOW DETAIL

JAMB
SUPPORT MULLION
NARROW MULLION
FIXED SCREEN
COMBINATION STORM SASH
PICTURE WINDOW

PLAN SECTION

NOTE

Spiral or reel spring balances or pressure weatherstrip operation. Glass size 12 x 12 in. to 44 x 40 in. for 1-light sash.

PLAIN RAIL WINDOW: No parting stop; movable sash slides against fixed sash with hold-open jamb bolts.

DOUBLE HUNG WINDOWS

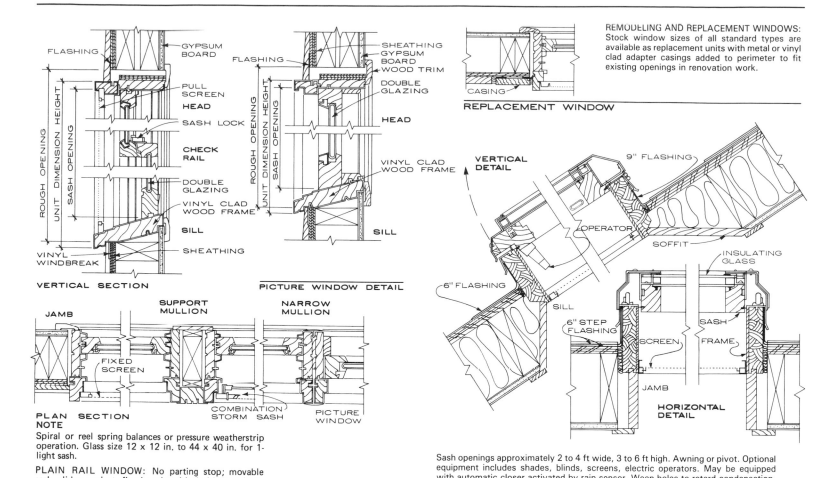

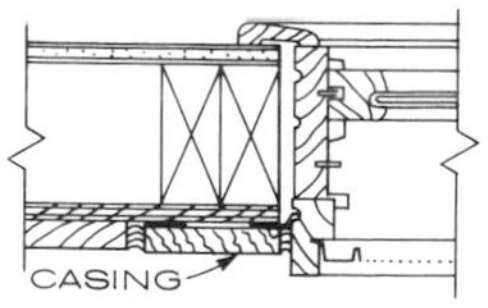

REMODELING AND REPLACEMENT WINDOWS: Stock window sizes of all standard types are available as replacement units with metal or vinyl clad adapter casings added to perimeter to fit existing openings in renovation work.

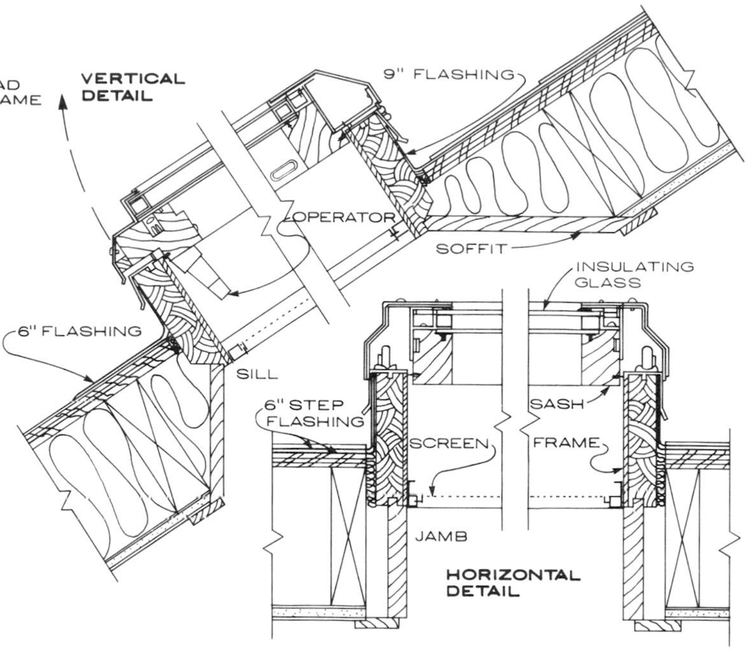

CASING

REPLACEMENT WINDOW

VERTICAL DETAIL
9" FLASHING
OPERATOR
SOFFIT
INSULATING GLASS
6" FLASHING
SILL
6" STEP FLASHING
SASH
SCREEN
FRAME
JAMB
HORIZONTAL DETAIL

Sash openings approximately 2 to 4 ft wide, 3 to 6 ft high. Awning or pivot. Optional equipment includes shades, blinds, screens, electric operators. May be equipped with automatic closer activated by rain sensor. Weep holes to retard condensation.

ROOF WINDOW

NOTE

CASEMENT WINDOWS: Stiles and top rail 1 to 2 in., bottom rail 3 in. nominal. Outswinging: screen inside, regular or self-storing flexible type with operation similar to window shade. Sash opening range for 1 sash per frame 1 ft 4 in. x 2 ft 2 in. to 2 x 6 ft. Extension hinges, friction arms, folding push bar or roto worm gear operator.

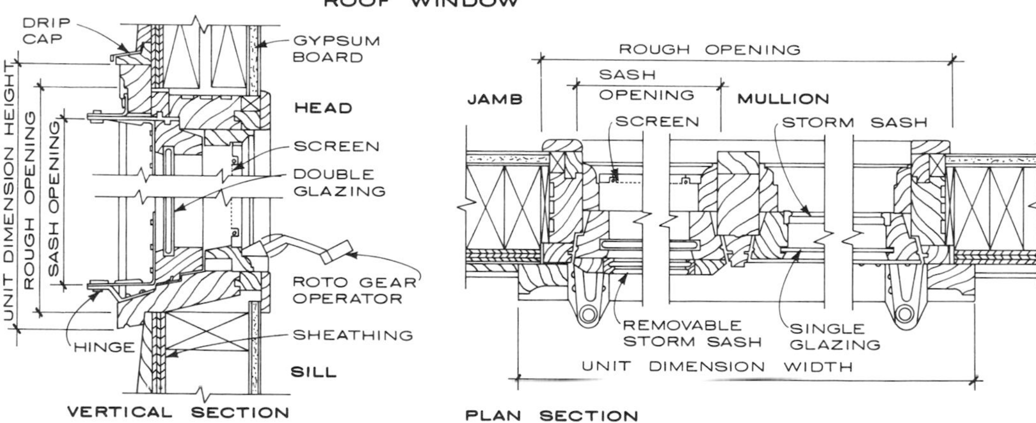

DRIP CAP
GYPSUM BOARD
HEAD
SCREEN
DOUBLE GLAZING
ROTO GEAR OPERATOR
SHEATHING
SILL
HINGE
UNIT DIMENSION HEIGHT
ROUGH OPENING
SASH OPENING
VERTICAL SECTION
ROUGH OPENING
SASH OPENING
JAMB
MULLION
SCREEN
STORM SASH
REMOVABLE STORM SASH
SINGLE GLAZING
UNIT DIMENSION WIDTH
PLAN SECTION

CASEMENT WINDOWS

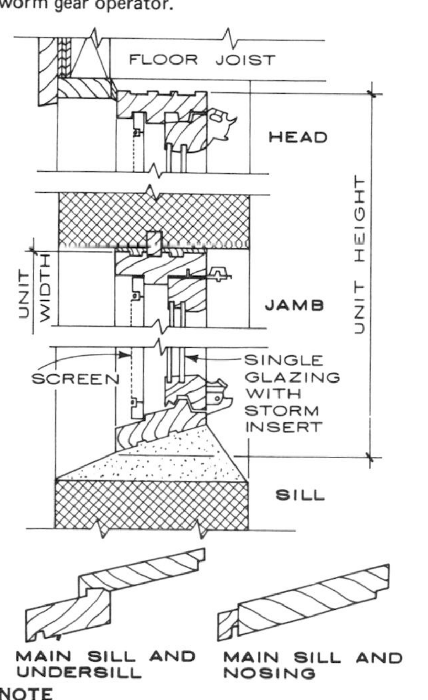

FLOOR JOIST
HEAD
UNIT WIDTH
JAMB
UNIT HEIGHT
SCREEN
SINGLE GLAZING WITH STORM INSERT
SILL
MAIN SILL AND UNDERSILL
MAIN SILL AND NOSING

NOTE

Removable sash and dual purpose hinges for opening from top or bottom.

BASEMENT WINDOWS

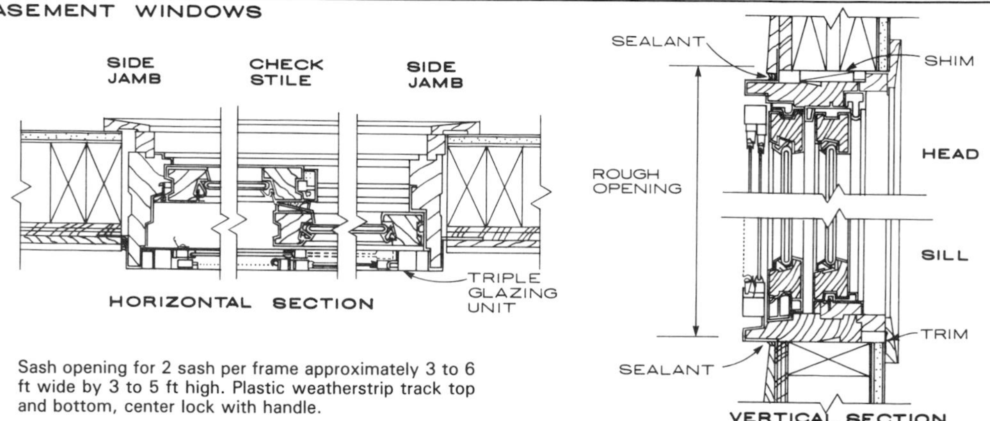

SIDE JAMB
CHECK STILE
SIDE JAMB
TRIPLE GLAZING UNIT
HORIZONTAL SECTION
SEALANT
SHIM
HEAD
ROUGH OPENING
SILL
TRIM
SEALANT
VERTICAL SECTION

Sash opening for 2 sash per frame approximately 3 to 6 ft wide by 3 to 5 ft high. Plastic weatherstrip track top and bottom, center lock with handle.

HORIZONTAL SLIDING WINDOWS

Carleton Granbery, FAIA; Guilford, Connecticut

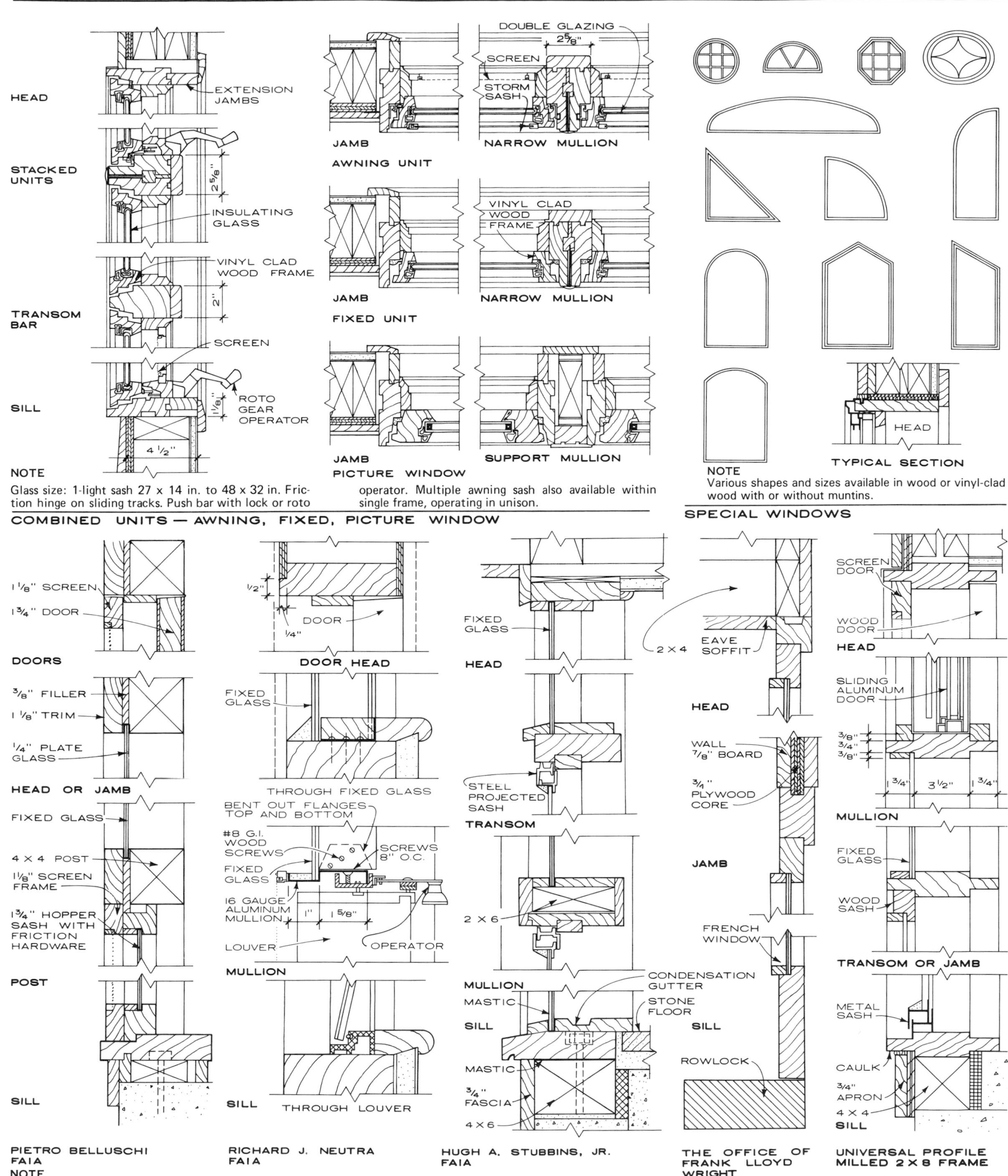
HEAD
EXTENSION JAMBS
STACKED UNITS
2 5/8"
INSULATING GLASS
VINYL CLAD WOOD FRAME
TRANSOM BAR
2"
SCREEN
SILL
1 1/8"
ROTO GEAR OPERATOR
4 1/2"
JAMB
AWNING UNIT
DOUBLE GLAZING
2 5/8"
SCREEN
STORM SASH
NARROW MULLION
JAMB
FIXED UNIT
VINYL CLAD WOOD FRAME
NARROW MULLION
JAMB
PICTURE WINDOW
SUPPORT MULLION
HEAD
TYPICAL SECTION
1 1/8" SCREEN
1 3/4" DOOR
DOORS
3/8" FILLER
1 1/8" TRIM
1/4" PLATE GLASS
HEAD OR JAMB
FIXED GLASS
4 X 4 POST
1 1/8" SCREEN FRAME
1 3/4" HOPPER SASH WITH FRICTION HARDWARE
POST
SILL
1/2"
DOOR
1/4"
DOOR HEAD
FIXED GLASS
THROUGH FIXED GLASS
BENT OUT FLANGES TOP AND BOTTOM
#8 G.I. WOOD SCREWS
SCREWS 8" O.C.
FIXED GLASS
16 GAUGE ALUMINUM MULLION
1"
1 5/8"
LOUVER
OPERATOR
MULLION
SILL
THROUGH LOUVER
FIXED GLASS
HEAD
STEEL PROJECTED SASH
TRANSOM
2 X 6
MULLION
MASTIC
SILL
MASTIC
3/4" FASCIA
4 X 6
CONDENSATION GUTTER
STONE FLOOR
2 X 4
EAVE SOFFIT
HEAD
WALL 7/8" BOARD
3/4" PLYWOOD CORE
JAMB
FRENCH WINDOW
SILL
ROWLOCK
SCREEN DOOR
WOOD DOOR
HEAD
SLIDING ALUMINUM DOOR
3/8"
3/4"
3/8"
3/4"
3 1/2"
3/4"
MULLION
FIXED GLASS
WOOD SASH
TRANSOM OR JAMB
METAL SASH
CAULK
3/4" APRON
4 X 4
SILL

NOTE

Glass size: 1-light sash 27 x 14 in. to 48 x 32 in. Friction hinge on sliding tracks. Push bar with lock or roto operator. Multiple awning sash also available within single frame, operating in unison.

COMBINED UNITS — AWNING, FIXED, PICTURE WINDOW

NOTE

Various shapes and sizes available in wood or vinyl-clad wood with or without muntins.

SPECIAL WINDOWS

PIETRO BELLUSCHI FAIA

RICHARD J. NEUTRA FAIA

HUGH A. STUBBINS, JR. FAIA

THE OFFICE OF FRANK LLOYD WRIGHT

UNIVERSAL PROFILE MILLED 2 X 8 FRAME

NOTE

Selected examples indicating joinery to achieve weathertight narrow profiles. Adaptable to insulating glass for energy conservation where dictated by local conditions. See also pages on metal windows.

CUSTOM DETAILS — FIXED GLASS, HOPPER, CASEMENTS, JALOUSIE, AWNING, AND TRANSOM SASH

Carleton Granbery, FAIA; Guilford, Connecticut

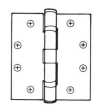

TOP HINGE 5" FROM JAMB RABBET TO TOP EDGE OF BARREL

THIRD HINGE CENTERED BETWEEN TOP AND BOTTOM HINGES

BOTTOM HINGE 10" FROM BOTTOM EDGE OF BARREL TO FINISHED FLOOR

5" EQUAL EQUAL 10"

NOTE: THE ABOVE IS U.S. STANDARD PROCEDURE. CERTAIN WESTERN STATES USE AS STANDARD 7" FROM TOP AND 11" FROM THE BOTTOM

LOCATION OF HINGES ON DOORS

FREQUENCY OF DOOR OPERATION

TYPE OF BUILDING AND DOOR	ESTIMATED FREQUENCY		HINGE TYPE
	DAILY	YEARLY	
HIGH FREQUENCY			
Large department store entrance	5,000	1,500,000	Heavy Weight
Large office building entrance	4,000	1,200,000	
School entrance	1,250	225,000	
School toilet door	1,250	225,000	
Store or bank entrance	500	150,000	
Office building toilet door	400	118,000	
AVERAGE FREQUENCY			
School corridor door	80	15,000	Standard Weight Antifriction Bearing (except on heavy doors)
Office building corridor door	75	22,000	
Store toilet door	60	18,000	
Dwelling entrance	40	15,000	
LOW FREQUENCY			
Dwelling toilet door	25	9,000	Plain Bearing Hinges may be used on light doors
Dwelling corridor door	10	3,600	
Dwelling closet door	6	2,200	

HINGE WIDTH

THICKNESS OF DOOR (IN.)	CLEARANCE REQUIRED* (IN.)	OPEN WIDTH OF HINGES (IN.)
1 3/8	1 1/4 1 3/4	3 1/2 4
1 3/4	1 1 1/2 2 3	4 4 1/2 5 6
2	1 1 1/2 2 1/2	4 1/2 5 6
2 1/4	1 2	5 6
2 1/2	3/4 1 3/4	5 6
3	3/4 2 3/4 4 3/4	6 8 10

*Note: Clearance is computed for door flush with casing.

HINGE HEIGHT

THICKNESS (IN.)	WIDTH OF DOORS (IN.)	HEIGHT OF HINGES (IN.)
Doors 3/4 to 1 1/8 cabinet	to 24	2 1/2
7/8 and 1 1/8 screen or combination	to 36	3
1 3/8	to 32 over 32	3 1/2 – 4 4 – 4 1/2
1 3/4	to 36 over 36 to 48 over 48	*4 1/2 *5 *6
2, 2 1/4 and 2 1/2	to 42 over 42	5 heavy 6 weight
Transoms 1 1/4 and 1 3/8 1 3/4 2, 2 1/4 and 2 1/2	....	3 3 1/2 4

*Note: Heavy weight hinges should be specified for heavy doors and for doors where high frequency service is expected. The heavy weight hinges should be of 4 1/2 in., 5 in. and 6 in. sizes as shown in table.

HINGE SELECTION DESIGN FACTORS

1. Material of door and frame
2. Size, thickness and weight of door with all hardware accessories
3. Clearance required
4. Use—exterior or interior exposure; frequency
5. Exposure to corrosive atmospheric elements (such as sea air, dust, etc.)
6. Quality desired
7. Special application or use (e.g., schools)
8. Door accessories (overhead holders, closers, stops, kick plates, etc.), which affect hinge performance
9. Hinge edge of door—beveled or squared

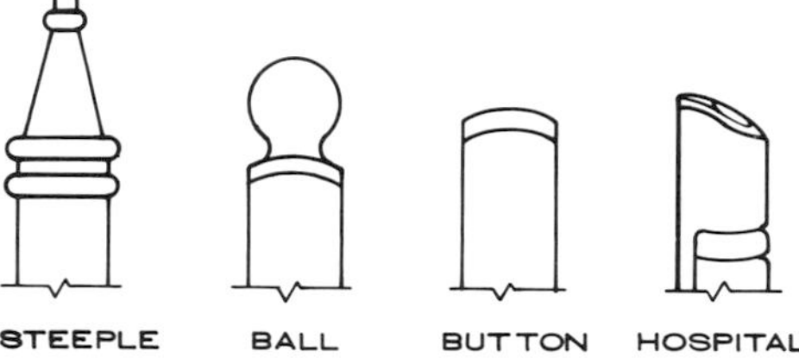
STEEPLE
BALL
BUTTON
HOSPITAL

NOTES
1. HOSPITAL TIPS ARE ROUNDED FOR EASE OF CLEANING.
2. CONSULT MANUFACTURERS FOR A WIDE VARIETY OF ORNAMENTAL TIPS

TYPES OF TIPS

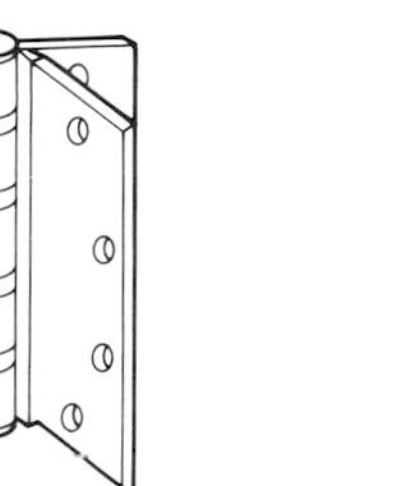

FULL MORTISE HALF MORTISE HALF SURFACE FULL SURFACE

TYPES OF HINGES

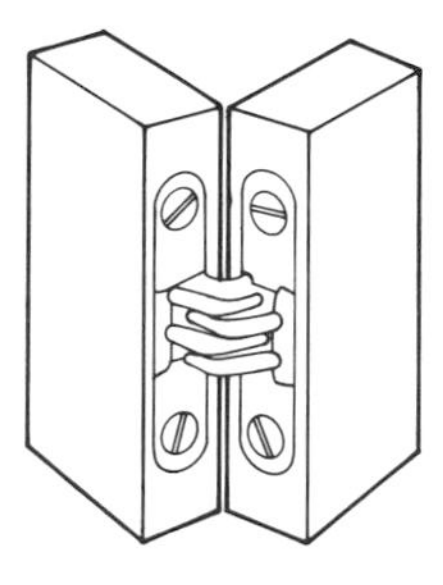

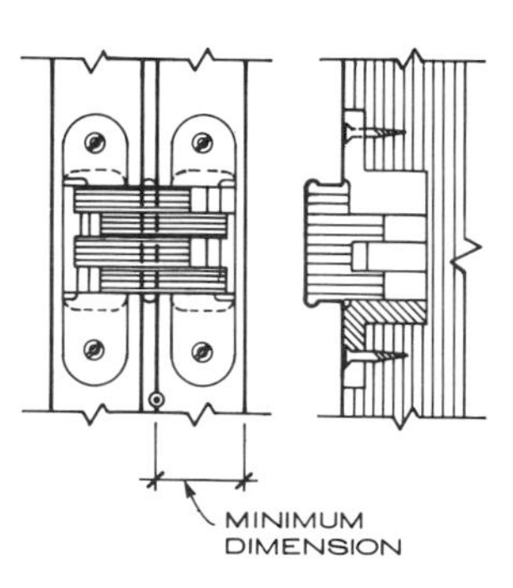

MINIMUM DIMENSION

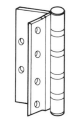

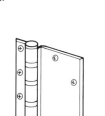

INVISIBLE HINGE

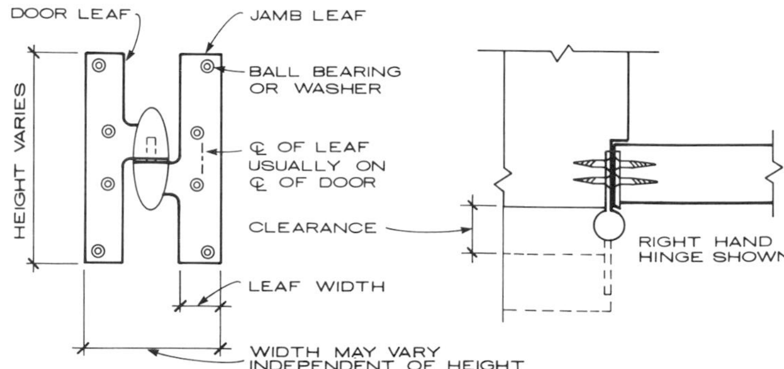
DOOR LEAF
JAMB LEAF
BALL BEARING OR WASHER
HEIGHT VARIES
℄ OF LEAF USUALLY ON ℄ OF DOOR
CLEARANCE
RIGHT HAND HINGE SHOWN
LEAF WIDTH
WIDTH MAY VARY INDEPENDENT OF HEIGHT

OLIVE KNUCKLE HINGE

Narcisa P. Sanchez; Sanchez & Sanchez; Falls Church, Virginia

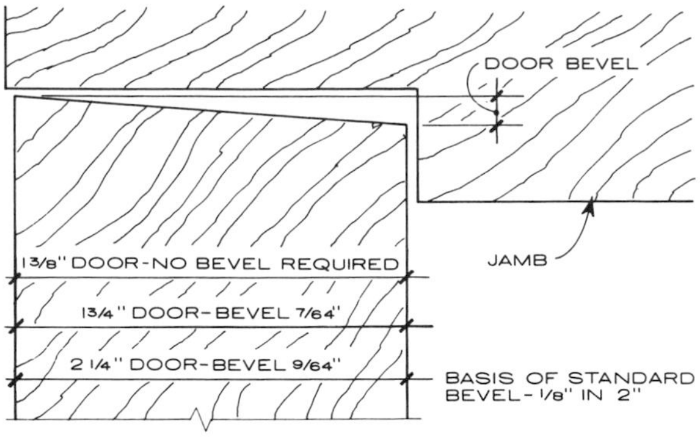

DOOR BEVEL
JAMB
1 3/8" DOOR-NO BEVEL REQUIRED
1 3/4" DOOR-BEVEL 7/64"
2 1/4" DOOR-BEVEL 9/64"
BASIS OF STANDARD BEVEL-1/8" IN 2"

DOOR BEVELS

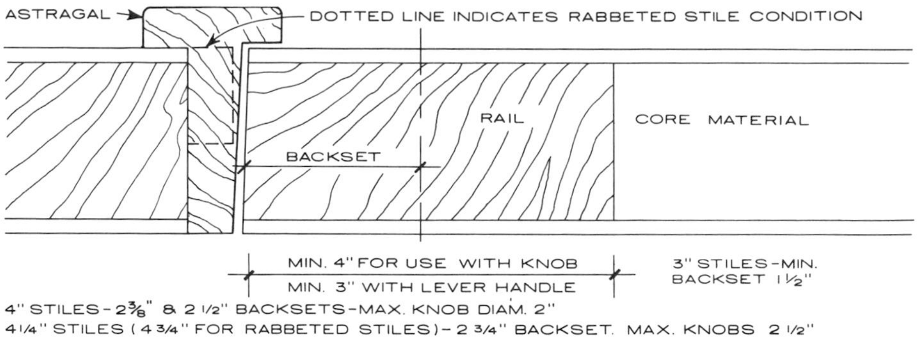

ASTRAGAL
DOTTED LINE INDICATES RABBETED STILE CONDITION
RAIL
CORE MATERIAL
BACKSET
MIN. 4" FOR USE WITH KNOB
MIN. 3" WITH LEVER HANDLE
3" STILES-MIN. BACKSET 1 1/2"
4" STILES-2 3/8" & 2 1/2" BACKSETS-MAX. KNOB DIAM. 2"
4 1/4" STILES (4 3/4" FOR RABBETED STILES)-2 3/4" BACKSET. MAX. KNOBS 2 1/2"

DOUBLE DOORS WITH FLAT ASTRAGAL (ALSO APPLIES TO DOORS WITH RABBETED MEETING STILES)

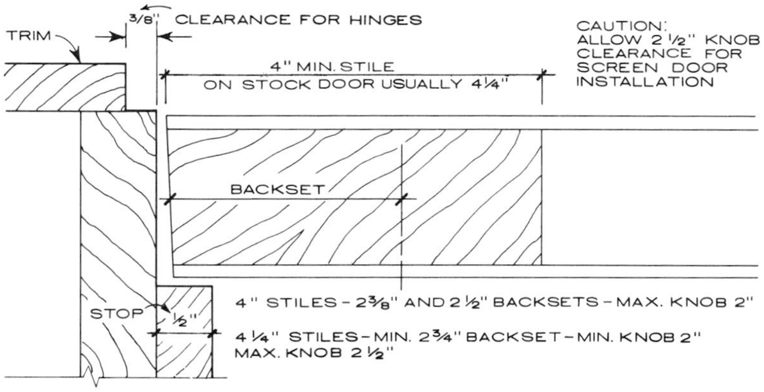

TRIM
3/8" CLEARANCE FOR HINGES
4" MIN. STILE
ON STOCK DOOR USUALLY 4 1/4"
CAUTION: ALLOW 2 1/2" KNOB CLEARANCE FOR SCREEN DOOR INSTALLATION
BACKSET
STOP
1/2"
4" STILES-2 3/8" AND 2 1/2" BACKSETS-MAX. KNOB 2"
4 1/4" STILES-MIN. 2 3/4" BACKSET-MIN. KNOB 2" MAX. KNOB 2 1/2"

DOOR WITH KNOB USING CYLINDER LOCK

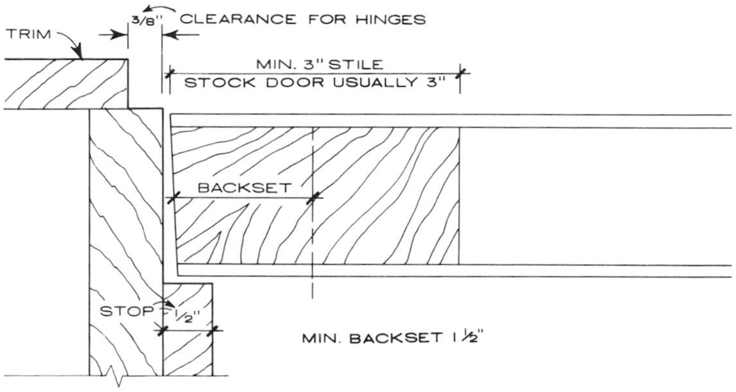

TRIM
3/8" CLEARANCE FOR HINGES
MIN. 3" STILE
STOCK DOOR USUALLY 3"
BACKSET
STOP
1/2"
MIN. BACKSET 1 1/2"

DOOR WITH LEVER HANDLE USING CYLINDER LOCK

DOOR STILES

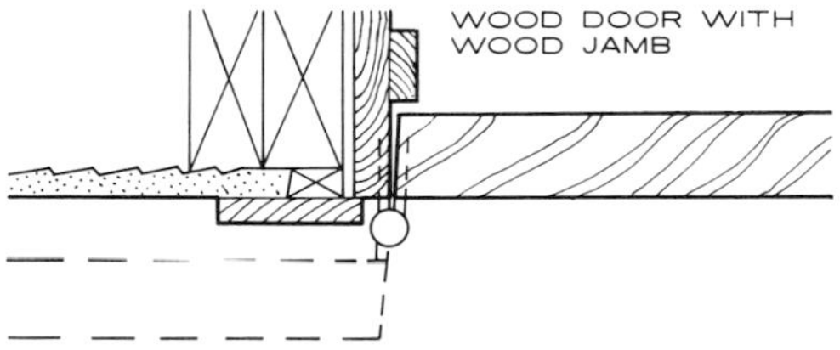

WOOD DOOR WITH WOOD JAMB

FULL MORTISE NON-TEMPLATE

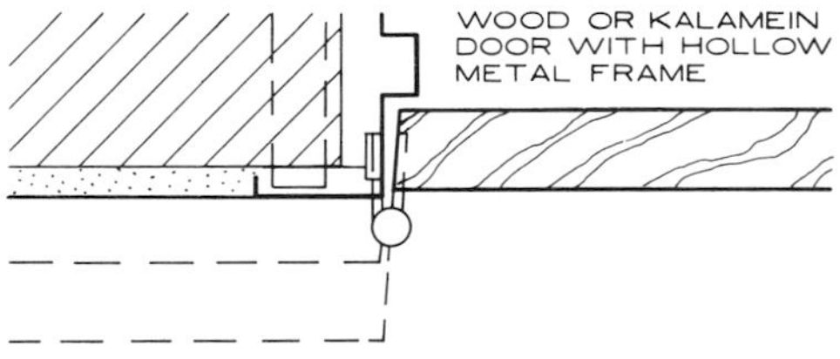

WOOD OR KALAMEIN DOOR WITH HOLLOW METAL FRAME

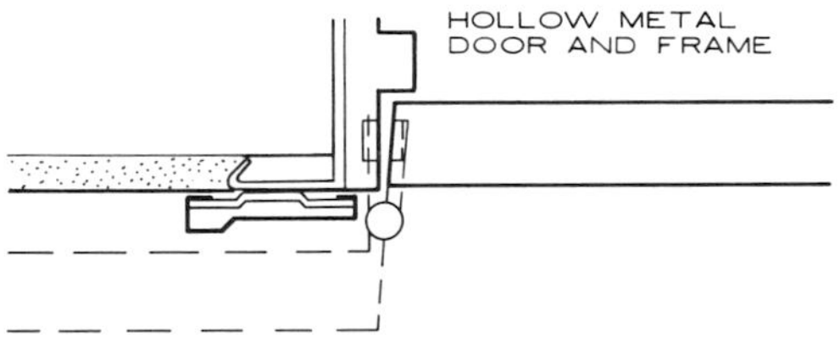

FULL MORTISE TEMPLATE

HOLLOW METAL DOOR AND FRAME

FULL MORTISE TEMPLATE

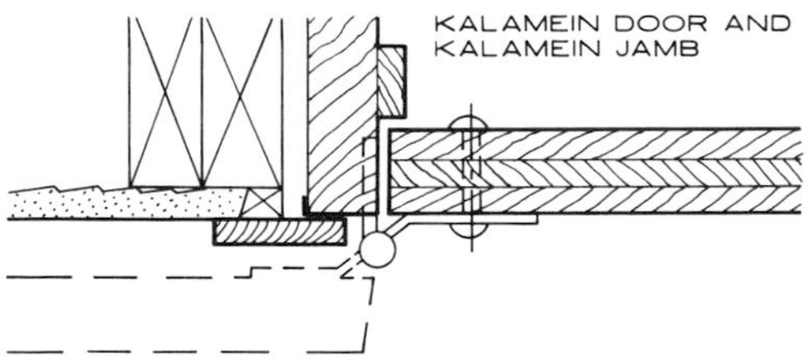

KALAMEIN DOOR AND KALAMEIN JAMB

HALF SURFACE TEMPLATE

KALAMEIN DOOR WITH HOLLOW METAL FRAME

HALF SURFACE TEMPLATE

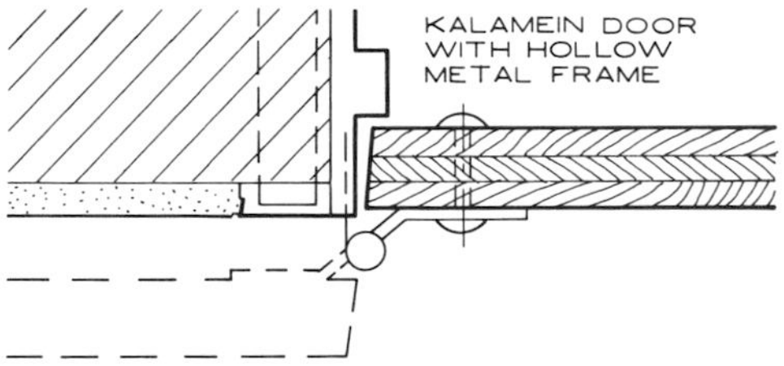

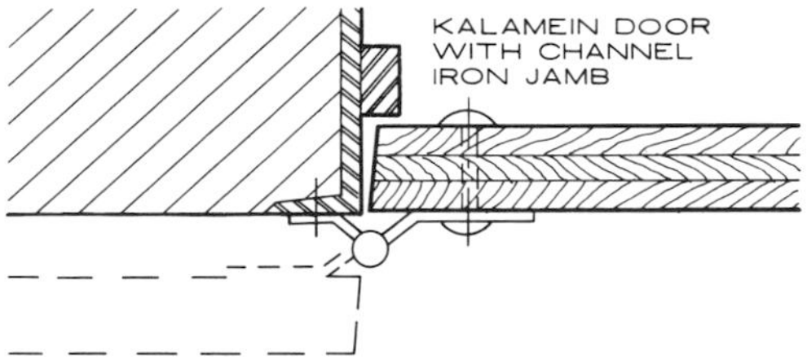

KALAMEIN DOOR WITH CHANNEL IRON JAMB

FULL SURFACE TEMPLATE

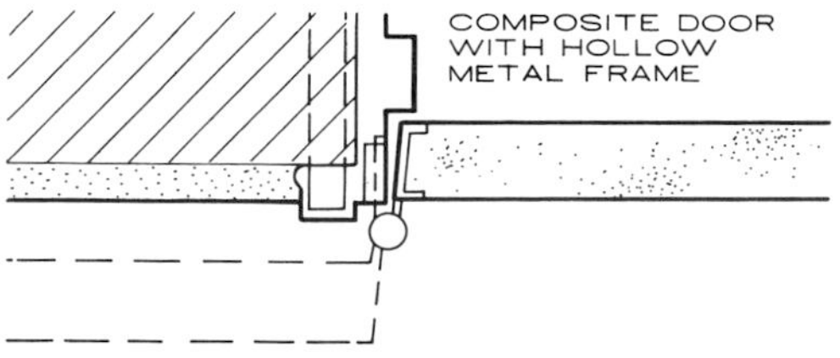

COMPOSITE DOOR WITH HOLLOW METAL FRAME

FULL MORTISE TEMPLATE

TUBULAR STEEL DOOR WITH CHANNEL IRON JAMB

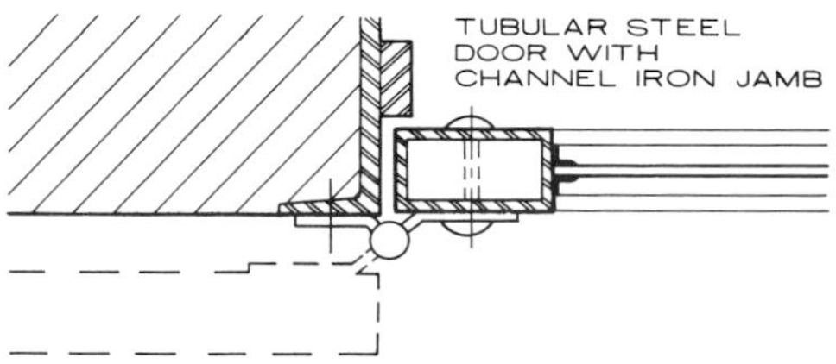

FULL SURFACE TEMPLATE

HOLLOW METAL DOOR WITH CHANNEL IRON JAMB

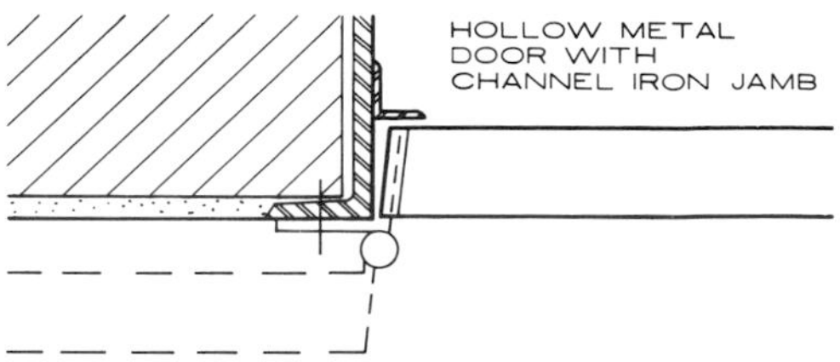

HALF MORTISE TEMPLATE

MORTISE TEMPLATES

F. J. Trost, SMS Architects; New Canaan, Connecticut
Door and Hardware Institute; Arlington, Virginia

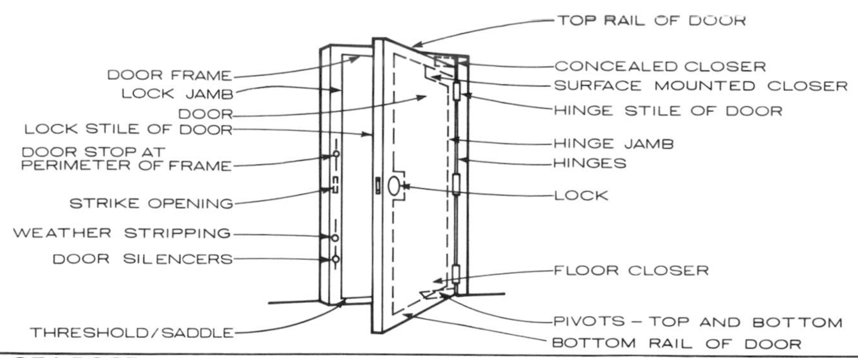
TOP RAIL OF DOOR
DOOR FRAME
LOCK JAMB
DOOR
LOCK STILE OF DOOR
DOOR STOP AT PERIMETER OF FRAME
STRIKE OPENING
WEATHER STRIPPING
DOOR SILENCERS
THRESHOLD/SADDLE
CONCEALED CLOSER
SURFACE MOUNTED CLOSER
HINGE STILE OF DOOR
HINGE JAMB
HINGES
LOCK
FLOOR CLOSER
PIVOTS – TOP AND BOTTOM
BOTTOM RAIL OF DOOR

PARTS OF A DOOR

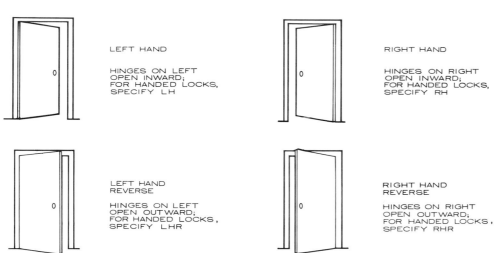

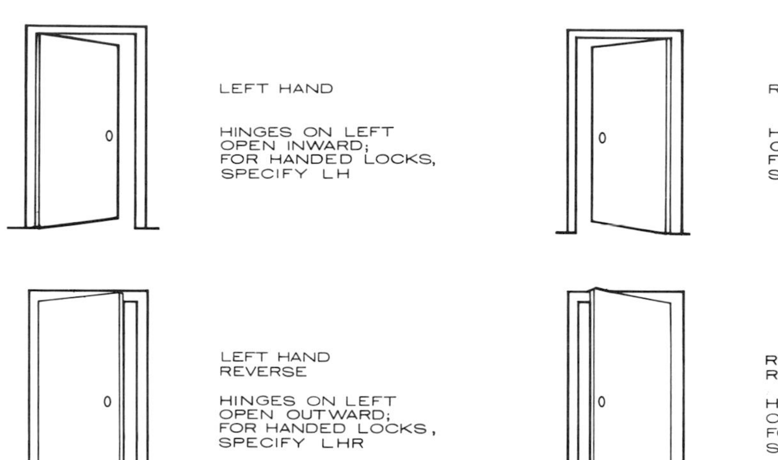
LEFT HAND
HINGES ON LEFT OPEN INWARD; FOR HANDED LOCKS, SPECIFY LH
RIGHT HAND
HINGES ON RIGHT OPEN INWARD; FOR HANDED LOCKS, SPECIFY RH

LEFT HAND REVERSE

HINGES ON LEFT OPEN OUTWARD; FOR HANDED LOCKS, SPECIFY LHR

RIGHT HAND REVERSE

HINGES ON RIGHT OPEN OUTWARD; FOR HANDED LOCKS, SPECIFY RHR

HANDS OF DOORS

DOOR FINISHES

NEAREST U.S. EQUIVALENT	BHMA CODE	FINISH DESCRIPTION	BASE MATERIAL
USP	600	Primed for painting	Steel
US1B	601	Bright japanned	Steel
US2C	602	Cadmium plated	Steel
US2G	603	Zinc plated	Steel
US3	605	Bright brass, clear coated	Brass*
US4	606	Satin brass, clear coated	Brass*
US9	611	Bright bronze, clear coated	Bronze*
US10	612	Satin bronze, clear coated	Bronze*
US10B	613	Oxidized satin bronze, oil rubbed	Bronze*
US14	618	Bright nickel plated, clear coated	Brass, Bronze*
US15	619	Satin nickel plated, clear coated	Brass, Bronze*
US19	622	Flat black coated	Brass, Bronze*
US20A	624	Dark oxidized, statuary bronze, clear coated	Bronze*
US26	625	Bright chromium plated	Brass, Bronze*
US26D	626	Satin chromium plated	Brass, Bronze*
US27	627	Satin aluminum, clear coated	Aluminum
US28	628	Satin aluminum, clear anodized	Aluminum
US32	629	Bright stainless steel	Stainless steel 300 series
US32D	630	Satin, stainless steel	Stainless steel 300 series
–	684	Black chrome, bright	Brass, Bronze*
–	685	Black chrome, satin	Brass, Bronze*

*Also applicable to other base metals under a different BHMA code number.
Note: BHMA—Builders' Hardware Manufacturers Association

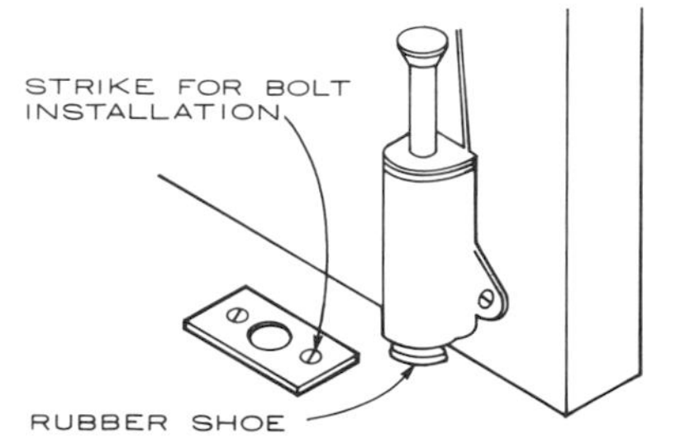
STRIKE FOR BOLT INSTALLATION
RUBBER SHOE

PLUNGER TYPE HOLDER OR BOLT

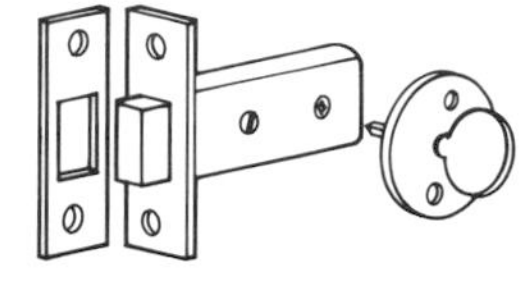

A MINIATURE DEADLOCK, WITH BOLT PROJECTED OR RETRACTED BY A TURN OF THE SMALL KNOB

MORTISE BOLT

GLOSSARY

Coordinator—A device used on a pair of doors to insure that the inactive leaf is permitted to close before the active leaf.

Cylinder (of a lock)—The cylindrical shaped assembly containing the tumbler mechanism and the keyway, which can be actuated only by the correct keys.

Cylinder Lock—A lock in which the locking mechanism is controlled by a cylinder.

Deadbolt (of a lock)—A lock bolt having no spring action or bevel, and which is operated by a key or a turn piece.

Door Bolt—A manually operated rod or bar attached to a door providing means of locking.

Door Holder—A device to hold a door open at selected positions.

Door Stop—A device to stop the swing or movement of a door at a certain point.

Electric Strike—An electrical device that permits releasing of the door from a remote control.

Exit Device—A door locking device which grants instant exit by pressing on a crossbar to release the locking bolt or latch.

Flush Bolt—A door bolt set flush with the face or edge of the door.

Hand (of a lock, etc.)—A term used to indicate the direction of swing or movement, and locking security side of a door.

Lock Set—A lock, complete with trim, such as knobs, escutcheons, or handles.

Mortise—A cavity made to receive a lock or other hardware; also the act of making such a cavity.

Mortise Lock (or Latch)—A lock designed to be installed in a mortise rather than applied to the door's surface.

Rabbet—The abutting edges of a pair of doors or windows, shaped to provide a tight fit.

Reversible Lock—A lock which, by reversing the latch bolt, may be used by any hand. On certain types of locks, other parts must also be changed.

Rose—A trim plate attached to the door under the knob. It sometimes acts as a knob bearing.

Shank (of a knob)—The projecting stem of knob into which the spindle is fastened.

Spindle (of a knob)—The bar or tube connected with the knob or lever handle that passes through the hub of the lock or otherwise engages the mechanism to transmit the knob action to the bolt(s).

Stop (of a lock)—The button, or other small device, which serves to lock the latch bolt against the outside knob or thumb piece or unlock it if locked. Another type holds the bolt retracted.

Strike—A metal plate or box which is pierced or recessed to receive the bolt or latch when projected. Sometimes called "keeper."

Three-Point Lock—A device sometimes required on three-hour fire doors to lock the active leaf of a pair of doors at three points.

NOTES

1. See also Hollow Metal Frames and Doors: Glossary.
2. Face the outside of the door to determine its hand. The outside of the door is the "key side" or that side which would be secured should a lock be used. This would usually be the exterior of an entrance or the corridor side of an office door.

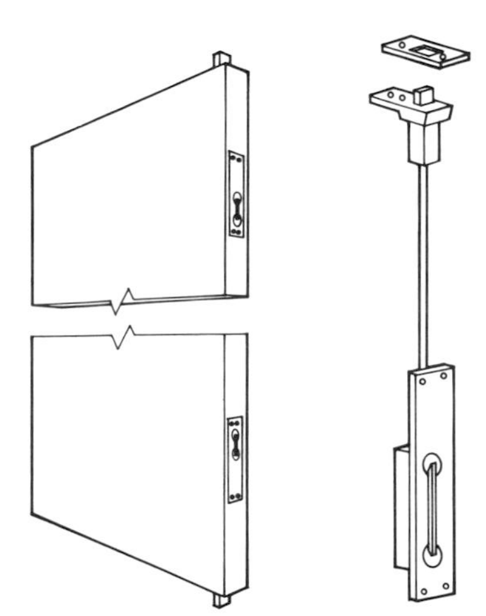

EXTENSION FLUSH BOLT

F. J. Trost, SMS Architects; New Canaan, Connecticut
Door and Hardware Institute; Arlington, Virginia

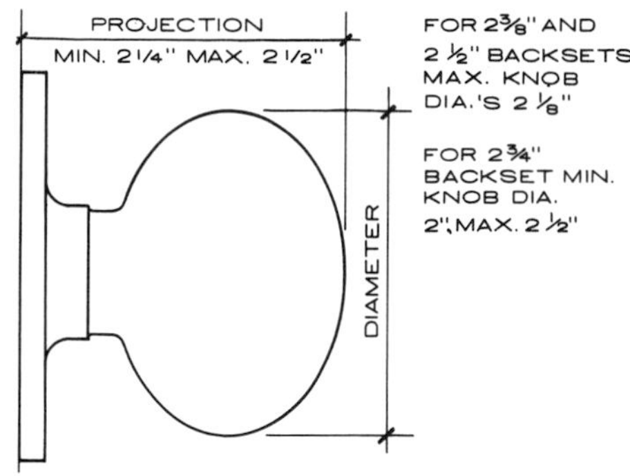
PROJECTION
MIN. 2 1/4" MAX. 2 1/2"
DIAMETER
FOR 2 3/8" AND 2 1/2" BACKSETS MAX. KNOB DIA.'S 2 1/8"
FOR 2 3/4" BACKSET MIN. KNOB DIA. 2", MAX. 2 1/2"

DOOR KNOB

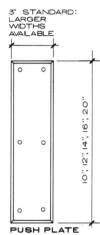

3" STANDARD: LARGER WIDTHS AVAILABLE

10", 12", 14", 16", 20"

PUSH PLATE

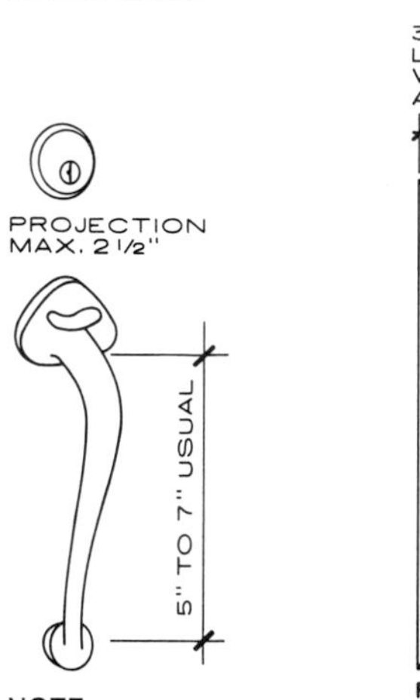
PROJECTION MAX. 2 1/2"
5" TO 7" USUAL

NOTE

Entrance door handle complete lockset includes mortise lock, handle outside, and knob and rose inside.

ENTRANCE HANDLE

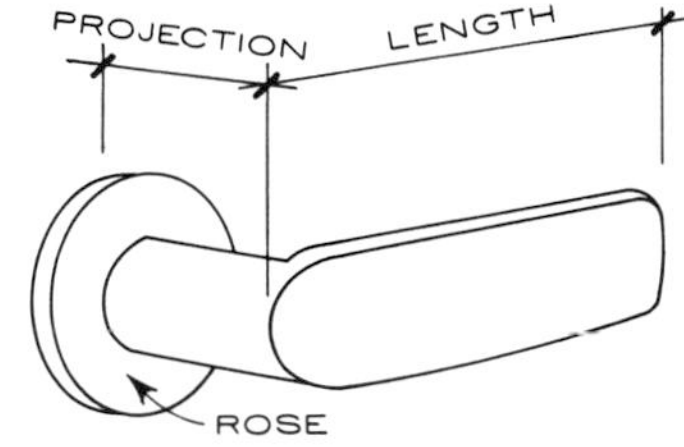
PROJECTION
LENGTH
ROSE

NOTES

Projection—1 3/4 in. to 2 1/2 in.
Length—2 in. to 4 in.
Rose—max. diameter 1 1/2 in. for 3 in.
Stile—larger stile takes larger rose.

LEVER HANDLE

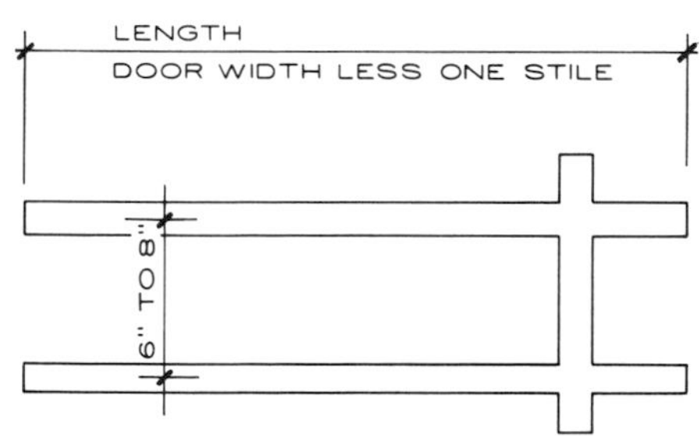
LENGTH
DOOR WIDTH LESS ONE STILE
6" TO 8"
MAX. PROJECTION 2 1/2"

NOTE

Double push-pull bars may be used on the pull side of single acting doors or on either side of double acting doors.

PUSH—PULL BAR

KNOB, HANDLES, PLATE AND BAR

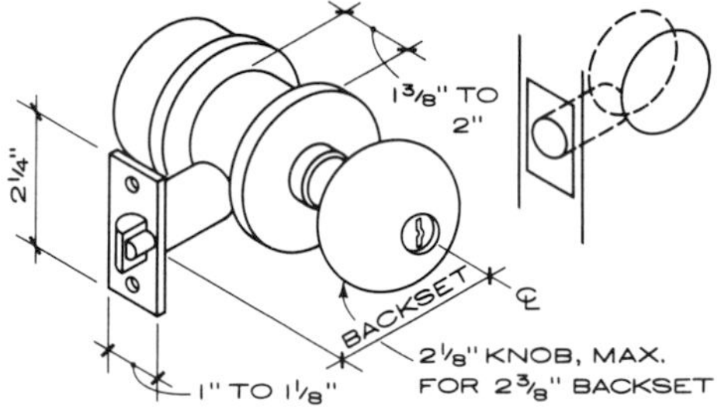
1 3/8" TO 2"
2 1/4"
BACKSET
℄
2 1/8" KNOB, MAX. FOR 2 3/8" BACKSET
1" TO 1 1/8"

NOTES

1. Installation requires 2 1/8 in. hole in door face. Door edge requires 7/8 in. or 15/16 in. hole for standard lock, 1 in. hole for heavy duty lock.
2. Backsets: standard lock—2 3/8 in. (regular), 2 in., 2 3/4 in., 3 3/4 in., 5 in., 7 in., 8 in., 10 in., 18 in. Heavy duty lock 2 3/4 in. (regular), 3 3/4 in., 5 in., 6 in., 7 in., 8 in., 18 in., 19 in. (42 in. special).

CYLINDER

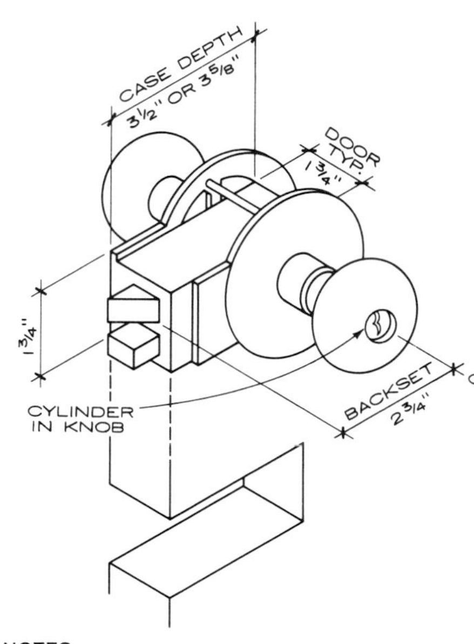
CASE DEPTH 3 1/2" OR 3 5/8"
DOOR TYP. 1 3/4"
1 3/4"
CYLINDER IN KNOB
BACKSET 2 3/4"
℄

NOTES

1. Also available for other door thicknesses.
2. Also available without deadbolt for use as latch.
3. Installation requires notch cut in lock side of door to suit case size. Complete factory assembly eliminates much adjustment on the job.

UNIT

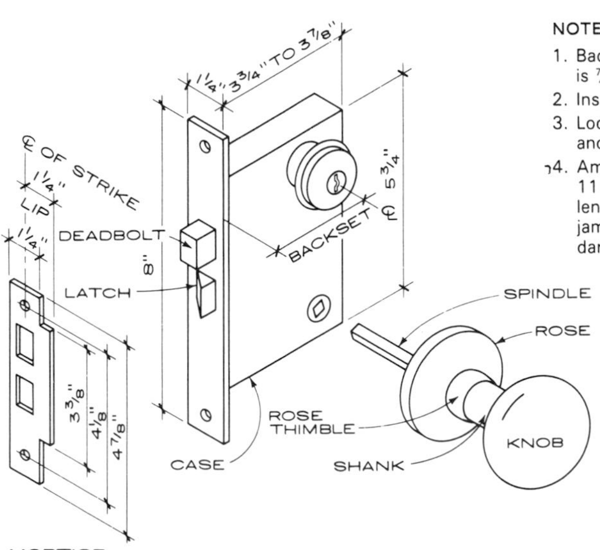
1 1/4", 3 3/4" TO 3 7/8"
℄ OF STRIKE
1 1/4"
LIP
1 1/4"
DEADBOLT
LATCH
8"
BACKSET
℄ 5 3/4"
SPINDLE
ROSE
3 3/8"
4 1/8"
4 7/8"
ROSE THIMBLE
CASE
SHANK
KNOB

MORTISE

LOCK TYPES

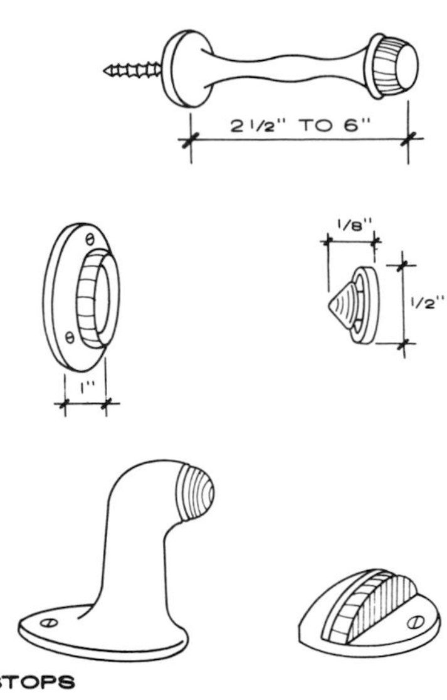
2 1/2" TO 6"
1/8"
1/2"
1"

STOPS

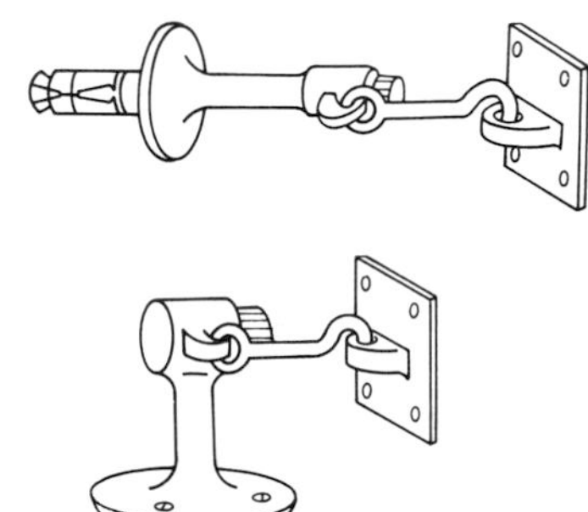

COMBINATION

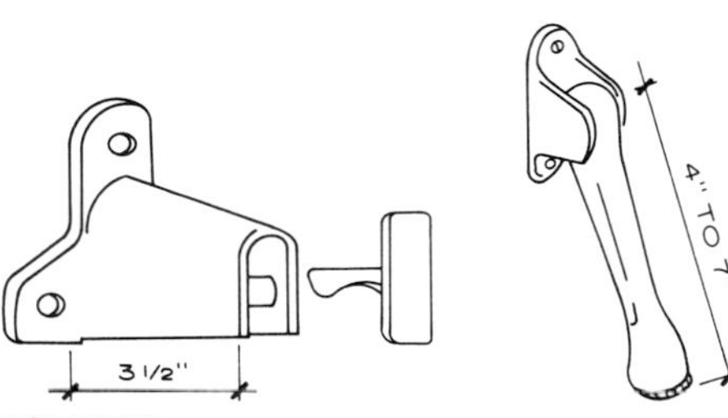
3 1/2"
4" TO 7"

HOLDERS

STOPS AND HOLDERS

NOTES

1. Backset 2 3/4 in. for 1 3/4 in. door. For 1 3/8 in. door, front is 7/8 in. or 1 in. and backset 2 1/2 in. or 2 3/4 in.
2. Installation requires mortise opening in door.
3. Locks available with rabbeted fronts and many key and latch functions.
4. American Standards Association Lock Strikes A-115V-1959 for metal door frames. To determine lip length measure from centerline of strike to edge of jamb and add 1/4 in. Outside strike dimensions standard for all lock types shown.

F. J. Trost, SMS Architects; New Canaan, Connecticut
Door and Hardware Institute; Arlington, Virginia

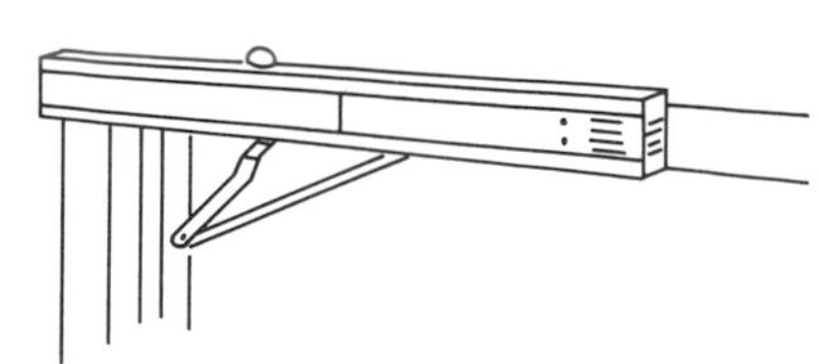

CLOSER, HOLDER, AND DETECTOR PUSH-SIDE MOUNTED

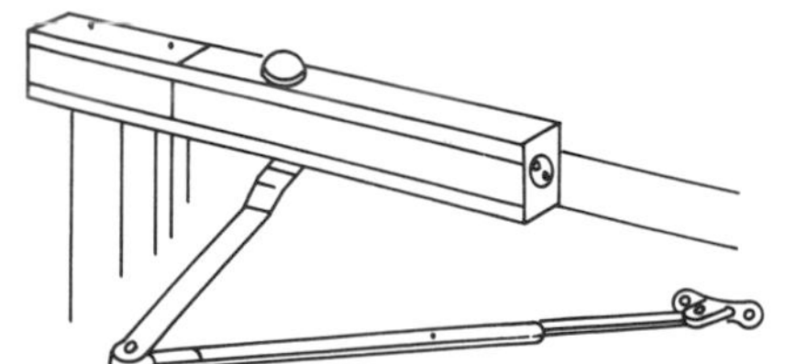

CLOSER AND HOLDER ONLY PUSH-SIDE MOUNTED

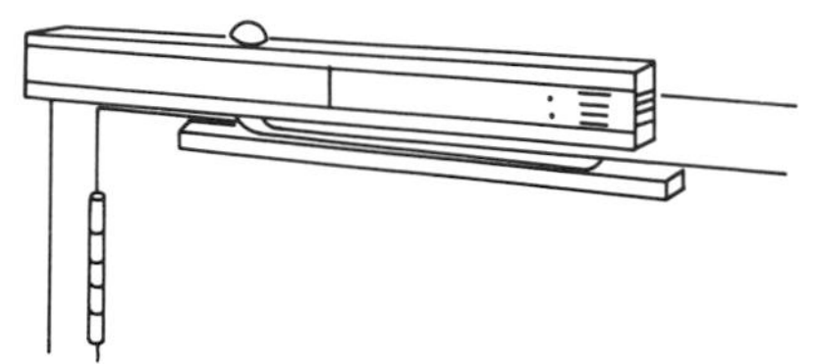

CLOSER, HOLDER, AND DETECTOR PULL-SIDE MOUNTED

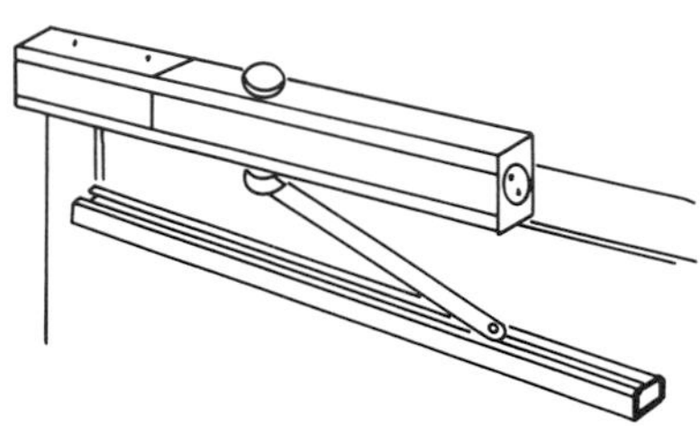

CLOSER AND HOLDER ONLY PULL-SIDE MOUNTED

A COMBINATION DOOR CLOSER, HOLDER, AND FIRE AND SMOKE DETECTOR is available with ionization, photoelectric, or heat sensing detectors for smoke or any combustion products and for holding the door open.

A COMBINATION CLOSER AND HOLDER (only) will hold door in open position when incorporated with an independent detector or when wired into any type of fire detecting system.

All these units have unlimited hold-open from 0° to approximately 170°, or limited hold-open from 85° to 170° for cross-corridor doors.

FIRE AND SMOKE DETECTION SYSTEMS

1. Heat sensing detectors operate on the basis of fixed temperature or a rate of temperature rise. Door closers are activated upon release of a heat activated device such as a fusible link. Closing mechanisms may consist of gravity operated weights or wound steel springs.
2. Smoke sensing detectors detect both visible and invisible airborne particles. Various operating principles include ionization, photoelectric, resistance, sampling, and cloud chamber detection.
3. Ionization detection closers contain a small quantity of radioactive material within the sensing chamber. The resulting ionized air permits an electric current flow between electrodes. When smoke particles reduce the flow of ionized air between electrodes to a certain level, the detection circuit responds. Closing mechanisms usually consist of a detector, electromechanical holding device, and a door closer.
4. Ionization detectors sense ordinary products of combustion from sources such as kitchens, motors, power tools, and automobile exhausts.
5. Photoelectric detection closers consist of a light source and a photoelectric cell. They activate when smoke becomes dense enough to change the reflectance of light reaching the photoelectric device. Photoelectric detectors may be spot or beam type. Closing mechanisms consist of a detector, electromechanical holding device, and a door closer.
6. Other types of smoke detectors include electrical bridging, sampling, and cloud chambers. Each has operating characteristics similar to ionization and photoelectric detectors.
7. Requirements for closers and detectors vary by code and governing jurisdiction. Refer to local building codes, the National Fire Protection Association's life safety code (NFPA) and other applicable regulations.

SURFACE MOUNTED COMBINATION CLOSERS, HOLDERS, AND DETECTORS

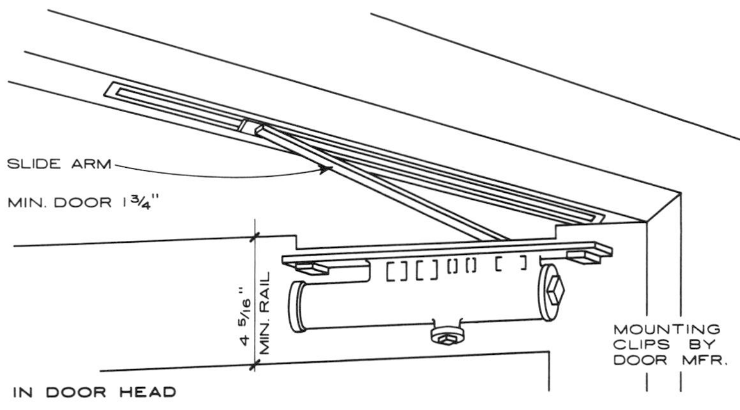
SLIDE ARM
MIN. DOOR 1¾"
4 5/16"
MIN. RAIL
MOUNTING CLIPS BY DOOR MFR.
IN DOOR HEAD

CONSULT MANUFACTURERS FOR MIN. SIZES
4 1/2" MAX.
LEVER ARM
SLIDING SHOE IN DOOR HEAD
IN FRAME HEAD

CONCEALED CLOSERS

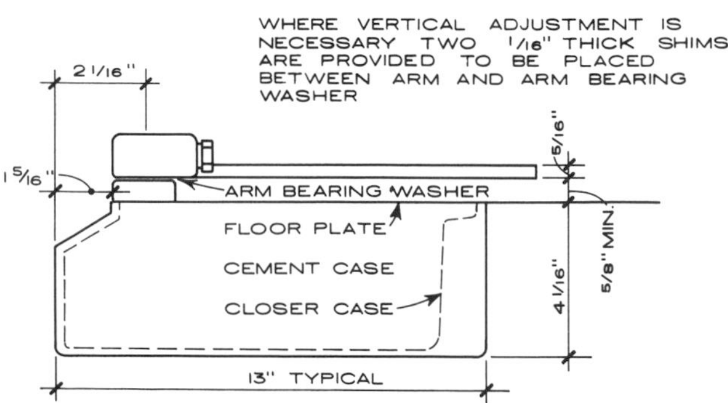
WHERE VERTICAL ADJUSTMENT IS NECESSARY TWO 1/16" THICK SHIMS ARE PROVIDED TO BE PLACED BETWEEN ARM AND ARM BEARING WASHER
2 1/16"
1 5/16"
5/16"
ARM BEARING WASHER
FLOOR PLATE
CEMENT CASE
CLOSER CASE
4 1/16"
5/8" MIN.
13" TYPICAL

EXTERIOR DOOR CLOSER CONCEALED IN FLOOR

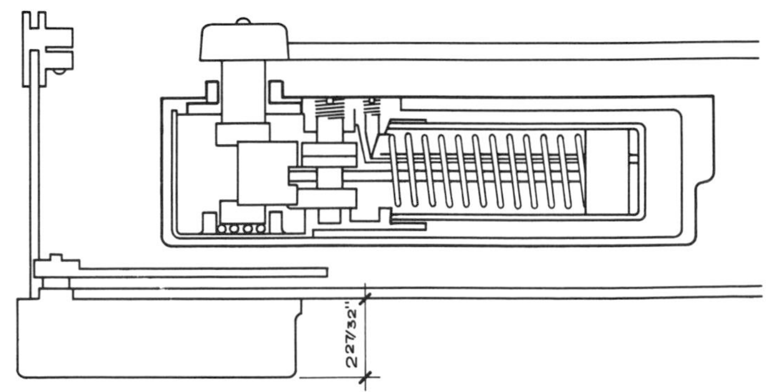
2 27/32"

CHECKING FLOOR HINGE FOR INTERIOR DOORS

Lee A. Anderson; SRGF, Inc., Architects; Champaign, Illinois
Sam A. Buzbee, AIA; Mott, Mobley, Richter, McGowan & Griffin; Fort Smith, Arkansas

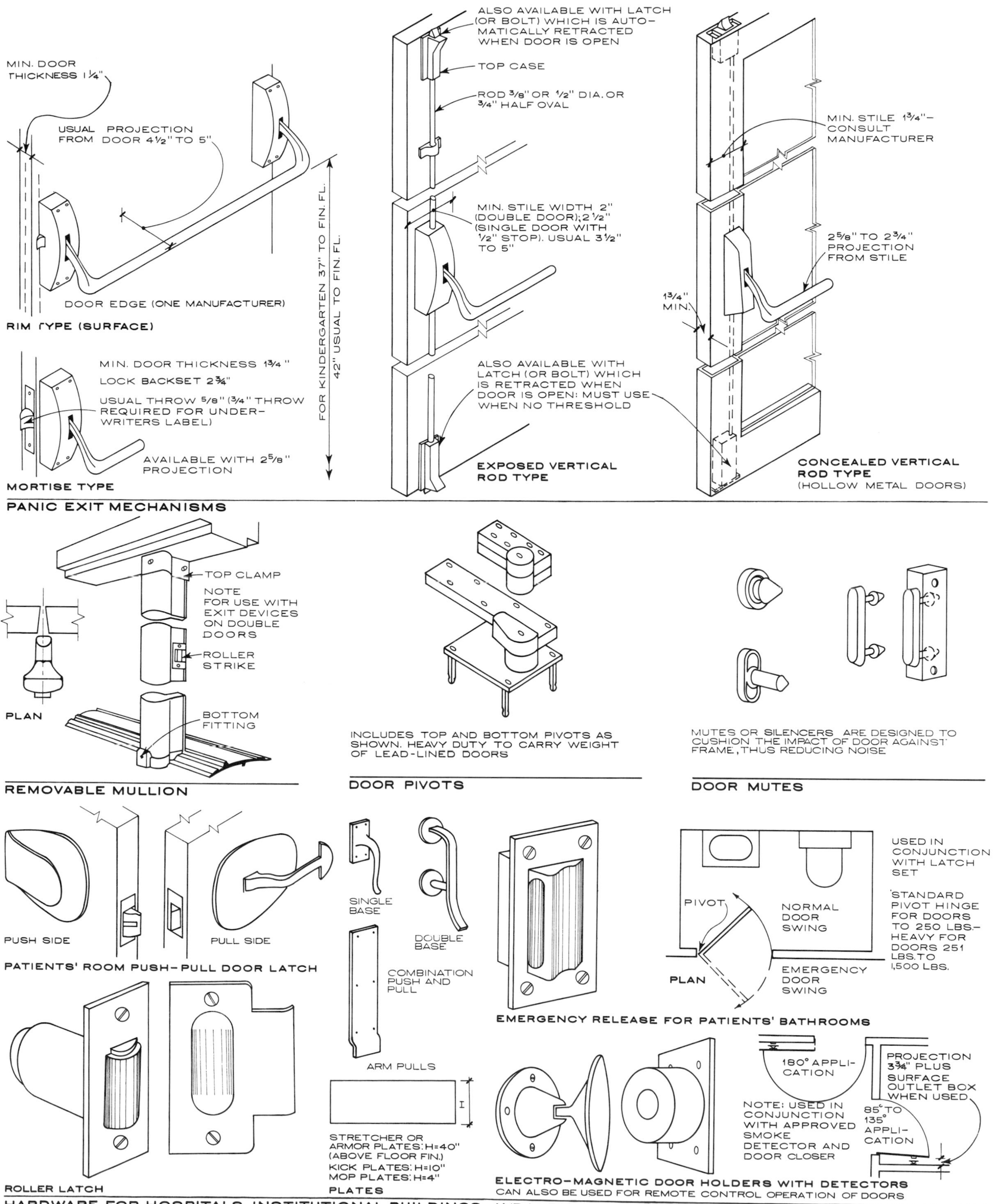
MIN. DOOR THICKNESS 1¼"
USUAL PROJECTION FROM DOOR 4½" TO 5"
DOOR EDGE (ONE MANUFACTURER)
RIM TYPE (SURFACE)
MIN. DOOR THICKNESS 1¾"
LOCK BACKSET 2¾"
USUAL THROW ⅝" (¾" THROW REQUIRED FOR UNDERWRITERS LABEL)
AVAILABLE WITH 2⅝" PROJECTION
MORTISE TYPE
FOR KINDERGARTEN 37" TO FIN. FL.
42" USUAL TO FIN. FL.
ALSO AVAILABLE WITH LATCH (OR BOLT) WHICH IS AUTOMATICALLY RETRACTED WHEN DOOR IS OPEN
TOP CASE
ROD ⅜" OR ½" DIA. OR ¾" HALF OVAL
MIN. STILE WIDTH 2" (DOUBLE DOOR); 2½" (SINGLE DOOR WITH ½" STOP). USUAL 3½" TO 5"
ALSO AVAILABLE WITH LATCH (OR BOLT) WHICH IS RETRACTED WHEN DOOR IS OPEN: MUST USE WHEN NO THRESHOLD
EXPOSED VERTICAL ROD TYPE
MIN. STILE 1¾" – CONSULT MANUFACTURER
2⅝" TO 2¾" PROJECTION FROM STILE
1¾" MIN.
CONCEALED VERTICAL ROD TYPE
(HOLLOW METAL DOORS)
PANIC EXIT MECHANISMS
TOP CLAMP
NOTE
FOR USE WITH EXIT DEVICES ON DOUBLE DOORS
ROLLER STRIKE
PLAN
BOTTOM FITTING
REMOVABLE MULLION
INCLUDES TOP AND BOTTOM PIVOTS AS SHOWN. HEAVY DUTY TO CARRY WEIGHT OF LEAD-LINED DOORS
DOOR PIVOTS
MUTES OR SILENCERS ARE DESIGNED TO CUSHION THE IMPACT OF DOOR AGAINST FRAME, THUS REDUCING NOISE
DOOR MUTES
PUSH SIDE
PULL SIDE
PATIENTS' ROOM PUSH-PULL DOOR LATCH
SINGLE BASE
DOUBLE BASE
COMBINATION PUSH AND PULL
ARM PULLS
STRETCHER OR ARMOR PLATES: H=40" (ABOVE FLOOR FIN.)
KICK PLATES: H=10"
MOP PLATES: H=4"
PLATES
ROLLER LATCH
USED IN CONJUNCTION WITH LATCH SET
STANDARD PIVOT HINGE FOR DOORS TO 250 LBS.– HEAVY FOR DOORS 251 LBS. TO 1,500 LBS.
PIVOT
NORMAL DOOR SWING
EMERGENCY DOOR SWING
PLAN
EMERGENCY RELEASE FOR PATIENTS' BATHROOMS
180° APPLICATION
PROJECTION 3¾" PLUS SURFACE OUTLET BOX WHEN USED
NOTE: USED IN CONJUNCTION WITH APPROVED SMOKE DETECTOR AND DOOR CLOSER
85° TO 135° APPLICATION
ELECTRO-MAGNETIC DOOR HOLDERS WITH DETECTORS
CAN ALSO BE USED FOR REMOTE CONTROL OPERATION OF DOORS

HARDWARE FOR HOSPITALS, INSTITUTIONAL BUILDINGS, AND NURSING HOMES

F. J. Trost, SMS Architects; New Canaan, Connecticut
Door and Hardware Institute; Arlington, Virginia

NOTE

Threshold profiles vary from mfr. to mfr. Consult mfr. catalog for additional sizes. Std. length is 18′ to 20′ or saddles may be cut to size. Anchors to wood floors are screws; to terrazzo or cement floors, screws in fiber plugs or expansive metal anchors; to concrete, screws tapped to clips set in concrete.

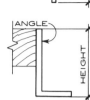

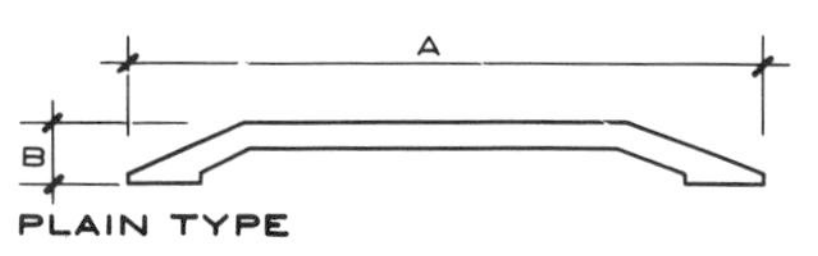
A
B

PLAIN TYPE

BRASS		ALUMINUM				BRONZE	
A	B	A	B	A	B	A	B
3″	1/4″	4 5/64″	3/32″	4″		2 1/2 & 3	1/4″
2 1/4″	3/16″	2 1/4″	3/16″	4 5/64″	1/2″	4, 5 & 6	1/2″
4,5 & 6	1/2″	2 1/2, 3″	1/4″	5 & 6			
		2 1/4″	3/16″	4″	7/16″		

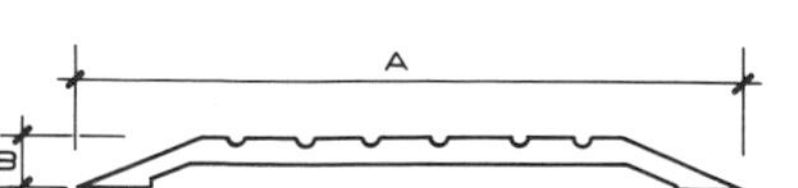
A
B

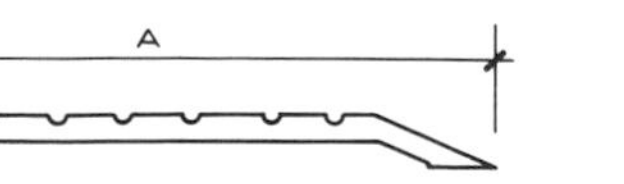

FLUTED TYPES

BRASS		ALUM.		BRONZE		STEEL	
A	B	A	B	A	B	A	B
3,3 1/2 4,5 & 6	1/2″	3, 4 5,6 6 1/4″ 7 7 1/2	1/2″	3	5/16″	3 & 4	1/2″
				3	3/8″	5 1/2″	9/16″
				4, 4 1/2 5, 6 & 7	1/2″	5 1/2 & 7	5/8″
		3, 4 5 & 6	5/8″	6 & 7	5/8″		

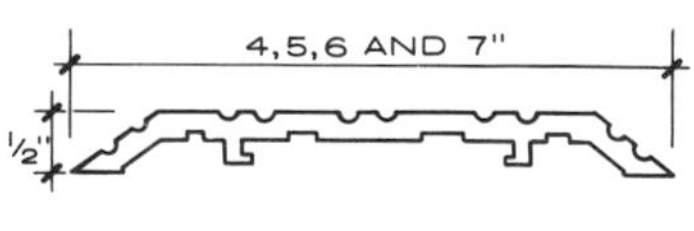
4,5,6 AND 7″
1/2″
3 7/8″
5/8″

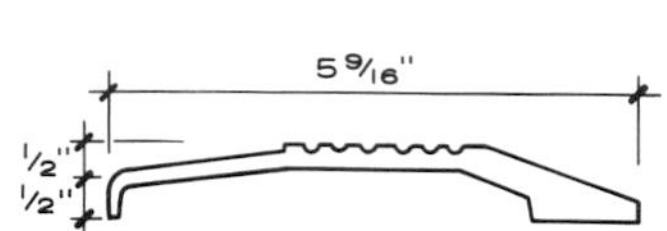
5 9/16″
1/2″
1/2″

FLOOR TILE
HEIGHT
ANGLE
HEIGHT

JOINT STRIP

Used for division of floors of different materials

PLAIN AND FLUTED SADDLES AND JOINT STRIPS FOR INTERIORS

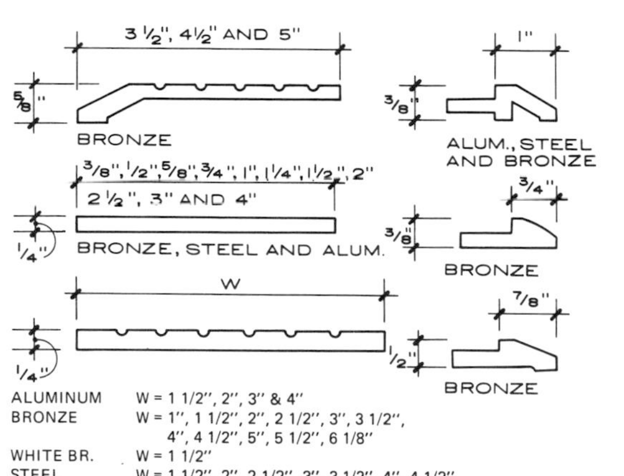
3 1/2″, 4 1/2″ AND 5″
5/8″
BRONZE
1″
3/8″
ALUM., STEEL AND BRONZE
1 3/8″, 1/2″, 5/8″, 3/4″, 1″, 1 1/4″, 1 1/2″, 2″
2 1/2″, 3″ AND 4″
1/4″
BRONZE, STEEL AND ALUM.
3/4″
3/8″
BRONZE
W
1/4″
7/8″
1/2″
BRONZE

ALUMINUM W = 1 1/2″, 2″, 3″ & 4″
BRONZE W = 1″, 1 1/2″, 2″, 2 1/2″, 3″, 3 1/2″, 4″, 4 1/2″, 5″, 5 1/2″, 6 1/8″
WHITE BR. W = 1 1/2″
STEEL W = 1 1/2″, 2″, 2 1/2″, 3″, 3 1/2″, 4″, 4 1/2″

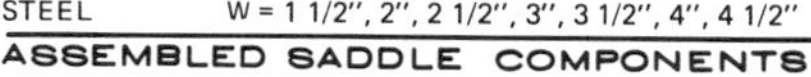

ASSEMBLED SADDLE COMPONENTS

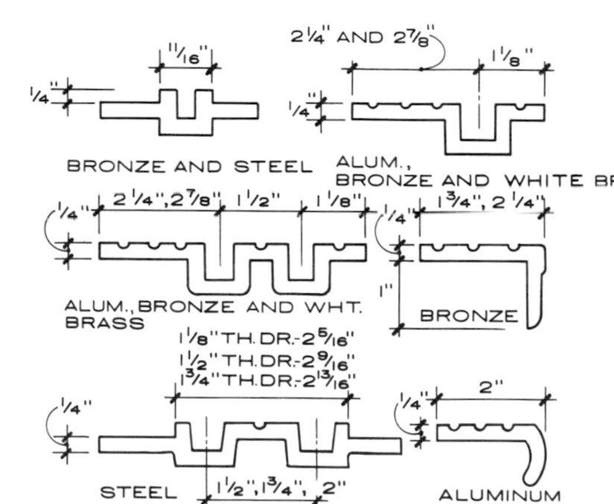
1 1/16″
1/4″
BRONZE AND STEEL
2 1/4″ AND 2 7/8″
1 1/8″
1/4″
ALUM., BRONZE AND WHITE BRASS
1/4″
2 1/4″, 2 7/8″, 1 1/2″, 1 1/8″
1/4″
1 3/4″, 2 1/4″
ALUM., BRONZE AND WHT. BRASS
1″
BRONZE
1 1/8″ TH. DR.-2 5/16″
1 1/2″ TH. DR.-2 9/16″
1 3/4″ TH. DR.-2 13/16″
1/4″
1/4″
2″
STEEL
1 1/2″, 1 3/4″, 2″
ALUMINUM

SLIDING DOOR SADDLE COMPONENTS

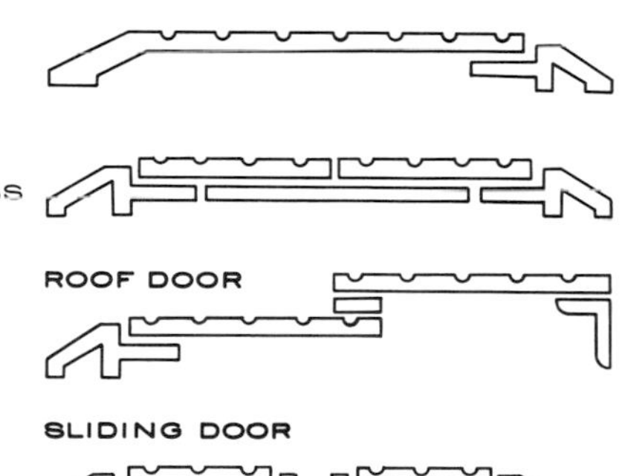
ROOF DOOR
SLIDING DOOR

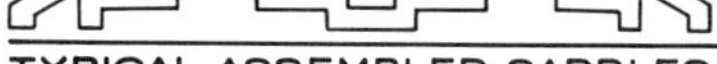

TYPICAL ASSEMBLED SADDLES

By combining components saddles may be made to any width, joints will not show as fluting pattern is identical.

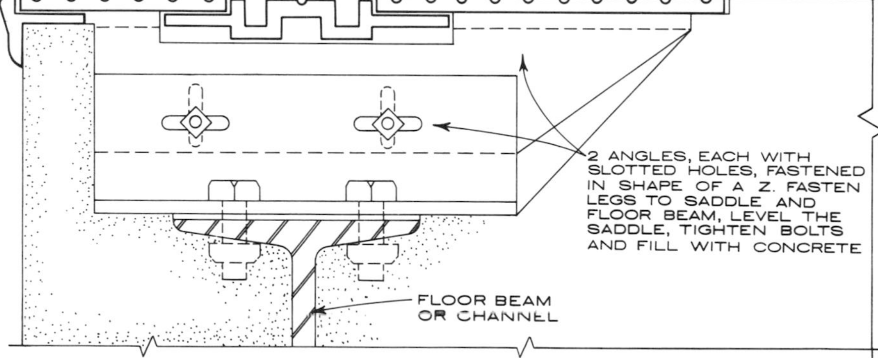
2 ANGLES, EACH WITH SLOTTED HOLES, FASTENED IN SHAPE OF A Z. FASTEN LEGS TO SADDLE AND FLOOR BEAM, LEVEL THE SADDLE, TIGHTEN BOLTS AND FILL WITH CONCRETE
FLOOR BEAM OR CHANNEL

ELEVATOR SADDLE CONSTRUCTION

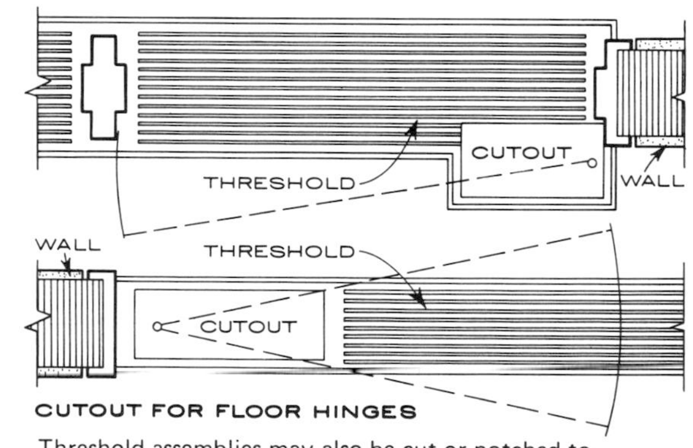
CUTOUT
THRESHOLD
WALL
WALL
THRESHOLD
CUTOUT

CUTOUT FOR FLOOR HINGES

Threshold assemblies may also be cut or notched to fit mullions or columns.

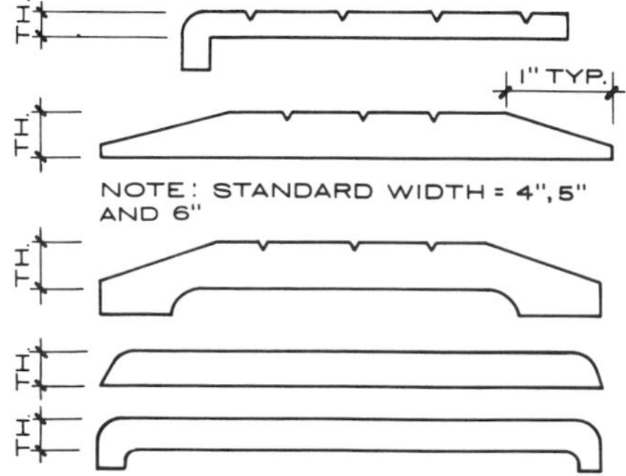
1″ TYP.
NOTE: STANDARD WIDTH = 4″, 5″ AND 6″

RECOMMENDED PRACTICE

TH.	IRON	BRONZE	ALUMINUM	NICKEL
1/4		to 6″ wide	to 10″ wide	to 6″ wide
5/16	to 6″ wide	to 10″ wide	to 18″ wide	to 10″ wide
3/8	to 12″ wide	to 18″ wide	to 24″ wide	to 14″ wide
7/16	to 24″ wide	to 24″ wide	to 36″ wide	to 18″ wide
1/2	to 30″ wide	to 30″ wide	to 42″ wide	to 24″ wide
5/8	to 42″ wide	to 42″ wide	to 42″ wide	to 30″ wide
3/4	to 42″ wide	to 42″ wide	to 42″ wide	to 30″ wide

Length, to 9′-6″. When width exceeds 32″, length should not exceed 7′-6″.

CAST METAL ABRASIVE SURFACE SADDLES

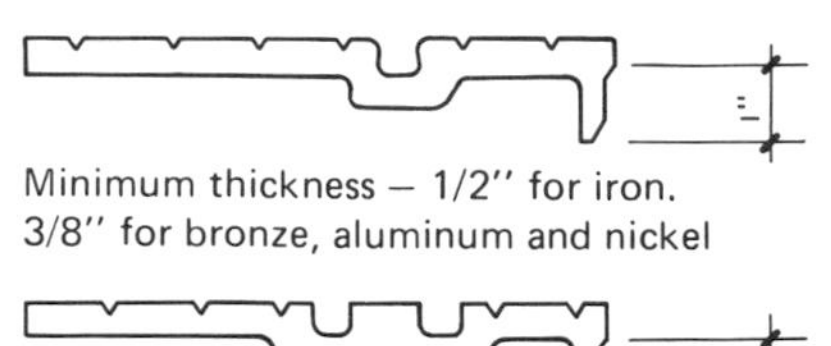

Minimum thickness — 1/2″ for iron. 3/8″ for bronze, aluminum and nickel

ELEVATOR DOOR SADDLE

Saddles with floor hinge cut-outs, as shown above also available.

Dan Cowling and Associates, Inc.; Little Rock, Arkansas

GLASS: DEFINITION

A hard, brittle amorphous substance made by fusing silica (sometimes combined with oxides of boron or phosphorus) with certain basic oxides (notably sodium, potassium, calcium, magnesium, and lead) and cooling rapidly to prevent crystallization or devitrification. Most glasses melt at 800°C to 950°C. Heat-resisting glass usually contains a high proportion of boric oxide. The brittleness of glass is such that minute surface scratches in manufacturing greatly reduce its strength.

INDUSTRY QUALITY STANDARDS

FEDERAL SPECIFICATION DD-G-451: Establishes thickness and dimensional tolerances and quality characteristics of flat glass products.

FEDERAL SPECIFICATION DD-G-1403: Establishes standards for tempered glass, heat strengthened glass, and spandrel glass.

AMERICAN NATIONAL STANDARD Z971: Establishes standards for testing safety glazing material.

INSULATING GLASS CERTIFICATION COUNCIL (IGCC): Conducts periodic inspection and independent laboratory tests of insulating glass products.

ASTM STANDARD E546: Test method for frost point of sealed insulating glass units (horizontal position).

ASTM STANDARD E576: Dew/frost point of sealed insulating glass units in vertical position.

ASTM STANDARD E773: Test method for seal durability of sealed insulating glass units.

ASTM STANDARD E774: Specification for sealed insulating glass units.

NOTE

Consult glass manufacturers for current information because processes, qualities, finishes, colors, sizes, thicknesses, and limitations are revised continuously. The following information represents one or more manufacturers' guidelines.

BASIC TYPES OF GLASS (CLEAR GLASS)

WINDOW AND SHEET GLASS

Manufactured by a horizontally flat or vertical draw process, then annealed slowly to produce natural flat fired, high gloss surfaces. Generally has residential and industrial applications. Inherent surface waves are noticeable in sizes larger than 4 sq. ft. For minimum distortion, larger sizes are installed with the wave running horizontally. The width is listed first when specifying.

FLOAT GLASS

Generally accepted as the successor to polished plate glass, float glass has become the quality standard of the glass industry in architectural, mirror, and specialty applications. It is manufactured by floating on a surface of molten tin, then annealing slowly to produce a transparent flat glass, thus eliminating grinding and polishing.

PLATE GLASS

Transparent flat glass is ground and polished after rolling. Within limits, cylindrical and conic shapes can be bent to desired curvature.

VARIATIONS OF BASIC TYPES OF GLASS

PATTERNED GLASS

Known also as rolled or figured glass, it is made by passing molten glass through rollers that are etched to produce the appropriate design. Most often only one side of the glass is imprinted with a pattern; however, it is possible to imprint both sides.

WIRE GLASS

Available as clear polished glass or in various patterns, most commonly with embedded welded square or diamond wire. Some distortion, wire discoloration, and misalignment are inherent. Some ¼ in. (6 mm) wired glass products are recognized as certified safety glazing materials for use in hazardous locations. For applicable fire and safety codes that govern their use, refer to ANSI Z97.1.

CATHEDRAL GLASS

Known also as art glass, stained glass, or opalescent glass. It is produced in many colors, textures, and patterns, is usually ⅛ in. thick, and is used primarily in decorating leaded glass windows. Specialty firms usually contract this highly exacting art.

OBSCURE GLASS

To obscure a view or create a design, the entire surface on one or both sides of the glass can be sandblasted, acid etched, or both. When a glass surface is altered by any of these methods, the glass is weakened and may be difficult to clean.

HEAT-ABSORBING OR TINTED GLASS

The glass absorbs a portion of the sun's energy because of admixture contents and thickness. It then dissipates the heat to both the exterior and interior. The exterior glass surface reflects a portion of energy depending on the sun's position. Heat-absorbing glass has a higher temperature when exposed to the sun than clear glass does; thus the central area expands more than the cooler shaded edges, causing edge tensile stress buildup.

DESIGN CONSIDERATIONS

1. To avoid shading problems, provide conditions so glass edges warm as rapidly as other lights. An example is framing systems with low heat capacity and minimal glass grip or stops. Structural rubber gaskets can be used.
2. The thicker the glass, the greater the solar energy absorption.
3. Indoor shading devices such as blinds and draperies reflect energy back through the glass, thus increasing the glass temperature. Spaces between indoor shading and the glass, including ceiling pockets, should be vented adequately. Heating elements always should be located on the interior side of shading devices, directing warm air away from the glass.

REFLECTIVE COATED GLASS

Reflective glass coatings may be applied to float plate, heat strengthened, tempered, laminated, insulated, or spandrel glass; the number is vast. Design considerations for heat absorbing glass also apply to reflective coated glass.

Reflective coating glass falls in three basic classifications:

1. Single glazing with a coating on one surface.
2. Laminated glass coated between the glass plies or on the exterior surface.
3. Insulating glass units with coating on the exterior surface or on either of the interior surfaces.

Application of a reflective coating on the exterior surface creates a visually uniform surface on any or all these glass classifications. Extreme care must be taken in handling, glazing, and cleaning this type of glass to avoid scratching the coating. Some reflective coatings are available only with insulating units.

HEAT STRENGTHENED AND TEMPERED GLASS

Produced by reheating and rapidly cooling annealed glass, it has greatly increased mechanical strength and resistance to thermal stresses. Neither type can be altered after fabrication; the manufacturer must furnish the exact size and shape. The inherent warpage may cause glazing problems. Refer to Federal Specifications DD-G-1404 for allowable tolerances.

HEAT STRENGTHENED GLASS

Twice as strong as annealed glass. Unlike tempered glass, it does not pulverize into crystal-like form when broken.

TEMPERED GLASS

Four to five times the strength of annealed glass; it breaks into innumerable small, cubed fragments. It can be much safer than annealed glass. Shallow patterned glass also may be tempered. Tong marks are visible near the edge on the short side when the glass is held vertically during tempering. Some manufacturers temper horizontally to eliminate these marks. Strain patterns are inherent and can be seen under some lighting conditions or through polarized eyeglasses.

SPANDREL GLASS

Heat strengthened by firefusing an opaque ceramic color to the interior surface of sheet, plate, or float glass. May be tempered fully if it conforms with GSA guide specification No. PBS-4-0885.

A variety of colors and special finishes are available. Supplied with a reflective coating, color frit, or opacifier film and with insulation or as part of an insulating glass unit. Pinholes and nonuniformity of color are apparent if used without solid opaque backup. If monolithic spandrel glass is supplied without integral insulation, at least 2 in. air space is required between glass back and insulation material.

SOUND CONTROL GLASS

Laminated, insulating, laminated insulating, and double laminated insulating glass products commonly are used for sound control. STC ratings from 31 to 51 are available depending on glass thicknesses, air space size, polyvinyl butyl film thickness, and number of laminated units used in insulating products.

LAMINATED GLASS

SAFETY GLASS

(See also Wire Glass, Mirrors)

A tough, clear plastic film sheet (interlayer) 0.015 in. (0.636 mm) thick minimum is sandwiched, under heat and pressure, between plies of sheet, plate, float, wired, heat absorbing, tinted, reflective, heat strengthened, full-tempered glass, or combinations of each.

When fractured, particles tend to adhere to the plastic film. Always weep the glazing cavity to the exterior.

SECURITY GLASS

Safety glass with a plastic film of 0.060 in. (1.5 mm) minimum thickness for bullet resistant and burglar resistant glass. Bullet resisting glass consists of three to five plies of glass and, in some cases, high performance plastics, with an overall ¾ in. to 3 in. thickness. Avoid sealants with organic solvents or oil, which can react with the plastic film. (See Plastics in Glazing.)

GENERAL CONSIDERATIONS FOR GLAZING ASSEMBLIES

1. Thermal movement in frame and glass.
2. Deflection, vertical framing members.
3. Deflection, horizontal framing members.
4. Clearances, shims, drainage.

Expansion and contraction of the glazing material and the resulting movement and stresses the glazing system must cope with are determined by:

1. Size of light to be glazed.
2. Maximum exposure temperatures for glazing materials.
3. Sealed insulating units (hotter trapped air.)

Consult manufacturer for load capacities.

Some factors impacting transfer of wind loads to surrounding structure are:

1. Proportion and size of opening, span between supports, and thickness and deflection of glass.
2. Method of support for the glass pane.
3. Movement of the surrounding structure.
4. Setting blocks placed under bottom edge of glass.
5. Spacer shims—to assure proper clearances between face of glazing material and framing channels.
6. Squareness, flatness tolerances surrounding channel.

INSULATING GLASS

Insulating glass, with high performance in thermal resistance and shading coefficient, is used primarily to control heat transfer. Insulating glass units are manufactured from two or more pieces of glass separated by a hermetically sealed air space. Two unit types are available:

1. GLASS EDGE OR GLASS SEAL UNIT: Primarily for residential use. Constructed by fusing edges of two glass lights together with 3/16 in. (5 mm) space filled with a dry gas at atmospheric pressure. Use at high altitudes is not recommended. Do not glaze with lockstrip structural gaskets.
2. ORGANIC SEALED EDGE UNIT: Primarily for commercial and industrial use, as well as for some residential applications. Constructed with two sheets of glass separated by a metal or organic spacer (filled with a moisture absorbing material) around the edges and hermetically sealed. Insulating units should be fabricated to IGCC AND ASTM E546, E576, E773, and E774 standards.

Available with 1/4 in. and 1/2 in. air space in float, patterned, heat absorbing, tinted, reflective coated, annealed, heat-strengthened, tempered, and laminated glass. The thickness of the two glass panes, however, should not differ by more than 1/16 in. Performance characteristics, glass thickness, maximum fabricated sizes, and a multitude of various combinations may be found in the manufacturer's literature.

The heat absorbing glass of a heat absorbing unit should be to the exterior. When sloped insulated glazing is used over occupied areas, heat-strengthened, laminated glass is advisable as the interior light; however, the glass manufacturer and governing codes and authorities on fire and safety should be consulted. Triple glazing units are available for special application. Moisture drainage that might collect in the glazing pocket, destroying the organic seal, must be provided for.

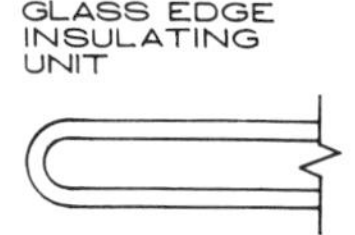
GLASS EDGE INSULATING UNIT

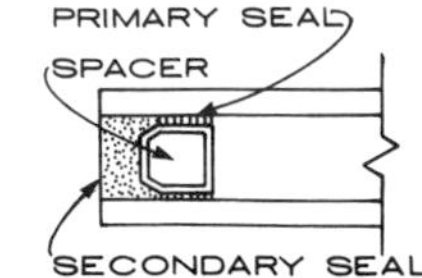
PRIMARY SEAL
SPACER
SECONDARY SEAL

INSULATING GLASS UNITS

ORGANIC SEALED EDGE INSULATING UNIT

INSULATING GLASS

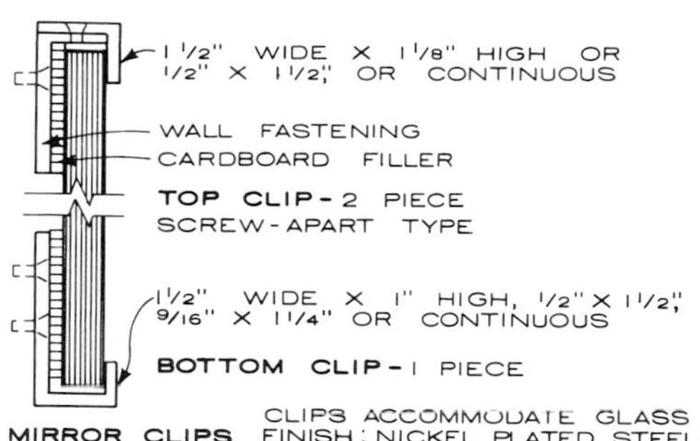
1 1/2" WIDE X 1 1/8" HIGH OR 1/2" X 1 1/2" OR CONTINUOUS
WALL FASTENING
CARDBOARD FILLER
TOP CLIP - 2 PIECE SCREW-APART TYPE
1 1/2" WIDE X 1" HIGH, 1/2" X 1 1/2" 9/16" X 1 1/4" OR CONTINUOUS
BOTTOM CLIP - 1 PIECE

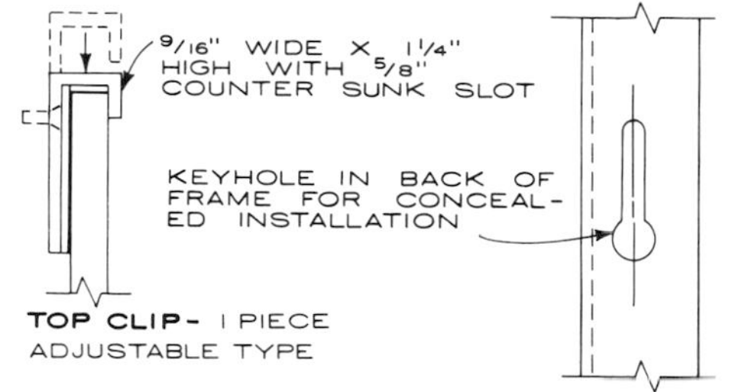
9/16" WIDE X 1 1/4" HIGH WITH 5/8" COUNTER SUNK SLOT
KEYHOLE IN BACK OF FRAME FOR CONCEALED INSTALLATION
TOP CLIP - 1 PIECE ADJUSTABLE TYPE

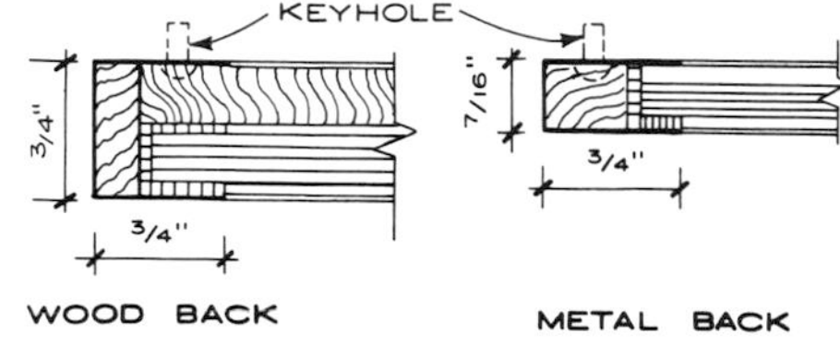
KEYHOLE
3/4"
3/4"
7/16"
3/4"
WOOD BACK
METAL BACK

MIRROR WITH METAL FRAME
AVAILABLE IN BRASS, BRONZE AND NICKEL SILVER WITH ANY POLISHED OR PLATED FINISH

MIRROR CLIPS
CLIPS ACCOMMODATE GLASS FROM 1/4" TO 3/8" AVAILABLE IN BRASS-BRIGHT CHROME FINISH; NICKEL PLATED STEEL; BRASS, NICKEL SILVER, BRONZE-ANY FINISH, BRASS-NICKEL PLATED

MIRROR GLAZING DETAILS

MIRRORS

Most commonly manufactured from surfacing sheet, float, or plate glass, hermetically sealing a silver coating with a uniform film of electrolytic copper plating. A protective coating of paint is then applied to seal out moisture from the silver. When sheet glass is used, the quality should be A-silvering or B-silvering. Float or plate glass should be selected for mirror glazing quality. Incidental applications include safety, observation (two-way), and institutional uses.

For applications of mirrored acrylic plastics, see Glazing with Plastics.

CONVEX AND CONCAVE MIRRORS

Mirrors can be used to provide both security and safety for "blind spots" from visual vantage points. Twisted or bent mirrors are used to create distorted images.

SAFETY MIRRORS

Used for cladding full height, hinged, pivoted, or sliding doors. Commonly manufactured by one of the following methods:

1. Silvering fully tempered glass—visually inferior to regular glass mirrors because of inherent warpage of tempered glass.
2. Silvering the back of laminated glass—visually inferior.
3. Silvering a light of glass and laminating it to another glass light with the silvering inside the unit—visually the best of the three.

OBSERVATION (ONE-WAY OR TWO-WAY) MIRRORS

Commonly used for research and security in observation areas. Designed to provide vision through one side while reflecting images when viewed from the opposite side. To facilitate this function, the observers' area should have dull, subdued colors and low lighting levels with controlled dimming. The area to be observed should have light colors and a high illumination level, as suggested in the light ratio table.

Light ratio = observed area : viewing area.

LIGHT RATIO TABLE

BASE		LIGHT RATIO	
GLASS	DESCRIPTION	PREFERRED	ACCEPTABLE
Float	Clear	10:1	5:1
	Laminated	10:1	5:1
	Gray	4:1	2:1

Observation mirrors can be manufactured in the following forms (for comments, see Safety Mirrors):

1. Single glazed, for interior applications. Extreme care must be taken to avoid damaging the reflective coating through abrasion.
2. Safety tempered.
3. Safety laminated. The mirror coating is usually located between the two bonded plys of glass, thus protecting it against abrasion.
4. Security laminated. A single light of observation mirror glass that is laminated between two lights of clear glass with a plastic film interlayer.

INSTITUTIONAL MIRRORS

Used in detention or security areas and in areas involving high risk to personal safety. Often made of highly polished noncorrosive metal with reinforced rounded corners and edges. Commonly made for attachment to masonry walls with flat head spanner screws.

MOUNTING APPLICATIONS

Mirrors can be mounted by way of frames or they can be surface mounted frameless by any of the following methods:

1. MASTIC: Mastic specifically made for mirrors is not generally recommended for use without clips, channels, or other auxiliary supportive devices. Certain design considerations, mirror sizes, and weights may, however, make this type of installation desirable. Mounting surfaces should be clean, dry, smooth, and plumb. Avoid applying to papered surfaces. Paint the back of the mirror with an extra coat of water resistant paint. Spot apply mastic to dry mirror back; it should not cover more than approximately 25% of the mirror area or exceed 1/2 to 5/8 in. in thickness, so as to allow for trueing the mirror and adequate ventilation. Always provide support along the bottom edge and brace the mirror until the mastic sets.
2. DOUBLE FACED TAPE: The tape must be compatible with the mirror backing and supportive surface. Thicknesses and quantities depend on adhesive qualities of the tape. A tape with a capability of 1 lb for every 1/2 sq in. is recommended. To prevent moisture collection, install tape vertically, cutting the top edge to a point. Provide a bottom edge support that allows for drainage.
3. BOTTOM CHANNEL AND CLIPS.
4. WOOD FRAME BACK: Used to level a single mirror or multiple mirrors in a uniform plane. Paint the surface facing the mirror back to prevent wood resins from spoiling the silver. All mechanical fastening devices should be countersunk into the frame. Use clips at the bottom edge; provide paper padding to prevent metal contact.
5. ROSETTES OR SCREWS: Only experienced glaziers should undertake this type of work, since extreme care is needed. To prevent the glass from coming in contact with the metal screw anchor, make the hole in the mirror of adequate size to accommodate a rubber sleeve fitting around the screw. A felt cushion should be placed behind the rosette on the face of the glass. It is recommended that mirrors up to 10 sq ft in area be supported at each corner, 4 in. in from the edges; mirrors over 10 sq ft in area should have holes about 36 in. on centers.

Surface mounted, frameless mirrors should have all exposed edges ground and polished. If a continuous bottom channel is used, the bottom edge should be ground and painted to protect it from possible moisture intrusion. The paint must be water resistant and compatible with the coating on the mirror's back, as it must overlap the back to seal the edge. To avoid moisture penetration, mirrors should not be mounted directly against felt or felt paper and unpainted plaster, wood, or plywood.

When walls are entirely covered with mirrors, either in vertical panels or rectilinear stacked panels, the mirror edges must be flat polished with an appropriate thin 1/16 in. divider strip placed between all butt joints. In working with large areas, use a wood frame system, with members behind each vertical and horizontal joint, to allow for proper leveling.

Skidmore, Owings & Merrill

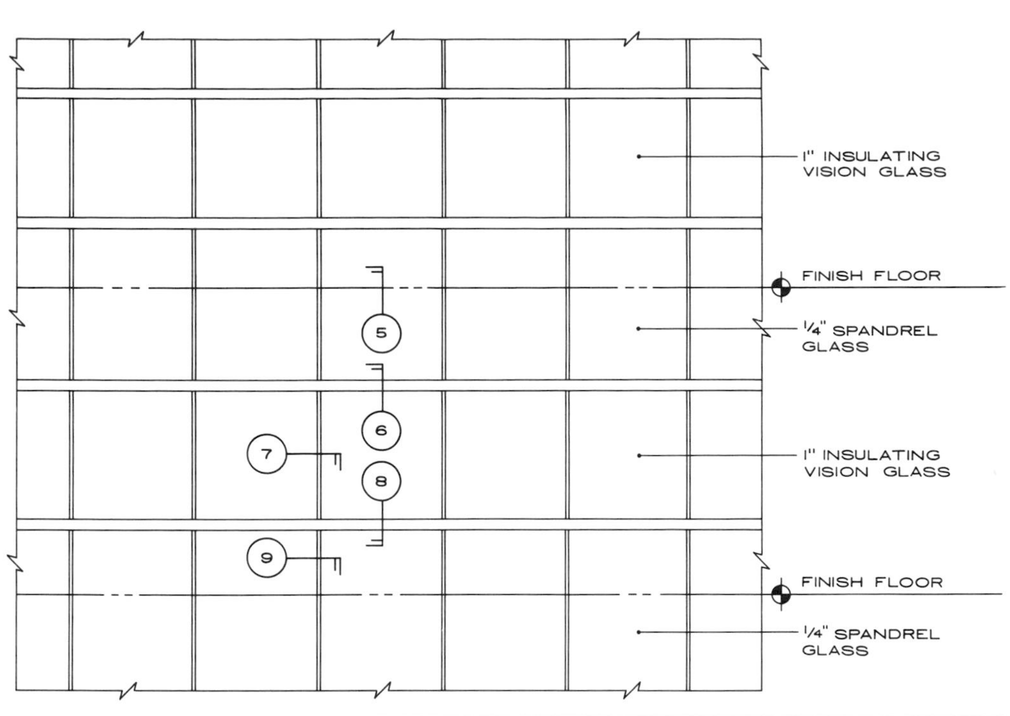
1" INSULATING VISION GLASS
FINISH FLOOR
¼" SPANDREL GLASS
1" INSULATING VISION GLASS
FINISH FLOOR
¼" SPANDREL GLASS
5
6
7
8
9

CURTAIN WALL ELEVATION

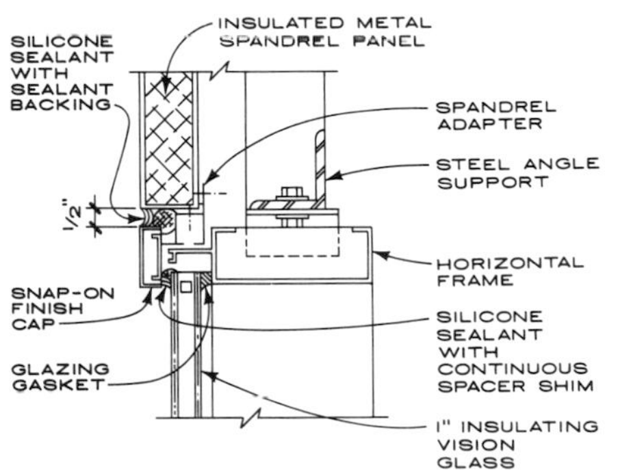
SILICONE SEALANT WITH SEALANT BACKING
INSULATED METAL SPANDREL PANEL
SPANDREL ADAPTER
STEEL ANGLE SUPPORT
HORIZONTAL FRAME
SNAP-ON FINISH CAP
SILICONE SEALANT WITH CONTINUOUS SPACER SHIM
GLAZING GASKET
1" INSULATING VISION GLASS

HEAD DETAIL 1 AT METAL SPANDREL

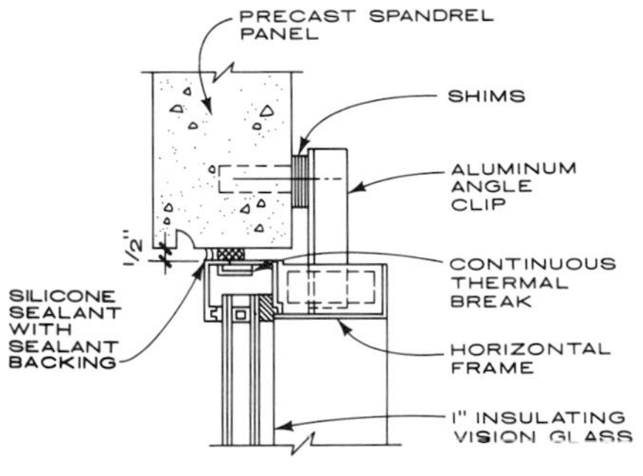
PRECAST SPANDREL PANEL
SHIMS
ALUMINUM ANGLE CLIP
CONTINUOUS THERMAL BREAK
SILICONE SEALANT WITH SEALANT BACKING
HORIZONTAL FRAME
1" INSULATING VISION GLASS

HEAD DETAIL 3 AT PRECAST SPANDREL

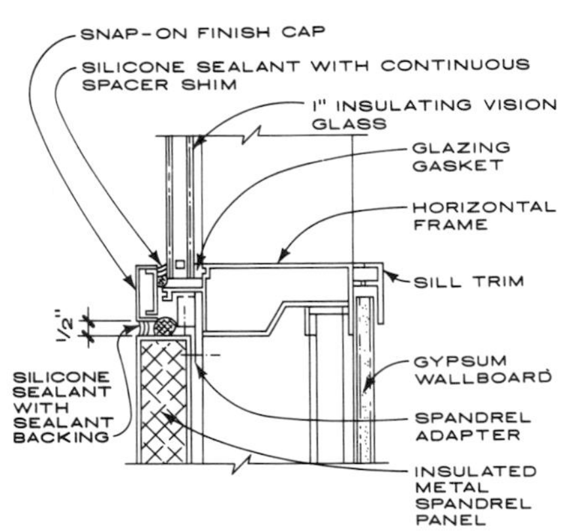
SNAP-ON FINISH CAP
SILICONE SEALANT WITH CONTINUOUS SPACER SHIM
1" INSULATING VISION GLASS
GLAZING GASKET
HORIZONTAL FRAME
SILL TRIM
GYPSUM WALLBOARD
SILICONE SEALANT WITH SEALANT BACKING
SPANDREL ADAPTER
INSULATED METAL SPANDREL PANEL

SILL DETAIL 2 AT METAL SPANDREL

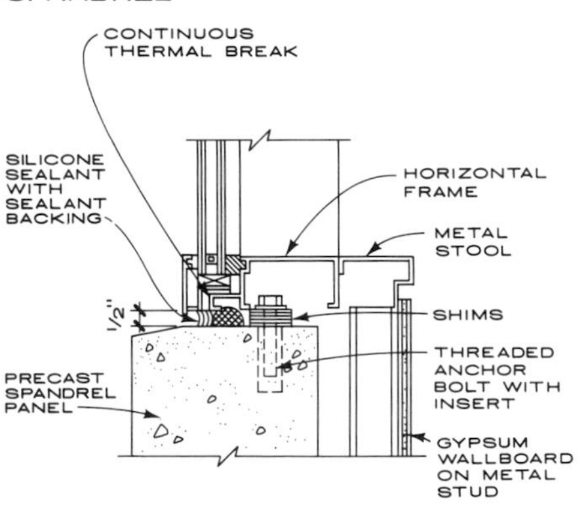
CONTINUOUS THERMAL BREAK
SILICONE SEALANT WITH SEALANT BACKING
HORIZONTAL FRAME
METAL STOOL
SHIMS
THREADED ANCHOR BOLT WITH INSERT
PRECAST SPANDREL PANEL
GYPSUM WALLBOARD ON METAL STUD

SILL DETAIL 4 AT PRECAST SPANDREL

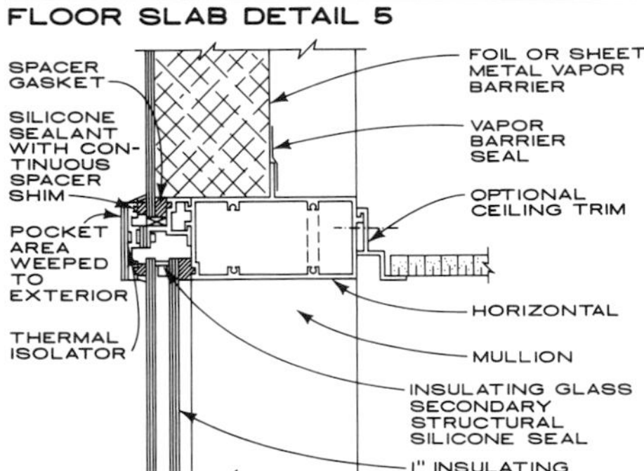
1/4" SPANDREL GLASS WITH OPACIFIER CUT BACK AT CONTACT WIDTH AREA OF THE STRUCTURAL SILICONE SEALANT
DEAD LOAD ANCHOR
CONTINUOUS FIRE-SAFING WITH IMPALING CLIPS
CONCRETE SLAB
FINISH FLOOR
INSULATION EITHER AGAINST GLASS WITH AN OPACIFIER OR AWAY FROM GLASS 2" WITHOUT AN OPACIFIER
DEAD AND WIND LOADS ANCHOR
STRUCTURAL BEAM

FLOOR SLAB DETAIL 5

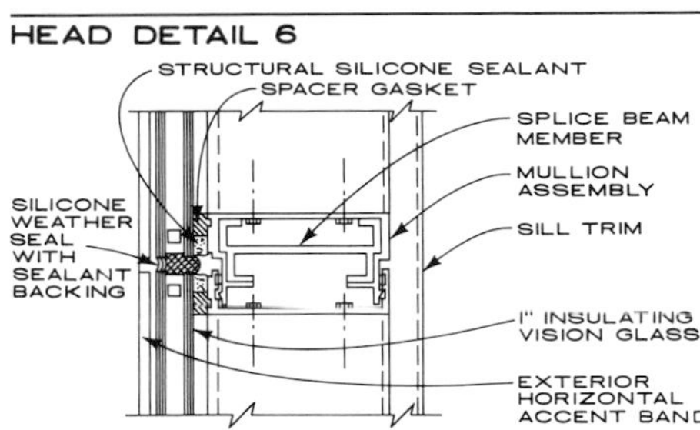
SPACER GASKET
SILICONE SEALANT WITH CONTINUOUS SPACER SHIM
POCKET AREA WEEPED TO EXTERIOR
THERMAL ISOLATOR
FOIL OR SHEET METAL VAPOR BARRIER
VAPOR BARRIER SEAL
OPTIONAL CEILING TRIM
HORIZONTAL
MULLION
INSULATING GLASS SECONDARY STRUCTURAL SILICONE SEAL
1" INSULATING VISION GLASS

HEAD DETAIL 6

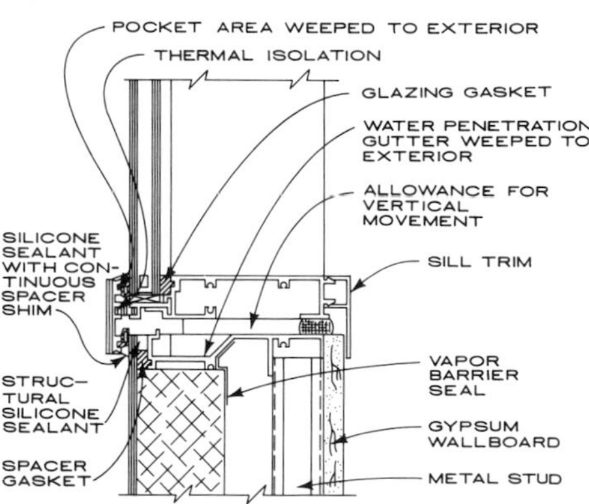
STRUCTURAL SILICONE SEALANT
SPACER GASKET
SILICONE WEATHER SEAL WITH SEALANT BACKING
SPLICE BEAM MEMBER
MULLION ASSEMBLY
SILL TRIM
1" INSULATING VISION GLASS
EXTERIOR HORIZONTAL ACCENT BAND

MULLION DETAIL 7 AT VISION GLASS

POCKET AREA WEEPED TO EXTERIOR
THERMAL ISOLATION
GLAZING GASKET
WATER PENETRATION GUTTER WEEPED TO EXTERIOR
ALLOWANCE FOR VERTICAL MOVEMENT
SILICONE SEALANT WITH CONTINUOUS SPACER SHIM
SILL TRIM
STRUCTURAL SILICONE SEALANT
VAPOR BARRIER SEAL
GYPSUM WALLBOARD
SPACER GASKET
METAL STUD

SILL DETAIL 8 AT SPANDREL GLASS

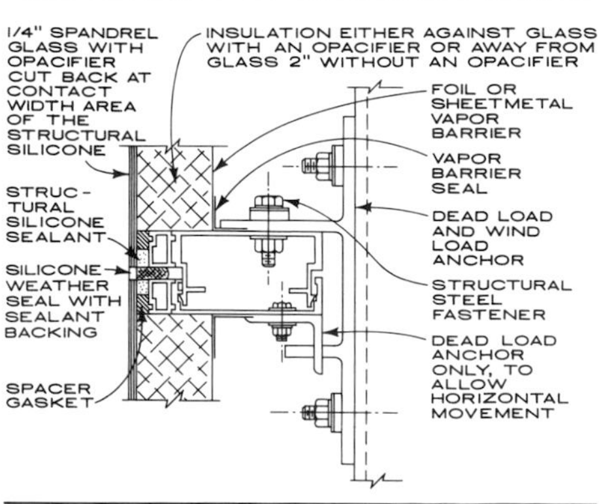
1/4" SPANDREL GLASS WITH OPACIFIER CUT BACK AT CONTACT WIDTH AREA OF THE STRUCTURAL SILICONE
INSULATION EITHER AGAINST GLASS WITH AN OPACIFIER OR AWAY FROM GLASS 2" WITHOUT AN OPACIFIER
FOIL OR SHEETMETAL VAPOR BARRIER
VAPOR BARRIER SEAL
STRUCTURAL SILICONE SEALANT
DEAD LOAD AND WIND LOAD ANCHOR
SILICONE WEATHER SEAL WITH SEALANT BACKING
STRUCTURAL STEEL FASTENER
DEAD LOAD ANCHOR ONLY, TO ALLOW HORIZONTAL MOVEMENT
SPACER GASKET

MULLION DETAIL 9 AT SPANDREL GLASS

NOTES

1. Coping detail and base detail similar to details 5 and 9 of four-sided structural curtain wall system.
2. Detail section cut numbers 1–4 are not shown on elevation, but represent its intended use for two-sided structural curtain wall system with precast and metal spandrel panel at the head and sill.
3. Detail section cut number 5 refers to note on four-sided structural sealant glazing system.

The Spector Group; North Hills, New York
Thomas F. O'Connor, AIA, ASTM; Smith, Hinchman & Grylls; Detroit, Michigan

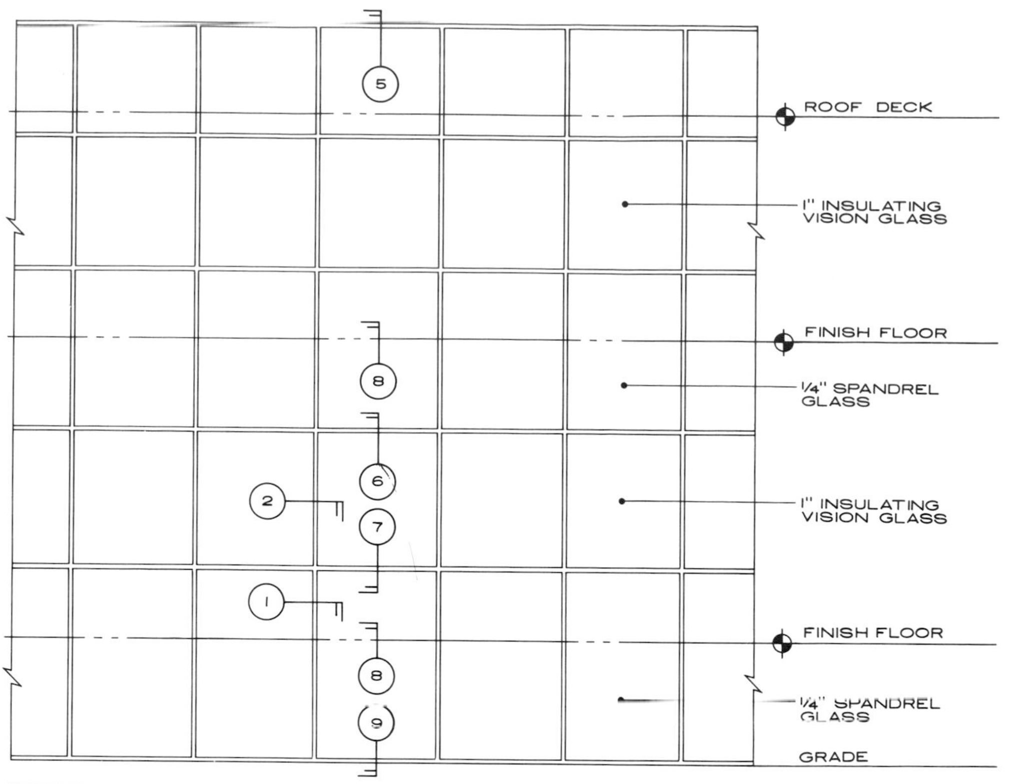
5
ROOF DECK
1" INSULATING VISION GLASS
FINISH FLOOR
8
1/4" SPANDREL GLASS
6
7
2
1" INSULATING VISION GLASS
1
FINISH FLOOR
8
9
1/4" SPANDREL GLASS
GRADE

CURTAIN WALL ELEVATION

NOTE

Detail section cut number 8 is for insulation with sheet metal vapor barrier and insulation against glass. If foil vapor barrier is used, then insulation must be of same material and rating as fire-safing material, and if insulation is 2 in. from glass, then a sheet metal vapor barrier with stiffeners is necessary.

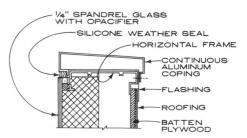

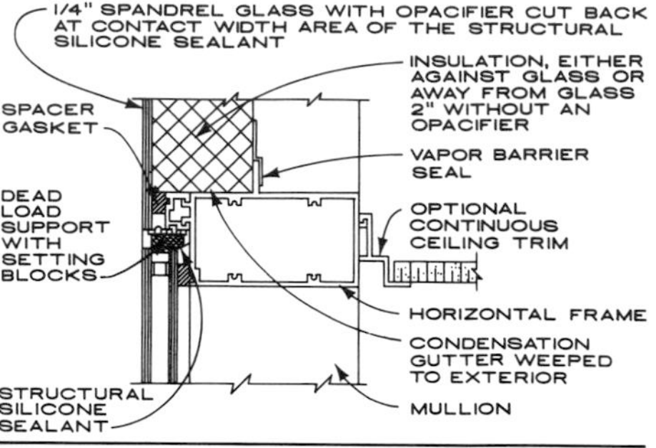
1/4" SPANDREL GLASS WITH OPACIFIER
SILICONE WEATHER SEAL
HORIZONTAL FRAME
CONTINUOUS ALUMINUM COPING
FLASHING
ROOFING
BATTEN PLYWOOD

COPING DETAIL 5

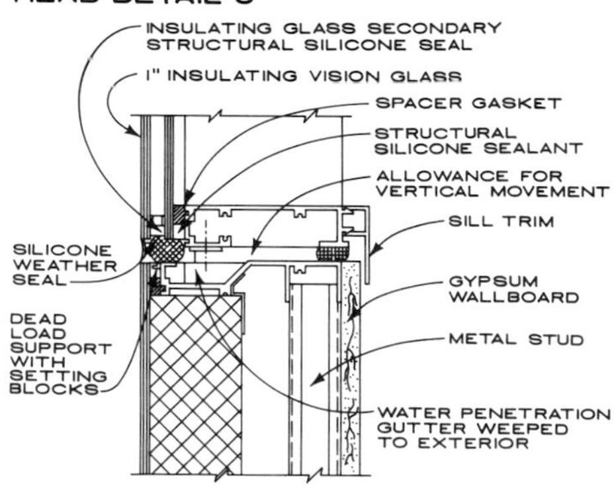
1/4" SPANDREL GLASS WITH OPACIFIER CUT BACK AT CONTACT WIDTH AREA OF THE STRUCTURAL SILICONE SEALANT
INSULATION, EITHER AGAINST GLASS OR AWAY FROM GLASS 2" WITHOUT AN OPACIFIER
SPACER GASKET
VAPOR BARRIER SEAL
DEAD LOAD SUPPORT WITH SETTING BLOCKS
OPTIONAL CONTINUOUS CEILING TRIM
HORIZONTAL FRAME
CONDENSATION GUTTER WEEPED TO EXTERIOR
STRUCTURAL SILICONE SEALANT
MULLION

HEAD DETAIL 6

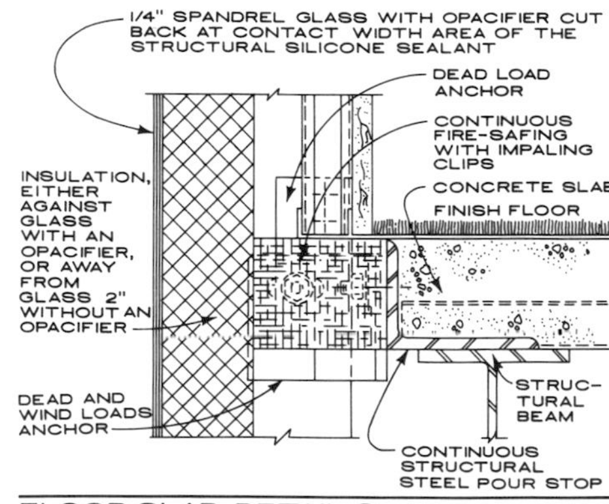
INSULATING GLASS SECONDARY STRUCTURAL SILICONE SEAL
1" INSULATING VISION GLASS
SPACER GASKET
STRUCTURAL SILICONE SEALANT
ALLOWANCE FOR VERTICAL MOVEMENT
SILL TRIM
SILICONE WEATHER SEAL
GYPSUM WALLBOARD
DEAD LOAD SUPPORT WITH SETTING BLOCKS
METAL STUD
WATER PENETRATION GUTTER WEEPED TO EXTERIOR

SILL DETAIL 7

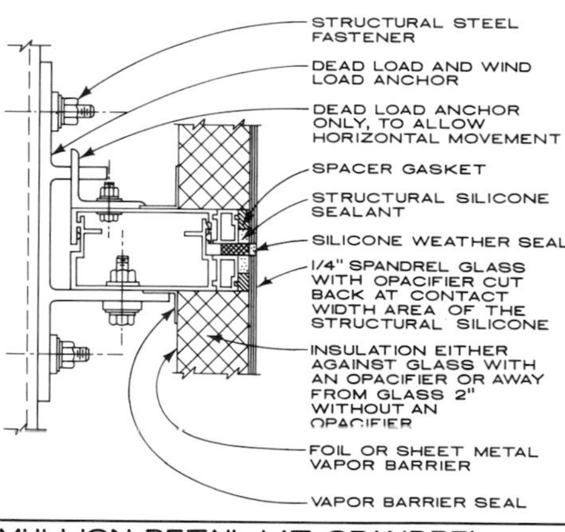
STRUCTURAL STEEL FASTENER
DEAD LOAD AND WIND LOAD ANCHOR
DEAD LOAD ANCHOR ONLY, TO ALLOW HORIZONTAL MOVEMENT
SPACER GASKET
STRUCTURAL SILICONE SEALANT
SILICONE WEATHER SEAL
1/4" SPANDREL GLASS WITH OPACIFIER CUT BACK AT CONTACT WIDTH AREA OF THE STRUCTURAL SILICONE
INSULATION EITHER AGAINST GLASS WITH AN OPACIFIER OR AWAY FROM GLASS 2" WITHOUT AN OPACIFIER
FOIL OR SHEET METAL VAPOR BARRIER
VAPOR BARRIER SEAL

MULLION DETAIL 1 AT SPANDREL GLASS

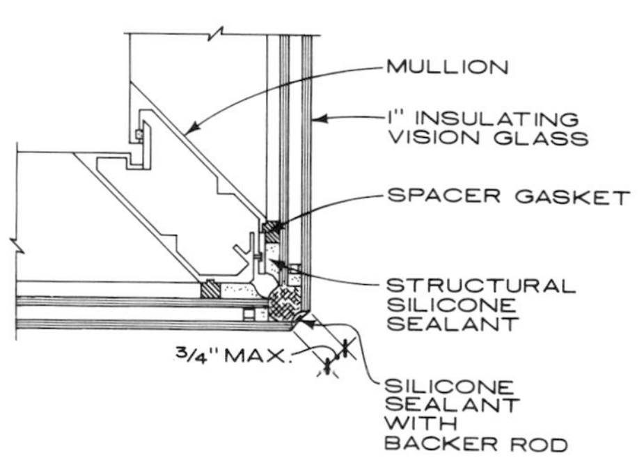
MULLION
1" INSULATING VISION GLASS
SPACER GASKET
STRUCTURAL SILICONE SEALANT
3/4" MAX.
SILICONE SEALANT WITH BACKER ROD

MULLION DETAIL 3 AT OUTSIDE CORNER

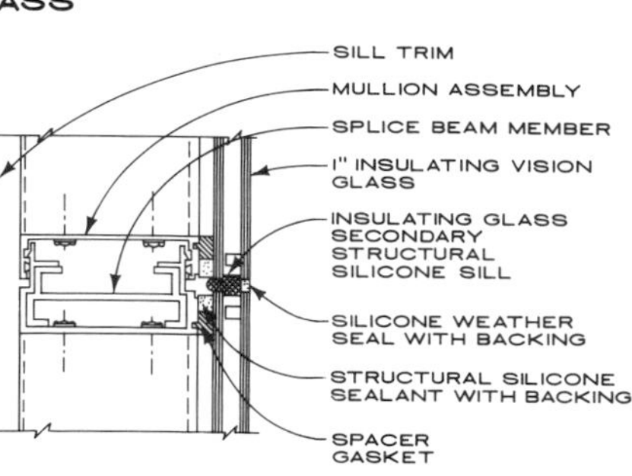
SILL TRIM
MULLION ASSEMBLY
SPLICE BEAM MEMBER
1" INSULATING VISION GLASS
INSULATING GLASS SECONDARY STRUCTURAL SILICONE SILL
SILICONE WEATHER SEAL WITH BACKING
STRUCTURAL SILICONE SEALANT WITH BACKING
SPACER GASKET

MULLION DETAIL 2 AT VISION GLASS

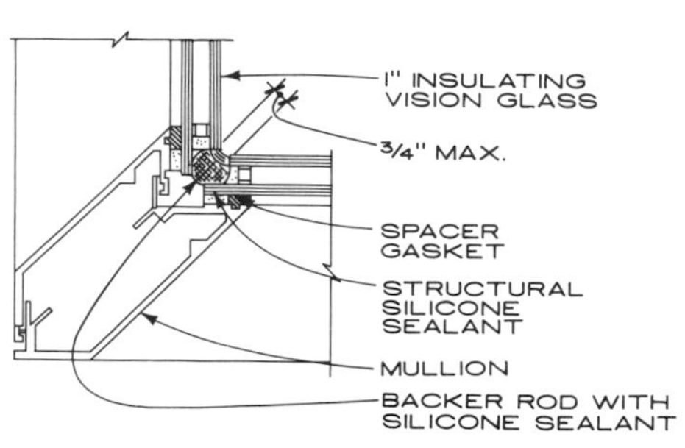
1" INSULATING VISION GLASS
3/4" MAX.
SPACER GASKET
STRUCTURAL SILICONE SEALANT
MULLION
BACKER ROD WITH SILICONE SEALANT

MULLION DETAIL 4 AT INSIDE CORNER

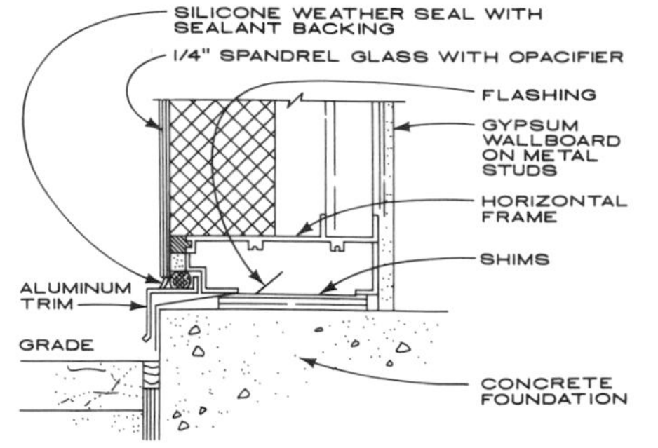
1/4" SPANDREL GLASS WITH OPACIFIER CUT BACK AT CONTACT WIDTH AREA OF THE STRUCTURAL SILICONE SEALANT
DEAD LOAD ANCHOR
CONTINUOUS FIRE-SAFING WITH IMPALING CLIPS
CONCRETE SLAB
FINISH FLOOR
INSULATION, EITHER AGAINST GLASS WITH AN OPACIFIER, OR AWAY FROM GLASS 2" WITHOUT AN OPACIFIER
DEAD AND WIND LOADS ANCHOR
STRUC-TURAL BEAM
CONTINUOUS STRUCTURAL STEEL POUR STOP

FLOOR SLAB DETAIL 8

SILICONE WEATHER SEAL WITH SEALANT BACKING
1/4" SPANDREL GLASS WITH OPACIFIER
FLASHING
GYPSUM WALLBOARD ON METAL STUDS
HORIZONTAL FRAME
SHIMS
ALUMINUM TRIM
GRADE
CONCRETE FOUNDATION

GRADE DETAIL 9

The Spector Group; North Hills, New York
Thomas F. O'Connor, AIA, ASTM; Smith, Hinchman & Grylls; Detroit, Michigan

GLAZING SYSTEMS NOTES

1. Only rubber materials formulated to recognized standards and of proven durability such as neoprene, EPDM; and silicone should be used for gaskets and blocking.
2. At least two ¼ to ⅜ in. diameter weep holes for the glazing pocket per glass lite or panel are necessary with access to weep holes not prevented by setting blocks or sealants.
3. Glazing compound or putty should not be used to glaze laminated or insulating glass in openings.
4. Sealants in contact or close proximity to gaskets, rubber blocking, and other sealants must be compatible with those materials to preclude loss of adhesion or lessened durability. Consult with the sealant manufacturer.
5. Sealant must be compatible with the insulating glass edge seal and the butyral laminate of laminated glass to preclude failure of the edge seal or delamination and discoloration of the laminate.
6. The dry glazing method requires careful design and control of tolerances of the frame opening and glazing materials to ensure the development of adequate compression sealing pressure (generally 4–10 lb/lin in. to achieve weathertightness.
7. Closed cell gaskets for dry glazing should have molded or vulcanized corners as the preferred method so as to form a continuous, joint-free glazing material around all sides of the opening.
8. The following table lists sources for specifications and installation practices for glazing materials which should be consulted when designing and specifying.

LOCK-STRIP GASKET NOTES

1. Lock-strip gasket glazing requires careful design and control of framing, gasket, and glazing tolerances to achieve the anticipated weather sealing pressures and structural capacity to resist lateral loads.
2. The best weather sealing performance is achieved with a continuous gasket having factory-formed, injection-molded joints.
3. Concrete gasket lugs require a draft on some surface of the lug to facilitate mold removal. Draft is permissible either on the sides or on top (preferred), not both. Draft on top should slope to the exterior.

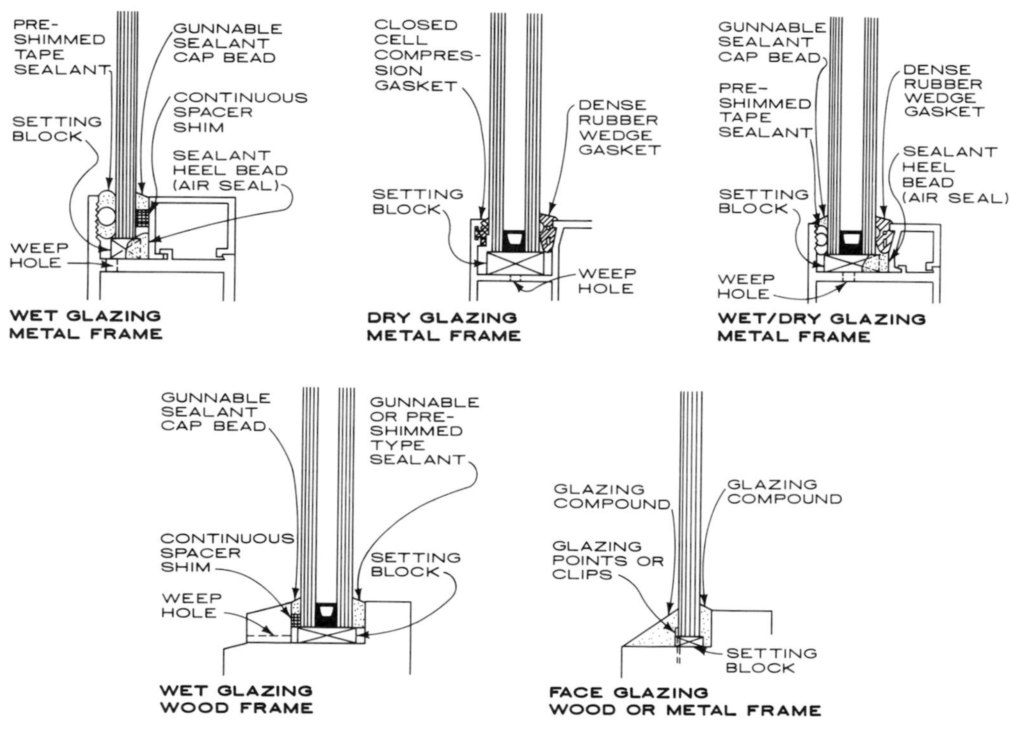
PRE-SHIMMED TAPE SEALANT
GUNNABLE SEALANT CAP BEAD
CONTINUOUS SPACER SHIM
SETTING BLOCK
SEALANT HEEL BEAD (AIR SEAL)
WEEP HOLE
WET GLAZING METAL FRAME
CLOSED CELL COMPRESSION GASKET
DENSE RUBBER WEDGE GASKET
SETTING BLOCK
WEEP HOLE
DRY GLAZING METAL FRAME
GUNNABLE SEALANT CAP BEAD
PRE-SHIMMED TAPE SEALANT
DENSE RUBBER WEDGE GASKET
SEALANT HEEL BEAD (AIR SEAL)
SETTING BLOCK
WEEP HOLE
WET/DRY GLAZING METAL FRAME
GUNNABLE SEALANT CAP BEAD
GUNNABLE OR PRE-SHIMMED TYPE SEALANT
CONTINUOUS SPACER SHIM
SETTING BLOCK
WEEP HOLE
WET GLAZING WOOD FRAME
GLAZING COMPOUND
GLAZING COMPOUND
GLAZING POINTS OR CLIPS
SETTING BLOCK
FACE GLAZING WOOD OR METAL FRAME

TYPICAL GLAZING SYSTEMS

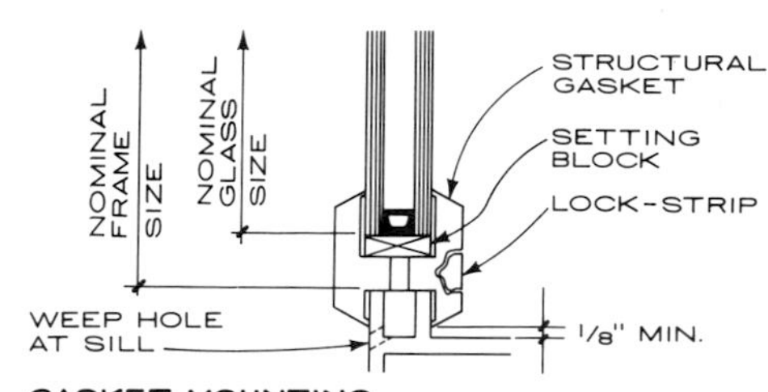
NOMINAL FRAME SIZE
NOMINAL GLASS SIZE
STRUCTURAL GASKET
SETTING BLOCK
LOCK-STRIP
WEEP HOLE AT SILL
1/8" MIN.

GASKET MOUNTING ON METAL FRAME

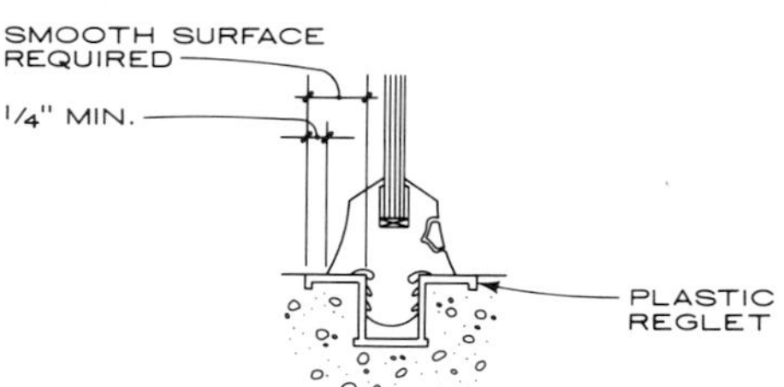
SMOOTH SURFACE REQUIRED
1/4" MIN.
PLASTIC REGLET

REGLET TYPE GASKET IN CONCRETE

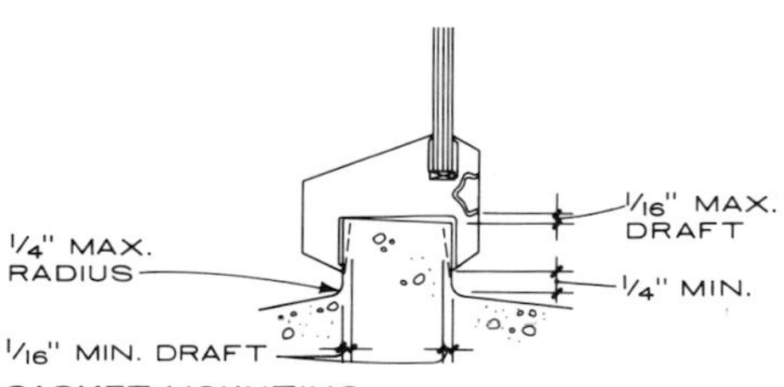
1/16" MAX. DRAFT
1/4" MAX. RADIUS
1/4" MIN.
1/16" MIN. DRAFT

GASKET MOUNTING ON CONCRETE LUG

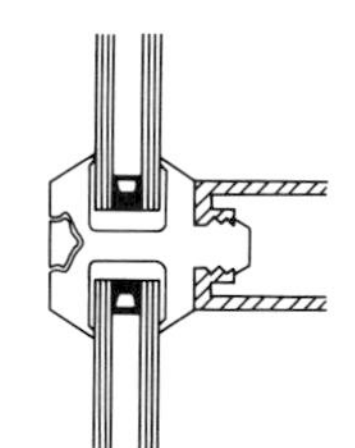

GASKET MOUNTING ON VERTICAL MULLION

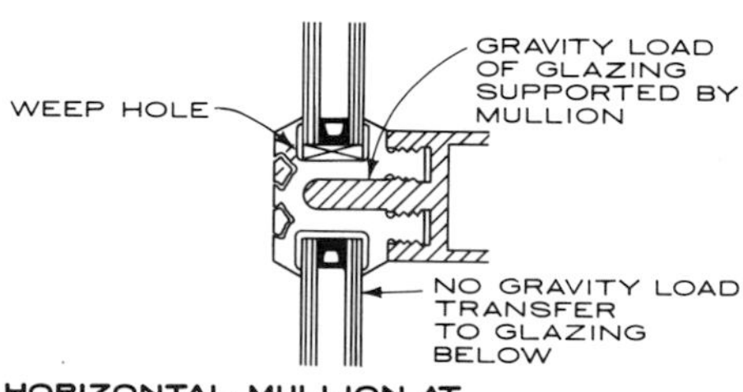
WEEP HOLE
GRAVITY LOAD OF GLAZING SUPPORTED BY MULLION
NO GRAVITY LOAD TRANSFER TO GLAZING BELOW

HORIZONTAL MULLION AT VERTICALLY STACKED GLAZING

LOCK-STRIP GASKETS

GLAZING SPECIFICATIONS*

PART	MATERIAL	SPECIFICATION	INSTALLATION PRACTICE
Closed cell rubber gasket	Neoprene Silicone EPDM	ASTM C0509	FGMA Glazing Manual
Dense wedge rubber gasket	Neoprene Silicone EPDM	ASTM C0864	FGMA Glazing Manual
Gunnable sealant	Silicone Polyurethane Polysulfide	ASTM C0920	ASTM C0962
Tape sealant	Butyl Polyisobutylene	AAMA 804.1, 806.1, 807.1	FGMA Glazing Manual
Lock-strip gasket	Neoprene EPDM	ASTM C0542	ASTM C0716, C0963, C0964
Setting and edge blocks	Neoprene Silicone EPDM	ASTM C0864	See setting block and edge block location details and FGMA Glazing Manual
Glazing compound	Oil or resin based	ASTM C0570, C0669	ASTM C0797

*AAMA, Architectural Aluminum Manufacturers Association.
ASTM, American Society for Testing and Materials.
FGMA, Flat Glass Marketing Association.

Thomas F. O'Connor, AIA, ASTM; Smith, Hinchman & Grylls; Detroit, Michigan

GENERAL NOTES

1. Information on this page is representative of industry recommendations for vertical glazing applications (within 15° of vertical). Consult with the applicable manufacturers and fabricators for specific applications or for applications at greater than 15° from vertical.
2. It is good practice to glaze at temperatures above 40°F (4°C) to preclude condensation and frost contamination of surfaces that will receive sealants. For sealant glazing below 40°F (4°C), consult the glazing sealant manufacturer.
3. Glazing materials should not be installed more than one day in advance of glass placement to avoid potential damage to the glazing materials by other trades or contamination of the materials.
4. Glazing materials used with high-performance reflective coated glass may require the consideration of additional factors for the glazing materials.
5. Glass should always be cushioned in the glazing opening by resilient glazing materials and should also be free to "float in the opening" so there is no direct contact of the glass with the perimeter framing system.
6. For glazing of polycarbonate and acrylic plastic sheet, particular attention should be given to thermal movement of the sheet and adhesion and compatibility of the sheet with glazing materials, as well as proper preparation of the glazing opening. Consult the manufacturer or fabricator for glazing recommendations.
7. Insulating, wired, and laminated glass must be installed in glazing pockets that are weeped to the exterior to preclude the detrimental effects of moisture.
8. For large glass lites the deflection characteristics of the glass should be investigated to preclude detrimental deflection which can cause glazing seal failure and glass breakage by contact of an edge or corner with the framing.
9. For setting and edge block requirements for casement, vertically pivoted and horizontally pivoted windows refer to the Flat Glass Marketing Association (FGMA) Glazing Manual.

SETTING BLOCK NOTES

1. Blocks should always be wider than the thickness of glass or panel, no more or less than two per glass or panel, and be of identical material.
2. For glass using the alternate method, verify acceptability of method with glass manufacturer or fabricator.
3. Setting block length per block
   a. Neoprene, EPDM, or silicone block = 0.1 in./sq ft of glass area; never less than 4 in. long.
   b. Lead block = 0.05 in./sq ft of glass area; never less than 4 in. long.
   c. Lock-strip gasket block = 0.5 in./sq ft of glass area; never less than 6 in. long.
4. For neoprene, EPDM, silicone, or lead blocks, the material should be 85 ± 5 shore A durometer.
5. Lead blocks should never be used with laminated, insulating, or wired glass or in lock-strip gaskets, nor should they be used with glass less than 1/2 in. thick.

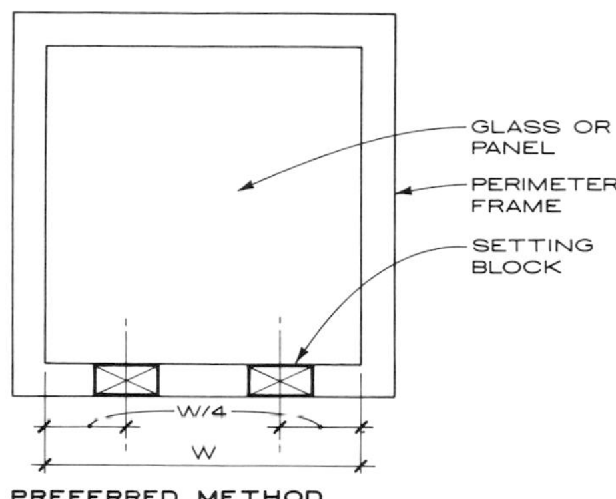
GLASS OR PANEL
PERIMETER FRAME
SETTING BLOCK
W/4
W

PREFERRED METHOD

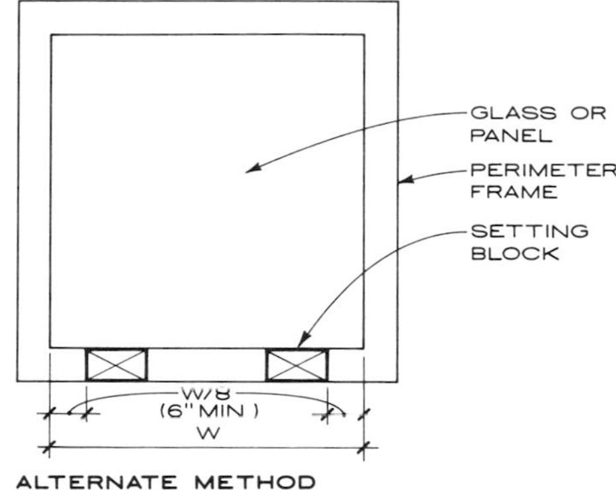
GLASS OR PANEL
PERIMETER FRAME
SETTING BLOCK
W/8
(6" MIN)
W

ALTERNATE METHOD

SETTING BLOCK LOCATIONS

EDGE BLOCK NOTES

1. Edge blocking is used to limit lateral movement of the glass or panel caused by horizontal thermal movement, building vibration, and other causes.
2. Method A is preferred.
3. Material should be neoprene, EPDM, or silicone rubber.
4. Hardness should be 65 ± 5 shore A durometer.
5. Blocks should be a minimum of 4 in. long.
6. Blocks should be placed in vertical frame spaces.
7. Blocks should be sized to permit a nominal 1/8 in. of clearance between the edge of the glass or panel and the block.

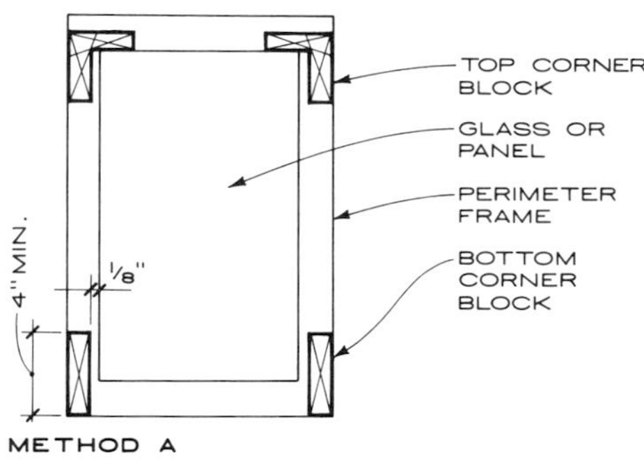
TOP CORNER BLOCK
GLASS OR PANEL
PERIMETER FRAME
BOTTOM CORNER BLOCK
4" MIN.
1/8"

METHOD A

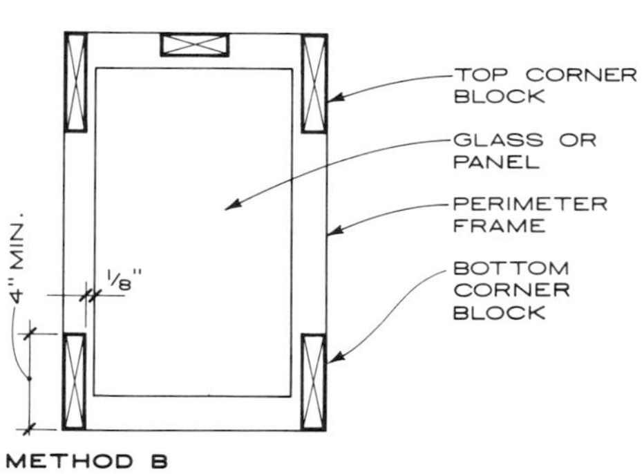
TOP CORNER BLOCK
GLASS OR PANEL
PERIMETER FRAME
BOTTOM CORNER BLOCK
4" MIN.
1/8"

METHOD B

EDGE BLOCK LOCATIONS

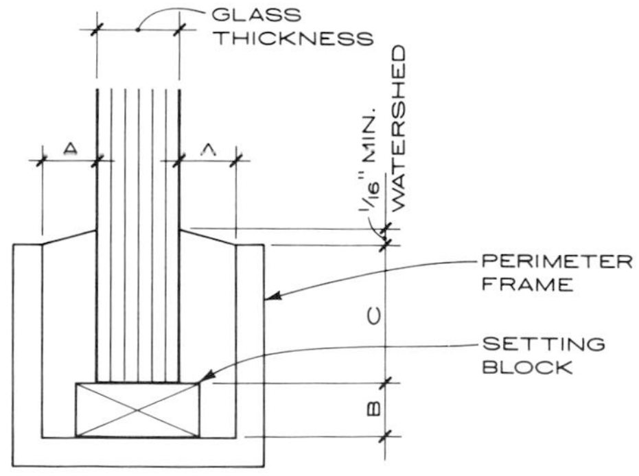
GLASS THICKNESS
A
1/16" MIN. WATERSHED
PERIMETER FRAME
SETTING BLOCK
C
B

NOTES

1. The typical clearances indicated in the adjacent table may vary by glass manufacturer or fabricator, particularly for special products or applications. Consult the glass manufacturer, fabricator, and sealing material supplier for those conditions.
2. The permissible bow and warp of large lites of heat-strengthened and tempered glass can be substantial, which may require extra face clearance.

TYPICAL FACE AND EDGE CLEARANCE AND BITE

GLASS THICKNESS		MINIMUM CLEARANCES		
IN.	MM	A = FACE	B = EDGE	C = BITE
MONOLITHIC GLASS				
SS*	2.5	1/16	1/8	1/4
1/8—DS†	3	1/8	1/8	1/4
1/8—DS‡	3	1/8	1/4	3/8
3/16†	5	1/8	3/16	5/16
3/16‡	5	1/8	1/4	3/8
1/4	6	1/8	1/4	3/8
5/16	8	3/16	5/16	7/16
3/8	10	3/16	5/16	7/16
1/2	12	1/4	3/8	7/16
5/8	15	1/4	3/8	1/2
3/4	19	1/4	1/2	5/8
7/8	22	1/4	1/2	3/4
INSULATING GLASS				
1/2	12	1/8	1/8	1/2
5/8	15	1/8	1/8	1/2
3/4	19	3/16	1/4	1/2
1	25	3/16	1/4	1/2
CERAMIC COATED SPANDREL GLASS				
1/4	6	3/16	1/4	1/2

*SS, Single strength; DS, double strength.
†Annealed glass only.
‡Tempered glass only.

FACE AND EDGE CLEARANCE AND BITE

Thomas F. O'Connor, AIA, ASTM; Smith, Hinchman & Grylls; Detroit, Michigan

ACRYLIC PLASTIC AND POLYCARBONATE SHEETS

Both materials are relatively tough, break, shatter, or crack resistant thermoplastics. They are commonly used in the clear transparent form for glazing in schools, factories, skylights, domes, display cases, and protective shields for stained glass assemblies. Certain conditions of varying temperatures and/or humidity on opposing surfaces of a single light may cause it to bow in the direction of the higher temperature and/or humidity. Though this does not affect visibility, it may cause distorted reflections. The surfaces of these materials are susceptible to scratching and abrasions. Progress is being made in developing abrasion resistant coatings. As compared with clear glass of equal size and thickness, they maintain greater resistance to impact and breakage and are lighter in weight. Polycarbonates have softer surfaces and are more impact resistant than acrylics. Acrylics generally weather better than polycarbonates. Because of a somewhat higher coefficient of thermal expansion than in clear glass and other materials with which they are used in construction, acrylics and polycarbonates are subject to a greater degree of dimensional change. In applications that must allow for wide ranges of thermal expansion, avoid inflexible installation methods. Both may be produced with or without light absorbing properties. The allowable continuous service temperature for polycarbonates is slightly higher than that for acrylics. Both may be cold formed to a smooth arc if the resulting radius of curvature is at least 100 times the thickness of the sheet for polycarbonates (180 times for acrylics) and both are supported by curved channel supports following this radius.

Mirrored coatings applied to acrylic sheets are available for interior applications and may be installed with recommended contact cements, double faced tape, clip and channel mounting, and through fastening. Distortion problems indicate that they should not be used for precise image reflectance requirements.

Certain polycarbonate sheets may be used in some bullet resisting and burglar resisting applications.

Consult the manufacturers for current information. Refer to and adhere to all applicable codes and governing authorities on fire and safety.

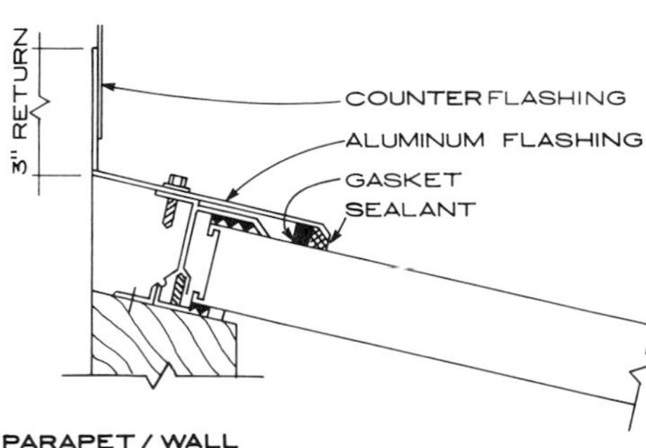
3" RETURN
COUNTER FLASHING
ALUMINUM FLASHING
GASKET
SEALANT

PARAPET / WALL

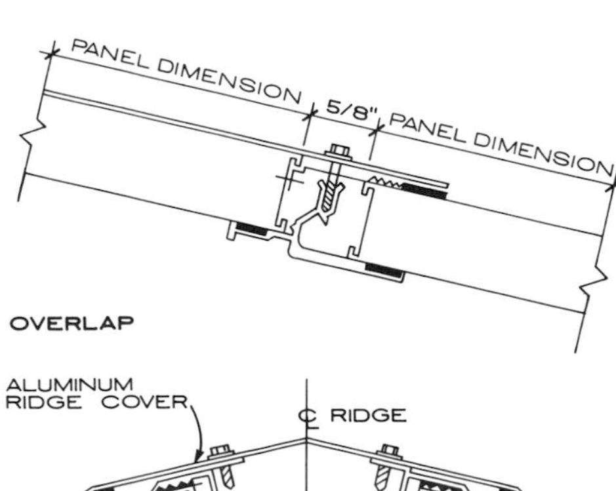
PANEL DIMENSION
5/8"
PANEL DIMENSION

OVERLAP

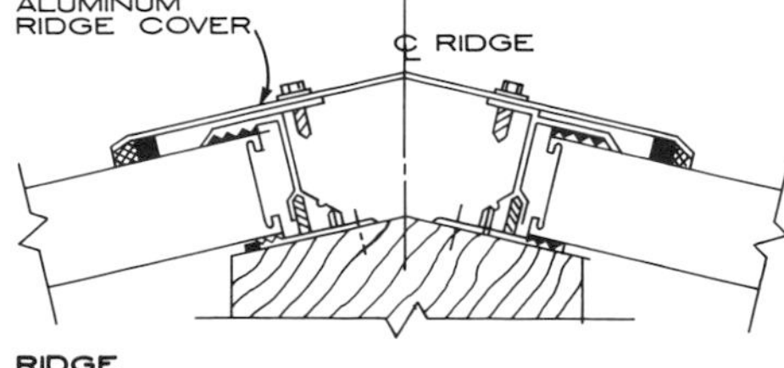
ALUMINUM RIDGE COVER
℄ RIDGE

RIDGE

SKYROOF SYSTEM DETAILS

POLYCARBONATE GLAZING

	POLY-CARBONATE SHEET THICKNESS	SHORT DIMENSION	RABBET DEPTH
Small lights	1/8″	24″	1/2″
Intermediate lights	3/16″ 1/4″	36″ 48″	3/4″ 3/4″
Large lights	3/8″ 1/2″	60″ 72″	1″ 1″

NOTES

1. Rabbet width is determined by sheet thickness plus sealant and tape as recommended by sealant tape manufacturers.
2. To select polycarbonate sheet thickness based on wind loads refer to manufacturers' information.

SMALL ACRYLIC LIGHTS

Maximum dimension to 24″
Minimum thickness—0.100″
Minimum rabbet depth 9/32″

INTERMEDIATE ACRYLIC LIGHTS

ACRYLIC THICKNESS	MAXIMUM SASH OPENING: SQUARE	MAXIMUM SASH OPENING: RECTANGULAR	RABBET DIMENSIONS: DEPTH	RABBET DIMENSIONS: WIDTH
0.125″	40″ x 40″	30″ x 42″	1/2″	3/8″
0.125″	55″ x 55″	36″ x 68″	3/4″	3/8″
0.187″	42″ x 42″	30″ x 45″	1/2″	7/16″
0.187″	63″ x 63″	36″ x 72″	3/4″	7/16″
0.250″	44″ x 44″	30″ x 46″	1/2″	1/2″
0.250″	69″ x 69″	36″ x 72″	3/4″	1/2″

LARGE ACRYLIC LIGHTS

ACRYLIC THICKNESS	LONG DIMENSIONS	RABBET DIMENSIONS*: DEPTH	RABBET DIMENSIONS*: WIDTH
0.187	57″ to 85″	3/4″	7/16″
0.250	78″ to 96″	1″	5/8″
0.250	108″ to 144″	1 1/8″	3/4″
0.375	72″ to 108″	1″	3/4″
0.375	108″ to 144″	1 1/8″	7/8″
0.500	114″ to 144″	1 1/8″	1″

* When darker (less than 60% light transmittance) transparent tints of acrylic plastic are used, rabbet depth shown above should be increased by 1/4″ to allow for greater thermal expansion resulting from solar energy absorption.

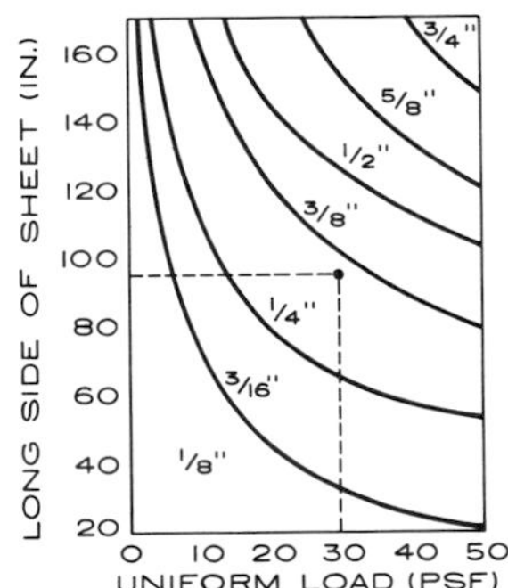
LONG SIDE OF SHEET (IN.)
160
140
120
100
80
60
40
20
0 10 20 30 40 50
UNIFORM LOAD (PSF)
3/4"
5/8"
1/2"
3/8"
1/4"
3/16"
1/8"

ACRYLIC GLAZING GRAPH
Design load data—large area acrylic glazing

Problem:
Size = 48 x 96 in.
Design load = 30 psf

Solution:
Select 1/4 in.
Sheet thickness

Data apply to square and rectangular lights of acrylic sheets when the length is no more than three times the width. All edges continuously held.

Sheet thickness section is based on total deflection under uniform load limited to 5% of the short side, or 3 in., whichever is smaller.

ACRYLIC SHEET EXPANSION ALLOWANCE

SASH LENGTH OR HEIGHT (IN.)	REDUCE ACRYLIC GLAZING LENGTH OR HEIGHT: CLEAR ACRYLIC (IN.)	REDUCE ACRYLIC GLAZING LENGTH OR HEIGHT: TINTED ACRYLIC (IN.)
0 to 36	1/16	1/16
36 to 60	1/8	3/16
60 to 96	3/16	5/16
96 to 132	1/4	3/8
132 to 144	5/16	1/2

Note: Both length and height must be reduced according to this table. For polycarbonate glazing expansion allowance, refer to manufacturer's literature.

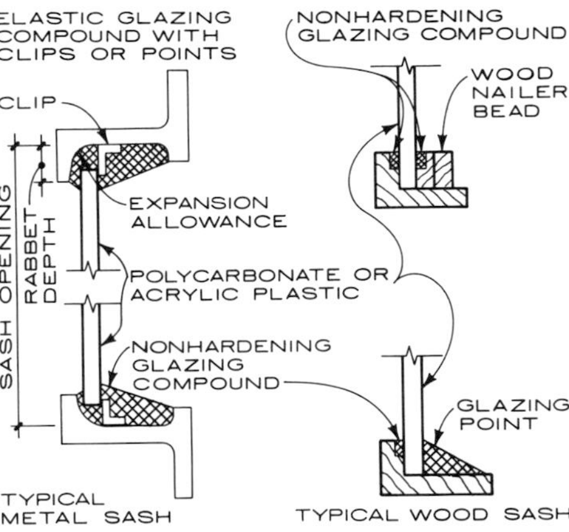
ELASTIC GLAZING COMPOUND WITH CLIPS OR POINTS
NONHARDENING GLAZING COMPOUND
CLIP
WOOD NAILER BEAD
SASH OPENING
RABBET DEPTH
EXPANSION ALLOWANCE
POLYCARBONATE OR ACRYLIC PLASTIC
NONHARDENING GLAZING COMPOUND
GLAZING POINT
TYPICAL METAL SASH
TYPICAL WOOD SASH

SMALL LIGHTS

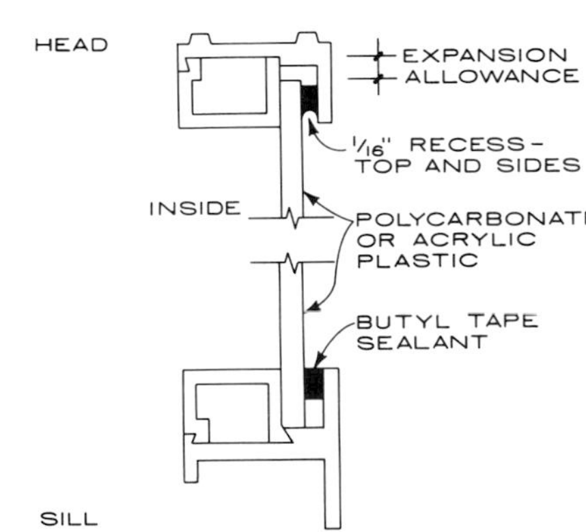
HEAD
EXPANSION ALLOWANCE
1/16" RECESS – TOP AND SIDES
INSIDE
POLYCARBONATE OR ACRYLIC PLASTIC
BUTYL TAPE SEALANT
SILL

INTERMEDIATE LIGHTS

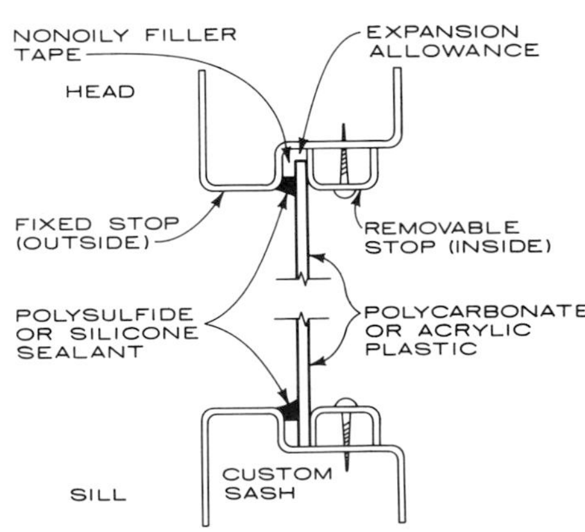
NONOILY FILLER TAPE
EXPANSION ALLOWANCE
HEAD
FIXED STOP (OUTSIDE)
REMOVABLE STOP (INSIDE)
POLYSULFIDE OR SILICONE SEALANT
POLYCARBONATE OR ACRYLIC PLASTIC
CUSTOM SASH
SILL

LARGE LIGHTS

PLASTIC GLAZING DETAILS

Skidmore, Owings & Merrill

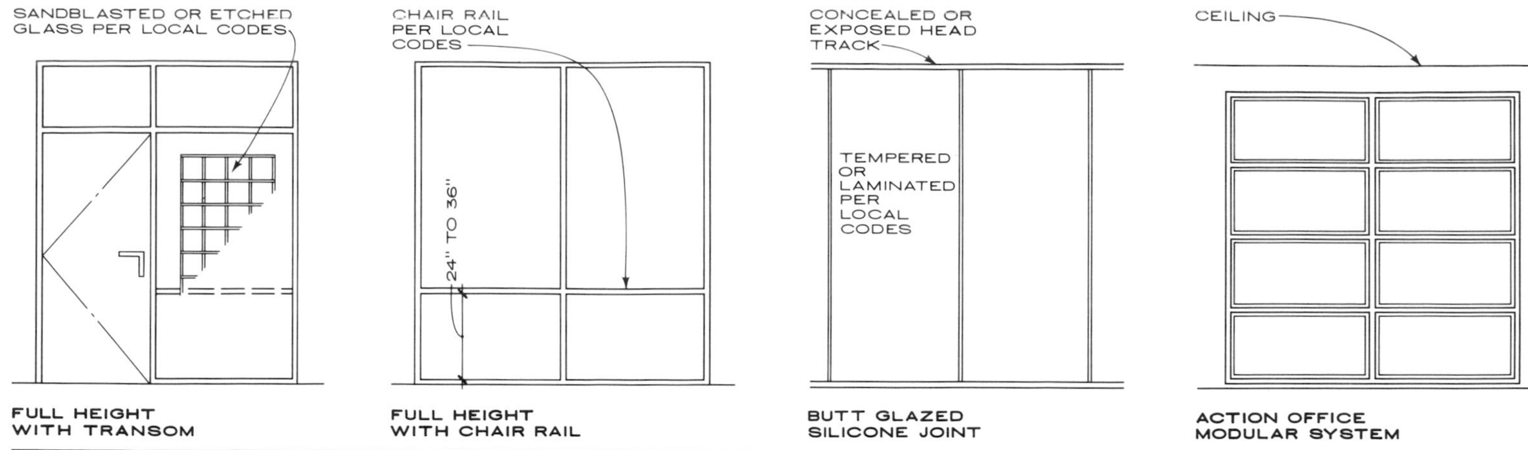
SANDBLASTED OR ETCHED GLASS PER LOCAL CODES
CHAIR RAIL PER LOCAL CODES
24" TO 36"
CONCEALED OR EXPOSED HEAD TRACK
TEMPERED OR LAMINATED PER LOCAL CODES
CEILING
FULL HEIGHT WITH TRANSOM
FULL HEIGHT WITH CHAIR RAIL
BUTT GLAZED SILICONE JOINT
ACTION OFFICE MODULAR SYSTEM

GLASS PARTITION ELEVATIONS

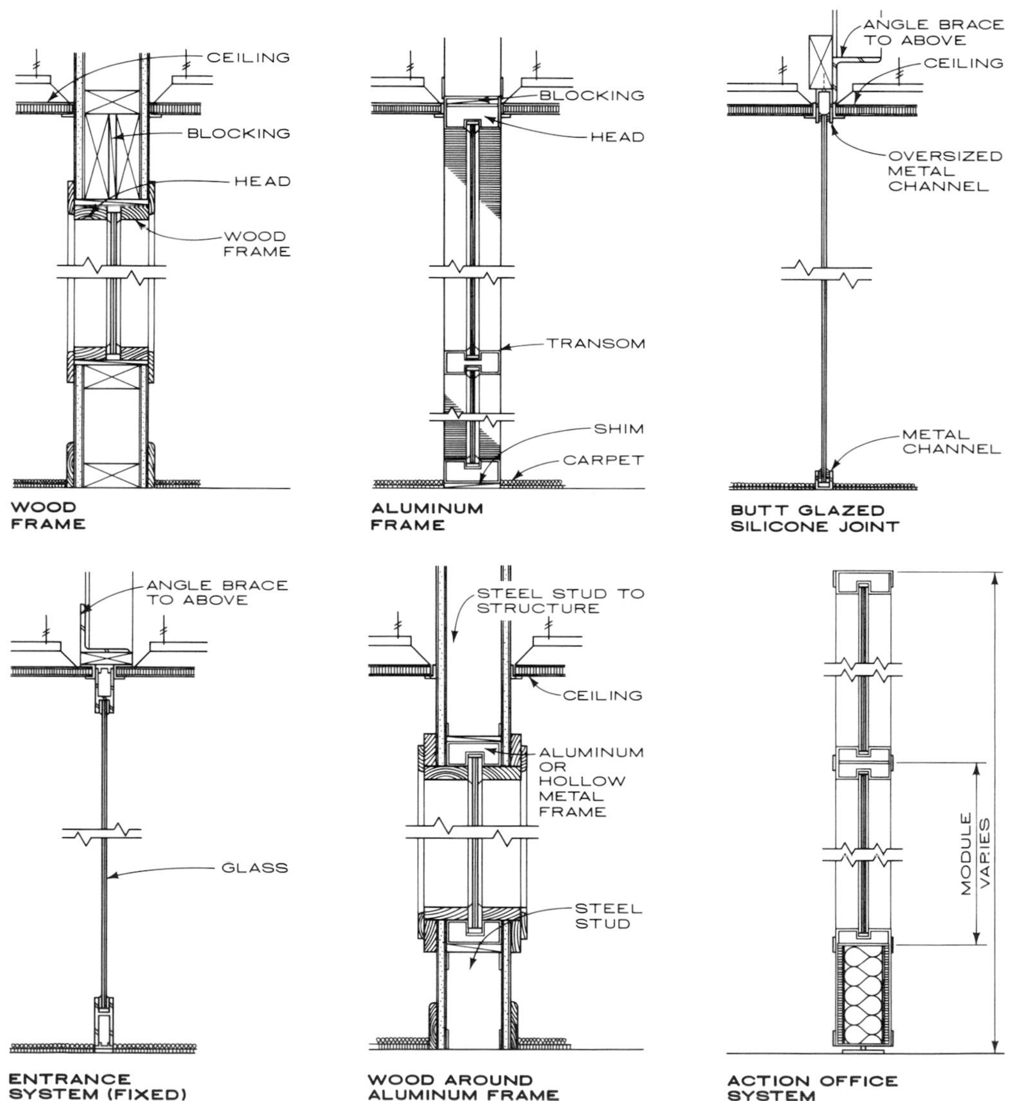
CEILING
BLOCKING
HEAD
WOOD FRAME
WOOD FRAME
BLOCKING
HEAD
TRANSOM
SHIM
CARPET
ALUMINUM FRAME
ANGLE BRACE TO ABOVE
CEILING
OVERSIZED METAL CHANNEL
METAL CHANNEL
BUTT GLAZED SILICONE JOINT
ANGLE BRACE TO ABOVE
GLASS
ENTRANCE SYSTEM (FIXED)
STEEL STUD TO STRUCTURE
CEILING
ALUMINUM OR HOLLOW METAL FRAME
STEEL STUD
WOOD AROUND ALUMINUM FRAME
MODULE VARIES
ACTION OFFICE SYSTEM

GLASS PARTITION SECTIONS

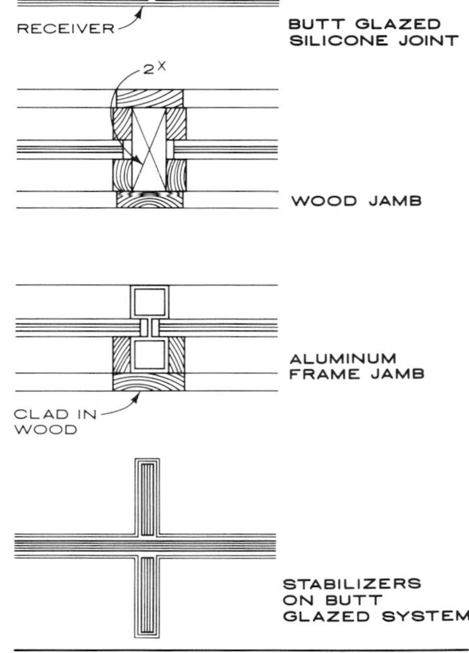
RECEIVER
BUTT GLAZED SILICONE JOINT
2X
WOOD JAMB
ALUMINUM FRAME JAMB
CLAD IN WOOD
STABILIZERS ON BUTT GLAZED SYSTEM

PLAN SECTIONS

GLAZED PARTITION NOTES

1. Interior glazed partitions are available in a variety of standard sizes, materials, and colors. Many manufacturers accommodate special or custom designs.
2. Finishes: Aluminum frames usually come in standard anodized or painted finishes. Many manufacturers now offer rich colors as well. Wood and hollow metal frames can be painted or finished in any tone or color. Action office systems are available in a wide array of colors and finishes, trimmed in wood, metal, or plastic.
3. Silicone glazing (butt glazing) partitions are framed at the top and bottom with either exposed or concealed frames. It is important that the glass thickness be in correct proportion to the unbraced length. If thickness alone cannot handle the span, then glass stabilizers should be used (see diagram).
4. Most manufacturers of action office systems offer a variety of glazed units to be incorporated in their system. Many systems are available with patterned, etched, or tinted glass for safety and privacy.

DRAPERIES

Draperies usually are custom made to specification. Drapery length is unlimited. Fabric width, usually 48 to 118 in. wide, does not limit final drapery width, but affects fabrication only. Considerations in drapery selection include: fabric weight, pleating (fullness), number of seams, track capacity, type of mounting track, type of draw, and control cords location.

SHADES

In addition to the common opaque shade, many shades with excellent shading coefficients that retain a high degree of transparency are available. Single shades usually are limited to 72 in. wide x 198 in. long (manual) or 312 in. long (motorized).

SHUTTERS

Interior shutters are available with fixed or operable vanes in all sizes up to 18 x 78 in. for 3/4 in. thick units and 48 x 96 in. for 1 1/4 in. thick units. Frames usually are painted or stained wood. Some styles use panels of cane, metal, plastic, or solid wood in lieu of vanes.

GLASS COATINGS

A full array of shading films and screens is available for use in new and existing glazing. Films range from totally reflective to slightly tinted. Many also provide excellent shading coefficients.

Sterling Thompson, AIA, and Larry Gawloski, AIA; ARCHIFORMS; Waco, Texas

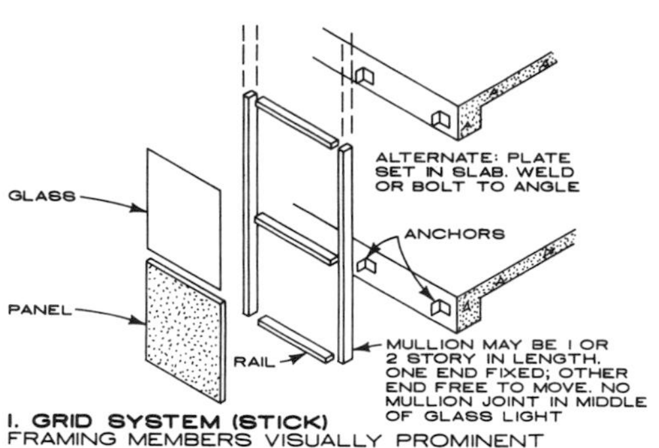
ALTERNATE: PLATE SET IN SLAB. WELD OR BOLT TO ANGLE
GLASS
ANCHORS
PANEL
RAIL
MULLION MAY BE 1 OR 2 STORY IN LENGTH. ONE END FIXED; OTHER END FREE TO MOVE. NO MULLION JOINT IN MIDDLE OF GLASS LIGHT

1. GRID SYSTEM (STICK)
FRAMING MEMBERS VISUALLY PROMINENT
COMPONENTS INSTALLED PIECE BY PIECE

CUSTOM TYPE

Walls designed specifically for one project, using specially designed parts and details. Such walls may be used on buildings of any height, but are more typical of multistoried structures. Included in this category are the highly publicized (and often more expensive) walls that serve as design pacesetters. Methods 1, 2, and 3 above are used for custom-type walls.

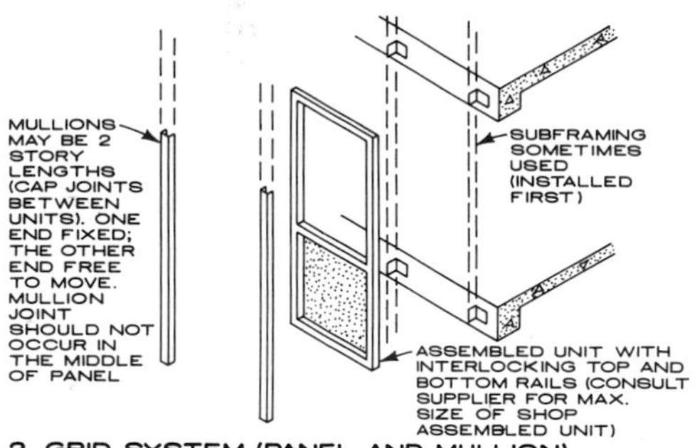
MULLIONS MAY BE 2 STORY LENGTHS (CAP JOINTS BETWEEN UNITS). ONE END FIXED; THE OTHER END FREE TO MOVE. MULLION JOINT SHOULD NOT OCCUR IN THE MIDDLE OF PANEL
SUBFRAMING SOMETIMES USED (INSTALLED FIRST)
ASSEMBLED UNIT WITH INTERLOCKING TOP AND BOTTOM RAILS (CONSULT SUPPLIER FOR MAX. SIZE OF SHOP ASSEMBLED UNIT)

2. GRID SYSTEM (PANEL AND MULLION)
FRAMING MEMBERS VISUALLY PROMINENT
PANEL PREASSEMBLED AND INSTALLED AS SHOWN

COMMERCIAL TYPE

Walls made up principally of parts and details standardized by the manufacturer and assembled either in the manufacturer's stock patterns or in accord with the architect's design. This type is commonly used on one- and two-story buildings and on taller structures. Commercial walls cost less because of quantity production and also offer the advantages of proven performance. Methods 1 and 2 above are used for commercial-type walls.

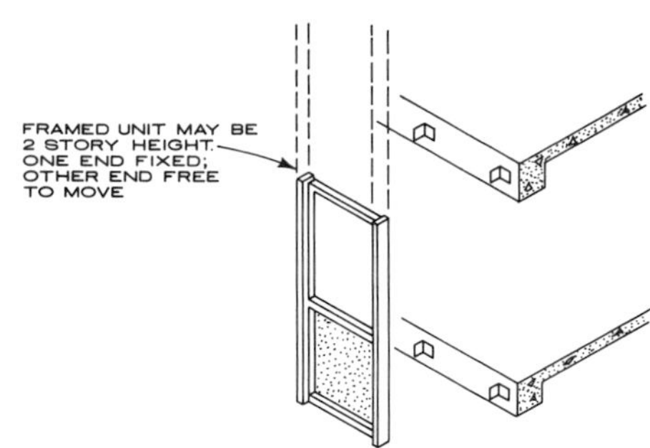
FRAMED UNIT MAY BE 2 STORY HEIGHT. ONE END FIXED; OTHER END FREE TO MOVE

3. PANEL SYSTEM
COMPLETELY PREASSEMBLED UNITS; MAY OR MAY NOT INCLUDE INTERIOR FINISH

INDUSTRIAL TYPE

Walls in which ribbed, fluted, or otherwise preformed metal sheets in stock sizes are used along with standard metal sash as the principal components. This type of metal curtain wall has a long history of satisfactory performance and, in its insulated form, is used in buildings other than industrial use-type buildings.

CLASSIFICATION BY CONSTRUCTION AND TYPE

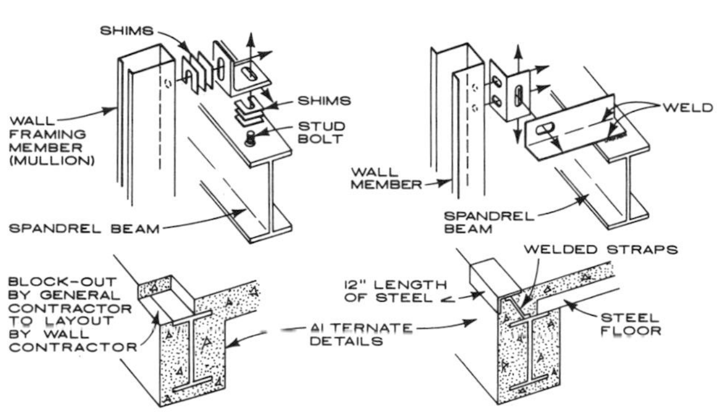
SHIMS
WALL FRAMING MEMBER (MULLION)
SHIMS
STUD BOLT
WALL MEMBER
WELD
SPANDREL BEAM
SPANDREL BEAM
WELDED STRAPS
BLOCK-OUT BY GENERAL CONTRACTOR TO LAYOUT BY WALL CONTRACTOR
12" LENGTH OF STEEL
ALTERNATE DETAILS
STEEL FLOOR

STEEL STRUCTURE

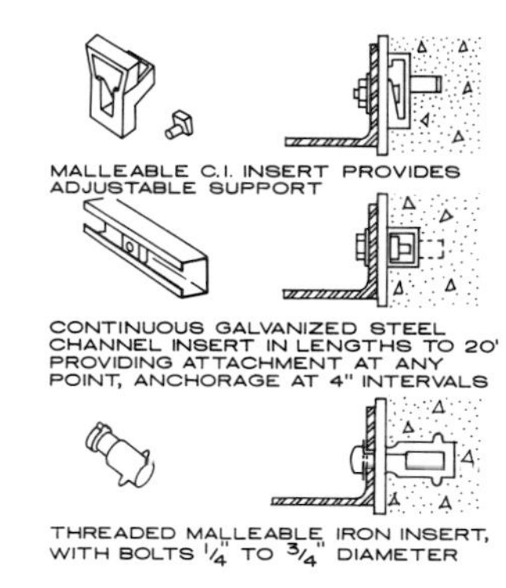
MALLEABLE C.I. INSERT PROVIDES ADJUSTABLE SUPPORT
CONTINUOUS GALVANIZED STEEL CHANNEL INSERT IN LENGTHS TO 20' PROVIDING ATTACHMENT AT ANY POINT, ANCHORAGE AT 4" INTERVALS
THREADED MALLEABLE IRON INSERT, WITH BOLTS 1/4" TO 3/4" DIAMETER

CONCRETE STRUCTURE

NOTES

1. Anchorage devices must permit three-dimensional adjustment. Metal-to-metal connections subject to intentional movement should be designed to eliminate noise caused by movement due to temperature change.
2. Anchors must be designed to withstand wind loads acting outward and inward as well as other required loads.
3. Anchors must be permanently secured in position after final assembly and adjustment of wall components.
4. All anchorage members must be corrosion resistant or protected against corrosive forces.
5. Shim plates may be installed between vertical leg of angle anchor and concrete structure, as required, for proper anchor alignment.

ATTACHMENT AND ANCHORAGE DETAILS

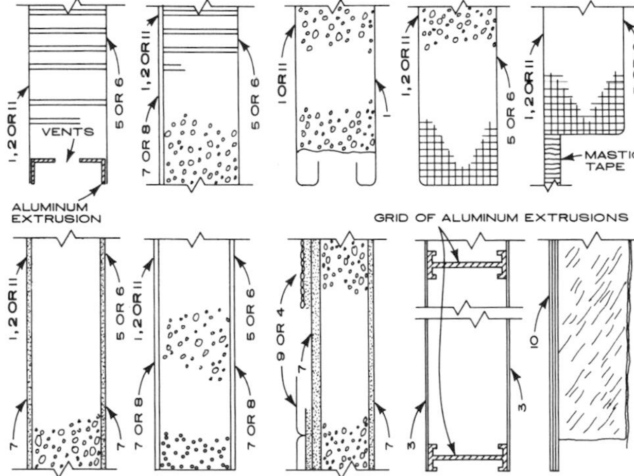
VENTS
ALUMINUM EXTRUSION
MASTIC TAPE
GRID OF ALUMINUM EXTRUSIONS
1,2 OR 11
5 OR 6
7 OR 8
9 OR 4

REPRESENTATIVE INSULATING PANEL TYPES
(EXTERIOR FACE ON LEFT)

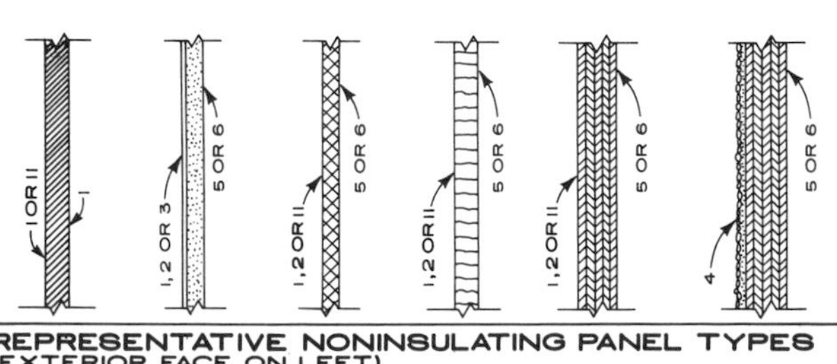
1 OR 11
1,2 OR 3
5 OR 6
1,2 OR 11

REPRESENTATIVE NONINSULATING PANEL TYPES
(EXTERIOR FACE ON LEFT)

TYPICAL CORE MATERIALS

- FIBER CEMENT
- TEMPERED HARDBOARD
- ALUMINUM HONEYCOMB
- EXTERIOR GRADE PLYWOOD
- PAPER HONEYCOMB
- FOAMED PLASTIC
- CELLULAR GLASS
- POLYETHYLENE
- PERLITE BEADS IN MINERAL BINDER
- FIBERGLASS ALUMINUM FOIL

TYPICAL FACING MATERIALS

1. Aluminum or stainless-steel sheet.
2. Porcelain enameled metal.
3. Glass-reinforced plastic sheet.
4. Stone chips in plastic matrix.
5. Galvanized bonderized steel sheet.
6. Aluminum sheet.
7. Fiber cementboard.
8. Tempered hardboard.
9. Ceramic tile in plastic matrix.
10. Opaque tinted glass.
11. Organic color coating on aluminum.

PROPERTIES OF COMMON INSULATING CORE MATERIALS

MATERIAL	DENSITY (LB/CU FT)	APPROXIMATE K VALUE
Paper honeycomb	2.5–7.0	0.45–0.55
Paper honeycomb, with foamed plastic fill	4.5–10.0	0.20–0.35
Paper honeycomb, with vermiculite fill	5–14	0.35–0.40
Polystyrene foam, extruded	1.7–3.5	0.20–0.26
Polyurethane foam	1.5–3.0	0.18
Polyisocyanurate foam	2.0	0.18
Phenolic foam	2.5	0.12
Fiberglass	0.3–2.0	0.23–0.27
Cellular glass	8.5	0.35
Perlite beads in mineral binder	11	0.36

GENERAL REMARKS

1. Local codes and ordinances should be consulted for fire resistance requirements of panel construction. This depends, in part, on conditions of use, degree of fire exposure, and core material type.
2. Choice of core material should be made with consideration of potential thermal bowing of panel, flatness of facing materials, oil-canning of facing materials, moisture resistance of panel, and thermal resistance aging characteristics of the core material.

Skidmore, Owings & Merrill
Thomas F. O'Connor, AIA, ASTM; Smith, Hinchman & Grylls; Detroit, Michigan

METAL CURTAIN WALLS

Exterior metal and glass enclosure walls require more careful development and skilled erection than traditional wall construction. Because metal and glass react differently to environmental conditions than do other wall materials, the technology is different from all other enclosure systems.

Errors in judgment can be avoided if behavior of the wall is understood. Some of the important considerations for successful curtain wall development are delineated below. Further in-depth material is available from the Architectural Aluminum Manufacturers Association (AAMA), the Flat Glass Marketing Association (FGMA), and standards developed by American Society for Testing and Materials (ASTM) committees C24 on building seals and sealants and E06 on performance of building constructions. See index under "Structural Sealant Glazing" for additional information that should be considered when developing a structural sealant curtain wall system.

FUNCTION OF THE WALL

The metal and glass curtain wall functions as an "enclosure system" which, when properly developed, can serve multiple functions: (1) withstand the action of the elements; (2) control the passage inward and outward of heat, light, air, and sound; (3) prevent or control access from outside.

NATURAL FORCES

Curtain wall development is determined in part by the impact of natural forces. Natural forces that cause the most concern and failures are (1) water, (2) wind, (3) sunlight, (4) temperature, (5) gravity, and (6) seismic forces. To understand the impact of these forces on curtain wall development, the effects of each should be separately examined.

WATER

The most frequent cause of problems with all enclosures is leakage from rain, snow, vapor, or condensate. Wind driven moisture can enter very small openings and may move within the wall, appearing far from its point of entry. Water vapor can penetrate microscopic pores and will condense on cool surfaces. Such moisture trapped within a wall can result in lessened durability of the wall which can result in serious damage that is difficult to detect. Leaks are usually limited to joints and openings, which must be designed to provide a weathertight enclosure.

WIND

Structural design development of the wall must take into account both positive and negative pressures caused by wind action, increasing in effect depending on the height and shape of the building. Increases in wind loading will occur in corner areas of the building and must be considered accordingly. Framing members, panels, and glass thicknesses should be determined by maximum wind load anticipated and permissible deflection allowable. Winds contribute to the movement of the wall, affecting joint seals and wall anchorage. The effect of positive or negative wind pressure can cause stress reversal on framing members and glass and will cause water to travel in any direction (including upward) across the face of the wall. The state of the art is to conduct scale model wind studies in a boundary layer wind tunnel to more realistically establish expected prevailing wind patterns and their effects on the building cladding. Wind is a major factor in potential water leakage.

SUNLIGHT

The ultraviolet spectrum of sunlight will cause breakdown of organic materials such as color pigments, various rubber gaskets, plastics, and sealants. Fading and failure of these materials will cause problems with the appearance and weathertightness of the curtain wall. Only quality organic materials should be used, and they should be tested for resistance to ultraviolet radiation and ozone attack.

Sunlight passing through glass can cause excessive brightness and glare and will cause fading of interior furnishings and finishes. Shading devices and the use of glare-reducing or high-performance types of glass should be considered in development of the wall.

TEMPERATURE

Change in temperature causes the expansion and contraction of materials. Control of the passage of heat or cold through the wall is also required. Thermal movement as a result of solar heating is one of the major problems in curtain wall development. Minimum outdoor temperatures vary about 80°F. Throughout the country, the maximum surface temperature of the darker colored surfaces on buildings can range as high as 170°F. This temperature fluctuation, both daily and seasonally, critically affects wall development. Thermal expansion and contraction is much greater in metals than in wood or masonry.

Heat passage through the wall causes heat gain in hot weather and heat loss in cold weather, the relative importance of the two varying with geographic location. Thermal insulation of opaque wall areas becomes an extremely important consideration, especially whenever these areas constitute a large portion of the total wall area. When vision glass areas predominate, the use of high-performance glasses and the minimizing of through metal or "cold bridges" (usually by inserting continuous nonmetallic breaks in the metal assembly) are more effective in lowering the heat transfer (U-value) through the wall.

GRAVITY

Because gravity is constant and static rather than variable and dynamic, gravity is a less critical force affecting the development of a window wall design, but is important in that it should be recognized. It causes deflection in horizontal load-carrying members, particularly under the weight of large sheets of heavy glass. However, because the weight of the wall is transferred at frequent intervals to the building frame, the structural effect of gravity is small in comparison with that imposed by wind action. Far greater gravity forces, in the form of floor and roof loads, are acting on the building frame to which the wall is attached. As these loads may cause deflections and displacements of the frame, connections of the wall to this frame must be designed to provide sufficient relative movement to ensure that the displacements do not impose vertical loads on the wall itself.

SEISMIC

Seismic (earthquake) loadings will produce additional static and dynamic loadings to the window wall system. Seismic loadings will produce both vertical and horizontal deflections of the wall. This will necessitate special energy absorption considerations in the detail of all wall anchorages and adequate consideration of the joints between curtain wall members.

DESIGN DEVELOPMENT CONSIDERATIONS: STRUCTURAL INTEGRITY

Structural integrity of the curtain wall is a prime concern involving the same design procedures used in any other exterior wall. However, deficiencies of weathertightness and temperature movements are more prevalent than deficiencies in strength, which will be elaborated upon further.

The structural integrity of the window wall must be evaluated using two criteria: strength and deflection. Based on numerous window wall tests, it has been found that the ultimate performance of the system is usually dependent on the elastic and inelastic deflections of the system rather than on just the strength of component parts.

Curtain wall fabrication and erection tolerances must be carefully reviewed in conjunction with structural frame tolerances. Many window wall failures have been caused by inadequate anchorage details and inadequate consideration of tolerances.

WEATHERTIGHTNESS

Weathertightness ensures protection against the penetration of water and an excessive amount of air through the wall. This depends on adequate provision for movement and is closely related to proper joint design. A major share of the problems experienced over the years has been due to the lack of weathertightness.

PROVISION FOR MOVEMENT

Development of the wall must accommodate relative movements of the wall components and also differential movements between the wall assembly and the building structure. Relative movements of the wall components will primarily be affected by thermal movements of the wall elements and erection tolerances of the individual wall elements. Erection tolerances may exceed the tolerance for thermal movement. The differential movements between the wall components and the building structure will be a direct function of the dead and live load deflections of the structure and also the creep, shrinkage, thermal, wind, and seismic deformations of the building structure. These differential movements may be of considerable magnitude, and the effects of such differential movements must not be transferred from the structure directly to the window wall system. Usually provisions for such differential movement are provided at the head and jamb anchorage locations between the wall jointery and/or joints between wall and adjacent cladding. Behavior of sealants must be considered. Current recommendations from sealant manufacturers are to limit movement of the joint to a percentage of the sealant's rated movement capacity. This will provide a safety factor to help prevent sealant failure. Temperature of metal parts at time of erection, as well as the anticipated design temperature range, will aid in predicting the extent of movement in a joint. Fabrication and erection tolerances must also be considered when establishing the joint opening width.

MOISTURE CONTROL

Control of condensation is essential because metal and glass are not only impermeable to moisture, but have low heat retention capacity. A vapor barrier should be provided on or near the room side wall face. Impervious surfaces within the wall should be insulated to keep them warmer than the dew point of the air contacting them. Provision should be made for the escape of water vapor to the outside. The wall should be detailed so that any condensation occurring within it will be collected and drained away via weeps to the exterior.

THERMAL INSULATION

High thermal and condensation resistance of the wall is a good long-term investment to minimize heat loss in cold weather or heat gain in hot weather. Such devices as minimizing the exposure of the framing members by using thermal breaks, employing high-performance glass, and insulating opaque surfaces are recommended.

SOUND TRANSMISSION

By careful selection of details and materials, sound transmission characteristics of the metal and glass wall can be made equal to traditional construction.

Use of insulating and laminated glass separately and in combination as well as increasing the mass of the wall will reduce the transmission of sound.

FIRE AND SMOKE STOPS

Prevention of the spread of fire and smoke by continuous firestopping between the curtain wall and the edge of each floor is necessary. Proper detailing and installation of a quality safing material not subject to breakdown by fire will help to avoid what can become an extremely dangerous condition.

CONCLUSION

The following items can be utilized to further refine the techniques of good curtain wall development and construction: It is very beneficial to work with contractors or manufacturers who have specialized for a period of not less than 5 years in the fabrication and installation of curtain walls. Visits to and interviews with owners or managers of buildings will help give an overall view of the performance of curtain wall systems. It is important at the start of design to work with the metal, glass, and sealant manufacturers' technical personnel when developing a metal curtain wall system. Before fabrication and construction starts, wall and component testing should be done under both laboratory and field conditions.

Skidmore, Owings & Merrill
Thomas F. O'Connor, AIA, ASTM; Smith, Hinchman & Grylls; Detroit, Michigan

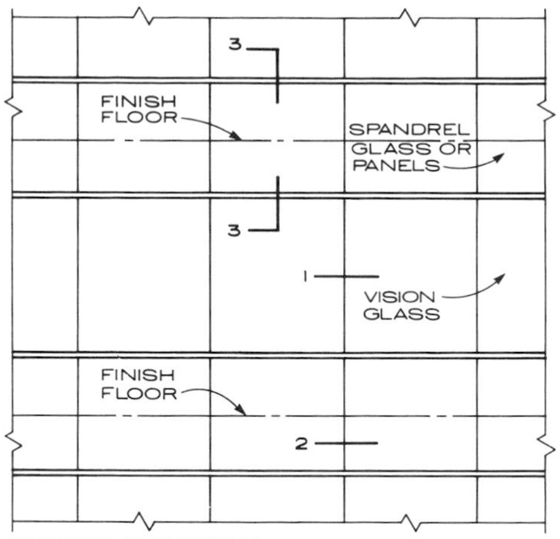

3
FINISH FLOOR
SPANDREL GLASS OR PANELS
3
1
VISION GLASS
FINISH FLOOR
2

TYPICAL ELEVATION

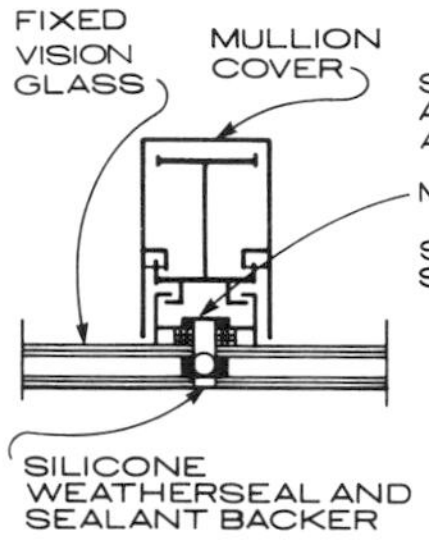

FIXED VISION GLASS
MULLION COVER
STEEL PLATE AND ANGLE ANCHORS
MULLION
SPANDREL GLASS
STRUCTURAL SILICONE
SILICONE WEATHERSEAL AND SEALANT BACKER
SILICONE WEATHERSEAL AND SEALANT BACKER

SECTION 1

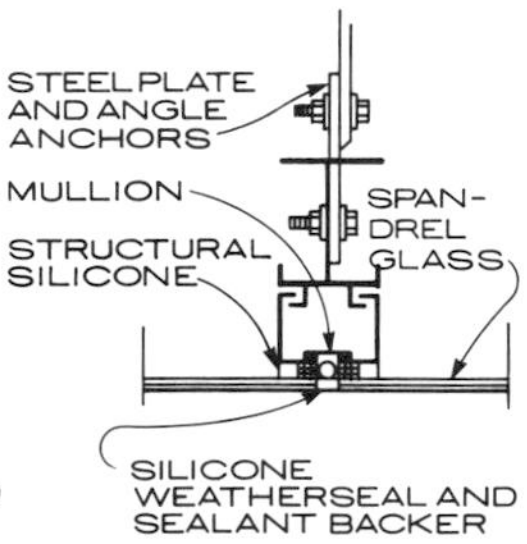

SECTION 2

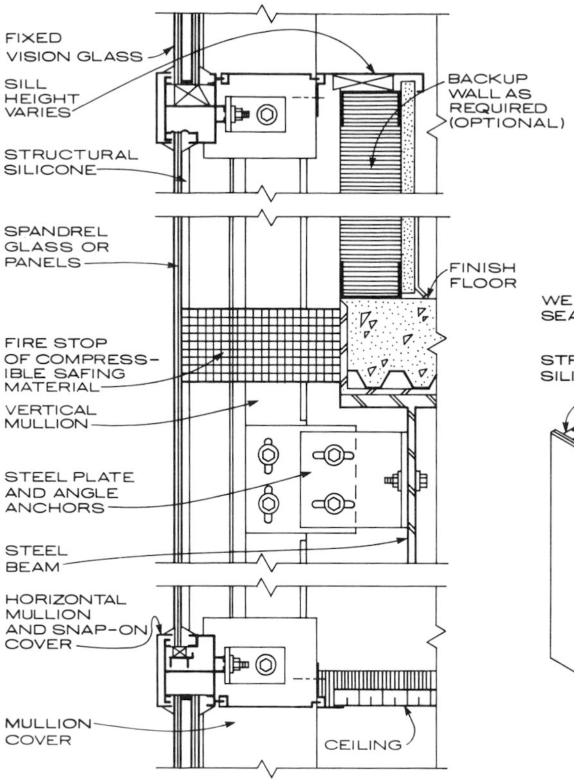

FIXED VISION GLASS
SILL HEIGHT VARIES
STRUCTURAL SILICONE
BACKUP WALL AS REQUIRED (OPTIONAL)
SPANDREL GLASS OR PANELS
FINISH FLOOR
FIRE STOP OF COMPRESSIBLE SAFING MATERIAL
VERTICAL MULLION
STEEL PLATE AND ANGLE ANCHORS
STEEL BEAM
HORIZONTAL MULLION AND SNAP-ON COVER
MULLION COVER
CEILING

SECTION 3-3

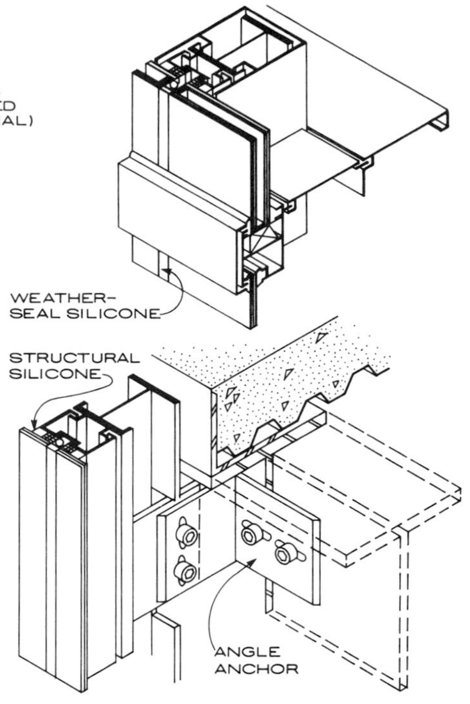

WEATHERSEAL SILICONE
STRUCTURAL SILICONE
ANGLE ANCHOR

ANCHORAGE AND MOVEMENT

STRUCTURAL GLAZING SYSTEM (STRIP WINDOW)-COMMERCIAL TYPE-ALUMINUM
SYSTEM WITH STRUCTURAL SILICONE SEALANT ATTACHMENT ON TWO SIDES

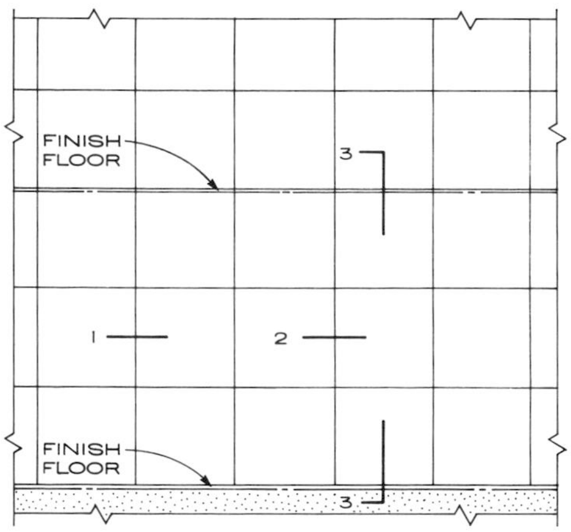

FINISH FLOOR
3
1
2
FINISH FLOOR
3

TYPICAL ELEVATION

NOTE

See index under "Structural Sealant Glazing" for additional information that should be considered when developing a structural sealant curtainwall system.

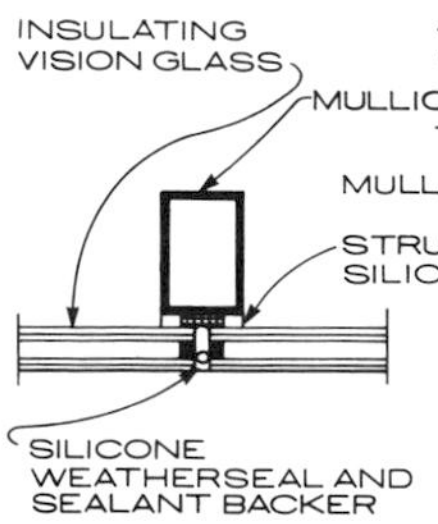

INSULATING VISION GLASS
ANGLE ANCHOR
MULLION STIFFENER
MULLION
MULLION
STRUCTURAL SILICONE
SILICONE WEATHERSEAL AND SEALANT BACKER
SILICONE WEATHERSEAL AND SEALANT BACKER

SECTION 1

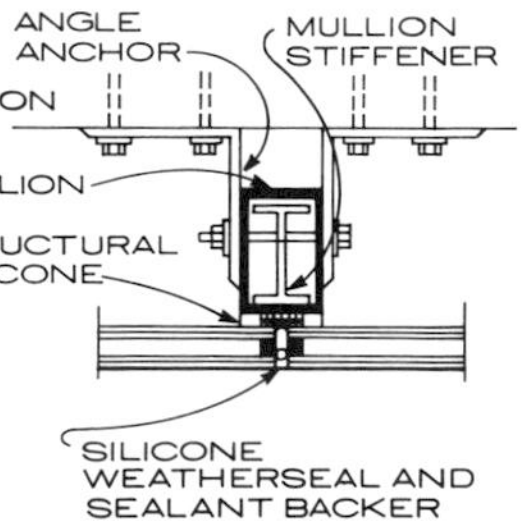

SECTION 2

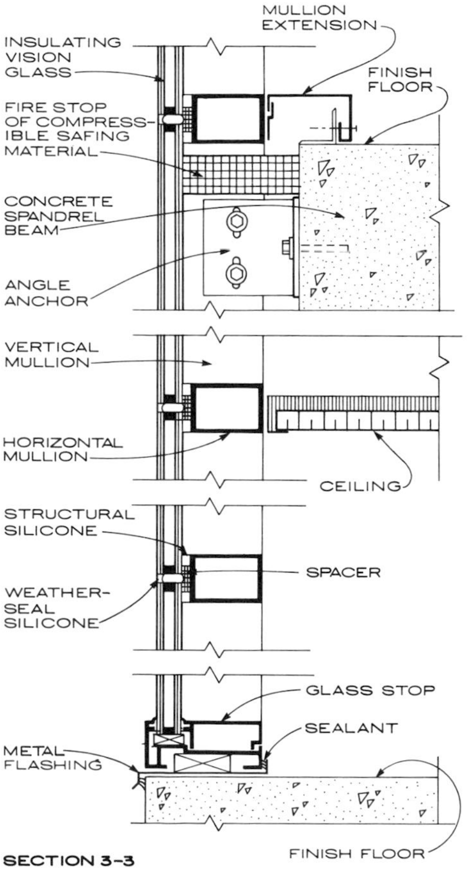

MULLION EXTENSION
INSULATING VISION GLASS
FINISH FLOOR
FIRE STOP OF COMPRESSIBLE SAFING MATERIAL
CONCRETE SPANDREL BEAM
ANGLE ANCHOR
VERTICAL MULLION
HORIZONTAL MULLION
CEILING
STRUCTURAL SILICONE
SPACER
WEATHERSEAL SILICONE
GLASS STOP
SEALANT
METAL FLASHING
FINISH FLOOR

SECTION 3-3

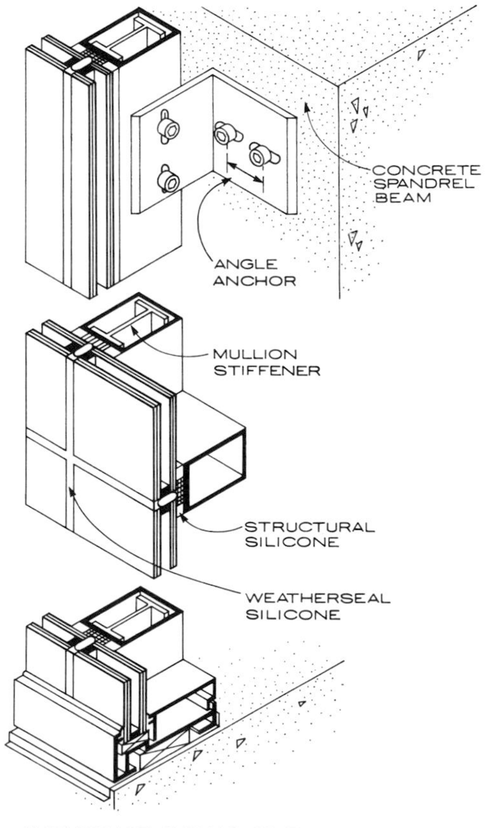

CONCRETE SPANDREL BEAM
ANGLE ANCHOR
MULLION STIFFENER
STRUCTURAL SILICONE
WEATHERSEAL SILICONE

ANCHORAGE AND MOVEMENT

STRUCTURAL GLAZING SYSTEM (STOPLESS)-COMMERCIAL TYPE-ALUMINUM
SYSTEM WITH STRUCTURAL SILICONE SEALANT ATTACHMENT ON FOUR SIDES

Bullock Tice Associates Architects, Inc.; Pensacola, Florida

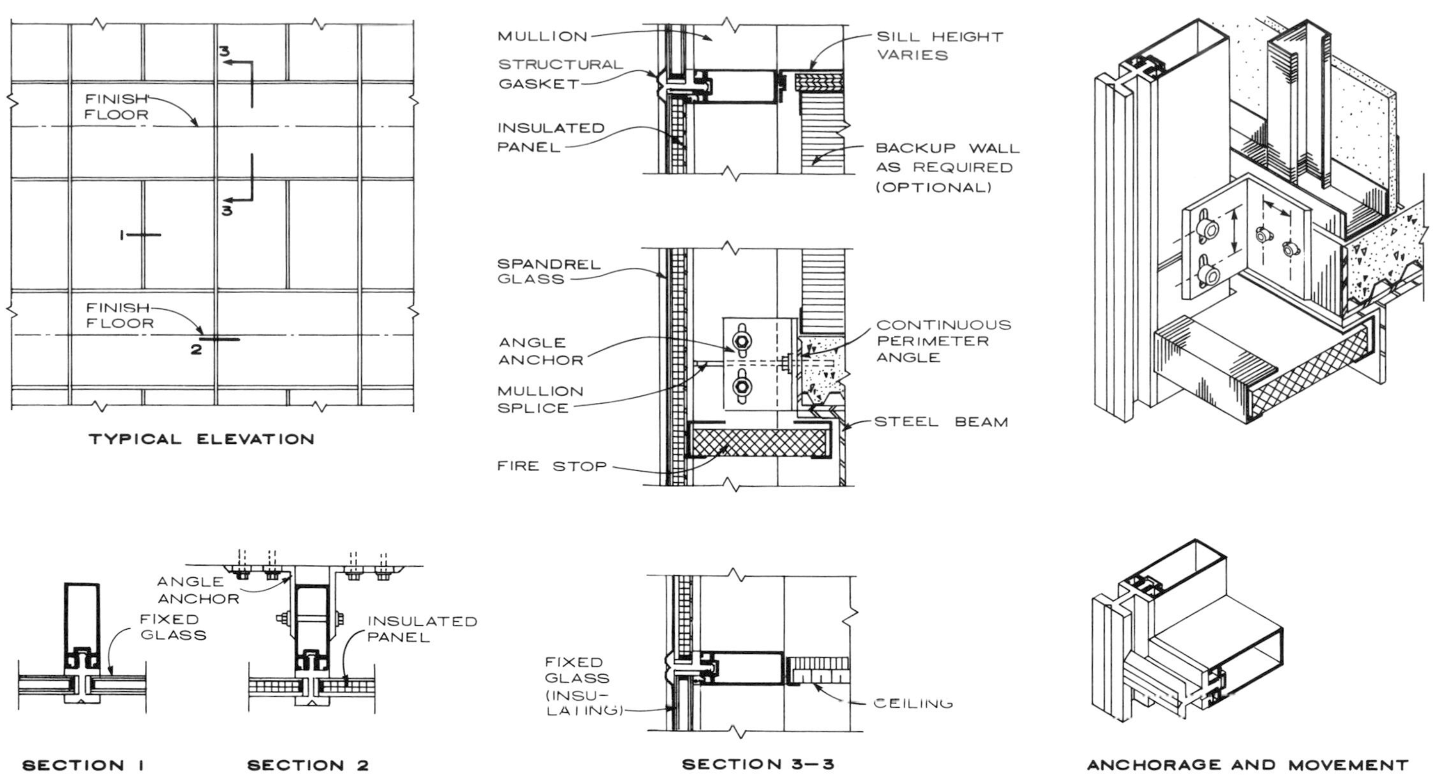

FINISH FLOOR
FINISH FLOOR
TYPICAL ELEVATION
MULLION
STRUCTURAL GASKET
INSULATED PANEL
SILL HEIGHT VARIES
BACKUP WALL AS REQUIRED (OPTIONAL)
SPANDREL GLASS
ANGLE ANCHOR
MULLION SPLICE
FIRE STOP
CONTINUOUS PERIMETER ANGLE
STEEL BEAM
ANGLE ANCHOR
FIXED GLASS
INSULATED PANEL
SECTION 1
SECTION 2
FIXED GLASS (INSULATING)
CEILING
SECTION 3-3
ANCHORAGE AND MOVEMENT

GRID SYSTEM (STICK OR STUD)—COMMERCIAL TYPE—ALUMINUM—GASKETED

MULTISTORY STICK OR STUD SYSTEM USING STRUCTURAL RUBBER GASKETS

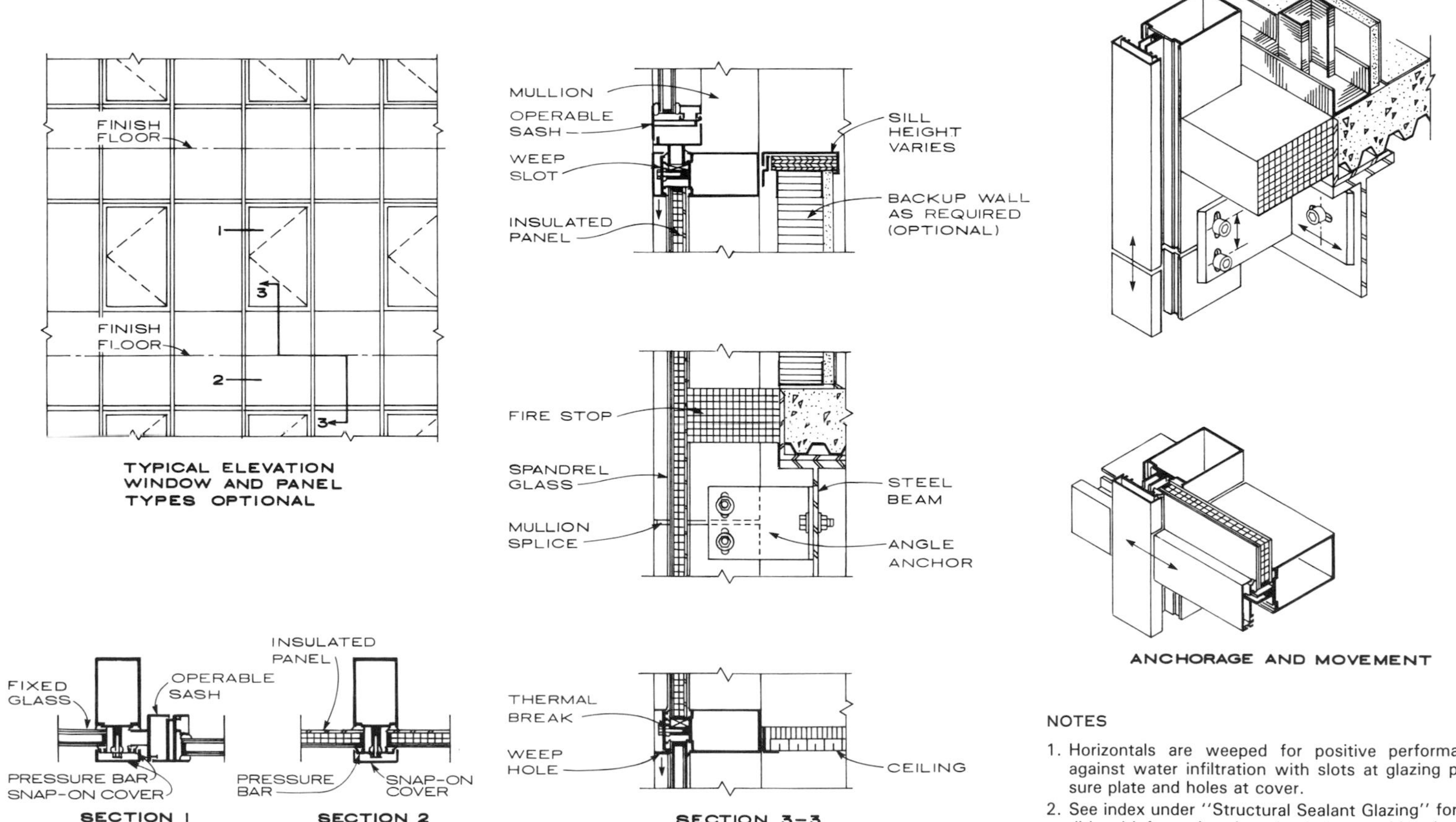

FINISH FLOOR
FINISH FLOOR
TYPICAL ELEVATION WINDOW AND PANEL TYPES OPTIONAL
MULLION
OPERABLE SASH
WEEP SLOT
INSULATED PANEL
SILL HEIGHT VARIES
BACKUP WALL AS REQUIRED (OPTIONAL)
FIRE STOP
SPANDREL GLASS
MULLION SPLICE
STEEL BEAM
ANGLE ANCHOR
FIXED GLASS
OPERABLE SASH
INSULATED PANEL
PRESSURE BAR
SNAP-ON COVER
PRESSURE BAR
SNAP-ON COVER
SECTION 1
SECTION 2
THERMAL BREAK
WEEP HOLE
CEILING
SECTION 3-3
ANCHORAGE AND MOVEMENT

NOTES

1. Horizontals are weeped for positive performance against water infiltration with slots at glazing pressure plate and holes at cover.
2. See index under "Structural Sealant Glazing" for additional information that should be considered when developing a structural sealant curtainwall system.

GRID SYSTEM (STICK OR STUD)—COMMERCIAL TYPE-ALUMINUM-PRESSURE BAR

TYPICAL MULTISTORY STICK OR STUD SYSTEM USING PRESSURE BARS

Bullock Tice Associates Architects, Inc.; Pensacola, Florida

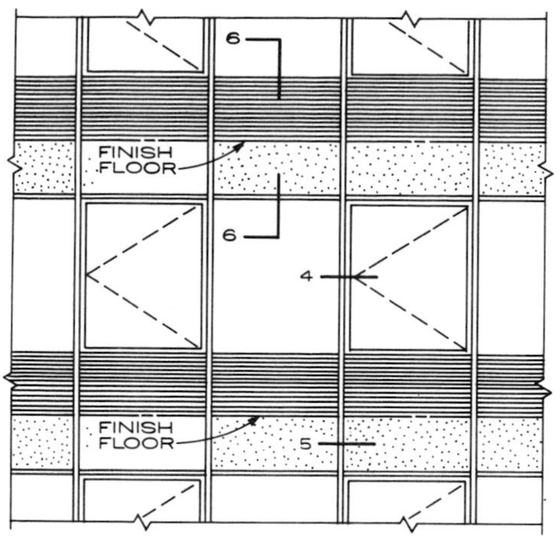
6
FINISH FLOOR
6
4
FINISH FLOOR
5

TYPICAL ELEVATION

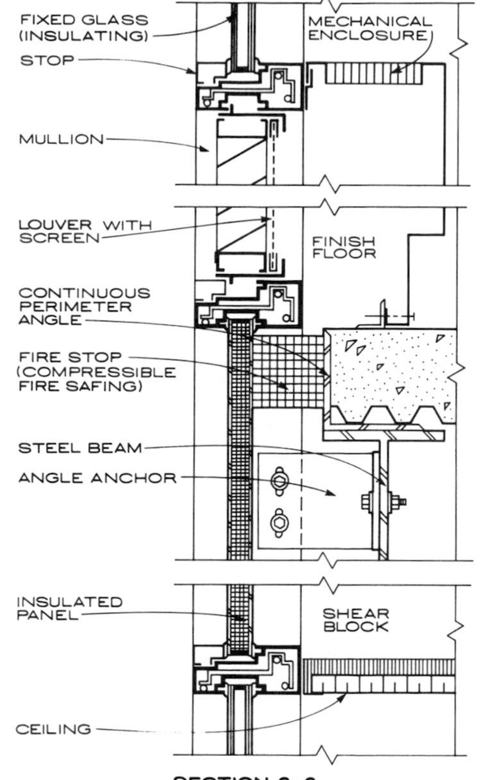
FIXED GLASS (INSULATING)
STOP
MULLION
MECHANICAL ENCLOSURE
LOUVER WITH SCREEN
FINISH FLOOR
CONTINUOUS PERIMETER ANGLE
FIRE STOP (COMPRESSIBLE FIRE SAFING)
STEEL BEAM
ANGLE ANCHOR
INSULATED PANEL
SHEAR BLOCK
CEILING

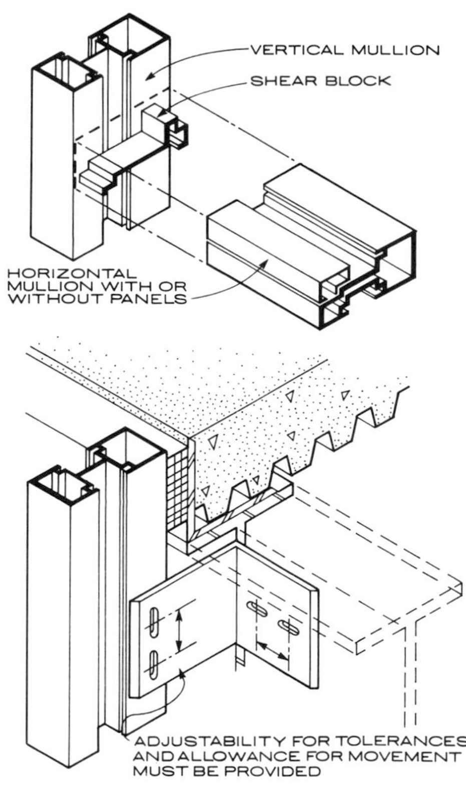
VERTICAL MULLION
SHEAR BLOCK
HORIZONTAL MULLION WITH OR WITHOUT PANELS
ADJUSTABILITY FOR TOLERANCES AND ALLOWANCE FOR MOVEMENT MUST BE PROVIDED

FIXED GLASS
OPERABLE SASH
ANGLE ANCHOR
INSULATED PANEL

SECTION 4 | SECTION 5 | SECTION 6-6 | ANCHORAGE

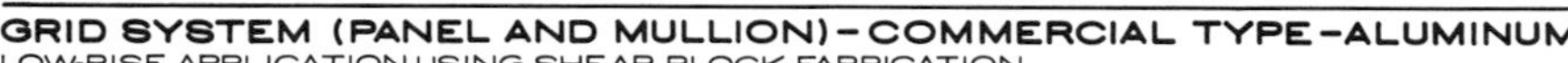

GRID SYSTEM (PANEL AND MULLION)–COMMERCIAL TYPE–ALUMINUM
LOW-RISE APPLICATION USING SHEAR BLOCK FABRICATION

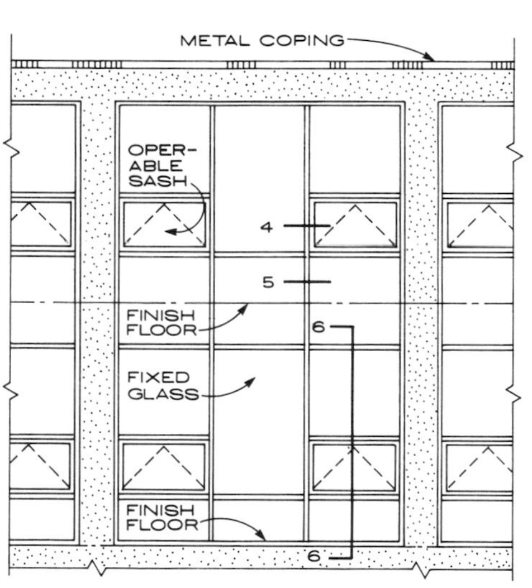
METAL COPING
OPERABLE SASH
4
5
FINISH FLOOR
6
FIXED GLASS
FINISH FLOOR
6

TYPICAL ELEVATION

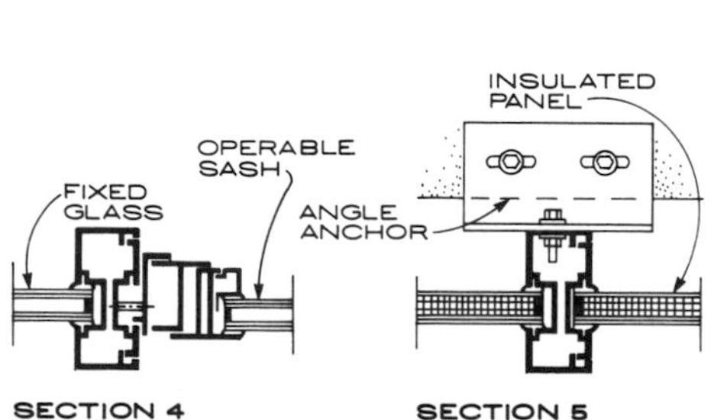
FIXED GLASS
OPERABLE SASH
ANGLE ANCHOR
INSULATED PANEL

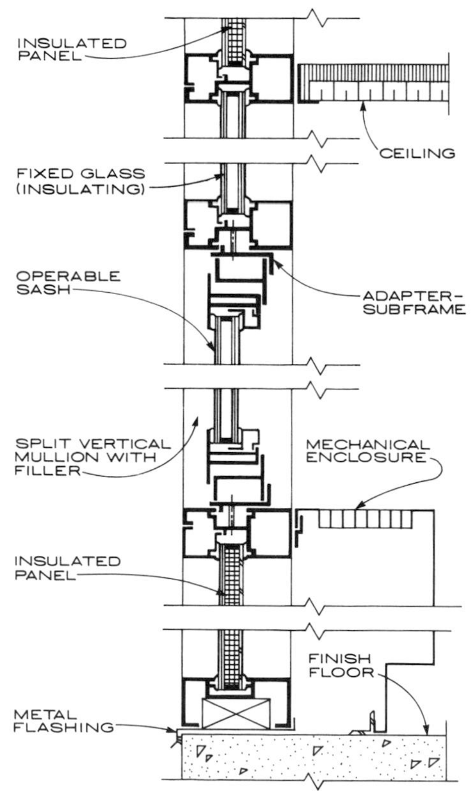
INSULATED PANEL
CEILING
FIXED GLASS (INSULATING)
OPERABLE SASH
ADAPTER-SUBFRAME
SPLIT VERTICAL MULLION WITH FILLER
MECHANICAL ENCLOSURE
INSULATED PANEL
FINISH FLOOR
METAL FLASHING

ADJUSTABILITY FOR TOLERANCES AND ALLOWANCE FOR MOVEMENT MUST BE PROVIDED

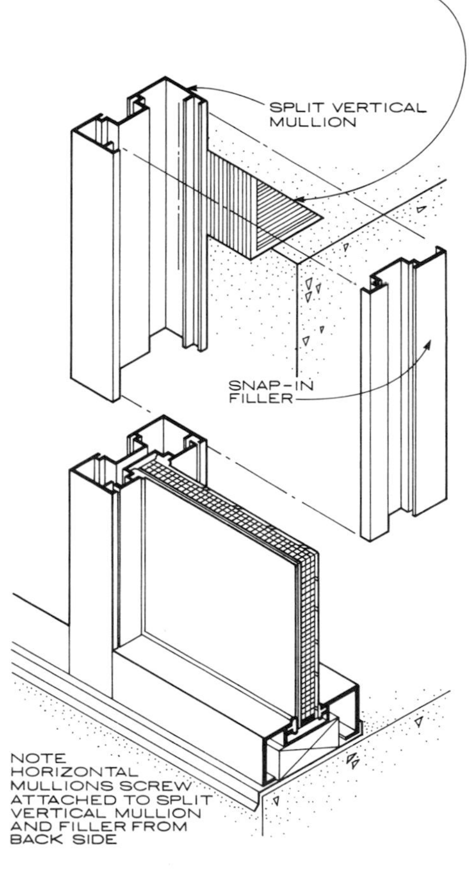
SPLIT VERTICAL MULLION
SNAP-IN FILLER
NOTE
HORIZONTAL MULLIONS SCREW ATTACHED TO SPLIT VERTICAL MULLION AND FILLER FROM BACK SIDE

SECTION 4 | SECTION 5 | SECTION 6-6 | ANCHORAGE

PANEL SYSTEM–COMMERCIAL TYPE–ALUMINUM
LOW-RISE APPLICATION USING SCREW SPLINE FABRICATION

Bullock Tice Associates Architects, Inc.; Pensacola, Florida

REFERENCES

DATA SOURCES: ORGANIZATIONS

Acorn Building Components, Inc., 267
Algoma Hardwoods, Inc., 262
American National Standards Institute (ANSI), 265, 293
American Society for Testing and Materials (ASTM), 265
Anderson Corporation, 267, 284, 285
Architectural Aluminum Manufacturers Association (AAMA), 277–281
Bilco Company, 274
Brosco, 285
Ceco Corporation, 255, 258–261
Darren John Castale Corporation, 296
Door and Hardware Institute, 288, 289, 291
Ellison Bronze Company, 275
Fentron Industries, Inc., 282
Flat Glass Marketing Association, 299
General Services Administration (GSA), 293
Hope's Windows, Inc., 278
House and Home, 285
Kawneer Architectural Products, 275, 276
Koppers Company, Inc., 254
Libbey-Owens Ford Company, 275, 276, 293
Malta Manufacturing Company, 284
National Association of Architectural Metal Manufacturers (NAANN), 255, 259, 260
National Wood Window and Door Association (NWWDA), 263
Northrop Architectural Systems, 268, 276, 279
Overhead Door Corporation, 270–272
Peachtree Doors, Inc., 285
Pioneer Industries, 255–261
PPG Industries, Inc., 276, 293, 294
Rolscreen Company, 285
Rusco Industries, Inc., 279
Steel Door Institute (SDI), 254, 259
Steel Window Institute (SWI), 277–281
Underwriters' Laboratories, Inc. (U.L.), 254, 301
Velux-America, Inc., 284
Western Integrated Materials, Inc., 255
Weyerhaeuser Company, 262
Woodco Corporation, 284

DATA SOURCES: PUBLICATIONS

Catalog 35, SUN-DOR-CO, 263
General Information Manual, Stanley Hardware, Division of The Stanley Works, 289
Industry Standard for Ponderosa Pine Doors, National Woodwork Manufacturers Association, 262, 263
Hinge Specification Guide, Stanley Hardware, Division of The Stanley Works, 289
Metal Curtain Wall Specifications Manual, National Association of Architectural Metal Manufacturers (NAAMM), 301, 302
NFPA 80-1983, National Fire Protection Association, 255

CHAPTER 9

FINISHES

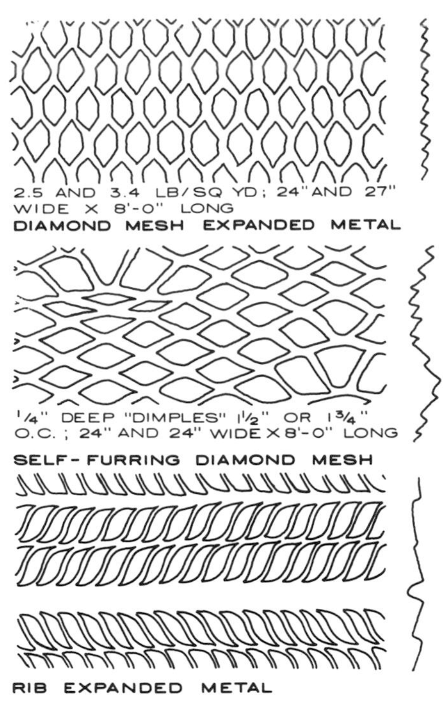
2.5 AND 3.4 LB/SQ YD; 24" AND 27" WIDE X 8'-0" LONG
DIAMOND MESH EXPANDED METAL
1/4" DEEP "DIMPLES" 1 1/2" OR 1 3/4" O.C.; 24" AND 24" WIDE X 8'-0" LONG
SELF-FURRING DIAMOND MESH
RIB EXPANDED METAL

LATHING SYSTEMS

NOTES

Self-furring paperbacked reinforcing is available in diamond mesh, welded wire, and hexagonal woven wire. Paperbacks are available to conform to Federal Specifications UU-B-790, Type 1, Grade A, Style 2 for highly water-vapor resistant paper.

Metal lath is also manufactured in large diamond mesh 27 x 96 in., 2.5 or 3.4 lb/sq yd, painted steel or galvanized; 1/8 in. flat rib 27 x 96 in., 2.75 or 3.4 lb/sq yd painted or galvanized; 3/8 in. rib expanded 27 x 96 in., 3.4 lb/sq yd painted or galvanized and 3/4 in. rib expanded 24 x 96 in., 5.4 lb/sq yd painted.

Other types of lath are available from some manufacturers.

GYPSUM LATH

Gypsum lath is composed of an air entrained gypsum core sandwiched between two sheets of fibrous absorbent paper and used as a basecoat for gypsum plaster.

1. PLAIN GYPSUM LATH: 3/8 and 1/2 in. thick, 48 in. long, and 16 in. wide (16 1/5 in. in the Western U.S.).
2. PERFORATED GYPSUM LATH: Plain gypsum lath with 3/4 in. diameter holes punched 4 in. o.c. in both directions to provide mechanical key to plaster.
3. INSULATING GYPSUM LATH: Plain gypsum lath with aluminum foil laminated to the backside as insulator or vapor barrier.
4. LONG LENGTH GYPSUM LATH: 16 and 24 in. wide, in lengths up to 12 ft, available insulated or plain with square or vee-jointed Tongue and Groove edges or interlocking as ship-lap edge.

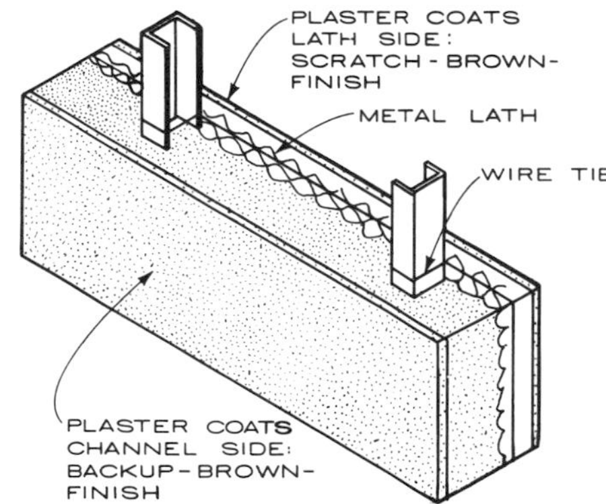
PLASTER COATS LATH SIDE: SCRATCH - BROWN - FINISH
METAL LATH
WIRE TIE
PLASTER COATS CHANNEL SIDE: BACKUP - BROWN - FINISH

SOLID PARTITION SYSTEMS

SOLID PLASTER PARTITION CONSTRUCTION

PARTITION CONSTRUCTION	THICKNESS	MAXIMUM HEIGHT
3/4" cold-rolled channels Diamond mesh lath and plaster	2"	12'-0"
3/4" cold-rolled channels Diamond mesh lath and plaster	2 1/2"	16'-0"
1 1/2" cold-rolled channels Diamond mesh lath and plaster	3"	20'-0"
1 1/2" cold-rolled channels Diamond mesh lath and plaster	3 1/2"	22'-0"

NOTE: Maximum partition length is unrestricted if less than 10 ft tall. Twice the height if over 10 ft tall; one and one half the height if over 14 ft tall and equal to the height if over 20 ft tall.

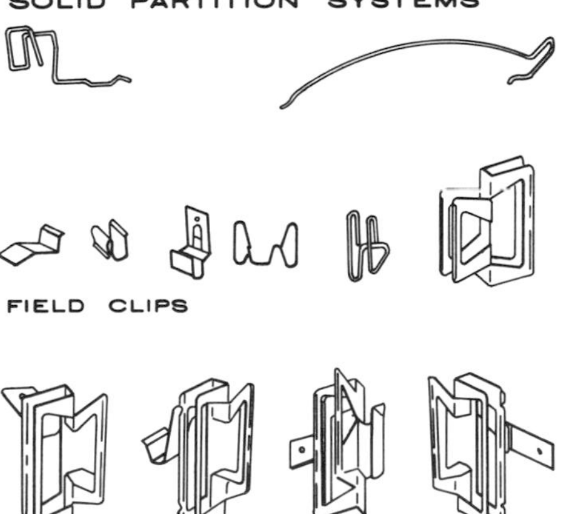
FIELD CLIPS
CORNER CLIPS

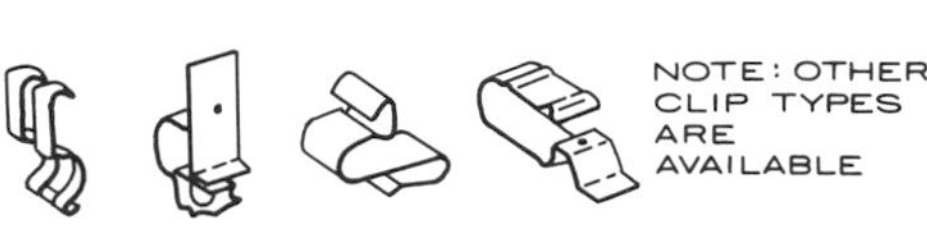
NOTE: OTHER CLIP TYPES ARE AVAILABLE
MISCELLANEOUS

CLIPS FOR GYPSUM LATH SYSTEM

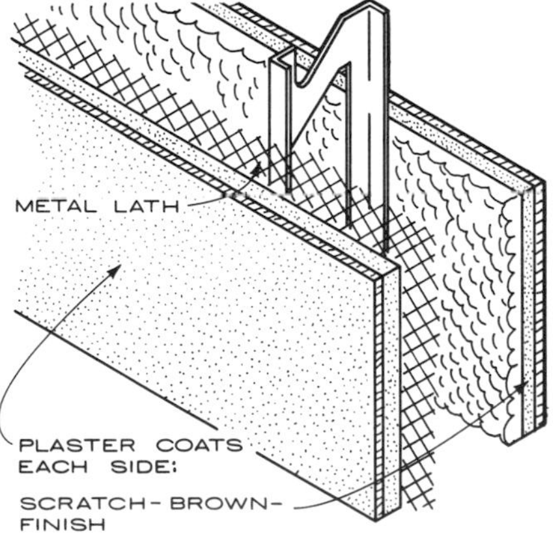
METAL LATH
PLASTER COATS EACH SIDE:
SCRATCH - BROWN - FINISH

NOTES

Prefabricated metal studs are used as the supporting elements of lath and plaster hollow partitions. They are available in 1 5/8, 2, 2 1/2, 3 1/4, 4, and 6 in. widths. Lengths are available in various increments up to 24 ft. Prefabricated studs are usually of the nonload bearing type, but load bearing metal studs also are manufactured. Designs vary with the manufacturer, and most manufacturers produce a line of related accessories, such as clips, runners, stud shoes, and similar articles.

HOLLOW PARTITION SYSTEMS

DEFINITIONS

AGGREGATE: Inert material used as filler with a cementitious material and water to produce plaster or concrete. Usually implies sand, perlite, or vermiculite.

BASECOAT: Any plaster coat applied before the finish coat.

BEAD: Light gauge metal strip with one or more expanded or short perforated flanges and variously shaped noses; used at the perimeter of plastered surfaces.

BROWN COAT: In three-coat plaster, the brown coat is the second coat; in two-coat plaster, the base coat.

CALCINED GYPSUM: Gypsum that has been partially dehydrated by heating.

CLIP: A device made of wire or sheet metal for attaching various types of lath to the substructure and lath sheets to one another.

FIBERED PLASTER: Gypsum plaster containing fibers of hair, glass, nylon, or sisal.

FINISH COAT: The final coat of plaster, which provides the decorative surface.

FURRING: Grillage for the attachment of gypsum or metal lath.

GAUGING: Cementitious material, usually calcined gypsum or portland cement combined with lime putty to control set.

GROUND: A formed metal shape or wood strip that acts as a combined edge and gauge for various thicknesses of plaster to be applied to a plaster base.

GYPSUM: Hydrous calcium sulphate, a natural mineral in crystalline form.

GYPSUM LATH: A base for plaster; a sheet having a gypsum core, faced with paper.

GYPSUM READY MIX PLASTER: Ground gypsum that has been calcined and then mixed with various additives to control its setting and working qualities; used, with the addition of aggregate and water, for basecoat plaster.

HYDRATED LIME: Quicklime mixed with water, on the job, to form a lime putty.

LIME: Obtained by burning various types of limestone, consisting of oxides or hydroxides of calcium and magnesium.

LIME PLASTER: Basecoat plaster of hydrated lime and an aggregate.

NEAT PLASTER: Basecoat plaster, fibered or unfibered, used for job mixing with aggregates.

PERLITE: Siliceous volcanic glass containing silica and alumina expanded by heat for use as a lightweight plaster aggregate.

PLASTER: Cementitious material or combination of cementitious materials and aggregate that, when mixed with water, forms a plastic mass that sets and hardens when applied to a surface.

PORTLAND CEMENT: Manufactured combination of limestone and an argillaceous substance.

SCRATCH COAT: In three-coat plastering, the first coat, which is then scratched to provide a bond for second or brown coat.

SCREED: A device secured to a surface which serves as a guide for subsequent applications of plaster. Thicknesses and widths vary with the thicknesses desired for each operation.

STUCCO PORTLAND CEMENT: Plaster used in exterior application.

VERMICULITE: Micaceous mineral of silica, magnesium, and alumina oxides made up in a series of parallel plates or laminae and expanded by heat for use as a lightweight plaster aggregate.

NOTES

Keene's cement plaster is a specialty finish coat of gypsum plaster primarily used where a smooth, dense, white finish is desired.

Thickness, proportions of mixes of various plastering materials, and finishes vary. Systems and methods of application vary widely depending on local traditions and innovations promoted by the industry.

The Marmon Mok Partnership; San Antonio, Texas

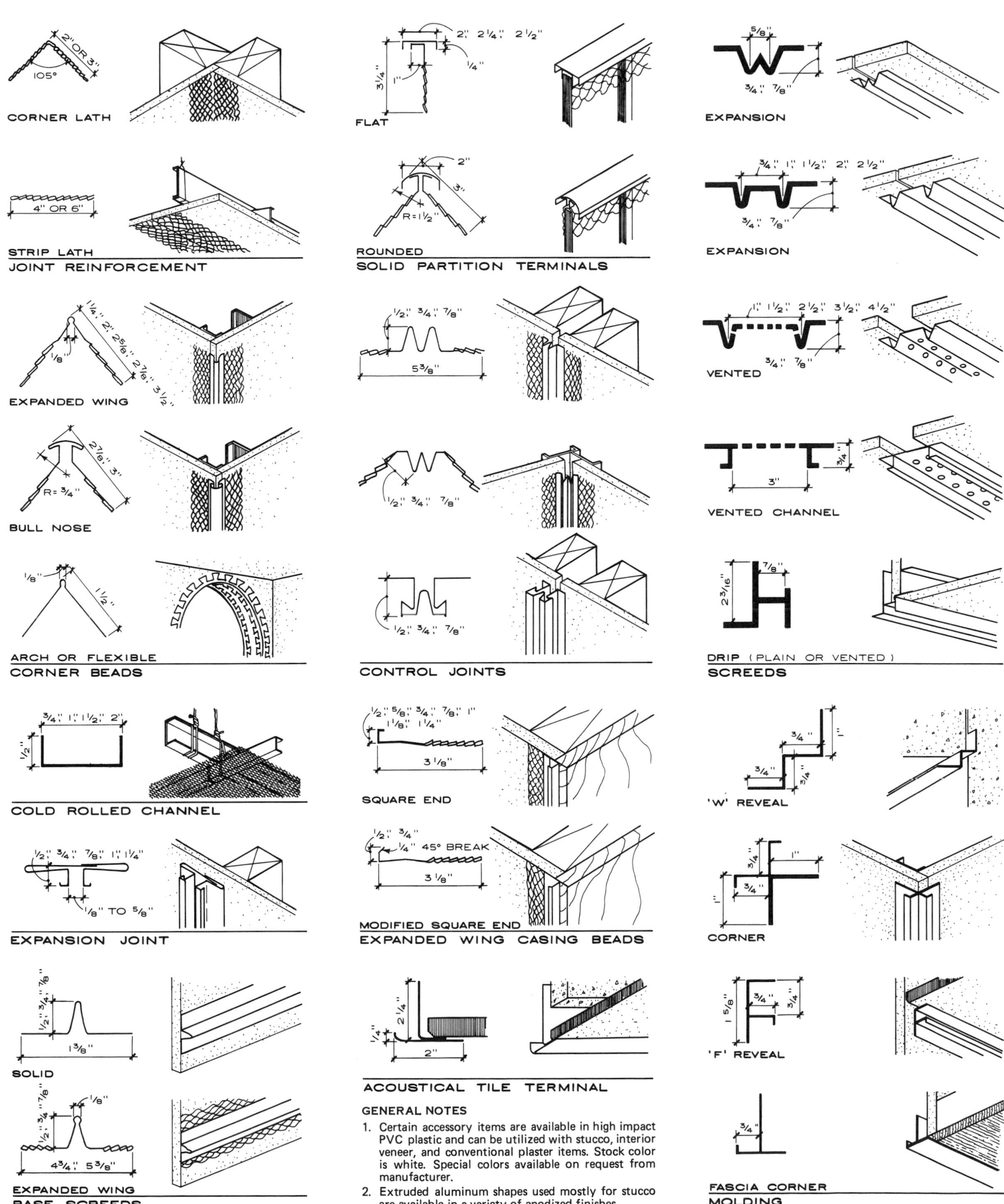

CORNER LATH
STRIP LATH
JOINT REINFORCEMENT
FLAT
ROUNDED
SOLID PARTITION TERMINALS
EXPANSION
EXPANSION
VENTED
VENTED CHANNEL
EXPANDED WING
BULL NOSE
ARCH OR FLEXIBLE
CORNER BEADS
CONTROL JOINTS
DRIP (PLAIN OR VENTED)
SCREEDS
COLD ROLLED CHANNEL
EXPANSION JOINT
SQUARE END
MODIFIED SQUARE END
EXPANDED WING CASING BEADS
'W' REVEAL
CORNER
SOLID
EXPANDED WING
BASE SCREEDS
ACOUSTICAL TILE TERMINAL
'F' REVEAL
FASCIA CORNER
MOLDING

GENERAL NOTES

1. Certain accessory items are available in high impact PVC plastic and can be utilized with stucco, interior veneer, and conventional plaster items. Stock color is white. Special colors available on request from manufacturer.
2. Extruded aluminum shapes used mostly for stucco are available in a variety of anodized finishes.

The Marmon Mok Partnership; San Antonio, Texas

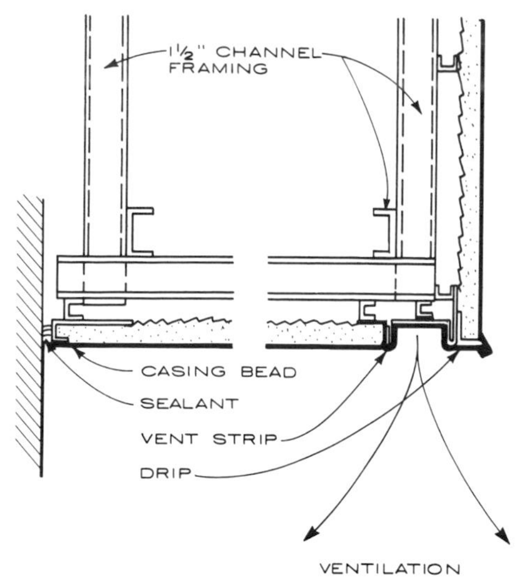

1½" CHANNEL FRAMING
CASING BEAD
SEALANT
VENT STRIP
DRIP
VENTILATION

SOFFIT DETAIL

NOTE

Framing details for exterior cement plaster (stucco) are similar to details shown. Wind loads must be considered in designing framing systems for exterior stucco work. Galvanized mesh is available for exterior applications and use in humid areas. Ventilation strips should be used for ventilating all dead airspaces. Where plenum or attic spaces are closed off by ceiling installation, ventilation shall be provided with a minimum of ½ sq. in./sq. ft. of horizontal surface.

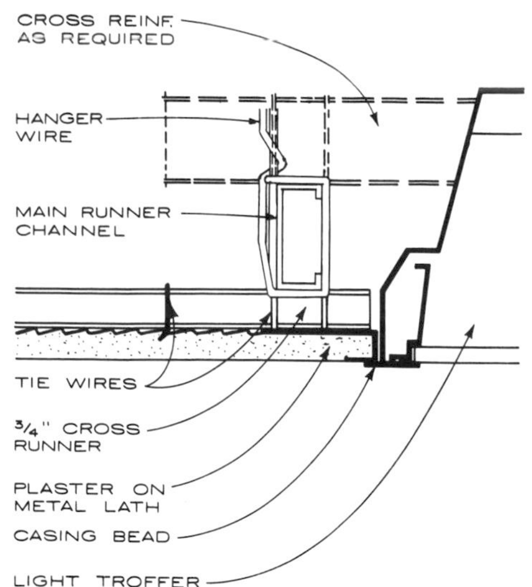

CROSS REINF. AS REQUIRED
HANGER WIRE
MAIN RUNNER CHANNEL
TIE WIRES
¾" CROSS RUNNER
PLASTER ON METAL LATH
CASING BEAD
LIGHT TROFFER

SUSPENDED PLASTER CEILING AT RECESSED LIGHT FIXTURE

NOTE

Penetrations of the lath and plaster ceiling—at borrowed light openings, vents, grilles, access panels, and light troffers, for example—require additional reinforcement to distribute concentrated stresses if a control joint is not used. Where a plaster surface is flush with metal, as at metal access panels, grilles, or light troffers, the plaster should be grooved between the two materials.

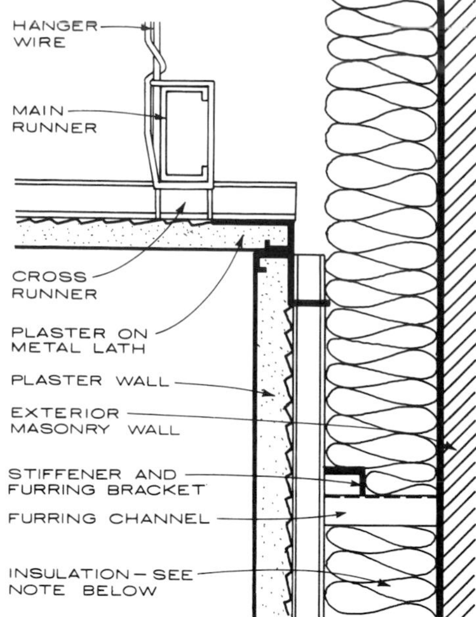

HANGER WIRE
MAIN RUNNER
CROSS RUNNER
PLASTER ON METAL LATH
PLASTER WALL
EXTERIOR MASONRY WALL
STIFFENER AND FURRING BRACKET
FURRING CHANNEL
INSULATION — SEE NOTE BELOW

SUSPENDED PLASTER CEILING AT FURRED MASONRY WALL

NOTE

When interior walls are furred from an exterior masonry wall and insulated, the ceiling should stop short of the furred space. This allows wall insulation to continue above the ceiling line to ceiling or roof insulation, thus forming a complete insulation envelope. In a suspension system that abuts masonry wall, provide 1 in. clearance between ends of main runners or furring channels and wall face.

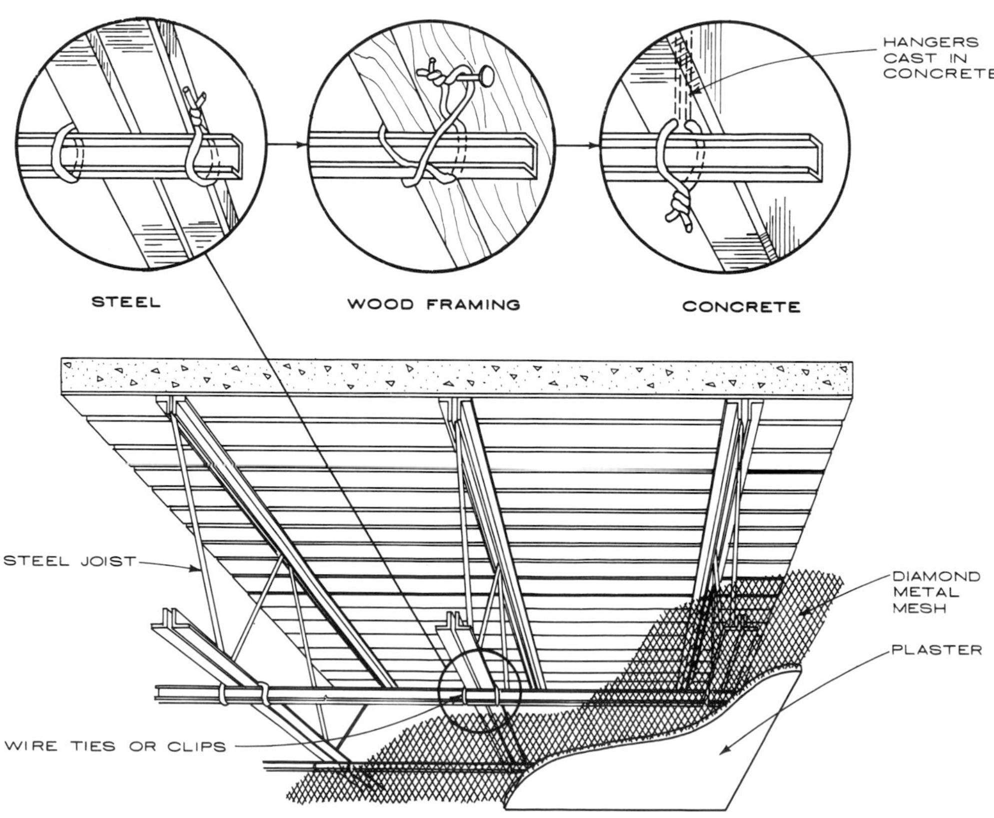

HANGERS CAST IN CONCRETE
STEEL
WOOD FRAMING
CONCRETE
STEEL JOIST
DIAMOND METAL MESH
PLASTER
WIRE TIES OR CLIPS

NOTE
RIB METAL LATH MAY BE USED IN LIEU OF DIAMOND MESH LATH AND FURRING CHANNELS IF LATH SPANS DO NOT EXCEED ALLOWABLE MAXIMUM. SEE TABLE I

FURRED METAL LATH ON STEEL JOIST

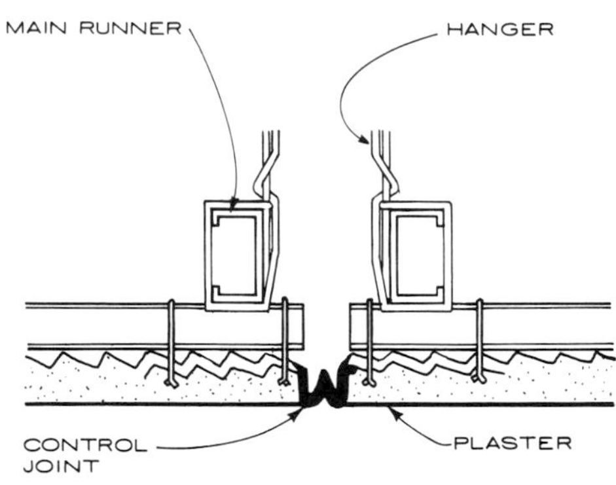

MAIN RUNNER
HANGER
CONTROL JOINT
PLASTER

CONTROL JOINT DETAIL

NOTE

Control joints shall be spaced no further than 30 ft on center in each direction for large plastered ceiling areas. Area shall not exceed 900 sq ft without provision for expansion control. Exterior plaster soffits should have control joints spaced no further than 25 ft on center. For portland cement plaster (stucco) areas, interior or exterior, control joints should be placed at 10 ft on center and areas should not exceed 100 sq ft without provisions for expansion/contraction control. Control joints are spaced closer for cement plaster because of its inherent shrinkage during curing.

NOTE

Details shown are for furred (contact) ceilings that are attached directly to the structural members. The architect or ceiling designer should give consideration to the deflection and movement of the structure, since movement and deflection of more than 1/360 of the span will cause cracking of plaster ceilings. If spacing of structural members exceeds the maximum span of furring members shown in the span charts, the addition of suspended main runners between structural members will be required. Flat rib lath may be attached directly to wood framing members, but is subjected to stresses created by the inherent properties of wood members.

James E. Phillips, AIA; Enwright Associates, Inc.; Greenville, South Carolina

DIRECTIONS FOR USING TABLES

1. Select lath and plaster system.
2. Determine spacing of cross furring channels from Table 1—Lath Span.
3. Determine spacing of main runners from Table 2—Maximum Spacing between Runners.
4. Determine hanger support spacing for main runner from Table 3—Maximum Spacing between Hangers.
5. Calculate area of ceiling supported per hanger.
6. Select hanger type from Table 4—Hanger Selection.
7. Select tie wire size from Table 5—Tie Wire Selection.

TABLE 1. LATH SPAN

	LATH TYPE	WEIGHT/SQ. FT.	SPAN (IN.)
Gypsum lath	3/8" plain	1.5#	16
	1/2" plain	2.0#	16
	1/2" veneer	1.8#	16
	5/8" veneer	2.25#	16
	3/8" perforated	1.4#	16
Metal lath	Diamond mesh	0.27#	12
	Diamond mesh	0.38#	16
	1/8" flat rib	0.31#	12
	1/8" flat rib	0.38#	19
	3/8" flat rib	0.38#	24

TABLE 2. MAXIMUM SPACING BETWEEN RUNNERS

CROSS FURRING TYPE	CROSS FURRING SPACING			
	12"	16"	19"	24"
1/4" diam. pencil rod	2'-0"	—	—	—
3/8" diam. pencil rod	2'-6"	—	2'-0"	—
3/4" CRC, HRC (0.3 lb/ft)	—	4'-6"	3'-6"	3'-0"
1" HRC (0.41 lb/ft)	5'-0"	—	4'-6"	4'-0"

CRC = Cold rolled channel
HRC = Hot rolled channel

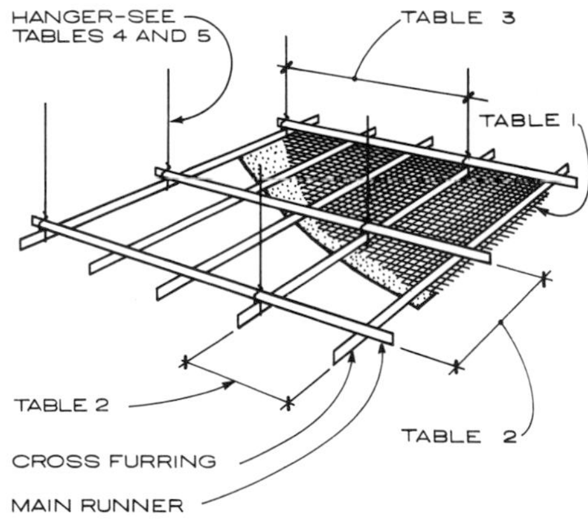
HANGER-SEE TABLES 4 AND 5
TABLE 3
TABLE 1
TABLE 2
TABLE 2
CROSS FURRING
MAIN RUNNER

FURRED AND SUSPENSION SYSTEM COMPONENT SELECTION DETAIL

TABLE 3. MAXIMUM SPACING BETWEEN HANGERS

MAIN RUNNER TYPE	MAIN RUNNER SPACING				
	3'-0"	3'-6"	4'-0"	4'-6"	5'-0"
3/4" CRC (0.3 lb/ft)	2'-0"	—	—	—	—
1 1/2" CRC (0.3 lb/ft)	3'-0"*	—	—	—	—
1 1/2" CRC (0.875 lb/ft)	4'-0"	3'-6"	3'-0"	—	—
1 1/2" HRC (1.12 lb/ft)	—	—	—	4'-0"	—
2" CRC (0.59 lb/ft)	—	—	5'-0"	—	—
2" HRC (1.26 lb/ft)	—	—	—	—	5'-0"
1/2" x 1/2" x 3/16" ST1	—	5'-0"	—	—	—

*For concrete construction only—a 10-gauge wire may be inserted in the joint before concrete is poured.

TABLE 4. HANGER SELECTION

MAX. CEILING AREA	MIN. HANGER SIZE
12 sq. ft.	9-gauge galvanized wire
16 sq. ft.	8-gauge galvanized wire
18 sq. ft.	3/16" mild steel rod*
25 sq. ft.	1/4" mild steel rod*
25 sq. ft.	3/16" x 1" steel flat*

*Rods galvanized or painted with rust inhibitive paint and galvanized straps are recommended under severe moisture conditions.

TABLE 5. TIE WIRE SELECTION

	SUPPORT	MAX. CEILING AREA	MIN. HANGER SIZE
Cross furring		8 sq. ft.	14-gauge wire
		8 sq. ft.	16-gauge wire (two loops)
Main runners	Single hangers between beams	8 sq. ft.	12-gauge wire
		12 sq. ft.	10-gauge wire
		16 sq. ft.	8-gauge wire
	Double wire loops at supports	8 sq. ft.	14-gauge wire
		12 sq. ft.	12-gauge wire
		16 sq. ft.	11-gauge wire

ERECTION OF METAL LATH SUSPENSIONS

Metal lath suspensions commonly are made below all types of construction for fire rated plaster ceilings. The lath is supported by framing channels and furring channels suspended with wire hangers from the floor or roof structure above. Framing channels normally are spaced up to 4 ft. o.c. perpendicular to joists and should be erected to conform with the contour of the finished ceiling. Framing channels normally are furred with 3/4 in. channels placed at right angles to the framing. Spacing varies by lath types and weights. The lath should be lapped at both sides and ends and secured to the 3/4 in. channels with wire ties every 6 in. Where plaster on metal lath ceilings abuts masonry walls, partitions, or arch soffits, galvanized casing beads should be installed at the periphery.

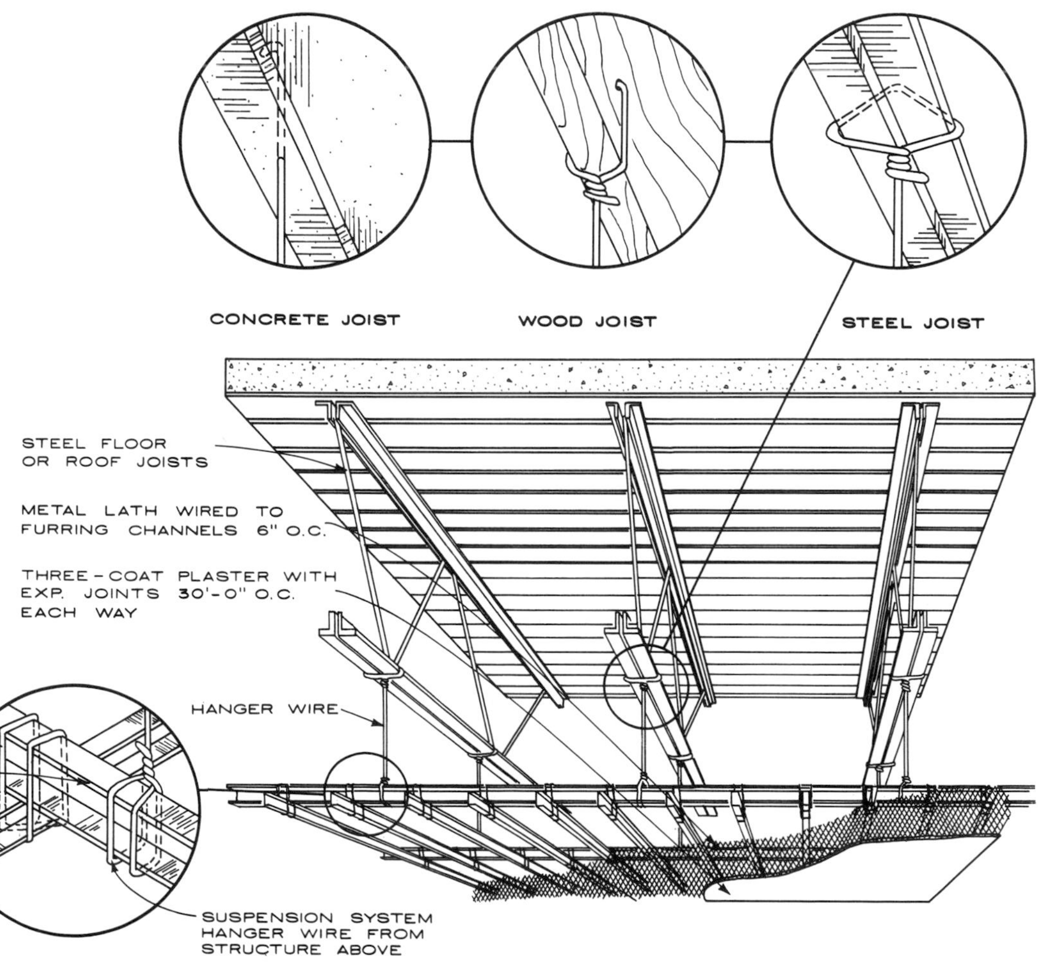
CONCRETE JOIST
WOOD JOIST
STEEL JOIST
STEEL FLOOR OR ROOF JOISTS
METAL LATH WIRED TO FURRING CHANNELS 6" O.C.
THREE-COAT PLASTER WITH EXP. JOINTS 30'-0" O.C. EACH WAY
HANGER WIRE
SUSPENSION SYSTEM TIE WIRES AS REQUIRED
MAIN RUNNER CHANNEL
3/4" CROSS FURRING CHANNEL
SUSPENSION SYSTEM HANGER WIRE FROM STRUCTURE ABOVE

METAL LATH SUSPENDED FROM STEEL JOISTS

NOTE

Dimensional requirements for support spacing, runner spacing, hanger spacing, hanger type selection, and tie wire selection are given in tables on this page.

James E. Phillips, AIA; Enwright Associates, Inc.; Greenville, South Carolina

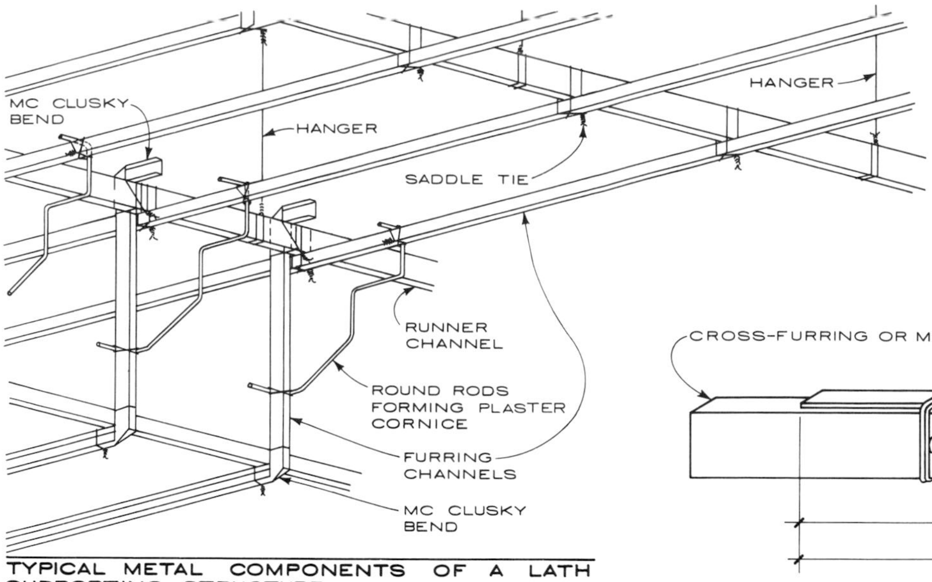

MC CLUSKY BEND
HANGER
HANGER
SADDLE TIE
RUNNER CHANNEL
ROUND RODS FORMING PLASTER CORNICE
FURRING CHANNELS
MC CLUSKY BEND

TYPICAL METAL COMPONENTS OF A LATH SUPPORTING STRUCTURE

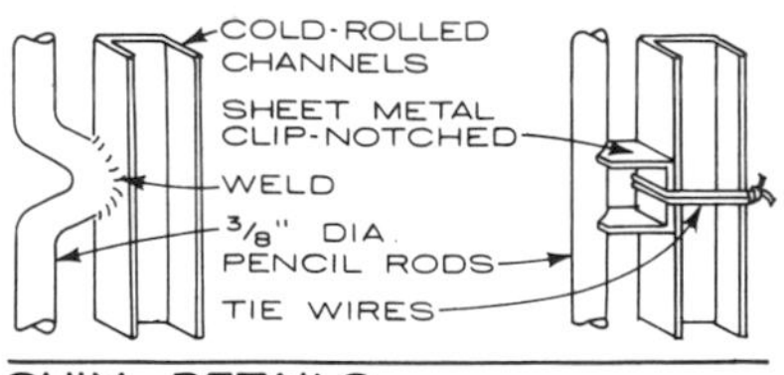

COLD-ROLLED CHANNELS
SHEET METAL CLIP-NOTCHED
WELD
3/8" DIA. PENCIL RODS
TIE WIRES

SHIM DETAILS

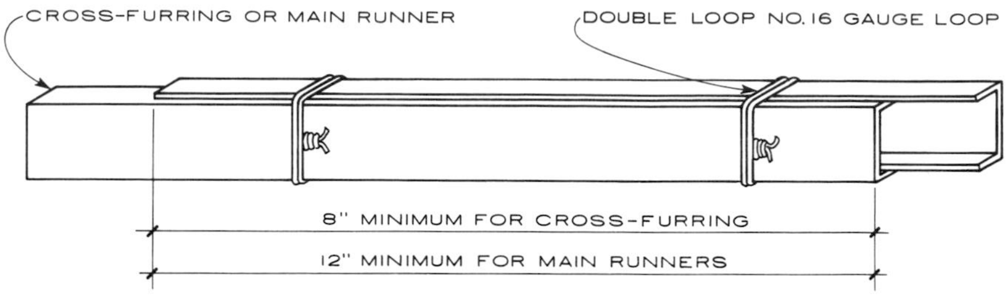

CROSS-FURRING OR MAIN RUNNER
DOUBLE LOOP NO. 16 GAUGE LOOP
8" MINIMUM FOR CROSS-FURRING
12" MINIMUM FOR MAIN RUNNERS

CHANNEL SPLICE

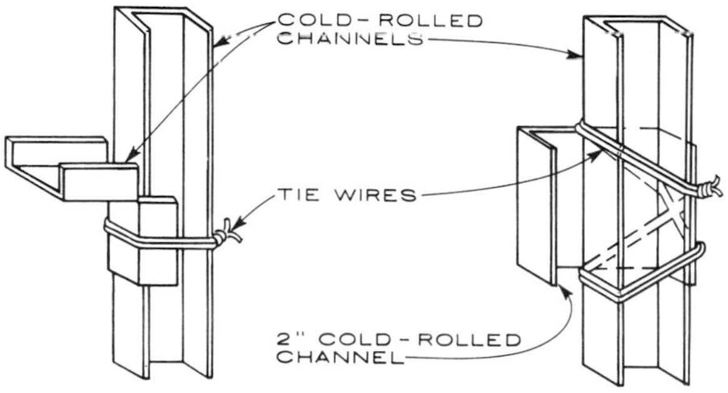

COLD-ROLLED CHANNELS
TIE WIRES
2" COLD-ROLLED CHANNEL

SPACER DETAILS

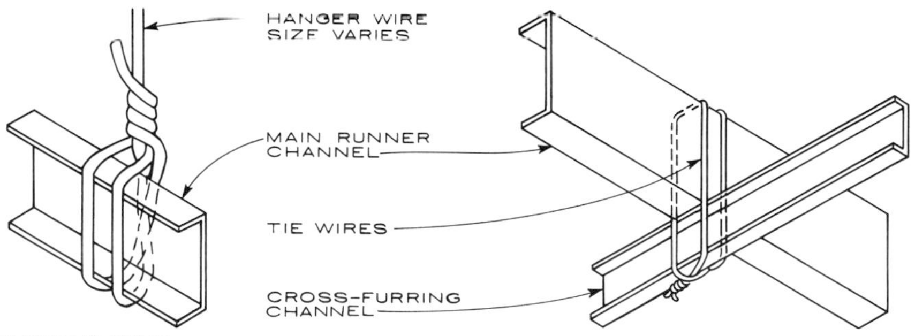

HANGER WIRE SIZE VARIES
MAIN RUNNER CHANNEL
TIE WIRES
CROSS-FURRING CHANNEL

SADDLE TIES

TYPICAL METAL CHANNEL SUSPENSION AND FURRING DETAILS

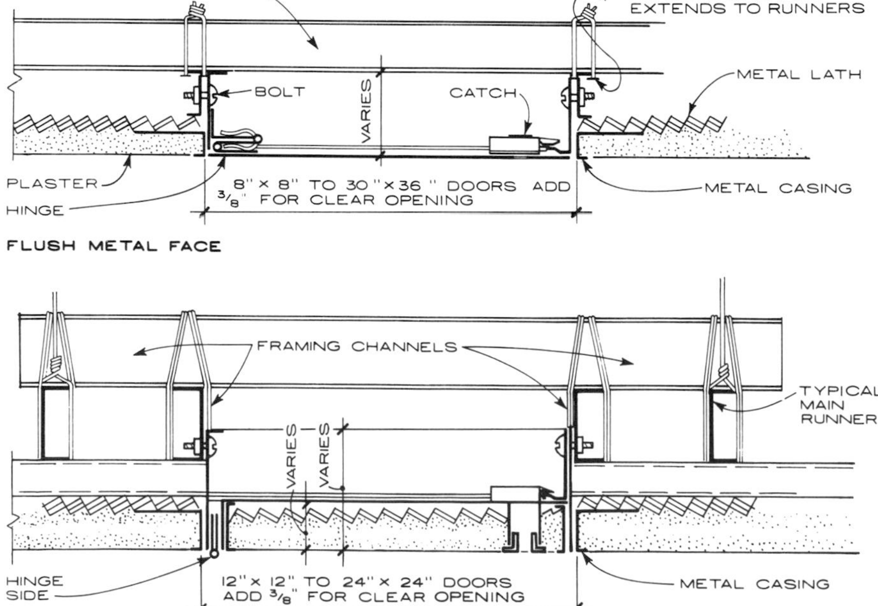
MAIN RUNNER CHANNEL
3/4" FRAMING CHANNEL EXTENDS TO RUNNERS
BOLT
VARIES
CATCH
METAL LATH
PLASTER
HINGE
8" x 8" TO 30" x 36" DOORS ADD 3/8" FOR CLEAR OPENING
METAL CASING
FLUSH METAL FACE
FRAMING CHANNELS
TYPICAL MAIN RUNNER
VARIES
VARIES
HINGE SIDE
12" x 12" TO 24" x 24" DOORS ADD 3/8" FOR CLEAR OPENING
METAL CASING
FLUSH PLASTER FACE

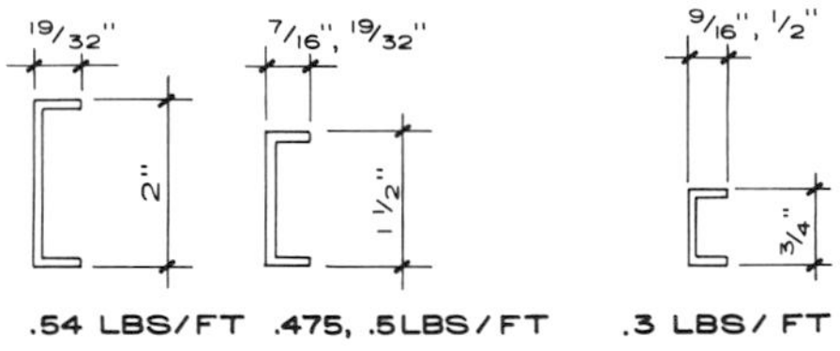

METAL ACCESS DOORS AND FRAMES

NOTE
GAUGE OF METAL, NO. OF LOCKS, HINGES VARY. FIRE-RATED DOORS AVAILABLE

19/32" 2" .54 LBS/FT
7/16", 19/32" 1 1/2" .475, .5 LBS/FT
9/16", 1/2" 3/4" .3 LBS/FT

RUNNERS
FURRING

TYPICAL COLD-ROLLED CHANNEL SHAPES

Heat-rolled channels (HRC) generally run heavier than cold-rolled channels (CRC). Shapes illustrated are available in 16 gauge, 16 ft. and 20 ft. standard lengths.

Galvanizing of all components is recommended where moisture is a factor. Extra heavy galvanizing is required for swimming pools.

See Suspended Ceiling Systems for instructions for selection of components.

Douglas S. Stenhouse, AIA; Los Angeles, California

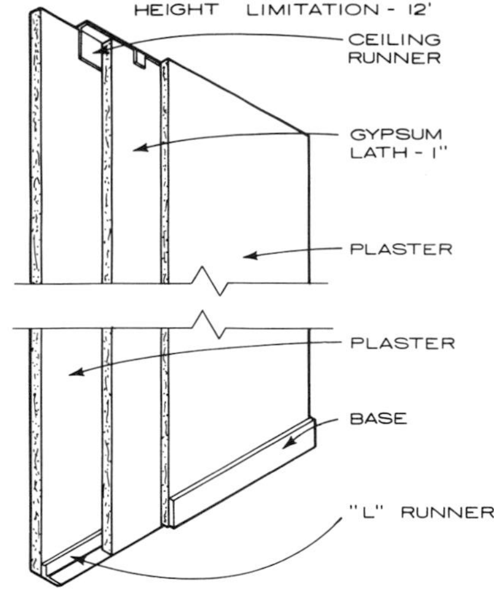
HEIGHT LIMITATION - 12'
CEILING RUNNER
GYPSUM LATH - 1"
PLASTER
PLASTER
BASE
"L" RUNNER

SECTION THROUGH TYPICAL WALL

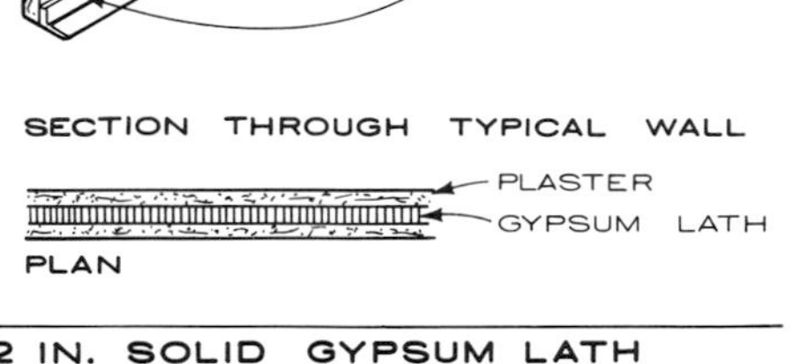
PLASTER
GYPSUM LATH

PLAN

2 IN. SOLID GYPSUM LATH

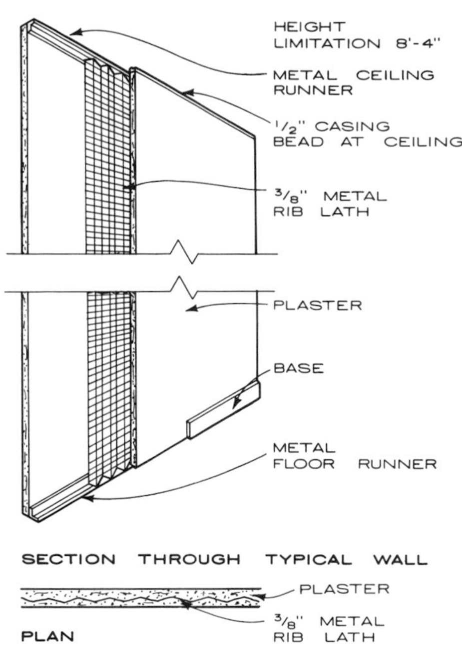
HEIGHT LIMITATION 8'-4"
METAL CEILING RUNNER
1/2" CASING BEAD AT CEILING
3/8" METAL RIB LATH
PLASTER
BASE
METAL FLOOR RUNNER

SECTION THROUGH TYPICAL WALL

PLASTER
3/8" METAL RIB LATH

PLAN

2 IN. SOLID METAL LATH AND PLASTER

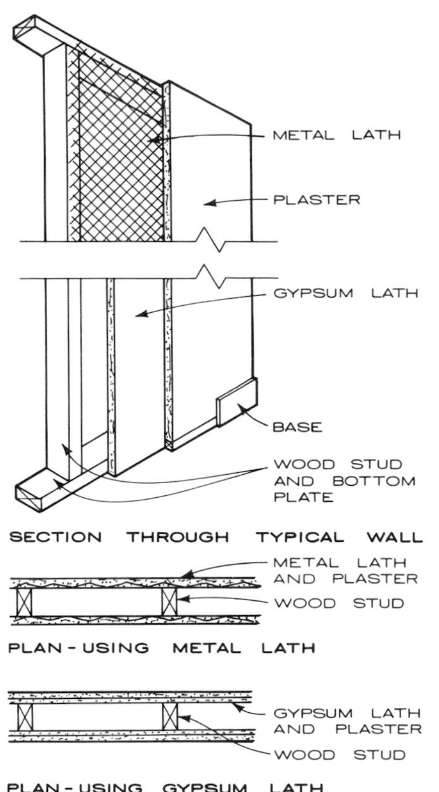
METAL LATH
PLASTER
GYPSUM LATH
BASE
WOOD STUD AND BOTTOM PLATE

SECTION THROUGH TYPICAL WALL

METAL LATH AND PLASTER
WOOD STUD

PLAN - USING METAL LATH

GYPSUM LATH AND PLASTER
WOOD STUD

PLAN - USING GYPSUM LATH

WOOD STUD AND LATH

CHANNEL STUD SPACING

TYPE OF LATH	WEIGHT #/SQ YD	SPACING OF SUPPORTS
Diamond mesh	2.5 3.4	16 16
Flat rib	2.75 3.4	16 24*

*Spacing for solid partitions not to exceed 16'-0" in height.

CHANNEL STUD SIZE

PARTITION HEIGHT	PARTITION THICKNESS	CHANNEL
12'	2"	
14'	2¼"	¾ in. 300 lb per 1000 ft
16'	2½"	
18'	2¾"	1½ in. 475 lb per 1000 ft

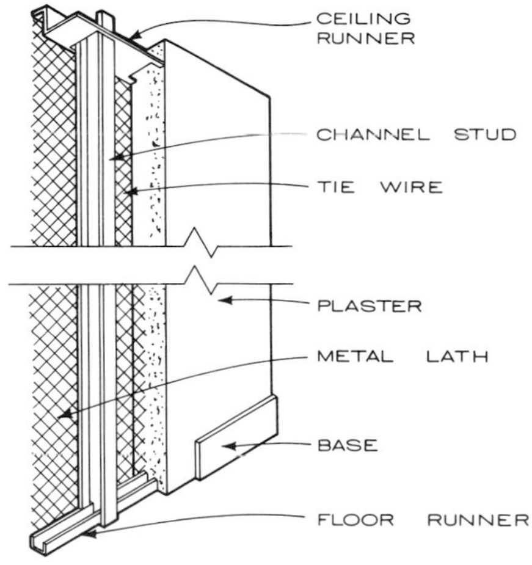
CEILING RUNNER
CHANNEL STUD
TIE WIRE
PLASTER
METAL LATH
BASE
FLOOR RUNNER

SECTION THROUGH TYPICAL WALL

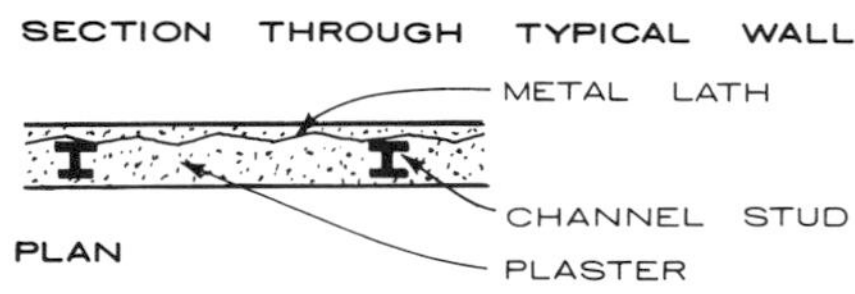
METAL LATH
CHANNEL STUD
PLASTER

PLAN

METAL LATH-CHANNEL STUD-PLASTER

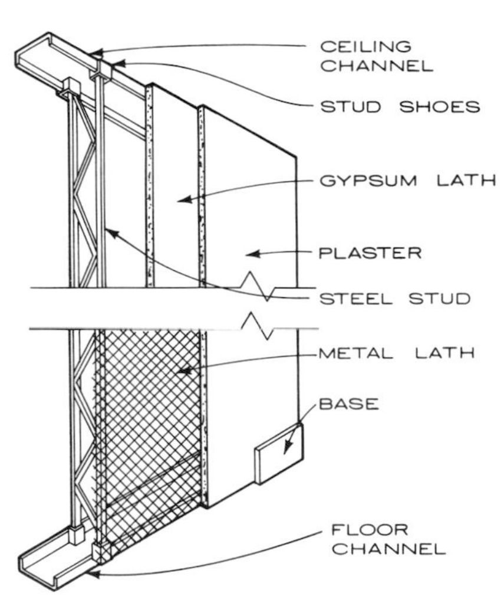
CEILING CHANNEL
STUD SHOES
GYPSUM LATH
PLASTER
STEEL STUD
METAL LATH
BASE
FLOOR CHANNEL

SECTION THROUGH TYPICAL WALL

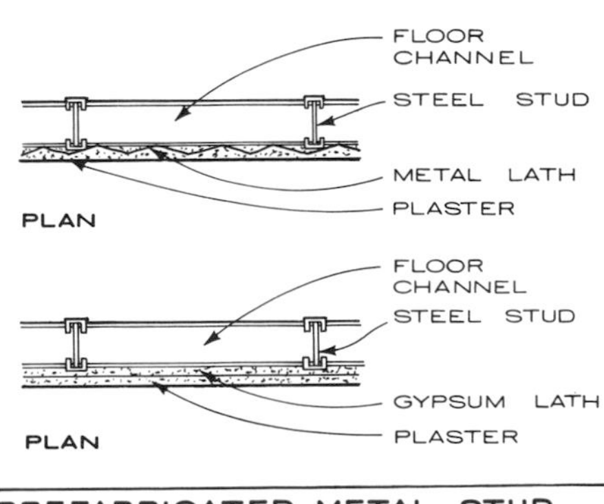
FLOOR CHANNEL
STEEL STUD
METAL LATH
PLASTER
PLAN
FLOOR CHANNEL
STEEL STUD
GYPSUM LATH
PLASTER
PLAN

PREFABRICATED METAL STUD

METAL STUD WITH METAL LATH STUD SPACING AND HEIGHT LIMITATION*

STUD WIDTH	THICKNESS	MAXIMUM HEIGHT 16" OC.	19" OC.	24" OC.
2½"	4"	15'	14'	9'
3¼"	4¾"	21'	18'	13'
4"	5½"	22'	20'	16'
6"	7½"	26'	24'	20'

*For length not exceeding 1½ times height; for lengths exceeding this, reduce 20%.

METAL STUD WITH ⅜" GYPSUM LATH HEIGHT LIMITATIONS

STUD WIDTH	THICKNESS STANDARD SYSTEM	MAX. HEIGHT STUDS 16" OC.
2½"	4¼"	15'
3¼"	5"	21'
4"	5¾"	22'
6"	7¾"	26'

Walter H. Sobel, FAIA & Associates; Chicago, Illinois

TYPES OF GYPSUM PANEL PRODUCTS

DESCRIPTION	THICKNESS (IN.)	WIDTH/EDGE (FT)	STOCK LENGTH (FT)
Regular gypsum wallboard used as a base layer for improving sound control; repair and remodeling	1/4	4, square or tapered	8-10
Regular gypsum wallboard used in a double wall system over wood framing; repair and remodeling	3/8	4, square or tapered	8-14
Regular gypsum wallboard for use in single layer construction	1/2, 5/8	4, square or tapered	8-16
Rounded taper edge system offers maximum joint strength and minimizes joint deformity problems	3/8 1/2, 5/8	4, rounded taper	8-16
Type X gypsum wallboard with core containing special additives to give increased fire resistance ratings. Consult manufacturer for approved assemblies	1/2, 5/8	4, tapered, rounded taper, or rounded	8-16
Aluminum foil backed board effective as a vapor barrier for exterior walls and ceilings and as a thermal insulator when foil faces 3/4" minimum air space. Not for use as a tile base or in air conditioned buildings in hot, humid climates (Southern Atlantic and Gulf Coasts)	3/8 1/2, 5/8	4, square or tapered	8-16
Water resistant board for use as a base for ceramic and other nonabsorbant wall tiles in bath and shower areas. Type X core is available	1/2, 5/8	4, tapered	8, 10, 12
Prefinished vinyl surface gypsum board in standard and special colors	1/2, 5/8	2, 2 1/2, 4, square and beveled	8, 9, 10
Prefinished board available in many colors and textures. See manufacturers' literature	5/16	4, square	8
Coreboard for use to enclose vent shafts and laminated gypsum partitions	1	2, tongue and groove or square	4-16
Shaft wall liner core board type X with gypsum core used to enclose elevator shafts and other vertical chases	1, 2	2, square or beveled	6-16
Sound underlayment gypsum wallboard attached to plywood subfloor acts as a base for any durable floor covering. When used with resiliently attached gypsum panel ceiling, the assembly meets HUD requirements for sound control in multifamily dwellings	3/4	4, square	6-8
Exterior ceiling/soffit panel for use on surfaces with indirect exposure to the weather	1/2	4, rounded taper	8, 12
Sheathing used as underlayment on exterior walls with type X or regular core	1/2	2, tongue and groove	8
	1/2, 5/8	4, square	8, 9, 10

NOTE: A large range of adhesives, sealants, joint treatments, and texture products are available from the manufacturers of most gypsum board products. Consult available literature for current recommendations and products.

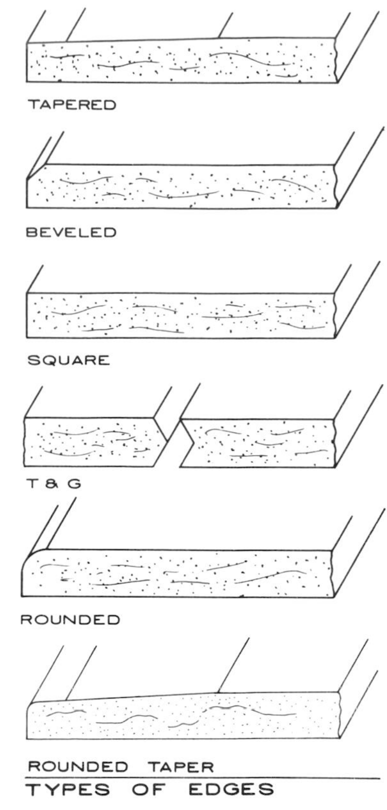
TAPERED
BEVELED
SQUARE
T & G
ROUNDED
ROUNDED TAPER
TYPES OF EDGES

MAX. BENDING FOR DRYWALL

THICKNESS	BENDING RADII LENGTHWISE	BENDING RADII WIDTH
1/4"	5'-0"	15'-0"
3/8"	7'-6"	25'-0"
1/2"	20'-0"	–

Shorter radii may be obtained by moistening face and back so that water will soak well into core of board.

MAXIMUM ALLOWABLE PARTITION HEIGHT

STUD SPACING (IN.) (FACING ON EACH SIDE)	STUD DEPTH (IN.) 1 5/8 *	2 1/2	3 1/4	3 5/8	4
	MAXIMUM ALLOWABLE HEIGHT				
16 (1/2 one-ply)	11'-0"	14'-8"	17'-10"	19'-5"	20'-8"
24 (1/2 one-ply)	10'-0"	13'-5"	16'-0"	17'-3"	18'-5"
24 (1/2 two-ply)	12'-4"	15'-10"	18'-3"	19'-5"	20'-8"

*1 5/8" stud with single layer of gypsum wallboard recommended for chase walls and closets only.

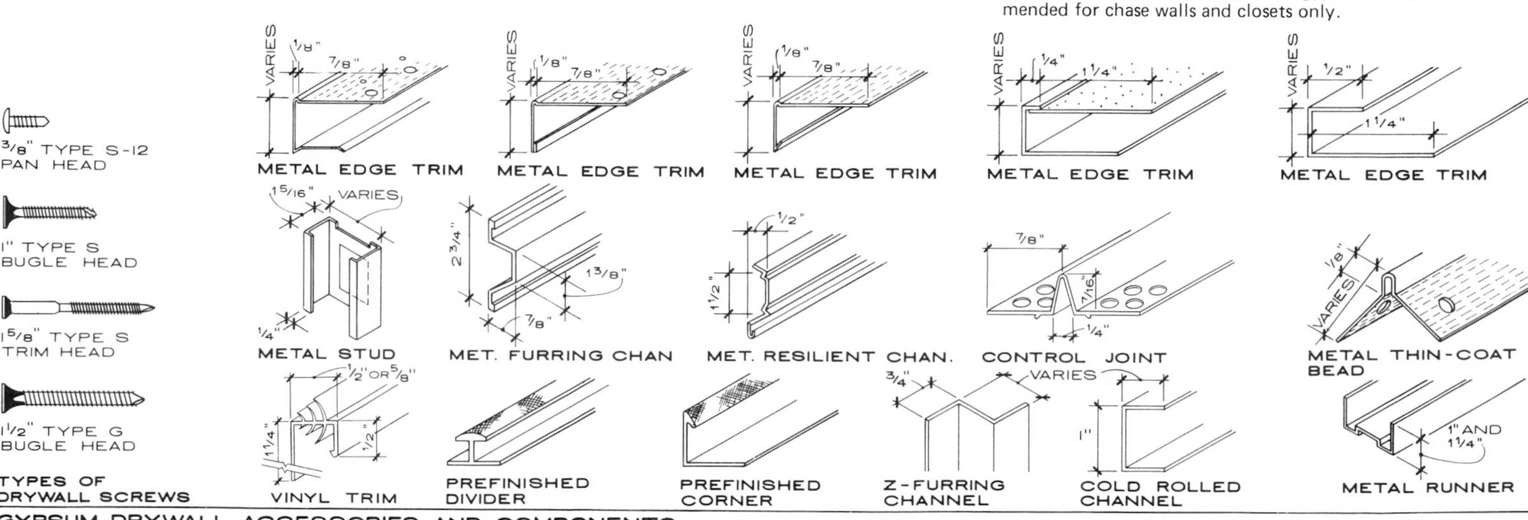
3/8" TYPE S-12 PAN HEAD
1" TYPE S BUGLE HEAD
1 5/8" TYPE S TRIM HEAD
1 1/2" TYPE G BUGLE HEAD
TYPES OF DRYWALL SCREWS
METAL EDGE TRIM
METAL EDGE TRIM
METAL EDGE TRIM
METAL EDGE TRIM
METAL EDGE TRIM
VARIES
METAL STUD
MET. FURRING CHAN
MET. RESILIENT CHAN.
CONTROL JOINT
METAL THIN-COAT BEAD
VINYL TRIM
PREFINISHED DIVIDER
PREFINISHED CORNER
Z-FURRING CHANNEL
COLD ROLLED CHANNEL
METAL RUNNER
1" AND 1 1/4"
GYPSUM DRYWALL ACCESSORIES AND COMPONENTS

Ferdinand R. Scheeler, AIA; Skidmore, Owings & Merrill; Chicago, Illinois
James Lloyd; Kennett Square, Pennsylvania

FIRE RATING	STC	WALL THICKNESS	CONSTRUCTION DESCRIPTION	WALL SECTIONS
1 HOUR	30 TO 34	4 7/8"	One layer 1/2 in. type X veneer base nailed to each side of 2 x 4 in. wood studs 16 in. o.c. with 5d coated nails 8 in. o.c. Minimum 3/32 in. gypsum veneer plaster. Joints staggered vertically 16 in. and horizontal joints each side at 12 in.	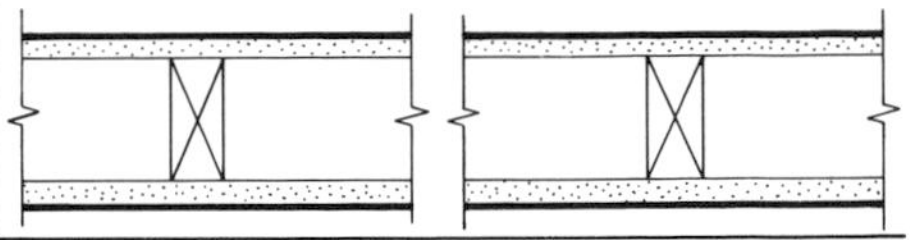
		4 7/8"	One layer 5/8 in. type X gypsum wallboard or veneer base nailed to each side of 2 x 4 in. wood studs 16 in. o.c. with 6d coated nails 7 in. o.c. Stagger joints 24 in. on each side.	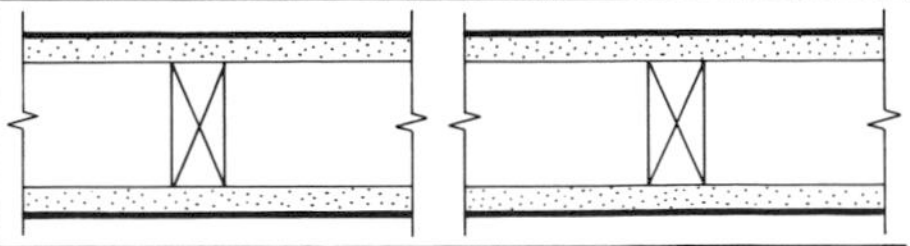
	35 TO 39	5 1/8"	Two layers 3/8 in. regular gypsum wallboard or veneer base nailed to each side of 2 x 4 in. wood studs 16 in. o.c. First layer attached with 4d coated nails, second layer applied with laminating compound and nailed with 5d coated nails 8 in. o.c. Stagger joints 16 in. o.c. each side.	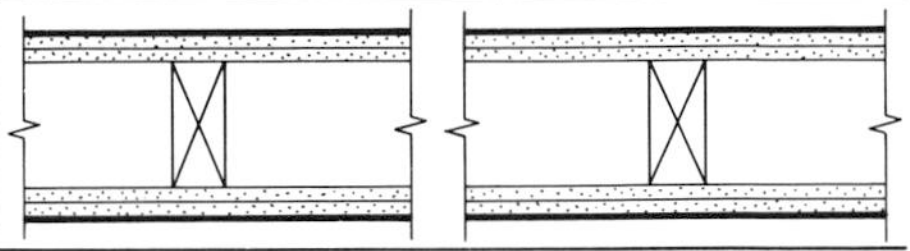
	45 TO 49	5 3/8"	Base layer 3/8 in. regular gypsum wallboard or veneer base nailed to each side of 2 x 4 in. wood studs 16 in. o.c. Face layer 1/2 in. (same as base layer). Use 5d coated nails 24 in. o.c. for base layer and 8d coated nails 12 in. o.c. to edge and 24 in. o.c. to intermediate studs. Stagger joints 16 in. o.c. each layer and side.	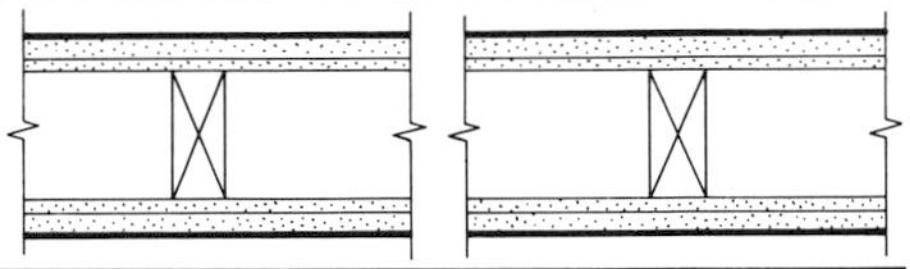
		5 7/8"	Base layer 1/2 in. wood fiberboard to each side of 2 x 4 in. wood studs 16 in. o.c. with 5d coated nails 24 in. o.c. on vertical joints and 16 in. o.c. to top and bottom plates. Face layer 5/8 in. type X gypsum wallboard or veneer base applied to each side with laminating compound and nailed with 8d coated nails 24 in. o.c. on vertical joints and 16 in. o.c. to top and bottom plates. Stagger joints 24 in. o.c. each layer and side.	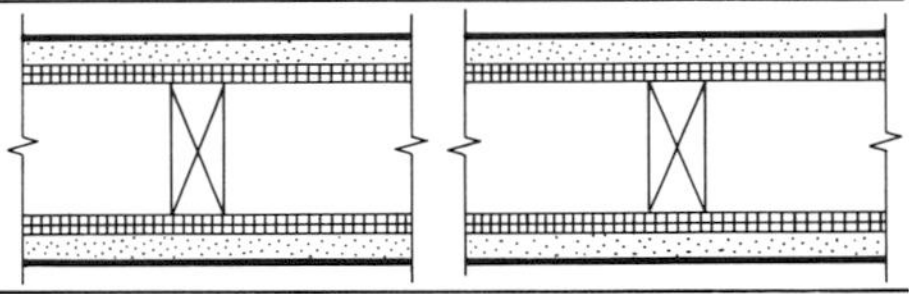
		5 7/8"	Both sides resilient channels 24 in. o.c. attached with GWB 54 drywall nails to each side of 2 x 4 in. wood studs 16 in. o.c. One layer 5/8 in. type X gypsum wallboard or veneer base attached with 1 in. type S drywall screws 12 in. o.c. to each side and vertical joints back-blocked. GWB filler strips along floor and ceiling both sides. Stagger joints 24 in. o.c. each side.	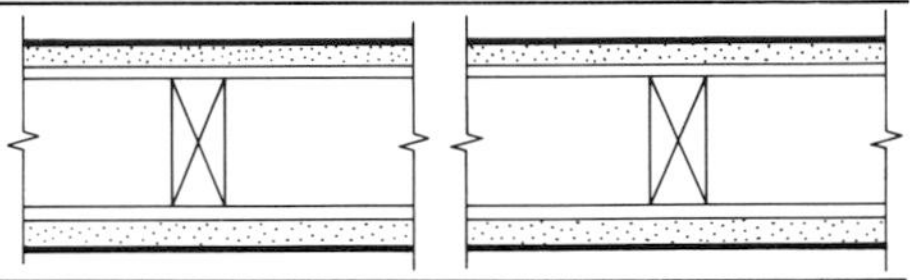
	50 TO 54	5 3/8"	Base layer 1/4 in. proprietary gypsum wallboard applied to each side of 2 x 4 in. wood studs 16 in. o.c. with 4d coated nails 12 in. o.c. Face layer 5/8 in. type X gypsum wallboard or veneer base applied with laminating compound and nailed with 6d coated nails 16 in. o.c. to each side. 1 1/2 in. mineral fiber insulation in cavity. Stagger joints 24 in. o.c. each side.	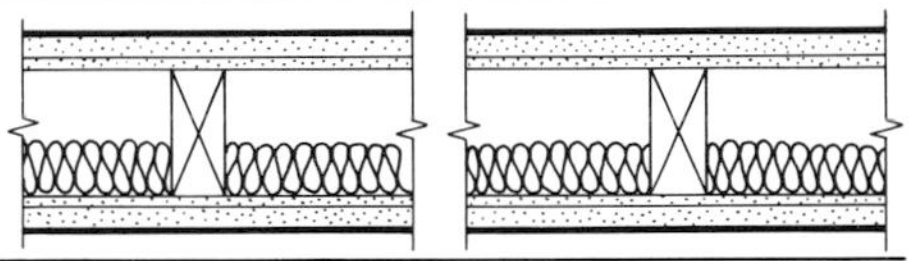
		5 3/8"	One side resilient channel 24 in. o.c. with 1 1/4 in. type S drywall screws to 2 x 4 in. wood studs 16 in. o.c. Both sides 5/8 in. gypsum wallboard or veneer base attached to resilient channel with 1 in. type S drywall screws 12 in. o.c. and GWB to stud with 1 1/4 in. type W drywall screws. 1 1/2 in. mineral fiber insulation in cavity. Stagger joints 48 in. o.c. each side.	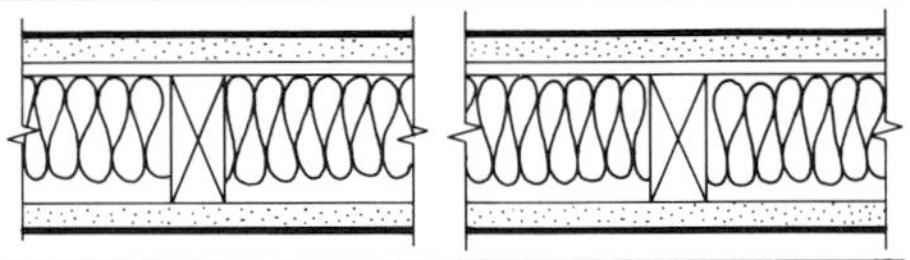
	60 TO 64	6 7/8"	One side resilient channels 24 in. o.c. attached with 1 in. type S drywall screws to 2 x 4 in. wood studs 16 in. o.c. Two layers of 5/8 in. type X gypsum wallboard or veneer base. First layer attached with 1 in. type S drywall screws, second layer applied with laminating compound. Other side one layer each of 5/8 in. and 1/2 in. gypsum wallboard or veneer base plus top 3/8 in. gypsum wallboard applied with laminating compound. Use 5d coated nails 32 in. o.c. for base, 8d for 1/2 in. center layer. 2 in. glass fiber insulation in cavity. Stagger all joints 16 in. o.c.	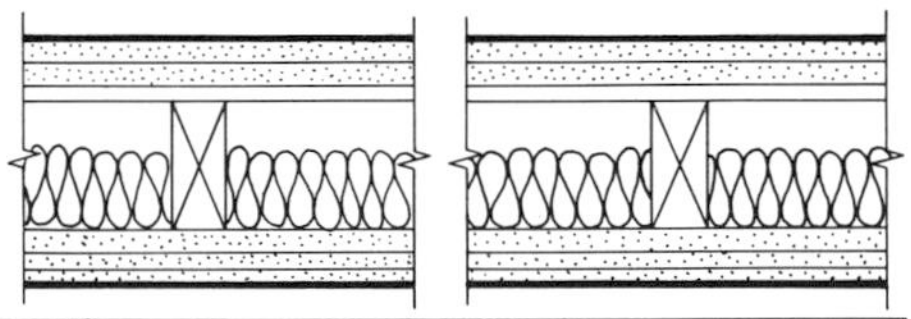
2 HOUR	40 TO 44	6 1/8"	Two layers 5/8 in. type X gypsum wallboard or veneer base applied to each side of 2 x 4 in. wood studs 24 in. o.c. Use 6d coated nails 24 in. o.c. for base layer and 8d coated nails 8 in. o.c. for face layer. Stagger joints 24 in. o.c. each layer and side.	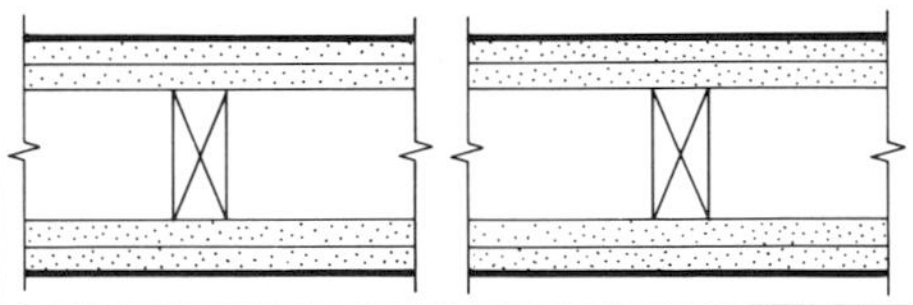
	50 TO 54	8"	Two layers 5/8 in. type X gypsum wallboard or veneer base applied to each side of 2 x 4 in. wood studs 16 in. o.c. staggered 8 in. o.c. on 2 x 6 in. wood plates. Use 6d coated nails 24 in. o.c. for base layer and 8d coated nails 8 in. o.c. for face layer. Stagger vertical joints 16 in. o.c. each layer and side.	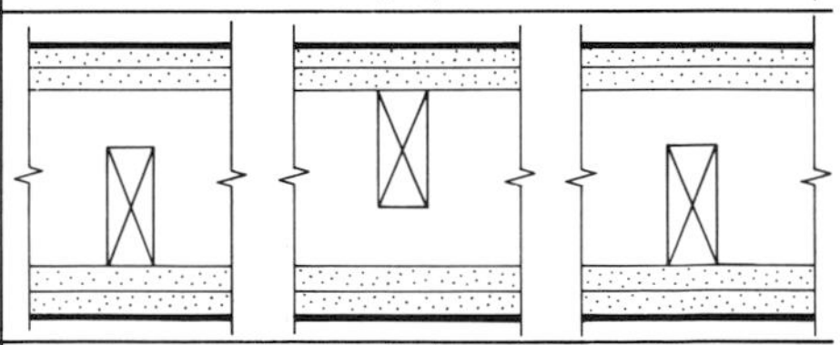
	55 TO 59	10 3/4"	Two layers 5/8 in. type X gypsum wallboard or veneer base applied to each side of double row of 2 x 4 in. wood studs 16 in. o.c. on separate plates 1 in. apart. Use 6d coated nails 24 in. o.c. for base layer and 8d coated nails 8 in. o.c. for face layer. 3 1/2 in. glass fiber insulation in cavity. Stagger joints 16 in. o.c. each layer and side. GWB fire stop continuous in space between plates.	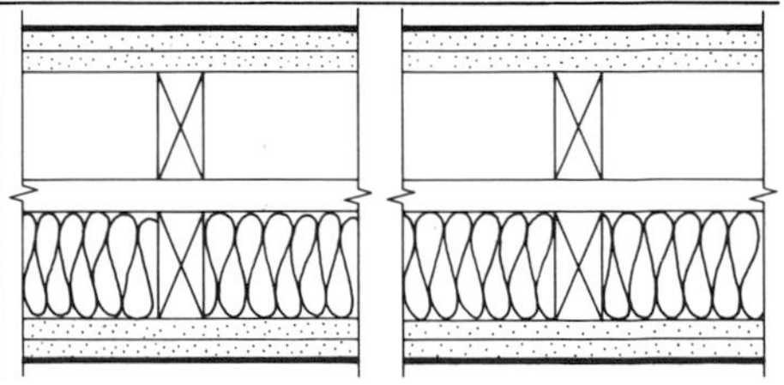

CONSULT MANUFACTURER OR GYPSUM ASSOCIATION FOR ADDITIONAL INFORMATION

FIRE RATING	STC	WALL THICKNESS	CONSTRUCTION DESCRIPTION	WALL SECTIONS
1 HOUR	35 TO 39	2 7/8"	One layer 5/8 in. type X gypsum wallboard or veneer base applied to each side of 1 5/8 in. metal studs 24 in. o.c. with 1 in. type S drywall screws 8 in. o.c. to edges and 12 in. o.c. to intermediate studs. Stagger joints 24 in. o.c. each side.	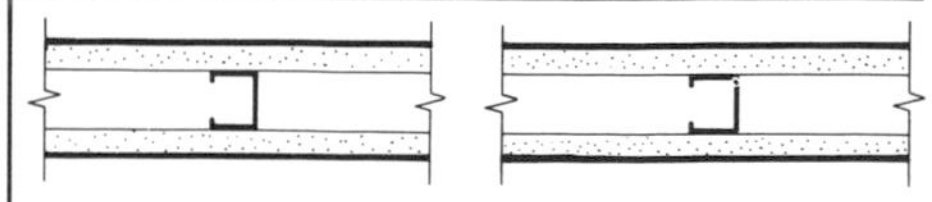
	40 TO 44	3 3/8"	Base layer 3/8 in. regular gypsum wallboard or veneer base applied to each side of 1 5/8 in. metal studs 24 in. o.c. with 1 in. type S drywall screws 27 in. o.c. to edges and 54 in. o.c. to intermediate studs. Face layer 1/2 in. attached on each side to studs with 1 5/8 in. type S drywall screws 12 in. o.c. to perimeter and 24 in. o.c. to intermediate studs. Stagger joints 24 in. o.c. each layer and side.	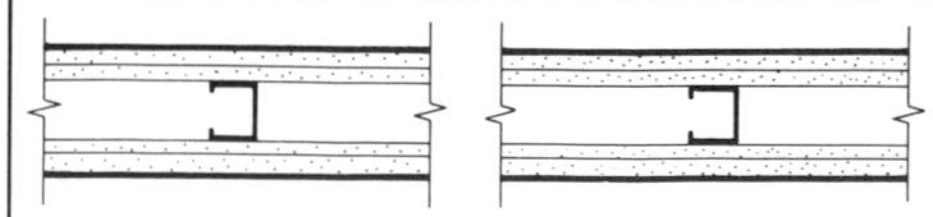
		4 7/8"	One layer 5/8 in. type X gypsum wallboard or veneer base applied to each side of 3 5/8 in. metal studs 24 in. o.c. with 1 in. type S drywall screws 8 in. o.c. to vertical edges and 12 in. o.c. to intermediate studs. Stagger joints 24 in. o.c. each side.	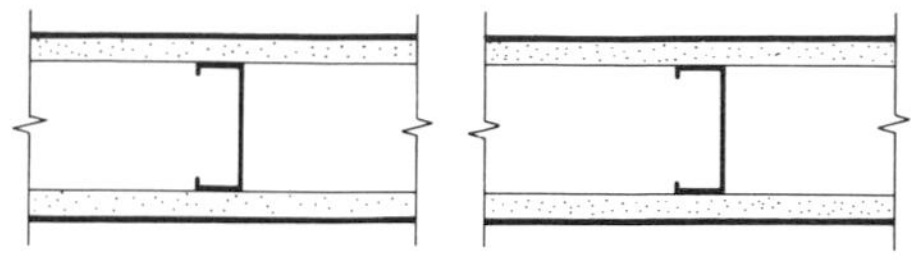
	45 TO 49	3 1/8"	Two layers 1/2 in. regular gypsum wallboard or veneer base applied to each side of 1 5/8 in. metal studs 24 in. o.c. Use 1 in. type S drywall screws 12 in. o.c. for base layer and 1 5/8 in. type S drywall screws 12 in. o.c. for face layer. Stagger joints 24 in. o.c. each layer and side.	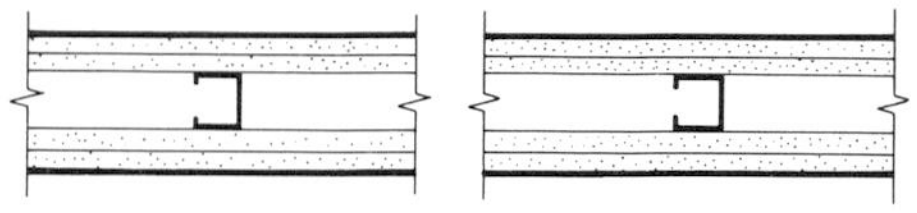
		3 1/8"	Base layer 1/4 in. gypsum wallboard applied to each side of 1 5/8 in. metal studs 24 in. o.c. with 1 in. type S drywall screws 24 in. o.c. to edges and 36 in. o.c. to intermediate studs. Face layer 1/2 in. type X gypsum wallboard or veneer base applied to each side of studs with 1 5/8 in. type S drywall screws 12 in. o.c. Stagger joints 24 in. o.c. each layer and side.	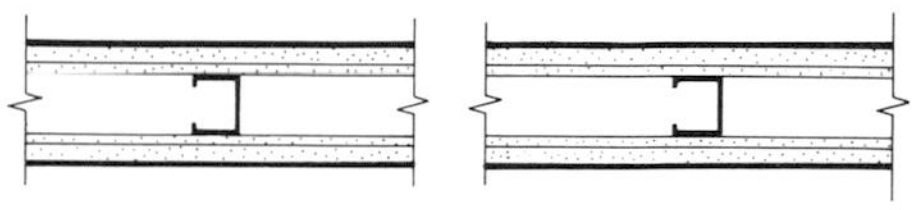
		5 1/2"	One layer 5/8 in. type X gypsum wallboard or veneer base applied to each side of 3 5/8 in. metal studs 24 in. o.c. with 1 in. type S drywall screws 8 in. o.c. to edge and vertical joints and 12 in. o.c. to intermediate stud. Face layer 5/8 in. (same as other layer) applied on one side to stud with laminating compound and attached with 1 5/8 in. type S drywall screws 8 in. o.c. to edges and sides and 12 in. o.c. to intermediate studs. 3 1/2 in. glass fiber insulation in cavity. Stagger joints 24 in. o.c. each layer and side.	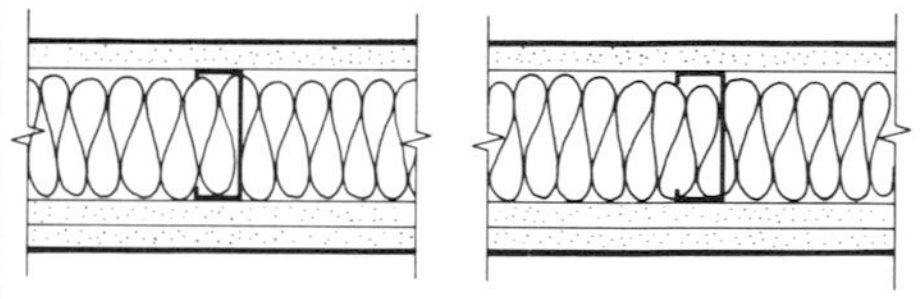
	50 TO 54	4"	Base layer 1/4 in. regular gypsum wallboard applied to each side of 2 1/2 in. metal studs 24 in. o.c. with 1 in. type S drywall screws 12 in. o.c. Face layer 1/2 in. type X gypsum wallboard or veneer base applied to each side of studs with laminating compound and with 1 5/8 in. type S drywall screws in top and bottom runners 8 in. o.c. 2 in. glass fiber insulation in cavity. Stagger joints 24 in. o.c. each layer and side.	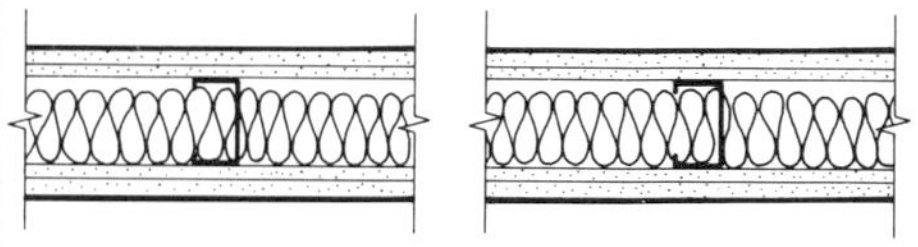
		4"	Two layers 1/2 in. type X gypsum wallboard or veneer base applied to one side of 2 1/2 in. metal studs 24 in. o.c. Base layer 1 in. and face layer 1 5/8 in. type S drywall screws 8 in. o.c. to edge and adhesive beads to intermediate studs. Opposite side layer 1/2 in. type X gypsum wallboard or veneer base applied with 1 in. type S drywall screws 8 in. o.c. to vertical edges and 12 in. o.c. to intermediate studs. 3 in. glass fiber insulation in cavity. Stagger joints 24 in. o.c. each layer and face.	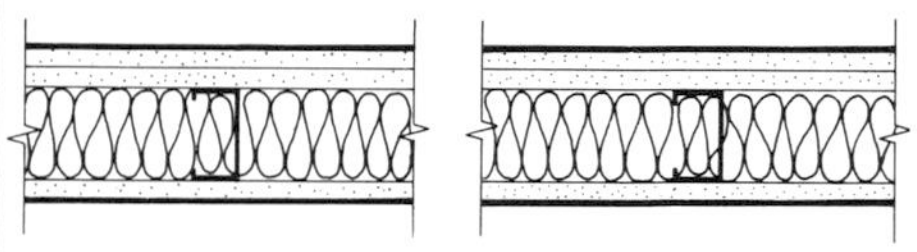
	55 TO 59	4 1/4"	Base layer 1/4 in. gypsum wallboard applied to each side of 2 1/2 in. metal studs 24 in. o.c. with 7/8 in. type S drywall screws 12 in. o.c. Face layer 5/8 in. type X gypsum wallboard or veneer base applied on each side of studs with 1 5/16 in. type S drywall screws 12 in. o.c. 1 1/2 in. glass fiber insulation in cavity. Stagger joints 24 in. o.c. each layer and side.	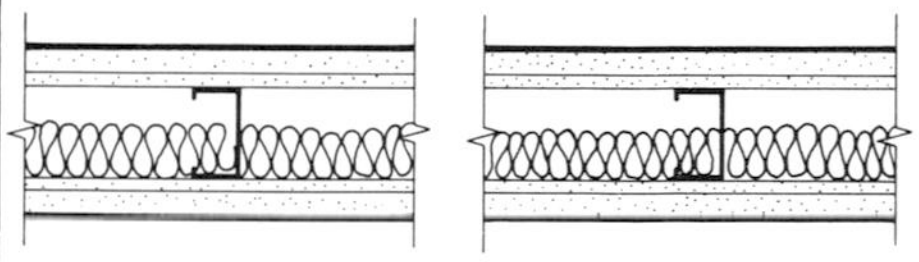
2 HOUR	40 TO 44	5"	Two layers 5/8 in. type X gypsum wallboard or veneer base applied to each side of 2 1/2 in. metal studs 16 in. o.c. braced laterally. Use 1 in. for base layer and 1 5/8 in. for facelayer type S-12 drywall screws 12 in. o.c. Stagger joints 16 in. o.c. each layer and side.	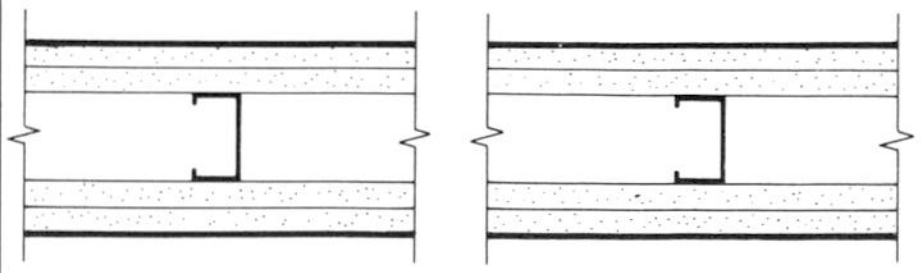
	50 TO 54	3 5/8"	Base layer 1/2 in. type X gypsum wallboard or veneer base applied to each side of 1 5/8 in. metal studs 24 in. o.c. Use 1 in. type S drywall screws 12 in. o.c. for base layer and 1 5/8 in. type S drywall screws 12 in. o.c. for face layer. 1 1/2 in. glass fiber insulation in cavity. Stagger joints 24 in. o.c. each layer and side.	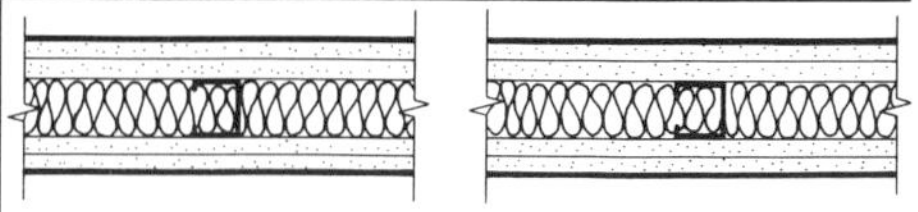
	55 TO 59	6 1/4"	Two layers 5/8 in. type X gypsum wallboard or veneer base applied to each side of 3 5/8 in. metal studs 24 in. o.c. Use 1 in. type S drywall screws 32 in. o.c. for base layer and 1 5/8 in. type S drywall screws 12 in. o.c. to edge and 24 in. o.c. to intermediate studs. One side third layer 1/4 or 3/8 in. gypsum wallboard or veneer base applied with laminating compound. Stagger joints 24 in. o.c. each layer and side.	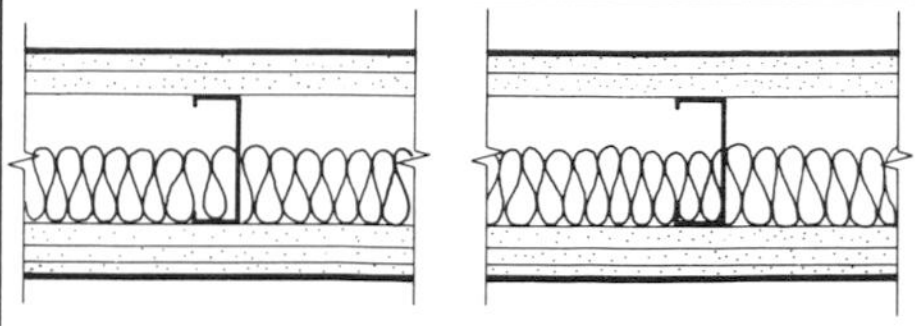

CONSULT MANUFACTURER OR GYPSUM ASSOCIATION FOR ADDITIONAL INFORMATION

FIRE RATING	STC	WALL THICKNESS	CONSTRUCTION DESCRIPTION	WALL SECTIONS
1 HOUR	35 TO 39	$3^1/_8$"	1 in. x 24 in. proprietary type X gypsum panels inserted between $2^1/_2$ in. floor and ceiling J runners with $2^1/_2$ in. proprietary vented C-H studs between panels. One layer $^5/_8$ in. proprietary type X gypsum wallboard or veneer base applied parallel to studs on side opposite proprietary gypsum panels with 1 in. type S drywall screws spaced 12 in. o.c. in studs and runners. STC estimate based on 1 in. mineral fiber in cavity. (NLB)	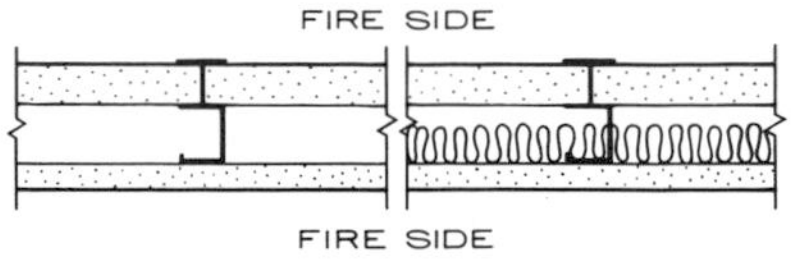 FIRE SIDE / FIRE SIDE
	40 TO 44	$2^7/_8$"	$^3/_4$ in. x 24 in. proprietary type X gypsum panels inserted between $2^1/_4$ in. floor and ceiling track and fitted to proprietary $2^1/_4$ in. slotted metal I studs with tab-flange. Face layer $^5/_8$ in. type X gypsum board applied at right angles to studs, with 1 in. type S drywall screws, 12 in. o.c. Sound tested with 1 in. glass fiber friction fit in stud space. (NLB)	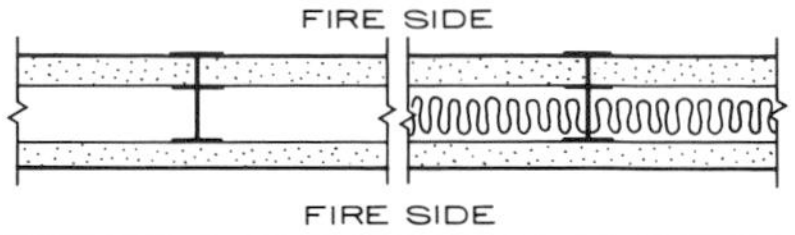 FIRE SIDE / FIRE SIDE
2 HOURS	30 TO 34	$2^1/_4$"	One layer $^5/_8$ in. type X gypsum wallboard or veneer base applied vertically to each side of 1 in. gypsum board panels (solid or laminated) with laminating compound combed over entire contact surface. Panel supported by metal runners at top and bottom and horizontal bracing angles of No. 22 gauge galvanized steel $^3/_4$ in. x $1^1/_4$ in. spaced 5 ft. 0 in. o.c. or less on shaft side. (NLB) *Limiting height shown is based on interior partition exposure conditions. Shaft wall exposure conditions may require reduction of limiting height.	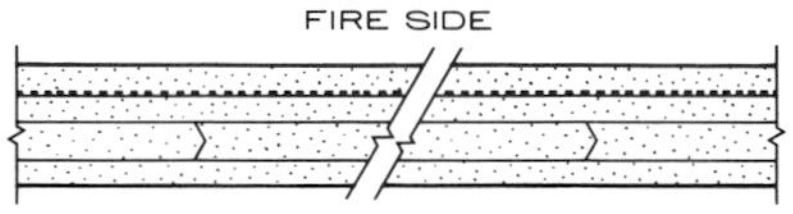 FIRE SIDE
	35 TO 39	$4^1/_8$"	Four layers $^5/_8$ in. type X gypsum wallboard or veneer base applied at right angles to one side of $1^5/_8$ in. metal studs 24 in. o.c. Base layer attached to studs with 1 in. type S drywall screws 12 in. o.c. Second layer attached to studs with $1^5/_8$ in. type S drywall screws using only two screws per board. Third layer attached with $2^5/_8$ in. type S drywall screws similar to second layer. Steel strips $1^1/_2$ in. wide vertically applied over third layer at stud lines and attached 12 in. o.c. to studs with $2^5/_8$ in. type S drywall screws. Third layer also attached to top and bottom track with $2^5/_8$ in. type S drywall screws placed midway between studs. Face layer attached to steel strips with 1 in. type S drywall screws 8 in. o.c. at each stud. Stagger joints of each layer. (NLB)	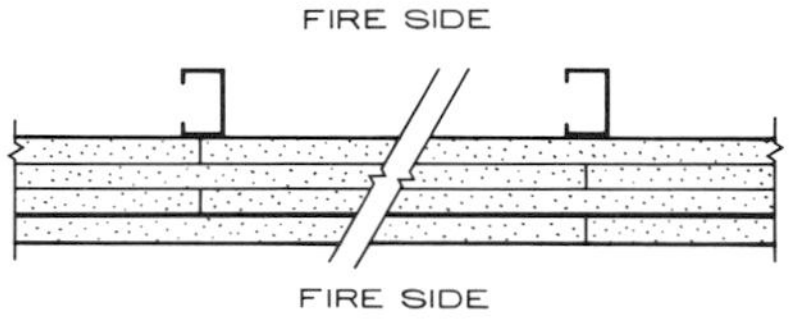 FIRE SIDE / FIRE SIDE
	40 TO 44	$3^1/_2$"	1 in. x 24 in. proprietary type X gypsum panels inserted between $2^1/_2$ in. floor and ceiling J track with T section of $2^1/_2$ in. proprietary C-T metal studs between proprietary gypsum panels. Two layers of $^1/_2$ in. type X gypsum wallboard applied to face of C–T studs. Base layer applied at right angles to studs with 1 in. type S drywall screws 24 in. o.c. and face layer applied at right angles to studs with $1^5/_8$ in. type S drywall screws 8 in. o.c. Stagger joints 24 in. o.c. each layer. (NLB)	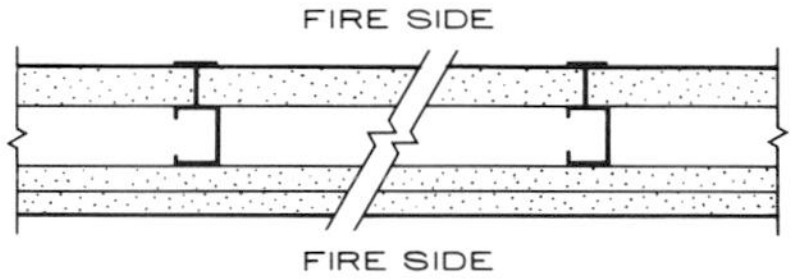 FIRE SIDE / FIRE SIDE
	45 TO 49	$3^1/_2$"	1 in. x 24 in. proprietary type X gypsum panels inserted between $2^1/_2$ in. floor and ceiling track with tab-flange section of $2^1/_2$ in. metal I studs between proprietary gypsum panels. One layer of $^1/_2$ in. proprietary type X gypsum wallboard or veneer base applied at right angles to each side of metal I studs with 1 in. type S drywall screws 12 in. o.c. Sound tested using $1^1/_2$ in. glass fiber friction fit in stud space. (NLB)	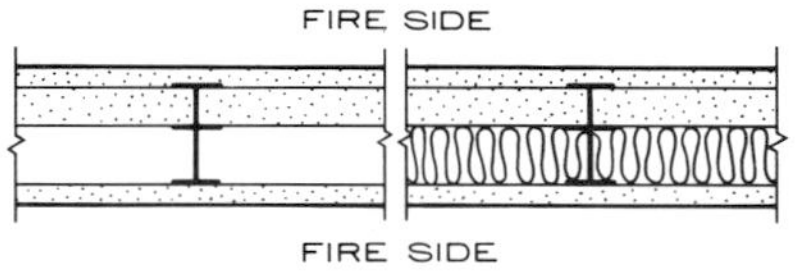 FIRE SIDE / FIRE SIDE
	50 TO 54	4"	1 in. x 24 in. proprietary type X gypsum panels inserted between $2^1/_2$ in. floor and ceiling track with tab-flange section of $2^1/_2$ in. metal I studs between proprietary gypsum panels. One layer of $^1/_2$ in. proprietary type X gypsum wallboard or veneer base applied at right angles to flanges of I studs adjacent to proprietary gypsum panels with 1 in. type S drywall screws 12 in. o.c. Resilient channels spaced 24 in. o.c. horizontally, screw attached to opposite flanges of I studs with $^3/_8$ in. type S screws, one per channel-stud intersection. $^1/_2$ in. proprietary type X gypsum wallboard or veneer base applied parallel to resilient furring channels with 1 in. type S drywall screws 12 in. o.c. Sound tested using 1 in. glass fiber friction fit in stud space. (NLB)	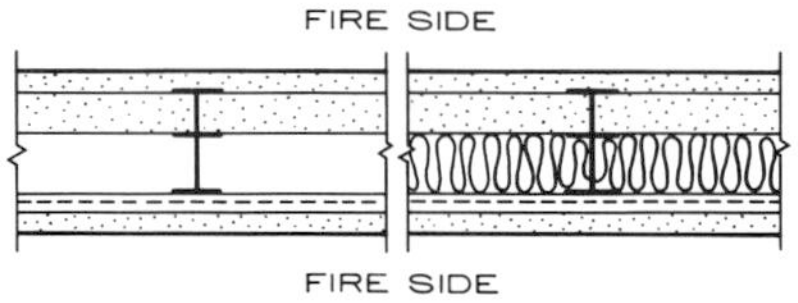 FIRE SIDE / FIRE SIDE
3 HOURS	40 TO 44	$4^1/_8$"	2 in. x 24 in. laminated gypsum board panels installed vertically between floor and ceiling 20 gauge J runners with 25 gauge steel H members between panels. Panels attached at midpoint to $2^1/_2$ in. leg of J runners with $2^3/_8$ in. type S-12 drywall screws. H studs formed from 20 or 25 gauge 2 in. x 1 in. channels placed back to back and spot welded 24 in. o.c. Base layer $^5/_8$ in. gypsum wallboard or veneer base applied parallel to one side of panels, with 1 in. type S drywall screws 12 in. o.c. to H studs. Rigid furring channels horizontally attached 24 in. o.c. to H studs with 1 in. type S drywall screws. Face layer $^5/_8$ in. gypsum wallboard or veneer base attached at right angles to furring channels with 1 in. type S drywall screws 12 in. o.c. Stagger joints 24 in. o.c. each layer and side. (NLB)	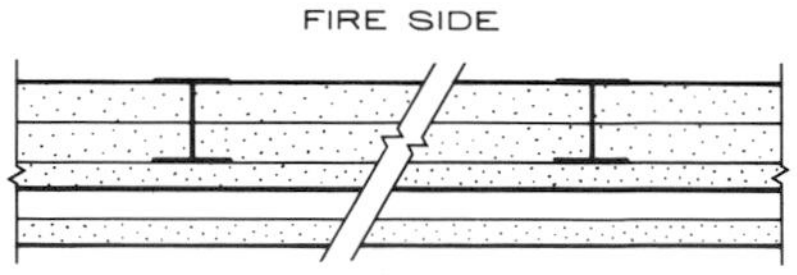 FIRE SIDE
	45 TO 49	$5^1/_4$"	$^3/_4$ in. x 24 in. proprietary type X gypsum panels inserted between $2^1/_4$ in. floor and ceiling tracks and fitted to $2^1/_4$ in. slotted metal I studs with tab-flange. First layer $^5/_8$ in. type X gypsum board applied at right angles to studs with 1 in. type S drywall screws 24 in. o.c. Second layer $^5/_8$ in. type X gypsum board applied parallel to studs with $1^5/_8$ in. type S drywall screws 42 in. o.c. starting 12 in. from bottom. Third layer $^5/_8$ in. type X gypsum board applied parallel to studs with $2^1/_4$ in. type S drywall screws 24 in. o.c. Resilient channels applied 24 in. o.c. at right angles to studs with $2^1/_4$ in. type S drywall screws. Fourth layer $^5/_8$ in. type X gypsum board applied at right angles to resilient channels with 1 in. type S drywall screws 12 in. o.c. Sound tested with 1 in. glass fiber friction fit in stud space. (NLB)	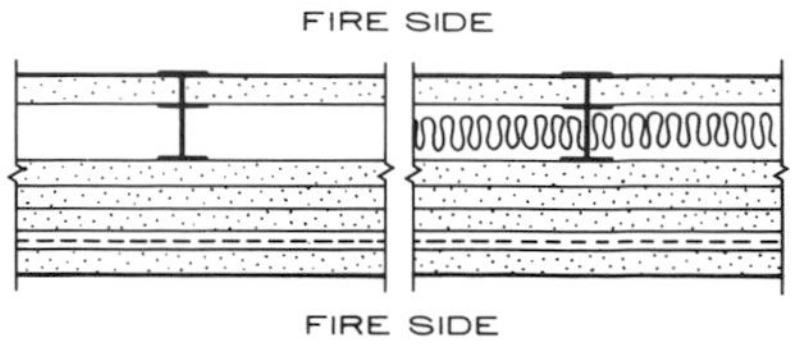 FIRE SIDE / FIRE SIDE

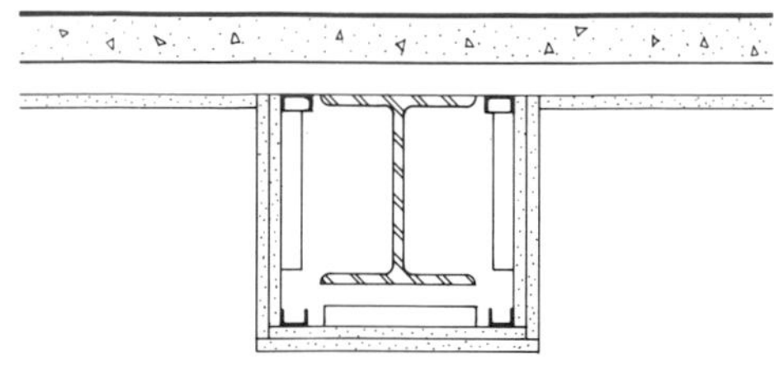

2 HOUR FIRE RATING

Two layers of 5/8 in. type X gypsum wallboard or veneer base around beam. Base layer attached with 1 1/4 in. type S drywall screws 16 in. o.c., face layer attached with 1 3/4 in. type S drywall screws 8 in. o.c. to horizontally installed U-shaped steel channels (25 gauge steel 1 11/16 in. wide and 1 in. legs) located not less than 1/2 in. from beam flanges. Upper channels secured to steel deck units with 1/2 in. type S pan head screws spaced 12 in. o.c. U-shaped brackets formed of steel channels spaced 24 in. o.c. suspended from the upper channels with 1/2 in. type S pan head screws and supported steel channels installed at lower corners of brackets. Outside corners of gypsum board protected by 0.020-in.-thick steel corner beads crimped or nailed. (2 hour restrained or unrestrained beam)

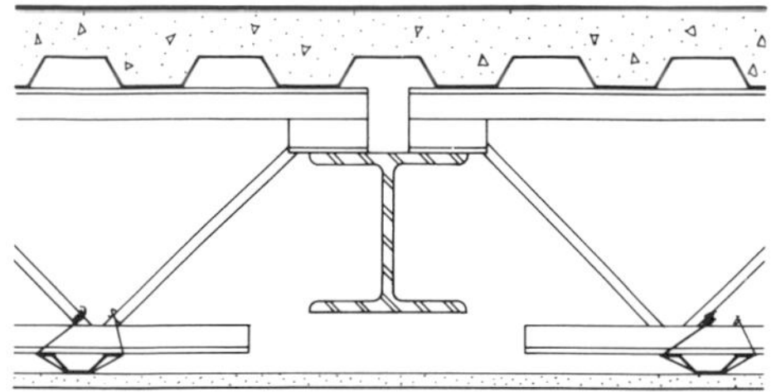

3 HOUR FIRE RATING

One layer 1/2 in. type X gypsum wallboard or veneer base applied at right angles to rigid furring channels with 1 in. type S drywall screws 12 in. o.c. Wallboard end joints located midway between continuous channels and attached to additional pieces of channel 54 in. long with screws at 12 in. o.c. Furring channels 24 in. o.c. attached with 18 gauge wire ties 48 in. o.c. to open web steel joists 24 in. o.c. supporting 3/8 in. rib metal lath or 9/16 in. deep, 28 gauge corrugated steel and 2 1/2 in. concrete slab measured from top of flute. Furring channels may be attached to 1 1/2 in. cold-rolled carrying channels 48 in. o.c. suspended from joists by 8 gauge wire hangers not over 48 in. o.c. (3 hour unrestrained beam)

BEAMS, GIRDERS AND TRUSSES

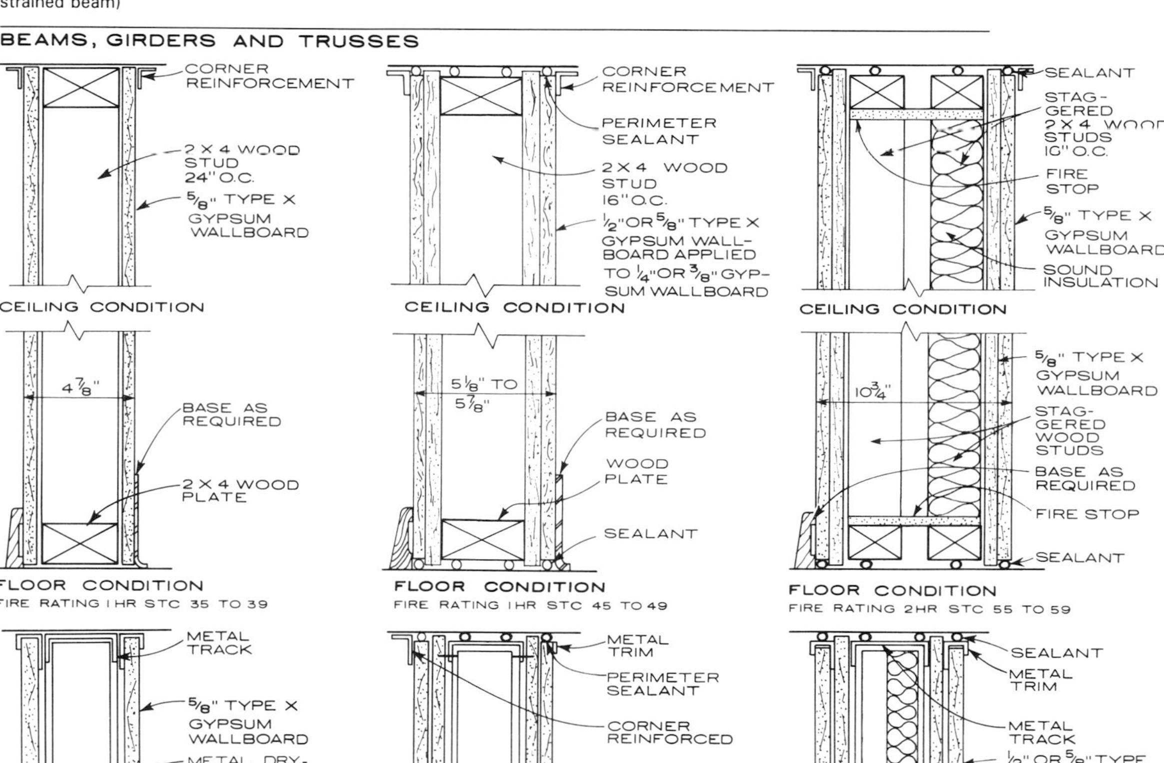
CORNER REINFORCEMENT
2 X 4 WOOD STUD 24" O.C.
5/8" TYPE X GYPSUM WALLBOARD
CEILING CONDITION
4 7/8"
BASE AS REQUIRED
2 X 4 WOOD PLATE
FLOOR CONDITION
FIRE RATING 1 HR STC 35 TO 39
CORNER REINFORCEMENT
PERIMETER SEALANT
2 X 4 WOOD STUD 16" O.C.
1/2" OR 5/8" TYPE X GYPSUM WALLBOARD APPLIED TO 1/4" OR 3/8" GYPSUM WALLBOARD
CEILING CONDITION
5 1/8" TO 5 7/8"
BASE AS REQUIRED
WOOD PLATE
SEALANT
FLOOR CONDITION
FIRE RATING 1 HR STC 45 TO 49
SEALANT
STAGGERED 2 X 4 WOOD STUDS 16" O.C.
FIRE STOP
5/8" TYPE X GYPSUM WALLBOARD
SOUND INSULATION
CEILING CONDITION
10 3/4"
5/8" TYPE X GYPSUM WALLBOARD
STAGGERED WOOD STUDS
BASE AS REQUIRED
FIRE STOP
SEALANT
FLOOR CONDITION
FIRE RATING 2 HR STC 55 TO 59
METAL TRACK
5/8" TYPE X GYPSUM WALLBOARD
METAL DRYWALL STUD 24" O.C.
CEILING CONDITION
METAL TRIM
PERIMETER SEALANT
CORNER REINFORCED
1/2" TYPE X GYPSUM WALLBOARD APPLIED TO 1/2" TYPE X GYPSUM WALLBOARD
CEILING CONDITION
SEALANT
METAL TRIM
METAL TRACK
1/2" OR 5/8" TYPE X GYPSUM WALLBOARD APPLIED TO 1/2" OR 5/8" TYPE X GYPSUM WALLBOARD
SOUND INSULATION
CEILING CONDITION
2 7/8"
METAL TRACK
BASE - AS REQUIRED
FLOOR CONDITION
FIRE RATING 1 HR STC 35 TO 39
METAL STUD 24" O.C.
4 1/2"
BASE - AS REQUIRED
METAL RUNNER
SEALANT
FLOOR CONDITION
FIRE RATING 2 HR STC 45 TO 49
METAL STUD 24" O.C.
3 5/8" TO 5"
METAL RUNNER
BASE - AS REQUIRED
SEALANT
FLOOR CONDITION
FIRE RATING 2 HR STC 50 TO 54

GYPSUM WOOD AND METAL FRAMED TYPE PARTITIONS

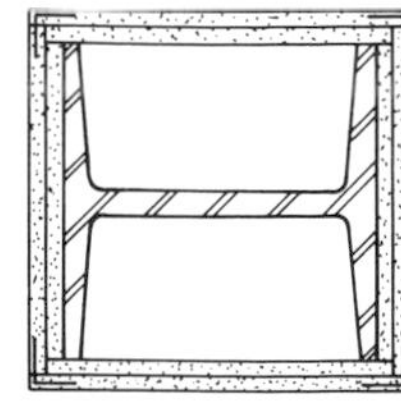

1 HOUR FIRE RATING

Base layer 1/2 in. gypsum wallboard or veneer base tied to column with 18 gauge wire 15 in. o.c. Face layer 1/2 in. gypsum wallboard or veneer base applied with laminating compound over entire contact surface.

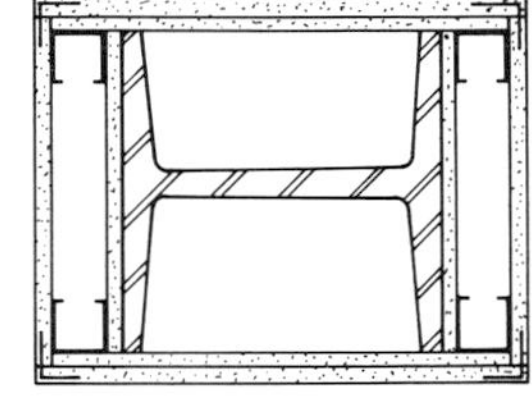

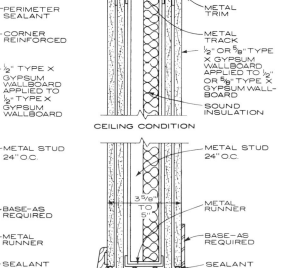

2 HOUR FIRE RATING

Base layer 1/2 in. type X gypsum wallboard or veneer base against flanges and across web openings fastened to 1 5/8 in. metal studs with 1 in. type S drywall screws 24 in. o.c. at corners. Face layers 1/2 in. type X gypsum wallboard or veneer base screw-attached to studs with 1 in. type S drywall screws 12 in. o.c. to provide a cavity between boards on the flange. Face layers across the web opening laid flat across the base layer and screw attached with 1 5/8 in. type S drywall screws 12 in. o.c. Metal corner beads nailed to outer layer with 4d nails 1 3/8 in. long, 0.067 in. shank, 13/64 in. heads, 12 in. o.c.

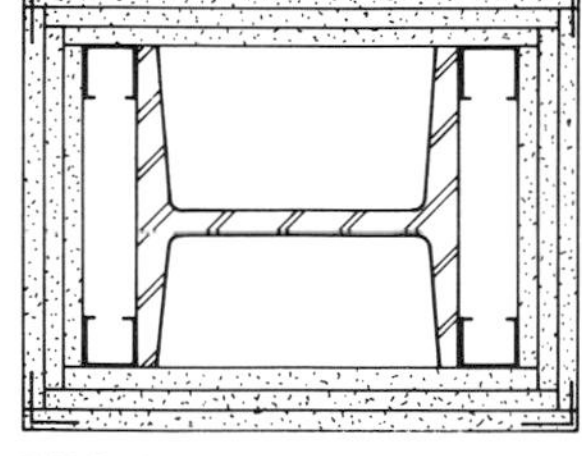

3 HOUR FIRE RATING

Three layers of 5/8 in. type X gypsum wallboard or veneer base screw attached to 1 5/8 in. metal studs located at each corner of column. Base layer attached with 1 in. type S drywall screws 24 in. o.c. Second layer with 1 5/8 in. type S drywall screws 12 in. o.c. and 18 gauge wire tied 24 in. o.c. Face layer attached with 2 1/4 in. type S drywall screws 12 in. o.c. and 1 1/4 in. corner bead at each corner nailed with 6d coated nails, 1 7/8 in. long, 0.0915 in. shank, 1/4 in. heads, 12 in. o.c.

COLUMNS FIRE-RESISTIVE CONSTRUCTION

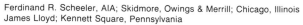

Ferdinand R. Scheeler, AIA; Skidmore, Owings & Merrill; Chicago, Illinois
James Lloyd; Kennett Square, Pennsylvania

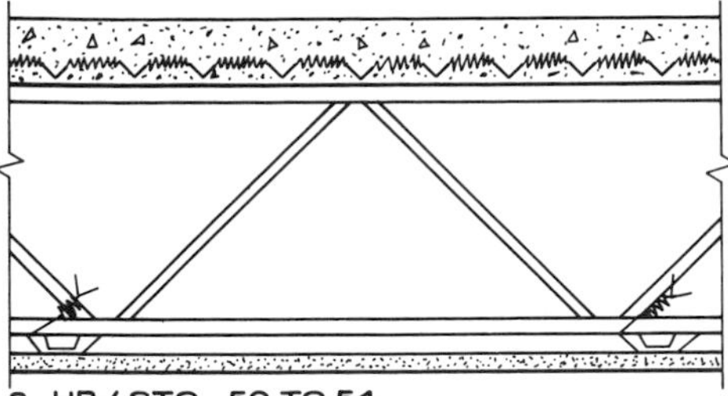

2 HR / STC 50 TO 54

1/2 in. type X gypsum wallboard or veneer base applied to drywall furring channels. Furring channels 24 in. o.c. attached with 18 gauge wire ties 48 in. o.c. to open web steel joists 24 in. o.c. supporting 3/8 in. rib metal lath or 9/16 in. deep, 28 gauge corrugated steel and 2 1/2 in. concrete slab measured from top of flute. Double channel at wallboard end joints.

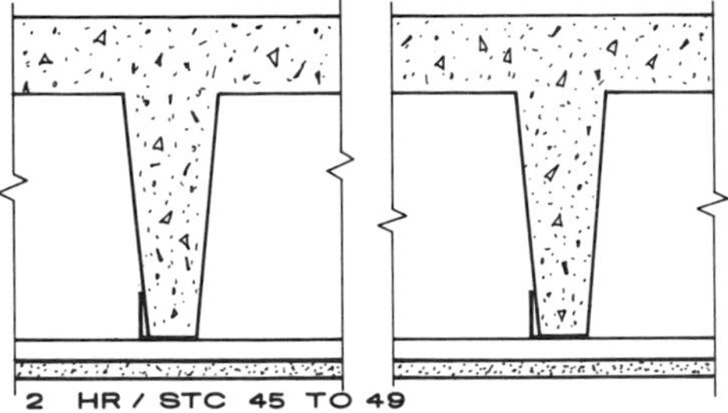

2 HR / STC 45 TO 49

5/8 in. type X gypsum wallboard or veneer base screw attached to drywall furring channels. Furring channels 24 in. o.c. suspended from 2 1/2 in. precast reinforced concrete joists 35 in. o.c. with 21 gauge galvanized steel hanger straps fastened to sides of joists. Joist leg depth, 10 in. Double channel at wallboard end joints.

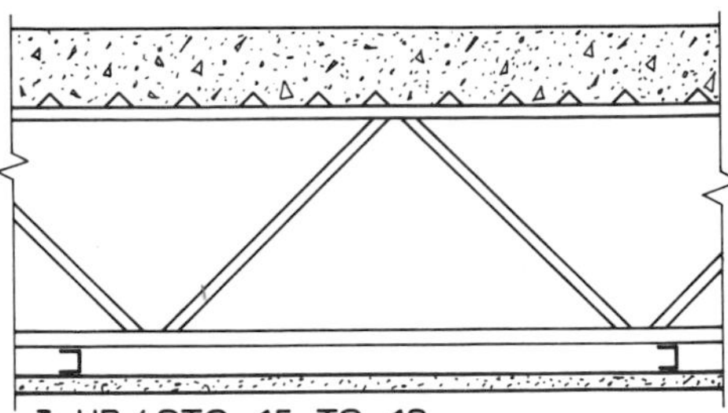

3 HR / STC 45 TO 49

5/8 in. proprietary type X gypsum wallboard or veneer base screw attached to furring channels 24 in. o.c. (double channels at end joints). Furring channel wire tied to open web steel joist 24 in. o.c. supporting 3 in. concrete slab over 3/8 in. rib metal lath. 5/8 x 2 3/4 in. type X gypsum wallboard strips over butt joints.

FLOOR/CEILING ASSEMBLIES, NONCOMBUSTIBLE

1 HR / STC 35 TO 39

5/8 in. type X gypsum wallboard or veneer base applied to wood joists 16 in. o.c. Joists supporting 1 in. nominal wood sub and finish floor, or 5/8 in. plywood finished floor with long edges T & G and 1/2 in. interior plywood with exterior glue subfloor perpendicular to joists with joints staggered.

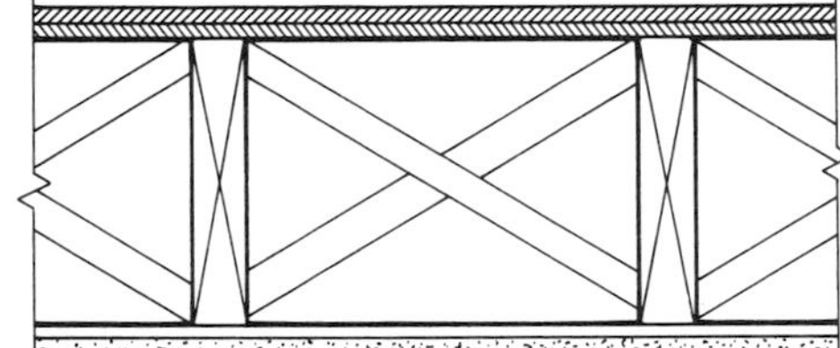

1 HR / STC 40 TO 44

1/2 in. type X gypsum wallboard or veneer base applied to drywall resilient furring channels 24 in. o.c. and nailed to wood joists 16 in. o.c. Wood joists supporting 1 in. nominal T & G wood sub and finish floor, or 5/8 in. plywood finished floor with long edges T & G and 1/2 in. interior plywood with exterior glue subfloor perpendicular to joists with joints staggered.

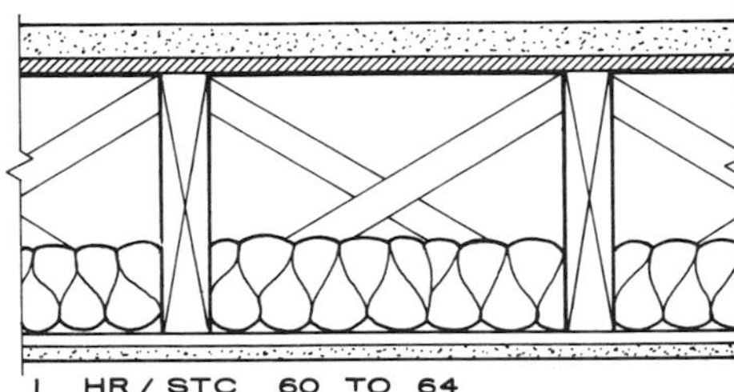

1 HR / STC 60 TO 64

1/2 in. type X gypsum wallboard or veneer base applied to resilient furring channels. Resilient channels applied 24 in. o.c. to wood joists 16 in. o.c. Wood joists support 1/2 in. plywood subfloor and 1 1/2 in. cellular or lightweight concrete over felt. 3 1/2 in. glass fiber batts in joist spaces. Sound tested with carpet and pad over 5/8 in. plywood subfloor.

FLOOR/CEILING ASSEMBLIES, WOOD FRAMED

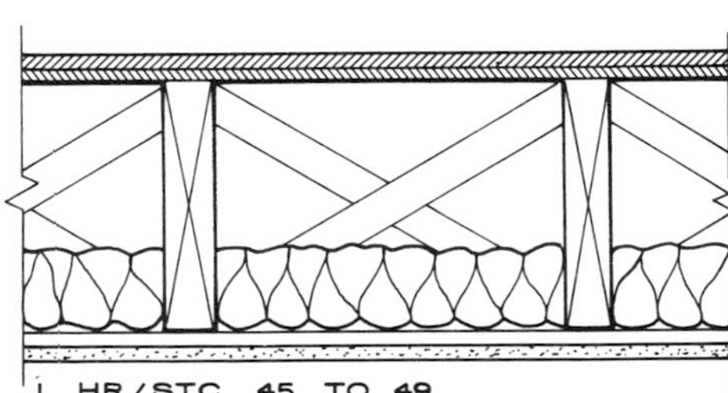

1 HR/STC 45 TO 49

ELECTRIC RADIANT HEAT PANEL

5/8 in. proprietary type X gypsum board electrical radiant heating panels attached to resilient furring channels spaced 24 in. o.c. installed to 2 x 10 in. wood joists 16 in. o.c. 3/12 in. glass fiber insulation friction fit in joist space. Wood floor of nominal 1 in. T & G or 1/2 in. plywood subfloor and nominal 1 in. T & G or 5/8 in. plywood finish floor.

FLOOR/CEILING ASSEMBLIES, WOOD FRAMED

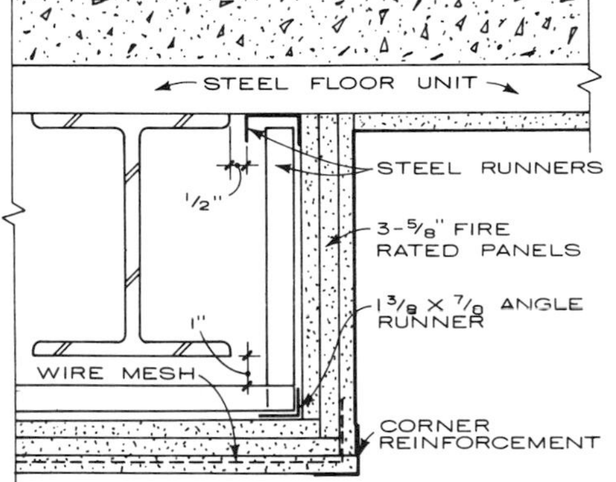
STEEL FLOOR UNIT
STEEL RUNNERS
1/2"
3-5/8" FIRE RATED PANELS
1 3/8 X 7/8 ANGLE RUNNER
1"
WIRE MESH
CORNER REINFORCEMENT

BEAM PROTECTION
3 HR. RESTRAINED 2 HR. UNRESTRAINED

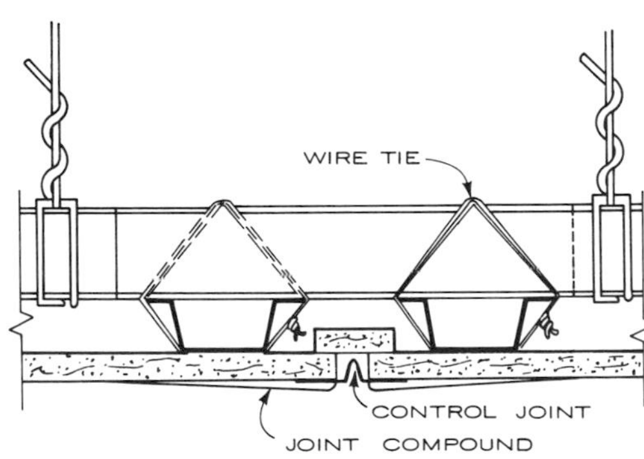
WIRE TIE
CONTROL JOINT
JOINT COMPOUND

CONTROL JOINT

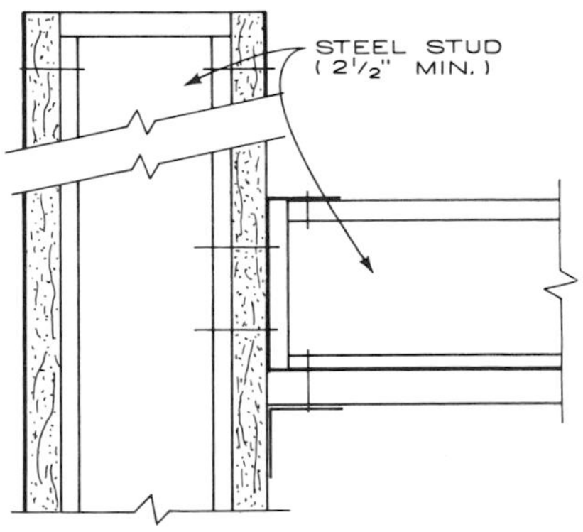

PARTITION ATTACHMENT
(SCREW ATTACHED)

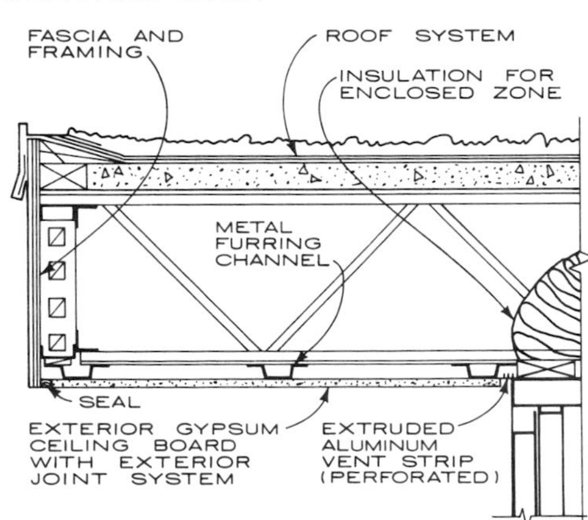
FASCIA AND FRAMING
ROOF SYSTEM
INSULATION FOR ENCLOSED ZONE
METAL FURRING CHANNEL
SEAL
EXTERIOR GYPSUM CEILING BOARD WITH EXTERIOR JOINT SYSTEM
EXTRUDED ALUMINUM VENT STRIP (PERFORATED)

EXTERIOR SOFFIT

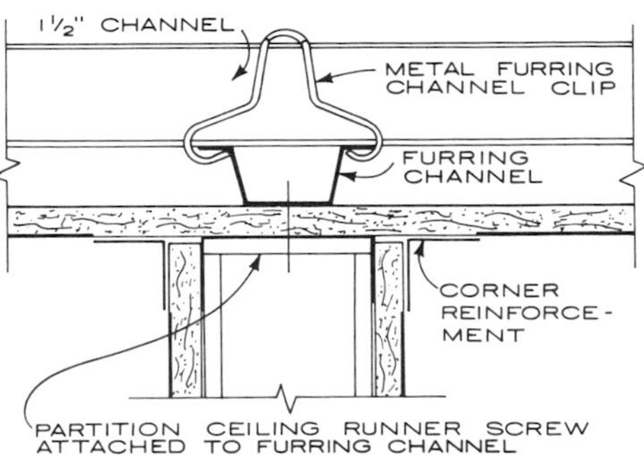
1 1/2" CHANNEL
METAL FURRING CHANNEL CLIP
FURRING CHANNEL
CORNER REINFORCE-MENT
PARTITION CEILING RUNNER SCREW ATTACHED TO FURRING CHANNEL

CONTINUOUS CEILING

James Lloyd; Kennett Square, Pennsylvania

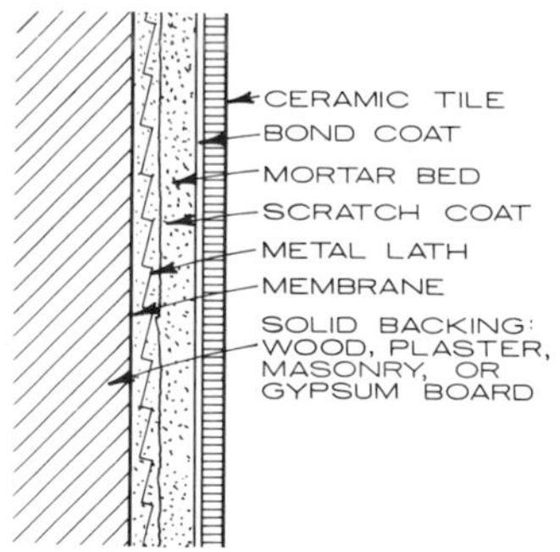
CERAMIC TILE
BOND COAT
MORTAR BED
SCRATCH COAT
METAL LATH
MEMBRANE
SOLID BACKING: WOOD, PLASTER, MASONRY, OR GYPSUM BOARD

CEMENT MORTAR

Use over solid backing, over wood or metal studs. Preferred method for showers and tub enclosures. Ideal for remodeling.

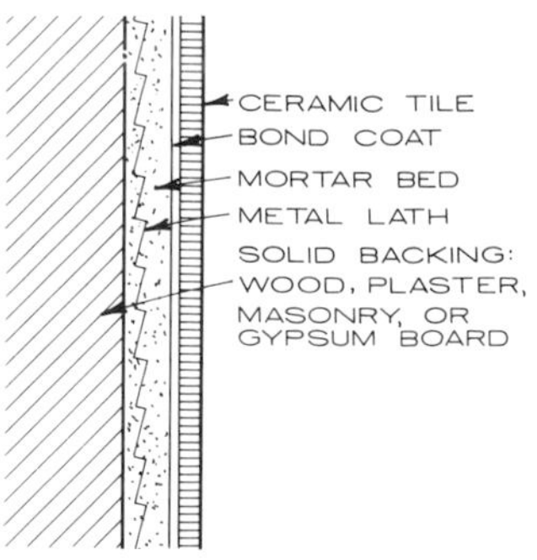
CERAMIC TILE
BOND COAT
MORTAR BED
METAL LATH
SOLID BACKING: WOOD, PLASTER, MASONRY, OR GYPSUM BOARD

ONE COAT METHOD

Use for remodeling or on surfaces that present bonding problems. Preferred method of applying tile over gypsum plaster or gypsum board in showers and tub enclosures.

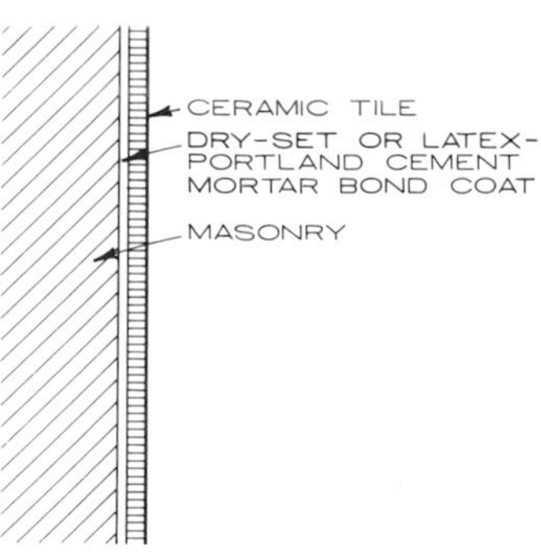
CERAMIC TILE
DRY-SET OR LATEX-PORTLAND CEMENT MORTAR BOND COAT
MASONRY

DRY-SET MORTAR

Use over gypsum board, plaster, exterior plywood, or other smooth, dimensionally stable surfaces. Use water-resistant gypsum board in wet areas.

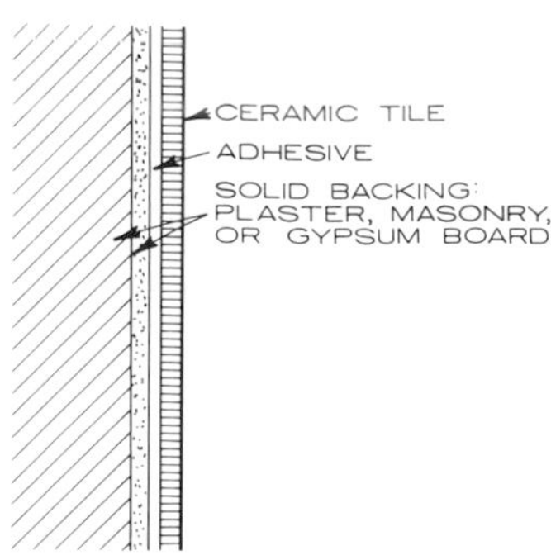
CERAMIC TILE
ADHESIVE
SOLID BACKING: PLASTER, MASONRY, OR GYPSUM BOARD

ORGANIC ADHESIVE

Use over gypsum board, plaster, exterior plywood, or other smooth, dimensionally stable surfaces. Use water-resistant gypsum board in wet areas.

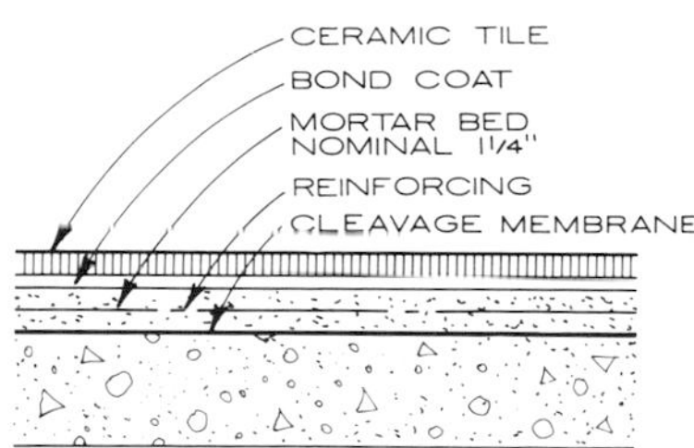
CERAMIC TILE
BOND COAT
MORTAR BED NOMINAL 1¼"
REINFORCING
CLEAVAGE MEMBRANE

CEMENT MORTAR

Use over structural floors subject to bending and deflection. Reinforcing mesh mandatory; mortar bed nominal 1¼ in. thick and uniform.

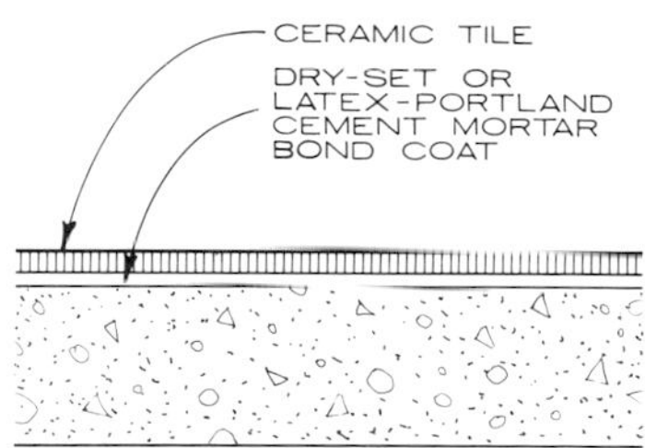
CERAMIC TILE
DRY-SET OR LATEX-PORTLAND CEMENT MORTAR BOND COAT

DRY-SET MORTAR

Use on level clean concrete where bending stresses do not exceed 1/360 of span and expansion joints are installed. Scarify existing concrete floors before installing tile.

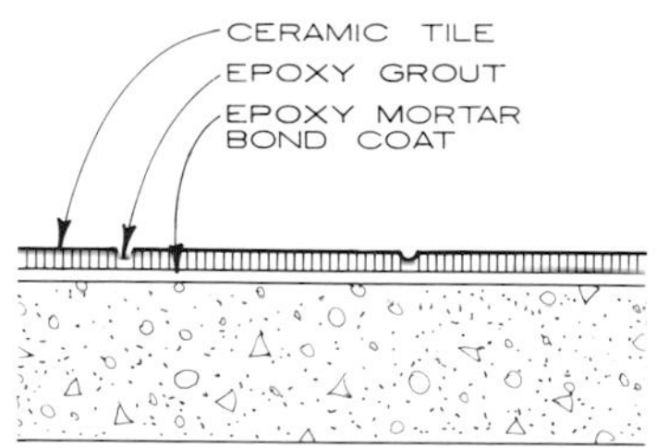
CERAMIC TILE
EPOXY GROUT
EPOXY MORTAR BOND COAT

EPOXY MORTAR & GROUT

Use where moderate chemical exposure and severe cleaning methods are used, such as in commercial kitchens, dairies, breweries and food plants.

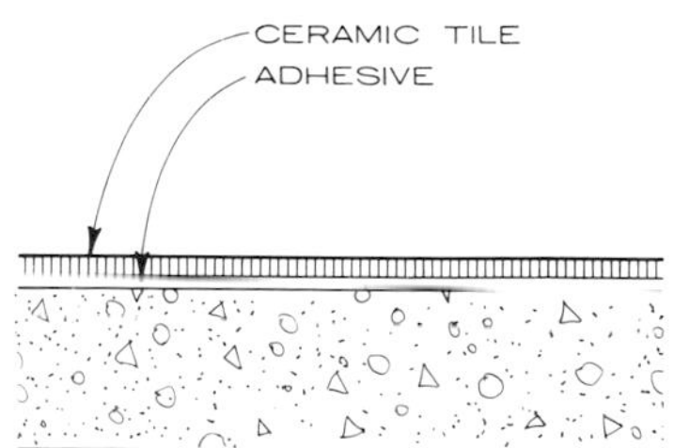
CERAMIC TILE
ADHESIVE

ORGANIC OR EPOXY ADHESIVE

Use over concrete floors in residential construction only. Will not withstand high impact or wheel loads. Not recommended in areas where temperatures exceed 140°F.

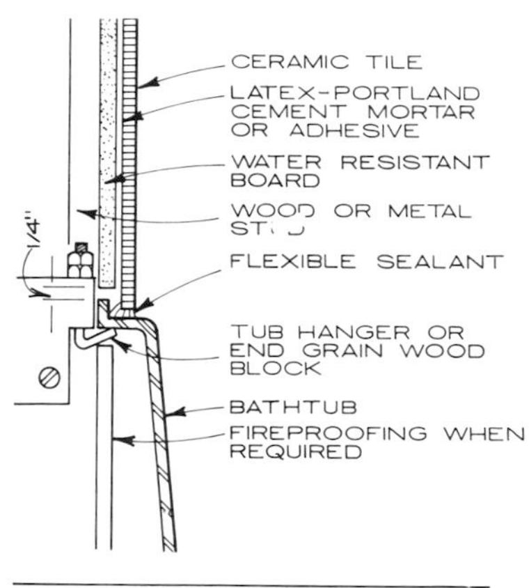
CERAMIC TILE
LATEX-PORTLAND CEMENT MORTAR OR ADHESIVE
WATER RESISTANT BOARD
WOOD OR METAL
FLEXIBLE SEALANT
1/4"
TUB HANGER OR END GRAIN WOOD BLOCK
BATHTUB
FIREPROOFING WHEN REQUIRED

CERAMIC TILE TUB ENCLOSURE

WOOD OR METAL STUD
CERAMIC TILE
EPOXY OR ORGANIC ADHESIVE
PLYWOOD OR GLASS MESH MORTAR UNIT

THIN-SET COUNTERTOP

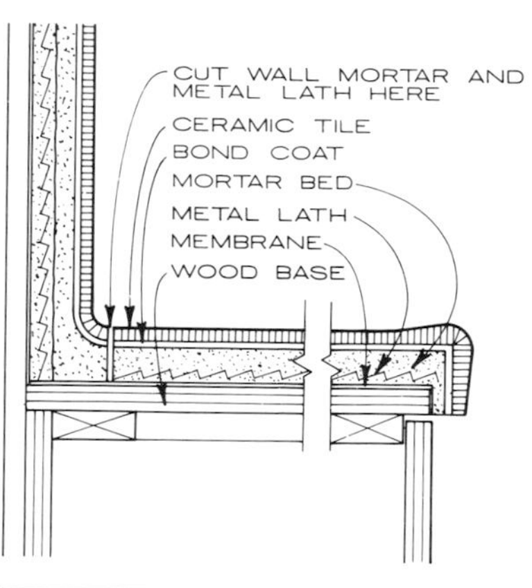
CUT WALL MORTAR AND METAL LATH HERE
CERAMIC TILE
BOND COAT
MORTAR BED
METAL LATH
MEMBRANE
WOOD BASE

CEMENT MORTAR COUNTERTOP

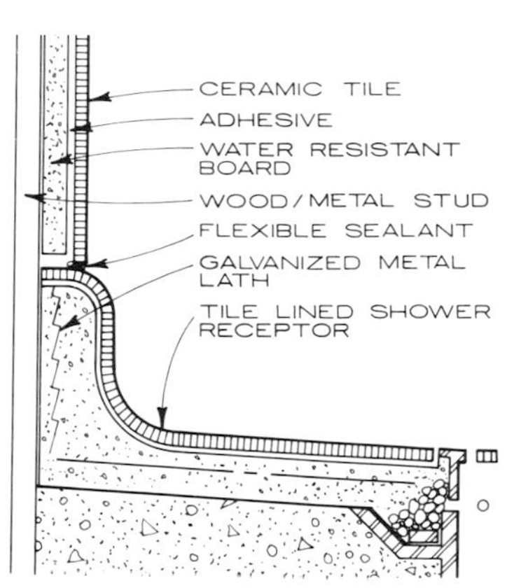
CERAMIC TILE
ADHESIVE
WATER RESISTANT BOARD
WOOD/METAL STUD
FLEXIBLE SEALANT
GALVANIZED METAL LATH
TILE LINED SHOWER RECEPTOR

CERAMIC TILE SHOWER RECEPTOR AND WALL

TYPES OF MORTAR

PORTLAND CEMENT MORTAR

A mixture of portland cement and sand (for floor) or sand and lime (for walls) used for thick-bed installation.

DRY-SET MORTAR

A mixture of portland cement with sand and additives, imparting water retention that eliminates the need to soak tiles.

LATEX-PORTLAND CEMENT MORTAR

A mixture similar to dry-set but with latex (an emulsion of rubber or resin particles in water) added to replace all or part of the water in the mortar. It provides better adhesion, density and impact strength than dry-set mortar, and it is more flexible and resistant to frost damage.

MODIFIED EPOXY EMULSION MORTAR

As with epoxy mortars, this mixture contains a resin and hardener along with portland cement and sand. Although it is not as chemically resistant as epoxy mortar, it binds well. Compared with straight portland cement, it allows little or no shrinkage.

METHODS OF INSTALLATION

In a thick-bed process, tiles usually are applied over a portland cement mortar bed ¾ in. to 1¼ in. thick. The thick-bed allows for accurate slopes or planes in the finished tile work and is not affected by prolonged contact with water. If the backing surface is damaged, cracked or unstable, a membrane should be used between the surface and the tile.

In a thin-set process, tiles are set or bonded to the surface with a thin coat of material varying from 1/32 in. to 1/8 in. thickness. Bonding materials used include dry-set mortar, latex-portland cement mortar, organic adhesive, and modified epoxy emulsion mortar. Thin-set application requires a continuous, stable and undamaged surface.

THIN-SET MORTAR WITHOUT PORTLAND CEMENT

EPOXY MORTAR

A two- or three-part mixture (resin and hardener with silica filler) used where chemical resistance is important. It has high bond strength and high resistance to impact. This mortar and furan mortar are the only two that can be recommended for use over steel plates.

EPOXY ADHESIVE

Mixture similar to epoxy mortar in bonding capability, but not as chemical or solvent resistant.

ORGANIC ADHESIVE

A one-part mastic mixture that requires no mixing. It remains somewhat flexible (as compared with portland cement mortar), and has good bond strength but should not be used for exterior or wet applications.

Tile Council of America, Inc.

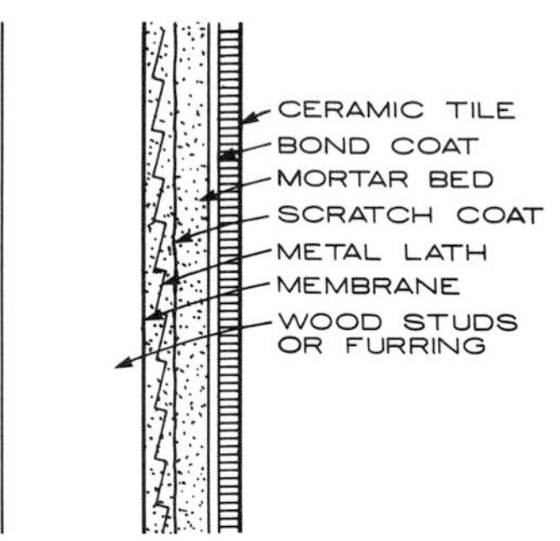
CERAMIC TILE
BOND COAT
MORTAR BED
SCRATCH COAT
METAL LATH
MEMBRANE
WOOD STUDS OR FURRING

CEMENT MORTAR

Use over dry, well-braced wood studs or furring. Preferred method of installation in showers and tub or enclosures.

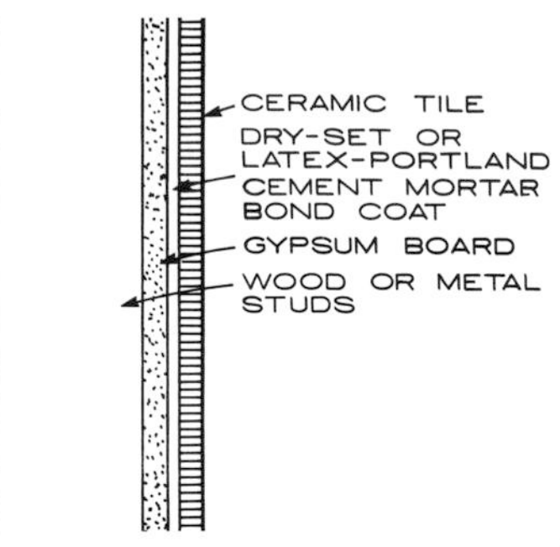
CERAMIC TILE
DRY-SET OR LATEX-PORTLAND CEMENT MORTAR BOND COAT
GYPSUM BOARD
WOOD OR METAL STUDS

DRY-SET MORTAR

Use in dry interior areas in schools, institutions and commercial buildings. Do not use in areas where temperatures exceed 125° F.

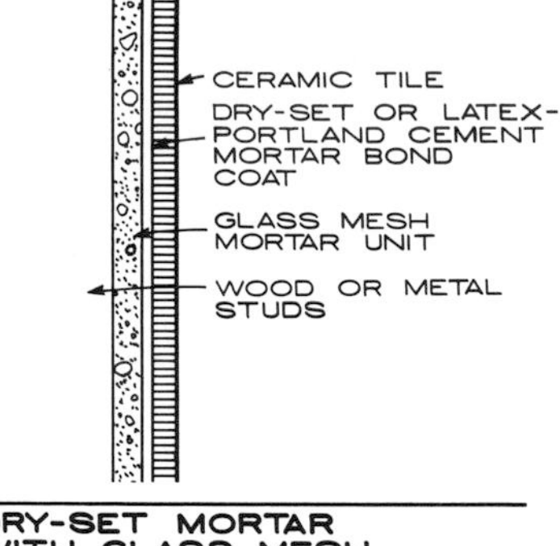
CERAMIC TILE
DRY-SET OR LATEX-PORTLAND CEMENT MORTAR BOND COAT
GLASS MESH MORTAR UNIT
WOOD OR METAL STUDS

DRY-SET MORTAR WITH GLASS MESH MORTAR UNIT

Use in wet areas over well-braced wood or metal studs. Stud spacing should not exceed 16 in. o.c., and metal studs should be 20 ga. or heavier.

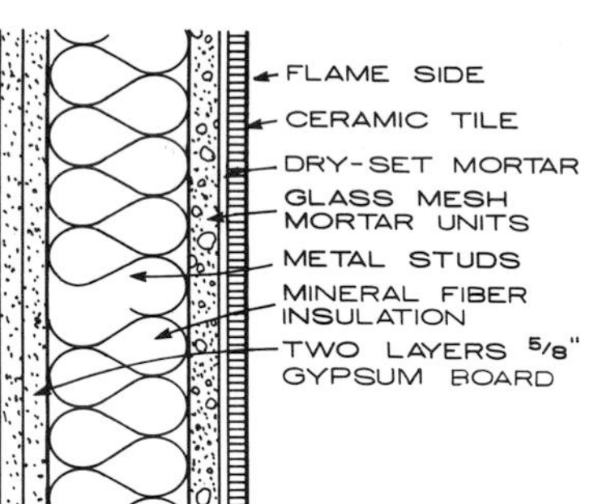
FLAME SIDE
CERAMIC TILE
DRY-SET MORTAR
GLASS MESH MORTAR UNITS
METAL STUDS
MINERAL FIBER INSULATION
TWO LAYERS 5/8" GYPSUM BOARD

DRY-SET MORTAR (FIRE-RATED WALL)

Use where a fire resistance rating of 2 hours is required with tile face exposed to flame. Stud spacing not to exceed 16 in. o.c. and mortar bed min. thickness 3/32 in.

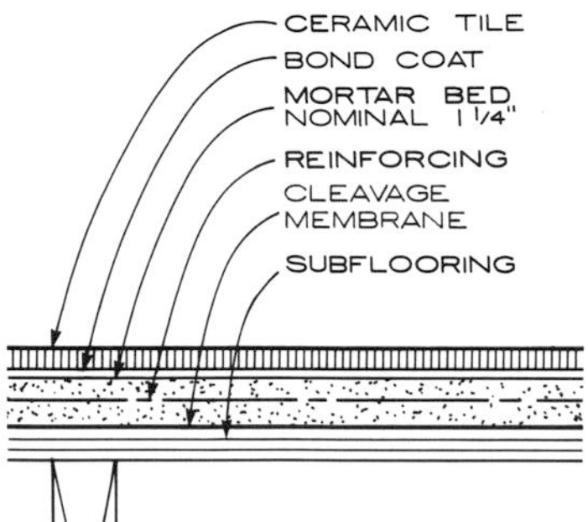
CERAMIC TILE
BOND COAT
MORTAR BED NOMINAL 1 1/4"
REINFORCING
CLEAVAGE MEMBRANE
SUBFLOORING

CEMENT MORTAR

Use over wood floors that are structurally sound and where deflection, including live and dead loads, does not exceed 1/360 of span.

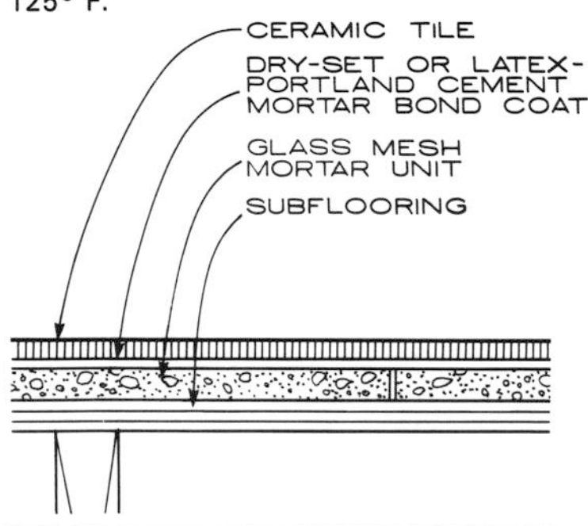
CERAMIC TILE
DRY-SET OR LATEX-PORTLAND CEMENT MORTAR BOND COAT
GLASS MESH MORTAR UNIT
SUBFLOORING

DRY-SET MORTAR

Use in light commercial and residential construction, deflection not to exceed 1/360, including live and dead loads. Waterproof membrane is required in wet areas.

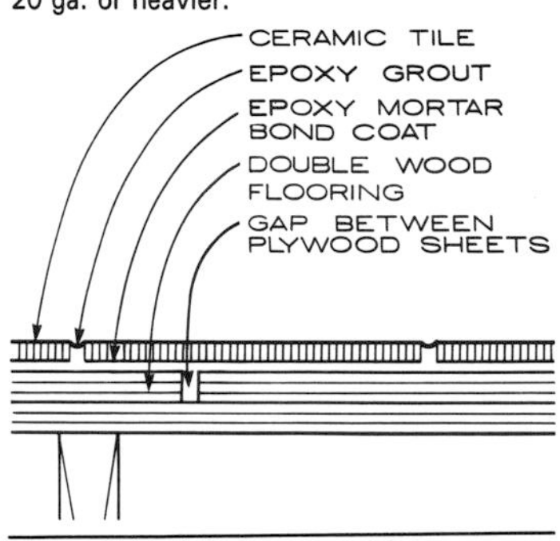
CERAMIC TILE
EPOXY GROUT
EPOXY MORTAR BOND COAT
DOUBLE WOOD FLOORING
GAP BETWEEN PLYWOOD SHEETS

EPOXY MORTAR AND GROUT

Use in residential, normal commercial and light institutional construction. Recommended where resistance to water, chemicals or staining is needed.

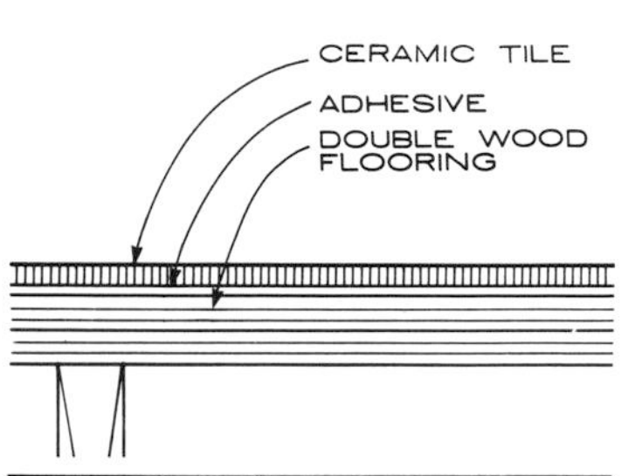
CERAMIC TILE
ADHESIVE
DOUBLE WOOD FLOORING

ORGANIC ADHESIVE

Use over wood or concrete floors in residential construction only. Not recommended in wet areas.

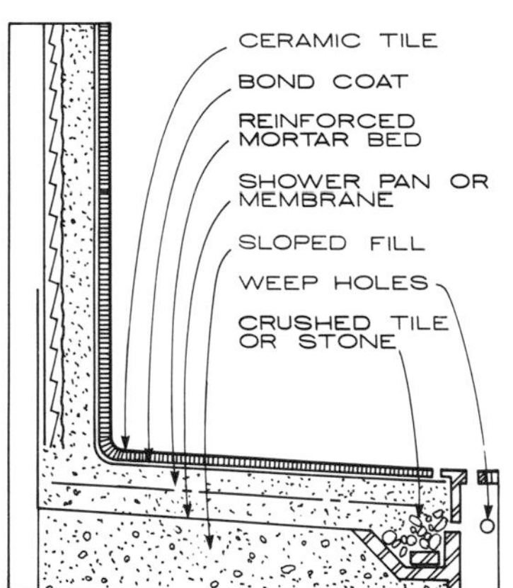
CERAMIC TILE
BOND COAT
REINFORCED MORTAR BED
SHOWER PAN OR MEMBRANE
SLOPED FILL
WEEP HOLES
CRUSHED TILE OR STONE

TILE SHOWER RECEPTOR

CERAMIC TILE
MORTAR BED
THRESHOLD
ADJACENT FLOOR

THRESHOLDS, SADDLES

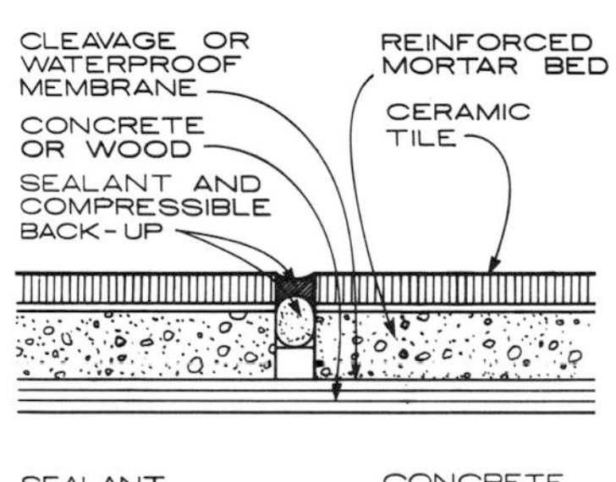
CLEAVAGE OR WATERPROOF MEMBRANE
CONCRETE OR WOOD
SEALANT AND COMPRESSIBLE BACK-UP
REINFORCED MORTAR BED
CERAMIC TILE

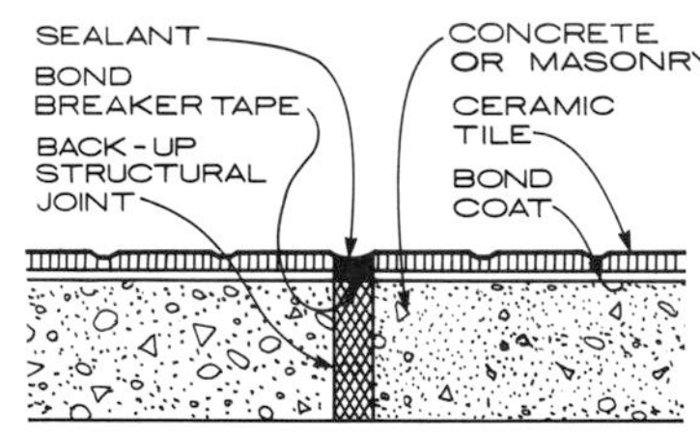
SEALANT
BOND BREAKER TAPE
BACK-UP STRUCTURAL JOINT
CONCRETE OR MASONRY
CERAMIC TILE
BOND COAT

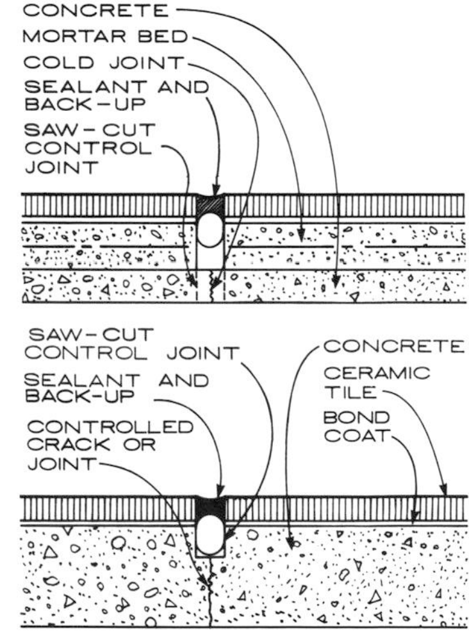
CONCRETE
MORTAR BED
COLD JOINT
SEALANT AND BACK-UP
SAW-CUT CONTROL JOINT
SAW-CUT CONTROL JOINT
SEALANT AND BACK-UP
CONTROLLED CRACK OR JOINT
CONCRETE
CERAMIC TILE
BOND COAT

VERTICAL AND HORIZONTAL EXPANSION JOINTS

FURAN MORTAR

A two-part mixture (furan resin and hardener) excellent for chemical resistant uses and its high temperatures (350°F.) tolerance.

GROUT

Grout is used to fill joints between tiles and is selected with a compatible mortar. Types include:

PORTLAND CEMENT BASED GROUTS

Include commercial portland cement grout, sand-portland cement grout, dry-set grout and latex-portland cement grout.

EPOXY GROUT

A two- or three-part mixture (epoxy resin hardener with silica sand filler) highly resistant to chemicals. It has great bond strength. This grout and furan grout are made for different chemical and solvent resistance.

FURAN RESIN GROUT

A two-part furan mixture (similar to furan mortar) that resists high temperatures and solvents.

MASTIC GROUT

A flexible one-part mixture.

SILICONE RUBBER GROUT

An elastomeric mixture based on silicone rubber. It has high bond strength, is resistant to water and staining, and remains flexible under freezing conditions.

Tile Council of America, Inc.

CERAMIC MOSAIC TILE

Ceramic mosaic tile may be either natural clay or porcelain in composition. Special abrasive or slip-resistant surfaces and conductive tile are available only in 1 in. x 1 in. size. Nominal thickness is ¼ in.

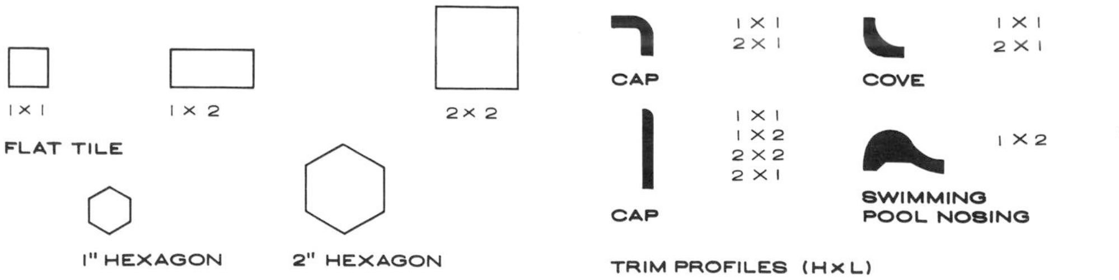

GLAZED WALL TILE

Traditional bright and matte glazed wall tile has been supplemented with tile of variegated appearance. Textured, sculptured, embossed, and engraved surface characteristics are coupled with accent designs. Imported tile has increased in availability, and it offers a wide range of variation from the native materials used in the manufacturing process as well as the process itself. Tile from Germany, France, Italy, Mexico, Switzerland, Austria, Brazil, and Spain currently are represented in manufacturer's literature. Nominal thickness is 5/16 in.

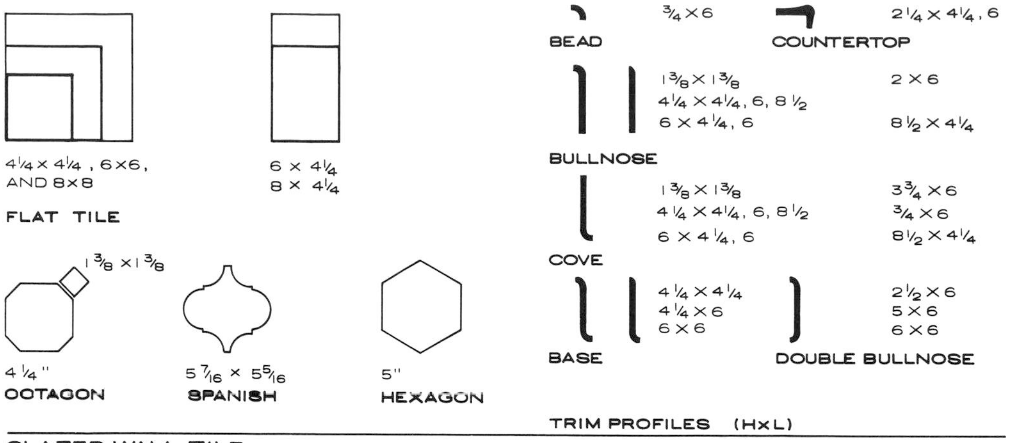

QUARRY AND PAVER TILE

Quarry and paver tile may be natural clay, shale, or porcelain in composition. These tile are characterized by their natural earth-tone coloration, high compressive strength, and slip and stain resistance. They are recommended for interior and exterior applications. Nominal thicknesses are ½ in. and ¾ in. for quarry tile and ⅜ in. and ½ in. for paver tile.

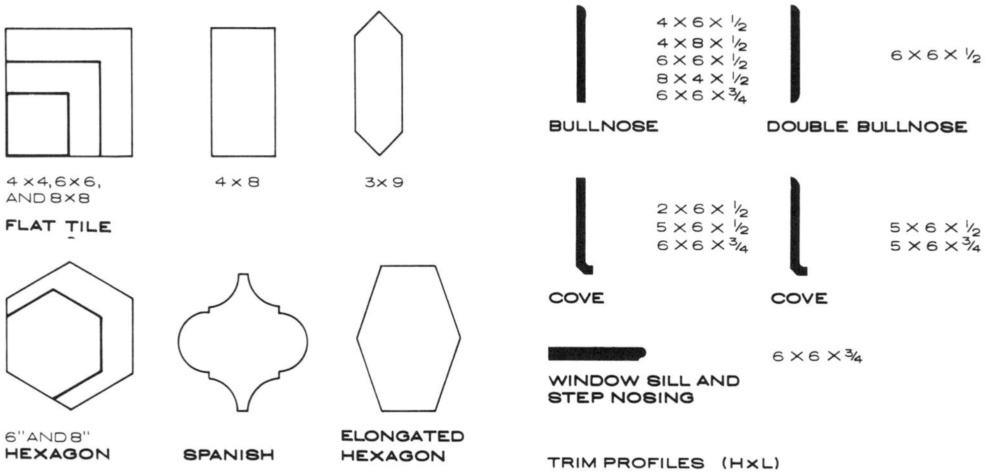

1 x 1
1 x 2
2 x 2
FLAT TILE
1" HEXAGON
2" HEXAGON
CAP
1 x 1
2 x 1
CAP
1 x 1
1 x 2
2 x 2
2 x 1
COVE
1 x 1
2 x 1
SWIMMING POOL NOSING
1 x 2
TRIM PROFILES (H x L)

CERAMIC MOSAIC TILE

4¼ x 4¼, 6x6, AND 8x8
6 x 4¼
8 x 4¼
FLAT TILE
1 3/8 x 1 3/8
4 ¼"
OOTAGON
5 7/16 x 5 5/16
SPANISH
5"
HEXAGON
BEAD
¾ x 6
COUNTERTOP
2¼ x 4¼, 6
BULLNOSE
1 3/8 x 1 3/8
4¼ x 4¼, 6, 8 ½
6 x 4¼, 6
2 x 6
8½ x 4¼
COVE
1 3/8 x 1 3/8
4¼ x 4¼, 6, 8 ½
6 x 4¼, 6
3¾ x 6
¾ x 6
8½ x 4¼
BASE
4¼ x 4¼
4¼ x 6
6 x 6
DOUBLE BULLNOSE
2½ x 6
5 x 6
6 x 6
TRIM PROFILES (H x L)

GLAZED WALL TILE

4 x 4, 6 x 6, AND 8 x 8
4 x 8
3 x 9
FLAT TILE
6" AND 8" HEXAGON
SPANISH
ELONGATED HEXAGON
BULLNOSE
4 x 6 x ½
4 x 8 x ½
6 x 6 x ½
8 x 4 x ½
6 x 6 x ¾
DOUBLE BULLNOSE
6 x 6 x ½
COVE
2 x 6 x ½
5 x 6 x ½
6 x 6 x ¾
COVE
5 x 6 x ½
5 x 6 x ¾
WINDOW SILL AND STEP NOSING
6 x 6 x ¾
TRIM PROFILES (H x L)

QUARRY TILE AND PAVER TILE

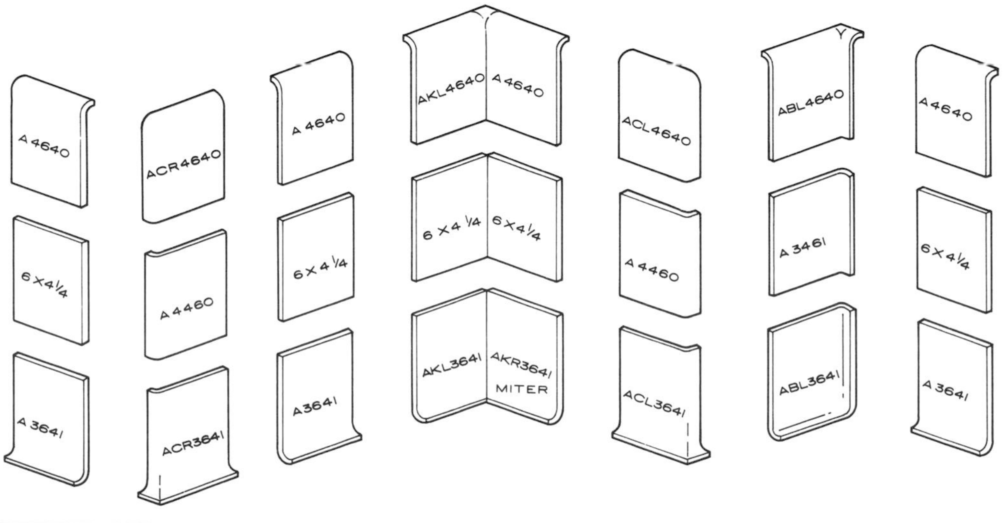

A 4640
6x4¼
A 3641
ACR4640
A 4460
ACR3641
A 4640
6x4¼
A3641
AKL4640
A4640
6 x 4¼
6x4¼
AKL3641
AKR3641
MITER
ACL4640
A 4460
ACL3641
ABL4640
A 3461
ABL3641
A4640
6x4¼
A 3641

PORTLAND CEMENT MORTAR TRIM SHAPES
VERTICAL INSTALLATION 6"x4¼" GLAZED WALL TILE

NOTES

1. The trim diagram shows typical shapes available for portland cement mortar installations of glazed wall tile. Similar types are available for thin-set installations and for ceramic mosaic tile, quarry tile, and paver tile. See manufacturer's literature for exact shapes, colors, and glazes available.
2. Mounted tile assemblies (sometimes referred to as ready-set systems) are available for glazed tile and ceramic mosaic applications. These assemblies consist of either pregrouted sheets using flexible silicone grout or backmounted sheets that are finished with dry-set grout after installation. Both provide approximately 2 sq ft of coverage per sheet. They are designed to simplify installation and improve uniformity.
3. Ceramic bathroom accessories usually are supplied in sets that include bath and lavatory soap holders, roll-paper holder, towel post, and toothbrush tumbler holder. Designs include surface-mounted and fully recessed models. They may be used with both conventional mortar and thin-set tile installations. Colors and glazes are available to match or harmonize with glazed wall tiles.

Ted B. Richey, AIA; The InterDesign Group; Indianapolis, Indiana

Terrazzo is a material composed of stone chips and cement matrix and is usually polished. There are four generally accepted types, classified by appearance:

1. STANDARD TERRAZZO: The most common type; relatively small chip sizes (#1 and #2 size chips).
2. VENETIAN TERRAZZO: Larger chips (size #3 through #8), with smaller chips filling the spaces between.
3. PALLADIANA: Random fractured slabs of marble up to approximately 15 in. greatest dimension, 3/8 to 1 in. thick, with smaller chips filling spaces between.
4. RUSTIC TERRAZZO: Uniformly textured terrazzo in which matrix is depressed to expose chips, not ground or only slightly ground.

MATRIX DATA

Two basic types exist: portland cement and chemical binders. Color pigments are added to create special effects. Limeproof mineral pigments or synthetic mineral pigments compatible with portland cement are required. Both white and grey portland cement is used depending on final color.

CHEMICAL BINDERS

All five types of chemical binders provide excellent chemical and abrasion resistance, except for latex, which is rated good.

1. EPOXY MATRIX: Two component resinous matrix.
2. POLYESTER MATRIX: Two component resinous matrix.
3. POLYACRYLATE MATRIX: Composite resinous matrix.
4. LATEX MATRIX: Synthetic latex matrix.
5. CONDUCTIVE MATRIX: Special formulated matrix to conduct electricity with regulated resistance, use in surgical areas and where explosive gases are a hazard.

PRECAST TERRAZZO

Several units are routinely available and almost any shape can be produced. Examples include: straight, coved, and splayed bases; window sills; stair treads and risers; shower receptors; floor tiles; and wall facings.

STONE CHIPS

Stone used in terrazzo includes all calcareous serpentine and other rocks capable of taking a good polish. Marble and onyx are the preferred materials. Quartz, granite, quartzite, and silica pebbles are used for rustic terrazzo and textured mosaics not requiring polishing.

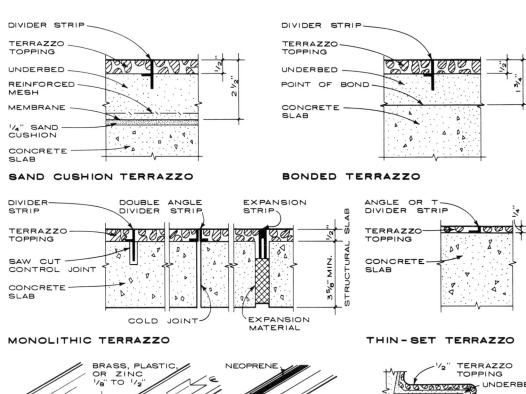

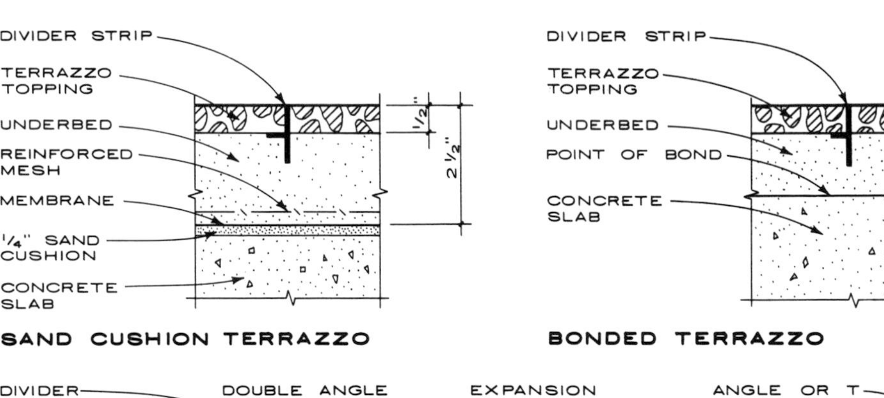

DIVIDER STRIP
TERRAZZO TOPPING
UNDERBED
REINFORCED MESH
MEMBRANE
1/4" SAND CUSHION
CONCRETE SLAB
1/2"
2 1/2"
DIVIDER STRIP
TERRAZZO TOPPING
UNDERBED
POINT OF BOND
CONCRETE SLAB
1/2"
1 3/4"

SAND CUSHION TERRAZZO

BONDED TERRAZZO

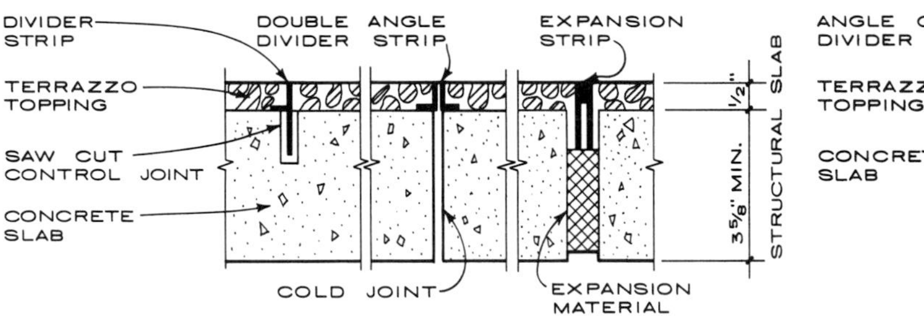

DIVIDER STRIP
DOUBLE ANGLE DIVIDER STRIP
EXPANSION STRIP
TERRAZZO TOPPING
SAW CUT CONTROL JOINT
CONCRETE SLAB
COLD JOINT
EXPANSION MATERIAL
1/2"
3 5/8" MIN.
STRUCTURAL SLAB

MONOLITHIC TERRAZZO

ANGLE OR T DIVIDER STRIP

TERRAZZO TOPPING

CONCRETE SLAB

1/4"

THIN-SET TERRAZZO

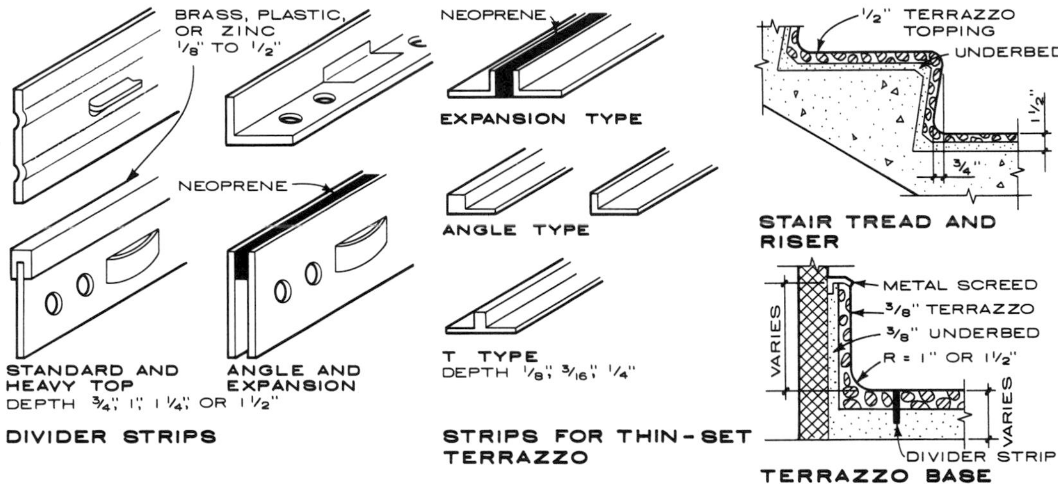

BRASS, PLASTIC, OR ZINC 1/8" TO 1/2"
NEOPRENE
NEOPRENE
EXPANSION TYPE
ANGLE TYPE
T TYPE
DEPTH 1/8", 3/16", 1/4"
1/2" TERRAZZO TOPPING
UNDERBED
1 1/2"
3/4"
METAL SCREED
3/8" TERRAZZO
3/8" UNDERBED
R = 1" OR 1 1/2"
VARIES
VARIES
DIVIDER STRIP

STANDARD AND HEAVY TOP
DEPTH 3/4", 1", 1 1/4", OR 1 1/2"

ANGLE AND EXPANSION

DIVIDER STRIPS

STRIPS FOR THIN-SET TERRAZZO

STAIR TREAD AND RISER

TERRAZZO BASE

TERRAZZO SYSTEMS

TERRAZZO SYSTEM	MINIMUM ALLOWANCE FOR FINISH	MINIMUM WEIGHT/ SQ FT	CONTROL JOINT STRIP LOCATION	SUGGESTED PANEL SIZE AND DIVIDER STRIP LOCATION	COMMENTS
Sand cushion terrazzo	2 1/2"	27 lb	At all control joints in structure	9 to 36 sq ft	Avoid narrow proportions (length no more than twice the width) and acute angles
Bonded underbed or strip terrazzo	1 3/4"	18 lb	At all control joints in structure	16 to 36 sq ft	Avoid narrow proportions as in sand cushion
Monolithic terrazzo	1/2"	7 lb	At all control joints in structure and at column centers or over grade beams where spans are great	At column centers in sawn or recessed slots maximum 24 x 24 ft	T or L strips usually provide decorative feature only
Thin-set terrazzo (chemical binders)	1/4"	3 lb	At all control joints	Only where structural crack can be anticipated	
Modified thin-set terrazzo	3/8"	4 1/2 lb	At all control joints	Only where structural crack can be anticipated	
Terrazzo over permanent metal forms	Varies, 3" minimum	Varies	Directly over beam	Directly over joist centers and at 3 to 5 ft on center in the opposite direction	
Structural terrazzo	Varies, 4" minimum	Varies	At all control joints at columns and at perimeter of floor	Deep strip (1 1/2 in. min.) at all column centers and over grade beams	Use divider strip at any location where structural crack can be anticipated

NOTES

1. Venetian and Palladiana require greater depth due to larger chip size; 2 3/4 in. minimum allowance for finish 28 lb/sq ft.
2. Divider and control joint strips are made of white alloy of zinc, brass, aluminum, or plastic. Aluminum is not satisfactory for portland cement matrix terrazzo; use brass and plastic in chemical binder matrix only with approval of binder manufacturer.
3. In exterior terrazzo, brass will tarnish and white alloy of zinc will deteriorate.

John C. Lunsford, AIA, Varney Sexton Sydnor Architects; Phoenix, Arizona

ACOUSTICAL CEILING SYSTEMS

CEILING TYPE	COMPONENTS										MATERIALS				FINISHES					ACOUSTIC TILE SIZES (IN.)									NOTES
	MAIN, CROSS T	ACCESS T's	Z CHANNEL	H CHANNEL	T SPLINE	FLAT SPLINE	SPACER	MODULAR T	METAL PAN T	SPECIAL	BENT STEEL	BENT STEEL ALUM. CAP	BENT ALUMINUM	EXTRUDED ALUMINUM	GALVANIZED	PAINTED	ANODIZED	EMBOSSED PATTERN	FIRE RATING AVAILABLE	12 x 12	12 x 24	24 x 24	24 x 48	24 x 60	20 x 60	30 x 60	60 x 60	48 x 48	
GYPSUM WALLBOARD																													
Suspended	●										●				●	●			●										
Exposed grid	●										●	●	●	●		●	●	●	●			●	●						
Semiconcealed grid	●				●		●				●				●	●			●			●	●						
Concealed H & T				●	●	●					●				●	●			●	●									
Concealed T & G			●								●				●	●			●	●									
Concealed Z			●			●					●				●	●			●	●									
Concealed access	●	●			●	●	●				●				●	●			●	●		●							
Modular	●				●	●		●			●					●			●				●	●	●	●	●	●	50 or 60″ sq main grid
Metal pan									●		●		●		●		●			●	●								12″ sq pattern
Linear metal										●			●			●													4″ o.c. typical
Perforated metal	●						●				●		●			●													1 way grid 4′–8′ o.c.
Luminous ceiling										●			●			●	●												1″ to 4″ sq grid

ACOUSTICAL CEILING MATERIALS

MATERIALS	SIZES (IN.)										THICKNESS (IN.)						EDGES				NRC RANGE					USES				
	12 x 12	12 x 24	24 x 24	24 x 48	24 x 60	20 x 60	30 x 60	60 x 60	48 x 48	CUSTOM SIZES	1/2	5/8	3/4	1	1 1/2	3	SQUARE	TEGULAR	T & G	KERFED AND RABBETED	.45–.60	.60–.70	.70–.80	.80–.90	.90–.95	HIGH HUMIDITY	EXTERIOR SOFFIT	HIGH ABUSE/IMPACT	SCRUBBABLE	FIRE RATING AVAILABLE
Mineral fiber:																														
Painted	●	●	●	●	●	●	●			●	●	●	●				●	●	●	●	●	●	●	●						●
Plastic face			●	●								●					●					●					●		●	●
Aluminum face	●		●	●								●					●				●	●				●			●	●
Ceramic face			●	●								●					●				●					●	●			●
Mineral face	●		●	●			●					●	●				●	●		●	●							●		●
Glass fiber:																														
Painted			●	●	●				●			●	●	●			●							●						
Film face			●	●	●					●		●	●	●		●	●						●	●						
Glass cloth face			●	●	●		●	●	●	●			●	●	●		●							●	●			●		
Molded				●	●			●	●	●	Varies						●													
Gypsum			●	●							●						●				●						●			●
Mylar face	●		●	●								●	●				●	●		●	●									
Tectum			●	●			●		●	●	1-3						●	●			●							●		

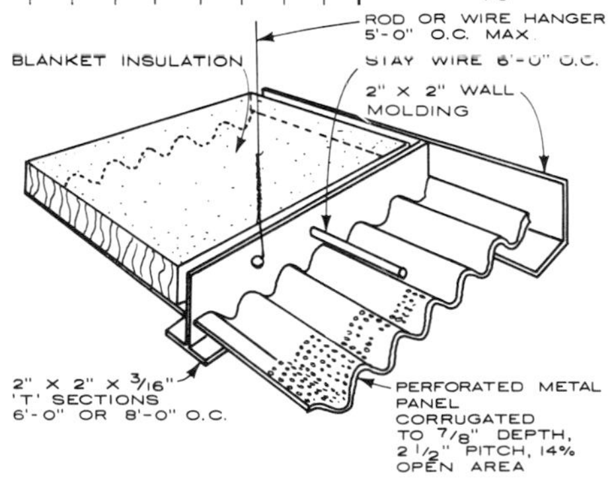

ROD OR WIRE HANGER 5′-0″ O.C. MAX
BLANKET INSULATION
STAY WIRE 6′-0″ O.C.
2″ x 2″ WALL MOLDING
2″ x 2″ x 3/16″ 'T' SECTIONS 6′-0″ OR 8′-0″ O.C.
PERFORATED METAL PANEL CORRUGATED TO 7/8″ DEPTH, 2 1/2″ PITCH, 14% OPEN AREA

PERFORATED METAL CEILING

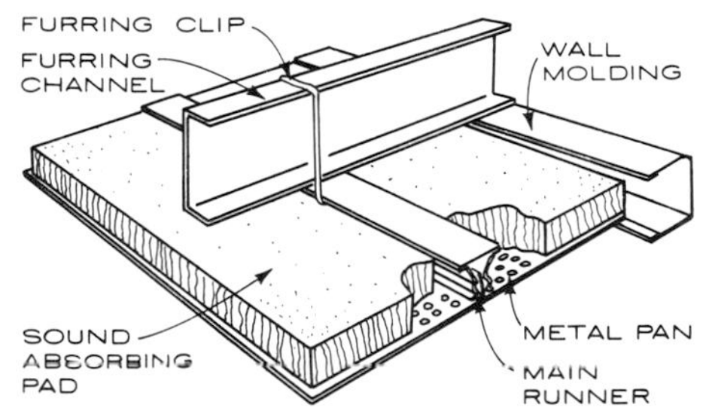

FURRING CLIP
FURRING CHANNEL
WALL MOLDING
SOUND ABSORBING PAD
METAL PAN
MAIN RUNNER

METAL PAN CEILING

SPECIAL ACOUSTICAL SYSTEMS

SOUND ISOLATION: When it is necessary to isolate a high noise area from a building or a "quiet room" from a high surrounding noise level; floors, walls, and ceilings should be built free of rigid contact with the building structure to reduce sound and vibration transmission.

CUSTOM WALLS: Auditoriums, concert halls, and other special acoustically conditioned space may require both absorptive and reflective surfaces and in some cases surfaces that can be adjusted for varying absorption coefficients to "tune" the space.

LOOSE BATTS

USE: Reduce sound transmission through or over partitions; installed over suspended acoustical tile. Also used between gypsum wall partitions.

MATERIALS: Expanded fiberglass or mineral fiber.

S.T.C.: Based on total designed system, can range from 40 to 60.

Setter, Leach & Lindstrom, Inc.; Minneapolis, Minnesota

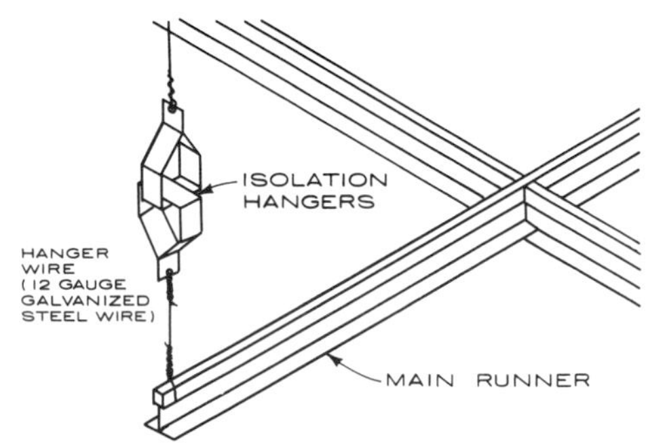

ISOLATION HANGERS
HANGER WIRE (12 GAUGE GALVANIZED STEEL WIRE)
MAIN RUNNER

ISOLATION HANGER

CEILING ISOLATION HANGER

Isolates ceilings from noise traveling through the building structure. Hangers also available for isolating ceiling systems to shield spaces from mechanical equipment and/or aircraft noise.

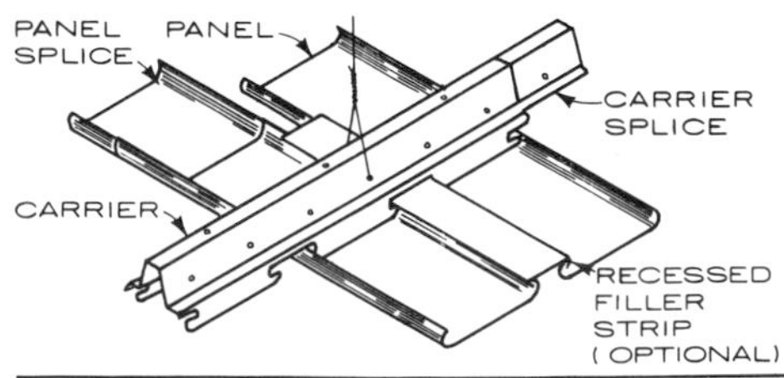

PANEL SPLICE
PANEL
CARRIER SPLICE
CARRIER
RECESSED FILLER STRIP (OPTIONAL)

LINEAR METAL CEILING

METAL CEILINGS

USE: Sound absorption depends on batt insulation.

MATERIALS: Bent steel, aluminum, or stainless steel.

N.R.C.: 0.70 to 0.90.

FINISH: Painted, anodized, or stainless steel.

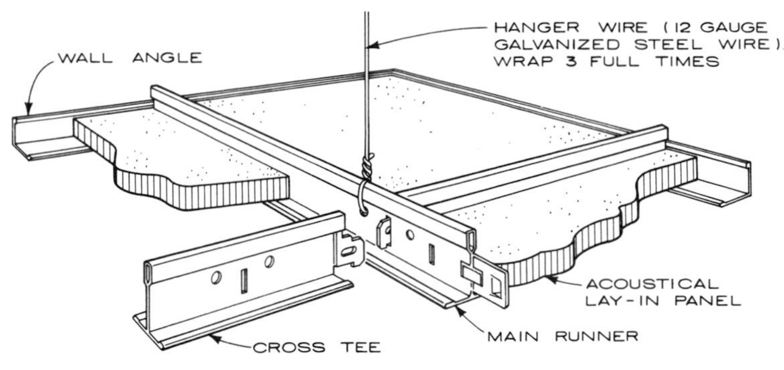
WALL ANGLE
HANGER WIRE (12 GAUGE GALVANIZED STEEL WIRE). WRAP 3 FULL TIMES
ACOUSTICAL LAY-IN PANEL
MAIN RUNNER
CROSS TEE

EXPOSED GRID

CONCEALED GRID

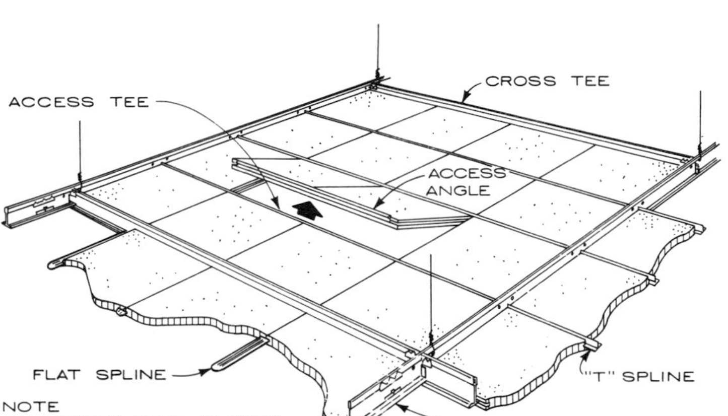
ACCESS TEE
CROSS TEE
ACCESS ANGLE
FLAT SPLINE
"T" SPLINE
NOTE
FIRE RATED GRID SHOWN
MAIN RUNNER

CONCEALED GRID – UPWARD ACCESS (SIDE PIVOT SHOWN – END PIVOT AVAILABLE)

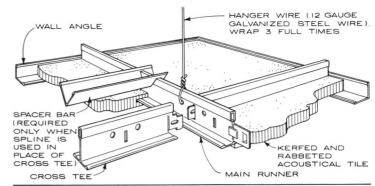

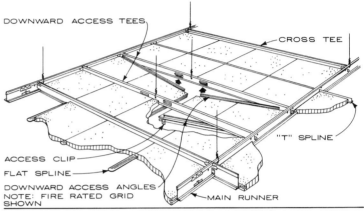

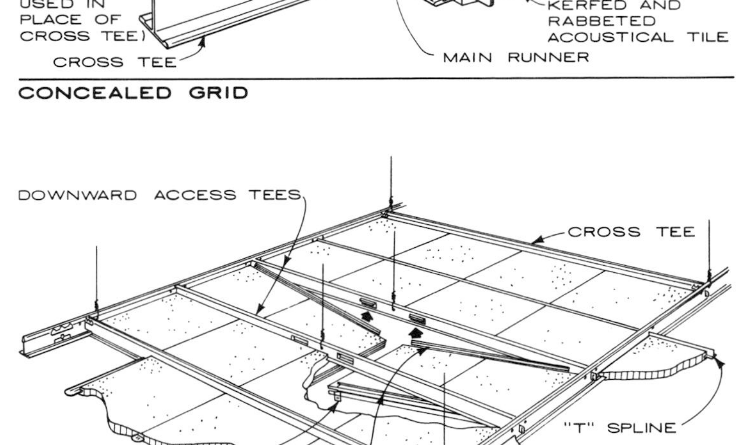
WALL ANGLE
HANGER WIRE (12 GAUGE GALVANIZED STEEL WIRE). WRAP 3 FULL TIMES
SPACER BAR (REQUIRED ONLY WHEN SPLINE IS USED IN PLACE OF CROSS TEE)
CROSS TEE
KERFED AND RABBETED ACOUSTICAL TILE
MAIN RUNNER
DOWNWARD ACCESS TEES
CROSS TEE
"T" SPLINE
ACCESS CLIP
FLAT SPLINE
DOWNWARD ACCESS ANGLES
NOTE: FIRE RATED GRID SHOWN
MAIN RUNNER

CONCEALED GRID – DOWNWARD ACCESS (END PIVOT SHOWN – SIDE PIVOT AVAILABLE)

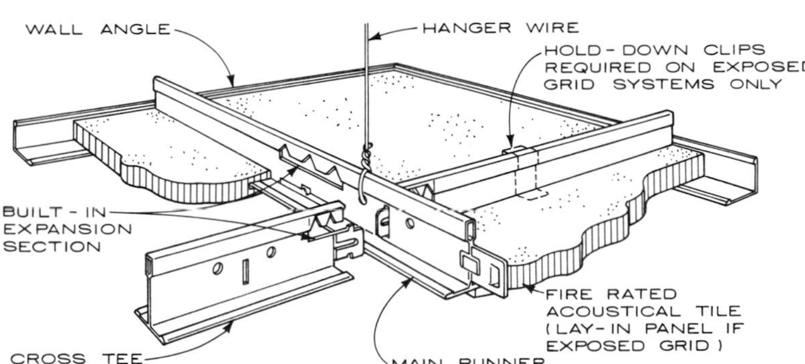
WALL ANGLE
HANGER WIRE
HOLD-DOWN CLIPS REQUIRED ON EXPOSED GRID SYSTEMS ONLY
BUILT-IN EXPANSION SECTION
FIRE RATED ACOUSTICAL TILE (LAY-IN PANEL IF EXPOSED GRID)
CROSS TEE
MAIN RUNNER

FIRE RATED GRID (CONCEALED GRID SHOWN)

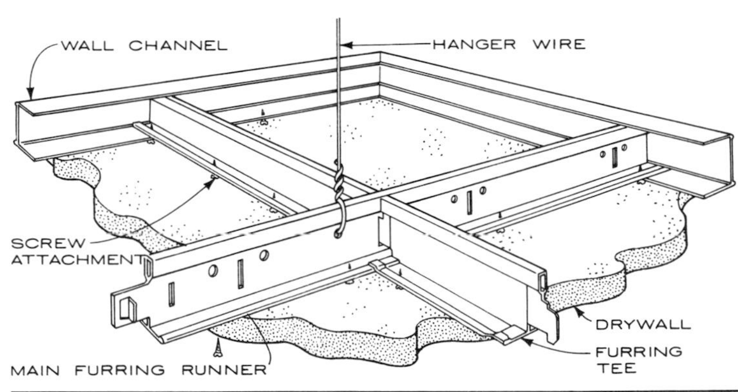
WALL CHANNEL
HANGER WIRE
SCREW ATTACHMENT
DRYWALL
FURRING TEE
MAIN FURRING RUNNER

DRYWALL FURRING SYSTEM

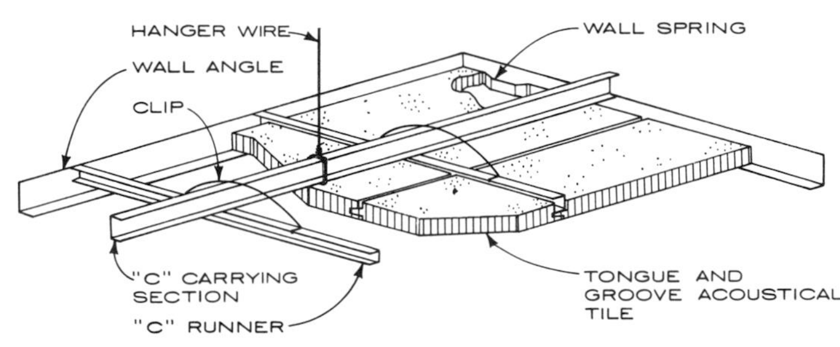
HANGER WIRE
WALL ANGLE
CLIP
WALL SPRING
"C" CARRYING SECTION
"C" RUNNER
TONGUE AND GROOVE ACOUSTICAL TILE

TONGUE AND GROOVE

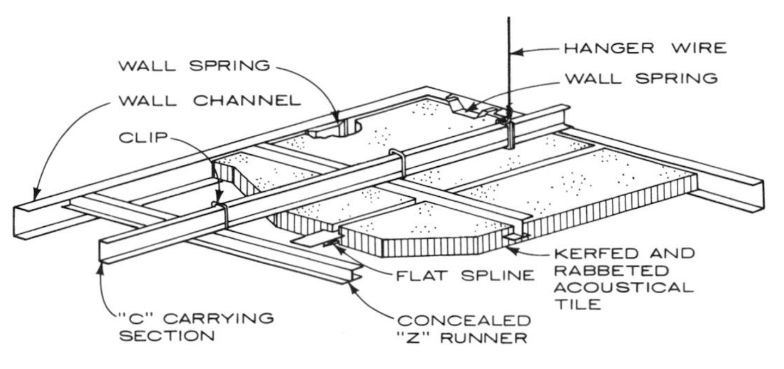
WALL SPRING
WALL CHANNEL
CLIP
HANGER WIRE
WALL SPRING
KERFED AND RABBETED ACOUSTICAL TILE
FLAT SPLINE
"C" CARRYING SECTION
CONCEALED "Z" RUNNER

CONCEALED "Z" SYSTEM

Setter, Leach & Lindstrom, Inc.; Minneapolis, Minnesota

NOTES

1. Flooring can be manufactured from practically every commercially available species of wood. In the United States wood flooring is grouped for marketing purposes roughly according to species and region. There are various grading systems used with various species, and often different specifications for different sized boards in a given species. For instance, nail size and spacing varies among the several board sizes typically available in oak.
2. Information given here should be used for preliminary decision making only. Precise specifications must be obtained from the supplier or from the appropriate industry organization named below.
3. Several considerations in wood flooring selection and installation are applicable industrywide. These are shown graphically at right.
4. The table below includes typical grades and sizes of boards for each species or regional group. Grade classifications vary, but in each case one can assume that the first grade listed is the highest quality, and that the quality decreases with each succeeding grade. The best grade will typically minimize or exclude features such as knots, streaks, spots, checks, and torn grain and will contain the highest percentage of longer boards. Grade standards have been reduced in recent years for practically all commercially produced flooring, hence a thorough review of exact grade specifications is in order when selecting wood flooring.
5. End matching gives a complete tongue and grooved joint all around each board. Board length is reduced as required to obtain the matched ends.

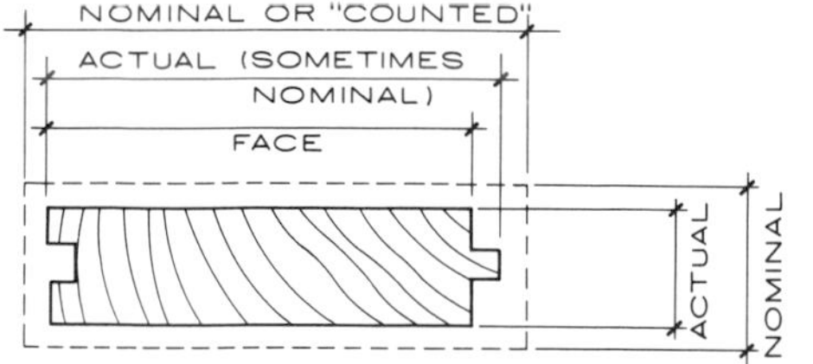
NOMINAL OR "COUNTED"
ACTUAL (SOMETIMES NOMINAL)
FACE
ACTUAL
NOMINAL

CROSS SECTIONAL DIMENSIONING SYSTEMS VARY AMONG SPECIES, PATTERNS, MANUFACTURERS. TRADE ORGANIZATIONS PROVIDE PERCENTAGE MULTIPLIERS FOR COMPUTING COVERAGE

CROSS SECTIONAL DIMENSIONS

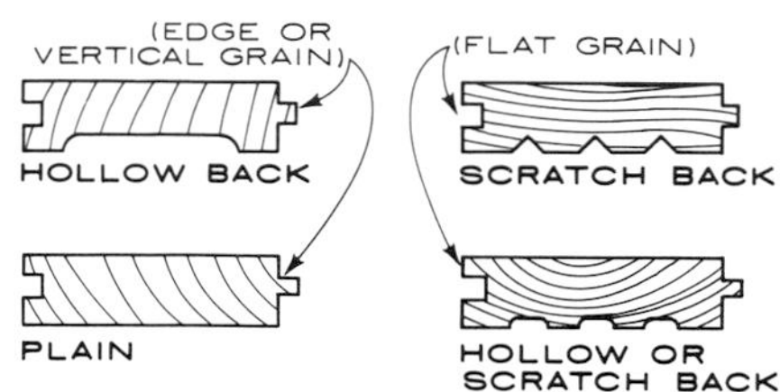
(EDGE OR VERTICAL GRAIN)
(FLAT GRAIN)
HOLLOW BACK
SCRATCH BACK
PLAIN
HOLLOW OR SCRATCH BACK

THE UNDERSIDE OF FLOORING BOARDS MAY BE PATTERNED AND OFTEN WILL CONTAIN MORE DEFECTS THAN ARE ALLOWED IN THE TOP FACE. GRAIN IS OFTEN MIXED IN ANY GIVEN RUN OF BOARDS

BOARD CHARACTERISTICS

FACE 3/8", 1/2", AND 5/8" LIGHT USE

FACE 25/32" NORMAL SERVICE

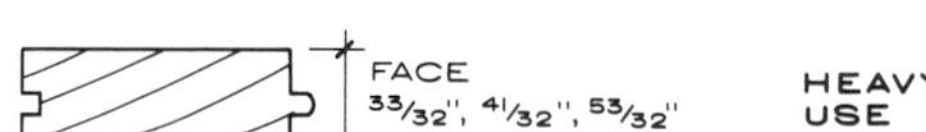
FACE
33/32", 41/32", 53/32"
HEAVY USE

MOST FLOORING MAY BE HAD IN VARYING THICKNESSES TO SUIT WEAR REQUIREMENTS. ACTUAL DIMENSIONS SHOWN ARE AVAILABLE IN MAPLE

VARIOUS THICKNESSES

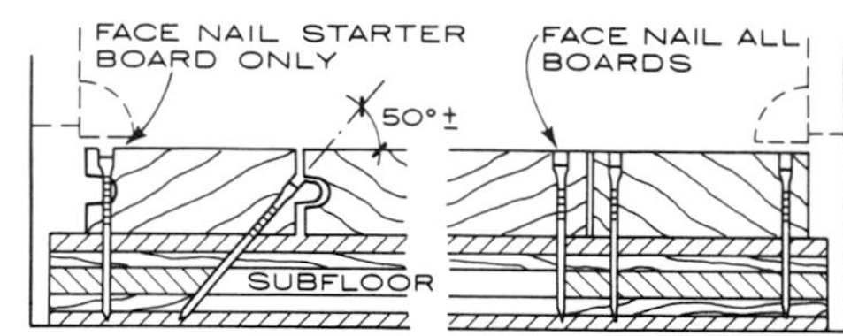
FACE NAIL STARTER BOARD ONLY
FACE NAIL ALL BOARDS
50° ±
SUBFLOOR
TONGUE AND GROOVED
JOINTED

JOINTED FLOORING MUST BE FACE NAILED, USUALLY WITH FULLY BARBED FLOORING BRADS
TONGUE AND GROOVED BOARDS ARE BLIND NAILED WITH SPIRAL FLOOR SCREWS, CEMENT COATED NAILS, CUT NAILS, MACHINE DRIVEN FASTENERS. USE MANUFACTURER'S RECOMMENDATIONS

FASTENING

PARQUET FLOORING—SQUARE PANELS

THICKNESS	FACE DIMENSIONS
5/16" (most common) 9/16", 11/16", 3/4"	6" x 6", 6 1/4" x 6 1/2", 12" x 12", 19" x 19" Other sizes are available from certain manufacturers

PARQUET FLOORING—INDIVIDUAL STRIPS

THICKNESS	FACE DIMENSIONS
5/16"	2" x 12" typical strips can be cut, mitered, etc., to obtain pieces required for special patterns

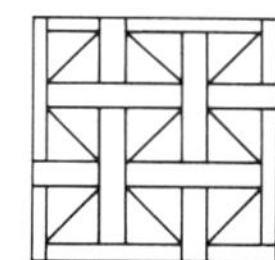
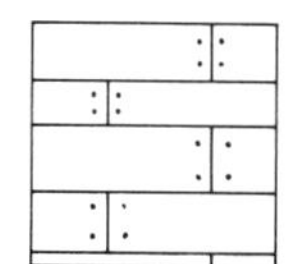

TYPICAL GRADES AND SIZES OF BOARDS BY SPECIES OR REGIONAL GROUP

GROUP	INDUSTRY ORGANIZATION	GRADE	THICKNESS	WIDTH		NOTES
Oak (also beech, birch, pecan, and hard maple)	National Oak Flooring Manufacturers' Assoc.	Quarter Sawn: Clear Select Plain Sawn: Clear Select No. 1 Common No. 2 Common	3/4", 1/2" Standard; also 3/8" 5/16"	Face 1 1/2" 2" 2 1/4"		This association grades birch, beech, and hard maple. First Grade, Second Grade, Third Grade, and "Special Grades." Pecan is graded: First Grade, First Grade Red, Second Grade, Second Grade Red, Third Grade.
Hard maple (also beech and birch) (acer saccharum—not soft maple)	Maple Flooring Manufacturers' Assoc. Inc.	First Grade Second Grade Third Grade Fourth Grade Combinations	3/8", 12/32" 41/32", 1/2" 33/32", 53/32", 5/8"	Face 1 1/2" 2" 2 1/4" 3 1/4"		Association states that beech and birch have physical properties that make them fully suitable as substitutes for hard maple. See manufacturer for available width and thickness combinations.
Southern pine	Southern Pine Inspection Bureau	B & B C C & Btr D No. 2	3/8", 1/2" 5/8", 1" 1 1/4", 1 1/2"	Nom. 2" 3" 4" 5" 6"	Face 1 1/8" 2 1/8" 3 1/8" 4 1/8" 5 1/8"	Grain may be specified as edge (rift), near-rift, or flat. If not specified, manufacturer will ship flat or mixed grain boards. See manufacturer for available width and thickness combinations.
Western woods (Douglas fir, hemlock, Englemann spruce, Idaho pine, incense cedar, lodgepole pine, Ponderosa pine, sugar pine, Western larch, Western red cedar)	Western Wood Products Association	Select: 1 & 2 clear- B & Btr C Select D Select Finish: Superior Prime E	2" and thinner	Nominal 3" 4" 6"		Flooring is machined tongue and groove and may be furnished in any grade agreeable to buyer and seller. Grain may be specified as vertical (VG), flat (FG), or mixed (MG). Basic size for flooring is 1" x 4" x 12'; standard lengths 4' and above.
Eastern white pine Norway pine Jack pine Eastern spruce Balsam fir Eastern hemlock Tamarack	Northern Hardwood & Pine Manufacturers' Association	C & Btr Select D Select Stained Select	3/8", 1/2" 5/8", 1", 1 1/4", 1 1/2"	Nom. 2" 3" 4" 5" 6"	Face 1 1/8" 2 1/8" 3 1/8" 4 1/8" 5 1/8"	The various species included in this "Lake States Region" group provide different visual features. Consult manufacturer or local supplier to determine precisely what is available in terms of species and appearance.

Darrel Downing Rippeteau, Architect; Washington, D.C.

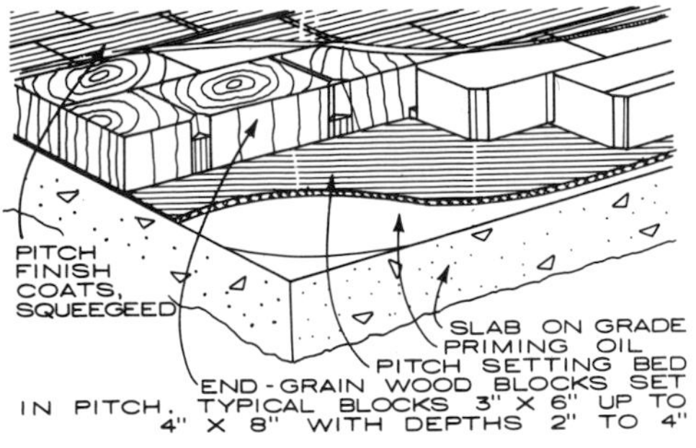
PITCH FINISH COATS, SQUEEGEED
SLAB ON GRADE
PRIMING OIL
PITCH SETTING BED
END-GRAIN WOOD BLOCKS SET IN PITCH. TYPICAL BLOCKS 3" X 6" UP TO 4" X 8" WITH DEPTHS 2" TO 4"

INDUSTRIAL WOOD BLOCK URETHANE FINISH COATS AVAILABLE FOR NONINDUSTRIAL USES

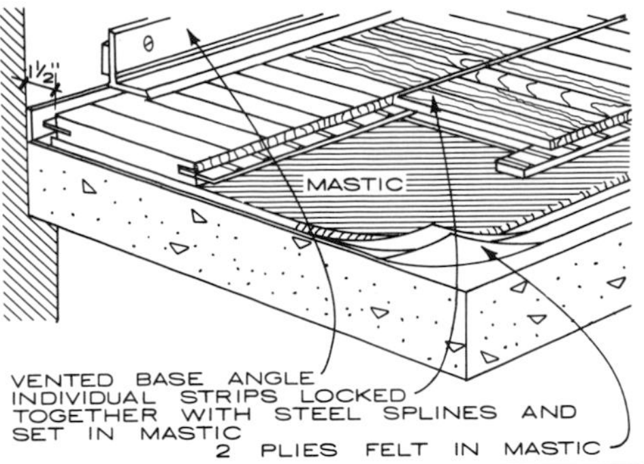
$1\frac{1}{2}$"
MASTIC
VENTED BASE ANGLE
INDIVIDUAL STRIPS LOCKED TOGETHER WITH STEEL SPLINES AND SET IN MASTIC
2 PLIES FELT IN MASTIC

STEEL SPLINED ROWS OF STRIPS CORK UNDERLAYMENT ADDED FOR NON-INDUSTRIAL USE

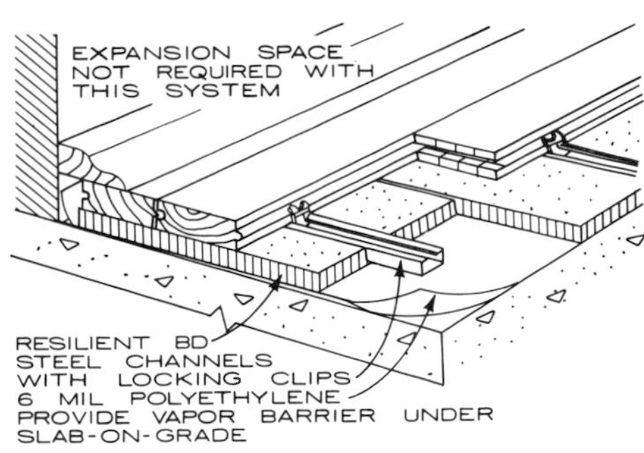
EXPANSION SPACE NOT REQUIRED WITH THIS SYSTEM
RESILIENT BD
STEEL CHANNELS WITH LOCKING CLIPS
6 MIL POLYETHYLENE
PROVIDE VAPOR BARRIER UNDER SLAB-ON-GRADE

METAL CHANNEL RUNNERS WITH CLIPS

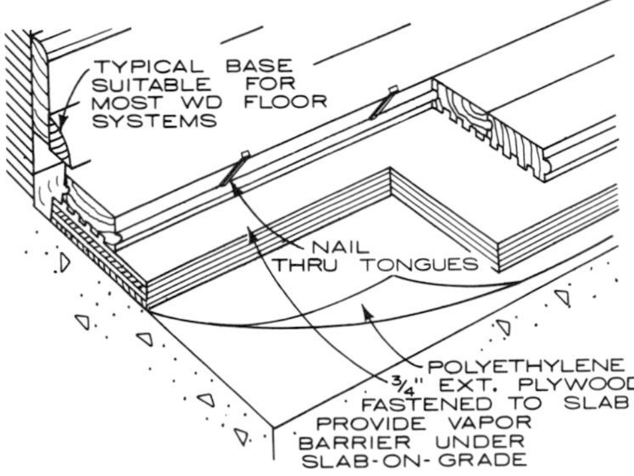
TYPICAL BASE SUITABLE FOR MOST WD FLOOR SYSTEMS
NAIL THRU TONGUES
POLYETHYLENE
$\frac{3}{4}$" EXT. PLYWOOD FASTENED TO SLAB
PROVIDE VAPOR BARRIER UNDER SLAB-ON-GRADE

STRIPS OVER PLYWOOD UNDERLAYMENT A NOFMA STANDARD

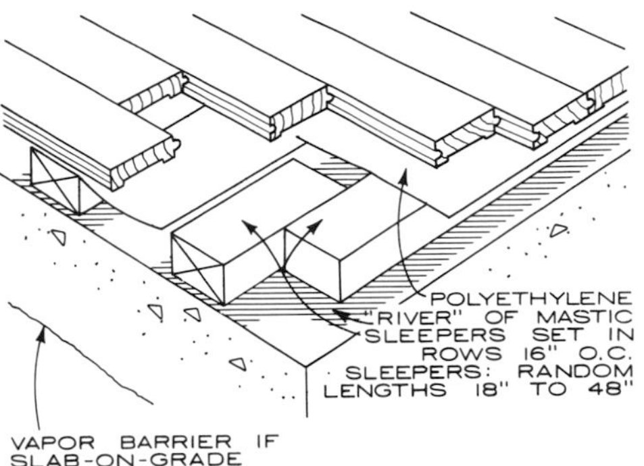
POLYETHYLENE
"RIVER" OF MASTIC
SLEEPERS SET IN ROWS 16" O.C.
SLEEPERS: RANDOM LENGTHS 18" TO 48"
VAPOR BARRIER IF SLAB-ON-GRADE

STRIPS OVER STAGGERED 2 X 4 SLEEPERS A NOFMA STANDARD

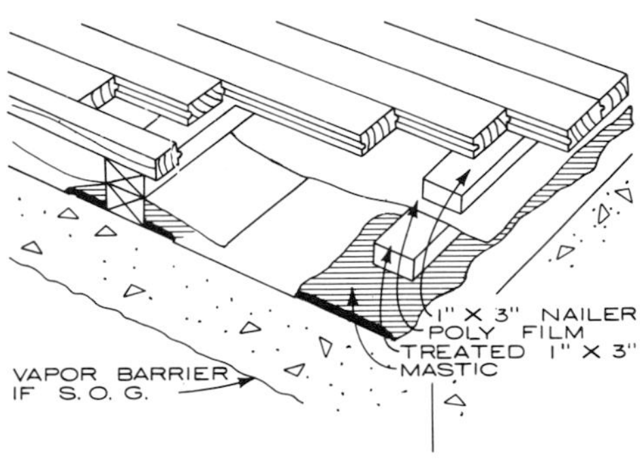
1" X 3" NAILER
POLY FILM
TREATED 1" X 3"
MASTIC
VAPOR BARRIER IF S.O.G.

DOUBLE COURSE OF SLEEPER STRIPS A NOFMA STANDARD

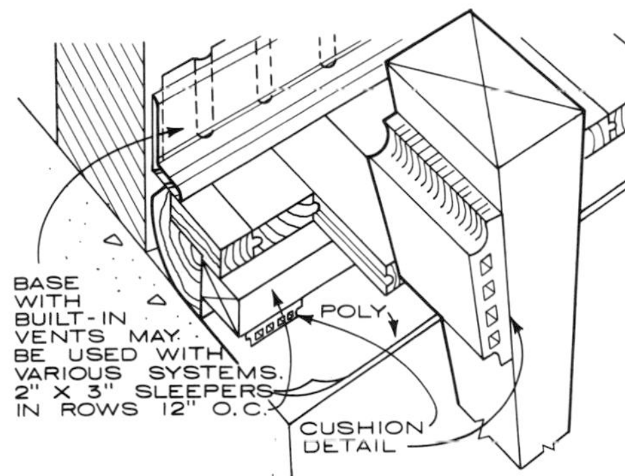
BASE WITH BUILT-IN VENTS MAY BE USED WITH VARIOUS SYSTEMS.
2" X 3" SLEEPERS IN ROWS 12" O.C.
POLY
CUSHION DETAIL

STRIPS OVER CUSHIONED SLEEPERS

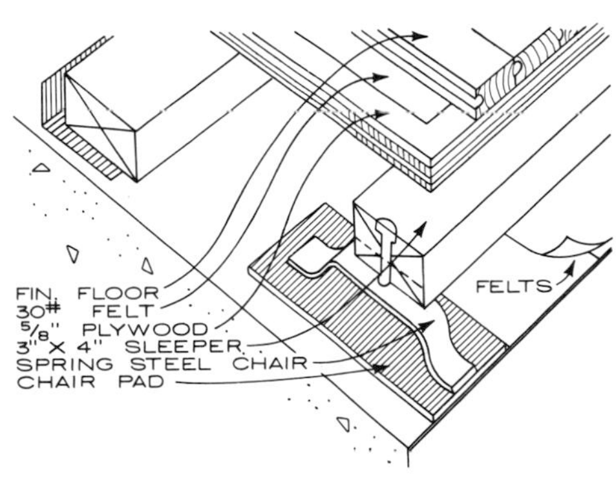
FIN. FLOOR
30# FELT
$\frac{5}{8}$" PLYWOOD
3" X 4" SLEEPER
SPRING STEEL CHAIR
CHAIR PAD
FELTS

STRIPS OVER SLEEPERS MOUNTED ON SPRING-STEEL CHAIRS

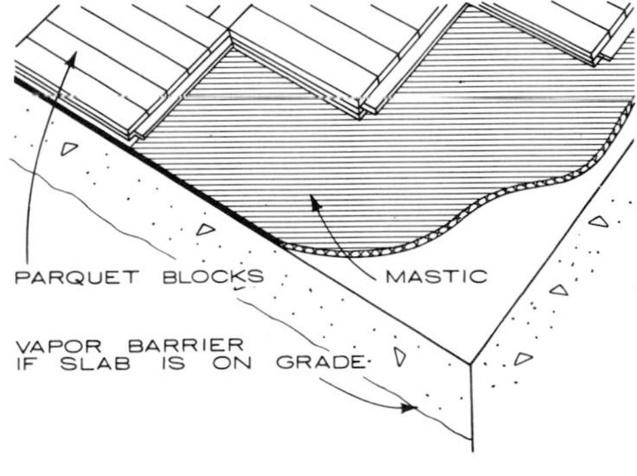
PARQUET BLOCKS
MASTIC
VAPOR BARRIER IF SLAB IS ON GRADE

PARQUET BLOCKS SET IN MASTIC

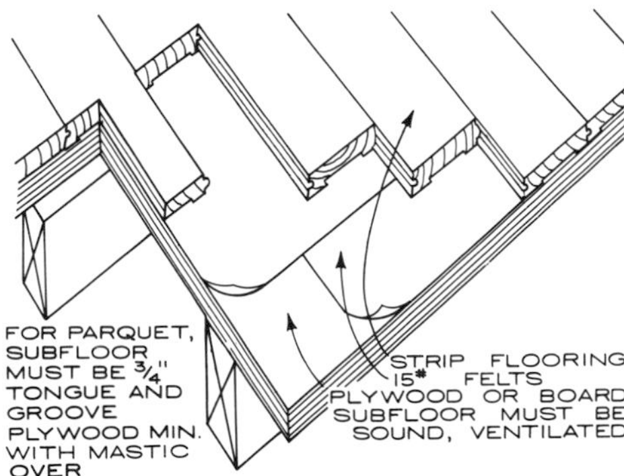
FOR PARQUET, SUBFLOOR MUST BE $\frac{3}{4}$" TONGUE AND GROOVE PLYWOOD MIN. WITH MASTIC OVER
STRIP FLOORING
15# FELTS
PLYWOOD OR BOARD SUBFLOOR MUST BE SOUND, VENTILATED

STRIPS OVER SUBFLOOR ON WOOD JOISTS

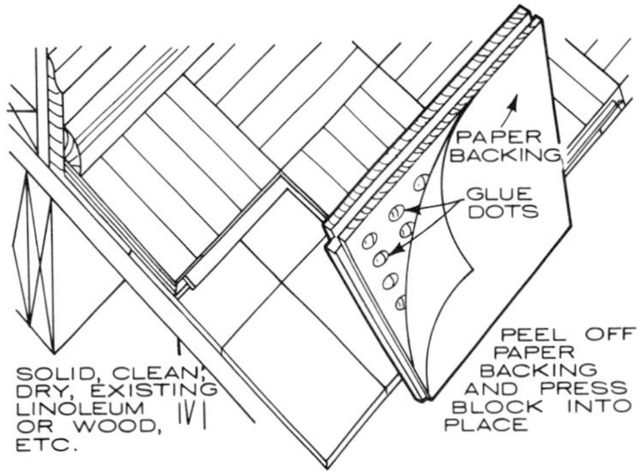
PAPER BACKING
GLUE DOTS
PEEL OFF PAPER BACKING AND PRESS BLOCK INTO PLACE
SOLID, CLEAN, DRY, EXISTING LINOLEUM OR WOOD, ETC.

PRESSURE-SENSITIVE "DO-IT-YOURSELF" PANELS (PRE-FINISHED)

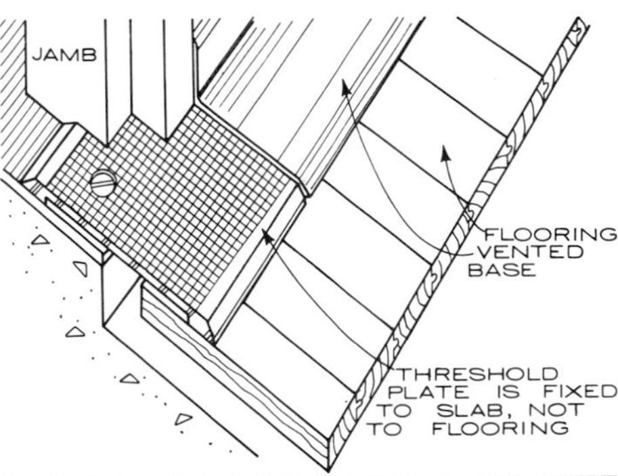
JAMB
FLOORING VENTED BASE
THRESHOLD PLATE IS FIXED TO SLAB, NOT TO FLOORING

EXPANSION PLATE AT DOORWAY /JOINT WITH DISSIMILAR CONSTRUCTION

Wood flooring is visually attractive and provides an excellent wearing surface. However, wood requires particular care in handling and installation to prevent moisture attack. Minimize moisture attack on wood floors by avoiding proximity to wet areas. Installation should occur after all "wet" jobs are completed. All the permanent lighting and heating plant should be installed to ensure constant temperature and humidity.

Expansion and contraction is a fact of life with most wood flooring. Perimeter base details that allow for movement and ventilation are included in the details above. Moisture control is further enhanced by use of a vapor barrier under a slab on or below grade. This provision should be carefully considered for each installation. Wood structures require adequate ventilation in basement and crawl space.

Wearing properties vary from species to species in wood flooring and should be considered along with appearance. In addition, grain pattern will affect a given species wearability. For instance, industrial wood blocks are typically placed with the end grain exposed because it presents the toughest wearing surface. The thickness of the wood above tongues in T & G flooring may be increased for extra service.

Darrel Downing Rippeteau, Architect; Washington, D.C.

RESILIENT FLOORING CHARACTERISTICS

TYPE OF RESILIENT FLOORING	BASIC COMPONENTS	SUBFLOOR APPLICATION*			RECOMMENDED LOAD LIMIT (PSI)	DURABILITY†	RESISTANCE TO HEEL DAMAGE	EASE OF MAINTENANCE	GREASE RESISTANCE	SURFACE ALKALI RESISTANCE	RESISTANCE TO STAINING	CIGARETTE BURN RESISTANCE	RESILIENCE	QUIETNESS
Vinyl sheet	Vinyl resins with fiber back	B	O	S	75-100	2-3	2-5	1-2	1	1-3	3-4	4	4	4
Homogeneous vinyl tile	Vinyl resins	B	O	S	150-200	1-3	1-4	2-4	1	1-2	1-5	2-5	2-5	2-5
Vinyl composition tile	Vinyl resins and fillers	B	O	S	25-50	2	4-5	2-3	2	4	2	6	6	6
Cork tile with vinyl coating	Raw cork and vinyl resins			S	150	4	3	2	1	1	5	3	3	3
Cork tile	Raw cork and resins			S	75	5	4	4	4	5	4	1	1	1
Rubber tile	Rubber compound	B	O	S	200	2	4	4	3	2	1	2	2	2
Linoleum	Cork, wood, floor, and oleoresins			S	75	3	4-5	4-5	1	4	2	4	4	4

*B: below grade; O: on grade; S: suspended.
†Numerals indicate subjective ratings (relative rank of each floor to others listed above), "1" indicating highest.
Bruce A. Kenan, AIA, Pederson, Hueber, Hares & Glavin; Syracuse, New York.

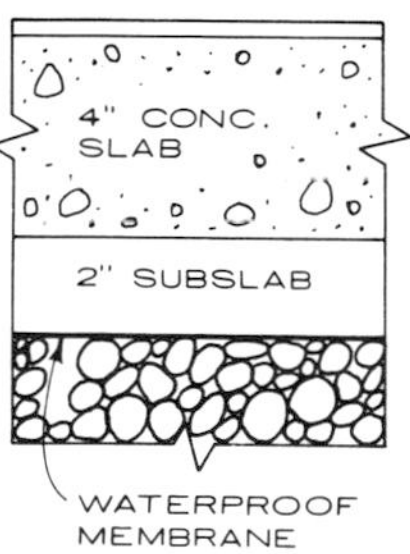
4" CONC. SLAB
2" SUBSLAB
WATERPROOF MEMBRANE
SLAB BELOW GRADE

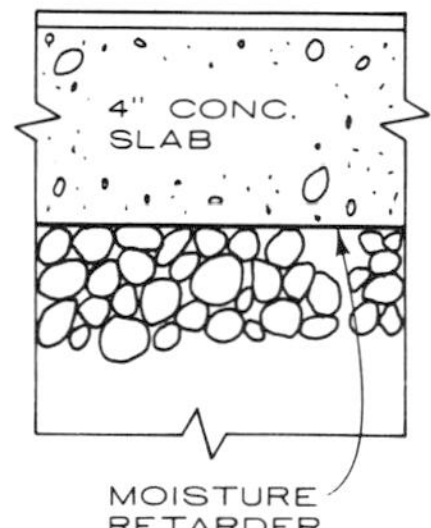
4" CONC. SLAB
MOISTURE RETARDER
SLAB ON GRADE

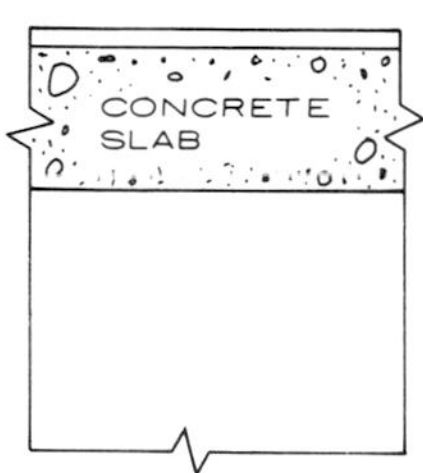
CONCRETE SLAB
SLAB ABOVE GRADE

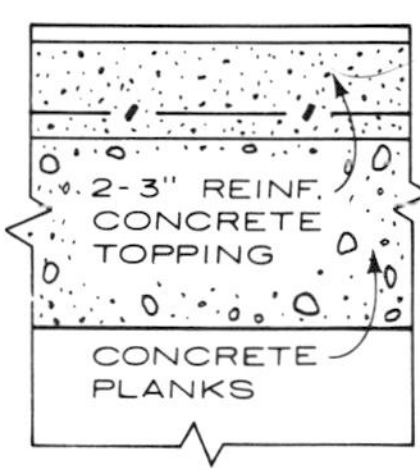
2-3" REINF. CONCRETE TOPPING
CONCRETE PLANKS
SLAB OVER PRECAST

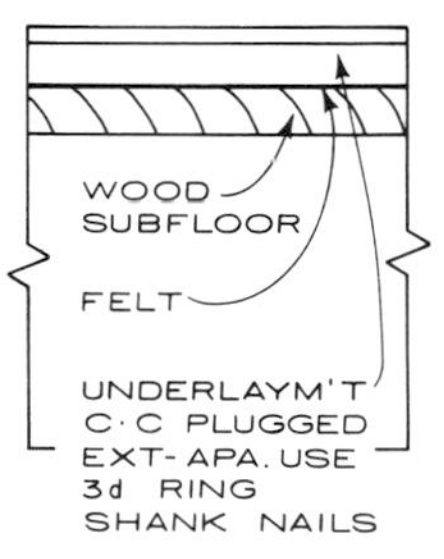
WOOD SUBFLOOR
FELT
UNDERLAYM'T C-C PLUGGED EXT-APA. USE 3d RING SHANK NAILS
WOOD SUBFLOOR

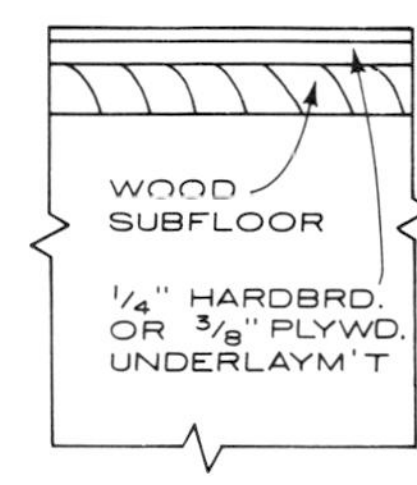
WOOD SUBFLOOR
1/4" HARDBRD. OR 3/8" PLYWD. UNDERLAYM'T
WOOD SUBFLOOR

RESILIENT FLOORING

PREPARING OLD WOOD FLOORS

TYPE OF SUBFLOOR		COVER WITH
Single wood floor	Tongue and groove not over 3"	Hardboard or plywood, 1/4" or heavier
	Not tongue and groove	Plywood 1/2" or heavier
Double wood floor	Strips 3" or more	Hardboard or plywood 1" or heavier
	Strips less than 3" tongue and groove	Renail or replace loose boards, remove surface irregularities

PREPARING OLD CONCRETE FLOORS

1. Check for dampness.
2. Remove all existing surface coatings.
3. Wirebrush and sweep dusty, porous surfaces. Apply primer.

PREPARING LIFT SLABS

Remove curing compounds prior to resilient flooring installation.

CONCRETE SLABS BY DENSITY

Density			
Light		Medium	Heavy
Pounds per cubic foot			
20/40	60/90	90/120	120/150
Type of concrete			
Expanded perlite, vermiculite, and others		Expanded slag shale, and clay	Standard concrete of sand, gravel, or stone
Recommendations			
Top with 1" thickness of standard concrete mix		Approved for use of resilient flooring if troweled smooth and even	

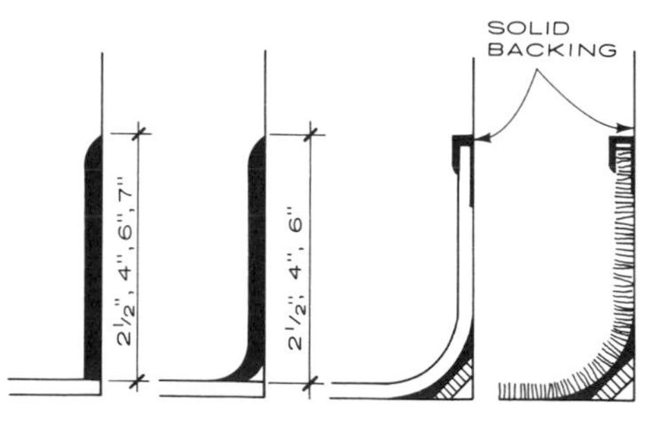
2 1/2", 4", 6", 7"
2 1/2", 4", 6"
SOLID BACKING
BASES - STRAIGHT OR COVED
COVE STRIP AND CAP STRIP

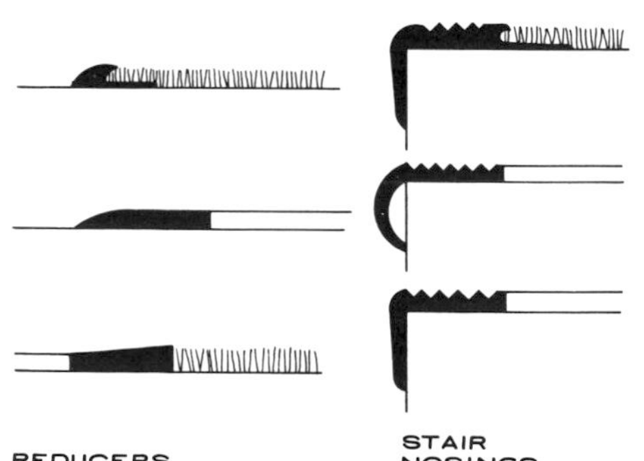
REDUCERS
STAIR NOSINGS

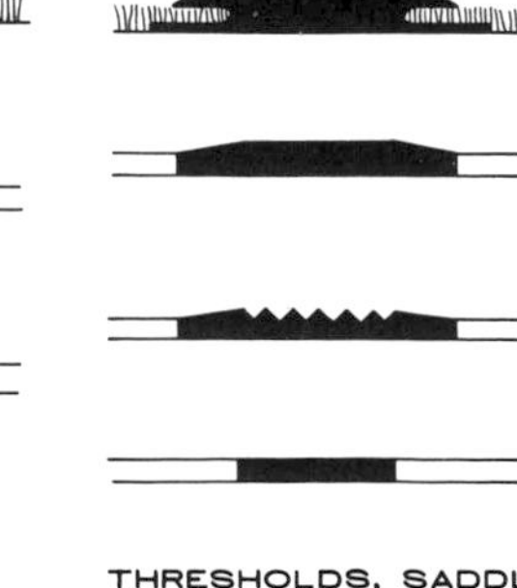
THRESHOLDS, SADDLES FEATURE STRIP

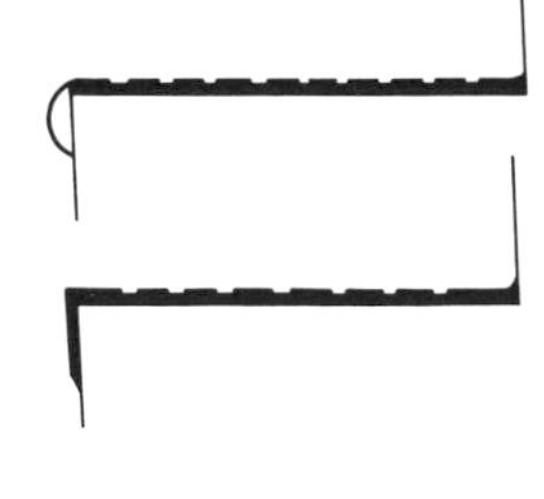
STAIR TREAD

RESILIENT FLOORING ACCESSORIES, CARPET ACCESSORIES

Broome, Oringdulph, O'Toole, Rudolf & Associates; Portland, Oregon

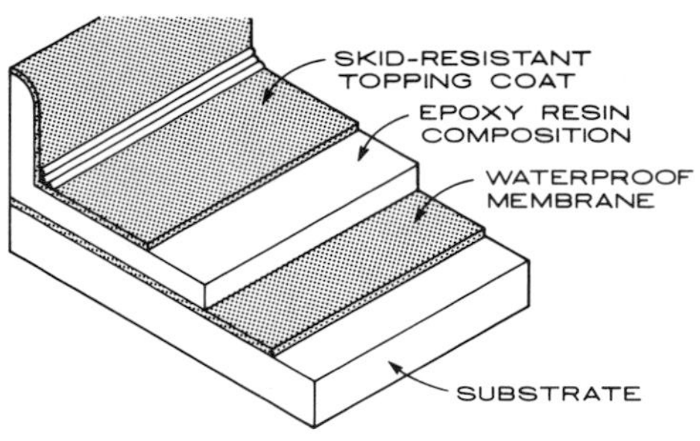
SKID-RESISTANT TOPPING COAT
EPOXY RESIN COMPOSITION
WATERPROOF MEMBRANE
SUBSTRATE

An epoxy resin composition flooring resistant to a large number of corrosive materials, 3/16 in. to 1/4 in. thickness, weight 3 psf. Used in manufacturing areas, food processing, hotel and restaurant kitchens, beverage bottling plants and loading docks.

EPOXY RESIN COMPOSITION FLOORING

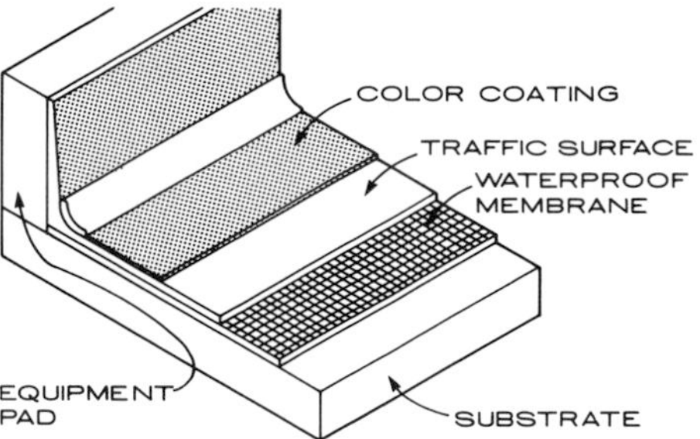
COLOR COATING
TRAFFIC SURFACE
WATERPROOF MEMBRANE
EQUIPMENT PAD
SUBSTRATE

A troweled surface over a fabric reinforced latex-type waterproof membrane. Flooring thickness 3/16 in., weight 2 1/2 psf. Used in mechanical equipment rooms and plenum rooms.

WATERPROOF LATEX MEMBRANE FLOORING

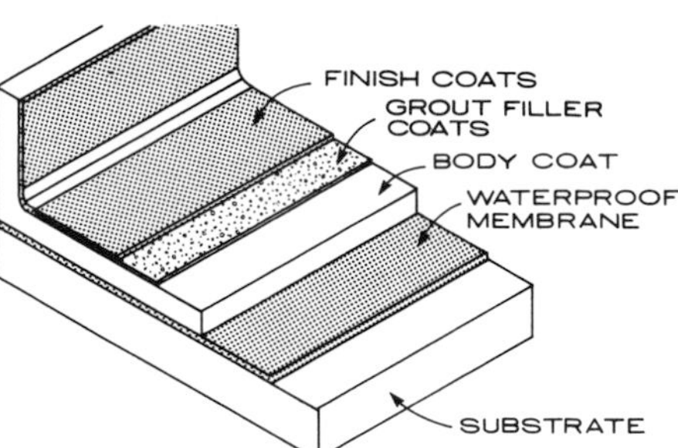
FINISH COATS
GROUT FILLER COATS
BODY COAT
WATERPROOF MEMBRANE
SUBSTRATE

A trowel-applied elastomeric latex resin forming a jointless floor with good chemical resistance, is waterproof in conjunction with membrane. Thickness 1/4 in., weight 3 psf. Used in showers and locker rooms, laboratories, pollution control facilities, TV studios.

ELASTOMERIC LATEX RESIN FLOORING

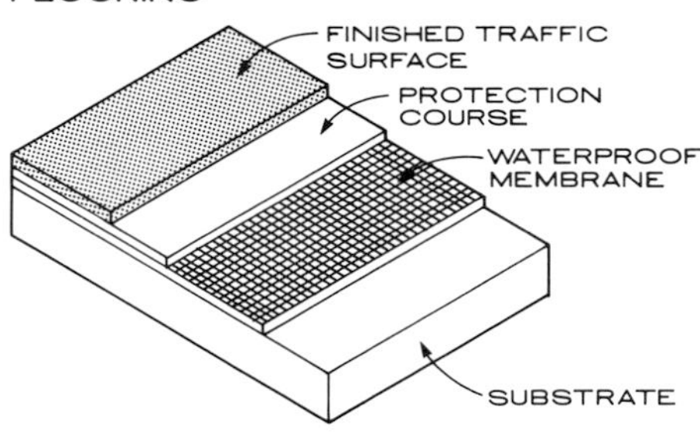
FINISHED TRAFFIC SURFACE
PROTECTION COURSE
WATERPROOF MEMBRANE
SUBSTRATE

A multicolored installation consisting of a fabric reinforced latex membrane, a neoprene-cement protection course, and a flexible, oil-resistant finish. Thickness 3/16 in., weight 1.5 psf. Used on interior or exterior auto parking facilities.

REINFORCED LATEX MEMBRANE

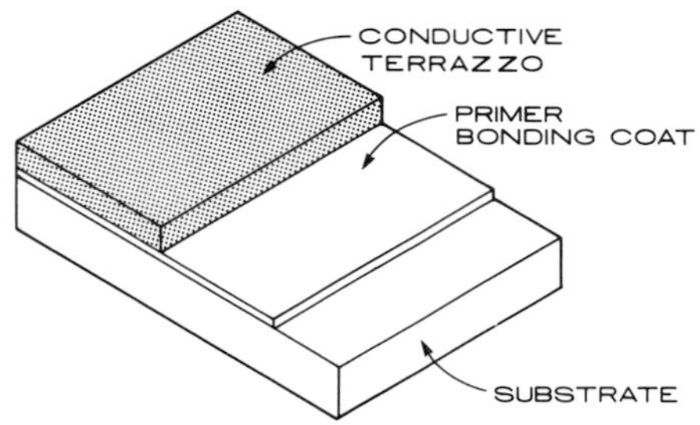
CONDUCTIVE TERRAZZO
PRIMER BONDING COAT
SUBSTRATE

Static-dissipating, nonsparking trowel-applied jointless flooring of elastomeric resin terrazzo, incorporating marble chips. Thickness 1/4 in. to 1/2 in., weighing 3 psf (1/4 in. thick). Used in hospital operating suites.

CONDUCTIVE FLOORING

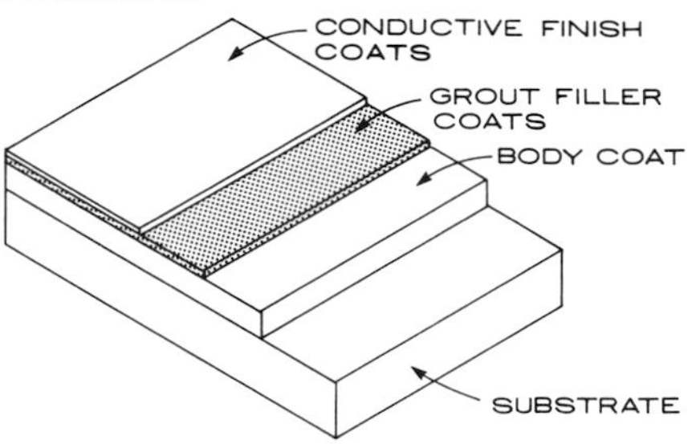
CONDUCTIVE FINISH COATS
GROUT FILLER COATS
BODY COAT
SUBSTRATE

Static-dissipating and nonsparking trowel-applied jointless flooring, 1/4 in. thick, weighing 3 psf. Used in arsenals and ammunition plants, flammable materials storage areas and explosion-hazardous industrial locations.

CONDUCTIVE FLOORING

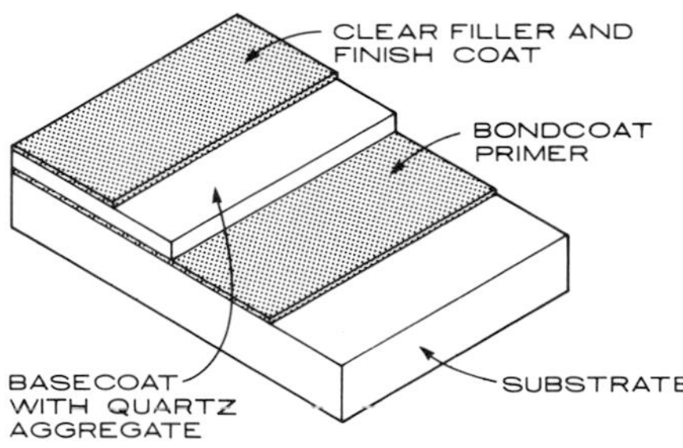
CLEAR FILLER AND FINISH COAT
BONDCOAT PRIMER
BASECOAT WITH QUARTZ AGGREGATE
SUBSTRATE

A jointless flooring in which quartz aggregates are embedded either by trowel or broadcast into a wet epoxy binding coat followed by clear filler coat. Used in laboratories, pollution control facilities, locker rooms, light manufacturing.

EPOXY/QUARTZ AGGREGATE

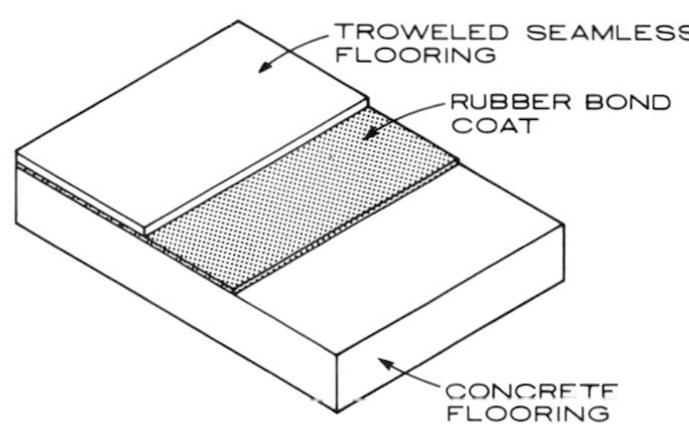
TROWELED SEAMLESS FLOORING
RUBBER BOND COAT
CONCRETE FLOORING

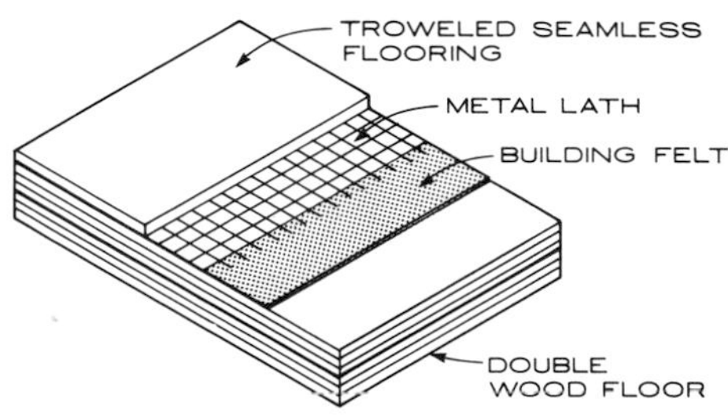
TROWELED SEAMLESS FLOORING
METAL LATH
BUILDING FELT
DOUBLE WOOD FLOOR

A trowel-applied cupric oxychloride flooring that is nonsparking and solvent resistant, weighing 3.2 psf at 3/8 in. thick. Used in hospitals, arsenals and ammunition plants, light manufacturing areas, warehouses, laboratories.

CUPRIC OXYCHLORIDE FLOORING

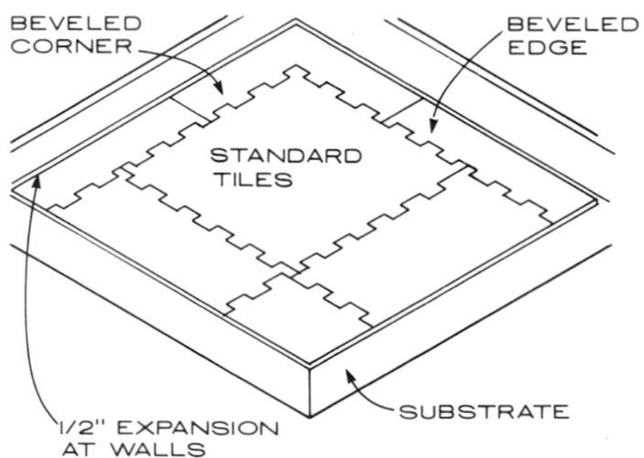
BEVELED CORNER
BEVELED EDGE
STANDARD TILES
1/2" EXPANSION AT WALLS
SUBSTRATE

An interlocking rubber tile flooring system made in various thicknesses and types according to user requirements. Can be used in saunas, deck areas, weight, exercise, and locker rooms, on assembly lines, in industrial art rooms.

INTERLOCKING RUBBER FLOORING

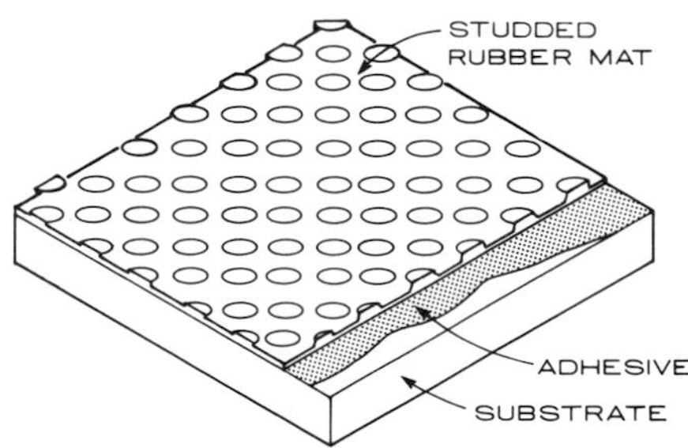
STUDDED RUBBER MAT
ADHESIVE
SUBSTRATE

A solid, nonconductive rubber flooring with a raised circular, square, "H" or ribbed pattern. Applied to substrate by use of an adhesive. Used in terminals, malls, recreation facilities, elevators and offices.

STUDDED RUBBER FLOORING

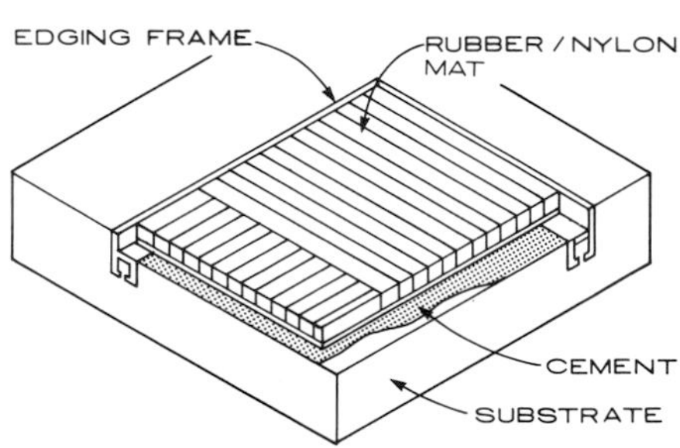
EDGING FRAME
RUBBER / NYLON MAT
CEMENT
SUBSTRATE

Manufactured from recycled synthetic rubber tires containing nylon fibers for strength and bonded to a glass-cloth backing. Applied to substrate cement adhesive. Used in golf clubs, stores, malls, and air terminals.

RUBBER/NYLON FLOORING

Timothy B. McDonald; Washington, D.C.

BACKGROUND

The word "carpet" comes from the Latin *carpere*, "to card wool." Carpet production in the U.S. has grown from 100 million square yards in 1910 to over 1 billion square yards per year in the 1980s. Three events account for the major increases:

1. Development of man-made fibers in the 1930s.
2. Replacement of weaving by tufting in the 1950s.
3. Combining of the tufting machine with piece dyeable bulked continuous filament (BCF) nylon in the period beginning 1960. This gave the industry the ability to produce carpet styles with long color lines of up to 50 or more colors without large inventory costs.

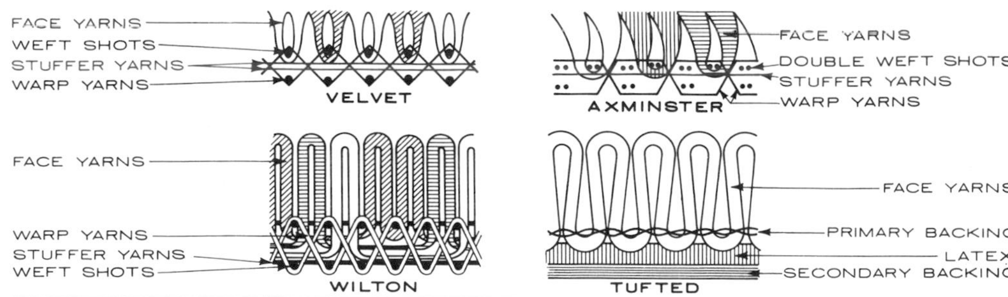
FACE YARNS
WEFT SHOTS
STUFFER YARNS
WARP YARNS
VELVET
FACE YARNS
DOUBLE WEFT SHOTS
STUFFER YARNS
WARP YARNS
AXMINSTER
FACE YARNS
WARP YARNS
STUFFER YARNS
WEFT SHOTS
WILTON
FACE YARNS
PRIMARY BACKING
LATEX
SECONDARY BACKING
TUFTED
CONSTRUCTION MODES

CARPET FIBERS

Nature accounted for 100% of face fiber production for floor coverings. The uncertainties of supply of desirable wools from about 20 countries, plus variation in fiber length and increasing costs of scouring and processing encouraged development of man-made fibers. Man-made fibers are easy to clean, mildew resistant, mothproof, and nonallergenic.

Wool: Of 1986 U.S.-produced carpet production, 1% was wool. Its qualities have been copied but never quite duplicated. The natural tendency of animal fibers to stretch and return to their original length makes wool carpet resilient, with excellent recovery from crushing. Problems of supply make it the most expensive fiber and the only one requiring antimoth treatment.

Cotton: Negligible current usage. Early tufted carpet was an offshoot of the "turfed" bedspread cottage industry in the South and had single color, loop, or cut pile fibers made of cotton.

Nylon: Of 1986 carpet production, 80% was nylon—a petrochemical engineered for carpet use, with easy dying characteristics. First successfully introduced into carpet in continuous filament, it was later cut and processed in staple lengths (like wool) to give more natural qualities to the finished product. Recent developments have combined topical treatments with modified extrusions to give antisoil properties to the fibers. Adequate maintenance provisions should accompany specifications for these products, since soil that remains hidden will cause fiber damage unless properly removed by regular vacuuming and cleaning.

Acrylic: Negligible current usage. This hydrocarbon synthetic is considered to be the most wool-like of all man-made fibers.

Polypropylene (olefin): Of 1986 production, 12% and growing. This man-made hydrocarbon normally lacks resilience and the ability to be post dyed. Its simplified extrusion capabilities plus the ability to be solution dyed prior to extrusion have encouraged many carpet makers to install their own polypropylene fiber-making facilities.

Polyester: Of 1986 production, 7%. A high tensile strength synthetic made by the esterification of ethyl glycol, having easy care and water-repellent qualities.

CARPET CONSTRUCTION

Woven carpet represents 2% of the total carpet production in the U.S. today. Whether hand-knotted, loomed, or mechanically produced, there are many similarities in production methods. The side-to-side progression in hand-knotted is accelerated in a loom as the shuttle propels the weft (or woof) yarn back and forth over the 12 or 15 ft width of the finished carpet. This is missing in tufted and later methods. Common to all, however, is a progression of the leading edge of this 12–15 ft finished width in the direction of manufacture. This sets up the direction of lay of the finished face fibers, always in the opposite direction. The exception is in hand-knotted, where the direction of lay of the face fibers falls to one side or the other, depending on the style of knot. In hand-knotted, it will also change after cleaning to follow the direction of brushing.

In all tufted or woven broadloom, it is imperative that the direction of lay be made to run in the same direction on all components of every installation. Otherwise, adjacent widths, although perfectly seamed, will appear to mismatch in perceived color and texture.

Oriental rugs: Defined by the Oriental Rug Retailers of America as "a rug of either wool or silk, knotted entirely by hand by native craftsmen in some parts of Asia, from the shores of the Persian Gulf, North to the Caspian Sea, and Eastward through Iran, the Soviet Union, Afghanistan, Pakistan, India, China, and Japan." An Oriental rug is classed an antique if it is over 75 years old, semiantique if less than 75 years old, and new if made in the past 15 years.

More than 60% of the hand-knotted rugs imported by the U.S. come from China and India. Most machine-made rugs are manufactured in the U.S. or imported from Belgium or Spain. They are available in traditional (floral or curvilinear) and contemporary (geometric) colors and designs.

Dhurrie and Kilim rugs are flat weaves costing less than hand-knotted Orientals. They can be either machine- or hand-made and have primitive as well as modern designs. Other types of rugs are ryas from Scandinavia, American Indian woven rugs, and Greek flotakis. Braided and rag rugs are also finding a niche in the market. Many carpet and rug makers offer custom designs (some computer aided) in a variety of fiber construction.

CONSTRUCTION MODES

Velvet: Simplest of all carpet weaves. Although the simplicity of the loom does not permit patterned designs, beautiful yarn color combinations can be used to produce tweed effects. Pile is formed as the warp yarns are looped over removable "wires" inserted consecutively across the loom (weft-wise). Requires additional space equal to the width of the loom for this rapid operation. Alternate height wires can be used to create high–low loop texture, while wires with a raised knife blade at the trailing end are used to create cut pile upon retraction.

Axminster: Has a smooth cut pile surface, with almost all of the yarn appearing on the surface. Colors and patterns are limited only by the number of tufts in the carpet. Identifying feature is the heavy ribbed backing that only allows the carpet to be rolled lengthwise.

Wilton: Basic velvet loom, improved in the early 1800s by the addition of a Jacquard mechanism to feed yarn through as many as six separate punched hole patterns to vary the texture or colored design. Uses only one color at a time on the surface; the other yarns remain buried; thus the reputation that Wiltons have a hidden quality because of the extra "hand" or feel that this gives to the finished carpet.

Tufted: This technique developed from an early method for making tufted bedspreads. Spacing of as many as 2000 needles on a huge sewing machine (12–15 ft wide) determines the carpet gauge. Face yarn is stitched through the primary backing, where it is bonded to a secondary backing with latex before curing in a drying oven. For energy saving, hot-melt adhesive is substituted for latex by some mills, though this results in a loss of ability to pass flammability tests. Some "single-needle" tufting machines exist having a small stitching head that moves from side to side during carpet construction. They are mainly used for special orders for multiple odd-shaped spaces to eliminate installation waste.

Knitted: Resembles weaving in that knitted carpet is a warp-knitted fabric comprised of warp chains, weft-forming yarns, and face yarns and is knitted in a single operation. Warp-chain stitches run longitudinally and parallel to each other. The backing yarns are laid weft-wise into the warp stitches and pass over 3 or 4 rows of warp stitches overlapping in the back of the carpet for strength and stiffness. As in tufted carpet, latex is applied to the back for stability and tuft lock. An additional backing may also be attached. Knitted carpets usually have solid or tweed colors, with level-loop textures.

Flocked: Made by propelling short strands of pile fiber (usually nylon) electrostatically against an adhesive-coated (usually jute), prefabricated backing sheet. As many as 18,000 pile fibers per inch become vertically embedded in the adhesive before a secondary backing is laminated to the fabric and the adhesive cured. The pile fibers can either be dyed prior to flocking or the finished surface can be printed after fabrication.

Needlepunched: First made of polypropylene fibers in solid colors for outdoor use (patios and swimming pools), they are now made for indoor and automotive use as well, using wool, nylon, acrylic, and/or olefin fibers in variegated colors and designs. They are made by impinging loose layers of random, staple carpet fibers into a solid sheet of polypropylene, from both sides, by means of thousands of barbed needles until the entire mass is compressed to a solid bonded fiber mass of indoor/outdoor carpet.

Fusion bonded: This process produces dense cut pile or level-loop carpet in solid or moresque colors. For cut pile, the face yarn, fed simultaneously from the total width of the supply roll, or "beam," is folded back and forth between two vertically emerging primary backings as they are coated with a viscous vinyl paste that hardens, binding the folded face yarns alternately to the vertical backing sheet on each side. Final operation is a mid-line cutting that separates the vertical "sandwich" into two identical cut pile finished rolls. To make loop pile fusion-bonded carpet, one primary backing and the cutting operation are omitted. Fusion bonding is especially suited to making carpet tiles.

SELECTION CRITERIA

FIBER	DURABILITY	SOIL RESISTANCE	RESILIENCE	ABRASION RESISTANCE	CLEANABILITY
Nylon	Excellent	Good	Good to excellent	Excellent	Very good
Polyester	Very good	Fair	Good	Excellent	Very good
Polypropylene	Excellent	Fair	Poor	Excellent	Very good
Acrylic	Good	Fair	Fair	Good	Very good
Wool	Very good	Good to excellent	Excellent	Good	Very good

Neil Spencer, AIA; North Canton, Ohio

DEFINITIONS

Carpet tiles: Square (from 18 to 36 in.) modules, dense cut pile or loop, heavy backed. Can be made to cover flat, regular wiring; low-voltage lighting systems ("safe-lites"); or underfloor utilities.

Carpet wear: As defined by fiber manufacturers refers to percent of face fiber lost over the life of a guarantee.

Commercial: Includes all contract, institutional, transportation; any use where carpet is specified by other than the end user.

Residential: Includes all carpet specified and purchased for residential use by the owner.

Life-cycle costing: Permits comparison of diverse flooring methods by totaling initial cost, installation, and detailed predictable maintenance expenses over the expected life of the carpet.

Traffic: Usage expressed in terms of foot traffics (person) per unit of time or as light, medium, or heavy, to define need for matching carpet construction, which normally increases in density as traffic increases. See recommendations below.

Pile height: Height of loop or tuft from the surface of the backing to the top of the pile, measured in fractions, or decimals, of an inch.

Pile weight (face weight): total weight of pile yarns in the carpet (measured in oz/sq yd, excluding backing).

Pile density: D = 36 times the finished pile weight, in oz/yd, divided by the average pile height.

$$\text{Weight density (WD)} = \frac{(\text{Face weight})^2 \times 36}{\text{Pile height}}$$

Pitch (in woven carpet): The number of yarn ends in a 27 in. finished width of carpet.

Gauge: In tufted carpet, the number of needles per inch across the width of the finished carpet (tufting machine).

Stitches: Number of rows of yarn ends per inch, finished carpet. Tufts per sq in.: Calculation made by multiplying pitch x wires for woven carpet, or gauge x stitches per in. for tufted.

Denier: Weight in grams of 9000 meters (9750 yd) of a single extruded filament of nylon. Based on the standard weight of 450 meters of silk weighing 5 centigrams.

Filament: Continuous strand of extruded synthetic fiber, combined into a "singles" yarn by simply twisting, without the need for spinning.

Ply: Refers to the number of strands of "singles" yarn twisted together for color or texture reasons to create a two-ply or three-ply yarn system.

Point: A single tuft of carpet pile.

BCF: Bulked continuous filament.

Cut pile pattern: Plush or saxony type carpet with woven, tufted, or printed design or pattern.

Level loop: Carpet made from uncut tufts in looped form and having all tufts the same pile height.

Cut pile velvet: Solid color, tweed, or heather blend yarns which give smooth velvety or velour texture.

Cut and loop: Carpet with areas of both cut pile and loop pile, most often with the cut pile being higher than the loop.

Frieze: Cut pile carpet made from highly twisted yarns that are heat set to give a curled random configuration to the pile yarns.

Primary backing: The matrix used in making tufted carpet, consisting of woven or nonwoven fabric, usually jute or polypropylene, into which pile yarn tufts are stitched.

Secondary backing: The woven or nonwoven material adhered to the underside of a carpet during construction to provide additional tuft bind for tufted carpet and dimensional stability and body. Usually jute, or polypropylene, latex foam, or vinyl.

Neil Spencer, AIA; North Canton, Ohio

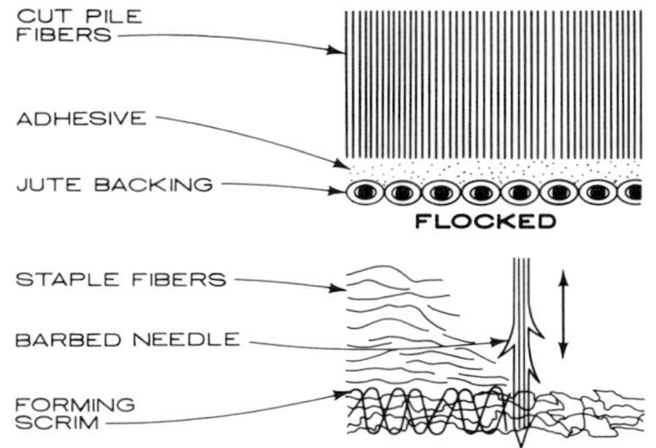
CUT PILE FIBERS
ADHESIVE
JUTE BACKING
FLOCKED
STAPLE FIBERS
BARBED NEEDLE
FORMING SCRIM
NEEDLEPUNCHED

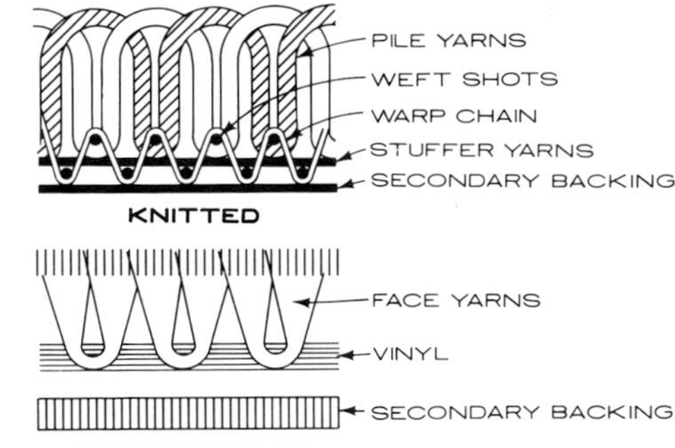
PILE YARNS
WEFT SHOTS
WARP CHAIN
STUFFER YARNS
SECONDARY BACKING
KNITTED
FACE YARNS
VINYL
SECONDARY BACKING
FUSION BONDED

CONSTRUCTION MODES

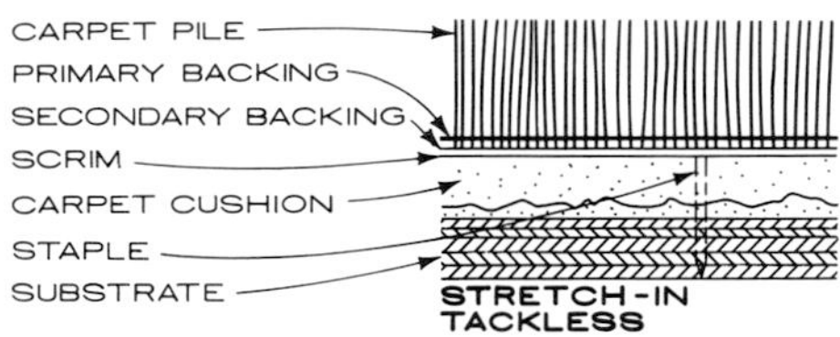
CARPET PILE
PRIMARY BACKING
SECONDARY BACKING
SCRIM
CARPET CUSHION
STAPLE
SUBSTRATE
STRETCH-IN TACKLESS

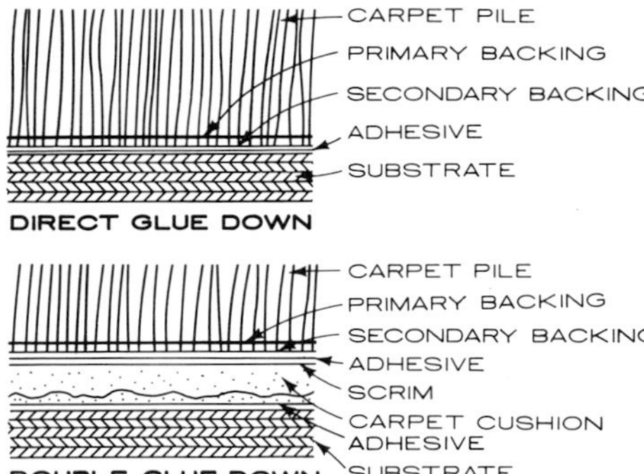
CARPET PILE
PRIMARY BACKING
SECONDARY BACKING
ADHESIVE
SUBSTRATE
DIRECT GLUE DOWN
CARPET PILE
PRIMARY BACKING
SECONDARY BACKING
ADHESIVE
SCRIM
CARPET CUSHION
ADHESIVE
SUBSTRATE
DOUBLE GLUE DOWN

INSTALLATION (THREE TYPES)

1. Stretch-in (tackless). Over separate cushion. Best condition for maximum carpet wear and most effective cleaning.
2. Direct glue down. For large surface areas which make power-stretching and tackless installations prohibitive. Adhesive must be tailored to match carpet backing and substrate, as recommended by carpet manufacturer.
3. Double glue down. Developed to counter early fiber failure, occurring in direct glue-down carpets in heavy traffic areas, due to lower than normal resilience level of man-made fibers. Provides ease of large area coverage plus benefits of separate pad.

INSTALLATION

CARPET CUSHION OR UNDERLAYMENT

Four reasons for considering separate carpet cushion in wall-to-wall installations are:

1. Adds as much as 50% to the life of the carpet.
2. Absorbs as much as 90% of the traffic noise.
3. Can reduce installation costs by eliminating need for repairs to less than perfect substrate.
4. Improves thermal environment by insulation, which varies depending on material.

Four major categories of carpet cushion are:

1. Felt padding
2. Sponge rubber
3. Urethane foam
4. Foam rubber

TRAFFIC CLASSIFICATION

	TRAFFIC RATING		
CARPETED AREAS	LIGHT	MEDIUM	HEAVY
Educational			
Schools and colleges			
Administration		•	
Classroom			•
Dormitory			•
Corridor			•
Libraries		•	
Museums and art galleries			
Display room			•
Lobby			•
Medical			
Health care			
Executive	•	•	
Patient's room			•
Lounge			•
Nurses' station			•
Corridor			•
Lobby			•
Commercial			
Retail establishments			
Aisle			•
Sales counter			•
Smaller boutiques, etc.			•

TRAFFIC CLASSIFICATION (CONTINUED)

	TRAFFIC RATING		
CARPETED AREAS	LIGHT	MEDIUM	HEAVY
Office buildings			
Executive		•	
Clerical			•
Corridor			•
Cafeteria			•
Supermarkets			•
Food services			•
Recreational			
Recreation areas			•
Club house			•
Locker room			•
Convention centers			
Auditorium			•
Corridor and lobby			•
Religious			
Churches/temples			
Worship	•	•	
Meeting room			•
Lobby			•

NOTE: If rolling traffic is a factor, carpet may be of maximum density for minimum resistance to rollers. Select only level loop or dense low cut pile for safety.

MAINTENANCE PROGRAMMING

The following maintenance-related factors should be considered in the selection of carpet:

Color: Carpets in the mid-value range show less soil than very dark or very light colors. Consider the typical regional soil color. Specify patterned or multicolored carpets for heavy traffic areas in hotels, hospitals, theaters, and restaurants.

Traffic: The heavier the traffic, the heavier the density of carpet construction.

Topical treatment: Note that the soil-hiding qualities of advanced generation fibers do not reduce the need for regular maintenance. They do make soil removal easier, but by disguising the presence of dirt, make it easier for the dirt that remains hidden to contribute to earlier fiber failure unless regularly removed.

Placement: The location of carpeted areas within a building affects the maintenance expense. Walk-off carpet areas can contribute effectively to reducing tracked-in soil near entrances.

WALL TREATMENT

1. USE: Sound absorption.
2. MATERIALS: Fabric-wrapped glass fiber or mineral wool.
3. N.R.C.: .55–.85
4. NOTES: Wall panels may be used individually or grouped to form an entire wall system. Noise reduction coefficient varies with material thickness and acoustical transparency of fabric facing. Maximum panel sizes vary with manufacturer up to 4 x 12 ft.

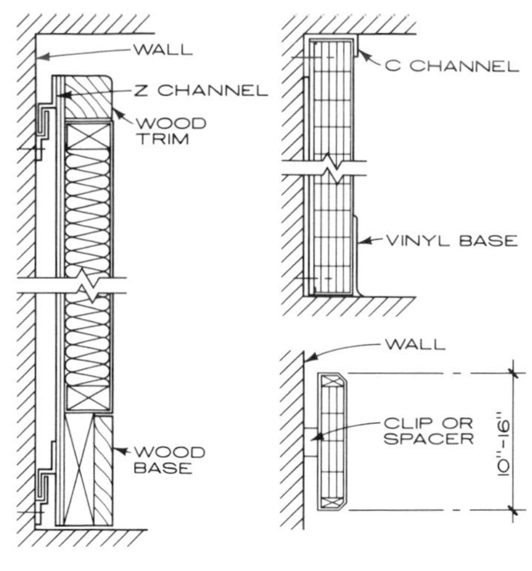
WALL
Z CHANNEL
WOOD TRIM
WOOD BASE
C CHANNEL
VINYL BASE
WALL
CLIP OR SPACER
10"-16"

SECTIONS

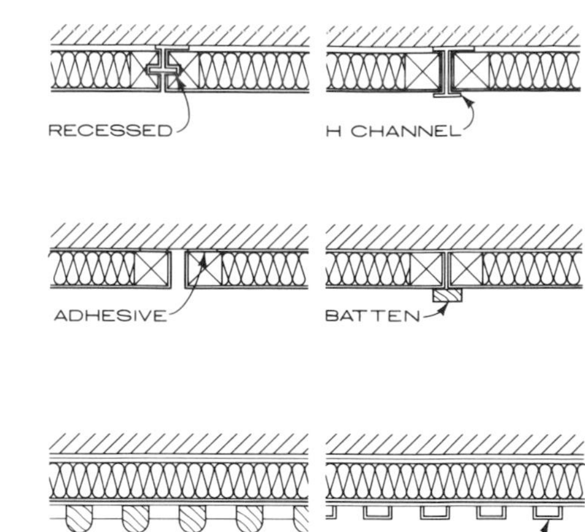
RECESSED
H CHANNEL
ADHESIVE
BATTEN
WOOD GRILLE
METAL GRILLE

PLAN SECTIONS

WALL TREATMENT

PLENUM BARRIER

1. USE: Reduce sound transmission through plenum above partitions.
2. MATERIALS: 1/64 in. sheet lead, lead-loaded vinyl, perforated aluminum, or foil-wrapped glass fiber.
3. S.T.C.: 18–41 dB improvement.
4. NOTES: All openings through barrier for pipes, ducts, etc., must be sealed airtight for maximum effectiveness.

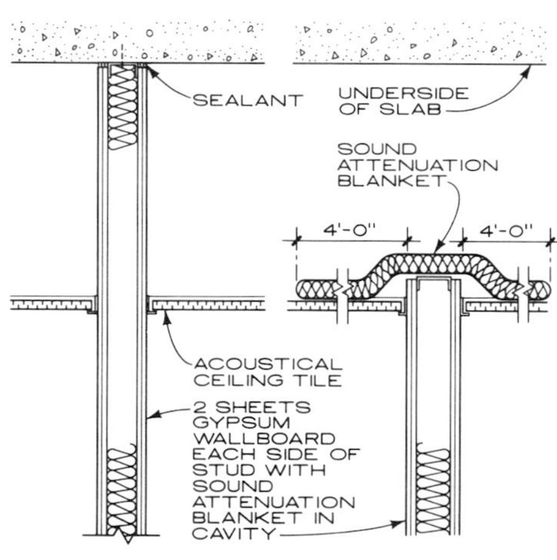
SEALANT
UNDERSIDE OF SLAB
SOUND ATTENUATION BLANKET
4'-0"
4'-0"
ACOUSTICAL CEILING TILE
2 SHEETS GYPSUM WALLBOARD EACH SIDE OF STUD WITH SOUND ATTENUATION BLANKET IN CAVITY

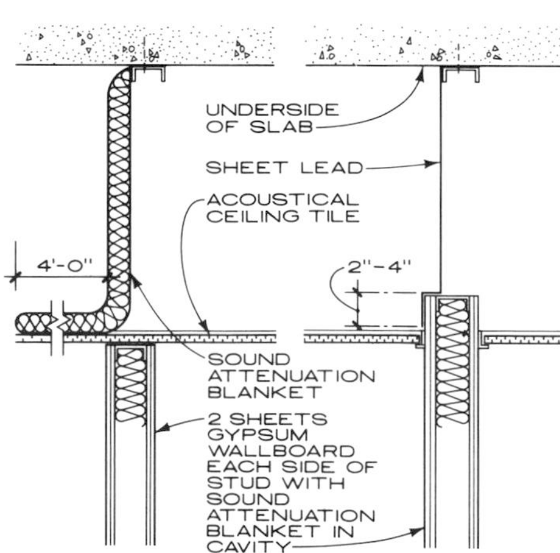
UNDERSIDE OF SLAB
SHEET LEAD
ACOUSTICAL CEILING TILE
4'-0"
2"-4"
SOUND ATTENUATION BLANKET
2 SHEETS GYPSUM WALLBOARD EACH SIDE OF STUD WITH SOUND ATTENUATION BLANKET IN CAVITY

PLENUM BARRIERS

SUSPENDED PANELS

1. USE: Sound absorption.
2. MATERIALS: Vertical suspension–glass fiber blanket wrapped with perforated aluminum foil or fabric stretched over frame. Horizontal suspension–perforated steel or aluminum with glass fiber blanket, or similar to vertical.
3. N.R.C.: .55–.85
4. NOTES: Panels may be suspended from structure or attached directly to ceiling grid. May be arranged in a variety of patterns including linear, square, zigzag vertical, or regular or random spaced horizontal panels.

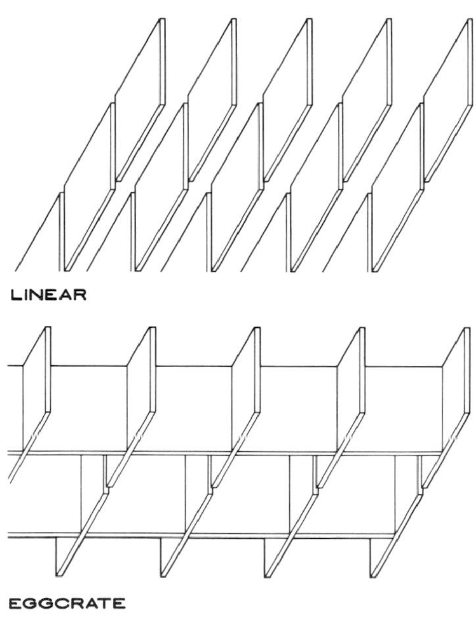

LINEAR

EGGCRATE

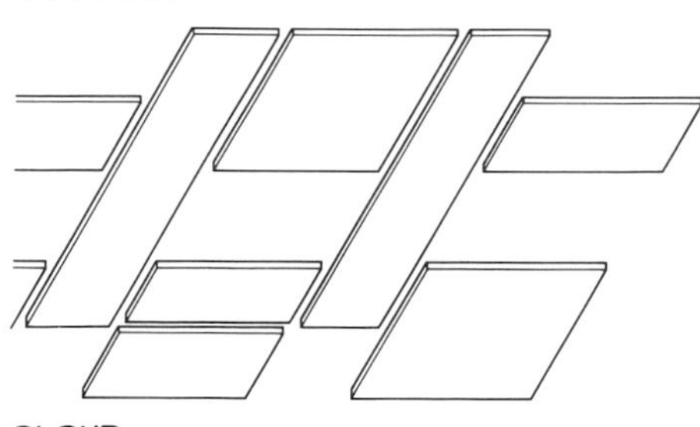

CLOUD

SUSPENDED PANELS

ACOUSTICAL MASONRY UNITS

1. USE: Sound absorption
2. MATERIALS: Concrete masonry unit, 4, 6, or 8 in. thick, with metal baffle and/or fibrous filler in slotted areas
   Structural glazed facing tile, 4, 6, or 8 in. thick; 8 x 8 in. or 8 x 16 in. (nominal) face dimensions, with fibrous filler in cores.
3. N.R.C.: .45–.65

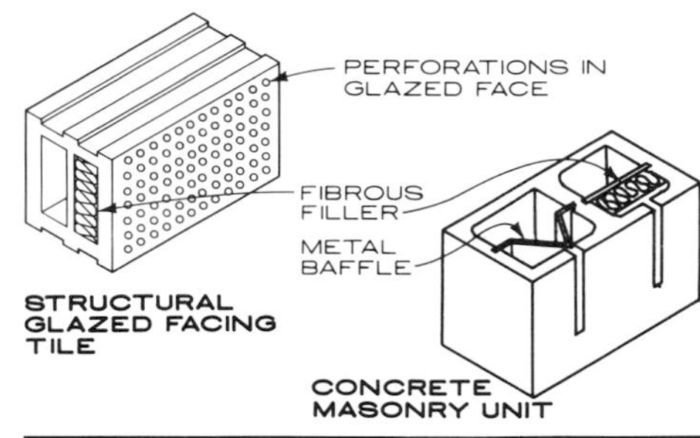
PERFORATIONS IN GLAZED FACE
FIBROUS FILLER
METAL BAFFLE
STRUCTURAL GLAZED FACING TILE
CONCRETE MASONRY UNIT

ACOUSTICAL MASONRY UNITS

SPRAY-ON ACOUSTICAL MATERIAL

1. USE: Sound absorption.
2. MATERIALS: Mineral or cellulose fibers spray applied to metal lath or directly to hard surfaces such as concrete, steel, masonry, or gypsum wallboard.
3. N.R.C.: .50–.95
4. NOTES: Application to metal lath provides slightly better sound absorption and permits irregular shapes. Available with a hard surface for wall applications. Available with fire protection rating.

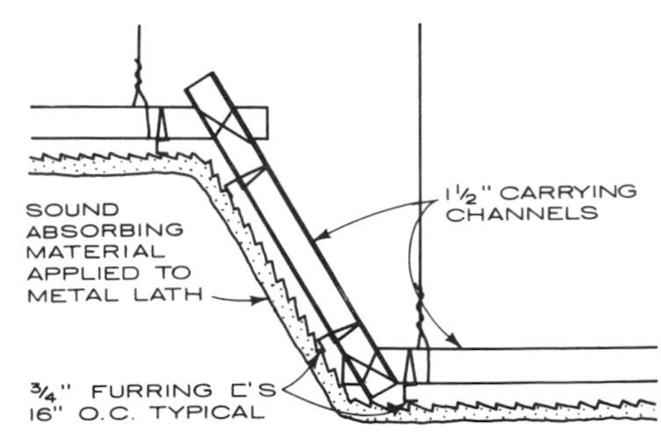
SOUND ABSORBING MATERIAL APPLIED TO METAL LATH
1 1/2" CARRYING CHANNELS
3/4" FURRING C'S 16" O.C. TYPICAL

SPRAY-ON ACOUSTICAL MATERIAL

Setter, Leach & Lindstrom, Inc.; Minneapolis, Minnesota
Blythe + Nazdin Architects, Ltd.; Bethesda, Maryland

PREFINISHED PANELS

MATERIAL TYPE	USE	THICKNESS 1/32	1/16	1/8	3/16	1/4	5/16	3/8	1/2	5/8	3/4
PLYWOOD											
Hardwood veneer	Cabinets, interior paneling, protective surfaces					●		●	●		●
Softwood veneer	Interior paneling					●		●	●	●	●
Printed/embossed	Interior paneling					●		●	●	●	●
Textured	Interior paneling, siding							●	●	●	●
Printed vinyl faced	Decorative interior finish							●	●	●	
HARDBOARD											
Standard	Interior use, cabinet liner			●	●	●	●	●	●		
Tempered	Interior and exterior use, underlayment where strength and wear count			●	●	●	●	●	●		
Plastic finished	Interior paneling, wearing surfaces			●		●		●		●	
Embossed factory finish	Interior decorative paneling				●	●					
FIBERBOARD											
Vinyl covered	Tackboard—interior decorative paneling								●		
Fabric covered	Acoustic, panels, tackboard								●		
LAMINATES											
Plastic laminates	Cabinets, countertops, protective wall finish	●	●	●							
Metal faced	Decorative paneling	●	●	●							
GYPSUM											
Vinyl covered	Interior walls					●		●	●	●	
Fabric covered	Interior walls					●		●	●	●	

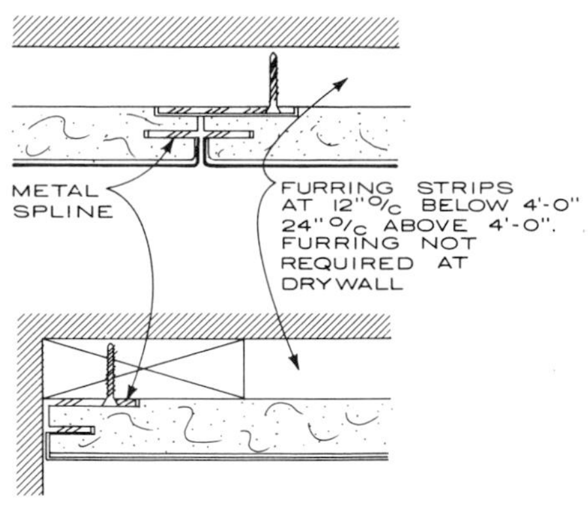
METAL SPLINE
FURRING STRIPS AT 12" O/C BELOW 4'-0" 24" O/C ABOVE 4'-0". FURRING NOT REQUIRED AT DRYWALL

FABRIC COVERED FIBERBOARD

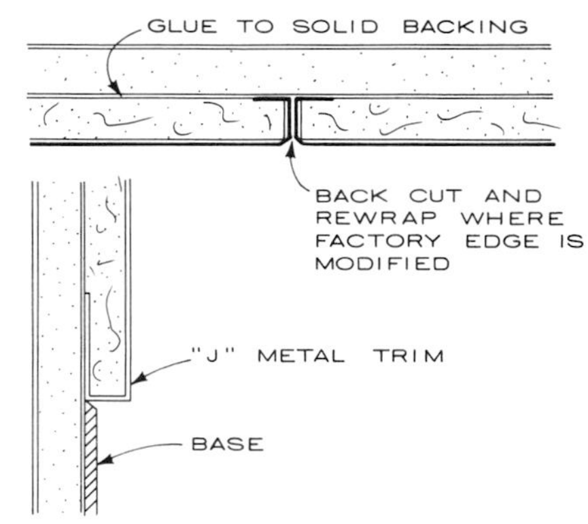
GLUE TO SOLID BACKING
BACK CUT AND REWRAP WHERE FACTORY EDGE IS MODIFIED
"J" METAL TRIM
BASE

VINYL COVERED FIBERBOARD

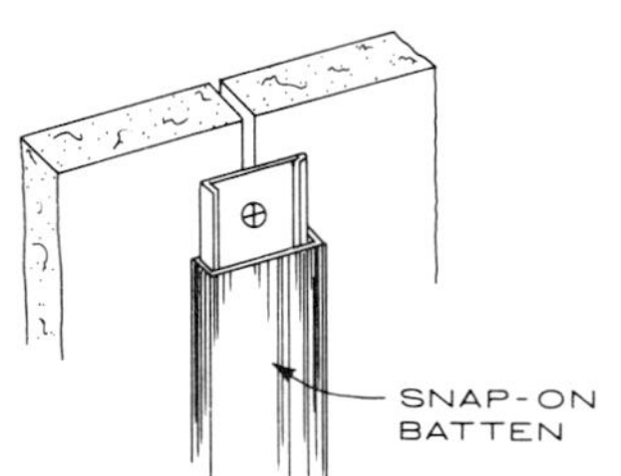
SNAP-ON BATTEN

VINYL COVERED GYPSUM BOARD

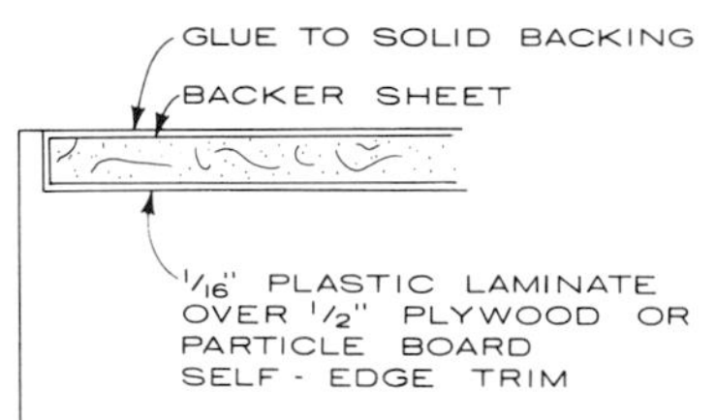
GLUE TO SOLID BACKING
BACKER SHEET
1/16" PLASTIC LAMINATE OVER 1/2" PLYWOOD OR PARTICLE BOARD SELF - EDGE TRIM

PLASTIC LAMINATE PANELS

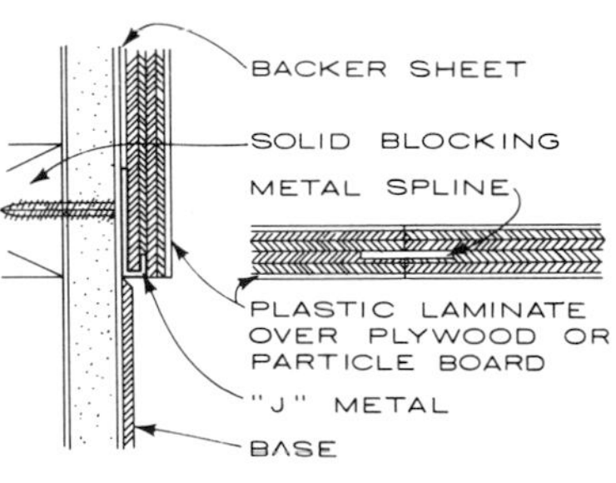
BACKER SHEET
SOLID BLOCKING
METAL SPLINE
PLASTIC LAMINATE OVER PLYWOOD OR PARTICLE BOARD
"J" METAL
BASE

PLASTIC LAMINATE PANELS

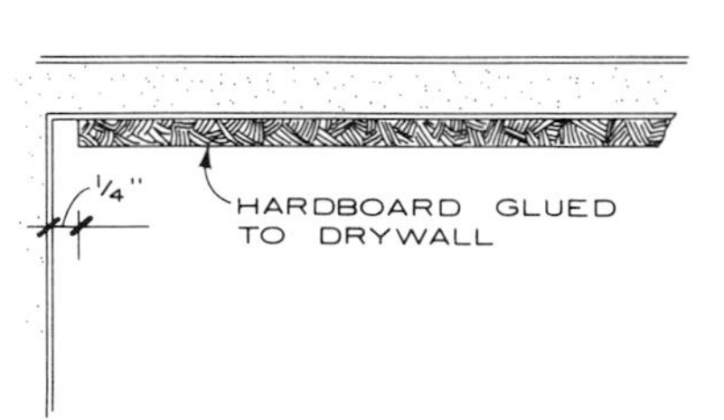
1/4"
HARDBOARD GLUED TO DRYWALL

TEMPERED HARDBOARD

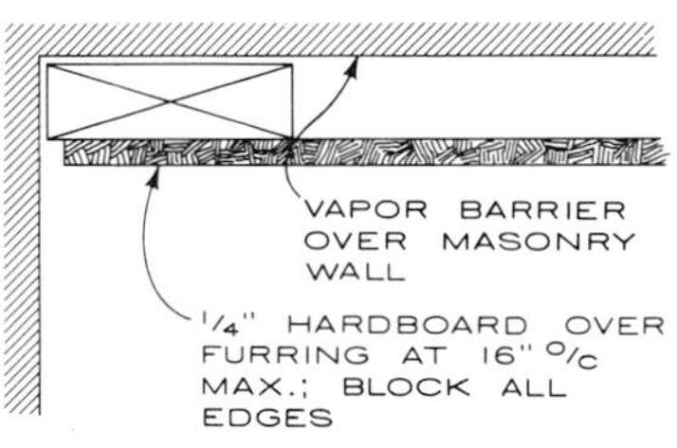
VAPOR BARRIER OVER MASONRY WALL
1/4" HARDBOARD OVER FURRING AT 16" O/C MAX.; BLOCK ALL EDGES

TEMPERED HARDBOARD

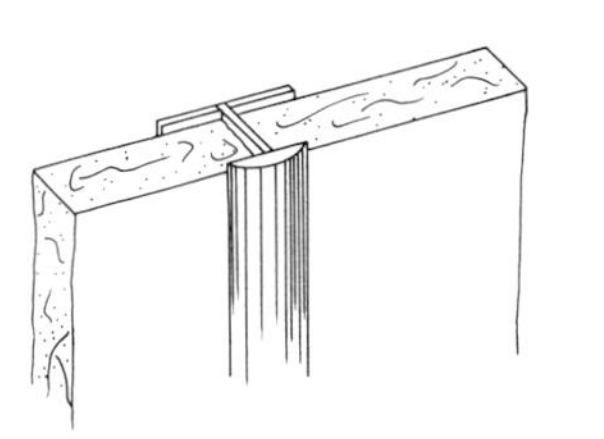

DIVIDER

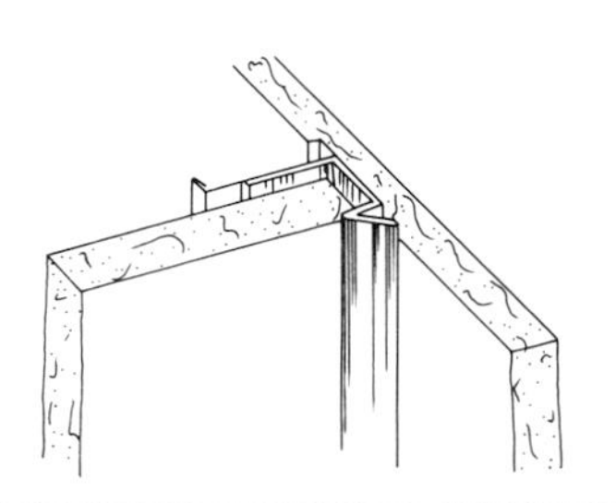

INSIDE CORNER TRIM

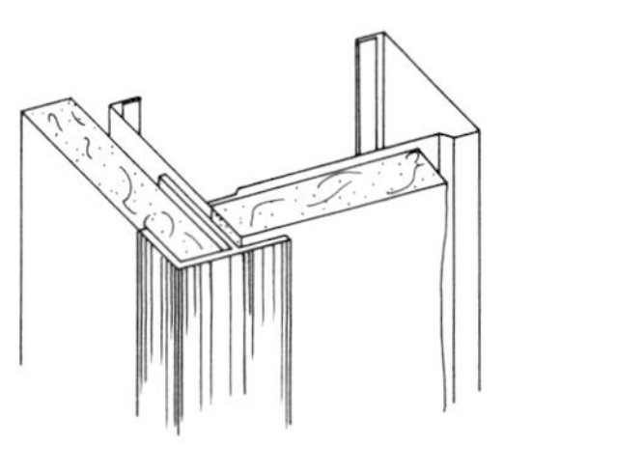

OUTSIDE CORNER TRIM

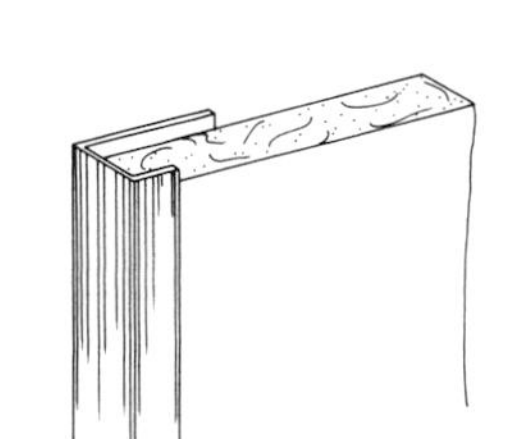

END CAP

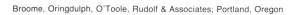

Broome, Oringdulph, O'Toole, Rudolf & Associates; Portland, Oregon

REFERENCES

GENERAL REFERENCES

Architectural Acoustics, 1988, M. Egan, McGraw-Hill
Ceiling Systems Handbook, Ceilings and Interior Contractors Association
Handbook for Ceramic Tile Installation, Tile Council of America
Manual of Lathing and Plastering, Gypsum Association
Plaster and Drywall Systems Manual, 3rd ed., 1988, J. P. Gorman, et al., McGraw-Hill

DATA SOURCES: ORGANIZATIONS

Alcan Aluminum Corporation, 324
Chicago Metallic Corporation, 325
Connor Forest Industries, 327
Dow Badische Company, 330
Keene Association, 308
Manhattan American Terrazzo Strip Company, 323
Maple Flooring Manufacturers' Association, Inc. (MFMA), 326
Metal Lath Institute (MLI), 308, 309
Monsanto Textiles Company, 330
National Gypsum Company, 313, 314, 318, 319
National Oak Flooring Manufacturers Association (NOFMA), 326
National Terrazzo and Mosaic Association, Inc. (NTMA), 323
Northern Hardwood and Pine Manufacturers Association, Inc. (NPHMA), 326
Southern Pine Inspection Bureau (SPIB), 326
Texas Lathing and Plastering Contractors' Association (TLPCA), 308, 309
Tile Council of America, Inc. (TCA), 320, 321
U.S. Gypsum Company, 308, 309, 314, 318, 319
Western Wood Products Association (WWPA), 326

DATA SOURCES: PUBLICATIONS

Carpet and Rugs, The Hoover Company, 330, 331
Specifications for Commercial Interiors, S. C. Reznikoff, Whitney Library of Design, 331

CHAPTER **10**

SPECIALTIES

TACKBOARD TYPES AND SIZES

TYPE	VARIATIONS	BACKING	THICKNESS	MAXIMUM SIZE WITHOUT JOINTS
Cork	Unfaced cork, plain or burlap backed	Unmounted	⅛", ¼"	4' x 130', 6' x 90'
		Particle board	½"	4' x 16'
		Hardboard		
	Vinyl covered cork	Unmounted	¼"	4' x 100'
		Particle board	½"	4' x 16'
		Hardboard		4 x 12' fire rated
	Vinyl impregnated cork	Unmounted	⅛", ¼"	6' x 90'
		Hardboard	½"	4' x 12'
Fiber-board	Vinyl covered		½"	4' x 12'
	Burlap covered			4' x 8', 4' x 14' spec.

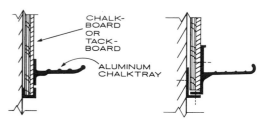

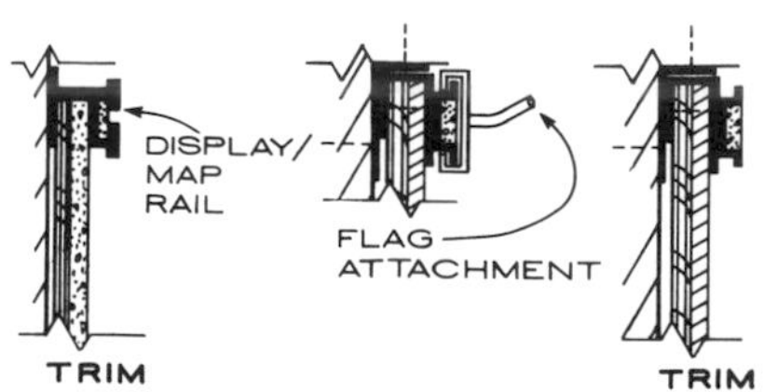
DISPLAY/
MAP
RAIL
FLAG
ATTACHMENT
TRIM
TRIM

ADDITIONAL VARIETIES OF TRIM AND CHALKTRAYS ARE AVAILABLE

CHALKBOARD TYPES AND SIZES

TYPE	CORE	THICKNESS	MAXIMUM SIZE WITHOUT JOINTS
Porcelain enamel steel (18-28 gauge)*	None	1/32"	4' x 12'
	Plywood	¼"-7/16"	4' x 12'
	Hardboard	¼", 7/16"	5' x 12', 4' x 16'
	Fiberboard	7/16", ½"	4' x 12'
	Particle board	⅜"-½"	4' x 16'
	Gypsum board	⅜", ½"	4' x 12'
	Honeycomb	⅜", 7/16"	4' x 16'
Painted-on composition	Hardboard	¼", ½"	4' x 16'
	Gypsum board	¼", ½"	4' x 12'
Natural slate		¼"-⅜"	4' x 6'

* Available in either chalkboard or liquid marker board.

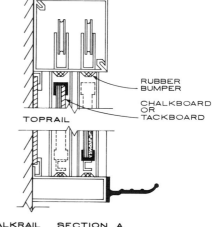

CHALK-BOARD OR TACK-BOARD
ALUMINUM CHALKTRAY

CHALKRAILS

CHALKBOARDS WITH ALUMINUM FRAMING

AVERAGE RECOMMENDED CHALKBOARD MOUNTING HEIGHT
(Chalkrail to Floor)

Nursery	20"
Kindergarten	24"
1st-3rd grade	30"
4th-6th grade	32"
Junior high	36"
Senior high	36"
Adult	36"

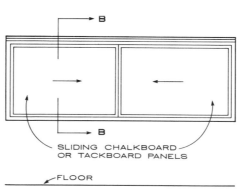

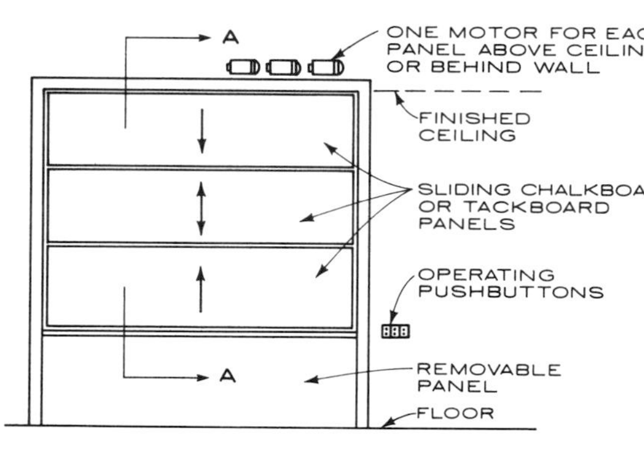
A
ONE MOTOR FOR EACH PANEL ABOVE CEILING OR BEHIND WALL
FINISHED CEILING
SLIDING CHALKBOARD OR TACKBOARD PANELS
OPERATING PUSHBUTTONS
REMOVABLE PANEL
FLOOR
A

VERTICAL SLIDING PANELS
(MANUAL OR MOTOR OPERATED)

RUBBER BUMPER
CHALKBOARD OR TACKBOARD
TOPRAIL

CHALKRAIL SECTION A

PIANO HINGE
PLATE GLASS

JAMB

B
SLIDING CHALKBOARD OR TACKBOARD PANELS
FLOOR

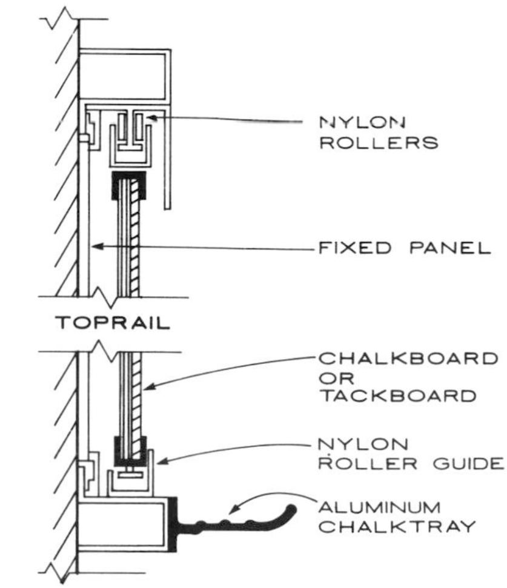
NYLON ROLLERS
FIXED PANEL
TOPRAIL
CHALKBOARD OR TACKBOARD
NYLON ROLLER GUIDE
ALUMINUM CHALKTRAY

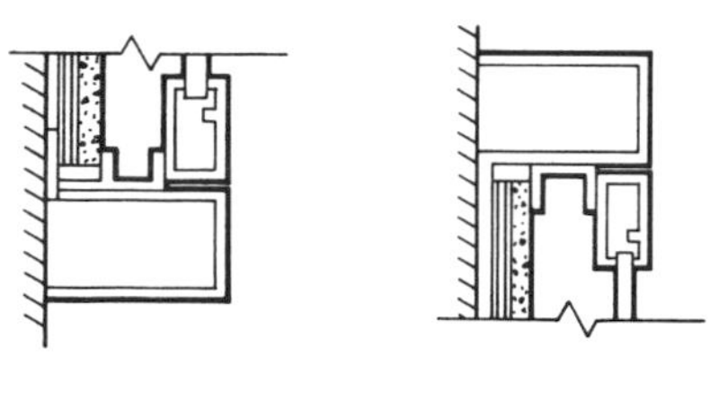

SILL HEAD

HORIZONTAL SLIDING PANELS

CHALKRAIL SECTION B

BULLETIN BOARD

SLIDING CHALKBOARDS AND TACKBOARDS

NOTES

1. Compartment types: ceiling hung (marble or metal), overhead braced, wall hung (metal only).
2. Metal finishes: baked-on enamel, porcelain enamel, stainless steel. Phenolic core, plastic laminate, solid polyethylene, tempered glass, and marble panels also are available.
3. A = standard compartment widths: 2 ft. 6 in., 2 ft. 8 in., 2 ft. 10 in., 3 ft. 0 in. (2 ft. 10 in. is used most frequently).
4. B = standard door widths: 1 ft. 8 in., 1 ft. 10 in., 2 ft. 0 in., 2 ft. 2 in., 2 ft. 4 in., 2 ft. 6 in. (2 ft. 0 in. metal doors are standard with marble compartments). Nonstandard sizes that sometimes are used: 1 ft. 11 in., 2 ft. 3 in., 2 ft. 5 in.
5. C = standard pilaster widths: 3 in., 4 in., 5 in., 6 in., 8 in., 10 in., 1 ft. 0 in. Nonstandard sizes that sometimes are used: 2 in., 7 in., 1 ft. 2 in.
6. D = standard panel widths: 18 in. to 57 in. in 1 in. increments. All panels are 58 in. high.
7. Wall hung models apply only to metal partitions.
8. Accessories include such items as paper holders, coat hooks, and purse shelves.

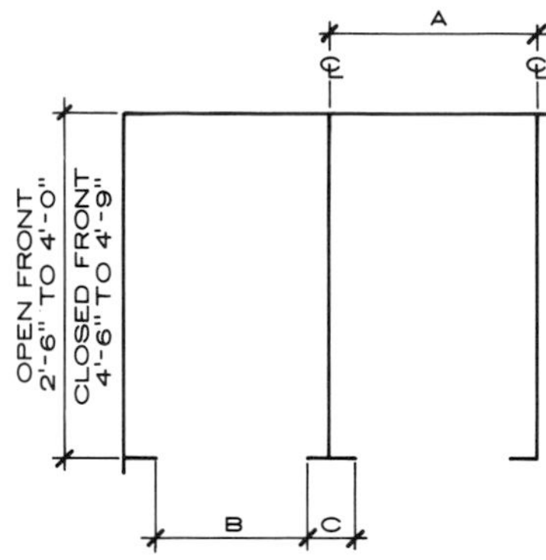
A
OPEN FRONT 2'-6" TO 4'-0"
CLOSED FRONT 4'-6" TO 4'-9"
B
C
PLAN OF STANDARD W.C. COMPARTMENT (TYPICAL FOR METAL OR PLASTIC LAMINATE)

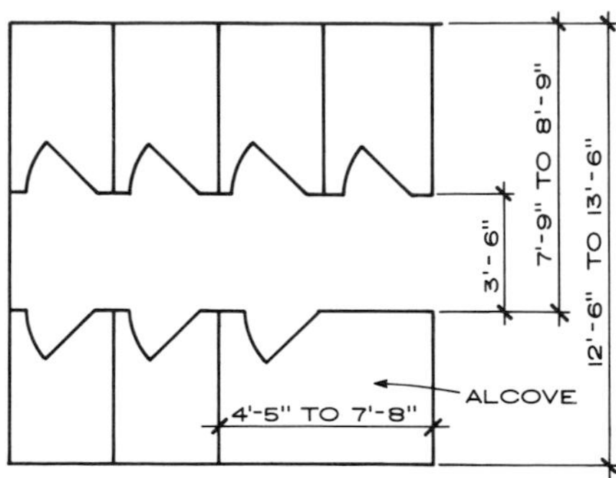
3'-6"
7'-9" TO 8'-9"
12'-6" TO 13'-6"
ALCOVE
4'-5" TO 7'-8"
SPACE REQUIREMENTS

GENERAL PLANNING DATA

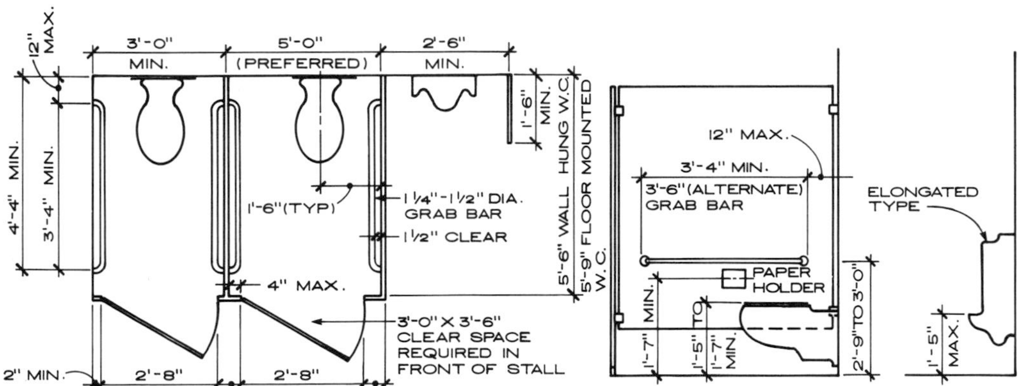
12" MAX.
3'-0" MIN.
5'-0" (PREFERRED)
2'-6" MIN.
4'-4" MIN.
3'-4" MIN.
1'-6" MIN.
5'-6" WALL HUNG W.C.
5'-9" FLOOR MOUNTED W.C.
1'-6"(TYP)
1 1/4"-1 1/2" DIA. GRAB BAR
1 1/2" CLEAR
4" MAX.
3'-0" X 3'-6" CLEAR SPACE REQUIRED IN FRONT OF STALL
2" MIN.
2'-8" MIN.
2'-8" MIN.
1'-4" MIN.
1'-4" MIN.
12" MAX.
3'-4" MIN.
3'-6"(ALTERNATE) GRAB BAR
PAPER HOLDER
1'-7" MIN.
1'-5" TO 1'-7" MIN.
2'-9" TO 3'-0"
ELONGATED TYPE
1'-5" MAX.
PLAN
SECTION
SECTION AT URINAL

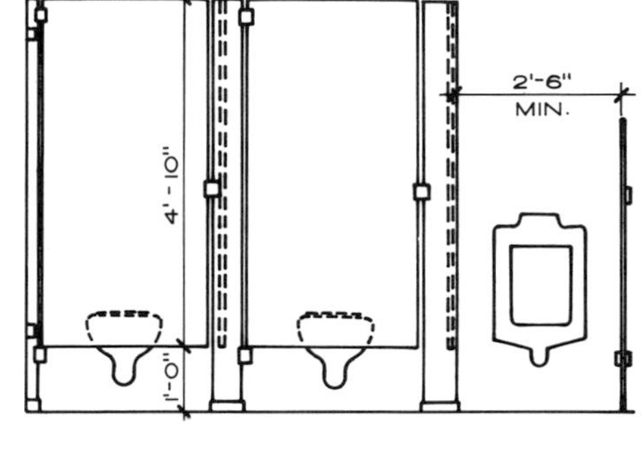
4'-10"
1'-0"
2'-6" MIN.
FRONT ELEVATION

HANDICAPPED TOILET LAYOUT

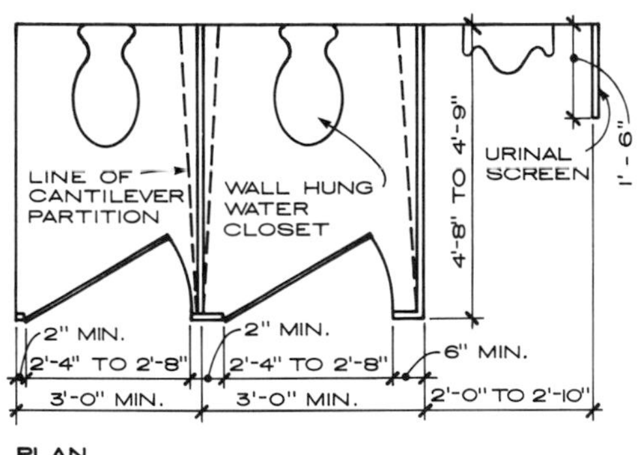
LINE OF CANTILEVER PARTITION
WALL HUNG WATER CLOSET
URINAL SCREEN
4'-8" TO 4'-9"
1'-6"
2" MIN.
2'-4" TO 2'-8"
2" MIN.
2'-4" TO 2'-8"
6" MIN.
3'-0" MIN.
3'-0" MIN.
2'-0" TO 2'-10"
PLAN

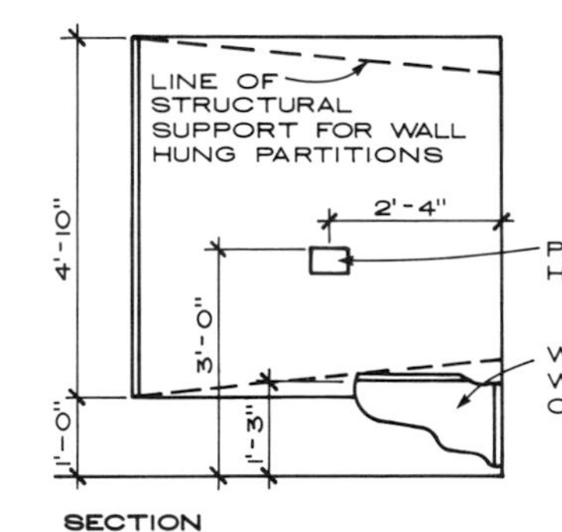
LINE OF STRUCTURAL SUPPORT FOR WALL HUNG PARTITIONS
2'-4"
PAPER HOLDER
WALL HUNG WATER CLOSET
4'-10"
3'-0"
1'-0"
1'-3"
SECTION

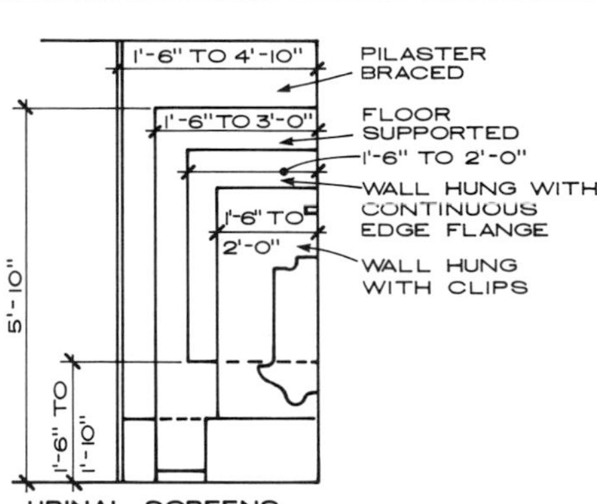
1'-6" TO 4'-10"
PILASTER BRACED
1'-6" TO 3'-0"
FLOOR SUPPORTED
1'-6" TO 2'-0"
WALL HUNG WITH CONTINUOUS EDGE FLANGE
1'-6" TO 2'-0"
WALL HUNG WITH CLIPS
5'-10"
1'-6" TO 1'-10"
URINAL SCREENS

1'-0"
4'-10"
1'-0"

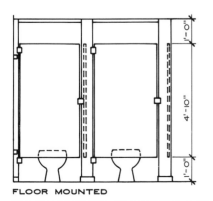

FLOOR MOUNTED

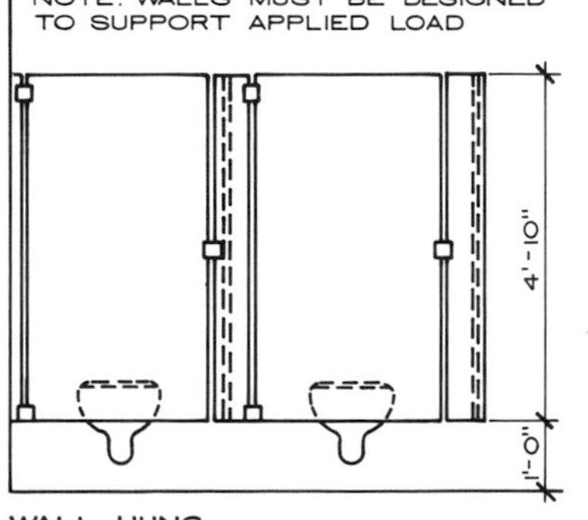
NOTE: WALLS MUST BE DESIGNED TO SUPPORT APPLIED LOAD
4'-10"
1'-0"
WALL HUNG

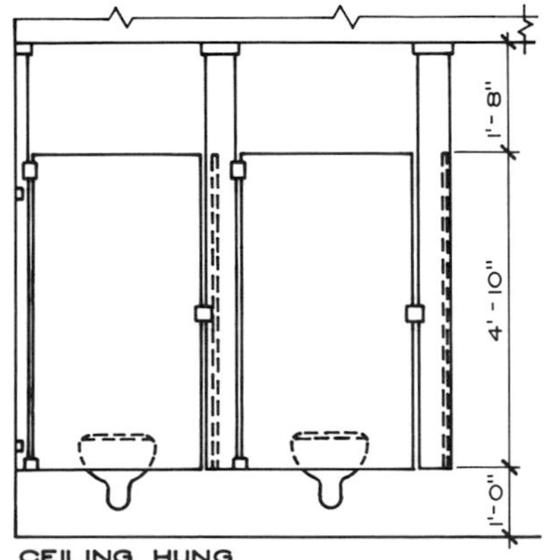
1'-8"
4'-10"
1'-0"
CEILING HUNG

METAL AND PLASTIC LAMINATE TOILET PARTITIONS

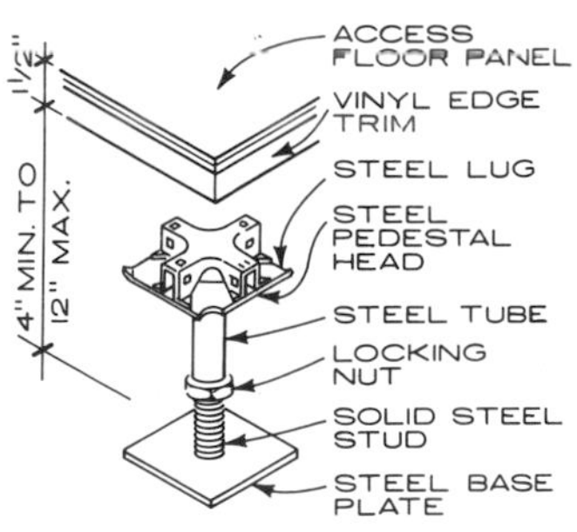

ACCESS FLOOR PANEL
VINYL EDGE TRIM
STEEL LUG
STEEL PEDESTAL HEAD
STEEL TUBE
LOCKING NUT
SOLID STEEL STUD
STEEL BASE PLATE
4" MIN. TO 12" MAX.

STRINGERLESS

This system is used in general construction or small computer rooms. It provides maximum accessibility, optimum underfloor space, and electrical continuity. Note that it is dependent on panels being restrained by perimeter walls. Maximum load: 150 psf. Concentrated load: 400 lb.

PANEL LOCK

This system is used in general construction and is designed without a stringer connection at the edge. Bolted at the corner, it provides added rigidity over stringerless systems and maximum access and flexibility.

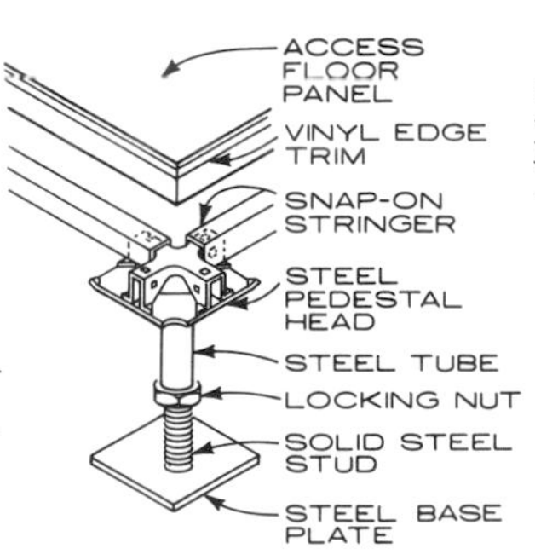

ACCESS FLOOR PANEL
VINYL EDGE TRIM
SNAP-ON STRINGER
STEEL PEDESTAL HEAD
STEEL TUBE
LOCKING NUT
SOLID STEEL STUD
STEEL BASE PLATE

SNAP-ON-GRID

This system is used in computer rooms and in general construction where frequent access is required. It provides improved lateral stability when compared to stringerless systems, electrical continuity, and plenum seal.

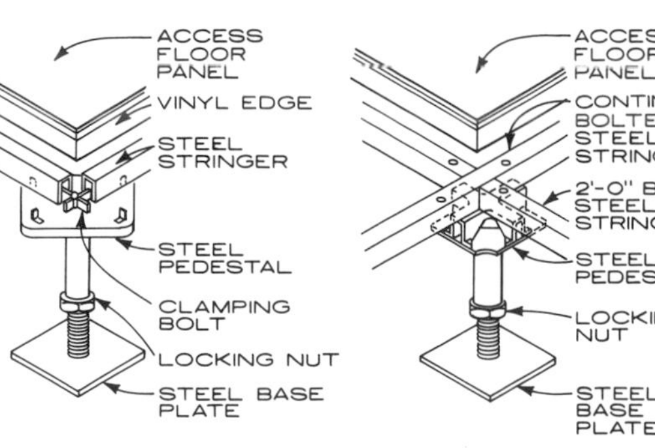

ACCESS FLOOR PANEL
VINYL EDGE
STEEL STRINGER
STEEL PEDESTAL
CLAMPING BOLT
LOCKING NUT
STEEL BASE PLATE
ACCESS FLOOR PANEL
CONTINUOUS BOLTED STEEL STRINGER
2'-0" BOLT STEEL STRINGER
STEEL PEDESTAL
LOCKING NUT
STEEL BASE PLATE

CLAMPED STRINGER

This system is used in computer rooms and provides high lateral stability, complete access to the below-floor cavity, electrical continuity for grounding, and static control. The system's contact between panel edge and stringer provides a plenum seal.

RIGID GRID

This system is used in computer rooms and areas of heavy loading. It provides maximum rigidity for seismic or dynamic loading, electrical continuity for grounding or static control, and plenum seal. Maximum load: 400 psf. Concentrated load: 1250 lb.

TYPES OF SUPPORT SYSTEMS—LEAST STABLE TO MOST STABLE

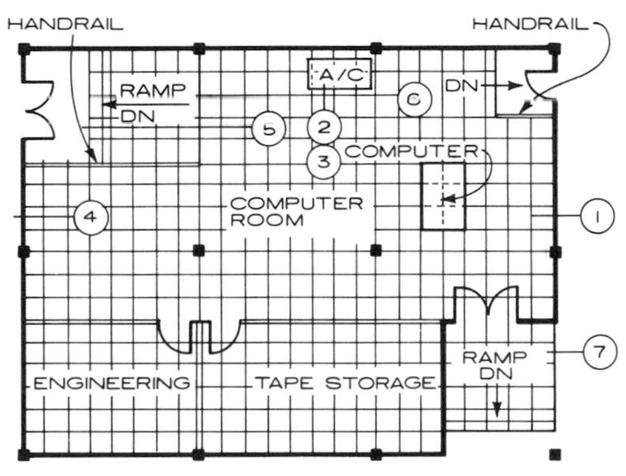

HANDRAIL
HANDRAIL
RAMP
DN
A/C
C
DN
COMPUTER
COMPUTER ROOM
ENGINEERING
TAPE STORAGE
RAMP DN

TYPICAL COMPUTER ROOM PLAN

WALL
COVE BASE
CUT PANEL
PERIMETER PEDESTAL
FIELD PEDESTAL
ELECTRICAL OUTLET BOX
SUBFLOOR
1 CONDITION AT WALL OR COLUMN
GALVANIZED SHEET METAL PLENUM DIVIDER
4" MIN.
PEDESTAL
SUBFLOOR
2 PLENUM
CHANNEL
DUCT
SUBFLOOR
3 DUCT OR OTHER OBSTRUCTIONS
METAL EDGE EMBEDDED IN
FIELD CUT TO MEET
PEDESTAL
SUBFLOOR
4 EDGE CONDITION

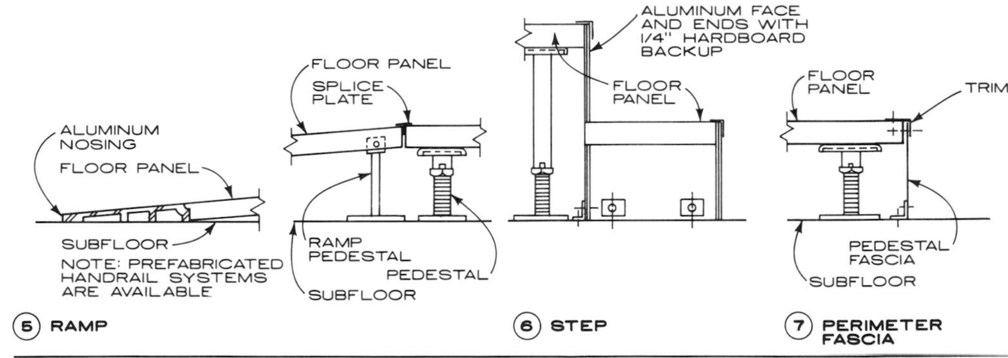

ALUMINUM NOSING
FLOOR PANEL
SUBFLOOR
NOTE: PREFABRICATED HANDRAIL SYSTEMS ARE AVAILABLE
FLOOR PANEL
SPLICE PLATE
RAMP PEDESTAL
PEDESTAL
SUBFLOOR
5 RAMP
ALUMINUM FACE AND ENDS WITH 1/4" HARDBOARD BACKUP
FLOOR PANEL
6 STEP
FLOOR PANEL
TRIM
PEDESTAL FASCIA
SUBFLOOR
7 PERIMETER FASCIA

TYPICAL ACCESS FLOOR CONDITIONS

COMPUTER ROOMS

Computers place high demands on electrical, mechanical and floor systems. The floor surface must be conductive and grounded to avoid static electricity and dust accumulation. An automatic fire detection system should be installed in below-floor plenums. Plenums may not exceed 10,000 sq. ft., and they must be divided by noncombustible bulkheads. Computer rooms should be separated from all other occupancies within buildings by fire-resistant walls, floors, and ceilings with a resistance rating of not less than 1 hour. Structural floors beneath access floors should provide for water drainage to reduce damage to computer systems. All access floor openings should be protected from debris. Computer rooms require precision temperature and humidity control. Package air-conditioning units suitable for computer rooms can supply air within a tolerance of $\pm 1.5°$ and $\pm 5\%$ humidity.

Computer room heat gains often are concentrated. For minimum room temperature gradients, supply air distribution should match closely the load distribution. The distribution system should be flexible enough to accommodate location changes and heat gain with minimum change in the basic distribution system. Supply air systems require about 74 litres per second per kilowatt of cooling to satisfy computer room conditions. This provides enough air change rate for even air temperature distribution. Packaged air-conditioning systems using the underfloor air supply plenum should supply the large computer area adequately. The zoning area is controlled by various floor registers and perforated floor panels.

Setter, Leach and Lindstrom, Inc.; Minneapolis, Minnesota

ACCESS FLOORS

Access floor systems are used in business offices, hospitals, laboratories, open area schools, television systems, computer rooms, and telephone-communication centers. They provide mechanical and electrical accessibility and flexibility in placing desks, telephone services, machines, and general office equipment. Equipment can be moved and reconnected quickly. Raised access floors in large areas offer maximum flexibility for future change. They also can be used in a recessed structural floor area.

Reinforced steel panels, aluminum, steel-encased wood core, and cementitious fill are available with finish surfaces of vinyl tile, plastic laminate, and carpet. Basic panel sizes are 24 in. x 24 in. Panel systems rely on gravity-held connections, but they can be held mechanically, increasing rigidity. Wraparound, butt, and protective plastic edge carpet systems are available; some are available with Class A flame-spread ratings. Panels are available in structural grades ranging from general office to light industrial construction.

Using modular wiring increases installation speed and simplifies panel variation. Space beneath floors can be used as an air-conditioning plenum. Special panels provide perforation for air distribution, cable slots, and sound and thermal insulation. Various support systems can be provided in steel. Possible difficulties encountered with access floor systems are restricted minimal floor heights and structural integrity of older buildings. Wet washing techniques cannot be used, and poor placement of exceedingly heavy loads can damage floor systems.

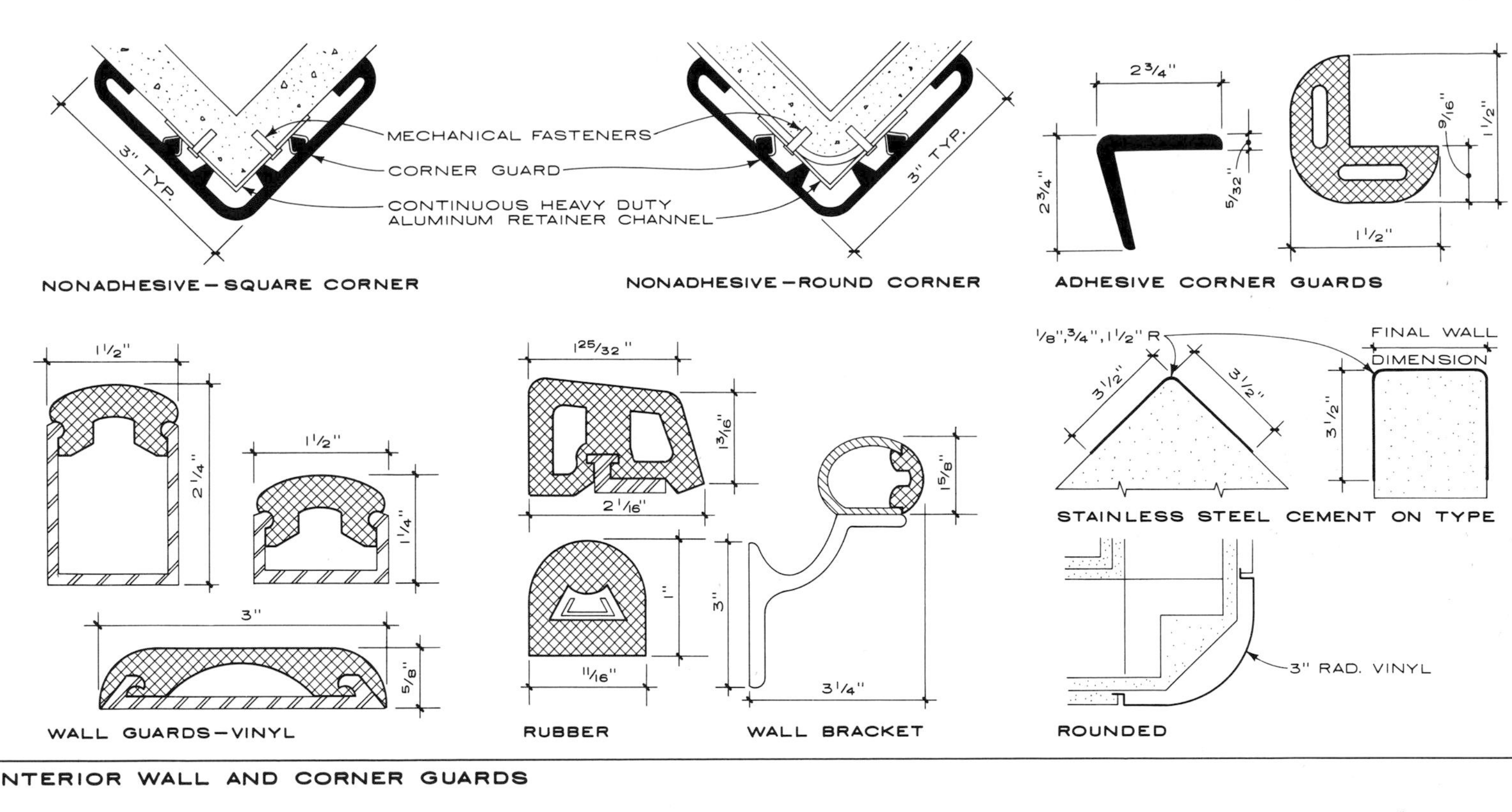
MECHANICAL FASTENERS
CORNER GUARD
CONTINUOUS HEAVY DUTY ALUMINUM RETAINER CHANNEL
3" TYP.
NONADHESIVE—SQUARE CORNER
NONADHESIVE—ROUND CORNER
ADHESIVE CORNER GUARDS
WALL GUARDS—VINYL
RUBBER
WALL BRACKET
STAINLESS STEEL CEMENT ON TYPE
FINAL WALL DIMENSION
3" RAD. VINYL
ROUNDED

INTERIOR WALL AND CORNER GUARDS

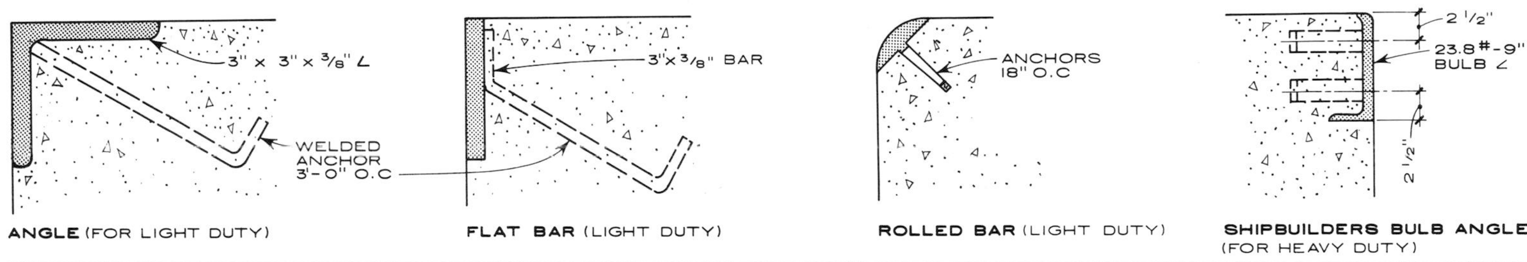
3" x 3" x 3/8" ∠
WELDED ANCHOR 3'-0" O.C
3"x 3/8" BAR
ANCHORS 18" O.C
2 1/2"
23.8#-9" BULB ∠
ANGLE (FOR LIGHT DUTY)
FLAT BAR (LIGHT DUTY)
ROLLED BAR (LIGHT DUTY)
SHIPBUILDERS BULB ANGLE (FOR HEAVY DUTY)

CURB GUARDS

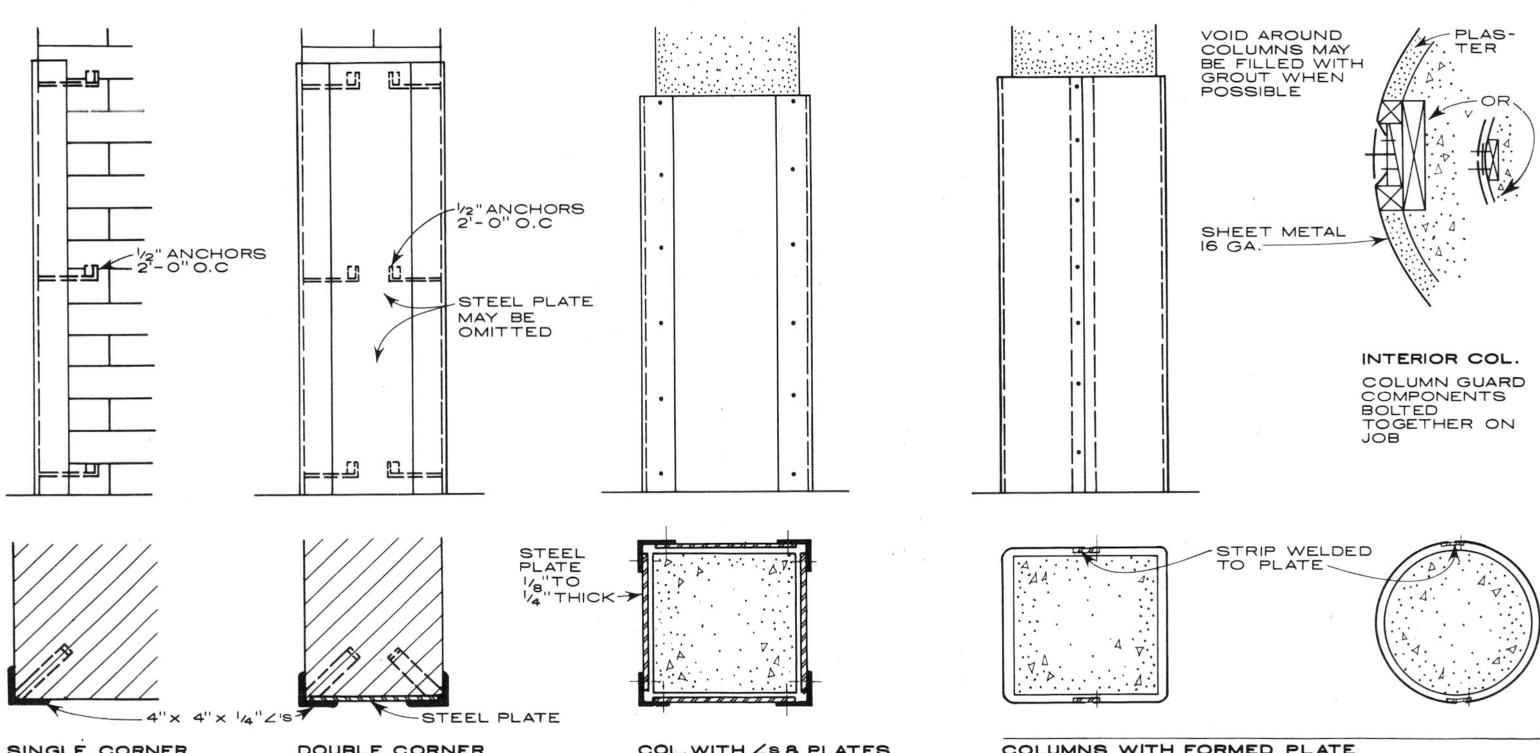
1/2" ANCHORS 2'-0" O.C
STEEL PLATE MAY BE OMITTED
VOID AROUND COLUMNS MAY BE FILLED WITH GROUT WHEN POSSIBLE
PLASTER
OR
SHEET METAL 16 GA.
INTERIOR COL.
COLUMN GUARD COMPONENTS BOLTED TOGETHER ON JOB
STEEL PLATE 1/8" TO 1/4" THICK
STRIP WELDED TO PLATE
4" x 4" x 1/4" ∠'s
STEEL PLATE
SINGLE CORNER
DOUBLE CORNER
COL. WITH ∠s & PLATES
COLUMNS WITH FORMED PLATE

CORNER AND COLUMN GUARDS

John Sava; The Architects Collaborative, Inc.; Cambridge, Massachusetts
Vicente Cordero, AIA; Arlington, Virginia

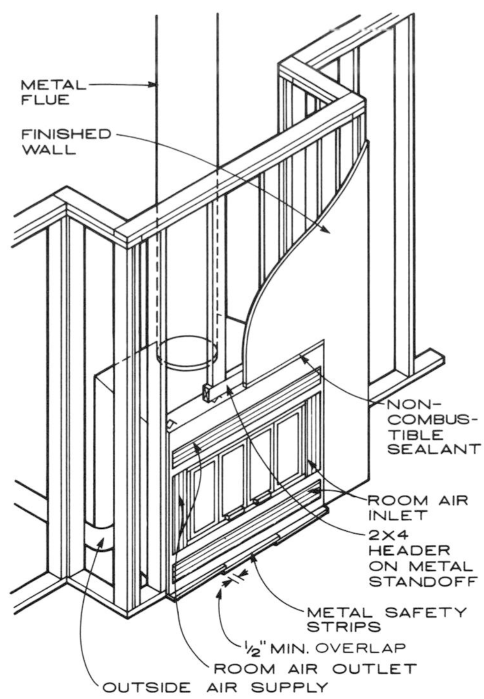
METAL FLUE
FINISHED WALL
NON-COMBUSTIBLE SEALANT
ROOM AIR INLET
2X4 HEADER ON METAL STANDOFF
METAL SAFETY STRIPS
½" MIN. OVERLAP
ROOM AIR OUTLET
OUTSIDE AIR SUPPLY

HEAT CIRCULATING FIREPLACE SET IN STUD WALL

HEAT CIRCULATING FIREPLACE

Specially constructed steel fireplaces must be properly enclosed in masonry to obtain a complete wood burning unit. When placed on a firebrick hearth, a steel fireplace includes all essential combustion and smoke handling spaces. A circulator provides a heat transfer chamber with inlets and outlets that draw in cool air, heat it, and expel warm air by natural convection. The air heating cycle can be augmented with electric fans in the intakes (not in the outlets). A steel shell provides a form for the masonry enclosure, but it is not a structural element. Enclosing masonry must be held at least ½ in. away from the shell to allow for expansion and contraction in the metal. The ½ in. space is taken up with fireproof insulation that covers the entire circulator. The fireplace rear wall should be at least 8 in. thick if exposed to the exterior. Placing the fireplace within the exterior stud wall gives better thermal insulation in exchange for some lost indoor floor space.

Steel circulatory fireplaces are manufactured in various sizes with proportions set for proper burning action and air heating. An incorrect flue size may negate the fireplace design. The flue must be independently supported.

NOTES

Circulator must be entirely wrapped in insulation to control heat and to help space the masonry away from the steel shell.

1. Some manufacturers recommend using a chimney cap with a heat-circulating fireplace.
2. Check local codes for minimum clearance requirements to combustible materials such as walls and mantles.

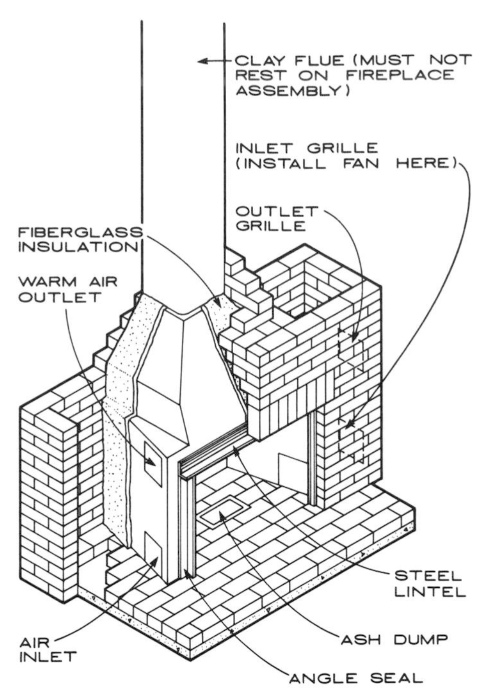
CLAY FLUE (MUST NOT REST ON FIREPLACE ASSEMBLY)
INLET GRILLE (INSTALL FAN HERE)
OUTLET GRILLE
FIBERGLASS INSULATION
WARM AIR OUTLET
STEEL LINTEL
ASH DUMP
AIR INLET
ANGLE SEAL

HEAT CIRCULATING FIREPLACE SET IN MASONRY

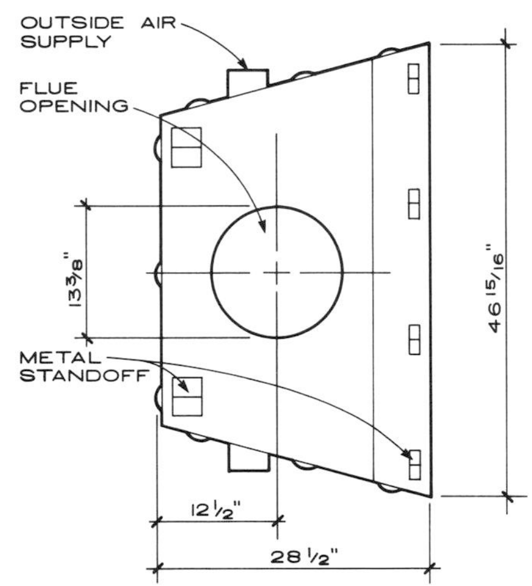
OUTSIDE AIR SUPPLY
FLUE OPENING
13⅜"
METAL STANDOFF
46 15/16"
12½"
28½"

PLAN

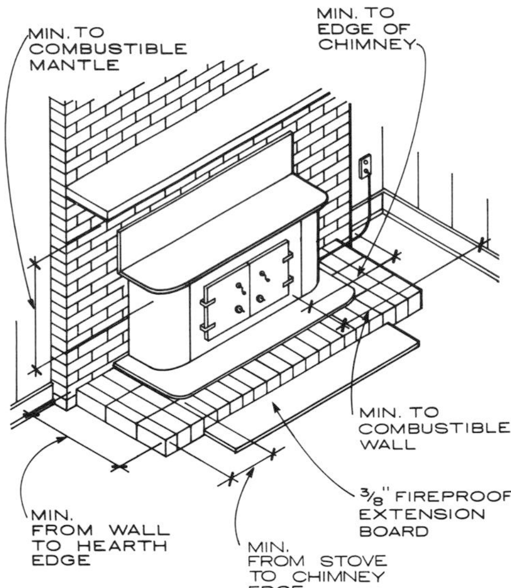
MIN. TO COMBUSTIBLE MANTLE
MIN. TO EDGE OF CHIMNEY
MIN. TO COMBUSTIBLE WALL
⅜" FIREPROOF EXTENSION BOARD
MIN. FROM WALL TO HEARTH EDGE
MIN. FROM STOVE TO CHIMNEY EDGE

HEAT CIRCULATING FIREPLACE

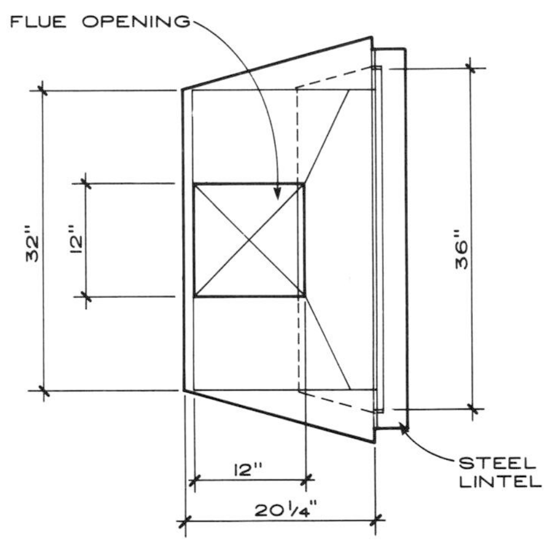
FLUE OPENING
32"
12"
36"
12"
20¼"
STEEL LINTEL

PLAN

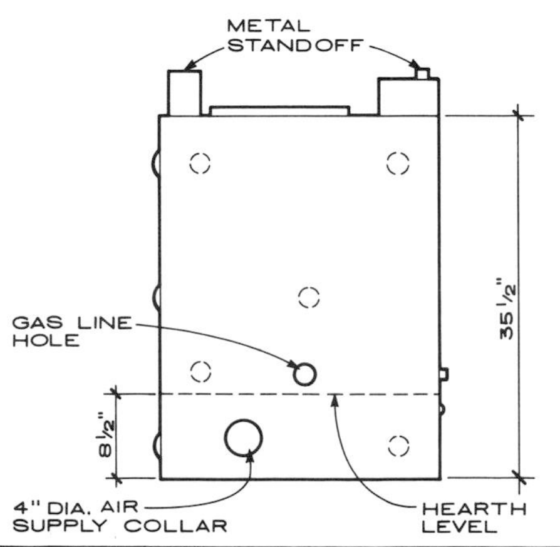
METAL STANDOFF
GAS LINE HOLE
35½"
8½"
4" DIA. AIR SUPPLY COLLAR
HEARTH LEVEL

SIDE ELEVATION

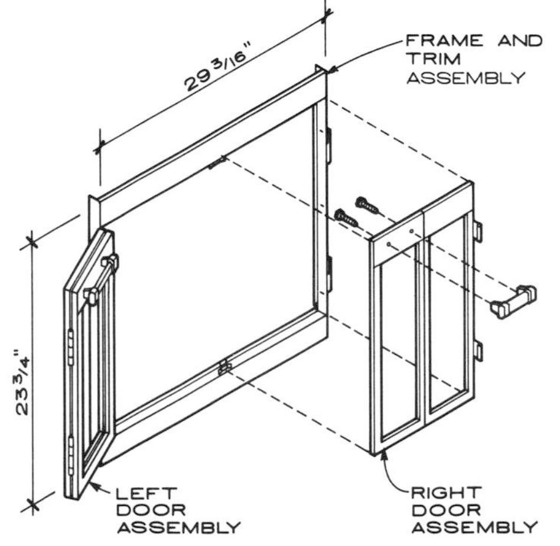
29 3/16"
FRAME AND TRIM ASSEMBLY
23¾"
LEFT DOOR ASSEMBLY
RIGHT DOOR ASSEMBLY

FIREPLACE DOOR ASSEMBLY

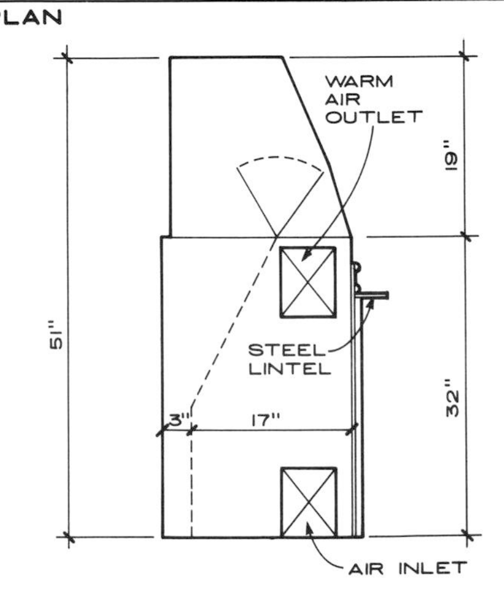
WARM AIR OUTLET
19"
51"
STEEL LINTEL
3"
17"
32"
AIR INLET

SIDE ELEVATION

Timothy B. McDonald; Washington, D.C.

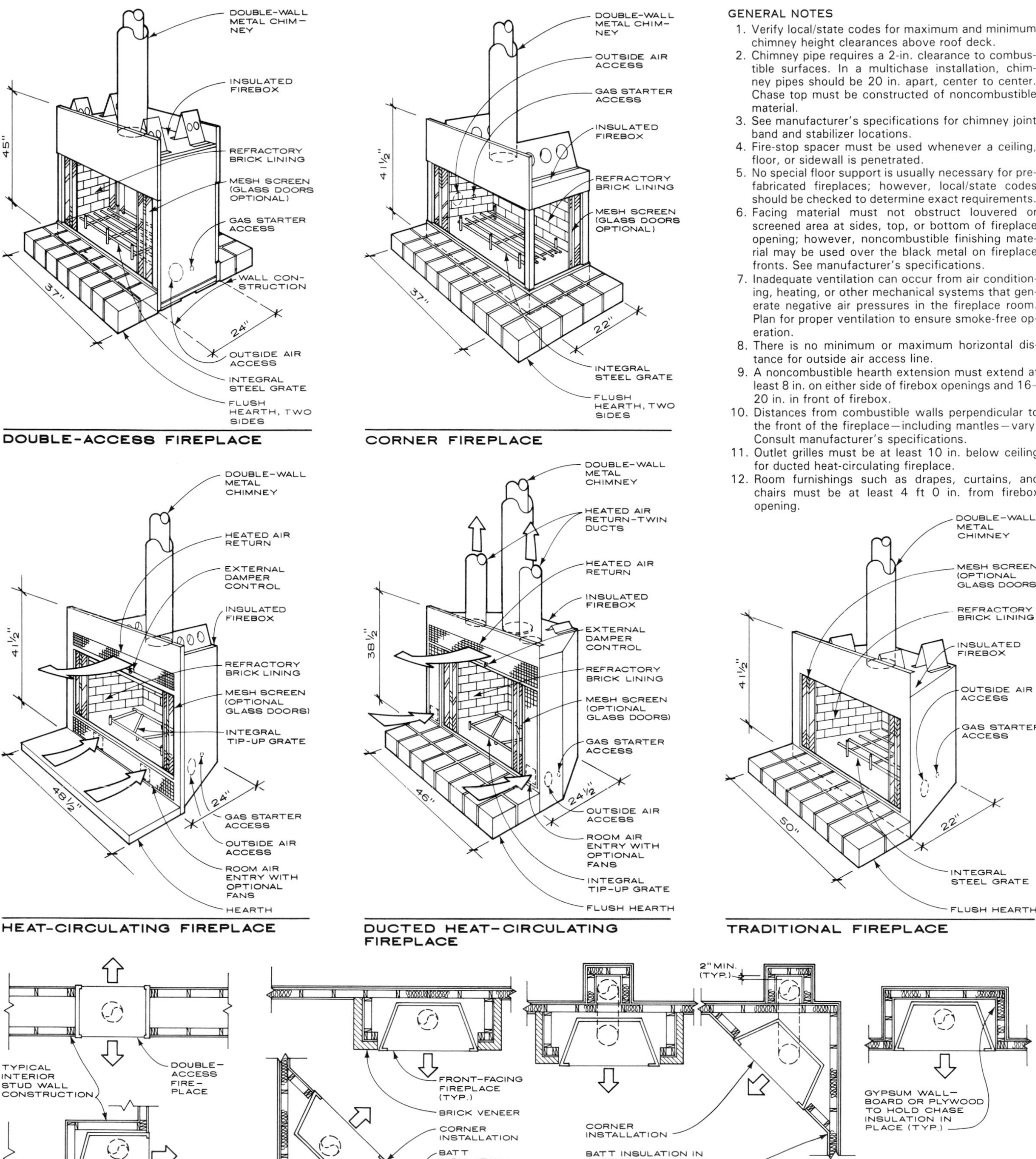
DOUBLE-WALL METAL CHIMNEY
INSULATED FIREBOX
45"
REFRACTORY BRICK LINING
MESH SCREEN (GLASS DOORS OPTIONAL)
GAS STARTER ACCESS
WALL CONSTRUCTION
37"
24"
OUTSIDE AIR ACCESS
INTEGRAL STEEL GRATE
FLUSH HEARTH, TWO SIDES
DOUBLE-ACCESS FIREPLACE
DOUBLE-WALL METAL CHIMNEY
OUTSIDE AIR ACCESS
GAS STARTER ACCESS
INSULATED FIREBOX
41 1/2"
REFRACTORY BRICK LINING
MESH SCREEN (GLASS DOORS OPTIONAL)
37"
22"
INTEGRAL STEEL GRATE
FLUSH HEARTH, TWO SIDES
CORNER FIREPLACE
DOUBLE-WALL METAL CHIMNEY
HEATED AIR RETURN
EXTERNAL DAMPER CONTROL
INSULATED FIREBOX
41 1/2"
REFRACTORY BRICK LINING
MESH SCREEN (OPTIONAL GLASS DOORS)
INTEGRAL TIP-UP GRATE
48 1/2"
24"
GAS STARTER ACCESS
OUTSIDE AIR ACCESS
ROOM AIR ENTRY WITH OPTIONAL FANS
HEARTH
HEAT-CIRCULATING FIREPLACE
DOUBLE-WALL METAL CHIMNEY
HEATED AIR RETURN-TWIN DUCTS
HEATED AIR RETURN
INSULATED FIREBOX
EXTERNAL DAMPER CONTROL
38 1/2"
REFRACTORY BRICK LINING
MESH SCREEN (OPTIONAL GLASS DOORS)
GAS STARTER ACCESS
46"
24 1/2"
OUTSIDE AIR ACCESS
ROOM AIR ENTRY WITH OPTIONAL FANS
INTEGRAL TIP-UP GRATE
FLUSH HEARTH
DUCTED HEAT-CIRCULATING FIREPLACE
DOUBLE-WALL METAL CHIMNEY
MESH SCREEN (OPTIONAL GLASS DOORS)
REFRACTORY BRICK LINING
INSULATED FIREBOX
41 1/2"
OUTSIDE AIR ACCESS
GAS STARTER ACCESS
50"
22"
INTEGRAL STEEL GRATE
FLUSH HEARTH
TRADITIONAL FIREPLACE
TYPICAL INTERIOR STUD WALL CONSTRUCTION
DOUBLE-ACCESS FIRE-PLACE
CORNER FIRE-PLACE
INTERIOR WALL CONDITION CHASE CONSTRUCTED ON ROOF
FRONT-FACING FIREPLACE (TYP.)
BRICK VENEER
CORNER INSTALLATION
BATT INSULATION IN EXTERIOR WALL (TYP.)
EXTERIOR WALL CONDITION CHASE CONSTRUCTED ON ROOF
2" MIN. (TYP.)
CORNER INSTALLATION
BATT INSULATION IN EXTERIOR WALL AND AROUND CHASE (TYP.)
EXTERIOR WALL CONDITION CHIMNEY OFFSET THROUGH EXTERIOR WALL AND ENCLOSED IN CHASE
GYPSUM WALLBOARD OR PLYWOOD TO HOLD CHASE INSULATION IN PLACE (TYP.)
EXTERIOR WALL CONDITION FIREPLACE AND CHIMNEY ENCLOSED IN CHASE
INSTALLATION CONDITIONS FOR PREFABRICATED FIREPLACES

GENERAL NOTES

1. Verify local/state codes for maximum and minimum chimney height clearances above roof deck.
2. Chimney pipe requires a 2-in. clearance to combustible surfaces. In a multichase installation, chimney pipes should be 20 in. apart, center to center. Chase top must be constructed of noncombustible material.
3. See manufacturer's specifications for chimney joint band and stabilizer locations.
4. Fire-stop spacer must be used whenever a ceiling, floor, or sidewall is penetrated.
5. No special floor support is usually necessary for prefabricated fireplaces; however, local/state codes should be checked to determine exact requirements.
6. Facing material must not obstruct louvered or screened area at sides, top, or bottom of fireplace opening; however, noncombustible finishing material may be used over the black metal on fireplace fronts. See manufacturer's specifications.
7. Inadequate ventilation can occur from air conditioning, heating, or other mechanical systems that generate negative air pressures in the fireplace room. Plan for proper ventilation to ensure smoke-free operation.
8. There is no minimum or maximum horizontal distance for outside air access line.
9. A noncombustible hearth extension must extend at least 8 in. on either side of firebox openings and 16–20 in. in front of firebox.
10. Distances from combustible walls perpendicular to the front of the fireplace—including mantles—vary. Consult manufacturer's specifications.
11. Outlet grilles must be at least 10 in. below ceiling for ducted heat-circulating fireplace.
12. Room furnishings such as drapes, curtains, and chairs must be at least 4 ft 0 in. from firebox opening.

Richard J. Vitullo; Washington Grove, Maryland

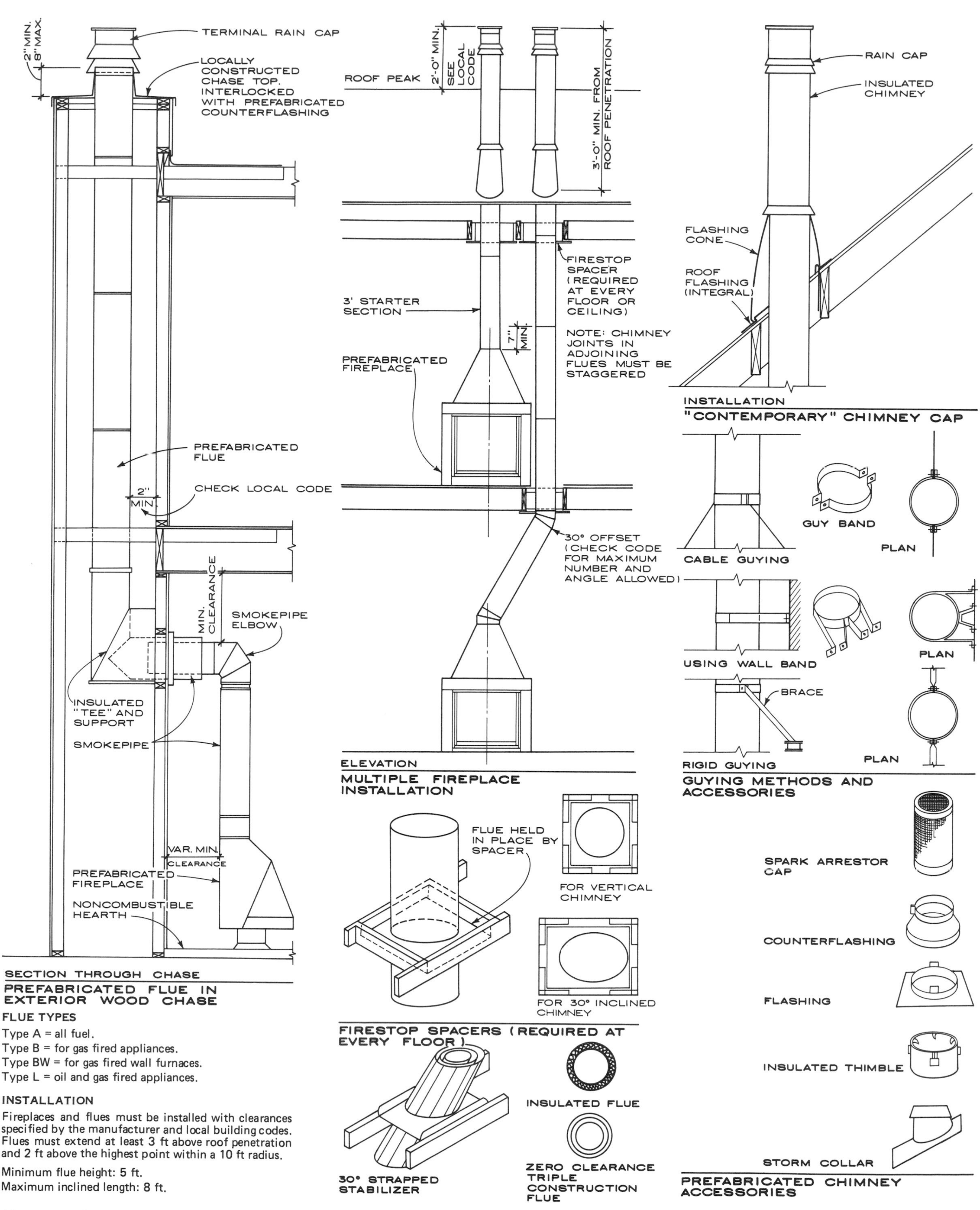

2" MIN. 8" MAX.
TERMINAL RAIN CAP
LOCALLY CONSTRUCTED CHASE TOP. INTERLOCKED WITH PREFABRICATED COUNTERFLASHING
PREFABRICATED FLUE
2" MIN.
CHECK LOCAL CODE
MIN. CLEARANCE
SMOKEPIPE ELBOW
INSULATED "TEE" AND SUPPORT
SMOKEPIPE
VAR. MIN. CLEARANCE
PREFABRICATED FIREPLACE
NONCOMBUSTIBLE HEARTH
SECTION THROUGH CHASE
PREFABRICATED FLUE IN EXTERIOR WOOD CHASE
ROOF PEAK
2'-0" MIN.
SEE LOCAL CODE
3'-0" MIN. FROM ROOF PENETRATION
FIRESTOP SPACER (REQUIRED AT EVERY FLOOR OR CEILING)
3' STARTER SECTION
7" MIN.
NOTE: CHIMNEY JOINTS IN ADJOINING FLUES MUST BE STAGGERED
PREFABRICATED FIREPLACE
30° OFFSET (CHECK CODE FOR MAXIMUM NUMBER AND ANGLE ALLOWED)
ELEVATION
MULTIPLE FIREPLACE INSTALLATION
RAIN CAP
INSULATED CHIMNEY
FLASHING CONE
ROOF FLASHING (INTEGRAL)
INSTALLATION
"CONTEMPORARY" CHIMNEY CAP
GUY BAND
PLAN
CABLE GUYING
PLAN
USING WALL BAND
BRACE
PLAN
RIGID GUYING
GUYING METHODS AND ACCESSORIES
FLUE HELD IN PLACE BY SPACER
FOR VERTICAL CHIMNEY
FOR 30° INCLINED CHIMNEY
FIRESTOP SPACERS (REQUIRED AT EVERY FLOOR)
30° STRAPPED STABILIZER
INSULATED FLUE
ZERO CLEARANCE TRIPLE CONSTRUCTION FLUE
SPARK ARRESTOR CAP
COUNTERFLASHING
FLASHING
INSULATED THIMBLE
STORM COLLAR
PREFABRICATED CHIMNEY ACCESSORIES

FLUE TYPES

Type A = all fuel.
Type B = for gas fired appliances.
Type BW = for gas fired wall furnaces.
Type L = oil and gas fired appliances.

INSTALLATION

Fireplaces and flues must be installed with clearances specified by the manufacturer and local building codes. Flues must extend at least 3 ft above roof penetration and 2 ft above the highest point within a 10 ft radius.

Minimum flue height: 5 ft.
Maximum inclined length: 8 ft.

Olga Barmine; Darrel Downing Rippeteau, Architect; Washington, D.C.

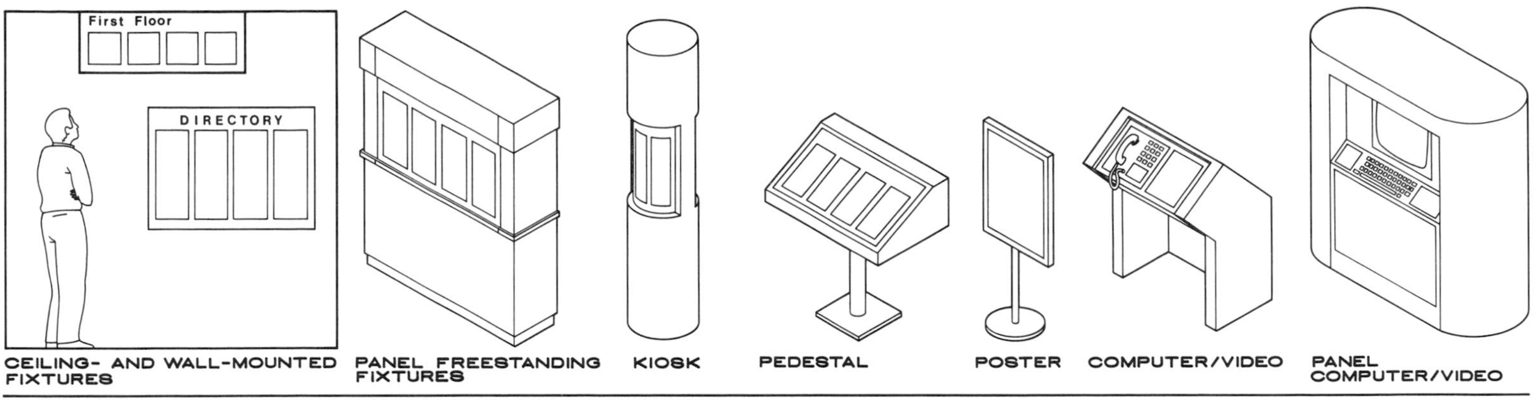
First Floor
DIRECTORY
CEILING- AND WALL-MOUNTED FIXTURES
PANEL FREESTANDING FIXTURES
KIOSK
PEDESTAL
POSTER
COMPUTER/VIDEO
PANEL COMPUTER/VIDEO

DIRECTORIES/ORIENTATION MAPS/INFORMATION SYSTEMS

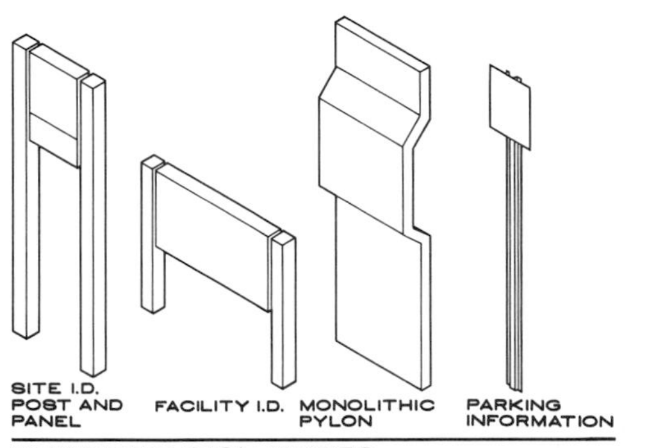

SITE I.D. POST AND PANEL
FACILITY I.D.
MONOLITHIC PYLON
PARKING INFORMATION

EXTERIOR SIGN TYPES

MEZZANINE
Registration →
Lobby →
Restaurant/Cafe ←
Shops →

RIGID VINYL INSERTS

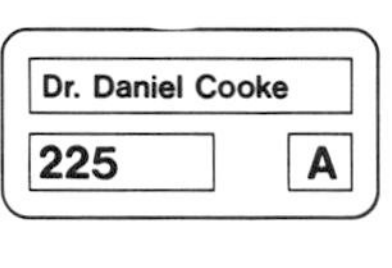
Dr. Daniel Cooke
225
A

MAGNETIC

Conference Room
206
IN USE

SLIDING

212

WINDOW

INTERIOR SIGN TYPES

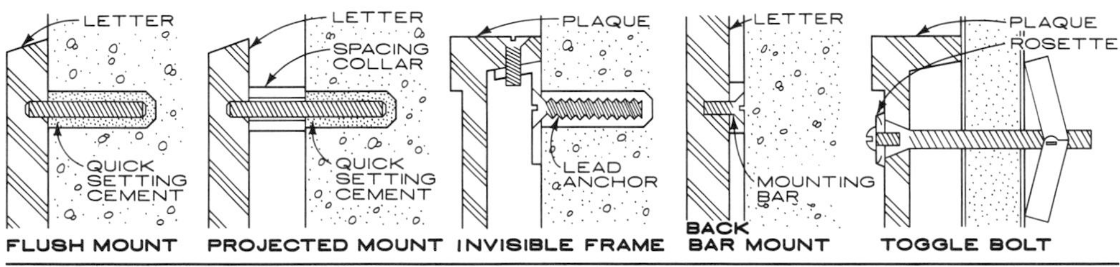
LETTER
QUICK SETTING CEMENT
FLUSH MOUNT
LETTER
SPACING COLLAR
QUICK SETTING CEMENT
PROJECTED MOUNT
PLAQUE
LEAD ANCHOR
INVISIBLE FRAME
LETTER
MOUNTING BAR
BACK BAR MOUNT
PLAQUE
ROSETTE
TOGGLE BOLT

MOUNTING METHODS/MATERIALS

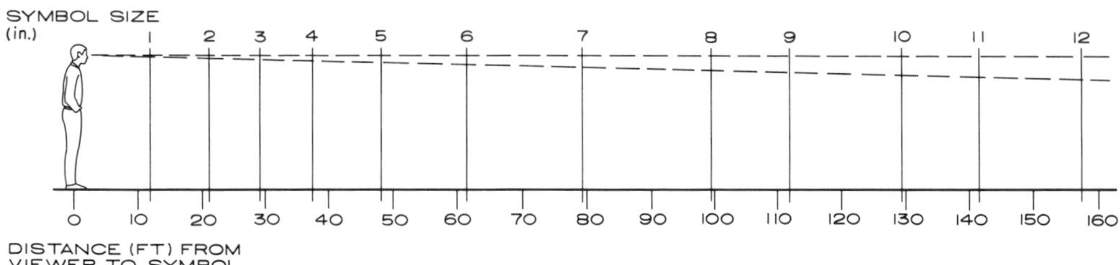
SYMBOL SIZE (in.)
1 2 3 4 5 6 7 8 9 10 11 12
0 10 20 30 40 50 60 70 80 90 100 110 120 130 140 150 160
DISTANCE (FT) FROM VIEWER TO SYMBOL

SYMBOL READABILITY

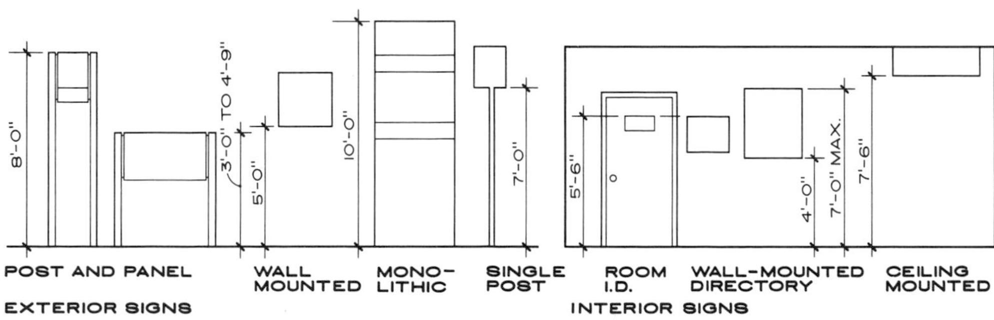
8'-0"
3'-0" TO 4'-9"
5'-0"
10'-0"
7'-0"
5'-6"
4'-0"
7'-0" MAX.
7'-6"
POST AND PANEL
WALL MOUNTED
MONO-LITHIC
SINGLE POST
EXTERIOR SIGNS
ROOM I.D.
WALL-MOUNTED DIRECTORY
CEILING MOUNTED
INTERIOR SIGNS

MOUNTING HEIGHTS

Marr Knapp Crawfis Associates, Inc.; Mansfield, Ohio
Richard J. Vitullo; Washington Grove, Maryland

GENERAL NOTES

EXTERIOR SIGNS

1. Identify entrance and exit of site and building, handicapped information, parking lot location, and facility identification.
2. Signs should be 6 ft 0 in. min. from face of curb, 7 ft 0 in. from grade to bottom of sign, and 100–200 ft from intersections.
3. Building signage materials: fabricated aluminum, illuminated plastic face, back lighted, cast aluminum, applied letter, die raised, engraved, and hot stamped.
4. Plaque and sign materials: cast bronze, cast aluminum, plastic/acrylic, stone (cornerstone), masonry, and wood.
5. For handicapped signage, designate building entrance access, identify parking areas, and direction to facilities. See ANSI 117.1 or state regulations for specific headings.

DIRECTORIES AND MAPS

1. Locate these in main entrances and/or lobbies with appropriate information for the handicapped.
2. Place directory information adjacent to "You are here" information.
3. Directories should be placed in stair/elevator lobbies of each floor.
4. Mounting choices: surface mounted, semirecessed, full recessed (flush), cantilevered, chain suspended, rigidly suspended, mechanically fastened, or track mounted.

INTERIOR SIGNS

1. Lightweight freestanding signs should not be used in high-traffic areas. Use when specific location/information maneuverability is required.
2. Electronic, computer, and videotex technologies can provide an innovative and highly flexible directory/sign display system for mapping and/or routing, information (facility and local), advertisement and messages, and management tie-in capabilities.
3. Where changeability and flexibility is a design priority, a modular system is recommended. Rigid vinyl, aluminum, and acrylic inserts as well as magnetic systems may be used.
4. For maximum ease of reading interior signs, any given line in a sign should not exceed 30 characters in width, including upper and lower case letters and spaces between words. To accommodate the visually handicapped, room numbers should be raised or accompanied with braille.
5. Choose the height and "weight" of letter styles and symbols for readability. Consider background materials and contrast when choosing a color scheme.
6. Permanent mounting:
   a. Vinyl tape/adhesive backing, usually factory applied.
   b. Silastic adhesive, usually supplied with vinyl tape strips to hold sign in place until adhesive cures.
   c. Mechanically fastened; specify hole locations.
7. Semipermanent: vinyl tape square can be used on inserts.
8. Changeable: dual-lock mating fasteners, magnets, magnetic tape, or tracks may be used.

L
W
U.S. GOVERNMENT STANDARD L=1.9 W.

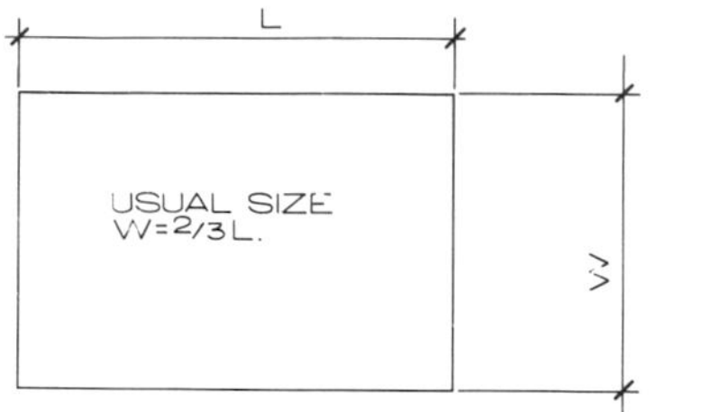

L
USUAL SIZE
W=2/3 L.
W

PROPORTIONS OF U.S. FLAG

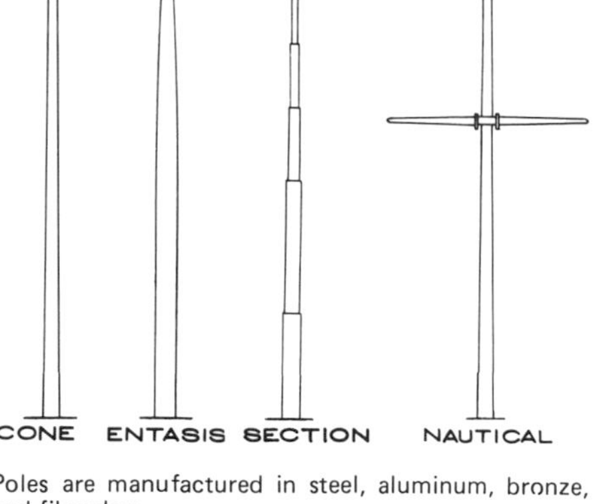

CONE
ENTASIS
SECTION
NAUTICAL

Poles are manufactured in steel, aluminum, bronze, and fiberglass.

Flagpoles must be designed to withstand wind loads while the flag is flying. Design dimensions are dictated by the maximum wind load a pole is exposed to depending on geographical location, whether it is located in a city or open country, whether it is mounted at ground or on top of a building, and size of the flag to be flown. The combination wind load on pole and flag should always be considered. Refer to wind load tests conducted by the National Association of Architectural Metal Manufacturers. (NAAMM)

POLE STYLES

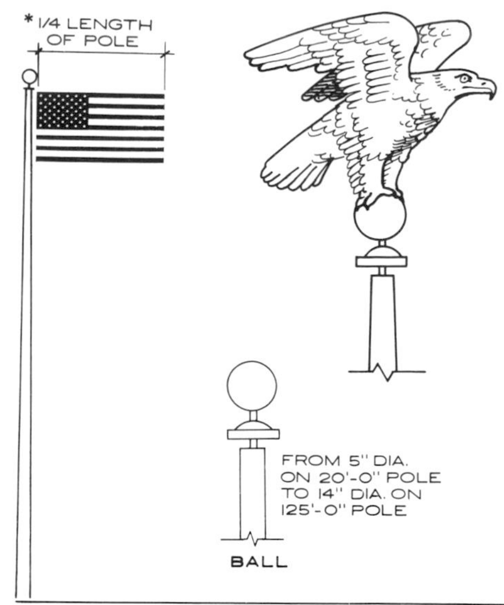

* 1/4 LENGTH OF POLE
FROM 5" DIA. ON 20'-0" POLE TO 14" DIA. ON 125'-0" POLE
BALL

POLE ON GROUND

U.S. FLAG SIZES AS MANUFACTURED AND USED

WIDTH	LENGTH	WIDTH	LENGTH
3'– 0"	5'– 0"	10'– 0"	18'– 0"
4'– 0"	6'– 0"	10'– 0"	19'– 0"
4'– 4"	5'– 6"	12'– 0"	20'– 0"
5'– 0"	8'– 0"	15'– 0"	25'– 0"
5'– 0"	9'– 6"	20'– 0"	30'– 0"
6'– 0"	10'– 0"	20'– 0"	38'– 0"
8'– 0"	12'– 0"	26'– 0"	45'– 0"
10'– 0"	15'– 0"		

RELATION OF HEIGHT OF POLE TO HEIGHT OF BLDG.

HEIGHT OF POLE	HEIGHT OF BLDG.
20'– 0"	1 to 2 stories
25'– 0"	3 to 5 stories
33'– 0" to 35'– 0"	6 to 10 stories
40'– 0" to 50'– 0"	11 to 15 stories
60'– 0" to 75'– 0"	over 15 stories

NOTE

This rule serves for preliminary assumptions.

SIZE OF FLAG IN RELATION TO POLE
RECOMMENDED FLAG SIZES

POLE	FLAG SIZE	POLE	FLAG SIZE
15'– 0"	3'– 0" x 5'– 0"	50'– 0"	8'– 0" x 12'– 0"
20'– 0"	4'– 0" x 6'– 0"	60'– 0"	8'– 0" x 12'– 0"
25'– 0"	4'– 0" x 6'– 0"	65'– 0"	9'– 0" x 15'– 0"
30'– 0"	5'– 0" x 8'– 0"	70'– 0"	9'– 0" x 15'– 0"
35'– 0"	5'– 0" x 8'– 0"	80'– 0"	10'– 0" x 15'-- 0"
40'– 0"	6'– 0" x 10'– 0"	90'– 0"	10'– 0" x 15'– 0"
45'– 0"	6'– 0" x 10'– 0"	100'– 0"	12'– 0" x 18'– 0"

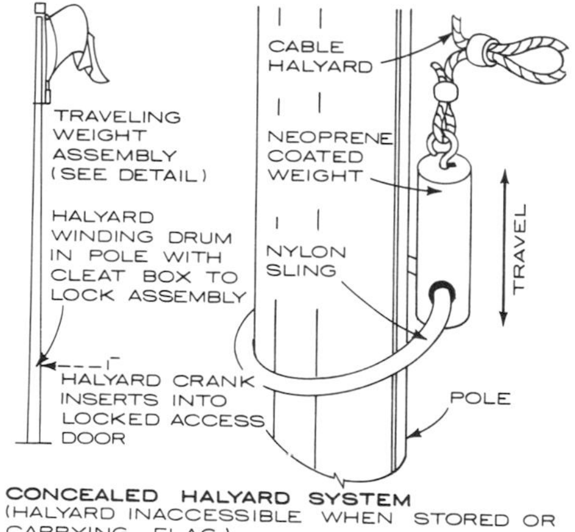

TRAVELING WEIGHT ASSEMBLY (SEE DETAIL)
HALYARD WINDING DRUM IN POLE WITH CLEAT BOX TO LOCK ASSEMBLY
CABLE HALYARD
NEOPRENE COATED WEIGHT
NYLON SLING
TRAVEL
HALYARD CRANK INSERTS INTO LOCKED ACCESS DOOR
POLE

CONCEALED HALYARD SYSTEM
(HALYARD INACCESSIBLE WHEN STORED OR CARRYING FLAG)

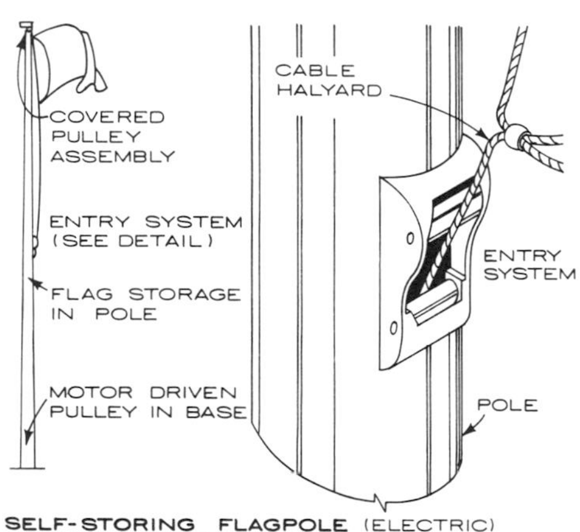

COVERED PULLEY ASSEMBLY
ENTRY SYSTEM (SEE DETAIL)
FLAG STORAGE IN POLE
MOTOR DRIVEN PULLEY IN BASE
CABLE HALYARD
ENTRY SYSTEM
POLE

SELF-STORING FLAGPOLE (ELECTRIC)
AUTOMATIC SOLAR CELL OR REMOTE SWITCH OPERATION

SPECIAL MECHANISMS FOR REMOTE OR VANDAL-PROOF OPERATION

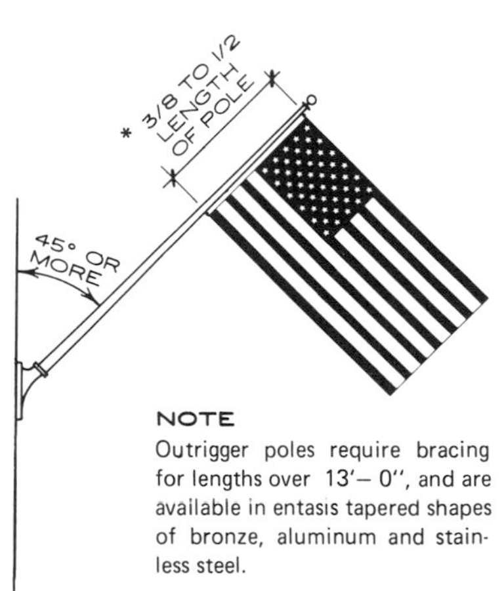

* 3/8 TO 1/2 LENGTH OF POLE
45° OR MORE

NOTE

Outrigger poles require bracing for lengths over 13'– 0", and are available in entasis tapered shapes of bronze, aluminum and stainless steel.

OUTRIGGER POLES FOR FLAGS ON BUILDING FRONTS

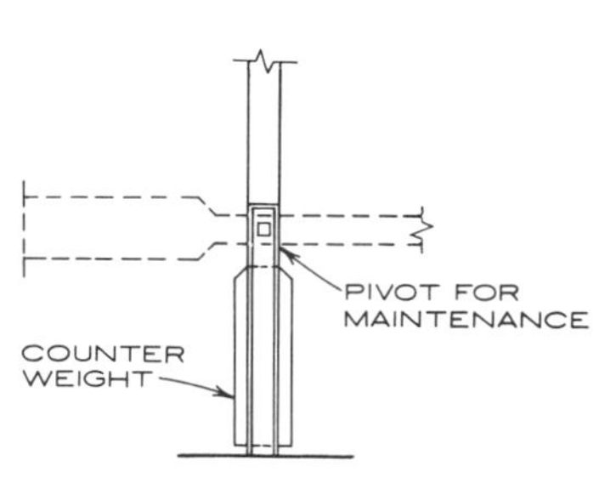

PIVOT FOR MAINTENANCE
COUNTER WEIGHT

TILTING POLE UNIT

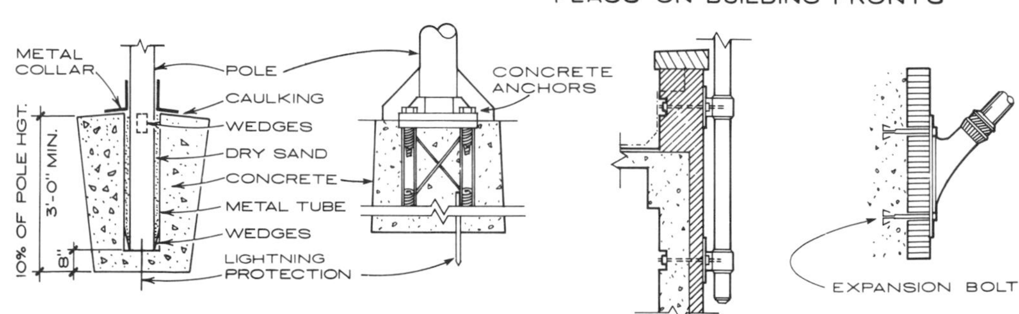

METAL COLLAR
POLE
CAULKING
WEDGES
DRY SAND
CONCRETE
METAL TUBE
WEDGES
LIGHTNING PROTECTION
10% OF POLE HGT.
3'-0" MIN.
8"
CONCRETE ANCHORS
EXPANSION BOLT
FOUNDATION FOR GROUND SET POLES
WALL MOUNTING FLAGPOLES

FOUNDATION AND SURFACE MOUNTING DETAILS

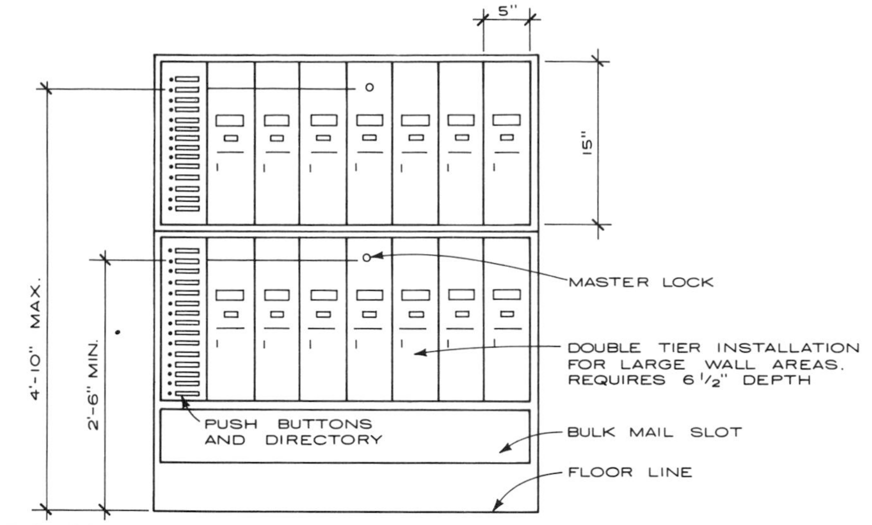

5"
15"
4'-10" MAX.
2'-6" MIN.
MASTER LOCK
DOUBLE TIER INSTALLATION FOR LARGE WALL AREAS. REQUIRES 6 1/2" DEPTH
PUSH BUTTONS AND DIRECTORY
BULK MAIL SLOT
FLOOR LINE

ELEVATION

VERTICAL COMPARTMENT TYPE
FRONT LOADING

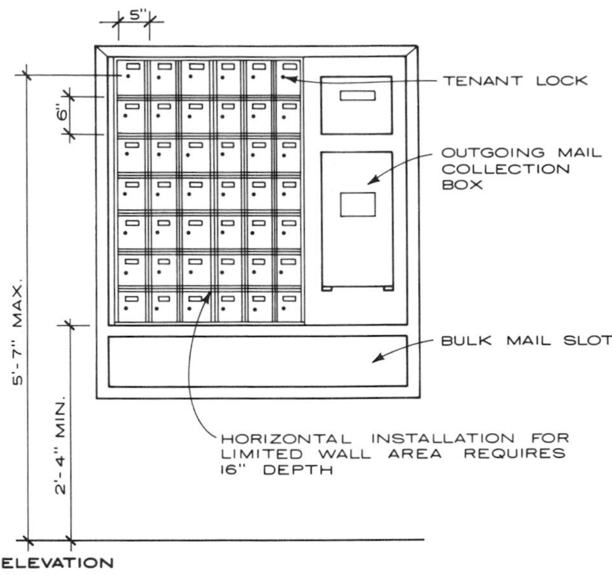
5"
6"
5'-7" MAX.
2'-4" MIN.
TENANT LOCK
OUTGOING MAIL COLLECTION BOX
BULK MAIL SLOT
HORIZONTAL INSTALLATION FOR LIMITED WALL AREA REQUIRES 16" DEPTH

ELEVATION

HORIZONTAL COMPARTMENT TYPE
FRONT OR REAR LOADING

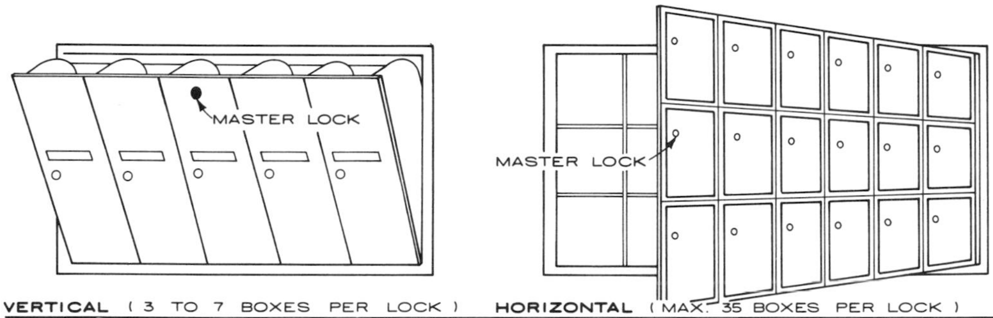

MASTER LOCK
MASTER LOCK

VERTICAL (3 TO 7 BOXES PER LOCK) HORIZONTAL (MAX. 35 BOXES PER LOCK)

FRONT LOADING COMPARTMENTS WITH MASTER LOCK

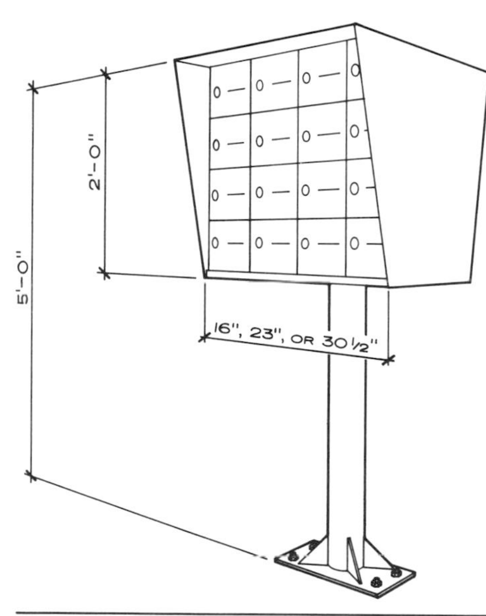
2'-0"
5'-0"
16", 23", OR 30 1/2"

PEDESTAL MOUNTED TYPE

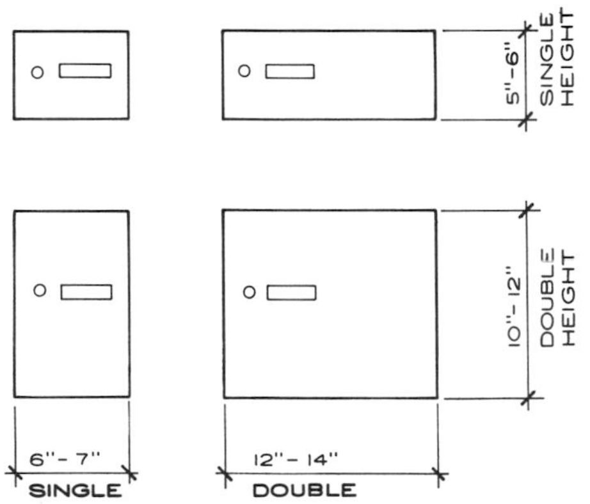

5"-6" SINGLE HEIGHT
10"-12" DOUBLE HEIGHT
6"-7" SINGLE
12"-14" DOUBLE

COMPARTMENT SIZES

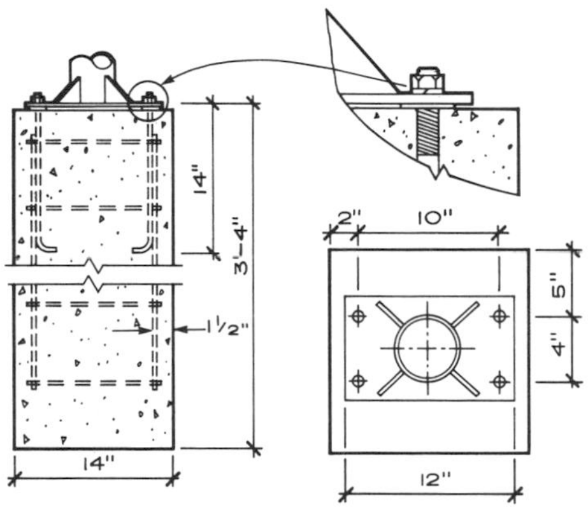

14"
3'-4"
1 1/2"
14"
2" 10"
5"
4"
12"

FOUNDATION DETAILS OF PEDESTAL MOUNTED TYPE

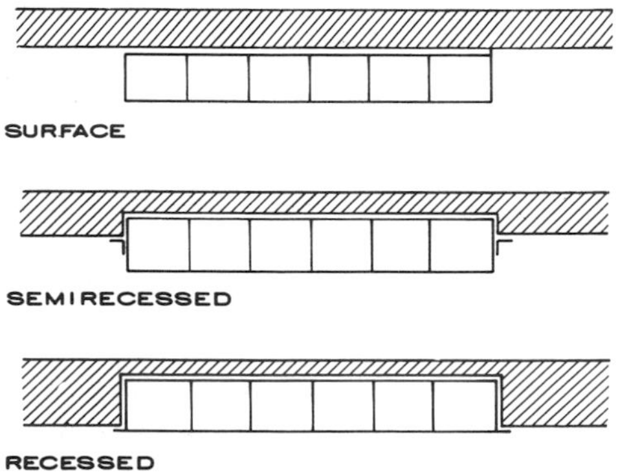

SURFACE

SEMIRECESSED

RECESSED

MOUNTING TYPES
FRONT LOADED COMPARTMENTS

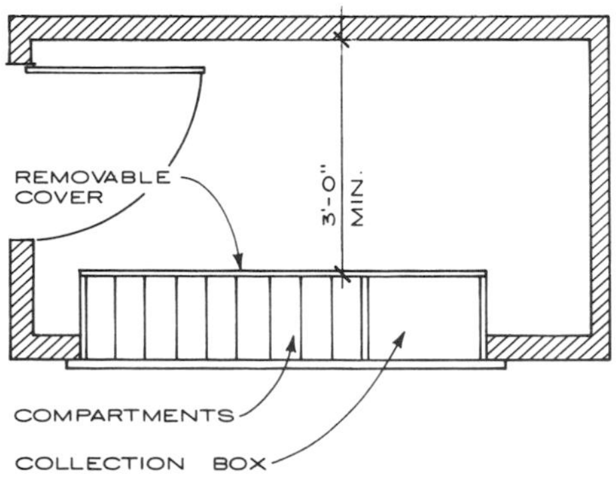

REMOVABLE COVER
3'-0" MIN.
COMPARTMENTS
COLLECTION BOX

MAILROOM PLAN
REAR LOADED COMPARTMENTS

GENERAL NOTES

1. Postal Service approved mail receptacles are required for apartment houses containing three or more apartments with a common building entrance and street number.
2. Individual compartments should be large enough to receive long letter mail 4 1/2 in. wide and bulky magazines 14 1/2 in. long and 3 1/2 in. in diameter.
3. An outdoor installation should preferably be at least 15 ft from a street or public sidewalk, protected from driving rain, and visible from at least one apartment window.
4. All installations must be adequately lighted to afford better protection to the mail and enable carriers to read addresses on mail and names on boxes.
5. A directory, in alphabetical order, is required for installations with more than 15 compartments.
6. Each compartment group is supplied with mounting hardware for master lock.
7. Call buttons with telephone can be integrated into frame with mailboxes.
8. Depending on occupancy, a certain number of compartments shall be assigned to handicapped tenants. Key slots shall be no more than 48 in. from floor.
9. Use of collection boxes is subject to approval by local offices of the United States Postal Service.

Cohen, Karydas & Associates, Chartered; Washington, D.C.

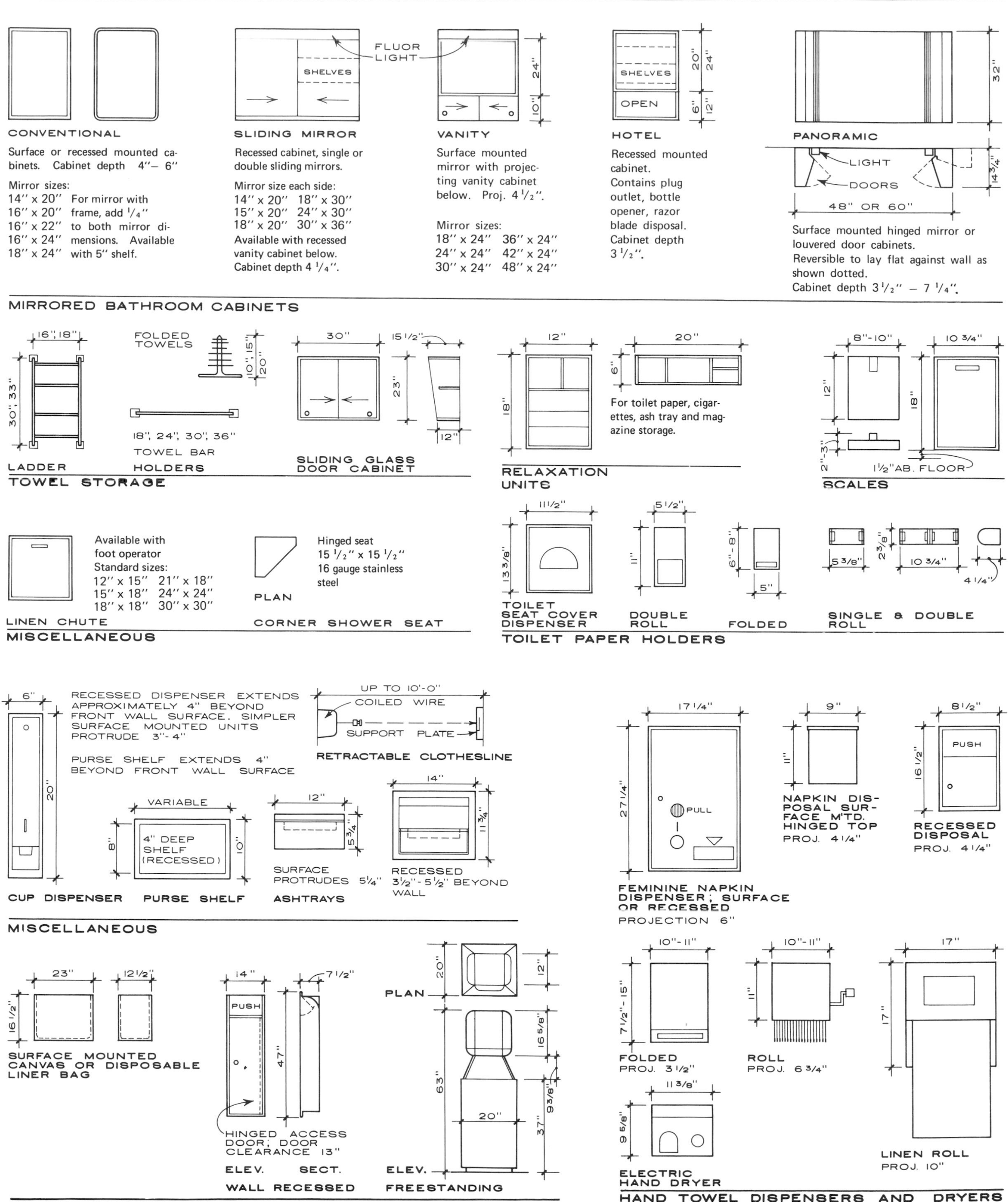

FLUOR LIGHT
SHELVES
OPEN
LIGHT
DOORS
48" OR 60"
CONVENTIONAL
Surface or recessed mounted cabinets. Cabinet depth 4"– 6"
Mirror sizes:
14" x 20"
16" x 20"
16" x 22"
16" x 24"
18" x 24"
For mirror with frame, add 1/4" to both mirror dimensions. Available with 5" shelf.
SLIDING MIRROR
Recessed cabinet, single or double sliding mirrors.
Mirror size each side:
14" x 20" 18" x 30"
15" x 20" 24" x 30"
18" x 20" 30" x 36"
Available with recessed vanity cabinet below.
Cabinet depth 4 1/4".
VANITY
Surface mounted mirror with projecting vanity cabinet below. Proj. 4 1/2".
Mirror sizes:
18" x 24" 36" x 24"
24" x 24" 42" x 24"
30" x 24" 48" x 24"
HOTEL
Recessed mounted cabinet. Contains plug outlet, bottle opener, razor blade disposal. Cabinet depth 3 1/2".
PANORAMIC
Surface mounted hinged mirror or louvered door cabinets.
Reversible to lay flat against wall as shown dotted.
Cabinet depth 3 1/2" – 7 1/4".
MIRRORED BATHROOM CABINETS
FOLDED TOWELS
18", 24", 30", 36"
TOWEL BAR
LADDER
HOLDERS
TOWEL STORAGE
SLIDING GLASS DOOR CABINET
For toilet paper, cigarettes, ash tray and magazine storage.
RELAXATION UNITS
1 1/2" AB. FLOOR
SCALES
Available with foot operator
Standard sizes:
12" x 15" 21" x 18"
15" x 18" 24" x 24"
18" x 18" 30" x 30"
LINEN CHUTE
Hinged seat
15 1/2" x 15 1/2"
16 gauge stainless steel
PLAN
CORNER SHOWER SEAT
MISCELLANEOUS
TOILET SEAT COVER DISPENSER
DOUBLE ROLL
FOLDED
SINGLE & DOUBLE ROLL
TOILET PAPER HOLDERS
RECESSED DISPENSER EXTENDS APPROXIMATELY 4" BEYOND FRONT WALL SURFACE. SIMPLER SURFACE MOUNTED UNITS PROTRUDE 3"- 4"
PURSE SHELF EXTENDS 4" BEYOND FRONT WALL SURFACE
UP TO 10'-0"
COILED WIRE
SUPPORT PLATE
RETRACTABLE CLOTHESLINE
VARIABLE
4" DEEP SHELF (RECESSED)
SURFACE PROTRUDES 5 1/4"
RECESSED 3 1/2"- 5 1/2" BEYOND WALL
CUP DISPENSER
PURSE SHELF
ASHTRAYS
MISCELLANEOUS
PULL
PUSH
FEMININE NAPKIN DISPENSER; SURFACE OR RECESSED
PROJECTION 6"
NAPKIN DISPOSAL SURFACE M'TD. HINGED TOP
PROJ. 4 1/4"
RECESSED DISPOSAL
PROJ. 4 1/4"
SURFACE MOUNTED CANVAS OR DISPOSABLE LINER BAG
HINGED ACCESS DOOR; DOOR CLEARANCE 13"
ELEV.
SECT.
WALL RECESSED
PLAN
ELEV.
FREESTANDING
WASTE RECEPTACLES
FOLDED
PROJ. 3 1/2"
ROLL
PROJ. 6 3/4"
LINEN ROLL
PROJ. 10"
ELECTRIC HAND DRYER
HAND TOWEL DISPENSERS AND DRYERS

H. E. Hallenbeck, Capuccilli-Bell Architects, AIA; Syracuse, New York

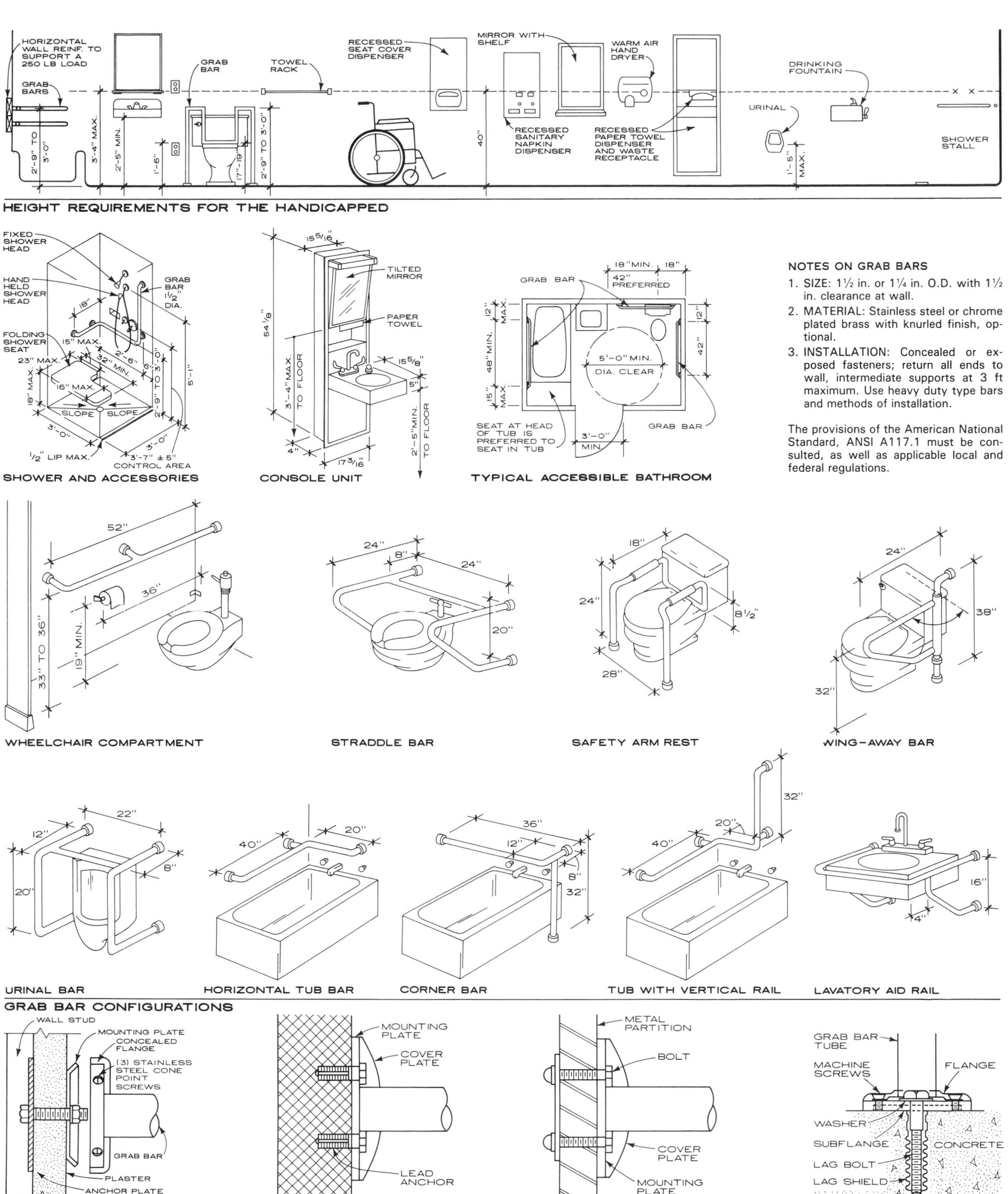
HORIZONTAL WALL REINF. TO SUPPORT A 250 LB LOAD
GRAB BARS
GRAB BAR
TOWEL RACK
RECESSED SEAT COVER DISPENSER
MIRROR WITH SHELF
WARM AIR HAND DRYER
DRINKING FOUNTAIN
URINAL
SHOWER STALL
RECESSED SANITARY NAPKIN DISPENSER
RECESSED PAPER TOWEL DISPENSER AND WASTE RECEPTACLE
2'-9" TO 3'-0"
3'-4" MAX.
2'-5" MIN.
1'-6"
17"-19"
2'-9" TO 3'-0"
40"
1'-5" MAX.
HEIGHT REQUIREMENTS FOR THE HANDICAPPED
FIXED SHOWER HEAD
HAND HELD SHOWER HEAD
GRAB BAR 1 1/2" DIA.
FOLDING SHOWER SEAT
15" MAX.
23" MAX.
16" MAX.
18" MAX.
SLOPE
1/2" LIP MAX.
3'-7" ± 5" CONTROL AREA
SHOWER AND ACCESSORIES
TILTED MIRROR
PAPER TOWEL
54 1/8"
15 5/16"
3'-4" MAX. TO FLOOR
2'-5" MIN. TO FLOOR
17 3/16"
CONSOLE UNIT
18" MIN.
18"
42" PREFERRED
GRAB BAR
48" MIN.
15" MAX.
12" MAX.
42"
5'-0" MIN. DIA. CLEAR
SEAT AT HEAD OF TUB IS PREFERRED TO SEAT IN TUB
3'-0" MIN.
TYPICAL ACCESSIBLE BATHROOM
52"
36"
33" TO 36"
19" MIN.
WHEELCHAIR COMPARTMENT
24"
8"
20"
STRADDLE BAR
18"
24"
28"
8 1/2"
SAFETY ARM REST
38"
32"
WING-AWAY BAR
22"
12"
20"
URINAL BAR
40"
HORIZONTAL TUB BAR
36"
CORNER BAR
TUB WITH VERTICAL RAIL
16"
4"
LAVATORY AID RAIL
GRAB BAR CONFIGURATIONS
WALL STUD
MOUNTING PLATE
CONCEALED FLANGE
(3) STAINLESS STEEL CONE POINT SCREWS
GRAB BAR
PLASTER
ANCHOR PLATE
STUD WALL
MOUNTING PLATE
COVER PLATE
LEAD ANCHOR
MASONRY WALL
METAL PARTITION
BOLT
COVER PLATE
MOUNTING PLATE
METAL PARTITION
GRAB BAR TUBE
MACHINE SCREWS
FLANGE
WASHER
SUBFLANGE
CONCRETE
LAG BOLT
LAG SHIELD
SLAB
ATTACHMENT DETAILS

NOTES ON GRAB BARS

1. SIZE: 1½ in. or 1¼ in. O.D. with 1½ in. clearance at wall.
2. MATERIAL: Stainless steel or chrome plated brass with knurled finish, optional.
3. INSTALLATION: Concealed or exposed fasteners; return all ends to wall, intermediate supports at 3 ft maximum. Use heavy duty type bars and methods of installation.

The provisions of the American National Standard, ANSI A117.1 must be consulted, as well as applicable local and federal regulations.

Jones/Richards and Associates; Ogden, Utah

REFERENCES

DATA SOURCES: ORGANIZATIONS

American Dispenser Company, 346, 347
American National Standards Institute (ANSI), 347
Bobrick Washroom Equipment, Inc., 347
Bommer Associates, 345
Bradley Corporation, 347
Heatilator, 341, 342
Liskey, Inc., 338
Nutone Housing Products, 346
Parker Company, 346
Pawling Rubber Company, 339
Tate Architectural Products, Inc., 338
Tubular Specialties Manufacturing, Inc., 347
U.S. Postal Service (USPS), 345
Van Packer Company, Inc., 342

CHAPTER 11

EQUIPMENT

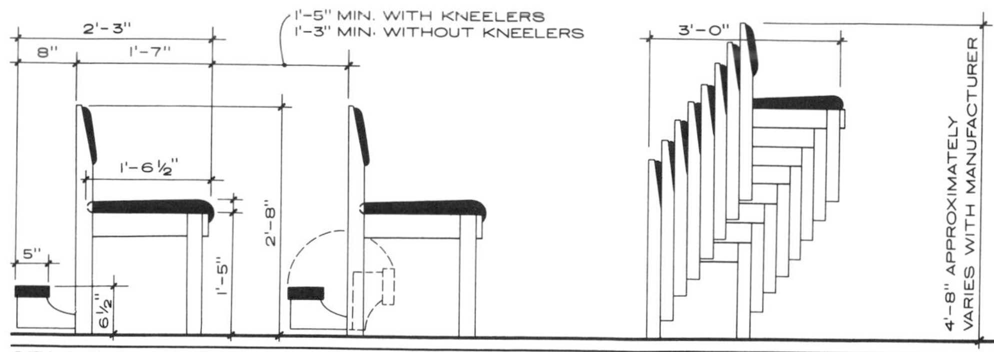
2'-3"
8"
1'-7"
1'-5" MIN. WITH KNEELERS
1'-3" MIN. WITHOUT KNEELERS
1'-6½"
5"
6½"
1'-5"
2'-8"
3'-0"
4'-8" APPROXIMATELY
VARIES WITH MANUFACTURER
STACKING CHAPEL/CHOIR CHAIRS

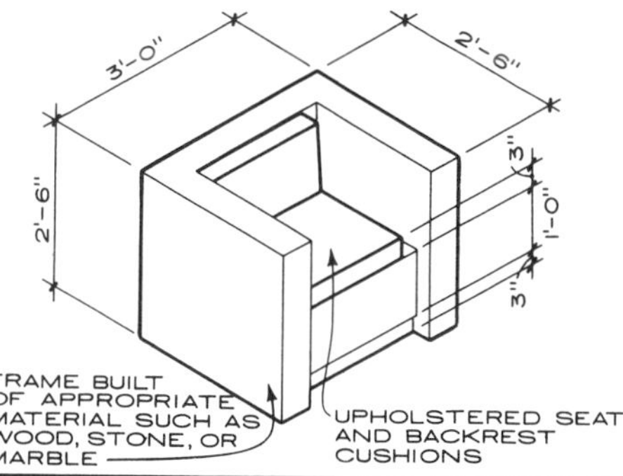
3'-0"
2'-6"
2'-6"
3"
1'-0"
3"
FRAME BUILT OF APPROPRIATE MATERIAL SUCH AS WOOD, STONE, OR MARBLE
UPHOLSTERED SEAT AND BACKREST CUSHIONS
CLERGY/PRESIDER CHAIR

STACK CHAIRS

A variety of stacking or modular chairs are available and well suited to uses such as small churches, chapels, and choir areas where flexibility of arrangement or complete removal is desired. Like pews, these chairs may be upholstered in differing degrees and equipped with kneelers, book holders, and other features. In addition, most manufacturers offer an interlocking device that enables the user to join rows of chairs together for temporarily fixed arrangements. Stacking capability allows efficient storage of chairs. When worship spaces become large enough to require a sloped floor for proper sight and sound lines, chairs are generally not advisable.

ALTAR/COMMUNION TABLE

In most churches, the altar or communion table is the primary focus and therefore the most visually prominent furnishing. Style and symbolism of the altar/table are deeply rooted in the liturgy of individual churches and usually require the participation and theological direction of both clergy and laity during design. Appropriateness of scale and material are particularly important and widely variable. The altar/table is among the most suitable furnishings for artist collaboration in design and execution.

BAPTISMAL FONT

A font for ceremonial sprinkling of infants and/or adults may be placed in various locations including at the chancel/sanctuary or at the entrance to the church in the narthex. In some cases, the font may be alternately moved between these locations. Usually space for gathering of family and friends is required around the font and, in many churches, the font is required to be in a position that permits general viewing of a baptism by the entire congregation. Churches practicing baptism by immersion or submersion require an altogether different style of baptistry involving a pool or tank that allows full entry by laity and clergy. Prefabricated baptistry tanks are available and custom installations possible.

TABERNACLE

The tabernacle generally associated with Roman Catholic, Orthodox, and Episcopalian ("ambry" rather than tabernacle) churches is a very significant element in the worship environment, acting as the place of repose for the consecrated Host—the body of Christ. It is often a highly artistic and custom furnishing. Careful attention to the liturgical attitudes of the individual church and review of the document *"Environment and Art in Catholic Worship"* (for Roman Catholic churches) should guide the design and placement of the tabernacle.

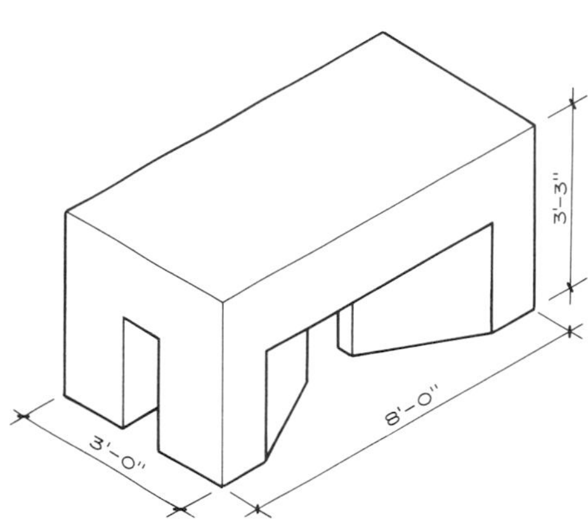
3'-3"
8'-0"
3'-0"
ALTAR

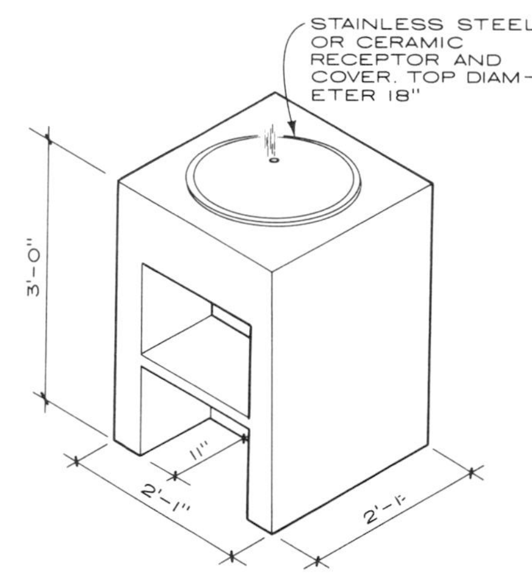
STAINLESS STEEL OR CERAMIC RECEPTOR AND COVER. TOP DIAMETER 18"
3'-0"
11"
2'-1"
2'-1"
BAPTISMAL FONT

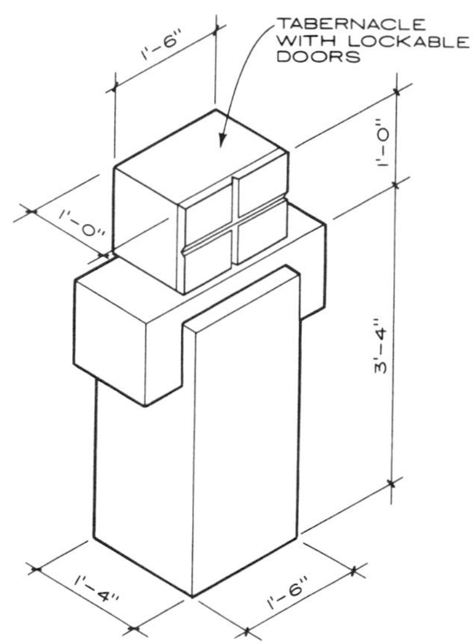
1'-6"
TABERNACLE WITH LOCKABLE DOORS
1'-0"
1'-0"
3'-4"
1'-4"
1'-6"
TABERNACLE

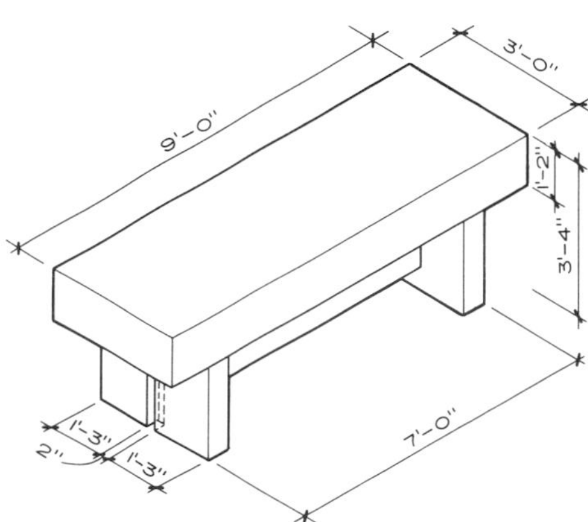
3'-0"
9'-0"
1'-2"
3'-4"
7'-0"
1'-3"
2"
1'-3"
COMMUNION TABLE

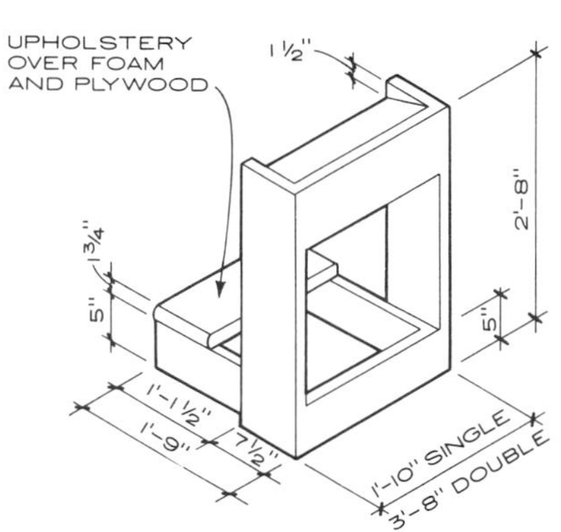
UPHOLSTERY OVER FOAM AND PLYWOOD
1½"
2'-8"
¾
5"
5"
1'-1½"
1'-9"
7½"
1'-10" SINGLE
3'-8" DOUBLE
INDIVIDUAL KNEELER

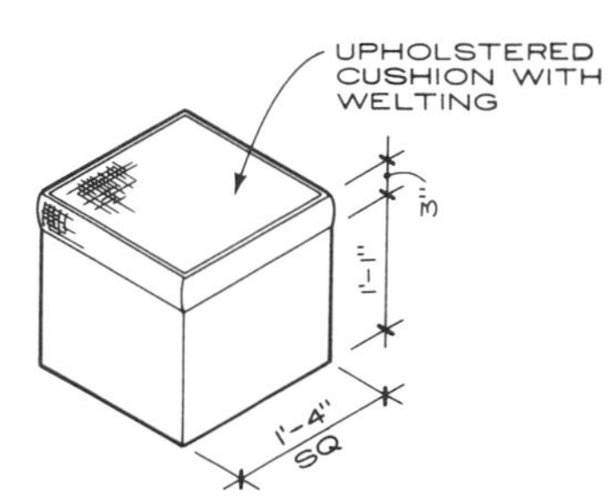
UPHOLSTERED CUSHION WITH WELTING
3"
1'-1"
1'-4" SQ
ACOLYTE STOOL

Randall S. Lindstrom, AIA; Ware Associates, Inc.; Rockford, Illinois

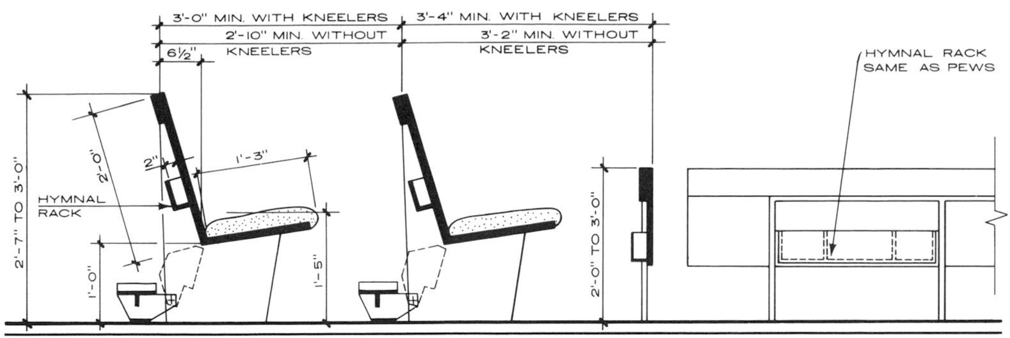
3'-0" MIN. WITH KNEELERS
2'-10" MIN. WITHOUT KNEELERS
3'-4" MIN. WITH KNEELERS
3'-2" MIN. WITHOUT KNEELERS
6½"
HYMNAL RACK SAME AS PEWS
2'-0"
2"
1'-3"
HYMNAL RACK
2'-7" TO 3'-0"
1'-0"
1'-5"
2'-0" TO 3'-0"

PEW AND FRONTAL

PEW SPACING

NO. OF SPACES	BACK-TO-BACK BETWEEN PEWS 2'-10" SPACING	3'-0" SPACING
5	14'-2"	15'-0"
10	28'-4"	30'-0"
20	56'-8"	60'-0"
30	85'-0"	90'-0"

PEW LENGTH* NO. OF PERSONS	1'-8" PER PERSON	1'-10" PER PERSON
3	5'-0"	5'-6"
5	8'-4"	9'-2"
7	11'-8"	12'-10"
9	15'-0"	16'-6"
11	18'-4"	20'-0"
12	20'-0"	

*Minimum space allowed per person is 1 ft 6 in. Based on NFPA 101 Life Safety Code (1985), the maximum number of seats allowed in a row with aisles at both ends of the row is 14; maximum length allowed for a row is 21 ft 0 in.

INTRODUCTION

Ecclesiastical furnishings are as much or more a part of the ambiance, symbolism, and meaning of a worship environment as the structure and architecture itself. Virtually all ecclesiastical furnishings are available from various manufacturers in predesigned, prefabricated form. In many cases, especially with regard to pews and chairs, such stock or semicustom items can be highly satisfactory and economical. Where special scale, material, or symbolism is desired, custom-designed and custom-built furnishings may be more appropriate, as is often true of chancel/sanctuary furnishings including pulpit, table, font, and clergy chairs. The illustrations on these pages provide information concerning the general size and character of such furnishings. The theology and liturgical attitudes of each church should provide primary guidance in the design and execution of ecclesiastical furnishings.

PEWS

Most pew manufacturers offer a diverse selection of styles, materials, and finishes, and many will custom build special designs prepared by the architect. Pew ends contribute most to style and are available in numerous designs from closed to semiopen to fully open. Kneelers are optional and some are available with hydraulic pistons to govern the speed (and noise) with which they are lowered and raised. Other options include book, card, pencil, and communion cup holders.

PULPIT/AMBO

The pulpit (Protestant) or ambo (Roman Catholic) has historically been a fixed chancel/sanctuary furnishing. However, with increasing demands for multiple uses of worship spaces, the need for flexibility often requires that all furnishings be movable.

Among the most important features of a pulpit/ambo is an adjustable top to accommodate the physical variations of speakers. A drop-down step may also be desirable. A pulpit should include a concealed reading lamp (especially where A/V darkening is employed) and a built-in clock. Although extensive use is being made of lavalier or wireless microphones, a concealed microphone cable raceway should be provided and the pulpit top padded to minimize the noise of rustling notes that sensitive microphones may amplify.

LECTERN

The lectern is almost always movable. In small churches or chapels, a lectern may be used as a pulpit. Features similar to those required of the pulpit should be provided.

COMMUNION RAIL

Communion rails should provide for comfortable kneeling. The rail may need to provide for the disposition of individual communion cups (as illustrated below). In worship spaces also used for concerts or drama, communion rails may need to be easily removable.

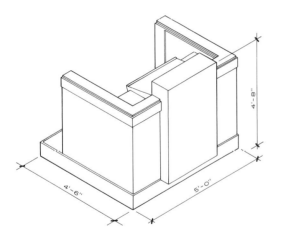

4'-8"
4'-6"
5'-0"

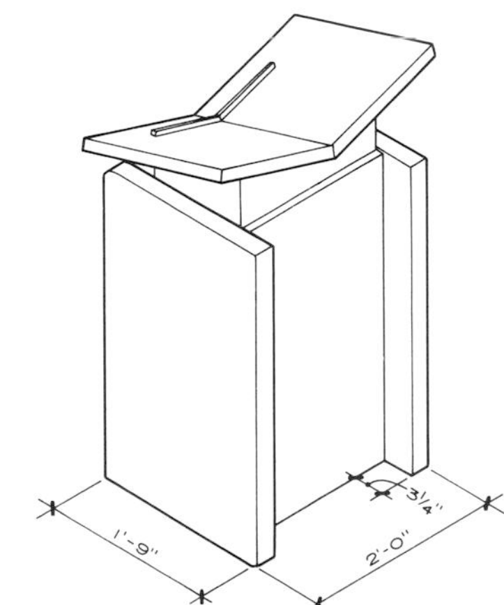
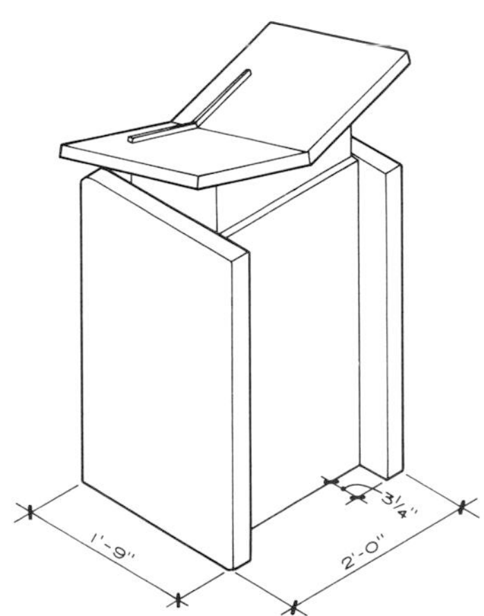
1'-9"
2'-0"
¾"

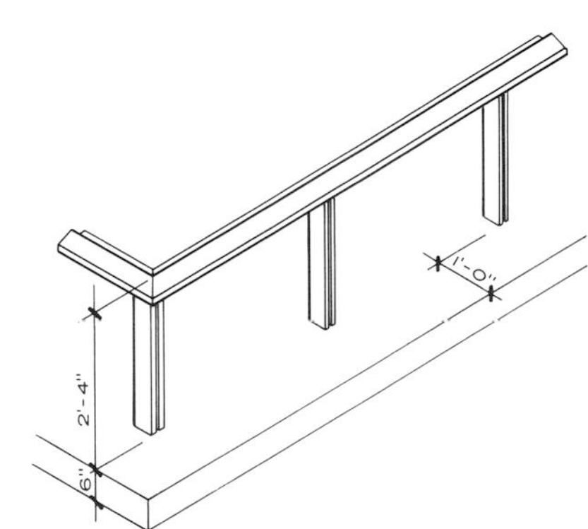
1'-0"
2'-4"
6"

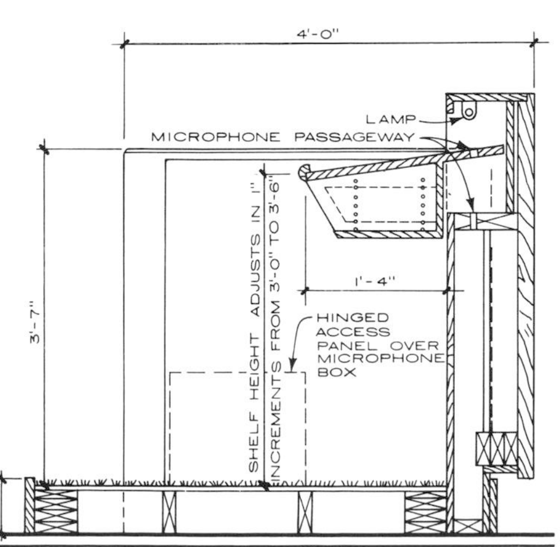
4'-0"
LAMP
MICROPHONE PASSAGEWAY
SHELF HEIGHT ADJUSTS IN 1" INCREMENTS FROM 3'-0" TO 3'-6"
1'-4"
HINGED ACCESS PANEL OVER MICROPHONE BOX
3'-7"
6½"

PULPIT / AMBO

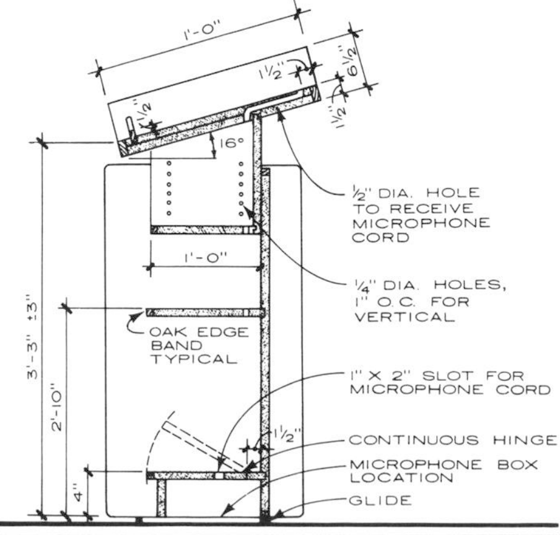
1'-0"
1½"
6½"
16°
½" DIA. HOLE TO RECEIVE MICROPHONE CORD
1'-0"
¼" DIA. HOLES, 1" O.C. FOR VERTICAL
OAK EDGE BAND TYPICAL
3'-3" ±3"
2'-10"
1" X 2" SLOT FOR MICROPHONE CORD
1½"
CONTINUOUS HINGE
MICROPHONE BOX LOCATION
4"
GLIDE

LECTERN

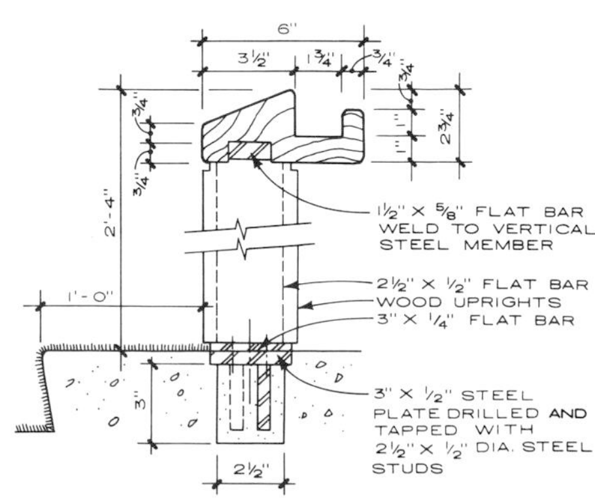
6"
3½"
1¾"
¾"
2¾"
1½" X ⅝" FLAT BAR WELD TO VERTICAL STEEL MEMBER
2'-4"
1'-0"
2½" X ½" FLAT BAR
WOOD UPRIGHTS
3" X ¼" FLAT BAR
3"
3" X ½" STEEL PLATE DRILLED AND TAPPED WITH 2½" X ½" DIA. STEEL STUDS
2½"

COMMUNION RAIL

Randall S. Lindstrom, AIA; Ware Associates, Inc.; Rockford, Illinois

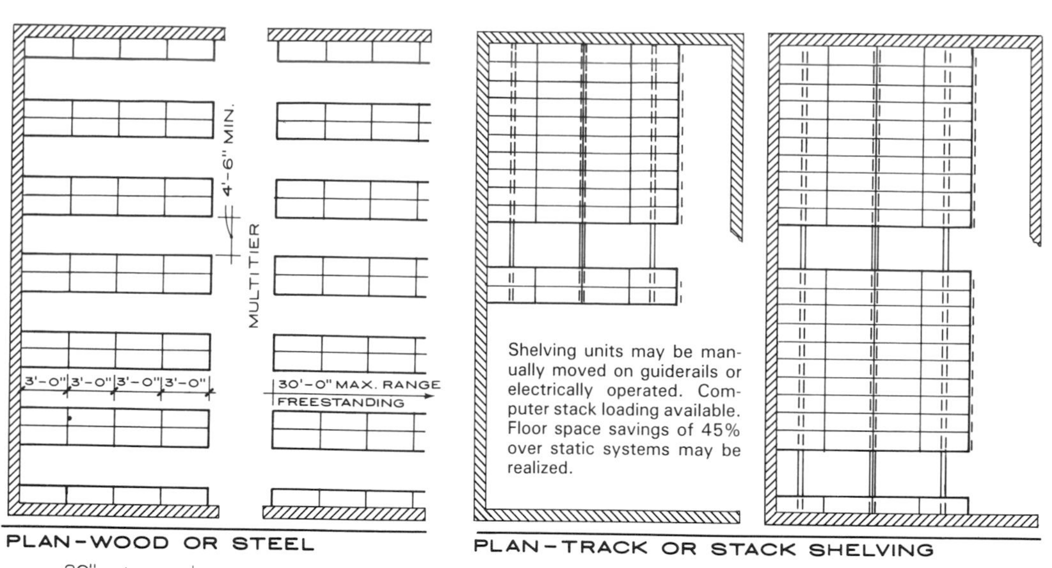
4'-6" MIN.
MULTITIER
3'-0" 3'-0" 3'-0" 3'-0"
30'-0" MAX. RANGE
FREESTANDING
Shelving units may be manually moved on guiderails or electrically operated. Computer stack loading available. Floor space savings of 45% over static systems may be realized.

PLAN–WOOD OR STEEL

PLAN–TRACK OR STACK SHELVING

SHELF CAPACITY AND DEPTH

TYPE OF BOOK	VOLUMES PER LINEAR FT	SHELF DEPTH (IN.)
Children's	10-12	8
Fiction and economics	7	8
History and General Literature	7	8
Reference	7	10
Technical and Scientific	6	8
Medical	5	10
Law and public documents	4-5	8
Bound periodicals	5	10-12
U.S. Patent spec.	2	8

BOOK CAPACITY PER GROSS FLOOR AREA

Many variables must be considered: size and kind of books, book lifts, carrels, number and width of aisles, ultimate capacity, and so on. Variances run from 13½ to 19 books/sq ft. For a rule of thumb allow 16 books/sq ft of gross area. The average dead load of books is 25 lb/cu ft.

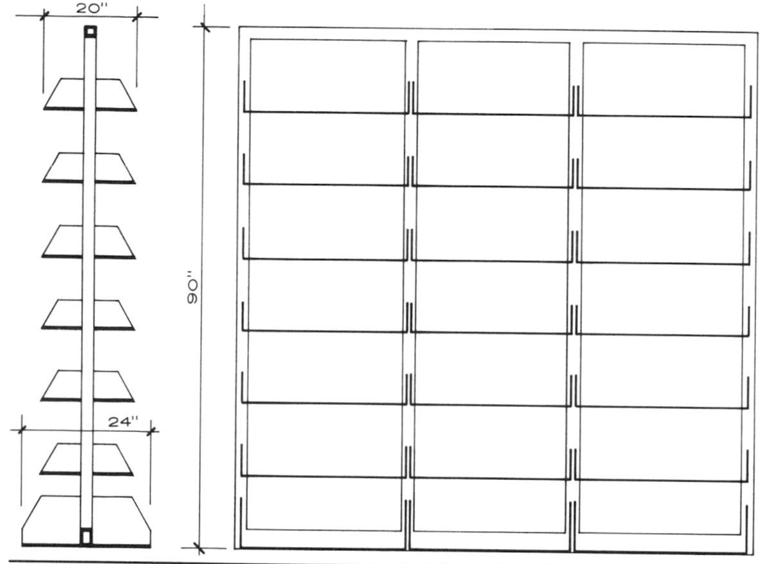
20"
24"
90"

ADJUSTABLE SHELF UNIT, STEEL

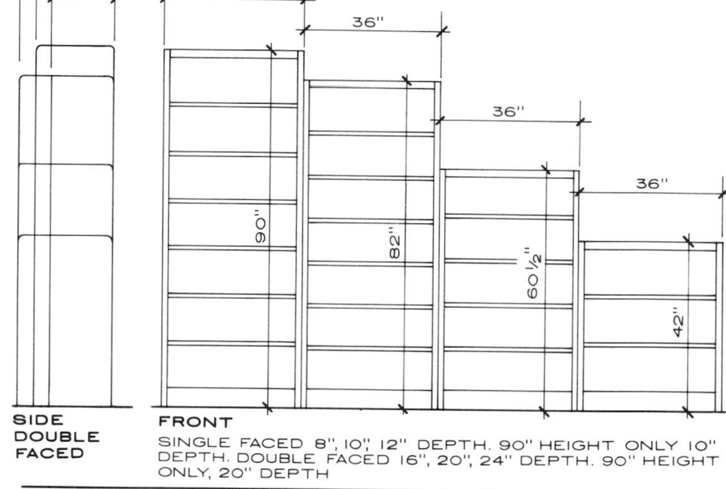
24"
20"
16"
36"
36"
36"
36"
90"
82"
60 ½"
42"
SIDE
DOUBLE
FACED
FRONT

SINGLE FACED 8", 10", 12" DEPTH. 90" HEIGHT ONLY 10" DEPTH. DOUBLE FACED 16", 20", 24" DEPTH. 90" HEIGHT ONLY, 20" DEPTH

ADJUSTABLE SHELF UNIT, WOOD

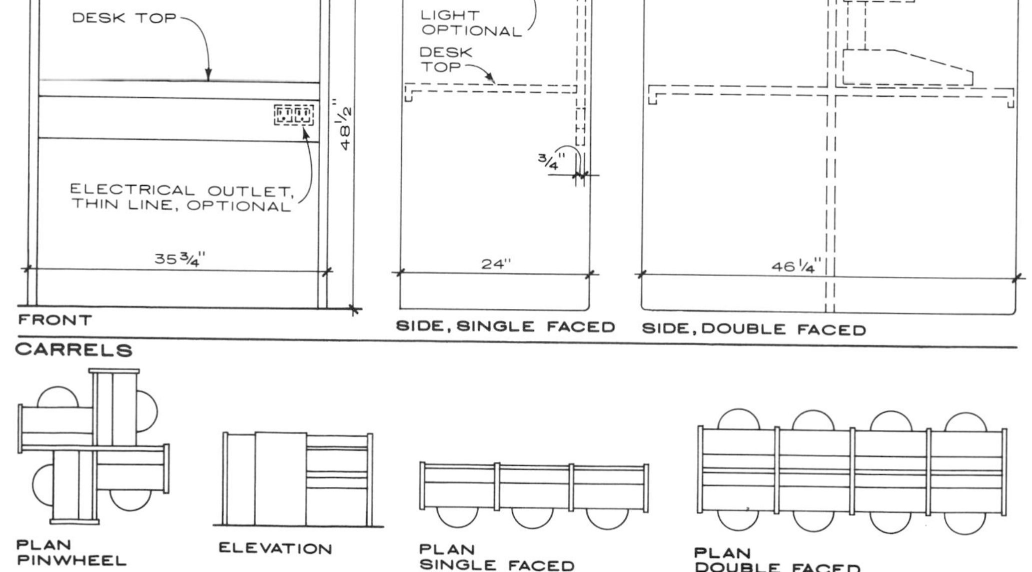
SHELF
DESK TOP
ELECTRICAL OUTLET, THIN LINE, OPTIONAL
48 ½"
35 ¾"
FRONT
SHELF
LIGHT OPTIONAL
DESK TOP
¾"
24"
SIDE, SINGLE FACED
46 ¼"
SIDE, DOUBLE FACED

CARRELS

PLAN PINWHEEL

ELEVATION

PLAN SINGLE FACED

PLAN DOUBLE FACED

CARREL ARRANGEMENTS

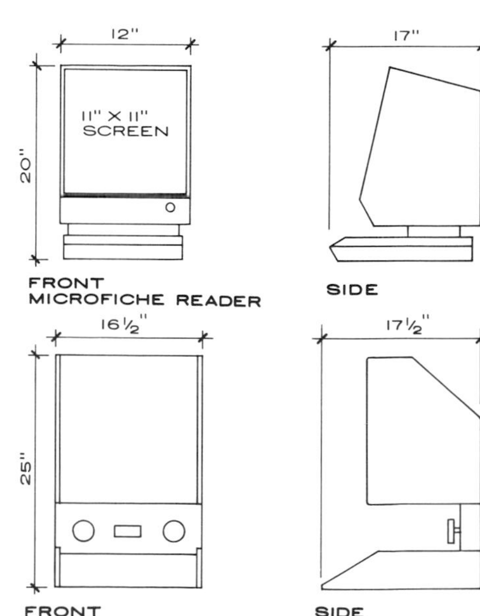
12"
11" X 11" SCREEN
20"
FRONT
MICROFICHE READER
17"
SIDE
16 ½"
17 ½"
25"
FRONT
SIDE
MICROREADER FOR FICHE OR FILM

NOTE

Generally microfilm and microfiche readers and video display terminals (VDT) are positioned on tables.

LIBRARY EQUIPMENT

Walter Hart Associates, AIA; White Plains, New York

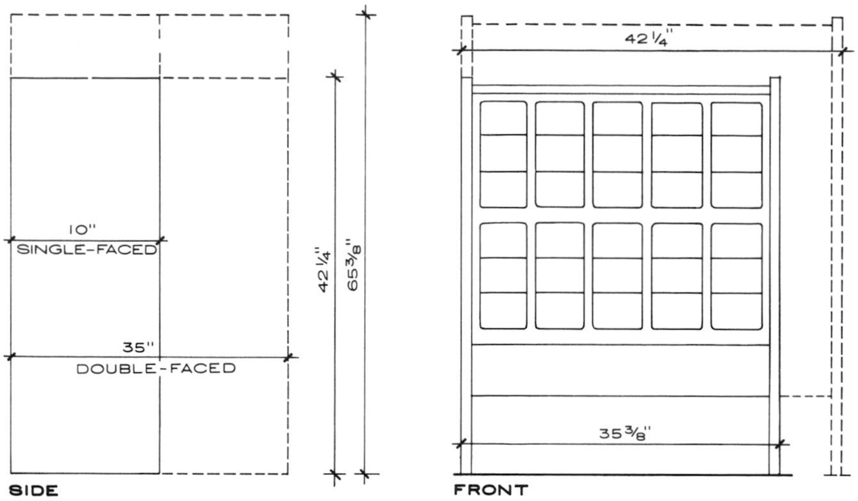

10"
SINGLE-FACED
35"
DOUBLE-FACED
42¼"
65⅜"

SIDE

42¼"
35⅜"

FRONT

NOTES

Card catalog cases are available in units:
Single-faced 15–60 trays, 42¼'' H; double-faced 30–120 trays, 42¼'' H; high, single, or double faced with pullout shelves, 72–144 trays, 65⅜'' H. Effective tray card filing depth 14¾'', tray capacity 1250–1300 standard cards of 3'' x 5''.

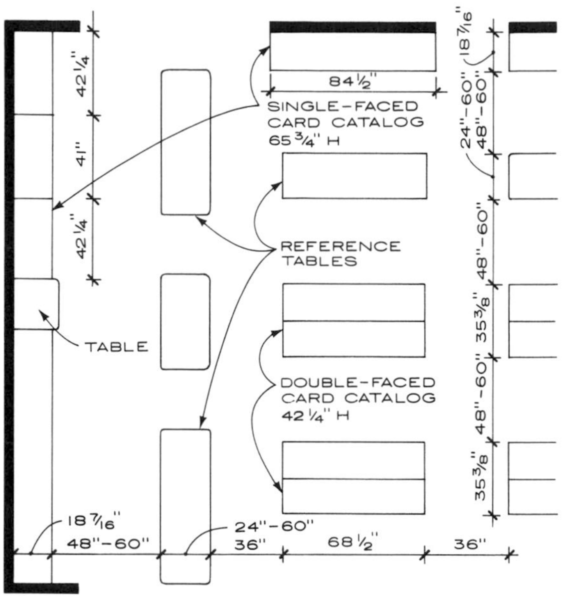

42¼"
41"
42¼"
84½"
SINGLE-FACED CARD CATALOG 65¾" H
REFERENCE TABLES
TABLE
DOUBLE-FACED CARD CATALOG 42¼" H
18 7/16"
48"–60"
24"–60"
36"
68½"
36"
18 7/16"
24"–60"
48"–60"
48"–60"
35⅜"
48"–60"
35⅜"

CARD CATALOG ARRANGEMENT PLAN

CARD CATALOG CASES

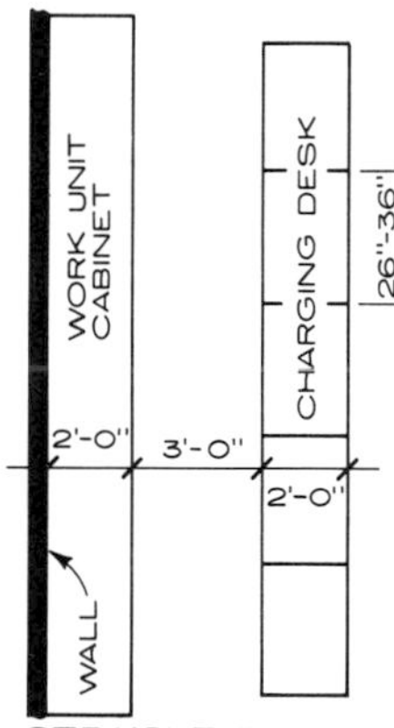

WORK UNIT CABINET
CHARGING DESK
26"–36"
2'–0"
3'–0"
2'–0"
WALL

STRAIGHT PLAN

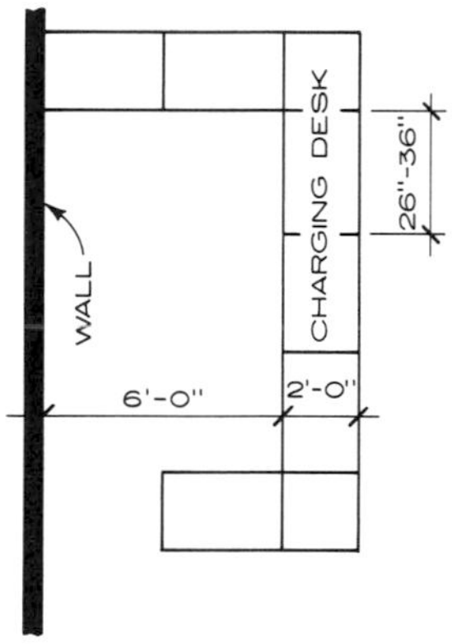

WALL
CHARGING DESK
26"–36"
6'–0"
2'–0"

'U' PLAN

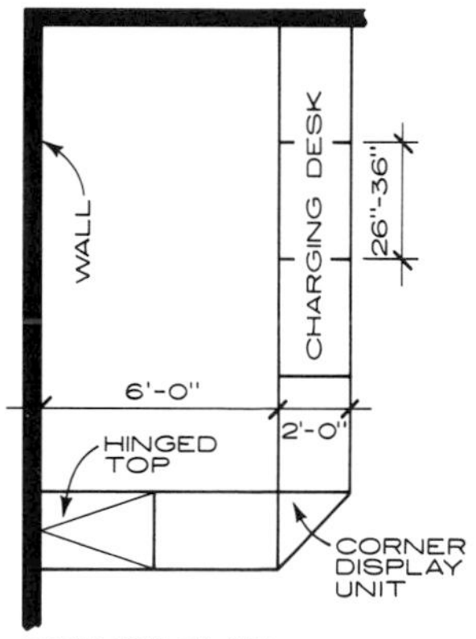

WALL
CHARGING DESK
26"–36"
6'–0"
2'–0"
HINGED TOP
CORNER DISPLAY UNIT

CORNER PLAN

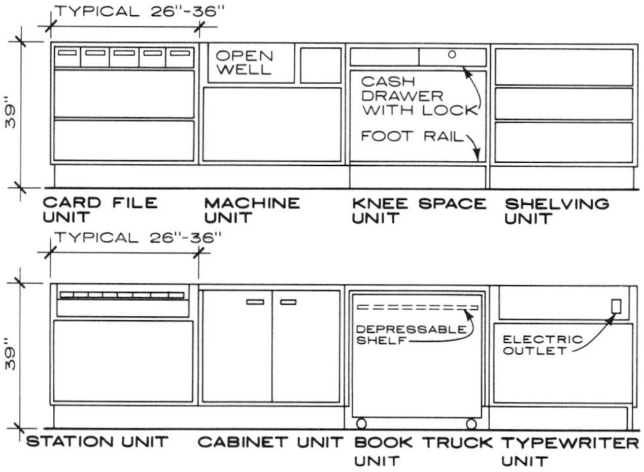

TYPICAL 26"–36"
39"
OPEN WELL
CASH DRAWER WITH LOCK
FOOT RAIL
CARD FILE UNIT
MACHINE UNIT
KNEE SPACE UNIT
SHELVING UNIT

TYPICAL 26"–36"
39"
DEPRESSABLE SHELF
ELECTRIC OUTLET
STATION UNIT
CABINET UNIT
BOOK TRUCK UNIT
TYPEWRITER UNIT

CHARGING DESKS

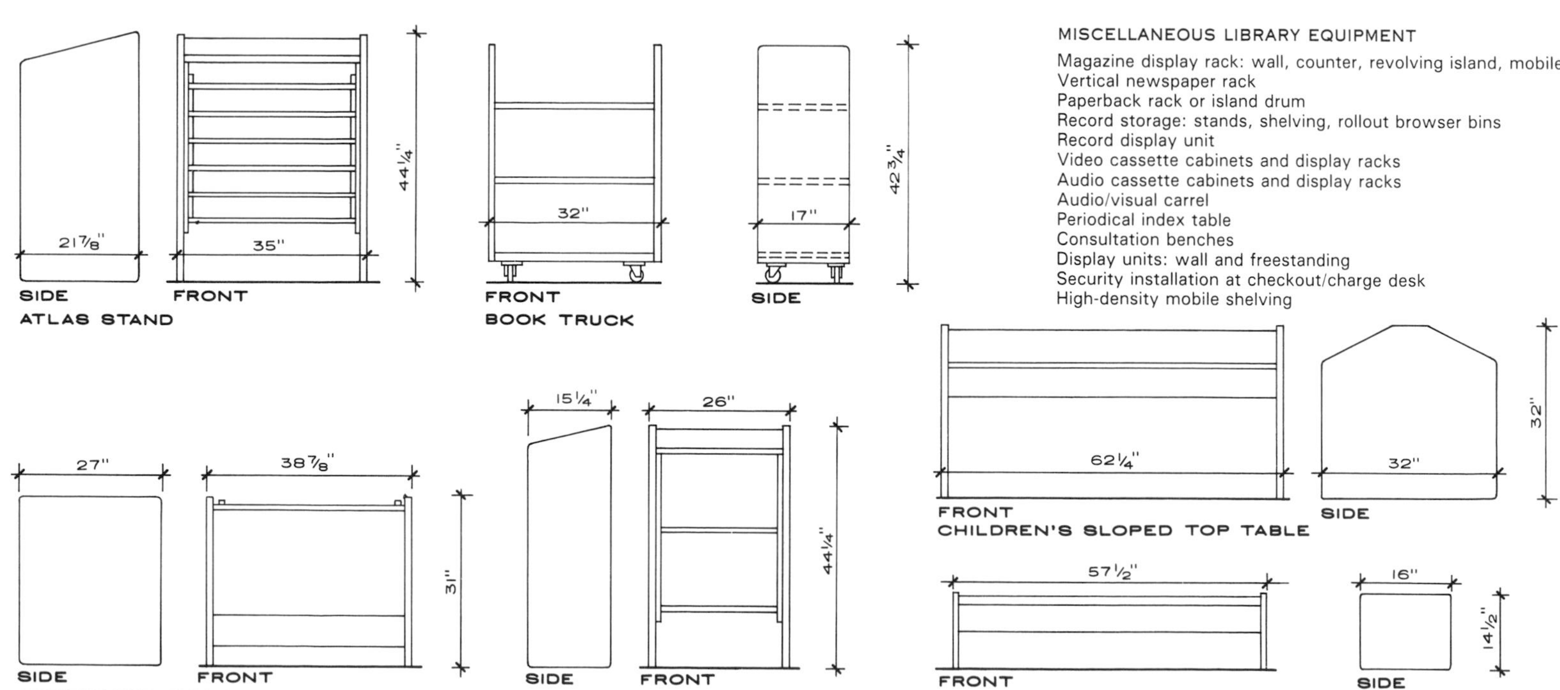

21⅞"
35"
44¼"
SIDE
FRONT
ATLAS STAND
32"
17"
42¾"
FRONT
SIDE
BOOK TRUCK
62¼"
32"
32"
FRONT
CHILDREN'S SLOPED TOP TABLE
SIDE
27"
38⅞"
31"
SIDE
FRONT
NEWSPAPER STAND
15¼"
26"
44¼"
SIDE
FRONT
57½"
16"
14½"
FRONT
CHILDREN'S BENCH
SIDE

MISCELLANEOUS LIBRARY EQUIPMENT

Magazine display rack: wall, counter, revolving island, mobile
Vertical newspaper rack
Paperback rack or island drum
Record storage: stands, shelving, rollout browser bins
Record display unit
Video cassette cabinets and display racks
Audio cassette cabinets and display racks
Audio/visual carrel
Periodical index table
Consultation benches
Display units: wall and freestanding
Security installation at checkout/charge desk
High-density mobile shelving

MISCELLANEOUS LIBRARY EQUIPMENT

Walter Hart Associates, AIA; White Plains, New York

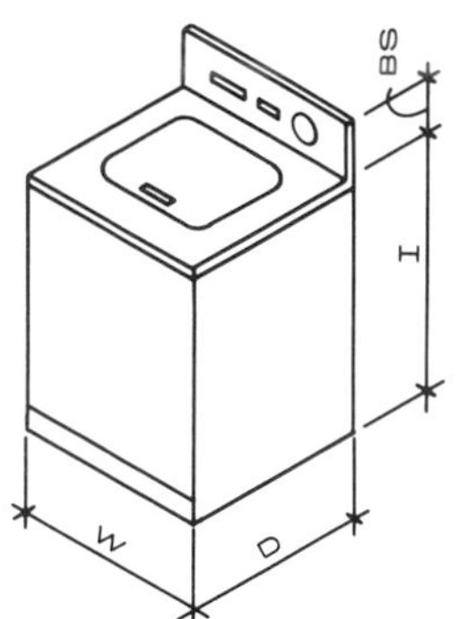
BS
H
W
D

FREESTANDING – TOP OR FRONT LOADING

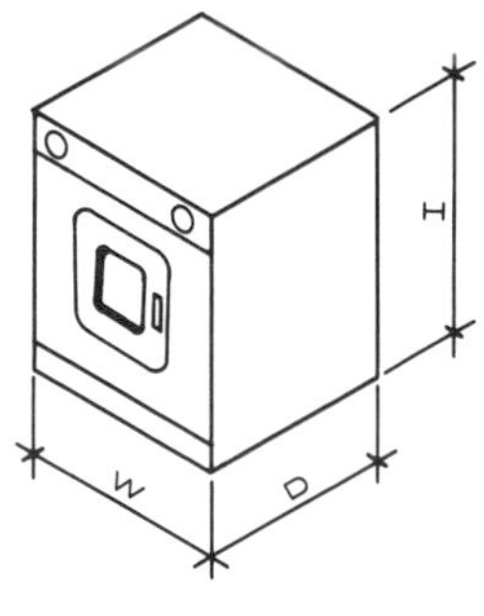
H
W
D

UNDER COUNTER

AUTOMATIC WASHERS (SOME HAVE KICK SPACES, SOME NOT)

	MIN.	MAX.	OTHER
W	25 1/2	27	25 5/8 - 26 3/4
D	24 7/8	28 23/32	25 - 28 5/16
H	36	36 1/2	36 1/8 - 36 1/4
BS	6 3/32	8 3/4	6 1/2 - 8 1/2

	MIN.	MAX.
W	26 3/4	30 1/4
D	24 7/8	24 7/8
H	34 1/2	

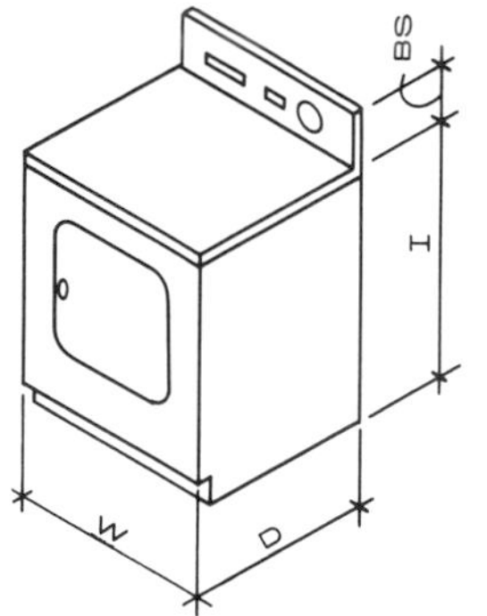
BS
H
W
D

FREESTANDING FRONT LOADING

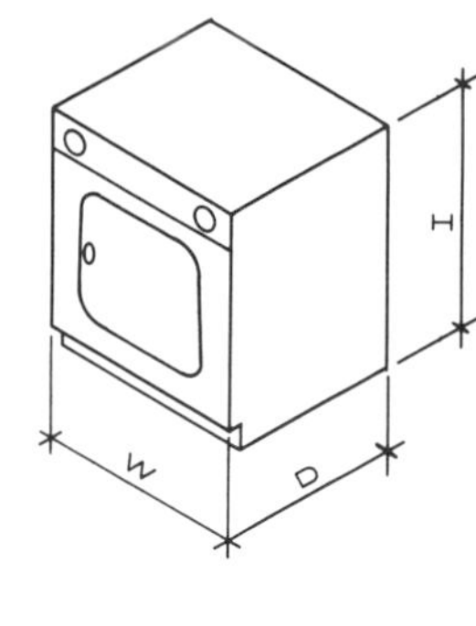
H
W
D

UNDER COUNTER

AUTOMATIC DRYERS (SOME HAVE KICK SPACES, SOME NOT)

	MIN.	MAX.	OTHER
W	26 3/4	31 1/2	27 - 31
D	24 7/8	28 23/32	25 - 28 5/16
H	36	36 1/2	36 1/8 - 36 1/4
BS	6 3/32	8 3/4	6 1/2 - 8 1/2

	MIN.	MAX.
W	26 3/4	
D	24 7/8	
H	34 1/2	

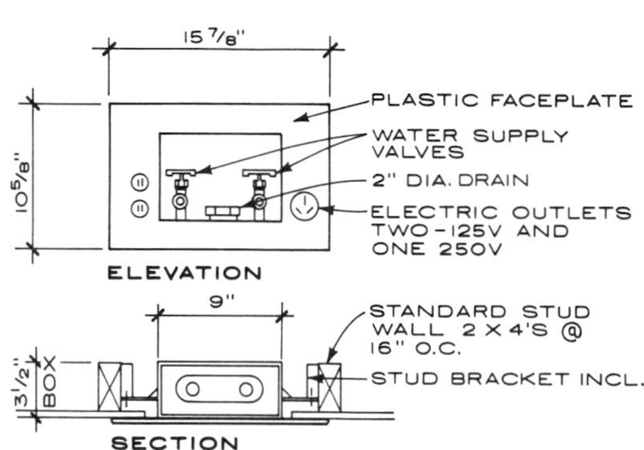
15 7/8"
10 5/8"
PLASTIC FACEPLATE
WATER SUPPLY VALVES
2" DIA. DRAIN
ELECTRIC OUTLETS TWO - 125V AND ONE 250V
ELEVATION
9"
3 1/2" BOX
STANDARD STUD WALL 2 X 4'S @ 16" O.C.
STUD BRACKET INCL.
SECTION

UTILITY CONNECTION BOX (RECESSED)

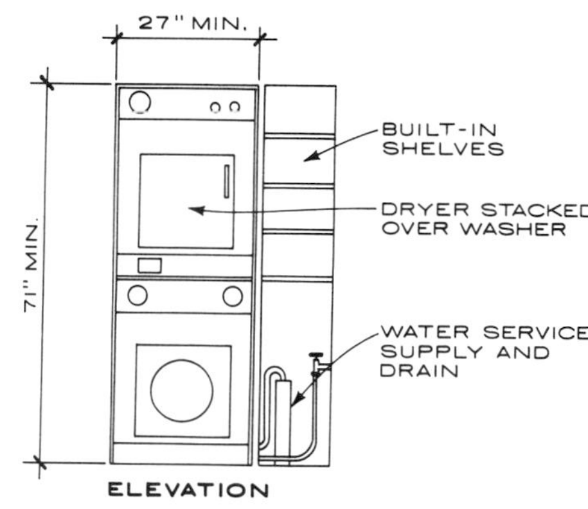
27" MIN.
71" MIN.
BUILT-IN SHELVES
DRYER STACKED OVER WASHER
WATER SERVICE SUPPLY AND DRAIN
ELEVATION

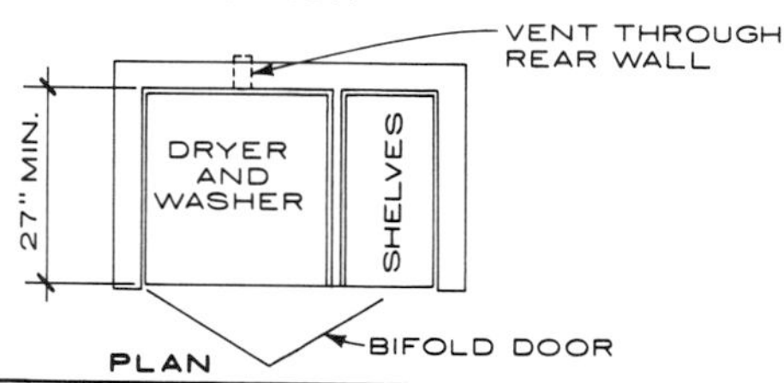
VENT THROUGH REAR WALL
27" MIN.
DRYER AND WASHER
SHELVES
BIFOLD DOOR
PLAN

WASHER AND DRYER STACKED IN CLOSET

GENERAL NOTES

See kitchen & laundry layout pages for locations of washers & dryers and wall chases for pipes & vents and for dishwasher locations.

Where clearances of doors of machines (when open) may be a problem, check manufacturers catalog for "open-door" dimension.

All dimensions given are actual ones but certain variations in body design may affect actual depths of models. Check all units for exact voltage. Some units available with gas.

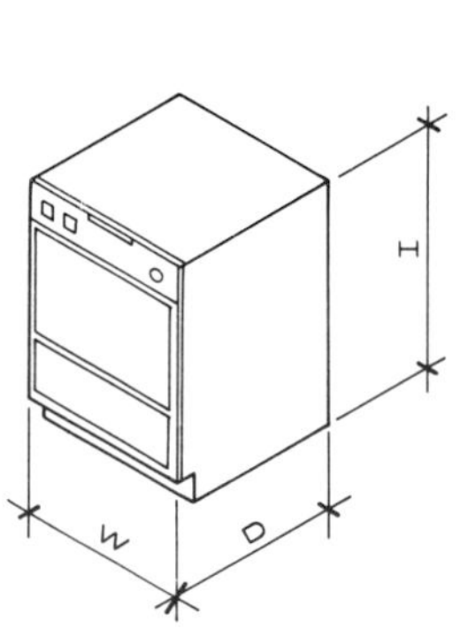
H
W
D

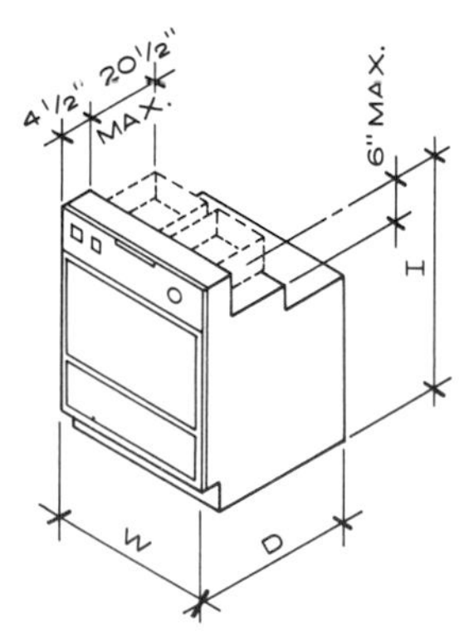
4 1/2" 20 1/2" MAX.
6" MAX.
H
W
D

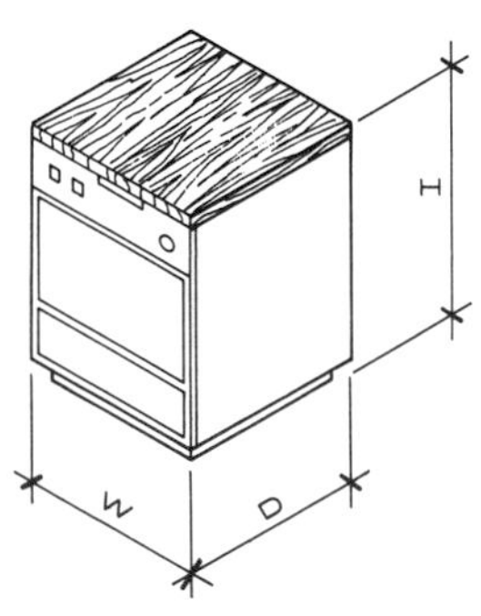
H
W
D

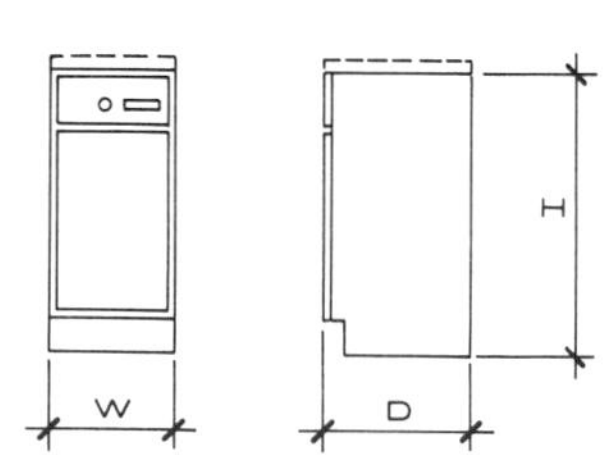
H
W
D

AUTOMATIC DISHWASHERS

UNDER COUNTER

	MIN.	MAX.	OTHER
W	23	24	23 7/8
D	23 11/16	26 1/4	25 1/2
H	33 1/2	34 1/2	34 1/8

UNDER SINK

	MIN.	MAX.	OTHER
W	24	24 1/4	24
D	24	25 1/2	25
H	34 1/2	34 1/2	34 1/2

MOBILE (WITH COUNTER TOP)

	MIN.	MAX.	OTHER
W	22 1/2	27	24 5/8
D	23 11/16	26 1/2	25
H	34 1/8	39	36

TRASH COMPACTOR: UNDER COUNTER OR FREESTANDING

	MIN.	MAX.	OTHER
W	11 7/8	17 3/4	14 7/8
D	18	24 3/16	18 1/4
H	33 1/2	35	34 1/2

William G. Miner, AIA, Architect; Washington, D.C.
R. E. Powe, Jr., AIA; Hugh Newell Jacobsen, FAIA; Washington, D.C.

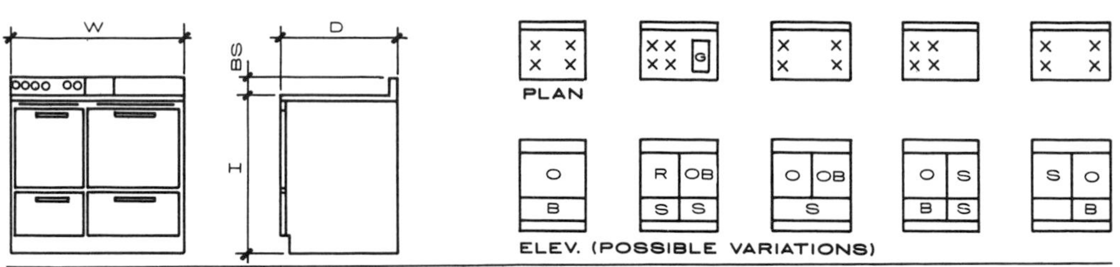
W
D
BS
H
PLAN
O
B
R
OB
S
G
ELEV. (POSSIBLE VARIATIONS)

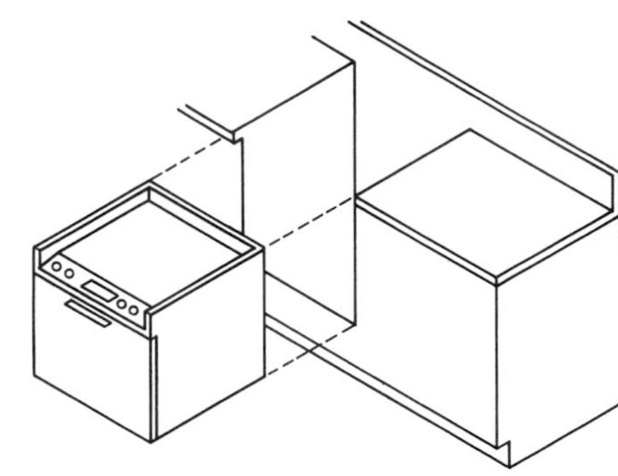

STANDARD RANGE (FREE STANDING)

ONE OVEN-FOUR UNITS

	MIN.	MAX.	OTHER
W	19 1/2	40	21-30
D	24 1/4	27 1/2	25-26 1/4
H	35 1/8	36 1/8	35 1/4-36
BS	4 11/16	12 1/2	8 1/4-11 1/2

TWO OVENS FOUR UNITS

	MIN.	MAX.	OTHER
W	40		
D	25	27 1/2	25 1/2-26 1/4
H	35 1/8	36	35 1/4
BS	8 1/4	11 1/8	8 1/8-10 3/8

SYMBOLS
O-OVEN
B-BROILER
G-REVOLVING GRILL
X-BURNER, GAS OR ELECTRIC
W-WARMING OVEN
S-STORAGE
R-ROTISSERIE

DROP-IN RANGE

	MIN.	MAX.	OTHER
W	22 7/8	30	23 7/8
D	22 1/8	25	22 1/2 24
H	23	24 1/16	23 1/2

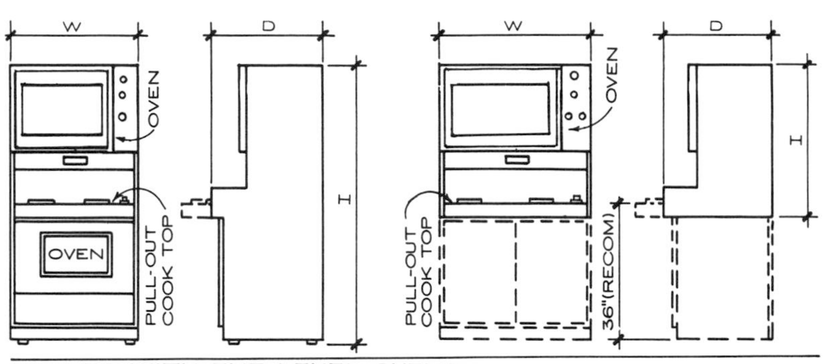
W
D
H
OVEN
PULL-OUT COOK TOP
36"(RECOM)

RANGES WITH EYE LEVEL OVENS

DOUBLE OVEN-4 UNITS

	MIN.	MAX.	OTHER
W	29 7/8	30	
D	25 1/2	27 5/8	25 5/8-27 1/2
H	61 1/2	71 1/4	63 3/4-67 7/16

SINGLE OVEN TOP ONLY-4 UNITS

	MIN.	MAX.	OTHER
W	29 13/16	38 7/8	29 7/8
D	25 1/2	27 5/8	27 1/4
H	33 1/2	41 1/16	36 3/4

DOUBLE OVEN TOP ONLY-4 UNITS

	MIN.	MAX.	OTHER
W	39	40 1/4	40
D	25 1/2	27 5/8	26 3/4
H	34 7/8	36 3/4	

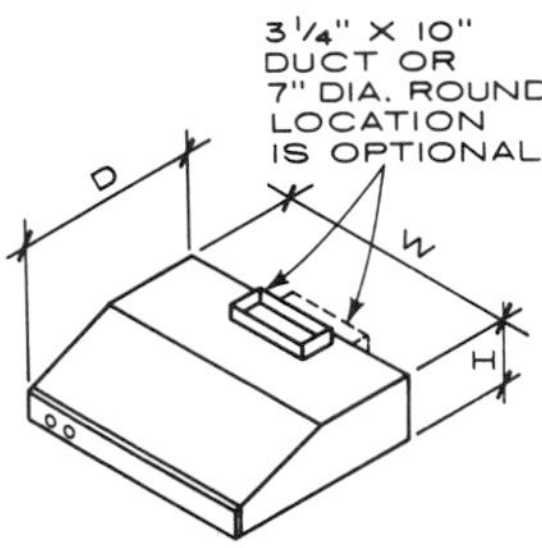
3 1/4" X 10" DUCT OR 7" DIA. ROUND LOCATION IS OPTIONAL
D
W
H

Range hoods are available with vents as shown or without vent. Manufacturers provide accessories such as fans, filters, and lights.

RANGE HOOD

	MIN.	MAX.	OTHER
W	24	72	30-66
D	12	27 1/2	17-26
H	5 1/2	8 5/8	5 5/8-7 1/2

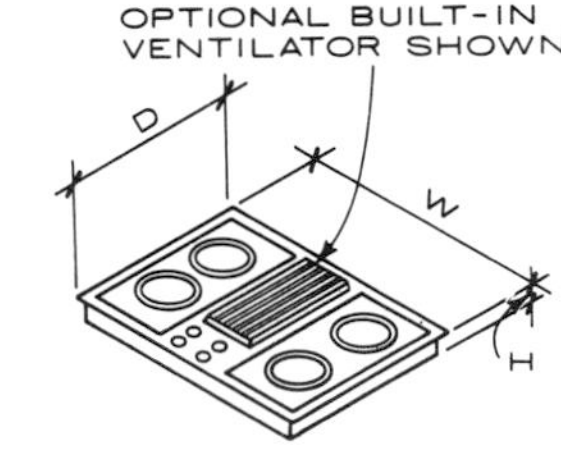
OPTIONAL BUILT-IN VENTILATOR SHOWN
D
W
H

Cook tops are available with two to seven heating elements. Griddles, grills, and built-in ventilators are optional.

BUILT-IN COOK TOP ELECTRIC OR GAS

	MIN.	MAX.
W	12	48
D	18	22
H	2	3

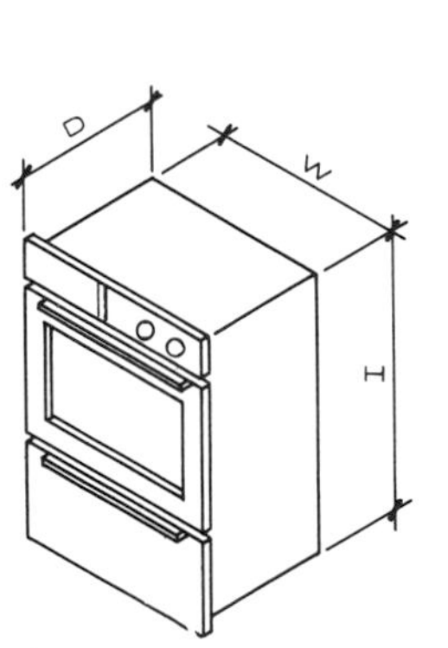
D
W
H

OVEN AND BROILER

	MIN.	MAX.	OTHER
W	21	24 1/4	22 1/2-24
D	21 1/8	24	22 1/2-22 11/16
H	38	40 7/16	40 3/16

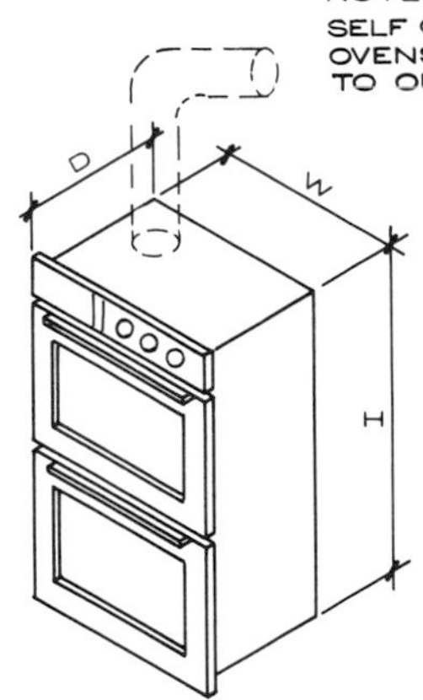
NOTE
SELF CLEANING OVENS MUST VENT TO OUTSIDE
D
W
H

DOUBLE OVEN

	MIN.	MAX.	OTHER
W	21	24 1/4	22 1/2-24
D	21 1/8	24	22 1/2-22 11/16
H	39 1/4	50 3/8	42-46 13/16

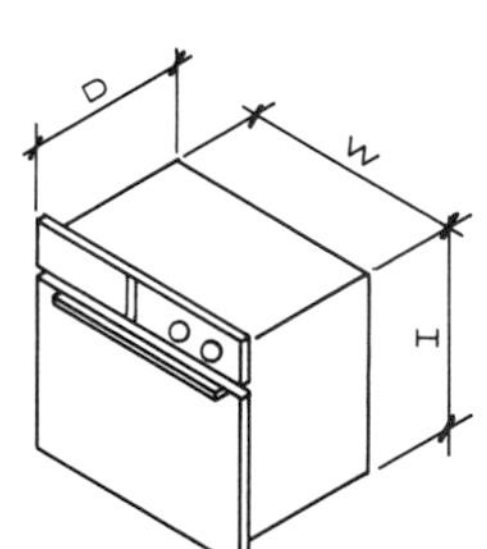
D
W
H

SINGLE OVEN

	MIN.	MAX.	OTHER
W	21	24 1/4	22 1/2-24
D	21 1/8	24	22 1/2-22 11/16
H	23 1/2	26 7/8	25

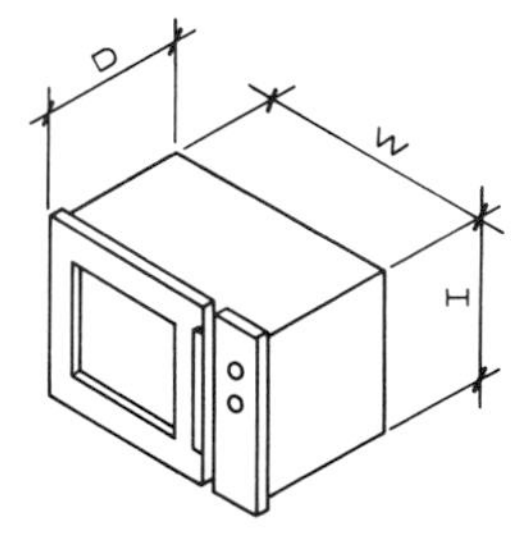
D
W
H

MICROWAVE OVEN

	MIN.	MAX.	OTHER
W	21 1/2	24 3/4	22 1/2
D	14 1/2	22	18 3/4
H	13 5/8	18	17

BUILT-IN WALL OVENS (GAS OR ELECTRIC)

NOTES

1. Check manufacturers requirements for rough clearances.
2. Dimensions shown are in inches.
3. Optional equipment available for ranges or wall ovens are broilers and rotisseries.

William G. Miner, AIA, Architect; Washington, D.C.
R. E. Powe, Jr., AIA; Hugh Newell Jacobsen, FAIA; Washington, D.C.

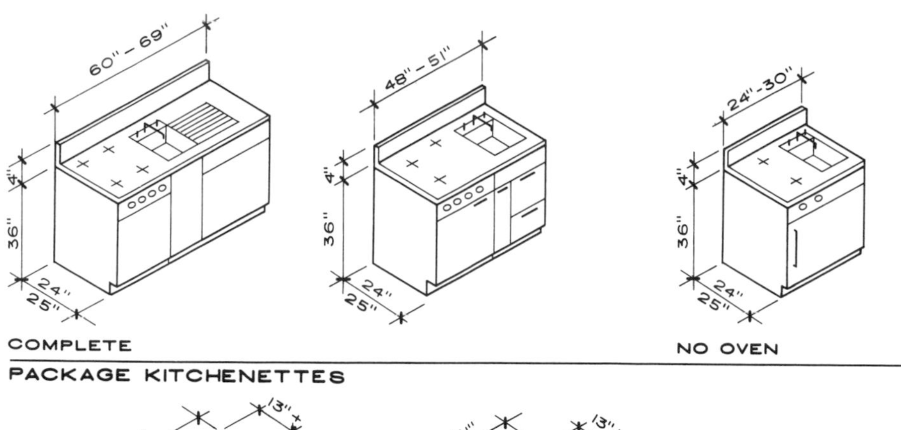
60" - 69"
48" - 51"
24" - 30"
4"
36"
24"
25"
COMPLETE
NO OVEN

PACKAGE KITCHENETTES

60", 69"
48" - 51"
39"
13"
30"
24", 30"
51"
36"
36" - 38"
24"
25"
REF.
COMPLETE
NO OVEN

KITCHENETTE UNITS

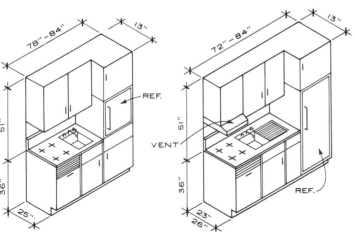

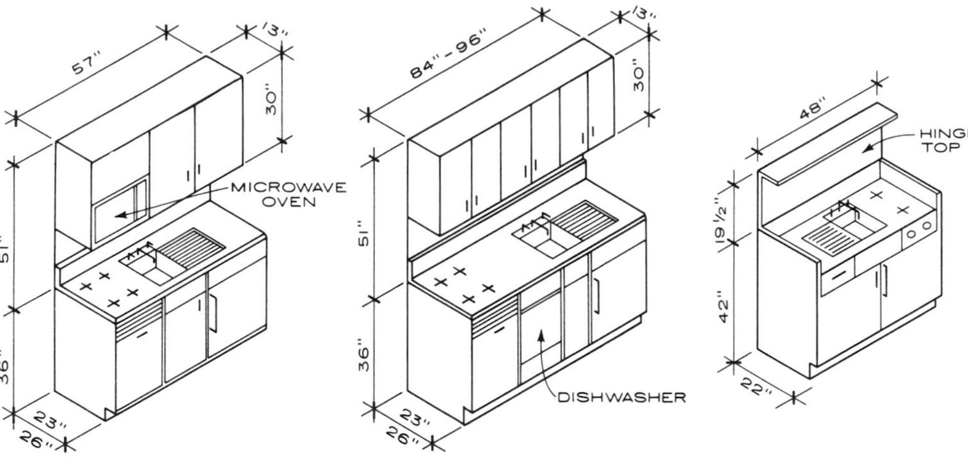
57"
84" - 96"
48"
13"
30"
51"
36"
19 1/2"
42"
23"
26"
22"
MICROWAVE OVEN
DISHWASHER
HINGED TOP

78" - 84"
72" - 84"
13"
51"
36"
25"
23"
26"
REF.
VENT

SPECIAL KITCHENETTE UNITS

NOTE

See manufacturers' catalogues for actual dimensions of specific units which may include: number of burners, size of refrigerator, size of sink, finish materials, and options such as garbage disposer, range hood, microwave oven, ice maker, dishwasher, or freezer.

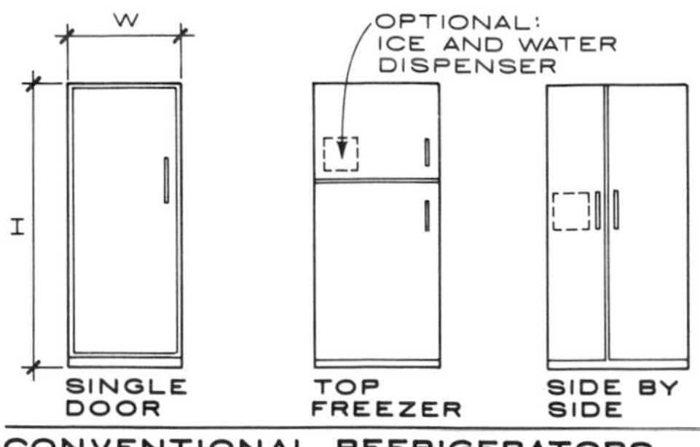
W
H
OPTIONAL: ICE AND WATER DISPENSER
SINGLE DOOR
TOP FREEZER
SIDE BY SIDE

CONVENTIONAL REFRIGERATORS

	MIN.	MAX.	MIN.	MAX.	MIN.	MAX.
W	24	32 3/4	28	32 3/4	30 1/2	35 3/4
D	26 9/16	31 5/8	28 3/4	31 5/8	29 1/2	32 7/8
H	55 1/2	63 1/2	—	66	64	68 7/8
cu ft	9.5	14.0	11.8	22.4	18.5	25.6

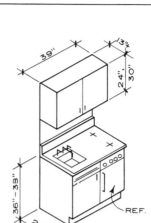

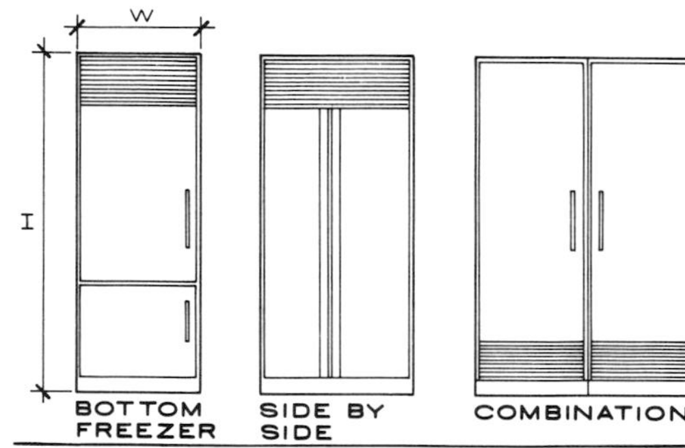
W
H
BOTTOM FREEZER
SIDE BY SIDE
COMBINATION

BUILT-IN REFRIGERATORS

	MIN.	MAX.	MIN.	MAX.	OVERALL
W	30	36	36	48	72
D	24	24	24	24	24
H	84	84	84	84	73
cu ft	19	23.6	24	32	42

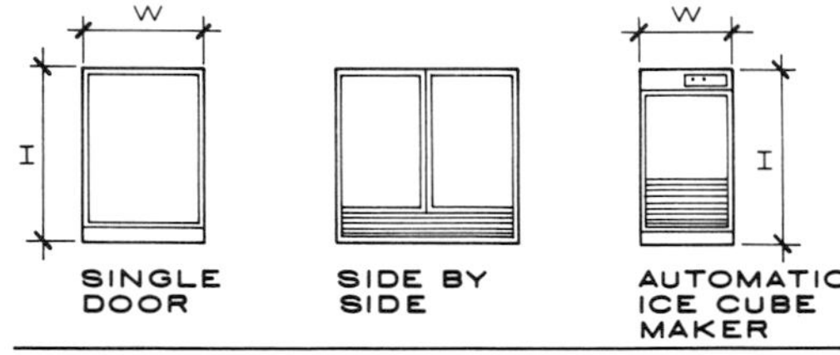
W
H
SINGLE DOOR
SIDE BY SIDE
AUTOMATIC ICE CUBE MAKER

UNDERCOUNTER REFRIGERATORS

	OVERALL	OVERALL	MIN.	MAX.
W	24	36	15	17 7/8
D	23 3/4	23 3/4	20 3/8	23 13/16
H	34 1/2	34 1/2	33 1/8	34 13/32
cu ft	5.2	6.0	35 lb of ice	

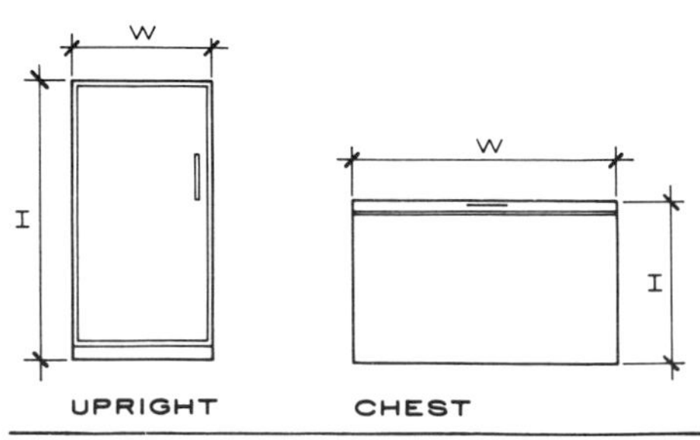
W
H
UPRIGHT
CHEST

FREEZERS

	MIN.	MAX.	MIN.	MAX.
W	28	32	25	69 1/2
D	28 7/8	30 11/16	23 1/4	31
H	59 1/8	70 1/8	34 11/16	35
cu ft	11.6	21.1		25.3

William G. Miner, AIA, Architect; Washington, D.C.

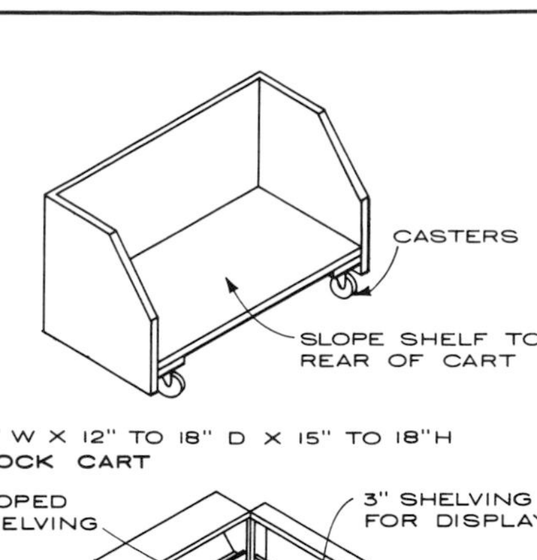
CASTERS
SLOPE SHELF TO REAR OF CART

24" W X 12" TO 18" D X 15" TO 18"H
BLOCK CART

SLOPED SHELVING
3" SHELVING FOR DISPLAY
10"SHELVING

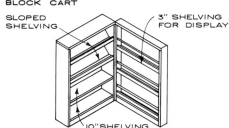

36" W X 52"H
FOLDING BOOKCASE

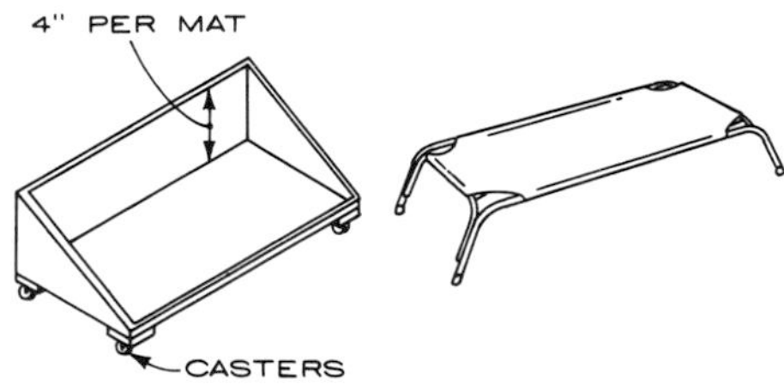

24" W X 3"D X 48"H SECTIONS
FOLDING BOOKSCREEN

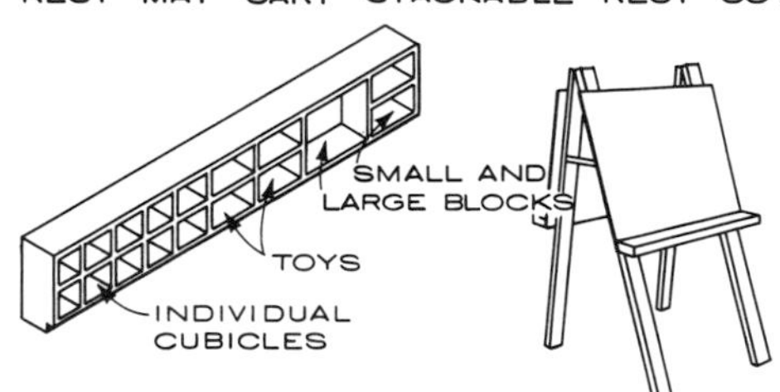
4" PER MAT
CASTERS

26"W X 14"D
REST MAT CART

22" TO 27"W X 54" TO 62"D X 12"H
STACKABLE REST COT

SMALL AND LARGE BLOCKS
TOYS
INDIVIDUAL CUBICLES

12" TO 18"D X 24"H
BUILT-IN STORAGE CUBICLES

FLOOR EASEL

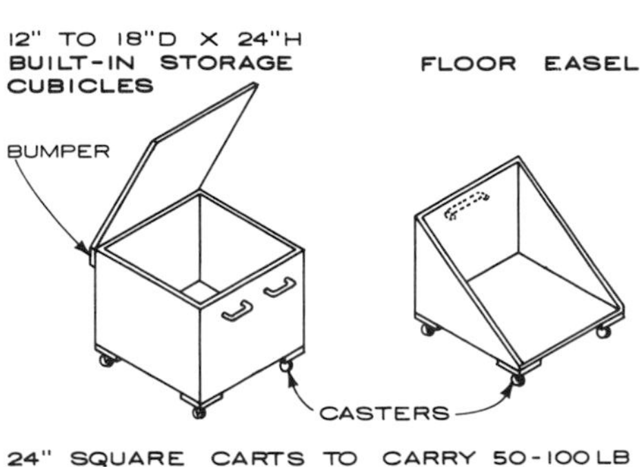
BUMPER
CASTERS

24" SQUARE CARTS TO CARRY 50-100 LB
CLAY CART

UNDERCOUNTER CLAY CART

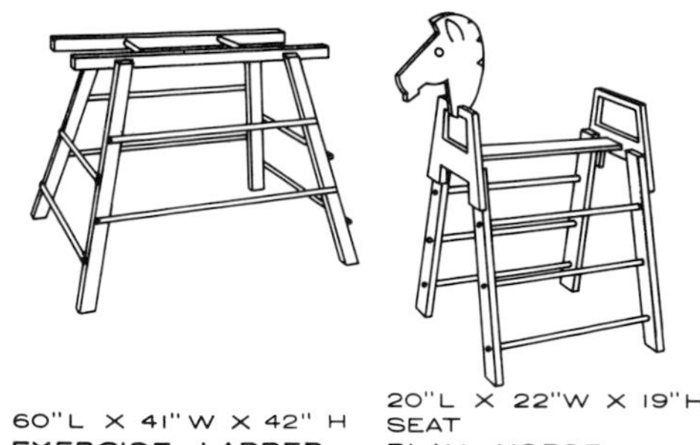

60"L X 41"W X 42" H
EXERCISE LADDER

20"L X 22"W X 19"H SEAT
PLAY HORSE

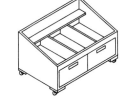

44"L X 20"W X 26"H
WORKBENCH

30"W X 24"D X 18" X 24"H
CARPENTRY TOOL CART

LARGE INSTRUMENT STORAGE
RECORD STORAGE
CASSETTE AND CASSETTE PLAYER STORAGE
RUBBER TIRES
SMALL INSTRUMENT STORAGE

54"W X 18"D X 28"H
MUSIC CART

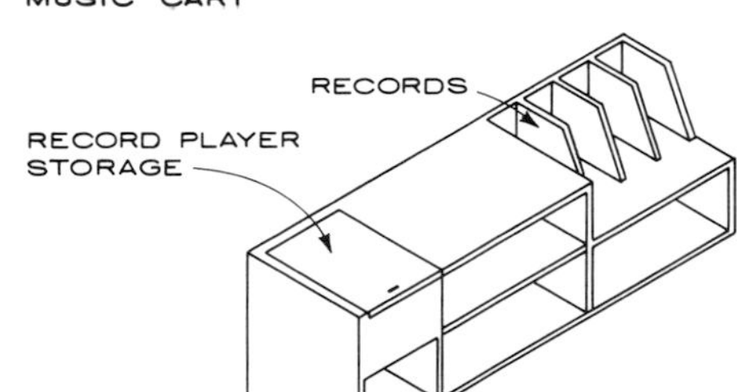
RECORDS
RECORD PLAYER STORAGE

20"D X 24"H
RECORD PLAYER AND STORAGE UNIT

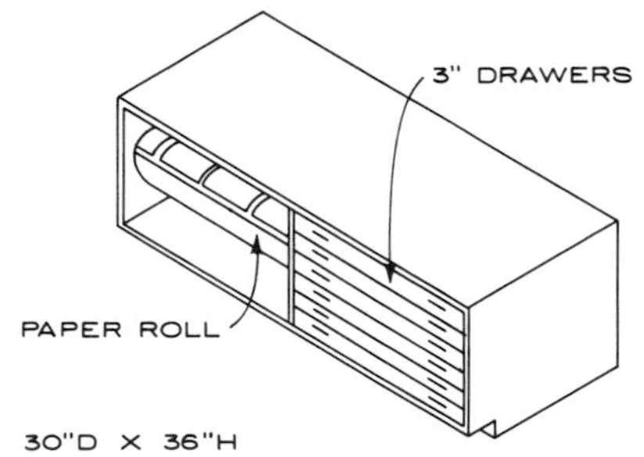
3" DRAWERS
PAPER ROLL

30"D X 36"H
PAPER STORAGE UNIT

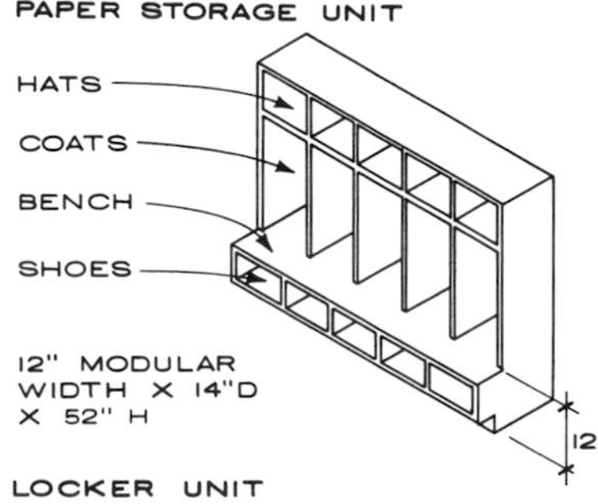
HATS
COATS
BENCH
SHOES
12"

12" MODULAR WIDTH X 14"D X 52" H
LOCKER UNIT

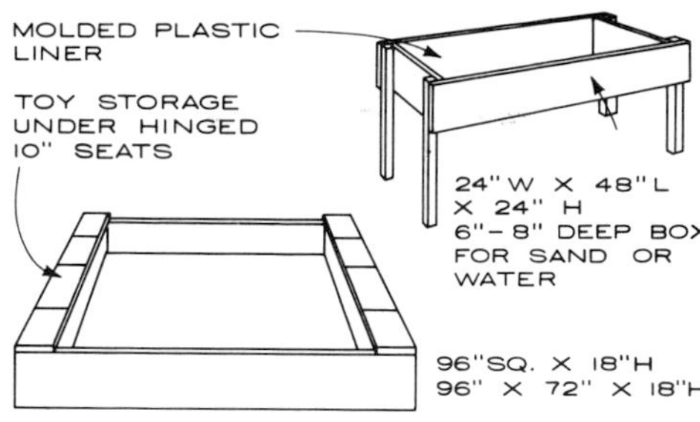
MOLDED PLASTIC LINER
TOY STORAGE UNDER HINGED 10" SEATS
24"W X 48"L X 24" H
6"–8" DEEP BOX FOR SAND OR WATER
96"SQ. X 18"H
96" X 72" X 18"H

SANDBOXES

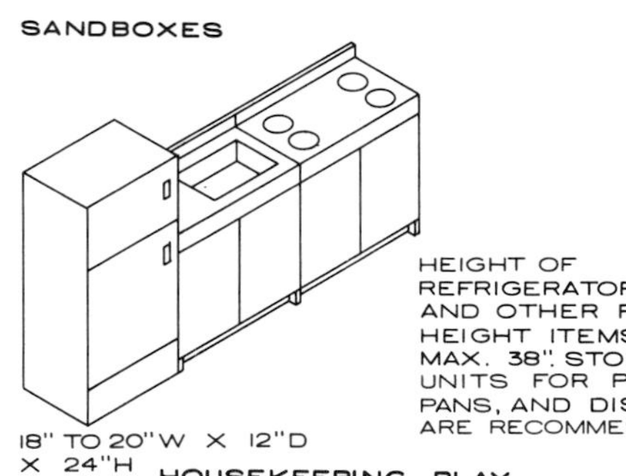
HEIGHT OF REFRIGERATOR AND OTHER FULL HEIGHT ITEMS MAX. 38". STORAGE UNITS FOR POTS, PANS, AND DISHES ARE RECOMMENDED

18" TO 20"W X 12"D X 24"H
HOUSEKEEPING PLAY

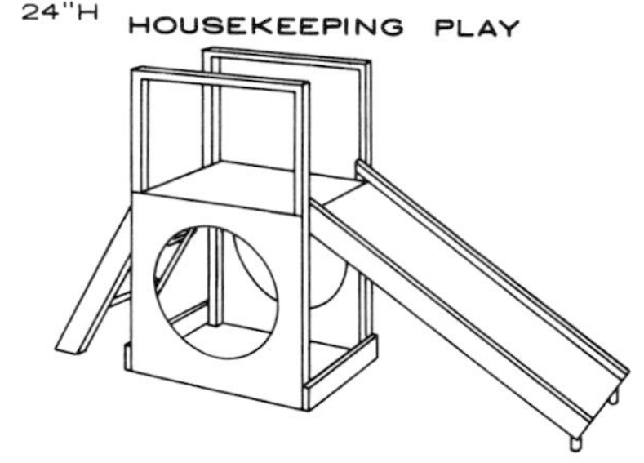

62"L X 24"W X 36"H
INDOOR SLIDE

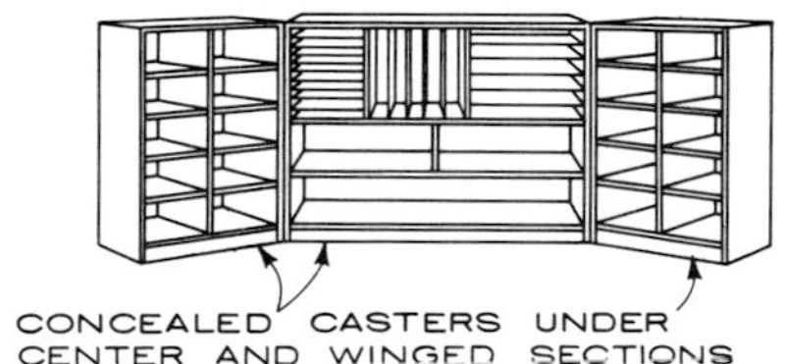
SHELVES MOVABLE IN 2" INTERVALS
CONCEALED CASTERS UNDER CENTER AND WINGED SECTIONS

46"W (CLOSED) X 14"D X 34"H
FOLDING STORAGE UNIT

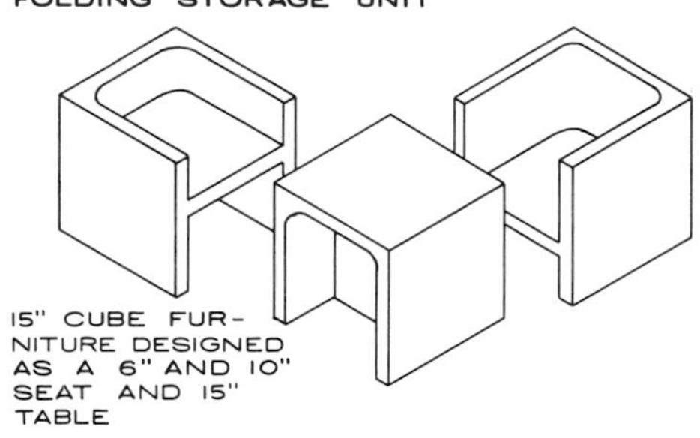

15" CUBE FURNITURE DESIGNED AS A 6" AND 10" SEAT AND 15" TABLE
PRESCHOOL AND KINDERGARTEN SEATING

GENERAL CHAIR AND TABLE REQUIREMENTS

	CHAIR SEAT HEIGHT				TABLE HEIGHT
AGE OF CHILD	8″	10″	12″	14″	
2 years	80%	20%			–
3 years	40%	50%	10%		18″
4 years		25%	75%		20″
5 years			75%	25%	22″

Kent Wong; Hewlett, Jamison, Atkinson & Luey; Portland, Oregon

REFERENCES

DATA SOURCES: ORGANIZATIONS

Carr Craft Manufacturing Company, 354
Community Playthings, 357
Creative Playthings, 357
Dwyer Products Corporation, 356
General Electric Company, 354–356
Herman Miller, Inc., 352, 353
Jenn-Air Corporation, 355
Learning World, Inc., 357
Library Bureau, Inc., Catalog LB-76, 352, 353
Library Bureau, Inc., Steel Book Stack Catalog, 352
Sub-Zero Freezer Company, 356
Westinghouse Electric Corporation, 354–356

CHAPTER 12

FURNISHINGS

OVERFILE STORAGE

TYPE	W	H	D	WEIGHT*
Over 2-drawer letter	30	26 or 37	29	170
Over 2-drawer legal	36		29	308
Over 3-drawer letter	43		29	377
Over 3-drawer legal	54		29	445

VERTICAL FILES

TYPE	W	H	D	WEIGHT*
5-drawer letter	15	60	29	405
5-drawer legal	18	60	29	430
4-drawer letter	15	50	29	324
4-drawer legal	18	50	29	344
3-drawer letter	15	41	29	258
3-drawer legal	18	41	29	162
2-drawer letter	15	30	29	162
2-drawer legal	18	30	29	172

INSIDE DRAWER DIMENSIONS

TYPE	W	H	D
Letter	12¼	10½	26¾
Legal	15¼	10½	26¾

*Weights = fully loaded file.

PLANNING

1. Users' filing needs should be tabulated in inches and in turn converted into number of cabinets. Consult manufacturer for inches available in specific cabinets.
2. For open space planning, the following square footage allowances should be used:

TYPES	SPACE ALLOWANCE (FT^2)
Vertical and 36 in. lateral files	10
Lateral file for computer printout	15

NOTE: All dimensions shown are approximate. Consult manufacturer for actual dimensions.

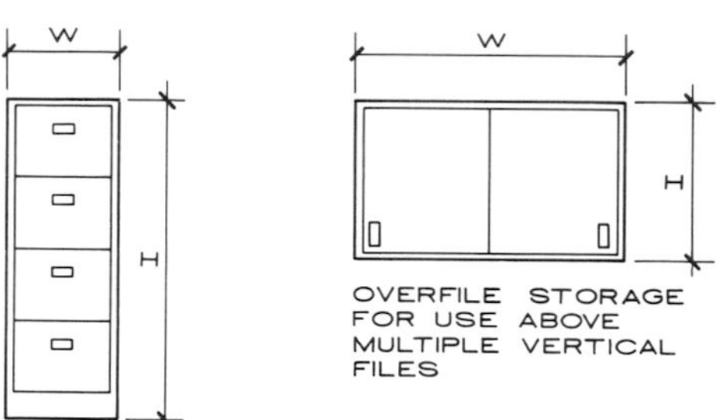
W
H
W
H
OVERFILE STORAGE FOR USE ABOVE MULTIPLE VERTICAL FILES

VERTICAL FILE CABINETS

FILE CLEARANCES

	VERTICAL FILES	LATERAL FILES
A	106–120	82–94
B	29	18
C	48–62	46–58
D	18–26	16–22
E	30–36	30–36

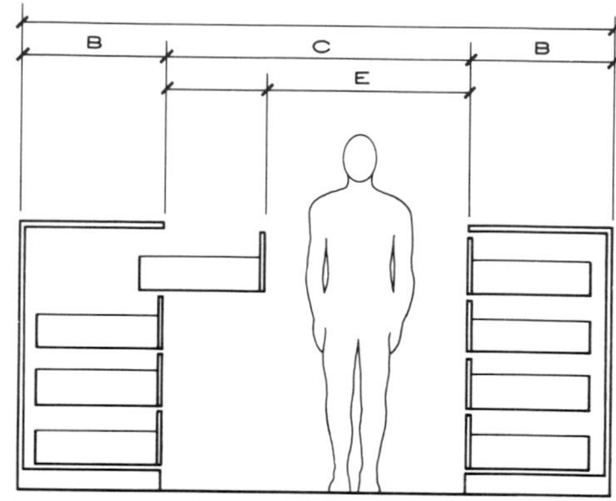
B
C
B
E
DIMENSIONS FOR PLANNING

LATERAL FILES

TYPE	W	H	D	WEIGHT*
5-drawer	30, 36, 42	64	18	610-843
4-drawer	30-36-42	52	18	524-720
3-drawer	30, 36, 42	40	18	401-553
2-drawer	30, 36, 42	32	18	285-391

*Weights = fully loaded file.

STANDARD

COMPUTER PRINTOUT

NOTES

1. Basic types accommodate multiple configurations of drawers, doors, and shelves.
2. 6 in. drawer accommodates cards and vouchers not exceeding 5 in. in one direction.
3. 12 in. drawer accommodates letter and legal files.
4. 15 in. drawer accommodates computer printouts.
5. Files are available to five-drawer height. Files more than five drawers high are not recommended.
6. Typical overfile storage is 26 or 37 in. high.

LATERAL FILE CABINETS

SPECIAL FILES

TYPE	W	H	D
A. Custom stack system	36	52	18
B. Check file	15	52	27
C. Special/double check	22	52	27
D. Card record file	22	52	27
6 drawer (3 × 5, 4 × 6 cards)	22	52	27
5 drawer (3 × 5, 4 × 6, 5 × 8)	22	52	27
E. Pedestal file	16	28	24
Library card file (see index)			

A

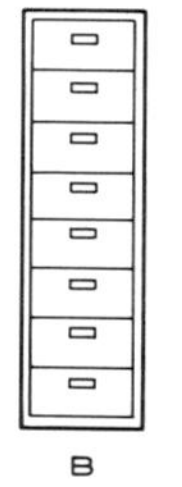
B

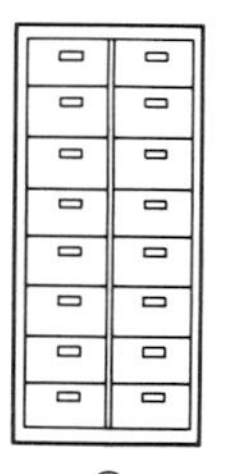
C

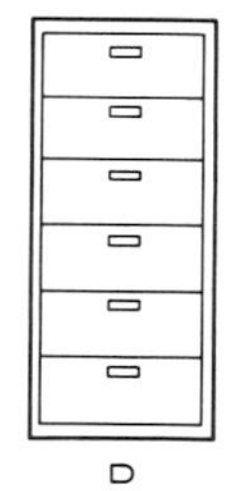
D

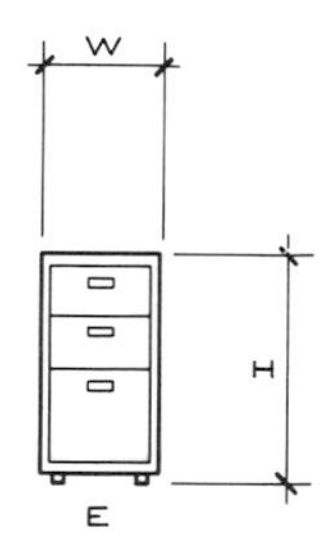
W
H
E

SPECIAL FILING CABINETS

FIRE INSULATED FILES

TYPE	W	H	D	WEIGHT*
4-drawer letter	17	52	30	600
4-drawer legal	20	52	30	660
3-drawer letter	17	51	30	465
3-drawer legal	20	41	30	515
2-drawer letter	17	28	30	330
2-drawer legal	20	28	30	370
3-drawer lateral	39	56	24	1220
2-drawer lateral	39	39	24	875

*Weight = fully loaded.

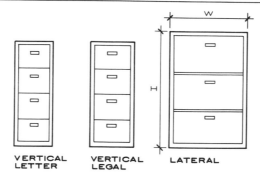

VERTICAL LETTER

VERTICAL LEGAL

LATERAL

FIRE INSULATED FILE CABINETS

These units are designed to resist forced entry and are fabricated from heavy gauge steel plate. They are available only in legal size vertical format and are essentially the same size as fire insulated cabinets. They are available with or without fire protection.

SECURITY FILES

TYPE	WEIGHT*
5-drawer	1350
5-drawer fire insulated	1650
4-drawer	1050
4-drawer fire insulated	1400
2-drawer	650
2-drawer fire insulated	825

*Weight = fully loaded

SECURITY FILE CABINETS

Associated Space Design, Inc.; Atlanta, Georgia

DESIGN RATIONALE

Systems furniture is designed primarily for utilization in an open office plan which uses few fixed floor-to-ceiling partitions as compared to conventional office layouts. Open office planning receives its impetus from its ability to respond to requirements for increased flexibility and lower long term expenses. Some of the major areas of response are the following:

1. FLEXIBILITY OF PLANNING: Systems furniture in an open plan maximizes the efficient use of net plannable space. This is the result of the use of more vertical space without fixed floor-to-ceiling partitions, thereby freeing floor area and reducing space planning inefficiencies.
2. FLEXIBILITY OF FUNCTION: Systems furniture allows individual workstation modification so that workstation design can reflect functional requirements of the task performed. In this way, changes in function can be accommodated without total furniture replacement.
3. FLEXIBILITY OF PLAN MODIFICATION: Systems furniture in open office planning allows institutions to respond more easily to organizational changes of size, structure, and function. Open planning allows institutions to respond to change at lower cost by reducing expenses related to partition relocation, HVAC modification, lighting relocation, construction, and moving time.

NOTES

1. Any open office plan as commonly applied will utilize some enclosed spaces having fixed, floor-to-ceiling partitions.
2. Systems furniture requires careful planning and engineering consultation to achieve the maximum functional advantage.
3. Systems furniture components are not compatible from one manufacturer to another regardless of generic type.
4. The generic types listed below are broad classifications for descriptive purposes only.

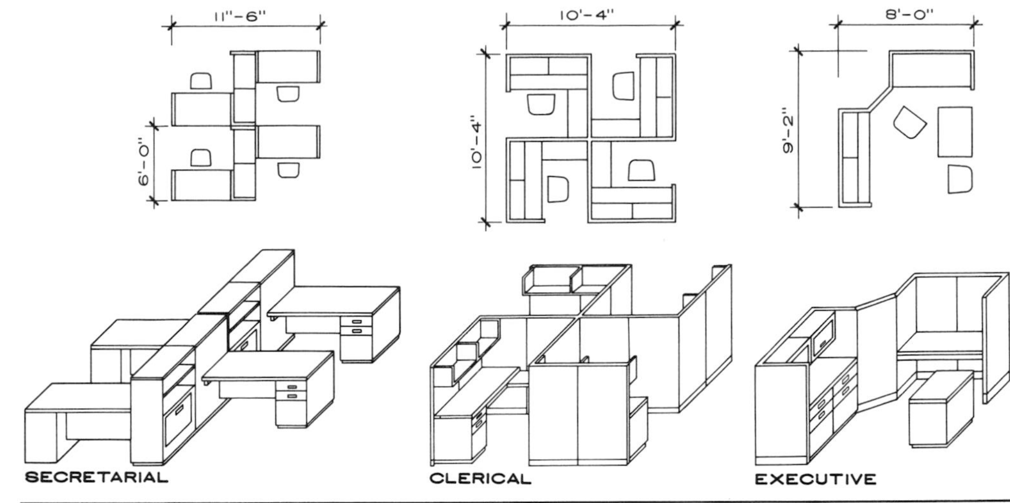
11'-6"
6'-0"
10'-4"
10'-4"
8'-0"
9'-2"
SECRETARIAL
CLERICAL
EXECUTIVE

CONFIGURATIONS

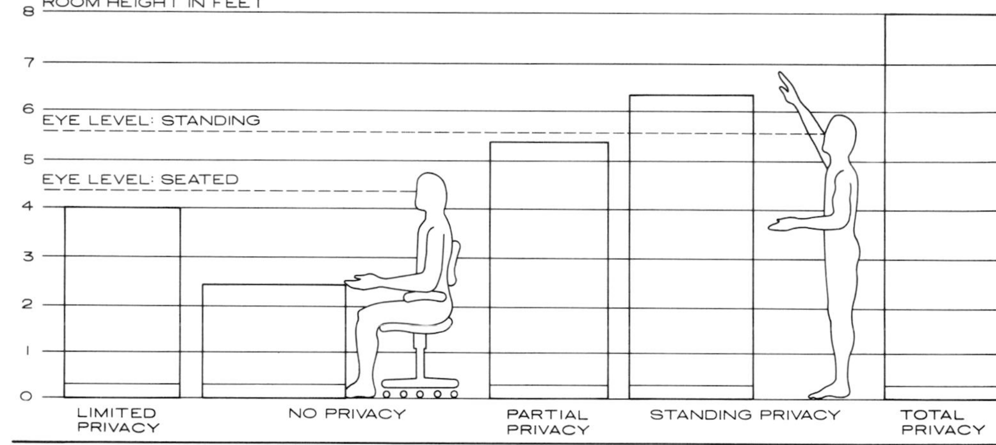
ROOM HEIGHT IN FEET
8
7
6
EYE LEVEL: STANDING
5
EYE LEVEL: SEATED
4
3
2
1
0
LIMITED PRIVACY
NO PRIVACY
PARTIAL PRIVACY
STANDING PRIVACY
TOTAL PRIVACY

RELATIONSHIP OF PANEL HEIGHT TO PRIVACY

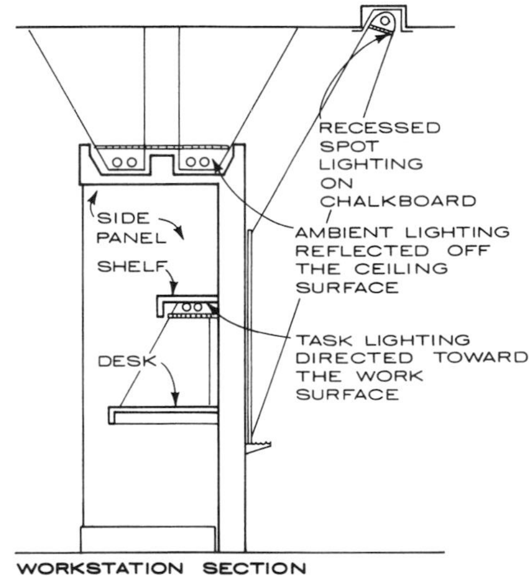
RECESSED SPOT LIGHTING ON CHALKBOARD
SIDE PANEL
SHELF
AMBIENT LIGHTING REFLECTED OFF THE CEILING SURFACE
DESK
TASK LIGHTING DIRECTED TOWARD THE WORK SURFACE

WORKSTATION SECTION

INTEGRATED LIGHTING

Artificial lighting is integrated into most open office furniture systems. The components consist of task oriented downlights located directly over work surfaces, which provide the user with control of intensity and direction of light. Uplights are mounted in the top of workstations to provide indirect light reflected off the ceiling to the ambient surroundings.

Task/ambient lighting provides more flexibility than do standard ceiling mounted fixtures. It can reduce energy consumption by decreasing general light levels and utilizing more efficient light sources. It can also improve acoustics, since fewer fixtures are installed in the acoustical ceiling.

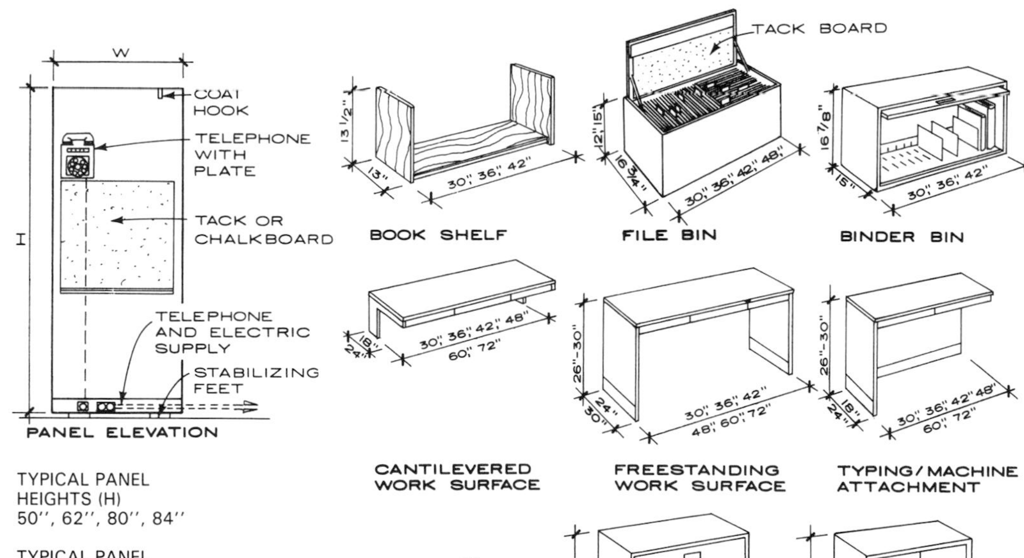
W
COAT HOOK
TELEPHONE WITH PLATE
H
TACK OR CHALKBOARD
TELEPHONE AND ELECTRIC SUPPLY
STABILIZING FEET
PANEL ELEVATION
13 1/2"
13"
30", 36", 42"
BOOK SHELF
TACK BOARD
12", 15"
16 3/4"
30", 36", 42", 48"
FILE BIN
16 7/8"
15"
30", 36", 42"
BINDER BIN
18", 24"
30", 36", 42", 48"
60", 72"
CANTILEVERED WORK SURFACE
26"-30"
24", 30"
30", 36", 42"
48", 60", 72"
FREESTANDING WORK SURFACE
26"-30"
18", 24"
30", 36", 42", 48"
60", 72"
TYPING/MACHINE ATTACHMENT

TYPICAL PANEL HEIGHTS (H)
50'', 62'', 80'', 84''

TYPICAL PANEL WIDTHS (W)
12'', 24'', 30'', 36'', 48''

PANEL FINISH OPTIONS
Plastic laminate
Wood veneer
Tempered safety glass
Acoustical fabric

NOTE: Consult manufacturer for specific sizes and finishes available.

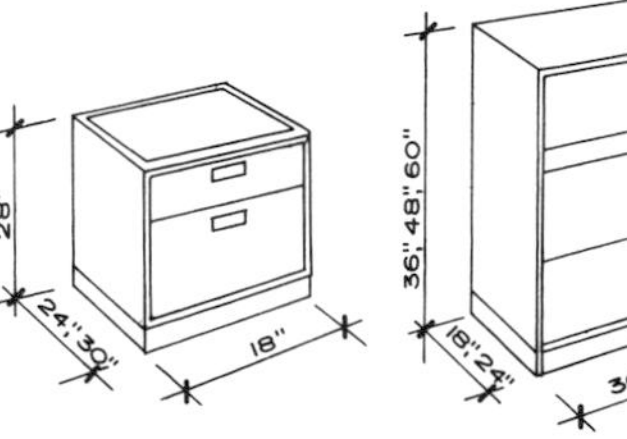
28"
24", 30"
18"
DRAWER BASE
36", 48", 60"
18", 24"
30", 36", 42"
FILE CASE

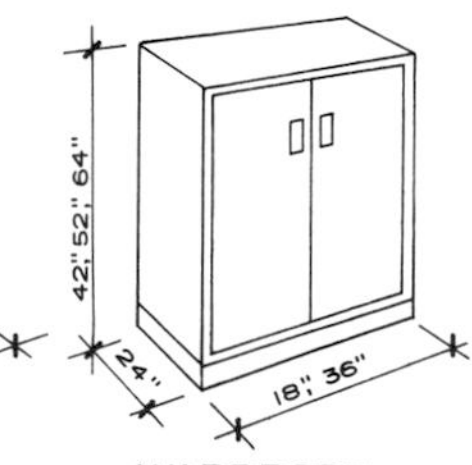
42", 52", 64"
24"
18", 36"
WARDROBE

SYSTEMS FURNITURE COMPONENTS

Interspace Incorporated; Washington, D.C.

TILT 90°

37"

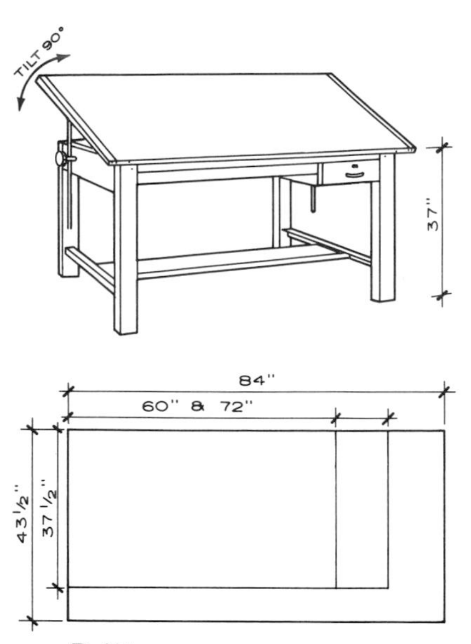
84"
60" & 72"
43 1/2"
37 1/2"
PLAN

Drafting and/or engineering table is available in wood, in steel, or in combination. Various drawer and pedestal arrangements are available.

DRAFTING TABLE WITH ADJUSTABLE TOP

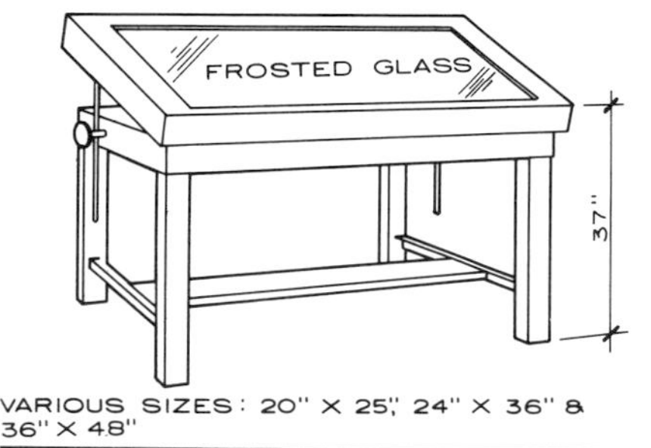
FROSTED GLASS
37"

VARIOUS SIZES: 20" X 25", 24" X 36" & 36" X 48"

FLUORESCENT TRACING TABLE

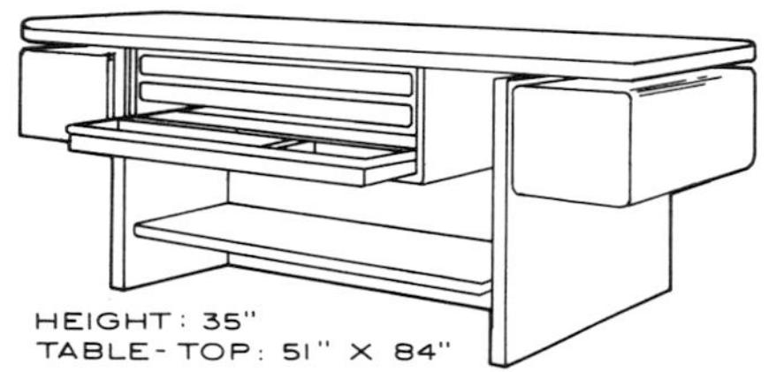
HEIGHT: 35"
TABLE-TOP: 51" X 84"

Service table provides a large worktop and integral storage compartments. Entire offices can be furnished with coordinated units.

SERVICE TABLE

TILT 15°

PENCIL TRAY

FOOTREST

29" OR 41" ADJUSTABLE

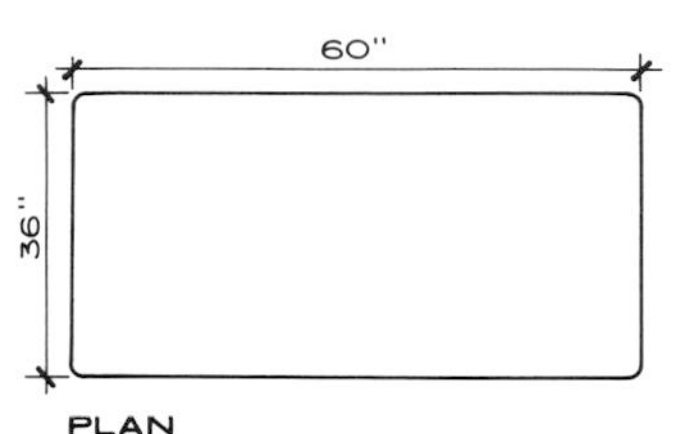
60"
36"
PLAN

ADJUSTABLE WORKING SURFACE

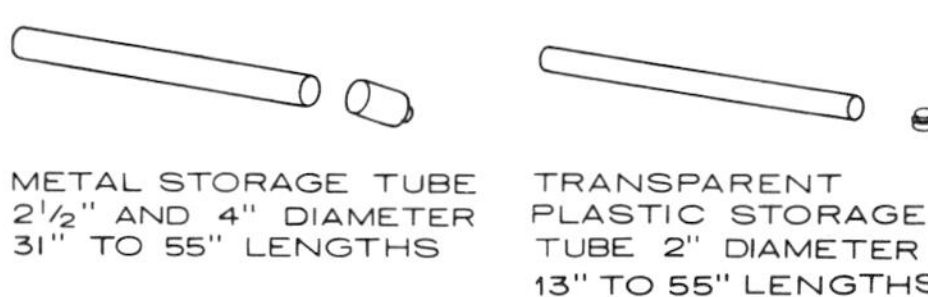

METAL STORAGE TUBE 2 1/2" AND 4" DIAMETER 31" TO 55" LENGTHS

TRANSPARENT PLASTIC STORAGE TUBE 2" DIAMETER 13" TO 55" LENGTHS

STORAGE TUBES

WALL MOUNTED DATA FILES 1 3/4" X 8" X 11 1/2" SHEET WIDTHS: 12" TO 48"

WALL MOUNTED RACK FILES FOR FRICTION TYPE BINDERS 18" TO 54" AT 6" INTERVALS

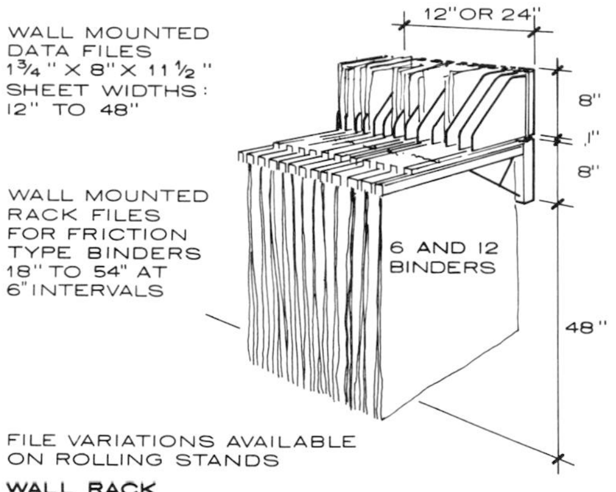
12" OR 24"
8"
1"
8"
6 AND 12 BINDERS
48"

FILE VARIATIONS AVAILABLE ON ROLLING STANDS

WALL RACK

ROTATES 360°

BOARD SIZES:
29.5" X 41.3" (75 X 105 CM)
31.5" X 47.3" (80 X 120 CM)
31.5" X 55" (80 X 140 CM)

ADJUSTABLE TILT TO 90°

ADJUSTABLE HEIGHT

Several manufacturers produce an array of drawing tables with adjustable tops, optional footrests, and pencil drawers.

COUNTERBALANCED AUTOMATIC DRAFTING TABLE

NO. OF TUBES: 27, 48, AND 108
SQ. TUBE SIZES: 4 1/2", 3 3/8", AND 2 1/8"

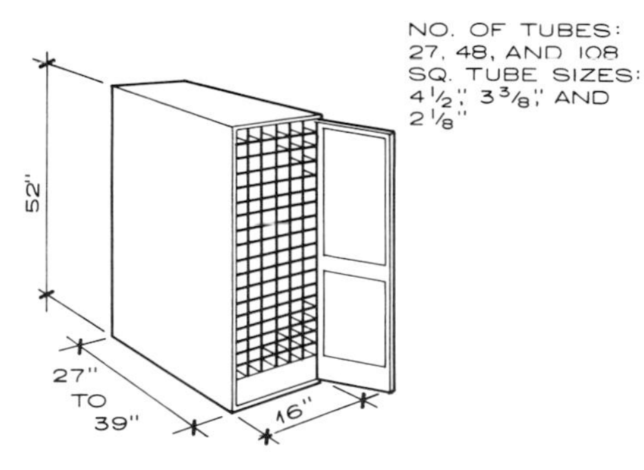
52"
27" TO 39"
16"

CABINET ROLL FILE

SHEET SIZES: LENGTH UP TO 52", WIDTH 18" TO 42"

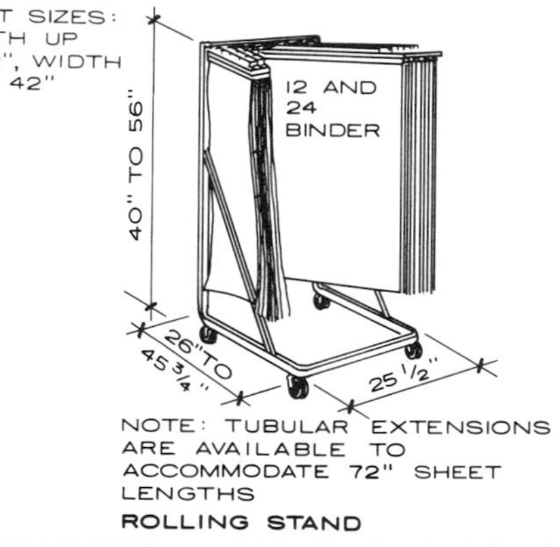
12 AND 24 BINDER
40" TO 56"
26" TO 45 3/4"
25 1/2"

NOTE: TUBULAR EXTENSIONS ARE AVAILABLE TO ACCOMMODATE 72" SHEET LENGTHS

ROLLING STAND

PIVOT FILING SYSTEM

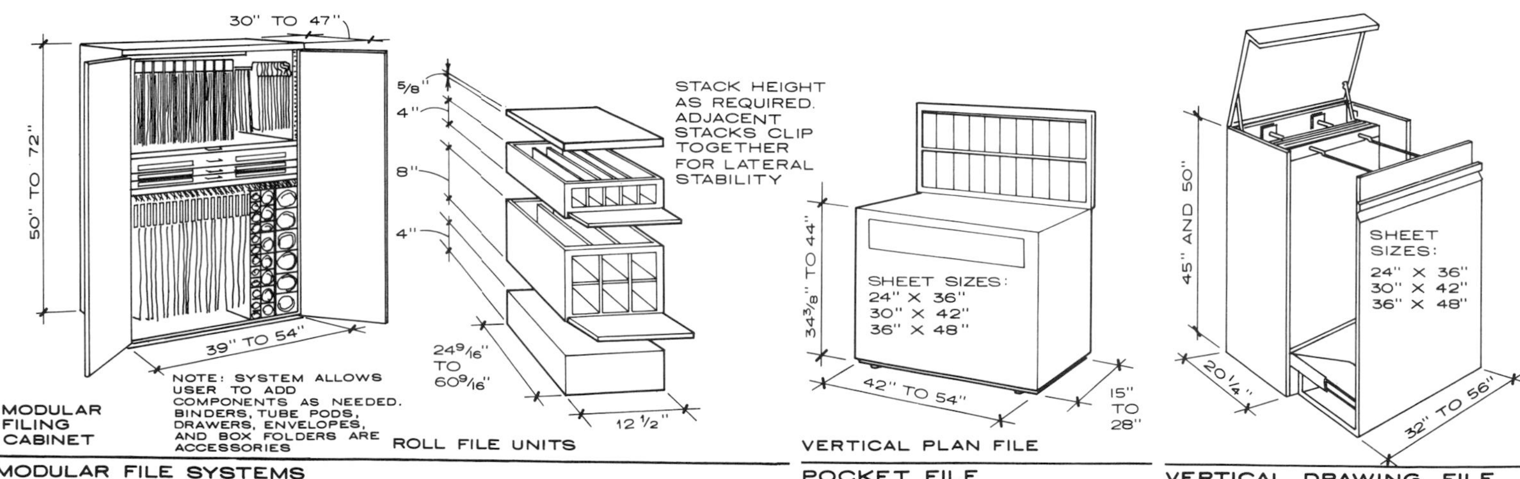
30" TO 47"
50" TO 72"
39" TO 54"
NOTE: SYSTEM ALLOWS USER TO ADD COMPONENTS AS NEEDED. BINDERS, TUBE PODS, DRAWERS, ENVELOPES, AND BOX FOLDERS ARE ACCESSORIES
MODULAR FILING CABINET
5/8"
4"
8"
4"
STACK HEIGHT AS REQUIRED. ADJACENT STACKS CLIP TOGETHER FOR LATERAL STABILITY
24 9/16" TO 60 9/16"
12 1/2"
ROLL FILE UNITS
34 3/8" TO 44"
SHEET SIZES:
24" X 36"
30" X 42"
36" X 48"
42" TO 54"
15" TO 28"
VERTICAL PLAN FILE
45" AND 50"
SHEET SIZES:
24" X 36"
30" X 42"
36" X 48"
20 1/4"
32" TO 56"

MODULAR FILE SYSTEMS

POCKET FILE

VERTICAL DRAWING FILE

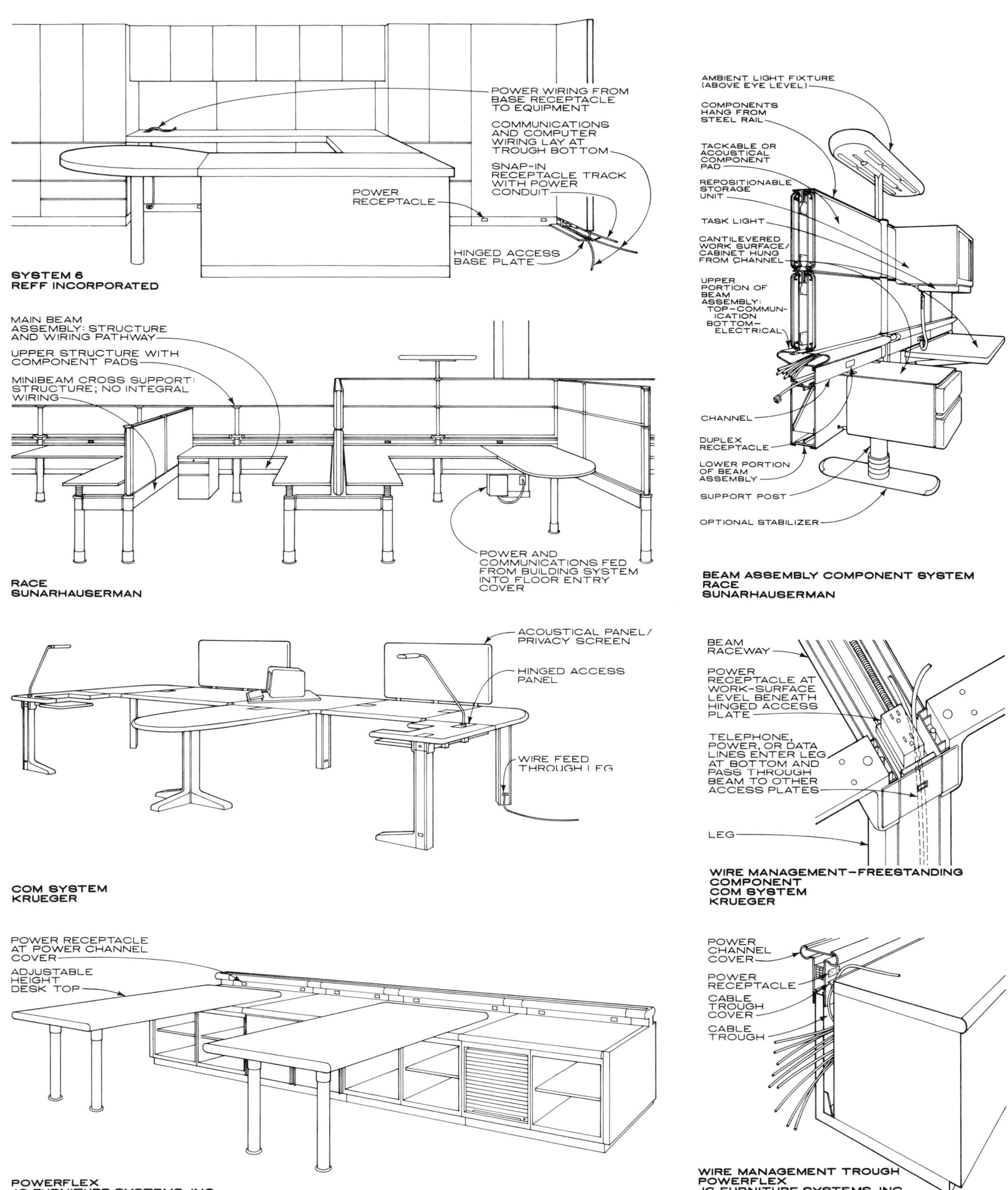
POWER WIRING FROM BASE RECEPTACLE TO EQUIPMENT
COMMUNICATIONS AND COMPUTER WIRING LAY AT TROUGH BOTTOM
SNAP-IN RECEPTACLE TRACK WITH POWER CONDUIT
POWER RECEPTACLE
HINGED ACCESS BASE PLATE
SYSTEM 6
REFF INCORPORATED
MAIN BEAM ASSEMBLY: STRUCTURE AND WIRING PATHWAY
UPPER STRUCTURE WITH COMPONENT PADS
MINIBEAM CROSS SUPPORT: STRUCTURE; NO INTEGRAL WIRING
POWER AND COMMUNICATIONS FED FROM BUILDING SYSTEM INTO FLOOR ENTRY COVER
RACE
SUNARHAUSERMAN
AMBIENT LIGHT FIXTURE (ABOVE EYE LEVEL)
COMPONENTS HANG FROM STEEL RAIL
TACKABLE OR ACOUSTICAL COMPONENT PAD
REPOSITIONABLE STORAGE UNIT
TASK LIGHT
CANTILEVERED WORK SURFACE/ CABINET HUNG FROM CHANNEL
UPPER PORTION OF BEAM ASSEMBLY: TOP-COMMUN- ICATION BOTTOM- ELECTRICAL
CHANNEL
DUPLEX RECEPTACLE
LOWER PORTION OF BEAM ASSEMBLY
SUPPORT POST
OPTIONAL STABILIZER
BEAM ASSEMBLY COMPONENT SYSTEM
RACE
SUNARHAUSERMAN
ACOUSTICAL PANEL/ PRIVACY SCREEN
HINGED ACCESS PANEL
WIRE FEED THROUGH LEG
COM SYSTEM
KRUEGER
BEAM RACEWAY
POWER RECEPTACLE AT WORK-SURFACE LEVEL BENEATH HINGED ACCESS PLATE
TELEPHONE, POWER, OR DATA LINES ENTER LEG AT BOTTOM AND PASS THROUGH BEAM TO OTHER ACCESS PLATES
LEG
WIRE MANAGEMENT—FREESTANDING COMPONENT
COM SYSTEM
KRUEGER
POWER RECEPTACLE AT POWER CHANNEL COVER
ADJUSTABLE HEIGHT DESK TOP
POWERFLEX
JG FURNITURE SYSTEMS, INC.
POWER CHANNEL COVER
POWER RECEPTACLE
CABLE TROUGH COVER
CABLE TROUGH
WIRE MANAGEMENT TROUGH
POWERFLEX
JG FURNITURE SYSTEMS, INC.

TYPICAL WIRE MANAGEMENT SYSTEMS

Robert Staples; Staples & Charles Ltd; Washington, D.C.
Richard J. Vitullo; Washington Grove, Maryland

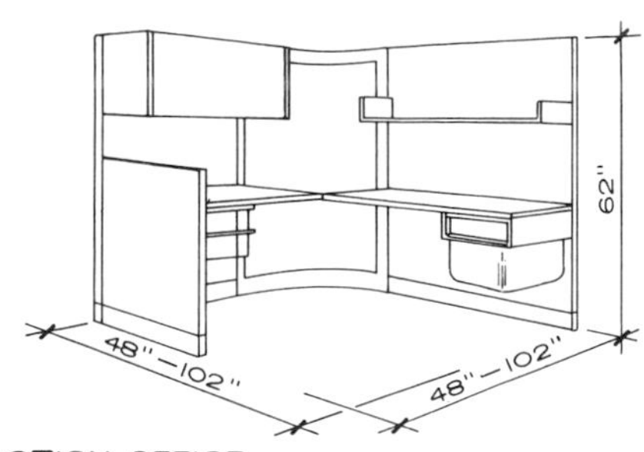

62"
48"—102"
48"—102"

ACTION OFFICE
HERMAN MILLER, INC.

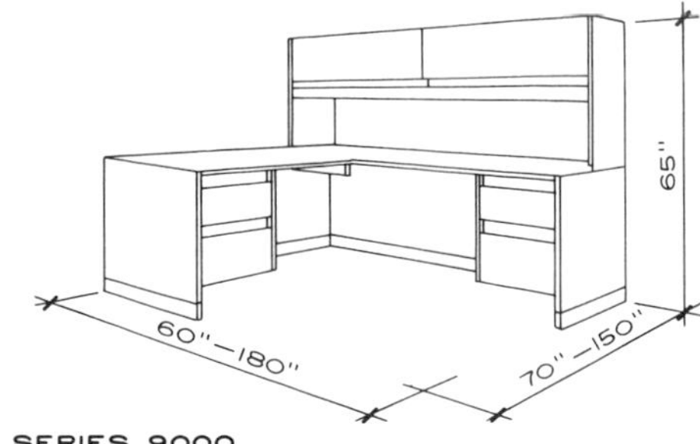

65"
60"—180"
70"—150"

SERIES 9000
STEELCASE, INC.

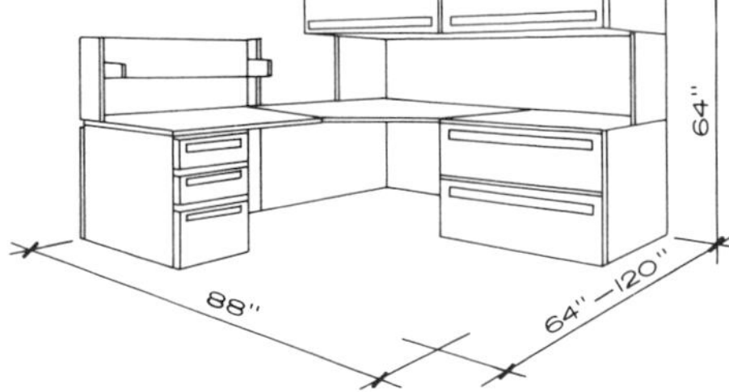

64"
88"
64"—120"

HANNAH DESK SYSTEM
KNOLL INTERNATIONAL

PANEL HUNG TYPE

These systems are based on panels that can be connected at various angles (angle options depend on manufacturer). Panels achieve stability through configuration or by attached stabilizing feet. Components are hung on panels at desired heights (usually on 1 in. increments).

SYSTEM ADVANTAGES

Panel hung systems usually have a large variety of components. They offer the highest degree of planning flexibility. These systems are easily modified and are relatively light.

OPTIONS OFFERED (VARY WITH MANUFACTURER)

1. Ability to hang components on fixed, full height partitions.
2. Specialized use components (i.e., hospitals, schools, libraries).
3. Integrated wiring in panels with fast connect or wire manager components for horizontal raceways.
4. Integrated task/ambient lighting components.
5. Multiple standard panel heights (dimensions vary).
6. Fabric covered acoustical panels as structural panel option.
7. Integrated file storage components.

PANEL ENCLOSURE TYPE

These systems are based on building rectilinear enclosures with panel components. Panels achieve stability through right angle panel-to-panel configuration. Components are hung in panel enclosures (usually at several predetermined mounting heights) and are supported by end panels rather than back panels.

SYSTEM ADVANTAGES

Assembled systems have a somewhat unitized appearance. They are stable and, when assembled, are not easily moved. They have a relatively high level of flexibility with a more limited number of components and accessories than in most panel hung systems.

OPTIONS OFFERED (VARY WITH MANUFACTURER)

1. Multiple standard panel heights.
2. Full panel high closed storage units (i.e., wardrobes, shelf).
3. Vertical power poles with lighting outlets, convenience outlets, circuit breakers, telephone raceway.
4. Wire manager components for vertical and horizontal raceways.
5. Integrated task/ambient lighting components and freestanding ambient light units.
6. Fabric covered acoustical panels are structural panel option.
7. Integrated file storage components.

UNITIZED PANEL TYPE

These systems are based on ganging assembled units and panels to form workstations and workstation groupings. Units are individually stable and panels achieve stability by attachment to units and right angle panel-to-panel configuration. Some of these systems are more componentized than others (similar to panel enclosure type) but are marketed as assembled units. Components within assembled units are usually supported by end panels.

SYSTEM ADVANTAGES

Assembled systems have a unitized appearance more closely resembling conventional furniture. They are very stable and, when assembled, are not easily moved. They have a relatively high level of flexibility depending on the degree to which they are unitized. These systems simplify purchase, inventory management, and installation because of their unitized character.

OPTIONS OFFERED (VARY WITH MANUFACTURER)

1. Multiple standard panel heights (dimensions vary).
2. Full panel high closed storage units (i.e., wardrobes, shelf).
3. Wire raceways (horizontal and vertical), convenience outlets, and switches are an integral part of system.
4. Integrated task/ambient light units.
5. Fabric covered acoustical panels usually as hang on or finish panel option.
6. Integrated flexible branch wiring system.
7. Can be used in conventional configurations.

GENERIC TYPES OF SYSTEM FURNITURE

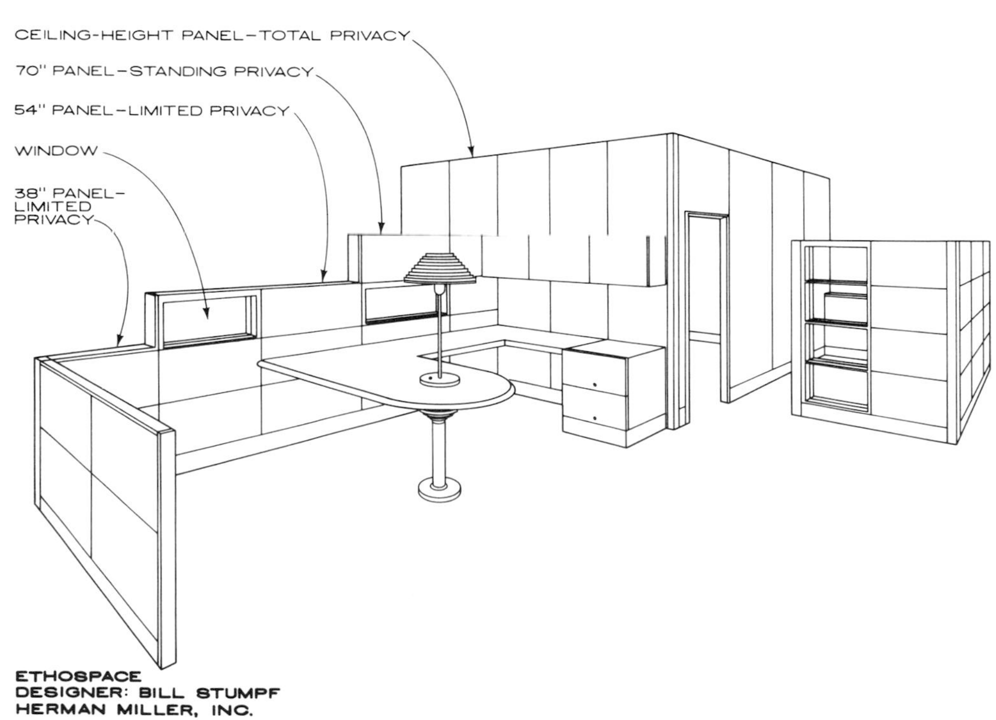

CEILING-HEIGHT PANEL—TOTAL PRIVACY
70" PANEL—STANDING PRIVACY
54" PANEL—LIMITED PRIVACY
WINDOW
38" PANEL—LIMITED PRIVACY

ETHOSPACE
DESIGNER: BILL STUMPF
HERMAN MILLER, INC.

COMPONENT WALL AND PARTITION SYSTEM

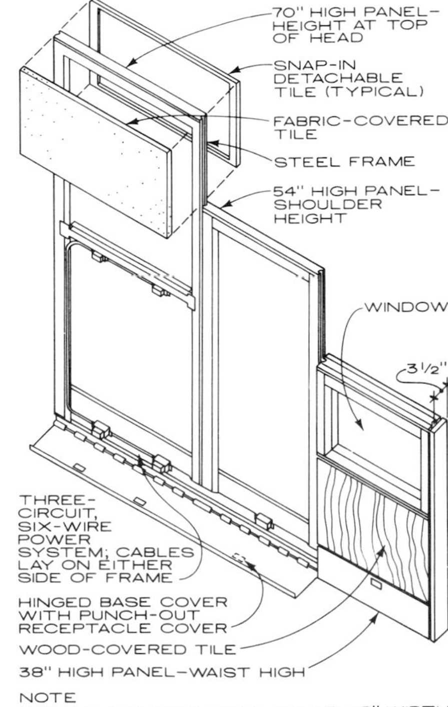

70" HIGH PANEL—HEIGHT AT TOP OF HEAD
SNAP-IN DETACHABLE TILE (TYPICAL)
FABRIC-COVERED TILE
STEEL FRAME
54" HIGH PANEL—SHOULDER HEIGHT
WINDOW
3 1/2"
THREE-CIRCUIT, SIX-WIRE POWER SYSTEM; CABLES LAY ON EITHER SIDE OF FRAME
HINGED BASE COVER WITH PUNCH-OUT RECEPTACLE COVER
WOOD-COVERED TILE
38" HIGH PANEL—WAIST HIGH

NOTE
PANELS ARE MADE IN 24, 30, OR 48" WIDTH. PANELS ARE BASED ON A 16" VERTICAL MODULE

PANEL COMPONENT

Interspace Incorporated; Washington, D.C.
Richard J. Vitullo; Washington Grove, Maryland

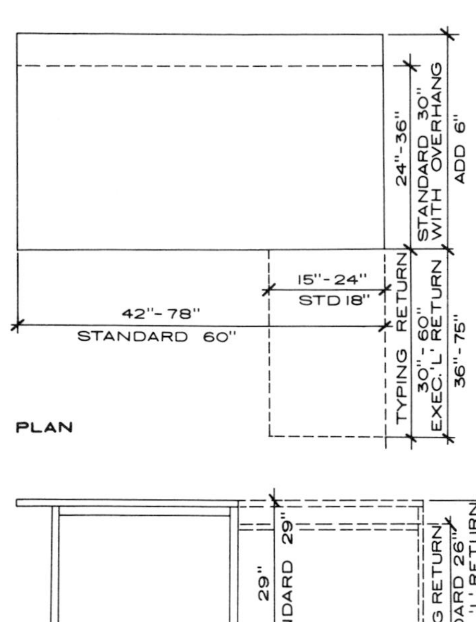
24"-36"
STANDARD 30"
WITH OVERHANG
ADD 6"
15"-24"
STD 18"
42"-78"
STANDARD 60"
TYPING RETURN
30"-60"
EXEC. 'L' RETURN
36"-75"

PLAN

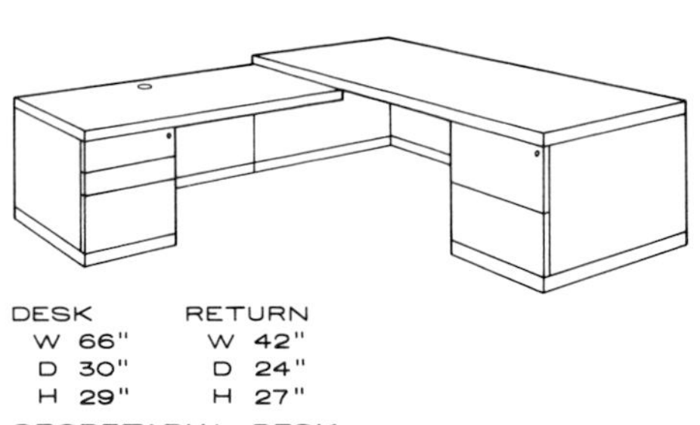

DESK
W 66"
D 30"
H 29"

RETURN
W 42"
D 24"
H 27"

SECRETARIAL DESK
CORRYHIEBERT CORP.

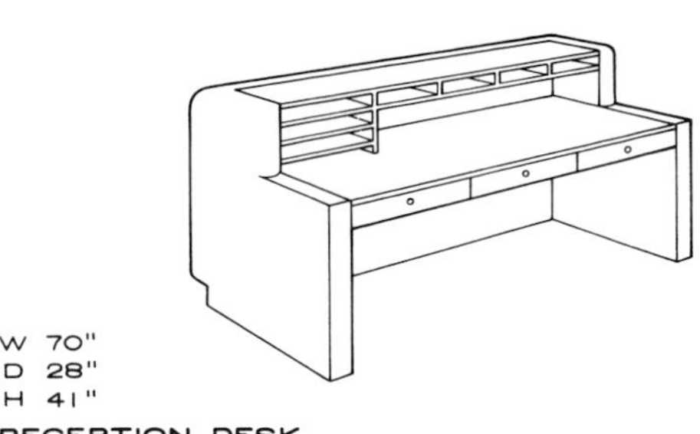

W 70"
D 28"
H 41"

RECEPTION DESK
THE PACE COLLECTION, INC.

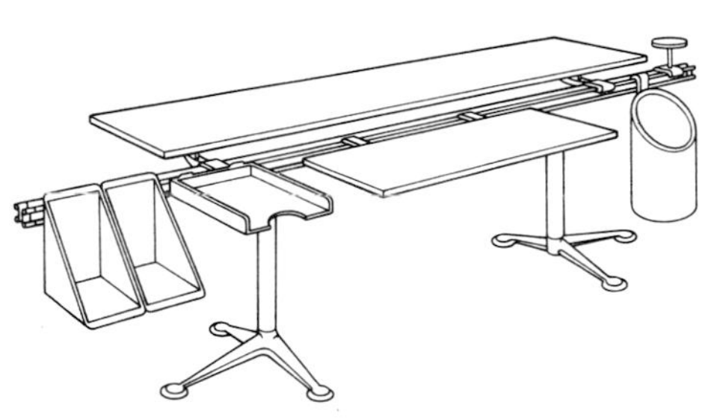
29"
STANDARD 29"
TYPING RETURN
STANDARD 26"
EXEC. 'L' RETURN
STANDARD 29"

ELEVATION
DESK: SINGLE OR DOUBLE PEDESTAL

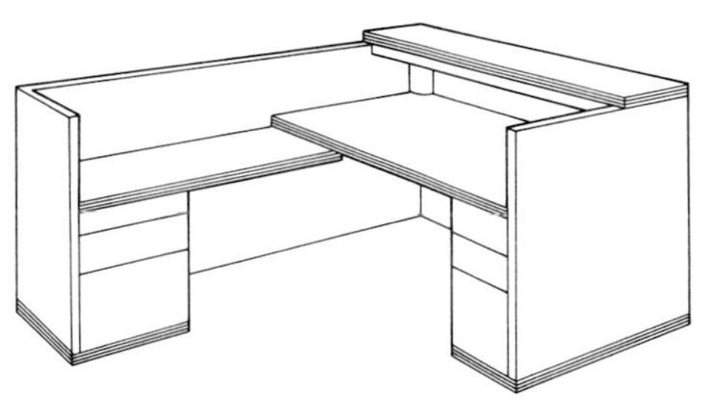

W 70"
D 36"
H 29"

DOUBLE PEDESTAL DESK,
SIDE OVERHANG 4200 SERIES
STEELCASE, INC.

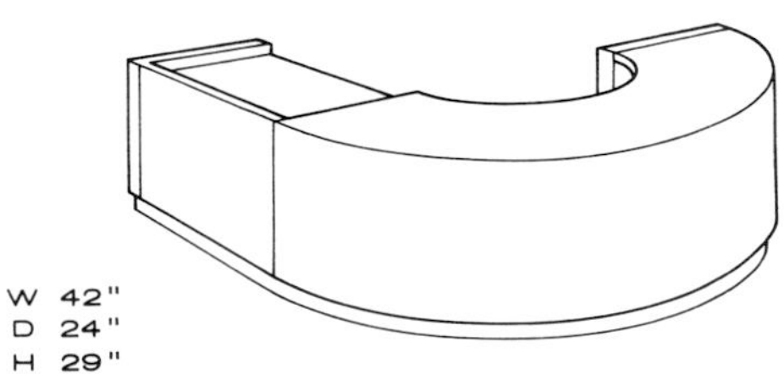

W 42"
D 24"
H 29"

CURVED SEGMENTED DESK
JG FURNITURE SYSTEMS, INC.

BURDICK GROUP
HERMAN MILLER, INC.

DESK, VARIA CASEGOODS
MUELLER

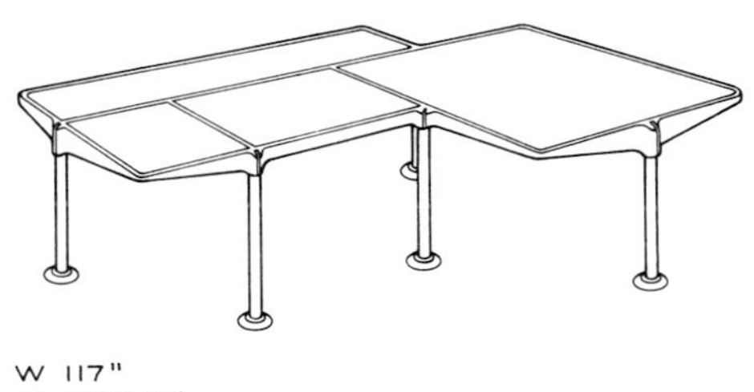

W 117"
D 66 3/4"
H 29"

MENHIR DESK
KRUEGER INTERNATIONAL DIVISION

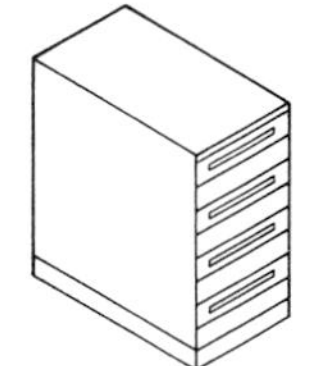

4 BOX DRAWERS

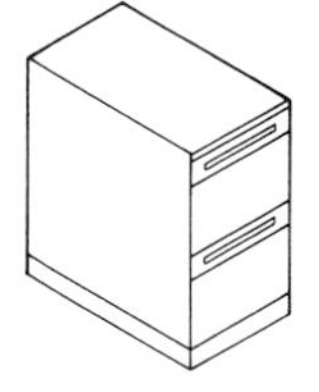

2 FILE DRAWERS

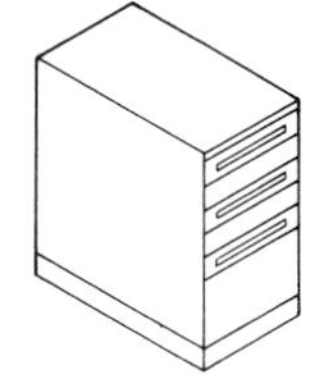

2 BOX DRAWERS
1 FILE DRAWER

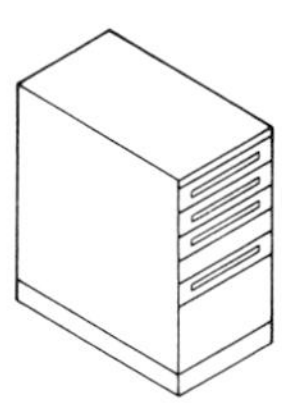

2 TRAY DRAWERS
1 BOX DRAWER
1 FILE DRAWER

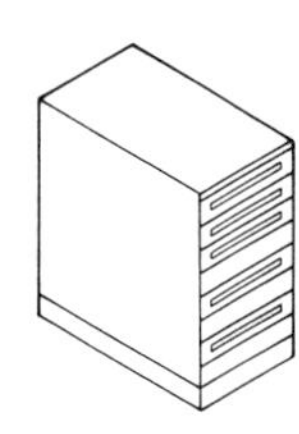

2 TRAY DRAWERS
3 BOX DRAWERS

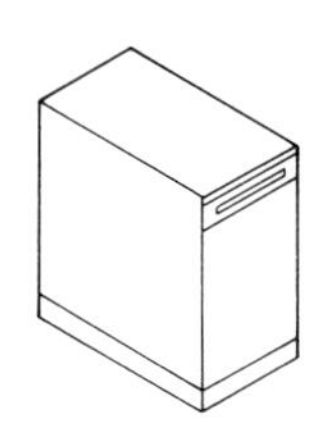

1 HINGED DOOR

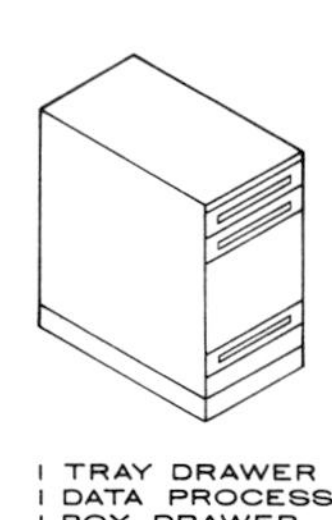

1 TRAY DRAWER
1 DATA PROCESSING
1 BOX DRAWER

NOTE: ALL PEDESTALS – W 15", D 24", H 29"

4600/8600 CREDENZA PEDESTALS
ALL-STEEL, INC.

TYPICAL CREDENZA DIMENSIONS

	WIDTH (IN.)	DEPTH (IN.)	HEIGHT (IN.)
One component	15–30	17¾–24	25½–29¾
Two component	30–41½		
Three component	45–60½	17¾–24	25½–29¾
Four component	60–79¾	17¾–24	25½–29¾
Five component	75–98½	17¾–24	25½–29¾

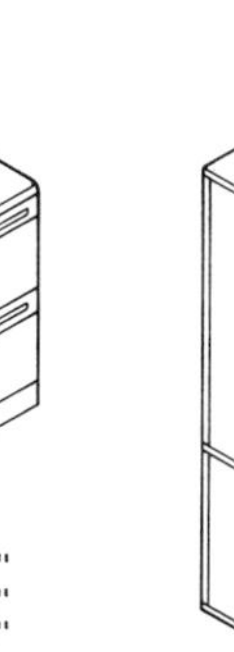

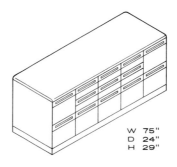

W 75"
D 24"
H 29"

4600/8600 SERIES CREDENZA
ALL-STEEL, INC.

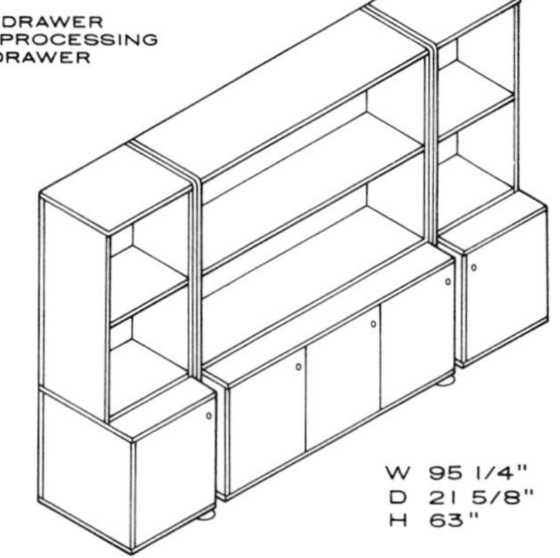

W 95 1/4"
D 21 5/8"
H 63"

MENHIR CABINET
KRUEGER INTERNATIONAL DIV.

Robert Staples; Staples & Charles Ltd; Washington, D.C.
Richard J. Vitullo; Washington Grove, Maryland

REFERENCES

DATA SOURCES: ORGANIZATIONS

All-Steel, Inc., 365
Corry Hiebert Corporation, 365
Herman Miller, Inc., 362, 364, 365
JG Furniture Systems, Inc., 363, 365
Knoll International, 364
Krueger, Inc., 363, 365
Luxo Lamp Corporation, 362
Martin Industries, 362
Mayline Company, 362
Mueller, 365
Pace Collection, Inc., 365
Reff Inc., 363
Steelcase, Inc., 360, 361, 364, 365
Sunar Hauserman, 363
Vemco, 362

DATA SOURCES: PUBLICATIONS

Designing the Automated Office, William Pulgram, Whitney Library of Design, 361

CHAPTER **13**

SPECIAL CONSTRUCTION

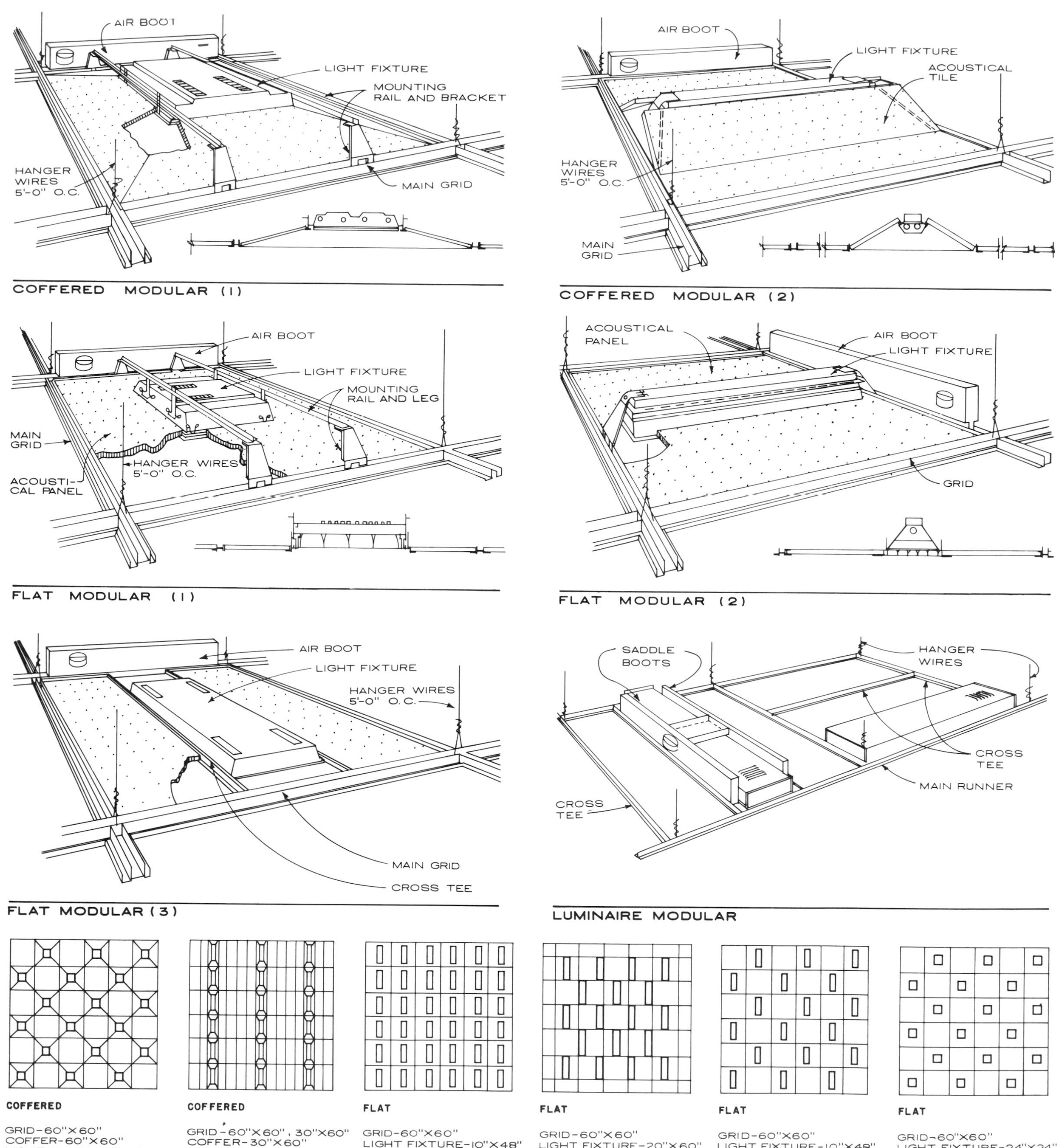
AIR BOOT
LIGHT FIXTURE
MOUNTING RAIL AND BRACKET
HANGER WIRES 5'-0" O.C.
MAIN GRID
COFFERED MODULAR (1)
AIR BOOT
LIGHT FIXTURE
ACOUSTICAL TILE
HANGER WIRES 5'-0" O.C.
MAIN GRID
COFFERED MODULAR (2)
AIR BOOT
LIGHT FIXTURE
MOUNTING RAIL AND LEG
MAIN GRID
HANGER WIRES 5'-0" O.C.
ACOUSTICAL PANEL
FLAT MODULAR (1)
ACOUSTICAL PANEL
AIR BOOT
LIGHT FIXTURE
GRID
FLAT MODULAR (2)
AIR BOOT
LIGHT FIXTURE
HANGER WIRES 5'-0" O.C.
MAIN GRID
CROSS TEE
FLAT MODULAR (3)
SADDLE BOOTS
HANGER WIRES
CROSS TEE
MAIN RUNNER
CROSS TEE
LUMINAIRE MODULAR
COFFERED
GRID-60"X60"
COFFER-60"X60"
LIGHT FIXTURE-1'X4'
2'X2', 2'X4' AND 30"X30"
COFFERED
GRID-60"X60", 30"X60"
COFFER-30"X60"
LIGHT FIXTURE-6½"X48"
FLAT
GRID-60"X60"
LIGHT FIXTURE-10"X48"
FLAT
GRID-60"X60"
LIGHT FIXTURE-20"X60"
FLAT
GRID-60"X60"
LIGHT FIXTURE-10"X48"
FLAT
GRID-60"X60"
LIGHT FIXTURE-24"X24"
OR 30"X30"

REFLECTED CEILING PLANS (INTEGRATED CEILINGS)

Timothy B. McDonald; Washington, D.C.

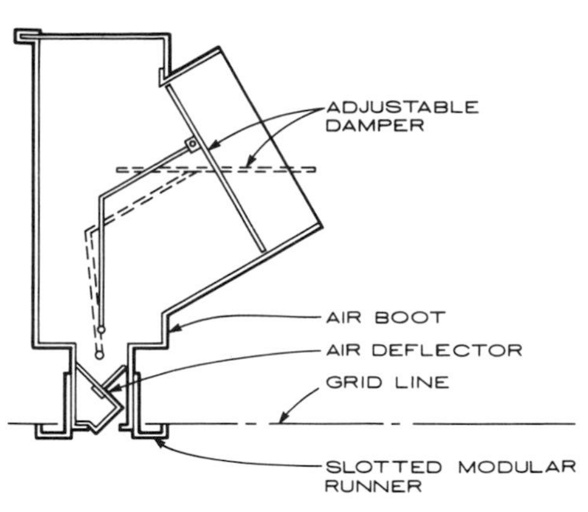
ADJUSTABLE DAMPER
AIR BOOT
AIR DEFLECTOR
GRID LINE
SLOTTED MODULAR RUNNER

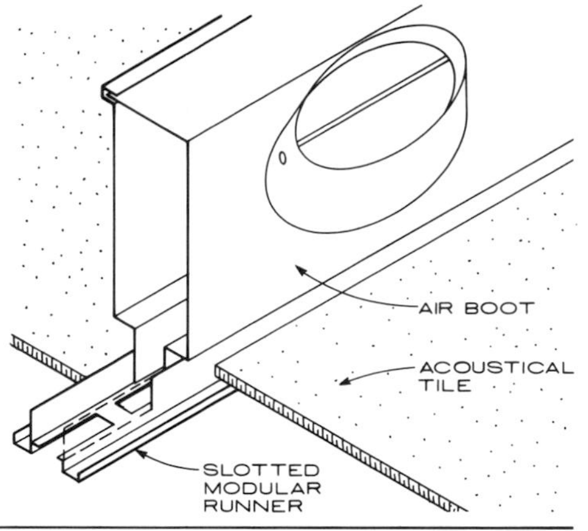
AIR BOOT
ACOUSTICAL TILE
SLOTTED MODULAR RUNNER

AIR BOOT SECTION AND DETAIL

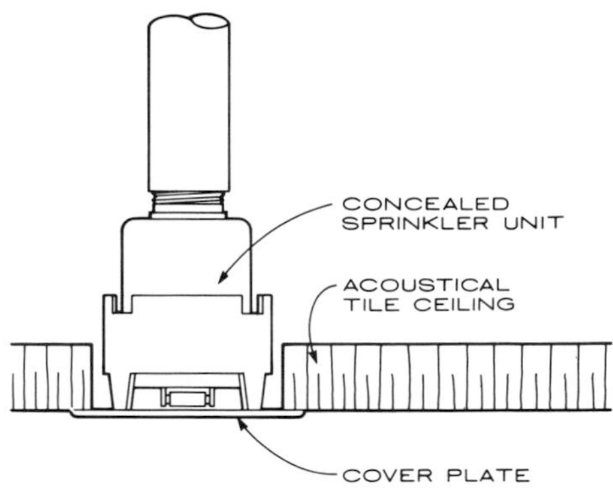
CONCEALED SPRINKLER UNIT
ACOUSTICAL TILE CEILING
COVER PLATE

CONCEALED SPRINKLER

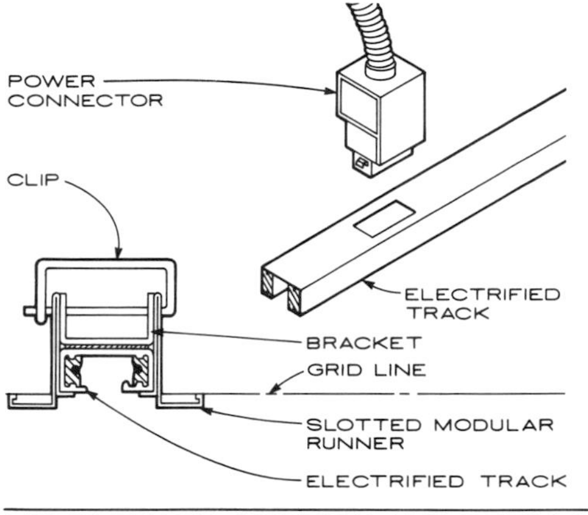
POWER CONNECTOR
CLIP
ELECTRIFIED TRACK
BRACKET
GRID LINE
SLOTTED MODULAR RUNNER
ELECTRIFIED TRACK

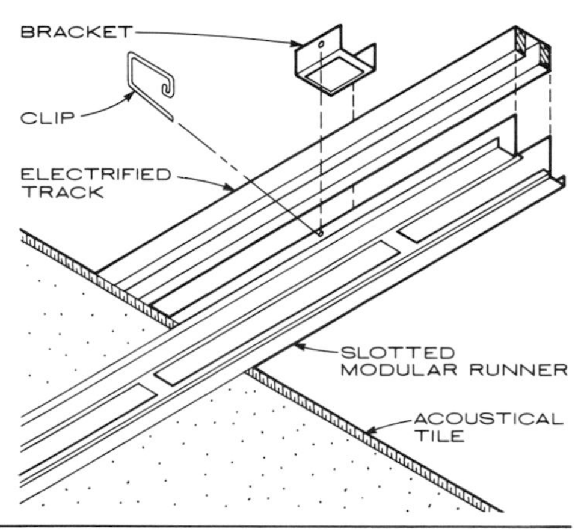
BRACKET
CLIP
ELECTRIFIED TRACK
SLOTTED MODULAR RUNNER
ACOUSTICAL TILE

LIGHT TRACK SECTION AND DETAILS

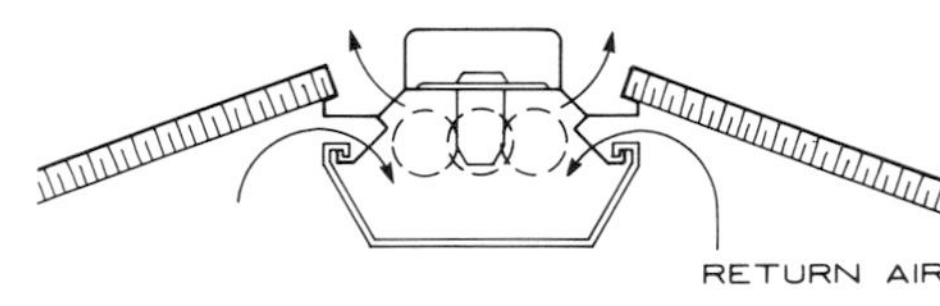
RETURN AIR

COFFERED FIXTURE

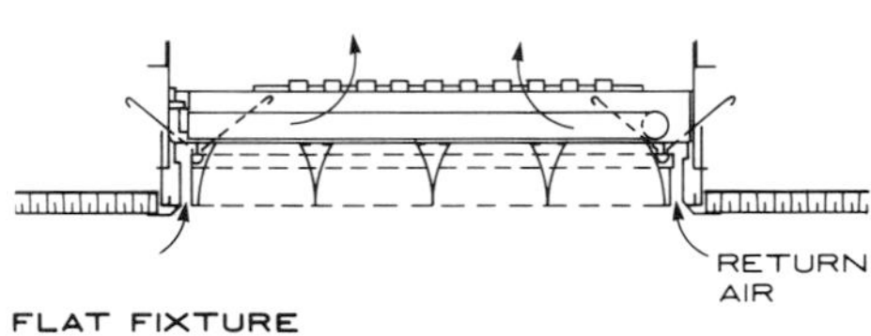
RETURN AIR

FLAT FIXTURE

LIGHTING FIXTURES

INTEGRATED CEILINGS

Integrated ceilings combine lighting, air diffusion, fire protection, and acoustical control into a single, unified unit. Demountable partitions can be accommodated by the use of an adaptor attached on the modular grid lines. A 60 x 60 in. module is basic to most integrated ceiling systems. Custom sized modules are also available.

LUMINAIRE MODULAR CEILING

The basic configuration is a 60 x 60 in. module divided into four 15 x 60 in. modules.

A recess in the modular defining grid will accommodate demountable partitions, sprinkler heads, and slots for air diffusion.

The basic lighting unit is a 14 1/2 x 48 in. recessed troffer. Air return is by return air light fixtures.

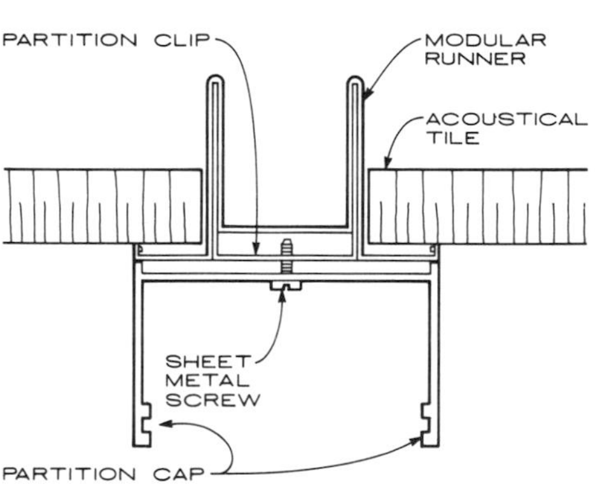
PARTITION CLIP
MODULAR RUNNER
ACOUSTICAL TILE
SHEET METAL SCREW
PARTITION CAP

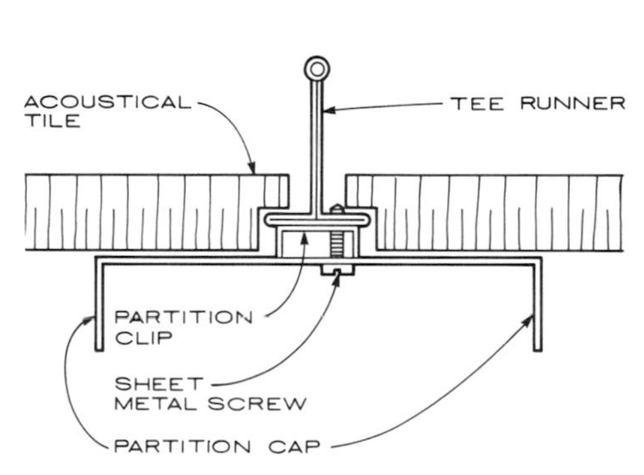
ACOUSTICAL TILE
TEE RUNNER
PARTITION CLIP
SHEET METAL SCREW
PARTITION CAP

PARTITION ASSEMBLIES

COMPONENTS

CEILING SYSTEMS	HANGER SPACING (o.c.)	WALL MOLDINGS			MAIN RUNNERS			SPACING	CROSS MEMBERS			SPACING (o.c.)	AIR BAR AIR BOOT			ACOUSTIC PANELS			LIGHT FIXTURES		
		L	W	H	L	W	H		L	W	H		L	W	H	L	W	H	L	W	H
Flat modular	2'-6"	10'	3/4"	3/4"	10'	3/4"	1 1/2"	5'	60"	3/4"	1 1/2"	20"	5'	3 1/8"	9 3/4"	5'	20"	5/8"	–	1.	–
Coffered lighting	30"	60"	1 1/4"	1 1/4"	5'	2 1/4"	1 1/4"	5'	60"	2 1/4"	1 1/4"	5'	5'	7 1/4"	8"	5'	15"	5/8"	48"	14 1/2"	5"
Luminair modular	5'	–	–	–	58 1/2"	3"	1 1/2"	5'	57"	15/16"	1 1/2"	5'	5'	7 1/4"	8"	5'	15"	5/8"	48"	14 1/2"	5"
Vertical screen	7' Max.	–	–	–	16'	1 1/2"	1 7/8"	7' Max.	16' Max.	5/8"	4"	2'-6"	–	2.	–	–	–	–	–	2.	–
Linear screen	5' Max.	–	–	–	16'	1 27/32"	1 1/4"	50"	3'-16'	3"	5/8"	2"	–	3.	–	–	4.	–	–	5.	–

NOTES

1. Size can vary.
2. No special type necessary.
3. Utilizes slots between panels for delivery and return.
4. Acoustic blanket.
5. Designed to fit panel width.

Timothy B. McDonald; Washington, D.C.

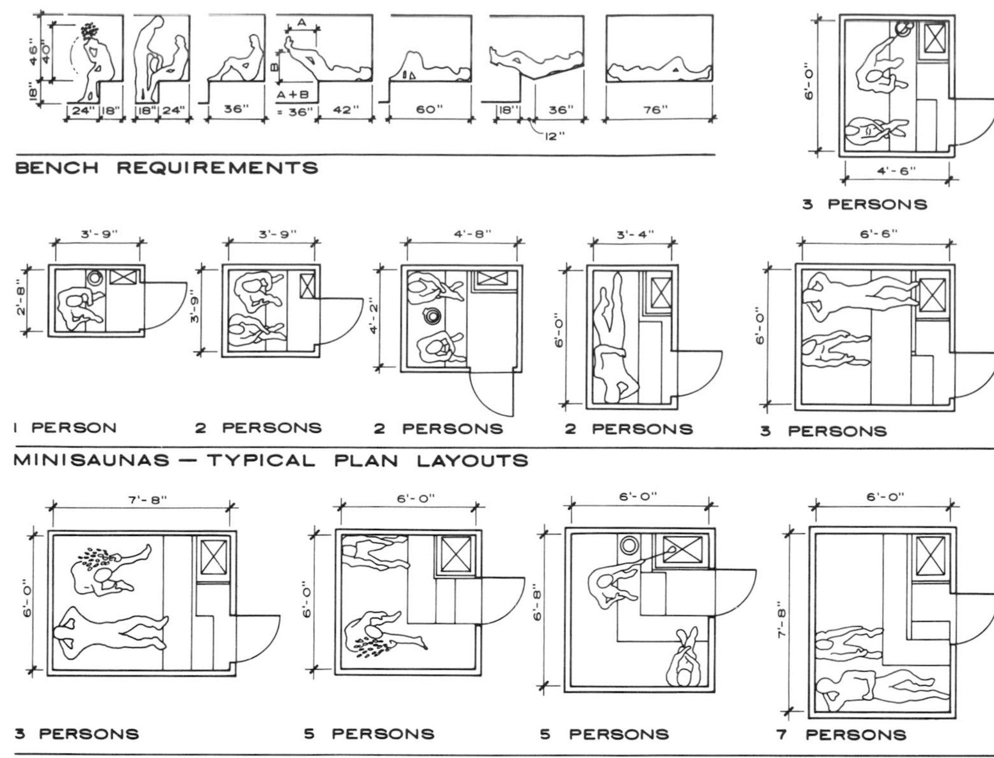

46"
40"
18"
24"
18"
18"
24"
A
B
A+B = 36"
36"
42"
60"
18"
36"
12"
76"
6'-0"
4'-6"
3'-9"
2'-8"
3'-9"
3'-9"
4'-8"
4'-2"
3'-4"
6'-0"
6'-6"
6'-0"
I PERSON
2 PERSONS
2 PERSONS
2 PERSONS
3 PERSONS
3 PERSONS
7'-8"
6'-0"
6'-0"
6'-0"
6'-0"
6'-0"
6'-8"
7'-8"
3 PERSONS
5 PERSONS
5 PERSONS
7 PERSONS

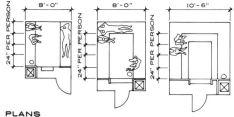

BENCH REQUIREMENTS

MINISAUNAS — TYPICAL PLAN LAYOUTS

FAMILY SAUNAS — TYPICAL PLAN LAYOUTS

8'-0" 8'-0" 10'-6"

24" PER PERSON

PLANS

PUBLIC SAUNAS

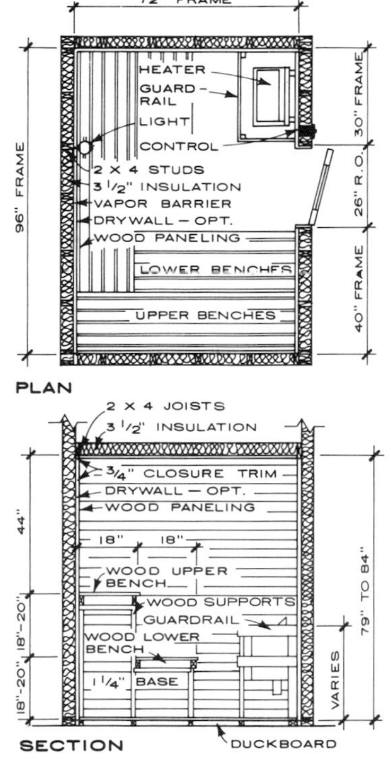

72" FRAME
HEATER
GUARD-RAIL
LIGHT
CONTROL
2 X 4 STUDS
3 1/2" INSULATION
VAPOR BARRIER
DRYWALL – OPT.
WOOD PANELING
LOWER BENCHES
UPPER BENCHES
96" FRAME
30" FRAME
26" R.O.
40" FRAME
PLAN
2 X 4 JOISTS
3 1/2" INSULATION
3/4" CLOSURE TRIM
DRYWALL – OPT.
WOOD PANELING
18"
18"
WOOD UPPER BENCH
WOOD SUPPORTS
GUARDRAIL
WOOD LOWER BENCH
1 1/4" BASE
44"
18"-20"
18"-20"
79" TO 84"
VARIES
SECTION
DUCKBOARD

SAUNA ROOM CONSTRUCTION

DESIGN CONSIDERATIONS

The fundamental purpose of the sauna is to induce perspiration; the higher the temperature, the more quickly perspiration will begin.

The drier the air, the more heat one can stand. Temperatures on the platform can be as high as 212°F, 230°F, and 240°F. A little warm water thrown over the stove stones just before leaving the sauna produces a slightly humid wave of air that suddenly seems hotter and envelops the bather with an invisible glowing cloud, pleasantly stinging the skin. It is usually better to lie than to sit, for the temperature rises roughly 18°F for every 1 ft above the floor level; if one lies, heat is equally dispensed over the entire body. When lying down one may wish to raise one's feet against the wall or ceiling.

The expanded hot air in the sauna contains proportionately less oxygen than the denser atmosphere outside. Bathers sometimes experience faintness unless the air is changed regularly. An amount of fresh air enters each time the door is opened; this is insufficient, however. Normally two adjustable ventilators are built into the walls. One, the air inlet, is usually placed low near the stove. Fresh air should be drawn from outside and not from adjoining rooms where odors can be present.

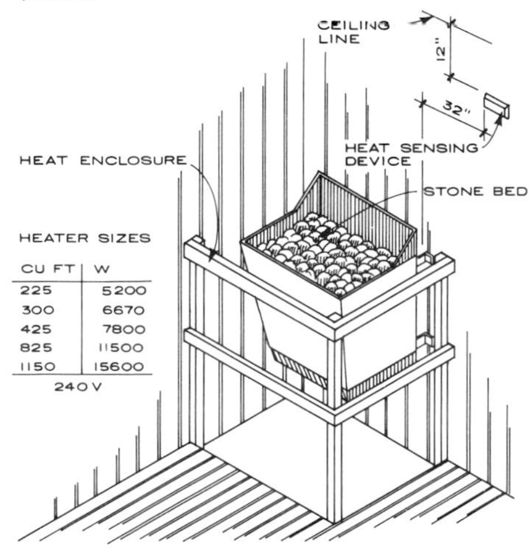

CEILING LINE
12"
32"
HEAT ENCLOSURE
HEAT SENSING DEVICE
STONE BED

HEATER SIZES

CU FT	W
225	5200
300	6670
425	7800
825	11500
1150	15600

240 V

STOVE AND THERMOSTAT LOCATION

A B C

SUGGESTED AIRFLOW PATTERNS

PANEL SAUNA VENTILATION

NATURAL VENTILATION

Air must flow freely into the room—inlet and outlet normally are on opposite walls and at approximately the same level. The inlet situated under the stove creates a strong updraft.

A. A flue or duct provides a chimney action that will pull air off the floor and out.

B. Inlet is low on the wall, with outlet high and directly above it. This ensures ventilation even if wind pressure exists on the wall containing the two ventilators because of the difference in air temperature at the two openings and the effect of normal convection.

C. Suggest fresh air from exterior with outlet through another room, fan, or fireplace.

HEATER: The heater depends on convection for air circulation. It is the preferred method, for the air in a sauna should be as static as possible to heat the sauna in 1 to 1½ hr.

INTERIOR PANELING: Tongue and grooved boards should be at least ⅝ in. thick, or thicker if possible because of the increased ability to absorb vapor and to retain the timber smell. Boards should not be wider than about six times their thickness. Blind nailing with galvanized or aluminum nails is common. Vapor barrier and insulation under the interior paneling must be completely vaporproof and heat resistant. Most conventional insulating materials are effective; mineral base is preferred; avoid using expanded polystyrene.

DOOR: The opening should be kept as small as possible to minimize loss of heat. Maximum height is 6 ft. Door must open outward as a safety measure. A close fitting rebate on all four sides is usually sufficient insurance against heat loss around the edges. The construction should approach the U value of the walls.

HARDWARE: Because of the weight of the door, a pair of 4 in. brass butt hinges with ball bearings are recommended. A heavy ball or roller catch keeps the door closed. Door handles are made of wood.

LIGHTING: The lighting must be indirect and the fitting unobtrusive. The best position for the light is above and slightly behind the bather's normal field of view. The switch is always outside the hot room.

TYPE OF WOOD: White or western red cedar and redwood are the materials suitable for sauna construction. They should be chosen based on their resistance to splitting and decay, color of the wood, and the thermal capacity of the wood. These woods stain badly by metal.

CEILING HEIGHT: The bigger the volume the more heat required; hence, keep the ceiling as low as possible within the limits imposed by the benches.

The main platform or bench will be about 39 in. above floor in a family sauna or at least 60 in. in a large public sauna. The ceiling is about 43 in. above the highest bench. Average family sauna ceiling height is 82 in., public 110 in.

Jerry Graham; CTA Architects Engineers; Billings, Montana

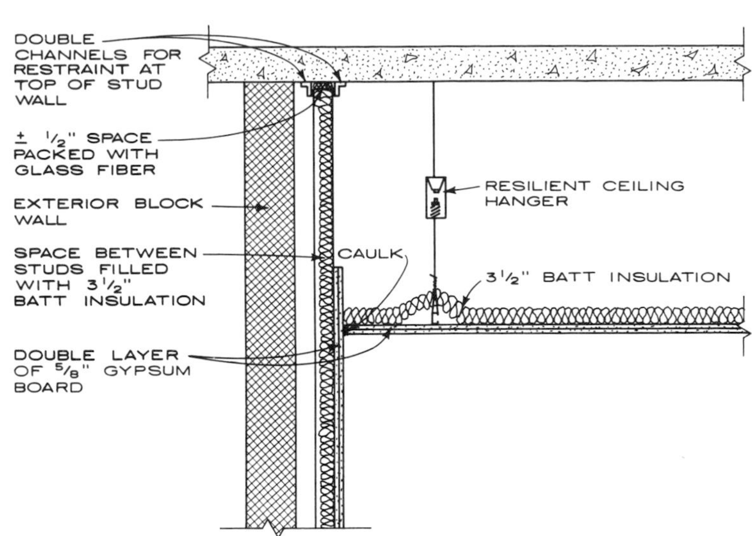
DOUBLE CHANNELS FOR RESTRAINT AT TOP OF STUD WALL
± 1/2" SPACE PACKED WITH GLASS FIBER
EXTERIOR BLOCK WALL
SPACE BETWEEN STUDS FILLED WITH 3 1/2" BATT INSULATION
DOUBLE LAYER OF 5/8" GYPSUM BOARD
RESILIENT CEILING HANGER
CAULK
3 1/2" BATT INSULATION

UPPER EXTERIOR WALL

FLEXIBLE DUCT CONNECTION REQUIRED IF PENETRATION THROUGH STUD WALL IS RIGID
± 1/2" SPACE PACKED WITH GLASS FIBER
RESILIENT DUCT HANGER
DOUBLE CHANNELS FOR RESTRAINT
CAULKING, TYPICAL
FLEXIBLE CONDUIT
TYPICAL DUCT
CAULKING
3 1/2" BATT INSULATION
INTERIOR BLOCK WALL
SURFACE MOUNTED LIGHTING FIXTURE

UPPER INTERIOR WALL WITH HVAC AND ELECTRICAL PENETRATIONS

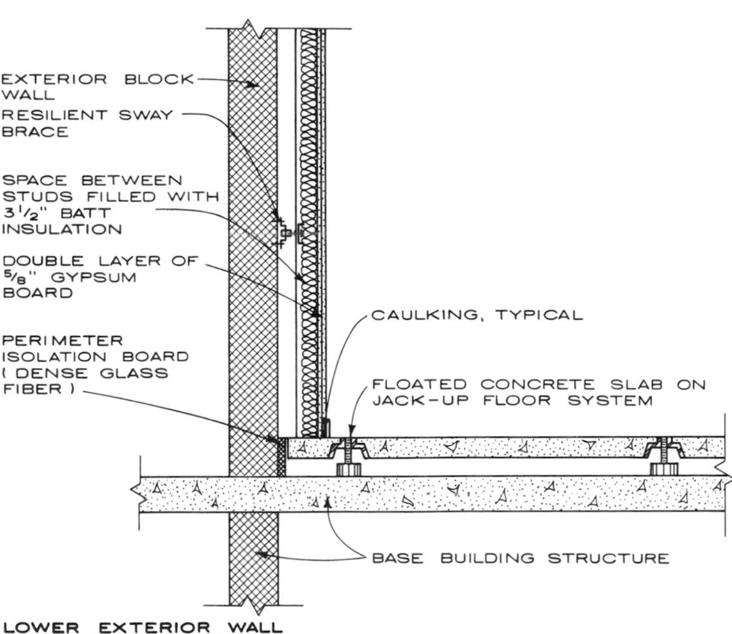
EXTERIOR BLOCK WALL
RESILIENT SWAY BRACE
SPACE BETWEEN STUDS FILLED WITH 3 1/2" BATT INSULATION
DOUBLE LAYER OF 5/8" GYPSUM BOARD
PERIMETER ISOLATION BOARD (DENSE GLASS FIBER)
CAULKING, TYPICAL
FLOATED CONCRETE SLAB ON JACK-UP FLOOR SYSTEM
BASE BUILDING STRUCTURE

LOWER EXTERIOR WALL WITH JACK – UP FLOOR

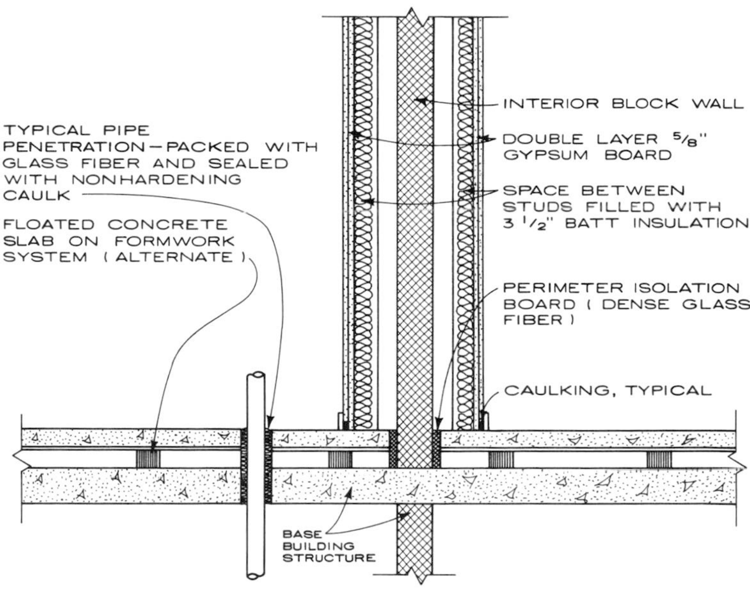
TYPICAL PIPE PENETRATION – PACKED WITH GLASS FIBER AND SEALED WITH NONHARDENING CAULK
FLOATED CONCRETE SLAB ON FORMWORK SYSTEM (ALTERNATE)
INTERIOR BLOCK WALL
DOUBLE LAYER 5/8" GYPSUM BOARD
SPACE BETWEEN STUDS FILLED WITH 3 1/2" BATT INSULATION
PERIMETER ISOLATION BOARD (DENSE GLASS FIBER)
CAULKING, TYPICAL
BASE BUILDING STRUCTURE

LOWER INTERIOR WALL

DETAILS

ISOLATED ROOMS

Isolated rooms incorporate special constructions to reduce intrusive noise and vibration from outside the room or to contain the sound and impact energy that is generated within the room. Typical applications include music practice rooms, sound studios, testing chambers, mechanical equipment rooms near sensitive areas, spaces exposed to nearby aircraft flyovers, and offices under gymnasiums. Isolated room construction can be very expensive; whenever possible, space planning and layout design should isolate high noise sources from acoustically critical uses so that the need for isolated rooms can be minimized.

The correct design of an isolated room is a "box-within-a-box." The inner box, which is the four walls, ceiling and floor of the isolated room, should be an airtight enclosure of dense impervious materials; this box must be isolated by resilient supports from the surrounding structure. It is also important that the base structure that supports the isolated room be as rigid and massive as possible.

The most effective floor construction is a "floated" concrete pad, which is separated from the base building structure by steel springs, neoprene, or glass fiber isolation mounts. Inner walls can be supported from this slab. Any necessary structural bracing to the base building structure should be with a resilient nonrigid connection. The ceiling of the box can be suspended from resilient hangers, or it can be supported from the walls of the inner box. The diagram shows typical construction details.

It is necessary to avoid all flanking paths between an isolated room and the base building structure. Any penetrations through the walls or connections to outside services must be as well isolated as the room itself. Therefore, there should be flexible connections in ducts and conduit between the inner and outer box, and all piping must be resiliently supported.

Weatherstripped or sound rated doors and double glazed windows should be part of the continuous airtight enclosure that defines the inner box.

The degree of noise reduction that can be attained by an isolated room depends on the type of constructions, their resiliency, the elimination of flanking paths, and the amount of dead airspace that surrounds the inner box. A well-built isolated room can achieve field performance ratings of STC 60 to 70 for airborne sound, and ratings of IIC 80 to 90 for impact noise. However, even minor flanking paths and short circuits can easily degrade these results by 10 points or more. The sound isolation between spaces will be only as great as the weakest sound path.

The advice and assistance of a qualified acoustical consultant should be sought in both the planning and design of isolated rooms and their related special constructions.

In addition to field erected isolated rooms as described above, several manufacturers make prefabricated units. These rooms are sold as self-contained music practice rooms, audiometric booths, and control booths for manufacturing plants. Although the detailing of their constructions is proprietary, one will find the same design approach as outlined here: a separate airtight box kept separate from the building structure. The degree of noise reduction that these prefabricated rooms can attain depends on the parameters used for field erected rooms.

Don Klabin, AIA; Bolt Beranek and Newman, Inc.; Cambridge, Massachusetts

REFERENCES

GENERAL REFERENCES

Architectural Acoustics, 1988, M. Egan, McGraw-Hill

Architectural Interior Systems: Lighting, Air-Conditioning, Acoustics, 1988, J. Flynn and A. Segil, Van Nostrand Reinhold

Building Configuration and Seismic Design, 1985, C. Arnold and R. Reitherman, Wiley

Noise and Vibration Control in Buildings, 1984, R. Jones, McGraw-Hill

The Seismic Design Handbook, 1989, F. Naiem, Van Nostrand Reinhold

CHAPTER **14**

CONVEYING SYSTEMS

GENERAL

An elevator system with its hoistway, machine room, and waiting lobbies is a major element in a building and requires special design consideration. Preengineered or custom-made elevator systems can be constructed to meet virtually all vertical transportation needs for passenger, freight, or service.

In all cases, design of an elevator system must be carefully considered throughout all stages of the building design process. During initial stages, the elevator handling capacity and quality of service desired determines the size, number, type, and location of elevator systems. Proper selection depends on type of tenancy, number of occupants, and the building design (number of floors, floor heights, building circulation, etc.). Elevator ARRANGEMENT locates the elevator within the building plan to provide efficient and accessible service. Each elevator system, once selected, requires OPERATIONAL SPACES, hoistway and machine room, and PASSENGER SPACES, lobby, and elevator car.

Proper planning and contact with representatives of the elevator industry and local code officials are essential to each of these design areas.

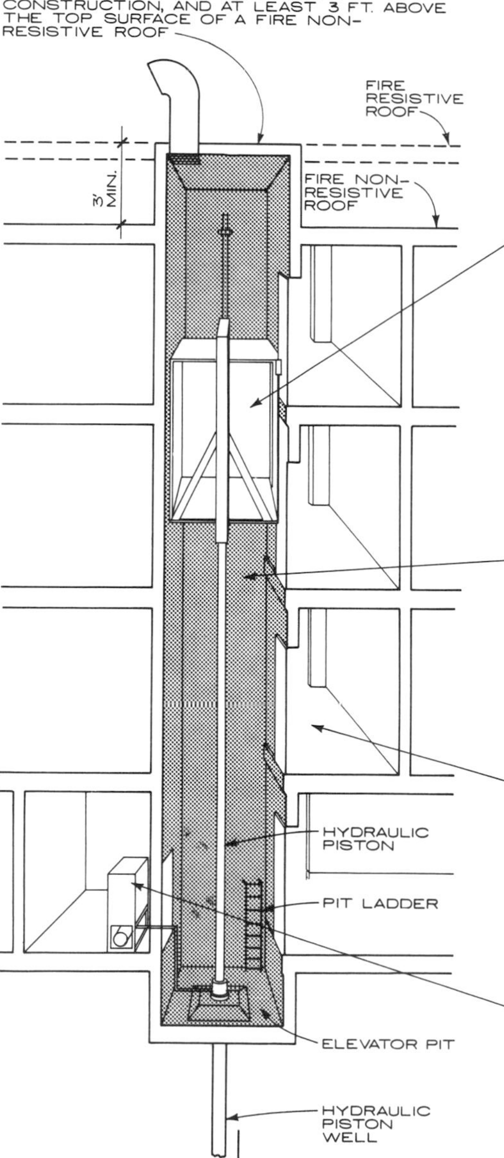
NOTE: WHERE A HOISTWAY EXTENDS INTO THE TOP FLOOR OF A BUILDING, FIRE RESISTIVE HOISTWAY OR MACHINERY SPACE ENCLOSURES, AS REQUIRED, SHALL BE CARRIED TO THE UNDERSIDE OF THE ROOF IF THE ROOF IS OF FIRE RESISTIVE CONSTRUCTION, AND AT LEAST 3 FT. ABOVE THE TOP SURFACE OF A FIRE NON-RESISTIVE ROOF
FIRE RESISTIVE ROOF
3' MIN.
FIRE NON-RESISTIVE ROOF
HYDRAULIC PISTON
PIT LADDER
ELEVATOR PIT
HYDRAULIC PISTON WELL

HYDRAULIC ELEVATOR

The two most common systems, the HYDRAULIC ELEVATOR and the ELECTRIC ELEVATOR, are shown in the two diagrams on this page. The systems are distinguished mainly by their hoisting mechanisms.

The HYDRAULIC ELEVATOR uses a hydraulic driving machine to raise and lower the elevator car and its load. A hydraulic driving machine is one in which the energy is applied by means of a liquid under pressure in a cylinder equipped with a plunger or piston. The car and driving machine are supported at the pit floor (hoistway base). Lower speeds and the piston length restrict the use of this system to approximately 60 ft. It generally requires the least initial installation expense, but more power is used during operation because of the greater loads imposed on the driving machine.

An ELECTRIC ELEVATOR is a power elevator where the energy is applied by means of an electric driving machine. In the electric driving machine the energy is applied by an electric motor. It includes the motor, brake, and the driving sheave or drum together with its connecting gearing, belt, or chain, if any. High speeds and virtually limitless rise allow this elevator to serve highrise, medium-rise, and lowrise buildings.

MACHINE ROOM (ELECTRIC ELEVATOR)

Normally located directly over the top of the hoistway—it could also be below at side or rear—the machine room is designed to contain elevator hoisting machine and control equipment. Adequate ventilation, soundproofing, and structural support for the elevator must be considered. Local codes may require that no other electrical or mechanical equipment, not associated with the elevator, be installed in the machine room.

ELEVATOR CAR

Guided by vertical guide rails, the elevator car conveys passenger or freight between floors. It consists of a car constructed within a supporting platform and frame. Design of the car focuses on the finished ceiling, walls, floor, and doors with lighting, ventilation, and elevator signal equipment.

The car of an hydraulic elevator system is supported by a piston or cylinder.

The car of a hydraulic elevator system is supported by a piston or cylinder.

HOISTWAY

The hoistway is a shaftway for the travel of one or more elevators. It includes the pit and terminates at the underside of the overhang machinery space floor or grating, or at the underside of the roof where the hoistway does not penetrate the roof. Access to the elevator car and hoistway is normally through hoistway doors located at each floor serviced by the elevator system. Hoistway design is determined by the characteristics of the elevator system selected and by requirements of the applicable code for fire separation, ventilation, soundproofing, or nonstructural elements.

LOBBY

Elevator waiting areas are designed to allow free circulation of passengers, rapid access to elevator cars, and clear visibility of elevator signals.

HANDICAP ACCESSIBILITY

Passenger elevators on accessible routes should comply with requirements of ANSI 117.1.

MACHINE ROOM (HYDRAULIC ELEVATOR)

Normally located near the base of the hoistway, the machine room contains hydraulic equipment and controls. Provisions of adequate ventilation and soundproofing must be considered. Local codes may require that no other electrical or mechanical equipment, not associated with the elevator, be installed in the machine room.

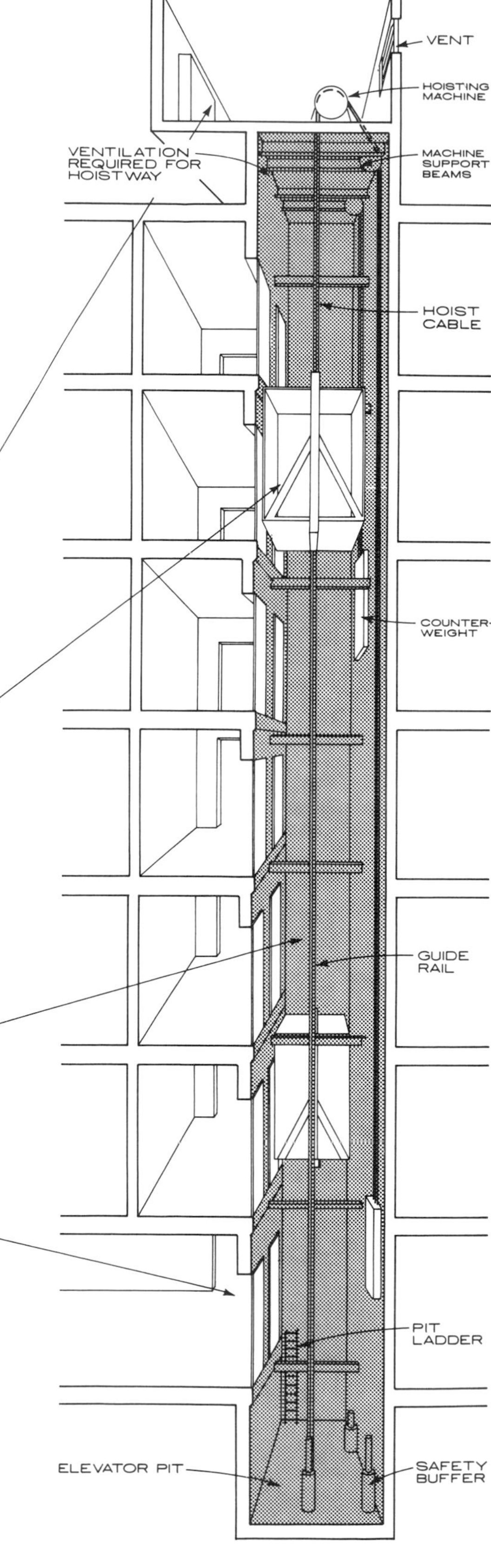
VENT
HOISTING MACHINE
VENTILATION REQUIRED FOR HOISTWAY
MACHINE SUPPORT BEAMS
HOIST CABLE
COUNTER-WEIGHT
GUIDE RAIL
PIT LADDER
ELEVATOR PIT
SAFETY BUFFER

ELECTRIC ELEVATOR

Alexander Keyes; Darrel Downing Rippeteau, Architect; Washington, D.C.

GENERAL

ELEVATOR SELECTION depends on several factors: the building's physical characteristics, available elevator systems, and code regulations. The functions that relate these selection parameters and indicate the number, size, and type of elevators are, in most cases, complex and are based on the performance of the elevator systems. Representatives of the elevator industry or consulting elevator engineers should be contacted during the selection process to ensure that the most suitable elevator system is chosen.

PRIVATE RESIDENCES

Elevator selection for private residences can be simplified to a few parameters. By code they are limited in size, capacity, rise, and speed and are installed only in a private residence or a multiple dwelling as a means of access to a single private dwelling.

AVAILABLE ELEVATOR SYSTEMS are outlined on another page. The speed, capacity type, and controls of preengineered systems are generally limited to only a few options.

BUILDING POPULATION analysis involves the identification of the needs of prospective users. Relevant information includes the number of passengers expected to occupy the elevator in one trip and elevator service in a given time period, as well as the number of passengers expected and the possible need for a wheelchair.

BUILDING CHARACTERISTICS affect elevator selection by establishing the building height (distance of elevator travel) and hoistway location. In private residences, the elevator may occupy a tier of closets, an exterior shaft, a room corner, or a stairwell.

ELEVATOR SELECTION–HOSPITAL

The accompanying diagram illustrates elevator selection parameters in the context of a hospital layout. Actual calculations relating these parameters are complex. Consultation with an elevator industry representative or consulting elevator engineer is recommended.

1. BUILDING HEIGHT: Floor-to-floor height and number of floors.
2. BUILDING POPULATION: Total number of building occupants and expected visitors and their expected distribution throughout the building.
3. BUILDING USE ANALYSIS: Location of offices, patients' rooms, service areas, and ancillary spaces conducive to mass assembly. Primary public circulation areas and primary staff circulation areas should be identified.
4. WAITING AREA: Peak loading and waiting time are two important concepts in providing the quality of elevator service expected by hospital visitors and staff. Different standards are applied according to building use. Consult an elevator engineer.
5. LOCATION OF MAJOR ENTRANCES
6. ELEVATOR SYSTEMS: A large selection of elevator capacities, speed, controls, and type are available. In this case, passenger and service elevators are shown. An elevator with a front and rear entrance serves as a passenger elevator during peak visiting hours. The wide variety of elevator alternatives should be discussed with an elevator engineer to select the system most suitable for each individual situation.

SERVICE REQUIREMENTS: Elevators must have sufficient capacity and speed to meet building service requirements. In this case, the elevator must accommodate a 24 x 76 in. ambulance type stretcher with attendants. Check local requirements.

For patient service in hospitals, to accommodate beds with their attachments, use 5000 lb elevators; platforms 6 ft wide x 9 ft 6 in. deep, doors at least 4 ft wide (4 ft 6 in. width is preferred).

CODE AND REGULATIONS: Recommendations and code restrictions regarding handicapped access, fire safety, elevator controls, and so on, may affect elevator selection. Consult with an elevator industry representative or consulting elevator engineer. As a minimum the ANSI A17.1 for Elevators, Dumbwaiters, Escalators and Moving Walks should be complied with.

NOTE: Elevators should not be considered as emergency exits.

ELEVATOR SYSTEMS IN BUILDINGS OTHER THAN PRIVATE HOMES

Selection of elevator systems increases in complexity with the size and complexity of the project. Even though the vertical transportation needs of lowrise residential and commercial projects may be simply met, all the parameters listed below should be considered and analyzed with a consulting elevator engineer to ensure proper selection.

BUILDING POPULATION

The elevator selection process must begin with a thorough analysis of how people will occupy the building.

1. TOTAL POPULATION AND DENSITY: The total number of occupants and visitors and their distribution by floors within a building.
2. PEAK LOADING: Periods when elevators carry the highest traffic loads. For example, peak loading in office buildings coincides with rush hours and/or lunch periods, while peak loading in hospitals may occur during visiting hours.
3. WAITING TIME: The length of time a passenger is expected to wait for the next elevator to arrive. These demands vary according to building use and building occupant expectations. A person willing to wait 50–70 sec in an apartment building may be willing to wait only 20–35 sec in an office building.
4. DEMAND FOR QUALITY: Sophistication of controls and elevator capacity may be varied to cater to the expected taste of passengers. Large elevator cars and the smooth, long life operation of a gearless elevator may convey an image of luxury even if a smaller elevator having a less sophisticated system would be technically sufficient.

BUILDING CHARACTERISTICS

Physical building characteristics are considered together with population characteristics to determine size, speed, type, and location of elevator systems.

1. HEIGHT: The distance of elevator travel (from lowest terminal to top terminal), number of floors, and floor height.
2. BUILDING USE ANALYSIS: Location of building entrance areas of heavy use such as cafeteria, restaurant, auditorium, and service areas must be identified. Typically, a building should be planned to ensure that no prospective passengers must walk more than 200 ft to reach an elevator.

ELEVATOR SYSTEMS AND REGULATIONS

The parameters previously described outline the environment in which the elevator operates. Local code regulations and ANSI A17.1 requirements provide further elevator guidelines.

Available elevator systems are analyzed to ensure that suitable speed, capacity, controls, and number of cars are selected.

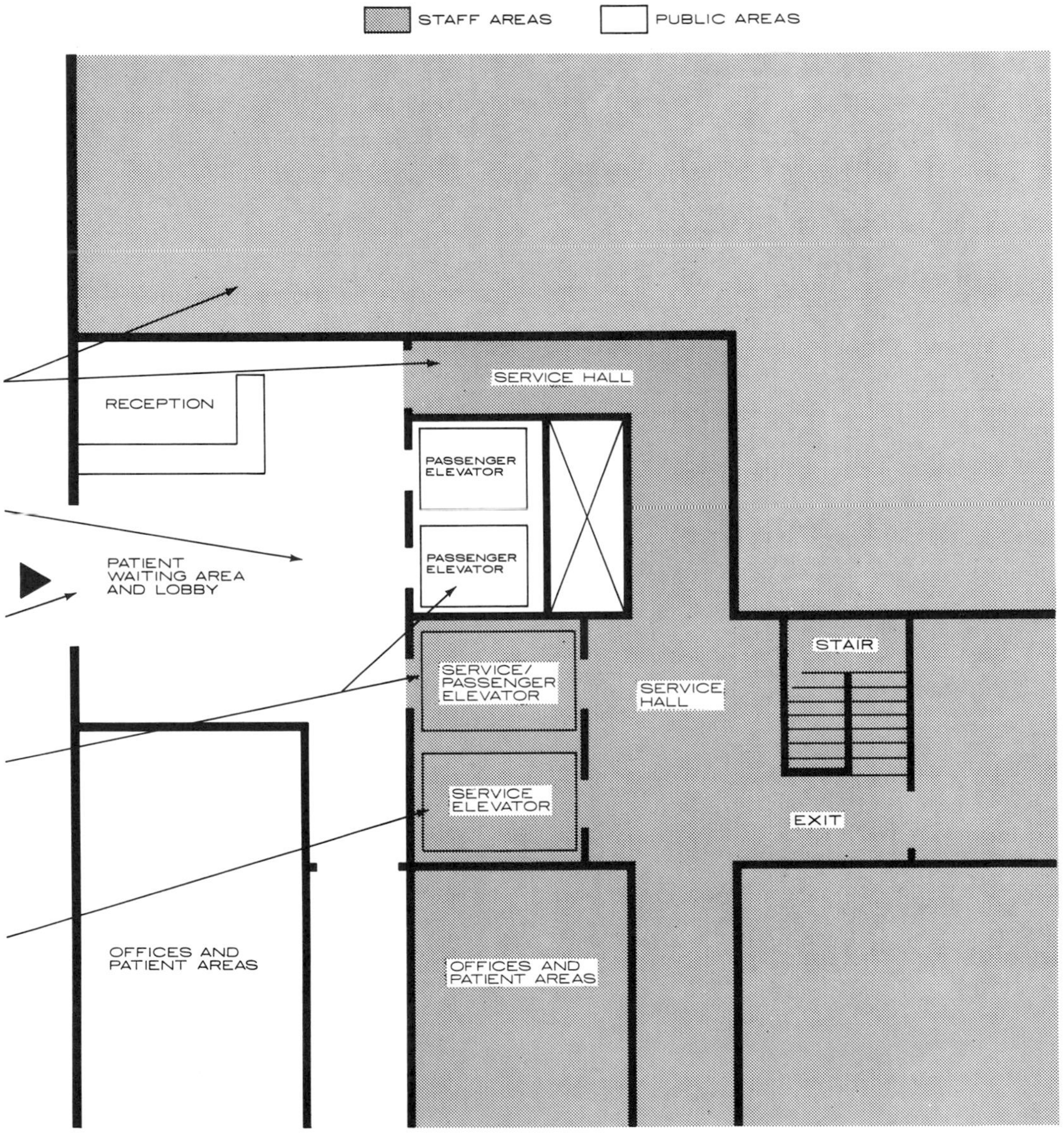

ELEVATOR SELECTION FACTORS — HOSPITAL

Alexander Keyes; Darrel Downing Rippeteau, Architect; Washington, D.C.

GENERAL NOTES

Lowrise buildings may use either the hydraulic or the electric elevator systems. Elevator selection, arrangement, and design of lobby and cars are similar in both cases. The primary differences between the two systems are in their operational requirements. The hydraulic elevator system is described below; the electric elevator system on the next page.

The major architectural considerations of the hydraulic elevator are the machine room, normally located at the base, and the hoistway serving as a fire protected, ventilated passageway for the elevator car. Adequate structure must be provided at the base of the hoistway to bear the load of the elevator car and its supporting piston or cylinder.

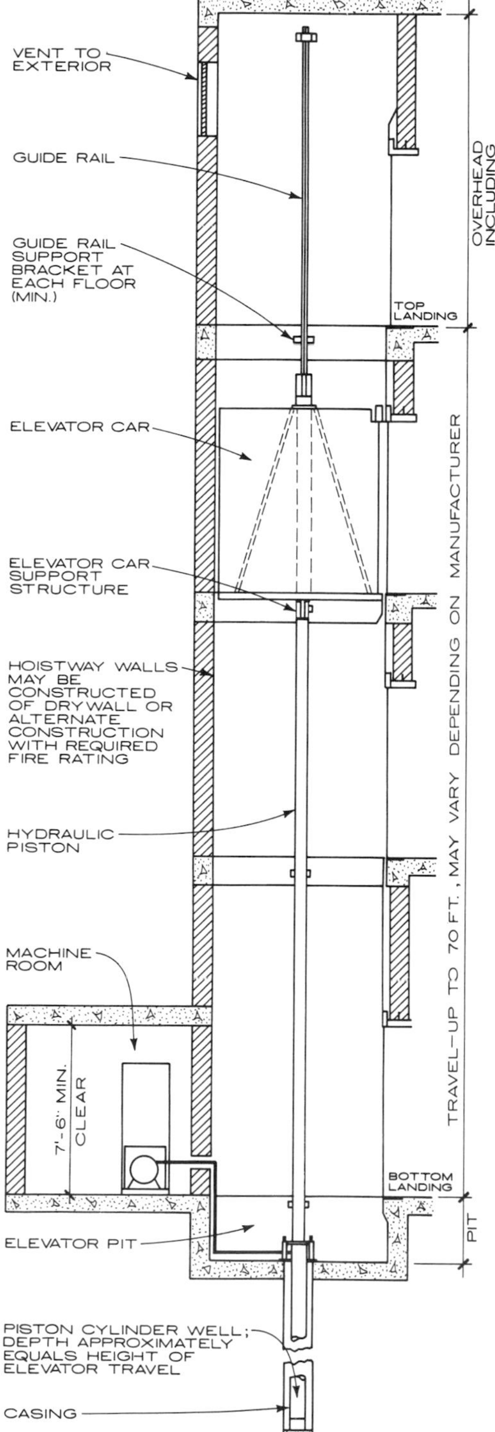
VENT TO EXTERIOR
GUIDE RAIL
GUIDE RAIL SUPPORT BRACKET AT EACH FLOOR (MIN.)
OVERHEAD INCLUDING CLEARANCE
TOP LANDING
ELEVATOR CAR
ELEVATOR CAR SUPPORT STRUCTURE
HOISTWAY WALLS MAY BE CONSTRUCTED OF DRYWALL OR ALTERNATE CONSTRUCTION WITH REQUIRED FIRE RATING
TRAVEL–UP TO 70 FT., MAY VARY DEPENDING ON MANUFACTURER
HYDRAULIC PISTON
MACHINE ROOM
7'-6" MIN. CLEAR
BOTTOM LANDING
PIT
ELEVATOR PIT
PISTON CYLINDER WELL; DEPTH APPROXIMATELY EQUALS HEIGHT OF ELEVATOR TRAVEL
CASING

HYDRAULIC ELEVATOR – SECTION

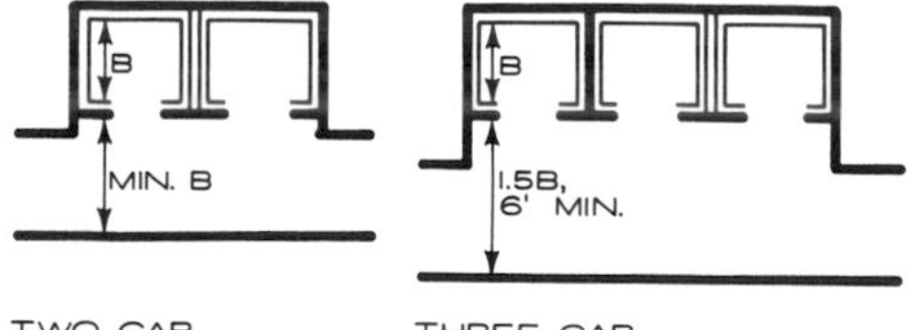
B
MIN. B
1.5B, 6' MIN.
TWO CAR, SIDE BY SIDE
THREE CAR, SIDE BY SIDE

B = DEPTH OF CAR

NOTES

Certain guidelines lead to effective placement, grouping, and arrangement of elevators within a building. Elevators should be: (a) centrally located, (b) near the main entrance, and (c) easily accessible on all floors. If a building requires more than one elevator, they should be grouped, with possible exception of service elevators.

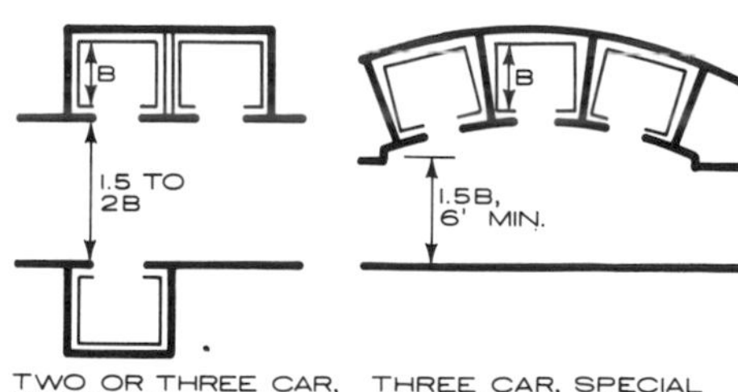
B
1.5 TO 2B
1.5B, 6' MIN.
TWO OR THREE CAR, OPPOSITE
THREE CAR, SPECIAL ARRANGEMENT

Within each grouping, elevators should be arranged to minimize walking distance between cars. Sufficient lobby space must be provided to accommodate group movement.

ELEVATOR ARRANGEMENT, TWO AND THREE CARS (TYPICAL FOR LOWRISE APPLICATIONS)

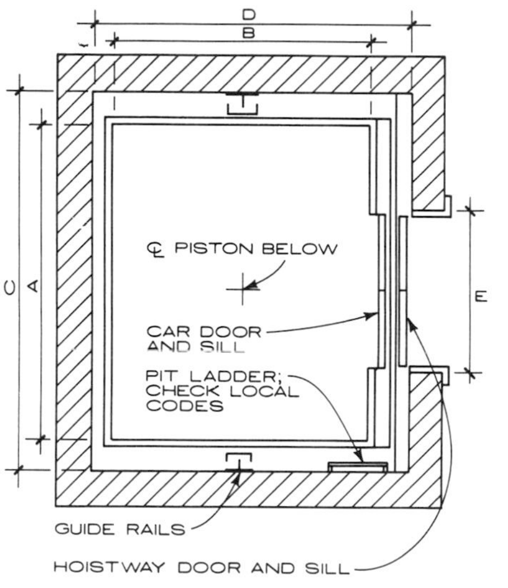
D
B
C
A
E
℄ PISTON BELOW
CAR DOOR AND SILL
PIT LADDER; CHECK LOCAL CODES
GUIDE RAILS
HOISTWAY DOOR AND SILL

HYDRAULIC ELEVATOR DIMENSIONS

RATED LOAD (LB)	DIMENSIONS (FT-IN.)				
	A	B	C	D	E
1500	4-10	5-0	6-8	5-9	2-8
2000	6-0	5-0	7-4	5-9	3-0
2500	7-0	5-0	8-4	5-9	3-6
3000	7-0	5-6	8-4	6-3	3-6
3500	7-0	6-2	8-4	6-11	3-6
4000	5-8	8-9	7-4	9-8	4-0

Rated speeds are 75 to 200 fpm.

NOTES

Elevator car and hoistway dimensions of the preengineered units listed above are for reference purposes only. A broad selection of units is available. Representatives of the elevator industry should be contacted for the dimensions of specific systems.

Hoistway walls normally serve primarily as fireproof enclosures. Check local codes for required fire ratings. Guide rails extend from the pit floor to the underside of the overhead. When excessive floor heights are encountered consult the elevator supplier for special requirements.

ELEVATOR CAR AND HOISTWAY

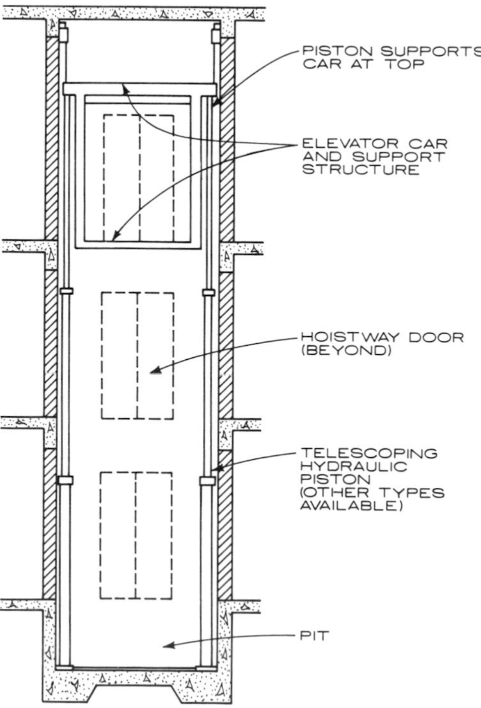
PISTON SUPPORTS CAR AT TOP
ELEVATOR CAR AND SUPPORT STRUCTURE
HOISTWAY DOOR (BEYOND)
TELESCOPING HYDRAULIC PISTON (OTHER TYPES AVAILABLE)
PIT

One type of holeless hydraulic elevator uses a telescoping hydraulic piston as the driving machine, eliminating the need for cylinder well excavation. This system is presently limited to a height of three stories or 21 ft 6 in. Other types of holeless hydraulic elevator units are also available using an inverted cylinder attached to the side of the elevator car.

HOLELESS HYDRAULIC ELEVATOR – SECTION

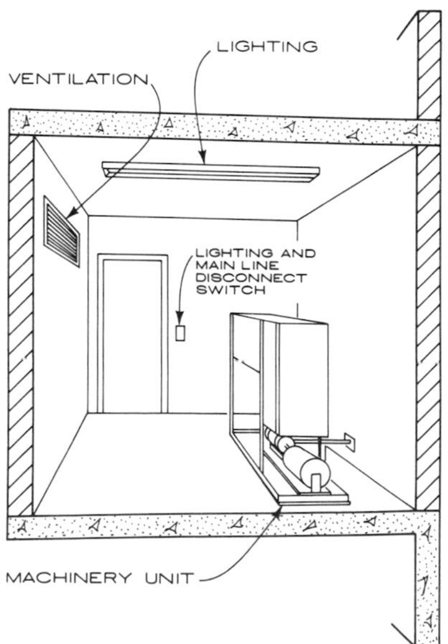
LIGHTING
VENTILATION
LIGHTING AND MAIN LINE DISCONNECT SWITCH
MACHINERY UNIT

The MACHINE ROOM of a hydraulic elevator system is usually located next to the hoistway at or near the bottom terminal landing. Consult with elevator manufacturers for required dimensions. Refer to local codes.

Machinery consists of a pump and motor drive unit, hydraulic fluid storage tank, and control panel. Adequate ventilation, lighting, and entrance access (usually 3 ft 6 in. x 7 ft) should be provided.

MACHINE ROOM

Alexander Keyes; Darrel Downing Rippeteau, Architect; Washington, D.C.

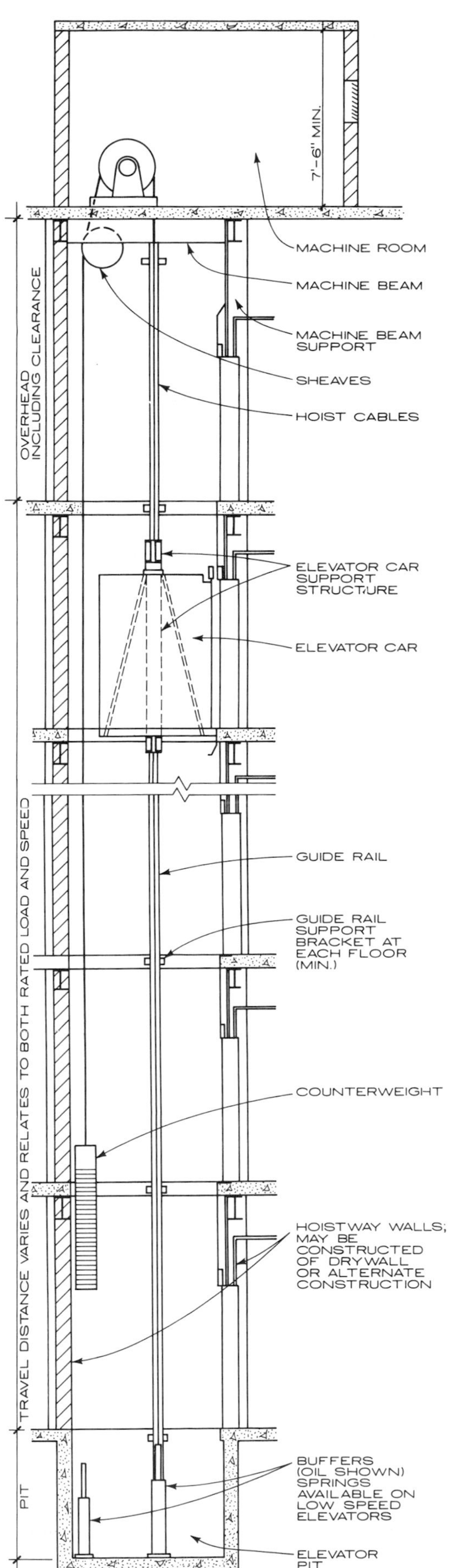
7'-6" MIN.
OVERHEAD INCLUDING CLEARANCE
MACHINE ROOM
MACHINE BEAM
MACHINE BEAM SUPPORT
SHEAVES
HOIST CABLES
ELEVATOR CAR SUPPORT STRUCTURE
ELEVATOR CAR
GUIDE RAIL
GUIDE RAIL SUPPORT BRACKET AT EACH FLOOR (MIN.)
TRAVEL DISTANCE VARIES AND RELATES TO BOTH RATED LOAD AND SPEED
COUNTERWEIGHT
HOISTWAY WALLS; MAY BE CONSTRUCTED OF DRYWALL OR ALTERNATE CONSTRUCTION
PIT
BUFFERS (OIL SHOWN) SPRINGS AVAILABLE ON LOW SPEED ELEVATORS
ELEVATOR PIT

ELECTRIC ELEVATOR – SECTION

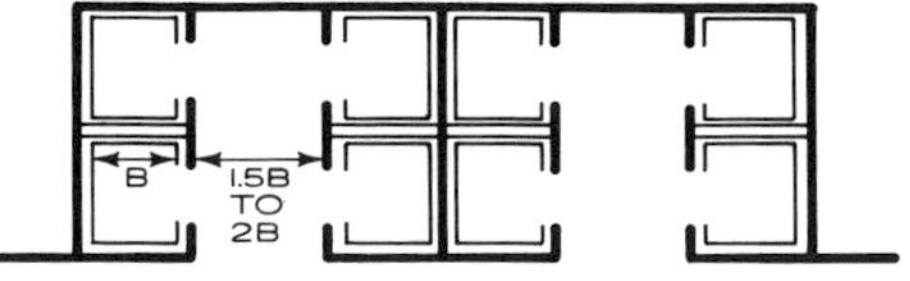
B
1.5B TO 2B

B = DEPTH OF CAR

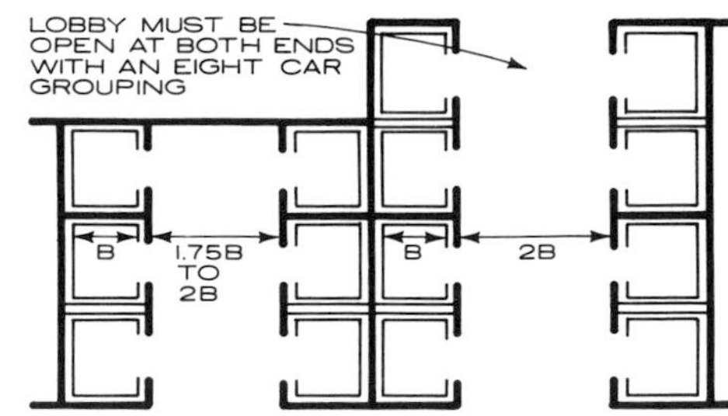
LOBBY MUST BE OPEN AT BOTH ENDS WITH AN EIGHT CAR GROUPING
B
1.75B TO 2B
B
2B

NOTES

The largest practical grouping of elevators in a building is eight cars. One row of more than four cars is generally unacceptable. With groupings of four or six cars, waiting lobbies may be alcoved (one end closed) or open at both ends. In case of several elevator groupings, one grouping may serve lower floors, while others are express elevators to upper floors.

Where 4 or more elevators serve all or the same portion of a building, they shall be located in not less than 2 hoistways, but in no case shall more than 4 elevators be located in any one hoistway.

ELEVATOR ARRANGEMENTS – FOUR, SIX, AND EIGHT CARS (TYPICAL FOR HIGHRISE APPLICATIONS)

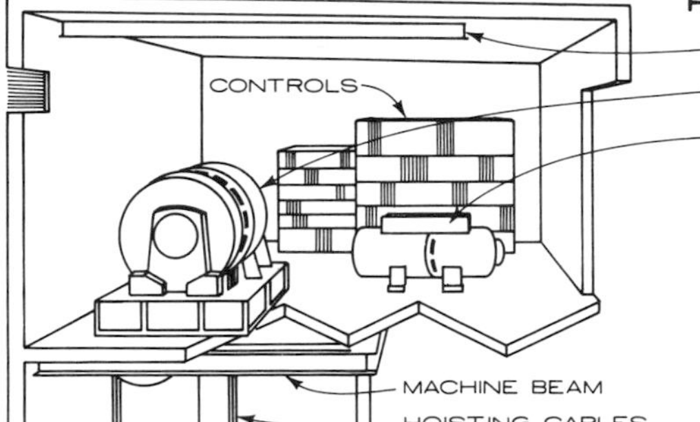
CONTROLS
MACHINE HOISTING BEAM
GEARLESS HOISTING MACHINE
MOTOR – GENERATOR SET
MACHINE BEAM
HOISTING CABLES
HOISTWAY WALL

NOTES

The MACHINE ROOM for electric elevators is normally located directly above the hoistway. Space must be provided for the elevator drive, control equipment, and governor with sufficient clearance for equipment installation, repair, or removal. Space requirements vary substantially according to code capacity and speed of the system selected. Adequate lighting and ventilation are required by codes, and sound insulation should be provided.

MACHINE ROOM (GEARLESS ELEVATOR)

C
A
COUNTERWEIGHT AND GUIDES
D
B
CAR
GUIDES
PIT LADDER; CHECK CODES
E
STEEL BEAM SUPPORT FOR GUIDE RAIL AT EACH FLOOR (MIN.)
HOISTWAY DOOR AND SILL

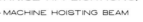

ELECTRIC ELEVATOR DIMENSIONS

RATED LOAD (LB)	DIMENSIONS (FT-IN.)				
	A	B	C	D	E
2000	6-0	5-0	7-4	6-10	3-0
2500	7-0	5-0	8-4	6-7	3-6
3000	7-0	5-6	8-4	7-1	3-6
3500	7-0	6-2	8-4	7-7	3-6
4000	5-8	8-9	7-8	9-8	4-0

NOTES

Dimensions of preengineered units, listed above, are for reference purposes only. Elevator manufacturers should be consulted for a complete selection.

ELEVATOR HOISTWAY AND CAR – ELECTRIC ELEVATOR

NOTES

Medium and highrise buildings utilize ELECTRIC GEARED TRACTION and ELECTRIC GEARLESS TRACTION elevator systems. The main difference between the two systems lies in the hoisting machinery. General design considerations involving hoistway, machine room, and elevator planning are similar.

ELECTRIC GEARLESS TRACTION ELEVATOR systems are available in preengineered units with speeds of 200 to 1200 fpm. Systems with greater speeds are also available. Gearless elevators, when used in conjunction with appropriate controls, offer the advantages of a long life and smoothness of ride.

ELECTRIC GEARED TRACTION ELEVATOR systems are designed to operate within the range of 100 to 350 fpm, which restricts their use to medium rise buildings.

Both geared and gearless drive units are governed by CONTROLS, which coordinate car leveling, passenger calls, collective operation of elevators, door operation, car acceleration and deceleration, and safety applications. A broad range of control systems are available to meet individual building requirements.

STRUCTURAL REQUIREMENTS call for the total weight of the elevator system to be supported by the MACHINE BEAMS and transmitted to the building (or hoistway) structure. Consult with elevator and structural engineers.

If the elevator machine is to be supported solely by the machine room floor slab, the floor slab shall be designed in accordance with the requirements of ANSI A17.1.

Check local codes for required fire enclosures.

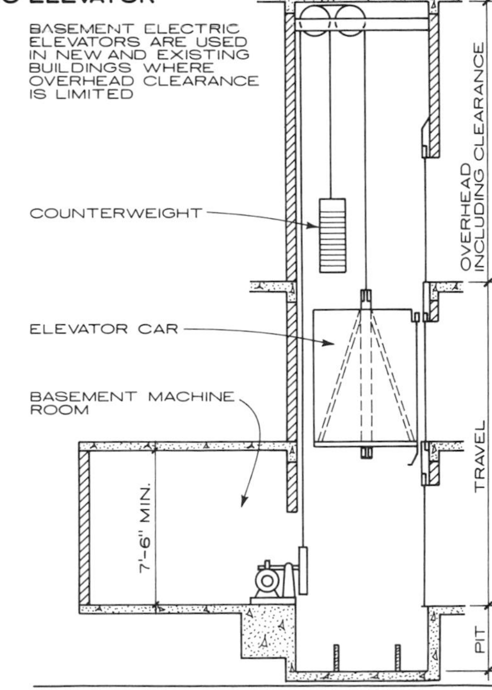
BASEMENT ELECTRIC ELEVATORS ARE USED IN NEW AND EXISTING BUILDINGS WHERE OVERHEAD CLEARANCE IS LIMITED
OVERHEAD INCLUDING CLEARANCE
COUNTERWEIGHT
ELEVATOR CAR
BASEMENT MACHINE ROOM
7'-6" MIN.
TRAVEL
PIT

BASEMENT ELECTRIC ELEVATOR – SECTION

Alexander Keyes; Darrel Downing Rippeteau, Architect; Washington, D.C.

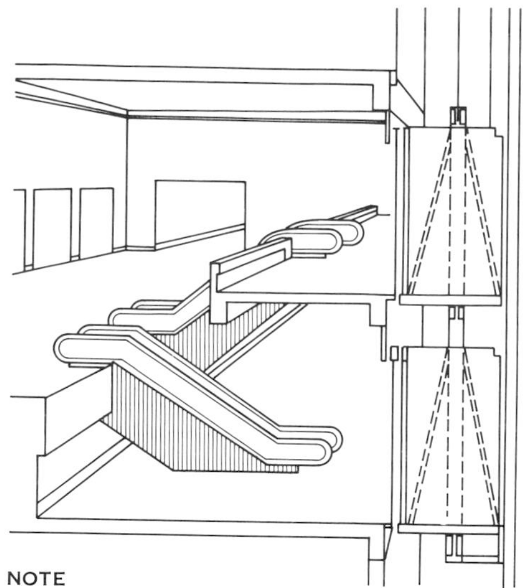

NOTE

In buildings with heavy populations double deck elevators permit an increase in handling capacity without increasing the number of elevators. Two cars in tandem operate simultaneously, one serving all floors. Escalators connect the two floors in 2-story lobbies.

DOUBLE DECK ELEVATOR

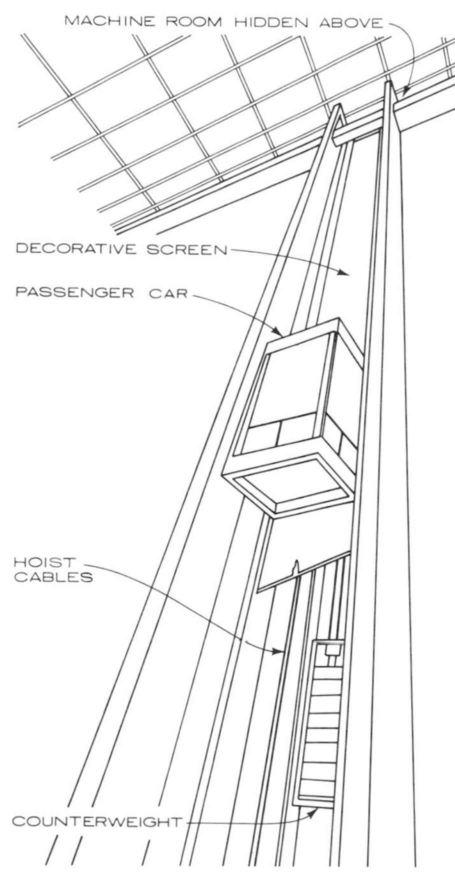
MACHINE ROOM HIDDEN ABOVE
DECORATIVE SCREEN
PASSENGER CAR
HOIST CABLES
COUNTERWEIGHT

NOTE

Observation and glassback elevators travel outside of a hoistway or in a hoistway open on one side. Machinery is concealed or designed to be inconspicuous. Elevators may be engineered for hydraulic, geared, or gearless use. Cabs can be custom designed with over 75% of wall area as glass. Glassback cabs provide glass rear panel only. Safety barriers must be provided at floor penetrations and ground floor, completely surrounding that part of elevator not enclosed by hoistway.

OBSERVATION ELEVATOR

FIRE RATED HOISTWAY ENCLOSURE
CAR DOOR
HOISTWAY DOOR
HANDRAILS 32" ABOVE FLOOR
GUIDE RAILS IN HOISTWAY
NONSLIP FLOOR COVERING
CONTROL PANEL ACCESSIBLE FROM WHEELCHAIR

PLAN OF ELEVATOR CAR WITH REAR DOOR

HORIZONTAL SLIDE BIPARTING DOORS
TWO SPEED HORIZONTAL SLIDE DOORS
SINGLE SLIDE CAR DOOR WITH SWING HOISTWAY DOOR

ELEVATOR DOOR TYPES

HALL LANTERNS — SHOW CAR DIRECTION; SHOULD BE CLEARLY VISIBLE FROM ANY POINT IN THE LOBBY AND EQUIPPED WITH A GONG FOR THE VISUALLY IMPAIRED
CAR POSITION INDICATOR
DOORS AND FRAMES OF HEAVY GAUGE METAL
CALL BUTTONS MOUNTED 42" ABOVE FLOOR
FLOOR INDICATION ON BOTH JAMBS, 5'-0" ABOVE FLOOR
TRAFFIC DIRECTOR'S PANEL IN MAIN LOBBY FOR OVERVIEW OF SYSTEM, WITH KEYED MANUAL OVERRIDE FOR EMERGENCIES
ENTRANCE SAFETY DEVICES (LIGHT BEAM PHOTOCELL, ELECTRONIC PROXIMITY DETECTOR, ETC.) MOUNTED ON CAR DOOR
B 1 2 3 4 5 6 7 8 9

ELEVATOR LOBBY

VENTILATION — CHANGE AIR TWICE EVERY MINUTE
LIGHTING — GLAREFREE, MIN. 5 FT-C
CAR POSITION INDICATOR
SIGN PROHIBITING USE OF ELEVATOR DURING EMERGENCIES
CONTROL PANEL: CALL BUTTONS, DOOR OPEN, EMERGENCY STOP, FLOOR ALARM, INTERCOM TO TRAFFIC DIRECTOR'S PANEL
HANDRAIL, MOUNTED 32" ABOVE FLOOR
TELEPHONE FOR EMERGENCY USE
NONSLIP FLOOR FINISH
LOAD WEIGHING DEVICE BELOW CAR

INTERIOR OF ELEVATOR CAR

Alexander Keyes; Darrel Downing Rippeteau, Architect; Washington, D.C.

SERVICE ELEVATORS

Service elevators in industrial, residential, and commercial buildings are often standard passenger elevator packages modified for service use. These modified systems, when compared with custom made freight elevator systems, are generally more economical, are delivered in less time, and have more stringent load ratings related to the platform area. Special provisions include interior cab protection (steel or oak rubbing strips or suitable abuse resistant finish surface) and a door and cab of sufficient size to handle expected loads. Standard horizontal sliding doors can often meet service needs. If the full width of the car platform is needed for loading, vertical biparting doors can be used. If bulky loads are expected only occasionally, a removable car front with swinging hoistway door panels can be provided.

Vertically sliding doors and vertically sliding gates, where permitted by ANSI A17.1, shall conform to the following requirements:

1. At entrances used by passengers they shall be:
   a. Of the balanced counterweighted type which slide in the up direction to open.
   b. Power operated.
2. At entrances used exclusively for freight, they shall be:
   a. Of the balanced counterweighted type or the biparting counterbalanced type.
   b. Manually or power operated.

CAPACITY: Size to largest expected load, with the exception of single one piece loading, which is restricted to 25% of the rated capacity.

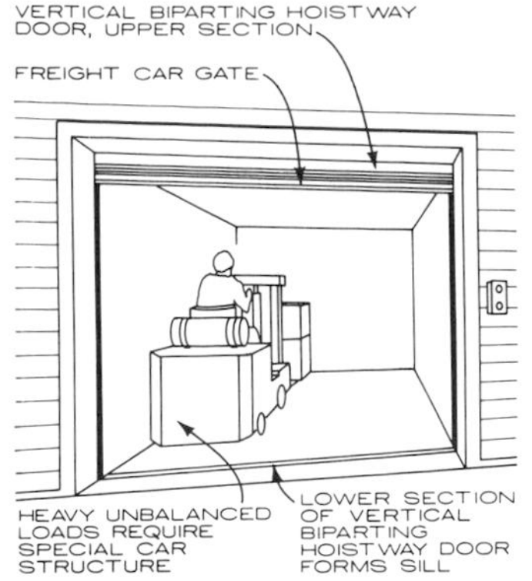
VERTICAL BIPARTING HOISTWAY DOOR, UPPER SECTION
FREIGHT CAR GATE
HEAVY UNBALANCED LOADS REQUIRE SPECIAL CAR STRUCTURE
LOWER SECTION OF VERTICAL BIPARTING HOISTWAY DOOR FORMS SILL

INTERIOR VIEW

FREIGHT ELEVATOR DIMENSIONS

CAPACITY (LB)	PLATFORM		HOISTWAY	
	WIDTH	DEPTH	WIDTH	DEPTH
2,500	5′-4″	7′-0″	7′-4″	8′-2″
6,000	8′-4″	10′-0″	10′-4″	11′-2″
10,000	8′-4″	12′-0″	11′-4″	13′-2″
16,000	10′-4″	14′-0″	14′-0″	15′-2″
20,000	12′-4″	20′-4″	16′-6″	21′-6″

FREIGHT ELEVATOR

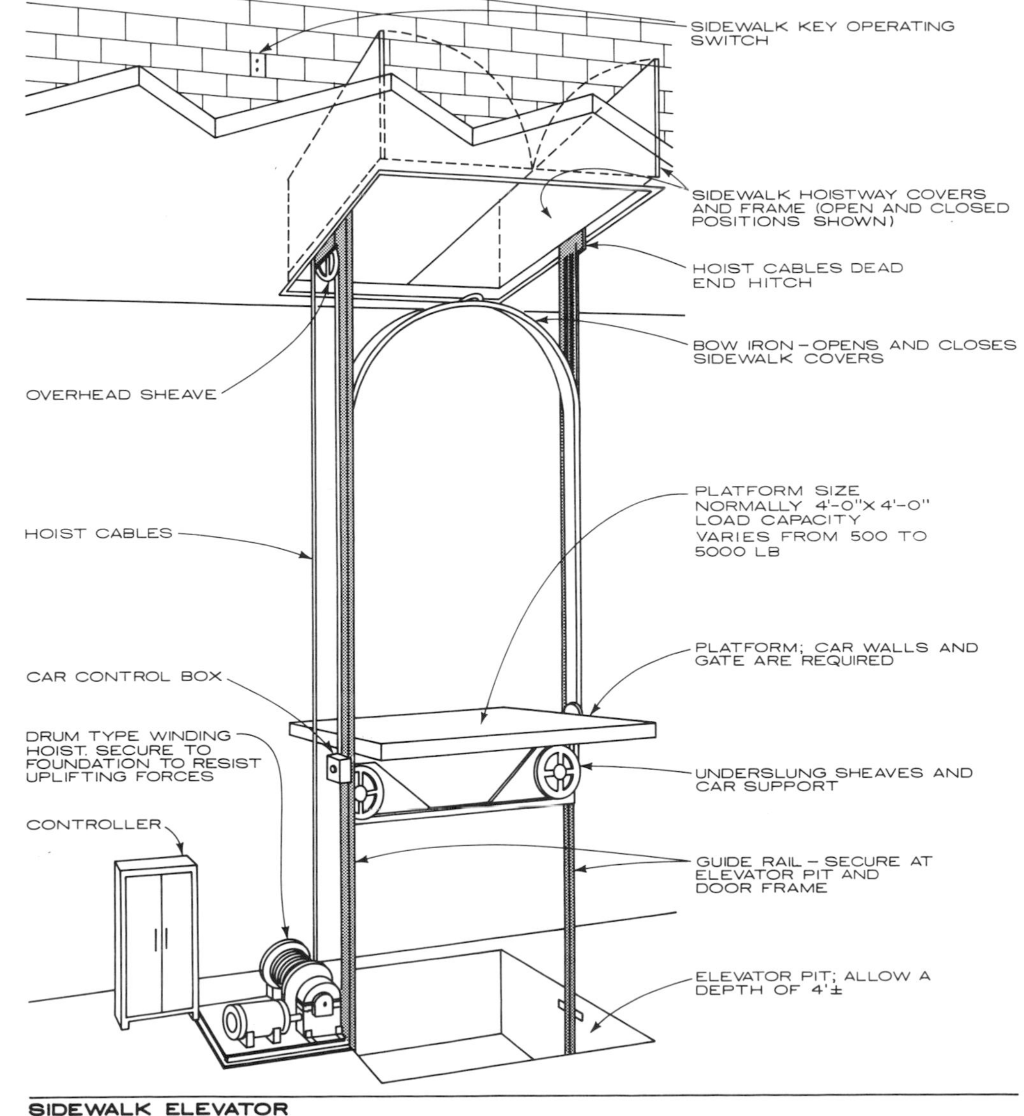
SIDEWALK KEY OPERATING SWITCH
SIDEWALK HOISTWAY COVERS AND FRAME (OPEN AND CLOSED POSITIONS SHOWN)
HOIST CABLES DEAD END HITCH
BOW IRON – OPENS AND CLOSES SIDEWALK COVERS
OVERHEAD SHEAVE
PLATFORM SIZE NORMALLY 4′-0″×4′-0″ LOAD CAPACITY VARIES FROM 500 TO 5000 LB
HOIST CABLES
PLATFORM; CAR WALLS AND GATE ARE REQUIRED
CAR CONTROL BOX
DRUM TYPE WINDING HOIST. SECURE TO FOUNDATION TO RESIST UPLIFTING FORCES
UNDERSLUNG SHEAVES AND CAR SUPPORT
CONTROLLER
GUIDE RAIL – SECURE AT ELEVATOR PIT AND DOOR FRAME
ELEVATOR PIT; ALLOW A DEPTH OF 4′±

SIDEWALK ELEVATOR

FREIGHT ELEVATORS

Freight elevators are usually classed as general freight loading, motor vehicle loading, industrial truck or concentrated loading elevators. General freight loading elevators, described below, may be electric drum type or traction or hydraulic elevators.

General freight loading elevators satisfy a variety of material handling requirements with capacities of 2000 to 8000 lb. Industrial truck loading freight elevators require special design considerations to handle truck loads of 10,000 to 20,000 lb or more.

General freight or industrial truck elevators may have either hydraulic or electric drive systems, similar to those described on previous pages. The units are usually custom designed with vertical biparting doors and special structural support to carry increased loads and eccentric loading conditions.

Freight elevators usually operate at slower speeds with simple control systems. Capacity must be sized for the largest expected load.

LIGHT DUTY FREIGHT ELEVATORS with capacities of 1000 to 2500 lb may utilize hydraulic or traction drives. Standard systems are illustrated on other pages of this section. Two special types of light freight elevators, with rises limited according to manufacturer, are the SIDEWALK ELEVATOR and the SELF-SUPPORTING ELEVATOR.

The SIDEWALK ELEVATOR, illustrated on this page with an electric winding drum type machine, rises to a top level through hatch doors. Note that local codes often forbid the raising of an elevator in a public sidewalk; elevators may have to be located within building lines.

The SELF-SUPPORTING FREIGHT ELEVATOR is similar to the sidewalk elevator illustrated and operates within a building up to three stories (rise varies with manufacturer). Weight of the car is transferred through the supporting guide rails to the elevator pit.

With the electric winding drum machine, machinery must lift the full weight of car and its load. The drum must be anchored to the floor to resist uplifting forces. Safety codes forbid use of electric winding drum machines for passenger elevators and restrict their use on freight elevators to a speed not exceeding 50 fpm and a travel not exceeding 40 ft; they shall not be provided with counterweights.

SELF-SUPPORTING ELEVATOR DIMENSIONS

CAPACITY (LB)	PLATFORM		HOISTWAY	
	WIDTH	DEPTH	WIDTH	DEPTH
1,500	5′-4″	6′-1″	6′-11″	6′-9″
2,000	6′-4″	7′-0″	7′-11″	7′-8″
2,500	6′-4″	8′-0″	7′-11″	8′-8″

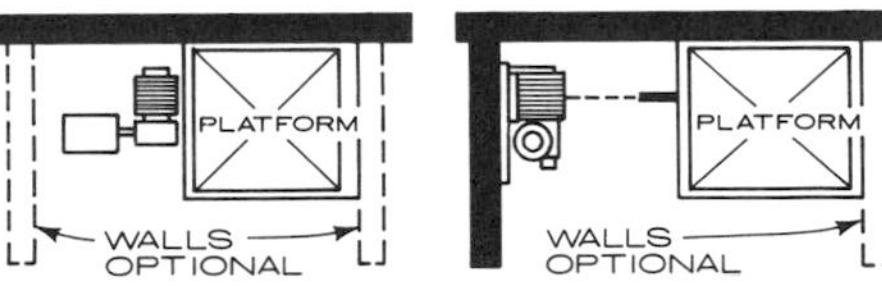
PLATFORM
WALLS OPTIONAL
PLATFORM
WALLS OPTIONAL

SIDE MOUNTED WALL MOUNTED

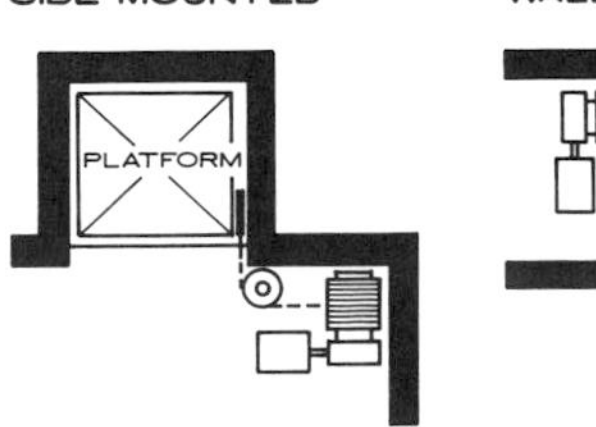
PLATFORM

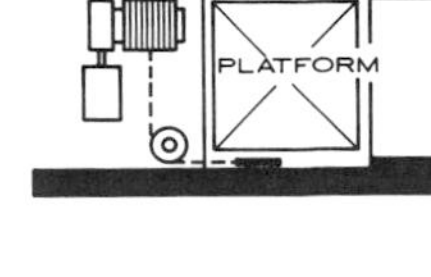
PLATFORM

AROUND THE CORNER MACHINE IN BACK

MACHINE LAYOUTS – WINDING DRUM TYPE

Alexander Keyes; Darrel Downing Rippeteau, Architect; Washington, D.C.

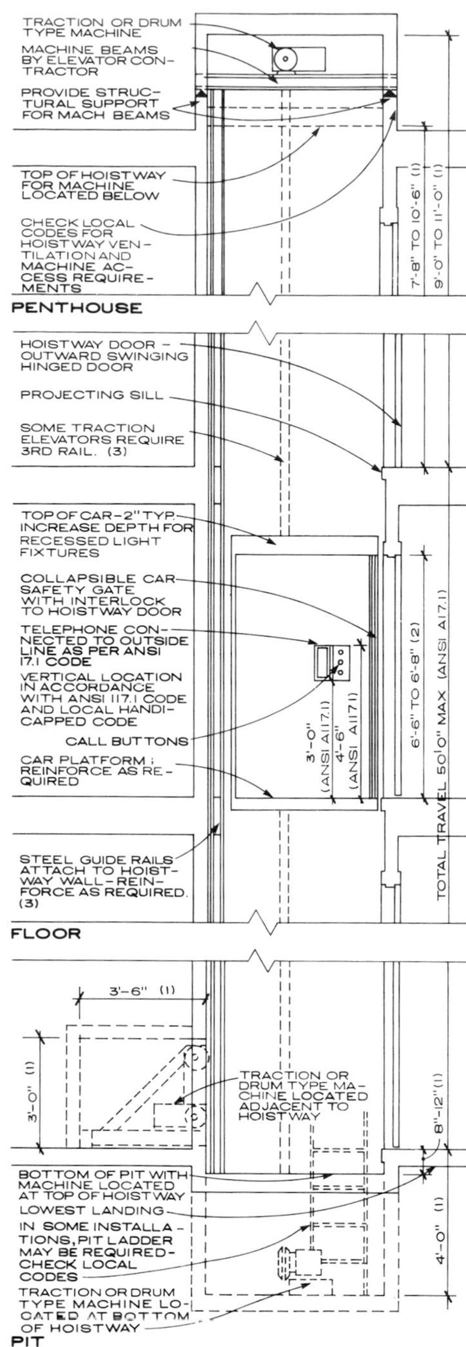
TRACTION OR DRUM TYPE MACHINE
MACHINE BEAMS BY ELEVATOR CONTRACTOR
PROVIDE STRUCTURAL SUPPORT FOR MACH BEAMS
TOP OF HOISTWAY FOR MACHINE LOCATED BELOW
CHECK LOCAL CODES FOR HOISTWAY VENTILATION AND MACHINE ACCESS REQUIREMENTS
7'-8" TO 10'-6" (1)
9'-0" TO 11'-0" (1)
PENTHOUSE
HOISTWAY DOOR - OUTWARD SWINGING HINGED DOOR
PROJECTING SILL
SOME TRACTION ELEVATORS REQUIRE 3RD RAIL. (3)
TOP OF CAR-2" TYP- INCREASE DEPTH FOR RECESSED LIGHT FIXTURES
COLLAPSIBLE CAR SAFETY GATE WITH INTERLOCK TO HOISTWAY DOOR
TELEPHONE CONNECTED TO OUTSIDE LINE AS PER ANSI 17.1 CODE
VERTICAL LOCATION IN ACCORDANCE WITH ANSI 117.1 CODE AND LOCAL HANDICAPPED CODE
CALL BUTTONS
CAR PLATFORM; REINFORCE AS REQUIRED
3'-0" (ANSI A117.1)
4'-6" (ANSI A117.1)
6'-6" TO 6'-8" (2)
TOTAL TRAVEL 50'0" MAX (ANSI A17.1)
STEEL GUIDE RAILS ATTACH TO HOISTWAY WALL - REINFORCE AS REQUIRED. (3)
FLOOR
3'-6" (1)
3'-0" (1)
TRACTION OR DRUM TYPE MACHINE LOCATED ADJACENT TO HOISTWAY
8'-12" (1)
BOTTOM OF PIT WITH MACHINE LOCATED AT TOP OF HOISTWAY
LOWEST LANDING
IN SOME INSTALLATIONS, PIT LADDER MAY BE REQUIRED - CHECK LOCAL CODES
TRACTION OR DRUM TYPE MACHINE LOCATED AT BOTTOM OF HOISTWAY
4'-0" (1)
PIT
ELEVATOR SECTION

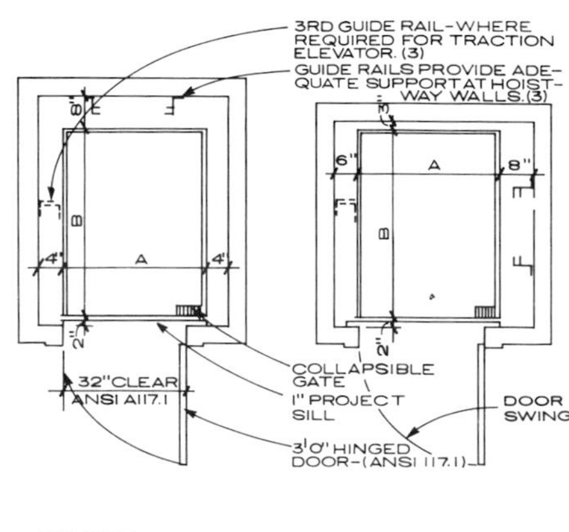
3RD GUIDE RAIL-WHERE REQUIRED FOR TRACTION ELEVATOR. (3)
GUIDE RAILS PROVIDE ADEQUATE SUPPORT AT HOISTWAY WALLS.(3)
A
B
4"
6"
8"
32"CLEAR ANSI A117.1
COLLAPSIBLE GATE
1" PROJECT SILL
DOOR SWING
3'0" HINGED DOOR-(ANSI 117.1)
CAR WITH RAILS AT REAR (4,5)
CAR WITH RAILS AT SIDE (4,5)
RESIDENTIAL ELEVATOR PLANS

RESIDENTIAL ELEVATORS

Typical car sizes, A x B: 36 in. x 36 in., 42 in. x 42 in., 36 in. x 48 in.

12 sq ft platform maximum size allowed by National Elevator Code for residential elevators, ANSI A17.1. This platform size does not meet the National Handicapped Access Code, ANSI A117.1, for use by an unassisted wheelchair-bound person.

Load capacity of drum-type machine is 450 lb. Speed is 30 ft per minute.

Load capacity of traction machine is 700 lb. Speed is 36 ft per minute.

Elevators operate on 220/230 volt, single phase power supply. A disconnect switch must be provided within sight of the machine. A 110V, single phase power supply is required for lighting of machine area of hoistway.

Enclosures are recommended for all hoistways. Fire rating of hoistway enclosure and access doors must be consistent with the fire rating of the building construction. See local codes.

NOTES

1. Dimensions may vary among manufacturers and according to system selected. Elevators carrying greater loads or operating at higher speeds require more clearance overhead and in pit areas.
2. Elevator cars may have higher interior clearances if desired, which increases overhead clearance required in the hoistway.
3. Guide rails usually are provided by the manufacturer in 5 ft sections. Some manufacturers supply rails that can span from floor structure to floor structure. If the existing structure cannot support the guide rails, manufacturers can provide a self-supporting tower that transmits the load to its base. Increased horizontal clearance in the hoistway is required. If a third guide rail is required, it is supplied in 3 ft 4 in. sections.
4. Dimensions given are appropriate for most applications. For exact dimensions required in specific circumstances, consult manufacturers.
5. Elevator cars can be provided with openings on two sides; guide rails must be located accordingly. Consult manufacturers.

DUMBWAITERS

Typical car sizes, A x B: 24 in. x 24 in., 30 in. x 30 in., 36 in. x 36 in., 30 in. x 48 in. Smaller sizes are available.

9 sq ft platform maximum size allowed by National Elevator Code for dumbwaiters, ANSI A17.1.

48 in. high car is maximum allowed by National Elevator Code for dumbwaiters, ANSI A17.1.

Load capacity for drum-type machines is 500 lb. Speed is 50 ft per minute.

Drum-type machines are not recommended for installations with total travel of more than 36 ft–40 ft. Maximum total travel 50 ft.

Load capacity of traction machines is 500 lb. Speeds to 500 ft per minute are available.

Dumbwaiters require 3 phase electrical power. For exact voltage consult manufacturer.

NOTES

1. Dimensions may vary among manufacturers and according to system selected. Dumbwaiters carrying greater loads or operating at higher speeds require more clearance overhead and in pit areas.
2. Guide rails usually are provided by the manufacturer in 5 ft sections. Some manufacturers supply rails that can span from floor structure to floor structure. If existing structure cannot support the guide rails, manufacturers can provide a self-supporting tower that transmits the load to its base. Increased horizontal clearance in the hoistway is required.
3. Vertical dimensions given assume the use of vertical bi-parting doors. The entire door may slide up or down; however, required clearances will vary. Swing hoistway doors also are available. Consult manufacturers.

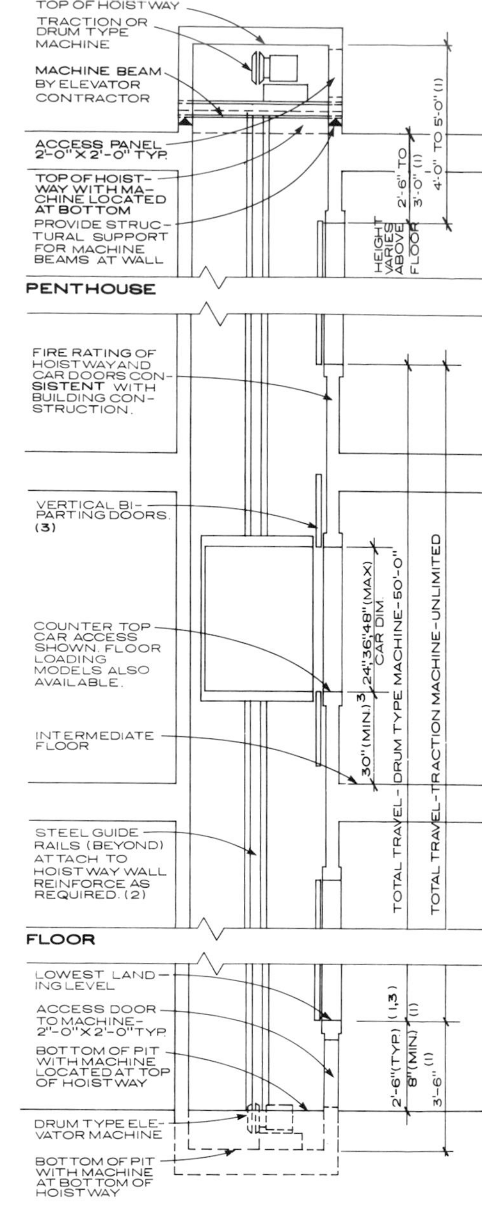
TOP OF HOISTWAY
TRACTION OR DRUM TYPE MACHINE
MACHINE BEAM BY ELEVATOR CONTRACTOR
ACCESS PANEL 2'-0" X 2'-0" TYP.
TOP OF HOISTWAY WITH MACHINE LOCATED AT BOTTOM
PROVIDE STRUCTURAL SUPPORT FOR MACHINE BEAMS AT WALL
HEIGHT VARIES ABOVE FLOOR
2'-6" TO 3'-0" (1)
4'-0" TO 5'-0" (1)
PENTHOUSE
FIRE RATING OF HOISTWAY AND CAR DOORS CONSISTENT WITH BUILDING CONSTRUCTION.
VERTICAL BI-PARTING DOORS (3)
COUNTER TOP CAR ACCESS SHOWN. FLOOR LOADING MODELS ALSO AVAILABLE.
INTERMEDIATE FLOOR
30" (MIN) 3
24"36"48" (MAX) CAR DIM
TOTAL TRAVEL-DRUM TYPE MACHINE-50'-0"
TOTAL TRAVEL-TRACTION MACHINE-UNLIMITED
STEEL GUIDE RAILS (BEYOND) ATTACH TO HOISTWAY WALL REINFORCE AS REQUIRED (2)
FLOOR
LOWEST LANDING LEVEL
ACCESS DOOR TO MACHINE 2'-0"X2'-0" TYP
BOTTOM OF PIT WITH MACHINE LOCATED AT TOP OF HOISTWAY
DRUM TYPE ELEVATOR MACHINE
BOTTOM OF PIT WITH MACHINE AT BOTTOM OF HOISTWAY
2'-6"(TYP) (1,3)
8"(MIN) (1)
3'-6" (1)
PIT
DUMBWAITER SECTION

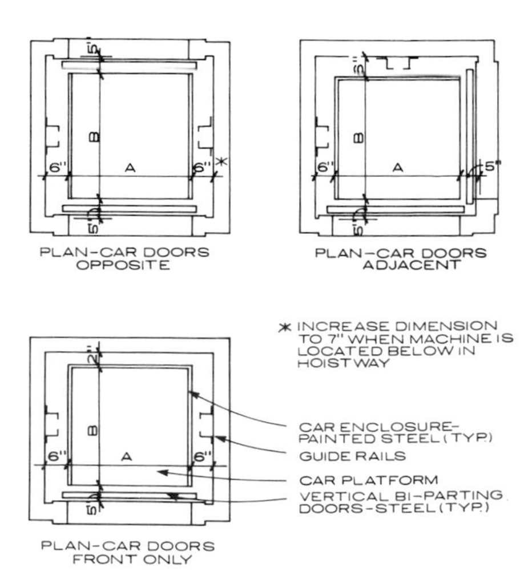
PLAN-CAR DOORS OPPOSITE
PLAN-CAR DOORS ADJACENT
* INCREASE DIMENSION TO 7" WHEN MACHINE IS LOCATED BELOW IN HOISTWAY
CAR ENCLOSURE-PAINTED STEEL (TYP)
GUIDE RAILS
CAR PLATFORM
VERTICAL BI-PARTING DOORS-STEEL (TYP)
PLAN-CAR DOORS FRONT ONLY
A
B
6"
5"
PLANS OF TYPICAL DUMBWAITERS

Beth D. Buffington, AIA; Wilkes, Faulkner, Jenkins, and Bass Architects; Washington, D.C.

Escalators are a very efficient form of vertical transportation for very heavy traffic where the number of floors served is limited, normally a maximum of five to six floors. Escalators are not usually accepted as a required exit.

Dimensions shown are general and will vary somewhat with the manufacturer. Consult manufacturers for structural support, electrical supply, and specific dimensional requirements.

Moving passenger conveyors are particularly useful in transportation terminals, sports arenas, and exposition centers where large numbers of people must move long distances horizontally. The conveyors may be arranged in any combination of horizontal runs and inclines with a practical maximum of 12°.

It is generally not economical to provide moving sidewalks for distances shorter than 100 ft; for distances greater than 300 ft they invoke passenger frustration by their slow operating speed. Narrower units (26 in.) accommodate one adult. 40 in. widths allow for both walking and standing passengers.

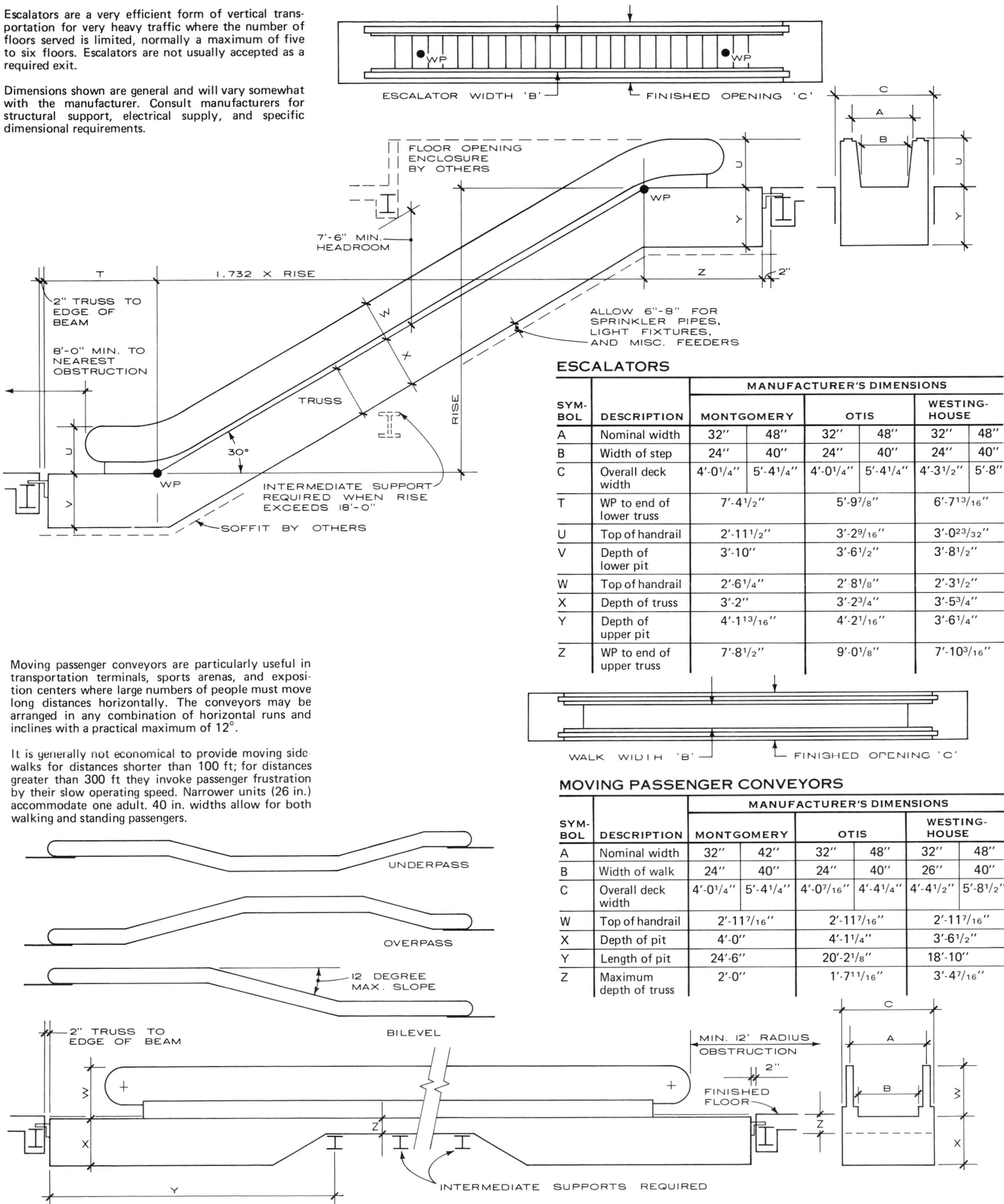
WP
ESCALATOR WIDTH 'B'
FINISHED OPENING 'C'
FLOOR OPENING ENCLOSURE BY OTHERS
7'-6" MIN. HEADROOM
T
1.732 X RISE
2" TRUSS TO EDGE OF BEAM
8'-0" MIN. TO NEAREST OBSTRUCTION
TRUSS
30°
RISE
INTERMEDIATE SUPPORT REQUIRED WHEN RISE EXCEEDS 18'-0"
SOFFIT BY OTHERS
ALLOW 6"-8" FOR SPRINKLER PIPES, LIGHT FIXTURES, AND MISC. FEEDERS
WALK WIDTH 'B'
UNDERPASS
OVERPASS
12 DEGREE MAX. SLOPE
BILEVEL
MIN. 12' RADIUS OBSTRUCTION
FINISHED FLOOR
INTERMEDIATE SUPPORTS REQUIRED

ESCALATORS

SYMBOL	DESCRIPTION	MANUFACTURER'S DIMENSIONS					
		MONTGOMERY		OTIS		WESTINGHOUSE	
A	Nominal width	32"	48"	32"	48"	32"	48"
B	Width of step	24"	40"	24"	40"	24"	40"
C	Overall deck width	4'-0 1/4"	5'-4 1/4"	4'-0 1/4"	5'-4 1/4"	4'-3 1/2"	5'-8"
T	WP to end of lower truss	7'-4 1/2"		5'-9 7/8"		6'-7 13/16"	
U	Top of handrail	2'-11 1/2"		3'-2 9/16"		3'-0 23/32"	
V	Depth of lower pit	3'-10"		3'-6 1/2"		3'-8 1/2"	
W	Top of handrail	2'-6 1/4"		2'-8 1/8"		2'-3 1/2"	
X	Depth of truss	3'-2"		3'-2 3/4"		3'-5 3/4"	
Y	Depth of upper pit	4'-1 13/16"		4'-2 1/16"		3'-6 1/4"	
Z	WP to end of upper truss	7'-8 1/2"		9'-0 1/8"		7'-10 3/16"	

MOVING PASSENGER CONVEYORS

SYMBOL	DESCRIPTION	MANUFACTURER'S DIMENSIONS					
		MONTGOMERY		OTIS		WESTINGHOUSE	
A	Nominal width	32"	42"	32"	48"	32"	48"
B	Width of walk	24"	40"	24"	40"	26"	40"
C	Overall deck width	4'-0 1/4"	5'-4 1/4"	4'-0 7/16"	4'-4 1/4"	4'-4 1/2"	5'-8 1/2"
W	Top of handrail	2'-11 7/16"		2'-11 7/16"		2'-11 7/16"	
X	Depth of pit	4'-0"		4'-1 1/4"		3'-6 1/2"	
Y	Length of pit	24'-6"		20'-2 1/8"		18'-10"	
Z	Maximum depth of truss	2'-0"		1'-7 11/16"		3'-4 7/16"	

Alan H. Rider, AIA; Daniel, Mann, Johnson & Mendenhall; Washington, D.C.

REFERENCES

GENERAL REFERENCES

National Electric Code Handbook, National Fire Protection Agency (NFPA)
Standard Elevator Layouts, National Elevator Industry
Vertical Transportation: Elevators and Escalators, 2nd ed., 1983, George R. Strakosch, Wiley

DATA SOURCES: ORGANIZATIONS

American National Standards Institute (ANSI), 375, 377, 379
Montgomery Elevator Company, 381
National Elevator Industry, Inc., 374–378, 379
Otis Elevator Company, 381
Westinghouse Electric Corporation, 381

CHAPTER **15**

MECHANICAL

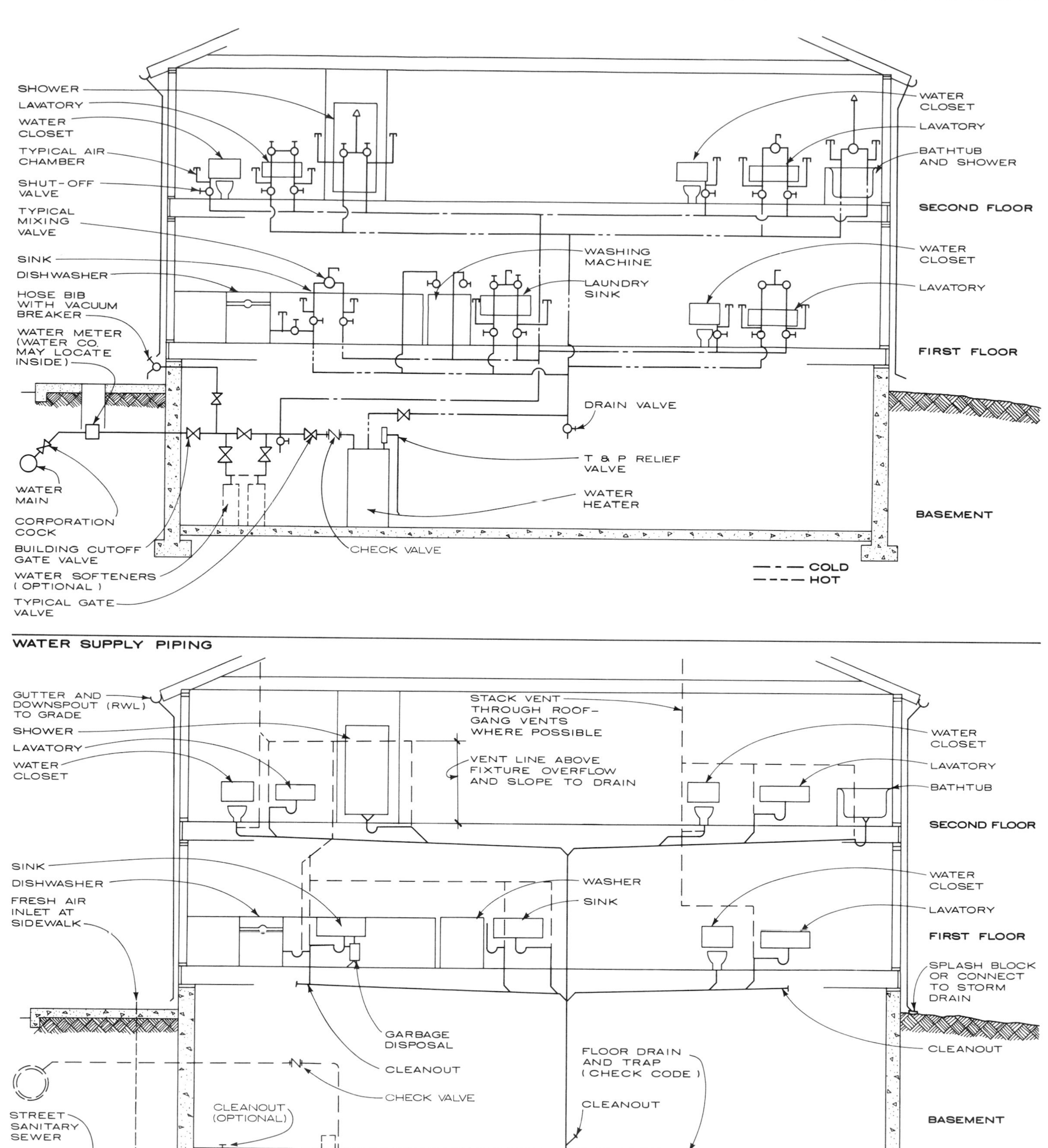
SHOWER
LAVATORY
WATER CLOSET
TYPICAL AIR CHAMBER
SHUT-OFF VALVE
TYPICAL MIXING VALVE
SINK
DISHWASHER
HOSE BIB WITH VACUUM BREAKER
WATER METER (WATER CO. MAY LOCATE INSIDE)
WATER MAIN
CORPORATION COCK
BUILDING CUTOFF GATE VALVE
WATER SOFTENERS (OPTIONAL)
TYPICAL GATE VALVE
WASHING MACHINE
LAUNDRY SINK
DRAIN VALVE
T & P RELIEF VALVE
WATER HEATER
CHECK VALVE
WATER CLOSET
LAVATORY
BATHTUB AND SHOWER
SECOND FLOOR
WATER CLOSET
LAVATORY
FIRST FLOOR
BASEMENT
COLD
HOT

WATER SUPPLY PIPING

GUTTER AND DOWNSPOUT (RWL) TO GRADE
SHOWER
LAVATORY
WATER CLOSET
STACK VENT THROUGH ROOF-GANG VENTS WHERE POSSIBLE
VENT LINE ABOVE FIXTURE OVERFLOW AND SLOPE TO DRAIN
WATER CLOSET
LAVATORY
BATHTUB
SECOND FLOOR
SINK
DISHWASHER
FRESH AIR INLET AT SIDEWALK
WASHER
SINK
WATER CLOSET
LAVATORY
FIRST FLOOR
SPLASH BLOCK OR CONNECT TO STORM DRAIN
GARBAGE DISPOSAL
CLEANOUT
CHECK VALVE
FLOOR DRAIN AND TRAP (CHECK CODE)
CLEANOUT
CLEANOUT
BASEMENT
STREET SANITARY SEWER
CLEANOUT (OPTIONAL)
SUMP PUMP WHEN STREET SEWER IS HIGHER THAN LOWEST DRAIN
SEWAGE EJECTOR AS REQUIRED BY ELEVATION OF SEWER

NOTE

Angle stop typical at all fixtures. Local codes should be consulted for pipe sizes, materials, and other requirements in plumbing system.

SOIL, WASTE AND VENT PIPING

Brent Dickens, AIA, Architect; San Rafael, California

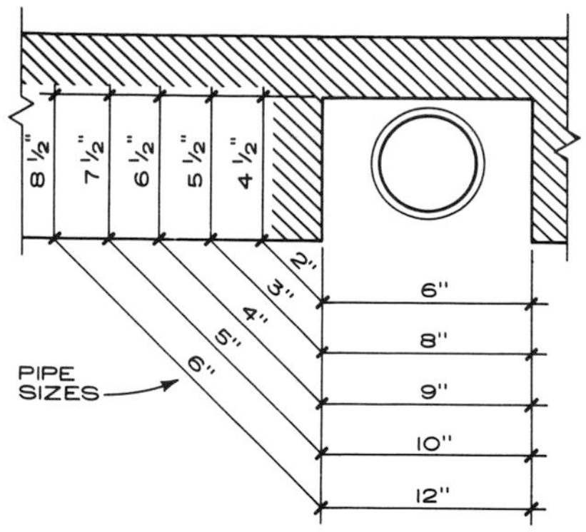

8 ½" 7 ½" 6 ½" 5 ½" 4 ½"
2" 3" 4" 5" 6"
6" 8" 9" 10" 12"
PIPE SIZES

ONE SOIL, WASTE, OR VENT

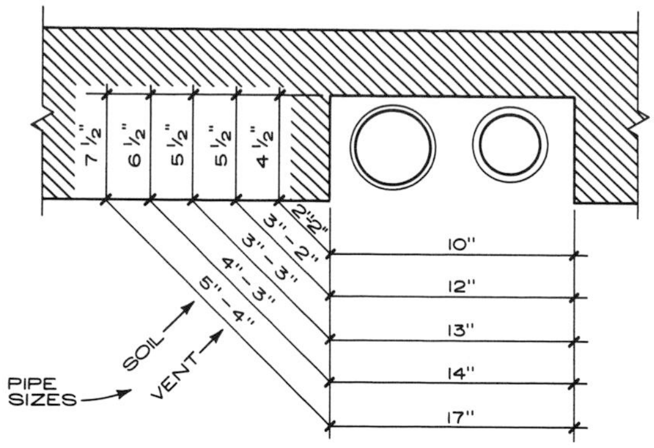

7 ½" 6 ½" 5 ½" 5 ½" 4 ½"
2"-2" 3"-2" 3"-3" 4"-3" 5"-4"
10" 12" 13" 14" 17"
SOIL VENT
PIPE SIZES

TWO SOILS, WASTES, OR VENTS

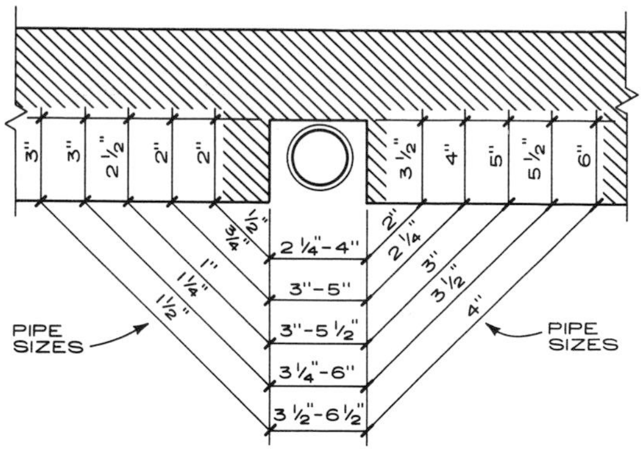

3" 3" 2 ½" 2" 2" 3 ½" 4" 5" 5 ½" 6"
¾" ½" 1" 1 ¼" 1 ½" 2" 2 ¼" 3" 3 ½" 4"
2 ¼"-4" 3"-5" 3"-5 ½" 3 ¼"-6" 3 ½"-6 ½"
PIPE SIZES

WATER PIPES

RECOMMENDED CHASE SIZES FOR VARIOUS PIPE SIZES WITH HUBS (SEE NOTES 2,3, AND 4 ON THIS PAGE)

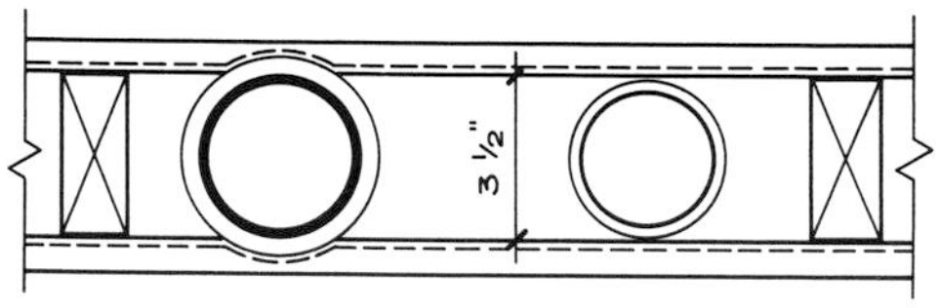

3 ½"

2" B & S WASTE PIPE
3" M.P. VENT OR WATER PIPE

3" C., P., OR N.H. VENT PIPE
3" C. WATER PIPE
2" M.P. VENT OR WATER PIPE

4" STUD

5 ½"

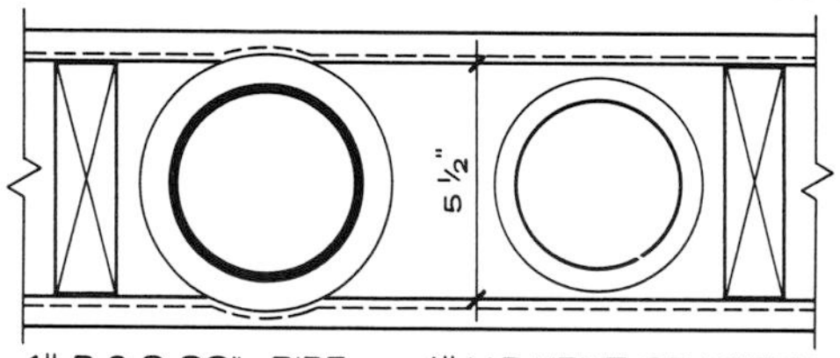

4" B & S SOIL PIPE
5" M.P. VENT PIPE

4" M.P. VENT OR WATER PIPE
4" OR 5" N.H. OR P. SOIL PIPE
4" OR 5" N.H., C., OR P. VENT PIPE
4" OR 5" C. WATER PIPE

6" STUD

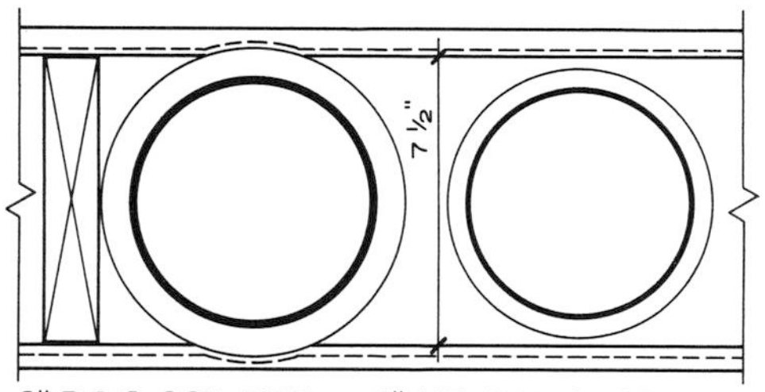

7 ½"

6" B & S SOIL PIPE

6" M.P., N.H., C., OR P. VENT PIPE
6" N.H. OR P. SOIL PIPE
6" M.P. OR C. WATER PIPE

8" STUD

WOOD STUD PARTITIONS WITH 3/4" METAL LATH AND PLASTER

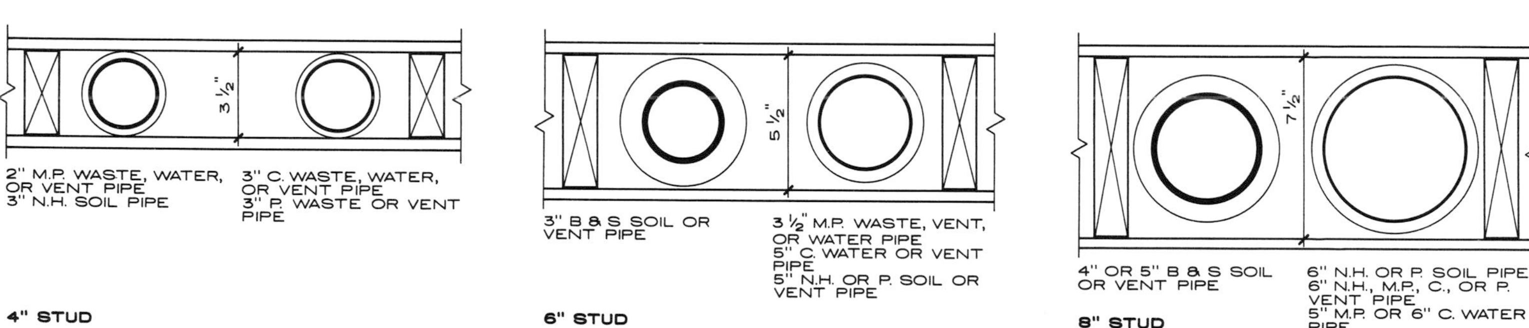
3 ½"
2" M.P. WASTE, WATER, OR VENT PIPE
3" N.H. SOIL PIPE
3" C. WASTE, WATER, OR VENT PIPE
3" P. WASTE OR VENT PIPE
4" STUD
5 ½"
3" B & S SOIL OR VENT PIPE
3 ½" M.P. WASTE, VENT, OR WATER PIPE
5" C. WATER OR VENT PIPE
5" N.H. OR P. SOIL OR VENT PIPE
6" STUD
7 ½"
4" OR 5" B & S SOIL OR VENT PIPE
6" N.H. OR P. SOIL PIPE
6" N.H., M.P., C., OR P. VENT PIPE
5" M.P. OR 6" C. WATER PIPE
8" STUD

WOOD STUD PARTITIONS WITH RIGID BOARD OR RIGID LATH

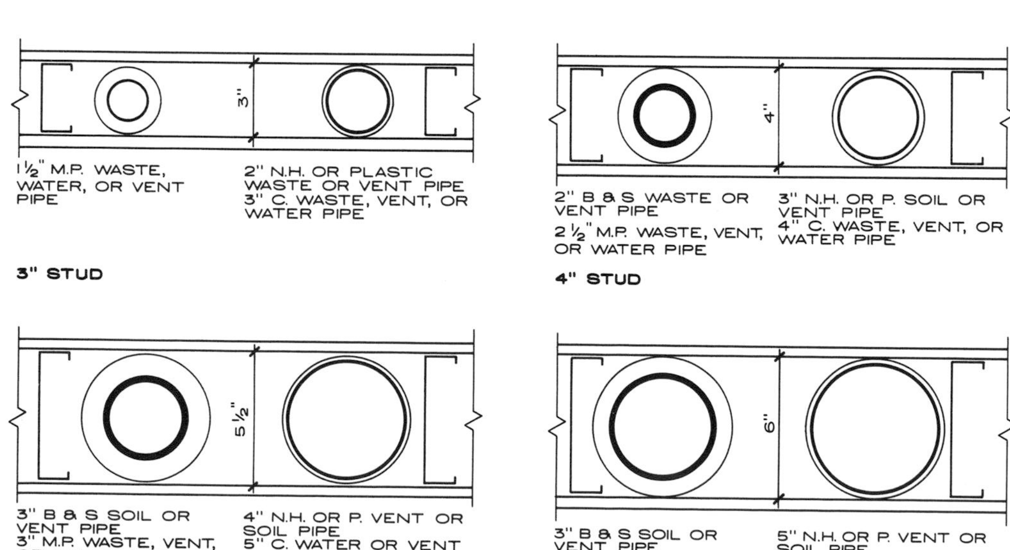
3"
1 ½" M.P. WASTE, WATER, OR VENT PIPE
2" N.H. OR PLASTIC WASTE OR VENT PIPE
3" C. WASTE, VENT, OR WATER PIPE
3" STUD
4"
2" B & S WASTE OR VENT PIPE
2 ½" M.P. WASTE, VENT, OR WATER PIPE
3" N.H. OR P. SOIL OR VENT PIPE
4" C. WASTE, VENT, OR WATER PIPE
4" STUD
5 ½"
3" B & S SOIL OR VENT PIPE
3" M.P. WASTE, VENT, OR WATER PIPE
4" N.H. OR P. VENT OR SOIL PIPE
5" C. WATER OR VENT PIPE
5 ½" STUD
6"
3" B & S SOIL OR VENT PIPE
4" M.P. VENT OR WATER PIPE
5" N.H. OR P. VENT OR SOIL PIPE
6" C. WATER OR VENT PIPE
6" STUD

STEEL STUD PARTITIONS WITH RIGID BOARD

NOTES

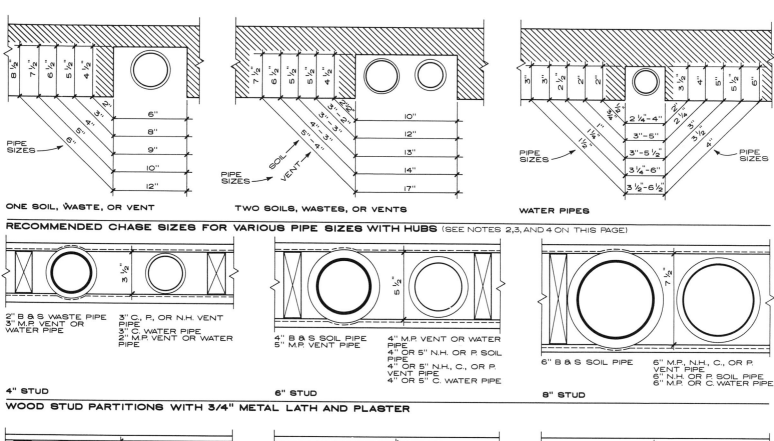

1. B&S: extra heavy cast iron bell and spigot (push or caulked joints). C: copper tubing. NH: extra heavy cast iron no-hub pipe. MP: malleable pattern (galvanized or nongalvanized). P: plastic pipe.
2. Recommended chase sizes for various pipes include a ¾ in. covering. For additional cover subtract ¾ in. from the amount of cover required; add the result to the desired pipe size dimension.
3. Chases may be provided with or without access. Chases for several pipes, especially those containing main water supply pipes, should be provided with a means of access in case repair is necessary.
4. To size a chase with several pipes, add required widths for each.
5. Partitions with ¾ in. lath and plaster are shown with certain maximum pipe sizes encroaching on the lath and plaster. Encroaching pipe portions should be coated with asphaltic paint to prevent staining the plaster.
6. When rigid board or lath, such as gypsum board, plaster board, or gypsum lath, is used, the extreme diameter of pipe fitting bead or bell should come within the actual clear dimension of the wall core.
7. Pipe spaces can be enlarged by placing piping between two back-to-back partitions with the required clear space between them.
8. Use steel pipe clearances for hubless pipe installation.

Kelly Sacher & Associates; Architects Engineers Planners; N. Babylon, Long Island, New York

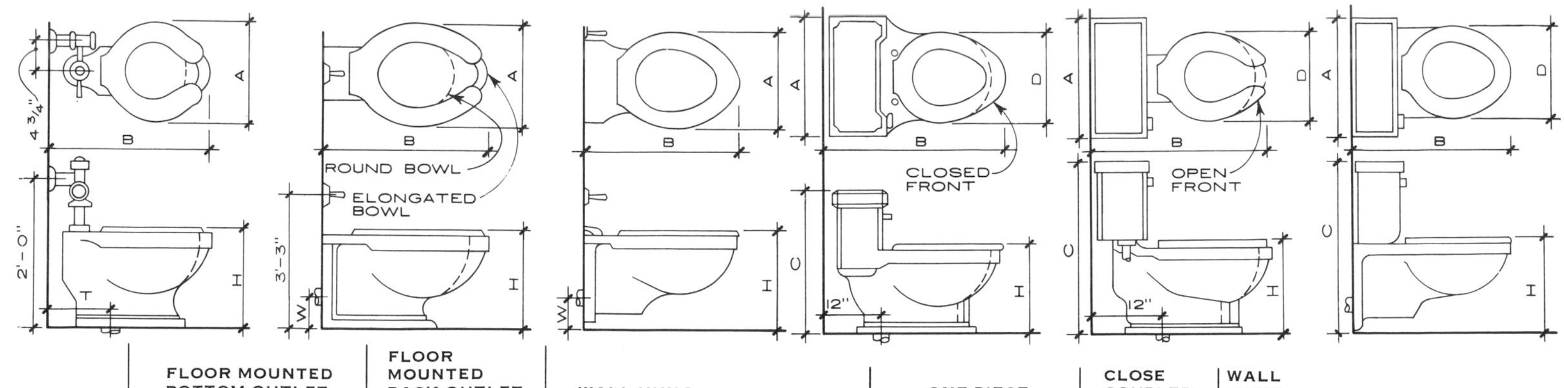

4 3/4"
A
B
2'-0"
T
H
ROUND BOWL
ELONGATED BOWL
3'-3"
W
C
D
CLOSED FRONT
OPEN FRONT
12"

	FLOOR MOUNTED BOTTOM OUTLET			FLOOR MOUNTED BACK OUTLET		WALL HUNG	
	SJ	WD	BO	SJ	BO	SJ	BO
A	14"	14"	14"	14"	14"	14"	14"
B Round	24"	27"		20 1/8"			
B Elongated	24 1/2" or 26 1/2"		26 1/4"	25 1/2" to 26"	21 1/2"	21 1/2" to 25 3/4"	24 1/4" to 26"
H	14" to 14 3/4" 10"* 17"† to 19"	15"	15"	14 1/2" to 15"	15"	15"	15" to 15 3/4"
W				4 1/4" or 4 1/2"	10 1/4"	4" to 5 1/2"	11 1/2" to 12 1/4"
T	10" or 12"	12" to 14"	9"	9" or 10"	9" or 10"		

*For children.
†For handicapped.

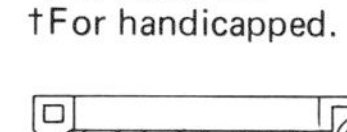

	ONE PIECE			CLOSE COUPLED		WALL HUNG
	SV	SJ	SA	SJ	RT	SJ
A	20 3/4" to 22"	20 5/8" to 23 3/4"	20 3/4" to 21"	20 7/8" to 21 1/2"	17" to 20 7/8"	20 7/8" to 23 3/4"
B Round	27 3/4"	24 3/4"	27 3/4"	27 1/2" to 29"	22" to 27 5/8"	26 1/2" to 29 3/4"
B Elongated	29 1/4"	28 1/2" to 29"	28 1/2" to 29 3/4"	29 1/8" to 29 7/8"		28 1/4"
C	20" to 23 3/4"	18 3/4" to 20 1/2"	18 3/4" to 19 1/2"	26 1/8" to 31 7/8"	28 1/4" to 31"	29" to 29 1/2"
D	14 3/4" to 15 1/2"	14 3/4" to 15 1/2"	14 3/4" to 15 1/2"	14 3/4" to 15 1/2"	14 3/4" to 15 1/2"	14 3/4" to 15 1/2"
H	14"	14" to 15"	14 1/2"	14" 17"† to 19" 10"*	14 1/2" to 15"	15"

NOTE: Dimensions include seat. For closed front seats, add 1 in. to B. With seat cover, add 3/4 in. to height. All fixtures are of vitreous china except where noted. For concealed carrier wall hung, allow 10 1/2 in. minimum from back of closet to outside edge of soil pipe.

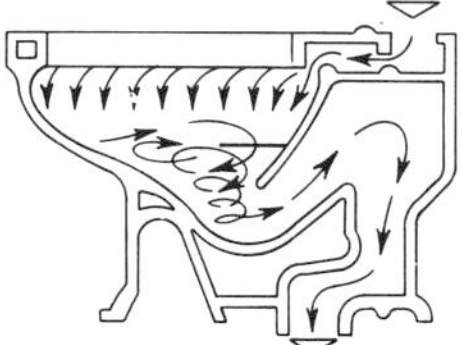

SIPHON - VORTEX (S-V)
Quiet, extremely sanitary. Water directed through rim to create vortex. Scours bowl. Folds over into jet; siphon.

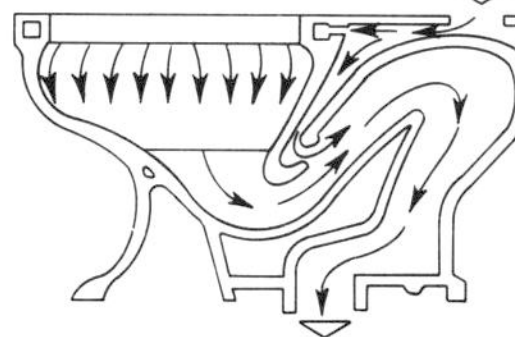

SIPHON - JET (S-J)
SIPHON - ACTION (S-A)
Sanitary, efficient, very quiet. Water enters through rim and siphons in down leg.

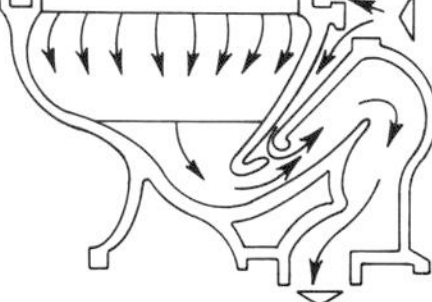

REVERSE - TRAP (R-T)
Similar to siphon-jet except that trap passageway and water surface area are smaller, moderately noisy.

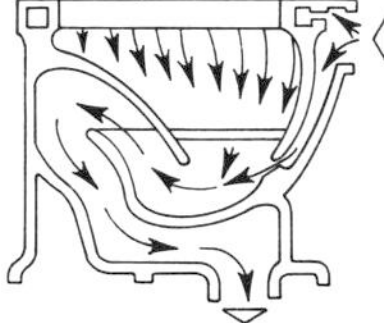

WASH - DOWN (W-D)
Minimum cost. Least efficient, subject to clogging, noisy. Simple washout action through small irregular passageway.

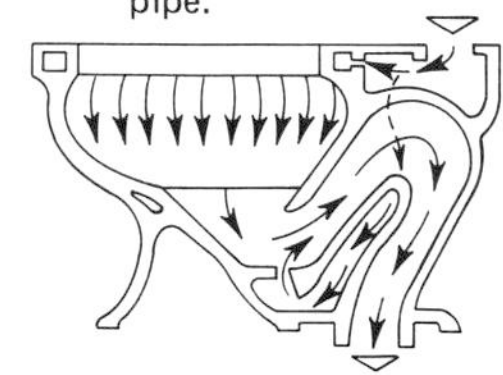

BLOWOUT (BO)
Noisy but highly efficient. Strong jet into up leg forces contents out. Use with FV only. Higher pressure required.

WATER CLOSETS

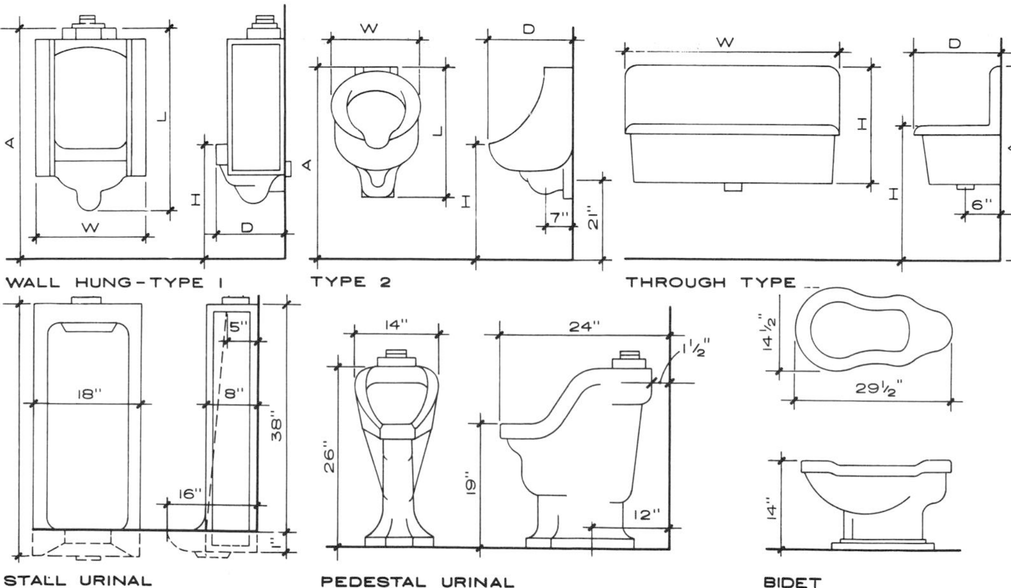

A
L
W
H
D
7"
21"
6"
18"
5"
8"
38"
16"
14"
24"
1 1/2"
26"
19"
12"
14 1/2"
29 1/2"
14"

WALL HUNG - TYPE I

TYPE 2

THROUGH TYPE

STALL URINAL

PEDESTAL URINAL

BIDET

	TYPE 1 (SJ, WD, BO)	TYPE 2			THROUGH TYPE
		SJ	BO	WD	
A	35", 42 1/2"	35 1/2" to 37 1/8"	26 1/2" to 27"	34 1/2" to 37 1/8"	32"-34"
W	13", 18"	13" to 14 1/4"	14"	12 3/4" to 14 1/4"	36", 48", 60", 72"
L	18" to 30"	17" to 20"	17" to 20"	17" to 20"	16", 17 3/4", 18 3/4"
D	11 3/4" to 13 1/4"	11 1/4" to 14"	11 1/2" to 14"	12 7/8" to 14"	14", 18"
H	24"	24", 17"*, 19"*			24"

*For handicapped.

NOTE: Provide minimum 4 in. clear pipe chase for urinal piping and support.

BATTERY STALLS

Stall urinals available with seam covers for battery installation on 1'- 9" or 2'- 0" centers.

URINALS AND BIDETS

K. Shahid Rab, AIA; Friesen International; Washington, D.C.
B. J. Baldwin; Giffels & Rossetti, Inc.; Detroit, Michigan

SINGLE BOWL

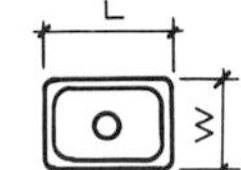
L
W

STAINLESS STEEL

	MIN.	MAX.	OTHER
L	11½	33	12½ → 31
W	13	22⅜	14 → 22¼
D	5½	12	6 → 7½

PORCELAIN ENAMELED STEEL

	MIN.	MAX.	OTHER
L	24	30	
W	21		
D	7⅜	8⅛	

ENAMELED CAST IRON

	MIN.	MAX.	OTHER
L	12	30	
W	12	21	18→20
D	6	8	6½→7½

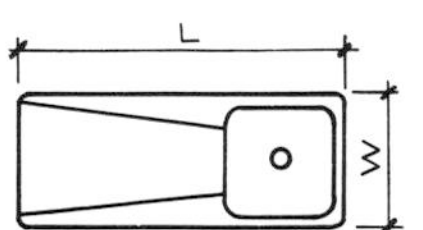
L
W

SINGLE BOWL AND DRAINBOARD (RIGHT OR LEFT)

STAINLESS STEEL

	MIN.	MAX.	OTHER
L	33	72	
W	21	25	
D	7	7½	

ENAMELED CAST IRON

	MIN.	MAX.	OTHER
L	42	72	
W	20	25	24
D	6	8	6½→7½

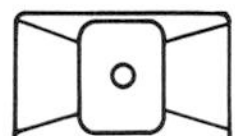

SINGLE BOWL DOUBLE DRAINBOARD

STAINLESS STEEL

	MIN.	MAX.	OTHER
L	54	72	
W	21	25	
D	7	7½	

ENAMELED CAST IRON

	MIN.	MAX.	OTHER
L	54	72	
W	21	25	24
D	6	8	6½→7½

DOUBLE BOWL

STAINLESS STEEL

	MIN.	MAX.	OTHER
L	28	46	30 → 42
W	16	22	17 → 21¼
D	5	10	6½ → 7½

PORCELAIN ENAMELED

	MIN.	MAX.	OTHER
L	32		
W	21		
D	7	8⅛	

ENAMELED CAST IRON STEEL

	MIN.	MAX.	OTHER
L	32	42	
W	20	25	
D	6	8	6½→7½

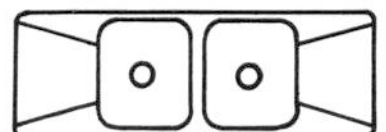

DOUBLE BOWL AND DRAINBOARD

STAINLESS STEEL

	MIN.	MAX.	OTHER
L	60	72	66
W	21	25	
D	7	7½	

ENAMELED CAST IRON

	MIN.	MAX.	OTHER
L	54	72	60
W	24	25	
D	6	8	6½→7½

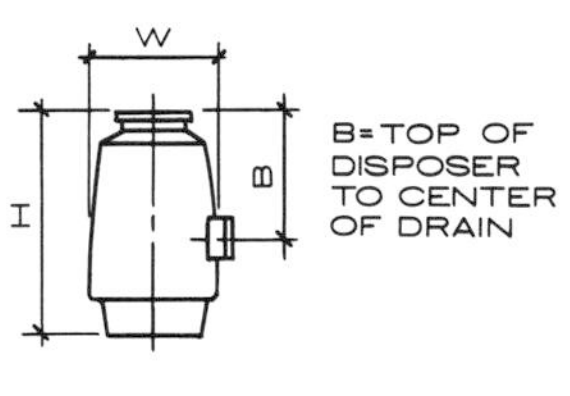
W
B
H
B=TOP OF DISPOSER TO CENTER OF DRAIN
13 5/16"
6" MIN.
5 5/8"
7" DIA.

GARBAGE DISPOSER

	MIN.	MAX.	OTHER
W	6¼	10⅛	7⅜→9½
B	6	9⅜	6⅝→8¾
H	12¾	9 3/16	12⅝→16

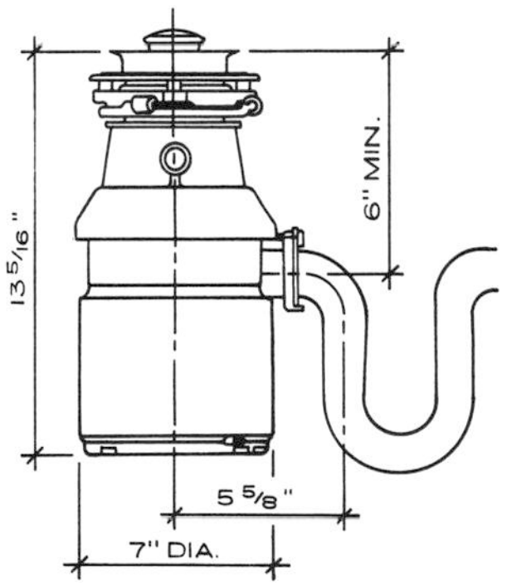

GARBAGE DISPOSER UNITS

TRIPLE BOWL

STAINLESS STEEL

	MIN.	MAX.	OTHER
L	43	54	45
W	22		
D	5	7½	

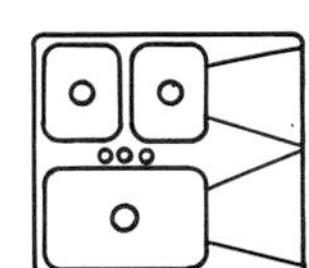

TRIPLE BOWL AND DRAINBOARD (ISLAND)

STAINLESS STEEL

	MIN.	MAX.	OTHER
L	54½	57	
W	40½		
D	4	7½	

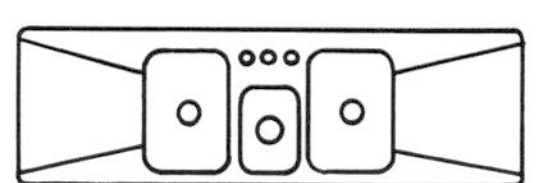

TRIPLE BOWL AND DOUBLE DRAINBOARD

STAINLESS STEEL

	MIN.	MAX.	OTHER
L		84	
W		25	
D		7½	

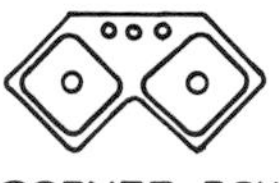

CORNER BOWL

STAINLESS STEEL

	MIN.	MAX.	OTHER
L	31⅞	32½	
W	31⅞	32½	
D	7	7½	

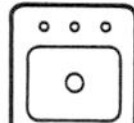

BAR SINK

STAINLESS STEEL

	MIN.	MAX.	OTHER
L	14	16¼	15
W	14	20¼	15
D	6	7⅜	6

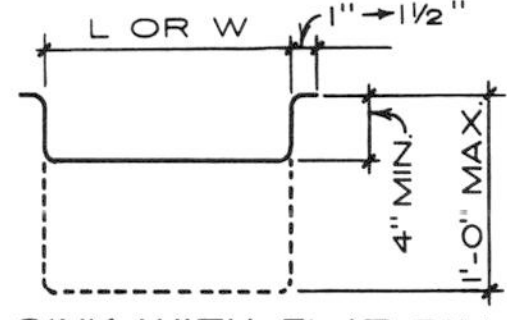
L OR W
1"→1½"
4" MIN.
1'-0" MAX.

SINK WITH FLAT RIM

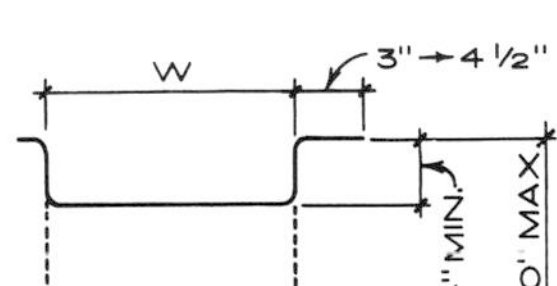
W
3"→4½"
4" MIN.
1'-0" MAX.

SINK WITH BACK LEDGE

W
4"
4" MIN.
1'-0" MAX.

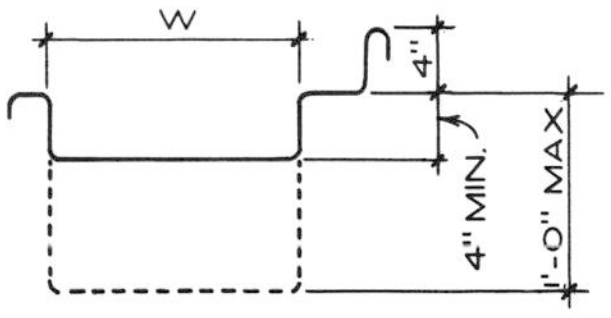

SINK WITH BACK LEDGE AND BACKSPLASH

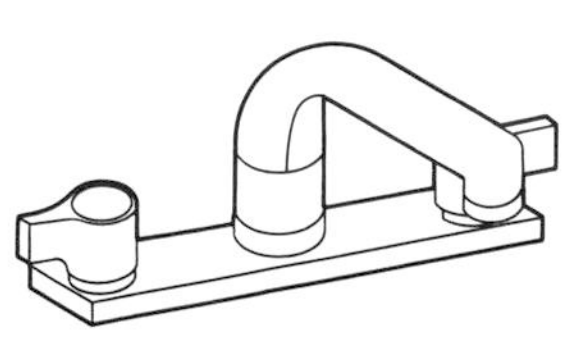

WASHER TYPE

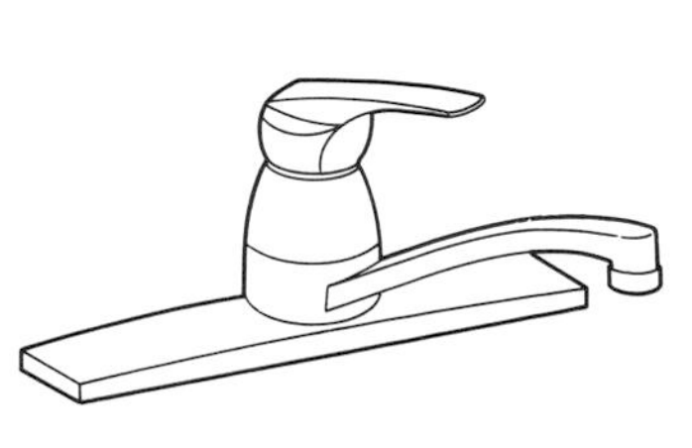

WASHERLESS

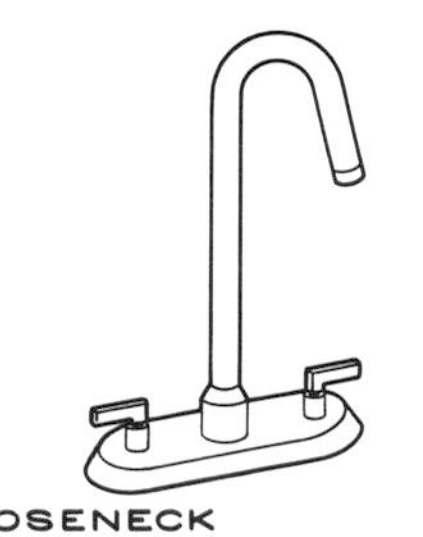

GOOSENECK

KITCHEN FAUCETS

Giffels & Rossetti, Inc.; Detroit, Michigan

NOTES

All dimensions shown on this page are in inches.

Consult manufacturers' literature for variations in bowl finish and available accessories, such as cup strainer, spray head, cutting boards, and trim.

See pages on handicapped accessibility for suggested modifications to mounting height and cabinetry.

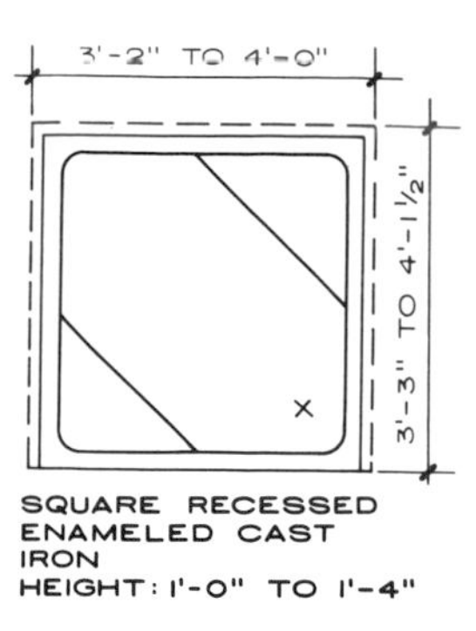
3'-2" TO 4'-0"
3'-3" TO 4'-1 1/2"

SQUARE RECESSED
ENAMELED CAST IRON
HEIGHT: 1'-0" TO 1'-4"

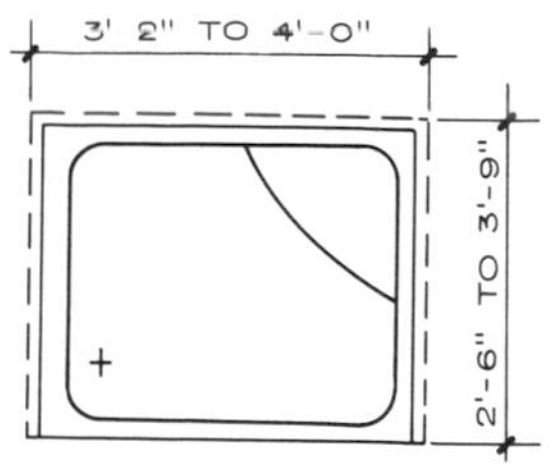
3' 2" TO 4'-0"
2'-6" TO 3'-9"

SQUARE
RECESSED
ENAMELED STEEL
HEIGHT: 1'-0" TO 1'-2"

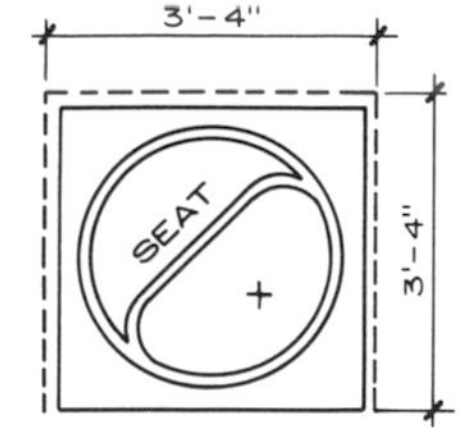
3'-4"
SEAT
3'-4"

SQUARE
RECESSED OR
PLATFORM
FIBERGLASS
HEIGHT: 2'-9"

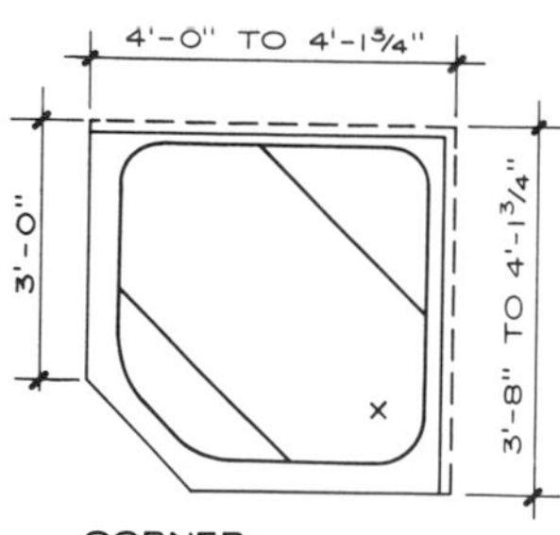
4'-0" TO 4'-1 3/4"
3'-0"
3'-8" TO 4'-1 3/4"

CORNER
ENAMELED CAST IRON
HEIGHT: 1'-4"

5'-0" TO 5'-1 1/4"
2'-8 1/2"
2'-6"

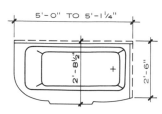

BUILT-IN-CORNER
ENAMELED CAST IRON,
VITREOUS CHINA, OR
EARTHENWARE
HEIGHT: 1'-4"

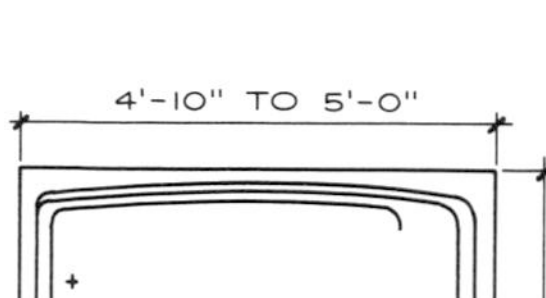
4'-10" TO 5'-0"
2'-8"

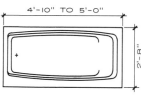

BUILT-IN-RECESS
FIBERGLASS
REINFORCED
POLYESTER
HEIGHT: 1'-4"

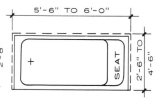

5'-6" TO 6'-0"
SEAT
2'-6" TO 4'-6"

BUILT-IN-RECESS
ENAMELED CAST IRON
HEIGHT: 1'-6" & 1'-8"

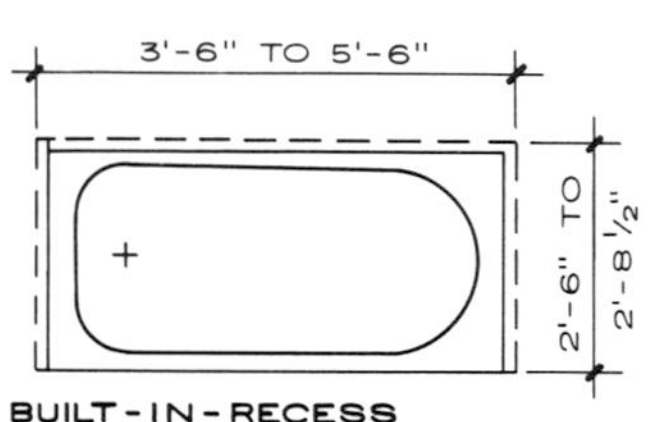
3'-6" TO 5'-6"
2'-6" TO 2'-8 1/2"

BUILT-IN-RECESS
ENAMELED CAST IRON,
ENAMELED STEEL, OR
FIBERGLASS
HEIGHT: 1'-0" & 1'-4"

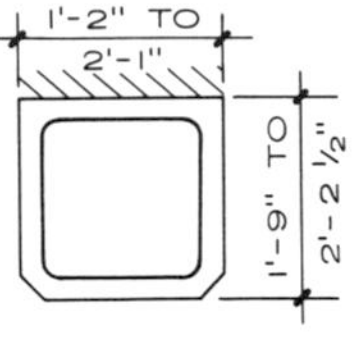
1'-2" TO 2'-1"
1'-9" TO 2'-2 1/2"

FOOT BATH
ENAMELED CAST
IRON, VITREOUS
CHINA, OR
EARTHENWARE
HEIGHT: 1'-3"

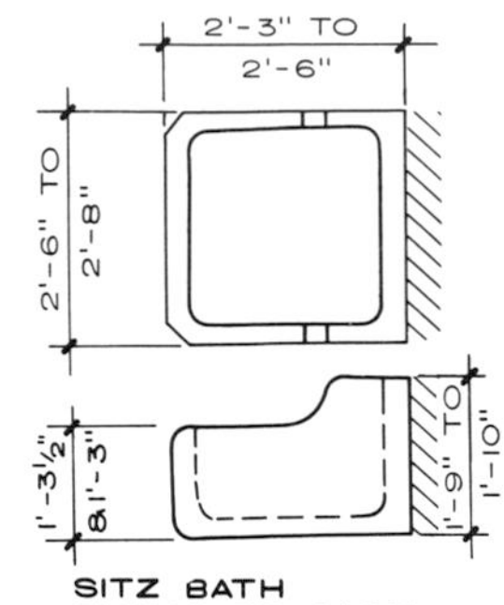
2'-3" TO 2'-6"
2'-6" TO 2'-8"
1'-3 1/2"
1'-3"
1'-9" TO 1'-10"

SITZ BATH
ENAMELED CAST
IRON, VITREOUS
CHINA, OR
EARTHENWARE

SQUARE AND RECTANGULAR SHOWERS AND BATHTUBS

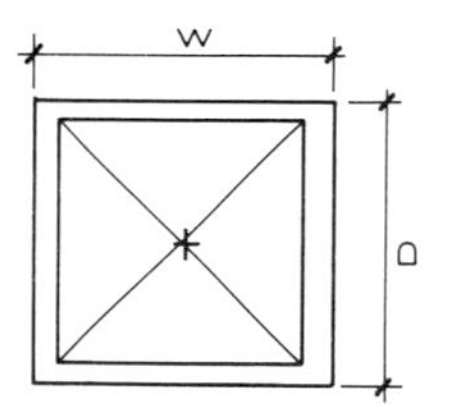
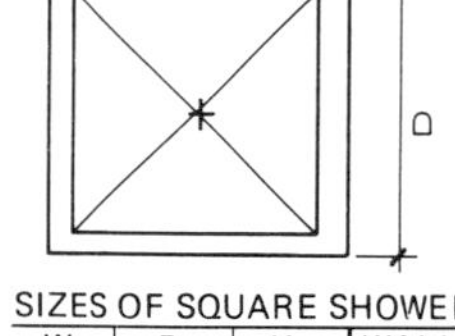
W
D

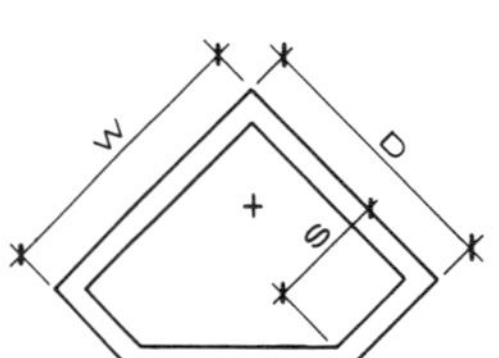
W
D
S

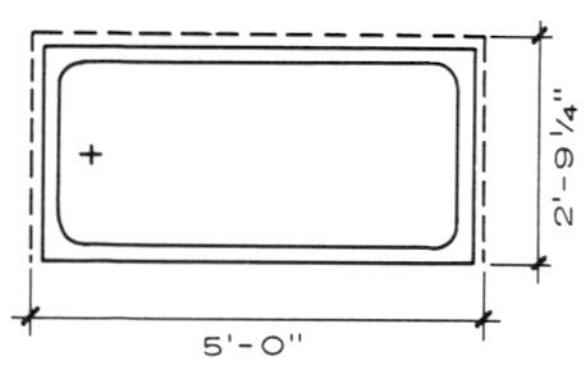
2'-9 1/4"
5'-0"

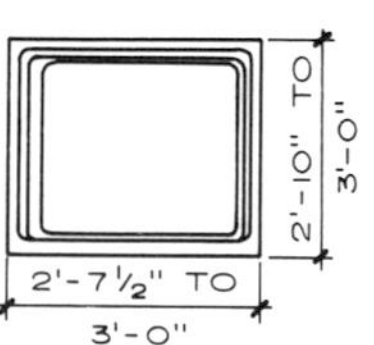
2'-10" TO 3'-0"
2'-7 1/2" TO 3'-0"

USED FOR HANDICAPPED

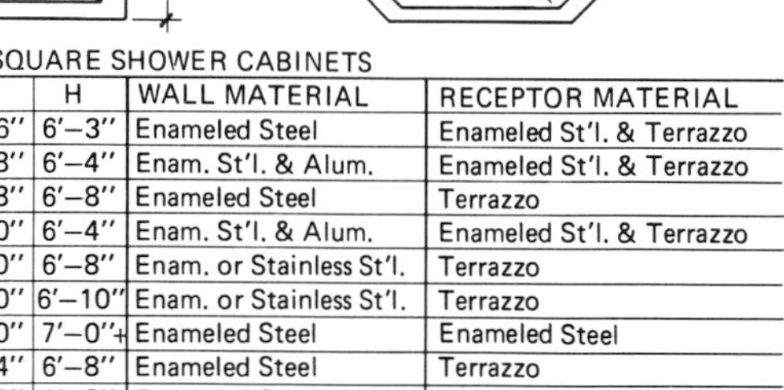

SIZES OF SQUARE SHOWER CABINETS

W	D	H	WALL MATERIAL	RECEPTOR MATERIAL
2'–6"	2'–6"	6'–3"	Enameled Steel	Enameled St'l. & Terrazzo
2'–8"	2'–8"	6'–4"	Enam. St'l. & Alum.	Enameled St'l. & Terrazzo
2'–8"	2'–8"	6'–8"	Enameled Steel	Terrazzo
3'–0"	3'–0"	6'–4"	Enam. St'l. & Alum.	Enameled St'l. & Terrazzo
3'–0"	3'–0"	6'–8"	Enam. or Stainless St'l.	Terrazzo
3'–0"	3'–0"	6'–10"	Enam. or Stainless St'l.	Terrazzo
3'–0"	3'–0"	7'–0"+	Enameled Steel	Enameled Steel
3'–4"	3'–4"	6'–8"	Enameled Steel	Terrazzo
3'–6"	3'–6"	6'–8"	Enameled Steel	Terrazzo

+ – AVAILABLE TO ORDER 2'–6", 2'–8" & 2'–10"

SIZES OF CORNER SHOWER CABINETS

W	D	H	S	WALL MAT'L.	PANEL MAT'L.	RECEPTOR
3'–0"	3'–0"	6'–8"	1'–5"	Enam. St'l.	Enam. St'l.	Terrazzo
3'–4"	3'–4"	6'–8"	1'–7"	Enam. St'l.	Glass	Terrazzo

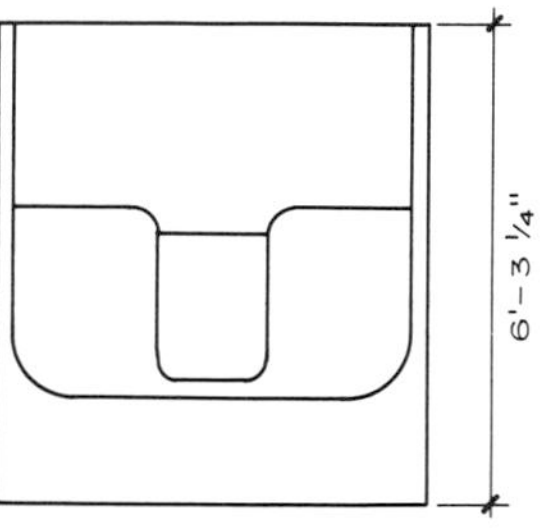
6'-3 1/4"

INTEGRAL BATH
FIBERGLASS
REINFORCED
POLYESTER

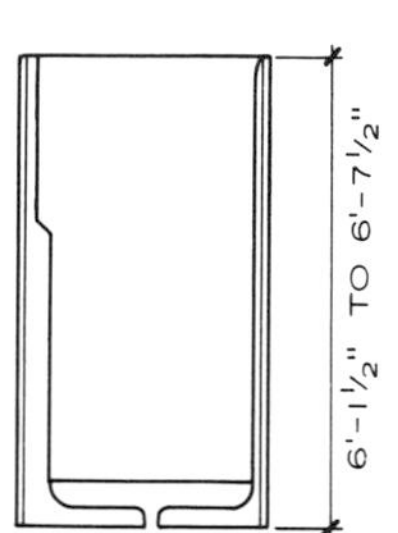
6'-1 1/2" TO 6'-7 1/2"

INTEGRAL
SHOWER
FIBERGLASS
REINFORCED
POLYESTER

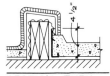

4 1/2"

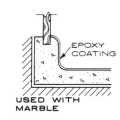

SECTION THRU THRESHOLD

EPOXY
COATING

USED WITH MARBLE

FREESTANDING SHOWER CABINETS AND BATHTUBS

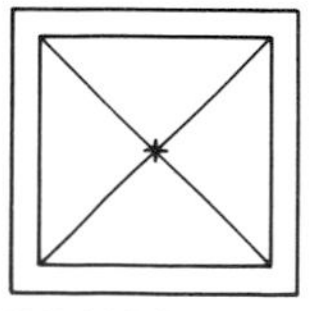

SQUARE

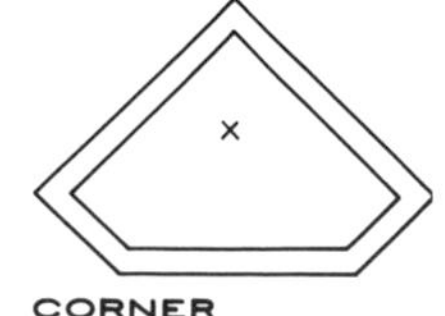

CORNER

MULTISTALL

Wedge Shaped Stalls Grouped in 2's, 3's, 4's, 5's & 6's, with 6'–0" Standard Ht., 5'–6" Intermediate Ht. & 5'–0" Junior Ht.

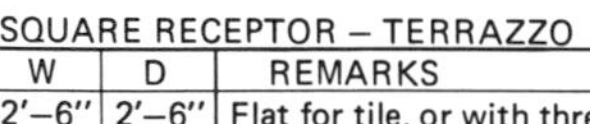

SQUARE RECEPTOR – TERRAZZO

W	D	REMARKS
2'–6"	2'–6"	Flat for tile, or with threshold
3'–0"	3'–0"	Flat for tile, or with threshold
3'–4"	3'–4"	Flat for tile, or with threshold
3'–0"	3'–0"	Rabbetted for marble wall
6'–0"	3'–0"	Rabbetted for marble wall

CORNER RECEPTOR – TERRAZZO

W	D	REMARKS
3'–0"	3'–0"	Flat for tile, or with threshold
3'–4"	3'–4"	Flat for tile, or with threshold

SHOWER RECEPTOR TYPES

3'-0"
2'-6"
1'-1"
7"
1'-0"
SEAT
6"

PLAN SHOWING FOLDING SHOWER SEAT

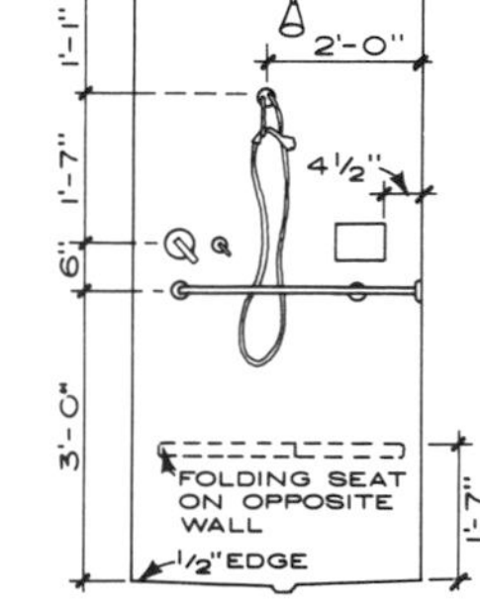
1'-4"
2'-0"
1'-1"
1'-7"
4 1/2"
6"
3'-0"
FOLDING SEAT ON OPPOSITE WALL
1/2" EDGE
1'-7"

ELEVATION OF PLUMBING WALL

SHOWER USED BY HANDICAPPED

4 1/2"

USED WITH TILE, PLASTER

SECTION THRU SIDE

NOTE

Adequate waterproofing should be added to each of the sections.

K. Shahid Rab, AIA; Friesen International; Washington, D.C.

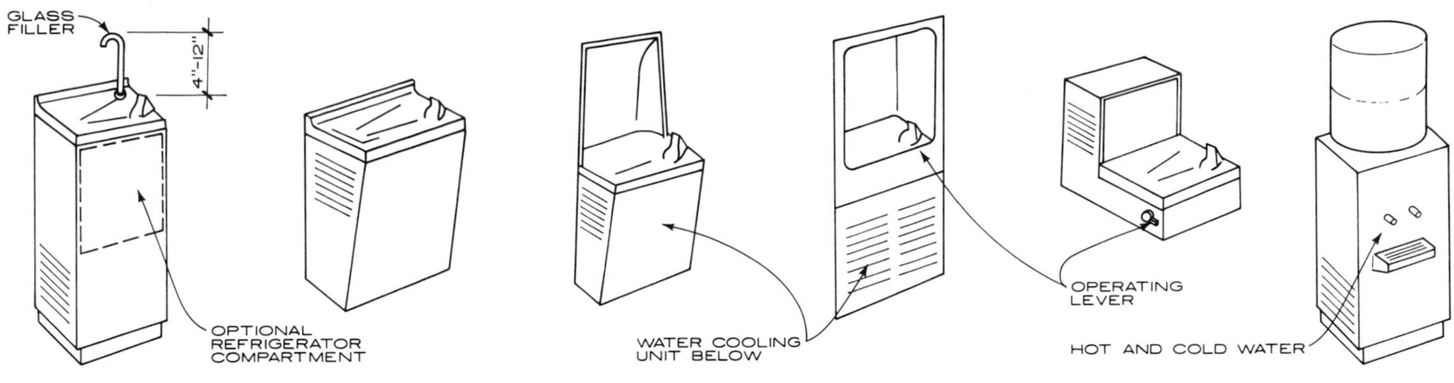
GLASS FILLER
4"-12"
OPTIONAL REFRIGERATOR COMPARTMENT
WATER COOLING UNIT BELOW
OPERATING LEVER
HOT AND COLD WATER

FLOOR MOUNTED (IN.) FLUSH TO WALL OR FREESTANDING				WALL MOUNTED (IN.)				SEMIRECESSED (IN.)				FULLY RECESSED (IN.)				HANDICAPPED (IN.)				BOTTLE TYPE (IN.)			
H	W	D	GPH	H	W	D	GPH	H	W	D	GPH	H	W	D	GPH	H	W	D	GPH	H	W	D	GPH
30½	15	15	7-12	16	17	13¼	2-5	35¾	17	13½	11-17	50¼	18	12	8-14	5	14	20	5-20	36	12	12	1
33½	18	14½	4-20	22	18	14½	4-14	37½	16½	14½	7-15	54¼	19	12¼	7-12	7	15	21	20-100	40	14	14	2
40	12	12	3-10	26	17	14	5-15	39¾	18	13½	7-12	55¼	21	13	5-10	25	18	18½	7-9	44	17	14	1
41½	18	14½	4-20	29½	18	14½	4-20	44¼	17¼	14	5-13					28	17¼	18½	7-10				

SELF-CONTAINED WATER COOLERS

Air cooled condensers are used for normal room temperatures; water cooled units for high room temperatures and larger capacities. Many fountain models are available with cold and hot water supply, a glass filler attachment, or refrigerated compartments. There is a wide selection of colors and finishes to choose from.

Floor and wall mounted fountains are made in lower heights for children's use and can be mounted low on the side of regular height models.

Recommended fountain rim heights, above the floor:

1. 40 in.—adults.
2. 30 in.—children.
3. 34-36 max. in.—handicapped.

Special explosionproof fountains are recommended for use in hazardous atmospheres. Corrosion resistant fountains are available as well as a water cooled type for excessively hot and dusty atmospheres.

Power requirements are 110, 115, 230 V; 50 to 60 cycles, single phase AC; otherwise a transformer is used.

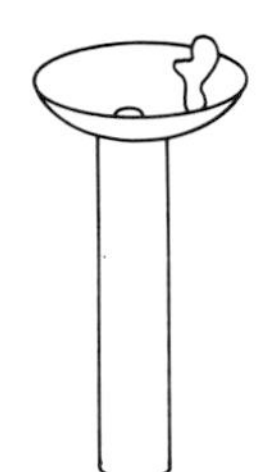
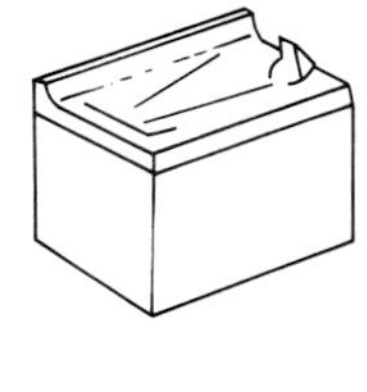
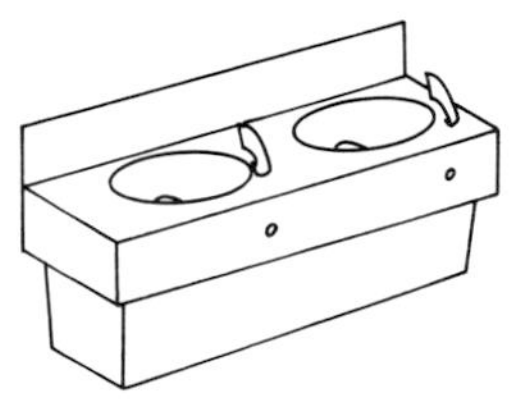
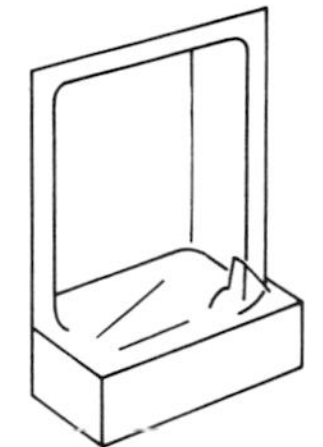
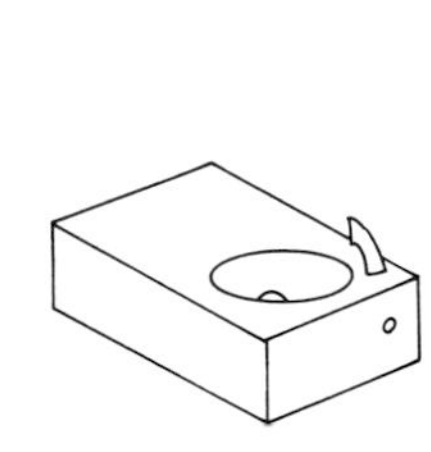
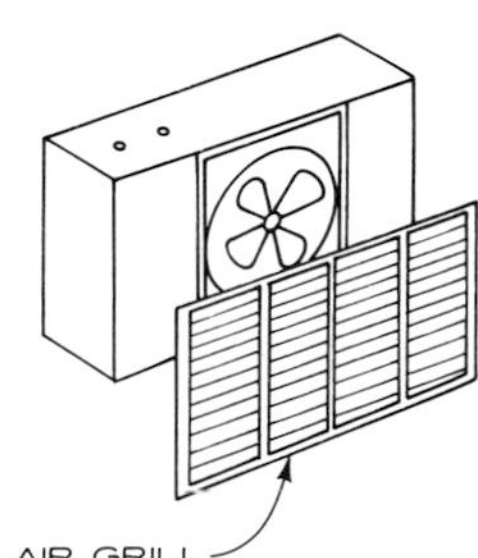
AIR GRILL

PEDESTAL DISH (IN.)			WALL MOUNTED (IN.)				TWO STATION (IN.)				SEMIRECESSED OR FULLY RECESSED (IN.)				HANDICAPPED (IN.)				REMOTE PACKAGE COOLER (IN.)			
H	D	SUPPLY/ WASTE	H	W	D	SUPPLY/ WASTE	H	W	D	SUPPLY/ WASTE	H	W	D	SUPPLY/ WASTE	H	W	D	SUPPLY/ WASTE	H	W	D	GPH
38¼	4	¼, 1½	7¾	10	10	⅜, 1¼	6	39	11¼	½, 1½	27¾	17½	13	⅜, 1¼	6	12	20	½, 1¼	16¼	15¾	8	5-6
38¼	14¼	¼, 1½	16	17	13¼	⅜, 1¼	15	31	14	½, 1½	29	21	13	⅜, 1¼	7	15	21	⅜, 1¼	22¼	30	6½	6-10

DRINKING FOUNTAINS (FOR USE WITH REMOTE STORAGE COOLERS)

DRINKING WATER REQUIREMENTS

	GPH PER PERSON	
TYPE OF SERVICE	CUP	BUBBLER
Offices, schools, cafeterias, hotels (per room), hospitals (per bed and per attendant)	0.033	0.083
Restaurants	0.04	0.1
Light manufacturing	0.0573	0.143
Heavy manufacturing	0.08	0.20
Hot, heavy manufacturing	0.10	0.25
Theaters per 100 seats	0.4 gph/ 100 seats	1.0 gph/ 100 seats
Department stores, lobbies, hotel and office buildings	1.6-2.0 gph/fountain	4-5 gph/ fountain

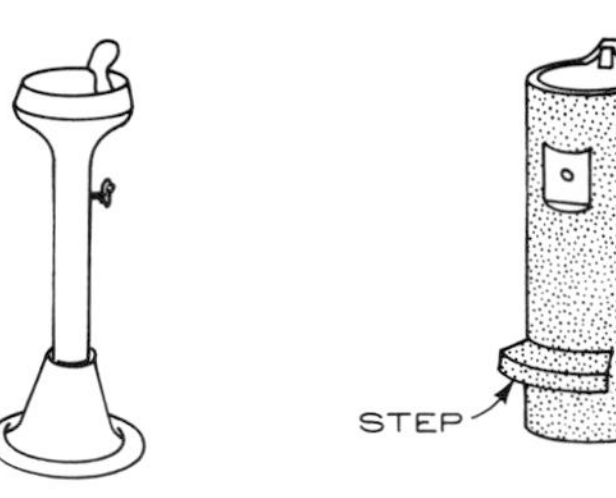
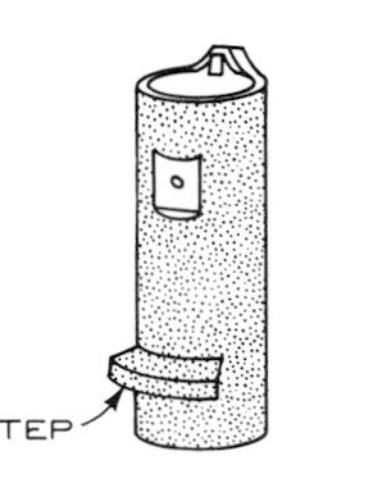
STEP
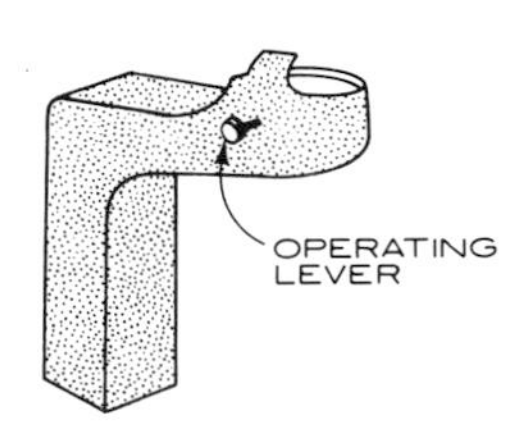
OPERATING LEVER
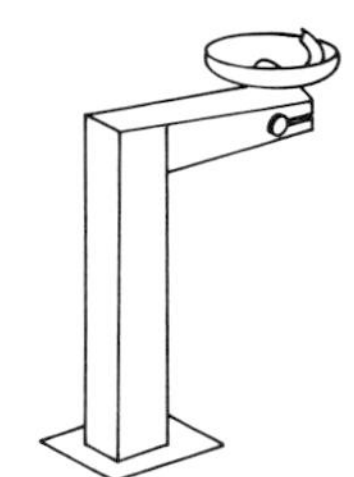

PEDESTAL (IN.)			CONCRETE CYLINDER (IN.)			CONCRETE HANDICAPPED (IN.)			PROJECTING PEDESTAL (IN.)		
H	DIA.	SUPPLY/ WASTE	H	DIA.	SUPPLY/ WASTE	H	L	SUPPLY/ WASTE	H	L	SUPPLY/ WASTE
36	12	⅜, 1	36	12	½, 1¼	33	30¾	½, 1¼	33	29¾	½, 1¼

OUTDOOR TYPE FOUNTAINS

William G. Miner, AIA, Architect, Washington, D.C.

GENERAL NOTES

Lavatories and work sinks are available in vitreous china (V.C.), enameled cast iron (E.C.I.), enameled steel (E.S.), and stainless steel (S.S.). Typically, floor to rim dimension is 2 ft. 7 in., unless otherwise noted. The most commonly used means of support is the chair or wall carrier with concealed arms. Other methods are detailed below. Consult manufacturer's data for specific fixture design and support recommendations.

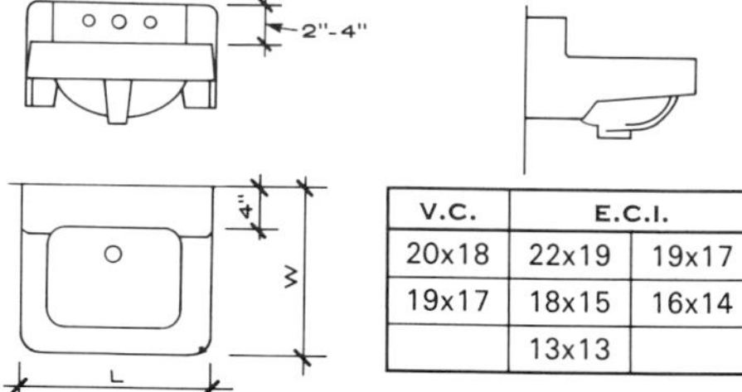

V.C.	E.C.I.	
20x18	22x19	19x17
19x17	18x15	16x14
	13x13	

Shelf-back lavatories generally are rectangular with semi-oval basins. Height of the shelf typically is 4 in.; depth is usually 5 in. Support with metal legs and brackets or concealed carrier.

SHELF BACK

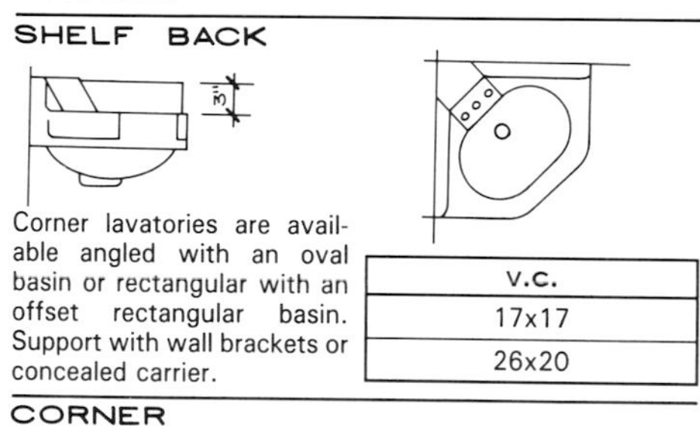

Corner lavatories are available angled with an oval basin or rectangular with an offset rectangular basin. Support with wall brackets or concealed carrier.

V.C.
17x17
26x20

CORNER

Wash sinks supported with concealed wall brackets for E.C.I. or with angle supports for S.S.

E.C.I.		S.S.		STATIONS
18x36	18x48	20x48		2
18x60	18x72	20x60	20x72	3
		20x96		4

WASH SINKS

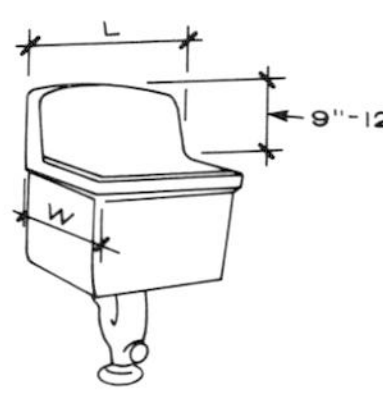

Wall-mounted service sinks are designed for janitorial requirements of hospitals, plants, institutions, office buildings, and schools. Floor to rim dimension is 2 ft. 3 in. to 2 ft. 5 in. Fittings are mounted either on or above the sink back. "H" designates flushing rim design for hospital use specifically.

V.C.		E.C.I.		S.S.	
28x22	26x20 H	24x20	24x18	25x19	23x18
24x22 H	20x20 H	22x18			
22x20					

SERVICE SINKS

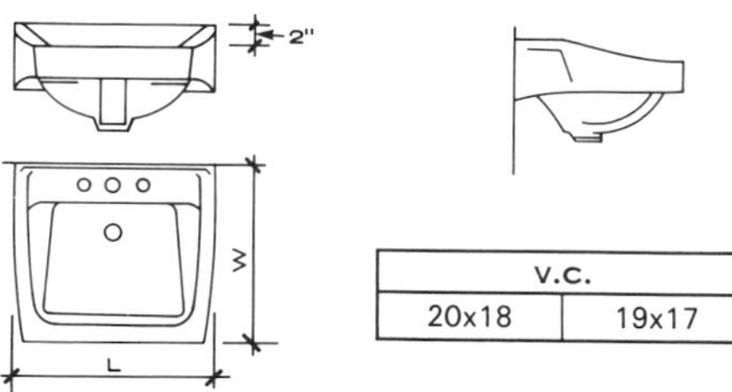

V.C.	
20x18	19x17

Ledge-back lavatories generally are rectangular with rectangular basins. Ledge width usually is 4 in. Typically supported with concealed carrier.

LEDGE BACK

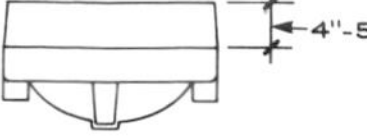

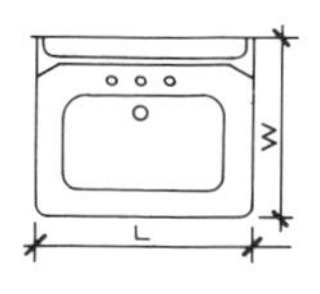

V.C.	E.C.I.	S.S.
20x18	20x18	23x20
18x15	19x17	22x19
24x21	(L x W)	
24x20		
18x16		

Most flat-back lavatories are rectangular with rectangular or semi-oval basins. Typically, floor to rim dimension is 2 ft. 7 in. Support using metal legs with brackets or with concealed carrier.

FLAT BACK

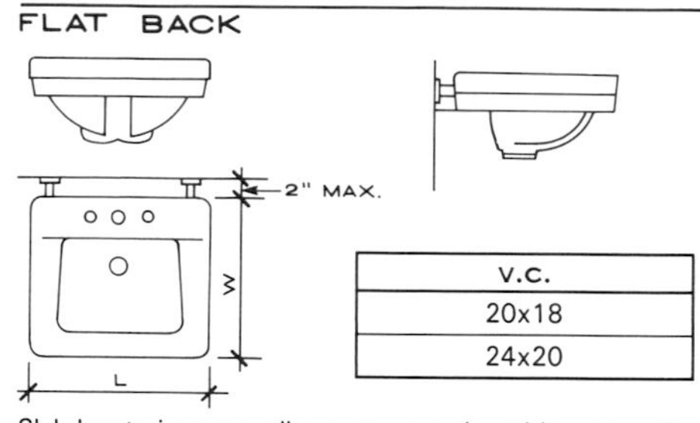

V.C.
20x18
24x20

Slab lavatories generally are rectangular with rectangular basins. A 2 in. escutcheon typically spaces lavatory from finish wall. (4 in. and 6 in. also are available.) Vitreous china leg with brackets can be used as alternate means of support.

SLAB

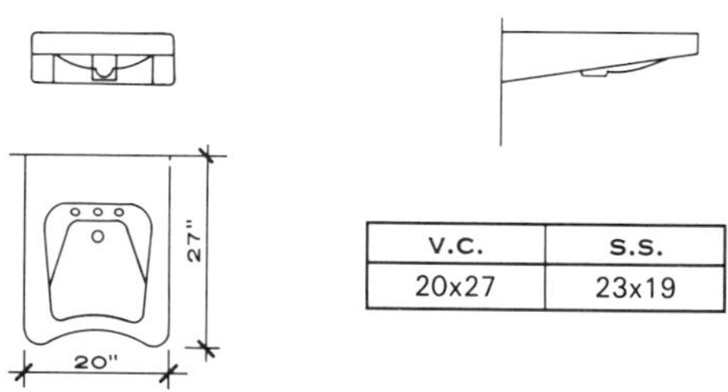

V.C.	S.S.
20x27	23x19

Wheelchair lavatories must be supported using a concealed arm carrier. Height from floor to rim is 2 ft. 10 in.

WHEELCHAIR LAVATORY

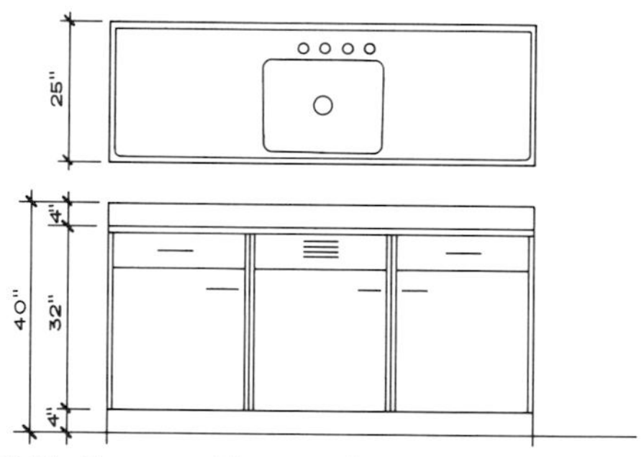

Sink/cabinet assemblies are available in stainless steel with single or double bowls, with or without adjacent drainboards. Lengths of cabinets vary from 42 in. to 96 in., depending on drawer, door, and bowl options.

CABINET

TYPE	DIAM. (IN.)	NO. USERS
Circ.	54 36	8 5
Semi-circ.	54 36	4 3
Corner	54	3

In addition to circular designs, semi-circular and corner types are available, most in precast terrazzo, stainless steel, and some in fiberglass. Most have foot controls, and some have hand controls. Supply from above, below, or through the wall. Vents many rise centrally or come off drain through wall or floor.

WASH SINK

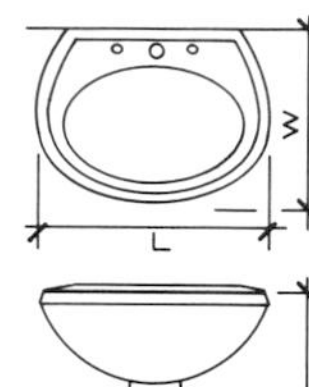

Pedestal lavatories are available in a wide variety of forms, sizes, and basin shapes. See manufacturer for specific designs.

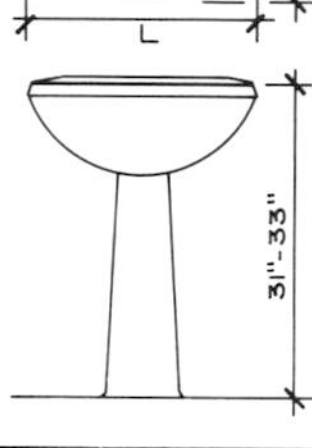

V.C.		
38x22	30x20	28x21
24x19	26x22	25x21
22x21	20x18	

PEDESTAL LAVATORY

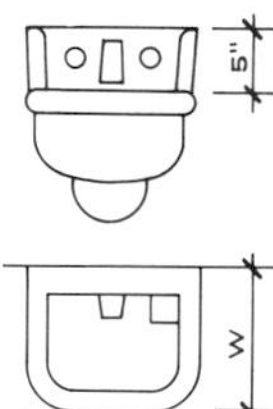

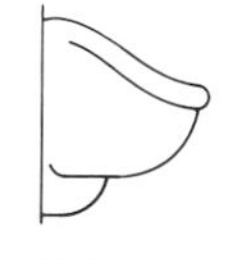

V.C.	E.C.I.
14x13	16x14
14x12	

Institutional lavatories have an integral supply channel to spout and drinking nozzle, strainer, and soap dish. Trap is enclosed in wall. Wall thickness must be specified.

INSTITUTIONAL LAVATORY

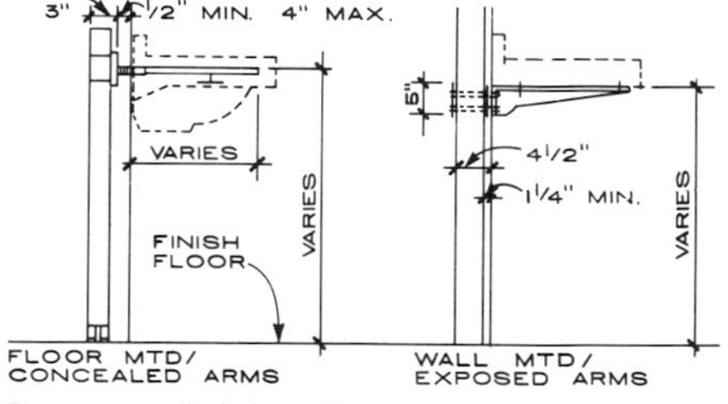
3"
1/2" MIN.
4" MAX.
VARIES
FINISH FLOOR
VARIES
FLOOR MTD/ CONCEALED ARMS
5"
4 1/2"
1 1/4" MIN.
VARIES
WALL MTD/ EXPOSED ARMS

Floor-mounted chair carriers support fixture independent of wall construction. Available with exposed or concealed arms. Wall-mounted carrier with exposed or concealed arms also is available. Additional methods include floor-mounted hanger plate types, floor-mounted bearing plate types, paired metal or single vitreous china leg, in addition to exposed, enameled wall brackets.

METHODS OF LAVATORY SUPPORT

Built-in lavatories are available oval, rectangular and circular in a variety of basin shapes. Typically, built-ins are now self-rimming but are available with metal rims, or rimless for undercounter installations.

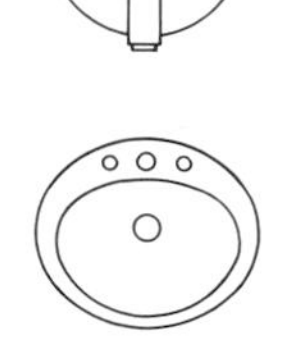

V.C.			E.S.			E.C.I.		
with Metal Rim								
19x16	19x15	17x14	19x16	18x18		26x18	18x18	
Self-rimming								
28x19	26x20	24x20	20x17	19x19		33x19	28x19	21x19
21x19	21x17	21x13				20x17	19x19	19x16
19x19	19x16							
Rimless								
21x17	19x16	17x14	19x16					

BUILT-IN

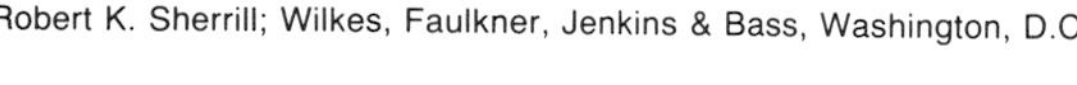
Robert K. Sherrill; Wilkes, Faulkner, Jenkins & Bass, Washington, D.C.

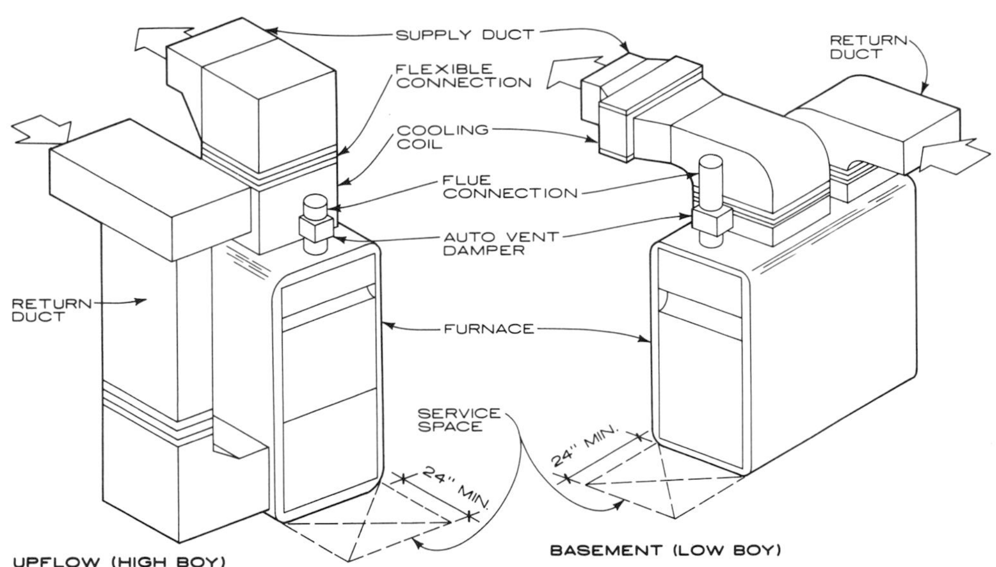
SUPPLY DUCT
FLEXIBLE CONNECTION
COOLING COIL
FLUE CONNECTION
AUTO VENT DAMPER
FURNACE
RETURN DUCT
RETURN DUCT
SERVICE SPACE
24" MIN.
24" MIN.
UPFLOW (HIGH BOY)

BASEMENT (LOW BOY)

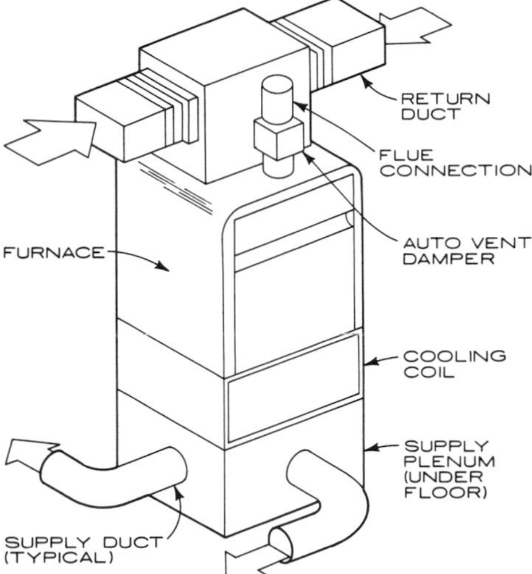
RETURN DUCT
FLUE CONNECTION
AUTO VENT DAMPER
FURNACE
COOLING COIL
SUPPLY PLENUM (UNDER FLOOR)
SUPPLY DUCT (TYPICAL)
DOWNFLOW (COUNTERFLOW)

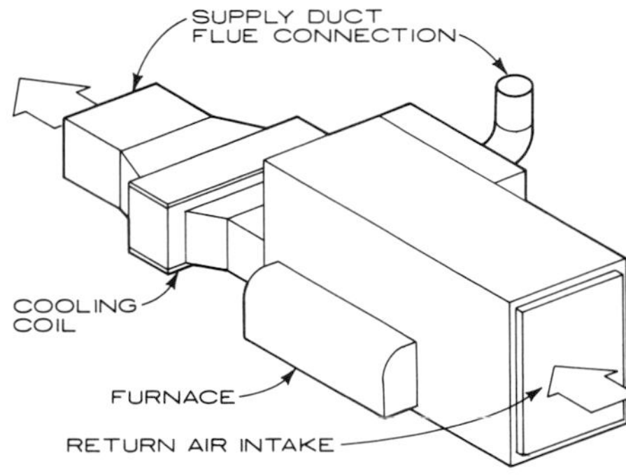
SUPPLY DUCT
FLUE CONNECTION
COOLING COIL
FURNACE
RETURN AIR INTAKE
HORIZONTAL

WARM AIR FURNACES

FLOOR AREA REQUIRED BY WARM AIR FURNACE

OUTPUT CAPACITY (BTU/HR)	FURNACE FLOOR AREA (SQ FT)*
Up to 52,000	2.4
52,000–84,000	4.2
84,000–120,000	6.6
120,000–200,000	13.1

*Based on net floor area occupied by the upflow or downflow furnace. Low boy unit requires 50% more floor area. Space for combustion air should be added as required by local codes. Adequate space should be provided for service.

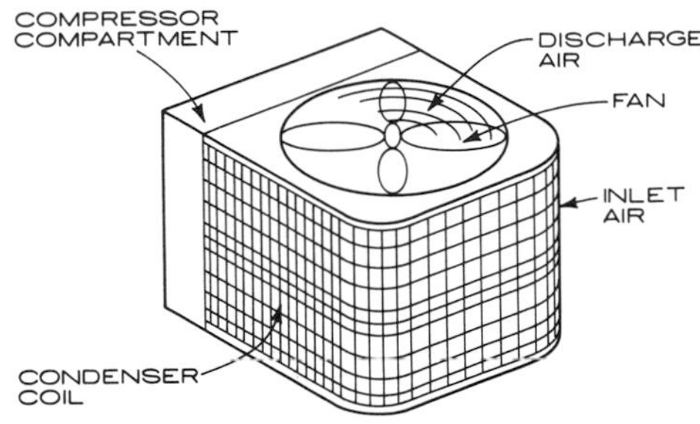
COMPRESSOR COMPARTMENT
DISCHARGE AIR
FAN
INLET AIR
CONDENSER COIL
CONDENSING UNIT

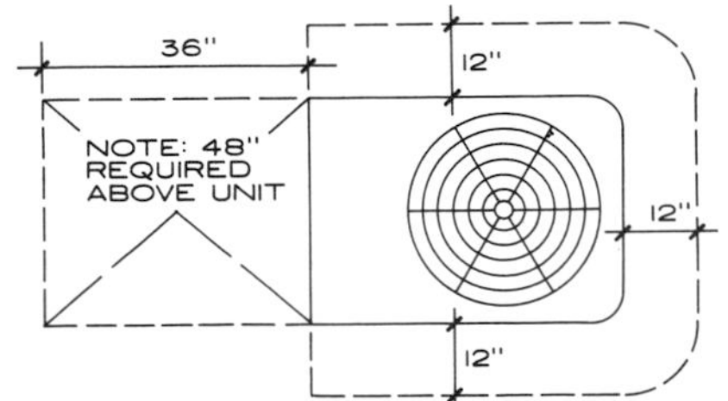
36"
12"
NOTE: 48" REQUIRED ABOVE UNIT
12"
12"
INSTALLATION CLEARANCES

CONDENSING UNIT

NOTES

1. Warm air furnace units are designed primarily for residential, small commercial, or classroom heating. Cooling can be added to these units by installing a cooling coil downstream from the furnace, with refrigerant compressor and condenser located remotely outside the building.
2. Duct system from the furnace unit can be either above the ceiling or in the floor slab. Above ceiling distribution systems are usually the radial type with high wall registers. Perimeter loop and extended plenum systems in floor slabs provide good air distribution. There are smaller temperature variations across the floor with perimeter loop systems than with radial or extended plenum systems.
3. Duct systems also may be installed below the living spaces, in a crawl space, or in a basement.
4. Two- or three-story buildings using similar warm air furnace and cooling coil combinations are centrally air conditioned via vertical extension of the branch ductwork through walls and partitions. Since all variations of the warm air heating/cooling systems recirculate their air within the building envelope, it is a crucial design requirement to leave return air passage, from each space supplied with air, to the furnace room.

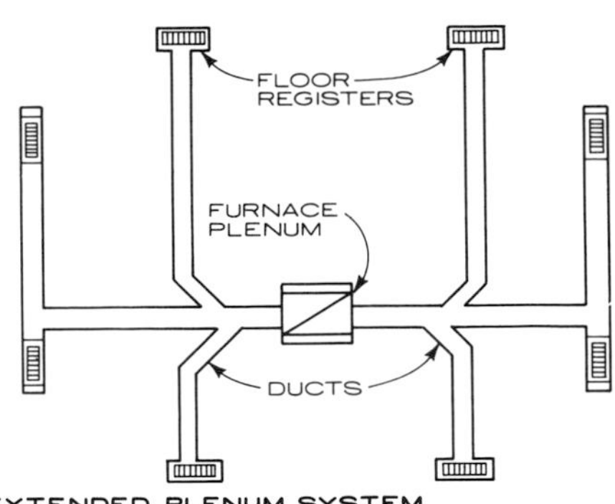
FLOOR REGISTERS
FURNACE PLENUM
DUCTS
EXTENDED PLENUM SYSTEM

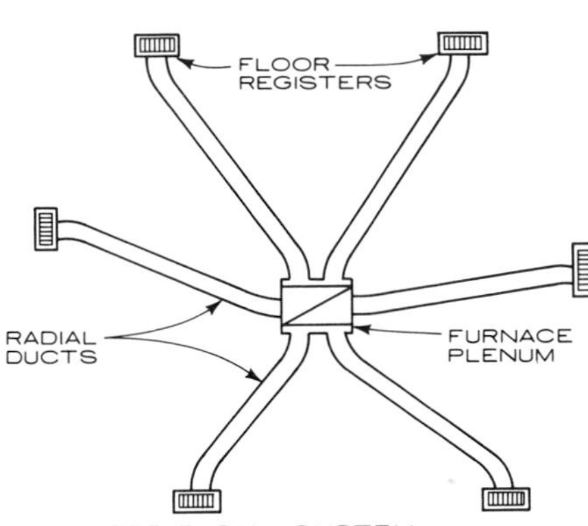
FLOOR REGISTERS
RADIAL DUCTS
FURNACE PLENUM
PERIMETER RADIAL SYSTEM

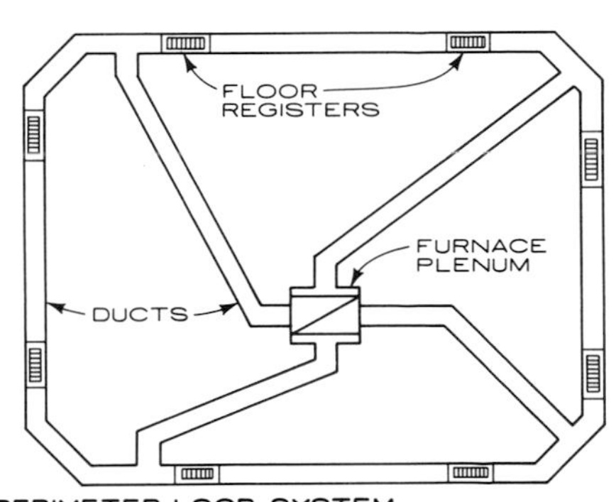
FLOOR REGISTERS
FURNACE PLENUM
DUCTS
PERIMETER LOOP SYSTEM

DUCT SYSTEMS

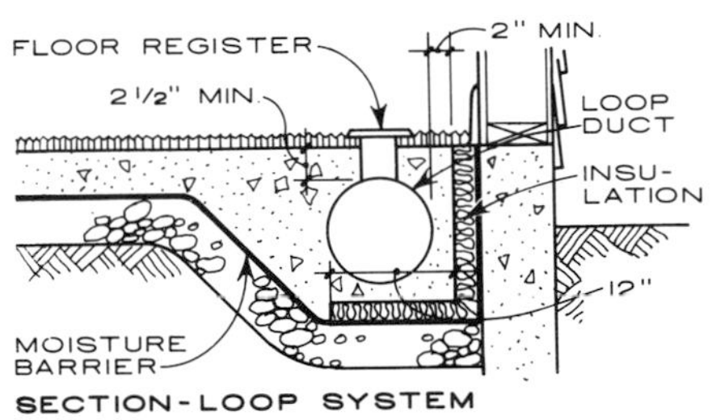
FLOOR REGISTER
2" MIN.
2 1/2" MIN.
LOOP DUCT
INSU-LATION
12"
MOISTURE BARRIER
SECTION-LOOP SYSTEM

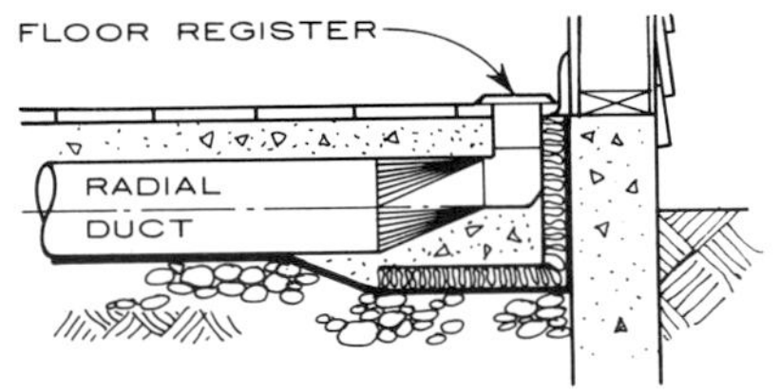
FLOOR REGISTER
RADIAL DUCT
SECTION-RADIAL SYSTEM

AIR OUTLETS

DiClemente-Siegel Engineering, Inc.; Southfield, Michigan

REFERENCES

GENERAL REFERENCES

Mechanical and Electric Equipment for Buildings, 7th ed., 1986, Benjamin Stein, John Reynolds, and William McGuinness, Wiley

Plumbing Design and Installation Reference Guide, 1986, T. G. Hicks, McGraw-Hill

DATA SOURCES: ORGANIZATIONS

Ebco Manufacturing Company, 389
Haws Drinking Faucet Company, 389
Jacuzzi Whirlpool Bath, 388
Leffler Engineering, 384

CHAPTER **16**

ELECTRICAL

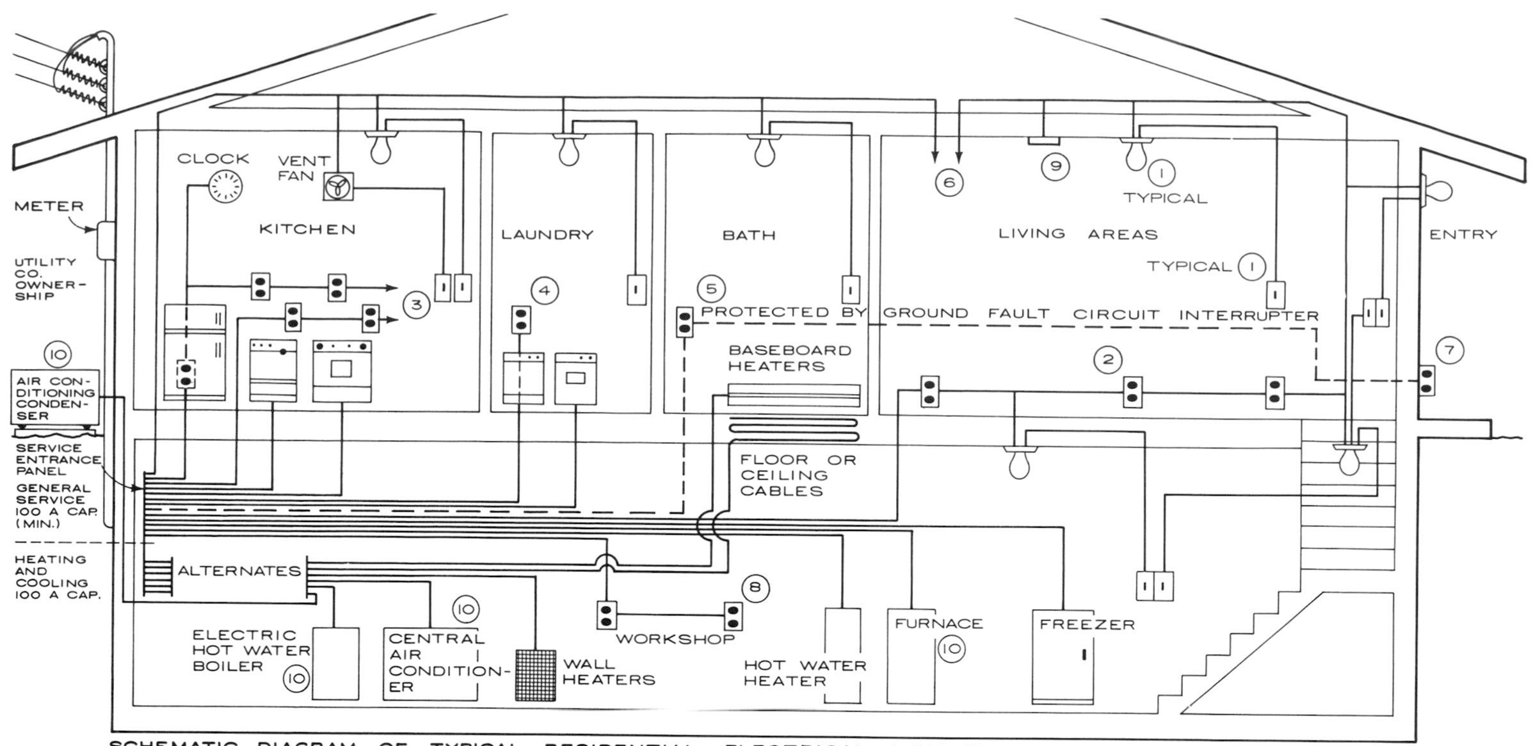

CLOCK
VENT FAN
KITCHEN
METER
UTILITY CO. OWNER-SHIP
10
AIR CON-DITIONING CONDEN-SER
SERVICE ENTRANCE PANEL
GENERAL SERVICE 100 A CAP. (MIN.)
HEATING AND COOLING 100 A CAP.
ALTERNATES
3
LAUNDRY
4
BATH
5
PROTECTED BY GROUND FAULT CIRCUIT INTERRUPTER
BASEBOARD HEATERS
FLOOR OR CEILING CABLES
6
9
1
TYPICAL
LIVING AREAS
TYPICAL 1
ENTRY
2
7
ELECTRIC HOT WATER BOILER
10
CENTRAL AIR CONDITION-ER
10
WALL HEATERS
WORKSHOP
8
HOT WATER HEATER
FURNACE
10
FREEZER

SCHEMATIC DIAGRAM OF TYPICAL RESIDENTIAL ELECTRICAL LAYOUT

GENERAL REQUIREMENTS

1. A minimum of one wall switch controlled lighting outlet is required in every habitable room, in hallways, stairways, and attached garages, and at outdoor entrances. Exception: in habitable rooms other than kitchens and bathrooms one or more receptacles controlled by a wall switch are permitted in lieu of lighting outlets.
2. In every kitchen, family room, dining room, den, breakfast room, living room, parlor, sunroom, bedroom, recreation room, and similar rooms, receptacle outlets are required such that no point along the floor line in any space is greater than 12 ft, measured horizontally, from an outlet in that space, including any wall space 2 ft or more wide and the wall space occupied by sliding panels in exterior walls.
3. A minimum of two #12 wire 20 A small appliance circuits are required to serve only small appliance outlets, including refrigeration equipment, in kitchen, pantry, dining room, breakfast room, and family room. Both circuits must extend to kitchen; the other rooms may be served by either one or both of them. No other outlets may be connected to these circuits, other than a receptacle installed solely for the supply to and support of an electric clock. In kitchen and dining areas receptacle outlets must be installed at each and every counter space wider than 12 in.
4. A minimum of one #12 wire 20 A circuit must be provided to supply the laundry receptacle(s), and it may have no other outlets.
5. A minimum of one receptacle outlet must be installed in bathroom near the basin and must be provided with ground fault circuit interrupter protection.
6. The code requires sufficient 15 and 20 A circuits to supply 3 W of power for every square foot of floor space, not including garage and open porch areas. Minimum code suggestion is one circuit per 600 sq ft; one circuit per 500 sq ft is desirable.
7. A minimum of one exterior receptacle outlet is required (two are desirable) and must be provided with ground fault circuit interrupter protection.
8. A minimum of one receptacle outlet is required in basement and garage, in addition to that in the laundry. In attached garages it must be provided with ground fault circuit interrupter protection.
9. Many building codes require a smoke detector in the hallway outside bedrooms or above the stairway leading to upper floor bedrooms.
10. Disconnect switches required.

NOTE

Refer to the National Electrical Code (NEC) for further information on residential requirements.

INDIVIDUAL APPLIANCE CIRCUITS

TYPE	VOLTS	TYPE	VOLTS
Range	240	Dishwasher	120
Separate oven or countertop cooking unit	240	Freezer	120
Water heater	240	Oil furnace motor	120
Automatic washer	240	Furnace blower motor	120
Clothes dryer	240	Water pump	240
Garbage disposal	240	Permanently connected appliances > 1000 W	Varies

BRANCH CIRCUIT PROTECTION

Lighting (general purpose)	#14 wires	15 A
Small appliance	#12 wires	20 A
Individual appliances	#12 wires	20 A
	#10 wires	30 A
	#8 wires	40 A
	#6 wires	50 A

AVERAGE WATTAGES OF COMMON RESIDENTIAL ELECTRICAL DEVICES

TYPE	WATTS	TYPE	WATTS	TYPE	WATTS
Air conditioner, central	2500-6000	Heating pad	50-75	Range oven (separate)	4000-5000
Air conditioner, room type	800-2500	Heat lamp (infrared)	250	Razor	8-12
Blanket, electric	150-200	Iron, hand	600-1200	Refrigerator	150-300
Clock	2-3	Knife, electric	100	Refrigerator, frostless	400-600
Clothes dryer	4000-6000	Lamp, incandescent	10 upward	Roaster	1200-1650
Deep fat fryer	1200-1650	Lamp, fluorescent	15-60	Rotisserie (broiler)	1200-1650
Dishwasher	1000-1500	Lights, Christmas tree	30-150	Sewing machine	60-90
Fan, portable	50-200	Microwave oven	1000-1500	Stereo (solid state)	30-100
Food blender	500-1000	Mixer	120-250	Sunlamp (ultraviolet)	275-400
Freezer	300-500	Percolator	500-1000	Television	50-450
Frying pan, electric	1000-1200	Power tools	Up to 1000	Toaster	500-1200
Furnace blower	380-670	Projector, slide or movie	300-500	Vacuum cleaner	250-1200
Garbage disposal	500-900	Radio	40-150	Waffle iron	600-1000
Hair dryer	350-1200	Range (all burners and oven "on")	8000-14000	Washer, automatic	500-800
Heater, portable	1000-1500	Range top (separate)	4000-8000	Water heater	2000-5000

Ed Hesner; Rasmussen & Hobbs Architects, AIA; Tacoma, Washington

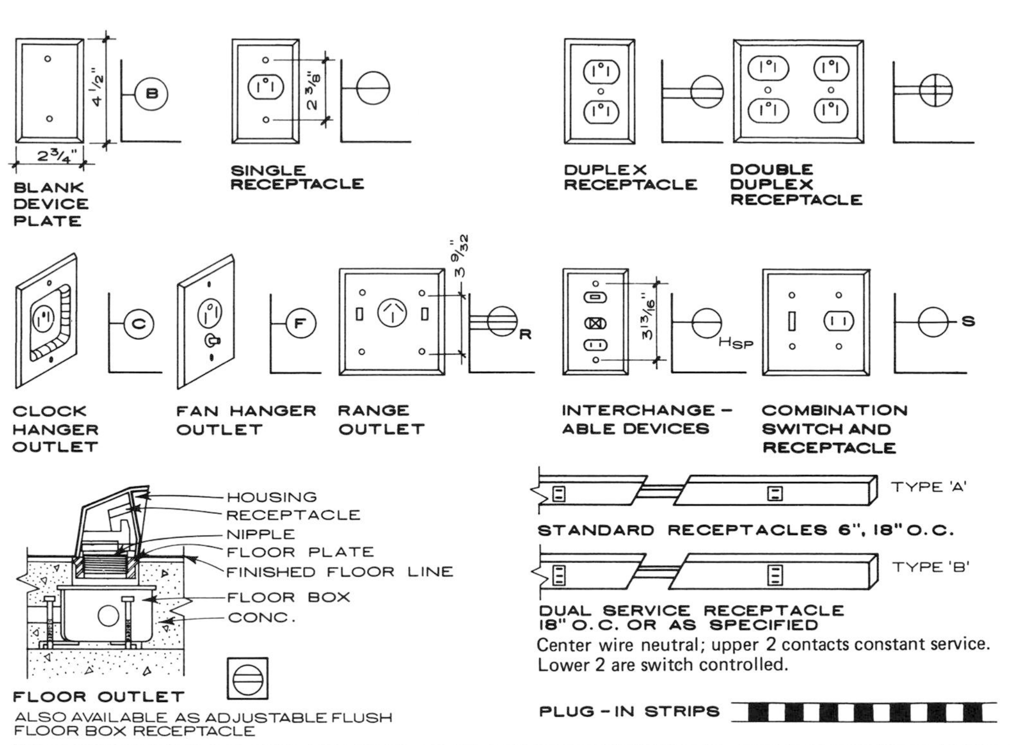

4 1/2"
2 3/4"
B
BLANK DEVICE PLATE
2 3/8"
SINGLE RECEPTACLE
DUPLEX RECEPTACLE
DOUBLE DUPLEX RECEPTACLE
C
CLOCK HANGER OUTLET
F
FAN HANGER OUTLET
3 9/32"
R
RANGE OUTLET
3 13/16"
HSP
INTERCHANGE-ABLE DEVICES
S
COMBINATION SWITCH AND RECEPTACLE
HOUSING
RECEPTACLE
NIPPLE
FLOOR PLATE
FINISHED FLOOR LINE
FLOOR BOX
CONC.
FLOOR OUTLET
ALSO AVAILABLE AS ADJUSTABLE FLUSH FLOOR BOX RECEPTACLE
TYPE 'A'
STANDARD RECEPTACLES 6", 18" O.C.
TYPE 'B'
DUAL SERVICE RECEPTACLE 18" O.C. OR AS SPECIFIED

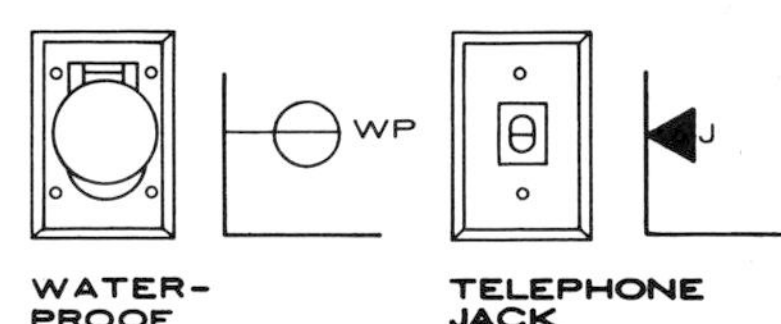

WP
J
WATER-PROOF
TELEPHONE JACK

Center wire neutral; upper 2 contacts constant service. Lower 2 are switch controlled.

PLUG-IN STRIPS 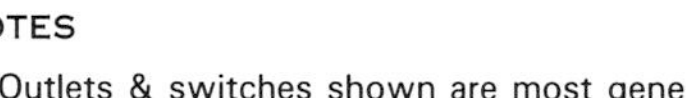

GANG SIZE

	HORIZONTAL		VERTICAL	
GANG	HEIGHT	WIDTH	HEIGHT	WIDTH
2	4 1/2"	4 9/16"	8 1/8"	2 3/4"
3	4 1/2"	6 3/8"	11 3/4"	2 3/4"
4	4 1/2"	8 3/16"	15 3/8"	2 3/4"
5	4 1/2"	10"	19"	2 3/4"
6	4 1/2"	11 13/16"	22 5/8"	2 3/4"
NOTE:	Add 1 13/16" each added gang. Screws 1 13/16" o.c.		Add 3 5/8" each added gang.	

Plates Made in Plastic, Brass (0.04 to 0.06 inches thick), Stainless Steel & Aluminum.

NOTES

1. All devices to be Underwriters Laboratory approved.
2. All devices to comply with requirements of National Electric Code.
3. All devices to be of NEMA configuration.

RECEPTACLES, OUTLET TYPES AND SIZES

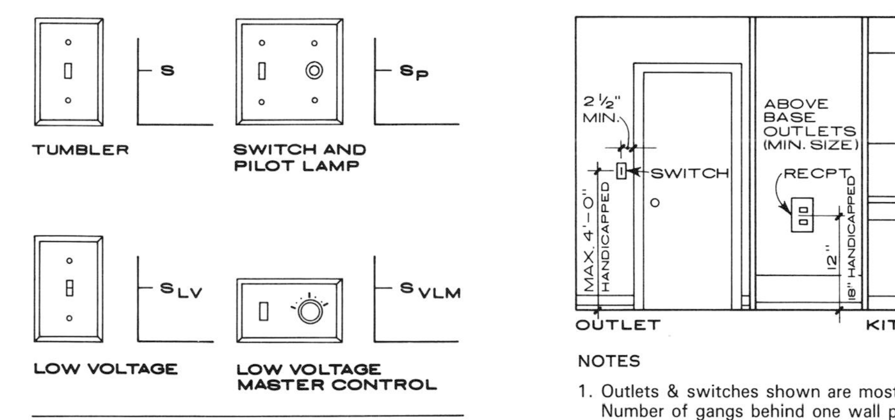

S
TUMBLER
SP
SWITCH AND PILOT LAMP
SLV
LOW VOLTAGE
SVLM
LOW VOLTAGE MASTER CONTROL
SWITCHES
2 1/2" MIN.
SWITCH
MAX. 4'-0" HANDICAPPED
ABOVE BASE OUTLETS (MIN. SIZE)
RECPT.
12"
18" HANDICAPPED
4'-0"
LIGHT FIXTURE
MIRROR
GFI RECEPTACLE
LAV.
4'-0"
7'-0"
3'-6"
(4'-0" IN GARAGES)
OUTLET
KITCHEN
BATHROOM
BASEMENT, LAUNDRY ROOM UTILITY ROOM

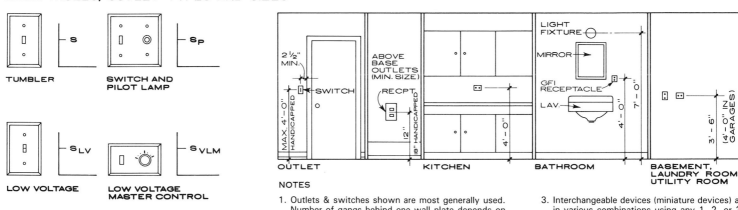

NOTES

1. Outlets & switches shown are most generally used. Number of gangs behind one wall plate depends on types of devices used.
2. Symbols used are ASA standard. See page on "Electric Symbols."
3. Interchangeable devices (miniature devices) available in various combinations using any 1, 2, or 3 of the following: switch, convenience outlet, radio outlet, pilot light, bell, button, in one gang. Combined gangs made.

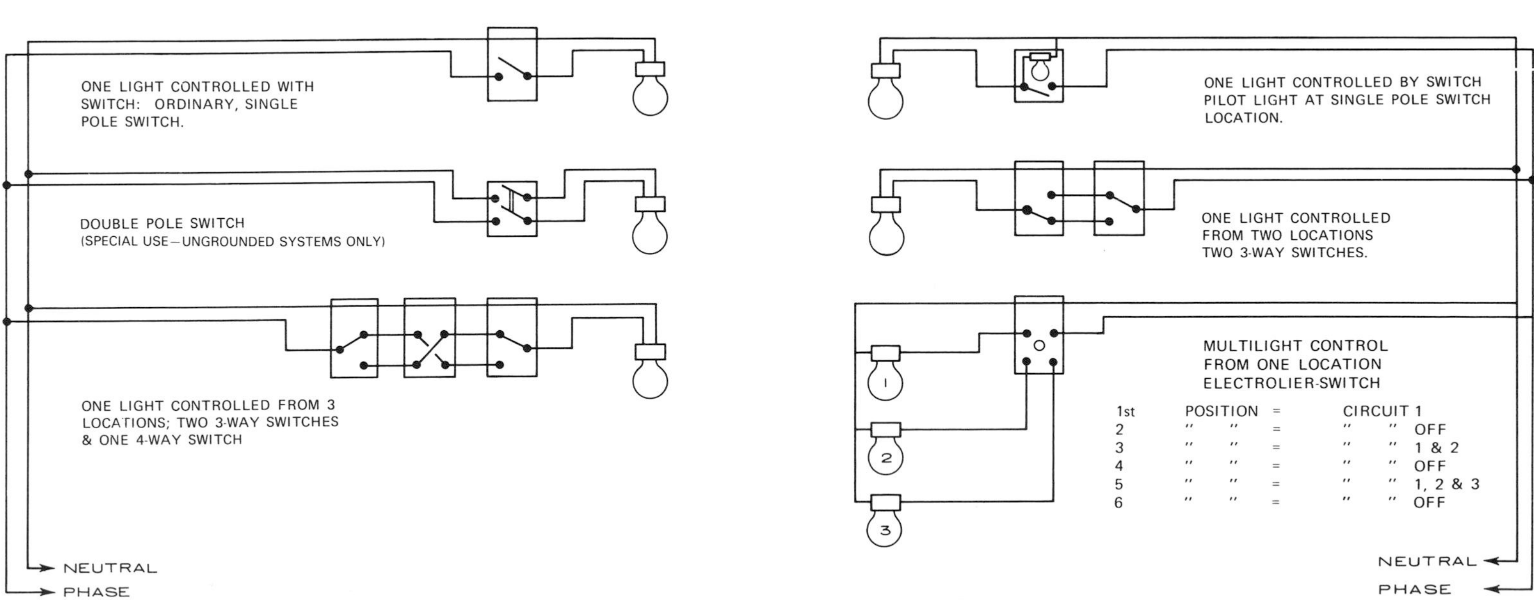

ONE LIGHT CONTROLLED WITH SWITCH: ORDINARY, SINGLE POLE SWITCH.
DOUBLE POLE SWITCH (SPECIAL USE—UNGROUNDED SYSTEMS ONLY)
ONE LIGHT CONTROLLED FROM 3 LOCATIONS; TWO 3-WAY SWITCHES & ONE 4-WAY SWITCH
NEUTRAL
PHASE
ONE LIGHT CONTROLLED BY SWITCH PILOT LIGHT AT SINGLE POLE SWITCH LOCATION.
ONE LIGHT CONTROLLED FROM TWO LOCATIONS TWO 3-WAY SWITCHES.
MULTILIGHT CONTROL FROM ONE LOCATION ELECTROLIER-SWITCH
1st POSITION = CIRCUIT 1
2 " " = " " OFF
3 " " = " " 1 & 2
4 " " = " " OFF
5 " " = " " 1, 2 & 3
6 " " = " " OFF
NEUTRAL
PHASE

SWITCH WIRING DIAGRAMS

B. J. Baldwin; Giffels & Rossetti, Inc.; Detroit, Michigan

NOTES

Poke-through systems are used in conjunction with overhead branch distribution systems run in accessible suspended ceiling cavities to serve outlets in full height partitions. When services are required at floor locations where adjacent partitions or columns are not available, as in open office planning, they must either be brought down from a wireway assembly (known as a power pole) or up through a floor penetration containing a fire-rated insert fitting and above-floor outlet assembly. To install a poke-through assembly, the floor slab must either be drilled or contain preset sleeves arranged in a modular array. Poke-through assemblies are used in conjunction with cellular deck and underfloor duct systems when precise service location required does not fall directly above its associated system raceway.

With one floor penetration, the single poke-through assembly can serve all the power, communications, and data requirements of a work station. Distribution wiring in the ceiling cavity can be run in raceways. The more cost-effective method is to use armored cable (bx) for power and approved plenum rated cable for communications and data when the ceiling cavity is used for return air. To minimize disturbance to the office space below when a poke-through assembly needs to be relocated or added, a modular system of prewired junction boxes for each service can be provided, although it is more common to elect this option for power only. A different type of wiring system must be selected for a floor slab on grade, above lobby or retail space, above mechanical equipment space, or above space exposed to atmosphere.

Low initial cost of a poke-through system makes it both viable and attractive for investor-owned buildings where tenants are responsible for future changes and for corporate buildings where construction budget is limited. It is effective when office planning includes interconnecting work station panels containing provisions to extend wiring above the floor, reducing the number of floor penetrations needed for services.

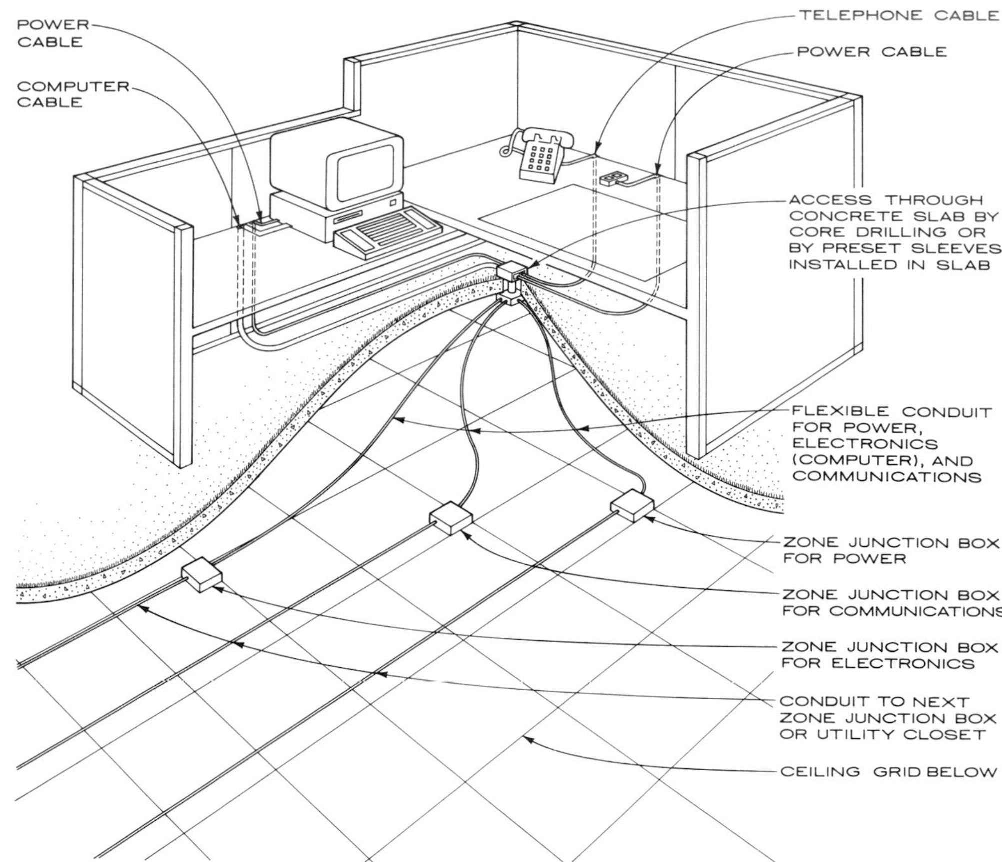
POWER CABLE
COMPUTER CABLE
TELEPHONE CABLE
POWER CABLE
ACCESS THROUGH CONCRETE SLAB BY CORE DRILLING OR BY PRESET SLEEVES INSTALLED IN SLAB
FLEXIBLE CONDUIT FOR POWER, ELECTRONICS (COMPUTER), AND COMMUNICATIONS
ZONE JUNCTION BOX FOR POWER
ZONE JUNCTION BOX FOR COMMUNICATIONS
ZONE JUNCTION BOX FOR ELECTRONICS
CONDUIT TO NEXT ZONE JUNCTION BOX OR UTILITY CLOSET
CEILING GRID BELOW

POKE-THROUGH HARDWIRE SYSTEM/ZONE JUNCTION BOXES

NOTES

Based on projected frequency of future changes in office furniture layouts, a corporate or government organization may elect to preinvest in a permanent raceway system to minimize cost and disturbance to occupants when changes or additions are made. When structural design dictates the use of metal decking, a cellular floor raceway system utilizing trench header ducts becomes the most likely candidate for selection.

Cellular raceways come in a variety of sizes and configurations ranging from 1½ to 3 in. high with cells 8 or 12 in. o.c. and 2 or 3 cells per section. An overall floor deck can be full cellular, where bottom plates are provided throughout, or blended as shown.

Trench header ducts come in various sizes and configurations. Height is adjustable for slab depths above cells of 2½–4 in. and widths vary from 9 to 36 in. Coverplates are ¼ in. thick, with lengths from 6 to 36 in., and can either be secured with spring clips or flush, flathead bolts. Two versions of trench design are available, one consisting of a compartmental bottom tray with a grommeted access hole for each cell it crosses and the other a bottomless trench duct consisting of side rails and a separate wireway in the middle, with grommeted access holes only for the power cells.

When service is needed, floor is core drilled above desired cell, the cell top is drilled into, and an afterset insert with above-floor fitting is attached. If data and communication wiring can occupy the same cell, with power wiring in an adjacent cell, two separate service fittings are required for each work station.

Where it is necessary to eliminate or minimize core drilling, a modular pattern combination of two or three preset service flush outlets can be provided along the cellular sections before the floor is poured, as shown. Upon activation, one flush outlet can serve all the power, communication, and data requirements of a work station.

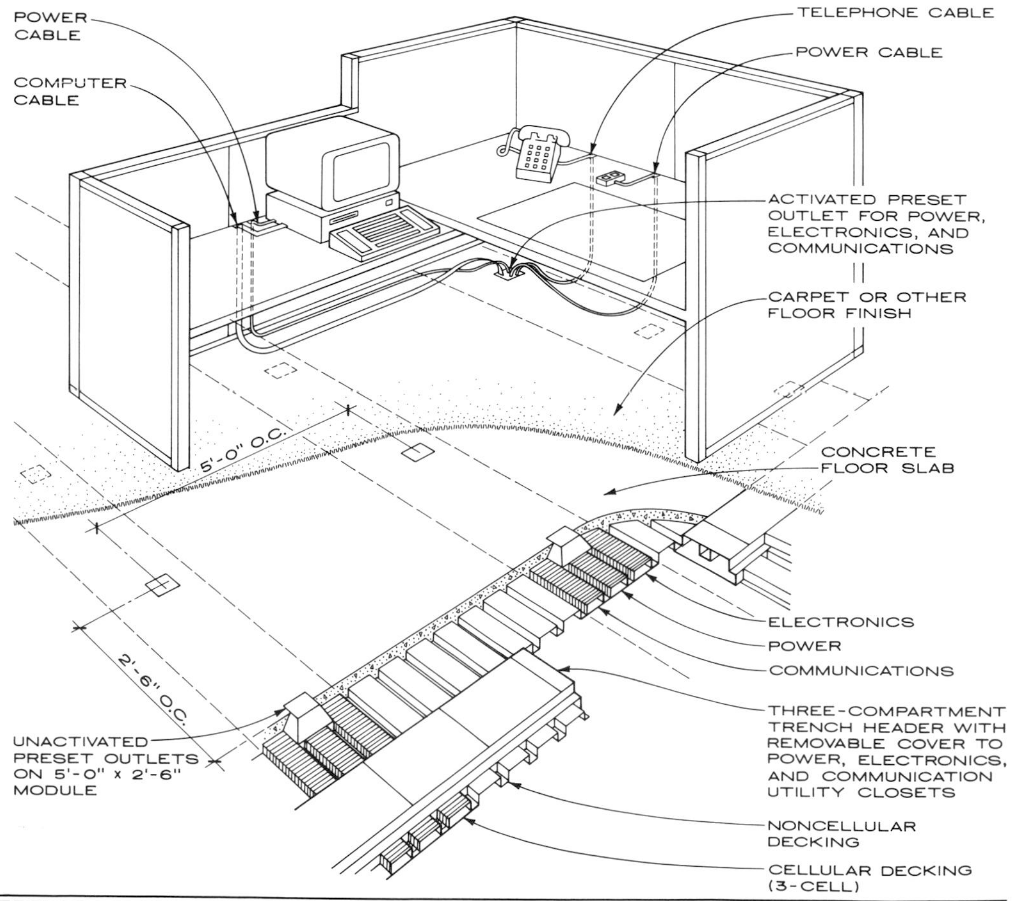
POWER CABLE
COMPUTER CABLE
TELEPHONE CABLE
POWER CABLE
ACTIVATED PRESET OUTLET FOR POWER, ELECTRONICS, AND COMMUNICATIONS
CARPET OR OTHER FLOOR FINISH
5'-0" O.C.
CONCRETE FLOOR SLAB
ELECTRONICS
POWER
COMMUNICATIONS
2'-6" O.C.
THREE-COMPARTMENT TRENCH HEADER WITH REMOVABLE COVER TO POWER, ELECTRONICS, AND COMMUNICATION UTILITY CLOSETS
UNACTIVATED PRESET OUTLETS ON 5'-0" x 2'-6" MODULE
NONCELLULAR DECKING
CELLULAR DECKING (3-CELL)

ELECTRIFIED CELLULAR DECK SYSTEM/TRENCH HEADER DUCT

Richard F. Humenn, PE; Joseph R. Loring & Associates, Inc., Consulting Engineers; New York, New York
Gary A. Hall; Hammel Green and Abrahamson; Minneapolis, Minnesota

NOTES

Where projected frequency of future changes is relatively high, a raised access floor system will provide the maximum flexibility and lowest cost to relocate or add services for work stations. When used in conjunction with a modular system of power, communication and data wiring plug-in receptacles, and cable connector sets, changes can be made without the need of an electrician or wiring technician. Advantages come at a premium, as access floor is the highest in initial cost of all systems described in this section.

Raised access floor is essentially a basic computer floor that is restricted in application to distribute only power, communication, and data services to work stations. The absence of air distribution and high density of cabling associated with computers permits raised floor height to be reduced to nominal 6 in. As the depth of standard 2 ft sq formed steel floor panel is less than 2 in., over 4 in. clear height under the panels provides sufficient clearance to accommodate hardware associated with distributing services. Virtually any variety of above-floor or flush outlets can be mounted on a floor panel and connected to lengths of cable with plug or connector fitting at the other end.

Access floor can be provided with or without stringers, which are used to minimize "creep" effect. Laser beam equipment speeds up accurate leveling of pedestal heights. For a custom installation without ramps or steps, the base floor is structurally designed to be depressed below permanent building elements such as lobbies, stairs, and toilets. Panels can be ordered with factory-installed carpeting or, alternatively, magnetic-backed carpet squares can be added after installation.

The introduction of an access floor does not necessarily require an increase in floor-to-floor height, and if so, the cubage added is at a much lower per unit cost than for the rest of the building. When special attention is given to coordinating lighting with other elements in the suspended ceiling or when lighting is provided below as from the work stations, the cavity can be compressed to compensate for the raised floor.

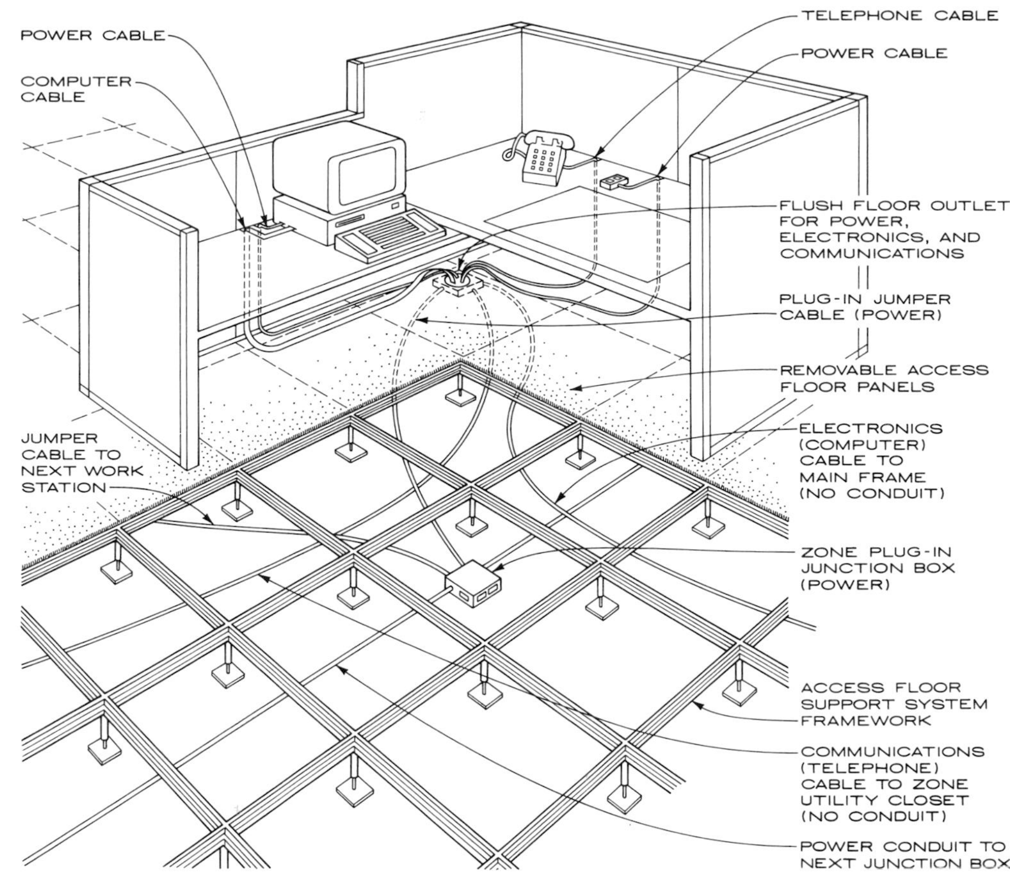
POWER CABLE
COMPUTER CABLE
TELEPHONE CABLE
POWER CABLE
FLUSH FLOOR OUTLET FOR POWER, ELECTRONICS, AND COMMUNICATIONS
PLUG-IN JUMPER CABLE (POWER)
REMOVABLE ACCESS FLOOR PANELS
JUMPER CABLE TO NEXT WORK STATION
ELECTRONICS (COMPUTER) CABLE TO MAIN FRAME (NO CONDUIT)
ZONE PLUG-IN JUNCTION BOX (POWER)
ACCESS FLOOR SUPPORT SYSTEM FRAMEWORK
COMMUNICATIONS (TELEPHONE) CABLE TO ZONE UTILITY CLOSET (NO CONDUIT)
POWER CONDUIT TO NEXT JUNCTION BOX

RAISED ACCESS FLOOR SYSTEM / MODULAR PLUG-IN DISTRIBUTION

NOTES

Undercarpet flat cable wiring has developed into a viable system to serve work stations. By code, it can only be used with carpet squares to afford an acceptable degree of access. Although there are some limitations in performance for flat communication and data cables, improvements are continually being made. Flat cables are now available for Local Area Network (LAN) distribution, applicable where communication and data requirements are extensive.

Cables originate at transition boxes located at various intervals along core corridor walls and/or columns that are individually served from distribution centers in utility closets. Boxes can also be cast in the floor or atop a poke-through insert. Cables are not permitted to pass under fixed partitions and must be carefully mapped out to minimize crossovers and clutter.

To install a service fitting, an interface base assembly must first be secured directly to the concrete floor at the flat cable location. The base assembly stabs into conductors of the flat cable and converts them to round wire. When the service fitting is attached, it is activated and ready for use.

Careful consideration must be given to the application of this system based on limitations that may or may not be acceptable under different conditions. For instance, it may be ideal for small areas or renovation of existing buildings where the poke-through or power pole systems are unacceptable or cannot be used. In new buildings where poke-through has been chosen as the base system, the flat cable system is a viable solution in areas where poke-through outlets cannot be installed, such as slab on grade.

Where frequent changes and additions are contemplated, the resulting wear and tear on expensive, glued down carpet tiles may become a distinct disadvantage.

Although this system appears to be simple and inexpensive, it is highly labor intensive and actual installed initial costs and outlet relocation costs are comparable to cellular deck with trench header ducts.

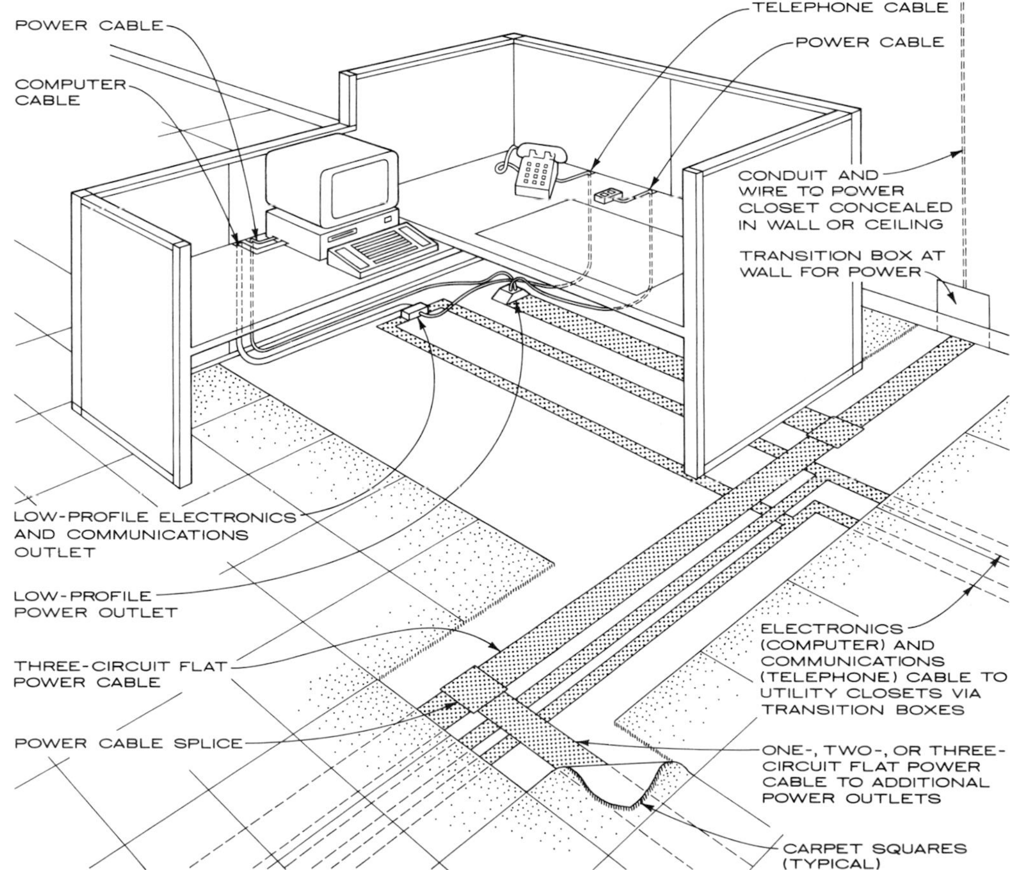
POWER CABLE
COMPUTER CABLE
TELEPHONE CABLE
POWER CABLE
CONDUIT AND WIRE TO POWER CLOSET CONCEALED IN WALL OR CEILING
TRANSITION BOX AT WALL FOR POWER
LOW-PROFILE ELECTRONICS AND COMMUNICATIONS OUTLET
LOW-PROFILE POWER OUTLET
THREE-CIRCUIT FLAT POWER CABLE
POWER CABLE SPLICE
ELECTRONICS (COMPUTER) AND COMMUNICATIONS (TELEPHONE) CABLE TO UTILITY CLOSETS VIA TRANSITION BOXES
ONE-, TWO-, OR THREE-CIRCUIT FLAT POWER CABLE TO ADDITIONAL POWER OUTLETS
CARPET SQUARES (TYPICAL)

FLAT CABLE WIRING SYSTEM

Richard F. Humenn, PE; Joseph R. Loring & Associates, Inc., Consulting Engineers; New York, New York
Gary A. Hall; Hammel Green and Abrahamson; Minneapolis, Minnesota

DECENTRALIZED HEATING SYSTEMS

Electric energy is ideally suited to space heating because it is simple to distribute and control. Complete electric heating systems are widely used in residences, schools, and commercial and industrial establishments.

A decentralized electric system applies heating units to individual rooms or spaces. Often the rooms are combined into zones with automatic temperature controls. In terms of heat output, electric in-space heating systems may be classified as natural convection, radiant, or forced air.

NATURAL CONVECTION UNITS

Heating units for wall mounting, recessed placement or surface placement are made with elements of incandescent bare wire or lower temperature bare wire or sheathed elements. An inner liner or reflector is usually placed between elements so that part of the heat is distributed by convection and part by radiation. Electric convectors should be located so that air movement across the elements is not impeded. Small units with ratings up to 1650 W operate at 120 V. Higher wattage units are made for 208 or higher voltages and require heavy duty receptacles.

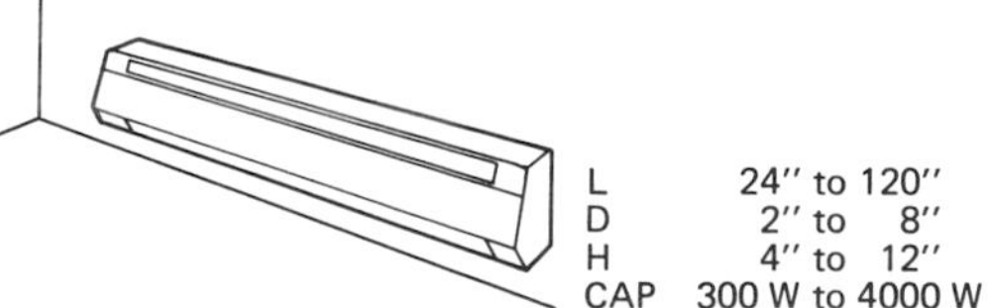

L 24″ to 120″
D 2″ to 8″
H 4″ to 12″
CAP 300 W to 4000 W

BASEBOARD HEATER (Wall Mounted)

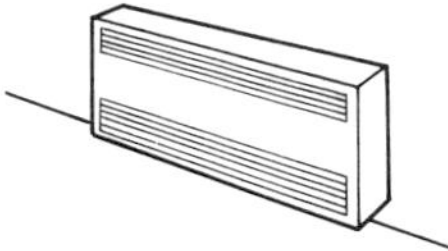

L 24″ to 96″
D 3″ to 8″
H 11″ to 32″
CAP 1000 W to 4000 W

CABINET CONVECTOR (Surface Mounted or Recessed)

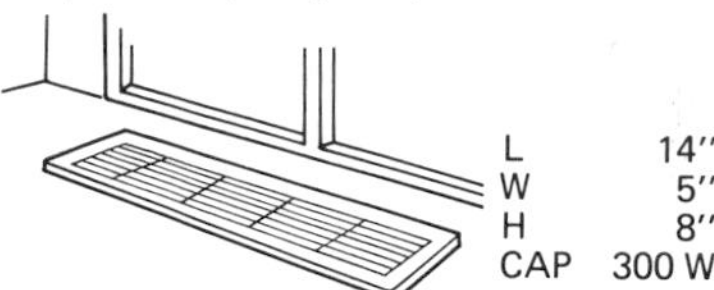

L 14″ to 108″
W 5″ to 8″
H 8″ to 11″
CAP 300 W to 2000 W

FLOOR HEATER (Recessed)

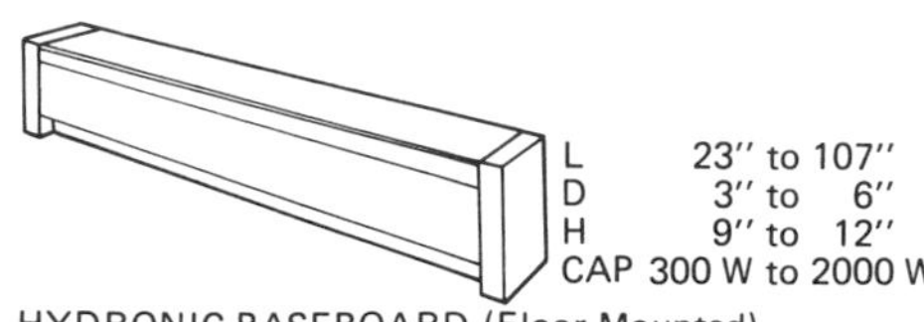

L 23″ to 107″
D 3″ to 6″
H 9″ to 12″
CAP 300 W to 2000 W

HYDRONIC BASEBOARD (Floor Mounted)

NATURAL CONVECTION UNITS

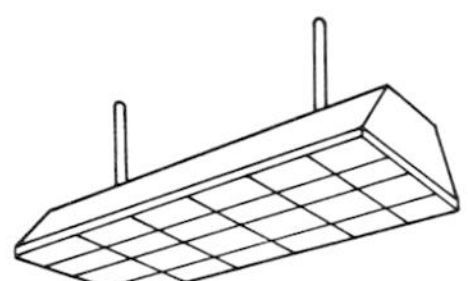

L 14″ to 86″
W 4″ to 12″
H 3″ to 16″
CAP 500 W to 7000 W

INFRARED HEATER (Pendant Mounted) Circular heat lamp is available

L 48″ to 144″
W 24″ to 48″
D 1″
CAP 500 W to 1000 W

RADIANT HEAT PANEL (Surface Mounted or Recessed) Decorative murals are available

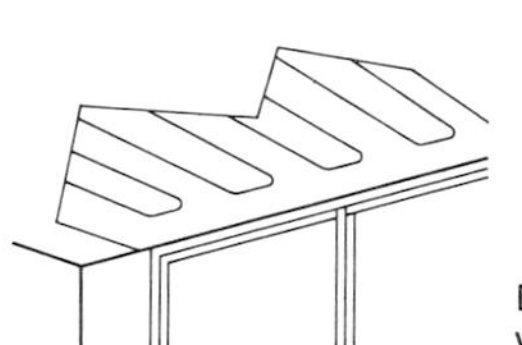

Dimensions and capacity vary with coverage

RADIANT CEILING WITH EMBEDDED CONDUCTORS

RADIANT HEATING UNITS

RADIANT HEATING

Heat is produced by a current that flows in a high resistance wire or ribbon and is then transferred by radiation to a heat absorbing body. Manufacturer's recommendations for clearance between a radiant fixture and combustible materials or occupants should be followed.

FORCED AIR UNITS

Unit ventilators and heaters combine common convective heating with controlled natural ventilation.

Unit ventilators are most often mounted on an outside wall for air intake and at windowsills to prevent the down draft of cold air.

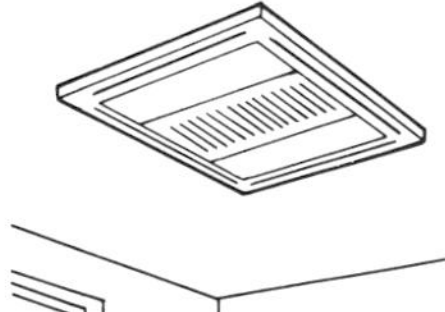

L 10″ to 14″
W 8″ to 14″
D 4″ to 8″
CAP 500 W to 1500 W

CEILING HEATER (Recessed) Circular unit with light is available

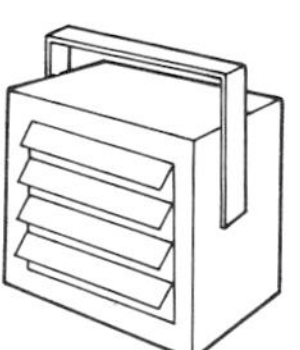

W 12″ to 52″
D 6″ to 22″
H 12″ to 26″
CAP 1.5 KW to 50 KW

UNIT HEATER (Bracket Mounted)

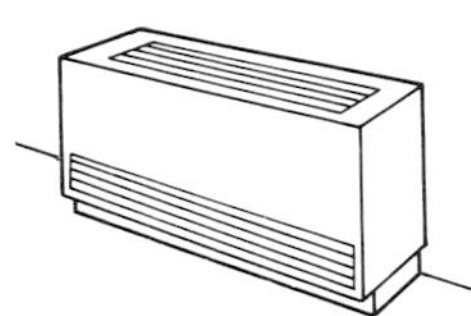

L 48″ to 104″
D 11″ to 26″
H 26″ to 32″
CAP 1 KW to 36 KW

UNIT VENTILATOR (Surface Mounted or Recessed)

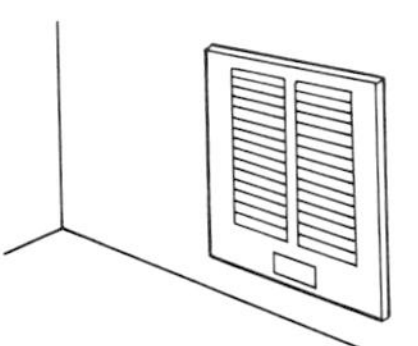

W 10″ to 18″
D 2″ to 6″
H 9″ to 24″
CAP 750 W to 4000 W

WALL HEATER (Recessed)

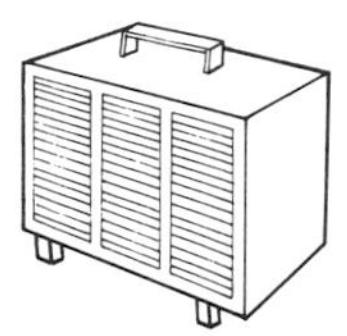

W 10″ to 72″
D 2″ to 12″
H 7″ to 24″
CAP 500 W to 5000 W

PORTABLE HEATER

FORCED AIR UNITS

CENTRALIZED HEATING SYSTEMS

A central hot water system with terminal radiators can be operated using an electric hot water boiler that contains immersion heating elements.

An electric furnace, consisting of resistance heating coils and a blower, can supply a ducted warm air system. Electric heating units are also installed in supply ducts to provide final temperatures and relative humidities in central air systems.

Integrated recovery systems make use of heat gains from electrical loads such as lights and motors. The excess heat accumulated from these sources can either be transferred or stored for later use.

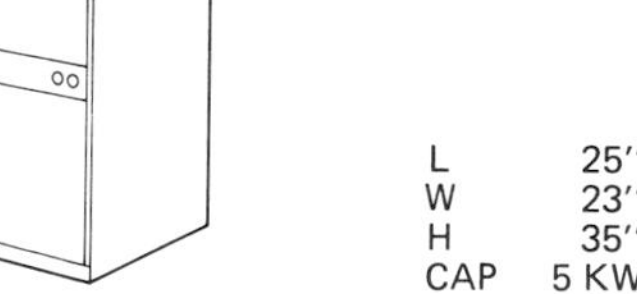

L 25″
W 23″
H 35″
CAP 5 KW to 60 KW

ELECTRIC FURNACE

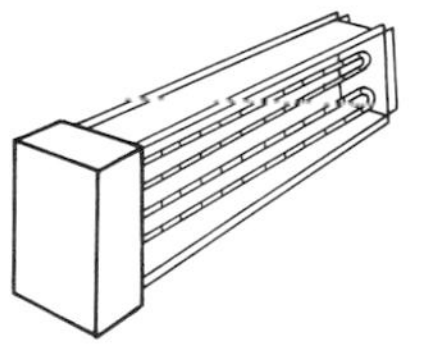

Size varies with duct dimensions
CAP 0.3 KW to 2000 KW

DUCT INSERT HEATER

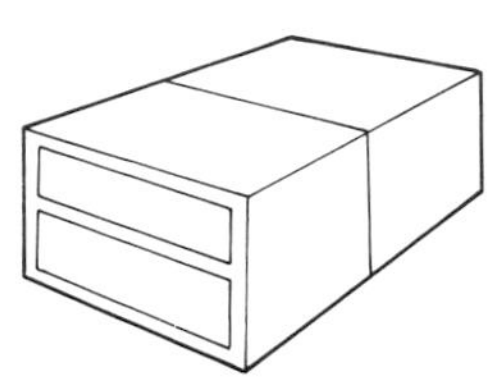

Size varies
CAP 2 KW to 100 KW

HEAT PUMP

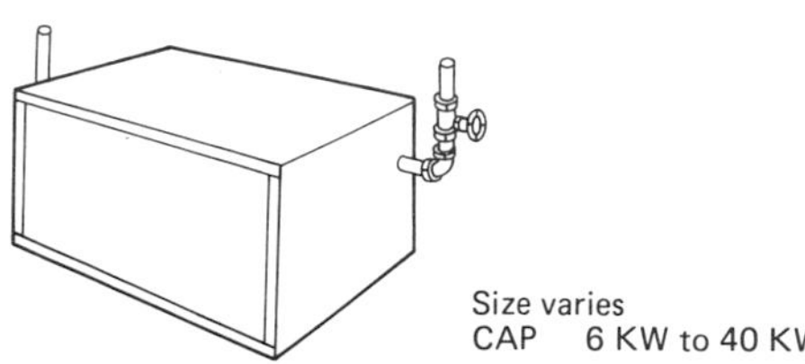

Size varies
CAP 6 KW to 40 KW

ELECTRIC BOILER

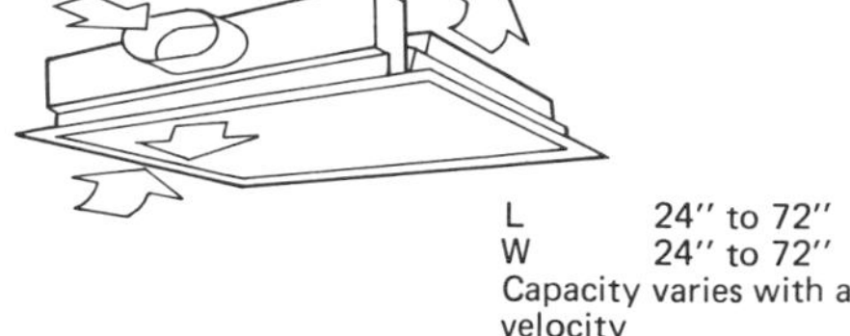

L 24″ to 72″
W 24″ to 72″
Capacity varies with air velocity

INTEGRATED HEAT RECOVERY Heat is gained from light fixtures

CENTRALIZED HEATING SYSTEMS

Tseng-Yao Sun, P.E. and Kyoung S. Park, P.E.; Ayres, Cohen and Hayakawa, Consulting Engineers; Los Angeles/San Francisco, California

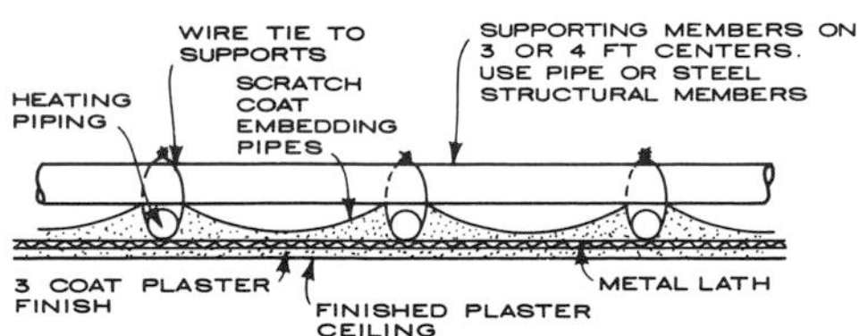
WIRE TIE TO SUPPORTS
SUPPORTING MEMBERS ON 3 OR 4 FT CENTERS. USE PIPE OR STEEL STRUCTURAL MEMBERS
HEATING PIPING
SCRATCH COAT
EMBEDDING PIPES
3 COAT PLASTER FINISH
FINISHED PLASTER CEILING
METAL LATH

PIPES IN SUSPENDED PLASTER CEILING

In a suspended plaster ceiling both the lath and the heating coils are securely wired to the support members so that the lath is below but in good contact with the coils. Plaster is then applied to the lath to embed the tubes. Some local codes may prohibit this assembly.

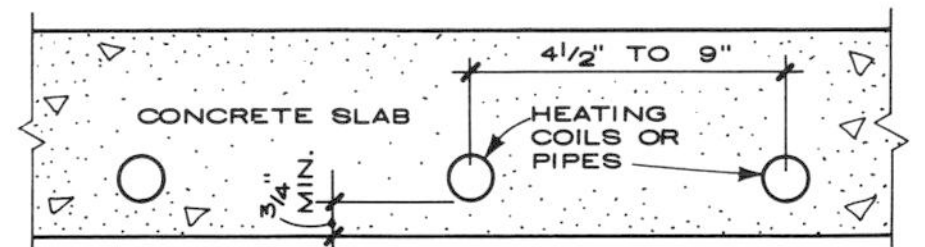
4 1/2" TO 9"
CONCRETE SLAB
HEATING COILS OR PIPES
3/4" MIN.

COILS IN STRUCTURAL CONCRETE SLAB

Heating pipes can be embedded in the lower portion of a concrete slab. If plaster is to be applied to the concrete, the piping may be placed directly on the wood forms. The minimum coverage for an exposed concrete slab is generally $^3/_4$ in. but may vary with local codes.

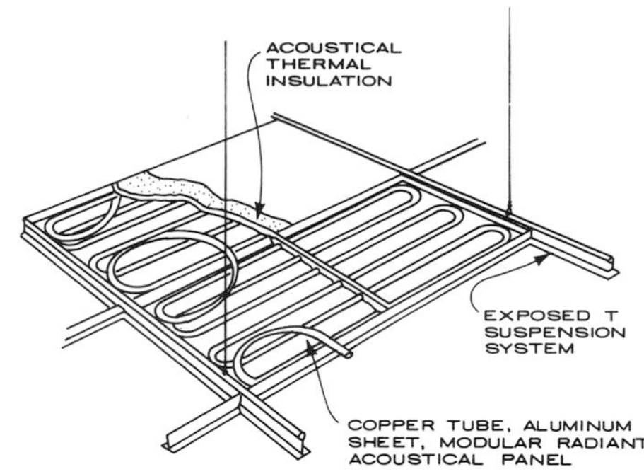
ACOUSTICAL THERMAL INSULATION
EXPOSED T SUSPENSION SYSTEM
COPPER TUBE, ALUMINUM SHEET, MODULAR RADIANT ACOUSTICAL PANEL

METAL CEILING PANELS

Metal panel ceiling systems use copper tubing bonded to an aluminum panel which can be mounted into a standard suspended ceiling grid. An insulating blanket is required to reduce the upward flow of heat from the metal panel. The heating pipes can be connected in either a sinuous or parallel flow welded system. A ceiling panel system can also be used for cooling purposes if chilled water is supplied through the tubes.

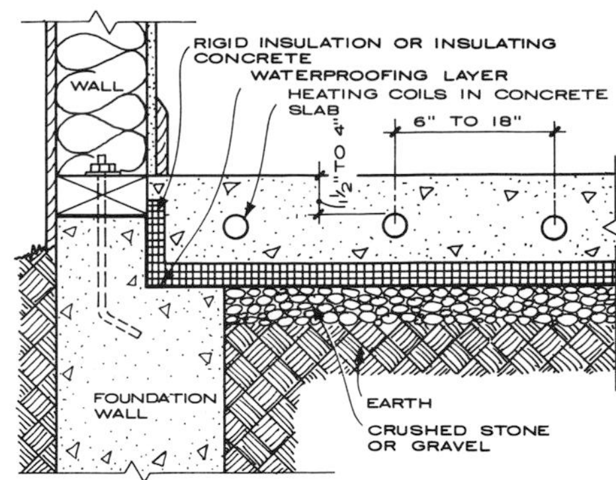
RIGID INSULATION OR INSULATING CONCRETE
WATERPROOFING LAYER
HEATING COILS IN CONCRETE SLAB
WALL
6" TO 18"
1 1/2" TO 4"
FOUNDATION WALL
EARTH
CRUSHED STONE OR GRAVEL

COILS IN FLOOR SLAB ON GRADE

Plastic, ferrous, or nonferrous heating pipes are used in floor slabs that rest on grade. It is recommended that perimeter insulation be used to reduce thermal losses at the edges. Coils should be embedded completely in the concrete slab and should not rest on an interface. Supports used to position the coils while pouring the slab should be nonabsorbent and inorganic. A layer of waterproofing should be placed above grade to protect insulation and piping.

LIQUID RADIANT HEATING SYSTEMS

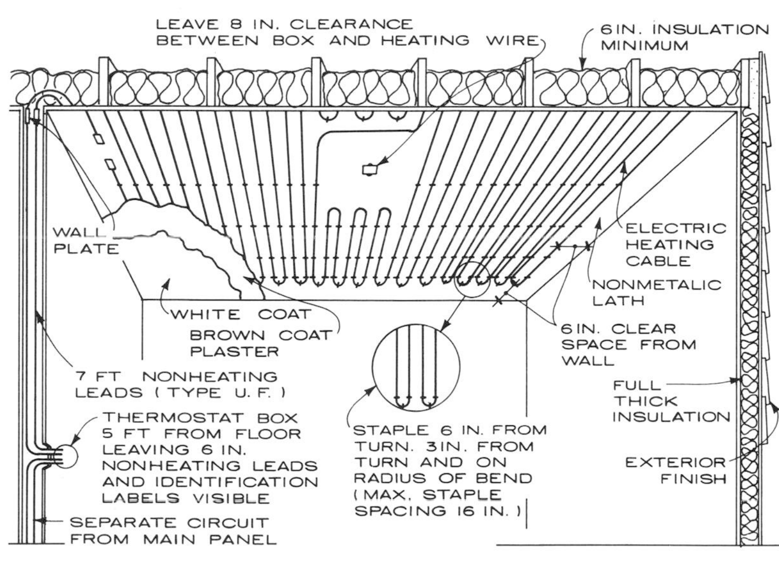
LEAVE 8 IN. CLEARANCE BETWEEN BOX AND HEATING WIRE
6 IN. INSULATION MINIMUM
WALL PLATE
ELECTRIC HEATING CABLE
NONMETALIC LATH
WHITE COAT
BROWN COAT PLASTER
6 IN. CLEAR SPACE FROM WALL
7 FT NONHEATING LEADS (TYPE U. F.)
FULL THICK INSULATION
THERMOSTAT BOX 5 FT FROM FLOOR LEAVING 6 IN. NONHEATING LEADS AND IDENTIFICATION LABELS VISIBLE
STAPLE 6 IN. FROM TURN. 3 IN. FROM TURN AND ON RADIUS OF BEND (MAX. STAPLE SPACING 16 IN.)
EXTERIOR FINISH
SEPARATE CIRCUIT FROM MAIN PANEL

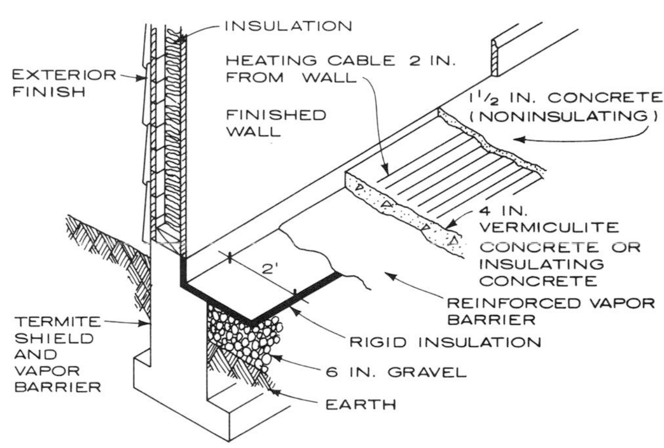
INSULATION
EXTERIOR FINISH
HEATING CABLE 2 IN. FROM WALL
FINISHED WALL
1 1/2 IN. CONCRETE (NONINSULATING)
4 IN. VERMICULITE CONCRETE OR INSULATING CONCRETE
2'
REINFORCED VAPOR BARRIER
TERMITE SHIELD AND VAPOR BARRIER
RIGID INSULATION
6 IN. GRAVEL
EARTH

ELECTRIC HEATING CABLE IN CONCRETE SLAB

Electric heating cables embedded in plaster ceilings or concrete floors or laminated in gypsum board construction are factory-assembled units furnished in standard lengths from 75 to 1800 ft. Standard cable assemblies are normally rated at 2.75 W/linear ft and are available for 120, 208 and 240 V.

ELECTRIC RADIANT HEATING SYSTEMS

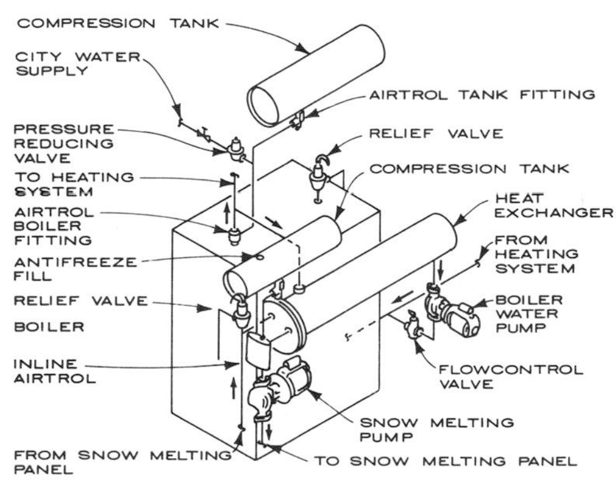
COMPRESSION TANK
CITY WATER SUPPLY
AIRTROL TANK FITTING
PRESSURE REDUCING VALVE
RELIEF VALVE
TO HEATING SYSTEM
COMPRESSION TANK
AIRTROL BOILER FITTING
HEAT EXCHANGER
ANTIFREEZE FILL
FROM HEATING SYSTEM
RELIEF VALVE
BOILER WATER PUMP
BOILER
INLINE AIRTROL
FLOWCONTROL VALVE
SNOW MELTING PUMP
FROM SNOW MELTING PANEL
TO SNOW MELTING PANEL

BOILER AND HEAT EXCHANGER

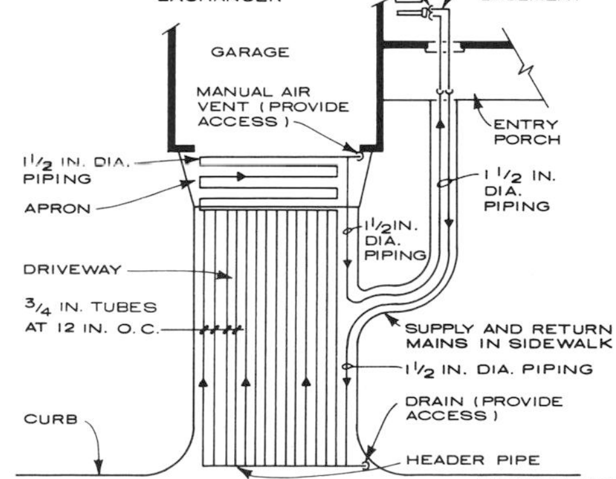
BOILER AND HEAT EXCHANGER
PIPES IN BASEMENT
GARAGE
MANUAL AIR VENT (PROVIDE ACCESS)
ENTRY PORCH
1 1/2 IN. DIA. PIPING
APRON
1 1/2 IN. DIA. PIPING
1 1/2 IN. DIA. PIPING
DRIVEWAY
3/4 IN. TUBES AT 12 IN. O. C.
SUPPLY AND RETURN MAINS IN SIDEWALK
1 1/2 IN. DIA. PIPING
DRAIN (PROVIDE ACCESS)
CURB
HEADER PIPE

DRIVEWAY PIPING PLAN

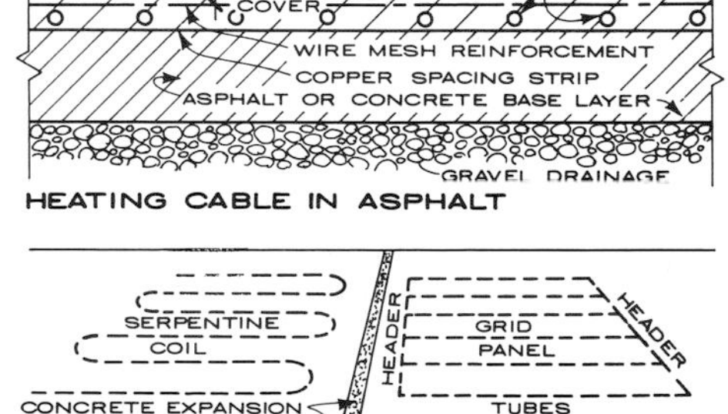
1 1/4" TO 1 1/2" ASPHALT COVER
CABLES
WIRE MESH REINFORCEMENT
COPPER SPACING STRIP
ASPHALT OR CONCRETE BASE LAYER
GRAVEL DRAINAGE

HEATING CABLE IN ASPHALT

SERPENTINE COIL
HEADER
GRID PANEL
TUBES
CONCRETE EXPANSION JOINT
CONCRETE SLAB
DISTRIBUTION MAIN
INSULATED PIPING

EXPANSION JOINT IN CONCRETE WALK OR DRIVEWAY

SNOW MELTING SYSTEMS

Snow melting systems for driveways and sidewalks can be of the ethylene-glycol type, hot oil or electric cables. The hot liquid types use a central hot water boiler with a heat exchanger that pumps the fluid through tubes embedded in the asphalt pavement.

Vents, drains, slab pitch, and expansion joints must be provided for in the initial design. A $^3/_4$ in. pipe or tube on 12 in. centers is used as a standard coil. Header pipes are normally $1^1/_2$ in. in diameter. Piping should be supported with a minimum of 2 in. of concrete above and below the pipe.

If piping must pass through a concrete expansion joint, provision should be made to avoid any stresses on the tubing. By dipping the tube below the expansion joint any movement or heaving in the slab can be accommodated. All piping below the level of the concrete slab must be waterproofed and covered with insulation.

W. S. Fleming and Associates, Inc.; Fayetteville, New York

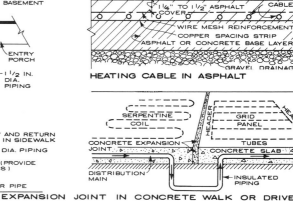

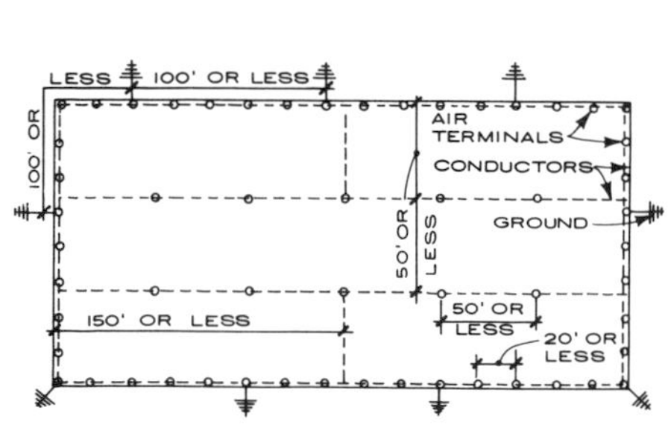

LESS
100' OR LESS
100' OR LESS
AIR TERMINALS
CONDUCTORS
GROUND
50' OR LESS
150' OR LESS
50' OR LESS
20' OR LESS

FLAT ROOF PLAN

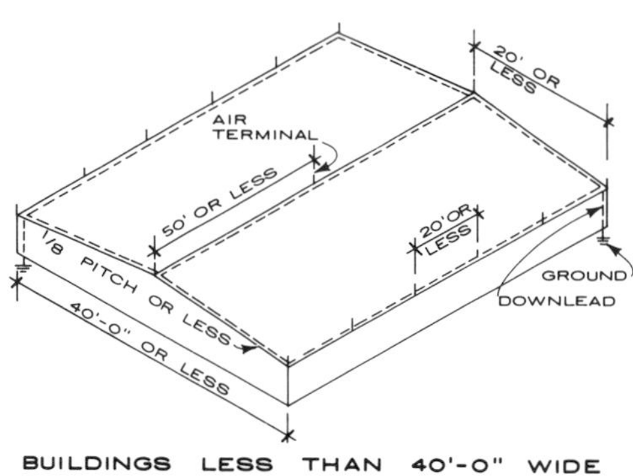

AIR TERMINAL
20' OR LESS
50' OR LESS
20' OR LESS
1/8 PITCH OR LESS
40'-0" OR LESS
GROUND
DOWNLEAD

BUILDINGS LESS THAN 40'-0" WIDE

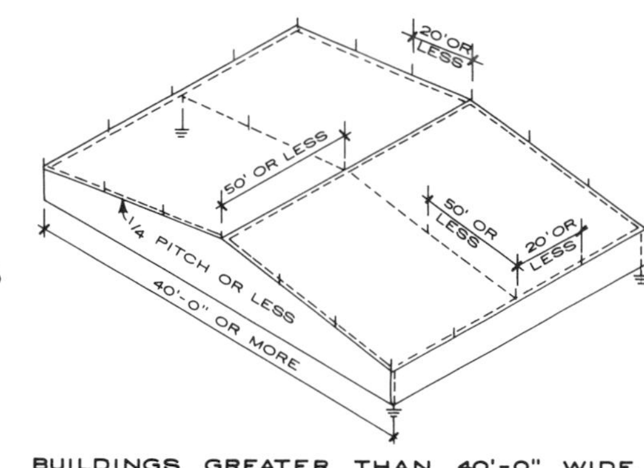

20' OR LESS
50' OR LESS
50' OR LESS
20' OR LESS
1/4 PITCH OR LESS
40'-0" OR MORE

BUILDINGS GREATER THAN 40'-0" WIDE

ROOF LAYOUT PLANS

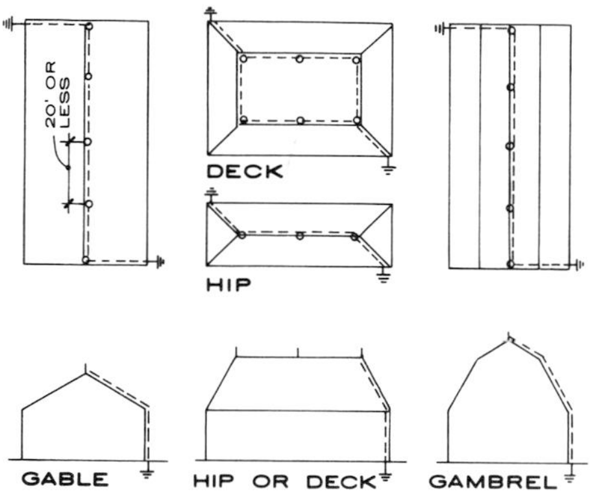

20' OR LESS
DECK
HIP
GABLE
HIP OR DECK
GAMBREL

PITCH ROOF TYPES

OVERALL SYSTEMS DESIGN

1. Air terminals shall be located around the perimeter of flat roof buildings and along the ridge of pitched roof buildings spaced at 20 ft on center maximum and located not more than 2 ft from ridge ends, outside corners, and edges of building walls.
2. Full size main conductors shall interconnect all air terminals.
3. Additional air terminals shall be located in the center of large open flat roofs at spacings not to exceed 50 ft maximum.
4. Cable runs connecting these center roof air terminals shall not exceed 150 ft in length without a lead back to the perimeter cable.
5. Gently sloping roofs are classed as flat under the rules shown above and are protected in the same fashion as flat roof.
6. Download cables to ground shall be connected to the roof perimeter cable at a maximum spacing of 100 ft on center. Buildings having a perimeter of 250 to 300 ft shall have three downleads. For each additional 100 ft or fraction thereof add one downlead.
7. No building or structure shall have less than two downleads.

GENERAL NOTES

A lightning protection system is an integrated arrangement of air terminals, bonding connections, arrestors, splicers, and other fittings installed on a structure in order to safely conduct to ground any lightning discharge to the structure.

Lightning protection systems and components are grouped into three categories (U.L. classes) based on building height and intended applications. Class I equipment and systems are for ordinary buildings under 75 ft in height, Class II is for those over 75 ft in height, and Class II Modified is a specialty area covering only large, heavy duty stacks and chimneys similar to those used at power plants, for example. Each of these types of systems consists of five or six major groups of components:

1. Air terminals (lightning rods) located on the roof and building projections.
2. Main conductors that tie the air terminals together and interconnect with the grounding system.
3. Bonds to metal roof structures and equipment.
4. Arrestors to prevent powerline surge damage.
5. Ground terminals, typically rods or plates driven or buried in the earth.
6. Tree protection (usually applicable only to residential work).

Each of these types of equipment and the methods for their installation are covered in the following drawings.

Beyond these material requirements, other factors to be considered relative to lightning protection systems include (a) selection of codes for compliance, (b) inspection criteria (again based on code), (c) criteria to evaluate competency of installing personnel, and (d) requirement for annual inspection and maintenance.

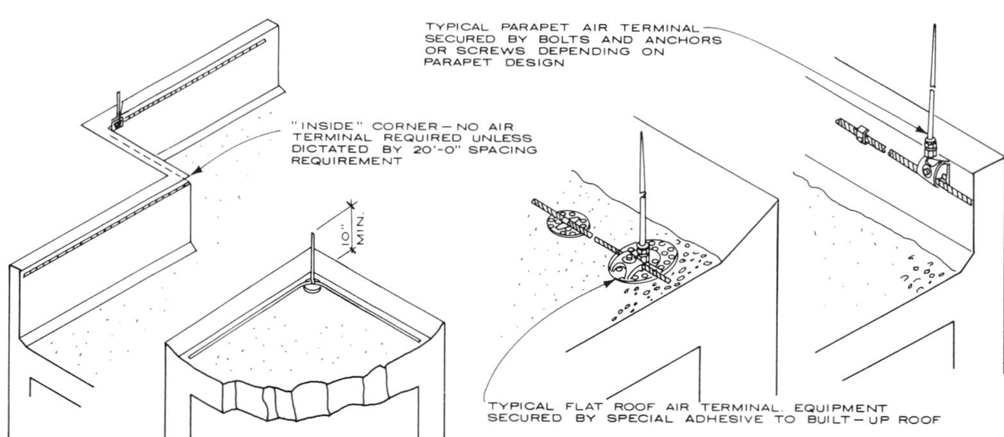

TYPICAL PARAPET AIR TERMINAL SECURED BY BOLTS AND ANCHORS OR SCREWS DEPENDING ON PARAPET DESIGN
"INSIDE" CORNER — NO AIR TERMINAL REQUIRED UNLESS DICTATED BY 20'-0" SPACING REQUIREMENT
10" MIN.
TYPICAL FLAT ROOF AIR TERMINAL. EQUIPMENT SECURED BY SPECIAL ADHESIVE TO BUILT-UP ROOF

AIR TERMINALS

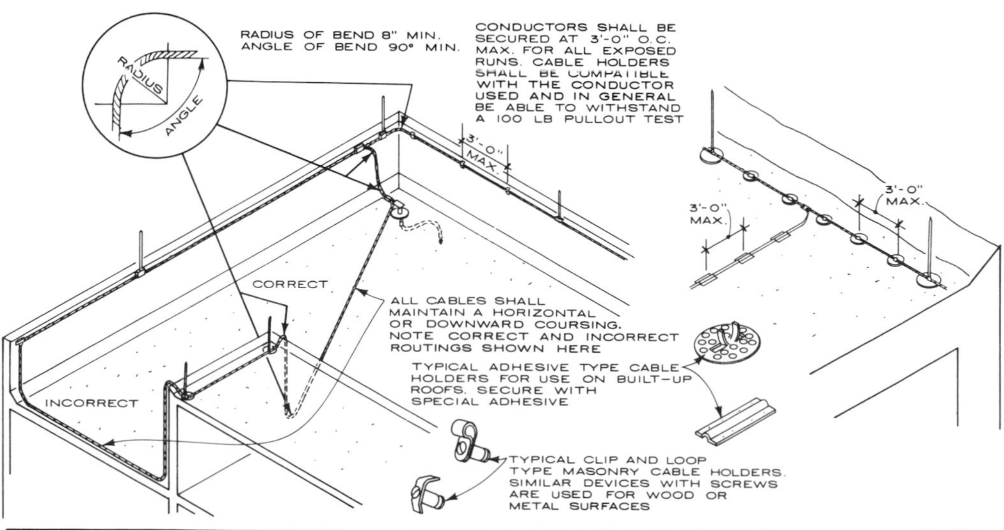

RADIUS
ANGLE
RADIUS OF BEND 8" MIN.
ANGLE OF BEND 90° MIN.
CONDUCTORS SHALL BE SECURED AT 3'-0" O.C. MAX. FOR ALL EXPOSED RUNS. CABLE HOLDERS SHALL BE COMPATIBLE WITH THE CONDUCTOR USED AND IN GENERAL BE ABLE TO WITHSTAND A 100 LB PULLOUT TEST
3'-0" MAX.
3'-0" MAX.
3'-0" MAX.
CORRECT
INCORRECT
ALL CABLES SHALL MAINTAIN A HORIZONTAL OR DOWNWARD COURSING. NOTE CORRECT AND INCORRECT ROUTINGS SHOWN HERE
TYPICAL ADHESIVE TYPE CABLE HOLDERS FOR USE ON BUILT-UP ROOFS. SECURE WITH SPECIAL ADHESIVE
TYPICAL CLIP AND LOOP TYPE MASONRY CABLE HOLDERS. SIMILAR DEVICES WITH SCREWS ARE USED FOR WOOD OR METAL SURFACES

CONDUCTORS

Douglas J. Franklin; Thompson Lightning Protection, Inc.; St. Paul, Minnesota

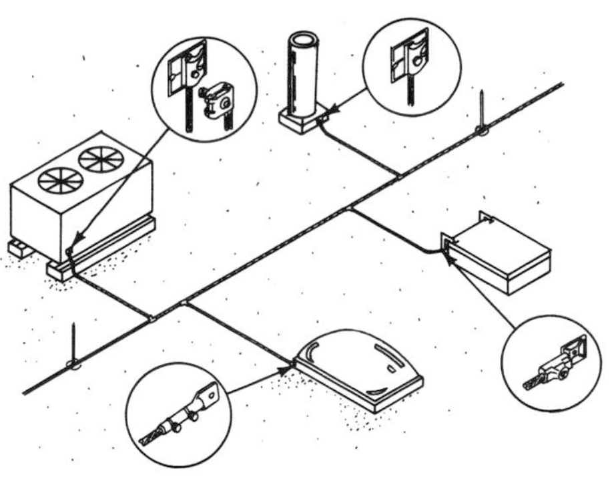

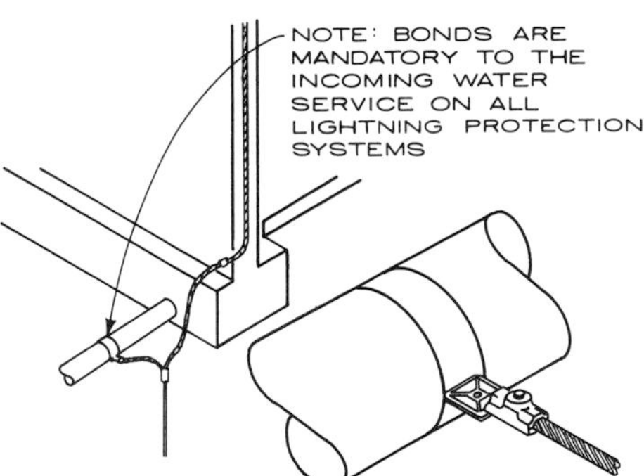
NOTE: BONDS ARE MANDATORY TO THE INCOMING WATER SERVICE ON ALL LIGHTNING PROTECTION SYSTEMS

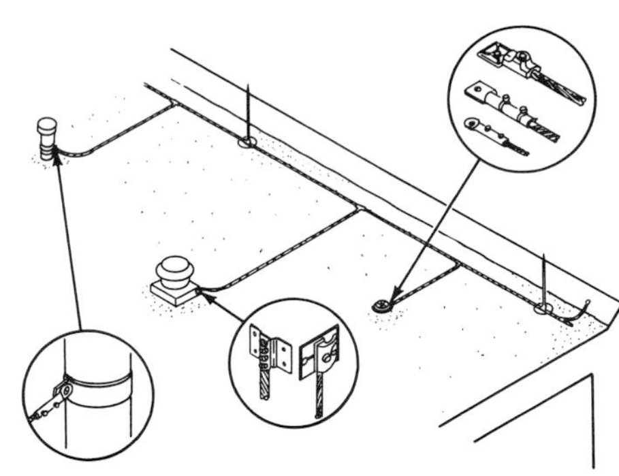

BONDING

NOTES

There are two classes of equipment that require bonding to the lightning protection systems.

1. METAL BODIES OF CONDUCTANCE: Larger metal objects located on the roof and subject to direct lightning strike. These objects must be bonded using full size conductor and fittings regardless of their location on the roof. Typical examples as shown include plumbing vents, exhaust fans, air-conditioning units, metal stacks, skylite frames, and roof hatches. Television and radio antennas must also be bonded.
2. METAL BODIES OF INDUCTANCE: Smaller objects such as roof drains, gutters, downspouts, flashings, coping, and expansion joint caps. These require bonding only if within 6 ft of the system.

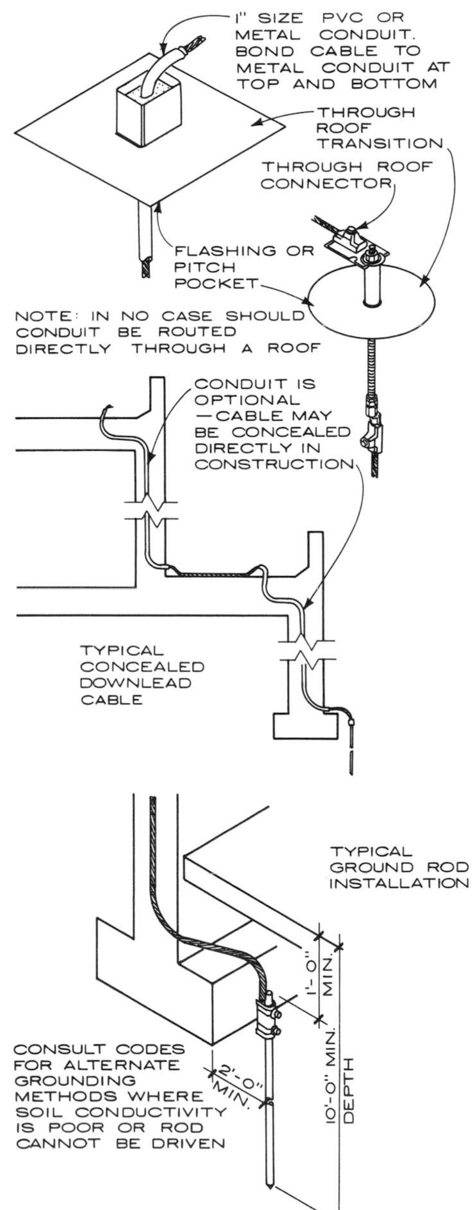
1" SIZE PVC OR METAL CONDUIT. BOND CABLE TO METAL CONDUIT AT TOP AND BOTTOM
THROUGH ROOF TRANSITION
THROUGH ROOF CONNECTOR
FLASHING OR PITCH POCKET
NOTE: IN NO CASE SHOULD CONDUIT BE ROUTED DIRECTLY THROUGH A ROOF
CONDUIT IS OPTIONAL —CABLE MAY BE CONCEALED DIRECTLY IN CONSTRUCTION
TYPICAL CONCEALED DOWNLEAD CABLE
TYPICAL GROUND ROD INSTALLATION
1'-0" MIN.
10'-0" MIN. DEPTH
2'-0" MIN.
CONSULT CODES FOR ALTERNATE GROUNDING METHODS WHERE SOIL CONDUCTIVITY IS POOR OR ROD CANNOT BE DRIVEN

DOWNLEADS AND GROUNDS

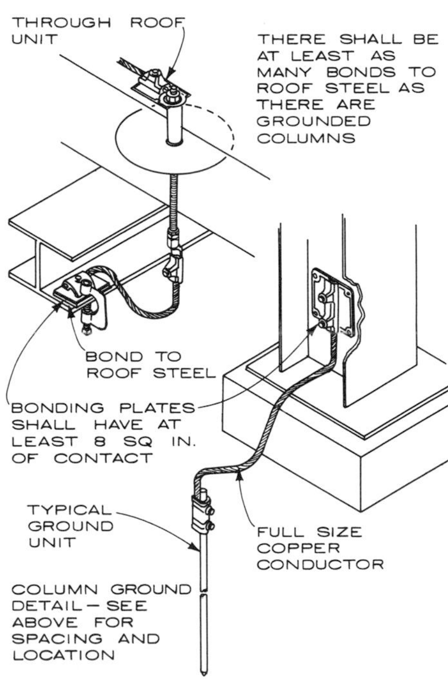
THROUGH ROOF UNIT
THERE SHALL BE AT LEAST AS MANY BONDS TO ROOF STEEL AS THERE ARE GROUNDED COLUMNS
BOND TO ROOF STEEL
BONDING PLATES SHALL HAVE AT LEAST 8 SQ IN. OF CONTACT
TYPICAL GROUND UNIT
FULL SIZE COPPER CONDUCTOR
COLUMN GROUND DETAIL — SEE ABOVE FOR SPACING AND LOCATION

STEEL FRAME AS CONDUCTOR

NOTE

In some cases, especially on tall structures, it may be advantageous to substitute the steel frame of a structure for portions of the usual conductor system, normally the downleads. Connections are made to cleaned areas of the building steel, at grade and roof level, and the columns serve to connect the roof and ground systems.

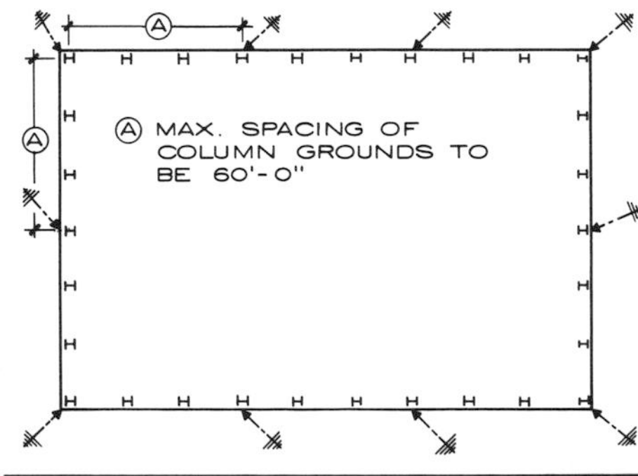
Ⓐ
Ⓐ MAX. SPACING OF COLUMN GROUNDS TO BE 60'-0"

COLUMN GROUND LOCATION

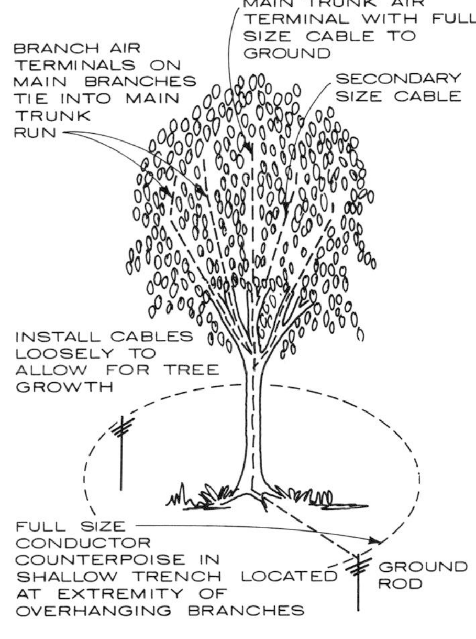
MAIN TRUNK AIR TERMINAL WITH FULL SIZE CABLE TO GROUND
BRANCH AIR TERMINALS ON MAIN BRANCHES TIE INTO MAIN TRUNK RUN
SECONDARY SIZE CABLE
INSTALL CABLES LOOSELY TO ALLOW FOR TREE GROWTH
FULL SIZE CONDUCTOR COUNTERPOISE IN SHALLOW TRENCH LOCATED AT EXTREMITY OF OVERHANGING BRANCHES
GROUND ROD

TREE INSTALLATION

OTHER CONSIDERATIONS

1. Arresters should be installed on the electric and telephone services and on all radio and television lead-ins to a structure. Responsibility and jurisdiction for the installation of these devices can vary with locality so that special consideration may have to be given to these items.
2. Trees adjacent to residences pose another special hazard. It is recommended that all trees taller than an adjacent structure that are within 10 ft be fully protected. Consult codes or manufacturer for recommendations on materials and installation requirements.
3. On-site inspections and certification of completed systems, installer competency certification, and guaranteed inspection/maintenance options are all available under existing standards. Consult codes and standards for specifics.

REFERENCES

The following codes, technical sources, and quality control procedures are standards for lightning protection systems.

1. LIGHTNING PROTECTION INSTITUTE: "Installation Code L.P.I.–175."
2. UNDERWRITERS LABORATORIES: Master Labeled program under "U.L. Installation Requirements 96A."
3. NATIONAL FIRE PROTECTION ASSOCIATION: "Lightning Protection Code N.F.P.A. 78."

Douglas J. Franklin; Thompson Lightning Protection, Inc.; St. Paul, Minnesota

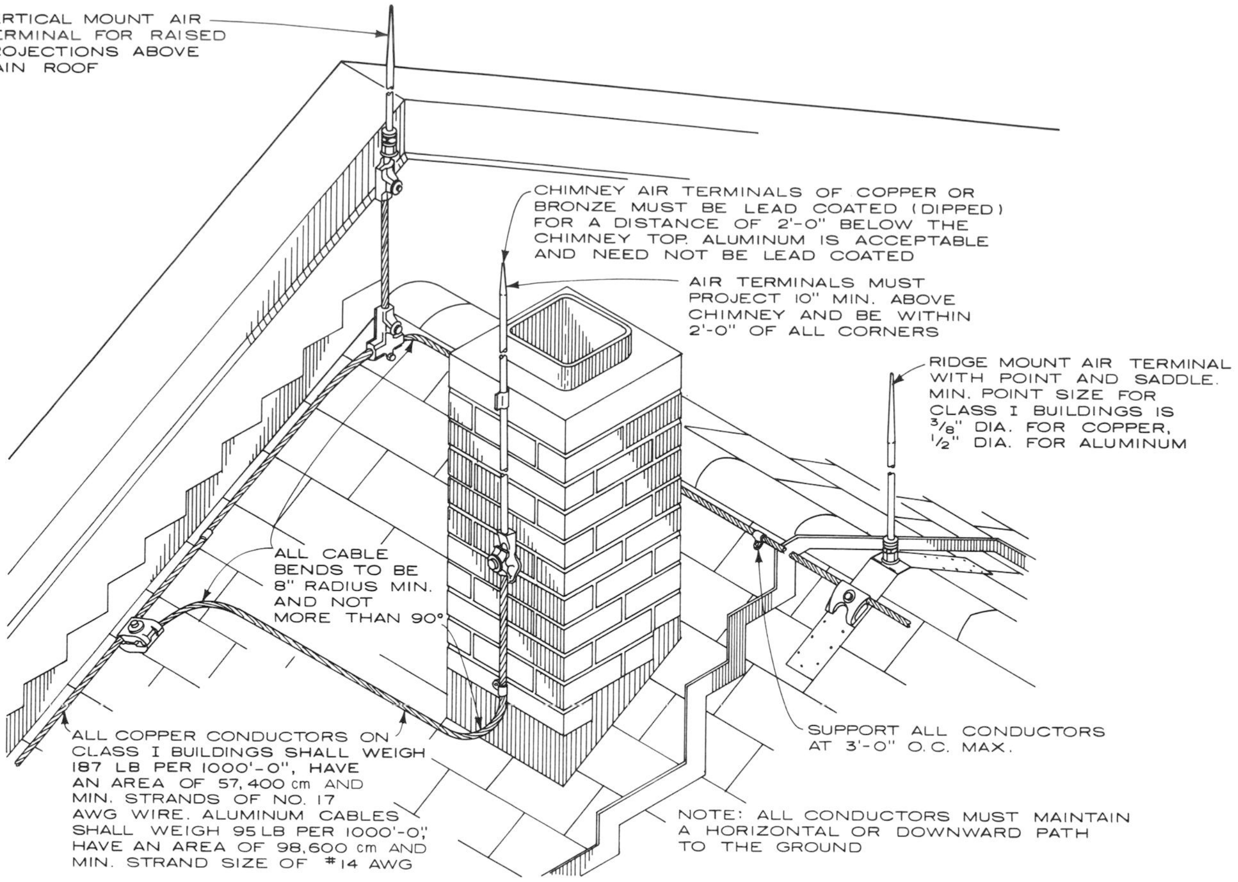

VERTICAL MOUNT AIR TERMINAL FOR RAISED PROJECTIONS ABOVE MAIN ROOF

CHIMNEY AIR TERMINALS OF COPPER OR BRONZE MUST BE LEAD COATED (DIPPED) FOR A DISTANCE OF 2'-0" BELOW THE CHIMNEY TOP. ALUMINUM IS ACCEPTABLE AND NEED NOT BE LEAD COATED

AIR TERMINALS MUST PROJECT 10" MIN. ABOVE CHIMNEY AND BE WITHIN 2'-0" OF ALL CORNERS

RIDGE MOUNT AIR TERMINAL WITH POINT AND SADDLE. MIN. POINT SIZE FOR CLASS I BUILDINGS IS 3/8" DIA. FOR COPPER, 1/2" DIA. FOR ALUMINUM

ALL CABLE BENDS TO BE 8" RADIUS MIN. AND NOT MORE THAN 90°

SUPPORT ALL CONDUCTORS AT 3'-0" O.C. MAX.

ALL COPPER CONDUCTORS ON CLASS I BUILDINGS SHALL WEIGH 187 LB PER 1000'-0", HAVE AN AREA OF 57,400 cm AND MIN. STRANDS OF NO. 17 AWG WIRE. ALUMINUM CABLES SHALL WEIGH 95 LB PER 1000'-0", HAVE AN AREA OF 98,600 cm AND MIN. STRAND SIZE OF #14 AWG

NOTE: ALL CONDUCTORS MUST MAINTAIN A HORIZONTAL OR DOWNWARD PATH TO THE GROUND

CLASS I SYSTEMS — TYPICAL DETAILS

ON HEAVY DUTY STACKS (OVER 75'-0" HIGH WITH FLUE OPENING OVER 500 SQ IN) ALL EQUIPMENT SHALL BE CLASS II MODIFIED. ALL POINTS MUST BE 5/8" DIA. OF COPPER OR STAINLESS STEEL. ALL COPPER / BRONZE FITTINGS AND CABLE MUST BE 1/16" LEAD COVERED WITHIN 25'-0" OF STACK TOP

CONFIGURATION SAME AS OTHER SIDE. ALL STACK POINTS MUST PROJECT A MIN. OF 18" ABOVE STACK, BE WITHIN 2'-0" OF ALL CORNERS, AND BE SPACED NOT MORE THAN 8'-0" APART. MOST LARGER STACKS REQUIRE FOUR OR MORE AIR TERMINALS. ALL STACKS MUST HAVE TWO DOWNLEADS TO GROUND

TOP MOUNT PARAPET AIR TERMINAL FOR CLASS II STRUCTURES. COPPER POINTS MUST BE 1/2" DIA. MIN. ALUMINUM POINTS MUST BE 5/8" DIA. MIN.

PARALLEL CABLE SPLICER. ALL CONNECTORS MUST CONTACT CABLE FOR 1 1/2" LENGTH

SUPPORT ALL CABLES ON STACKS AT 2'-0" O.C. HORIZONTALLY AND 4'-0" O.C. VERTICALLY

ALL CABLE BENDS TO BE 8" RADIUS MIN. AND NOT MORE THAN 90°

FOR CLASS II STRUCTURES, COPPER CONDUCTORS SHALL WEIGH 375 LB PER 1000'-0", HAVE AN AREA OF 115,000 cm AND STRANDS OF NOT LESS THAN #16 AWG.
ALUMINUM CONDUCTORS SHALL WEIGH 190 LB PER 1000'-0", HAVE AN AREA OF 192,000 cm AND STRANDS OF NOT LESS THAN # 13 AWG

SUPPORT CABLES ON BUILDING AT 3'-0" O.C. MAX.

FOR EXPOSED DOWNLEADS LOCATED IN SCHOOL YARDS, DRIVEWAYS, WALK AREAS, ETC., WHERE SUBJECT TO DAMAGE OR DISPLACEMENT, PROPER GUARDS SHALL BE PROVIDED. TUBULAR METAL GUARDS MUST BE BONDED TO THE CABLE AT BOTH ENDS

CONDUCTOR ON THE TOP 25'-0" OF A STACK OR TO ROOF LEVEL SHALL MEET CLASS II COPPER CRITERIA AND MUST BE COVERED WITH LEAD 1/16" THICK

STRAIGHT SPLICE TRANSITION FROM LEAD COVERED TO BARE CONDUCTOR

SEE GROUNDING REQUIREMENTS ON OTHER PAGE

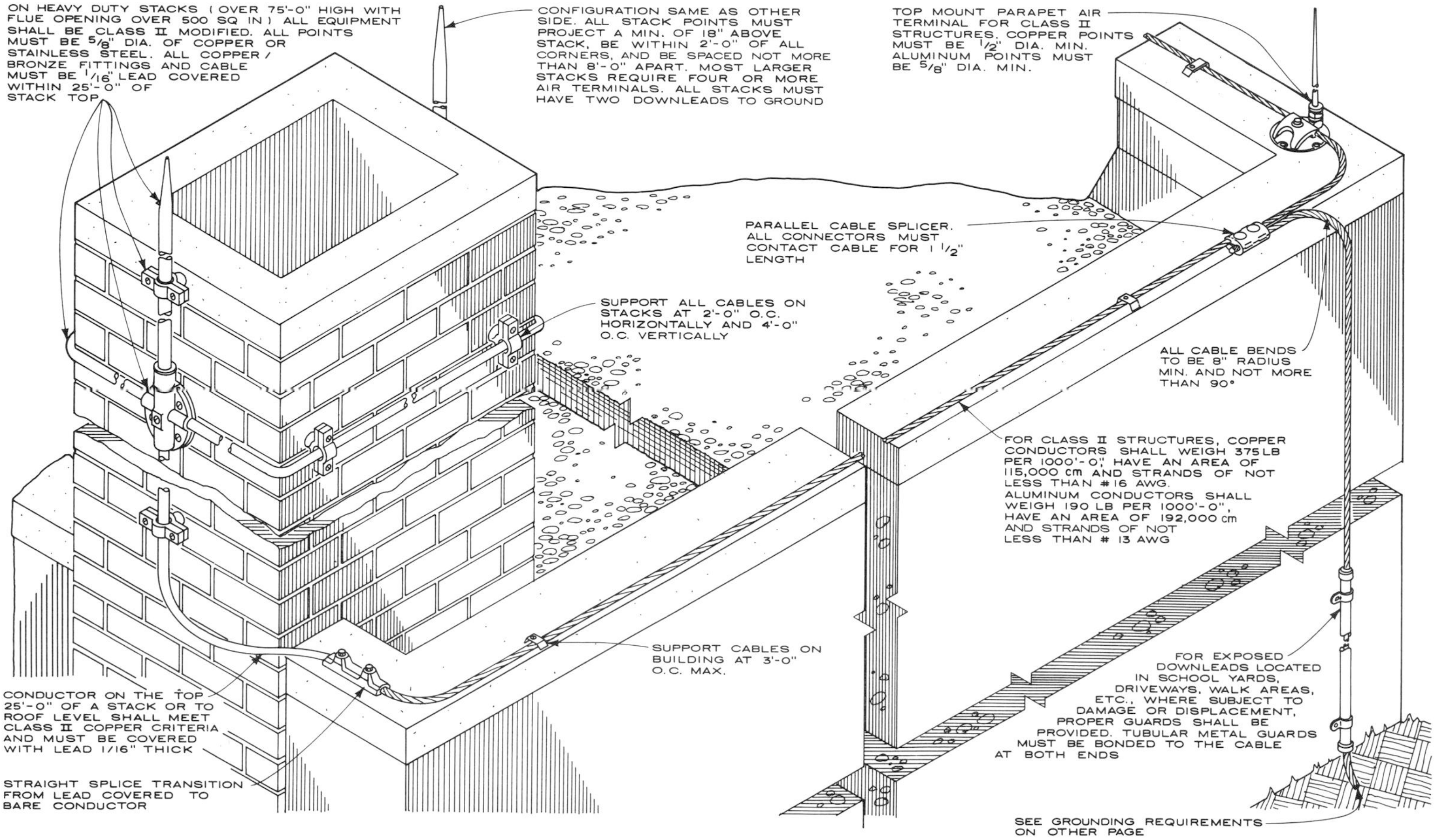

CLASS II SYSTEMS — TYPICAL DETAILS

Douglas J. Franklin; Thompson Lightning Protection, Inc.; St. Paul, Minnesota

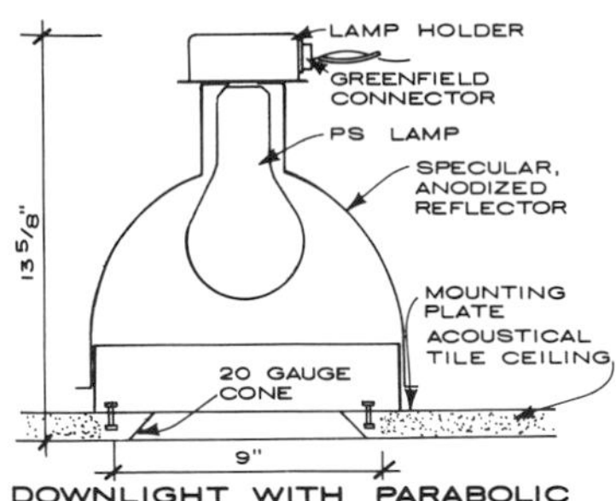
LAMP HOLDER
GREENFIELD CONNECTOR
PS LAMP
SPECULAR, ANODIZED REFLECTOR
MOUNTING PLATE
ACOUSTICAL TILE CEILING
20 GAUGE CONE
13 5/8"
9"

DOWNLIGHT WITH PARABOLIC REFLECTOR

The open reflector downlight uses general service lamps in a polished parabolic reflector to produce controlled light without a lens. The reflector efficiently redirects the upward component of the light source down through the aperture.

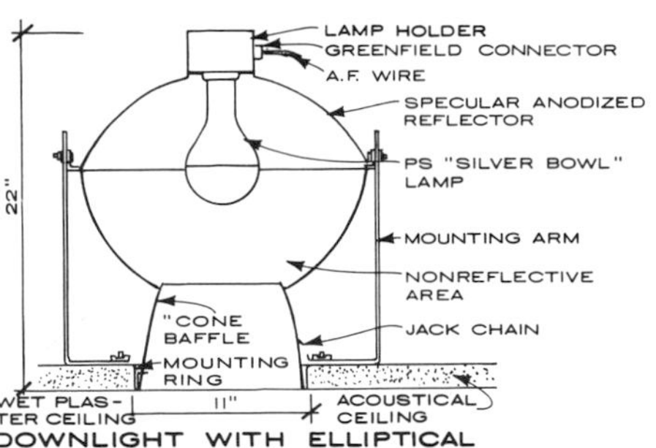
LAMP HOLDER
GREENFIELD CONNECTOR
A.F. WIRE
SPECULAR ANODIZED REFLECTOR
PS "SILVER BOWL" LAMP
MOUNTING ARM
NONREFLECTIVE AREA
JACK CHAIN
"CONE" BAFFLE
MOUNTING RING
22"
WET PLASTER CEILING
11"
ACOUSTICAL CEILING

DOWNLIGHT WITH ELLIPTICAL REFLECTOR

A more sophisticated downlight uses a silver bowl lamp to project light up into an elliptical reflector. When the light source is located at one focal point the output light converges and can be redirected through a constricted aperture at the other focal point.

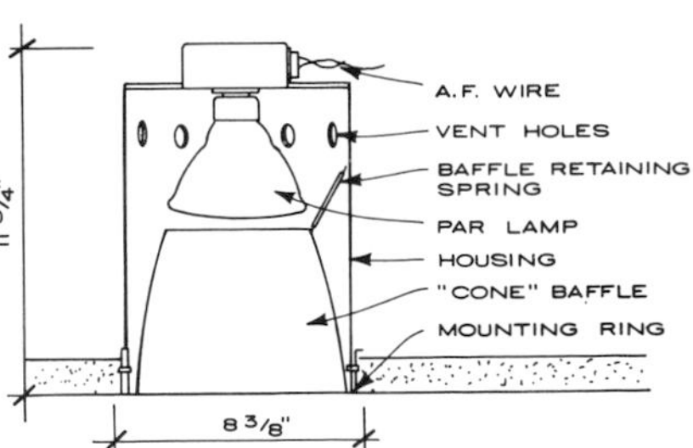
A.F. WIRE
VENT HOLES
BAFFLE RETAINING SPRING
PAR LAMP
HOUSING
"CONE" BAFFLE
MOUNTING RING
11 3/4"
8 3/8"

DOWNLIGHT WITH REFLECTOR LAMP

Downlights without reflectors or lenses are commonly called "cans." They have cylindrical housings and rely on a PAR or R lamp for optical control. Cones, annular rings, or lower type baffles will shield an observer from glare in the normal field of view.

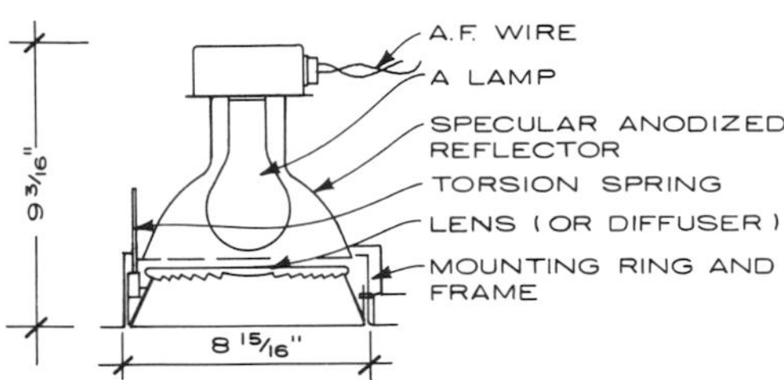
A.F. WIRE
A LAMP
SPECULAR ANODIZED REFLECTOR
TORSION SPRING
LENS (OR DIFFUSER)
MOUNTING RING AND FRAME
9 3/16"
8 15/16"

DOWNLIGHT WITH FRESNEL LENS

One downlight type combines a general service lamp with a reflector housing and a diffusing lens. The lens provides directional control of the light as it leaves the luminaire. The lens covers the ceiling aperture, thus keeping dust from the reflector and providing a heat shield.

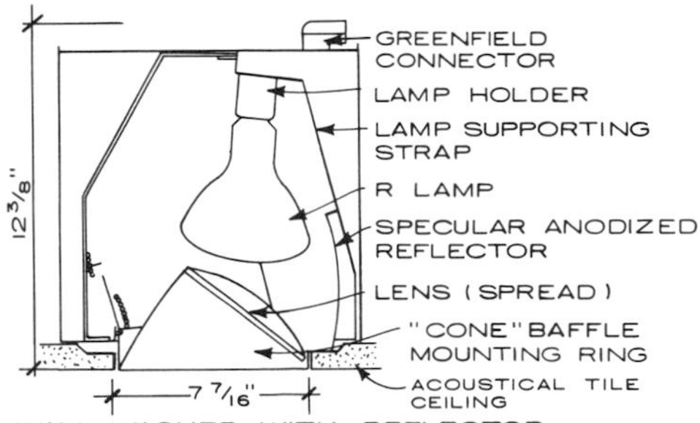
GREENFIELD CONNECTOR
LAMP HOLDER
LAMP SUPPORTING STRAP
R LAMP
SPECULAR ANODIZED REFLECTOR
LENS (SPREAD)
"CONE" BAFFLE
MOUNTING RING
ACOUSTICAL TILE CEILING
12 3/8"
7 7/16"

WALL WASHER WITH REFLECTOR LAMP AND LENS

Wall washers provide shadowless coverage of vertical surfaces with an even "wash" of light. They are used to set a mood within a space, to accent surrounding walls, or to obscure undesirable unevenness of the surface.

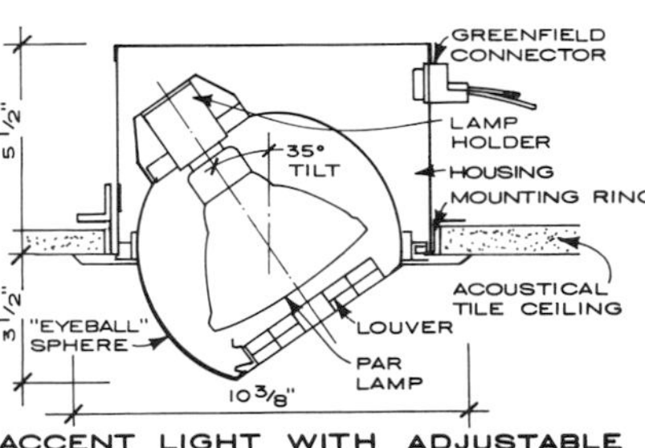
GREENFIELD CONNECTOR
LAMP HOLDER
35° TILT
HOUSING
MOUNTING RING
ACOUSTICAL TILE CEILING
LOUVER
PAR LAMP
"EYEBALL" SPHERE
5 1/2"
3 1/2"
10 3/8"

ACCENT LIGHT WITH ADJUSTABLE REFLECTOR LAMP

The accent light produces an asymmetrical distribution of light and normally allows for adjustments in the lamp position. It is used for gallery lighting to emphasize objects or small wall areas.

INCANDESCENT FIXTURES

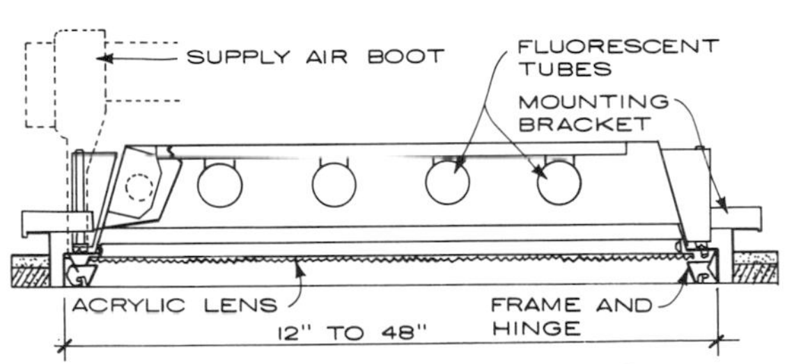
SUPPLY AIR BOOT
FLUORESCENT TUBES
MOUNTING BRACKET
ACRYLIC LENS
FRAME AND HINGE
12" TO 48"

RECESSED UNIT WITH PRISMATIC LENS

The recessed fluorescent luminaire is usually designed to fit into a standard ceiling grid. A transparent, prismatic lens usually encloses the fixture and directs useful light to the work surface.

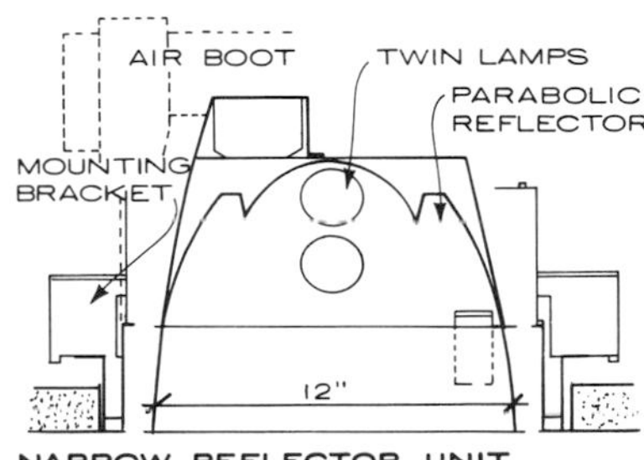
AIR BOOT
TWIN LAMPS
PARABOLIC REFLECTOR
MOUNTING BRACKET
12"

NARROW REFLECTOR UNIT

Parabolic reflectors are used in narrow profile fixtures to redirect the upward component of the light source down to the task area. The fluorescent lamps are stacked so that one may be switched off without sacrificing the even distribution of light.

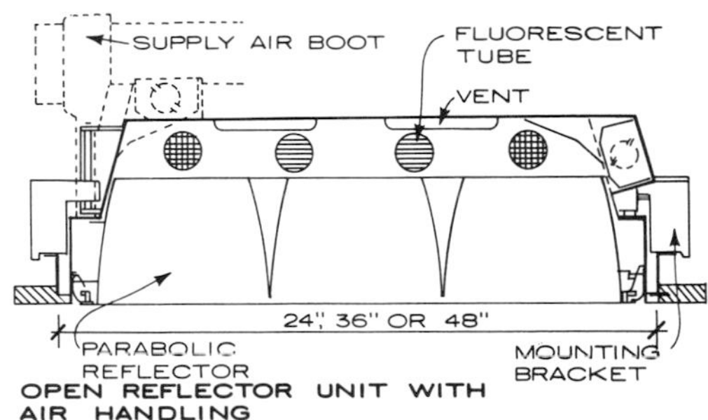
SUPPLY AIR BOOT
FLUORESCENT TUBE
VENT
24", 36" OR 48"
PARABOLIC REFLECTOR
MOUNTING BRACKET

OPEN REFLECTOR UNIT WITH AIR HANDLING

Some open reflector units are fitted with parabola shaped louver blades to better control glare and veiling reflections. Air fittings are also integrated into the lamp housing for ducted air supply or return.

FLUORESCENT FIXTURES

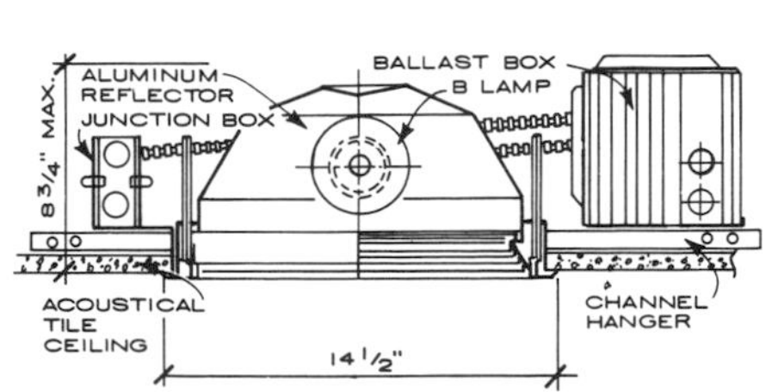
ALUMINUM REFLECTOR
JUNCTION BOX
BALLAST BOX
B LAMP
8 3/4" MAX.
ACOUSTICAL TILE CEILING
CHANNEL HANGER
14 1/2"

SQUARE LENS AND REFLECTOR UNIT

HID fixtures are usually preassembled and wired for fast installation. A recessed reflector with a fresnel or prismatic lens will maximize the utilization and control of the high lamp output.

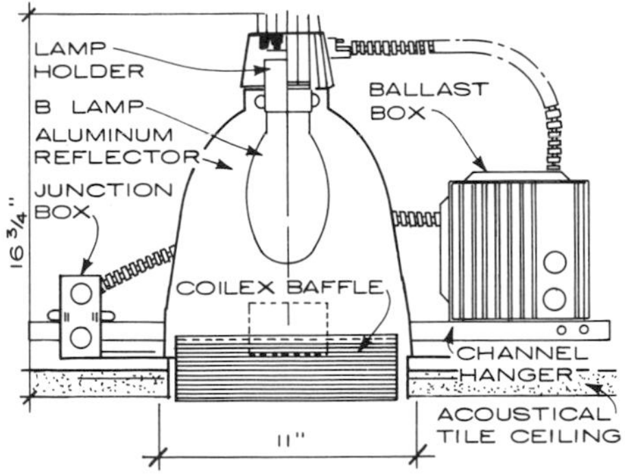
LAMP HOLDER
B LAMP
ALUMINUM REFLECTOR
JUNCTION BOX
BALLAST BOX
COILEX BAFFLE
CHANNEL HANGER
ACOUSTICAL TILE CEILING
16 3/4"
11"

OPEN REFLECTOR DOWNLIGHT

HID luminaires require a deep ceiling space to fully recess the large lamp housing. Open reflector downlights often use elliptical reflectors that focus the lamp light through a small aperture. Coil or cone baffles help reduce fixture surface brightness.

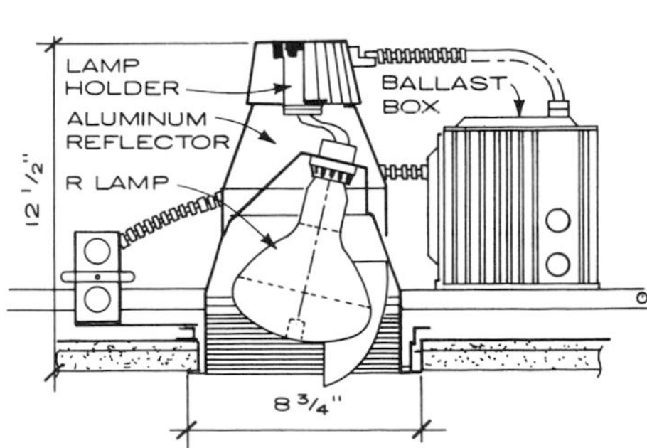
LAMP HOLDER
ALUMINUM REFLECTOR
R LAMP
BALLAST BOX
12 1/2"
8 3/4"

ADJUSTABLE WALL WASHER

A special scoop insert can be added to a standard downlight fixture to create a HID wall washer unit. The reflector and lamp socket can be rotated for desired positioning of light throw.

HIGH INTENSITY DISCHARGE FIXTURES

William G. Miner, AIA, Architect; Washington, D.C.

REFERENCES

GENERAL REFERENCES

Architectural Lighting Design, 1987, F. H. Jones, William Kaufmann

Architectural Lighting for Contract Interiors, 1987, P. Sorcar, Wiley

Mechanical and Electrical Equipment for Buildings, 7th ed., 1986, Benjamin Stein, John Reynolds, and William McGuinness, Wiley

National Electric Code Handbook, National Fire Protection Agency (NFPA)

DATA SOURCES: ORGANIZATIONS

American Society of Heating, Refrigerating and Air Conditioning Engineers (ASHRAE), 399
American Standards Association, 395
Bell & Gossett (ITT), 399
Halo Lighting Company, 403
Lighting and Electronics Company, 403
Lightning Protection Institute (LPI), 400–402
Lightolier, Inc., 403
National Electric Code (NEC), 394
National Electrical Manufacturers' Association (NEMA), 395
National Fire Protection Association (NFPA), 400–402
Underwriters Laboratories, Inc. (U.L.), 395, 398, 400–402

DATA SOURCES: PUBLICATIONS

Wiring Simplified, H. P. Richter, Park Publishing, 394

CHAPTER 17

ENERGY DESIGN

STRATEGIES OF CLIMATE CONTROL

Underheated conditions occur in both humid and arid regions and dominate much of the U.S. The strategies are to minimize conduction and infiltration losses and to take advantage of winter solar gain. Humidity affects sky clearness and availability of solar radiation, making optimization of solar glazing area one of the main opportunities of regional design. Moisture movement through the building shell must be controlled. It is driven by air leakage (exfiltration) and by vapor diffusion, which is related to temperature differences.

MINIMIZE CONDUCTION LOSSES

Minimize ratio of envelope to heated floor area. Minimize foundation perimeter length. Insulate envelope components in proportion to indoor–outdoor temperature difference. Minimize areas of windows, doors, and other envelope components of inherently low R value. Detail to avoid thermal bridging. Provide movable insulation for glazed areas.

MINIMIZE INFILTRATION LOSSES

Plant vegetation to create wind-sheltered building sites. Shape building to minimize exposure to winter wind. Orient doors and windows away from winter wind. Specify weatherstripping and infiltration barrier.

CAPTURE SOLAR GAIN

Provide high-transmittance south-facing glazing. Provide thermal mass indoors to store solar gains.

INSULATION

Insulation requirements are proportional to heating loads. The foundation is often underinsulated and can be a major source of heat loss. The desirable insulation level depends on basement temperature and insulation levels in the rest of the building. An approximate thermal optimum is:

$$R_{ins} = \frac{T_{bsmt} - T_0}{T_1 - T_0} R_{ref} - R_{wall}$$

R_{ins} = R value to be added to basement wall above grade

R_{ref} = R value of superstructure wall

R_{wall} = R value of uninsulated basement foundation wall

T_{bsmt} = average seasonal temperature of basement

T_1 = average seasonal temperature of living space

T_0 = average seasonal outdoor temperature

The added foundation insulation above grade is R_{ins}. It should decrease with depth by R − 2 per foot in ordinary soils and R − 1.5 in wet soils. A horizontal skirt can be used to reduce floor perimeter losses. Exterior insulation keeps the wall warm and eliminates condensation and thermal bridges. As seasonal basement temperature decreases, losses to it from the superstructure increase, and basement ceiling R value should increase. As a very rough rule, the basement ceiling R value should be greater than ($R_{ref} - R_{ins}$).

SOLAR DESIGN AND DAYLIGHTING

The most advantageous south glazing area depends on thermal and climatic factors. Rules of thumb have been prepared (Los Alamos National Laboratory) and more sophisticated methods are available for desktop computers.

The advantage of glazing for daylighting has to be weighed against the penalty of winter heat loss. In predominantly cloudy climates, skylighting can be designed without significant shading, but not without concern for glare. In clear, sunny climates and in warmer regions, daylight glazing may require shading to reduce undesired heat gain. South glazing has the combined advantages of daylighting, winter heat gain, and economical summer shading.

REFERENCES

1. Los Alamos National Laboratory, *Passive Solar Heating Analysis*, ASHRAE, Atlanta, 1984.
2. National Research Council, Canada, Ottawa, Ontario, K1A OR6: *Construction Details for Air Tightness* (nonresidential), NRCC 18291, 1980; *Exterior Walls: Understanding the Problems*, NRCC 21203, 1983; *Humidity, Condensation and Ventilation in Houses*, NRCC 23293, 1984; J. Latta, *The Principles and Dilemmas of Designing Durable House Envelopes for the North*, Building Practice Note 52, 1985.

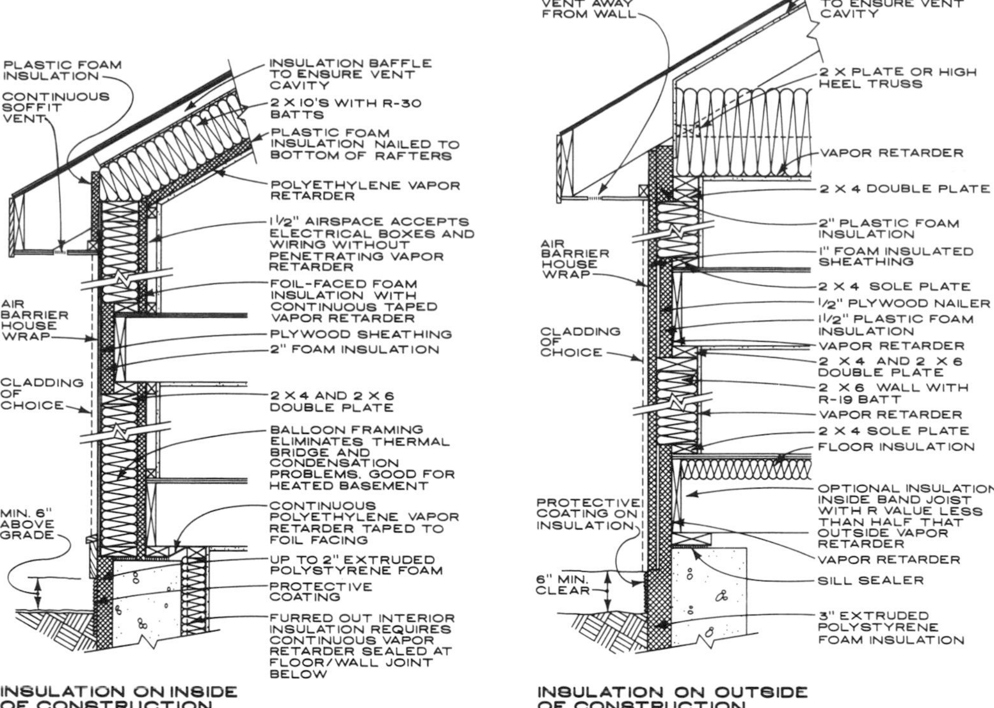

PLASTIC FOAM INSULATION
CONTINUOUS SOFFIT VENT
INSULATION BAFFLE TO ENSURE VENT CAVITY
2 X 10'S WITH R-30 BATTS
PLASTIC FOAM INSULATION NAILED TO BOTTOM OF RAFTERS
POLYETHYLENE VAPOR RETARDER
1 1/2" AIRSPACE ACCEPTS ELECTRICAL BOXES AND WIRING WITHOUT PENETRATING VAPOR RETARDER
AIR BARRIER HOUSE WRAP
FOIL-FACED FOAM INSULATION WITH CONTINUOUS TAPED VAPOR RETARDER
PLYWOOD SHEATHING
2" FOAM INSULATION
CLADDING OF CHOICE
2 X 4 AND 2 X 6 DOUBLE PLATE
BALLOON FRAMING ELIMINATES THERMAL BRIDGE AND CONDENSATION PROBLEMS. GOOD FOR HEATED BASEMENT
MIN. 6" ABOVE GRADE
CONTINUOUS POLYETHYLENE VAPOR RETARDER TAPED TO FOIL FACING
UP TO 2" EXTRUDED POLYSTYRENE FOAM
PROTECTIVE COATING
FURRED OUT INTERIOR INSULATION REQUIRES CONTINUOUS VAPOR RETARDER SEALED AT FLOOR/WALL JOINT BELOW
LOCATE SOFFIT VENT AWAY FROM WALL
INSULATION BAFFLE TO ENSURE VENT CAVITY
2 X PLATE OR HIGH HEEL TRUSS
VAPOR RETARDER
2 X 4 DOUBLE PLATE
2" PLASTIC FOAM INSULATION
AIR BARRIER HOUSE WRAP
1" FOAM INSULATED SHEATHING
2 X 4 SOLE PLATE
1/2" PLYWOOD NAILER
1 1/2" PLASTIC FOAM INSULATION
CLADDING OF CHOICE
VAPOR RETARDER
2 X 4 AND 2 X 6 DOUBLE PLATE
2 X 6 WALL WITH R-19 BATT
VAPOR RETARDER
2 X 4 SOLE PLATE
FLOOR INSULATION
PROTECTIVE COATING ON INSULATION
OPTIONAL INSULATION INSIDE BAND JOIST WITH R VALUE LESS THAN HALF THAT OUTSIDE VAPOR RETARDER
VAPOR RETARDER
6" MIN. CLEAR
SILL SEALER
3" EXTRUDED POLYSTYRENE FOAM INSULATION

INSULATION ON INSIDE OF CONSTRUCTION

INSULATION ON OUTSIDE OF CONSTRUCTION

ENERGY-EFFICIENT WALL SECTIONS

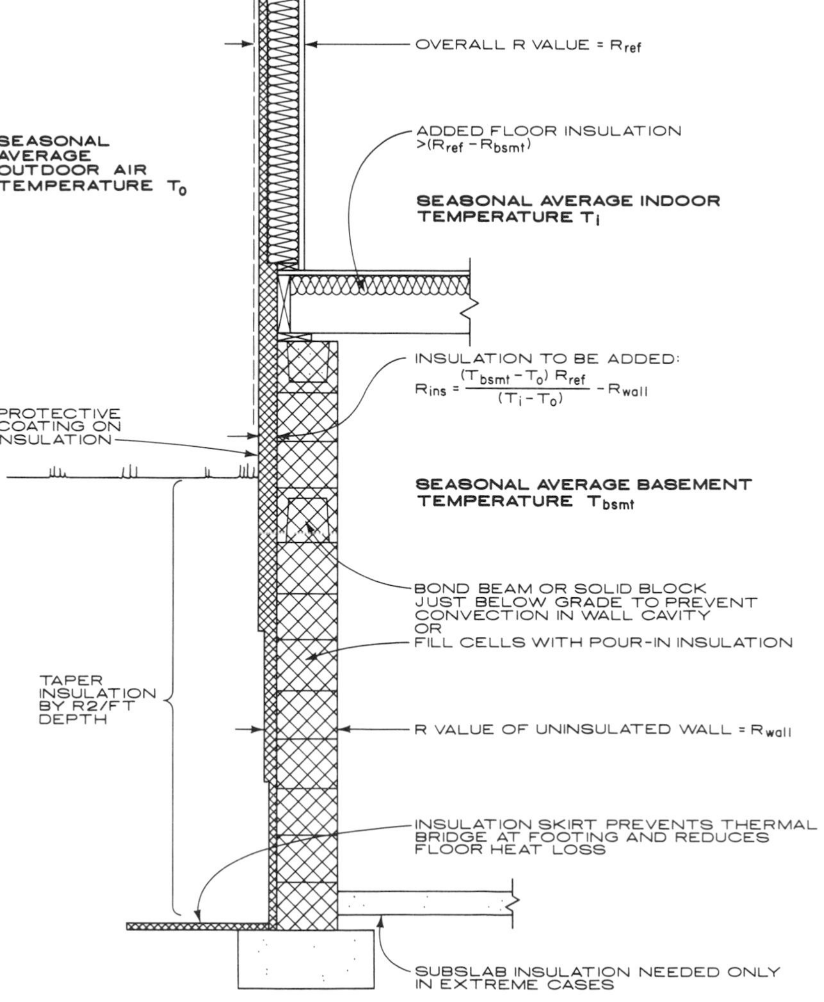

OVERALL R VALUE = R_{ref}
SEASONAL AVERAGE OUTDOOR AIR TEMPERATURE T_0
ADDED FLOOR INSULATION >($R_{ref} - R_{bsmt}$)
SEASONAL AVERAGE INDOOR TEMPERATURE T_i
INSULATION TO BE ADDED: $R_{ins} = \frac{(T_{bsmt} - T_0) R_{ref}}{(T_i - T_0)} - R_{wall}$
PROTECTIVE COATING ON INSULATION
SEASONAL AVERAGE BASEMENT TEMPERATURE T_{bsmt}
BOND BEAM OR SOLID BLOCK JUST BELOW GRADE TO PREVENT CONVECTION IN WALL CAVITY OR FILL CELLS WITH POUR-IN INSULATION
TAPER INSULATION BY R2/FT DEPTH
R VALUE OF UNINSULATED WALL = R_{wall}
INSULATION SKIRT PREVENTS THERMAL BRIDGE AT FOOTING AND REDUCES FLOOR HEAT LOSS
SUBSLAB INSULATION NEEDED ONLY IN EXTREME CASES

BASEMENT FOUNDATION AND FLOOR INSULATION

Donald Watson, FAIA; Trumbull, Connecticut
Kenneth Labs; New Haven, Connecticut

STRATEGIES OF CLIMATE CONTROL

Dry, clear atmospheres lead to high insolation levels, high daytime air temperatures, very high sol-air temperatures, and large thermal radiation losses. These factors produce daily temperature ranges in excess of 30°F. Although daytime air temperatures may be too high for ventilation, nighttime temperatures often fall below comfort limits and are useful for cooling. Arid regions in the U.S. have winter heating requirements, especially at night. Clear skies greatly favor passive solar heating.

High daytime temperatures and solar loads require measures that reduce heat gain. Evaporative roof spray systems dissipate absorbed solar heat, but consume large quantities of water and decrease in value with increases in roof insulation. Evaporative space cooling systems are often effective substitutes for refrigerant air conditioning. Deep ground temperatures are too high and soil thermal conductivity too low in hot, arid regions for the earth to be a useful cooling sink in conventional construction. Low conductivity makes the soil a good buffer against surface conditions, and earth-integrated design can take advantage of seasonal cold storage, so earth coupling does offer opportunities.

MINIMIZE SOLAR GAINS

Plant trees to shade roof and east and west walls. Shape building to minimize solar load on envelope. Cluster buildings to shade one another. Provide shading for outdoor pedestrian and living areas (ramadas and pergolas), and shade all glazing during overheated period. Use carport or garage as buffer on west side. Use light-colored surfacing on walls and roof.

MINIMIZE CONDUCTIVE GAINS

Insulate envelope components in proportion to (sol-air–indoor) temperature difference. Use radiant barrier in attic or cathedral ceiling. Use thermally massive envelope materials. Insulate perimeter of slab-on-grade floors.

PROMOTE VENTILATION LOSSES

Site building to exploit nighttime breezes. Arrange floor plan for internal air movement, especially to cool thermal mass. Consider a whole-house fan for night cooling. Ventilate building envelope (attic or roof, walls).

THERMAL MASS AND INSULATION CONCEPTS

Massive walls of sufficient thickness can average daily outdoor temperatures and maintain nearly constant indoor surface temperatures. This thickness (in feet) for an uninsulated homogeneous wall must be greater than 6.4 $(k/wc)^{1/2}$, where k is thermal conductivity in Btu/ft(hr)F, w is density in lb/cu ft, and c is specific heat in Btu/(lb)F. The minimum thickness is 14 in. for poured concrete, 12 in. for brick, 9 in. for adobe, and 6 in. for pine log. Less thick walls reduce, but do not eliminate, the temperature swing. The ratio of interior to exterior fluctuation is termed the "decrement factor." Values for some composite walls are given in the table.

A completely shaded, uninsulated massive wall can do no better than maintain a temperature near the outdoor daily average at the interior, unless the space is ventilated at night. Uninsulated mass walls have low R values and are not economically suitable for heated and air-conditioned buildings. Insulating outside the mass has the greatest benefit: It reduces heat gain while allowing the wall to store "coolth" from nighttime ventilation. Insulation also allows less mass to be used. The thermally optimal storage thickness (in feet) of mass that is well insulated on the outside is 3.3 $(k/wc)^{1/2}$. Less thickness is still beneficial.

Insulating inside the mass or adding mass outside an insulated frame wall (brick veneer) improves performance over either case alone. Both are inferior to outside insulation and slightly less effective than walls with integral insulation (masonry with core insulation). The optimal insulation and mass combinations vary with climate and conditioning hours of the building.

THERMAL MASS TIME DELAY

Mass delays the transfer of heat to the interior. Its usefulness depends on occupancy and air-conditioning schedules. While a masonry west wall can relieve an office building of peak loads during business hours, for example, it would be inappropriate for a west-facing bedroom. The delay rate in hours per foot for a homogeneous wall is about 1.4$(wc/k)^{1/2}$ in thickness.

INTERIOR ZONING AND DAYLIGHTING

Vernacular house design in hot, arid regions uses low mass construction for sleeping areas and high mass for daytime activity areas. The low mass zone is ventilated and cools off quickly at night, while the massive zone has little window area. Evaporative space coolers can provide comfort more than 90% of the time at elevations above 1500 ft and more than 50% at elevations below 1500 ft throughout the Southwest. Ducts should be sized for 1200 fpm (for silence and efficiency) to 1600 fpm.

Clear, sunny skies make daylighting dependable and predictable for design. Small window and skylight areas are effective. Apertures should be shaded at the exterior. Reflected light from the ground and from light shelves is useful, but glare from uncontrolled reflecting surfaces must be kept from view.

REFERENCES

1. K. Clark and P. Paylore, *Desert Housing: Balancing Experience and Technology for Dwelling in Hot Arid Zones*, Office of Arid Land Studies, University of Arizona, Tucson.
2. J. Cook, *Cool Houses for Desert Suburbs*, Arizona Solar Energy Commission, Phoenix, 1984.
3. H. Kessler, *Passive Solar Design for Arizona*, Arizona Solar Energy Commission, Phoenix, 1983.
4. A. Olgyay and V. Olgyay, *Solar Control and Shading Devices*, Princeton University Press, Princeton, 1957.
5. S. Byrne and R. Ritschard, "A Parametric Analysis of Thermal Mass in Residential Buildings," LBL-20288, Lawrence Berkeley Laboratory, Berkeley, CA 94720, 1985.

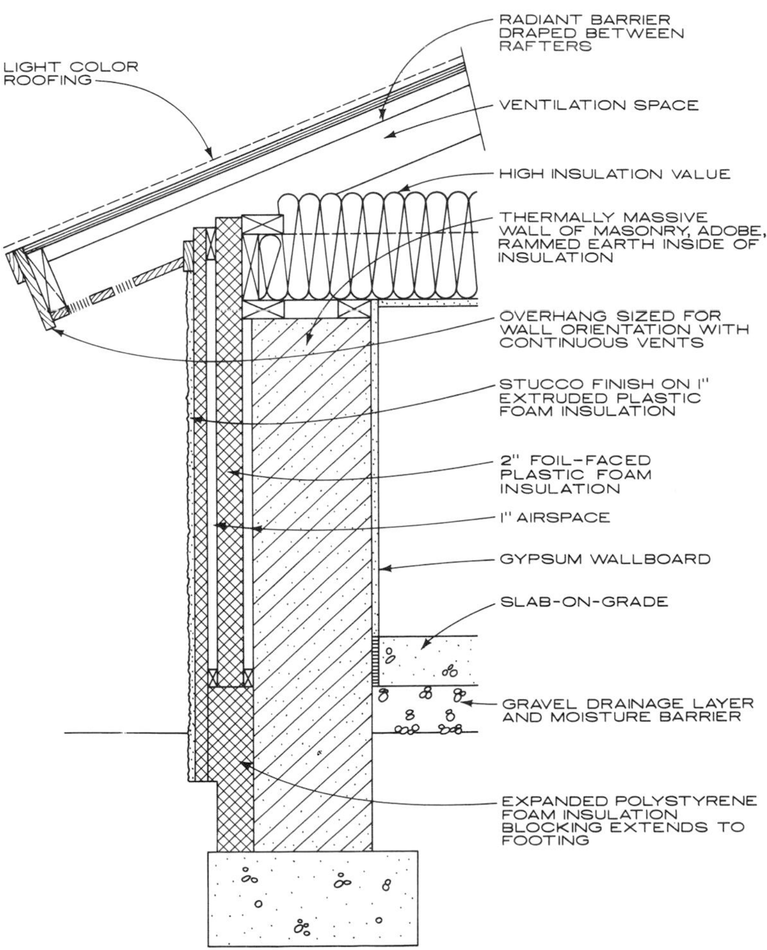

RADIANT BARRIER DRAPED BETWEEN RAFTERS
LIGHT COLOR ROOFING
VENTILATION SPACE
HIGH INSULATION VALUE
THERMALLY MASSIVE WALL OF MASONRY, ADOBE, RAMMED EARTH INSIDE OF INSULATION
OVERHANG SIZED FOR WALL ORIENTATION WITH CONTINUOUS VENTS
STUCCO FINISH ON 1" EXTRUDED PLASTIC FOAM INSULATION
2" FOIL-FACED PLASTIC FOAM INSULATION
1" AIRSPACE
GYPSUM WALLBOARD
SLAB-ON-GRADE
GRAVEL DRAINAGE LAYER AND MOISTURE BARRIER
EXPANDED POLYSTYRENE FOAM INSULATION BLOCKING EXTENDS TO FOOTING

ENERGY-EFFICIENT WALL SECTION
INTERIOR MASS WITH OUTSIDE INSULATION

THERMAL PERFORMANCE (TIME LAG) OF VARIOUS WALL SECTIONS

WALL DESCRIPTION	U VALUE (WINTER)	HEAT GAIN BTU/HR/SQ FT (DARK COLOR) AVERAGE ORIENTATION	HEAT GAIN BTU/HR/SQ FT (DARK COLOR) WEST ORIENTATION	TIME LAG (HR)	AMPLITUDE DECREMENT FACTOR
8″ brick and lightweight concrete (100 lb density) block 2″ polystyrene insulation board ½″ gypsum wallboard	0.073	2.06	1.75	4	0.40
6″ precast concrete (140 lb density) sandwich panel 2″ polyurethane core	0.065	1.82	1.55	4	0.40
½″ plywood siding ½″ insulation board sheathing, wood studs. Full batt (R-11) insulation ½″ gypsum wallboard	0.076	3.05	4.60	2	0.75
4″ brick veneer ½″ insulation board sheathing. Wood studs full batt (R-11) insulation ½″ gypsum wallboard	0.077	2.18	1.95	4	0.62
8″ brick wall (hollow units) 1″ x 2″ furring. ½″ gypsum wallboard	0.316	7.37	5.90	6	0.25

Donald Watson, FAIA; Trumbull, Connecticut
Kenneth Labs; New Haven, Connecticut

STRATEGIES OF CLIMATE CONTROL

Humid overheated conditions are most severe along the Gulf Coast, but occur across the entire southeastern U.S. Atmospheric moisture limits radiation exchange, resulting in daily temperature ranges less than 20°F. High insolation gives first priority to shading. Much of the overheated period is only a few degrees above comfort limits, so air movement can cool the body. Ground temperatures are generally too high for the earth to be useful as a heat sink, although slab-on-grade floor mass is useful. The strategies are to resist solar and conductive heat gains and to take best advantage of ventilation.

MINIMIZE SOLAR GAINS

1. Plant trees to shade roof and east and west walls.
2. Shape building to minimize solar load on envelope.
3. Shade all glazing during overheated period.
4. Shade north elevation in subtropical latitudes.
5. Use light-colored surfacing on walls and roof.

MINIMIZE CONDUCTIVE GAINS

1. Insulate envelope components in proportion to sol-air–indoor temperature difference.
2. Use radiant barrier in attic space.
3. Consider thermally massive envelope materials to reduce peak air-conditioning loads.
4. Use slab-on-grade instead of crawl space and insulate only at perimeter.

PROMOTE VENTILATION LOSSES

1. Orient building to benefit from breezes.
2. Use plantings to funnel breezes into building, but be careful not to obstruct vent openings.
3. Use wing walls and overhangs to direct breezes into building.
4. Locate openings and arrange floor plan to promote cross ventilation.
5. Plan interior for effective use of whole-house fan.
6. Ventilate building envelope (attic or roof, walls).

SPACE VENTILATION

"Air-change ventilation" brings outdoor temperatures indoors by breezes or whole-house exhaust fans. Whole-house fans yield about 60 air changes per hour (ACH) and are useful only as long as outdoor conditions are within comfort limits (72°–82°F). They may offer 30–50% savings in electricity costs over air conditioning. Whole-house fans do not provide high enough airflow rates for body ventilation. Ceiling (paddle) fans are recommended for air movement and can maintain comfort with indoor temperatures up to 85°F ET*. Air conditioning is necessary above 85°F ET*. The issue of when to ventilate and when to air condition is a function of building type, occupancy hours, heat and moisture capacity of the structure, and climatic subregion. Humidity is a factor, as night air may be cool but excessively humid.

ROOFS AND ATTICS

The attic should be designed to ventilate naturally. Most of the heat gain to the attic floor is by radiation from the underside of the roof. While ventilation is unable to interrupt this transfer, most of it can be stopped by an aluminum foil radiant barrier. Foil facings on rigid insulation and sheathing can be used as radiant barriers when installed facing an airspace.

Roof spray systems can dissipate most of the solar load, leaving the roof temperature near the ambient dry-bulb instead of the sol-air temperature. The theoretical lowest temperature that the roof can be cooled to by evaporation is the wet-bulb, but is not attainable under real daytime conditions. The cost-effectiveness of spray systems depends on the roof section, R value, building type, climatic region, and other factors. Spray systems are most advantageous for poorly insulated flat roofs.

WALLS

Radiant barriers enhance the performance of walls by reducing solar gain. They are most effective on east and west walls and are recommended for predominantly overheated regions [<2000 heating degree days (HDD), >2500 cooling degree days (CDD)]. They are not recommended on south walls except where CDD exceed 3500. Radiant barriers must face an airspace and can be located on either side of the wall structure. Outside placement allows the cavity to be vented. This enhances summer wall performance, but admitting cold air degrades it during winter. Venting is recommended for regions having more than 3500 CDD. Discharging the cavity into the attic ensures best vent action. Thermal mass in walls reduces peak air-conditioning loads and delays peak heat gain. By damping off some of the peak load, massive walls help keep indoor temperatures in the range where ceiling (paddle) fans and airflow from cross ventilation provide comfort.

DAYLIGHTING

Windows and skylights should be shaded to prevent undesired heat gain. North- and south-facing glazing is shaded most easily for predictable daylighting. Light-colored reflective sunshades and ground surfaces will bounce the light and minimize direct gain. Cloudy or hazy sky conditions are a source of brightness and glare.

REFERENCES

1. S. Chandra et al. *Cooling with Ventilation*, Solar Energy Research Institute, Golden, CO, 1982.
2. P. Fairey, "Radiant Barrier Systems," Design Notes 6 and 7, Florida Solar Energy Center, Cape Canaveral, 1984.
3. P. Fairey, S. Chandra, A. Kerestecioglu, "Ventilative Cooling in Southern Residences: A Parametric Analysis," PF-108-86, Florida Solar Energy Center, Cape Canaveral, 1986.

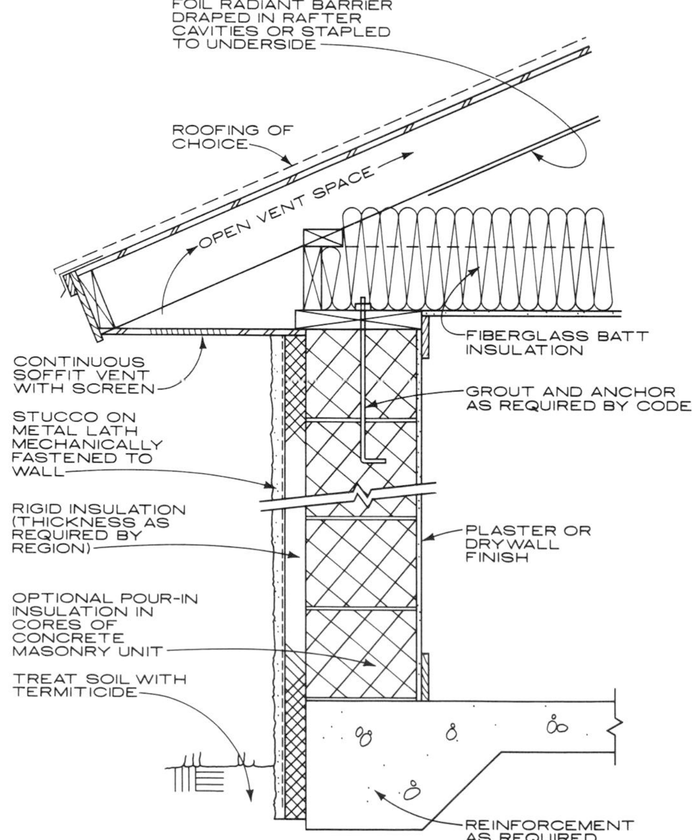

FOIL RADIANT BARRIER DRAPED IN RAFTER CAVITIES OR STAPLED TO UNDERSIDE
ROOFING OF CHOICE
OPEN VENT SPACE
CONTINUOUS SOFFIT VENT WITH SCREEN
STUCCO ON METAL LATH MECHANICALLY FASTENED TO WALL
RIGID INSULATION (THICKNESS AS REQUIRED BY REGION)
OPTIONAL POUR-IN INSULATION IN CORES OF CONCRETE MASONRY UNIT
TREAT SOIL WITH TERMITICIDE
FIBERGLASS BATT INSULATION
GROUT AND ANCHOR AS REQUIRED BY CODE
PLASTER OR DRYWALL FINISH
REINFORCEMENT AS REQUIRED

ENERGY-EFFICIENT WALL SECTION: VENTED SKIN MASONRY WALL WITH INSIDE INSULATION

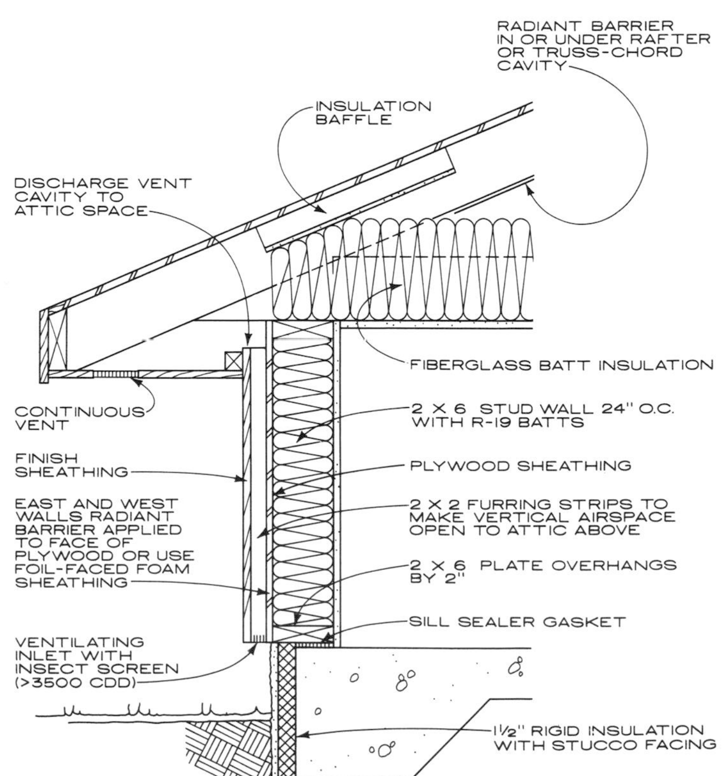

RADIANT BARRIER IN OR UNDER RAFTER OR TRUSS-CHORD CAVITY
INSULATION BAFFLE
DISCHARGE VENT CAVITY TO ATTIC SPACE
FIBERGLASS BATT INSULATION
CONTINUOUS VENT
2 × 6 STUD WALL 24" O.C. WITH R-19 BATTS
FINISH SHEATHING
PLYWOOD SHEATHING
EAST AND WEST WALLS RADIANT BARRIER APPLIED TO FACE OF PLYWOOD OR USE FOIL-FACED FOAM SHEATHING
2 × 2 FURRING STRIPS TO MAKE VERTICAL AIRSPACE OPEN TO ATTIC ABOVE
2 × 6 PLATE OVERHANGS BY 2"
SILL SEALER GASKET
VENTILATING INLET WITH INSECT SCREEN (>3500 CDD)
1½" RIGID INSULATION WITH STUCCO FACING

ENERGY-EFFICIENT WALL SECTION: VENTED SKIN WALL WITH RADIANT BARRIER

Donald Watson, FAIA; Trumbull, Connecticut
Kenneth Labs; New Haven, Connecticut

ENERGY-EFFICIENT ATRIUM DESIGN

In its original meaning, an atrium was the open courtyard of a Roman house. Today an atrium is a glazed courtyard on the side of or within a building. If issues of heating, cooling, and lighting are ignored, atrium designs can add significantly to the energy cost of the building as well as require above-average energy to maintain comfort within them. On the other hand, energy-efficient atrium spaces can contribute savings through natural lighting, passive heating, and natural cooling strategies. (Any multistoried space raises concerns for fire safety and requires special attention.)

Atrium spaces are more responsive to the influence of the outside climate than conventional buildings, and their design therefore will follow local climate requirements. Design also will depend on the specific function and goals of the atrium: to supply daylighting for itself or to adjacent spaces; to provide comfort for sedentary human occupancy or plants; or to serve only as a semiconditioned space for circulation. The challenge of energy-efficient atrium design is to combine various and perhaps conflicting requirements for passive heating, natural cooling, and daylighting using the geometry of the atrium, its orientation, and solar and insulation controls at the glazing surfaces. These architectural choices need to be integrated with the mechanical engineering to assure that the passive energy opportunities will in fact effectively reduce building energy use.

PASSIVE SOLAR HEATING OPPORTUNITIES

Atriums designed with large glass areas overheat during the day, providing potentially recoverable heat to parts of the adjacent building, such as its outer perimeter, which can be transferred by air or by an air-to-water heat pump. In cool climates and in buildings with a predominant heat load (such as a residential or hotel structure), using this solar heat gain can be cost-effective. In such a case, vertical glass facing the south captures winter sun while incurring minimum summer heat gain liability. If the atrium space requires sedentary occupant comfort, heat storage within the space and energy-efficient glazing also is beneficial.

NATURAL COOLING OPPORTUNITIES

To reduce required cooling in an atrium, protection from the summer sun is essential. It can be accomplished by glass orientation, protective coatings as part of the glazing, and shading devices, which may or may not be movable. In hot, sunny climates, relatively small amounts of glass can meet daylighting objectives while reducing the solar gain liability. In warm, humid climates with predominantly cloudy skies (the sky is nonetheless a source of undesirable heat gain), the north-facing orientation should be favored for large glazed areas. Mechanical ventilation should facilitate the upward flow of natural ventilation. Spot cooling by air-conditioning lower atrium areas is a relatively efficient means of keeping some areas comfortable for occupancy without fully conditioning the entire volume of air.

DAYLIGHTING OPPORTUNITIES

An atrium with the predominant function to provide natural lighting takes its shape from the predominant sky condition. In cool, cloudy climates, the atrium cross section ideally would be stepped outward as it gets higher in order to increase overhead lighting. In hot, sunny locations with clear sunny skies, the cross section is like a large lighting fixture designed to reflect, diffuse, and make usable the light from above. This purpose is complicated by the light source—the sun—as it changes position with respect to the building throughout the day and the year.

WINTERGARDEN ATRIUM DESIGN

Healthy greenery can be incorporated in atrium design. The designer needs to know the unique horticultural requirements for the plant species for lighting, heating, and cooling, which could be quite different from those for human occupancy. Generally, plants need higher light levels and cooler temperatures than might be comfortable for humans. The most efficient manner to keep plants heated is with plant bed or root heating, as with water tubes or air tubes in gravel or earth. Plants also benefit from gentle air movement, which reduces excessive moisture that might rot the plants and circulates CO_2 needed for growth.

Donald Watson, FAIA; Trumbull, Connecticut

RELATIVE IMPORTANCE OF DESIGN PRINCIPLES IN VARIOUS CLIMATES

ATRIUM ENERGY-DESIGN PRINCIPLE		COLD/CLOUDY SEATTLE CHICAGO MINNEAPOLIS	COOL/SUNNY DENVER ST. LOUIS BOSTON	WARM/DRY LOS ANGELES PHOENIX MIDLAND, TX	HOT/WET HOUSTON NEW ORLEANS MIAMI
	HEATING				
H1	To maximize winter solar heat gain, orient the atrium aperture to the south.	●	□	▼	
H2	For radiant heat storage and distribution, place interior masonry directly in the path of the winter sun.	▼	□	●	
H3	To prevent excessive nighttime heat loss, consider an insulating system for the glazing.	●	□		
H4	To recover heat, place a return air duct high in the space, directly in the sun.	□	●	▼	
	COOLING				
C1	To minimize solar gain, provide shade from the summer sun.		□	□	●
C2	Use the atrium as an air plenum in the mechanical system of the building.	□	□	□	□
C3	To facilitate natural ventilation, create a vertical "chimney" effect with high outlets and low inlets.	□	□	□	●
	LIGHTING				
L1	To maximize daylight, use a stepped section (in predominantly cloudy areas).	□	▼		
L2	To maximize daylight, select skylight glazing for predominant sky condition (clear and horizontal in predominantly cloudy areas).	□	□	□	□
L3	Provide sun and glare control.	□	□	●	□

Key: ● = Very important; □ = positive benefit; ▼ = discretionary use.

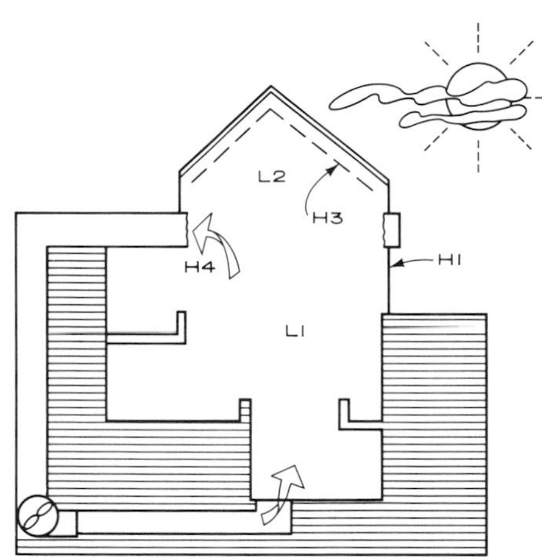
L2
H3
H1
H4
L1
COLD/CLOUDY

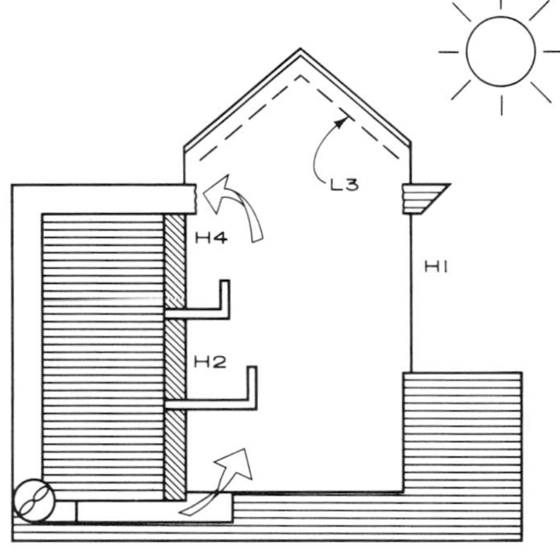
H4
L3
H1
H2
COOL/SUNNY

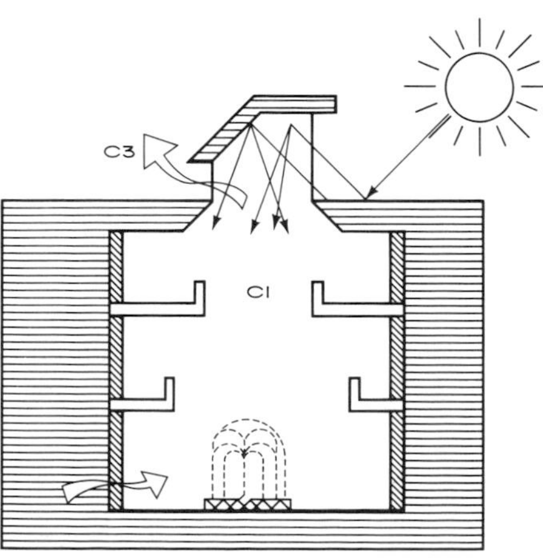
C3
C1
WARM/DRY

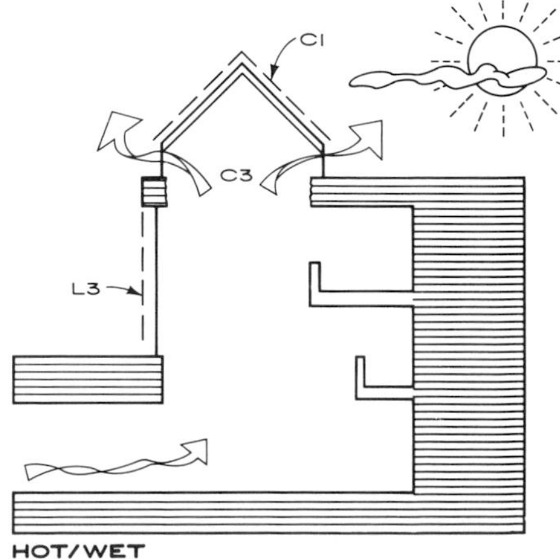
C1
C3
L3
HOT/WET

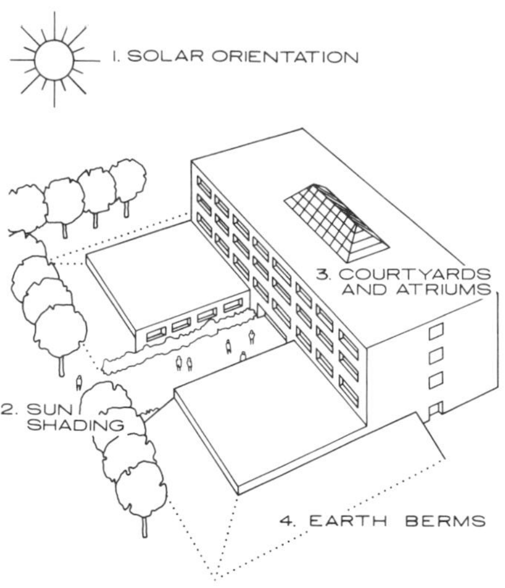

1. SOLAR ORIENTATION
3. COURTYARDS AND ATRIUMS
2. SUN SHADING
4. EARTH BERMS

SITE PLANNING AND ORIENTATION

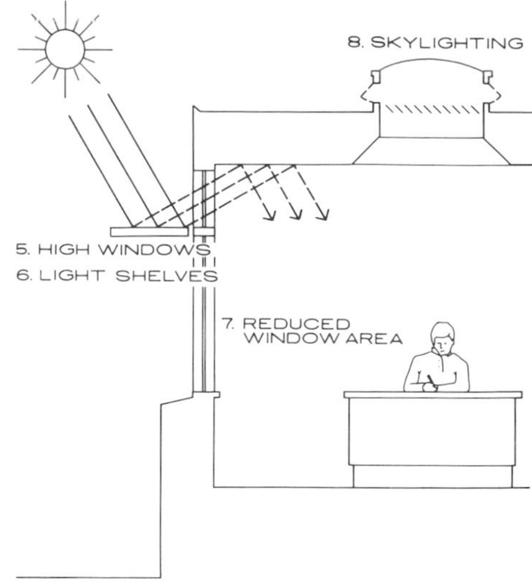

8. SKYLIGHTING
5. HIGH WINDOWS
6. LIGHT SHELVES
7. REDUCED WINDOW AREA

DAYLIGHTING

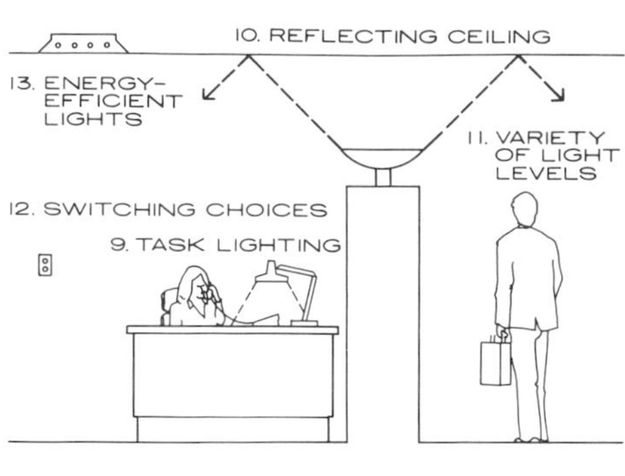

10. REFLECTING CEILING
13. ENERGY-EFFICIENT LIGHTS
11. VARIETY OF LIGHT LEVELS
12. SWITCHING CHOICES
9. TASK LIGHTING

ENERGY-EFFICIENT LIGHTING

ENERGY-CONSERVING DESIGN: NONRESIDENTIAL BUILDINGS

Energy-conserving design for nonresidential buildings is justified by savings in operating costs which result in a lower "life-cycle" investment. For large buildings of all types, the best opportunities are most likely to be found in electricity costs; depending upon the demand charges of the local utility, "peak load" reduction and/or "shifting" (diurnal or seasonal) measures may prove to be cost-effective. Concurrently, lower electric use by effective daylighting and by cooling load reduction (window orientation and solar controls) will be cost-effective, since these loads are typically interrelated and use expensive forms of energy. When these loads and costs are reduced, heating cost reduction by solar and energy-conserving techniques also applies to larger buildings. Energy-conserving opportunities are best addressed by a whole-systems team approach of architecture, HVAC, lighting, and controls engineering. For example, high levels of insulation or of thermal mass may be cost justified when these also result in substantially reduced mechanical system sizes and power requirements.

The architect should consider the following items in designing an energy-efficient nonresidential building, regardless of size and building type.

SITE PLANNING AND ORIENTATION

1. ORIENT THE LONGER WALLS OF A BUILDING TO FACE NORTH–SOUTH

Walls that face the equator (e.g., the noonday sun) are ideal for windows oriented to admit daylighting with minimum cost for shading or sun control (i.e., relatively small horizontal overhangs create effective shading). Walls and windows facing east and west, on the other hand, are sources of undesirable overheating and are difficult to shade effectively. In a cool climate, windows facing the equator can gain useful wintertime heating from the sun. (See also "Daylighting" criteria.)

2. PROVIDE SUN SHADING TO SUIT CLIMATE AND USE VARIATIONS

Buildings can be located in groups to shade one another. Landscaping and sun shading can be used to shade building surfaces, especially windows, during overheated hours. Functions can be located within a building to coincide with solar gain benefit or liability. For example, cafeterias are ideally exposed to noontime winter sun in cool and temperate climates or placed in the midday shade in warm climates; low-use areas (storage areas) can be used as climatic buffers placed on the east or west in hot climates or on the north in cool climates.

3. CREATE COURTYARDS AND ENCLOSED ATRIUMS

Semienclosed courtyards (in warm climates) and enclosed atriums (in temperate and cool climates) can be formed by groups of buildings to provide areas for planting, shading, water fountains, and other microclimatic benefits. Atriums can also be used as light courts and ventilating shafts. Indoor or outdoor planted areas provide evaporative cooling for local breezes when located near buildings.

4. USE EARTH BERMS FOR CLIMATIC BUFFERING

Earth berms (sloped or terraced, formed simply by grading earth against the wall of a building) help to buffer the building against temperature extremes of both heat and cold. The planting on earth berms also provides evaporative cooling near the building. Earth berms can be construction cost savers because the foundation does not have to be as deep (in single-storied construction); the earth and ground cover is often less costly than other wall finishing materials. Its long-term maintenance can also be lower than conventional materials.

DAYLIGHTING

5. PLACE WINDOWS HIGH IN THE WALL OF EACH FLOOR

Windows placed high in the wall near the ceiling provide the most daylight for any given window area, permitting daylight to penetrate more deeply into the interior.

6. USE LIGHT SHELVES

Light shelves are horizontal projections placed on the outside and below a window to reflect sunlight into the interior. Typically placed just above eye level, the light shelf reflects daylight onto the interior ceiling, making it a light-reflecting surface (instead of a dark, shaded surface typical of a conventional interior ceiling). At the same time, the light shelf shades the lower portion of the window, reducing the amount of light near the window, which is typically overlit. The result is more balanced daylighting with less glare and contrast between light levels in the interior.

7. SIZE WINDOWS ACCORDING TO USE AND ORIENTATION

Because window glass has little or no resistance to heat flow, it is one of the primary sources of energy waste and discomfort. Window areas should be shaded against direct solar gain during overheated hours. Even when shaded, windows gain undesired heat when the outdoor temperature exceeds the human comfort limit. Window areas should therefore be kept to a reasonable minimum, justified by clearly defined needs for view, visual relief, ventilation, and/or daylighting. Double glazing should be considered for all windows for energy efficiency and comfort in cool and temperate climates. In warm climates, double, tinted, or reflective glass should be considered, depending upon building size and use.

8. USE SKYLIGHTING FOR DAYLIGHTING, WITH PROPER SOLAR CONTROLS

Skylighting that is properly sized and oriented is an efficient and cost-effective source of lighting. Consider that for most office buildings, sunlight is available for nearly the entire period of occupancy and that the lighting requirement for interior lighting is only about 1% of the amount of light available outside. Electric lighting costs, peak demand charges, and work interruptions during power brownouts can be greatly reduced by using daylight. Cost-effective, energy-efficient skylights can be small, spaced widely, with "splayed" interior light wells that help reflect and diffuse the light. White-painted ceilings and walls further improve the efficiency of daylighting (by as much as 300% if compared with dark interior finishes). Skylights should include some means to control undesired solar gain by one or more of the following means: (a) Face the skylight to the polar orientation; (b) provide exterior light-reflecting shading; (c) provide movable sunshades on the inside, with a means to vent the heat above the shade.

ENERGY-EFFICIENT LIGHTING

9. USE TASK LIGHTING, WITH INDIVIDUAL CONTROLS

Lamps for task lighting are ideally located near the work surface and are adjustable to eliminate reflective glare. The energy-efficient advantages are that less light output is required (reduced geometrically as a function of its closer distance to the task) and the lamp can be switched off when not needed.

Note: General light levels should be reduced below conventional standards and sources of reflective glare from ceiling lights and windows eliminated in areas where cathode ray tubes (CRTs) are used.

10. USE THE CEILING AS A LIGHT-REFLECTIVE SURFACE

By using "uplights," either ceiling pendants or lamps mounted on partitions and/or cabinets, the ceiling surface can be used as a light reflector. This has several advantages: (a) fewer fixtures are required for general area ("ambient") lighting; (b) the light is indirect, eliminating the sources of visual discomfort due to glare and reflection, (c) if light shelves are used, the ceiling is the light reflector for both natural and artificial light, an advantage for the occupant's sense of visual order.

11. EMPLOY A VARIETY OF LIGHT LEVELS

In any given interior, a variety of light levels improves visual comfort. Light levels can be reduced in low-use areas, storage, circulation, and lounge areas. Daylighting can also be used to provide variety of lighting, thereby reducing monotone interiors.

12. PROVIDE SWITCHING CHOICES, TO ACCOMMODATE SCHEDULE AND DAYLIGHT AVAILABILITY

Areas near windows that can be naturally lit should have continuous dimming controls to dim lights that are not needed. Other areas should have separate switching to coincide with different schedules and uses. Consider occupant-sensing light switches in areas of occasional use, such as washrooms, storage, and warehouse areas.

Donald Watson, FAIA; Trumbull, Connecticut

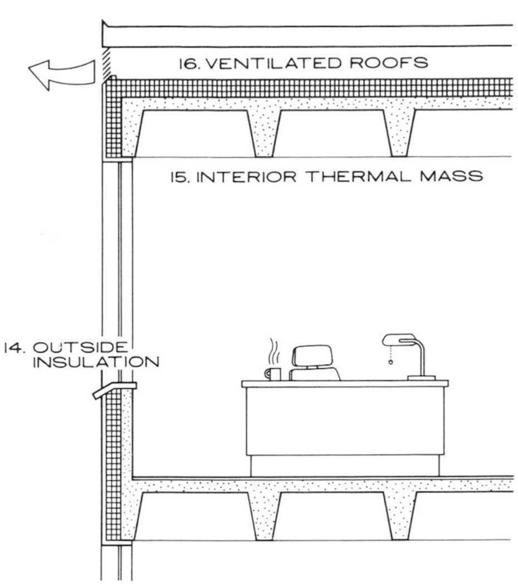
16. VENTILATED ROOFS
15. INTERIOR THERMAL MASS
14. OUTSIDE INSULATION

THERMAL CONSTRUCTION

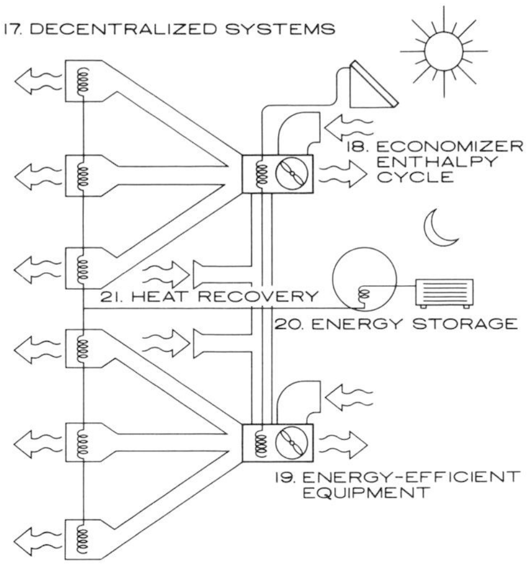
17. DECENTRALIZED SYSTEMS
18. ECONOMIZER ENTHALPY CYCLE
21. HEAT RECOVERY
20. ENERGY STORAGE
19. ENERGY-EFFICIENT EQUIPMENT

ENERGY-EFFICIENT MECHANICAL SYSTEMS

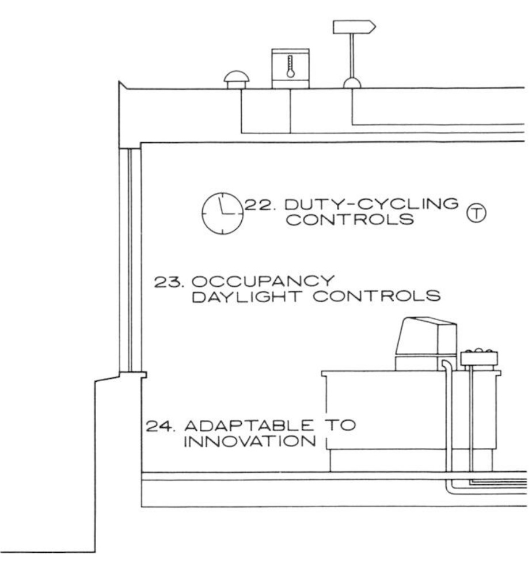
22. DUTY-CYCLING CONTROLS
23. OCCUPANCY DAYLIGHT CONTROLS
24. ADAPTABLE TO INNOVATION

SMART BUILDING CONTROLS

13. USE ENERGY-EFFICIENT LIGHTS AND LUMINAIRES

Use the most efficient light source for the requirement: these might be fluorescent bulbs, high-intensity discharge lamps, or high-voltage/high-frequency lights. Compact fluorescent lights with high-efficiency ballasts have advantages of low wattage, low waste heat, long life, and good color rendering. Incandescent lights use less energy when switched on, so these are appropriate for occasional use and short-term lighting. Luminaires should also be evaluated for how efficiently they diffuse, direct, or reflect the available light.

THERMAL CONSTRUCTION

14. PLACE INSULATION ON THE OUTSIDE OF THE STRUCTURE

Insulation is one of the most cost-effective means of energy conservation. Insulation placed on the outer face of a wall or roof protects the structure from the extremes of the outside temperature (with the added benefit of lengthening the life of the roof waterproofing membrane) and adds the massiveness of the structure to the thermal response of the interior (see Criteria 15). In localities where "resistance insulation" is not available, the combination of airspaces and high capacitance materials (such as masonry and/or earth berms) should be designed for effective thermal dampening or time lag (the delay and diffusion of outside temperature extremes that are transmitted to the interior). As an alternative to insulating roof structures in hot climates, a "radiant barrier" consisting of a continuous sheet of reflective foil with a low emissivity coating and an airspace around it serves as an effective shield against undesired heat gain.

15. UTILIZE THERMAL MASS ON BUILDING INTERIOR

In office buildings, thermally massive construction (such as masonry and concrete which have good heat storage capacity) benefits the energy-efficient operation of heating and cooling equipment as follows:

(a) Cooling benefits: Thermal mass absorbs the "overheating" that is inevitable in an office space due to the buildup of heat from people, equipment, lighting, rising afternoon temperature, and solar gain. The more thermal mass that is effectively exposed to an interior space (ceiling and walls), the greater is the saving on air conditioning in the afternoon, with the potential to delay the overheating until early evening when electric rates may be lower and/or outdoor air may be low enough to cool the mass by night ventilation. (The "night cooling" option is especially favorable in warm, dry climates due to predictably cooler nighttime temperatures.)

(b) Heating benefits: In temperate and cool climates, thermal mass helps absorb and store wintertime passive solar heat. This is especially effective if the thermal mass is on the building interior and directly heated by the sun (made possible by design of various corridor, stairway, and half-height partition arrangements).

16. USE LIGHT-CONSTRUCTED VENTILATED ROOFS IN HOT CLIMATES

In hot climates, the roof is the primary source of undesired heat gain. Energy-efficient roof designs should be considered. One of the best for hot climates is a ventilated double roof wherein the outside layer is a light-colored and lightweight material which shades the solar heat from the inner roof, which should be well insulated. As described in Strategy 14, a "radiant barrier" can be considered as an alternative to resistance insulation to serve as a shield against thermal transfer through the ceiling portion of the roof structure.

ENERGY-EFFICIENT MECHANICAL SYSTEMS

17. USE DECENTRALIZED AND MODULAR SYSTEMS

Heating and cooling equipment is most efficient when sized to the average load condition, not the "peak" or extreme condition. Use modular unit boilers, chillers, pumps, and fans in series so that the average operating load can be met by a few modules operating at peak efficiency rather than a single unit that is oversized for normal conditions. Zone the distribution systems to meet different loads due to orientation, use, and schedule. Use variable-air-volume (VAV) systems to reduce fan energy requirements and to lower duct sizes and costs (the system can be designed for the predominant load, not the sum of the peak loads). Decentralized air-handling systems have smaller trunk lines and duct losses. Dispersed air handlers, located close to their end use, can be reduced in size from conventional system sizes if hot and chilled water is piped to them (a decentralized air-handling system with a centralized plant).

18. USE ECONOMIZER/ENTHALPY CYCLE COOLING

Economizer/enthalpy cycle cooling uses outdoor air when it is cool enough for direct ventilation and/or when the outdoor air has a lower heat content than indoor air (so that it can be cooled evaporatively without raising indoor humidity). Although useful in all climates, direct or indirect evaporative cooling systems are especially effective in hot, dry climates.

19. USE ENERGY-EFFICIENT EQUIPMENT

The energy efficiency of mechanical equipment varies greatly. Consider heat pumps for cooling and for heating to replace separate chiller and boiler units. Heat pumps can also use local water sources or water storage (see Criteria 20 below). Newly developed mechanical heating equipment, such as gas-fired pulse combustion boilers, is achieving very high (up to 85%) annual operating efficiencies.

20. USE ENERGY STORAGE FOR COOLING

Chilled water storage has several advantages: It permits water chilling or ice-making at night under more favorable ambient conditions and possible lower electric rates; perhaps more important, it reduces or eliminates peak-hour energy consumption, thereby reducing demand charges.

21. USE HEAT RECOVERY FOR HEATING

In cool and temperate climates, heat can be recovered from warm zones of a building and recirculated to underheated areas. Recoverable heat sources include equipment, process heat, and passive solar gain. Heat recovery wheels or coils can be used where indoor air needs to be ventilated, transferring heat into the incoming fresh airstream. In all climates, process heat or active solar heat (e.g., from solar collectors) can be used for domestic hot water or for tempering incoming fresh air.

"SMART BUILDING" CONTROLS

22. USE SMART THERMOSTATS

"Duty-cycling" temperature controls can be programmed for different time schedules and thermal conditions, the simplest being the day–night setback. Newer controls are "predictive," sensing outdoor temperature trends and then selecting the system operation most appropriate to the condition.

23. USE OCCUPANCY- AND DAYLIGHT-SENSING LIGHTING CONTROLS

Automatic switching of lights according to the building occupant schedule and the daylight condition is recommended, with manual override for nighttime occupancy. Photosensors should be placed in areas that can be predictably lit by natural light.

24. BE PREPARED FOR RAPID INNOVATION IN BUILDING CONTROL SYSTEMS

Newly developing "smart" building systems include microprocessing for thermal and light control, fire and air-quality precautions, equipment failure, and operations/maintenance requirements (along with new communication and office management systems). These innovations require that electric wiring be easily changed, such as through "double-floor" construction.

REFERENCES

Burt Hill Kosar Rittelmann Associates: *Small Office Building Handbook*, New York: Van Nostrand Reinhold, 1985.

Burt Hill Kosar Rittelmann Associates: *Commercial Building Design*, New York: Van Nostrand Reinhold, 1987.

McGuiness, Stein, and Reynolds: *Mechanical and Electric Equipment for Buildings*, New York: John Wiley & Sons, 7th Edition, 1986

Solar Energy Research Institute: *Design of Energy-Responsive Commercial Buildings*, New York: John Wiley Interscience, 1985.

Watson, Donald, editor: *Energy Conservation through Building Design*, New York: McGraw-Hill Book Company, 1979.

Donald Watson, FAIA; Trumbull, Connecticut

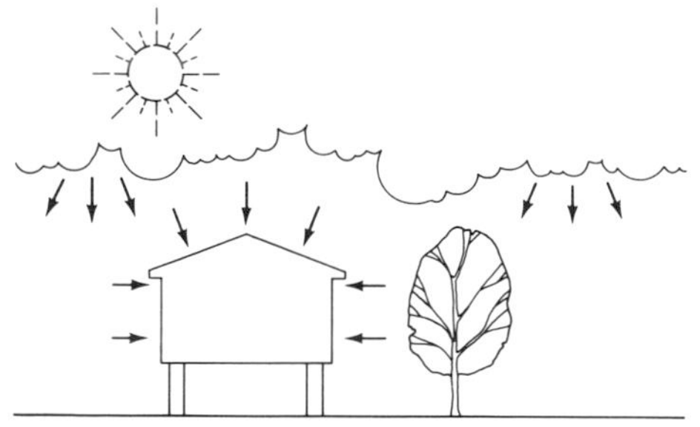

OVERCAST: DIFFUSE, STEADY; BRIGHT OR DARK

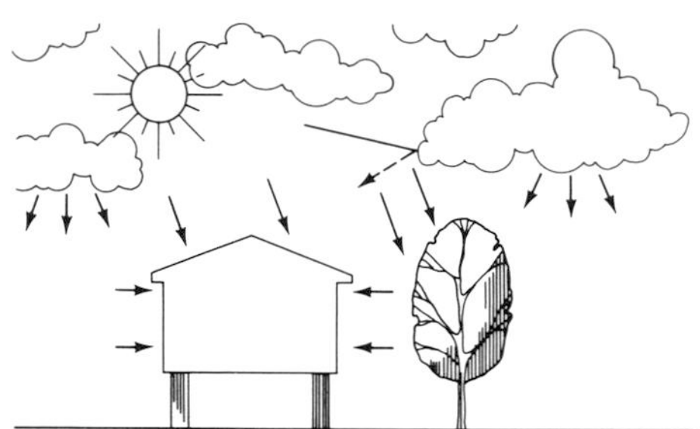

PARTLY CLOUDY: INTENSE/DIFFUSE; DIRECT BRIGHT

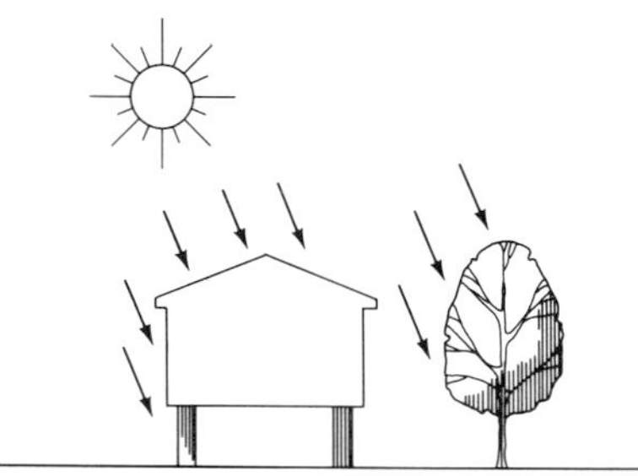

CLEAR: INTENSE, DIRECT BRIGHT, BLUE

DAYLIGHT

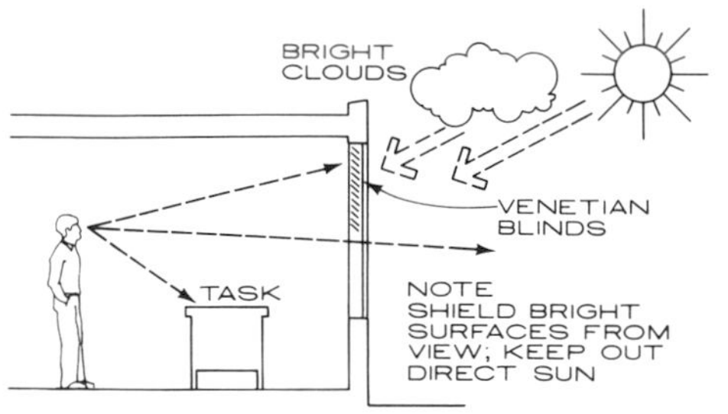
BRIGHT CLOUDS
VENETIAN BLINDS
TASK
NOTE
SHIELD BRIGHT SURFACES FROM VIEW; KEEP OUT DIRECT SUN

QUALITY DAYLIGHTING

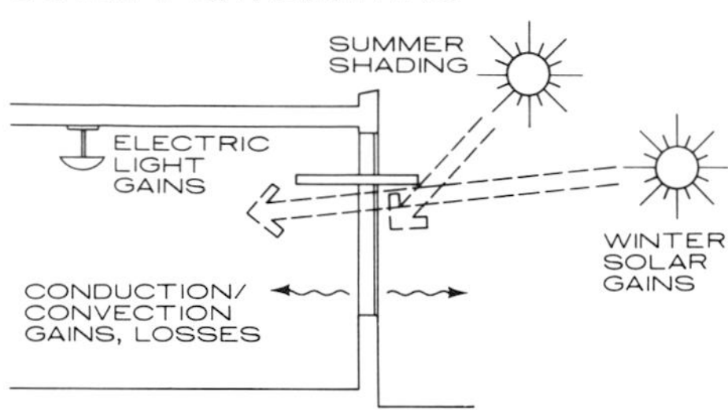
SUMMER SHADING
ELECTRIC LIGHT GAINS
WINTER SOLAR GAINS
CONDUCTION/ CONVECTION GAINS, LOSSES

SOLAR GAIN OPTIMIZATION

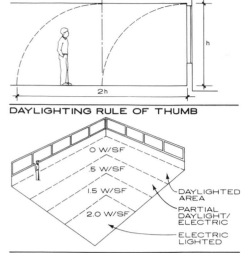

DAYLIGHTING RULE OF THUMB

DAYLIGHTING BY ZONE/ THREE-STEP SWITCHING

INTRODUCTION

Ample daylight is available throughout most of North America for lighting interior spaces during a large portion of the working day. This daylight may be used for critical visual tasks or for ambient lighting, to be supplemented with electric task lights. Daylight is thought by most to be psychologically desirable and there is much evidence that it is biologically beneficial. The variability of daylight from one moment to the next produces visual stimulus and provides a psychological contact with the outdoors which most people find extremely satisfying. Its use in place of, or in conjunction with, other lighting sources can conserve energy, but energy is conserved only if electric light sources are adequately controlled through on–off switching and/or dimming.

SOURCE

Daylight comes from the sun, bright and direct; it often comes filtered, diffused, and scattered by clouds, and it is reflected by the ground and other surfaces. The availability of daylight for a particular location can be determined from charts published by the Illuminating Engineering Society (IES), "Recommended Practice of Daylighting"; from the Solar Energy Research Institute (SERI), "Daylight Availability Data for Selected Cities in the U.S."; and from "Daylight in Architecture," by Benjamin Evans, McGraw-Hill, 1981.

It has been traditional, particularly in Europe, to consider the overcast sky as the minimum daylighting condition and to design buildings accordingly, but in North America the clear sky with sun and the partly cloudy sky are more common and generally more critical to building design for good daylighting.

Direct sun contains the maximum quantity of all wavelengths of radiation, including infrared which causes the sensation of heat. Smaller quantities of infrared as well as ultraviolet, which can cause material deterioration, come from the diffuse light of the sky and clouds.

QUALITY IN DAYLIGHTING

The principles of good lighting apply equally to daylight and electric light. Of principal concern in daylighting is the glare that may result when building occupants peripherally see bright clouds or sunlighted surfaces while trying to perform visual tasks.

Direct sun in interiors where critical visual tasks are performed is generally to be avoided. Thus, apertures that allow vision to the exterior must provide for shielding (or filtering) of exterior excessive brightnesses, or work stations must be oriented away from the apertures. Partly cloudy skies may contribute major quantities of daylight but also can be excessively bright and, therefore, should be shielded from view. Energy savings from switching or dimming of electric lights depend on daylight intensity and on the percentage of the year that daylight is available.

SOLAR-THERMAL GAINS/LOSSES

Daylight includes a significant amount of radiation that produces heat. This may be beneficial during the heating season, allowing for a reduction in other interior heating, or it may be detrimental during the cooling season, requiring additional air conditioning. Shading can be configured to reduce direct sun heating during warm weather while allowing some sun penetration in winter.

The quantity of radiant heat gain from the direct sun through glazing can be determined using the following formula:

Solar heat gain (Btu/hr) = insolation* x exposed area of glazing x transmissivity of glazing x hours of exposure

(* in Btu/hr/sq ft)

Glazing also allows for transmission of heat between outdoors and indoors via conductivity and convection. These heat losses or gains can be determined with the following formula:

Thermal gains/losses (Btu/hr) = exposed area of glazing x outdoor temperature x maintained indoor temperature x U factor of glazing x hours of exposure

ENERGY USE CONTROLS

Energy-efficient lighting design requires that electric lights remain off when daylighting levels are sufficient. The two principal types of lighting controls are selective switching (on/off) and dimming. These controls can eliminate or reduce work plane footcandles from electric lights by task, area, or zone. The simplest version of this is switching off the luminaires near the windows or at other points when and where the daylight is sufficient. Automatic dimming of luminaires can ensure that the total quantity of illumination on the work plane is maintained even as the daylight disappears or is reduced by clouds.

Switches can be controlled manually or by photosensors that switch luminaires off or on depending on the levels of daylight available; by timers that switch lights according to some preselected times (e.g., off at 8:00 am and on at 6:00 pm); by a sensor that responds to the presence of occupants.

Switching can be categorized as two, three, four, or five step. The two step is a simple on/off of all lamps on the circuit. The three-step mode requires a luminaire with two lamps or multiples of two. The three steps are all on, all off, or half on. Similar switching can be with luminaires with multiples of three or four lamps. Multilevel switching can maintain illumination levels more evenly and increase energy savings over two-step systems.

Most incandescent lamps can be dimmed, and lamps that require ballasts (e.g., fluorescent) can be dimmed if equipped with an appropriate ballast. Automatic switching and dimming controls combined with thoughtfully selected control zones allow electric lighting levels to reliably and economically respond to available daylight levels.

Energy-efficient design is a function of not only the energy used by electric lights, but also of the effect of heat given off by lights on cooling and heating systems. The approximate heat gain from an average electric lighting system can be calculated as follows:

Heat gain (Btu/hr) = footcandles/sq ft x area x .06 watt/footcandle x 3.41 Btu/hr/watt

Calculation of the electric energy used in the operation of a lighting system can be determined by the following equation:

Energy (watts/hr) = watts per luminaire* x number of luminaires x hours of operation

(* including watts for ballast)

Determining the amount of daylight that any interior space will receive during the course of the day or year is a complex process involving the determination of (1) the amount of daylight available on any aperture at appropriate times, (2) the amount of daylight that will reach interior areas, through calculations or by studies using scale models, (3) the results of step two modified by local weather data according to the percentage of cloud cover expected, and (4) the percentage of electric lighting that can be reduced or eliminated. (For scale model studies see "Daylight in Architecture," by Benjamin Evans, McGraw-Hill, 1981; see also "A Method for Predicting Energy Savings Attributed to Daylighting," by Claude L. Robbins and Kerry C. Hunter, Solar Energy Research Institute, 1982.)

Benjamin Evans, FAIA; Blacksburg, Virginia

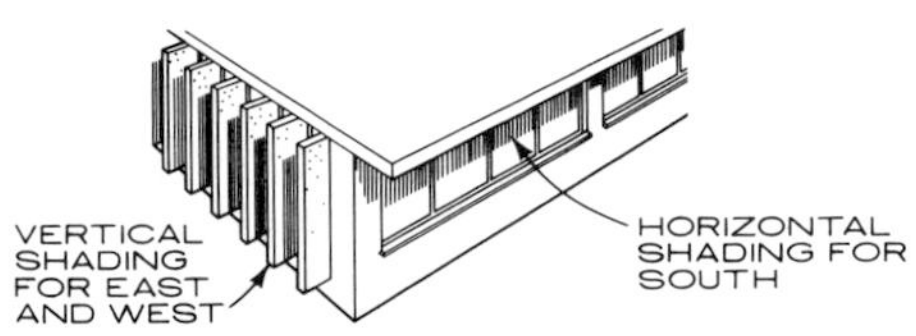
VERTICAL SHADING FOR EAST AND WEST
HORIZONTAL SHADING FOR SOUTH

SHADING DEVICES BY ORIENTATION

ORIENTATION

Usable daylight is available to apertures oriented in any direction, although the amount will differ with each orientation. Of principal concern is the location of the sun relative to a building fenestration. Apertures to the north receive only sky-contributed illumination and so will require larger areas of glazing than orientations with exposure to direct sun. Advantages of north apertures include the resulting soft, diffuse north sky light and lack of need for sun controls. However, sky glare controls still need to be considered.

East and west facades require treatment to avoid the bright early and late direct sun. This is usually best accomplished with vertical louvers or a mix of vertical and horizontal (eggcrate) louvers. The location of the sun at any time relative to any aperture can be determined using the charts on the Solar Angles pages.

South facades provide the best opportunity for daylighting. Horizontal controls (e.g., overhangs, light shelves, louvers, venetian blinds) respond best to the sun in the southern sky quadrant. Apertures can be designed such that when the sun is high in the sky during the summer there is no sun penetration, but in the winter some low-altitude sun can be admitted.

CONFIGURATION

Building configuration is also important in daylighting. Multistory buildings will be most effective if they are long and narrow, allowing maximum vertical glazing per square foot of floor space. A rule of thumb is that daylighting (allowing electric lights to be turned off) can be achieved to a depth of about 2.5 times the height of the windows, or about 15–20 ft from the windows.

Buildings wrapped around courtyards, light wells, and atria can be effectively daylighted if properly designed. Open spaces must be large enough so as not to block light from the sky from reaching interior spaces. The effectiveness of such light wells can be improved by using high-reflecting, diffuse exterior finishes such as white paint, light-colored tile, or concrete. Direct sun illuminating these surfaces, however, may make them very bright when viewed from the building interior.

In single-story buildings the configuration is not so important, since roof apertures (e.g., skylights, clerestories) can be used to illuminate interior spaces, with or without peripheral windows.

ARCHITECTURAL CONTROLS

Shading/Reflecting Devices: Shading devices can be used to prevent penetration of direct sun and to shield view of the sky. Some shading devices also reflect daylight toward the interior (e.g., light shelves). Light shelves, however, are not very effective in reflecting diffuse light from the sky and are cost-effective only when necessary to shade direct sun. Venetian blinds are very effective for shading direct sun, and they can be adjusted for total blackout and raised and lowered as needed. Sun screen consisting of tiny horizontal louvers can also be effective in shading.

Glazing: Tinted glazing (glass or plastic) reduces the apparent brightness of exterior objects from the interior, but it also reduces the amount of transmitted daylight, which must be supplemented by electric light. Heat-reflecting and other variable spectrum transmission glazing is available that tends to reduce the transmission of heat more than light, but may produce only a small advantage (check manufacturer's data). Directional glass block is useful in directing incoming light toward the ceiling, providing a low brightness image from the interior. Translucent materials exposed to direct sun diffuse incoming light and can be excessively bright when viewed from the interior.

Benjamin Evans, FAIA; Blacksburg, Virginia

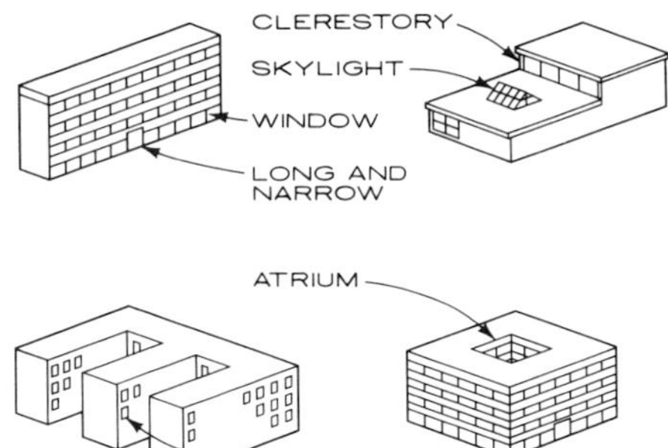
CLERESTORY
SKYLIGHT
WINDOW
LONG AND NARROW
ATRIUM
LIGHT WELL

BUILDING CONFIGURATIONS

Finishes/Surfaces: All surfaces absorb and reflect light to varying degrees. Light-colored surfaces, particularly the ceiling, generally increase the light available on the interior. Floors are usually the least effective surface in reflecting light to the work plane. Avoid highly reflective or slick finishes on large areas.

Apertures: Windows, clerestories, and skylights can be used for effective daylighting, provided they are equipped with proper shading devices. Glazing located above the work plane (e.g., high windows) is more effective in producing work plane illumination than glazing close to the floor. Clerestories and skylights are valuable in single-story buildings. The effect of clerestories can be improved by using light-colored roof surfaces to reflect exterior daylight into the aperture, but direct sun penetration may still be a concern. Clerestories and skylights both may produce glare if the sky is not properly shielded from interior view.

Geometry: The geometry or shape of interior spaces is generally not significant in achieving good daylighting. Interior walls and partitions, of course, can prevent or reduce daylight penetration into other areas, but this can often be offset by using glass in the upper portions of interior partitions. The shape and slope of the ceiling can increase interior daylight by very small amounts, but usually not enough to be cost-effective.

Spectral Transmission: The amount of light radiation received on earth depends on the amount and content of atmosphere through which the light must pass. Therefore, the color of the daylight received in buildings varies by time of day and quantity of air pollution. Generally, daylight tends to be warm (i.e., more light from the red/orange end of the spectrum) early and late in the day and cooler (i.e., blue/violet) toward midday.

Coordination of daylighting with electric lighting requires selection of interior lamps that will produce colors compatible with that of daylight. Some fluorescent lamps, particularly the new triphosphorus lamps, and metal halides are similar to daylight in color.

Ultraviolet radiation is considered to cause damage to materials such as paintings, drapes, carpets, and furniture coverings. While regular glass eliminates much of the ultraviolet energy, additional protection can be achieved by using ultraviolet filters. This is especially useful in museums.

ANALYSIS

Physical Scale Models: Daylight in a scale model will behave exactly as in the full-scale building provided that all details are identical and the model is tested under an identical sky. Relatively simple models can be used to compare design alternatives (e.g., horizontal vs. vertical window) and to determine approximate footcandle levels. Certain details and surface finishes, however, are critical for meaningful model studies, and proper instruments must be used.

Computers: Several computer programs have been developed for analyzing building designs. Each program is designed to produce a particular sophistication of analysis using a limited variety of parameters.

For further discussion of these issues, see Benjamin Evans, "Daylight in Architecture" (McGraw-Hill, 1981) and Fuller Moore, "Concepts and Practice of Architectural Daylighting" (Van Nostrand Reinhold, 1985).

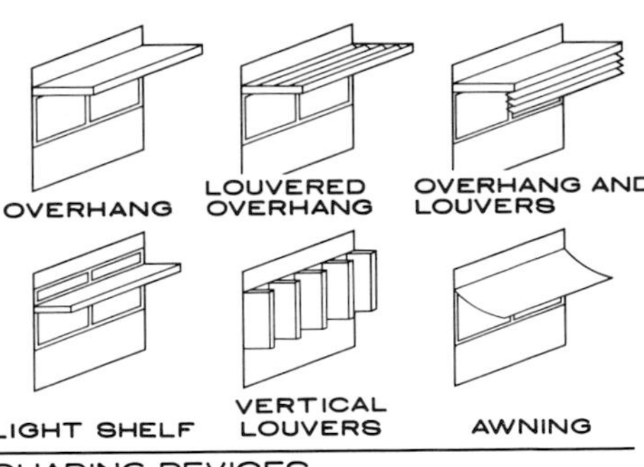
OVERHANG
LOUVERED OVERHANG
OVERHANG AND LOUVERS
LIGHT SHELF
VERTICAL LOUVERS
AWNING

SHADING DEVICES

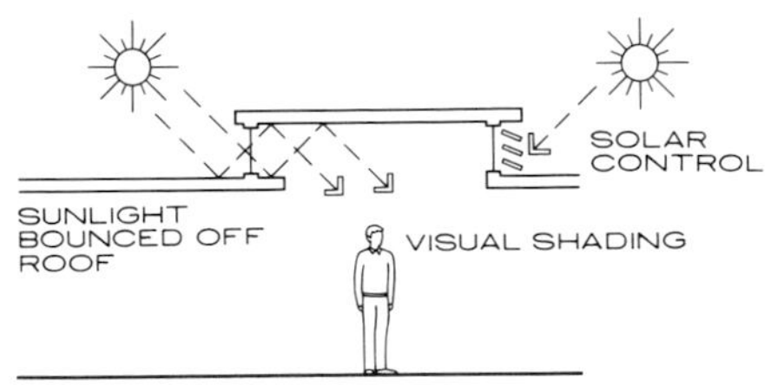
SOLAR CONTROL
SUNLIGHT BOUNCED OFF ROOF
VISUAL SHADING

CLERESTORY

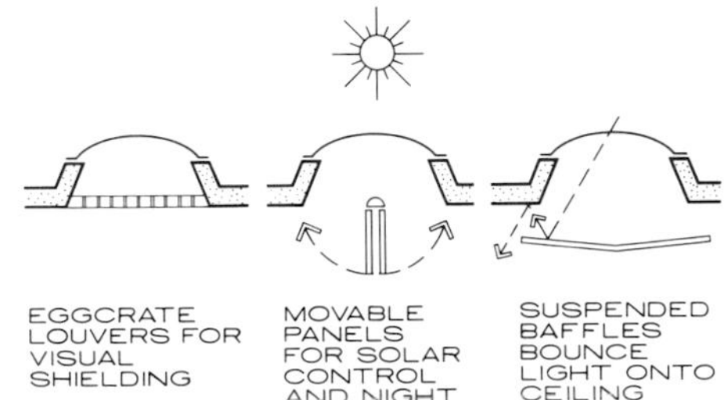
EGGCRATE LOUVERS FOR VISUAL SHIELDING
MOVABLE PANELS FOR SOLAR CONTROL AND NIGHT INSULATION
SUSPENDED BAFFLES BOUNCE LIGHT ONTO CEILING

SKYLIGHT CONTROLS

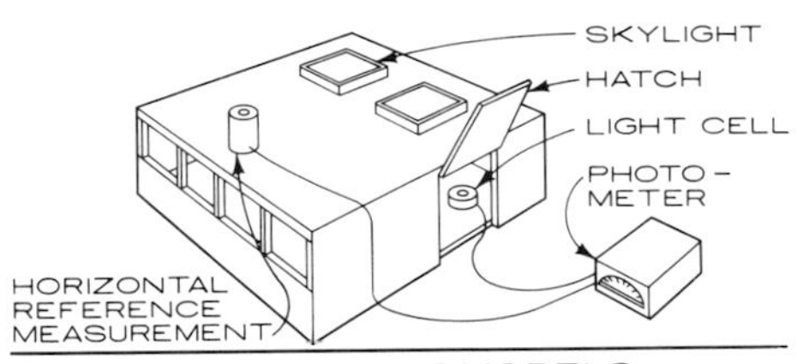
SKYLIGHT
HATCH
LIGHT CELL
PHOTO-METER
HORIZONTAL REFERENCE MEASUREMENT

DAYLIGHTING SCALE MODELS

REFLECTION FACTORS OF TYPICAL SURFACES

SURFACE TYPE	PERCENT
Concrete	20–40
Red brick	10–25
Dark stone	10–30
Light stone	20–50
Grass	5–10
Dirt	10–20
Snow	70–80
White ceiling	75–80
Wood floor	20–30
Tile floor	15–20

TRANSMISSIVITY OF TYPICAL GLAZING 1/8" THICK

GLAZING MATERIAL	PERCENT
Clear glass	85–90
Tinted glass	30–60
Bronze glass	65–75
Reflective glass	8–50
Heat-absorbing glass	70–80
Glass block	60–80
Clear plastic	80–92
Translucent plastic	10–80

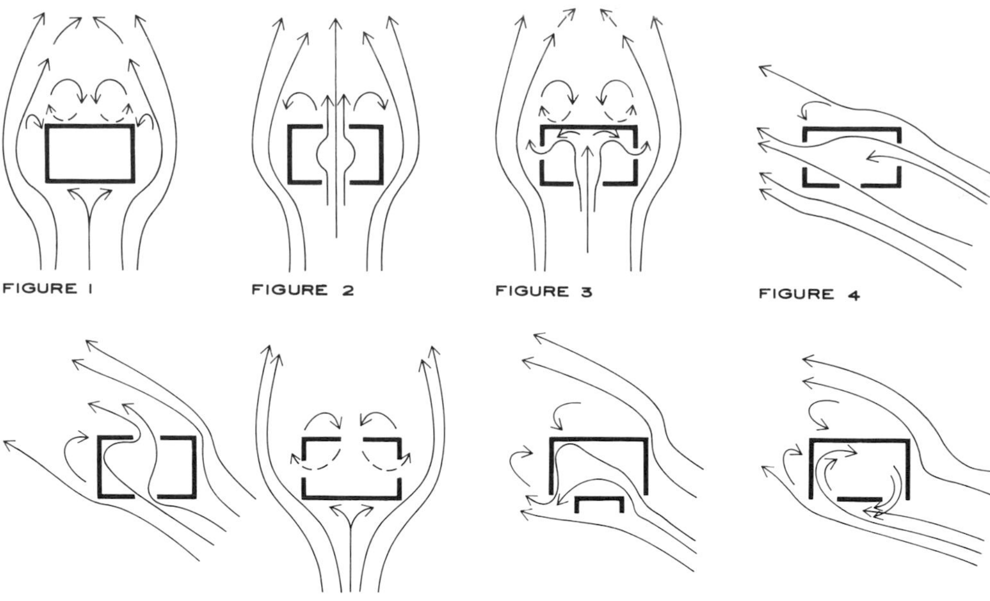

FIGURE 1 FIGURE 2 FIGURE 3 FIGURE 4

FIGURE 5 FIGURE 6 FIGURE 7 FIGURE 8

BASIC PRINCIPLES

The diagrams presented in this discussion are based on an isolated building. Neighboring buildings and landscaping can substantially affect airflow and should be taken into account when evaluating ventilation strategies.

As wind approaches the face of a building the airflow is slowed, creating positive pressure and a cushion of air on the building's windward face. This cushion of air, in turn, diverts the wind toward the building sides. Airflow as it passes along the sidewalls separates from building wall surfaces and, coupled with high-speed airflow, creates suction (negative pressure) along these wall surfaces. On the building leeward side a big slow-moving eddy is created. Suction on the leeward side of the building is less than on the sidewalls (see Figure 1).

If windows are placed in both windward and leeward faces, the building would be cross ventilated and eddies will develop against the main airflow direction (see Figure 2). Ventilation can be enhanced by placing windows in sidewalls due to the increased suction at this location; also, greater air recirculation within the building will occur due to air inertia (see Figure 3). Winds often shift direction, and for oblique winds, ventilation is best for rooms with windows on three adjacent walls (see Figure 4) than on two opposite walls (see Figure 5). However, if wind is from the one windowless side, then ventilation is poor, since all openings are in suction (see Figure 6).

If the building configuration only allows for windows in one wall, then negligible ventilation will occur with the use of a single window, because there is not a distinct inlet and outlet. Ventilation can be improved slightly with two widely spaced windows. Airflow can be enhanced in these situations by creating positive and negative pressure zones by use of architectural features such as wing walls (see Figure 7). Care must be exercised in developing these features to avoid counteracting the natural airflow, thereby weakening ventilation (see Figure 8).

AIR JETS

As airflow passes through a well-ventilated room, it forms an "air jet." If the windows are centered in a room, it forms a free jet (see Figure 9). If, however, the openings are near the room walls, ceiling, or floor, the airstream attaches itself to the surface, forming a wall jet (see Figure 10). Since heat removal from building surfaces is enhanced with increased airflow, the formation of wall jets is important in effecting rapid structure cooling. To improve the overall airflow within a room, offsetting the inlet and outlet will promote greater mixing of room air (see Figure 11).

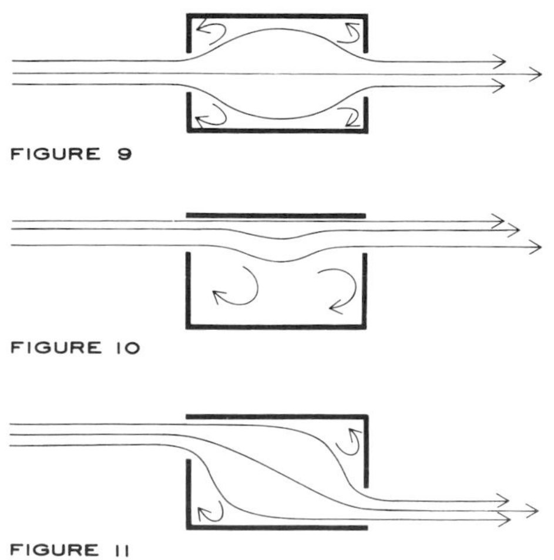

FIGURE 9

FIGURE 10

FIGURE 11

WINDOW SIZE

Airflow within a given room increases as window size increases, and to maximize airflow, the inlet and outlet opening should be the same size. Reducing the inlet size relative to the outlet increases inlet velocities. Making the outlet smaller than the inlet creates low but more uniform airspeed.

VENTILATION AIR CHANGE RATE

The natural air change rate within a building depends on several factors: speed and direction of winds at building site; the external geometry of building and adjacent surroundings; window type, size, location, and geometry; and the building's internal partition layout. Each of these factors may have an overriding influence on the air change rate of a given building.

Natural ventilation can be accomplished by wind-driven methods or by solar chimneys (stack effect). However, the stack effect is weak and works best during hours when air temperatures are highest and ventilation may not be desirable. In many areas ventilation is best accomplished during the night hours when temperatures are lowest. The night average wind speed is generally about 75% of the 24-hr average wind speed reported by weather bureaus. Often wind speeds are insufficient to accomplish effective people cooling; therefore, ventilating for structure cooling rather than people cooling should be the first design goal. As a rule of thumb, an average of 30 air changes per hour should provide adequate structure cooling, maintaining air temperatures most of the time within 1.5°F of outdoor temperatures.

EXTERNAL EFFECTS

The leeward wake of typical residential buildings extends roughly four and one-half times the ground-to-eave height. For buildings spaced greater than this distance, the general wind direction will remain unchanged. For design purposes, vegetation should be considered for its effect on wind speed, which can be as great as 30–40% in the vegetation's immediate vicinity. Its effect on wind direction is not well established and should not be relied upon in establishing ventilation strategies.

RULE OF THUMB EXAMPLE

Determine inlet window opening area to achieve 30 air changes per hour in a house of 1200 sq ft with a ceiling height of 8 ft and awning windows with insect screens.

Required airflow (CFM)

= House volume x air changes per hr/60

Required airflow = (1200 x 8) x 30/60 = 4800 CFM

From local National Oceanic and Atmospheric Administration (NOAA) weather data, determine site wind conditions for design month. For the example above, average wind speed at 10 m above ground level = 7 mph or 616 ft/min at 30° incidence angle to the house face. Note that site wind speeds are generally less than NOAA data, usually collected at airports.

To determine the required inlet area, divide the house airflow by the wind speed passing through openings in the windward building face. To establish this wind speed, the site wind speed must be modified by the effects of building angle relative to wind direction and porosity of the window opening.

Figure 12 charts the effect of wind incidence angle on airflow rates (based on wind tunnel tests on model buildings with equal inlet and outlet areas equaling 12% of inlet wall areas). Table 1 establishes porosity factors for typical window arrangements. By multiplying the site wind speed by the window air speed factor (WAF) and window porosity factor (WPF), the effective wind speed can be determined. Therefore:

$$\text{Inlet window area} = \frac{\text{Airflow}}{\text{Wind speed x WAF x WPF}}$$

$$\text{Inlet window area} = \frac{4800}{616 \times 0.35 \times 0.75} = 29.7 \text{ sq ft}$$

In the example above, therefore, providing a total of 60 sq ft of insect screened awning windows will provide the required ventilation of 30 air changes per hour.

For best results, the 60 sq ft of windows should be split equally between inlets and outlets. However, adequate airflows can be maintained for anywhere from 40/60 to 60/40 split between inlets and outlets.

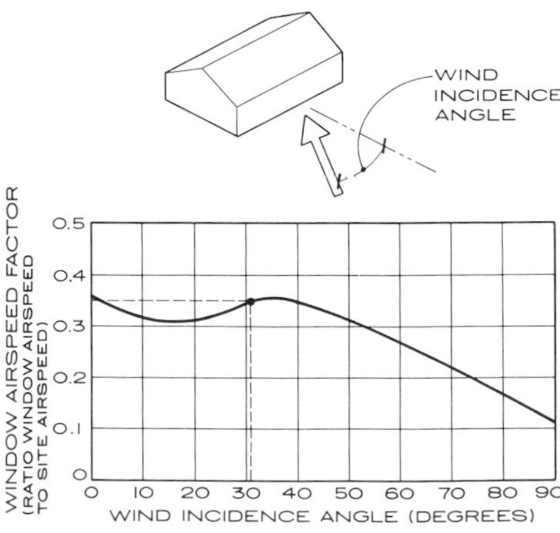
WIND INCIDENCE ANGLE
WINDOW AIRSPEED FACTOR (RATIO WINDOW AIRSPEED TO SITE AIRSPEED)
0.5
0.4
0.3
0.2
0.1
0
0 10 20 30 40 50 60 70 80 90
WIND INCIDENCE ANGLE (DEGREES)

FIGURE 12

TABLE 1 POROSITY FACTORS

WINDOW TYPE	FACTOR
Fully open awning or projecting window	C.75
Awning window with 60% porosity insect screen	0.65
60% porosity insect screen only	0.85

W. Fred Roberts Jr., AIA; Roberts & Kirchner Architects; Lexington, Virginia

GENERAL NOTES

Building attics, crawl spaces, and basements must be ventilated to remove moisture and water vapor resulting from human activity within the building. Moisture in basements and crawl spaces can occur, in addition, from water in the surrounding soil. The quantity of water vapor depends on building type (e.g., residence, school, hospital), activity (e.g., kitchen, bathroom, laundry), and air temperature and relative humidity. Proper ventilation and insulation must be combined so that the temperature of the ventilated space does not fall below the dew point; this is especially critical with low outdoor temperatures and high inside humidity. Inadequate ventilation will cause condensation and eventual deterioration of framing, insulation, and interior finishes.

The vent types shown allow natural ventilation of roofs and crawl spaces. Mechanical methods (e.g., power attic ventilators, whole house fans) can combine living space and attic ventilation, but openings for natural roof ventilation must still be provided. Protect all vents against insects and vermin with metal or fiberglass screen cloth. Increase net vent areas as noted in table.

VENTILATION REQUIREMENTS TO PREVENT CONDENSATION

SPACE	ROOF TYPE	TOTAL NET AREA OF VENTILATION	REMARKS
Joist (ceiling on underside of joists)	Flat	1/300. Uniformly distributed at eaves	Vent each joist space at both ends. Provide at least 1 1/2" free space above insulation for ventilation
	Sloped	Ditto	Ditto. On gable roofs, drill 1" diameter holes through ridge beam in each joist space to provide through-ventilation to both sides of roof
Attic (unheated)	Gable	1/300. At least two louvers on opposite sides near ridge	
	Hip	1/300. Uniformly distributed at eaves. Provide additional 1/600 at ridge, with all vents interconnected	Ridge vents create stack effect from eaves; both are recommended over eaves vents alone

Total net vent area = 1/300 of building area at eaves line. With screens increase net area by: 1/4" screen, 1.0; #8 screen, 1.25; #16 screen, 2.00.

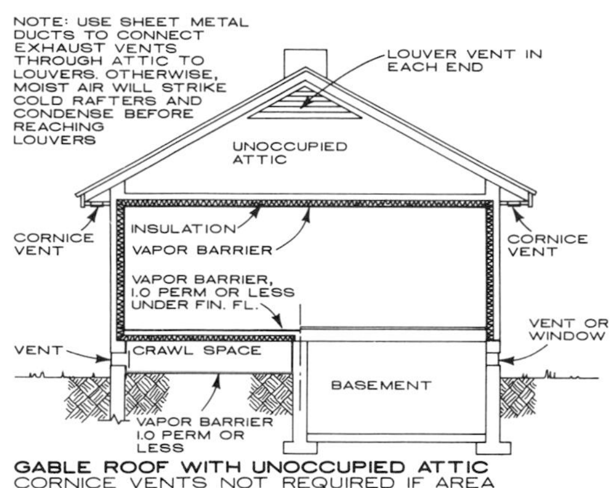
NOTE: USE SHEET METAL DUCTS TO CONNECT EXHAUST VENTS THROUGH ATTIC TO LOUVERS. OTHERWISE, MOIST AIR WILL STRIKE COLD RAFTERS AND CONDENSE BEFORE REACHING LOUVERS
LOUVER VENT IN EACH END
UNOCCUPIED ATTIC
CORNICE VENT
INSULATION
VAPOR BARRIER
CORNICE VENT
VAPOR BARRIER, 1.0 PERM OR LESS UNDER FIN. FL.
VENT OR WINDOW
VENT
CRAWL SPACE
BASEMENT
VAPOR BARRIER 1.0 PERM OR LESS

GABLE ROOF WITH UNOCCUPIED ATTIC
CORNICE VENTS NOT REQUIRED IF AREA IS SMALL

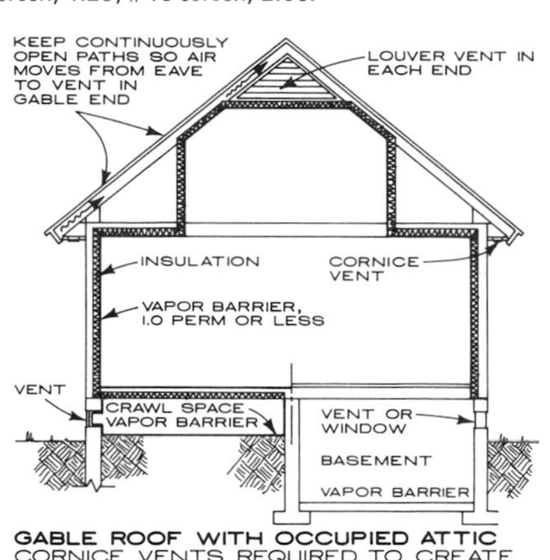
KEEP CONTINUOUSLY OPEN PATHS SO AIR MOVES FROM EAVE TO VENT IN GABLE END
LOUVER VENT IN EACH END
INSULATION
CORNICE VENT
VAPOR BARRIER, 1.0 PERM OR LESS
VENT
CRAWL SPACE
VAPOR BARRIER
VENT OR WINDOW
BASEMENT
VAPOR BARRIER

GABLE ROOF WITH OCCUPIED ATTIC
CORNICE VENTS REQUIRED TO CREATE "STACK EFFECT" TO RIDGE

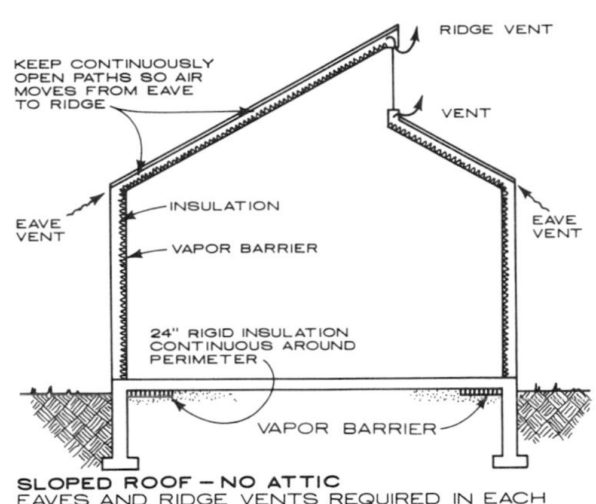
RIDGE VENT
KEEP CONTINUOUSLY OPEN PATHS SO AIR MOVES FROM EAVE TO RIDGE
VENT
EAVE VENT
INSULATION
EAVE VENT
VAPOR BARRIER
24" RIGID INSULATION CONTINUOUS AROUND PERIMETER
VAPOR BARRIER

SLOPED ROOF – NO ATTIC
EAVES AND RIDGE VENTS REQUIRED IN EACH JOIST SPACE

TYPICAL ATTIC AND CRAWL SPACE VENTILATION APPLICATIONS

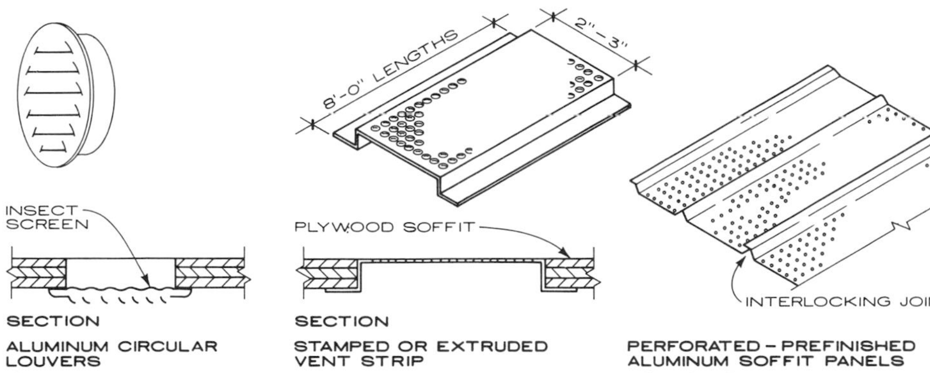
8'-0" LENGTHS
2"-3"
INSECT SCREEN
PLYWOOD SOFFIT
INTERLOCKING JOINT
SECTION
SECTION

ALUMINUM CIRCULAR LOUVERS
1"-3" DIA.

STAMPED OR EXTRUDED VENT STRIP

PERFORATED – PREFINISHED ALUMINUM SOFFIT PANELS
10" x 10' - 0" LONG. ALSO IN ROLLS

EAVES VENTILATING MATERIALS

NOTE

Vapor barriers minimize moisture migration to attics and crawl spaces; their use is required for all conditions. Always locate vapor barriers on the warm (room) side of insulation. Provide ventilation on the cold side; this permits cold/hot weather ventilation while minimizing heat gain/loss.

CRAWL SPACES VENTILATION

Crawl spaces under dwellings where earth is damp and uncovered require a high rate of ventilation. Provide at least one opening per side, as high as possible. Calculate total net area by the formula:

$$a = \frac{2L}{100} + \frac{A}{300}$$

where

L = crawl space perimeter (linear ft)
A = crawl space area (sq ft)
a = total net vent area (sq ft)

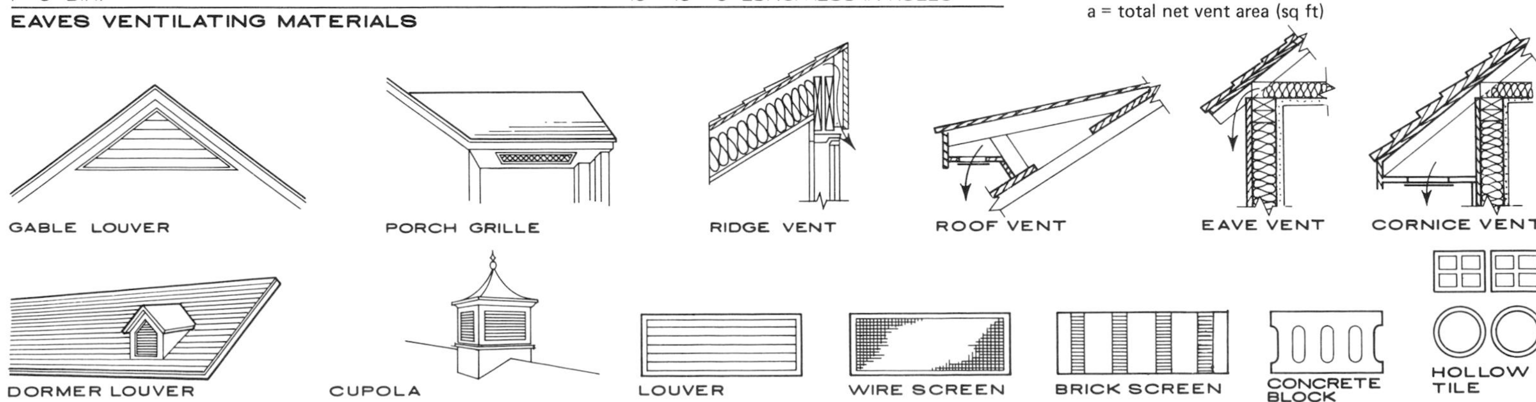
GABLE LOUVER
PORCH GRILLE
RIDGE VENT
ROOF VENT
EAVE VENT
CORNICE VENT
DORMER LOUVER
CUPOLA
LOUVER
WIRE SCREEN
BRICK SCREEN
CONCRETE BLOCK
HOLLOW TILE

TYPICAL ATTIC AND CRAWL SPACE VENT OPENINGS

David Metzger, Architect, CSI; Wilkes and Faulkner Associates; Washington, D.C.

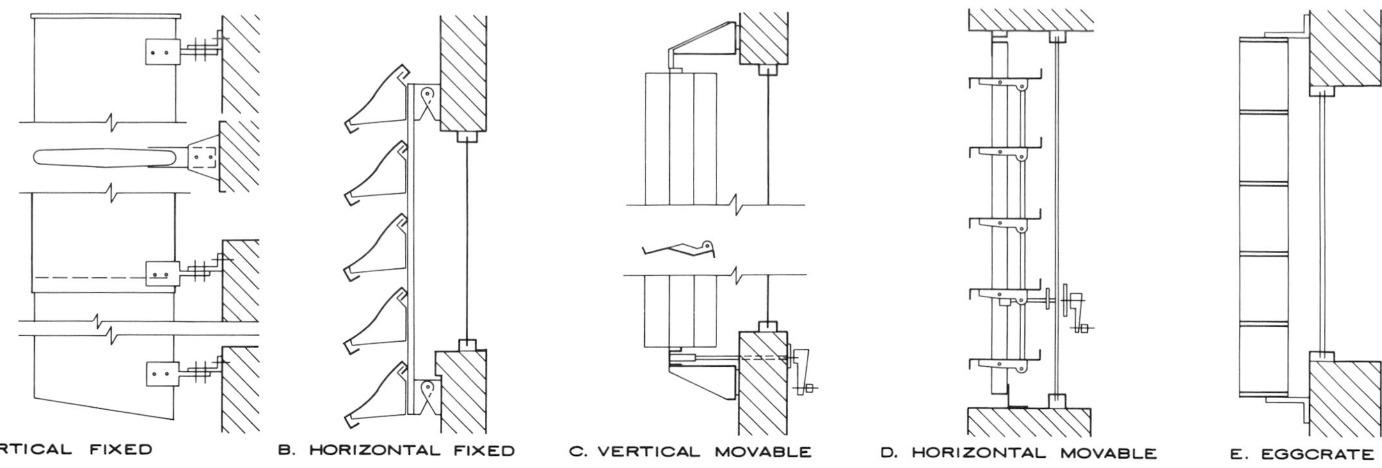

A. VERTICAL FIXED B. HORIZONTAL FIXED C. VERTICAL MOVABLE D. HORIZONTAL MOVABLE E. EGGCRATE

TYPICAL SUN SHADES AND CONTROLS

A. This device is effective on an east or west wall and can be attached at any degree of angle to facade. If slanted, it should incline to north. Fins are made in floor-to-floor lengths, capped at top and bottom, and telescoped top into bottom at intermediate levels.

B. This device is effective on any side of a building. Blades have a maximum length of 20 ft with supports of 6 ft on center.

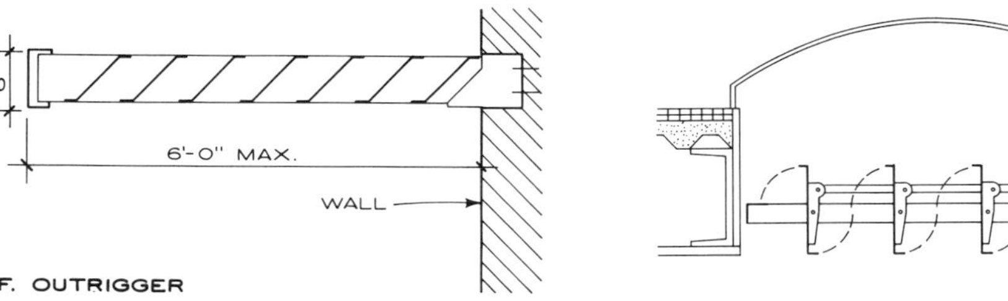
6"
6'-0" MAX.
WALL

F. OUTRIGGER

F. Overhangs are most effectively used on the south side of a building. Wall brackets are made of cast aluminum. Projections greater than 6 ft require structural support or hangers.

C. Used on east or west side of building. This type may interfere with view. Many models are available up to 27 in. wide and 12 ft high.

D. Although this is effective on any side of a building, it is the least restrictive to view when used on the south side. It is usually hinged at the head for emergency exit and window washing. Blades are 9 in. deep; maximum width is 6 ft.

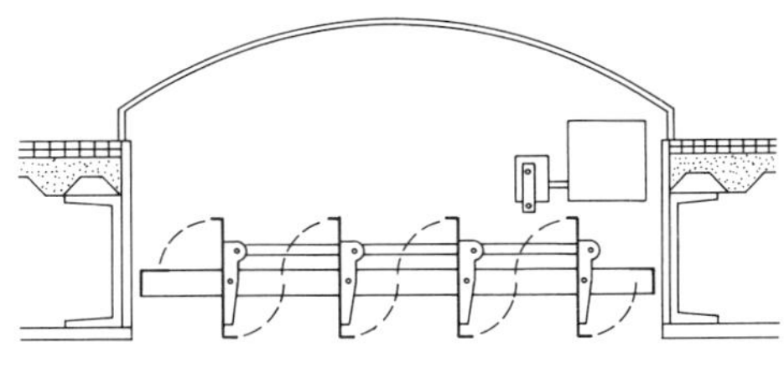

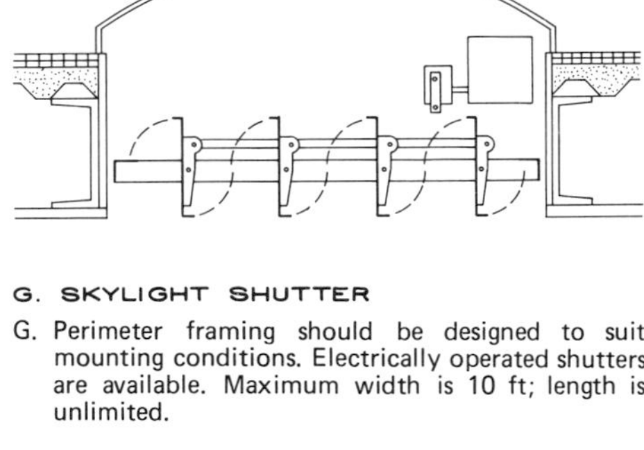

G. SKYLIGHT SHUTTER

G. Perimeter framing should be designed to suit mounting conditions. Electrically operated shutters are available. Maximum width is 10 ft; length is unlimited.

E. This type is very effective on southeast and southwest orientations. It is efficient in hot climates especially if bars can be tilted to more effective angles. All dimensions are variable according to desired function.

EXTERIOR SUN CONTROLS

The incidence of the sun's rays on a building transmits solar energy to the interior of the building. Since the heat gain through glass is particularly high, various forms of solar control for fenestration have been developed to reduce the use of mechanical equipment for cooling.

The most efficient of these is exterior shading, that is, avoiding the penetration of solar heat through the skin of the building. Exterior shading devices vary according to climate, orientation, and building function and are manufactured to suit specific conditions. They are strong design elements.

Sunshades (fixed horizontal or vertical fins, outriggers, and grills) shade glass completely or partially at critical times. Sun controls (movable horizontal or vertical fins) regulate the quantity of solar heat and light admitted through the glass, which is clear. Adjusting mechanisms can be manual or electric and can be automatically operated with time or photoelectric controls.

Aluminum, either sheet or extruded, is the standard material. Anodic and baked enamel coatings are available as finishes.

SLAT
STRINGER
45°
$22\frac{1}{2}$°
PROJECTED
VERTICAL

H. SHUTTER PANELS

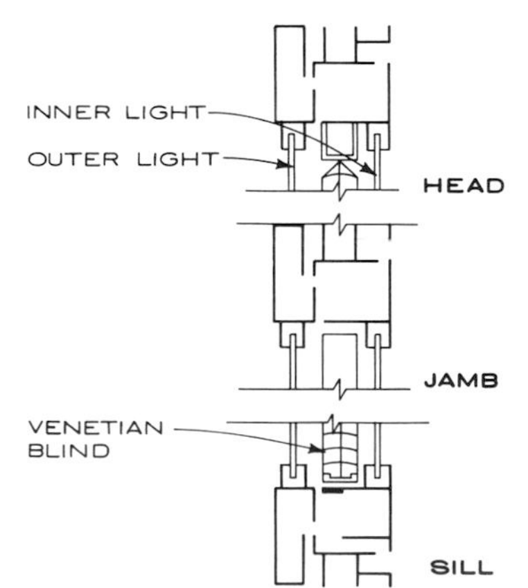
INNER LIGHT
OUTER LIGHT
HEAD
JAMB
VENETIAN BLIND
SILL

I. INTEGRAL VENETIAN BLINDS

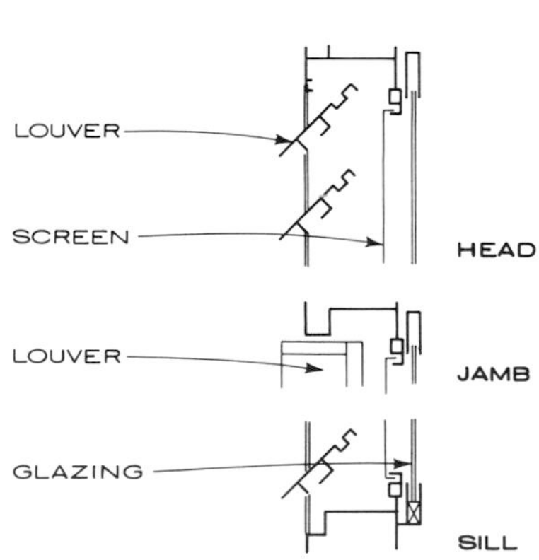
LOUVER
SCREEN
HEAD
LOUVER
JAMB
GLAZING
SILL

J. INTEGRAL HORIZONTAL SHADES

SPECIAL WINDOW TREATMENT

H. These panels are effective solar screens. The aluminum louvers are spaced to preserve the outside view and admit soft, diffused light while eliminating heat and glare. Horizontal slats snap onto stringer supports which can be easily attached to most structures.

I. This window type combines the thermal insulating values of dual glazing with the advantage of semi-external shading. An aluminum blind is provided between two pieces of glass, each in its own frame and each frame pivoted horizontally or vertically to make cleaning possible. The cavity between the two pieces of glass is ventilated to avoid condensation and to equalize air pressure.

The venetian blind can be tilted and, in some models, raised with controls on the interior window frame.

Window frames are constructed of aluminum, teak or pine.

J. A combination of exterior adjustable horizontal louvers and window frame, this window can be double hung, sliding, jalousie, or fixed. Louvers can be aluminum alloy extrusions, redwood, or glass.

Graham Davidson, Architect; Washington, D.C.

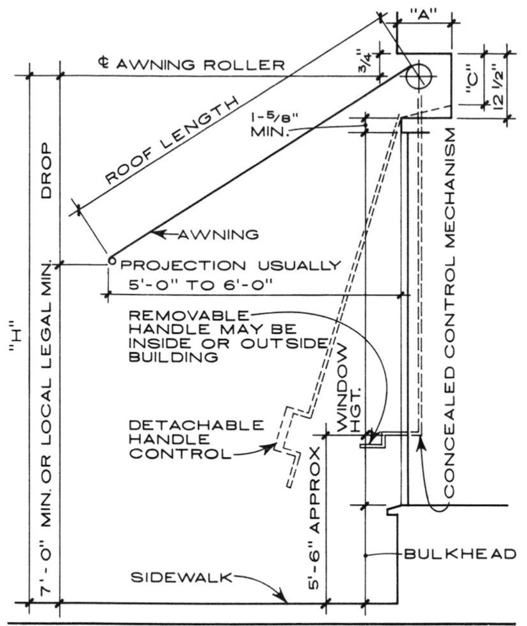
"A"
℄ AWNING ROLLER
3/4"
"C"
12 1/2"
ROOF LENGTH
1-5/8" MIN.
DROP
CONCEALED CONTROL MECHANISM
AWNING
PROJECTION USUALLY 5'-0" TO 6'-0"
REMOVABLE HANDLE MAY BE INSIDE OR OUTSIDE BUILDING
"H"
7'-0" MIN. OR LOCAL LEGAL MIN.
WINDOW HGT.
DETACHABLE HANDLE CONTROL
5'-6" APPROX.
BULKHEAD
SIDEWALK

DIAGRAMMATIC SECTION RECESSED BOX INSTALLATION

AWNING MATERIALS:

1. Canvas
2. Interlocking metal slats
   a. aluminum
   b. bronze
   c. stainless steel
3. Fiberglass

AWNING OPERATORS:

1. Detachable handle control
2. Gear box & shaft (concealed or exposed) with removable handle inside or outside of building
3. Electric control

AWNING BOX CLEARANCES:

Recessed box sizes	"H"	"A"	"B"	"C"
A. lateral arm type	9'–6" to 11'–0"	10"	10 1/2"	10"
	9'–6" to 12'–0"	10 1/2"	12"	10"
	9'–6" to 14'–0"	11"	13 1/2"	10"
B. outrigger arm type	varies	6'–2"	6'–2"	6'–2"

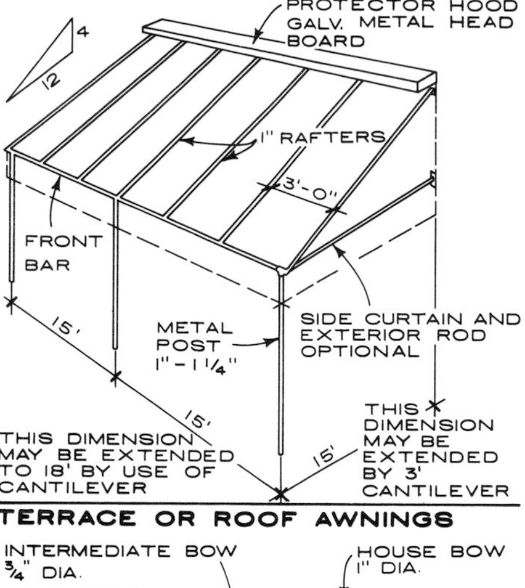
4
12
PROTECTOR HOOD GALV. METAL HEAD BOARD
1" RAFTERS
3'-0"
FRONT BAR
METAL POST 1"-1 1/4"
SIDE CURTAIN AND EXTERIOR ROD OPTIONAL
15'
15'
THIS DIMENSION MAY BE EXTENDED TO 18' BY USE OF CANTILEVER
THIS DIMENSION MAY BE EXTENDED BY 3' CANTILEVER
15'

TERRACE OR ROOF AWNINGS

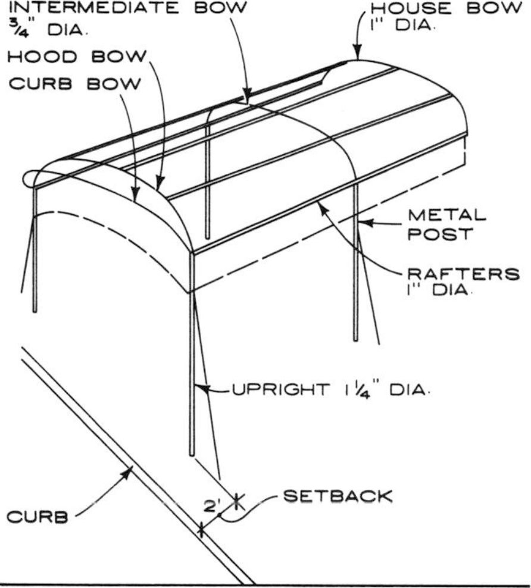
INTERMEDIATE BOW 3/4" DIA.
HOUSE BOW 1" DIA.
HOOD BOW
CURB BOW
METAL POST
RAFTERS 1" DIA.
UPRIGHT 1 1/4" DIA.
CURB
2'
SETBACK

CANOPIES - LOW CURVED BOW SHOWN

TERRACE OR ROOF AWNINGS

To provide complete sun protection and shade, the overall length of the awning bar should extend 3 in. past the glass line on both sides. For proper sunshade protection, awnings should project at least as far forward from the face of the window as the bottom of the window is below the front bar of the awning.

The wall measurement of an awning is the distance down the face of the building from the point where the awning attaches to the face of the building (or from the center of the roller in the case of the roller type awning).

The projection of an awning is the distance from the face of the building to the front bar of the awning in its correct projected position.

Right and left of an awning are your right and left as you are facing the awning looking into the building.

Framework consists of galvanized steel pipe, with non-rattling fittings. Awning is lace-on type canvas with rope reinforced eave. Protector hood is galvanized sheet metal or either bronze, copper, or aluminum.

Sizes of members should be checked by calculation for conditions not similar to those shown on this page.

Consult local building code for limitations on height and setback.

COVERED WALKWAYS

Covered walkways are available with aluminum fascia and soffit panels in a number of profiles. The fascia panels are supported with pipe columns and steel or aluminum structural members if necessary. Panels can cantilever up to 30% of span. Canopy designs can be supported from above.

Another method of providing covered exterior space is with stressed membrane structures. Using highly tensile synthetic fabric and cable in collaboration with compression members, usually metal, dynamic and versatile tentlike coverings can be created. Membrane structures are especially suited to temporary installations.

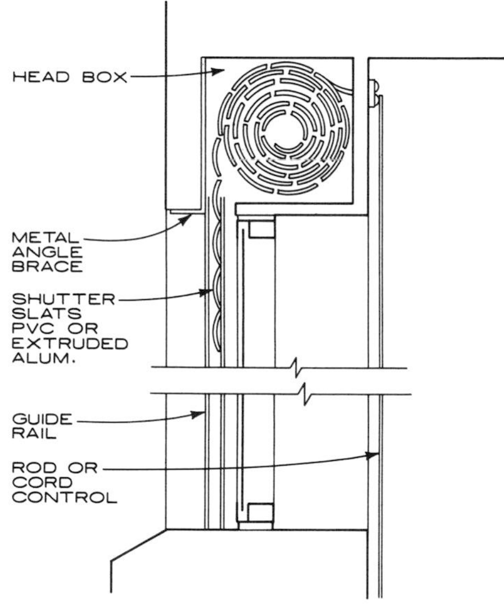
HEAD BOX
METAL ANGLE BRACE
SHUTTER SLATS PVC OR EXTRUDED ALUM.
GUIDE RAIL
ROD OR CORD CONTROL

NOTE

Rolling shutters provide sun control not only by shading windows from direct sun rays but also by way of two dead airspaces—one between shutter and window, the other within the shutter extrusions to serve as insulation. The dead airspaces work as well in winter to prevent the escape of heat from the interior. In addition, shutters are useful as privacy and security measures. They can be installed in new or existing construction and are manufactured in standard window sizes.

ROLLING SHUTTERS

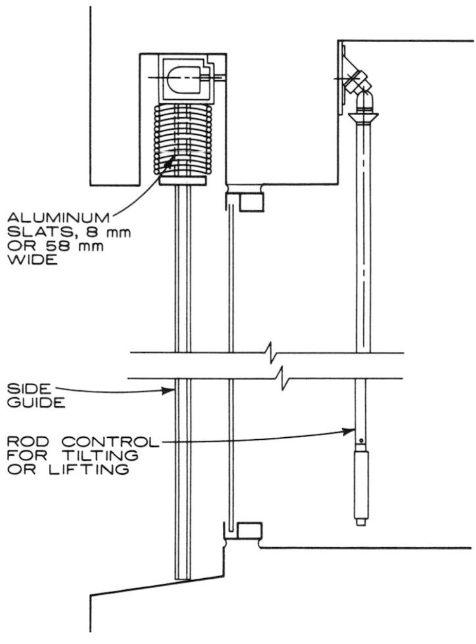
ALUMINUM SLATS, 8 mm OR 58 mm WIDE
SIDE GUIDE
ROD CONTROL FOR TILTING OR LIFTING

NOTE

External blinds protect the building interior from solar gain and glare, but can be raised partially or fully to the head when not needed. Manual or electric control is from inside the building.

EXTERNAL VENETIAN BLINDS

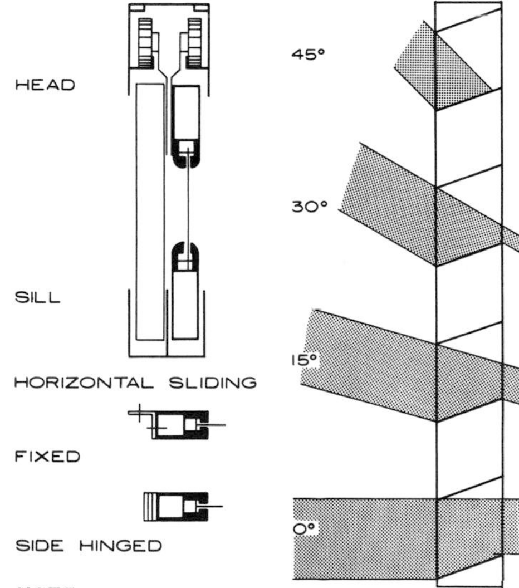
HEAD
SILL
HORIZONTAL SLIDING
FIXED
SIDE HINGED
45°
30°
15°
0°

NOTE

These miniature external louvers shade windows from direct sunlight and glare while allowing a high degree of visibility, light, ventilation, insect protection, and daytime privacy. Much like a woven metal fabric, they are not strong architectural elements but present a uniform appearance in the areas covered. The solar screen is installed in aluminum frames and can be adapted to suit most applications.

SOLAR SCREEN SIZES

MATERIAL	LOUVERS	TILT	VERTICAL SPACING	SIZE (WIDTHS)
Aluminum	17"	17°	1" o.c.	18"–48"
Bronze	17", 23"	20°	1/2" o.c.	Up to 72 1/2"

Aluminum screens are available in black or light green. Bronze screens come in black only.

SOLAR SCREENS

Graham Davidson, Architect; Washington, D.C.

STRUCTURAL CONSIDERATIONS

Earth sheltered structures are usually deeper and the loads greater than for basements. Hydrostatic and compaction loads add to the triangular soil loading on walls (Figure 1). Floors below water level are subjected to uplift of 62.4 psf per foot depth below water level and may require special design (Figure 2) to resist the load and to provide a uniform support plane for the waterproof membrane. Roof live loads in urban areas may include public assembly at 100 psf, in addition to soil, plants, and furnishings. Saturated soils and gravel are usually taken at 120 pcf. Tree loads are related to species and size. Tree weights can be estimated for preliminary design by the logarithmic relation

$$\log(\text{wt}) = x + 2.223 \log(\text{dia.}) + 0.339 \log(\text{ht})$$

where (wt) is in pounds, (dia.) is trunk diameter in inches at breast height, and (ht) is in feet. Forest trees range in x from 0.6 for fir to 0.8 for birch, with spruce and maple at about 0.7. The equation has not been tested for lawn trees, so it must be used with caution. Site investigation is important to determine soil bearing and drainage capacity, shearing strength, and water level. Hillside designs produce unbalanced lateral loads that may recommend interior wall buttressing.

LANDSCAPE CONSIDERATIONS

Rooftop plantings require adequate soil depth (Figure 3), underdrainage, and irrigation. Lightweight soil mixes reduce roof loads, but are not suitable under foot. Highly trafficked roofs may require special sandy soil mixes used for golf greens and athletic fields to resist compaction and root damage. Plant materials should be drought-resistant and hardier than normal, since roof soil may be colder than lawn soil.

DRAINAGE AND MOISTURE CONSIDERATIONS

Footing drains draw down the water table and prevent ponding in the backfill. Exterior location is more effective, but is subject to abuse during backfilling and to subsequent settlement. Underslab drains are easier to install correctly and are less likely to fail. Unless both are used, weep holes should be installed through the footing to connect underfloor and perimeter systems. A polyethylene sheet keeps water vapor from entering the slab, and through-joint flashing prevents capillary transfer of soil moisture through the footing to the wall. The waterproofing system must be suited to the structural system and the surface condition of the substrate. Plastic waterstops complicate joint forming and may conceal the source of leaks, disadvantages that usually outweigh whatever benefit they may provide. Chemical (e.g., bentonite base) waterstops do not have these disadvantages.

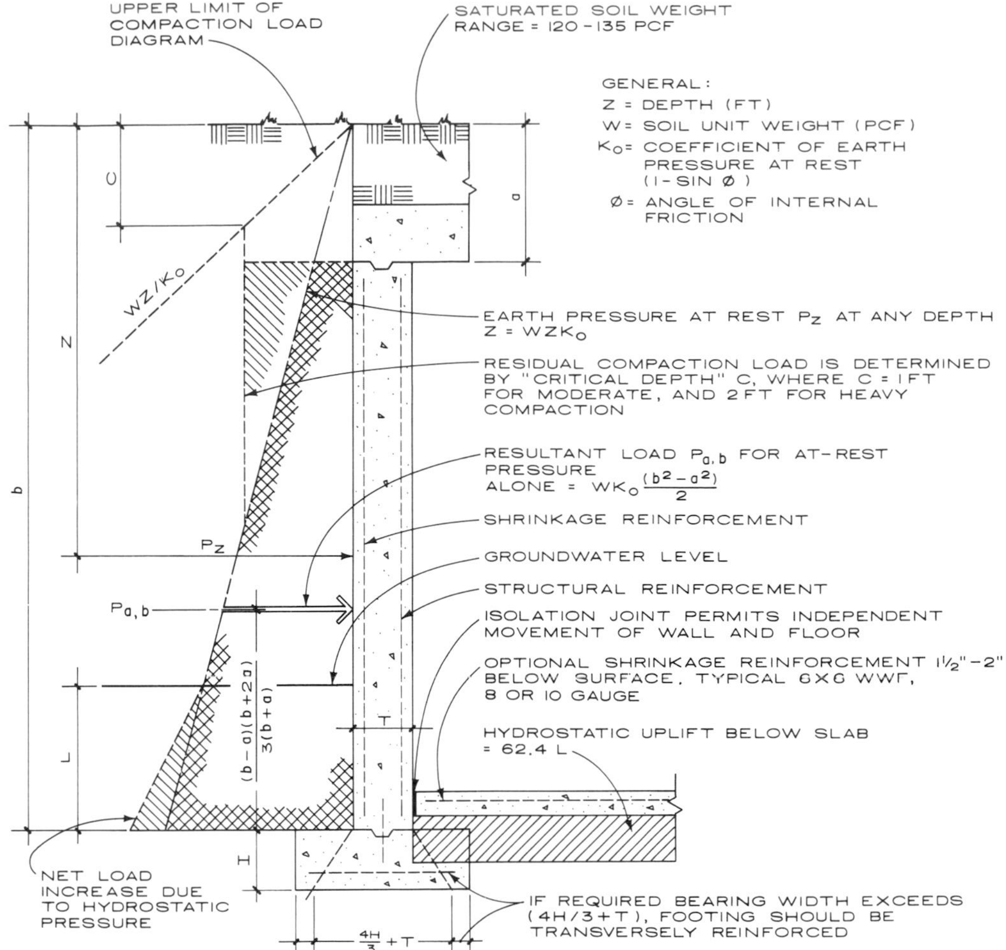
UPPER LIMIT OF COMPACTION LOAD DIAGRAM
SATURATED SOIL WEIGHT RANGE = 120 - 135 PCF
GENERAL:
Z = DEPTH (FT)
W = SOIL UNIT WEIGHT (PCF)
K_O = COEFFICIENT OF EARTH PRESSURE AT REST (1 - SIN Ø)
Ø = ANGLE OF INTERNAL FRICTION
C
a
N
b
L
H
T
WZ/K_O
P_Z
$P_{a,b}$
$\frac{(b-a)(b+2a)}{3(b+a)}$
EARTH PRESSURE AT REST P_Z AT ANY DEPTH $Z = WZK_O$
RESIDUAL COMPACTION LOAD IS DETERMINED BY "CRITICAL DEPTH" C, WHERE C = 1 FT FOR MODERATE, AND 2 FT FOR HEAVY COMPACTION
RESULTANT LOAD $P_{a,b}$ FOR AT-REST PRESSURE ALONE = $WK_O\frac{(b^2-a^2)}{2}$
SHRINKAGE REINFORCEMENT
GROUNDWATER LEVEL
STRUCTURAL REINFORCEMENT
ISOLATION JOINT PERMITS INDEPENDENT MOVEMENT OF WALL AND FLOOR
OPTIONAL SHRINKAGE REINFORCEMENT 1½"-2" BELOW SURFACE, TYPICAL 6X6 WWF, 8 OR 10 GAUGE
HYDROSTATIC UPLIFT BELOW SLAB = 62.4 L
NET LOAD INCREASE DUE TO HYDROSTATIC PRESSURE
IF REQUIRED BEARING WIDTH EXCEEDS (4H/3+T), FOOTING SHOULD BE TRANSVERSELY REINFORCED
$\frac{4H}{3}+T$

FIGURE 1 COMPOSITE LOAD DIAGRAM

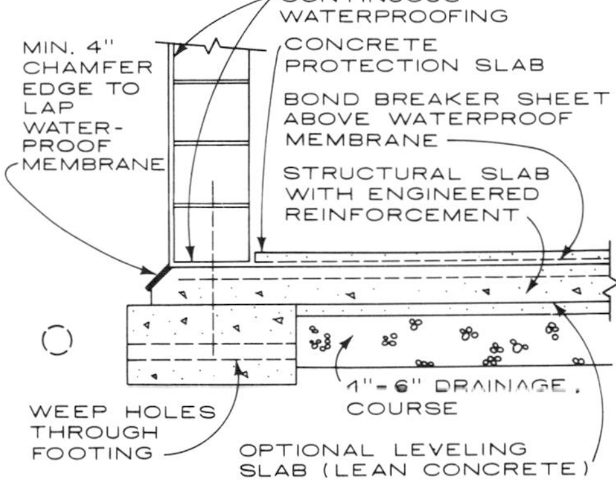
CONTINUOUS WATERPROOFING
MIN. 4" CHAMFER EDGE TO LAP WATER-PROOF MEMBRANE
CONCRETE PROTECTION SLAB
BOND BREAKER SHEET ABOVE WATERPROOF MEMBRANE
STRUCTURAL SLAB WITH ENGINEERED REINFORCEMENT
WEEP HOLES THROUGH FOOTING
4"-6" DRAINAGE COURSE
OPTIONAL LEVELING SLAB (LEAN CONCRETE)

FIGURE 2 REINFORCED SLAB (GERMAN APPROACH)

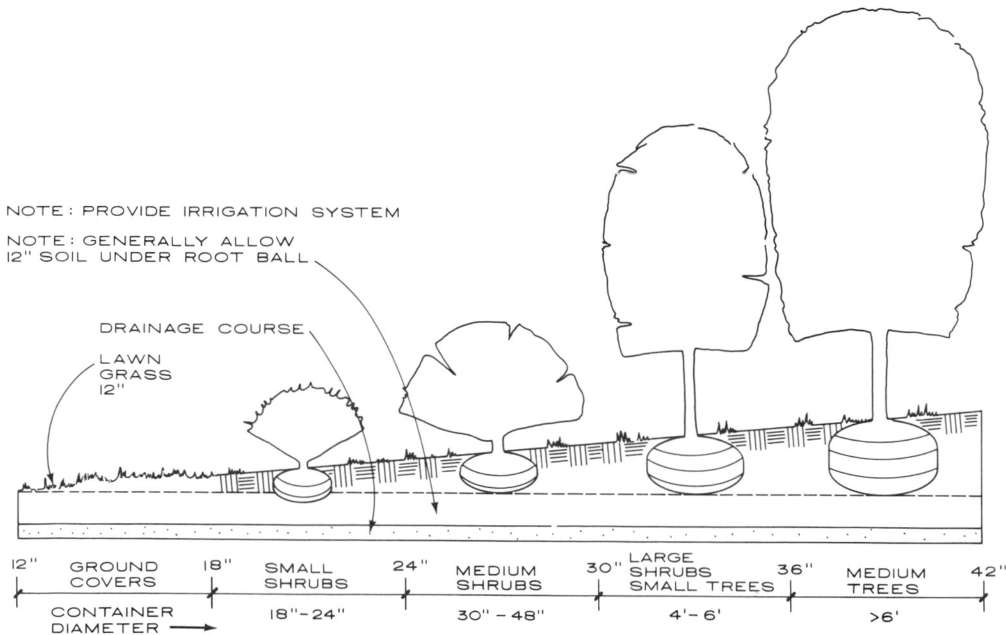
NOTE: PROVIDE IRRIGATION SYSTEM
NOTE: GENERALLY ALLOW 12" SOIL UNDER ROOT BALL
DRAINAGE COURSE
LAWN GRASS 12"
12"
GROUND COVERS
18"
SMALL SHRUBS
24"
MEDIUM SHRUBS
30"
LARGE SHRUBS SMALL TREES
36"
MEDIUM TREES
42"
CONTAINER DIAMETER
18"-24"
30" - 48"
4'-6'
>6'

FIGURE 3 PLANT SOIL COVER REQUIREMENTS

Kenneth Labs; New Haven, Connecticut

RECOMMENDED REFERENCES

1. B. Anderson, "Waterproofing and the Design Professional," *The Construction Specifier*, March 1986, pp. 84–97.
2. J. Carmody and R. Sterling, *Earth Sheltered Housing Design*, 2nd Ed., Van Nostrand Reinhold, New York, 1985, 350 pp.
3. R. Sterling, W. Farnan, J. Carmody, *Earth Sheltered Residential Design Manual*, Van Nostrand Reinhold, New York, 1982, 252 pp.
4. U.S. Navy, *Earth Sheltered Buildings*, NAVFAC Design Manual 1.4, U.S. Government Printing Office, 1983.
5. Moreland Associates, *Earth Covered Buildings: An Exploratory Analysis for Hazard and Energy Performance*, Federal Emergency Management Agency, 1981.

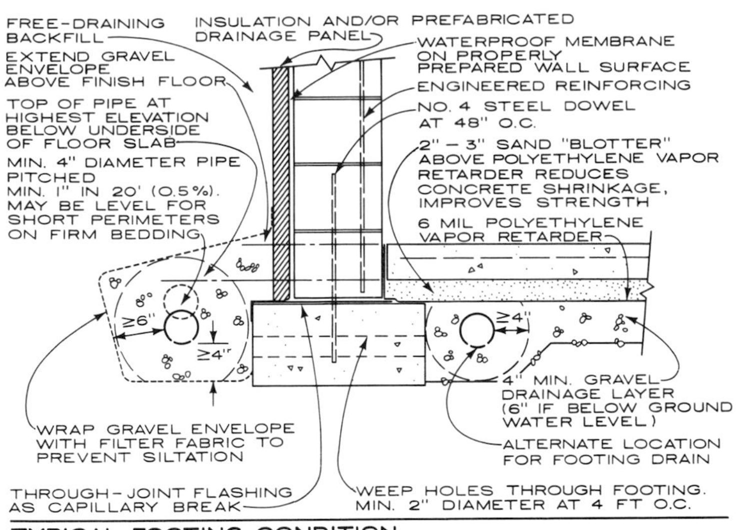
FREE-DRAINING BACKFILL
INSULATION AND/OR PREFABRICATED DRAINAGE PANEL
EXTEND GRAVEL ENVELOPE ABOVE FINISH FLOOR
WATERPROOF MEMBRANE ON PROPERLY PREPARED WALL SURFACE
ENGINEERED REINFORCING
TOP OF PIPE AT HIGHEST ELEVATION BELOW UNDERSIDE OF FLOOR SLAB
NO. 4 STEEL DOWEL AT 48" O.C.
MIN. 4" DIAMETER PIPE PITCHED MIN. 1" IN 20' (0.5%). MAY BE LEVEL FOR SHORT PERIMETERS ON FIRM BEDDING
2" – 3" SAND "BLOTTER" ABOVE POLYETHYLENE VAPOR RETARDER REDUCES CONCRETE SHRINKAGE, IMPROVES STRENGTH
6 MIL POLYETHYLENE VAPOR RETARDER
≥6"
≥4"
≥4"
4" MIN. GRAVEL DRAINAGE LAYER (6" IF BELOW GROUND WATER LEVEL)
WRAP GRAVEL ENVELOPE WITH FILTER FABRIC TO PREVENT SILTATION
ALTERNATE LOCATION FOR FOOTING DRAIN
THROUGH-JOINT FLASHING AS CAPILLARY BREAK
WEEP HOLES THROUGH FOOTING. MIN. 2" DIAMETER AT 4 FT O.C.

TYPICAL FOOTING CONDITION

FORM "GUTTER" WITH POLYETHYLENE SHEET. PROVIDE FOLDS TO ALLOW SETTLEMENT
4" PERFORATED PIPE PITCHED TO DRAIN
1" – 2"
EXTEND POLYETHYLENE SHEET OVER BACKFILL MIN. 4'
OPTIONAL POLYETHYLENE SLIP SHEET
RIGID INSULATION WITH OPTIONAL TAPER OF R-2 PER FOOT
SYNTHETIC DRAINAGE PANEL COUPLED TO LOWER ROOF DRAIN LAYER
WATERPROOFING OVER WALL SURFACE PREPARED AS REQUIRED BY MANUFACTURER
SYNTHETIC FABRIC FILTER
EARTH COVER TO DEPTH DESIRED (USUALLY 12" MIN.)
PRIMARY DRAINAGE LAYER OF PEA GRAVEL, MIN. 4" THICK
10-20 MIL POLYETHYLENE "WATERSHED" SHINGLE-LAPPED
RIGID INSULATION, BUTTED
SECONDARY (OPTIONAL, BUT PREFERRED) DRAINAGE LAYER, 2" MIN.
WATERPROOFING WITH PROTECTION BOARD RECOMMENDED BY MANUFACTURER
POURED CONCRETE TOPPING SLAB FINISHED TO WATERPROOF MEMBRANE MANUFACTURER'S SPECIFICATIONS
ENGINEERED ROOF DECK AND SYSTEM DETAILS
ENGINEERED REINFORCED WALL SYSTEM
NOTE: DECK, INSULATION WATERSHED, AND GROUND SURFACE ALL SLOPED MIN. 2% (1" IN 4') TO DRAIN TO COLLECTION DEVICES

ROOF EDGE DETAIL

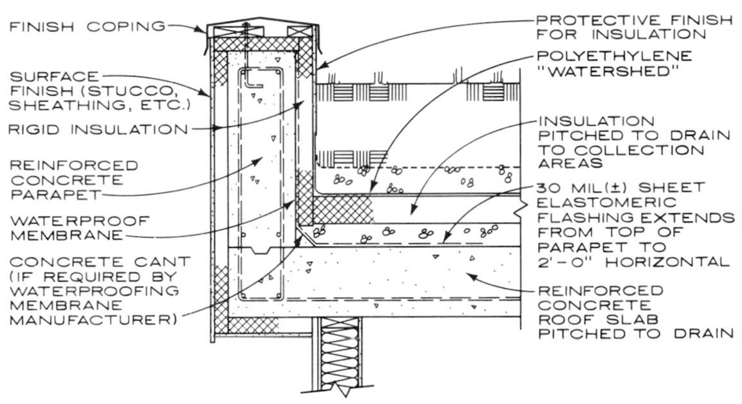
FINISH COPING
SURFACE FINISH (STUCCO, SHEATHING, ETC.)
RIGID INSULATION
REINFORCED CONCRETE PARAPET
WATERPROOF MEMBRANE
CONCRETE CANT (IF REQUIRED BY WATERPROOFING MEMBRANE MANUFACTURER)
PROTECTIVE FINISH FOR INSULATION
POLYETHYLENE "WATERSHED"
INSULATION PITCHED TO DRAIN TO COLLECTION AREAS
30 MIL(±) SHEET ELASTOMERIC FLASHING EXTENDS FROM TOP OF PARAPET TO 2'-0" HORIZONTAL
REINFORCED CONCRETE ROOF SLAB PITCHED TO DRAIN

CONCRETE PERIMETER PARAPET

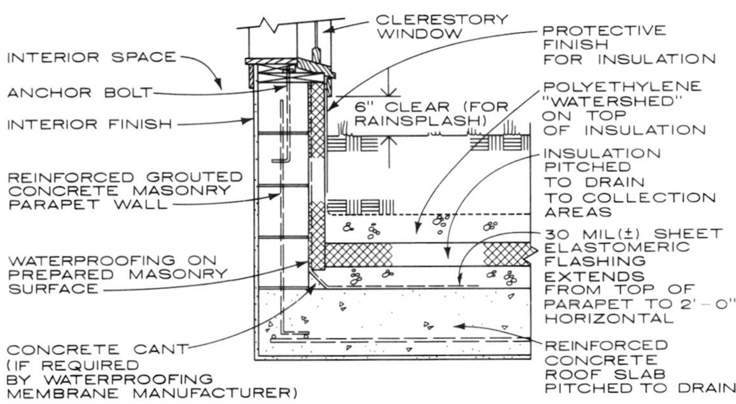
INTERIOR SPACE
ANCHOR BOLT
INTERIOR FINISH
REINFORCED GROUTED CONCRETE MASONRY PARAPET WALL
WATERPROOFING ON PREPARED MASONRY SURFACE
CONCRETE CANT (IF REQUIRED BY WATERPROOFING MEMBRANE MANUFACTURER)
CLERESTORY WINDOW
6" CLEAR (FOR RAINSPLASH)
PROTECTIVE FINISH FOR INSULATION
POLYETHYLENE "WATERSHED" ON TOP OF INSULATION
INSULATION PITCHED TO DRAIN TO COLLECTION AREAS
30 MIL(±) SHEET ELASTOMERIC FLASHING EXTENDS FROM TOP OF PARAPET TO 2'-0" HORIZONTAL
REINFORCED CONCRETE ROOF SLAB PITCHED TO DRAIN

MASONRY INTERIOR PARAPET

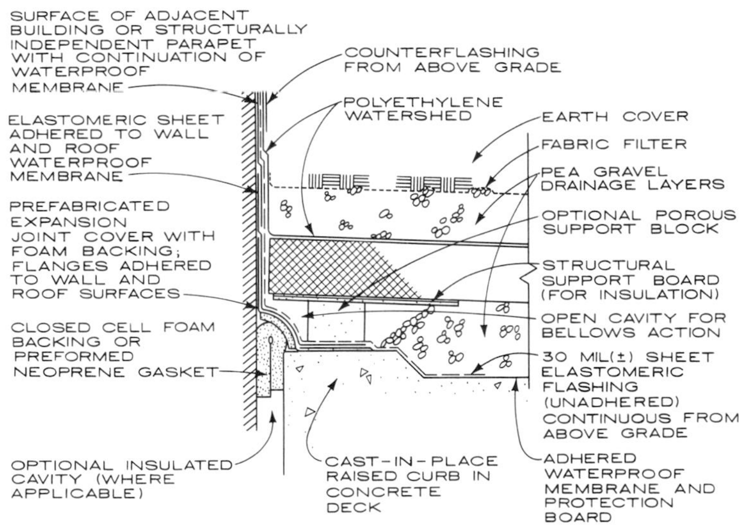
SURFACE OF ADJACENT BUILDING OR STRUCTURALLY INDEPENDENT PARAPET WITH CONTINUATION OF WATERPROOF MEMBRANE
COUNTERFLASHING FROM ABOVE GRADE
ELASTOMERIC SHEET ADHERED TO WALL AND ROOF WATERPROOF MEMBRANE
POLYETHYLENE WATERSHED
EARTH COVER
FABRIC FILTER
PEA GRAVEL DRAINAGE LAYERS
PREFABRICATED EXPANSION JOINT COVER WITH FOAM BACKING; FLANGES ADHERED TO WALL AND ROOF SURFACES
OPTIONAL POROUS SUPPORT BLOCK
STRUCTURAL SUPPORT BOARD (FOR INSULATION)
CLOSED CELL FOAM BACKING OR PREFORMED NEOPRENE GASKET
OPEN CAVITY FOR BELLOWS ACTION
30 MIL(±) SHEET ELASTOMERIC FLASHING (UNADHERED) CONTINUOUS FROM ABOVE GRADE
OPTIONAL INSULATED CAVITY (WHERE APPLICABLE)
CAST-IN-PLACE RAISED CURB IN CONCRETE DECK
ADHERED WATERPROOF MEMBRANE AND PROTECTION BOARD

FLEXIBLE JOINT AT ROOF EDGE

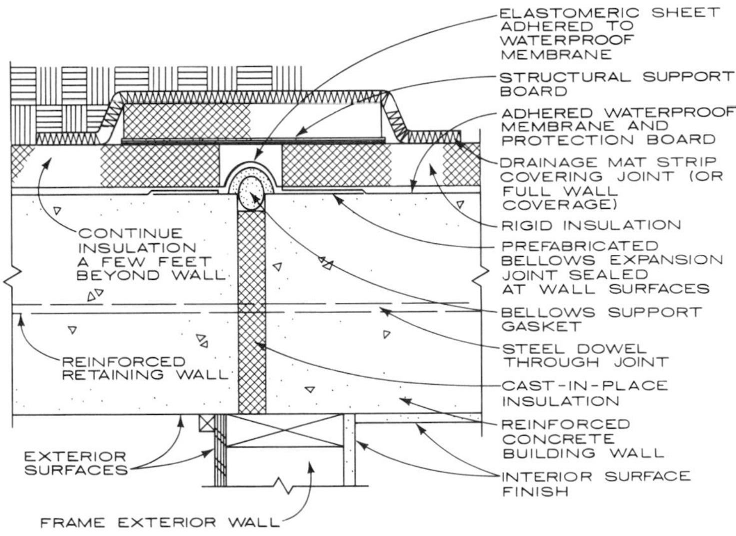
ELASTOMERIC SHEET ADHERED TO WATERPROOF MEMBRANE
STRUCTURAL SUPPORT BOARD
ADHERED WATERPROOF MEMBRANE AND PROTECTION BOARD
DRAINAGE MAT STRIP COVERING JOINT (OR FULL WALL COVERAGE)
RIGID INSULATION
CONTINUE INSULATION A FEW FEET BEYOND WALL
PREFABRICATED BELLOWS EXPANSION JOINT SEALED AT WALL SURFACES
BELLOWS SUPPORT GASKET
STEEL DOWEL THROUGH JOINT
REINFORCED RETAINING WALL
CAST-IN-PLACE INSULATION
REINFORCED CONCRETE BUILDING WALL
EXTERIOR SURFACES
INTERIOR SURFACE FINISH
FRAME EXTERIOR WALL

THERMAL BREAK AT RETAINING WING WALL (PLAN)

THERMAL CONSIDERATIONS

Exterior insulation keeps walls and roofs warm and at a stable temperature. This minimizes dimensional change and indoor surface condensation and keeps elastomeric waterproofing pliable. Exterior insulation consumes no indoor space, but it is sometimes attacked by rodents and insects. Extruded polystyrene is usually preferred for its resistance to water absorption. Roof insulation should be placed within the drainage layer so that it does not sit in water or impede drainage. Gravel is not always needed under the insulation, especially if the insulation is pitched to drain and is covered with polyethylene sheets. All seepage planes should be sloped a minimum of 1 in. in 4 ft.

Soil has little thermal resistance, so roof winter thermal performance depends largely on added insulation. Heat loss from earth-covered roofs is nearly constant at

$$Q = (T_1 - T_0)/R$$

where Q is heat loss in Btu/ft^2[hr]°F, T_1 and T_0 are indoor and outdoor air temperatures (°F) averaged over the preceding few days, and R is the thermal resistance of the overall roof assembly. Wet soil has an R value of slightly less than 1.0 per foot thickness.

Kenneth Labs; New Haven, Connecticut

TYPES OF UNDERGROUND SPACE

Commercial underground buildings can be classified in a number of ways:

1. Cut-and-cover buildings: Buildings relatively near the surface. The structure supports earth loads from above and on the sides. The term "earth-sheltered" usually refers to cut-and-cover buildings. Also, distinctions can be made between buildings that are fully beneath existing grade and those that are bermed.
2. Mined space: Building area is created by excavating in self-supporting soil or rock.

Underground building type is determined primarily by the site, topography, and program requirements. The ability to create mined space is determined by local soils and geology. Further classification of underground buildings often is based on the surface opening. Categories include windowless chambers, atrium designs, and elevational designs (windows along a single wall).

GENERAL ADVANTAGES

Some of the many advantages associated with underground buildings are:

1. Limited visual impact of the building in natural or historical settings.
2. Preservation of surface open space above the building in dense urban or campus settings.
3. Efficient land use by extending buildings beyond normal setbacks or by building into otherwise unbuildable slopes.
4. Environmental benefits such as reducing water runoff and preserving or increasing plant and animal habitat.
5. Protection from tornadoes, storms, and fire.
6. Provision of civil defense shelters.
7. Increased security against vandalism and theft.
8. Insulation from noise and vibration, permitting some incompatible uses to be located in closer proximity.
9. Reduced exterior maintenance.
10. Reduced construction costs for exterior finishing materials and mechanical equipment.
11. Reduced life-cycle costs of the building based on reduced heating, cooling, maintenance, and insurance costs.

ENERGY-RELATED ADVANTAGES AND LIMITATIONS

In most climates underground buildings have characteristics that reduce heating and cooling loads when compared with above-ground structures. Advantages from improved energy efficiency include:

1. Reduced winter heat loss because of moderate below-grade temperatures and reduced cold infiltration.
2. Reduced summer heat gain especially when earth-bermed walls are planted with grass or ground cover. Peak cooling loads are reduced.
3. Direct cooling from earth in summer.
4. Daily and seasonal temperature fluctuations are reduced, resulting in smaller HVAC equipment sizes.
5. Large mass below-grade concrete buildings can store sun heat and off-peak electric power.

The U.S. deep-ground temperature map illustrates variations in the below-grade environment. At about 25 ft. and deeper, temperatures of undisturbed ground remain approximately constant. Ground temperatures around an in-ground building rise. Buildings nearer to the surface initially experience some temperature variations that stabilize in time.

Energy-conserving benefits are affected by climate, ground temperatures, degree of exposure, building depth, mechanical system design, and building use. Buildings requiring high levels of mechanical ventilation are less likely to benefit from below-grade placement than buildings with low to moderate ventilation requirements. Maximum energy benefits are derived from building uses such as cold storage, or precision temperature and humidity conditions control (i.e., laboratories, libraries, and special materials storage).

DISADVANTAGES

Underground building limitations present a number of disadvantages over conventional construction. Most of these can be overcome by design. Among the limitations are:

1. Limited opportunities for natural light and exterior views;
2. Limited entrance and service access;
3. Limited view of the building and its entrance;
4. Increased costs on sites that have water tables, bedrock near the surface, or adjacent buildings with shallow foundations;
5. Increased construction costs for heavier structures (especially if earth is placed on the roof), and high-quality waterproofing systems.

SPECIAL DESIGN CONCERNS

Entrance design: Entrances should be visible and clear from the exterior. Descending may occur inside or outside the building. If possible, large spaces and natural light should be provided in the entrance area. Various underground building entrance approaches are shown in drawings at the right.

Natural light and view: A primary concern in designing underground buildings is offsetting the possible negative psychological and physiological effects of windowless environments. In addition to admitting sunlight, windows provide orientation, variety, and a similarity to above-ground space. As shown in drawings at the right conventional windows, skylights, and courtyards are effective means of providing light and view in near-surface underground buildings. Where these techniques are inadequate, beamed or reflected daylighting systems may be explored.

Interior design: In underground spaces with limited opportunities for natural light and view, building interior should be organized to provide maximum exposure to light and view for the greatest number of users at each opportunity. Design techniques include large interior courtyards, high ceilings, glass walls, plants, warm colors, variety in design and lighting, and full spectrum artificial lights.

ENTRY

ENTRANCE INTO A BERMED STRUCTURE

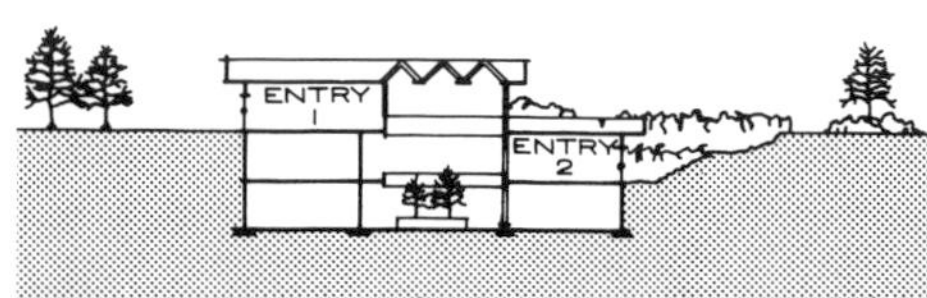
ENTRY 1
ENTRY 2

ENTRANCES AT GRADE AND SUBGRADE LEVELS

BUILDING ENTRANCE DESIGN

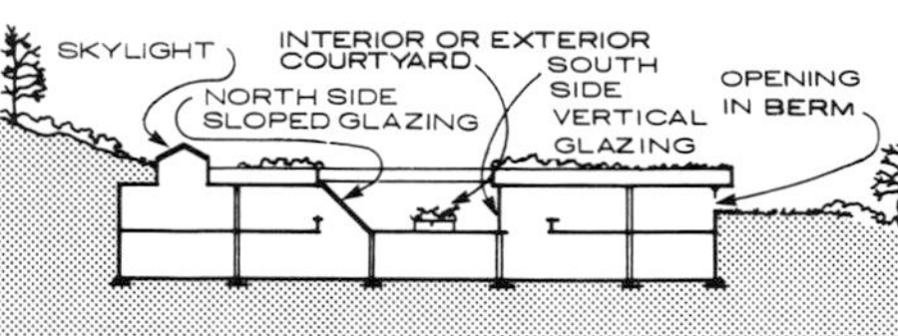
SKYLIGHT
INTERIOR OR EXTERIOR COURTYARD
SOUTH SIDE VERTICAL GLAZING
OPENING IN BERM
NORTH SIDE SLOPED GLAZING

BUILDING SET INTO A SLOPING SITE

NATURAL LIGHT AND VIEW

INSULATION AND WATERPROOFING

Generally, waterproofing should be applied to all below-grade roofs and walls. When a building floor is below the water table level, waterproofing must be placed beneath the floor as well. On below-grade roofs and walls, waterproofing applied directly on the substrate (concrete, wood) is recommended. Insulation and drainage layers then can be placed over the waterproofing (see roof detail below).

When insulation is used in a below-grade application outside of the waterproofing, two characteristics are crucial:

1. Ability to resist structural loads from the earth (this limits selection to rigid board products).
2. Ability to maintain R-value and to resist degradation during constant and severe exposure to water and moisture.

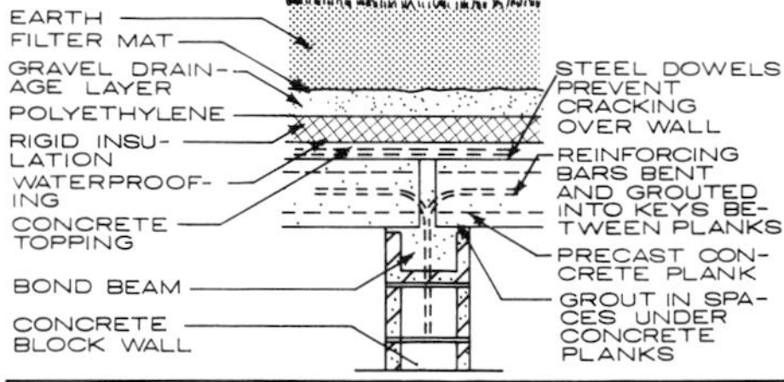
EARTH
FILTER MAT
GRAVEL DRAINAGE LAYER
POLYETHYLENE
RIGID INSULATION
WATERPROOFING
CONCRETE TOPPING
BOND BEAM
CONCRETE BLOCK WALL
STEEL DOWELS PREVENT CRACKING OVER WALL
REINFORCING BARS BENT AND GROUTED INTO KEYS BETWEEN PLANKS
PRECAST CONCRETE PLANK
GROUT IN SPACES UNDER CONCRETE PLANKS

ROOF DETAIL

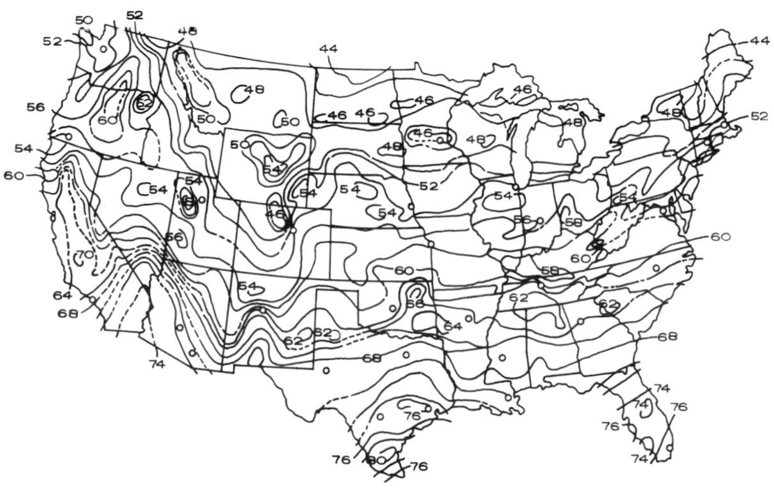

U.S. DEEP-GROUND TEMPERATURE MAP

SUGGESTED AMOUNTS OF BELOW-GRADE INSULATION

HEATING/COOLING DEGREE DAYS (BASE; 65°F)	SUGGESTED RANGE OF BELOW-GRADE INSULATION[1] ROOFS AND[2] UPPER WALL	LOWER WALL[3]	REMOTE FLOOR[4] AREAS
8,000–11,000/0–500	R-20–R-40	R-5–R-20	0–R-5
5,000–8,000/500–1,500	R-20–R-30	R-5–R-10	0–R-5
2,000–5,000/1,500–2,500	R-10–R-20	0–R-5	0
over 2,000/under 2,000	R-10–R-20	0	0

NOTES

1. This table is a general guide only and assumes an earth cover thickness in the range of 12 in. to 30 in. for the earth-covered roof.
2. Earth-covered roof with 12 in. to 30 in. of cover and walls within 8 ft of the ground surface.
3. Earth-covered wall surfaces farther than 8 ft from the ground surface.
4. Floor areas remote (i.e., more than 10 ft from the ground surface) not used as a solar storage area or for heat distribution.

David Eijadi, AIA, and Kyle Williams; BRW, Inc.; Minneapolis, Minnesota

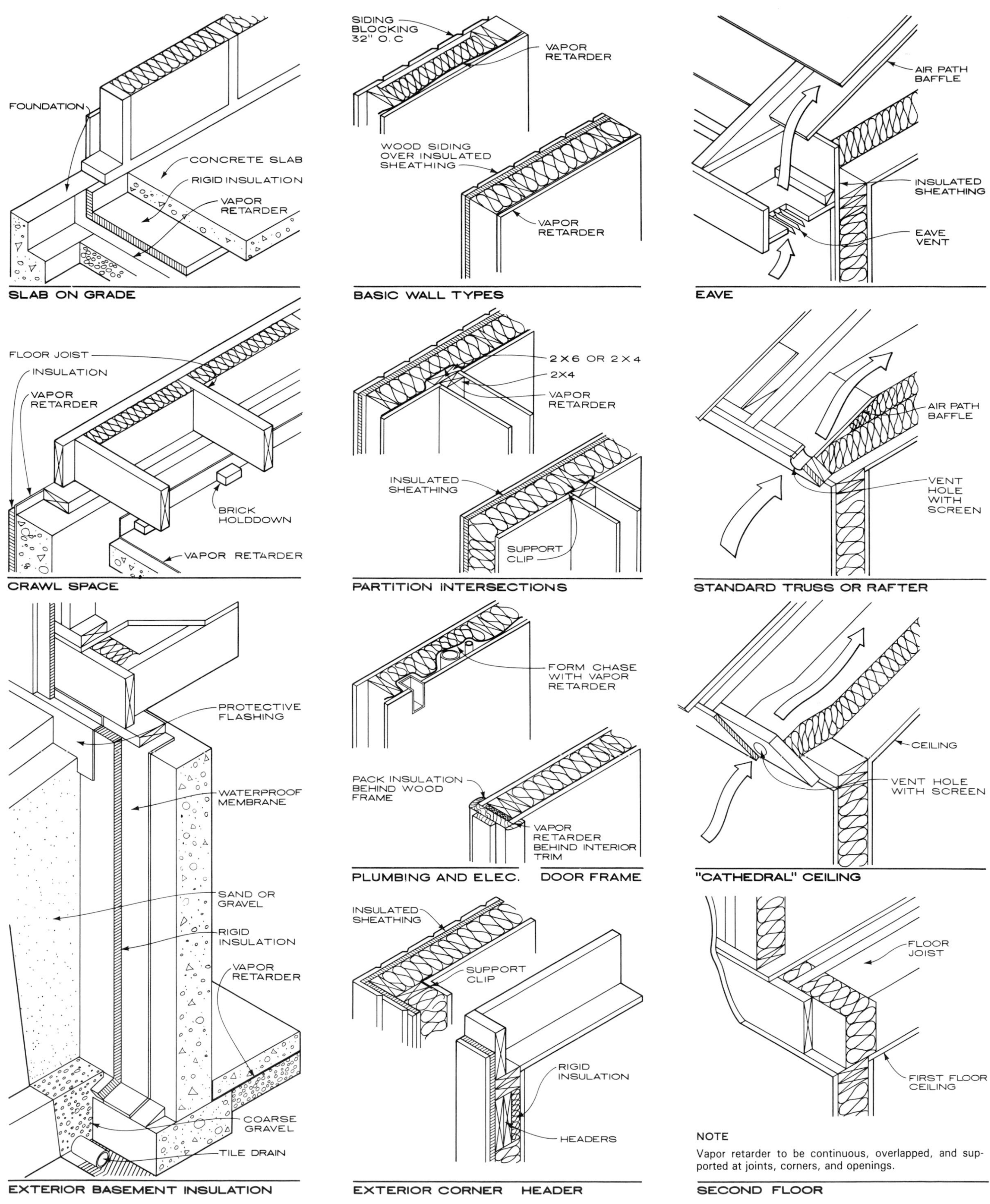
FOUNDATION
CONCRETE SLAB
RIGID INSULATION
VAPOR RETARDER
SLAB ON GRADE
SIDING BLOCKING 32" O.C
VAPOR RETARDER
WOOD SIDING OVER INSULATED SHEATHING
VAPOR RETARDER
BASIC WALL TYPES
AIR PATH BAFFLE
INSULATED SHEATHING
EAVE VENT
EAVE
FLOOR JOIST
INSULATION
VAPOR RETARDER
BRICK HOLDDOWN
VAPOR RETARDER
CRAWL SPACE
2X6 OR 2X4
2X4
VAPOR RETARDER
INSULATED SHEATHING
SUPPORT CLIP
PARTITION INTERSECTIONS
AIR PATH BAFFLE
VENT HOLE WITH SCREEN
STANDARD TRUSS OR RAFTER
PROTECTIVE FLASHING
WATERPROOF MEMBRANE
SAND OR GRAVEL
RIGID INSULATION
VAPOR RETARDER
COARSE GRAVEL
TILE DRAIN
EXTERIOR BASEMENT INSULATION
FORM CHASE WITH VAPOR RETARDER
PACK INSULATION BEHIND WOOD FRAME
VAPOR RETARDER BEHIND INTERIOR TRIM
PLUMBING AND ELEC.
DOOR FRAME
CEILING
VENT HOLE WITH SCREEN
"CATHEDRAL" CEILING
INSULATED SHEATHING
SUPPORT CLIP
RIGID INSULATION
HEADERS
EXTERIOR CORNER
HEADER
FLOOR JOIST
FIRST FLOOR CEILING
SECOND FLOOR

NOTE

Vapor retarder to be continuous, overlapped, and supported at joints, corners, and openings.

Timothy B. McDonald; Washington, D.C.

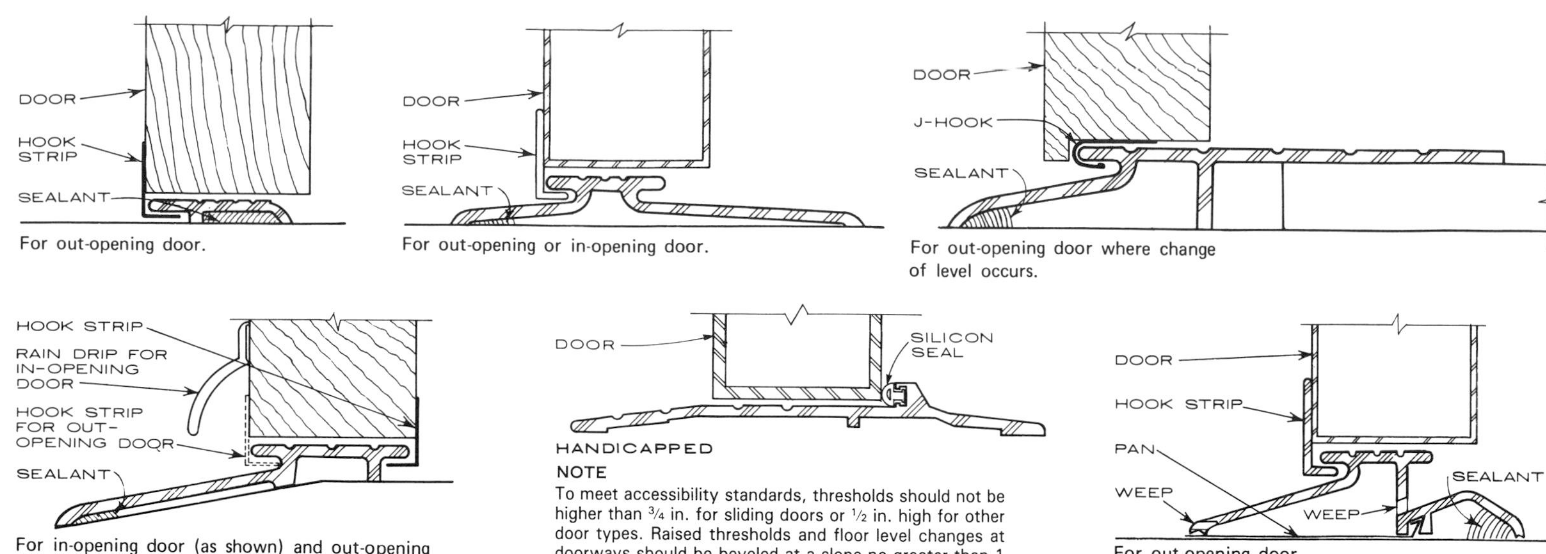
DOOR
HOOK STRIP
SEALANT
DOOR
HOOK STRIP
SEALANT
DOOR
J-HOOK
SEALANT
HOOK STRIP
RAIN DRIP FOR IN-OPENING DOOR
HOOK STRIP FOR OUT-OPENING DOOR
SEALANT
DOOR
SILICON SEAL
HANDICAPPED
DOOR
HOOK STRIP
PAN
WEEP
WEEP
SEALANT

For out-opening door.

For out-opening or in-opening door.

For out-opening door where change of level occurs.

For in-opening door (as shown) and out-opening door where change of level occurs.

HANDICAPPED

NOTE

To meet accessibility standards, thresholds should not be higher than 3/4 in. for sliding doors or 1/2 in. high for other door types. Raised thresholds and floor level changes at doorways should be beveled at a slope no greater than 1 in 2.

For out-opening door.

INTERLOCKING THRESHOLDS

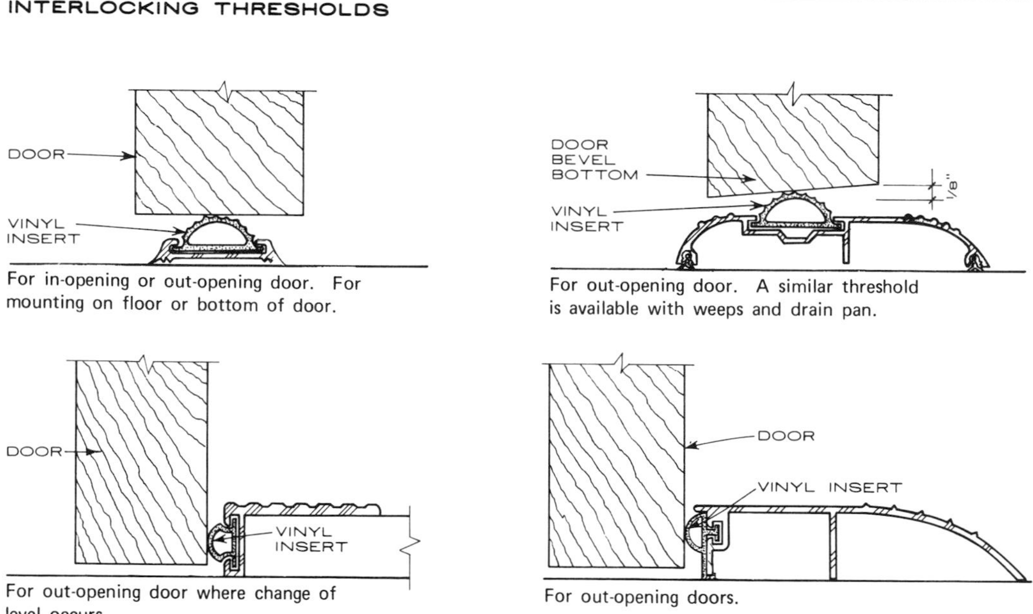
DOOR
VINYL INSERT
DOOR BEVEL BOTTOM
VINYL INSERT
1/8"
DOOR
VINYL INSERT
DOOR
VINYL INSERT

For in-opening or out-opening door. For mounting on floor or bottom of door.

For out-opening door. A similar threshold is available with weeps and drain pan.

For out-opening door where change of level occurs.

For out-opening doors.

VINYL INSERT THRESHOLDS

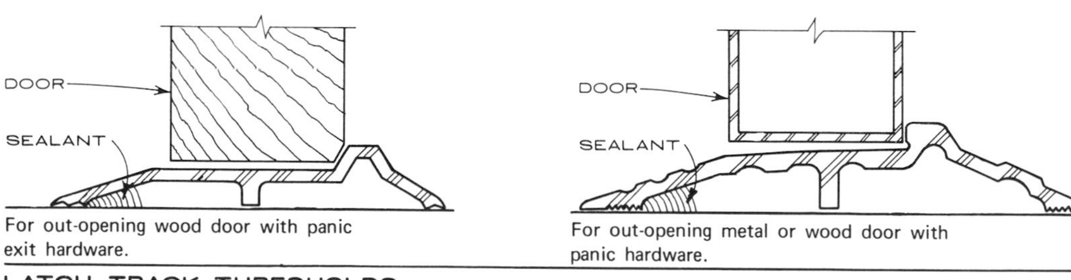
DOOR
SEALANT
DOOR
SEALANT

For out-opening wood door with panic exit hardware.

For out-opening metal or wood door with panic hardware.

LATCH TRACK THRESHOLDS

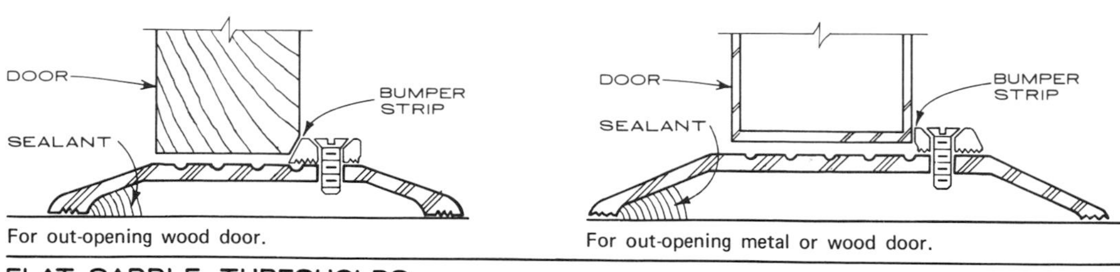
DOOR
SEALANT
BUMPER STRIP
DOOR
SEALANT
BUMPER STRIP

For out-opening wood door.

For out-opening metal or wood door.

FLAT SADDLE THRESHOLDS

Dan Cowling & Associates, Inc.; Little Rock, Arkansas

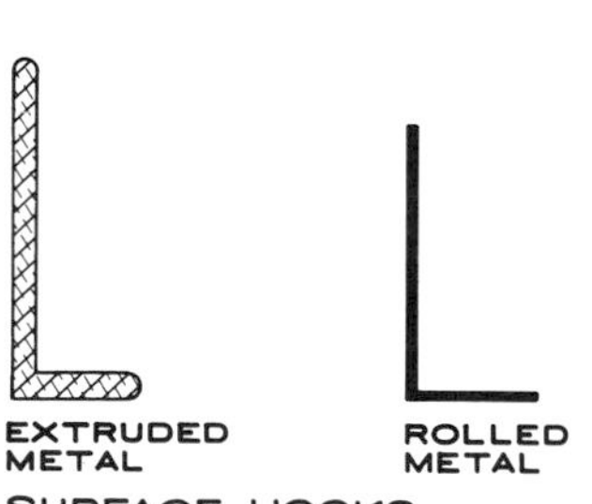

EXTRUDED METAL ROLLED METAL

SURFACE HOOKS

EXTRUDED METAL

ROLLED METAL

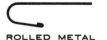

CONCEALED HOOKS

INTERLOCKING HOOK STRIPS

NOTE

Hook strips are available in aluminum, brass, bronze, and zinc, and vary in thickness and dimensions. Consult manufacturers' catalogs.

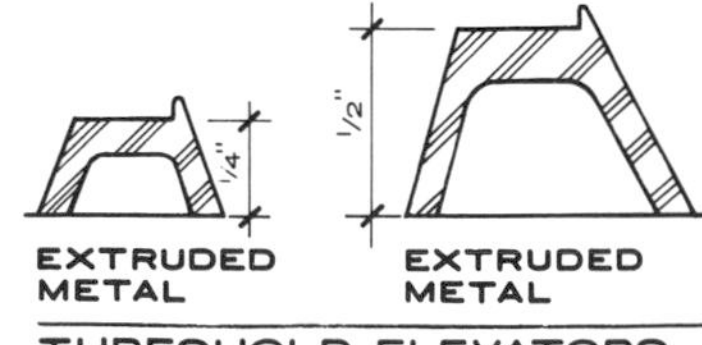
1/4"
1/2"

EXTRUDED METAL EXTRUDED METAL

THRESHOLD ELEVATORS

NOTE

Available in alum. and bronze. Consult manufacturers' catalogs.

GENERAL NOTE

Thresholds are available in bronze and aluminum with a wide selection of shapes and dimensions.

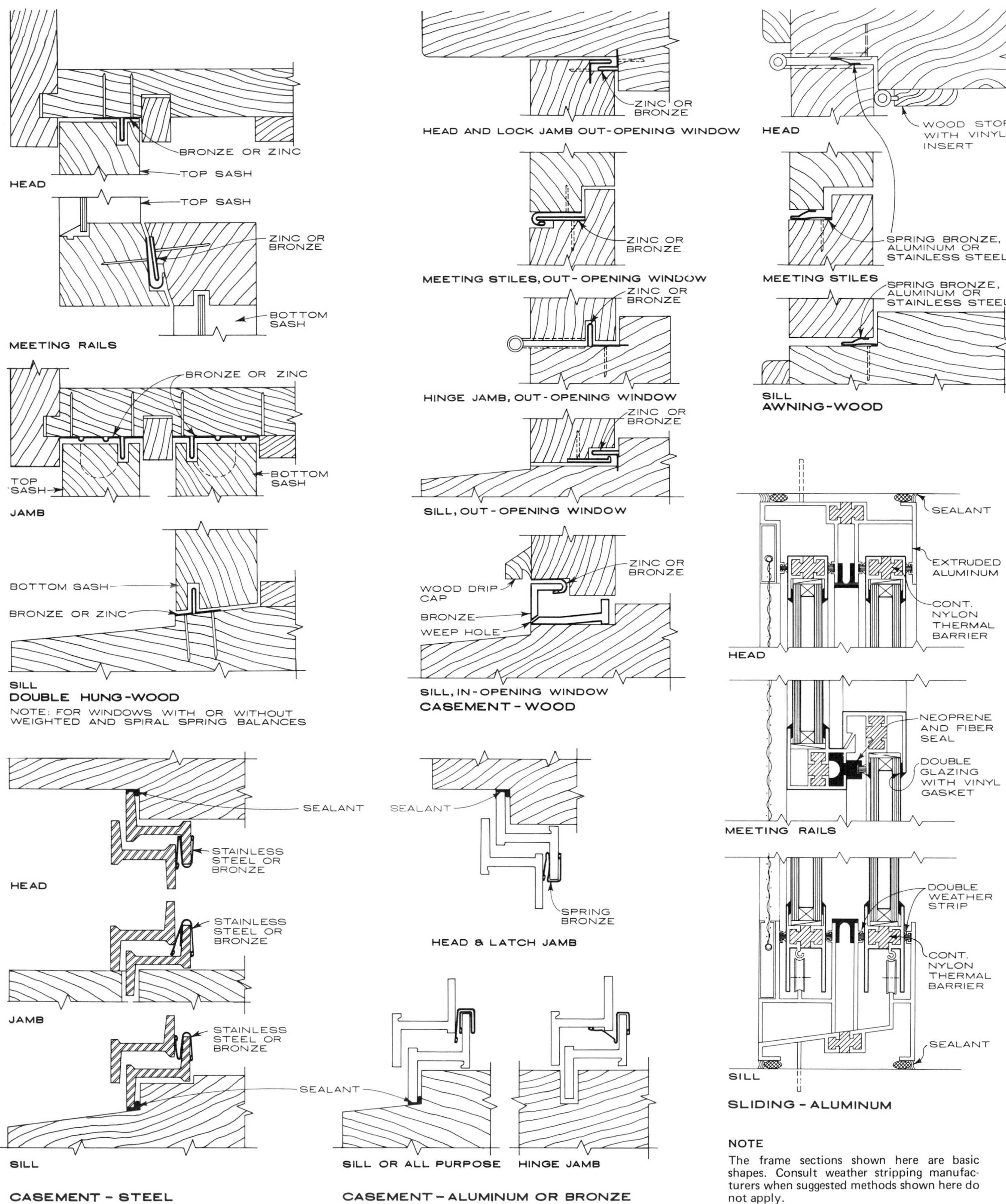
BRONZE OR ZINC
TOP SASH
HEAD
TOP SASH
ZINC OR BRONZE
BOTTOM SASH
MEETING RAILS
BRONZE OR ZINC
TOP SASH
BOTTOM SASH
JAMB
BOTTOM SASH
BRONZE OR ZINC
SILL
DOUBLE HUNG-WOOD
NOTE: FOR WINDOWS WITH OR WITHOUT WEIGHTED AND SPIRAL SPRING BALANCES
ZINC OR BRONZE
HEAD AND LOCK JAMB OUT-OPENING WINDOW
ZINC OR BRONZE
MEETING STILES, OUT-OPENING WINDOW
ZINC OR BRONZE
HINGE JAMB, OUT-OPENING WINDOW
ZINC OR BRONZE
SILL, OUT-OPENING WINDOW
ZINC OR BRONZE
WOOD DRIP CAP
BRONZE
WEEP HOLE
SILL, IN-OPENING WINDOW
CASEMENT - WOOD
HEAD
WOOD STOP WITH VINYL INSERT
SPRING BRONZE, ALUMINUM OR STAINLESS STEEL
MEETING STILES
SPRING BRONZE, ALUMINUM OR STAINLESS STEEL
SILL
AWNING-WOOD
SEALANT
EXTRUDED ALUMINUM
CONT. NYLON THERMAL BARRIER
HEAD
NEOPRENE AND FIBER SEAL
DOUBLE GLAZING WITH VINYL GASKET
MEETING RAILS
DOUBLE WEATHER STRIP
CONT. NYLON THERMAL BARRIER
SEALANT
SILL
SLIDING - ALUMINUM
SEALANT
STAINLESS STEEL OR BRONZE
HEAD
STAINLESS STEEL OR BRONZE
JAMB
STAINLESS STEEL OR BRONZE
SEALANT
SILL
CASEMENT - STEEL
SEALANT
SPRING BRONZE
HEAD & LATCH JAMB
SILL OR ALL PURPOSE
HINGE JAMB
CASEMENT - ALUMINUM OR BRONZE

NOTE

The frame sections shown here are basic shapes. Consult weather stripping manufacturers when suggested methods shown here do not apply.

Dan Cowling & Associates, Inc.; Little Rock, Arkansas

REFERENCES

GENERAL REFERENCES

Mechanical and Electrical Equipment for Buildings, 7th ed., 1986, Benjamin Stein, John Reynolds, and William McGuinness, Wiley

DATA SOURCES: ORGANIZATIONS

American-German Industries, 417
Brown Manufacturing Company, 416
Clearview Corporation, 416
Disco Aluminum Products Company, 416
Fisher-Insley Corporation, 423
Koolshade Corporation, 417
Remco Weatherstripping, 421, 423
Willard Shutter Corporation, 416
Zero Weatherstripping Company, Inc., 421, 423

DATA SOURCES: PUBLICATIONS

Wiring Simplified, H. P. Richter, Park Publishing, 394

APPENDIXES

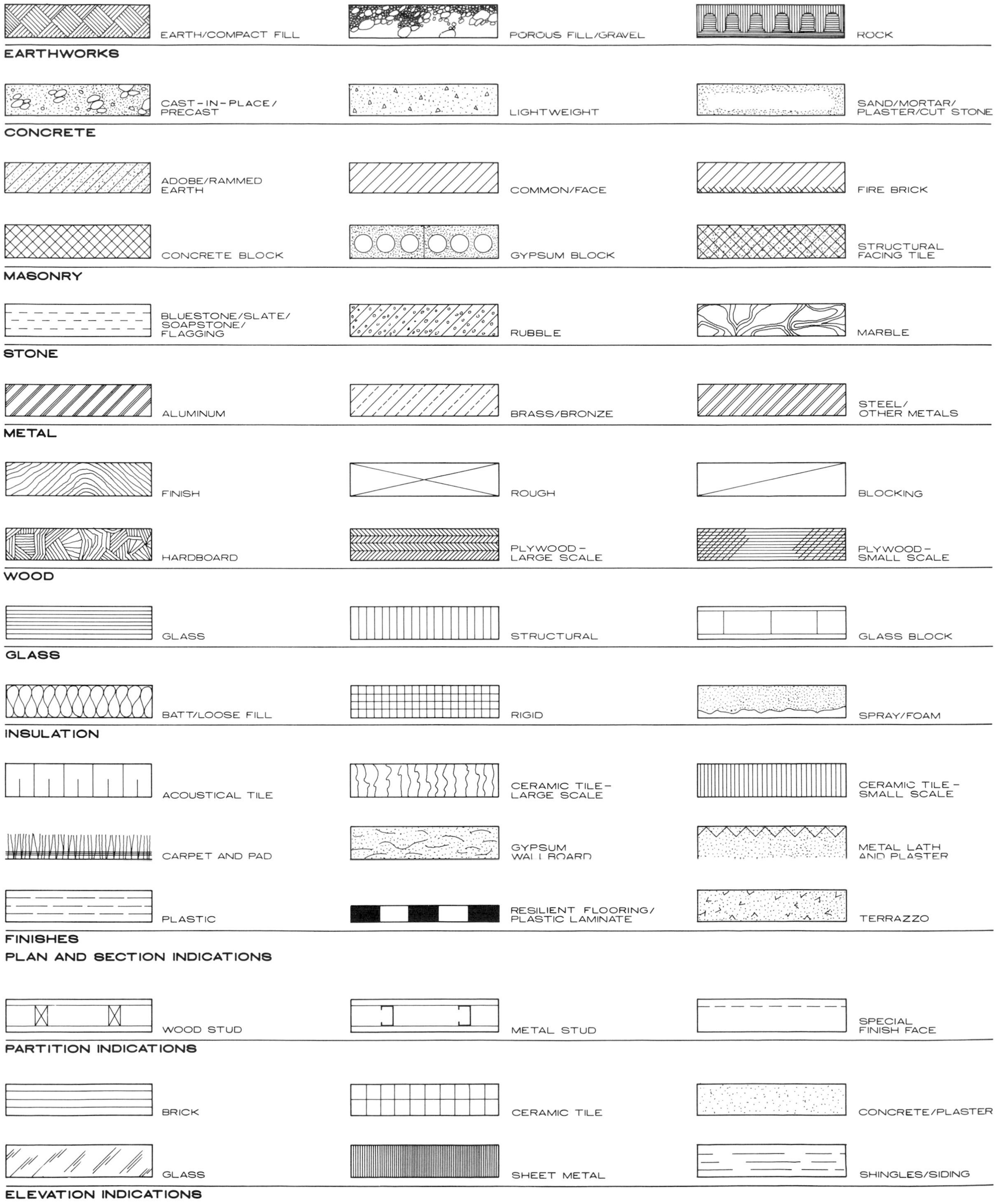

EARTH/COMPACT FILL
POROUS FILL/GRAVEL
ROCK

EARTHWORKS

CAST-IN-PLACE/PRECAST
LIGHTWEIGHT
SAND/MORTAR/PLASTER/CUT STONE

CONCRETE

ADOBE/RAMMED EARTH
COMMON/FACE
FIRE BRICK
CONCRETE BLOCK
GYPSUM BLOCK
STRUCTURAL FACING TILE

MASONRY

BLUESTONE/SLATE/SOAPSTONE/FLAGGING
RUBBLE
MARBLE

STONE

ALUMINUM
BRASS/BRONZE
STEEL/OTHER METALS

METAL

FINISH
ROUGH
BLOCKING
HARDBOARD
PLYWOOD—LARGE SCALE
PLYWOOD—SMALL SCALE

WOOD

GLASS
STRUCTURAL
GLASS BLOCK

GLASS

BATT/LOOSE FILL
RIGID
SPRAY/FOAM

INSULATION

ACOUSTICAL TILE
CERAMIC TILE—LARGE SCALE
CERAMIC TILE—SMALL SCALE
CARPET AND PAD
GYPSUM WALLBOARD
METAL LATH AND PLASTER
PLASTIC
RESILIENT FLOORING/PLASTIC LAMINATE
TERRAZZO

FINISHES

PLAN AND SECTION INDICATIONS

WOOD STUD
METAL STUD
SPECIAL FINISH FACE

PARTITION INDICATIONS

BRICK
CERAMIC TILE
CONCRETE/PLASTER
GLASS
SHEET METAL
SHINGLES/SIDING

ELEVATION INDICATIONS

John Ray Hoke, Jr., AIA; Washington, D.C.

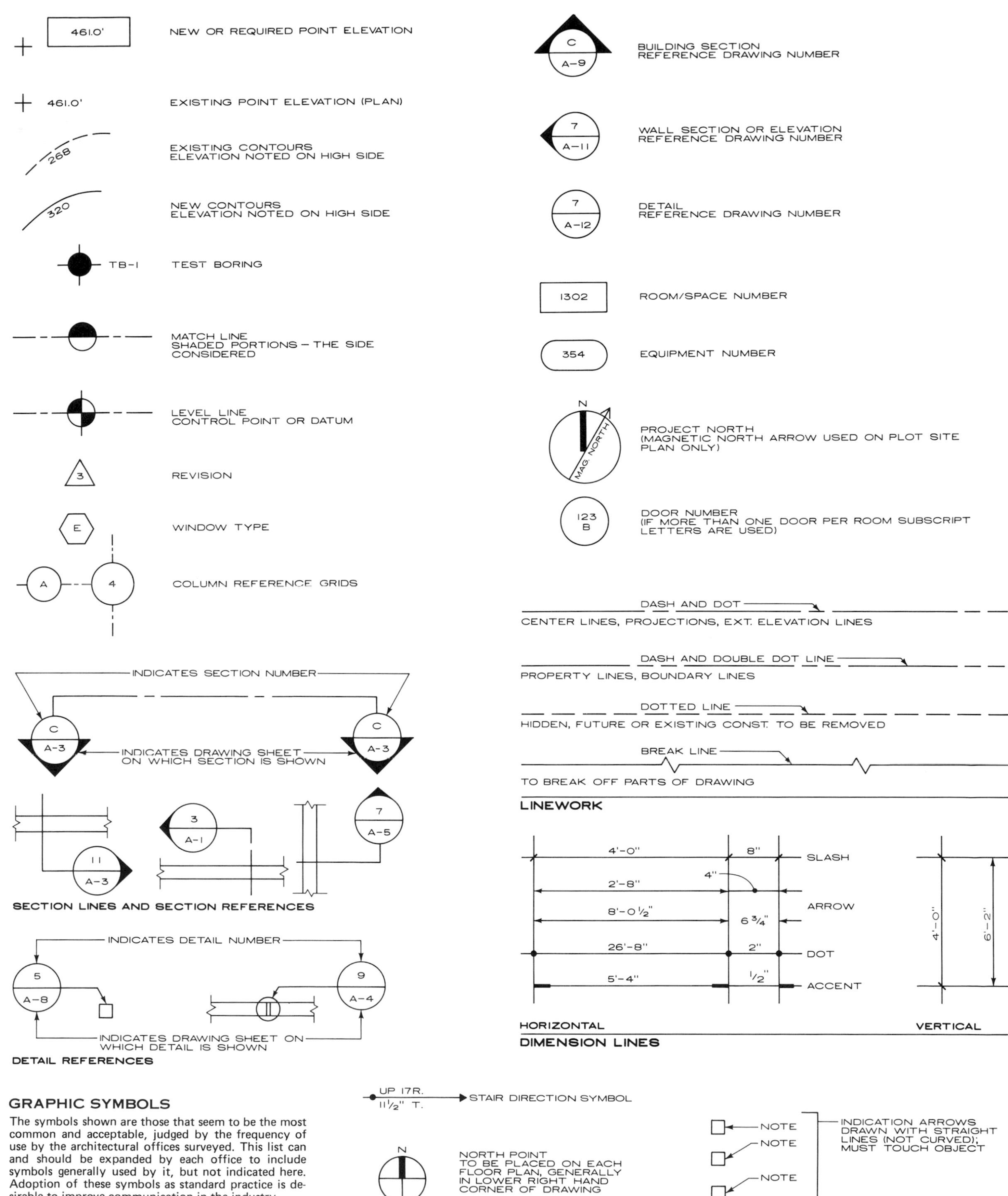
461.0'
NEW OR REQUIRED POINT ELEVATION
461.0'
EXISTING POINT ELEVATION (PLAN)
268
EXISTING CONTOURS
ELEVATION NOTED ON HIGH SIDE
320
NEW CONTOURS
ELEVATION NOTED ON HIGH SIDE
TB-1
TEST BORING
MATCH LINE
SHADED PORTIONS – THE SIDE CONSIDERED
LEVEL LINE
CONTROL POINT OR DATUM
3
REVISION
E
WINDOW TYPE
A
4
COLUMN REFERENCE GRIDS
INDICATES SECTION NUMBER
C
A-3
INDICATES DRAWING SHEET ON WHICH SECTION IS SHOWN
3
A-1
7
A-5
11
A-3
SECTION LINES AND SECTION REFERENCES
INDICATES DETAIL NUMBER
5
A-8
9
A-4
INDICATES DRAWING SHEET ON WHICH DETAIL IS SHOWN
DETAIL REFERENCES
C
A-9
BUILDING SECTION
REFERENCE DRAWING NUMBER
7
A-11
WALL SECTION OR ELEVATION
REFERENCE DRAWING NUMBER
7
A-12
DETAIL
REFERENCE DRAWING NUMBER
1302
ROOM/SPACE NUMBER
354
EQUIPMENT NUMBER
N
MAG. NORTH
PROJECT NORTH
(MAGNETIC NORTH ARROW USED ON PLOT SITE PLAN ONLY)
123
B
DOOR NUMBER
(IF MORE THAN ONE DOOR PER ROOM SUBSCRIPT LETTERS ARE USED)
DASH AND DOT
CENTER LINES, PROJECTIONS, EXT. ELEVATION LINES
DASH AND DOUBLE DOT LINE
PROPERTY LINES, BOUNDARY LINES
DOTTED LINE
HIDDEN, FUTURE OR EXISTING CONST. TO BE REMOVED
BREAK LINE
TO BREAK OFF PARTS OF DRAWING
LINEWORK
4'-0"
8"
SLASH
4"
2'-8"
ARROW
8'-0 1/2"
6 3/4"
26'-8"
2"
DOT
5'-4"
1/2"
ACCENT
4'-0"
6'-2"
HORIZONTAL
VERTICAL
DIMENSION LINES

GRAPHIC SYMBOLS

The symbols shown are those that seem to be the most common and acceptable, judged by the frequency of use by the architectural offices surveyed. This list can and should be expanded by each office to include symbols generally used by it, but not indicated here. Adoption of these symbols as standard practice is desirable to improve communication in the industry.

UP 17R.
11 1/2" T.
STAIR DIRECTION SYMBOL

N
NORTH POINT
TO BE PLACED ON EACH FLOOR PLAN, GENERALLY IN LOWER RIGHT HAND CORNER OF DRAWING

NOTE
NOTE
NOTE
INDICATION ARROWS DRAWN WITH STRAIGHT LINES (NOT CURVED); MUST TOUCH OBJECT

John Ray Hoke, Jr., AIA; Washington, D.C.

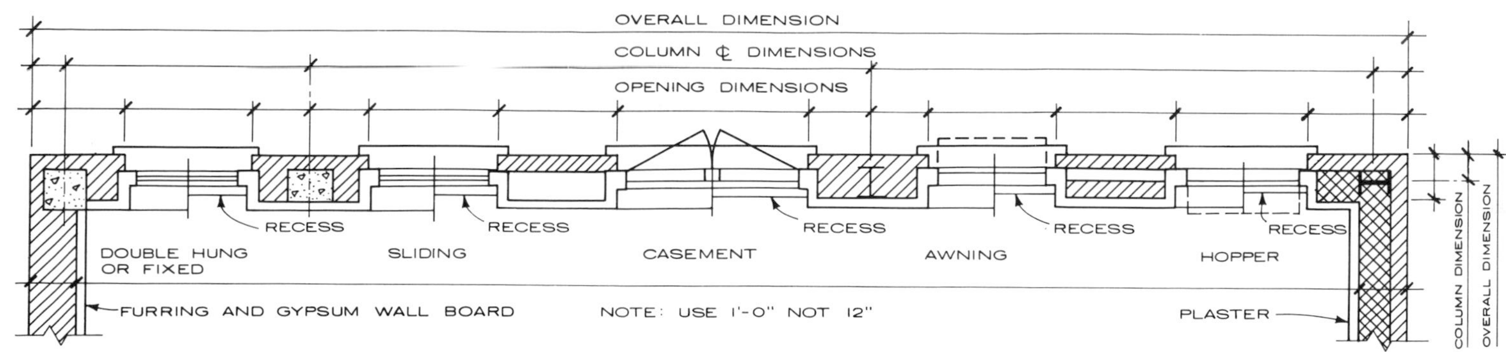
OVERALL DIMENSION
COLUMN ℄ DIMENSIONS
OPENING DIMENSIONS
RECESS
RECESS
RECESS
RECESS
RECESS
DOUBLE HUNG
OR FIXED
SLIDING
CASEMENT
AWNING
HOPPER
FURRING AND GYPSUM WALL BOARD
NOTE: USE 1'-0" NOT 12"
PLASTER
COLUMN DIMENSION
OVERALL DIMENSION

METHOD FOR DIMENSIONING EXTERIOR WINDOW OPENINGS IN MASONRY WALLS (DOORS SIMILAR)

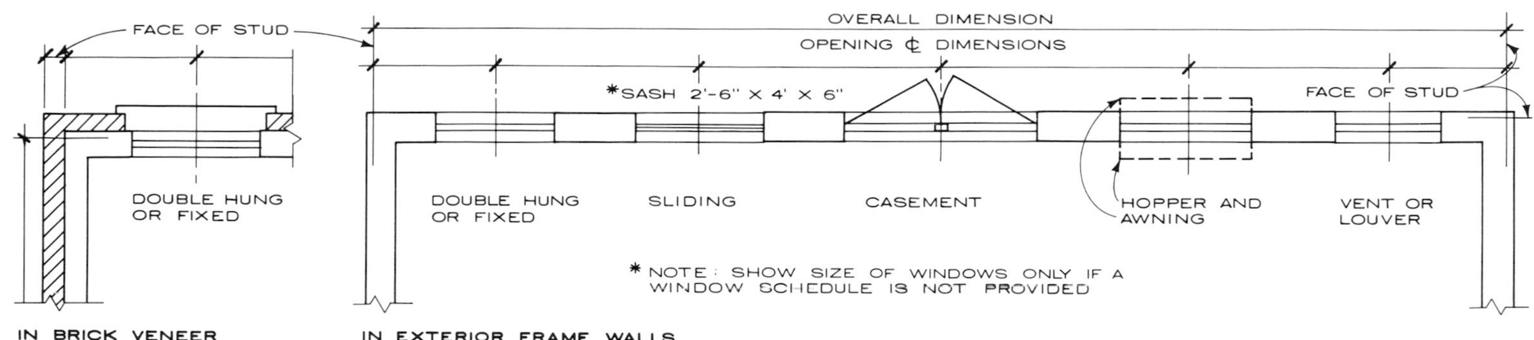
FACE OF STUD
DOUBLE HUNG
OR FIXED
IN BRICK VENEER
OVERALL DIMENSION
OPENING ℄ DIMENSIONS
*SASH 2'-6" X 4' X 6"
FACE OF STUD
DOUBLE HUNG
OR FIXED
SLIDING
CASEMENT
HOPPER AND
AWNING
VENT OR
LOUVER
* NOTE: SHOW SIZE OF WINDOWS ONLY IF A
WINDOW SCHEDULE IS NOT PROVIDED
IN EXTERIOR FRAME WALLS

METHOD FOR DIMENSIONING EXTERIOR WINDOW OPENINGS IN FRAME WALLS (DOORS SIMILAR)

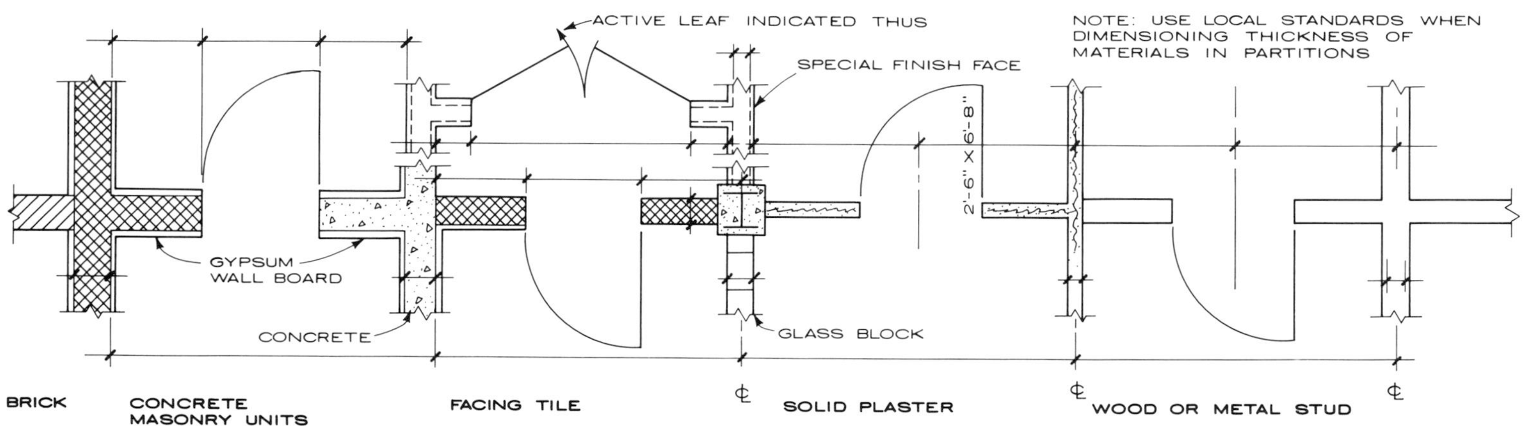
ACTIVE LEAF INDICATED THUS
SPECIAL FINISH FACE
NOTE: USE LOCAL STANDARDS WHEN
DIMENSIONING THICKNESS OF
MATERIALS IN PARTITIONS
2'-6" X 6'-8"
GYPSUM
WALL BOARD
CONCRETE
GLASS BLOCK
BRICK
CONCRETE
MASONRY UNITS
FACING TILE
SOLID PLASTER
WOOD OR METAL STUD

METHOD FOR DIMENSIONING AND INDICATIONS OF INTERIOR PARTITIONS AND DOORS

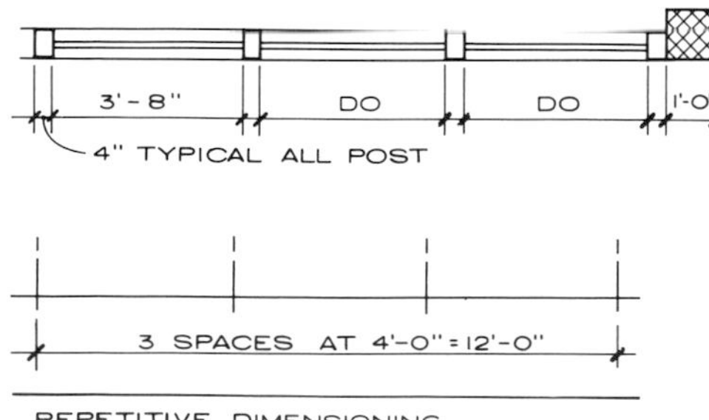
3'-8"
DO
DO
1'-0"
4" TYPICAL ALL POST
3 SPACES AT 4'-0" = 12'-0"

REPETITIVE DIMENSIONING

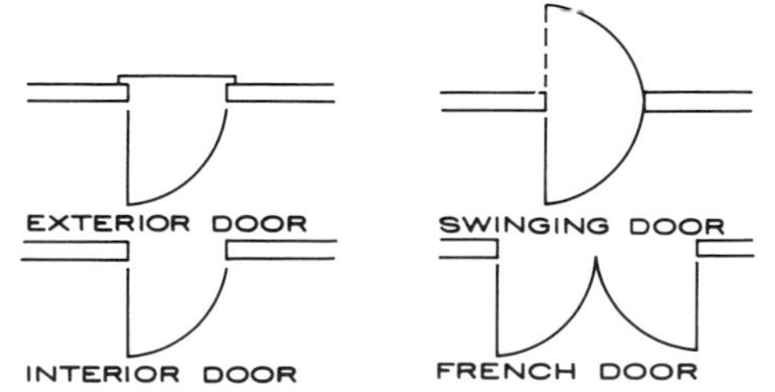
EXTERIOR DOOR
SWINGING DOOR
INTERIOR DOOR
FRENCH DOOR

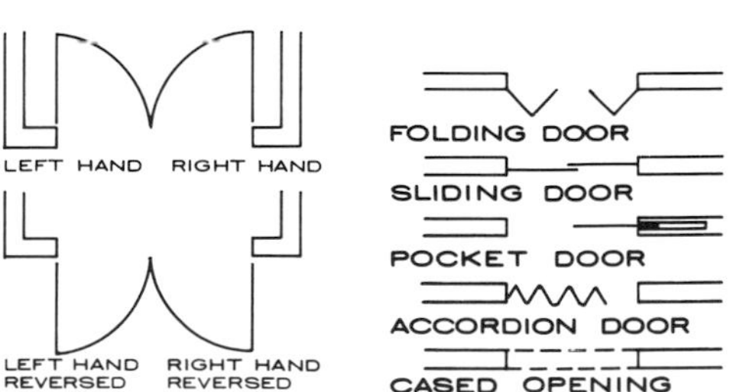
LEFT HAND
RIGHT HAND
LEFT HAND
REVERSED
RIGHT HAND
REVERSED
FOLDING DOOR
SLIDING DOOR
POCKET DOOR
ACCORDION DOOR
CASED OPENING

GENERAL NOTES

Dimensioning should start with critical dimensions and should be kept to a minimum. Consideration must be given to the trades using them and the sequencing adjusted to their respective work. It is also necessary to bear in mind that tolerances in actual construction will be varied. This means that as-built dimensions do not always coincide with design dimensions. Dimensioning from established grids or structural elements, such as columns and structural walls, assists the trades that must locate their work prior to that of others.

RECOMMENDATIONS

1. Dimensions under 1 ft shall be noted in inches. Dimensions 1 ft and over shall be expressed in feet.
2. Fractions under 1 in. shall NOT be preceded by a zero. Fractions must have a diagonal dividing line between numerator and denominator.
3. Dimension points to be noted with a short blunt 45° line. Dash to be oriented differently for vertical (⋆) and horizontal (⋆) runs of dimensions. Modular dimension points may be designated with an arrow or a dot.
4. Dimension all items from an established grid or reference point and do not close the string of dimensions to the next grid or reference point.
5. Dimension: to face of concrete or masonry work; to centerlines of columns or other grid points; to centerlines of partitions. In nonmodular wood construction dimension to critical face of studs. When a clear dimension is required, dimension to the finish faces and note as such. Do not use the word "clear."
6. Dimension as much as possible from structural elements.
7. Overall readability, conciseness, completeness, and accuracy must be foremost in any dimensional system. It takes experience to determine how to use dimensions to the best advantage.

John Ray Hoke, Jr., AIA; Washington, D.C.

PLUMBING PIPING

SOIL, WASTE OR LEADER (ABOVE GRADE)	————
SOIL, WASTE OR LEADER (BELOW GRADE)	— — — -
VENT	- - - - - - -
COMBINATION WASTE AND VENT	——SV——
ACID WASTE	——AW——
ACID VENT	– – –AV– – –
INDIRECT DRAIN	——IW——
STORM DRAIN	——S——
COLD WATER	—— - —— - —— -
SOFT COLD WATER	——SW——
INDUSTRIALIZED COLD WATER	——ICW——
CHILLED DRINKING WATER SUPPLY	——DWS——
CHILLED DRINKING WATER RETURN	——DWR——
HOT WATER	—— -- —— -- ——
HOT WATER RETURN	—— --- —— --- ——
SANITIZING HOT WATER SUPPLY (180° F.)	—/— - - —/— - - —/
SANITIZING HOT WATER RETURN (180° F.)	—/— - - - —/— - -
INDUSTRIALIZED HOT WATER SUPPLY	——IHW——
INDUSTRIALIZED HOT WATER RETURN	——IHR——
TEMPERED WATER SUPPLY	——TWS——
TEMPERED WATER RETURN	——TWR——
FIRE LINE	—F——F—
WET STANDPIPE	——WSP——
DRY STANDPIPE	——DSP——
COMBINATION STANDPIPE	——CSP——
MAIN SUPPLIES SPRINKLER	——S——
BRANCH AND HEAD SPRINKLER	——o——o——
GAS - LOW PRESSURE	—G——G—
GAS - MEDIUM PRESSURE	——MG——
GAS - HIGH PRESSURE	——HG——
COMPRESSED AIR	——A——
VACUUM	——V——
VACUUM CLEANING	——VC——
OXYGEN	——O——
LIQUID OXYGEN	——LOX——
NITROGEN	——N——
LIQUID NITROGEN	——LN——
NITROUS OXIDE	——NO——
HYDROGEN	——H——
HELIUM	——HE——
ARGON	——AR——
LIQUID PETROLEUM GAS	——LPG——
INDUSTRIAL WASTE	——INW——
PNEUMATIC TUBES TUBE RUNS	——PN——
CAST IRON	——CI——
CULVERT PIPE	——CP——
CLAY TILE	——CT——
DUCTILE IRON	——DI——
REINFORCED CONCRETE	——RCP——
DRAIN - OPEN TILE OR AGRICULTURAL TILE	== == == ==

HEATING PIPING

HIGH PRESSURE STEAM	——HPS——
MEDIUM PRESSURE STEAM	——MPS——
LOW PRESSURE STEAM	——LPS——
HIGH PRESSURE RETURN	——HPR——
MEDIUM PRESSURE RETURN	——MPR——
LOW PRESSURE RETURN	——LPR——
BOILER BLOW OFF	——BD——
CONDENSATE OR VACUUM PUMP DISCHARGE	——VPD——
FEEDWATER PUMP DISCHARGE	——PPD——
MAKE UP WATER	——MU——
AIR RELIEF LINE	——V——
FUEL OIL SUCTION	——FOS——
FUEL OIL RETURN	——FOR——
FUEL OIL VENT	——FOV——
COMPRESSED AIR	——A——
HOT WATER HEATING SUPPLY	——HW——
HOT WATER HEATING RETURN	——HWR——

AIR CONDITIONING PIPING

REFRIGERANT LIQUID	——RL——
REFRIGERANT DISCHARGE	——RD——
REFRIGERANT SUCTION	——RS——
CONDENSER WATER SUPPLY	——CWS——
CONDENSER WATER RETURN	——CWR——
CHILLED WATER SUPPLY	——CHWS——
CHILLED WATER RETURN	——CHWR——
MAKE UP WATER	——MU——
HUMIDIFICATION LINE	——H——
DRAIN	——D——
BRINE SUPPLY	——B——
BRINE RETURN	——BR——

Amor Halperin, PE; Ayres, Cohen, and Hayakawa; Consulting Engineers; Los Angeles/San Francisco, California
Joseph R. Loring & Associates, Inc., Consulting Engineers; New York, New York

FITTINGS	VALVES	MISCELLANEOUS
ELBOW—90°	GATE	FLANGED CONNECTION
ELBOW—45°	GLOBE	SCREWED CONNECTION
ELBOW—TURNED UP	HOSE GATE	BELL AND SPIGOT JOINT
ELBOW—TURNED DOWN	HOSE GLOBE	WELD CONNECTION
ELBOW—LONG RAD.	ANGLE GATE—ELEV.	SOLDER CONNECTION
ELBOW—SIDE OUTLET DOWN	ANGLE GATE—PLAN	EXPANSION JOINT
ELBOW—SIDE OUTLET UP	ANGLE GLOBE—ELEV.	UNION
BASE ELBOW	ANGLE GLOBE—PLAN	ALIGNMENT GUIDE
DOUBLE BRANCH ELBOW	SWING CHECK	REDUCER
REDUCING ELBOW	ANGLE CHECK	BALL JOINT
SINGLE SWEEP TEE	SAFETY	PIPE ANCHOR
DOUBLE SWEEP TEE	COCK	EXPANSION LOOP
STRAIGHT TEE	QUICK OPEN	REDUCING FLANGE
TEE OUTLET UP	FLOAT	AIR VENT, AUTOMATIC
TEE OUTLET DOWN	MOTOR OPERATION GATE	AIR VENT, MANUAL
TEE—SIDE OUTLET UP	MOTOR OPERATION GLOBE	CAPS
TEE—SIDE OUTLET DOWN	DIAPHRAGM	CROSSOVER
STRAIGHT CROSS	AUTO BYPASS	CONCENTRIC REDUCER
LATERAL	AUTO GOVERNOR OPERATION	ECCENTRIC REDUCER

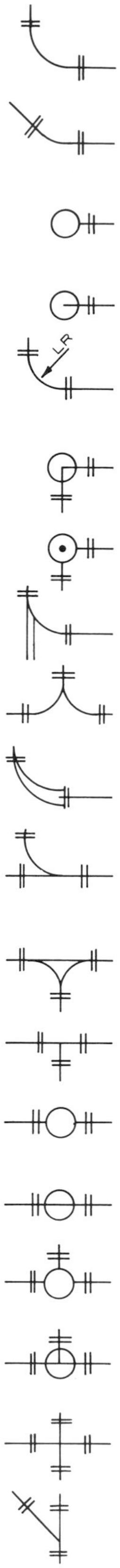

LR
M
M
EJ 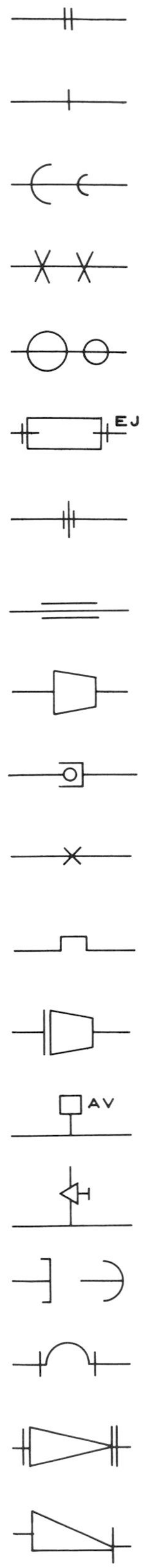
AV

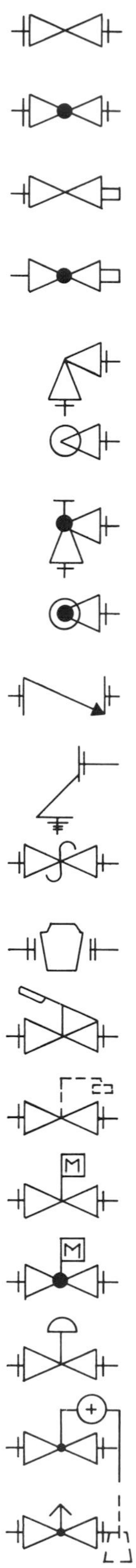

NOTE: FITTINGS AND VALVES ARE SHOWN WITH FLANGED CONNECTIONS

Sargent, Webster, Crenshaw & Folley, Architects Engineers Planners; Syracuse, New York
Harrison D. Goodman, PE; Joseph R. Loring & Associates, Inc., Consulting Engineers; New York, New York

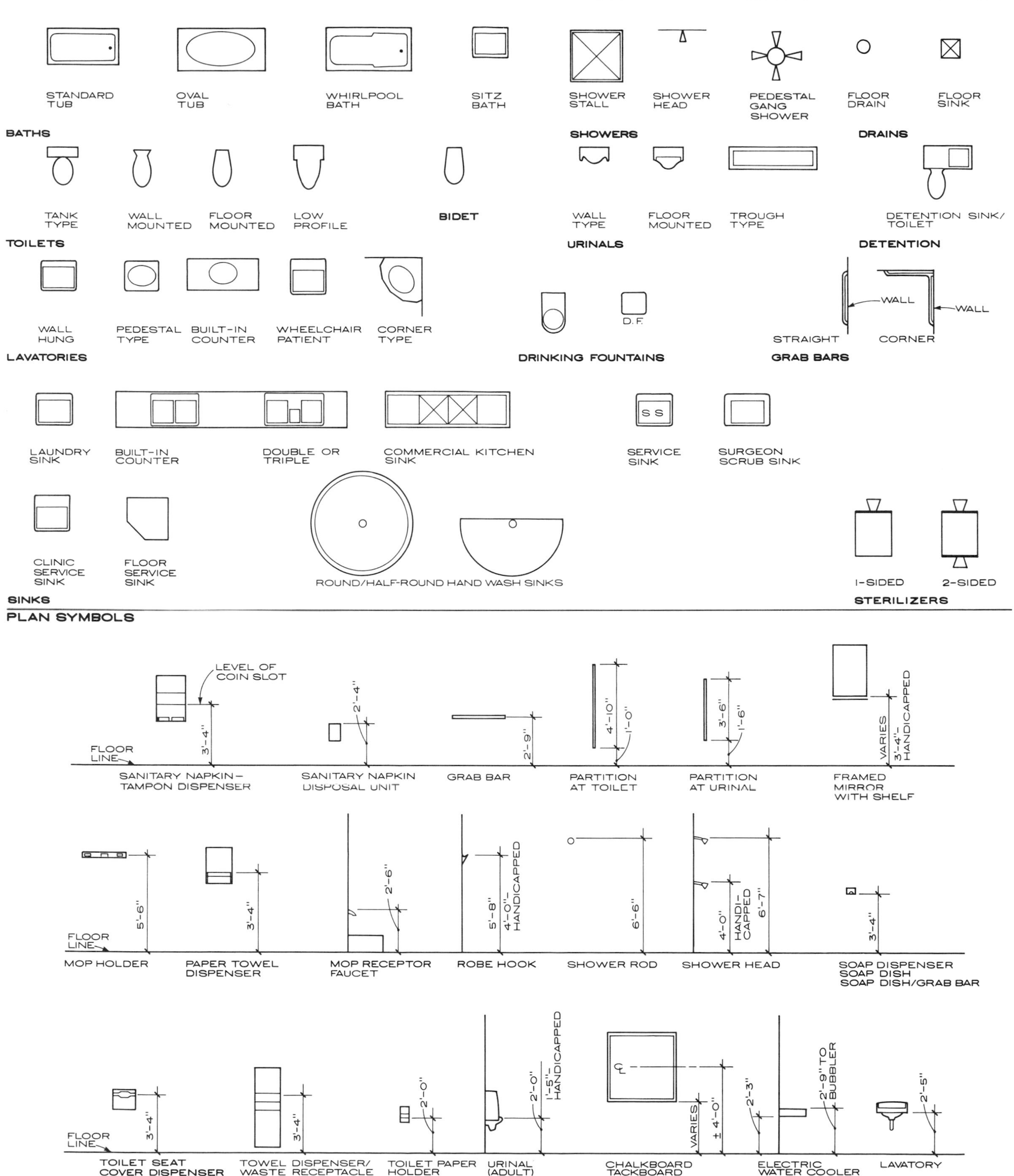
STANDARD TUB
OVAL TUB
WHIRLPOOL BATH
SITZ BATH
SHOWER STALL
SHOWER HEAD
PEDESTAL GANG SHOWER
FLOOR DRAIN
FLOOR SINK
BATHS
SHOWERS
DRAINS
TANK TYPE
WALL MOUNTED
FLOOR MOUNTED
LOW PROFILE
BIDET
WALL TYPE
FLOOR MOUNTED
TROUGH TYPE
DETENTION SINK/ TOILET
TOILETS
URINALS
DETENTION
WALL HUNG
PEDESTAL TYPE
BUILT-IN COUNTER
WHEELCHAIR PATIENT
CORNER TYPE
D.F.
WALL
WALL
STRAIGHT
CORNER
LAVATORIES
DRINKING FOUNTAINS
GRAB BARS
LAUNDRY SINK
BUILT-IN COUNTER
DOUBLE OR TRIPLE
COMMERCIAL KITCHEN SINK
SS
SERVICE SINK
SURGEON SCRUB SINK
CLINIC SERVICE SINK
FLOOR SERVICE SINK
ROUND/HALF-ROUND HAND WASH SINKS
1-SIDED
2-SIDED
SINKS
STERILIZERS
PLAN SYMBOLS
LEVEL OF COIN SLOT
FLOOR LINE
3'-4"
2'-4"
2'-9"
4'-10"
1'-0"
3'-6"
1'-6"
VARIES
3'-4"-HANDICAPPED
SANITARY NAPKIN-TAMPON DISPENSER
SANITARY NAPKIN DISPOSAL UNIT
GRAB BAR
PARTITION AT TOILET
PARTITION AT URINAL
FRAMED MIRROR WITH SHELF
FLOOR LINE
5'-6"
3'-4"
2'-6"
5'-8"
4'-0"-HANDICAPPED
6'-6"
4'-0"
HANDI-CAPPED
6'-7"
3'-4"
MOP HOLDER
PAPER TOWEL DISPENSER
MOP RECEPTOR FAUCET
ROBE HOOK
SHOWER ROD
SHOWER HEAD
SOAP DISPENSER
SOAP DISH
SOAP DISH/GRAB BAR
FLOOR LINE
3'-4"
3'-4"
2'-0"
2'-0"
1'-5"-HANDICAPPED
VARIES
± 4'-0"
2'-3"
2'-9" TO BUBBLER
2'-5"
TOILET SEAT COVER DISPENSER
TOWEL DISPENSER/ WASTE RECEPTACLE
TOILET PAPER HOLDER
URINAL (ADULT)
CHALKBOARD TACKBOARD
ELECTRIC WATER COOLER
LAVATORY
MOUNTING HEIGHTS

Dale Switzer, AIA; Hope Architects & Engineers; San Diego, California

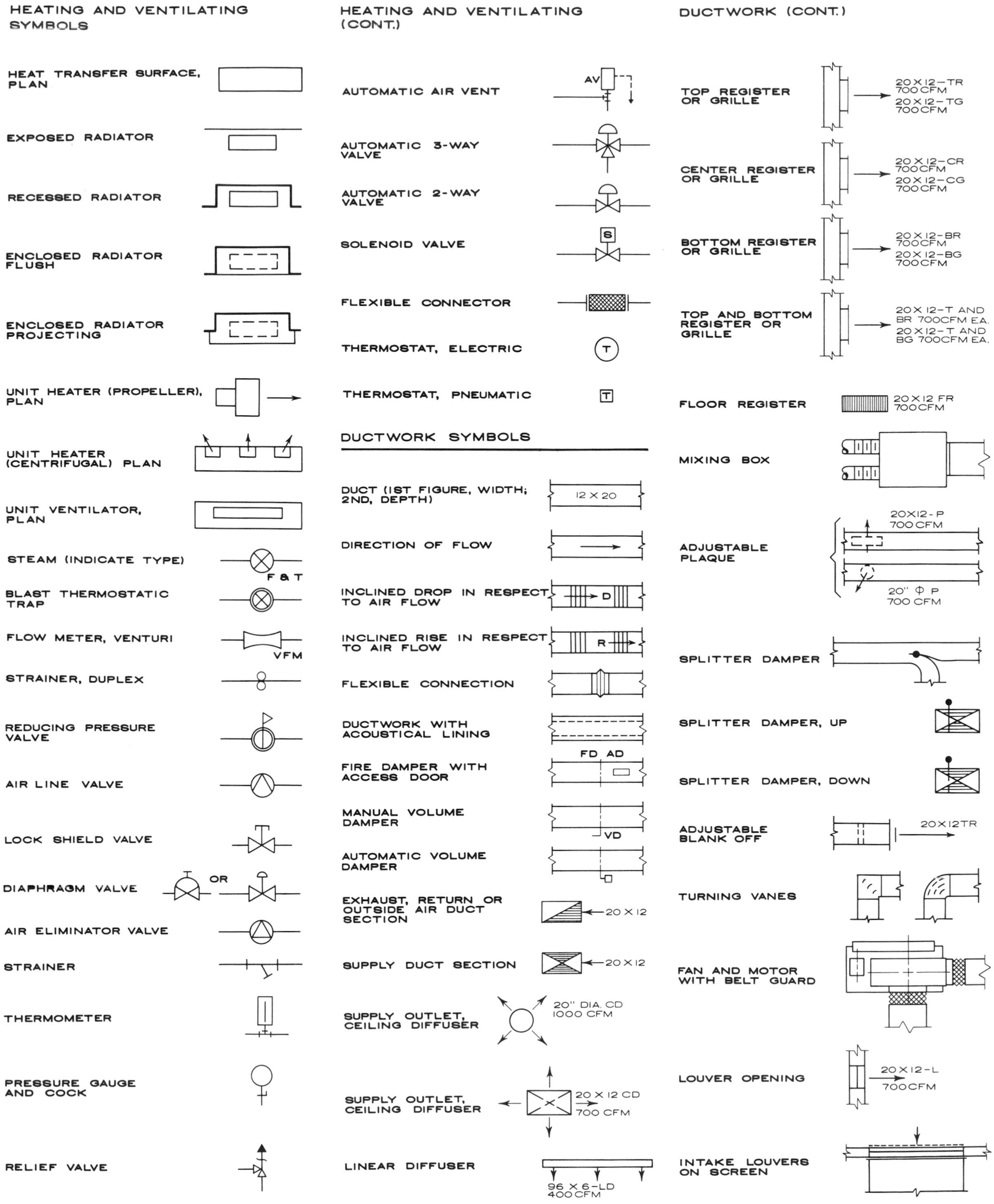

HEATING AND VENTILATING SYMBOLS

HEAT TRANSFER SURFACE, PLAN

EXPOSED RADIATOR

RECESSED RADIATOR

ENCLOSED RADIATOR FLUSH

ENCLOSED RADIATOR PROJECTING

UNIT HEATER (PROPELLER), PLAN

UNIT HEATER (CENTRIFUGAL) PLAN

UNIT VENTILATOR, PLAN

STEAM (INDICATE TYPE) — F & T

BLAST THERMOSTATIC TRAP

FLOW METER, VENTURI — VFM

STRAINER, DUPLEX

REDUCING PRESSURE VALVE

AIR LINE VALVE

LOCK SHIELD VALVE

DIAPHRAGM VALVE — OR

AIR ELIMINATOR VALVE

STRAINER

THERMOMETER

PRESSURE GAUGE AND COCK

RELIEF VALVE

HEATING AND VENTILATING (CONT.)

AUTOMATIC AIR VENT — AV

AUTOMATIC 3-WAY VALVE

AUTOMATIC 2-WAY VALVE

SOLENOID VALVE — S

FLEXIBLE CONNECTOR

THERMOSTAT, ELECTRIC — T

THERMOSTAT, PNEUMATIC — T

DUCTWORK SYMBOLS

DUCT (1ST FIGURE, WIDTH; 2ND, DEPTH) — 12 X 20

DIRECTION OF FLOW

INCLINED DROP IN RESPECT TO AIR FLOW — D

INCLINED RISE IN RESPECT TO AIR FLOW — R

FLEXIBLE CONNECTION

DUCTWORK WITH ACOUSTICAL LINING

FIRE DAMPER WITH ACCESS DOOR — FD AD

MANUAL VOLUME DAMPER — VD

AUTOMATIC VOLUME DAMPER

EXHAUST, RETURN OR OUTSIDE AIR DUCT SECTION — 20 X 12

SUPPLY DUCT SECTION — 20 X 12

SUPPLY OUTLET, CEILING DIFFUSER — 20" DIA. CD 1000 CFM

SUPPLY OUTLET, CEILING DIFFUSER — 20 X 12 CD 700 CFM

LINEAR DIFFUSER — 96 X 6-LD 400 CFM

DUCTWORK (CONT.)

TOP REGISTER OR GRILLE — 20 X 12-TR 700 CFM; 20 X 12-TG 700 CFM

CENTER REGISTER OR GRILLE — 20 X 12-CR 700 CFM; 20 X 12-CG 700 CFM

BOTTOM REGISTER OR GRILLE — 20 X 12-BR 700 CFM; 20 X 12-BG 700 CFM

TOP AND BOTTOM REGISTER OR GRILLE — 20 X 12-T AND BR 700 CFM EA.; 20 X 12-T AND BG 700 CFM EA.

FLOOR REGISTER — 20 X 12 FR 700 CFM

MIXING BOX

ADJUSTABLE PLAQUE — 20 X 12-P 700 CFM; 20" Φ P 700 CFM

SPLITTER DAMPER

SPLITTER DAMPER, UP

SPLITTER DAMPER, DOWN

ADJUSTABLE BLANK OFF — 20 X 12 TR

TURNING VANES

FAN AND MOTOR WITH BELT GUARD

LOUVER OPENING — 20 X 12-L 700 CFM

INTAKE LOUVERS ON SCREEN

Amor Halperin, PE; Ayres, Cohen and Hayakawa; Consulting Engineers; Los Angeles/San Francisco, California
Joseph R. Loring & Associates, Inc., Consulting Engineers; New York, New York

INSTITUTIONAL COMMERCIAL AND INDUSTRIAL OCCUPANCIES

NURSES CALL SYSTEM DEVICES. (ANY TYPE)

PAGING SYSTEM DEVICES (ANY TYPE)

FIRE ALARM SYSTEM DEVICES (ANY TYPE)

STAFF REGISTER SYSTEM (ANY TYPE)

ELECTRICAL CLOCK SYSTEM DEVICES (ANY TYPE)

COMPUTER DATA SYSTEM DEVICES

PRIVATE TELEPHONE SYSTEM DEVICES

WATCHMAN SYSTEM DEVICES

SOUND SYSTEM

FACP — FIRE ALARM CONTROL PANEL

SC — SIGNAL CENTRAL STATION

CR — CARD READER

AUXILIARY SYSTEM CIRCUITS

Any line without further designation indicates two-wire system. For a greater number of wires, designate with numerals in manner similar to: 12- no. 18W - ¾" C. Designate by numbers corresponding to listing in schedule.

A, B, C, ETC. — SPECIAL AUXILIARY OUTLETS

Subscript lettering refers to notes on drawings or detailed description in specifications.

PANELBOARDS

FLUSH MOUNTED PANELBOARD AND CABINET

SURFACE - MOUNTED PANELBOARD AND CABINET

BUSDUCTS AND WIREWAYS

T T T — TROLLEY DUCT

B B B — BUSWAY (SERVICE, FEEDER OR PLUG-IN)

C C C — CABLE THROUGH LADDER OR CHANNEL

W W W — WIREWAY

SIGNALING SYSTEM OUTLETS RESIDENTIAL OCCUPANCIES

PUSH BUTTON

BUZZER

BELL

BELL AND BUZZER COMBINATION

ANNUNCIATOR

COMPUTER DATA OUTLET

INTERCONNECTING TELEPHONE

TELEPHONE SWITCHBOARD

BT — BELL RINGING TRANSFORMER

D — ELECTRIC DOOR OPENER

CH — CHIME

TV — TELEVISION OUTLET

T — THERMOSTAT

UNDERGROUND ELECTRICAL DISTRIBUTION OR LIGHTING SYSTEM

M — MANHOLE

H — HANDHOLE

TM — TRANSFORMER- MANHOLE OR VAULT

TP — TRANSFORMER PAD

UNDERGROUND DIRECT BURIAL CABLE

UNDERGROUND DUCT LINE

STREET LIGHT STANDARD FED FROM UNDERGROUND CIRCUIT

ELECTRICAL DISTRIBUTION OR LIGHTING SYSTEM, AERIAL

POLE

STREET LIGHT AND BRACKET

TRANSFORMER

PRIMARY CIRCUIT

SECONDARY CIRCUIT

DOWN GUY

HEAD GUY

SIDEWALK GUY

SERVICE WEATHER

PANELS CIRCUITS AND MISCELLANEOUS

LIGHTING PANEL

POWER PANEL

WIRING, CONCEALED IN CEILING OR WALL

WIRING, CONCEALED IN FLOOR

WIRING EXPOSED

HOME RUN TO PANEL BOARD.

Indicate number of circuits by number of arrows. Any circuit without such designation indicates a two-wire circuit. For a greater number of wires indicate as follows: (3 wires) (4 wires), etc.

FEEDERS

Use heavy lines and designate by number corresponding to listing in feeder schedule.

WIRING TURNED UP

WIRING TURNED DOWN

G — GENERATOR

M — MOTOR

I — INSTRUMENT (SPECIFY)

T — TRANSFORMER (OR DRAW TO SCALE)

CONTROLLER

EXTERNALLY OPERATED DISCONNECT SWITCH

PULL BOX

Frederick R. Brown, PE; Ayres, Cohen and Hayakawa; Consulting Engineers; Los Angeles/San Francisco, California
Richard F. Humenn, PE; Joseph R. Loring & Associates, Inc., Consulting Engineers; New York, New York

LIGHTING OUTLETS

CEILING, WALL

- OUTLET BOX AND INCANDESCENT LIGHTING FIXTURE. SLASH INDICATES FIXTURE ON EMERGENCY SERVICE
- INCANDESCENT LIGHTING TRACK
- B BLANKED OUTLET
- D DROP CORD
- EXIT LIGHT AND OUTLET BOX, DIRECTIONAL ARROWS AS INDICATED. SHADED AREAS DENOTE FACES
- OUTDOOR POLE ARM MOUNTED FIXTURES
- J JUNCTION BOX
- L PS LAMP HOLDER WITH PULL SWITCH
- MULTIPLE FLOODLIGHT ASSEMBLY
- B EMERGENCY BATTERY PACK WITH CHARGER AND SEALED BEAM HEADS
- REMOTE EMERGENCY SEALED BEAM HEAD WITH OUTLET BOX
- L OUTLET CONTROLLED BY LOW VOLTAGE SWITCHING WHEN RELAY IS INSTALLED IN OUTLET BOX
- INDIVIDUAL FLUORESCENT FIXTURE. SLASH INDICATES FIXTURE ON EMERGENCY SERVICE
- OUTLET BOX AND FLUORESCENT LIGHTING STRIP FIXTURE
- CONTINUOUS ROW FLUORESCENT FIXTURE
- SURFACE-MOUNTED FLUORESCENT

RECEPTACLE OUTLETS

- SINGLE RECEPTACLE OUTLET
- DUPLEX RECEPTACLE OUTLET
- TRIPLEX RECEPTACLE OUTLET
- QUADRUPLEX RECEPTACLE OUTLET
- DUPLEX RECEPTACLE OUTLET-SPLIT WIRED
- TRIPLEX RECEPTACLE OUTLET-SPLIT WIRED
- SINGLE SPECIAL PURPOSE RECEPTACLE OUTLET
- DUPLEX SPECIAL PURPOSE RECEPTACLE OUTLET
- R RANGE OUTLET
- DW SPECIAL PURPOSE CONNECTION
- CLOSED CIRCUIT TELEVISION CAMERA
- C CLOCK HANGER RECEPTACLE
- F FAN HANGER RECEPTACLE
- FLOOR SINGLE RECEPTACLE OUTLET
- FLOOR DUPLEX RECEPTACLE OUTLET
- FLOOR SPECIAL PURPOSE OUTLET
- DATA OUTLET IN FLOOR
- FLOOR TELEPHONE OUTLET-PRIVATE
- UNDERFLOOR DUCT AND JUNCTION BOX FOR TRIPLE, DOUBLE, OR SINGLE DUCT SYSTEM AS INDICATED BY NUMBER OF PARALLEL LINES
- CELLULAR FLOOR HEADER DUCT

SWITCH OUTLETS

S	SINGLE POLE SWITCH
S_2	DOUBLE POLE SWITCH
S_3	THREE-WAY SWITCH
S_4	FOUR-WAY SWITCH
S_D	AUTOMATIC DOOR SWITCH
S_K	KEY OPERATED SWITCH
S_P	SWITCH AND PILOT LAMP
S_{CB}	CIRCUIT BREAKER
S_{WCB}	WEATHERPROOF CIRCUIT BREAKER
S_{DM}	DIMMER
S_{RC}	REMOTE CONTROL SWITCH
S_{WP}	WEATHERPROOF SWITCH
S_F	FUSED SWITCH
S_{WF}	WEATHERPROOF FUSED SWITCH
S_L	SWITCH FOR LOW VOLTAGE SWITCHING SYSTEM
S_{LM}	MASTER SWITCH FOR LOW VOLTAGE SWITCHING SYSTEM
S_T	TIME SWITCH
(S)	CEILING PULL SWITCH
S	SWITCH AND SINGLE RECEPTACLE
S	SWITCH AND DOUBLE RECEPTACLE

A,B,C ETC.
A,B,C ETC. } SPECIAL OUTLETS
S A,B,C ETC.

Any standard symbol given above with the addition of lowercase subscript lettering may be used to designate some special variation of standard equipment of particular interest in a specific set of architectural plans.

When used they must be listed in the schedule of symbols on each drawing and if necessary further described in the specifications.

Frederick R. Brown, PE; Ayres, Cohen and Hayakawa; Consulting Engineers; Los Angeles/San Francisco, California
Richard F. Humenn, PE; Joseph R. Loring & Associates, Inc., Consulting Engineers; New York, New York

HEAT-POWER APPARATUS

STEAM GENERATOR (BOILER) .....

FLUE GAS REHEATER (INTERMEDIATE SUPERHEATER) . .

LIVE STEAM SUPERHEATER OR REHEATER ......

FEED HEATER WITH AIR OUTLET ....

CONDENSER, SURFACE ....

STEAM TURBINE ....

CONDENSING TURBINE ....

OPEN TANK ....

CLOSED TANK ....

AUTOMATIC REDUCING VALVE ....

AUTOMATIC BYPASS VALVE .....

AUTOMATIC VALVE OPERATED BY GOVERNOR ......

BOILER FEED PUMP ....

SERVICE PUMP ....

CONDENSATE PUMP ....

CIRCULATING WATER PUMP ......

AIR PUMP ....

OIL PUMP ....

RECIPROCATING PUMP ....

AIR EJECTOR (DYNAMIC PUMP)

VACUUM TRAP ....

REFRIGERATION

THERMOSTAT, SELF-CONTAINED

THERMOSTAT, REMOTE BULB ...

PRESSURE SWITCH ....

EXPANSION VALVE, HAND......

EXPANSION VALVE, AUTOMATIC .

EXPANSION VALVE, THERMOSTATIC ....

EVAPORATOR PRESSURE REGULATING VALVE, THROTTLING TYPE (EVAPORATOR SIDE)

EVAPORATOR PRESSURE REGULATING VALVE, THERMOSTATIC, THROTTLING TYPE

EVAPORATOR PRESSURE REGULATING VALVE SNAP-ACTION

COMPRESSOR SUCTION VALVE, PRESSURE LIMITING, THROTTLING TYPE (COMPRESSOR SIDE)

CONSTANT PRESSURE VALVE, SUCTION

THERMAL BULB ....

SCALE TRAP ....

DRYER ....

FILTER AND STRAINER ....

COMBINATION STRAINER AND DRYER

SIGHT GLASS

FLOAT VALVE HIGH SIDE

FLOAT VALVE LOW SIDE

GAUGE ....

COOLING TOWER ....

EVAPORATOR, FINNED TYPE, NATURAL CONVECTION

EVAPORATOR, FORCED CONVECTION ....

IMMERSION COOLING UNIT ....

CONDENSER, AIR-COOLED, FINNED, FORCED AIR

CONDENSER, WATER-COOLED, SHELL AND TUBE

CONDENSER EVAPORATIVE

HEAT EXCHANGER

CONDENSING UNIT AIR COOLED

CONDENSING UNIT WATER COOLED

PRESSURE SWITCH WITH HIGH PRESSURE CUT-OUT

COMPRESSOR

COMPRESSOR OPEN CRANKCASE RECIPROCATING, DIRECT DRIVE

COMPRESSOR OPEN CRANKCASE RECIPROCATING BELTED

COMPRESSOR ENCLOSED CRANKCASE, ROTARY, BELTED

Amor Halperin, PE; Ayres, Cohen and Hayakawa; Consulting Engineers; Los Angeles/San Francisco, California

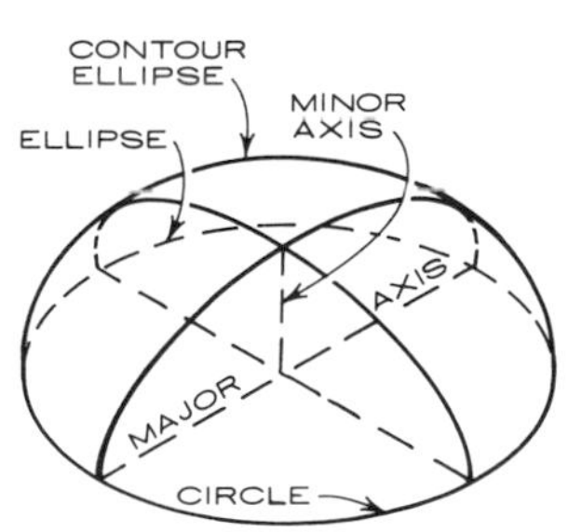
CONTOUR ELLIPSE
MINOR AXIS
ELLIPSE
AXIS
MAJOR
CIRCLE

OBLATE SPHEROID

An ellipse rotated about its minor axis.

ELLIPSE
CONTOUR ELLIPSE
MAJOR AXIS
AXIS
MINOR
CIRCLE

PROLATE SPHEROID

An ellipse rotated about its major axis.

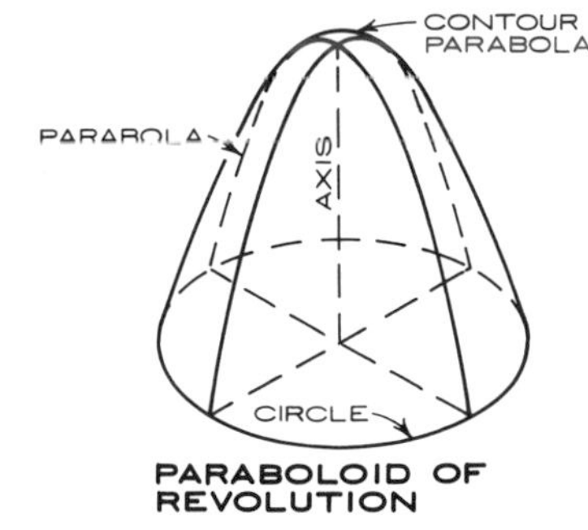
CONTOUR PARABOLA
PARABOLA
AXIS
CIRCLE

PARABOLOID OF REVOLUTION

A parabola rotated about its axis.

The elliptic paraboloid is similar, but its plan is an ellipse instead of circle, and vertical sections are varying parabolas.

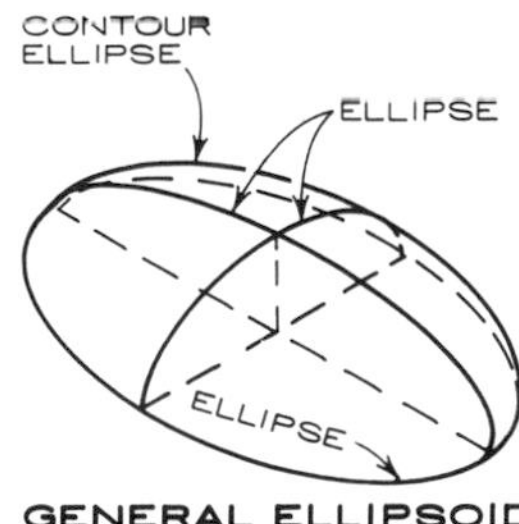
CONTOUR ELLIPSE
ELLIPSE
ELLIPSE

GENERAL ELLIPSOID

NOTES

1. The dome shapes shown above are SURFACES OF POSITIVE CURVATURE, that is, the centers of both principal radii of curvature are on the same side of the surface.

2. SURFACES OF NEGATIVE CURVATURE (saddle shapes) such as those shown below, are surfaces in which the centers of the two principal radii of curvature are on opposite sides of the surface.

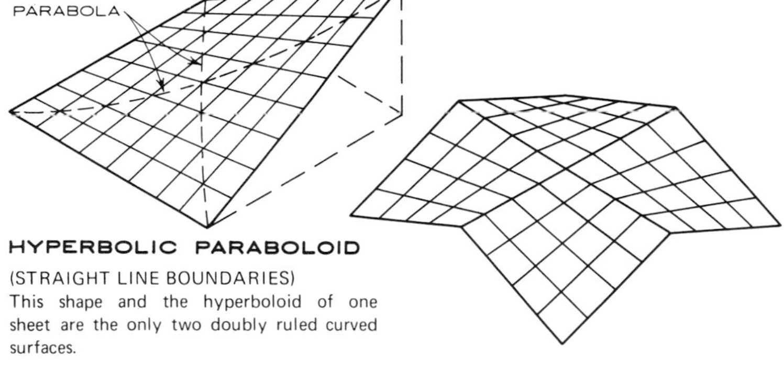
PARABOLA

HYPERBOLIC PARABOLOID

(STRAIGHT LINE BOUNDARIES)

This shape and the hyperboloid of one sheet are the only two doubly ruled curved surfaces.

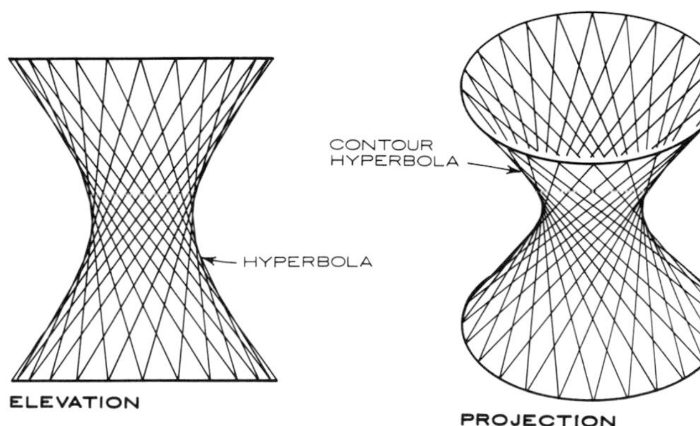
HYPERBOLA
CONTOUR HYPERBOLA

ELEVATION

PROJECTION

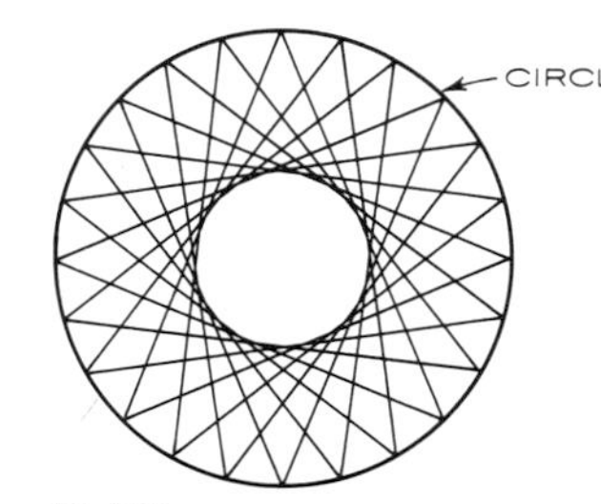
CIRCLE

PLAN

HYPERBOLOID OF REVOLUTION

(OR HYPERBOLOID OF ONE SHEET)

NOTE

This shape is a doubly ruled surface, which can also be drawn with ellipses as plan sections instead of the circles shown.

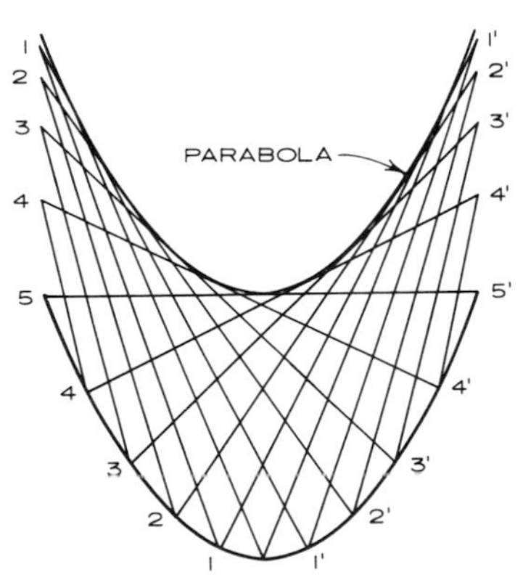
PARABOLA
1 2 3 4 5 4 3 2 1
1' 2' 3' 4' 5' 4' 3' 2' 1'

SECTION A-A

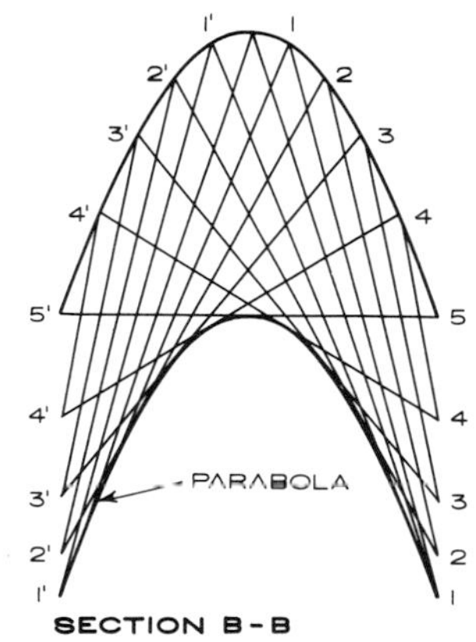
PARABOLA
1' 2' 3' 4' 5' 4' 3' 2' 1'
1 2 3 4 5 4 3 2 1

SECTION B-B

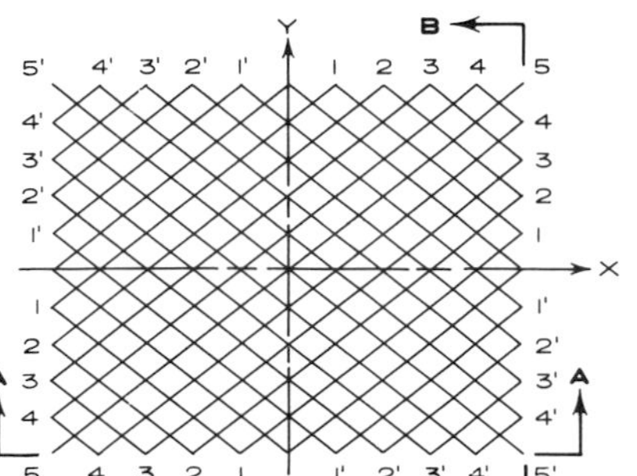
Y
X
B
A
5' 4' 3' 2' 1' 1 2 3 4 5
5 4 3 2 1 1' 2' 3' 4' 5'

PLAN

HYPERBOLIC PARABOLOID

(PARABOLA BOUNDARIES)

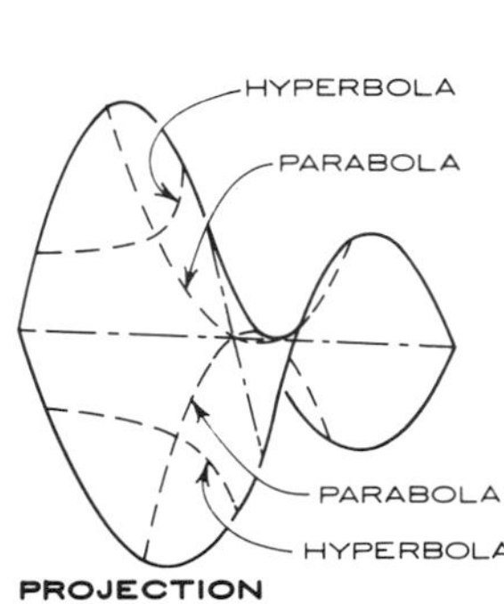
HYPERBOLA
PARABOLA
PARABOLA
HYPERBOLA

PROJECTION

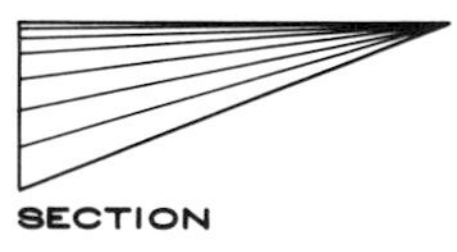

SECTION

ELEVATION

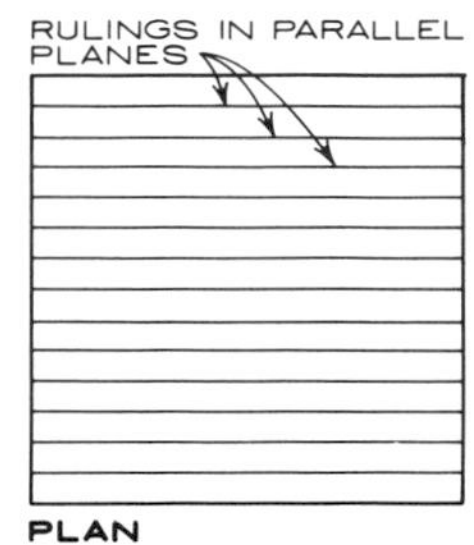
RULINGS IN PARALLEL PLANES

PLAN

CONOID

(SINGLY RULED SURFACE)

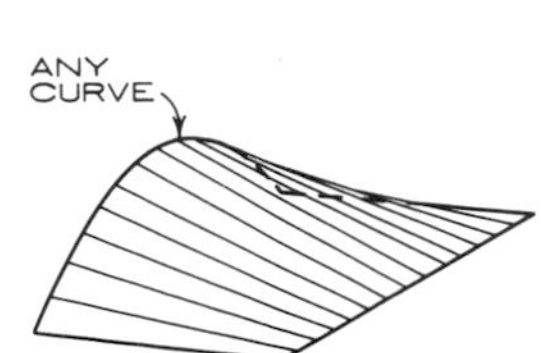
ANY CURVE

PROJECTION

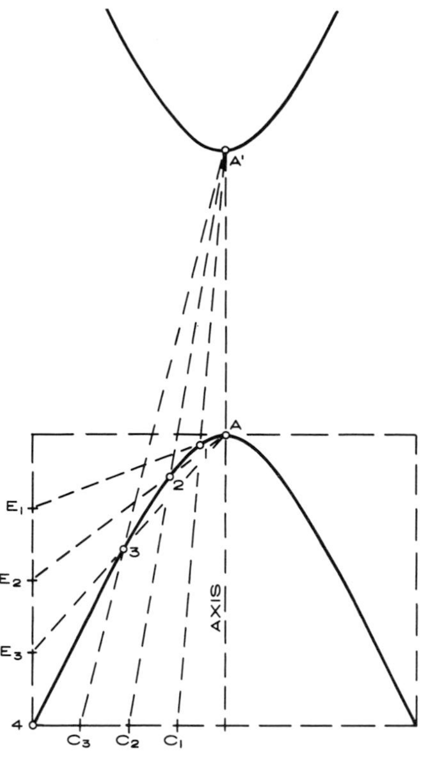
A'
A
2
3
AXIS
E1
E2
E3
4
C3 C2 C1

HYPERBOLA

PARALLELOGRAM METHOD

GIVEN:

Axis, two apexes (A and A') and a chord.

1. Draw surrounding parallelogram.
2. Divide chord in whole number of equal spaces (C_1, C_2, C_3, etc.).
3. Divide edge of parallelogram into same integral number of equal spaces (E_1, E_2, E_3, etc.).
4. Join A to points E on edge; join A' to points C on chord. Intersection of these rays are points on curve.

This method can be used equally well for any type of orthogonal or perspective projection, as shown by example of ellipse.

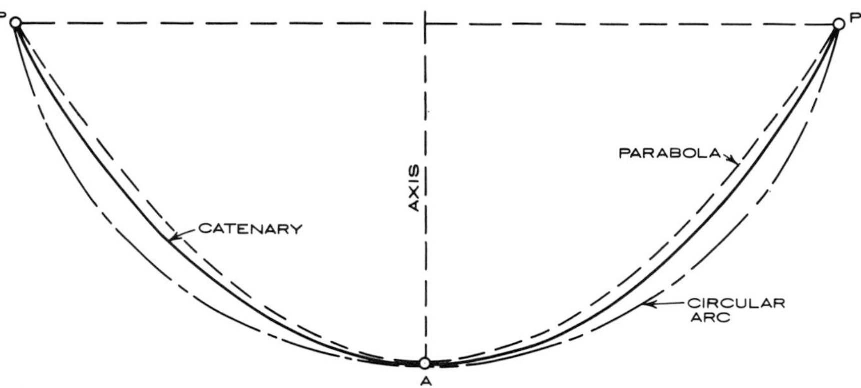
P
P'
AXIS
PARABOLA
CATENARY
CIRCULAR ARC
A

CATENARY

A catenary curve lies between a parabola and a circular arc drawn through the same three points, but is closer to the parabola. The catenary is not a conic section. The easiest method of drawing it is to tilt the drafting board and hang a very fine chain on it, and then prick guide points through the links of the chain.

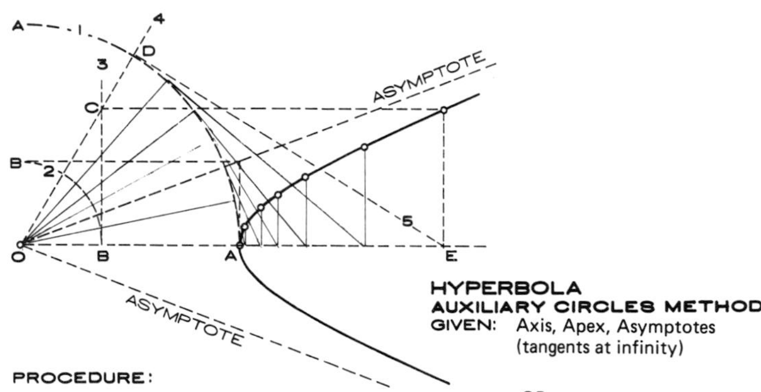
A
4
D
3
C
ASYMPTOTE
B
2
5
O
B
A
E
ASYMPTOTE

HYPERBOLA

AUXILIARY CIRCLES METHOD

GIVEN: Axis, Apex, Asymptotes (tangents at infinity)

PROCEDURE:

1. Draw auxiliary circles with OB and OA as radii: note $\frac{OB}{OA}$ = slope of asymptote.
2. Erect perpendicular 3 where circle 2 intersects axis.
3. Draw any line 4 through O, intersecting circle 1 at B and line 3 at C.
4. Draw line 5 through C parallel to axis.
5. Draw tangent 6 at D, intersecting axis at E.
6. Erect perpendicular 7 at E, intersecting 5 at P, a point on hyperbola.

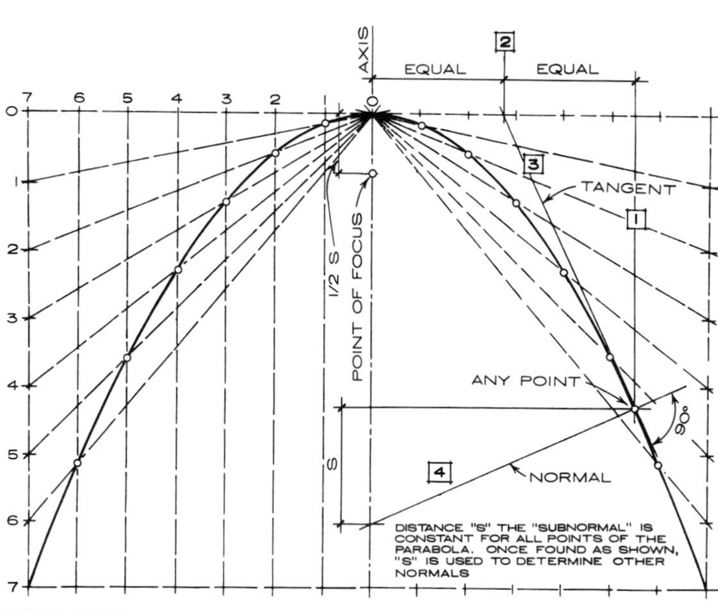
AXIS
EQUAL
EQUAL
2
3
TANGENT
1
1/2 S
POINT OF FOCUS
ANY POINT
90°
S
4
NORMAL
DISTANCE "S" THE "SUBNORMAL" IS CONSTANT FOR ALL POINTS OF THE PARABOLA. ONCE FOUND AS SHOWN, "S" IS USED TO DETERMINE OTHER NORMALS

PARABOLA

PARALLELOGRAM METHOD

This method is comparable to the "Parallelogram Method" shown for the hyperbola above and the ellipse on previous page. The other apex 'A' is at infinity.

ANY NUMBER OF EQUAL PARTS

EQUAL TO RISE

AXIS

RISE

EQUAL EQUAL

PARABOLA

ENVELOPE OF TANGENTS

This method does not give points on the curve, but a series of tangents within which the parabola can be drawn.

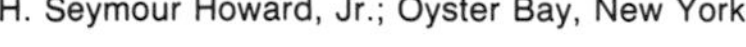
H. Seymour Howard, Jr.; Oyster Bay, New York

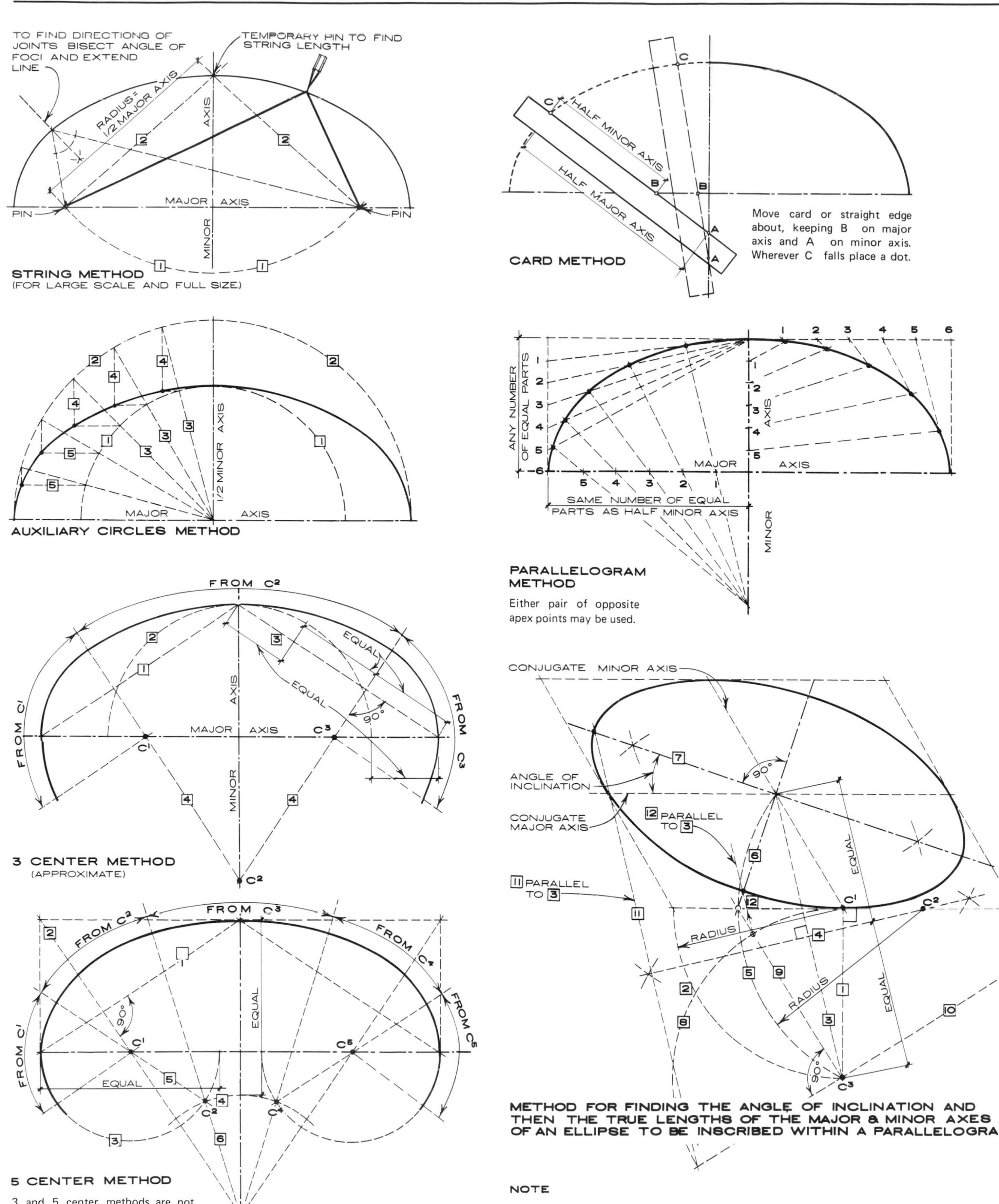
TO FIND DIRECTIONS OF JOINTS BISECT ANGLE OF FOCI AND EXTEND LINE
TEMPORARY PIN TO FIND STRING LENGTH
RADIUS = 1/2 MAJOR AXIS
MAJOR AXIS
MINOR AXIS
PIN
PIN
STRING METHOD
(FOR LARGE SCALE AND FULL SIZE)
HALF MINOR AXIS
HALF MAJOR AXIS
Move card or straight edge about, keeping B on major axis and A on minor axis. Wherever C falls place a dot.
CARD METHOD
1/2 MINOR AXIS
MAJOR AXIS
AUXILIARY CIRCLES METHOD
ANY NUMBER OF EQUAL PARTS
SAME NUMBER OF EQUAL PARTS AS HALF MINOR AXIS
MAJOR AXIS
MINOR AXIS
PARALLELOGRAM METHOD
Either pair of opposite apex points may be used.
FROM C²
FROM C¹
FROM C³
EQUAL
EQUAL
90°
MAJOR AXIS
MINOR AXIS
3 CENTER METHOD
(APPROXIMATE)
CONJUGATE MINOR AXIS
ANGLE OF INCLINATION
CONJUGATE MAJOR AXIS
PARALLEL TO 3
PARALLEL TO 3
RADIUS
RADIUS
EQUAL
EQUAL
90°
FROM C³
FROM C²
FROM C⁴
FROM C¹
FROM C⁵
EQUAL
EQUAL
90°
METHOD FOR FINDING THE ANGLE OF INCLINATION AND THEN THE TRUE LENGTHS OF THE MAJOR & MINOR AXES OF AN ELLIPSE TO BE INSCRIBED WITHIN A PARALLELOGRAM
5 CENTER METHOD

3 and 5 center methods are not true ellipses, but only approximations which are useful for small scale drawings.

NOTE

1. Using the conjugate axes, the ellipse can be drawn directly by using the parallelogram method.
2. Using the true lengths of the axes, the ellipse may be drawn with any one of the methods illustrated on this page.

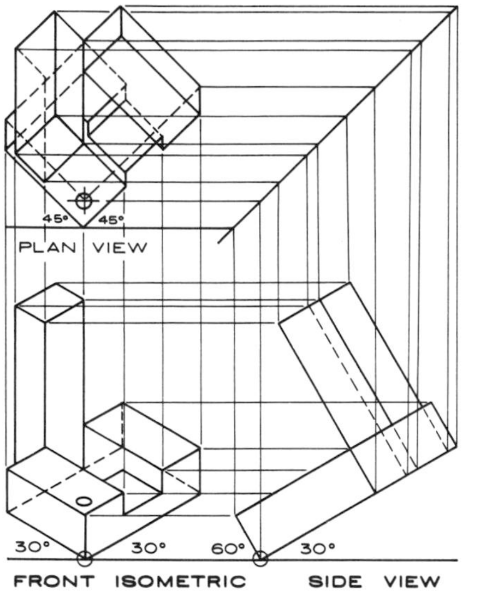

PLAN VIEW

FRONT ISOMETRIC SIDE VIEW

PROJECTED METHOD

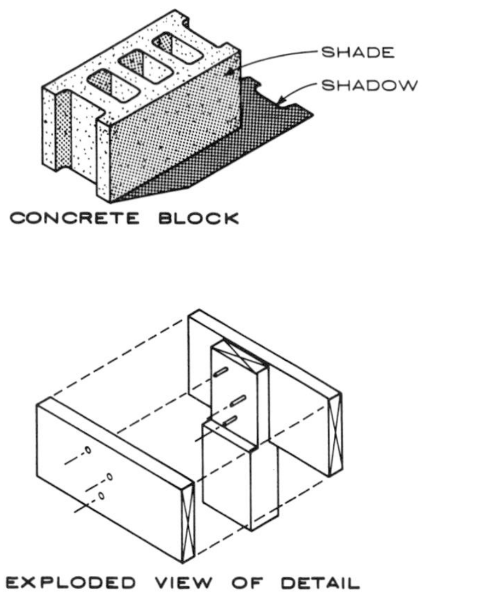

CONCRETE BLOCK

EXPLODED VIEW OF DETAIL

ISOMETRIC

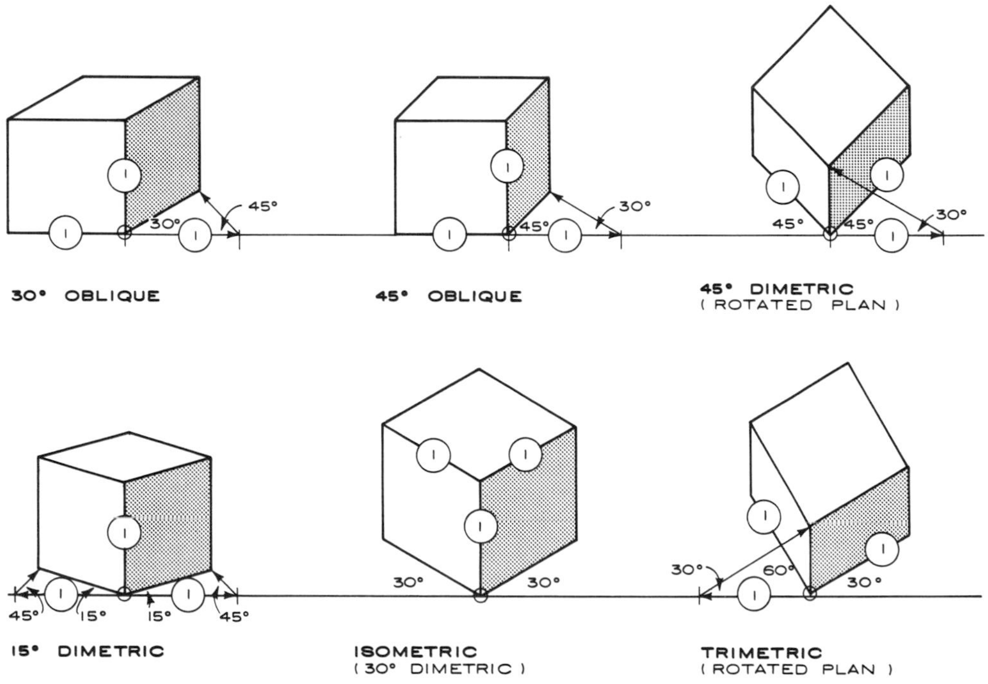

30° OBLIQUE

45° OBLIQUE

45° DIMETRIC (ROTATED PLAN)

15° DIMETRIC

ISOMETRIC (30° DIMETRIC)

TRIMETRIC (ROTATED PLAN)

AXIOMETRIC — MEASURED METHOD

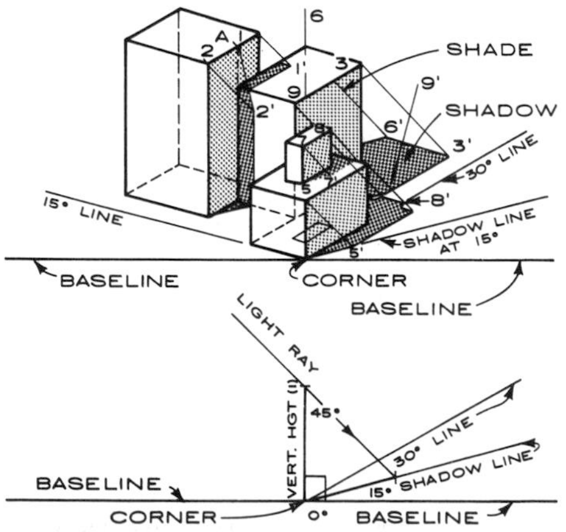

15 / 30° TRIMETRIC SHADOW

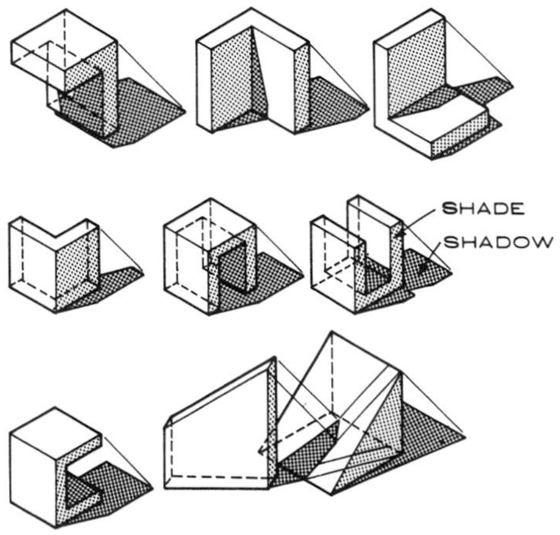

SHADES AND SHADOWS

Jim Maeda; Samuel J. De Santo and Associates; New York, New York

PARALINE DRAWINGS

Paraline drawings are sometimes referred to as AXONOMETRIC (Greek) or AXIOMETRIC (English) drawings. These drawings are projected pictorial representations of an object which give a three-dimensional quality. They can be classified as orthographic projections inasmuch as the plan view is rotated and the side view is tilted. The resulting "front" view is projected at a 90° angle to the picture plane (as illustrated in the projected method). These drawings differ from perspective drawings, since the projection lines remain parallel instead of converging to a point on the horizon.

Drawings prepared by using the projection method require three views of the object, which tends to be more time-consuming and complex than drawing by the direct measuring method. The following drawings utilize this method; they are simple to draw and represent reasonably accurate proportions.

OBLIQUE

In an oblique drawing one face (either plan or elevation) of the object is drawn directly on the picture plane. Projected lines are drawn at a 30 or 45° angle to the picture plane. The length of the projecting lines is determined as illustrated and varies according to the angle chosen.

DIMETRIC

A dimetric drawing is similar to oblique, with one exception—the object is rotated so that only one of its corners touches the picture plane. The most frequently used angle for the projecting lines is an equal division of 45° on either side of the leading edge. A 15° angle is sometimes used when it is less important to show the "roof view" of the object.

ISOMETRIC

The isometric, a special type of dimetric drawing, is the easiest and most popular paraline drawing. All axes of the object are simultaneously rotated away from the picture plane and kept at the same angle of projection (30° from the picture plane). All legs are equally distorted in length at a given scale and therefore maintain an exact proportion of 1:1:1.

TRIMETRIC

The trimetric drawing is similar to the dimetric, except that the plan of the object is rotated so that the two exposed sides of the object are not at equal angles to the picture plane. The plan is usually positioned at 30/60° angle to the ground plane. The height of the object is reduced proportionately as illustrated (similar to the 45° dimetric).

SHADES AND SHADOWS

Shades and shadows are easily constructed and can be very effective in paraline drawings. The location of the light source will determine the direction of the shadows cast by the object. The shade line is the line (or the edge) that separates the light area from the shaded areas of the object. Shadows are constructed by drawing a line, representing a light ray, from a corner of the lighted surface at a 45° angle to the ground plane. Shadows cast by a vertical edge of the object will be drawn midway in the angle created by the intersection of the projected line of the object and the ground, or baseline (the baseline represents the intersection of the picture plane). The 45° light ray is extended until it meets the shadow line (as illustrated), and this point determines the length of the shadow for any given vertical height of the object. Shadow lines of all vertical edges of the object are drawn parallel to one another.

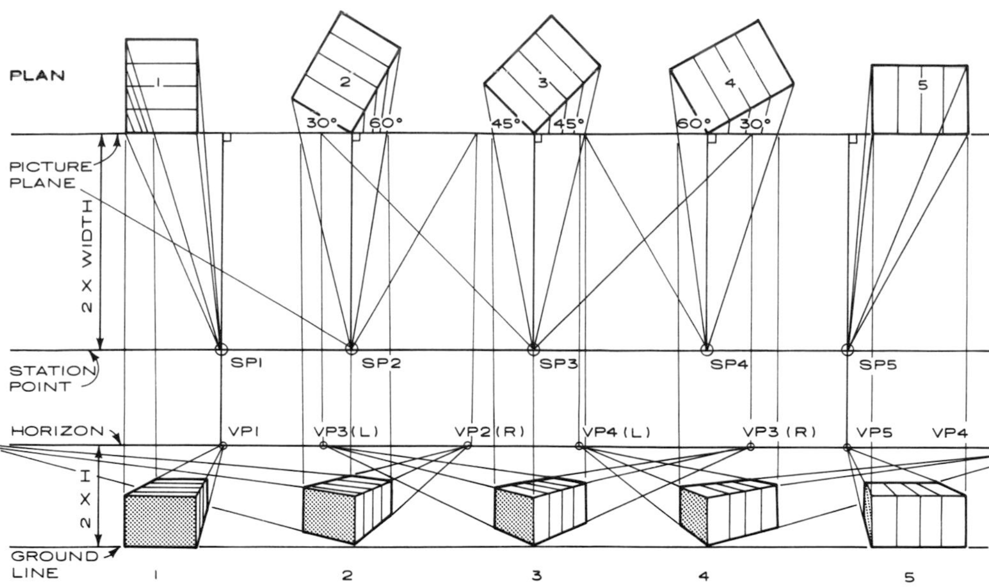
PLAN
PICTURE PLANE
2 X WIDTH
STATION POINT
HORIZON
2 X H
GROUND LINE
SP1
SP2
SP3
SP4
SP5
VP1
VP3 (L)
VP2 (R)
VP4 (L)
VP3 (R)
VP5
VP4
30°
60°
45°
1
2
3
4
5

PERSPECTIVE — PROJECTION METHOD

GENERAL NOTES

Before the drawing can be laid out, the following information must be obtained:

1. An approximation of the overall dimensions of the building.
2. The location of the building in relation to the picture plane.
3. The orientation of the building, either in front of or behind the picture plane.

While the building can be located anywhere in the drawing—in front of, behind, or at any angle to the picture plane—the simplest approach is to place the building at the picture plane. The horizontal lines of the building would be parallel to the picture plane in a one-point perspective or placed at an angle to the picture plane. Usually this will be a 30/60 or 45° angle in a two-point perspective.

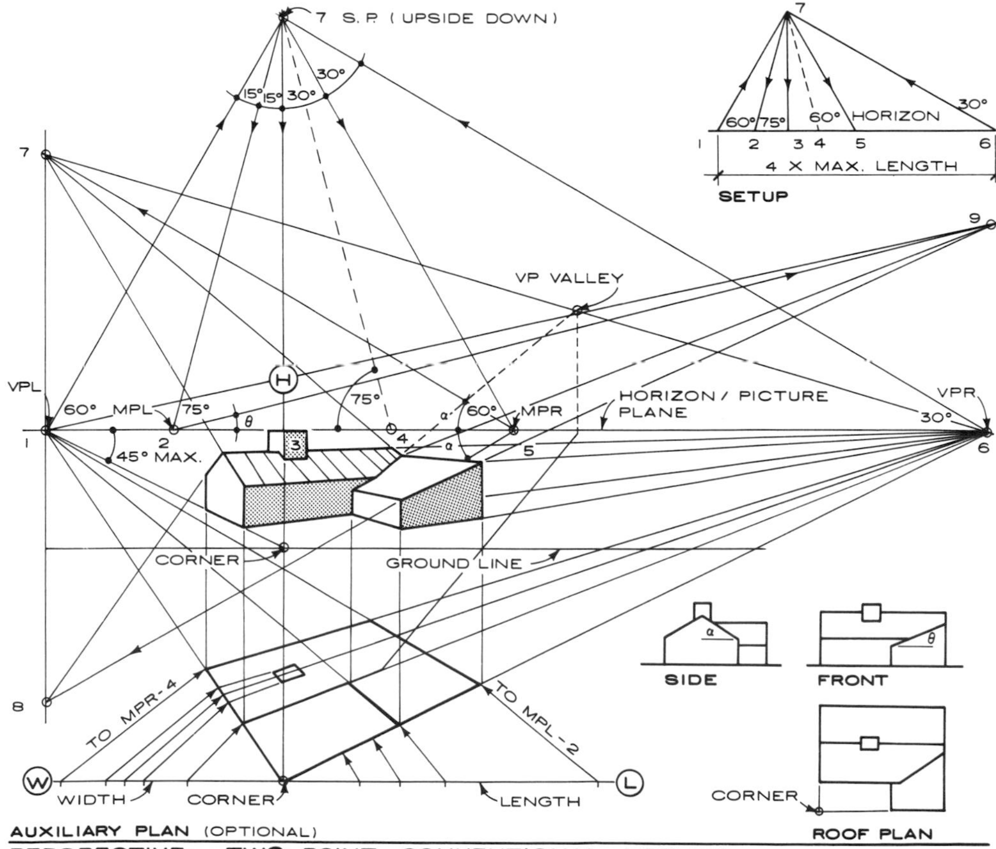
7 S. P. (UPSIDE DOWN)
15°
15°
30°
30°
SETUP
60°
75°
60°
HORIZON
30°
1 2 3 4 5 6
4 X MAX. LENGTH
VP VALLEY
VPL
60°
MPL
75°
θ
MPR
α
HORIZON / PICTURE PLANE
VPR
2
45° MAX.
CORNER
GROUND LINE
TO MPR-4
TO MPL-2
WIDTH
CORNER
LENGTH
SIDE
FRONT
ROOF PLAN
W
L
H
7
8
9

AUXILIARY PLAN (OPTIONAL)

PERSPECTIVE — TWO-POINT CONVENTIONAL METHOD

TERMS AND CONCEPTS

1. THE OBJECT: Called a building in this example.
2. THE PICTURE PLANE: An imaginary, transparent plane, onto or through which the object is perceived in a perspective rendering. It is:
   a. Parallel to one face of the drawing paper, if it is a one-point perspective.
   b. Perpendicular to the ground line and at any angle to the building if it is a two-point perspective.
   c. Tilted and placed at any angle to the building if it is a three-point perspective.
   d. A curved plane if it is a wide angle perspective view.
3. HORIZON LINE: A line drawn on the picture plane to represent the horizon. It is usually located at the point where all parallel lines recede away from the viewer and finally converge. This point is aptly designated as the vanishing point. Note that although the horizon is generally thought of as a horizontal line, in certain applications it could be vertical, or even at an angle, to the picture plane. For example, in drawing shades and shadows it appears to be at a 90° angle and in a three-point perspective it appears to be slanted.
4. STATION POINT: The point from which the object is being viewed or, in other words the point from which the viewer is seeing the building. The location of this point will be the factor that determines the width of the drawing. A 30° cone of vision is drawn from the station point; as the viewer moves away from the object, the cone widens, the object becomes smaller, and more material is included in the area surrounding the object. A common way of determining the distance between the station point and the picture plane is by referring to the following parameters:
   Minimum—1.73 times the width of the drawing.
   Average—2.00 times the width of the drawing.
   Maximum—2.50 times the width of the drawing.
5. VANISHING POINT(S): A specific point or points located on the horizon line, where all parallel lines, drawn in perspective, converge or terminate. The location of the vanishing point varies with the type of perspective drawing. In a two-point perspective, the distance between the vanishing point left and the vanishing point right is estimated as being approximately four times the overall size of the building.
6. VISUAL RAY: An imaginary line drawn from the station point to any specific point lying within the designated scope of the plan layout of the object. The point at which this projected line passes through the picture plane will determine the location of that point in the perspective drawing.
7. GROUND PLANE: The ground on which the viewer is standing. In plan, this is determined at the station point. In perspective, it is the primary plane on which the building is sited. When the lines of this plane are extended to infinity, it becomes the horizon line. The intersection formed when the picture plane and the ground plane come together is called the ground line. In this way the horizontal dimension of the drawing is determined. The vertical dimension is determined by the vertical distance from the ground line to the horizon line. This should be approximately twice the height of object, in perspective, or a 30° cone in elevation.
8. ONE-POINT INTERIOR PERSPECTIVE: The most frequently used application of a one-point perspective. This is the same method as that used in setting up a one-point exterior perspective, except for the limitations that the confinement of space places on the location of the vanishing points. The vanishing point is usually located at the sitting or standing height of an average person within the space (eye level can be considered to be at 5 ft 4 in. from the floor. In most cases, the vanishing point is located within the confines of the enclosed space being represented in the drawing.
9. TWO-POINT PERSPECTIVE USING THE MEASURING POINT METHOD: This is a simplified alternative to the conventional method of laying out the plan picture plane and projecting the vanishing lines. The measuring point method of drawing a two-point perspective eliminates the necessity of the preliminary layout of the plan. One of the obvious advantages of this method is the ease with which the size of the drawing can be adjusted. A perspective can be made larger by simply increasing the scale of the drawing.

Jim Maeda; Samuel J. De Santo and Associates; New York, New York

GIVEN:
HEIGHT = 5'-0"
WIDTH = 6'-0"
DEPTH = 4'-0"
HGT = 5'-0"
TO DESIRED SCALE
1 FRONT ELEVATION
HORIZON
VP
MAX. 2 X HEIGHT
GROUND LINE
2 LOCATE HORIZON AND VP
SP
30°
45°
60° HORIZON
VP
START FROM MOST REMOTE POINT FROM VP
GROUND LINE
3 LOCATE 45° POINT
45° POINT
HORIZON
VP
GROUND LINE
CORNER
4 CONNECT CORNERS TO VP
45° POINT
HORIZON
VP
LOCATES BACK WALL
GROUND LINE
0 1 2 3 4
5 MEASURE DEPTH
45° POINT
HORIZON
VP
GROUND LINE
DEPTH
6 COMPLETE

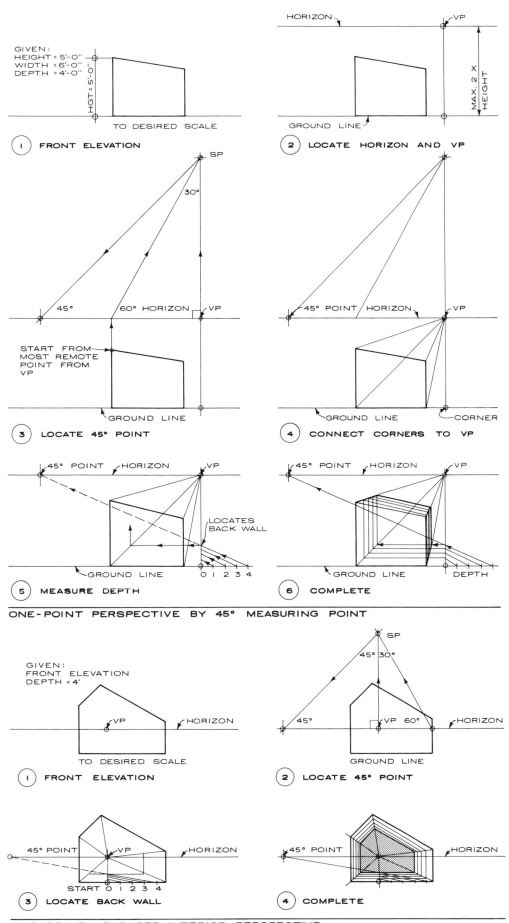

ONE-POINT PERSPECTIVE BY 45° MEASURING POINT

GIVEN:
FRONT ELEVATION
DEPTH = 4'
VP
HORIZON
TO DESIRED SCALE
1 FRONT ELEVATION
SP
45°
30°
45°
VP
60°
HORIZON
GROUND LINE
2 LOCATE 45° POINT
45° POINT
VP
HORIZON
START 0 1 2 3 4
3 LOCATE BACK WALL
45° POINT
HORIZON
4 COMPLETE

ONE-POINT MEASURED INTERIOR PERSPECTIVE

Jim Maeda; Samuel J. De Santo and Associates; New York, New York

ONE-POINT PERSPECTIVE

The one-point perspective is probably the least complicated of the projected perspective methods. The primary face of the building or object is placed directly on the picture plane. The adjacent planes, generally connected to the primary plane at right angles, converge to the vanishing point—which can be either in front of or behind the picture plane. The vanishing point, located on the horizon line, also determines the height from which the building is viewed.

The conventional method of laying out a one-point exterior perspective is illustrated on the preceding page. A plan view, roof view, and elevation are required for the layout. The size of the object, and therefore the drawing, can be increased or decreased by moving the plan further in front of or behind the picture plane. This method is more flexible but much more complicated and time-consuming than the method that follows.

EXTERIOR ONE-POINT PERSPECTIVE

① Draw the primary elevation of the building to scale.

② Locate the horizon above the ground line at the desired level (eye level is at approximately 5 ft 4 in.). To ensure that the final perspective will fall within the 60° cone vision, the height should not exceed 2X the height of the building. The VP is located left or right arbitrarily depending on the view desired.

③ A 45° vanishing point can be graphically located by starting at the most remote point of the roof and extending a vertical line to the horizon line. From this point, draw a line upward, at a 60° angle. Another line should be drawn vertically upward from the vanishing point. The station point (upside down) is located at the point where these two lines intersect. From the station point, draw a line at a 45° angle to meet the horizon line. This point will be the vanishing point for all lines that are positioned at 45° angle and parallel to the picture plane.

④ From each corner of the primary elevation, draw a line to the vanishing point.

⑤ The correct building depth (drawn at 6 ft in the illustration) is measured along the ground line—on the picture plane—starting at point 0. Draw a line connecting this point to the 45° point on the horizon line. The point at which this line intersects the line extended between the lower corner of the elevation to the vanishing point will determine the location of the back wall of the building.

⑥ The perspective is completed by constructing the back wall at the location established in step 5 and connecting it to the front wall. Note that the lines that are drawn at a 45° angle in the drawing remain parallel to each other as they are extended in perspective.

ONE-POINT INTERIOR AND SECTIONAL PERSPECTIVE

① Draw the primary elevation, or section, to scale. Locate the horizon line and vanishing point within the confines of the interior space.

② A 45° point is located in a similar manner to the one-point exterior perspective. The station point is established by drawing a line, at a 60° angle, from the most remote point in the elevation to intersect another line extended upward at a perpendicular from the vanishing point.

③ The room depth is determined by starting at point 0 on the ground line and measuring the appropriate distance to the 45° point on the horizon line. The back wall is located where these two lines come together.

④ Complete the back wall as illustrated. Note that all lines occurring at a 45° angle in the elevation remain parallel in perspective. All surfaces that are parallel to the picture plane will remain parallel in perspective.

A

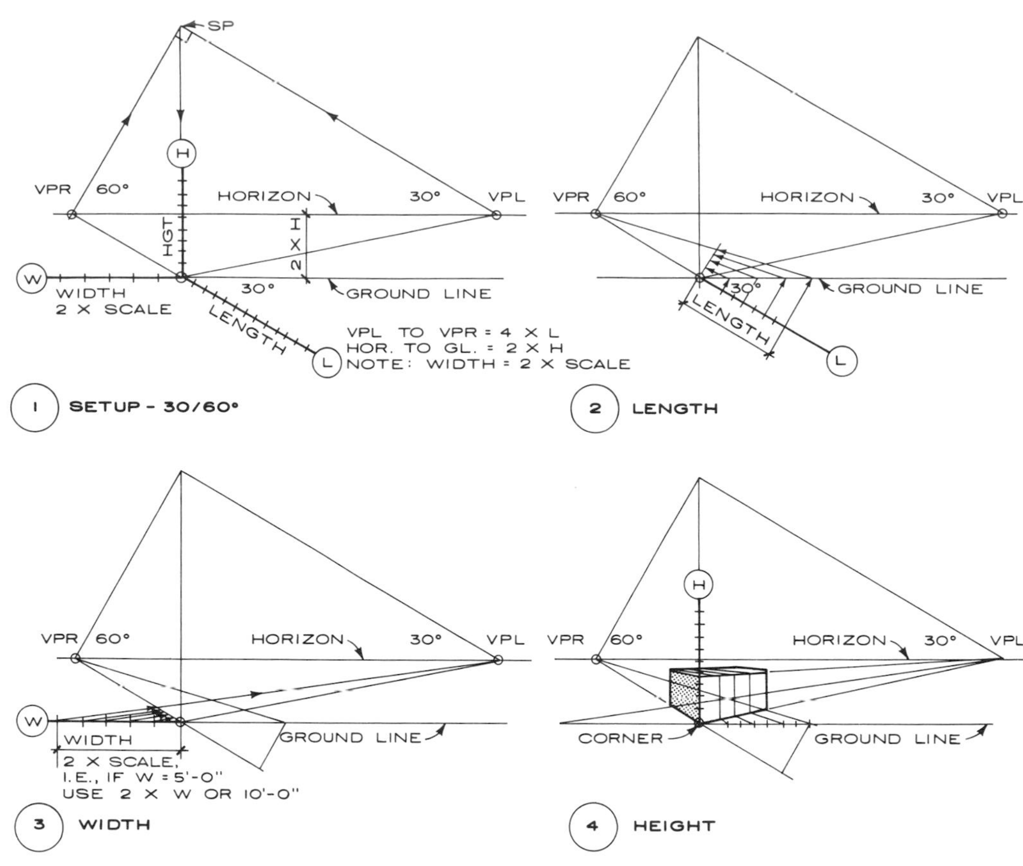

SP
H
VPR
60°
HORIZON
30°
VPL
HGT
2 X H
W
WIDTH
2 X SCALE
30°
GROUND LINE
LENGTH
VPL TO VPR = 4 X L
HOR. TO GL. = 2 X H
L
NOTE: WIDTH = 2 X SCALE
1 SETUP - 30/60°
2 LENGTH
WIDTH
2 X SCALE,
I.E., IF W = 5'-0"
USE 2 X W OR 10'-0"
3 WIDTH
CORNER
4 HEIGHT

TWO-POINT PERSPECTIVE — 30/60° MEASURED SYSTEM

TWO-POINT PERSPECTIVE

The projection method of constructing a two-point perspective is illustrated on the preceding page. This is the most widely used and most flexible method of drawing a two-point perspective. It can be taken from any viewpoint by simply turning the plan to the desired position in the preliminary layout. The size of the perspective can also be adjusted by moving the plan in front of the picture plane for a larger drawing and behind the picture plane for a smaller drawing. As in all projected methods, an inordinate amount of time and energy is devoted to the layout. The measured method is equally accurate, less time-consuming, and much easier to construct, since it eliminates the need to lay out the drawing in plan. The desired size of the drawing is determined by drawing the primary elevation at the desired scale.

30/60° MEASURED SYSTEM

(1) SET-UP: Draw a horizon line and locate VPR and VPL separated at a distance that is approximately 4 to 4.5 × the maximum width of the building. Follow the illustration to locate the station point and leading corner of the building.

(2) LENGTH: Measure, to scale, the length of the building along length line L. A perpendicular line is drawn from these designated points to the ground line. The vanishing perspective lines are then drawn directly from these points to the appropriate vanishing point (VPL). In this way the correct length of the line can be determined. Note what happens when equally spaced points are projected from the ground line to the vanishing point. The visual distance (length) between them, as they get closer to the vanishing point, is progressively foreshortened.

(3) WIDTH: The width is measured along the width line (see illustration) at double the scale. That is, if the perspective is drawn at a scale of ⅛ in. = 1 ft and a particular line is to be drawn at 5 ft, measure 5 ft at ¼-in. scale starting at the corner and measure to the left of the corner horizontally. A line is drawn from each point on the width line to the appropriate vanishing point (VPR). The intersections of the length and width vanishing lines will define the "plan" in perspective.

(4) HEIGHT: Since the leading corner of the building is placed directly on the picture plane, the height is measured, to scale, directly on the H line. It is then carried to VPL and VPR as illustrated.

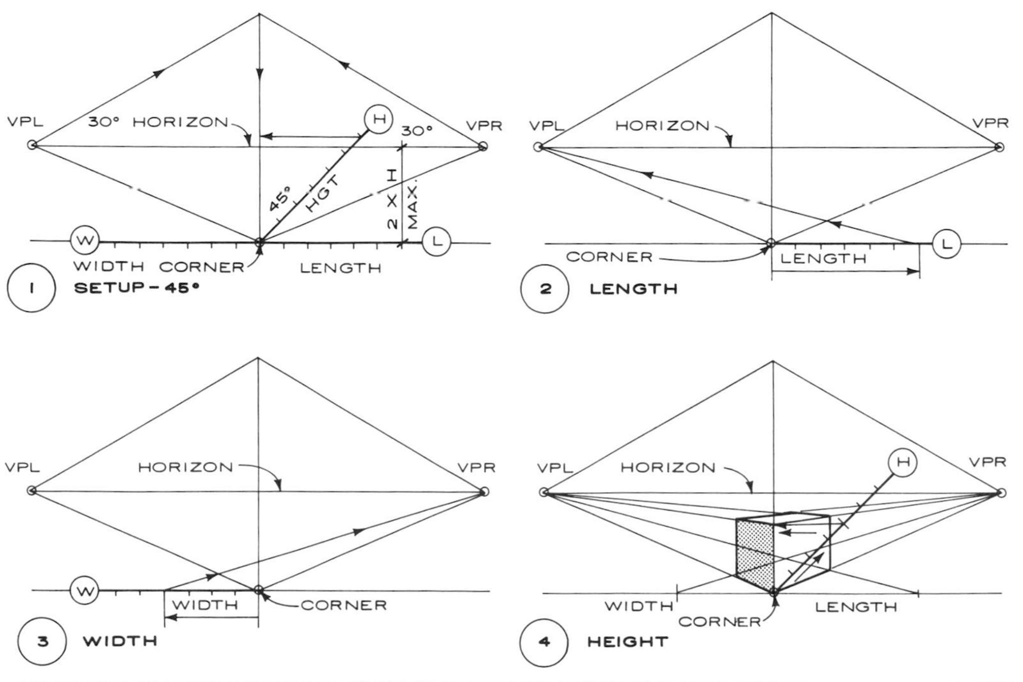

VPL
30° HORIZON
H
30°
VPR
45°
HGT
2 X H MAX.
W
L
WIDTH CORNER
LENGTH
1 SETUP - 45°
CORNER
LENGTH
2 LENGTH
HORIZON
WIDTH
CORNER
3 WIDTH
4 HEIGHT

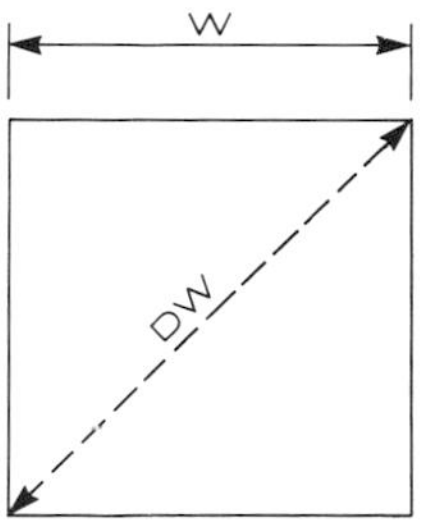

W
DW

45° METHOD SYSTEM

(1) SET-UP: Similar to the method used in the 30/60° set-up, the vanishing points are placed on the horizon line and separated by 2.5 × the diagonal width plus the maximum width of the building. Complete the set-up as illustrated.

(2) LENGTH: Measure, to scale, the length of the building along the length line L. Connect the points directly to VPL.

(3) WIDTH: In this set-up, the width is the same as the length scale. Measure the width of the building along the width line W. The length and width lines will form an outline of the "plan" in perspective.

(4) HEIGHT: The height line is positioned at a 45° angle and marked off to scale. A line representing the leading corner of the building is drawn perpendicular to the ground line. Connect or draw a line from the measurement points along the height line to the vertical corner line. As in the 30/60° setup, these points are then carried to VPR and VPL.

TWO-POINT PERSPECTIVE — 45° MEASURED SYSTEM

Jim Maeda; Samuel J. De Santo and Associates; New York, New York

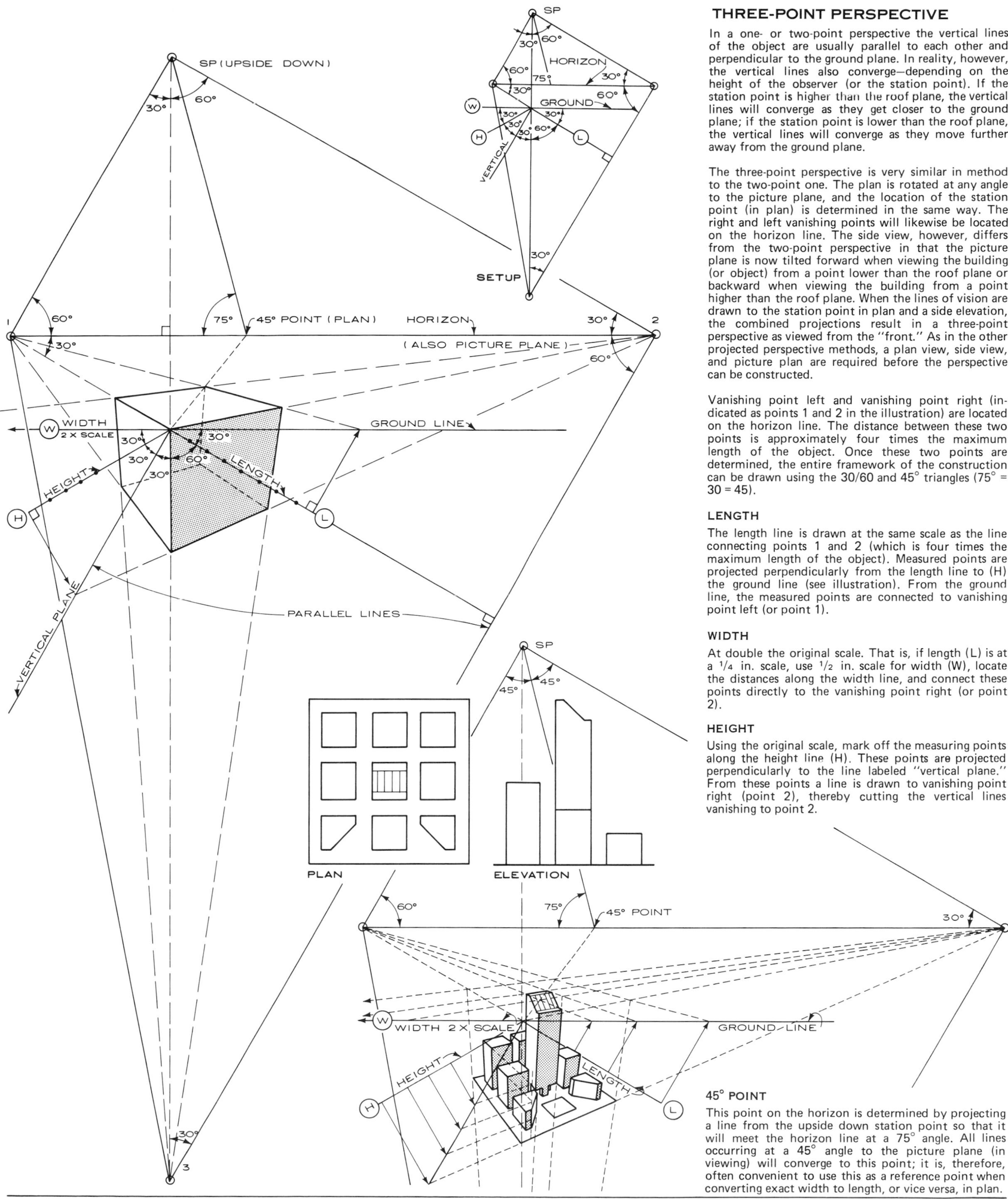
SP
SETUP
HORIZON
GROUND
VERTICAL
SP (UPSIDE DOWN)
45° POINT (PLAN)
HORIZON
(ALSO PICTURE PLANE)
WIDTH
2 X SCALE
GROUND LINE
HEIGHT
LENGTH
VERTICAL PLANE
PARALLEL LINES
PLAN
ELEVATION
45° POINT
WIDTH 2 X SCALE
GROUND LINE

PROJECTING THE PERSPECTIVE

THREE-POINT PERSPECTIVE

In a one- or two-point perspective the vertical lines of the object are usually parallel to each other and perpendicular to the ground plane. In reality, however, the vertical lines also converge—depending on the height of the observer (or the station point). If the station point is higher than the roof plane, the vertical lines will converge as they get closer to the ground plane; if the station point is lower than the roof plane, the vertical lines will converge as they move further away from the ground plane.

The three-point perspective is very similar in method to the two-point one. The plan is rotated at any angle to the picture plane, and the location of the station point (in plan) is determined in the same way. The right and left vanishing points will likewise be located on the horizon line. The side view, however, differs from the two-point perspective in that the picture plane is now tilted forward when viewing the building (or object) from a point lower than the roof plane or backward when viewing the building from a point higher than the roof plane. When the lines of vision are drawn to the station point in plan and a side elevation, the combined projections result in a three-point perspective as viewed from the "front." As in the other projected perspective methods, a plan view, side view, and picture plan are required before the perspective can be constructed.

Vanishing point left and vanishing point right (indicated as points 1 and 2 in the illustration) are located on the horizon line. The distance between these two points is approximately four times the maximum length of the object. Once these two points are determined, the entire framework of the construction can be drawn using the 30/60 and 45° triangles (75° = 30 = 45).

LENGTH

The length line is drawn at the same scale as the line connecting points 1 and 2 (which is four times the maximum length of the object). Measured points are projected perpendicularly from the length line to (H) the ground line (see illustration). From the ground line, the measured points are connected to vanishing point left (or point 1).

WIDTH

At double the original scale. That is, if length (L) is at a 1/4 in. scale, use 1/2 in. scale for width (W), locate the distances along the width line, and connect these points directly to the vanishing point right (or point 2).

HEIGHT

Using the original scale, mark off the measuring points along the height line (H). These points are projected perpendicularly to the line labeled "vertical plane." From these points a line is drawn to vanishing point right (point 2), thereby cutting the vertical lines vanishing to point 2.

45° POINT

This point on the horizon is determined by projecting a line from the upside down station point so that it will meet the horizon line at a 75° angle. All lines occurring at a 45° angle to the picture plane (in viewing) will converge to this point; it is, therefore, often convenient to use this as a reference point when converting exact width to length, or vice versa, in plan.

Jim Maeda; Samuel J. De Santo and Associates; New York, New York

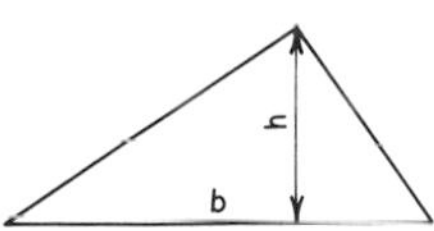
h
b

TRIANGLE
AREA = ½ ANY ALTITUDE × ITS BASE (ALTITUDE IS PERPENDICULAR DISTANCE TO OPPOSITE VERTEX OR CORNER.)
$A = \frac{1}{2} b \times h$

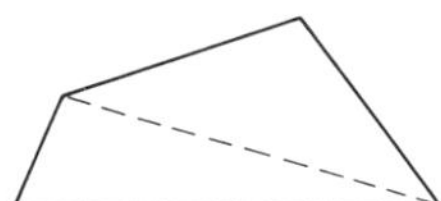

TRAPEZUM (IRREGULAR QUADRILATERAL)
AREA = DIVIDE FIGURE INTO TWO TRIANGLES AND FIND AREAS AS ABOVE

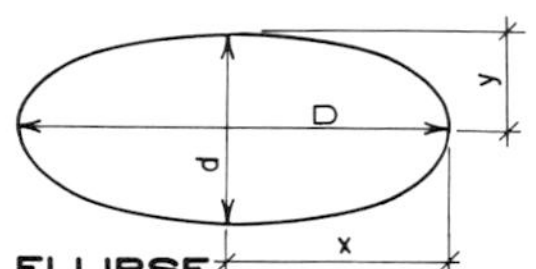
D
d
y
x

ELLIPSE
AREA = .7854 Dd
APPROX. PERIMETER
$= \pi\sqrt{2(x^2+y^2)}$

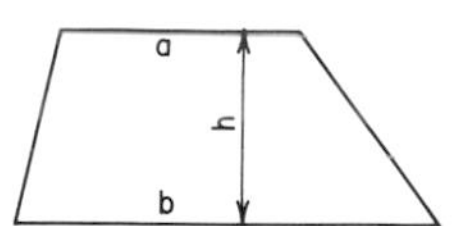
a
h
b

TRAPEZOID
AREA = ½ SUM OF PARALLEL SIDES × ALTITUDE
$A = \frac{h(a+b)}{2}$

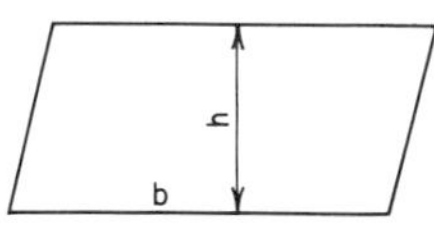
h
b

PARALLELOGRAM
AREA = EITHER SIDE × ALTITUDE

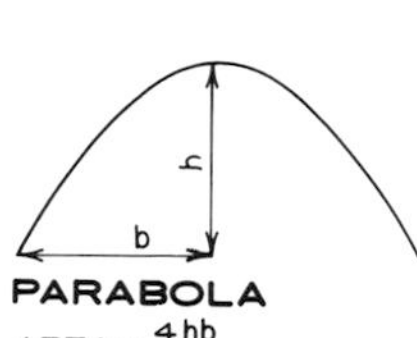
h
b

PARABOLA
AREA = $\frac{4hb}{3}$

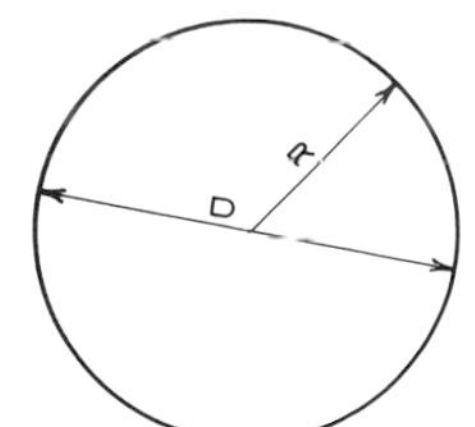
R
D

CIRCLE
AREA = $\frac{\pi D^2}{4} = \pi R^2$
CIRCUMFERENCE = $2\pi R = \pi D$
(π = 3.14159265359)

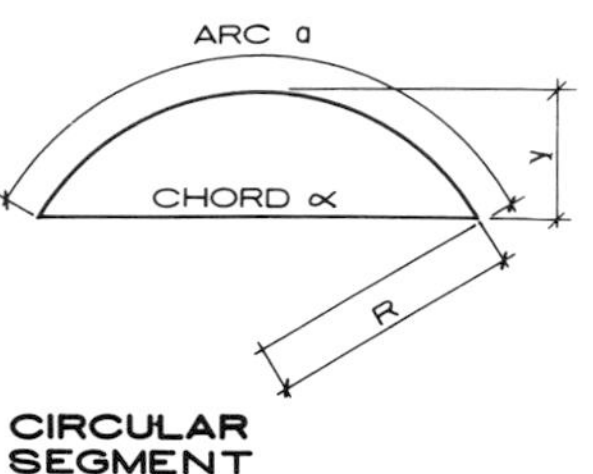
ARC a
CHORD ∝
y
R

CIRCULAR SEGMENT
AREA = $\frac{(\text{LENGTH OF ARC } a \times R - \alpha(R-y)}{2}$
CHORD $\alpha = 2\sqrt{2yR - y^2}$
$= 2R \sin \frac{A°}{2}$

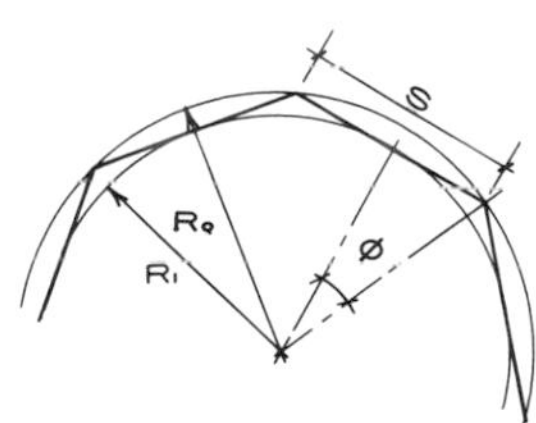
S
R₀
R₁
Ø

REGULAR POLYGON
AREA = $\frac{nSR_1}{2}$
(n = NUMBER OF SIDES)
ANY SIDE $S = 2\sqrt{R_0^2 - R_1^2}$
$R_1 = \frac{S}{2 \tan \emptyset}$ $R_0 = \frac{S}{2 \sin \emptyset}$

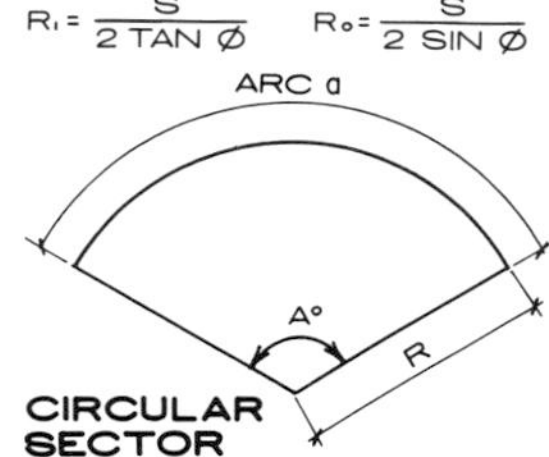
ARC a
A°
R

CIRCULAR SECTOR
AREA = ½ LENGTH OF ARC a × R
= AREA OF CIRCLE × $\frac{A°}{360}$
$= 0.0087 R^2 A°$
ARC $a = \frac{\pi R A°}{180°} = 0.0175\, RA°$

GEOMETRIC PROPERTIES OF PLANE FIGURES

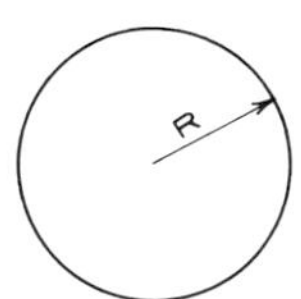
R

SPHERE
VOLUME = $\frac{4\pi R^3}{3}$
$= 0.5236 D^3$
SURFACE = $4\pi R^2$
$= \pi D^2$

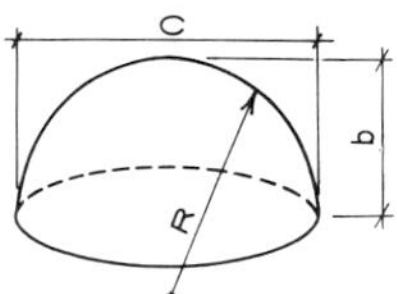
C
b
R

SEGMENT OF SPHERE
VOLUME = $\frac{1\pi b^2(3R-b)}{3}$
(OR SECTOR - CONE)
SURFACE = $2\pi Rb$
(NOT INCLUDING SURFACE OF CIRCULAR BASE)

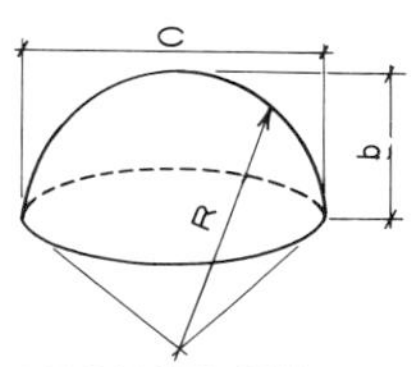
C
b
R

SECTOR OF SPHERE
VOLUME = $\frac{2\pi R^2 b}{3}$
SURFACE = $\frac{\pi R(4b+c)}{2}$
(OR: SEGMENT + CONE)

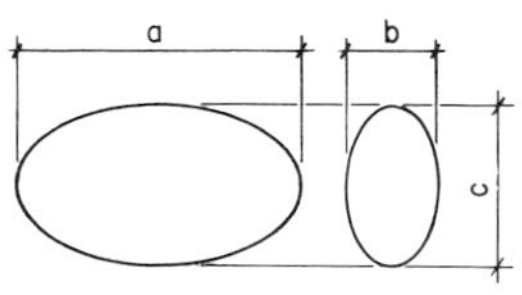
a
b
c

ELLIPSOID
VOLUME = $\frac{\pi abc}{6}$
SURFACE: NO SIMPLE RULE

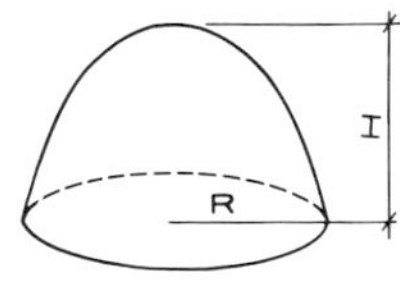
H
R

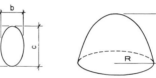

PARABOLOID OF REVOLUTION
VOLUME = AREA OF CIRCULAR BASE × ½ ALTITUDE.
SURFACE: NO SIMPLE RULE

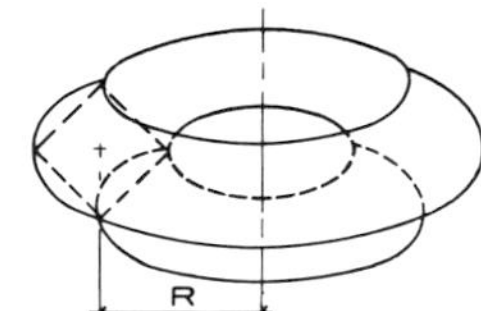
R

CIRCULAR RING OF ANY SECTION
R = DISTANCE FROM AXIS OF RING TO TRUE CENTER OF SECTION
VOLUME = AREA OF SECTION × $2\pi R$
SURFACE = PERIMETER OF SECTION × $2\pi R$
(CONSIDER THE SECTION ON ONE SIDE OF AXIS ONLY)

VOLUMES AND SURFACES OF DOUBLE - CURVED SOLIDS

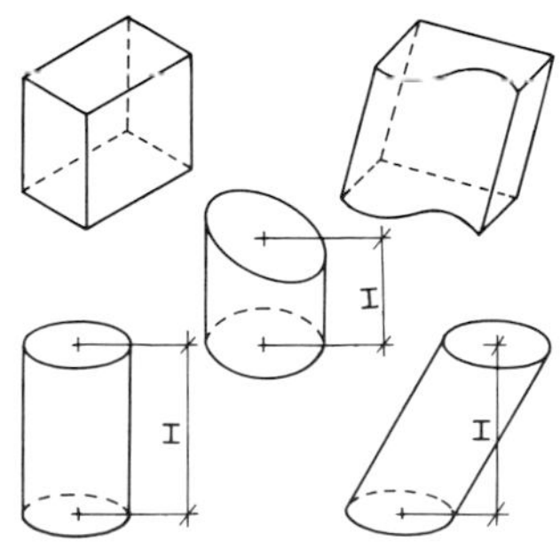
I
I
I

ANY PRISM OR CYLINDER, RIGHT OR OBLIQUE, REGULAR OR IRREGULAR.

Volume = area of base x altitude

Altitude = distance between parallel bases, measured perpendicular to the bases. When bases are not parallel, then Altitude = perpendicular distance from one base to the center of the other.

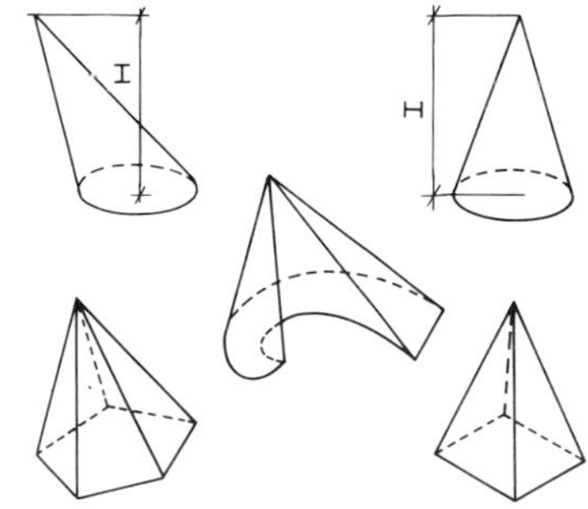
I
H

ANY PYRAMID OR CONE, RIGHT OR OBLIQUE, REGULAR OR IRREGULAR.

Volume = area of base x 1/3 altitude

Altitude = distance from base to apex, measured perpendicular to base.

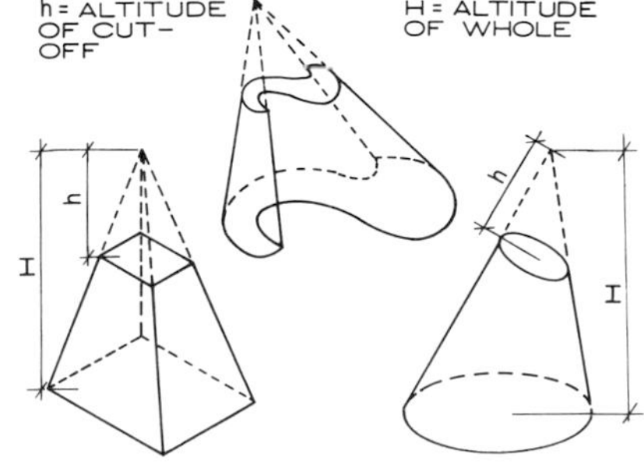
h = ALTITUDE OF CUT-OFF
H = ALTITUDE OF WHOLE
h
I
h
I

ANY FRUSTUM OR TRUNCATED PORTION OF THE SOLIDS SHOWN

Volume: From the volume of the whole solid, if complete, subtract the volume of the portion cut off.

The altitude of the cut-off part must be measured perpendicular to its own base.

SURFACES OF SOLIDS

The area of the surface is best found by adding together the areas of all the faces.

The area of a right cylindrical surface = perimeter of base x length of elements (average length if other base is oblique).

The area of a right conical surface = perimeter of base x 1/2 length of elements.

There is no simple rule for the area of an oblique conical surface, or for a cylindrical one where neither base is perpendicular to the elments. The best method is to construct a development, as if making a paper model, and measure its area by one of the methods given on the next page.

VOLUMES AND SURFACES OF TYPICAL SOLIDS

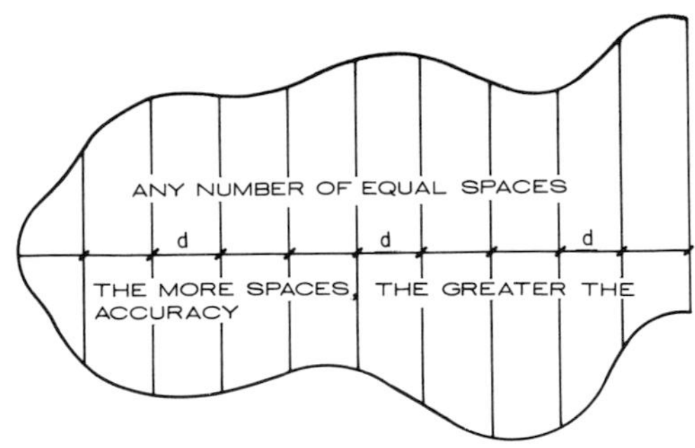
ANY NUMBER OF EQUAL SPACES
d
d
d
THE MORE SPACES, THE GREATER THE ACCURACY

TO FIND THE AREA OF AN IRREGULAR PLANE FIGURE

1. Divide the figure into parallel strips by equally spaced parallel lines.
2. Measure the length of each of the parallel lines.
3. Obtain a summation of the unit areas by one of these 3 "rules".

TRAPEZOID RULE

Add together the length of the parallels, taking the first and last at $^1/_2$ value, and multiply by the width of the internal "d". This rule is sufficiently accurate for estimating and other ordinary purposes.

SIMPSON'S RULE

Add the parallels, taking the first and last at full value, second, the fourth, sixth, etc. from each end at 4 times full value, and the third, fifth, seventh, etc. from each end at 2 times the value, then multiply by $^1/_3$d. This rule works only for an even number of spaces and is accurate for areas bounded by smooth curves.

DURAND'S RULE

Add the parallels taking the first and last at $^5/_{12}$ value, the second from each end at $^{13}/_{12}$ value, and all others at full value, then multiply by d. This rule is the most accurate for very irregular shapes.

NOTE

Irregular areas may be directly read off by means of a simple instrument called a Planimeter.

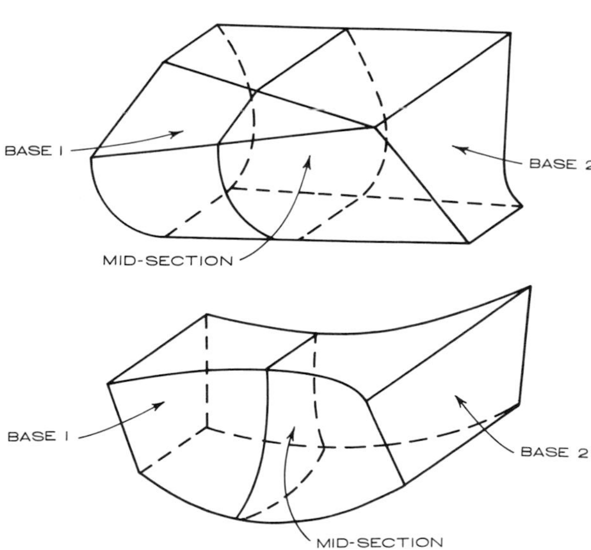
BASE I
BASE 2
MID-SECTION
BASE I
BASE 2
MID-SECTION

TO FIND THE VOLUME OF AN IRREGULAR FIGURE BY THE PRISMATOID FORMULA

Construct a section midway between the bases. Add 4 to the sum of the areas of the 2 bases and multiply the quantity by the area of the mid-section. Then multiply the total by $^1/_6$ the perpendicular distance between the bases.

V = [(area of base$_1$ + area of base$_2$ + 4) (area of midsection) x $^1/_6$ perpendicular distance between bases.

This formula is quite accurate for any solid with two parallel bases connected by a surface of straight line elements (upper figure), or smooth simple curves (lower figure).

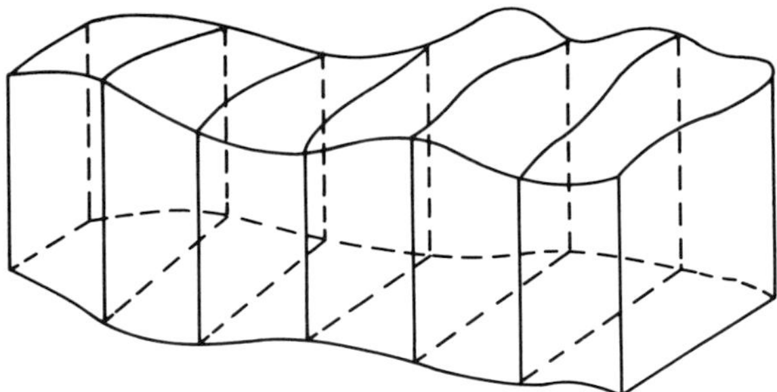

TO FIND THE VOLUME OF A VERY IRREGULAR FIGURE BY THE SECTIONING METHOD

1. Construct a series of equally spaced sections or profiles.
2. Determine the area of each section by any of the methods shown at left (preferably with a Planimeter).
3. Apply any one of the 3 summation "rules" given at left, to determine the total volume.

This method is in general use for estimating quantities of earthwork, etc.

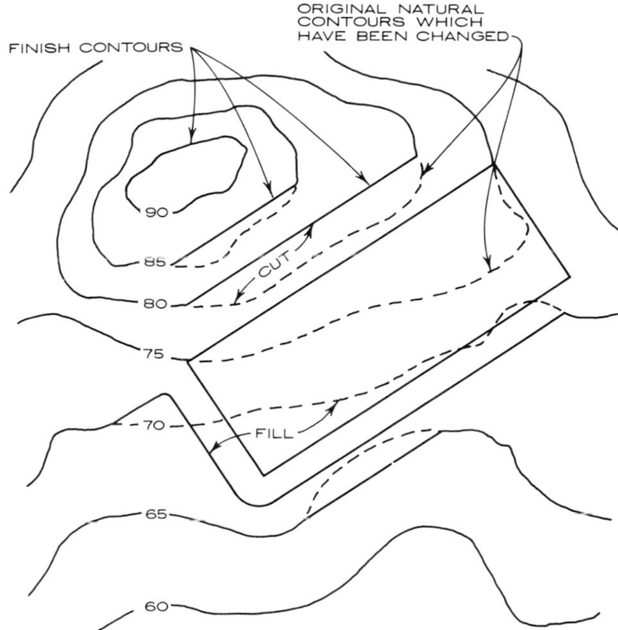
ORIGINAL NATURAL CONTOURS WHICH HAVE BEEN CHANGED
FINISH CONTOURS
90
85
80
75
70
65
60
CUT
FILL

TO FIND THE VOLUME OF CUT AND FILL DIRECTLY FROM THE CONTOUR PLAN

1. Draw "finish" and "original" contours on same contour map.
2. Measure the differential areas between new and old contours of each contour and enter in columns according to whether cut or fill.
3. Add up each column and multiply by the contour interval to determine the volume in cubic feet.

EXAMPLE

CONTOUR	CUT	FILL
85	300	
80	960	
75	2,460 − 2 = 1,230	3,800 − 2 = 1,900
70	20	2,200
	9,200	6,800
	x5	x5
TOTALS	46,000 cu. ft.	34,000 cu. ft.

NOTE

1. Where a cut or fill ends directly on a contour level use $^1/_2$ value.
2. The closer the contour interval, the greater the accuracy.

This method is more rapid than the sectioning method, and is sufficiently accurate for simple estimating purposes and for balancing of cut and fill.

BRICK AND BLOCK MASONRY		PSF
4″ brickwork		40
4″ concrete block, stone or gravel		34
4″ concrete block, lightweight		22
4″ concrete brick, stone or gravel		46
4″ concrete brick, lightweight		33
6″ concrete block, stone or gravel		50
6″ concrete block, lightweight		31
8″ concrete block, stone or gravel		55
8″ concrete block, lightweight		35
12″ concrete block, stone or gravel		85
12″ concrete block, lightweight		55
CONCRETE		**PCF**
Plain	Cinder	108
	Expanded slag aggregate	100
	Expanded clay	90
	Slag	132
	Stone and cast stone	144
Reinforced	Cinder	111
	Slag	138
	Stone	150
FINISH MATERIALS		**PSF**
Acoustical tile unsupported per 1/2″		0.8
Building board, 1/2″		0.8
Cement finish, 1″		12
Fiberboard, 1/2″		0.75
Gypsum wallboard, 1/2″		2
Marble and setting bed		25-30
Plaster, 1/2″		4.5
Plaster on wood lath		8
Plaster suspended with lath		10
Plywood, 1/2″		1.5
Tile, glazed wall 3/8″		3
Tile, ceramic mosaic, 1/4″		2.5
Quarry tile, 1/2″		5.8
Quarry tile, 3/4″		8.6
Terrazzo 1″, 2″ in stone concrete		25
Vinyl tile, 1/8″		1.33
Hardwood flooring, 25/32″		4
Wood block flooring, 3″ on mastic		15
FLOOR AND ROOF (CONCRETE)		**PSF**
Flexicore, 6″ precast lightweight concrete		30
Flexicore, 6″ precast stone concrete		40
Plank, cinder concrete, 2″		15
Plank, gypsum, 2″		12
Concrete, reinforced, 1″	Stone	12.5
	Slag	11.5
	Lightweight	6-10
Concrete, plain, 1″	Stone	12
	Slag	11
	Lightweight	3-9
FUELS AND LIQUIDS		**PCF**
Coal, piled anthracite		47-58
Coal, piled bituminous		40-54
Ice		57.2
Gasoline		75
Snow		8
Water, fresh		62.4
Water, sea		64
GLASS		**PSF**
Polished plate, 1/4″		3.28
Polished plate, 1/2″		6.56
Double strength, 1/8″		26 oz
Sheet A, B, 1/32″		45 oz
Sheet A, B, 1/4″		52 oz

Material	
Insulating glass 5/8″ plate with airspace	3.25
1/4″ wire glass	3.5
Glass block	18
INSULATION AND WATERPROOFING	**PSF**
Batt, blankets per 1″ thickness	0.1-0.4
Corkboard per 1″ thickness	0.58
Foamed board insulation per 1″ thickness	2.6 oz
Five-ply membrane	5
Rigid insulation	0.75
LIGHTWEIGHT CONCRETE	**PSF**
Concrete, aerocrete	50-80
Concrete, cinder fill	60
Concrete, expanded clay	85-100
Concrete, expanded shale-sand	105-120
Concrete, perlite	35-50
Concrete, pumice	60-90
METALS	**PCF**
Aluminum, cast	165
Brass, cast, rolled	534
Bronze, commercial	552
Bronze, statuary	509
Copper, cast or rolled	556
Gold, cast, solid	1205
Gold coin in bags	509
Iron, cast gray, pig	450
Iron, wrought	480
Lead	710
Nickel	565
Silver, cast, solid	656
Silver coin in bags	590
Tin	459
Stainless steel, rolled	492-510
Steel, rolled, cold drawn	490
Zinc, rolled, cast or sheet	449
MORTAR AND PLASTER	**PCF**
Mortar, masonry	116
Plaster, gypsum, sand	104-120
PARTITIONS	**PSF**
2 x 4 wood stud, GWB, two sides	8
4″ metal stud, GWB, two sides	6
4″ concrete block, lightweight, GWB	26
6″ concrete block, lightweight, GWB	35
2″ solid plaster	20
4″ solid plaster	32
ROOFING MATERIALS	**PSF**
Built up	6.5
Concrete roof tile	9.5
Copper	1.5-2.5
Corrugated iron	2
Deck, steel without roofing or insulation	2.2-3.6
Fiberglass panels (2 1/2″ corrugated)	5-8 oz
Galvanized iron	1.2-1.7
Lead, 1/8″	6-8
Plastic sandwich panel, 2 1/2″ thick	2.6
Shingles, asphalt	1.7-2.8
Shingles, wood	2-3
Slate, 3/16″ to 1/4″	7-9.5
Slate, 3/8″ to 1/2″	14-18
Stainless steel	2.5
Tile, cement flat	13
Tile, cement ribbed	16
Tile, clay shingle type	8-16
Tile, clay flat with setting bed	15-20

Material	
Wood sheathing per inch	3
SOIL, SAND, AND GRAVEL	**PCF**
Ashes or cinder	40-50
Clay, damp and plastic	110
Clay, dry	63
Clay and gravel, dry	100
Earth, dry and loose	76
Earth, dry and packed	95
Earth, moist and loose	78
Earth, moist and packed	96
Earth, mud, packed	115
Sand or gravel, dry and loose	90-105
Sand or gravel, dry and packed	100-120
Sand or gravel, dry and wet	118-120
Silt, moist, loose	78
Silt, moist, packed	96
STONE (ASHLAR)	**PCF**
Granite, limestone, crystalline	165
Limestone, oolitic	135
Marble	173
Sandstone, bluestone	144
Slate	172
STONE VENEER	**PSF**
2″ granite, 1/2″ parging	30
4″ granite, 1/2″ parging	59
6″ limestone facing, 1/2″ parging	55
4″ sandstone or bluestone, 1/2″ parging	49
1″ marble	13
1″ slate	14
STRUCTURAL CLAY TILE	**PSF**
4″ hollow	23
6″ hollow	38
8″ hollow	45
STRUCTURAL FACING TILE	**PSF**
2″ facing tile	14
4″ facing tile	24
6″ facing tile	34
8″ facing tile	44
SUSPENDED CEILINGS	**PSF**
Mineral fiber tile 3/4″, 12″ x 12″	1.2-1.57
Mineral fiberboard 5/8″, 24″ x 24″	1.4
Acoustic plaster on gypsum lath base	10-11
WOOD	**PCF**
Ash, commercial white	40.5
Birch, red oak, sweet and yellow	44
Cedar, northern white	22.2
Cedar, western red	24.2
Cypress, southern	33.5
Douglas fir (coast region)	32.7
Fir, commercial white; Idaho white pine	27
Hemlock	28-29
Maple, hard (black and sugar)	44.5
Oak, white and red	47.3
Pine, northern white sugar	25
Pine, southern yellow	37.3
Pine, ponderosa, spruce: eastern and sitka	28.6
Poplar, yellow	29.4
Redwood	26
Walnut, black	38

NOTE

To establish uniform practice among designers, it is desirable to present a list of materials generally used in building construction, together with their proper weights. Many building codes prescribe the minimum weights of only a few building materials. It should be noted that there is a difference of more than 25% in some cases.

GENERAL REFERENCES

References for the individual chapters of this book are given at the end of each chapter. Those lists include both general references for additional information and the sources for information used in developing the chapter contents.

This group of publications consists of references with additional information that spans the topics of several chapters of this book.

Architectural Graphic Standards, 8th ed., 1988, Ramsey/Sleeper and the American Institute of Architects, John Ray Hoke, Jr., Editor in Chief for the 8th edition, Wiley.
This book (the Light Construction Edition) consists of approximately one half of the 8th edition; as a result, the full copy of the 8th edition should be considered as a resource for additional information on many special topics.

Construction Principles, Materials, and Methods, 5th ed., 1983, Harold B. Olin, John L. Schmidt, and Walter H. Lewis, Van Nostrand Reinhold.
Although somewhat dated, this book represents a rich resource of information for the general topic of light and residential construction.

Time-Saver Standards for Architectural Design Data, 6th ed., 1982, John Hancock Callendar, McGraw-Hill.
A general reference for data and details for building construction and planning.

Building Design and Construction Handbook, 4th ed., 1982, Frederick S. Merritt, McGraw-Hill.
A general technical reference on all aspects of the design of building construction and the various building subsystems.

Mechanical and Electric Equipment for Buildings, 7th ed., 1986, Benjamin Stein, John Reynolds, and William McGuinness, Wiley.
The most comprehensive reference on design of building subsystems for all topics other than structures and general building construction.

Building Structures, 1988, James Ambrose, Wiley.
The most comprehensive single volume on building structures, from basic concepts through systems design.

The following books contain presentations of details of building construction—a topic of endless variety.

House Construction Details, 7th ed., 1986, Nelson Burbank, Arnold Romney, and Charles Phelps, McGraw-Hill.

Building Construction Illustrated, 1975, Francis Ching, Van Nostrand Reinhold.

Means Graphic Construction Standards, 1986, R. S. Means Co.

Wall Systems: Analysis by Detail, 1986, Herman Sands, McGraw-Hill. (Analysis of the curtain wall systems of ten buildings.)

Construction Details for Commercial Buildings, 1988, Glenn E. Wiggins, Whitney.

Architect's Detail Library, 1990, Fred A. Stitt, Van Nostrand Reinhold. (Computer-generated details.)

Professional Handbook of Architectural Detailing, 2nd ed., 1987, Osamu A. Wakita and Richard M. Linde, Wiley.

Architectural Drafting and Construction, 4th ed., 1989, Ernest R. Weidhaas, Allyn and Bacon.

Handbook of Architectural Details for Commercial Buildings, 1980, Joseph De Chiara, McGraw-Hill.

INDEX